# USA

## THE ROUGH GUIDE

There are more than one hundred and fifty Rough Guide titles
covering destinations from Amsterdam to Zimbabwe

**Forthcoming titles include**
Argentina • Cape Town • Croatia • Ecuador • Southeast Asia

**Rough Guide Reference Series**
Classical Music • Drum 'n' Bass • English Football • European Football
House • The Internet • Jazz • Music USA • Opera • Reggae
Rock Music • Techno • World Music

**Rough Guide Phrasebooks**
Czech • Dutch • Egyptian Arabic • European Languages • French • German
Greek • Hindi & Urdu • Hungarian • Indonesian • Italian • Japanese
Mandarin Chinese • Mexican Spanish • Polish • Portuguese • Russian
Spanish • Swahili • Thai • Turkish • Vietnamese

**Rough Guides on the Internet**
www.roughguides.com

# ROUGH GUIDE CREDITS

**Text editors:** Mary Beth Maioli and Kelly Cross
**Series editor:** Mark Ellingham
**Editorial:** Martin Dunford, Jonathan Buckley, Jo Mead, Kate Berens, Amanda Tomlin, Ann-Marie Shaw, Paul Gray, Helena Smith, Judith Bamber, Orla Duane, Olivia Eccleshall, Ruth Blackmore, Sophie Martin, Geoff Howard, Claire Saunders, Gavin Thomas, Alexander Mark Rogers, Polly Thomas, Joe Staines, Lisa Nellis, Andrew Tomičić, Claire Fogg, Richard Lim, Duncan Clark, Peter Buckley (UK); Andrew Rosenberg (US)
**Production:** Susanne Hillen, Andy Hilliard, Link Hall, Helen Ostick, Julia Bovis, Michelle Draycott, Katie Pringle, Robert Evers, Neil Cooper

**Cartography:** Melissa Baker, Maxine Repath, Nichola Goodliffe, Ed Wright
**Picture research:** Louise Boulton, Sharon Martins
**Online editors:** Kelly Cross, Loretta Chilcoat (US)
**Finance:** John Fisher, Gary Singh, Edward Downey, Mark Hall, Tim Bill
**Marketing & Publicity:** Richard Trillo, Niki Smith, David Wearn, Jemima Broadbridge (UK); Jean Marie Kelly, Myra Campolo, Simon Carloss (US)
**Administration:** Tania Hummel, Charlotte Marriott, Demelza Dallow

# ACKNOWLEDGEMENTS

**The editors** would like to thank all those who contributed to this and the last four editions; also, thanks to Susanne Hillen and Katie Pringle for smooth production, Russell Walton for superb proofreading, Melissa Baker for great mapmaking, Antonia Hebbert and Silke Kerwick for Basics research and Andrew Rosenberg for support.

**Sam**: Thanks to Mary Beth and Kelly at Rough Guides, to Christine de Cuir at the New Orleans CVB, and at home, as ever, to Greg Ward, Jim Cook and Pam Cook.

**Tim**: Thanks again to Isabel Castro and Barry Carroll for supreme hospitality in Austin, Texas; to Nadine Kennedy for being a cheery co-pilot of the Chrysler Sebrine and her help in researching the all-important nightlife sections; to Mary Beth Maioli for editing this beast with humor and patience; and to all the people who helped out on the road, particularly Cindy Saunders in Nashville, Greg Staley in Fort Worth, Dee Dee Potette in San Antonio, Denise DuBois in Memphis and Christine Hopkins in Galveston.

**Greg**: Thanks once again to Sam Cook, for ten great years; to my parents and family; to Tim; to Annie for her work on the last two editions; to road companions Edie Jarolim, Jules Brown, Rob Jones and Jamie Jensen; to Steve Lewis in Santa Fe, Pamela Westwood in Salt Lake City, Marion DeLay in Moab, and Jean McKnight in Tucson; and to everyone in the New York office.

# PUBLISHING INFORMATION

This fifth edition published March 2000 by Rough Guides Ltd, 62–70 Shorts Gardens, London WC2H 9AB.
Distributed by the Penguin Group:
Penguin Books Ltd, 27 Wrights Lane, London W8 5TZ
Penguin Books USA Inc., 345 Hudson Street, New York 10014, USA
Penguin Books Australia Ltd, 487 Maroondah Highway, PO Box 257, Ringwood, Victoria 3134, Australia
Penguin Books Canada Ltd, 10 Alcorn Avenue, Toronto, Ontario, Canada M4V 1E4
Penguin Books (NZ) Ltd, 182–190 Wairau Road, Auckland 10, New Zealand
Typeset in Linotron Univers and Century Old Style to an original design by Andrew Oliver.
Printed in England by Clays Ltd, St Ives PLC

Illustrations in Part One and Part Three by Edward Briant.
© Samantha Cook, Tim Perry and Greg Ward 2000
No part of this book may be reproduced in any form without permission from the publisher except for the quotation of brief passages in reviews.
1232pp – Includes index
A catalogue record for this book is available from the British Library
ISBN 1-85828-527-5

# USA

## THE ROUGH GUIDE

written and researched by

## Samantha Cook, Tim Perry
## and Greg Ward

With additional contributions by

JP Anderson, Don Bapst, Justin Bell, Amy Brown, Jules Brown, Loretta Chilcoat, Jeff Dickey, Heather Elton, Donald Hutera, Cam Jeffreys, Rob Mackey, Olivia Mandel, Mike Meyer, Ken Miller, Tim Nollen, Diana Wells and Paul Whitfield

THE ROUGH GUIDES

# THE ROUGH GUIDES

## TRAVEL GUIDES • PHRASEBOOKS • MUSIC AND REFERENCE GUIDES

 We set out to do something different when the first Rough Guide was published in 1982. Mark Ellingham, just out of university, was traveling in Greece. He brought along the popular guides of the day, but found they were all lacking in some way. They were either strong on ruins and museums but went on for pages without mentioning a beach or taverna. Or they were so conscious of the need to save money that they lost sight of Greece's cultural and historical significance. Also, none of the books told him anything about Greece's contemporary life – its politics, its culture, its people, and how they lived.

So with no job in prospect, Mark decided to write his own guidebook, one which aimed to provide practical information that was second to none, detailing the best beaches and the hottest clubs and restaurants, while also giving hard-hitting accounts of every sight, both famous and obscure, and providing up-to-the-minute information on contemporary culture. It was a guide that encouraged independent travelers to find the best of Greece, and was a great success, getting shortlisted for the Thomas Cook travel guide award, and encouraging Mark, along with three friends, to expand the series.

The Rough Guide list grew rapidly and the letters flooded in, indicating a much broader readership than had been anticipated, but one which uniformly appreciated the Rough Guide mix of practical detail and humor, irreverence and enthusiasm. Things haven't changed. The same four friends who began the series are still the caretakers of the Rough Guide mission today: to provide the most reliable, up-to-date and entertaining information to independent-minded travelers of all ages, on all budgets.

We now publish more than 150 titles and have offices in London and New York. The travel guides are written and researched by a dedicated team of more than 100 authors, based in Britain, Europe, the USA and Australia. We have also created a unique series of phrasebooks to accompany the travel series, along with an acclaimed series of music guides, and a best-selling pocket guide to the Internet and World Wide Web. We also publish comprehensive travel information on our Web site:

### www.roughguides.com

## HELP US UPDATE

We've gone to a lot of effort to ensure that the fifth edition of *The Rough Guide to the USA* is accurate and up-to-date. However, things change – places get "discovered," opening hours are notoriously fickle, restaurants and rooms raise prices or lower standards. If you feel we've got it wrong or left something out, we'd like to know, and if you can remember the address, the price, the time, the phone number, so much the better.

We'll credit all contributions, and send a copy of the next edition (or any other *Rough Guide* if you prefer) for the best letters. Please mark letters: "Rough Guide to the USA Update" and send to:
Rough Guides, 62–70 Shorts Gardens, London WC2H 9AB, or Rough Guides, 4th Floor, 345 Hudson St, New York, NY 10014.
Or send email to: mail@roughguides.co.uk
Online updates about this book can be found on Rough Guides' Web site at www.roughguides.com

## THE AUTHORS

**Sam Cook** first visited the USA in 1988, fell in love with the place, and has returned at least once a year since, roaming from Lubbock to Las Vegas, New Orleans to Memphis, Key West to Kauai and pretty much everywhere in between. She has been involved with Rough Guides for more than ten years, as an author and, for several years, as an editor and managing editor. In 1998 she returned to full-time writing, since when she has written the *Rough Guide to New Orleans*. She lives in London.

**Tim Perry** has co-written Fodor's *Rock & Roll Traveler USA* and contributes regularly on music to the *Independent* newspaper and various magazines. He lives in London.

**Greg Ward**, who lives in London, has worked for Rough Guides since 1985, in which time he has also written *Rough Guides* to Southwest USA, Las Vegas, Hawaii, Honolulu, Maui, the Big Island, Brittany and Normandy, and Essential Blues CDs, edited the first two editions of the *Rough Guide to the USA*, contributed to and edited several others, and set up the company's DTP department.

## READERS' LETTERS

We'd like to thank all the readers who wrote in with comments and updates: Caroline and Panos Alevizakis, Anne Bailey, Sakna Bates, Anne Burrows, Geraldine Cummins, Dudley Curtis, Rachel Fahey, Ginny Flower, Richard Germany, Hans Christian Hansen, Eileen and Phillip Hawkins, David Jessop, Nicholas MacCabe, Tim McGogney, Dean Marvin, Rachel Millman, Lars Moller Nielson, Barbara O'Boyle, Els van Ooigen, Ann Parker, Robert Peel, Kelly Perkel, Phil Riley, Andrew Rodger, Simon Skarritt, Lara Solomon, Kim Still, Lana Thomson, Steve Walton, Charlotte White and the many folks who contacted us via email but preferred to remain anonymous.

# CONTENTS

Introduction ix

## *PART THREE* CONTEXTS 1153

# LIST OF MAPS

## MAP SYMBOLS

| | | | |
|---|---|---|---|
| ═⟨80⟩═ | Interstate | 🏛 | Historic house |
| ═⟨30⟩═ | U.S. Highway | ⚲ | Lighthouse |
| ═⟨1⟩═ | Highway | ⚶ | Viewpoint |
| ▫▫▫▫▫ | Tunnel | ✕ | Battlefield |
| ▪▪▪▪▪ | Track | ⌃⌃ | Mountain range |
| ----- | Path | ▲ | Mountain peak |
| ▬▬▬ | Railway | ⇃ | Waterfall |
| — — | Ferry route | ⩊ | Marshland |
| ▪━▪━▪ | International border | ⓘ | Information center |
| ▬ ▪ ▪ ▬ | State border | ⊠ | Post office |
| ▬ ▬ ▬ | Chapter division boundary | ▪▪▪▪▪ | Wall |
| ——— | River | ■ | Building |
| ✗ | Airport | ⊞ | Church |
| ◉ | Hotel | ⁺⁺⁺ | Cemetery |
| △ | Campsite | ▨ | National Park |
| ⛪ | Church (regional maps) | ▨ | Park |
| ♦ | Museum | ▨ | Beach |
| 🏛 | Monument | | |

# INTRODUCTION

For five centuries, travelers have brought their hopes and dreams to America. For the earliest pioneers, it was a virgin wilderness ready to be shaped into a "New World," a potential paradise wasted on its native peoples. Millions of immigrants followed, to share in the building of the new nation and to better their lives, far from the hidebound societies of Europe and Asia. Eventually, slaves, who had been shipped over from Africa and the Caribbean, joined them as free citizens. As the United States expanded to fill the continent, something genuinely new was created: a vast country that took pride in defining itself in the eyes of the world.

Every traveler in the United States has some idea of what to expect. American culture has become so thoroughly shared throughout the globe that one of the principal joys of getting to know the country is not so much the difference of the place as the repeated delicious shock of the familiar. Yellow taxis on busy city streets; roadside mailboxes straight out of *Peanuts* cartoons; wooden porches overlooking the cotton-fields; tumbleweed skittering across the desert; endless highways dotted with pick-up trucks and chrome-plated diners; the first sight of the Grand Canyon, or the Manhattan skyline.

In this book, we've picked out the highlights for travelers across the entire USA, from Maine to Hawaii, and Alaska to Florida. We've divided the country region by region and state by state, and covered every area of every state. As well as the big cities and national parks, we've explored the highways and byways, singling out detours worth making, and places to avoid. On every area written about, we've done more than simply provide up-to-date practicalities for visitors: we've delved into the history and provided background on the people who have made America what it is. Our hope is to inform and entertain travelers, and to point in unexpected directions as well as to the obvious landmarks, no matter whether you've lived here all your life or are seeing it all for the first time.

Traveling in the United States is extremely easy; in a country where everyone seems to be forever on the move, there's rarely any problem finding a room for the night, and you can almost invariably depend on being able to eat well and inexpensively. The development of transportation has played a major role in the growth of the nation; the railroad opened the way for transcontinental migrations, while most of the great cities have been shaped by the automobile. Your experience of the country will be very much flavored by how you choose to get around. By far the best way to explore the country is to **drive your own vehicle**: it takes a long time before the sheer pleasure of cruising down the interstate, with the radio blaring rock or country music and the signs to Chicago or Nashville flashing past, begins to pall. Car rental is an absolute bargain, every main road is lined with budget motels charging around $30 per night for a good room, and the price of gasoline remains relatively low.

We have also detailed public transportation options throughout; with the aid of the excellent-value nationwide rail, bus and air passes, you can get to wherever you choose, foreign visitors in particular. However, if you do travel this way, there's a real temptation to see America as a succession of big **cities**. True enough, **New York** and **Los Angeles** have an exhilarating dynamism and excitement, and among their worthy rivals are **New Orleans**, the flamboyant home of jazz, **Chicago**, at the cutting edge of modern architecture, and **San Francisco**, on its beautiful Pacific bay. Few other cities – with the possible, and idiosyncratic, exception of neon-laden **Las Vegas** – can quite match this level of interest, however, and following a heavily urban itinerary will cut you off from the astonishing **landscapes** that make the USA truly distinctive. Especially in

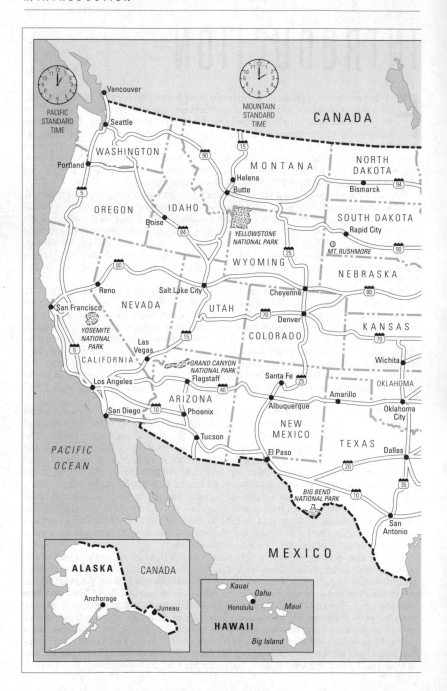

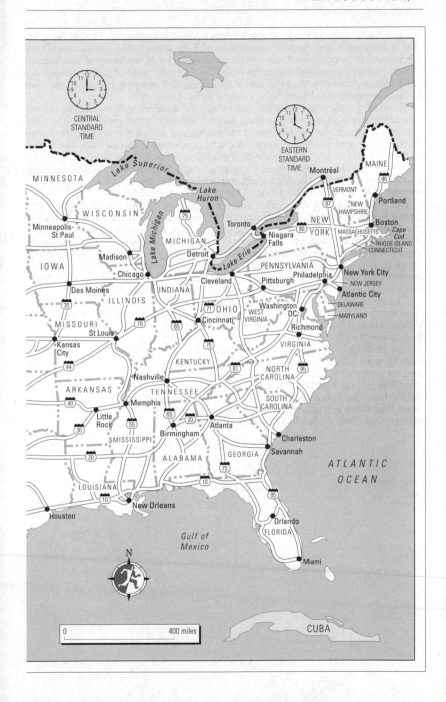

the vast open spaces of the West, the scenery is often breathtaking. The glacial splendor of **Yosemite**, the thermal wonderland of **Yellowstone**, the awesome red-rock **canyons** of Arizona and Utah, and the spectacular **Rocky Mountains** are among many of the treasures preserved and protected in the splendid national park system. Once you reach such wilderness, the potential for **hiking** and **camping** is magnificent – but it's usually essential to have a car to get near these spots.

Above all, travelers can enjoy the sheer thrill of experiencing American popular culture in the places where it began. Place names from rock 'n' roll songs spring into life; panoramas straight out of Hollywood movies spread across the horizon; road trips taken by your favorite literary characters can be re-created. For **music** fans, the chance to hear country music in Nashville or rhythm and blues in New Orleans, or to visit Elvis's shrine in Memphis, verges on a religious experience; readers brought up on the **books** of Mark Twain can ride a paddle-wheeler on the Mississippi; **moviegoers** can live out their Western fantasies in the Utah desert.

The United States is all too often dismissed, even by its own inhabitants, as a land almost devoid of **history**. Though mainstream America tends to trace its roots back to the Pilgrims and Puritans of New England, the rest of the continent has a longer history, stretching back way beyond the French culture of Louisiana and the Spanish presence in California to the majestic cliff palaces built by the Anasazi in the Southwest a thousand years ago. There are also any number of fascinating strands to America's post-revolutionary history: relics of the Gold Rush in California, of the Civil Rights years in the South, or of the Civil War anywhere east of the Mississippi.

Though we've had to structure this book regionally, the most invigorating expeditions are those that take in more than one area. You do not, however, have to cross the entire continent from shore to shore in order to appreciate its amazing diversity, or to be impressed by the way in which such an extraordinary range of topography and people has been melded into one nation. It would take a long time to see the whole place, and the more time you spend on the road simply getting from place to place – no matter how enjoyable in itself that can be – the less time you'll have to savor the small-town pleasures and backroads oddities that may well provide your strongest memories. It doesn't take long to realize that there is no such thing as a typical American person, any more than there is a typical American landscape, but there can be few places where strangers can feel so confident of a warm reception.

# PART ONE
## THE
# BASICS

THE
BASICS

# GETTING THERE FROM BRITAIN AND IRELAND

**More than twenty US cities are accessible by nonstop flights from the UK (see overleaf). At these "gateway cities," airport hubs for US air carriers, you can connect with extensive networks of domestic flights on into the** rest of the country. "Direct" services (which may land once or twice on the way, but are called direct if they keep the same flight number throughout their journey) fly from Britain to nearly every other major US city.

Nonstop flights to **Los Angeles** from London take eleven or twelve hours; the London–**Miami** flight takes eight hours; while flying time to **New York** is seven or so hours. Following winds ensure that return flights are always an hour or two shorter than outward journeys. One-stop direct flights to destinations beyond the East Coast add time to the journey, but can work out cheaper than nonstop flights. They can even save you time, because customs and immigration are cleared on first touchdown into the US rather than the final destination, which may be a busy international gateway. Because of the time difference between Europe and the US, flights usually leave Britain in mid-morning, while flights back from the US tend to arrive in Britain early in the morning.

## SAMPLE AIRFARES FROM BRITAIN

The prices given below (in £ sterling) are a general indication of the (minimum) transatlantic airfares obtainable from specialist companies; remember to add £45–60 airport tax to these figures. Each airline decides the exact dates of its own seasons.

| | LOW Nov–Mar (except Christmas and Easter) | | SHOULDER April (except Easter) –June, Oct | | HIGH Easter, July–Sept, Christmas | |
|---|---|---|---|---|---|---|
| **London to** | one-way | return | one-way | return | one-way | return |
| New York | 108 | 160 | 108 | 182 | 222 | 375 |
| Boston | 106 | 198 | 150 | 254 | 240 | 398 |
| Washington | 102 | 170 | 132 | 206 | 222 | 374 |
| Miami | 150 | 252 | 186 | 312 | 270 | 456 |
| Denver | 146 | 288 | 195 | 387 | 246 | 487 |
| Chicago | 143 | 286 | 199 | 397 | 264 | 527 |
| Houston | 132 | 264 | 186 | 372 | 240 | 480 |
| Seattle | 146 | 288 | 172 | 343 | 187 | 502 |
| Los Angeles | 156 | 260 | 204 | 330 | 288 | 480 |
| San Francisco | 144 | 250 | 204 | 338 | 288 | 480 |
| **Manchester to** | | | | | | |
| New York | 108 | 172 | 138 | 196 | 228 | 426 |
| Chicago | 126 | 196 | 162 | 299 | 252 | 472 |
| Los Angeles | 149 | 252 | 176 | 252 | 255 | 505 |

## FARES AND AIRLINES

Britain remains one of the best places in Europe to obtain flight bargains, though **fares** vary widely according to season, availability and the current level of inter-airline competition. The chart overleaf will give you a broad idea of typical rates offered by the operators listed opposite.

The comments that follow can act only as a general guide. The lowest-priced tickets usually have to be booked in advance and may carry restrictions, with heavy penalties for changes. The travel ads in the weekend papers and the holiday pages of ITV's *Teletext* give an idea of what's available; in London, scour *Time Out* and the *Evening Standard*. A good local travel agent will give you cost-saving advice as well as competitive quotes. Giveaway magazines aimed at young travelers, such as *TNT*, are also useful resources.

## NONSTOP FLIGHTS TO THE US FROM BRITAIN

**FROM LONDON**
(Heathrow or Gatwick)

**Atlanta** British Airways, Delta

**Baltimore** British Airways

**Boston** American Airlines, British Airways, United, Virgin Atlantic

**Charlotte** British Airways

**Chicago** Air India, American Airlines, British Airways, United, Virgin Atlantic

**Cincinnati** Delta

**Cleveland** Continental

**Dallas/Fort Worth** American Airlines, British Airways

**Detroit** Northwest, British Airways

**Houston** British Airways, Continental

**Los Angeles** Air New Zealand, American Airlines, British Airways, United, Virgin Atlantic

**Miami** American Airlines, British Airways, Virgin Atlantic

**Minneapolis** Northwest

**New York** Air India, American Airlines, British Airways, Continental, Kuwait Airways, United, Virgin Atlantic

**Orlando** British Airways, Virgin Atlantic

**Philadelphia** British Airways

**Phoenix** British Airways

**Raleigh/Durham** American Airlines

**St Louis** TWA

**San Francisco** British Airways, United, Virgin Atlantic

**Seattle** British Airways

**Washington DC** British Airways, United, Virgin Atlantic

**FROM BIRMINGHAM**

**Chicago** American Airlines

**New York** Continental

**FROM MANCHESTER**

**Atlanta** Delta

**Chicago** American Airlines

**Dallas** American Airlines (seasonal)

**New York** British Airways, Continental, Delta

**Orlando** Virgin Atlantic

**FROM GLASGOW**

**Chicago** American Airlines (seasonal)

**New York** British Airways, Continental

## AIRLINES

| | | | |
|---|---|---|---|
| **Aer Lingus** (Ireland) | ☎0645/737747 | **Delta** (Ireland) | ☎01/676 8080 |
| **Air India** | ☎020/8560 9996 | **Kuwait Airways** | ☎020/7412 0006 |
| **Air New Zealand** | ☎020/8741 2299 | **Northwest** | ☎0990/561000 |
| **American Airlines** | ☎0345/789789 | **TWA** | ☎0345/333333 |
| **British Airways** | ☎0345/222111 | **United** | ☎0845/844 4777 |
| **Continental** | ☎0800/776464 | **Virgin Atlantic** | ☎01293/747747 |
| **Delta** (UK) | ☎0800/414767 | | |

For airline numbers in the US, and Web site addresses, see p.28.

## FLIGHT AGENTS AND TOUR OPERATORS IN BRITAIN & IRELAND

### FLIGHT AGENTS

| | | | |
|---|---|---|---|
| **Bridge The World** | | Birmingham | ☎0121/236 1234 |
| London | ☎020/7916 0990 | Bristol | ☎0117/929 9000 |
| **Joe Walsh Tours** | | Glasgow | ☎0141/353 2224 |
| Dublin | ☎01/676 0991 | Manchester | ☎0161/839 6969 |
| **STA Travel** | | **The Travel Bug** | |
| London | ☎020/7361 6262 | London | ☎020/7835 2000 |
| Bristol | ☎0117/929 4399 | Manchester | ☎0161/721 4000 |
| Cambridge | ☎01223/366966 | **Twohigs** | |
| Leeds | ☎0113/244 9212 | Dublin | ☎01/670 9750 |
| Manchester | ☎0161/834 0668 | **USIT Campus** | |
| Oxford | ☎01865/792800 | National Call Centre | ☎0870/240 1010 |
| **Student & Group Travel** | | London | ☎020/7730 2101 |
| (student groups, New York and Boston) | | **USIT Now** | |
| Dublin | ☎01/677 7834 | Belfast | ☎028/9032 4073 |
| **Trailfinders** | | Cork | ☎021/270900 |
| London | ☎020/7628 7628 | Dublin | ☎01/679 8833 |

### TOUR OPERATORS

| | | | |
|---|---|---|---|
| **AmeriCan Adventures** | | **Greyhound International** | |
| Tunbridge Wells | ☎01892/512700 | East Grinstead | ☎01342/317317 |
| *www.americanadventures.com* | | *www.greyhound.com* | |
| **American Holidays** | | **North America Travel Service** | |
| Belfast ☎ | 028/9031 0000 | Leeds | ☎0113/246 1466 |
| Dublin ☎ | 01/679 8800 | **Trans Atlantic Vacations** | |
| **Bon Voyage** | | Horley | ☎01293/789400 |
| Southampton | ☎023/8024 8248 | **TrekAmerica** | |
| **British Airways Holidays** | | Banbury | ☎01295/256777 |
| Crawley | ☎0870/242 4245 | **Unijet** | |
| US cities | ☎0870/242 4243 | Haywards Heath | ☎0990/114114 |
| **Destination USA** | | **United Vacations** | |
| London | ☎020/7400 7000 | Heathrow Airport | ☎020/8313 0999 |
| **Explore Worldwide** | | **Virgin Holidays** | |
| Aldershot | ☎01252/760000 | Crawley | ☎01293/456789 |

Generally, the most expensive time to fly – **high season** – is from July to the end of September, and around Easter and Christmas. Fares during April, May, June and October – **shoulder** or **mid season** – are slightly less pricey, while the rest of the year, **low season**, is cheaper still. Remember, however, that high season in the UK can sometimes be the least costly and crowded season at your destination. For example, southern Florida and New Orleans are both extremely hot – almost swampy – in the summer, so the extra you might spend on a summer flight can be more than compensated for by low prices once you're on the ground – as long as you can handle the heat. Keep an eye out for slack season bargains, and, additionally, make sure to check the exact dates of the seasons with your operator or airline; you might be able to make major savings by shifting your departure date by a week – or even a day. **Taxes** vary almost monthly, but move relentlessly upwards.

For an overview of the various offers, and unofficially discounted tickets, go straight to an **agent** specializing in low-cost flights. Especially if you're under 26 or a student, they may be able to knock up to thirty percent off the regular fares. In low or shoulder season, you should be able to find a return flight to East Coast destinations such as New York for around £200, or to California for more like £300, while high-season rates tend to be from £100 to £150 more expensive. A **Visit USA airpass** (VUSA) can be a good idea if you want to see a lot of the country. These are available only to non-US residents, and must be bought before reaching the States (see p.25).

With an **open-jaw ticket** you can fly into one city and out of another; fares are calculated by halving the return fares to each destination and adding the two figures together. Remember to check whether there is a high drop-off fee for returning a rental car in a different state to the one where you picked it up (see p.28).

If you're on a really tight budget you may want to consider flying as a **courier**, although these days the savings to be made are virtually negligible. Most of the major courier firms offer opportunities to travel cheaply in return for delivering a package, at rates of around £150 for a return to New York. As a rule, you're required to sacrifice your baggage allowance (only hand baggage is allowed) and fit in with some tight restrictions on when you travel – stays of much more than a fortnight are rare. For addresses look in the Yellow Pages.

## PACKAGES

**Packages** – fly-drive, flight-accommodation deals and guided tours (or a combination of all three) – can work out cheaper than arranging the same trip yourself, especially for a short-term stay. High-street travel agents have plenty of brochures and information.

### FLIGHT AND ACCOMMODATION DEALS

There are countless **flight and accommodation** packages to all the major American cities; although you can often do things cheaper independently, these allow you to leave the organizational hassles to someone else. Drawbacks include the loss of flexibility and the fact that you'll probably be made to stay in hotels in the mid-range to expensive bracket, even though less expensive accommodation is almost always readily available.

To take a typical example, a low-season return flight plus middle-range Midtown hotel accommodation for three nights in New York City starts at around £400–450 per person, rising to more like £650 at peak periods. Among the many tour

operators, Virgin Holidays is about the least expensive (www.virginholidays.co.uk): for example, seven nights in San Francisco plus return flight costs around £629–849 per person, and the same deal for a Florida destination, with car rental included, can be as low as £400. Pre-booked accommodation schemes, where you buy vouchers for use in a specific group of hotels, are not normally good value – see p.39.

### FLY-DRIVE DEALS

**Fly-drive** deals, which give cut-rate (sometimes free) car rental when buying a transatlantic ticket from an airline or tour operator, are always cheaper than renting on the spot and give great value if you intend to do a lot of driving. On the other hand, you'll probably have to pay more for the flight than if you booked it through a discount agent. Competition between airlines and tour operators means that it's well worth phoning to check on current special promotions.

Getaway (☎020/8313 0550) arranges fly-drive deals with various carriers. Northwest Flydrive (☎01424/224400) offers excellent deals for not much more than an ordinary Apex fare; buy a return flight to Boston for £200 in low season, for example, and a week's car rental might cost a mere £49 extra (but £170 with insurance). Several of the companies listed in the box overleaf offer similar, and sometimes cheaper, packages. A good travel agent will put one together for you. There will often be little to choose between prices; the most important determining factors are the current strength of the dollar against the pound, and your destination in the US. Florida and California usually offer the lowest rates, ridiculously cheap in off-peak times (and all year in Florida), starting at around £16 per week for a small family saloon or £116 for a seven-seat passenger van (Northwest Flydrive). Watch out for hidden extras, such as taxes, "drop-off" charges and insurance; all are detailed on p.27 onwards.

Several of the operators listed overleaf go one stage further and book accommodation for self-drive tours. Bon Voyage, for example, arranges tailor-made packages in the Southwest, with two weeks in Arizona, including the flight to Phoenix and standard hotels, costing £1000–1200 per person.

### TOURING AND ADVENTURE PACKAGES

A simple and exciting way to see a chunk of America's Great Outdoors, without being hassled by too many practical considerations, is to take a specialist **touring and adventure package**, which includes transportation, accommodation, food and a guide. Some of the more adventurous, such as AmeriCan Adventures and TrekAmerica, carry small groups around on minibuses and use a combination of budget hotels and camping (all equipment, except sleeping bags, is provided), or hostels on AmeriCan Adventures Roadrunner Hostelling Treks. Most concentrate on the West – ranging from Arizona to Alaska, and from seven days to five weeks; AmeriCan Adventures also covers the East, including the Florida Keys. Typical rates for a two-week trip – excluding transatlantic flights – range from £450 in low season up to £650 in midsummer.

## FLIGHTS FROM IRELAND

Only two airlines run nonstop scheduled services to the US **from Ireland**. From both Dublin and Shannon airports, Aer Lingus flies to New York, Chicago, Los Angeles and Boston, while Delta flies to New York and Atlanta. Both can arrange onward flights to any American destination, and may have good-value special deals. Otherwise the cheapest flights – if you're under 26 or a student – are available from USIT. Student-only return fares to New York or Boston go for around IR£315 in the low season and IR£379 in the high season, while fares to Chicago range from IR£331 to IR£440, and those to San Francisco range from IR£389 to IR£569. Ordinary Apex fares may be only marginally higher.

# GETTING THERE FROM AUSTRALIA & NEW ZEALAND

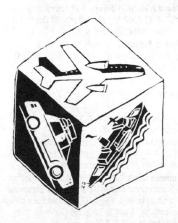

**Other than seasonal bargains and all-in packages that may be on offer from time to time, the best deals from Australasia are available from the travel agents listed overleaf. Various add-on fares and airpasses valid in the continental US are available with your main ticket, allowing you to fly to destinations across the States. These must be bought before you go, though.**

## FARES AND TICKETS

Whatever kind of ticket you're after, first call should be to one of the **travel agents** listed in

the box overleaf, who can fill you in on all the latest fares and any special offers. The **most expensive** time to fly is during the northern summer (mid-May to end-Aug) and over the Christmas period (Dec to mid-Jan); shoulder seasons cover March to mid-May and September, while the rest of the year is **low season**. The exact dates vary slightly between the airlines, so it's worth shopping around, especially if you have the flexibility to change your departure date by a day or two. Los Angeles is the main US gateway airport for flights **from Australia**; when they have surplus capacity, airlines frequently offer special fares to Los Angeles, which can be as low as A$1499 from the eastern states, sometimes with bonus A$99 return add-on fares to New York, Boston, Washington, Dallas, Chicago or Miami. Otherwise, the best you're likely to find are the regular Air New Zealand, Qantas and United flights to Los Angeles: low-season return fares cost around A$1650 from the eastern states, rising to A$1999 from Western Australia; flying during peak season will add at least another A$500. Through-flights to New York start at A$1350, on Japan Airlines midweek special from Sydney, Brisbane or Cairns, including an overnight stop in Tokyo. Korean Air offers a similar deal, via Seoul, starting at A$1700. Expect to pay upwards of A$1990 from Perth to New York via Johannesburg on South African Airways.

**From New Zealand**, low-season fares from Auckland or Christchurch (add another NZ$100 for Wellington departures) start at around NZ$1485 to LA or San Francisco, NZ$1899 to New York.

## AIRLINES AND AGENTS IN AUSTRALIA & NEW ZEALAND

### AIRLINES

**Air New Zealand**, 5 Elizabeth St, Sydney ☎13/2476; 139 Queen St, Auckland ☎09/357 3000; *www.airnz.co.nz*

**America West Airlines**, 364 Kent St, Sydney ☎02/9290 2232

**American Airlines**, 8/80 Clarence St, Sydney ☎1300/650 747; Level 15, Jetset Centre, 48 Emily Place, Auckland ☎09/308 9150 or 0800/887 997

**British Airways**, Qantas Centre, 70 Hunter St, Sydney ☎02/8904 8800; 154 Queen St, Auckland ☎09/356 8690

**Garuda**, 55 Hunter St, Sydney ☎1300/365 330; 120 Albert St, Auckland ☎09/366 1855 or 1800/128 510

**Japan Airlines**, 14/201 Sussex St, Sydney ☎02/9272 1111; 12/120 Albert St, Auckland ☎09/379 3202

**KLM**, 5 Elizabeth St, Sydney ☎02/9231 6333 or 1800/505 747

**Korean Air**, 36 Carrington St, Sydney ☎02/9262 6000; 63 Albert St, Auckland ☎09/303 0166

**Malaysian Airlines**, 16 Spring St, Sydney ☎13/2627; 12/12 Swanson St, Auckland ☎09/373 2741 or 0800/657 472

**Qantas**, 70 Hunter St, Sydney ☎13/1313; 154 Queen St, Auckland ☎09/357 8900 or 0800/808 767; *www.qantas.com.au*

**Singapore Airlines**, 17 Bridge St, Sydney ☎13/1011; cnr Albert and Fanshawe sts, Auckland ☎09/303 2129 or 0800/808 909.

**South African Airways**, 5 Elizabeth St, Sydney ☎02/9223 4402; Walshes World, 87 Queen St, Auckland ☎09/379 3708

**United Airlines**, 10 Barrack St, Sydney ☎13/1777; 7 City Rd, Auckland ☎09/379 3800; *www.ual.com*

### TRAVEL AGENTS

**Anywhere Travel**, 345 Anzac Parade, Kingsford, Sydney ☎02/9663 0411; *anywhere@ozemail.com.au*

**Budget Travel**, 16 Fort St, Auckland, plus branches around the city ☎09/366 0061 or 0800/808 040

**Destinations Unlimited**, 87 Albert St, Auckland ☎09/373 4033

**Flight Centres**, 82 Elizabeth St, Sydney, plus branches throughout Australia ☎13/1600; 350 Queen St, Auckland ☎09/358 4310, plus branches throughout New Zealand; *www.flightcentre.com.au*

**Northern Gateway**, 22 Cavenagh St, Darwin ☎08/8941 1394; *oztravel@norgate.com.au*

**STA Travel**, 855 George St, Sydney; 256 Flinders St, Melbourne; other offices in state capitals and major universities (nearest branch ☎13/1776, fastfare telesales ☎1300/360 960); 10 High St, Auckland (☎09/309 0458, fastfare telesales ☎09/366 6673), plus branches in Wellington, Christchurch, Dunedin, Palmerston North, Hamilton and at major universities.

*traveller@statravel.com.au; www.statravel.com.au*

**Student Uni Travel**, 92 Pitt St, Sydney ☎02/9232 8444, plus branches in Brisbane, Cairns, Darwin, Melbourne and Perth.

**Thomas Cook**, 175 Pitt St, Sydney; 257 Collins St, Melbourne; plus branches in other state capitals (local branch ☎13/1771, Thomas Cook Direct telesales ☎1800/801 002); 191 Queen St, Auckland ☎09/379 3920; *www.thomascook.com.au*

**Trailfinders**, 8 Spring St, Sydney ☎02/9247 7666; 91 Elizabeth St, Brisbane ☎07/3229 0887; Hides Corner, Shield St, Cairns ☎07/4041 1199

**Travel.com**, 76-80 Clarence St, Sydney ☎02/9262 3555; *consultant@travel.com.au; www.travel.com.au*

**Usit Beyond**, cnr Shortland St and Jean Batten Place, Auckland ☎09/379 4224 or 0800/788 336, plus branches in Christchurch, Dunedin, Palmerston North, Hamilton and Wellington. *www.usitbeyond.co.nz*

## AIRPASSES AND RTW TICKETS

Unless you're combining your US trip with jaunts to Europe and/or Asia, US **airpasses** (see box on p.25) and add-on fares generally offer greater savings and more flexibility than round-the-world (RTW) tickets. However, if the US is just one port of call on your big trip, there are endless possibilities for **RTW routings**; for example, prices for Sydney to Tahiti to Los Angeles, traveling overland to New York, then continuing to Frankfurt and Bangkok on the way back to Sydney, start at A$2679, flying with the "Star Alliance" which includes Air New Zealand, Lufthansa, United Airlines, Thai, Varig, SAS, Air Canada and Ansett Australia. The "Star Alliance" works on a mileage basis and is a flat rate year-round. If you're departing in low season, cheaper still is the "One World" fare offered by Qantas and British Airways, in conjunction with American Airlines, Canadian Airlines and Cathay Pacific, which covers four continents from A$2399. Kiwi travelers could start in Auckland and take in Sydney, Harare, Nairobi, London, New York, LA and Brisbane for around NZ$2899. Agents such as STA (see box opposite) specialize in putting together RTW airfares using various airlines, and can help you plan your trip.

## PACKAGES AND TOURS

There are many variations on **package deals** available to Australasian travelers, from **fly-drive** deals to fully escorted bus tours, skiing packages and camping treks, which can work out cheaper than making the same arrangements yourself. Some of the no-frills fly-drive packages, for example, can cost less than a flight alone, and you'll often get extras, such as stopovers in Hawaii or Tahiti and passes to Disneyland, thrown in. Insight's eight-day "West Coast" coach tour costs A$1180, while Creative Holidays tours start at A$1750 for seven days, including all your accommodation, but excluding flights.

Small-group **hotel** and **camping tours** can get you further off the beaten track. TrekAmerica offers several itineraries ranging from one to nine weeks; its ten-day "Wild West" tour starts and ends in LA, taking in Death Valley, Las Vegas and the Grand Canyon, and costs from A$944/NZ$1170, not including flights, while its 28-day "Continental Explorer," which crosses the continent from Miami to San Francisco, starts at A$2085/NZ$2585 (again, airfares are extra).

## SPECIALIST AGENTS AND OPERATORS

**Adventure Specialists** 1/69 Liverpool St, Sydney ☎02/9261 2927

**Adventure Travel Company**, 164 Parnell Rd, Parnell, Auckland ☎09/379 9755

**Adventure World** 73 Walker St, North Sydney ☎02/9956 7766 or 1800/221 931, plus branches in Adelaide, Brisbane, Melbourne and Perth; 101 Great South Rd, Remuera, Auckland ☎09/524 5118

**Canada & America Travel Specialists**,343 Pacific Highway, Crows Nest, Sydney ☎02/9922 4600

**Creative Holidays** 3/55 Grafton St, Woollahra, Sydney ☎02/9386 2111

**Insight** Level 2, 39–41 Chandos St, St Leonards, Sydney ☎02/9512 0767

**Peregrine** 258 Lonsdale St, Melbourne ☎03/9662 2700; *www.peregrine.net.au*

**Snow Bookings Only** 1141 Toorak Rd, Camberwell, Melbourne ☎03/9809 2699 or 1800/623 266

**Wiltrans** 10/189 Kent St, Sydney ☎02/9255 0899

# ENTRY REQUIREMENTS FOR FOREIGN VISITORS

## VISAS

Under the **Visa Waiver Scheme**, designed to speed up immigration procedures, citizens of Britain, Ireland, Australia, New Zealand and most European countries in possession of **full passports** do not require visas for trips to the United States of less than ninety days. **Visa waiver forms** are handed out on incoming planes, and are processed during immigration control at your initial point of arrival on US soil. The form requires details of where you are staying on your first night, and the date you intend to leave the US. You should be able to prove that you have enough money to support yourself while in the US, and may experience difficulties if you admit to being HIV-positive or having AIDS or TB. Part of the form will be attached to your passport, where it must stay until you leave. The same form also covers entry across the land borders with Canada and Mexico.

Citizens of all other countries should contact their local US embassy or consulate for details of current entry requirements. Even those eligible for the visa waiver scheme *must* apply for a free tourist visa if they intend to stay in the US for more than ninety days; for advice on working or studying in the US, see p.12. Whatever your nationality, visas are not issued to convicted felons and anybody who owns up to being a communist, fascist or drug dealer.

## CUSTOMS

All passengers arriving in the US must present a completed **customs declaration form** (also handed out on incoming planes). Customs officers check whether you're carrying any fresh foods and ask if you've visited a farm in the last month: if you have, you could well lose your shoes. As well as foods and anything agricultural, it's prohibited to carry into the country any articles from such places as North Korea, Cambodia, Iraq, Libya or Cuba, obscene publications, lottery tickets, chocolate liqueurs or pre-Columbian artifacts. Anyone caught bringing drugs into the country will not only face prosecution but be entered in the records as an undesirable and probably denied entry for all time. The **duty-free allowance** if you're over 17 is 200 cigarettes and 100 cigars (*not* Cuban) and, if you're over 21, a liter of spirits.

## EXTENSIONS

The date stamped on your passport is the latest you're legally allowed to stay. Leaving a few days later may not matter, especially if you're heading home, but more than a week or so can result in a

## CANADIAN VISITORS

**Canadian** citizens are in a particularly privileged position when it comes to crossing the border into the US. For a brief excursion, you do not necessarily need even a passport, just some form of ID; if you're obviously setting off on a longer trip, you should carry a passport, and if you plan to stay for more than ninety days you need a visa too.

Bear in mind that if you cross into the States in your car, trunks and passenger compartments are subject to spot searches by US Customs personnel, though this sort of surveillance is likely to decrease as remaining tariff barriers fall over the next few years. Remember, too, that Canadians are legally barred from seeking gainful employment in the US.

## US EMBASSY AND CONSULATES IN CANADA

**Embassy:** 100 Wellington St,
Ottawa, ON K1P 5A1 ☎613/238-5335

**Consulates**:

615 Macleod Trail SE, 10th Floor,
Calgary, AB T2G 4T8 ☎403/266-8962

2000 Barrington St,
Suite 910, Cogswell Tower,
Scotia Square,
Halifax, NS B3J 3K1 ☎902/429-2480

PO Box 65,
Station Desjardins, South Tower,
Montréal, PQ H5B 1G1 ☎514/398-9695

2 Place Terrasse Dufferin,
Québec City, PQ G1R 4T9 ☎418/692-2095

360 University Ave,
Toronto, ON M5G 1S4 ☎416/595-1700

1095 W Pender St, 21st Floor,
Vancouver, BC V6E 2M6 ☎604/685-4311

## US EMBASSIES AND CONSULATES ELSEWHERE

**UK**

5 Upper Grosvenor St,
London W1A 1AE ☎020/7499 9000
visa hotline ☎0891/200290

3 Regent Terrace,
Edinburgh EH7 5BW ☎0131/556 8315

Queens House, 14 Queen St,
Belfast BT1 6EQ ☎028/9032 8239

**AUSTRALIA**

**Embassy:** 21 Moonah Place,
Canberra, ACT 2600 ☎02/6270 5000

**Consulate:** 19–29 Martin Place,
Sydney, NSW 2000 ☎02/9373 9200

Visa hotline ☎1902/262 682
(premium rated, $1.50 per minute)

**IRELAND**

42 Elgin Rd, Ballsbridge, Dublin ☎01/472 2068

**NEW ZEALAND**

**Embassy:** 29 Fitzherbert Terrace,
Thorndon, Wellington ☎04/472 2068

**Consulate:** cnr Shortland and
O'Connell sts, Auckland ☎09/303 2724

Address for visa applications:
Non-Immigrant Visas, Private Bag 92022,
Auckland 1

## EMBASSIES AND CONSULATES IN THE US

**UK**

**Embassy:** 3100 Massachusetts Ave,
NW Washington DC, 20008 ☎202/462-1340

**Consulates:**

The Wrigley Building, 400 N
Michigan Ave, Suite 1306,
Chicago, IL 60611 ☎312/346-1810

11766 Wilshire Blvd,
Suite 400, Los Angeles,
CA 90025 ☎310/477-3322

1001 Brickell Bay Drive,
Suite 2800, Miami, FL 33131 ☎305/374-1522

845 3rd Ave, New York,
NY 10022 ☎212/745-0200

1 Sansome St,
Suite 850, San Francisco,
CA 94104 ☎415/981-3030

**AUSTRALIA**

1601 Massachusetts Ave,
NW Washington DC, 20036 ☎202/797-3000

**CANADA**

501 Pennsylvania Ave,
NW Washington DC, 20001 ☎202/682-1740

**IRELAND**

2234 Massachusetts Ave,
NW Washington DC, 20008 ☎202/462-3939

**NEW ZEALAND**

37 Observatory Circle,
NW Washington DC, 20008 ☎202/328-4800

protracted, rather unpleasant, interrogation from officials, which may cause you to miss your flight. Overstaying may also cause you to be turned away next time you try to enter the US.

To get an extension before your time is up, apply at the nearest **US Immigration and Naturalization Service** (INS) office (addresses appear in the Federal Government Offices listings at the front of local phone books). They will assume that you're working illegally and it's up to you to convince them otherwise. Do this by providing evidence of ample finances, and, if you can, bring along an upstanding American citizen to vouch for you. You'll also have to explain why you didn't plan for the extra time initially.

### WORK AND STUDY

Permission to work in the country can only be granted by the Immigration and Naturalization Service in the US itself. Contact your local embassy or consulate for advice on current regulations, and INS addresses, but be warned that unless you've got relatives (parents or children over 21) or a prospective employer to sponsor you, your chances are at best slim.

**Illegal work** is nothing like as easy to find as it used to be, now that the government has introduced fines as high as $10,000 for companies caught employing anyone without the legal right to work in the US. Even in the traditionally more casual establishments, like restaurants and bars, things have really tightened up, and if you do find work it's likely to be of the less visible, poorly paid kind – washer-up instead of waiter.

**Students** have the best chance of prolonging their stay in the US. One way is to get onto an Exchange Visitor Program, for which participants are given a J-1 visa that entitles them to accept paid summer employment and apply for a social security number. However, you should note that most of these visas are issued for jobs in American **summer camps**, which aren't everybody's idea of a good time; they fly you over, and after a summer's work you end up with around $500 and a month to six weeks to blow it in. If you live in Britain and are interested, contact BUNAC (16 Bowling Green Lane, London EC1; ☎020/7251 3472) or Camp America (37 Queens Gate, London SW7; ☎020/7581 7373). If you want to **study** at an American university, apply to that institution directly; if they accept you, you're more or less entitled to unlimited visas so long as you remain enrolled in full-time education.

Applicants for **au pair visas** have to prove that they have at least 200 hours' experience with infants, 24 hours' training in child development and eight hours' child safety training; prospective employers must provide a written description of the job they expect their au pair to perform, so there is protection on both sides. Camp America runs a scheme known as Au Pair in America (☎207/581-7322), open to men and women aged 18 to 26. There is a placement fee of £35, a £67 contribution towards insurance and a good-faith deposit of £268; the combined amount covers the interviewing and selection process, visa and flight to the US. On-the-job payment while in the US is about US$139 per week; if you last the whole year you get your good-faith deposit back in dollars.

# INSURANCE, HEALTH AND PERSONAL SAFETY

## INSURANCE

Though not compulsory, **travel insurance** is *essential* for **foreign travelers**. The US has no national health system and you can lose an arm and a leg (so to speak) having even minor medical treatment. Bank and credit cards (particularly American Express) often have certain levels of medical or other insurance included, especially if you use them to pay for your trip.

If you plan to participate in watersports, or do some hiking or skiing, you'll probably have to pay an extra premium; check carefully that your policy will cover you in case of an accident. Note also that very few insurers will arrange on-the-spot payments in the event of a major expense or loss; you will usually be reimbursed only after going home. In all cases of loss or theft of goods, you will have to contact the local police to have a report made out so that your insurer can process the claim.

## BRITISH COVER

Most **travel agents** and tour operators will offer you insurance when you book your flight or holiday, and some will insist you take it. These policies are usually reasonable value, though, as ever, you should check the small print. If you feel the suggested cover is inadequate, or you want to compare prices, any travel agent, insurance broker or bank should be able to help: call Columbus Travel Insurance (☎020/7375 0011), Endsleigh Insurance (☎020/7436 4451), or Frizzell Insurance

(☎01202/292333). Two weeks' cover for a trip to the US should cost around £40, a month more like £60. If you have a good "all risks" home insurance policy it may well cover your possessions against loss or theft even when overseas, and many private medical schemes also cover you while abroad – make sure you know the procedure and the helpline number. On all policies, read the small print to ensure the cover includes a sensible amount for medical expenses – this should be at least £1,000,000, which will cover the cost of an air ambulance to fly you home in the event of serious injury or hospitalization.

## AUSTRALASIAN COVER

In **Australia**, travel insurance is available from most travel agents (see p.8) or direct from insurance companies such as Cover More (☎1800/251 881) and Ready Plan (☎1800/337 462), with prices averaging A$190 for 31 days. In **New Zealand**, a good range of policies are offered by STA and Flight Centres (see p.8), or direct from Ready Plan in Auckland (☎09/379 3203), with a month's cover costing around NZ$220.

## NORTH AMERICAN COVER

Before buying an insurance policy, **North American** travelers should check that they're not already covered – some **homeowners' or renters' policies** are valid on vacation, and **credit cards** such as American Express often include some medical or other insurance, while most **Canadians** are covered for medical mishaps away from home by their **provincial health plans**. If you need only trip cancellation/interruption coverage (to supplement your existing plan), this generally costs around $6 per $100. If you aren't already covered, the best premiums can usually be obtained through **student/youth travel agencies** – STA Travel (☎212/627-3111 or 1-800/777-0112) now offers ISIS policies for travelers under the age of 60. Coverage is worldwide and comes in packages covering 7 days ($35), 15 days ($55), 1 month ($115), 45 days ($155), 2 months ($180) and 1 year ($730) – add an extra $35–50 for each additional month on longer stays. Other reliable agents include Access America (☎1-800/284-8300), Travel Guard (☎1-800/826-1300), and, in Canada, Desjardins Travel Insurance (☎1-800/463-7830).

## HEALTH ADVICE FOR FOREIGN TRAVELERS

If you have a serious **accident** while in the US, emergency medical services will get to you quickly and charge you later. For emergencies or ambulances, dial ☎911, the nationwide emergency number (or whatever variant may be on the information plate of the pay phone).

Should you need to see a doctor, lists can be found in the *Yellow Pages* under "Clinics" or "Physicians and Surgeons." The basic consultation fee is $50–100, payable in advance. Medications aren't cheap either – keep all your receipts for later claims on your insurance policy.

Foreign visitors should bear in mind that many pills available over the counter at home require a **prescription** in the US – most codeine-based painkillers, for example – and that local brand names can be confusing; ask for advice at the **pharmacy** in any **drugstore**.

Travelers from Europe do not require **inoculations** to enter the US.

## CRIME AND PERSONAL SAFETY

No one could pretend that America is trouble-free, although away from the urban centers **crime** is often remarkably low-key. Even the lawless reputation of New York, Detroit or Los Angeles is far in excess of the truth, and most parts of these cities, by day at least, are safe; at night, though, some areas are completely off limits. All the major tourist areas and the main nightlife zones in cities are invariably brightly lit and well policed. By being careful, planning ahead and taking good care of your possessions, you should, generally speaking, have few real problems.

Foreign visitors tend to report that the **police** are helpful and obliging when things go wrong, although they'll be less sympathetic if they think you brought the trouble on yourself through carelessness.

## MUGGING AND THEFT

The biggest fear for most travelers is the threat of **mugging**, though it's nothing to get overly paranoid about. It's impossible to give hard and fast rules about what to do if confronted by a mugger. Whether to run, scream or fight depends on the situation – but most locals would just hand over their money.

Of course, the best thing is simply to avoid being mugged, and a few basic rules are worth remembering: *don't* flash money around; *don't* peer at your map (or this book) at every street corner, thereby announcing that you're a lost stranger; even if you're terrified or drunk (or both), try not to appear so; avoid dark streets, especially ones you can't see the end of; and in the early hours stick to the roadside edge of the sidewalk, so that it's easier to run into the road to attract attention. If you have to ask for directions, choose your target carefully. Another idea is to carry a wad of cash, perhaps $50 or so, separate from the bulk of your holdings so that if you do get confronted you can hand over something of value without losing everything.

If the worst happens and your assailant is toting a gun or (more likely) a knife, try to stay calm: remember that he (for this is generally a male pursuit) is probably scared, too. Keep still, don't make any sudden movements – and hand over your money. When he's gone, find a phone and dial ☎911, or hail a cab and ask the driver to take you to the nearest police station. Here, report the theft and get a reference number on the report to claim insurance and travelers' check refunds. If you're in a big city, ring the local Travelers Aid (their numbers are listed in the phone book) for sympathy and practical advice. For specific advice for women in the case of mugging or attack, see p.35.

Another potential source of trouble is having your **hotel room burgled**. Always store valuables in the hotel safe when you go out; when

| TO REPORT STOLEN TRAVELERS' CHECKS AND CREDIT CARDS, CALL: | |
|---|---|
| **American Express checks** | ☎1-800/221-7282 |
| **American Express cards** | ☎1-800/528-4800 |
| **Citicorp** | ☎1-800/645-6556 |
| **Diners Club** | ☎1-800/234-6377 |
| **MasterCard** | ☎1-800/826-2181 |
| **Thomas Cook/ MasterCard** | ☎1-800/223-9920 |
| **Visa checks** | ☎1-800/227-6811 |
| **Visa cards** | ☎1-800/336-8472 |

inside, keep your door locked and don't open it to anyone you are suspicious of; if they claim to be hotel staff and you don't believe them, call reception to check.

Needless to say, having bags that contain travel documents snatched can be a big headache, none more so for foreign travelers than **losing your passport**. If the worst happens, go to the nearest consulate and get them to issue you a **temporary passport**, basically a sheet of paper saying you've reported the loss, which will get you out of America and back home.

## CAR CRIME

Crimes committed against tourists driving **rented cars** have garnered headlines around the world in recent years. In major urban areas, any car you rent should have nothing on it – such as a particular license plate – that makes it easy to spot as a rental car. When driving, under no circumstances stop in any unlit or seemingly deserted urban area – and especially not if someone is waving you down and suggesting that there is something wrong with your car. Similarly, if you are "accidentally" rammed by the driver behind, do not stop immediately but drive on to the nearest well-lit, busy area and **call ☎911** for assistance. Keep your doors locked and windows never more than slightly open. Do not open your door or window if someone approaches your car on the pretext of asking directions. Hide any valuables out of sight, preferably locked in the trunk or in the glove compartment.

# COSTS AND MONEY

**This book contains detailed price information for lodging and eating throughout the United States. Accommodation rates are coded according to the system explained on p.37, which excludes any local taxes that may apply, while restaurant prices include food only and not drinks or tip. For museums and similar attractions, the entrance fees quoted are for adults; unless we say otherwise, you can assume that children get in half-price. Naturally, costs will increase slightly overall during the life of this edition.**

## COSTS

Even when the exchange rate is at its least advantageous (see box, overleaf), most western European visitors find virtually everything – accommodation, food, gas, cameras, clothes and more – to be better value in the US than it is at home. However, if you're used to traveling in the less expensive countries of Europe, let alone in the rest of the world, you shouldn't expect to scrape by on the same minuscule budget once you're in the US. You should also be prepared for regional variances; most New York prices, for example, are well above those in rural America. New England, Hawaii and Alaska, among others, can also be quite pricey areas.

**Accommodation** is likely to be your biggest single expense. Typical motel rooms in rural areas cost a few dollars either side of $40 per night, while hotel and motel rates in cities tend to start around $60. Hostels offering dorm beds – usually for $10 to $20 – are reasonably common, but don't save all that much money for two or more people traveling together. Camping, of course, is cheap, ranging from free to perhaps $20 per night, but is rarely practical in or around the big cities.

As for **food**, $20 a day is enough to get an adequate life-support diet, consisting of perhaps one full-scale meal in a local diner supplemented by a stash of groceries, while for a daily total of around $30 you can dine pretty well. Beyond this, everything hinges on how much sightseeing, taxi-taking, drinking and socializing you do. Much of any of these – especially in a major city – and you're likely to be getting through upwards of $50 a day. If you're visiting a significant number of national parks and monuments, buy a Golden Eagle pass (see p.43); the $50 fee covers all passengers in your vehicle.

**Renting a car**, at around $150 per week, is a far more efficient way to explore the country than public transportation, and for a group of two or more it's no more expensive either. Having your own vehicle also enables you to stay in budget motels along the interstates instead of expensive city-center hotels.

In almost every state, **sales tax**, at rates varying up to ten percent, is added to virtually everything you buy in shops, but it isn't part of the marked price (for more details, see p.57). The most economical possible vacation, therefore, with two people sharing a rental car, camping in state and federal parks most nights, and eating one restaurant meal per day, will work out at something over $200 per person per week.

## TAKING, CHANGING AND ACCESSING MONEY

Expect to pay most of your major expenses by **credit or debit card**; hotels and car rental agencies usually demand a credit card imprint as security, even if you intend to settle the bill in cash, and you'll be at a serious disadvantage if you don't have one. Visa, MasterCard, Diners Club, American Express and Discover are the most widely used.

You'll also need to carry a certain amount of **cash**. If you have a MasterCard or Visa, or a cash-dispensing card linked to an international network such as Cirrus or Plus – check with your home bank before you set off – you can withdraw cash from appropriate automatic teller machines (**ATMs**). For both American and foreign visitors, US dollar **travelers' checks** are a better way to carry money than ordinary bills; they offer the great security of knowing that lost or stolen checks will be replaced. Checks such as American Express, Visa and Thomas Cook are universally

### MONEY: A NOTE FOR FOREIGN TRAVELERS

**US currency** comes in **bills** of $1, $5, $10, $20, $50 and $100, plus various larger (and rarer) denominations. Confusingly, all are the same size and same green color, making it necessary to check each bill carefully. The dollar is made up of 100 cents in **coins** of 1 cent (known as a **penny**), 5 cents (a **nickel**), 10 cents (a **dime**) and 25 cents (a **quarter**). Change – especially quarters – is needed for buses, vending machines and telephones, so always carry plenty.

Generally speaking, one pound sterling will buy between $1.50 and $1.70; one Canadian dollar is worth between 70¢ and 90¢; one Australian dollar is worth between 70¢ and 80¢; and one New Zealand dollar is worth between 60¢ and 70¢.

accepted as cash in shops, restaurants and gas stations, and change from your transactions will be rendered in hard currency. Be sure to have plenty of $10 and $20 denominations, and don't be put off by "no checks" signs, which refer only to personal checks. Foreign travelers should not bring travelers' checks issued in their own currencies; it can be hard to find a bank prepared to change them, and no other business is likely to accept them.

## EMERGENCIES

Assuming you know someone who is prepared to send you money in a crisis, the quickest way is to have them take the cash to the nearest **American Express Moneygram** (☎1-800/543-4080) office and have it instantaneously **wired** to the office nearest you. In the US this process should take no longer than ten minutes. They charge according to the amount sent (ranging from $12 to wire $100, to $66 for $1000). The fees are slightly different if the money is being sent from outside the US (from the UK, for example, it costs $20 to wire $100, and $50 to wire $1000). **Western Union** offers a similar service, at slightly higher rates (US ☎1-800/325-6000; UK ☎0800/833833); if credit cards are involved they charge an extra $10.

If you have a few days' leeway, it's cheaper to mail a **postal money order**, which is exchangeable at any post office. The equivalent for foreign travelers is the **international money order**, for which you need to allow up to seven days in the mail before arrival. An ordinary check sent from overseas takes two to three weeks to clear.

Foreign travelers in real difficulties also have the final option of throwing themselves on the mercy of their nearest national **consulate** (see p.11), who will – in worst cases only – repatriate you, but will never, under any circumstances, lend you money.

# TELEPHONES, TIME ZONES, US MAIL AND EMAIL

**Visitors from overseas tend to be impressed by the speed and efficiency of communications in the US (with the exception of the US mail, which is incredibly slow and careless). In rural areas you may find it slightly frustrating just getting to the nearest public phone – which may be many miles away – but in general keeping in touch is easy.**

US **telephones** are run by a huge variety of local companies, many of which were hived off from the previous Bell System monopoly – the successor to which is the nationwide AT&T network.

**Public telephones** usually work, and in cities at any rate can be found everywhere – on street corners, in train and bus stations, hotel lobbies, bars and restaurants. They take 25¢, 10¢ and 5¢ coins. The cost of a **local call** from a public phone is usually 25¢ – when necessary, a voice comes on the line telling you to pay more.

Some numbers covered by the same area code are considered so far apart that calls between them count as **non-local** (zone calls). These cost much more and sometimes require you to dial 1 before the seven-digit number. Pricier still are **long-distance calls** (ie to a different area code,

again with the 1 in front), for which you'll need plenty of change. Non-local calls and long-distance calls are much less expensive if made between 6pm and 8am – the cheapest rates are 11pm–8am – and calls from **private phones** are always much cheaper than those from public phones. Detailed rates are listed at the front of the **telephone directory** (the *White Pages*, a copious source of information on many matters).

Making telephone calls from **hotel rooms** is usually generally more expensive than from a pay phone, though some budget hotels offer free local calls from rooms – ask when you check in. An increasing number of phones accept **credit cards**, while anyone who holds a credit card issued by an American bank can obtain an **AT&T calling card** (information on ☎1-800/225-5288).

Many government agencies, car rental firms, hotels and so on have **toll-free numbers**, which usually have the prefix ☎1-800 (or increasingly, ☎1-888 or ☎1-877). From within the US, you can dial any number that starts with those digits free of charge. Phone numbers with the prefix ☎1-900 are pay-per-call lines, generally quite expensive and almost always involving either sports or phone sex.

The US currently has around one hundred **area codes** – three-digit numbers that must precede the seven-figure number if you're calling from abroad or from a region with a different code. It can get confusing, especially as certain cities have several different area codes within their boundaries; for clarity, in this book, we've included the local area codes in all telephone numbers.

## US MAIL

**Post offices** are usually open Monday to Friday from 9am until 5pm, and Saturday from 9am to noon, and there are blue **mail boxes** on many street corners. Ordinary **mail within the US** costs 33¢ for a letter weighing up to an ounce; addresses must include the **zip code**, and a

## INTERNATIONAL TELEPHONE CALLS

**International calls** can be dialled direct from private or (more expensively) public phones. Most expensive of all is dialling direct from your hotel room, which often gets billed at the highest rate and then has a surcharge of up to forty percent slapped on top – so avoid doing this if at all possible. You can get assistance from the **international operator (☎ 00)**, who may also interrupt every three minutes asking for more money. The **lowest rates** for international calls to Europe are between 6pm and 7am, when the rate is about $5 for the first three minutes. In Britain, it's possible to obtain a free BT Chargecard (☎0800/800838), with which all calls from overseas can be charged to your quarterly domestic account. To use these cards in the US, or to make a **collect call** (to "reverse the charges"), dial one of the following access numbers to get a British operator: ☎1-800/445-5667; ☎1-800/444-2162; or ☎1-800/800-0008. British visitors who are going to be making a number of calls **to the US**, and who

want to be able to call toll-free ☎1-800 numbers, otherwise inaccessible from outside the US, should take advantage of **Swiftcall** telephone club (☎0800/769 0800). As long as you have a touch-tone phone, and pay for however many units you want in advance (minimum £25), you will be given a local access number to call and a PIN. Then when you want to make calls to the US, you simply dial the local number, punch in your PIN and then dial just as you would from within the US, remembering to put a 1 before the area code at the start of the number. Calls to the US are 5 1/2p per minute, from the US to the UK 23p per minute and calls within the US 23 1/2p per minute.

Visitors from **Australia** or **New Zealand** can also arrange to get a calling card which will allow them to make calls from the US. Options include: the **Telstra Telecard** (☎1800/626 008), the **Optus Calling Card** (☎1300/300 300), or the **New Zealand Telecom Calling Card** (☎04/382 5818).

To make international calls **TO THE US**, remember to add the country code, which is 1, before the area code and number.

To make international calls **FROM THE US**, dial 011 followed by the appropriate country code:
**Australia** 61     **New Zealand** 64     **United Kingdom** 44     **Ireland** 353

---

return address must be written on the envelope. **Air mail** between the US and Europe generally takes about a week. Postcards cost 55¢, aerograms are 60¢, while letters weighing up to half an ounce (a single thin sheet) are 60¢.

The last line of the address is made up of an abbreviation denoting the state (California is "CA," Texas is "TX," for example, though you can spell it in full if you're unsure; each abbreviation appears with the State Tourist Office addresses given on pp.20–22) and a five-figure number – the **zip code** – denoting the local post office. (The additional four digits you will sometimes see appended to zip codes are not essential.) Letters that don't carry the zip code are liable to get lost or at least delayed; if you don't know it, phone books carry a list for their service area, and post offices – even in Britain – have directories.

Letters can be sent c/o **General Delivery** (what's known elsewhere as **poste restante**) to the one relevant post office in each city (which we've listed in the *Guide*), but *must* include the

zip code and will be held for only thirty days before being returned to sender – so make sure there's a return address on the envelope. If you're receiving mail at someone else's address, it should include "c/o" and the regular occupant's name; otherwise it, too, is likely to be returned.

Rules on sending **parcels** are very rigid: packages must be in special containers bought from post offices and sealed according to their instructions, which are given at the start of the *Yellow Pages*. To send anything out of the country, you'll need a green **customs declaration form**, available from a post office.

## EMAIL

More and more, **email** is the way to keep in touch with friends and family when you're on the road. You'll find **cybercafes** (generally speaking, cafes in which you can access the Internet) in plenty of US cities, usually at rates of $7–10 an hour for computer use and Internet access. If you don't already have an email account, the best idea is to set up a **free account** before you leave, through a provider such as *hotmail.com, juno.com,* or *yahoo.com.*

## TELEGRAMS AND FAXES

To send a **telegram** (sometimes called a wire), don't go to a post office but to a Western Union office (listed in the *Yellow Pages*). Credit card holders can dictate messages over the phone. **International telegrams** cost slightly less than the cheapest international phone call: one sent in the morning from the US should arrive at its overseas destination the following day. For domestic telegrams ask for a **mailgram**, which will be delivered to any address in the country the next morning.

Public **fax** machines, which may require your credit card to be "swiped" through an attached device, are found at photocopy centers and, occasionally, bookstores.

## TIME ZONES

The continental US is so big that it spreads over four different time zones, plus another one for Alaska and Hawaii; these are shown on the map at the start of this book. The **Eastern** zone, which covers the area inland to the Great Lakes and the Appalachian Mountains, is five hours behind Greenwich Mean Time, so 10am London time is 5am in New York City. The **Central** zone, starting at Chicago and spreading west to Texas and the Great Plains, is an hour behind the East; the **Mountain** zone covers the Rocky Mountains and the Southwest states and is two behind the East Coast, seven behind Britain; and the **Pacific** zone includes the three coastal states and Nevada and is three hours behind New York, eight behind London. **Alaska** is another two hours behind the **Pacific** zone, as is Hawaii.

# INFORMATION AND MAPS

Each state in this book has its own tourist office, as listed on pp.20–22, which offers prospective visitors a colossal range of free maps, leaflets and brochures. Either contact them before you set off, or as you travel around the country look out for the state-run Welcome Centers, usually located along main highways close to the state borders. In the more heavily touristed states, these often have piles of valuable discount coupons for cut-price accommodation and food. In addition, visitor centers in most

towns and cities – often known as the "Convention and Visitors Bureau," or CVB, and listed throughout this book – provide details on the area.

The **USTTA** – United States Travel and Tourism Administration – has offices all over the world, usually in US embassies and consulates. These serve mainly as clearing houses, stocking vast quantities of printed material, but are unable to help with queries on specific states or cities. In Britain, you can contact them only by telephone, on ☎020/7495 4466 (Mon–Fri 10am–4pm).

## MAPS

The **free road maps** distributed by each state through its tourist offices and Welcome Centers are usually fine for general driving and route planning. For something more detailed, say for **hiking** purposes, camping shops generally have a good selection, and park ranger stations in national parks, state parks and wilderness areas all sell good-quality local hiking maps for $1–3.

Rand McNally produces good commercial maps, printed separately for each state, and bound together in the *Rand McNally Road Atlas*. They also run 24 stores across the US; call

## STATE TOURIST OFFICES

### Alabama
Alabama Bureau of Tourism &
Travel
PO Box 4927, Montgomery
AL 36103-4927 ☎334/242-4169
☎1-800/ALABAMA
www.touralabama.org

### Alaska
Alaska Division of Tourism
PO Box 110801, Juneau
AK 99811
☎907/465-2010
www.commerce.state.ak.us
/tourism

### Arizona
Arizona Office of Tourism
2702 N 3rd St, Suite 4015
Phoenix AZ 85004
☎602/230-7733
☎1-888/520-3434
www.arizonaguide.com

### Arkansas
Arkansas Dept of Parks &
Tourism
One Capitol Mall
Little Rock AR 72201
☎501/682-7777
☎1-800/628-8725
www.1800natural.com

### California
California Office of Tourism
801 K Street, Suite 1600
Sacramento CA 95814
☎916/322-2881
☎1-800/862-2543
www.gocalif.com

### Colorado
Colorado Tourism Board
1127 Pennsylvania St
Denver CO 80203
☎303/832-6171
☎1-800/433-2656
www.colorado.com

### Connecticut
Connecticut Tourism Division
505 Hudson St
Hartford CT 06106
☎860/270-8081
☎1-800/282-6863
www.ctbound.org

### Delaware
Delaware State Tourism Office
99 Kings Hwy
Dover DE 19901
☎302/739-4271
☎1-800/441-8846
www.state.de.us/tourism

### Florida
Florida Division of Tourism
Tallahassee FL 32399
☎850/488-5607
☎1-888/735-2872
www.flausa.com

### Georgia
Georgia Dept of Industry, Trade
& Tourism
285 Peachtree Center Ave,
Suite 1000
Atlanta GA 30303
☎404/656-3590
☎1-800/847-4842
www.georgia.org

### Hawaii
Hawaii Visitors Bureau
2270 Kalakaua Ave, Suite 801
Honolulu HI 96815
☎808/923-1811
☎1-800/464-2924
www.gohawaii.com

### Idaho
Idaho Travel Council
200 W State St
Boise ID 83720
☎208/334-2470
☎1-800/635-7820
www.visitid.org

### Illinois
Illinois Bureau of Tourism
100 W Randolph St, Suite
3–400
Chicago IL 60601
☎312/814-4732
☎1-800/226-6632
www.enjoyillinois.com

### Indiana
Indiana Dept of Tourism
1 N Capitol Ave, Suite 100
Indianapolis IN 46204-2288
☎317/232-8860
☎1-800/824-8376
www.indianatourism.com

### Iowa
Iowa Division of Tourism
200 E Grand Ave
Des Moines IA 50309
☎515/242-4705
☎1-888/472-6035
www.state.ia.us/tourism

### Kansas
Kansas Travel & Tourism
Division
700 SW Harrison St, Suite
1300
Topeka KS 66603
☎785/296-2009
☎1-800/252-6727
www.kansascommerce.com

### Kentucky
Kentucky Dept of Travel
500 Mero St, Suite 2200
Frankfort KY 40601
☎502/564-4930
☎1-800/225-8747
www.kentuckytourism.com

### Louisiana
Louisiana Office of Tourism
Box 94361
Baton Rouge LA 70804-4291
☎225/342-8100
☎1-800/677-4082
www.louisianatravel.com

### Maine
Maine Office of Tourism
33 Stone St, SHS59
Augusta ME 04333
☎207/623-0363
☎1-888/624-6345
www.visitmaine.com

### Maryland
Maryland Office of Tourism
100 Light St, 12th Floor
Baltimore MD 21202
☎410/659-7300
☎1-800/543-1036
www.mdisfun.org

### Massachusetts
Massachusetts Division of
Tourism
10 Park Plaza, Suite 8510
Boston MA 02116
☎617/727-3201

☎1-800/447-6277
*www.massvacation.com*

**Michigan**
Travel Michigan
201 N Washington Square, 2nd
Floor
Lansing MI 48913
☎517/373-0670
☎1-888/784-7328
*www.michigan.org*

**Minnesota**
Minnesota Office of Tourism
500 Metro Square
121 7th Place E
St Paul MN 55101
☎651/296-5029
☎1-800/657-3700
*www.exploreminnesota.com*

**Mississippi**
Mississippi Division of Tourism
PO Box 849
Jackson MS 39205-0849
☎601/359-3297
☎1-800/927-6378
*www.visitmississippi.org*

**Missouri**
Missouri Division of Tourism
PO Box 1055
Jefferson City MO 65102
☎573/751-4133
☎1-800/877-1234
*www.missouritourism.org*

**Montana**
Travel Montana
PO Box 200533
Helena MT 59620
☎406/422-1962
☎1-800/541-1447
*www.visitmt.org*

**Nebraska**
Nebraska Travel & Tourism
PO Box 98907
Lincoln NE 68509
☎402/471-3796
☎1-800/228-4307
*www.visitnebraska.org*

**Nevada**
Nevada Commission on
Tourism
401 N Carson St
Carson City NV 89701
☎775/687-4322

☎1-800/638-2328
*www.travelnevada.com*

**New Hampshire**
New Hampshire Office of
Travel
PO Box 1856
Concord NH 03302
☎603/271-2343
☎1-800/386-4664
*www.visitnh.gov*

**New Jersey**
New Jersey Division of Travel
& Tourism
PO Box 820
Trenton NJ 08625-820
☎609/292-2470
☎1-800/847-4865
*www.visitnj.org*

**New Mexico**
New Mexico Department of
Tourism
491 Old Santa Fe Trail
PO Box 20002
Santa Fe NM 87501
☎505/827-7400
☎1-800/733-6396
*www.newmexico.org*

**New York City**
New York City CVB
810 7th Ave
New York NY 10019
☎212/484-1222
☎1-877/446-8313
*www.nycvisit.com*

**New York State**
New York Division of Tourism
PO Box 2603
Albany NY 12220
☎518/474-4116
☎1-800/225-5697
*www.iloveny.state.ny.us*

**North Carolina**
North Carolina Travel &
Tourism
301 N Wilmington St
Raleigh NC 27601-2825
☎919/733-4171
☎1-800/847-4862
*www.visitnc.com*

**North Dakota**
North Dakota Tourism Division
604 E Boulevard Ave

Bismarck ND 58505
☎701/328-2525
☎1-800/435-5663
*www.ndtourism.com*

**Ohio**
Ohio Office of Travel & Tourism
PO Box 1001
Columbus OH 43266
☎614/466-8844
☎1-800/848-1300
*www.ohiotourism.com*

**Oklahoma**
Oklahoma Tourism &
Recreation
15 N Robinson St, Suite 801
Oklahoma City OK 73102
☎405/521-2409
☎1-800/652-6552
*www.touroklahoma.com*

**Oregon**
Oregon Tourism Commission
775 Summer St NE
Salem OR 97310
☎503/986-0000
☎1-800/547-7842
*www.traveloregon.com*

**Pennsylvania**
Pennsylvania Bureau of Travel
Room 404, Forum Building
Harrisburg PA 17120
☎717/787-5453
☎1-800/847-4872
*www.state.pa.us*

**Rhode Island**
Rhode Island Tourism Division
One W Exchange St
Providence RI 02903
☎401/222-2601
☎1-800/556-2484
*www.visitrhodeisland.com*

**South Carolina**
South Carolina Parks,
Recreation and Tourism
Dept of International
Marketing
1205 Pendleton St
Columbia SC 29201
☎803/734-0129
☎1-800/346-3634
*www.travelsc.com*

*continued overleaf*

**South Dakota**
South Dakota Dept of Tourism
711 E Wells Ave
Pierre SD 57501
☎605/773-3301
☎1-800/732-5682
www.travelsd.com

**Tennessee**
Tennessee Dept of Tourism
Rachel Jackson Building
320 6th Ave, 5th Floor
Nashville TN 37243
☎615/741-2158
☎1-800/462-8366
www.tourism.state.tn.us

**Texas**
Texas Dept of Commerce,
Tourism Division
Box 141009
Austin TX 78714-1009
☎512/462-9191
☎1-800/888-8839
www.traveltex.com

**Utah**
Utah Travel Council
Council Hall
Capitol Hill
Salt Lake City UT 84114

☎801/538-1030
☎1-800/200-1160
www.utah.com

**Vermont**
Vermont Travel Division
134 State St
Montpelier VT 05602
☎802/828-3236
☎1-800/837-6668
www.1-800-vermont.com

**Virginia**
Virginia Division of Tourism
901 E Bird St
Richmond VA 23219
☎804/786-4484
☎1-800/847-4882
www.virginia.org

**Washington**
Washington State Tourism
PO Box 42500
Olympia WA 98504
☎360/586-2102
☎1-800/544-1800
www.tourism.wa.gov

**Washington DC**
Washington DC Visitor
Information
1212 New York Ave NW, Suite

200
Washington DC 20005
☎202/789-7000
☎1-800/422-8644
www.washington.org

**West Virginia**
West Virginia Division of
Tourism
2101 Washington St E
PO Box 50312
Charleston WV 25305
☎304/558-2766
☎1-800/225-5982
www.callwva.com

**Wisconsin**
Wisconsin Department of
Tourism
PO Box 7606
Madison WI 53707
☎608/266-2161
☎1-800/432-8747
www.travelwiscon.com

**Wyoming**
Wyoming Division of Tourism
I-25 at College Drive
Cheyenne WY 82002
☎307/777-7777
☎1-800/225-5996
www.wyomingtourism.org

☎1-800/333-0136 (ext 2111) for their locations, or for direct-mail maps. Britain's best source of maps is Stanfords, at 12–14 Long Acre, London WC2E 9LP (☎020/7836 1321), who have a mail-order service.

The American Automobile Association (AAA; ☎1-800/222-4357 or 303/753-8800), based at 4100 E Arkansas Drive, Denver, CO 80222, provides free maps and assistance to its members, and to British members of the AA and RAC. Call the main number to get the location of a branch close to your point of arrival, and remember to bring your membership card, or at least know your membership number.

# GETTING AROUND

**Distances in the US are so great that it's essential to think carefully in advance about how you plan to get from place to place. Your choice of transportation will have a crucial impact on your trip. Amtrak provides a skeletal but often scenic rail service, and there are usually good bus links between the major cities – though Greyhound, the mainstay of the US bus network, has cut back on non-profitable routes of late. Things are liable to get difficult only in isolated rural areas – and even here, by adroit forward planning, you'll usually be able to reach the main points of interest without too much trouble by using local buses and charter services, as detailed state-by-state throughout this book.**

It has to be said, however, that things are always easier if you have a **car**. Many of the most worthwhile and memorable destinations in the United States are far removed from the cities. Even if a bus or train can take you to the general vicinity of one of the great national parks, for example, it can be nearly impossible to explore the area without your own vehicle. For that matter, the cities themselves can be so vast, and so heavily car-oriented, that the lack of a car can seriously impair your enjoyment.

At the end of the introduction to each individual state in this book, a "**Getting Around**" section summarizes local transportation options.

For all information on **Amtrak fares and schedules** in the US, and to make reservations, use the toll-free number:
**☎1-800/USA-RAIL**
Alternatively, check out the Amtrak **Web site:** *www.amtrak.com*
Do not phone individual stations.

## BY TRAIN

Traveling by **rail** is rarely the fastest way of getting from A to B, though if you have the time it can be a pleasant and relaxing experience. As you will see from our map, overleaf, the Amtrak system isn't at all comprehensive – such popular destinations as Nashville and Santa Fe, and even some entire states, are missed out altogether. What's more, the cross-country routes tend to be served by one or at most two trains per day, so in large areas of the nation the only train of the day passes through at three or four in the morning. That said, the train is by far the most comfortable way to travel, and especially on long-distance rides it can be a great way to meet people. There are also a number of local train services that connect stops on the Amtrak lines with towns and cities not on the main grid.

Amtrak also runs the coordinated Thruway bus service which connects some cities that their trains don't reach. However, this network is not in the least comprehensive.

For any one specific journey, the train can be more expensive than taking a Greyhound or even a plane – the standard fare from New York to Los Angeles, for example, is around $300 one-way – though special deals, especially in the off-peak seasons (Sept–May), bring the cost of a coast-to-coast round-trip down to well under $350 (closer to $250 at certain times). In addition to these, Amtrak's **All Aboard America** fares, allowing three stopovers en route, are available by region (Florida, for some reason, is excluded). Foreign travelers can benefit from the **passes** detailed on p.25.

Always **reserve** as far in advance as possible; all passengers must have seats, and some trains, especially between major East Coast cities, are booked solid. Supplements are also payable, for

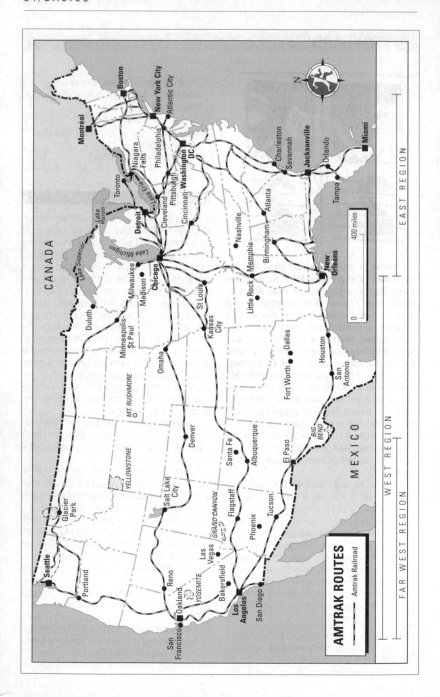

AMTRAK ROUTES

——— Amtrak Railroad

**sleeping compartments** (which cost around $100 per night for one or two people, including three full meals), and for the plush Metroliner carriages, for example. Even standard Amtrak carriages are surprisingly spacious, and there are additional dining cars and lounge cars (with full bars and sometimes glass-domed 360° viewing compartments).

## ADVANCE PLANNING FOR OVERSEAS TRAVELERS

### AMTRAK USA RAIL PASSES

Overseas travelers have a choice of the following **USA Rail Passes**, covering the areas shown on our map; the **Coastal Pass** permits unlimited train travel on the East and West coasts, but not between the two.

|  | 15-day (June–Aug) | 15-day (Sept–May) | 30-day (June–Aug) | 30-day (Sept–May) |
|---|---|---|---|---|
| **East** | $260 | $210 | $320 | $265 |
| **Far West** | $245 | $190 | $320 | $250 |
| **Northeast** | $205 | $185 | $240 | $225 |
| **West** | $325 | $200 | $405 | $270 |
| **Coastal** | – | – | $285 | $235 |
| **National** | $440 | $295 | $550 | $385 |

On production of a passport issued outside the US or Canada, the passes can be bought at Amtrak stations in the US. The Amtrak Web site lists several places you can buy them across the **UK**, including Destination Marketing, Molasses House, Clove Hitch Quay, Plantation Wharf, London SW11 3TN (☎020/7400 7099, fax 7400 7088); in **Ireland**, contact Campus Travel/Eurotrain (☎01/874 1777); in **Australia**, Thomas Cook World Rail (☎1300/361 941); and in **New Zealand**, Walshes World (☎09/379 3708).

### GREYHOUND AMERIPASSES

Foreign visitors intending to travel virtually every day by bus (which is unlikely), or to venture further around the US, can buy a Greyhound **Ameripass**, offering unlimited travel within a set time limit, before leaving home: most travel agents can oblige. In the UK, they cost £75 (4-day), £85 (5-day), £110 (7-day), £170 (15-day), £230 (30-day) or £340 (60-day). No daily extensions are available. Greyhound's **UK** office is at Sussex House, London Road, East Grinstead, West Sussex RH19 1LD (☎01342/317317).

Walshes World (☎02/9232 7499 or 1800/227 122 in **Australia**; ☎09/379 3708 in **New Zealand**) are the Greyhound agents down under, though you can also get passes from most travel agents.

The first time you use your pass, it will be dated by the ticket clerk (this becomes the commencement date of the ticket), and your destination is written on a page which the driver will tear out and keep as you board the bus. Repeat this procedure for every subsequent journey.

### AIRPASSES

All the main American airlines (and British Airways in conjunction with various carriers) offer airpasses for visitors who plan to fly a lot within the US: these have to be bought in advance, and in the UK are usually sold with the proviso that you cross the Atlantic with the relevant airline. All the deals are broadly similar, involving the purchase of between three and ten coupons; United, for instance, charges British travelers between £249 and £279 for three **Visit USA** coupons and £479 to £499 for ten depending on the season. Each coupon is valid for a flight of any duration in the 48 contiguous US states – you purchase additional coupons for flights to Alaska, Hawaii, the Caribbean and Mexico at varying rates. The situation is similar for Australasian visitors.

Other schemes entitle foreign travelers to discounts on regular US domestic fares, again with the proviso that you buy the ticket before you leave home. However you do it, flying within the US is only a wise choice for travel in regions where fares are low anyway; flights within Florida, for example, are very expensive.

Beautiful East Coast Amtrak rides include the Hudson River Valley north of New York City (on the Adirondack route among others); along the Potomac River at Harpers Ferry, West Virginia (on the *Capitol Limited* out of Washington DC); and the New River Gorge (on the *Cardinal*). In the West the sights only get bigger and better: the *California Zephyr*, between Chicago and San Francisco, follows a stunning route up and over the Rockies west of Denver, rivaled a day later by the towering Sierra Nevada, while the *Coast Starlight* gives unsurpassed views of the California coast on its journey between San Luis Obispo and Santa Barbara. Try to make sure when you book your journey that the train passes through during daylight hours.

## HISTORIC RAILROADS

While Amtrak has a monopoly on long-distance rail travel, a number of **historic** or **scenic railways**, some of them steam-powered or running along narrow-gauge mining tracks, do much to bring back the glory days of train travel. Many are purely tourist attractions, doing a full circuit through beautiful countryside in two or three hours, though some can drop you off in otherwise hard-to-reach wilderness areas. Popular lines include the **Cass**

**Scenic Railroad** in West Virginia (☎304/456-4300; *www.neumedia.net/~cassar*); the **Cumbres and Toltec** line in Chama, New Mexico (☎505/756-2151; *www.cumbresandtoltec.com*); **Durango & Silverton Narrow Gauge Railroad** in Colorado (☎970/247-2733; *www.durangotrain.com*); the **Big Trees and Roaring Camp Railroad** in Santa Cruz (☎831/335-4400; *www.roaringcamprr.com*), and the **Fort Bragg–Willits** line (☎707/964-6371; *www.skunktrain.com*), both in California; and the **Mount Hood Railroad** (☎541/386-3556; *www.mthoodrr.com*) outside Portland, Oregon

## BY BUS

If you're traveling on your own, and making a lot of stops, **buses** are by far the cheapest way to get around. The main long-distance operator is **Greyhound**, which links all major cities and many smaller towns. Out in the country, buses are fairly scarce, sometimes appearing only once a day, and here you'll need to plot your route with care. But along the main highways, buses run around the clock to a fairly full timetable, stopping only for meal breaks (almost always fast-food dives) and driver changeovers. Greyhound buses are slightly less uncomfortable than you

## GREEN TORTOISE

One alternative to Long-Distance Bus Hell is the slightly countercultural **Green Tortoise**, whose buses, complete with foam cushions, bunks, fridges and rock music, ply the major cities of the West Coast, running between Los Angeles, San Francisco and Seattle. In summer, they also cross the country to New York and Boston, transcontinental trips which amount to mini-tours of the nation, taking around a dozen days (at a current cost of between $349 and $389, not including food), and allowing plenty of stops for hiking, river-rafting, and hot springs. Other Green Tortoise trips include excursions to the major national parks (in 16 days for $499), and north to Alaska ($1500 for 28 days). Main Office: 494 Broadway, San Francisco, CA 94133 (☎415/956-7500 or 1-800/TORTOISE; *www.greentortoise.com*).

## EAST COAST EXPLORER

Another alternative to Greyhound, the **East Coast Explorer** runs budget-priced buses between Boston and Washington DC, picking up and dropping off passengers at hostels, hotels, motels, airports and just about anywhere else along the way. Avoiding the freeways, and stopping off at points of historic, natural or cultural interest en route, the East Coast Explorer is a great way for car-less visitors to get around the otherwise frustrating northeastern USA.

Buses run about once a week on a variety of routes, and cost little more than Greyhound – the trip from New York to Washington DC via the Pennsylvania Dutch Country, for instance, costs around $35. There's also a three-day return trip from New York City to Niagara Falls. Main Office: 210 Congress St, Brooklyn, NY 10011 (☎1-800/610-2680).

Greyhound's nationwide **toll-free informa-tion service** can give you routes and times, plus phone numbers and addresses of local ter-minals. You can also make reservations.

**☎1-800/231-2222**

Alternatively, check out the Greyhound **Web site**: *www.greyhound.com*.

might expect, too, and it's feasible to save on a night's accommodation by traveling overnight and sleeping on the bus – though you may not feel up to much the next day.

To avoid possible hassle, lone female travelers in particular should take care to sit as near to the driver as possible, and to arrive during daylight hours – many bus stations are in fairly dodgy areas. It used to be that any sizeable community would have a Greyhound station; in some places the post office or a filling station doubles as the bus stop and ticket office, and in many others the bus ser-vice has been canceled altogether. **Reservations**, either in person at the station or on the toll-free number, are not essential, but recommended – if a bus is full you may be forced to wait until the next one, sometimes overnight or longer.

**Fares** on shorter journeys average about 10¢ a mile, but discounts are common on longer hauls (for example it will cost you $69 to get a round-trip ticket from Los Angeles to San Francisco, but for $205 you could get all the way to New York and back). For long-trip travel though, considering the time expended (around 75 hours coast-to-coast, if you eat and sleep on the bus), riding the bus is not necessarily a much better deal than flying. However, the bus is the best deal if you plan to visit a lot of places: Greyhound's **Ameripasses** for domestic travelers are good for unlimited travel nationwide for 7 days ($199), 15 days ($309) and 30 days ($419); the reduced rates for foreign travelers (typically a saving of $20–40 per pass) are given in the box on p.25.

Greyhound produces a condensed **timetable** of major countrywide routes, but this is not dis-tributed to travelers; to plan your route, pick up the free route-by-route timetables from larger stations.

## BY PLANE

Don't be too misled by the scenes from the movies in which characters stroll into large air-ports and casually buy cross-country air tickets;

that kind of plane travel is outrageously expensive – $1000 for a one-way flight is not unheard of. However, if you plan ahead, **air travel** can work out reasonably cheap, as well as obviously being the quickest way to get around. Indeed, it can cost less than the train – especially if you take into account how much you save not having to pay for food and drink while on the move – and only a lit-tle more than the bus. Flying can also make sense for relatively short local hops, turning a full day's cross-desert $25 bus journey, for example, into a quick and scenic $50 flight of under an hour. We mention such options wherever appropriate.

Most airlines offer comparable Apex fares, but any good **travel agent**, especially student and youth-oriented ones like Council Travel and STA, can usually get you a much better deal. Phone the airlines to find out routes and schedules, then buy your ticket using the **Fare Assurance Program**, which processes all the ticket options to find the cheapest fare, taking into account the require-ments of individual travelers. One agent using the service is Travel Avenue (☎1-800/333-3335). Few standby fares are available, and the best discounts are usually offered on tickets booked and paid for at least two weeks in advance, which are almost always non-refundable and hard to change.

## BY CAR

For many people, the concept of cruising down the highway, preferably in an open-top convert-ible with the radio blaring, is one of the main rea-sons to set out on a tour of the US. The romantic images of countless road movies, from *Bonnie and Clyde* to *Thelma and Louise*, are not far from the truth, though you don't have to embark on a wild spree of drink, drugs, crime and murder to enjoy driving across America. Apart from anything else, a car makes it possible to choose your own itinerary and to explore the wide-open landscapes that may well provide your most enduring memo-ries of the continent.

Driving in the **cities**, on the other hand, is not exactly fun, but places tend to be so large that a car is by far the most convenient way to negotiate your way around, especially as public transporta-tion is all but nonexistent outside the major metropolises. Many cities, especially in the West, have grown up and assumed their present shape since cars were invented, sprawling for so many miles in all directions – Los Angeles and Houston are classic examples – that your hotel may be fif-

## TOLL-FREE AIRLINE NUMBERS IN THE US

| | | | |
|---|---|---|---|
| **Aer Lingus**<br>www.aerlingus.ie | ☎1-800/474-7424 | **Iberia**<br>www.iberia.com | ☎1-800/772-4642 |
| **Air Canada**<br>www.aircanada.ca | ☎1-800/776-3000 | **Icelandair**<br>www.icelandair.com | ☎1-800/223-5500 |
| **Air France**<br>www.airfrance.fr | ☎1-800/237-2747 | **Japan Air Lines**<br>www.jal.co.jp | ☎1-800/525-3663 |
| **Alaska Airlines**<br>www.alaskaair.com | ☎1-800/426-0333 | **KLM**<br>www.klm.com | ☎1-800/374-7747 |
| **Alitalia**<br>www.alitalia.it | ☎1-800/223-5730 | **Lufthansa**<br>www.lufthansa.com | ☎1-800/645-3880 |
| **America West**<br>www.americawest.com | ☎1-800/235-9292 | **Northwest Airlines**<br>www.nwa.com | ☎1-800/447-4747 |
| **American Airlines**<br>www.americanair.com | ☎1-800/433-7300 | **Qantas Airways**<br>www.qantas.com | ☎1-800/227-4500 |
| **American Trans Air**<br>www.ata.com | ☎1-800/435-9282 | **SAS**<br>www.flysas.com | ☎1-800/221-2350 |
| **British Airways**<br>www.british-airways.com | ☎1-800/247-9297 | **Skywest**<br>www.delta-air.com | ☎1-800/453-9417 |
| **Canadian Airlines**<br>www.cdnair.ca | ☎1-800/426-7000 | **Southwest**<br>www.southwest.com | ☎1-800/435-9792 |
| **Cathay Pacific**<br>www.cathay-usa.com | ☎1-800/233-2742 | **Swissair**<br>www.swissair.com | ☎1-800/221-4750 |
| **Continental Airlines**<br>www.continental.com | ☎1-800/231-0856 | **Tower Air**<br>www.towerair.com | ☎1-800/348-6937 |
| **Delta Air Lines**<br>www.delta-air.com | ☎1-800/241-4141 | **TWA**<br>www.twa.com | ☎1-800/221-2000 |
| **El Al**<br>www.elal.com | ☎1-800/223-6700 | **United Airlines**<br>www.ual.com | ☎1-800/538-2929 |
| **Garuda Indonesia**<br>www.garuda.co.id | ☎1-800/342-7832 | **US Airways**<br>www.usairways.com | ☎1-800/622-1015 |
| **Hawaiian Airlines**<br>www.hawaiianair.com | ☎1-800/367-5320 | **Virgin Atlantic**<br>www.virgin-atlantic.com | ☎1-800/862-8621 |

teen or twenty miles from the sights you came to see, or perhaps simply on the other side of a freeway which can't be crossed on foot. Only on the East Coast, and perhaps Chicago, are the main attractions and facilities concentrated within walking distance of each other. Even in smaller towns the motels may be six miles or more out along the interstate, and the restaurants in a brand-new shopping mall on the far side of town.

Drivers wishing to **rent** cars are supposed to have held their licenses for at least one year (though this is rarely checked); people under 25 years old may encounter problems, and will probably get lumbered with a higher than normal insurance premium. Car rental companies (listed opposite) will also expect you to have a credit card; if you don't have one they may let you leave

a hefty deposit (at least $200), but don't count on it. The likeliest tactic for getting a good deal is to phone the major firms' toll-free numbers and ask for their best rate – most will try to beat the offers of their competitors, so it's worth haggling.

In general the lowest rates are available at the airport branches – $149 a week for a compact is a fairly standard budget rate. Always be sure to get free unlimited mileage, and be aware that leaving the car in a different city to the one in which you rent it will incur a **drop-off charge** that can be as much as $200 or more. Also, don't automatically go for the cheapest rate, as there's a big difference in the quality of cars from company to company; industry leaders like Alamo, Hertz and Avis tend to have newer, lower-mileage cars, often with air conditioning and stereo cassette decks as standard equipment – no small consideration on a 2000-mile desert drive.

Alternatively, various **local** companies rent out new – and not so new (try Rent-a-Wreck) – vehicles. They are certainly cheaper than the big chains if you just want to spin around a city for a day, but free mileage is not included, so they work out far more costly for long-distance travel. Addresses and phone numbers are documented in the *Yellow Pages*.

When you rent a car, read the small print carefully for details on **Collision Damage Waiver (CDW)**, sometimes called Liability Damage Waiver (LDW) usually included in the price if you pre-pay outside the US, but well worth considering if it isn't. This form of insurance specifically covers the car that you are driving yourself – you are in any case insured for damage to other vehicles. At $9–13 a day, it can add substantially to the total cost, but without it you're liable for every scratch to the car – even those that aren't your fault. Some credit card companies offer automatic CDW coverage to Americans and Canadians using their card; read the fine print beforehand in any case.

Increasing numbers of states (New York for one) are requiring that this insurance be included in the weekly rental rate, and are regulating the amounts charged to cut down on rental-car company profiteering. Companies are also becoming more particular about checking up on the driving records of would-be renters and refusing to rent to high-risk drivers.

## CAR RENTAL COMPANIES

| | US | UK | Ireland | Australia | New Zealand |
|---|---|---|---|---|---|
| **Alamo**<br>*www.goalamo.com* | ☎1-800/354-2322 | ☎0800/272200 | | | |
| **Avis**<br>*www.avis.com* | ☎1-800/331-1084 | ☎0990/900500 | ☎028/9024 0404 | ☎1800/225 533 | ☎09/526 2847 |
| **Budget**<br>*www.drivebudget.com* | ☎1-800/527-0700 | ☎0800/181181 | ☎028/9023 0700 | ☎13/2727 | ☎09/375 2222 |
| **Dollar**<br>*www.dollar.com* | ☎1-800/800-6000 | ☎01895/233300 | | | |
| **Enterprise**<br>*www.pickenterprise.com* | ☎1-800/325-8007 | | | | |
| **Hertz**<br>*www.hertz.com* | ☎1-800/654-3001 | ☎0990/996699 | ☎01/660 2255 | ☎13/3039 | ☎09/309 0989 |
| **Holiday Autos**<br>*www.kemwel.com* | ☎1-800/422-7737 | ☎0990/300400 | ☎01/454 9090 | | |
| **National**<br>*www.nationalcar.com* | ☎1-800/227-7368 | ☎01345/222525 | ☎028/9045 0904 | | |
| **Rent-a-Wreck**<br>*www.rent-a-wreck.com* | ☎1-800/535-1391 | | | | |
| **Thrifty**<br>*www.thrifty.com* | ☎1-800/367-2277 | ☎01494/442110 | | | |

## DRIVING FOR FOREIGNERS

UK nationals can drive in the US on a **full UK driving license** (International Driving Permits are not always regarded as sufficient). Fly-drive deals are good value if you want to **rent** a car (see p.6), though you can save up to sixty percent simply by booking in advance with a major firm. If you choose not to pay until you arrive, be sure you take a written confirmation of the price with you. Remember that it's safer not to drive straight after a long transatlantic flight; and that most standard rental cars have **automatic transmissions**.

It's also easier and cheaper to book **RVs** in advance from Britain. Most travel agents who specialize in the US can arrange RV rental, and usually do it cheaper if you book a flight through them as well. A price of £400 for a five-berth van for two weeks is fairly typical.

Specific information on public transportation and car rental for travelers with disabilities can be found on p.33.

Another policy that rental companies try to get you to accept (and they've trained their staff to drive fear deep into your soul about this one) is **liability cover** if you cause injury to others whilst in a rental car. This usually costs around the same as CDW and when both these are taken together with taxes can double the cost of the rental. It's worth reading the small print of your holiday insurance to see if you are covered: the American Express annual policy includes up to $1 million coverage (☎0800/700707 in the UK) and the policy pays for itself in a fortnight.

In case you **break down** in a rented car, there's an emergency number pinned to the dashboard. Otherwise you should sit tight and wait for the highway patrol or state police, who cruise by regularly. Raising your car hood is recognized as a call for assistance, although women traveling alone should be wary of doing this. Another tip, for women especially, is to rent a **mobile telephone** from the car rental agency – you often have to pay only a nominal amount until you actually use it, and in larger cities they increasingly come built into the car. Having a phone can be reassuring at least, and a potential lifesaver should something go wrong (see p.15)

## DRIVEAWAYS

One variation on renting is a **driveaway**, whereby you drive a car from one place to another on behalf of the owner, paying only for the petrol you use. The same rules as for renting apply, but look the car over before you take it, as you'll be lumbered with any repair costs, and a large fuel bill if the vehicle's a big drinker. Some driveaway companies want a personal reference from someone either in the town you're leaving or in the car's eventual destination, and it makes obvious sense to get in touch in advance, to spare yourself a week's wait for a car to turn up. The most common routes are between the coasts, although there's a fair chance of finding something that needs shifting to where you want to go. You needn't drive flat out, although four hundred miles a day is expected. Look under "Automobile Transporters" in the *Yellow Pages* and phone around for current offers; or try one of the sixty

branches of Auto Driveaway, based at 310 S Michigan Ave, Chicago, IL 60604 (☎312/341-1900; *www.autodriveaway.com*).

## RENTING AN RV

Besides cars, Recreational Vehicles or **RVs** – those huge juggernauts that rumble down the highway complete with multiple bedrooms, bathrooms and kitchens – can be rented from around $400 per week (plus mileage charges) for a basic camper on the back of a pickup truck. Though good for groups or families traveling together, these can be unwieldy on the road. Also, rental outlets are not as common as you might expect, as people tend to own their RVs. On top of the rental fees, take into account the cost of gas (some RVs do twelve miles to the gallon or less) and any drop-off charges, in case you plan to do a one-way trip across the country. Also, it is rarely legal simply to pull up in an RV and spend the night at the roadside; you are expected to stay in designated parks that cost up to $20 per night. The Recreational Vehicle Dealers Association, 3930 University Drive, Fairfax, VA 22030 (☎703/591-7130 or 1-800/336-0355; *www.rvda.com*), publishes a newsletter and a directory of rental firms. Among the larger companies offering RV rentals are Cruise America (☎1-800/327-7799; *www.cruiseamerica.com*) and Grand Travel Systems (☎602/939-6909 or 1-877/478-7368).

## BY BIKE

In general, **cycling** is a cheap and healthy method of getting around all the big **cities**, some of which have cycle lanes and local buses equipped to carry bikes (strapped to the outside). For a $10 fee, Greyhound will take bikes (so long as they're in a box), and Amtrak charges $5 every time you board with one. In **country areas**, roads are usually well maintained and have wide shoulders. A number of companies organize multiday cycle tours, either camping out or staying in country inns; we've mentioned local firms where appropriate. The biggest of the nationwide organizations is the

The usual advice given to **hitchhikers** is that they should use their common sense; but common sense should tell anyone that hitchhiking in the United States is a **bad idea**. We do not recommend it under any circumstances.

# Driving Distances In Miles

The distances shown on this chart represent the total mileages between selected cities and national parks in the US and Canada. They are calculated according to the shortest available route by road, and are thus higher than figures obtained by drawing a straight line on a map.

| From \ To | Albuquerque | Atlanta | Boston | Chicago | Dallas | Denver | Grand Canyon NP | Great Smoky Mtns NP | Las Vegas | Los Angeles | Memphis | Miami | Nashville | New Orleans | New York | Orlando | St Louis | Salt Lake City | San Francisco | Seattle | Washington DC | Yellowstone NP | Yosemite NP | Montréal |
|---|---|---|---|---|---|---|---|---|---|---|---|---|---|---|---|---|---|---|---|---|---|---|---|---|
| Albuquerque NM | | | | | | | | | | | | | | | | | | | | | | | | |
| Atlanta GA | 1404 | | | | | | | | | | | | | | | | | | | | | | | |
| Boston MA | 2220 | 1108 | | | | | | | | | | | | | | | | | | | | | | |
| Chicago IL | 1312 | 708 | 994 | | | | | | | | | | | | | | | | | | | | | |
| Dallas TX | 644 | 822 | 1753 | 921 | | | | | | | | | | | | | | | | | | | | |
| Denver CO | 437 | 1430 | 1998 | 1021 | 784 | | | | | | | | | | | | | | | | | | | |
| Grand Canyon NP AZ | 407 | 1818 | 2627 | 1732 | 1051 | 708 | | | | | | | | | | | | | | | | | | |
| Great Smoky Mtns NP | 1457 | 177 | 917 | 585 | 905 | 1385 | 1831 | | | | | | | | | | | | | | | | | |
| Las Vegas NV | 586 | 1979 | 2752 | 1780 | 1230 | 758 | 283 | 2036 | | | | | | | | | | | | | | | | |
| Los Angeles CA | 811 | 2191 | 3017 | 2046 | 1399 | 1031 | 555 | 2254 | 272 | | | | | | | | | | | | | | | |
| Memphis TN | 1010 | 382 | 1341 | 537 | 454 | 1043 | 1416 | 450 | 1603 | 1807 | | | | | | | | | | | | | | |
| Miami FL | 1970 | 663 | 1520 | 1397 | 1343 | 2107 | 2499 | 614 | 2570 | 2716 | 997 | | | | | | | | | | | | | |
| Nashville TN | 1225 | 246 | 1092 | 466 | 659 | 1184 | 1610 | 221 | 2011 | 1811 | 209 | 910 | | | | | | | | | | | | |
| New Orleans LA | 1157 | 480 | 1507 | 919 | 517 | 1277 | 1548 | 622 | 1858 | 1732 | 414 | 860 | 532 | | | | | | | | | | | |
| New York NY | 1997 | 854 | 208 | 809 | 1559 | 1794 | 2401 | 706 | 2572 | 2794 | 1102 | 1334 | 900 | 1335 | | | | | | | | | | |
| Orlando FL | 1741 | 426 | 1301 | 1147 | 1098 | 1879 | 2271 | 614 | 2350 | 2429 | 776 | 229 | 688 | 648 | 1092 | | | | | | | | | |
| St Louis MO | 1042 | 565 | 1207 | 289 | 655 | 863 | 1449 | 522 | 1620 | 1836 | 283 | 1226 | 321 | 698 | 976 | 1004 | | | | | | | | |
| Salt Lake City UT | 604 | 1934 | 2376 | 1417 | 1257 | 534 | 365 | 1910 | 419 | 691 | 1551 | 2566 | 1703 | 1775 | 2189 | 2337 | 1362 | | | | | | | |
| San Francisco CA | 1109 | 2483 | 3128 | 2173 | 1752 | 1255 | 954 | 2592 | 570 | 387 | 2116 | 3093 | 2325 | 2278 | 2930 | 2871 | 2118 | 752 | | | | | | |
| Seattle WA | 1453 | 2625 | 3016 | 2052 | 2131 | 1341 | 1213 | 2630 | 1180 | 1134 | 2317 | 3303 | 2442 | 2590 | 2841 | 3088 | 2135 | 848 | 810 | | | | | |
| Washington DC | 1849 | 618 | 448 | 709 | 1307 | 1616 | 2304 | 469 | 2420 | 2646 | 854 | 1057 | 659 | 1099 | 237 | 856 | 862 | 2048 | 2843 | 2721 | | | | |
| Yellowstone NP WY | 973 | 1944 | 2382 | 1388 | 1343 | 563 | 755 | 1907 | 809 | 1081 | 1604 | 2568 | 1712 | 1840 | 2213 | 2432 | 1385 | 390 | 1027 | 827 | 2081 | | | |
| Yosemite NP CA | 971 | 2375 | 2961 | 2021 | 1634 | 1000 | 641 | 2384 | 358 | 348 | 1946 | 2928 | 2184 | 2096 | 2777 | 2708 | 1863 | 558 | 182 | 928 | 2616 | 1003 | | |
| Montréal Canada | 2131 | 1199 | 310 | 847 | 1770 | 1824 | 2542 | 1035 | 2583 | 2855 | 1315 | 1649 | 1112 | 1651 | 382 | 1462 | 1101 | 2225 | 2959 | 2714 | 607 | 2009 | 2644 | |
| Toronto Canada | 1787 | 1011 | 609 | 515 | 1435 | 1492 | 2198 | 807 | 2251 | 2523 | 956 | 1494 | 776 | 1307 | 516 | 1346 | 749 | 1910 | 2823 | 2564 | 571 | 1910 | 2303 | 344 |
| Vancouver Canada | 1590 | 2756 | 3155 | 2173 | 2234 | 1484 | 1357 | 2774 | 1322 | 1278 | 2461 | 3447 | 2566 | 2734 | 2943 | 3232 | 2191 | 990 | 954 | 144 | 2887 | 971 | 1072 | 3014 |

Note: Vancouver Canada to Toronto Canada = 2820 miles.

nonprofit Adventure Cycling Association (formerly Bikecentennial), at 150 E Pine St, PO Box 8308, Missoula, MT 59807 (☎406/721-1776; *www .adv-cycling.org*), founded in 1974 as part of the national bicentennial celebrations, to promote transcontinental cycle trips. It publishes **maps** ($10.50 each) of several 400-mile routes, detailing campgrounds, motels, restaurants, bike shops and sites of interest. Many individual states issue their own cycling guides; contact the tourist offices listed on pp.20–22. Backroads Bicycle Tours, 1516 Fifth St, Berkeley, CA 94704 (☎510/527-1555 or 1-800/462-2848; *www.backroads.com*), and the HI-AYH hosteling group (see p.39) also arrange group tours.

For more casual riding, bikes can be **rented** for $15 to $30 per day, or at discounted weekly rates, from outlets that are usually found close to beaches, university campuses, or simply in areas that are good for cycling, although rates in heavily touristed areas can be much higher. Local visitor centers should have details. Before setting out on a **long-distance cycling** trip, you'll need a good-quality, multispeed bike, panniers, tools and spares, maps, padded shorts, a **helmet** (not a legal obligation but a very good idea), and a route avoiding interstates (on which cycling is unpleasant and usually illegal). Of **problems** you'll encounter, the main one is traffic – RVs driven by buffoons who can't judge their width, and huge eighteen-wheelers (or in the western states, logging trucks) that scream past and create intense backdrafts capable of pulling you out into the middle of the road.

## TRAVELERS WITH DISABILITIES

**By international standards, the US is exceptionally accommodating for travelers with mobility problems or other physical disabilities. All public buildings, including hotels and restaurants, have to be wheelchair accessible and provide suitable toilet facilities. Almost all street corners have dropped curbs, and most public transportation systems have such facilities as subways with elevators, and buses that "kneel" to let people board.**

Most states provide information for disabled travelers – contact the tourism departments on pp.20–22. Among **national organizations** are SATH, the Society for the Advancement of Travel for the Handicapped (347 5th Ave, #610, New York, NY 10016 ☎212/447-7284; *www.sath.org*), a non-profit travel-industry grouping that includes travel agents, tour operators, hotel and airline management, and people with disabilities. They will pass on any inquiry to the appropriate member; allow plenty of time for a response. Mobility International USA (PO Box 10767, Eugene, OR 97440; ☎541/343-1284; *www.miusa.org*) offers travel tips to members ($35 a year) and operates an exchange program for disabled people.

The **Golden Access Passport**, issued without charge to permanently disabled US citizens, gives free lifetime admission to all national parks. *Easy Access to National Parks*, by Wendy Roth and Michael Tompane ($15), details every national park for people with disabilities, senior citizens and families with children. It's published by the Sierra Club, 730 Polk St, San Francisco, CA 94110 (☎415/977-5653; *www.sierraclubbookstore.com*). *Disabled Outdoors* is a quarterly magazine specializing in facilities for disabled travelers who wish to explore the great outdoors; its friendly office (see "Tour Operators," opposite) serves as a clearing house for all related information.

Other publications include *Travel for the Disabled* ($19.95), *Wheelchair Vagabond* ($14.95) and *Directory for Travel Agencies for the Disabled* ($19.95), all produced by Twin Peaks Press, PO Box 129, Vancouver, WA 98666 (☎1-800 /637-2256 or 360/694-2462; *www.pacifier.com /twinpeak*).

### GETTING AROUND

Most **airlines**, transatlantic and within the US, do whatever they can to ease your journey, and will usually let attendants of more seriously disabled people accompany them at no extra charge. The Americans with Disabilities Act 1990 obliged all air carriers to make the majority of their services accessible to travelers with disabilities.

Almost every Amtrak train includes one or more coaches with accommodation for handicapped passengers. Guide dogs travel free and may accompany blind, deaf or disabled passengers in the carriage. Be sure to give 24 hours' notice. Hearing-impaired passengers can get information on ☎1-800/654-5988 (though it can take a while to get through since the service is poorly staffed).

Greyhound, however, is not to be recommended. Buses are not equipped with lifts for wheelchairs, though staff will assist with boarding (intercity carriers are required by law to do this), and the "Helping Hand" scheme offers two-for-the-price-of-one tickets to passengers unable to travel alone (carry a doctor's certificate).

The American Public Transit Association, 1201 New York Ave NW, Suite 400, Washington, DC 20005 (☎202/898-4000), provides information about the accessibility of public transportation in cities.

The American Automobile Association produces the *Handicapped Driver's Mobility Guide* for disabled drivers (AAA ☎1-800/222-4357). The larger car rental companies provide cars with hand-controls at no extra charge, though only on their full-size (ie most expensive) models; reserve well in advance.

## TOUR OPERATORS

A few **tour operators** cater for disabled travelers or arrange disabled group tours. A good place to start is with Directions Unlimited, 720 N Bedford Rd, Bedford Hills, NY 10507 (☎914/241-1700 or 1-800/533-5343; *cruisesusa@aol.com*).

# SENIOR TRAVELERS

**For many senior citizens, retirement brings the opportunity to explore the world in a style and at a pace that is the envy of younger travelers. As well as the obvious advantages of being free to travel during the quieter, more congenial and less expensive seasons, and for longer periods, anyone over the age of 62 with the appropriate ID can enjoy a vast range of discounts. Both Amtrak and Greyhound, for example, offer (smallish) percentage reductions on fares to older passengers.**

Any US citizen or permanent resident aged 62 or over is entitled to free admission for life to all national parks, monuments and historic sites, using a **Golden Age Passport**, which can be issued for a one-off fee of $10 at any such site. This free admission applies to all accompanying travelers in the same vehicle – a welcome encouragement to families to travel together –

and also gives a fifty percent reduction on park user fees such as camping charges.

The **American Association of Retired Persons**, 601 E St NW, Washington, DC 20049 (☎202/434-2277 or 1-800/424-3410; *www.aarp.org*), membership of which is open to US residents aged 50 or over for an annual fee of $8, organizes group travel for senior citizens and can provide discounts on accommodation and vehicle rental. The more politically active **National Council of Senior Citizens**, 8403 Colesville Rd, Suite 1200, Silver Spring, MD 20910 (☎1-800/333-7212; *www.ncscinc.org*), which has a yearly membership fee of $13, provides a similar service. **Elderhostel**, 75 Federal St, Boston, MA 02110 (☎1-877/426-8056; *www.elderhostel.com*), runs an extensive network of educational and activity programs for people over sixty throughout the US, at prices broadly in line with those of commercial tours.

# TRAVELING WITH CHILDREN

**Traveling with kids in the United States is relatively problem-free; children are readily accepted – indeed welcomed – in public places across the country.**

Hotels and motels are well used to them, most state and national parks organize children's activities, every town or city has clean and safe playgrounds – and of course Disneyland in Los Angeles, and Disney World in Florida, are the ultimate in kids' entertainment.

**Restaurants** make considerable efforts to encourage parents in with their offspring. All the national chains offer bolster chairs and a special kids' menu, packed with huge, excellent-value (if not necessarily healthy) meals – cheeseburger and fries for 99¢, and so on.

Virtually all **museums** and tourist attractions offer reduced rates for kids. Most large cities have natural history museums or aquariums, and quite a few also have hands-on children's museums.

State tourist offices can provide specific information, and various **guidebooks** have been written for parents traveling with children – such as *California With Kids* ($18) and *The Candy Apple – NY With Kids* ($18), both in the Frommer's Family Guides list, and the very helpful *Trouble Free Travel with Children* ($6.95), available through Publishers Group West. Travel With Your Children, 40 Fifth Ave, New York, NY 10011 (☎212/477-5524; *www.familytraveltimes.com*), publishes *Family Travel Times*, a newsletter that comes out ten times a year ($40 annually), plus a series of books on travel with children, including *Great Adventure Vacations With Your Kids* ($11.95).

Each of John Muir Publications' *Kidding Around* series covers the history and sights of a major US city.

## GETTING AROUND

Children under two years old **fly** free on domestic routes, and for ten percent of the adult fare on international flights – though that doesn't mean they get a seat, let alone frequent-flier miles. When aged from two to twelve they are usually entitled to half-price tickets.

Traveling by **bus** may be the cheapest way to go, but it's also the most uncomfortable for kids. Under-twos travel (on your lap) for free; ages two to four are charged ten percent of the adult fare, as are any toddlers who take up a seat. Children under twelve are charged half the standard fare.

Even if you discount the romance of the railroad, taking the **train** is by far the best option for long journeys – not only does everyone get to enjoy the scenery, but you can get up and walk around. Most cross-country trains have sleeping compartments, which may be quite expensive but are likely to be seen as a great adventure. Children's discounts are much the same as for bus or plane travel.

Most families choose to travel by **car**; if you're hoping to enjoy a driving vacation with your kids, it's essential to plan ahead. Don't set yourself unrealistic targets; pack plenty of sensible snacks and drinks; plan to stop (ie don't make your kids make you stop) every couple of hours; arrive at your destination well before sunset; and avoid traveling through big cities during rush hour. If you're on a fly-drive vacation, note that car rental companies can usually provide **kids' car seats** for around $4 a day. You would, however, be advised to check, or bring your own, as they are not always available.

Recreational Vehicles (RVs) are also a good option for family travel, combining the convenience of built-in kitchens and bedrooms with the freedom of the road (see "Getting Around", p.30).

# WOMEN TRAVELERS

**Practically speaking, a woman traveling alone in America is not usually made to feel conspicuous, or liable to attract unwelcome attention. The cities can feel a lot safer than you might expect from recurrent media images of demented urban jungles, simply because there are so many people about. But like anywhere, particular care has to be taken at night: walking through unlit, empty streets is never a good idea, and if there's no bus service, take cabs. It's true that women who look confident are less likely to encounter trouble – those who stand around looking lost and a bit scared are prime targets.**

In the major urban centers, provided you stick to the better parts of town, going into bars and clubs alone should pose few problems: there's generally a pretty healthy attitude towards women who do so and your privacy will be respected. Gay and lesbian bars are usually a trouble-free and welcoming alternative.

However, **small towns** tend not to be blessed with the same liberal or indifferent attitudes toward lone women travelers. People seem to jump immediately to the conclusion that your car has broken down, or that you've suffered some strange misfortune; in fact, you may get fed up with well-meant offers of help. If your **vehicle** does **break down** on interstate highways or heavily traveled roads, wait in the car for a police or highway patrol car to arrive. One increasingly available option is to rent a portable telephone with your car, for a small additional charge – a potential lifesaver.

**Rape** statistics in the US are high, and it goes without saying that you should *never* hitch alone – this is widely interpreted as an invitation for trouble, and there's no shortage of weirdos to give it. Similarly, if you have a car, be careful who you pick up: just because you're in the driving seat doesn't mean you're safe. Avoid traveling at night by public transportation – deserted bus stations, if not actually threatening, will do little to make you feel secure – and where possible try and team up with a fellow traveler (there really is safety in numbers).

## WOMEN'S TRAVEL SPECIALISTS IN THE US

**Call of the Wild**, 2519 Cedar St, Berkeley, CA 94708 (☎510/849-9292; *www.callwild.com*). Established outfitter offering hiking adventures for women of all ages and abilities. Trips include visits to Native American ruins, backpacking in Californian national parks, cross-country skiing, dogsledding and some jaunts to Hawaii.

**Outdoor Vacations for Women over 40**, PO Box 200, Groton, MA 01450 (☎978/448-3331; *ov40fun@aol.com*). Cross-country skiing, rafting, canoeing, biking, hiking and snorkeling. No previous experience required.

**Outward Bound**, 100 Mystery Point Rd, Garrison, NY 10524 (☎1-800/243-8520 or 914/424-4000; *www.outwardbound.com*). Year-round programs including canoeing, sledding, desert- and canyon-hiking. No previous experience required.

**Prairie Women Adventures and Retreats**, RR Matfield Green, KS 66862 (☎316/753-3416). A 5000-acre cattle ranch, owned by women. Guests can work alongside ranch hands, with free time for horse-riding, hiking and biking.

**Womanship**, The Boathouse, 410 Severn Ave, Annapolis, MD 21403 (☎410/267-6661; *www.womanship.com*). Live-aboard, learn-to-sail cruises for women of all ages. Destinations include the Chesapeake Bay, Florida, the Pacific Northwest and Mystic, Connecticut. Choice of 3-, 5- or 7-day trips.

On Greyhound buses, follow the example of other lone women and sit as near to the front – and the driver – as possible. Should disaster strike, all major towns have some kind of rape counselling service; if not, the local sheriff's office will make adequate arrangements for you to get help and counseling, and, if necessary, get you home.

The **National Organization for Women** is a central women's issues group whose lobbying has done much to effect positive legislation. NOW branches, listed in local phone directories, can provide referrals for specific concerns such as rape crisis centers and counselling services, feminist bookstores and lesbian bars.

Further material can be found in *Ferrari Guides: Women's Travel in Your Pocket* ($14; Ferrari Publications, PO Box 37887, Phoenix, AZ 85069; ☎602/863-2408; *www.q-net.com*), an annual guide for women traveling in the US, Canada, the Caribbean and Mexico.

# GAY AND LESBIAN TRAVELERS

**The gay scene in America is huge, albeit heavily concentrated in the major cities. San Francisco, where between a quarter and a third of the voting population is reckoned to be gay or lesbian, is arguably the premier gay city of the world; New York runs a close second; and up and down both coasts gay men and women enjoy the kind of visibility and influence those in other places can only dream about. Gay politicians, and even police officers, are more than a novelty, and representation at every level is for real. Resources, facilities and organizations are endless.**

However, head into the heartland and life more than looks like the Fifties – away from large cities homosexuals are still oppressed and commonly reviled, and gay travelers would be well advised to watch their step to avoid hassles and possible aggression.

Ghettoization is no longer the self-defensive manoeuvre it used to be, but virtually every major city has its own sizeable, predominantly gay area – **Christopher Street** in New York City, Los Angeles' **West Hollywood**, San Francisco's **Castro** district, Houston's **Montrose**, Seattle's **Capitol Hill**, and so on.

However, although gay life exploded into the public eye in the 1970s, in the face of the AIDS pandemic the energies of gay men and women have been directed to the protection of existing rights and to increasing support and help for victims of the disease. Activist groups like ACT-UP (the AIDS Coalition To Unleash Power) and Queer Nation hold sit-ins (and kiss-ins) as part of continuing efforts to maintain a high profile in the face of continued intolerance and isolation.

Things change as quickly in the gay and lesbian (and emerging bisexual) scene as they do everywhere else, but we've tried to give an overview of local **resources**, **bars** and **clubs** in each of the major cities.

Of national **publications** to look out for, most of which are available from any good bookstore, by far the best are the range produced by Bob Damron in San Francisco (PO Box 4222458, San Francisco, CA 94142; ☎415/255-0404 or 1-800/462-6654; *www.damron.com*). These include the *Men's Travel Guide*, a pocket-sized yearbook full of listings of hotels, bars, clubs and resources for gay men, costing $17.95; the *Women's Traveler*, which provides similar listings for lesbians ($13.05); the *Road Atlas*, which shows lodging and entertainment in major cities ($17.95); and *Damron Accommodations*, which provides detailed listings of over 1000 accommodations for gays and lesbians worldwide ($18.95). All of these titles are offered for less on the Web site.

Gayellow Pages (PO Box 533, Village Station, New York, NY 10014; ☎212/674-0120; *www.gayellowpages.com*) publishes a useful directory of businesses in the US and Canada ($16), plus regional directories for New England, New York and the South. *The Advocate* (Liberation Publications, 6922 Hollywood Blvd, Los Angeles, CA 90028; $2.95) is a bimonthly national gay news magazine, with features, general info and classified ads (not to be confused with *Advocate Men*, which is a soft-porn magazine).

Another useful lesbian publication is *Gaia's Guide* (132 W 24th St, New York, NY 10014; $6.95), a yearly international directory with a lot of US information.

# ACCOMMODATION

**Accommodation costs form a significant proportion of the expenses for any traveler exploring the United States – in part, at least, because the standards of comfort and service are so dependably high.**

If you're on your own, it's possible to pare down what you pay by sleeping in dormitory-style hostels, where a bed usually costs between $10 and $20. However, with basic room prices away from the major cities tending to start at around $40 per night, groups of two or more will find it little more expensive to stay in the far more abundant motels and hotels. Many hotels will set up a third single bed for around $15 on top of the regular price, reducing costs for three people sharing. On the other hand, the lone traveler will have a hard time of it: "singles" are usually double rooms at an only slightly reduced rate.

Wherever you stay, you'll be expected to **pay in advance**, at least for the first night and perhaps for further nights too. Most places ask for a

credit card imprint when you arrive, but they'll also accept cash or dollar travelers' checks. **Reservations** – essential in busy areas in summer – are only held until 5 or 6pm unless you've warned the hotel you'll be arriving late.

## HOTELS & MOTELS

It is consistently easy to find a basic motel room in the United States. Drivers approaching any significant town are confronted by endless lines of motels along the highway, while the choice along major cross-country routes is phenomenal. Most towns mentioned in this book hold more motels than there's room to review; the very few that have none at all are clearly indicated.

**Hotels** and **motels** are essentially the same thing, although motels tend to be located beside the main roads away from city centers – and thus are much more accessible to drivers. The budget ones are pretty basic affairs, but in general there's a uniform standard of comfort everywhere – each room comes with a double bed (often two), a TV and phone, and an attached bathroom – and you don't get a much better deal by paying, say, $60 instead of $40. Over $60, the room and its fittings simply get bigger and more luxurious, and there'll probably be a swimming pool which guests can use for free.

The very cheapest properties tend to be family-run, independent motels, but there's a lot to be said for paying a few dollars more to stay in motels belonging to the **national chains**. After a

---

### ACCOMMODATION PRICE CODES

**Throughout this book, accommodation prices have been graded with the symbols below, according to the cost of the least expensive double room throughout most of the year.**

However, with the exception of the budget interstate motels, there's rarely such a thing as a set rate for a room. A basic motel in a seaside or mountain resort may double its prices according to the season, while a big-city hotel which charges $200 per room during the week will often slash its tariff at the weekend. As the high and low seasons for tourists vary widely across the country, astute planning can save a lot of money. Watch out also for local events, ranging from big spectacles such as Mardi Gras in New Orleans, through Spring Break in Myrtle Beach, down to college football games – which can raise rates far above normal.

Only where we explicitly say so do these room rates include local taxes.

| | | |
|---|---|---|
| ① up to $30 | ④ $60–80 | ⑦ $130–175 |
| ② $30–45 | ⑤ $80–100 | ⑧ $175–250 |
| ③ $45–60 | ⑥ $100–130 | ⑨ $250+ |

## NATIONAL HOTEL, HOSTEL AND MOTEL CHAINS

Most of the hotel and lodging chains listed below publish handy free directories (with maps and illustrations) of their properties. Although we have indicated typical room rates (using the codes explained overleaf), bear in mind that the location of a particular hotel or motel has a huge impact on the price.

**Best Western (③–⑥)** ☎1-800/528-1234
www.bestwestern.com

**Budgetel (③)** ☎1-800/428-3438
www.baymontinns.com

**Comfort Inns (③–⑤)** ☎1-800/221-2222
www.hotelchoice.com

**Courtyard by Marriott (⑤/⑥)** ☎1-800/321-2211
www.marriott.com

**Days Inn (④/⑤)** ☎1-800/329-7466
www.daysinn.com

**Econolodge (②–④)** ☎1-800/424-4777
www.econolodge.com

**Embassy Suites Hotels (⑥)** ☎1-800/362-2779
www.embassysuites.com

**Fairfield Inns (④/⑤)** ☎1-800/228-2800
www.marriot.com

**Friendship Inns (③)** ☎1-800/424-4777
www.roadway.com

**Hallmark Inns (②/③)** ☎1-800/251-3294

**Hampton Inns (④/⑤)** ☎1-800/426-7866
www.hampton-inn.com

**Hilton Hotels (⑤ and up)** ☎1-800/445-8667
www.hilton.com

**Holiday Inns (⑤ and up)** ☎1-800/465-4329
www.holiday-inn.com

**Hostelling International – American Youth Hostels (①)** ☎1-800/909-4776
www.hiayh.org

**Howard Johnson (②–④)** ☎1-800/446-4656
www.hojo.com

**ITT Sheraton (⑤ and up)** ☎1-800/325-3535
www.starwoodhotels.com

**La Quinta Inns (④)** ☎1-800/531-5900
www.laquinta.com

**Marriott Hotels (⑥ and up)** ☎1-800/228-9290
www.marriott.com

**Motel 6 (②)** ☎1-800/466-8356
www.motel6.com

**Ramada Inns (④ and up)** ☎1-800/272-6232
www.ramada.com

**Red Carpet Inns (②)** ☎1-800/251-1962
www.reservahost.com

**Red Roof Inns (③)** ☎1-800/843-7663
www.redroof.com

**Renaissance Hotels (⑤ and up)** ☎1-800/468-3571
www.renaissancehotels.com

**Scottish Inns (②)** ☎1-800/251-1962
www.reservahost.com

**Select Inns (②)** ☎1-800/641-1000
www.selectinn.com

**Sleep Inns (③)** ☎1-800/627-5337
www.sleepinn.com

**YMCA (②/③)** ☎212/308-2899
www.ymcanyc.org

few days on the road, if you find that a particular chain consistently suits your requirements, you can use its central reservation number, listed above, to book ahead, and possibly obtain discounts as a regular guest.

During **off-peak periods** many motels and hotels struggle to fill their rooms, and it's worth **haggling** to get a few dollars off the asking price. Staying in the same place for more than one night will bring further reductions. Additionally look out for **discount coupons**, especially in the free magazines distributed by local visitor centers and interstate Welcome Centers. These can offer amazing value – $20 for a double room in a comfortable mid-range chain – but read the small print, as rates sometimes turn out to be a per-person charge for two people sharing and are often limited to midweek.

Few budget hotels or motels bother to compete with the ubiquitous diners by offering **breakfast**, although many provide free self-service coffee and sticky buns.

### BED AND BREAKFAST

Over the last decade or so, **bed and breakfast** has become an ever more popular option, often as a luxurious alternative to conventional hotels – if not necessarily any more expensive. Some B&Bs consist of no more than a couple of furnished rooms in someone's home, and even the larger establishments tend to have fewer than ten rooms, without TV or phone but often laden with flowers, stuffed cushions and an almost over-contrived homey atmosphere.

The price you pay for a B&B – which varies from around $50 to $200 for a double room – always includes a huge and wholesome breakfast (sometimes a buffet on a sideboard, but more often a full-blown cooked meal). The crucial determining factor is whether or not each room has an en-suite bathroom; most B&Bs feel obliged to provide private bath facilities, although that can damage the authenticity of a fine old house. Prices in those that do tend to start at more like $60 or $70. At the top end of the spectrum, the distinction between a "hotel" and a "bed and breakfast inn" may amount to no more than that the B&B is owned by a private individual rather than a chain.

In many areas, B&Bs have grouped together to form central **booking agencies**, making it much easier to find a room at short notice; we've given addresses and numbers for these where appropriate.

## YS AND YOUTH HOSTELS

Although hostel-type accommodation is not as plentiful in the US as it is in Europe and elsewhere, provision for backpackers and low-budget travelers is on the increase. Unless you're traveling alone, most hostels work out little cheaper than motels, so there's only much point staying in them if you prefer their youthful ambiance and sociability. Note also that many are not accessible on public transportation, or particularly convenient for sightseeing in the towns and cities, let alone in rural areas.

The official **HI-AYH (Hostelling International–American Youth Hostels)** network has over 150 hostels in major cities and rural locations throughout the US. Urban hostels tend to have 24-hour access, while rural ones may have a curfew and limited daytime hours. Rates range from $8 to $22 for HI members; nonmembers generally pay an additional $3 per night. Check the HI-AYH Web site (*www.hiayh.org*) for comprehensive listings.

There's also a growing number of **independent** hostels, of which some may have failed to meet the HI's (fairly rigid) criteria, but most simply choose not to be tied down by HI regulations. Many are no more than converted motels, where the "dorms" consist of a couple of sets of bunk beds in a musty room, which is also let out as a private room on demand; others may be purpose-built rural properties, or at least converted and modernized to a high standard. The AAIH (American Association of Independent Hostels) is a loose affiliation of independent hostels.

In addition, **YMCA/YWCA** hostels (known as "Ys"), provide mixed-sex or, in a few cases, women-only accommodation, at prices ranging from around $12 for a dormitory bed to $20–35 for a single or double room. *Ys* offering accommodation (and not all do, many being basically health clubs) are often in older buildings in less than ideal neighborhoods, but facilities can include a gym, a swimming pool and an inexpensive cafeteria.

Especially in high season, it's advisable to **reserve ahead** by writing to the relevant hostel and enclosing a deposit. Some hostels will allow you to use a **sleeping bag**, though officially HI affiliates should insist on a **sheet sleeping bag**. The **maximum stay** is often restricted to three days, though this rule is often ignored if there's space. Few hostels provide meals but most have **cooking** facilities.

For advice on **camping**, see the "Outdoors" section beginning overleaf.

All the information in this book was accurate at the time of going to press; however, youth hostels are often shoestring organizations, prone to changing address or closing down altogether. Similarly, new ones appear each year; check the noticeboards of other hostels for news. The *Hostel Handbook for the USA and Canada*, produced each May, lists over four hundred hostels and is available for $3 from Jim Williams, *Sugar Hill House International House Hostel*, 722 St Nicholas Ave, New York, NY 10031 (☎212/926-7030; *www.hostelhandbook.com*). *Hostelling North America*, the HI guide to hostels in the USA and Canada, is available free of charge to any overnight guest at HI-AYH hostels or direct from the HI National Office, 733 15th St NW, Suite 840, Washington, DC 20005 (☎202/783-6161; *www.hiayh.org*).

Overseas travelers will find a comprehensive list of hostels in the *International Youth Hostel Handbook*. In the UK, it's available from the **Youth Hostel Association (YHA)**, Trevelyan House, 8 St Stephen's Hill, St Albans, Herts AL1 2DY (☎01727/855215), from whom annual HI membership costs £9.50 (under-18s £3).

# OUTDOORS

The United States is scattered with fabulous backcountry and wilderness areas, coated by dense forests, cut by deep canyons and capped by great mountains. Even the heavily populated East Coast has its share of open space, notably along the Appalachian Trail, which winds from Mount Katahdin in Maine to the Blue Ridge Mountains of Tennessee – some two thousand miles of untrammeled forest. In order to experience the full breathtaking sweep of America's wide-open stretches, however, head west to the Rockies, to the red-rock deserts of the Southwest, or right across the continent to the amazing wild spaces of the West Coast states. The shoreline itself, however, is often disappointingly hard to access, with a high proportion firmly under private ownership.

## NATIONAL PARKS AND MONUMENTS

The **National Park Service** administers both national parks and national monuments. The park service is sadly underfunded – it doesn't even get to keep park entrance fees, which are absorbed into the general federal treasury – and in style and design most of its visitor centers and other facilities still date conspicuously from the 1950s. Nonetheless, its rangers do a superb job of providing information and advice to visitors, maintaining trails, and organizing such activities as free guided hikes and campfire talks.

In principle, a **national park** preserves an area of outstanding natural beauty, encompassing a wide range of terrain as well as sites of historic interest – **Yellowstone**, with its teeming geysers and wildlife, **Yosemite**, with its towering granite walls, and the awesome **Grand Canyon** are the most famous examples – while a **national monument** is much smaller, focusing perhaps on just one archeological site or geological phenomenon, such as **Devil's Tower** in Wyoming.

National parks tend to be perfect places to **hike** – almost all have extensive trail networks – but they're all far too large to tour on foot.

For up-to-the-minute **information** on the national park system, access the official park-service Web site at *www.nps.gov*

It features full details of the main attractions of the national parks, plus opening hours, the best times to visit, admission fees, hiking trails and visitor facilities.

(Yellowstone, for example, is bigger than the states of Delaware and Rhode Island combined.) Even in those rare cases where you can use public transportation to reach a park, you'll almost certainly need some sort of vehicle to explore it once you're there.

Most parks and monuments charge **admission fees** ranging from $4 to $20, which cover a vehicle and all its occupants. For $50, they also sell the **Golden Eagle pass**, which gives a named driver, and all passengers in the same vehicle, a year's unlimited access to (almost) every national park and monument. Separate passes are available for disabled travelers and senior citizens – see p.32 and p.33 respectively.

While hotel-style **lodges** are found only in major parks such as Yosemite or the Grand Canyon, every park or monument tends to have at least one well-organized **campground** for visitors. With appropriate free permits – subject to number restrictions in popular parks – backpackers can also usually camp in the **backcountry** (a general term for areas inaccessible by road).

## OTHER PUBLIC LANDS

National parks and monuments are often surrounded by tracts of **national forest**, also federally administered, but much less protected. These too tend to hold appealing rural campgrounds, but in the words of the slogan each is a "Land Of Many Uses," and usually allows some limited logging and other land-based industry – ski resorts more often than strip mines, fortunately.

Further government departments administer a whole range of wildlife refuges, national scenic rivers, recreation areas and the like – such administration consisting basically of leaving the natural landscape alone. The **Bureau of Land Management** (BLM) has the largest holdings of all, most of it open rangeland, such as in Nevada and Utah, but also including some enticingly out-of-the-way reaches.

**State parks** and **state monuments**, administered by individual states, are a mirror-image of the federal system, preserving sites of more limited, local significance. Many are explicitly designed for recreational use, and thus hold better campgrounds than their federal equivalents.

## CAMPING AND BACKPACKING

The ideal way to see the great outdoors – especially if you're on a low budget – is to tour by car,

and **camp** at night in state and federal campgrounds, which tend to be far more peaceful and scenic than their commercially run equivalents. Typical public campgrounds range in price from free (usually when there's no water available, which may be seasonal) to around $8 per night; fees at the commercial campgrounds abundant near major towns – many of which resemble open-air hotels, complete with shops and restaurants – are more like $15–20. There may be plenty of campgrounds, but there are also plenty of people who want to use them: if you're camping in high season, either reserve in advance or avoid the most popular areas.

**Backcountry camping** in the national parks is usually free, by permit only. Before you set off on anything more than a half-day hike, and whenever you're headed for anywhere at all isolated, be sure to inform a ranger of your plans, and ask about weather conditions and specific local tips. Carry sufficient food and drink to cover emergencies, as well as all the necessary equipment and maps. Check that fires are permitted before you start one; even if they are, try to use a camp stove in preference to local materials – in some places firewood is scarce, although you may be allowed to use deadwood. In wilderness areas, try to camp on previously used sites. Where there are no toilets, bury human waste at least six inches into the ground and a hundred feet from the nearest water supply and campground. Burn what trash you can, and take the rest away.

Backpackers should **never drink** from rivers and streams, however clear and inviting they may look; you never know what unspeakable acts people – or animals – have performed further upstream. **Giardia** – a water-borne bacteria that causes an intestinal disease, characterized by chronic diarrhoea, abdominal cramps, fatigue and weight loss – is a serious problem. Water that doesn't come from a tap should be boiled for at least five minutes, or cleansed with an iodine-based purifier (such as Portable Aqua) or a Giardia-rated filter, available from any camping or sports store.

Hiking at lower elevations should present few problems, though the thick swarms of **mosquitoes** you're likely to encounter near water can drive you crazy; Avon Skin-so-soft handcream or anything containing DEET are fairly reliable repellents. **Ticks** – tiny beetles that plunge their heads into your skin and swell up – are another hazard.

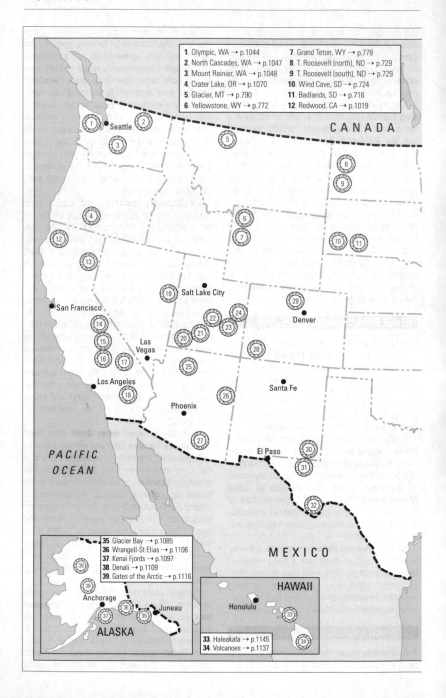

1. Olympic, WA → p.1044
2. North Cascades, WA → p.1047
3. Mount Rainier, WA → p.1048
4. Crater Lake, OR → p.1070
5. Glacier, MT → p.790
6. Yellowstone, WY → p.772
7. Grand Teton, WY → p.778
8. T. Roosevelt (north), ND → p.729
9. T. Roosevelt (south), ND → p.729
10. Wind Cave, SD → p.724
11. Badlands, SD → p.716
12. Redwood, CA → p.1019

35. Glacier Bay → p.1085
36. Wrangell-St Elias → p.1106
37. Kenai Fjords → p.1097
38. Denali → p.1109
39. Gates of the Arctic → p.1116

33. Haleakala → p.1145
34. Volcanoes → p.1137

**13**. Lassen Volcanic, CA → p.1021
**14**. Yosemite, CA → p.972
**15**. Kings Canyon, CA → p.970
**16**. Sequoia, CA → p.970
**17**. Death Valley, CA → p.954
**18**. Joshua Tree, CA → p.953
**19**. Great Basin, NV → p.905

**20**. Zion, UT → p.872
**21**. Bryce Canyon, UT → p.875
**22**. Capitol Reef, UT → p.872
**23**. Canyonlands, UT → p.878
**24**. Arches, UT → p.881
**25**. Grand Canyon, AZ → p.854
**26**. Petrified Forest, AZ → p.848

**27**. Saguaro, AZ → p.838
**28**. Mesa Verde, CO → p.760
**29**. Rocky Mountain, CO → p.740
**30**. Carlsbad Caverns, NM → p.829
**31**. Guadalupe Mtns, TX → p.671
**32**. Big Bend, TX → p.667

**40**. Voyageurs, MN → p.346
**41**. Isle Royale, MI → p.293
**42**. Acadia, ME → p.246
**43**. Mammoth Cave, KY → p.486
**44**. Great Smoky Mtns, TN → p.447, 508
**45**. Shenandoah, VA → p.395
**46**. Hot Springs, AR → p.533
**47**. Everglades, FL → p.585
**48**. Biscayne, FL → p.544

**US NATIONAL PARKS**

For a detailed description of each park
see the page indicated

0                    400 miles

They sometimes leave their heads inside, causing blood clots or infections, so get advice from a park ranger if you've been bitten. Beware, too, of **poison oak**, an allergenic shrub that grows all over the western states, usually among oak trees. Its leaves come in groups of three and are distinguished by prominent veins and shiny surfaces. If you come into contact with this, wash your skin (with soap and cold water) and clothes as soon as possible – and don't scratch. In serious cases, hospital emergency rooms can give antihistamine or adrenaline jabs.

## MOUNTAIN HIKES

Hiking at **higher elevations**, for instance in the 14,000ft peaks of the Rockies or California's Sierra Nevada, and certainly in Alaska, you need to take especial care: late snows are common, even into July, and in spring there's a real danger of avalanches, not to mention meltwaters making otherwise simple stream crossings hazardous. Altitude sickness, brought on by the depletion of oxygen in the atmosphere, can affect even the fittest of athletes. Take it easy for the first few days you go above seven thousand feet; drink lots of water, avoid alcohol, eat plenty of carbohydrates, and protect yourself from the increased power of the sun.

## DESERT HIKES

If you intend to hike in the **desert**, plan ahead. Tell somebody where you are going, and write down all pertinent information, including your expected time of return. Carry an extra two days' food and water and never go anywhere without a map. Try and cover most of your ground early morning: the midday heat is too debilitating, and you shouldn't even think about it when the mercury goes over 90°F (temperatures in California's Death Valley, for example, can reach 136°F). If you get lost, find some shade and wait. As long as you've registered, the rangers will eventually come and fetch you.

Not only can you anticipate battling with incredible heat, but at high elevations at night you should also be prepared for below-freezing temperatures. At any time of year, you'll stay cooler during the day if you wear full-length sleeves and trousers: shorts and a vest will expose you to far too much sun – something you won't be aware of until it's too late. A wide-brimmed hat and a pair of good sunglasses will spare you the blinding

headaches that can result from the desert light. You may also have to contend with **flash floods**, which can appear from nowhere: an innocent-looking dark cloud can turn a dry wash into a raging river. Never camp in a dry wash, and don't attempt to cross flooded areas until the water has receded.

It's essential to carry – and **drink** – large quantities of liquid in the desert. An eight-hour hike in typical summer temperatures of over 100°F would require you to drink a phenomenal thirty pints of water. Loss of appetite and thirst are early symptoms of heat exhaustion, so it's possible to become seriously dehydrated without feeling thirsty. Watch out for signs of dizziness or nausea; if you feel weak and stop sweating, it's time to get to the doctor. You should always know whether water will be available on your chosen trail – park rangers keep abreast of the latest conditions – and carry at least a quart per person even if it is.

When **driving** in the desert, be sure to carry two gallons of water per person in the car, and take along an emergency pack with flares, a first-aid and snakebite kit, matches and a compass. A shovel, tire pump and extra gas are always a good idea. If the car's engine overheats, don't turn it off; instead, try to cool the engine quickly by turning the front end towards the wind. Carefully pour some water on the front of the radiator, and turn the air conditioning off and heating up full blast. In an emergency, never panic and leave the car: you'll be harder to find wandering around alone.

## ADVENTURE TRAVEL

The opportunities for active traveling in the US are all but endless, from whitewater rafting down the Colorado River, to mountain biking in the volcanic Cascades, canoeing down the headwaters of the Mississippi River, horseback riding in the Big Bend on the Rio Grande in Texas, and Big Wall rock-climbing on the sheer granite monoliths of Yosemite Valley.

While an exhaustive listing of the possibilities could fill another volume of this book, certain places have an especially high concentration of adventure opportunities, such as Moab, Utah (p.882), or New Hampshire's White Mountains (p.222). Throughout the book we recommend guides, outfitters and local adventure tour operators.

## WILDLIFE

Watch out for bears, deer, moose, mountain lions and rattlesnakes in the backcountry, and consider the effect your presence can have on their environment.

Other than in a national park, you're highly unlikely to encounter a **bear**. Even there, it's rare to stumble across one in the wilderness. If you do, don't try to run, just back away slowly. As friendly as they appear, they are *wild* animals. Most fundamentally, they will be after your food, which should be stored in airtight containers when camping. Ideally, you should hang both food and garbage from a high branch (too weak to support the weight of a bear) some distance from your camp. Never attempt to feed bears (frequently they'll beg, but once fed will become aggressive in their demands for more), and never get between a mother and her young. Young animals are cute; irate mothers are not.

## SNAKES AND CREEPY-CRAWLIES

Though the deserts in particular are home to a wide assortment of **poisonous creatures**, these are rarely aggressive towards humans. By observing obvious precautions – don't attempt to handle wildlife; keep your eyes open as you walk, and watch where you put your hands when scrambling over obstacles; shake out shoes, clothing and bedding before use; and back off if you do spot a creature, to give it room to escape – you should be able to avoid trouble.

If you are bitten or stung, current medical thinking rejects the concept of cutting yourself open and attempting to suck out the venom; whether snake, scorpion or spider is responsible, you should apply a cold compress to the wound, constrict the area with a tourniquet to prevent the spread of venom, drink lots of water, and bring your temperature down by resting in a shady area. Stay as calm as possible and seek medical help immediately.

# FOOD AND DRINK

**"Fast food" may be America's most enduring contribution to the modern culinary world, but most travelers find the sheer variety – and, for the most part, quality – of the foods available around the United States quite staggering.**

Whether it's for basic sustenance or for a special social occasion, most Americans love to **dine out**, and in the cities at least you can pretty much eat whatever you want, whenever you want. Along all the highways and on every main street, restaurants, fast-food places and coffee shops try to outdo one another with flashing neon signs as well as bargains and special offers.

## REGIONAL SPECIALTIES

While the predictable enormous steaks, burgers, piles of ribs or half a chicken, served up with salads, cooked vegetables and bread, are found everywhere, many visitors find it more rewarding to explore the diverse regional and **ethnic cuisines** around the country. **Beef** is especially prominent in the Midwest and Texas, while **fish** and **seafood** dominate the menus in Florida, Louisiana, around the Chesapeake Bay, and in the Pacific Northwest. **Shellfish**, such as the highly rated Dungeness crab – smoother and creamier than the average crab – and the Chesapeake's unique soft-shell crab, highly spiced and eaten whole, is popular too. Maine lobsters and steamers (clams), eaten alone or mixed up in a chowder, are a great reason to visit New England.

**Cajun** food, which originated in the bayous of Louisiana as a way of using up leftovers, is centered on red beans and rice, enlivened with unusual seafood like crawfish and catfish, and always highly spiced. The often misunderstood distinction between Cajun and **Creole** cooking is explained in our "Louisiana" chapter, on p.606.

**Southern American** cooking – also known as "**soul food**" – is not always easy to find away from the South, but is well worth seeking out. You may not fancy eating **grits** for breakfast (ground white corn served hot, mixed with butter), but full meals can be delicious, and incredibly filling. Vegetables such as **collard greens**, **black-eyed peas**, fried **eggplant** and **okra** (a principal ingredient of the Cajun gumbo) are added to staples such as fried chicken, roast beef and **hogjaw** – meat from the mouth of a pig. **Chitterlings** (or chitlins) are a delicacy prepared from the innards of a pig. Meat dishes are usually accompanied by **cornbread** to soak up the thick gravy poured over everything; with fried fish, you'll often get **hush puppies** – fried corn balls with tiny bits of chopped onion.

By contrast, **California cuisine** is geared towards health and aesthetics. It's basically a development of French *nouvelle cuisine*, utilizing the wide mix of fresh, locally available ingredients. The theory is to eat only what you need, and what your body can process. Vegetables are harvested before maturity and steamed to preserve both vitamins and flavor. Seafood comes from oyster farms and the catches of small-time fishers, and what little meat there is tends to be from animals reared on organic farms. The result is small but beautifully presented portions, and high, high prices: not unusually $50 a head (or much more) for a full dinner with wine.

---

**COPING AS A VEGETARIAN**

In the big cities at least, being a **vegetarian** in the United States presents few problems. Most towns of any size boast at least one wholefood or vegetarian cafe. However, don't be too surprised in rural areas if you find yourself restricted to a diet of eggs, cheese sandwiches (you might have to ask them to leave the ham out), salads and pizza. In the southeast, most soul-food cafes offer great-value vegetable plates (four different vegetables, including potatoes) for around $5, but these are often cooked with pork fat. Similarly, baked beans, and the nutritious-sounding red beans and rice, usually contain bits of diced pork. Of the major fast-food chains, the Mexicanesque *Taco Bell* is your best bet, selling good meatless tostadas and burritos.

---

**TIPPING**

Whatever you eat and wherever you eat, service is usually enthusiastic – thanks in large part to the institution of **tipping**. Wait staff depend on tips for the bulk of their earnings; fifteen to twenty percent is the standard rate.

---

A spin-off from California cuisine is the so-called New New Mexican or **Santa Fe-style** food, again emphasizing ultrafresh and unusual ingredients, and spiced with chilis to reflect the Spanish and Mexican heritage of the Southwest desert region.

Although technically ethnic, **Mexican** food is so common it often seems like an indigenous cuisine, especially in southern California. In Texas, **Tex-Mex** food is a somewhat less spicy local version, whose distinguishing dish is beef and bean chili con carne. Day or night, this is the cheapest type of food to eat: even a full dinner with a few drinks will rarely be over $10 anywhere except in the most upmarket establishment.

Mexican food in the States is different from that found in Mexico, making more use of fresh meats and vegetables, but the essentials are the same: lots of rice and pinto beans, often served refried (ie boiled, mashed and fried), with variations on the **tortilla**, a very thin corndough or flour pancake that can be wrapped around the food and eaten by hand (a **burrito**); folded, fried and filled (a **taco**); rolled, filled and baked in sauce (an **enchilada**); or fried flat and topped with a stack of filling (a **tostada**). Meals are usually served with complimentary **nachos** (chips) and a hot **salsa** dip. The **chile relleno** is a good vegetarian option – a green pepper stuffed with cheese, dipped in egg batter and fried.

Local variations are endless. Many farming and ranching regions – Nevada in particular – have a surprising number of **Basque** restaurants; the **Amish** communities of Pennsylvania have their own traditions; and **Portuguese** restaurants, dating from whaling days, abound in New England. **Chinese** food is everywhere, and can often be as cheap as Mexican; **Japanese**, found especially on the coasts but increasingly in all big cities, is rather more expensive and fashionable. **Italian** food is popular – in fact, the pizza is an American invention – and specialist Italian regional cooking is catching on fast in the major cities. **French** food, too, is available, though always pricey, the

## AMERICAN FOOD TERMS FOR OVERSEAS VISITORS

| | | | |
|---|---|---|---|
| *A la mode* | With ice cream | *Gumbo* | Thick Cajun soup of seafood, chicken and vegetables |
| *Au jus* | Meat served with a gravy made from its own juices | *Half-and-half* | Half cream, half milk |
| *Biscuit* | Similar to a scone, eaten as an accompaniment to a meal | *Hash browns* | Fried chopped or grated potato |
| *BLT* | Bacon, lettuce and tomato toasted sandwich | *Hero* | French-bread sandwich |
| *Broiled* | Grilled | *Hoagie* | Another French-bread sandwich |
| *Check* | Bill | *Home fries* | Thick-cut fried potatoes |
| *Chicken-fried steak* | Steak deep-fried in batter | *Hot cakes* | Pancakes |
| *Chips* | Potato crisps | *Jambalaya* | A sort of Cajun paella, containing seafood, chicken, sausage and vegetables |
| *Chitterlings* | Pig's intestines | | |
| *Cilantro* | Coriander | | |
| *Clam chowder* | Thick seafood soup | *Jello* | Gelatinous pudding |
| *Club sandwich* | Large, three-layered, over-stuffed sandwich | *Jelly* | Jam |
| | | *Muffin* | Small cake made with bran and/or fruit and other sweeteners |
| *Cookie* | Sweet biscuit | | |
| *Crawfish* (also *crayfish*) | Crustacean resembling a baby lobster | | |
| | | *Muffuletta* | Huge French-bread sandwich, served in Louisiana |
| *Eggs:* | | | |
| sunny side up | fried on one side only | *Navajo taco* | Fry-bread covered with beans |
| over | flipped over to stiffen the yolk | *Pecan pie* | Pastry shell filled with pecan nuts and syrupy goo |
| over easy | flipped for a few seconds only | | |
| | | *Po'Boy* | Southern equivalent of a sub sandwich, often filled with deep-fried seafood |
| *Eggplant* | Aubergine | | |
| *English muffin* | Crumpet | | |
| *Fajita* | Soft, taco-like flour tortilla stuffed with shrimp, chicken or beef | *Pretzels* | Savory circles of glazed pastry |
| | | *Quahog* | Large clam, served in New England |
| *Frank* | Frankfurter (hot dog) | | |
| *Fries* | Chips | *Seltzer* | Fizzy/soda water |
| *Frijoles* | Refried beans, ie mashed, fried pinto beans | *Sherbet* | Sorbet |
| | | *Steamers* | Steamed clams, served with butter |
| *Fry bread* | Puffy, deep-fried slab of bread | | |
| | | *Sub* | French-bread sandwich |
| *Gravy* | White, lard-like sauce poured over biscuits for breakfast | *Tab* | Bill |
| | | *Tamales* | Cornmeal dough with meat and chili, baked in a corn husk |
| *Grits* | Ground white corn, served hot with butter | | |
| | | *Zucchini* | Courgettes |

cuisine of social climbers and power-lunchers and rarely found outside the larger cities. **Thai**, **Korean** and **Indonesian** food is similarly city-based, though usually cheaper. **Indian** restaurants, on the other hand, are thin on the ground just about everywhere except New York – although as Indian cuisine catches on, the situation is gradually changing for the better, with a sprinkling of moderately priced Southern Indian food outlets.

## DRINKING

Across the country, **bars** and **cocktail lounges** are pretty true to their *Cheers*-celebrated popular image: long, dimly lit counters with a few punters perched on stools before a bartender-cum-guru, and tables and booths for those who don't want to join in the drunken bar-side debates. New York, Baltimore, Chicago, New Orleans and San Francisco are the consummate boozing towns, but almost anywhere, men, at any rate, shouldn't have to search very hard for a comfortable place to drink.

To **buy and consume alcohol** in the US, you need to be 21, and could well be asked for ID even if you look much older. Mormon Utah has the most byzantine restrictions, while many other states have prohibitions about selling alcohol on Sunday, during elections, or – in the case of various counties in the Midwest – at all, ever. The famous **distilleries** of Tennessee and Kentucky, including Jack Daniels (see p.505), can be visited – though maddeningly, several are in "dry" counties so they don't offer samples. A few states – Vermont, Oklahoma, and, once more, Utah – restrict the alcohol content in beer to just 3.2 percent, half the usual strength. In more liberal areas, alcohol can be bought and drunk any time between 6am and 2am, seven days a week (New Orleans is a law unto itself, with certain bars open 24 hours and a far from rigid policy on ID).

Though for the most part American **beer** is limited to fizzy, light national brands like Budweiser, Miller and Coors, there are alternatives: on the East Coast look out for Boston-based Samuel Adams or New Amsterdam Bitter, not to mention the budget-beer-turned-style-accessory Rolling Rock. The Texan brand Lone Star has its dedicated followers, as do Minnesota's Pete's Wicked Ales; out in California, the full-bodied, San Francisco-brewed Anchor Steam beer is available all over, while the rarer Red Sail Ale is among the finest brews in the country.

Of special interest to travelers are **microbreweries** and **brewpubs**, originating in the West but now found in virtually every sizeable US city and college town, in which you can drink excellent beers, brewed on the premises and often not available anywhere else. These are usually friendly and welcoming places, and almost all serve a wide range of good-value, hearty **food** to help soak up the drink.

As for **wine** and wineries, you'll find details of tours and tastings for visitors scattered throughout the book, for example in California on p.1016, Texas on p.664, Ohio on p.265, and even Hawaii on p.1146.

# SPORTS

Besides being good fun, catching a baseball game at Chicago's Wrigley Field on a summer afternoon, or joining in with the screaming throngs at an Oilers game in Houston, can give visitors an unforgettable insight into a town and its people. Professional teams almost always put on the most spectacular shows, but big games between college rivals, minor league baseball games, even Friday-night high-school football, provide an easy and enjoyable way to get on intimate terms with a place. The major professional sports leagues all have Web sites that list the whole year's schedules and provide links to individual teams.

**Baseball**, because the teams play so many games – 162 in total, usually five or so a week throughout the summer – is probably the easiest sport to catch when traveling. The ballparks – such as Wrigley Field, Boston's Fenway Park, LA's glamorous Dodger Stadium, or Baltimore's evocative new Camden Yards – are great places to spend time. It's also among the cheapest sports to watch (from around $7 a seat), and tickets are usually easy to come by.

**Pro football** is quite the opposite. Tickets are exorbitantly expensive and almost impossible to obtain (if the team is any good), and most games are played in anonymous municipal bunkers; you'll do better stopping in a bar to watch it on TV.

**College football** is a whole lot better and more exciting, with chanting crowds, cheerleaders, and cheaper tickets; while New Year's Day games such as the Rose Bowl or the Cotton Bowl are all but impossible to see in the flesh, big games like Nebraska vs Oklahoma, Michigan vs Ohio State, or Notre Dame vs anybody are not to be missed if you're anywhere nearby.

**Basketball**, on both the college and pro level, also focuses local attention and emotions. We've listed the major league teams for all three sports in the box on p.51; local tourist offices can also help with schedules and ticket information.

**Hockey**, long the preserve of Canada and cities in the far north of the US, is now penetrating the rest of the country, with teams as far south as LA and Dallas. Tickets, particularly for successful teams, are very hard to get.

The **Kentucky Derby**, held in Louisville on the first Saturday in May (see p.484), is the biggest event in the **horse-racing** calendar. Also in May, the **Indianapolis 500**, the largest **motor-racing** event in the world, fills that city with visitors throughout the month, with practice sessions and carnival events building up to the big race.

## SKIING

**Skiing** is the biggest mass-market participant sport, and downhill resorts can be found all over

## SKIING: HOW TO SAVE MONEY

Especially in the Rocky Mountains, the US features some of the best **ski terrain** in the world, but without careful planning a ski vacation can be horribly expensive. In addition to the tips listed below, phone (toll-free) or write in advance to resorts for brochures, and, when you get there, scan local newspapers for money-saving offers.

• Visit during early or late season to take advantage of lower accommodation rates.

• The more people in your party, the more money you save on lodgings. For groups of four to six, a condo unit costs much less than a standard motel.

• Before setting a date, ask the resort about package deals including flights, rooms and ski passes. This is the no-fuss and often highly economical way to book a ski vacation.

• Shop around for the best boot and ski rentals – prices often vary enormously.

• Purchase advance sale lift tickets; for example, gas stations and supermarkets in Colorado offer savings of around thirty percent on ski-slope rates.

• If you have to buy tickets at the resort, save money by purchasing multiday tickets.

• If you're an absolute beginner, look out for resorts that offer free "never-ever" lessons with the purchase of a lift ticket.

• Finish your day's skiing in time to take advantage of happy hours and dining specials, which usually last from 4pm until 7pm.

## THE RULES OF BASEBALL

The field of play for **baseball** still looks something like that of the English game of rounders, from which it was derived, with four **bases** set at the corners of a 90-foot-square **diamond**. The base at the bottom corner is called **home plate**, and serves much the same purpose as do the stumps in cricket. Play begins when the **pitcher**, standing on a low pitcher's mound in the middle of the diamond, throws a ball at up to a hundred miles an hour, often making it curve or bend as it travels towards the **catcher**, who crouches behind home plate; seven other defensive players take up **positions**, four guarding the bases of the **infield** and three others spread out around the **outfield**.

A **batter** from the opposing team stands beside home plate and tries to hit the pitched ball. If the batter swings and misses, or if the pitched ball crosses the plate above the batter's knees and below his chest, it counts as a **strike**; if he doesn't swing and the ball passes outside of this **strike zone**, it counts as a **ball**. If the batter gets **three strikes** against him he is **out** and has to retire; if he is thrown **four balls**, he gets a free **walk**, and takes his place as a **runner** on first base.

If he succeeds in hitting the pitched ball into **fair territory**, the wedge between the first and third bases, the batter runs towards first base; if the opposing players catch the ball before it hits the ground, the batter is **out**. Otherwise they field the ball and attempt to relay it to first base before the batter gets there; if they do he is **out**, if they don't the batter is **safe** – and stays there, being moved along by subsequent batters until he makes a complete circuit of the bases and scores a **run**. The most exciting moment in baseball is the **home run**, when a batter hits the ball over the outfield fence, a boundary about 400ft away from home plate; he and any runners on base when he hits the ball each score a run. If there are runners on all three bases it's called a **grand slam**, and earns four runs.

The nine players per side bat in rotation; each side gets **three outs** per **inning**, and there are **nine innings** per **game**. Games normally last two to three hours, and never end in a tie; if the scores are level after nine innings, extra innings are played until one side pulls ahead and wins.

## THE RULES OF FOOTBALL

The **rules of American football** are fairly simple, though slightly more complicated than those of rugby, from which the game evolved. The **field** is 100 yards long by 40 yards wide, plus two **endzones** beyond the **goal-lines** at each end. There are two teams of eleven men on the field at any one time – one the **offense** and the other the **defense**. The game begins with a **kickoff**, after which the team in possession of the ball tries to move downfield to score a **touchdown**, while the opposing team tries to stop them. The attacking team has four chances to move the ball forward ten yards and gain a **first down**. If they manage this, they are rewarded with another four chances to move the ball forward, if not, they forfeit possession to the opposition. Play begins for the team with the ball when the **quarterback**, the leader of the attack, either passes the ball to a **running back**, or throws the ball through the air downfield to a receiver. Play ends when the man with the ball is tackled to the ground, or if the pass attempt falls incomplete. Despite the name of the sport, there is very little kicking involved, the offense advances primarily by running with the ball or throwing it.

A **touchdown**, worth six points, is made when a player crosses into the defending team's endzone carrying the ball; an **extra** point is awarded if the team then manages to make a fairly simple kick after the touchdown; a **field goal**, worth three points, is scored when the **placekicker** – always the smallest man on the team and often the lone foreigner – kicks the ball, as in rugby, through the **goalposts** that stand in the endzone. If the attacking team has failed to move the ball within scoring range, and seems unlikely to gain the required ten yards for another first down, they can elect to **punt** the ball, kicking it to the other team.

A change of possession can also occur if the opposition players manage to **intercept** an attempted pass. All changes of possession are automatically followed by each team sending in an entirely new squad to play **offense** or **defense**. This high degree of specialization, and the consequent interruptions in play for mass substitutions, is what makes this game so different from sports like rugby and soccer to which it is distantly related.

## BASEBALL

| | | | |
|---|---|---|---|
| Major League Baseball | ☎212/931-7800 | American League | ☎212/931-7600 |
| www.majorleaguebaseball.com | | **Anaheim Angels** | ☎714/940-2000 |
| National League | ☎212/931-7700 | **Baltimore Orioles** | ☎410/685-9800 |
| **Arizona Diamondbacks** | ☎602/514-8500 | **Boston Red Sox** | ☎617/267-1700 |
| **Atlanta Braves** | ☎404/522-7630 | **Chicago White Sox** | ☎312/674-1000 |
| **Chicago Cubs** | ☎773/404-2827 | **Cleveland Indians** | ☎216/420-4200 |
| **Cincinnati Reds** | ☎513/421-4510 | **Detroit Tigers** | ☎313/962-4000 |
| **Colorado Rockies** | ☎303/292-0200 | **Kansas City Royals** | ☎816/921-8000 |
| **Florida Marlins** | ☎305/626-7400 | **Milwaukee Brewers** | ☎414/933-4114 |
| **Houston Astros** | ☎713/799-9555 | **Minnesota Twins** | ☎612/375-1366 |
| **Los Angeles Dodgers** | ☎323/224-1500 | **New York Yankees** | ☎718/293-4300 |
| **New York Mets** | ☎718/507-6387 | **Oakland Athletics** | ☎510/762-2255 |
| **Philadelphia Phillies** | ☎215/463-1000 | **Seattle Mariners** | ☎206/622-4487 |
| **Pittsburgh Pirates** | ☎412/323-5000 | **Tampa Bay Devil Rays** | ☎727/825-3137 |
| **St Louis Cardinals** | ☎314/421-3060 | **Texas Rangers** | ☎817/273-5100 |
| **San Diego Padres** | ☎619/283-4494 | | |
| **San Francisco Giants** | ☎415/467-8000 | | |

## BASKETBALL

| | | | |
|---|---|---|---|
| National Basketball | | **Los Angeles Lakers** | ☎310/419-3100 |
| Association (NBA) | ☎212/407-8000 | **Miami Heat** | ☎305/577-4328 |
| www.nba.com | | **Milwaukee Bucks** | ☎414/227-0500 |
| **Atlanta Hawks** | ☎404/827-3865 | **Minnesota Timberwolves** | ☎612/673-1600 |
| **Boston Celtics** | ☎617/523-6050 | **New Jersey Nets** | ☎201/935-8888 |
| **Charlotte Hornets** | ☎704/357-0252 | **New York Knicks** | ☎212/465-6000 |
| **Chicago Bulls** | ☎312/455-4000 | **Orlando Magic** | ☎407/896-2442 |
| **Cleveland Cavaliers** | ☎216/420-2287 | **Philadelphia 76ers** | ☎215/339-7600 |
| **Dallas Mavericks** | ☎214/748-1808 | **Phoenix Suns** | ☎602/379-7867 |
| **Denver Nuggets** | ☎303/405-1100 | **Portland Trailblazers** | ☎503/224-4400 |
| **Detroit Pistons** | ☎248/377-0100 | **Sacramento Kings** | ☎916/928-6900 |
| **Golden State Warriors** | ☎510/986-2200 | **San Antonio Spurs** | ☎210/554-7787 |
| **Houston Rockets** | ☎713/627-3865 | **Seattle Supersonics** | ☎206/281-5800 |
| **Indiana Pacers** | ☎317/263-2100 | **Utah Jazz** | ☎801/325-7328 |
| **Los Angeles Clippers** | ☎213/745-0400 | **Washington Wizards** | ☎202/628-3200 |

## FOOTBALL

| | | | |
|---|---|---|---|
| National Football League (NFL) | ☎212/450-2000 | **Miami Dolphins** | ☎305/620-2578 |
| www.nfl.com | | **Minnesota Vikings** | ☎612/828-6500 |
| **Arizona Cardinals** | ☎602/379-0102 | **New England Patriots** | ☎508/543-1776 |
| **Atlanta Falcons** | ☎770/945-1111 | **New Orleans Saints** | ☎504/733-0255 |
| **Baltimore Ravens** | ☎410/261-7283 | **New York Giants** | ☎201/935-8222 |
| **Buffalo Bills** | ☎716/649-0015 | **New York Jets** | ☎516/560-8200 |
| **Carolina Panthers** | ☎704/358-7800 | **Oakland Raiders** | ☎510/864-5000 |
| **Chicago Bears** | ☎847/295-6600 | **Philadelphia Eagles** | ☎215/463-5500 |
| **Cincinnati Bengals** | ☎513/621-3550 | **Pittsburgh Steelers** | ☎412/323-1200 |
| **Cleveland Browns** | ☎440/891-5050 | **St Louis Rams** | ☎314/982-7267 |
| **Dallas Cowboys** | ☎972/556-9900 | **San Diego Chargers** | ☎619/280-2121 |
| **Denver Broncos** | ☎303/649-9000 | **San Francisco 49ers** | ☎408/562-4949 |
| **Detroit Lions** | ☎248/335-4151 | **Seattle Seahawks** | ☎206/682-2800 |
| **Green Bay Packers** | ☎920/496-5719 | **Tampa Bay Buccaneers** | ☎813/870-2700 |
| **Indianapolis Colts** | ☎317/297-7000 | **Tennessee Titans** | ☎615/341-7627 |
| **Jacksonville Jaguars** | ☎904/633-6000 | **Washington Redskins** | ☎301/276-8326 |
| **Kansas City Chiefs** | ☎816/920-9300 | | |

the US. The eastern resorts of Vermont and New York State, however, pale by comparison with those of the Rockies, such as Vail and Aspen in Colorado, and the Californian Sierra Nevada. You can usually rent equipment for about $20 per day, and expect to pay another $20 to $45 a day for lift tickets.

A cheaper option is **cross-country skiing**, or ski-touring. Backcountry ski lodges dot mountainous areas along both coasts and in the Rockies, offering a range of rustic accommodation, equipment rental and lessons, from as little as $10 a day for skis, boots and poles, up to about $150 for an all-inclusive weekend tour.

# ENTERTAINMENT

**Even first-time visitors touring the United States are liable to find themselves traveling through a landscape that is already intensely familiar, where the place names come from classic rock'n'roll songs and the wide-open spaces seem straight out of Hollywood Westerns. Exploring the reality behind the glamorous media images, and experiencing at first hand the mighty entertainment industry responsible for so many preconceptions, are two of the greatest pleasures of getting to know America.**

Whether you want to follow in the footsteps of Bob Dylan in north-country Minnesota or Robert Johnson in Mississippi, see Woody Allen's Manhattan or the film noir of LA, there's nowhere like the US for living out musical and movie fantasies. Mickey Mouse and Dolly Parton have their own theme parks, the buffalo still roam the Great Plains, Route 66 still winds from Chicago to LA, and Elvis still lives in Graceland.

## MUSIC

Music fans make pilgrimages from all over the world to the cities that spawned jazz, blues, country, soul and rap. No country devotee could fail to enjoy the rhinestone glitter, halls of fame, honky-tonks and stars' homes of **Nashville**, while **Memphis**, the home of Sun, Stax and the Reverend Al Green, and **Chicago** are the prime destinations for live blues. The party town of **New Orleans** boasts an unrivaled jazz and R&B scene; hardcore rock fans head for **Los Angeles**, **Boston**, **Seattle** or **Cleveland**, home of the Rock and Roll Hall of Fame (see p.260). Not everywhere lives up to the myth, however; Motown fans, for example, may well be disappointed by **Detroit**.

The musical excitement is by no means confined to the big cities. Travel through rural Appalachia and you may find ensembles of backwoods **fiddlers**; the otherwise sleepy bayous of southern Louisiana are enlivened by foot-stomping **Cajun** and **zydeco** sounds; and the little jookjoints of Mississippi Delta hamlets enrapture **blues** purists. The influence of **country** music extends well beyond Tennessee; the South, particularly Texas, is awash with unpretentious honky-tonk bars, and the cowboy bars of southern Wyoming play nothing but good old C&W. Towns as far flung as **Bakersfield**, California, with its gutsy honky-tonk style, and tiny but more mainstream **Branson**, Missouri, boast almost as many live country venues as Nashville.

Today's rock and soul superstars may play virtually all their gigs in huge 30,000-seater stadia, but there are innumerable smaller venues where you can see the latest up-and-coming groups. College towns in particular play a major role in introducing new artists to wider audiences, and you shouldn't pass through **Ann Arbor**, Michigan, **Austin**, Texas (also the home of progressive country music), or **Athens**, Georgia (where REM and the B-52's come from), without checking out what's going on.

## CINEMA AND THEATER

Foreign visitors who want to be ahead of the crowds back home should take in a film or two while in the States; Hollywood **movies** are generally on show three to six months before they reach the rest of the world. Most cities have good cinemas downtown, though in smaller places you often have to make your way out to the multiscreen venues in the malls on the edge of town. Sadly, you don't come across many drive-ins these days.

**Theater** is very hit and miss in the big cities. The international reputation of New York's

Broadway theaters is generally well deserved but it costs a small fortune to get a seat even for most of the Off-Broadway productions. The larger college towns tend to feature well-funded performances of Shakespeare and the usual canon, while throughout the country – in Minneapolis, for example – local companies provide their own stimulating alternatives.

## FESTIVALS AND PUBLIC HOLIDAYS

**Someone, somewhere is always celebrating something in the US, although apart from national holidays, few festivities are shared throughout the country. Instead, there is a disparate multitude of local events: art and craft shows, county fairs, ethnic celebrations, music festivals, rodeos, sandcastle-building competitions, and many others of every hue and shade.**

The box overleaf contains a selection of the best of the local festivals covered in this book. In addition, tourist offices for each state (see pp.20–22) can provide full lists, or you can just phone the visitor center in a particular region ahead of your arrival and ask what's coming up. Certain festivities, such as **Mardi Gras** in New Orleans (p.612), are well worth planning your vacation around; obviously other people will have the same idea, and visiting during these times requires an extra amount of advance effort.

### PUBLIC HOLIDAYS

The biggest and most all-American of the **national festivals and holidays** is **Independence Day**, on the Fourth of July, when the entire country grinds to a standstill as people get drunk, salute the flag and partake in firework displays, marches, beauty pageants and more, all in commemoration of the signing of the Declaration of Independence in 1776. **Halloween** (October 31) lacks any such patriotic overtones, and is not a public holiday despite being one of the most popular yearly flings. Traditionally, kids run around the streets banging on doors demanding "trick or treat," and are given pieces of candy. These days that sort of activity is mostly confined to rural and suburban areas, while in bigger cities Halloween has grown into a massive gay celebration: in West Hollywood in LA, in New York's Greenwich Village and San Francisco's Castro district, the night is marked by mass cross-dressing, huge block parties and general licentiousness. More sedate is **Thanksgiving Day**, on the last Thursday in November. The third big event of the year is essentially a domestic affair, when relatives return to the familial nest to stuff themselves with roast turkey, and (supposedly) fondly recall the first harvest of the Pilgrims in Massachusetts – though in fact Thanksgiving was already a national holiday before anyone thought to make that connection.

On the national **public holidays** listed below, shops, banks and offices are liable to be closed all day. Many states also have their own additional holidays, and in some places Good Friday is a half-day holiday. The traditional **summer season** for tourism runs from **Memorial Day** to **Labor Day**; some tourist attractions are only open during that period.

Jan 1 **New Year's Day**
Third Mon in Jan **Martin Luther King's Birthday**
Third Mon in Feb **President's Day**
Last Mon in May **Memorial Day**
July 4 **Independence Day**
First Mon in Sept **Labor Day**
Second Mon in Oct **Columbus Day**
Nov 11 **Veterans' Day**
Fourth Thurs in Nov **Thanksgiving Day**
December 25 **Christmas Day**

## ANNUAL FESTIVALS AND EVENTS

For further details of the selected festivals and events listed below, including more precise dates, see the relevant page of the *Guide*, or contact the local authorities direct. The state tourist boards listed on pp.20–22 can provide fuller calendars for each area.

*JANUARY*

| | |
|---|---|
| **Aspen** CO: Winterskol | p.751 |
| **Elko** NV: Cowboy Poetry Gathering | p.906 |
| **St Paul** MN: Winter Carnival | p.341 |

*FEBRUARY*

| | |
|---|---|
| **Cordova** AK: Iceworm Festival | p.1105 |
| **Daytona Beach** FL: Daytona 500 Race | p.563 |
| **Fort Worden** WA: Hot Jazz Festival | p.1043 |

*MARCH*

| | |
|---|---|
| **Austin** TX: South by Southwest | p.648 |
| **Butte** MT: St Patrick's Day | p.786 |
| **Fairbanks** AK: Ice Festival | p.1112 |
| **Los Angeles** CA: Academy Awards | p.947 |
| **New Orleans** LA: Mardi Gras | p.612 |
| also elsewhere in Louisiana | p.617 |

*APRIL*

| | |
|---|---|
| **Boston** MA: Patriot's Day – Marathon | p.186 |
| **Lafayette** LA: Festival International de Louisiane | p.617 |
| **New Orleans** LA: French Quarter Festival and Jazz & Heritage Festival (into May) | p.612 |
| **Santuario de Chimayó** NM: Easter Pilgrimage | p.817 |

*MAY*

| | |
|---|---|
| **Black Mountain** NC: Folk Festival | p.447 |
| **Breaux Bridge** LA: Crawfish Festival | p.617 |
| **Charleston** WV: Vandalia Festival of Appalachian Culture | p.404 |
| **Flagstaff** AZ: Zuni Crafts Show | p.850 |
| **Indianapolis** IN: Indianapolis 500 Race | p.296 |
| **Los Angeles** CA: Cinco de Mayo (May 5) | p.947 |
| **Louisville** KY: Kentucky Derby | p.484 |
| **Memphis** TN: Memphis in May, including Barbecue Cook-out | p.497 |
| **San Antonio** TX: International Conjunto Festival | p.644 |

*JUNE*

| | |
|---|---|
| **Fort Worth** TX: Chisholm Trail Round-up | p.661 |
| **Hardin** MT: Little Bighorn Days | p.783 |
| **Nashville** TN: Fan Fair | p.504 |
| **Shreveport** LA: Good Times Festival | p.624 |
| **Telluride** CO: Bluegrass Festival | p.758 |

*JULY*

| | |
|---|---|
| **Blowing Rock** NC: Highland Games | p.446 |
| **Cheyenne** WY: Cheyenne Frontier Days | p.763 |
| **Elko** NV: National Basque Festival | p.906 |
| **Fairbanks** AK: Eskimo/Indian Olympics | p.1112 |
| **Flagstaff** AZ: Hopi Crafts Show | p.850 |
| Navajo Crafts Show (into Aug) | p.850 |
| **Fort Totten** ND: Powwow and Rodeo | p.727 |
| **Milwaukee** WI: Great Circus Parade | p.326 |
| **Minneapolis** MN: Aquatennial | p.339 |
| **Philadelphia** PA: Freedom Fest | p.145 |
| Riverblues | p.145 |
| **St Paul** MN: Taste of Minnesota | p.341 |
| **Talkeetna** AK: Moose Dropping Festival | p.1108 |
| **Traverse City** MI: Cherry Festival | p.287 |

*AUGUST*

| | |
|---|---|
| **Asheville** NC: Mountain Dance & Folk Festival | p.447 |
| **Elkins** WV: Augusta Festival of Appalachian Culture | p.401 |
| **Gallup** NM: Inter-tribal Indian Ceremonial | p.828 |
| **Memphis** TN: Anniversary of Elvis's Death | p.488 |
| **Newport** RI: Folk & Jazz Festivals | p.209 |
| **San Antonio** TX: Texas Folklife Festival | p.644 |
| **Santa Fe** NM: Indian Market | p.809 |
| **Sturgis** SD: Motorcycle Rally & Races | p.720 |

*SEPTEMBER*

| | |
|---|---|
| **Fort Worth** TX: Pioneer Days | p.661 |
| **Greenville** MS: Delta Blues Festival | p.522 |
| **Lafayette** LA: Festivals Acadiens | p.617 |
| **Los Angeles** CA: LA's Birthday (Sept 4) | p.947 |
| LA County Fair | p.947 |
| **Lubbock** TX: Panhandle South Plains Fair | p.665 |
| **Monterey** CA: Monterey Jazz Festival | p.966 |
| **New York** NY: Festa di San Gennaro | p.75 |
| **Opelousas** LA: Zydeco Festival | p.617 |
| **Pendleton** OR: Pendelton Round-up | p.1073 |
| **Santa Fe** NM: Fiestas de Santa Fe | p.810 |
| **Savannah** GA: Jazz Festival | p.475 |
| **Tulsa** OK: Chile Cookoff & Bluegrass Festival | p.677 |

*OCTOBER*

| | |
|---|---|
| **Albuquerque** NM: Hot-air Balloon Rally | p.823 |
| **Charleston** SC: Moja Arts Festival | p.456 |
| **Custer State Park** SD: Round-up of Bison | p.723 |
| **Helena** AR: Blues Festival | p.531 |
| **Opelousas** LA: Louisiana Yambilee | p.617 |
| **Tombstone** AZ: Helldorado Days | p.841 |

# CLIMATE AND WHEN TO GO

**The climate of the United States is characterized by wide variations, not just from region to region and season to season, but also day to day and even hour to hour. Even setting aside the exceptionally far-flung states of Alaska and Hawaii, the main body of the US is subject to dramatically shifting weather patterns, most notably produced by westerly winds sweeping across the continent from the Pacific.**

It is, of course, possible to make certain generalizations. Temperatures tend to rise the further south you go, and to fall the higher you climb, while the climate along either coast is, on the whole, milder and more equable than inland.

Starting a brief survey of the nation's weather in the east, the **Northeast**, from Maine down to Washington DC, experiences relatively low precipitation as a rule, but temperatures can range from bitterly cold in winter to stiflingly hot (made worse by humidity) in the short summer. Further south, summers get warmer and longer. Though **Florida**'s air temperatures are not necessarily dramatically high in summer, being kept down by the proximity of the sea both east and west, it's warm and sunny enough in winter to attract visitors from all over the country.

The **Great Plains**, which for climatic purposes can be said to extend from the Appalachians to the Rockies, are alternately exposed to icy

Arctic winds streaming down from Canada, and humid tropical airflows from the Caribbean and the Gulf of Mexico. Winters in the north, around the Great Lakes, can be abjectly cold, with driving winds and freezing rain. It can freeze or even snow in winter as far south as the Gulf of Mexico, though spring and fall get progressively longer and milder further south through the Plains. Summer is much the wettest season in the **South** as a whole, the time when thunderstorms are most likely to strike. One or two **hurricanes** each year rage across Florida and/or the **Southeast**, from obscure origins somewhere in the Gulf of Mexico on the way to extinction out in the Atlantic. **Tornadoes** (or "twisters") are usually a much more local phenomenon, tending to cut a narrow swath of destruction in the wake of violent spring or summer thunderstorms. Average rainfall dwindles to lower and lower levels the further west you head across the Plains.

Temperatures in the **Rockies** correlate closely with altitude; beyond the mountains in the south lie the extensive arid and inhospitable deserts of the **Southwest**, much of which lies in the rainshadow of the Californian ranges. In cities such as Las Vegas and Phoenix, the mercury regularly soars above 100°F, though the atmosphere is not usually humid enough to be as enervating as that might sound.

Once across the barrier of the Cascade Mountains, the fertile Pacific Northwest is the only region of the country where winter is the wettest season, and throughout the year the European-style climate is wet, mild and seldom hot. Californian weather more or less lives up to the popular idyllic image, though the climate is markedly hotter and drier in the south than in the north, and there's enough snow to make the mountains a major skiing destination. There are also noteworthy local variations. San Francisco is kept milder and colder than the immediately surrounding district by the propensity of the Bay Area to attract sea fogs, while the basin of Los Angeles is prone to fill up with smog, trapping pollution and fog beneath a layer of warm air.

## AVERAGE TEMPERATURES (°F AND RAINFALL)

|  |  | Jan | Feb | March | April | May | June | July | Aug | Sept | Oct | Nov | Dec |
|---|---|---|---|---|---|---|---|---|---|---|---|---|---|
| **Anchorage** | av. max temp | 19 | 27 | 33 | 44 | 54 | 62 | 65 | 64 | 57 | 43 | 30 | 20 |
|  | av. min temp | 5 | 9 | 13 | 27 | 36 | 44 | 49 | 47 | 39 | 29 | 15 | 6 |
|  | days of rain | 7 | 6 | 5 | 4 | 5 | 6 | 10 | 15 | 14 | 12 | 7 | 6 |
| **Atlanta** | av. max temp | 51 | 54 | 62 | 71 | 79 | 86 | 87 | 86 | 82 | 72 | 61 | 52 |
|  | av. min temp | 35 | 37 | 43 | 51 | 60 | 67 | 70 | 69 | 64 | 54 | 43 | 37 |
|  | days of rain | 12 | 11 | 11 | 10 | 10 | 11 | 13 | 12 | 8 | 7 | 8 | 11 |
| **Boston** | av. max temp | 36 | 37 | 43 | 54 | 66 | 75 | 80 | 78 | 71 | 62 | 49 | 40 |
|  | av. min temp | 20 | 21 | 28 | 39 | 49 | 58 | 63 | 62 | 55 | 46 | 35 | 25 |
|  | days of rain | 12 | 10 | 12 | 11 | 11 | 10 | 10 | 10 | 9 | 9 | 10 | 11 |
| **Chicago** | av. max temp | 32 | 34 | 43 | 55 | 65 | 75 | 81 | 79 | 73 | 61 | 47 | 36 |
|  | av. min temp | 18 | 20 | 29 | 40 | 50 | 60 | 66 | 65 | 58 | 47 | 34 | 23 |
|  | days of rain | 11 | 10 | 12 | 11 | 12 | 11 | 9 | 9 | 9 | 9 | 10 | 11 |
| **Honolulu** | av. max temp | 76 | 76 | 77 | 78 | 80 | 81 | 82 | 83 | 83 | 82 | 80 | 78 |
|  | av. min temp | 69 | 67 | 67 | 68 | 70 | 72 | 73 | 74 | 74 | 72 | 70 | 69 |
|  | days of rain | 14 | 11 | 13 | 12 | 11 | 12 | 14 | 13 | 13 | 13 | 13 | 15 |
| **Las Vegas** | av. max temp | 60 | 67 | 72 | 81 | 89 | 99 | 103 | 102 | 95 | 84 | 71 | 61 |
|  | av. min temp | 29 | 34 | 39 | 45 | 52 | 61 | 68 | 66 | 57 | 47 | 36 | 30 |
|  | days of rain | 2 | 2 | 2 | 1 | 1 | 1 | 2 | 2 | 1 | 1 | 1 | 2 |
| **Los Angeles** | av. max temp | 65 | 66 | 67 | 70 | 72 | 76 | 81 | 82 | 81 | 76 | 73 | 67 |
|  | av. min temp | 46 | 47 | 48 | 50 | 53 | 56 | 60 | 60 | 58 | 54 | 50 | 47 |
|  | days of rain | 6 | 6 | 6 | 4 | 2 | 1 | 0 | 0 | 1 | 2 | 3 | 6 |
| **Miami** | av. max temp | 74 | 75 | 78 | 80 | 84 | 86 | 88 | 88 | 87 | 83 | 78 | 76 |
|  | av. min temp | 61 | 61 | 64 | 67 | 71 | 74 | 76 | 76 | 75 | 72 | 66 | 62 |
|  | days of rain | 9 | 6 | 7 | 7 | 12 | 13 | 15 | 15 | 18 | 16 | 10 | 7 |
| **Nashville** | av. max temp | 47 | 50 | 59 | 69 | 78 | 86 | 89 | 88 | 82 | 72 | 58 | 49 |
|  | av. min temp | 31 | 33 | 40 | 49 | 58 | 67 | 70 | 68 | 62 | 60 | 40 | 33 |
|  | days of rain | 12 | 11 | 12 | 11 | 11 | 11 | 11 | 9 | 8 | 7 | 9 | 11 |
| **New Orleans** | av. max temp | 62 | 65 | 71 | 77 | 83 | 88 | 90 | 90 | 86 | 79 | 70 | 64 |
|  | av. min temp | 47 | 50 | 55 | 61 | 68 | 74 | 76 | 76 | 73 | 64 | 55 | 48 |
|  | days of rain | 10 | 12 | 9 | 7 | 8 | 13 | 15 | 14 | 10 | 7 | 7 | 10 |
| **New York City** | av. max temp | 37 | 38 | 45 | 57 | 68 | 77 | 82 | 80 | 79 | 69 | 51 | 41 |
|  | av. min temp | 24 | 24 | 30 | 42 | 53 | 60 | 66 | 66 | 60 | 49 | 37 | 29 |
|  | days of rain | 12 | 10 | 12 | 11 | 11 | 10 | 12 | 10 | 9 | 9 | 9 | 10 |
| **San Francisco** | av. max temp | 55 | 59 | 61 | 62 | 63 | 66 | 65 | 65 | 69 | 68 | 63 | 57 |
|  | av. min temp | 45 | 47 | 48 | 49 | 51 | 52 | 53 | 53 | 55 | 54 | 51 | 47 |
|  | days of rain | 11 | 11 | 10 | 6 | 4 | 2 | 0 | 0 | 2 | 4 | 7 | 10 |
| **Seattle** | av. max temp | 45 | 48 | 52 | 58 | 64 | 69 | 72 | 73 | 67 | 59 | 51 | 47 |
|  | av. min temp | 36 | 37 | 39 | 43 | 47 | 52 | 54 | 55 | 52 | 47 | 41 | 38 |
|  | days of rain | 18 | 16 | 16 | 13 | 12 | 9 | 4 | 5 | 8 | 13 | 17 | 19 |
| **Washington DC** | av. max temp | 42 | 44 | 53 | 64 | 75 | 83 | 87 | 84 | 78 | 67 | 55 | 45 |
|  | av. min temp | 27 | 28 | 35 | 44 | 54 | 63 | 68 | 66 | 58 | 48 | 38 | 29 |
|  | days of rain | 11 | 10 | 12 | 11 | 12 | 11 | 11 | 11 | 8 | 8 | 9 | 10 |

To convert °F to °C, subtract 32 and multiply by 5/9

# DIRECTORY

**ADDRESSES** Generally speaking, roads in built-up areas in the US are laid out on a grid system, creating "blocks" of buildings. The first one or two digits of a specific address refer to the block, which will be numbered in sequence from a central point, usually downtown; for example, 620 S Cedar Avenue will be six blocks south of downtown. It is crucial, therefore, to take note of components such as "NW" or "SE" in addresses; 3620 SW Washington Boulevard will be a very long way indeed from 3620 NE Washington Boulevard.

**AIRPORT TAX** This is invariably included in the price of your ticket.

**CIGARETTES AND SMOKING** The country that first gave tobacco to the world is now probably the most concerned about its detrimental effects on health, and smoking is severely frowned upon. Most cinemas are non-smoking, restaurants are usually divided into non-smoking and smoking sections (California and New York City have banned smoking altogether in most restaurants) and smoking is forbidden on public transportation and flights.

**DATES** In the American style, the date 1.8.99 means not August 1 but January 8.

**ELECTRICITY** 110V AC. All plugs are two-pronged and rather insubstantial. Some travel plug adapters don't fit American sockets.

**FLOORS** The first floor in the US is what would be the ground floor in Britain; the second floor would be the first floor, and so on.

**ID** Should be carried at all times. Two pieces should suffice, one of which should have a photo: a passport and credit card(s) are your best bets. Not having your license with you while driving is an arrestable offence.

**MEASUREMENTS AND SIZES** US measurements are in inches, feet, yards and miles; weight in ounces, pounds and tons. American pints and gallons are about four-fifths of Imperial ones. Clothing sizes are two figures less what they would be in the UK – a British women's size 12 is a US size 10 – while British shoe sizes are 1/2 below American ones for women, and one size below for men.

**TAX** Be warned that sales tax is added to virtually everything you buy in a shop, but isn't included in the marked price. The actual rate varies from place to place: in New York and parts of California it's over eight percent, while some states – Alaska, Delaware, Montana and Oregon – have no sales tax at all. Hotel tax will add five to fifteen percent to most bills. You also often have to pay tax on top of the cost of car rental if you pick the vehicle up from an airport.

**TEMPERATURES** Always given in Fahrenheit.

**TIME ZONES** See p.19.

**TIPPING** Expected for all bar and restaurant service, at a rate of fifteen percent or so on the bill (unless the service is utterly abominable). About the same amount should be added to taxi fares. A hotel porter who has lugged your suitcases up several flights of stairs should get $3 to $5.

**VIDEOS** The standard format used for video cassettes in the US is different from that used in Britain. This means that you cannot buy videotapes in the US compatible with a video player bought in Britain. Despite this, there is no problem with buying blank tapes in the US for use with a video camera bought in Britain. The camera will format the blank tape so that it will record and play in the British standard.

# PART TWO

## THE

# GUIDE

# CHAPTER ONE

# NEW YORK CITY

**N**EW YORK CITY is one of the most exciting cities in the world. You may not think so at first – for the place is nothing short of mad, epitomizing the extremes of modern America. But spend even a few days here and the adrenalin takes hold. Just walking through the canyon-like city streets is an experience, eyes forever drawn upwards by the soaring architecture, the buildings like icons of the modern age. And despite the hype and the movie-image sentimentality, the island of **Manhattan** is massively romantic. Whether it's the flickering lights of the Midtown skyscrapers, the 4am half-life in Greenwich Village, or just wasting the morning on the Staten Island Ferry, you'd have to be made of stone not to be moved by it all.

New York is not a conventionally pleasing city – or for that matter conventional in any respect. The divisions between rich and poor – especially in Manhattan – are starkly underscored on the street: the homeless pick through the trash of manicured brownstone apartment buildings, and seedy hostels linger in gentrifying neighborhoods. In a perverse way, though, these tangible and potent contrasts give New York much of its excitement. That said, late-Nineties New York seems to have emerged, though wearily, from a long period defined by racial strife, urban blight and general despair. Indeed, recent statistics that put crime rates at their lowest level for 25 years, with murders and shootings down by over thirty percent, have citizens and visitors alike breathing a sigh of relief.

The city's most unique pleasures come from the **neighborhoods** of downtown Manhattan: Chinatown and the Lower East Side, the arty concentrations of SoHo and TriBeCa, and Greenwich and East Village; its **architecture** (the whole city reads like an illustrated history of modern design); and its **visual art**, which you can spend weeks exploring in the Metropolitan and Modern Art museums and countless smaller collections. On top of that there's **dance, theater** and **music**, from grass-roots productions to top-shelf names, as well as a formidable **club scene**. And, of course, there's the opportunity to consume. You can **eat** anything, cooked in any style; **drink** in any kind of company; sit through any amount of **movies**. And as for **shops**, the choice in this heartland of the great capitalist dream is almost numbingly exhaustive.

## Some history

The first European to see Manhattan Island, then inhabited by the Algonquin Indians, was the Italian navigator Verrazano, in 1524. Dutch colonists established the settlement of **New Amsterdam** exactly one hundred years later; its first governor, Peter Minuit, was the man who "bought" the whole island for a handful of trinkets, though considering the Indians he actually paid were not locals but only passing through, it might be said that they received a fine deal too. The colony was surrounded by a strong defensive wall – today's Wall Street follows its course – but by the time the British laid claim to the area in 1664, the heavy-handed rule of governor **Peter Stuyvesant** had so alienated its inhabitants that control was handed over without a fight.

Renamed New York, the city prospered and grew, its population reaching 33,000 by the time of the Revolution. The opening of the Erie Canal in 1825 facilitated trade further inland, spurring the city to become the economic powerhouse of the nation, the base later in the century of **financiers** such as Cornelius Vanderbilt and J Pierpont Morgan. The **Statue of Liberty** arrived in 1886, a symbol of the city's role as the gateway for generations of immigrants, and the early twentieth century saw the sudden proliferation of Manhattan's extraordinary **skyscrapers**, which cast New York as the city of the future in the eyes of an astonished world.

# ARRIVAL, INFORMATION AND GETTING AROUND

New York City is served by two **international airports**: most flights use **John F Kennedy (JFK)** (☎718/244-4444) in Queens, but some Virgin, British Airways and Continental flights touch down at **Newark** (☎973/961-6000) in New Jersey. In addition, most domestic arrivals come in at **La Guardia** (☎718/533-3400), also in Queens. From all the airports, the cheapest and most straightforward way into Manhattan is by **bus**.

From **JFK**, New York Airport Service buses run to the Port Authority Bus Terminal, Grand Central Station, Penn Station and major Midtown hotels in Manhattan ($13; students $6; every 15–20min 6am–midnight; journey time 45min–1hr; ☎718/706-9658). The alternative bus/subway link (☎718/330-1234) costs just the $1.50 subway fare: take the free shuttle bus (labeled "Long-term parking") to Howard Beach station on the #A subway line, a ninety-minute train ride from central Manhattan (every 20min 6am–1am).

Olympia Airport Express buses take up to forty minutes to get from **Newark** to Manhattan, where they stop at the World Trade Center, Grand Central and Penn stations ($10; every 20–30min 6.15am–midnight; ☎212/964-6233 or in NJ ☎908/354-3330). New Jersey Transit buses also run to the Port Authority Terminal in Manhattan ($3.25; every 15–30min; ☎201/762-5100).

New York Airport Service buses (see above) from **La Guardia** take 45 minutes to Grand Central and Port Authority. The fare is $10 (students $6); buses run every 15–30min 6am–midnight (to Grand Central and Port Authority) with a somewhat more limited schedule in the other direction (☎718/706-9658). New York Airport Service buses also link **JFK and La Guardia**, taking 45 minutes or so ($11; every 30min 5.40am–11pm).

**Taxis** are pricey from any of the airports; reckon on paying $20-plus from La Guardia, a flat rate of $30 from JFK and $35–55 from Newark (airport taxis at Newark will tell you their flat fares to different parts of Manhattan before you leave). **Car services** may cost a few dollars more. **Minibus shuttle services** are a decent mid-priced option if you are staying in midtown and don't mind multiple stops along the way. Gray Line Air Shuttles run from all three airports between 7am–11.30pm. Prices are roughly $15–20 per person depending on the airport. (☎212/315-3006 or 1-800/451-0455); Super Shuttle minivans are a similar 24-hour option (☎1-800/258-3826 or 212/258-3826). For **general information** on getting to and from the airports, call ☎1-800/AIR-RIDE.

**Greyhound** buses pull in at the Port Authority Bus Terminal, 42nd Street and Eighth Avenue (☎212/564-8484). By Amtrak train, you'll be coming in to **Penn Station**, at Seventh Avenue and 33rd Street (☎1-800/872-7245).

## Information

The best place for information is the **New York Convention and Visitors Bureau** at 810 7th Ave at 53rd St (Mon–Fri 8.30am–6pm, Sat & Sun 9am–5pm; ☎212/484-1222; *www.nycvisit.com*). It has up-to-date leaflets on what's going on in the arts and elsewhere, bus and subway maps, and information on accommodations – though they can't

actually book anything for you. You can also find lots of up-to-date listings at *www
.citysearchnyc.com* and *www.newyork.sidewalk.com*.

The main Manhattan **post office** is at 421 8th Ave, between West 31st and 33rd
streets (Mon–Sat 24hr for important services; zip code 10001).

## City transportation

Few cities equal New York for sheer street-level stimulation, and **walking** is the most
exciting method of exploring. However, it's also exhausting, and you'll need to use
some form of **public transportation**. The fastest way to get from A to B in Manhattan
and the boroughs is the **subway**. Intimidating at first glance, the subway system is
actually quite user-friendly. Each subway train and route is identified by a number or
letter; the majority of routes run Uptown or Downtown, following the great avenues,
rather than crosstown. The subway is open 24 hours a day. Every journey, whether on
the **express** lines, which stop only at major stations, or the **locals**, which stop at them
all, costs $1.50, bought in the form of a token or the newer, more convenient
**MetroCard** from station booths or from any branch of *McDonald's*; both are also valid
on the buses (the MetroCard also allows free transfers within a two-hour period from
bus to subway or vice-versa). MetroCards can be purchased in any amount from $3 to
$80; a $15 purchase allows 11 rides for the cost of 10. You can also get a 7-day pass for
$17 which allows unlimited rides during the 7-day period and a 30-day pass for $63.
The daily "Fun Pass" is valid for 24-hours of unlimited rides but is unaccountably not
sold at subway booths; you can usually find them in hotels and certain businesses
such as Gristedes supermarkets. Call ☎212/638-7622 to find the nearest location that
sells them.

Once you get past the turnstile, forget everything you've seen in the movies. New
York City subways are generally quite safe in part because they are almost always
crowded, even at night. The key to being safe is to simply use common sense. Always
use the crowded center subway cars late at night and while you're waiting, keep to the
area marked in yellow, where you can be seen by the booth attendants.

New York's **bus system** is clean, efficient and fairly frequent. Its one disadvantage
is that it can be extremely slow – in peak hours almost down to walking pace. Buses
stop every two or three blocks, at five- to ten-minute intervals. Anywhere in Manhattan
the fare is $1.50, payable on entry with either a subway token, a MetroCard or with the
correct change – but not pennies or dollar bills. If you're using a token, ask for a transfer if you need to change buses anywhere along your journey; transfers can only be
used to continue in your direction, not for return trips. You can only transfer from bus
to subway for free if you use the MetroCard; it has to be used within two hours.

Route **maps** for both the **subway** and **bus** networks are available at all token booths
or from the New York Convention and Visitor's Bureau at Seventh Avenue and 53rd
Street, or the concourse office at Grand Central.

**Taxis** in New York are pretty reasonably priced, and although the rudimentary
English of many of the drivers is notorious, they can normally get you where you want
to go. Knowing the exact address and its cross street is helpful.

## Guided tours

There are countless businesses and individuals vying to help you make sense of the
city, with all manner of **guided tours** available. One of the more original – and least
expensive – ways to get oriented is with Big Apple Greeters (1 Centre St, New York, NY
10007; ☎212/669-8159, fax 669-3685), a nonprofit group that matches you up with a local
volunteer and points you to places that interest you – and it's free (so get in touch well
ahead of time).

## WALKING TOURS

**Big Onion Walking Tours** (☎212/439-1090; *www.bigonion.com*) unveil the many layers of the city's history (all guides hold advanced degrees in American History). From $10; call for schedules and meeting places.

**Harlem Heritage Tours**, 230 W 116th St, Suite 5C (☎212/280-7888). Cultural tours of Harlem, general and specific (such as Harlem Jazz Clubs) are led midday and evenings for $15–20; reservations are recommended.

**Municipal Arts Society**, 457 Madison Ave (☎212/935-3960 or 439-1049). Architectural and cultural tours. Weekday walking tours from $10–15; free Wednesday lunchtime tours of Grand Central Station begin at 12.30pm from the main information booth; Saturday walking and bus tours may need reservations.

**The 92nd Street Y**, 1395 Lexington Ave (☎212/996-1100). None better, with a mixed bag of walking tours, from art tours to political New York and pre-dawn visits to the wholesale meat and fish markets. $20 and up.

Grayline is the biggest operator of guided **bus tours**, based in midtown Manhattan at the corner of Eighth Avenue and 42nd Street, in the Port Authority Bus Terminal (☎1-800/669-0051). Half-day tours, taking in the main sights of Manhattan, go for around $29, and a full day costs $36, bookable through any travel agent. New York Apple Tours, located at 1040 6th Ave, also offers double-decker bus tours for about the same prices; call ☎1-800/876-9868.

The **Circle Line Ferry** takes three hours to sail right round Manhattan from Pier 83 at the far west end of 42nd Street (at 12th Ave), taking in everything from soaring views of downtown Manhattan to the bleaker stretches of Harlem, with a commentary and on-board bar ($22; March–Dec with varying regularity; ☎212/563-3200; *www.circleline.com*). The **Staten Island Ferry** (see p.96) provides a staggering panorama of the Downtown skyline for free.

Island Helicopter, at the far eastern end of East 34th Street (☎212/683-4575), and Liberty Helicopter Tours, at the western end of 30th Street, near the Jacob Javits Convention Center (☎212/967-4550), offer helicopter flights from around $46 for 4 and a half minutes to $149 for 15 minutes.

# ACCOMMODATION

Prices for **accommodation** in New York are well above the norm for the US as a whole, with the majority of hotels charging over $100 a night (although exceptions and decent double rooms from $75 a night do exist). If you're just here for a few days, you may well be away from your lodgings for all your waking hours anyway, so spending $150 on a bed doesn't make all that much sense. On the other hand, there's a lot of high-standard accommodation about, and if you pay that bit more you can stay in a much more central location. Getting yourself a room with a **TV** is also a definite plus: New York's cable stations have to be seen to be believed. Booking accommodation in advance is strongly recommended.

## Hostels

**Chelsea Center Hostel**, 313 W 29th St at 8th Ave (☎212/643-0214, fax 473-3945). Small, clean and safe private Downtown hostel, with beds for $25, sheets, blankets and breakfast included. Reservations essential in high season. Cash only. ①.

---

**ACCOMMODATION PRICE CODES**

All accommodation prices in this book have been coded using the symbols below. Prices are for the least expensive double rooms in each establishment, and in this section include New York State tax at 8.25 percent, city tax at five percent and occupancy tax of $2. Note that hotels never include taxes when quoting dollar rates. For a full explanation see p.37 in Basics.

|   |   |   |
|---|---|---|
| ① up to $30 | ④ $60–80 | ⑦ $130–175 |
| ② $30–45 | ⑤ $80–100 | ⑧ $175–250 |
| ③ $45–60 | ⑥ $100–130 | ⑨ $250+ |

---

**Chelsea International Hostel**, 251 W 20th St, between 7th and 8th aves (☎212/647-0010, fax 727-7289). Located in the heart of Chelsea, this is the closest hostel to Downtown. Beds are $23 a night, with four or six sharing the clean, rudimentary rooms. Private double rooms $55 a night. Guests must leave a $10 key deposit. No curfew. ①.

**Gershwin**, 7 E 27th St, off 5th Ave (☎212/545-8000, fax 684-5546). New hostel/hotel geared toward young travelers. Pop Art decor, small bar, well-priced restaurant, beds from $27 a night, and private rooms from $95. Reservations accepted for private rooms only. ①/②.

**Hostelling International-New York**, 891 Amsterdam Ave at W 103rd St (☎212/932-2300, fax 932-2574). Dorms $22–29, plus restaurant, library, travel shop and theater. Reserve well in advance – they're very busy. ①.

**International House – Sugar Hill**, 722 St Nicholas Ave at 145th St (☎212/926-7030, fax 283-0108) and its jointly run neighbor, **The Blue Rabbit**, at no. 730 (☎ & Fax 212/491-3892). Noisy but adequate dorms in friendly, well-run hostels way up on the border of Harlem and Washington Heights, opposite 145th St subway station (A or D train). $20 a night, limited number of doubles $25 per person; no curfew, no chores and no lockout. Both ①.

**Jazz in the Park**, 36 W 106th St at Central Park W (☎212/932-1600). Just over a year old, this groovy bunkhouse boasts a TV/games room, rooftop barbecues, the *Java Joint Cafe* and lots of activities. The rooms sleep between 2 and 14, and are clean, bright and air-conditioned. Reservations essential June–October and over Christmas and New Year. ②.

**Vanderbilt YMCA**, 224 E 47th St, between 2nd and 3rd aves (☎212/756-9600). Smaller and quieter than its handy Midtown location (a 5min walk from Grand Central Station) might suggest. Inexpensive restaurant, swimming pool, gym and laundry. All rooms are air-conditioned. Singles $68, doubles $81. ④.

# Bed and breakfast

**Bed and breakfast** – staying in a New Yorker's spare room or subletting an apartment – is an increasingly popular (and somewhat less inexpensive) option. Normally arranged through an agency such as those listed below, rates run about $80–100 for a double, or $100 and up a night for a studio apartment. It is essential to book well in advance.

**Bed and Breakfast Manhattan**, PO Box 533, NY 10150-0533 (☎212/472-2528, fax 988-9818). Friendly agency for excellent rooms in hosted ⑤ and unhosted ⑥–⑨ apartments all over the city. Standards are consistently high, and properties range from characterful Greenwich Village townhouses to convenient uptown pieds-à-terre. Highly recommended.

**Bed and Breakfast Network of New York**, Suite 602, 134 W 32nd St, NY 10001 (☎212/645-8134). Write at least a month in advance. Hosted doubles ⑤; unhosted accommodation ⑥/⑦.

**Colby International**, 139 Round Hey, Liverpool L28 1RG, England (in the UK ☎0151/220 5848). Guaranteed B&B accommodations which can be arranged from the UK. Book at least a fortnight ahead in high season. Excellent value doubles ⑤ and studios ⑥.

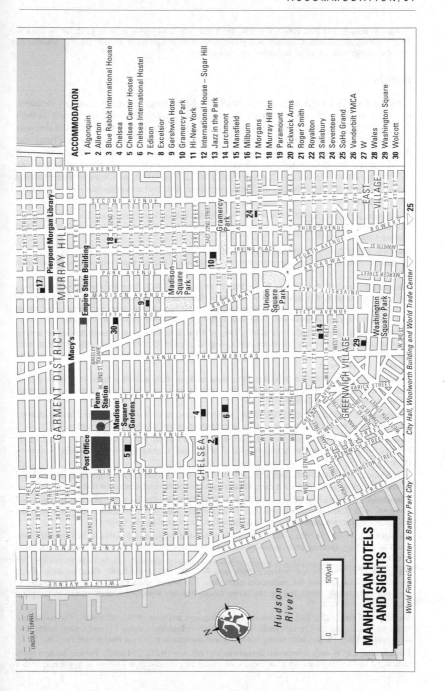

## ACCOMMODATION

1 Algonquin
2 Allerton
3 Blue Rabbit International House
4 Chelsea
5 Chelsea Center Hostel
6 Chelsea International Hostel
7 Edison
8 Excelsior
9 Gershwin Hotel
10 Gramercy Park
11 HI-New York
12 International House – Sugar Hill
13 Jazz in the Park
14 Larchmont
15 Mansfield
16 Milburn
17 Morgans
18 Murray Hill Inn
19 Paramount
20 Pickwick Arms
21 Roger Smith
22 Royalton
23 Salisbury
24 Seventeen
25 SoHo Grand
26 Vanderbilt YMCA
27 W
28 Wales
29 Washington Square
30 Wolcott

# MANHATTAN HOTELS AND SIGHTS

**Urban Ventures**, PO Box 426, NY 10024. Personal callers welcome at Suite 1412, 38 W 32nd St (☎212/594-5650). No minimum stay, and you can book up until the last minute. Budget doubles ④, "comfort range" rooms ⑤/⑥, unhosted apartments ⑥.

# Hotels

Most of New York's **hotels** are in midtown Manhattan – a good enough location, though you may well want to travel Downtown for less expensive (and usually better) food and nightlife. **Booking ahead** is very strongly advised; at certain times of the year – Christmas and early summer particularly – everything is likely to be full. Phone the hotels directly, or contact a booking service to reserve rooms at no extra charge, such as Meegan's (☎718/995-9292 or 1-800/441-1115); CRS (☎305/408-6100 or 1-800/950-0232); The Room Exchange (Mon–Fri only ☎212/760-1000); or Express Reservations (Mon–Fri only ☎1-800/356-1123). Rates are often reduced at weekends – so it's always worth asking.

**Algonquin**, 59 W 44th St (☎212/840-6800). New York's classic literary hangout. The decor remains little changed, though the bedrooms have been refurbished to good effect. Ask about summer and weekend specials. ⑧/⑨.

**Allerton**, 302 W 22nd St at 8th Ave (☎212/243-6017). This family-run hotel on a quiet, tree-lined residential street in Chelsea has decent-sized, well-maintained rooms, some with kitchenettes. Good value. ⑥.

**Amsterdam Inn**, 340 Amsterdam Ave at 76th St (☎212/579-7500). From the owners of the *Murray Hill Inn* (see below), this new hotel is located within walking distance of Central Park, Lincoln Center and the American Museum of Natural History. Rooms are very basic (no closets) but clean, with TVs, phones and maid service. The staff is friendly and there's a 24-hour concierge. ⑤.

**Chelsea**, 222 W 23rd St (☎212/243-3700). One of New York's most noted landmarks, this ageing neo-Gothic building boasts a notorious past (see p.81). Avoid the older rooms; ask for a renovated one, with wood floors, log-burning fireplaces and plenty of space for a few extra friends. ⑦ for a studio room, ⑨ for a suite.

**Edison**, 228 W 47th St (☎212/840-5000). The most striking thing about the funky 1000-room *Edison* is its beautifully restored Art Deco lobby. The rooms aren't fancy, but they've been recently renovated. A good value for Midtown. ⑦.

**Excelsior**, 45 W 81st St (☎212/362-9200). Old-fashioned hotel across from the Natural History Museum in the lively Columbus Ave area. Decent-sized rooms and four-person suites. ⑥/⑦.

**Gramercy Park**, 2 Lexington Ave at E 21st St (☎212/475-4320). Pleasant enough hotel in a lovely location, with a mixture of newly renovated and tatty rooms. Guests get a key to the adjacent private park. ⑦/⑧.

**Larchmont**, 27 W 11th St, between 5th and 6th aves (☎212/989-9333). Budget hotel in tree-lined Greenwich Village, with small but nice, clean rooms. Good find. ④ singles, ⑤ doubles.

**Mansfield**, 12 W 44th St at 5th Ave (☎212/944-6050). Value alternative to the nearby *Algonquin* and *Royalton*, with above-average rooms (some triples and quads), and luxuries like thermo-vapor whirlpools and steambaths. Good deli off the lobby, and a steakhouse. ⑦/⑧.

**Milburn**, 242 W 76th St (☎212/362-1006). Welcoming and well-situated hotel that has recently been renovated in very gracious style; great for families. Doubles ⑦/⑧; large two-room suites, with kitchenettes ⑧.

**Morgans**, 237 Madison Ave between 36th and 37th sts (☎212/686-0300). Chic creation of the founders of *Studio 54* and the *Palladium* nightclub. The black, white and gray decor is starting to look self-consciously 1980s, but for the steep prices you get a jacuzzi, a great stereo system and cable TV in your room. ⑨.

**Murray Hill Inn**, 143 E 30th St between Lexington and 3rd aves (☎212/683-6900). The rooms are small and basic, but they're air-conditioned and have telephones, cable TV and a sink; some also have private bath. Packed with young travelers and backpackers. Great weekly rates too. ④/⑤.

**Paramount**, 235 W 46th St between Broadway and 8th Ave (☎212/764-5500). Former budget hotel renovated by the *Morgans/Royalton* crew. One of the hippest places in town to stay, popular with a pop and media crowd, who come to enjoy the Philippe Starck interior and to be waited on by sleek young things. Also boasts a trendy *Dean and DeLuca* coffee shop, plus a quality bar and restaurant. ⑨; with summer specials at ⑧.

**Pickwick Arms**, 230 E 51st St (☎212/355-0300). Thoroughly pleasant budget hotel, and one of the best deals near the Upper East Side. All 400 rooms are air-conditioned, with cable TV, direct dial phones and room service. Open-air roof deck with stunning views, and *Torremolino's* restaurant. A single room with shared bath is $75. ④.

**Roger Smith**, 501 Lexington Ave at E 47th St (☎212/755-1400). One of the best Midtown hotels, offering both style and helpful service. Individually decorated rooms, a great restaurant that doubles as a jazz club and art works on display in public spaces. Breakfast is included. Popular with bands. ⑨.

**Royalton**, 44 W 44th St (☎212/869-4400). Attempting to capture the market for the style arbiter, the Philippe Starck-designed *Royalton* aimed to be the *Algonquin* of the 1990s and beyond. As much a power-lunch venue for NYC's media and publishing set as a place to stay. ⑨.

**Salisbury**, 123 W 57th St (☎212/246-1300). Good service, large rooms with kitchenettes and proximity to Central Park are the attractions here. Price includes continental breakfast. ⑧.

**Seventeen**, 225 E 17th St between 2nd and 3rd aves (☎212/475-2845). Budget accommodation as you'd expect to find it: rudimentary bedrooms and bathrooms in the hall that have seen better days. But it's clean and friendly and its location can't be beat – on a pleasant tree-lined street minutes from Union Square and the East Village. Check out the excellent weekly rates. Nightly rates ④/⑤.

**SoHo Grand**, 310 W Broadway at Grand St (☎212/965-3000). Great location at the edge of SoHo, with guests of the model/media-star/actor variety. Small but stylish rooms, with decor by Philippe Starck, a good bar, restaurant and fitness center. ⑨.

**W**, 541 Lexington Ave between 49th and 50th sts (☎212/755-1200). If the crowd hanging out in the *Whisky Blue Bar*, dining at *Heartbeat* or just posing on the sidewalk are any indication, the *W*, which opened in December 1998, might well be the hippest hotel in town. Stylish rooms. ⑨.

**Wales**, 1295 Madison Ave at 92nd St (☎212/876-6000). Very Upper East Side refined in feel. Excellent prices for the lovingly restored accommodation. Ask about the weekend specials. ⑧.

**Washington Square**, 103 Waverly Place (☎212/777-9515). Ideal location right in the heart of Greenwich Village, and a stone's throw from the NYU campus. Don't be deceived by the posh-looking lobby – the rooms are what you'd expect for the price, and the staff can be surly. Continental breakfast is included. ⑥/⑦.

**Wolcott**, 4 W 31st St at 5th Ave (☎212/268-2900). Surprisingly relaxing, moderately priced hotel, with a gilded, ornamented lobby and decent rooms, all with bathrooms. A very good deal. ⑦.

# THE CITY

New York City comprises the central island of Manhattan and four outer boroughs – Brooklyn, Queens, the Bronx and Staten Island. **Manhattan**, to many, *is* New York; certainly, this is where you're likely to spend most time, and to stay. The island is broadly divided into three areas: **downtown** (below 14th St); **midtown** (from 14th St to Central Park/57th St); and **uptown Manhattan** (north of 57th St). The southern (Downtown) part of Manhattan was the first to be settled, which means that its streets have names and are somewhat randomly arranged. Above Houston Street (pronounced *How-stun*, not *Hew-stun*) on the east side and 14th on the west side, the streets follow a sensible grid pattern, numbers increasing as you move north.

**Fifth Avenue**, the greatest of the main avenues, begins Downtown at the arch in Washington Square Park and cuts along the east side of Central Park, serving as a dividing line between east streets ("the East Side") and west streets ("the West Side"). House numbers increase as you walk away from Fifth Avenue to either side; numbers on avenues increase as you move north. Traffic runs from east to west on **odd**-numbered streets, from west to east on **even**-numbered streets, and in both directions on

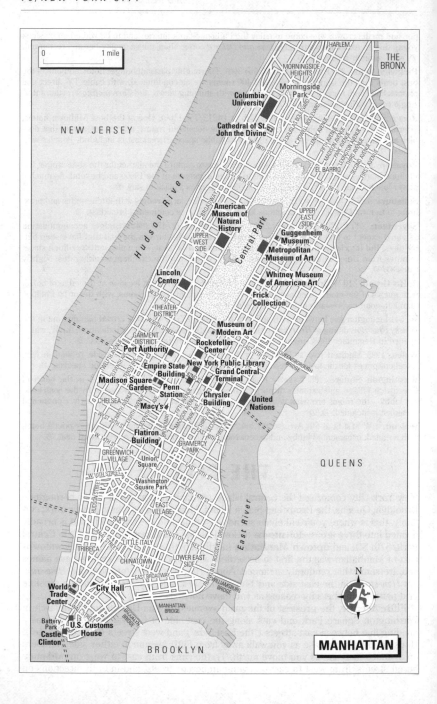

0      1 mile

NEW JERSEY

THE BRONX

HARLEM

MORNINGSIDE HEIGHTS

Morningside Park

Columbia University

Cathedral of St. John the Divine

EL BARRIO

UPPER EAST SIDE

American Museum of Natural History

UPPER WEST SIDE

Central Park

Guggenheim Museum

Metropolitan Museum of Art

Whitney Museum of American Art

Lincoln Center

Frick Collection

THEATER DISTRICT

GARMENT DISTRICT

Museum of Modern Art

Port Authority

Rockefeller Center

New York Public Library

Empire State Building

Grand Central Terminal

QUEENSBOROUGH BRIDGE

Madison Square Garden

Penn Station

Chrysler Building

United Nations

CHELSEA

Macy's

Flatiron Building

GRAMERCY PARK

GREENWICH VILLAGE

Union Square

QUEENS

Washington Square Park

EAST VILLAGE

SOHO

HOUSTON STREET

TRIBECA

LITTLE ITALY

CHINATOWN

LOWER EAST SIDE

EAST BROADWAY

FRANKLIN D. ROOSEVELT DRIVE

WILLIAMSBURG BRIDGE

East River

Hudson River

World Trade Center

City Hall

MANHATTAN BRIDGE

Battery Park

U.S. Customs House

Castle Clinton

BROOKLYN BRIDGE

N

BROOKLYN

**MANHATTAN**

major crosstown streets. Apart from Park, Broadway and Eleventh Avenue, which run both ways in most stretches, avenues run in alternate directions.

Manhattan is a hard act to follow, and the four **outer boroughs** inevitably pale in comparison, essentially residential in character. However, **Brooklyn Heights** is one of the city's most beautiful neighborhoods, and both the faded resort of **Coney Island** and nearby **Brighton Beach**, both in Brooklyn, deserve trips out on the subway, while a ride on the **Staten Island Ferry** is an attraction in itself.

# Downtown Manhattan

DOWNTOWN MANHATTAN harbors its extremes in close proximity. For some it's the most spectacular, most glamorous skyline in the world, for others a somewhat run-down and seedy home. But whatever your perspective, it is undeniably archetypal New York.

The **Statue of Liberty** is the obvious focus – not so much for the vaunted symbol (though this is hard to ignore) as for the views of southern Manhattan. This lower part of the island begins with the **Financial District** – Wall Street at its center – and then drifts, within half a mile, into the first of the city's ethnic districts: bustling, insular **Chinatown**, fast expanding into adjacent **Little Italy**. Over to the west, the one-time industrial areas of **SoHo** and **TriBeCa** are now expensive residential blocks, home to Manhattan's art and film scenes, while further north come **Greenwich Village** and the **East Village**, former bohemian enclaves now more traditional than their residents would like to believe. Further down is the **Lower East Side**, a hotbed of artistic innovation that quickly fades into areas of real poverty, quite unhidden and occasionally threatening.

## The Statue of Liberty and Ellis Island

The tip of Manhattan Island, and the shores of New Jersey, Staten Island and Brooklyn, form the broad expanse of **New York Harbor**, one of the finest natural harbors in the world, stretching as far as the Verrazano Narrows – the narrow neck of land between Staten Island and Long Island. It's possible to appreciate it by simply gazing out from the promenade in Battery Park, but to get the best views of the classic skyline you should really take to the water. You can do this on the Staten Island Ferry, or from the islands in the bay.

**Ferries**, run by Circle Line, go to both the Statue of Liberty and Ellis Island from the pier in Battery Park (sailings every 20min in summer, 8.30am–4.30pm; $7 round-trip; tickets from Castle Clinton in the park; ticket and schedule information ☎212/269-5755). If you take the last ferry, you can't visit both islands, so try and leave as early as possible, which will also help you to avoid the long queues. Each island deserves a couple of hours at least, and Liberty Island makes a pleasant place to spend an entire afternoon. There are no admission fees for either island. (Governor's Island, the third island in the bay, is currently inaccessible. It is expected to be sold to a private interest by 2001: call the New York Convention and Visitors Bureau ☎212/484-1222 for developments.)

The **Statue of Liberty**, torch in hand and clutching a stone tablet, has for a century served as a figurehead for the American Dream, with probably the most instantly recognizable profile in existence. Depicting Liberty throwing off her shackles and holding a beacon to light the world, it was the creation of the French sculptor Frédéric Auguste Bartholdi, crafted a hundred years after the American Revolution in recognition of fraternity between the French and American people (though he originally intended it for Alexandria in Egypt). Liberty, which consists of thin copper sheets bolted together and supported by an iron framework designed by Gustave Eiffel, was built in Paris between

1874 and 1884. Bartholdi enlarged his original terracotta model through four successive versions – one of which stands beside the Seine in Paris – to its present size. It was
formally dedicated by President Cleveland on October 28, 1886. You can climb up to the
crown, though the cramped stairway to the torch sadly remains closed to the public.
Don't be surprised if you have to wait more than an hour to ascend; while you do so,
you can always enjoy Liberty Park's views of the downtown Manhattan skyline.

Just across the water, a few minutes by ferry, sits **Ellis Island**, the first stop for over
twelve million prospective immigrants. Originally called Gibbet Island by the English
(who used it for punishing unfortunate pirates), it became an immigration station in
1894, mainly to handle the massive influx from Southern and Eastern Europe. It
remained open until 1954, when it was left to fall into atmospheric ruin.

The immigrants who arrived at Ellis Island were all steerage class passengers; richer voyagers were processed at their leisure on board ship. Most families arrived hungry and penniless; con men preyed on them from all sides, stealing their baggage as it
was checked and offering rip-off exchange rates for whatever money they had managed
to bring. Each family was split up – men sent to one area, women and children to another – while a series of checks weeded out the undesirables and the infirm. Steamship
carriers were obliged to return any immigrants not accepted to their original port, but
according to official records only two percent were ever rejected, and many of those
jumped into the sea and tried to swim to Manhattan rather than face going home.

By the time of its closure, Ellis Island was a formidable complex, the island having
been expanded by landfill. In the turreted central building, **The Museum of
Immigration** (daily 9.30am–5pm; free) tries hard to recapture the spirit of the place
with features such as "Ellis Island Stories", a half-hour dramatic reenactment of the
immigrant experience based on oral histories (April–Sept only, $3 for adults, $2.50 for
children); the Wall of Honor, with the names of many of those that came through Ellis
Island; and Treasures From Home, a collection of family heirlooms, photos and other
artifacts.

## The Financial District

The skyline of Manhattan's **Financial District** is the one you see in all the movies –
dramatic skyscrapers crammed into the southern tip of the island and framed by the
monumental elegance of the Brooklyn Bridge. At the heart of the nation's wheeler-deal-
ing, this is the place where Manhattan began, though precious few leftovers of those
early days remain, most having been bulldozed by big corporations eager to boost their
images with headquarters at the right address. A nascent residential community –
housed in converted office space and formerly abandoned buildings along the waterfront – has helped the area begin to shed its nine-to-five existence. Still, don't expect too
much here outside of business hours.

The Dutch arrived in this part of New York first, building a wooden wall at the edge
of their small settlement to protect themselves from pro-British settlers to the north.
Hence, the narrow canyon of Wall Street gained its name. It's here, behind the
Neoclassical mask of the **New York Stock Exchange** at Broad and Wall streets, that
the purse strings of the world are pulled – a process you can view from the visitors'
gallery on the 3rd floor (Mon–Fri 9.15am–4pm; free). The **Federal Hall National
Memorial**, at 26 Wall St, looks a little foolish surrounded by skyscrapers. The building
was once the Customs House, but the exhibition inside (Mon–Fri 9am–5pm; free)
relates to the headier days of 1789, when George Washington was sworn in as president from a balcony on this site. Washington's statue stands, very properly, on the steps
outside the daintily rotunded hall. At Wall Street's other end, **Trinity Church**
(Broadway between Rector and Church sts; guided tours daily at 2pm) is an ironic
onlooker to the street's dealings, a knobbly neo-Gothic structure erected in 1846 which,

for fifty years, was the city's tallest building. It has much of the air of an English church, especially in its sheltered graveyard, the resting place of such early luminaries as the first Secretary to the Treasury, Alexander Hamilton.

Broadway comes to a gentle end at the **Bowling Green**, an oval of turf used for the game by eighteenth-century colonial Brits on a lease of "one peppercorn per year". Earlier still, the green was the site of one of Manhattan's more memorable business deals, when Peter Minuit, first director general of the Dutch colony of New Amsterdam, bought the whole island from the Indians for a handful of baubles worth sixty guilders (about $25). Today the green is a spot for office people picnicking in the shadow of Cass Gilbert's 1907 **US Customs House**, a monument to New York's booming maritime economy. Four statues at the front (sculpted by Daniel Chester French, who also created the Lincoln Memorial in Washington DC) represent the four continents, while the twelve near the top personify the world's commercial centers. The Customs House contains the superb **National Museum of the American Indian** (daily 10am–5pm; free; ☎212/514-3700), a fascinating assembly of artifacts from almost every tribe native to the Americas. The curators have been creative with the presentation of their material, which includes large wood and stone carvings from the Pacific Northwest; elegant featherwork from Amazonia; a large array of masks, Aztec mosaics; Mayan textiles; seven-foot house posts shaped like animals, some scalps and a tribe's worth of elaborately beaded moccasins. Downtown Manhattan lets out its breath in **Battery Park**, where the nineteenth-century **Castle Clinton** (daily 9am–5pm) once protected the southern tip of Manhattan and now sells ferry tickets to the Statue of Liberty and Ellis Island. A new edition to Battery Park is the **Museum of Jewish Heritage** (April–Sept: Sun–Fri 9am–5pm, Thurs until 8pm; Oct–March Fri closes at 3pm, otherwise same hours; closed Sat and Jewish holidays; $7), where three floors of exhibits range from the practical accoutrements of everyday Eastern European Jewish life to the prison garb survivors wore in Nazi concentration camps, along with photographs, personal belongings, multimedia presentations and narratives. Recent acquisitions include Himmler's own annotated copy of *Mein Kampf*.

North up Water Street, at Pearl and Broad, the partially reconstructed **Fraunces Tavern** (Mon–Fri 10am–4.45pm, Sat noon–4pm; $2.50) was where, on December 4, 1783, with the British conclusively beaten, a weeping George Washington took leave of his assembled officers, intent on returning to rural life in Virginia. The second floor recreates the simple colonial dining room where this took place – all probably as genuine as the relics of Washington's teeth and hair in the adjacent museum.

Further up Water Street, at the far eastern end of Fulton Street, is the renovated **South Street Seaport**, formerly New York's sailship port, from where Robert Fulton started a ferry service to Brooklyn. Trade eventually moved elsewhere, and the blocks of warehouses and ship's chandlers were left to rot until being renovated in the late 1970s. Regular guided tours of the Seaport run from the visitor center at 207 Water St, but the best place to start looking around is the so-called **Museum Block**, where upmarket shops lurk behind Water Street's hotchpotch of Greek Revival and Italianate facades. You might also look in on the **Fulton Fish Market**, a tatty building that wears its eighty years as the city's wholesale outlet with no pretensions. The enclave generates over a billion dollars annually, and has recently come under the jurisdiction of municipal authorities, intent upon stemming the corruption and Mafia influence in the area. These back-room dealings are of no threat to the casual visitor, though, and if you can manage it, you should visit here around 6am, when buyers' lorries park up beneath the highway to collect the catches – invigorating stuff. The adjacent **Pier 17 Pavilion**, an overdeveloped complex of restaurants and shops, sticks out like a sore thumb, though more interesting and germane are piers 15 and 16, which house the **South Street Museum**'s collection of soaring sailships and chubby ferries (April–Sept daily 10am–6pm, Thurs until 8pm; Oct–March daily except Tues 10am–5pm; $6).

From just about anywhere in the Seaport you can see the much-loved **Brooklyn Bridge**. Now just one of several spans across the East River, it was in its day a technological quantum leap. The first bridge to use steel cables, it towered over the low brick structures around it, and for twenty years after it opened in 1883 was the world's largest suspension bridge. It didn't go up easily, though. John Augustus Roebling, its architect and engineer, crushed his foot taking measurements for the piers and died of gangrene three weeks later; his son Washington took over, only to be crippled by the bends from working in an insecure underwater caisson, and subsequently directed the work from his sick bed. Yet the result of their efforts, coupled with the spectacular views of Manhattan that the bridge offers, seems worth the trouble.

Wherever you are in downtown Manhattan, the twin towers of the **World Trade Center** dominate the landscape. Spirited down to a tenth of their size, the towers – actually a five-building complex – wouldn't get a second glance. But the fact is they're so big that a walk across the plaza below in summer makes your head reel (it's closed in winter, since icicles falling from the towers can kill). The World Trade Center was quickly surpassed as the world's tallest building by the Sears Tower in Chicago, and remained half-empty for several years. But despite the damage wrought by a terrorist bomb explosion on February 26, 1993, in which six people were killed, the Center is now full and successful, and has become one of the city's emblems. With courage, a trip to the 107th-floor **observation deck** of Two World Trade Center (June–Sept daily 9.30am–11.30pm; Oct–May daily 9.30am–9.30pm; $12.50) gives a mind-blowing view from a height of 1350ft. From the open-air **rooftop promenade**, the silent panorama is more dramatic still – even Jersey City looks exciting. As you timidly edge your way around, ponder the fact that one Philippe Petit once walked a tightrope between the two towers – nerve indeed.

Across from the World Trade Center on Vesey Street and Broadway, **St Paul's Chapel** comes from a very different order of things. It's the oldest church in Manhattan, dating from 1766 – eighty years earlier than Trinity Church and almost prehistoric by New York standards. And to the west is **Battery Park City**, a self-sufficient section of office buildings, luxury apartments and boutiques built on the million cubic yards of earth and rock thrown up when digging the foundations for the World Trade Center.

## City Hall Park and the Civic Center

Immediately north of St Paul's Chapel, Broadway and Park Row form the apex of **City Hall Park**, a noisy, pigeon-splattered triangle of green with Cass Gilbert's 1913 **Woolworth Building** (233 Broadway between Barclay St and Park Place) as a venerable onlooker. For many, this is New York's definitive skyscraper, its soaring lines fringed with Gothic decoration. Frank Woolworth made his fortune from "five and dime" stores, and true to his philosophy he paid cash for his skyscraper. The whimsical reliefs at each corner of the lobby show him doing just that, counting out the money in nickels and dimes. Facing him in caricature are the architect (medievally clutching a model of his building), renting agent and builder. Within, vaulted ceilings ooze honeygold mosaics, and even the mailboxes are magnificent.

At the top of the park, marking the beginning of the **Civic Center** and its incoherent jumble of municipal offices and courts, stands **City Hall** (Mon–Fri 10am–4pm), completed in 1812. After the city's 1927 feting of returned aviator Charles Lindbergh, it became the traditional finishing point for Broadway tickertape parades, given for astronauts, returned hostages and, more recently, the city's triumphant baseball team. Inside, it's an elegant meeting of arrogance and authority, with the sweeping spiral staircase delivering you to the precise geometry of the **Governor's Room** and the self-important section that formerly contained the **Board of Estimates Chamber**.

If City Hall is the acceptable face of municipal bureaucracy, the **New York Courthouse** (known unofficially as the **Tweed Courthouse**) behind it at 52 Chambers St is a reminder of a seamier underbelly. William Marcy "Boss" Tweed worked his way from nowhere to become chairman of the Democratic Central Committee at Tammany Hall in 1856, and manipulated the city's revenues through his own and his supporters' pockets. For a while his grip strangled all dissent, until a political cartoonist, Thomas Nast, and the editor of the *New York Times* (who'd refused a half-million-dollar bribe to keep quiet) turned public opinion against him. With suitable irony Tweed died in 1878 in Ludlow Street jail – which he'd had built as Commissioner of Public Works.

## Chinatown and Little Italy

A short stroll north from the Civic Center is **Chinatown**, Manhattan's most thriving ethnic neighborhood, which over recent years has extended north across Canal Street into Little Italy and east into the Lower East Side. With more than 100,000 residents, seven Chinese newspapers, around 150 restaurants and over 300 garment factories, it is a "model slum," with the lowest crime rate, highest employment and least juvenile delinquency of any city district.

The Chinese began to arrive in New York in the mid-nineteenth century. Most had previously worked out West, building railroads and digging gold mines, and few intended to stay: their idea was simply to make a nest egg and retire to a life of leisure with their families (99 percent of the workers were men) back in China. Some did go back, but on the whole the big money took rather longer to accumulate than expected, and so Chinatown took shape as a permanent settlement. Budget restaurants boomed, thanks in part to the increase in working women who had no time to cook and bought food to take home. **Mott Street** is the main thoroughfare and the streets around – Canal, Pell, Bayard, Doyers and Bowery – host a positive glut of restaurants, tea and rice shops and grocers.

On the other side of Canal Street, **Little Italy** is light years away from the solid ethnic enclave of old. Originally settled by the huge nineteenth-century influx of Italian immigrants, the neighborhood has few Italians living here now, with families driven away by the high rents or the encroaching expanse of Chinatown, and the restaurants (of which there are plenty) tend to have high prices and a touristy feel. However, some original bakeries and *salumerias* (Italian specialty food stores) do survive, and you can still indulge yourself with a cappuccino and pastry. September's **Festa di San Gennaro** is a wild and raucous splurge to celebrate the saint's day, when Italians from all over the city turn up and **Mulberry Street**, the main strip, is transformed by street stalls and food outlets.

## SoHo and TriBeCa

Since the mid-1960s, **SoHo**, the grid of streets that runs *So*uth of *Ho*uston Street, has meant **art**. Squashed between the Financial District and Greenwich Village, it had long been a wasteland of manufacturers and wholesalers; but as the Village declined in hipness, SoHo was suddenly "in." Its loft spaces were ideal for low-rent studios, and galleries quickly followed, attracting crowds, boutiques and restaurants. Gentrification came next, and what remains is a mix of chichi antique, art and clothes shops, overpriced galleries and numerous **museums**, like the SoHo branch of the Guggenheim at 575 Broadway (Thurs–Mon 11am–6pm, closed Tues & Wed; free), and the New Museum of Contemporary Art at 583 Broadway (Wed & Sun noon–6pm, Thurs–Sat noon–8pm, closed Mon & Tues; $5, students, seniors and artists $3; ☎212/219-1355). SoHo now carries the veneer of the chic establishment – a loft in the area means money (and lots of it) – but it is still home to some good art galleries and some of the best cast-iron facades in America.

The technique of **cast-iron architecture** originated as a way of assembling buildings quickly and inexpensively, with iron beams rather than heavy walls carrying the weight of the floors. The result was the removal of supporting walls, greater space for windows and, most noticeably, decorative facades. Almost any style or whim could be cast in iron and pinned to a building, and architects indulged themselves in Baroque balustrades, forests of Renaissance columns and all the effusion of the French Second Empire to glorify SoHo's sweatshops. Have a look at 72–76 Greene St, a neat extravagance whose Corinthian portico stretches the whole five stories, all in painted metal, and at the strongly composed elaborations of its sister building at nos. 28–30. At the northeast corner of Broome Street and Broadway the magnificent **Haughwout Building** is perhaps the ultimate in the genre, with rhythmically repeated motifs of colonnaded arches framed behind taller columns in a thin sliver of a Venetian palace.

**TriBeCa**, the *Tri*angle *Be*low *Ca*nal Street, has caught the fallout of SoHo's artists, and has rapidly changed from a wholesale garment district to an upscale community. Less a triangle than a crumpled rectangle – the area bounded by Canal and Chambers streets, Broadway and the Hudson – its spacious industrial buildings house the apartments of TriBeCa's new gentry, among them Robert De Niro (whose film production company, TriBeCa Film Center, and restaurant, *TriBeCa Grill*, are located at 375 Greenwich St) and, until his death in 1999, John F Kennedy Jr.

## Greenwich Village

**Greenwich Village** (or simply "the Village") is at the top of most visitor's list of favorite neighborhoods in New York, despite the fact that while its bohemian image endures well enough if you don't live in New York, the Village has long since lost any radical edge. Yet to a great extent, it still sports many of the attractions that brought people here in the first place: a busy street life that lasts later than in any other part of the city, more restaurants per head than anywhere else, and bars cluttering every corner.

Greenwich Village grew up as a rural retreat from the early and frenetic nucleus of New York City, given impetus during the yellow fever epidemic of 1822 when it served as a refuge from the infected streets Downtown. Refined Federal and Greek Revival townhouses lured some of the city's highest society names and later proved fertile ground for struggling artists and intellectuals. By the turn of the century Greenwich Village was on its way to becoming New York's Left Bank.

The natural center of the Village, **Washington Square** is not exactly elegant, but it does retain its northern edging of redbrick rowhouses – the "solid, honorable dwellings" of Henry James's eponymous novel – and Stanford White's imposing **Triumphal Arch**, built in 1892 to commemorate the centenary of George Washington's inauguration. It's also the heart of the truly urban campus of New York University. As soon as the weather gets warm, the park becomes sports field, theater, drug den and social club, boiling over with life as buskers perform, skateboards flip and the pulsing bass of hip-hop resounds through the whispered offers of dope peddlers and the honking taxi horns.

Follow **MacDougal Street** south and you hit **Bleecker Street** – the Village's main drag, packed with shops, bars, people and restaurants. This junction is also the area's best-known meeting place, a vibrant corner whose mock-European sidewalk cafes have been turned from literary hangouts to overpriced tourist traps. Turning right takes you through the hubbub of Village life, stretching up **Sixth Avenue** to the unmistakeable nineteenth-century bulk of the **Jefferson Market Courthouse**, voted, in 1885, fifth most beautiful building in America and now serving as the local public library. Cut through from here to **Seventh Avenue** and you'll pass by **Bedford Street**, one of the Village's quietest and most desirable living areas. Nearby, **Christopher Street** joins Seventh at **Sheridan Square**, site of the **Stonewall** gay bar where, in 1969, a police raid precipitated a siege that lasted the best part of an hour. If not a victory for gay rights, it was the first time that gay men had stood up to the police en masse, and as such represents a turning point in the struggle for equal rights, remembered by the annual **Gay Pride march**, held on the last Sunday in June.

## The East Village

The **East Village** is quite different in look and feel to its western counterpart, Greenwich Village. Once, like the Lower East Side proper which it abuts, the East Village was a refuge of immigrants and solidly working-class. Home to New York's non-conformist fringe in the earlier part of this century, it later became the haunt of the Beats – Kerouac, Burroughs, Ginsberg, et al – who would get together at Ginsberg's house on East Seventh Street for declamatory readings. Later, Andy Warhol debuted the Velvet Underground here; the Fillmore East hosted almost every band under the sun; and Richard Hell, Patti Smith and the Ramones invented punk rock in a hole-in-the-wall called **CBGB** (see p.103). Further East is **Alphabet City** (avenues A, B, C, D) a former Slavic enclave – and erstwhile turf of drug dealers and gangs – which has since gentrified at an alarming rate. If you walk along Avenue A, you'll pass a number of worthwhile fashion and design shops as well as cafes and record stores, including the excellent Etherea Records (66 Ave A). **Tompkins Square Park** begins at East Seventh Street between avenues A and B and is considered the center of Alphabet City. The area surrounding the park is welcoming, with plenty of offbeat restaurants and bars, like *Drinkland* (339 E Tenth St), with its psychedelic interior. Be warned, though: venture beyond Avenue C and the mood turns dangerously edgy, especially at night.

Much of the East Village has changed since the economic boom of the mid-1980s, not the least of which has been its escalating rents and encroaching "yuppification." The East Village isn't the hotbed of creativity it once was, but **St Mark's Place** is still one of downtown Manhattan's more vibrant strips, even if the thrift shops, panhandlers and political hustlers have given way to more sanitized forms of rebellion and even a Gap.

Though it's hard to believe now, **Astor Place**, at the western end of St Mark's Place, was one of the city's most desirable neighborhoods in the 1830s. Undistinguished-looking Lafayette Street was home to such wealthy names as John Jacob Astor himself, one of New York's most hideously greedy tycoons. The Astor Place **subway station**, in the middle of the junction, discreetly remembers the man on its platforms, where colored reliefs of beavers recall Astor's first big killings – in the fur trade. More recently, Astor Place has begun looking like a mall, with chain superstore outlets – like the city's first K-Mart, a giant American discounter – hawking household goods, books and records.

## The Lower East Side

South of Tompkins Square, the **Lower East Side** began life towards the end of the last century as an insular slum for over half a million Jewish immigrants. Since then it has changed considerably, with the inhabitants now largely Puerto Rican or Chinese rather than Jewish. Yet the neighborhood is moving up the social ladder: south of East Houston Street is wholesomely seedy and borderline trendy, with new nightspots popping up almost weekly.

You can still **buy** just about anything cut-price in the Lower East Side, especially on Sunday mornings, when **Orchard Street** is filled with stalls and stores selling off hats, clothes and designer labels at hefty discounts. Located next to this melee is the **Lower**

**East Side Tenement Museum**, 90 Orchard St between Broome and Delancey (Tues–Fri 1–5pm, Thurs until 8pm, Sat & Sun 11am–4.30pm; $8, students $6) which offers the lowdown on the neighborhood's immigrant past. The museum gives tours through a tenement building, whose restored rooms re-create the poverty that many area residents withstood while trying to build a new life in America.

The **Bowery** spears up as far as Cooper Square on the edge of the East Village. This wide thoroughfare has gone through many changes over the years: it took its name from "Bouwerie," the Dutch word for farm, when it was the city's main agricultural supplier; later, in the closing decades of the last century, it was lined with music halls, theaters, hotels and middle-market restaurants, drawing people from all parts of Manhattan. Currently it's a skid row for the homeless, flanked by a demoralizing line of boarded-up shops and long-stay hotels, where few New Yorkers venture of their own accord, although it's rarely all that dangerous. The one – bizarre – focus is the **Bowery Savings Bank** on the corner of Grand Street. Designed by Stanford White in 1894, it rises out of the neighborhood's debris like a god, much as does its sister bank on 42nd Street, a shrine to the virtue of thrift.

# Midtown Manhattan

**MIDTOWN MANHATTAN** is in many ways the center of the city. Most of the hotels are here, and it's where you're most likely to arrive – at Penn or Grand Central Station, or the Port Authority Bus Terminal. New York's most glamorous (and most expensive) street, **Fifth Avenue**, cuts through its heart, with the neon theater strip of **Broadway** just to the west for much of the way. The character of Midtown undergoes a radical transformation depending on which side of Fifth you find yourself. To the east are the corporate businesses and prestigious skyscrapers – the Chrysler, the Empire State, the Seagram Building – as well as the residential neighborhoods of **Gramercy Park** and **Murray Hill**. West of Fifth, and in particular west of Broadway, the area progressively declines from the recently revitalized **Chelsea** – a new magnet for art galleries and commercial development – to the **Garment District**, whose wholesale apparel shops still roll their racks of clothing through the streets. The **Theater District** is no longer sleazy, having benefited from the multimillion-dollar cleanup of **Times Square**. Even the folks at Disney have been impressed by the transformation, judging the area sanitized enough to be the home of their flagship store, located at 42nd Street and Seventh Avenue, and a new Disney Hotel, currently under construction. **Clinton**, the former Hell's Kitchen neighborhood located to the west of Broadway in the 40s and low 50s, has also been improved by the crackdown on porn shops and sleazy businesses, gentrifying slowly though still rough near the West Side Highway.

## The East Side: Union Square to 42nd Street

Downtown Manhattan ends at 14th Street, which slices across from the housing projects of the east side through rows of cut-price shops to the meat-packing warehouses on the Hudson. In the middle is **Union Square**, until the mid-1980s the unpleasant scene of dope pushing and street violence but recently remodeled and much more inviting now, its spill of shallow steps enticing you in to stroll the paths, feed the squirrels and admire the statuary. Wander through on any Monday, Wednesday, Friday or Saturday, and you'll find a terrific farmers' market. The stretch of **Broadway** north of here used to be known as "Ladies' Mile" for its fancy stores and boutiques, and has recently been reinvented as an urban mall, with large chain stores on every block in the 20s. There is also some interesting architecture on view here, with sculpted facades, massive windows and curvy lintels.

## THE SKYSCRAPERS OF NEW YORK

Along with Chicago and Hong Kong, Manhattan holds one of the world's greatest concentrations of **skyscrapers**. Yet there are only two main clusters – in the **Financial District**, where the narrow streets and tall buildings form lightless canyons, and **midtown Manhattan**, where the big skyscrapers, flanking the wide central avenues between the Thirties and the Sixties, compete for height and prestige.

New York's first recognized skyscraper was the oddly shaped **Flatiron Building**, designed in 1902 and wedged between Fifth and Broadway on W 23rd Street. A few years later, in 1913, the city clinched the title of the world's tallest building with the sixty-story **Woolworth Building** on lower Broadway, then later produced such landmarks as the **Chrysler** and **Empire State** buildings, as well as the **World Trade Center** – though the latter has since been dwarfed by Chicago's Sears Tower. Styles over the years have been influenced by stringent zoning laws. At first skyscrapers were sheer vertical monsters, maximizing the floor space with no regard for the effect on neighboring buildings that, more often than not, were thrown into dark shade. The authorities came up with the concept of "air rights," putting a restriction on how high a building could be before it had to be set back from its base. This forced skyscrapers to be designed in a series of steps – a pattern repeated all over the city but seen at its most elegant in the Empire State Building, which has no fewer than ten steps.

Due to the pressure on space in Manhattan's narrow confines, and the price of real estate, which makes the speculative building of office blocks so potentially lucrative, the skyscrapers continue to rise, and some steel frame is always slowly going up somewhere in the city. There seems to be almost no limit to the heights envisaged in the future, and even in times of recession skyscrapers remain the "machines for making money" that Le Corbusier originally proclaimed them to be.

Turn right on East 20th Street for **Theodore Roosevelt's Birthplace** at no. 28 (Wed–Sun 9am–5pm; $1) – or at least a reconstruction of it: a grim brownstone mansion that boasts a few rooms with their original furnishings, some of Teddy's hunting trophies and a small gallery documenting the president's life.

Past here, Manhattan's clutter breaks into the ordered open space of **Gramercy Park** (between 20th and 21st sts where Lexington Ave becomes Irving Place), a former swamp reclaimed in 1831 that is one of the city's best squares, its center tidily planted and, most noticeably, completely empty for much of the day – principally because the only people who can gain access are those rich enough to live here and possess keys to the gate.

Broadway and Fifth Avenue meet at 23rd Street at **Madison Square**, by day a maelstrom of dodging cars and cabs, but with a monumentality and serenity that Union Square has long since lost. Most notable among the grand structures that surround it is the **Flatiron Building** (175 Fifth Ave, between 22nd and 23rd sts), set cheekily on a triangular plot of land on the square's southern side, its full twenty stories dwarfing all the other structures around when it was built in 1902. Its tapered shape creates unusual wind currents at ground level, and years ago police officers were posted to prevent men gathering to watch the wind raise the skirts of women passing on 23rd Street. The cry they gave to warn off voyeurs – "23 Skidoo!" – has passed into the language.

Further up Fifth Avenue is New York's prime **shopping territory**, home to some heavyweight department stores including Lord & Taylor, which stretches between 38th and 39th streets. Overshadowing them all, however, is the **Empire State Building** at 34th Street and Fifth Avenue, a potent symbol of New York since the structure was completed in 1931. After two years in the making, its 102 stories and 1472 feet – from base to TV mast – render it the world's third tallest building; but the height is deceptive, for it rises in stately tiers with steady panache. Inside, its basement is an underground marbled shopping precinct, finished everywhere with delicate Deco touches. The first elevator towards the top takes you to the 86th floor, summit of the building before the radio and TV mast was added. The views from the outside walkways here are as stunning as you'd expect – better than the World Trade Center because Manhattan spreads on all sides. If you're feeling brave, and can stand the queues for the small single elevator, go up to the Empire State's last reachable zenith, a small cylinder at the foot of the TV mast (part of a harebrained scheme to erect a mooring post for airships – a plan subsequently abandoned after some local VIPs almost got swept away by the wind). You can't go outside and the extra sixteen stories don't really add a great deal to the view, but you will at least have been to the top. Make sure that you visit during the week if you are intent upon traveling up to that apex: due to crowding, the 102nd Floor Observatory is closed on weekends during the summer (otherwise daily 9.30am–midnight; $6).

East of the Empire State lies **Murray Hill**, a residential district formerly dominated by the crusty old financier J P Morgan and his offspring, Morgan Jr; the latter's brownstone, on the corner of 37th Street and Madison Avenue, is now headquarters of the American Lutheran Church. Morgan Senior's place, which used to abut his son's, was razed to make way for the **Pierpont Morgan Library** (Tues–Fri 10.30am–5pm, Sat 10.30am–6pm, Sun noon–6pm; July & Aug closed Sun; suggested donation $5). A gracious Italian-style nest built in 1917, the Library, at 29 E 36th St, is filled with the fruits of the Morgans' magpie-like trips to Europe. Its two main rooms are reached along a corridor usually (though not always) lined with Rembrandt prints. The first, the **West Room**, remains much as it looked when it was Morgan's study, with a carved sixteenth-century Italian ceiling, paintings by Memling and Perugino, and a custom-carved desk. Through a domed and pillared hallway lies the **East Room** or library, a sumptuous three-tiered cocoon of rare books, autographed musical manuscripts and trinkets culled from European households and churches. A changing exhibit holds original manuscripts by Mahler (the museum has the world's largest collection of his work); a Gutenburg Bible from 1455 (one of eleven surviving); and literary relics ranging from the letters of Vasari and George Washington to works by Keats and Dickens.

North up Fifth Avenue, on the corner of **42nd Street**, stands the Beaux Arts **New York Public Library** (Mon & Thurs–Sat 9am–6pm, Tues & Wed 11am–6pm; free guided tours Mon–Sat at 11am & 2pm; meet in Astor Hall). Trotsky worked on and off in the large coffered Reading Room at the back of the building during his brief sojourn in New York, just prior to the 1917 Revolution, having been introduced to the place by his friend Bukharin, who was bowled over by a library you could use so late in the evening. The opening times are less impressive now, but the library still boasts one of the five largest collections of books in the world. East on 42nd Street at Park Avenue looms the huge bulk of **Grand Central Station**, constructed around a basic iron frame but clothed with a Beaux Arts skin. The most spectacular aspect of the building is its size, now cowed by the soaring airplane wing of the Met Life building behind it. Yet the main station's **concourse** is a sight to behold – 470ft long and 150ft high, it boasts a barrel-vaulted ceiling speckled like a Baroque church with a painted representation of the winter night sky, its 2500 stars shown back to front: "As God would have seen them," the painter is reputed to have explained. For the best view of the concourse – as well as the flow of commuters and commerce, the cogs in the American dream machine – climb up to the catwalks that span the sixty-foot-high windows on the Vanderbilt Avenue side. After that, explore the station's more esoteric reaches, such as the **Oyster Bar** – one of the city's most highly regarded seafood restaurants, located in the terminal's bowels and crammed every lunchtime. You can also stand on opposite sides of any of the vaulted spaces in the station and hold a conversation just by whispering, an acoustic fluke that makes this the loudest place in town.

Across the street, the **Bowery Savings Bank** echoes Grand Central's grandeur, extravagantly lauding the shibboleths of sound investment and savings. A Roman-style basilica, it has a floor paved with mosaics, columns (each fashioned from a different kind of marble), and bronze bas-reliefs on the elevator doors. The more famous **Chrysler Building**, at 405 Lexington Ave, also dates from a time (1930) when architects carried off prestige with grace and style. This was for a short while the world's tallest building, and, since the rediscovery of Art Deco, has become one of Manhattan's best-loved structures, its car-motif friezes, jutting gargoyles and arched stainless-steel pinnacle giving the solemn Midtown skyline a welcome touch of whimsy. Chrysler moved out some time ago, and for a while the building was left to degenerate by a company that didn't fully appreciate its spirited silliness, but the new owner has pledged to keep it lovingly intact. The lobby, once a car showroom, is for the moment all you can see, with its opulently inlaid elevators, walls covered in African marble and murals showing airplanes, machines and brawny builders who worked on the tower.

At the eastern end of 42nd Street is the **United Nations** complex, comprising the glass-curtained **Secretariat**, the curving sweep of **the General Assembly**, and, connecting them, the low-rising **Conference Wing**. Guided tours leave from the monumental General Assembly lobby (daily, every 20min, 9.15am–4.45pm; $7.50, students ☎212/963-7539; $4.50) and take in the UN conference chambers and its constituent parts.

## The West Side: Chelsea, the Garment District and Times Square

**Chelsea** took shape in 1830 when its owner, Charles Clarke Moore, laid out his land for sale in broad lots. Enough remains to indicate Chelsea's middle-class suburban origins, though in fact the area never quite achieved the desirability it sought. Instead, Manhattan's chic residential focus leapfrogged Chelsea, stuck between the ritziness of Fifth Avenue and the poverty of Hell's Kitchen, straight to the East Forties and Fifties.

During the nineteenth century the area was a focus of New York's theater district. Nothing remains of that now, but the hotel that put up all the actors, writers and attendant entourages – the **Chelsea Hotel** – remains a New York landmark, with a down-at-heel Edwardian grandeur all its own. Mark Twain and Tennessee Williams lived here, Brendan Behan and Dylan Thomas staggered in and out during their New York visits, and in 1951 Jack Kerouac, armed with a customized typewriter (and a lot of Benzedrine), typed the first draft of *On the Road* nonstop onto a 120ft roll of paper. In the 1960s Andy Warhol and his doomed protégée Edie Sedgwick holed up here and made the film *Chelsea Girls* in (sort of) homage; and in October 1978 Sid Vicious stabbed Nancy Spungen to death in their suite, a few months before his own life ended with an overdose of heroin. It also inspired Joni Mitchell to write *Chelsea Morning* – which in turn inspired Bill and Hillary Clinton in naming their daughter.

The last decade has seen Chelsea revitalized, especially along Eighth Avenue between West 14th and West 23rd Streets. A new **gay** community is especially apparent here: muscular, well-groomed "Chelsea Boys," who have fled the Village's soaring rents and now live amongst the Puerto Rican and Cuban families long-established in the neighborhood. The area is a great mix, where fashionable restaurants, bars and clubs catering to all persuasions have grown up alongside thrift shops, bodegas and liquor stores straight out of a B-movie.

Also renewing the neighborhood's vigor are new entertainment and arts developments. **Chelsea Piers**, a 1.7 million-square-foot sports complex, was recently built along the Hudson River around West 23rd Street; extending over four piers, it offers a host of indoor and outdoor facilities as well as some good spots to eat and drink. A block over, at West 22nd Street between Tenth and Eleventh avenues, is a patch of established **galleries**, many of which have relocated here from SoHo, driven away by rising rents and a lack of space.

A few blocks north at 32nd Street, Sixth Avenue collides with Broadway at **Greeley Square**, an overblown name for a trashy triangle celebrating Horace Greeley, founder of the *Tribune* newspaper, and known for his rallying call to "Go West, young man!"

In a way this part of Broadway is the storefront to the **Garment District**, a loosely defined patch between 34th and 42nd streets and Sixth and Eighth avenues that produces around three-quarters of all the women's and children's clothes in America – you'd never believe it, as the outlets are strictly wholesale with no need to woo customers. There are also lots of retail stores in the area, however. Macy's, the famed old department store with some two million square feet of floor space and $5 million of turnover a day, is located on Herald Square at 34th Street and Seventh Avenue. The dominant landmark is the **Pennsylvania Station and Madison Square Garden complex**, a combined box and drum structure that swallows up millions of commuters in its train station below and accommodates the Knicks and Liberty basketball – and Rangers hockey – teams up top. The original Penn Station, demolished to make way for this, is now hailed as a lost masterpiece, which reworked the ideas of the Roman Baths of Caracalla to awesome effect: "Through it one entered the city like a god . . . One scuttles in now like a rat," mourned one observer. Immediately behind Penn Station, the same architects – McKim, Mead and White – were responsible for the **General Post Office**. The old joke is that it had to be this big to fit in the sonorous inscription above the columns – "Neither snow nor rain nor heat nor gloom of night stays these couriers from the swift completion of their appointed rounds." The Post Office still has a branch here, though a plan to reconfigure the building as a new Penn Station is in the works, with bureaucracy and money troubles tying up progress.

The Port Authority Bus Terminal at 40th Street and Eighth Avenue serves as a gateway to the garish stretch of 42nd Street beyond, a former strip of prostitution and petty vice. For years, **Times Square** at Broadway was in its excess and brashness a distillation of the city itself, an increasingly sleazy, sometimes dangerous area that has recently undergone a massive cleanup. Almost all of the peep shows and sex shops have gone, replaced by gaudy neon billboards, corporate office blocks, and a Virgin Megastore.

Further north, the **Equitable Center**, 757 7th Ave, houses Roy Lichtenstein's 68ft *Mural with Blue Brush Stroke*, which pokes you in the eye as you enter; also look for Thomas Hart Benton's *America Today* murals, a magnificent portrayal of ordinary American life in the days before the Depression. Otherwise **Carnegie Hall**, an overblown, warehouse-like venue for opera and concerts at 154 W 57th St, is the thing to see. Tchaikovsky conducted the program on opening night and Mahler, Rachmaninov, Toscanini, Frank Sinatra and Judy Garland have played here; it has dropped in status since Lincoln Center opened (see pp.90 & 107), but the superb acoustics still ensure full houses most of the year (mid-Sept to end June; tours available Mon, Tues, Thurs & Fri at 11.30am, 2pm & 3pm; $6; ☎212/247-7800).

A block east, **Sixth Avenue** is properly named "Avenue of the Americas," though no New Yorker ever calls it this and the only manifestation are the flags of Central and South American countries. If nothing else, Sixth's distinction is its width, a result of the Elevated Railway that once ran along here, now replaced by the Sixth Avenue subway underground. In its day the Sixth Avenue "El" marked the borderline between respectability to the east and vice to the west, and it still separates the glamorous strips of Fifth, Madison and Park avenues from the less salubrious western districts. Worth a stop is the **Royalton** (44 W 44th St), one of the three New York hotels designed by Philippe Starck (the *SoHo Grand* and the *Paramount* are the others; see pp.68–69 for reviews of all), and whose decor – which includes fountains and hidden doors in the toilets – seems straight out of *Alice in Wonderland*. Another unexpected treasure is **Diamond Row**, located on West 47th Street between Fifth and Sixth avenues. It's a short strip of shops chock-full of expensive stones, watches and jewelry, largely managed by ultra-Orthodox Hassidic Jews.

Further up, Sixth Avenue is solidly corporate, especially between 47th and 50th streets, where the towers of **Rockefeller Center Extension** don't have the romance of their predecessor (see below) but do possess some of its monumentality, and across the avenue at 49th Street, the **Radio City Music Hall** is the last word in 1930s luxury. The staircase is regally resplendent with the world's largest chandeliers, the original murals from the men's toilets are now in the Museum of Modern Art, and the huge auditorium looks like an extravagant scalloped shell.

## Fifth Avenue and east: 42nd Street to Central Park

**Fifth Avenue** has been a great strip for as long as New York has been a great city, and its very name evokes wealth and opulence. All who consider themselves suave and cosmopolitan end up here, and the stores showcase New York's most conspicuous consumerism. That the shopping is beyond the means of most people needn't put you off, for Fifth Avenue has some of the city's best architecture; the boutiques and stores are just the icing on the cake.

At the heart of Fifth Avenue's glamour is **Rockefeller Center**, built between 1932 and 1940 by John D Rockefeller, son of the oil magnate. One of the finest pieces of urban planning anywhere, it balances office space with cafes, a theater, underground concourses and rooftop gardens that work together with a rare intelligence and grace. It's a combination that shows every other city-center shopping mall the way; Cyril Connolly's snide description of it as "that sinister Stonehenge of Economic Man" was way off the mark. The **GE Building** here rises 850ft, its monumental lines matching the scale of Manhattan itself, though softened by symmetrical setbacks to prevent an overpowering expanse of wall. At its foot, the **Lower Plaza** holds a sunken restaurant in summer, linked visually to the downward flow of the building by Paul Manship's sparkling *Prometheus*; in winter, the plaza becomes an ice rink, allowing skaters to show off their skills to passing shoppers and tourists. Inside, the Center is no less impressive. In the lobby are José Maria Sert's murals, *American Progress* and *Time*, a little faded but eagerly in tune with the Thirties Deco ambiance – presumably more so than the original paintings by Diego Rivera, which were removed by John D's son Nelson when the artist refused to scrap a panel glorifying Lenin. A leaflet available from the lobby desk details a **self-guided tour** of the Center. Among the GE Building's many offices are the **NBC Studios** (daily 1hr tours leave regularly, 9.15am–5pm; reservations at the desk in the foyer; $10). If you're a TV freak, pick up a free ticket for a **show recording** from the mezzanine lobby or out on the street. The most popular tickets evaporate before 9am. The newer glass-enclosed **Today Show** studio is located at the southwest corner of the plaza at 49th Street, usually surrounded by avid fans waiting outside, eager to get on TV by way of the cameras that obligingly pan the crowds from time to time.

Almost opposite Rockefeller Center on 51st Street and Fifth Avenue, **St Patrick's Cathedral**, designed by James Renwick and completed in 1888, seems the result of a painstaking academic tour of the Gothic cathedrals of Europe – perfect in detail, but lifeless in spirit, with a sterility made all the more striking by the glass-black **Olympic Tower** next door, an exclusive apartment block where Jackie Onassis once resided. Between Fifth and Sixth avenues at 25 W 52nd St, is the **Museum of Television and Radio** (Tues–Wed & Fri–Sun noon–6pm, Thurs noon–8pm; $6), an excellent archive of American TV and radio broadcasts. The museum's computerized reference system allows you to research programs ranging from news to documentaries to sitcoms to adverts, then watch them on one of the 96 video consoles.

Continuing north, the **Trump Tower** at 57th Street is the last word in Fifth Avenue opulence, with an outrageously over-the-top atrium, filled with designer stores, that is just short of repellent. Perfumed air, polished marble paneling and a five-story waterfall are calculated to knock you senseless with expensive yet somewhat garish taste. But the building is clever: a neat little outdoor garden is squeezed high in a corner, and each of the 230 apartments above the atrium gets views in three directions.

To the east, **Madison Avenue** makes for pleasant strolling, especially north of here, where it is filled with expensive galleries, haute couture shops and elegantly dressed Eastsiders. The next big avenue east, **Park Avenue**, was said in 1929 to be the place "where wealth is so swollen that it almost bursts." Things haven't changed much: corporate headquarters and four-star hotels jostle in triumphal procession, led by the massive **New York Central Building** (now the Helmsley Building) that literally sits above Park Avenue at 46th Street and boasts a lewdly excessive Rococo lobby. In its day this formed a skilled punctuation mark to the avenue, but its thunder was stolen in 1963 by the **Met Life Building** (200 Park Ave at 45th St) that looms behind it. Former headquarters of the (now defunct) airline Pan Am, the building has a profile meant to suggest an aircraft wing; the blue-gray mass certainly adds drama to the cityscape, but it robs Park Avenue of the views south it deserves. Another black mark was the rooftop helipad, closed in the 1970s after a helicopter undercarriage collapsed shortly after landing, killing four people and injuring several others.

Wherever you placed it, the solid mass of the **Waldorf Astoria Hotel** (Park Ave between 49th and 50th sts) would hold its own, a resplendent statement of Art Deco elegance. Crouched behind it is **St Bartholomew's Church**, a low-slung Byzantine hybrid that adds immeasurably to the street and gives the lumbering skyscrapers a much-needed sense of scale. The spiky-topped **General Electric Building** behind seems like a wild extension of the church, its slender shaft rising to a meshed crown of abstract sparks and lightning strokes that symbolizes the radio waves used by its original occupier, RCA. The lobby (entrance at 570 Lexington) is yet another Deco delight. Among all this it's difficult at first to see the originality of the **Seagram Building** between 52nd and 53rd. Designed by Mies van der Rohe with Philip Johnson and built in 1958, this was the seminal curtain-wall skyscraper, the floors supported internally, allowing a skin of smoky glass and whisky-bronze metal (Seagram are distillers), now weathered to a dull black. Every interior detail – from the fixtures to the lettering on the mailboxes – was specially designed. It was the supreme example of Modernist reason, and its opening was met by a wave of approval. The plaza, an open forecourt designed to set the building apart from its neighbors, was such a success as a public space that the city revised the zoning laws to encourage other high-rise builders to supply plazas – the result being the windswept, sterile places now found all over Manhattan.

A block east, the chisel-topped **Citicorp Center** on **Lexington Avenue** (between 53rd and 54th sts) was finished in 1979 and is now one of Manhattan's most conspicuous landmarks. The slanted roof was designed to house solar panels and provide power, but the idea was ahead of the technology and Citicorp had to content itself with adopting the distinctive top as a corporate logo.

## The Museum of Modern Art

Founded in 1929, moved to its present home ten years later, and extensively updated in the mid-1980s so that its gallery space was doubled, the **Museum of Modern Art** (MoMA) at 11 W 53rd St offers probably the finest and most complete account of late nineteenth- and twentieth-century art you're likely to find (Sat–Tues & Thurs 10.30am–6pm, Fri 10.30am–8.30pm, closed Wed; $9.50, students $6.50). MoMA covers every medium – illustration and design, architecture and photography – but focuses primarily on painting and sculpture. It also has an outdoor **sculpture garden**, where works by Rodin and Matisse are juxtaposed with such artifacts as an Art Nouveau *métro* sign. MoMA is justly famous for its 14,000 plus **film archive**, often showing retrospectives and rare films you have little chance of seeing elsewhere.

MoMA's exhibits and layout are currently in flux as the museum launches its ambitious **MoMA 2000** exhibit, and soon afterwards begins another round of renovation and expansion. The entire museum, including its film programming, is being given over to this special integrated exhibit of all aspects of the permanent collection. MoMA 2000 will be held through March 2001 in three successive chronological stages: **Cycle I: Modern Starts** from October 1999 to March 2000 – studying 1880 to 1920, the beginning of Modernism. **Cycle II** from March to September 2000, focusing on 1920 to 1960, featuring themes of war, social and political upheaval, and the advance of technology; with artists from the Dada and Surrealist schools to the abstract artists such as Mondrian, Malevitch and others. **Cycle III: Open Ends** from September 2000 through March 2001, concentrates on 1960 to the present, and is the first time that the bulk of MoMA's holdings of contemporary art will be on display at one time – works by Warhol, Rothko, Twombly and Jasper John.

# Uptown Manhattan

UPTOWN MANHATTAN begins above 57th Street, where the businesslike bustle of Midtown gives way abruptly to the comfortable domesticity of the Upper East and West sides. People come to **Central Park** in between, the city's back garden, to play, jog and escape Midtown's crowds in a particularly intelligent piece of urban landscaping.

The **Upper East Side** is at its most opulent in the mansions of Fifth and Madison avenues, and at its most prestigious in the Metropolitan and other great museums of "Museum Mile." The **Upper West Side** is less refined, though its Lincoln Center hosts New York's most prestigious arts performances. It is again predominantly residential, well heeled on its southern fringe, especially along Columbus Avenue, but less so as you move north to its top end, marked at the edge by the monolithic Cathedral of St John the Divine and Columbia University – the last gasp of Manhattan's wealth, which is creeping ever further into the streets of **Harlem**. Further north is one of the city's most intriguing museums, the medieval arts collection of **The Cloisters**.

## Central Park

"All radiant in the magic atmosphere of art and taste." So enthused *Harper's* magazine on the opening of **Central Park** in 1876, and to this day, few New Yorkers could imagine life without it. Set just about smack in the middle of Manhattan, extending from 59th to 110th streets, it provides residents (and street-weary tourists) with a much-needed refuge from the noise, crowds and general harshness of big-city life. Whether you're into jogging, baseball, boating, botany or just plain walking, or even if you rarely go near the place, there's no question that Central Park is one of the things that makes New York a bearable place to live.

The poet and newspaper editor William Cullen Bryant had the idea for an open public space back in 1844, and spent seven years trying to persuade City Hall to carry it out. Eventually 840 desolate and swampy acres north of the city limits, then occupied by a shantytown of squatters, were set aside. The two architects commissioned to design the landscape, Frederick Olmsted and Calvert Vaux, planned to create a rural paradise, a complete illusion of the countryside bang in the heart of Manhattan – even then growing at a fantastic rate. At its opening in 1876, Central Park was declared a "people's park" – though most of the impoverished masses it was allegedly built to serve had neither the time nor the carfare to come up from their Downtown slums and enjoy it. But as New York grew and workers' leisure time increased, people began flooding in, and the park began to live up to its mission, sometimes in ways that might have scandalized its original builders. Today, in spite of the advent of motorized traffic, the sense of disorderly nature they intended largely survives, although the skyline has changed greatly and some of the open space has been turned into asphalted playground. The park has suffered some periods of terrible neglect, most ruinously during the city's financial crisis in the mid-1970s; but since the Central Park Conservancy, a city-assisted nonprofit group, started working on the place in 1980, it has been wonderfully restored. For general park information call ☎212/360-3444 or call ☎1-888/NYPARKS for special events information.

One of the best ways to explore is to rent a **bicycle** (roughly $6 an hour) from either the Loeb Boathouse or Metro Bicycles (Lexington at 88th St; ☎212/427-4450). The other is **on foot**, along the many footpaths that crisscross the park. There's little chance of getting lost, but to know exactly where you are, find the nearest lamppost: the first two figures signify the number of the nearest street. After dark, however, it's ill-advised to enter on foot. If you want to see the buildings of Central Park West lit up, à la Woody Allen's *Manhattan*, one option is to fork out for a **carriage ride**. You can pick up a hack along Central Park South, between Fifth and Sixth avenues, or call ☎212/246-0520 for pickup anywhere between 42nd and 57th streets and Seventh and Ninth avenues. If you worry that the carriage business is cruel to the horses, bear in mind that city law requires that they cannot work more than nine hours per day, and must get fifteen-minute breaks every two hours; you might better worry about the damage to your wallet – a twenty-minute trot costs $40, excluding tip.

Most things of interest lie in the southern reaches of the park. Near Grand Army Plaza, the main entrance to the park at Fifth Avenue and 59th Street, is the recently refurbished **Central Park Zoo**, which tries to keep caging to a minimum and the animals as close to the viewer as possible ((Mon–Fri 10am–5pm, Sat, Sun & holidays 10.30am–5.30pm; ☎212/439-6500; $3.50 adults, 50¢ children aged 3–12, free for children under 3) Beyond here, the **Dairy**, once a ranch building intended to provide milk for nursing mothers, now houses one of the Park's **Visitor Centers** (Tues–Sun 10am–5pm; ☎212/794-6564), distributing free leaflets and maps, selling books and putting on exhibitions. Weekend walking tours often leave from here; call for times.

Nearby, the **Wollman Rink** is a lovely place to skate in winter (63rd St at mid-park; ☎212/396-1010; in winter open daily for ice skating, skate rental $3; in summer open for rollerblading Thurs & Fri 11am–6pm, Sat & Sun 11am–8pm). The most obvious route onwards – after a brief westward sojourn to people-watch at **Sheep Meadow**, one of the park's giant open areas – is north up the formal **Mall** to the **Bandshell**, and the terrace and sculpted birds and animals of **Bethesda Fountain,** on the shore of the Central Park Lake. To your left (west) is **Strawberry Fields**, a tranquil, shady spot dedicated to John Lennon by his widow, Yoko Ono. Rent a boat from the **Loeb Boathouse** on the eastern bank of the lake (March–Nov daily 10am–6pm, weather permitting; ☎212/517-2233 for more information; rowboats are $10 for the first hour, $2.50 per each hour after, with a $30 refundable deposit; gondola rides are given 5–10pm at a cost of $30 per 30min per group and require reservations) or cross the water by the elegant cast-iron **Bow Bridge** and delve into the wild woods of **The Ramble** along a maze of paths and bridges. At 81st Street near the West Side stands the mock citadel of **Belvedere Castle**, another Visitor's Center which sometimes hosts small exhibitions and boasts great views of the park from its terraces. Next to the Castle is the **Delacorte Theater**, home to free Shakespeare in the Park performances in summer, and the immense **Great Lawn**, traditionally the preferred sprawling ground of sun-loving New Yorkers. An unexpected treat at the north end of the park is the beautifully terraced and landscaped **Conservatory Garden** at 103rd Street, off Fifth Avenue.

## The Metropolitan Museum of Art

Jutting into the park from the east is one of the great art museums of the world, the **Metropolitan Museum of Art** (usually simply the "Met"), on Fifth Avenue at 82nd Street (Tues–Thurs & Sun 9.30am–5.15pm, Fri & Sat 9.30am–8.45pm, closed Mon; suggested donation $10, students $5, includes same-day admission to The Cloisters, see p.93). Its all-embracing collection amounts to over two-million works of art, spanning not just America and Europe but also China, Africa, the Far East, and the classical and Islamic worlds. You could spend weeks in here and still not see everything, and the choice of works that follows – among the Met's greatest hits – is inevitably selective in the extreme.

If you're obliged to make just one visit, head first for the **European Painting** galleries. Of the **early Flemish and Netherlandish paintings**, the best are by Jan van Eyck, who is generally credited with having started the tradition of North European realism, and Rogier van der Weyden, whose *Christ Appearing to His Mother* is one of his most beautiful works. Later canvases include Brueghel's *Harvesters*, part of the series of twelve paintings that included his familiar Christmas-card *Hunters in the Snow*. Cutting left at this point brings you to the Spanish paintings and the very different landscape of El Greco's extraordinary *View of Toledo*, and Velázquez's *Portrait of Juan de Parej* – "All the rest are art, this alone is truth," remarked a critic of this sombre portrait when it was first exhibited. The **Italian Renaissance** is less spectacularly represented here but a worthy selection includes an early *Madonna and Child Enthroned with Saints* by Raphael, a late Botticelli and Fra Filippo Lippi's *Madonna and Child Enthroned with Two Angels*. The culmination of the European Galleries is the **Dutch paintings** section, dominated by the major works of Rembrandt, Vermeer and Hals. Vermeer, genius of the domestic interior, is represented by five works, most haunting of which is the *Portrait of a Young Woman*, and there are some fine portraits by Rembrandt – a beautiful painting of his common-law wife, Hendrike Stoffjels, painted three years before her early death, and a superb *Self-portrait* from 1660, the year he was declared bankrupt.

The **nineteenth-century galleries** house a startling array of **Impressionist and Post-Impressionist** art, beginning with Edouard Manet, the movement's most influential precursor, and his striking *Woman with a Parrot*. The prolific Monet is widely represented, from his early *Garden at Sainte Adresse* to *Poplars*, in which you can detect the beginnings of his final phase of near-Abstract Impressionism. Courbet's *Young Ladies from the Village* constitutes a virtual manifesto of his idea of realism; nearby is his own superbly erotic *Woman with a Parrot*, along with a casting of Degas' *Little Dancer*, complete with real tutu, bodice and shoes.

Tacked on to the rear of the Met in 1975 to house the collection of banker Robert Lehman, the two-storey **Lehman Pavilion** fills the gaps in the Met's **Italian Renaissance** paintings, most notably with a small Botticelli *Annunciation* and a sculptural *Madonna and Child* by Giovanni Bellini. There are also works from the **Northern Renaissance**, notably Hans Holbein the Younger's *Portrait of Erasmus of Rotterdam* and Rembrandt's *Portrait of Gerard de Lairesse*. By all accounts de Lairesse was disliked for his luxurious tastes and unpleasant character, but mainly for his face, which had been ravaged by congenital syphilis. Boldly colored canvases such as *Reclining Nude* by Suzanne Valadon – largely neglected today, or remembered simply as a model for Toulouse-Lautrec, Renoir and Degas – show her originality and influence on her son, Utrillo, whom she taught to paint as an attempt to wean him off drink and drugs. Utrillo's *Rue Ravignon* stands beside his mother's painting.

Housed over two floors in the **Lila Acheson Wallace Wing**, the Met's compact **twentieth-century collection** features paintings such as Picasso's *Portrait of Gertrude*

*Stein* alongside works by Klee, Matisse, Braque and Klimt, and postwar pieces such as Pollock's masterly *Autumn Rhythm (Number 30)*, Thomas Hart Benton's rural idyll of *July Hay*, Charles DeMuth's *The Figure 5 in Gold*, and Andy Warhol's *Last Self Portrait*, as well as works by Max Beckmann, Roy Lichtenstein and Gilbert and George.

The **American Wing**, in the northwest corner of the Met, is virtually a museum in its own right, with furnished historical rooms, starting with the Early Colonial period and the Hart room of around 1674, and ending with Frank Lloyd Wright's *Room from the Little House, Minneapolis*, originally windowed on all four sides, in line with Wright's concept of minimizing interior–exterior division. The **American paintings** on display include the nineteenth-century canvases of William Sidney Mount, who depicted genre scenes on his native Long Island, and the landscape artists of the Hudson Valley School – Thomas Cole and his pupil Frederick Church. Winslow Homer is allowed a gallery to himself, while later rooms bring the Met's American art into the twentieth century with work by Thomas Eakin (including the melancholic *Max Schmitt in a Single Scull*) and John Singer Sargent, whose *Portrait of Madam X* was one of the most famous pictures of its day, exhibited at the 1884 Paris salon and considered so improper that Sargent had to leave the city.

The Met's **Medieval Galleries** are no less exhaustive, with displays of sumptuous Byzantine metalwork and jewelry donated by J P Morgan and a main sculpture hall piled high with religious statuary and carvings, as well as later period rooms – paneled Tudor bedrooms, florid Rococo boudoirs and salons from France, and an entire Renaissance patio from Vélez Blanco in Spain. The **Egyptian rooms** also have as much to see – huge statuary, smaller sculptural pieces and jewelry – although the most prominent exhibit is the **Temple of Dendur**, housed in its own huge gallery, designed to symbolize its original site on the banks of the Nile. Built by the Emperor Augustus in 15 BC for the Goddess Isis of Philae, the temple was moved here as a gift from the Egyptian people during the construction of the Aswan High Dam – it would otherwise have been drowned.

Greatly expanded in recent years are the **Asian Art galleries**, with plenty of murals, sculptures, and textile art from Japan, China, Southeast and Central Asia, and Korea, all centered around the galleries' highlight – the exquisite **Chinese Garden Court**, lovingly assembled by experts from the People's Republic. The Met has also just completely expanded and redesigned its **Greek and Roman** galleries; always rich in classical artifacts (including a near-fully-restored Roman Cubiculum, replete with an uncomfortable-looking chaise), it now also boasts a formidable array of earlier Cypriot, Mycenaean, Etruscan and Italic painting, ornaments, vases and other objects. The new exhibits are truly stunning.

Finally, if you have plenty of time on your hands, consider the Met's minor glories: stately rows of human and equine dummies clad for battle in the **Arms and Armor** exhibit; and the second-floor **Musical Instruments** collection, featuring eighteenth-century spinets and clavichords in surprisingly good condition. There is also a **Costume Institute** on the ground floor that puts on wonderfully imaginative special exhibits that can be worthwhile.

# The Upper East Side

A two-square-mile grid, scored by the great avenues of Madison, Park and Lexington, the **Upper East Side** has wealth as its defining characteristic, as you'll appreciate if you've seen any of the many Woody Allen movies set here. **Fifth Avenue** up here has been the patrician face of Manhattan since the opening of Central Park attracted the Carnegies, Astors and Whitneys to migrate north and build fashionable residences. **Grand Army Plaza**, at the junction of Central Park South and Fifth Avenue, serves as the introduction, flanked by the extended chateau of the swanky **Plaza Hotel**. Fifth

Avenue continues with Henry Clay Frick's house at 70th Street, marginally less ostentatious than its neighbors and now the tranquil home of the **Frick Collection**
(Tues–Sat 10am–6pm, Sun 1–6pm; closed Mon; $7, students $5), the first of many
prestigious museums in the area. The Frick is perhaps the most enjoyable of the big
New York galleries, made up of the art treasures hoarded by Frick during his years as
probably the most ruthless of New York's robber barons. The legacy of his self-
aggrandizement is a revealing glimpse of the sumptuous life enjoyed by New York's
big industrialists. The collection includes paintings by Reynolds, Hogarth,
Gainsborough's *St James's Park* – "Watteau far outdone," wrote a critic at the time –
and Bellini's *St Francis*, which suggests his vision of Christ by means of pervading
light, a bent tree and an enraptured stare. El Greco's *St Jerome*, above the fireplace,
reproachfully surveys the riches all around, and looks out to the South Hall, where
one of Boucher's very intimate depictions of his wife hangs near an early Vermeer,
*Officer and Laughing Girl*. In the opposite direction are the Library's British works,
most notably one of Constable's *Salisbury Cathedral* series, and the North Hall, which
holds an engaging and sensitive portrait of the Comtesse de Haussonville by Ingres.
But the West Gallery holds Frick's greatest prizes: two Turners, views of Cologne and
Dieppe; van Dyck's informal portraits of Frans Snyders and his wife – paintings only
reunited when Frick purchased them; and a set of piercing self-portraits by
Rembrandt, along with the enigmatic *Polish Rider*. A tiny room on the other side of the
West Gallery houses an exquisite set of Limoges enamels and a collection of small-
scale paintings that includes a *Virgin and Child* by Jan van Eyck.

The **Guggenheim Museum**, further up Fifth Avenue at 89th Street (Sun–Wed
9am–6pm, Fri & Sat 9am–8pm; closed Thurs; $12, seniors, students $7, children under
12 free, Fri 6–8pm pay what you wish) is better known for the building than its collection. This structure, designed by Frank Lloyd Wright, caused a storm of controversy
when it was unveiled in 1959. Its centripetal spiral ramp, which wends you continuously all the way to its top floor (affording a vertiginous view of the lobby at the center), is
still thought by some to favor Wright's talents over those of the exhibited artists. More
outrage accompanied the recent construction of a tower extension, but new visitors will
have difficulty understanding the fuss; it melds seamlessly with the ramp, and its galleries allow a much greater part of the museum's collection to be on rotational display.
One of the new spaces is the Mapplethorpe Gallery, fittingly housing some of the museum's odder pieces, including Louise Bourgeois' wood-chip sculpture *Femme Volage* –
and several Calder mobiles. Much of the building is still given over to temporary exhibitions, but the permanent collection includes work by Chagall, Léger, the major
Cubists, and, most completely, Kandinsky. Additionally, there are some late nineteenth-
century paintings, not least the exquisite Degas' *Dancers*, Modigliani's *Jeanne Héburene
with Yellow Sweater,* and some sensitive early Picassos.

South of here, the **Whitney Museum of American Art**, 945 Madison Ave at 75th
Street (Tues, Wed & Fri–Sun 11am–6pm, Thurs 1–8pm, closed Mon; $12.50, students
$10.50; the first Thurs of every month 6–8pm pay what you wish), brings things up to
date: a preeminent collection of twentieth-century American art and a superb exhibition
locale that every other year mounts the Whitney biennial show of contemporary
American art – an event that has become a lightning rod for critical abuse since the 1995
show, when a giant mound of cooking fat presented as sculpture set right-wing aesthetes
into a frenzy. When that's not on, you can view the somewhat arbitrary Highlights of the
Permanent Collection, arranged by both chronology and theme, and enjoy the prominent Abstract Expressionists collection, with great works by high priests Pollock and de
Kooning, leading on to Rothko and the Color Field painters, and the later Pop Art works
of Warhol, Johns and Oldenburg. The museum is particularly strong on Edward Hopper,
Georgia O'Keeffe and Alexander Calder, and a recent renovation, which increased
gallery space by thirty percent, includes galleries concentrating on each.

The **Museum of the City of New York**, on the corner of 103rd Street (Wed–Sat 10am–5pm, Sun 1–5pm; closed Mon; ☎212/534-1672; suggested donation $5), might also grab your interest, with an informative rundown on the history of the city from Dutch times to the present day; it also runs Sunday walking tours of various New York neighborhoods.

## The Upper West Side

North of 59th Street, midtown Manhattan's glitzy west side becomes less commercial, fading north of Lincoln Center into a residential area of mixed charms. This is the **Upper West Side**, now one of the city's most desirable addresses, though in truth an area long favored by artists and intellectuals – streets have been rechristened in honor of erstwhile residents like Isaac Bashevis Singer and Edgar Allan Poe. However, gentrification during the 1990s has seen it become a bit yuppified and noticeably less funky than it once was.

Broadway sheers north from Columbus Circle to the **Lincoln Center for the Performing Arts**, a marble assembly of buildings put up in the early 1960s on the site of some of the city's worst slums. Home to the Metropolitan Opera and the New York Philharmonic, as well as a host of other smaller companies – see p.107 – this is worth seeing even if you don't catch a performance (**tours** leave daily at 10.30am, 12.30pm, 2.30pm and 4.30pm from the ticket booth at the Met; phone to reserve; ☎212/875-5350; $9.50). At the center of the complex, the **Metropolitan Opera House** is an impressive marble and glass building, with murals by Marc Chagall behind each of its high front windows. On the left, *Le Triomphe de la Musique* is cast with a variety of well-known performers, landmarks snipped from the New York skyline and a portrait of Sir Rudolph Bing, the man who ran the Met for more than three decades, garbed as a gypsy. The other mural, *Les Sources de la Musique*, is reminiscent of Chagall's renowned Met production of *The Magic Flute*: the god of music strums a lyre while a Tree of Life, Verdi and Wagner all float down the Hudson River.

The most famous of the monumental apartment buildings of **Central Park West** is the **Dakota**, a grandiose Renaissance-style mansion on 72nd Street, built in the late nineteenth century to persuade wealthy New Yorkers that life in an apartment could be just as luxurious as in a private house. Over the years, big-time tenants have included Lauren Bacall and Leonard Bernstein, and in the late 1960s the building was used as the setting for Polanski's film *Rosemary's Baby*. Most people now know the building as the former home of **John Lennon** – and (still) of his wife Yoko Ono, who owns a number of the apartments. It was outside the Dakota, on the night of December 8, 1980, that Lennon was murdered – shot by a man who professed to be one of his greatest admirers. Fans may want to light a stick of incense for Lennon across the road in **Strawberry Fields**, a section of Central Park that has been restored and maintained in his memory through an endowment by Yoko Ono; trees and shrubs were donated by a number of countries as a gesture towards world peace.

North up Central Park West, the often-overlooked **New York Historical Society** at 77th Street (Tues–Sun 11am–5pm; ☎212/873-3400; $5) is more a museum of American than of New York history, with a collection that includes the paintings of James Audubon, the Harlem artist and naturalist who specialized in lovingly detailed watercolors of birds; a broad sweep of nineteenth-century American portraiture (including the picture of Alexander Hamilton that found its way onto the $10 bill) and Hudson River School landscapes (among them Thomas Cole's fantastically pompous *Course of Empire* series); and a glittering display of Tiffany glass, providing an excellent all-round view of Louis Tiffany's attempts "to provide good art for American homes."

Across the street looms the **American Museum of Natural History** (Central Park West at 79th St; Sun–Thurs 10am–5.45pm, Fri & Sat 10am–8.45pm; suggested donation

$8, students $6, children $4.50; IMAX films, the Hayden Planetarium and certain special exhibits cost extra, call for details; ☎212/769-5100). The largest such museum in the world, it is a strange architectural melange of heavy Neoclassical and rustic Romanesque styles covering four city blocks. Spectacularly restored in the mid-1990s, the museum boasts superb nature dioramas and anthropological collections; interactive and multimedia displays, lively signage and an awesome assemblage of bones, fossils and models.

Top attractions range from the spectacular **Dinosaur Halls** to the new **Hall of Biodiversity**, which focuses on both the ecological and evolutionary aspects of nature. Other delights include the massive totems of the **Hall of African Peoples**, the taxidermical marvels of **North American Mammals** (including a vividly staged bull moose fight), and the two thousand gems of the **Hall of Meteorites**, among them a dazzling two-ton hunk of raw copper. The **Rose Center for Earth and Space**, made up of the new **Hall of the Universe** and the **Hayden Planetarium**, is due to open in early spring 2000. Bearing no resemblance to the rather fusty old planetarium which was torn down, the new center boasts all the latest technology and a truly innovative design.

The Upper West Side's second best address after Central Park West is **Riverside Drive**, which weaves its way from 72nd Street up the western edge of Manhattan Island, flanked by palatial townhouses put up in the early part of this century by those not quite rich enough to compete with the folks down on Fifth Avenue, and by **Riverside Park**, landscaped in 1873 by Frederick Olmsted of Central Park fame. Riverside Drive makes the most pleasant route up to the prestigious **Columbia University**, whose campus fills seven blocks between 114th and 121st streets and Amsterdam and Morningside Drive, and boasts a set of plazas laid out by McKim, Mead and White in grand Beaux Arts style. Regular guided **tours** start from the information office on the corner of 116th Street and Broadway.

The **Cathedral Church of St John the Divine** rises up at Amsterdam Avenue and 111th Street with a solid kind of majesty – far from finished but still one of New York's main tourist hot spots. A curious mixture of Romanesque and Gothic styles, the church was begun in 1892, but building stopped with the outbreak of war in 1939 and only sporadically resumed in the early 1990s, albeit fraught with funding difficulties and controversy. St John's is intended as very much a community church, housing a soup kitchen and shelter for the homeless, studios for graphics and sculpture, a gym and a (planned) amphitheater for drama and concerts. A little over two-thirds of the cathedral is finished, and completion isn't due until around 2050, when it will be the largest cathedral structure in the world, its floor space – at 600ft long, and 320ft wide at the transepts – big enough to swallow both the cathedrals of Notre Dame and Chartres whole.

## Harlem, El Barrio and the North

**Harlem** is the side of Manhattan that few visitors bother to see. Home to a culturally and historically – if not economically – rich **black** community, Harlem is still a focus of black activism and culture, and worth seeing if you can. Up until recently, because of a near-total lack of support from federal and municipal funds, Harlem formed a self-reliant and inward-looking community. For many downtown Manhattanites, white and black, 125th Street was a physical and mental border not willingly crossed. Today, the fruits of a cooperative effort involving businesses, residents and City Hall funding are manifest in new housing, retail and community projects. But while brownstones triple in value and Harlem's physical proximity to the Upper West Side is touted, poverty and unemployment are still evident in large patches of Harlem. Though it's unlikely you'll be hassled in daytime, 125th Street, 145th Street, Convent Avenue and Malcolm X Boulevard (formerly Lenox Avenue) are the safest areas; at night, stick to the clubs.

Harlem's **sights** are very spread out; it's not a bad idea to get acquainted with the area via a **guided tour** (see p.64), and follow that up with further trips. 125th Street between Broadway and Fifth Avenue is Harlem's working center, a flattened expanse spiked with the occasional skyscraper. Number 253 is the famous **Apollo Theater** – not much from the outside, but for many years the center of black entertainment in northeastern America. Almost all the great figures of jazz and blues played here – James Brown recorded his seminal *Live At The Apollo* album in 1962 – though a larger attraction today is the Wednesday Amateur Night, open to all. At no. 144 is the **Studio Museum in Harlem** (Wed–Fri 10am–5pm, Sat & Sun 1–6pm, closed Mon & Tues; $5, students $2, free on the first Sat of every month) a small but vibrant collection of African and African-American art from all eras.

Close by, **Adam Clayton Powell Jr Boulevard** pushes north, a broad and busy thoroughfare named after the 1930s minister who helped force the white-owned stores of Harlem to employ the blacks on whom their economic survival depended. Powell later became the first black on the city council, then New York's first black representative at Congress, a career which came to an embittered end in 1967, when amid rumors of the misuse of public funds he was excluded from Congress by majority vote. This failed to diminish his standing in Harlem, where voters twice reelected him before his death in 1972. A block east, the **Schomburg Center for Research in Black Culture**, 515 Malcolm X Blvd at 135th Street (Mon–Wed noon–8pm, Thurs–Sat 10am–6pm; free), has thought-provoking displays on black history. Just north at 132 W 138th St, the **Abyssinian Baptist Church** was where Powell preached, and a small **museum** inside records his life (minus the scandal). The church is also famed for its revival-style Sunday morning services and a gospel choir of gut-busting vivacity. Cross over to 138th Street between Powell and Eighth, and you're in what many consider the finest, most articulate block of rowhouses in Manhattan – **Strivers' Row** – commissioned during the 1890s housing boom and taking in designs by three sets of architects. Within the burgeoning black community of the turn of the century this came to be the desirable place for ambitious professionals to reside; hence its nickname.

From Park Avenue to the East River, Spanish Harlem, or **El Barrio**, dips down as far as East 96th Street to collide head on with the affluence of the Upper East Side. The center of a large Puerto Rican community, it is quite different from Harlem in look and feel. El Barrio was originally a working-class Italian neighborhood (a small pocket of Italian families survives around 116th St and First Ave) and the quality of building here are nowhere as good as that immediately to the west. The result is a shabbier and more intimidating atmosphere. In the early 1950s the government's "Operation Bootstrap" policy offered Puerto Ricans incentives to emigrate to the US. But the occupants have had little opportunity to evolve Latino culture in any meaningful way, and the only space where cultural roots are in evidence is **La Marqueta** on Park Avenue between 111th and 116th, a five-block street market of tropical produce, sinister-looking meats and much shouting, and the **Museo del Barrio** at Fifth Avenue and 104th Street (Wed–Sun 11am–5pm; suggested donation $4), which showcases Latin American and Caribbean art and culture.

North of Harlem, but easily reached by the #A train to 157th and Broadway or the #A to 155th, **Audubon Terrace** at 155th and Broadway is a complex of nineteenth-century Beaux Arts buildings housing an odd array of museums. The best of these is the **Hispanic Museum**, 3753 Broadway between 155th and 156th streets (Tues–Sat 10am–4.30pm, Sun 1–4pm, closed Mon, Library closed Aug; free), which houses one of the largest collections of Hispanic art outside Spain, with more than three thousand paintings, including works by Spanish masters such as Goya, El Greco and Velázquez, and more than 6000 decorative works of art.

The **Morris-Jumel Mansion**, within easy walking distance on 160th Street between Amsterdam and Edgecombe (Wed–Sun 10am–4pm; closed Mon & Tues; $3), is another

Uptown surprise, its proud Georgian outlines faced with a later Federal portico. Built as a rural retreat in 1765 by Colonel Roger Morris, it was briefly Washington's headquarters before falling into the hands of the British. Later, wine merchant Stephen Jumel bought the mansion and refurbished it for his wife Eliza, formerly a prostitute and his mistress. When Jumel died in 1832, Eliza married ex-Vice President Aaron Burr, twenty years her senior. The marriage lasted six months before old Burr upped and left, to die on the day of their divorce. Eliza battled on to the age of 91, and on the top floor of the house you'll find her obituary, a magnificently fictionalized account of a "scandalous" life.

From most western stretches of Washington Heights you get a glimpse of the **George Washington Bridge** that links Manhattan to New Jersey, a dazzling concoction of metalwork and graceful lines. You can get even better views from **The Cloisters** in Fort Tryon Park, a reconstruction of a monastic complex which houses the pick of the Metropolitan Museum's medieval collection (Tues–Sun 9.30am–5.15pm, closes 4.45pm Nov–Feb, closed Mon; suggested donation $10, students $4, includes admission to Metropolitan Museum (see p.87) on same day; also reachable by hourly direct shuttle bus from the Met Fri & Sat in June, July & Aug for $5). The collection is the handiwork of collectors George Barnard and John D Rockefeller, who spent the early years of this century shipping over all they could buy of medieval Europe. Among its larger artifacts are a monumental Romanesque Hall made up of French remnants and a frescoed Spanish Fuentiduena Chapel, both thirteenth-century and cornering on the prettiest of the four sets of cloisters here, from St Guilhelm in thirteenth-century France. At the center of the museum is the Cuxa cloister from a twelfth-century Benedictine monastery in the French Pyrenees, whose capitals are brilliant works of art, carved with weird, self-devouring grotesque creatures. Among smaller sculpture, the Early Gothic Hall houses a memorably tender *Virgin and Child*, carved in England in the fourteenth century. Tapestries on show include the spectacular *Unicorn Tapestries*. Campin's Merode Altarpiece, housed in its own antechamber, depicts the Annunciation in a typical Flemish interior of the day, beyond which life goes on in a fifteenth-century market square, perhaps Campin's native Tournai. The amazing downstairs Treasury houses the *Belles Heures de Jean, Duc de Berry* – perhaps the greatest of all medieval Books of Hours, executed by the Limburg Brothers with dazzling genre miniatures of seasonal life – and the twelfth-century altar cross from Bury St Edmunds in England, a mass of tiny expressive characters from biblical stories.

# The outer boroughs

Most visitors to New York don't stray off Manhattan. But if you're staying a while, choose to investigate the **outer boroughs** and you'll be well rewarded. **Brooklyn** is certainly worth a trip, primarily for the salubrious neighborhood of Brooklyn Heights just across the East River, bucolic Prospect Park and the Brooklyn Botanical Garden, and the Brooklyn Museum. For inveterate nostalgics, Coney Island and its Russian neighbor, Brighton Beach, lie at the far end of the subway line. Few indeed make it to **Queens**, though it holds the bustling Greek community of Astoria and the Museum of the Moving Image. **Staten Island** boasts a couple of unusual museums, and the ferry ride is fun in itself. Even the **Bronx**, renowned for the desolate and bleak environs of its southern reaches, which are in fact slowly improving, has the city's largest zoo and another glorious botanical garden.

## Brooklyn

If it were still a separate city, **Brooklyn** would be the fourth largest in the US, but until as recently as the early 1800s it was no more than a group of autonomous towns and villages distinct from the already thriving Manhattan. Robert Fulton's steamship service across the water first changed the shape of Brooklyn, starting with the establishment of a leafy retreat at Brooklyn Heights. What really transformed things, though, was the opening of the Brooklyn Bridge. Thereafter development spread deeper inland, as housing was needed to service a more commercialized Manhattan. By the turn of the century, Brooklyn was fully established as part of the newly incorporated New York City, and its fate as Manhattan's perennial kid brother was sealed.

**Brooklyn Heights**, now one of New York City's most beautiful neighborhoods, has little in common with the rest of the borough – a peaceful, tree-lined enclave originally settled by financiers from Wall Street across the water and today still very exclusive. There isn't much to see as you wander its perfectly preserved terraces and breathe in the air of civilized calm, but students of urban architecture can have a field day. The obvious place to begin a tour is the so-called **Esplanade** – more commonly known as the **Promenade** – with its fine views of downtown Manhattan across the water, east of which **Pierrepoint** and **Montague** streets are the Heights' main arteries, studded with delightful brownstones, restaurants, bars and shops.

Further into Brooklyn, Flatbush Avenue leads up to **Grand Army Plaza**, a grandiose junction laid out by Calvert and Vaux late in the nineteenth century as a dramatic approach to their new Prospect Park just beyond. The triumphal **Soldiers and Sailors' Memorial Arch** was added thirty years later, topped with a fiery sculpture of Victory in tribute to the Northern triumph in the Civil War. **Prospect Park** itself was landscaped in the early 1890s, and remains for the most part remarkably bucolic – far more so than Central Park – as does the adjacent **Brooklyn Botanic Garden** (April–Sept Tues–Fri 8am–6pm, Sat & Sun 10am–6pm; Oct–March Tues–Fri 8am–4.30pm, Sat & Sun 10am–4.30pm), one of the most enticing park and garden spaces in the city, smaller and more immediately likeable than its more celebrated rival in the Bronx.

**The Brooklyn Museum**, 220 Eastern Parkway (Wed–Fri 10am–5pm, Sat & Sun 11am–6pm, first Sat of every month 11am–11pm, closed Mon & Tues; $4, students $2), though doomed to stand perpetually in the shadow of the Met, is a major museum and a good reason in itself for forsaking Manhattan for an afternoon, with five demanding floors of miscellaneous artifacts. Highlights include the ethnographic department on the ground floor, with arts and applied arts from Oceania and the Americas, the classical and Egyptian antiquities on the second floor, and the evocative American period rooms on the fourth floor. Be sure, too, to look in on the top-story American and European picture galleries, where the eighteenth-century portraits include one of George Washington by Gilbert Stuart. Pastoral canvases by William Sidney Mount, alongside the heavily romantic Hudson River School and paintings by Eastman Johnson (such as the curious *Not at Home*) and John Singer Sargent, lead up to twentieth-century work by Charles Sheeler and Georgia O'Keeffe. European artists featured include Degas, Cézanne, Toulouse-Lautrec, Monet and Dufy. The giftshop sells ethnic items from around the world at reasonable prices.

Generations of working-class New Yorkers came to relax at one of Brooklyn's furthest points, **Coney Island**, reachable from Manhattan on the #B, #D, #F or #N subway lines. At its height it was visited by 100,000 people a day; now, however, it's one of the city's poorest districts, and not a little threatening. The amusement park is peeling and run-down, and until recently the boardwalk was cracked and broken – although if you like down-at-heel seaside resorts there's no better place on earth. The beach at least is beautiful, a broad swath of golden sand. The **New York Aquarium** on the boardwalk opened in 1896 and is still going strong, displaying fish and invertebrates from the world over in its darkened halls, along with frequent open-air shows of marine mammals (daily 10am–6pm; $7.75).

Further along, **Brighton Beach**, or "Little Odessa," is home to the country's largest community of Russian émigrés – around 20,000, who arrived in the 1970s – and a long-established and now largely elderly Jewish population. Livelier than Coney Island, it's also more prosperous, especially along its main drag, **Brighton Beach Avenue**, which runs underneath the El in a hotchpotch of food shops and appetizing restaurants. In the evening, the restaurants really heat up, becoming a near-parody of a rowdy Russian night out with loud live music, much glass-clinking and the frenzied knocking back of vodka. Definitely worth a visit.

## The Bronx

The city's northernmost borough, **The Bronx** was for a long time believed to be its toughest and most notoriously crime-ridden district, and presented as such in films like *Fort Apache, The Bronx* and books like *Bonfire of the Vanities,* even after urban renewal was underway. In fact, it's not much different than the other New York outer boroughs, and has proved less vulnerable to the racial tensions that surfaced elsewhere during the late 1980s and early 1990s. Geographically, the Bronx has more in common with Westchester County to the north than it does with the island regions of New York City: steep hills, deep valleys and rocky outcroppings to the west, and marshy flatlands along Long Island Sound to the east. First settled in the seventeenth century by the Swedish Jonas Bronk, like Brooklyn it only became part of the city proper around the end of the nineteenth century. From 1900 onwards things moved fast, and the Bronx became one of the most sought-after residential areas of the city, its main thoroughfare, **Grand Concourse**, becoming edged with increasingly luxurious Art Deco apartment blocks – many of which, though greatly run-down, still stand.

The **Bronx Zoo** (Apr–Oct Mon–Fri 10am–5pm, Sat & Sun 10am–5.30pm; Nov–Mar daily 10am–4.30pm; admission Apr–Oct $7.75, $4 for kids; Nov–Dec $6 and $3; Jan–Mar $4 and $2; free every Wed) is accessible either by its main gate on Fordham Road or by a second entrance on Bronx Park South. The latter is the entrance to use if you come directly here by subway (to E Tremont Ave). Even if you don't like zoos, the largest urban zoo in the US is better than most, and one of the first to realize that animals both looked and felt better out in the open. Its "Wild Asia" exhibit is an almost forty-acre wilderness through which tigers, elephants and deer roam relatively free, viewable from a monorail (May–Oct; $2). Look in also on the "World of Darkness," which holds nocturnal species, and the simulation of a Himalayan mountain area, holding endangered species such as the giant panda and snow leopard.

Across the road from the zoo's main entrance is the back turnstile of the **New York Botanical Gardens** (Tues–Sun 10am–6pm; $3, $2 students and $1 kids, free Wed) which in parts is as wild as anything you're likely to see upstate. West of its main entrance, the **Poe Cottage** (Grand Concourse and Kingsbridge Rd; Sat 10am–4pm, Sun 1–5pm; $2) is a tiny white clapboard shack that was Edgar Allan Poe's home for the last three, unhappy years of his life, which saw his wife's death and very little writing beyond the short, touching poem, *Annabel Lee.* Poe left the cottage for the last time in 1849 to secure backing for his long-held dream – his own literary magazine – but got entangled in the election furore in Baltimore, disappeared, and was eventually found delirious, dying in hospital a few days later. What actually happened no one knows, and the house, with its few meagre furnishings spread thinly through half a dozen rooms, tells you little more about the man.

## Queens

Of the four outer boroughs, **Queens**, named after the wife of Charles II of England, is the most consistently ignored. Though considerably more accessible than Staten Island, a great deal larger than Brooklyn, and more interesting and ethnically diverse than the Bronx, it is simply not seen as a desirable place to live. People who live in

Queens, the thinking seems to run, are either excruciatingly dull or just can't afford to live anywhere else.

This belittles its role as one of the rare places where postwar immigrants could buy their own homes and establish their own communities. **Astoria**, for example, holds the largest concentration of Greeks outside Greece (Melbourne included). It also has a long **filmmaking** tradition: Paramount had its studios here until it was lured away by Hollywood's reliable weather. Astoria was then left empty and disused by all except the US Army, until Hollywood's stranglehold on the industry finally weakened. The new studios here – not open to the public – now rank as the country's fourth largest and are set for a major expansion. The **American Museum of the Moving Image** in the old Paramount complex at 34–31 35th St near Broadway (Tues–Fri noon–5pm, Sat & Sun 11am–6pm, closed Mon; $8.50, students/seniors $5.50, children 5–12 $4.50, children under 5 free; price includes all film and video programs) is devoted to the history of film, video and TV. In addition to viewing posters and kitsch movie souvenirs from the 1930s and 1940s you can listen in on directors explaining sequences from famous movies; watch fun short films made up of well-known clips; add your own sound effects to movies; and see some original sets and costumes. A wonderful, mock-Egyptian pastiche of a 1920s movie theater shows kids' movies and TV classics.

If you're really keen on exploring Queens, the **Queens Museum**, at Flushing Meadows-Corona Park (Wed–Fri 10am–5pm, Sat & Sun noon–5pm; suggested donation $4, students $2) is another possible destination. Its one permanent item is an 18,000-square-foot model of the five boroughs of New York City, spectacularly lit, recently updated and originally conceived for the 1964 World's Fair by Robert Moses. Great fun if you know the city well, and useful orientation if you don't. Take the subway #7 to Willets Point–Shea Stadium.

## Staten Island

Until 1964 **Staten Island** was isolated – getting to it meant a ferry trip or a long ride through New Jersey, and commuting into town was almost an eccentricity. The opening of the Verrazano Narrows Bridge changed things: upwardly mobile Brooklynites found inexpensive property on the island and swarmed over the bridge to buy their parcel of suburbia. Today Staten Island has swollen to accommodate dense residential neighborhoods amid the rambling greenery, endless backwaters of neat look-don't-touch homes; and residents pining for a lost sense of isolation voted in November 1993 to begin the long process of divorcing their borough from New York City altogether (though that seems unlikely to happen anytime soon).

The **Staten Island Ferry** sails from Battery Park, with half-hourly departures 24 hours a day, giving great wide-angled views of the city – absolutely free. The ferry terminal quickly dispels any romance, but it's easy to escape to the adjoining bus station and catch the #4 bus to the **Jacques Marchais Center of Tibetan Art** at 338 Lighthouse Ave (April–Nov Wed–Sun 1–5pm; other times by appointment, call ☎718/987-3500; $3). Jacques Marchais was the alias of Jacqueline Kleber, a New York art dealer who reckoned she'd get on better with a French name. She assembled the largest collection of Tibetan art in the Western world and housed it in a hillside "Buddhist temple." The exhibition is small enough to be accessible, with magnificent bronze Bodhisattvas, fearsome deities in union with each other, musical instruments, costumes and decorations from Tibet. During the first or second week of October it hosts a **harvest festival**: Tibetan monks in saffron robes perform the traditional ceremonies, and Tibetan food and crafts are sold.

Back on the main Richmond Road, a short walk leads to the **Richmondstown Restoration** (July & Aug Wed–Fri 10am–5pm, Sat & Sun 1–5pm; Sept–June Wed–Sun 1–5pm; $4, students $2.50), where a dozen or so old buildings have been transplanted from their original sites and grafted on to the eighteenth-century village of Richmond. Half-hourly tours negotiate the best of these – including the oldest elementary school in the country, a picture-book general store, and the atmospheric Guyon-Lake-Tyson House of 1740 – and craftspeople use old techniques to weave cloth and fire kilns. It's all carried off to picturesque and ungimmicky effect in rustic surroundings, a mere twelve miles from downtown Manhattan.

# EATING

There isn't anything you can't **eat** in New York. The city has more restaurants per head than anywhere else in the States, and many New Yorkers not only eat out often but take their food incredibly seriously, obsessed with new cuisines, new dishes and new restaurants. Certain areas are pockets of ethnic restaurants: **Chinatown** (including Vietnamese) below Canal Street; **Little Italy** just to the north; and **Little India**, Sixth Street east of Second Avenue. On the **Upper West Side**, quite a few places offer the surprising combination of Cuban and Chinese. Due to space restrictions, only restaurants in Manhattan are listed here.

## Downtown Manhattan

**Baby Jupiter**, 170 Orchard St at Stanton St (☎212/982-2229). The front room boasts big booths and a well-stocked bar with ample portions of Cajun treats flying out of the kitchen to a smart crowd. The back room hosts local music talent and pulls in a decent crowd almost every night of the week.

**Balthazar**, 80 Spring St between Crosby St and Broadway (☎212/965-1414). After two years this is still one of the hottest reservations in town. The tastefully ornate Parisian decor and nonstop beautiful people keep your eyes busy until the food arrives; then all you can do is savor the fresh oysters and mussels, the exquisite pastries and everything in between.

**Cafe Le Figaro**, 184 Bleecker St at MacDougal St (☎212/677-1100). Former Beat hangout during the 1950s; the ersatz Left Bank at its finest. Good people-watching, and first-rate snacks and meals.

**Corner Bistro**, 331 W 4th St at Jane St (☎212/242-9502). Down-home pub with cavernous booths serving some of the best burgers and fries in town. An excellent place to unwind and refuel in a friendly neighborhood atmosphere – it's also a longstanding literary haunt.

**Cowgirl Hall of Fame**, 519 Hudson St at 10th Ave (☎212/633-1133). Don't let the theme-bar ambiance put you off this great-value Tex Mex treat. A rowdy atmosphere, great margaritas and a different cowgirl celebrated every week.

**Cupping Room Cafe**, 359 W Broadway, between Broome and Grand sts (☎212/925-2898). American/Continental restaurant which hosts live jazz on Friday and Saturday nights. An eclectic and creative mix of food, from good steaks to Cajun to French, mostly well pulled off. Good for brunch but be prepared to wait.

**Day-O**, 103 Greenwich Ave at W 12th St (☎212/924-3161). A young crowd enjoys the food and lively atmosphere at this Downtown Caribbean/Southern joint. Highlights include fried catfish, jerk chicken, coconut shrimp and a choice of two veggie dishes. Deadly tropical drinks too.

In 1995, New York City passed some of the most stringent **public smoking laws** in the country. Smoking is now allowed only in restaurants that seat fewer than 35 people, in separate bars of larger restaurants, and in stand-alone bars. Some restaurants prepared for the laws in advance, adapting themselves to satisfy long-term customers. Perhaps the most extreme example of this is *Marylou's* restaurant in Greenwich Village, which spent more than $30,000 in renovations for a room with separate air conditioning, ventilation and air-quality monitors. Why? Favored customer Jack Nicholson is an avid cigar-smoker. If smoking is important to you, call ahead to check if it's allowed.

**Florent**, 69 Gansevoort St, near W 14th St and 9th Ave (☎212/989-5779). See and be seen at this 24hr ultrafashionable diner-cum-bistro in the heart of the meat-packing district, serving good French food. Moderate to pricey.

**Gandhi**, 345 E 6th St, between 1st and 2nd aves (☎212/614-9718). E 6th St is Manhattan's curry capital, and this inexpensive place is one of its stars. Though there's a bar here, you may still bring your own wine or beer.

**Il Fornaio**, 132a Mulberry St between Hester and Grand sts (☎212/226-8306). Stylish, bright, tiled Italian restaurant with good lunch deals – fine calzone and pizza for $4. Affordable and tasty Southern Italian cooking: pastas, Italian stews and the like.

**Japonica**, 100 University Place at E 12th St (☎212/243-7752). Some of the freshest sushi in the city, at very reasonable prices. But the word's out and there can be queues.

**Jerry's**, 101 Prince St, between Greene and Mercer sts (☎212/966-9464). American–French restaurant, with an upscale diner atmosphere and moderate prices, that's one of SoHo's trendier spots. Casual and good for people-watching.

**Jules,** 65 St Mark's Place at 1st Ave (☎212/477-5560). Step down into this relaxed, yet unmistakeably hip, French bistro where live jazz on Thursdays accompanies the steak frites and salad *frisee aux lardons*. Weekend brunch is also unbeatable.

**Katz's**, 205 E Houston St at Ludlow St (☎212/254-2246). Wisecracking Lower East Side Jewish deli serving archetypal overstuffed pastrami and corned beef sandwiches. Best known as the scene of the orgasm scene in *When Harry Met Sally*.

**Kelley and Ping**, 127 Greene St between Houston and Prince sts (☎212/228-1212). If you're in the midst of a SoHo shopping spree there aren't too many affordable options in the area – but this noodle oasis will put your stomach and your wallet at ease. This Pan-Asian noodle spot will set you right – $13 for dinner entrees; $8 lunch specials.

**Life Cafe**, 343 E 10th St at Ave B (☎212/477-8791). Peaceful East Village haunt on Tompkins Square that hosts sporadic concerts. Sandwiches, or Tex-Mex and vegetarian full meals for around $8–10. Good happy hour too.

**Lupe's East LA Diner**, 110 6th Ave at Watts St (☎212/966-1326). Very laid-back hole-in-the-wall restaurant serving great beer and burritos. Good fun and inexpensive.

**Moustache**, 90 Bedford St, between Grove and Barrow sts (☎212/229-2220); 265 E 10th St between 1st Ave and Ave A (☎212/228-2022). Small, cheap, nicely decorated Middle Eastern spot with a "pitza" specialty (pizzas of pita bread and eclectic toppings) and great hummus and falafel.

**Rio Mar**, 7 9th Ave at W 12th St (☎212/243-9015). Hearty Spanish food at the edge of the seedy meat-packing district. Worth the trip for the paella alone.

**Sala**, 344 Bowery at Great Jones St (☎212/979-6606). Terra cotta-tiled Spanish eatery serving delicious tapas, as well as full entrees; good sangrias as well. Large appetizers for about $7; entrees are $14 and up.

**Second Avenue Deli**, 156 2nd Ave at E 10th St (☎212/677-0606). East Village deli with marvelous burgers, pastrami and other goodies served in an ebullient, snap-happy style.

**Spring Street Natural Restaurant**, 62 Spring St at Lafayette St (☎212/966-0290). Not wholly vegetarian, but very good, freshly prepared health food served in a large airy space. Moderately priced, with entrees from $9.

**Thailand Restaurant**, 106 Bayard St at Baxter St (☎212/349-3132). This Chinatown restaurant is a standout in the neighborhood – the deep sea bass, crispy and spicy, is delicious.

**Time Cafe**, 380 Lafayette St at Great Jones St (☎212/533-7000). Consistently great food with an organic edge. Great salads, pasta and fish specials in a comfortable, airy setting at moderate to expensive prices, with a popular outdoor cafe. Also on the premises is the *Fez Lounge*, a faux Moroccan back-room bar, and a downstairs club with nightly live music. Gets quite crowded at weekends.

**Tortilla Flats**, 767 Washington St at W 12th St (☎212/243-1053). This over-decorated Mexican spot is a must-see. Check out the Elvis room and sample the potent margaritas and heaped portions of food. Theme nights include Ernest Borgnine Night, Vegas Night and Bingo for Shots.

**Two Boots**, 37 Ave A, between E 2nd and 3rd sts (☎212/505-2276). Raucous, inexpensive pizza joint where anything goes on great, thin-crust pizza. Other dishes served as well as pizza.

# Midtown Manhattan

**B Smith's**, 771 8th Ave at 47th St (☎212/247-2222). Great Southern food (pricey) and a happening bar scene attracting the black urban professional set.

**Cabana Carioca**, 123 W 45th St, between 6th and 7th aves (☎212/581-8088). Great Brazilian food and atmosphere at reasonable prices for Midtown. The *caipirinha* cocktails are excellent, and portions are big enough for two. Best black beans and rice in town.

**Carnegie Deli**, 854 7th Ave, between W 54th and 55th sts (☎212/757-2245). Famous Jewish deli serving the most generously stuffed sandwiches in the city.

**Eighteenth and Eighth**, 159 8th Ave at 18th St (☎212/242-5000). A hip little upscale diner in the heart of Chelsea. The prices are moderate, the crowd is trendy, and even breakfast is trendy.

**Hallo Berlin**, 402 W 51st St, between 9th and 10th aves (☎212/541-6248). On the west side, the best for wursts. The owner used to sell this stuff from a pushcart, and made enough to open a restaurant. Pleasant bench-and-table beer-garden setting.

**Jezebel**, W 45th St and 9th Ave (☎212/582-1045). Good, old-fashioned Southern cooking and a bordello atmosphere make this place stand out amid the Theater District clones on Restaurant Row, as this block of 45th is known.

**Julian's**, 802 9th Ave, between W 53rd and 54th sts (☎212/262-4800). Light and inventive Mediterranean fare in a bright, pleasing room and clever dining garden tucked in an alley.

**Negril**, 362 W 23rd St off 9th Ave (☎212/807-6411). Lively Jamaican restaurant serving spicy jerk chicken or goat stews and other dishes at reasonable prices (especially the lunch specials). Dinner entrees are around $10–12.

**Oyster Bar**, Lower Level, Grand Central Terminal (☎212/490-6650). Wonderfully atmospheric old place, down in the vaulted dungeons of Grand Central, where Midtown office workers break for lunch (see p.80). Clam chowder and fresh oyster selections daily. Moderate to expensive prices, but if you eat at the bar you can eat more cheaply.

**Pad Thai**, 114 8th Ave at 16th St (☎212/691-6226). Good noodle dishes, curries and other Thai classics, all at reasonable prices. Also a wide array of vegetarian choices.

**Sushi Zen**, 57 W 46th St, between 5th and 6th aves (☎212/302-0707). Swimmingly fresh sushi and tranquility-inducing decor. Very attentive service, but the food's on the expensive side.

**Union Square Café**, 21 E 16th St, between 5th Ave and Union Square W (☎212/243-4020). Choice California-style dining with a classy but comfortable Downtown atmosphere. No one does salmon like Chef Danny Meyer. Prices average $100 for two – but the creative menu (and great people-watching) is a real treat.

**Vong**, 200 E 54th St, between 2nd and 3rd aves (☎212/486-9592). Eccentrically decorated, still hot restaurant with a French colonial approach to Thai cooking – the chefs put mango in foie gras, and sesame and tamarind on Muscovy duck. Somehow, it works. Expensive.

**Zen Palate**, 663 9th Ave at W 46th St (☎212/582-1669). Ultra-vegetarian Chinese in a beautifully decorated setting. With dishes like "Jewels of Happiness," how can you go wrong? Moderately priced.

# Uptown Manhattan

**Amsterdam's**, 428 Amsterdam Ave, between W 80th and 81st sts (☎212/874-1377). Popular in the neighborhood for consistently great roasted half-chicken served with mountains of fries and its packed bar. Moderate.

**Barking Dog Luncheonette**, 1678 3rd Ave at E 94th St (☎212/831-1800). Diner-like place with outstanding, cheap American food (like mashed potatoes and gravy). Kids will feel at home.

**Big Nick's**, 2175 Broadway, between 76th and 77th sts (☎212/362-9238). An Upper West Side institution, Big Nick has been serving mini-pizzas and maxi-burgers, all night long, to locals for over twenty years. Wash the stuff down with 12-ounce draft beers at $1 a pop.

**Brother Jimmy's BBQ**, 1461 1st Ave at E 76th St (☎212/545-RIBS). Casual, fun barbecue restaurant whose motto is "Pig Out!" Quite a happening bar scene, if you're into its frat-party atmosphere.

**Carmine's**, 2450 Broadway, between W 90th and W 91st sts (☎212/362-2200). Mountainous portions of tasty home-style Southern Italian food made to share, served at a large and loud Upper West Side favorite. Be prepared to wait; only parties of six or more can make reservations.

**Dock's Oyster Bar**, 2427 Broadway, between W 89th and W 90th sts (☎212/724-5588) and 633 3rd Ave at E 40th St (☎212/986-8080). Ultrafresh, moderate to expensive seafood. The Upper West Side branch is a bit cozier, but both can be noisy and the service can be slow.

**Ecco-la**, 1660 3rd Ave, between E 92nd and E 93rd sts (☎212/860-5609). Unique pasta combinations at very moderate prices make this one of the Upper East Side's most popular Italians. A real find if you don't mind waiting.

**EJ's Luncheonette**, 447 Amsterdam Ave, between W 81st and W 82nd sts (☎212/873-3444) and 1271 3rd Ave at E 73rd St (☎212/472-0600). Retro diner food and atmosphere at great prices. Both are popular so come early or be ready to wait. Don't miss the French-fried sweet potatoes.

**El Pollo**, 1746 1st Ave, between E 90th and E 91st sts (☎212/996-7810). An Upper East Side find for fast food Peruvian-style, like rotisserie chicken – tasty and cheap. Bring your own wine.

**Fujiyama Mama**, 467 Columbus Ave, between W 82nd and 83rd sts (☎212/769-1144). The West Side's best – and most boisterous – sushi bar, with high-tech decor and loud music.

**Gabriela's**, 685 Amsterdam Ave at 93rd St (☎212/961-0574). Terrific, inexpensive, authentic Mexican – not just your usual enchiladas and burritos, but also a wide array of regional chicken and seafood dishes. Large crowded room, noisy, lively and thoroughly enjoyable, but be prepared to wait.

**Heidelburg**, 1648 2nd Ave between E 85th and 86th sts (☎212/628-2332). One of the last of the Yorkville German joints. The food is the real deal, with excellent liver dumpling soup, *Bauernfruestuck* omelettes, and pancakes (both sweet and potato). Have a huge, boot-shaped glass of Weissbeer with anything.

**La Caridad**, 2199 Broadway at W 78th St (☎212/874-2780). Upper West Side institution, doling out plentiful and inexpensive Cuban–Chinese food. Bring your own beer and expect to wait.

**Malaga**, 406 E 73rd St, between First and York aves (☎212/737-7659). Intimate local Spanish restaurant with good, wholesome food at moderate prices.

**Piccolo Pomodoro**, 1742 2nd Ave, between E 90th and E 91st sts (☎212/831-8167). Great Italian serving giant portions at quite slender prices.

**Ruby Foo's**, 2182 Broadway at 77th St (☎212/724-6700). Pan-Asian cuisine in an enjoyable setting, with new twists on dim sum, dumplings and sushi.

**Sylvia's Restaurant**, 328 Lenox Ave, between 126th and 127th sts (☎212/996-0660). The downhome Southern cooking at this Harlem institution makes it worth the trek Uptown. Now with a gospel brunch on Sundays.

**Tom's Restaurant**, 2880 Broadway at W 112th St (☎212/864-6137). Cheap, greasy-spoon diner fare. This is the *Tom's* of *Seinfeld* and Suzanne Vega fame, usually filled with students from Columbia. Great breakfast deals – a large meal for under $5.

**Vince & Eddie's**, 70 W 68th St, between Columbus Ave and Central Park W (☎212/721-0068). Slightly pseudo-country-style restaurant serving home-cooking like granny used to make – hearty, wholesome and delicious.

**Vinnie's Pizza**, 285 Amsterdam Ave at W 73rd St (☎212/874-4382). For those who prefer their pizza thick, doughy, loaded with cheese and cheap, this Upper West Side place is for you.

# DRINKING

New York's best **bars** are in **downtown Manhattan** – Greenwich Village, the East Village and SoHo. The **Midtown** places tend to be geared to an after-hours office crowd and (with a few exceptions) are pricey and rather dull; **Uptown**, the Upper West Side at least, between 60th and 85th streets along Amsterdam and Columbus avenues, has several good places to drink. Most of the bars listed below serve food of some kind. See also the bars listed in "Gay and Lesbian New York" (p.108).

# Downtown Manhattan

**Barmacy** 538 E 14th St, between aves A and B (☎212/228-2240). Cross a dive-bar and a pharmacy circa 1950 and this is what you get. Plus cheap beer, good DJs and a devoted regular crowd.

**Blind Tiger Ale House**, 518 Hudson St at W 10th St (☎212/675-3848). The name is fitting as you could easily leave here with things looking a bit foggy: 24 beers on tap, eclectic bottled selection, and assorted liquors.

**Blue and Gold**, 74 E 7th St, between 1st and 2nd aves (☎212/473-8918). Popular dive with cheap beer and a great 1980s pop jukebox.

**Broome Street Bar**, 363 W Broadway at Broome St (☎212/925-2086). A popular and long-established local haunt, also serving reasonably priced burgers and salads in a dimly lit setting.

**Chumley's**, 86 Bedford St at Barrow St (☎212/675-4449). As much fun to find (there's no sign) as it is to drink in, this atmospheric former speakeasy has a great selection of beers and good bar food.

**d.b.a.**, 41 1st Ave, between E 2nd and 3rd sts (☎212/475-5097). A beer lover's paradise, *d.b.a.* has at least 60 bottled beers, 14 varieties on tap, and an authentic hand pump. Garden seating in the summer.

**Drinkland**, 339 E 10th St, between aves A and B (☎212/228-2435). Dizzying psychedelic decor fused with DJs spinning big-beat and trip-hop make this place a favorite among Downtown dwellers – plus strong mixed drinks.

**Ear Inn**, 326 Spring St, between Washington and Greenwich St (☎212/226-9060). 'Ear' as in 'Bar' with half the neon 'B' chipped off. Be that as it may, this cozy pub, a stone's throw from the Hudson River, has a good mix of beers on tap, serves basic, reasonably priced, American food and claims to be the second oldest bar in the city. It may also be one of the best.

**Fanelli**, 94 Prince St at Mercer St (☎212/226-9412). Cozy bar, SoHo's oldest, with cheap and hearty food.

**Lakeside Lounge**, 162 Ave B, between 10th and 11th sts (☎212/529-8463). Opened by a local DJ and a record producer who have stocked the jukebox with old rock, country and R&B. A down-home hangout, with live music four nights a week.

**Lansky Lounge**, 38 Delancey St, between Norfolk and Suffolk sts (☎212/677-5588). The venerable dairy restaurant *Ratner's* has spun its back room into a retro cocktail lounge, to which jaded urban sophisticates flock.

**Liquor Store**, 225 W Broadway at White St (☎212/226-7121). Cozy little pub with sidewalk seating that feels like it's been around since colonial times. A welcome respite from the trendy local scene.

**Ñ**, 33 Crosby St between Broome and Grand sts (☎212/219-8856). This colorful long and narrow bar serves tasty tapas and $15 pitchers of strong sangria. A favorite of the SoHo scene.

**St Dymphna's**, 118 St Marks Place between 1st Ave and Ave A (☎212/254-6636). With a pleasant garden out back, a tempting menu and some of the city's best Guinness, this snug Irish watering hole is a favorite among young East Villagers.

**Sweet and Vicious**, 5 Spring St between Bowery and Elizabeth (☎212/334-7915). Although this gem of a bar is said to be named after the owner's cats, it could just as easily refer to the peachy-pink lighting and the two decrepit pistols (found while excavating the site) that hang next to the door.

**White Horse Tavern**, 567 Hudson St at W 11th St (☎212/243-9260). Convivial, inexpensive old-time Village bar where Dylan Thomas supped his last. Excellent jukebox.

# Midtown Manhattan

**Belmont Lounge**, 117 E 15th St between Park Ave S and Irving Place (☎212/533-0009). Oversized couches, dark cavernous rooms and an attractive waitstaff reel in a continuous stream of twenty-somethings. Strong drinks too.

**The Blue Bar** at **The Algonquin Hotel**, 59 W 44th St, between 5th and 6th aves (☎212/840-6800). The *Algonquin's* not quite the chic literary haunt of yore, but this sleek monochrome bar still packs in power-suit tipplers knocking back their Absolut Gimlets. If it gets too crowded, try *Figaro* 28 W 44th St (☎212/840-1010) across the street.

**Candy Bar and Grill**, 131 8th Ave (☎212/229-9702). Stylish hangout for a mixed, well-dressed crowd. Amazing martinis and cocktails plus an excellent menu of munchies and meals.

**The Coffee Shop**, 29 Union Square W at 16th St (☎212/243-7969). Former coffee shop turned trendy bar and restaurant. Brazilian-style food in the noisy adjacent restaurant, and bar grub too.

**5757, The Four Seasons**, 57 E 57th St, between Madison and Park aves (☎212/758-5700) *Very* upscale, but a great way to experience the *Four Seasons'* elegance without splurging for a meal. Dress sharp.

**McHale's**, 750 8th Ave at 46th St (no phone). A good, old-fashioned bar offering respite from tawdry Times Square. A regular menu of bar food (burgers, fries, nachos, wings) at affordable prices.

**Murphy's**, 977 2nd Ave (☎212/751-5400). Irish bar which attracts the Midtown singles set. Drinks are costly but food less so – a rare and useful standby in this part of town.

**Old Town Bar and Restaurant**, 45 E 18th St between Broadway and Park Ave S (☎212/473-8874). Atmospheric bar popular with publishing types, models and photographers from the surrounding Flatiron district. Unpretentious and old-world, with a good pub menu.

**P J Clarke's**, 915 3rd Ave at E 55th St (☎212/759-1650). Legendary spit-and-sawdust alehouse with a not-so-cheap restaurant out back. You may recognize it as the location of the movie *The Lost Weekend*.

**Paddy Reilly's** 519 2nd Ave between 29th and 30th sts (☎212/686-1210). A good place to enjoy a few Guinness drafts, listen to live music and pretend you're Irish. $5 cover some nights.

**Rudy's Bar and Grill**, 627 9th Ave between W 44th and 45th sts (☎212/974-9169). One of New York's cheapest, friendliest and liveliest dive bars, a favorite with local actors and musicians. Great jukebox and free hot dogs.

**Siberia**, 250 W 50th St in the IRT subway station (☎212/333-4141). A genuine New York oddity: a small bar – in look and feel, like a rec room – located in the 1/9 subway station at 50th St.

# Uptown Manhattan

**Bear Bar**, 1770 2nd Ave, between 92nd and 93rd sts (☎212/987-7580). When happy hour starts at 4pm, drafts and buffalo wings are 25¢ apiece; prices go up 25¢ every half-hour thereafter until they reach full price around 7 or 8pm. Wild.

**Border Cafe**, 244 E 79th St (☎212/535-4347). Friendly neighborhood hangout with good frozen margaritas. Down to earth despite its upscale location.

**Dublin House Tap Room**, 225 W 79th St, between Broadway and Amsterdam Ave (☎212/874-9528). Lively Upper West Side Irish pub, pouring a very nice Black & Tan, and dominated at night by the young and rowdy.

**Hi-Life**, 477 Amsterdam Ave at W 83rd St (☎212/874-8037). A lively, crowded joint harking back to the 1940s.

**Lenox Lounge**, 288 Lenox Ave and 125th St (☎212/722-9566). Infamous Harlem jazz hangout with a great Art Deco interior and always a cool vibe throughout.

**Lucy's Retired Surfers**, 503 Columbus Ave, between W 84th and 85th sts (☎212/787-3009). Day-Glo painted, surfboard-decorated bar with killer cocktails with names like "Shark Attack." Inevitably popular with upwardly mobile Upper West Siders.

**Ruby's River Road Cafe & Bar**, 1754 2nd Ave (☎212/348-2328). Home of the famous jello-shots (shots of liquor made with different colored jello), and a fun bar with a Cajun cafe in the back.

**Rusty's**, 1271 3rd Ave (☎212/861-4518). Small bar, good for burgers and brew, that's run by an ex-Mets baseball player and is packed with sporting paraphernalia.

**The Saloon**, 1920 Broadway (☎212/874-1500). Large bar/restaurant with a vast, if indifferent, menu. Bonuses include outside seating and waiters serving on roller skates.

**Smoke**, 2751 Broadway at 105th St (☎212/864-9834). Unpretentious, mellow lounge, favored by local jazz fans for its live music from 10pm (formerly *Augie's*). $8 cover charge on weekends.

**Subway Inn**, 143 E 60th St at Lexington Ave (☎212/223-8929). Downscale neighborhood dive bar surprisingly located across the street from Bloomingdale's. Great for a late afternoon beer.

**Twins**, 1712 2nd Ave at E 87th St (☎212/987-1111 or 1-800/RU-TWINS). Who can resist visiting a bar where everyone who works there is a twin, down to the matching bouncers?

# NIGHTLIFE AND ENTERTAINMENT

Considering New York's everyday energy and diversity it is an awesome feat that it continues into the night – every night. Excellent traditional and contemporary **jazz** is still concentrated in Greenwich Village, and you'll find a scattering of blues, hip-hop, Brazilian and West Indian music in Manhattan as well. Straight **rock music** is led these days by an enhanced indie scene, and there's also a widely unreliable range of **electronic music** clubs. Admission **prices** to venues vary, but most jazz clubs have a hefty cover and a minimum charge for food and drinks; rock venues and dance clubs ask from nothing (rare) to around $20.

*New York Magazine* carries good **what's on listings**, though the *Village Voice* is better for things Downtown and anything vaguely "alternative." The Sunday *New York Times Weekly Guide* is also good for mainstream events: on Friday, the paper's "Weekend" section lists "ticket availability" for the major shows. The monthly *Paper Magazine* features club, bar and restaurant guides, offering a hip, "downtown" perspective. Your best bet is probably *Time Out New York*, which simplifies the city with comprehensive listings and consumer information.

## Larger performance venues

**Beacon Theater**, 2124 Broadway at W 74th St (☎212/496-7070). A restored theater hosting big, off-the-mainstream names.

**Madison Square Garden**, W 31st–33rd sts, between 7th and 8th aves(☎212/465-6741). New York's principal large stage plays host to big rock acts. Not the most atmospheric place to see a band, with seating for yourself and 20,000 of your closest friends.

**Radio City Music Hall**, 6th Ave and 50th St (☎212/247-4777). Not as prestigious a venue as it used to be, although the building itself still has the same sense of occasion.

**Roseland**, 239 W 52nd St, between Broadway and 8th Ave (☎212/249-8870). This club has retained the grand ballroom feel of its heyday (take a gander at the shoes in the entryway and the elaborate powder rooms). The sound system's not the best, but this is still a great place to catch big names before they hit the arena/stadium circuit.

## Rock and pop venues

**Arlene Grocery**, 95 Stanton St, between Ludlow and Orchard sts (☎212/473-9831). Intimate, erstwhile bodega that hosts free gigs by local indie talent seven nights a week; Monday is "Heavy Metal Karaoke" night.

**Baby Jupiter**, 170 Orchard St at Stanton St (☎212/982-2229). Restaurant in front, performance space in back. Hosts a spectrum of rock (indie to avant-garde) bands and experimental performances. $2–5.

**The Bottom Line**, 15 W 4th St at Mercer St (☎212/228-7880). Established singer-songwriters in a cabaret setup, with tables crowding out any suggestion of a dance floor. $15–20, cash only.

**Bowery Ballroom**, 6 Delancey St, corner of Bowery (☎212/533-2111). A minimum of attitude, great sound, and even better sightlines makes this a local favorite to see well-known Britpop and indie rock bands. Shows $10–20.

**Brownies**, 169 Ave A, between E 10th and 11th sts (☎212/420-8392). The place to see major-label one-offs and bands on the cusp of making it big. Around $8.

**CBGB**, 315 Bowery at Bleecker St (☎212/982-4052). This legendary punk/art noise bastion has seen far better days. Run-of-the-mill rock bands crowd today's bills, often four or five acts playing a night. $3–9.

**The Cooler**, 416 W 14th St, between 9th and 10th aves (☎212/645-5189). Adventurous indie rock and avant-garde music attract a twentysomething crowd to this meat refrigerator-turned-club. $5–10.

**Fez (Under Time Cafe)**, 380 Lafayette St at Great Jones St (☎212/533-2680). The mirrored bar and sparkling gold stage curtain suggest a disco fantasy; the poetry readings and acoustic performances are high caliber. Around $10.

**Irving Plaza**, 17 Irving Place, between E 15th and E 16th sts (☎212/777-6800). Once home to off-Broadway musicals, now host to an impressive array of rock, electronic music and techno acts. Good place to see popular bands in a manageable setting. $10–25.

**Mercury Lounge**, 217 E Houston St at Essex St (☎212/260-7400). Dark, medium-sized, innocuous space which hosts a mix of local, national and international pop and rock acts. It's owned by the same crew as Bowery Ballroom – who lately get the better bands. Around $7–12.

**SOB's ("Sounds of Brazil")**, 204 Varick St at W Houston St (☎212/243-4940). Lively club/restaurant, with regular Caribbean, salsa and world music acts. Two performances a night. $12–20.

## Jazz venues

**The Blue Note**, 131 W 3rd St at 6th Ave (☎212/475-8592). Famous names at the attendant high prices. Covers vary from $7.50–65 ($5 for 1am set on Fri & Sat); plus a $5 minimum per person at the tables, a one-drink minimum at the bar.

**Detour**, 349 E 13th St at Ave A (☎212/533-6212). Coffee and cocktail bar that fancies itself as a bit of the Left Bank in the East Village. Modern jazz and experimental music. No cover.

**Knickerbocker's**, 33 University Place at 9th St (☎212/228-8490) High-caliber bass/piano duos. Cover free–$4; minimum $5–17, depending on whether or not you're there for dinner.

**The Knitting Factory**, 74 Leonard St, between Broadway and Church St (☎212/219-3006). Venerable Downtown club hosting live jazz and rock upstairs and more experimental music in its Alter-knit room. Good place to see popular acts in an intimate setting, and boasts 18 beers on draft. $15–20.

**Smalls**, 183 W 10th St at 7th Ave S (☎212/929-7565). Cozy West Village club that offers ten hours of music for $10. Hosts well-knowns and unknowns. Free juice and non-alcoholic beverages, or BYOB.

**Sweet Basil**, 88 7th Ave, between Grove and Bleecker sts (☎212/242-1785). One of New York's major jazz spots. $17.50 cover during the week and a $10 minimum at the tables ($18 at the bar including a drink); Fri and Sat $20–25 cover plus the $10 minimum.

**Village Vanguard**, 178 7th Ave at Greenwich St (☎212/255-4037). Jazz landmark that still lays on a regular diet of big names. Admission $15; $10 drink minimum weekdays, $20 cover and $10 minimum at weekends.

**Visiones**, 125 MacDougal St at W 3rd St (☎212/673-5576). A Spanish restaurant four doors down from *The Blue Note* that hosts an eclectic range of acts. The atmosphere is looser and the clientele younger than many of NY's jazz venues. Cover $10–12, with $10 minimum at the tables, and $12–15 (plus a free drink) at the bar.

**Zinc Bar**, 90 W Houston at LaGuardia (☎212/477-8337). Great jazz venue with strong drinks and a loyal bunch of regulars. The blackboard above the entrance announces the evening's featured band. Cover is $5 with a one-drink minimum. Hosts new talent and established greats such as Max Roach and Grant Green.

## Clubs and discos

New York's **club life** is an amorphous creature. Parties change at a rapid pace, so be sure to check *Paper Magazine* or *Time Out New York* before you make any plans. Musically, **techno** and **house** hold sway at the moment – with the emphasis on the deep, vocal style that's always been popular in the city – but Latin freestyle, dancehall reggae, funk, drum 'n' bass and hip-hop all retain interest. Nothing gets going much before midnight, so there's no point turning up earlier. During the week is the best time to club – prices are cheaper, crowds are smaller and service is better. All venues tend to be strict about **ID**.

**Baktun**, 418 W 14th St (☎212/206-1590). If you're in the mood to make the trek this far west the rewards are vast in one of the city's most unpretentious nightclubs. "Direct Drive" Sat feature drum 'n' bass with DJ's Lion, Seoul, Cassien, Reid Speed and Chris Thomas. Great time guaranteed.

**Don Hill's**, 511 Greenwich St at corner of Spring (☎212/219-2850). Drag queens, creative types, and slumming stars congregate at this dive on the outskirts of SoHo. Less trendy than it used to be, but still the place where your rubber gear won't get a second glance. Fri is "Squeezebox," a cauldron of glam, punk and disco ($10); on Sat, Tiswas, featuring cutting-edge Britpop, is $7. Live bands both nights; other parties during the week.

**Life**, 138 Bleecker St at Thompson St (☎212/420-1999). Mirrored pillars and a huge dance floor make this trendy spot antiseptic and anachronistic, executed without a trace of humor. But the people (and celebrities) still come. $20.

**Limelight**, 660 6th Ave at 20th St (☎212/807-7850). Back in business, and its drug-bustee owner, Peter Gatien, is even on the door some nights. The building is splendid: a church designed by Trinity Church-builder Richard Upjohn. Looking to the 1980s for inspiration, Gatien and his new partner, Irv Johnson, have added an art gallery/lounge behind the main dance floor, but moveable video screens still rule the day. Suffers from weekender syndrome. $25.

**Meow Mix**, 269 E Houston St at Suffolk St (☎212/254-0688). Lipstick lesbians, leather ladies and all types in between dance at this temple to *les femmes*. Free–$5.

**Mother**, 432 W 14th St at Washington St (☎212/366-5680). Located in the meat-packing district, this is probably one of the last New York clubs where anything goes. Inventive parties skewed toward gay clientele but all welcome. $10 (Sat $15).

**Ohm**, 16 W 22nd St between 5th and 6th aves (☎212/229-2000). Formerly *Les Poulets*, this glam supper club with three-level lounge area, an upstairs dance floor and a mellower black-lacquered dance floor downstairs is always lively and crowded. Prix-fixe breakfast served starting at 2am. Open for dinner and dancing Thurs–Sat; admission $20.

**Tunnel**, 220 12th Ave at W 27th St (☎212/695-4682). This club's a survivor from the 1980s. Plenty of house keeps this old underground train station popular in clubbing circles. $15–20.

**Twilo**, 530 W 27th St, between 10th and 11th aves (☎212/462-9422). House and trance pump out the speakers, and gay boys galore pack the floor. Features name European DJs each Fri. $15–25.

**Vanity**, 28 E 23rd St (☎212/989-1038 ext 219). Friday nights are "GBH" (Great British House) while Saturday's rock with "Sticky," a big-beat night featuring drum 'n' bass mega-stars like David Holmes and Deejay Punk Roc. $20–25.

**Vinyl**, 6 Hubert St, between Hudson and Greenwich sts (☎212/343-1379). This big warehouse is a techno sweatshop: full of rave kids and other slaves to the beat. Expect a lengthy queue. $12–20.

# Comedy clubs

**Caroline's Comedy Club**, 1626 Broadway at W 49th St (☎212/757-4100). Glitzy room that books some of the best acts in town. Two-drink minimum. $10–20 cover.

**Catch a Rising Star**, 253 W 28th St, between 7th and 8th aves (☎212/462-2824). New talent showcase twice nightly, three times on Saturday. Two-drink minimum, cover $8–15.

**Comic Strip**, 1568 2nd Ave, between E 81st and E 82nd sts (☎212/861-9386). Famed showcase for stand-up comics going for the big time. Weeknight shows begin at 8.30pm, weekends at 8pm. Three shows Fri & Sat. Cover $10–15, with a $9 drink minimum.

**Dangerfield's**, 1118 1st Ave at E 61st St (☎212/593-1650). New talent showcase run by the established comedian Rodney Dangerfield. Cover $12.50–15, no minimum.

**Don't Tell Mama**, 343 W 46th St, between 8th and 9th aves (☎212/757-0788). Lively, convivial piano bar and cabaret featuring rising stars. Shows at 8 and 10pm. Two-drink minimum, cover $8–15.

**Duplex**, 61 Christopher St at 7th Ave (☎212/255-5438). Village cabaret popular with a gay crowd. Two-drink minimum. Cover $12. The rowdy piano bar downstairs is also worth catching.

**Improvisation**, 433 W 34th St, between 8th and 9th aves (☎212/279-3446). New comic and singing talent, mostly improvised. Shows at 9pm during the week; two on Saturday. Cover $7.50–10, plus $9 minimum at table in food or drink.

**Stand Up New York**, 236 W 78th St at Broadway (☎212/595-0850). Upper West Side club that's a forum for established acts. Nightly shows, two, sometimes three, at weekends. Two-drink minimum, cover $8, weeknights; $12 weekends.

## Theater

New York is one of the world's great **theater** centers. You can find just about any kind of production here, from lavish, over-the-top musicals to experimental productions in converted garages. Venues are referred to as **Broadway**, **Off Broadway** or **Off-Off Broadway**, representing a descending order of ticket price, production polish, elegance and comfort – but it doesn't necessarily have much to do with the address.

**Broadway** offerings consist primarily of large-scale musicals, comedies and dramas with big-name actors, with the occasional classic and one-person show. **Off Broadway** theaters tend to combine high production qualities with a greater willingness to experiment. Off Broadway is social and political drama, satire, ethnic plays and repertory: in short, anything that Broadway wouldn't consider a sure-fire money-spinner. **Off-Off Broadway** is the fringe – drama on a shoestring, perhaps with sensitive or uncommercial subjects. Most Broadway theaters are located just east or west of Broadway between 40th and 52nd streets; Off and Off-Off Broadway theaters are sprinkled throughout Manhattan, with a concentration in the East and West Villages, Union Square, Chelsea and several in the 40s and 50s west of the Broadway Theater District. Specific Broadway listings appear in the free, widely available *Official Broadway Theater Guide*.

Nowhere are regular **tickets** inexpensive on Broadway; they range from $50–100; Off Broadway prices have risen recently too, to as much as $50 in some cases: in general, expect to pay upwards of $20 Off Broadway and $15 Off-Off. These prices can, however, be cut considerably if you can wait in line on the day of the performance at the **TKTS** booth in Times Square (W 47th St at Broadway). The booth (open Mon–Sat 3–8pm, 10am–2pm for Wed & Sat matinees, 10–11am for Sun matinees) has at least one pair of tickets for every performance of every Broadway and Off Broadway show available, at fifty to 75 percent off (plus a $2.50 ticket service charge), payable in cash or travelers' checks. There's another TKTS booth on the mezzanine of 2 World Trade Center (same-day tickets Mon–Fri 11am–5.30pm & Sat 11am–3pm; matinee tickets must be purchased the day before the performance).

**Twofer discount coupons** are available at New York Convention and Visitors Bureau, as well as many shops, banks, restaurants and hotel lobbies. The days are long gone when they really did offer two-for-the-price-of-one, but they still entitle two people to a hefty discount. Unlike TKTS, twofers make it possible to book ahead, though don't expect to find coupons for the latest shows.

If you're prepared to pay **full price** you can, of course, either go directly to the theater, or Tickets Central, 406 W 42nd St (daily 1–8pm; ☎212/279-4200). Ticketron (☎1-800/SOLD-OUT) books seats for those with credit cards for a $2.50 charge.

## Classical music, opera and dance

New Yorkers take **serious music** seriously. Long queues form for anything popular, many concerts sell out, and on summer evenings a quarter of a million people may turn up in Central Park for free performances by the New York Philharmonic.

Besides Lincoln Center (see box, opposite), the most important venue is **Carnegie Hall**, 154 W 57th St (☎212/247-7800), where the greatest names from all schools of music have performed. The acoustics remain superb, and a recent renovation has amended years of structural neglect, restoring the place to its former glory.

As for **dance**, for which Lincoln Center once again serves as a showcase, a number of other venues regularly host events. The **Brooklyn Academy of Music** (or BAM),

## LINCOLN CENTER

**Lincoln Center**, on Broadway at 64th St, is New York's powerhouse of performing art. Each of its major auditoria is in active use throughout the year.

**New York State Theater** (☎212/870-5770). Six months of the year home to the New York City Ballet – considered by many to be the greatest dance company in existence – this accessible venue is also where the New York City Opera plays David to the Met's Goliath. Seats go for less than half the Met's prices, and standing-room tickets are available if a performance sells out.

**Avery Fisher Hall** (☎212/875-5030). The permanent base of the New York Philharmonic, now conducted by Kurt Masur, and a temporary one for visiting orchestras and soloists. Tickets $15–50.

**Metropolitan Opera House** (☎212/362-6000). Hosts the Metropolitan Opera Company from September until late April, and the American Ballet Theater early May to July. Tickets are outrageously expensive and difficult to get hold of. Last-minute cancellations and standing-room tickets can, in theory, be picked up from the box office, but queues form the night before any significant occasion.

**Alice Tully Hall** (☎212/875-5050). Smaller venue used by chamber orchestras, string quartets and instrumentalists. Prices similar to those in the Avery Fisher Hall.

30 Lafayette St, Brooklyn (☎718/636-4100), is America's oldest performing arts academy and one of the most daring producers in New York – definitely worth crossing the river for. Five dance troupes are in residence at the **City Center**, 131 W 55th St (☎212/581-1212), including America's two undisputed choreographic giants, the Merce Cunningham Dance Company and the Paul Taylor Dance Company, as well as the Joffrey and Dance Theatre of Harlem. The most important space in Manhattan for small and mid-sized dance companies is the **Joyce Theater**, 175 8th Ave (☎212/242-0800), home to the Eliot Feld Ballet. The Joyce hosts companies from around the world, and its success has led it recently to open a small satellite – Joyce SoHo – at 155 Mercer St (☎212/431-9233).

## Film

Revival cinemas are increasingly giving way to multiscreen "plexes," but some alternatives still exist.

**Angelika Film Center**, W Houston St at Mercer St (☎212/995-2000). Latest non-Hollywood offerings and European art-house movies.

**Anthology Film Archives**, 32–34 2nd Ave (☎212/505-5181). Shows many films you thought you'd never have the chance to see again.

**Film Forum**, 209 W Houston St, between Varick St and 6th Ave (☎212/727-8110). Showing the best in independent film and documentary, as well as themed revivals.

**Museum of the Moving Image**, 35th Ave and 36th St, Queens (☎718/784-0077). Foreign and avant-garde films.

# GAY AND LESBIAN NEW YORK

Gay refugees from all over America and the world come to New York, home to a large **lesbian and gay** population. **Greenwich Village** is the traditional and most established gay neighborhood, but the **East Village**, too, has a growing scene, especially for younger, more politically active, gay men and lesbians. A more upmarket gay population has moved into **Chelsea** in the West 20s, establishing a growing, funky scene. Other promising locales include the **East 20s and 30s**, and the **Upper West Side**. Gay and lesbian bars are listed below, clubs on p.105. For more information, get hold of the **Gayellow Pages** (New York is in the *Northeast* edition; $9.95), available from the bookstores below. Up-to-the-minute news can be found in *HomoXtra (HX)*, a provocative free listings magazine, or the monthly lesbian/feminist *Sappho's Isle*.

# Resources

**Community Health Project**, 208 W 13th St, 2nd Floor (☎212/675-3559). Low-priced gay clinic.

**A Different Light Bookstore and Cafe**, 151 W 19th St (☎212/989-4850). Excellent range of gay and lesbian publications. Open late all week, and often hosts book-signing parties and readings.

**Gay & Lesbian Visitors' Center**, 135 W 20th St (☎212/463-9030 or 1-800/395-2315). A full travel service for visitors to NYC, including hotel and entertainment reservations, plus guided tours.

**Gay Men's Health Crisis (GMHC)**, 129 W 20th St (☎212/807-6664). Despite the name, this organization – the oldest and largest not-for-profit AIDS organization in the world – provides information and referrals to everyone.

**Gay Switchboard** (daily 10.30am–midnight; ☎212/777-1800). Help and what's on information.

**Lesbian and Gay Community Services Center**, 208 W 13th St (☎212/620-7310). Umbrella group and meeting space for more than eighty gay organizations, which holds regular social events.

**Lesbian Switchboard** (Mon–Fri 6–10pm; ☎212/741-2610). Information on events, happenings and contacts in the New York City community.

**The Oscar Wilde Memorial Bookshop**, 15 Christopher St (☎212/255-8097). The first gay bookstore in the US. Unbeatable.

# Bars

**The Bar**, 68 2nd Ave at E 4th St (☎212/674-9714); **The Boiler Room**, 86 E 4th St at 2nd Ave (☎212/254-7536). Two connected bars, very popular on the East Village scene, with an especially good mixing of gay and lesbian patrons.

**Champs**, 17 W 19th St, between 5th and 6th aves (☎212/633-1717). Cruisy sports bar, for the young Chelsea boy crowd. Live DJs and dancers nightly; Sunday tea dances.

**Crazy Nanny's**, 21 7th Ave (☎212/366-6312). Hardcore lesbian bar with dancing nightly. A Village institution.

**G**, 223 W 19th St between 7th and 8th aves (☎212/929-1085). Nearly as stylish as its "guppie" clientele, this large and deservedly very popular lounge also features a regular DJ and juice bar.

**Hell**, 59 Gansevoort St between Greenwich and Washington sts (☎212/727-1666). Upscale lounge, male-dominated, on the upper fringes of the West Village.

**Henrietta Hudson**, 438 Hudson St at Morton St (☎212/924-3347). Lesbian hangout that gets fairly brimming at night. Serves food. Handy Village location, too.

**Julie's**, 204 E 58th St (☎212/688-1294). Not super-happening, but the choices are limited in Midtown. Wed and Sat are Latin nights.

**Keller's**, 384 West St at Christopher St (☎212/243-1907). Friendly West Village bar that draws a largely African-American crowd.

**King**, 579 6th Ave at W 16th St (☎212/366-5464). A three-floor lounge/bar with theme nights including Amateur Strip Night, Sunday Tea Dance and Fridaze DJ dance party.

**Meow Mix**, 269 E Houston St at Suffolk St (☎212/254-0688). This place remains the girl-club of the moment, way east Downtown. Bands or performances most nights; men are welcome if they behave themselves. See also p.105.

**The Monster**, 80 Grove St (☎212/924-3558). Venerable West Village institution. With dance floor, campy piano bar and cabaret.

**Spike**, 120 11th Ave at 20th St (☎212/243-9688). Chelsea area leather bar for mostly middle-aged in- and out-of-towners.

**Stonewall**, 53 Christopher St between Waverly Place and 7th Ave S (☎212/463-0950). Yes, *that Stonewall*, mostly refurbished and flying the pride flag like they own it – which, one supposes, they do.

**Wonderbar**, 505 E 6th St, between aves A and B (☎212/777-9105). A festive hangout that's friendly to all, but still boy-dominated, despite the punning implication of its name.

# SHOPPING

New York is the consumer capital of the world. You can **shop** for every possible taste, creed or perversity, in any combination and at any time of day or night – and, in the markets of **Greenwich Village**, for example, it can be extraordinarily cheap as well as phenomenally expensive. **Midtown Manhattan** is mainstream territory, with its department stores, big-name clothes designers and branches of the larger chains; Downtown plays host to a wide variety of more offbeat stores – **SoHo** is perhaps the most popular shopping neighborhood in these parts, and generally the most expensive, although with some affordable alternatives for the young and trendy. **Uptown**, the Upper East Side is uncompromisingly upmarket, while the funkier **Upper West Side** has an array of off-the-wall stores to compare with anything SoHo or the Village can offer.

Overseas visitors looking for bargain rates on **electrical goods** should head for the discount stores on Seventh Avenue, a little north of Times Square in the 50s; for **cameras**, try Midtown from 30th to 50th streets between Park and Seventh avenues.

## Department stores

**Bloomingdale's**, 1000 3rd Ave (☎212/355-5900). Perhaps Manhattan's most famous department store, packed with designer clothiers, perfume concessions and the like.

**Macy's**, Broadway at 34th St (☎212/695-4400). The largest department store in the world: two buildings, two million square feet of floor space, ten floors, and, lest we forget, the setting for the holiday tearjerker, *Miracle on 34th Street*.

**Saks Fifth Avenue**, 611 5th Ave at W 49th St (☎212/753-4000). Although Saks remains virtually synonymous with style, it has also updated itself to carry the merchandise of all the big designers.

## Books

**Barnes & Noble**, nine superstore locations at 1972 Broadway at Columbus (☎212/595-6859); Broadway and W 82nd St (☎212/362-8835); 6th Ave and W 22nd St (☎212/727-1227); Lexington Ave and E 86th St (☎212/423-9900); 240 E 86th St at 2nd Ave (☎794-1962); Union Square at 33 E 17th St (☎212/253-0810); 4 Astor Place at Broadway (☎212/420-1322); Citicorp building, E 54th St and 3rd Ave (☎212/750-8033); and 600 5th Ave at W 48th St (☎212/765-0590). These megasized bookstores, part of a nationwide chain, offer generous selection, comfortable fittings and coffee bars.

**Coliseum Books**, 1771 Broadway (☎212/757-8381). Huge, if not flashy, general bookstore; knowledgeable staff and late hours.

**Complete Traveler**, 199 Madison Ave at W 35th St (☎212/685-9007). Manhattan's premier travel bookshop, well stocked with both secondhand and new titles.

**Drama Book Shop**, 723 7th Ave between W 48th and 49th sts (☎212/944-0595). The best theater and film bookstore around, with over 50,000 titles and a very knowledgeable staff.

**Gotham Book Mart**, 41 W 47th St (☎212/719-4448). Literary bookstore, good on drama and theater.

**Murder Ink**, 2486 Broadway between 92nd and 93rd sts (☎212/362-8905). First store to specialize in mystery and detective fiction in the city, and it's still the best.

## SPORT IN NEW YORK

Seeing either of New York's two **baseball** teams involves a trip across the East River to the outer boroughs. The **Yankees** play in the Bronx, at **Yankee Stadium**, 161st Street and River Avenue (☎718/293-6000). Get there on subway #C, #D or #4 direct to 161st St station. The **Mets** are based in Queens, at **Shea Stadium**, 126th Street at Roosevelt Avenue (☎718/507-8499). Take subway #7 to Willets Point/Shea Stadium station. Tickets are priced between $6.50 and $25, depending on where you sit. For an unbelievably raucous New York experience, show up on game day for bleacher seats at Yankee Stadium: the hooligan regulars and the bouncers who keep an eye on them are often more fun to watch than the baseball game.

Both of New York's **football** teams – the **Jets** and the **Giants** – play at the **Meadowlands Sports Complex**, East Rutherford, New Jersey (☎201/935-3900). The stadium is served by regular buses from the Port Authority Bus Terminal on 42nd Street and 8th Avenue (☎212/564-8484). Call ahead to check ticket availability as they are hard to come by. If all else fails, you can simply catch the action on the big screen in any sports bar.

**Basketball** has two New York representatives: the **Knicks** and the **Liberty**, the latter members of the newly formed **WNBA**, a women's professional league. Both play at **Madison Square Garden** (☎212/465-6741), West 33rd and 7th Avenue; served by the #1, #2, #3, #9, #A, #C and #E trains. Tickets for the Knicks are very expensive and hard to come by, but the women's games are fairly exciting and a deal at $10–45. Another area team, the New Jersey **Nets**, play in an arena at the Meadowlands Complex (see above).

**Rizzoli**, 31 W 57th St (☎212/759-2424); 3 World Financial Center (☎212/385-1400); and 454 W Broadway between Prince and Houston sts (☎212/674-1616). Manhattan branches of Italian store, with a good selection of foreign newspapers and magazines and high-quality art and photography books.

**St Mark's Bookshop**, 31 3rd Ave (☎212/260-7853). Best-known "alternative" bookstore in the city, with a good array of titles on politics, feminism, literary criticism and journals, as well as more obscure subjects. Open late.

**Strand Bookstore**, 828 Broadway at W 12th St (☎212/473-1452). Gigantic place, one of the few surviving secondhand stores in an area that used to be full of them. Also offers half-price review copies.

## Records

**Etherea**, 66 Ave A between 4th and 5th sts (☎212/358-1126). Specializing in indie rock and electronica; domestic and imports, CDs and vinyl, this is one of the best shops in the city. Good used selection.

**Footlight Records**, 113 E 12th St (☎212/533-1572). *The* place for show tunes.

**The Golden Disc**, 239 Bleecker St (☎212/255-7899). Jazz, rock oldies, blues and gospel.

**House of Oldies**, 35 Carmine St (☎212/243-0500). What the name says – oldies but goldies of all kinds.

**Mondo Kim's**, 6 St Mark's Place between 2nd and 3rd aves (☎212/598-9985); other location at 144 Bleecker at LaGuardia St (☎212/260-1010). Extensive selection of new and used indie obscurities on CD and vinyl, some real cheap. Esoteric videos upstairs. Staff has a serious attitude problem – and they like it that way.

**Other Music**, 15 E 4th St (☎212/477-8150). Great selection of indie, alternative and lost relics.

**Reggae Land**, 125 E 7th St between 1st Ave and Ave A (☎212/353-2071). Only reggae here, mainly vinyl, some CDs, good selection of the latest releases.

**Sounds**, 20 St Mark's Place between 2nd and 3rd aves (☎212/677-2727). New and used CDs; good prices (you won't find cheaper new releases anywhere else) and selection. Cash only.

**Vinyl Mania**, 41 Carmine St (☎212/924-7223). Where DJs go for the newest, rarest releases.

**Virgin Megastore**, 1540 Broadway (☎212/921-1020). Row upon row of pricey CDs; has cafe and travel agency in-store.

# CHAPTER TWO

# THE MID-ATLANTIC

The three Mid-Atlantic states – **NEW YORK, PENNSYLVANIA** and **NEW JERSEY** – stand at the heart of the most populated and industrialized corner of the US. Although dominated in the popular imagination by the gray smokestacks of New Jersey and the coalfields and steel factories of Pennsylvania, these states also encompass lakes, forests, farmland, rolling green countryside, and, in places, expanses of virtual wilderness.

European settlement was characterized by considerable shifts and turns: the **Dutch**, who arrived in the 1620s, were methodically squeezed out by the **English**, who in turn fought off the **French** challenge to secure control of the region by the mid-eighteenth century. The Native American population, including the **Iroquois Confederacy** and Lenni Lenape, had sided with the French against the English, and were soon confined to reservations or pushed north into Canada. At first the economy depended on the fur trade, though by the 1730s English **Quakers**, along with **Amish** and **Mennonites** from Germany and a few Presbyterian **Irish**, had made farming a significant force, their holdings extending to the western limits of Pennsylvania and New York.

All three states were important during the **Revolution**: over half the battles were fought here, including major American victories at **Trenton** and **Princeton** in New Jersey. Upstate New York was geographically crucial, as the British forces knew that control of the Hudson River would effectively divide New England from the other colonies, and the long winter spent at **Valley Forge** outside Philadelphia turned the rag-tag Continental Army into a well-organized force.

After the Revolution, industry became the region's prime economic force, with **mill towns** springing up along the numerous rivers. By the mid-1850s the large **coalfields** of northeast Pennsylvania were powering the smoky steel mills of Pittsburgh, and the discovery of high-grade **crude oil** in 1859 marked the beginning of the automobile age. Though still significant, especially in the regions near New York City, heavy industry has now by and large been replaced by tourism as the economic engine.

Although many travelers to the East Coast may not consider venturing much further than New York City itself – covered in Chapter One of this book – the region is much more than just an overspill of the Big Apple. Each region has a distinct personality. Just thirty minutes outside of Manhattan, **Long Island** offers both the crashing surf of the Atlantic Ocean and the cool calm of the Long Island Sound. **Upstate New York** is for outdoors enthusiasts: the wooded **Catskill Mountains** line the Hudson River (which Henry James claimed was "in the geography of the ideal"), the imposing **Adirondack**

## ACCOMMODATION PRICE CODES

All accommodation prices in this book have been coded using the symbols below. Note that prices are for the least expensive double rooms in each establishment. For a full explanation see p.37 in Basics.

| | | |
|---|---|---|
| ① up to $30 | ④ $60–80 | ⑦ $130–175 |
| ② $30–45 | ⑤ $80–100 | ⑧ $175–250 |
| ③ $45–60 | ⑥ $100–130 | ⑨ $250+ |

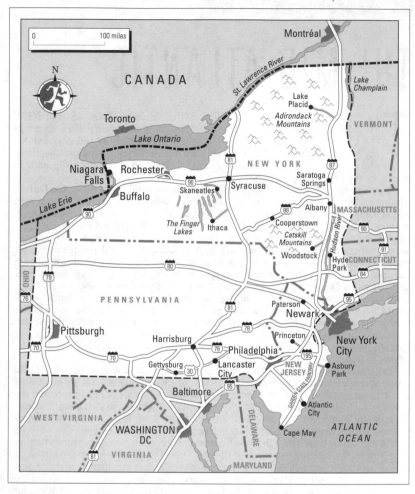

**Mountains** spread over a quarter of the state, and the **Finger Lakes** region offers a pastoral alternative to the industrial Erie Canal cities along I-90. In the northwest corner of the state, on the Canadian border, are the awesome **Niagara Falls**. **Pennsylvania** is best known for the fertile **Pennsylvania Dutch** country and the two great cities of **Philadelphia** and **Pittsburgh**. **New Jersey**, often pictured as one big industrial carbuncle, offers shameless tourist pleasures along the shore: day-trippers in their millions flock to the Boardwalk and casinos of **Atlantic City**.

The entire region is well covered by **public transportation**, with New York's JFK and New Jersey's Newark airports acting as important international gateways, and New York's La Guardia Airport serving domestic flights. In Pennsylvania, both Philadelphia and Pittsburgh have reasonably busy airports with a growing number of international flights. Amtrak **trains** run Northeast Corridor routes north–south through New York, New Jersey and Pennsylvania, while the New Jersey Transit rail and bus network serves all of New Jersey, extending from Atlantic City west to Philadelphia and north to Manhattan. Greyhound **buses** follow the major interstates, with a few subsidiary lines running to more out-of-the-way places.

# NEW YORK STATE

However much the tourist authorities try to encourage visitors, the large and rambling state of **NEW YORK** stands inevitably in the shadow of America's most celebrated city. The words "New York" bring to mind soaring skyscrapers and congested streets, not the 50,000 square miles of rolling dairy farmland, colonial villages, workaday towns, lakes, waterfalls and towering mountains that spread north and west from New York City and constitute **upstate New York**. Their strongest appeal is to the outdoors fanatic. Just an hour's drive north of Manhattan, the valley of the **Hudson River**, with the moody **Catskill Mountains** rising stealthily from the west bank, offers a respite from the intensity of the city. Much wilder and more rugged are the peaks of the vast **Adirondack Mountains** further north – far beyond the scope of a casual excursion, but holding some of eastern America's most enticing scenery. To the west, the slender Finger Lakes and endless miles of dairy farms and vineyards occupy the central portion of the state. Few of the cities hold much of interest, but the smaller towns, like Ivy League **Ithaca**, can be quite charming for a day or two, while the venerable spa town of **Saratoga Springs** attracts thousands of punters during the August racing season.

In the seventeenth and eighteenth centuries, as nation-molding political and military battles were taking place, semi-feudal **Dutch landowning dynasties** such as the Van Rensselaers held sway upstate. Their control over tens of thousands of tenant farmers was barely affected by the transfer of colonial power from Holland to Britain, or even by American independence. Only with the completion of the **Erie Canal** in 1825, linking New York City with the Great Lakes, did the interior start to open up; improved opportunities for trade enabled canal-side cities like **Rochester, Syracuse** and especially **Buffalo** to undergo massive expansion. On the other hand, this industrial and agricultural growth in the hinterland served, inevitably, to increase the financial standing of the Wall Street capitalists. The story of the past century and a half has been one of New York City's political and economic domination of New York State, though upstate politicians have been buoyed by Govenor George Pataki's popularity, if not fully redressing its imbalance.

## Getting around New York State

From New York City, the Long Island Railroad leaving from Penn Station and Metro North leaving from Grand Central Station shuttle commuters to and from the suburbs of Long Island and Westchester County respectively. For journeys further north, Greyhound and Adirondack Trailways **buses** run to all the major towns, while Amtrak operates a **train** service along a beautiful route through the Hudson Valley to the state capital, **Albany**; from there trains continue north to Montréal via the Adirondacks, and west along the Erie Canal to Buffalo and Niagara Falls. Many bus and train **stations** are several miles out from the town centers; the necessary walking can be unpleasant in the muggy heat of summer (not to mention the freezing winter).

**Car rental** in and around New York City is expensive, and restricted to drivers over 25 years of age; lower rates can be found by taking public transportation away from the metropolitan area. Be aware as well that the New York State Thruway (I-95 and I-87) is a **toll road**, which adds up to around $15 end-to-end. **Flying**, with occasional special deals of $150 for a New York to Buffalo round-trip, is another option, though you'll miss a lot of nice scenery. **Cycling** is best enjoyed as a means of exploring areas such as the

Finger Lakes or Catskills, and if you have a lot of time you may want to consider renting a **canal boat** and cruising the Erie or Champlain canals; contact the state tourist office (see p.21) for details on either of these options, and for general information on visiting New York.

# Long Island

Just east of New York City, **Long Island** unfurls for 125 miles of lush farmland and broad sandy beaches, perhaps best explored as an excursion of perhaps a few days from the metropolis. Its western end abuts the urban boroughs of Brooklyn and Queens, and for a while continues in a suburban sprawl of shopping malls and fast-food outlets; but further east, the settlements begin to thin out and the countryside can get surprisingly remote. The **north** and **south shores** differ greatly – the former more immediately beautiful, its cliffs topped with luxurious mansions and estates, while the South Shore is fringed by almost continuous sand, interspersed with holiday resorts such as **Jones Beach** and **Fire Island**. At its far end Long Island splits in two, the **North Fork** retaining a marked rural aspect while the **South Fork**, much of which is known as **The Hamptons**, has long been an enclave of New York's richest and most famous.

The quickest way to reach Long Island is via the reliable if rather worn **Long Island Railroad** from Penn Station (☎718/217-LIRR), though numerous **bus services** (operated by major companies and the Hampton Jitney, ☎1-800/936-0440) cover most destinations. **Parking permits** for most of Long Island's beaches are issued only to local residents, so on the whole it works out to be less expensive to head down to the beach on foot. There's plenty of **accommodation**, listed in the text; A Reasonable Alternative (117 Spring St, Port Jefferson, NY 11777; ☎516/928-4034) offers a good range of alternative B&B lodging throughout Long Island.

## The South Shore and Fire Island

Long Island's **South Shore** merges gently with the wild Atlantic, with shallow, creamy sand beaches and rolling dunes like those at Long Beach and **Jones Beach,** which together run along fifty miles of seashore. These get less crowded the further east you go; once you get as far as **Gilgo** or **Oak Beach**, or cross the water to **Robert Moses State Park** on the western tip of Fire Island, you can find solitude. **Long Beach** has a die-hard surfer contingent that gathers at the **Long Beach Surf Shop** (651 E Park Ave; ☎516/897-7873); you can purchase a used board here for about $250. **Ocean Parkway** leads along the narrow offshore strand from Jones Beach to **Captree**, a good base for whale-watching expeditions (☎516/669-0449), before crossing back to **Bay Shore**, a dull town that serves as a **ferry** terminal for Fire Island. This way you bypass the sprawling mess of **Amityville**, famous for its "horror" of twenty years ago. The house on the hill, from which a family was driven by some mysterious supernatural force, still stands.

### Fire Island
**Fire Island**, a slim spit of land parallel to the South Shore, is in many ways a microcosm of New York City. On summer weekends half of Manhattan seems to be holed up in its tiny settlements. Though the population is definitely mixed, certain parts of the island are primarily known as a **gay** resort: older gay men and women make for **Cherry Grove**; the wealthier gay males for **The Pines**, where the social scene revolves around private house parties as opposed to bars. **Ocean Beach** is considered trendy and has a very active (straight) nightlife; **Point O Woods** is the most exclusive of the lot. A

mixed crowd hangs out in the **Sunken Forest** (aka Sailor's Haven), so called because it's the only part of the island that lies below sea level – and the pressure, barometric and otherwise, is less intense.

The **season** is as rigidly defined as the people. From Memorial Day onwards Fire Island hums with activity and is swamped with crowds, though it's always possible to escape for gorgeous wild walks along the sand (there is a national seashore here, with a beautiful restored lighthouse); after Labor Day, the weather may still be very warm, but the throngs diminish dramatically.

Most **ferries** dock at Ocean Beach, where trippers pile up groceries on trolleys (cars are forbidden) and set off for their vacation pads. Ferry schedules are subject to change; Fire Island Ferries (☎516/665-3600 or 665-2115) and the Sayville Ferry Service (☎516/589-0810) leave from Bay Shore, while the Davis Park Ferries (☎516/475-1665) leave from Patchogue; one-way rates are around $5 and the journey takes half an hour. All **accommodation** should be booked well in advance; options include *Jerry's*, 168 Cottage Walk, Ocean Beach (☎516/583-8870; ④), which doubles its rates at weekends; *Cleggs Hotel*, 478 Bayberry Walk, Ocean Beach (☎516/583-5399; ⑤), which offers garden apartments with full kitchens and baths as well as rooms; *Fire Island Hotel* (same location as *Flynn's*), in nearby Ocean Bay Park (☎516/583-8000; ⑥), which used to be a Coast Guard station; and the famous *Fire Island Pines*, Harbor Walk, Fire Island Pines (☎516/597-6500; ③–⑥). *Giovanni's*, opposite the ferry terminal, is the best and most convivial place to **eat** for under $10; at weekends, the *Ice Palace*, at the *Cherry Grove Beach Motel* on Main Walk, *Flynn's*, and *Leo's* on Bay Walk, are good for riotous boozing and dancing. Pick up the *Fire Island News* at a newsstand to find out what's happening while you're there.

## The North Shore and North Fork

Along the rugged **North Shore**, Long Island drops to the sea in a series of bluffs, coves and wooded headlands. The expressway beyond Queens leads straight onto the **Gold Coast**, where **Great Neck** was F Scott Fitzgerald's *West Egg* in *The Great Gatsby*, home of Gatsby himself. Some of this real estate is so expensive that no one can afford to live here. The motley French Norman-style buildings at Falaise in **Sands Point**, on the sharp tip of the next peninsula, were once owned by the Guggenheims; they now house a self-celebratory **museum** (May–Oct Wed–Sun noon–3pm; tours $4). The 209 acres of unkempt parkland offer great views over what Fitzgerald called "the most domesticated body of salt water in the Western hemisphere, the great barnyard of Long Island Sound." In Old Westbury, at 71 Old Westbury Rd, **Westbury Gardens** is a classier attraction: a Georgian mansion with beautiful, well-tended gardens and some pleasant works of art, including a few Gainsboroughs (April–Dec daily except Tues 10am–5pm; tours $6; ☎516/333-0048).

**Sagamore Hill**, on the coast road six miles beyond Glen Cove, is the heavily touristed former country retreat where **Teddy Roosevelt** lived for thirty-odd years (daily 9am–5pm; $5; ☎516/922-4788). Its 23 rooms are adorned everywhere with the great man's trophies, sprouting horns from walls or grinning toothily up from the firesides. The **Old Orchard Museum** near the parking lot recounts Teddy's political and personal life, but the real reason to come is to stroll the gorgeous grounds, where springy lawns drop to Oyster Bay and the sea. It's a very pleasant trip altogether – with helpful and knowledgeable tour guides (often Roosevelt descendants) to take you around.

Nearby **COLD SPRING HARBOR** grew up as a whaling port, and retains some of its looks. A fully equipped whaleboat and a 400-piece assembly of scrimshaw work help its **Whaling Museum** (Tues–Sun 11am–5pm; $2) to recapture that era. The **Vanderbilt Mansion** just outside Centerport (April–Oct Tues–Sat 10am–4pm, Sun noon–5pm; Nov–March Tues–Sun noon–4pm; $5) displays the dubious taste typical of

Vanderbilt residences. In the style of a Baroque Spanish palace, it's heavily ornate both outside and in, with marble-encased galleries, swirling staircases and gaudy fireplaces. For some reason, they also have planetarium shows here.

On the less touristed **North Fork** – once an independent colony – the scenery has something of the feel of New England at its wildest. In **GREENPORT**, its most picturesque town, a clutter of narrow streets and alleys lead down to a harbor pierced by the masts of visiting yachts with an adjacent small **maritime museum** (May–Dec daily 10am–4pm; free). Plentiful **accommodation** includes the *Bartlett House*, 503 Front St (☎516/477-0371; ④), and the *White Lions Inn*, 433 Main St (☎516/477-8819; ⑤), where you'll get lovely homemade buttermilk biscuits for breakfast. Regular **ferries** connect with Shelter Island and the South Fork every fifteen minutes (foot passengers $1 each way; cars $6.50 one-way, $7 round-trip); others cross to New London, Connecticut, described on p.213.

# The South Fork

The US holds few wealthier quarters than the small towns of Long Island's **South Fork**, where huge mansions lurk in the trees or stand boldly on the flats behind the dunes. Nowhere is consumption as deliberately conspicuous as in **The Hamptons** – among the oldest communities in the state, settled by restless New Englanders in the mid-1650s, but relatively isolated until the rich began to turn up in their motor cars. The current generation of high rollers clog the roads in Range Rovers and Mercedes, and the sidewalks in slow, sauntering processions; pretty as the Hamptons are, avoid them if you are at all antisocial. Nightlife venues are expensive and notoriously changeable; pick up *Dan's Papers* or the *East Hampton Star* to find out what's happening.

## Southampton

Long association with the smart set has left **SOUTHAMPTON** unashamedly upper class. Its streets are lined with galleries and clothing and jewelry stores, but the nearby beaches are superb. The **visitor center** at 76 Main St (daily 9am–5pm; ☎516/283-0402) has lists of **B&Bs**, such as the *Hill Guest House*, 535 Hill St (May–Oct; ☎516/283-9889; ④). You can get marvelous fresh seafood in a number of **restaurants**, notably *Barrister's* at 36 Main St (☎516/283-6206) and the venerable *Southampton Publick House* at 40 Bowden Square (☎516/283-2800), which operated during Prohibition as "Mrs Cavanaugh's Speakeasy." There are **nightspots** galore, from the relatively casual – like *Southampton Tavern* on Tuckahoe Lane, which has occasional pool parties – to the impossibly upscale, like *Jet East* on North Sea Road, where super-rich regulars shell out hundreds of dollars to reserve Saturday night tables.

## Sag Harbor

Historic **SAG HARBOR**, in its heyday a harbor second only to that of New York, was designated first Port of Entry to the New Country by George Washington; the **Old Custom House** (July–Aug daily except Mon 10am–5pm; June & Sept Sat–Sun 10am–5pm; $3) dates from this era. The **Whaling Museum** on Main Street (mid-May to Sept Mon–Sat 10am–5pm, Sun 1–5pm; $3) commemorates the town's brief whaling days with guns and scrimshaw. Nearby the **Whaler's Presbyterian Church** is crenellated with jutting rows of whale blubber spades, and beautiful memorials in **Oakland Cemetery** commemorate young whalers.

In summer, the windmill where John Steinbeck once lived serves as a **visitor center** (June–Sept daily 10am–5pm; rest of year Sat & Sun only 10am–5pm; ☎516/725-0011). You can get a nice room at the *Baron's Cove Inn* (☎516/725-2100; ⑤), but at the well-heeled *American Hotel* at 25 Main St (☎516/725-3535; ⑦) you can also get a splendid French meal and a good cigar from the hotel's humidor. There are several good, less expensive **restaurants** along Main Street, such as the superb sushi bar *Sen* (☎516/725-1774). For **nightlife**, the *Boom Bistro,* right across from *Baron's Cove,* is the club of the moment and wildly popular.

### East Hampton and Amagansett

**East Hampton** is the trendiest of the Hamptons, filled with the mansions of celebrities like Stephen Spielberg, and Alec Baldwin and Kim Basinger, as well as obnoxiously chic shops and restaurants. However if you're there, it's worth driving or biking around **Further Lane**, **Lily Pond** and some of the other exclusive neighborhoods just to catch sight of some of the spectacular (and just plain beautiful) homes. **Amagansett** is a village within East Hampton and though crowded in the summer, tends to be more down to earth. Note the old shingle homes along quiet leafy side streets and enjoy the lively weekend scene (and fresh muffins) at *Farmer's Market* on Main Street and the partying at *Stephen Talkhouse,* a terrific bar and music joint that gets well-known folk, jazz and rock performers year-round (☎516/267-3117).

### Montauk

Blustery, wind-battered **MONTAUK**, beyond Amagansett on the furthest tip of Long Island, never quite made it as a resort; plans to develop it were shattered by the Wall Street Crash of 1929. This town isn't chic or quaint, but real people actually live here and it provides access to the rocky wilds of **Montauk Point**, whose rare beauty figures in all the tourist brochures. A **lighthouse** – New York state's oldest, dating from 1796 – forms an almost symbolic finale to this stretch of the American coast.

**Motels** in the town center offer fairly priced rooms (a rarity in the eastern end of Long Island); rates at the *Oceanside Beach Resort* (☎516/668-9825; ④/⑤) at the junction of the Old Montauk Highway and Main Street, vary seasonally but reasonably; if you want something fancier, try *Gurney's Inn* on Old Montauk Highway (☎516/668-2345; ⑨). The ultimate Montauk **dining** experience is *The Lobster Roll* on the highway, which serves excellent fresh fish, including the eponymous sandwich.

# The Hudson Valley and the Catskills

To the average commuter, the **Hudson River** is just an inconvenient barrier en route to New Jersey. However, you only need to travel a few miles north of Manhattan before the valley takes on a Rhine-like charm, with prodigious historic homes, such as those of the Roosevelt, Vanderbilt and van Cortland families, rising from its steep and thickly wooded banks. A little further on come the forests of the **Catskill Mountains**, whose brilliant fall colors rival anything to be seen in New England. Few of the cities along the Hudson, including the large but lackluster state capital of **Albany**, hold much to attract the visitor, but some of the small towns are worth checking out, most notably the New Agey village of **Woodstock**, nestled among the Catskills.

## The lower Hudson Valley

A mere 25 miles north of central New York City, leafy **TARRYTOWN** was the original setting for Washington Irving's tales of *Rip Van Winkle* and *The Legend of Sleepy Hollow.* In 1835 the author rebuilt a farm cottage just south of town on West Sunnyside Lane (off US-9), which he named **Sunnyside**: "a little old-fashioned stone mansion, all made up of gable ends, and as full of angles and corners as an old cocked hat." Tours squeeze around its cozy rooms, enjoyable even if you've never read a word of Irving

(March–Dec, daily except Tues 10am–5pm; $6; ☎914/591-8763). It's also worth looking around the neighboring village of **LYNDHURST**, where the spikily crenellated **Lyndhurst Castle** is as dapper a piece of nineteenth-century Gothic revivalism as you'll find (May–Oct Tues–Sun 10am–5pm; Nov–April Sat & Sun 10am–5pm; $9; ☎914/631-4481). Also of interest here is **Kykuit**, the old Rockefeller Estate that was only recently reopened to the public; the mansion is filled with modern artwork (particularly sculpture) and the gardens and grounds are just as impressive (tours only, ☎914/631-9491; reservations are a must).

About ten miles north of Tarrytown along US-9, the town of **OSSINING** holds two impressive mid-Victorian creations: one is a huge bridge carrying the **Old Croton Aqueduct**, New York City's first water supply; the other, just south of town, is **Sing Sing Prison**, which for over 150 years has been the place where New York City criminals get sent "up the river."

## The west bank and Catskill Mountains

Rising above the west bank of the Hudson River, the magnificent crests of the **Catskills**, cloaked with maple and beech that turn orange, ochre and gold each fall, have a rich and absorbing beauty. This dislocated branch of the Appalachians is inspiring country, filled with amenities – campgrounds, hiking, fishing and, especially, skiing. To enjoy it to the full, venture onto the trails; the mountains are so tightly packed that good roadside overlooks are rare.

### West Point
The first real place of interest on the west bank of the Hudson, sixty miles out of New York City, is the United States Military Academy at **WEST POINT**, which Congress established in 1802 after realizing that the ragged troops who had won the Revolutionary War had been knocked into shape almost exclusively by European officers. Homegrown skills had to be cultivated in case foreign help wasn't so readily forthcoming again. Since then, West Point has provided the military training for US Army generals Grant, Lee, MacArthur, Eisenhower, Patton and Schwarzkopf, to name but a famous few. Today, four-thousand-odd candidates on a tough four-year course fill the smart showpiece campus, which protectively overlooks the Hudson from a wide, strategic bluff. What draws most people are the stirringly patriotic parade ground drills, at their most frequent during spring and late summer/early fall; West Point's **visitor center** (daily 9am–4.45pm; ☎914/938-2638) can provide a full schedule. The free **West Point Museum** (daily 10.30am–4.15pm) shows trophies of war including pistols that belonged to George Washington, Napoleon Bonaparte and Adolf Hitler and, disturbingly, the pin from the Nagasaki bomb.

### Kingston
Of the various towns on the fringes of the mountains, **KINGSTON** is one of the most pleasant and convenient places to stop. An agreeable mix of well-preserved old houses and neat little businesses line **Green and Crown streets** at the center of town, much of which dates from the late eighteenth century, when Kingston played a vital political and military role in the fight for American independence.

Kingston is very easy to reach – it's just off I-87 (exit 19), and Adirondack Trailways buses heading north from New York City stop ten minutes walk from the center. The town's two **visitor centers**, on Clinton Avenue (☎914/331-9506) and Broadway (☎914/331-7517), have leaflets for suggested walking tours around the historic sights. If you want to **stay**, the large *Holiday Inn*, 503 Washington Ave (☎914/338-0400; ⑥), is probably the best option, complete with sauna, pool and games area, though its rates rise on summer weekends. *Schneller's*, 61 John St (☎914/331-9800), has a mid-priced German menu that's strong on sausages – it makes 25 different varieties – and has occasional evening entertainment that runs from polka to classic rock. The *Market Basket Deli*, 308 Wall St (☎914/338-2755), serves fresh breads and bagels, while the town's brewpub, the *Woodstock Brewing Co*, 20 St James St (☎914/331-2810), does good big platters of food as well as a range of home-brewed ale. Further **food and drink** options can be found across the river in Rhinebeck (see p.121).

## Woodstock

West from Kingston, Hwy-28 meanders into the Catskills, looping past the lovely Ashokan Reservoir where Hwy-375 branches off to **WOODSTOCK**. The village, carved out of the lush deciduous woodlands and cut by fast-rushing creeks, was not actually the venue of the famed **psychedelic picnic** of August 1969. That was some sixty miles southwest in Bethel, where a monument at Herd and West Shore roads marks the site on Max Yasgur's farm. However, Woodstock has enjoyed a bohemian reputation since the foundation in 1902 of the **Byrdcliffe Arts Colony** (which runs summer residency courses; ☎914/679-2079), and during the 1960s it was a favorite stomping ground for the likes of Dylan, Hendrix and Van Morrison. It still bears signs of its **hippie** past with shops selling tie-dyed T-shirts and crystals, and there's even the odd commune out in the woods, but in the cafes you're just as likely to bump into a successful Manhattanite who owns a second home here as a long-haired beatnik (not that these two categories are necessarily mutually exclusive). Woodstock's galleries and craftshops command a regional reputation and the village is also a hub for the performing arts: the **Maverick Concert** series (late June–Aug; around $8 per concert; ☎914/679-8217 or 679-7558) has played host to some of the world's finest chamber musicians since 1916.

Woodstock makes a great base for exploring the Catskills, and the best **accommodation** is the cozy *Twin Gables Guest House* (☎914/679-9479; ④/⑤), in the center of the village at 73 Tinker St. If this is full, as is often the case, the higher rates at *Woodstock Lodge* on Country Club Lane (☎914/679-2814; ⑤/⑥), get you a cabin and breakfast. Alternatively, there are *HoJo* and *Super 8* chain motels ten miles northeast in **SAUGERTIES**, as well as the renovated *Solway Inn* on Old Hwy-21 (☎914/246-4021; ④). Between Saugerties and Woodstock are the *Rip Van Winkle* (☎914/246-8334) and *KOA* (☎914/246-4089) **campgrounds**. The best **places to eat** are a little way out of the village: the menu at the *New World Home Cooking Company*, 424 Zena Rd (☎914/246-0900), has Caribbean and Creole-influenced dishes for under $10, while two miles west of Woodstock on Hwy-212 in tiny **Bearsville**, the *Bear Cafe* (☎914/679-5555) serves French bistro food unparalleled in these parts. In the village itself, the *Tinker Street Cafe*, 59 Tinker St (☎914/679-2487), and the *Joyous Lake*, 42 Mill Hill Rd (☎914/679-1234), both feature **live music** at the weekend. Several **buses** each day take two and a half hours to reach Woodstock from New York City's Port Authority Bus Terminal (Adirondack Trailways; ☎1-800/858-8555). Sturdy **bikes** can be rented from Overlook Mountain Bikes, 93 Tinker St (☎914/679-2122).

For more **information** visit the Chamber of Commerce booth, which keeps erratic hours, on Rock City Road just off the village green (☎914/679-6234), tune into the local radio station, WDST (100.1 FM), or pick up the weekly *Woodstock Times*.

## On through Catskill Park

As you continue along Hwy-28, the picturesque hamlet of **PHOENICIA**, in a hollow to the right of the road, is an ideal resting place and a great base for hiking trails in the area. You can catch the circular **Catskill Mountain Railroad** (summer & fall; ☎914/688-7400) through scenic Esopus Creek. The *Phoenicia Inn*, on Main Street

(☎914/688-7500 or 1-800/560-4505; ③), is a basic and inexpensive place to stay with an inviting (and cheap) bar attached. Next door is the *American Café* with great burgers plus a tasty selection of Mexican fare. A few miles further west, Hwy-49A affords a good vista of the rambling Catskills from the parking lot of the Belleayre ski resort. The *HI-AYH Hostel*, Bonnieview Ave, Pine Hill (☎914/254-4200), has beds for $10 ($13 in winter); other accommodation in the village includes two large budget Victorian places on Main Street – the *Colonial Inn* (☎914/254-5577; ④) and the *Pine Hill Arms Century Old Inn* (☎914/254-9811; ③) – plus the six-room *Birchcreek Inn* (☎914/254-5222; ⑤), in a wooded setting out on Hwy-28.

The return route to I-90 along Hwy-23A includes a breathtaking view of the dramatic **gorge** between the villages of Hunter and Catskill, along with the area's premier **ski runs** on Hunter Mountain. The resort's chair lifts also operate after the snow has melted (June–Aug and weekends during fall foliage season; $8; ☎518/263-4223). Accommodation rates rise significantly during the ski season: *Scribner Hollow Lodge*, half a mile from the mountain on Hwy-23A (☎518/263-4211; ⑧/⑨), boasts fireplaces in most of its 38 deluxe rooms and a fine-dining restaurant with great views, though places in the hamlet of Catskill, such as the few-frills *Pioneer Motel* on Hwy-32 (☎518/678-3376; ③), are much more affordable.

## The east bank

**HYDE PARK**, set on a peaceful plateau on the east bank of the Hudson twenty miles south of Kingston, is not an especially attractive town, but is worth a stop for the homes of **Franklin D** and **Eleanor Roosevelt**. Well-signposted off US-9 at 519 Albany Post Rd, the house where the "New Deal" president was born and spent much of his adult life is preserved here along with a library and a good **museum** (May–Oct daily 9am–6pm; Nov–April daily 9am–5pm; no charge for the grounds, guided house tour $10, combination pass Hyde Park, Val-Kill and the Vanderbilt estate $18; ☎914/229-9115). The museum contains extensive photos and artifacts, including the specially adapted car he drove after being struck down by polio in 1921, and the letter from Einstein that led to the development of the atomic bomb.

FDR lies buried in the Rose Garden, beside his wife (and distant cousin) Eleanor, a gifted and influential Democratic politician without whose help his career might well not have survived his long bouts of illness. She broke away from the tradition that the president's wife should merely serve as a hostess at society functions by playing a prominent role in the New Deal programs, touring the country and reporting to FDR on the living conditions of the poor. After FDR's death in 1945 she moved to the nearby cottage, **Val-Kill**, from where she carried on her work as chair of the United Nations Human Rights Commission, receiving dignitaries such as Tito, Nehru, Khrushchev and John F Kennedy until her death in 1962. Shuttle buses leave the FDR house every half-hour for free **tours** (May–Oct daily 9am–5pm; April, Nov & Dec Sat & Sun 9am–5pm; ☎914/229-9115).

A three-mile-long clifftop **path** along the Hudson from the Roosevelt complex winds up at the Beaux Arts **Vanderbilt Mansion**. This virtual palace is, believe it or not, the smallest of the family's residences, built for Frederick, a grandson of railroad baron Cornelius. The furnishings are quite garish, but the formal gardens are very pretty and offer a fine view of the Hudson River (May–Oct daily 9am–5pm; Nov–April Mon & Thurs–Sun 9am–5pm; $2). The grounds are open year-round, from dawn to dusk, at no charge.

Apart from these historic homes, Hyde Park has one other huge tourist draw, the excellent public dining rooms of the **Culinary Institute of America**, the largest and most prestigious cooking school in the country. Housed in a huge Gothic-style red-brick castle along US-9, south of Hyde Park at 433 Albany Post Rd, the various restaurants here – ranging from the casual atmosphere and healthy new American menu of the *St Andrew's Cafe* to the $25 fixed-price Italian dinners at *Caterina De Medici* and the four-star *American Bounty* and *Escoffier* rooms, where jackets are required – have trained some of America's best chefs; for reservations phone ☎914/471-6608.

Beyond Hyde Park, US-9 cuts slightly inland from the Hudson, passing through a number of sleepy towns on its way north towards Albany. **RHINEBECK**, six miles north of Hyde Park, is the first and most worthwhile of these, holding a number of good restaurants as well as **America's oldest hotel**. The lovely, white colonial *Beekman Arms*, in the center of town at Mill and Market, has been hosting and feeding travelers in its warm, wood-paneled rooms since 1766 (☎914/876-7077; ⑤/⑦). Two other good places to eat on the same block of Mill Street are the *Calico Restaurant & Patisserie* (☎914/876-2749), which offers good breakfast pastries and a lunch and dinner menu with strong Northern Italian and regional French influences at around $10 for a main course, and the all-American *Foster's Coachhouse Tavern*, at 22 Montgomery St (☎914/876-8052). Nearby is the pricier but very authentic French *Le Petit Bistro* at 8 E Market St (☎914/876-7400). Rhinebeck is also home to the New Agey **Omega Institute for Holistic Studies**, which runs a wide range of self-improvement workshops at a large campus east of town on Lake Drive; find out more at its bookshop, 22 E Market St (☎914/876-5701).

The other good stop on the east bank of the Hudson is **Olana**, the hilltop home of **Frederick Church** (1826–1900), one of the foremost artists of the Hudson River School. High above a bend in the river, across the bridge from the town of Catskill, the quirky but very attractive house rises in an odd blend of Persian and Moorish motifs; obligatory (and very popular) guided **tours** (April–Aug Wed–Sun 10am–4pm; Sept & Oct Wed–Sun noon–4pm; $3; for reservations call ☎518/828-0135) take in the bric-a-brac clogged rooms, as well as a number of his picturesque paintings.

## Albany

Founded by Dutch fur trappers in the early seventeenth century, **ALBANY** made its money by controlling trade along the Erie Canal, and its reputation by being capital of the state. It's not an unpleasant town, just rather boring, with its contemporary character almost exclusively shaped by political and bureaucratic affairs, though there are a few livelier areas on the fringes.

A good place to start a tour is the **Quackenbush House**, the city's oldest building, built along the river in 1736 and now serving as part of the **Albany Urban Culture Park**. The modern **visitor center** next door at Broadway and Clinton (daily 10am–4pm; ☎518/434-6311) has free maps and occasionally leads guided **tours** of the downtown area, where there are a number of revolutionary-era homes. It also has engaging displays tracing Albany's history, with a special emphasis on the impact of the Erie Canal, and maps detailing driving tours of the surrounding area, taking in a still-functioning set of **locks** from the original canal along with the impressive industrial legacy of **Troy**, across the Hudson via I-787 N.

Uphill from the waterfront, piercing like an arrowhead into downtown Albany, Nelson A Rockefeller's **Empire State Plaza** went up in the 1960s and 1970s, replacing 98 acres of nineteenth-century buildings (and displacing hundreds of Albanian families) with a complex that includes a subterranean retail arcade lined with impressive modern art. The view from the **Corning Tower** 42nd floor observation deck (Mon–Fri 9am–3.45pm, Sat & Sun 10am–3.45pm; free) seems designed to make you feel like the conqueror of an invaded territory, looking out beyond the twisting Hudson to the Adirondack foothills, the Catskills and the Massachusetts Berkshires. It also peers down on the neighboring Performing Arts Center, known locally as "The Egg" – which adds the only curves to the Plaza's harsh angularity (call ☎518/473-1845 for performance information).

The **New York State Museum** (daily 10am–5pm; free; ☎518/474-5877), one level down at the south end of the plaza, reveals everything you could want to know about

New York State in imaginative if static tableaux. The excellent section on New York City is better than anything in Manhattan itself, with histories of immigration and sky-scraper construction, storefronts and trolley cars, and the original set of *Sesame Street*.

The most engaging part of Albany is the few blocks west of the plaza, stretching between Washington and Madison avenues to the open green spaces of **Washington Park**, laid out by Frederick Law Olmsted. The **Albany Institute of History and Art**, 125 Washington Ave (Wed–Sun noon–5pm; $3, free Wed; ☎518/463-4478), has a good range of Hudson River School paintings, and the neighborhood is full of the same sort of nineteenth-century brick-built homes Rockefeller had pulled down.

### Practicalities

Arrive by Greyhound (☎518/434-0121) or Adirondack Trailways (☎518/436-9651) and it's a short, hilly walk to the heart of downtown; come in by Amtrak and you face a two-mile bus ride (☎518/462-5763) across the river in Rensselaer. If you intend to **stay** the night, bear in mind that downtown lodging is not particularly cheap. Suburban chain motels start at $50; a small **youth hostel** offers budget rates at 46 Elm St (☎518/434-4963; ①). Downtown options amount to the *Ramada Inn*, 300 Broadway (☎518/434-4111; ④), the more comfortable *Omni Albany Hotel*, at State and Lodge (☎518/462-6611; ⑦), and the exceptionally nice *Mansion Hill Inn*, 115 Philip St (☎518/465-2038; ⑥), a B&B in a restored home just down the hill from the state governor's mansion; it also has a fine restaurant. Other good **places to eat** include *Jack's Oyster House*, 42 State St (☎518/465-8854), and the Indonesian *Yono's*, 289 Hamilton Ave (☎518/436-7747). **Lark Street**, a few blocks west of the plaza, lit up by fairy lights between Washington and Madison, is the place to be at night. *Justin's* at no. 301 (☎518/436-7008) and *Cafe Hollywood* at no. 275 (☎518/472-9043) serve good progressive American food at moderate prices, while the welcoming *MaMoun's*, 206 Washington Ave (☎518/434-3901), has great inexpensive lamb, chicken and vegetarian dishes. The *Lionheart Blues Cafe*, 258 Lark St (☎518/436-9530), puts on live music most nights. The college town of **TROY**, across the river, also has a number of lively spots. The *Half Moon Cafe*, 154 Madison Ave (☎518/436-0329), hosts a good range of mostly acoustic folk, jazz and bluegrass.

# North through the Adirondacks

Mountaineers, skiers and dedicated hikers form the majority of visitors to the vast northern region between Albany and the Canadian border. Outdoor pursuits are certainly the main attractions in the rugged wilderness of the **Adirondack Mountains**, though a few small resorts, especially the former Winter Olympic venue of **Lake Placid**, have a bit of life to offer, and the elegant spa town of **Saratoga Springs** nestles invitingly in the delicate countryside of the southern foothills.

## Saratoga Springs

For well over a century, **SARATOGA SPRINGS**, just 42 miles north of Albany on I-87, was very much the place to be seen for the northeast's richest and most glittering names. At first, the town's curative waters were the main attraction; then John Morrisey, an Irish boxer, transformed things by opening a **racecourse** and **casino** during the 1860s. The Morgans, Vanderbilts and Whitneys all had houses in the town at one time, and Diamond Jim Brady was one of its most ostentatious visitors. Saratoga Springs retains the feel of an exclusive vintage resort during the August racing season, but for the rest of the summer it is accessible, affordable and fun. **Broadway**, the main axis, takes in just about every aspect of the modern town from lurid motel signs to the Gothic and Renaissance residential palaces on the northern tip of downtown; most of the town's many good bars are here or in the few blocks just east. The carefully cultivated **Congress Park**, off South Broadway, laid out for the *curistes*, remains a shady retreat from town center traffic. Three of the original mineral springs still flow up to the surface here, funneled out into drinking fountains (the water is tepid and salty, but some people swear by it). Also here is the original **casino**, which when built formed part of a whole city block; it now houses a small historical **museum** (May–Sept Mon–Sat 10am–4pm, Sun 1–4pm; Oct–April Wed–Sat 10am–4pm, Sun 1–4pm; $3).The **racetrack** (season runs late July through August; post time 1pm; ☎518/584-6200; grandstand $2) still functions in a rather grand, old-fashioned manner, though there is no longer a strict dress code (beyond shirt and shoes) for the grandstand or the clubhouse (no shorts or tank tops). There's no such pretension at the **harness track** on nearby Crescent Avenue (evening meetings several times a week May–Nov; $2). If you can't get to either, visit the array of paintings, trophies and audiovisual displays at the **National Museum of Racing and Thoroughbred Hall of Fame** on Union Avenue at Ludlow Street (Mon–Sat 10am–4.30pm, Sun noon–4.30pm; $3, $10 including tour of track; ☎518/584-0400). On the southern edge of town, green **Saratoga State Park** (daily 8am–dusk; $4 per car) presents opportunities to swim in great old Victorian pools, picnic, hike or even bathe in one of two bathhouses (☎518/583-2880). The **Saratoga Performing Arts Center** (☎518/587-3330) – or SPAC – was built during the 1960s in a successful attempt to revive the town's fortunes. As well as being home to the New York City Opera in June, the New York City Ballet in July and the Philadelphia Orchestra in August, it hosts the Newport Jazz Festival – Saratoga in late June and promotes rock concerts by big-name stars.

### Practicalities

Central Saratoga Springs is easily explored on foot. **Accommodation** is only a problem during August's race season, or if there's a big gig on at SPAC, when prices can more than double. Central motels include the *Spa Motel*, 73 Ballston Ave (☎518/587-5280; ③), and the *Turf and Spa*, 140 Broadway (☎518/584-2550 or 1-800/972-1779; ③). The lavishly restored landmark *Adelphi Hotel*, 365 Broadway (☎518/587-4688; ⑥), the *Sheraton*, a little further north at no. 534 Broadway (☎518/584-4000; ⑥), and the grand *Gideon Putnam Hotel*, located right in Saratoga Springs State Park, have more character (☎518/584-1354; ⑦/⑧). The **Chamber of Commerce**, 494 Broadway (☎518/584-3255 or 1-800/526-8970), has full lists, with prices. **Eating** is also easy. One longtime favorite is the soul food at *Hattie's*, 45 Phila St (☎518/584-4790), where huge dinners cost under $15; another good bet is *Wheat Fields*, 440 Broadway (☎518/587-0534), with good salads and pasta on an outdoor patio. *Beverly's*, 47 Phila St (☎518/583-2755), serves great but pricey breakfasts. There's usually good Irish **music** at the *Parting Glass Pub*, 40 Lake Ave (☎518/583-1916). *Nine Maple Avenue*, logically enough at 9 Maple Ave (☎518/583-2582), offers live jazz and blues until 1am, and the folksy *Caffe Lena*, 47 Phila St (Thurs–Sun; ☎518/583-0022) – where Don McLean first inflicted *American Pie* on the world – still pulls in the crowds.

## The Adirondacks

Covering a larger area than Connecticut and Rhode Island combined, the **Adirondacks** have until recent decades been the almost exclusive preserve of loggers, fur trappers and a few select New York millionaires who really knew how to get away from it all (E L Doctorow's novels *Loon Lake* and *Billy Bathgate* both describe the bucolic retreats of Manhattan mobsters). For sheer grandeur, the region is hard to beat. Forty-six peaks reach to over 4000ft; in summer the purple-green mountains span far into the distance in shaggy tiers, in fall the trees form a russet-red kaleidoscope.

Though Adirondack Trailways buses serve the area, you'll find it hard-going without a **car**. General **information** can be had from the Adirondack Region tourist office

(☎1-800/487-6867), or the Welcome Center along I-87 south of Lake George (☎518/761-6366 or 1-800/365-1050). The Adirondack Mountain Club (ADK), PO Box 3055, Lake George, NY 12845 (☎518/668-4447), or the Adirondack Park **Visitor Interpretive Centers** (daily: May–Sept 9am–7pm; Oct–April 9am–5pm) in Paul Smiths, north of Saranac Lake (☎518/327-3000), and in Newcomb on Hwy-28 N right in the heart of the park (☎518/582-2000), can provide details on hiking and camping.

## Lake George

Though the undulating scenery around **LAKE GEORGE**, 25 miles up I-87 from Saratoga Springs, is undeniably some of the most gorgeous in the region, the village itself is overrun with cheap souvenir shops catering to the thousands of tourists who come here in search of a quick taste of the Adirondacks. The numerous sightseeing cruises, fun parks, factory outlet stores and other diversions now on offer, here and in neighboring Glens Falls, obscure the natural splendor, as well as the region's considerable history. James Fenimore Cooper's *Last of the Mohicans* was based on the Battle of **Fort William Henry**, which was fought here between the British and the French in 1757, but the replica fort (July & Aug daily 9am–10pm; May, June, Sept & Oct daily 10am–5pm; $8), along the lakeshore on Canada Street in the center of town, does little to evoke the era when this was the distant frontier.

## Blue Mountain Lake

While Lake George and the eastern fringes of the Adirondacks in general hold little to compete with the interior, an hour's drive northwest along Hwy-28 takes you past the headwaters of the Hudson River to the tiny resort of **BLUE MOUNTAIN LAKE**. A handful of **motels** and lakeside **cabins** provide accommodation, and you can swim at the pretty little **beach** that fronts the village center. **Sagamore Great Camp**, about fifteen miles west, in the woods above Raquette Lake, is the sole survivor of the many "Great Camps" wealthy Easterners constructed in the Adirondacks around the end of the nineteenth century. Not to be confused with the four-star *Sagamore Resort* on an island in Lake George, this was a summer home of the **Vanderbilts**, basically a huge and luxurious log cabin in which they entertained illustrious guests – including Hoagie Carmichael, who supposedly wrote *Stardust* while driving the four-mile dirt road that leads up to the house. The still-intact house and grounds are now used as a conference and educational center, and for cross-country skiing in winter; call for details of summer art and photography **classes**, or to reserve a place on a guided two-hour **tour** (10.30am & 1.30pm daily in the summer, Sat & Sun the rest of the year; ☎315/354-4303; $8).

Just north of Blue Mountain Lake on Hwy-30, the twenty-building **Adirondack Museum** (late May to mid-Oct daily 9.30am–5.30pm; $10) has 22 exhibit areas spread over thirty acres on aspects of regional life, including art, sports, mining and wildlife, but is perhaps most memorable for its grand views out over the lake and surrounding mountains.

## Lake Placid

The winter sports center of **LAKE PLACID**, twice the proud host of the Winter Olympics, lies thirty miles west of I-87 on Hwy-73. In winter there's thrilling alpine skiing at imposing Whiteface Mountain and all manner of Nordic disciplines at Mount Van Hoevenberg, and in summer you can watch luge athletes practice on refrigerated runs, freestyle skiers somersaulting off dry slopes into swimming pools, and top amateur ice hockey games; ask at the **information center** in the Olympic Center on Main Street (☎518/523-2445 or 1-800/2-PLACID). The mountain slopes also provide challenging terrain for hikers and cyclists; good **mountain bikes**, maps of local trails, and **guided tours** are available from the very helpful Adirondack Adventure Tours, 126 Main St

(☎518/523-1475). In summer, the self-guided **Olympic Site Tour** package (☎1-800/ 44-PLACID; $18) takes you to the top of the 393ft ski jump (via chair lift) and eight miles up the sheer Whiteface Mountain toll road. At **Mount Van Hoevenberg**, you can do a bobsled run ($20 in summer, $30 in winter) or bike the extensive trail network ($20 bike rental; $4 trail fee; ☎518/523-4436). Less exhaustingly, you can take a **trolley tour** around town (☎518/523-4431; $2 per day) and hop on or off at designated spots.

The town itself is set on two lakes: **Mirror Lake**, which you can sail on in summer and skate on in winter, and larger **Lake Placid**, just to the west, on which you can take a narrated **cruise** in summer ($8.75; ☎518/523-9704). Other attractions include the **Olympic Center** at 216 Main St (☎518/523-1655), which houses four ice rinks and the informative **1932 and 1980 Lake Placid Winter Olympic Museum** ($3). **John Brown's Farm and Grave**, on Hwy-73 outside the village, was where the famous abolitionist brought his family in 1849 to aid a small colony of black farmers and where he conceived his ill-fated raid on Harper's Ferry in an attempt to end slavery. The house is less interesting than his story (see p.399), but at least it's free (late May to late Oct Wed–Sat 10am–5pm, Sun 1–5pm; ☎518/523-3900).

Lake Placid's **accommodation** options range from the somewhat economical to the opulent. The casually elegant *Mirror Lake Inn*, 5 Mirror Lake Drive (☎518/523-2544; ⑤–⑨), has over 120 rooms, the best of them palatial, but is as cozy as a small B&B. Facilities include pool, sauna, health club, private beach/skating rink and a top-notch restaurant. *High Peaks Base Camp*, Springfield Rd, Wilmington (☎518/946-2133; ②), is a friendly hostel-like place, with private rooms and dorm beds from $15, close to the Whiteface Mountain ski slopes. *Alpine Motor Inn*, on Hwy-86 on the edge of town (☎518/523-2180 or 1-800/257-4638; ②), is a spotlessly clean and friendly motel with a great Swiss/German restaurant.

Lake Placid is virtually a fast-food-free zone and it's possible to **eat well** for comparatively little. *Leslie's* is a much-loved local bakery at 99 Main St (☎518/523-4279), while *Nicola's Over Main*, at no. 90 (☎518/523-4430), does Greek and Italian dinners, including good wood-fired pizza; there's also the convivial, German-themed *Alpine Cellar Restaurant* on Hwy-86 (☎518/523-2180). The waterfront *Cottage Cafe*, 5 Mirror Lake Drive (☎518/523-9845), is a cafe/pub, serving snacks and unusual specials (chilled strawberry soup). It's also the town's top apres-ski spot, while the central *Hilton* is the main place for **live music**.

## Saranac Lake

**SARANAC LAKE**, ten miles northwest of Lake Placid, is a smaller, more laid-back community. The tranquil lakeshore is lined by lovely gingerbread cottages, most of them built during the late 1800s when this was a popular middle-class retreat. Robert Louis Stevenson spent the winter of 1888 in a small cottage here, now preserved as a **museum** (☎518/891-1990); or contact the **Saranac Area Chamber of Commerce**, 30 Main St (☎518/891-1990 or 1-800/347-1992), for details and directions. Saranac Lake is still a rather quiet year-round resort, the main attraction for budget travelers being the large, $12-a-night **youth hostel**, housed in the grand old *Hotel Saranac* at 101 Main St (☎518/891-2200; ①–③).

# The Thousand Islands

Beyond the Adirondacks, on the broad St Lawrence River that forms the border with Canada, are 1800 barely populated hunks of earth known as the **Thousand Islands**. They share their name with a salad dressing because one c.1900 visitor, George Boldt, president of New York's *Waldorf-Astoria Hotel*, is said to have asked the steward on his yacht to concoct something different for a special luncheon. The resultant orange goo is now famous the world over.

From both **Alexandria Bay** and the smaller fishing port of **Clayton**, boat excursions set out to explore the waterway; the tiny craft are all but swamped by the huge passing cargo ships, larger than many of the islands. For departure times, contact Uncle Sam's Tours (April–Oct daily; in Clayton ☎315/686-3511, in Alexandria Bay ☎315/482-2611 or 1-800/ALEXBAY).

# The Finger Lakes

At the heart of the state, southwest of Syracuse on the far side of the Catskills from New York City, are the eleven **Finger Lakes**, narrow channels gouged out by glaciers that have left tell-tale signs in the form of drumlins, steep gorges and any number of waterfalls. With the exception of well-to-do **Ithaca** and tiny **Skaneatles**, few towns compete with the lakeshore scenery, but the area as a whole is a relaxing place to spend some time, particularly if you enjoy sampling **wine**: it comes as a surprise to many people, but the Finger Lakes region – and much of upstate New York – produces a number of good vintages.

## Skaneatles and Seneca Falls

**SKANEATLES** (pronounced "Skinny-Atlas"), crouching at the neck of Skaneatles Lake, is perhaps the prettiest Finger Lakes town. It's also the best place to go swimming in the region: just a block from the town center, and lined by huge resort homes, the appealing bay sports a **beach** and a marina where you can take boat trips and rent watersports equipment. **Accommodation** is sparse, but the handful of motels includes the *Hi-Way Host*, 834 W Genessee St (☎315/685-7633; ③), and the *Colonial Motel*, one mile west on Hwy-20 (☎315/685-5751; ④), while the *Sherwood Inn* (☎315/685-3405; ④), overlooking the lake, is not as expensive as it looks. It also has two good restaurants; cheaper but still scrumptious meals can be had at the ever-popular *Doug's Fish Fry*, 8 Jordan St (☎315/685-3288).

At **SENECA FALLS**, just west of the northern tip of Cayuga Lake, Elizabeth Cady Stanton and a few colleagues planned and held the first Women's Rights Convention in 1848 – 72 years before the Nineteenth Amendment gave all US women the right to vote. On the site of the **Wesleyan Chapel**, 136 Fall St, where the first campaign meeting was held, is the **Women's Rights National Historical Park** (daily 9am–5pm; free; ☎315/568-2991), setting the early women's movement in its historical context. The center also offers a **walking tour** that takes in the small museum at the Cady Stanton house and passes the (privately owned) former home of **Amelia Bloomer**, whose crusade to urge women out of their cumbersome undergarments won her a place in the dictionary. A block east of the visitor center, the **National Women's Hall of Fame** (May–Oct daily 9.30am–5pm; Nov–April Wed–Sat 10am–4pm, Sun noon–4pm; free; ☎315/568-2703) at 76 Fall St, where over a hundred women, including Emily Dickinson and Sojourner Truth, have been honored for their efforts in fields such as humanitarianism, sports and the arts, makes an interesting stop.

The town itself is a blend of old mills and different-styled homes, tucked away among the mature trees. If you want to stop over, the best **place to stay** is the *Guion House* B&B, at 32 Cayuga St (☎315/568-8129; ⑤). **Eat** at one of the cafes along Fall Street.

Hwy-89, between Seneca Falls and Ithaca, has been dubbed the **Cayuga Wine Trail**, with dozens of small wineries operating along the west shore of the largest of the Finger Lakes.

## Ithaca

Cayuga Lake comes to a halt at its southern end at picturesque **ITHACA**, piled like a diminutive San Francisco high above the lakeshore and culminating in the towers, sweeping lawns and shaded parks of the Ivy League **Cornell University**. On campus, which is cut by striking gorges, creeks and lakes, the sleek, I M Pei-designed **Herbert F Johnson Museum of Art** (Tues–Sun 10am–5pm; free) merits a visit more for its fifth-floor view of the town and lake than for the unspectacular collection of Asian and contemporary art. The pick of the countless **waterfalls** within a few miles of town is the slender 210ft **Taughannock Falls**, ten miles north, just off Hwy-89, which has a swimming beach close at hand. **Buttermilk Falls State Park**, two miles south of town on Route 13, is another delightful spot. Cayuga Lake provides excellent boating and windsurfing opportunities; boards and boats can be rented from the nearby **visitor center** at 904 East Shore Drive, off Hwy-34 N (☎607/272-1313 or 1-800/28-ITHACA).

Greyhound and other **buses** operate out of the terminal at W State and N Fulton. Budget **places to stay** are scarce, though accommodation is on the whole reasonably priced; try the cramped *Hillside Inn*, 518 Stewart Ave (☎607/273-6864; ④), the *Elmshade Guest House*, 402 S Albany St (☎607/273-1707; ④), or, best of the three, the *Collegetown Motor Lodge*, 312 College Ave (☎607/273-3542; ③/④), in **Collegetown**, further up the hill on the doorstep of Cornell. The larger rooms at the *Best Western University Inn*, 1020 Ellis Hollow Rd, on the east edge of campus (☎607/272-6100; ⑤), are probably worth the extra expense.

Ithaca boasts two dining and entertainment zones. Downtown, centered around the vehicle-free **Commons**, is the larger and better, and features the top-rated vegetarian **restaurant** of cookbook fame, *Moosewood* (☎607/273-9610), in DeWitt Mall. A block away, *Just a Taste*, 116 N Aurora St (☎607/277-9463), is a lively wine-and-tapas bar, while *Simeon's on the Commons*, 224 E State St (☎607/272-2212), does gourmet sandwiches. Numerous cheap student-oriented places to eat line the streets of Collegetown: check out the Italian *Little Joe's*, 410 Eddy St (☎607/273-2771) or *The Nines*, serving up the best deep-dish pizza around and has live music, on 311 College Ave (☎607/272-1888). For news of the lively **music** scene – and gigs at the *Haunt*, 114 W Green St (☎607/273-3355) – get the free *Ithaca Times*.

## Corning

Forty miles southwest of Ithaca, world-famous **Steuben Glass** has been manufactured in the otherwise undistinguished town of **CORNING** since Frederick Carder started making his characteristic Art Nouveau pieces in 1903. The excellent **Museum of Glass** in the Corning Glass Center traces its history from ancient heads and amulets to modern sculptures and paperweights. Also in the complex, where glass is omnipresent in mirrors and motifs, are the Hall of Science and Technology, full of push-button exhibits, and the Steuben Glass factory itself, where every stage of the production process can be viewed from behind (glass) screens (daily: July & Aug 9am–8pm; Sept–June 9am–5pm; ☎607/974-8271; $6).

The **Rockwell Museum**, ten minutes' stroll away at 111 Cedar St and Denison Parkway (Mon–Sat 9am–5pm, Sun noon–5pm; $4), has more than two thousand pieces of Steuben glass, plus antique toys and a strong collection of Western art – and is not to be confused with the Norman Rockwell Museum in Stockbridge, Massachusetts.

# Towards Niagara Falls: the Erie Canal towns

The fertile farming country stretching from Albany at the head of the Hudson to Buffalo on Lake Erie, along the route of **Erie Canal**, comprises the agricultural heartland of New York State. The eastern parts – also known as **Central Leatherstocking**, after the protective leggings worn by the area's first settlers – are well off the conventional tourist trails. Unless you want to check out one of the specialist sports museums, like the Baseball Hall of Fame at **Cooperstown**, this is not a high-priority destination.

With the captivating exception of **Niagara Falls**, one of the continent's biggest crowd pullers, there's little to see in the northwest reaches of New York State. Standing out from the mostly flat farmland, the industrial giants of **Rochester**, **Syracuse** and **Buffalo** each possess a couple of worthy museums, but are best approached as bases for seeing the surrounding area (Buffalo, for example, is a good base for Niagara Falls).

## Cooperstown

Seventy miles west of Albany, sitting gracefully on the wooded banks of tranquil Otsego Lake, is the almost aggressively pretty **COOPERSTOWN**, christened "Glimmerglass" by novelist James Fenimore Cooper, son of the town's founder. The fact that baseball is said to have originated here on Doubleday Field is commemorated by the inspired and spacious **National Baseball Hall of Fame**, on Main Street. Everything is displayed in such an attention-grabbing manner that even if you know nothing about the game it's difficult to remain uninterested. Babe Ruth gets a whole display to himself, while more of the greats are shown in action in photographs and videos (daily: May–Sept 9am–9pm; Oct–April 9am–5pm; ☎607/547-7200; $9.50). In summer, Cooperstown hosts classical concerts and the Glimmerglass Opera, north on Hwy-80 by the lake.

The local chamber of commerce runs a really helpful little **visitor center** at 31 Chestnut St (daily 10am–4.45pm; ☎607/547-9983). If you're here in high season, leave the car at one of the free parking lots on the edge of town and take the trolley around the various sights ($1.50 all-day pass). **Accommodation** in the town itself is expensive, but there's a cluster of clean motels right on gorgeous Otsego Lake, a few miles north on Hwy-80; the *Lake'N Pines* (☎607/547-2790 or 1-800/615-5253; ④) offers superb value. For **eating**, *Obie's Brot und Bier*, 46 Pioneer Alley (☎607/547-5601), serves sandwiches with a Germanic influence, while the *Hamburger Hall of Fame*, three miles south on Hwy-28 (☎607/547-4113), is enjoyably gimmicky and the food's not bad, either.

## Canastota

Just before Syracuse, at exit 34 from I-90, nondescript **CANASTOTA** is the home of the **International Boxing Hall of Fame** (daily 9am–5pm; $4). Canastota's links with boxing go back to early in the nineteenth century, and this ten-thousand-strong village has produced two postwar world champions: Carmen Basilio, who took away the middleweight crown of Sugar Ray Robinson in an epic 1958 encounter, and Billy Backus, a welterweight title-holder during the early 1970s. All the greats are represented in the two-room museum, whether by picture, dressing-gown, mouthpiece, handwraps, gloves or bronze fist impressions, and there's a selection of big-fight videos.

## Syracuse

A lively but largely unattractive modern city, busy **SYRACUSE** made its name first for the production of salt and, more importantly, for its central position on the Erie Canal. Despite a population nudging half a million, there's little to see, though the presence of Syracuse University gives downtown an active and youthful feel. The redevelopment of **Armory Square**, around Franklin and Fayette streets, as an area of specialty shops, galleries and cafes has gone some way towards adding character to the city center, but the city still feels dominated by the highways and railroads that slice through it.

The **Erie Canal Museum** (daily 10am–5pm; donation), housed in one of the few surviving canal-era buildings, an 1850s weighing station at 318 E Erie Blvd, tells the story of the long battle between politicians and taxpayers before work on the canal began in 1810. The waterway was designed to link the Great Lakes with New York City via the Hudson, thereby cutting hefty transportation costs – which it did by an average of ninety percent. At first, however, not everyone was in favor, critics speaking of a "big ditch" in which "would be buried the treasure of the state." The project eventually took fifteen years and one thousand lives, and went three million dollars over budget, but it spawned America's first generation of engineers, and after it opened in 1825, prosperous towns arose alongside the canal almost overnight. Erie Boulevard itself was created by filling in the old canal bed, and the industrial surroundings do little to evoke the era, though the reconstructed **canal boat** inside the museum is definitely worth a look.

Good-value **rooms** can be found in downtown's *Comfort Inn*, 454 James St (☎315/425-0015; ③), and the fairly central *HI-Downing International Hostel*, 535 Oak St (☎315/472-5788; ①), has $10 dorm beds. For **food**, *Clark's Ale House*, 122 W Jefferson St (☎315/479-9859), is locally famous for its roast beef sandwiches and cheese plates. The *Empire Brewing Co*, 120 Walton St (☎315/475-2337), has an eclectic menu and good beer brewed on the premises, while *Pastabilities*, 311 S Franklin St (☎315/474-1153), is health-conscious and popular. Student numbers insure a lively **music** scene; consult the resourceful *Syracuse New Times* freesheet. Good hangouts include the loud, bluesy *Dinosaur Bar Barbecue*, 246 W Willow St (☎315/476-4937) which also serves ribs, and the small, punky *Lost Horizon*, 5863 Thompson Rd (☎315/446-1052). The city's **visitor center** is at 572 S Salina St (Mon–Fri 8.30am–5pm; ☎315/470-1800 or 1-800/234-4SYR).

# Rochester

In contrast to its sprawling suburbs, downtown **ROCHESTER** is a salubrious place, with its central office-block area bordered by well-heeled mansions on spacious boulevards. High-tech companies such as Bausch & Lomb and Xerox have brought capital to the city, but by far the most conspicuous names on view are those of **Kodak** and its founder, George Eastman. Legacies throughout the metropolitan area include Kodak Park, the Eastman Theater, and above all the **International Museum of Photography** at George Eastman House, two miles from downtown at 900 East Ave (Tues–Sat 10am–5pm, Sun 1–5pm; $7). A first-rate exhibition of photographic history ranges from unbelievably clear Civil War prints to modern experimental works, and the twentieth-century gallery forms an A to Z of modern greats: Ansel Adams, Cartier-Bresson, Steiglitz, Weston and lots more. Upstairs is the fun, hands-on Discovery Room, plus cabinets of unusual **cameras**. Nonetheless, with Kodak cash behind it, you would expect the museum to be much bigger; a visit will leave most people thirsting for more and frustrated that a large part is given over to research and storage rather than exhibition space.

Assorted domestic artifacts collected by another wealthy former resident, Margaret Woodbury Strong (1897–1969), are gathered in the **Strong Museum** on Manhattan Square (Mon–Sat 10am–5pm, Sun 1–5pm; $5). With everything from stuffed toys to porcelain plates and Shaker furniture, it is seen by many as an over-the-top souvenir hypermarket, but aficionados of Victoriana will have a field day. Of more general interest are the well-presented temporary exhibits on American consumer society. The theme of celebrating former Rochester denizens continues at the **Susan B Anthony House** at 17 Madison St, where this groundbreaking suffragist lived from 1866–1906 (Labor day–Memorial day Wed–Sun 11am–4pm; ☎716/235-6124; $6).

## Practicalities
Greyhound drops off at Broad and Chestnut streets downtown. The Amtrak station, 320 Central Ave, is on the north side beyond the I-490 inner loop road; it's served by RTS **buses** (☎716/654-0200). Rochester's **visitor center** is at 126 Andrews St (Mon–Fri 8am–6pm, Sat 9am–5pm, Sun 10am–3pm; ☎716/546-3070). **Accommodation** is not

inexpensive. Downtown choices include the excellent *428 Mt Vernon* B&B (☎716/271-0792; ⑥), at the entrance to lush Highland Park, with private baths in all rooms. Among budget options in the south of the city, near the I-90 Thruway, is the *Red Roof Inn*, 4820 W Henrietta Rd, off I-90 exit 46 (☎716/359-1100; ③).

Popular **places to eat** in the fairly lively downtown include *Aladdin's Natural Eatery*, 141 State St (☎716/546-5000), serving inexpensive Middle Eastern food, the pub-style *Old Toad*, 277 Alexander St (☎716/232-2626), where British staff serve beer and cheap meals, and the restored Art Deco *Highland Park Diner*, 960 S Clinton Ave (☎716/461-5040). Keep an eye out for the local soft drink Jolt, which tastes like a normal cola but packs a big wallop of caffeine.

## Out from Rochester

The **Lake Ontario State Parkway** is a quiet, scenic way of driving to Niagara Falls from Rochester, taking about an hour longer than the standard route along I-90 via Buffalo. The parkway starts eight miles from downtown at the end of Lake Avenue, near the popular **Ontario Beach Park**. This short golden strand of shore, rimmed by exclusive holiday homes, is a real poseur's paradise; you may well feel self-conscious if your shades don't match up to the ubiquitous (locally manufactured) Ray-Bans.

If big crowds and the churning noise of speedboats are not your thing, head twenty miles along the parkway to the more secluded **Hamlin Beach State Park** ($3 per car). The parkway passes through few towns, and the best place to stop for refreshments is the small and attractive Point Breeze harbor, ten miles on from Hamlin.

## Buffalo

As I-90 sweeps down into the state's second largest city, **BUFFALO**, downtown looms up in a cluster of Art Deco spires and glass-box skyscrapers – Manhattan in miniature on Lake Erie. The city's early twentieth-century prosperity is reflected in such architecturally significant structures as the towering 1928 **City Hall** (the tallest in the country, and with a free observation deck on the top floor), and the deep red terra-cotta relief of Louis Sullivan's **Guaranty Building** on Church Street, as well as major buildings by H H Richardson, Eliel Saarinen and Frank Lloyd Wright. However, the dereliction of the immediate environs suggests this may now be the beginning of the Rust Belt. Buffalo has only distant memories of the boom years, when the massive **grain elevators** along the Erie waterfront were busy 24 hours a day.

That Buffalo's wealthy merchants were a cultured lot is also apparent in the excellent **Albright-Knox Art Gallery**, 1285 Elmwood Ave (Tues–Sat 11am–5pm, Sun noon–5pm; ☎716/882-8700; $4), two miles north of downtown amid the green spaces of the F L Olmsted-designed **Delaware Park**. One of the top modern collections in the world, it's especially strong on recent American and European art: the Color Field painters, Abstract Expressionism, Pop, Op and Kinetic Art, with Pollock, Rothko, Warhol and Rauschenberg among the names. Other highlights include thirty large paintings by Clyfford Still, and a fine selection of pieces by earlier artists such as Matisse, Picasso and Monet.

The area around Delaware Park is Buffalo's choicest neighborhood, featuring several homes designed by Frank Lloyd Wright (call ☎716/884-0095 for guided architectural tour information). Between here and downtown is **Allentown**, Buffalo's most bohemian quarter, its leafy streets lined by lovely Victorian homes as well as numerous good cafes, bars and restaurants. Allen Street between Main and Elmwood holds some of the best; the area around Theatre Place downtown is also good (see opposite).

Being a staunchly blue-collar city, Buffalo loves its professional **sports** teams: football's Bills (☎716/649-0015), ice hockey's Sabres (☎716/856-7300) and baseball's

Bisons (☎716/846-2003), who as the top farm team for the Cleveland Indians attract over a million fans per season to downtown's modern and very pleasant ballpark.

The **Lake Erie shoreline** west of Buffalo is lined by numerous beaches where **windsurfers** skim across the water and do flips in the waves, while the Miss Buffalo boat tours (☎716/856-6696; $8 and up), which leave from 79 Marine Drive next to the Naval and Servicemen's Park, provide a good view of the city skyline. To the south, in the town of Orchard Park, the **Burgwardt Bicycle Museum** (Mon, Fri & Sat 11am–5pm, Sun 1.30–5pm; $4.50; ☎716/662-3853) holds over two hundred antique bikes and engaging displays of cycling memorabilia.

### Practicalities

Greyhound, Empire Trailways (☎716/852-1750), Metro Bus and Metro Rail, the city's new tramway (both ☎716/855-7211), all operate from the downtown depot at Ellicott and Church. To get to **Niagara Falls**, take bus #40 (1hr; hourly 7am–10pm; $1.70). Amtrak **trains** to and from Niagara Falls and Toronto stop some six blocks away at Exchange and Washington; Chicago-bound trains only stop in the eastern suburb of Depew, eight miles from town but close to the **airport** (☎716/632-3115). There's a helpful **visitor center** at 107 Delaware Ave (☎716/852-0511 or 1-800/BUFFALO).

The one moderately priced **place to stay** near downtown – except for the very central *HI-Buffalo Hostel*, 667 Main St (☎716/884-4761; ①), where beds are $15 – is the *Hotel Lenox*, 140 North St (☎716/884-1700 or 1-800/82-LENOX; ④; $10 discount for students). The *Holiday Inn*, 620 Delaware Ave (☎716/886-2121; ⑤), is a safe bet, while the recently renovated *Hilton*, 120 Church St (☎716/845-5100; ⑥), gives you free use of its extensive health club. An unusual place to stay, a half-hour drive east in the gorgeous village of **EAST AURORA**, is the *Roycroft Inn* at 40 S Grove St (☎716/652-5552 or 1-800/267-0525; ⑦): what was once the centerpiece of the fourteen-building campus of Elbert Hubbard's c.1900 Roycroft Arts and Crafts Community has been immaculately refurbished. It also does great food.

The city's specialty of **buffalo** (spicy chicken) **wings** with blue cheese dressing is said to have been invented at the *Anchor Bar*, 1047 Main St (☎716/886-8920), where lunch costs around $7; at night they sometimes have live jazz. For snacks, the cheap food stalls and tiny Polish cafes of ancient **Broadway Market**, 999 Broadway, are well worth perusing. Good **restaurants** include the upscale, eclectic *Biac's World Bistro*, 581 Delaware Ave (☎716/884-6595) in Allentown, and hearty *Hemingway's*, 492 Pearl St (☎716/852-1937); the late-night *Calumet Arts Cafe*, 56 W Chippewa St (☎716/855-2220), is also good. The *Sport City Grill by Jim Kelly*, 100 Main Place Tower (☎716/849-1201), owned by the Bills' one-time quarterback, is stuffed with sporting memorabilia, serves big portions of good food, and has the jumping *Network* club next door. Among the liveliest of Allentown's bars and cafes are *Nietzsche's*, 248 Allen St (☎716/886-8539), and *Colter Bay*, 561 Delaware Ave (☎716/882-1330). The majority of theaters and venues that house the city's burgeoning **arts scene** are handily grouped along Main Street between Chippewa and Tupper. Further listings are given in *Art Voice*, a biweekly free sheet.

# Niagara Falls

Every second, over half a million gallons of water explode over the knife-edge **NIAGARA FALLS**, right on the border with Canada some twenty miles north of Buffalo on I-190. This awesome spectacle is made even more so by the variety of methods laid on to help you get closer: boats, catwalks, observation towers and helicopters all push as near to the curtain of gushing water as they dare. At night the falls are lit up, and the colored waters tumble dramatically into blackness, while in winter the whole scene changes as the falls freeze to form gigantic razor-tipped icicles.

Many visitors will, however, find the whole experience a bit too gimmicky; no commercial opening has been left unexploited (Oscar Wilde quipped that he would have been more impressed if the falls ran upwards; at least no one's tried that yet) and now corporate big-hitters like the *Hard Rock Cafe* have joined in the action, pushing the place closer to an aquatic Vegas (there's already a **casino** on the Canadian side). Don't expect too much; neither the small city of **Niagara Falls**, still a smelly, shabby industrial eyesore despite recent efforts to spruce it up, nor the more developed tinsel town of **Niagara, Canada**, is a place to savor in any way. Once you've seen the falls, from as many different angles as you can manage, there's no point in sticking around, and you'll have a better time heading on to Buffalo (or Rochester, or anywhere) rather than trying to rustle up some fun here. However, one of the biggest **factory outlet malls** in the country is just north of the city, and seems to be almost as big a draw as the falls these days.

### Arrival and information

Amtrak **trains**, en route between New York and Toronto, stop a long two miles from downtown at 27th Street and Lockwood Road. If you arrive at the **bus station** (☎716/285-9391), on Fourth and Niagara, you're next door to the official **Welcome Center** (daily: July & Aug 9am–8pm; Sept–June 9am–5pm; ☎716/285-2400 or 1-800/338-7890). There's also a kiosk in Prospect Park by the falls, as well as countless other places in town that claim to be visitor centers but are in fact just fronts for tour companies.

Arriving **by car**, follow the signs to the main parking lot, which is right next to the falls and costs $3. Local Metro Transit System **buses** (☎716/285-9319) run to all areas of the city ($1.20) and to Buffalo (bus #40 or #60 express; $1.70 each way). To send the

obligatory postcards, you'll need the **post office** at 615 Main St (Mon–Fri 8.30am–5pm, Sat 9am–noon; ☎716/285-7561; zip code 14302).

## Accommodation

**Places to stay** in central Niagara can be quite expensive if you don't plan ahead or shop around, but US-62, east of Hwy-190, is lined with dozens of motels with rates beginning at $30. Many of these are pretty tacky, targeting the thousands of honeymoon couples who come here every year (despite Wilde's assertion that the falls "must be one of the earliest if not keenest disappointments of American married life"). With the falls under an hour's drive away, both **Rochester** and **Buffalo** make better bases.

The closest place to **camp** is seven miles from downtown at the **Niagara Falls Campground & Lodging**, 2405 Niagara Falls Blvd in Wheatfield (☎716/731-3434), for $18 a night.

**All Tucked Inn B&B**, 574 3rd St (☎716/282-0919). Cozy B&B. No credit cards. ③.

**Budget Inns**, 492 Main St (☎716/285-8366). No-frills downtown motel. ③.

**Days Inn Falls View**, 201 Rainbow Blvd (☎716/285-9321 or 1-800/876-3297). Landmark hotel with grand lobby but rather plain rooms. The rates fluctuate, dropping dramatically off-season. ⑤.

**HI-Niagara Falls**, 1101 Ferry Ave (☎716/282-3700). Friendly, well-run hostel with beds for $13 ($15 nonmembers). Facilities include showers, kitchen and TV lounge. Preference is given to HI members and reservations are necessary in summer. ①.

**Park Place B&B**, 740 Park Place (☎716/282-4626). Comfortable home near downtown with full breakfast and afternoon pastries. ④.

## The Falls

**Niagara Falls** comprises three distinct cataracts. The tallest are the **American** and **Bridal Veil** falls on the American side, separated by tiny Luna Island and plunging over jagged rocks in a 180ft drop; the broad **Horseshoe Falls** which curve their way over to Canada are probably the most impressive. They date back a mere twelve thousand years, when the retreat of melting glaciers allowed water trapped in Lake Erie to gush north to Lake Ontario. Back then the falls were seven miles down river, but constant erosion has cut them back to their present site. The falls are colorfully lit up at night, and many say they're most beautiful in winter, when the grounds are covered in snow and the waters turn to ice.

The best views on the American side are from the **Prospect Point Observation Tower** (daily 10am–5pm; 50¢), and from the area at its base where the water rushes past; Terrapin Point on **Goat Island** in the middle of the river has similar views of Horseshoe Falls. The nineteenth-century tightrope-walker Blondin crossed the Niagara repeatedly near here, and even carried passengers across on his back; other suicidal fools over the years have taken the plunge in barrels. One survivor among the many fatalities was the Englishman Bobby Leach, who went over in a steel barrel in July 1911 and had to spend the rest of the year in hospital. That practice has since been banned (though a couple of maniacs did it in summer 1995 and came away with minor bruises), for reasons which become self-evident when you approach the towering cascade on the not-to-be-missed **Maid of the Mist** boat trip from the foot of the observation tower (April–Oct Mon–Fri 10am–5pm, Sat & Sun 10am–6pm; $8.50; ☎716/284-4233). From Goat Island, the **Cave of the Winds** tour leads down to the base of the falls by elevator to within almost touching distance of the water (mid-May to late Oct; $5.50). A combination pass for these and other attractions costs $16. Rainbow **helicopter** tours (☎716/284-2800) are a more expensive proposition at $40 per person for a ten-minute ride. To check the view out from Niagara, Ontario, it's a twenty-minute walk across the **Rainbow Bridge** to the Canadian side (25¢ each way; bring ID, and check with US Immigration officials before heading across), where you get an arguably better view, bigger crowds and even more tawdry commercialism. Driving across is inadvisable: the toll for a car is just 75¢, but parking on the other side is upwards of $15.

As you look on in awe, reflect that you're seeing only about half the volume of water – the rest is diverted to hydroelectric power stations. The full story of this engineering feat is related at the free **Niagara Power Project Visitors Center** in nearby Lewiston (daily: July & Aug 9am–6pm; Sept–June daily 10am–5pm; ☎716/285-3211). With your own transportation it's also possible to trace the inhospitable Niagara Gorge two miles along the dramatic Robert Moses Parkway to the **Whirlpool Rapids**, a violent maelstrom swollen by broken trees and other flotsam. Ten miles east of Niagara Falls, the town of **LOCKPORT** takes its name from the series of locks that raise and lower boats some 65ft at the western end of the Erie Canal. You can see the impressive flight of locks from the Pine Street Bridge, or up close on canal boat **tours** (May–Nov daily at 12.30 & 3pm, also 10am on Sat; ☎716/693-3260; $9).

## Eating and drinking

Though most of the **eating options** in Niagara Falls are fast-food joints of indifferent quality, there are a few decent local bars and restaurants – with some better places over in Canada.

**Arterial Restaurant**, 314 Niagara St (☎716/782-9459). Tasty burgers for under $2 and generous portions of spicy chicken wings at $3 make this an excellent downtown alternative to the fast-food emporia.

**Atrium**, 219 4th St (☎716/282-17134). Affordable American standards and pasta in the *Ramada Inn*.

**The Bakery and Ports of Call Restaurant**, 3004 Niagara St (☎716/282-9498). A bit out of the way but a wide variety of European dishes for $10–20. The bar is good for a quiet drink.

**Riverside Inn**, 115 S Water St, Lewiston (☎716/754-8206). Waterfront 1871 property, ten minutes' drive north of the falls, with a menu that approaches fine dining.

# PENNSYLVANIA

**PENNSYLVANIA**, which but for a small stretch on Lake Erie is the only landlocked state in the northeast, was explored by the Dutch in the early 1600s, settled by the Swedes forty years later, and claimed by the British in 1664. Charles II of England, who owed a debt to the Penn family, rid himself of the potentially troublesome young **William Penn**, an enthusiastic advocate of religious freedom, by granting him land in the colony in 1682. Penn Jr immediately established a "holy experiment" of "brotherly" love and tolerance, naming the state for his father and setting a good example by signing a peaceful cohabitation treaty with the Native Americans. Most of the early agricultural settlers were religious refugees: Quakers like Penn himself, Mennonites from Germany and Switzerland, and Irish Catholics.

"The keystone state" was crucial in the development of the US. Politicians and thinkers like **Benjamin Franklin** congregated in Philadelphia – home of both the Declaration of Independence and the Constitution – and were prominent in articulating the ideas behind the Revolution. Later, the battle in Gettysburg, south Pennsylvania – best remembered for Abraham Lincoln's immortal **Gettysburg Address** – marked a turning point in the Civil War. Pennsylvania was also vital industrially: Pittsburgh, in the west, was the world's leading steel producer in the nineteenth century, and nearly all the nation's anthracite coal is still mined here.

The two great urban centers of **Philadelphia** and **Pittsburgh**, both lively and vibrant tourist destinations, are at opposite ends of the state. The three hundred miles between them, though predominantly agricultural, are topographically diverse. There are over one hundred state parks, with green rolling countryside in the east, brooding forests in the west, and in the northeast, the rivers, lakes and valleys of the Poconos. **Lancaster County**, home to traditional Amish farmers, and the **Gettysburg** battlefield both heave with busloads of day-trippers, while the Hershey chocolate factory, minutes away from **Harrisburg**, the capital, draws thousands of cocoa-loving visitors.

## Getting around Pennsylvania

Although to appreciate the less-populated stretches of Pennsylvania you really need a **car**, public transportation is adequate if you organize yourself carefully. Both I-76 (the Pennsylvania Turnpike) and I-80 sweep right the way across to Ohio, nearly five hundred miles east to west. US-30 (the Lincoln Highway) also runs east–west between Philadelphia and Pittsburgh, past Lancaster City, York and Gettysburg, while the prettiest north–south route is US-15, from Maryland to New York State, which follows the Susquehanna River for about fifty miles.

**Amtrak** crosses daily from Philadelphia to Pittsburgh, stopping at Lancaster City, Harrisburg and other smaller towns. **Greyhound** covers all the major cities and some small towns not served by rail, but its routes can be circuitous; check arrival times when buying your ticket, especially if you need to make a connection.

# Philadelphia

The original capital of the nation, **PHILADELPHIA** was laid out by William Penn Jr in 1682, on a grid system that was to provide the pattern for most American cities. It was envisaged as a "greene countrie towne" and today, for all its historical and cultural significance, it still manages to retain a certain quaintness. Just a few blocks away from the noise, crowds, heat and dust of downtown, shady cobbled alleys stand lined with red-brick colonial houses, while the peace and quiet of huge Fairmount Park make it easy to forget you're in a major metropolis.

Settled by **Quakers**, Philadelphia prospered swiftly on the back of trade and commerce, and by the 1750s had become the second largest city in the British Empire. Economic power fueled strong revolutionary feeling, and the city was the capital during the **War of Independence** (except for nine months under British occupation in 1777–78). It also served as the US capital until 1800, while Washington DC was being built. The **Declaration of Independence** was written, signed and first publicly read here in 1776, as was the **US Constitution** ten years later. Philadelphia was also a hotbed of new ideas in the arts and sciences, as epitomized by the scientist, philosopher, statesman, inventor and printer **Benjamin Franklin**.

Philadelphia, which translated from Greek means "City of Brotherly Love," is in fact one of the most **ethnically mixed** US cities, with substantial communities of Italians, Irish, Eastern Europeans and Asians living side by side among the majority black population. Many of the city's **black** residents are descendants of the migrants who flocked here after the Civil War when, like Chicago, Philadelphia was seen as a place of tolerance and liberalism. More recently, it voted in the nation's first black mayor, and has the country's best museum dedicated to African-American history and culture. On the downside, Philadelphia is also the place where, as part of a huge police effort to dislodge the black separatist group MOVE, a bomb dropped from a helicopter set fire to entire city blocks, killing women and children and leaving many hundreds homeless.

Once known as "Filthydelphia," and the butt of endless derision from W C Fields in the 1930s (as in his famous epitaph: "On the whole, I'd rather be in Philadelphia"), the city underwent a remarkable resurgence preparing for the nation's bicentennial celebrations in 1976. Philadelphia's strength today is its great energy – fueled by history, strong cultural institutions, and a new influx of income due to its new downtown convention center – grounded in its many staunchly traditional neighborhoods, especially Italian South Philadelphia. An impressive amount of new construction and revitalization is currently being undertaken in the downtown area, further testimony of the city's economic boom.

## Arrival and information

Philadelphia's **International Airport** (☎215/937-6800) is eight miles southwest of the city off I-95. Taxis into town cost around $20 (try Yellow Cab; ☎215/829-4222), and the South East Pennsylvania Transit Authority (SEPTA) runs **trains** every thirty minutes (6am–midnight; $4; see transportation below) to three downtown destinations: 30th Street near the university, Suburban Station near City Hall, and Market East, adjacent to the Greyhound terminal at 1001 Filbert St (☎215/931-4000). The very grand 30th Street Amtrak station, the second busiest in the US, is just across the Schuylkill River in the university area (Amtrak passengers can transfer downtown on SEPTA for free; ask when you purchase your ticket), opposite the city's main (24-hour) **post office** at 30th and Market (zip code 19104).

The excellent **visitor center**, 1525 JFK Blvd (daily: summer 9am–6pm; rest of year 9am–5pm; ☎215/636-1666 or 1-800/537-7676) at the Penn Center subway station in the heart of downtown, supplies a wealth of information and can help with accommodation.

## City transportation

SEPTA (☎215/580-7800) runs an extensive **bus** system and a **subway** (both 6.30am–1am). The most useful subway lines cross the city east–west (Market–Frankford line) and north–south (Broad Street line); the handiest bus route is **#76**, which runs from Penn's Landing and the Independence Hall area out along Market Street past City Hall to the museums and Fairmount Park and costs only 50¢. All other bus and subway services require exact fares of $1.60; **day passes**, which are also good for a ride to or from the airport, go for $6. Bright purple PHLASH buses run a handy downtown loop (☎215/474-5274; $1.50 one way, $3 day pass).

### City tours
Philadelphia Trolley Works (☎215/925-TOUR) cruises the historic area and Fairmount Park in fake streetcars on ninety-minute narrated jaunts ($14 for a day pass – board at any of the trolley's 20 stops); you'd do much better to get a map and wander around on your own. The best guided **walking tours** are offered by the Foundation for Architecture (☎215/569-3187 or 569-TOUR for recorded information; $6); Candlelight Tours through the hidden gardens and courtyards of Society Hill leave from the *City Tavern* (May–Oct Thurs–Sat 6.30pm; ☎215/735-3123; $5). Gray Line **coach tours** (☎215/569-3666; from $16) range from three-hour historical tours to all-day bashes and trips to Pennsylvania Dutch Country. Companies such as the 76 Carriage Co (☎215/923-8516) run narrated thirty-minute horse-drawn tours around the historic district for $25 (1–4 people).

## Accommodation

Philadelphia's luxury downtown **hotels** are prohibitively expensive, though at weekends there's a chance of getting a reduced rate. The visitor center is a great resource for accommodation discounts. **B&Bs** are a good option, but often need to be arranged in advance. **B&B Center City**, 1804 Pine St (☎215/735-1137), can arrange rooms throughout the metropolitan area for between $50 and $100 per night.

**Comfort Inn**, 100 N Christopher Columbus Blvd (☎215/627-7900). High-rise hotel in a good location near Penn's Landing; rates include continental breakfast. ⑤.

**HI-Bank Street Hostel**, 32 S Bank St (☎215/922-0222 or 1-800/392-HOST). Friendly hostel wedged between INHP and Old City, with bunk beds for $16–19 and free tea and coffee. Closed 10am–4.30pm; curfew 12.30am, 1am Fri & Sat. ①.

**HI-Chamounix Mansion Philadelphia**, West Fairmount Park (☎215/878-3676 or 1-800/379-0017). Quaker country estate in a gorgeous park setting, but a bit of a trek from downtown (take bus #38 from Market St to Ford and Cranston and then walk for a mile). Midnight curfew, closed 11am–4.30pm and mid-Dec to mid-Jan; beds $11 HI members, $14 others. ①.

**Holiday Inn Cityline**, 4100 Presidential Blvd at City Ave (☎215/477-0200 or 1-800/642-8982). Comfortable hotel with bar, restaurant and indoor pool in exclusive Maine Line district, 10 miles from downtown. Handy for restaurants and stores in Manayunk and a 15-min drive from downtown. ⑥.

**International House**, 3701 Chestnut St (☎215/387-5125). Rooms with shared baths adjacent to the University of Pennsylvania. ③.

**Penn's View Inn**, 14 N Front St (☎215/922-7600). Exceptional service and clean, comfortable rooms in Old City, with a very fine wine bar next to the lobby. ⑥.

**Shippen Way Inn**, 418 Bainbridge St (☎215/627-7266). Newly renovated, family-run B&B a block from South St with nine cozy rooms. ⑤/⑥.

**Thomas Bond House**, 129 S 2nd St (☎215/923-8523 or 1-800/845-BOND). Twelve-room 1769 B&B near INHP, slightly marred by an ugly parking lot at the rear. ⑦.

# The City

Philadelphia stretches for about two miles from the Schuylkill (pronounced *Schoolkill*) River on the west to the Delaware on the east; the urban area extends for many miles to the north and south, but everything you're likely to want to see is right in the central swath. The city's central districts are compact, walkable and readily accessible from each other; Penn's sensibly planned grid system makes for easy sightseeing.

## Independence Hall National Park

Any tour of Philadelphia should start with **Independence National Historic Park**, or **INHP**, "America's most historic square mile," which covers a mere four blocks just west of the Delaware River between Walnut and Arch, but can take more than a day to explore in full. The solid redbrick buildings here, not all of which are open to the public, epitomize the Georgian (and after the Revolution, Federalist) obsession with balance and symmetry.

All INHP sites (unless otherwise specified) are open 365 days a year and admission is free; hours are usually 9am to 5pm, sometimes longer in summer. The **visitor center** at Third and Chestnut (daily 9am–5pm, open until 6pm July & Aug; ☎215/597-8974) has maps and shows a short, somewhat ghostly film, *Independence*, directed by John Huston. Free **tours** set off from the rear of the east wing of Independence Hall, the single most important site.

It's best to reach **Independence Hall** early, to avoid the hordes of tourists and school parties. Built in 1732 as the Pennsylvania State House, this was where the Declaration of Independence was prepared and signed and, after the pealing of the Liberty Bell, given its first public reading on July 8, 1776. Today, in the room in which Jefferson et al drafted and signed the United States Constitution, you can see George Washington's high-backed chair with the half-sun on the back – Franklin, in optimistic spirit, called it "the rising sun."

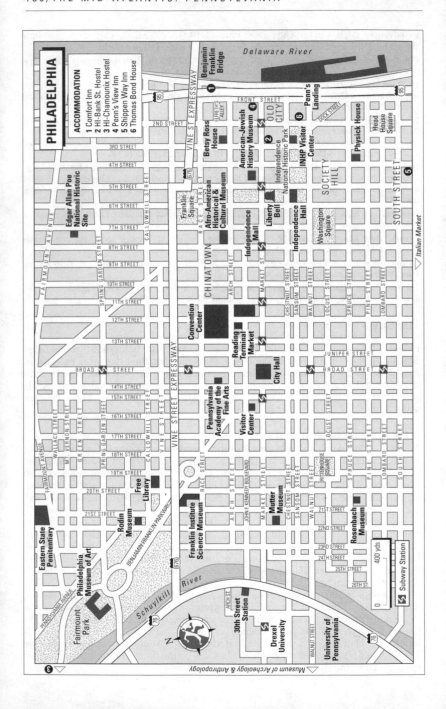

**PHILADELPHIA**

ACCOMMODATION
1 Comfort Inn
2 HI-Bank St. Hostel
3 HI-Chamounix Hostel
4 Penn's View Inn
5 Shippen Way Inn
6 Thomas Bond House

The **Liberty Bell** itself hung in Independence Hall from 1753, ringing to herald vital announcements such as victories and defeats in the Revolutionary War. Stories as to how it received its famous crack vary; one tells that it occurred while tolling the funeral of Chief Justice Marshall in 1835. Whatever the truth, it rang publicly for the very last time on George Washington's birthday in 1846.

Later in the century, the bell's inscription from Leviticus, advocating liberty "throughout all the land unto all the inhabitants," made it an anti-slavery symbol for the New England abolitionists – the first to call it the Liberty Bell. After the Civil War the silent bell was adopted as a symbol of reconciliation and embarked on a national rail tour. The well-traveled and somewhat lumpen icon now rests at eye level in a purpose-built concrete-and-glass **pavilion** on Market Street between Fifth and Sixth.

Next door to Independence Hall on Sixth and Chestnut, **Congress Hall**, built in 1787 as the Philadelphia county courthouse, is where members of the new United States Congress first took their places, and where all the patterns for today's government were established. The US Supreme Court sat from 1791 until 1800 in **Old City Hall**, on the other side of Independence Hall on Fifth and Chestnut.

In 1774, delegates of the first Continental Congress – predecessor of the US Congress – chose defiantly to meet at **Carpenter's Hall**, 320 Chestnut St, rather than the more commodious State House, to air their grievances against the English king. Today the building exhibits early tools and furniture (Tues–Sun 10am–4pm). Directly north, **Franklin Court**, 313 Market St, is a tribute, on the site of his home, to Benjamin Franklin. The house no longer stands, but steel frames outline the original structure. An underground museum has dial-a-quote recordings of his pithy sayings and the musings of his contemporaries, and there's a working printshop. The **B Free Franklin Post Office**, 316 Market St, sells stamps and includes a small postal museum. Other buildings in the park include the **Philosophical Hall**, 104 S Fifth St, still used today by the nation's first philosophical debating society (founded by Franklin). The building is closed to the public, but features a statue of Ben in intellectual mode, garbed in a fetching toga. The original **Free Quaker Meeting House**, two blocks north of Market at Fifth and Arch, was built in 1783 by the small group of Quakers who actually fought in the Revolutionary War.

## Old City

INHP runs north into **Old City**, Philadelphia's earliest commercial area, above Market Street near the riverfront. Washington, Franklin and Betsy Ross all worshipped at **Christ Church**, on Second Street just north of Market Street. Dating from 1727, it is surrounded by the gravestones of signatories to the Declaration of Independence (Mon–Sat 9am–5pm, Sun 1–5pm; donation). The church's official burial ground, two blocks west at Fifth and Arch, includes **Benjamin Franklin's grave**. At 239 Arch St, the **Betsy Ross House** (Tues–Sun 10am–5pm; donation; ☎215/627-5343), by means of unimpressive wax dummies, salutes the woman credited with making the first American flag. There's a gift shop and shady **garden**, an oasis away from the busy streets outside.

The claim of **Elfreth's Alley** – a pretty little cobbled way off Second Street between Arch and Race to be the "oldest street in the United States" is somewhat nebulous, but it has been in continuous residential use since 1727, and its thirty houses, notable for their wrought-iron gates, water pumps, wooden shutters and attic rooms, all date from the eighteenth century. No. 126 is the **Mantua Maker's Museum** where furniture was made for Philadelphia's elite in the eighteenth century (daily 10am–4pm, weekends only in Jan; $2; ☎215/574-0560).

The area north of Market Street also holds two excellent museums: the **National Museum of American-Jewish History**, 55 N Fifth St (Mon–Thurs 10am–5pm, Fri 10am–3pm, Sun noon–5pm; ☎215/923-3811; $2.50), which is dedicated to the experiences of Jews in the States and includes a synagogue, and the emotive and politically informed **Afro-American Historical and Cultural Museum**, Seventh and Arch (Tues–Sat 10am–6pm, Sun noon–6pm; ☎215/574-0380; $4). The latter tells the stories of the thousands of blacks who migrated north to Philadelphia after Reconstruction and in the early twentieth century. As well as lectures, films and concerts, there are photos, personal memorabilia, poems by black poet Langston Hughes and a Billie Holiday soundtrack.

The **Edgar Allan Poe House**, 532 N Seventh St, just north of Spring Garden Street (daily 9am–5pm; free; ☎215/597-8780), is the only one of five Philadelphia houses Poe lived in that survives; it's also where he wrote *The Black Cat* in 1843. The stripped-down walls and bare wood floors do little to evoke Poe's presence (plans to restore the house fully are as yet unfulfilled), but the staff in the small **museum** adjacent to the house can answer almost any Poe-related question. If you're keen on literary pilgrimages, you might also want to visit the grave of another key figure of American letters, **Walt Whitman**; he's buried in the Harleigh Cemetery, on Haddon Avenue across the river in Camden, New Jersey.

## Penn's Landing

Just to the east of Old City along the Delaware River, where William Penn stepped off in 1682, spreads the huge and heavily industrialized port of Philadelphia. Along the port's southern reaches, on the river side of the I-95 freeway, the old docklands have been renovated as part of the **Penn's Landing** development, which includes the **Independence Seaport Museum** (daily 10am–5pm; $5, $7.50 with ships) and a variety of historical **ships**, including the flagship *USS Olympia* and World War II submarine *Becuna* (both daily 10am–5pm; $5), and the three-masted Portuguese Tall Ship *Gazela*, built in 1883 (while in port Sat & Sun 12.30–5.30pm; check ☎215/923-9030; donation). All along the riverfront promenade are food stalls, landscaped pools and fountains, and there are regular outdoor concerts and festivals. A ferry crosses the Delaware (Riverbus Ferry; ☎1-800/634-4027; $5 round-trip) to the down-at-heel town of Camden, where the main attraction is the New Jersey State Aquarium (daily: mid-March to mid-Sept 9.30am–5.30pm; mid-Sept to mid-March 10am–5pm; ☎609/365-3300; $10.95) – good for kids but otherwise eminently missable. A $15 River Pass covers the museum, ships, aquarium and a round-trip on the ferry.

## Society Hill

Society Hill, an elegant residential area west of the Delaware and directly south of INHP, spreads between Walnut and Lombard streets. Though it is indeed Philadelphia's high society who live here now, the area was named for its first inhabitants, the Free Society of Traders – a rather more fun-loving bunch than the strict Quakers who lived to the north. After falling into disrepair, the Hill itself was flattened in the early 1970s to provide a building site for the huge condominium development near the waterfront, but the rest of the neighborhood has been restored to form one of the city's most picturesque districts: cobbled gas-lit streets are lined with immaculately kept colonial, Federal and Georgian homes, and markers everywhere point out the area's rich history. One of the few buildings open to the public is the **Physick House**, 321 S Fourth St, home to Dr Philip Syng Physick, "the Father of American Surgery," and filled with eighteenth- and nineteenth-century decorative arts (Thurs–Sat noon–4pm, Sun 1–4pm; $4).

## Center City

Center City, Philadelphia's main business and commercial area, stretches from Eighth Street west to the Schuylkill River, dominated by the endearing Baroque wedding cake of **City Hall** and its 37ft bronze statue of Penn. Before ascending thirty stories to the observation deck at Penn's feet, check out the quirky sculptures and carvings around the building, including the cats and mice at the south entrance. A couple of blocks north at Broad and Cherry streets, the **Museum of American Art** at the Pennsylvania Academy of the Fine Arts (Mon–Sat 10am–5pm, Sun 11am–5pm; $5.95, free on Sun 3–5pm), housed in an elaborate, multicolored Victorian pile at Broad and Cherry, exhibits three hundred years of American art, including works by Mary Cassatt and Thomas Eakins.

Beginning at Eighth Street, Chinatown, marked by a 40ft oriental gate, has some of the best budget food in the city. A block over on Twelfth Street is the century-old Reading Terminal Market – always good for a lively time (p.143 for specific recommendations). The $500-million Convention Center, which opened next door in 1993, signaled major changes for this once dodgy area, as flashy hotels, coffeehouses and restaurants replace the once derelict shops and offices.

## Rittenhouse Square

Grassy **Rittenhouse Square**, one of Penn's original city squares, is in a very fashionable part of town. On one side it borders chic Walnut Street, on the other a residential area of solid brownstones with beautifully carved doors and windows. The redbrick 1860 **Rosenbach Museum**, 2010 Delancey Place, holds over thirty thousand rare books and James Joyce's original hand-scrawled manuscripts of Ulysses (Tues–Sun 11am–4pm, tours at 2.45pm; $3.50). On summer evenings there are free outdoor jazz and R&B concerts in the square itself.

Three blocks northwest from the square, the **Mutter Museum** (Tues–Fri 10am–4pm; $2), 19 S 22nd St in the College of Physicians (between Chestnut and Market), is not for the squeamish. Filled with weird pathological and medical oddities, including sickeningly lifelike wax models of tumours and infections, alongside closets full of skeletons, syphilitic skulls, pickled internal organs and the death cast of a pair of Siamese twins, it's unique to say the least.

## The museums

The mile-long Benjamin Franklin Parkway, known as Museum Row – or, less convincingly, as "America's Champs-Elysees" – sweeps northwest from City Hall to the colossal Museum of Art in **Fairmount Park**, an area of countryside annexed by the city in the nineteenth century. Spanning nine hundred scenic acres on both sides of the Schuylkill River, this is the world's largest landscaped city park, with jogging, biking and hiking trails, early American homes, an all-wars memorial to the state's black soldiers, and a zoo – the country's first – at 3400 Girard Ave (daily 9.30am–5.45pm; $8.50). In the late 1960s, local residents **Muhammad Ali** and Joe Frazier all but brought the city to a standstill with the announcement one afternoon that they were heading for Fairmount for an informal slug-out.

Sylvester Stallone later immortalized the steps of the **Philadelphia Museum of Art** (Tues & Thurs–Sun 10am–5pm, Wed 10am–8.45pm; $7, free Sun 10am–1pm), 26th Street and Franklin Parkway, by running up them in the film *Rocky*, but he missed out on a real treat inside: one of the finest collections in the US, with a twelfth-century French cloister, Renaissance art, a complete **Robert Adam** interior from a 1765 house in London's Berkeley Square, Rubin tapestries, Pennsylvania Dutch crafts and **Shaker furniture**, a strong **Impressionist** collection, and the world's most extensive gathering of the works of **Marcel Duchamp**. Exhibits are displayed in an easy-to-follow chronological order. On Wednesday nights, there are excellent programs of live jazz and classical music along with film showings and artistic debate – all included in the admission price.

A statue of Stallone as Rocky stood for a while on the steps, but the museum authorities shunted it away as soon as discreetly possible, considering it out of keeping with the general theme of their decor. Statuary addicts may find some consolation for that loss in the exquisite **Rodin Museum**, a few blocks away at Franklin Parkway and 22nd Street (Tues–Sun 10am–5pm; donation). Marble-walled, and set in a shady garden with a green pool, it holds the largest collection of Rodin's Impressionistic sculptures and casts outside Paris, including *The Thinker, The Burghers of Calais* and *The Gates of Hell.* Among the rare books at the **Free Library of Philadelphia**, 19th and Vine (Mon–Fri 9am–5pm, tours at 11am; free), are cuneiform tablets from 3000 BC, medieval manuscripts, first editions of Dickens and Poe, and such intriguing titles as the 1807 *Inquiry into the Conduct of the Princess of Wales.*

Over the road in the vast **Franklin Institute Science Museum** (N 20th St and Benjamin Franklin Parkway; daily 9.30am–5pm) are a **Planetarium** ($6), the four-story **OMNIVERSE movie theater** ($7.50), and the **Mandell Futures Center** (open until 9pm Wed–Sun; $9.50) – a state-of-the-art facility filled with entertaining gadgets such as a hugely popular machine on which you can see (disappointingly hazy) images of your face aged by 25 years. A **combination ticket** ($14.50) covers admission to all three. Continuing the educational theme, the nearby **Academy of Natural Sciences** exhibits dinosaurs, mummies and gems (Mon–Fri 10am–4.30pm, Sat, Sun & holidays 10am–5pm; $7.75), while the **Please Touch Museum**, 210 N 21st St (daily 9am–4.30pm; $6.95), is a hands-on adventureland aimed at youngsters.

## Eastern State Penitentiary

One of Philadelphia's most significant historic sites stands, all but forgotten, just a short walk from the Fairmount Park museums. The **Eastern State Penitentiary**, whose gloomy Gothic fortifications fill an entire block of the residential neighborhood along Fairmount Avenue at 22nd Street, embodies an almost complete history of attitudes towards crime and punishment in the US. Since it opened in 1829, the Quaker-inspired prison's efforts to rehabilitate inmates rather than punish them attracted visitors from around the world; when Charles Dickens came to America in 1842, he wanted to see two things, this prison and Niagara Falls. Though it underwent substantial changes in its 140-year history, and has slowly decayed since its final closure in 1970, the bulk of the Panopticon-style radial prison survives, and preservationists have recently completed a major restoration program. **Guided tours** leave on the hour (June–Sept Wed–Sun 10am–6pm, May–June & Oct–Nov Sat & Sun 10am–6pm; $7; ☎215/236-7326), and point out its many novel architectural features, as well as the cell where Al Capone cooled his heels and the block where Tina Turner filmed a music video.

## West Philadelphia

Across the Schuylkill River, **West Philadelphia** is home to the Ivy League **University of Pennsylvania**, where Franklin established the country's first medical school. The compact campus blends into fairly gritty urban areas, but has some great museums: the small **Institute of Contemporary Art**, 36th and Sansom, which displays cutting-edge traveling exhibitions in an airy white space (Wed & Fri–Sun 10am–5pm, Thurs 10am–7pm; $3, free Sun 10am–noon), and the intriguing **Arthur Ross Gallery** (call ☎215/898-2083 for hours; free), 220 S 34th St, which has changing student displays. The superlative **Museum of Archeology and Anthropology**, 33rd and Spruce (Tues–Sat 10am–4.30pm, Sun 1–5pm; $5), is the university's top draw. Regarded by experts as one of the world's finest science museums, its exhibits span all the continents and their major epochs – from Nigerian Benin bronzes to Chinese crystal balls. Most astonishing is the priceless twelve-ton granite Sphinx of Rameses II, circa

1293–1185 BC, in the **Lower Egyptian Gallery**, though the **Meso-American** and **Greco-Roman Galleries** also hold plenty of highlights.

## South Philadelphia

**South Philadelphia**, center of Philadelphia's black community since the Civil War, is also home to many of the city's Italians; opera singer **Mario Lanza** (who has his own museum at 416 Queen St) and pop stars Fabian and Chubby Checker grew up here. It's also where to come for an authentic – and very messy – **cheesesteak**, and to rummage through the wonderful **Italian Market** (another *Rocky* location) which runs along Ninth Street south from Christian Street. One of the last surviving urban markets in the US, the wooden market stalls that have stood here for generations are packed to over-flowing with bargain-basement flowers, fabrics, secondhand Levis, live seafood and fragrant olive oils.

**South Street**, the original boundary of the city, is now Philadelphia's main **nightlife** district, with dozens of cafes, bars, restaurants and nightclubs lined up along the few blocks west from Front Street, with an ambiance not unlike Greenwich Village or Haight-Ashbury. During the day you can wander amongst the many good book, record and clothing **shops** (the Book Trader, 501 South St, is open daily until midnight), and it's lively almost every night – on summer weekends almost uncomfortably so.

## Eating

**Eating out** in Philadelphia is a real treat: try Chinatown, Reading Terminal Market near the Convention Center and the Italian Market for ethnic food, South Street for trendy and reasonably priced restaurants, and the ubiquitous street stands for **soft pretzels** with mustard (around 50¢). The Bourse building next to the INHP has a reasonable food hall. The South Philly **cheesesteak** varies from joint to joint around town, though logically enough some of the best are to be found in the Italian cafes around Ninth and Passyunk in South Philadelphia. And bear in mind that a cheesesteak is hot, a **hoagie** is not.

**Alyan's**, 603 S 4th St (☎215/922-3553). Small Middle Eastern restaurant off South St. Dinner from $7. Bring your own bottle.

**Brasil's**, 112 Chestnut St (☎215/413-1700). Good Brazilian food, with live Latin and salsa music and friendly service. Great atmosphere.

**Circa**, 1518 Walnut St (☎215/545-6800). A stylish Center City restaurant decked out in marble, mirrors and chandeliers. Offers meat and seafood dinners with innovative twists for around $10. Great happy hours on Thurs & Fri; techno music later at night.

**City Tavern**, 2nd and Walnut sts (☎215/413-1443). Reconstructed 1773 tavern in INHP, familiar to the city's founders, and called by John Adams "the most genteel tavern in America." Costumed staff serve "olde style" food (pasties, turkey rarebit) to a harpsichord accompaniment, but the prices, unfortunately, are as modern as they get, from about $16 for dinner. Lunch is less expensive.

**Delilah's**, Reading Terminal Market, 12th and Spruce (☎215/574-0929). Superb soul food, scatty service. Nigerian stew with cornbread for under $5; beans and rice even less.

**Diner on the Square**, 1839 Spruce St (☎215/735-5787). 24hr diner off Rittenhouse Square serving staple foods (including a good cheesesteak) from $4 and with a circular soda and ice-cream bar.

**Jim's Steaks**, 400 South St (☎215/928-1911). Black-and-white-tiled Art Deco diner serving some of the biggest and best cheesesteaks in the city. Try and beat the record – 11 cheesesteaks in 90 minutes.

**Lee's Hoagies**, 44 S 17th St (☎215/564-1264). Downtown lunch place; a thousand variations on a single theme. The regular hoagies (from $3.95) are giant; the giants (from $7.50) truly gargantuan.

**Montserrat**, 623 South St (☎215/627-4224). Wide variety of fresh, healthy food, with a vegetarian emphasis, served inside or on a large deck overlooking the South St parade.

**Serrano**, 20 S 2nd St (☎215/928-0770). Intimate Old City cafe. Creative international cooking, with good fresh seafood. Try the appetizer tasting menu. Diners get preferential seating at the *Tin Angel* folk club upstairs (see p.145).

**Sonoma**, 4411 Main St, Manayunk (☎215/483-9400). Pleasant, reasonably priced Cal-Ital restaurant.

**South Street Diner**, 140 South St (☎215/627-5258). Huge menu with Greek and Italian specialties from $6. Open 24hr seven days a week.

**White Dog Cafe**, 3420 Sansom St (☎215/386-9224). Trendy, creative food in an antique-filled room near the universities. Arty, student crowd; dinners cost $12–25.

# Drinking

A trail of theme **bars** has sprung up along Penn's Landing and the Delaware River, but by far the most popular place for bar-hopping is **South Street; Second Street** in the Old City also has a few good places. Philly's growing number of **cafes** are spread around the city; South Street and Second Street again have the densest concentrations, though several have opened in Center City over the past couple of years.

**BeatHaus**, 12th and Ellsworth (☎215/465-6106). "Where Art Lives" – late-night South Philly coffee bar with jazz, folk and spoken-word performances.

**Dickens Inn**, 421 S 2nd St (☎215/928-9307). English-style pub in Head House Square, with four large bars and over 130 different single-malt whiskeys. The exceptionally welcoming staff make it a great night out, and a decent lunch stop, too.

**Irish Pub**, 2007 Walnut St (☎215/568-5603). Good music and atmosphere near Rittenhouse Square.

**The Khyber Pass**, 56 S 2nd St (☎215/440-9683). Philly's oldest and most congenial bar, with a huge range of beers; it's also a good place to hear local bands (see opposite).

**Last Drop Coffeehouse**, 1300 Pine St (☎215/893-0434). Trendy cafe, serving Philly's best espresso.

**Love Lounge**, 230 South St (☎215/922-3956). Small bar with the feel of a living room above the *Knave of Hearts* restaurant. Arty crowd.

**Samuel Adam's Brew House**, 1516 Sansom St (☎215/563-2326). Traditional tavern, traditional beer, darts and good sandwiches.

**Society Hill**, 3rd and Chestnut (☎215/925-1919). Great sandwiches in a bar with plenty of atmosphere, a stone's throw from the *Bank Street Hostel*. Live jazz piano music nightly.

**Sugar Mom's Church Street Lounge**, 225 Church St (☎215/925-8219). Popular basement bar where music ranges from Tony Bennett to Sonic Youth, with a dozen international beers on tap. Those carrying HI cards get a 20 percent food discount.

**Who's on Third**, 700 S 3rd St (☎215/625-2835). Irish pub just below South St. Happy hour 7–9pm.

**Woody's Bar and Restaurant**, 202 S 13th St (☎215/545-1893). Friendly downtown beer bar popular with Philly's gay community.

# Nightlife and entertainment

Few reminders are left of the 1970s "Philly Sound"; stars like Patti LaBelle, the O'Jays and Harold *If You Don't Love Me By Now* Melvin and the Blue Notes have waned, though their legacy is readily apparent in the smooth vocals of contemporary artists like Boyz II Men. It's also a decent place to get to see rock bands: most of the names that play New York come down here and tickets are half the price or even less. The world-famous **Philadelphia Orchestra** performs at the grand Academy of Music on Broad Street (☎215/893-1999), modeled after Milan's La Scala; nosebleed seats cost just $5 on the day, and they give free summer concerts at the Mann Music Center in Fairmount Park (☎215/567-0707). Philadelphia's other great strength is its **theater** scene: small venues abound. Check the **listings** in Friday's free *City Paper*, or call the

24-hour **event hotline** (☎215/573-2787). TIXSTOP, in the visitor center, sells half-price standby tickets (Tues–Thurs 11.30am–3.30pm, Fri & Sat 11.30am–5pm).

**Annual events** in Philadelphia include the fortnight-long Freedom Fest that leads up to the Fourth of July, and the superb Riverblues weekend festival on the Delaware River, at the end of July, which features top-name blues artists.

**Katmandu**, Pier 25, N Delaware Ave (☎215/629-1101). World music in "exotic" surroundings just north of the decidedly unexotic Franklin Bridge. Bar and nightly outdoor barbecue.

**The Khyber Pass**, 56 S 2nd St (☎215/440-9683). Small, mainly alternative, rock venue with a gargoyle-lined bar, bluesy jukebox and casual young clientele. Cover $3–6 when bands are on.

**Painted Bride Art Center**, 230 Vine St (☎215/925-9914). Art gallery with live folk, jazz and poetry performances after dark.

**Silk City Lounge**, 5th and Spring Garden (☎215/592-8838). Very mixed musical bag – Sinatra, hip-hop, acid jazz, indie dance – in ultratrendy but unflashy club. Live local bands at the weekend.

**Theater of Living Arts**, 334 South St (☎215/922-1011). Converted movie palace that's the best place to catch "alternative" rock bands.

**Tin Angel**, 20 S 2nd St (☎215/928-0978). Intimate upstairs bar and coffeehouse, featuring top local and nationally known folk and acoustic acts.

**Trocadero**, 10th and Arch sts (☎215/922-LIVE). Trendy downtown dance club with occasional live alternative bands. Cover varies, ID essential.

**Warmdaddy's**, 4 S Front St (☎215/627-2500). Live blues every night and a normally buzzing atmosphere; something of a Penn's Landing institution.

**Zanzibar Blue**, 200 S Broad St in the *Bellevue Hotel* (☎215/829-0300). Classy club with contemporary New York-style jazz nightly, often from famous names, so expect a hefty cover charge and two-drink minimum.

# Central Pennsylvania

**Central Pennsylvania**, cut north to south by the broad **Susquehanna River**, has no major cities, though the state capital, **Harrisburg**, is an excellent base from which to explore sights that include the **Hershey** chocolate empire and the rolling Amish farmlands of **Lancaster County** to the east, and the Civil War site of **Gettysburg** on the state's southern border. To the north, the mighty forests of the "Grand Canyon of Pennsylvania," around **Williamsport**, reveal the legacy of its great nineteenth-century lumber wealth in mansion-lined streets. **Johnstown**, beyond the dramatic Allegheny Mountains in the west, is a tough survivor, subject of many folk songs due to its tragic history of floods (the most destructive in 1889 when the South Fork Dam, ten miles east, collapsed and killed over two thousand in ten minutes; the most recent occurred in 1977). Northeastern Pennsylvania is also hard-rock **coal mining** country, remembered in cities like **Scranton** by a number of museums, preserved mines, blast furnaces and the country's largest remaining stock of coal-fired railroad machinery at **Steamtown USA National Historic Site**.

## Lancaster County – Pennsylvania Dutch Country

**Lancaster County**, fifty miles west of Philadelphia, stretches for about 45 miles from Churchtown in the east to the Susquehanna River in the west. Although Lancaster City, ten miles east of the river, was US capital for a day in September 1777, the region is famed more for its preponderance of agricultural religious communities, known collectively as the **Pennsylvania Dutch** (a mistaken derivation of *Deutsch*, or German).

An extremely touristy place, even before it was brought to international fame by the movie *Witness*, Lancaster County has maintained its natural beauty in the face of encroaching commercialization. It is a region of gentle countryside and fertile farm-

## THE PENNSYLVANIA DUTCH

The people now known as the Pennsylvania Dutch originated as **Anabaptists** in six-teenth-century Switzerland, under the leadership of Menno Simons. His unorthodox advocacy of adult baptism and literal interpretation of the Bible led to the order's perse-cution; they were invited by William Penn to settle in Lancaster County in the 1720s. Today the twenty thousand or so Pennsylvania Dutch include the "plain" Old Order **Amish** (a strict order that originally broke away from Simons in 1693) and freer-living **Mennonites**, as well as the "fancy" **Lutheran** groups (distinguished by the colorful cir-cular "hex" signs on their barns). The Amish are the best known, the men with their wide-brimmed straw hats and beards (but no "military" moustaches), the women in bonnets, plain dresses (with no fripperies like buttons) and aprons. Shunning electricity and any exposure to the corrupting influence of the outside world, the Amish power their farms with generators, and travel (at roughly ten miles per hour) in handmade horse-drawn bug-gies. For all their insularity, the Amish are very friendly and helpful; resist the temptation to photograph them, however, as the making of "graven images" offends their beliefs.

lands, mule-drawn ploughs, tiny roadside bakeries crammed with jams and pies, Amish children wending on old-fashioned scooters to and from their one-room schoolhouses, and flower-filled, immaculate farmhouses. However, attempting to live a simple life away from the pressures of the outside world has proved too much for many Pennsylvania Dutch. A few (mainly Mennonites) have succumbed to commercial need by offering rides in their buggies and meals in their homes. Members of the stricter orders in particular have moved away from the ceaseless intrusions of privacy – as well as soaring land prices – to less touristed Ohio and Iowa.

### Arrival and information

The Pennsylvania Turnpike sweeps across the north of the region, but most activity is concentrated further south near the east–west US-30. Trailways arrives in Lancaster City at 22 W Clay St (daily 7am–5.15pm; ☎717/387-4861), Amtrak at 53 McGovern Ave. The bustling **Pennsylvania Dutch Visitors Bureau**, just off US-30 at 501 Greenfield Rd (daily 8.30am–5pm; ☎717/299-8901), does an excellent job of providing orientation and advice on accommodation. In Lancaster City itself, the smaller and less resource-ful **visitor center** at 100 S Queen St in the Southern Farmers' Market (April–Oct Mon–Fri 8.30am–5pm, Sat 9am–4pm, Sun 10am–3pm; ☎717/397-3531) has maps for self-guided walking tours. It also organizes **guided tours** (April–Oct Mon–Sat 10am & 1.30pm, Sun 1.30pm; $5).

Visitors keen to learn about Pennsylvania Dutch culture should head to the excellent **People's Place**, Main Street, Intercourse, eleven miles east of Lancaster City, which has a well-stocked bookstore, an informative if sentimental slide show, an Amish world museum, and the film *Hazel's People*, plus displays of quilts and artwork (June–Aug Mon–Sat 9.30am–9.30pm, Sept–May Mon–Sat 9.30am–4pm; ☎717/768-7171). The **Mennonite Information Center**, 2209 Millstream Rd off US-30, organizes lodging with Mennonite families. Call at least two hours ahead for a guide to take you on a two-hour, $19.50 tour in your car (April–Oct Mon–Sat 9.30am–9.30pm, Nov–March Mon–Sat 8am–5pm; ☎717/299-0954).

### Getting around

Winding country lanes weave through Pennsylvania Dutch Country, passing small vil-lages with eccentric-sounding names such as **Intercourse** (source of many droll post-cards, but supposedly named for its location on the junction of two main roads). Although a car will get you to the quieter back roads the tour buses miss, it's more fun to **ride a bike**. Only then can you feel the benefits of all that pure fresh air – and it shows more consideration for the horse-drawn buggies with which you share the road. Strasburg Bike Rental, by the railroad in Strasburg (☎717/687-8222), rents bikes by the day or hour.

For those without transportation, Red Rose Transit, 47 N Queen St in Lancaster City (☎717/397-4246), runs an extensive **bus** system. Amish Country Tours, on US-30 (☎717/392-8622), does four-and-a-half-hour farmlands **tours** ($25; though some accommodation places offer a similar service for free) and limited-number "VIP" tours ($36), which stop at Amish properties – a rare opportunity to talk to the people rather than merely gawk at them. Ed's Buggy Rides on US-896, north of Strasburg, runs lolloping three-mile countryside excursions for $6.50 (☎717/687-0360).

## Accommodation

**Accommodation** options in Pennsylvania Dutch Country range from reasonably priced **hotels** in and around Lancaster City, through **farm vacations** (ask at the Pennsylvania Dutch CVB) to **campgrounds**. *White Oak Campgrounds*, 372 White Oak Rd, Quarryville, four miles north of Strasburg, overlooks the heart of the Dutch farmlands and hosts a county auction on Saturdays (reservations recommended; $12; ☎717/687-6207).

**Brunswick**, Chestnut and Queen (☎717/397-4801 or 1-800/233-0182). Seventies-style luxury hotel in the center of downtown Lancaster City, with spacious, comfortable rooms. ④.

**Countryside Motel**, 134 Hartman Bridge Rd (☎717/687-8431). Clean and simple place six miles east of Lancaster City on Hwy-896. ③.

**Historic Strasburg Inn**, Rte-896, Strasburg (☎717/687-7691 or 1-800/872-0201). One hundred luxury rooms tucked away in sixty rolling acres of land. ⑥.

**O'Flaherty's Dingledein House**, 1105 E King St (☎717/293-1723 or 1-800/779-7765). Friendly B&B near Lancaster City. Only four rooms, so call ahead. Rates include a huge country breakfast. ④.

**Patchwork Inn**, 2319 Old Philadelphia Pike (☎717/293-9078). Nineteenth-century farm between Lancaster City and Smoketown. ④.

**Red Caboose Motel**, Paradise Lane, Strasburg (☎717/687-5000). Quirky accommodation in converted train cabooses. ③.

**Village Inn**, 2695 Old Philadelphia Pike, Bird-in-Hand (☎717/293-8369 or 1-800/914-2473). Excellent old inn with modern amenities, large breakfast, patio, lawn and back pasture. Price includes 2hr tour of Amish Country and use of adjacent motel's pool. Off-season discounts. Book ahead. ⑤.

## Touring Pennsylvania Dutch Country

Though useful for a general overview and historical insight, the attractions that interpret Amish culture tend toward overkill. It's far more satisfying just to explore the countryside for yourself. Here, among the streams with their covered bridges and fields striped with corn, alfalfa and tobacco, the reality hits you – these aren't actors re-creating an ancient lifestyle, but a living, working community. There's no guarantee as to what you'll see: on Sunday, for example, there are no quilt sales or bake shops, and the farmers don't work the fields, but there may well be a large gathering of buggies outside one of the farms, indicating an Amish church service (in High German) or a "visiting day."

Among the widely spread formal "attractions," the **Ephrata Cloister**, 632 W Main St, Ephrata (on US-272 and 322), re-creates the eighteenth-century settlement of German Protestant celibates that acted, amongst other things, as an early publishing and printing center (April–Oct Mon–Sat 9am–5pm, Sun noon–5pm; $5). Further south, about three miles northeast of Lancaster City, the **Landis Valley Museum**, 2451 Kissell Hill Rd, is a living history museum of rural life (Tues–Sat 9am–5pm, Sun noon–5pm; $7; ☎717/569-0401).

In Lancaster City itself, a stolid redbrick town with tree-lined avenues, the **Heritage Center Museum**, in Penn Square (Tues–Sat 10am–4pm; free; ☎717/299-6440), exhibits Lancaster master crafts, including wagons and rifles, ancient fraktur calligraphy, clocks, wooden toys, weathervanes and quilts. At **Strasburg**, a mixture of tourist kitsch and historical authenticity southeast of Lancaster City on US-896, the **Strasburg Railroad** gives 45-minute round-trip rides in original steam trains through patchwork farmland to Paradise (daily; $8; ☎717/687-7522). Disappointingly, **Paradise** holds no heavenly delights, but there are some good views on the way (if little that couldn't be seen by bike or car), and the train makes regular picnic stops. The oldest building in the county, the **Hans Herr House**, 1849 Hans Herr Drive, five miles south of downtown Lancaster City off US-222, is a 1719 Mennonite church with a pretty garden and orchard, a medieval German facade and exhibits on early farm life (April–Dec Mon–Sat 9am–4pm; $3.50).

### Eating and nightlife

Lancaster County **food** is delicious: Germanic and served in vast quantities. There are no Amish-owned restaurants, but Amish roadside stalls sell fresh homemade root beer, jams, pickles, breads and pies. The huge "all-you-can-eat" **tourist restaurants** on US-30 and US-340 may look off-putting, all pseudo-rusticism with costumed waitresses, but most serve good meals (for around $13.50), "family-style" – you share long tables and limitless mountains of fried chicken, sauerkraut, noodles, pickles, cottage cheese and apple butter, corn, hickory-smoked ham, *schnitz*, *knepp*, apple dumplings and shoo-fly pie with crowds of other tourists. None stays open later than 8pm.

Rural Lancaster County, where people get up at the crack of dawn, is not known for its wild **nightlife** – or any nightlife for that matter; even the streets of Lancaster City are strangely quiet after dark. Options are not totally limited to early nights or cable TV, however: a couple of good – and very friendly – bars are worth exploring downtown. The *Fulton Opera House*, 12 N Prince St (☎717/397-7425), is a plush red-and-gold restored Victorian theater, hosting dance, plays and special events.

**Central Market**, Penn Square, Lancaster City (☎717/291-4739). Covered market selling fresh farm produce and sandwiches. Tues & Fri 6am–4.30pm, Sat 6am–2pm.

**Family Style Restaurant**, 2323 E Lincoln Hwy (☎717/393-2323). One of the few "family-style" restaurants to open on Sunday and serve alcohol, as well as absolutely colossal portions. Also does breakfast.

**Good 'n Plenty**, East Brook Rd, US-896, Smoketown (☎717/394-7111). Not Amish-owned, but Amish women cook and serve food in the best of the family-style restaurants. Open Mon–Sat 11.30am–8pm. Closed mid-Dec to end of Jan.

**Lancaster Dispensing Co**, 33–35 N Market St, Lancaster City (☎717/299-4602). Downtown Lancaster's trendiest, friendliest bar. Live weekend jazz and blues, plus food.

**Lancaster Malt Brewing Co**, Plum and Walnut, Lancaster City (☎717/391-MALT). Newish brew-pub serving good food and three different microbrews. Tours by appointment. Open daily.

**Molly's Pub**, 53 E Chestnut St, Lancaster City (☎717/396-0225). Neighborhood bar with lively atmosphere and good burgers. Closed Sun.

**Zinn's Diner**, Route 272, Denver (☎717/336-2500). Well-established premises serving authentic Dutch and American favorites. Adjacent recreation park ideal for an after-dinner stroll.

## Harrisburg and Hershey

**HARRISBURG**, Pennsylvania's capital, lies on the Susquehanna River thirty or so miles northwest of Lancaster City. It's a surprisingly attractive small city, lined with shuttered colonial buildings and well complemented by its kitsch Chocolatetown neighbor **Hershey**. Harrisburg is also known as the site of **Three Mile Island** nuclear facility, which stands along the river on the east side of town.

The ornate **capitol** at Third and State is undeniably beautiful; at its dedication in 1906, Theodore Roosevelt called it "the handsomest building I ever saw". Italian Renaissance in style, it has a dome modeled after St Peter's in Rome (Mon–Sat 9am–4pm; free). The complex includes the archeological and military artifacts, decorative arts, tools and machinery exhibited in the free four-floor **State Museum of Pennsylvania**, a cylindrical building that holds a planetarium, at Third and North (Tues–Sat 9am–5pm, Sun noon–5pm; free).

One of the best ways to spend a Harrisburg afternoon is to cross the Susquehanna along the Walnut Street footbridge and stroll through **City Island**, a waterfront development with vast sports facilities (including a family-filled concrete beach, a baseball stadium and a football ground), shady picnic areas, regular festivals and concerts and **paddlewheeler rides** (May–Oct; call ☎717/234-6500 for schedule; $5).

**HERSHEY**, ten miles east, was built in 1903 by candy magnate Milton S Hershey for his chocolate factory – so it has streets named Chocolate and Cocoa Avenue, streetlamps in the shape of Hershey's Chocolate Kisses and air rich with the smell of cocoa. **Hershey Chocolate World** (daily 9am–4.45pm; longer hours in summer; ☎717/534-4900) offers a free mini-train ride through a simulated chocolate factory (accompanied by sugary, piped warblings of *It's a Chocolate, Chocolate World*). Those not content with the free sample given out at the end can gorge themselves in the vast gift and souvenir shops and cafes.

**Hersheypark**, which began in 1907 as a picnic ground for Hershey factory workers, is now a huge **amusement park** with roller coasters and sundry other rides (mid-May to Sept daily hours vary; ☎717/534-3090 or 1-800/HERSHEY; $27.95). The adjacent **Hershey Museum of American Life** has exhibits on the Pennsylvania Dutch and tells the Milton S Hershey story (daily 10am–5pm; $4.25).

Twenty-five miles south of Harrisburg, the blue-collar town of **YORK** is home to the final assembly plant of **Harley-Davidson**. The company runs free tours of its factory and museum (Mon–Fri; call ☎717/848-1177 ext 5900 for times).

### Practicalities

Amtrak **trains** share the central new station at Fourth and Chestnut with Greyhound, whose buses also stop in Hershey at 337 W Chocolate St (☎717/397-4861). Harrisburg's **visitor center** at 114 Walnut St (☎717/232-1377) provides maps and a suggested downtown **walking tour**. Hotels on the outskirts of town, aimed towards business travelers and politicians, are a snip compared to prices in DC or Philly. *Quality Inn Riverfront*, 525 S Front St (☎717/233-1611; ③), is in downtown Harrisburg, while just across the river in leafy Camp Hill is the *Radisson Penn Harris* (☎717/763-7117; ④), with good-value rooms in relaxing surroundings. Alternatives in Hershey include the *Spinners Motor Inn*, 845 E Chocolate Ave (☎717/533-9157 or 1-800/800-5845; ④), with a decent restaurant, and (yes, really) the *Chocolatetown Motel* (March–Oct; ☎717/533-2330; ④), a mile further on at no. 1806. Call the Hershey Visitor's Information line ☎717/534-4900 for more listings.

Budget **restaurants** line Second Street in downtown Harrisburg, the best being *Zephyr Express*, 402 N Second St (☎717/257-1328), which serves superb gourmet pasta from $5.25 in a lively chrome Art Deco setting. *Deweys Dry Dock & Deli*, 33 N Second St (☎717/233-3700), does good sandwiches and fries, while *Nick's*, 1014 N Third St (☎717/238-8844), and *Scott's*, 212 Locust St (☎717/234-7599), are popular bar/grills with music some nights.

## Gettysburg

The small town of **GETTYSBURG**, thirty miles south of Harrisburg near the Maryland border, gained tragic notoriety in July 1863 for the cataclysmic **Civil War** battle in which fifty thousand men died. There were more casualties during these three days than in any American battle before or since – a full third of those who fought were killed or wounded – and entire regiments were wiped out when the tide finally turned against the South.

Four months later, on November 19, Abraham Lincoln delivered his **Gettysburg Address** at the dedication of the National Cemetery. His two-minute speech, in memory of all the soldiers who died, is acknowledged as one of the most powerful orations in American history. Lincoln himself was convinced that it was a "flat failure," and prefaced his remarks with the words "the world will little note nor long remember what we say here . . ."; you'll be muttering it in your sleep by the time you leave.

Gettysburg, by far the most baldly commercialized of all the Civil War sites, is overwhelmingly geared towards **tourism**, relentlessly replaying the most minute details of the battle. Fortunately, it is perfectly feasible to avoid the crowds and commercial overkill and explore for yourself the rolling hills of the battlefield (now a national park) and the tidy town streets with their shuttered historic houses.

## Information and getting around

**Gettysburg Travel Council**, 35 Carlisle St (☎717/334-6274), is housed in the tiny historic train depot where Lincoln disembarked in November 1863 and should be the first stop on any visit. Though the town is compact, and easy to walk around, there is no public transportation, and a car helps when touring the huge battlefield. **Bikes** can be rented in the battleground at 610 Taneytown Rd (April–Oct; from $2 per hour to $16 per day; ☎717/334-1258). Two-hour Battlefield Bus Tours, running through the town and making numerous stops in the battlefield, depart from 778 Baltimore St (daily every 30min; ☎717/334-6296; $26.75).

## Accommodation

There are plenty of lodgings in and around Gettysburg, including many **B&Bs**. The most central place to **camp** is at Artillery Ridge Resort, 610 Taneytown Rd (☎717/334-1288).

**Blue Sky Motel**, 2585 Biglerville Rd (☎717/677-7736). Good-value motel four miles north of town. ②.

**Doubleday Inn**, 104 Doubleday Ave (☎717/334-9119). A memorabilia-packed luxury B&B, the only one within the battlefield. ⑥.

**Heritage Motor Lodge**, 64 Steinwehr Ave (☎717/334-9281). Standard motel between downtown and the battlefield. ③.

**Historic Farnsworth House Inn**, 401 Baltimore St (☎717/334-8838). An 1810 townhouse, used as Union HQ in the war and still riddled with bullet holes. Four rooms, with breakfast, afternoon tea and ghost stories in the cellar. ⑤.

**The Tannery B&B**, 449 Baltimore St (☎717/334-2454). Gothic facade and interior, with friendly hosts doubling as Civil War guides. ④.

## The Town

Pick just a couple of the numerous museums in town and follow the Travel Council's fourteen-block downtown walking tour for a sense of the history of the place. The **National Civil War Wax Museum**, 297 Steinwehr Ave (summer daily 9am–8.15pm; rest of year daily 9am–6.15pm; $4.50), uses dreadful dummies in its displays on the lead-up to the Civil War, the Underground Railroad for escapee slaves, abolitionist John Brown, and the famous Southern belle spies Rose Greenhow and Belle Boyd. Across the National Cemetery in the battlefield, there are yet more dummies in the **Hall of Presidents and their First Ladies**, 504 Baltimore St (summer daily 9am–9pm; rest of year daily 9am–5pm; $5.25), complete with pearls of presidential wisdom and stirring patriotic music. The only civilian to die in the battle, twenty-year-old Jennie Wade, was killed by a stray bullet as she made bread for the Union troops in her sister's kitchen. The **Jennie Wade House**, next to the Gettysburg Tour Center on Baltimore Street (daily 9am–7pm; $5.25), looks exactly as it did on July 3, 1863, with bullet holes in the front door and on the bedpost, an artillery shell hole ripped through the wall adjoining the neighboring house, and a macabre model of Jennie's corpse lying under a sheet in the cellar.

President Eisenhower, who retired to Gettysburg, is commemorated to the west of the park at the **Eisenhower National Historic Site**, where his Georgian-style mansion holds an array of memorabilia. The site is accessible only on shuttle bus tours from the National Park Visitor Center in Taneytown (daily 9am–4.15pm; ☎717/334-1124; $4).

### The battleground

It takes most of a day to see the 3500-acre **Gettysburg National Military Park**, which surrounds the town (daily 6am–10pm; free). The **visitor center** on Taneytown Road (daily 8am–5pm; ☎717/334-1124) doubles as the best **museum**, with guns, uniforms, surgical and musical instruments, tents and flags, as well as touching photos of the 1938 Joint Soldiers Reunion. A thirty-minute, painstakingly thorough **electric map show** ($2) plots the intricacies of the battle; you can pick up details of a self-guided **driving route** or a **guide** will join you in your car for a personalized two-hour tour ($25).

Directly opposite the visitor center, the **Gettysburg National Cemetery** contains thousands of graves arranged in a semicircle around the Soldiers' National Monument on the site where Lincoln gave the Gettysburg Address. Most stirring of all are the hundreds of small marble gravestones marked only with numbers. A short walk away, the **Cyclorama Center** holds a 356ft circular painting of **Pickett's Charge**, the suicidal Confederate thrust across open wheat fields in broad daylight, and is accompanied by a recitation of the Gettysburg Address (daily 9am–5pm; $2). The earliest existing draft of the Address (not, as commonly believed, scrawled on the back of an envelope) sits in a hallowed cabinet in a dark room on the lower story. If you're dissatisfied with mere representations of the battlefield, the unsightly **National Tower** opposite the visitor center gives views of the real thing from 300ft observation decks (summer daily 9am–7.30pm; rest of year daily 9am–5.30pm; $4.90). The battlegrounds themselves, golden fields reminiscent of an English country landscape, are peaceful now except for the names: **Valley of Death**, **Bloody Run**, **Cemetery Hill**. Uncanny statues of key figures stand at appropriate points and heavy stone monuments honor different regiments.

### Eating and nightlife

Evenings in Gettysburg tend to be quiet; the tour buses have gone home and many people choose to drink in their hotel bars. However, there are some good **restaurants**, many in historically important buildings, and for those still hungry for battle trivia, James Getty, an Abe Lincoln lookalike, gives summer evening performances, answering questions and recounting his "memories," at the Conflict Theater, 213 Steinwehr Ave (Mon–Thurs 8pm; ☎717/334-8003; $5).

**Blue Parrot Bistro**, 35 Chambersburg St (☎717/337-3739). Pasta and steaks with a good choice of sauces. Like most restaurants in town, things wind down soon after 8.30pm.

**Dobbin House Tavern**, 89 Steinwehr Ave (☎717/334-2100). The oldest house in the city, dating from 1776 and once an underground slave hideout. Lunch from $6, candlelit dinners more expensive. Food veers between Pennsylvania Dutch and early American.

**Krackerjacks**, 619 Baltimore St (☎717/334-5648). Gourmet sandwiches; happy hour 6–8pm.

# Western Pennsylvania

**Western Pennsylvania**, a key point for frontier trade and an important thoroughfare to the West, was the focus of the fighting between English and French in the seven-year French and Indian War for colonial and maritime power (1756–63). It grew to industrial prominence in the nineteenth century, with the exploitation of its coal resources gathering pace after the Civil War, and the opening of the world's first oil well at Titusville (now Drake Well Memorial Park) in northwestern Pennsylvania in 1859.

Today, tourism in western Pennsylvania, like the now-quiet coal and steel industries, is concentrated around the surprisingly appealing city of **Pittsburgh**. If you're after a more rural experience, however, the lush **Allegheny National Forest** in the north, which begins twenty miles from I-80, is a great place to explore. The summer-only Kinzua Point Information Center on Hwy-59 way up on the north side of the forest (☎814/726-1291) has details on campgrounds and trails.

## Pittsburgh

The vibrant ten-block district, known as the "Golden Triangle," at the heart of downtown **PITTSBURGH** stands at the confluence of the Monongahela, Allegheny and Ohio rivers, once bitterly fought over as the gateway to the West. The French built Fort Duquesne on the site in 1754, only for it to be destroyed four years later by the British, who replaced it with **Fort Pitt**. Industry began with the development of iron foundries in the early 1800s, and by the time of the Civil War Pittsburgh was producing half of the

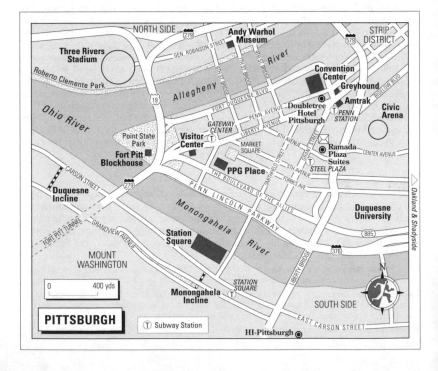

iron and one third of the glass in the US. Soon after, Pittsburgh became the world's leading producer of steel, thanks to the vigorous expansion programs of **Andrew Carnegie**, who, by 1870, was the richest man in the world. Present-day Pittsburgh is dotted with his cultural bequests, along with those of other rich forefathers including the Mellon bankers, the Frick coal merchants and the Heinz food company.

Though saddled with a Victorian reputation for dirt and pollution, the city has been transformed by two "renaissances" since the 1950s. The first face-lift involved large-scale demolition of abandoned steel mills, freeing up much of the downtown water-front, but all-out yuppification has been kept in check by the student population and the small-town feel of the older ethnic neighborhoods to the north and south. Pittsburgh today is one of America's best-looking and most liveable cities; resilience and enthusiasm rather than coal fumes fill the air, and sleek architecture and green parks supplant smokestacks and slums. The **Andy Warhol Museum**, opened in 1994, has further bolstered its image as a destination city.

Each of Pittsburgh's close-knit neighborhoods – the **South Side** and **Mount Washington**, across the Monongahela River from the **Golden Triangle** downtown, the **North Side** across the Allegheny River, and **Oakland**, the university area in the east – attests in its own way to the city's history and its resurgence. Easily accessible from each other, they retain individual identities while remaining part of a proud whole.

## Arrival, information and getting around

Greyhound pulls in at Eleventh Street and Liberty Avenue downtown, across from Amtrak. From the modern, efficient **Pittsburgh International Airport** (☎412/472-3500), fifteen miles west, Airlines Transportation (☎412/471-8900) runs half-hourly **shuttles** downtown (daily 5am–10pm; $12 one-way, $20 round-trip) and to Oakland (daily 7am–8pm; $12.50 one-way, $21 round-trip). Pittsburgh has two main **visitor centers**: downtown on Liberty Avenue, adjacent to the Gateway Center (Mon–Fri 9.30am–5pm, Sat & Sun 9.30am–3pm; ☎412/281-9222), and in Oakland at Forbes Avenue on the University of Pittsburgh campus behind the Cathedral of Learning (Mon 9am–4pm, Tues–Sun 10am–4pm; ☎412/624-4660). The main **post office** is at Seventh and Grant (Mon–Fri 7am–6pm, Sat 7am–2.30pm; ☎412/642-4472; zip code 15230).

Though Pittsburgh is a city of distinct districts, **transportation** between them is simple. **Buses** through town ($1.25), the Monongahela trolley incline to Mount Washington (daily until late; $1) and a small "T" **subway** system (free downtown, 75¢ to cross the river to the South Side) are all run by PAT (☎412/442-2000 or 255-1356). Useful routes run to Oakland and Shady Side along the **East Busway**, avoiding the traffic-clogged city streets. For **taxis**, call Yellow Cab (☎412/665-8100).

## Accommodation

Pittsburgh's **hotels** are usually pricey, although weekend packages at luxury downtown hotels can bring rates down to under $100. **Oakland** has a couple of reasonably priced business hotels and some student accommodation, and the Pittsburgh B&B Registry, 2190 Ben Franklin Drive (☎412/367-8080), has details of rooms from $50.

**Best Western University Center Hotel**, 3401 Blvd of the Allies (☎412/683-6100). Standard motel rooms, but one of the best deals in Oakland. ④.

**Carnegie-Mellon University**, 1060 Morewood St (☎412/268-2939). College dorm rooms in Oakland, available during the summer for $25, with a $5 reduction for students. Office hours 8am–5pm. ①.

**Doubletree Hotel Pittsburgh**, 1000 Penn Ave (☎412/281-3700). Flashy downtown tower with pool and gym. ⑦.

**Hampton Inn**, 3315 Hamlet St, Oakland (☎412/681-1000). Large continental self-service breakfast bar and free van shuttle to downtown and surrounding areas. ⑤.

**HI-Pittsburgh**, 830 Arlington Ave (☎412/431-1267). Sixty beds ($14–16) in a new hostel housed in a former bank vault on the South Side close to Union Station. ①.

**The Priory–A City Inn**, 614 Pressley St (☎412/231-3338). Recently restored 1880s inn, originally built to house traveling Benedictine monks and now offering North Side's nicest B&B. ⑤/⑥.

**Ramada Plaza Suites**, One Bigelow Square (☎412/281-5800). Convenient downtown suites with kitchens. ⑥.

## Downtown: the Golden Triangle

The *New York Times* once described Pittsburgh as "the only city with an entrance," and the view of the **Golden Triangle** skyline on emerging from the tunnel on the Fort Pitt Bridge is undeniably breathtaking. Surrounded by water and fronted with a huge fountain, Pittsburgh's downtown pays tribute to both its coal-grimed past and sunny future. In the core of the original city, the Triangle's imaginative contemporary architecture stands next to Gothic churches and redbrick warehouses. Philip Johnson's magnificent postmodern concoction, the black-glass Gothic **PPG Place** complex, looms incongruously over the old **Market Square**, lined with historic restaurants and shops. More recent history is apparent on the faded buildings along Liberty Avenue, with 1940s and 1950s fronts left in peace during successive face-lifts.

**Point State Park**, at the peak of the Triangle, is where it all began, the site of five different forts during the French and Indian War. This popular gathering area has a 150ft fountain with a pool, as well as great views of port activity and across to the colorful old buildings on verdant Mount Washington. The park, a great place to view sunsets and an excellent venue for the city's outdoor festivals, contains the 1764 **Fort Pitt Blockhouse**, the city's oldest structure, a lookout of sandstone and rough brick.

Northeast of downtown along Penn Avenue, the **Strip District** is an anarchic early-morning market with wholesale outlets and fresh produce stalls, popular with bargain hunters and good for cheap breakfasts; it's also a place to head for at night. Down by the river is a growing entertainment complex, with restaurants, bars, a marina and a floating boardwalk. The new seven-floor **Senator John Heinz Regional History Center**, at 1212 Smallman St (daily 10am–5pm; $6; ☎412/454-6000), does a good job of telling the city's story, paying particular attention to immigrants of various eras.

## South Side

In the nineteenth century, 400ft **Mount Washington**, across the Monongahela River, was the site of most of the city's coal mines. No longer dominated by belching steel mills and industry, the South Side, banked by the green "mountain," is an area of many churches, colorful houses nestling on steep hills, and old neighborhoods. These days only two survive of the twelve cable cars which, at the height of steel production, used to carry coal up the trolley inclines. The 1877 **Duquesne Incline**, from 1197 W Carson St to 1220 Grandview Ave, is the most interesting for its small **museum** of Pittsburgh history in the waiting room at the top: old photos of the city show workers struggling blindly through the streets in pitch-black midday smog (daily 7am–12.45pm; $1). The outdoor observation platform is a prime spot for **views** over the Golden Triangle to the hills on the horizon; the prospect is absolutely awesome after dark. Not surprisingly, many (expensive) bars and restaurants here take advantage of the vista.

The best way to get to the South Side is across the 1883 blue-and-cream **Smithfield Street Bridge**, the oldest of fifteen downtown bridges and the most unusual-looking, thanks to its elliptical "fisheye" truss. Just to the west of the bridge stands redbrick **Station Square**, a complex of renovated railroad warehouses filled with restaurants and shops. Its showpiece is the beautiful stained glass and marble of the *Grand Concourse* seafood restaurant (see Eating p.157), filling the huge waiting room of the old Pittsburgh and Lake Erie train station.

Along the banks of the Monongahela at the foot of Mount Washington, East Carson Street is the main drag of the lively mixed residential and commercial **South Side**, where a longstanding community of Polish and Ukrainian steelworkers has gradually absorbed an offbeat mix of cafes, bars and bookstores. Onion-domed churches stand alongside thrift stores and galleries, and the narrow backstreets are lined by brick rowhouses. This is also one of Pittsburgh's prime **nightlife** centers.

## North Side

The star attraction on the **North Side**, annexed by Pittsburgh only in 1907, is undoubtedly the **Andy Warhol Museum**, 117 Sandusky St, just over the Seventh Street Bridge from downtown, which documents the life and work of Pittsburgh's most celebrated son over eight floors of a spacious Victorian warehouse (Wed & Sun 11am–6pm, Thurs–Sat 11am–8pm; $6, students and children $4).

Born in Pittsburgh in 1928, Andy Warhol (born Andrew Warhola, the youngest son of working-class Carpatho-Rusyn immigrants) moved to New York at the age of 21, after graduating from the Carnegie-Mellon University. By the end of the 1950s, he was one of the most successful commercial artists in the nation, before turning his attention to fine and Pop arts. During the early 1960s he started shooting 16mm films – *Empire*, *Chelsea Girls* and *Lonesome Cowboys* – and developed the "Exploding Plastic Inevitable" multimedia show, featuring erotic dancers and music by the Velvet Underground, whom he managed. After founding *Interview* magazine in 1969, Warhol became transfixed with the rich and famous and, up until his death in 1987, was perhaps best known for his celebrity portraits and his appearances at society events.

Although the majority of Warhol's most famous pieces are in the hands of private collectors, the museum boasts an impressive selection of work, with over five hundred items on display at any one time, including Pop Art (*Campbell's Soup Cans*) and portraiture (Elvis, Marilyn, Jackie Kennedy). It pays equal attention to archival material, and chronological self-guided tours give a good idea of Warhol's artistic development and his eventful lifestyle. A cinema shows two films or videos daily, one of which is usually a Warhol production. There's an excellent, informative Archives Study Department, and a popular free **Weekend Factory** (call ☎412/237-8300 for details), where Warhol's techniques are explained and visitors can have a go themselves. There's also a well-stocked gift shop and a good cafe.

Elsewhere on the North Side, revitalization centers around the intriguingly named **Mexican War Streets** on the northern edge of Allegheny Commons. In this unevenly restored, tree-lined area of nineteenth-century gray-brick and limestone terraces, old families, descendants of German and Scandinavian immigrants, live in an uneasy truce alongside young professionals. The excellent and highly unusual **Mattress Factory**, 500 Sampsonia Way (Tues–Sat 10am–5pm, Sun 1–5pm, closed Aug; ☎412/231-3169; $4, free on Thurs), has contemporary installations by top mixed-media artists, and is a must on any visit to the city. The **National Aviary**, Allegheny Commons West (daily 9am–4.30pm; $4; ☎412/323-7235), is a huge indoor bird sanctuary with over three hundred species, including foul-mouthed parrots, in free flight under a showpiece 30ft glass dome.

The **USS Requin**, a 1945 submarine, bobs on the shores of the Allegheny River (daily 10am–5pm; $4), outside the huge state-of-the-art **Carnegie Science Center**, 1 Allegheny Ave, most of whose exhibits are aimed at children (daily 10am–5pm, Sat till 9pm; ☎412/237-3400; $6.50, children $4). One, "The Works," explores Pittsburgh's past by means of a working foundry, and it holds such wonders as the world's largest cockroach (from Florida). The Center also contains an impressive OMNIMAX theater and a planetarium; combination tickets are available ($10 for exhibits and one attraction; $12 for all). **Three Rivers Stadium**, next to the Science Center, is home to the Pittsburgh Pirates baseball and Steelers football teams, and open for hour-long "behind the scenes" tours when no games are scheduled; if you come for a game, be sure to climb up to the top levels for a grand panorama of downtown Pittsburgh. However, the stadium's future is in doubt as both clubs currently want to move to new premises.

## Oakland and the East Side

**Oakland**, Pittsburgh's university area (dotted with the mansions of wealthy industrialists), today houses a strong mixture of Italian and Greek families. Sights concentrate around the campuses of **Carnegie-Mellon University** and the **University of Pittsburgh** (always known as "Pitt"). The 42-story Gothic-revival **Cathedral of Learning**, Fifth Avenue at Bigelow Boulevard, called by Frank Lloyd Wright "the world's largest Keep Off the Grass sign," is a university building with a difference: over twenty classrooms are furnished with antiques and specially crafted items donated by the city's different ethnic groups, from Lithuanian through Chinese to Irish. These beautiful rooms, far more interesting than they may sound, have been used by students since the 1930s; all are open to the public except the exotic Syria-Lebanon room and the Early American room, complete with trap door and secret passage, which are shown on ninety-minute **guided tours** only (Mon–Fri 9am–3pm, Sat 9.30am–3pm, Sun 11am–4.30pm; $2). Alternatively, you can do your own tape-recorded tour (also $2) or follow the useful booklet ($1.50). Also in the Cathedral of Learning is the French Gothic **Heinz Memorial Chapel**, notable for its long, skinny, stained-glass windows.

Across from the cathedral at 4400 Forbes Ave, the **Carnegie** cultural complex holds two great museums – the **Museum of Natural History**, famed for its extensive dinosaur relics and sparkling gems, and the **Museum of Art**, with Impressionist, Post-Impressionist and American regional art, as well as a really excellent modern collection (Mon–Sat 10am–5pm, Sun 1–5pm, closed Mon Sept–June; $6, students $4). Schenley Park nearby includes the colorful flower gardens of **Phipps Conservatory** (Tues–Sun 9am–5pm, extended hours during shows; $3).

If you're coming to the East Side from downtown, be sure to avoid the area along Center Avenue known as "The Hill"; this is one of Pittsburgh's toughest districts, especially after dark. Many cab drivers avoid it, but as it neighbors the college precincts tourists can easily stumble into it.

**Shady Side**, on the eastern fringes of Oakland, is an upmarket residential district with a villagey feel, especially along Walnut Street. The **Pittsburgh Center for the Arts**, at 6300 Fifth Ave in Mellon Park, showcases innovative Pittsburgh art in various media (Mon–Sat 10am–5.30pm, Sun noon–5pm; free).

Further east, the small **Frick Art Museum**, 7227 Reynolds St (Tues–Sat 10am–5.30pm, Sun noon–6pm; free), shows Italian, Flemish and French art from the fifteenth to the nineteenth century; its collection of decorative art includes two of Marie Antoinette's chairs. On the same grounds, **Clayton** is a mansion furnished exactly as it was when industrialist Henry Clay Frick lived there. Obligatory guided **tours** ($5) walk you around the house, pointing out the various late-Victorian decorative touches, as well as the bed where Frick recovered after being stabbed by an anarchist during the bitter Homestead Steel Strike. Frick and most of his family are buried, under tons of protective concrete and steel, just south of the family home, on the highest hill in **Homestead Cemetery**, which also holds the tombs of H J Heinz (of the ketchup and baked beans fortune) and sundry Mellons.

## Eating

**Eating** downtown can prove expensive, but there's a growing range of places in the adjacent **Strip** district and good neighborhood Italian and Eastern European places along and around **Carson Street** on the South Side. Station Square and Mount Washington cater to a more upmarket crowd, while **Oakland** is, as you might expect, home to an array of cheap student hangouts. A little further out, **Shady Side** has a number of good mid-priced places.

**Grand Concourse**, 1 Station Square (☎412/261-1717). Pricey and plush seafood restaurant in a gorgeous setting inside the Station Square complex.

**Grandview Saloon**, 1212 Grandview Ave (☎412/431-1400). Cheap, relaxed Mount Washington restaurant, usually packed with a young crowd enjoying huge plates of pasta. Arrive early for a deck table with a view.

**India Garden**, 328 Atwood St (☎412/682-3000). Pittsburgh's favorite Indian restaurant, offering solid North Indian cooking and great lunch buffet.

**Java River Kaffe**, 14th and Bingham (☎412/481-9077). Unpretentious bistro with a great line in huge, healthy sandwiches and entrees. Dozens of coffees and teas but no alcohol.

**Kaya**, 2000 Smallman St (☎412/261-6565). Stylish Caribbean restaurant in the Strip district with a good vegetarian selection. Huge range of beers, rums and other spirits.

**Mad Mex**, 370 Atwood St (☎412/681-5656). Lively Southwestern cafe with good vegetarian options (like spicy spinach burritos) and many microbrewed ales. Half-price food 11pm–1am.

**Mallorca**, 2228 E Carson St (☎412/488-1818). Excellent paella and Mediterranean dishes in a smart setting on South Side.

**Papa J's Mercato**, 1900 Smallman St (☎412/261-7272). A market-cum-food court in the Strip that's a fun way of doing lunch. Over 20 vendors, selling ethnic, mostly Mediterranean food.

**Penn Brewery**, Troy Hill and Vinial (☎412/237-9402). On the North Side, this is Pittsburgh's longest-established brewpub, serving decent German food.

**Seventh Street Grille**, 130 7th St, Century Building (☎412/338-0303). Excellent Californian- and Italian-influenced menus strong on pasta and seafood. Very popular. Open 11am–1am.

**Union Grille**, 413 Craig St (☎412/683-1450). Dark pub and restaurant near the Carnegie Cultural Center in Oakland.

## Nightlife and entertainment

With its recent cultural resurgence, Pittsburgh's **nightlife** offers rich pickings in everything from the classics to jazz and alternative rock. The nationally regarded City Theater, 57 S 13th St (☎412/431-4900), puts on groundbreaking productions in a converted South Side church; TIX booth, 209 Ninth St (☎412/580-1313), offers half-price theater and concert **tickets** on the day. The widely traveled Pittsburgh Symphony Orchestra, under the baton of Lorin Maazel, plays at the Heinz Hall, 600 Pennsylvania Ave (☎412/392-4900). The city's ballet, dance and opera companies perform at the downtown Benedum Center for the Performing Arts, 719 Liberty Ave (☎412/456-2600). *In Pittsburgh*, a free news weekly, has extensive **listings**, as does the *City Paper*.

**Balcony**, 5520 Walnut St (☎412/687-0110). Shady Side jazz club. No cover, excellent food.

**Beehive Coffeehouse**, 3807 Forbes Ave (☎412/488-HIVE). Oakland's liveliest late-night coffeehouse, drawing a young, artsy-alternative crowd. Also at 1327 E Carson St on the South Side.

**Bloomfield Bridge Tavern**, 4412 Liberty Ave (☎412/682-8611). Super-friendly Polish local just over the bridge from Oakland. Live music Thurs–Sat, from punk to polka, and there's also food: mostly greasy stuff, though the potato pancakes are great when washed down with vodka.

**Buffalo Blues**, 216 S Highland Ave (☎412/36-BLUES). Shady Side blues club with cheap food and drink. Showtimes at 9.30pm, 11pm and 12.30am.

**Dee's**, 1314 Carson St (☎412/431-5400). South Side institution; great jukebox, pool, darts and a lively crowd.

**Heaven**, 107 6th St (☎412/338-2727). Self-consciously upscale cocktail bar and nightclub downtown.

**Metropol**, 1600 Smallman St (☎412/261-4512). Huge, popular Strip district dance club (mainly techno and industrial) that also promotes some live rock. Next door to *Rosebud* (see overleaf).

**Nick's Fat City**, 1601 E Carson St (☎412/481-6880). Popular South Side pool bar with (usually) good live bands. Happy hour 10pm–midnight.

**Rosebud,** 1650 Smallman St (☎412/261-2221). Venue and cafe putting on acoustic, rockabilly and Americana acts.

# NEW JERSEY

The long, skinny state of **NEW JERSEY**, squashed between Philadelphia and New York on the Atlantic coast, suffers a severe image problem. Most travelers only see "the Garden State" (so called for the rich market garden territory at the state's heart) from the stupendously ugly New Jersey Turnpike toll road, which, heavy with truck traffic, cuts through a landscape of gray smokestacks and industrial estates. Even the songs of **Bruce Springsteen**, Asbury Park's golden boy, paint his home state as a gritty **urban wasteland** of empty lots, gray highways, lost dreams and blue-collar tragedy. In reality, the majority of the refineries and factories hug a mere fifteen-mile-wide swath along the turnpike, but bleak cities like **Newark**, home to the major airport, and **Trenton**, the capital, do little to improve the look of the place.

The Dutch, who had snatched New Jersey from the peaceful Lenni Lenape Indians, turned the land over to the English in the 1660s. During the **Revolution** a battle was fought at **Princeton**, and George Washington spent two bleak winters at **Morristown**. When the **Civil War** came, the state's obvious industrial future ensured that, despite its border location along the Mason–Dixon line, it fought with the Union.

There's more to New Jersey than factories and pollution. Both Thomas Paine and Walt Whitman wrote of their years here with fond nostalgia; the **northwest corner** near the **Delaware Water Gap** is traced with picturesque lakes, streams and woodlands, while the **Atlantic shore** offers many bustling resorts.

## Getting around New Jersey

With a **car**, New Jersey is easily accessible from New York City, via I-95, while the **New Jersey Turnpike** (a $4 toll road) sweeps from the northeast down to Philadelphia. The **Garden State Parkway** runs parallel to the Atlantic from New York to Cape May (with a 35¢ toll every twenty miles), and gives easy access to the shoreline resorts. One nice route in the north of the state is US-29, from Trenton along the Delaware River. Driving soon becomes unpleasureable, though, as New Jersey must have the worst and most confusing set of roadsigns in the States.

**Newark International Airport** (☎973/961-6000) is the fastest-growing gateway to the US, served by all the major international carriers and popular for its convenient access to Manhattan (a 30min bus ride away) rather than for being in New Jersey.

Numerous Amtrak **trains** pass through Newark, Princeton and Trenton, en route between Philadelphia, New York and Washington DC. There's also a service that links Philadelphia and Atlantic City. Greyhound covers most of the state, while New Jersey Transit (☎973/762-5100 or 1-800/772-2222) also provides a good train and bus service, extending to Philadelphia and New York as well as out to the coast. New Jersey's south coast is connected to Delaware by the Cape May–Lewes **ferry** (in Cape May ☎609/886-1725; in Lewes ☎302/645-6313).

# Inland New Jersey

Traveling west on the interstates from the shore or from New York City, visitors see the New Jersey of popular imagination: heavily industrialized, a cultural and visual desert. **Newark**, the state's largest city, is perhaps the nation's drabbest, redeemed only by its efficient airport, new performing arts center, and views over the Hudson to the Statue of Liberty (which is, incidentally, in New Jersey waters). Northwest of Newark, on

I-287, **Morristown**, where Washington spent two harsh winters, is now a national historic park. **Trenton**, the state capital, sits on the Delaware River at the border with Pennsylvania, something of a national joke for its motto "Trenton makes, the world takes." Nearby **Princeton**, an Ivy League town that makes a pretty if limited stopoff, is one place worth visiting.

## Paterson

Though in some ways it's the sort of New Jersey place most people do their best to avoid, **PATERSON** is perhaps the state's most significant city. Though it last made the news in the 1970s, when Bob Dylan campaigned against the trumped-up murder conviction of local boxer **Rubin "Hurricane" Carter**, its historic importance dates back to Revolutionary times, when Alexander Hamilton established the young nation's largest manufacturing complex here in 1791, taking advantage of the immense waterpower of the 70ft **Great Falls** of the Passaic River. For 150 years Paterson was at the forefront of American **industry**, its mills responsible for the first Colt revolvers, as well as silk fabrics, its millworkers on the front lines of the American Labor movement.

While most of the old looms have been silent since the 1950s, the millraces and buildings survive intact awaiting creative reuse. An expanding **museum** (Tues–Fri 10am–4pm, Sat & Sun 12.30–4.30pm; $2) is housed inside the renovated Rogers Locomotive factory at Market and Spruce, but the best first stop is the **Great Falls Visitor Center**, a block away at 65 McBride Ave (Mon–Fri 9am–4pm, Sun noon–4pm; ☎201/279-9587), for a wealth of maps and background information. Don't miss the **waterfalls** themselves, across the street; after a good rain they roar like a mini-Niagara.

Like many old mill towns, Paterson now suffers from serious decay, poverty and unemployment, so it's not really a place to linger. Still, it's easy to reach on a day-trip: regular **buses** run from New York's Port Authority building (see p.62); if you're driving, take the Grand Street exit off the I-80 freeway. Once here, there are a couple of good **bars** (such as the *Question Mark* on Van Houten and Cianci, where journalist and labor activist John Reed used to drink) and **cafes** in the historic district where you can get a feel for Paterson's proudly blue-collar character.

## Princeton

Self-satisfied **PRINCETON**, on US-206 eleven miles north of Trenton, is home to the Ivy League **Princeton University** – the nation's fourth oldest, which broke away from the overly religious Yale in 1756. It began its days inauspiciously as Stony Brook, and then in 1724 as Princes Town, a coach stop between New York and Philadelphia. In January 1777, a week after Washington's triumph against the British at Trenton, the **Battle of Princeton** occurred southwest of town. This victory, a turning point in the Revolutionary effort, bolstered the morale of Washington's troops before their long winter encampment at Morristown to the north. After the war, in 1783, the **Continental Congress**, fearful of potential attack from incensed unpaid veterans in Philadelphia, met here for four months; the leafy, well-kept town was then left in peace to follow its academic pursuits. Graduates of the university include actor James Stewart, jazz-age writer F Scott Fitzgerald, and presidents Wilson and Madison. Today, there is little to do in this sleepy place other than tour the university and see the historic sites.

### Arrival, information and getting around

A shuttle bus, the Princeton Airporter, makes the run from Newark (1hr 30min) and JFK (2hr 40min) airports to town (daily 7am–10pm; ☎609/587-6600). The in-town train terminal, on campus at University Place, a block north of Alexander Road, is connected by SEPTA shuttles (☎215/580-7800) to Princeton Junction, three miles south, where both Amtrak and New Jersey Transit stop on their New York–Philadelphia runs. Suburban Transit **buses** (☎201/249-1100) from New York stop every thirty minutes at Nassau Street.

**Information** is available from Stanhope Hall at the university (Mon–Fri 8.30am–4.30pm; ☎609/258-3600) or from the **CVB**, 20 Nassau St (☎609/683-1760). The **Historical Society museum**, 158 Nassau St (Tues–Sun noon–4pm; ☎609/921-6748), organizes **walking tours** through town (Sun 2pm; $3), and also provides **maps** so you can do it yourself.

## The Town and the University

**Mercer Street**, the long road that sweeps southwest past the university campus to Nassau Street, is lined with elegant colonial houses, graced with shutters, columns and wrought-iron fences. The **Princeton Battlefield State Park**, a mile out, includes the **Thomas Clarke House**, 500 Mercer St, a Quaker farmhouse that served as a hospital during the battle (Wed–Sat 10am–noon & 1–4pm, Sun 1–4pm). The simple house at 112 Mercer St, back towards town, is where **Albert Einstein** lived while teaching at the Institute of Advanced Study (however, it is not open to the public).

Princeton University's tranquil and shaded campus is a beautiful place for a stroll. Just inside the main gates on Nassau Street, **Nassau Hall** (Mon–Fri 2–5pm, Sat 9am–5pm, Sun 1–5pm; free) was, when constructed in 1756, the largest stone building in the nation; its 26-inch-thick walls (now patterned with plaques and patches of ivy placed by graduating classes) withstood American and British fire during the Revolution. It was also the seat of government during Princeton's brief spell as national capital. The 1925 **chapel**, based on Kings College Cambridge, has stained-glass windows showing scenes from works by Dante, Shakespeare and Milton, as well as the Bible, and the Prospect Gardens, a flowerbed in the shape of the university emblem, are a blaze of orange in summer. In the middle of the campus, fronted by the Picasso sculpture *Head of a Woman*, the **University Art Museum**, not included on the standard tours, is well worth a look for its collection from the Renaissance to the present, including Modigliani, Van Gogh and Warhol, and Chinese and pre-Columbian art (Tues–Sat 10am–5pm, Sun 1–5pm; tours Sat 2pm, museum talks Fri 12.30pm & Sun 3pm; ☎609/452-3787; free).

While Princeton has found itself acting as a sanctuary and gathering place for exiled members of China's democracy movement since the **Tiananmen Square** massacre of 1989, a substantial number of those who visit are disarmingly conservative prospective students and their proud parents, soaking up the tales of old-boy pranks and superstitions (for example, that no student should pass through the main gates for fear of being tarnished by the ugly outside world) that prop up the Ivy League tradition. The student-led **tours** may be complacent, but they are free; they leave from the rear of the yellow **Maclean House** at 73 Nassau St (Mon–Sat 10am, 11am, 1.30pm & 3.30pm, Sun 1.30pm & 3.30pm; ☎609/258-3603).

## Accommodation, eating and drinking

The only **hotel** in the center of Princeton is the pompous, ersatz-colonial *Nassau Inn* on Palmer Square (☎609/921-7500; ⑦). Budget **motels** can be found along US-1 and in the suburb of **Lawrenceville** a few miles south of town; there's the functional *Sleep-e-Hollow*, 3000 US-1 (☎609/896-0900; ②), and the *McIntosh Inn* (☎609/896-2544; ③), by the Quaker Bridge Mall on US-1, along with the more relaxing *Best Western Palmer Inn*, 3499 US-1 at Alexander Road (☎609/452-2500; ⑤).

There's cheap diner-type **food** along Witherspoon Street: the *Tempting Tiger* at no. 14 (☎609/924-0644) serves vegetarian salads, soups and sandwiches, accompanied by classical music, from around $4; for a more upmarket feast, the popular *Annex*, 128 Nassau St, serves quality Italian dinners by candlelight from $7. *Mediterra* at 29 Hulfish St (☎609/252-9680) is an upscale Mediterranean restaurant with a welcoming atmosphere and well-prepared food. **Nightlife** is limited, especially out of term time, but the *Tap Room* bar downstairs at the *Nassau Inn* is usually full of ancient revelers drinking, reminiscing and enjoying live jazz.

# New Jersey shore

New Jersey's Atlantic coast, a 130-mile stretch of almost uninterrupted **resorts** – some rowdy, many pitifully run-down and faded, a few undeveloped and peaceful – has long been reliant on farming and tourism. No profitable ports were established, nor did short-lived attempts at whaling come to anything. In the late 1980s the whole coastline suffered severe and well-publicized pollution from ocean dumping, but today the beaches, if occasionally somewhat crowded, are safe and clean: sandy, broad and lined by characteristic wooden **boardwalks**, some of which, in an attempt to maintain their condition, charge admission during the summer. The casinos of the tackily surreal **Atlantic City** are the most brazenly obvious attraction, with the restorative **Spring Lake** and historic Victorian **Cape May** offering quieter charms.

## Spring Lake and Asbury Park

**SPRING LAKE**, about twenty miles down the Jersey coast, is one of the smallest, most uncommercial communities on the shore, a gentle respite on the road south to Atlantic City. Tourism in this elegant Victorian resort evolved slowly, without the booms, crises, resurgence and depressions of other seaside towns – partly due to the strict zoning laws prohibiting new building; and stressed-out city dwellers coming here to get away from it all. You can walk the totally undeveloped two-mile **boardwalk** and watch the crashing ocean from battered gazebos, swim and bask on the white beaches (in summer, compulsory beach tags cost $3.50 per day, but most guesthouses provide them free) or sit in the shade by the town's namesake, **Spring Lake** itself. Wooden footbridges, swans and geese, and the grand St Catherine's Catholic Church on the banks of the lake give it the feel of a country village. For the moment, what little activity there is centers on the upmarket shops of Third Avenue.

Bruce **Springsteen** fans can use the town as a base for visiting nearby **ASBURY PARK**, a decaying old seaside town where The Boss lived for many years and played his first gigs. Almost nothing remains of the carousels and seaside arcades that Springsteen wrote about on early albums such as his debut *Greetings from Asbury Park*; the sole survivor is Madame Marie's fortune-telling salon, which still stands amid the rubble and half-completed condominium developments that line the boardwalk. Also of interest is the *Stone Pony*, 913 Ocean Ave, where Springsteen played dozens of times in the mid-1970s and to which he returned even after becoming famous, for impromptu jam sessions and, in 1999, for his most recent reunion tour with the E Street Band.

### Practicalities

Spring Lake is accessible by US-34 from the New Jersey Turnpike, and served by New Jersey Transit from New York. The Spring Lake Hotel and Guest House Association (☎732/449-1332) can help find lodging, especially on summer weekends. There are no cheap **motels**, and **B&Bs** can be expensive. The easygoing *Sea Crest by the Sea*, 19 Tuttle Ave (☎732/449-9031; ⑦), is an 1885 inn with rooms furnished individually on quirky themes, and an excellent all-you-can-eat home-cooked breakfast. *Ashling*

*Cottage*, 106 Sussex Ave (☎732/449-3553; closed Jan–March; ⑤), overlooks the lake, while the *Carriage House*, 208 Jersey Ave (☎732/449-1332; ④), is slightly less expensive. Adjacent to Asbury Park, in the much more attractive Victorian resort of **OCEAN GROVE**, friendly *Lillagaard B&B*, 5 Abbot Ave (☎732/774-4049; ⑤), is right on the beach. Most of Spring Lake's **restaurants** are in the elegant Victorian hotels along the seafront, and can be pricey. The **North Pavilion** on the boardwalk sells cheap breakfasts and snacks, but there are no fast-food stands along the walk itself. *Who's On Third*, 1300 Third Ave (☎732/449-4233), is a no-nonsense cafe serving breakfast from $2 and lunch from $4. *The Beach House*, 901 Ocean Ave (☎732/449-9646), is more upmarket, with screened-in veranda seating and healthy lunches from $5, dinner from $16. For a blowout, the *Sandpiper*, 7 Atlantic Ave (☎732/449-6060), serves superb fresh fish and seafood in elegant, candlelit surroundings. Dinner costs around $20; bring your own bottle.

# Atlantic City

*What they wanted was Monte Carlo. They didn't want Las Vegas.*
*What they got was Las Vegas. We always knew that they would get Las Vegas.*
Stuart Mendelson, *Philadelphia Journal*, 1978.

**ATLANTIC CITY**, on Absecon Island just off the midpoint of the Jersey shoreline, has been a tourist magnet since 1854, when Philadelphia speculators created it as a rail terminal resort. In 1909, at the peak of the seaside town's popularity, Baedeker wrote "there is something colossal about its vulgarity" – a quality which it sustains today, even while beset by bankruptcy and decay. The real-life model for the board game **Monopoly**, it has an impressive popular cultural history, boasting the nation's first **Boardwalk** (1870), the first color **postcards** (1893), the world's first **Big Wheel** (1869) and the first **Miss America Beauty Pageant** (cunningly devised to extend the tourist season in 1921, and still held here yearly). During Prohibition and the Depression, Atlantic City was a center for rum-running, packed with speakeasies and illegal gambling dens. Thereafter, in the face of increasing competition from Florida, it slipped into apparently terminal decline, until desperate city officials decided in 1976 to open up the decrepit resort to legal **gambling**.

The monster **casinos** that replaced the grand old hotels dominate not just the Boardwalk and the skyline, but the whole culture of the city. Their tackiness puts the lie to the would-be glamorous image; pace Stuart Mendelson, Atlantic City didn't even quite "get" Las Vegas. The place is not so much limousines and roulette as hamburgers and slot machines. As eighty percent of Atlantic City's millions of visitors are day-trippers, there's definitely more glitz than glamour, and the neglected areas inland from the casinos betray the fact that only a very few property developers have benefited from the influx of cash.

## Arrival, information and getting around

Traveling to Atlantic City by bus can be a real money-spinner; casino-sponsored **buses** from New York, Philadelphia and other points along the coast give away vouchers exchangeable for cash and free meals to a value well above the fare. It's hoped that you will spend all this money and more in the casinos, but you can easily cash it and leave. The bus terminal (☎609/347-5413) at Arctic and Arkansas avenues is served by Greyhound and New Jersey Transit (☎973/762-5100 or 1-800/772-3606).

Amtrak runs express **trains** from New York, Philadelphia, Washington and Baltimore, and New Jersey Transit trains (☎1-800/772-3606; $6 one-way, $12 round-trip) run between Atlantic City and Philadelphia, from 1 Atlantic City Expressway (☎344-9013). **Atlantic City International Airport** is thirteen miles from downtown in

Pleasantville (☎609/645-8882); the smaller Bader Field Airport (☎609/345-6402), in the center of town, has connections to Boston, Baltimore, Philadelphia and Pittsburgh. For maps and information, head for the **CVB**, 2314 Pacific Ave (Mon–Fri 9am–5pm; ☎609/348-7100 or 1-888/228-4748), or the **visitor information desk** in the old Convention Hall on the Boardwalk between Florida and Mississippi avenues (daily 10am–7pm; ☎609/348-7044).

Atlantic City is easy to **walk** around, although it is unwise to stray further from the five-mile Boardwalk along the ocean than the parallel Pacific, Atlantic and Arctic avenues. Ventnor and Margate, to the south on Absecon Island, are served by **buses** along Atlantic Avenue. Jitneys (☎609/344-8642) offers a 24-hour minibus service the length of Pacific Avenue, the #1 route traveling as far as Ventnor ($1).

Various **bike rental** stands along the Boardwalk charge about $3 per hour, although cycling is only permitted from 6am until 10am in the summer.

## Accommodation

Atlantic City is not Vegas – there's no chance of getting a $40 room at one of the casinos. The already high **accommodation** rates rise at weekends and in summer, though if you book ahead and business is slow many places will offer discounted **package deals**, with $200 suites going for under half-price. Otherwise room prices at the casinos are astronomical, but **motels** line Pacific and Atlantic avenues behind the Boardwalk, and things are cheaper in quiet Ocean City, a family resort to the south. The massive new **Convention Center** above the train terminal offers over 12,000 hotel rooms: bland but convenient.

**The Dunes Motel**, 2819 Pacific Ave (☎609/344-5271 or 1-800/423-8858). Reasonable rooms near the Boardwalk. ④.

**Econolodge Boardwalk**, 117 S Kentucky Ave (☎609/344-9093 or 1-800/323-6410). Standard chain motel next to the Boardwalk and *Sands Casino*. ④.

**The Irish Pub**, 164 St James Place (☎609/344-9063). Basic rooms above one of the town's best bars. ②.

**Shamrock**, 133 St James Place (☎609/348-9832). Budget rooms; weekly rates from $200. ②.

**Showboat Casino**, on the Boardwalk at Delaware Ave (☎609/343-4000 or 1-800/621-0200). The most pleasant of the huge casino hotels, with luxury ocean-view rooms. ⑦.

**Trump Taj Mahal Casino Resort**, 1000 Boardwalk (☎609/449-1000 or 1-800/825-8786). Nothing terribly exciting, but the closest Atlantic City gets to the way-out theme casinos of Vegas (see box, overleaf). ⑦.

## The Town

Arriving by train, you'll be confronted by the monstrous **Convention Center**, which opened above the station in 1997, and houses a massive food court and standard mall shops, along with its meeting spaces and countless hotel rooms. Most of the hopeful new arrivals, however, head straight for the casinos, with an ample overspill flooding the Boardwalk and beach. Beyond the Boardwalk there is little to see in Atlantic City, although a quick walk around the eerily quiet slums of the South Inlet district makes a chilling contrast to the manic jollity a mere block away. This is not an area in which to linger for any length of time, or indeed at all at night – the **danger** is very real, though police have made considerable inroads over the past few years.

Atlantic City's wooden **Boardwalk** was originally built as a temporary walkway, raised above the beach so that vacationers could take a seaside stroll without treading sand into the grand hotels. Alongside the brash 99¢ shops and exotically named palm-readers, a few beautiful Victorian buildings that survived the wrecker's ball invoke past elegance, despite being dwarfed by the casinos and housing fast-food joints. Early in the morning, when the breezes from the ocean are at their most pleasant, the Boardwalk is peaceful, peopled only by keen cyclists and a few lost souls down on their luck.

The **Central Pier** offers all the fun of a fair, with rides, games and old-fashioned "guess your weight" challenges. A few blocks south, another pier has been remodeled into an ocean-liner-shaped shopping center. The small and faded **Arts Center and Historic Museum**, on the Garden Pier, at the quiet northern end of the Boardwalk, has a free collection of seaside memorabilia, postcards, photos and a special exhibit on Miss America, as well as traveling art shows. A block off the Boardwalk, where Pacific Avenue meets Rhode Island Avenue, and at the heart of some of the city's worst deprivation, the **Absecon Lighthouse** was active until 1933, but is now a small free marine museum, with separate entrance to the 167ft tower (June–Oct Thurs–Tues 10am–5pm, Nov–May Mon & Fri–Sun 10am–5pm; 50¢).

Atlantic City's **beach** is free, family filled and surprisingly clean considering its proximity to the Boardwalk. Beaches at neighboring **Ventnor**, a jitney ride away, are quieter, but charge users $3.50 per week. For the same fee, New Jersey's beautiful people pose on the beaches of **Margate**, three miles south of Atlantic City; all watched over by Lucy, the Margate Elephant at 9200 Atlantic Ave. A 65ft wood and tin Victorian oddity, Lucy was built as a seaside attraction in 1881 and used variously as a tavern and a hotel. Today her huge belly is filled with a **museum** of Atlantic City memorabilia, and photos and artifacts from her own history (mid-May to Oct daily 10am–9pm; rest of year Sat & Sun 10am–5pm; $2; ☎609/823-6473).

### Eating

One side-effect of Atlantic City's rabid commercialization is an abundance of **fast food**. The Boardwalk is lined with pizza, burger and sandwich joints, and the diners on

---

### THE CASINOS OF ATLANTIC CITY

Each of Atlantic City's dozen **casinos**, which also act as luxury hotels, conference centers and concert halls, has a slightly different personality, despite the apparent uniformity of vast, richly ornamented halls, slot machines, relentless flashing lights and incessant noise, chandeliers, mirrors, and a disorienting absence of clocks or windows. Apart from a quick flutter, the real pleasure here is in people-watching: from the frisky pensioners cashing in their chips to the shady-looking compulsive types lurking at the roulette wheel. All casinos are **open 24 hours** a day, though things get pretty quiet in the wee hours. Casino **restaurants** keep their own hours, and costumed waitresses serve drinks at the tables and will supply newcomers with rule books. Although officially jeans and T-shirts are frowned upon, in practice most of the punters are extremely **casual**, even after 6pm; during the day many people seem to have just wandered in off the sands. One rule that is never waived is the **age requirement**; you must be 21 to gamble and will be asked to show **ID**.

As time goes on, these overblown amusement arcades have become more and more outrageous in order to compete with each other. By far the most ostentatious (and "The Don" wouldn't have it any other way) is Donald Trump's Disneyesque **Taj Mahal**. Occupying nearly twenty acres and over forty stories high, with glittering minarets and onion domes, this gigantic piece of Far Eastern kitsch stands opposite the arcade-packed Steel Pier at the north end of the Boardwalk. It is one of the largest gambling casinos on earth, precariously tottering on the edge of bankruptcy. At the other end of the scale, the **Claridge**, Indiana Avenue and the Boardwalk, dubs itself "the friendly casino" and is smaller, darker and more downmarket than the others. **Sands**, next door at South Indiana Avenue, is a noisy and popular venue on a pink flamingo theme. Both these properties are slightly off the Boardwalk, accessible by a glass-covered slow-moving sidewalk with accompanying taped music from the various stars who have played Atlantic City. **Caesars**, Arkansas Avenue and the Boardwalk, has an uninspired Roman theme, with statues of Greek gods, marble columns and laurel wreaths at every turn.

Atlantic and Pacific avenues serve soul food and cheap breakfasts. All the large casinos boast several restaurants, ranging in price and menu, as well as all-you-can-eat **buffets**: the *Claridge* ($7) is the least expensive, while *Bally's Park Place* ($14) is slightly better and more extensive. Some of the casinos offer half-price buffets to "members" or "VIPs" – all you have to do to join is fill in a form and give some proof of address.

**Hunan Chinese Restaurant**, 2323 Atlantic Ave (☎609/348-5946). Reasonably priced Chinese food two blocks from the Boardwalk. Combination plates from $6.

**Los Amigos**, 1926 Atlantic Ave (☎609/344-2293). Mexican restaurant and bar, with good tortillas and enchilada meals from $7. Open until 6am.

**Planet Hollywood**, at *Caesars*, 2100 Pacific Ave on the Boardwalk (☎609/347-STAR). Decent burgers and salads at hyped-up prices in a hyped-up atmosphere.

**Tony's Little Italy**, S Carolina Ave and the Boardwalk. One of the better cheap and cheerful Boardwalk joints, with pizza and breakfast from $2.

**White House Sub Shop**, Mississippi and Arctic aves (☎609/345-8599). This bright and super-efficient sandwich bar is where Bill Cosby gets his subs when in town. Prices range from $3 for half a French loaf crammed with omelette, to $7 for a full steak sandwich.

## Entertainment and nightlife
Atlantic City sells itself as the fun nighttime city; but the **nightlife** centers on the casinos and Boardwalk amusements. Once you get bored with slot machines there is little else to do. Big-name entertainers perform regularly at the casinos, with tickets in the $20 range. Both the *Claridge* (☎609/340-3400) and the *Trop World Casino* (☎609/340-4000) have **comedy clubs** with shows from $10. For cheaper informal fun, good neighborhood **bars** include the friendly, dark-paneled *Irish Pub*, 164 St James Place (☎609/345-9613), which serves cheap food and often has live Irish music, and *McGuire's Pittsburgh Cafe*, 142 S Tennessee Ave (☎609/345-9607).

## Cape May
**CAPE MAY** was founded in 1620 by the Dutch Captain Mey, on the small hook at the very southern tip of the Jersey coast, jutting out into the Atlantic and washed by the Delaware Bay on the west. After being briefly settled by New England whalers in the late 1600s, it turned in the eighteenth century to more profitable farming and, soon after, to tourism. In 1745 the first advertisement for Cape May's restorative air and fine accommodation appeared in the Philadelphia press, heralding a period of great prosperity, when Southern plantation owners, desiring cool sea breezes without having to venture into Yankee land, flocked to the fashionable boarding houses of this genteel "resort of Presidents."

The Victorian era was Cape May's finest; nearly all its gingerbread architecture dates from a mass rebuilding after a severe fire in 1878. However, the increase in car travel after World War I meant that vacationers could go further, more quickly and more cheaply, and the little town found itself something of an anachronism, while the gaudier charms of Atlantic City became the brightest stars on the Jersey coast. During the 1950s, Cape May began to dust off its most valuable commodity: its history. Today the whole town is a National Historic Landmark, with over six hundred **Victorian buildings**, tree-lined streets and beautifully kept **gardens**, and a lucrative B&B industry. Avoid the few inevitable cutesy olde shoppes, and concentrate instead on the appealing combination of historical authenticity and good **beaches**.

### Arrival, information and getting around
New Jersey Transit (☎973/762-5100 or 1-800/772-3606) runs an express **bus** from Philadelphia and the south Jersey coast, and services from New York and Atlantic City. **Flights** from New York, Philadelphia and Atlantic City touch down at the Cape May

County airport (☎609/886-1500), five miles north on US-47, and **ferries** connect the town to Lewes, Delaware (15 a day in the summer, 6 off-season; $4.50 per person, $18 per car; schedules on ☎609/886-1725 or 1-800/64-FERRY). The ferry **dock** is in west Cape May, at the end of US-9, and **shuttle buses** take foot passengers into town (every 30min, $2 one-way, $4 round-trip).

Maps and **information** are available from the friendly **Mid-Atlantic Center for the Arts**, 1048 Washington St, the nonprofit organization that masterminded Cape May's preservation move (Mon–Fri 9am–5pm; ☎609/884-5404). It also organizes guided **walking tours** of the town's central mansions and thirty-minute historical trolley tours of the area, and issues details of self-guided cycling tours. The **Welcome Center** at 405 Lafayette St (April–Oct Mon–Sat 9am–4pm, Sun 1–3pm; ☎609/884-9562) can help with finding accommodation; other sources of information include a small booth in the paved mall at the southern end of Washington Street, and the tiny Chamber of Commerce, in the bus depot, 609 Lafayette St (Mon–Fri 9am–5pm; ☎609/884-5508).

Though Cape May itself is best enjoyed on foot, to venture out a bit further rent a **bike** from Shields, 11 Gurney St (daily 7am–7pm; $17 per day; ☎609/898-1818). The Cape May Whale Watcher (☎609/884-5445 or 1-800/786-5445), at Second Avenue and Wilson Drive, offers three trips around Cape May Point daily: two **dolphin-watches** (2hr; 10am & 6.30pm; $12) and a **whale-watching voyage** (3hr; 1pm; $15). Boats leave from an inlet of the Cape May Canal, behind Wilson Drive.

## Accommodation

Most of Cape May's pastel Victorian homes seem to be (pricey) **B&Bs** or **guest-houses**, and the resort is so popular that choice plummets on summer weekends. During July and August even old motor inns can command over $100 a night; June and September rates are often around half that. Standard **hotels** front the ocean on Beach Drive, and you can **camp** at *Seashore Campsites*, 720 Seashore Rd (reservations recommended July & Aug; ☎609/884-4010).

**Abigail Adams Bed and Breakfast**, 12 Jackson St (☎609/884-1371). High-quality lodging 100ft from the beach. Rates include afternoon tea. ⑥.

**Inn of Cape May**, Beach Drive and Ocean Ave (☎1-800/582-5933). Once a fashionable Victorian shorefront hotel, now with small adjoining modern motel wing. The cheapest rooms are those with shared baths in the main building. ⑤–⑦.

**Manor House**, 612 Hughes St (☎609/884-4710). Great breakfasts and a relaxing porch in the heart of the historic district. ⑥/⑦.

**The Montreal Inn**, Beach Drive and Madison Ave (☎609/884-7011 or 1/800-525-7011). Modern motel with standard rooms. ⑤/⑥.

**Queen Victoria**, 102 Ocean St (☎609/884-8702). Twenty-plus rooms in four buildings, including a cottage and a carriage house. Rates include bicycle loans and beach passes, as well as breakfast (in bed if desired) and afternoon tea. ⑤–⑧.

**Sea Breeze Motel**, Pittsburgh and New York aves (☎609/884-3352). No-nonsense budget motel in a residential street a couple of blocks from the beach, a mile from downtown. ⑤.

**Summer Cottage Inn**, 613 Columbia Ave (☎609/884-4948). 1867 inn with verandas and cupola. ⑥/⑦.

## The Town

Cape May's brightly colored houses were built by nouveau riche Victorians with a healthy disrespect for subtlety. Cluttered with cupolas, gazebos, balconies and "widow's walks," the houses follow no architectural rules except excess. They were known as "patternbook homes," with designs and features chosen from catalogs and thrown together in accordance with the owner's taste. The Victorian obsession with the Orient is everywhere: Moorish arches and onion domes sit comfortably next to gingerbread-and Queen Anne-style turrets.

The only old home open as a museum, the eighteen-room **Emlen Physick House**, 1048 Washington St (daily 10am–4pm; $6; ☎609/884-5404), was built by the popular Philadelphia architect Frank Furness. It has been restored to its 1879 glory, with whimsical "upside down" chimneys, a mock Tudor half-timbered facade, and much original furniture. Various B&Bs and hotels, given enough notice, also conduct informal tours of their premises: the *Mainstay Inn*, 635 Columbia Ave, was an elaborate Italianate 1872 gambling club (guided tour and tea Tues, Thurs, Sat and Sun at 4pm; ☎609/884-8690; $7.50), and the *Abbey*, Columbia Avenue and Gurney Street, is a Gothic mansion with a 60ft tower and blood-red etched windows (tours Mon, Wed and Fri; ☎609/884-4506; $5).

West of town, where the Delaware Bay and the ocean meet, the 1859 **Cape May Lighthouse**, visible from 25 miles at sea, offers great views from a gallery below the lantern (199 steps up) and a small exhibit on its history at ground level (daily 10am–5pm; $3.50). Three miles north of town on US-9, **Historic Cold Spring Village**, 735 Seashore Rd (June–Sept daily 10am–4.30pm; $3; ☎609/898-2300), depicts a typical nineteenth-century south Jersey farming community. Restored buildings from the region house a jail, school, inn and shops, and there are various craft shows and special events.

Cape May's excellent **beaches** literally sparkle with quartz pebbles. Beach tags ($4 per day, $9 per week) must be worn from 10am until 6pm in the summer, and are available from B&Bs, official vendors or from **City Hall**, 643 Washington St (☎609/884-9525).

## Eating

Cape May lacks the usual boardwalk snack bars, but it has plenty of cheap **lunch** places. **Dinner**, however, is far more expensive. If you're staying at a B&B, you can always fill up there with homemade goodies, and make do with bar snacks at night.

**Bella Rosa,** 414 Washington St mall (☎609/898-2100). Tasty Italian specialties and lunch snacks from $5.

**Bellevue Tavern,** 7–9 S Main St (☎609/463-1738). Functional c.1900 bar with inexpensive hot sandwiches at lunchtime; dinners average $14.

**The Lemon Tree,** Washington St mall (☎609/884-2704). Cheap, cheerful deli where nothing's over $6; the cheesesteaks are Philadelphia-quality.

**Louie's Pizza,** 7 Gurney St (☎609/884-0305). Fresh pizza opposite the beach from $8, or $2 per slice.

**Mad Batter,** 19 Jackson St (☎609/884-5970). Splash out on international meals (baked clams in a tomato pesto sauce) served by candlelight in the garden, from $16. Lunch from $8.

**Van Scoys,** Carpenter's Square mall (☎609/898-9898). Bistro cafe with a wide-ranging menu and a patio. Also serves as a late-night cappuccino bar.

## Nightlife and entertainment

Cape May is a friendly and laid-back place to be after dark; the day-trippers have gone home and the **bars** and **music venues** are enjoyed by locals and tourists alike. If you're after something a bit more lively, head a few miles north to the raucous nightclubs of **Wildwood**.

**Carney's,** 401 Beach Ave (☎609/884-4424). Spacious and relaxed Irish bar, with raucous live music.

**Ugly Mug,** Washington St mall and Decatur St (☎609/884-3459). Local favorite, with a friendly bar, plus chowder, sandwiches and seafood from $4.

# CHAPTER THREE

# NEW ENGLAND

T he six New England states of **MASSACHUSETTS, RHODE ISLAND, CON-NECTICUT, NEW HAMPSHIRE, VERMONT** and **MAINE** like to view themselves as the repository of all that is intrinsically American. In this version of history, the tangled streets of old Boston, the farms of Connecticut and the village greens of Vermont are the cradle of the nation. Certainly, nostalgia is at the root of the region's tourist trade; while the real business of making a living goes on in cities for the most part well off the tourist trail, innumerable small towns have been dolled up to recapture a past that is at best wishful, and at times purely fictional. Picturesque they may be, with white-spired churches beside immaculate rolling greens, but they're not always authentic: there's little to distinguish a clapboard house built last year from another, two hundred years old, which has just had its annual fresh coat of white paint.

The genteel seaside towns of modern Cape Cod and Rhode Island are a far cry from the first European settlements in New England. While the Pilgrims congregated in neat and pristine communities, later arrivals, with so much land to choose from, felt no need to reconstruct the compact little villages they had left behind in Europe. Instead, they fanned out across the Native American fields, or straggled their farmhouses in endless strips along the newly built roadways (thus establishing a more genuinely American style of development). As the European foothold on the continent became more certain, the coastline came increasingly to be viewed as prime real estate, to be lined with grand patrician homes – from the Vanderbilt mansions of Newport to the presidential compounds of the Bush and Kennedy families.

The Ivy League colleges – Harvard, Yale, Brown, Dartmouth, et al – still embody New England's strong sense of its own superiority, though in fact the region's traditional role as home to the WASP elite is due more to the vagaries of history and ideology than to economic or cultural realities. Its thin soil and harsh climate made it difficult for the first pioneers to sustain an agricultural way of life, while the industrial prosperity of the nineteenth and early twentieth centuries is now for the most part a distant memory. Indeed, New England has pockets, mostly in rural Vermont and New Hampshire, that are as poor as any in the US economic base, yet, as a whole it has managed to diversify in recent years especially in high-tech industry in the southern states.

New England can be a rather pricey place to visit, especially in late September and October, when visitors flock to see the magnificent **fall foliage**. Its tourist facilities are aimed at weekenders from the big cities as much as outsiders; places like **Cape Cod** make convenient short breaks for locals, but they're not the bucolic retreats you might

---

## ACCOMMODATION PRICE CODES

All accommodation prices in this book have been coded using the symbols below. Note that prices are for the least expensive double rooms in each establishment. For a full explanation see p.37 in Basics.

| | | |
|---|---|---|
| ① up to $30 | ④ $60–80 | ⑦ $130–175 |
| ② $30–45 | ⑤ $80–100 | ⑧ $175–250 |
| ③ $45–60 | ⑥ $100–130 | ⑨ $250+ |

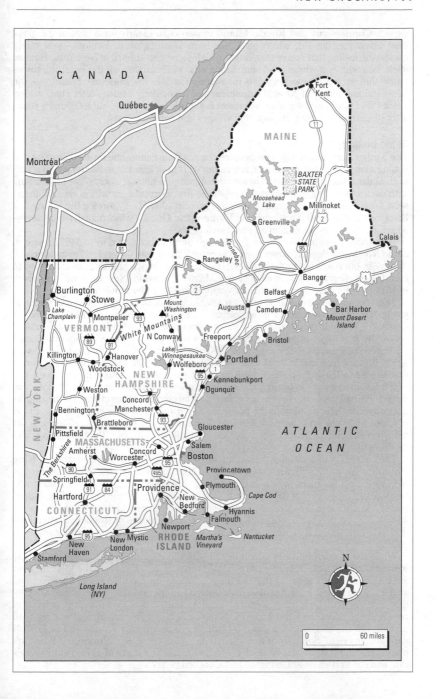

expect. **Connecticut** and **Rhode Island** in particular clearly form part of the great East Coast megalopolis, which stretches from Washington to Boston – you rarely escape the feeling that you're traveling through some vast suburb of New York. **Boston** itself, however, is a vibrant and stimulating city, while further up the coast the towns finally thin out and the scenery gets interesting (as does the **seafood**). Inland, too, the lakes and mountains of **New Hampshire**, and particularly **Maine**, offer rural wildernesses to rival any in the nation. **Vermont** is slightly less diverse, but its country roads offer pleasant wandering through tiny villages and serene forests.

## Some history

The **Native Americans** who first peopled the northeast shoreline lived by farming and fishing along the coast in summer, retreating with their animals to the relative warmth of the inland valleys in winter. Though the Algonquin did not always live in harmony with each other, they did manage to repel the first European invaders, earning themselves five hundred years' grace, some time around 1000 AD, by forcing the Viking Leif Ericsson to abandon the settlement of **Vinland the Good** – which may have been anywhere between Newfoundland and Massachusetts.

Within five years of Columbus's first voyage, John Cabot nosed by in 1497, in search of the Northwest Passage. Over the next century, European fishermen began to return each year, but it was not until the early 1600s that the French and English attempted to found permanent colonies, in what is now Maine. The name "New England" was given in 1614 by John Smith, who particularly appreciated the plentiful lobsters.

This was not promising land: as a character in Robert Lowell's *Endecott and the Cross* put it, "I'm not a birdwatcher or an Indian . . . I don't see the point of this outpost of England." Without precious metals to be mined, or the potential to grow lucrative crops, the first major impetus for emigration was **religion**. Refugees from intolerance – notably the Puritans, beginning with the **Pilgrims** in 1620 – made the arduous voyage to find the freedom to build their own communities. The Pilgrims only survived at first thanks to the Indians: they were aided by a certain Squanto, who had been kidnapped, sold as a slave in Spain and returned home via England. In return, the Pilgrims forced the natives from the terraces they had farmed for generations, dismissing as inappropriate their solution to the problems of survival in such terrain: "Their land is spacious and void, and there are few and do but run over the grass . . . They are not industrious, neither have art, science, skill or faculty to use either the land or the commodities of it."

The possibility of a serious Native American threat was removed by victory in **King Philip's War** of 1675–76, when a leader of the Narragansett persuaded feuding groups to bury their differences in one last despairing throw. By then, white colonization was beyond the stage where it could be controlled by a few high-minded zealots. The **Salem witch trials** of 1692 provided a salutary lesson on the potential dangers of fanaticism, and as immigration became less English-based, with influxes of Huguenots after 1680 and Irish in 1708, Puritan domination decreased and a definite class structure began to emerge.

While the strand of history which began with the Pilgrims is just one among many in the colonization of America – the Spanish were in Santa Fe before the Pilgrims ever left England – it is true to say that the metropolis of **Boston** deserves to be celebrated as the place where the great project of American **independence** first captured the popular imagination. The leading port of colonial America was always the likeliest focus of resentment against the latest impositions of the British government, and was ready to take up the challenge thrown down by British Prime Minister Townshend in 1766: "I dare tax America." So many of the seminal moments of the **Revolutionary War** took place here: the Boston Massacre of 1770, the Boston Tea Party of 1773, Paul Revere's ride and the first shots at Lexington and Concord in 1775.

Nationhood secured, however, New England's prosperity was ironically hit hard by the loss of trade with England, and Boston was slowly eclipsed by Philadelphia, New York and the new capital, Washington. The **Triangular Trade** in slaves, sugar and rum provided one substitute source of income, the brief heyday of **whaling** another. New England was also momentarily at the forefront of the **Industrial Revolution**, when water-powered mills created a booming textile industry, most of which quickly moved south where wages were scandalously cheaper. The attempt to farm the north, however, foundered: careless techniques served to exhaust the land, and as the vast spaces of the west opened to settlement many of the inland towns fell silent.

# MASSACHUSETTS

To the first colonists of the **Massachusetts Bay Company**, their arrival near the site of modern Salem in 1630 marked a crucial moment in history. **Puritans** who had decided to leave England before it was engulfed by the clearly imminent chaos of civil war, saw their purpose, in the words of Governor John Winthrop, as the establishment of a Utopian "**City upon a hill.**" Their new colony of **MASSACHUSETTS** was to be a beacon to the rest of humanity, an exemplar of sober government along sound spiritual principles. Not all those who followed, however, shared the same motivation; the story is often told of the preacher who told his congregation that they had come to New England to build a new kingdom of God, only to be challenged by a vociferous element who said that they personally had come to fish.

In their own terms, the Puritans were not successful: as waves of immigration brought all kinds of dissenters and free-thinkers from Europe, society in New England inevitably became secular. However, their **influence** remained. A clarity of thought and forcefulness of purpose can be traced from the foundation of Harvard College in 1636, through the intellectual impetus behind the Revolution and the crusade against slavery, to the nineteenth-century achievements of **writers** such as Melville, Emerson, Hawthorne and Thoreau.

Other traditions, too, have helped shape the state – poor migrants from **Ireland** and **Italy**, freed and escaped **slaves** from the Southern states, **Portuguese** seamen – even if they have not always been welcome. The anti-immigrant "Know-Nothings" of the 1850s acquired considerable public support; in 1927, the Italian anarchists **Sacco and Vanzetti** came up against conservative old Massachusetts, and were framed and executed on murder charges. As recently as the 1970s, Boston experienced racial conflicts, that matched the bitterness of those erupting throughout the nation. There is, however, a cosmopolitan side to Massachusetts – witness the extraordinary blend of nationalities involved in the transglobal **whaling** industry of nineteenth-century Nantucket – and a strong liberal undercurrent. The high-tech promise of former Governor Michael Dukakis's "Massachusetts Miracle" may not quite have delivered lasting prosperity, but optimism and resilience still shine through.

Spending a few days in **Boston** is strongly recommended: the city is East Coast America at its best. It's a place that feels no need to rest on its laurels – the history is there and visible, but there's a great deal of modern life and energy besides, thanks in part to the presence of **Cambridge**, the home of Harvard University, just across the river. Several further historic towns are within easy reach – **Salem** to the north, **Concord** and **Lexington** just inland, and **Plymouth** to the south. **Provincetown**, a three-hour ferry ride across the bay at the tip of Cape Cod, is a lot of fun to visit, and the rest of the Cape offers historic towns, lovely beaches – and huge crowds. Except for a handful of college towns, **inland Massachusetts** is much quieter; its settlements are naturally concentrated where the land gets fertile, such as along the Connecticut River valley and in the **Berkshires** to the west.

## Getting around Massachusetts

With the single proviso that all roads in Massachusetts seem to lead to Boston, this is an easy state to tour on **public transportation**. Planes, trains and buses all radiate out from the one great city; the connections to **Cape Cod** in particular (see p.190) are absolutely legion. The Amtrak line which connects Boston with New York, Philadelphia and Washington is the best regional **train** service in the nation, and the east–west line via Worcester and Springfield gives access to Montréal, Toronto and Chicago. With the exception of local commuter lines, trains do not, however, continue north of Boston: the only service along the coast is the summer-only service south to Hyannis on Cape Cod. **Buses** from Boston are also plentiful, but the only major north–south route inland is that which runs up Route 91 along the Connecticut River valley.

# Boston

Although the metropolitan area of **BOSTON** has long since expanded to fill the shoreline of **Massachusetts Bay**, and stretches for miles inland as well, the seventeenth-century port at its heart is still discernible. Forget the neat grids of modern urban America; the twisting streets clustered around **Boston Common** are a reminder of how the nation started out, and the city is enjoyably human in scale.

Boston was until 1755 the biggest city in America; as the one most directly affected by the latest whims of the British Crown, it was the natural focus for the opposition that culminated in the **Revolutionary War**. Numerous evocative sites from that era are preserved along the **Freedom Trail** through downtown. Since then, however, Boston has in effect turned its back on the sea. As the third busiest port in the British Empire (after London and Bristol), it stood on a narrow peninsula. What is now Washington Street provided the only access by land, and when the British set off to Lexington in 1775 they embarked in ships from the Common itself. During the nineteenth century, the Charles River marshlands were filled in to create the posh Back Bay residential area. Central Boston is now slightly but significantly set back from the water, separated by the psychological barrier of the hideous John Fitzgerald Expressway that carries I-93 across downtown. The city is currently working on routing the traffic underground and disposing of this eyesore, though that won't happen until at least 2002.

There is a certain truth in the charge leveled by other Americans that Boston likes to live in the past; echoes of the "Brahmins" of a century ago can be heard in the upper-class drawl of the posher districts. But this is by no means just a city of WASPs: the Irish who began to arrive in quantity after the Great Famine had produced their first mayor as early as 1885, and the president of the whole country within a hundred years. The liberal tradition that spawned the Kennedys remains alive, fed in part by the presence in the city of more than one hundred universities and colleges, the most famous of which – **Harvard University** – actually stands in the city of Cambridge, just over the Charles River and is fully integrated into the tourist experience thanks to the area's excellent subway system.

The slump of the Depression seemed to linger in Boston for years – even in the 1950s, the population was actually dwindling – but these days the place definitely has a rejuvenated feel to it. **Quincy Market** has served as a blueprint for urban development worldwide, and with its busy street life, imaginative museums and galleries, fine architecture and palpable history, Boston is the one destination in New England there's no excuse for missing.

## Arrival and information

Boston may not be the "hub of the universe," as Oliver Wendell Holmes liked to think, but it is at any rate the center of New England's transportation networks. An increasing number of direct flights from Europe means that it provides many travelers with their first taste of America, while efficient rail and bus services from New York, Montréal and further afield make this an obvious starting point, wherever you're heading in New England.

## Air

**Logan Airport** (☎617/561-1800 or 1-800/23-LOGAN), constantly busy with both international and domestic services, is a mere three miles from downtown Boston. It stands on an artificial peninsula jutting into Boston Harbor, created by leveling three islands and destroying Revolution Wharf. As driving within the city is not to be recommended (see overleaf), it makes little sense to rent a car at the airport. A **taxi** into town costs between $10 and $20, plus an extra $4.50 in fees and tolls; the trip should take twenty minutes, but most traffic passes through the Sumner or Callahan tunnels, which can get very congested. The recent construction of the Ted Williams Tunnel has alleviated the problem somewhat. Between 5.30am and 1am, free shuttle **buses** run every few minutes from all terminals to the airport **subway** station on the MBTA Blue line (see overleaf), from where it's an easy ten-minute ride to the city center. Just as quick, and a lot more fun, is the **water shuttle**, which connects the terminal buses with Rowes Wharf across the harbor (Mon–Fri every 15min 6am–8pm, Fri also every 30min 8am–11pm, Sat every 30min 10am–11pm, Sun every 30min 10am–8pm; $8 one-way, $14 round-trip; ☎1-800/23-LOGAN).

## Trains

Amtrak (☎1-800/USA-RAIL) trains along the Northeast Corridor from Providence, Washington DC and New York, and from Chicago and Canada via Springfield, as well as the summer-only Cape Cod specials, arrive a short walk from downtown Boston near the waterfront at **South Station**, Summer Street and Atlantic Avenue. The newly renovated station houses information booths, newsstands, restaurants, and a fantastic old clock, though no currency exchange. The easily accessible Red subway line can whisk you to the center of town or out to Cambridge. Some Amtrak services also make an extra stop at **Back Bay Station**, 145 Dartmouth St, on the Orange subway line near Copley Square. **North Station** is used only by MBTA commuter trains.

## Buses

Several **bus** companies provide direct links between Boston and the rest of New England. Vermont Transit (☎1-800/451-3292) covers western Massachusetts, New Hampshire's White Mountains, Vermont and Montréal; while Concord Trailways (☎1-800/639-3317) runs to southern New Hampshire and up the Maine coast. Heading south, Bonanza Bus Lines (☎1-800/556-3815) connects Providence and Newport, Cape Cod and New York City; and Peter Pan Bus Lines (☎617/343-9999) services New York and western Massachusetts. Greyhound (☎1-800/231-2222), with its many connections, offers nationwide service. Plymouth and Brockton Bus Co (☎508/746-0378), serving Hyannis, is the only service to make stops at Logan Airport; all other buses leave from South Station (see above).

## Information

The most convenient place to get advice and maps is the **Visitor Information Center** (Mon–Sat 8.30am–5pm, Sun 9am–5pm; ☎617/536-4100 or 1-800/888-5515) at Park Street subway on the Tremont Street side of Boston Common. There are also information kiosks in **Quincy Market**, the **John Hancock Tower** at Copley Square in the Back Bay area, and in the **Prudential Center**, also in the Back Bay. For advance information, the **Boston By Phone** service (☎1-800/888-5515 or 1-800/SEE-BOSTON) allows visitors anywhere in North America to connect directly with a wide range of hotels and services.

The city's main **post office** is at McCormack Station, Post Office Square (Mon–Fri 8am–5pm; ☎617/720-4754; zip code 02109).

# Getting around

Much of the pleasure of visiting Boston comes from being in a city that was built long before cars were invented. Walking around it can be a joy; conversely, driving is an absolute nightmare. The freeways won't take you where you want to be, the one-way traffic systems can have you circling for hours without getting any nearer your destination, and if you ever do arrive, parking lots are thin on the ground and very expensive. There's no point renting a car in Boston until the day you leave, especially since the city's public transportation is so good.

The Massachusetts Bay Transportation Authority (MBTA, known as the "**T**") is responsible for Boston's **subway** system and **trolleybuses**. The subway, which opened in 1897, is the oldest in the US; its first station, **Park Street**, remains its center (any train marked "inbound" is headed here), and is the place to pick up all schedules and information. Four lines – Red, Green, Blue and Orange – operate daily from 5am until 1am, although certain routes begin to shut down earlier. Away from downtown, the trains emerge from tunnels to run along the city's major arteries. Though maps are posted at each station, it's a good idea to pick up the widely available Rapid Transit maps for reference. Trains are fast and safe; only some parts of the Orange line might be said to be unsafe after dark.

Within the city, the standard fare is 85¢, paid with tokens inserted into turnstiles, but on some incoming overground routes you have to pay extra, up to $2 (conversely, some outbound overground routes are free). You can buy eleven tokens for the price of ten, and a **tourist pass** covers all subway and local bus journeys at a cost of $5 for a day, $9 for three days, or $18 for a week. (All MBTA **information** is on ☎617/722-3200.)

The normal fare on MBTA's **local buses** is 60¢, but longer distances, such as out to Salem or Marblehead, cost up to $2.50. MBTA also runs **commuter rail lines**, extending as far as Salem, Ipswich and Concord; these are based at the unlovely **North Station** (☎617/222-3200) on Causeway Street, under the Fleet Center (on the site of what was until recently the Boston Garden).

In and around Boston are some eighty miles of **bike trails**, making it an excellent city to explore on two wheels. Bicycles can be rented from the Community Bike Shop at 490 Tremont St (☎617/542-8623) and **Back Bay Bikes & Boards**, 333 Newbury St (☎617/247-2336), from mid-March through mid-October.

### City tours

It's easy enough to get to know Boston by following the **Freedom Trail** on foot (see p.176). If you prefer to be guided, narrated trips run throughout the day aboard the hundred-minute Old Town Trolley Tours (☎617/269-7010; $20, $7 kids aged 4–12) or the similarly priced Beantown Trolley/Gray Line (☎781/986-6100). Boston By Foot, 77 N Washington St (☎617/367-2345), conducts ninety-minute walking tours for $8. Also useful are the bus excursions further afield to Lexington, Concord, Salem and Plymouth with Brush Hill Tours/Gray Line (☎617/720-6342).

# Accommodation

Good-quality budget **accommodation** is hard to find in Boston – any hotel room in walking distance of downtown for under $100 has to be considered a bargain. Central

Reservation Service (☎617/569-3800 or 1-800/332-3026) can often get discounts of ten percent or more at major hotels, though a more enjoyable and affordable way of staying in the Boston area is to use a **B&B agency**. The excellent B&B Agency of Boston (47 Commercial Wharf, Boston, MA 02110; ☎617/720-3540 or 1-800/248-9262; in the UK ☎0800/895128) offers hundreds of properties across the city for between $70 and $100. Host Homes of Boston (PO Box 117, Waban Branch, Boston, MA 02468; ☎617/244-1308) and Boston Reservations (☎617/332-4199) provide a similar service.

## Hostels

**Back Bay Summer Hostel**, 519 Beacon St (☎617/353-3294). A well-located Boston University dorm used as a hostel in the summer months. HI members pay $20, others pay $23. ③.

**Charlestown YMCA**, 150 2nd Ave, Charleston Navy Yard (☎617/241-8400). Rooms near the *USS Constitution*, popular with military personnel. Free use of the excellent gym. ④.

**Greater Boston YMCA**, 316 Huntington Ave (☎617/536-7800). Best budget rooms in the Back Bay, next to Northeastern "T" station. Mixed accommodation. Rates – around $40 for one person, $56 for two – include breakfast. Co-ed June–Sept, otherwise men-only. ③.

**HI-Boston**, 12 Hemenway St (☎617/536-1027). In the Fenway area (Hynes Convention Center "T" station), close to the hip end of Newbury St and the Lansdowne St clubs. Dorms $20 for members, $23 nonmembers. In summer book ahead, or check in at 8am, to be sure of a place. ①.

**Irish Embassy Hostel**, 232 Friend St (☎617/973-4841). Dorm beds for $15 above the *Irish Embassy* pub, about 5 minutes' walk north of Faneuil Hall. Free admission to pub gigs on most nights, and free barbecues Tues and Sun. ①.

**YWCA**, 40 Berkeley St (☎617/482-8850). Women-only singles ($42), doubles ($64) and triples ($75) in convenient South End location, near Arlington or Back Bay "T" stations. Non-YWCA cardholders pay $2 for temporary membership. Nightly and weekly rates. ③.

## Hotels, motels and B&Bs

**Best Western - Inn at Longwood Medical**, 342 Longwood Ave (☎617/731-4700 or 1-800/528-1234). Above-average motel rooms near Longwood "T" station and within walking distance of Fenway Park. ⑥.

**Boston Park Plaza**, 64 Arlington St (☎617/426-2000 or 1-800/225-2008). Spacious, high-ceilinged rooms in Bill Clinton's favorite grand old Boston hotel, in the Back Bay. The presence of the original *Legal Seafoods* restaurant and several airline offices in the hotel ensure that it's always a hub of activity. ⑦.

**A Cambridge House**, 2218 Massachusetts Ave, Cambridge (☎617/491-6300 or 1-800/232-9989). Classy restored B&B near Porter Square, a 30min walk from Harvard Square. Tasty breakfasts, served on the patio in summer, and early-evening nibbles and wine. ⑥.

**Copley Square Hotel**, 47 Huntington Ave (☎617/536-9000 or 1-800/225-7062). Situated on the eastern fringe of Copley Square, this is a quiet hotel and home to the *Café Budapest*, widely considered the most romantic restaurant in Boston. ⑧/⑨.

**82 Chandler Street**, 82 Chandler St (☎617/482-0408). One of Boston's best in-town B&Bs, this refreshingly restored 1863 brownstone sits on one of the most up-and-coming streets of the South End. Breakfasts are good, served communally on the sun-splashed top floor – where you'll find the best room in the house. ⑤/⑥.

**Eliot Hotel**, 370 Commonwealth Ave at Massachusetts Ave (☎617/267-1607 or 1-800/443-5468). West Back Bay's answer to the *Ritz*, at the busy crossroads of Boston's upscale student ghetto. Rooms have luxurious Italian marble bathrooms and kitchenettes. Nice breakfasts, too. ⑨.

**Harborside Inn**, 185 State St (☎617/723-7500). Newish hotel with a Victorian accent in a renovated mercantile warehouse across from Quincy Market and the Custom House. ⑥/⑦.

**Howard Johnson Lodge**, 1271 Boylston St (☎617/267-8300 or 1-800/654-2000). Reasonably priced motel rooms next to Fenway Park. The free parking's a definite plus point. ⑤.

**Lenox Hotel**, 710 Boylston St (☎617/536-5300 or 1-800/225-7676). Lovingly maintained, medium-sized hotel in the heart of the Back Bay. ⑨.

**Newbury Guest House**, 261 Newbury St (☎617/437-7666 or 1-800/383-1550). Big, 32-room Victorian brownstone house, with rates at the lower end of the price range. $10 parking and free continental breakfast. ⑥.

**Tremont House**, 275 Tremont St (☎617/426-1400 or 1-800/331-9998). Well-restored, 281-room Art Deco hotel, in the Theater District two blocks from the Common. ⑨.

# The City

Boston has grown up around **Boston Common**, which was set aside as common land in 1634. The obvious first stop on any tour of the city, it is also one of the gems in the string of nine parks (six of which were designed by Frederick Law Olmsted, America's foremost landscape architect) known as Boston's **Emerald Necklace**. Another gem is the lovely **Public Garden**, across Charles Street, where the two-ton **swan boats** ($1.50), which paddle across the main pond, are a less-than-natural, though whimsical, focal point.

The **visitor center** – the start of the **Freedom Trail** – is near the tapering north end of the Common. As you stand here, facing up Tremont Street with the **State House** away to your left, the main **shopping** district, **Quincy Market**, and the **waterfront** are slightly ahead but down to the right. The modern concrete wasteland of **Government Center** is straight up Tremont Street, with the **North End** beyond – first Irish, then Jewish, and now very definitely Italian. A short way behind you on the left rises **Beacon Hill**, every bit as elegant as when Henry James called Mount Vernon Street "the most prestigious address in America" (and far removed from its eighteenth-century nickname of "Mount Whoredom"). Heading away from the center down Tremont Street brings you to **Chinatown** and the **Theater District**, while grand boulevards such as Commonwealth Avenue lead west from the Public Garden into the **Back Bay**, where Harvard Bridge runs across the Charles River into **Cambridge**.

## The Freedom Trail

Much the best way to orientate yourself in downtown Boston – and to appreciate the city's role in American history – is to walk some or all of the **Freedom Trail**. You can pick up or leave this easy self-guided route anywhere – a line of red bricks marking the trail is embedded in the pavement – but technically it begins on Boston Common at the **Visitor Information Center**.

From here, head for the golden dome of the **Massachusetts State House** (free tours Mon–Fri 10am–4pm), which was completed in 1798 to a design by Charles Bulfinch. It remains the seat of Massachusetts' government; its most famous feature, the wooden Sacred Cod symbolizing the wealth Boston accrued from its fisheries, hangs in front of the Speaker, and faces in different directions according to which party is in office.

Though **Park Street Church** (July & Aug daily 9am–3pm; rest of year by appointment; free) is by no means "the most interesting mass of bricks and mortar in America" that Henry James claimed, its ornate white steeple is undeniably impressive. This was where the orator William Lloyd Garrison launched his campaign to free the slaves on July 4, 1829. The 1600 graves of the **Old Granary Burying Ground** just around the corner (daily during daylight hours; free) include those of Paul Revere, Samuel Adams and John Hancock, as well as the reputed original Mother Goose, while **King's Chapel Burying Ground** (June–Oct daily 9.30am–4pm; Nov–May Mon–Sat 10am–4pm; free) contains Boston's earliest colonists and the first governor, John Winthrop. A statue of Benjamin Franklin marks the site of **Boston Latin**, America's first public school, attended by Franklin and Samuel Adams. Guests at the nearby **Omni Parker House Hotel** (not officially on the Trail) have included Charles Dickens and John Kennedy; employees, Malcolm X, Red Foxx and Ho Chi Minh. The **Old Corner Bookstore** at

School and Washington was a literary salon frequented by Longfellow, Thoreau and Hawthorne.

Next come the Trail's two most striking and significant buildings. At the **Old South Meeting House** (daily: April–Oct 9.30am–5pm; Nov–March 10am–4pm; $3), Samuel Adams addressed the patriots about to carry out the Boston Tea Party on December 16, 1773. This was no raucous and unruly mob: they were solemn men, well aware of the likely impact of their actions. The elegant **Old State House**, built in 1712 and still proud, although dwarfed by surrounding skyscrapers, was the seat of colonial government. From its balcony the Declaration of Independence was read on July 18, 1776; exactly two hundred years later Queen Elizabeth II appeared on that same balcony. Inside is a **museum** of Boston history (daily 9.30am–5pm; $3). Outside, a ring of cobblestones marks the site of the **Boston Massacre** on March 5, 1770, when British soldiers fired on a crowd which was pelting them with stone-filled snowballs, and killed five, including the black Crispus Attucks.

Modern visitors gravitate to **Quincy Market** and **Faneuil Hall** (it rhymes with Daniel; daily 9am–9pm; free) for the lively shops, restaurants and takeaways which made this a pioneer example of successful urban renewal (by the developer who went on to transform London's Covent Garden). Faneuil Hall was, however, once known as the "Cradle of Liberty," a meeting place for Revolutionaries and, later, abolitionists.

Passing under the six-lane John Fitzgerald Expressway and into the North End, you reach **Paul Revere House**, Boston's last surviving seventeenth-century house (daily: mid-April to Oct 9.30am–5.15pm; Nov to mid-April 9.30am–4.15pm; closed Mon Jan–March; $2.50), built after the Great Fire of 1676, and home to Paul Revere – patriot, silversmith, Freemason and father of sixteen children – from 1770 until 1800. When Revere embarked upon his famous **ride** of April 18, 1775, to warn Lexington of imminent British attack, two lanterns were hung from the belfry of **Old North Church**, 193 Salem St (daily: June–Oct 9am–6pm; Nov–May 9am–5pm), to alert Charlestown in case he got caught. A little further up, from **Copp's Hill Burial Ground** (daily 8am–5pm; free) you can see across the harbor to Charlestown; as indeed could the British, who planted their artillery here for the Battle of Bunker Hill.

## THE BLACK HERITAGE TRAIL

Massachusetts was the first state to declare slavery illegal, in 1783 – partly as a result of black participation in the Revolutionary War – and a large community of free blacks and escaped slaves swiftly grew up in the North End and on Beacon Hill. Ironically, very few blacks now live on Beacon Hill, but the **Black Heritage Trail** through the area celebrates important sites in local black history (the various visitor centers provide maps).

Pick up the Trail either at 46 Joy St, where the **Abiel Smith School** contains a **Museum of Afro-American History** (daily 10am–4pm; $5), illustrating the national civil rights campaign as well as local history, or at the **African Meeting House** at 8 Smith Court (off Joy St), for displays and talks from well-informed rangers. Built in 1806 as the first African-American church in the United States, this became known as "Black Faneuil Hall" during the abolitionist campaign; Frederick Douglass issued his call here for all blacks to take up arms in the Civil War. Among those who responded were the volunteers of the **Massachusetts 54th Regiment**, commemorated by a monument at the edge of Boston Common, opposite the State House, which depicts their farewell march down Beacon Street. Robert Lowell won a Pulitzer Prize for his poem, *For the Union Dead*, about this monument, and the regiment's tragic end at Fort Wagner was depicted in the movie *Glory*. The Trail then winds around Beacon Hill, passing schools, other institutions, and residences ranging from the small, cream clapboard houses of Smith Court to the imposing **Lewis and Harriet Hayden House** at 66 Phillips St, once a stop on the famous "Underground Railroad," sheltering runaway slaves from pursuing bounty-hunters.

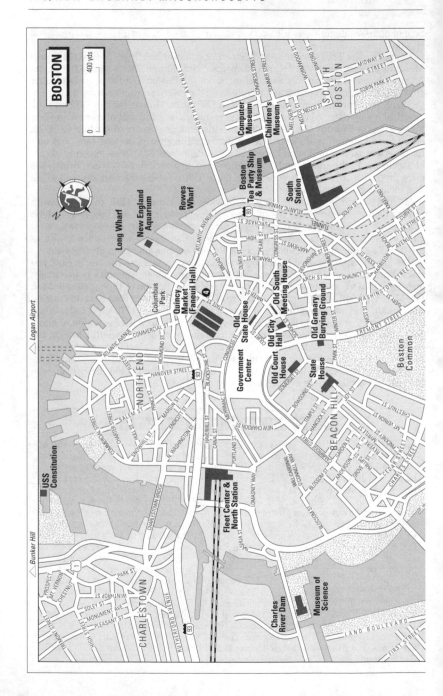

**BOSTON**

0       400 yds

△ Logan Airport
△ Bunker Hill

USS Constitution

CHARLESTOWN

PROSPECT
MT VERNON
CHESTNUT
WINTHROP ST
SOLEY ST
MONUMENT AVE
PLEASANT ST
HIGH STREET
TREMONT STREET
PARK ST
ADAMS STREET

CHARLESTOWN BRIDGE

RUTHERFORD AVENUE

NORTH END

COMMERCIAL STREET
CHARTER STREET
SNOWHILL ST
HULL ST
SALEM ST
PRINCE ST
HANOVER STREET
MARGIN ST
ENDICOTT ST
N WASHINGTON ST

ATLANTIC AVENUE
RICHMOND ST

Columbus Park

Quincy Market (Faneuil Hall)

Long Wharf

New England Aquarium

Rowes Wharf

NORTHERN AVENUE

Computer Museum

Children's Museum

Boston Tea Party Ship & Museum

South Station

SOUTH BOSTON

MIDWAY ST
A STREET
SUMMER STREET
WORMWOOD ST
BINFORD ST
SOBIN PARK ST

MELCHER ST
NECCO ST
NECCO CT

ATLANTIC AVENUE
PURCHASE ST
HIGH ST
OLIVER ST
PEARL ST
FRANKLIN ST
CONGRESS ST
MATHEWS STREET
DEVONSHIRE ST
SUMMER STREET
ARCH ST
CHAUNCY ST
WASHINGTON ST
AVERY ST
WEST ST
TREMONT STREET

TUNNEL

PHASE ST
CURVE ST
TYLER STREET
BEACH ST
HARRISON AVENUE
ESSEX ST

Old South Meeting House

Old State House

Old City Hall

Old Granary Burying Ground

WATER ST
STATE ST
DEVONSHIRE ST
COURT ST
SCHOOL ST
WINTER ST
PARK ST

Government Center

Old Court House

State House

Boston Common

BEACON HILL

SOMERSET ST
BOWDOIN ST
TEMPLE ST
HANCOCK ST
DERNE ST
MYRTLE ST
REVERE ST
PINCKNEY ST
MT VERNON ST
CHESTNUT ST
BEACON ST
CEDAR STREET
CHARLES STREET
BRIMMER STREET

BOWDOINS ST
CAMBRIDGE ST
GARDEN ST
ANDERSON ST
PHILLIPS ST
GROVE ST
BLOSSOM ST
S RUSSELL ST

NEW CHARDON ST

HAVERHILL ST
CANAL ST
MERRIMAC ST
BLACKSTONE ST
CONGRESS ST
PORTLAND ST
LOMASNEY WAY
WM CARDINAL O'CONNELL WAY

Fleet Center & North Station

MARTHA RD
NASHUA ST

Charles River Dam

Museum of Science

LAND BOULEVARD

FIRST ST

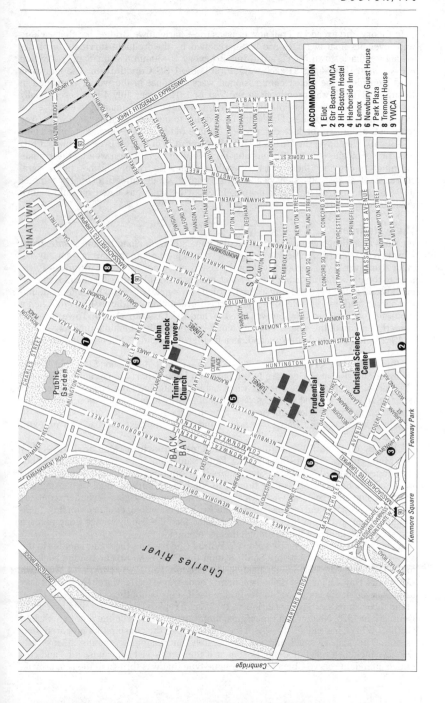

**ACCOMMODATION**
1 Eliot
2 Gtr Boston YMCA
3 HI-Boston Hostel
4 Harborside Inn
5 Lenox
6 Newbury Guest House
7 Park Plaza
8 Tremont House
9 YWCA

In theory, the Freedom Trail now crosses the Charlestown Bridge, but that's a long walk over. Its final two sites are better reached by the frequent **ferries** from Long Wharf to Charlestown Navy Yard (Mon–Fri every 15–30min 6.30am–8pm, Sat & Sun every 30min 10am–6pm; $1 each way). First is the **USS Constitution**, also known as "Old Ironsides," the oldest commissioned warship afloat in the world. Launched in Boston in 1797, it was prominent in the War of 1812. Every July 4 it is ceremonially turned around – sailed out into the bay and its cannon fired – mainly to equalize the weathering on its two sides. Unless it's closed due to ongoing rehabilitation work, free tours of the ship are conducted in period costume (daily 9.30am–dusk; last guided tour at 3.30pm). Up above, the **Bunker Hill Monument** is in fact on Breed's Hill, but this was the actual site of the battle on June 17, 1775, which, although won by the British, did much to convince them that they could not hope to triumph in the end. A spiral staircase of almost 300 steps leads to the top; a small **museum** (daily: summer 9.30am–5pm; rest of year 9.30am–4pm; free) at the base has dated but informative exhibits on the battle.

## The waterfront

It comes as a disappointment to realize that you can't walk along Boston's **waterfront** – broken by over a dozen heavily developed wharfs jutting into the harbor – for any distance. However, if you head straight for the sea from Quincy Market, **Columbus Park**, next to the ugly *Marriott Long Wharf Hotel*, makes a nice place to sit. Faneuil Hall originally stood at the head of **Long Wharf**, which stuck nearly two thousand feet out into the harbor, and was the site of the final British evacuation on March 17, 1776. Then a thousand-foot expanse of water was filled in, and the **Custom House Tower** erected to mark the end of the wharf. That remained Boston's tallest building until as recently as 1962; it too now finds itself inland, as a further thousand feet of new land has been added.

**Boston Harbor Cruises** (☎617/227-4321; inner and outer harbor $15, inner harbor $8, inner and stop at St George's Island $8) from Long Wharf are not all that exciting. The port is nothing like as busy as when fishing boats lined the quays three or four deep on all sides. Instead you pass vast rows of freshly imported Japanese cars on the quayside, and get a close-up view of the airport. You can get off one cruise in Charlestown, to see the *USS Constitution*, and catch the next one back for no extra charge.

Close by on Central Wharf, the **New England Aquarium** (Memorial Day–Labor Day Mon, Tues & Fri 9am–6pm, Wed & Thurs 9am–8pm, Sat & Sun 9am–7pm; Labor Day–June Mon–Wed & Fri 9am–5pm, Thurs 9am–8pm, Sat & Sun 9am–6pm; summer weekends & holidays $12, other times $10.50) has an outdoor pool of basking sea otters. Inside, the colossal Giant Ocean Tank, a four-story glass cylinder, contains sharks, giant turtles and tropical marine life (with an unsettling emphasis on how "delicious" certain specimens are). Scuba divers hand-feed the fish five times a day, and sea lion shows are held in a floating amphitheater alongside.

If you follow the shoreline past **Rowe's Wharf** (the base for the water shuttles to the airport), a short distance before South Station the **Congress Street Bridge** leads off to the left across the Fort Point Channel. The **Boston Tea Party Ship and Museum** (Memorial Day–Labor Day daily 9am–6pm; Labor Day–Dec & March–Memorial Day daily 9am–5pm; $7) is moored to the bridge itself. This is not the original *Beaver*, one of the three ships stormed by patriots in 1773, but a replica, *Beaver II*, sailed here from Denmark in 1973. Neither is it the original mooring, which was on the now-demolished Griffin's Wharf; instead it's the site of the house where the conspirators prepared their assault. The ship is small and not desperately interesting, for adults at any rate. Displays include a relief model of Boston as it then was – virtually an island – and costumed attendants serve China tea of the same type that was thrown in the sea, provoking the British to close the port and place Boston under martial law. From time to time throughout the day there are reenactments of the Tea Party itself.

On the far side of the bridge, a forty-foot **milk bottle**, which serves as an ice-cream parlor and sandwich bar, marks **Museum Wharf**. The **Children's Museum**, 300 Congress St (Tues–Thurs, Sat & Sun 10am–5pm, Fri 10am–9pm; $7, children $6, Fri 5–9pm $1 for all), comprises five floors of educational exhibits designed to entice kids into learning by doing. Action and interaction are encouraged by the sheer abundance of marbles, costumes, water toys, blocks, video cameras, climbing structures, buttons to push, strings to pull and tunnels to crawl through. A cool shop on the second floor lets kids stuff a brown bag with recycled treasures, such as bits of rubber, odd-shaped styrofoam, nuts, bolts and plastic tubing, for a couple of bucks.

Next door, the **Computer Museum** (Tues–Thurs, Sat & Sun 10am–5pm, Fri 10am–9pm; $7, children $5, Sun 3–5pm half-price) has two floors of displays aimed at educating folks about the history and capabilities of computers. If the kids are busy playing virtual reality games, then head to the engaging artificial intelligence display or take a stroll through the museum's proudest attraction, the Walk-Through Computer, which allows visitors to experience a PC from the vantage point of a microchip. You get the most out of the place when you aren't jostling in line with six-year-olds, so if you can, come during the week and avoid holidays.

The **Museum of Science**, in the Science Park on the Charles River Dam at the northern end of the waterfront, not far from North Station (summer daily 9am–7pm; rest of year Mon–Thurs, Sat & Sun 9am–5pm, Fri 9am–9pm; $8, children $6), is full of hands-on exhibits designed for all age groups. The impressive OMNIMAX cinema takes up the full height of one end of the building, and the Hayden Planetarium pays its way with Pink Floyd laser shows and the like ($7.50, children $5.50; call ☎617/723-2500 for show times).

## Back Bay and beyond

As each portion of the tidal flats of the Charles River was filled in, from 1857 onwards, more of the spacious boulevards and grand houses of **Back Bay** were built. Thus a walk through the area from east to west provides an object lesson in Victorian architecture. One of the most architecturally significant – if not the prettiest – of its buildings is the Romanesque **Trinity Church** on Clarendon Street, supported on four thousand wooden pilings that have to be kept permanently moist. Today the church can always be seen reflected in the gleaming windows of the adjacent **John Hancock Tower**, whose rooftop observatory provides a glorious overall view of Boston (Mon–Sat 9am–10pm, Sun noon–10pm; $5). Construction defects caused Hancock Tower to shed three thousand panes of glass during its first year; the cost of insuring a neighboring hotel against damage was so prohibitive that it was cheaper for the developers to buy it outright. **Copley Square** nearby is an upmarket shopping mall with several good snack bars and restaurants.

The **Christian Science Center** at Huntington and Massachusetts avenues is the "Mother Church" of the First Church of Christ, Scientist, and the home of the *Christian Science Monitor* newspaper; Nelson Mandela made a point of paying a personal visit in 1990 to thank the paper for its support. The complex houses the **Mapparium** (Mon–Sat 10am–4pm; free), an impressive glass globe of the world, which you can walk inside on a footbridge. Part of its interest is that it was built in 1932, and thus shows national boundaries as they were then.

Further south, beyond the boundaries of Back Bay and a long enough walk to warrant taking the Green subway line instead (get on a car marked "E"), is the **Museum of Fine Arts** at 465 Huntington Ave (Mon, Tues & Thurs–Sun 10am–5pm, Wed 10am–10pm, West Wing also open Thurs & Fri until 10pm; $10, under-17s free, donation Wed 4–10pm). From its magnificent collections of Asian and ancient Egyptian art onwards, this holds sufficient marvels to detain you all day. High points include Edward Hopper's tranquil, hopeful *Room in Brooklyn* (American Modern); Andrew Wyeth's *Corner of the Woods* (William Coolidge); Degas' *The Little Dancer*, Gauguin's *Where do we come from, What are we, Where are we going?* (Impressionists), and Millet's *The Sower* (English and French). Don't miss the **American Decorative Arts**, either: a gloriously nostalgic jamboree of coffee urns, speak-your-weight machines and reconstructed living rooms. The I M Pei-designed West Wing holds special exhibits and the contemporary art collection.

A smaller-scale and rather more idiosyncratic collection of fine arts can be found at the **Isabella Stewart Gardner Museum**, down the road at 280 The Fenway (Tues–Sun 11am–5pm; $10). This reconstructed Italian Renaissance villa, complete with indoor fountain, is crammed with the eclectic harvest of a lifetime spent in pursuit of the sublime – a breathtaking hotchpotch of anything from modern American to fifteenth-century Italian. Some of the most interesting works are "unlisted," such as the tapestry of a lion, a sea lion and an elephant above the door of the Italian room, or the sculpted pigeon on the nearby windowsill. Relaxing weekend music concerts are held Sat and Sun at 1.30pm and cost an additional $5.

## Cambridge

The excursion across the Charles River to **Cambridge** merits at least half a day, starting with a fifteen-minute ride on the Red "T" line from Park Street to **Harvard Square**. This is not so much a square as a number of interlocking streets, filled with shopping malls and bookstores, at the point where Massachusetts Avenue runs into JFK and Brattle streets. It's an exceptionally lively area, filled with students from nearby Harvard University and MIT; its cafe terraces, such as *Au Bon Pain*, make for enjoyable people-watching. The **Cambridge Visitor Information Booth** here (Mon–Sat 9am–5pm, Sun 1–5pm; ☎617/497-1630) sporadically organizes walking tours in summer, and sells local maps and guides. More thorough information is available from **Cambridge Tourism**, 18 Brattle St (Mon–Fri 9am–5pm; ☎617/441-2884).

Feel free to wander into **Harvard Yard** and around the core of the university, founded in 1636; its enormous Widener Library (named for a victim of the *Titanic*) boasts a Gutenberg Bible and a first folio of Shakespeare. Five minutes' walk west along Brattle Street is the imposing yellow-fronted mansion at no. 105, known as **Longfellow House** (Wed–Sun 10.30am–4.30pm; $2), after the author of *Hiawatha,* who lived here until 1882. A century earlier it was briefly the headquarters of General George Washington. Dexter Pratt, immortalized in Longfellow's *Under the spreading chestnut tree, the village blacksmith stands,* lived at 56 Brattle St, now a popular bakery and cafe.

## Lexington and Concord

On the night of April 18, 1775, **Paul Revere** rode down what is now Massachusetts Avenue from Boston, racing through Cambridge and Arlington on his way to warn the American patriots gathered at **Lexington** of an impending British attack. Close behind him was a force of more than four hundred British soldiers, intent on seizing the supplies which they knew the "rebels" had hoarded at **Concord**.

Although much of Revere's route has been turned into major freeways, and you are barely out of the Boston suburbs when you arrive in Lexington, the various scenes of the first military confrontation of the Revolutionary War – "the shot heard round the world" – remain much as they were then. The triangular **Town Common** at Lexington was where the British encountered the opposition. Captain John Parker ordered his 77 American "**Minutemen**" to "stand your ground. Don't fire unless fired upon, but if they mean to have a war let it begin here." No one knows who fired the first shot – it may have come from one of the venerable houses around the green – but the Minuteman

Statue commemorates the eight Americans who died. Guides in period costume lead tours of the **Buckman Tavern**, where the Minutemen waited for the British to arrive; the **Hancock-Clarke House** a quarter of a mile north, where Samuel Adams and John Hancock were awakened by Paul Revere, is now a **museum**. All three sites are open Monday to Saturday from 10am to 5pm, on Sunday from noon to 5pm, and admission to each is $4.

There were no British casualties in Lexington, but by the time they marched on Concord the next morning the surrounding countryside was up in arms. In running battles in the town itself, and along the still-evocative **Battle Road** leading back towards Boston, 73 British soldiers and 49 colonials were killed over the next two days. The relevant sites now form the **Minuteman National Historic Park**, with visitor centers at the scenic North Bridge (174 Liberty St) in Concord and at Battle Road in Lexington. Paul Revere's ride is re-enacted annually on Patriot's Day, a city holiday on the third Monday in April, along with the Battle of Lexington (and the Boston Marathon).

South of Concord, **Walden Pond** was where Henry David Thoreau conducted the experiment in solitude and self-sufficiency described in his 1854 book *Walden*. "I did not feel crowded or confined in the least," he wrote of life in his simple log cabin. The site where it stood is now marked with stones, and at dawn you can still watch the pond "throwing off its nightly clothing of mist." This pretty and popular state park was saved from development by a band of Hollywood types led by ex-Eagle Don Henley. Thoreau is interred, along with Ralph Waldo Emerson, Nathaniel Hawthorne and Louisa May Alcott, atop a hill in **Sleepy Hollow Cemetery**, just east of the center of Concord.

As well as guided **bus tours** from Boston (see p.174), **buses** run to Lexington from Alewife Station, at the northern end of the Red "T" line, and **trains** to Concord from North Station ($3.60 one-way).

# Eating

There is far more to eating in Boston than its image as "Beantown" might suggest. Above all, there's the **seafood**, especially lobsters, scrod (a generic term for young, white-fleshed fish), clams (served as steamers, dipped in butter, or as creamy chowder) and oysters (some of the world's best come fresh daily from Wellfleet and other Cape Cod spots). You could base a day's tour of the different neighborhoods around the foods on offer: breakfast in the cafes of **Beacon Hill** or **Cambridge**; lunch in the food plazas of **Quincy Market** or **The Garage** on JFK Street in Cambridge, or dim sum in **Chinatown**; for dinner, a budget **Indian** in Cambridge, an **Italian** around Hanover Street in the North End, or expensive seafood overlooking the Harbor.

The central aisle of **Quincy Market** is superb for all kinds of takeaways, including fresh clams and lobster, ethnic dishes, fruit cocktails and cookies (all over the city, you'll find marvelous chocolate and ice cream), which you can buy from different vendors and eat in the central seating area. There are restaurants and brasseries on all sides.

Chinatown, where restaurants stay open until 2 or 3am, is best for **late-night** eating.

## Boston

**The Blue Diner**, 150 Kneeland St (☎617/695-0087). Classic restored Fifties diner with lively juke-box, slowly inching its way upmarket but with excellent traditional and unpretentious American food. Open till 4am on weekends.

**Buzzy's**, 327 Cambridge St (☎617/242-7722) and 647 Massachusetts Ave, Cambridge (☎617/864-2333). Locally famous for fabulous roast beef sandwiches, hand-cut french fries, and the fact that they never close.

**Daily Catch**, 323 Hanover St (☎617/523-8567) and 261 Northern Ave (☎617/338-3093). Sicilian-style seafood restaurant, noted for its many styles of calamari. Expect to pay up to $20.

**Division Sixteen**, 855 Boylston St (☎617/353-0870). The food is so-so, but the real draw is being able to sip martinis and any number of frozen concoctions in this converted police stable with a decidedly 1920s feel.

**Durgin Park**, 340 N Market St, Faneuil Hall (☎617/227-2038). Crowded, hurried and priding itself on surly service, but a Boston institution for its chunky prime ribs and seafood specialties – not to mention the baked beans. Shared tables, no reservations. Anything from $7 upwards.

**Gabriele's**, 1 1st Ave, Charlestown Navy Yard (☎617/242-4040). Excellent upscale Italian, with a terrace for outdoor dining.

**Giacomo's**, 355 Hanover St (☎617/523-9026). Fresh, flavorful food, with an emphasis on seafood and pasta specialties – the pumpkin tortellini in a sage butter sauce is a North End classic.

**Golden Palace**, 14–20 Tyler St (☎617/423-4559). Chinese restaurant open until 11.30pm, with excellent and reasonably priced dim sum daily until 3pm. $7 and upwards.

**Legal Sea Foods**, at the *Park Plaza Hotel*, 50 Park Plaza (☎617/426-4444). Citywide chain deservedly renowned for its top-quality seafood. Excellent oysters.

**Mamma Maria**, 3 North Square (☎617/523-0077). Widely acknowledged as the best of the North End's traditional-style Italian restaurants, noted for seafood dishes and fresh breads. Expensive and popular for special occasions.

**Mucho Gusto Café**, 1124 Boylston St (☎617/236-1020). Good-sized portions of Cuban cuisine in a room brimming with bric-a-brac. If you sit on the terrace, try not to face the Mass Turnpike.

**Rabia's**, 73 Salem St (☎617/227-6637). The best thing about this small restaurant is its Express Lunch special from noon till 2pm, when you can pay under $5 for a heaping plateful of filling leftovers.

**Steve's Greek-American Cuisine**, 316 Newbury St (☎617/267-1817). One of Boston's classic cheap eats, with heavenly Greek food and divine grilled chicken sandwiches.

**Tremont 647**, 647 Tremont St (☎617/266-4600). Recent addition to the burgeoning South End dining scene, with big portions of New American food, much of it grilled, and superb desserts.

## Cambridge

**Bombay Club**, 57 JFK St, second floor, Harvard Square (☎617/661-8100). One of the very best of Cambridge's many Indian restaurants, with a good-value lunch buffet.

**Cambridge Sail Loft**, 1 Memorial Drive, Kendall Square (☎617/225-2222). Fine array of inexpensive seafood.

**Dali**, 415 Washington St, Somerville (☎617/661-3254). Excellent tapas and Spanish entrees amid decor nearly as surreal as its namesake. Lively sangria bar makes long waits tolerable.

**East Coast Grill**, 1271 Cambridge St, Inman Square (☎617/491-6568). Fairly pricey, but tasty Southern-style food – BBQ and the like – in the midst of a surprisingly good restaurant area.

**Elephant Walk**, 2067 Massachusetts Ave, Porter Square (☎617/623-9939) and 900 Beacon St, Boston (☎617/247-1500). Their French fare is very good, but the adventurous Cambodian side of the menu steals the show: try the *poulet dhomei* – chicken with basil, bamboo shoots and pineapple.

**John Harvard's Brew House**, 33 Dunster St, Harvard Square (☎617/868-3585). Cozy brewpub, serving a good menu with exciting little twists on American grill standards. $25 should suffice for a big meal with a couple of drinks.

**Mr and Mrs Bartley's Burger Cottage**, 1246 Massachusetts Ave, Porter Square (☎617/354-6559). Delicious, shamelessly unhealthy burgers and other diner fare served in an Americana-festooned atmosphere.

**Redbone's**, 55 Chester St, Somerville (☎617/628-2200). Excellent, inexpensive ribs, chicken and catfish with a big range of vegetable side dishes. Just off Davis Square, two "T" stops from Harvard Square.

**Rhythm & Spice**, 315 Massachusetts Ave, Central Square (☎617/497-0977). Lively restaurant with a young clientele not far from MIT, serving good-value Caribbean food.

# Nightlife and entertainment

Mainstream Boston's pride and joy, the **Boston Symphony Orchestra**, under the youthful directorship of Keith Lockhart, is based at the Symphony Hall, 301 Huntington Ave (☎617/266-1200), which Stravinsky called the best auditorium in the world – with a winter season followed by the **Boston Pops** concerts in May, June and on July 4. The city's **theater** scene divides into the safe productions of the Theater District (often Broadway cast-offs) and more experimental companies in Cambridge. The **Bostix** kiosks (☎617/482-BTIX) at Faneuil Hall and in Copley Square sell tickets for all major events – as well as tours, "T" passes, and so on – with some half-price same-day tickets.

Seattle bands may have attracted much of the music business hype during the 1990s, but arguably Boston has made a more innovative and substantial contribution to **rock music**. The emergence in the late 1980s of the Pixies, Dinosaur Jr and Buffalo Tom has been followed by a fresh batch of guitar rock acts like Tracy Bonham and Letters to Cleo, and the live music circuit is dominated by the very best local and touring indie bands. Key nightlife zones include **Lansdowne Street**, an entire block of nightclubs next to Fenway Park, **Boylston Place**, on the south side of Boston Common, and Cambridge's **Central Square** district.

Note that the city's **bars** are unusually officious in demanding ID. Though not permitted to offer cut-price happy hours, some provide free early-evening snacks instead. The weekly *Boston Phoenix* ($1.50) is the best source of up-to-date **listings**.

## Boston bars, cafes and clubs

**Avalon**, 15 Lansdowne St (☎617/262-2424). An anchor on the Lansdowne St club scene, *Avalon* is a local favorite for late-night dancing.

**The Black Rose**, 160 State St (☎617/742-2286). Large Irish pub right beside Faneuil Hall, with traditional music every night and Guinness galore.

**Bull and Finch Pub**, 84 Beacon St, Beacon Hill (☎617/227-9605). Its status as the original setting of TV's *Cheers* makes this place totally touristy, but at least it's central and lively.

**Chaps**, 100 Warrenton St, off Stuart St (☎617/266-7778). Glitzy gay club filled with lots of decked-out young men.

**Commonwealth Brewery Company**, 138 Portland St (☎617/523-8383). Brewpub right by the Fleet Center near North Station, serving good pub food and its own real ale.

**Mercury Bar**, 116 Boylston St (☎617/482-7799). More of a place to see and be seen than to taste the tapas, which are generally quite good. There's a dance club in the back.

**Other Side Cosmic Café**, 407 Newbury St (☎617/536-9477). Popular and trendy cafe with great salads, sandwiches, beer, wine, coffee and tea. Across from Tower Records and Mass Turnpike, and open late.

**Seven's Ale House**, 77 Charles St, Beacon Hill (☎617/523-9074). It may not look like much, but that's the point at this centrally located local watering hole.

## Cambridge

**The Cellar**, 991 Massachusetts Ave (☎617/876-2580). An eclectic mix of students and locals gather in a laid-back niche between Harvard and Central squares. Two stories, two bars, and some live entertainment on weekends.

**House of Blues**, 96 Winthrop St, Harvard Square (☎617/497-2229). The original, surprisingly small branch of this popular chain of live music venues. High-quality blues nightly, a decent Cajun-themed restaurant and a heaving bar.

**Man Ray**, 21 Brookline Ave, Central Square (☎617/864-0400). Nightly themes draw very different crowds to Cambridge's most popular dance club. Wed is gothic/industrial, Thurs and Sat (when the club is known as *Campus*) draw a lively gay crowd, and Fri is reserved for the fetish/bondage scene.

**Middle East**, 472/480 Massachusetts Ave, Central Square (☎617/864-EAST). Cambridge's best alternative music venue with three stages and a good, inexpensive Arabic restaurant. Cover usually $3–10 in the main rooms with free music in the restaurant – bands to have played here gratis include Morphine, Buffalo Tom and Tracy Bonham.

**Passim**, 47 Palmer St, Harvard Square (☎617/492-5300). Longstanding "coffeehouse" folk/blues venue.

**Phoenix Landing**, 512 Massachusetts Ave, Central Square (☎617/576-6260). Affable neighborhood bar and restaurant with soccer piped in from Europe and a down-to-earth mix of music at weekends.

**Plough & Stars**, 912 Massachusetts Ave, between Harvard and Central squares (☎617/441-3455). Time-worn Irish pub with music most nights. Cover free or up to $6.

**Western Front**, 343 Western Ave, Central Square (☎617/492-7772). Live music every night, reggae at weekends.

## Sport

The legendary Red Sox play **baseball** at Fenway Park (Kenmore subway on the Green "T" line). The whole stadium, squeezed in 1912 into the odd-shaped plot that was all its builders could buy, is painted green, including the 37ft, six-inch wall in the left field known as the "**Green Monster**" (☎617/267-8661; ☎617/267-1700 tickets, $10–26). **Basketball**'s Celtics and **hockey**'s Bruins both play at the Fleet Center, 150 Causeway near North Station (box office ☎617/624-1000).

The **Boston Marathon**, first run in 1897, is now held on Patriot's Day, the third week in April, and finishes on Boylston Street at Copley Square (details ☎617/236-1652).

# The North Shore

As you head northwards out of Boston, you pass through a succession of rich little ports that have been all but swallowed up by the suburbs. The most obvious day-trip from Boston is the half-hour ride out to witch-hunting **Salem**. Nearby **Marblehead**, on the other hand, gave us the **US Navy**: George Washington's first five vessels were built there. If you have the time, the atmospheric old fishing ports of **Gloucester** and **Rockport**, further out on **Cape Ann**, have strong literary and artistic identities: T S Eliot used to come here for his family vacations, and the *Dry Salvages* of the third of his *Four Quartets* are a group of offshore rocks. They're also the best places on the East Coast for **whale-watching** trips: Cape Ann Whale Watch (☎978/283-5110 or 1-800/877-5110) offers four-hour trips for around $25 between May and October.

## Salem and Marblehead

Ironically, **SALEM** is remembered less as the site where the colony of Massachusetts was first established, with the most elevated of intentions, than as the place where just sixty years later Puritan self-righteousness reached its apogee in the horrific **witch trials** of 1692. While the town itself was to prosper as a port – as evidenced by its fine old buildings – the witch scare did much to discredit the idea that the New World conducted its affairs on a different moral plane than the Old. Nineteen Salem women were hanged as witches (and one man, Giles Corry, pressed to death with a boulder), thanks to a group of impressionable teenage girls who reported as truth a garbled mixture of fireside tales told by a West Indian slave, Tituba, and half-digested scare stories published by Cotton Mather, a pillar of the Puritan community.

That this unpleasant history is now the basis of a child-oriented tourist industry – all black hats and broomsticks – makes Salem an unsettling place. The **Salem Witch Museum** in Washington Square (daily: July & Aug 10am–7pm; rest of year 10am–5pm;

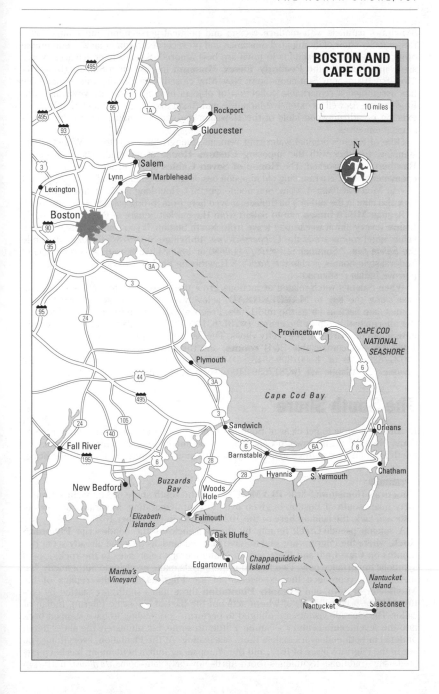

**BOSTON AND CAPE COD**

0 _____ 10 miles

N

Rockport
Gloucester
Salem
Lynn
Marblehead
Lexington
Boston
Provincetown
CAPE COD
NATIONAL
SEASHORE
Plymouth
Cape Cod Bay
Sandwich
Orleans
Barnstable
Fall River
New Bedford
Buzzards
Bay
Woods
Hole
Hyannis
S. Yarmouth
Chatham
Elizabeth
Islands
Falmouth
Oak Bluffs
Martha's
Vineyard
Edgartown
Chappaquiddick
Island
Nantucket
Island
Nantucket
Siasconset

$4) draws parallels with modern racism and political persecution, but is at heart a rather tacky show of illuminated dioramas and prerecorded commentary. Innumerable other witch-related attractions in town are best ignored. Salem's later seafaring years are remembered in the **Peabody Essex Museum** in East India Square (June–Oct Mon–Sat 10am–5pm, Sun noon–5pm; Nov–May closed Mon; $8.50), which since 1799 has assembled a remarkable collection of objects brought home by voyaging New Englanders. As well as extensive Japanese and Asian displays, it has one of only three existing breadfruit-wood idols of the Hawaiian god Ku, and details about the town's ships themselves.

Little of Salem's original waterfront remains, though the long **Derby Wharf** is still standing, together with the imposing **Custom House** at its head, where Nathaniel Hawthorne once worked. The **House of Seven Gables** at 54 Turner St, the star of his eponymous novel, is a rambling old mansion beside the sea (summer daily 9am–5pm; rest of year Mon–Sat 10am–4.30pm, Sun noon–5pm; $7). Hour-long guided tours of the complex also take in the author's birthplace, moved here from its original site on Union Street.

Regular MBTA **buses** run to Salem from Haymarket Square in Boston, and hourly **trains** (every 2hr at weekends) leave from North Station. If you want to **stay**, the best-value motel rooms are at the *Clippership Inn*, 40 Bridge St (☎978/745-8022; ③), while the *Salem Inn*, 7 Summer St (☎978/741-0680 or 1-800/446-2995; ⑥), a 39-room trio of Federal-style homes, is classier. *Ravi's*, 6 Hawthorne Blvd (☎978/744-6570), is an inexpensive Indian restaurant.

When Salem's witch-related attractions grow tiresome, head five miles south and east along the bay to **MARBLEHEAD**, a lovely waterfront village whose historic homes date back as far as the mid-1700s. Free walking tour **maps** are available from the information booth in the center (☎781/631-2868), while 250-year-old **Fort Sewall**, jutting into the harbor, gives pretty views. The *Seagull Inn*, 106 Harbor Ave (☎781/631-1893; ⑥), has comfortable B&B **rooms**, and the *Marblehead Inn*, 264 Pleasant St (☎781/639-9999 or 1-800/399-5843; ⑦) offers newly renovated two-room suites; *Flynnie's*, 28 Atlantic Ave (☎781/639-2100), serves fresh, inexpensive **seafood**.

# The South Shore

It can take a while to get clear of Boston heading south – especially on summer weekends, when the traffic down to Cape Cod can be horrendous. Two historic towns, one north and one west of the Cape, are worth exploring – **Plymouth** and **New Bedford**.

## Plymouth

"America's Hometown," little **PLYMOUTH**, on the south shore of Massachusetts Bay forty miles south of Boston, is given over to commemorating, in various degrees of taste and tack, the landing here of the 102 **Pilgrims** in December 1620.

A solemn pseudo-Greek temple by the sea encloses the nondescript **Plymouth Rock**, where the Pilgrims are said to have touched land; as they had already spent two months on Cape Cod, and there are no contemporary references to the rock, it is of symbolic importance only. Two worthier memorials make no claim to authenticity, but meticulously reproduce the experience of the Pilgrims. Both the replica of the **Mayflower** in town, and **Plimoth Plantation** three miles south, are staffed by costumed "interpreters," each of whom acts out the part of a specific Pilgrim, Indian or sailor. The charade visitors are obliged to perform – pretending to have stepped back into the seventeenth century – can be a little tiresome, but ultimately the sheer depth of detail in both endeavors makes them fascinating. At the Plantation, everything you see in the Pilgrim Village of 1627, and the Wampanoag Indian Settlement, has been created using traditional techniques (both April–Nov daily 9am–5pm; *Mayflower* until 7pm in July & Aug; ☎508/746-1622; *Mayflower* alone $6.50 and Plantation alone $16.50, Plantation and *Mayflower* $19). A reasonably interesting way to pass time for free is at **Cranberry World** (May–Nov daily 9.30am–5pm), a slick little museum sponsored by Ocean Spray, which details how the tart crimson berries are harvested from local bogs and then processed into various products. The frequent tours end with free samples of juice; if you've always wondered what "Cran-Raspberry" or "Cranicot" taste like, here's your chance to find out.

Plymouth's **visitor center** is located on the Waterfront at no. 130 (☎508/747-7525 or 1-800/USA-1620). Plymouth & Brockton (☎508/746-0378) provides a regular **bus** service to and from Boston. Standard **motels** include the *Blue Spruce Motel*, 710 State Rd (☎508/224-3990 or 1-800/370-7080; ④), the *Cold Spring*, 188 Court St (☎508/746-2222; ④), and the *Sleepy Pilgrim*, 182 Court St (☎508/746-1962; ④), while the *Governor Bradford Motor Inn*, 98 Water St (☎508/746-6200 or 1-800/641-1620; ⑤), overlooking the harbor, has slightly better facilities, including a heated outdoor pool. The *Lobster Hut* (☎508/746-2270) and *McGrath's* (☎508/746-9751) are good, reasonably priced **seafood** places on the waterfront.

## New Bedford

The famous old whaling port of **NEW BEDFORD**, 45 miles due south of Boston, is still home to one of the nation's most prosperous fishing fleets which, each year, haul in the largest catch on the East Coast. New development, and a waterfront highway, have obscured some of its past, but on County Street the fine old houses still stand of which Melville commented:

> *New Bedford is a queer place. Had it not been for us whalemen, that tract of land would this day perhaps have been in as howling condition as the coast of Labrador . . . all these brave houses and flowery gardens came up from the Atlantic, Pacific and Indian oceans. One and all, they were harpooned and dragged hither from the bottom of the sea.*

The roster of the whaling ship *Acushnet*, in the **New Bedford Whaling Museum** at 18 Johnny Cake Hill (daily 9am–5pm, summer Thurs until 8pm; $4.50), shows Melville as one of the crew. Other evocative displays include a half-size replica of a whaling vessel. Immediately opposite stands the **Seamen's Bethel**; it really does have the ship-shaped pulpit described in *Moby Dick*, but this one was rebuilt after a later fire.

The town's **visitor centers** at 47 N Second St (☎508/991-6200) and at Pier 3 (☎508/979-1745) can prebook **accommodation**; *The 1875 House* is an atmospheric little B&B at 36 Seventh St (☎508/997-6433; ③). **Ferries** to Martha's Vineyard are detailed on p.195.

# Cape Cod and the islands

> *Here a man may stand, and put all America behind him.*
>
> Henry David Thoreau

The trouble with standing on **Cape Cod** these days is that "all America" tends to be a lot closer behind you than you might prefer. Its main tourist haunts are packed in summer, its roads circled by a grim procession of crawling vehicles, searching in vain for some "unspoiled" bit of beach or "undiscovered" old town. Unless you have your own, preferably very secluded, place to stay, it's barely worth turning up at weekends, especially between June and August, and putting yourself through the hassle of trying to find what little available accommodation there is, invariably at premium prices. However, the place is undeniably beautiful and if you find yourself in the region midweek in May or September – when hotel prices are much lower, the crowds have thinned, and the weather usually very pleasant – it's certainly worth a visit.

Cape Cod was named by Bartholomew Gosnold in 1602, on account of the prodigious quantities of cod caught by his crew off Provincetown. Less than twenty years later the Pilgrims landed nearby; in the few months before moving on to Plymouth, they began the process, continued by generations of Europeans, of stripping the interior of the Cape bare of its original covering of thick woods. Today, much of the land on the Cape – from its salt marshes to its ever-eroding dunes – is considered a fragile and endangered ecosystem, designation, however, that hasn't especially dampened the persistence of developers.

Thinking of the Cape, as everyone does, as an arm, its **upper** section, the thirty-mile eastward stretch closest to mainland Massachusetts would be represented by the biceps. Much of the worst beachfront development lies along the southern shore, and **Hwy-28**, running from Falmouth via Hyannis to Chatham, gets especially clogged. Only once you get beyond the "elbow" and head north to the **Outer Cape** or, anatomically speaking, the forearm, past the spectacular dunes of **Cape Cod National Seashore** do you get a feeling for why the Cape still has a reputation as a seaside wilderness. **Provincetown**, right at the end, is the one town on the Cape that can be unreservedly recommended.

Sadly, the islands of **Martha's Vineyard** and **Nantucket**, off the Cape to the south, are dependent on summer tourism for their livelihood. However, a trip out to Nantucket in particular does still evoke haunting memories of its proud seafaring days. Again, the off-season has a charm all it's own, a time when you can sink into the rhythms of life on the island without the distraction of hordes of day-trippers toting beach chairs.

## Getting to the Cape

It was the Pilgrims who first suggested the construction of a canal between Cape Cod Bay and Buzzards Bay, so that coastal shipping could avoid the dangers of the open ocean; when finally completed at the start of the twentieth century, it left the peninsula as an island. Now all traffic to the Cape bottlenecks at one or other of the two enormous bridges – Bourne on Hwy-28 and Sagamore on Hwy-6 – across the canal, and you may regret trying to **drive** there on a summer Friday (or back on a Sunday). Each has an **information office** for the Cape (daily 9am–7pm) on its mainland side.

One way to dodge the traffic is to **fly**. Delta's Business Express (☎1-800/345-3400) serves Hyannis and Nantucket from Boston and New York; and Continental affiliate Colgan Air (☎1-800/272-5488) serves Hyannis and Nantucket from New York; and Cape Air (☎1-800/352-0714) flies several times daily from Boston and New Bedford to Hyannis, Provincetown and the islands. Bonanza **buses** run regularly from New York and Boston(☎617/345-0539 or 1-800/556-3815), and the Plymouth & Brockton Bus Co (☎508/746-0378) runs to Hyannis and Provincetown from Rhode Island, Boston and New York daily (for other Boston services, see p.174). **Ferries** take three hours to cross from Boston to Provincetown (see p.192); for boats to the various islands, see p.195.

You can also **cycle** from Boston on the 135-mile Boston–Cape Cod Bikeway, which extends all the way to Provincetown.

## The Upper Cape

The **Upper Cape**, just across the bridges, was the first part of the peninsula to attract tourists in any numbers – and it shows. To see the various communities of the south coast as "pretty little villages" – the image they hope to project – you'd have to be wearing exceptionally rose-tinted spectacles, or blinders. In theory, each is coyly arranged around a prim central green; but you have to fight your way through thickets of malls, motels and fast-food joints to reach their artificial hearts.

It only makes sense to **stay** in one of these places if you're catching a **ferry** to the islands (see p.195). Thus one obvious base is **FALMOUTH**, where central motels include the comfortable *Shoreway Acres Inn*, 59 Shore St (☎508/540-3000 or 1-800/352-7100; ⑤), with indoor and outdoor pools, and the harborfront *Best Western Marina Tradewinds* on Robbins Road (☎508/548-4300 or 1-800/341-5700; ⑤). The luxurious clapboard *Village Green Inn*, 40 W Main St (☎508/548-5621 or 1-800/237-1119; ⑤), is a bargain in Cape terms; the oceanfront *Grafton Inn*, 261 Grand Ave (☎508/540-8688 or 1-800/642-4069; ⑤), in the Falmouth Heights district, is also good. The *Sippewissett Campground*, a couple of miles out at 836 Palmer Ave (☎508/548-2542), offers a free shuttle service to the ferries and beaches. Restaurants abound, though with the possible exception of *Betsy's Diner*, 457 Main St (☎508/540-0060), built in the Fifties and serving no-nonsense food from that era, the best food is to be found in the assorted moderately priced seafood places along the waterfront at **WOODS HOLE**, four miles southwest; the *Fishmonger's Cafe* at 56 Water St (☎508/548-9148) is recommended. An **exhibition** at 15 School St, near Little Harbor (May–Oct Tues–Sat 10am–4.30pm, Sun noon–4.30pm; Nov, Dec, March & April Fri & Sat 10am–4.30pm, Sun noon–4.30; free), focuses on the sensational rediscovery of the *Titanic* in 1986 by the well-respected **Woods Hole Oceanographic Institute**. Ocean Quest offers ninety-minute science-based ocean cruises (reservations recommended; ☎1-800/37-OCEAN; $17).

The largest port on the Cape, and its main commercial hub, **HYANNIS** clings a little desperately to the glamour it earned when the **Kennedy compound** at Hyannisport placed it at the center of world affairs. Hence the existence of the **John F Kennedy Museum**, 397 Main St (Mon–Sat 10am–4pm, Sun 1–4pm; $2), which shows photographs, newsclips and film footage of the days JFK spent on the Cape. The Kennedys are still here, though their property can only be glimpsed, from a considerable distance, from the sea – Hy-Line Cruises, Ocean Street Docks (☎508/778-2600; $8), runs one-hour harbor cruises that peek in at the compound. Coincidentally, the town itself has become a rather anonymous playground for the over-privileged young.

Sightseeing trips on the **Cape Cod Central Railroad** (May–Oct Tues–Sun; ☎508/771-3800; $11.75) run from Center Street in Hyannis along a meandering route west through cranberry bogs to Sandwich, Buzzards Bay and Falmouth.

There are many hotels in Hyannis, but you would have to find a pretty compelling reason for wanting to stay in one. A good **B&B** in Hyannis Port – and the only one – is the *Simmons Homestead Inn*, 288 Scudder Ave (☎508/778-4999 or 1-800/637-1649; ⑥). *The Egg & I*, 521 Main St (☎508/771-1596), does a decent breakfast, while *Alberto's* at no. 360 (☎508/778-1770) is a good but pricey Italian; *Paisan's*, 530 Main St (☎508/775-0344), is cheaper.

## The Mid-Cape

The middle stretch of Cape Cod holds some of its prettiest, most unspoiled places. Time-worn old fishing communities like Wellfleet and Chatham, along with dozens of carefully maintained, mildly touristy hamlets along the many winding roads, are what most people hope to find when they come to the Cape. Cutting across the middle, the **Cape Cod Rail Trail** follows a paved-over railroad track from Dennis to Eastham, through cranberry bogs and forests. It makes a good **cycling** trip; bikes can be rented in all the main towns.

One desirable destination is the whitewashed old fishing community of **CHATHAM**, tucked on a protected harbor between Nantucket Sound and the open Atlantic Ocean. Hang out at the **Fish Pier** on Shore Road and wait for the fleet to come in mid-afternoon, or head a mile south on Hwy-28 to **Chatham Light**, one of many lighthouses built to protect mariners from the treacherous shoals. Tour **maps** are available from the booth at 533 Main St (☎508/945-5199 or 1-800/715-5567). Just off Main Street at 15 Chatham Bars Ave, the *Impudent Oyster* (☎508/945-3545) serves excellent seafood. One of the nicest **places to stay** on the whole East Coast is the *Whalewalk Inn*, at 220

## CAPE COD NATIONAL SEASHORE

After the bustle of Cape Cod's towns, the **Cape Cod National Seashore** really does come as the proverbial "breath of fresh air." These protected lands, spared by President Kennedy from the rampant development further south, take up virtually the entire Atlantic side of the Cape, from Chatham north to Provincetown. Most of the way you can park by the road, sometimes for a fee, and strike off across the dunes to windswept beaches – though in places parking is limited to local residents. A program of grass-planting helps to hold the whole place together; three feet of the lower Cape is washed away each year, and much of it is carried here by the sea to extend the endless beaches.

It was on these shifting sands, not then as denuded as today, that the **Pilgrims** made their first home. They obtained their water from Pilgrim Spring near Truro; at Corn Hill Beach they uncovered the freshly buried cache of Indian corn that kept them alive. After a couple of months, which they survived with the help of the Wampanoag Indians, they moved on to Plymouth (where the reconstructed Indian village at Plimoth Plantation, covered on p.188, is based on one found at Eastham).

Displays and movies at the main **Salt Pond Visitor Center**, on US-6 just north of Eastham (March–June, Sept–Dec & weekends in Jan and Feb 9am–4.30pm; July & Aug daily 9am–5pm ☎508/255-3421), trace the geology and history of the Cape. A road and a hiking/cycling trail head east to the sands of **Coast Guard Beach** and **Nauset Light Beach**, both of which offer excellent swimming. Another fine beach is the **Head of the Meadow**, halfway between Truro and Provincetown on the northeast shore.

Bridge Rd in the town of **EASTHAM** (☎508/255-0617; ④), where rates for the lovely B&B rooms include free use of bicycles to ride the many nearby trails. Out on Queen Anne Road, a five-minute walk from downtown, the *Chatham Guest House* at no. 49 (☎508/945-3274; ④) and the *Bow Roof House* at no. 59 (☎508/945-1346; ③) are two B&Bs where all rooms have private baths. The nearest **hostel**, with beds from $14, is the *HI-Mid Cape*, between Chatham and Provincetown at 75 Goody Hallet Drive, Eastham (☎508/255-2785; ①).

## Provincetown

The compact fishing village of **PROVINCETOWN** ("P-Town") is right on the knuckle of Cape Cod's clenched fist. Silvery clapboard houses, with gloriously unruly gardens, line its tiny winding streets. Provincetown is far from secluded: its population of five thousand rises tenfold in summer. Self-professed **bohemians** and **artists** have always flocked here for the dazzling light and vast beaches, and in 1914 Eugene O'Neill established the Provincetown Playhouse in a small hut. It has also become renowned, since the beatnik 1950s, as a **gay** and **lesbian** center. Commercialism, though rampant, is countercultural: gay, environmentalist and feminist giftshops join arty (not craftsy) galleries, restaurants and bars on the aptly named **Commercial Street**.

Provincetown retains a firm grip on its past. Strict zoning ensures that there are few new buildings in town, and there is barely a sign of ugly development. Albeit crowded and raucous from July onwards, P-Town remains a place where history, natural beauty and, above all, difference, are respected and celebrated.

### Arrival, information and getting around

Provincetown lies 120 miles from Boston by land, but less than fifty by sea, nestled in the second largest natural harbor in the world (after Le Havre in France). By far the nicest way to arrive is on the **ferry**. Bay State Cruises leave Commonwealth Pier in Boston at 9am, arriving at MacMillan Wharf three hours later, and return at 3pm (daily mid-June to Labor Day, weekends only in early June and rest of Sept; ☎617/723-8012; $18 one-way, $30 same-day round-trip, $75 two-hour express). The tiny **information center** in the Chamber of Commerce, at the end of the wharf at 307 Commercial St, sells ferry tickets (summer daily 9am–5pm; rest of year Mon–Sat 10am–4pm; ☎508/487-3424).

It couldn't be easier to **walk** around tiny P-town, but many visitors prefer to **cycle** the narrow streets, hills and the undulating Province Lands Bike Trail, a difficult six-mile route with great vistas. Rental outlets in town include Arnold's, 329 Commercial St (☎508/487-0844). For those without transportation, **tours** to the more isolated dunes and moors include the Provincetown Trolley Inc from the town hall on Commercial Street (daily 10am–6pm; ☎508/487-9483; $8); Art's Dune Tours are based at Commercial and Standish (April–Oct 10am–dusk; $12 daytime tour and $15 sunset tour; ☎508/487-1950). **Whale-watching** cruises leave from MacMillan Wharf between April and October 31; recommended is the Dolphin Fleet Whale Watch (☎508/349-1900 or 1-800/826-9300). All sell tickets in the harbor for about $20.

## Accommodation

As well as the few motels on the outskirts, every second picturesque cottage in town seems to be a guesthouse. Prices are reasonable until mid-June, and off-season you can find real bargains. The Provincetown Reservation Service (☎508/487-2400 or 1-800/648-0364) and the gay-oriented Intown Reservations (☎508/487-1883 or 1-800/67P-TOWN) can usually rustle up lodging at busy times. The welcoming *Dunes' Edge Campground*, on Hwy-6 just east of the central stop lights (☎508/487-9815), charges $25 for its wooded sites and is only in operation May–Sept.

**Elephant Walk Inn**, 156 Bradford St (☎508/487-2543 or 1-800/889-WALK). Central, spacious rooms with private baths. Free parking. ⑤.

**Gull Walk Inn**, 300A Commercial St (☎508/487-9027). All-women guesthouse in a quiet lane off the town center, with sun deck and sea views. ④.

**HI-Truro**, North Pamet Rd, Truro (☎508/349-3889). Ten miles south of Provincetown in a former coastguard station. Dorm beds $12 a night. Open mid-June–early Sept. Office hours 7.30–9.30am & 5–10.30pm. ①.

**Land's End Inn**, 22 Commercial St (☎508/487-0706). Meticulously decorated rooms and suites, many with sweeping ocean views. ⑤–⑦.

**Outermost Hostel**, 28 Winslow St (☎508/487-4378). Five-dorm cabins with $15 beds. ①.

**Revere Guesthouse**, 14 Court St (☎508/487-2292 or 1-800/487-2292). B&B with relaxing garden patio and continental breakfast, and rooms with shared baths for around $65 in summer. ④.

**Sunset Inn**, 142 Bradford St (☎508/487-9810 or 1-800/965-1801). Clean, quiet rooms in an artistic house close to the center. ④.

**Watership Inn**, 7 Winthrop St (☎508/487-0094 or 1-800/330-9413). Fifteen rooms with private bath in an 1820 sea captain's home; rates include a good continental breakfast. ④.

## The town and the beaches

Visitors who head straight for the beaches miss out on Provincetown's tiny core, centered on the three narrow miles of **Commercial Street**. **MacMillan Wharf**, always busy with charters, yachts and fishing boats (which unload their catch each afternoon), splits the town in half. Not far away in the quieter **East End**, the **Heritage Museum**, 356 Commercial St (daily: summer 10am–6pm; rest of year 10am–5pm; $3), stands in an 1860 Methodist church. This well-loved collection of Provincetown memorabilia includes a 68-inch striped bass, a Portuguese altar, a model fishing schooner and a reconstruction of the beach hut of Harry Kemp, beach-bum poet and crony of Eugene O'Neill. It also provides leaflets detailing walking tours. Further out, the delightful **Provincetown Art Association and Museum**, 460 Commercial St (April–Oct daily noon–5pm & 8–10pm; Nov–March Sat & Sun noon–4pm; $3), displays paintings by local artists.

The 252ft granite tower of the **Pilgrim Monument and Provincetown Museum** on Town Hill, in the pretty **West End** of P-Town, has an observation deck (only accessible by stairs and ramps) which looks out over the whole of the Cape (July & Aug daily 9am–7pm; May, June, Sept & Oct daily 9am–5pm; $5). At the bottom of the hill on Bradford Street, there's a bas-relief monument to the Pilgrims' **Mayflower Compact**. Further from the wharf, the weathered clapboard houses have colored blinds, white picket fences, and wildflowers spilling out of every possible crevice. The 1746 **Seth Nickerson House**, 72 Commercial St (June–Oct daily 10am–5pm; $2.50), is the oldest house in town, built by a ship's carpenter. Tours lead through cabin-like rooms with slanting doors and crazed floorboards. A modest bronze plaque on a boulder at the western end of Commercial Street commemorates the Pilgrims' actual landing place.

A little way beyond the town's narrow strip of sand, undeveloped **beaches** are marked only by dunes and a few shabby beach huts. You can swim in the clear water from the uneven rocks of the two-mile breakwater, where the sea bed crunches with soft-shell clams, or head onwards through scented wild roses and beach plums to find blissful isolation. West of town, **Herring Cove Beach**, easily reached by bike or through the dunes, is more crowded but never unbearably so. In the wild **Province Lands**, at the Cape's northern tip, vast sweeping moors and bushy dunes are buffeted by a deadly sea, site of 3000 known shipwrecks. The **visitor center** (April–Nov daily 9am–5pm; ☎508/487-1256), in the middle of the dunes on Race Point Road, has an observation deck from which you might spot a whale.

## Eating

**Food** in Provincetown can be expensive: the snack bars around MacMillan Wharf are generally extortionate, and the – undeniably good – *nouvelle cuisine* in the trendy gay restaurants can hit $10 for a salad and a coffee. Portuguese bakeries, relics of early settlement, and bland family restaurants abound on Commercial Street.

**Cafe Blase**, 328 Commercial St (☎508/487-9465). Touristy pastel cafe, one of the few places with outdoor seating for people-watching. Pricey for dinner, but delicious $6 fresh fruit and waffle breakfasts.

**Cafe Heaven**, 199 Commercial St (☎508/487-9639). Light and airy, upmarket-looking cafe serving all-day breakfasts, cappuccino and creative salads from $5. Closed 3–6.30pm, then reopens until 10pm.

**Ciro & Sal's**, 4 Kiley Court (☎508/487-0049). Traditional Italian cooking, though quite expensive.

**Fat Jack's**, 335 Commercial St (☎508/487-4822). Low-priced, no-nonsense breakfasts, and lunch and dinner specials.

**Post Office Cafe**, 303 Commercial St (☎508/487-3892). Small, gay-run restaurant serving healthy lunches and dinners for $5–10. Gay/feminist cabaret nightly.

**Spiritus**, 190 Commercial St (☎508/487-2808). Combination pizza place and coffee bar with a scene that gets more intense as the night marches on.

## Nightlife and entertainment

Each weekend, boatloads of revelers seek out P-Town's notoriously wild nightlife. From house music raves to drag cabarets, from torch singing to R&B, the variety is huge.

**The Atlantic House**, 6 Masonic Place, behind Commercial St (☎508/487-3821). The "A-House" – a dark drinking hole of Tennessee Williams and Eugene O'Neill – is now a trendy gay music club and bar.

**Crown and Anchor**, 247 Commercial St (☎508/487-1430). Noisy pub with nightly drag cabaret.

**Governor Bradford**, 312 Commercial St (☎508/487-2781). Popular bar with live jazz, reggae and R&B.

**Student Union**, 9–11 Carver St (☎508/487-3490). Popular dance club and video bar.

**Vixen**, 336 Commercial St (☎508/487-6424). High-energy lesbian club.

## Martha's Vineyard

The island of **MARTHA'S VINEYARD**, just seven miles south of Cape Cod and twenty-four miles long by ten wide, may or may not have been named for Bartholomew Gosnold's daughter Martha (some ancient maps call it *Martin's* Vineyard). The "Vineyard" part, however, was for its "incredible store of vines"; considerably more fertile than bleak little Nantucket, it has never been quite so dependent on the sea to make a living. Now more than ever, tourism is at the root of the island's economy, boosted by the gaggle of celebrities, not least the Clintons, who shown up year after year. The popularity of the island with the rich, famous, and/or well-connected has driven up housing prices and lowered availability to extremes. The many second-homeowners who spend the summer here get a better deal than mere day-trippers, though – some of the best beaches are off-limits to non-residents.

Ferries to the island arrive either at **Oak Bluffs**, where genteel Victorian terraced cottages look down on the harbor and there's a colorful century-old fairground carousel near the jetty, or at the more upmarket **Vineyard Haven**. **Edgartown**, over to the east, is the oldest settlement on the island, and has been extravagantly dolled up for visitors (you may recognize it as the location for the *Jaws* films). A little ferry shuttles back and forth from Edgartown to adjacent **Chappaquiddick Island** (the bridge that Senator Edward Kennedy made infamous is on the far side).

The three principal island communities are connected by a regular bus service and offer full facilities and shops of every kind. They're quite mellow places to pass a summer's day, but exploring on your own can yield unexpected pleasures. Bringing a car

---

### FERRIES TO MARTHA'S VINEYARD AND NANTUCKET

Unless otherwise specified, all the ferries below run several times daily in midsummer (mid-June to mid-Sept). Most have fewer services from May to mid-June, and between mid-September and October. There is at least a skeleton service to each island, though not on all routes, all year round. Round-trip passenger **fares** from Woods Hole and Falmouth to Martha's Vineyard are around $12; from Hyannis $22. Round-trip costs for cars (mid-May to mid-Sept) are around $80, not including passengers.

**To Martha's Vineyard**

From **Falmouth** to Oak Bluffs. Passengers only. The *Island Queen* (☎508/548-4800).

From **Falmouth** to Edgartown. Passengers only. Falmouth Ferry Service (☎508/548-9400).

From **Woods Hole** to both Vineyard Haven and Oak Bluffs. Car ferry. Steamship Authority (☎508/447-8600).

From **Hyannis** to Oak Bluffs. Passengers only. Hy-Line (☎508/778-2600 in Hyannis; ☎508/693-0112 on Martha's Vineyard).

From **New Bedford** to Vineyard Haven. Passengers only, $19 round-trip. Martha's Island Ferries (☎508/997-1688).

From **Montauk**, Long Island, to Oak Bluffs. Passengers only, summer Thursdays only, $40. Viking Ferry (☎516/668-5709).

**To Nantucket**

From **Hyannis**. Cars on Steamship Authority (☎508/477-8600 for auto reservations; ☎508/548-5011 on the mainland; ☎508/228-0262 on Nantucket). Also Hy-Line (☎440/891-5000; ☎508/778-2600 in Hyannis; ☎508/228-3949 on Nantucket).

From **Harwich Port**. Passengers only. Freedom Cruise Line (☎508/432-8999).

The Hy-Line ferry company in summer also runs one daily connecting service, for passengers only, between Martha's Vineyard and Nantucket.

over is expensive and rather pointless, but as soon as you get off the ferry you encounter rows of **bike** rental places. The best ride is along the State Beach Park between Oak Bluffs and Edgartown, with the dunes to one side and marshy Sengekontacket Pond to the other; purpose-built cycle routes continue to the youth hostel at West Tisbury (see below).

Trips around the west side of the island ("up-island") can be disappointing, with not a peep at the ocean beyond the private estates; however, you do eventually come to the **lighthouse** at **Gay Head Cliffs**, where the multicolored clay was once the main source of paint for the island's houses – anyone caught removing any clay faces a sizeable fine. The cliffs are not vast, and they're crumbling away so fast that it's not safe to approach them too closely. From Gay Head public beach below, however, you can get some great views of this spectacular mass. Gay Head was once famous for its Wampanoag harpooneers, such as Tashtego in *Moby Dick*.

## Accommodation

If accommodation is booked up, as is very likely, the main **Chamber of Commerce** office at Beach Road in Vineyard Haven (☎508/693-0085) may be able to help. There are **campgrounds** in Vineyard Haven (☎508/693-3772).

**Attleboro House**, 42 Lake Ave, Oak Bluffs (☎508/693-4346). Charming, old-fashioned guesthouse in a distinguished harbor-view terrace – no private bathrooms. ④.

**Colonial Inn**, 38 N Water St, Edgartown (☎508/627-4711 or 1-800/627-4701). Extremely central white clapboard inn, part of a largish mall. Some off-season bargains, but midsummer rates are high. ⑦.

**HI-Martha's Vineyard**, Edgartown–West Tisbury Rd (☎508/693-2665). A very nice setting. Shuttle buses available at the ferry terminal. April to mid-Nov. $14 members, $17 nonmembers. ①.

**Nashua House B&B**, Kennebec Ave across from the Post Office, Oak Bluffs (☎508/693-0043). Small rooms, shared baths. ④.

**Shiretown Inn**, 44 N Water St, Edgartown (☎508/627-3353 or 1-800/541-0090). Variety of different-styled B&B rooms, including some very costly ones, right in the center of town. ⑥.

**Tuscany Inn**, 22 N Water St, Edgartown (☎508/625-5999). Savor an unexpected slice of Italy in the center of (somewhat stuffy) Edgartown. ⑥.

**Wesley Hotel**, 70 Lake Ave, Oak Bluffs (☎508/693-6611 or 1-800/638-9027). Large but characterful hotel near the ferries. Most rooms are $130-plus, but a few with shared bathrooms cost less. ⑤.

## Eating and drinking

It's not at all hard to find something to **eat** on Martha's Vineyard. The ports in particular have rows of places to tempt tourists just off the ferries. Only in Edgartown and Oak Bluffs can you order alcohol with meals, but you can bring your own elsewhere. Many pubs, too, serve inexpensive food, though the people partaking of it often look like they're on a break from a Ralph Lauren photo shoot. Wear Nautica if you want to blend in with the locals.

**The Black Dog Bakery**, Water St, Vineyard Haven (☎508/693-4786). Skip the overrated *Black Dog Tavern* next door and stock up on delicious muffins and breads for the ferry ride back.

**Giordano's**, Circuit Ave, Oak Bluffs (☎508/693-0184). Crowded and reasonably priced Italian.

**Lambert's Cove**, West Tisbury (☎508/693-2298). The restaurant at this hideaway country inn – surrounded by forest and apple orchards – is a gem; try the delectable soups. Reservations suggested.

**Louis'**, 102 State Rd, Vineyard Haven (☎508/693-3255). Lively, well-priced Italian place.

**The Newes from America**, attached to the *Kelley House Inn*, 23 Kelley St, Edgartown (☎508/627-7000). Swill 500 beers in this atmospheric pub (not necessarily all in the same night) and they'll name a stool after you.

**The Wharf**, Lower Main St, Edgartown (☎508/627-9966). One of the better-priced seafood joints on the island, on the east side of town.

**Zapotec**, 10 Kennebec Ave, Oak Bluffs (☎508/693-6800). Exciting seafood variations on Mexican cuisine.

# Nantucket

The thirty-mile, two-hour sea crossing to **NANTUCKET** may not be an oceangoing odyssey, but it does set the "Little Grey Lady" apart from her larger, shore-hugging sister, Martha. Halfway here from Hyannis, neither mainland nor island is in sight, and once you've landed you can avert your eyes from the smart-money double-deck cruisers with names like *Pier Pressure* and *Loan Star* and let the place remind you that it hasn't always been a rich folk's playground. Indeed, despite the formidable prowess of its seamen (see box overleaf), survival for early settlers on the island's scrubby soil was always a struggle.

The tiny cobbled carriageways of **Nantucket Town** itself, once one of the largest cities in Massachusetts, were frozen in time by economic decline 150 years ago. Today, this area of delightful old restored houses – the town has more buildings on the National Register of Historic Places than Boston – is very much the center of activity. From the moment you get off the ferry you are besieged by bike rental places and tour companies. **Straight Wharf** leads directly onto **Main Street** with its shops and restaurants; the **information office** – which has a daily list of accommodation vacancies, but doesn't make reservations – is nearby at 25 Federal St (☎508/228-0925). The **Chamber of Commerce**, 48 Main St (☎508/228-1700), carries the best range of island information. The main sights in town are the excellent **Whaling Museum** (summer daily 10am–5pm; $5) on Broad Street at the head of Steamboat Wharf, where you should look out especially for such scrimshaw artefacts as a set of 21 whale types carved from whales' teeth, and the astonishing harpoon corkscrewed in the "flurry" or last struggle of a dying whale, and the **Peter Foulger Museum** ($4) of island history next door.

After a stroll around Nantucket Town, the usual procedure is to cycle the seven flat miles east to the village of **Siasconset** (always abbreviated to 'Sconset), where the venerable cottages stand literally encrusted with salt, and then to meander back at will across the heaths and moorland. Buses also link Nantucket Town and 'Sconset.

## Accommodation

But for the **youth hostel**, accommodation on Nantucket is invariably expensive; the going rate in B&Bs and guesthouses starts at $75. There are no campgrounds.

**Cliff Lodge**, 9 Cliff Rd (☎508/228-9480). B&B with some low-priced singles. ⑧.

**Hawthorn House**, 2 Chestnut St (☎508/228-1468). Central, well-appointed guesthouse. ⑨.

**HI-Nantucket, Star of the Sea**, Surfside (☎508/228-0433). Dorm beds at Surfside Beach, just over 3 miles south of town. $12 members, $15 nonmembers. Lockout 10am–5pm, curfew 11pm. April–Oct only. ①.

**Hungry Whale**, 8 Derrymore Rd (☎508/228-0793). Good-value, friendly B&B a short walk from the center. Five rooms, one with private bath. ④.

**Jared Coffin House**, 29 Broad St (☎508/228-2400 or 1-800/248-2405). Sixty rooms, all with period furniture in four adjacent buildings in the town center. Superb restaurant and likeable bar. ⑥.

**The Nesbitt Inn**, 21 Broad St (☎508/228-0156). The central location and affordable rooms, most with original furniture, compensate for the shared baths in this Victorian inn, built in 1872. ④.

## Eating

Crèvecoeur (see box overleaf) reported that on Nantucket "music, singing and dancing are holden in equal detestation." **Seafood** fortunately is not; the only trouble is that Nantucket's restaurants, good as they may be, tend to be exceptionally expensive.

## THE WHALERS OF NANTUCKET

*Scores of anonymous Captains have sailed out of Nantucket, that were as great, and greater than your Cook . . . For in their succorless empty-handedness, they, in the heathenish sharked waters, and by the beaches of unrecorded, javelin islands, battled with virgin wonders and terrors that Cook with all his marines and muskets would not have willingly dared.*

Herman Melville, *Moby Dick*

In 1659, a sober group of 27 Quaker and Presbyterian families arrived on Nantucket and set about imposing order on the haphazard business of **whaling**. Whales had always beached themselves on the treacherous sandy shoals all around – up to a dozen might be washed ashore in a major storm – and the local **Indians** had become skilled in hunting them in nearby waters. At first, the white settlers treated the island itself as their vessel, erecting tall masts from which a permanent watch was kept for passing whales. As the years went by, they stopped waiting at home, and sent large ships out into the ocean to pursue their prey. The Wampanoag played an integral part in the process: the actual kill was effected by two rowboats working in tandem, and at least five of each thirteen-man crew, usually including the crucial **harpooneer**, would be Indian. (The common occurrence when an injured whale would speed away, dragging a boat helterskelter behind it for endless terrifying hours, was known as a "**Nantucket Sleighride.**")

The early chronicler Crèvecoeur provides an extensive account of Nantucket as it was in 1782 in his *Letters from an American Farmer*. Although perturbed by the islanders' universal habit of taking a dose of opium every morning, he held them up as a model of diligence and good self-government. Whaling was a disciplined profession, unmarred by the stereotyped debauchery of sailors elsewhere, and to feed themselves and equip their ships the islanders kept up a shrewd and extensive trade with the mainland. At that time there were already more than a hundred ships. The whalemen were not paid; instead each had a share (a *lay*) of the final proceeds of the voyage. Crèvecoeur was impressed by the Nantucketers' ambition: "Would you believe that they have already gone to the Falkland Islands and I have heard several of them talk of going to the South Sea."

They did indeed reach the Pacific – see Chapter Sixteen, Hawaii, for an account of their experiences there. The great days of Nantucket were immortalized by Herman Melville:

*And thus have these naked Nantucketers, these sea hermits, issuing from their ant-hill in the sea, overrun and conquered the watery world like so many Alexanders . . . Two thirds of this terra-queous globe are the Nantucketer's. For the sea is his; he owns it, as Emperors own empires.*

In fact *Moby Dick* is a valediction; by the time it was published in 1851, Nantucket's fortunes had gone into an abrupt decline. Soon after a devastating fire in 1846, reports of the Californian Gold Rush lured young men westwards; the discovery of underground oil in Pennsylvania came as the final blow. A magazine article of 1873 reported, "Let no traveler visit Nantucket with the expectation of witnessing the marks of a flourishing trade . . . of the great fleet of ships which dotted every sea, scarcely a vestige remains."

**Arno's**, 41 Main St (☎508/228-7001). Good-value snacks and lunches.

**Espresso Cafe**, 40 Main St (☎508/228-6930). Inexpensive, healthy lunches. Some vegetarian dishes.

**Rose and Crown**, 23 S Water St (☎508/228-2595). Seafood saloon with music and comedy.

**Sea Grille**, 45 Sparks Ave (☎508/325-5700). One of the best places for seafood and not too badly priced.

**Topper's**, 120 Wauwinet Rd (☎508/228-8768). Pricey but outstanding New American cuisine in this quiet, upscale flagship restaurant at the *Wauwinet* hotel and resort a few miles outside Nantucket town.

# Central and western Massachusetts

The 150 miles of Massachusetts that stretch inland to the west of Boston have always been obliged to play second fiddle to the state capital. Just ten years after the Revolution, the farmers who struggled to make a living from this indifferent soil so resented the imposition of taxes by the prosperous merchants of the east that they rose in **Shay's Rebellion**; their pitchforks were no match for the guns of the new nation.

These days the citizens of the west are eager to promote themselves as cultural rivals to the big city, with the **Berkshires** hosting the celebrated **Tanglewood** music festival in summer. **Amherst**, the home of such diverse talents as Emily Dickinson and Dinosaur Jr, is a stimulating little college community, as is its larger neighbor, **Northampton**; both have all the cafes, restaurants and bookstores you could want. Another delightful college town is **Williamstown** in the far northwest corner, set at the end of the incredibly scenic Mohawk Trail.

## Worcester

Forty miles west of Boston on I-90, **WORCESTER** is Massachusetts' second largest city and the only industrial city in the US beside neither sea, lake nor river. Abbie Hoffman's home town is definitely not a place to spend a great deal of time, but if you're nearby you could visit the remarkable **Higgins Armory Museum**, at 100 Barber Ave (Tues–Sat 10am–4pm, Sun noon–4pm; $4.75), which houses weapons and armor from all over the world in a bizarre steel and glass office-cum-museum (note the conspicuous riveting). The enthusiasm for metalworking of the founder of the Worcester Pressed Steel Company led him to tour Europe after World War I, buying vast quantities of ancient armor. You might also drop in at the **American Antiquarian Society**, 185 Salisbury St (Mon–Fri 9am–5pm, tours Wed 2pm), which holds copies of two-thirds of all the material published in America before 1821, more even than the Library of Congress. The **Worcester Art Museum**, 55 Salisbury St (Tues, Wed & Fri 11am–4pm, Thurs 11am–8pm, Sat 11am–5pm, Sun 1–5pm; $5) is worth a stop, as is its cafe. A more consumerist attraction is the new **Worcester Common Fashion Outlet Mall**, just off I-290 exit 14 or 16, with over a hundred designer and designer-like stores under one roof; one reason for its popularity is that there is no state sales tax on clothing purchases under $175.

Of local **accommodation**, the *Hampton Inn*, 110 Summer St (☎508/757-0400 or 1-800/426-7866; ⑤), has good clean rooms; the *Econolodge*, 531 Lincoln St at Lincoln Plaza (☎508/852-5800; ③), is less expensive. The *Sole Proprietor*, 118 Highland St (☎508/798-3474), is a reliable fish **restaurant**. Outside Worcester but worth a detour is the *Salem Cross Inn* (off Route 9 in West Brookfield; ☎508/867-8337), a rambling restaurant in a restored 1705 farmhouse that serves consistently high-quality Yankee cooking.

## Springfield

**SPRINGFIELD**, at the point where I-90 crosses I-91 – in an extremely confusing way – ninety miles from Boston at the southern end of the Pioneer Valley, has an odd assortment of claims to fame, including being the home of the Springfield rifle and the late children's author Dr Seuss. However, visitors are drawn to this unwieldy and unattractive city, split by the wide Connecticut River, by the 1890s invention of Dr James Naismith – the sport of **basketball**. Naismith designed the game as a way of providing exercise for athletes at the YMCA, and its popularity spread with amazing rapidity. After a trip to the Berlin Olympics in 1936 Naismith came up with another bright idea and established the **Basketball Hall of Fame** at 1150 W Columbus Ave, next to the river just south of Memorial Bridge (Mon–Tues, Thurs & Sun 9am–6pm, Wed, Fri & Sat

## OLD STURBRIDGE VILLAGE

Halfway between Worcester and Springfield on US-20, near the junction of I-90 and I-84, the restored and reconstructed **Old Sturbridge Village** (daily 9am–5pm; $15), made up of preserved buildings brought from all over the region, gives a somewhat idealized but still engaging portrait of a small New England town of the 1830s. As in other similar places, costumed interpreters act out roles – working in blacksmiths' shops, planting and harvesting vegetables, tending cows and the like – but they pull it off in an unusually convincing manner. The 200-acre site itself, with mature trees, ponds and dirt footpaths, is very pretty, and with all its crafts and diversions you could easily spend half a day here. The nearby *Old Sturbridge Village Lodges* (☎508/347-3327; ⑤), owned by the museum, is a reasonable place to stay; the *American Motor Lodge*, on Hwy-20 W at I-84 exit 3B, Sturbridge (☎508/347-9121; ④), costs a bit less.

9am–8pm; $8). This enjoyably traces the history of the game with movies, videos and plenty of memorabilia, and also lets you test your own skills.

Springfield's Amtrak station is very central, at 66 Lyman St. Several bus lines, including Peter Pan (☎413/781-2900), which provides daily services to and from Boston and New York, operate out of the nearby bus station at 1776 Main St (☎413/781-7882). The **CVB** is downtown at 34 Boland Way (☎413/787-1548 or 1-800/723-1548). **Motels** include the *Rodeway Inn*, 1356 Boston Rd (☎413/783-7750; ③), and there are a number of budget motels over the river in West Springfield. The *Cityspace YMCA*, 275 Chestnut St (☎413/739-6951; ③), has rooms for men and women. If you're hungry, tiny Fort Street has been home to *The Fort/Student Prince* (☎413/734-7475) for over 60 years – a local favorite serving German wiener schnitzel, goulash and sauerbraten.

## The Berkshires

The **Berkshire Hills**, where Massachusetts borders New York, are a cross between the English Lake District and the grand seafront resort of Newport, Rhode Island. Especially in the area nearest the Massachusetts Turnpike (I-90), the green hillsides are dotted with ostentatious Victorian mansions, while the towns are chic, arty – if not snooty – summer tourist magnets. Further north, it's easier to escape civilization and get deep into the woods. The **Mohawk Trail** in the northwest corner passes through North Adams and **WILLIAMSTOWN**, following the very scenic route the Native Americans used to travel between the valleys of the Connecticut and Hudson rivers. Williamstown, in the northwest corner of the state, has two worthy, free art museums: the highlight of the **Sterling and Francine Clark Art Institute**, 225 South St (Tues–Sun 10am–5pm), is the thirty-strong collection of Renoir paintings, while the **Williams College Museum of Art** on Main Street (Tues–Sun 10am–5pm) has good exhibits of ancient Middle Eastern and modern American art.

**STOCKBRIDGE**, just south of I-90 fifty miles west of Springfield, started out as "Indian Town." The Reverend John Sergeant built the simple wooden **Mission House**, now located on Main Street, in 1739 in an attempt to live in close proximity with the local Native Americans and convert them to Christianity by sheer force of example. His success barely lasted beyond his own death; later settlers were far less keen on having the natives around.

That Stockbridge today looks the archetypal New England small town – above all when there's snow on the ground – is due largely to the artist **Norman Rockwell**, who lived here for 25 years until his death in 1978. Many of his *Saturday Evening Post* covers, whose sentimentality was made palatable by his sharp wit, featured the town; a collection can be seen at the $10 million **museum** on Hwy-183 (daily 10am–5pm; $9). Some of the tour guides modeled for Rockwell as children and recall that for every few minutes they managed to hold still he'd slip them one more from his large pile of nickels.

Magnificent houses in the hills around Stockbridge include **Chesterwood**, the luxurious home and studio of Daniel Chester French, sculptor of the Lincoln Memorial (late May to Oct daily 10am–5pm), half a mile south of the new Rockwell Museum, and **Naumkeag**, which belonged to Joseph Choate, US ambassador to Queen Victoria (summer daily 10am–4.15pm). Stockbridge was also the setting for Arlo Guthrie's song, and movie, *Alice's Restaurant*.

Well-heeled tourists flock to nearby **LENOX** each year for the summer season of the Boston Symphony Orchestra at **Tanglewood**. Open-air symphonic concerts are held every Friday, Saturday and Sunday in July and August, with chamber music and recitals given on other days; covered seats are pricey and often hard to get, but you can sit and picnic on the lush lawns for an admission fee of around $15. Some midweek rehearsals are also open to the public (☎413/637-1666 for details), and there's a jazz festival on the weekend of Labor Day.

Further north on US-7, **Arrowhead** (daily 10am–5pm; $5), near Pittsfield, was Herman Melville's home while he wrote *Moby Dick*; declining popularity eventually obliged him to sell up and move to New York. The **Hancock Shaker Village**, five miles west of Pittsfield, survived from 1790 to 1960 (May–Oct daily 9.30am–5pm; April & Nov daily 10am–3pm; $9). Its legacy includes the large dwelling place, in which almost one hundred people slept and ate; a round stone barn for their cattle; and the garage where the last Shakers kept their cars. A more important, and much less commercialized, Shaker village, **Mount Lebanon**, is another five miles west on US-20, just over the New York state border; much has been dismantled and moved to museums, but self-guided **tours** give a sense of the Shaker way of life ($5).

### Practicalities

Much of the **accommodation** in the Berkshires is concentrated in Lenox and neighboring Lee; when the Tanglewood concerts are on, prices naturally go through the roof and a last-minute vacancy is almost impossible to find. The only rooms in Lee for under $60 are in the *Super 8 Motel* at 170 Housatonic St (☎413/243-0143 or 1-800/800-8000; ④). For slightly more, you can stay at the historic *Merell Inn* in South Lee, an atmospheric 200-year-old roadside inn (Route 102; ☎413/243-1794; ⑦). In Lenox, the *Brook Farm Inn* at 15 Hawthorne St (☎413/637-3013; ⑤–⑦) is a welcoming B&B with some luxury rooms at over $100; the *Best Western Black Swan Inn* (☎413/243-2700 or 1-800/876-7926; ⑤) on Rte-20 in Lee has lakefront doubles. Williamstown has several mid-priced motels, as well as some stately accommodation – like the 100-room *Williams Inn* on Main Street (☎413/458-9371 or 1-800/828-0133; ⑦). The *Red Lion Inn* is one of the grander edifices on Main Street, Stockbridge (☎413/298-5545; ⑦); rooms are expensive, but the *Lion's Den* bar and restaurant downstairs is fun. If you're hungry, the *Church Street Cafe*, 59 Church St, Lenox (☎413/637-2745), is good value and the friendly *Sullivan Station*, a converted railroad station in Lee (☎413/243-2082), serves food plus a selection of beers on tap.

# RHODE ISLAND

**RHODE ISLAND** is the smallest state of the Union, at a mere 48 miles long by 37 miles wide, and tends to be overlooked as a destination, even if it is home to more than twenty percent of the nation's historical landmarks. It was established by Roger Williams in 1635 as a "lively experiment" in religious freedom. He had been expelled from Puritan Salem for his radical ideas (including the notion that Indians should be paid for their land and that there should be a complete separation of church from state), and the Massachusetts Puritans liked to call the state "**Rogues Island**."

Despite its size, Rhode Island has over four hundred miles of coastline, hacked out of the Narragansett Bay; it is, in fact, made up of over thirty tiny islands, including Hope and Despair. The **"Ocean State"** therefore developed through sea trade, whaling and smuggling. Partly due to this commercial interest, Rhode Islanders, resenting the stringent economic pressures placed on them from England, were in the front rank of Revolutionary groundswell. However, no Revolutionary battles were fought on Rhode Island soil and unwilling at first to abandon its new-found freedom, it turned out to be the last state to ratify the Constitution. Between the Revolution and the Civil War, Rhode Island shifted from a maritime economy and led the **Industrial Revolution** with Samuel Slater's creation of the nation's first water-powered **textile mill** in Pawtucket, just outside Providence. Today, although still heavily industrialized, the state's principal destinations are its two original ports: well-heeled **Newport**, yachting capital of the world, with good beaches and outrageously extravagant mansions, and the colonial college town of **Providence**. **Block Island**, about thirty miles south of Newport, has a popular state beach, while the rest of Rhode Island is largely made up of sleepy small towns and fishing ports.

### Getting around Rhode Island

Rhode Island is tiny enough to make getting around ridiculously easy. I-95, the major interstate, runs through **Providence** on its way from Massachusetts to Connecticut. The more scenic US-1 follows the coast of Narragansett Bay into Connecticut. **Newport** is accessible from Hwy-138, which connects the small islands in Narragansett Bay to the mainland. **Public transportation** is good: local buses connect Providence and Newport, and Amtrak stops regularly in Providence. **Ferries** link Block Island and Newport.

# Providence

Splayed across seven hills on the Providence and Seekonk rivers, **PROVIDENCE** was Rhode Island's first settlement, founded "in commemoration of God's providence" on land given to Roger Williams by the Narragansett Indians (his insistence that Indians should be paid for their land being waived in his own case). Now New England's fourth largest city, it has been the **state capital** since 1901, and flourished as one of the most important ports of call in the notorious "triangle trade," where New England rum was exchanged for African slaves to be sold for West Indian molasses. Since Slater's invention of the water-powered textile mill, port trade and industry have been the mainstays of the economy. Today Ivy League **Brown University** and the **Rhode Island School of Design** (RISD or "Rizdee") give the place a certain cultural verve (although this admittedly doesn't stray far beyond the immediate environs of College Hill on the east bank of the river), and the many original colonial homes on **Benefit Street** emphasize a historical importance almost absent from the somewhat drab downtown across the river. Ethnic diversity is provided by **Little Italy** on Federal Hill, west of the river, and by fairly voluble Greek and Portuguese – and especially Cape Verdean – communities.

## Arrival, information and getting around

**T F Green Airport** is in Warwick, nine miles south of Providence. In town, there's a brand-new Amtrak station at 100 Gaspee St, in a domed building a short walk southwest of the capitol. Greyhound and Bonanza (☎401/751-8800) **buses** stop downtown at Kennedy Plaza, while Plymouth & Brockton (☎508/746-0378) buses stop considerably further out at 1 Bonanza Way, exit 25 off I-95. Bus transportation within the city, and to the rest of the state, is provided by RIPTA (Mon–Sat 7am–7pm; ☎401/781-9400), with most local and all longer-distance buses leaving from Kennedy Plaza, where schedules are available from a rarely staffed information booth (Mon–Fri 7am–6pm). However, sightseeing is best done on foot.

The **CVB**, 1 W Exchange (Mon–Fri 10am–5pm; ☎401/751-1177 or 1-800/233-1636), provides maps and brochures, as does the useful **Providence Preservation Society**, in the 1772 Shakespeare's Head building at 21 Meeting St, which has self-guided walking tours of the city's historic areas (Mon–Fri 9am–5pm; ☎401/831-7440). There's another **information center** in the Roger Williams National Memorial Park Zoo, 282 N Main St (daily: summer 9am–5pm; rest of year 9am–4.30pm; ☎401/785-3510).

## Accommodation

Downtown Providence has few budget **rooms**, although **B&B**'s are a viable option. Anna's Victorian Connection (☎1-800/884-4288), books rooms for $5. Motorists can take advantage of the mid-priced **motels** along I-95, or north in Pawtucket, and south near the airport at Warwick.

**C C Ledbetter Bed & Breakfast**, 326 Benefit St (☎401/351-4699). Clean rooms in a new house with harbor views. ④.

**Comfort Inn**, 2 George St, Pawtucket (☎401/723-6700), and 1940 Post Rd, Warwick (☎401/732-0470). Decent rooms near exit 27 off of I-95 and Slater's Mill, or by the airport. ④.

**Days Hotel on the Harbor**, 220 India Point (☎401/272-5577). Private home with clean rooms, shared baths and several pets. ③.

**Holiday Inn Downtown**, 21 Atwells Ave (☎401/831-3900). Next to the Civic Center near Little Italy. ⑤.

**The Old Court**, 144 Benefit St (☎401/751-2002). Luxury ten-room B&B in an old rectory. ⑥.

**State House Inn**, 43 Jewett St (☎401/785-1235). Pleasant, central B&B rooms in a restored old home. ④.

## The City

Providence's main attractions focus around three of its seven hills. Downtown, which centers on **Kennedy Plaza**, is sited just below **Constitution Hill**. **City Hall**, at the western end of the plaza, is mainly notable for a star-spangled midnight blue ceiling in the Alderman's Chamber. Though no longer used as a train terminal, the nearby 1898 Beaux Arts **Union Station** is a fine example of the historic restoration at which the city excels. Southeast of the plaza, the 1828 **Westminster Arcade**, the oldest enclosed shopping mall in the nation, features expensive clothes shops and a food court in a small, bright, skylit hall. The **Roger Williams National Memorial**, at N Main and Smith, at the foot of Constitution Hill, includes an original well said to be used by Williams and his followers (daily 9am–4.30pm; free), while at the top of the hill, the white marble **Rhode Island Statehouse** boasts a huge unsupported dome, the fourth largest in the world, topped with a statue of "independent man." A handsome full-length portrait of Washington adorns the Reception Room (Mon–Fri 8.30am–4.30pm; free tours at 10am & 11am; ☎401/222-2357).

Laid-back **College Hill**, across the river, is an attractive district of colonial buildings and museums. Part of Williams' holy experiment was the establishment of the Baptist Church in 1638. The white clapboard **First Baptist Meeting House**, at the foot of the hill at 75 N Main St, dates from 1775, and is remarkable for its very tall steeple. This street leads into **South Main Street**, once bustling with waterfront activity, now a small stretch of potpourri and pottery shops. **Benefit Street**, a block up the hill, is Providence's **"mile of history,"** lined with the ice cream-colored former clapboard homes of merchants and sea captains. Now beautifully restored, the street was just a dirt path leading to graveyards until it was improved in the nineteenth century for the "benefit of the people of Providence" – hence its name. The elegant **John Brown House**, 52 Power St at Benefit Street (March–Dec Tues–Sat 10am–5pm, Sun noon–4pm; Jan–Feb Sat & Sun only; $6), was home to the Donald Trump of the eighteenth century, who made his wealth from trading in slaves and with China. The first house built on the hill (nicely conspicuous from the river), it retains its original furnishings and holds displays on the formidable Brown family and the city itself.

Ivy League **Brown University** sets the tone for this three-centuries-old district with its relaxed, intellectual feel; for free tours, contact the admissions office, 45 Prospect St (Mon–Fri 8am–4pm; tours 10am, 11am, 1pm, 3pm & 4pm; 11am & 3pm only during Christmas & spring break). At the eastern edge of College Hill, **Wickenden Street** buzzes with a creative assortment of bookstores, cafes, and antique and thrift stores.

The small but excellent collection of the **RISD Museum of Art**, 224 Benefit St, is worthy of its status as one of the best art schools in the country, and includes ancient and Oriental works, Impressionists and Post-Impressionists, American art and Rodin's statue of Balzac (Wed, Thurs, Sat, & Sun 10am–5pm, Fri 10am–8pm; $2, free Sat). Also on the RISD campus, the **Woods-Gerry Gallery**, 62 Prospect St (Mon–Sat 10am–4pm, Sun 2–5pm; free), is a solid redbrick mansion set in a tree-shaded garden with heavy stone benches, exhibiting innovative student art.

Across the road, the Greek Revival **Providence Athenaeum**, 251 Benefit St (Mon, Tues, Thurs & Fri 8.30am–5.30pm, Wed 8.30am–8.30pm, Sat 9.30am–5.30pm; free), is where Edgar Allan Poe unsuccessfully wooed fellow poet Sarah Whitman. Today the library holds original Audubon prints and rare books, and the piano and hand-painted chairs in the cozy reading rooms give it the feel of someone's living room.

**Federal Hill**, west of downtown, is Providence's **Little Italy**, entered through a large arch topped by a bronze pinecone at Atwells Avenue. Long a powerful Mafia stronghold, this area is one of the friendliest and safest in the city – alive with cafes, delis, bakeries and bars, and with a large Italianate fountain in the Piazza de Pasquale.

## Pawtucket

In 1793, Samuel Slater used technology surreptitiously imported from England to shove Rhode Island into the industrial age. His landmark **Old Slater Mill** is still in operation, in suburban Pawtucket. A ten-minute drive north to exit 28 on I-95, the **Slater Mill Historical Site**, on Roosevelt Avenue, also includes in its living museum of the Industrial Revolution the 1810 Wilkinson Mill and the 1758 **Sylvanus Brown House** (June–Oct Mon–Sat 10am–5pm, Sun 1–5pm; Nov–Dec & March–May Sat & Sun 1–5pm; closed Jan & Feb; $6.50).

# Eating

Studenty **Thayer Street** is lined with inexpensive lunch places, almost all of which remain open until late. **Wickenden Street** is more alternative, and more expensive. The family-run Italian restaurants on Federal Hill serve good food at reasonable prices, and the Westminster Arcade downtown is your best bet for a quick breakfast or lunch.

**Angelo's**, 141 Atwells Ave (☎401/621-8171). Family-style restaurant offering Italian standards at low cost.

**CAV Restaurant, Antiques and Gifts**, 14 Imperial Place (☎401/751-9164). A trendy restaurant with a great atmosphere and live entertainment after 9.30pm Thurs–Mon.

**Coffee Exchange**, 207 Wickenden St (☎401/273-1198). Trendy coffee bar. A popular meeting place for arty intellectuals. Deckchairs and barrels act as pavement seating and tables.

**Kabob 'n' Curry**, 261 Thayer St (☎401/273-8844). Above-average Indian meals in trendy Thayer St.

**Le Grecque**, 24 Arcade Mall (☎401/351-3454). The cheapest and most interesting food in the mall. Greek specialties include marinated chickpeas and rice or spinach pies.

**New Japan**, 145 Washington St (☎401/351-0300). Reasonably priced Japanese place, with sashimi six days a week, and sushi on Sunday.

## Nightlife and entertainment

As Providence's **nightlife** is largely student-generated, things get quiet during the vacations, though Thayer Street is always lively. On summer evenings, a **party trolley** with balloons and noisy music rumbles through downtown. The $6 fee includes entrance to six nightclubs on its route, and a half-price drink (Fri & Sat 8.30pm–2am; ☎401/861-1385). The Cable Car Cinema at 204 S Main St (☎401/272-3970), and the Avon Rep Cinema, at 250 Thayer St (☎401/421-3315), show good independent and art **films**. The Providence Performing Arts Center, downtown at 220 Weybosset St, hosts various shows in a grand old Art Deco movie house (☎401/421-2787). The free weekly *Providence Phoenix* has complete entertainment listings.

**AS220**, 115 Empire St (☎401/831-9327). Unabashedly artsy cafe-bar hangout for locals and students. Also a music venue featuring everything from mellow jazz to performance art. Gallery on second floor. Cover $2–5.

**Finnegan's Wake**, 397 Westminster St (☎401/751-0290). Authentic Irish pub, right down to the corned beef and cabbage.

**Snooker's Cafe**, 145 Clifford St (☎401/351-7665). Lively pool hall with a variety of table games. Its green room features alternative DJs and is one of the city's most sociable spots. No cover.

**Trinity Brewhouse**, 186 Fountain St (☎401/453-2337). Hang out here after a Providence Bruins (minor league hockey) or Friars (college basketball) game to imbibe microbrews either in celebration or despair.

# Newport

Thirty miles south of Providence, **NEWPORT** stands at the southern tip of the largest island in Narragansett Bay, **Aquidneck** (or **Rhode**) **Island**. It was established as a colony by William Coddington of Providence in 1639. Due to its excellent harbor, it grew rapidly as a port for the triangle trade, a privateering center, and a hotbed of Revolutionary feeling. **Religious tolerance** led to an influx of Jews, Quakers and Baptists who formed lucrative international trade links, but this great prosperity was severely knocked back by the **British occupation** of 1776–79, when half the population fled and much of the town was burned down. Fortunately, enough buildings survived for Newport now to rival Boston for its number of original eighteenth-century homes.

In the 1850s the town became fashionable again as a resort for wealthy Southern merchants, and very soon nouveau riche industrialists such as the Astors, Belmonts and Vanderbilts were building **"summer cottages"** – better described as mansions – along the rocky coastline. The obscene ostentation of this era, now known by Mark Twain's disparaging phrase as the **Gilded Age**, shocked Massachusetts' old wealth to the core.

Depression killed off the decadence, but Newport kept going as a naval town until the 1970s. Today the town feeds off tourism; much of it caters to the tennis and yachting set, but there are as many people looking at – and envying – the wealth as enjoying it. Though sanitized by the ugly new **America's Cup Avenue**, which replaced the sea-salt rawness of the waterfront with bars and boutiques, the rough old port still rears its boozy head, with beer and R&B clubs as evident as cocktails and cruises, making it an essential urban stop, especially during the summer **festival season**.

## Arrival, information and getting around

There are actually three towns on Aquidneck Island: **Portsmouth** is at the northern edge, and then comes the appropriately named **Middletown**, with **Newport**, the southernmost, just below it. The mainland is connected to the island from I-95 on US-138 by the **Jamestown Bridge** to Conanincut Island, and from there by the **Newport Bridge**.

Newport itself, spanning only ten miles, is easy to walk around. **Thames** (pronounced *Thaymz*) Street is the main road, with Bellevue Avenue, or Mansion Row, parallel to the east. Maps and advice are available from the large **visitor center** at 23 America's Cup Ave (daily: summer 8am–8pm; rest of year 9am–5pm; ☎401/849-8048 or 1-800/326-6030).

The adjacent **Gateway Center**, the least expensive place to park a car, is also the terminal for Bonanza (☎401/846-1820) and RIPTA **buses**; the latter run regularly through town, to the beaches and on to Providence ($1–3; ☎401/781-9400 or 1-800/244-0444). Also based at the Center are free summer **shuttle buses** connecting the main sights and shopping areas (daily 10am–7pm); and Viking Tours, whose bus and harbor excursions take in admission to one or more mansions (☎401/847-6921). Rented **bikes**, good for getting to the quieter beaches, cost $5 per hour ($25 a day) from Ten Speed Spokes, 18 Elm St, next to the visitor center (Mon–Sat 9.30am–5.30pm, summer also Sun noon–5pm; ☎401/847-5609). The Newport Historical Society organizes **walking tours** through colonial Newport on Friday and Saturday in summer at 10am (usually $5). Easily the best and most relaxing way of getting a good look at the mansions and town is on the beautiful *Madeleine* **schooner** (☎401/849-3033), which leaves several times daily from Bannisters Wharf; the $15 price for a ninety-minute tour is ultimately better value than the cheaper motorboat tours.

## Accommodation

There are plenty of reasonably priced **guesthouses** in Newport, but it's a good idea to book ahead, especially on summer weekends (when prices rocket). The visitor center (see above) has free phone links to inns and motels in all price ranges. By far the most prevalent form of accommodation is **B&B**, and it's usually possible to get a decent room for $60. Two established agencies are Bed and Breakfast of Rhode Island (☎401/849-1298 or 1-800/828-0000; free), which can find rooms from around $65, and Anna's Victorian Connection, 5 Fowler Ave (☎401/849-2489 or 1-800/884-4288; $5), whose range starts at $40.

**Admiral Fitzroy Inn**, 398 Thames St (☎401/848-8000 or 1-800/343-2863). Cheerfully decorated B&B in the heart of the action, with a roof deck overlooking the harbor and excellent breakfasts. ⑦.

**Cliffside Inn**, 2 Seaview Ave (☎401/847-1811 or 1-800/845-1811). Gorgeous and romantic Victorian manor house, one minute from the Cliff Walk and First Beach. ⑦.

**Howard Johnson Lodge**, 351 W Main Rd, Middletown (☎401/849-2000 or 1-800/446-4656). Just two miles from downtown Newport, this represents the best hotel value in the area. Rates heavily reduced outside of July & August. ⑤.

**The Melville House**, 39 Clarke St (☎401/847-0640). Colonial B&B two blocks from the harbor in Newport's Hill District. ⑤.

**Villa Liberté**, 22 Liberty St (☎401/846-7444 or 1-800/392-3717). Fifteen comfortably appointed rooms, with black-and-white tiled baths, in a cheerfully restored one-time "house of the evening." ④–⑦.

**The Willows Romantic Inn**, 8–10 Willow St (☎401/846-5486). If you liked Beechwood (see opposite), you'll feel right at home with the daily "living history lessons" which come with your breakfast in bed. ④.

# The Town

Newport's main attractions are obviously its **mansions**, but there is nothing to be gained by attempting to tour them all, and although it is pleasant enough to stroll around the predominantly colonial **downtown**, the ever-growing profusion of souvenir shops is somewhat off-putting. Otherwise, if you don't fancy beautiful-people-spotting on the harbor, you'll do better following the crowds to one of the **beaches**.

## The mansions

The phrase "**conspicuous consumption**" was coined by sociologist Thorstein Veblen, who visited Newport c.1900 and witnessed the desperate need felt by new entrepreneurial **millionaires** to bolster their fragile identities by flaunting their wealth. More than just a summer resort, Newport became an arena in which families competed with increasing mania to outdo each other – though the "**season**" of wild and decadent parties lasted only a few weeks, and many of the ten-million-dollar mansions lay empty for years at a time.

It's difficult to grasp the sheer wealth involved by merely gawking at the mansions' facades, but after being herded in and rushed through more than a couple, the opulence rapidly begins to pall. Choose one to see, or two at the most. The most important stand on **Bellevue Avenue**, **Ocean Drive** and **Harrison Avenue**. The Astors' **Beechwood**, 580 Bellevue Ave (mid-May to Oct daily 10am–5pm; Nov & Dec daily 10am–4pm; Feb to mid-May Sat & Sun 10am–4pm; $8.75), is an entertaining antidote to the drier historical drills given on other tours. Costumed actors welcome visitors as house guests who have arrived for a party held by Mrs Astor, the self-proclaimed queen of American society (she devised the notion of the **Four Hundred**, an elite of individuals whose lineage had to go back at least three generations). Anecdotes, bitchy asides and a constant stream of activity – as well as strawberry tea in the servants' kitchen – make it all great fun.

Also on Bellevue Avenue, the **Marble House** is the most over-the-top example of Gilded Age excess, with a golden ballroom and a Chinese teahouse in the grounds; both this and **Rosecliff**, with its colorful rose garden and heart-shaped staircase, were used as sets during the filming of *The Great Gatsby*. **Kingscote**, on Bellevue Avenue, is a quirky Arts and Crafts cottage with a lovely interior, while the biggest and best of the lot, Cornelius Vanderbilt's **The Breakers**, on Ochre Point Avenue, is a sumptuous Italian Renaissance palace, overlooking the ocean. All except Beechwood are run by the **Preservation Society of Newport County**, 424 Bellevue Ave (☎401/847-1000), whose combination tickets slightly help to beat the hefty individual admission prices of at least $7 (April–Sept daily 10am–5pm; rest of year schedules vary; Breakers costs $12, all others $9; any three buildings $24, five $34, seven $40, all eight Society properties $47; ☎401/847-1000).

One way to see the Bellevue Avenue mansions on the cheap is to peer in the back gardens from the **Cliff Walk**, which begins on Memorial Avenue where it meets First Beach. This three-and-a-half-mile oceanside path alternates from jasmine and wild roses to unappealing concrete underpasses through perilous rocks. For those with a car, Ocean Drive continues from Bellevue Avenue where the Cliff Walk ends, following the coast eastwards and passing **Hammersmith Farm**, John and Jackie Kennedy's 28-room shingled summer home, originally owned by Jackie's mother (April to mid-Nov daily 10am–5pm; $8.50; ☎401/846-7346). Be sure to call first, since the property is currently up for sale and might close to the public. If it's open, then meander around the beautiful grounds, where the First Couple's wedding reception was held. The interior of the house, meanwhile, is English Country style and includes Jackie's childhood bedroom and only a smattering of JFK mementos, among them his "summer White House" office.

## Downtown

Newport's colonial political and business center, **Washington Square**, lies just south of the Gateway Center, beginning where Thames Street meets the Brick Market. The 1762 market, off **Long Wharf** (the most important of Newport's colonial wharves), has been reconstructed to include fairly ordinary galleries and pricey giftshops. The **Old Colony House**, one of Rhode Island's few pre-Revolutionary brick buildings and seat of government from 1739 to 1900, stands across the square (July–Sept Mon–Fri 9.30am–noon & 1–4pm, Sat & Sun 9.30am–noon; free). To the north, the **Easton's Point** district, between Washington Street on the water and Spring Street to the east, is lined with the eighteenth-century homes of ships' captains; only the 1748 **Hunter House**, 54 Washington St, is open to the public (May–Oct daily 10am–5pm; $7).

The oldest religious building in town is the shabby 1699 **Quaker House**, at Marlborough and Farewell, restored to its nineteenth-century appearance and completely free of adornment (tours by appointment; donation). In 1790, Newport's Jewish community wrote to George Washington expressing their hopes for his new government. His enthusiastic reply advocating religious liberty is exhibited at the Georgian **Touro Synagogue**, 85 Touro St, built in 1763 and the oldest in the nation (July 4 to Labor Day daily except Sat 10am–4pm; Labor Day to mid-Oct Mon–Fri 1–2pm Sun 11am–3pm; rest of year daily except Sat 1–3pm; ☎401/847-4794; free). Down the hill, the newly opened **Museum of Newport History**, 127 Thames St (Mon & Wed–Sat 10am–5pm, Sun 1–5pm; $5), may be small, but it has a superb understanding of the evolution of not just Newport but the whole of maritime New England, displayed through photographs, artifacts and a huge computer database. A $7 combination ticket covers admission and **walking tours** organized by the **Newport Historical Society** (see p.206). The Society's offices at 82 Touro St also feature changing exhibits on Newport's past (Tues–Fri 9.30am–4.30pm, Sat 9.30am–noon; free).

Washington himself worshipped at the 1726 **Trinity Church** on Queen Anne Square, a colonial structure based on the Old North Church in Boston and the designs of Sir Christopher Wren (daily: mid-June to early Sept 10am–4pm; May & mid-Sept to mid-Oct 1–4pm; rest of year 10am–1pm; free). A few blocks south, **St Mary's Church**, Spring Street and Memorial Boulevard, is the oldest Catholic Church in Rhode Island and the place where Jackie Bouvier married John Kennedy (Mon–Fri 7–11.30am; free).

Bellevue Avenue, the street lined with most of Newport's famous mansions, also has two museums of note. The **Newport Art Museum**, at no. 76, is housed in the 1864 mock-medieval Griswold House and exhibits New England art from the last two centuries (Mon–Sat 10am–5pm, Sun noon–5pm; $4). At no. 194, the grand **Newport Casino** was an early country club, which held the first national tennis championship in 1881. It is now the **International Tennis Hall of Fame**, and still keeps its grass courts open to the public. The museum includes exhibits on tennis fashion – or what has passed for it – and trophies (daily 9.30am–5pm; $8).

## The beaches

The indubitable attraction of Newport's shoreline, with its many coves and gently sloping beaches, is slightly marred by the fact that many are strictly private. **Gooseberry Beach**, on the southern edge of the island, is surrounded by grand houses and charges $1 admission. The town beach, **First** (or Newport, or Easton's) **Beach**, is at the east end of Memorial Boulevard. **Second** and **Third** beaches are further along the same route towards Middletown. The visitor center provides a guide to them all.

## Eating

Many of Newport's restaurants are smug and overpriced, with the result that visitors on a budget have to make do with snacks. However, there are some gems, even along touristy Thames Street, and the seafood here is well worth the blowout if you have the extra cash.

**Anthony's Shore Dinner Hall**, Waites Wharf (☎401/848-5058). Inexpensive, family-style clams, lobster and fish, with outdoor tables.

**Asterix & Obelisk**, 599 Thames St (☎401/841-8833). Happening, moderately priced eatery in a former garage, with abstract paintings on the walls and Oriental rugs on an orange cement floor. Food is American Eclectic with a touch of Asian.

**The Black Pearl**, Bannisters Wharf (☎401/846-5264). A Newport institution famous for its chunky clam chowder; repair to the Commodore Room for more formal dining.

**Brick Alley Pub & Restaurant**, 140 Thames St (☎401/849-6334). Attracts a good mix of locals and tourists for lunch, dinner and cocktails.

**Ocean Coffee Roasters**, 22 Washington Square (☎401/846-6060). Hip, upbeat cafe serving aspiring artists and poets rather than the yacht club. Crepes from $4, lunch specials with an international edge from $5.50, flavored coffees and teas. Occasional poetry readings and exhibitions.

**Via Via I**, 112 William St (☎401/846-4074). Specialty oven-fired pizza – shrimp pesto or chicken and goat's cheese, for example – that can also be delivered until 2am. The slightly better situated *Via Via II* is nearby at 372 Thames St (☎401/848-0880).

**White Horse Tavern**, Marlborough and Farewell sts (☎401/849-3600). Intensely atmospheric restaurant (the building dates from 1687) serving solid American fare, such as New York sirloin, sauteed lobster and rack of lamb. More affordably priced at lunchtime.

## Live music

Newport is historically famed for its duo of music festivals: the **Ben & Jerry's Folk Festival** in late July or early August, followed by the **August Jazz Festival**. Both are held in Fort Adams State Park (☎401/847-2400), as is the **Rhythm & Blues Festival**. The lesser-known but arguably more memorable **Newport Music Festival**, with a focus on classical music, unfolds in the mansions during July (☎401/846-1133).

Otherwise, there is plenty of shamelessly unrefined **nightlife**. Noisy bars abound near the waterfront, and among the **live music venues** in town, two of the best are the *Red Parrot*, 348 Thames St (☎401/847-3800), for live jazz and world music nightly, and the *Wharf Deli & Pub*, 37 Bowen's Wharf (☎401/846-9233), which puts on R&B and jazz.

# CONNECTICUT

**CONNECTICUT** was named *Quinnehtukqut* by the Native Americans for the "great tidal river" which splits it in two before spilling out into the Long Island Sound and washing the old whaling ports of the coast. This small and densely populated state is a sort of conservative, high-rent suburb of New York City, enabling commuters to earn Big Apple salaries while avoiding New York state and city taxes. Its first white settlers arrived in the 1630s: refugees from Massachusetts seeking liberty, good farmland and trading opportunities (not necessarily in that order). Connecticut soon became a center for **"Yankee ingenuity,"** prospering through the invention and marketing (often by the notorious and not always honorable Yankee peddlers) of many a useful little household object. Although hit very badly by English raids in the Revolutionary War, its role in providing the war effort with crucial supplies made it known as "the **provisions state**." After the war, the original charter of Connecticut's first colonists was used as a model for the American Constitution and gave rise to another nickname: "the

**Constitution state.**" It continued to prosper during the eighteenth and nineteenth centuries, with steady industrialization and lucrative whaling along the southeastern coast. Today, much of the old industry, especially in the north, has withered away, leaving areas of green countryside, untroubled by noisy interstates, many verdant forests and the idyllic rural villages that typify New England's PR image – but also unemployment, poverty, and a degree of displacement. **New Haven** in particular, home to Yale University, faces distinctly urban problems like drug wars, homelessness and violent crime, which belie New England's myth of rural tranquility.

The linchpins of Connecticut's economy – insurance companies, medical research and military bases – hardly make for pleasing aesthetics, as demonstrated by the rather dull capital city, **Hartford**; and even the historic and otherwise attractive coastline is marred by some unfortunate stretches of sprawling gray concrete.

### Getting around Connecticut

Except for a few isolated areas in the north, Connecticut is well provided with major **roads**: I-95 is the main interstate, running from New York to Rhode Island along the shore of the Long Island Sound. I-91 travels north from I-95 at New Haven, weaving its way along the Connecticut River to Vermont. However, in Connecticut, as with the other New England states, it's a shame to miss out on the quiet countryside scenery along the side roads. Although it's easy to get lost on poorly labeled back roads, distances are so small that this is unlikely to be a major problem.

All the major East Coast air carriers **fly** to Bradley International Airport near Hartford, and Greyhound, Bonanza (☎1-800/556-3815) and Peter Pan Trailways (☎1-800/343-9999) **buses** run to most of the main towns. Connecticut Transit buses (☎203/327-7433) serve the inland area around Hartford. Metro North (☎1-800/638-7646) **trains** carry passengers between New Haven and New York City, with connecting services to numerous other towns; Amtrak's line runs between New York City and Boston with various stops along the shore and a connection to Hartford.

# Southeastern Connecticut

The much-visited **southeastern coast** of Connecticut spans fifteen miles from Stonington in the east to Niantic in the west, bisected by the Thames (pronounced *Thaymz*) River. Each of the handful of tiny, picturesque colonial communities and old whaling villages along the Long Island Sound is a mere stone's throw from the next. No longer are they the iniquitous and rumbustious ports that so inspired Melville, but they're still keen to preserve a sense of their history. The restored nineteenth-century **Mystic Seaport** justifies at least a day's visit; nearby are the less lovely US Naval submarine base at **Groton** and the pretty fishing harbor of **Stonington Borough**.

## Mystic

The old whaling port and shipbuilding center of **MYSTIC**, the purists will tell you, does not in fact exist; it is an area governed partly by Groton and partly by Stonington. Nonetheless, it does have a small, well-kept, and somewhat touristy **downtown**, lined with typical New England-quaint clapboard galleries and antique shops. The old bridge across the bustling **Mystic River** which divides it down the middle still opens hourly, and self-guided walking tours take in the many old houses built by well-off sea captains. The **Olde Mistick Village**, at the intersection of I-95 and US-27, is a pleasant enough outdoor mall with over sixty upmarket shops in colonial-style buildings. For a scenic walk or bike ride away from the tourists, the four-mile river road is protected from cars and development and passes by Downes Marsh, a sanctuary for osprey.

What brings the tourists to Mystic is the impeccably reconstructed seventeen-acre waterfront village of **Mystic Seaport**, at the mouth of the river, where more than sixty weathered buildings house old-style workshops, stores and a printing press. Its **Stillman Building** exhibits exquisitely carved scrimshaw and a vast amount of products made from whales' wax-like spermaceti, as well as showing film of a bloody whale capture. Demonstrations of shanty-singing, fish-splitting and sail-setting, among other sea-salty pastimes, vie with storytelling and theater, while in the **shipyard** you can watch the building, restoration and maintenance of wooden ships. The *pièce de résistance* is the restored *Charles W Morgan*, a three-masted wooden Yankee **whaling ship** built in 1841 (daily: summer 9am–6pm; rest of year 9am–5pm; ☎860/572-0711; $16, late-afternoon arrivals are granted free entrance on the next day). The last of its kind, the *Morgan* is an elegy to an age of exploration and arrogant expansion remembered now with a mixture of nostalgia and shame. Done up ready to embark on a two-year voyage, the ship is filled with whaling memorabilia; below deck, accessible by perilously narrow stairs, the blubber room is crowded with huge iron try-pots for melting down the stinking blubber.

Over six thousand weird and wonderful sea creatures glug about the **Marinelife Aquarium**, at exit 90 off I-95. The hourly Marine Theater, with porpoises and a beluga whale, is more educational than the usual performing seal show and there are various gooey-eyed baby seals and cute penguins to coo at (daily 9am–7pm, last seal show 5.30pm; $12).

## Practicalities

Mystic has an **information office** in the Olde Mistick Village shopping mall (Mon–Sat 9.30am–6.30pm, Sun 10am–6pm; ☎860/536-1641). The office lists current rates for **accommodation**: places to stay in town are at a premium in July and August. Options include the *Comfort Inn* (☎860/572-8531 or 1-800/221-2222; ⑤), *Days Inn* (☎860/572-0574 or 1-800/325-2525; ⑤) and the *Best Western Sovereign Hotel* (☎860/536-4281 or 1-800/528-1234; ⑤), which are all handy for the Seaport, on Whitehall Avenue just off I-95 exit 90. The rural colonial farmhouse *Applewood Farms Inn* is five minutes north of town at 528 Colonel Ledyard Highway, Ledyard (☎860/536-2022; ⑤); its owners will collect you from the train station if given notice. The *Seaport* **campground** is on US-184 in Old Mystic, three miles from the Seaport (☎860/536-4044).

Much the best-known **restaurant** is *Mystic Pizza*, at 56 W Main St (☎860/536-3700), a small, family-run pizza place which continues to serve huge, inexpensive and fresh "pies," unruffled by its movie-star status. The *Sea View Snack Bar*, on Hwy-27 between the visitor center and downtown (☎860/572-0096), serves semi-fast seafood and sandwiches in a covered picnic area overlooking the Mystic River, while *The Green Marble*, 8 Steamboat Wharf (☎860/572-0012), roasts its own coffee. Ten minutes' drive south in the small fishing port of **Noank**, the casual summer-only *Abbott's Lobster in the Rough*, 117 Pearl St (☎860/536-7719), serves superb fresh steamed lobster and seafood at outdoor picnic tables. A giant New England dinner for four costs $22 per person, a lobster plate around $14; bring your own alcohol.

# Stonington Borough

**STONINGTON BOROUGH**, five miles east of Mystic, is an overwhelmingly pretty old fishing village, originally Portuguese but now very New England, characterized by desirable whitewashed cottages (which were once factory houses), white picket fences and colorful flower gardens. Its main street, **Water Street**, is chock-a-block with antique shops and upmarket thrift stores, crowded with well-heeled bargain hunters at the weekend. The **Lighthouse Museum** at no. 7 dates from 1823 and is full of local memorabilia, maps and drawings; fresh flowers everywhere add a nice touch. You can climb the stone steps and iron staircase to the top for views over the water and Connecticut's neighboring states (July & Aug daily 11am–5pm; May, June, Sept & Oct Tues–Sun 11am–5pm; $3). The waterside itself is a great place to pass a few sunny hours, peaceful and quiet with a few bobbing fishing boats and clean water for swimming.

Authentic New England clam chowder, and full meals, can be had at *Noah's*, 115 Water St (☎860/535-3925), an old Portuguese **restaurant** with a friendly, pine-table-trendy atmosphere and delicious home-baked cakes. Two seafood restaurants – *Water Street Cafe* and *Skipper's Dock* – share the premises at 60 Water St (☎860/535-8544); the former is elegant, the latter less expensive and rowdier, with an open deck sporting fabulous views of the ocean.

## Groton

Seven miles west of Mystic Seaport, **GROTON** is a suitably unpleasant name for the home town of the hideous **US Naval Submarine Base**, headquarters for the North Atlantic fleet. The **USS Nautilus**, America's first nuclear-powered submarine, was built in Groton. In 1958, four years after it was launched, it became the first vessel to sail under the polar icecap. It's now moored on the Thames, and self-guided tours allow access to its terrifyingly claustrophobic corridors, one-person-wide in many places. The sub looks pretty much as it did in the 1950s, complete with pin-ups of Marilyn Monroe. The **Submarine Force Museum** next door has exhibits on the history of submersibles from the minuscule *American Turtle*, built in 1775, to the frighteningly powerful *Trident* (mid-April to Oct Mon & Wed–Sun 9am–5pm, Tues 1–5pm; Nov to mid-April Mon & Wed–Sun 9am–4pm; free; ☎860/449-3174 or 1-800/343-0079).

## New London

**NEW LONDON**, opposite Groton on the west side of the Thames, is the closest thing the region has to a city, although it spreads over only six square miles. Originally settled in 1646, it was a wealthy whaling port in the nineteenth century and is today home to the **US Coast Guard Academy**, Mohegan Avenue off I-95, where visitors can wander around a museum of Coast Guard history (Mon & Wed–Fri 9am–4.30pm, Tues 9am–8pm, Sat 10am–5pm, Sun noon–5pm; free) and, when it is in port, visit the tall ship *USS Eagle* (Fri–Sun 1–5pm; when in port call ☎860/444-8595). A self-guided walking tour of downtown passes along the prosperous Huntington Street, where four adjacent Greek Revival mansions are known as **Whale Oil Row**. For swimming and sunbathing, the **Ocean Beach Park**, Ocean Avenue, has a sand beach and huge saltwater pool, as well as a wooden boardwalk (summer daily 9am–midnight; $2).

New London was the birthplace of boozy playwright **Eugene O'Neill**. His childhood home, the **Monte Cristo Cottage**, 325 Pequot Ave, is open for tours, complete with juicy details of his trauma-ridden early life – though they may already be familiar to you from his *Long Day's Journey into Night* (April–Dec Mon–Fri 1–4pm; tours noon, 2pm & 4pm; $3). The writer's influence is felt further at the O'Neill Memorial Theater Center, 305 Great Neck Rd (I-95 exit 82) in nearby **Waterford**, an acclaimed testing ground for playwrights and actors, where audiences can take pot luck and watch new, often experimental, shows in rehearsal (performances held sporadically May–Aug; ☎860/443-5378).

### Groton and New London practicalities

**Groton–New London Airport** (☎860/445-8549) has a limited service to the rest of New England (and several car rental outlets); you can also arrive in New London by **car**

**ferry** from Orient Point on Long Island (Cross Sound Ferry; ☎860/443-5281). Greyhound and Bonanza both serve the town, which is also the center of SEAT's far from comprehensive local **bus** system (☎860/886-2631).

The **Southeastern Connecticut Chamber of Commerce** has offices at 1 Whale Oil Row (☎860/443-8332). New London is generally a less expensive place to stay than Mystic, with reasonably priced **motels** along I-95, including the *Holiday Inn*, I-95 and Frontage Road (☎860/442-0631; ⑤), and the *Red Roof Inn*, 707 Colman St (☎860/444-0001 or 1-800/843-7663; ③). Additionally, in Groton there are plenty of budget motels off I-95 exit 86, including a *Super 8* (☎860/448-2818 or 1-800/800-8000; ③).

# Central Connecticut

Though **central Connecticut** is dominated by **Hartford**, the state's largest city is possibly one of the nation's dullest destinations. There's not a great deal of point in straying away from the coast, where **New Haven** is a whole lot more interesting.

## Hartford

The unattractive modern capital of Connecticut, **HARTFORD**, on the Connecticut River, is also the insurance center of the United States. Its central gold-domed **state capitol**, sitting on a hill in Bushnell Park, houses a small museum of Connecticut history; free tours are available during the week from 9.15am until 2.15pm. Marginally more thrilling is the antique merry-go-round in the park, which gives jangling rides for a mere 25¢. The **Museum of Connecticut History**, across the road at 231 Capitol Ave, holds Colt rifles and revolvers and the desk at which Abraham Lincoln signed the paper that emancipated all slaves during the Civil War (Mon–Fri 9.30am–4pm; free).

Hartford's pride and joy is the Greek Revival **Wadsworth Atheneum** 600 Main St, the nation's oldest continuously operating public art museum, holding some 45,000 pieces, among which are many fine and decorative arts, as well as Old Masters including Rubens' *The Return of the Holy family from Egypt* and, in the French Impressionists collection, Pierre-Auguste Renoir's *Monet Painting in His Garden at Argenteuil*. Lectures and films are put on at the Atheneum Theater, and there's an excellent cafe, too (Tues–Sat 11am–5pm; $5, free all day Thurs & before noon Sat).

About a mile west of downtown Hartford on Hwy-4, a hilltop community known as Nook Farm was home in the 1880s to next-door neighbors **Mark Twain** and **Harriet Beecher Stowe**. Today their Victorian homes, furnished much as they were then, are open for tours (Twain house summer Mon–Sat 9.30am–5pm, Sun noon–5pm; rest of year Mon & Wed–Sat 9.30am–5pm, Sun noon–5pm; $6.50; Stowe house summer Mon–Sat 9.30am–4pm, Sun noon–4pm; rest of year closed Mon; $6.50). Twain lived at 351 Farmington Ave from 1874 until 1891, writing many of his classic works including *Huckleberry Finn*, and he spent a fair portion of his publishing royalties building and redecorating this outrageously ornate home, with its unusual black-and-orange brickwork and luxurious Tiffany-filled interior.

### Practicalities

Hartford, which lies at the junction of I-91 (north–south) and I-84 (east–west), is easily accessible by car. Greyhound, Peter Pan and Bonanza **buses** and Amtrak **trains** all pull into the terminal at Union Place. If you have to stay the night, there are budget **motels** along I-91, including *Susse Chalet* at exit 27 (☎860/525-9306 or 1-800/524-2538; ③) and the *Super 8* at exit 33 (☎860/246-8888 or 1-800/800-8000; ③); hotels in Hartford itself cater mainly to business visitors and are correspondingly pricey, though it's possible to get a room for around $130 at the central *Sheraton*, 315 Trumbell St (☎860/728-5151 or 1-800/325-3535; ⑥). The *YMCA*, 160 Jewell St (☎860/522-4183; ②), often has rooms with shared bath for $19 and with private bath for $24, and the *1895 House B&B*, 97 Girard Ave, off I-84 exit 46 (☎860/232-0014; ③), has inexpensive rooms with shared bathrooms near the Twain House. A popular **restaurant** is *Black Eyed Sally's*, 350 Asylum St (☎860/278-7427), which serves hearty Cajun cooking with great selections of Cajun beer, plus live blues music Thursday through Sunday. For tasty, inexpensive home-cooking check out *Timothy's*, 243 Zion St (☎860/728-9822), a popular hangout with local artists and musicians, feasting on classic American dishes. For further information, try Hartford's **CVB**, downtown on Civic Center Plaza (Mon–Fri 9am–4.30pm; ☎860/728-6789); or pick up a copy of the free local weekly, *The Hartford Advocate*.

# New Haven

**NEW HAVEN**, founded in 1638 by a group of wealthy Puritans from London on a large natural harbor at the mouth of the Quinnipiac River, developed a solid economy based on shipping and, later, industry. In 1716 it became the seat of **Yale University**, the third oldest college in the States, but it was manufacturing in the nineteenth century that really brought the city into its own. New Haven churned out Winchester rifles, musical instruments, tools, carriages and corsets, and **Eli Whitney**, inventor of the revolutionary cotton gin, discovered in his workshop here a method of mass production that did away with expensive skilled labor. Today, however, there is little manufacturing activity left in New Haven, which is facing a damaging and profound depression.

It's an uneasy place, half tension-ridden urban wasteland and half Ivy League idyll. Town-versus-gown conflicts are so marked as to give the city a crackling energy, and New Haven is certainly less WASPish and smug than many other Ivy League towns. Drug pushing, gang wars and homelessness notwithstanding, blacks and whites – and Italians, Irish and Asians – co-exist, ambivalently. Even the students themselves seem a different, slightly less self-satisfied, breed from those at Princeton, say, or Harvard. The city's ethnic diversity, and the undeniable vitality provided by the much-maligned Yalies, make it a stimulating place to spend some time.

### Arrival, information and getting around

New Haven lies where the interstates I-91 and I-95 fork apart, and is on the main **train** line between Washington and Boston; services also run to Canada and New York. The Amtrak terminal is in the colossal and newly renovated **Union Station**, on Union Avenue six blocks southeast of the Yale campus downtown. To or from New York, the Metro-North Commuter Railroad (☎203/497-2089 or 1-800/638-7646) is a better deal than Amtrak. Greyhound, Bonanza and Peter Pan (to Boston) **buses** arrive at 45 George St (☎203/772-2470). On arrival, it's advisable to catch a cab to your hotel, as the bus and train terminals are in potentially dodgy areas. One reputable firm is Metro Taxi (☎203/777-7777).

**Public transportation** to areas outside downtown is provided by Connecticut Transit (☎203/624-0151), 470 James St, but service is poor after 6pm. An **information booth** at 200 Orange St, two blocks east of the Green, has schedules (Mon–Fri 9am–5pm). The **Greater New Haven CVB** is at 195 Church St, on the Green (Mon–Fri 8.30am–5pm; ☎203/787-8822).

### Accommodation

New Haven has surprisingly few **hotels** for a city of its size; not even expensive ones for visiting Yalie parents. **B&B** from around $50 can be arranged in advance through Nutmeg Bed and Breakfast, 222 Girard Ave, Hartford, CT 06105 (☎860/236-6698). The downtown hotels, although slightly overpriced, are worth it for their convenient location and safety. Because of the shortage of rooms, be sure to book ahead if you're going to be visiting during graduation.

**Best Western–West Haven**, 490 Sawmill Rd, West Haven (☎203/933-0344). Standard rooms not far from downtown New Haven at I-95 exit 42. Hotel features indoor pool and fitness center. ④.

**Colony Inn**, 1157 Chapel St (☎203/776-1234). Luxury hotel in the center of things. ④.

**Holiday Inn**, 30 Whalley Ave (☎203/777-6221). Generic rooms in good central Yale location. ④.

**Hotel Duncan**, 1151 Chapel St (☎203/787-1273). Comfortable rooms in an old-fashioned hotel, a few steps away from Yale, with singles in the $40 range. ③.

**New Haven Hotel**, 229 George St (☎203/498-3100). Central hotel with nice rooms and health club. ⑤.

## The City

A succession of remarkably ugly buildings put up during the 1950s rather blighted New Haven, but its **downtown**, centering on the **Green**, remains both attractive and walkable, thanks in part to some sensitive restoration. This area, laid out in 1638, was the site of the city's original settlement; around the Green are three churches, a grand library and a number of stately government buildings. The park itself is now home to a handful of harmless itinerants, and borders the student-filled College and Chapel Street district. The surrounding five blocks are a genuinely lively place in which to hang out, filled with bookstores, cafes, clubs and hip clothes stores; the **Neon Garage**, an art exhibit in a real parking lot on Crown Street, is especially notable. There are some very rough pockets, but in general New Haven is reasonably safe to wander around, even at night, especially during term time.

New Haven's prime attraction, **Yale University**, stands proudly right in the center of things. You can wander at will, though free hour-long student-led **tours** set off daily from the Yale Visitor Information Center at 149 Elm St (☎203/432-2300), across from the north side of the Green (Mon–Fri 9am–4.45pm, Sat & Sun 10am–4pm; tours Mon–Fri 10.30am & 2pm, Sat & Sun 1.30pm); it also supplies maps for self-guided tours. Tours entail quite a bit of trooping to and fro, starting with the beautiful old spires and ivy-strewn cobbled courtyards of the old campus (mostly built in the 1930s, but painstakingly distressed to look suitably ancient) and ending up at the remarkable **Beinecke Rare Books Library**, 121 Wall St, where venerable manuscripts and hand-printed books can be seen with the aid of natural light seeping through the translucent marble walls (Mon–Fri 8.30am–5pm, Sat 10am–5pm, closed Sat in summer; free). Other buildings of interest include the modernist, Louis Kahn-designed **Center for British Art**, 1080 Chapel St, where British paintings range from Elizabethan portraits to modern works by Peter Blake and Francis Bacon (Tues–Sat 10am–5pm, Sun noon–5pm; free). The impressive **Yale University Art Gallery**, just across the road at 1111 Chapel St (Tues–Sat 10am–5pm, Sun 2–5pm; closed mid-July to Aug; free), and the nation's oldest university art collection, holds American decorative arts, regional design and furniture, and African and pre-Columbian works. Among major European paintings is Van Gogh's famous *Night Cafe*, said by the artist to be "one of the ugliest pictures I have done." A quirky **Collection of Musical Instruments** is at 15 Hillhouse Ave (Tues–Thurs 1–4pm; closed summer; $1 suggested donation), and the **Peabody Museum of Natural History**, 170 Whitney Ave, is a solid nineteenth-century collection of fossils, skeletons and gems (Tues–Sat 10am–5pm, Sun noon–5pm; $5).

Since 1900, New Haven's close-knit **Italian District** has been based among the well-kept brownstones and colorful window boxes of **Wooster Street**, just beyond Crown Street southeast of the Green. This was where the city's original Italian immigrants settled when they came to work on the railroad. There's little to see here, but there are some incredibly popular restaurants, and it's well worth stopping by when there's a festival on.

## Eating

You can't leave New Haven without trying the local **pizza** (known by the cognoscenti as tomato pies). The *New York Times* discovered New Haven's pizzas a few years ago, and since then there have been queues down the street at all the family restaurants in Wooster Square. There are also plenty of reasonably priced and innovative restaurants around the Green, on College and Chapel streets.

**Atticus Bookstore Cafe**, 1082 Chapel St, next to the Yale Center for British Art (☎203/776-4040). Salads, soups, sandwiches, brioches and good coffee, in a relaxed bookstore open until midnight.

**Claire's Corner Copia**, 1000 Chapel St (☎203/562-3888). Eclectic Mexican and Middle Eastern food at moderate prices. Quite vegetarian-friendly.

**India Palace**, 65 Howe St (☎203/776-9010). Serviceable Indian restaurant, most notable for its huge $6 lunch buffet.

**Louis' Lunch**, 261–263 Crown St (☎203/562-5507). Small, dark and ancient burger house that claims to have served the first hamburger in the US, and presents the meat between two slices of toast. Highly popular, but worth the inevitable wait.

**Pepe's Pizzeria**, 157 Wooster St (☎203/865-5762). Most popular of the Wooster St places; plain, functional and friendly, with huge "combination pies" starting at $5. The secret is apparently in the coal-fired ovens and the Italian tomatoes.

**Willoughby's**, 1006 Chapel St (☎203/789-8400). Self-consciously trendy gourmet coffee bar frequented by hip intellectuals and fashionable townies. Superb coffee from $1, sticky cakes for slightly more.

**Yankee Doodle**, 260 Elm St (☎203/865-1074). Yalies' favorite low-cost caff, with original Fifties fittings and shop sign.

## Nightlife and entertainment

New Haven has an undeniably rich **cultural scene**, and is especially strong on **theater**. The Yale Rep Company, 1120 Chapel St (☎203/432-1234), which boasts among its eminent past members Jodie Foster and Meryl Streep, turns out consistently good shows during the school year. The Long Wharf Theater (☎203/787-4282), 222 Sargent Drive, just off I-95, has a nationwide reputation for quality performances, as does the refurbished Schubert Performing Arts Center, 247 College St (☎203/562-5666).

Additionally, there are several good **bars** and **clubs**, concentrated on Chapel and College streets. The free biweekly paper *Hip*, available from the clothes shops along Chapel Street, has details of all the happening happenings in and around New Haven, while the *New Haven Advocate*, a free news and arts weekly paper, has more comprehensive listings.

**Anchor Bar**, 272 College St (☎203/865-1512). Authentic Fifties bar, one of the best spots in town. Snug plastic booths, dim orange lighting, frosted windows and a formidable matronly hostess.

**Bar**, 254 Crown St (☎203/495-8924), Plain name, outrageous place – this is where the New Haven gay community lets its collective hair down.

**Café Nine**, 250 State St (☎203/789-8281). Intimate club with live jazz Sat and Sun nights.

**Toad's**, 300 York St (☎203/624-8623). Mid-sized nationally renowned live music venue, where the likes of Dylan and the Stones "pop in" occasionally to play impromptu gigs. Tickets $10–25.

# NEW HAMPSHIRE

Long after sailors, fishermen and agricultural colonists had domesticated the entire coastline of New England, the harsh, glacier-scarred interior of **NEW HAMPSHIRE**, with its dense forests and forbidding mountains, remained the exclusive preserve of the Algonquin Indians. Only the few miles of seashore held sizeable seventeenth-century communities of European settlers, such as Strawbery Banke at **Portsmouth**.

Even when the Indians were finally driven back, following the defeat of their French allies in Canada, the settlers could make little agricultural impact on the rocky terrain of this "granite state." Towns such as Nashua, Manchester and Concord grew up in the fertile Merrimack Valley, but not until the Industrial Revolution made possible the development of water-powered **textile** mills did the economy take off. For a while, ruthless **timber** companies looked set to strip all northern New Hampshire bare – very few of the trees you see now are original growth – but they were brought under control when it was appreciated that the pristine landscape of the **White Mountains** might turn out to be the state's greatest asset. Large-scale **tourism** began towards the end of last century; at one stage fifty trains daily brought travelers up to Mount Washington.

Ever since becoming the first American state to declare independence, in January 1776, New Hampshire has been proud to go its own idiosyncratic way. The absence of a sales tax, or even a personal income tax, is seen as a fulfilment of the state motto, "Live Free or Die." Alternative sources of revenue include state-owned **liquor stores** in which, unlike in neighboring states, you are able to purchase alcohol on Sundays – set up after the failure of Prohibition, and enthusiastically promoted: they even have them in freeway rest areas. The state has long gained inordinate political clout as the venue of the first **primary election** of each presidential campaign, with its villages well used to playing host to would-be world leaders.

One less ideological aspect of New Hampshire's individualism is the emphasis on a healthy outdoor lifestyle. Hiking, climbing, cycling and **skiing** are enjoyed both by energetic locals and by the many visitors who drive up from Boston and New York. The major destinations are **Lake Winnipesaukee**, and **Conway**, **Lincoln** and **Franconia** in the mountains further north. Some have grown rather too large and commercial for their own good, but if you steer clear of the paying "attractions," the lakes, islands and snowcapped peaks themselves remain spectacular. To see the bucolic rural scenery more usually associated with New England, take a detour off the main roads up the Merrimack Valley – to **Canterbury Shaker Village** near Concord, for example.

### Getting around New Hampshire

Manchester has a small **airport**, but travelers coming to New Hampshire from far afield usually do so via Boston's Logan Airport, approximately 45 minutes to the south. Concord Trailways (☎1-800/639-3317; ☎603/228-3300 in NH) runs **buses** from there to Manchester, Concord, Conway and Franconia. Vermont Transit (☎1-800/451-3292) runs from Boston to Conway and Franconia, and at weekends (Fri, Sat & Sun) also connects Conway with Burlington and Montréal. The closest Amtrak service is to White River Junction in Vermont, across the state line from Hanover. A surprising number of **cyclists** set out to tour the mountains.

# The coast

Of all the US states with ocean access, New Hampshire has the shortest coastline – just eighteen miles. Driving north from Boston along either I-95 or the quieter US-1, you enter New Hampshire after roughly forty miles, to be confronted almost immediately by the nuclear power plant at **Seabrook Station**, which opened in 1990 after years of determined opposition, not least from the irate state of Massachusetts over the border.

**HAMPTON BEACH**, a little further on, is a traditional family, if somewhat tacky, seaside resort (its free information line has the optimistic number ☎1-800/GET-A-TAN). The usual assortment of motels and fast-food places lines the approaches to the boardwalk and crowded beaches, but in a place this close to Boston summer **accommodation** rates are high. The *Pine Haven* at 183 Lafayette Rd (☎603/964-8187; ④), on

US-1 four miles north of town, is one of the least expensive options; for a bit more atmosphere try the *Oceanside Hotel* at 365 Ocean Blvd (☎603/926-3542; ④). Large local **campgrounds** include *Tuxbury Pond* in South Hampton (☎603/394-7660).

# Portsmouth

New Hampshire's oldest community, **PORTSMOUTH**, might look like a major city on the map, but once you're there it has much more of the feel of a country town, and a pleasant lived-in atmosphere that places it well above some of the smaller, more tourist-focused communities along the coast. Its position at the mouth of the Piscataqua River has always made it an important port – it was the state capital until 1808 – but it has barely grown, and the spire of **North Church** in the central **Market Square** remains the highest building you'll see in town.

Of a striking selection of grand timber mansions, the 1758 gambrel-roofed, cream-and-white clapboard **John Paul Jones House** at 43 Middle St, on the corner of State Street, is the most distinctive (June to mid-Oct Mon–Sat 10am–4pm, Sun noon–4pm; $4). However, with so many old houses to see you can contentedly walk at random (or, better, get a *Harbor Trail* leaflet from the visitor center), and a visit to **Strawbery Banke** (see below) provides a better overview of local history. In **Prescott Park** along the waterfront, the **Sheafe Warehouse Museum** has a fascinating free collection of mostly nautical ephemera.

Indeed Portsmouth's fortunes have long rested with its **naval shipyard**, visible across the bay (in Kittery, Maine; see p.236). Founded in 1800 by John Paul Jones as the US government's first shipyard, it has remained active ever since – it launched 31 submarines in 1944 alone, and built the first Polaris in 1962. During World War I, **Humphrey Bogart**, as a junior naval rating, received injuries while attempting to prevent the escape of a prisoner that left him with his trademark permanent sneer and a slight lisp.

### Strawbery Banke

The lack of any great pressure on space has made it possible to preserve ten acres of Portsmouth's original site as **STRAWBERY BANKE**, Hancock and Marcy streets at I-95 exit 7 (May–Oct & Thanksgiving weekend daily 10am–5pm; $10 adults, $7 children, $25 family; tickets good for two consecutive days). This area began life as the home of wealthy shipbuilders, and was successively the lair of privateers and a red-light district before turning into respectable – and, in the 1950s, ultimately decaying – suburbia. It was then decided to re-create its former appearance, mainly by clearing away the newer buildings (only two of the houses on display had to be moved here). One or two people still live here, tucked away on the upper floors, but the whole complex serves as a living museum, which you can explore either on a guided tour or at your own whim; in either case, several of the houses have well-informed attendants.

Each building is shown in its most interesting former incarnation, whether that be 1695 or 1955; in the **Drisco House**, the first you come to, each individual room dates from a different era. The 1766 **Pitt Tavern** holds most historic significance, having acted as a meeting place during the Revolution for patriots and loyalists (it still functions as a Masonic lodge, one of the four oldest in the US – which explains why you can't go upstairs). Tiny glasses remind you that its clientele drank gin rather than beer.

Although you may have to struggle to keep ahead of school groups, Strawbery Banke continues to undertake serious academic research. Traditional **crafts** are studied and practiced; in the **Dinsmore Shop**, an infinitely patient cooper manufactures barrels with the tools and methods of 1800. The Mills Zoldak **pottery** shop, open year-round, produces attractive low-priced ceramics; you can visit without paying admission.

## Practicalities

C&J Trailways **buses** (☎1-800/258-7111) halt at 5 Congress St, on Market Square, en route between Boston and Portland. You can pick up information from the **visitor center** at 500 Market St (Mon–Fri 9.30am–5pm; ☎603/436-1118), and the outside tables of the *Café Brioche* in Market Square make an obvious point from which to get your bearings. Portsmouth Harbor Cruises (☎603/436-8084) is among operators offering boat trips from $7.50.

**Accommodation** in the town center is restricted to expensive places such as the grand *Sise Inn* at 40 Court St (☎603/433-1200 or 1-800/267-0525; ⑥), a nicely preserved Queen Anne-style house with large rooms, and **B&Bs** like the peaceful, rambling seven-room *Inn at Strawbery Banke*, 314 Court St (☎603/436-7242; ⑤), and the more formal *Martin Hill Inn*, 404 Islington St (☎603/436-2287; ⑤). Hotels and motels along US-1 include the *Comfort Inn at Yoken's* (☎603/433-3338 or 1-800/552-8484; ④), which has a pool. The adjacent *Yoken's* (☎603/436-8224) is a popular and inexpensive ribs restaurant, housed in New England's largest **giftshop**, a veritable gold mine of trivia.

Of the in-town **restaurants**, the *Stockpot*, overlooking the river at 53 Bow St (☎603/431-1851), specializes in paella and stir-fries; *Porto Bello*, 67 Bow St (☎603/431-2989), does superb Italian dishes at reasonable prices and funky *Friendly Toast*, 121 Congress St (☎603/430-2154) makes for an inexpensive breakfast and lunch spot featuring generous portions and homemade bread. At night, the *Portsmouth Brewery*, 56 Market St (☎603/431-1115), is raucous with live music and *The Press Room*, 77 Daniel St (☎603/431-5186), has live jazz and good bar food.

## Odiorne Point State Park

The one brief patch of semi-wilderness along the New Hampshire coast was, ironically, where the first white settlers landed in 1623. Some of the scattered ruins in the marshy duneland of **Odiorne Point State Park** date from those early days; others, far more modern, were World War II defences. The two park entrances are on Hwy-1A near **Rye**, four miles southeast of Portsmouth, where a summer-only visitor center is open daily from 10am until 4pm. The offshore **Isles of Shoals**, a supposed haunt of Blackbeard the pirate, can be seen up close on boat trips from Portsmouth Harbor (☎603/431-5500).

# The Merrimack Valley

The financial and political heartland of New Hampshire is the **Merrimack Valley**, which – first by water and now by road – has always been the main thoroughfare north to the White Mountains and Québec. None of its towns is of any great interest to tourists, though all are pleasant enough, and equipped with relatively inexpensive motels.

The southernmost town on the river, **Nashua**, was rated by *Money* magazine in 1987 as the number one place to live in America. Plenty of its citizens still choose to work in Boston, though Massachusetts no longer allows employees to escape state taxes by living across the border in New Hampshire. **Manchester**, like its namesake in England, was a major nineteenth-century cotton producer. Although its massive Amoskeag Mills closed in the 1930s, it remains the largest city in the state, and is now notable mainly for the glassware, furniture and paintings in the **Currier Gallery of Art** at 201 Myrtle Way (Mon, Wed–Thurs & Sat–Sun 11am–5pm, Fri 9am–11pm; free). The focal point of **Concord** is the gold dome of the State House, the seat of New Hampshire's state legislature; despite its small size it has 424 members, making it the fourth largest such body in the world (after the parliaments of the United States, Britain and India). Local schoolteacher Christa McAuliffe, a victim of the *Challenger* tragedy, is commemorated by a planetarium.

Fifteen miles north of Concord on Hwy-106, **Canterbury Shaker Village** (May–Oct daily 10am–5pm; $8.50) was the sixth Shaker community (see pp.201, 481 and 486) to be founded by Ann Lee in the 1780s, and had grown to 300-strong by 1860. Ninety-minute tours show Shaker crafts and techniques – such as box-making – and the attached *Creamery* restaurant serves Shaker food. South of Concord, outside Derry on Hwy-28, the **Robert Frost Farm** (summer daily 10am–6pm; rest of year Sat & Sun 10am–6pm; $2.50) has been evocatively restored to its condition when New England's poet laureate lived here from 1900 to 1911. Displays in the barn discuss his work, and a half-mile "poetry nature trail" leads past the sites that inspired many of his best-known poems.

# The Lakes Region

Of the literally hundreds of lakes created by the snowmelt flowing south from the White Mountains, much the biggest is **Lake Winnipesaukee**, which forms the center of the vacation-oriented Lakes Region. Long segments of its 300-mile shoreline, especially in the east, consist of thick forests sweeping down to waters dotted with little islands, which are disturbed only by pleasure craft. The most sophisticated of the towns is **Wolfeboro**; the most fun to visit has to be **Weirs Beach**.

Ideally, you would bring your own small boat and get thoroughly lost in the maze of small channels and islets. Failing that, the **cruise ship** *Mount Washington* does daily two-and-a-half-hour tours of the more open stretches in summer, leaving Weirs Beach daily at 10am and 12.30pm, and Wolfeboro (except Mon & Thurs) at 11.15am. The tours cost $16, and also call at either Center Harbor (Mon 11am) or Alton Bay (Thurs 11.15am). It's certainly a pretty ride, though it can seem a little long in the heat of the day and you might prefer to take a (more expensive) evening dinner cruise (July & Aug Mon–Sat). A smaller mail-boat does more local round-trips from Weirs Beach for $12 (Mon–Sat 11am & 1.30pm). For all inquiries, call ☎603/366-BOAT.

## Wolfeboro

Because Governor Wentworth of New Hampshire built his summer home nearby in 1768, tiny **WOLFEBORO** claims to be "the oldest summer resort in America." Sandwiched between lakes Winnipesaukee and Wentworth, it has little to show for that history, but it's a relaxing place to spend a few hours, along the short but bustling main street, next to the quay where the *Mount Washington* comes in.

The 1812 *Wolfeboro Inn* (☎603/569-3016 or 1-800/451-2389; ⑤) stands in a dignified waterfront position at 44 N Main St, just a few yards from the town proper; its tavern serves good-value meals. The *Tuc' Me Inn B&B*, 118 N Main St (☎603/569-5702; ④), is a relaxing place with lots of Victoriana, close to both town and lake. *Wolfeboro Campground* is on Haines Hill Road (☎603/569-9881). Two branches of *Bailey's* (☎603/569-3662), one on the quayside and one on Main Street, serve basic good-value **food**; *West Lake Asian Cuisine* (☎603/569-6700), on Hwy-28 in Wolfeboro Center, is an excellent, affordable Chinese restaurant.

The eastern shore of Lake Winnipesaukee is considerably less developed than the area around Weirs Beach, and makes for much better walking. One fascinating stopoff, a few miles north of Wolfeboro on Hwy-109, is the **Libby Museum** (summer Tues–Sun 10am–4pm; $2), where the obsession of c.1900 dentist Henry Forest Libby with evolution is illustrated by various ineptly stuffed animals (one can only hope that he was a better dentist than he was a taxidermist) and the skeletons of bears, orang-utans and humans. There's also a mastodon's tooth, a "Niddy Noddy" spinning device, and a fingernail supposedly pulled out by its Chinese owner to demonstrate his new Christian faith. The front steps command a superb view over the lake itself.

## Weirs Beach and Laconia

The short boardwalk at **WEIRS BEACH**, the very essence of seaside tackiness even if it is fifty miles inland, is in summer the social center of the Lakes Region. Its little wooden jetty throngs with vacationers, the amusement arcades jingle with cash, and there's even a neat little crescent of sandy beach, suitable for family swimming. The better of its two competing **water parks** is Surf Coaster (summer daily 10am–8pm, weather permitting; $20, cheaper if you are under 4ft tall) on Hwy-11B just south of town, which offers dramatic rides and a powerful wave machine.

Nearby **LACONIA** controls the purse-strings for Weirs Beach. **Belknap Mill** here claims to be "the oldest unaltered brick textile mill building in the United States." You might think the fact that it is now an arts center would count as some sort of alteration, but the mill machinery is still in working order in amongst the gallery space, which is the venue for evening concerts and lecture programs.

On Father's Day weekend (the third in June), at least twenty thousand **bikers** cruise up for a gigantic motorcycle race and rally in **Loudon**. Even at quieter times, room rates in Laconia are high; choices include the beachfront *Birch Knoll Motel*, 867 Weirs Blvd (April–Oct; ☎603/366-4958; ④), *Monaco Beach Motel*, 94 Lake St/Rte-3 (☎603/524-5972; ④), and the restaurant and B&B *Hickory Stick Farm* (☎603/524-3333; ④), 60 Bean Hill Rd, in the woods four miles south. The nearest **campground** is the *Gunstock* (☎603/293-4344), near Gilford six miles south (a ski resort in winter).

## Meredith

**MEREDITH**, four miles north of Weirs Beach, is the last of Lake Winnipesaukee's resorts. In the new waterfront mall, the *Millworks Restaurant* (☎603/279-4116) is a nice place to eat seafood, while the *Inn at Mill Falls,* Rte-3, (☎603/279-7006 or 1-800/622-MILL; ⑤) is an exceptionally comfortable place to overnight; rooms at the *Olmec Motor Lodge*, 95 Pleasant St (☎603/279-8584; ④) are much more basic, though the lakeside setting is nice enough.

The **Winnipesaukee Railroad** (☎603/279-5253) operates scenic trips ($8.50) along the lakeshore between Meredith and Weirs Beach, at weekends from Memorial Day and then daily from mid-June to mid-October, including special fall foliage excursions (and even a Santa Claus special).

The only thing to admire at **Annalee's Doll Museum** (summer daily 9am–5pm; rest of year slightly shorter hours), just outside Meredith, is its effrontery in calling itself a museum. In fact it's a hard-sell toy store, specializing in painted-felt dolls of quite stunning ugliness. Those items onto which they've managed to stitch the heads back to front are offered at a 25 percent reduction.

## Northwards to the mountains

Hwy-25 northeast from Meredith leads to Conway in the White Mountains; US-3 northwest, on the other hand, keeps you in the Lakes Region a little longer, leading past **Squam Lake**, where portions of the movie *On Golden Pond* were filmed. Educational tours of the **Science Center of New Hampshire** at **Holderness** (May–Nov daily 9.30am–4.30pm; $8) lead through a largely natural landscape, in which animals such as deer, bobcat, otters, bears and foxes are kept (mostly short-term) in enclosures.

Five miles on from Holderness at **Plymouth**, you can either rejoin I-93 as it heads into the mountains, or continue another five miles west to the **Polar Caves** mid-May to Oct daily 9am–5pm; $9.50). Frankly, that would not be a good idea; whatever else the Polar Caves may be, they are not caves. They are no more than a cascade of clammy granite boulders tumbled against a hillside, between which visitors are for no discernible reason expected to find pleasure in squeezing themselves – while paying handsomely for the privilege. A large giftshop sells supremely irrelevant "souvenirs."

# The White Mountains

Thanks to their accessibility from both Montréal to the north and Boston to the south, the **White Mountains** have become a year-round tourist destination, popular with summer hikers and winter skiers alike. Commercialized they may be, in built-up strips along the main highways, but the great granite massifs retain much of their majesty and power. **Mount Washington** can claim the severest weather in the world, and conditions are harsh enough for the timberline to be at four thousand feet, as compared to the norm in the Rockies of ten thousand.

Just a few high passes – here called "**notches**," only discovered with infinite pains by the early pioneers – pierce the range, and the roads through these gaps, such as the **Kancamagus Highway** between Lincoln and Conway, make for an enjoyable driving tour. However, you won't really have made the most of the White Mountains unless you also set off, on foot or on skis, across the long expanses of thick evergreen forest that separate them, with snowcapped peaks poking out in all directions. The best source of **information** in the region is the White Mountains Attractions visitor center at I-93 exit 32 in North Woodstock (☎603/745-8720 or 1-800/FIND-MTS).

## White Mountains accommodation

So many youthful hikers and skiers come to the White Mountains that for once there is a great deal of **low-budget accommodation**. However, there's quite a chasm between the hostels, costing under $20, and the inns and B&Bs, which tend to start at over $80, although haggling sometimes pays dividends at quiet times. **Campers** can pitch their tents anywhere in the White Mountains National Forest below the treeline and away from the roads, so long as they show consideration for the environment; there are also more than twenty official campgrounds ($14–16 per night; National Forest information ☎1-888/CAMPS-NH, reservations ☎877/444-6777; State Park Reservations ☎603/271-3628).

### Hostels and mountain huts

Apart from the hostels at Crawford Notch and Pinkham Notch, accessible to motorists, the ten **Appalachian Mountain Club** huts along the Appalachian Trail can be reached only on foot. In summer, they provide meals and bedding for up to one hundred people per night. Prices in all of them range from $20 to $60, according to the amount of privacy (and food) you desire. It's extremely advisable to book ahead and reservations can be made by phone (☎603/466-2727) or fax (203/466-3871). A deposit is often required to hold a reservation.

**Bowman's Base Camp**, Randolph (☎603/466-5130). Very basic summer-only hostel, roughly ten miles by road north of Pinkham Notch. $13 beds. ①.

**Crawford Notch Depot**, US-302, Carroll (☎603/466-2727). AMC hostel; two dorms and three cabins in the heart of the mountains. See above for rates. Daily information in summer 8.30am–4.30pm. ②.

**Pinkham Notch Huts and Lodges**, Hwy-16, Gorham (☎603/466-2727). One of the more expensive AMC lodges (see above for rates), near the base of the Mount Washington Auto Rd. Daily information in summer 7am–10pm. ④.

### Motels, hotels and B&Bs

**The Bungay Jar**, Easton Valley Rd/Hwy-116, Franconia (☎603/823-7775). B&B in superb woodland setting. ④.

**Eagle Mountain House**, 2 Carter Notch Rd, Jackson (☎603/383-9111 or 1-800/966-5779). Highly atmospheric inn, recently rebuilt, far above the bustle of North Conway. ⑥.

## HIKING, CYCLING & SKIING IN THE WHITE MOUNTAINS

**Hiking** in the mountains is coordinated by the **Appalachian Mountain Club** (AMC), whose chain of information centers, hostels and huts along the Appalachian Trail, traversing the region from northeast to southwest, is detailed opposite; ring ☎603/466-2727 for further information, and pick up a copy of the *AMC White Mountain Guide* ($20) before you attempt any serious expedition.

Downhill and cross-country skiers can choose from several resorts that double up as summertime activity centers. Both Loon Mountain (☎603/745-8111 or 1-800/229-LOON) and Ski Bretton Woods (☎603/278-5000 or 1-800/258-0330) keep the chair lifts open through summer, have decent mountain-bike trails and offer pastimes including rollerblading and horseback riding. General information on the skiing centers along I-93 is available from Ski 93 (PO Box 517, Lincoln, NH 03251; ☎603/745-8101); those further east are covered by the very helpful Mount Washington Valley Chamber of Commerce (PO Box 2300, North Conway, NH 03860; ☎603/356-3171 or 1-800/367-3364). Once you're in the area, North Conway is the best place to rent equipment and other supplies.

**Bikes** can be rented from the Loon Mountain Bike Center on the Kancamagus Highway in Lincoln, the Bretton Woods ski resort on Hwy-302, or Joe Jones on Main Street in North Conway (☎603/356-9411).

**The Forest – A Country Inn**, Hwy-16A, Intervale (☎603/356-9772 or 1-800/448-3534). Very welcoming B&B between North Conway and Jackson. Organizes inn-to-inn cross-country skiing and biking holidays in conjunction with other B&Bs in the region. ⑤.

**Franconia Inn**, Easton Valley Rd/Hwy-116, Franconia (☎603/823-5542 or 1-800/473-5299). Thirty-bed inn two miles south of town, with great views. A good cross-country ski base. ⑤.

**Gale River Motel**, 1 Main St, Franconia (☎603/823-5655 or 1-800/255-7989). Sweet little ten-room motel; three cottages, sleeping 4 to 6 people, also available. ④.

**Hillwinds Lodge**, Hwy-18, Franconia (☎603/823-5551 or 1-800/906-5292). Standard rooms at a good price. ③.

**The Inn at Jackson**, Thorn Hill Rd, Jackson (☎603/383-4321 or 1-800/289-8600). A nonsmoking inn in an 1895 Stanford White-designed building near Jackson Village. ⑥/⑦.

**Mount Washington Hotel**, Bretton Woods (☎603/278-1000 or 1-800/258-0330). Beautiful hotel dating from 1902 (see p.224). ⑦.

**New England Inn**, Hwy-16A, Intervale (☎603/356-5541 or 1-800/826-3466). Comfortable traditional white-clapboard inn, near North Conway; rooms vary in quality so check them out first; cottages are good value. ⑥.

**Northern Zermatt Inn**, Hwy-3, Twin Mountain (☎603/846-5533 or 1-800/535-3214). Inn and motel rooms plus a few cottages at value-for-money prices. ③.

**Snowvillage Inn**, Snowville (☎603/447-2818 or 1-800/447-4345). Peaceful setting, on Stuart Rd 12 miles south of North Conway. Big, country-style breakfasts. ⑤.

**Stony Brook Motor Lodge**, one mile south of Franconia on Hwy-18 (☎603/823-8192 or 1-800/722-3552). Comfortable, well-priced motel near the interstate. ④.

**Swiss Chalets**, Hwy-16A, Intervale (☎603/356-2232). One of the nicest motels in the North Conway area, away from the bustle of the main drag. ④.

**Village House**, Hwy-16A, Jackson (☎603/383-6666 or 1-800/972-8343). B&B just beyond the covered bridge, with private baths and a great big porch. ⑤.

**Woodstock Inn**, Hwy-3, North Woodstock (☎603/745-3951 or 1-800/321-3985). Sumptuous Victorian inn, with its own brewpub and good seafood restaurant. ⑤.

## Franconia Notch and the Old Man of the Mountains

I-93, speeding up towards Canada, and the more leisurely US-3 merge briefly about ten miles beyond **Lincoln**, to pass through **Franconia Notch State Park**. From a roadside pullout you can look back and upwards to the **Old Man of the Mountains**. This natural rock formation, resembling an old man's profile, will no doubt already be familiar from powerfully magnified photographs – and New Hampshire's license plates. Seen from a thousand feet below, it's absolutely tiny. It all has to be held together with wires, and one particular family has the annual responsibility of climbing up to plug the cracks made by the winter's ice.

**Franconia Notch** itself is a slender valley crammed between two great walls of stone. From the park **visitor center** (May–Oct daily 9am–4.30pm; ☎603/745-8391), you can, for $7, walk along a two-mile boardwalk-cum-nature trail to the **Flume**, to look down on the Pemigewasset River as it rages through a narrow, rock-filled gorge, take a $9 **cable-car** ride up the sheer granite face of **Cannon Mountain** (May–Oct daily 9am–4.30pm; ☎603/823-8800), or hike the various, well-marked trails up to panoramic views for free.

Further on, one mile south of **FRANCONIA**, the **Frost Place** on Ridge Road (Memorial Day to Columbus Day daily except Tues 1–5pm; $3) is a former home of poet Robert Frost, memorable largely for an inspiring panorama of mountains that can look almost undisturbed by human interference. If you're interested in his poetry, his farm outside Concord (see p.220) makes a better destination.

## Bretton Woods

The ease with which US-302 now crosses the middle of the mountains belies the effort that went into cutting a road through **Crawford Notch**, halfway between Franconia and Conway. Just north, the magnificent **Mount Washington Hotel** (see overleaf) stands in splendid isolation in the wide mountain valley of **BRETTON WOODS**. Its glistening white facade, capped by red cupolas and framed by the western slopes of Mount Washington rising behind, has barely changed since the hotel opened in 1902. In its heyday, a stream of horse-drawn carriages brought families (and their servants) up from the train station, deliberately located at a distance in order to increase the sense of grandeur. Displays in the grand lobby commemorate the Bretton Woods Conference of 1944, which laid the groundwork for the postwar financial structure of the capitalist world, by setting the gold standard at $35 an ounce – it's now $350 – and creating the International Monetary Fund and the World Bank.

Recent restoration has ensured that the hotel remains marvelously – somewhat eerily – evocative, with its quarter-mile terrace and white wicker furniture. It's not the one featured in the movie *The Shining* (see p.1062), but it's said to have inspired it; it's worth checking out even if you're not staying. Weekend golfing and tennis packages are available, and there's skiing in winter.

## Mount Washington

The 6288ft **Mount Washington** was named for George Washington before he became president, but over the years other mountains in this "Presidential Range" have taken the names of Madison, Jefferson, and even Eisenhower. (Mount Nancy was called that long before the Reagans; and Mount Deception just happens to be close by.)

You can see all the way to the Atlantic – and right into Canada – from the top of Mount Washington on a clear day, but the real interest in making the ascent lies in the extraordinary severity of the weather up there. The wind exceeds hurricane strength on over a hundred days of the year, and in 1934 it reached the highest speed ever recorded anywhere in the world – 231mph. On the very summit, you'll see the remarkable spectacle of buildings actually held down with great chains; many have been blown away over the years, including the old observatory, said to be the strongest wooden building ever constructed. There's now a viewing platform, with a weatherproof museum and cafe just below. A roll call of the 103 victims to die on the mountain includes two who attempted to slide down the Cog Railway on "improvised boards."

On the way to the top, you pass through four separate climatic zones, with century-old fir and ash trees so stunted as to be below waist-height, before coming out finally amid Arctic tundra. The drive up the **Mount Washington Auto Road** (mid-May to late Oct only – weather permitting, 7.30am–6pm in peak season, and 7.30am–5.30pm after Labor Day; call ☎603/466-2222 to check weather conditions) is not quite as hair-raising as you may be led to expect, though the hairpin bends and lack of guard-rails certainly keep you alert. There is, however, a $16 **toll** for private cars and driver (plus $6 for each additional adult and $4 for kids). Specially adapted minibuses, still known as "stages" in honor of the twelve-person horse-drawn carriages which first used the road, give **narrated tours** ($20). Driving takes thirty or forty minutes under sane conditions, though rally-drivers have done it in under ten. The record for the annual **running** race each June – heading up the mountain – now stands at an incredible 58 minutes 20 seconds.

Last but far from least, you can also ride to the top on the coal-fired steam train of the **Mount Washington Cog Railway**, which noisily climbs the exposed western flank of the mountain, ascending gradients of up to 38 percent on a track that was completed in 1869. It's truly a unique experience, inching up the steep wooden trestles while avoiding descending showers of coal smut – although anyone who's not a bona fide antique train aficionado might find it not really worth the money. The three-hour round-trip costs $44 and trains leave hourly (late May to late Oct 8am–5pm, weather permitting; ☎603/846-5404 or 1-800/922-8825) from a station off Rte-302 six miles northeast of Bretton Woods. Reservations are recommended.

## North Conway

A few miles south of Mount Washington, heading past **Glen**, US-302 and Hwy-16 as they approach **NORTH CONWAY** become a veritable turmoil of shopping malls, fast-food places and theme parks such as Heritage USA and Storyland. The strip between North Conway and **Conway** proper offers all sorts of "factory outlets" (including a branch of Maine's L L Bean's – see p.240) for discount shopping. The towns are not terribly interesting, but there are plenty of secluded lodging options in the foothills to either side, and bars and restaurants in the malls (detailed below). If you're traveling through here in high season, be warned that it can take over half an hour to drive five miles.

## The Kancamagus Highway

The **Kancamagus Highway** (Hwy-112) connecting Conway and Lincoln is the least busy road through the mountains, and makes for a very pleasant drive. Several campgrounds are situated in the woods to either side, and various walking trails are signposted. The half-mile hike to **Sabbaday Falls**, off to the south roughly halfway along, leads up a narrow rocky cleft in the forest to a succession of idyllic waterfalls.

## White Mountains eating and drinking

Family restaurants and fast-food places line the main drags of major centers such as North Woodstock and North Conway. The best places are less conspicuous and worth rooting out. Some of the hotels and B&Bs recommended on pp.222–223 also serve food.

**1785 Inn & Restaurant**, 3582 Hwy-16, just north of North Conway (☎603/356-9025 or 1-800/421-1785). The area's premier fine-dining experience, with prices to match – $40–50 a head with wine.

**Polly's Pancake Parlor**, I-93 exit 38, Hwy-117, Sugar Hill (☎603/823-5575). Yes, it's in the middle of nowhere, but it's a scenic nowhere and well worth the schlep if you love pancakes.

**Red Parka Pub**, US-302, Glen (☎603/383-4344). Evening-only barbecue restaurant with bar until 1am, live rock music at weekends.

**The Thompson House Eatery**, Hwy-16, Jackson (☎603/383-9341). Huge portions of very reasonably priced American comfort food.

**Truant's Taverne**, Main St, North Woodstock (☎603/745-2239). Cozy, affordable restaurant, serving well-cooked American grill fare.

# West to Vermont

Much of the western side of New Hampshire, as you approach the Connecticut River that forms the entire border with Vermont, amounts to a less developed – and therefore less touristy – version of the Lakes Region. For a tranquil day or two the area around **Lake Sunapee** can be very appealing. Good bets for local inns include *The Backside Inn*, 1171 Brook Rd, Goshen, behind Mount Sunapee (☎603/863-5161; ④), and the upmarket *Goddard Mansion* on Hillstead Road in Claremont (☎603/543-0603 or 1-800/736-0603; ⑤).

## Hanover

**HANOVER**, near Lebanon just across from Vermont, is home to the venerable and elegant **Dartmouth College**, founded in this remote spot in the eighteenth century "for the instruction of the Youth of Indian tribes . . . and others." The main attraction here is the small **Hood Museum of Art** on the college green (Tues & Thurs–Sat 10am–5pm, Wed 10am–9pm, Sun noon–5pm; free), which contains works by Picasso and Monet alongside genuine Assyrian bas-reliefs. In the adjacent cultural complex, the Dartmouth Film Society screens international art and classic movies year-round ($5).

Hanover is enjoyable to wander around, with lively places to **eat and drink** such as *Molly's Balloon*, 43 S Main St (☎603/643-2570), and the paneled cellar of *Old Pete's Tavern* at 39 S Main St (☎603/643-2345). Its best **accommodation** is in the *Hanover Inn* (☎603/643-4300 or 1-800/443-7024; ⑦), overlooking Dartmouth Green from the corner of Main and Wheelock; the *Chieftain Motor Inn*, 84 Lyme Rd (☎603/643-2550 or 1-800/845-3557; ④), represents the best of the few budget options.

One unforgettable place to stay nearby is *Moose Mountain Lodge* (☎603/643-3529; ⑦), a steep climb up in the hills above **Etna**, looking over Vermont. All year it feels marvelously remote from the world below, but it really comes into its own for **cross-country skiing** in winter. The friendly owners expect their guests to share their enthusiasm for the country life, and charge $85 per day per person, which includes a hearty breakfast and dinner.

# VERMONT

**VERMONT** comes closer than any New England state to fulfilling the quintessential image of small-town Yankee America, with its white churches and red barns, covered bridges and clapboard houses, snowy woods and maple syrup. No city manages a population of forty thousand (only **Burlington** even comes close) and the chief tourist attraction is Ben and Jerry's ice-cream factory in Waterbury. Though rural, the landscape is not all that agricultural, as much is covered by mountainous forests (the state's name comes from the French *vert mont*, or green mountain). The people who choose to live here hold a lot in common: hippies and diehard conservatives, working together to preserve their environment and lamenting the advent of yet more ski resorts. One striking feature of Vermont is the absence of billboards, but the cutesy "country stores" which seem to grace every other crossroads can become tedious.

This was the last area of New England to be settled, early in the eighteenth century. As French explorers worked their way down from Canada, American colonists began to spread north; but even as that rivalry died down, a further antipathy developed between settlers from New Hampshire and those from New York. The wealthy New York merchants who built fine homes along the Connecticut River valley thought of themselves as the "River Gods," but the hardy settlers of the lakes and mountains to the west had little time for their patrician ways. Their leader was the now-legendary **Ethan Allen**, who formed his **Green Mountain Boys** in 1770, proclaiming that "the gods of the hills are not the gods of the valley." When the Revolutionary War superseded such conflicts, this all-but-autonomous force captured Fort Ticonderoga from the British and helped to win the decisive Battle of Bennington. For fourteen years from 1777, Vermont was an independent republic, with the first constitution in the world explicitly to forbid slavery and grant universal (male) suffrage, but once its boundaries with New York were finally agreed, it joined the Union in 1791. Curiously, the two seminal figures of the **Mormon** religion were both born in Vermont shortly thereafter – Joseph Smith in 1805, and his lieutenant and successor Brigham Young in 1801.

With the occasional exception, such as the extraordinary assortment of Americana at the **Shelburne Museum** near Burlington, there are few specific goals for tourists. Visitors come in great numbers during two well-defined seasons: to see the **fall foliage** in the first two weeks of October, and to **ski** in the depths of winter, when the resorts of **Killington**, and **Stowe** further north (home of *The Sound of Music*'s Von Trapp family), spring into life. For the rest of the year, you might just as well explore any of the state's minor roads which take your fancy, confident that some picturesque village will be around the next corner. There are far too many to list; we've had to leave out such prime examples as **Peru**, **Grafton** and **Middlebury**. Further information can be picked up from the official Welcome Center on each interstate as it enters Vermont.

### Getting around Vermont

Vermont Transit Lines (☎1-800/642-3133 in Vermont; ☎1-800/451-3292 elsewhere in New England) **buses** connect Montréal with Boston and New York, passing through Burlington, Montpelier, Rutland, White River Junction and Brattleboro. Other services link Stowe with Burlington, cross the north from Newport to Portland, Maine, and traverse the Green Mountains. Amtrak-affiliated Vermonter **trains** between Washington DC and St Albans stop at Brattleboro, White River Junction, Montpelier, Waterbury and Burlington – in the early morning southbound and mid-evening going north. The main **airport** is in Burlington.

Lake Champlain Ferries (☎802/864-9804) carries cars to New York at three points, including Burlington, and a six-minute ferry journey links Larrabee's Point with Ticonderoga further south. Vermont Mountain Bike Tours (PO Box 541, Pittsfield, VT 05762; ☎802/746-8580) and Adventure Guides of Vermont (PO Box 3, North Ferrisburgh, VT 05473; ☎802/425-6211 or 1-800/425-8747) organize **cycling tours**.

# Southern Vermont

Of the two low-key towns at either end of Vermont's southern corridor – a mere forty miles from east to west and linked by Hwy-9 – **Brattleboro** has the atmosphere of a college town, but not the college, while **Bennington** has the college but not the atmosphere. The birthplace of Mormon prophet Brigham Young is marked by a monument at **Whitingham**, halfway between the two.

## Brattleboro

If **BRATTLEBORO**, in the southeast corner of the state, is your first taste of Vermont, it may come as a surprise. Not the Fifties throwback you might expect, its style owes more to the central Massachusetts college towns, with numerous little stores catering to the youthful and vaguely "alternative" population which has moved into the surrounding hills over the last two decades. The town's one unlikely claim to fame is that this was where **Rudyard Kipling** wrote his two *Jungle Book*s.

**Trains** follow the river into town and stop behind the Old Railroad Station, which as the **Brattleboro Museum & Art Center** (mid-May through Oct Tues–Sun noon–6pm; $3) now displays locally made Estey organs and works of art. **Buses**, on the other hand, pick up and set down next to exit 3 off the interstate, a couple of miles north. Much the best place to **stay** is in one of the lovely river-view rooms at the Art Deco *Latchis Hotel*, 50 Main St (☎802/254-6300; ④). There's also a good restaurant, the *Latchis Grille*, serving beer from the on-site Windham Brewery (restaurant & brewery ☎802/254-4747). The nearby *Common Ground Community Restaurant* at 25 Elliot St (☎802/257-0855) is a long-established **wholefood restaurant**, serving vegetarian specialties in a very pleasant glassed-in conservatory. Homemade baked goods and specialty coffee make *Mocha Joe's* at 82 Main St (☎802/257-7794) a good place for a morning snack or evening dessert.

## Bennington

Little has happened in **BENNINGTON** in the past two hundred years to match the excitement of the days when Ethan Allen's Green Mountain Boys were based here, known as the "Bennington Mob." A 306ft hilltop obelisk (mid-April to Oct daily 9am–5pm; $2) commemorates the **Battle of Bennington** in August 1777, in which they were a crucial factor in defeating the British under General Burgoyne (though the battle itself was fought just across the border in New York).

About a mile north of the sleepy intersection at the town center, three **covered bridges** cross the Walloomsac River. Walkers set out from the southern end of the Long Trail (see below) roughly five miles east. Students from the small and exclusive arts-oriented Bennington College crowd into the *Blue Benn* **diner** at 102 Hunt St (☎802/442-5140). The *Fife 'n' Drum* **motel** (☎802/442-4074; ③) is one of many south of town on US-7. Eight miles east of town on Hwy-9, by the Prospect Ski Mountain, is the *HI-Greenwood Lodge* **hostel** (open mid-May to mid-Oct; ☎802/442-2547; ①), with beds for $15.

# The Green Mountains

The **Green Mountains** that form the backbone of Vermont are not as harsh as New Hampshire's White Mountains, though the forests for which they are named are invariably buried in snow for most of the winter, and the higher roads are liable to be blocked for long periods. Here and there, denuded patches mark where trees have been shaved away to create ski-runs, but for the most part the usually peaceful **Hwy-100** running up from the south offers unspoiled mountain views to either side.

In summer, hikers take up the challenge of the **Long Trail** along the central ridge, 264 miles from north to south. This predates the Appalachian Trail, which now joins its southern portion, and was constructed by the **Green Mountain Club** (4711 Waterbury-Stowe Rd, Waterbury Center, VT 05677; ☎802/244-7037). The Club's *Guidebook to the Long Trail* ($9.95) is invaluable.

## Hwy-100 Scenic Drive: Weston

One of the prettiest villages along Hwy-100 is **WESTON**, spreading beside a little river and centering on a perfect green, where a somber stone slab commemorates the seventeen local soldiers who were killed on the same day during the Civil War, at Alexandria in Virginia. Nearby, the **Farrar-Mansur House** (July & Aug Wed–Sun 1–4pm; May, June, Sept & Oct Sat–Sun 1–4pm; donations) is an early tavern which has been restored to show the lives of early settlers, while the **Weston Playhouse** is a typical little Vermont theater, putting on light summer performances (Tues–Sun; ☎802/824-5288).

Stores selling antiques, toys and fudge are scattered up and down the main street. The spell is slightly broken when you realize just how vast the **Vermont Country Store** south of the green really is, artfully concealed behind its modest facade. The original Weston Village Store tends to lean more on the side of kitsch but still offers a fun look into Vermont crafts.

Weston's nicest **accommodation** has to be the lovely *Inn at Weston* (☎802/824-6789; ⑤), with an excellent on-site restaurant as well as a cozy pub; among decent alternatives are the *Colonial House Inn & Motel* (☎802/824-6286 or 1-800/639-5033; ④), less than two miles south on Hwy-100, and the *Friendly Acres Motel & Inn* (☎802/824-5851; ④), a little closer to town on the same road. A small, but magnificent soda fountain dominates the 1885 mahogany bar of the lunch-only *Bryant House* **restaurant** (closed Sun; ☎802/824-6287), two doors down from the Vermont Country Store and run by the same management; the menu includes such country goodies as "johnny cakes" of cornbread with molasses.

## Killington

The ski resort of **KILLINGTON**, in the center of the Green Mountains halfway between Woodstock to the east and Rutland to the west, has grown out of nothing since 1957. Despite a permanent population of perhaps fifty, it's estimated that in season there are enough beds within twenty miles to accommodate over ten thousand people each night. The resort sprawls over six peaks and is especially good for beginners and intermediates (for skiing information, call ☎802/422-3333 Mon–Fri 9am–5pm).

In winter, the Killington Access Road up from US-4 is jammed with bars and restaurants; most close in summer, though you can still take the **cable car** (☎802/422-3333) up to the observation deck and cafeteria on the bleak summit. Hiking routes which meet here include the Long and Appalachian Trails. The *Cortina Inn* (☎802/773-3333 or 1-800/451-6108; ⑤) is one of several luxury **inns** on Hwy-4 to offer reduced summer rates; the quiet *Val Roc Motel*, out on Hwy-4 just after the junction with Hwy-100 S (☎802/422-3881 or 1-800/238-8762; ③), is reasonably priced except during the busiest ski weekends.

## Woodstock

Since the 1790s, **WOODSTOCK**, a few miles west of the Connecticut River up US-4, has been one of Vermont's more refined centers. Hence the distinguished houses around its oval green, now largely taken over by antiques stores and tearooms. It should most certainly not be confused with Woodstock, New York, of festival fame; the closest it came to radical action in the Sixties was to build a new covered bridge.

Both of Woodstock's two main paying attractions are geared towards seeing animals close up. Part of **Billings Farm and Museum** (May–Oct daily 10am–5pm; Nov Sat–Sun 10am–4pm; $7) is maintained as it was on the death of its former owner in 1890, while the rest is run as a modern dairy farm; the **Vermont Raptor Center** on Church Hill Road (May–Oct daily 10am–4pm; Nov–April Mon–Sat 10am–4pm; $5) treats injured birds of prey.

An information booth on the green in summer (☎802/457-3555) conducts free **walking tours** of the village (Mon, Wed & Sat 10.30am), and can help with **accommodation**, which includes the *Shire Motel*, 46 Pleasant St (☎802/457-2211; ④), the *Village Inn of*

*Woodstock*, 41 Pleasant St (☎802/457-1255 or 1-800/722-4571; ⑥), and the cozy *Applebutter Inn* (☎802/457-4158; ④), just east on Hwy-4 in Taftsville. You don't have to be a guest at the riverside *Lincoln Inn* (☎802/457-3312; ⑥), three miles west on Hwy-4, to **eat** in its very reasonable dining room (Wed–Sun only); in Woodstock itself, *Bentley's*, 3 Elm St (☎802/457-3232), has a range of microbrews and upscale bar fare, as well as live music on weekends, while *The Prince and the Pauper*, 24 Elm St (☎802/457-1818), serves more expensive continental cuisine in a casual setting. *Pane Salute*, 61 Central (☎802/457-4882), has the area's best cappuccino and pastries. The nearest **hostel** is over twenty miles south in Ludlow: beds at the HI-affiliated *Trojan Horse Hostel*, 44 Andover St (☎802/228-5244 or 1-800/547-7475; ①), cost $12 in summer and $17 in winter.

## Quechee

In recent years, the grand houses on the hills around **QUECHEE**, six miles east of Woodstock, have been joined by a proliferation of new condos and second homes. It's all reasonably well landscaped, but a shame nonetheless, and adds nothing to the environs of **Quechee State Park**, which was fortunately created in time to spare the splendors of the **Quechee Gorge**. A delicate bridge spans the 165ft chasm of the Ottauquechee River, and hiking trails lead down through the fir trees, where you'll find Quechee Gorge State Park, one of Vermont's many state-run **campgrounds** (☎802/295-2990). The *Quality Inn*, on Hwy-4 between Quechee Gorge and the Timber Village antiques mart (☎802/295-7600 or 1-800/732-4376; ④), offers the best value **accommodation**.

A waterfall on the river turns the turbines of **Simon Pearce Glass** (daily 9am–9pm; ☎802/295-2711), on Main Street in Quechee itself. Housed in a former woollen mill, this is an unusual combination of glass-blowing center and restaurant, where you can watch bowls and pots being made and then eat off them. Adventurous meals start at $12.

## White River Junction

Probably the most exciting thing ever to happen in **WHITE RIVER JUNCTION** was the first use of laughing gas as an anesthetic, in 1844. But it's an invaluable transportation hub: weary Amtrak trains stop right by North Main Street, and buses run east into New Hampshire – **Hanover** (see p.226) is just across the river – and throughout Vermont.

A good old-fashioned railroad hotel – the *Hotel Coolidge* at 17 S Main St (☎802/295-3118 or 1-800/622-1124; ③) – still survives in the town center, and has recently added an HI-affiliated hostel wing with kitchen space and $15 dorm beds. In the same building, the *River City Cafe* serves good soups and sandwiches at bargain rates. Except for the *Super 8 Motel*, at I-91 exit 11 (☎802/295-7577 or 1-800/800-8000; ③), other places to stay are pricey. The Catamount Brewery down the road at 58 S Main St (☎802/296-2248) serves free samples of its tasty microbrews.

## Montpelier and Barre

Another fifty miles north up I-89, **MONTPELIER** is the smallest state capital in the nation, with fewer than ten thousand inhabitants. The golden dome of the **capitol** is appealing in its leafy gardens, and recent remodeling makes its marble-floored, mural-lined hallways well worth a free tour. Copious information on accommodation possibilities, here and throughout the state, is available from the **Vermont Travel Division** at 134 State St (Mon–Fri 7.45am–4.30pm; ☎1-800/VERMONT). Budget rooms can be had at the central Montpelier Guest Home, 22 North St (☎802/229-0878; ②), which has a relaxing deck and gardens, or the *Vermonter Hotel* (☎802/479-9014; ③), southeast on US-302. There's also the *Capitol Home Hostel* (HI/AYH), out on RD1 (phone for directions: ☎802/223-2104 before 9pm; ①), with beds for $12.

Students from the local New England Culinary Institute run both the *Main St Grill & Bar* at 118 Main St (☎802/223-3188) and the more upmarket *Chef's Table* at the same address (☎802/229-9202), serving excellent and inexpensive – if experimental – dishes from all over the world. The *Horn of the Moon Cafe*, 8 Langdon St (☎802/223-2895), is a wholefood bakery, while *Julio's*, 44 Main St (☎802/229-9348), cooks up delicious Mexican specialties.

The immigrant stoneworkers of the adjacent town of **BARRE** (pronounced *BA-rie*) were around 1900 famed for their militancy. Their most enduring memorials are the gravestones they carved themselves, in **Mount Hope Cemetery** on Hwy-14, though the Scots among them did also erect a rather incongruous statue of Robert Burns downtown. Southeast of town, you can watch workers cut huge blocks out of the earth at the world's biggest granite quarry, the **Rock of Ages** (May–Oct Mon–Sat 8.30am–5pm, Sun noon–5pm; free). The *Hollow Inn & Motel* at 278 S Main St (☎802/479-9313 or 1-800/998-9444; ④) has a fitness center and provides complimentary continental breakfast. For other **meals**, the *Country House*, 276 N Main St (☎802/476-4282), serves affordable pasta and fish dishes.

## Waterbury

Few people paid much attention to **WATERBURY** before 1978; even then, the opening of a homemade ice-cream stand run by a pair of hippies on the forecourt of a gas station excited little interest. However, **Ben & Jerry's Ice Cream Factory**, one mile north of I-89 on Rte-100 in Waterbury Center, on the way up to Stowe, has grown so huge, so fast, that it is now the number-one tourist destination in Vermont. Half-hour tours (daily: July–Aug 9am–8pm; Sept–Oct 9am–6pm; Nov–May 10am–5pm; June 9am–6pm; ☎802/882-1260; $2) feature a short film, a chance to look down on the workforce from an observation platform, and a free mini-scoop of the stuff that made it all possible – you can buy more at the top-price giftshop and ice-cream stall outside. The omnipresent black-and-white cow logo, and the sanctimonious reminders to recycle, eat organic and buy your milk from farming co-ops can get a bit much; if the summer crowds seem intolerable, bear in mind there are better things to do in Burlington and Stowe.

Waterbury is the closest Amtrak stop to Stowe – the station is just south of the interstate – and Vermont Transit buses also pass through.

## Stowe

There is still a beautiful nineteenth-century village at the heart of **STOWE**, with a white-spired meeting house and a green to stroll around, although a century's experience of catering to large crowds of skiers, summertime hikers, bikers and golfers, and autumn leaf-peepers has rather swamped the approach road to the main ski area with resort spas, equipment stores and sprawling condominium complexes. Nonetheless, the setting remains spectacular, at the foot of Vermont's highest mountain, the 4393ft **Mount Mansfield**.

Hwy-108 – **Mountain Road** – leads close to the mountain through the dramatic **Smugglers' Notch**, which is closed by snow through the winter. Weather permitting, you can get to the very top either by driving up the **Toll Road**, which starts seven miles up (late May to mid-Oct daily 10am–5pm; $12 per car), or by taking the **gondola** (mid-June to mid-Oct daily 10am–5pm; ☎802/253-7311; $10) up to Cliff House, and hiking for another half-hour from there. There's also a rollerblading skate park ($10 a day) that offers lessons and rentals, plus an Alpine Slide ($7.50 a ride). What really made Stowe's name as a **cross-country ski resort** was its connection with the **Von Trapp family**, of *The Sound of Music* fame. After fleeing Austria during the war, they established the *Trapp Family Lodge* on Luce Hill Road (☎802/253-8511 or 1-800/826-7000; ⑦). The original lodge, where Maria Von Trapp held her singing camps, has burned down, and she herself died in 1987, but a new and equally luxurious building has taken its place; its *Austrian Tea Room* serves incredibly heavy Germanic cakes and pastries.

Plentiful **accommodation**, mostly on Mountain Road, includes the streamside *Inn at Turner Mill* (☎802/253-2062; ④); the *Stoweflake Inn & Resort* (☎1-800/253-7355 or 253-2232; ⑤); the *Riverside Inn* (☎802/253-4217 or 1-800/966-4217; ③), where rates rise about $15 in winter; the small *Charbonneau Guest House* (☎802/253-7701; ③); and the central 1833 *Green Mountain Inn* (☎802/253-7301 or 1-800/253-7302; ⑦). Vermont's **State Ski Dorm**, 6992 Mountain Rd, is just past the foot of the Toll Road (☎802/253-4010; ①). From the end of August through early March, it serves as *The Mount Mansfield Hostel*, a **youth hostel** renting dorm beds for $15 to $25, with available breakfast ($5) and dinner ($7). The *Gold Brook* **campground** is two miles south on Hwy-100 (☎802/253-7683). Also on Hwy-100, the sunken lounge of *Hapeltons* (☎802/253-4653) is a nice place for a snack and a drink, and very snug in winter.

There's a big choice of places to **eat** in and around Stowe. Best for breakfast is *McCarthy's* up on Mountain Road (☎802/253-8626); *Gracie's* in the Carlson Building on Main Street (☎802/253-8741) does a good job with sandwiches, burgers, and salads. In the evening, the *Shed Restaurant & Brew Pub* on Mountain Road (☎802/253-4364) has moderately priced dinners, while the *Blue Moon Café*, 35 School St (☎802/253-7006), offers an innovative menu with prices in the $15–20 range. The constantly crowded *Pie in the Sky*, 492 Mountain Rd (☎802/253-5100), serves relatively inexpensive family-style pizza and pasta dishes.

The **visitor center** is on Main Street (Mon–Fri 9am–5pm, Sat–Sun 10am–5pm; ☎802/253-7321 or 1-800/24-STOWE); for **skiing information**, contact Mount Mansfield (☎802/253-7311) or Smuggler's Notch (☎802/664-8851 or 1-800/451-8752). **Bikes** can be rented from the Mountain Bike Shop on Mountain Road (☎802/253-7919); an excellent biking trail climbs the mountain.

# Lake Champlain

The 150-mile-long **Lake Champlain**, which forms the boundary between the states of New York and Vermont, and just nudges its way into Canada in the north, never exceeds twelve miles in width. Across the water from the flatlands of the Champlain Valley, the impassive Adirondacks are always visible, looming up in the west. The first non-native to see the lake, Samuel de Champlain in 1609, who named it in his own honor, was also the first to claim that it held a sinuous Loch-Ness-type monster. "Champ" is now familiar as an informal symbol of the region.

The life and soul of the valley is the French-influenced city of **Burlington**, whose longstanding trade connections with Montréal have filled it with elegant nineteenth-century architecture. Within just a few miles of the center, US-2 leads north onto the supremely rural **Champlain Isles**, covered in meadows and orchards.

Vermont is one of the few states with designated Underwater Historic Preserves (details on ☎802/828-3226), where divers can see wrecks on the lake floor. There are several of these underwater "state parks" close to Burlington, and the best place to find out about them is at the **Lake Champlain Maritime Museum** in Basin Harbor, six miles east of Vergennes (May–Oct daily 10am–5pm; $5), which also has details of the horse-powered ferry that plied the lake c.1900. The museum is in the grounds of the *Basin Harbor Club* (☎802/475-2311 or 1-800/622-4000), part down-home family resort, part well-heeled country club, with a golf course, which supplies three meals a day in summer (⑧) and breakfast only at other times (⑦).

Lake Champlain Ferries (☎802/864-9804) cross the lake from Vermont to New York from **Burlington** (to Port Kent; hourly; $12.75); **Charlotte** (to Essex; every 30min; $7);

and **Grand Isle** (to Plattsburgh; every 20min; $6.75). All these rates are one-way for a car and driver; additional passengers, cyclists and walk-ons pay $2–3.25.

# Burlington

Lakeside **BURLINGTON**, Vermont's largest "city" with a population nudging forty thousand, is one of the most purely enjoyable towns in New England, a hip, relaxed and open-minded fusion of Montréal, eighty miles to the north, and Boston, over two hundred miles southeast. In fact, from its earliest days Burlington looked as much to Canada as to the south. Shipping connections with the St Lawrence River were far easier than the land routes across the mountains, and the harbor became a major supply center. The city's founders included Ethan Allen and family – far from being some impoverished Robin Hood figure, Ethan was a wealthy landowner, and his brother Ira set up the University of Vermont.

Burlington today is the definitive youthful, outward-looking university town. From the bandstands to the brewpubs, this is simply a nice place to be. It's one of the few American cities to offer something approaching a cafe society, with a downtown, especially around the Church Street Marketplace, you can stroll around on foot, and plenty of open-air terraces. Politically, too, it's unusual: Bernard Saunders, the former "socialist" mayor of Burlington, was in 1990 elected to the House of Representatives from Vermont – the first political independent to go to Congress in forty years.

### Arrival, information and getting around

Vermont Transit **buses** stop in downtown Burlington, beside City Hall Park at the corner of St Paul and Main, but the Amtrak station is an inconvenient five miles northeast, in the small community of Essex Junction (connecting buses every half-hour; $1). The airport is two miles out along US-2, in the same general direction. Practical **information** is available from the **visitor center** at 60 Main St (July–Sept Mon–Fri 8.30am–5pm, Sat & Sun 11am–3pm; Oct–June Mon–Fri 8.30am–5pm; ☎802/863-3489), or the kiosk in Church Street. The local CCTA **bus** company (☎802/864-CCTA) runs a free shuttle (Mon–Fri 6.30am–7pm, Sat–Sun 11am–6pm) connecting the university campus, downtown and the waterfront.

Lake Champlain Ferries (see opposite) leave from the jetty at the end of King Street; as do Lake Cruise and Charter (☎802/864-9804; $7). Ski Rack, 85 Main St (☎802/658-3313), rents **bikes**.

### Accommodation

Burlington has no shortage of moderate accommodation, while for **camping** the lakeside *Northbeach Campsites* (☎802/862-0942) is less than two miles north on Institute Road.

**B&B Burlington Redstone**, 497 S Willard St (☎802/862-0508). Redstone home a few blocks south of town center. Doubles from $80.

**Colonial Motor Inn**, 462 Shelburne Rd (☎802/862-5754). Sixties-era decor lends a campy touch to this clean motel with pool and cable TV. ③.

**Econolodge**, 1076 Williston Rd (☎802/863-1125 or 1 800/55 ECONO). On US-2 just east of I-89, with clean basic rooms and continental breakfast. ④.

**Ho-Hum Motel**, 1660 Williston Rd (☎802/863-4551). Simple, reasonably priced motel, three miles east of downtown on US-2. ④.

**Mid-Town Motel**, 230 Main St (☎802/862-9686). Spartan, inexpensive quarters in the heart of downtown. No phones. ②.

**Mrs Farrell's Home Hostel (HI/AYH)**, 27 Arlington Court (☎802/865-3730). A few dorm beds. $15 members, $18 others. Three miles out from the center. 10pm curfew; reservations essential. ①.

**YWCA**, 278 Main St (☎802/862-7520). Women-only budget option. Dorms $11, doubles $24. ①.

## The City

Your natural inclination on setting out to explore Burlington might be to head for the **waterfront**. In fact, this is surprisingly undeveloped, though Battery Park at its northern end makes a good place to watch the sun go down over the Adirondacks – especially when there's a band playing, as there often is at weekends.

A better target is the pedestrianized **Church Street Marketplace**, a few blocks back, which holds Burlington's finest old buildings and all its modern cafes and boutiques. The free **Robert Hull Fleming Museum** on Colchester Avenue (Tues–Fri 9am–4pm, Sun 1–5pm) has an interesting collection of art and artifacts from all over the world, including pre-Columbian pieces, while north on Hwy-127, the **Ethan Allen Homestead** (mid-May to mid-June daily 1–5pm; mid-June to mid-Oct Mon–Sat 10am–5pm, Sun 1–5pm; $4) offers a multifaceted look at the life and history of Vermont's controversial founding father.

## The Shelburne Museum

It takes a whole day, if not more, fully to appreciate the remarkable fifty-acre collection of unalloyed **Americana** gathered at the **Shelburne Museum**, on Hwy-7 in Shelburne, three miles south of Burlington (June–Oct daily 9am–5pm, guided tours at 1pm; Nov–May guided tours only; ☎802/985-3346; $17.50, valid for two successive days). Created in 1947 by heiress Electra Webb, it centers on her parents' French Impressionist paintings, including works by Degas and Monet, displayed in a meticulous reconstruction of their New York apartment. However, Electra's own interests ranged far wider, and she put together what is probably the nation's finest celebration of its own inventive past.

More than thirty buildings, some original and some newly constructed, focus on aspects of everyday life over the past two centuries; most are staffed by well-informed attendants. The village includes a general store, complete with painted "**cigar store Indians**," an apothecary, an early print shop, a doctor's, a dentist's and a blacksmith's. There's a **Shaker barn**, a schoolhouse, a meeting house, a covered bridge, a railroad station, and even an enormous **steam paddlewheeler** from Lake Champlain, the *SS Ticonderoga*, with its own rock-surrounded lighthouse.

## Eating, drinking and entertainment

The presence of ten thousand students during term time ensures Burlington offers any number of inexpensive and good restaurants, as well as some pretty raucous night spots. Note that this is one of the most vehement **anti-smoking** towns in the East, and smoking is banned in most restaurants and some bars.

**Bourbon Street Grill**, 213 College St (☎802/865-2800). Crowded and dimly lit place, with Cajun specials from $8.

**Daily Planet**, 15 Center St behind Church Street Marketplace (☎802/862-9647). Innovative menu combining Asian and Mediterranean cooking with old-fashioned American comfort food.

**Five Spice Cafe**, 175 Church St (☎802/864-4045). Excellent Southeast Asian food: dim sum and vegetarian.

**Muddy Waters**, 184 Main St (☎802/658-0466). Crazy interior and colorful clientele adorn this popular coffeehouse. The caffeine beverages pack quite a kick.

**NECI Commons**, 25 Church St (☎802/862-6324). The Burlington outpost of the New England Culinary Institute. Wonderful food and attentive service. Brunch is a bargain.

**Pauline's Cafe & Restaurant**, 1834 Shelburne Rd, South Burlington (☎802/862-1081). Innovative American cuisine with a continental flavor, using much local produce. Light meals in a casual setting downstairs, more formality and higher prices upstairs.

**Shanty on the Shore**, 181 Battery St (☎802/864-0238). Absolutely fresh seafood in a laid-back setting with views of Lake Champlain.

**Smoke Jack's**, 156 Church St (☎802/658-1119). Innovative American food smoked over an oak-wood grill.

**Sweetwaters**, 120 Church St (☎802/864-9800). American grill standards in a converted bank with sidewalk dining; most notable for its Sunday brunch and salads.

# MAINE

As big as the other five New England states combined, **MAINE** has barely the population of Rhode Island. In principle, therefore, there's plenty of room for its massive summer influx of visitors; in practice, the majority of these make for the southern stretches of the extravagantly corrugated **coast**. You only really begin to appreciate the size and space of the state further north, or **inland**, where vast tracts of mountainous forest are dotted with lakes, and barely pierced by roads – more like the Alaskan interior than the RV-clustered roads of the Vermont and New Hampshire mountains, and ideal territory for hiking and canoeing (and spotting moose).

Although Maine is in many ways inhospitable – the **Algonquin** called it "Land of the Frozen Ground" – it has been in contact with Europe ever since the **Vikings**, around 1000 AD. For the navigator Verrazano, in 1524, the "crudity and evil manners" of the Indians made this the "Land of Bad People," but before long European fishermen were setting up camps each summer to dry their catch. Francis Bacon in turn said that the English were "worse than the very Savages, impudently lying with their Women, teaching their men to drink drunke, and . . . to fall together by the eares."

North America's first agricultural **colonies** were in Maine: de Champlain's **French** Protestants near Mount Desert Island in 1604, and an **English** group that survived one winter at the mouth of the Kennebec three years later. In the face of the unwillingness of subsequent English settlers to let them farm in peace, the local Indians formed a long-term alliance with the French, and until as late as 1700 regularly drove out streams of impoverished English refugees. By 1764, however, the official census could claim that even Maine's black population was more numerous than its Native Americans.

At first considered part of Massachusetts, Maine became a separate entity only in 1820, when the Missouri Compromise made Maine a Free and Missouri a Slave state. In the nineteenth century, its people had a reputation for conservatism and resistance to immigration, manifested in anti-Irish riots. Today, the **economy** remains heavily based on the sea, although many of those who fish also farm, and long expeditions are rare. Recently they have been selling their catch direct to Russian factory ships anchored just offshore. Lobster fishing in particular has defied gloomy predictions and has boomed again, as evidenced by the many thriving **lobster pounds**.

In winter, most of Maine is under ice; summer is short and usually heralded in early June by an infestation of tiny black flies. **Fall colors** begin to spread from the north in late September – when, unlike elsewhere in New England, off-season prices apply – but temperatures drop sharply, becoming quite frosty by mid-October.

## Getting around Maine

The vast majority of visitors to Maine **drive**. Much the most enjoyable route to follow is US-1, running within a few miles of the coast all the way to Canada, with innumerable side turnings to hidden seaside villages. If you're in a hurry, I-95, initially the (tolled) Maine Turnpike, offers speedy access to Portland and beyond. In the **interior**, the roads are quiet and the views spectacular; many belong to the lumber companies, who keep careful track of who you are and where you're going (and charge you for the privilege). At any time of year bad weather can render these roads suddenly impassable; be sure to check before setting off.

   **Public transportation,** on the other hand, falls a long way short of meeting travelers' needs. The six-times-daily Greyhound service from Boston to Portland, three of which continue to Bangor, at least links the main towns of the southern coast, as does Concord Trailways (☎1-800/639-3317), but that's about all. Except in high summer, you can't get a bus any nearer to Acadia National Park or Bar Harbor than Bangor or Belfast, and nothing at all runs north. Sadly, in a state whose industry and tourism were once built on its railroads, there is no longer any Amtrak service. A Canadian train runs across the middle of the state to reach New Brunswick, but doesn't connect anywhere useful within Maine itself.

# The Maine coast

Considering that the state has a **coastline** of three thousand miles, finding access to the sea in Maine can be a frustrating business. The oceanfront is monopolized by an endless succession of private homes and vacation residences – most famously that of former president Bush at Kennebunkport. In fact, only two percent of the shore is publicly owned – and not all of that is beach. Rather than long walks on coastal footpaths, travelers can expect attractive if rather commercial harbor villages, linked mostly by roads set well back from the water and packed with diners, motels and factory outlets.

   Europeans tend to find the landscape pretty, but not strikingly different to the Atlantic coast back home, and occasionally a bit too well manicured. The liveliest destinations are **Portland** and **Bar Harbor** (at the edge of **Acadia National Park**); there's a wide choice of smaller seaside towns, such as **Belfast** and **Wiscasset**, if you're looking for a more peaceful base. **Beaches** are more common (and the sea is warmer) further south, for example at **Ogunquit**.

   The best way to see the coast itself must be by **boat**: ferries and excursions operate from even the smallest harbors, with major routes including the ferries to **Canada** from Portland and Bar Harbor, and the shorter trips to **Monhegan** and **Vinalhaven** islands from Boothbay Harbor and Rockland respectively.

## South of Portland

I-95 crosses from Portsmouth, New Hampshire (see p.218), into an area of Maine so dense with little communities that Mark Twain alleged one couldn't "throw a brick without danger of disabling a postmaster." Three miles over the border, an **information center** at **Kittery** provides copious details on the whole state (daily: July–Aug 7am–9pm; Sept 9am–6pm; rest of year 9am–5pm; ☎207/439-1319).

   If you want to avoid the tolls on the interstate and follow more scenic US-1 instead, you'll soon find yourself in **YORK**, which was in 1639 the first English city to be chartered in North America. Its seventeenth-century **Old Gaol** now serves as a museum, commemorating its own past and that of the local Native Americans.

### Ogunquit
The three-mile spit of sand that shields **OGUNQUIT** from the open ocean is Maine's finest **beach**, but the town remains small enough to be a pleasant resort. The summer season at the **Ogunquit Playhouse** (☎207/646-5511) usually attracts a few big-name performers. Among dozens of **motels**, most of which close for the winter, are the *Sea View* (☎207/646-7064; ⑤) and the *Holiday House* (☎207/646-5020; ④), which also has a few cottages. *Dixon's* (May–Sept; ☎207/363-2131), the closest **campground** to town, is five miles north on US-1 and operates a free shuttle to Ogunquit Beach in July and August. The Marginal Way, a not very rural clifftop path, leads from central Ogunquit

to **Perkins Cove** a mile south, where well-priced **seafront restaurants** include *Barnacle Billy's* (☎207/646-5575).

## Kennebunkport

**KENNEBUNKPORT** was perfectly happy as a self-contained and exclusive residential district, before its worldwide exposure as the home of **George Bush's** "summer White House." If anything, locals seem to feel that George lowered the tone of the place by becoming president. There were complaints at having to bear the extra cost of policing (the far smaller and poorer Plains, Georgia, home of Jimmy Carter, paid up with pride), and talk of a "lower class" of gawking visitor clogging the streets and driving the old money away. However, Kennebunkport is not actually all that different from anywhere else along the coast – which is presumably what's really bothering the locals. The best place to hang out (and eat seafood) is *Alisson's* at 8 Dock Square (☎207/967-4841), where dinner is served until 10pm and a pub menu available until 11pm, and the bar stays open until 1am. There's no great point paying in-town hotel rates when there are so many motels along the highways.

Five miles south of Portland is the **Cape Elizabeth lighthouse**, commissioned by George Washington in 1791 and familiar from postcards and posters. The *Lobster Shack* (☎207/799-1677) just below the light (and above the horn) is great for fresh seafood.

# Portland

The largest city in Maine, **PORTLAND** was founded in 1632 in a superb position on the Casco Bay Peninsula, and quickly prospered, building ships and exporting the great inland pines for use as masts. A long line of wooden **wharves** stretched along the seafront, with the merchants' houses on the hillside above. From the earliest days it was a cosmopolitan city, with a large free black population who traditionally worked as longshoremen; there was great bitterness when Irish immigrants began to muscle in on the scene in the 1830s. When the **railroads** came, the Canada Trunk Line had its terminus right on Portland's quayside, bringing the produce of Canada and the Great Plains one hundred miles closer to Europe than it would have been at any other major US port. Some of the wharves are now taken up by new condo developments, though **Custom House Wharf** remains much as it must have looked when Anthony Trollope passed through in 1861 and said, "I doubt whether I ever saw a town with more evident signs of prosperity." Most of the town he saw was destroyed by an accidental **fire** in 1866 (Indians in 1675, and the British in 1775, had previously burned Portland deliberately).

Grand Trunk Station was torn down in 1966, and downtown Portland appeared to be in terminal decline until a group of committed residents undertook the energetic redevelopment of the area now known as **Old Port Exchange**. Their success has revitalized the city, keeping it at the heart of Maine life – but you shouldn't expect a hive of energy. Portland is simply a pleasant, sophisticated, and in places very attractive town, not a major urban center.

## Arrival, information and getting around

Both I-95 and US-1 skirt the promontory of Portland, within a very few miles of the city center; **Portland International Jetport** (☎207/774-7301) is next to I-95, and connected with downtown by regular city buses. Congress Street is the main central thoroughfare, while Fore Street runs along the harbor just to the south. Concord Trailways (☎1-800/639-3317) and Greyhound are the principal **bus** operators along the coast, with frequent services to Boston, as well as north to Bangor (and, in summer, Bar Harbor). Vermont Transit Lines (☎207/772-6587 or 1-800/552-8737) runs to Montréal,

New Hampshire and Vermont; the station is at 950 Congress St, on the eastern edge of downtown. The **visitor center** is at 305 Commercial St (mid-May to mid-Oct Mon–Fri 8am–6pm, Sat & Sun 10am–6pm; rest of year Mon–Fri 8am–5pm, Sat & Sun 10am–3pm; ☎207/772-5800).

Downtown Portland, though served by buses ($1) and trolleys, is compact enough to stroll around; Cyclemania, 59 Federal St (☎207/774-2933), rents **bicycles** for $15 a day.

Between mid-May and October, the Prince of Fundy Company's *Scotia Prince* **ferry** leaves Portland for **Yarmouth** in Nova Scotia at 9pm each evening, returning the next day. The standard high-season fare is $93 per car, $68 per person, plus extra for a cabin, though there are various discount and excursion fares (details on ☎207/775-5616 or 1-800/482-0955 in Maine, ☎1-800/437-3270 elsewhere in the US).

## Accommodation

Finding a room in Portland is no great problem, though you can expect to pay more to stay in town than in the **budget motels** around exit 8 off I-95. The closest (May to mid-Oct only) **campground** is *Wassamki Springs* (☎207/839-4276), off Hwy-114 towards Westbrook.

**The Danforth**, 163 Danforth St (☎207/879-8755 or 1-800/991-6557). Twelve rooms, ten with private baths and working fireplaces, in an 1820s Federal-style home near the Old Port. Full breakfast served. ⑥.

**Embassy Suites**, 1050 Westbrook St (☎207/775-2200 or 1-800/EMBASSY). Spacious suites for the price of a hotel room, overlooking Portland's tiny Jetport. Rates include full breakfast and afternoon cocktails. ⑦.

**HI-Portland Summer Hostel**, 645 Congress St, in Portland Hall (☎207/874-3281). Open June through late August. Office hours 6–11am & 5pm–midnight. $14 members, $17 nonmembers. ①.

**Hotel Everett**, 51A Oak St (☎207/773-7882). Cozy rooms, near the Wadsworth-Longfellow House. ④.

**Inn at St John**, 939 Congress St (☎207/773-6481 or 1-800/636-9127). Small, central rooms near the museums. ③.

**Radisson Eastland Hotel**, 157 High St (☎207/775-5411 or 1-800/333-3333). Luxury central accommodation. ⑤.

**Susse Chalet Inn**, 340 Park Ave (☎207/871-0611 or 1-800/5-CHALET). Good-value doubles on the western edge of the peninsula near the Maine Medical Center; there's another *Susse Chalet* at 1200 Brighton Ave (☎207/774-6101; ③), further north and so slightly less expensive. ⑤.

**YMCA**, 70 Forest Ave (☎207/874-1105). Men-only hostel accommodation north of Congress St near Deering Oaks Park. $26.25 per night; often full. ①.

**YWCA**, 87 Spring St (☎207/874-1130). Very near the Museum of Art, charging $25 single, or $20 per bed in a double room. Women only. ①.

## The City

Thanks to the various fires, not all that much of old Portland survives, though various grand mansions can be seen along Congress and Danforth streets. The **Wadsworth-Longfellow House/Maine History Gallery** at 489 Congress St was Portland's first brick house when built in 1785 by Peleg Wadsworth, but owes its fame primarily to Peleg's grandson, the poet Henry Longfellow, who spent his boyhood here. The gallery features changing displays of state history and art. Tours start on the hour and half-hour and last around 45 minutes (June–Oct Tues–Sun 10am–4pm; $4, gallery only $2).

The **Portland Museum of Art** at 7 Congress Square is a much more modern affair, built in 1988 by the I M Pei partnership (Mon–Wed & Sat 10am–5pm, Thurs–Fri 10am–9pm, Sat noon–5pm; tours at 2pm daily & 6pm Thurs–Fri; $6). All parts of the museum give superb views over the bay, including some through porthole windows; indeed, on occasions the collection seems subordinate to the design, which does not allow much room for extensive displays. Normally the lower stories are occupied by temporary exhibitions – though there's a lovely open-air garden cafe as well – while the works upstairs include a lively and flirtatious set of 1880s Winslow Homer engravings, some Andrew Wyeths, and an array of early nineteenth-century European ceramics commemorating heroes of the American Revolution.

For relaxed wandering, the restored **Old Port Exchange** near the quayside, between Exchange and Pearl, is quite entertaining, with all sorts of redbrick antiquarian shops, specialist book and music stores (particularly on Exchange St), and other esoterica. Several companies operate **boat trips** from the nearby wharves: the *Palawan*, a vintage 58ft ocean racer, sails around the harbor and Casco Bay islands and lighthouses from DiMillo's Marina off Commercial Street (daily in summer; 2hr trip; ☎207/773-2163; $20), and Bay View Cruises, 184 Commercial St, offers **seal-watching** tours (daily May–Oct; ☎207/642-3270; $8). Casco Bay Lines runs a twice-daily mailboat all year, and additional cruises in summer, to six of the innumerable **Calendar Islands** in Casco Bay, from its terminal at Commercial and Franklin (☎207/774-7871; $8). **Long, Peaks** and **Cliff islands** all have accommodation or camping facilities.

If you follow Portland's waterfront to the end of the peninsula, you'll come to the **Eastern Promenade**, which became almost exclusively residential after the last fire, and is remarkably peaceful for so close to downtown. A big beach lies below the headland, while above, at the top of Munjoy Hill, is the eight-sided shingled 1807 **Portland Observatory** (June Fri–Sun 1–5pm; July to Labor Day Wed–Sun noon–5pm; $2), which affords an exhilarating view of the bay.

## Eating

Not only is Portland rich in affordable **restaurants**, but most of its entertainment venues and bars, listed separately below, serve food as well. The bountiful Farmer's Market, in Monument Square on Wednesdays May through November, offers the perfect opportunity to sample local produce and culture.

**Boone's**, 6 Custom House Wharf (☎207/774-5725). Traditional waterfront restaurant in old wharf buildings, overlooking the fishing docks. Good lobster and grilled seafood in general.

**Federal Spice**, 225 Federal St (☎207/774-6404). Eclectic international fare influenced by South American, Southeast Asian and Caribbean cuisine, all very hot and spicy.

**Fresh Market**, 43 Exchange St (☎207/773-7146). All kinds of fresh pasta and noodles, including ginger and squid's ink, at reasonable prices.

**Seaman's Club**, 375 Fore St (☎207/774-7777). Standard seafare in the heart of downtown, overlooking the harbor.

**Shalimar of India**, 675 Congress St (☎207/874-6342). Good tandoori dishes and lunchtime and evening specials. The outdoor deck is the place to sit in summer.

**Silly's**, 40 Washington St (☎207/772-0360). Burgers, pies and particularly fine milkshakes in a space adorned with wacky Americana.

**Village Cafe**, 112 Newbury St (☎207/772-5320). No-nonsense, well-priced family dining; well-cooked steak and seafood plus several Italian dishes.

### Nightlife and entertainment

Portland's formal entertainment possibilities range from the tiny and adventurous Mad Horse Theater Company at 955 Forest Ave (☎207/797-3338) up to the large productions at the Portland Performing Arts Center, 25A Forest Ave (☎207/774-0465). The free *Casco Bay Weekly* has listings of all local events; Maine's biggest gigs take place each summer roughly ten miles south of Portland at **Old Orchard Beach**.

**Gritty McDuff's**, 396 Fore St (☎207/772-2739). Portland's first brewpub, making Portland Head Pale Ale and Black Fly Stout. Food, folk music, long wooden benches, and a friendly (if a little self-consciously British) atmosphere, which gets rowdy on a Saturday night.

**Three Dollar Dewey's**, 241 Commercial St (☎207/772-3310). Raucous beer hall, with a wide selection of draft beers.

**Zootz**, 31 Forest Ave (☎207/773-8187). "Progressive" dance club hosting world-beat discos and concerts.

# North along the coast from Portland

The coastal towns immediately north of Portland are no less commercialized than those to the south; **Freeport**, for example, is one long shopping mall, albeit a good one. However, soon after **Brunswick** I-95 veers away inland towards Augusta (see p.249), and US-1 is left to run on alone parallel to the ocean. Things become much less frenetic, and prices a whole lot lower; even on the main road you'll find pleasant communities such as **Bath** and **Belfast**, while the many headlands can be even more peaceful. There's really no need to race the full 160 miles to Acadia National Park in one go.

## Freeport

Much of the current prosperity of **FREEPORT**, fifteen miles north of Portland, rests on the invention by Leon L Bean, in 1912, of a particularly ugly rubber-soled fishing boot. That original boot is still selling, and **L L Bean's** has grown into an enormous clothing store on Main Street that literally never closes. In theory, this is so predawn hunting expeditions can stock up; all the relevant equipment is available for rent or sale, and the store runs regular workshops to teach backcountry lore and has a quaint trout pond in its grounds. However, with the outdoor look in vogue, L L Bean's is now more of a fashion emporium. Freeport has expanded to welcome its 2.5 million annual customers a year with a mile-long strip of top-name **factory outlets** along US-1, most of which do give genuine reductions on usual shop prices (though coastal North Hampton, New Hampshire, offers much the same selection without Maine's sales tax).

Freeport is not an ideal place to stay – everything falls quiet once the shoppers have gone home – but the *Harraseeket Inn* at 162 Main St (☎207/865-9377 or 1-800/342-6423; ⑧) is a wonderful clapboard B&B inn with some fifty rooms. The *Freeport Inn & Cafe*, 335 Hwy-1 S (☎207/865-3106 or 1-800/99-VALUE; ⑤), provides good-value rooms and no-frills food, including all-day breakfasts.

For a complete change of pace, head a mile south of Freeport to the sea, where the *Harraseeket Lunch & Lobster Co* (☎207/865-4888), extending on its wooden jetty into the peaceful bay, makes a great outdoor lunch spot. The very green promontory visible just across the water is **Wolfe's Neck Woods State Park**. In summer, for $1, you can follow hiking and nature trails along the unspoiled fringes of the headland.

## Brunswick

Only a few miles further on from Freeport is **BRUNSWICK**, home since 1794 of the private Bowdoin College. Free tours of the college itself (Mon–Fri at 9am, 11am, 2pm & 4pm, Sat at 11am & noon; ☎207/725-3375) take in the intriguing **Peary-Macmillan Arctic Museum** (Tues–Fri 10am–4pm, Sat 10am–5pm, Sun 2–5pm). After decades of controversy, experts are now generally agreed that former student Admiral Robert Peary really was the first man to reach the North Pole in 1909; whatever the truth, his assembled equipment and notebooks have a powerful fascination.

It was while her husband Calvin was teaching here in the early 1850s that Harriet Beecher Stowe wrote *Uncle Tom's Cabin*, a book whose portrait of slavery had such an impact that Lincoln is said to have greeted her with the words "so this is the little lady that made this big war." The rambling old **Harriet Beecher Stowe House** at 63 Federal St (☎1-800/698-5548; ④) is now a motel; guests stay in modern rooms around the back, but can use the lounge of the original house. Alternatives include the friendly

*Traveler's Inn*, 130 US-1 (☎207/729-3364 or 1-800/457-3364; ④). The *Great Impasta* at 42 Maine St (☎207/729-5858) serves excellent, well-priced Italian **food**; the *Broadway Deli*, 142 Maine St (☎207/729-7781), does all-day breakfasts; and *Bohemian*, 111 Maine St (☎207/725-9095), is a pleasant sidewalk **cafe** with good coffee.

The ideal moment to visit Brunswick is Labor Day Weekend, when the town hosts a **Bluegrass Festival** (☎207/725-6009) a little way on at Thomas Point Beach, reached by following Hwy-24 from Cook's Corner. On the same road, **Orrs Island** has a well-equipped oceanfront **campground** (☎207/833-5595).

## Bath

The small town of **BATH** has an exceptionally long history of **shipbuilding**: the first vessel to be constructed and launched here was the *Virginia* in 1607, by Sir George Popham's short-lived colony. **Bath Iron Works**, founded in 1833, attracted job-seeking Irishmen in such numbers as to provoke a mob of anti-immigrant "Know-Nothings" to burn down the local Catholic church in July 1854. The works continue to produce ships – during World War II, more destroyers were built here than in all Japan – and only admit visitors for special occasions such as ceremonial launchings. However, at the **Maine Maritime Museum**, 243 Washington St, next to the Iron Works two miles south of the town center (May–Oct daily 10am–5pm; $6), you can tour a functioning shipyard where apprentices learn to build wooden schooners using traditional techniques.

As you head up the coast, **accommodation** starts to be better value. West on Bath Road, the *New Meadows Inn* (☎207/443-3921; ④) serves good basic meals, and has bargain four-person cottages. For a more rural experience, try the *Fairhaven Inn* on North Bath Road (☎207/443-4391 or 1-888/443-4391; ⑤), which features shared and private bathrooms, serves a fine full breakfast, and has hiking and cross-country skiing in season.

The *Harbor Lights Cafe*, 164 Front St (☎207/443-9883), is a Mexican restaurant putting on live music at weekends. *Kristina's*, 160 Centre St (☎207/442-8577), specializes in inventive American dishes and serves up great breads and desserts. *Montsweag Restaurant* (☎207/443-6563), on US-1 in **Woolwich** just to the east, is a very inexpensive and lively seafood place, open for both lunch and dinner. Be warned that everything in Bath closes very early in the evenings.

## Wiscasset and Boothbay Harbor

Achingly quaint, tiny **WISCASSET**, ten miles on from Bath, is dominated by the bridge, which carries US-1 over the Sheepscot River. Tourism is catching on here, perhaps partially on account of Wiscasset's easily accessible town center, right where the bridge meets the river's west bank; in fact, the town lumberyard, grocery, and newsstand have all been replaced by antique shops and art galleries to welcome visitors (changes that have been unwelcome to locals). Further removal of the town's character occurred in 1997, when two famous shipwrecks, the *Luther Little* and the *Hesper*, which had sat in the shallow waters for more than sixty years were carted away – rotted beyond recognition.

**Accommodation** possibilities in the area include the comfortable and modern *Wiscasset Motor Lodge* (☎207/882-7137 or 1-800/732-8168; ③), approximately three miles south on US-1 and open from April to October. The lakeside **campground** *Downeast Family Camping* (☎207/882-5431), at Gardiner Pond, four miles north on Hwy-27, features an impressive cathedral stand of Norway pines.

For no obvious reason, **BOOTHBAY HARBOR**, at the southern tip of Hwy-27, is one of Maine's most crowded resorts and it lays on lots of different boat trips. Don't plan to stay, but if you do pass by, the *Lobstermen's Co-op* at 99 Atlantic Ave (☎207/633-4900), a working lobster pound, dishes up ultrafresh lobsters at minimal prices, as well as a range of sandwiches. *Fisherman's Wharf Inn* at Pier 6, 22 Commercial St, serves good seafood in a more formal setting and also has waterfront rooms (☎207/633-5090 or 1-800/628-6872; ⑤). *Moody's Diner* (☎207/832-7785) in **Waldoboro**, back on the main road east, is a longstanding haunt of police and truckers, open 24 hours and oozing nostalgia.

## Rockland and Vinalhaven

**ROCKLAND**, where US-1 reaches Penobscot Bay roughly halfway between Portland and Bar Harbor, is the world's largest distributor of **lobsters**, and holds the Maine Lobster Festival over the first weekend of August (for more info call ☎207/596-0376 or 1-800/LOB-CLAW). One of the best of its traditional lobster pounds is *Miller's* (☎207/594-7406), on the shore of Wheeler's Bay in an isolated cove at Spruce Head on Hwy-73, which is open from 10am until 7pm in season, for succulent lobsters and steamers. The *Brown Bag* bakery, 606 Main St (☎207/596-6372), has low-fat breads and lunches. The *White Gates*, four miles north on US-1 (☎207/594-4625; ③), is the best budget **motel** in the area.

South of Rockland, the pretty **St George Peninsula**, in particular the village of Tenants Harbor, inspired writer Sarah Orne Jewett's classic Maine novel *Country of the Pointed Firs*. Boats leave from the hamlet of Port Clyde at the tip of the peninsula, fourteen miles south of Rockland, to tiny **Monhegan Island**, eleven miles off the coast and with a year-round population of less than a hundred. Lobsters are the main business on this rocky outcrop, though the stunning cliffs and isolated coves have long attracted artists – including Edward Hopper. Fifteen miles of hiking trails twist through the wilderness and past a magnificent 1824 lighthouse. **Accommodation** such as the *Island Inn* (May to mid-Oct; ☎207/596-0371; ⑦) is pricey, though there are self-catering units available: try *Shining Sails* (☎207/596-0041; ⑤). However, it's a great day-trip away from the tourist bustle of the mainland, aboard the *Laura B* (May–Oct daily; Nov–April Mon, Wed & Fri; three sailings a day in summer, fewer at other times; ☎207/372-8848; $25 round-trip).

Between three and six **ferries** run daily throughout the year from Rockland to the island of **Vinalhaven**, which has one or two inns (but no campgrounds), a few shops, a museum and an impressive lighthouse; slightly fewer serve neighboring **North Haven**. The boats do carry cars, though the chance to hike is what attracts many visitors. The Maine State Ferry Service at 517A Main St (☎207/863-4421 for Vinalhaven; ☎207/867-4441 for North Haven) has full schedules; they also operate several daily services from **Lincolnville**, six miles north of Camden – where there's also a small but pleasant beach – across to **Islesboro**.

## Camden and Rockport

The adjacent communities of **CAMDEN** and **ROCKPORT** split into two separate towns in 1891, over a dispute as to who should pay for a new bridge over the Goose River between them. Rockport was at that time a major lime producer, but a fire at the kilns in 1907 not only put an end to that business but also destroyed the ice-houses that were the town's other main source of income. Now it's a quiet working port, among the prettiest on the Maine coast, home to numerous lobster boats, pleasure cruisers and little else; clearly, over-cute Camden has won the competition for tourists. The one essential stop in the area is **Camden Hills State Park**, two miles north of Camden ($2), where you can hike or drive up to a tower that affords one of the best views of the Maine coastline; on a clear day it's possible to see as far as Acadia National Park. It is also one of the best places to **camp** on the coast.

Camden's specialty is organizing sailing expeditions of up to six days in the large schooners known as **windjammers**. Vessels include the *Stephen Taber* (☎207/236-3520 or 1-800/999-7352) for three- and six-day trips ($390–720) and the *Appledore* (☎207/236-

8353), which does two-hour cruises for $20. Among busy **eating and drinking** spots in Camden are *Marigold Grill* at 21 Bayview St (☎207/236-3272), for pizzas and seafood, and the nearby *Waterfront* (☎207/236-3747), for gourmet sandwiches and a great harbor location. *Gilbert's Publick House* on Sharps Wharf (☎207/236-4320) has pool tables and microbrews on tap, while the *Sea Dog*, 44 Mechanic St (☎207/236-6863), is the town's popular brewpub.

Camden's information office is at the Public Landing (☎207/236-4404). The classy **place to stay** is the *Whitehall Inn*, 400 yards north of the center at 52 High St (☎207/236-3391 or 1-800/789-6565), which in summer provides great evening meals (⑦) and during the rest of the year operates on a B&B basis (⑤). The nearby *Maine Stay*, 22 High St (☎207/236-9636; ⑦), is a cozy 1813 white-clapboard inn, while the *Snow Hill Lodge*, north on Hwy-1 near Lincolnville Beach (☎207/236-3452; ④), ranks as a good budget option.

## Belfast

Homely **BELFAST** feels like the most lived-in and liveable of the towns along the Maine coast. Here the shipbuilding boom is long since over (and the chicken-processing plant that regularly turned the bay blood red has also gone), but the inhabitants have had the waterfront declared a historic district, sparing it from over-commercialization and condo development. As you stroll around, look out for the old-fashioned Greyhound and Western Union office (complete with jukebox) and any number of whitewashed Greek Revival houses. Belfast was a lively center in the 1960s, a fact still reflected in its stores, community theater groups, festivals and the WBYA (101.7 FM) radio station. However, except for its several eating establishments and one cinema, most businesses close early in the evening.

The convivial **information office** (☎207/338-2896), at the foot of Main Street by the bay, is next to the old **railroad station** used by the Belfast and Moosehead Lake Railroad (☎207/948-5500 or 1-800/392-5500). Hour-long excursions ($14) in reconditioned Pullman cars run from here up the lush banks of the Passagassawakeag River, along track laid in 1870 to connect logging operations with the sea – though whatever impression you might get from their advertisements, the trains are pulled by diesel not steam. En route to the villages of Brooks and Burnham Junction, you pass through thick forests, at their most colorful in the fall. The same company offers **cruises** on an old-style paddleboat in Penobscot Bay ($14); a combination ticket saves $3.

Also right beside the rail terminal, *Weathervane's* seafood **restaurant** (☎207/338-1774) has tables on the wooden jetty outside; across the bay, *Young's Lobster Pound* (☎207/338-1160) serves $10 fresh-boiled lobster dinners, among the best in the state, with sunset views. Up the street, *Krazy Kones* scoops locally made Cranberry Tiger **ice cream** in its family-friendly parlor. Between them, historic *Darby's Restaurant* and *Whitcomb's* on High Street serve tasty, inventive breakfasts, lunches and dinners to a congenial mix of locals and visitors. *Belfast Co-op Store and Deli*, 123 High St (☎207/338-2532), offers a huge range of vegetarian food and picnic fixin's. For **accommodation**, try the *Hiram Alden Inn*, 19 Church St (☎207/338-2151; ④), a beautiful 1840 Greek Revival house run as a B&B by the genial Jim Lovejoy, the comfortable *Thomas Pitcher House*, 5 Franklin St (☎207/338-6454; ④), or the *Kingsbury House*, 35 Northport Ave (☎207/338-2419; ③), which serves macrobiotic breakfasts. Along Hwy-1 across the Passagassawakeag River in East Belfast are several inexpensive motels, including the *Gull* (☎207/338-4030; ④).

# Mount Desert Island

Considering that five million visitors come to **Mount Desert Island** each year, that it contains most of New England's only national park, and that it boasts not only a genuine fjord but also the highest headland on the entire Atlantic coast north of Rio de Janeiro, it is quite an astonishingly small place, measuring just sixteen miles by thirteen. It is, of course, simply one among innumerable rugged granite islands along the Maine coast; the reason to come here is that it is the most accessible, linked to the mainland by bridge since 1836, and has the best facilities. The social center, **Bar Harbor**, has accommodation and restaurants to suit all pockets, there are lower-key communities all over the island, and **Acadia National Park** can offer less sedate travelers camping, cycling, canoeing, kayaking and bird-watching.

The island was named *Monts Deserts* (bare mountains) by Samuel de Champlain in 1604 and fought over by the French and English for the rest of the century. Although all existing settlements date from long after the final defeat of the French, the name remains, still pronounced in French (more like *dessert*, actually).

## Getting there

If you're **driving**, Mount Desert is easy enough to get to, along Hwy-3 off US-1, though in high summer roads on the island itself get congested (and the horse-drawn tours don't help). **Public transportation**, however, is minimal. Greyhound buses run to Bar

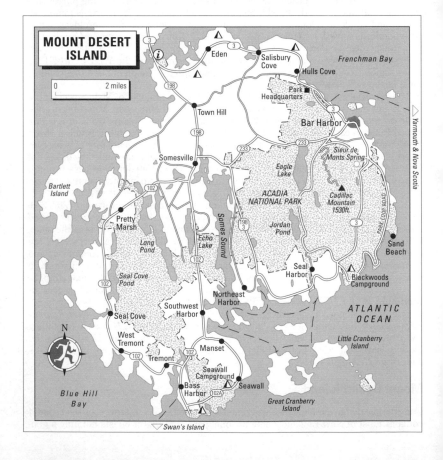

Harbor from Bangor for perhaps a couple of months in summer, starting in mid-June, though even that can't be guaranteed; West Coastal Connections (☎207/546-2823 or 1-800/596-2823) goes as far as Ellsworth and Bar Harbor, as does Downeast Transportation (Mon, Wed & Fri; ☎207/667-5796), which also runs buses across the island from Bar Harbor to Southwest Harbor (Mon & Thurs) and Northeast Harbor (Tues & Wed).

Nearby Hancock City/Bar Harbor Airport (☎207/667-7432) has a limited service run by Colgan Air (☎1-800/272-5488); Bangor International Airport, 45 miles away, is served by Northwest, Delta and Continental. The *Bluenose* **ferry** takes six hours to link Bar Harbor with Yarmouth, Nova Scotia (June–Aug cars $55, people $41.50; Sept to mid-Oct cars $50, people $27.25; ferries leave Bar Harbor daily 8am, return from Yarmouth 4.30pm). For reservations, contact Bay Ferries (☎207/249-7245).

## Accommodation on Mount Desert Island

Hwy-3 into and out of Bar Harbor (which becomes Main Street on the way south) is lined with budget **motels**, which do little to improve the look of the place but satisfy an enormous demand for accommodation. Rates increase drastically in July and August, and anywhere offering sea views will cost a whole lot more. The quieter places elsewhere on the island tend to be booked up early.

**Bar Harbor Inn**, Newport Drive, Bar Harbor (☎207/248-3351 or 1-800/248-3351). The nicest place to stay bar none, with spacious rooms looking out over the bay from the heart of town. ⑦.

**Bass Cottage in the Field**, The Field, just off Main St, Bar Harbor (☎207/288-3705). Ten-room, old-fashioned white-clapboard inn, very near the center. ④.

**Emery's Cottages on the Shore**, Sand Point Rd, five miles north of Bar Harbor (☎207/288-3432). Sweet little cottages on a private pebble beach just off Hwy-3. Weekly stays in high season cost $440–630. ④.

**HI-Bar Harbor**, 27 Kennebec St, Bar Harbor (☎207/288-5587). Beds in large dormitories for $12 HI members, $15 nonmembers. Mid-June to Aug only; reservations strongly advised. ①.

**Johnson Cottage**, 108 Cottage St, Bar Harbor (☎207/288-3743 or 667-5142). Clean and basic guesthouse with shared baths. ②.

**Maine Street Motel**, 315 Main St, Bar Harbor (☎207/288-3188). Recently refurbished place, with its own restaurant next door. ⑤.

**Moorings Inn**, Shore Rd, Manset (☎207/244-5523). Lovely 200-year-old inn, two miles east of Southwest Harbor. Private beach, boats for rent next door. Open May–Oct. ⑤.

**YWCA**, 36 Mount Desert St, Bar Harbor (☎207/288-5008). Very central, women-only accommodation. Open sporadically – call ahead. Beds in shared rooms start at $20, and go as high as $50. ②.

## Bar Harbor

The town of **BAR HARBOR** began life as an exclusive resort, summer home to the Vanderbilts and the Astors; the great fire of October 1947 which destroyed their opulent "cottages" ended all that. It's now firmly geared towards tourists, though it's by no means downmarket. There's not all that much to do in town, even in high summer. However, the ambiance is sufficient for it to take a while to realize that once you've strolled around the village green, and walked past the headland of the *Bar Harbor Inn* for views of the ocean and Frenchman Bay, you've seen most of what Bar Harbor has to offer.

In high season up to 21 different **sea trips** set off each day, for purposes ranging from deep-sea fishing to cocktail cruises. Among the most popular are the *Atlantis* **whale-watching** expeditions, departing from Harbor Place, next to the Town Pier (May–Oct three daily; ☎207/288-3322 or 1-800/508-1499), and the two-hour cruises on the impressive **two-masted schooners** *Young America* and *Sylvania Beal* from the *Bar Harbor Inn* (daily June–Oct; *America* 10.30am, 2pm & 6.15pm; $22; *Sylvania* noon & 3.30pm, $14; summer ☎207/288-4585, winter ☎207/546-2927).

One of the town sights in its heyday was the "Indian village," a summer encampment where Native Americans came to sell to tourists; it was cleared away in the 1930s to make room for a new ballpark. Now the only signs of the island's first inhabitants are the artifacts at the **Robert Abbe Museum**, which were found at Fernald Point near Southwest Harbor and attributed to a nomadic people who made birch-bark canoes. What became of them is encapsulated by a classic understatement on a map contrasting the tribal areas of 1600 with the modern reservations: "The native population did not view territorial boundaries as we do today." The museum is a couple of miles south of Bar Harbor – not a particularly pleasant walk – at Sieur de Monts Spring, just off the Park Loop Road (July & Aug daily 9am–5pm; mid-May to June, Sept & Oct daily 10am–4pm; $2).

Bar Harbor's main **tourist information** office is at the ferry terminal (☎207/288-5103); in summer there's another in the basement of the Municipal Building on Cottage Street which offers many free and comprehensive maps of the area.

## Acadia National Park

Not all of **ACADIA NATIONAL PARK** is on Mount Desert Island – there are sections on the Isle au Haut to the west, reached by ferry from Stonington, and on the Schoodic peninsula to the east – but there's all you could want here in terms of mountains and lakes for secluded rambling, and **wildlife** such as seals, beavers, puffins and bald eagles. The two main geographical features are the narrow fjord of **Somes Sound**, which almost splits the island in two, and **Mount Cadillac**, only 1530ft high but offering tremendous ocean views. The summit, the first place in the United States to see the sun rise each morning, can be reached either by a moderately strenuous climb – more than you'd want to do before breakfast – or by a very leisurely drive, winding up a low-gradient road.

Much the most enjoyable way to explore is to ride a rented **bicycle** around the fifty miles of gravel-surfaced "**carriage roads**," built by John D Rockefeller as a protest against the 1917 vote that allowed "infernal combustion engines" onto the island. Two Bar Harbor companies rent mountain bikes between 8am and 6pm, at around $10 for half a day, $16 all day: Bar Harbor Bicycle Shop, at 141 Cottage St on the edge of town (☎207/288-3886), and Acadia Bike & Coastal Kayaking, across from the post office at 48 Cottage St (☎207/288-9605). Southwest Cycle does the same in Main Street, Southwest Harbor (☎207/244-5856). All provide excellent maps. Carry water, as there are very few refreshment stops inside the park. **Kayaks** can be rented ($50 all day), from mid-May to mid-October from National Park Outdoor Activities Center, 137 Cottage St in Bar Harbor (☎207/288-0342), which also offers guided sea kayaking trips and downhill bike rides from the top of Mount Cadillac.

The park is open all year, with a summer-only **visitor center** in Hull's Cove at the entrance to the Loop Road north of Bar Harbor (mid-April to June & Sept–Oct daily 8am–4.30pm; July–Aug daily 8am–6pm; ☎207/288-3338), and the headquarters at Eagle Lake (mid-April to Oct Mon–Fri 8am–4.30pm; Nov to mid-April daily 8am–4.30pm; same phone). The entrance fee is $10 per vehicle or $7 per cycle, and is good for a four-day stay. There are two official **campgrounds**: *Blackwoods*, five miles south of Bar Harbor off Route 3 (reserve through Destinet, 9450 Canal Park Drive, San Diego, CA 92121-1256 or on ☎207/288-3338), and *Seawall* on Hwy-102A, four miles south of Southwest Harbor (first-come, first-served). Both are in woods, near the ocean, and have full facilities in summer; only *Blackwoods* is open in winter, with minimal facilities.

The one and only sizeable beach, five miles south of Bar Harbor, is a stunner: called simply **Sand Beach**, it's a gorgeous strand bounded by twin headlands, with restrooms, a parking lot and a few short hiking trails. The water, sadly, is usually arctic.

## Eating, drinking and nightlife on Mount Desert Island

Mount Desert's most memorable **eating** experiences are to be found in the many **lobster pounds** all over the island, but for nightlife as such, Bar Harbor is where the people are. Cottage Street is a much more promising area to look for food and evening atmosphere than the surprisingly subdued waterfront. The Art Deco Criterion cinema at 35 Cottage St (☎207/288-3441) puts on 2pm matinees on rainy days.

**The Alternative Market**, 16 Mount Desert St (☎207/288-8225). Bag lunches, big sandwiches, soups, smoothies and fresh squeezed juices.

**Beal's Lobster Pier**, Clark Point Rd, Southwest Harbor (☎207/244-7178). Fresh seafood for under $10, on a rickety wooden pier crammed full of lobsters.

**Chef Marc & Eat a Pita**, 326 Main St, Southwest Harbor (☎207/244-4344) A great casual, cozy, and affordable spot with delicious, healthy gourmet food (pastas, salads, pita sandwiches, seafood), candlelit tables, and friendly service. Lunch and dinner served. Credit cards not accepted.

**Galyn's**, 17 Main St, Bar Harbor (☎207/288-9706). Delicious fish and prime ribs in unpretentious setting.

**Jordan Pond House**, Park Loop Rd (☎207/276-3316). Worthy concession restaurant in the heart of Acadia National Park between Bar Harbor and Northeast Harbor. Serves light meals, ice cream and popovers (light, puffy egg muffins). Tea is served in the beautiful lakeside garden 11.30am–8pm, until 9pm during July and August.

**Lompoc Brewpub & Cafe**, 36 Rodick St, Bar Harbor (☎207/288-9392). A healthy Middle Eastern menu for $10–15, with local Thunder Hole Ale on draft and live music every night. Open 11.30am–1am.

**Preble Grill**, 14 Clark Point Rd, Southwest Harbor (☎207/244-7463). Classy and deservedly popular spot with flavorfully grilled meats for $15–19 or pastas for about $12.

**Rupununi**, 119 Main St (☎207/288-2886). Late-night overpriced pub grub – stick to the burgers. The bar stays open until 1am.

**Seafood Ketch**, Bass Harbor (☎207/244-7463). Great super-fresh fish and seafood overlooking Bass Harbor. Reservations recommended.

**Thirsty Whale**, 44 Cottage St, Bar Harbor (☎207/288-9335). Bar Harbor's busiest late-night bar.

**Village Green Bakery Cafe**, 150 Main St, Bar Harbor (☎207/288-9450). Great pastries, plus a full range of lunches and dinners, including the requisite boiled lobsters. Low prices, good for families.

**XYZ Dockside Restaurant**, across from Manset Town Dock, Shore Rd, Manset (☎207/244-5221). Ocean views from every table, seafood from $7.

# Downeast Maine: the coast to Canada

Looking at a typical map of the United States, you'd never dream that Canada stretches for five hundred miles beyond Maine to the east. In fact, few travelers venture far beyond Acadia National Park, which is one reason why what's known as **Downeast Maine** remains so little touched by change. Another reason is that this is bleak and windswept country, where high cliffs are battered by harsh seas. In summer, though, the weather is no worse than in the rest of Maine, and the coastal drive can be exhilarating. At those points where the road runs next to the sea, you get a real sense of the overwhelming power of the ocean, sweeping in to create the highest tides in the nation.

A short way northeast of Acadia, a loop road leads from US-1 to the rocky outcrop of **Schoodic Point**, which offers good bird-watching, great views, and a splendid sense of solitude. Tourism is not big business in these parts, but each village has one or two B&Bs and low-priced restaurants. The fishing harbor at **JONESPORT** on Hwy-187, which deserves a detour, holds *Tootsies Bed and Breakfast* (☎207/497-5414; ③). A glorious high-arched iron bridge leads to the nature reserve of **Beal's Island**. **MACHIAS**, back on US-1, is even more picturesque, with a little waterfall right in the middle, and was the unlikely scene of the first naval battle of the Revolutionary War, in 1775. The townsfolk commandeered the British schooner *Margaretta* and proceeded to terrorize all passing British shipping. The attack was planned in the still-standing gambrel-roofed

**Burnham Tavern**. Meals are good value at *Helen's Restaurant*, 32 Main St (☎207/255-8423), part of the *Machias Motor Inn* (☎207/255-4861; ④) which has sun decks and superb views; the *Mainland Motel*, a mile east on Hwy-1 (☎207/255-3334; ③), is comfortable.

Continuing east, and abandoning US-1 for Hwy-189, you come to the prominently striped **lighthouse** at **West Quoddy Head**, the easternmost point of the US, where an international bridge crosses to Campobello Island in Canada. The nearby settlement of **Bailey's Mistake** is named for a sea captain who beached his lumber vessel in thick fog in 1830, and chose to settle here with his crew, building homes with their erstwhile cargo, rather than face the wrath of the ship's owners back in Boston.

The border between the United States and Canada weaves through the center of **Passamaquoddy Bay**; the towns to either side get on so well that they refused to fight in the US–UK war of 1812, and promote themselves jointly to tourists as the **Quoddy Loop** (information on ☎207/454-2597). It's perfectly feasible to take a "two-nation vacation," but each passage through customs and immigration between **CALAIS** (pronounced *callous*) in the States and **St Stephen** in Canada does take a little while – and watch out for confusion stemming from the fact that they're in different time zones. No trace now remains of Samuel de Champlain's 1604 attempt to found a colony on the diminutive St Croix Island, which you can see from an overlook on the main road. In town, the *Wickachee*, on Main Street (☎207/454-3400), serves big plates of seafood and steak. West Coastal Connections (☎207/546-2823 or 1-800/596-2823) runs a once-daily van from Calais to Ellsworth and Bar Harbor.

# Inland Maine

The vast expanses of the **Maine interior**, stretching up into the cold far north, consist mostly of evergreen forests of pine, spruce and fir, interspersed by the white birches and maples responsible for the spectacular fall colors. Only in the remote north is much of it genuine wilderness, however; elsewhere, what you see is more likely to be woodlands cultivated by the timber companies.

Distances are large. Once you get away from the two largest cities nearer the sea – **Augusta**, the State capital, and **Bangor** – it's roughly two hundred miles by road to the northern border at **Fort Kent**, while to drive between the two most likely inland bases, **Greenville** and **Rangeley** (where exiled psychologist Wilhelm Reich lived and is buried), takes three hours or more. Driving (there's no public transportation) through this mountainous scenery can be a great pleasure, but you do need to know where you're going. There are few places to stay, and beyond Bangor many roads are tolled access routes belonging to the lumber companies: gravel-surfaced, vulnerable to bad weather, and in any case often not heading anywhere in particular.

This landscape has evolved in a very unusual way. Many waterfront communities grew up without roads to serve them, in the days when the timber harvest was floated downriver to the sea; other more recent settlements have only ever been accessible by seaplane. Now that mighty trucks carry the tree-trunks instead, roads are finally being pushed through, amid complaints that they are ruining the whole feel of the place.

If you have the time, this is great territory in which to **hike** – the **Appalachian Trail** starts its 2000-mile course down to Georgia at the top of Mount Katahdin – or **raft** on the **Allagash Wilderness Waterway**. Especially around **Baxter State Park**, the forests are home to deer, beaver, a few bears, some recently introduced caribou – and plenty of **moose**. These endearingly gawky creatures (they look like badly drawn horses, and are virtually blind), tend to be seen at early morning or dusk; in spring they come to lick the winter's salt off the roads, while in summer you may spot them feeding in shallow water. They do, however, cause major havoc on the roads, particularly at night, and each year significant numbers of drivers are killed in collisions with these hefty creatures.

## Augusta

The capital of Maine since 1832, **AUGUSTA** is much quieter and less visited now than it was a hundred years ago. The lumber industry here really took off after the technique of making paper from wood was rediscovered in 1844, and Augusta also had a lucrative sideline – each winter hundreds of thousands of tons of **ice**, cut from the Kennebec River, were shipped out, as far south as the Caribbean, in a trade now all but forgotten by history. There are informative displays on Maine's landscape and industrial past at the lively **Maine State Museum**, a short way south of the capitol on State Street (Mon–Fri 9am–5pm, Sat 10am–4pm, Sun 1–4pm).

If you plan to stay in Augusta, the best-value **accommodation** is the *Susse Chalet Motor Lodge* (☎207/622-3776; ③), on Whitten Road at the Maine Turnpike's Augusta-Winthrop exit. For **food**, the lobster rolls at *Burnsie's Homestyle Sandwiches* (☎207/622-6425), on Hitchborn Street next to the capitol, are favorites with the politicians, while *Curly's*, 750 Main St (☎207/933-2745), does good, moderately priced seafood.

## Bangor

In its prime, **BANGOR**, 120 miles northeast of Portland, was the undisputed "Lumber Capital of the World." Every winter its raucous population of "River Tigers" went upstream to brand the felled logs, which they then maneuvered down the Penobscot as the thaw came in April, reaching Bangor in time to carouse the summer away in the grog shops of Peppermint Row. (Bangor, too, exported ice to the West Indies – and got rum in return.) Those days were coming to an end when in October 1882 Oscar Wilde addressed a large crowd at the new Opera House and spoke diplomatically of "such advancement . . . in so small a city."

Bangor today is not a place to spend much time, although its plentiful motels and the big new Bangor Mall on Hogan Road north of town make it a good last stop before the interior. Its twin claims to fame are that it's the unlikely home of Stephen King, the horror fiction writer (Betts Bookstore at 26 Main St stocks King paraphernalia), and that it possesses what, at 31ft, may well be the largest statue of **Paul Bunyan** in the world, excepting perhaps one or two in Minnesota – though it looks more like a brightly painted model airplane kit than a statue.

From mid-May until the end of July there's **harness racing** at Bass Park on Main Street (☎207/947-6744), just behind the statue; admission is $1 but the potential to lose money is unlimited. The same venue hosts the **Bangor State Fair**, in the last week of July and the first in August. A few miles north of Bangor, the Maine Center for the Arts (☎207/581-1755), at the University of Maine in **Orono**, runs a series of big-name concerts each summer. Orono is named after the eighteenth-century Chief Joseph Orono; a small island nearby is now a rather sad reservation running summer bingo sessions.

### Practicalities

Bangor is the last sizeable town along I-95, before it finally veers from the coast and heads up the Penobscot towards Canada. It's also the end of the line for Greyhound, the three daily services from Boston and Portland terminating at 158 Main St.

**Accommodation** possibilities include the *Main Street Inn*, opposite Paul Bunyan at 480 Main St (☎207/942-5282; ③), and the *Phoenix Inn*, right downtown at 20 Westmarket Square (☎207/947-0411; ③). The *Holiday Inn* at 500 Main St (☎207/947-8651; ⑤) houses Bangor's liveliest dance venue, the *Bounty Taverne*. The best breakfasts in Bangor are at the *Bagel Shop*, 1 Main St (☎207/947-1654), the state's only kosher deli; other, equally incongruous options include a handful of Indian and Pakistani places, and the massive Mexican *Pepino's* at 520 Stillwater Ave (☎207/947-1233). *Margarita's*, 15 Mill St in Orono (☎207/866-4863), is another lively, if unimaginatively named, Mexican place.

## Baxter State Park and the far north

Driving through northern Maine can feel as though you're trespassing on the private fiefdoms of the logging companies; only **Baxter State Park** is public land. However, you're pretty much free to hike, camp and explore anywhere you like, so long as you let people know what you're doing (only a sensible precaution, after all). The scenery is pretty much the same everywhere, although of course to get the best of it – to experience what Thoreau described in his *Maine Woods* – you need to leave your car at some point and set off into the backwoods.

Five miles north of Brownsville Junction on Hwy-11, an inconspicuous left turn leads to the **Katahdin Iron Works** at Silver Lake (summer daily 9am–5pm), built in 1843. It's remarkable quite how little remains of what one hundred years ago was a thriving industrial community: one solitary brick oven and the tower of the blast furnace, stark and forlorn at the end of a few miles of gravel track. In good summer weather it's possible to continue along the track across the hills to Greenville.

Further north, **MILLINOCKET** is a genuine company town, built on a wilderness site by the Great Northern Paper Company in 1899–1900 as the "magic city of the North." Public curiosity was so great that three hundred people came on a special train from Bangor to see what was happening. Since then it has produced massive quantities of newsprint, but in 1990 the company was taken over by the Georgia Pacific Corporation, and although the townspeople made a killing from cashing in their stock, their homes are almost unsaleable, and their jobs may well not last.

Next to **Millinocket Lake**, ten miles northwest, the splendidly ramshackle old *Big Moose Inn* (Box 98, Millinocket, ME 04462; ☎207/723-8391; ②) with adjacent campground makes a great place to stay; it also has some four-person cabins. Unicorn Expeditions (☎207/725-2255) uses the inn as a base for day **rafting** and **kayaking** expeditions, and there are **dogsled races** in February and March, as well as seaplane tours. A more standard place to stay is the clean *Pamola Motel*, 973 Central St/Hwy-11 (☎207/723-9746; ③), which provides a free continental breakfast.

By now you're approaching the southern end of **Baxter State Park** itself, with on a clear day the 5268ft peak of **Mount Katahdin** visible from afar. The park was the single-handed creation of former Maine Governor Percival P Baxter, who having failed to persuade the state to buy Katahdin and the land around it, bought it himself between the 1930s and 1960s and deeded it bit by bit to the state on condition that it remain "forever wild."

### North to Canada

The northernmost tip of Maine is taken up by Aroostook County, which covers an area larger than several individual states. Although its main activity is the large-scale cultivation of potatoes, it is also the location of the **Allagash Wilderness Waterway**; this is where most of the **whitewater rafting** companies mentioned in this section actually carry out their expeditions.

Britain and the United States all but went to war over Aroostook in 1839; at **Fort Kent**, the northern terminus of US-1 (which runs all the way from Key West, Florida), the main sight is the solid cedar **Fort Kent Blockhouse**, built to defend American integrity and looking like a throwback to early pioneer days. *Doris' Cafe* (☎207/834-6262), at Fort Kent Mills on Hwy-161, just off Hwy-11 towards Eagle Lake, can provide big breakfasts.

## Greenville

**GREENVILLE**, at the southern end of Moosehead Lake, is another nineteenth-century lumber town which now makes its living primarily from tourism. It's not exceptionally pretty and it's certainly not very large, but it is well positioned for explorations throughout the Maine woods. In town, the main attraction is the restored **steamboat** *Katahdin*, which tours the lake and also serves as the (nonprofit) Moosehead Marine Museum (cruises at 10am & 2pm daily July–Sept, Sat & Sun only in May & June; ☎207/695-2716).

The **Chamber of Commerce** on Main Street near the T-junction at the lake (summer daily 10am–5pm; rest of year Thurs–Tues 10am–4pm; ☎207/695-2702) has details about **accommodation** such as the *Kineo View Motor Lodge* (☎207/695-4470 or 1-800/659-VIEW; ④), overlooking the lake from deep in the woods on the hill three miles above town, the *Chalet Moosehead*, Birch Street (☎207/695-2950 or 1-800/290-3645; ④), the only motel right on the lake, and the antique-filled *Greenville Inn* on Norris Street (☎207/695-2206; ⑥). Among local **rafting** companies charging $90–110 for a day in the water is Wilderness Expeditions, The Birches, PO Box 41GC, North Rockwood, ME 04478 (☎207/534-7305 or 1-800/825-WILD). Greenville is also the largest **seaplane** base in New England; contact Currier's Flying Service (☎207/695-2778) or Folsom's (☎207/695-2821).

## Rangeley

**RANGELEY** is only just in Maine, a little way east of New Hampshire and an even shorter distance south of the border with Québec. Furthermore, as the cafe-bar *Doc Grant's* (☎207/864-3449) on Main Street makes a great show of telling you, it's equidistant (at 3107.5 miles) from the North Pole and the Equator. That doesn't mean it's on the main road to anywhere, although if you're avoiding the coast altogether you can get here direct from the northern side of the White Mountains (see p.222). It has always been a resort, served in 1900 by two train lines and several steamships, with the main attraction then being the fishing in the spectacularly named Mooselookmeguntic Lake.

This small and very cozy one-street town, nestling amid a complex system of lakes and waterways, serves as base for summer explorations, and in winter as the nearest town to the **ski** area at **Saddleback Mountain**.

Rangeley also has one unlikely and not exactly orthodox tourist attraction. About halfway along the north side of Rangeley Lake, a mile up a side track off Route 16, the remote **Wilhelm Reich Museum** at **Orgonon** (PO Box 687, Rangeley, ME 04970; July & Aug Tues–Sun 1–5pm; Sept Sun 1–5pm; $3; ☎207/864-3443) is where Wilhelm Reich eventually made his American home after fleeing Germany in 1933. Although he was an associate of Freud in Vienna, and wrote the acclaimed *Mass Psychology of Fascism*, Reich is best remembered for developing the orgone energy accumulator. He claimed it could create rain and dissipate nuclear radiation; skeptical authorities focused on the not very specific way in which it was said to collect and harness human sexual energy. In a tragic end to his career, Reich was imprisoned after a wayward student broke an injunction forbidding the transportation of his accumulators across state lines, and he died in the federal penitentiary in Lewisberg, Pennsylvania in November 1957. He is buried here, amid the neat lawns and darting hummingbirds, and his house remains a center for the study of his work.

### Practicalities

The *Rangeley Inn* on Main Street (☎207/864-3341; ⑤) stands between Rangeley Lake and the smaller bird sanctuary of Haley Pond, so you can stay right in town and have a room that backs onto a scene of utter tranquility; there's also a gorgeous old wooden dining room. *Northwoods B&B* on Main Street (☎207/864-2440; ⑤) is a good second choice. Otherwise, the Chamber of Commerce (see below), can provide lists of private home/condo rentals and "remote campsites" around the lake – which really are remote, several of them inaccessible by road. For **food**, try the *People's Choice Cafe* on Rte-4 (☎207/864-5220) where the portions are huge and the desserts divine.

Twenty miles north of Rangeley, the peaceful *Grants Camps* beside Kennebago Lake (PO Box 687, Rangeley, ME 04970; ☎207/864-3608) arranges fishing, canoeing and windsurfing, with accommodation in comfortable cabins, including all meals, costing around $90 per person per day; there are lower weekly rates. A more accessible campground is *Cathedral Pines* (☎207/246-3491), just north of **Stratton** on Eustis Road. At its entrance stands a memorial to Benedict Arnold's expedition to Québec in 1775, which passed this way, and to Colonel Timothy Bigelow, who climbed the mountain in a "vain endeavor to see the city of Québec."

Rangeley Lakes' **Chamber of Commerce**, down by Lakeside Park (☎207/864-5364 or 1-800/MT-LAKES), has details of various activities, including snowmobiling and dawn moose-watching **canoeing** expeditions (☎207/864-5136; $38). One really fun thing to do is to take a **seaplane** trip with the Mountain Air Service (☎207/864-5307) – a fifteen-minute tour, flying low over vast forests and tiny lakes, costs $25 per person. Boat cruises are also available, and various outfits along Main Street rent out canoes and mountain bikes.

## Sugarloaf USA and Kingfield

The road east of Rangeley cuts through prime moose-watching territory – locals call Hwy-16 E "Moose Alley." After about fifty miles, in the Carrabassett Valley, looms the huge mountain of the **SUGARLOAF USA** ski resort (1-800/THE-LOAF). A brilliant place for skiers of all abilities, this condo-studded center would be a more popular destination if it wasn't for the fact that the nearest airport is a two-hour drive away in Portland. In summer, one of the most likely places to spot a gangling **moose** is behind the check-in building on the resort's approach road. Other summer activities include guided **mountain bike tours** with the Sugarloaf Outdoor Center (☎207/237-6830).

The best base for Sugarloaf is fifteen miles south in the tiny town of **KINGFIELD**. The gorgeous *Inn on Winter Hill*, Winter Hill (☎207/265-5421 or 1-800/233-WNTR; ⑤), is a lovingly restored Georgian Revival house with big rooms, an outdoor pool, hot tub, tennis court and the excellent *Julia's* dining room (winter only). Down on the main street, the big white *Herbert Hotel* (☎207/265-2000; ④) has less attractive but functional rooms. *Anni's Cafe*, next to the gas station, is an inexpensive place to **eat**. Kingfield was the birthplace of twins Francis and Freelan Stanley, who invented, among other things, a steam-powered car and the dry plate photographic process (which they sold to Kodak). The **Stanley Museum** on School Street (Tues–Sun 1–4pm; $2) celebrates their story. Part of the main room is given over to their sister, Chansonetta, a remarkable photographer whose studies of c.1900 rural and urban workers have been widely published.

# CHAPTER FOUR

# THE GREAT LAKES

S wept by tumultuous storms and traversed by fleets of oceangoing tankers, the interconnected **Great Lakes** form the largest body of fresh water in the world; Lake Superior alone is over three hundred miles from east to west. Left untouched, the shores of these inland seas can rival any coastline: Superior and the northern reaches of Lake Michigan offer stunning rocky peninsulas, craggy cliffs, tree-covered islands, mammoth dunes and deserted beaches. For lengthy stretches along Lake Erie, and the bottom lips of lakes Michigan and Huron, however, sluggish waters lap against grimy cities and the unused wharves of decaying ports.

To varying degrees, all the states that line the American side of the lakes – **OHIO, MICHIGAN, INDIANA, ILLINOIS, WISCONSIN** and **MINNESOTA** – share this mixture of natural beauty and industrial blight. Cities such as Chicago and Detroit, with all their good and bad points – and **Chicago** in particular, with its magnificent architecture, museums, music and restaurants, is an unmissable destination – should not be seen as characterizing the entire region. Within the first hundred miles or so of the lakeshores, especially in Wisconsin and Minnesota, tens of thousands of smaller lakes and tumbling streams are scattered through a spectacular rural wilderness; beyond that, you are soon in the heart of the Corn Belt, where you can drive for hours and encounter nothing more than a succession of crossroads communities, grain silos and giant barns. Garrison Keillor's wry stories about the fictional backwater town of Lake Wobegon (where "all the women are strong and all the men are beautiful"), set in Minnesota, carry more than a ring of truth.

The first foreigner to reach the Great Lakes, the French explorer Champlain in 1603, found the region inhabited mostly by tribes of Huron, Iroquois and Algonquin. France soon established a network of military forts, Jesuit missions and fur-trading posts – which entailed treating the native people as allies rather than subjects. Territorial disputes with their colonial rivals, however, culminated in the **French and Indian War** with Britain from 1754 to 1761. The victorious British felt no constraints to deal equitably with the Native Americans, and things grew worse with large-scale American settlement after independence. The **Black Hawk War** of 1832 put a bloody end to traditional life.

Settlers from the east were followed to Wisconsin and Minnesota by waves of **Scandinavians** and **Germans**, while the lower halves of Illinois and Indiana attracted **Southerners**, who attempted to maintain slavery and resisted Union conscription during the Civil War. These areas often still have more in common with neighboring Kentucky and Tennessee than with the industrial cities of their own states.

## ACCOMMODATION PRICE CODES

All accommodation prices in this book have been coded using the symbols below. Note that prices are for the least expensive double rooms in each establishment. For a full explanation see p.37 in Basics.

| | | |
|---|---|---|
| ① up to $30 | ④ $60–80 | ⑦ $130–175 |
| ② $30–45 | ⑤ $80–100 | ⑧ $175–250 |
| ③ $45–60 | ⑥ $100–130 | ⑨ $250+ |

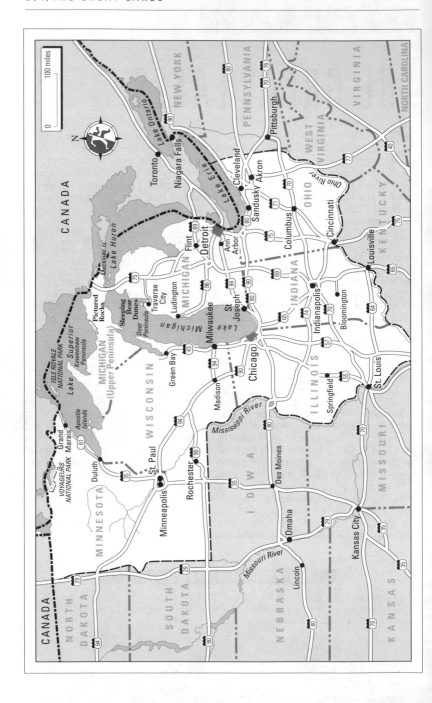

The impetus given to **industry** by the Civil War was encouraged by abundant supplies of ores and fuel and efficient transportation connections by water and rail. As lakeshore cities like Chicago, Detroit and Cleveland grew, their populations swelled with hundreds of thousands of poor **blacks** brought in from the Deep South as cheap labor, particularly to work in munitions during the two world wars. But a complete lack of planning, inadequate housing provision and mass lay-offs at times of low demand bred conditions that led to the riots of the late 1960s and current inner-city deprivation. Depression in the 1970s ravaged the economy – especially the **automobile** industry, on which so much else depended – and brought the unwanted title of "**Rust Belt.**" Since then, urban centers have battled back, with **Cleveland**, Ohio, perhaps the most dramatic example of a turnaround in fortunes.

During the summer, breezes coming off the Great Lakes keep the **temperature** down to a comfortable average of 70°F, though heatwaves can push temperatures over 100°F. Even in spring and fall it often slips below freezing in the northern reaches of the region, where winter readings of -50°F are not uncommon and parts of the lakes are frozen solid.

All the major towns of the region are easily reached by public transportation. **Amtrak**'s national hub is in Chicago and its routes spread across the entire region; **Greyhound** operates reasonably frequent services to nearly all urban centers. The best way to appreciate the sculpted shorelines of the lakes themselves, however, is to travel the lonely minor roads by **car**, while **cycling** in the northwest, alongside Superior and the northern parts of Lake Michigan, can be hugely enjoyable.

# OHIO

**OHIO**, the furthest east of the Great Lakes states, clings to the southern edge of shallow Lake Erie. This is known as one of the nation's most industrialized regions, but the industry is largely concentrated in the east, near the Ohio River, and to the south the landscape becomes less populated and more forested. Ohio also has the largest **Amish** population in the world, who farm in the northeast and west into mid-Indiana, and are much less of a tourist attraction than the highly publicized Pennsylvania Dutch (see p.146).

Enigmatic traces of Ohio's earliest inhabitants can be seen at the **Great Serpent Mound**, a grassy state park sixty miles east of Cincinnati, where a cleared hilltop high above a river was reshaped to represent a giant snake swallowing an egg, possibly by the Adena Indians around 800 BC. When the French claimed the area in 1699, it was inhabited by the **Iroquois**, in whose language Ohio means "something great." In the eighteenth century, its prime position between Lake Erie and the Ohio River made it the subject of fierce contention between the French and British; once the British had acquired control of most of the French land east of the Mississippi, settlers from New England began to establish communities both along the Iroquois War Trail paths on the shores of the lake and along the Ohio River.

During the Civil War, Ohio was at the forefront of the struggle, producing two great Union generals, Ulysses Grant and William Sherman, and sending more than twice its quota of volunteers to fight for the North. Its progress thereafter has followed the classic "Rust Belt" pattern: rapid industrialization, aided by its natural resources and crucial location, which during the 1970s foundered alarmingly and has only recently shown any signs of resurgence.

Although the state is dominated by its triumvirate of "C"s (**Cleveland**, **Columbus** and **Cincinnati**), its most visited destinations are the **Lake Erie Islands**, which have benefited from the recent cleanup of the polluted lake and now attract thousands of partying mainlanders. Cincinnati and Cleveland, the latter hit especially hard by the recession, have both undergone major face-lifts and are surprisingly attractive, as is the comparatively unassuming state capital of Columbus.

### Getting around Ohio
Amtrak **trains** between New York or Washington and Chicago stop at either Cincinnati or Cleveland and Toledo. Ohio is well served by Greyhound **buses**, and there are major **airports** at Cleveland and Cincinnati.

# Cleveland and around

Today, the great industrial port of **CLEVELAND** – for so long the butt of jokes after the heavily polluted Cuyahoga River caught fire in the early 1970s – is no longer the "Mistake on the Lake." Although the path back from acute recession (another 1970s legacy) is by no means complete on a citywide basis, the downtown area is now a hub of energy. Cleveland boasts a sensitive and fond restoration of the Lake Erie/Cuyahoga River waterfront, a superb constellation of museums, glittering city center malls and new downtown super-stadia. Add to that the recent arrival of several major corporate headquarters and classy hotels – and, of course, the **Rock and Roll Hall of Fame** – and there's an unmistakeable buzz about the place.

Founded in 1796, Cleveland profited greatly, thirty years later, from the opening of the **Ohio Canal** between the Ohio River and Lake Erie. During the city's heyday, which began with the Civil War and lasted until the 1920s, its vast iron and coal supplies made it one of the most important **steel** and **shipbuilding centers** in the world. **John D Rockefeller** made his billions here, as did the many others whose now-decrepit old mansions line "Millionaires' Row." This has become a no-go area, along with several other bleak and faceless danger spots; despite the investment of billions of dollars during the past decade, the scars of deprivation are still visible if you wander too far off the tourist path.

South and west of the city are several spots of interest, including the quaint lakeshore community of **Vermilion**, the tiny liberal college sanctuary of **Oberlin**, and the charming hamlet of **Peninsula**.

### Arrival, information and getting around
**Cleveland Hopkins International Airport** (☎216/265-6030) is ten miles southwest of downtown. The twenty-minute **taxi** ride into town costs around $20, but the Regional Transit Authority (RTA; ☎216/621-9500) **train** is only $1.50 and takes just ten minutes longer. Greyhound arrives at 1465 Chester Ave, at the back of Playhouse Square, and the Amtrak station is on the lakefront at 200 Cleveland Memorial Shoreway NE.

Cleveland is concentrated in different pockets, and as the potentially dangerous areas are scattered pretty wide (it is not safe, for example, to stray into the streets around the three-block-deep Cleveland Clinic, very close to the much-frequented University Circle), you're safest in a **car**. The RTA runs an efficient **bus** service ($1.25 or $1.50 for express services; 50¢ within downtown) and a small Rapid train line ($1.50) until about 12.30am. A **light rail** system – the Waterfront Line – connects Terminal Tower, the Flats, the Rock and Roll Hall of Fame and other downtown sights; it costs $1.50 and runs every fifteen minutes between 7am and midnight. **City tours** are run by Trolley Tours of Cleveland, and leave from the Powerhouse on the west bank of the Flats (May–Oct daily; Nov–Apr Fri & Sat; $9 for 1hr, $14 for 2hr, reservations required; ☎216/771-4484 or 1-800/848-0173).

**Maps** and **information** can be had in advance from the Cleveland **CVB** (Mon–Fri 9am–9pm; ☎1-800/321-1004). The handiest **visitor centers** are in the lobby of the Terminal Tower in Public Square (summer daily 10am–5pm; rest of year Mon–Fri

9.30am–4.30pm, Sat & Sun 11am–4pm; ☎216/621-7981) and on the east bank of the Flats next to *Hooter's* (summer daily 11am–7pm; winter daily 11am–4pm; ☎216/621-2218).

# Accommodation

Travelers without cars in Cleveland are limited to the somewhat expensive downtown hotels, a small cluster of places next to the train station at West 150th Street out by the airport, or a long bus ride into town. Most hotels now offer packages that include admission to the Rock and Roll Hall of Fame or other attractions. **B&Bs** can be arranged through Private Lodgings, Box 18590, Cleveland, OH 44118 (☎216/321-3213).

**Baymont Inn**, 4222 W 150th St (☎216/251-8500). Standard motel rooms; easy downtown access via train and only two miles to the airport. ④.

**Comfort Inn Downtown**, 1800 Euclid Ave (☎216/861-0001). Standard *Comfort Inn* rooms on the edge of downtown: a little far to walk to bars and restaurants. ⑤.

**Days Inn – Lakewood**, 12019 Lake Ave (☎216/226-4800). Plain but adequate rooms, located out in the western suburb of Lakewood five miles from downtown, though accessible by bus #55CX. ④.

**Embassy Suites Hotel**, 1701 E 12th St (☎216/523-8000). Quality downtown rooms near Playhouse Square. ⑦.

**Glidden House**, 1901 Ford Drive (☎216/231-8900). Bed and large continental breakfast in a huge Gothic mansion – it has 60 rooms – very handy for University Circle. ⑦.

**Holiday Inn – Lakeside**, 1111 Lakeside Ave (☎216/241-5100). Functional, unexciting downtown hotel on the edge of the Warehouse District and near the Rock and Roll Hall of Fame. ⑥.

**Omni International Hotel**, 2065 E 96th St (☎216/791-1900). Clean, luxury hotel in University Circle. Handy for Little Italy and Coventry Village. Rooms are over $200 during the week – ask about weekend discounts. ⑦.

**Red Roof Inn**, 6020 Quarry Lane, Independence (☎216/447-0030). Eleven miles south from downtown, but served by public transportation. ③/④.

# The City

All the main streets in Cleveland lead to the stately nineteenth-century Beaux Arts **Public Square**, at the very center of downtown, dominated by the landmark **Terminal Tower** in its southwestern corner. **Ontario Street**, which runs north–south through the Square, divides the city into east and west. Cleveland's most interesting areas are at two opposite ends of the spectrum: the industrial romance of the **Flats** in the northwest, and the cultural institutions of **University Circle**, east of the river.

## Downtown and around

**Downtown Cleveland** is once again a bustling place, and its recent redevelopment has seen the emergence of several distinct subsections. In its traditional heart, amongst the banks and corporate headquarters, stand glamorous shopping malls, such as the **Avenue at Tower City** in the Terminal Tower – which has an **observation deck** on the 42nd floor (summer Sat & Sun 11am–4.30pm; rest of year Sat & Sun 11am–3.30pm; $2; tickets from the visitor center in the lobby) and the **Arcade**, a skylit hall built in 1890. The **Playhouse Square Center** (☎216/241-6000), twelve blocks away at 1501 Euclid Ave, is an impressive complex of four renovated old theaters. Take a look at the gorgeous lobby of the small Ohio Theatre, with its starlit-sky ceiling.

Just to the southwest, in what just five years ago were mostly vacant lots, is what's now called the **Gateway District**. New restaurants and bars surround **Jacob's Field** stadium (☎216/420-4200) – home of the Indians baseball team – and the equally modern multipurpose **Gund Arena** (☎216/420-2000), which hosts the Cavaliers basketball club as well as major sporting and entertainment events.

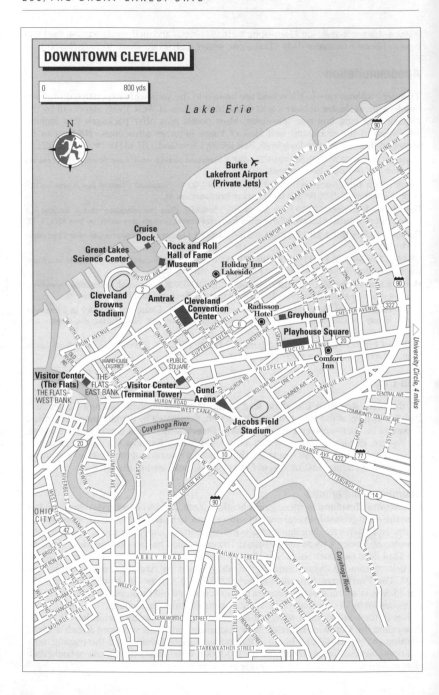

# DOWNTOWN CLEVELAND

0      800 yds

N

*Lake Erie*

Burke
Lakefront Airport
(Private Jets)

NORTH MARGINAL ROAD

SOUTH MARGINAL AVE

DAVENPORT AVE

KING AVE

LAKESIDE AVE

E. 3RD ST
E. 26TH ST
E. 25TH ST
E. 30TH ST

90

Cruise
Dock

Great Lakes
Science Center

Rock and Roll
Hall of Fame
Museum

Holiday Inn
Lakeside

HAMILTON AVE
FLAIR AVE
PAYNE AVE

E. 22ND ST
E. 23RD ST
E. 18TH ST
E. 19TH ST
E. 21ST ST
E. 17TH ST
E. 24TH ST

90

ERIESIDE AVE

Cleveland
Browns
Stadium

Amtrak

2

Cleveland
Convention
Center

LAKESIDE

E. 9TH ST
E. 6TH ST

Radisson
Hotel

Greyhound

CHESTER AVENUE

322

E. MALL DR
ST CLAIR AVE

ROCKWELL

Playhouse Square

EUCLID AVENUE

20

W. 10TH ST
FRONT AVENUE

SUPERIOR AVENUE

6

CHESTER AVE

PROSPECT AVE

Comfort
Inn

WAREHOUSE
DISTRICT

N. 3RD ST

PUBLIC
SQUARE

HURON RD

ERIE CT
SUMNER AVE

CARNEGIE AVE

CENTRAL AVE

EAST 22ND ST
E. 25TH ST

Visitor Center
(The Flats)

THE
FLATS—
EAST BANK

Visitor Center
(Terminal Tower)

Gund
Arena

BOLIVAR RD

COMMUNITY COLLEGE AVE

THE FLATS—
WEST BANK

OLD
RIVER RD

HURON ROAD

WEST CANAL RD

Jacobs Field
Stadium

*Cuyahoga River*

EAGLE AVE

ORANGE AVE

A22

77

COLUMBUS AVE

20

CARTER RD

SCRANTON RD

W. 47TH ST

10

PITTSBURGH AVE

14

RIVERBED ST
MERWIN AVE

90

*Cuyahoga River*

OHIO
CITY

42

FRANKLIN AVE
WEST 25TH ST

LORAIN AVE

BROADWAY

BRIDGE ST
CARR RON AVE

ABBEY ROAD

RAILWAY STREET

WEST 3RD STREET

KEENE ST

WILLEY ST

WEST 7TH STREET
WEST 5TH STREET
WEST 4TH STREET

WEST 20TH ST
WEST 22ND ST
CHATAM ST
HANDCOCK STREET

KENILWORTH
C STREET

PROFESSOR STREET
JEFFERSON STREET
TREMONT STREET
WEST 10TH STREET

MONROE STREET

STARKWEATHER STREET

△ University Circle, 4 miles

West of the Gund is the **riverfront**, where one of the nation's busiest waterways shares space with excellent bars, clubs and restaurants strung out along a boardwalk. On both banks of the Cuyahoga River, the **Flats**, long known for its nightlife, relishes its industrial setting: magnificent grimy old buildings, warehouses and slag heaps, set in amongst fourteen **bridges**, appear powerful and romantic rather than depressing, a proud testimony to Cleveland's manufacturing history.

It's a short but steep walk uphill to the **Warehouse District**, a nicely developing stretch of nineteenth-century commercial buildings between West Third and West Tenth streets, given over to shops, galleries and cafes. North, on the other side of the busy Cleveland Memorial Shoreway (Hwy-2), the waters of Lake Erie lap gently into **North Coast Harbor**, the new showpiece of Midwest regeneration. To see the city from the water, try a two-hour cruise on the *Goodtime III* (☎216/861-5110; $12.50) from the dock at East Ninth Street Pier, just beyond the I M Pei-designed **Rock and Roll Hall of Fame and Museum** (see box, overleaf). Next door to the Rock Hall – as Clevelanders refer to it – is the giant **Great Lakes Science Center** (daily 9.30am–5.30pm; OMNIMAX open until 9pm with shows on the hour; $7.75 for museum; $7.75 OMNIMAX theater; $10.95 combo ticket), its white paneling and glass frontage perfectly complementing its neighbor. There are no stand-out displays, though the cumulative effect of the 350 interactive exhibits (many on meteorological and aquatic themes) makes this a very enjoyable place to spend a few hours. Across the road, the futuristic, 72,000-seat **Cleveland Stadium** is the brand new home of the reincarnated Browns pro football team (☎440/891-5000). After living in NFL limbo for three years, Cleveland football fans joyously welcomed their team back for the 1999 season.

To the west of the river, **Ohio City** is one of Cleveland's hipper neighborhoods, with junk stores, Victorian clapboard houses and the busy **West Side Market** at Lorain Avenue and West 25th Street, selling all manner of ethnic foods (Mon & Wed 7am–4pm, Fri & Sat 7am–6pm). It's easily spotted by its redbrick Victorian clock tower.

## Out from downtown

Five miles east of downtown, **University Circle** is a cluster of over seventy cultural and medical institutions, and is also home to several major performing arts companies (see p.261). The eclectic **Museum of Art**, fronted by a lagoon at 11150 East Blvd (Tues, Thurs & Fri 10am–6pm, Wed 10am–10pm, Sat 9am–5pm, Sun 1–6pm; free), ranges from Renaissance armor to African art, and has a good cafe. Also notable is the **Museum of Natural History**, Wade Oval, with exhibits on dinosaurs and Native American culture (Mon–Sat 10am–5pm, Sun noon–5pm; Wed until 10pm from Sept–May; $6.50). The modest **Cleveland Botanical Garden**, 11030 East Blvd (daily dawn to dusk; free), is trying to increase its profile, with a $37 million face-lift planned for 2001. Meanwhile, dotted along East and Martin Luther King boulevards in Rockefeller Park, 24 small landscaped cultural **gardens** are dedicated to and tended by Cleveland's diverse ethnic groups, including Croatians, Estonians and Finns. **Murray Hill**, Cleveland's Little Italy, is adjacent to University Circle: an attractive area of brick streets, small delis and galleries, beyond which is the trendy **Coventry Village** neighborhood.

Five miles southwest of downtown via I-71 (exit at W 25th or Fulton Rd), the **Cleveland Metroparks Zoo**, 3900 Brookside Drive (summer Mon–Fri 9am–5pm, Sat & Sun 9am–7pm; rest of year daily 9am–5pm; rainforest also open Wed until 8pm; $7, or $5 zoo only), features "Wolf Wilderness," plus a spectacular 165-acre **rainforest** building populated by seven thousand plants and 118 species of animal, including orangutans, American crocodiles and Madagascan hissing cockroaches. RTA runs special buses from downtown during summer.

Thirty miles southeast of downtown is **Seaworld**, the region's top family attraction; performing sharks, dolphins and killer whales delight the crowds, and there's a

## THE ROCK AND ROLL HALL OF FAME AND MUSEUM

Cleveland, not the most obvious candidate, convincingly won a hotly contested bid to host the **Rock and Roll Hall of Fame and Museum** largely because **Alan Freed**, a local disc jockey, popularized the phrase "rock and roll" here back in 1951. Since then, Cleveland has hardly produced a roll call of rock icons – Joe Walsh, Pere Ubu, Nine Inch Nails and Bone Thugs 'N' Harmony are about the biggest names – but the city embraced the idea of the museum with such enthusiasm that few can now argue that it was not the correct choice. However, cynics are quick to snipe that Cleveland won out over Memphis, New York and other cities with a richer musical heritage because, quite simply, it stumped up the most cash – a financial package that some put as high as $65 million.

The idea for a definitive rock museum was first mooted in 1983, with the establishment of the **Rock Hall of Fame Foundation** to honor all those who have made "an exceptional contribution to modern music." The inductees are selected annually by an international panel of rock "experts," but only those performers who have released a record 25 years prior to their nomination are eligible.

The museum's septuagenarian architect – **I M Pei** – wanted the building "to echo the energy of rock and roll." One of Pei's trademark tinted-glass pyramids (a smaller version of the one he did at the Louvre), the resultant white concrete, steel and glass structure strikes a bold pose right on the shore of Lake Erie. A tall main tower supports sweeping geometric extensions and dramatic cantilevered offshoots in cylindrical, triangular and rectangular shapes, all fronted by the pyramid (or tent, as Pei likes to call it), which looks spectacular when lit up at night. The base of the pyramid extends into an impressive entrance plaza shaped like a turntable, complete with a stylus arm attachment. It might all look good but Pei's lavish design means that most of the exhibits have to be placed in the basement.

The museum itself is much more than an array of mementos and artifacts. Right from the start – the excellent twelve-minute films *Mystery Train* and *Kick Out the Jams* – the emphasis is on the contextualization of rock. The exhibits chart the art form's evolution and progress, acknowledging influences ranging from the blues singers of the Delta to the hillbilly wailers of the Appalachians. Look for "The Beat Goes On" display – a bank of interactive computers that reveals the inspirational earlier artists who shaped the sound of a series of contemporary bands.

Elsewhere in the subterranean main exhibition hall, there's an in-depth look at seven crucial rock genres through the cities that spawned them: rockabilly (Memphis), R&B (New Orleans), Motown (Detroit), psychedelia (San Francisco), punk (London and New York), hip-hop (New York) and grunge (Seattle). Much space is taken up by exhibits on what the museum sees as key artists of all time, including Elvis Presley, the Beatles (featuring a collection of John Lennon's possessions donated by Yoko Ono), U2, George Clinton and the Rolling Stones. In November 1999, the new exhibit "Beats and Rhymes" opened at the museum, tracing the development of hip-hop and rap with costumes, artifacts and special programs.

Above ground, Pei's airy structure feels like a modern art gallery: several U2 Trabants are suspended from the ceiling, a giant inflatable teacher from Pink Floyd's *Wall* tour bursts forth every five minutes, and photographic portraits by Annie Leibovitz et al adorn the area by the stairwells.

On the top floor is the **Hall of Fame** itself. Compared to the racket elsewhere, this is a self-consciously reverential darkened space; the images of the hundred-plus inductees are flicked up on tiny screens, beside which are their autographs etched on glass.

The museum is at North Coast Harbor (daily 10am–5.30pm, Wed until 9pm; $14.95; reservations ☎1-800/493-ROLL). It gets particularly crowded at weekends: if that's the only time you can make it, you'll have to book in advance and you'll be given a time to turn up. However, since it takes a good half-day to see just a decent proportion of the exhibits, it's much better to go on a weekday morning, when you can take full advantage of the interactive displays. It's worth planning a visit to coincide with the extensive series of seminars and workshops that feature Hall of Fame inductees and leading rock writers. Full details of these events can be called up on the Rock Hall's Web site (*www.rockhall.com*).

*Baywatch*-themed action show (June–Sept hours vary; ☎330/995-2121 or 1-800/63-SHAMU; $30.95).

# Eating

At first sight, corporate chains seem to dominate Cleveland – especially in the Flats – but the city has many culinary delights on offer, many of them ethnic. The **West Side Market** in Ohio City is one of the best places for cheap and unusual picnic food, but there are also some excellent (if pricey) fine-dining restaurants downtown. Little Italy and the Coventry Village area, both just east of University Circle, are worth exploring for authentic food and coffee bars respectively. The *Arabica* chain also serves up good quality espresso at locations around the city, and can be found downtown at 856 Euclid Ave (☎216/771-6869).

**Flat Iron Cafe**, 1114 Center St (☎216/696-6968). Landmark tavern on the east (downtown) bank of the Flats, with an Irish-American edge, that serves up good sandwiches, salads and desserts, plus a smooth pint of Guinness.

**Hornblower's Barge & Grille**, 1151 N Marginal Rd (☎216/363-1151). Reasonable-value pastas, sandwiches and seafood. Good location overlooking Lake Erie and a short stroll from the Rock Hall.

**Mama Santa**, 12301-05 Mayfield Rd (☎216/231-9567). Unpretentious and inexpensive Southern Italian home cooking in Little Italy.

**Nate's Deli & Restaurant**, 1923 W 25th St (☎216/696-7529). Daytime Middle Eastern cafe serving great gyros and plenty of vegetarian dishes. The hummus, in particular, has quite a reputation.

**New York Spaghetti House**, 2173 E 9th St (☎216/696-6624). Inexpensive and extremely popular, family-owned Italian restaurant.

**Ruthie & Moe's Diner**, 4002 Prospect Ave (☎216/431-8063). Clean, friendly, traditional diner, well worth the 5min drive from downtown for its breakfasts, lunches and huge desserts.

**Tommy's**, 1824 Coventry Rd (☎216/321-7757). Great-value food, much of it Middle Eastern vegetarian, in a trendy, bright setting in lively Coventry Village.

**Watermark Restaurant**, 1250 Old River Rd (☎216/241-1600). Excellent and extensive seafood menu in a classy Flats location overlooking the river.

# Nightlife and entertainment

For after-dark entertainment, the **Flats** area boasts the greatest conglomeration of drinking, live music and dancing venues, although they tend to be cheesier than their counterparts in the **Warehouse District** and the more bohemian **Ohio City** across the river. Five miles east, both the **University Circle** and the youthful **Coventry Village** neighborhoods have good venues and bars, though the Circle contains no-go zones you shouldn't wander into. Cleveland's **rave** scene remains strong and mostly underground; if you're interested, look for flyers at Record Revolution (☎216/321-7661), 1828 Coventry Rd.

As for more refined entertainments, the **Cleveland Opera** (☎216/575-0900) and **Ballet** (☎216/426-2500) perform in **Playhouse Square Center** (☎216/241-6000), which also hosts drama. The well-respected **Cleveland Orchestra** (☎216/231-1111) is based in University Circle at Severance Hall, 11001 Euclid Ave, close to the leading regional theater of **Cleveland Play House** (☎216/795-7000). For **what's on** information, try one of Cleveland's two free weeklies: the well-written *Free Times* covers all of the arts, while *Scene* concentrates mostly on music.

**The Basement**, 1078 Old River Rd (☎216/344-0001). Eighties dance-rock and occasional concerts in this club on the Flats east bank. Voted Cleveland's best dance club four years running.

**Club Isabella**, 2025 University Hospitals Drive, University Circle (☎216/229-1177). Popular, reasonably priced Italian restaurant, featuring live jazz.

**Euclid Tavern**, 11629 Euclid Ave, University Circle (☎216/229-7788). One of America's great rock bars, this beloved dive puts on alternative and blues bands with occasional big-name surprises.

**Great Lakes Brewing Co**, 2516 Market St, Ohio City (☎216/771-4404). Famous old joint whose huge mahogany bar still bears the bullet holes made during a 1920s shootout involving Elliot Ness. Cleveland's best brewpub.

**Grog Shop**, 1765 Coventry Rd, Cleveland Heights (☎216/321-5588). Dark, dank and sweaty collegiate punk and alternative venue near Coventry Village.

**Harbor Inn**, 1219 Main Ave (☎216/241-3232). Great old-fashioned bar amid the hyped chain outfits of the Flats. 180 beers, video games, lotsa character.

**Peabody's Down Under**, 1059 Old River Rd (☎216/241-2451). Long-running rock club in the Flats, showcasing local and national bands.

**Trilogy**, 2325 Elm St (☎216/241-4007). This old warehouse on the west bank of the Flats hosts rock and dance on Friday and Saturday, and hugely popular techno on Sunday.

**Wilbert's Bar & Grille**, 1360 W 9th St (☎216/771-2583). Friendly place between the Flats and the Warehouse District, hosting good touring blues and roots bands and serving highly rated Southwestern food.

## Around Cleveland

Less than an hour outside the city are several small towns and sights well worth exploring. **VERMILION**, beyond the western suburbs of Cleveland, is also known as Harbor Town because of its attractive lakeside area, which has thrived since 1837. Today it's a quaint old hamlet lined with clapboard houses, cedar trees and tidy gardens. Old-style galleries and shops hug the small downtown, a stone's throw from the boat rides, seafood restaurants and fishing boats on the dockside. Through models, pictures and artifacts, the **Inland Seas Maritime Museum**, 480 Main St (daily 10am–5pm; $5), does a worthy job of exploring shipping on the Great Lakes from the late seventeenth century to the wreckage of the *Edmund Fitzgerald* freighter almost 300 years later. Vermilion's **visitor center** is at 5741 Liberty Ave (Tues–Sat 10am–5pm; ☎440/967-4262). The best place to **stay in town** is the comfortable *Motel Plaza*, 4645 Liberty Ave (☎440/967-3191; ④), while just east in the industrial port town of **LORAIN**, the *Spitzer Plaza Hotel*, 301 Broadway Ave (☎440/246-5767 or 1-800/446-7452; ⑤), offers big rooms and good value.

Some twenty miles southeast of Vermilion, the famously liberal college town of **OBERLIN** clusters around the green acres of Tappan Square. Founded in 1834, **Oberlin College**, on the square's north and east sides, was America's first co-ed university and one of the first to enroll black students. From the start, it played a pivotal role in facilitating the movement of black slaves from the Deep South to Canada on the Underground Railroad. A **sculpture** of railroad tracks emerging from the earth, opposite the Conservatory of Music at South Professor Street, is one of several such commemorative sights detailed in a fascinating **walking tour** leaflet available from the **Chamber of Commerce**, 20 E College St (Mon–Fri 8.30am–5pm; ☎440/774-6262). Also of interest is the **Allen Memorial Art Museum**, 87 Main St (Tues–Sat 10am–5pm, Sun 1–5pm; free). Recognized as one of the best college museums in the US, it holds over 14,000 objects, from ancient Egyptian icons to Japanese woodblock prints and a fine array of contemporary art.

There are plenty of good places to **stay** in town. The pleasant *Oberlin Inn* motel (☎440/775-1111; ⑥) is right on campus, and the **Ivy Tree Inn & Garden**, 195 S Professor St (☎440/774-4510; ⑤), offers a well-tended garden in a comfortable B&B atmosphere. Oberlin also boasts half a dozen hip coffeehouses and bars, with good organic **food** dished up at the *Two Trees Cafe* in the Co-op Bookstore, 37 W College St (☎440/774-3741).

Twenty miles south of Cleveland off US-77, the village of **PENINSULA** is nestled in the heart of the **Cuyahoga Valley National Recreation Area** (☎1-800/445-9667), where the Ohio & Erie Canal Towpath's hiking and biking trail follows the meandering Cuyahoga River for twenty miles. A few miles south of town off Riverview Road, the sprawling **Hale Farm and Village** (Tues–Sat 10am–5pm, Sun noon–5pm; $9) brings to life the fictional 1848 Ohio township of Wheatfield, complete with good-natured role-playing townsfolk and artisans who demonstrate skills like brick-making and glass-blowing.

The best place to stay in the area is at *Stanford House* (☎330/467-8711; ①), 6093 Stanford Rd, a hostel in a lovely old farmhouse. Bike rental is easy to come by at Century Cycles, 1621 Main St ($5 first hour, $4 second hour, $3 each additional hour); the **Chamber of Commerce,** 1663 Main St (☎330/849-0677), is just down the block.

A few miles further south in **AKRON**, visitors can tour Goodyear co-founder F.A. Seiberling's palatial **Stan Hywet Hall and Gardens**, 714 N Portage Path (Jan–March Tues–Sat 10am–4pm, Sun 1–4pm; Apr–Dec daily 10am–4.30pm; $8, only gardens $4), a magnificent 65-room Tudor Revival country house finished in 1915, featuring secret passageways, hand-carved linenfold wood paneling, and an indoor swimming pool.

# The Lake Erie Islands

The **LAKE ERIE ISLANDS** – Kelleys Island, and the three **Bass Islands** further north – were early stepping stones for the **Iroquois** on the route to what is now Ontario. French attempts to claim the islands in the 1640s met with considerable hostility, and they were left more or less in peace until 1813, when in the **Battle of Lake Erie**, fought off South Bass Island, the Americans established their control over the Great Lakes by destroying the entire English fleet (for the first time in history).

The islands first tasted prosperity in the 1860s, when a boom in **wine production** meant that nearly every available acre was planted with grapes. Tourism arrived almost simultaneously, with steamboats bringing wealthy visitors to spend their summers in the grand hotels. However, the economy was hit hard by Prohibition and the emergence of the California wineries, as well as by the advent of car travel. In the 1970s, Lake Erie's appalling pollution was the final straw for many inhabitants, who undertook a huge cleanup, both literally, of the lake, and figuratively, of the islands' image. Their plan has worked; today the islands are heavily touristed, especially in summer, with fishing, swimming and partying the main attractions. Those mainland towns, like **Sandusky**, that act as jump-off points for the islands, are destinations in themselves.

## The mainland

The large coal-shipping port of **SANDUSKY**, fifty miles west of Cleveland on US-2, is probably the most visited of the lakeshore towns, thanks to **Cedar Point Amusement Park**, five miles southeast of town (May–Sept daily 9am–10pm; $32.95, $20.95 after 5pm). The largest ride park in the nation – and widely considered the best in the world – Cedar Point boasts no less than thirteen roller coasters. The neighboring **Soak City** water park provides a good way to cool off, with eighteen acres of water slides and a wave pool (May–Sept daily 10am–9pm; $19.95, both parks $44.95). Otherwise, Sandusky is a nice enough town in a pleasant farmland setting, but there's not much to it apart from its pretty downtown square and the fast-food spots lining US-2.

The smaller resort town of **PORT CLINTON**, twelve miles west across the Sandusky Bay Bridge, is another departure point for the islands, its pleasant lakefront dotted with decent cafes and jet ski-rental outlets. Try not to leave the area without exploring the rest of the peninsula, with glorious views particularly around tiny **MARBLEHEAD**, fourteen miles east of Port Clinton.

Eight miles south of Sandusky, tiny **MILAN** (pronounced *MY-lan*) boasts a pleasant, leafy village square and many well-preserved Greek Revival-style homes. Its most famous building is the two-story brick **Thomas Edison Birthplace**, 9 Edison Drive (summer Tues–Sat 10am–5pm, Sun 1–5pm; rest of year Tues–Sun 1–5pm; $5), with guided tours and an adjacent museum dedicated to the inventor of the light bulb.

## Practicalities

Amtrak **trains** pass through Sandusky once daily en route between Chicago and Boston or New York, via Cleveland; the station, at North Depot and Hayes avenues, is in a dodgy area, and unstaffed. Greyhound **buses** call way out at 6513 Milan Rd. Sandusky's **visitor center** is at 4424 Milan Rd, Suite A (summer daily 8am–9pm; rest of year daily 8.30am–5pm; ☎419/625-2984 or 1-800/255-ERIE).

**Accommodation** in Sandusky can be frighteningly expensive in high season – it's not unheard-of for a standard motel room to cost $200-plus on peak weekends. The *Coronado Motel*, 4319 Venice Rd (☎419/625-2954; ③), two miles west of downtown, is affordable, its clean rooms equipped with microwaves and fridges. Along the main drag of Cleveland Road (US-6), try the *Mecca* at no. 2227 (☎419/626-1284; ④) or the *Best Western Cedar Point* at no. 1530 (☎419/625-9234; ⑤), which has a pool and mini-golf course. **Camping** is available at the *Bayshore Estates* at 2311 Cleveland Rd (☎419/625-7906) and at the *Milan Travel Park* just off US-80 at 11404 US 250 N (☎419/433-4277), which has laundry facilities, free showers and a pool. Also in **Milan**, the *Colonial Inn South*, 12111 Rte-250 (☎419/499-3403 or 1-800/886-9010; ④), is a recently refurbished family-owned motel, while in **Lakeside**, a quiet Methodist retreat across Sandusky Bay, the *Lakeside Hotel*, 236 Walnut Ave (☎419/798-4461; ④), offers decent, simple rooms at great prices.

For a good **meal** and live music in fun surroundings (there's an on-site waterfall), head for *Margaritaville* in Sandusky, at the junction of Highways 6 and 2 (☎419/627-8903).

---

### GETTING TO THE ISLANDS

**Ferries** to **Kelleys Island** are operated by Neuman Boats from the foot of Frances Street in **Marblehead** every hour from dawn until dusk, more frequently at weekends and during peak times (April–Nov; $9.50 round-trip, bikes $3.50; ☎419/798-5800 or 1-800/876-1907). Kelleys Island Ferry Boat Lines (☎419/798-9763) offers a year-round service from Main Street, Marblehead, for the same prices. The *Island Rocket* (☎419/627-1500 or 1-800/854-8121), a powerful "cigarette" boat, whisks through the water from Jackson Street Pier in **Sandusky** for $9 one-way.

You can also take the *Island Rocket* from **Sandusky** to **South Bass Island** for a one-way fare of $11. A better value is the *Island Rocket* same-day "island hopper" ticket, which allows you to visit both islands for $28. The *Jet Express* (April–Nov; $10 one-way; ☎1-800/2451-JET) takes a mere 22 minutes to reach **South Bass Island** from Port Clinton, and runs until 11.30pm in the summer. Look out for their discount days or take the boat after 4pm any day but Saturday and return before the end of the evening and the fare is $13 round-trip. Ferry boats are hourly by Miller Boats (March–Nov daily 7am–7.30pm; $5 one-way; ☎419/285-2421) from **Catawba Point**, at the end of US-53 N, to Lime Kiln Dock on the island's southern tip. **Cruises**, run by Goodtime (☎419/625-9692) from Sandusky's Jackson Street Pier, depart daily at 9.30am and call at both Kelleys Island and South Bass Island, for a round-trip fare of $21.95.

All crossings generally operate from late March to early November, though weather can interfere with these plans.

**Flights** to both Kelleys Island and South Bass Island leave daily from Sandusky and Port Clinton and cost about $50 round-trip. Contact Griffing Airlines (☎419/626-5161 or 1-800/368-3743).

# Kelleys Island

**KELLEYS ISLAND** is about nine miles north of Sandusky, in the western basin of Lake Erie. Seven miles across at its widest, it's the largest American island on the lake, but it's also one of the most peaceful and picturesque, home to just 175 permanent residents. The whole island, green, sleepy and with few buildings less than a century old, is a National Historic District. Its seventy-plus archeological sites include **Inscription Rock**, a limestone slab carved with four-hundred-year-old pictographs, east of the dock on the southern shore. The **Glacial Grooves State Memorial**, on the west shore, is a four-hundred foot trough of solid limestone, scoured with deep ridges by the glacier that carved the Great Lakes.

Settled in the 1830s, Kelleys was initially a working island, its economy based on lumber, then wine, and later limestone quarrying. All but the last have collapsed, though a steady tourist industry also developed. Today, hundreds of Clevelanders come here at weekends to swim from the sandy public beach on the north shore, bird-watch with the island's active Audubon Society, and hike through some dramatic disused quarries, which now sprout cedars.

## Practicalities

Kelleys Island's **Chamber of Commerce** (summer daily 10am–5pm; ☎419/746-2360) is on Division Street straight up from the *Island Rocket* dock. Getting around is easy; cars are heavily discouraged, and most people, when not strolling, use **bikes** ($2 per hour/$8 per day) or **golf carts** ($12 per hour/$65 per day), available from First Place Rentals, at the top of the Neuman ferry dock (☎419/746-2314). There are a few B&Bs and inns, which can be reserved through the chamber. One comfortable option is *The Inn on Kelleys Island,* 317 W Lakeshore Drive (☎419/746-2258; ④), a restored nineteenth-century Victorian home with a great lake view and a private beach. You can **camp** for $15 at the first-come, first-served state park on the north bay near the beach. The jovial *Village Pump* (☎419/746-2281) serves good home-style **food and drink** until 2am; the menu at the *Island Café & Brew Pub* (☎419/746-2314) includes several options for vegetarians.

# South Bass Island

**SOUTH BASS ISLAND** is the largest and southernmost of the Bass Island chain, three miles from the mainland northwest of Kelleys Island, and named for the excellent bass fishing in the surrounding waters. Also referred to as **Put-in-Bay** (the name of its one and only village), this is the most visited of the American Lake Erie Islands, with its permanent population of 450 swelling to ten times that in summer.

Just a year after its first white settlers arrived, British troops invaded the island as part of the 1812 war for control of the lakes. The Battle of Lake Erie, which took place on the island's southeastern edge, is commemorated by **Perry's Victory and International Peace Memorial** in a 25-acre park where the island dramatically nips in at the waist. You can see the ten miles to the battle site from an observation deck near the top of the 352ft stone Doric column (May–Oct daily 10am–7pm; $3).

After the war, with the lake safe from Canadian invasion, South Bass Island grew both as a port (transporting cedar to the mainland for the construction of steamboats) and as a tourist destination: in the 1890s its *Victory Hotel* was one of the largest hotels in the world. Wine was also big business, though only one of its 26 vineyards survived Prohibition (by producing grape juice) – the **Heineman Winery** (☎419/285-2811), on Catawba Avenue. The winery gives tours which include a glass of wine or grape juice (May–Sept daily 11am–5pm; $4).

All this history is well documented at the **Lake Erie Islands Historical Society**, 441 Catawba Ave, which features dozens of model ships, exhibits on the shipping and fishing industries, and memorabilia of life on the islands.

Despite the colorful past, and the island's undeniable beauty, visitors today may well be struck most by the hordes of boozers staggering between bars whose repertoire extends little beyond Jimmy Buffet songs.

### Practicalities

Put-in-Bay's **visitor center** (summer daily 9am–6pm, call for hours out of season; ☎419/285-2832) is in Harbor Square, downtown, just next to the northern dock. To get around, as on Kelleys Island, most people either rent **golf carts** from Baycarts Rental on Harbor Square ($10–20 per hour; ☎419/285-5785), or bikes, from Island Bike Rental at both docks (☎419/285-2016; $9 per day). A **shuttle bus** runs between the northern dock, the winery and the state park ($1), and a narrated jump-on/jump-off **tram tour** ($6) sets off from the dock every thirty minutes. The local **taxi** will take you anywhere on the island for $3 per person (8am–3am; ☎419/285-2311).

**Hotel** rooms are heavily booked at the weekends and during the summer, and B&Bs often require a two-night minimum stay at the weekend. The *Stagger Inn B&B*, 182 Concord (☎419/285-2521; ④), and the *Commodore Motel*, 272 Delaware Ave (☎419/285-3101; ⑤), which has a pool, offer some of the most competitive rates. There's **camping** for $12 in the state park (get there by 9am) and at the *Fox's Den Campground* (☎419/285-5001; $25 for one or two) on the southern shore.

**Food** on the island is expensive everywhere. The grill meals and seafood sandwiches at *The Boardwalk* (☎419/285-3695) are no exception, but this is the only downtown restaurant directly on the water. Just over the street, *Frosty's* (☎419/285-3278) does good pizza. Put-in-Bay's wild **nightlife** – it really does get raucous here – pulls in revelers from the other islands and the mainland. Numerous **live music** venues include the *Beer Barrel Saloon* (☎419/289-0996) – said to have the longest uninterrupted bar in the world complete with 160 bar stools – and the appropriately named *Round House*. *The Brewer*, just round the corner from the main drag on Catawba Avenue, is a reasonable brewpub.

# Columbus

Ohio's largest city, state capital and home to the massive Ohio State University, **COLUMBUS** is a likeable place to visit. Its position in the rural heart of the state also makes it the only center of culture for a good three-hour drive in any direction.

Ohio became a state in 1803, and after trying Zanesville and Chillicothe, legislators designated this former patch of rolling farmland on the high east bank of the Scioto River its capital in 1812. The fledgling city was built from scratch, and its considered town planning is evident today in broad thoroughfares and green spaces. Statuary forms another part of the cityscape, with monuments seemingly erected on any spare scrap of land, most of them of its namesake, **Christopher Columbus**; there's even a replica of his ship, the *Santa Maria*, docked downtown on the Scioto River. For the 1992 quincentennial of the explorer's discovery of North America, some city officials erroneously felt that a full-scale celebration would put their city (which has lagged behind Cincinnati and Cleveland in terms of public recognition) on the map; it bombed, with Native American and other ethnic groups branding the festivities as exploitive.

After that failure to capture national recognition, city boosters have pinned their hopes on **sport**. The Columbus Crew of professional soccer (who play in the nation's only stadium built specifically for pro soccer) have a huge following, as does the Ohio

State Buckeyes college football team; and the year 2000 welcomes Ohio's first NHL hockey team, the Columbus Blue Jackets.

However, until Columbus does manage to make it big, it's best enjoyed for what it is – a lively college city with a smattering of good **museums**, some gorgeous Germanic **architecture**, and a particularly vibrant **nightlife**, including Ohio's most active **gay scene**. The spacious, orderly and easygoing **downtown** area holds several attractions and the giant Columbus City Center mall, while the main entertainment districts – the bohemian **Short North** and the more mainstream **Brewery District** – are located right on the north and south fringes respectively.

## Arrival, information and getting around

**Port Columbus International Airport** (☎614/239-4083) is seven miles northeast of downtown; **taxis** into the center cost around $15, while cheaper alternatives include the Airport Express **shuttle** (☎614/476-3004; $8.50) and the COTA **bus** (☎614/228-1776; $1.10). Greyhound calls at East Town and Third streets. COTA also runs a good central bus service connecting downtown with German Village, the Short North and North Campus; a day pass costs $2.50. The main **visitor center** is at 90 N High St (Mon–Fri 9am–5.30pm; ☎614/221-CITY or 1-800/345-4FUN), with another branch on the second level of the Columbus City Center mall, just south of the Ohio Statehouse at High and Rich streets (Mon–Sat 10am–9pm, Sun noon–6pm).

## Accommodation

Compared to other cities in the region, Columbus offers a good choice of mid-range places to **stay** that are well placed to let you discover the city by day and night. Downtown rates are good while even more savings can be made by staying in the German Village/Brewery District locales.

**Best Western Clarmont**, 650 S High St (☎614/228-6511). A 2min walk from the Brewery District and German Village, and a key location in the Jodie Foster movie *Little Man Tate*. A little run-down but good-value nonetheless. ④.

**German Village Inn**, 920 S High St (☎614/443-6506). Family-run motel on the south edge of German Village/Brewery District. Similar to the *Clarmont*. ④.

**Harrison House B&B**, 313 W 5th Ave (☎614/421-2202 or 1-800/827-4203). Welcoming big home in Victorian Village, an upcoming district close to the Short North. Private bath, cable TV, phone. ⑤.

**Holiday Inn City Center**, 175 E Town St (☎614/221-3281). Reliable motel with pool and bar in easy walking distance of the main museums, German Village and the Statehouse. ⑥.

**Hostelling International – Columbus**, 95 E 12th Ave (☎614/294-7157). Excellent location on campus. Reservations advisable. $14 per night, $17 for non-HI members. ①.

**Inn on City Park**, 1023 City Park Ave (☎614/443-3048). Light, airy rooms in a sunny B&B on Schiller Park at the southern edge of the German Village. No smoking, no credit cards. ④.

**The Westin Columbus**, 310 S High St (☎614/228-3800). Columbus's grand downtown Victorian hotel. ⑦.

## Downtown

As good a place as any to start a walking tour of downtown is the **Ohio Statehouse** (Mon–Fri 7am–7pm, Sat & Sun 10am–5pm; tours Mon–Fri 9.30am–3pm, Sat & Sun 11.15am–3pm; free), pleasantly set in ten acres of park at the intersection of Broad and High streets, the two main downtown arteries. Highlights of the free guided tours in this recently renovated 1839 Greek Revival structure – one of the very few state capitols without a dome – are the ornate Senate and House chambers.

From here, most places of interest lie a few blocks east and west along Broad Street. The new incarnation of Columbus' **COSI** (Center of Science and Industry) is housed in a streamlined structure across the river at 333 W Broad St (Mon–Sat 10am–5pm, Sun noon–5.30pm; adults $8, kids $6, family ticket $28), and boasts more than 300,000 square feet of exhibit space, most of it geared toward children. Across from COSI's former location, the **Wendy's Original Restaurant** at 257 E Broad St (Mon–Fri 10am–8pm, Sat 10am–7pm, Sun 11am–6pm), pays homage to Dave Thomas' enduringly down-home national burger chain, started here in 1969. There's the usual menu, plus pictures of famous patrons, glass cases full of *Wendy* dolls, the original homemade dress Thomas's daughter Wendy wore when she posed for the logo that's still used today, and other memorabilia. Incidentally, the city also introduced the **White Castle** burger chain to the world in 1921, but some enthusiast of the greasy patties bought up the first castellated diner and moved it elsewhere as a private residence.

Three blocks east, a giant Henry Moore sculpture stands at the entrance to the inviting **Columbus Museum of Art**, 480 E Broad St (Tues–Wed & Fri–Sun 10am–5.30pm, Thurs 10am–8.30pm, closed Mon; $4, free Thurs 5.30–8.30pm), which also has a pleasant sculpture garden. Indoors, this airy space holds particularly good collections of Western and modernist art, including a dramatic mixed-media piece by Anselm Keifer just by the entrance, a renowned photography gallery and touring exhibits.

The **Topiary Garden** in Old Deaf School Park (daylight hours; free), at the corner of Washington Avenue and East Town Street south of the museum, provides a quirky photo opportunity. In the center of this verdant little park, a group of locals have re-created in topiary Georges Seurat's famous post-Impressionist work, *Sunday Afternoon on the Island of La Grande Jatte*. Believed to be the only painting reinterpreted in evergreen shrubbery, it features fifty pruned humans, three dogs, a monkey, a cat and eight leafy boats floating in a pond.

### German Village and Brewery District

Just six blocks south of the Statehouse, I-70 separates downtown from the delightful **German Village** neighborhood. During the mid-nineteenth century, thousands of German immigrants settled in this part of Columbus, building neat redbrick homes, the most lavish of which surround the 23-acre **Schiller Park**. Their descendants, however, started leaving the area during World War I, and with Prohibition and World War II further depleting their numbers, few were left by the 1950s. The area, then known as the Old South End, soon became run-down, and by the 1960s the big corporations were eyeing it for office developments until a group of local preservationists, determined to save these gorgeous homes from the wrecker's ball, decided to designate the area as the German Village. They formed a preservation society, drew up a list of renovation guidelines for residents, and won a place on the National Register of Historic Places.

Today the eighteen-block village is the biggest privately funded body on that register, a professional residential district with a sizeable gay community. The best way to explore its brick-paved streets, corner bars, old-style restaurants, Lutheran churches and grand homes is to call at the **German Village Meeting Haus**, 588 S 3rd St (April–Sept Mon–Fri 9am–4pm, Sat 10am–2pm; rest of year closed Sun; ☎614/221-8888), where popular walking tours run by the German Village Society start with a twelve-minute video presentation. The Society also oversees the immensely popular **Haus und Garten Tour** on the last Sunday in June, and the **Oktoberfest** celebrations in early September. The Village caters to book lovers; the **Book Loft**, 631 S 3rd St (daily 10am–11pm; ☎614/464-1774), crams its books, many of them discounted, into 32 rooms of a former residence.

Just across High Street (US-23) are the warehouses of the **Brewery District**, where until Prohibition, the German immigrants brewed beer by traditional methods. Many of the original buildings still stand, but today the beer is produced by a handful of microbreweries such as **Columbus Brewing Co**, 525 Short St, which sometimes fixes up free tours of the operation (by appointment on ☎614/224-3626). The area is also the focus of Columbus's more mainstream nightlife, with several restaurants, theme pubs, music venues and, inevitably, brewpubs.

## North of downtown

Across Nationwide Boulevard at the top end of downtown is the **Short North**, a former red-light area that's now Columbus's most vibrant enclave. Standing either side of High Street – the main north–south thoroughfare – two landmark buildings mark the transition into the area. To the left is the restored Victorian warehouse of **North Market** (see "Eating," below), while to the right is the strikingly deconstructivist **Greater Columbus Convention Center**, a massive pile of angled blocks designed by Peter Eisenman and completed in 1993. A few blocks further north across I-670 is the start of the trail of galleries, bars and restaurants that makes the area so popular with locals. The first Saturday of each month sees the **Gallery Hop**, when all the local art dealers throw open their doors – complementing the art works with wine, snacks and occasional performance pieces – and the socializing goes on well into the evening.

Businesses become a little more low-rent for a mile before High Street cuts through the **university campus** and suddenly sprouts cheap eating places and funky shopping emporia. For bargain vinyl, head to the basement Used Kids Records, 1992 North High Street On the other side of the street, the **Wexner Center for the Arts**, North High Street at 15th Avenue (Tues–Wed & Fri–Sun 10am–6pm, Thurs 10am–9pm; ☎614/292-3535), is another recent Eisenman construction – even more extreme than the Convention Center – and it's home to cutting-edge contemporary art exhibitions, movies, mixed-media performances, a cafe and a bookstore.

## Eating

The Short North and German Village neighborhoods are crammed with places to **eat**, be they bottom-dollar snack-bars or stylish and adventurous bistros. For a wide range of ethnic and organic snacks during the day, try the **North Market** downtown at 59 Spruce St (Tues–Fri 9am–7pm, Sat 8am–5pm, Sun noon–5pm; ☎614/463-9664), which also sells fresh produce.

**Barcelona**, 263 E Whittier St, German Village (☎614/444-1130). Noted for its tapas and desserts, this stylishly decorated local favorite also does tasty Mediterranean entrees.

**Cap City Fine Diner**, 1229 Olentangy River Rd (☎614/291-3663). A self-proclaimed "upscale diner," this big, lively joint just off downtown serves up traditional food (meatloaf) with new twists (chili-onion rings and buttermilk mash). Huge portions, especially the desserts; lunch entrees around $8, dinner $14.

**Cup O' Joe Coffee & Dessert House**, 627 S 3rd St, German Village (☎614/221-1JOE). Great desserts and coffees and comfy sofas. Voted Columbus' best coffeehouse.

**Katzinger's**, 475 S 3rd St, German Village (☎614/228-3354). A mesmeric range of sandwiches, Jewish munchies and cheesecakes, though prices are high for a deli.

**Out on Main**, 122 E Main St (☎614/224-9520). Hot new gay-themed restaurant with fabulous atmosphere and a great menu to match. *Planet Hollywood*esque exhibits include Melissa Etheridge's guitar, Greg Louganis' Speedo and a Liberace display.

**Schmidt's Restaurant und Sausage Haus**, 240 E Kossuth St, German Village (☎614/444-6808). A Columbus landmark since 1886, serving schnitzel and strudel in a former slaughterhouse.

**Tapatio**, 491 N Park St, Short North (☎614/221-1085). Inventive Caribbean and South American food and a great patio.

## Nightlife

A few years back, Columbus was being tipped as "the next Seattle"; while that didn't happen, this youthful university town has a rich source of local **bands**, from country revivalists to experimental alternative acts. The **gay scene** is concentrated in the Short North on and around North High Street, with a few additional bars and clubs downtown – the biweekly *OUTlook* has complete listings. On most summer Friday evenings there are free concerts in downtown Bicentennial Park on the Scioto River. The *Other Paper* and *Columbus Alive* provide free details of what's happening.

**Chelsie's**, 980 N High St, Short North (☎614/297-1682). Tatty bar with good regional rock and reggae. Plus cheap drinks.

**Dick's Den**, 2417 N High St (☎614/268-9573). Campus dive bar with good jazz at the weekends.

**Little Brother's**, 1100 N High St, Short North (☎614/421-2025). Underground sounds from alternative rock to swing and spoken word.

**Ludlow's**, 485 S Front St, Brewery District (☎614/341-7284). Pick of the more mainstream Brewery District venues with live bands Thurs–Sat.

**Mekka**, 382 Dublin Ave (☎614/621-2582). Close to the Brewery District, in a backstreet next to the gruesome old State Pen, this vastly popular club plays progressive techno and house.

**Oldfield's On High**, 2590 N High St (☎614/784-0477). Predominantly collegiate campus bar with eclectic live music tastes.

**Short North Tavern**, 674 N High St, Short North (☎614/221-2432). Oldest bar in the neighborhood; live bands at the weekend.

**Union Station Video Cafe**, 630 N High St, Short North (☎614/228-3740). Popular gay video bar with a decent selection of appetizers and sandwiches, plus a pool table and Internet access.

# Cincinnati

CINCINNATI, just across the Ohio River from Kentucky and roughly three hundred miles from both Detroit and Chicago, is a dynamic commercial metropolis with a definite European flavor and a sense of the South. Its tidy center, rich in architecture and culture, lies within a few minutes' easy walk of the arty **Mount Adams** district, the attractive **riverfront** and the lively **Over-the-Rhine** area in the north end of downtown.

The city was founded in 1788 at the point where a Native American trading route crossed the river. Its name comes from a group of Revolutionary War admirers of the Roman general Cincinnatus, who saved Rome in 458 BC and then returned to his small farm and refused to accept any reward or glory. Cincinnati quickly became an important supply point for pioneers heading west on flatboats and rafts, and its population skyrocketed with the establishment of a major steamboat **riverport** in 1811. Tens of thousands of **German** immigrants poured in during the 1830s.

Loyalties were split by the **Civil War**. At first, merchants were perturbed by the loss of important markets; then they began to pick up lucrative government contracts, and the city decided its future lay with the Union. In the prosperous postwar decade, Cincinnati acquired Fountain Square, the prodigious Music and Exhibition Hall, a zoo, art museum, public library and the country's first professional baseball team. **Sport** remains a great source of pride: downtown gift shops are decked out in the orange and black of the woeful **Bengals** football team, and the red and white of the more competitive baseball-playing **Reds**.

A Cincinnati success story is the **Rookwood Pottery**, started by Maria Storer in Mount Adams in 1880. Its distinctive tiles adorn countless downtown Art Deco landmarks, as well as the Union and Dixie train terminals.

Charles Dickens, Winston Churchill and Longfellow all admired Cincinnati; Mark Twain, on the other hand, said that he hoped to be in Cincinnati when the world ended, as it's always twenty years behind everywhere else.

### Arrival, information and getting around

**Cincinnati-Northern Kentucky International Airport** (☎606/767-3151) is twelve miles south of downtown, in Covington, Kentucky. **Taxis** to the city center (☎606/586-5236) cost $22, and JetPort Express (☎606/767-3702) **shuttle buses** $12. The Greyhound station is on the eastern fringe of the center, just off Broadway, at 1005 Gilbert Ave. Amtrak **trains** arrive a mile northwest of downtown at the Union Terminal museum complex, which is on the daytime citywide Metro **bus** network (50¢; ☎513/621-4455). The best way to move between downtown Cincy and the sights across the river in Covington and Newport, KY, is via the South Bank Shuttle Tank **shuttle bus**, which picks up at Fountain Square in front of the *Westin* – and costs only 25¢. The city's taxis enforce a $3 minimum fare, though that will usually get you from downtown to most places of interest.

Cincinnati's main **visitor center** is at 300 W 6th St (Mon–Fri 9am–5pm; ☎513/621-2142 or 1-800/CINCY-USA); there are also information booths in Fountain Square and at 605 Philadelphia St in Covington (daily 9am–5pm; ☎606/655-4159).

## Accommodation

Although Cincinnati's quality **hotels** are reasonable by big-city standards, budget travelers may have problems finding affordable downtown rooms. Uptown **motels** – about two miles north – are much cheaper, but you'll need a car to get around safely at night.

**Budget Host Inn**, 3356 Central Parkway (☎513/559-1600). Just about the cheapest place in uptown Cincinnati, though doubles vary greatly in price. Three miles from downtown. ③.

**Gateway B&B**, 326 E 6th St, Newport, KY (☎606/581-6447). Comfortable, affordable Victorian place, five minutes from downtown Cincy and Covington, KY. ⑤.

**Holiday Inn Downtown**, 800 W 8th St (☎513/241-8660). Fairly priced downtown rooms. ⑤.

**Marriott at River Center**, 10 W River Center Blvd, Covington, KY (☎606/261-2900 or 1-800/228-9290). Brand new luxury hotel on the river with spacious rooms and great service. On-site pool and spa. ⑥–⑧.

**Regal Cincinnati Hotel**, 150 W 5th St (☎513/352-2100 or 1-800/876-2100). Twin-towered hotel with hundreds of rooms and a legion of staff that provide excellent service. Best downtown option. ⑤–⑦.

**Riverview Hotel**, 668 5th St, Covington, KY (☎513/491-1200). Strange-looking tower hotel with comfortable rooms, very near the interstates just south of downtown. The expensive revolving *Riverview* restaurant offers amazing views of the river. ⑥.

**Vernon Manor Hotel**, 400 Oak St (☎513/281-3300). Huge suite rooms in old-style hotel. Good location for the university and zoo but not somewhere you'd walk around at night. ⑦.

## Downtown

**Downtown Cincinnati** rolls back from the Ohio River to fill the flat Basin area, ringed by a disarray of steep hills. During the city's emergent industrial years, the filth, disease, crime and general commotion of the so-called Sausage and Rat rows led the middle classes to abandon downtown en masse, an early instance of what became a common phenomenon. Nowadays, however, it has been taken over by an abundance of attractive stores, street vendors, restaurants, cafes, open spaces and gardens. The city's rich blend of architecture is best appreciated on the **walking tour** detailed in an excellent free booklet from the visitor centers, while over, among and even right through the hotel plazas, office lobbies and retail areas, the **Skywalk** network of air-conditioned passages and flyovers spans sixteen city blocks.

At the geographic center of downtown, the **Genius of the Waters** in **Fountain Square** sprays a cascade of hundreds of jets to symbolize the city's trading links; surrounded by a tree-dotted plaza and all but enclosed by soaring facades of glass and steel, the area is a popular lunch spot and venue for daytime concerts. Looming above at Fifth and Vine streets, the 48-story Art Deco **Carew Tower** has a viewing gallery on its top floor that gives a wonderful panorama of the tight bends of the Ohio and the surrounding hillsides (Mon–Thurs 9.30am–5.30pm, Fri & Sat 9.30am–9pm, Sun 11am–5pm; $2).

Just east of Fountain Square are the Art Deco headquarters of the detergents giant **Procter and Gamble**. The company was formed in 1837 by candlemaker William

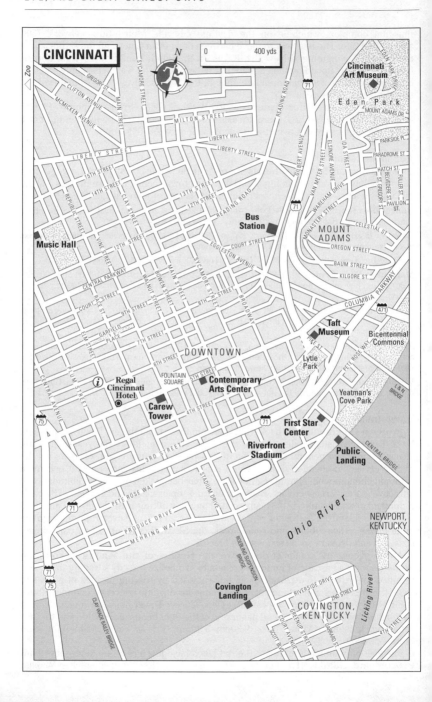

# CINCINNATI

N

0                    400 yds

Cincinnati
Art Museum

Eden Park

MOUNT ADAMS DR

Zoo

GREGORY ST

CLIFTON AVENUE

MCMICKEN AVENUE

MAIN STREET

SYCAMORE STREET

MILTON STREET

LIBERTY HILL

LIBERTY STREET

LIBERTY STREET

15TH STREET

14TH STREET

13TH STREET

12TH STREET

READING ROAD

READING ROAD

GILBERT AVENUE

VAN METER STREET

ELSINORE AVENUE

IDA STREET

PARKSIDE PL

PARADROME ST

HATCH ST

ST GREGORY ST

BELVEDERE ST

FULLER ST

PAVILION ST

WARHAM DRIVE

MONASTERY STREET

CELESTIAL ST

MOUNT
ADAMS

OREGON STREET

BAUM STREET

KILGORE ST.

COLUMBIA PARKWAY

Bus
Station

COURT STREET

EGGLESTON AVENUE

**Music Hall**

REPUBLIC STREET

VINE STREET

CLAY STREET

12TH STREET

CENTRAL PARKWAY

BOWEN STREET

MAIN STREET

WALNUT STREET

SYCAMORE STREET

BROADWAY

9TH STREET

8TH STREET

COURT ST.

RACE ST.

ELM STREET

GARFIELD
PLACE

7TH STREET

5TH STREET

Taft
Museum

PINE ST.

Bicentennial
Commons

471

Lytle
Park

DOWNTOWN

PETE ROSE WAY

PLUM STREET

CENTRAL AVENUE

75

(i)  **Regal
Cincinnati
Hotel**

FOUNTAIN
SQUARE

5TH STREET

**Contemporary
Arts Center**

4TH STREET

**Carew
Tower**

Yeatman's
Cove Park

L & N
BRIDGE

71

**First Star
Center**

CENTRAL BRIDGE

3RD STREET

**Riverfront
Stadium**

STADIUM DRIVE

**Public
Landing**

PETE ROSE WAY

71

PRODUCE DRIVE

MEHRING WAY

RIVERSIDE SUSPENSION BRIDGE

*Ohio River*

NEWPORT,
KENTUCKY

71
75

CLAY WADE BAILEY BRIDGE

**Covington
Landing**

RIVERSIDE DRIVE

2ND STREET

*Licking River*

COVINGTON,
KENTUCKY

GREENUP STREET

COURT AVENUE

SCOTT BLVD

GARRARD ST.

4TH STREET

Procter and soapmaker James Gamble, to exploit the copious supply of animal fat from the slaughterhouses of **"Porkopolis,"** as Cincinnati was then known. A shady style of management has spawned tales of dubious religious and political links; the corporate logo even had to be changed to counter accusations that it was a satanic symbol. By sponsoring radio's "Puddle Family" in 1932, the company was responsible for creating the world's first **soap opera**.

Nearby, the left-field multimedia modern art exhibitions at the superb **Contemporary Arts Center**, in the Mercantile Center at 115 E Fifth St (Mon–Sat 10am–6pm, Sun noon–5pm; $3.50, free Mon), lead to continual run-ins with Cincy's more conservative citizens. By contrast, the **Taft Museum**, just east of downtown in an immaculate 1820 Federal-style mansion at 316 Pike St (Mon–Sat 10am–5pm, Sun 1–5pm; $4), contains a priceless collection of works by Rembrandt, Goya, Turner and Gainsborough, plus some staggering Ming porcelain and French enamels. The statue of a weary Abraham Lincoln in **Lytle Park**, in front of the museum, was criticized as unpatriotic when unveiled in 1917; it's now seen as a great example of sculptural realism.

## Mount Adams and Eden Park

Just over a mile from downtown, the land rises suddenly and the streets – narrow courses with tight corners and abrupt dead ends – start to conform to the contours of **Mount Adams**. Century-old townhouses coexist with avant-garde galleries, stylish boutiques, trendy gift shops and international restaurants. During the late nineteenth century, the elegant dining rooms of Mount Adams entertained the rich and famous who wished to escape the squalor and noise of the Basin. Today its lively bars attract yuppies, students, hedonists and iconoclasts from all over the city. From downtown, take a taxi or #49 bus.

Adjacent to this tightly packed neighborhood recline the rolling lawns, verdant copses and scenic overlooks of **Eden Park**, its features reflected in the new **Mirror Lake**, a man-made pool installed as part of the city's Millenium Project. A loop road at the northern end of the park leads to the **Cincinnati Art Museum** on Art Museum Drive (Tues–Sat 10am–5pm, Sun noon–5pm; $5, free Sat). Its one hundred labyrinthine galleries span five thousand years, taking in an excellent Islamic collection as well as a solid selection of European and American paintings by the likes of Matisse, Monet, Picasso, Edward Hopper and Grant Wood.

## Riverside

The Cincinnati side of the Ohio River has been a mess recently, due to the massive redevelopment project underway to build two new stadiums for the Bengals and the Reds. But just to the east, the riverside takes on a greater serenity – the mile-long **riverside walk** begins near the stadium at **Public Landing**, at the bottom of Broadway. The cobbled wharf here, on the original site of the city, is a great place to take a look at immaculately painted showboats and other river craft. Further west, **Bicentennial Commons** was a two-hundredth-birthday present from the city to itself in 1988.

## The Museum Center at Union Terminal

Cincinnati's latest attraction is its **Museum Center** (☎513/287 7000), housed in the magnificent Art Deco **Union Terminal** northwest of downtown, approached via a stately driveway off Ezzard Charles Drive. The newly restored lobby is absolutely stunning, complete with extraordinary mosaic murals and a Rookwood-tiled ice-cream parlor. Highlights of the **Museum of Natural History** are dioramas of Ice Age Cincinnati and "The Cavern," which houses a living bat colony. The **Historical Society** holds a succession of well-presented, short-term exhibitions, and the **Cinergy Children's Museum** has a two-story treehouse and eight other interactive exhibit areas (Mon–Sat 10am–5pm, Sun 11am–6pm; museums $5.50 each, any two $9, all three

$12, with OMNIMAX $15). The museums are time-consuming, so it's best to get a combination ticket (valid for six months) and use it over two days.

### Covington and Newport, Kentucky

**Covington**, directly across the Ohio River on the Kentucky side, is very much a part of the Cincinnati hinterland. It can be reached from downtown Cincinnati by walking over the bright-blue 355-yard 1867 **John A Roebling Suspension Bridge**, at the bottom of Walnut Street, which served as a prototype for the Brooklyn Bridge. Once across, you're confronted by the much-hyped **Covington Landing** – "the largest waterfront complex on inland waters" – a collection of cafes, shops and clubs on permanently moored boats that's little more than an upmarket mall on water. The BB riverboat company (☎606/261-8500) runs sightseeing cruises ($9) from the Landing – reservations are recommended.

Ten minutes' walk southwest of the bridge brings you to the attractive, narrow, tree-lined streets and nineteenth-century houses of **MainStrasse Village**. It's a Germanic neighborhood of antique shops, bars and restaurants that plays host to the lively **Maifest** on the third weekend of each May, and is the centerpiece of the citywide **Oktoberfest** on the weekend after Labor Day. At Sixth and Philadelphia streets, 21 mechanical figures accompanied by glockenspiel music toll the hour on the German Gothic **Carroll Chimes Bell Tower**. Just beyond Covington at I-75 exit 186 is the **Oldenberg Brewery**, crammed with boozing memorabilia; tours of the microbrewery and its museum cost $3 (daily 10am–5pm).

Across the Licking River from Covington, the subdued town of **Newport** has gotten a lot livelier since the recent opening of the impressive **Newport Aquarium**, One Aquarium Way (June–Aug daily 10am–9pm, Sept–May daily 10am–6pm; ☎606/491-FINS or 1-800/406-FISH). Clear underwater tunnels and see-through floors allow visitors to literally be surrounded by sharks and snapping gators.

### Eating

Cincinnati boasts enough excellent home-grown gourmet and continental restaurants to ensure that national chains have a low profile in the city. It's also famous for fast-food **Cincinnati chili** with chains such as *Skyline Chili*, open from breakfast to midnight at over forty sites, including Vine and Seventh streets downtown.

**Aralia**, 815 Elm St (☎513/723-1217). Excellent Sri Lankan curries in a handy downtown location.

**Arboreta**, 1133 Sycamore St, Over-the-Rhine (☎513/721-1133). Stylish, moderately priced restaurant with seafood specials the locals rave about.

**Courtyard Cafe**, 1211 Main St, Over-the-Rhine (☎513/723-1119). Good grill food, burgers and desserts at value-for-money prices.

**Dee Felice**, 529 Main St, Covington, K (☎606/261-2365). Small and atmospheric restaurant/jazz venue, specializing in Cajun cuisine, with lots of fresh seafood dishes.

**Longworth's**, 1108 St Gregory St, Mount Adams (☎513/579-0900). Good meals at attractive prices in a delightful garden setting. Food served all day until midnight, and music until 2.30am.

**Mullane's Parkside Cafe**, 723 Race St (☎513/381-1331). Friendly joint bedecked with local art, and with an excellent choice of vegetarian options.

**Pigall's Cafe**, 127 W 4th St (☎513/651-2233). Inventive angles on traditional dishes like meatloaf and fried fish, plus pizza, pasta and sandwiches.

**Rookwood Pottery**, 1077 Celestial St, Mount Adams (☎513/721-5456). Snacks and burgers right inside the former kilns of Cincinnati's celebrated pottery.

**Scalea's Ristorante**, 320 Greenup St, Covington, KY (☎606/491-3334). An atmospheric and inventive Italian eatery, with entrees between $12–25; the restaurant's attached deli/market offers cheaper options.

**Tucker's**, 1637 Vine St (☎513/721-7123) and 18 E 13th St, Over-the-Rhine (☎513/241-3354). A perfect start to the day with traditional and gourmet breakfasts in a 1950s setting.

## Nightlife

After dark, the hottest area with the widest appeal is the **Over-the-Rhine** district, which fans out from Main Street, around 12th and 14th, and buzzes every night – though be careful where you park or walk as it backs onto some dodgy areas. The bars, restaurants and cafes of scenic **Mount Adams** offer a good choice of music, food and atmosphere, especially on warm summer nights, when the narrow streets are full of revelers. The studenty **Corryville** neighborhood, a five-minute drive northwest from downtown, has a lively undergraduate edge, while **Covington Landing**, Kentucky, is busy but bland. A proliferation of **brewpubs** has sprung up all over town in the past few years, always dependable for a good drink in friendly surroundings. What's-on **listings** for the whole city can be found in the free *Cincinnati CityBeat*.

**Arnold's**, 210 E 8th St (☎513/421-6234). Fun and funky downtown spot. A favorite with jazz fans, though it also puts on roots and acoustic acts. Good restaurant upstairs.

**Blind Lemon**, 936 Hatch St, Mount Adams (☎513/241-3885). Intimate, low-ceilinged bar with a relaxed crowd on the patio. Music (mostly acoustic) every night at 9.30pm.

**Bogart's**, 2621 Vine St, Corryville (☎513/281-8400). Established indie acts play this mid-sized venue directly opposite *Sudsy Malone's*.

**BrewWorks**, 1115 Main St, Covington, KY (☎606/581-2739). Big, boisterous brewpub pouring the best microbrewed ales in town.

**Main Street Brewery**, 1203 Main St, Over-the-Rhine (☎513/665-4677). Cincy's first brewpub, serving good imaginative food (up to 11pm) and drinks until 2.30am. Live jazz at weekends.

**The Pavilion**, 949 Pavilion St, Mount Adams (☎513/744-9200). Bar with great view of the city and the Ohio River from its terraced outdoor deck.

**Rhythm & Blues Cafe**, 1142 Main St, Over-the-Rhine (☎513/684-0080). Good food and great atmosphere. Live jazz happy hour every Fri 5–8pm and blues, jazz and roots at the weekend.

**Sudsy Malone's Rock & Roll Laundry & Bar**, 2626 Vine St, Corryville (☎513/751-2300). You can drink beer, catch a live indie act and wash your clothes all at the same time in this fun Corryville landmark. Daily 7am–12.30am.

**Warehouse**, 1313 Vine St, Over-the-Rhine (☎513/684-9313). Popular dance club playing alternative and industrial sounds midweek and the latest house at weekends.

## Classical music, opera and theater

**Music Hall**, at 1243 Elm St (☎513/621-1919), an 1870s conglomeration of spires, arched windows and cornices, is said to have near-perfect acoustics. Home to Cincinnati's Opera and Symphony Orchestra, it also hosts the May Festival of choral music. The **Cincinnati Playhouse in the Park** (☎513/421-3888), in Eden Park, puts on drama, musicals and comedies, with performances throughout the year (except Mon).

# MICHIGAN

Mention **MICHIGAN** and most people think of cars, heavy industry and inner-city Detroit. Midwesterners prefer to focus on its magnificent scenery: the beaches, dunes and cliffs along the 3200-mile shoreline of its two vividly contrasting **peninsulas** – bordering four of the five Great Lakes – rival many an oceanfront state.

The mitten-shaped **Lower Peninsula** is dominated from its southeastern corner by the industrial giant of **Detroit**, surrounded by satellite cities almost exclusively devoted to the automotive industry. In the west, the scenic 350-mile Lake Michigan shore drive passes through likeable little ports before reaching the stunning **Sleeping Bear Dunes** and resort towns such as **Traverse City** in the peninsula's balmy northwest corner. The desolate, dramatic and thinly populated **Upper Peninsula**, reaching out from Wisconsin like a claw to separate lakes Superior and Michigan, is a far cry indeed from the cosmopolitan south.

In the mid-seventeenth century, **French explorers** forged a successful trading relationship with the Chippewa, Ontario and other tribes. The **British**, who acquired control after 1763, were far more brutal: Governor Henry Hamilton was known as the "Hair Buyer of Detroit" for his advocacy of taking scalps rather than prisoners. Ever since, Michigan's economy has developed in waves, the eighteenth-century fur, timber and copper booms culminating in the state establishing itself at the forefront of the nation's manufacturing capacity, thanks to its abundant raw materials, good transportation links, and the genius of innovators such as **Henry Ford**. Despite the slumps of the Seventies and Eighties, car production remains the major source of Michigan income – and tourism is now a four-season money-spinner.

## Getting around Michigan

It's easy to be caught out by Michigan's sheer **size**: Detroit is over seven hundred miles from Ironwood on the Wisconsin border (a **ferry** between Ludington and Manitowoc, Wisconsin, helps to cut driving time – see p.286). Greyhound **buses** run regularly throughout the south, but services elsewhere are less frequent, and those few buses that serve the remote Upper Peninsula travel through at night. Amtrak **trains** between New York and Chicago stop at Detroit, Dearborn and Ann Arbor; trains into Canada leave from Windsor, just over the river from Detroit. Michigan's principal **airport**, a hub for Northwest Airlines, is just outside Detroit. **Cycling** is both feasible and rewarding, particularly with the abundance of bike paths in and around Traverse City; Michigan Bicycle Touring (☎616/463-5885) in Kingsley organizes tours and can help with routes.

# Detroit

**DETROIT**, the birthplace of the mass-production car industry and the Motown sound, has long been a city with an image problem. It boasts a billion-dollar downtown development, ultramodern motor-manufacturing plants, some excellent museums and one of the nation's biggest art galleries. But since the 1960s, media attention has dwelt instead on its huge tracts of urban wasteland, where block after block there's nothing but the occasional heavily fortified loan shop or food store. Despite the fact that cities like Atlanta, Newark and Washington DC regularly post much worse crime statistics, the press has seemed intent on painting Detroit as some kind of war zone.

Such views have incurred the wrath of many Detroiters, who claim that the press has magnified the city's problems for the simple reason that blacks run Detroit and account for 75 percent of its population. That assertion certainly carries weight, but Detroit – which has lost nearly half its citizens, almost a million people, in less than forty years – has unarguably suffered. However, following the resurgence of Cleveland, Pittsburgh and other Rust Belt cities, Detroit, under the leadership of Mayor Dennis Archer, is showing signs of having turned the corner. Plans are afoot to enhance the waterfront, new state-of-the-art sports stadia are primed to play ball, and three big-time casinos could open as soon as 2001 – with temporary casinos already up and running. While these developments won't wipe out the city's problems in one fell swoop, they're an exciting start.

Founded in 1701 by Antoine de Mothe **Cadillac**, as a trading post for the French to do business with the Chippewa, Detroit was no more than a medium-sized port two hundred years later. Then **Ford**, **Olds**, the **Chevrolets** and the **Dodge** brothers began to build their automobile empires. Thanks to the introduction of the mass assembly line, Detroit sped into full gear in the 1920s, expanding into the countryside and booming like a mining town – fast, compulsive and indifferent to the needs of its population. The auto barons sponsored the construction of segregated neighborhoods and unceremoniously dispensed with workers during times of low demand. Such policies created huge ghettos, and the city came to the boil in July 1967 in the bloodiest **riot** in the USA for fifty years. More than forty people died and over 1300 buildings were destroyed. Nothing was solved, and little even improved; the inner city was left to fend for itself, and the all-important motor industry was rocked by the oil crises and Japanese competition.

No visitor to Detroit could fail to be disturbed by the divisions between rich and poor, and the fact that other industrial towns have been hit equally hard by the recession is little consolation. However, while heavily scarred and bruised, Detroit is not the apocalyptic mess some would have it. New businesses and theaters have already opened downtown, and suburban residents have started to return to its festivals, theaters, clubs and restaurants; but it makes more sense to think of Detroit as a region rather than a European-style city and, so long as you plan your time and don't mind driving, it holds plenty to see and do. For the moment, **downtown** is not so much the heart of the giant as just another segment, along with the huge **Cultural Center**, attractive pockets such as freewheeling **Royal Oak**, posh **Birmingham** and the Ford-town of **Dearborn**, and even nearby towns such as **Windsor, Ontario** and **Ann Arbor**, a short drive west.

## Arrival, information and getting around

**Flights** come into **Detroit Wayne County Metropolitan Airport** in Romulus (☎734/942-3550), eighteen miles southwest of downtown and a hefty $30-plus taxi ride, though CTC (☎734/941-3252) runs a shuttle for $19.

The main Greyhound (1001 Howard Ave) and Amtrak (2601 Rose St) terminals are in areas where it's inadvisable to walk around at night. Amtrak also stops ten miles out at 16121 Michigan Ave, Dearborn, near the Henry Ford Museum and several mid-range motels, and at unstaffed suburban stations at Birmingham, Pontiac and Royal Oak. The People Mover elevated **railway** loops around thirteen art-adorned stations downtown (Mon–Thurs 7am–11pm, Fri 7am–midnight, Sat 9am–midnight, Sun noon–8pm; 50¢). Otherwise, public transportation is inadequate. DOT **buses** (☎313/933-1300) runs a patchy inner-city service for $1.25 per ride, while the slightly better SMART buses (☎313/962-5515; $1.50) serve suburbia. Transportation in the Motor City is geared firmly towards the **car**; driving in Detroit is not too much of a challenge, but you do need to know where you're heading. During the day, the Attractions Shuttle minibuses (April–Aug; ☎313/259-8726) run between the major sights with unlimited stops for $4.

Detroit's main **visitor center** is downtown at 211 W Fort St on the tenth floor (Mon–Fri 9am–5pm; ☎1-800/DETROIT). There is also an information booth at the entrance to the Henry Ford Greenfield Village (May–Sept daily 9am–6pm; ☎313/271-1620). The main **post office** is at 1401 W Fort St, at Eighth Street (Mon–Fri 8.30am–5pm, Sat 8am–noon; zip code 48200).

## Accommodation

Downtown Detroit caters well for expense-account travelers – its top-range hotels are as secure as any city's – but if your budget is restricted it's harder to find lodging that is both cheap and safe at night. A fifteen percent tax comes slapped onto room bills; if exchange rates are favorable it may be worth considering staying in Windsor, Ontario.

**The Atheneum**, 1000 Brush St (☎313/962-2323 or 1-800/772-2323). Swish, newish, all-suite hotel in Greektown. Some units fetch over $300 a night; others are around a third of that price. ⑦.

**Blanche House Inn B&B**, 506 Parkview Drive (☎313/822-7090). Large Victorian home, handy for Belle Isle and downtown. Comfortable rooms and a friendly, relaxed atmosphere. ⑤.

**Dobson House**, 1439 Bagley Ave (☎313/965-1887). Functional Victorian B&B near Tiger Stadium, with continental breakfast included in the price. ⑤.

## THE MOTOWN SOUND

**Mo.town** (*mo'toun*) adj [< a trademark for phonograph records, etc. <Mo(tor) Town, nickname for Detroit, Mich] designating or of style of rhythm and blues characterized by a strong, even beat.

*Webster's New World Dictionary of the American Language*

The legend that is Tamla Motown started in 1959 when Ford worker and part-time songwriter **Berry Gordy Jr** borrowed $800 to set up a studio. From his first hit onwards – the prophetic *Money (That's What I Want)* – he set out to create a crossover style, targeting his records at white and black consumers alike.

Early Motown hits were pure **formula**. Gordy softened the blue notes of most contemporary black music, in favor of a more danceable, poppy beat, with **gospel**-influenced singing and clapping. Prime examples of the early approach featured all-female groups like the **Marvelettes** (*Needle in a Haystack*), the **Supremes** (*Baby Love*) and **Martha Reeves and the Vandellas** (*Nowhere to Run*), as well as the all-male **Miracles** (*Tracks of My Tears*) featuring the sophisticated love lyrics of lead singer **Smokey Robinson**. Gordy's "Quality Control Department" scrutinized every beat, playing all recordings through speakers modeled on cheap transistor radios before the final mix.

The Motown organization was an intense, close-knit community: **Marvin Gaye** married Gordy's sister, "Little" **Stevie Wonder** was the baby of the family. It did, however, move with the times, utilizing such innovations as the wah-wah pedal and synthesizer. By the late 1960s its output had acquired a harder sound, crowned by the acid soul productions of Norman Whitfield with the versatile **Temptations**. In 1968 the organization outgrew its premises on Grand Avenue; four years later it abandoned Detroit altogether for LA, to be closer to Hollywood. Befitting the MOR tastes of the 1970s, the top sellers now were the high-society soul of **Diana Ross** and the ballads of the **Commodores**. White artists began to appear on the label: Tom Jones is said to have turned down a contract, though R Dean Taylor (*Indiana Wants Me*) and the less successful Kiki Dee accepted.

The 1970s saw many top artists, dissatisfied with Gordy's constant intervention, leave the label. The crack songwriting team of Holland-Dozier-Holland, responsible for most of the **Four Tops**' hits, stayed in Detroit to produce the seminal **Chairmen of the Board** (*Gimme Just A Little More Time*), along with **Aretha Franklin** and **Jackie Wilson**.

Today Motown is owned by the giant **PolyGram** corporation; artists on the label include Boyz II Men, Queen Latifah and, to this day, Stevie Wonder.

**Fairfield Inn – Auburn Hills**, 1294 Opdyke Rd (☎248/373-2228). Clean new motel on the north edge of the metro area, close to Pontiac Silverdome. ④.

**Fairfield Inn – Metro Airport**, 31119 Flynn Drive, Romulus (☎734/728-2322). The pick of the budget motels near the airport. ④.

**HI-Country Grandma's Home Hostel**, 22330 Bell Rd, New Boston (☎734/753-4901). Friendly home hostel on the outskirts of Dearborn, halfway between Detroit and Ann Arbor. Beds $11 for HI-AYH members; $14 nonmembers. ①.

**Holiday Inn Express**, 34952 Woodward Ave, Birmingham (☎248/646-7300). Recently renovated and reasonably placed for Birmingham and Royal Oak restaurants and bars. ⑦.

**Hotel St Regis**, 3071 W Grand Blvd (☎313/873-3000). Nice old hotel, about four miles from downtown. Besides the Motown Museum, there's little to see in the immediate area, though it is well placed for those with a car. Weekend rates see a price drop of around $35. ⑤.

**Hyatt Regency Dearborn**, Fairlane Town Centre, Dearborn (☎313/593-1234 or 1-800/233-1234). Candy-brown colossus with every imaginable amenity. Not cheap, but lots of special deals. ⑦.

**Marriott Renaissance Center**, downtown (☎313/568-8000 or 1-800/228-3000). A fun place to stay towering over the city by the river – ask for a room on the upper floors. ⑥.

**Ramada Plaza Hotel & Suites**, 430 Ouellette Ave, Windsor, ON (☎519/256-4656 or 1-800/769-0949). Renovated hotel next to the Windsor Tunnel, with a bar, restaurant and indoor pool. ④.

**Red Roof Inn**, 24130 Michigan Ave, Dearborn (☎313/278-9732 or 1-800/843-7663). Clean, budget lodgings near the Henry Ford Museum. ④.

**Sagamore Motor Lodge**, 30776 N Woodward Ave (☎248/549-1600). Have a look at the room first; if it's all right you've got a bargain, close to trendy Royal Oak. ③.

**Shorecrest Motor Inn**, 1316 E Jefferson Ave (☎313/568-3000 or 1-800/992-9231). Friendly, family-run place in lively Rivertown, just off downtown. The dingy exterior masks clean, good-value rooms. ④.

## Downtown

Futuristic glass-box office blocks and a tastefully revamped park overlook the deodor-ant-green **Detroit River**, but for the most part downtown seems rather empty – even in the middle of the day, its streets are quiet and uncrowded. Part of the reason is that most offices and stores are squeezed into the six gleaming towers of the **Renaissance Center**, a virtual city within a city. Zooming up 73 stories from the riverbank, the towers offer a great view of the metropolis from an observation deck ($3). This giant business, convention and retail center, known locally as the RenCen, was one of many complexes developed by **Detroit Renaissance** (a joint public/private sector project) to rejuvenate downtown in the aftermath of the 1967 riot. Seen by some as the savior of the city, the consortium is viewed less favorably by those whose small businesses and homes were compulsorily purchased to make way for its multimillion-dollar projects. In 1996, General Motors bought the RenCen, promising to take down the concrete ramparts that made it so fort-like and alienated from the rest of the city center. Among the landscaping plans are a glass-enclosed "Winter Garden" on the river and a riverfront boardwalk to Belle Isle (see below).

Rare green space comes among the fountains and sculptures of **Hart Plaza**, which rolls down to the river in the shade of the RenCen. It hosts free lunchtime concerts, as well as lively weekend ethnic festivals, all summer long. The US leg of the annual **Montreux–Detroit Jazz Festival** takes place here in early September (☎313/963-7622). The plaza nestles between the towering RenCen and another massive chunk of steel and concrete, the **Cobo Convention Center**. This in turn is next to **Joe Louis Arena** (☎313/983-6606), home of Detroit's beloved Red Wings hockey team, 1997 and 1998 Stanley Cup champions.

Ten long blocks north up Woodward Avenue is the **Theater District**, downtown's prime nightlife spot, currently focused around the magnificently restored Siamese-Byzantine **Fox Theatre**, 2211 Woodward Ave (☎313/983-6611), a huge old movie palace that is the city's top concert and drama venue, and the grand Italian Renaissance **State Theatre** nearby (☎313/961-5450). This area is at the center of the city's massive **Columbia Street** redevelopment project, with new baseball and football stadiums in the works (see "Sport," p.284), alongside microbreweries, coffeehouses and the inevitable themed restaurants, including a *Hard Rock Café*.

Three miles further east, **Belle Isle** public park is a quiet inner-city island retreat with twenty miles of walkways, sports facilities, a marina, and free attractions including an aquarium, a Great Lakes Museum and elaborate gardens. It's also home to the annu-al **Detroit Grand Prix** for Indy cars. Diamond Jack's River Tours (June–Sept; $12; ☎313/843-7676) depart from Hart Plaza downtown, last two hours and loop round Belle Isle; alternatively, take DOT bus #25 and transfer to #12 at MacArthur Bridge.

## The Detroit Cultural Center

Three miles northwest of downtown, next to Wayne State University, the top-class museums of the **Detroit Cultural Center** cluster within easy walking distance of each other, and there's so much to do in them, you can easily spend a whole day here.

One hundred galleries in the colossal **Detroit Institute of Arts**, 5200 Woodward Ave (Wed–Fri 11am–4pm, Sat & Sun 11am–5pm; $4), trace a history of civilization, most notably Chinese, Persian, Egyptian, Greek, Roman, Italian, Dutch and American.

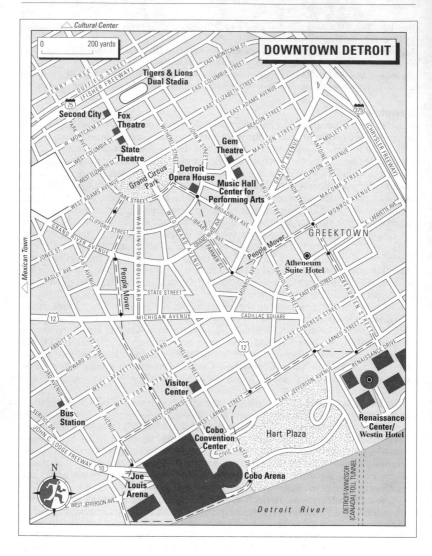

No fewer than 93 Rembrandts, 77 Matisses and 67 Picassos are in its collection, as are masterpieces such as a Van Gogh self-portrait and Joos Van Cleeve's *Adoration of the Magi*; but Diego Rivera's enormous 1932 mural *Detroit Industry* steals the show. Guided tours of what ranks as one of America's most prestigious art museums take place at 1pm with an extra tour at 2.30pm on Sunday, for no additional charge.

The impressive new Charles H. Wright **Museum of African-American History**, 315 E Warren St (daily except Mon 9.30am–5pm; $5), is the largest African-American museum in the world. Its massive core exhibit covers 600 years of history in eight distinct segments, starting with a chilling sculpture of a slave boat, before moving through the Civil War, the Depression, and the respective work of Dr Martin Luther King and Malcolm X before settling on contemporary African-American society. Also in the Cultural Center, the **Detroit Historical Museum**, 5401 Woodward Ave (Wed–Fri 9.30am–5pm, Sat & Sun 10am–5pm; $3), interprets the city's past through its "**Streets of Old Detroit**" display; its most interesting exhibit, not surprisingly, examines the automobile, with an automated display of the "body drop" process on an assembly line.

## The Motown Museum

Unlike cities such as Memphis, Nashville and New Orleans, Detroit is devoid of the bars, clubs and homes of its musical heroes. The golden age of Motown was very much confined to a time and a place, and, disappointingly, only at the **Motown Museum**, 2648 W Grand Blvd (Tues–Sat 10am–5pm, Sun & Mon noon–5pm; $6), can Tamla fans now pay homage to the world's most celebrated record label. The museum, run independently as a nonprofit organization, is housed in the small white-and-blue-clapboard house that served as Motown's recording studio from 1959 to 1972. On the ground floor, Studio A remains just as it was left: battered instruments stand piled up against the nicotine-stained acoustic wall-tiles, and a well-scuffed Steinway piano all but fills the room. Upstairs are the former living quarters of label founder Berry Gordy, while in the adjoining house (once Motown's publishing office) are displayed record sleeves, gold and platinum discs and various pieces of memorabilia. The enthusiastic and knowledgeable staff will quite happily give one person the full tour. The museum was restored and expanded in 1995 and each October, Motown legends contribute to its upkeep by performing at the annual 2648 Grand fundraiser.

## The Henry Ford Museum, Greenfield Village and the Automotive Hall of Fame

The enormous **Henry Ford Museum**, ten miles from downtown at 20900 Oakwood Blvd, Dearborn, pays fulsome tribute to its founder (an inveterate collector of Americana) as a brilliant industrialist and do-gooder. The former is certainly true. The hero of the "second industrial revolution" and inventor of the assembly line didn't succeed by being a philanthropist. His Service Department of 3500 private policemen prompted the *New York Times* in 1928 to call him "an industrialist fascist – the Mussolini of Detroit." To Ford, unions were "the worst things that ever struck the earth," though he was forced to let the UAW into his factories in 1943, after only 34 out of 78,000 workers voted against joining a union. Ford also bowed to the economic necessity of employing blacks, though he banned them from the model communities he built for his white workers. Instead, the company constructed a separate town, which he sardonically named Inkster.

Besides the massive "**The Automobile in American Life**" exhibit, the twelve-acre museum amounts to a giant curiosity shop, holding several planes and trains, rows and rows of domestic inventions, and cabinets full of schoolchild collectibles like dime novels, comics and baseball cards. Real oddities include the chair Lincoln was sitting in and the car Kennedy was riding in when each was shot, and even a test tube holding Edison's last breath. One pertinent item not on view, however, is the Iron Cross that Hitler presented to Ford (a notorious anti-Semite) in 1938.

Ford uprooted the houses of famous Americans from all over the country to relocate them in **Greenfield Village**. Among the 240 buildings, you'll find Ford's own birthplace, the Wright Brothers' cycle shop, Edison's laboratory and Firestone's farm. Costumed staff demonstrate everything from weaving to puncture repairing.

Reached on SMART bus routes #200 and #250, the museum and village are open daily from 9am to 5pm, although the interiors of the village buildings are closed from January 4–March. Tickets are $12.50 for the museum or village, $22 for a two-day combination ticket. For further information, call ☎313/271-1620 or 1-800/835-5237.

Directly next door to the Ford sprawl, the **Automotive Hall of Fame**, 21400 Oakwood Blvd, (summer daily 10am–5pm; rest of year closed Mon; $6) is more interesting than it might at first sound. In paying homage to the innovators and inventors of the global (not just the Detroit) auto industry, the interactive exhibits let visitors see how they would have handled problems encountered by Buick, Honda and the like. It's not just for mechanical types, either – there's a chance to pit your wits against the deal makers who set up General Motors.

New additions include the **Spirit of Ford** at 1151 Village Rd (daily 9am–5pm; $9), which takes a fun, highly interactive look behind the scenes at Ford Motor Company.

## Windsor, Ontario

The riverside cafes of the easygoing Canadian city of **WINDSOR**, due south of Detroit across the river, offer surprisingly pleasant views of their larger neighbor's skyline. Like Detroit's, Windsor's main industry is auto-manufacturing, but it's much smaller and more relaxed, and makes a good place simply to hang out. However, two new downtown **casinos** have added significant traffic to the streets. For those not hooked on slots and blackjack, the most interesting attraction in the town is booze-oriented: the **Hiram Walker plant**, where Canadian Club whisky is distilled, stands just a short stroll from downtown at Riverside and Walker (free tours and samplings Mon–Fri; ☎519/254-5171).

Transit Windsor **buses** (☎519/944-4111) connect downtown Detroit and downtown Windsor for $2.35 each way. Be sure to bring the proper identification for customs and immigration officials. To drive, take the tunnel and pay the $2 toll. The **visitor center** has two locations, across the Ambassador Bridge at 1235 Huron Church Rd, and at 110 Park St E in the city center (both open Sun–Thurs 8.30am–6pm, Fri–Sat 8am–8pm; ☎519/973-1338 or 1-800/265-3633).

## Eating

Detroit's **ethnic** restaurants dish up the best (and least expensive) food in the city. **Greektown**, basically one block of Monroe Avenue between Beaubien and St Antoine streets, is crammed with authentic Greek places, and also contains Trappers Alley, a small mall brimming with good stalls and shops. Less commercial, but offering just as high a standard, are the bakeries, bars and cantinas of **Mexican Town**, five minutes from downtown. **Royal Oak**, ten miles north, has a wide range of vaguely alternative wholefood places, along with bars, record and bookstores, making it the liveliest suburban hangout in this massive sprawling metropolis.

**Alabazam!**, 1515 Ottawa St, Windsor, ON (☎519/252-8264). Trendy Creole restaurant with live jazz, close to the tunnel.

**Atwater Block Brewery**, 237 Joseph Campau St (☎313/393-2073). New, spacious Rivertown brewpub with excellent beer-battered fish, mushrooms, mussels, wings and whatever else the chefs can think of.

**Elwood Grill**, 2100 Woodward Ave (☎313/961-7485). Wonderful Art Deco building that's a popular post-theater stop – it's open to 2am at weekends. Gourmet burgers, sandwiches and main courses from $8 to $15.

**Fishbone's Rhythm Kitchen Cafe**, 400 Monroe Ave, Greektown (☎313/965-4600). Noisy, fun and often packed-out Cajun joint.

**Intermezzo**, 1435 Randolph St (☎313/961-0707). Flash modern Italian downtown place, where the cigar-and-martini set like to dwell. Good food.

**La-Shish**, 12918 Michigan Ave, Dearborn (☎313/584-4477). Brilliant juice bar with good, inexpensive Lebanese dishes.

**New Hellas Cafe**, 583 Monroe St, Greektown (☎313/961-5544). Very authentic, reasonably priced Greektown institution. Also includes the *Top of the Hellas* cafe, serving coffees and desserts in grand, relaxing surroundings.

**Original Pancake House**, 1360 S Woodward Ave, Birmingham (☎248/642-5775). Uninspired decor, but a huge variety of superb crepes, waffles, omelettes and pancakes. Top breakfast spot.

**Pronto!**, 608 S Washington, Royal Oak (☎248/544-0123). Big salads and a huge selection of sandwiches in a soothing pastel space.

**Rattlesnake Club**, 300 River Place, Rivertown (☎313/567-4400). Owned by creative Detroit masterchef Jimmy Schmidt, with a setting to match the exquisite food. Dinner will set you back $15–25 per main course; lunch costs a lot less.

**Woodbridge Tavern**, 289 St Aubin St, Rivertown (☎313/259-0578). Excellent burgers and sandwiches, with 1920s decor and a great outdoor terrace. Also live rock music Thurs–Sun.

**Xochimilco**, 3409 Bagley Ave (☎313/843-0179). The cornerstone restaurant of Detroit's authentic Mexican Town area. Huge portions, great service and superb value. Open to 4am, but if it's full try *El Zocala* across the street.

## Nightlife

There's lots to do late at night in Detroit – the city where the techno beat originated and is still going strong – though if you're unfamiliar with the layout it's best to travel by taxi. In the past few years young whites from the suburbs have started to come back downtown for nights out, particularly to the bars and clubs of the **Theater District**, while the **Rivertown** area is renowned for its chic bistros and funky jazz and blues bars, tucked in among rambling warehouses. The suburbs of upmarket **Birmingham** and youthful **Royal Oak** are good places to hang out, while there are a couple of fun establishments in the blue-collar neighborhood of **Hamtramck**. Way up on the northern fringe, once-deserted **Pontiac** now has a range of well-attended rock venues, dance clubs and lounges. Canadian **Windsor** also has some good nightlife, with an age limit of 19 as opposed to Michigan's 21.

For details of events in Detroit, Ann Arbor and Windsor, pick up the free weekly *Metro Times*.

**Gusoline Alley**, 309 S Center St, Royal Oak (☎248/545-2235). Cramped and dark with a loaded jukebox, this is a legend among Detroit bars. Go early for a seat; the wildly mixed crowd is a people-watcher's dream.

**Lili's 21**, 2390 Jacob St, Hamtramck (☎313/875-6555). Cool and quirky rock venue, five miles from downtown.

**Magic Bag**, 22920 Woodward Ave, Ferndale (☎248/544-3030). About two miles south of Royal Oak, this popular club boasts a huge range of beers, top blues artists and regular roots acts.

**Magic Stick**, 4120 Woodward Ave (☎313/833-9700). Great venue that incorporates a bowling alley and billiards lounge. Next to the Majestic Theater, a venue for big rock shows and huge techno nights.

**Motor**, 3515 Caniff St, Hamtramck (☎313/369-0090). The place to see and be seen, and to dance to techno and funk; occasional live acts.

**Rhinoceros**, 265 Riopelle St, Rivertown (☎313/259-2208). Poppy jazz hangout – a tight squeeze but fun.

**Saint Andrew's Hall/Shelter**, 431 E Congress St (☎313/961-MELT). Cramped downtown club promoting top bands on the alternative circuit. Only holds 800, so get a ticket in advance. Downstairs is the *Shelter* club, with lesser-known touring bands followed by dance music.

**Soup Kitchen Saloon**, 1585 Franklin St, Rivertown (☎313/259-2643). Detroit's premier venue for gutsy, low-down blues. A great old bar but the capacity of just 130 makes it sweaty, smoky and squashed.

**Velvet Lounge**, 29 S Saginaw St, Pontiac (☎248/334-7411). Part of the cigar and martini craze but good swing, mambo and Latin sounds, with free or inexpensive dance lessons on offer.

## Classical music, theater and opera

Most of Detroit's major arts venues are handily grouped together in the northwest sector of downtown. A sweeping staircase and giant chandeliers are part of the splendor of the new **Detroit Opera House**, 1526 Broadway (☎313/237-7464). Close by, the **Music Hall Center for Performing Arts**, 350 Madison Ave (☎313/963-7622), is the primary venue for **dance** in the city and also promotes rock concerts, youth theater and Broadway shows. In the Theater District, the gorgeous **Fox Theatre**, 2211 Woodward Ave (☎313/983-6611), is the biggest draw, hosting the big Broadway shows, while the cozy 450-seater **Gem Theatre**, 58 E Columbia St (☎313/963-9800), and the **Masonic Temple Theatre**, a little north at 500 Temple St (☎313/832-2232), a hall with near-perfect acoustics, are also worth a visit. A little further on toward the Cultural Center, the Detroit Symphony Orchestra performs at the **Orchestra Hall**, 3711 Woodward Ave (☎313/576-5100).

## Sport

Detroit is one of the few cities with franchises competing at the highest level in all four major team sports, and the toast of the local fans are the 1997 and 1998 **hockey** champions Red Wings, who entertain at the downtown Joe Louis Arena (☎313/983-6606). Tickets are virtually impossible to get, but plenty of bars put on promotions for games. **Baseball**'s Tigers (☎313/962-4000) said their goodbyes to venerable Tiger Stadium at Michigan and Trumbull, to move east to snazzy **Comerica Park** for the 2000 season. In a couple years, they'll be joined by the **football**-playing Lions (☎248/335-4131), who will move into a $225-million domed venue next door. In the meantime, the Lions and **basketball**'s Pistons (☎248/377-0100) are based 25 miles north in the Pontiac Silverdome and Palace of Auburn Hills.

# Out from Detroit: Ann Arbor

Although its population just tops 100,000, **ANN ARBOR**, 45 minutes' drive west of Detroit along I-94, offers a greater choice of restaurants, live music venues and cultural activities than most towns ten times its size. The **University of Michigan** has shaped the economy and character of the town ever since it was moved here from Detroit in 1837, providing the city with a very conspicuous radical edge.

Much the best thing to do in Ann Arbor is to stroll round downtown and the campus, which meet at South State and Liberty streets. Downtown's twelve blocks of brightly painted shops and sidewalk cafes offer all you would expect from a college town, with over forty bookshops and more than a dozen record stores. Don't miss the huge flagship store of Border's Books at 612 E Liberty St (☎734/663-7248), or Encore Recordings, 417 E Liberty St (☎313/994-8031).

Though the huge university campus doesn't look particularly appealing, it does emanate a sense of excitement especially around the central meeting place of the **Diag**. Worth a look are the **Museum of Natural History**, 1109 Geddes Ave (Mon–Sat 9am–5pm, Sun noon–5pm; free), packed with huge dinosaur skeletons, rare Native American artifacts and a planetarium, and the small but eclectic **Museum of Art**, 525 S State St (Tues–Sat 10am–4pm, Thurs until 9pm, Sun noon–5pm; free).

## Practicalities

Frequent Greyhound services to both Detroit and Chicago stop at 116 W Huron St; Amtrak is on the north edge of downtown at 325 Depot St. The **visitor center** is at 120 W Huron St (Mon–Fri 9am–5pm; ☎734/995-7281).

Although most Ann Arbor **motels** target their rates at conventioneers and academics, the *Lamp Post Inn*, 2424 Stadium Blvd (☎734/971-8000; ②), is a good-value motel about a mile from campus. The choice place to stay is the *Campus Inn*, right downtown at 615 E Huron St (☎734/769-2200 or 1-800/666-8693; ⑦). There are also several good **B&Bs**, like the unusual *Artful Lodger* on the edge of the university campus at 1547

Washtenaw Ave (☎734/769-0653; ④), decorated with art, theater and music memorabilia. The modern downtown *YMCA*, 350 S Fifth Ave (☎734/663-0536; ②), is open to both sexes. The nearest **campground** is ten miles east, at the *KOA*, 6680 Bunton Rd, in blue-collar Ypsilanti.

**Restaurants** worth trying include the good-value Indian *Raja Rani*, 400 S Division St (☎734/995-1545), and the wholefood *Seva*, 314 E Liberty Ave (☎734/662-1111). *Jerusalem Garden*, 307 S Fifth St (☎734/995-5060), serves the best falafel in town, while *Zingerman's*, 422 Detroit St (☎734/663-DELI), is an excellent if expensive deli. A pair of popular **brewpubs** – the *Arbor Brewing Co*, 114 E Washington St (☎734/213-1393), and the *Grizzly Peak Brewing Co*, 120 W Washington St (☎734/741-7325) – lie within a couple of blocks of each other.

Ann Arbor's **live music** scene has enjoyed a nationwide reputation ever since the Stooges, MC5 and Bob Seger made their names here; and, unlike many college towns, the place doesn't go to sleep during the summer. For news of gigs, grab a copy of *Current*, a free monthly. Likely venues include the jazzy *Bird of Paradise*, 207 S Ashley Ave (☎734/662-8310), and the often-crowded *Del Rio*, 122 W Washington Ave (☎734/761-2530), which serves good Mexican food and hosts free Sunday jazz sessions. The *Blind Pig*, 208 S First St (☎734/996-8555), is the best place to watch live rock, alternative and blues while *The Ark*, 316 S Main St (☎734/761-1451), is a nationally significant venue for folk, acoustic and roots music. From time to time there are also live bands at the beautiful Art Deco *Michigan Theater*, 603 E Liberty St (☎734/668-8480), otherwise a great place to watch movies on the cheap.

**Festivals** are a key part of Ann Arbor life. The orchestral May Festival kicks off activities, followed by the Frog Island Festival in Ypsilanti, that focuses on jazz and world music in mid-June. The following month sees the hectic Street Art Fair with hundreds of stalls, while early September sees the recently revived Ann Arbor Blues and Jazz Festival.

# The rest of the Lower Peninsula

Between Ann Arbor and the Lake Michigan coast there's not a whole lot worth stopping for, though Kellogg's new **Cereal City USA**, 171 W Michigan Ave (☎616/962-6230), in Battle Creek is a fun diversion that traces the history of cereal – and of course, magnate Kellogg's impact on it (summer Mon–Fri 9.30am–5pm, Sat 9.30am–6pm, Sun 11am–5pm; call for winter hours; $6.50). Further west, **St Joseph** is just the first of many small ports on the 350-mile trip north along Lake Michigan's eastern shore, the northwest reaches of the peninsula attract sportspeople and tourists from all over the Midwest. Within striking distance of **Traverse City** are the beautiful **Sleeping Bear Dunes** and the charming towns of **Charlevoix** and **Petoskey**. At the northern tip, a revitalized **Mackinaw City** is the departure point for the state's major tour-bus attraction, old-world **Mackinac Island**.

## Along Lake Michigan

Less than thirty miles north of Indiana, **ST JOSEPH** marks the start of "Harbor Country" – a string of small towns offering good swimming, boating and fishing opportunities. St Joseph's neat downtown perches on a high bluff, from which steep steps lead down to sandy Silver Beach, where each of the two parallel piers has its own lighthouse. When not swimming, pass the time watching the yachts go by while eating great **food** at *Clementine's Too* (☎616/983-0990), 1235 Broad St, or at a sidewalk table at *Schu's*, 501 Pleasant St (☎616/983-7248). **Places to stay** include the classy lakeside *Boulevard Suite Hotel*, 521 Lake Blvd (☎616/983-6600; ⑥), where all the rooms are suites, and the good-value *Best Western Golden Link*, two miles from downtown at 2723 Niles Ave (☎616/983-6321; ③). For general information on the area, call into the **visitor center** just off I-94 exit 29 (☎616/925-6301).

Fifty miles north, **HOLLAND** was settled in 1847 by Dutch religious dissidents. Today's residents lose no opportunity to let visitors know of their roots: tens of thousands of tulips brighten the town in early summer, while the Netherlands museum, a Dutch village, a clog factory and the inevitable windmill all attract tourist dollars. A further twenty miles up the shoreline, **GRAND HAVEN** boasts one of the largest and best sandy beaches on the Great Lakes, seen on a leisurely stroll along the one-and-a-half-mile boardwalk (for the most part a concrete path). At the top of Dewey Hill stands a huge, electronically controlled musical fountain.

Just under one hundred miles further north, a string of pleasant small villages starts with **LUDINGTON**, where **Ludington State Park**, eight miles north on Hwy-116, offers great hiking and sightseeing amid sweeping sand dunes and virgin pine forests; admission is $4 per car and **camping** in some beautiful sites costs $15 a night. From downtown, the **Lake Michigan Car Ferry** departs for Manitowoc, Wisconsin (☎231/845-5555 or 1-800/841-4243; $38 per adult, $46 per car, not including driver) – a comparative bargain when you weigh up the cost of braving the cross-Chicago traffic. The best place to **stay overnight** is *Snyder's Shoreline Inn*, 903 W Ludington Ave (☎231/845-1261 or 1-800/843-2177; ④), the only downtown property with uninterrupted views of the lakeshore. *House of Flavors*, 402 W Ludington Ave (☎231/845-5785), is a chrome-heavy diner serving breakfasts, burgers and a huge range of ice cream. *Scotty's*, 5910 E Ludington Ave (☎231/843-4033), is reliable for lunch and does steaks and seafood in the evenings. The **visitor center** is on the east side of town at 5827 US-10 (☎231/845-0324 or 1-800/542-4600).

Surrounded by forest, **MANISTEE**, 32 miles north, boasts an attractive Victorian downtown and a mile-long **boardwalk** that runs alongside the Manistee River onto Lake Michigan. One of several pretty lakeside areas is **Douglas Park** – with a good sandy beach, small marina and picnic area – next to the *Lake Shore Motel*, 101 S Lakeshore Drive (☎231/723-2667; ⑤). To stay downtown, try the *Maples B&B*, 435 Fifth St (☎231/723-2904; ③). The **Chamber of Commerce** is at 11 Cypress St (Mon–Fri 8am–5.30pm; ☎231/723-2575).

A further thirty miles north, tiny **FRANKFORT** nestles under bluffs overlooking Lake Michigan. With a grassy park and a small beach at either end of its main street, it not only makes a charming stop for lunch or a picnic, but also provides cheaper **accommodation** than the Leelanau Peninsula towns just to the north. The *Harbor Lights Motel and Condos*, 15 Second St (☎231/352-9614; ④), stands right on the beach, while the *Still Grinning Inn*, 670 Crystal Ave (☎231/352-7669; ②), provides great value B&B. Along the main drag, the *Frankfort Deli*, 327 Main St (☎231/352-3354), has good sandwiches; directly across the street, the *Coho Cafe* (☎231/352-6053) serves up well-priced modern food. The **visitor center** (Mon–Fri 9am–noon & 1–5pm; ☎231/352-7251) is also on Main Street, opposite the park.

## The Leelanau Peninsula

The southwestern edge of the heavily wooded **Leelanau Peninsula**, beyond the small port of **Frankfort**, 61 miles north of Ludington, is taken up by the **Sleeping Bear Dunes National Lakeshore**, a constantly resculpted area of towering dunes and precipitous 400ft drops. The area was named by the Chippewa, who saw the mist-shrouded North and South Manitou islands as the graves of two drowned bear cubs, and the massive mainland dune, covered with dark trees, as their grieving mother. Fierce winds off Lake Michigan cause the dunes to edge inland, burying trees that reappear years later stripped of foliage, while the continual attack of high water undercuts the massive sand banks, occasionally sending massive chunks into the lake. Stunning overlooks can be had along the hilly, nine-mile loop of the **Pierce Stocking Scenic Drive**, off Hwy-109; you can also clamber up the strenuous but enjoyable **Dune Climb**, four miles further north on Hwy-109 (best done barefoot, as shoes soon fill with sand).

The **visitor center** (☎231/326-5134), at the junction of highways 22 and 109, provides details on trails, campgrounds and beaches. Nearby, the village of **GLEN ARBOR**, dotted with some interesting galleries, is the closest community to the dunes. Decent places to **eat** here include *Le Bear*, 5707 Lake St (☎231/334-4640), where affordable lunches and costly seafood dinners are served on a waterfront deck, and *Art's Bar*, 6487 Western Ave (☎231/334-3754), a pleasant tavern dishing up great hamburgers and inexpensive fried fish.

**LELAND**, fifteen miles north, makes an even better base. Its harbor, crammed with expensive launches, holds a quaint collection of well-weathered sheds, known as **Fishtown**, where the day's catch used to be hauled in for gutting and smoking; most are now touristy knickknack shops. *The Cove*, at 111 River St (☎231/256-9834), serves up tasty Great Lakes fish dishes and a superb key lime pie. **Ferries** from Leland (☎231/256-9061; $20 round-trip) go to the uninhabited North and South Manitou islands. **NORTHPORT**, on the tip of the peninsula, is another relaxing fishing village, where the *Beech Tree*, 202 Waukazoo St (☎231/386-5200), an art gallery/cafe with outdoor seating, does good trade in espresso, sandwiches and chocolate desserts. Eleven miles south on the peninsula's east coast, **SUTTONS BAY** may not be as pretty but its main artery, St Joseph Avenue, has some of the area's best places to eat: *Hatties*, at no. 111 (☎231/271-6222), serves fine meals along the lines of chicken with cherry sauce and Thai scallops; *Cafe Bliss*, at no. 420 (☎231/271-5000), specializes in vegetarian and Native American cuisine with entrees around $12; and the *Hose House Deli*, in a restored 1913 fire station at no. 303 (☎231/271-6303), serves large good-value sandwiches and coffee.

Nowhere on the peninsula is **accommodation** inexpensive. The best option is the *Leelanau Country Inn*, midway between Glen Arbor and Leland at 149 East Harbor Hwy, Maple City (☎231/228-5060; ③), a good-value Victorian B&B serving large breakfasts.

## Traverse City

Smooth beaches and striking bay views help make lively **TRAVERSE CITY**, 242 miles northwest of Detroit, the favorite in-state resort for Michigan natives. A town of just over 15,000 year-round residents, it was saved from the stagnation that overtook many north Michigan communities when their lumber mills closed down, as the stripped fields proved to be ideal for fruit-growing. Today, the area's claim to be "**Cherry Capital of the World**" is no idle boast: thousands of acres of cherry orchards envelop the town, their wispy, pink blossoms bringing a delicate beauty each May. The annual **National Cherry Festival** is held during the first full week in July. In addition to parades, fireworks and concerts, there's a chance to sample every imaginable cherry product; Coca-Cola chose the event to launch its cherry flavor in the 1980s.

Traverse City's neat **downtown** rests along the bottom of the west arm of **Grand Traverse Bay**, below the Old Mission Peninsula. This slender seventeen-mile strip of land, which divides the bay into two inlets, makes for a pleasant short driving tour; narrow roads slice through miles of cherry orchards and vineyards, with tremendous simultaneous views of the bay on either side. Five sandy public beaches and a small harbor can be found around the town itself. Various companies offer boat, windsurfer, jet ski and mountain bike rental (the surrounding countryside is excellent for cycling), and there are no fewer than 36 **golf courses** – some of them among the most beautiful in the country – in the immediate area.

## Practicalities

Greyhound stops near downtown at 3233 Cass Rd. The **visitor center**, downtown at 101 Grandview Parkway (summer Mon–Fri 9am–7pm, Sat 9am–6pm, Sun noon–4pm; rest of year Mon–Fri 9am–5pm, weekends vary; ☎231/947-1120 or 1-800/TRAVERS), can help with finding **accommodation**, though there's a dearth of central budget lodgings in summer. The attractive little *Bay Shore Motel*, near downtown at 833 E Front St (☎231/935-4400; ⑥), has a private beach and nice rooms. The remodeled and very central *Park Place Hotel*, 300 E State St (☎231/946-5000 or 1-800/748-0133; ⑥), is reliable, as are the well-maintained *Days Inn & Suites*, 420 Munson Ave (☎231/941-0208; ⑤), and the basic but clean *Sierra Motel*, 230 Munson Ave (☎231/946-7720; ④), both a couple of miles southeast. There's **camping** at Traverse City State Park, just outside town at 1132 US-31 N (☎231/922-5270).

Traverse City brochures may tout its exclusive country clubs, but more affordable **places to eat** are easy to find. Big breakfasts with home-baked bread are served at *Mabel's*, 472 Munson Ave (☎231/947-0252), while *Mode's Bum Steer*, 125 E State St (☎231/947-9832), is Traverse's premier rib joint. The best bet for a meal, particularly in the evening, is to drive north onto the Mission Peninsula where the *Boathouse*, 14039 Peninsula Drive (☎231/223-4030), dishes up fresh seafood, pasta and vegetarian food right by the lake. Further up, on the peninsula's central spine road, the popular *Old Mission Tavern*, 17015 Center Rd (☎231/223-7280), has classic European dishes and lots of local art.

The *U & I Lounge*, 214 E Front St (☎231/946-8932), is the best **bar** in town; besides the drink it serves up great gyros plus burgers and salads. *Union Street Station*, 117 S Union St (☎231/941-1930), has pool tables and **live music** of all sorts most nights. *Larry's Place* at the *Bay Winds*, 1265 US-31 N (☎231/929-1044), is a hectic beach bar a couple of miles north that's popular with students and great fun – even if there is a limit to the number of Jimmy Buffet songs you can stomach in one night.

# North of Traverse City

Scenic Hwy-31 skims along Lake Michigan and through **Charlevoix** and other pretty lakeside towns on its way north from Traverse City. The northern tip of the peninsula is occupied by the much improved **Mackinaw City**, where ferries take excursionists to much-hyped **Mackinac Island** – roadside hoardings advertise its attractions for a good fifty miles before you arrive.

## Charlevoix, Petoskey and Harbor Springs

**CHARLEVOIX** boasts a positively idyllic setting, fronting onto three separate lakes: Michigan, Charlevoix and the beautiful, bowl-shaped Round Lake. Petunia-lined **Bridge Street**, the two-block downtown, looks over a picturesque, almost landlocked **harbor** on Round Lake, hemmed in on other sides by terraced ridges. It's an undeniably beautiful place but in recent years has become just that bit too fancy. Various companies offer boat trips, including cruises on a schooner ($25–40 for 2hrs) – call in at the **visitor center**, 408 E Bridge St (☎231/547-2101 or 1-800/367-8557), for details. There are two sandy beaches on the Michigan shoreline – great places to watch the sunset.

Lakeside **hotels**, such as the turreted *Weathervane Terrace*, 111 Pine River Lane (☎231/547-9955; ⑦), may charge more than $300 on peak weekends, though the *Charleboyne Motel*, at US-31 and Boyne City Road a mile north of town (☎231/547-9340; ③), is small, basic and clean. One of the best value **B&Bs** is the *MacDougall House*, 109 Petoskey Ave (☎231/547-5788; ④) offering private bathrooms and huge breakfasts. *Whitney's Oyster Bar*, 305 Bridge St (☎231/547-0818) serves fresh seafood and snacks until 2am with lots of beers and upstairs seating.

Bigger and busier **PETOSKEY**, sixteen miles north along US-31, high above Lake Michigan, feels more like a real town, with its grand Victorian houses encircling the nicely restored **Gaslight District** downtown. Ernest Hemingway spent many of his teenage summers here – his novel *The Torrents of Spring* alludes to several local landmarks. The most central and welcoming hotel is the venerable *Perry's Hotel*, Bay and Lewis streets (☎231/347-4000 or 1-800/456-1917; ⑤); its *Noggin Room Pub* has good snacks and pizza. The award-winning *Montgomery Place B&B*, 618 E Lake St (☎231/347-1338; ⑥), is a big Victorian house serving superb full breakfasts. Budget lodging is sometimes available in the clean dorms at North Central Michigan College, 1515 Howard St (☎231/348-6611; ①). One of Hemingway's favorite hangouts was *Jesperson's*, 312 Howard St (☎231/347-3601), which still does great pies and sandwiches. The locally popular *Mitchell Street Pub*, 426 E Mitchell St (☎231/347-1801), also offers decent snacks. The town's helpful **visitor center** is located at 401 E Mitchell St (Mon–Fri 8am–4pm; ☎1-800/845-2828).

Another twelve miles along Hwy-119, **HARBOR SPRINGS** is a favorite with the Midwestern elite. Its charming main street and small shaded beach with adjacent park are certainly captivating, but the sheer ostentation puts many off this "Cornbelt Riviera" resort. The comfy *Harbor Springs Cottage Inn*, at Bay and Zoll streets (☎231/526-5431; ⑤), has the only reasonably affordable rooms in town.

## Mackinaw City

Forty miles northeast of Petoskey, **MACKINAW CITY** has long enjoyed a steady tourist trade as the major embarkation point for Mackinac Island (the other is the sleepier town of **St Ignace** just across the bridge).

Until just a few years ago, Mackinaw City was little more than a bland colony of cheap motels and fudge shops touting for trade from those who couldn't get a place to stay on the island. Part of the reason for this was that the city used to be a terminus for freight trains; the oil and other detritus they dumped put the city's sewer system under strain and for a decade or so there was a moratorium on new developments. The situation has been sorted, the streets have been landscaped with trees that are lit up at night, and visitors now flock to the new **Mackinaw Crossings** on South Huron Street. This mall-cum-entertainment zone has given the town a lift, offering vacationers several dozen niche retail stores, a food court, a multiscreen cinema and an amphitheater that hosts nightly live acts and a laser show at 10pm during the summer.

Several mid-priced **motels** have been newly built alongside the shore, among them the *Ramada Limited Waterfront*, 723 S Huron St (☎231/436-5055; ⑤) and the *Best Western Dockside Waterfront* (☎231/436-5001; ④–⑧). A couple blocks north at 111 Langlade St, the *Welcome Inn* (☎231/436-5525; ③) offers simple, clean rooms for a much better rate. A good **meal** can be had outdoors at the *Depot* (☎231/436-7060), a refurbished rail station in the Courtyards of Mackinaw City; not only will you get tasty grill food and seafood dips, but you'll have a good view of the entertainment in the adjacent amphitheater.

## Mackinac Island

Viewed from an approaching boat, the tree-blanketed rocky limestone outcrop of **MACKINAC ISLAND** (pronounced "Mackinaw"), suddenly thrusting out from the swirling waters, is an unforgettable sight. As you near the harbor, large Victorian houses come into view, dappling the hillsides with white and pastel. The most conspicuous is the imposing $250-plus-a-night *Grand Hotel* (☎906/847-3331; ⑨), where just to enter the foyer costs $5. On disembarking, your attention is grabbed by the rows of horses and buggies (all motorized transportation is banned from the island, except for emergency vehicles) and the omnipresent smell of fresh manure. Also ubiquitous on the island is **fudge**, relentlessly marketed as a Mackinac "delicacy."

Mackinac's crowded Main Street and the contrived nostalgia can get irritating, but the island is still worth visiting, not least for the ferry ride over and the chance to cycle along the hilly backroads. Underneath the tourist trimmings is a rich history. French priests established a mission to the Huron Indians here during the winter of 1670–71, and the French army built a fort in 1715 but within fifty years had lost control of the island to the British. Since independence Mackinac has been a base for John Jacob Astor's American Fur Company, a fishing port, and a jail for Confederate officers during the Civil War. The government acknowledged its beauty by designating it as the country's second national park, two years after Yellowstone in 1875, though management was handed over to the state of Michigan twenty years later. To get a feel for the history, hike or cycle up to the whitewashed stone **Fort Mackinac**, a US Army outpost until 1890. Its ramparts afford a great view of the village and lake below, though admission is a steep $7.25 (May to mid-Oct 9.30am–6.30pm).

### Practicalities

Arnold Transit (☎906/847-3351 or 1-800/542-8528; $13.50; $5.50 for bikes) is the only one of the three ferry companies to offer a high-speed catamaran crossing from Mackinaw City to the island.

Though the average **room** on Mackinac costs more than $130 per night – the least costly hotel is *Murray's* (☎906/847-3360 or 1-800/462-2546; ⑤), which serves a large continental breakfast buffet – unpretentious B&Bs such as the *Bogan Lane Inn* (☎906/847-3439; ③) and the secluded *Small Point* (☎906/847-3758; ④) are more affordable. *Haan's 1830 Inn* (☎906/847-6244; ⑥) is a big Greek Revival home close by the harbor. The **information kiosk** on Main Street (☎906/847-3783) provides full details of accommodation, horseback rides and bike rental.

# The Upper Peninsula

From the map, it would seem logical for Michigan's **Upper Peninsula**, separated from the rest of the state by the **Mackinac Straits**, to be part of Wisconsin. However, when Michigan entered the Union in 1837 (eleven years before Wisconsin), its legislators, keen to tap the peninsula's huge mineral wealth, incorporated it into their new state.

Before then the UP, as it's commonly known, figured prominently in French plans to create an empire in North America. Missionaries such as Father Jacques Marquette made peace with the native people and established settlements like the port of Sault Ste Marie in 1688. The French hoped to press further south, but before they could get much past Detroit, the British inflicted a severe military defeat in 1763.

Vast, lonesome and wild, the Upper Peninsula is full of stunning landmarks, exemplified by the **Pictured Rocks National Lakeshore**. Most of the eastern section is marked by low-lying, sometimes swampy land in between softly undulating limestone hills. The northwest corner is the most desolate, especially the rough and broken **Keewanaw Peninsula**, and **Isle Royale National Park** fifty miles offshore. The UP's only real city is **Marquette**, a college town with a quiet buzz about it that makes a good base from which to explore the UP's rugged terrain. Until 1957 you could only get to the UP from lower Michigan by ferry. Today, the five-mile **Mackinac Bridge** ($1.50 toll), lit up beautifully at night, stretches elegantly across the bottleneck Straits of Mackinac, with lakes Superior and Huron to either side.

## Sault Ste Marie

Perched at the northeast corner of the UP, 340 miles from Detroit, **SAULT STE MARIE** (known locally as *The Soo*) lies across St Mary's Rapids from the Canadian town bearing the same name. It's one of the oldest settlements in the US, not that you'd guess that from its bedraggled, Fifties-looking downtown and the industrial sprawl of the waterfront. The Soo owes most of its trade and industry to the St Mary's Locks, the only water connection between Superior and the other Great Lakes, built in 1855 and later expanded to take oceangoing vessels. Four giant reservoirs raise upbound boats 21 feet to the level of Lake Superior. To see this impressive operation, which accounts for more tonnage than the Suez and Panama canals combined, take one of the **Soo Locks boat tours** ($15; ☎906/632-6301) from Dock #1 or Dock #2 on East Portage Avenue, or watch for free from the visitor center (daily 7am–11pm).

Despite efforts to increase its tourist trade, the Soo is not a place where you'd want to spend much time, though the *Crestview Thrifty Inn*, 1200 Ashmun St (☎906/635-5213; ④), has clean, comfortable rooms, and the *Bambi Motel*, further along at no. 1801 (☎906/632-7881; ③), has one of the most garish signs you'll ever clap eyes on. *Antler's*, 804 E Portage Ave (☎906/632-3571), looks like a dive bar but is in fact an historic **pub**, where you can also get reasonable steaks and fish.

## Paradise

Native Americans who lived in this area sixty miles west and north of the Soo called it *Tahquamenon* (Marsh of the Blueberries). Now it's called **PARADISE**, and in summer this elongated lakeside village can live up to its name, cut as it is out of thick, dark green forests and surrounded by small, reed-cluttered ultramarine lakes. Life is slow and easy here, but the choppy waters of Superior deny absolute calm to the beach. In winter temperatures drop to -40°F and snowmobiles are the usual mode of transportation. Ten miles west on Hwy-123, one of the most popular spots on the UP for hiking, boating and camping is the gorgeous **Tahquamenon Falls State Park** (daily; $3 per car), where waters, dyed a translucent brown by tannic acid, spill over two sets of cataracts.

Whitefish Road winds eleven miles north of town to where shingly **Whitefish Point** nudges into the harsh waters of Lake Superior. Raging northwesterly winds building up over almost four hundred miles of open lake have contributed to more than five hundred shipwrecks along the eighty-mile stretch of lakeshore to Munising, a story told by the **Great Lakes Shipwreck Historical Museum** (mid-May to mid-Oct daily 10am–6pm; $7) with the help of subtle lighting and atmospheric background music. It's not all ancient history; the cargo ship *Edmund Fitzgerald* foundered in 96mph gusts on November 10, 1975, with the loss of its 29-strong crew.

*Curley's Motel & Cabins* (☎906/492-3445; ③) is your best bet for **accommodation**: six-person cabins cost under $100, and there's a nice beach on site – plus the *Yukon Inn*, full of stuffed trophies, across the road. A clean budget option is the *Vagabond Motel* (☎906/492-3477; ②), while you can pitch a tent at the *Superior Campground* (☎906/492-3249), a mile south of town near *The Penguin*, a restaurant popular for its whitefish.

## Pictured Rocks National Lakeshore

The 42 miles between the attractive fishing villages of **Grand Marais** and **Munising** form the **Pictured Rocks National Lakeshore**, a splendid array of multicolored cliffs, rolling dunes and secluded sandy beaches. Rain, wind, ice and sun have carved and gouged arches, columns and caves into the face of the lakeshore, all stained different hues. Hiking trails run along the clifftops and the partially unpaved Hwy-58 takes you close to the water, but the best way to see the cliffs is by **boat**. Pictured Rocks Cruises offers a three-hour narrated tour that leaves from the left of the City Pier in Munising (July & Aug 5–7 trips daily; June, Sept & early Oct 2 trips daily; $22; ☎906/387-2379); less than a mile further along the lake at 1204 Commercial St, Shipwreck Tours gives two-hour narrated cruises in a glass-bottom boat with surprisingly clear views of three shipwrecks – one intact (June to early Oct 2–3 trips daily; $20; ☎906/387-4477). Those in a hurry can get a glimpse by visiting the **Miners Castle Overlook**, just east of Munising, or **Munising Falls**, near the village's well-posted **visitor center** (☎906/387-2138). In Munising, *Scotty's Motel*, 415 Cedar St (☎906/387-2449; ③), and the *Munising Motel*, 332 E Onota St (☎906/387-3187; ④), are comfortable enough places to stay.

## Marquette

Forty miles west of Munising lies the unofficial capital of the UP, the bustling college town of **MARQUETTE**, also the center of the area's massive ore industry.

The helpful **state welcome center** (summer daily 9am–6pm, rest of year daily 9am–5pm; ☎906/249-9066), 2201 US-41 S just south of town, has vouchers for local hotel discounts and lots of information about Marquette's sights, premier among which is rugged **Presque Isle Park**, north of town on Lakeshore Boulevard, almost completely surrounded by Lake Superior and with stunning views of the lake. Back at East Ridge and Lakeshore, the **Marquette Maritime Museum** (late May–Sept daily 10am–5pm; $3) has exhibits on the fishing and freighting industries, as well as a video about the fabled Superior wrecking of the *Edmund Fitzgerald*. The area's most curious sight, however, is the **Superior Dome**, on Northern Michigan University's campus at 1401 Presque Isle Ave, the largest wooden dome in the world.

**Accommodations** in Marquette are abundant and generally inexpensive. Cheap motels cluster west of town on US-41, but there are better, equally affordable options downtown. The *Village Inn* at 1301 N Third St (☎906/225-5000; ③/④), offers high-quality, good-value rooms (some with kitchen), but by far the nicest place to stay is the grand **Landmark Inn** at 230 N Front St (☎906/228-2580; ⑤/⑥), with rooms overlooking the lake. You can camp at the *Tourist Park Campground* (☎906/228-0465) on Sugarloaf Avenue.

Downtown, *JJ's Shamrock,* 113 S Front St (☎906/226-6734), serves no-nonsense bar food along with occasional live music; for a more formal dining experience, locals favor the *Northwoods Supper Club* (☎906/228-4343), just west of town off US-41, with a meat-and-potatoes menu in a rustic setting. Popular drinkspots include *Remie's Bar*, 111 Third St (☎906/226-9133), with a rowdy local crowd and live music on Wednesdays.

# The Keewanaw Peninsula

Beyond Marquette, the land becomes progressively more rough-hewn, culminating in the **Keewanaw Peninsula**, which juts like a dorsal fin eighty miles out into Lake Superior. Encircled by a dramatic shoreline and potted with crags and precipices, it's a great place for a short driving tour, with roads winding through forests, past old copper workings and up and down steep hills.

Halfway up the peninsula in the small college town of **HOUGHTON** on Lake Portage, the *College Motel* at 1308 College Ave next to campus (☎906/482-2202; ②) is good value; the luxury option is the 100-year-old *Charleston House Inn B&B*, 918 College Ave (☎906/482-7790; ⑦), downtown by the water. The *Suomi Home Bakery and Restaurant* (☎906/482-3220), under the covered street downtown, serves cheap pasties and Finnish food. At the northern tip of Keewanaw, best reached along Hwy-26 (the Brockway Mountain Drive) from Eagle River, handsome little **COPPER HARBOR** was once so rich in minerals that early miners could pick up chunks of pure copper from the lakeshore. Today you can go on an underground tour at the **Delaware Mine** (☎906/289-4688), ten miles west on US-41. Budget **accommodation** is available at the *Norland Motel* (☎906/289-4815; ②), two miles east on US-41, next to Fort Wilkins State Park.

## Isle Royale National Park

Much closer to Canada than the US, the 45-mile sliver of **ISLE ROYALE NATIONAL PARK**, fifty miles out in Lake Superior, is in a double sense as far as you can get in Michigan from Detroit: all cars are banned and, instead of freeways, 166 miles of hiking trails lead past windswept trees, swampy lakes and grazing moose. The park is open from mid-May until the end of September, but besides other outdoors types the only traces of human life you're likely to see are ancient mineworks (thought to be two millennia old), shacks left behind by commercial fishermen in the 1940s, and a few lighthouses and park buildings. Trekking, canoeing, fishing and scuba-diving among shipwrecks are the principal leisure activities. Camping is free, but visit the **park headquarters** at 800 E Lakeshore Drive (☎906/482-0984) in Houghton (see opposite) before you leave the mainland, for advice on water purity, mosquitoes and temperatures that can drop well below freezing even in summer. You can also stay in a self-catering cottage or a more expensive lodge room (including all meals) at the *Rock Harbor Lodge* (PO Box 605, Houghton, MI 49931; ☎906/337-4993, Oct–April ☎270/773-2191; ⑥), where they rent canoes and motorboats for $22 and $48 per day, respectively, and offer cruises for $11.

**Ferries** leave from Copper Harbor ($40 one-way; ☎906/289-4437), Houghton ($47 one-way; ☎906/482-0984) and Grand Portage, Minnesota ($32–52 one-way; ☎715/392-5551). If there are enough in your party, it may be just as economical to charter a **plane** from *Isle Royale Seaplane Service* in Houghton (☎906/482-8850).

# INDIANA

Thanks to an early nineteenth-century influx of northward migrants, much of **INDIANA** still displays vestiges of the easygoing South. Among these early settlers was the family of Abraham Lincoln, who set up home near the present village of Santa Claus in 1816 and stayed for fourteen years before moving to Illinois. Unlike the abolitionist Lincolns, many brought slaves to this new territory; Indiana allowed a system of "voluntary servitude" to operate right up to 1843. At the outbreak of the Civil War, thousands of ex-Southerners rioted against the draft, in part expressing a concern that Indiana was every bit as subservient to the northeast as Deep South slaves were to their masters. However, since the 1870s, industrialization has integrated Indiana into the regional economy.

Despite some beautiful dunes and beaches, the most lasting memories provided by Indiana's fifty-mile **lakeshore** (by far the shortest of the Great Lake states) are of the grimy steel mills and poverty-stricken neighborhoods of towns like **Gary** and **East Chicago**. Elsewhere, the state holds only a few landmarks of interest to travelers. In northern Indiana, the area in and around **Elkhart** and **Goshen** is among the nation's largest **Amish settlements**. The central plains are characterized by small market towns, except for the sprawling capital, **Indianapolis**, which has brightened up its downtown in recent years to the point that it's not a bad stopover. Hilly southern Indiana, at its most appealing in the fall, is a welcome contrast to the central cornbelt, boasting several quaint towns such as **Vincennes**, **Madison** and **Corydon**. Thriving **Columbus** exhibits a great array of contemporary architecture for such a small city, and former resort town **West Baden Springs** is restoring the elegant hotel that made it famous.

Dozens of explanations have been offered as to why Indianans are called "Hoosiers"; the most believable is that its use spread from the days of the Ohio Falls Canal construction in the 1820s, when a contractor, Samuel Hoosier, gave employment preference to those living on the Indiana side of the Ohio River.

## Getting around Indiana

Nine different interstates – seven of them slicing through Indianapolis – provide boring but fast ways of traversing Indiana. Greyhound runs frequent services, particularly on I-65 between Chicago and Louisville and I-70 between the east and St Louis. **Indianapolis, Michigan City** and **South Bend** are the major stops on the three different Amtrak routes that cut through the state. Flights from most Midwestern and Eastern cities come in at **Indianapolis International Airport**.

# Northern Indiana

Lying just off I-80/90, halfway along the northern fringe of Indiana, **SOUTH BEND** briefly rivaled Detroit as the country's leading car manufacturer during the early 1920s, when the now-defunct Studebaker marque was going strong. These days it's better known for the **University of Notre Dame**, the most famous Roman Catholic college in the US and home of the widely supported Fighting Irish **football** team. Free tours of the campus (☎219/237-4872) take in the gold-domed Administration Building and sights such as a replica of the grotto at Lourdes. Budget **motels** are grouped along US-31 N while the *Book Inn B&B*, 508 W Washington St (☎219/288-1990; ⑤) offers gourmet breakfasts and has a used bookstore in the basement.

Forty miles west, smaller **MICHIGAN CITY** marks the start of the twenty-mile **Indiana Dunes National Lakeshore**, intended to prevent further encroachment on the state's shoreline. There's not much to the "city" itself but it is the handiest place to stay near the lake; the *Knights Inn*, 201 W Kieffer Rd (☎219/874-9500; ③), offers the best value. Just to the west of town, the impressive **Mount Baldy** is, in fact, a giant sand dune. Good swimming beaches, and hiking trails through woods and marshes, can be found at **Indiana Dunes State Park**, twelve miles further along.

From here it's another fifteen miles west to the industrial mess of **GARY**, the largest US city founded this century and mildly famous as the birthplace of Michael Jackson. Until the US Steel Corporation built a giant foundry here in 1906, this was uninhabited bogland. These days it's basically a depressed suburb of Chicago.

# Indianapolis

**INDIANAPOLIS** began life in 1821, when a tract of barely inhabited marshes was designated state capital. Its location in the middle of Indiana's rich farmland bore terrific commercial advantages, but the absence of a navigable river prohibited the transportation of bulky materials such as coal and iron to sustain heavy industry. Though home to over sixty car manufacturers by 1910, the city never seriously threatened Detroit's supremacy. Nevertheless, it has become one of the biggest cities in the world not to be accessible by water, attracting food, paper and pharmaceutical industries, including the giant Eli Lilly Corporation.

Today the city has shaken off such nicknames as Naptown, India-no-place and Brickhouse in the Cornfield in favor of its chosen designation as the country's unofficial amateur sports capital – "amateur" events like the Pan-American Games and national Olympic trials being worth big money these days. In recent years, it has constructed several world-class sports stadia (including the retro-styled **Conseco Fieldhouse** downtown) along with new hotels, a gaggle of top-class museums and a zoo – and its old downtown landmarks have become cultural, shopping and dining complexes. No longer is it (quite) true that nothing happens here except for the glamorous **Indianapolis 500 car race** each May – "the most televised annual event in the world" (see box, p.296).

## Arrival and information

**Indianapolis International Airport** (☎317/487-9594) is twelve miles west of downtown, on the #8 bus route (☎317/635-3344; $1). A **taxi** (Yellow Cabs; ☎317/487-7777) into the center costs around $25. Greyhound arrives at 127 N Capital Ave (☎1-800/231-2222), just off Monument Circle, while Amtrak, 350 S Illinois St (☎317/267-3071), is next to the fairly central Union Station complex. The **visitor center** is at 201 S Capitol St (Mon–Fri 10am–5.30pm, Sat 10am–5pm, Sun noon–5pm; ☎317/237-5200 or 1-800/824-INDY), beside the RCA Dome.

## Accommodation

Indianapolis has plenty of quality **places to stay**, but few real budget downtown options, and prices can double during the race months of May, August and September.

**Canterbury Hotel**, 123 S Illinois St (☎317/634-3000 or 1-800/538-8186). Gracious landmark hotel in the heart of downtown, built in 1928. Includes continental breakfast. ⑦.

**Crowne Plaza Union Station**, 123 W Louisiana St (☎317/631-2221). Regular hotel rooms plus suites in converted railway carriages. ⑥.

**Days Inn Downtown**, 401 E Washington St (☎317/637-6464 or 1-800/325-2525). Centrally located lodgings. ④.

**Fall Creek YMCA**, 860 W 10th St (☎317/634-2478). Single rooms for men and women; $25. ①.

**Hampton Inn Downtown**, 105 S Meridian St (☎317/261-1200 or 1-800/HAMPTON). Clean new rooms, next to Circle Centre. ⑤.

**Ramada Plaza Waterbury Hotel**, 108 N Pennsylvania (☎317/614-1400 or 1-800/272-6232). New rooms downtown in a recently converted, grand old bank building. Free parking. ⑤.

**Renaissance Tower Historic Inn**, 230 E 9th St (☎317/261-1652). Just off central downtown. Rooms are occasionally very inexpensive, but at all times come complete with four-poster bed, toaster, coffeemaker and popcorn popper. ⑤.

## Downtown

Though spacious and unhurried, downtown Indianapolis lacked a nerve center until the opening of the relatively tasteful **Circle Centre** shopping and entertainment complex in winter 1995. That year also saw the completion of the spectacular **Indianapolis Artsgarden**, an eight-story glass rotunda illuminated with fairy lights and suspended over the busy Washington and Illinois intersection. A performance and exhibition space, it also acts as a walkway to Circle Centre and several downtown hotels. One block north, streets radiate from **Monument Circle**, the starting point for a lengthy series of memorials and plazas dedicated to veterans. The challenge of climbing 32 flights of steep stairs up the just-renovated 284ft **Soldiers and Sailors Monument** (there are often queues for the tiny elevator) is rewarded by an unspectacular view of the city (daily 10am–7pm; free).

Five blocks east, the serene tree-shaded **Lockerbie Square Historic District**, starting at New York and East streets, is a small enclave of picturesque charm. Small wood-frame cottages, once home to nineteenth-century artisans, line the cobblestone streets, many of them painted in bright pinks, blues and yellows, with ornately carved porches. The nearby **Indiana State Museum**, 202 N Alabama St (Mon–Sat 9am–4.45pm, Sun noon–4.45pm; free), gives a useful insight to the state's history through exhibits on everything from geology to sport.

Indianapolis seems a strange setting for the spectacular **Eiteljorg Museum of American Indians and Western Art** (June–Aug Mon–Sat 10am–5pm, Sun noon–5pm; rest of year closed Mon; tours at 2pm; $5), housed in a stone, wood and adobe building on the western edge of downtown at 500 W Washington St. Harrison Eiteljorg, an industrialist who went West in the 1940s to speculate in minerals, fell so deeply in love with the art of the region that he brought as much of it back with him as possible. The work on display ranges from Georgia O'Keeffe to Frederic Remington and Andy Warhol. Tribal artifacts from all over North America are displayed on the upper level, while a 38ft Haida totem pole stands in the grounds. There are also frequent displays of beading and basket weaving, superb touring exhibits and a gorgeous gift shop. The Eiteljorg stands amid the rolling greenery of **White River State Park**, which is also home to the sizeable **Indianapolis Zoo** and the lush new **White River Gardens** (Mon–Fri 9am–4pm, Sat–Sun 9am–5pm; $10). In the park's southeast corner stands the superb new **Victory Field**, home of the Indianapolis Indians (☎317/269-3545), the farm team for the Cincinnati Reds.

## Out from downtown

Although the bodies of former president Benjamin Harrison and Hoosier poet James Whitcomb Riley lie in the enormous **Crown Hill Cemetery**, at 38th Street and Michigan Road, the most visited grave belongs to 1930s bank robber **John Dillinger**, supposedly buried at Section 44 Lot 94 (though some researchers allege another man was killed in his place). Designated Public Enemy Number One, he completed thirteen bank raids – killing four policemen, three FBI agents, one sheriff and an undetermined number of innocent bystanders – in a single-year career. Something of a folk hero, he escaped from jail twice, but was eventually ambushed by the FBI outside a Chicago theater in 1934 (see p.312).

Opposite the cemetery at 1200 W 38th St, over 150 lush wooded acres accommodate the capacious **Indianapolis Museum of Art** (Tues, Wed, Fri & Sat 10am–5pm, Thurs 10am–8.30pm, Sun noon–5pm; free). The main building, surrounded by a lake, botanical garden, sculpture courtyard and concert terrace, is fronted by the original of Robert Indiana's Pop Art sculpture *LOVE*. Inside, the exceptional displays include neo-

---

### THE INDIANAPOLIS 500

Seven miles north of downtown, the **Indianapolis Speedway** race track only stages two events per year; but one does happen to be the legendary **Indianapolis 500** (the other is the prestigious NASCAR Brickyard 400 in August).

Held on the last Sunday in May, the Indy 500 is preceded by two weeks of practice to whittle the hopeful entrants down to a final field of 33 drivers, one of whom will scoop the million-dollar first prize. The two-and-a-half-mile circuit was originally built as a test track for the city's motor manufacturers, but the first 500-mile race held in 1911 – won in a time of 6hr 42min, at an average speed of 74.6mph – was a huge success, vindicating the organizers' belief that the distance was the optimum length for spectators' enjoyment. The winner's speed is now likely to touch 225mph.

The big race crowns one of the nation's largest festivals, watched by up to 450,000. At first, the city's conservative hierarchy saw it as an infringement on the traditional observance of Memorial Day weekend. However, it brings so much money into the city, with thousands of "Indy Racing" fanatics staying for the fortnight, that it is now exploited to the full, with civic events such as the crowning of the Speedway Queen, a Mayor's Ball and street parade. Seats for the race usually sell out well in advance, but you may gain admittance to the infield, where the atmosphere makes up for the poor view, on the day.

Adjoining the track, the impressive display of race car history at the **Indianapolis Motor Speedway Hall of Fame Museum**, 4790 W 16th St, provides a good background to the hysteria (daily 9am–5pm; $3). For an extra two dollars, a rickety old bus saunters around the super-smooth asphalt track, ringed by huge banked grandstands. The circuit also holds four of the eighteen holes of the unique **Brickyard Crossing** golf course (☎317/484-6572), home to the annual Senior PGA Tournament; green fees are $90.

Impressionist works, the Eiteljorg Collection of African Art, the largest collection of Turner paintings outside Britain, and an array of paintings and prints from Gauguin's Pont Aven school.

The city's most offbeat museum, the **Indiana Medical History Museum**, 3045 W Vermont St (Wed–Sat 10am–4pm, or by appointment ☎317/635-7329; $5), is housed in the old Pathology Building of what was once a huge psychiatric hospital. Pointing out the cabinets of preserved brains and similarly gruesome exhibits, the guides give a fascinating account of medical practice in the late nineteenth century.

The **Children's Museum of Indianapolis**, 3000 N Meridian St (☎317/921-4000), is arguably the best of its kind in the country (summer daily 10am–5pm; rest of year closed Mon; $8, children $3.50). There's a carousel, an excellent exhibit on African-American storytelling, a big-screen IWERKS theater, interactive gadgets, and a planetarium that mounts laser shows to a Lollapalooza soundtrack.

## Eating

**Circle Centre**, the swish mall at Illinois and Washington, houses dozens of places to eat, but most of these are chains and you'd do better to stick to the more established restaurants downtown or head up to **Broad Ripple Village** (bus #17) at College Avenue and 62nd Street, packed with bars, cafes, galleries and shops. At lunchtime, **City Market**, 222 E Market St, is a maze of lunch counters and tables where you can feast cheaply on all sorts of international food amid a cacophonous din.

**Bazbeaux**, 334 Massachusetts Ave, downtown (☎317/636-7662), and 832 E Westfield Blvd, Broad Ripple Village (☎317/255-5711). The best pizzas in town, with a great range of toppings.

**Elbow Room**, 605 N Pennsylvania St (☎317/635-3354). Pub serving specialty sandwiches and lots of import beers.

**India Garden**, 830 Broad Ripple Ave (☎317/253-6060). Good Indian curries with a noted lunchtime buffet.

**Rathskeller Restaurant**, 401 E Michigan St (☎317/636-0396). Continental dishes including lots of German specialties, set in the historic Atheneum, built in 1892 as a cultural center for the city's German-speaking population.

**Ruthellen's**, 825 N Pennsylvania (☎317/631-RUTH). Wildly baroque yet cozy atmosphere for upscale dining; attracts a mixed clientele. Fri–Sat night piano bar. Closed Mon.

**St Elmo Steak House**, 127 S Illinois St (☎317/635-0636). One of the most famous steak restaurants in the meat-mad Midwest, though rather pompous and expensive. Expect to pay $25–30 for a meal.

**Shapiro's**, 808 S Meridian St (☎317/631-4041). Landmark deli, just a few blocks off downtown. Fill up at the counter with lox, tongue or other specialties and eat in an old-style cafeteria atmosphere. Leave room for the huge desserts.

## Nightlife and entertainment

The emerging area in downtown is Massachusetts Avenue, where along with some good bars and restaurants, the 3000-seater **Murat Centre** (502 N Jersey St; ☎317/231-0000) makes a special venue for gigs and Broadway musicals; decorated in outlandish Byzantine style, the center is part of a huge Shriner temple. In summer, head north to chic **Broad Ripple Village**. See the free paper *NUVO* for full details of gigs and events.

The 1927 Spanish Baroque Indiana Repertory Theatre, 140 W Washington St (☎317/635-5252), puts on dramatic productions between October and May; the Indianapolis Symphony Orchestra has weekly concerts at the equally elaborate 1916 Hilbert Circle Theatre, 45 Monument Circle (☎317/639-4300).

**Broad Ripple Brew Pub**, 840 E 65th St (☎317/253-2739). Atmospheric brewpub, six miles north.

**Chatterbox**, 435 Massachusetts Ave (☎317/636-0584). Lively local bar, with jazz nightly except Sun.

**Madame Walker Theatre Center**, 617 Indiana Ave (☎317/236-2099). Black cultural and heritage center. *Jazz on the Avenue* every Fri plus regular dance events, plays and concerts.

**Slippery Noodle**, 372 S Meridian St (☎317/631-6968). Indiana's oldest bar, established in 1850, next to Union Station. Cheap beer Mon and Tues, live blues Wed–Sat.

**Vogue**, 6259 N College Ave (☎317/255-2828). Popular Broad Ripple rock and indie venue with retro club nights.

## Out from Indianapolis: Bloomington

**BLOOMINGTON**, by far the liveliest small city in Indiana, lies 45 miles southwest of Indianapolis on Hwy-37. It owes its vibrancy to the 33,000-student Indiana University, east of downtown – best-known former pupil, J Danforth Quayle – where the I M Pei-designed **Indiana University Art Museum** on East Seventh Street (Wed–Sat 10am–5pm, Sun noon–5pm; free) holds a fine international collection of painting and sculpture. The architecturally rich downtown also features a host of good shops.

### Practicalities
Greyhound, 409 S Walnut St (☎812/332-1522), runs a reliable **bus** service to Indianapolis. Bloomington's friendly **visitor center** can be found at 2855 N Walnut St (☎812/334-8900 or 1-800/678-9828).

The best budget **place to stay** in central Bloomington is the *Motel 6 – Bloomington University*, 1800 N Walnut St (☎812/332-0820; ②), or there's the central Victorian *Grant Street Inn*, 310 N Grant St (☎812/334-2353; ⑤). The *Indiana Memorial Union* on Seventh and Park (☎812/856-6381), a good source of campus information, also offers a range of cheap places to **eat**. Student bars and cafes are strung out along Kirkwood Avenue, including the vegetarian *Laughing Planet*, at no. 322 E Fifth St (☎812/323-2233). Among the wide range of ethnic restaurants in town are the Tibetan *Snow Lion*, 113 S Grant Ave (☎812/336-0835), and the wonderful *Siam House*, 430 E Fourth St (☎812/331-1233). The *Runcible Spoon*, 412 E Sixth St (☎812/334-3997), is a favorite place for breakfast, coffee and dessert, while the *Brepub at Lennie's*, 1795 E Tenth St (☎812/323-2112), is the best place in town for microbrewed ales.

# ILLINOIS

Nearly everything in **ILLINOIS** revolves around **Chicago**, the largest and most exciting of all the Great Lakes cities. Set at the state's northeastern corner, on the shores of **Lake Michigan**, Chicago has a skyline to rival New York City's, plus a gamut of top-rated museums, restaurants and cafes, and innumerable bars and nightclubs paying homage to the city's strong jazz and blues heritage. Seventy-five percent of the state's twelve million population live within commuting distance of Chicago's energetic center, which controls the bulk of the state economy – Illinois is the third largest agricultural producer in the US. The sole exception to the endless flat prairies elsewhere is far to the south, where the forested **Shawnee Hills** rise between the Mississippi and Ohio rivers.

The contrast between the quiet rural hinterlands and the buzzing urban center could hardly be greater. That said, Illinois does hold a few places to look out for, though apart from a couple of mildly exciting college towns, most are of historic rather than current interest. First explored and settled by the French, in 1763 the area that's now Illinois was sold to the English, farming the western extent of their vast Virginia colony. Granted statehood in 1818, Illinois remained a distant frontier until the mid-1830s when, after a series of uprisings, the native **Sauk** and **Black Hawk** were subjugated and settlers began to arrive in sizeable numbers. Among these were the first followers of Joseph Smith, founder of the Mormon Church, who established a large colony along the Mississippi at Nauvoo. The **Mormons** met with suspicion and persecution and, after Smith was murdered by a lynch mob in 1844, fled west to Utah.

Other early immigrants included the young **Abraham Lincoln**, who practiced law from 1837 onwards in **Springfield**, the state capital and home of a wide range of Lincolniana, including his restored home, his law offices and various other period buildings and artifacts, as well as his monumental tomb. Indeed, Illinois' self-proclaimed nickname – emblazoned on its car license plates – is "Land of Lincoln," and many other central Illinois towns claim important roles in the making of the sixteenth US president.

### Getting around Illinois
Since Chicago is the site of **O'Hare Airport**, (the world's busiest, as well as the hub of the national Amtrak **train** network, you're likely at least to pass through it. If you plan to spend time in the rest of Illinois, Amtrak, numerous commuter railroads and to a lesser extent Greyhound make getting around on public transportation feasible, and **cycling** is generally easy on these endless flat plains.

Half a dozen **interstates** fan out across the country from Chicago; the famous Chicago-to-LA Route 66 has been defunct since the 1960s, though I-55 southwest to St Louis, followed by I-44 and I-40, follow its general route.

# Chicago

**CHICAGO** is in many ways the nation's last great city. Sarah Bernhardt called it "the pulse of America" and, though long eclipsed by Los Angeles as the United States' largest center after New York, Chicago really does have it all, with less of the hassle and infrastructural problems of its coastal rivals.

Founded in the early 1800s, Chicago grew up with the country, serving as the main connection between the established East Coast cities and the wide open Wild West frontier. This position on the sharp edge between civilization and wilderness made the city into a crucible of innovation; and many aspects of modern life, from skyscrapers to suburbia, had their start, and perhaps their finest expression, here on the shores of Lake Michigan.

Despite burning to the ground in the legendary fire of 1871, Chicago boomed thereafter, doubling in population every decade and reaching two million around 1900, swollen by **Irish** and **Eastern European** immigrants (Chicago still has the largest Polish population in the world outside Warsaw). In the early years of this century, it cemented a reputation as a place of apparently limitless opportunity, with jobs aplenty for those willing to work. The attraction was strongest among Deep South **blacks**: from 1900 to 1920 African-Americans poured in, with over 75,000 arriving during the war years of 1916–18 alone. Long hours, poor pay and squalid working conditions were the catalysts that made Chicago the cradle of American **trade unions**. By the turn of the century most workers were organized under the American Federation of Labor, and the 1894 Pullman strike saw black and white workers unite for almost the first time in the US. As hostilities intensified, the city's workers became the driving force behind the left-wing "Wobblies." Chicago has also long been an important center for black organization – both the Reverend Jesse Jackson's **Operation PUSH** (People United to Save Humanity) and the more militant **Nation of Islam**, founded by Elijah Mohammed in the 1940s, have their national headquarters on the city's South Side.

During the Roaring Twenties, Chicago's self-image as a no-holds-barred free market was pushed to the limit by a new breed of entrepreneur: criminal syndicates, ruthlessly and brazenly run by the likes of **gangsters** John Dillinger and Al Capone, took advantage of Prohibition to sell bootleg alcohol. Shootouts in the street between sharp-suited, Tommy-gun wielding mobsters were not as common as legend would have it, but the backroom dealing and iron-handed control they pioneered was later perfected

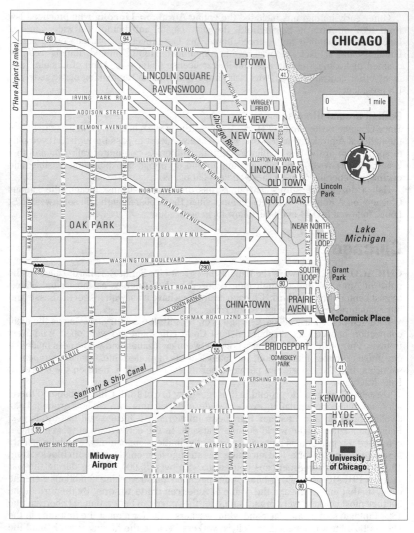

by politicians such as former mayor **Richard Daley** – father of the present mayor – who ran Chicago single-handedly from the 1950s until his death in 1976. His brutal handling of student anti-war demonstrators at the **1968 Democratic convention** remains notorious. These days, the tourist authorities play down the mobster era; few traces of the hoodlum years exist, and those that do owe more to Hollywood than contemporary Chicago.

Today, Chicago's towering **skyline** – the city has one of the world's best collections of **modern architecture**, from Frank Lloyd Wright houses to the 110-story **Sears Tower** – dominates the pancake-flat prairies for hundreds of miles around, and its status as the cultural and financial heart of middle America is beyond question. **The Loop** downtown holds the head offices of many major US companies and some of the nation's most important **commodity markets**, which together handle the buying and selling of one-third of the world's agricultural and industrial products.

For visitors, Chicago offers the **Art Institute of Chicago**, and a wide range of excellent **museums** (many of which have one day of free admission per week), restaurants, sports and highbrow cultural activities, but its strongest suit is **live music**, with a phenomenal array of **jazz** and **blues** clubs packed into the backrooms of its amiable bars and cafes. The **rock** scene is also one of the healthiest in the country with a prolific number of bands having come out of the city in the 1990s, including Smashing Pumpkins, Material Issue, Veruca Salt and Wilco. And almost everything is noticeably less expensive than in other US cities – **eating out**, for example, costs much less than in New York or LA, but is every bit as good. Though locals might deny it, the city has a surprisingly low-key and generally welcoming population – Chicagoans on the whole are proud of their city and usually keen to point out its best features. Two great ways to get a real feel for the city are to head out to ivy-covered **Wrigley Field** on a sunny summer afternoon to catch baseball's Cubs in action, or take a cruise boat under the bridges of the Chicago River at sunset.

## Arrival, information and getting around

Chicago's **O'Hare International Airport** (☎773/686-2200), the national HQ for United, American and several other airlines, is seventeen miles northwest of downtown Chicago. It is connected to the center by 24-hour CTA (Blue Line) **trains** from the station under Terminal 4, which take around forty minutes and cost $1.50 (see overleaf). **Midway Airport**, smaller than O'Hare but used by an increasing number of domestic airlines, is eleven miles southwest of downtown; take one of CTA's Midway (Orange Line) trains, which take thirty minutes, or the #99M Midway Express bus (weekday rush hours only). **Taxis** into town from O'Hare cost around $25–30 (there's also a shared ride program with a flat rate of $15), and take thirty minutes to an hour; from Midway the fare is about $25 (shared rides are $10) and the journey time twenty to forty minutes. Another option is Continental Air Transport's **express bus and van** service between the airports and downtown hotels (☎312/454-7799; $16 from O'Hare, $11.50 from Midway). The highways are often clogged, so allow at least an hour for the trip from either airport.

Chicago is the hub of the nationwide Amtrak rail system, and almost every cross-country route passes through **Union Station** (☎312/558-1075) at Canal and Adams, west of the Loop. Greyhound and a number of regional bus companies pull into the large 24-hour **bus station** at 630 W Harrison, three blocks southwest.

Arriving in Chicago **by road** can be memorable, racing towards the gleaming glass towers of the Loop. Bear in mind, though, that traffic on the expressways to and from downtown can be bumper-to-bumper during rush hours. **Parking** can also be a problem. Meters are expensive (25¢ for 15min) and usually have a two-hour limit. Check street signs for additional restrictions, which are rigidly enforced – violations may result in your car being towed and impounded. Perhaps the best place to leave a car in the downtown area is in the garage under Grant Park at Columbus and Monroe ($8 for 24hr; ☎312/742-7644), close to the east side of the Art Institute.

### Information

Pick up information and maps from the **Chicago Tourism Council**, in the lobby of the Chicago Cultural Center at the entrance on 77 E Randolph St (Mon–Wed 10am–7pm, Thurs 10am–9pm, Fri 10am–6pm, Sat 10am–5pm, Sun 11am–5pm; ☎312/744-6630 or 346-3278). There are also **information centers** in the Historic Water Tower, 800 N Michigan Ave on the Magnificent Mile (Mon–Sat 9.30am–7pm, Sun 10am–6pm) and in the Illinois Market Place Visitor Information Center at Navy Pier, 700 E Grand Ave (Mon–Thurs 10am–9pm, Sun 10am–7pm).

Chicago's new main **post office** is the largest in the world; it's at 433 W Harrison St (Mon–Sat 8am–5pm; ☎312/654-3895; zip code 60607). The Loop Station is at 211 S Clark St (Mon–Fri 7am–7pm).

## City transportation

Getting around Chicago is simple and quick, thanks to buses and the "El," a system of elevated trains operated 24 hours a day by the Chicago Transit Authority (CTA; ☎312/836-7000). Pick up a CTA System Map, available at most subway stations and visitor centers or from the CTA office on the seventh floor of the Merchandise Mart. **Buses** run every five to fifteen minutes during rush hours and every eight to twenty minutes at most other times. **Rapid transit trains** run every five to fifteen minutes during the day and every fifteen to sixty minutes all night. Lines are color-coded and denoted by route rather than destination. The Howard–Dan Ryan is the Red Line; Lake Englewood–Jackson Park is the Green Line; the O'Hare–Congress–Douglas is the Blue Line; the Ravenswood is the Brown Line (whose trains circle the Loop, giving the area its name); the Evanston Express is the Purple Line; and the Skokie Swift is the Yellow Line.

The CTA no longer accepts tokens; instead, riders purchase a **transit card** (available in all El stations) and add value to it. One ride costs $1.50; another ride within two hours costs just 30¢. If you're planning to be on the move, passes good for one ($5), two ($9), three ($12) or five ($18) days of unlimited rides might be a good idea. They're available at O'Hare, Midway and Amtrak subway stations.

Chicago's **taxis**, despite a recent increase in fares, are more reasonable than those of many other major US cities. Charges are $1.50 at the drop of the flag, $1.20 per mile and 50¢ for each additional passenger. Cabs can be hailed anytime in the Loop and other central neighborhoods; otherwise call Yellow (☎312/829-4222) or Checker taxis (☎312/243-2537).

---

### GUIDED TOURS

Various sightseeing companies run **guided bus tours** of the city center, among them Double Decker Bus Rides (daily 9.30am–5pm; $15 good for two days, hop-on; ☎312/922-8919), whose hour-long tours begin at the Sears Tower, and Trolley Tours ($12 for 90min, $15 for day pass; ☎312/663-0260), which picks up at Sears Tower, the Art Institute and Navy Pier.

The **Chicago Architecture Foundation**, in the Santa Fe Building at 224 S Michigan Ave (☎312/922-3432), runs a number of highly recommended tours throughout the city. Among these are two information-packed walking tours of the Loop, giving a friendly in-depth introduction to Chicago's buildings and history ($10 for 2hr, $15 for both tours). It also offers walking tours of Frank Lloyd Wright's buildings in Oak Park, Historic Pullman and other neighborhoods; bus tours of the Loop and Near North ($15; 2hr), Hyde Park and Frank Lloyd Wright's Robie House ($25; 3hr 30min). Perhaps the most popular of all are the excellent ninety-minute Chicago Architecture by Boat tours, which leave from Michigan Avenue and Lower Wacker Drive (May–Oct Mon–Sat 3 departures, Sun 2 trips; $18). **Other sightseeing boat tours** include those offered along the river by Mercury (☎312/332-1368; $14) and Wendella (☎312/337-1446) during the summer season; Spirit of Chicago Harbor Cruises (☎312/321-1241; $14), who continue year-round, sailing from Navy Pier; and the Chicago Duck Tours (☎312/461-1133; $20), which roll through the city for 45 minutes before plunging into the lake for another 35. Tours depart every half-hour from the corner of Clark and Ontario streets.

A **shuttle boat** (April–Oct; $1.50; ☎312/337-1446) operates on the river during rush hour in summer, running from the Michigan Avenue Bridge to Union Station.

# Accommodation

Most central **accommodation** is oriented towards business and convention trade rather than tourism, but there are still plenty of moderately priced rooms. A good selection of clean (if unexciting) prewar hotels in and around the Loop offer reasonable rates, especially at weekends, and motorists can pick from scores of motels along the interstates. Even top-class downtown hotels are, comparatively, not that expensive. Under the Chicago's Got It program, hotels in all price ranges offer discounts of fifteen to forty percent on Thursday to Sunday nights, when the business types have gone home, so you can often get a room in a really plush place for around $100. If you're stuck, Hot Rooms is a reservation service offering hotel rooms at discount rates (☎773/468-7666 or 1-800/468-3500). While they're not as prominent as elsewhere, **bed and breakfast** rooms are available from $75 per night through Chicago B&B, PO Box 14088, IL 60614 (☎312/951-0085). Just under fifteen percent room tax is added to all bills.

**Allegro**, 171 W Randolph St (☎312/236-0123). The old *Bismarck Hotel* has been given a total facelift and new name, and turned into a comfortable, business-class hotel. ⑧.

**Arlington House International Hostel**, 231 W Arlington Place (☎773/929-5380 or 1-800/538-0074). Easygoing hostel open 24hr, close to Wrigley Field and loads of good bars. Segregated and mixed dorms. Members pay $19.50; others $3 extra. ①.

**Best Western Grant Park**, 1100 S Michigan Ave (☎312/922-2900 or 1-800/528-1234). Large hotel with outdoor pool, handy for Grant Park and lakeside attractions. Good value if a little far south. ⑥.

**Blackstone**, 636 S Michigan Ave (☎312/427-4300). Resurgent, once elegant c.1900 hotel (featured in *The Untouchables*), overlooking the lake near Grant Park. ⑤.

**Cass**, 640 N Wabash Ave (☎312/787-4030). Clean and basic hotel offering the best value in the Near North area. ⑤.

**Chicago International Hostel**, 6318 N Winthrop Ave (☎773/262-1011). Big hostel a short walk from Loyola El station, open 24hr, 365 days a year, Dorm beds cost $15. ①.

**Comfort Inn Lincoln Park**, 601 W Diversey Parkway (☎773/348-2810 or 1-800/228-5150). Medium-sized motel, with free continental breakfast. ⑥.

**Days Inn Lincoln Park North**, 644 W Diversey Parkway at Clark (☎773/525-7010). Good, friendly motel popular with visiting musicians and a good base for North Side nightlife. Free continental breakfast. ⑤.

**The Drake**, 140 E Walton Place (☎312/787-2200 or 1-800/553-7256). Chicago's society hotel, modernized without sacrificing its sedate charms. Off the Magnificent Mile; you can always just pop in for a drink. ⑧/⑨.

**Executive Plaza Hotel**, 71 E Wacker Drive (☎312/346-7100). Magnificent setting by the Michigan Avenue Bridge; an extra $10 gets a river view. Big weekend discounts. ⑦.

**Hampton Suites Hotel**, 33 W Illinois Ave (☎312/832-0330). New, clean motel in good River North location. ⑦.

**HI-Chicago Summer Hostel**, 731 S Plymouth Court (☎773/327-5350). On the south side of downtown. Open 24hr, with dorm beds from $19 for members, otherwise $22. ①.

**HoJo Inn**, 720 N LaSalle St (☎312/664-8100 or 1-800/446-4656). Standard *HoJo* rooms in a good Near North location. ⑤.

**Lenox House Suites**, 231 N Rush St (☎312/337-1000). Great all-suite hotel just a few blocks north of the river. ⑦.

**International House of Chicago**, 1414 E 59th St (☎773/753-2270). Plain, pleasant rooms in summer on the University of Chicago campus; not a nice part of town. $37. Reservations essential. ②.

**Monaco**, 225 N Wabash (☎312/960-8500 or 1-800/397-7661). A stylish and luxurious French Deco hotel. ⑧.

**Motel 6**, 162 E Ontario St (☎312/787-3580 or 1-800/621-8055). A few yards off the Magnificent Mile, this is clean, no-frills accommodation in the center of the shopping action. ⑤.

**Three Arts Club of Chicago**, 1300 N Dearborn Parkway (☎312/944-6250). This women's residence doubles as a co-ed hostel in summer. Breakfast and dinner, linens and towels included. ②.

**Wright's Cheney House B&B**, 520 N East Ave, Oak Park (☎708/524-2067). Frank Lloyd Wright designed this Prairie-style house in 1904 and most of the furnishings and fabrics in the lovely two-bedroom suites are Wright designs too. ⑦.

# The City

Chicago is an easy city to negotiate: streets are generally arranged in four-block grids and numbering is consistent, beginning at State and Madison streets – State is at zero east and west and Madison at zero north and south. **Lake Michigan**, which provides Chicago with some of its most attractive open space (twenty miles of lakeshore lie within the city limits), serves as a clear point of reference for getting your bearings – the lake is always to the east of the urban grid. **Michigan Avenue** is the city's main thoroughfare, running between the lakeside museums and parklands, the densely packed skyscrapers of downtown and the diverse low-rise neighborhoods that spread to the north, south and west. It's here that you might experience the full force of "The Hawk," the nickname given to the strong wind that blows off the lake – although the nickname "**Windy City**" was coined by a New York newspaper editor describing the boastful claims of the city's promoters when pitching for the World's Columbian exhibition of 1893. The **Chicago River**, which cuts through the heart of downtown Chicago out of Lake Michigan, separates the business district from the shopping and entertainment areas of the North Side, which range from the upscale **Near North** and **Gold Coast** neighborhoods to the artists' lofts and galleries of **River North**, plus the modestly charming area of **Old Town**, the young professional enclaves of **Lincoln Park**, **Wrigleyville** and **Lakeview**, and hip **Wicker Park** – Chicago's hottest spots for nights out on a budget.

In contrast to the wealth and prosperity of the North Side, the deprived **South Side** is more like New York's South Bronx, a huge and, in places, desperately poor expanse with a justifiably dangerous reputation. But while large areas are definitely unsafe after dark and dodgy even at midday, a few corners of the South Side are well worth visiting – particularly the Gothic campus of the **University of Chicago**, and neighboring **Hyde Park**, site of the **Museum of Science and Industry** – one of the largest and most popular museums in the US. Apart from **Oak Park** to the west, which holds the childhood home of **Ernest Hemingway** and over a dozen well-maintained examples of the influential architecture of **Frank Lloyd Wright**, suburban Chicago has little to offer.

## Downtown Chicago: The Loop

It may not have anything like the sheer mass of Manhattan or the dense warrens of the City of London, but **downtown Chicago** puts on what is perhaps the finest display of **modern architecture** in the world, from the prototype skyscrapers of the 1890s to Mies van der Rohe's modernist masterpieces, and the second tallest building in the world, the quarter-mile-high **Sears Tower**. Just about all these edifices are workplaces of one kind or another; the whole place is bustling in the day and virtually empty later on.

The compact heart of Chicago is known as **the Loop**, because it's circled by the elevated tracks of the CTA "El" trains; for a first impression of downtown, you can't beat riding a train into any of the dozen stations, and starting your explorations by seeing the energy, drive and unmasked greed exposed in the trading pits of its various **commodity marketplaces**. Half the world's wheat and corn (and pork belly futures) are bought and sold amid the cacophonic roar of the **Chicago Board of Trade**, housed in a gorgeous Art Deco tower, appropriately topped by a 30ft stainless steel statue of

0      800 yds

N

GOETHE STREET

E. SCOTT ST.

N. CLYBORN AVE.

DIVISION STREET

DIVISION STREET

STATE PARKWAY

E. ELM ST.

GOLD COAST

E. CEDAR ST.

**ACCOMMODATION**

1 Blackstone
2 Clarion Executive Plaza
3 Drake
4 Grant Park
5 Lenox House Suites
6 Motel 6

E. BELLEVUE PL.

E. OAK STREET

E. WALTON ST.

**3 John Hancock Center**

E. CHESTNUT ST.

Lake Michigan

N. FRANKLIN STREET

N. WELLS STREET

N. LASALLE STREET

N. CLARK STREET

N. DEARBORN STREET

N. STATE STREET

**Historic Water Tower**

E. PEARSON ST.

**Museum of Contemporary Art**

MAGNIFICENT MILE

NORTH MICHIGAN AVENUE

N. RUSH ST.

W. CHICAGO AVENUE

E. SUPERIOR STREET

Ohio Street Beach

N. LARRABEE STREET

W. SUPERIOR STREET

W. HURON ST.

**Terra Museum of Art**

W. ERIE STREET

N. ORLEANS STREET

N. WABASH

**6**

W. ONTARIO STREET

**5**

W. OHIO STREET

N. McCLURG CT.

N. FAIRBANKS CT.

N. LAKE SHORE DRIVE

41

Navy Pier

W. GRAND AVENUE

W. ILLINOIS STREET

**Tribune Tower**

W. HUBBARD STREET

**Wrigley Building**

MILWAUKEE AVENUE

W. KINZIE STREET

**Merchandise Mart**

Chicago River

E. NORTH WATER ST.

**IBM Building**

Chicago River

**2**

EAST WACKER DRIVE

WEST WACKER DRIVE

**Illinois Center**

GEORGE HALES DRIVE

FIELD BOULEVARD

LAKE STREET

SOUTH JEFFERSON STREET

S. CLINTON STREET

S. FRANKLIN STREET

SOUTH WACKER DRIVE

E. RANDOLPH STREET

**Marshall Field**

E. WASHINGTON STREET

**Chicago Mercantile Exchange**

E. MADISON STREET

**Carson Pirie Scott**

E. MONROE STREET

NORTH MICHIGAN AVENUE

**Art Institute**

Grant Park

**Sears Tower**

THE LOOP

E. ADAMS STREET

**Union Station (Amtrak)**

E. JACKSON BOULEVARD

**Board of Trade**

**Symphony Center**

VAN BUREN STREET

290

CONGRESS PARKWAY

**Auditorium Theater**

41

Lake Michigan

**Buckingham Fountain**

W. HARRISON STREET

Chicago River

S. CANAL STREET

S. WELLS STREET

S. CLARK STREET

S. FEDERAL STREET

S. PLYMOUTH COURT

S. DEARBORN ST.

S. STATE STREET

S. WABASH AVENUE

**1**

S. COLUMBUS DRIVE

SOUTH LAKE SHORE DRIVE

E. BALBO DRIVE

**Greyhound Terminal**

W. POLK STREET

E. 8TH ST.

W. TAYLOR ST.

E. 9TH ST.

W. TAYLOR ST.

E. 11TH ST.

**4**

W. ROOSEVELT ROAD

E. ROOSEVELT ROAD

**Shedd Aquarium**

McFETRIDGE

**Field Museum of Natural History**

**Soldier Field Stadium**

**DOWNTOWN CHICAGO**

Ceres, Roman goddess of grain. From the entrance at 141 W Jackson St, at the south end of LaSalle Street, take the lift to the fifth-floor visitors' gallery (Mon–Fri 8am–1.15pm; free), where displays trace the evolution of the various frantic shouts and signals by which trade is actually carried out. A similarly energetic ballet goes on from the early hours on Chicago's stock options exchange, the largest in the US. At the **Chicago Mercantile Exchange**, three blocks away at 30 S Wacker Drive (Mon–Fri 7.30am–3.15pm; free), precious metals, currencies and commodities are bought and sold to the tune of some $50 billion a day. The **best time to visit** any of the exchanges is just before the close of trade, when the pressure is at its peak and tempers are most frayed.

A couple of other buildings in the immediate vicinity are worth nosing around. Half a block from the Board of Trade, **The Rookery**, 209 S LaSalle St, built in 1886 by Burnham and Root, is one of the city's most celebrated and photographed edifices. Its forbidding Moorish Gothic exterior gives way to a wonderfully airy lobby, decked out in cool Italian marble and gold leaf in 1905 during a major remodeling by Frank Lloyd Wright and restored in 1992; the spiral cantilever staircase rising from the second floor has to be seen to be appreciated. A couple of doors towards the Board of Trade, call in at the **Continental Illinois Bank** lobby, with its 28 Ionic marble columns and intricate murals.

Looking up at the proud facade of the **Reliance Building**, 32 N State St, you'd be forgiven for thinking it dated from the Art Deco 1930s, but it was in fact completed way back in 1895 by Daniel Burnham, who did much to shape the face of Chicago; his **Fisher Building**, with its tongue-in-cheek, aquatic-inspired ornamental terra cotta, stands at 343 S Dearborn St. A block further south, the 1890 **Manhattan Building** was the world's first tall all-steel-frame building, and is generally acknowledged as the progenitor of the modern curtain-walled skyscraper; now converted into luxury apartments, it preserves some noteworthy exterior ornament.

Besides office buildings, the Loop also holds some of Chicago's grandest c.1900 **department stores**. The best-looking of these, the 1889 **Carson Pirie Scott** store at 1 S State St, boasts a magnificent ironwork facade that blends botanic and geometric forms in an intuitive version of Art Moderne; its architect, Louis Sullivan, was also responsible for the gorgeous spherical bronze clocks suspended from the corners of the **Marshall Field's** department store, two blocks north, at State and Washington streets. The comparatively bland exterior of Marshall Field's oldest and grandest branch masks one of the world's great stores, with seven floors of merchandise corralling a multistory, escalator-filled atrium.

Further on, a newly resurrected stretch of the riverfront walk follows the western bank of the river, with open-air cafes and gardens. Further south, and back on the Loop side at South Wacker Drive and Adams Street, is the 1468ft **Sears Tower**, the tallest building in the world until 1997, when Malaysia's Petronas Towers controversially nudged it from the top by the length of an antenna. The tower is occupied by various companies (the Sears corporation recently moved out to the suburbs), and it's so huge that it has over one hundred different elevators. Two of them ascend, in little over a minute, all the way from the ground-level shopping mall to the 103rd-floor **Skydeck Observatory** (March–Sept daily 9am–11pm; Oct–Feb daily 9am–10pm; $8), for predictably breathtaking views that on a clear day take in four states – Illinois, Michigan, Wisconsin and Indiana – and allow you to pick out the city's landmarks. Look for the distinctive triangular **Metropolitan Detention Center**, where prisoners exercise on the grassy roof, beneath wire netting to ensure they don't get whisked away by helicopter.

## The Chicago River

The Loop is usually said to end at the "El" tracks, but the blocks beyond this core, to either side of the Chicago River, hold plenty more of interest. Broad, double-decked

**Wacker Drive**, parallel to the water, was designed as a sophisticated promenade, lined by benches and obelisk-shaped lanterns, by Daniel Burnham in 1909. It was never completed but, despite the almost constant intrusion of construction works, it makes for a nice extended walk. The river itself had its direction reversed c.1900, in an engineering project more extensive than the digging of the Panama Canal. As a result, rather than letting its sewage and industrial waste flow east into Lake Michigan, Chicago now sends it all south into the Corn Belt.

The best way to enjoy the riverfront is on a **boat tour** from beneath the Michigan Avenue Bridge, giving magnificent views of downtown and a good insight into the city's history (see "Guided Tours" box, p.302). However, half an hour's walk, especially at lunchtime when the office workers are out in force, will do the trick. Burnham's promenade runs along both sides of the river, crossing back and forth over the twenty-odd drawbridges that open and close to let barges and an occasional sailboat pass. The **State Street Bridge** is a superb vantage point. On the south bank, at 35 E Wacker Drive, the elegant Beaux Arts **Jewelers Building** was built in 1926 and is capped on the seventeenth floor by a domed rotunda that once housed Al Capone's favorite speakeasy. Across the river stands what's commonly considered the masterpiece of Ludwig Mies van der Rohe – the 1971 **IBM Building** at 330 N Wabash Ave. The gentle play of light and shadow across the detailed bronze and smoked-glass facade has been the model for countless other less considered copies worldwide. The building is so huge that it acts as a funnel for winter winds off Lake Michigan, and heavy ropes sometimes have to be tied across the broad plaza at its base to protect people from getting blown away.

Perhaps Chicago's most successful and acclaimed building of recent years stands four blocks west at **333 W Wacker Drive**. Towering over a broad bend in the river, and bowed to follow its curve, the green glass facade reflects the almost fluorescent green of the river (recently upgraded from "toxic" to merely "polluted"); on the lower floors, a more classically detailed stone base actively addresses its stalwart elder neighbours.

Further west, the huge **Merchandise Mart**, a hulking retail building hugging the river, was the world's largest building when it opened in 1931. Shrewd business tycoon Joseph P Kennedy snapped up the structure after the war just by paying its back taxes.

## South Michigan Avenue and the Art Institute of Chicago

Many of Chicago's major cultural attractions are gathered on the eastern edge of the Loop, along Michigan Avenue between the city's commercial core and the shores of Lake Michigan. On the lake side of South Michigan Avenue, at the east end of Adams Street, the **Art Institute of Chicago** (Mon–Fri 10.30am–4.30pm, Tues until 8pm, Sat 10am–5pm, Sun noon–5pm; $8 suggested donation, free Tues) has an excellent collection of Impressionist and Post-Impressionist paintings, Asian art (particularly Japanese prints), photography and architectural drawings. The Neoclassical facade of the main entrance does its best to look dignified, but the numerous added-on wings can make it hard to find your way around inside.

Most visitors head straight upstairs to the Impressionist works, which include a wall full of Monet's *Haystacks* captured in various lights, next to Seurat's immediately familiar pointillist *Sunday Afternoon on La Grande Jatte*; a handful of Post-Impressionist masterpieces by Van Gogh, Gauguin and Matisse are arrayed nearby. Beyond here, a tortured, tuxedoed self-portrait by **Max Beckmann** – his last Berlin painting before fleeing the Nazis – welcomes you into a crowded gallery of early twentieth-century American and European works, in which moody portraits by Balthus and Picasso, and Surrealist landscapes by Max Ernst and Yves Tanguy, hang side by side with Edward Hopper's lonely *Nighthawks* and Georgia O'Keeffe's *Black Cross, New Mexico*.

Elsewhere in the museum, keep an eye out for the pitchfork-holding farmer of Grant Woods' oft-reproduced *American Gothic* – a picture he painted as a student at the Art Institute school, and sold to the museum for $300 in 1930 – and for the delightful seventh-century Indonesian sculpted stone monkeys, in the Southeast Asian collections displayed around the McKinlock Court Garden, which in summer serves as an attractive **open-air cafe**. Also here, in the far east end of the complex, is the immaculately reconstructed Art Moderne trading room of the Chicago Stock Exchange, designed by Louis Sullivan in 1893 and moved here in the 1970s.

A few blocks north, the **Chicago Cultural Center** takes up most of the splendid old Public Library building at 78 E Washington St, and holds a range of free activities. As well as the city's main **visitor center**, it features various galleries (including some great photos of Chicago's most famous landmarks), major touring exhibits, and free lunchtime and evening recitals, readings and concerts (☎312/346-3278 for details). The highlight is the **Museum of Broadcast Communications**, where you can while away a few hours watching old adverts, newsreels and sporting moments (Mon–Sat 10am–4.30pm, Sun noon–5pm; free).

Around 1900 this lakefront strip around the Art Institute on South Michigan Avenue was the city's prime entertainment district. Many of that era's grand structures preserve a sense of its unabashed artistic aspirations. The world-renowned **Chicago Symphony Orchestra**, now run by Daniel Barenboim after many successful years under the baton of Sir Georg Solti, performs to sell-out crowds at the new **Symphony Center** at 220 S Michigan Ave. Down the street, the **Fine Arts Building** at no. 410 once held the offices of *Wizard of Oz* author L Frank Baum and the drafting studio of the young Frank Lloyd Wright. Further along at no. 430, the stately 1889 **Auditorium Theater** was originally funded by a group of Chicago's civic leaders who were embarrassed by the derision of the more established Eastern cities. They hoped this performance center, incorporating lavish use of gold, mosaics and murals, in addition to the acoustically perfect theater, would overcome the stigma.

Yet further along stand two of Chicago's most famous old **hotels**, including the recently renovated *Hilton* – the world's largest hotel when it opened in 1927 – and the more affordable and atmospheric *Blackstone*. South of here, the neighborhood income levels drop off sharply, and, apart from the Prairie Avenue Historic District described on p.314, there's little of interest before the Hyde Park district three miles south – though R&B fans may like to know that the southwest corner of Michigan Avenue and 21st Street held the studios and offices of **Chess Records**, immortalized in the early Rolling Stones song *2120 S Michigan Avenue*. Plans to turn this hallowed building into a museum and resource center for local musicians has so far failed to get beyond the argument stage.

## Grant Park

East of the Art Institute towards Lake Michigan, **Grant Park** provides a welcome but not entirely complete break from the downtown urban grid – wide strips of high-speed road and railroad slice through it, so casual rambling can be frustrating. The northern half of the park centers around the immense **Buckingham Fountain**, which features daily light and water shows from dusk to 11pm. The whole two-hundred-acre swath is liberally sprinkled with sculptures and monuments, from a moping Columbus to a proud Plains Indian on horseback. Practically every weekend in summer sees a musical festival (be it gospel, blues, country, jazz or classical) held in the area around Petrillo Music Shell, just behind the Art Institute. The **Taste of Chicago** in early July attracts more than two million people to a week-long feeding frenzy, garnished with concerts and other live entertainments.

The major attractions are gathered in the newly landscaped southern half of Grant Park, known as **Museum Campus**. The extensive and engaging **Field Museum of**

**Natural History**, 1200 S Lake Shore Drive at Roosevelt Road (daily 9am–5pm; $7, free Wed), is ten minutes' walk south of the Art Institute, in a huge marble-clad, Daniel Burnham-designed Greek temple. "Natural history" here includes anything non-white and non-European: the collection ranges from Egyptian tombs – the entire burial chamber of the son of a Fifth Dynasty Pharaoh was brought here in 1908 – to the man-eating lions of Tsavo. Folklorists in an earthen lodge in the Native American section tell myths and legends – intended for young kids but not overly sentimental or simple-minded. Also kid-oriented is "Underground Adventure," a simulated environment that "shrinks" you to 1/100th your size, giving you an entirely new perspective of the soil.

Just across busy Lake Shore Drive, on the shores of Lake Michigan, the **Shedd Aquarium** (summer daily 9am–6pm; rest of year Mon–Fri 9am–5pm, Sat & Sun 9am–6pm; $11, $6 on Mon, when Aquarium section only is free) proclaims itself, in true Chicago style, the largest indoor aquarium in the world. The 1930s structure itself is rather old-fashioned, but the lighthearted and often tongue-in-cheek displays – some use *Far Side* cartoons, while others describe a Joycean *Portrait of an Otter* – are at once informative and entertaining. The central exhibit, a 90,000-gallon re-creation of a coral reef complete with sharks (who get fed at 11am and 2pm daily), turtles and thousands of tropical fish, is surrounded by over a hundred lesser tanks. Highlights include the sluggish and comical South American freckled sideneck turtles, housed across from a 4ft, 250lb alligator snapping turtle, who trundles to the surface to breathe every half-hour. The recently added **Oceanarium** provides an enormous contrast, with its modern lake-view home for marine mammals such as Pacific dolphins and beluga whales. Designed to replicate a rocky Alaskan coastline, it's a carefully disguised amphitheater for such demonstrations of the animals' "natural behaviour" as jumping out of the water and fetching plastic rings. Performances are four times daily and you need a ticket; at other times you can watch from underwater galleries as the animals cruise around the tank, and listen to the clicks, beeps and whistles they use to communicate with each other. Get to the Shedd early to beat the long lines and school groups.

In summer, Shoreline Marine Sightseeing ($9; ☎312/222-9328) runs hour-long **cruises** along the lakeshore from a jetty just north of the Aquarium. Nearby, the expanded and renovated **Adler Planetarium** (Mon–Thurs 9am–5pm, Fri 9am–9pm, Sat & Sun 9am–5pm; $5, free Tues) has added an interactive 360-degree movie theater; and offers one of the best views of the city skyline. The small Meigs Field Airport is just to the south, so don't be surprised if low-flying planes seem about to crash into the lake.

## Chinatown

Close by the gentrified blocks of the South Loop neighborhoods, **Chinatown**, with an estimated population of nine thousand individuals within a narrow ten-block radius, is surprisingly unchanged, looking much as it did fifty or sixty years ago. There's a colorful tile-covered gate at Wentworth and Cermak that marks the edge of the district, and once through here you could just as well be in downtown Hong Kong as central Chicago – indeed, some of the older residents speak no English and very rarely pass through the gate to the outer world. There's nothing much to see, but over forty **restaurants** (the best of them listed on p.316) serving Mandarin, Szechuan, Shanghai and Cantonese cuisine mean it's a good place to come to eat, and in any case it's fun to poke around the little groceries filled with spices, teas, herbs and vegetables.

## The Near North Side

Chicago's **Near North Side**, where you're likely to spend much of your time, has few big-name attractions, but it's great for simply wandering around, chancing upon odd **shops**, neighborhood bars, and historic sites in a generally low-rise tangle containing some of the city's most characteristic corners.

When the Michigan Avenue Bridge was built over the Chicago River in 1920, the warehouse district along its north bank quickly changed into one of the city's most upmarket quarters, now known as the **Magnificent Mile** and famed for its increasingly fashionable shops and department stores. Throughout the Roaring Twenties one glitzy tower after another was thrown up along Michigan Avenue, starting in the north with the opulent **Drake Hotel** off Lincoln Park, and in the south with the white terracotta, wedding-cake colossus of the **Wrigley Building**, just over the river at 400 N Michigan Ave, that's spectacularly lit up at night. Built by the Chicago-based chewing-gum magnate, the latter was eclipsed almost immediately by the "Mag Mile's" most famous structure, the **Tribune Tower**. Still housing the editorial offices of Chicago's morning newspaper, as well as, on the ground floor, the studios of its main AM radio station, WGN (you can peer in from the street and watch the DJs in action), the tower was completed in 1925, its flying buttresses and Gothic detailing turning their back on the then-prevalent Moderne style. Look closely at its lower floors and you'll see pieces of historic buildings – like the Parthenon and the Great Pyramid – pilfered from around the world by *Tribune* staffers and embedded here.

While the Tribune Tower anchors its southern end, the Mag Mile's northern reaches are dominated by the quarter-mile-high, cross-braced steel **John Hancock Center** at 875 N Michigan Ave. Though it's 125ft shorter than the Empire State Building, and has since been pushed out of the top ten by New York's World Trade Center, the Sears Tower and a host of structures in Asia, the 360° panorama you get on a clear day from its 94th-floor **Skydeck Observatory** (daily 9am–midnight; $8) is unforgettable.

Back at ground level, you're right at the heart of Chicago's prime **shopping district**, where Neiman-Marcus and Tiffany & Co rub shoulders with Benetton and Nike Town. Some front straight onto Michigan Avenue, but most of the shops are enclosed within multistory complexes, or "vertical shopping malls." The oldest of these – and still the best – is **Water Tower Place**, 835 N Michigan Ave, with more than a hundred stores on seven floors plus a bustling food-court. The **900 N Michigan Avenue** mall offers a less-cramped space and more upscale shops, anchored by Bloomingdale's and including Gucci and Aquascutum.

Across from Water Tower Place, at the very center of this consumer paradise, stands the **Historic Water Tower** – a building you'll feel is either beautiful or grotesque. An exuberant but naive example of frontier Gothic, the stone castle, topped by a 100ft tower, was built in 1869 and is one of the very few structures to have survived the Chicago Fire of 1871. Two other museums are close at hand: the **Terra Museum of American Art**, 664 N Michigan Ave (Tues 10am–8pm, Wed–Sat 10am–6pm, Sun noon–5pm; $7, free on Tues), holds some good landscape paintings by Church and Cole, but it's the extensive collection of American Impressionist works that makes it stand out. The **Museum of Contemporary Art** recently moved to a huge facility at 200 E Chicago Ave (Tues & Thurs–Sun 11am–6pm, Wed 11am–9pm; $6.50), with lots of space for its wacky interactive displays, video presentations, and a permanent collection featuring pieces by Calder, Nauman, Warhol and others; at the rear is a sculpture garden and patio where you can enjoy the good bistro food served at the cafe.

Off Michigan Avenue at Ohio and Rush streets, the new five-story indoor, interactive theme park **DisneyQuest** has just opened its doors. One ride, CyberSpace Mountain lets you design your own roller coaster, complete with loops and corkscrews and then hop into a motion simulator to ride it (Mon–Wed 11am–11pm, Fri–Sat 10am–midnight, Thurs and Sun 10am–11pm; one day of unlimited play $32, one day pay for play $16). Disney is unfortunately further spreading its wings here: a Disney Store is being constructed around the corner, and next door they've opened the sports bar *ESPNZone* (see p.319).

Away from the Magnificent Mile, the area along the river between Michigan Avenue and the lake is at the center of a massive redevelopment project, at least partially attributed to the success of the renovated **Navy Pier**, at East Illinois Street; since undergoing a face-lift in 1995, it has become the city's premier tourist destination, attracting more than eight million visitors annually to its shops, chain restaurants, 3D-IMAX theater, and fifteen-story Ferris wheel. The pier is home to the **Chicago Children's Museum** (daily 10am–5pm; $6.50, free family night Thurs 5–8pm), also a venue for concerts and weekend festivals in summer and an embarkation point for several boat tours, including Shoreline Sightseeing Co ($9; ☎312/222-9328), which runs thirty-minute **cruises** along the lakeshore from Navy Pier (weather permitting) year-round.

The more heavily industrial area west of Michigan Avenue is also experiencing a revival of sorts, though on a smaller scale and with a different character. Rechristened **River North**, the many old brick warehouses and factory premises here have been converted to house avant-garde art galleries, restaurants and nightclubs. Huron and Superior streets, around their intersection with Wells Street, hold the most concentrated collection; if you're interested in doing any degree of serious gallery-hopping, pick up a copy of the free *Chicago Gallery News*.

## The Gold Coast and Old Town

As its name suggests, the **Gold Coast** is one of Chicago's wealthiest and most desirable neighborhoods, stretching north from the Magnificent Mile along the lakeshore. This residential district is primarily notable for Chicago's most central (and style-conscious) beach, the broad strand of **Oak Street Beach**, reached via a walkway under Lake Shore Drive, across from the *Drake Hotel*. After dark, the summertime crowds are apt to be found in the myriad bars of Rush and Division streets. The more northerly reaches of the Gold Coast, approaching Lincoln Park, are also its most exclusive, nowhere more so than the stretch of Astor Street running south from the park. **Old Town**, west of LaSalle Street to either side of North Avenue, has a much more lived-in look than does the dandified Gold Coast. Originally a German immigrant community based around the 1873 **St Michael's Church** – whose carillon is to Old Towners what Bow Bells are to Cockneys – today the neighborhood boasts a broad ethnic and cultural mix. While its many century-old rowhouses and workers' cottages are now prime real estate, as recently as thirty years ago its then-shabby housing stock and derelict factories attracted a variety of creative types. **Wells Street**, the main drag, emerged in the late 1960s as a mini-Haight Ashbury, and while almost all signs of that era have vanished (or, as in the case of the folk club *Earl of Old Town*, moved uptown), at least one survivor, the Second City comedy club (see p.322), is still going strong. The rest of the neighborhood is packed with some of the city's best bars, galleries and barbecue joints, and makes for a diverting afternoon's wander. Especially noteworthy are the House of Glunz, at 1206 N Wells St, a wine shop dating to 1888, and neighborhood landmark Barbara's Bookstore at 1350 N Wells St, an independent bookstore with an impressive fiction and children's section and frequent author readings.

## Lincoln Park and Wrigleyville

In summer, Chicago's largest green space, **Lincoln Park**, gives a much-needed respite from the gridded pavements of the rest of the city. Unlike Grant Park to the south, Lincoln Park is packed with leafy nooks and crannies, monuments and sculptures, and has a couple of friendly, family-oriented **beaches**, at the eastern ends of North Avenue and Fullerton Avenue. Near the small **zoo** (daily 9am–5pm; free) at the heart of the park, you can rent paddleboats or bikes. If the weather's bad, head for the **conservatory**, 2400 N Stockton Drive (free), or visit the **Chicago Historical Society museum** (Mon–Sat 9.30am–4.30pm, Sun noon–5pm; $5), at the south end of the park at 1601 N Clark St, and bone up on Chicago's captivating past; it also has a nice, skylit cafe.

The Lincoln Park neighborhood, inland from the lake between North Avenue and Diversey Parkway, centers on **Lincoln Avenue** and **Clark Street**, which run diagonally from near the Historical Society; **Halsted Street**, with its blues bars and nightclubs, runs north–south through its heart. Any of these main roads merits an extended stroll, popping in to the many book and record stores, while smaller side streets show off why Lincoln Park is such a popular place to live. Look out for the **Biograph Theatre** movie house, 2433 N Lincoln Ave, where **John Dillinger** was ambushed and killed by the FBI in 1934, thanks to a tip-off from his companion, the legendary Lady in Red; and **Oz Park**, at Lincoln and Webster avenues, which was the namesake, if not the inspiration, for Chicago author L Frank Baum's stories, set somewhere over the rainbow.

Chicago spreads north from Lincoln Park for block after low-rise block of houses and shops, many of which date from the late 1800s, when thousands of German immigrants settled in what was then the separate enclave of Lake View. It's now dubbed **Wrigleyville**, in honor of **Wrigley Field**, the ivy-covered 75-year-old stadium of baseball's much-loved Cubs. Along with Boston's Fenway Park (see p.186), this remains the best place to get a real feel for the game – the club is so traditional it fought the installation of floodlights right up to 1988. Even if you know nothing about the rules, there are few more pleasant and relaxing ways to spend an afternoon than drinking beer, eating hot dogs, watching the Cubs struggle to win a ball game (they haven't won anything important since World War II but oh, how close they've come) and joining in the ritual seventh-inning singing of *Take Me Out to the Ballgame*: once led by gravel-voiced announcer Harry Caray (who passed away in 1998), now the tune is sung in Caray's honor by a different celebrity guest each game.

## The West Side and Oak Park

Chicago's **West Side**, west of the Chicago River, was where the **Great Fire of 1871** started – supposedly when Mrs O'Leary's cow kicked over a lantern. The flames spread quickly east to engulf the entire central city, which was built of wood and fed the fire for three full days. Appropriately enough, the O'Leary cottage is now the site of the Chicago Fire Department training academy. The West Side also saw 1886's **Haymarket Riots**, when striking workers assembled at the old city market at Desplaines and Randolph streets; after a peaceful demonstration, as police began to break up the crowd, a bomb exploded, killing an officer. Another six policemen and four of the workers died in the resulting panic; four labor leaders were later found guilty of murder and hanged, despite the fact that none of them had been present at the event.

Though the West Side has little to see compared to the rest of the city, it does provide a good look at its day-to-day realities, having served as the port of entry for Chicago's myriad ethnic groups, now congregated in its distinct neighborhoods. **Milwaukee Avenue**, which stretches under the "El" tracks diagonally from the Loop out towards O'Hare Airport, has long been home to a sizeable eastern European community, mainly Poles – over a million altogether, including some 60,000 who came to Chicago during the martial law era of the 1980s. For an introduction, stop by the **Polish Museum of America** (daily noon–5pm; free) at 984 N Milwaukee Ave, or the **Ukrainian National Museum** (Thurs–Sun 11am–4pm; free), half a mile west at 2453 W Chicago Ave. **Greektown**, the few blocks of Halsted Street north of the I-290 freeway, and **Little Italy**, along Taylor Street west of Halsted, are both just a short walk from the University of Illinois subway station, on the CTA Congress line. On a Sunday morning, the liveliest spot on the West Side is **Maxwell Street market**, four blocks southeast of Little Italy, where blues bands busk on street corners and *kielbasa* replaces bagels among the stallholders.

Ten miles west of the Loop, the affluent and attractive c.1900 suburb of **Oak Park** has been preserved as a national historic district, thanks in part to its early influence on two very different but very American figures, **Ernest Hemingway** and **Frank**

**Lloyd Wright**. Oak Park is easily accessible by public transportation: take the Green Line west to the Harlem Avenue stop. The **visitor center**, just over two blocks east of the station at 158 N Forest Ave (summer daily 10am–5pm; rest of year daily 10am–4pm; ☎708/848-1500), has an excellent architectural walking tour map as well as guidebooks and free brochures.

Hemingway was born and bred in Oak Park, editing his high school newspaper and living a normal middle-class life; both his birthplace (at 339 N Oak Park Ave) and his boyhood home (600 N Kenilworth Ave) bear commemorative plaques, and there's an engaging collection of memorabilia at the **Oak Park and River Forest Historical Society** (Thurs–Sun 1–4pm; $5) at 217 Home Ave, a block south of the station.

In 1889, a decade before Hemingway's birth, an ambitious young architect named Frank Lloyd Wright arrived in Oak Park, which he used for the next twenty years as a testing ground for his innovative design theories. Most of the 25 buildings he put up here are in keeping with conventional Victorian design, and few are open to the public; fortunately, however, his most interesting and groundbreaking edifices are maintained as monuments. His ideal of an "organic architecture," in which all aspects of the design derive from a single unifying concept – quite at odds with the fussy "gingerbread" popular at the time – is exemplified by **Unity Temple** at 875 Lake St. Though the simplicity of this angular, reinforced-concrete structure was largely dictated by economics, its unembellished surfaces contribute to a masterful manipulation of space, especially in the skylit interior, where the subtle interplay of overlapping planes and volumes creates a dynamic spatial flow. Though little noticed in the US, Unity Temple was very influential in Europe as a precursor of modern architecture.

Wright built his small, brown-shingled **home and studio**, nearby at 951 Chicago Ave on the corner of Forest Avenue, at the age of 22 in 1889, and remodeled it repeatedly thereafter. It shows all his hallmarks: large fireplaces to symbolize the heart of the home and family; free-flowing, open-plan rooms; and the visual linking of interior and exterior spaces. The furniture of the kitchen and dining rooms is Wright's own design; he added a two-story studio in 1898, with a mezzanine drafting area suspended by chains from the roof beams. In 1909 Wright abandoned Oak Park and his family for new pastures; he was eventually to design such landmarks as New York's Guggenheim Museum. You can see the house itself on a 45-minute guided tour (Mon–Fri 11am, 1pm & 3pm, Sat & Sun every 15min between 11am–3.30pm; $8); lengthier walking tours, costing $8 including use of Walkman, take in the dozen other Wright-designed houses within a two-block radius. Booking the walking and house tours at the same time will save you $2.

## The South Side

The **South Side** of Chicago has always had a raw deal, cursed with the presence of bad-neighbor heavy industries like the sprawling **Chicago Stockyards**, the slaughter-houses and meatpackers which Upton Sinclair exposed in his 1906 novel *The Jungle* and whose stink covered most of the South Side up through the 1950s. The overriding impression is one of misery and downtrodden poverty, with block after block of deprived and dangerous neighborhoods. That said, there are exceptions: not just the **Prairie Avenue** and **Hyde Park** districts described overleaf, but also the buzzing **Chinatown** around Wentworth Avenue and 22nd Street; the artsy, predominantly Mexican **Pilsen** district, a few blocks north and west; and the predominantly Irish, blue-collar **Bridgeport**, around Halsted and 37th – Mayor Daley's old fiefdom, the home of Comiskey Park and baseball's White Sox (see p.322). To reach the South Side, double-decker Illinois Central commuter trains run beside the lake to Prairie Avenue (a block from the 18th St station) and Hyde Park (near the 59th St station); CTA bus #1 follows Michigan Avenue to the same places, while bus #8 runs every fifteen minutes, 24 hours a day, south through Pilsen to Bridgeport.

Two blocks east of Michigan Avenue, a mile from the Loop and only a quarter of a mile from the lake, **Prairie Avenue** started life as an exclusive suburb. Though just ten minutes' walk from Grant Park and the Field Museum, it's best reached by cab, bus or train; the route is confusing and the streets are just not safe. As the one part of Chicago to remain unscathed in the Great Fire of 1871, this area had a brief moment of glory as the city's finest address. However, by 1900 the railroads had cut it off from Lake Michigan, and the expansion of the stockyards had encouraged the wealthy to flee back to their traditional North Side haunts.

One of the few structures to have survived the intervening years is the Romanesque 1886 **Glessner House**, Chicago's only surviving H H Richardson-designed house, standing sentry on the southwest corner of Prairie Avenue and 18th Street. Behind the forbidding stone facade, the house opens onto a garden court, its interior filled with Arts and Crafts furniture and swathed in William Morris fabrics and wall coverings. The place is maintained by the Chicago Architecture Foundation, who give guided tours (Wed–Sun noon–4pm; $11 joint admission with Clarke House). A block away stands Chicago's oldest building, the **Clarke House** at 1855 S Indiana Ave (details as for Glessner House), a plain white 1836 Greek Revival pioneer home that spent many years as a community center before being gussied up as a minor museum of interior decor. Much more interesting, and proof of the wealth once concentrated here, is the lavish Gothic **Presbyterian Church**, a block away at 1936 S Michigan Ave, with its Burne-Jones and Tiffany stained-glass windows.

An island of middle-class prosperity surrounded by urban poverty, **Hyde Park** is the most attractive and sophisticated South Side Chicago neighborhood. It's also one of the more racially integrated areas of the city, and among its more erudite: the **University of Chicago**, endowed by Rockefeller in 1892 and now among the top institutions in the US, has encouraged a college-town atmosphere, with bookshops and numerous cafes around its compact campus, especially along East 57th Street. On the campus itself, two buildings are well worth searching out: the massive Gothic pile of the **Rockefeller Memorial Chapel**, at 59th Street and Woodlawn Avenue, and the Prairie-style **Robie House**, designed by Frank Lloyd Wright, two blocks north at 5757 S Woodlawn Ave. Campus tours start from the Ida Noyes Hall, 1212 E 59th St (Mon–Sat 10am).

**Woodlawn Avenue** runs north from the University of Chicago campus, passing one of the South Side's most popular taverns, *Jimmy's Woodlawn Tap* at 1172 E 55th St, before turning a whole lot grander. Besides its enormous mansions, Woodlawn Avenue illustrates the social and racial mix for which Hyde Park is renowned: within two blocks of each other are the Midwest's largest Jewish temple, the ornate **Isaiah Israel** at 1100 E Hyde Park Blvd, and the home of **Minister Louis Farrakhan**, leader of the Nation of Islam, which was started here on the South Side in the 1940s by the late Elijah Muhammad. In between, at 4944 S Woodlawn Ave, stands the huge brick manor where boxer Muhammad Ali lived for many years.

Just west of the university, on the edge of lush Washington Park, the **Du Sable Museum of African-American History**, 740 E 56th Place, takes a look at the experience of Americans of African descent, from slavery to the present day (Mon–Sat 9am–5pm, Sun noon–5pm; $3). Named for Jean Du Sable, the Haitian-born Francophone who was Chicago's first permanent settler, it focuses on the works of WPA-sponsored artists of the 1930s and on the Black Power-era of the 1960s.

Washington Park wraps around the south of the University of Chicago campus, to join the long green strip of the **Midway** – one of the few reminders that a hundred years ago Chicago was the site of the **World's Columbian Exposition**. Attracting some thirty million spectators in the summer of 1893 (45 percent of the USA's population at the time), the Midway was then filled with full-sized model villages from around the globe, including an Irish market town and a mock-up of Cairo complete with belly dancers; these days it's used mainly by joggers and students tossing

Frisbees. The cavernous **Museum of Science and Industry**, 57th Street at Lake Shore Drive (summer Mon–Fri 9.30am–5.30pm; rest of year Mon–Fri 9.30am–4pm, Sat & Sun 9.30am–5.30pm; $7; free on Thurs), was Chicago's single most popular tourist destination (and ranked second in the US) until it started charging admission in 1991. Besides interactive computer displays, the best of which explores the inner workings of the brain, exhibits include a captured German U-boat, a trip down a replica coal mine, and a simulated space-shuttle journey; it's fun for kids, but adults may not feel like staying very long. The complex also hosts a giant OMNIMAX movie dome; admission is $7.50 extra.

**Promontory Point** juts into Lake Michigan just east of the museum, giving great views of the Chicago skyline, including a close-up look at Mies van der Rohe's first high-rise, the Promontory Apartments at 5530 S Lake Shore Drive.

# Eating

Chicago's cosmopolitan make-up is reflected in its plethora of ethnic restaurants. **Italian** food, ranging from hearty **deep-dish pizza** (developed in 1953 at *Pizzeria Uno*, see p.317) to delicately crafted creations presented at stylish trattorias, continues to dominate a very dynamic scene. In recent years there's been a surge of popularity for **New American** cuisine. **Thai** restaurants still thrive, as do ones with a broad **Mediterranean** slant, many of which serve tapas; and there are still plenty of opportunities to sample more longstanding Chicago cuisines – Eastern European, German, Mexican, Chinese, Indian, even Burmese and Ethiopian. Of course, there are a number of establishments that serve good old-fashioned barbecue **ribs**, a legacy of Chicago's days as the nation's meatpacker. And no visit to the city is complete without sampling a messy Italian beef sandwich, or a Chicago-style hot dog, laden with tomatoes, onions, hot peppers and a pickle.

The largest concentration of restaurants is found north and west of the **Loop**. To the west, **Greektown**, around Halsted Street at Jackson Boulevard, and **Little Italy**, on and around Taylor Street, are worth a look; the **Near North** and **River North** areas harbor a good number of upscale places; and **Chinatown**, though not pretty, is a predictably good neighborhood for Cantonese and Szechuan food. Many of the bars and cafes listed in the "Nightlife and entertainment" section also serve snacks and light meals, and dozens of places in the Loop offer great breakfast and lunch specials.

## Downtown

**The Berghoff**, 17 W Adams St (☎312/427-3170). A beautifully preserved Chicago landmark dating from 1893. Plentiful Germanic specialties plus fish dishes and corned beef and cabbage; try the draft or root beer. A bargain.

**Billy Goat Tavern**, 430 N Michigan Ave, lower level (☎312/222-1525). This legendary journalists' haunt opens early and closes late, serving the "cheezborgers" made famous by John Belushi's comedy skit. Very reasonable.

**Everest**, One Financial Place, 440 S LaSalle St (☎312/663-8920). Take in the stunning vista from the 40th floor and tuck into chef Jean Joho's wild mushroom consommé and roasted Maine lobster. Very expensive.

**Italian Village**, 71 W Monroe St (☎312/332-7005). Three Italian establishments under one roof. The *Village* has traditional Italian-American food and a world-class wine cellar; the basement *La Cantina* serves chicken Vesuvio, a Chicago creation, among its reasonably priced dishes; while the expensive *Vivere* (☎312/332-4040) has an adventurous menu, a mesmerizing wine list and a large pre-theater crowd (so arrive after 8pm).

**Lou Mitchell's**, 565 W Jackson Ave (☎312/939-3111). Near Union Station, *Lou's* has been around since 1923, serving terrific omelettes, waffles and hash browns all day long. Try the pecan-laden cookies.

**Marché**, 833 W Randolph St (☎312/226-8399). Creative French cuisine – try the porcini crusted Chilean sea bass – in an eclectic atmosphere in the Market District. Entrees $16–28.

**Prairie**, 500 S Dearborn St, in the *Hyatt* (☎312/663-1143). Modeled on a Frank Lloyd Wright interior, this place uses only fresh Midwestern ingredients in dishes such as sirloin of buffalo and brandied loaf of duck.

**Printers Row**, 550 S Dearborn St (☎312/461-0780). Seafood and game are highlights among the captivating New American concoctions devised by owner/chef Michael Foley. Quite pricey.

**Russian Tea Time**, 77 E Adams St (☎312/360-0000). This Midwestern nod to New York's *Russian Tea Room* serves a sampling of authentic fare from the former Soviet empire. Pricey, but lunch can be a bargain.

**Sorriso**, 312 N Clark St (☎312/644-0283). Alfresco dining with a spectacular view of the Loop riverfront and skyline. The menu features Italian and American dishes including *scungilli* (conch) salad. Piano bar occasionally serves free pizza during cocktail hour.

**Trattoria No 10**, 10 N Dearborn St (☎312/984-1718). A charming surprise in a series of underground rooms. Delicious warm bread (stuffed with sun-dried tomatoes), grilled sea scallops and risotto.

**Wishbone**, 1001 W Washington Blvd (☎312/850-2663) and 1800 W Grand (☎312/829-3597). Rich, down-home Southern cooking, with large portions and reasonable prices. Yardbird chicken (served with a red-pepper sauce), baked ham and sweet potato pie are wonderful.

## Greektown and Little Italy

**Costa's**, 340 S Halsted St (☎312/263-9707). Casual Greek place that's reasonably priced. Try the Mussels Salonika, or the cheese-stuffed roasted peppers.

**Gennaro's**, 1352 W Taylor St (☎312/243-1035). The speakeasy atmosphere is enhanced by the locked front door, opened after you're checked out through the peephole. Fine *gnocchi*.

**Greek Islands**, 200 S Halsted St (☎312/782-9855). A large place with several rustic "taverna" nooks; grilled sea bass and red snapper are fresh and flavorful.

**Parthenon**, 314 S Halsted St (☎312/726-2407). One of the oldest places in Greektown: *saganaki* (fried cheese doused with Metaxa brandy and ignited) was invented here.

**Pegasus**, 130 S Halsted St (☎312/226-3377). True hospitality and evocative wall murals add to the appeal of this popular establishment. Stuffed squid and *pastitsio* (macaroni, meat and cheese casserole) are recommended. The rooftop garden has a superb view of the Loop skyline.

**Santorini**, 800 W Adams St (☎312/829-8820). The decor re-creates a Greek island village, and the food is beguiling too; grilled octopus and lamb *exohiko* (wrapped in filo pastry and fried) are highlights.

**Tufano's Vernon Park Tap**, 1073 W Vernon Park Place (☎312/733-3393), near the United Center. A neighborhood landmark for over 60 years; its recent face-lift has eroded some of the original charm, but the chalkboard specials, good service and moderate prices remain. The antipasto and homemade ravioli are standouts.

**Tuscany**, 1014 W Taylor St (☎312/829-1990). The creative menu here includes wood-roasted chicken and terrific risottos. Service is very attentive, and there's a huge, bustling bar.

## Chinatown

**Emperor's Choice**, 2238 S Wentworth Ave (☎312/225-8800). Attractive storefront serving delicious egg rolls and seafood dishes: try steamed clams, poached shrimp or the lobster.

**Hong Min**, 221 W Cermak Rd (☎312/842-5026). Superb dim sum, with more than 36 lunch items. Cantonese and Mandarin specialties include West Lake duck with barbecued pork.

**Seven Treasures**, 2312 S Wentworth Ave (☎312/225-2668). Cantonese and some spicier Szechuan dishes concentrate on soups, dumplings and noodles. Reasonable prices.

**Sixty-Five**, 2414 S Wentworth Ave (☎312/225-7060). Two-story Cantonese with the emphasis on exceptional seafood. Try the family-style meals.

## Near North Side and River North

**Big Bowl Cafe**, 159 E Erie St (☎312/787-8297). Diner with an Asian accent. Filling soups and pot stickers make it a budget choice for weary shoppers.

**Cafe Iberico**, 739 N LaSalle Blvd (☎312/573-1510). Authentic and reasonably priced tapas bar where you can share plates of eggplant stuffed with goat's cheese or grilled octopus on potatoes.

**Celebrity Cafe**, 320 N Dearborn St (☎312/744-1900). A jazz combo entertains Sunday brunchers over a superb cold buffet, grilled fish and poached eggs with corned-beef hash cakes.

**Eli's The Place For Steak**, 215 E Chicago Ave (☎312/642-1393). Glitzy room perfect for celebrity-spotting; great steaks plus seafood and other nicely rendered dishes, and famous cheesecake.

**Frontera Grill & Topolobampo**, 445 N Clark St (☎312/661-1434). Wildly imaginative Mexican food: *La Frontera* is crowded and boisterous; *Topolobampo* is more refined and pricier.

**Gino's East**, 160 E Superior St (☎312/943-1124). A Chicago tradition: huge deep-dish pizzas (no need for appetizers here) and graffiti-covered walls. Expect to wait.

**Nacional 27**, 325 W Huron St (☎312/664-2727). Popular new Latin place serving food from a variety of Central American cuisines. Salsa dancing on weekends.

**Pizzeria Uno**, 29 E Ohio St (☎312/321-1000). The place that put Chicago deep-dish pizza on the map.

**Portillo's**, 100 W Ontario St (☎312/587-8930). This Chicago-area chain serves good Chicago hot dogs and the best Italian beef sandwich in the city.

**Scoozi!**, 410 W Huron St (☎312/943-5900). Ebullient mixture of nostalgic (there's an accordion player) and trendy (it's a place to be seen). Emphasis on Northern Italian, with splendid pizza and risotto.

**Shaw's Crab House**, 21 E Hubbard St (☎312/527-2722). This large 1930s Key West-style dining room is crowded at lunch and after work; its consistently high-quality fare includes baked crab cakes, Dungeness crab in garlic butter, seafood gumbo and popcorn shrimp. Not cheap.

**Star of Siam**, 11 E Illinois St (☎312/670-0100). Terrific Thai food served in a spacious, inviting setting. The *Tom yom* soup, Pad Thai noodle dish and curries are top-notch.

## Old Town

**Blue Mesa** 1729 N Halsted St (☎312/944-5990) near the Steppenwolf Theater. Bountiful and delicious Southwestern brunch served on Sunday in the pueblo-style interior or on the patio in warm weather. Great margaritas, too.

**Café Ba-Ba-Reeba!**, 2024 N Halsted (☎773/935-5000). One of the city's Spanish hot spots, with a good variety of hot and cold tapas, filling paella and, of course, sangria.

**Flat Top Grill**, 319 W North Ave (☎312/787-7676). Create-your-own stir-fry with a wide variety of meats, vegetables, and mild-to-spicy sauces.

**Old Jerusalem**, 1411 N Wells St (☎312/944-0459). Old-time favourite serves reasonable Middle Eastern dishes; the falafel is great. Bring your own beer or wine.

**Topo Gigio**, 1516 N Wells St (☎312/266-9355). Well-prepared Italian cuisine served by the very friendly staff in a peaceful garden amid the Old Town bustle. The homemade tiramisu is fabulous.

**Twin Anchors**, 1655 N Sedgwick St (☎312/266-1231). You'll wait for a seat in a neighborhood spot that's famed for its BBQ ribs, but the interesting clientele and 1950s-style bar make it worth it.

## Lincoln Park and around

**Ann Sather**, 929 W Belmont Ave (☎773/348-2378) and four other locations. A Chicago institution for breakfast, brunch and some of the finest Scandinavian food in the city.

**Brother Jimmy's BBQ**, 2909 N Sheffield Ave (☎773/528-0888). The BBQ chicken and three kinds of ribs (aficionados say Northern are the best) come with side orders such as candied yams or collard greens and corn bread. Moderate prices, and loud live music Thurs–Sun.

**Charlie Trotter's**, 816 W Armitage Ave (☎773/248-6228). Prepare for a superb, and appropriately pricey, experience. Chef Trotter is a true artist and his daring creations, such as caviar-stuffed quail eggs or Maine salmon with blood sausage, are constantly evolving.

**Chicago Diner**, 3411 N Halsted St (☎773/935-6696). Open over 20 years, this vegetarian restaurant incorporates international influences in its expansive menu. Soup, salads, "Future Burgers" (rice, couscous and vegetables) and the macrobiotic plate are popular. Vegan dishes served as well.

**Little Bucharest**, 3001 N Ashland Ave (☎773/929-8640). A Romanian inn serving huge stews, roasts and sweetbreads. Rich desserts are served with a complimentary *slibovitz* (plum brandy). A bargain.

**Mia Francesca**, 3311 N Clark St (☎773/281-3310). Huge servings of pasta and tasty pizzas (try the *quattro formaggi*) ensure that this cozy Italian place with a no-reservations policy is always packed.

**RJ Grunts**, 2056 Lincoln Park W (☎773/929-5363). Great burgers and a top-notch salad bar – purported to be the nation's first – in a casual neighborhood atmosphere.

**Yoshi's Cafe**, 3257 N Halsted St (☎773/248-2310). East–West fusion with a French accent, which works especially well with tuna or fluke (sea urchin). More Asian is the three-course *kaiseki* menu of tiny dishes. Very expensive.

**Zum Deutschen Eck**, 2924 N Southport Ave (☎773/525-8121). Charmingly old-fashioned, family-run place serving vast helpings of roast pork loin, sausages and schnitzels at relatively low prices. An oompah singalong duo performs Thurs–Sun.

### Wicker Park

**Cafe Absinthe**, 1954 W North Ave (☎773/278-4488). Fine French dining in a romantic, casual setting. One of the city's best.

**Irazu**, 1865 N Milwaukee Ave (☎773/252-5687). Wonderful Costa Rican diner; great burritos plus a small selection of authentic main courses.

**Smoke Daddy**, 1804 W Division St (☎773/772-6656). Arguably Chicago's best BBQ, with jazz and blues nightly. Vegetarian options too.

**Soul Kitchen**, 1576 N Milwaukee Ave (☎773/342-9742). Loud joint where a youthful crowd munches on the likes of pecan-breaded catfish and fire-and-spice lamb.

### The South Side: Hyde Park

**Dixie Kitchen**, 5225 S Harper, Harper Court (☎773/363-4943). Great soul food, including pulled pork sandwiches, breaded oysters with chili sauce, and desserts like peach cobbler and pecan pie.

**Medici on 57th**, 1327 S 57th St (☎773/667-7394). Quintessential collegiate hangout right next to the University of Chicago. Chummy crowd chows down on burgers, pizza, salads and ice cream.

**Mellow Yellow**, 1508 E 53rd St (☎773/667-2000). A soul food emphasis is evident in the catfish, steaks, seafood and rotisserie chicken served at this casual, popular place – it does crepes and quiche, too.

**TJ's**, 5500 S Lake Shore Drive (☎773/752-6191). Fresh Cajun-style swordfish, rack of lamb and prime rib are highlights in this comfortable establishment opposite the Museum of Science and Industry.

**Valois Cafeteria**, 1518 E 53rd St (☎773/667-0647). A budget-priced menu featuring baked chicken, barbecue ribs and pork sandwiches. Don't skip the freshly baked biscuits.

## Drinking

If not quite as wild as in the bootlegging days of speakeasies and Prohibition, Chicago remains a consummate boozer's town and is one of the best US cities for **bars**, catering to just about every group and interest and many open to 3 or 4am, some until 5am. One thing Chicago has more of than anywhere else on earth is "**sports bars**," where banks of TV screens broadcast Cubs, Sox, Bears, Bulls and Blackhawks games – great places for beer drinking and male bonding, but not for thoughtful conversation. **Division Street**, in the two blocks west of State Street, is unreconstructed breeder-bar territory, with a handful of more subtle joints tucked away on side streets off the main drag. **Wicker Park**, a couple of miles north of Lincoln Park, is the trendiest hangout zone, while Halsted Street between Belmont and Addison is known as **Boystown** for its gay bars and clubs.

There are over a hundred **cafes and coffeehouses** across the city as well; they may not have taken the place of the traditional tavern, but they're a growing alternative.

## Saloons, pubs and bars

**Bar Louie**, 226 W Chicago Ave (☎312/337-3313). Friendly, casual place in River North with tables out front and cheap bar food.

**Berghoff's**, 17 W Adams St (☎312/427-3170). Former men-only stand-up bar in a showcase c.1900 tavern next to *The Berghoff* restaurant. Lunchtime and after work is crowded and congenial.

**Cavanaugh's**, 53 W Jackson St (☎312/939-3125). In the historic Monadnock Building, a Loop favorite for an after-work drink. Warm interior with antique woodwork, Harp on draft and a full menu.

**Delilah's**, 2771 N Lincoln Ave (☎773/472-2771). Murkily lit bar playing underground records – from alternative country to ambient techno – at night. Great selection of beers and bourbons.

**Goose Island Brewing Co**, 1800 N Clybourn Ave (☎773/915-0071). Forty ales and lagers, including the popular Honker's Ale, are brewed on the premises at this convivial Lincoln Park haunt.

**Green Door Tavern**, 678 N Orleans St (☎312/664-5496). In an unlikely spot near the galleries of River North, this historic place is chock-full of Chicago memorabilia: some pure kitsch, others genuine antiques. Drink at the long bar or settle into a cozy back room to sample "home-style cooking."

**Howard's**, 152 E Ontario St (☎312/787-5269). This dark little Near North space is popular with media types and serves good burgers. Its ace card is the patio out back.

**John Barleycorn**, 658 W Belden Ave (☎773/348-8899). Dimly lit Lincoln Park pub that has retained its character. A lovely garden open in summer. Daily all-you-can-eat specials.

**Old Town Ale House**, 219 W North Ave (☎312/944-7020). An eclectic crowd of scruffy regulars and yuppies mingle in this convivial haunt, complete with pinball and a library of paperbacks.

**O'Rourke's Pub**, 1625 N Halsted St (☎773/335-1806). Photos of Irish writers line the walls of this dark Old Town theatrical haunt. Guinness and Bass on draft; the jukebox plays vintage jazz.

**Rainbo Club**, 1150 N Damen Ave (☎773/489–5999). Busy Wicker Park bar and hangout for indie-rock types.

**The Red Lion Pub**, 2446 N Lincoln Ave (☎773/348-2695). British ales and ciders, fish and chips and shepherd's pie in an authentic pub atmosphere, complete with singalong piano.

**Resis' Beerstube**, 2034 W Irving Park Rd (☎773/472-1749). Old-time German tavern featuring good imported draft and bottled beers, platters of wurst and a delightful shaded beer garden.

## Sports bars

**ESPNZone**, 43 E Ohio St (☎312/644-3776). Part futuristic game parlor, part megalithic sports bar/restaurant, the *Zone's* food is just so-so, and service is sluggish, but sports fans will probably still pack it up.

**Harry Caray's**, 33 W Kinzie St (☎312/465-9269). Great sports bar/Italian restaurant in an old River North brick warehouse. Founded by former Cub radio and TV announcer Caray, the huge bar is packed with beer drinkers until the early hours and has floor to ceiling Cubs memorabilia.

**Michael Jordan's**, 500 N LaSalle St (☎312/644-3865). The bar has one TV screen, but it's the biggest in town. Laid-back atmosphere, and Michael makes the odd appearance in the pricey restaurant upstairs.

**Slugger's**, 3540 N Clark St (☎773/248-0055). Probably the only bar in the world with its own indoor batting cage, this raucous beer bar fairly rattles and hums during Cubs, Bears and Bulls games. Ridiculously inexpensive beer during happy hour.

**Wrigleyville Tap**, 3724 N Clark St (☎773/528-4422). The pick of the bars near Wrigley Field. Less boisterous than most, it gets a pleasant mix of sports fans and people from the *Metro* club next door.

## Gay & lesbian bars

**Big Chicks**, 5024 N Sheridan Rd, Andersonville (☎773/728-5511). Friendly place that has a free jukebox and free barbecues out back on summer Sundays.

**The Closet**, 3325 N Broadway (☎773/477-8533). Tiny, cramped but congenial lesbian bar that attracts its share of gay men as well.

**Gentry**, 440 N State St (☎773/836-0933). Cabaret and piano bar popular with corporate types after work.

**Sidetrack**, 3349 N Halsted St (☎773/477-9189). One of the most popular bars along Halsted's gay strip in Lakeview.

## Cafés

**The Bourgeois Pig**, 738 W Fullerton Ave (☎773/883-5282). Inventive sandwiches in a laid-back student atmosphere.

**Caffe Pergolesi**, 3404 N Halsted St (☎773/472-8602). A mostly vegetarian cafe with a distinctly laid-back, Greenwich Village-style atmosphere. Call to check on their quirky opening hours.

**Caffe Trevi**, 2275 N Lincoln Ave (☎773/871-4310). Old-fashioned coffeehouse that hosts poetry and prose readings one Sun a month, and live jazz every Wed and Sun.

**Equinox Cafe**, 2300 N Lincoln Ave (☎773/477-5126). In an Art Nouveau building – originally an apothecary/ice-cream parlor – with wonderful mahogany cabinets and original tiled floor. Classical piano music on Mon, while Tues is devoted to blues and jazz piano. Extensive menu.

**Kopi, A Traveler's Cafe**, 5317 N Clark St, Andersonville (☎773/989-5374). A bit of a trek from downtown, but a really splendid combo coffee-and-tea house, Indonesian art gallery, boutique and bookstore stocked with travel guides and literature. Live music and prose/poetry readings.

# Nightlife and entertainment

From its earliest frontier days, Chicago has had some of the best **nightlife** in the US. Sweet Home Chicago, birthplace of Muddy Waters' **urban blues**, as well as R&B's Chess Records, is still going strong, inspiring the energetic dance beat of 1980s **house music** as well as the groundbreaking **jazz** of the Art Ensemble of Chicago. **Nightclubs** aplenty are all over town, especially along Halsted Street, Lincoln Avenue and Clark Street on the North Side; **uptown**, at the intersection of North Broadway and Lawrence, is a bit down-at-heel, but has half a dozen good venues; the best **gay clubs** congregate in the Lincoln Park area. More highbrow pursuits are also well provided for: Chicago's **classical music**, **dance** and **theater** are world class.

For what's on information, Chicagoans pick up the excellent **free newspaper** *The Reader* (copies comes out Thursday afternoon and are usually all gone by Saturday); the weekly *New City* and the gay and lesbian *Windy City Times* are good sources as well. Full listings also appear in the Friday issues of the *Chicago Sun-Times* and the *Chicago Tribune*, and *Chicago* magazine has useful arts and restaurant listings. The Gramaphone Ltd record store at 2663 N Clark St (☎773/472-3683) is the best place for details of one-off **dance** nights.

## Blues

**B.L.U.E.S.**, 2519 N Halsted St (☎773/528-1012). Opened over two decades ago and still going strong, though a little over-touristed. The tiny stage has been graced by all the greats.

**Blue Chicago**, 536 N Clark St (☎312/661-0100). Touristy blues joint featuring mostly female performers.

**Buddy Guy's Legends**, 754 S Wabash Ave (☎312/427-0333). South Loop club owned by veteran guitarist and vocalist Buddy Guy. It aims to present the very best local and national acts. Great acoustics and atmosphere, and not as touristy as other downtown blues clubs.

**Checkerboard Lounge**, 423 E 43rd St (☎773/624-3240). Way down on the South Side, the *Checkerboard* has a fabulous history and retains the support of the best local acts.

**Kingston Mines**, 2548 N Halsted St (☎773/477-4646). Top-notch local and national acts on two stages play to an up-for-it partying crowd.

**Rosa's**, 3420 W Armitage Ave (☎773/342-0452). Run by Mama Rosa and her son, this is undoubtedly the friendliest blues joint around, hosting lectures and courses for real aficionados.

## Jazz

**Andy's**, 11 E Hubbard St (☎312/642-6805). Very popular with the after-work crowd; informal with moderate prices.

**The Cotton Club**, 1710 S Michigan Ave (☎312/341-9787). Sophisticated, live-music venue and disco; attracts a well-dressed, mellow crowd.

**Green Dolphin Street**, 2200 N Ashland Ave (☎773/395-0066). Swanky, pricey restaurant and jazz club with a solid line-up of regular performers.

**The Green Mill**, 4802 N Broadway (☎773/878-5552). This place had a checkered past during Prohibition and is in the tough uptown neighborhood, but is one of the best – and most beautiful – rooms for local and national talent.

**Joe Segal's Jazz Showcase**, 59 W Grand Ave (☎312/670-2473). Classy, dressy room hosting premier jazz by top names.

**Toulouse Cognac Bar**, 2140 N Lincoln Park W (☎773/665-9071). Upscale room where the friendly crowd shouts out requests. Inimitable jazz violinist Johnny Frigo plays with pianist Joe Vito on Mon.

## Rock clubs

**Cubby Bear**, 1059 W Addison St (☎773/327-1662). A sports bar during the day – right next to Wrigley Field – after dark this place transforms itself into one of the city's most boisterous and eclectic live venues, popular with ageing dinosaurs more than new bands, but still fun.

**Double Door**, 1572 N Milwaukee Ave (☎773/489-3160). Happening eclectic venue in the Wicker district with good sound and sight lines. Sundays feature Chicago acid jazz legends Liquid Soul.

**Elbo Room**, 2871 N Lincoln Ave (☎773/549-5549). Mostly indie/alternative bands on the way up.

**Empty Bottle**, 1035 N Western Ave (☎773/276-3600). More up-and-coming indie, along with avant-garde jazz, and progressive country.

**House of Blues**, 329 N Dearborn St (☎312/527-2583). Despite its name, this swish Near North venue puts on all kinds of music.

**Lounge Ax**, 2438 N Lincoln Ave (☎773/525-6620). Small, old bar room, with a nationwide reputation, that hosts some of the best new alternative bands. Always crowded at weekends.

**Metro**, 3730 N Clark St (☎773/549-0203). Arguably the top spot in the city, this club, in an old cinema building, regularly hosts young English bands trying to break in Stateside, and DJ mixes.

## Folk, country and world music clubs

**Baby Doll Polka Club**, 6102 S Central Ave (☎773/582-9706). For 40 years, this Southwest Side club has been full of locals doing the polka, two-step and the occasional tango.

**Equator Club**, 4715 N Broadway (☎773/728-2411). West African dance music, and appearances by top artists, in a gorgeous old building that once housed a speakeasy owned by Al Capone.

**Fitzgerald's**, 6615 W Roosevelt, Berwyn (☎708/788-2118). Excellent venue for alternative country, Americana, Cajun and zydeco in the western suburb of Berwyn.

**Old Town School of Folk Music**, 909 W Armitage Ave (☎773/525-7793). Established in 1959, this place presents about 80 concerts a year, including just about every type of folk.

**Schuba's**, 3159 N Southport Ave at Belmont Ave (☎773/525-2508). Some of the best alternative country and roots revival bands play this likeable bar at weekends.

## Dance

**Circus**, 901 W Weed St (☎312/266-1200). Hot new celebrity hangout featuring cartoonish, technicolor decor and a live trapeze act.

**Crobar**, 1543 N Kingsbury St (☎312/413-7000). Exclusive, hyper-trendy warehouse club near the river spinning the newest techno and house. Gay night Sun.

**Drink**, 702 W Fulton St (☎312/733-7800). Three huge floors with eight bars (including one in an elevator). Disco Thurs with the Afrodisiacs.

**Excalibur**, 632 N Dearborn St (☎312/266-1944). An institution in the city, blasting out rock, R&B and Motown on several floors.

**Iggy's**, 700 N Milwaukee Ave (☎312/829-4449). This place gets lively at about 3am at the weekend; the red-velvet interior looks like a bordello, and there's a cute patio.

**Karma**, 318 W Grand Ave (☎312/321-1331). Cutting-edge house and techno in a Hindi-funk setting in River North.

**Red Dog**, 1958 W North Ave (☎773/278-1009). Small Wicker Park club, or "funk parlor" as they like to call it, playing acid jazz, house, soul and funk. The entrance is in the alley.

**Smart Bar**, underneath the *Metro*, 3730 N Clark St (☎773/549-0203). Great techno and house at the weekend in post-industrial Wrigleyville surrounds. Weekdays see a mix of punk, goth and Eighties. The whole complex is open late – until 5am Fri and Sat.

**Voyeur**, 151 W Ohio St (☎312/832-1717). For clubgoers who take their people-watching seriously, this popular space offers two-way mirrors, fish-eye lenses, and closed-circuit TV cameras trained on the stainless-steel dance floor.

## Theater and comedy

While it was once every Chicago actor's and playwright's ambition to end up in New York, many are now quite content to remain here. The city now supports numerous **theater** companies, many of them – notably Steppenwolf, John Malkovich's former company, at 1650 N Halsted St (☎312/335-1888) – with reputations as good as any in the US. Notable Chicago theaters include the Court Theater, 5535 S Ellis St (☎773/753-4472), and Goodman Theater, 200 S Columbus Ave (☎312/443-3800). **Comedy**, too, is particularly vibrant; Chicago's improvisational scene is considered the best in the nation, with the troupe at Second City, 1231 N Wells St (☎312/337-3992), especially renowned.

## Classical music, opera and dance

Under Daniel Barenboim, who is committed to including more contemporary music in its repertoire, the profile of the world-renowned **Chicago Symphony Orchestra** – based at the Orchestra Hall, 220 S Michigan Ave (☎312/435-8122 or 435-8172) – looks like being raised yet higher. The 186-member **Symphony Chorus** performs both classical and contemporary choral works with the CSO, specifically in summer at the open-air **Ravinia Festival**, 25 miles north of downtown Chicago. The **Lyric Opera of Chicago**, 20 N Wacker Drive (☎312/332-2244), now under the directorship of William Mason, performs in the beautiful Civic Opera House; its season is from mid-September to early February, and most performances are sold out.

The **Joffrey Ballet** is the city's prime classically oriented dance company, based at 70 E Lake St (☎312/739-0120). **Hubbard Street Dance Chicago**, 218 S Wabash Ave (☎312/663-0853), is more contemporary but equally talented.

## Sports

Staunchly blue-collar Chicago must be among the best US cities for watching **sports**, as Chicagoans are, for better or worse, loyally supportive of their sports teams. The city's most successful outfit of late has been the Michael Jordan-led **Chicago Bulls** basketball team, winner of six NBA championships in the '90s. Now that Jordan has retired, however, Bulls fans have little to cheer about. The Bulls play in the ultramodern United Center, 1901 W Madison St, as do hockey's **Blackhawks** (both ☎312/559-1212). The **Chicago Bears** football team (☎847/615-2327) can be seen at the 66,000-capacity Soldier's Field at 425 E McFetridge Drive, at the south end of Grant Park.

As for baseball, the two Chicago teams – the Cubs and the White Sox – have not won a World Series since 1917. The **Chicago White Sox** (☎312/831-1SOX) play at the modern Comiskey Park at 333 W 35th St on the South Side. To fans, the real tragedy of

1994's baseball strike was the squelching of the then top-placed Sox' dreams of bringing the World Series to Chicago for the first time in almost eighty years. The **Chicago Cubs** (☎312/831-CUBS), meanwhile, are more consistent – they break North-Siders' hearts every year – but their games remain well-attended thanks to marquis players like Sammy Sosa and to the atmosphere conjured up at grand old Wrigley Field (described on p.312), near Lincoln Park.

# Central Illinois

Interstates 55 and 57 slice south through the Corn Belt of **central Illinois** from Chicago. Parallel to I-55, the legendary **Route 66** began its run here, cutting through the state and onto the Pacific Coast – you might try to catch a glimpse of it, as some old-time diners and other Americana still stand. One worthwhile stop, reachable by either interstate, is the state capital, **Springfield**, which interestingly commemorates President and former resident **Abraham Lincoln**. Otherwise, if you're on your way south, the college towns of **Bloomington-Normal** and **Champaign-Urbana** are the only rational urban stops, while if you're heading west from Chicago it's well worth pausing at the delightful old river town of **Galena**.

## Springfield

The Illinois state capital, **SPRINGFIELD**, spreads out from a neat, leafy downtown grid, 199 miles south of Chicago. Abraham Lincoln honed his legal and political skills here, and tourists flock to his old homes, haunts and final resting place. What they find is neither tacky nor pompous, portraying not only the life of the sixteenth president of the USA, but also the uncertainty and turmoil of a nation on the brink of civil war.

Twenty miles northwest of Springfield on Hwy-97, **Lincoln's New Salem State Historical Site** marks where the future president first came to live in this area in 1831. In this backwoods clearing he clerked in a store, volunteered for the Black Hawk War, served as postmaster and failed in business before taking up legal studies and moving to Springfield to pursue his political career. Today the authentically re-created village features simple homes, workshops, a store and a tavern. The **visitor center** hosts a worthwhile exhibit on pioneer lifestyles (March–Oct daily 9am–5pm; Nov–Feb daily 8am–4pm). On summer weekends the park presents *Abraham!*, a musical that dramatizes Lincoln's New Salem years.

Pick up tickets at the **Lincoln Home Visitor Center**, at Eighth and Jackson in Springfield itself, for a narrated tour of the only house Lincoln ever owned, which he shared with his wife Mary from 1844 to 1861. Though tours are free (daily 8.30am–5pm, though often later) you can expect to wait: various displays and a brief film at the visitor center are good ways of passing time.

In the restored Greek Revival **Old State Capitol**, three blocks away at Sixth and Adams (March–Oct daily 9am–5pm; Nov–Feb daily 9am–4pm; free), Lincoln attended at least 240 Supreme Court hearings, and proclaimed in 1858 that "A house divided against itself cannot stand. I believe that this government cannot endure, permanently, half-slavery, half-freedom." Objects, busts and papers relating to Lincoln and the Democrat Stephen Douglas, whom he beat in the 1860 presidential election, can be found throughout the building. At the tastefully renovated **Lincoln Depot** on Tenth and Monroe (April–Aug daily 10am–4pm; free), the newly elected president said goodbye to Springfield in February 1861 and boarded a train for his inauguration in Washington DC (a slide show illustrates the twelve-day journey). The next time he returned was in his funeral train. **Lincoln's Tomb** stands in Oak Ridge Cemetery on the north side of town. The vault, adorned with busts and statuettes, is open to the public (March–Oct daily 9am–5pm; Nov–Feb daily 9am–4pm; free).

At the current **Illinois State Capitol**, in majestic limestone at Second and Capitol, tour highlights include the chambers of the state Senate and House of Representatives, in striking red and blue, respectively (Mon–Fri 8am–4pm; free). The **Illinois State Museum**, on Spring and Edwards, is crammed with natural history and Native American and contemporary art exhibits, along with the interactive "**At Home in the Heartland**" display tracing Illinois family life from 1700 to 1970 (Mon–Sat 8.30am–5pm, Sun noon–5pm; free). The **Dana-Thomas House**, 301 E Lawrence Ave, completed in 1904, survives as the best-preserved and most completely furnished example of **Frank Lloyd Wright**'s early Prairie house, with over four hundred pieces of glasswork, original art and light fixtures (tours Wed–Sun 9am–4pm; $3). Just north of town, Bill Shea proudly displays 50 years worth of road signs, gas pumps, and Route 66 memorabilia at **Shea's Gas Station Museum** (Tues–Fri 9am–4pm, Sat 9am–noon; free).

### Practicalities

Amtrak **trains** from Chicago and St Louis roll in at Third and Washington downtown, at manageable times; Greyhound drops off two miles east of downtown at 2351 S Dirksen Parkway. The **CVB**, 109 N Seventh St (Mon–Fri 8am–5pm; ☎217/789-2360 or 1-800/545-7300), has brochures and maps. The best selection of budget **accommodation**, including a *Days Inn* (☎217/753-4000; ③), lies off I-55 at the Dirksen Parkway exit, though downtown accommodation is reasonably priced – even the swanky politicians' hotels offer affordable deals at the weekend. Central options include the *Best Western Lincoln Plaza*, 101 E Adams St (☎217/523-5661 or 1-800/528-1234; ④), right next to the capitol and Amtrak, and the *Mansion View Inn & Suites*, 529 S Fourth St (☎217/544-7411 or 1-800/252-1083; ④). *The Inn at 835*, 835 S Second Ave (☎217/523-4466; ⑤), is a charming eleven-room **B&B** converted from a 1900 downtown apartment block.

Springfield's cafes seem to have exclusive rights to a phenomenon known as the **Horseshoe** – ostensibly a sandwich, but fried, covered in melted cheese and very tasty. *Norb Andy's*, 518 E Capitol Ave (☎217/523-7777), musters up the best Horseshoes around. The *Cozy Dog Drive-In* at 2935 S Sixth St (☎217/525-1992) claims to be the birthplace of the **Cozy Dog** (also known as the corn dog), a deep-fried, batter-drenched hot dog on a stick. At the other end of the health spectrum, *Augie's Front Burner*, 2 W Old State Capitol Plaza (☎217/544-6979), serves up good California-style and vegetarian meals, while *Sebastian's Hideout*, 221 S Fifth St (☎217/789–8988), has a wide-ranging Mediterranean menu with good couscous dishes and occasional jazz or blues. Just north of New Salem on Hwy-97, the pleasant *New Salem Restaurant* (☎217/632-2232) serves up sandwiches and salads at reasonable prices.

## Galena

The neat little town of **GALENA**, ten miles short of both Iowa and Wisconsin in the far northwest corner of Illinois, can have changed little since its nineteenth-century heyday. Thanks to its sheltered location just a few miles up the Galena River, it was a major port of call for Mississippi steamboats. These days the only traffic it gets are the day-trippers who come to admire the gentle crescent of Main Street, tucked in behind an immaculate grassy levee. Its impeccable redbrick facades and graceful skyline of spires and crosses place it among the most attractive river towns in the US. With the aid of the free *Galenian* guide from the visitor center (see opposite), you can spend an enjoyable few hours on a walking tour of the various historic sites along both Main Street and Bench Street, which squeezes onto the steep bluff immediately above it.

JERRY DENNIS

Brooklyn Bridge, New York City

CHARLES BOWMAN

Billboard, New York City

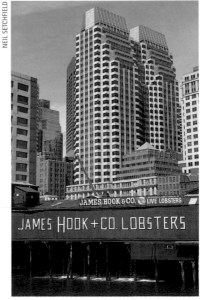

NEIL SETCHFIELD

Boston, MA

Fall colors, New England

Sun Studio, Memphis TN

The 'El', Chicago IL

Sears Tower, Chicago IL

Lighthouse, ME

Community church on the appalachian trail, Laurel Valley, Virginia

Capitol Building, Washington DC

Adams Morgan district, Washington DC

Agriculture and Forestry Musuem, Jackson MS

Galena boasts of having contributed nine generals to the Union army during the Civil War, much the most significant of whom was **Ulysses Simpson Grant**. Grant moved to the town in 1860, working as a clerk in a leather store owned by his father and operated by his two brothers. Some contemporary accounts speak of him as the town lush, the kind of person decent folk crossed the street to avoid. However, his West Point education encouraged the townspeople to appoint him as colonel when they raised the 21st Illinois regiment on the outbreak of war. When he came home, in August 1865, it was as overall commander of the victorious army.

The grateful citizens of Galena presented Grant with a **house**, a couple of blocks up Bouthillier Street on the far side of the river (daily 9am–5pm; $2 suggested donation). It's not a grand place by any means, but it was in the plainly furnished downstairs drawing room that Grant received the news of his election as president in 1868. Although he went on to serve two terms, he is commonly agreed to have been a better general than president: his administrations were plagued by scandal, and he lost all his own money through unwise investments. The family fortunes were only restored just before his death in 1885, when Mark Twain first persuaded him to write, and then published, Grant's best-selling *Memoirs*.

## Practicalities

The 1857 Railroad Museum, across the river from the town proper at 101 Bouthillier St, serves as the local **visitor center** (Mon–Thurs 9am–5pm, Fri & Sat 9am-7pm, Sun 10am–5pm; ☎815/777-0203 or 1-800/777-4390), and provides the most convenient short-term parking lot.

The plush *DeSoto House Hotel*, 230 S Main St (☎815/777-0090 or 1-800/343-6562; ⑦), was Grant's campaign headquarters in 1868; its grand *Generals' Restaurant* serves steak and seafood dinners. If your budget won't stretch that far, the *Triangle Motel*, at highways 20 and 84 (☎815/777-2897; ③), makes a good-value alternative. As for inexpensive spots to **eat**, *Boone's Place*, 305 S Main St (☎815/777-4488), is a reliable espresso and sandwich bar.

# WISCONSIN

As many cows as humans call **WISCONSIN** home. About four million of each eat to their hearts' content in this rich, rolling farmland, which has a higher proportion of overweight people than any other state. However, America's self-proclaimed "Dairyland" is more than just one giant pasture. Beyond the massive red barns and silvery silos lie endless pine forests, some 15,000 sky-blue lakes, postcard-pretty valleys and dramatic bluffs. The state, whose Ojibway name means "gathering of the waters," is bordered by Lake Michigan to the east, Lake Superior in the north and, to the west, the Mississippi and St Croix rivers; only the southern, Illinois, demarcation is dry.

The **history** of Wisconsin exemplifies the standard formula for westward expansion. Seventeenth-century French and British explorers began by trading with the Native Americans and soon ousted them from their land. The European settlers who followed – predominantly Germans, Scandinavians and Poles – tended to be liberal and progressive; such major national social programs as labor laws for women and children, assistance for the elderly and the disabled, and unemployment compensation were rooted here. On the downside, Joseph McCarthy, the infamous 1950s witch-hunter, was born in Grand Chute, former headquarters of the right-wing John Birch Society.

Wisconsin today is best known for its liquids. The **milk** from all those cattle yields cheeses of all kinds, while the **beer**, as the song says, is what made **Milwaukee** famous. Sparkling Madison apart, Wisconsin's other cities – **LaCrosse, Green Bay,**

**Oshkosh** – can veer towards the dull side, but they're also clean, safe and amiable, while its smaller towns can be distinctive and charming.

## Getting around Wisconsin

You'll be hard put to explore Wisconsin's remote north, or key locales like the Door County peninsula, without a vehicle. Public transportation is better in the south. Milwaukee and, to a lesser extent, Madison are hubs for Greyhound and Amtrak. Five **trains** daily connect Milwaukee and Chicago, a ninety-minute journey, while one crosses the state in the south en route for Seattle, via Columbus (near Madison), Portage, Wisconsin Dells, Tomah and LaCrosse.

# Milwaukee

Bustling **MILWAUKEE**, the "Deutsch Athens" of southeastern Wisconsin, is a combination of the down-home and the sophisticated, known for its lakeside and ethnic **festivals** and huge **breweries**. Visually it's a mix of elegant Teutonic architecture, rambling Victorian warehouses and tasteful waterfront developments. Its prime position on the shores of Lake Michigan, at the confluence of three rivers, made it a meeting place for Native groups long before white settlers moved in, while the opulent mansions lining the lake commemorate the industrialists who helped make this Wisconsin's economic and manufacturing capital. By 1850, less than two decades old and with a population of twenty thousand, Milwaukee already had a dozen breweries and 225 saloons. The contemporary estimate of six thousand bars – one per hundred residents – is not necessarily apocryphal.

## Arrival, information and getting around

Milwaukee is well served by air, rail and bus. Its **airport**, eight miles south of downtown at 5300 S Howell Ave, is connected with the city center by bus #80 ($1.35), and by limousine service ($8.50). A taxi will set you back about $15. Amtrak is at 433 W St Paul Ave, while Greyhound and Wisconsin Coach (☎414/542-7434), serving southeastern Wisconsin, operate out of the same terminal at 606 N James Lovell Drive. Badger Bus (☎414/276-7490), across the street at no. 635, runs an express service to Madison (six daily, $18 round-trip). Take care in and around the stations at night. **Getting around** Milwaukee is easy and inexpensive via the county's extensive **transportation system** (24-hour info ☎414/344-6711; flat fare $1.35). The Milwaukee Loop is a special trolley service connecting 18 stops in the city's center (Wed–Sat 10am–10pm, Sun till 6pm; $1 to hop on and off all day).

Milwaukee's **CVB**, 510 W Kilbourn Ave (Mon–Fri 8am–5pm, Sat 9am–2pm; ☎414/273-3950 or 1-800/554-1448), has details on such **festivals** as the eleven-day Summerfest (late June to early July), Great Circus Parade (usually mid-July) and the Wisconsin State Fair (early Aug). The main **post office** is at 345 W St Paul Ave (Mon–Fri 7.30am–8pm; ☎414/270-2000; zip code 53203).

## Accommodation

**Lodgings** in Milwaukee run the gamut from low-budget to upmarket chains to luxury hotels. Alternatively, **Cedarburg** is a tranquil and attractive Currier & Ives-type village twenty miles north; the *Washington House* (☎414/375-3550; ④) and *Stagecoach* (☎414/375-0208 or 1-888/375-0208; ④) inns here are charming.

**The Astor**, 924 E Juneau Ave (☎414/271-4220 or 1-800/558-0200; in Wisconsin 1-800/242-0355). Classy, historic 1920s hotel, offering free continental breakfast and health club passes. Extended stays available. ⑤.

**HI-Red Barn**, 6750 W Loomis Rd (☎414/529-3299). Hostel 13 miles southwest, via Hwy-894 or buses #10 and #35 (best avoided at night). Hiking and biking trails. May–Oct only; $10 members, $13 others. Check-in 5–10pm. ①.

**Crane House B&B**, 346 E Wilson St (☎414/483-1512). Handsome B&B in self-contained suburb-that's-not-a-suburb Bay View. Excellent breakfasts. ④.

**Park East Hotel**, 916 E State St (☎414/276-8800 or 1-800/328-PARK). Clean, very comfortable rooms in a nice part of downtown. Good value compared to the bigger hotels. ⑤.

# The City

**Downtown Milwaukee**, split north to south by the **Milwaukee River**, is only a mile long and a few blocks wide. Handsome old buildings and gleaming, modern steel-and-glass structures are comfortably corralled together on three sides by spaghetti-like strands of freeway. **Lake Michigan** forms the fourth boundary, with its parkland, marina and the **Summerfest** grounds. To bolster the allure of downtown, the city has successfully poured millions into its **Riverwalk** development, now something of a nightlife center and the site of many public entertainment events. The **Milwaukee Art Museum**, 750 N Lincoln Memorial Drive (Tues, Wed, Fri & Sat 10am–5pm, Thurs noon–9pm, Sun noon–5pm; $5), contains works by European masters and twentieth-century Americans. One wing – with stunning views of the lake – is devoted to a dazzlingly comprehensive collection of Post-Impressionist paintings. Architect Santiago Calatrava's spectacular expansion project opens in 2000. The **Museum Center** complex, downtown at 800 W Wells St, is a three-attraction entity (combination ticket $12), comprising the **Milwaukee Public Museum** (daily 9am–5pm; $5.50), where the intertwined histories and mysteries of the earth, nature and humankind are imaginatively presented through dioramas such as "The Streets of Old Milwaukee" and a battle of the dinosaurs; **Discovery World – The James Lovell Museum of Science, Economics and Technology** (daily 9am–5pm; $5), featuring popular hands-on exhibits and laser light shows; and the **Humphrey IMAX Dome Theater**, with a giant, wraparound screen (Mon–Wed 11.30am–4.30pm, Thurs & Fri 11.30am–8.30pm, Sat 10.30am–8.30pm, Sun 10.30am–5.30pm; shows on the half-hour; weekday matinees $4, evenings $6.50).

The blue-domed, neo-Byzantine **Annunciation Greek Orthodox Church** stands like a mushroom crossed with a spaceship at 9400 W Congress St. Completed in 1961, it was one of the last major works by native Wisconsin architect Frank Lloyd Wright. The interior is a jaw-dropping blend of the streamlined and the ornate. Unfortunately, tours have been phased out and visits discouraged. About the only way to see inside is to attend the Sunday service (9am summer, 9.30am rest of year; bus #57). Warmly gorgeous and surprisingly modestly-scaled, the 37-room **Pabst Mansion**, 2000 W Wisconsin Ave (Mon–Sat 10am–3.30pm, Sun noon–3.30pm; $7), was completed in 1893 as the castle of a local beer baron and is a knockout example of ornate Flemish Renaissance architecture, featuring exquisite wood, glass and ironwork. Pabst Brewery has shut down, but the **Miller Brewing Company** at 4251 W State St still offers free behind-the-scenes tours (Mon–Sat, usually 10am–4pm but times updated daily; phone ☎414/931-2467 or 1-800/944-LITE; bus #71), culminating in generous samples for over-21s. The more primitive microbrewery **Sprecher**, 701 W Glendale Ave (Sat 1pm, 2pm & 3pm, also Mon–Fri 4pm in June, July, Aug & holiday weeks; reservations ☎414/964-2739; $2), serves samples straight out of the barrel. Schlitz, the "beer that made Milwaukee famous," was bought out by Stroh's in the late 1980s and is now produced in Detroit. Riverwalk Boat Rentals (☎414/283-9999) conducts a fun, good-value microbrewery tour-cruise on Sat & Sun afternoons, 1–4pm ($10).

You can also take one-hour tours of the engine plant responsible for Milwaukee's other legendary brand name, **Harley-Davidson**, out in a rough area of town on 11700 W Capitol Drive at Hwy-45. It's really for Harley devotees; bikes aren't assembled hére and if you don't know your shovelheads from your knuckleheads you might feel out of place (free tours Mon–Fri 9.30am, 11am & 1pm June–Aug; Mon, Wed and Fri in Sept–Dec; ☎414/535-3666). For those more interested in Harley chic, there's ample opportunity to purchase all kinds of merchandise throughout Milwaukee. Milwaukee Iron Motorcycle Tours (☎414/628-9421 or 305-1946) provides safe, friendly chauffeured tours aboard Harleys at reasonable rates and tailored to clients' needs.

## Eating

The Germans who first settled in Milwaukee determined its **eating** style – heavy on bratwurst, rye bread and beer. Subsequent immigrants threw the collective kitchen wide open, making for a culinary cornucopia. With Lake Michigan lapping the city's feet, freshwater fish can hardly be overlooked, especially on a Friday night when fish boils (see p.331) break out all over the place. Wherever you go, portions tend to be big.

**J Pandl's Whitefish Bay Inn**, 1319 E Henry Clay St (☎414/964-3800). Suburban landmark famous for reasonably priced grilled whitefish, colossal oven-baked pancakes and stein collection.

**John Ernst's**, 600 E Ogden Ave (☎414/273-5918). One of the city's top, but pricey, German institutions. Assiduous service, excellent Wiener schnitzel and lots of seafood.

**The King & I**, 823 N 2nd St (☎414/276-4181). Good medium-priced Thai food, downtown.

**Milwaukee Ale House**, 233 N Water St (☎414/226-BEER). Milwaukee's sole all-grain, old-style brewpub serves filling food and fresh Wisconsin-only beer.

**Mimma's Café**, 1307 E Brady St (☎414/271-7737). Unmissable Italian restaurant, classy yet casual with imaginative, mouthwatering cuisine and extensive wine list.

**Old Town Serbian Gourmet House**, 522 W Lincoln Ave (☎414/672-0206). Tasty Serbian food on the Pole-dominated south side. Try a burek, a meat or spinach-filled pie the size of a Frisbee. Live music Fri–Sun.

## Nightlife and entertainment

The concept of neighborhoods is vital to Milwaukee's nightlife. **Brady Street** in the near northeast, a counterculture haven in the 1960s, is now filled with Italian restaurants and bars. **Walker's Point**, on the edge of downtown, has all sorts of gay and straight watering holes, while the Polish locals can be found further south. Downtown gets busy at the weekend, especially either side of the river on **Water** and **Old World Third** streets between Juneau and State.

High culture in downtown Milwaukee revolves around the **Marcus Center for the Performing Arts**, 929 N Water St (☎414/273-7206 or 1-800/472-4458), and the plush, historic **Pabst Theater**, 144 E Wells St (☎414/286-3663). Nearby, the **Milwaukee Repertory Theater**, 108 E Wells St (☎414/224-9490), has a reputation for risk-taking productions, as does the arty, eclectic **Theatre X** (☎414/278-0555), in the Broadway Theater Center in the Third Ward, a restored warehouse district on the edge of downtown. The Center, 158 N Broadway, is also home to the adventurous Skylight Opera (☎414/291-7811) and **Milwaukee Chamber Theatre** (☎414/276-8842), where the focus is split between classical and contemporary plays.

**Cafe Vecchio**, 1137 N Old World 3rd St (☎414/273-5700). Upscale European-style coffee/wine bar features 100-plus-bottle wine list, espresso drinks and twenty different martinis.

**John Hawk's Pub**, 100 E Wisconsin Ave (☎414/272-3199). Riverside Brit-style establishment downtown. Food all day, jazz on Sat.

**Safe House,** 779 N Front St (☎414/271-2007). Unique, tongue-in-cheek nightclub straight out of a spy film. Open from 11am, with light meals served.

**Up and Under Pub,** 1216 Brady St (☎414/276-2677). Milwaukee's top blues bar.

**Velvet Room,** 730 N Old World 3rd St (☎414/319-1190). Premier cocktail lounge with fun, plush decor, billiards and "New American" menu.

**Von Trier,** 2235 N Farwell Ave (☎414/272-1775). Black Forest decor and lots of imported beers – the Weise is a house specialty.

**Zur Krone,** 839 S 2nd St (☎414/647-1910). Blue-collar bar with good atmosphere and beer selection.

# Wisconsin's eastern shores

North of Milwaukee, **eastern Wisconsin** is a melange of the industrial and the maritime, with a nod to agriculture, shaped by its proximity to **Lake Michigan** and the smaller **Lake Winnebago**. Of its towns, Appleton was the birthplace of escapologist Harry Houdini, **Green Bay** is home to the legendary Packers, and **Oshkosh** is a household name for its overalls and baby clothes, but it's all best seen as a prelude to the most romanticized part of the state, **Door County**.

## Green Bay

Few cities can be as closely associated with a sports team as **GREEN BAY** is with the footballing Packers: 108 miles north of Milwaukee, it's the smallest city in the US to have a professional sports franchise and the only one to own it. **The Green Bay Packer Hall of Fame,** 855 Lombardi Ave (June–Aug daily 9am–6pm; rest of year daily 10am–5pm; $7.50), celebrates the dynastic years of the 1960s when the Pack won Superbowls I and II, as well as such stars of today as Antonio Freeman and Brett Favre. Stuffed with hands-on displays, movie theaters and memorabilia, the museum offers more than enough to satisfy any football fan. Packer fanatics can also tour adjacent **Lambeau Field** (summer daily 9.30am–4.30pm; $7.50, or $10 combination ticket with Hall of Fame).

Also in this busy but not particularly attractive port, pride of place at the **National Railroad Museum,** 2285 S Broadway (May to Oct daily 9am–5pm; rest of year Mon–Fri 9am–5pm; $6 in summer including train ride, $5 in winter) goes to the 1.1 million-ton 1941 Union Pacific Big Boy locomotive, one of many such trains which served Green Bay's still-enormous freight depot. West on Hwy-172, opposite the airport, stands Wisconsin's biggest casino – **Oneida Bingo & Casino** (☎920/497-8118 or 1-800/238-4263). Tribal history, and the way in which profits from blackjack, video poker and bingo have improved education, social and health facilities, are examined at the **Oneida Nation Museum,** seven miles west of Hwy-41 as it runs south from downtown (Tues–Fri 10am–6pm, Sat 10am–5pm; $2).

The city's visitor center (☎920/494-9507 or 1-888/867-3342) sits in the shadow of the football stadium, off Lombardi Avenue, near the *Best Western Midway Hotel,* 780 Packer Drive (☎920/499-3161 or 1-800/528 1234; ④). *Titletown Brewing Company,* 200 Dousman St (☎920/437-2337), has a great setting for drinks in a former railroad depot downtown, while *Brett Favre's Steakhouse,* 1020 Advance St (☎920/490-9663) is an upscale family restaurant/sportsbar serving Southern cuisine.

## Door County

From **Sturgeon Bay,** 140 miles north of Milwaukee, **Door County** sticks into Lake Michigan like a gradually tapering candle for 42 miles. With thirteen lighthouses and a dozen fishing villages, its coastline smacks more of New England than the Midwest. The name derives from "Porte des Morts" or "**Door of the Dead**," the French name for the treacherous eight-mile strait that severs Washington Island at its tip. Despite drawing a million-plus warm-weather tourists, the peninsula (actually an island split off from Wisconsin by a canal) is not an extended theme park. Prices can get a little steep, but you get what you pay for – a small sliver of America devoid, for the most part, of crude billboards, sloppy diners, bland chain motels and tacky amusements. Activities include browsing around galleries and attending arts festivals, as well as hiking, fishing and boating. Renting a **bicycle** (Fish Creek's Nor-Door Cyclery has the best models; ☎920/868-2275) gives you the chance to follow an excellent **cycle trail**. Winter is considerably quieter. Ice fishing, cross-country skiing and snowmobiling are the predominant outdoor activities.

Pick up road and trail maps at the visitor center at 1015 Green Bay Rd in Sturgeon Bay (☎920/743-4456 or 1-800/52-RELAX), where you can also phone local lodgings for free.

## Exploring Door County

Door County begins at its only sizeable town, **STURGEON BAY** – a pleasant enough shipbuilding community, if not exactly abundant in small-town splendor. Ten miles north on Hwy-57 is the rolling **Whitefish Dunes State Park**, with its wispy sand dunes and popular mile-long beach (daily; $7 per car). A short trail leads to the spectacular rocky **Cave Point County Park** (free), studded with wind- and wave-sculpted caves that are particularly dramatic in winter. In general beaches are better this side of the peninsula; **Jacksonport's** (free) Lakeside Park ranks as the best of the lot. You can also swim in several placid inland lakes.

Over on the western side, biking and hiking trails traverse the thickly forested hills of **Peninsula State Park** (situated between tiny **Fish Creek** and elegant Mennonite **Ephraim**, with its resplendent white-clapboard architecture). An observation tower and lighthouse stand on the park's extensive shoreline, while just outside it on Hwy-42 is the anachronistic Skyway Drive-In movie theater (☎920/854-9938).

**Washington Island**, off the peninsula's northern tip, offers a different cultural perspective. During Prohibition, the Icelandic community here convinced authorities that (40 percent alcohol) bitters were an ancient cure for rheumatism and dyspepsia. Cases of the stuff were shipped in, and the habit stuck; go into the historic Nelsen's Hall Bitters Pub and Restaurant (☎920/847-2496), about two miles from the Detroit Harbor dock, and you're likely to find old-timers shifting bitters by the pint. Motel rooms are available on Washington, but there's no such luxury on the primitive neighboring 950-acre Rock Island. Once the private estate of a millionaire, it's dotted with stark, stone buildings; no cars are allowed, so see them by foot or bike.

The islands are served by the Washington Island Ferry from Northport at the tip of the peninsula (daily; $7.50 round-trip, cars $17, bikes $3; ☎920/847-2546 or 1-800/223-2094) and the Rock Island Ferry out of Jackson Harbor (June to mid-Oct daily; $7 round-trip; ☎920/847-2252).

## Accommodation

Door County has a full range of accommodation, including some overpriced resorts. Prices given are for shoulder seasons (the best time to come); expect to pay up to 25 percent extra at the grander hotels in July and August, and a small weekend premium. Camping is idyllic; state park sites cost $10–15 (plus $9.50 reservation fee and $7 daily admission, annual $25), while among recommended private campgrounds, one is *Path of Pines*, County Road F off Hwy-42, near Fish Creek (mid-May to mid-Oct; $17–28; ☎920/868-3332 or 1-800/868-7802).

**Century Farm Motel**, 10068 Hwy-57 (☎920/854-4069). Basic cottages (sleeping up to six people), set in farmland halfway between Sister Bay and Ephraim. Among the lowest prices on the peninsula. ③.

**Chal-A-Motel**, 3910 Hwy-42, 57 Sturgeon Bay (☎920/743-6788). Offbeat, clean, year-round budget motel with huge collection of dolls, toys and old autos you can see for $1 ($2 for nonguests). ③.

**Liberty Park Lodge and Shore Cottages**, Hwy-42 N, Sister Bay (☎920/854-2025). Spotless complex with a lakeside porch and sandy beach. Good value. ③.

**Twin Oaks Lodge**, City Rd/Hwy-42 (☎920/854-2633). Cordial motor hotel conveniently located on the edge of Fish Creek at the quiet end of Peninsula State Park. Free use of bikes. ③.

**Waterbury Inn**, Hwy-42, Ephraim (☎920/854-2821 or 1-800/720-1624). This newish luxury property has suites with fully equipped kitchens. ⑤.

**White Gull Inn**, 4225 Main St, Fish Creek (☎920/868-3517). Elegant old inn, next to delightful Sunset Park, is the county's crown jewel. Good restaurant (breakfast not included), and fish boil every night in summer. ⑥.

## Eating

One reward of a midsummer visit to Door County is the chance to sample the cherry in all its guises. Another traditional treat is the **fish boil**, a delicious outdoor ritual involving whitefish steaks, potatoes and onions cooked in a cauldron over a wood fire. Rounded off with coleslaw and cherry pie, it's widely available for between $9 and $15.

**Al Johnson's Swedish Restaurant**, Hwy-42, Sister Bay (☎920/854-2626). Pancakes, meatballs and other fine Scandinavian dishes; and there are goats tethered atop the sod roof.

**Bayside Tavern**, Main St, Fish Creek (☎920/868-3441). Convivial pub serving a celebrated chili, burgers and a mean Friday night perch-fry.

**Dal Santo's**, 341 N 3rd Ave, Sturgeon Bay (☎920/743-6100). Pizza, pasta and bar snacks in an old railroad depot with a good microbrewery. The cherry ale is surprisingly palatable and refreshing.

**Square Rigger Lodge and Galley**, 6332 Hwy 57, Jacksonport (☎920/823-2408). Cocktail lounge and restaurant, plus one of the county's best-fun fish boils set on a private sandy beach.

**Wilson's**, Hwy-42, Ephraim (☎920/854-2041). Burgers, sandwiches and (along with the Door County Ice Cream Factory in Sister Bay) the top ice cream on the peninsula.

# Upstate Wisconsin

Sparsely settled **northern Wisconsin** has no large cities (and few small ones), and no interstates; it's a lake-studded wilderness, covered by enormous tracts of forest. You can canoe its rivers, fish for record-breakers, or ski or snowmobile cross-country trails without having to fight for space. **Bayfield** and the **Apostle Islands** in the northwest are the obvious destinations, but Hayward, 76 miles southeast of Superior, is home to the amazing **National Freshwater Fishing Hall of Fame** (mid-April to Nov daily 10am–5pm; $4.50), where you're invited to "Walk through the biggest fish in the world!" – a four-story, 500-ton, fiberglass monster.

## The Apostle Islands

All but one of the 22 **Apostle Islands**, scattered off **Bayfield Peninsula** eighty miles east of Duluth, Minnesota (see p.344), are designated as national lakeshore – a prized preserve for outdoors enthusiasts seeking to recharge depleted spiritual batteries.

The jumping-off point for the islands, **BAYFIELD**, once a lumbering and fishing village, is now a pleasant soft-sell tourist trap. Its sumptuous *Old Rittenhouse Inn*, 301 Rittenhouse Ave (☎715/779-5111 or 1-888/644-4667; ⑥), offers gourmet meals and swank **rooms**; *Tree Top House*, 225 N Fourth St (☎715/779-3293; ②), has clean, simple doubles. *Island View Place*, Route 1, Box 46 (☎715/779-5307 or 1-800/484-8189; ④), a half-mile outside of town, is one of many waterside condominiums with nightly and weekly accommodations. Lodges and cottages are the centerpiece for the thirty gorgeous lakeside acres of Rocky Run (☎715/373-2551; ⑨), a resort outside **Washburn** eleven miles south. Bayfield's visitor center is at 42 S Broad St (☎715/779-3335 or 1-800/447-4094). Campers heading for the islands require permits ($10; tent sites $15–30) from the visitor center at 410 Washington Ave (summer daily, weekdays in winter; ☎715/779-3397). Apostle Island Cruise Service boats (☎715/779-3925; $22.95) twist their way past all of the islands, and will set down and pick up campers.

## Madeline Island

By the fifteenth century **Madeline Island** was known to the Ojibway as Mon-a waun-a-kauning – home of the golden-shafted woodpecker. Frenchman Michel Cadotte founded a fur trading post there for the British in 1793, and subsequently married Equaysayway, daughter of a tribal leader, who took the name the island bears today. Madeline is now the only commercially developed Apostle island, but it all remains pretty low-key. Cadotte is buried in an overgrown cemetery in its sole town, **LA POINTE**.

La Pointe is accessible in summer via the twenty-minute ride on the Madeline Island Ferry Line from Bayfield (every 30min in peak season; passengers $3.50, bikes $1.75, cars $7.75; ☎715/747-2051). Its 180 year-round residents maintain an interesting little **historical museum** (May–Oct daily 10am–6pm; $5), while assorted sandy beaches, wide bays, scenic points and forests can be explored along 45 miles of sometimes rough road. **Bikes** can be rented near the dock for $22 per day, **mopeds** from Motion to Go (☎715/747-6585) at around $50. The Ferry Line conducts two-hour bus tours (10.30am and 1.30pm; $8) mid-June till September.

A **visitor center** on Main Street (☎715/747-2801 or 1-888/ISLE-FUN) can offer advice on places to stay; the *Madeline Island Motel* (☎715/747-3000; ③) and *The Island Inn* (☎715/747-2000; ④), both near the ferry dock, are probably the best value. Camping sites, on top of a bluff and close to caves at Big Bay State Park (☎715/779-3346), cost $8–10 plus $9.50 reservation fee, and include park admission. A wooden footbridge across the lagoon leads to **Big Bay Town Park** ($10–13; no reservations); the campgrounds share a splendid mile-long beach. Eating options include the new pub in *The Inn on Madeline Island* (☎715/747-6315 or 1-800/822-6315; ⑨), home-style meals in a casual harborside setting at *The Beach Club* (☎715/747-3955), or the low-cost *Grampa Tony's* (☎715/747-3911).

# Southern Wisconsin

Assorted highways and back roads lace up **southern Wisconsin**, passing over rolling hills and deep dales. The main conurbation of Wisconsin's most populated region, still mainly farmland, is the immensely likeable lakeside college town of **Madison**, which doubles as the state capital. Cozy Madison area communities like **New Glarus** or **Mount Horeb**, and historic settlements like **Little Norway**, attest to a mixed European heritage. **Wisconsin Dells** has a picturesque setting, but may appeal only to those who revel in tacky attractions and Americana. Stretches of the **Mississippi River**, undulating down the western border, are designated as **The Great River Road**, a scenic highway that runs from near Canada to the Gulf of Mexico.

## Madison

The history books record that **MADISON**, just over an hour west of Milwaukee, was little more than a wooded, mosquito-infested swamp when it was selected to be the political nucleus of Wisconsin Territory in 1836. Today this stimulating, youthful metropolis is one of the most beautifully set cities in the US, with a handful of diverting museums.

Downtown is neatly laid out on an isthmus between lakes Mendota and Monona, with the sumptuous white granite State Capitol sitting benignly on a hill at its center, surrounded by shady trees, lawns and park benches. Capitol Square itself is the site of a fun farmers' market (May–Oct Sat 6am–2pm); browse late for bargains. Madison Civic Center, close by at 211 State St (☎608/266-6550), houses a professional repertory theater (box office ☎608/266-9055) and art museum (☎608/257-0158) as well as presenting concerts and touring shows. Frank Lloyd Wright designed the Unitarian Meeting House, 900 University Bay Drive, in the late 1940s. With its sweeping, dramatically curved ceiling and triangle motif, it's definitely worth a look (May–Oct Tues–Fri 10am–4pm, Sat 9am–noon; $3). The lakeside Monona Terrace Community and Convention Center, 1 John Nolen Drive, is a more recently realized example of Wright's grand vision (daily tours 11am & 1pm; $2, free Mon & Tues); surprisingly intimate and full of architectural detail, its motif of curves, arches and domes echoes the State Capitol building just a few blocks away.

If the capitol is the city's governmental heart, the University of Wisconsin (average enrolment 46,000) is its spirited, liberal-thinking head, now mellowed since its protest heyday in the late 1960s. The campus "living room," Memorial Union, 800 Langdon St ☎608/262-1583), holds a budget cafeteria and pub, the *Rathskeller*, with tables strewn beneath huge, vaulted ceilings and live music most nights. Out back, the spacious UW Terrace offers beautiful sunset views over Lake Mendota. Capitol and campus are arterially connected by State Street, eight tree-lined, pedestrianized blocks of restaurants, cafes, bars and funky stores. Williamson Street, on the city's near-east side a few blocks from Monona Terrace, happily evinces its countercultural community roots.

## Practicalities

Greyhound does regular runs to Milwaukee, Green Bay and beyond, while Badger Coaches make six trips daily to Milwaukee ($18 round-trip; ☎608/255-6771). Both operate out of the terminal at 2 S Bedford St. Van Galder buses depart from Memorial Union to Chicago's O'Hare Airport (10 daily; $19; ☎608/752-5407 or 1-800/747-0994). The visitor center is at 615 E Washington Ave (Mon–Fri 8am–4.30pm; ☎608/258-4959 or 1-800/373-MDSN).

Accommodation can be had all over the city, though the budget chains lie to the east, off I-90/94. *Collins House*, 704 E Gorham St (☎608/255-4230; ⑤), is a beautiful B&B a few blocks from the capitol, while the upscale *Madison Concourse Hotel*, 1 W Dayton St (☎608/257-6000 or 1-800/356-8293; ⑤), is even closer. *Canterbury Inn*, 315 W Gorham St (☎608/258-8899 or 1-800/838-3850; ⑦), has six splendid Chaucer-inspired rooms above a welcoming bookstore-cum-coffeehouse.

State Street is a veritable smorgasbord of food and drink, from the tiny *Nepalese Himal Chuli* at no. 318 (☎608/251-9225) and its sister restaurant, *Chautara*, at no. 334 (☎608/251-3626) to the veteran *Ella's Deli* at no. 425 (☎608/257-8611), with its kosher-style food and rich ice creams. *Deb & Lola's* at no. 227 (☎608/255-0820) serves fresh, eclectic Southwestern-influenced cuisine. The *Essen Haus*, 514 E Wilson St (☎608/255-4674), is a raucous *biergarten* with a phenomenal selection of beers. *Dotty Dumpling's Dowry*, 116 N Fairchild St (☎608/255-3175), is a local landmark thanks to its great burgers and kooky nostalgic decor.

There's plenty of entertainment, often free, on campus (call the events line on ☎608/265-3000). The soulful neighborhood *Crystal Corner*, 1302 Williamson St (☎608/256-2953), puts on blues acts, while *O'Cayz Corral*, 504 E Wilson St (☎608/256-1348), ranges through heavy metal, folk and acoustic. *The Cardinal*, 418 E Wilson St

(☎608/251-0080), with its handsome 1908 decor, is one of the best dance club-cum-bars. Full listings are carried by the free weekly *Isthmus*.

## Baraboo

Between 1884 and 1912, the **Ringling Brothers' Circus** kept winter quarters in **BARABOO**, thirty miles northwest of Madison (see also Sarasota, p.582). The **Circus World Museum**, 426 Water St, successfully recaptures the pre-TV glory days of big-top history, via an enormous collection of memorabilia and daily performances including an old-time circus show that is both tawdry (elephants with bows on their tails doing leg kicks to *New York, New York*) and irresistible (mid-July and Aug daily 9am–9pm, $11.95, with shows at 11am, 3pm and 7.30pm; May, June, early July daily 9am–6pm, same schedule, without 7.30pm show; Sept–April Mon–Sat 9am–5pm, Sun 11am–5pm museum only, no shows, $4.95). Every summer, usually in the first half of July, 75 meticulously restored circus wagons set out on a four-day rail journey through small-town Wisconsin and Illinois, culminating in a horse-drawn parade through down-town Milwaukee – an unbeatable extravaganza of Americana. Built in 1915 and modeled after the grand opera house at Versailles, the **Al Ringling Theatre** (summer tours, noon Thurs–Sun; $2) in the town center is one of America's prettiest small playhouses.

Baraboo itself is calmer, quieter and more affordable than nearby Wisconsin Dells. The elegant *Victorian Gollmar Guest House B&B*, 422 Third St (☎608/356-9432; ④), plays up the fact that it was once home to a circus family. More basic rooms are on offer at the *Spinning Wheel*, 809 Eighth St (☎608/356-3933; ②). *Kristina's Family Cafe*, 113 Third St (☎608/356-3430), serves low-cost meals. Baraboo's **visitor center** is at 124 Second St (Mon–Fri 9am–4.30pm; ☎608/356-8333 or 1-800/227-2266) until late in 2000, when it relocates near the intersections of Highways 12, 33 and 136.

## Spring Green

During his seventy-year career, Wisconsin-born architect and social philosopher **Frank Lloyd Wright** designed such structures as New York's spiralling Guggenheim Museum and Tokyo's earthquake-proof *Imperial Hotel*. Three miles south of **SPRING GREEN**, itself forty miles west of Madison on Hwy-14, stand Wright's magnificent for-mer residence, **Taliesin**, and his **Hillside Home School**. The streamlined geometry and functional grandeur of the latter, opened in 1932, exemplify Wright's break away from the boxy, fustian Victorian style (May–Oct daily, tours on the hour 10am–4pm; $10). His actual studio is imposing; there's also a jewel-like theater space. Extensive and varied tours are also available of the house (daily except Wed at 9.30am & 1.30pm; reservation only; $40) and grounds (May–Oct daily at 10.45am & 1.45pm; $15). These and other, pricier, tours leave from the **Frank Lloyd Wright Visitor Center** (☎608/588-7900), designed by Wright in 1953 as a restaurant; it now features displays, a cafe and a bookstore. Among numerous other Wright-influenced buildings are the bank, pharmacy and the lounge of a mid-priced restaurant called the *Post House* (☎608/588-2595), on Jefferson Street downtown.

From 1944 onwards, Alex Jordan built the **House on the Rock**, six miles beyond Taliesin on Hwy-23, on and out of a natural, 60ft, chimney-like rock – for no discernible reason. He certainly never lived in it, nor did he intend it to become Wisconsin's num-ber one tourist attraction (mid-March to Oct daily 9am–dusk; Nov–Dec holiday tour daily 10am–6pm; $15.40, or $9.95 Nov–Dec). Only the first section of this multileveled series of furnished nooks and chambers bears any resemblance to a house of any kind. With its low ceilings, indirect lighting, indoor pools, waterfalls, trees and pervasive shag carpeting, the style is a sort of Frank Lloyd Wright meets *The Flintstones*. The rest of the house is a logic-free labyrinth, containing Jordan's astounding collection of collections (antiques, nickelodeons and pneumatic music machines, miniature circuses, dolls and dolls' houses, maritime memorabilia, armor and firearms, ad infinitum), with little to indicate what is genuine or imitation, and no clue as to what it all means. The net effect is overwhelming and disorienting, alternately great fun and ghastly. Highlights include the **Infinity Room**, composed of three thousand small glass panels tapering to a point and cantilevered several hundred feet above the Wyoming Valley. A complex of other attractions has been added to the fifty-acre grounds, including the utterly dazzling **World's Largest Carousel** (with 269 fabulous figures and some 20,000 lights), a circus building, a giant doll's house and an old-style shopping street.

### Practicalities

Spring Green is a pretty **place to stay**, but prices can be high in summer. *Round Barn Lodge*, Hwy-14 (☎608/588-2568; ④), has a pool, sauna and family dining on a former dairy farm. *The Usonian Inn*, Hwy-14/Hwy-23 (☎608/588-2323; ③), offers alternative, Taliesin-style lodgings. Locals and thespians hang out at *The Shed* (☎608/588-9049), an easygoing diner and bar on Lexington Street downtown. The **American Players Theatre** (☎608/588-2361) performs Shakespeare and other classics in a wooded amphitheater each evening from mid-June to October. For information, stop by the Winsted Shop on Hwy-23 or call ☎608/588-2054 or 1-800/588-2042.

# MINNESOTA

Though **MINNESOTA** is about a thousand miles from either coast, it's virtually a seaboard state, thanks to **Lake Superior**, connected to the Atlantic via the St Lawrence Seaway. The glaciers that, millions of years ago, flattened all but its southeast corner gouged out more than 15,000 **lakes**, and major **rivers** run along the eastern and western borders. Ninety-five percent of the population lives within ten minutes of a body of water, and the very name Minnesota is a Sioux word meaning "land of sky-tinted water."

French explorers in the sixteenth century encountered prairies to the south and, in the north, dense forests whose abundant waterways were an ideal breeding ground for beavers and muskrats. **Fur trading**, **fishing** and **lumbering** flourished, and the Ojibway and Sioux were eased out by waves of French, British and American immigrants. Admitted to the Union in 1858, the new state of Minnesota was at first settled by Germans and Scandinavians, who farmed in the west and south. Other ethnic groups followed, many drawn by the massive **iron ore** deposits of north central Minnesota, which are expected to hold out for another two hundred years.

Minnesota still thrives on its natural resources and on a progressive social outlook typified by such Democratic heavyweights as Hubert Humphrey, Walter Mondale and Eugene McCarthy. Current governor, **Jesse Ventura**, a former professional wrestler, has garnered attention nationally and beyond for his unconventional and even outspoken approach to politics.

More than half of Minnesota's hardy inhabitants, who endure some of the fiercest winters in the nation, live in the southeast, around the so-called Twin Cities of **Minneapolis** and **St Paul**, attractive and basically friendly rivals who together rank as the Midwest's great civic double act for their combined cultural, recreational and business opportunities. Smaller cities include the northern shipping port of **Duluth**, the gateway to the **Scenic Hwy-61** lakeshore drive, and **Rochester**, near pretty river towns like Red Wing and Winona. The tranquil waters **of Voyageurs National Park** lie halfway along the state's boundary with Canada.

In recent years, the state has earned a reputation as the "Hollywood of the North," thanks to its increased use as an affordable, talent-rich filmmaking locale.

Internationally acclaimed fraternal filmmakers Joel and Ethan Coen, responsible for the Oscar-winning, Minnesota-set *Fargo*, were raised in the Twin Cities' suburb of St Louis Park.

### Getting around Minnesota

Minneapolis/St Paul airport, home base for Northwest Airlines, handles routes to Europe as well as domestic flights, and there are daily flights between the Twin Cities on local budget airlines Sun Country (☎612/686-4411 or 1-800/752-1218) and Vanguard (☎1-800/826-4827). Amtrak **trains** cross the state once a day east and west from Chicago and Seattle, with stops in Winona, Red Wing, St Paul, St Cloud, Staples and Detroit Lakes. Greyhound, founded upstate in Hibbing although no longer based there, is the largest of the several **bus** companies plying Minnesota's roads. Seven buses per day make the nine-hour journey to Chicago from the Twin Cities; Duluth, St Louis and Kansas City are also served several times daily from the state's major metropolises.

# Minneapolis and St Paul

Commonly known as the **Twin Cities**, **MINNEAPOLIS** (a hybrid Sioux/Greek word meaning "water city") and **ST PAUL** are competitive yet complementary. Fraternally rather than identically twinned, they may be even better places to live than they are to visit, thanks to their good looks, cleanliness, cultural activity, social awareness and relatively low crime rates. About thirty of *Fortune Magazine's* 500 top-ranking corporations are based here; many extend substantial financial support to local arts, community projects and sports. Life for a majority of Twin Citians seems so vibrantly wholesome that the most significant threat would appear to be their own creeping complacency.

St Paul has been called "the last city of the east," making Minneapolis across the curving Mississippi "the first city of the west." Only a twenty-minute expressway ride separates their respective downtowns, but each has its own character, style and strengths. **St Paul**, the state capital – originally called Pig's Eye, after a scurrilous French-Canadian fur trader who sold whisky at a Mississippi river landing in the 1840s – is the staid, slightly older sibling, careful to preserve its buildings and traditions. Its residents are mainly German, Irish and Catholic. The compact but stately downtown is built, like Rome, on seven hills: the **Capitol** and the **Cathedral** occupy one each, august monuments that keep the city mindful of its responsibilities.

**Minneapolis**, founded on money generated by the Mississippi's hundreds of flour and saw mills, is livelier, artier and more modern, with skyscraping, up-to-date architecture and an upbeat and even brash attitude that never quite jeopardizes its essential affability. The mostly Slavonic, Nordic and Lutheran residents are spread over wider ground than in St Paul, with dozens of lakes and parks to underscore the city's appeal. The home-grown superstar formerly known as **Prince** and the recording company Flyte Tyme cast a global spotlight on the local music scene.

## Arrival, information and getting around

**Twin Cities International Airport** lies about ten miles south of either city in suburban Bloomington. Airport Express (☎612/827-7777 or 1-800/333-1532) shuttles travelers between the airport and major hotels for around $10, and some lodgings lay on their own transportation. **Taxis** to Minneapolis will set you back close to $25, to St Paul $15. Bus #7 goes to Minneapolis; #54 to St Paul (6am–midnight: $1–1.50). Amtrak is midway between the cities at 730 Transfer Rd, off University Avenue. The Greyhound terminals, both in convenient downtown locations, are at 29 Ninth St in Minneapolis, and, less used, Seventh and St Peter streets in St Paul. Metropolitan Council Transit Operations **buses** (☎612/349-7000 or 373-3333) make both cities relatively easy to explore without a car; money-saving multiple-ride tickets can be bought at 719 Marquette Ave in Minneapolis or numerous locations in either city. Old-style **trolleys** run through both downtowns; St Paul's is a bargain 50¢ per ride, but in Minneapolis it costs $5 for a two-hour pass or $6 all day.

In Minneapolis, the **visitor center** is at 4000 Multifoods Tower, 33 S Sixth St (☎612/661-4700 or 1-800/445-7412), with an additional location on the second level of the City Center shopping complex (☎612/335-5827); in St Paul it's at 102 Norwest Center, 55 E Fifth St (☎612/297-6985 or 1-800/627-6101). The main Minneapolis **post office** is on First and Marquette (zip code 55401); St Paul's at 180 E Kellogg Blvd (zip code 55101).

# Accommodation

You're likely to pay more for lodgings downtown than in the suburbs, where dozens of cheap **motels** line I-494 near the airport, though some of the pricier central hotels offer reduced rates and special package deals at weekends. The pretty riverside community of **Stillwater**, 25 miles from St Paul via I-35 N and Hwy-36 E, has many grand old B&Bs and motels – call ☎612/439-7700 for information.

## Minneapolis
**Christopher Inn**, 201 Mill St, Excelsior (☎612/474-6816). Year-round suburban B&B on Lake Minnetonka. Good discounts off-season and midweek. ⑤.

**City of Lakes International House**, 2400 Stevens Ave (☎612/871-3210). Conveniently located independent hostel. Private rooms $32, dorm beds $16. Bicycles $3. Reservations required. ①/②.

**Evelo's B&B**, 2301 Bryant Ave S (☎612/374-9656). Three comfortable rooms in a well-preserved Victorian home near bus lines, lakes and downtown. Nonsmokers preferred. ③.

**Hotel Amsterdam**, 830 Hennepin Ave (☎612/288-0459 or 1-800/649-9500). Friendly, low-cost gay/lesbian-owned hotel above a noise-controlled saloon bar/disco downtown. ②.

**Le Blanc House**, 302 University Ave NE (☎612/379-2570). Gourmet breakfasts and fine rooms in a fancy Victorian home minutes from downtown. Two-night minimum on summer weekends. ⑤.

**Minneapolis Hilton and Towers**, 1001 Marquette Ave (☎612/376-1000). The newest and classiest downtown lodgings, featuring a great gym and pool. Weekend rates around $100 a night. ⑥.

**Nicollet Island Inn**, 95 Merriam St (☎612/331-1800). This pricey, mid-river establishment has the edge on other downtown hotels due to its delightful location and Minnesota-grown menu. ⑥.

**Rodeway Inn**, 2335 3rd Ave S (☎612/871-2000 or 1-800/228-2000). Friendly, unpretentious motor hotel near downtown, across from the Art Institute. ④.

## St Paul
**Chatsworth B&B**, 984 Ashland Ave (☎612/227-4288). Beautiful c.1900 home now run as a welcoming B&B. ④.

**Como Villa**, 1371 W Nebraska Ave (☎612/647-0471). Antique-filled Victorian B&B by Como Park, with hospitable, hometown host. ④.

**The Covington Inn**, Pier 1, Harriet Island (☎612/292-1411). Compact, one-of-a-kind B&B on a converted towboat facing downtown, with a cafe on the premises. ⑥.

**Embassy Suites**, 175 E 10th St (☎612/224-5400 or 1-800/EMBASSY). The tropical atrium is the outstanding feature of this comfortable chain hotel on the edge of downtown. ⑥.

**Holiday Inn Express**, 1010 Bandana Blvd W (☎612/647-1637 or 1-800/HOLIDAY). This is a unique lodging in former railroad car repair shop attached to mall complex. Indoor pool and sauna. ⑤.

## Exploring Minneapolis

Laid out on a simple grid, **downtown Minneapolis** is bounded by the Mississippi River on the north side and by lovely Loring Park to the south. The riverfront, dubbed the "**Mississippi Mile**," continues to be developed as a place for strolling, dining and entertainment. Each city has its own landing site for narrated summertime **paddleboat** cruises (☎612/227-1100 or 1-800/543-3908; $8.50). The vast Third Avenue bridge makes an ideal vantage point for viewing **St Anthony Falls**, a controlled torrent in a wide stretch of the river. The missionary Father Hennepin discovered the Falls in 1680; the first permanent settlement of present-day Minneapolis was begun nearby in the early nineteenth century.

Downtown's major stores line up along the pedestrianized **Nicollet Mall**. **Hennepin Avenue**, the other main drag, is a block west. It has been revitalized as an entertainment district in recent years thanks, in part, to the beautifully restored

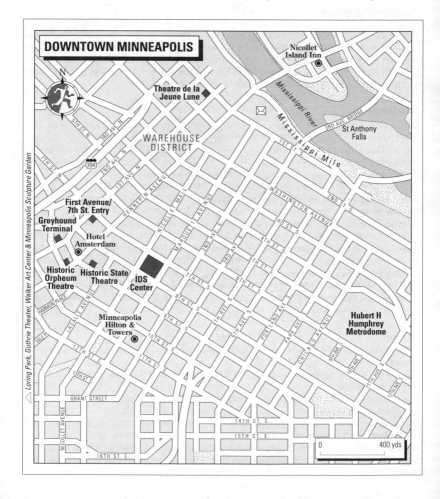

**Historic Orpheum** and **State Theatres**, twin hosts to top-quality Broadway shows and concerts. The **IDS Center**, on the Mall, is the tallest building in either city; its indoor glass atrium, the Crystal Court, is essentially modern Minneapolis's town square. Citizens escape weather extremes via a "skyway" system of elevated, climate-controlled glass walkways, connecting over forty buildings. Culturally, Minneapolis would be poorer without the **Walker Art Center**, Vineland Place (Tues, Wed, Fri & Sat 10am–5pm, Thurs 10am–8pm, Sun 11am–5pm; $4, free Thurs), on the edge of downtown, a multipurpose contemporary art and performance space which balances its permanent collection of sculpture and paintings (such as German Expressionist Franz Marc's *Blue Horses*) with exciting temporary exhibitions. The seven-acre outdoor **Sculpture Garden** is a work of genius, its most popular piece the gigantic whimsical *Spoonbridge and Cherry* (not exactly a bridge, more like a fountain) by Claes Oldenburg and Coosje van Bruggen. One mile from downtown, at 2400 Third Ave S (bus #9), the huge **Minneapolis Institute of Arts** hosts a huge and thoroughly comprehensive collection of art from 2000 BC to the present (Tues, Wed, Fri & Sat 10am–5pm, Thurs 10am–9pm, Sun noon–5pm; free). Antiques, crafts and artifacts fill the exquisite c.1900 mansion setting of the nearby **American Swedish Institute**, 2600 Park Ave S (Tues, Thurs, Fri & Sat noon–4pm, Wed noon–8pm, Sun 1–5pm; $3). In stark contrast, changing exhibitions and the University of Minnesota's permanent art collection share space in the controversial **Frederick R Weisman Museum**, on campus at 333 E River Rd (Tues, Wed & Fri 10am–5pm, Thurs 10am–8pm, Sat & Sun 11am–5pm; free). Architect Frank O Gehry's airy structure, with its boldly irregular stainless steel west facade overlooking the Mississippi, is the most startling love-it-or-hate-it design in the cities.

Arctic winters apart, hordes of Minneapolitans flock to the shores of the "big three," lakes **Calhoun** and **Harriet** and **Lake of the Isles**, all in residential areas within two miles south of downtown. The **Hubert H Humphrey Metrodome**, 900 S Fifth St (☎612/332-0386), squats on the eastern edge of downtown like a giant white pincushion; the dome is home to the state's pro baseball and football teams, the Twins and the Vikings. Each July the **Minneapolis Aquatennial** celebrates the lifestyle fostered by the lakes with two huge downtown parades and water-based events such as milk-carton boat races. Illuminated floats with storybook themes dominate the evening **Holidazzle** parades, on Nicollet Mall in the run-up to Christmas. **Minnehaha Falls**, south of downtown on bus #7, was featured in Longfellow's 1855 poem *Song of Hiawatha* without his ever having laid eyes on it. The adjacent park is a favorite haunt for hikes and picnics.

## Exploring St Paul

**St Paul**, reached along I-94 (and served by buses #16A, #21A or downtown express route #94BCD), has more wealthy old homes and civic monuments than Minneapolis. Call in at the jazzy Art Deco lobby of the **City Hall and Courthouse**, Fourth and Wabasha, to see Swedish sculptor Carl Milles' revolving 36ft *Vision of Peace*, carved in the 1930s from white Mexican onyx. The castle-like **Landmark Center**, a couple of blocks away at Fifth and Market, and the glittering **Ordway Music Theatre** both overlook Rice Park, probably the prettiest little square in either city. Here, too, downtown buildings are linked via "skyways"; but evenings and weekends in St Paul can get very quiet. **Town Square Park** is a lush, multilevel indoor garden in a shopping complex. The gorgeous granite and limestone **Minnesota History Center**, 345 W Kellogg Blvd (Tues, Wed, Fri & Sat 10am–5pm, Thurs 10am–9pm, Sun noon–5pm; free), with its extensive research facilities and some inventive exhibits for the more casual visitor, is the best place to grasp the state's story. An immense steel iguana is the doorkeeper at the exciting hands-on **Science Museum of Minnesota**, 30 E Tenth St (Mon–Sat 9.30am–9pm, Sun 10am–9pm; $8), which also has a domed Omnitheater (entry includ-

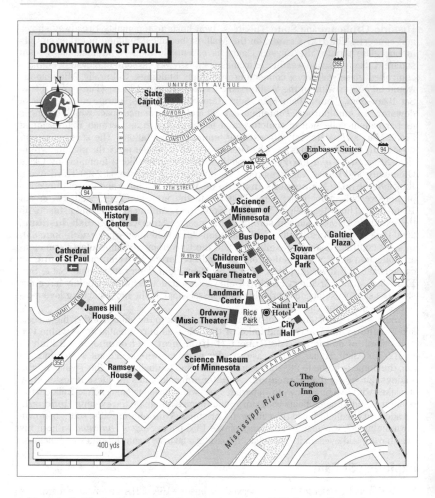

**DOWNTOWN ST PAUL**

ed in ticket). It's due to expand into new quarters in 1999, but until then its status as the cities' most imaginative museum is rivaled by the new **Minnesota Children's Museum**, 10 W Seventh St (summer daily 9am–5pm, Thurs till 8pm; rest of year closed Mon; $5.95), where even big kids will be diverted by the five interactive galleries.

A well-preserved five-mile Victorian boulevard, Summit Avenue, leads away from downtown. **F Scott Fitzgerald**, born close by, finished his first success, *This Side of Paradise*, in 1918 while living in a modest rowhouse at no. 599; he disparaged the avenue as a "museum of American architectural failures." Look for the coffin atop no. 465, once the home of an undertaker, and visit the **James J Hill House** at no. 240, a railroad baron's sumptuous mansion from around 1891 (tours every half-hour Wed–Sat 10am–3.30pm; reservations recommended ☎612/297-2555; $4). Pioneer politico **Alexander Ramsey's** house (tours on the hour May–Dec Tues–Sat 10am–3pm, Sun 1pm, 2pm & 3pm; $4), nearby at 265 S Exchange St in the fashionable Irvine Park district, remains a showcase of Victorian high style.

Costumed staff do a fine job of interpreting Minnesota's frontier past at **Fort Snelling** (May–Oct Mon–Sat 10am–5pm, Sun noon–5pm; $4), near the airport off highways 5 and 55. Built between 1819 and 1825 on a strategic bluff at the confluence of the Mississippi and Minnesota rivers, this was Minnesota's first permanent structure – a successful attempt by the US government to establish an official presence in the wilderness that had recently been won from Great Britain. Another good bet is the venerable and picturesque **Como Park Zoo and Conservatory**, reached by taking I-94 to the Lexington Ave exit, then continuing north on Lexington for about three miles (summer daily 10am–6pm; rest of year daily 10am–4pm; free). Further afield still, in suburban Apple Valley, off Hwy-775 (take bus #77Z from the Mall of America), is the spacious, highly regarded **Minnesota Zoo** (May–Sept Mon–Sat 9am–6pm, Sun 9am–8pm; Oct–April daily 9am–4pm; $8, or $14 combination ticket). The animals reside in reconstructions of their natural habitats; the Komodo dragon exhibit, Imation IMAX Theater and new Discovery Bay aquatic center are outstanding.

Annual celebrations in St Paul include a beanfeast called **Taste of Minnesota** (tons of food, live entertainment, rides and fireworks) running from late June to July 4, the nation's largest **State Fair** (end of Aug to early Sept), and the **Winter Carnival** (late Jan to early Feb), a frosty gala designed to make the most of the seasonal freeze with ice and snow sculpting, hot-air ballooning, team sports, parades and more.

## The Mall of America

Shopping addicts make the pilgrimage to the Mall of America from all over the Midwest – and far beyond, including parties from Japan and the regular "Shop 'Til You Drop" packages run by British operator Major Travel (£300; ☎020/7485-7017). Opened in 1992, this mind-boggling 4.2-million-square-foot, four-story monument to squeaky-clean consumerism has fast become the country's most-visited destination. It incorporates over five hundred stores, with a seven-acre theme park (the pay-per-ride Camp Snoopy) bang in the center. As an **entertainment** complex, the Mall features **UnderWater World** ($9.95), 1.2 million gallons of water with amazing Gulf of Mexico and Caribbean tanks, and **NASCAR Silicon Motor Speedway** ($7.50), for simulated stock-car racing. There's also a comedy club, several dance and music bars, a multiscreen cinema and a vast array of eateries – including *Hotel Discovery*, the latest in "diner-tainment," with international foods served in simulated global and mythological settings. The science and educational store **Brainstorms**, the custom-made **Basic Brown Bear Factory** (where you can custom-design a cuddly ursine companion), **Lake Wobegon USA** (an eclectic giftstore inspired by folksy Minnesota humorist Garrison Keillor's fictional community) and the hands-on demonstrations at Oshman's Super Sports USA are the highlights of a tour, while evidence of the Mall's all-under-one-roof convenience is provided by the **Chapel of Love** retail store (where over 1500 couples have legitimately tied the knot) and a National College campus. The futuristic superstructure contains twice as much steel as the Eiffel Tower, and there's enough room to play a week's NFL games side by side.

The Mall is twenty minutes south of the cities on I-494 at 24th Avenue, Bloomington; take bus #54M from St Paul's West Sixth Street, and #80AB, #5E, #7DEF or #19EFG from various locations in downtown Minneapolis.

## Eating

Preconceptions of Midwestern blandness are swiftly put to rest by an almost bewildering array of **restaurants** in the Twin Cities. In Minneapolis, head for the downtown warehouse district, the southerly **Nicollet** neighborhood, the funky **Uptown** and **Lyn-Lake** areas, or the university's Dinkytown; in St Paul, try Galtier Plaza downtown, the

Asian restaurants on University Avenue, or the horde of ethnic options all along **Grand Avenue**. Of local chains, *Lotus* serves budget Vietnamese meals, *LeeAnn Chin* has adequate Chinese cuisine, while *Keys* offers great breakfasts and fresh lunches. Be sure to sample **wild rice**, a Minnesota specialty.

## Minneapolis

**Broder's Cucina Italiana**, 2308 W 50th St (☎612/925-3113). Terrific deli for eat-in or takeaway. There's a full-service restaurant across the street.

**Buca**, 1204 Harmon Place (☎612/638-2225). Irresistibly festive Italian restaurant dishing out massive portions. There's another branch in St Paul.

**Cafe Brenda**, 300 1st Ave N (☎612/342-9230). Excellent, moderately priced *nouvelle* vegetarian cuisine in arty downtown warehouse district.

**Chez Bananas**, 129 N 4th St (☎612/340-0032). Spicy, Caribbean-influenced food, and toys on the tables.

**Emily's Lebanese Deli**, 641 University Ave NE (☎612/379-4069). Warm, low-cost local place.

**Goodfellows**, 40 S 7th St (☎612/332-4800). Award-winning (and pricey) American cuisine in posh setting.

**Modern Cafe**, 337 13th Ave NE (☎612/378-9882). Eclectic, cheap, flavorsome food in a former neighborhood diner gone hip.

**Odaa**, 408 Cedar Ave S (☎612/338-4459). Tasty all-you-can-eat Ethiopian finger food for $10 or less.

**Palomino**, 825 Hennepin Ave (☎612/339-3800). Stylish, popular downtown Euro-bistro specializing in Mediterranean fare.

**Peter's Grill**, 114 S 8th St (☎612/333-1981). Downtown lunch/early dinner institution – old-style, uncomplicated and quintessentially American. Past diners include President Clinton.

**Sawatdee**, 607 Washington Ave S (☎612/338-6451). Toothsome Thai food, always well prepared, with main courses $8–15. There's another branch in St Paul.

## St Paul

**Cafe DaVinci**, 400 Sibley St (☎612/222-4050). Exceptional Northern Italian cuisine in Leonardoesque setting.

**Caravan Serai**, 2175 Ford Parkway (☎612/690-1935). Afghani food, tent-like space, pillow seats.

**Mickey's Diner**, 36 W 7th St (☎612/222-5633). Landmark 24hr diner in 1930s dining car.

**Moscow on the Hill**, 371 Selby Ave (☎612/291-1236). Exquisite Russo-European food, modest ambiance.

**St Paul Grill**, 350 Market St (☎612/292-9292). Traditional but inventive food in classic downtown hotel.

**Taste of Scandinavia**, 75 W 5th St (☎612/222-1100). Delicious, authentic lunches and daytime snacks served cafeteria-style in Landmark Center. The most central of three locations.

**W A Frost**, Selby and Western aves (☎612/224-5715). Former pharmacy and F Scott Fitzgerald hangout converted into plush restaurant with garden patio.

# Nightlife and entertainment

The Greater Twin Cities have been dubbed a "cultural Eden on the prairie," where 2.5 million people support upwards of one hundred **theater** companies, over forty **dance** troupes, twenty **classical music** ensembles, and more than a hundred art galleries. Sir Tyrone Guthrie began the theatrical boom back in 1963, enrolling large-scale local assistance to establish the classical repertory company (☎612/377-2224 or 1-800/848-4912) named after him. The cities now have more theaters per capita than anywhere in the US apart from New York City.

Unusually, **nightlife** in Minneapolis (and, to a lesser extent, St Paul) hasn't been siphoned off by suburbia, with one hundred thousand students to ensure a vibrant club scene. Before the Seattle music explosion, Minneapolis natives Bob Mould and Paul Westerberg pioneered the grunge sound with their seminal bands **Hüsker Dü** and **The Replacements**. The city still churns out great guitar bands like Soul Asylum, while erstwhile **Prince Rogers Nelson** continues to meddle around in his multimedia **Paisley Park** studio in suburban Chanhassen. For complete entertainment information and listings, check out the ubiquitous free weekly *City Pages*. *Lavender* and *focus*POINT provide a similar service from a lesbian and gay perspective.

## Minneapolis and St Paul theaters

**Bryant-Lake Bowl Theatre**, 810 W Lake St Minneapolis (☎612/825-8949). Performances, bowling, cafe and bar all under one funky roof.

**Chanhassen Dinner Theater**, 521 W 78th St, Minneapolis (☎612/934-1525 or 1-800/362-3515). Mainstream musicals, popular comedies and drama on four stages, plus meals. Thirty minutes from downtown.

**Dudley Riggs' Brave New Workshop**, 2605 Hennepin Ave S, Minneapolis (☎612/332-6620). The grandparent of local satirical comedy troupes.

**Great American History Theater**, 30 E 10th St, St Paul (☎612/292-4323). Original plays dealing with events and personalities from the region's past.

**Jungle Theater**, 709 W Lake St, Minneapolis (☎612/822-7063). Hole-in-the-wall theater/cabaret.

**Park Square**, 408 St Peter St, St Paul (☎612/291-7005). Well-executed classic and contemporary plays.

**Penumbra**, 270 N Kent St, St Paul (☎612/224-3180). Professional African-American company.

**Red Eye Collaboration**, 15 W 14th St, Minneapolis (☎612/870-0309). Challenging experimental theater.

**Theatre de la Jeune Lune**, 1st St and 1st Ave, Minneapolis (☎612/333-6200). Unique ensemble of Parisians and Minneapolitans offering dynamic, highly physical productions from a commedia base.

## Minneapolis bars and clubs

**Backstage at BRAVO!**, 900 Hennepin Ave (☎612/338-0062). New three-story restaurant/piano bar with theatrical leanings.

**Figlio, Calhoun Square**, 3001 Hennepin Ave (☎612/822-1688). Top late-night dining and people-watching.

**Fine Line**, 318 1st Ave (☎612/338-8100). Sleek, small and musically eclectic downtown club.

**First Avenue and 7th St Entry**, 701 1st Ave (☎612/338-8388 or 332-1775). Landmark rock venue where TAFKAP's *Purple Rain* was shot. Still packs 'em in with top bands and dance music.

**Gay 90s**, 408 Hennepin Ave S (☎612/333-7755). Sprawling, predominantly but not exclusively gay club with two dance floors, piano lounge, dining, and polished weekend drag shows.

**Ground Zero**, 15 NE 4th St (☎612/375-5115). Great space, varied themes, mixed clientele.

**Kieran's Irish Pub**, 330 2nd Ave S (☎612/339-4499). Friendly atmosphere built round good food, grog, music and poetry. Downtown location.

**Loon Cafe**, 500 1st Ave N (☎612/332-8342). Noisy, likeable sports bar with great grub (try the chilis).

**Loring Bohemian Bar and Cafe**, 1624 Harmon Place (☎612/338-6258 or 332-1617). Beautiful people with attitude drink, dine or drift upstairs to the dance/theater Playhouse.

**New French Cafe & Bar**, 128 N 4th St (☎612/338-3790). Cozy warehouse district mainstay.

**Nye's Polonaise Room**, 112 E Hennepin Ave (☎612/379-2021). Plenty of old-time atmosphere with both piano and polka bars, plus Polish–American restaurant.

**Quest**, 110 N 5th St (☎612/338-3383). State-of-the-art dance club, with live acts. Dress flash.

## St Paul bars and clubs

**The Dakota Bar and Grill**, 1021 Bandana Blvd (☎612/642-1442). Gourmet Midwestern food and great local and national jazz in converted shopping mall locale.

**Gallivan's**, 354 Wabasha St (☎612/227-6688). Downtown white-collar pub with neighborhood feel.

**O'Gara's Bar and Grill**, 164 N Snelling Ave (☎612/644-3333). Mixed clientele drawn by grub, grog and live bands in the adjoining *Garage*.

**Rumors**, 490 N Robert St (☎612/224-0703). Downtown gay/lesbian club; exudes camaraderie.

**Town House**, 1415 University Ave (☎612/646-7087). Gay/lesbian bar with dance, drag and C&W evenings, plus piano lounge.

# Northern Minnesota

Minnesota's substantial **northern** half, overrun with forested lakes, remains much as it was when the Europeans first traded with the Indians. The northwest – **the Arrowhead**, poking into Lake Superior – holds the greatest charm: most visitors choose secluded outdoor vacations centered around fishing, canoeing and snowmobiling, but there's infinite potential for driving tours in a wilderness comparable to the Alaskan interior.

The Arrowhead is anchored by busy **Duluth**, from where **Scenic Hwy-61** skirts the clifftops around Lake Superior, passing waterfalls, state parks and neat little towns on the way north to the Canadian border. Sleepy little **Grand Marais** is poised at the edge of the wild **Boundary Waters Canoe Area Wilderness (BWCAW)** and the **Gunflint Trail**. Inland, the **Iron Range** makes a scenic route north to the idyllic **Voyageurs National Park**. To the west lies **Lake Itassa State Park**, where the Mississippi River begins its great 31-state roll down to the Gulf of Mexico; you can cross the headwaters on stepping stones. Everywhere you'll find campgrounds and "Ma and Pa" lakeside **resorts**, havens of homely simplicity dedicated to soothing urban-ravaged souls.

## Duluth

**DULUTH**, at the western extremity of Lake Superior 150 miles north of Minneapolis/St Paul, forms a long crescent at the base of the Arrowhead. Named for a seventeenth-century French officer, Daniel Greysolon, Sieur du Lhut, it cascades down from the granite bluffs surrounding **Skyline Drive** (an exhilarating thirty-mile route) to a busy **harbor**, shared with inferior Superior, Wisconsin. Together these "twin ports" constitute the largest inland port in the US. Originally the main cargo was fur; now it ships grain, lumber and ore to the Atlantic via the St Lawrence Seaway.

In the 1980s, Duluth had a face-lift and began to encourage tourism. The main drawback is that it's **cold**. The seaway is frozen through the winter, and even spring and fall evenings can be chilly. Temperatures are always significantly cooler near the lake – as fate would have it, the location of nearly all the attractions and activities.

A short walk down Lake Avenue from the **CVB office**, 100 Lake Place Drive (☎218/722-4011 or 1-800/4-DULUTH), leads to the free **Marine Museum** in Canal Park, a vantage point to watch big boats from around the world pass under the delightfully archaic Aerial Lift Bridge (June to early Sept daily 10am–9pm; rest of year times vary). Originating at Canal Park, Duluth's **Lakewalk** is the free way to take in the view, though in summer you can also take two-hour **harbor cruises** (☎218/722-6218; $9). Also worthwhile is a visit to the stately lakeside Jacobean Revival mansion **Glensheen**, 3300 London Rd (May–Oct daily 9.30am–4pm; Nov–April 11am–2pm Fri–Sun only; two separate tours $8.75/$10, reservations required on ☎218/724-8863 or 1-888/454-

GLEN). Both the grounds and interior are impressive. On a grislier note, aged heiress Elisabeth Congdon was murdered on the premises in 1977, but the crisply efficient guide deflects any queries.

**Rail excursions** along the Superior shoreline to pretty **Two Harbors** (mid-May to mid-Oct; ☎218/722-1273 or 1-800/423-1273; $17 for 6hr, $9 for 90min) run from **The Depot** complex at 506 W Michigan St. This also houses the Lake Superior Railroad Museum, a children's museum, cultural heritage center and art museum (summer 9.30am–6pm; winter 10am–5pm; $8), and is home to performing companies at night. The historic Lake Superior and Mississippi Railroad takes a ninety-minute journey along the scenic St Louis River 11am and 2pm on weekends, mid-June to early Sept ($7; departs from the parking lot on Grand Ave and 71st Ave W, across from the zoo). Duluth's Spirit Mountain **ski area** (☎1-800/642-6377) boasts the best downhill runs in the Midwest.

### Practicalities

From 4426 Grand Ave, Greyhound buses connect with the upper Midwest. **Accommodation** rates and availability fluctuate in summer; Victorian-styled B&Bs include the *A Charles Weiss Inn*, 1615 E Superior St (☎218/724-7016 or 1-800/525-5243; ⑤), while among choice **motels** are the *Best Western Edgewater East*, 2400 London Rd (☎218/728-3601 or 1-800/777-7925; ④), which has a good pool, and the central *Canal Park Inn*, 250 Canal Park Drive (☎218/727-8821 or 1-800/777-8560; ④). *Indian Point* **campground**, at 75th and Grand, west off Hwy-23 (☎218/624-5637), has summer bay-side sites.

The Italian–American **food** at *Grandma's Saloon And Deli*, in view of the bridge at 522 Lake Ave S (☎218/727-4192), is not for dieters. *Grandma's Sports Garden* (☎218/722-4724), across a parking lot at no. 425, is similarly convivial, dishing up tasty food when not functioning as either dance floor or basketball court. Classiest of all is the revolving *Top of the Harbor* (☎218/727-8981), atop the *Radisson Hotel*, 505 W Superior St, and there's also the lovely *Bennett's on the Lake*, 600 E Superior St (☎218/722-2829), featuring a superb lake view.

## North from Duluth: Highway 61

Memorialized on vinyl by Minnesota native Bob Dylan, stunning Scenic Hwy-61 follows Lake Superior for 150 miles from Duluth to the border, its precipitous cliffs interspersed with pretty little ports and picture-postcard picnic sites.

At **Gooseberry River State Park**, forty miles out from Duluth, the river splashes over volcanic rock through waterfalls and cascades to its outlet in Lake Superior. Like all but one of the seven other state parks along Hwy-61, it provides access to the rugged two-hundred-mile **Superior Hiking Trail** (☎218/834-2700), divided into easily manageable segments for day-trekkers. To camp at any of the state parks, reserve on ☎1-800/246-CAMP.

Just beyond **Cascade River State Park**, the road dips into the somnolent little port of **GRAND MARAIS**, where a walk around the photogenic Circular Harbor will soon cure car-stiff legs. The visitor center at 13 N Broadway (☎218/387-2524 or 1-888/922-5000) has lists of outfitters for those going into the BWCAW. Inexpensive **room** options include the ultraclean *Sandgren Motel*, by the lights on Hwy-61 (☎218/387-2975 or 1-800/796-2975; ③), and the characterful *Harbor Inn Motel* (☎218/387-1191 or 1-800/595-4566; ③). *Naniboujou Lodge*, fifteen miles east on Hwy-61 (☎218/387-2688; ⑤), is a bit pricier, but it's worth dropping by this former 1920s private club just to gawp at the restaurant's eye-poppingly brilliant Cree Indian designs. A backpacker haunt with a difference is *Spirit of the Land Island Hostel* (☎218/388-2241 or 1-800/454-2922; ①), 58 miles inland from Grand Marais on an island in Seagull Lake; bunks cost $16–18, plus $2 extra for nonmembers. For herrings and imported beer, or just a well-priced snack, head for *Sven & Ole's Pizza*, 9 W Wisconsin St (☎218/387-1713).

Ferries from **GRAND PORTAGE**, 136 miles nearer the Canadian border and site of an Indian-operated casino and a superbly reconstructed eighteenth-century stockade, run daily in summer to the **desolate Isle Royale National Park** (see p.293), 22 miles out among the sweeping waves of Lake Superior.

## The BWCAW and the Gunflint Trail

The huge **Boundary Waters Canoe Area Wilderness**, west of Grand Marais, is also accessible from Tofte and especially from easygoing ELY, home of the intriguing **International Wolf Center** (May–Oct daily 9am–5.30pm; Nov–April Fri–Sun 10am–5pm; $5.50). The BWCAW is a canoe, backpack and fishing enthusiast's paradise, where overland trails or "portages" link over a thousand lakes; in winter you can ski and dogsled cross-country. The unpaved sixty-mile Gunflint Trail from Grand Marais cuts the BWCAW in two; otherwise there are no roads in this outback, let alone electricity, telephones or trash cans. Most lakes remain motor-free. Stringent rules limit entry to the BWCAW; in summer you need a date-specific permit (☎1-800/745-3399, 1-877/550-6777 or 218/365-7561/2; $9 reservation fee, plus $20 deposit), which local outfitters can issue. For those who don't want to rough it, several rustic lodges lie strung out along the Gunflint. The **Gunflint Trail Association** can offer good advice on ☎1-800/338-6932 or 218/387-2870.

## The Iron Range

Valiant attempts have been made to reclaim and restore the once-inhospitable **Iron Range**, a few miles west of Ely. Here a number of fabulously rich mines continue to function over a century after their inception. If you're interested in surveying old workings, it's possible to descend 2300ft at the **Soudan Underground Mine State Park** on Hwy-169 (summer daily 10am–4pm; $6, plus $4 vehicle fee).

Seventy miles south on Hwy-169 in **CHISHOLM**, the **Ironworld USA** cultural theme park (June 11–Sept 12 9.30am–5pm; $7) turns ecological disaster into tourist spectacle, inviting you on a trolley ride to see "the scenic wonder of an open pit mine." Further opportunities to view such wonders (this time for free) occur during the ten-minute drive to **HIBBING** – a plain little community, of interest mainly as the birthplace of Robert Zimmerman in 1941. His adult persona of **Bob Dylan** debars the local **museum** in City Hall from showing any exhibits on his career.

Hibbing was also the home of America's biggest bus company. With the help of model buses and old adverts the Greyhound Bus Origin Center, 1201 Greyhound Blvd, looks back to its roots transporting local miners to and from the pits (mid-May to Sept 30 Mon–Sat 9am–5pm; $3). The Hull-Rust Mahoning Mine, once the world's largest open pit iron ore mine, can be toured or viewed from an overlook (mid-April to Sept 30 daily 9am–7pm; free).

## Voyageurs National Park

Made up of border lakes between Minnesota and Canada, **VOYAGEURS NATIONAL PARK** is like no other in the national park system. To see it properly, or indeed to grasp its immense beauty at all, you need to leave your car behind and venture into the wild by boat. Once out on the lakes, you're in a great, silent world where kingfishers, osprey and eagles swoop down for their share of the abundant walleye; moose and bear stalk the banks; and sunrises and sunsets conjure up a photographer's dream.

The park's name comes from the intrepid eighteenth-century French-Canadian trappers, who took almost a year to get their pelts back to Montréal in primitive birchbark canoes, paddling for sixteen hours a day and fighting off attacks from Native Americans – and each other. Their "customary waterway" became so established that the treaty of 1783 ending the American Revolution specified it as the international border.

You can't do Voyageurs justice on a day-trip, though daily cruises from Rainy Lake visitor center, ten miles east of International Falls, do at least allow a peek at the lakelands (late May to early Sept; ☎218/286-5470; $35 or more for a range of special tours). If you're here for a few days, rent a **boat** (reckon on $40 a day) and camp out. It's easy to get lost in this maze of islands and rocky outcrops, and unseen sandbanks lurk beneath the surface – if you're at all unsure, hire a guide from one of the resorts for the first day (around $200 per 8hr day). During **freeze-up** – usually from December until March – the park takes on a whole new aura, as a prime destination for skiers and snowmobilers (rentals from $115 per day).

**INTERNATIONAL FALLS**, the only sizeable nearby community, might sound attractive, but it's a messy array of motels, duty-free shops, fast-food joints and lumber yards; the falls, never more than glorified rapids anyway, were dammed in 1906.

### Practicalities

Most travelers access Voyageurs from Hwy-53, which runs northwest from Duluth. After just over one hundred miles comes the first entrance to the park, at Orr, 25 miles from **Crane Lake** on the eastern extreme. About 28 and 31 miles further along Hwy-53, highways 129 and 122 lead respectively to the **visitor centers** at **Ash River** (May–Sept daily 9am–5pm; ☎218/374-3221) and **Kabetogama** Lake (May–Sept daily 9am–5pm; ☎218/875-2111). Another prime visitor center is at **Rainy Lake** (May–Sept daily 9am–5pm; rest of year times vary; ☎218/286-5258), at the westernmost entrance 36 miles further on via International Falls.

Once inside the park, you have to take a few **precautions**: check (natural) mercury levels in fish before eating them, don't pick wild rice (only Native Americans can do this), be wary of Lyme's Disease (a tick-induced gastric illness), boil drinking water, and watch out for bears. Discuss such matters, along with customs procedures in case you venture into Canadian waters, with a ranger before venturing out.

The definitive way to experience the park is to **camp** on one of its many scattered islands, most plentiful around Crane Lake (if you don't have your own boat, cruise operators can drop you off and pick you up at a later date). There are also first-come, first-served state-owned campgrounds on the mainland at Ash River and Woodenfrog, near Kabetogama. However, most visitors shack up in one of over sixty **resorts**. Basically family-run cottages, these usually cater for weekly stays, with all meals, though you can rent rooms nightly. Most popular are those around Kabetogama, such as *Watson's Harmony Beach* (☎218/875-2811; ③), a great place for picking up tips on the park; *Arrowhead Lodge* (☎218/875-2141; ③), well known for its restaurant; and the basic, cheap and cheerful *Driftwood Lodge* (☎218/875-3841; ①). You can book through the Kabetogama Lake Association (☎1-800/524-9085). Resort associations for Crane Lake (☎218/993-2346), Ash River (☎1-800/950-2061) and Rainy Lake/International Falls (☎218/283-9400) can also fix you up with lodgings, including houseboats (usually $1000 and up per week).

# Southern Minnesota

**Southern Minnesota** is split between high plains, timbered ravines and slow-flowing Mississippi tributaries in the east, and the drier, flatter prairie and checkerboard farmland of the west. In the scenic **southeast**, spared a filing down by the last glacial advance, attractive small towns sit along the Mississippi, or on bluffs above it, in the ninety-mile **Hiawatha Valley**. Mississippi shipping helped sustain easygoing communities like **Winona**, **Red Wing**, **Lake City** (where waterskiing was invented circa 1922) and **Wabasha**, all of which share well-preserved old homes and hotels.

The agricultural and college center of **Northfield**, on I-35 a mere thirty miles south of the Twin Cities, annually commemorates the Jesse James gang's foiled attempt to rob the town bank in September 1876. **Harmony**, almost in Iowa and near Minnesota's largest **Amish colony**, **Lanesboro**, with a storybook setting on the hillsides of the Root River, and **Mantorville** have all kept at least one foot in the nineteenth century. Further west, **New Prague** and **New Ulm** were prime targets for the beleaguered Sioux during a six-week war with the US government in 1862.

## Rochester

The metropolis of **ROCHESTER**, a white-collar community in a rural setting about eighty miles southeast of Minneapolis/St Paul, was settled in the 1850s by migrants from Rochester, New York, as a humble crossroads campground for wagon trains. After a tornado devastated the town in 1883, Dr William Worral Mayo established the huge **Mayo Clinic**, 200 First St SW (☎507/284-2511). Free tours of its skyways and subways serve as ninety-minute pedestrianized adverts for "the first and largest private group medical practice in the world" (Mon–Fri 10am; art tour Tues–Thurs 1.30pm). You can also tour the sprawling family home, **Mayowood**, 3720 Mayowood Rd southwest of Hwy-52 (☎507/282-9447; Sat and Sun, May to mid-June at 1pm, 2pm and 3pm, plus Sat at 11am; mid-June to Oct on Tues, Thurs, Sat and Sun, same hours; $10).

Rochester is rife with chain and budget **accommodation**, especially within the five-block radius of downtown, such as the *I*, 20 SW Second Ave (☎507/282-2581 or 1-800/533-1655; ④). *The Broadstreet Cafe and Bar*, 300 NW First Ave (☎507/281-2451), a bistro in a renovated warehouse, serves excellent meals; there's live music in the cozy *Redwood Room* downstairs.

Jefferson Union Bus Depot, 405 SW First Ave (☎507/289-4037), is the hub for bus services. Rochester Express (☎507/282-8673 or 1-800/479-7824) and Rochester Direct (☎507/280-9270 or 1-800/280-9270) make between eight and eleven van runs daily to the Twin Cities' Airport or the Mall of America for $19 one-way, $36 round-trip. Rochester's **visitor center** is at 150 S Broadway (☎507/288-4331 or 1-800/634-8277).

## Pipestone

**PIPESTONE**, eight miles east of the South Dakota border, is named for a soft red rock within the local quartzite, which was used for centuries by Great Plains Indians to make ceremonial calumets, or peace pipes. The quarry site, a kind of neutral, inter-tribal United Nations, is now the **Pipestone National Monument** (daily 8am–5pm, longer on summer weekends; $2). A self-guided trail winds from the visitor center through stands of trees, past rock formations and exposed quarry pits, and over a creek, complete with picturesque falls.

Pipestone's small historic district includes a sleepy county museum and a building with several amusing sandstone gargoyles; pick up a walking-tour brochure from the **visitor center** (☎507/825-3316 or 1-800/336-6125), near the junction of highways 75 and 23. You can sleep and eat at the grand old *Calumet Inn*, 104 W Main St (☎507/825-5871 or 1-800/535-7610; ④), though the *Arrow Motel*, Hwy-75 N, is less expensive (☎507/825-3331 or 1-888/825-9599; ②). Each late July to early August the town puts on the nine-day "Song of Hiawatha" **Indian pageant** in an outdoor amphitheater.

From a distance the red rocks at **Blue Mounds State Park**, sloping into a long cliff a few miles north of the junction of I-90 and US-75 at Luverne, create a great hump that appeared blue at sunset to approaching pioneers. Twice a year, at the equinoxes, the sun lines up with a curious 1250ft row of rocks, aligned on an east–west axis. There are seasonal **campgrounds** (☎1-800/246-CAMP) and a permanent small herd of buffalo. Ring the same number for picturesque **Split Rock Creek State Park**, only seven miles south of Pipestone and the site of a dam dating from 1935.

# CHAPTER FIVE

# THE CAPITAL REGION

T he city of **WASHINGTON DC**, and the four states of **VIRGINIA, WEST VIR-GINIA, MARYLAND** and **DELAWARE**, constitute a cross-section of the nation. Since the days of the first American colonies, US history has been shaped here, from agitation towards independence to the battles of the Revolutionary and Civil wars. Now, the contrasts and incongruities of contemporary America are shown in high relief: the corridors of power in Washington are literally a stone's throw away from dire inner-city poverty, while nearby dozens of time-worn farming and fishing towns seem straight out of some Norman Rockwell idyll.

Early in the seventeenth century, the first British settlements began to take root along the rich estuary of the **Chesapeake Bay**; the colonists hoped for gold, but found their fortunes growing tobacco. **Virginia**, the first settlement, was the largest and most populous; it originally included most of what are now Kentucky, Tennessee and Ohio, and as late as the 1790s had double the population of any other state. Fully half of these people were **slaves**, brought from Africa to do the backbreaking work of harvesting the tobacco. Despite its central position on the East Coast, the whole region lies below the Mason-Dixon Line – the symbolic border between North and South, drawn up in 1763 as the boundary between slave and free states – and until the Civil War one of the country's busiest slave markets was just two blocks from the White House.

Besides generating the bulk of colonial wealth, the region also produced many of early America's great leaders, from firebrand politicians like **Patrick Henry** ("Give me Liberty or Give me Death") to patrician intellectuals such as **Thomas Jefferson**. Another Virginian, **George Washington**, led the Continental Army against the British in the Revolutionary War and served as the first president, while **James Madison** was the primary author of the Constitution.

For all its colonial importance, by the mid-nineteenth century the region had lost power and status to the industrial and mercantile centers of Philadelphia and New York. Tensions between North and South finally erupted into the **Civil War**, of which traces are still visible everywhere. The hundred miles between the capital of the Union – Washington DC – and that of the Confederacy – Richmond, Virginia – were a constant and bloody battleground for four long years. This sense of a nation divided against itself is especially acute at the grand manor of **Robert E Lee**, the Confederacy's military leader: high on a hill overlooking the heart of Washington DC, its grounds are now filled with the war dead of the Arlington National Cemetery.

---

## ACCOMMODATION PRICE CODES

All accommodation prices in this book have been coded using the symbols below. Note that prices are for the least expensive double rooms in each establishment. For a full explanation see p.37 in Basics.

| | | |
|---|---|---|
| ① up to $30 | ④ $60–80 | ⑦ $130–175 |
| ② $30–45 | ⑤ $80–100 | ⑧ $175–250 |
| ③ $45–60 | ⑥ $100–130 | ⑨ $250+ |

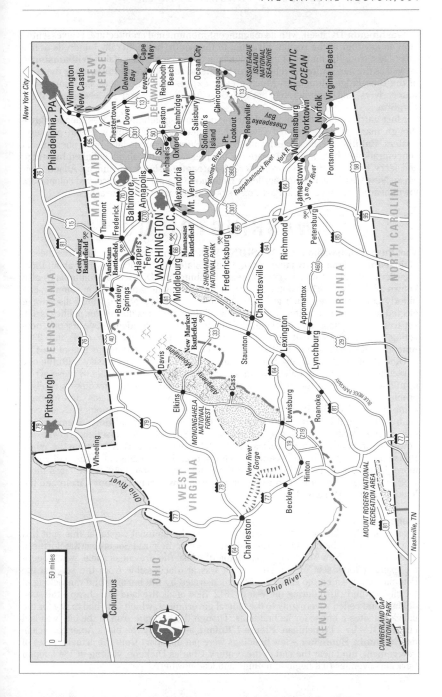

Washington DC itself, with its magnificent monumental architecture, is an essential stop on any tour of the region. **Virginia**, to the south, holds literally hundreds of historic sites, from the homes of early politicians to the colonial capital of **Williamsburg**, as well as the narrow forested heights of **Shenandoah National Park**, along the crest of the Blue Ridge Mountains. Much greater expanses of wilderness, crashing whitewater rivers and innumerable backwoods villages await you in less-visited **West Virginia**.

Most tourists come to **Maryland** for the maritime traditions of **Chesapeake Bay** – though many of its quaint old villages have been gentrified by weekend pleasureboaters. **Baltimore** is characterful and enjoyably unpretentious (and has a phenomenal concentration of bars), while **Annapolis**, the pleasant state capital, is linked by bridge and ferry to the **eastern shore**, where **Assateague Island** remains an Atlantic paradise. **New Castle**, across the border in **Delaware**, is a perfectly preserved colonial-era town; nearby are some of the East Coast's best and least crowded beaches.

# WASHINGTON DC

That the marshy swamp where **WASHINGTON DC** now stands was chosen as the site of the **capital** of the newly independent United States of America says a lot about then-prevalent attitudes towards government. Washington, District of Columbia – also known as **"DC"** and **"The District"** – can be unbearably hot and humid in summer, and bitterly cold in winter. Such an unpleasant climate, it was hoped, would discourage elected leaders from making government a full-time job. This disdain for politics is still apparent: DC is run as a virtual colony of Congress, where residents have just one, non-voting representative and couldn't vote in presidential elections until the 23rd Amendment was passed in 1961 – the first one they participated in was that of 1964.

Other than the federal government, **tourism** is DC's biggest industry, with the city attracting almost twenty million visitors each year. Conveniently, most of these arrive in midsummer, when the law-makers have gone home, so overcrowding is rarely a problem. The nation's showcase puts on quite a display for its guests, and for once admission to virtually all the major attractions is free. The most famous sites are concentrated along the central **Mall**, including the White House, individual memorials to four of the greatest presidents, and the superb Smithsonian museums. Downtown, however (broadly speaking the area immediately north of the Mall, between the White House and the Capitol), can seem very empty, even intimidating, at night, and you're more likely to spend your evenings in the hotels and restaurants of the city's more motherly neighborhoods, such as historic **Georgetown**, arty **Dupont Circle** and the funkier **Adams-Morgan** district.

## Some history

Apart from the climate, the decision to establish the national capital at this spot had much to do with the fact that it lies midway between the rural South and the northern cities of Boston, New York and Philadelphia (the last, the previous capital, was thought too exciting for a seat of government). It was also accessible from the sea, via the Potomac River – a bit too easily so, as demonstrated by the burning and ransacking of the city by the British during the War of 1812. Best of all, the land was cheap – the state of Maryland ceded sovereignty to the federal government, which only had to pay for the individual sites it chose for its buildings. Though the baroque plan of the city was laid out in 1791 – by a Frenchman, **Pierre L'Enfant**, assisted by the black American scientist **Benjamin Banneker** – few buildings were put up, apart from the actual houses of government, until near the end of the century. Charles Dickens, visiting in 1842, found "spacious avenues that begin in nothing and lead nowhere."

After the Civil War, thousands of Southern **blacks** arrived in search of a sanctuary from racial oppression; to some extent, they found one. Segregation was banned in public places, and **Howard University**, the only US institution of higher learning that enrolled black people, was set up in 1867. By the 1870s African-Americans made up over a third of the 150,000 population, but economic resources were soon stretched to breaking point. As poverty and squalor worsened, official **segregation** was reintroduced in 1920, banning blacks from government buildings – including, in an ironic twist, the Lincoln Memorial – and the jobs they had come to find.

The years after World War II saw the city's economy and population boom, but although segregation of public facilities was declared illegal in the 1950s, civil rights protests divided the city during the 1960s – culminating in the destructive downtown riots of 1968. The city's problems have changed little since: DC has one of the country's highest murder rates, as well as appalling levels of unemployment, illiteracy and drug abuse. A Congressionally appointed control board has jurisdiction over the city's finances until 2003, in an attempt to turn round the massive budget deficit, while the continuing middle-class flight to the suburbs has left the city population at its lowest since the 1930s, a situation which further shrinks the tax base and hinders any immediate economic improvement. However, new mayor **Anthony Williams** has made a positive start in an attempt to rescue the city from what many saw as the folly of the long years under the picaresque leadership of the notorious Marion Barry.

# Arrival, information and getting around

Washington DC is served by three major **airports**, two on the outskirts and one right in the city center. **Dulles International Airport**, 26 miles west in the depths of northern Virginia, and **Baltimore-Washington International** (BWI), halfway between DC and Baltimore, get the majority of the international traffic; **National Airport**, and its major state-of-the-art terminal, along the Potomac River just west of the Mall, is mostly used by domestic flights. Taking a **cab** downtown from BWI or Dulles costs around $50, but **express buses** run from both airports to a downtown terminal at 1517 K St NW, just three blocks north of the White House: Washington Flyer Express (☎1-800/927-4359) serves Dulles (every 30min; 40min journey; $16 one-way, $26 round-trip); and the SuperShuttle (☎1-800/BLUE-VAN) runs from BWI (every 30min; 1hr journey; $28 one-way). From Dulles, the very cheapest method, though more time-consuming, is to take the Washington Flyer Express as far as West Falls Church Metro station ($8) and the Metro subway system (see overleaf) from there. There's also a SuperShuttle from National (every 30–60min; $9 one-way, $18 round-trip), though this airport is on the Metro system, just a short ride from downtown. Taxis downtown from National cost around $15.

By **train** – from Philadelphia, New York and Boston, as well as direct from **BWI Airport** – you arrive amid the gleaming malls of bustling **Union Station**, 50 Massachusetts Ave NE, two blocks north of the US Capitol and with its own Metro station. Greyhound and other **buses** stop at a modern station at 1005 First St NE, in a fairly dodgy part of the city, ten blocks from downtown – take a cab, especially at night, at least as far as Union Station Metro (around $6). **Driving** into DC is a sure way to experience some of the worst traffic on the East Coast – the main I-95 and I-495 freeways circuit Washington on what's known as the **Beltway**, jammed eighteen hours a day.

Once in the city, first stop should be the **DC Chamber of Commerce Visitor Center**, Ronald Reagan Building, 1300 Pennsylvania Ave NW (Mon–Sat 8am–6pm, Sun noon–5pm; ☎202/328-4748), which can help with maps, tours, bookings and citywide information. There are also visitor information desks at the airports and Union Station, while the **White House Visitor Information Center**, 1450 Pennsylvania Ave NW (daily 7.30am–4pm; ☎202/208-1631), supplies free city maps and handy guides to all the museums and attractions, the most useful of which is the free *Washington DC Visitors Guide*, available from the above sources.

The main **post office** is across from Union Station on Massachusetts Avenue and Capitol Street NE (Mon–Fri 7am–midnight, Sat & Sun 7am–8pm; ☎202/523-2628; zip code 20002).

## City transportation

**Getting around** DC is a cinch. Most places downtown, including the Mall museums, the major monuments and the White House, are within walking distance of each other, and an excellent **public transportation** system reaches outlying sights and neighborhoods. The clean, efficient and still-growing **Metro subway** is the envy of other cities; one-way fares start at $1.10 (base rate, off-peak), with a slight rush-hour surcharge from 5.30–9.30am and 3–7pm, while a One Day Pass, only valid after 9.30am on weekdays, costs just $5 (trains run Mon–Fri 5.30am–midnight, Sat & Sun 8am–midnight; route information from the Metro Center Sales Office, Metro Center station, 12th and F sts NW; ☎202/637-7000). The standard fare on the more extensive **bus** network is also $1.10, while **taxis** are a good-value alternative with most cross-town fares ranging from $4 to $12.50. There are taxi ranks at major hotels and transportation terminals (like Union Station), or call Yellow Cab (☎202/544-1212).

## City tours

During the day, open-sided **Tourmobiles** (☎202/554-5100) connect the major museums and sites, allowing you to stop for as long as you choose at any of a dozen different locations. A $14 one-day ticket covers downtown DC and Arlington Cemetery, while an extra $22 gets you to Mount Vernon (see p.377) and back; two-day tickets for unlimited travel on both routes cost $37. All can be bought from the main office on the Ellipse, just south of the White House, at kiosks on the Mall and in Union Station, or on the tram itself.

If you want to **cycle** or **cruise** along the Potomac River or the historic C&O Canal, both Thompson's Boat Center, 2900 Virginia Ave NW at Rock Creek Parkway (☎202/333-4861), near the Watergate complex, and Fletcher's Boat House, 4940 Canal Rd NW, two miles further up the canal towpath (☎202/244-0461), rent out touring bikes, rowboats and canoes. You could also get to know the city on a three-hour cycling trip with Bike the Sites Inc ($35 per person including bike and helmet; ☎202/966-8662); or call Better Bikes (☎202/293-2080), who will deliver rental bikes anywhere in DC ($25 a day). In addition, mule-drawn **canal boats**, with costumed National Park Service guides, follow the old C&O Canal from behind 30th and M streets in Georgetown on a ninety-minute narrated cruise (April–Oct; $6; ☎202/653-5190). The city's best **walking tours** are led by Anthony S Pitch ($10; ☎301/294-9514), who ambles around Adams-Morgan and Georgetown a couple of times a week.

# Accommodation

Most DC **hotels** cater to business travelers and political lobbyists, and during the week are quite expensive. At weekends, however, and throughout July and August, when Congress is in recess, many cut their rates by up to fifty percent – it's always worth asking about special rates. For a list of properties contact one of the city information offices or call Washington DC Accommodations (☎202/289-2220 or 1-800/554-2220), which provides a general hotel reservation and travel planning service.

Similarly, a number of **B&B** agencies offer comfortable doubles from around $55–65: try the B&B League (☎202/363-7767) or Bed & Breakfast Ltd (☎202/328-3510). There's no good **camping** anywhere near DC, but besides the **youth hostel**, both the Catholic University (☎202/319-5277) and Georgetown University (☎202/687-4560) offer **budget rooms** in summer; these must be arranged well in advance.

One thing to keep in mind: DC in summer is hot and humid, and **air conditioning** is essential for a good night's rest.

**Adams Inn**, 1744 Lanier Place NW (☎202/745-3600 or 1-800/578-6807). Clean, simply furnished B&B rooms, with and without bath, spread across three adjoining Victorian townhouses in quiet Woodley Park street, near the zoo. ③/④.

**Allen Lee Hotel**, 2224 F St NW (☎202/331-1224 or 1-800/462-0186). Slightly faded, musty rooms with clunky air conditioning. It's seen much better days, but is handy and cheap, two blocks from Foggy Bottom-GWU Metro; it's worth paying the extra ten bucks or so for a private bath. ③.

**Brickskeller Inn**, 1523 22nd St NW (☎202/293-1885). Simple rooms, some with private baths, above a raucous late-opening bar near Dupont Circle. ④.

**Connecticut-Woodley Guest House**, 2647 Woodley Rd NW (☎202/667-0218). Friendly guesthouse with 15 rooms (including a couple of singles), opposite the *Sheraton Washington* and near the zoo and plenty of restaurants. ④.

**Doubletree Hotel Park Terrace**, 1515 Rhode Island Ave NW (☎202/232-7000 or 1-800/222-TREE). European elegance six blocks north of the White House, with comfortable rooms, marble bathrooms, and free coffee-making facilities; closest Metro is Dupont Circle. ⑥.

**Embassy Inn**, 1627 16th St NW (☎202/234-7800 or 1-800/423-9111). Welcoming inn on a residential side street in northern Dupont Circle. Good-value rooms (with attractive weekend rates), free continental breakfast, plus an early evening sherry to speed you on your way. ⑤.

**Four Seasons**, 2800 Pennsylvania Ave NW (☎202/342-0444 or 1-800/332-3442). DC's most luxurious hotel, a sympathetic modern redbrick at the eastern end of Georgetown, stuffed with leisure facilities. ⑨.

**Harrington Hotel**, 1100 E St NW (☎202/628-8140 or 1-800/424-8532). Popular with groups, this large, old-fashioned hotel has a great situation, halfway between the Capitol and the White House, off Pennsylvania Ave. ⑤.

**Hay-Adams Hotel**, 1 Lafayette Square NW (☎202/638-6600 or 1-800/424-5054). Historic (and very expensive) townhouse hotel overlooking the White House. ⑨.

**Hereford House**, 604 South Carolina Ave SE (☎202/543-0102). Attractive townhouse B&B, with bright, reasonably sized rooms run in the "true British tradition"; one block from Eastern Market Metro. ⑤.

**HI-Washington DC**, 1009 11th St NW (☎202/737-2333). Huge (250 beds), clean and very central hostel, three blocks north of Metro Center. $20 a night for HI members, $23 nonmembers. May only accept members in busy spring and summer months. ①.

**India House Too**, 300 Carroll St NW (☎202/291-1195). A little way out in Upper Northwest (though near Takoma Park Metro), this few-frills townhouse-hostel has the cheapest dorm beds in DC ($14) and two equally affordable (though sought-after) doubles. Take passport or ID. ①/②.

**Kalorama Guest House**, 1854 Mintwood Place NW (☎202/667-6369) and 2700 Cathedral Ave NW (☎202/328-0860). Cozy, nicely furnished rooms (no TVs though) in several restored Victorian townhouses; rates include breakfast, coffee and evening sherry. The first group is located in the grander part of the lively Adams-Morgan neighborhood, the second across Rock Creek near the zoo. ③/④.

**Omni Shoreham**, 2500 Calvert St NW (☎202/234-0700). Plush Washington institution, near Woodley Park Metro and bursting with history. Every president since FDR has held an inaugural ball here; Bill Clinton played the sax at his. ⑧.

**Simpkins' B&B**, 1601 19th St NW (☎202/387-1328). Welcoming Victorian townhouse at Dupont Circle, with a range of shared and private rooms, morning toast and tea included. Rates double if you can't produce a passport, whether US or foreign. ①–③.

**State Plaza**, 2117 E St NW (☎202/861-8200 or 1-800/424-2859). Spacious suites with fully-equipped kitchens, close to Foggy Bottom Metro; excellent weekend rates. ⑥.

**Tabard Inn**, 1739 N St NW (☎202/785-1277). Very pleasant small hotel, with exceptionally well furnished rooms and a decent restaurant, well located two blocks from Dupont Circle Metro. Rates, for doubles with shared bath, include breakfast. ⑥.

**Windsor Inn**, 1842 16th St NW (☎202/667-0300 or 1-800/423-9111). Under the same management as the *Embassy Inn*, the *Windsor* is a few blocks further north, its rooms a shade larger. ⑤/⑥.

# The City

Because the city was built from scratch, Washington's regular **town plan** is easy to grasp. Centered on Capitol Hill and its governmental monoliths, the District is divided into four **quadrants** – northeast, northwest, southeast and southwest. Dozens of broad **avenues**, all named after states, run diagonally across a standard grid of **streets**, meeting up at monumental traffic circles like Dupont Circle. North–south streets are numbered, east–west ones are lettered (there's no J Street, an intentional slight to early Supreme Court Justice John Jay, or X, Y or Z Street, and I Street is often written Eye Street). Be very sure to note the relevant two-letter code in any **address** (NW, NE, SW, SE), which shows its quadrant; 1600 Pennsylvania Ave NW is a *long* way from 1600 Pennsylvania Ave SE.

Until you get your bearings, it's wise to stick to the established tourist trail; almost all the most famous sights are on **Capitol Hill** or in the comparatively affluent northwest quarter. To the west of the Capitol, the broad, green **Mall** holds monuments to presidents **Washington, Jefferson, Lincoln** and **Franklin D Roosevelt**, as well as the **White House**, official home of the current incumbent. Also here are the bulk of the city's many marvelous museums, including the national collections of the **Smithsonian Institution**.

However, there is more to Washington than an endless succession of museums and monuments, and it's well worth searching out its many attractive **neighborhoods**. Despite its reputation, most of the city is in surprisingly good shape, with row after row of nineteenth-century brick-fronted houses set along leafy boulevards. Between the Mall and the main spine of **Pennsylvania Avenue** – the parade route connecting Capitol to White House – the Neoclassical buildings of **Federal Triangle** offer a sobering contrast to the rest of the city's neighborhoods. North and east of here, what's known as **Old Downtown** has been revitalized after years of neglect and features new plazas, galleries and restaurants alongside its traditional attractions, like the FBI Building, Old Post Office and the theater associated with President Lincoln's assassination. The area around the **MCI Center**, particularly along Seventh St NW, is fast developing as an entertainment and nightlife scene, with several rated bars and restaurants. The oldest area, **Georgetown**, where popular bars and restaurants now line M Street and Wisconsin Avenue above the **Potomac River**, actually precedes the establishment of the District; it's a 15-minute walk from the Foggy Bottom-GWU Metro but its Federal-era and Victorian townhouses and the towpath along the **C&O Canal** make it a fine target for a day's pottering about. Other neighborhoods to check out – especially for eating and drinking – are **Dupont Circle** at the intersection of Massachusetts, Connecticut and New Hampshire avenues, which pulls a dynamic mix of yuppies, guppies and buppies; and the lower-rent, Latin American immigrant community of **Adams-Morgan**, a short walk from Dupont Circle up 18th Street at Columbia Road.

Outside DC, most visitors also take the short Metro ride to **Arlington** in Virginia to see the National Cemetery – JFK's burial place – and the Pentagon.

## Capitol Hill

Though there's more than one hill in Washington DC, when people talk about what's happening on "**The Hill**" they mean **Capitol Hill** – a shallow knoll topped by the giant white dome of the US Capitol building and rising at the very center of the city. When Washington DC was first laid out, Capitol Hill was intended to be both the symbolic and real seat of the federal government. Home of both the legislature – **Congress** – and the judiciary – the **Supreme Court** – this is still the place where the law of the land is made and refined; it also holds the newly refurbished **Library of Congress**.

## US Capitol

*Between Constitution and Independence aves at the eastern end of the Mall; closest Metro Capitol South or Union Station. Summer daily 9am–8pm; rest of year daily 9am–4.30pm. Tour information ☎202/225-6827, general information ☎202/224-3121. Admission free.*

Visible from all over the city, and housing the nation's law-makers and tax-takers, the **Senate** and the **House of Representatives**, the **US Capitol** is one of the few places in the District where you can get a sense of the immense power wielded by the nation's elected officials – and watch them at work. The grand halls and public spaces are packed with monuments and statues of ex-politicians, while the current crop of legislators can be seen arguing over the finer points of law and policy in committee rooms and the ornate main chambers. When the lantern above the dome is lit, Congress is in session.

Begun in 1793 – George Washington, in Masonic garb, laid the cornerstone – the Capitol was repeatedly expanded over the ensuing years, and is now a confusing hybrid, hard to find your way around, though the omnipresent Capitol police officers keep you on the right track. There's free, walk-in access to the building all year (from the East Front), though between April and September you can expect to have to wait in line first, for up to two hours. Once inside, the **free tours** (every 15min, 9am–3.45pm) are basically just a walk around the building; US citizens who want to see inside the legislative chambers have to arrange "VIP tours" through their representatives, while foreigners can simply show their passports at the House or Senate appointments desks, both on the first floor. Nine presidents, most recently JFK (Nixon declined in advance), have lain in state before burial in the impressive **Rotunda**, which, capped by a 180ft dome, links the two halves of the Capitol – the Senate is in the north wing, the House in the south.

Armed Forces' **bands** perform for free four nights a week (June–Aug) on the East Terrace of the Capitol; the National Symphony Orchestra follows suit on the West Terrace on Memorial Day, July 4 and Labor Day.

## Library of Congress

*Jefferson Building, 10 First St SE; Madison Building, 101 Independence Ave SE; closest Metro Capitol South. Mon–Sat 10am–5.30pm. ☎202/707-8000. Admission free.*

In the **Library of Congress**, the largest in the world, over 95 million books and manuscripts, and countless thousands of microfilm rolls and computer disks, are arrayed on six hundred miles of shelves. Set up in 1800, the entire library was burned by the British in 1814; to replace the loss, Thomas Jefferson sold the country his six-thousand-volume personal collection. In 1870, when the Library of Congress was declared the national copyright library, the need was felt to build a suitable home; the result, the exuberantly eclectic **Thomas Jefferson Building**, opened in 1897 across from the Capitol, complete with a domed octagonal **Reading Room**, and hundreds of mosaics, murals and sculptures in its stunning Great Hall. The second floor holds the **American Treasures** exhibit, which includes a vast array of original documents and manuscripts, including the "I have a dream" typescript and Maya Lin's drawing of the Vietnam Veteran's Memorial. Documents of special significance – those associated with Washington, Lincoln and Jefferson, among others – are shown in an environmentally controlled cabinet for short periods at a time. Free library **tours** – the only way to see

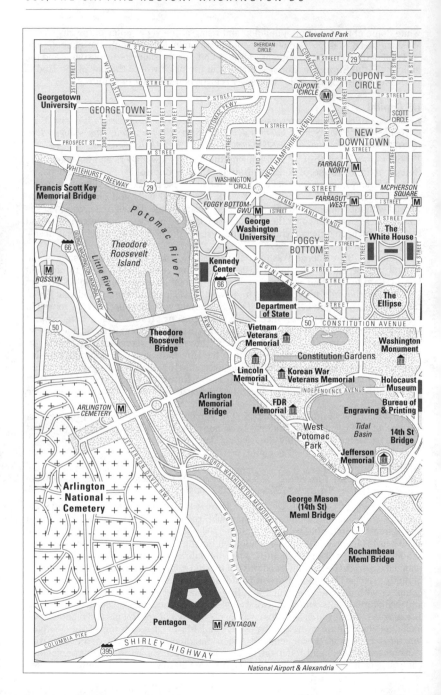

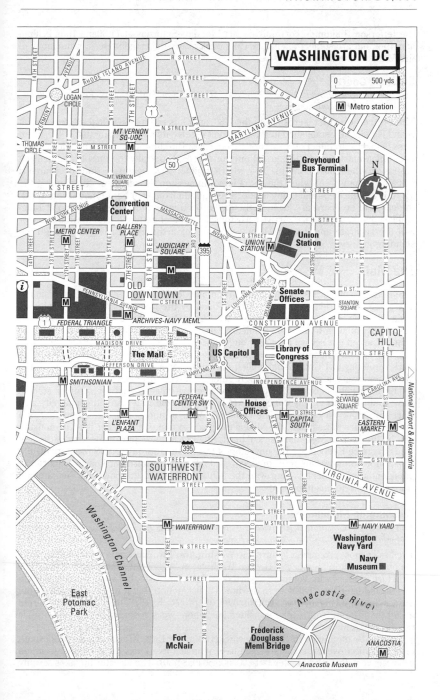

# WASHINGTON DC

0       500 yds

**M** Metro station

N

LOGAN CIRCLE

THOMAS CIRCLE

14TH STREET
VERMONT AVENUE
RHODE ISLAND AVENUE
9TH STREET
7TH STREET
R STREET
Q STREET
P STREET
N STREET
FLORIDA AVENUE

MARYLAND AVENUE

MT VERNON SQ-UDC **M**
13TH STREET
12TH STREET
11TH STREET
M STREET
MT VERNON SQUARE
50

K STREET

**Greyhound Bus Terminal**
1ST STREET
NORTH CAPITOL ST
K STREET
H STREET

**Convention Center**
NEW YORK AVENUE
MASSACHUSETTS AVENUE
3RD STREET

**Union Station**
G STREET
UNION STATION **M**
2ND STREET
F ST.
7TH STREET

METRO CENTER **M**
14TH STREET
13TH STREET
12TH STREET
11TH STREET
GALLERY PLACE **M**
9TH STREET
7TH STREET
6TH STREET

**JUDICIARY SQUARE** **M**

395

**Senate Offices**
DELAWARE AVE
LOUISIANA AVENUE
D ST.
STANTON SQUARE

ℹ

OLD DOWNTOWN
PENNSYLVANIA AVENUE
C STREET

**M**

1
**FEDERAL TRIANGLE**
ARCHIVES-NAVY MEML

1ST STREET
CONSTITUTION AVENUE

CAPITOL HILL

MADISON DRIVE

**The Mall**
JEFFERSON DRIVE
4TH STREET
MARYLAND AVE

**US Capitol**

**Library of Congress**
EAST CAPITOL STREET

SEWARD SQUARE
NORTH CAROLINA AVE

**M** SMITHSONIAN
12TH STREET
10TH STREET
9TH STREET
C STREET

INDEPENDENCE AVENUE

**FEDERAL CENTER SW** **M**

**House Offices**
C STREET
**M** CAPITOL SOUTH
D ST.

EASTERN MARKET **M**

**L'ENFANT PLAZA** **M**
3RD ST
WASHINGTON AVE
2ND STREET
NEW JERSEY AVE
E STREET

E STREET

G STREET

National Airport & Alexandria ▷

MAINE AVENUE
WATER STREET
7TH STREET
6TH STREET
SOUTHWEST/ WATERFRONT
I STREET
1ST STREET
SOUTH CAPITOL STREET

VIRGINIA AVENUE

*Washington Channel*
OHIO DRIVE

K STREET
L STREET
M STREET

4TH STREET
N STREET

**M** WATERFRONT
4TH STREET
1ST STREET

**M** *NAVY YARD*

**Washington Navy Yard**

**Navy Museum** ■

P STREET
2ND STREET

*Anacostia River*

East Potomac Park

Fort McNair

**Frederick Douglass Meml Bridge**

ANACOSTIA **M**

▽ *Anacostia Museum*

the Jefferson Building – currently depart Monday–Saturday at 11.30am, 1pm, 2.30pm and 4pm, but are subject to change; call or ask at the information desk in the lobby of the Madison Building.

## Supreme Court

*First St NE and Maryland Ave NE; closest Metro Union Station. Mon–Fri 9am–4.30pm. ☎202/479-3211. Admission free.*

The **Supreme Court**, across from the US Capitol, is the nation's final arbiter of what is and isn't legal. Established in 1787, it didn't receive its own building until 1935, when Cass Gilbert – architect of New York's Woolworth Building – was chosen to design this Corinthian masterpiece. The grand interior spaces, especially the marble and damask drapes of the courtroom itself – where guides give lectures (hourly, Mon–Fri 9.30am–3.30pm; free) when the court is not in session – make it worth climbing the gleaming white steps and going inside. Sessions run from October to June (Mon–Wed), the cases to be heard are listed in the day's *Washington Post*; sessions begin at 10am and last one hour per case. Arrive early to be assured of getting one of the 150 seats, or join the separate line if you're happy to settle for a three-minute stroll through the standing gallery.

# The Mall

One of the main features of L'Enfant's grand plan for Washington was the provision of a large central parkland, a Grand Avenue lined by the mansions of the political elite. Today the two-mile-long **Mall** stretches west from the Capitol to the Potomac River. It wasn't always such a carefully manicured park, however: when the Capitol was first built, it looked out across a muddy, bug-infested swamp, and by the 1870s, the south side was lined by meat-markets and warehouses and crisscrossed by railroad tracks. A stark reminder of L'Enfant's unfulfilled dream, for over twenty years the Washington Monument was left unfinished, an ugly stone stump cut off halfway.

The Mall has become DC's most popular green space, used for summer softball games and Fourth of July concerts. Yet its central role in a planned capital city also places it at the very heart of the country's political and social life. When there's a protest gesture to be made, the Mall is the place to make it, whether it's a demonstration by the Million Men marchers of black America, a mass prayer meeting of the religious Promise Keepers, or the unveiling of the commemorative AIDS Memorial Quilt. In addition to numerous museums, covered on p.363 onwards, it boasts a quartet of presidential monuments, along with the White House and the powerful Vietnam and Korean War Veterans memorials.

## Washington Monument

*15th St NW at Constitution Ave; closest Metro Smithsonian. April–Aug daily 8am–midnight; Sept–March daily 9am–5pm. Admission free.*

The Mall's most prominent feature, the **Washington Monument** is an unadorned marble obelisk built in memory of George Washington. At 555ft it's the tallest all-masonry structure in the world. Volunteers started work on it in 1848, but various internal arguments, and later the Civil War, so disrupted construction that it wasn't completed until 1884. When the US Government took over the project in 1876, they used marble from a slightly different source; the transition line where work resumed at the 150ft level is readily apparent.

To visit the monument pick up a free ticket from the 15th St kiosk (on the Mall, south of Constitution Ave), which allows you to turn up at a fixed time later in the day, or you can reserve with TicketMaster (☎1-800/505-5040; $1.50). The elevator up takes seventy seconds and deposits you at the 500ft level in order to enjoy the monument's panoramic 360° views of the city.

## The White House

*1600 Pennsylvania Ave NW; closest Metro McPherson Square or Farragut West. Continuous free tours Tues–Sat 10am–noon; additional tours in summer. Tours (☎202/456-7041) start from the bleachers on the Ellipse, south of the White House; in winter simply join the queues, but in late spring and summer you have to pick up tickets, as early as possible (they've usually all gone by 8.30am), from the Visitor Center at 1450 Pennsylvania Ave (daily 7.30am–4pm; ☎202/208-1631).*

For nearly two hundred years, the **White House** has been the residence and office of the President of the United States. Standing at the edge of the Mall, due north from the Washington Monument, this grand, Neoclassical edifice was completed in 1800 by Irish immigrant James Hoban, who modeled it on the Georgian manors of Dublin. Each of its presidential occupants has made his mark: Thomas Jefferson added the first toilets, just before the British burned the place down during the War of 1812. It was quickly rebuilt and expanded, often in such a hurry that the whole building was on the verge of collapse. Harry Truman had to move out for four years from 1948 while the structure was stabilized: all the rooms were dismantled and a modern steel frame inserted. Truman also added the balcony to the familiar south side portico.

Though many visitors are surprised by how small and homey it is, security at the White House is every bit as tight as you'd imagine. Protesters are still allowed to set up camp opposite the main entrance, but the stretch of Pennsylvania Avenue immediately outside was permanently closed to traffic in 1995, shortly after the Oklahoma bombing.

**Tours** of the White House consist of a lot of waiting around followed by a quick shuffle through the basement and up to the ground-floor reception rooms, peeping in at a succession of plush, railed-off rooms filled with portraits of ex-presidents. In summer, the gardens are sometimes opened for afternoon tours, and at Christmas there are special evening tours of the festively decorated interior.

If you're interested in the history of the place and its occupants, you may well find the **Visitor Center**, a couple of blocks southeast on Pennsylvania Avenue, more rewarding than the White House itself. It's filled with photos and film footage of First Families and their distinguished guests, including a portly President Hoover playing "Hooverball" with a group of lumbering judges, and the Wright Brothers showing off their latest airplane. In one inaugural portrait after another, a drawn and exhausted president hands over power to his beaming successor.

## Lincoln Memorial

*West Potomac Park, at 23rd St between Constitution and Independence aves; closest Metro Foggy Bottom-GWU. Daily 24hr, staffed 8am–midnight. Admission free.*

At the far west end of the Mall, the **Lincoln Memorial** is modeled upon a Doric temple, enclosed by a colonnade and fronted by a long reflecting pool. During the Civil Rights march on Washington in 1963, Dr Martin Luther King Jr delivered his epic "I Have a Dream" speech, not from the steps of the White House or the US Capitol, but here. Ironically, when this monument to the Great Emancipator was dedicated in 1922, the crowds were segregated by color – even black leader Dr Robert Moton, who gave an address, was forced to watch from a roped-off area to the side.

The Lincoln Memorial is a fitting tribute to the man who held the country together during the Civil War and thereby put an end to slavery in the US. A craggy likeness of Abraham Lincoln sits firmly grasping the arms of his throne-like chair, apparently deep in thought, while inscriptions of Lincoln's two most celebrated speeches – the Gettysburg Address and the Second Inaugural Address – are carved on north and south walls.

## Vietnam Veterans Memorial

*Constitution Ave at 21st St NW; closest Metro Foggy Bottom-GWU. Daily 24hr, staffed 8am–midnight. Admission free.*

Cutting sharply into the green lawn of the Mall, the small and simple **Vietnam Veterans Memorial** serves as a somber and powerful reminder of the nearly 60,000 US soldiers who died in Vietnam. The pathway that slopes down from the grass forms a gash in the earth, its increasing depth symbolizing the increasing involvement of US forces in the war. Alongside, a black marble wall is carved with the names of every soldier who died, in chronological order from 1959 to 1975.

The memorial was designed by Maya Lin, as a 21-year-old architecture student. When it was first erected in 1982, there was some outcry from veterans groups about its anti-war connotations. By way of appeasement, in 1984 a more traditional statue of three heroic soldiers was placed nearby, under a floodlit American flag. More lobbying led to the establishment of the **Vietnam Women's Memorial** in 1993, which stands in a grove of trees at the eastern end of the main site, to mark the 11,000 American women who served in the conflict.

## Korean War Veterans Memorial

*West Potomac Park, south of Lincoln Memorial Reflecting Pool; closest Metro Smithsonian. Daily 24hr, staffed 8am–midnight. Admission free.*

The **Korean War Veterans Memorial**, dedicated in 1995, incorporates a dramatic Field of Remembrance in which nineteen life-sized stainless steel combat troops advance across an open field towards the Stars and Stripes. Between 1950 and 1953, almost 55,000 Americans were killed in Korea (with another 8000 missing in action and over 103,000 wounded), a harbinger of the slaughter to begin in Vietnam a decade later. It's an affecting memorial to an often-forgotten conflict and a plaque at the flagstand proclaims: "Our nation honors her sons and daughters who answered the call to defend a country they never knew and a people they never met."

## Jefferson Memorial

*West Potomac Park, Tidal Basin near 15th St SW and Ohio Drive; closest Metro Smithsonian. Daily 8am–midnight. Admission free.*

Completed in 1943 and modeled on his country home, Monticello (see p.393), the **Jefferson Memorial** consists of a shallow dome hovering over a bronze statue of Thomas Jefferson, the author of the Declaration of Independence and the third US president. The interior walls, encircled by an Ionic colonnade, are carved with Jefferson's words, and an inscription around the frieze reads: "I have sworn upon the altar of God eternal hostility against every form of tyranny over the mind of man."

The **Tidal Basin**, which fills most of the space between the Lincoln and Jefferson memorials, was created in order to prevent the western end of the Mall, including the spots where the two memorials sit, from being inundated by Potomac floods. The reflections off it are especially pretty in spring (usually late April), when the rows of Japanese cherry trees come out in full bloom.

## FDR Memorial

*West Potomac Park, south of the Korean Memorial, near the Tidal Basin. Daily 24hr, staffed 8am–midnight. Admission free.*

The most recently constructed of the major Mall monuments, the **FDR Memorial** was opened in 1997, its four outdoor "gallery" rooms designed to highlight the achievements of Franklin Delano Roosevelt's twelve years as President. Bronze sculptures of FDR and his wife, Eleanor, along with waterfalls and remembrance pools, offset inscriptions from the President's best-known speeches – and in a belated nod to the fact that FDR was crippled by polio (a fact kept from the American people throughout his presidency), it's the first memorial in DC purposely designed to be wheelchair-accessible.

# The Smithsonian Institution

The cream of Washington DC's remarkable panoply of historical artifacts and fine art works comes under the general auspices of the **Smithsonian Institution**, which holds the US national collections of everything under the sun. Endowed by an Englishman – James Smithson, bastard son of the first Duke of Northumberland, who never even visited the US – the Smithsonian was established in 1846 "for the increase and diffusion of Knowledge." This broad brief is reflected in its impressive range of research centers and museums. Nine line up along the Mall, four more are located just north, and the zoo is a few miles north beyond Rock Creek.

The original home of the Smithsonian, the 1849 Norman-style Smithsonian Institution Building, known as **The Castle**, stands on the Mall halfway between the Capitol and the Washington Monument. It was at first devoted to scientific research, but as the Smithsonian became more of a museum, the sheer accumulation of items necessitated the construction of the various other buildings along the Mall. The old Castle is now the Smithsonian headquarters and main **visitor center**, 1000 Jefferson Drive SW (daily 9am–5.30pm; ☎202/357-2700), with the latest details on all the galleries available from the high-tech information desk. The ornate tomb of James Smithson is in an alcove just off the Mall entrance, and the lovely flower-filled Enid A Haupt Garden (daily: summer 7am–8pm; winter 7am–5.45pm) fronts the Castle on the south side. You can still get a feel for the days when the Smithsonian was known as "the nation's attic," by visiting the adjacent **Arts and Industries Building**, DC's first "National Museum," which once displayed the hundreds of objects sent here for safekeeping after the 1876 Centennial Exhibition in Philadelphia. Although some of the Victoriana artifacts remain on display, the building's main focus is now temporary exhibitions by the African-American History Center, and the American Indian and Anacostia museums.

## National Air and Space Museum

*South side of the Mall between Fourth and Seventh sts SW; closest Metro L'Enfant Plaza.*

The **National Air and Space Museum** is by far DC's most popular attraction, drawing nearly ten million people every year. Most of them may seem to be here on the day you come, but the hangar-like building can accommodate everyone without feeling crowded, and you can always see the hundreds of historic aircraft close up. Hanging from the rafters in the main entrance gallery, the "**Milestones in Flight**" include the handmade plane in which the **Wright Brothers** made the first powered flight in 1903; **Charles Lindbergh**'s *Spirit of St Louis*, in which he made the first solo transatlantic

---

### SMITHSONIAN DETAILS

All the Smithsonian museums and galleries are open daily all year (except 25 December) from **10am** until **5.30pm**. To cope with the summer crowds, however, several of the museums – including the **Air and Space**, **Natural History** and **American History** museums – open daily from **10am** until **6.30pm** from the first Monday in June to the first Monday in September. **Admission** to all the galleries is **free**. For details on current exhibitions and events, or a copy of the *Smithsonian Access* brochure for disabled visitors, call the visitor center on ☎202/357-2700, or access the Smithsonian's homepage at *www.si.edu*.

crossing in 1927; the claustrophobic *Mercury* capsule in which **John Glenn** orbited the earth in 1962; and the ultralight *Voyager*, which flew around the world nonstop in 1986.

Most of the museum is taken up with exploring the space race from both American and Soviet perspectives, using models and actual spacecraft to show the development from von Braun's V1 rockets up to a gawky-looking lunar module. "**Apollo to the Moon**" is one of the most fascinating galleries, centering on the Apollo 11 (1969) and 17 (1972) missions, the first and last respectively – there's Neil Armstrong's and Buzz Aldrin's spacesuits, navigation aids, space-food, clothes and charts, and an astronaut's survival kit (complete with shark repellant). Further galleries include "**Stars**," a history of astronomy; "**Looking at Earth**," where the aerial photographs include Boston snapped from a balloon in 1860 and German castles recorded by camera-toting pigeons; and "**The Great War in the Air**," bursting with dogfighting biplanes.

The museum also shows a rotating program of super-large-screen **IMAX** movies ($5.50; ☎202/357-1686 for times), all of which have some connection with flying; the most spectacular, *The Dream is Alive*, was shot from an orbiting space shuttle. The *Flight Line* **cafeteria** and the *Wright Place* **restaurant** enable star-struck families to stay in the building all day.

## National Museum of Natural History
*North side of the Mall, Tenth St NW and Constitution Ave; closest Metro Smithsonian.*

The imposing three-story entrance rotunda of the **National Museum of Natural History** feels like the busiest and most boisterous crossroads in all of DC, with troops of screeching schoolkids endlessly chasing each other around a colossal African elephant. Hundreds of other stuffed animals, tracing evolution from fossilized four-billion-year-old plankton to dinosaurs' eggs and beyond, are on display all over the place – pick up floor plans and guides at the information desk at the elephant's feet.

Naturally enough, the "**Dinosaurs**" section is the most popular part of the museum, with hulking skeletons reassembled in imaginative poses and accompanied by informative text, written with a light touch, accessible to children. "**Exploring Marine Ecosystems**" uses videos, aquariums and the odd furry seal to illustrate life on the "Rocky Shore of Maine" and a "Coral Reef from the Caribbean." Nearby you can admire a rare specimen of the giant squid; scientists don't know quite where it lives, but reckon it grows to fifty feet in length.

Elsewhere, the museum seems firmly locked into a 1950s-style approach to natural history, with a lot of very dated anthropology. Displays on "**Native Cultures of the Americas**" include the Lucayans (originally from the Bahamas), said to have "vanished" shortly after encountering Columbus, and dioramas of the "primitive" pueblos of the Southwest stand alongside bison, bighorn sheep and other once-wild things. Similarly static exhibits cover peoples of the Pacific and Asia, as well as ancient Greece and Egypt.

Upstairs are hundreds of creepy-crawly critters – lizards, snakes, tarantulas and the like – as well as an **Insect Zoo**, filled with hundreds of bugs, which you can play with should you so desire. The museum also boasts a truly exceptional array of gemstones, on display in a new **Gem and Mineral Hall**, featuring natural and reconstructed environments, interactive exhibits and hands-on specimens – though you'll have to be content with just a longing gaze at the legendary 45-carat **Hope Diamond**, which once belonged to Marie Antoinette.

## National Museum of American History
*North side of the Mall, 14th St NW and Constitution Ave; closest Metro Smithsonian.*

If you like kitsch, you won't want to miss the bizarre melange of cultural artifacts at the **National Museum of American History**. George Washington's wooden teeth,

Muhammad Ali's boxing gloves, and the ruby slippers Judy Garland wore in the *Wizard of Oz* are set among didactic displays tracing the country's development. It's not so much a center for scholarly study as a sanctuary for vanishing Americana, incorporating Model T Fords, old post offices and even a restored, c.1900 ice-cream parlor, which still serves up banana splits.

As you enter from the Mall, directly on to the second floor, a display showcases the battered red, white and blue flag that inspired the US national anthem – the **Star-Spangled Banner** itself, which survived the British bombing of Baltimore harbor during the War of 1812. It's under long-term restoration until 2002 but will remain on display while the work is carried out. The worthier exhibits are also on this floor: an account of the rural farm-based society of the early US stands across from an examination of the mass movement of African-Americans from Southern farms to the wartime industries of northern cities. A lunch counter from Woolworths in Greensboro, North Carolina, evokes the sit-in of 1960, while "American Encounters" focuses on New Mexico, looking at how tourism has affected communities such as the pueblo of Santa Clara and Hispanic Chimayo. On the first floor, the **"Information Age"** gallery traces communications from Morse's first telegraph to virtual reality tours of the Smithsonian, while separate galleries display in glorious profusion the artifacts and machines that have shaped modern America – from lightbulbs and motorbikes to trains and atomic clocks. The top floor holds political memorabilia (much of it over a century old), stamp and coin collections, old TV sets and typewriters, though two final outstanding exhibits inject a serious tone – **"Personal Legacy: the Healing of a Nation"** brings together some of the 25,000 items left by relatives at the Vietnam Memorial in DC, while **"A More Perfect Union"** deals candidly with the shameful internment of Japanese-American citizens during World War II.

## Hirshhorn Museum

*South side of the Mall, Independence Ave at Seventh St SW; closest Metro L'Enfant Plaza.*

Next to the Air and Space museum, and housed in the most clearly modern building on the Mall – a windowless cylinder balanced on fifteen-foot stilts above a concrete plaza, it looks like a spaceship poised for takeoff – the **Hirshhorn Museum** holds the Smithsonian's extensive collection of late nineteenth- and twentieth-century art. From the main entrance on Independence Avenue, escalators climb to the upper-floor galleries, where major works by Picasso, de Kooning, Mondrian, Pollock, Matisse and many more are on display. The gallery downstairs hosts touring exhibitions, and critically acclaimed films are shown in the evenings (☎202/357-1300 for details).

A stimulating collection of modern **sculpture** is displayed in an open-air garden across from Jefferson Drive, on the Mall side of the museum. Alongside assorted Moores, Rodins, Smiths and Malliols are two expressive abstract figures by Marino Marini, and a stalwart *Yucatán Woman* by Mexican sculptor Francisco Zuniga. The landscaped garden, sunk below ground level to spare Congress members from having to look at modern art, is also a nice place for a picnic lunch.

## National Museum of African Art

*South side of the Mall at 950 Independence Ave SW; closest Metro Smithsonian.*

Built in 1987, the curved and domed **National Museum of African Art** holds more than six thousand sculptures and artifacts, both spiritual and functional, from the numerous tribal cultures of sub-Saharan Africa. The permanent collection ranges from Nigerian carved-ivory cult figures to Zairean mother-and-child fertility fetishes and puppet heads from eastern Mali. Look out for an extraordinary seventeenth-century bronze from the Lower Niger, consisting of a vase swarmed over by eight bizarre chameleons, all cast in one piece. While the museum celebrates the **"Art of the**

Personal Object," highlighting the grace of everyday objects such as combs and pipes, much of its sculpture is highly abstract, and its influence on the Cubists is obvious.

Around half the space is devoted to changing exhibitions on specific regions, and the giftshop sells woven and dyed fabrics and clothes, as well as books and postcards.

## Arthur M Sackler Gallery

*South side of the Mall at 1050 Independence Ave SW; closest Metro Smithsonian.*

The angular and pyramidal counterpart of the African Art museum, the **Arthur M Sackler Gallery** contains art works and devotional objects from Asia and the Middle East. Most of the exhibitions are temporary, and occasionally draw from other museums' collections, so it's not possible to predict what will be on display at any one time. However, exhibitions might take in the Sackler's noted collection of translucent jade dragons and intricate, three-thousand-year-old bronzes from China; stone deities from India and Tibet; and lushly illustrated early Islamic texts from Iran, gorgeously colored in gilt, silver and crushed stone pigments. Inexpensive posters and prints are sold in the giftshop; while underground galleries – featuring temporary exhibitions – connect the Sackler to the Freer Gallery and the African Art museum.

## Freer Gallery of Art

*South side of the Mall, Jefferson Drive at 12th St SW; closest Metro Smithsonian.*

From the day it opened in 1923, the **Freer Gallery** has been one of the more unusual Smithsonian museums. Put together and paid for by railroad millionaire Charles Freer, it revolves around over one thousand prints, drawings and paintings by London-based American artist **James McNeil Whistler** – the largest collection of his works anywhere – but also includes Chinese jades and bronzes, Byzantine illuminated manuscripts, Buddhist wall sculptures and pieces of Persian metalwork, all collected by Freer under Whistler's tutelage. Among other works are pieces by Whistler's contemporaries Winslow Homer, Albert Pinkham Ryder and John Singer Sargent.

Besides his portraits and landscapes, Whistler himself is represented by an entire room – the **Peacock Room**. Its original owner commissioned Whistler to execute a painting for the mantelpiece; the artist later covered the walls and furnishings with blue and gold painted peacock feathers. His patron hated it, so Freer bought it and shipped it over from London (he also kept live peacocks in the museum's central courtyard).

## National Museum of American Art

*Eighth and G sts NW; closest Metro Gallery Place-Chinatown.*

Separated from the main Mall galleries, the **National Museum of American Art** may not get the traffic of the other museums, but it's perhaps the most worthwhile of all. As well as mounting the most thought-provoking shows – one exhibition examining the distortion and deceit underlying early images of the American frontier earned it national notoriety – its galleries are pleasant places to be in their own right.

When it opened in 1829, the museum was known as the National Gallery of Art – Andrew Mellon later usurped that name (see opposite). Since 1968, it has shared the Greek Revival-style **Old Patent Office** with the National Portrait Gallery. Works range from splendid nineteenth-century examples of "Art of the American West" – including almost 400 paintings by George Catlin, who spent six years touring the Great Plains – to Revolutionary portraits, dramatic American landscapes (notably a startling grouping by Thomas Moran at the top of the main staircase), WPA-style social realism and modern works by Helen Frankenthaler, Willem de Kooning, Robert Rauschenberg and Clyfford Still. More recent pieces have been displayed on the top floor in the vaulted and colonnaded **Lincoln Gallery**, which in 1865 hosted President Lincoln's post-Civil War Inaugural Ball. It's still one of DC's most celebrated interior spaces but may be closed for restoration for the next couple of years. Free daily **guided tours** set off around the gallery, Monday to Friday at noon, weekends at 2pm.

## National Portrait Gallery
*Eighth and F sts NW; closest Metro Gallery Place.*

The **National Portrait Gallery**, which shares its premises with the Museum of American Art, holds pretty much what you'd expect: paintings, sculptures and photographs of famous and not-so-famous people. Themed galleries downstairs take in "Performing Arts" and "Champions of American Sport," which provide an excuse to search for heroes and icons, but it's upstairs where the more serious works are congregated. In the Rotunda, Gilbert Stuart's famous "Lansdowne" portrait of George Washington gives way to the celebrated "Hall of Presidents," where there are portraits and sculptures of every President, with a separate gallery for George Washington. The rest of the floor is taken up with the "Galleries of Notable Americans," basically a parade of the great and the good, from Pocahontas to Mark Twain, with the odd masterpiece on show – like Edgar Degas's severe portrait of his friend, Impressionist Mary Cassatt.

## The National Zoo
*3001 Connecticut Ave NW; closest Metro Woodley Park-Zoo. Buildings open daily May to mid-Sept 10am–6pm; rest of year 10am–4.30pm. Grounds daily May to mid-Sept 6am–8pm; rest of year 6am–6pm. Admission free.*

Few people realize that the **National Zoo**, up in the north of town but a short walk from the Metro, forms part of the Smithsonian ensemble – which at least means that admission is free. It sprawls down the steep slopes of the gorge cut by Rock Creek, with trails through lush vegetation and comparatively humane simulations of the home environments of more than three thousand creatures. Among the zoo's star attractions is the **panda** Hsing Hsing, one of a pair presented by the People's Republic of China during Richard Nixon's 1972 visit; his mate, Ling Ling, died in 1992. You can usually see him only at feeding times (11am & 3pm). As well as the expected menagerie of giraffes and elephants, birds and bees, and lions and tigers, the zoo (or BioPark as it likes to call itself) boasts an unusual feature in its **Think Tank**, where orangutans assemble, commuting to and from their cages as they please by means of overhead cables across public areas of the zoo.

# Other museums and attractions

While you could quite easily spend a week wandering around the Smithsonian, the national collections are by no means the only worthwhile museums in DC – or, for that matter, along the Mall. The large **National Gallery**, at the foot of the US Capitol, is the best art museum in the city, and one of the top ten in the world. Besides further top-quality art galleries, you can tour various **federal buildings** – to watch the FBI track down criminals, or count brand-new dollar bills as they roll off the presses – or honor the nation's dead, including the Kennedy brothers, at **Arlington National Cemetery**.

## National Gallery of Art
*North side of the Mall, Constitution Ave between Third and Seventh sts NW; closest Metro Archives-Navy Memorial. Mon–Sat 10am–5pm, Sun 11am–6pm. ☎202/737-4215. Admission free.*

Though the visually stunning **National Gallery of Art**, the nearest of the Mall museums to the Capitol, is not in fact a government institution, it fully deserves its name. It owes its prominence to the efforts of industrialist **Andrew Mellon**, who bought the building and donated most of the paintings (many were purchased from the cash-poor post-revolutionary government of the USSR, where they had previously hung in the Hermitage). His family have continued as benefactors, raising countless millions to build I M Pei's modernistic East Building in 1978.

The original Neoclassical gallery, designed by John Russell Pope in 1941, is now called the **West Building** and holds the bulk of the permanent collection. Note that parts of the collection are rotated or sent out on tour, while some rooms may be closed for renovation. To track down the specific location of a particular work, visit the interactive **Micro Gallery** in the West Building (main floor, Mall entrance).

From the domed central rotunda, where you can pick up a floor plan and gallery guide, a vaulted corridor runs the length of the building. If you only have limited time, latch onto one of the informative daily **free tours** – ask for a schedule at the information desk. Galleries to the west on the main floor display major works by Renaissance masters, arranged by nationality: half a dozen Rembrandts fill the **Dutch** gallery, Van Eyck and Rubens dominate the **Flemish**, and El Greco and Velázquez face off in the **Spanish**, near eight progressively darker Goyas. There's also the only Leonardo in the US, the 1474 *Ginevra de' Benci*, painted in oil on wood, plus works by Botticelli, Crivelli and Raphael – including the latter's celebrated *Alba Madonna* (1520), one of Mellon's purchases from the Hermitage. The other half of the West Building holds an exceptional collection of nineteenth-century **French** paintings – Gauguin from Pont-Aven to Tahiti, a couple of Van Goghs, some Monet studies of Rouen Cathedral and water lilies, Cézanne still-lifes et al. At either end of the building, the skylit, fountain-filled **Garden Courts** make an ideal place to rest weary feet, while Salvador Dalí's *Last Supper* guards the escalators down to the cafe.

The triangular **East Building** houses **twentieth-century** paintings and sculpture. As in the Guggenheim in New York, the attention-grabbing spatial choreography of the architecture all but overpowers the works of art. You emerge from under the oppressively low entrance into a central atrium, from where an escalator, literally carved out of a 40ft granite wall, climbs to the main galleries – which, squeezed into the corners, can seem like an afterthought. Changing and touring exhibitions throughout the year mean that the bulk of the permanent collection is rarely on display, though you may catch Picasso's haunting *Family of Saltimbanques* and the very blue *The Tragedy*, as well as Giacometti bronzes and paintings, plenty of Alexander Calder (whose huge red-and-black mobile is usually in place), early Mirós, some Warhol soup cans and Chuck Close's finger painting *par excellence, Fanny*. The underground concourse that links the two buildings contains a good bookstore, an espresso bar and a large cafeteria – topped by pyramidal skylights and bordered by a glassed-in waterfall.

## National Archives

*North side of the Mall at Seventh St and Constitution Ave NW; closest Metro Archives-Navy Memorial. April to Labor Day daily 10am–9pm; rest of year daily 10am–5.30pm. ☎202/501-5000. Admission free.*

As well as a copy of the **Magna Carta**, dating from 1297, the **National Archives** hold exhibitions and serve as the official repository of all US national records – census data, treaties (including the surrender of Japan in World War II), passport applications, as well as genealogical records – most of which are kept in storage. On display inside the impressive Neoclassical Greek temple – designed by the National Gallery's John Russell Pope – are the three short texts upon which the United States is founded: the **Declaration of Independence**, the **Constitution** and the **Bill of Rights**. These three original sheets of parchment (the three further pages of the Constitution are not on display), drafted respectively in 1776, 1787 and 1789, are now contained in helium-filled glass cases, which drop underground in case of fire or other threat. You can usually look at them as long as you like, but if there's a crowd you have to shuffle on past.

## The FBI

*On Pennsylvania Ave between Ninth and Tenth sts NW, just north of the Mall; closest Metro Federal Triangle. Hour-long tours every 20–30min, Mon–Fri 8.45am–4.15pm, no reservations. ☎202/324-3447. Admission free.*

A fortress-like modern building on Pennsylvania Avenue holds the headquarters of the FBI – the **Federal Bureau of Investigation**, the nation's elite law-enforcement organization. Set up in 1908, the FBI came into its own chasing bootleggers and bank robbers like Al Capone and Machine Gun Kelly during the 1930s. Hordes of visitors queue outside, sometimes for well over an hour, to join tours through displays on the famous gangsters and dangerous Communists and subversives from whom the FBI shields the American people (they kept extensive files on Dr Martin Luther King Jr). Ideology aside (the FBI has only just begun to emerge from the shadow of its longtime führer, J Edgar Hoover), the tours rush you through an overview of fingerprinting, ballistics testing and other crime-fighting techniques. What really brings the crowds in, however, is the culminating display of sharpshooting and firepower: agents blast away at cut-out targets with a battery of small arms and automatic weapons.

## Old Post Office

*1100 Pennsylvania Ave NW, at 12th St. Closest Metro Federal Triangle. Mid-April to mid-Sept Mon–Sat 10am–9pm, Sun noon–8pm; rest of year Mon–Sat 10am–7pm, Sun noon–6pm. ☎202/289-4224. Admission free.*

Built in 1899, the fanciful Romanesque **Old Post Office**, just across from the FBI, is one of the most recognizable of downtown's monuments. Its glorious galleried interior is now known as the Pavilion, in which guise it supports hundreds of shops, stalls and a food court – though the more clued-up visitors make a beeline here, rather than the Washington Monument, for a first aerial view of the city. The building's **clock tower** (mid-April to mid-Sept daily 8am–11pm; closed Thurs 6.30–9.30pm; rest of year daily 10am–5.45pm; free; ☎202/606-8691) stands 270ft above Pennsylvania Avenue, and the glass elevator ride allows you to see the iron, glass and wood interior in all its fine glory.

## Ford's Theatre

*511 Tenth St NW; closest Metro Metro Center. Daily 9am–5pm; theater is closed during rehearsals or matinees, but Lincoln Museum and Petersen House remain open. ☎202/426-6924. Admission free.*

**Ford's Theatre** is a beautiful reconstruction of a nineteenth-century playhouse, which continues to stage regular productions of contemporary and period drama (see p.375). However, thanks to its role in one of the greatest national tragedies, it lives a double life as a tourist attraction in its own right. It was here, on April 14, 1865, a mere five days after the end of the Civil War, that **Abraham Lincoln** was shot by John Wilkes Booth during a performance of *Our American Cousin*.

Entertaining talks (hourly 9.15am–4.15pm; free) set the scene in the theater itself, after which you can file up to the circle for a view of the presidential box where it all happened, and finally go down to the basement Lincoln Museum. Macabre relics here include the clothes that Lincoln was wearing, Booth's .44 single-shot Derringer pistol, and the assassin's diary, in which he wrote: "I hoped for no gain. I knew no private wrong. I struck for my country and that alone." The mortally wounded president was carried across the street to the **Petersen House**, where he died the next morning. That, too, is open to the public, who troop through its gloomy parlor rooms to see a replica of the bed on which Lincoln breathed his last.

## Corcoran Gallery of Art

*500 17th St NW; closest Metro Farragut North or Farragut West. Mon, Wed & Fri–Sun 10am–5pm, Thurs 10am–9pm. ☎202/639-1700. Suggested donation $3.*

Just down the street from the White House, the **Corcoran Gallery** is one of the oldest and most respected art museums in the US – and one of the nicest to visit in DC, with good guided tours (daily except Tues), an excellent gallery shop, and cafe (featuring rousing gospel Sunday brunches). Especially strong on American art – from frontier artists like Remington and Bierstadt, to portraiture by Mary Cassatt and Thomas Eakins, and modern works by Calder, Warhol and Rothko – it also includes a sampling of Dutch masters, medieval tapestries and French Impressionists. In the *Salon Doré* (Gilded Room), an eighteenth-century Parisian interior has been re-created to stunning effect, with floor-to-ceiling hand-carved paneling, gold-leaf decor and ceiling murals.

## Phillips Collection

*1600 21st St at Q St NW; closest Metro Dupont Circle. Tues–Sat 10am–5pm, Sun noon–7pm. ☎202/387-2151. Admission $6.50.*

The **Phillips Collection**, one of the country's most extensive assemblies of modern paintings, starts off with a variety of proto-modern artists such as El Greco and Turner, before hurrying via French Impressionism to the real heart of the show – hundreds of works by Picasso, Matisse, Kandinsky, Van Gogh, Rothko, O'Keeffe, Klee and many others. The building adds to the experience: part is displayed in the Phillips family's ornate 1890s mansion, the rest in a 1960s purpose-built gallery space, all of it recently renovated. Popular free concerts take place in the oak-paneled Music Room on Sundays (Sept–May 5pm); and there are free gallery tours on Wednesdays and Saturdays at 2pm (reserve in advance).

## National Museum of Women in the Arts

*1250 New York Ave NW; closest Metro Metro Center. Mon–Sat 10am–5pm, Sun noon–5pm. ☎202/783-5000. Suggested donation $3.*

Housed in a converted Masonic Temple, the **National Museum of Women in the Arts**, which opened in 1987, is the country's only museum dedicated to women artists. It includes hundreds of works by "unknown" painters – a policy inspired by the fact that, just 25 years ago, not one female artist was mentioned in the main American art history textbook. It also features sculptures by Barbara Hepworth and Camille Claudel (Rodin's mistress and assistant) and paintings by Helen Frankenthaler, Georgia O'Keeffe, Mary Cassatt and Elaine de Kooning – and has one of DC's better museum cafes, the *Mezzanine Café*.

## US Holocaust Memorial Museum

*100 Raoul Wallenburg Place SW, off 14th St at Independence Ave. Closest Metro Smithsonian. Daily 10am–5.30pm. ☎202/488-0400. Admission free.*

Nothing in DC is more disturbing than the large and generously laid-out **US Holocaust Memorial Museum**. Commemorating the persecution and murder of six million Jews by the Nazis, it places Hitler in historical perspective while personalizing the suffering of the individual victims.

Besides case after case of newspapers and newsreels documenting Nazi activities from the early 1930s through the Final Solution, chillingly evocative reconstructions and in many cases actual relics of Warsaw Ghetto streets, railroad cattle-cars and concentration camp barracks fill the top floors. The sheer numbers of people killed is evoked throughout, first by a whole room filled with shoes stolen from deportees, later by a crisp glass wall etched with the names of the hundreds of Eastern European Jewish communities wiped off the map.

Tickets for specific entry times are available free of charge from 10am each day – with a limit of four per person – at the 14th Street entrance. You can also reserve in advance through Protix (☎1-800/400-9373; fee charged). If you arrive without a ticket any later than mid-morning, you're unlikely to get into the permanent exhibition, but a certain number of temporary displays are usually open to all visitors.

## The Bureau of Engraving and Printing

*One block south of the Mall at 14th and C sts SW; closest Metro Smithsonian. Mon–Fri 9am–2pm; May–Aug arrive early to pick up a timed ticket; Sept–April no ticket necessary. Closed Christmas to New Year. ☎202/622-2000. Admission free.*

In most ways, a tour of the **Bureau of Engraving and Printing** is like visiting any other printing plant. The difference is that the presses here crank out millions of dollars in currency every day, $120 billion a year. It's a surprisingly low-tech operation: the bills come off in huge sheets, which are sliced up into single bills by ordinary paper cutters, checked for defects and loaded into large wheelbarrows. The Bureau also produces all US postage stamps. A short film explains the basics of intaglio printing, and you can watch it all happen from a glassed-in upstairs gallery.

## Arlington National Cemetery

*Across the Potomac River in Arlington, Virginia; closest Metro Arlington Cemetery. April–Sept daily 8am–7pm; rest of year daily 8am–5pm. ☎703/979-0690. Admission free.*

A poignant contrast to the grand monuments of the capital is provided by the vast sea of identical white headstones on the hillsides of **Arlington National Cemetery**. The country's most honoured final resting place was first used during the Civil War, when the grand mansion at the top of the hill, and all the surrounding land, belonged to Confederate leader **Robert E Lee**. Nearly 200,000 US war dead lie here, and the **Tomb of the Unknown Soldier** remembers thousands more whose bodies were never recovered or identified. An eternal flame marks the grave of **President John F Kennedy**, near his brother Robert and next to his widow, Jacqueline Kennedy Onassis. Among other well-known names is Pierre L'Enfant, whose grave site offers a superb view over the Mall and the District he designed; while the new Women in Military Service Memorial, by the main gate, is just one of several high-profile **memorials** to celebrated personnel, like the doomed crew of the Space Shuttle *Challenger*.

Unless you have strong legs and lots of time, the best way to see the vast cemetery is by Tourmobile (see p.354), which leaves from the visitor center at the entrance. You can also walk here from the Lincoln Memorial across the Arlington Bridge.

## The Pentagon

*Across the Potomac along I-395. Closest Metro Pentagon. Mon–Fri 9.30am–5pm, last tour 3.30pm. ☎703/695-1776. Admission free.*

The headquarters of the US military establishment is one of the largest chunks of architecture in the world: though it's only five stories tall, the total floor area of over 6.5 million square feet is three times that of the Empire State Building. Each of the five sides is over 900ft long, and the combined length of all the internal corridors totals more than seventeen miles. These and other useless factoids are about all you get from visiting the behemoth building, apart from the opportunity to see at firsthand the people responsible for spending billions of tax dollars on those proverbial $50,000 toilet seats. In the one novel departure from the norm, the service-personnel guides who accompany you walk backwards the entire time to ensure that disguised foreign agents don't slip off into the restrooms.

Ninety-minute **guided tours** leave every half-hour from the small waiting area inside the entrance; take photo ID.

### The Newseum

*1101 Wilson Blvd, Arlington, VA. Closest Metro Rosslyn. Wed–Sun 10am–5pm. ☎703/284-3544. Admission free.*

Under the auspices of the Freedom Forum, in whose headquarters it stands, the **Newseum** provides an interactive look at the history, theory and practice of news. A 126-foot-long video wall displays live satellite newsfeeds and daily front pages from around the world, and the News History Gallery features a storyboard timeline with historic front pages (*Jesse James Assassinated! Nixon Resigns!*). If you can beat the crowds you can also try your hand at editing, reporting or TV announcing. Outside, the **Freedom Park** (daily dawn to dusk; free) features various "icons" of freedom – parts of the Berlin Wall, a South African ballot box, and a toppled statue of Lenin among them – and culminates in the world's first **Journalists Memorial**, a 24-foot-high spiraling glass prism etched with the names of nearly a thousand journalists killed while reporting.

# Eating

Just as the faces in government change with every election, so too do **restaurants** come and go quickly in Washington DC than just about anywhere else in the US. Within this constant flux a few longstanding favorites endure; and certain neighborhoods – Connecticut Avenue around **Dupont Circle**, 18th Street and Columbia Road in **Adams-Morgan**, M Street in **Georgetown**, and downtown's **Seventh Street** and **Chinatown** – always seem to hold a good range of dining options. There are handy **food courts** in Union Station, and at the Old Post Office and National Place, the last two both on Pennsylvania Avenue. A few citywide chains, like *Starbucks*, *Vie de France* and the *Chesapeake Bagel Bakery* offer good coffee and quick snacks; otherwise, the cafes in the main **museums** are good for downtown lunch breaks.

### Downtown

**America**, Union Station, 50 Massachusetts Ave NE (☎202/682-9555); Union Station Metro. Huge, reasonably priced menu culled from all over the US; double-decker restaurant inside, concourse seating outside.

**The Breadline**, 1751 Pennsylvania Ave NW (☎202/822-8900); Farragut West Metro. DC's best sandwiches made with DC's best bread. Mon–Fri 7am–6pm.

**Burma**, 740 6th St NW (☎202/638-1280); Gallery Place-Chinatown Metro. A change from the usual Chinatown offerings – finely judged, moderately priced Burmese food. Great noodles.

**Café Asia**, 1134 19th St NW (☎202/659-2696); Farragut North Metro. Situated in an old townhouse and serving excellent value dishes such as sashimi, Thai noodles and lemongrass-grilled chicken, with reasonable drink prices too. Sushi happy hour Mon–Sat 5.30–7.30pm.

**Coco Loco**, 810 7th St NW (☎202/289-2626); Gallery Place-Chinatown Metro. In-crowd restaurant where you can choose from superb Mexican tapas or all-you-can-eat Brazilian grills.

**Grillfish**, 1200 New Hampshire Ave NW (☎202/331-7310); Dupont Circle or Foggy Bottom-GWU Metro. One of the best finds in DC – offering casual dining, perfectly cooked fish and seafood, and excellent desserts.

**Jaleo**, 480 7th St NW (☎202/628-7949); Gallery Place-Chinatown Metro. Fashionable, upscale tapas bar; reserve for dinner or call in early for a glass of wine and nibbles.

**The Mark**, 401 7th St NW (☎202/783-3133); Gallery Place-Chinatown Metro. Chic, and expensive, Modern American dining with seasonally changing menu and select choice of wines by the glass.

**Old Ebbitt Grill**, 675 15th St NW (☎202/347-4801); Metro Center Metro. Very plush, old-style downtown tavern, with an immaculate mahogany bar, gilt mirrors and stylish clientele. Everything from burgers to oysters.

**Patent Pending**, Museum of American Art, 8th and G St (☎202/357-2700); Gallery Place-Chinatown Metro. Located just off the sunny central courtyard in the ornate old Patent Building, with good pastries and sandwiches. Only open 10am–3.30pm.

**Red Sage**, 605 14th St NW (☎202/638-4444); Metro Center Metro. Renowned and expensive Southwestern restaurant (reservations essential), dripping with Santa Fe chic; or eat for less at the funky *Chili Bar*.

**Reeve's Restaurant and Bakery**, 1306 G St NW (☎202/628-6350); Metro Center Metro. Classic daytime diner, with big fried breakfasts, crisp-coated chicken at lunchtime and strawberry pies. Mon–Sat 7am–6pm.

**Sholl's Colonial Cafeteria**, 1990 K St NW (☎202/296-3065); Farragut West Metro. The last of a disappearing breed – remarkably cheap self-service cafe, dishing out home-cooked food, cakes and pies to long lines. Closes at 8pm (Sun 3pm).

**Zuki Moon**, 824 New Hampshire Ave NW (☎202/333-3312); Foggy Bottom-GWU Metro. Spiffy Japanese-style noodle bar, with great value noodle soups, tempura appetizers and green-tea ice cream. Closed Sat & Sun lunch.

## Dupont Circle
*Dupont Circle Metro for all the places listed below.*

**Afterwords Café**, 1517 Connecticut Ave NW (☎202/387-1462). Located in the back of Kramerbooks, serving imaginative meals and a fine Sunday brunch; live music Wed–Sat. Open late every night, and all night Fri & Sat.

**Il Radicchio**, 1509 17th St NW (☎202/986-2627). Designer-rustic pizza-and-pasta emporium, tossing out superb wood-fired pizzas (under $10) or all the spaghetti you can eat, dressed with one of twenty sauces.

**Lauriol Plaza**, 1801 18th St NW (☎202/387-0035). Lines form early in this packed, family-run Mexican-Spanish restaurant – try the excellent fajitas.

**Pizzeria Paradiso**, 2029 P St NW (☎202/223-1245). Arguably DC's best pizzeria – certainly the most fun, though you can expect to wait in line.

**SoHo Tea & Coffee**, 2150 P St NW (☎202/463-6350). Late-night hangout for P street clubbers re-fueling on coffee, cakes and sandwiches.

**Straits of Malaya**, 1836 18th St NW (☎202/483-1483). Neighborhood Southeast Asian restaurant; great noodles and seafood.

## Adams-Morgan
*Nearest Metros for Adams-Morgan are Woodley Park-Zoo or Dupont Circle.*

**Bukom Café**, 2442 18th St NW (☎202/265-4600). Delicious West African dishes such as *obe ila*, a soup with okra and smoked fish, and *nkatikwan*, chicken with peanuts, for around $10. All washed down with African beer and music.

**Cities**, 2424 18th St NW (☎202/328-7194). Trendy restaurant-bar with regularly switching (cities-of-the-world) decor and menu, and a nice outdoor terrace.

**Las Placitas**, 1828 Columbia Rd NW (☎202/745-3751). Good-value Mexican and Salvadorean food with friendly service.

**Meskerem**, 2434 18th St NW (☎202/462-4100). The district's favorite Ethiopian hangout – the *messob* platter gives you a taste of everything.

**Mixtec**, 1792 Columbia Rd NW (☎202/332-1011). Great-tasting, low-priced Mexican food. Superb tacos and tortillas, plus spit-roasted chicken, mussels steamed with chilis, and a soothing *menudo*.

**Peyote Café**, 2319 18th St NW (☎202/462-8830). Lively basement Southwestern bar and grill; the pricier *Roxanne's* upstairs is a bit more adventurous and has a roof terrace.

**Red Sea**, 2463 18th St NW (☎202/483-5000). Inexpensive and plentiful portions of spicy food at the oldest Ethiopian place in town.

**Saigonnais**, 2307 18th St NW (☎202/232-5300). Gourmet-quality Vietnamese food, with such specialties as whole steamed fish and an amazing fish soup. Worth paying a little extra for.

**Tom Tom**, 2333 18th St NW (☎202/588-1300). Street-facing windows, cozy booths and a popular roof terrace bring in the crowds for wood-fired pizza, tapas and mix-and-match pastas.

## Georgetown

*Buses #30, #32, #34, #35 or #36 from Pennsylvania Ave NW; or Foggy Bottom-GWU Metro and 20min walk.*

**Au Pied du Cochon**, 1335 Wisconsin Ave NW (☎202/333-5440). Casual, enjoyable 24hr bistro with conservatory dining, breakfasts and great-value early-bird dinners (around $10).

**Dean & Deluca**, 3276 M St NW (☎202/342-2500). Conservatory-style cafe and attached deli-market in one of Georgetown's handsomest redbrick buildings; open until 8pm (weekends until 10pm).

**Enriqueta's**, 2811 M St NW (☎202/338-7772). An interesting menu showcasing authentic Mexican food – try the generous mussels appetizer – and excellent margaritas. Closed Sat lunch and Sun.

**J Paul's**, 3218 M St NW (☎202/333-3450). The best of Georgetown's saloons – not cheap, but worth it for the famous crab cakes and house-brewed Amber Ale.

**Old Glory**, 3139 M St NW (☎202/337-3406). Rollicking barbecue restaurant with hickory smoke rising in earnest from the kitchen – a good-time place with live R&B bands three nights a week.

**Paolo's**, 1303 Wisconsin Ave NW (☎202/333-7353). Designer Italian dining with a few, hotly contested sidewalk tables. Gourmet pizzas and even better pasta.

**Patisserie Café Didier**, 3206 Grace St NW (☎202/342-9083). Outrageously good (and quite expensive) cakes, pastries, teas and coffees. Just off Wisconsin Ave, across from the C&O Canal.

**Saigon Inn**, 2928 M St NW (☎202/337-5588). Bargain lunch deals bring in the punters – though the Vietnamese food is a bit too Westernized for authenticity's sake.

# Entertainment and nightlife

DC's **bar** and **nightlife** scene is less developed than in more settled cities. Peak times for drinking tend to be the rush hours, and comparatively few people who work in the District during the week venture back into town at the weekend. However, things are slowly improving, and in the well-worn haunts of collegiate **Georgetown**, yuppified **Dupont Circle** and harder-edged **Adams-Morgan** you should be able to pass a pleasant evening or two. For clubs, expect to pay a cover of $5 to $15 (highest at weekends); ticket prices for most gigs run $5 to $20. See the free weekly *CityPaper* for up-to-date **listings** of music, theater and other events in the area – as well as good alternative features and reporting. The *Washington Blade* focuses on **gay** and **lesbian** life, which is at its most outgoing in Dupont Circle.

**The Black Cat**, 1831 14th St NW (☎202/667-7960); U St-Cardozo Metro. Likeable showcase for new bands and veteran alternative acts; the separate bar has no cover charge.

**The Brickskeller**, 1523 22nd St NW (☎202/293-1885); Dupont Circle Metro. Brick-lined basement saloon serving "the world's largest selection of beer" – more than 800 different types.

**Capitol City Brewing Company**, 1100 New York Ave NW (☎202/628-2222); Metro Center Metro. DC's oldest microbrewery serving a changing menu of beers to an excitable crowd; there's a second branch at 2 Massachusetts Ave NE, near Union Station.

**The Circle**, 1629 Connecticut Ave NW (☎202/462-5575); Dupont Circle Metro. Welcoming gay bar/club where a wealthy crowd jostles for posing space.

**The Dubliner**, 520 N Capitol St NW, at the *Phoenix Park* (☎202/737-3773); Union Station Metro. Bare-bones Irish bar, with Guinness on draft, live music and no end of boisterous conversation.

**Hawk and Dove**, 329 Pennsylvania Ave SE (☎202/543-3300); Capitol South Metro. Famous old pub with battered bar and a young, loud crowd.

**Heaven & Hell**, 2327 18th St NW (☎202/234-3455). Split-level Adams-Morgan hangout with grungy *Hell* downstairs and dancing upstairs in *Heaven* to techno, dance and indie.

**Irish Times**, 14 F St NW (☎202/543-5433); Union Station Metro. Crowded but comfortable pub with a good range of beers and above-average bar food.

**Lulu's**, 1217 22nd St NW (☎202/861-5858); Foggy Bottom-GWU Metro. Large, loud and extremely busy bar/club/cattle market with Cajun restaurant.

**Mr P's**, 2147 P St NW (☎202/293-1064); Dupont Circle Metro. Longest-serving gay bar in the neighborhood with a mellow clientele.

**Mr Smith's**, 3104 M St NW (☎202/333-3104). Brick-walled saloon bar on the Georgetown drag, with decent burgers and beer, and live bands Fri & Sat.

**9:30 Club**, 815 V St NW (☎202/393-0930); U St-Cardozo Metro. Excellent indie, rock and pop venue with a good bar.

**Polly Esther's**, 605 12th St NW (☎202/737-1970); Metro Center Metro. Enthusiastic retro dance club, with extended happy hour on Fri.

**Republic Gardens**, 1355 U St NW (☎202/232-2710); U St-Cardozo Metro. Hip-hop, soul and jazz in one of U St's hottest clubs.

**The Tombs**, 1226 36th St NW (☎202/337-6668). Basement Georgetown haunt for burgers and beers; Clinton, it's said, used to drink here as a student.

**Tracks**, 1111 1st St SE (☎202/488-3320); Navy Yard Metro. Hugely popular gay and mixed dance club, it even has its own beach and volleyball area.

## Culture and sports

With five different theater spaces, the **Kennedy Center**, 2700 F St NW (☎202/467-4600; Foggy Bottom Metro), next to the Watergate complex, hosts most of the capital's high-brow cultural events (including Washington Opera and Washington Ballet company performances), as well as nightly **film** screenings organized by the American Film Institute (☎202/785-4600). The **Arena Stage**, Sixth Street and Maine Avenue SW (☎202/488-3300; Waterfront Metro), puts on contemporary **theater** and performance pieces, while the historic Ford's Theatre, 511 Tenth St NW (☎202/347-4833; Metro Center Metro), has a varied program of plays, too. The celebrated **Shakespeare Theater**, 450 Seventh St NW (☎202/547-1122; Archives-Navy Memorial Metro) stages four productions a year, plus a free summer performance in Rock Creek Park; while **Woolly Mammoth**, 1401 Church St NW (☎202/393-3939; Dupont Circle Metro), and **Source Theater Company**, 1815 14th St NW (☎202/462-1073; U St-Cardozo Metro), are also worth seeking out. Out of the city, **Wolf Trap Farm Park** (1551 Trap Rd, Vienna, VA) is the country's first national park for the performing arts, with a program of concerts, opera, ballet and dance at the outdoor **Filene Center** (☎703/255-1860) or the indoor **Barns** (☎703/938-2404) – there's a Metro-shuttle bus service for most performances. For half-price, same-day theater **tickets**, call ☎202/TICKETS or visit the TicketPlace booth on the ground floor of the Old Post Office Pavilion on Pennsylvania Avenue NW; otherwise TicketMaster (☎202/432-7328 or 1-800/551-7328) has full-price tickets for all arts, music and sports events.

Tickets to watch the Washington Redskins **football** team at the Jack Kent Cooke Stadium, just inside the Capital Beltway near US-50 in Raljon, MD (☎202/546-2222) are expensive, and games usually sell out. You'll have better luck catching the DC United **soccer** team at RFK Stadium, 2400 E Capitol St SE (☎202/478-6600; Stadium-Armory Metro); while the huge downtown **MCI Center** (☎202/628-3200; next to Gallery Place-Chinatown Metro) hosts home games of the Washington Wizards (**basketball**) and Washington Capitals (**hockey**).

# VIRGINIA

Traveling through **VIRGINIA**, the oldest, largest and wealthiest of the American colonies and the single most powerful influence on the early United States, is a nonstop history lesson. Pretty and rural it may be, but the past predominates: wherever you go you're pointed towards this or that painstakingly restored two-hundred-year-old building, where something or other happened a long time ago. The more you know about it all, the more rewarding Virginia is to visit, but the historical plaques get a bit ridiculous after a while, marking every spot where George Washington slept, Thomas Jefferson thought or Robert E Lee tied his horse to a tree. You can see why Disney chose northern Virginia as the site of its proposed theme park of American history a few years back; and you'll also soon realize that Virginia takes itself a bit too seriously to allow such a project to get off the ground.

Virginia's recorded history began at **Jamestown**, just off the Chesapeake Bay, with the establishment in 1607 of the first successful British colony in North America. Though the first colonists hoped to find gold, it was **tobacco** that made their fortunes. The native strain – used for hundreds of years by Virginia's indigenous population, of whom almost no trace remains – was too strongly flavored for European tastes. When a smoother, more palatable variety was introduced in 1615 by John Rolfe – the same man whose shipwreck on Bermuda inspired Shakespeare's *The Tempest* – tobacco quickly became the colony's major cash crop. Before long, vast plantations, owned by a very few aristocratic families, sprang up along the many broad rivers that flow into the Chesapeake Bay. To grow and harvest tobacco required both an immense amount of land – so the Native Americans had to go – and intensive labor – so the plantation owners brought in **slaves** from Africa. By the end of the seventeenth century, enslaved African-Americans accounted for nearly half of the colony's 75,000 people; a hundred years later, they numbered over 300,000.

Virginians had an enormous impact on the foundation of the nascent United States: George Mason, Thomas Jefferson and James Madison wrote the Declaration of Independence and the Constitution, and four of the first five US presidents were from Virginia. However, by the mid-1800s the state was in decline, its once fertile fields depleted by overuse and its agrarian economy increasingly eclipsed by the urban and industrialized North.

As the confrontation between North and South over slavery and related economic and political issues grew more divisive, Virginia was caught in the middle. Though this slaveholding state initially voted against secession from the Union, it joined the Confederacy when the **Civil War** broke out, providing its military leader, Robert E Lee, and its capital, Richmond. Four long years later, Virginia was ravaged, its towns and cities wrecked, its farmlands ruined and most of its youth dead. It has never regained its early prosperity, nor its prominence in national affairs.

**Richmond** itself was largely destroyed in the war; today it's a small city, with some good museums, and is the best starting point for seeing Virginia. The bulk of the **colonial** sites are concentrated just to the east, in what's known as the **Historic Triangle**. Here the remains of **Jamestown**, the original colony, **Williamsburg**, the restored colonial capital, and **Yorktown**, site of the final battle of the Revolutionary War, lie within half an hour's drive of each other.

Another historic center, Thomas Jefferson's **Charlottesville**, sits at the foot of the gorgeous **Blue Ridge Mountains**, an hour west of Richmond. An attractive small college town in its own right, it's also within easy reach of the natural splendors of **Shenandoah National Park** and the small towns of the western valleys. **Northern Virginia**, often visited as a day out from Washington DC, holds a number of restored homes and several preserved Civil War **battlefields**.

## Getting around Virginia

Virginia is not difficult to explore. Two north–south Amtrak routes from Washington DC cross the state, one through Charlottesville towards Atlanta and the other through Fredericksburg and Richmond on the way to Florida; in addition, daily connections run east from Richmond to the Historic Triangle, and west from Charlottesville towards Chicago. Greyhound reaches dozens of smaller towns. **Drivers** heading south can take the stunning Blue Ridge Parkway along the Appalachians. If you've got the time, there's ample opportunity for **cycling**, whether on quiet country roads or up in the mountains, and **hiking** or **walking** tours are also worth thinking about.

# Northern Virginia

**Northern Virginia**, almost all of which lies within commuting distance of Washington DC, holds some extremely exclusive suburbs – McLean and the rest of Fairfax County, for example, house an inordinate number of US senators. The anglophile heartland of Virginia's landed gentry – often called "Hunt Country" for their love of horses and fancy-dress blood sports – it holds well-preserved eighteenth- and nineteenth-century stately homes, cottages, churches, barns and taverns tucked away along the quiet back roads. It's all very popular with tourists, nowhere more so than **Mount Vernon**, the longtime home of George Washington. During the Civil War, **Fredericksburg** to the south witnessed the battles of Chancellorsville, Spotsylvania and the Wilderness, while **Manassas** to the west was the site of the bloody battles of Bull Run.

## Mount Vernon – George Washington's home

Set on a shallow bluff overlooking the broad Potomac River, **Mount Vernon** (daily: March & Sept–Oct 9am–5pm; April–Aug 8am–5pm; Nov–Feb 9am–4pm; $8) is among the most attractive historic houses in the US. The country estate of **George Washington**, with its eight thousand acres of landscaped and planted grounds, has been maintained virtually intact since his death in 1799. At just fifteen miles from downtown DC, it's close enough to be reached as a day-trip on the city's Tourmobiles ($22; see p.354), or by bus from Huntington Metro station. Besides illuminating the life and times of the leader of the revolutionary armies, and the first US president, Mount Vernon also provides an eye-opening look into the lifestyle of the colonial gentlemen who founded the USA.

A small museum gives an overview of Mount Vernon's history; in the house itself, the furnishings and decoration reflect Washington's preference for plain living, but few items – a reading chair with built-in fan, and a key to the destroyed Bastille, presented by Thomas Paine on behalf of Lafayette – give much of a sense of his character. The four-poster bed upon which he died stands in an upstairs bedroom; he and his wife Martha are buried in a simple tomb on the south side of the house.

## Gunston Hall – George Mason's home

The plain brick 1755 **Gunston Hall**, home of Washington's contemporary **George Mason**, stands just around a bend in the river, ten minutes' drive south along Hwy-1 at the east end of Hwy-242 (daily 9.30am–5pm; $5). It was Mason's revolutionary idea "that all men are by nature equally free and independent and have certain inherent rights" which Jefferson incorporated into the Declaration of Independence. Mason was later one of the main framers of the US Constitution, which he then refused to support because it neither included a Bill of Rights nor abolished slavery. Unlike Washington and Jefferson, Mason eschewed public power, preferring to stay here with his family – which is understandable once you've seen the place, one of the most impressive pieces of architecture in Virginia. Most of it was designed and constructed by William Buckland; the masterful interiors, particularly in the stately drawing room, feature some beautiful carved ornamentation. The house fronts onto a large formal garden, and the extensive grounds are in turn surrounded by two riverfront state parks and wildlife refuges.

## Manassas Battlefield National Park

MANASSAS BATTLEFIELD NATIONAL PARK spreads on grassy hills at the western fringes of the Washington DC suburban belt, just off I-66. Though the modern world is just outside its boundaries – after a lengthy court battle, developers were prevented in 1991 from building a tract of battle-view homes on its fringes – you don't have to know the details of what happened here to feel the power of these brooding hillsides.

Soon after the first shots were fired at Fort Sumter, the first major land battle of the Civil War, known as the **Battle of Bull Run**, was fought here on the morning of July 21, 1861. Expecting an easy victory, some 25,000 Union troops attacked a Confederate detachment that controlled a vital railroad link to the Shenandoah Valley. The rebels proved powerful opponents, their strength in battle earning their commander, General Thomas Jackson, the famous nickname "Stonewall." Displays in the small **visitor center** at the entrance (daily 8.30am–5pm; Jun–Aug Sat & Sun until 6pm; park admission $2) describe how the battle took shape, and detail the other battles fought here over the course of the war.

# Fredericksburg

Only a mile off the I-95 freeway, and easy to reach on Amtrak or Greyhound, **FRED-ERICKSBURG** is one of Virginia's prettiest historic towns, its elegant downtown streets backed by residential avenues lined with white picket fences. In colonial days, this was an important inland port, loading tobacco and other plantation products onto boats that sailed down the Rappahanock River. Dozens of eighteenth- and nineteenth-century buildings along the waterfront now hold antique stores and secondhand bookshops.

Two blocks away, in the 1816 town hall, the **Fredericksburg Area Museum**, 907 Princess Anne St (March–Nov Mon–Sat 9am–5pm, Sun 1–5pm; Dec–Feb Mon–Sat 10am–4pm, Sun 1–4pm; $4), has a broad range of displays tracing local history from Native American settlements to the present day. The **Rising Sun Tavern**, by the river at 1304 Caroline St, was built as a home in the mid-1700s by George Washington's brother Charles. As an inn, it became a key meeting place for patriots and a hotbed of sedition. It is now a small "living history" **museum** (March–Nov daily 9am–5pm; Dec–Feb daily 10am–4pm; $4), where costumed "wenches" guide visitors around a collection of pub games and ancient pewterware. They don't, however, serve food or drink anymore, except for the glass of spiced herbal punch you get on the tour.

Fredericksburg's important strategic location made it vital during the **Civil War**, and the land around the town was heavily fought over. Over 100,000 men lost their lives in the major battles of Fredericksburg, Chancellorsville, Spotsylvania and countless other bloody skirmishes. The **Fredericksburg and Spotsylvania National Battlefield Park**, south of town at 1013 Lafayette Blvd (visitor center summer daily 8.30am–6.30pm; rest of year daily 9am–5pm; $3 for a weekly pass), has informative exhibits and rents three-hour audio tours ($3 for tape and player) of the various battlefield sites.

## Practicalities

Fredericksburg's **visitor center** at 706 Caroline St (summer daily 9am–7pm; rest of year daily 9am–5pm; ☎540/373-1776 or 1-800/678-4748) can provide maps of walking tours and details of discounted tickets to the area's attractions. The town gets a lot of weekend trade, and so has several good places to **eat** and **drink**. The closest contemporary equivalent to the bawdy *Rising Sun* is probably *Sammy T's*, 801 Caroline St (☎540/371-2008), a popular bar and diner with substantial sandwiches and a huge range of bottled beers. For a cappuccino, head diagonally across from the visitor center to *Java Connection* at 615 Caroline St. The cozy pub at the eighteenth-century *Kenmore Inn*, 1200 Princess Anne St (restaurant closed Sun, and Mon lunchtime; ☎540/371-7622; ⑤), serves old-fashioned steaks and fish accompanied by occasional live jazz, and has B&B rooms furnished with antiques. Fredericksburg abounds in old-fashioned **B&Bs** like the *Richard Johnston Inn*, 711 Caroline St (☎540/899-7606; ④); good **motels** include the *Fredericksburg Colonial Inn*, 1707 Princess Anne St (☎540/371-5666; ③).

# Richmond and the tidewater

At the very heart of Virginia, **Richmond** and the **Chesapeake Bay tidewater** are, in many ways, where the US was born. Not only does this fairly compact area hold some of the most important surviving colonial-era sites, it is also where the strength of the nation was tested by the Civil War. The greatest interest is to be found in the compact **Historic Triangle**, east of Richmond, and along the **Atlantic coast** beyond.

## Richmond and around

Founded in 1737 at the furthest navigable point on the James River, **RICHMOND** remained a small outpost until just before the end of the colonial era, when independence-minded Virginians, realizing that their capital at Williamsburg was open to British attack, shifted it fifty miles further inland. The move to Richmond failed to offer much protection – the city was raided many times and twice put to the torch, once by troops under the command of Benedict Arnold.

Richmond subsequently flourished, its population reaching 100,000 by the time of the Civil War. When war broke out it was named the **capital of the Confederacy**, despite the fact that Virginia had voted two-to-one against secession from the Union just a month before. The massive **Tredegar Iron Works** became the main engine of the Confederate war machine. For four years the city was the focus of Southern defences and Union attacks, but despite an almost constant state of siege – General McClellan came within six miles as early as 1862, and General Grant steamrollered remorselessly towards it through the last months of the war – it held on until the very end. It was less than a week after the fall of Richmond, on April 3, 1865, that General Lee surrendered to General Grant at Appomattox, a hundred miles west.

After the war, Richmond was devastated. Much of its downtown was burned, allegedly by fleeing Confederates who wanted to keep its stores of weapons, and its warehouses full of tobacco, out of the victors' hands. Rebuilding, however, was quick, and the city's economy has remained among the strongest in the South. Today's Richmond is a remarkably elegant city, with an extensive inventory of architecturally significant older buildings alongside its modern office towers. **Tobacco** is still a major industry – machine-rolled cigarettes were invented here in the 1870s, and Marlboro-makers **Phillip Morris** runs a huge manufacturing plant just south of downtown – and Richmond is also a leading **banking** center. It is not, however, a place you'd choose to stroll around at night, being firmly established as America's number-one murder metropolis.

### Arrival, information and getting around

Two hours' drive from Washington DC via I-95, which cuts through the east side of downtown, Richmond is also served by Amtrak, pulling into 7519 Staples Mill Rd, five miles northwest of downtown, and Greyhound, which stops just off I-64 at 2910 N Blvd, also a good way from the center. The large **airport** ten miles east of downtown is served by major carriers and has a small visitor center (Mon–Fri 9am–5pm; ☎804/236-2360) in the arrivals terminal.

There's a larger **visitor center** near Greyhound at 1710 Robin Hood Rd, off I-95, which can provide accommodation discounts for some of the area's hotels (June–Aug daily 9am–7pm; Sept–May daily 9am–5pm; ☎804/358-5511); and another in the bell tower on the state capitol grounds (Mon–Fri 10am–4pm; ☎804/786-4484), while the **CVB** head office is in the Sixth Street Marketplace at 550 E Marshall St (☎804/782-2777 or 1-800/370-9004).

Most of Richmond is compact enough to walk around in the daytime, but to get to outlying places (like the stations or the Fine Art Museum) you might want to take a GRTC **bus** (most fares $1.25; ☎804/358-GRTC). More convenient for museum-hopping is the weekend-only Cultural Connection bus ($1; service runs June–Nov Sat 10am–5.30pm, Sun noon–5.30pm; ☎1-888/RICHMOND), whose three separate routes link all major sites. **Bikes** are available for rent at Two Wheel Travel, quite a distance from downtown at 2934 W Cary St (☎804/359-2453), while **city tours** run by the Historic Richmond Foundation, 707a E Franklin St (☎804/780-0107), include some on foot (April–Oct Mon–Sat 10am–noon; $13–16; reserve a day in advance).

## Accommodation

Finding well-priced **accommodation** in Richmond isn't difficult, with no shortage of anonymous downtown hotels catering to the business and government trade. Contact the city's **central reservation service** on ☎1-800/RICHMOND, or get a feel for the old city by staying the night in a **B&B** in one of the historic quarters.

**The Berkeley**, 1200 E Cary St (☎804/780-1300). Elegant small hotel on historic Shockoe Slip. ⑦.

**Jefferson**, Franklin and Adams sts (☎804/788-8000 or 1-800/424-8014). Beautifully maintained, spacious grand hotel, with fabulous marble-columned lobby. ⑦.

**Linden Row Inn**, 100 E Franklin St (☎804/783-7000 or 1-800/348-7424). A magnificent row of red-brick Georgian terrace houses, now a comfortable modern hotel with antique furnishings. ⑤.

**Massad House**, 11 N 4th St (☎804/648-2893). Cheerful old hotel in Court End District, with pleasant staff and clean rooms. Downtown's best value by a long chalk. ③.

**Midtown Inn and Conference Center**, 3200 W Broad St (☎804/359-4061 or 1-800/866-0553). Good location, near the Fan District and Fine Arts Museum. The usual hotel chain amenities. ③.

**William Catlin House**, 2304 E Broad St (☎804/780-3746). Small, comfortable and upmarket B&B on Church Hill, across from St John's Church. ④.

## Downtown Richmond

Richmond's **downtown** centers on a few blocks rising up from the James River to either side of Broad Street. Modern office towers front onto a riverside park, while up the shallow hill in the **Court End** district, dozens of well-preserved antebellum homes provide a suitable backdrop for some important museums and historic sites. A **thirty-day pass**, giving access to all of downtown's attractions, is available from any visitor center and the ticket desks of each attraction for $15 – well worth considering if you're in town for a few days.

The **Virginia State Capitol** (daily 9am–5pm; Jan–March closed Sun, last tour 4.15pm; free), which has been in use since 1788 as the seat of the state (and, during the Civil War, Confederate) government, is the focal point, visible from all over Richmond and offering a sweeping view from its columned portico. Thomas Jefferson had a hand in the design, based on his favorite building, the Roman Maison Carré in Nímes, France. The domed central rotunda, not visible from outside, holds the only marble statue of George Washington modeled from life, and busts of Jefferson and the seven other Virginia-born US presidents line the walls. Likenesses of famous Virginians, including a solemn bronze Robert E Lee, fill the adjacent **Old House Chamber**, where Aaron Burr was tried and acquitted of treason in 1807.

Just two blocks north of the capitol, the **Museum of the Confederacy**, 1201 E Clay St (Mon–Sat 10am–5pm, Sun noon–5pm; $5), gives an even-handed history of the Civil War. Personal effects of Confederate leaders include J E B Stuart's plumed hat, the tools used to amputate Stonewall Jackson's arms at Chancellorsville (he died), and Robert E Lee's revolver and the pen he used to sign the surrender. An exhibition entitled "From Sunup to Sunup" highlights the reality of slavery. Next door, the so-called **White House of the Confederacy** (same hours; $5.50), a Neoclassical mansion where Jefferson Davis lived as Confederate president, has recently been restored to its 1860s appearance. Tours of the house itself are reverential and rather dull, though it's strange to reflect that Abraham Lincoln came for a look just days before his death; far more interesting is the exhibition on Davis's staff, telling how some of his slaves were supposedly "bribed" into escaping north, and a small collection of domestic memorabilia with captions hurriedly written by Davis's wife. An $8 **combination ticket** allows access to both the house and museum.

Two blocks to the west, the 1812 **Wickham House** now forms part of the excellent **Valentine Museum** at 1015 E Clay St (Mon–Sat 10am–5pm, Sun noon–5pm; $5). This Neoclassical monolith houses a small local history museum, focusing on the experience of working-class and black Americans, as well as an extensive array of furniture and pre-Civil War clothing – whalebone corsets and other *Gone with the Wind*-era apparel.

West of the Convention Center on Sixth Street is a neighborhood of early nineteenth-century houses, many fronted by ornate wrought-iron balconies similar to those in New Orleans' French Quarter. Known as **Jackson Ward**, and filling a dozen blocks around First and Clay streets, this has been the center of Richmond's African-American community since well before the Civil War, when Richmond had the largest free black population in the US. As well as covering local history, the **Maggie L Walker House**, 110 E Leigh St (Wed–Sun 9am–5pm; free), traces the working life of the physically disabled black Richmond woman who, during the 1920s, founded and ran the first non-white-male-owned bank in the US, now the Consolidated Bank and Trust. Nearby, the **Black History Museum** at 00 Clay St (Tues–Sat 10am–5pm, Sun 1–5pm; $4) houses displays on Richmond's role as a center of Southern black society, and includes a well-presented gallery of the civil rights movement.

## Shockoe Bottom, the Poe Museum and Church Hill

A short walk southeast from the Court End District, a very different neighborhood allows a glimpse at another side of the Richmond story. Split down the middle by the raised I-95 freeway, the increasingly gentrified (and regularly flooded) riverfront warehouse district of **Shockoe Bottom** still holds a few palpable reminders of Richmond's industrial past among the restaurants and nightclubs on its cobblestone streets. From **Shockoe Slip**, a prettified old wharf area rebuilt in the 1890s after being destroyed in the Civil War, Cary Street runs east along the waterfront, lined by a wall of brick warehouses known as **Tobacco Row**.

Nearby, Richmond's oldest building, an appropriately gloomy 250-year-old stone house at 1914 E Main St, serves as the **Edgar Allan Poe Museum** (Tues–Sat 10am–4pm, Mon & Sun noon–4pm; $6). Poe spent much of his life in Richmond and considered it his hometown; he wrote the *Narrative of Arthur Gordon Pym* while working on the Richmond-based magazine *Southern Literary Messenger*. The museum displays Poe memorabilia plus a model of Richmond as it was in his day.

**Church Hill**, a few blocks northeast, is one of Richmond's oldest surviving residential districts, its decorative eighteenth-century houses, adorned with cast-iron porches and rambling magnolia-filled front gardens, looking out over the James River.

Capping the hill at the heart of the neighborhood, **St John's Church** at 2401 E Broad St (Mon–Sat 10am–4pm, Sun 1–4pm, last tour 3.30pm; $3), which dates back to 1741, is best known as the place where, during a 1775 debate on whether the Virginia colony should raise a militia against the British, **Patrick Henry** made the impassioned plea: "Is life so dear, or peace so sweet, to be purchased at the price of chains of slavery? I know not what course others may take, but as for me, give me liberty or give me death." His speech is reenacted by an actor every Sunday between Memorial and Labor days at 2pm, after the religious services.

## Monument Avenue and the Virginia Museum of Fine Arts

The newest and most opulent of Richmond's neighborhoods, called the **Fan District** because its tree-lined avenues fan out at oblique angles, spreads west from the downtown area, beyond Belvidere Street (US-1). Its centerpiece is **Monument Avenue**, lined with garish c.1900 mansions. Richmond's most imposing boulevard was laid out by unabashed city planners from 1889 onwards to commemorate key figures of the Confederacy. Four successive grand intersections hold statues of J E B Stuart, Robert E Lee, Stonewall Jackson and Jefferson Davis. In recent times, many of the city's black population expressed dissatisfaction with this choice of heroes, and in 1996 a statue of the late tennis champion **Arthur Ashe** was duly erected. A native of Richmond, Ashe felt himself obliged to leave the city in 1961 because its tennis courts were segregated. The statue shows Ashe's dedication to education – he's encircled with children and holds books and tennis racket aloft.

South of Monument Avenue, at 2800 Grove Ave, stands the **Virginia Museum of Fine Arts** (Tues–Sun 11am–5pm, Thurs until 8pm; $4 donation). Paul Mellon donated an extensive collection of Impressionist and Post-Impressionist paintings, displayed alongside American paintings ranging from George Catlin's romantic images of Plains Indians to the Pop Art creations of Roy Lichtenstein and Claes Oldenburg in the vast new West Wing. Other galleries contain such diverse items as Frank Lloyd Wright furniture, Lalique jewelry, and Hindu and Buddhist sculpture from the Himalayas, but perhaps the most popular part of the museum is a world-class array of over three hundred Carl Fabergé works, including four of his trademark jewel-encrusted Easter eggs crafted in the 1890s for the Russian tsars.

## Eating

Richmond has a good choice of **eating** options at either end of the price spectrum, with barbecue a specialty.

**Awful Arthur's Oyster Bar**, 101 N 18th St (☎804/643-1700). Shockoe Bottom hangout, with raw oysters and clams, plus shrimp and crabs, and steak for the squeamish. All budgets catered for.

**Millie's Diner**, 2603 E Main St (☎804/643-5512). Refurbished diner, complete with mini-jukeboxes on each table, somewhat adrift of downtown beyond Shockoe Bottom. A changing menu of fairly expensive but very tasty fine cuisine.

**Peking Pavilion**, 1302 E Cary St (☎804/649-8888). Very good, inexpensive (especially at lunchtime) Chinese place in Shockoe Slip. Szechuan and Mandarin specialties. Also a branch at 5710 Grove Ave in the West End.

**Sea Breeze Cafe**, 3 S 15th St (☎804/649-8516). Great Caribbean food, some dishes very hot and spicy.

**Strawberry Street Cafe**, 421 N Strawberry St (☎804/353-6860). Casual and comfortable Fan District neighborhood cafe – mainly quiches, pastas and salads.

**Third Street Diner**, 218 E Main St (☎804/788-4750). Relaxed all-American 24hr diner; splendid breakfasts and Greek dishes. Stylish student crowd, especially at night when it's also a bar.

**The Tobacco Company**, 1201 E Cary St (☎804/782-9431). Inventive New American food in stunningly restored three-story tobacco warehouse, with antique elevator. Cocktail bar with nightly live entertainment in the leafy first-floor atrium.

## Drinking and nightlife

Richmond's main **drinking and nightlife** spots are concentrated around the riverside Shockoe Slip and Shockoe Bottom areas, just east of downtown, where you'll find the likes of the *Richbrau Brewery*, 1214 E Cary St (☎804/644-3018), a watering hole that's especially lively at weekends; the *Cobblestone Brewery & Pub*, 110 N 18th St, offering over thirty microbrewed beers plus a small menu of steaks and Cajun specialties; and the *Have a Nice Day Café*, 18th and Main (☎804/771-1700), a cheesy but fun retro-1970s cafe and nightclub. In the Fan District, try *Buddy's Place,* 325 N Robinson St (☎804/355-3701), or the *Border Chophouse and Bar,* 1501 W Main St (☎804/355-2907).

Between October and June, Theater Virginia (☎804/367-0831), in the Museum of Fine Arts, is Richmond's best bet for live **theater**. For news on music and events check the listings in the free *Style Weekly* newspaper.

# The Historic Triangle: Jamestown, Williamsburg and Yorktown

The **Historic Triangle**, on the thin peninsula that stretches east of Richmond between the James and York rivers, holds by far the richest concentration of colonial-era sites in the US. **Jamestown**, founded in 1607, was Virginia's first settlement; **Williamsburg** is an animated if theatrical resurrection of the colonial capital; and it was at **Yorktown** that American independence from the English crown was finally secured. All three sites are within an hour by car, bus or train from the capital.

Although I-64 is the quickest way to cover the fifty miles from Richmond to Williamsburg, a far more pleasing drive along US-5 rolls through **plantation** country, where many eighteenth-century mansions, with invariably lovely grounds, are open to the public. Once you're in the Historic Triangle area the best way to get around is along the lushly landscaped **Colonial Parkway**, which winds west to Jamestown and east to Yorktown, twenty miles end-to-end. Most of the area's numerous tourist facilities – this is the most visited destination in the state – are to be found around Williamsburg. We've listed a few suggestions under "Historic Triangle practicalities" on p.387.

## Jamestown National Historic Site

The first successful English colony in the New World, **JAMESTOWN** was established as a commercial venture, sponsored by King James I but paid for and owned by the **Virginia Company**. On April 26, 1607, the colonists, thirty adventure-minded aristocrats and 75 indentured servants, arrived at the mouth of the Chesapeake Bay after

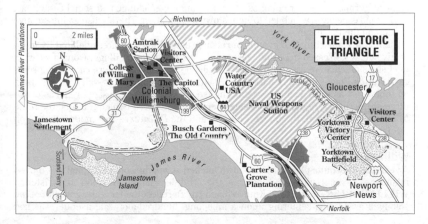

four months at sea, and within two weeks had established a fortified settlement on a low-lying island forty miles up the James River.

Despite the fact that Jamestown was intended to be self-supporting, not one of the party had any experience of farming or fishing – their leader, **John Smith**, wrote in 1608 that "though there be Fish in the Sea, and Foules in the ayre, and Beasts in the woods, their bounds are so large, they are so wilde, and we so weake and ignorant, we cannot much trouble them." The Virginia Company continued to send new recruits, but the loss of life was extreme: of more than seven thousand settlers who came to Jamestown in its first decade, six thousand perished within a year of arriving.

What saved Jamestown, besides the provisions brought by new settlers, was **tobacco**: by 1619 the colony was shipping some twenty tons a year back to England. As it expanded, the colony began to encroach upon the **Powhatan**, an Algonquin-speaking people who controlled most of tidewater Virginia and who until then had been fairly peaceable. In 1622 and again in 1644 provocations caused the Powhatan to attack the Jamestown colonists, killing some five hundred settlers each time. The most serious damage to Jamestown, however, was caused by the colonists themselves, when they burned the fort to the ground in 1675 in protest at the lack of protection offered them by the crown. Rather than rebuild the tiny island outpost, by the end of the 1600s they had shifted the capital and most of the commercial activity inland to Williamsburg, and Jamestown slowly disappeared.

The one bit of seventeenth-century Jamestown to survive, protected within the **Jamestown National Historic Site**, is the 50ft tower of the first brick church, built in 1639 – the rest was destroyed by fire in 1698. Around it are sundry unearthed foundations, as well as numerous memorial shrines and monuments.

From the **visitor center** (June–Sept daily 8.30am–5.30pm; Oct–May daily 9am–5pm; $5 per car, or $7 if combined with the Yorktown battlefield, see p.387; ☎757/229-1733), where artists' drawings and audiovisual exhibits endeavor to conjure up the past, a footpath leads down to the river, where the remains of the original fortress, now underwater, are vaguely visible.

## Jamestown Settlement

Next to the authentic site of Jamestown, the state of Virginia has created the **Jamestown Settlement** (daily 9am–5pm; $10.25, or $14 with Yorktown Victory Center, see p.387), a complex of museums and full-size replicas that elucidates the details of what went on here. A short film dramatizes Jamestown's early days, and displays explore Europe's need for colonies, documenting the economic and social conditions, in England especially, which led to Jamestown's foundation. There's also an informative section on the Powhatan.

Behind the museum, two groups of reconstructed buildings are inhabited by interpretive guides, dressed in period costume. In the **Powhatan Village**, women wearing buckskins practice weaving and pottery, while in the larger and more convincing replica of **James Fort**, some fifteen thatched, wattle-and-daub buildings – all built with period tools – act as a blacksmith's, a storehouse and a church. Full-sized replicas of the three **ships** that carried the first settlers here – the *Godspeed* (which retraced the route from England in 1985), the *Susan Constant* and the *Discovery* – are moored below on the James River.

## Williamsburg

A year after mosquito-plagued Jamestown burned down, the colonial capital was moved inland to a small village known as the Middle Plantation, soon rechristened **WILLIAMSBURG** in honor of King William III. To reflect the increasing wealth of the colony, a grand city, centering upon a mile-long, hundred-foot-wide avenue, was laid out. Suitable buildings were constructed, beginning with the **capitol** in 1704 and culminating in the opulent **Governor's Palace** in 1720. By the mid-1700s tobacco-rich Virginia was the most prosperous of the American colonies, and Williamsburg was its largest city, though with some two thousand residents not on the scale of Philadelphia, New York or Boston. Williamsburg remained the seat of colonial government, and emerged as one of the leading centers of **revolutionary thought**: at the College of William and Mary, George Wythe, Thomas Jefferson, James Monroe and George Mason argued the finer points of law and democracy, while in the capitol, and in the many raucous taverns that surrounded it, firebrand politicians like Patrick Henry held forth on the iniquities of colonialism and organized the first resistance to British rule. When the Revolutionary War broke out, the government moved to the more secure Richmond, and Williamsburg slowly faded from view, all but unrecognized for its place in American history.

Fortunately, many of the colonial structures survived intact until the 1920s, when oil baron **John D Rockefeller** answered the pleas of a local priest, W A R Goodwin, to support Williamsburg's restoration. (Goodwin, who considered that cars were going to ruin American towns, and that the men who were making millions out of the car industry might feel guilty about this, had initially approached Henry Ford, who sent him packing.) Over the ensuing years, Rockefeller, with Goodwin acting as his agent, spent some $90 million buying and restoring the surviving fragments to their original condition, in many cases building replicas from scratch. In 1934 **Colonial Williamsburg** opened as the first theme park in the US to use American history for amusement, with costumed guides as interpreters. While you have to buy a (very expensive) ticket to look inside most of the buildings (see box overleaf), the entire historic area, which includes many fine gardens, is open all the time, and you can wander freely down the cobbled streets and across the lush green commons. Cars are banned, and Williamsburg as a whole is a remarkably pleasant – if very crowded – place.

From the **Wren Building** on the William and Mary campus, built in 1716 at the west end of Williamsburg and now separated from the historic area by a mock-colonial shopping center, **Duke of Gloucester Street** runs east through the historic area to the rebuilt capitol. The first of its eighteenth-century buildings, a hundred yards along, is the Episcopalian **Bruton Parish Church** where Goodwin preached (Mon–Sat 9am–5pm, Sun noon–5pm; donation). It was built in 1715, when all white Virginians were required by law to attend services at least once a month. Behind it, the broad **Palace Green** spreads north to the rebuilt Governor's Palace (see overleaf). West of the church, the **courthouse** – built in 1770 and still in use when Rockefeller bought it – and the octagonal **Powder Magazine** face each other in the midst of the Market Square. Further along, **Chowning's Tavern**, a reconstruction of an alehouse that stood here in 1766, is one of four functioning pubs in the district. As a law student, Thomas Jefferson rented a room in the (no longer used) **Market Square Tavern** across the street.

Various other buildings along Duke of Gloucester Street house blacksmiths' shops, printers and milliners, open only to Colonial Williamsburg ticket-holders. At the east end of the street, fife-and-drum corps and members of the militia assemble in front of the reconstructed capitol (see overleaf) before the evening's march through town.

## Colonial Williamsburg

Crowds flock to **COLONIAL WILLIAMSBURG** in high summer, and tickets are expensive, but a visit really is worth including in your itinerary. The meticulously restored buildings and the various interpretive activities and crafts workshops – encompassing over thirty colonial trades, from apothecary to wig-maker – are both entertaining and true to life. As Rockefeller's tidy influence has waned (his idea of restoration was that everything should be made to look new), Williamsburg has tried to come to

---

### TICKETS FOR COLONIAL WILLIAMSBURG

To set foot inside any of the more than two hundred assorted buildings that have been restored or rebuilt as part of Colonial Williamsburg, you need to buy a ticket, either from the main **visitor center** (daily 8.30am–8pm; ☎1-800/HISTORY), north of center off the Colonial Parkway, or from a smaller office at the west end of Duke of Gloucester Street.

The **Basic Ticket** ($27), valid for one day only, gets you into everything except the Carter's Grove Plantation ($15, closed Mon), Governor's Palace ($18) and the Bassett Hall Museum ($10, closed Wed); the better-value **Patriot's Pass** ($35) gives you unlimited access to everything in Williamsburg for an entire year. Additional charges are made for the various special entertainment and educational events offered by Colonial Williamsburg, such as staged trials in the courthouse, evening dances and candlelit walking tours, but you can get a 25 percent discount on these with a Patriot's Pass. If you're in town for a couple of days, it's worth considering the **Colonial Pass** ($31), which offers the same access as the Basic Ticket with the addition of the Governor's Palace, and is valid for two consecutive days. All three tickets include an introductory guided tour.

---

grips with the less savory realities of colonial life. Thus people previously referred to as servants are now acknowledged to have been slaves – fully half of Williamsburg's population was African-American – and their lives and conditions are well covered. On another level, houses and outbuildings, formerly repainted every year, are now left to age naturally, and once-manicured lawns are now allowed to get (slightly at least) overgrown.

The real architectural highlight is the **capitol**, at the east end of Duke of Gloucester Street. The current building, a 1945 reconstruction of the 1705 original, has an open-air ground-floor **arcade** linking two keyhole-shaped wings. The east wing housed the elected, legislative body of the colonial government, the **House of Burgesses**, while the other held the chambers of the **General Court** – where alleged felons, including thirteen of Blackbeard's pirates, were tried. The eleven justices of the General Court, all of whom were appointed by the king, served as a second legislative body, much as the US House and Senate work today; if the two became deadlocked, they'd meet jointly in a conference chamber bridging the two wings.

A number of fully stocked giftshops along **Duke of Gloucester Street** have been done up as olde worlde apothecaries and silversmiths. The **Raleigh Tavern** was where the independence-minded colonial government reconvened after being dissolved by the loyalist governors in 1769 and again in 1774; the original tavern burned down in 1859. Considering that most Virginians of the time, even well-to-do landowners, lived in one- or two-room log cabins, the imposing two-story **Governor's Palace** at the north end of the Palace Green, with its grand ballroom and opulent furnishings, must have served as a telling declaration of the power vested within.

The smaller of the two conventional museums in Williamsburg, the recently expanded **Abby Aldrich Rockefeller Folk Art Center** on the south side of town, has an intriguing collection of household implements, children's toys, and general bric-a-brac, as well as fascinating paintings and sculptures by so-called primitive or natural artists. The other, the **DeWitt Wallace Decorative Arts Museum**, features fine furniture, porcelain and portraits. Its modern galleries are underground; the entrance is through the reconstructed facade of the **Public Hospital**, two blocks south of Bruton Parish Church. The first asylum in North America, the hospital now has reconstructions of the wire cages in which many early patients were kept, and exhibits tracing the evolution of the treatment of mental illness in the US.

## Yorktown battlefield

**YORKTOWN**, along the York River on the north side of the peninsula, is not much of a town, but gave its name to the decisive final battle of the **Revolutionary War**. The smallest and least visited of the Historic Triangle sites, Yorktown was little more than farmland when, on October 18, 1781, overwhelmed and besieged British (and German) troops under the command of Cornwallis surrendered to the joint American and French forces commanded by George Washington. At the heart of the battlefield, a **visitor center** (daily 9am–5pm; $5 per car, or $7 combined with the Jamestown National Historic Site, see p.383) has informative interpretive displays, racks of military artifacts and a short audiovisual presentation on the war. The **Siege Line Overlook** on the roof gives good views of strategic points; maps and a cassette-taped tour ($3) are available if you want to explore in greater detail.

The **Moore House**, where the British surrender was agreed, survived later Civil War battles (and eventual use as a barn) before John D Rockefeller had it restored; it stands along the York River, a mile east of the visitor center.

## Yorktown Victory Center

Though Yorktown survived the battle more or less unscathed – the fighting took place on open fields to the east, and in the waters of Chesapeake Bay – much of the town was destroyed by fire in 1814, and very little of substance survives from the colonial days. Many of the surviving homes are privately owned, and not open to visitors. To make up for this, as at Jamestown the state of Virginia and the National Park Service have constructed a mini-theme park – this time a re-created Continental Army encampment – as part of the **Yorktown Victory Center** (daily 9am–5pm; $8.25, or $14 with Jamestown Settlement, see p.384), west of the battlefield on US-17. It's not as extensive or convincing as the one at Jamestown, but the museum is better, focusing on the tobacco wealth of now-vanished York River towns and covering both sides, British and American, of events leading up to the Revolution. A final gallery deals with the course and impact of the war itself.

## Historic Triangle practicalities

Of the three main sites, only Williamsburg is easily reached without a car. Amtrak **trains** and Greyhound **buses** stop at the **Transportation Center** at 408 N Boundary St, two blocks from the Governor's Palace. An airport shuttle from Norfolk Airport runs to Williamsburg for $17 (☎757/587-6958). Once there, the Colonial Parkway makes an excellent cycling route to Jamestown or Yorktown, but there's no other transportation available; rent a **bike** for $14 a day from Bikes Unlimited at 759 Scotland St in Williamsburg (☎757/229-4620). In Colonial Williamsburg, hop-on, hop-off **shuttle buses** with an execrable recorded commentary leave from the visitor center every ten minutes or so and stop at convenient points in the historic area.

Considering the wealth of historic structures, it's surprising how few hotels or B&Bs there are with any character. All central **accommodation** is handled by Colonial Williamsburg (☎1-800/HISTORY), which includes the range from motel to four-star luxury, and they even offer rooms in some of the restored eighteenth-century homes and inns within the historic area – for which you must reserve well in advance. Good-value packages are available, with meals, two nights' lodging and admission, from around $150 per person. Otherwise **places to stay** around the Historic Triangle are generally anodyne and rarely cheap; to make your search easier, the Williamsburg Hotel/Motel Association (☎757/220-3330 or 1-800/899-9462) can find you a bed at no extra charge. West of center (and too far to walk) US-60 is lined with endless motels, and there are several lower-end places just a few blocks east of the capitol, including the *Bassett Motel*, 800 York St (☎757/229-5175; ③) and the recommended *Quarterpath Inn*, 620 York St ☎1-800/446-9222; ③/④). For a change of pace, the *Duke of York Motel*, 508 E Water St in Yorktown (☎757/898-3232; ③/④), has bargain beachfront doubles along the York River. Finally, there are several **campgrounds** along US-5 and US-60 west of Williamsburg.

The various old-style **restaurants** and taverns along Duke of Gloucester Street in Colonial Williamsburg feature good (though ludicrously overpriced) pub food as well as strolling entertainment, and can be fun; all except *Chowning's Tavern* must be reserved well in advance (☎1-800/HISTORY). West of the historic area, in the **Merchants Square** shopping mall, the excellent *Trellis Cafe* (☎757/229-8610) serves international food in an upmarket setting. There is also a clutch of restaurants near the William & Mary campus, including the *Green Leafe Café*, 765 Scotland St (☎757/220-3405), with a solid dose of hearty fare and good beers.

# The Atlantic coast

One of the busiest of the East Coast ports, **Norfolk** sits midway along the coast at the point where the Chesapeake Bay empties into the Atlantic Ocean. Virginia's sole heavily industrial center, it is not a particularly pretty place but it does have a rich maritime and naval heritage, as well as the Chrysler Museum, one of the nation's best art galleries. Fifteen miles east of Norfolk, along the open Atlantic, low-key **Virginia Beach** draws summer sun-seekers to the state's only real resort, surrounded by broad beaches and tidal marshlands.

The rest of Virginia's Atlantic coast is on its isolated and sparsely populated **Eastern Shore**, where the attractive little island town of **Chincoteague** serves as the headquarters of a wildlife refuge that straddles the Maryland border and forms part of the Assateague Island National Seashore.

## Norfolk

A strategic location at the broad mouth of the Chesapeake Bay, and an extensive deep-water harbor, made colonial **NORFOLK** the main American port for trade with England and the West Indies – in the mid-eighteenth century it was the largest city in Virginia. After being burned by the British in 1775, and suffering naval bombardments during the Civil War, Norfolk never regained much character, and despite recent efforts to redevelop its waterfront the modern city is little more than a supply depot for the vast naval shipyards. Along with Hampton and Newport News on the north side of the James River, Norfolk is home to the largest naval base outside Russia, and carriers, cruisers and all manner of gray-steel behemoths steam past incessantly. Hour-long tours take in top-secret centers and top-brass naval officers' homes.

### The Town
Five minutes from the naval base, an extraordinary array of oriental antiquities is displayed in the intimate and accessible Tudor-style former home of the Sloane family, on the Lafayette River at 7637 N Shore Rd (Mon–Sat 10am–5pm, Sun 1–5pm; $4, guided tours only). Now known as the **Hermitage Foundation Museum**, it ranges through medieval tapestries and Art Nouveau to Roman glass, Persian rugs and rare ancient Chinese ceremonial vessels.

A small **ferry** (daily 10am–midnight; 75¢; ☎757/640-6300) shuttles from Town Point Park, at the heart of the downtown waterfront, across the harbor to the historic **Portsmouth** neighborhood, where brick-paved streets are lined by eighteenth- and nineteenth-century houses. The **Chrysler Museum**, Olney Road and Mowlbray Arch

(Tues–Sat 10am–5pm, Sun 1–5pm; $6), half a mile north of the downtown waterfront, holds the collection of car magnate Walter Chrysler Jr, who was on drinking terms with Picasso. It includes a little bit of everything, from ancient Greek statuary to French Impressionist paintings, Franz Klein abstractions and Mayan funerary objects, as well as a world-class collection of Tiffany and Lalique glassware.

Two blocks from the harbor, amid the parking lots and vacant lots of downtown, the **Douglas MacArthur Memorial** on Bank Street (Mon–Sat 10am–5pm, Sun 11am–5pm; free) houses the mortal remains and personal papers of the flamboyant US general. The leader of the Allied armies in the Pacific during World War II, who as head of the occupying armies wrote the constitution of Japan, MacArthur was relieved of his command during the Korean War, apparently because of his alarming desire to bomb China. Objects in the Memorial include his trademark corncob pipe and dark glasses, along with some entertaining grainy old newsreel. On the downtown waterfront is Norfolk's premier attraction, **Nauticus: The National Maritime Center** (mid-May to mid-Sept daily 10am–5pm; rest of year closed Mon; $7.50), housed in a formidable replica battleship. The center's steep admission price is justified by the interactive oceanography exhibits, the giant-screen films and the country's first group virtual reality experience, where goggled visitors sink into Loch Ness and protect Nessie's eggs from unwelcome scientists. The more serious-minded will enjoy the on-site **Hampton Roads Naval Museum** (same hours; free), which documents the beginnings and growth of naval operations in the area. The adjacent **International Pier** is frequented by colossal US and foreign ships, which can be toured if they're docked for any length of time (call ☎757/664-1000 or 1-800/664-1080 for information).

The rest of downtown isn't up to much; head for **Colley Avenue and 21st Street**, lined with upmarket and innovative boutiques, bookstores and restaurants.

### Practicalities

Inexpensive Airport Shuttle (☎757/857-1231) services connect downtown Norfolk with both **Norfolk International Airport**, five miles northeast, and **Patrick Henry International Airport**, twelve miles north. Amtrak bus connections from Newport News stop at the *Howard Johnson Waterside*, 700 Monticello Ave, and Greyhound halts opposite at no. 701. Norfolk's downtown **visitor center** is in the Nauticus Center on the waterfront (daily 10am–5pm; ☎757/441-1852 or 1-800/368-3097); drivers can use a larger one at Fourth View Street, at exit 273 off I-64 (daily 9am–7pm; same phone numbers).

Cheap **accommodation** is limited to the highway motels. With credit card in hand, though, stay at the historic, renovated *James Madison,* 345 Granby St (☎757/622-6682; ⑤) downtown, or the lovely *Page House Inn,* 323 Fairfax Ave (☎757/625-5033 or 1-800/599-7659; ⑤–⑦), a Georgian Revival B&B near the Chrysler Museum – the proprietors also run a "boat and breakfast" on a nearby harbored yacht (⑧). **Eat** Cajun-style seafood at the *Bienville Grille,* 723 W 21st St downtown (☎757/625-5427), or try the eclectic Cajun–Asian blend at *The 219,* 219 Granby St (☎757/627-2896). Waterside Park, downtown at the mouth of the Elizabeth River, has something of a party atmosphere during summer weekends with live music, cheap beer and heaps of atmosphere. Also downtown, the ornate Art Nouveau Wells Theater (☎757/627-1234) puts on plays and small concerts.

## Virginia Beach

In both character and geography **VIRGINIA BEACH** is about halfway between Maryland's huge, frenzied Ocean City and North Carolina's wild, open Outer Bank. Virginia's only summer resort has grown to become the largest city in the state, but takes care to pitch itself as a family destination; among steps to deter the Spring Break crowd, the home of evangelist/politician Pat Robertson's Regent College has enacted anti-cruising laws that make it illegal to drive past the same spot twice within three hours. That said, the oceanfront vicinity can be a monument to tackiness, and the packed beaches and testosterone-filled surfer bars make Virginia Beach a place of less appeal than the tourism brochures suggest; it's not really a place for a long stay.

## The City

The city's focus is its long straight beach, lined with all the usual hotels and motels, and backed by a boardwalk strip of bars, restaurants and nightclubs. It barely matters that the forty-block downtown area is too spread out to walk along and too congested with traffic to drive through, as the same shops pop up every five blocks or so. During the day at least, there's not a lot to do other than lie in the sun and play in the waves: Virginia Beach is one of the main East Coast surfing centers, hosting the summer-long Billabong competitions. You can rent surf, skim and boogie boards from Wave Riding Vehicles, at 19th and Cypress (☎757/422-8823). Away from the sands, most of the action is along Atlantic Avenue, the main beachfront drag.

High-tech interactive exhibits and an IMAX theater combine at the lovely **Virginia Marine Museum**, 717 General Booth Blvd (mid-June to Labor Day daily 9am–9pm; rest of year daily 9am–5pm; $8.95, or $11.95 with IMAX show), illustrate all things aquatic, from submarines to seabirds. The museum organizes regular **dolphin-watching** expeditions in summer ($14; reserve a day in advance at ☎757/437-BOAT).

The eccentric **ARE Visitor Center**, at 67th Street and Atlantic Avenue (Mon–Sat 9am–8pm, Sun 11am–8pm; free), focuses on Edgar Cayce (1877–1945), a pioneer in hypnotism and ESP, known as "the sleeping prophet" because of his alleged ability, while in a trance, to diagnose and heal the ailments of individuals anywhere in the world. Visitors can use an enormous parapsychological library, or join "testings" of group ESP (June–Aug daily at 1pm; free).

Once the people-watching on the town beach starts to pall, head a few miles up or down the coast to find some beautiful and much more peaceful stretches of golden sand. To the south lie the four-mile-long **Back Bay National Wildlife Refuge**, where you can walk or fish but not swim or sunbathe, and **False Cape State Park**. Closer at hand to the north, the thick woodlands of **First Landing/Seashore State Park** was the site at which the first English settlers touched land in 1607 before moving on to Jamestown; it is now popular with weekend boaters and cyclists, and has a far less crowded beach on Chesapeake Bay.

## Practicalities

Greyhound drops off at 1017 Laskin Rd, off 31st Street, while the Amtrak bus connection from Newport News arrives at 19th Street and Arctic Avenue. The **visitor center** is at the east end of I-44, half a mile west of the beach on 21st Street (daily 9am–8pm; ☎757/437-4888 or 1-800/446-8038). Beach **trolleys** are the best mode of transportation in the area; there are four different routes covering the city, the most useful being up and down Atlantic Avenue (daily noon–midnight; ☎757/640-6300; 50¢).

Virginia Beach has one great boon for **budget travelers** – just a block from the beach, there are dorm beds from $14.45 and bargain B&B singles and doubles at *HI-Angie's Guest Cottage Hostel*, 302 24th St (☎757/428-4690; ①–③). Typical rates in the seafront hotels tend to approach $100 in high summer, with cheaper options including the appealingly old-styled *Thunderbird Motor Lodge* at 35th and Oceanfront (☎757/428-3024 or 1-800/633-6669; ②–⑥), which has a nice cafe, and the smallish *Sea Side* at 27th and Atlantic Avenue (☎757/428-9341 or 1-800/348-7263; ②–⑥) – a nice break from the surrounding high-rises. For details of the lovely oceanside **campground** at First Landing/Seashore State Park, call ☎757/412-2300 or 1-800/933-7275.

The town also offers a frenetic nightlife and some great **restaurants**. Hostelers congregate most nights at the *Jewish Mother*, 3108 Pacific Ave (☎757/422-5430), a daytime deli and late-night beer bar with free live music; *Chicho's*, 2112 Atlantic Ave (☎757/422-6011), is an Italian eating and drinking spot for exuberant twenty-something surfers, open until 2am. The *Lynnhaven Fish House*, at the top of the Lynnhaven Fishing Pier at the mouth of the Chesapeake Bay (☎757/481-0003), dishes out splendid soups, oysters and fish dinners, while *Mahi Mah's*, by the ocean at Seventh and Atlantic (☎757/437-8030), has a creative menu of sushi, sashimi and other seafood, plus a wide selection of beers. Check *Port Folio*, the listings newspaper, for details of live **music** events; the *Abbey Road Pub* at 203 22nd St (☎757/425-6330), has a humming bar with over a hundred different beers and live rock music every night.

# The eastern shore

Virginia's longest and least visited stretch of Atlantic coastline, the **eastern shore**, lies separated from the rest of the state on the far side of Chesapeake Bay. Only the southernmost segment of what's known as the Delmarva peninsula (see p.417) belongs to Virginia, by which point it has narrowed to become a flat spit of sand protected by a fringe of low-lying islands.

    **US-13**, which runs straight down the center of the peninsula and provides a handy short cut from Philadelphia or points north, crosses seventeen miles of open sea at the mouth of Chesapeake Bay, via the **Chesapeake Bay Bridge-Tunnel** ($10 per car). For most of its length, the roadway runs just a few yards above the water, bringing you almost eye-to-eye with passing ships; it twice burrows beneath the surface between artificial islands, before reaching its southern extremity halfway between Norfolk and Virginia Beach. To either side of US-13, bizarrely named little villages and fishing harbors such as Nassawadox, Assawoman and Accomac are tucked away on rambling back roads.

## Chincoteague

Much the most appealing destination on the eastern shore, **CHINCOTEAGUE** occupies a beautiful barrier island just south of the Maryland border. Although it's little more than a village, its two principal streets hold a fair assortment of motels and restaurants, and it makes an appropriately relaxed base for explorations of **Assateague Island National Seashore**. The northern half of Assateague, which holds some popular hiking trails, can only be reached from Maryland (see p.420); the southern half, just a mile onwards from Chincoteague, is taken up by the **Chincoteague National Wildlife Refuge**, notable for its seabirds and wild ponies. Call in at the **visitor center** (daily 9am–5pm; ☎757/336-6122; $5 per car) for a schedule of ranger-guided wildlife safaris ($8); or if you just want a day at the beach, drive straight past to **Tom's Cove**. Families fill the area nearest the parking lot, but set off walking north and you may end up with several miles of sand to yourself. If you're in Chincoteague on the last Wednesday and Thursday of July, don't miss the annual **Pony Penning Carnival**, when the wild ponies that roam Assateague Island to the north are herded together and directed on a swim through the channel to Chincoteague Memorial Park at the southern tip of the island. The ponies are then sold by auction to raise money for the local community. It can be a crowded event, but the sight of dozens of ponies swimming in convoy in such pristine surroundings is unforgettable.

    Central **accommodation** options in Chincoteague include the grand *Island Manor House*, 4160 Main St (☎757/336-5436; ⑤/⑥), an antique-furnished B&B, and the large but peaceful *Mariner Motel*, 6273 Maddox Rd (☎757/336-6565; ②–⑤), on the main road to Assateague. Next door, at no. 6251, is *Steamers* (☎757/336-5478), a brightly lit **restaurant** serving all-you-can-eat spiced crab and/or shrimp meals for around $20.

Copious quantities of soup, salad, fried chicken and so on are included in the price, all designed to ensure you eat as few crustaceans as possible.

# Charlottesville and the Shenandoah Valley

The densely forested four-thousand-foot peaks of the **Blue Ridge Mountains** form a definite barrier between the history-rich worlds of tidewater Virginia to the east and the rougher river-and-valley country to the west. In between the two, at the geographical center of the state, the friendly, manageably small college town of **Charlottesville** holds two great monuments to the mind of **Thomas Jefferson**. South of Charlottesville, the village of **Appommattox** is the sight at which papers were signed to officially end the **Civil War**, and is now preserved as an engaging national historic site. To the west, the northern Blue Ridge Mountains, crowned by the dense forests of **Shenandoah National Park**, run south to Tennessee, culminating in 5729ft Mount Rogers. Little seems to have changed in the lush Shenandoah Valley, on the far side of the mountains, since it was a vital battleground during the Civil War.

The main highway, I-81 through the Shenandoah Valley, is joined in the north by I-66 from Washington DC and in the middle by I-64 from Richmond through Charlottesville. Numerous scenic routes are slower but more worthwhile, such as **Skyline Drive** and the **Blue Ridge Parkway**, which weave along the four-hundred-mile-long mountain crest. You'll need a car to get the most out of the region, though cycling is a good option along the many back roads and, for hikers, the **Appalachian Trail** runs right down the middle. There are plenty of roadside motels, so you needn't be too concerned about advance planning – it's a great place for aimless exploration.

## Charlottesville

If you only have a couple of days to see Virginia, **CHARLOTTESVILLE**, seventy miles west of Richmond, should be near the top of your itinerary. Abounding in history, and holding some of the finest examples of early American architecture, it is at once small enough to feel comfortable in and large enough to have good restaurants and nightspots. Its compact, low-rise center is crisscrossed by magnolia-shaded streets, and makes a fine area to amble around, particularly the six pedestrianized blocks of **Main Street**, site of the nightly town promenade. However pleasant the town, the compelling attraction is the legacy of Thomas Jefferson, whose home and final resting place, **Monticello**, stands atop a hill just east of town, overlooking the beautifully landscaped Neoclassical campus of the University of Virginia.

### The University of Virginia

Though he wrote the Declaration of Independence and served as the third US president, Thomas Jefferson took more pride in having established the **University of Virginia** than in any of his other achievements, and after a visit you may well share his view. In 1976 the university was officially designated the greatest piece of architecture in the US, but it also reveals the ideology of its patron, who, besides designing every building down to the most minute detail, also planned the curriculum and selected the faculty. Uniquely for universities of the time, which functioned primarily as seminaries, the University of Virginia was not rooted in religious training – Jefferson having been one of the prime proponents of the separation of church from the affairs of state – but emphasized instead a broadly based liberal arts education.

The highlight and architectural focus is the redbrick, white-domed **Rotunda**, modeled on the Pantheon and completed in 1821 to house the university library and classrooms. A basement gallery tells the story of the university, while upstairs three elliptical classrooms are linked by a voluptuous central hall. A staircase winds up to the **Dome Room**, where, in place of the planetarium Jefferson wanted to install, Corinthian columns rise to an ocular skylight. From the Rotunda, where 45-minute guided tours of the campus begin (daily 10am–4pm; free), twin colonnades stretch along either side of a lushly landscaped quadrangle, linking together a string of single-story student apartments and taller pavilions, in which professors live and hold tutorials. While the overall feel is harmonious, each individual block is unique, the differing facades and rooflines designed to show off the various orders and styles of Neoclassical architecture.

Parallel to the quadrangle buildings, two further rows of dormitory buildings, the East and West Ranges, front on to serpentine walled gardens. **Edgar Allan Poe** stayed in one of these rooms while studying at the University of Virginia in 1826, but was forced to drop out after his stepfather cut off his allowance, apparently because Edgar had lost all his money gambling. His room – Number 13, of course, in the West Range – is now restored to how it would have looked during his occupancy, and is virtually the only campus interior, apart from the Rotunda, that you can visit.

## Monticello – Thomas Jefferson's home

One of America's most familiar buildings – it graces the back of the nickel coin – **Monticello**, three miles southeast of Charlottesville on Hwy-53, was the home of Thomas Jefferson for most of his life. A visit provides a distinctive insight into the most intriguing of America's founding fathers. Surrounded by acres of beautifully landscaped hilltop grounds with fine views out over the Virginia countryside, Monticello is a handsome house, whose symmetrical brick facade, centered upon a white Doric portico, belies the quirky irregularities of the interior – furnished as it was when Jefferson lived, and died, here.

To see Monticello you have to join one of the **guided tours** (March–Oct daily 8am–5pm; rest of year daily 9am–4.30pm; $9) that leave continuously from the parking lot at the bottom of the hill. There's often a queue, especially at weekends, so try to get there as early as possible in the morning. From the outside, Monticello looks like an elegant, Palladian-style country home, but as soon as you enter the domed entrance hall, with its funhouse mirror – which reflects an upside-down image – and displays of fossilized bones and elk antlers (from Lewis and Clark's epic 1804 journey across North America, which Jefferson sponsored as president), you begin to get a sense that Jefferson was a somewhat more interesting character than the sober statesman portrayed by most histories. His love of gadgets marked him as something of an eccentric: the weather vane over the front porch is connected to a dial, so he could see which way the wind was blowing without having to step outside, and the house is filled with odd little contraptions such as the elaborate dual-pen device Jefferson used to make automatic copies of all his letters. Jefferson's **private chambers** can also be seen on the tour: he slept in a tiny alcove linking his dressing room and his study, and would get up on the right side of the bed if he wanted to make some late-night notes, on the left if he wanted to get dressed.

The upstairs rooms, where Jefferson's daughter lived, are not open to the public, but in the grounds around the house you begin to see how Monticello, a 5000-acre plantation, really functioned. Extensive flower and vegetable gardens spread to the south and west, and a dank passage runs under the house from the kitchen and beer cellar (Jefferson was a keen home-brewer) to the remains of Mulberry Row, Monticello's **slave quarters** – despite calling slavery an "abominable crime," Jefferson owned almost two hundred of his fellow human beings; recent research indicates that he may have also sired a child with one of his slaves. At the south end of Mulberry Row, a grove of ancient hardwood trees surrounds Jefferson's grave, marked by a simple stone obelisk; a footpath beyond winds back down to the bottom of the hill.

## Charlottesville practicalities

Amtrak trains from DC stop in Charlottesville at 810 W Main St, and Greyhound pulls in a few blocks away at 310 W Main St. Once you arrive, you can get to everything on foot, apart from the **visitor center** (daily 9am–5pm; ☎804/977-1783), well-signposted just south of I-64 – take bus #8 from Market Street downtown. The center houses a superb free exhibit called "Thomas Jefferson at Monticello," and is an excellent starting point for a trip to Monticello.

For its size, Charlottesville has quite a good range of **accommodation**. The usual motels line Emmet Street (US-29) at the west end of town, the least expensive being the *Budget Inn*, 140 Emmet St (☎804/293-5141 or 1-800/293-5144; ②). *Hampton Inn & Suites* (☎804/923-8600 or 1-800/426-7866; ⑤) offers standard rooms right near the university at 900 W Main St, or good-value **B&B** is available at the two beautifully restored houses of the *200 South Street Inn*, 200 South St (☎804/979-0200; ⑥), and at the *1817 Historic Bed and Breakfast*, 1211 W Main St (☎804/979-7353; ⑤). To arrange a stay in a bed and breakfast, call Guesthouses (☎804/979-7264).

The best **eating** and **drinking** is to be had near the university and on the downtown mall. In between the two, *Southern Culture*, 633 W Main St (☎804/979-1990) is an inexpensive local favorite, with a slightly retro-1950s feel and fabulous tuna steak. *Metropolitan*, 214 W Water St (☎804/977-1043), is a suitably pricey downtown restaurant, but the fresh fish is worth every dollar. Just north of the downtown mall at Fifth and Market streets, *Tastings* (☎804/293-3663) offers grilled meats and a grand selection of wines, including many from the vineyards surrounding Charlottesville, while Virginia's best selection of beers, plus a range of light meals, can be sampled a block further north at the *Court Square Tavern*, 500 E Jefferson St (☎804/296-6111). The *C&O Restaurant*, 515 E Water St (☎804/971-7044), housed in an old railroad engineers' diner, offers bistro-style food in its humming bar and more upscale French *nouvelle cuisine* in the upstairs dining room.

As a college town, Charlottesville isn't short of **nightlife**, whether at bars like the *Outback Lounge*, 110 N Fourth St (☎804/979-7211), or in its two main nightclubs, *Max's*, 120 S 11th St (☎804/295-6299), and, just three doors down, *Trax*, 127 S 11th St (☎804/295-8729).

# Appommattox

Settled amid the mild, roaming hills of central Virginia, some sixty miles south of Charlottesville on US-24, **APPOMMATTOX**, marks the spot at which Robert E Lee and Ulysses S Grant met on April 9, 1865 to mark the end of the Civil War. After four years of enormous bloodshed on both sides, the Confederacy bowed out with a mere whimper. Grant's Union troops had cut off a nearby railroad line upon which Lee's final battalion depended for vital supplies, and the half-starved Confederate army had no choice but to submit. Final papers were signed in a private home near the Appommattox Court House. This event, a defining moment in American history, is remembered in the **Appommattox Court House National Historical Park** (daily 9am–5.30pm; $2), a place refreshingly free of the usual tourist baggage that accompanies most such important sites in the state. The tiny village has been handsomely restored, though the home and court house, containing a museum, are merely reconstructions of the original.

Getting to Appommattox requires a car, and the nearest accommodation is available in the newer city of the same name, a few miles west. You're better off driving 20 miles further west to **LYNCHBURG**, whose dramatic hills and clean historic center make a fine place to spend an evening. Try the *Lynchburg Mansion Inn*, 405 Madison St (☎804/528-5400; ⑤), a cozy Victorian B&B.

# Shenandoah National Park

SHENANDOAH NATIONAL PARK, which contains seemingly endless acres of dark forests, deep rocky ravines and precipitous, surging waterfalls, has one of the most unusual histories of any US national park. Far from being untouched for the past three hundred years, this "natural" landscape was created when hundreds of small family farms and homesteads were bought up by the state and federal governments during the Depression, and the land was left to revert to its natural state.

Shenandoah, meaning "river of high mountains," has one of the most scenic byways in the US, the **Skyline Drive**; a thin ribbon of pavement curving along the crest of the Blue Ridge Mountains. It starts just off I-66 near the town of **Front Royal**, 75 miles west of DC, and winds south through the park, giving great views over the Piedmont to the east and lovely Shenandoah Valley to the west.

**Admission** to the park is $10 for cars and $5 for pedestrians, cyclists and motorcyclists; permits last for six days. The views are especially fine, and the crowds especially large, in the fall, but any time of year you can get the best out of the park's open spaces by following one of the many **hiking trails** that split off from the ridge. One favorite leaves from the parking area of Big Meadows Lodge in the southern half of the park and winds along to tumbling **Dark Hollow Falls**; another, leaving Skyline Drive at milemarker 45, climbs up a fairly treacherous incline to the top of **Old Rag Mountain** for 360° views out over the whole of Virginia and the Allegheny Mountains in the west. More ambitious hikers, or those who want to spend the night out in the backcountry, head for the **Appalachian Trail**; details on any of these hikes, and free overnight camping permits, can be picked up at either of the **visitor centers** (☎540/999-3500), located along Skyline Drive four miles beyond the north entrance and at milemarker 50, in the middle of the park.

Three rustic **lodges**, near the center of the park, offer food and beds; reservations for all are handled by ARAMARK Services (☎540/743-5108 or 1-800/999-4714). The northernmost and oldest, the 1894 *Skyland Lodge*, has cabins (②) and modern hotel rooms (⑤), as well as a large restaurant with panoramic views; *Big Meadows Lodge*, next to the larger visitor center ten miles south, has similar facilities and a campground (☎1-800/365-2267); and Lewis Mountain has cabins and a first-come, first-served campground.

# The Shenandoah Valley

The small and characterful towns of the Shenandoah Valley, down below Skyline Drive, are as rich in human history as any in Virginia. Many were left in ruins after the war, but have since been restored to their original antebellum state, and numerous memorials, monuments and cemeteries line the back roads, surrounded by spacious horse farms and apple orchards.

Given its strategic importance and fertility, the Shenandoah Valley was inevitably one of the most fought-over battlegrounds in the Civil War, changing hands over seventy times at a cost of some 100,000 dead and maimed. The whole bloody story is told in evocative detail in the small but outstanding **museum** (mid-March to Nov daily 9am–5pm; $6.50) at the **New Market Battlefield**, just off I-81, thirty miles south of the I-66 junction. This was the scene of the legendary 1864 confrontation that involved a company of fourteen-year-old cadet soldiers from the Virginia Military Institute.

Besides its Civil War history, the northern Shenandoah Valley also holds half a dozen of Virginia's many underground **limestone caverns**. All are privately owned and cost $6–13.50 to enter. You'll no doubt see billboards advertising each one as the best: that title really belongs to the largest, **Luray Caverns**, twelve miles east of New Market off Hwy-211 (guided 1hr tours daily, every 20min, last tour 6pm, 4pm in winter; $13.50), a subterranean wonderland featuring a bizarre underground "organ" with stalagmites as "pipes." Your ticket also gives access to the adjacent **Historic Car and Carriage** exhibit (open until 7.30pm), a collection of vintage automobiles starring an 1892 Benz.

Further south, off Hwy-250 northwest of the town of **STAUNTON**, the **Museum of Frontier American Culture** (daily 9am–5pm; $8) brings to light how the various immigrants who settled here melded their traditions to develop a joint American culture. Most of the exhibits are about farming techniques and other somewhat mundane activities, but it's all engagingly presented and well worth a look.

## Lexington

Though it's one of the region's smaller towns, **LEXINGTON**, in the heart of the Shenandoah Valley, easily has the most to offer visitors. From horse-drawn carriages parading along its quiet, brick-paved streets, to the fine rolling countryside all around – displayed to great effect in the movie *Sommersby* – Lexington makes a great place to sit back and relax or, if you prefer, delve deep into Civil War and assorted other military arcana at its small museums and memorials.

The most engaging of these, the **Lee Chapel** (Mon–Sat 9am–5pm, Sun 2–5pm; free), is on the attractive colonnaded campus of **Washington and Lee University**, a short walk north of the town center. A commodious and somber building, the chapel is named in honor of Confederate general Robert E Lee, who taught here after the Civil War. Behind the pulpit is a marble statue of Lee in repose, surrounded by an array of authentic battle flags; along with many members of his family, Lee is interred downstairs in the chapel crypt, and his horse Traveller is buried just outside.

On the comparatively bland but formidable campus of the **Virginia Military Institute**, just east of the Lee Chapel, the **Military Museum** (daily 9am–5pm; free) tells the story of the state-supported, male-only military academy, which was founded in 1836 and has the dubious claim to fame of being the only university in US history to have sent its entire student body into battle. If possible, time your visit to coincide with the 4pm Friday full-dress parade – a bit like the changing of the guard, American-style – held on the field in front of the museum.

At the opposite end of the parade ground, the **George C Marshall Museum** (March–Oct daily 9am–5pm; Nov–Feb daily 9am–4pm; $3) documents the life of World War II US general and later secretary of state George Marshall, whose plan for the reconstruction of postwar Europe earned him the Nobel Peace Prize in 1953.

The **Stonewall Jackson House**, 8 E Washington St (June–Aug Mon–Sat 9am–6pm, Sun 1–6pm; Sept–May Mon–Sat 9am–5pm, Sun 1–5pm; $5), is where the noted Confederate general and Virginia Military Institute philosophy professor lived for fifteen years before his death at the battle of Chancellorsville. His spartan brick townhouse is furnished as it was in the years before the war, and Stonewall himself is buried, along with hundreds of his fellow soldiers, in the **Stonewall Jackson Memorial Cemetery** off South Main Street. This is now the prime destination for twilight **ghost tours**, leaving from the visitor center every evening at 8.30pm (May–Oct only; $8) and great if you're traveling with kids.

Twenty miles south of Lexington on US-11 is the spectacular **Natural Bridge**, where meandering Cedar Creek has gradually carved away at the softer limestone forming a 215ft archway that has dazzled several distinguished visitors over the years. George Washington allegedly carved his initials into the rock (though it may take a keen eye to see them), and Thomas Jefferson was so impressed that he bought the site and owned it for fifty years. It's worth the hefty admission price, but don't expect it to be "one of the Seven Natural Wonders of the World" as its publicists suggest (June–Sept daily 9am–10pm; Oct–May daily 9am–5pm; $8). The Natural Bridge **Caverns** are also on site ($7), but it's best to save your money for the more spectacular Luray Caverns, further north (see opposite).

Even if you're not thrilled by war stories and natural bridges, Lexington still makes a good stop, with dozens of fine old homes; pick up a walking tour map from the friendly **visitor center**, 102 E Washington St (June–Aug daily 8.30am–6pm; Sept–May daily 9am–5pm; ☎540/463-3777). For **food**, the *Southern Inn Restaurant*, bang in the center at 37 S Main St (☎540/463-3612) offers Southern cooking such as a scrumptious meatloaf; it's attached to a bar that churns out live music Friday and Saturday nights. If your taste tends towards tofu, you may prefer the *Blue Heron Cafe*, 4 E Washington St (☎540/463-1163), across from the Washington and Lee campus. A few blocks west stands Lexington's one remarkably cheap **place to stay**, Ms Ruth Rees's $10-a-night *Overnight Guests*, 216 W Washington St (☎540/463-3075; ①); in addition to the usual motels along the highways, the comfy German- and French-speaking *Asherowe B&B*, 314 S Jefferson St (☎540/463-4219; ③), stands in the Golden Triangle six blocks southwest of the visitor center. There is also a **campground** along Route 11 south of town, near Natural Bridge.

# The Blue Ridge Parkway

Once out of Shenandoah National Park, Skyline Drive becomes the **Blue Ridge Parkway**, which winds southwest along the crest of the Appalachians at an average elevation of three thousand feet. It's a beautiful drive, though **I-81**, sweeping along the flank of the mountains, is a more efficient way of getting from Virginia to North Carolina and on to the Great Smokies, a route covered in detail on p.444. In summer the *Rocky Knob Cabins* (☎540/593-3503; ③), at milepost 174 on the Parkway itself, offers a memorable night's stay in the idyllic Meadows of Dan. Not far beyond milepost 214, the rambling old *HI-Blue Ridge Country* **hostel** (☎540/236-4962; ①) has dorm beds for $13 ($16 for nonmembers). Of the nearby towns, **ROANOKE**, sandwiched between I-81 and the Parkway and the largest community in western Virginia, is the nicest. Its leisurely, old-fashioned streets make for a very pleasant stopoff, focusing around its still-functioning farmers' market (Mon–Sat) and the modern Center In The Square mall, which contains several museums such as the engaging **Roanoke Valley History Museum** (Mon–Sat 10am–5pm, Sun 1–5pm; $2), which documents settlement of the region by the Scottish, Welsh and Germans. The **Virginia Museum of Transportation**, 303 Norfolk Ave (Mon–Sat 10am–5pm, Sun noon–5pm; $5), has the largest collection of steam locomotives in America, and hints at Roanoke's railroad foundations.

An excellent, helpful **visitor center** at 114 Market St (daily 9am–5pm; ☎540/345-8622 or 1-800/635-5535) can provide full details and walking tour maps. The *Mary Bladon House* at 381 Washington Ave SW (☎540/344-5361; ④), a few blocks southwest, is a welcoming **B&B**, while the least expensive of the interstate motels is the *Rodeway Inn*, 526 Orange Ave NE, at exit 4E off I-581 (☎540/981-9341; ③). Campbell Avenue downtown sports a number of appealing restaurants, including *Awful Arthur's Seafood Co*, 108 Campbell Ave (☎540/344-2997), a good lunch or dinner spot with interesting specials. *Carlos*, opposite at 312 Market St (☎540/345-7661), serves superb "international cuisine," predominantly Brazilian, while *O'Dell's on the Market*, 19 E Salem Ave (☎540/342-9340), is a lively music venue with blues jam sessions at weekends.

# WEST VIRGINIA

The people of **WEST VIRGINIA** are only half joking when they call their state the Ireland of the US. Generally poor and almost entirely rural, it shares a similar history of exploitation by outside powers, with **timber** and **coal-mining** companies taking advantage of the rich natural resources while giving little in return. But, quite apart from the almost Third World deprivation which endures in some areas (and which, along with John Denver songs and the barefoot hillbillies supposed to inhabit its backwoods reaches, still colors most outsiders' preconceptions), West Virginia is also, in places at least, incredibly beautiful, holding the longest whitewater rivers and most extensive wilderness areas in the eastern US. The extreme topography which has historically isolated its inhabitants now makes this a popular destination for hikers and outdoors enthusiasts, and the moonshiners of old have been replaced by ski instructors and mountain-bike guides.

Pioneer settlers only started to cross the mountains of western Virginia in significant numbers during the middle of the seventeenth century. Farming small plots of land with their own labor, they came to have ever less in common with the slave-holding plantation owners of old Virginia, and when the Civil War broke out the area declined to secede from the Union. The Supreme Court never ruled whether West Virginia was legally entitled to declare itself a state, and Virginia itself has still not officially recognized the split. West Virginia has, however, developed a political and economic identity of its own. Around 1900, when railroads from the East Coast first reached into the mountainous interior, timber companies clear-cut stand after stand of forest, setting up a succession of mill towns, each dismantled in its turn when they moved on somewhere new – **Cass**, now preserved within the Allegheny National Forest, is one of the few that was left intact. Later on, coal-mining conglomerates, especially in the south, perfected the "company town" approach, wherein workers were paid a little bit less each month than the amount they owed for their company-provided food and lodging. Coal companies still exert immense power in West Virginia, but the real key to the state's future prosperity is tourism, which in places now accounts for over half its income.

The most popular destination, the restored 1850s town of **Harpers Ferry**, is barely in West Virginia at all, standing just across the broad rivers which form its Maryland and Virginia borders. To the west, the **Allegheny Mountains** stretch for over 150 miles; more than a million acres of hardwood forest rival New England for brilliant autumnal color. West Virginia's oldest and most attractive town, **Lewisburg**, sits just off I-64 at the mountains' southern foot, while the capital, **Charleston**, lies in the comparatively flat Ohio River valley of the west.

## Getting around West Virginia

With its many mountains and rivers making straight, flat roads virtually nonexistent, getting around West Virginia is as much a part of its attraction as is any specific destination – a bike and a stout pair of legs, or a motorcycle, would be ideal, but a car is pretty necessary if you really want to see the state. Greyhound is basically useless, and Amtrak, apart from serving Harpers Ferry from Washington DC, has only one, albeit spectacular, route, running through the New River Gorge to the capital, Charleston.

## Harpers Ferry

**HARPERS FERRY**, a ruggedly sited eighteenth-century town now restored as a national historic park, gives many visitors their first and only look at West Virginia. Clinging to steep hillsides above the rocky confluence of the Potomac and Shenandoah rivers, many of its forty-odd brick and stone buildings date from the days when George

Washington set up the country's first **national munitions factory** here to arm the young Republic. During the mid-1800s Harpers Ferry was a thriving industrial complex, home to some five thousand workers and linked to the capital by the B&O Railroad and the Chesapeake & Ohio Canal, but after suffering the ravages of the Civil War and a series of torrential floods it was all but abandoned, the empty shells of its homes and factories slowly becoming overgrown by the dense forest that covers the surrounding hills. Almost all of Harpers Ferry has since been reconstructed as an outdoor museum, combining historical importance and natural beauty.

However pretty Harpers Ferry may be – and in the fall, when the leaves blaze with color, it's hard to imagine a more picture-perfect setting – it's best known for its place in US history. The 1859 raid on its huge US arsenal by anti-slavery revolutionary **John Brown**, which rocked the already fragmenting nation, was the clearest foreshadowing of the Civil War which broke out just sixteen months later. In the hope of fomenting a widespread slave revolt, Brown and 21 other abolitionist radicals, including two of his sons and five black men, seized the munitions factory and its large store of weapons on the night of October 16. They held out for two days before US troops, under the command of Robert E Lee, stormed the buildings, killing many of the raiders and capturing Brown. He was taken to nearby Charles Town, put on trial just nine days later, and convicted of treason; by the time he was hanged on December 2, he was far from alone in regarding himself as a martyr to the abolitionist cause.

As one of only two places in the US with the capacity to manufacture munitions, Harpers Ferry was a major prize in the Civil War, and never got back on its feet after the resultant devastation. The arsenal buildings were burned in 1861 to keep the weapons out of Confederate hands, while in 1862 Stonewall Jackson captured the town along with 12,500 Union soldiers. Enough of the original buildings and cobbled streets survive, however, to give a good sense of how things used to be, and the restoration project has so far managed to re-create the townscape without making it feel too much like a theme park.

## The Town

Almost everyone who comes to Harpers Ferry drives. Parking is virtually banned in the old town area; shuttle buses run from the large **visitor center** on US-340 (daily 8am–5pm; buses run until 6.30pm; ☎304/535-6298) – where you pay the $3 per person, $5 per car entry fee – to the old town, dropping off outside the balconied old **Stagecoach Inn**, at the end of gas-lit Shenandoah Street in the heart of the restored area; inside there's an information desk with maps and a small bookshop. Across the street, displays in the **Master Armorer's House** will tell you everything you want to know about gun-making; adjacent buildings include a restored blacksmith's shop, a general store and a tavern, often peopled with costumed guides who describe and act out events from the town's history.

John Brown's **fort** – actually the armory's engine room, where he and his raiders were captured – originally stood directly across from the tavern, and has been rebuilt a block away, near the point where the rivers meet. It's no more than an empty shell, however, and if you want to get the full story of the raid you'd do better to spend half an hour in the **John Brown Museum** opposite. Here, as throughout Harpers Ferry, debate continues to rage over Brown's sanity or sanctity; many regard him as a borderline psychotic. One monument on the wall of the building, erected by the Daughters of the Confederacy, salutes the attack's first victim, a free black railroad baggage master named Hayward Shepherd, as epitomizing the "character and faithfulness of thousands of negroes" in the old South; across from it stands another honoring Brown's "heroism."

Further museums, housing exhibits on the Civil War and local black history, line both sides of **High Street** as it climbs away from the river. At one point, a set of stone steps climbs away between them, through the residential area, to the 1782 **Harper House**, preserved as a typical worker's rooming house of the period.

A footpath continues uphill, past overgrown churchyards hemmed in by drystone walls, to **Jefferson Rock**, a huge gray boulder giving a great view over the two rivers – Thomas Jefferson said that the outlook was worth a voyage across the Atlantic. For a longer hike, two trails lead onwards into the surrounding forest: the **Appalachian Trail** continues from Jefferson Rock across the Shenandoah River into the Blue Ridge Mountains of Virginia, while the **Maryland Heights Trail** makes a four-mile round-trip around the headlands across the Potomac River. You can also float down the river in a **raft** or inner-tube provided by one of the many outfitters along the rivers east and south of town.

### Practicalities

Harpers Ferry makes a popular excursion from Washington DC, served by several trains daily on the Maryland Rail Commuter network (☎1-800/325-7245), and by one daily Amtrak service, which arrives at 5.15pm, en route to Chicago. Greyhound, however, comes no closer than Frederick, Maryland (see p.413).

If you want to **spend the night**, the century-old *Hilltop House Hotel and Restaurant* on Ridge Street (☎304/535-2132 or 1-800/338-8319; ④) may be showing its age, but still has reasonable prices and good views, while amiable B&Bs are sprinkled throughout the surrounding region; nearby budget motels include the *Comfort Inn* on US-340 (☎304/535-6391 or 1-800/228-5150; ③). The *HI-Harpers Ferry Lodge*, a couple of miles east at 19123 Sandy Hook Rd in Knoxville, MA (☎301/834-7652; closed Nov–March; ①), has dorm beds from $13, and its own campground; there's plenty more **camping** along the Potomac River in the C&O Canal Historic Park. The **park visitor center** has further details, as does the **Jefferson County tourist bureau** (☎304/535-2627 or 1-800/848-TOUR), across US-340. As for **eating**, old-style cafes line High Street up from the historic area – both the *Mountain House Cafe* (☎304/535-2339) and the *Garden of Food* (☎304/535-2202) are good and relatively inexpensive.

## Around Harpers Ferry

Among small towns worth seeing nearby is **CHARLES TOWN**, four miles south of Harpers Ferry on US-340, where John Brown was tried and hanged; the **Jefferson County Museum** at Washington and Samuel (Mon–Sat 10am–4pm; free) tells the story of his trial, conviction and execution, and remembers his last words: "I, John Brown, am now quite certain that the crimes of this guilty land will never be purged away but with blood." The cozy village of **SHEPHERDSTOWN**, along the Potomac ten miles to the north, is prettier and better for wandering, its quaint ancient shops and cafes looking across the river to Maryland's bloody **Antietam Battlefield** (see p.413).

Further afield, and of more salubrious interest, is the old spa town of **BERKELEY SPRINGS**, now preserved intact as a state historic park, thirty miles west of Harpers Ferry on Hwy-9, seven miles south of I-70. The nearest early America ever came to having resorts like Bath in England, Berkeley Springs was a favorite summer retreat of the colonial elite – George Washington and Lord Fairfax were among the regulars who came here to take the waters – and assorted massage and steam bath treatments are still available at its many health farms. In summer, you can soak yourself in the old **Roman Baths**, in active use since 1815 and now run by the state. The town's **central square** is leafy and green, with footpaths fanning out in all directions, one climbing the hill up to **Berkeley Castle**, a fortress-like mid-Victorian folly above the town that originally held a large ballroom and is now used mostly for weddings. Among **B&Bs** in Berkeley Springs are the *Highlawn Inn*, 304 Market St (☎304/258-5700; ⑤), and the *Manor Inn*, 415 Fairfax St (☎304/258-1552; ⑤).

# The Allegheny Mountains

Considering that it's the most extensive wilderness area near the East Coast, within a few hours' drive of a dozen big cities, surprisingly few people have heard about, much less bothered to visit, the backcountry reaches of the **Allegheny Mountains**, West Virginia's segment of the Appalachian chain. The entire 140-mile crest is protected as part of the **Monongahela National Forest**, within which numerous state parks highlight the most spectacular sights. There are no cities and few towns, public transportation is nonexistent, and not much goes on after dark – to give an idea of how rural it is, whole counties do without a single traffic light – but if you like to backpack, ski, cycle, climb, canoe or just wander around the great outdoors, the Alleghenies are well worth a visit. For maps and more detailed information, contact the state tourist office (see p.22) or the Monongahela National Forest, 200 Sycamore St, Elkins, WV 26241 (Mon–Fri 8am–4.45pm; ☎304/636-1800).

## Blackwater Falls, the Canaan Valley and Seneca Rocks

Some of the most beautiful stretches of the Monongahela National Forest are in the northern corner of the state, where the thundering torrents of the **Blackwater Falls** pour over a 60ft limestone cliff before crashing down through a steeply walled canyon. South from here spreads the dense maple, oak, walnut and birch forest of broad **Canaan Valley**, while to the east rise the barren subarctic highlands of the **Dolly Sods Wilderness**, the whole area crisscrossed by hiking, cycling and skiing trails.

Rising up at the far end of the Canaan Valley, the state's highest point, the 4861ft **Spruce Knob** stands out over the headwaters of the Potomac River – you can actually drive all the way to the summit. Even more impressive views can be had from the top of **Seneca Rocks**, some twenty miles to the northeast, whose 1000ft limestone cliffs are commonly considered to present the most challenging rock-climb on the East Coast. A good trail leads around the back of the North Peak if you want to take the easy way up, and the helpful **visitor center** at the junction of US-33 and Hwy-28 (summer daily 9am–5.30pm; rest of year Sat & Sun only; ☎304/257-4488) has details of outdoor recreation opportunities in the entire region. *Yokum's* (☎304/567-2351 or 1-800/772-8342) near the base of the rocks, takes care of all your vital needs, with a cheap **motel** (②), self-service **cabins** (④), and a pretty riverside **campground** (about $10), plus a down-home **restaurant** and country store.

The old logging town of **DAVIS** (population 1000), just east of US-219 at the north end of the Canaan Valley, makes another obvious base, with a couple of **places to stay**: the *Best Western Alpine Lodge* (☎304/259-5245; ④) has good motel rooms, and the *Bright Morning Inn* (☎304/259-5119; ③) on Williams Avenue doubles as the town **cafe**. Among local **outdoor guides and outfitters**, the Blackwater Outdoor Center (☎304/478-4456) runs rafting, caving and canoeing trips and rents out bikes; and Timberline Resort (☎304/866-4801 or 1-800/SNOWING) runs the state's largest downhill ski area. For more information, contact the **visitor center** on Main Street (daily 9am–5pm; ☎304/259-5315 or 1-800/782-2775).

## Elkins and the Augusta Festival

One of the best places for visitors to experience the vibrant folkways of the West Virginia mountains is **ELKINS**, the biggest town in northern West Virginia, which lies just west of the Canaan Valley. The **Augusta Heritage Center** here, which is part of Davis and Elkins College (100 Sycamore St, Elkins, WV 26241; ☎304/637-1209), works to keep Appalachian cultural traditions alive in music, arts and crafts. Concerts and events are held throughout the summer, and there are celebrations of dulcimer-playing in April and fiddle music in October, but its major annual showcase is mid-August's

**Augusta Festival**. This offers public workshops in such diverse down-home pursuits as banjo-playing, blacksmithing, quilt-making and folk dancing, and after dark performers get together for a nightly hoedown, featuring storytellers, bluegrass bands and all-round good times.

Elkins's main **visitor center**, half a mile east of the center at the intersection where Hwy-33 starts to climb into the mountains (Mon–Fri 8.30am–5.30pm, Sat–Sun 9am–6pm; ☎304/636-2717 or 1-800/422-3304), can provide full details on local **accommodation**, including several B&Bs, while the *Super 8*, at the intersection of US-219 and US-250 (☎304/636-6800; ②), has inexpensive, clean motel rooms. The *Happy Trails Hostel* at 218 Randolph Ave (☎304/636-9670; ①) offers bunk beds for $12 and rents out bikes. The *Starr Cafe and Augusta Bookshop*, 224 Davis Ave (☎304/636-7273), is a friendly place to stop off for a coffee or snack in the center of town.

## Pocahontas County

The southern half of the Monongahela National Forest is contained within hilly **Pocahontas County**, known as "the birthplace of rivers" because it holds the headwaters of the Greenbrier, Cheat, Gauley and other great West Virginia rivers. Like most of the Alleghenies, it's a mountainous, fairly inaccessible region – two roads, US-219 and Hwy-92, wind north-to-south, with a handful of narrow tracks twisting between them – offering outstanding outdoor recreation as well as endless scenic vistas.

Besides gorgeous scenery, Pocahontas County is also home to the state-run **Cass Scenic Railroad**, a restored, steam-powered logging railroad built in 1902. Running on narrow-gauge tracks, the chugging Shay locomotive carries visitors up to the top of 4842ft Bald Knob on a converted logging train, starting at the old lumber-mill village of **CASS**, five miles west of Hwy-28 near the town of **Greenbank** (summer daily 10.50am, 1pm & 3pm; $10, $12 weekends; ☎304/456-4300 or 1-800/CALL-WVA). Cass has been preserved in its entirety as a historic park; the town was built by the local logging company to provide subsidized housing for its workers, thereby ensuring their faithful economic dependence. You can wander around the eerily monotonous, white loggers' cabins, or even **stay the night** in one of several converted into self-service accommodation (☎1-800/CALL-WVA; ④/⑤); they hold up to six people.

An energetic five-mile walk downhill from Cass leads along the tracks to the start of the cycle-friendly **Greenbrier River Trail**, which follows the river and the railroad for 75 miles, coming out near Lewisburg (see below). You can also rent a **mountain bike** from Elk River Touring Center (☎304/572-3771), fifteen miles north of **Marlinton**, the county seat, off US-219 in the hamlet of **Slatyfork**, and set off into the mountains. The company runs a shuttle service to the trailheads and organizes backcountry cycling trips and ski tours in winter, and its lovely year-round **hotel** (③) has a hot tub and good-value restaurant. Pocahontas County **tourist bureau** (☎304/799-4636 or 1-800/336-7009) provides maps.

The other main attraction in this part of the Alleghenies is the birthplace of **Pearl S Buck**, author of *The Good Earth* and one of only two American women – the other being Toni Morrison – to win the Nobel Prize for Literature. Her **home** at **HILLSBORO**, on US-219 halfway between Marlinton and Lewisburg, is packed with memorabilia.

## Lewisburg and the Greenbrier Resort

Located just off I-64 on the southern edge of the Monongahela National Forest wilderness, **LEWISBURG** is the archetypal West Virginia town, its few square blocks of old buildings surrounded by rich pastureland, with good roads allowing quick access to the wilder mountain reaches. Originally a frontier outpost during the Indian Wars of the 1770s, Lewisburg was greatly prized during the Civil War for its location at the head of the Greenbrier Valley, but nowadays its attractions are those of a classic American small town, where everyone seems to know everyone else and where the houses and shops have remained in the same hands for generations. In mid-August each year, Lewisburg plays host to the West Virginia State Fair (call ☎304/645-1090 for exact dates).

**Washington Street**, the four-block business district, is lined on both sides by brick-fronted early nineteenth-century houses, and makes for pleasant wandering; no. 106 has been a two-chair barber shop for over a hundred years. A block away, in a small park at 200 N Jefferson St, stands the oldest surviving structure in Lewisburg, a rough-hewn limestone shed built in 1770 to protect the still-flowing freshwater spring.

The **visitor center**, 105 Church St (Mon–Fri 9am–5pm, Sat 10am–4pm; ☎304/645-1000 or 1-800/833-2068), hands out walking tour maps of the town and can suggest driving tours around Greenbrier Valley. It can also put you in touch with various cozy **hotels**, such as the *General Lewis Inn*, 301 E Washington St (☎304/645-2600 or 1-800/628-4454; ⑨), which also has a fine **restaurant**.

Just east of Lewisburg, outside the faded spa of **WHITE SULPHUR SPRINGS**, two dozen US presidents have escaped the pressures of politics in *The Greenbrier* (☎304/536-1110 or 1-800/624-6070; ⑨). The grandest and plushest hotel in West Virginia, it's five-star all the way, from the pillared entrance hall to the 6500 acres of lush grounds and golf courses.

## The New River Gorge

One of West Virginia's most spectacular river canyons, the **New River Gorge** lies just thirty miles west of Lewisburg along I-64. Stretching for over fifty miles, and now protected as a national park, the thousand-foot cleft was carved through the limestone West Virginia mountains by the New River – despite its name, one of the oldest rivers in North America. Apart from one daily train (see below), there's no easy access to most of the gorge – to see it, you have to get out on the water, with the help of any of over fifty professional rafting companies; but visitor centers located near the most impressive spots give details of recreation opportunities. Just off US-19 in **Fayetteville**, the **Canyon Rim visitor center** sits alongside the New River Gorge Bridge (June–Aug daily 9am–8pm; Sept–May daily 8am–5pm; ☎304/574-2115), a single-span steel arch that rises nine hundred feet above the river; the smaller **Grandview visitor center** is located at an elbow bend in the river, five miles north of I-64 near Beckley (same hours; ☎304/763-3715).

Fortunately for car-less travelers, Amtrak **trains** from Washington DC pass right through the gorge on one of the most stunning railway journeys in the East. Though the ride itself is memorable enough, for a close-up look you can get off at the southern end of the gorge at the c.1900 railroad town of **HINTON**. The train's only stop, it's a fascinating, if somewhat dilapidated remnant of the glory days of the railroads. An almost perfectly preserved purpose-built company town – the National Park Service intends someday to restore it as a living museum – it is beautifully sited, with brick-paved streets angling up from the water, lined by dozens of grand civic buildings as well as row after row of slowly decaying workers' houses. A walking tour map of Hinton is available from the Chamber of Commerce, 206 Temple St (☎304/466-5420).

Although the town has definitely seen better days, Hinton still makes a workable base for visitors to the gorge, with a pair of budget **motels**, the Coast-to-Coast (☎304/466-2040; ②) and the *Sandman* (☎304/466-1700; ③), and a couple of riverfront taverns on Hwy-20 just south of town. Local **river-rafting** firms include New River Tours (☎304/466-2288 or 1-800/292-0880) and Cantrell Canoes (☎304/466-0595 or 1-800/470-RAFT), both charging $45–75 per person for trips through the gorge.

## Charleston

After leaving the gorge, the New River flows west into the Ohio and eventually the Mississippi, but not before passing through **CHARLESTON**, West Virginia's state capital and largest city. Charleston isn't a place many people set out to visit, mainly because there's not very much to see or do: the riverfront **state capitol**, designed by Lincoln Memorial architect Cass Gilbert and completed in 1932, is pleasant enough, with a small monument to black activist Booker T Washington in its grounds, but nothing really grabs you. The **West Virginia Cultural Center** (Mon–Fri 9am–8pm, Sat & Sun 1–5pm; free), in the same compound as the capitol, showcases traditional West Virginian culture, especially during the annual **Vandalia Festival**, Appalachia's largest celebration of folk arts and crafts, held on Memorial Day weekend and featuring lively bluegrass music and tall-tale-telling contests. A shop in the lobby of the Cultural Center sells a wide selection of local crafts, while the basement is given over to an informative museum on the state's history.

There are three hundred very central **rooms** at the *Elk River Town Center Inn*, 2 Kanawha Blvd E (☎304/343-4521 or 1-800/765-6566; ③), which also has a sauna and swimming pool, and motels abound on the interstates. *General Seafood*, 213 Broad St (Tues–Sat; ☎304/343-5671), is a restaurant conveniently attached to a fish market. On the western edge of downtown, almost alongside I-64 between Lee and Quarrier streets, the gleaming new **Charleston Civic Center** mall is the liveliest area to while away a couple of hours.

# MARYLAND

Founded as the sole Catholic colony in strongly Protestant America, and isolated as the northernmost slave state, **MARYLAND** has always been unusual. Within its small but irregular area, it ranges from the frantic, boardwalk beaches of **Ocean City** to sleepy fishing villages of the **Chesapeake Bay**, and the bustling urban center of **Baltimore** to Appalachian hill country. Once one of the world's most productive fishing areas, the Chesapeake has recently been brought back from the brink of complete annihilation due to pollution and overfishing. Its abundant oyster stocks are a thing of the past, but legendary **soft-shell blue crabs** and sweet rockfish are more plentiful than ever, and now support a diverse, decentralized economy, buoyed by the hundreds of weekend watermen who cruise from one to another of its colonial-era towns.

Maryland's heritage isn't quite as obvious as Virginia's, with nowhere near as many historical sites, but it boasts plenty of firsts for the United States, including the first Catholic Cathedral, gas-lit street and telegraph line between Baltimore and Washington DC. Kent Island on Maryland's **Eastern Shore** was the third permanent English settlement (behind Jamestown and Plymouth Rock) in 1631. And during the War of 1812, the British forces attempted a last-ditch effort to wrest back the colonies, in which they burned down much of Washington DC and moved onto the shipyards of Baltimore. In a valiant battle, they were staved off at **Fort McHenry**; the fort's resistance inspired an onlooker, Francis Scott Key, to write the words to the United States' national anthem, **The Star-Spangled Banner**.

Maryland's largest city is the busy port of **Baltimore**, a quirky and engaging metropolis with a revitalized urban waterfront, thriving cultural scene and eclectic neighborhoods that characterize its diverse residents. **Western Maryland** stretches over a hundred miles to the Appalachian foothills, its rolling farmlands noteworthy chiefly for the Civil War battlefield at **Antietam**. Just twenty miles south of Baltimore, along the Chesapeake Bay, picturesque **Annapolis** has served as Maryland's capital since 1694. Some of the state's most worthwhile destinations, from the pretty fishing and yachting town of **St Michaels** to the untouched wilderness of **Assateague Island**, are across the Chesapeake Bay on the eastern shore, connected to the rest of the state by the US-50 bridge but otherwise still a world apart – except for the sprawling resort of **Ocean City**.

## Getting around Maryland

The best way to get around Maryland is by **boat**, sailing around the gorgeous Chesapeake Bay. If you lack either the money or the good luck needed to do this, you can hop aboard the *Chesapeake Flyer* **catamaran** (☎304/639-7241), which cruises the bay from Baltimore to Annapolis and the eastern shore towns of St Michaels and Rock Hall. **Cycling** is also a good option, especially on the eastern shore, where the roads are wide-shouldered and little-traveled, winding through cornfields from one colonial-era hamlet to another – the state tourist office (see p.20) puts out an excellent free map of the safest and most scenic routes. Baltimore is on the main Amtrak line between New York, Philadelphia and Washington DC, and is linked by regular buses with Annapolis.

# Baltimore

> *I would never want to live anywhere but Baltimore. You can look far and wide, but you'll never discover a stranger city with such extreme style. It's as if every eccentric in the South decided to move north, ran out of gas in Baltimore, and decided to stay.*
>
> John Waters, *Shock Value*

**BALTIMORE** is among the more enjoyable stops on the East Coast, and its closely knit neighborhoods and historic quarters provide an engaging backdrop to many diverse attractions – like the Inner Harbor's **National Aquarium**, Pier 6 Concert Pavilion and Power Plant entertainment complex along its celebrated **waterfront** – and top-rated **museums**, like the Walters Art Gallery and child-oriented Port Discovery interactive museum, which cover everything from fine arts through black history to urban archeology. That Baltimore has been home to such diverse figures as writers Edgar Allan Poe and Anne Tyler and civil rights activists Frederick Douglass and Thurgood Marshall goes some way to explaining its sometimes bizarrely varied character, but it's still hard to pin down exactly what makes it such an engaging city to visit, and to live in.

## Arrival, information and getting around

The spacious, modern **Baltimore-Washington International Airport** (BWI), ten miles south of the city center and 25 miles northeast of DC, is one of the busier East Coast hubs. Airport Shuttle **vans** ($13–18 one-way, $20 round-trip; ☎410/821-5387 or 1-800/BLUE-VAN) into Baltimore leave the terminal every twenty minutes, taking half an hour to reach downtown. **Taxis** cost around $20. Amtrak **trains** (☎1-800/872-7245 or USA-RAIL) stop every hour or so at the restored **Pennsylvania Station** (commonly known as Penn Station), half a mile north of downtown at 1525 N Charles St, while **MARC** commuter trains (☎410/539-5000 or 1-800/325-RAIL), operating weekdays from DC, stop at BWI airport before continuing on to Penn (23 daily; $5.75 one-way, $10.25 round-trip). Greyhound **buses** stop on the west side of downtown at 210 W Fayette St, but be careful in this area at night since it borders on the rougher part of the city.

Pick up free maps and the seasonal *Quick Guide* at the **Baltimore Area Convention and Visitors Association**, on the main jetty at the Inner Harbor (☎410/837-4636 or 1-800/282-6632), or from its booths at the airport and train station.

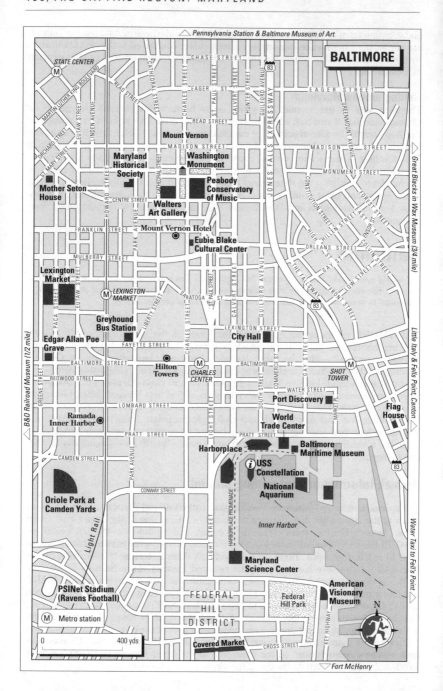

△ Pennsylvania Station & Baltimore Museum of Art

**BALTIMORE**

STATE CENTER

Ⓜ

CHASE STREET

EAGER ST

READ STREET

EAGER STREET

Mount Vernon

MADISON STREET

Maryland Historical Society

Washington Monument

Peabody Conservatory of Music

Mother Seton House

CENTRE STREET

Walters Art Gallery

Mount Vernon Hotel ◉

FRANKLIN STREET

Eubie Blake Cultural Center

MULBERRY STREET

Lexington Market

Ⓜ LEXINGTON MARKET

SARATOGA ST

ORLEANS ST

GAY ST

Greyhound Bus Station

LEXINGTON STREET

Edgar Allan Poe Grave

FAYETTE STREET

City Hall

BALTIMORE STREET

Hilton Towers ◉

Ⓜ CHARLES CENTER

BALTIMORE ST

SHOT TOWER

Ⓜ

REDWOOD STREET

WATER STREET

Port Discovery

Flag House

Ramada Inner Harbor ◉

LOMBARD STREET

World Trade Center

PRATT STREET

PRATT STREET

CAMDEN STREET

Harborplace

Baltimore Maritime Museum

ⓘ USS Constellation

Oriole Park at Camden Yards

CONWAY STREET

National Aquarium

Inner Harbor

Maryland Science Center

American Visionary Museum

PSINet Stadium (Ravens Football)

FEDERAL

HILL

DISTRICT

Federal Hill Park

N

Ⓜ Metro station

0        400 yds

Covered Market

CROSS STREET

▽ Fort McHenry

B&O Railroad Museum (1/2 mile)

Great Blacks in Wax Museum (3/4 mile)

Little Italy & Fell's Point, Canton

Water Taxi to Fell's Point

## City transportation

Because the city is so compact – everything of interest is within a mile of the center – you could get around quite happily on foot. A **water taxi** nips between the Inner Harbor and more than forty area attractions, including the National Aquarium, Fell's Point, the Civil War Museum and Canton – an all-day ticket includes a trolley ride to Fort McHenry (April–Oct Mon–Fri 10am–11pm, Sat & Sun 10am–midnight; Nov–March Mon–Fri 11am–6pm, Sat & Sun 10am–11pm; all-day pass $4.50; ☎410/563-3901 or 1-800/658-8947). Several other operators run **harbor cruises**, including the *Baltimore Patriot*, which docks next to the visitor center (April–Oct; 5 daily, first at 11am; $6.50). The city-operated **MTA** bus, subway and light-rail system ($1.35, day passes $3; ☎410/539-5000) is more useful for commuters than for visitors, but runs from 6am (8am at weekends) until midnight. On buses, have the exact change ready. **Taxi** companies include Yellow Cab (☎410/685-1212) and Royal Cab (☎410/327-0330).

## Accommodation

Unfortunately, Baltimore has few budget options since the city's only youth hostel shut down, but the usual chain **hotels** provide moderately priced accommodation downtown. A more pleasant alternative – and certainly worth the price if barhopping is on your agenda – are the quaint **B&B's** clustered around the historic waterfront area of Fell's Point. The Maryland Reservation Center (☎410/269-7550 or 1-800/654-9303) lists area inns and rooms in private homes from $50 per night.

**Admiral Fell Inn**, 888 S Broadway (☎410/522-7377 or 1-800/292-4667). Nicely restored historic hotel in the heart of Fell's Point, with breakfast and free parking. ⑨.

**Celie's Waterfront B&B**, 1714 Thames St (☎410/522-2323 or 1-800/432-0184). Seven exquisite rooms, some with private balcony, and a rooftop deck with superb views of Fell's Point harbor. Celie is a welcoming and knowledgeable host, and a continental breakfast is included in the price. ⑥–⑧.

**Days Inn Inner Harbor**, 100 Hopkins Place (☎410/576-1000 or 1-800/DAYSINN). Standard hotel chain with cheaper rates than the rest and a central location within walking distance to most sights, including Harborplace. ③/④.

**Hilton and Towers**, 20–30 W Baltimore St (☎410/539-8400). Plush downtown hotel, two blocks from the Inner Harbor. ⑥.

**The Inn at Government House**, 1125 N Calvert St (☎410/539-0566). Elaborate Victorian mansion with antique-filled rooms, and breakfast included. The mayor of Baltimore is a regular in the splendid dining room. Substantially cheaper Oct–May. ④–⑥.

**Mount Vernon Hotel**, 24 W Franklin St (☎410/727-2000 or 1-800/245-5256). With comfortable rooms and a great location at a flat $66 (incl. tax), the *Mount Vernon* has taken over for the defunct youth hostel. Book ahead in summer. ④.

## Downtown Baltimore

When the whole of **downtown Baltimore** burned to the ground in 1904, everything from the waterfront to Mount Vernon was destroyed, except for the domed 1867 **City Hall** at 100 N Holiday St. And though it wasn't a place to spend much time a few years ago, Baltimore has undergone a dramatic face-lift, especially in the **Inner Harbor** area. The old power plant station is now outfitted with the country's first *ESPNZone* sports bar/restaurant and gaming center, as well as a Barnes & Noble bookstore and *Hard Rock Café*. Injected with new restaurants and bars, **Harborplace** – originally a tourist magnet for shopping – is now a pleasant stroll along the brick-lined waterfront, with attractions like the National Aquarium, Science Center and Baltimore-built Navy frigate *USS Constellation*, not to mention its walking proximity to the two **sports stadiums**, where baseball and football fans can meet for a pre-game meal or post-game drink.

West of the central **Charles Street** – where you'll find the main cluster of business-es, restaurants and cafes – is Baltimore's original **shopping** district, now in decline as consumers head for the huge Harborplace Mall (see below). Though many of the premises are boarded up and abandoned, there are a few remaining, including the old-est and loudest of the city's covered markets, **Lexington Market**, at the center of which *Faidley's* is the best (and cheapest) place to sample oysters, clams, crabs and other Chesapeake Bay produce, though not the safest place to linger, even in daylight. The surrounding streets can be threatening even during the day, so it's best to stick with the crowds after leaving the market.

Three blocks up, at 600 N Paca St, the **Mother Seton House** (Sat & Sun 1–4pm; free) is a small, late eighteenth-century brick house, now a museum, where **Elizabeth Seton**, the first American woman to achieve sainthood, founded the Daughters of Charity Catholic order.

Just south of the market, **Westminster Church** was built in 1852 on top of the main Baltimore cemetery, and many ornate tombs now stand in dark catacombs underneath. Among the prominent citizens buried here is **Edgar Allan Poe**, who lived in Baltimore for three years in the 1830s, marrying his thirteen-year-old cousin and beginning a career in journalism before moving on to Richmond, Virginia. In 1849, while passing through Baltimore, Poe was found incoherent in a polling place and died soon after-wards. In 1875 his remains were moved from a pauper's grave and entombed within the stone memorial that stands along Green Street on the north side of the church.

Much more fun than either of these is the narrow brick rowhouse where baseball great **Babe Ruth** was born in 1895, at 216 Emory St (☎410/727-1539; April–Oct daily 10am–5pm; Nov–March daily 10am–4pm; 10am–7pm on days when the Orioles have a home game; $6). Filled to bursting point with photographs, film clips and baseball memorabilia, it not only traces the life and achievements of the much-loved home run hitter, but also serves as an enjoyable introduction to the game and its per-sonalities.

Appropriately enough, the beautiful baseball stadium of the Baltimore Orioles, **Oriole Park at Camden Yards**, is just two blocks west, on the site of the old railroad terminus at Camden Yards (for tickets to a game, phone Ticketmaster ☎410/481-7328). Guided tours of the ballpark cost $5 (daily April–Sept; last tour 2pm; information on ☎410/547-6234), leaving from the ticket office at Eutaw and Camden streets, and tick-ets can only be purchased in person. The centenary of the Babe's birth was marked by the unveiling of a bronze statue in the summer of 1995; see if you can spot the mistake, which was immediately picked up on by hardcore baseball buffs.

Just next door, looking very much like the mother ship just landed, is the absurdly named PSI Net Stadium – home to the **Baltimore Ravens** football team – which opened its 68,400 seats to a professional football team-hungry crowd in September 1998. Tickets can be purchased through Ticketmaster (☎410/481-7328), and tours are offered daily (☎410/261-RAVE).

## The Inner Harbor and the National Aquarium

Sooner or later, if you're in Baltimore you're bound to be drawn down to the **Inner Harbor**, a success story of urban regeneration. The rotting wharves and derelict warehouses that stood here through the 1970s have been replaced by the sparkling steel-and-glass **Harborplace** shopping mall, crammed with thriving restaurants like the *Cheesecake Factory*, *Wayne's BBQ* and seafood specialty, *Phillips*, as well as sports souvenirs and bric-a-brac shops that swarm day and night with tourists and locals. Nothing here dates from before the rebuilding, but it's still quite an enjoyable place, the waterfront promenade enlivened by busking guitar players and the occasional fire-eating juggler.

To lend an air of authenticity, remnants from the city's proud maritime past have been assembled in the Inner Harbor, including the graceful **USS Constellation** (daily 10am–6pm; ☎410/539-1797; $6), an eighteenth-century, Baltimore-built frigate that was the first ship in the US Navy, and which has just undergone a $9 million renovation. Another collection of ships – a Coast Guard cutter that survived Pearl Harbor, a Chesapeake Bay lightship and a World War II submarine – and a charming lighthouse make up the **Baltimore Maritime Museum** (Sun–Thurs 10am–5pm, Fri & Sat 10am–6pm; $5.50) on the next pier.

## The National Aquarium

Far and away the biggest tourist attraction in Baltimore – on national holidays it rivals Walt Disney World as the most popular destination in the US – the **National Aquarium** (July & Aug daily 9am–8pm; Sept–Oct & Mar–June Sat–Thurs 9am–5pm, Fri 9am–8pm; Nov–Feb Sat–Thurs 10am–5pm, Fri 10am–8pm; always open for 2hr after last admission; $14) is certainly well worth seeing, so long as you avoid the weekend throngs. The main exhibition building, a rather gray, 1970s concrete space with a confusing jumble of escalators and ramps, rises in levels from a tankful of bat rays past a simulated South Pacific reef up to the rooftop rainforest garden. From here, another ramp winds down past the **Open Ocean Exhibit**, which features a number of slow-moving sharks.

While the displays in the main building are generally educational, if not all that innovative or thought-provoking, the separate **Marine Mammal Pavilion**, at the end of an adjacent pier, is a lot more entertaining: this is where the aquarium's trained **dolphins** and beluga **whales** are put through their paces. Half-hour shows are every ninety minutes, with the best views to be had from either side, where transparent acrylic panels allow you to watch the animals above and below the water as they run the gamut of tail-walking, breaching and spitting water into the audience. A slithery **snake** exhibit has recently been added, and judging from the squeals of onlookers, it's a hit as well.

Incidentally, this is a privately run, profit-making institution – a clever Maryland politician had a special decree passed in Congress so that it could be called the National Aquarium.

# Mount Vernon

Baltimore's most elegant quarter is just north of downtown on the shallow rise known as **Mount Vernon**, where a couple of good museums sit among rows of eighteenth-century brick townhouses. It takes its name from the country home of George Washington, whose likeness tops the 165ft marble column of the central **Washington Monument**, in a small leafy park next to the aspirational spire of the sham-Gothic Mount Vernon Methodist Church at Charles Street and Monument Place. You can climb the monument for a great view over the city, but it opens only on random days.

At the foot of the monument, the solemn stone facade of the Peabody Conservatory of Music hides one of the city's best interior spaces: the beautiful, skylit atrium of the **Peabody Library** (Mon–Fri 9am–3pm; free). Five tiers of intricate wrought-iron balconies rise above ground-floor displays of sixteenth-century books, including a wonderful illustrated 1555 edition of Boccaccio's *Decameron* and a 1493 printing of the *Nuremburg Chronicles*. Two blocks west, the **Maryland Historical Society museum** (Tues–Fri 10am–5pm, Sat 9am–5pm, closed Sun; $4, free on Sat 9–11am) has a fairly tame collection of portraits of Maryland society and documents tracing local history, though its antique-filled chambers give a strong sense of the maritime wealth created here through nineteenth-century trade. A small room off the lobby holds some nifty models of Chesapeake Bay boats, and upstairs the "War of 1812 Gallery" displays the original manuscript of the lyrics to *The Star-Spangled Banner*.

## Walters Art Gallery

Baltimore's best museum, the **Walters Art Gallery** at 600 N Charles St, a block south of the Washington Monument, provides a comprehensive survey of art from ancient statuary to French Impressionist painting (Tues–Fri 10am–4pm, Sat & Sun 11am–5pm; open the first Thurs of every month until 8pm; $5, free Sat 11am–1pm and first Thurs of month 5–8pm). Its core is a large sculpture court, modeled upon an Italian Renaissance palazzo, beyond which modern galleries show off Greek and Roman antiquities, medieval illuminated manuscripts, Islamic ceramics and some very fine Byzantine silver. The top floor has the oddest organization, with pre-Columbian stone carvings displayed in a narrow corridor, at the end of a grand hall filled with late nineteenth-century paintings, including Manet's beer-drinking *At the Cafe*.

Almost everything on show was bought by William Walters, one of the first US collectors of **Chinese** and **Southeast Asian** art. The restored **Hackerman House** holds some especially fine pieces, including a roomful of Chinese jade figurines, a Ming dynasty handscroll, some lovely Japanese prints and a pair of polychrome and gilt temple doors, carved to look like peacock feathers. A seventh-century lacquered wood statue of a svelte Buddha is perhaps the oldest such image in the world.

## The Flag House and 1812 Museum and Little Italy

A quarter of a mile east of downtown and the Inner Harbor, across the busy Falls Expressway, the intriguing **Flag House and 1812 Museum** (Tues–Sat 10am–4pm; last tour at 3.30pm; $4) was where in 1813 Mary Pickersgill sewed the 30ft by 45ft US flag whose presence at the harbor fort attack inspired Francis Scott Key to write *The Star-Spangled Banner*. The actual banner is now in the Museum of American History in Washington DC (see p.404), but the house is full of other such patriotic tributes.

The densely tangled streets of **Little Italy**, still a strongly Italian neighborhood, spread to the south and east. Besides dozens of usually very good restaurants and cafes, the area holds plenty of Baltimore's trademark stone-fronted rowhouses, almost all with highly polished marble steps. As a sort of traditional local substitute for air conditioning, in the heat of summer residents move their furniture outdoors, thereby turning each entire street into an extended living room.

## Fell's Point and Canton

Beyond Little Italy, separated from the renovated Inner Harbor by acres of derelict wharves and warehouses, stands Baltimore's oldest and liveliest quarter, **Fell's Point**. Projecting into the main harbor, its deepwater frontage made it the heart of the city's extensive shipbuilding industry; the shipyards are long gone, but many old bars and pubs have hung on to form one of the best nightlife districts in the country. Specific places of interest are hard to pinpoint, though the **Pink Flamingoes** junk shop owned and run by Edith Massey, inspiration for many of John Waters' offbeat films, was at 728 S Broadway, a block from the water; it's now a novelty shop specializing in Divine memorabilia. The now scrapped NBC cop drama, *Homicide*, also called this area home for a while, using the abandoned police station and local coffee shops as a backdrop.

**Canton** is also an area awakening to new businesses and restaurants, quickly rivaling Fell's Point and Federal Hill for top billing in nightly entertainment. Heading east from Fell's Point, you'll see the first wave of trendy restaurants and bookstore cafes along Boston Street, but the main concentration of bars and eateries surround the square off O'Donnell Street.

## Other Baltimore attractions

The city's newest museum, designated by Congress as "America's official National Museum, Repository, and Education Center for the Best in original, self-taught artistry," is the **American Visionary Art Museum**, 800 Key Hwy (Tues–Sun 10am–6pm; $6), which holds an array of creatively displayed art handcrafted from everyday objects such as sand and stone; there's also a good organic cafe on site.

The **B&O Railroad Museum**, housed in an 1830 passenger station at 901 W Pratt St, just under a mile west of the Inner Harbor (daily 10am–5pm; $6.50), commemorates the first large-scale railroad in the US, founded in 1827. It holds dozens of ornate carriages, including some wacky parasol-covered early models, and row upon row of locomotives, from steam engines to sleek 1940s diesels.

Perhaps Baltimore's most unusual museum is about a mile northeast of the center, in an old fire station off Broadway at 1601 E North Ave. The **Great Blacks in Wax Museum** (mid-Jan to mid-Oct Tues–Sat 9am–6pm, Sun noon–6pm; mid-Oct to mid-Jan Tues–Sat 9am–5pm, Sun noon–5pm; $5.75) uses wax models to illustrate black history, from Egyptian pharaohs and early Muslims through to Dr Martin Luther King Jr, Marcus Garvey and Malcolm X. The models are posed in prop-filled dioramas – Rosa Parks being dragged off a Montgomery bus, for example, stands across from a pair of Jim Crow-era drinking fountains, a spotless enamel one labeled "Whites Only" and a rusty spigot for "Colored People." Upstairs, figures in the Maryland Room include Baltimore-born ragtime piano player and composer Eubie Blake, and blues diva Billie Holiday, who was born and raised on Dallas Street just around the corner.

Further out on the north side, at the top of Charles Street, two miles from downtown (bus #3), are the pseudoclassical modern galleries of the **Baltimore Museum of Art** (Wed–Fri 11am–5pm, Sat & Sun 11am–6pm; $5.50, free on first Thurs of the month). As well as great Italian and Dutch works by Botticelli, Raphael, Rembrandt and Van Dyck, an overview of contemporary art spotlights Gilbert and George's *Hellish* self-portrait. One gallery in the West Wing is devoted to Warhol, while the American Wing holds furniture and decorative arts, as well as paintings. The highlight is the Cone Collection of works by Delacroix, Degas, Cézanne and Picasso, with over a hundred drawings and paintings by Henri Matisse.

A short walk south of the Inner Harbor, the predominantly residential **Federal Hill District** is a great place to escape from the crowds. Lined with interesting shops, its main thoroughfare, Light Street, leads to the **Cross Street Market**, which, though smaller than its downtown counterpart, is considerably more welcoming, and boasts some excellent delis, seafood bars and fruit stalls. **Federal Hill Park** in the northeast is a quiet public space with fine views over the harbor and the downtown cityscape – in the summer months, it's a popular spot for sunset canoodling.

As part of the city's regeneration, the decrepit fish market across from the Harbor at 35 Market Place was relaunched as the gleaming **Port Discovery** (Tues–Sun 10am–5.30pm; $10), an interactive children's museum packed to the ceiling with hands-on exhibits and – surprisingly – fun for visitors of all ages.

## Eating

Baltimore is affectionately known as **Crab City**, and locals will argue to their graves that Maryland produces the best steamed crabs this side of heaven. The city has dozens of reasonably priced fresh **seafood** places, as well as the usual range of diners and more than a dozen good family-run restaurants side by side in Little Italy, just east of the Inner Harbor. Canton holds a wider selection, ranging from Irish to Mexican, while Fell's Point boasts numerous vegetarian and waterfront restaurants and even high tea at *Bertha's* pub. The Colonnade Market in the Light Street Pavilion of **Harborplace Mall** holds a wide selection of fast-food outlets, including several *Phillips* counters offering steamed clams, soft-shell crab sandwiches and so on. Otherwise, the city's restaurants tend to be unpretentious and family oriented, with prices lower than elsewhere.

**Bertha's**, 734 S Broadway (☎410/327-5795). Casual, inexpensive but stylish seafood restaurant, tucked away behind a tiny Fell's Point bar.

**Da Mimmo**, 217 S High St (☎410/727-6876). Intimate, romantic Little Italy cafe, with live piano music, a wide-ranging menu, and even a complimentary limo service from any downtown location. Main dishes $9–15.

**Donna's Coffee Bar**, 2 W Madison at Charles (☎410/385-0180). Espressos and pastries in elegant Mount Vernon, with sidewalk seating.

**Helmand**, 806 N Charles St (☎410/752-0311). Inexpensive but chic dinner-only Afghan restaurant in Mount Vernon. Plenty of lamb dishes, plus *aushak* (leek-filled vegetarian ravioli) and the delicious *kaddo borawani*, a fried-pumpkin appetizer.

**John Steven Ltd**, 1800 Thames St (☎410/327-5561). Fresh seafood, including good sushi – $5 for 6 pieces – in a cozy Fell's Point pub.

**Louie's Bookstore Café**, 518 N Charles St (☎410/962-1224). Busy Mount Vernon bar which also does a range of good $6–10 meals. Open late, with regular live music.

**Obrycki's**, 1727 E Pratt St (☎410/732-6399). Baltimore's best and longest established fish restaurant, with delicious fresh crabs at premium prices. Closed in winter.

**Women's Industrial Exchange Restaurant**, 333 N Charles St (☎410/685-4388). Excellent-value 1940s cafe with full breakfasts for under $2, huge plates of chicken gumbo for $4, and great crabcakes.

## Drinking and nightlife

Baltimore's waterfront **Fell's Point** neighborhood may well have the densest assembly of drinking places in the US. One bar after another lines up along Broadway and the many smaller side streets; almost all feature some sort of entertainment, usually live bands, and on summer nights the pavements are packed solid with revelers. But crowds tired of long wait lines are heading to the up-and-coming area around Canton, which offers plenty of venues – and more room – for the thirsty. The city's highbrow culture is concentrated northwest of the center, in the Mount Royal Avenue area, home to both the **Meyerhoff Symphony Hall** (☎410/783-8000) and the **Lyric Opera House** (☎410/727-6000).

For a full rundown of what's on and where, pick up a copy of the excellent free *City Paper*, at newsstands and book and record stores all over town.

**Bohagers/Parrot Island**, 515 S Eden St (☎410/563-7220). Raucous bar and grill, with country/R&B bands several times a week and crabcakes every night.

**Buddy's Jazz Pub**, 313 N Charles St (☎410/332-4200). Evening jazz, for the price of a drink or two.

**Cat's Eye Pub**, 1730 Thames St (☎410/276-9085). Cozy, crowded bar, with a good range of beers and live music nightly.

**Eight by Ten**, 10 E Cross St (☎410/625-2000). Just west of Inner Harbor, this Federal Hill joint puts on live bands every night, with the emphasis on indie rock and reggae.

**Max's on Broadway**, 735 S Broadway (☎410/675-6297). Huge corner venue with a very long bar, requisite pool tables and a rainbow of beer taps. Upstairs is a more refined atmosphere in the leather upholstered cigar lounge. Live bands play occasionally.

**Mount Royal Tavern**, 1204 W Mount Royal Ave (☎410/669-6686). Welcoming bar, popular with art students as well as nightcapping musicians.

**Sisson's**, 36 E Cross St (☎410/539-2093). A Federal Hill watering hole featuring six handcrafted beers, homemade root beer and Cajun/Creole munchies.

**Wharf Rat Bar**, 801 S Ann St (☎410/276-9034). A well-stocked and convivial bar that packs in a local yuppie crowd.

# Western Maryland

Stretched between West Virginia and the razor-straight Pennsylvania border, western Maryland ranges for some two hundred miles east to west, but is in places well under five miles across. In general, the further west you go, the more mountainous and back-woodsy the feel – with a strong affinity to Maryland's Appalachian neighbors.

Though the countryside is very pretty, specific points of interest are few unless you love to camp and hike. Apart from the Civil War battlefield at **Antietam**, west of the only sizeable town, **Frederick**, the best reason to come is to cycle or hike the footpath of the restored old **Chesapeake and Ohio Canal**, which winds along the Maryland side of the Potomac River from Washington DC for over 180 miles to **Cumberland** in the western mountains. Even further west is the state's largest freshwater lake, **Deep Creek Lake**, popular with watersports enthusiasts and with more than 70,000 acres of public parks and forests surrounding it – some of which makes smooth cross-country skiing during the winter.

## Frederick and around

One of the first towns settled in northwestern Maryland, **FREDERICK**, at the junction of I-70 and I-270 an hour west of Baltimore, was laid out in 1745 by German farmers lured from Pennsylvania by the promise of cheap fertile land. It grew to become a main stopover on the route west to the Ohio Valley, and the bulk of today's tidy town survives from the early 1800s. A **visitor center** (☎301/663-8687 or 1-800/999-3613) at 19 E Church St has walking tour maps of the town, pointing out such places as the **Schifferstadt House** (Tues–Sat 10am–4pm, Sun noon–4pm; donation), just off US-15, a stonewalled farmhouse built in 1753 and largely unaltered since.

According to a romantic poem popular with c.1900 schoolchildren, 95-year-old Barbara Fritchie defiantly waved the US flag while Confederate soldiers marched past her home, the tiny **Barbara Fritchie House** (April–Sept Mon & Thurs–Sun; Oct–Nov Sat & Sun; closed Dec–March) along Carroll Creek on the west side of town. When Winston Churchill passed through, he stopped at the house and recited the poem from memory.

**Camp David**, the mountain retreat used by US presidents since FDR, where Jimmy Carter brought Menachem Begin and Anwar Sadat together in 1978 to sign the historic Camp David accords between Israel and Egypt, is hidden away in the mountains north of Frederick. Nearby **Cunningham Falls State Park** and the **Catoctin Mountain Park** both hold seemingly endless hardwood forests – great for fall color – in the midst of which are numerous preserved remnants of early homesteaders. Pick up details on hiking and camping at the main **visitor center** (daily 10am–4pm; ☎301/663-9388), off Hwy-77 two miles west of US-15.

Besides being a nice detour off the highway, Frederick is a good base for exploring places such as **Antietam** (see below) and **Harpers Ferry** in West Virginia (see p.398). There are **motels** along both I-70 and US-15, and in town the *Tyler Spite House*, 112 W Church St (☎301/831-4455; ⑥), is a pleasant **B&B** in an elegant 1814 mansion. For a bite to **eat**, try the soups and steaks at the *Brown Pelican*, 5 E Church St, or the burgers and steamed crabs at *Cactus Flats*, three miles north off US-15.

## Antietam National Battlefield

The site of the single bloodiest battle in the Civil War, **Antietam National Battlefield** spreads over unaltered farmlands outside the whitewashed and balconied village of

**Sharpsburg.** Here, fifteen miles west of Frederick, on the morning of September 17, 1862, in an effort to consolidate rebel gains after their victory at Manassas, 40,000 troops faced a Union army twice that number. Hours later, some 25,000 from both sides lay dead or dying. The fiercest fighting, and the worst bloodshed, occurred in cornfields to the north; Union general Joseph Hooker recorded: "In the time that I am writing, every stalk of corn in the northern and greater part of the field was cut as closely as could have been done with a knife, and the slain lay in rows precisely as they had stood in their ranks a few moments before."

The battle continued throughout the day without a clear result. It may not have been decisive, but the Confederates' lack of success lost them the support of their erstwhile ally Great Britain, while the Union performance encouraged Lincoln to issue the Emancipation Proclamation. Pick up a brochure and driving tour map of the park at the **visitor center**, a mile north of Sharpsburg off Hwy-65 (daily 8.30am–5pm; ☎301/432-5124). Numerous plaques and memorials have been constructed around the fields, but otherwise the site, with its various farm buildings and country churches, is unchanged, and the entire park serves as a mute but evocative memorial to the conflict.

## Cumberland and the C&O Canal

The only large town in the far west of Maryland, **CUMBERLAND** started life as a coal-mining center in the late 1700s. Often confused with Daniel Boone's Cumberland Gap in southwest Virginia, this Cumberland was also an important trans-Appalachian crossing, but its main place in history is as the terminus of the ill-fated **C&O (Chesapeake and Ohio) Canal**, an impressive engineering feat begun in 1813 but not completed until 1850, by which time the railroads had already made it obsolete.

The **Western Maryland Station Center** (Mon–Fri 9am–5pm, Sat & Sun 10am–4pm; ☎301/777-5905), beside the canal, can provide information on hiking, cycling, canoeing and camping; in summer, the historic trains of the **Western Maryland Scenic Railroad** set off on ninety-minute rides through the surrounding mountains (May–Sept Tues–Sun; Oct daily; Nov–Dec 14 Sat–Sun 11.30am; ☎301/759-4400 or 1-800/872-4650; $16).

About twenty miles before Cumberland, I-68 slices straight through a wedge of sedimentary rock, exposing a dramatic syncline that can be viewed from a platform at the excellent **Sideling Hill Exhibit Center** (☎301/842-2155); there's a special **geologic exhibit** staffed by an on-site geologist, and the views east of the hill from the parking lot are quite stunning.

# Annapolis and southern Maryland

While Baltimore has grown into the state's largest and busiest city, **Annapolis**, Maryland's colonial and current capital, has remained more or less unchanged. Before the US broke free from English rule, this was considered to be one of the most genteel and attractive colonial centers, and though its time-worn streets are now always crowded, Annapolis is still among the more engaging small US cities. Its once-vital Chesapeake Bay **waterfront** now has little of the feel of colonial maritime life, but the real attractions of Annapolis, among its narrow streets, include fine homes, the Beaux Arts campus of the US Naval Academy, and the beautiful state capitol.

If you like the look of Annapolis, and want to get a better feel for the Chesapeake Bay region away from the crowds, head south to places like **St Mary's City** – the first capital of Maryland, completely reconstructed in the 1960s – or **Solomons Island**, one of many small Chesapeake Bay towns that seem not to have changed for decades.

# Annapolis

At the center of **ANNAPOLIS**, overlooking the town's baroque web of streets, the **Maryland State House** (daily 9am–5pm, tours at 11am & 3pm; free) was completed in 1779 and soon after served as an early capitol of the United States. The **Old Senate Chamber**, to the right of the grand entrance hall, is where the Treaty of Paris was ratified in 1784, officially ending the Revolutionary War; a statue of George Washington stands on the spot where he resigned his commission as head of the Continental Army, and displays document the role Annapolis played in the life of the young Republic. Free guided tours are given twice a day, or you can wander around on your own, perhaps stopping by to listen to the proceedings of Maryland's current crop of legislators, who hold court from January to April in the more modern wing to the north of the old building. Also on the grounds of the State House is the cottage-sized **Old Treasury Building**, built in 1735 to hold colonial Maryland's currency reserves.

Grand late eighteenth-century brick homes line the streets of Annapolis, but for substance and grace none surpasses the **Hammond-Harwood House**, two blocks west of the State House at 19 Maryland Ave, off King George Street (Mon–Sat 10am–4pm, Sun noon–4pm; $4). The warm redbrick Palladian villa, which consists of two symmetrical wings connected by a central hall, was built in 1774 to the designs of William Buckland, and is most notable for its beautifully carved decorative woodwork, especially evident in the intricate front doorway. Despite its architectural harmony, the house has had an unfortunate history, the original owner becoming so obsessed with its construction that his fiancée left him, breaking his heart and causing his untimely death at the age of 38; Buckland also died in mysterious circumstances before the house was completed.

Another historic Annapolis mansion, the 1765 **William Paca House**, 186 Prince George St (March–Dec Mon–Sat 10am–4pm, Sun noon–4pm; Jan–Feb Fri & Sat 10am–4pm, Sun noon–4pm; $4), was a downmarket rooming house until the 1960s; it was restored to its period appearance in time for the 1976 Bicentennial, and boasts a splendid formal garden (a parking lot twenty years ago), which you can peer into from King George Street.

Besides such elite manors, dozens of pastel eighteenth-century clapboard cottages and commercial structures fill the narrow streets that run down to the waterfront. Of those that have escaped the gentrifiers, the **Tobacco Prise House**, 4 Pinkney St (by appointment, ☎410/267-7619; $2), is a colonial tobacco warehouse that now sets out to explain the handling and storage of the valuable leaves. Further along, the **Shiplap House**, 18 Pinkney St (Mon–Fri 2–4pm; free), was built in 1715 as a tavern; now it's a small museum of Annapolis history, with a herb garden to the rear containing assorted medicinal plants grown in colonial times.

## The waterfront and US Naval Academy

Although few colonial sites survive along the modern **Chesapeake Bay waterfront** to give a sense of the port's former maritime strength, the rebuilt 1850s dockside city **Market House** is an early nineteenth-century replacement of a colonial warehouse used by the revolutionary army. Today, with its sidewalk cafes and stalls, it's a good spot for people-watching.

The rest of the waterfront is pleasant enough for an afternoon's wandering, especially on summer weekends when the harbor and bay are full of clanging halyards and billowing sails. In among the boat supply shops and harborside bars, the gray stone walls of the **US Naval Academy** (March–Nov daily 9am–5pm; Dec–Feb daily 9am–4pm; free) seem designed to exacerbate the sensory deprivation endured by the over four thousand crew-cut young men and handful of women (all of whom line up in formation outside **King Hall**, the dining commons, every day at noon) who spend four strictly disciplined years here before embarking on careers as naval officers. The moment of transition, at the end of each summer's graduation ceremony, is marked by the traditional "Hat Toss." A small museum holds models of various British and US warships and other naval memorabilia. Superb guided tours of the Academy ($5.50) leave every half-hour from the **Armel-Leftwich Visitor Center** (hours as for Academy) in Halsey Field House, through Gate 1 at the end of King George Street.

### Practicalities

Compared to the rest of Maryland, Annapolis is easy to reach, on Greyhound and MTA (#210) buses from Baltimore. By road it's about half an hour from Washington (via US-50) or Baltimore (via I-97), though parking can be difficult. A trolleybus (75¢) loops around the small and very walkable central area. Annapolis's **visitor center**, 26 West St (Mon–Fri 9am–5pm; ☎410/280-0445), can provide free maps and practical information, including lists of **walking tour** operators; if you'd rather see the city on your own, consider picking up one of the *Historic Annapolis* audio-cassette tours, narrated by newsman Walter Cronkite, from the Maritime Museum at 77 Main St.

Finding a **place to stay** is not usually a problem, though prices are fairly steep. There's a free accommodation bureau (☎1-800/715-1000), or you can choose from **B&Bs** like the central and characterful *Scot-Laur Inn*, 165 Main St (☎410/268-5665; ⑤); the pricier *Prince George Inn*, 232 Prince George St (☎410/263-6418; ⑤); or the small *Corner Cupboard*, 30 Randall St (☎410/263-4970; ③). Dozens of motels are to be found along US-50 on the west side of town.

**Restaurants** and **bars** are both plentiful and good: the no-frills, 24-hour *Chick and Ruth's Delly*, 165 Main St (☎410/269-6737), does big breakfasts and has a booth on permanent reserve for Maryland's governor; the ritzier *Harry Browne's*, 66 State Circle (☎410/263-4332), is popular with politicos and expense-account lobbyists. You can tuck into fish and chips while people-watching from the sunny porch of the waterfront *Middleton Tavern*, 2 Market Space (☎410/263-3323), one of the city's oldest buildings. The *King of France Tavern* in the historic *Maryland Inn*, 16 Church Circle (☎410/263-2641), puts on live jazz, while *Marmaduke's*, 301 Severn Ave (☎410/269-5420), is a waterfront bar popular with the yachting brigade, who turn out to watch videos of themselves racing around the bay.

## Southern Maryland

The little-visited back roads (there are no big roads) of **southern Maryland** in many ways resemble the agricultural Deep South. All along both main routes, US-301 from Baltimore and Hwy-2 from Annapolis, lush fields of corn and tobacco, dotted with ageing wooden barns, fill the arable lands in scattered parcels, and narrow, tree-lined country lanes open suddenly onto rivers or the broad Chesapeake Bay.

### Solomons Island

Towns in southern Maryland are few and far between, but a couple are worth searching out. The old shipbuilding community of **SOLOMONS ISLAND**, sixty miles south of Annapolis via Hwy-2, is not actually an island but a narrow two-mile peninsula between the Patuxent River and Back Creek Bay. The entire waterfront is dotted with cozy **B&Bs**, like the *Locust Inn* (☎410/326-9817; ③), and fresh seafood **restaurants** – the *Lighthouse Inn* (☎410/326-2444) on the bay side, and *Solomon's Pier* (☎410/326-2424) across the road both have sunny outdoor decks – but the best reason to stop is the **Calvert Marine Museum** (daily 10am–5pm; $5), on Hwy-2 at the north end of town. This focuses specifically on the Patuxent River, and on the unique estuarine ecosystem of the Chesapeake Bay tidal areas. Its two protected marshland wildlife areas, one saltwater and one freshwater, can be explored on raised walkways. Inside the main building, exhibits follow the development of local boat-building and commercial fishing, and dozens of historic boats are on show. In summer, an old oyster bay-boat, the *William B Tennison*, leaves from the museum dock on hour-long **cruises** (May–Oct Wed–Sun at 2pm; $5) around the bay.

### St Mary's City and Point Lookout State Park
The reconstructed village of **ST MARY'S CITY** is well worth a look, both for its lovely position and the exemplary attention to detail in all the buildings and archeological sites. Set on a broad Potomac cove near the southern tip of the Maryland peninsula, twenty miles south of Solomons Island, St Mary's City is a small-scale but accurate reconstruction of Maryland's first colonial capital, established here in 1634 before being moved to Annapolis sixty years later. The entire complex, including a working tobacco plantation and a replica of the tiny *Maryland Dove* ship on which the first colonists arrived from England, is run as a sort of theme park, complete with costumed tour guides who are approachable and very knowledgeable, even if their English accents need a bit of work (Wed–Sun 10am–5pm; $6.50). Its main feature is a reconstruction of the long-vanished **State House**, where in 1689 Protestant rebels seized control of what had been a Catholic-run colony, but it's all a bit too manicured to provide much sense of history. Nearby, and much more fun, living history **performances** are staged at the *Maryland Dove* dock, which are well acted and sensitive to the fact that this was British America, and long before Independence was even a thought; to a modern American, truly prehistoric.

South from St Mary's City, the very tip of the southern Maryland peninsula was used during the Civil War as a **prisoner-of-war camp** for rebel forces captured at the battle of Gettysburg. In just over a year, from March 1864 to June 1865, more than four thousand died due to the appalling conditions, including some seven hundred Union guards. Most of the Confederate soldiers were buried in a mass grave, now marked by a granite obelisk; the actual camp (the ramparts have been rebuilt and there's a small and somewhat gruesome museum) was a mile south. The point where the Potomac flows into the Chesapeake is a good place to watch the sun rise or set.

# The eastern shore

Maryland's compelling **eastern shore** occupies something over half of the broad Delmarva (*Del*aware, *Mary*land, *Vir*ginia) peninsula that protects the Chesapeake from the open Atlantic. Its miles of back roads are perfectly suited to aimless exploration and sudden discovery, such as coming across the odd wooden farmhouse or tobacco barn marooned in the middle of a field, or an old sailboat tied up at an apparently decrepit dock that springs to life when the fishing craft return. The US-50 bridge/tunnel, built across the Chesapeake Bay in the early 1960s, may have made the eastern shore more accessible, but it hasn't affected its air of somnolence. Quiet country lanes head away from US-50 as it races down to the beach resort of **Ocean City**, to two-hundred-year-old waterfront towns like **Chestertown**, **St Michaels** and **Oxford**.

### Chestertown and Rock Hall
A stopping place for travelers since colonial days, when it was a prime Chesapeake port, **CHESTERTOWN** is the northernmost center on the eastern shore. Stretching west along High Street from the Chester River, it's surprisingly intact, with its fine old riverfront homes, a courthouse square lined with ornate wooden cottages, and a generally languorous feel that makes it a popular weekend escape from Baltimore or DC. Many

of the old houses, like the *Widow's Walk Inn*, 402 High St (☎410/778-6455 or 1-888/778-6455; ⑤), have been converted into **B&Bs**, while others now house top-rated **restaurants** like the *Feast of Reason*, 203 High St (☎410/778-3828; closed Mon), and the swanky dining room of the *Imperial Hotel* (☎410/778-2100) across the street. The **visitor center**, 400 S Cross St (Mon–Fri 9am–4pm, Sat 10am–2pm; ☎410/778-0416), has details of walking and cycling tours.

To the west of town, fifteen miles of country lanes lead down to the wharves and dockside restaurants of **ROCK HALL**, an old fishing port where you can watch the day's catch being unloaded while chewing on crab legs at the bare-bones *Waterman's Crabhouse* (☎410/778-1803) on the main pier. The *Chesapeake Flyer* catamaran service lands here (see p.405), and bikes can be rented from the marina office.

## St Michaels

A contender for prettiest harbor on the Chesapeake Bay, tiny **ST MICHAELS**, twelve miles west of US-50 on Hwy-33, is also one of its oldest ports. Founded during the mid-1600s, it grew into one of colonial America's prime shipbuilding centers; its fast sloops and shallow-draft "bugeyes" evaded British blockades during the Revolutionary War. St Michaels languished as Baltimore bloomed, but since the early 1960s it has been rediscovered, its old buildings now gentrified into art galleries, boutiques and cozy B&Bs.

Some corners survive intact, however; among them the old town green, **St Mary's Square**, a block off the main Talbot Street on Mulberry Street. To get a clear sense of the human and natural history of Chesapeake Bay, head north along the docks to the extensive modern **Chesapeake Bay Maritime Museum** (March–Dec daily 9am–5pm; Jan–Feb Sat & Sun 10am–4pm; $7.50). This focuses on the restored **Hooper Strait Lighthouse**, at the foot of which float a few Chesapeake Bay sailboats – designed to make the most of the bay's shallow waters. Nearby, some two hundred other boats include a Native American dugout canoe, while in the museum workshop skilled artisans and legions of volunteers restore and maintain historic boats using painstaking traditional techniques.

Among St Michaels' revered seafood **restaurants**, the *Crab Claw* (☎410/745-2900; March to mid-Dec) occupies a prime chunk of the waterfront alongside the Maritime Museum and boasts an extensive menu. Though many of its customers turn up for the beer and the views rather than anything else, the prime reason to come is to enjoy one of its huge piles of all-you-can-eat **steamed crabs**. At weekends especially, the rest of the town's wharves and docks are filled with sailors, who flock to restaurant-cum-bars such as the *Town Dock* (☎410/745-5577) and *St Michaels Crab House* (☎410/745-3737), both at the end of Mulberry Street. As a result, **B&Bs** such as the period-furnished *Hambleton Inn*, 202 Cherry St (☎410/745-3350; ⑤), and the *Kemp House Inn*, 412 S Talbot St (☎410/745-2243) charge high rates and tend to be fully booked; for cheaper rooms your choice is restricted to the *St Michaels Motor Inn* (☎410/745-3333 or 1-800/528-1234; ④), a *Best Western* at 1228 S Talbot St on the rather featureless main road into town.

## Tilghman Island

If you want to see the real, workaday Chesapeake, **Tilghman Island**, west from St Michaels across the Knapps Narrows drawbridge (which rules over vehicle traffic and opens for every single boat coming through), was once home to most of the Chesapeake's skipjack fleet. Partly in response to the continued depletion of oyster stocks, the government has made it illegal to harvest oysters except from small, graceful and hopelessly outmoded sailing boats called **skipjacks**, of which there are just a handful still in use. Most are moored at **Dogwood Harbor**, on the east side of the island; during the fall and winter harvest, they unload at the Harrison Oyster Packing Company, at the foot of the bridge. You can buy oysters fresh off the boat, or sample them and other local delicacies at two very good restaurants on either side of the bridge: the *Bay Hundred* (☎410/886-2622) and the more upscale *Bridge Restaurant* (☎410/886-2500). However, many locals and visiting weekend fisherman head straight for *Harrison's*, directly across from the bridge (☎410/886-2121), for a traditional Eastern Shore dinner stacked with corn on the cob and fresh fried chicken.

## Oxford

Just west of US-50, or seven miles south of St Michaels via country lanes and the ferry, the leafy waterfront hamlet of **OXFORD** seems to have slumbered peacefully since colonial days. Along with Annapolis, this was one of the two ports of entry for all colonial Maryland, a role remembered by the reconstructed one-room **Customs House** next to the ferry landing on the north side of town. After Independence, Oxford was all but forgotten; its full-time population is under a thousand and there's hardly any tourist trade. Wandering the quiet streets, however, or lolling on the lawns of the lengthy riverfront promenade, can be quite relaxing and enjoyable. A trip on the small **ferry** across the Tred Avon River, which made its maiden voyage in 1683 and has been in continuous service since 1836, makes for a nice excursion en route to or from St Michaels (every 20min; June to Labor Day Mon–Fri 7am–9pm, Sat & Sun 9am–9pm; Labor Day to mid-Dec & March–June Mon–Fri 7am–sunset, Sat & Sun 9am–sunset; $5 per car, $1 per passenger; ☎410/745-9023).

*Schooner's Landing* (☎410/226-0160) is a friendly, inexpensive seafood **restaurant** with a large deck right on the main harbor, at the end of Tilghman Street; at the *Pier Street Marina & Restaurant* (☎410/226-5411), further south, you can sample fresh crabs in a spectacular waterfront setting. The ancient *Robert Morris Inn*, on Morris Street at The Strand (☎410/226-5111; ⑤), named for the Oxford man who personally financed the Continental Army during the Revolutionary War, serves James Michener's favorite crabcakes. In the larger but less interesting US-50 town of **EASTON**, the ancient *Bishop's House B&B*, 214 Goldsborough St (☎410/820-7290 or 1-800/223-7290; ⑤), provides a comfortable alternative to the highway motels.

## Ocean City

With more than ten miles of broad Atlantic beach, a boisterous boardwalk amusement park and hundreds of thousands of visitors every weekend, **OCEAN CITY** is Maryland's number one summer resort. No matter how you get here, down the coast from Delaware or across the rural eastern shore along US-50, its tower-block hotels and overcrowding will come as a shock. If you're after a quiet weekend by the sea, avoid it like the plague, and take extra care to avoid college vacations.

Ocean City might be good for a day out, or even a long weekend, but it's hard to imagine anyone wanting to stay very long. It is, at least, easy to reach: Carolina Trailways **buses** from DC end up in the southern end of town at Second Street and Hwy-1 (☎410/289-9307). Places to **stay** are plentiful except on summer weekends, and off-season rates are at least half prime-time ones, but pleasant accommodation is rare indeed. The *Summer Place*, a privately run **hostel** near the bus station and boardwalk at 104 Dorchester St (April–Oct; ☎410/289-4542; ②), rents rooms at a flat rate of $18 per person and does not accept reservations; if you're unlucky there, and want a **motel** in the same area, try the *Oceanic* at the south end of Baltimore Street (☎410/289-6498; ③). Alternatives range from the faded seaside grandeur of the *Commander Hotel*, on the boardwalk at 14th Street (☎410/289-6166 or 1-800/543-6986; ④), to the gleaming marble and glass of the *Cocoanut Malorie*, at 60th Street and The Bay (☎410/723-6100 or 1-800/767-6060; ⑦). If you get stuck, the **Chamber of Commerce**, on Hwy-1 at 40th Street (June–Aug Mon–Sat 8am–6pm, Sun 9am–5.30pm; rest of year daily 8.30am–5.30pm; ☎410/289-8181 or 1-800/62-OCEAN), can usually help out.

Apart from the boardwalk fast-food joints and the national franchises along Hwy-1 (there are three all-night *McDonald's*, for example), Ocean City has few good **eating** options. The *Angler Restaurant*, on the bay at Talbot Street (☎410/289-7424), has fresh seafood and an all-you-can-eat salad bar; it also offers nice beers, wild tropical cocktails and nightly live bands. Other **nightspots** include the frenetic *Big Kahuna Surf Club*, 18th and Hwy-1 (☎410/289-6331), and *Terrapin Station*, at 125th and Coastal (☎410/250-0095), which puts on some of the bigger-name bands in town and also serves vegetarian food.

### Assateague Island National Seashore

If you find yourself in the Ocean City area in the peak of summer and want to escape the crowds, head just down the coast to **Assateague Island National Seashore** – a twenty-mile stretch of entirely undeveloped beach and marshland. Until 1933 Assateague Island was attached to Ocean City; then a hurricane drove a wedge between them, and it became a separate barrier island, which is progressively being pushed by the elements back towards the mainland. A further storm in 1962 led to the abandonment of construction plans, under which nine thousand residential lots had been set aside, and instead the island became a national seashore.

The main **visitor center** for Assateague is eight miles from Ocean City, just before the humpback bridge across to the island (☎410/641-3030; $5). If you plan to do any walking, pick up the $1.50 booklet here detailing the park's three main trails. Of these, the **Life of the Marsh Trail** guides you along half a mile of boardwalks through low-lying leeward wetlands, while **Life of the Dunes** is a little longer, and harder going, on the thick white sands just back from the beach. Most visitors, however, come strictly for the beaches themselves, which feel a world away from Ocean City. The state of Maryland provides seashore **camping facilities** at Assateague State Park (☎410/641-2120), but if you want a bit more comfort the best **lodging** is to be found near the southern half of the island, across the Virginia border in **Chincoteague** (see p.391).

# DELAWARE

Though **DELAWARE** has its beauty spots – including some of the mid-Atlantic's best beaches – its tourist boards and PR people have their work cut out. About the only images potential visitors have of the state are negative: Delaware is known for the massive chemical plants of the **Du Pont** Corporation and **Dover Air Force Base**, as well as for tolerating shady business practices – half of America's largest companies have their official bases in this tiny state, thanks to its permissive tax, banking and incorporation laws (there's no sales tax either).

None of the above is likely to make you want to visit, so instead Delaware's promoters emphasize its past – for example, as the first ex-colony to ratify the Constitution, it claims the title of **America's First State**. Dutch whalers established a settlement at the mouth of the Delaware Bay in 1631, and soon afterwards the Swedes built a larger colony at present-day **Wilmington**. The two groups fought among themselves until the British took over in 1664. Delaware was part of neighboring Pennsylvania – Philadelphia is only ten miles north of the present, arching state border – until hiving itself off in 1776.

Much of Delaware's fortunes (and misfortunes) since then can be traced directly to the du Pont family, who, fleeing the wrath of revolutionary France, set up a gunpowder mill that became, and has remained, the main supplier of conventional explosives to the US Government. After World War I, the du Ponts went public and made millions in the stock market frenzies of the Roaring Twenties, since when the company has diversified, its labs inventing such modern essentials as nylon and Cellophane.

The du Ponts built huge mansions for themselves in the **Brandywine Valley** north of Wilmington, near the perfectly preserved old colonial capital, **New Castle**, on the Delaware Bay just five miles south of I-95. Further south, **Dover**, the capital, may not detain you long, but beyond it the small and amiable resorts of **Lewes** and **Rehoboth Beach** mark the northern extent of over twenty miles of unspoiled Atlantic beaches.

### Getting around Delaware

Apart from Wilmington, which is on the main East Coast **train** and **bus** lines, Delaware is hard to get around without a car. Greyhound services are limited to a summer-only route from DC to **Rehoboth**, and local transportation is nonexistent.

I-95 and the New Jersey Turnpike converge at Wilmington, from where US-13 runs south through the state. More often called the **Du Pont Highway**, it was paid for and constructed by the industrialists so that they could ride in comfort between their Wilmington mansions and Dover. A direct car **ferry** connects Cape May, the southern tip of New Jersey and Lewes, at the mouth of the Delaware Bay (see p.424).

## Wilmington and around

**WILMINGTON** may not be the most compelling place in America, but this much-maligned, medium-sized city can make for a refreshing break from the tourist trail: not only does it boast the excellent Delaware Art Museum and some pretty waterside parks, but the surrounding Brandywine Valley holds the manor homes and gardens (and factories) of the First State's First Family, the du Ponts, all open to the public and providing an inside look at America's de facto aristocracy.

If you arrive in Wilmington by train, on the Amtrak line between New York and Washington, you'll pull in to the quirky 1907 terra-cotta station on the somewhat dodgy south side of the city. From here, the two main streets, Market and King, run north for about a mile to the Brandywine River, their partly pedestrianized lengths holding a standard array of stores and other small businesses, as well as a handful of restored eighteenth-century rowhouses clustered around the Georgian **Old Town Hall**, 505 Market St (March–Dec Tues–Fri noon–4pm, Sat 10am–4pm; free), now a small museum of local history. The faceless gray monoliths that tower over the cityscape house the headquarters of hundreds of national companies.

A short walk north of the downtown commercial district, at the top end of Market Street, **Brandywine Park** comes as a welcome relief from the concrete pavements, its grassy knolls lining both banks of the Brandywine River. In the residential districts to the north are some of the city's oldest and poshest houses, many dating from the Revolutionary War, when Wilmington's flour mills fed the American forces. The nearby **Delaware Art Museum**, 2301 Kentmere Parkway (Wed–Sat 10am–5pm, Tues 10am–9pm, Sun noon–5pm; free), has a good range of works by American painters like Thomas Eakins, Winslow Homer and Edward Hopper, as well as a comprehensive collection of English Pre-Raphaelite painting and drawing.

Most of Wilmington's surprising number of important colonial sites are hidden away amid the decrepit and heavily industrialized waterfront to the east of downtown. A poorly signposted "historic Wilmington" loop stops first at the foot of Seventh Street, where a small monument marks the site of Delaware's first European colony, **Fort Christina**, set up by Swedish settlers in 1638. Nearby, at 606 Church St, the **Hendrickson House Museum** and **Old Swedes Church** (Mon–Sat 10am–4pm; free) is one of the oldest houses of worship in the US, built in 1690 and still retaining its impressive black walnut pulpit.

The **CVB** at the corner of 10th and Orange St (Mon–Sat 9am–5pm; ☎302/652-4088 or 1-800/422-1181) downtown has walking and driving tour maps and practical information, but unless you want to **eat at** the excellent *Waterworks Café*, 16th and French streets in Brandywine Park (☎302/652-6022), or blow $289 on a night at the splendidly ornate *Hotel du Pont,* 100 W 11th and Market St (☎302/594-3100 or 1-800/441-9019; ⑤), there's no reason to linger.

## The du Pont mansions

Various generations of the du Pont family built opulent homes in the rural Brandywine Valley northwest of Wilmington. To learn how their fortune was made, stop first at the **Hagley Museum**, off Hwy-141 just north of Wilmington (mid-March to Dec daily 9.30am–4.30pm; Jan to mid-March Sat & Sun 9.30am–4.30pm; $9.75). Pierre du Pont, the patriarch, was minister of finance to Louis XVI, but the museum begins with the foundation in 1802 of a small water-powered gunpowder mill along the banks of the Brandywine River. Mirroring the development of nineteenth-century American industry, the complex grew over the next hundred years to include ever-larger steam-powered and eventually electrically powered factories – almost all of which are still in working order.

The enormous pink **Nemours Mansion**, just a mile up the road, gives an idea of the wealth and power the family garnered (May–Nov; tours every two hours, Tues–Sat 9am–3pm, Sun 11am–3pm; $8). It was thrown up by Alfred du Pont in 1910, modeled upon the family's ancestral home in France and surrounded by a 300-acre, Versailles-style formal garden. Two miles northwest, off Hwy-52, the one-time du Pont family estate of **Winterthur** (Mon–Sat 9am–5pm, Sun noon–5pm; $8, gardens only $5) has evolved into the country's finest museum of early American decorative arts. Since 1927, when Henry du Pont took over the twelve-room cottage to house himself and his antique furniture, Winterthur has grown into a vast private museum, each of its two hundred rooms showcasing a particular decorative style. Ranging from the simplicity of a Shaker cottage to a beautiful three-story elliptical staircase taken from a North Carolina plantation home, the various pieces of furniture, textiles, silverwork and paintings – all made in America between 1640 and 1860 – form a rich catalog of the diversity of American applied arts.

## New Castle

Delaware's magnificently preserved first capital, **NEW CASTLE**, fronts the broad Delaware River, just six miles south of Wilmington via Hwy-141. Founded in the 1650s by the Dutch, intent on expanding from their colony at New Amsterdam, and taken over by the British in 1664, New Castle was the main stopping point between Baltimore and Philadelphia. Though largely bypassed when railroads and highways replaced the riverboats, it has somehow managed to survive intact, its quiet cobbled streets and immaculate eighteenth-century brick houses shaded by ancient hardwood trees.

The heart of New Castle is the tree-filled **town green** that spreads east from the shops of Delaware Street. Laid out in 1655 by Peter Stuyvesant, and ringed by a cracked and lumpy red-brick sidewalk, it is dominated by the stalwart tower of the **Immanuel Episcopal Church**, built in 1703 and bordered by tidy rows of two-hundred-year-old gravestones. The church's pristine white interior, however, is more recent, reconstructed after a disastrous 1980s fire. On the west edge of the green, the **Old Court House** (Tues–Sat 10am–3.30pm, Sun 1.30–4.30pm; free) was built in 1732 and served as the first state capitol. Its dainty cupola was the centerpoint from which surveyors determined the state's curved northern border, drawn up when Delaware seceded from Pennsylvania in 1776.

Fine colonial houses fill the few blocks around the town green. The largest, and the only one regularly open to the public, is the **George Read II House** (March–Dec Tues–Sat 10am–4pm, Sun noon–4pm; Jan & Feb Sat 10am–4pm, Sun noon–4pm; $4), two blocks south along the river at 42 The Strand. Built between 1797 and 1804 for a signatory of the **Declaration of Independence**, the original house burned down in 1824, but the sumptuously detailed rebuilt version holds marble fireplaces, brightly painted walls, elaborately carved woodwork and some of the finest plasterwork ornament of the Federal period. The spacious gardens behind were laid out in 1847 to the picturesque designs of Andrew Jackson Downing. The large houses across the street, backing onto the Delaware River, also date from the early nineteenth century, and many are now run as B&Bs. A large riverfront park spreads south from the foot of Delaware Street, with rolling lawns and sheltered benches. Its pride and joy is a tiny white-clapboard ticket office that dates from the opening of the town's first railroad, in 1832, and stands next to a small piece of track.

## Practicalities

Many visitors are content to see New Castle, just off the interstate, as a day out from Washington DC or Philadelphia, but there's enough here to merit a longer trip. For further information, or to pick up the self-guided **walking tour** map, call in at the **visitor center** at the courthouse on 211 Delaware St (☎302/323-4453) or call the Historic New Castle Visitor's Bureau on ☎1-800/758-1550. Comfortable **B&Bs** line the Delaware riverfront, varying from the cozy, hospitable *Armitage Inn*, 2 The Strand (☎302/328-6618; ③), to the more luxurious *Olde Canal Inn*, 30 Clinton St (☎302/832-5100; ⑤). There's good beer, and pub grub including crabs and clams, at the popular *Green Frog Tavern*, 114 Delaware St (☎302/656-9917), while more refined tastes will enjoy the French-influenced seafood dishes at the grand *Arsenal on the Green*, next to the Church on Market Street (☎302/328-1290).

# Dover

**DOVER**, the capital of Delaware, struggles to attract visitors as they bypass the town en route to the beach resorts of Rehoboth and Ocean City. Located in the mostly agricultural center of the state, just west of US-13, it's basically a very small town, with a low-rise business district hemmed in by blocks of suburban detached houses. South of **Lockerman Street**, the main route through town, a few strangely somnolent governmental buildings center upon the 1792 **Old State House**, its old legislative chambers now restored as a museum (Tues–Sat 10am–4.30pm, Sun 1.30–4.30pm; free; ☎302/739-4266) and furnished with early American antiques. To the west, around the oval **town green**, lawyers and insurance brokers have taken over historic buildings such as the *Golden Fleece Tavern*, where Delaware's early legislators agreed to ratify the Constitution.

A short walk west of the green, a couple of the small **Delaware State Museums** (Tues–Sat 10am–3.30pm; free) are worth a look, not for the fairly tedious displays of anthropological detritus – Native American shell necklaces, wooden water pipes from early Wilmington and the like – but because a small building across the graveyard holds the **Johnson Victrola Museum**. This large and enjoyable collection of phonographs, dedicated to the memory of Dover-born engineer Eldridge Reeves Johnson, who helped to invent the **Victrola**, is laid out like a 1920s music store. Dozens of "talking machines," from early wind-ups to prototype jukeboxes, play period recordings, and comical photographs document early, pre-electric recording techniques – entire orchestras crowd together around huge megaphones. Pride of place goes to a painting of a dog, Nipper, listening to a Victrola, an image made familiar as "His Master's Voice." In 1929 Johnson sold the rights to his machine, and to his trademark dog, to RCA for $29 million.

Every Tuesday and Friday for over fifty years, **Spence's Bazaar**, two blocks south on Queen Street at New Burton Road, has hosted a free-for-all **flea market**. All of Dover turns out for this, including dozens of local **Amish**, who ride here in their ancient horse-drawn buggies to sell home-grown fruits and vegetables. Though it's not as well known as the Amish community of **Lancaster County** (see p.146), the area around Dover has nearly as large an Amish population, concentrated in the farmlands to the west of town; happily for them, their presence has yet to become a tourist attraction.

## Practicalities
Most of Dover's **restaurants** and **hotels** are concentrated on Lockerman Street and State Street in the town center, just north of the green. State Street in particular holds the *Tudor House B&B* at no. 228 (☎302/736-1763; ⑥) and the more pub-like *W T Smithers* (☎302/674-8875) further down at no. 140. The US-13 highway also has some budget accommodation, such as the *Comfort Inn* (☎302/674-3300; ③), two blocks south of Lockerman Street. A **visitor center** (☎302/739-4266) at the corner of Duke of York and Federal streets next to the Old State House has the usual tourist information and helpful staff.

# The Delaware coast

The thirty-mile-long Delaware coast is one of the little-known jewels of the East Coast. Its one built-up resort, **Rehoboth Beach**, is a traditional seaside town, packed solid in summer, and the fishing community of **Lewes** is attractive and historic, but what really sets the area apart is the ease with which you can find long stretches of sand to yourself. For every developed stretch, about ten times more has been preserved as open space, most extensively at **Delaware Seashore State Park**, which stretches south from Rehoboth to the Maryland border.

## Lewes
Whether you come down Hwy-1, or cruise across on the ferry from Cape May, New Jersey, **LEWES** makes a good introduction to the Delaware coast. Its natural harbor at the mouth of the Delaware Bay has attracted seafarers ever since a Dutch whaling company set up a small colony here in 1631. Lewes' current role as a summer resort hasn't obscured its substantial history, outlined in the mock-Dutch **Zwaanendael Museum**, in the heart of town on Savannah Road at Kings Highway (Tues–Sat 10am–4.30pm, Sun 1.30–4.30pm; free). The **CVB** next door (Mon–Fri 10am–4pm, Sat 10am–2pm; ☎302/645-8073), housed inside a gambrel-roofed 1730s farmhouse, has walking tour maps of the rest of the town, pointing out the handful of eighteenth-century houses and outbuildings collected from around the area to form the **Lewes Historical Complex** (mid June–early Sept Tues–Sat; $4) on Front Street three blocks north. Along the canal, keep an eye out also for the **Overfalls Lightship**, which lit the entrance to Delaware Bay until 1961, and the array of cannons, one said to be from an old pirate ship, that are lined up along the top of **Memorial Park**.

Though Lewes can justly boast of being "the First Town in the First State," most people come here for the beach rather than history. There's an extensive strand along the usually calm Delaware Bay at the foot of the town, while **Cape Henlopen State Park** (☎302/645-6852), a three-thousand-acre open space where the bay meets the open ocean just a mile east of the town center, is even better, and has the biggest sand dunes north of Cape Hatteras. For a nice day out, or a possible next leg of your journey, take the seventy-minute **ferry trip** across the Delaware Bay from beyond the state park to the pleasant Victorian beach resort of **CAPE MAY**, New Jersey (6–15 services daily all year, first at 8am, last at 8pm, or 9.20pm mid-May to mid-Oct; $4.50 per person, $18 per car; ☎302/645-6030 or 1-800/64-FERRY; see also p.165).

Except on peak summer weekends, Lewes is quiet enough that you should have no trouble finding a room in motels along Savannah Road, such as *Vesuvio's* (☎302/645-2224; ③), just before the bridge, or *The Captain's Quarters* (☎302/645-7924; ③), on the far side. Most of the **restaurants**, not surprisingly, feature seafood, with giant plates of spiced crab at bargain prices unceremoniously doled out at the bright pink *Lewes Crab House* at Bay and Henlopen, a block from the beach as the main road veers right towards the ferry terminal, and more formal Italian dining at *La Rosa Negra* at 128 Second St (☎302/645-1980), back in the town center. You can walk almost everywhere in town, or **rent a bike** from Lewes Cycle Sports, 514 Savannah Rd (☎302/645-4544).

## Rehoboth Beach

A nonstop parade of motels and shopping malls along the six miles of Hwy-1 links Lewes with **REHOBOTH BEACH**, Delaware's largest and liveliest beach resort. Crowded all summer, but nearly empty the rest of the year, Rehoboth – which started life as a Methodist revival camp, and attracts so many escapees from DC that it's known as the Nation's Summer Capital – is more family oriented than other beach towns, lacking the nightlife of Ocean City but making up for it with miles of clean and uncrowded sands.

Rehoboth has less of a history than Lewes, though its wooden **boardwalk** is one of the last on the East Coast. It stretches along the Atlantic to either side of Rehoboth Avenue – always "**The Avenue**" – which acts as the main drag, its four short blocks clogged with souvenir shoppers browsing though the usual array of T-shirts and seaside kitsch. Most of the **restaurants** and **nightspots** are concentrated here, with *Thrashers French Fries* stands mixed in with the mock-Caribbean beach shack decor of the *Back Porch Café*, 59 Rehoboth Ave (☎302/227-3674), and boardwalk burger bars like *Obie's-by-the-Sea* (☎302/227-6261), three blocks north; after dark, the action shifts to the Anglophile environs of the *Country Squire*, 19 Rehoboth Ave (☎302/227-3985), which has the largest beer selection for miles.

Of course if shopping is your passion, Rehoboth has the largest concentration of **outlet stores** in the Delmarva area, with more than 140 famous name shops (like Nike, Donna Karan, Gap and Coach). You can't miss the blatant consumerism along Route 1 – just follow the tide of cars inching toward the latest bargains.

Apart from the peak times of July and August, you shouldn't have much trouble finding a bed in one of Rehoboth's many **motels**: the *Sandcastle*, 123 Second St (☎302/227-0400 or 1-800/372-2112; ③), or the *Admiral*, a block south at 2 Baltimore Ave (☎1-888/882-4188; ③), are just off the boardwalk, or if you want to avoid the crowds try *Adams Oceanfront*, a mile south of the center at 4 Read St in Dewey Beach (☎1-800/448-8080; ③). **B&B's** are a nice alternative at the beach: try the *Corner Cupboard Inn*, 50 Park Ave (☎302/227-8553), just four blocks from the beach, or the *Rehoboth Guest House*, 40 Maryland Ave (☎302/227-4117). Room rates at all of the above can rise as high as $100 on summer weekends. For more information, contact the **Chamber of Commerce**, 501 Rehoboth Ave (☎302/227-2233 or 1-800/441-1329).

South of Rehoboth, **Delaware Seashore State Park** (☎302/227-2800) stretches for miles along a thin, sandy peninsula, split by Hwy-1 and bounded on the east by the Atlantic and on the west by various freshwater marshlands. There's little here apart from beachfront parking areas until you approach the Maryland border, where the concrete tower blocks of **Bethany Beach** do little to prepare you for the Costa del Sol-like concentrations of hotels and condos in Ocean City, ten miles further along (ooo p.419).

# CHAPTER SIX

# THE SOUTH

A s Mark Twain put it in 1882, "In the South, the [Civil] war is what AD is elsewhere; they date everything from it." Five generations later, the legacies of years of slavery and the "War Between the States" are still evident throughout the southern heartland states of **NORTH CAROLINA, SOUTH CAROLINA, GEORGIA, KENTUCKY, TENNESSEE, ALABAMA, MISSISSIPPI** and **ARKANSAS**. The war is the focus point for countless museums and shrines, and the Confederate "Stars and Bars" flag remains conspicuous everywhere.

It's not, however, an area that's entirely stuck in its ways. How far the "New South" differs from the old is still a matter for debate; but the last few decades have unquestionably seen the influx of high-tech industries, the emergence of liberal white politicians such as Jimmy Carter and Bill Clinton, and the growth of such dynamic urban centers as the black city of **Atlanta**, the birthplace of Dr Martin Luther King Jr and venue for the 1996 Olympics. It took suffering and bloodshed to effect the changes of the 1950s and 1960s, but relations between black and white have improved, in the cities, at least; though driving through the countryside can reveal levels of shocking iniquity and poverty where racial tension lies uneasily close to the surface.

The South has never been one uniform, homogenous unit; even during the Civil War there were substantial pockets of pro-Union support, particularly in the mountains. Today the culture and make-up of the overwhelmingly black Mississippi Delta or South Carolina are markedly different from the white hill farms in Kentucky and Tennessee. Likewise, the Sun Belt industries of North Carolina and northern Alabama are far removed from the rural backwaters of southern Georgia.

The most exciting aspect of the Southern heritage is undoubtedly its **music**. Hundreds of thousands of fans make pilgrimages each year to the country and blues meccas of **Nashville** and **Memphis**, the homelands of Elvis Presley, Hank Williams, Robert Johnson, Dolly Parton and Otis Redding, and a substantial number of visitors seek out the backwoods barn dances in Appalachia or the blues jook-joints of the Mississippi Delta and South Carolina. The Southern experience is also reflected in a rich regional **literature**, its communities and people well documented by the likes of William Faulkner, Carson McCullers, Flannery O'Connor, Alice Walker, Eudora Welty, and the one-book-wonders Margaret Mitchell and Harper Lee.

Other major destinations for travelers include the elegant coastal cities of **Charleston** and **Savannah**, frenzied beach resorts such as **Myrtle Beach**, college towns like **Athens** and **Chapel Hill**, and the historic Mississippi riverports of **Natchez**

## ACCOMMODATION PRICE CODES

All accommodation prices in this book have been coded using the symbols below. Note that prices are for the least expensive double rooms in each establishment. For a full explanation see p.37 in Basics.

| | | |
|---|---|---|
| ① up to $30 | ④ $60–80 | ⑦ $130–175 |
| ② $30–45 | ⑤ $80–100 | ⑧ $175–250 |
| ③ $45–60 | ⑥ $100–130 | ⑨ $250+ |

and **Vicksburg**. Away from the urban areas, much Southern scenery consists of undulating, sun-scorched hillsides dotted with wooden shacks and rust-red barns, broken by occasional forests. Highlights include the misty Appalachian **mountains** of Kentucky, Tennessee and North Carolina, the subtropical **beaches** and tranquil **barrier islands** along both the Atlantic and Gulf coasts, and the river road through the tiny settlements of the flat Mississippi Delta.

During July and August, the **temperature** is mostly a very humid 90°F; virtually every motel, bar, restaurant and museum is air-conditioned, but you might want to schedule your visit a little to either side of these months. On the coast, where the beaches offer a less expensive alternative to neighboring Florida, the main season is from Memorial Day to Labor Day, and outside these dates many attractions are closed. The fall colors in the mountains (just as beautiful and a lot less expensive and congested than New England) are at their headiest during October.

**Public transportation** through the large rural expanses is poor. In any case, it's best to take things at your own pace – you'll find things to see and do in the most unlikely places – so renting a car is a good idea. **Accommodation** in the South is generally good value, while its varied **cuisine**, much of it dished out at simple roadside shacks, ranges from the ubiquitous grits (maize porridge) to highly calorific, irresistible **soul food** – fried chicken, wood-smoked barbecue and the like, along with turnip greens, spinach, macaroni and all manner of tasty vegetables. Fish is also good, from catfish (which has a sort of mild trout flavor), to the wonderful **Low Country Boils**, seafood stews served with rice, traditionally prepared on the sea islands. Look out, too, for the peculiarly Southern Krispy Kreme doughnut outlets, especially in the Carolinas and Georgia. The doughnuts are great, but it's the decor that steals the show, all turquoise Formica, shiny chrome counter stools and fabulous 1950s signs.

## Some history

The **Spanish** and **French** had begun to build settlements throughout the South as early as the 1520s. However, by the early seventeenth century the **British** had pushed them back to what are now Florida and Louisiana, and steered the region toward a role as supplier of **raw materials** to its **cotton** mills and **tobacco** factories. Both climate and soil favored staple agriculture, and massive labor-intensive **plantations** started to spring up. No self-respecting European would cross the Atlantic to pick cotton on a plantation, so the big landowners turned to **slavery** as the most profitable source of labor, importing Africans in their millions through the port of Charleston.

As the South became increasingly set in its ways, with little incentive to diversify, the Northern states surged ahead in both agriculture and industry. By the early nineteenth century the Southern economy was clearly subservient to that of the North: the South grew the crops, but Northern factories monopolized the more lucrative manufacturing of finished goods. Southern politicians and plantation-owners accused the North of political and economic aggression, and felt that unless slavery continued to spread into the Territories and even the free states, they would progressively lose all say in the future of the nation. The election as president in late 1860 of **Abraham Lincoln**, a hardline pro-Northern candidate, brought the crisis to a head, and in February 1861 six Southern states broke away to form the Confederate States of America. Jefferson Davis was sworn in as president of the Confederacy on February 18, 1861 – an occasion on which his vice-president proudly proclaimed that this government was "the first in the history of the world, based upon this great physical and moral truth . . . that the Negro is not equal to the white man." **Secession** radically upped the stakes in the controversy. Most Northerners had been indifferent to the issue of slavery – even Lincoln, as late as mid-1861, said "I have no purpose . . . to interfere with slavery in the States where it exists" – but the potential destruction of the Union was seen as a far more serious, and treacherous, threat.

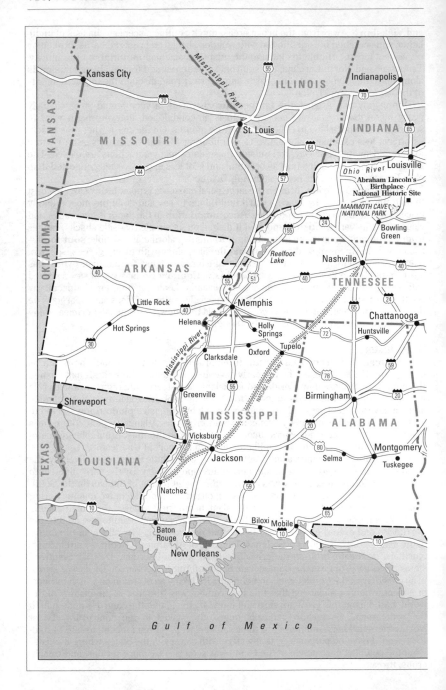

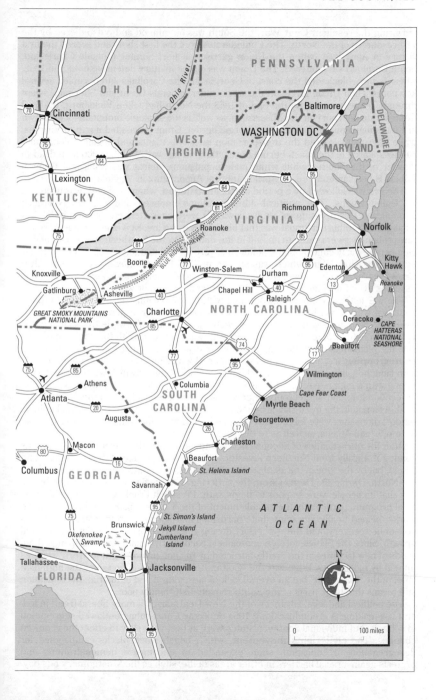

During the resultant **Civil War**, the South was outgunned and outsoldiered by the vast resources of the North. The Confederates fired the first shots and scored the first victory in April 1861, when the Union garrison at Fort Sumter (outside Charleston, South Carolina) surrendered. The Union was on the military defensive until mid-1862, when its navy blockaded the coast of Georgia and the Carolinas and occupied several key ports. Then Union forces in the west, under generals Grant and Sherman, swept through Tennessee, and by the end of 1863 the North had taken Vicksburg, the final Confederate-held port on the Mississippi, as well as the strategic mountain-locked town of Chattanooga on the Tennessee–Georgia border. Grant proceeded north to Virginia, while Sherman captured the transportation nexus of Atlanta and began a bloody and ruthless march to the coast, burning everything in his way. With 228,000 men dead (a quarter of the South's adult white male population), defeat was total, and General Robert E Lee surrendered on April 9, 1865, at Appomattox in Virginia.

The war was followed by a period of **Reconstruction**, when the South was occupied by Union troops. The political administrations imposed and run by Northern Republicans ("carpetbaggers" or "scalawags") were characterized by corruption, but what galled Southerners most was that blacks were also involved in government. When this probationary era came to an end in the mid-1870s, the Southern states returned to Democratic Party control; black politicians were intimidated out of office, in particular by the **Ku Klux Klan**, which was started in 1865 by ex-Confederate officers. "**Jim Crow**" segregation laws were imposed, and poll taxes, literacy tests and property qual-ifications disenfranchised virtually all blacks (and many poor whites).

The war left the South in chaos. Along with the devastating death toll, two-thirds of Southern wealth had been destroyed. From controlling thirty percent of the nation's assets in 1860, the South was down to twelve percent in 1870, while the spur the war gave to industrialization meant that the North was booming. With the abolition of slav-ery, the plantations were no longer viable. Instead, the Southern economy turned to **sharecropping**, a crude barter system under which landowners provided their tenants with land, housing and even food and implements, the cost of which was later deducted (along with a high rate of interest) from the sale of crops. Most farms were too small to be economical, and sharecropping encouraged production of cash crops rather than food. As a result, the freed slaves benefited little from the abolition of the "peculiar insti-tution": thousands were forced into debt, and there were mass migrations to cities like Memphis and Atlanta, as well as to the North.

After the uncertainties of Reconstruction, industrial growth accelerated (the impetus coming ironically from Northern investors, who took advantage of the cheap land and labor), but by the time of the 1929 stock market crash the South still lagged well behind the North. During the **Depression**, the suffering of the region was exacerbated by the fact that its people were so poor to begin with. President Franklin D Roosevelt's New Deal program, particularly the establishment of the TVA (see p.487) and road-building works, helped to alleviate immediate hardships and lay down an infrastructure to aid economic recovery, and the war effort during the early Forties stimulated industrial growth. Since the Sixties, foreign companies, particularly Japanese, have opened thou-sands of new factories in the South, attracted by the anti-union "Right to Work" statutes upheld by most states. What was the "Cotton Belt" now likes to go under the high-tech label of the "**Sun Belt**" but an overall lack of agricultural and industrial diversification still means that huge parts of the South remain disturbingly poor.

The political and legal advances of the New Deal started a more liberal trend in fed-eral law-making. A groundbreaking 1954 Supreme Court ruling outlawed segregation in schools, but individual Southern states were at best very slow to effect the required changes. The **civil rights movement**, which began when blacks campaigned for desegregation in education, soon expanded to encompass demonstrations and protests against racial barriers in other areas of life, such as the Montgomery bus boycott and the Greensboro lunch-counter sit-in. Before civil rights legislation was finally imposed in the late Sixties, Southern whites, led by firebrand politicians, put up a bloody resistance to change, and left behind a catalog of murder, attacks and harassment – particularly in Mississippi and Alabama. Modern travelers can follow in the footsteps of **Dr Martin Luther King Jr** throughout the South, from his birthplace in Atlanta, through his church in Montgomery, to the site of his assassination in Memphis, commemorated (some think rather inappropriately) by the National Civil Rights Museum.

The civil rights years had a marked effect on **party politics** in the South. Since the Civil War the region had voted almost *en bloc* for the **Democrats**, but as that party has become more identified with liberal reforms, greater government intervention and, especially, racial integration, there has been a marked shift toward the **Republican** Party, especially in presidential elections. Right-wing politicians have been forced to search for a party political home; dinosaur Strom Thurmond of South Carolina and the equally vitriolic George Wallace campaigned for the US presidency under the banners of small segregationist parties, while more recently, Senate Majority Leader Trent Lott has added to the traditional Southern demagoguery typified by Senator Jesse Helms of North Carolina. Nevertheless, many unreconstructed backwoodsmen still fight for white supremacy under the umbrella of the Democratic Party.

The dispossession of the **Native Americans** is often the forgotten chapter of Southern history. Colonial powers at best tolerated the Indians, for the most part peaceful agrarian tribes, and used them as allies in their imperialist wars with each other. However, after the Revolution, pressure from plantation-owners and small farmers led to the forced removal in the 1830s of the "five civilized tribes" – the Cherokee, Creek, Choctaw, Chickasaw and Seminole – to malarial Oklahoma. Today only a few thousand Native Americans live in the South.

# NORTH CAROLINA

**NORTH CAROLINA**, though the most industrialized of the Southern states, remains relatively rural and poor, with just six million people spread over an area larger than England. It suffered heavily during the **Civil War**, and **Reconstruction** brought mixed fortunes: although the Democrats regained control in 1870, they ran a liberal administration and were effective in stamping out the Ku Klux Klan. Since then there have been parallel traditions of radical black, and white racist, activity. **Greensboro**, for example, where **Jesse Jackson** served his political apprenticeship, was the site of the 1960 lunch-counter sit-in by black students, and also of the Greensboro Massacre of 1979, when Klansmen killed five people at a Communist Workers Party demonstration.

Geographically, North Carolina breaks down into three distinct areas – running from east to west, the coast, the Piedmont and the mountains – that help make it one of the more interesting states to tour around. For visitors, the **coast** is the most promising area, with good beaches, beautiful landscapes and a fascinating history. The inner coast consists largely of the less developed **Albemarle Peninsula**, with colonial **Edenton** nearby. The central **Piedmont** is dominated by manufacturing cities, and by the academic institutions of the Research Triangle: **Raleigh**, the state capital, **Durham**, home of prestigious Duke University, and trendy **Chapel Hill**. **Winston-Salem** combines tobacco culture and Moravian heritage, while **Charlotte** bills itself as the next boom city of the South, though for the moment it's distinguished by little but its downtown skyscrapers. In the **mountains**, one of the most stunning stretches of Appalachia, the only towns of any size, **Boone** and **Asheville**, are linked by the spectacular **Blue Ridge Parkway**, while **Great Smoky Mountains National Park** overlaps the border with Tennessee.

## Getting around North Carolina

North Carolina's major **airports** are at Raleigh-Durham, a hub for American Airlines, and Charlotte, an arrival point for transatlantic flights on British Airways. A tiny airport at Manteo in the Outer Banks (☎1-800/352-0714) serves Norfolk Virginia, four times daily or you can call for charter flights to the Outer Banks, but driving would be easier. Charlotte, Raleigh, Durham and Greensboro (with an express bus link to Winston-Salem) are served by **Amtrak**, but unfortunately there is no coastal route. Plenty of **buses** run within the Piedmont; schedules are much less frequent in the mountains and along the coast, both of which are best explored by car. North Carolinan **interstates** are some of the most attractive in the country, the medians carpeted with poppies and wildflowers. The state has a good network of **cycling** routes along quiet country roads; for information, contact the Department of Transportation (☎919/733-2804).

# The North Carolina coast

The **North Carolina coast**, which ranges through salt marshes, beaches, barrier islands and estuaries, holds most of the state's more interesting **historic sites**. The continent's earliest English colonists vanished inexplicably from **Roanoke Island** in 1590; just over three centuries later, the Wright brothers achieved the first powered flight a few miles up the road. The **Outer Banks**, the long reef of barrier islands which stretches down from Virginia, are in parts tacky and elsewhere beautifully unspoiled.

## Edenton and the Albemarle

The huge and generally relaxed **Albemarle Peninsula** remains largely unexploited. Local towns try to make much of their **colonial history** – this was the first part of North Carolina to have permanent European settlements, around the end of the seventeenth century – but often there's not a lot left to see, except for restored eighteenth-century buildings that get a bit similar after a while.

### Edenton

**EDENTON**, set along a beautiful, placid Albemarle Sound **waterfront** roughly forty miles back from the ocean and the same distance south of the Virginia border, was established as North Carolina's first state capital in 1722. A major center of unrest in the American Revolution, it remained a prosperous port until the early nineteenth century, when it began to fade. Today Edenton feels frozen, not unpleasantly, some time around 1961.

As you stroll around the town – possibly aided by the self-guided walking tour issued by the **Historic Edenton Visitor Center** (April–Oct Mon–Sat 9am–5pm, Sun 1–5pm; Nov–March Tues–Sat 10am–4pm, Sun 1–4pm; guided tours available, call ahead for times ☎252/482-2637; $3–5) – you'll come across an exceptional number of colonial and pre-Civil War **houses**, and the magnificent wooden **Cupola House**; **St Paul's Parish Church** and the **Georgian Chowan County Courthouse** overlooking the waterfront are fine mid-seventeenth-century structures. The main road, **Broad Street**, is also interesting in an offbeat way, with its Victorian facades, old-fashioned drugstores selling home-mixed sodas, and Fifties chrome signs.

A narrated slide show at the visitor center covers colonial history well, but is less explicit about slavery. There's no mention of the remarkable **Harriet Jacobs**, a runaway slave who hid for seven years in her grandmother's attic. She finally escaped to the North through such ruses as disguising herself as a male sailor, and was eventually reunited in Boston with the two children she had had by a white man in Edenton. She wrote this amazing story as *Incidents in the Life of a Slave Girl*, which became one of the most famous published slave narratives of the nineteenth century. None of the buildings mentioned in the book is still standing, although you can get an idea of where places were from the map in the Harvard UP edition (1987) and some historic markers. The visitor center, with some lead-time, can arrange a special tour.

If you like peace and quiet, Edenton is not a bad base for explorations of the coast. Among luxurious **B&Bs** are the *Trestle House Inn*, 1114 Soundside Rd (☎919/482-2282; ⑤), and the bizarre *Granville Queen Themed Inn*, 108 S Granville St (☎919/482-5296; ⑤), in which every room is done out on a "queen" theme – ask for the Egyptian Queen, with its resident sphinxes. You won't need to eat for the rest of the day after their spectacular five-course breakfast. A reliable budget **motel** is the *Coach House*, 919 N Broad St (☎919/482-2107; ③). For **eating,** The *Creekside Restaurant & Bar*, 406 W Queen St (☎252/482-0118) has a good, varied menu, for Carolina bar-b-que try *Lane's Family BBQ and Seafood*, 421 E Church St (☎252/482-4008), closer to the water, there is *Waterman's Grill*, 427 S Broad St (☎252/482-7733), and for good pasta check out the *Dram Tree*, 112 W Water St (☎252/482-2711).

## Exploring the Albemarle

**ALBEMARLE plantation life** can be sampled at **Hope**, the home of David Stone, a state governor and US senator of the revolutionary and Federal period. It's off Hwy-308, a few miles west of **Windsor**, about 25 miles southwest of Edenton (Jan to late Dec Mon–Sat 10am–4pm, Sun 2–5pm; $6.50). The house, built in 1803, is classic Southern myth: white, with a double balcony at the front, and filled with hand-carved wooden furniture. Admission includes entrance to the 1763 **King-Bazemore House**, a simple planter's home, which holds demonstrations of colonial cooking in its working kitchen.

A clearer picture of slave life is given by **Somerset Place State Historic Site**, a plantation 25 miles southeast of Edenton at **Cresswell** on US-64 (summer Mon–Sat 9am–5pm, Sun 1–5pm; rest of year Tues–Sat 10am–4pm, Sun 1–4pm; free). This is how the lowland plantations must have looked, with fields dissolving into marshland beyond huge oaks. The wooden shacks of the slaves' quarters have gone, although you can see the foundations of the tiny shed-sized slave "hospital." The director of the site is descended from slaves who worked here and there are guided tours available.

There's a **campground** at the neighboring **Pettigrew State Park** on Phelps Lake (☎919/797-4475; $12), an area of mighty trees ranged around a shallow rainwater-fed lake, ideal for fishing. Even if you don't stay, take time to go down to the tiny museum at the water's edge, where the interesting display on local Native Americans includes a couple of 4000-year-old dugout canoes raised from the lake. Close by both is the Tyrrell County **Visitor's Center**, 203 S Ludington Drive, (☎252/796-0723) who can aid in further exploring.

The southern shore of the Albemarle holds less to see, though the marshy countryside and tree-lined roads make for a pleasant drive, and **Lake Mattamuskeet Wildlife Refuge**, off Hwy-94 on the causeway across the lake, or off US-264 near New Holland, is an amazing sight in winter, when thousands of swans migrate here from Canada. It's also a sanctuary for endangered osprey.

# The Outer Banks

The **OUTER BANKS** are a series of long sand bars, sprinkled with wispy sea oats, that stretch around 180 miles from the Virginia border to Cape Lookout, near Beaufort. They are a great place to wander at your own speed, although unfortunately there's no public transportation apart from the ferries between islands and to the mainland.

The main road from the north, US-158, crosses from the mainland on a low bridge, where you're greeted by a roadside **visitor center** (☎252/261-4644). South along US-158 and the parallel shoreline Beach Road, the coastal towns of **Kitty Hawk, Kill Devil Hills** and **Nags Head** are strung out without a break, and the fine warm-water **beaches** are lined with motels and fast-food places mixed in with huge vacation "cottages." Note that when Outer Banks hotels describe themselves as "waterfront," it simply means they are on the coastal side of the road, not that they necessarily have ocean views.

## Kill Devil Hills, Nags Head and Roanoke Island

The **Wright Brothers National Memorial** (summer daily 9am–7pm; rest of year daily 9am–5pm; $4 per car, $2 pedestrians), a large granite fin atop a hill just off the main road at **KILL DEVIL HILLS**, commemorates the plucky Orville Wright's **first powered flight**, on December 17, 1903. While most histories accredit the incident with having taken place at **Kitty Hawk**, a town eight miles north, that was just the name of the nearest post office. The flight in fact took place off Kill Devil Hill, in what is now the city of Kill Devil Hills. A boulder on the left-hand side of the **visitor center** marks where his first aircraft hit the ground, and successive numbered markers show the distance of each of his subsequent flights. A museum in the visitor center records the brothers' various experiments; after several years of trials with kites and gliders, visiting the Outer Banks for a few weeks at a time and living in makeshift shacks on the beach, Orville and Wilbur finally shook hands before launching their powered plane on a cold December morning. As one of the local lifeboatmen acting as ground crew remarked, "We couldn't help notice how they held on to each other's hand, sort o' like folks parting who weren't sure they'd ever see one another again." Wilbur asked the men "not to look too sad, but to . . . laugh and holler and clap . . . and try to cheer Orville up when he started." The phlegmatic Orville recorded the historic moment of take-off in his diary: "The machine lifted from the truck . . . I found control of the front rudder quite difficult . . . the machine would rise suddenly to about 10ft and then as suddenly, on turning the rudder, dart for the ground . . . time about 12 seconds."

A few miles south in **NAGS HEAD**, at Hwy-158 milepost 12, **Jockey's Ridge State Park** boasts the largest sand dunes on the east coast. It's a particularly great place to be at sunset, while during the day instructors from Kitty Hawk Kites (☎252/441-4124) will teach you the basics of hang-gliding for $55.

**ROANOKE ISLAND**, between Bodie Island and the mainland via US-64/264 and another bridge, was the **first English settlement** in North America, founded by **Sir Walter Raleigh** in 1585. The colonists survived initial difficulties with weather, disease and Indians, and were joined by one hundred more settlers brought over by John White in 1587. When White returned three years later, however, all trace of the colony had disappeared, except for the one mysterious word "Croatoan" carved on a tree. Theories as to the fate of the "Lost Colony" have varied, although it is generally assumed that the settlers were massacred by hostile natives – a key piece of early anti-Indian mythology. A rather fanciful but happier version has it that settlers and Indians banded together and marched inland, forming what is now the small and very racially mixed Lumbee tribe in southwest North Carolina.

Nothing authentic survives of the Roanoke settlement, but **Fort Raleigh**, three miles north of **Manteo** off US-64, is a conjectural and very tiny reconstruction of the colonists' earthwork fort, set in a wooded glade with a canopy of Spanish moss (summer Sun–Fri 9am–8pm, Sat 9am–6pm; rest of the year daily 9am–5pm; free). Its museum explains local Indian interaction with colonists, and an outdoor amphitheater on the ocean hosts performances of *The Lost Colony*, an undeniably impressive drama (June–Aug daily except Sat 8.30pm; ☎1-800/488-5012; $12–18). Adjacent to the fort, the **Elizabethan Gardens** are elegantly landscaped with walkways, statues and subtropical blooms – the shade provided by the trees makes it a great place to go in high summer (daily 9am–dusk; until 8pm when *The Lost Colony* is being performed; $3).

In Manteo itself, the recently renovated **Roanoke Island Festival Park** has a slew of well-done historical attractions that, if seen in full, take about a half day (daily:

summer 9am–7pm; rest of the year 10am–5pm, last tickets sold an hour before close; $8). Of particular note is the **Exhibit Hall**, where costumed employees walk you through the history of Virginia; also here is the *Elizabeth II*, a reconstruction of a sixteenth-century English **ship**, and more folks in period dress provide a "first person account" of the ship's trip to Roanoke. A changing schedule of films, dance, music and dramatic presentations are hosted here; call ☎252/475-1506 for a current schedule.

**Motels** line the beaches north of Oregon Inlet, separating the mainland and Cape Hatteras National Seashore. The *Blue Heron Motel*, on Hwy-12 at Nags Head (☎252/441-7447; summer ⑤, winter ③), is one of the cleanest, with an oceanfront pool; the *First Colony Inn* is a great B&B at 6720 S Virginia Dare Trail, Nags Head (☎252/441-2343; summer ⑦/⑧, winter ⑤/⑥), with friendly, knowledgeable staff. There's also a nice **hostel** accommodation at *HI-Outerbanks* in Kitty Hawk (☎252/261-2294; ①–③), with dorms for $15–18 a night, camping and some private rooms available. The standard of **food** varies considerably, but the *Flying Fish Cafe*, on Hwy-158 in Kill Devil Hills (☎252/441-6894), and the *Lone Cedar Cafe*, on the Manteo-Nags Causeway, Nag's Head (☎252/441-5405), both serve reasonably priced fresh seafood.

## Cape Hatteras National Seashore

**CAPE HATTERAS NATIONAL SEASHORE** stretches south onto **Hatteras** and **Ocracoke** islands, with wonderful unspoiled beaches on its seawardside. Most tourists just drive straight through on Hwy-12, and even in high season you can pull off the road and walk across the dunes to deserted beaches. The salt marshes on the western side are also beautiful, and at the northern end of Hatteras Island the **Pea Island National Wildlife Refuge** has trails and observation platforms from which you can see a wide variety of birdlife.

Over six hundred ships have been wrecked along this treacherous stretch of coast since the sixteenth century. At the south end of Hatteras Island, near the early nineteenth-century black-and-white-striped **Cape Hatteras Lighthouse**, a **visitor center** (summer daily 9am–6pm; rest of the year daily 9am–5pm) holds displays on the island's maritime history. At the village of **Frisco**, the **Native American Museum** is a loving collection of arts and crafts, including a drum from a Hopi *kiva* (Tues–Sun 11am–5pm; Mon by appointment; ☎252/995-4440; free).

Various **motels**, food shops and adequate **restaurants** are scattered through the fly-blown settlements along Hwy-12. The *Cape Hatteras Motel* in Buxton (☎252/995-5611; summer ⑤, winter ③) is a big hit with windsurfers and has a relaxed, friendly atmosphere plus a fish-cleaning station. *Diamond Shoals* on Hwy-12 (☎252/995-5217) is a good central place for breakfast. **Camping** is best at one of the summer-only, first-come, first-served, National Park Service campgrounds near Salvo, Buxton and Frisco. Ocracoke and Bodie Island ranger stations at the entrances to the seashore keep daily lists of what's available (call ☎252/473-2111).

## Ocracoke island

**OCRACOKE ISLAND** (pronounced *oke-ruhcoke*) is forty minutes by ferry from Hatteras – and is even more beautiful. This 14-mile ribbon of land is bisected by Hwy-12, and it's perfectly possible to drive along and pull over to find yourself a deserted patch of beach. Despite the crowds of tourists in the village of **OCRACOKE** itself, at its southern tip, the island somehow seems to have hung on to its atmosphere. There's nothing in particular to see on the island, except perhaps the harbor and squat brown lighthouse (you can't go in), and a tiny British World War II naval cemetery. It's nicer instead just to catch some rays, take a stroll or enjoy a cycle ride; **bike rental** places include Island Rentals on Silver Lake Road (☎252/928-5480).

---

**OCRACOKE FERRIES**

In summer, **ferries between Ocracoke and Hatteras** leave both islands on the hour and half-hour all day, except between 5 and 7am and from 6.30pm until midnight when they are hourly. Winter sailings from Ocracoke and Hatteras are hourly between 5am and midnight. The crossing takes forty minutes, although you may have to wait to get on in a car as there's limited space (30 cars only), and it's loaded on a first-come, first-served basis.

Ferries from Ocracoke also head south down the coast to **Cedar Island** (2hr 15min; 8 daily each way between 7am and 8.30pm in summer, 4–6 ferries daily in winter; $1 foot passenger, $2 bike, $10 car), and to **Swan Quarter**, on the Albemarle (2hr 30min; 3 daily all year; same fares). Both require motorists to reserve in summer (☎1-800/293-3779); at short notice you should get the day you want, if not the time.

---

**Hotels** and **B&Bs** in Ocracoke village get full in summer, and are fairly expensive; as elsewhere on the Outer Banks, rates drop in September. There is also a recently opened small, scenic **hostel** at **The Ocracoke Island Wayfarer Hostel**, 125 Lighthouse Rd (☎252/928-3411; ①/②) Dorms are $19 and there is a private room available. The *Anchorage Inn*, on Front Street (☎252/928-1101; ④–⑥), is comfortable, with a pool and complimentary continental breakfast; or you could sleep in one of the unusual "crow's-nest" rooms in the 1901 *Island Inn and Dining Room*, on Hwy-12 (☎1-877/456-3466; ②), whose **restaurant** is renowned for its crabcakes (☎252/928-7821). Other, less expensive restaurants include the *Back Porch*, on the main street (☎252/928-6401), which serves great fish, and the lively *Howard's Pub & Raw Bar*, a mile north of the village on Hwy-12 (☎252/928-4441), which has over 200 beers and serves a full menu until 2am. The fairly isolated Park Service **campground**, a few miles north, tends to be the first of the Outer Banks sites to fill up.

### Cape Lookout National Seashore

The mainland between Cedar Island and Beaufort is a rural backwater, sparsely settled and hardly touched by tourists. It's reasonably attractive to wander around, but towns such as **Davis** and **Smyrna** don't have any accommodation, and the most likely reason to pass through is to get to the all-but-deserted **CAPE LOOKOUT NATIONAL SEASHORE**, a narrow ribbon of sand stretching south of Ocracoke Island along three undeveloped Outer Banks, with no roads or habitation (park headquarters at the eastern end of Harker's Island; ☎252/728-2250). Its few visitors share a total of around 56 miles of beach along all three islands, with the marshes on the landward side supporting rich and unusual plant and birdlife adapted to the harsh, salty conditions.

At the northern tip of the **north core banks**, across from Ocracoke, stand the pretty, strangely eerie ruins of the abandoned village of **Portsmouth Village**, whose last two residents left in 1971. The main ferry for the island, from **Atlantic** (Morris Marina, call for times/fare ☎252/225-4261), lands seventeen miles south of Portsmouth Village, which you can only reach on foot. Groups of travelers are taken by ferries to or from Ocracoke (Rudy Austin at ☎252/928-4361, around $15 per person). **Cabins** on the island, operated by the marina cost around $10 per person; otherwise there's only primitive **camping**, with neither drinking water nor food available.

The **south core banks** is served in summer by one private ferry each way per day from Davis ($13 round-trip; call Alger Willis on ☎252/729-2791). Here, too, the ferry company manages some wood **cabins** (the smallest sleeps four people; all work out at $12 per head if full). Camping is as primitive as on the north island, but the ferry will buy food for you on the mainland and bring it across. At the cabin area, showers and water are available. Three passenger ferries run to the southern tip of the south island from low-key **Harker's Island**, south of Smyrna, to within two miles or three miles of **Cape Lookout** itself and its lighthouse. Ferries also go to the peaceful **Shackleford Banks**, inhabited by feral horses since the early 1500s. Check with park headquarters for scheduling details (☎252/728-2250).

## Beaufort

**BEAUFORT**, about 150 miles southeast of Raleigh, is probably the nicest of North Carolina's coastal towns: a relaxing place to hang out and drink cold beer, or just sit around on the waterfront, which hots up at night. The **Maritime Museum** has good displays on local ecology and shipping history (Mon–Fri 9am–5pm, Sat 10am–5pm, Sun 2–5pm; free). In the restored area on Turner Street, off the waterfront, you'll find handsome **old houses**, an apothecary and the city jail. Across from the museum, you can take a more active excursion with AB Kayaks (☎252/728-6330), who have guided kayak eco-tours of the surrounding waterways including the **Shackleford Banks**; (tours start at $40, kayak rentals $10 hour, $30 half-day, $55 full day). The main house serves as the town **welcome center** (Mon–Sat 9am–5pm; ☎919/728-5225 or 1-800/575-SITE).

Among the many historic **B&Bs** in the shady residential streets off Turner Street, *Langdon House*, 135 Craven St (☎919/728-5499; ⑥), is friendly and relaxed, as is the *Cedars Inn*, 305 Front St (☎919/728-7036; ⑤ summer). The *Inlet Inn*, on the waterfront at 601 Front St (☎919/728-3600; ⑤ summer), has huge hotel rooms, and also offers a continental breakfast served to your room. **Rates** everywhere increase considerably in summer. **Morehead City**, a couple of miles down the coast, and the Bogue Bank resorts boast plenty of **motels**.

As for **eating and nightlife**, Beaufort's waterfront is vibrant at night, milling with yachties and vacationers drinking, listening to the live music and simply strolling. There are a number of decent bar-restaurants on the wooden **boardwalk** right on the water, but for exquisite – if pricey – food, Southwestern with a Mediterranean twist, head for the stylish *Front Street Grill*, set back from the waterfront at 419 Front St (☎919/728-3118). The notable *Beaufort Grocery Co*, 117 Queen St (☎919/728-3899), prides itself on inventive dishes made from superbly fresh ingredients.

### The beaches

South of Beaufort, the **beaches** along the twenty-mile offshore **Bogue Bank** are always pretty crowded, especially **Atlantic Beach** at the east end, with **Emerald Isle**, to the west, marginally less so. On **Bear Island** to the south, though – reached by ferry (April–Oct; various hours ☎910/326-4881; $2) with a strict limit on the number of daily passengers – the stunning **Hammocks Beach State Park** has high sand dunes, a wooded shore and perfect beaches. The entrance is four miles west of **Swansboro**; register at the small park center if you want to **camp** (☎910/326-4881; $8). No camping is permitted on the few days around each full moon, when **loggerhead sea turtles** come ashore to lay their eggs.

On the far side of the Camp Lejeune US Marine base, **Topsail Island**, yet another sand bar of resorts, is considerably less built up than Bogue Bank, presumably because its beaches aren't quite as good. **Surf City** and **Topsail** were once both slightly run-down family resorts, but seem to have improved nicely, possibly in part to a beating from a couple of hurricanes. Public beach access points are signposted from the main road, but in practice you can get down at lots of other places.

# Wilmington

Though it's the largest town on North Carolina's coast, **WILMINGTON**, set back along the **Cape Fear River** fifty miles short of the southern border, has a welcoming down-home feel. During the Civil War, it was briefly the Confederacy's most important harbor, exporting cotton all over the world. "**Blockade-runners**" would attempt to outrun the Union navy, racing into the safety of Fort Fisher's guns some twenty miles to the south of town; "Rebel Rose" Greenhow, glamorous Confederate spy, drowned here during a run in 1864. Dozens of blacks were murdered in Wilmington by white mobs in the **Race Riot** of 1898 – a backlash to the election of a "Fusionist" (Republican-Populist-black) governor two years earlier.

Wilmington today is attractive and friendly, with a historic district, starting on the south side of Market Street and stretching east along Third Street, that feels genuinely lived in. At 814 Market St, the **Cape Fear Museum** (summer Mon–Sat 9am–5pm, Sun 2–5pm; rest of year closed Mon; $4, free 1st of the month and 1st and 3rd Sun) gives a lively account of local history, while **St John's Art Museum**, 114 Orange St (Tues–Sat 10am–5pm, Sun noon–4pm; $3), features works by the nineteenth-century Impressionist Mary Cassatt. Architecture fans should head for the **Bellamy Mansion Museum of History and Design Arts**, in an ornate antebellum mansion at Fifth and Market (Wed–Sat 10am–5pm, Sun 1–5pm; $6), which concentrates on restoration, preservation and local design. The extravagant houses, ornate **City Hall** and lovely old **Thalian Theatre** demonstrate Wilmington's former wealth, but it's the cobbled streets of the weathered, boardwalked **waterfront**, dotted with laid-back cafes and restaurants, that really appeal. **Chandler's Wharf**, an upmarket shopping mall in a restored warehouse, is typical of the area's revitalization, while the **Old City Market** (daily, varied hours) sells crafts and food in a more authentic atmosphere. The blocks back from the waterfront are lined with quirky thrift shops and memorabilia troves. Wilmington has also gained some notoriety as a popular film setting – *Blue Velvet* and *Teenage Mutant Ninja Turtles* were shot in the area, and EUE/Screen Gems Studios, at N 23rd Street, boasts the set of the hit teen-drama *Dawson's Creek* (weekend tours, call Silver Screen Tours to reserve ☎910/675-8479; $10). A self- guided tour of locations used in the show can also be picked up at the visitor center.

Twenty miles south on Hwy-421, near Kure Beach, **Fort Fisher State Historic Site** commands a spectacular rocky position overlooking both the sea and the mouth of the Cape Fear River. A small **museum** focuses on its days as a Confederate stronghold, with relics from sunken blockade runners and various weaponry (April–Oct Mon–Sat 9am–5pm, Sun 1–5pm; Nov–March Tues–Sat 10am–4pm, Sun 1–4pm; free).

## Practicalities

The **bus** station is at 201 Harnett St, a mile north of downtown off Third Street. Wilmington's **visitor center**, 24 N Third St (Mon–Fri 8.30am–5pm, Sat 9am–4pm, Sun 1–4pm; ☎910/341-4030 or 1-800/222-4757), has maps and walking tours; the funniest, most informative overviews of the city are given by Adventure Tours, which leave from the flagpole at Market and Water streets (April–Oct 10am & 2pm; ☎910/763-1785; $10). There's also an **information** kiosk (April–Oct daily 9am–4.30pm) at the foot of Market Street, from where riverboat tours ($6) depart.

Accommodation is concentrated in **B&Bs**: when the movie stars come to town, they stay at the *Graystone Inn* on Dock and Third, with its comfortable library and shady patio (☎910/763-2000; ⑦); another nice alternative is the *Inn on Orange*, 410 Orange St (☎910/815-0035; ⑤), which has spacious rooms, a pool and garden. You could also head a dozen miles east to **Wrightsville Beach**, where among the string of weather-worn condos and pricey resort hotels, the *Silver Gull*, 20 E Salisbury St, offers comfortable motel rooms next to the fishing pier (☎910/256-3728; ⑤), though nowhere is particularly cheap, apart from the usual budget **motels** on Hwy-17.

For a quick **meal** try the *Underground Sandwich Shoppe*, 103 Market St (☎910/763-9686), or *Mollye's Fresh Market*, 118 Princess St (☎910/772-9989), which has a good selection of vegetarian fare and occasional live music plus other events. For dinner *Paleo Sun Cafe*, 35 N Front St (☎910/762-7700), has something for almost everyone as well as live jazz on weekends. The same can be said for the *Cafe Phoenix*, 9 S Front St (☎910/343-1395), with pasta, seafood, steaks and vegetarian selections, and possibly, the occasional film star. Wilmington, has a fairly thriving **nightlife** – as well as a small gay scene. A fun-loving crowd heads to the *Reel Cafe*, 100 S Front St (☎910/251-1832), to hear live music on the restaurant's third floor patio, while the nearby *Barbary Coast*, 116 Front St (☎910/762-8996), is a rough hole-in-the-wall that gains some cachet from being Mickey Rourke's favorite spot in town. The excellent *Thalian Hall*, Third and Chestnut streets (☎910/343-3664), built in 1858, hosts many well-known bands touring through the area and shows art-house movies.

# The North Carolina Piedmont

North Carolina's **PIEDMONT** is a fairly industrialized area of textile and tobacco towns, mostly in decline. However, even close to the towns it can still be very rural, little changed since the 1950s. The main area of interest is the **Research Triangle** trio of neighboring college towns: **Raleigh**, the state capital; relaxed **Durham**, with its strong black community; and countercultural **Chapel Hill**. **Winston-Salem**, famous for its tobacco industry, boasts the excellent Old Salem village, while **Charlotte**'s international airport is the point of arrival for many European visitors.

## Raleigh

**RALEIGH**, North Carolina's capital, stands on I-40 at the very heart of the state, focusing around the central, pedestrianized **Capitol Square**. The **Capitol** itself is worth a look if only to see the copy of Canova's bizarre statue of George Washington in Roman garb (Mon–Fri 8am–5pm, Sat 9am–5pm, Sun 1–5pm; free). Almost next door, the **North Carolina Museum of History**, 109 E Jones St (Tues–Sat 9am–5pm, Sun noon–5pm; free), is impressively far-reaching, a chronological trot through the state's history from the viewpoint of its people, with particularly strong sections on women. Opposite is the **North Carolina Museum of Natural Sciences** (Mon–Sat 9am–5pm, Sun 1–5pm; free), which is undergoing a massive redevelopment to include more interactive exhibits.

The four-block **City Market**, south of the capitol, arranged around Martin Street and Moore Square, holds a number of good shops and restaurants; check out the local artists and sculptors at work in **Artspace**, 201 E Davie St (Mon–Sat 9am–5pm). US President **Andrew Johnson** was born in a tiny hut just north of where the capitol now stands; his birthplace has since been moved to **Mordecai Historic Park**, north of town at 1 Mimosa St (Mon & Wed–Sat 10am–3pm, Sun 1–3pm; $4). Here you can also see the **Mordecai House**, built by a wealthy plantation-owner and continuously inhabited by the same family for the next two centuries. A little way out to the northwest via I-40, the impressive **North Carolina Museum of Art**, 2110 Blue Ridge Blvd (Tues–Thurs & Sat 9am–5pm, Fri 9am–9pm, Sun 11am–6pm; tours Tues–Sun 1.30pm; free), has an eclectic display of works from Africa and the US. It also boasts a particularly good restaurant open for lunch from Tuesday to Friday, brunch at the weekend, and dinner on Friday (☎919/833-3548).

## Practicalities

Raleigh-Durham **airport** (☎919/840-2123) is off I-40, fifteen minutes northwest of town. The **taxi** ride into town costs around $15, various circuitous shuttle services about $10. One daily Amtrak train passes through on its way to New York, another on the way to Florida, pulling in downtown at 320 W Cabarrus St. The Greyhound station is in a seedy part of downtown at 321 W Jones St. A patchy local **bus** service (☎919/828-7228) operates out of the transit mall at Blount and Martin streets. The **visitor center** at 301 N Blount St (Mon–Fri 8am–5pm, Sat 9am–5pm, Sun 1–5pm; ☎919/733-3456) co-ordinates local walking and driving tours.

If you want to **stay**, avoid the more anonymous downtown hotels and try instead the central *William Thomas House B&B*, 530 N Blount St (☎919/755-9400; ⑤), or head out to Hillsborough Street near North Carolina State University, where the *Velvet Cloak Inn* at no. 1505 offers comfortable rooms, free coffee and an indoor pool, plus has good weekend rates (☎919/828-0333; ④–⑤).

*Big Ed's*, in the City Market at 220 Wolfe St (☎919/836-9909), does a fair job of Southern **home-cooking**, especially at breakfast. Across the street, *Greenshields Brewery*, 214 E Martin St (☎919/829-0214), serves very good English-style beer and pub food. More upmarket, but just as popular, the huge *42nd St Oyster Bar*, downtown at West and Jones (☎919/831-2811), is always buzzing with journalists, politicians and students enjoying fresh fish and seafood. **Hillsborough Street**, lined with bars, clubs and cafes, has some great places to eat and is the epicenter of Raleigh's excellent **nightlife**. *Rathskeller* at no. 2412 (☎919/821-5342) serves healthy, creative food in intimate wooden booths, and there's a lively bar. Or try *Cup a Joe* at no. 3100 (☎919/828-9665), a bohemian coffee bar with live folk music on Friday and Saturday. For techno and house, make for the *Five O Cafe*, above the Studio arts cinema at no. 2526 (☎919/821-4419), while *The Brewery* at no. 3009 (☎919/834-7018) is a good venue in which to see the best regional rock and alternative bands. Away from Hillsborough Street, the *Berkeley Cafe*, at 217 W Martin (☎919/821-0777), specializes in roots and alternative country as well as rock. The *Tir Na Nog Irish Pub* on 218 S Blount (☎919/833-7795), is a lively bar with live music Tuesday–Saturday, that also serves Irish cuisine and a Sunday brunch. Pick up the free *Spectator* for some current information.

# Durham

Twenty miles northwest of Raleigh, **DURHAM** found itself at the center of the nation's tobacco industry after farmer Washington Duke came home from the Civil War with the idea of producing cigarettes – by 1890 he and his three sons had formed the **America Tobacco Company**, one of the nation's most powerful businesses. The **Duke Homestead Historical Site**, 2828 Duke Homestead Rd, about a half-mile north of I-85 (April–Oct Mon–Sat 9am–5pm, Sun 1–5pm; Nov–March Tues–Sat 10am–4pm, Sun 1–4pm; free), incorporates an even-handed and lively museum covering the social history of tobacco farming.

In 1924 the Duke family's $40 million endowment to the previously small-scale Trinity College enabled it to expand into a world-respected medical research facility, swiftly changing its name to **Duke University**. It's well worth visiting the campus: on the original, eastside, the **Museum of Art** (Tues–Fri 9am–5pm, Sat 11am–2pm, Sun 2–5pm; free) has good African, pre-Columbian, medieval and Asian collections. The Gothic west campus centers on the soaring cathedral-style **chapel** (daily 8.30am–5pm), which boasts one of the most powerful Flentrop organs in the world. Still on campus, the terraces and bowers of the beautifully landscaped **Sarah P Duke Gardens** are a blaze of fragrance and color surrounded by pine forest.

Elsewhere, the city has more of a blue-collar feel and takes pride in its vibrant **black heritage**. Based in a number of surprisingly small old plantation homes, set in 71 acres seven miles north of town in rural Treyburn Park, the **Stagville Preservation Center** (Mon–Fri 9am–4pm; ☎919/620-0120; free) is not a museum as such, but hosts various workshops and living history demonstrations, illustrating plantation life from the early 1800s to Reconstruction through the work of local black craftworkers.

On Farrington Road, between Hwy-54 and Old Chapel Hill Road, and worth a detour, **Patterson's Mill Country Store**, at the end of a rutted country lane, looks straight out of *The Waltons*, selling everything from old signs and used books to crafts, candy, soap and spices. A back room is stuffed with vials and potions; upstairs there's a bewildering panoply of tobacco memorabilia.

### Practicalities

Greyhound **buses** stop in Durham at 820 W Morgan St. Pick up maps and local information from the Durham **visitor center**, at 101 E Morgan St (Mon–Fri 8.30am–5pm, Sat 10am–2pm; ☎919/687-0288).

Durham's **Brightleaf Square**, an upbeat, upmarket shopping area of restored tobacco warehouses off Main Street downtown, is a good bet for **restaurants**: try *Anotherthyme*, 109 N Gregson St (☎919/682-5225), which serves creative California-style food. Durham has historically been at the center of the North Carolina Piedmont **blues** scene, with musicians such as Reverend Gary Davis playing for tips in the 1920s at the tobacco markets in town. It hosts the **Bull Durham Blues Festival** in mid-September. You can hear jazz at *Talk of the Town*, 108 E Main St (☎919/682-7747).

# Chapel Hill

The hip, villagey atmosphere of **CHAPEL HILL**, on the southwest outskirts of Durham, has benefited from the rise to national prominence of such local bands as Superchunk, Archers of Loaf and Ben Folds Five. It's also the hometown of James "Carolina On My Mind" Taylor. About fifty percent of the 45,000 population are students, and its position as a bastion of white liberalism in a poor rural state brings the town its detractors; that said, it's a pleasant enough place to hang out for a while, joining the hordes of students in the laid-back bars and coffeehouses along **Franklin Street**, which fringes the north side of campus. Franklin continues west into the adjacent city of **Carrboro**, though there's very little to distinguish the transition.

The **University of North Carolina**, dating from 1789, was the nation's first state university and holds some fine eighteenth-century buildings. The earliest is **Old East**, its original brick painted a fashionable tan in the 1840s. Evidence of the university's wealth can be seen at the splendid **Morehead Planetarium**, E Franklin Street (surrounding exhibits free, star shows $4; ☎919/549-6863), which serves as a NASA training center, and at the **Ackland Art Museum**, South Columbia and Franklin streets (Wed–Sat 10am–5pm, Sun 1–5pm; suggested donation $3), that's strong on Greek and Roman antiquities. The UNC **visitor center** (☎919/962-1630) is in the west lobby of the Planetarium, and they lend out Walkmans that allow you to do a self-guided tour of the campus.

### Practicalities

Greyhound **buses** stop downtown at 311 W Franklin St, and the downtown **welcome center** is at 179 E Franklin St (Tues–Sat 10am–4pm; ☎919/929-9700 or 1-800/968-2060). Chapel Hill has few places to **stay**, and is often booked up; one of the most popular spots is the 1920s *The Carolina Inn* at 211 Pittsboro St, on campus (☎919/933-2001; ⑦). The *Hampton Inn*, 1740 Hwy-15/501 (☎919/968-3000; ④), is a comfortable motel just out of town, while *Travel Time Inn*, 4145 Garrett Rd (☎919/489-9146; ②/③) actually in Durham is a budget option conveniently located between both cities.

For **food**, *Crooks Corner*, 610 W Franklin St (☎919/929-7643), serves cordon bleu Southern cooking such as shrimp and grits or fried chicken and greens in smart surroundings. *Four Eleven West*, 411 W Franklin St (☎919/967-2782), is an excellent modern Italian restaurant. One of the best breakfast spots is *Elmo's Diner*, in the Carr Mill Mall in Carrboro at 200 N Greensboro St (☎919/929-2909). Adjacent to the mall is the community-owned *Weaver Street Market*, 101 E Weaver St (☎919/929-0010), featuring an inexpensive, tasty vegetarian buffet where you pay by the weight. For Chapel Hill **nightlife**, stay on Franklin Street: *The Cave*, 452 W Franklin St (☎919/968-9308), has live music from bluegrass to indie, with *Local 506*, 506 W Franklin St (☎919/942-5506), the next step up. Over in Carrboro, the *Cat's Cradle*, 300 E Main St (☎919/967-9053), has a reputation for booking the best bands on the national touring circuit, while the cozy 300-seater ArtsCenter, 300 E Main St (☎919/929-2787), stages plays, dance shows and concerts.

## Winston-Salem

Though synonymous with the brand names of its cigarettes, **WINSTON-SALEM**, 105 miles west of Raleigh, instead owes its spot on the tourist itinerary to the delightful **Old Salem**, a well-preserved twenty-block area that honors the heritage of the city's first Moravian settlers. Escaping religious persecution in what are now the Czech and Slovak republics, the first Moravians settled in this rolling area of the Piedmont in the mid-seventeenth century. They soon established trading links with the frontier settlers and founded the town of Salem on a communal basis – they permitted only those of the same religious faith to live here. The demand for their crafts helped establish the adjacent community of Winston, which, accruing tremendous wealth from tobacco, soon outgrew the older community. The two merged in 1913 to form Winston-Salem.

Today visitors can tour ten of Old Salem's buildings and, with the help of costumed guides, learn about the skills, trades and customs of the Moravians. Start at the **visitor center** between Academy and West streets (Mon–Sat 9am–5pm, Sun 12.30–5pm), and if time is tight, prioritize the **Single Brothers House**, built in 1771, where unmarried men would sleep, worship and make items such as silverware, hats and paper. There's also a **tavern** (☎336/748-8585) where beers and large lunches and dinners are served, and a **bakery** that produces great cookies.

There isn't too much to see in Winston-Salem's downtown, although the city is trying to liven things up by introducing live music outdoors from April to October, Thursday through Saturday nights. On Thurdays, Live after Five is at The Winston Square Park, Friday 4th Street is blocked off for jazz performances, and Saturdays, Trade Street hosts a variety of music programs. Three miles northwest of downtown, the **Reynolda House Museum of American Art**, 2500 Reynolda Rd (Tues–Sat 9.30am–4.30pm, Sun 1.30–4.30pm; $6, free to college students), uniquely throws together pieces by all the top American artists from the eighteenth century to the present day in what was the home of tobacco baron Richard Joshua Reynolds. The mansion, designed by Charles Barton Keen, is set in lush, landscaped gardens, with a number of its surrounding buildings converted into fancy stores collectively known as **Historic Reynolda Village**. Close by, and integrating the former home of underwear manufacturer Charles Hanes, is the occasionally controversial **Southeastern Center for Contemporary Art (SECCA)**, 750 Marguerite Drive, which gets all the area's major shows. About a mile east, **Whitaker Park**, off Reynolds Boulevard (museum Mon–Fri 8am–5pm; free), is the impressive, fully automated factory that churns out up to 275 million Winston, Salem and Camel cigarettes per day, unfortunately a video has replaced the previous tours and there's not much of a reason to stop by anymore. At Winston-Salem State University, the renowned **Diggs Gallery** (Tues–Sat 11am–5pm;

☎336/750-2458; free), has ten to fifteen different exhibits yearly, primarily on African-American art and various educational programs. Be sure to check out the colorful and somewhat perplexing murals *Origins* and *Ascension*, by John Biggers, in the nearby O'Kelly library.

## Practicalities

Greyhound **buses** stop at 250 Greyhound Court on the east side of town by Hwy-52. Amtrak lays on buses to the *Salem Inn* for the short ride from the nearest station in Greensboro. Winston-Salem's resourceful **visitor center** is on the north edge of downtown at 601 N Cherry St (☎910/777-3796 or 1-800/331-7018).

*Brookstown Inn*, 200 Brookstown Ave (☎336/725-1120 or 1-800/845-4262; ⑥), is a highly recommended small **hotel** in a former cotton warehouse, dishing up complimentary cheese and wine, cookies and milk, and continental breakfast. A less expensive option across the street, the *Salem Inn*, 127 S Cherry St (☎336/725-8561 or 1-800/533-8760; ④), offers clean and central motel rooms.

**Eating** options aren't that exciting, though the *Twin City Diner*, 1425 W First St (☎336/724-4462), is a popular place for sandwiches and grill food. The more upmarket *Bistro 900,* 900 S Marshall St (☎336/721-1336), serves good Southern cuisine. The *Village Tavern*, in Reynolda Village (☎336/760-8686), is a great spot for a beer and some pub food. Touring roots, rock and reggae bands play the atmospheric *Ziggy's*, 433 Baity St (☎336/748-0810), out by Wake Forest University campus.

# Charlotte

More than anywhere else in the region, **CHARLOTTE**, at the junction of I-77 and I-85 near the South Carolina border, can genuinely claim to have made it: a banking and transportation center that has become the largest city in the state, "boosted," in much the same way as Atlanta, by ambitious business and city leaders. They like to project the image of a sophisticated, fast-lane cultural metropolis – in fact its center is somewhat soulless, though many nearby neighborhoods are delightful and stuffed with good places to eat. Served by direct British Airways flights from London, however, it does make one of the best and most manageable arrival points in the region.

The chief attraction in **downtown** Charlotte, an unlovely mass of skyscrapers and concrete known as "uptown," is **Discovery Place**, 301 N Tryon St, a kids-oriented science museum with an indoor rainforest and an OMNIMAX theater hosting the nation's largest planetarium (Mon–Sat 9am–6pm, Sun 1–6pm, except Mon–Fri 9am–5pm from Sept–May; $6.50, kids (6–12) $5; call ☎704/372-6261 for evening theater shows). Another major landmark, on the eastside is the massive **Ericsson Stadium,** home of the fairly new NFL team, the Carolina Panthers.

Although most restaurants and stores are tucked away inside the city's skyscrapers, Tryon Street is downtown's busiest thoroughfare. At the intersection of Tryon and Trade streets is **Independence Square**, where at each corner giant modern statues stand – depicting transportation, commerce, industry and the future. Just a few blocks away, the **Museum of the New South**, 324 N College St (Tues–Fri 11am–5pm; $2), looks at the growth of the region from Reconstruction onwards. Interesting vignettes examine musical history, with the spotlight falling on local names such as gospel legends the Golden Gate Quartet. The **Mint Museum of Art**, three miles further southeast at 2730 Randolph Rd on bus #15 (Tues 10am–10pm, Wed–Sat 10am–5pm, Sun noon–5pm; $6), has a good array of Indian, pre-Columbian and African art, plus a noted collection of pottery and porcelain. The **Mint Museum of Craft and Design** on 220 N Tryon St, is also worth a stop for its eclectic collection of metal, glass, wood, fiber and ceramic works (Tues–Thurs 10am–7pm, Fri 10am–9pm, Sat 10am–7pm, Sun noon–5pm; $6).

For those interested in **NASCAR** racing, fifteen minutes from downtown in the suburb of Concord is the **Lowe's Motor Speedway**, where guided tours are available, and in late May the Coca-Cola 600 comes to town.

### Practicalities

**Charlotte/Douglas International Airport** (☎704/359-4000), seven miles west of town on Old Dowd Road or I-85, is served by the #5 **bus** running every 45min from downtown to the airport from 5.25am–1.30am; **taxis** cost about $12, and **shuttle buses**, which leave from the lower level, $8. Greyhound stops centrally at 601 W Trade St, while Amtrak trains pull in at 1914 N Tryon St. The expansive **visitor center** is at 330 S Tryon St (Mon–Fri 8.30am–5pm, Sat 10am–4pm, Sun 1–4pm; ☎704/331-2700 or 1-800/231-4636).

Most of Charlotte's **hotels** are aimed at the conference trade, though the *Dunhill Inn*, 237 N Tryon St (☎704/332-4141; ⑦), possesses old-world charm. The *Holiday Inn City Center*, 230 N College St (☎704/335-5400; ⑤/⑥), has good facilities, and the *Days Inn*, 601 N Tryon St (☎704/333-4733; ④), is the cheapest central option. The *Morehead Inn B&B*, 1122 E Morehead St (☎704/376-3357; ⑤), offers a great location in the **Dilworth/South End** neighborhood, a pleasing mix of renovated commercial buildings and broad, tree-lined avenues. Just a mile southeast of uptown, is where you'll find the best range of **restaurants**, from the upscale *Lamplighter*, 1065 E Morehead St (☎704/372-5343), to the more casual *Castaldi's Italian Bistro*, at 311 East Blvd (☎704/333-6999), and the *Southend Brewery & Smokehouse*, 2100 South Blvd (☎704/358-HOPS). *Lupie's Cafe*, 2718 Monroe Rd, (☎704/374-1232) is an inexpensive option where you will find lipsmacking chili and other homemade dishes. **Nightlife** is concentrated between the easily walked grid of Tryon, College, Seventh and Fifth streets, particularly around the Mint Museum of Art.

# The North Carolina mountains

The best way to see the **mountains** of North Carolina is from the pristine **Blue Ridge Parkway**, which runs across the northwest from Virginia (see p.397) to the **Great Smoky Mountains National Park**. It's a delight to drive; the vast panoramic expanses of forested hillside, with barely a settlement in sight, may astonish travelers fresh from the crowded centers of the East Coast. This predominantly poor region has been a breeding ground for **bluegrass** music, as played by Doc Watson and Earl Scruggs. The North Carolina High Country Host, 1700 Blowing Rock Rd, in Boone (☎1-800-438-7500) is a helpful visitor center that services most of the mountain area.

## The Blue Ridge Parkway

The peak tourist season for the **BLUE RIDGE PARKWAY** is October, when the leaves of the deciduous trees which cover the landscape turn from bright yellow and gold through browns to vivid red. All year round, however, this magnificent, twisting mountain road – largely built in the 1930s by Roosevelt's Civilian Conservation Corps volunteers – is a worthwhile vacation destination in itself, peppered with state-run campgrounds, short hiking trails and dramatic overlooks. When planning your itinerary, take note that though the Parkway is closed to commercial vehicles, and only particularly crowded near one or two hyped beauty spots, the constant curves make it difficult to average anything approaching the 45mph speed limit.

## MOUNTAIN ACTIVITIES

Organized **outdoor pursuits** available along the Blue Ridge Parkway include excellent **whitewater rafting** and **canoeing**, most of it on the Nolichucky River near the Tennessee border south of Johnson City, Tennessee, but also on the Watauga River and Wilson Creek. Companies running trips include Wahoo's Adventures (☎1-800/444-7238), based near Boone, and High Mountain Expeditions (☎1-800/262-9036), in Blowing Rock. Expect to pay $65 for a full day (safety equipment included).

Winter sees **skiing** at a number of slopes and resorts, particularly around **Banner Elk**, twelve miles southwest of Boone. Resort accommodation is expensive, ski passes less so ($20–30 for each weekday). Appalachian Ski Mountain (☎1-800/322-2373) is near Blowing Rock, and Ski Beech (☎1-800/222-2293) is at Beech Mountain; you can pick up full listings at visitor centers. **Cross-country skiing** availability has declined in recent years due to lack of snow.

## Boone

**BOONE** is the most obvious northern base for exploring the mountains; the town itself holds little of interest, though as home to the Appalachian State University it does have a life of its own. On campus, just off Hwy-321, the small **Appalachian Cultural Museum** (Tues–Sat 10am–5pm, Sun 1–5pm; $2, free Tues) gives a good overview of the area, concentrating on such mountain pastimes as music, storytelling, stock-car racing and making moonshine whiskey. Corny family entertainments dot US-321 – the three-mile steam-driven Tweetsie Railroad which also has other attractions, is all that remains of a line across the mountains to Johnson City, Tennessee (summer–fall daily 9am–6pm; $18) – while pretty back roads hold offbeat settlements such as **Valle Crucis** on US-194, where the 1883 Mast General Store (summer Mon–Sat 7am–6.30pm, Sun 1–6pm, winter hours vary) is well worth a look around.

Local public transportation is dire, so you'll need a **car** to get here and around. The **visitor center** is downtown at 208 Howard St (☎828/264-2225 or 1-800/852-9506). Bargain central **accommodation** can be had at the *Boone Trail Motel*, 275 E King St (☎828/264-8839; ①/②). The *High Country Inn*, 1785 Hwy-105 (☎828/264-1000 or 1-800/334-5605; ③), is a clean motel with a decent cafe and a sports bar, while the *Cat Pause Inn*, Broadstone Road, Valle Crucis (☎828/963-7297; ④), is great value as long as you like felines. Back in Boone, the *Lovill House Inn* at 404 Old Bristol Rd (☎704/264-4204 or 1-800/849-9466; ⑤) is a pleasant **B&B**. Most of the best places to **eat** or to have a beer are along King Street; the *Caribbean Cafe*, 489 W King St (☎828/265-2233), serves good, spicy food including vegetarian dishes; the gourmet pizzas, pasta and Mexican food at the *Red Onion Cafe* (☎828/264-5470) are favorites among locals. For great vegetarian cuisine and powerful smoothies try *Angelica's*, 506 W King St (☎828/265-0809) and the *Cottonwood Brewery*, 179 Howard St (☎828/266-1004), is a relaxing place to sip a local brew and take in some local music.

## South along the Parkway

Eight miles south of Boone, **BLOWING ROCK** is a pleasant if touristy resort just south of the Parkway, though the "Blowing Rock" itself (summer daily 8am–8pm; rest of year daily 10am–5pm; $4) is nothing as impressive as photos suggest. At the nearby **Parkway Craft Center** (☎704/295-7938), you can see traditional folk crafts being made. The **visitor center** (Mon–Sat 9am–5pm; ☎828/295-7851) is on the main street, together with **hotels** such as the *Boxwood Lodge* (☎828/295-9984; ④). The least expensive local **campground** is at Julian Price Park, milepost 297 on the Parkway (☎828/963-

5911; no reservations, electricity or showers; $12). At *Woodland's*, on Hwy-321 Bypass (☎828/295-3651), the pork barbecue is excellent; it's also a good spot to drink beer, as is the back porch of *The Emporium*, a comfy restaurant on Hwy-321 (☎828/295-7661).

*The Emporium* also has a fine view of the privately owned **Grandfather Mountain** (5964ft), fifteen miles further south with access near milepost 304 (summer daily 8am–7pm; rest of year daily 8am–5pm; $10). The price may be high, but the owners make a genuine attempt to protect this unique environment, and the prospect from the top – especially on the "mile-high swinging bridge" between the peaks – is superb, as are some of the trails. Bears, otters and other animals, including golden and bald eagles that were wounded by gunshot in their western homelands, are held in habitat settings. During the **Highland Games** and "Gathering of the Clans" in the second full week in July, distantly Scottish Americans (take a look at the local phone book and see just how many names begin with "Mc") dress up in kilts, toss cabers and tootle away on bagpipes.

Of various short and easy **trails** off the Parkway hereabouts, the one leading half a mile or so up to **Rough Ridge**, near milepost 301, is especially enjoyable. Rough Ridge is one of several access points to the 13.5-mile **Tanawha Trail**, which runs along the ridge above the Parkway from Beacon Heights to Julian Price Park, looking out over the lush, dense forests to the east. If you plan a longer backpacking trip, equip yourself with a large-scale visitor center map; though the actual walking is not that difficult, it's not hard to lose yourself in the woods.

Another good hike heads through the **Linville Gorge Wilderness**, near milepost 316 a couple of miles outside Linville Falls village. The high and spectacular **Linville Falls** themselves are at one end of the wilderness where the gorge begins. Breathtaking views from either side of the gorge look down 2000ft to the **Linville River** below, which has perfect, long, deep swimming pools. Be warned that ascents are steep, and some of the fainter paths are near-jungle. You can also climb **Hawksbill** or **Table Rock** mountains from the nearest unsurfaced forest road, which leaves Hwy-181 south of the village of Jonas Ridge (signposted "Gingercake Acres," with a small, low sign to Table Rock). The unremarkable but amiable villages of **Linville** and **Linville Falls** have the usual **motels** and restaurants; Linville Falls also has a **campground** (☎828/765-2681), and *Spears Restaurant* (☎828/765-0026) is worth a detour for its hickory-smoked pork barbecue. Alternatively, travel south along the Parkway to milepost 328.3 and stock up on apple cider, homemade honey and fudge at the **Orchard at Altapass** (open Memorial Day–Nov 1; ☎828/765-9531; call for hayride details), where there's also live mountain music in the store at weekends.

The views from the Parkway in the **Mount Mitchell State Park** area, south toward Asheville, are tremendous. Sadly, however, this is largely because the trees around the summit of Mount Mitchell – the highest point in the eastern US, at 6684ft – have been ravaged by acid rain from coal-burning industries in the Chattanooga Basin to the west, and the large barren patches leave the horizon clear.

## Asheville and Black Mountain

Encircled by a ring of interstates, and skirted to the east and south by the Parkway, modest **ASHEVILLE**, roughly 100 miles southwest of Boone, retains an appealing downtown core. It's also something of a New Age center, with ephemera stores, holistic healing sessions, and a tradition among the region's farmers of growing medicinal herbs. Two miles south on Biltmore Avenue, the **Biltmore Estate** is the largest private mansion in the US (daily 9am–5pm; $30). Built in the late nineteenth century by George Vanderbilt and loosely modeled on a Loire chateau, it's a wild piece of nouveau riche folly from the Victorian chic of the indoor palm court to the landscaped gardens.

Asheville's Greyhound/Trailways terminal is inconveniently located at 2 Tunnel Rd, two miles out of downtown on bus #13 or #4 stopping at the Innsbruck Mall. Central

**motels** include the *American Court*, 85 Merrimon Ave (☎1-800/233-3582; ③/④); for a bit of pampering, head for the luxurious *Cedar Crest* **B&B**, 674 Biltmore Ave (☎828/252-1389; ⑦). The *Wolfe Den*, 22 Ravenscroft Drive (☎828/285-0230; ①), is a friendly hostel with an occasional creative workshop, close to downtown and has dorm beds for $15–18 depending on how long you stay. The nearest **campground** is *Bear Creek RV Park*, 81 S Bear Creek Rd, off I-40 to the west (☎828/253-0798).

There are several upmarket **places to eat**, among them tiny *Salsas*, 6 Patton Ave (☎828/252-9805), serving up an aromatic blend of Mexican and Caribbean dishes, though tables can be hard to come by. The *Laughing Seed Cafe*, 40 Wall St (☎828/252-3445), has wonderful vegetarian food (check out the "meatloaf"), while *Beanstreets Coffee*, 3 Broadway (☎828/255-8180), is a fun place to hang out. Although Asheville is small, there are enough students to keep a reasonable **nightlife** scene going; *Barley's*, 42 Biltmore Ave (☎828/255-0504), is the best brewpub in town and offers good food and live music. *Be Here Now*, further along at no. 5 (☎828/258-2071) is a nonsmoking venue hosting a lot of alternative country and reggae bands. *Jack in the Wood*, 95 Patton Ave (☎828/233-3582), is an enjoyable pub.

Pick up information on the numerous local summer music and craft festivals from the downtown **visitor center**, 151 Haywood St (☎828/258-6101 or 1-800/257-1300). August's **Mountain Dance and Folk Festival** features bluegrass and traditional dancing, while the hugely enjoyable **Folk Festival**, held in mid-May and October in **BLACK MOUNTAIN**, fourteen miles east on I-40 (one bus a day), showcases Appalachian and world folk music, usually attracting major European and African musicians. There's little to do in Black Mountain otherwise, though the clear fresh air, pretty views and relaxed pace make a stroll worthwhile. The *Monte Vista* there, at 308 W State St (☎828/669-2119; ③–⑤), is a small, very comfortable **hotel** with regional decor, while the *Town Pump*, 143 Cherry St (☎828/669-9151), promotes top local musicians.

Twenty miles southeast of the Parkway on US-64/74, the natural granite tower of **Chimney Rock** sticks out from the almost-sheer side of Hickory Nut Gorge (summer daily 8.30am–5.30pm; rest of year daily 8.30am–4.30pm; park stay about an hour and a half past ticket sale; $10). After taking the elevator to the top, you can clamber up and down steps and walk along protected walkways atop the impressive cliffs. Many of the climactic moments of *The Last of the Mohicans* were filmed here; you may recognize the mighty waterfall that drops 400ft from the western end of the gorge. From the top you can see **Lake Lure**, where the movie *Dirty Dancing* was filmed.

## Great Smoky Mountains National Park

West of Asheville, **GREAT SMOKY MOUNTAINS NATIONAL PARK** is the most visited national park in the US. It straddles the border with Tennessee, and is covered in more detail – with a map – in our Tennessee section on p.508. In summer and fall, the North Carolina approaches to the park are every bit as clogged with traffic as those in Tennessee, and all accommodation can be booked up weeks in advance.

The largest of the possible bases for touring the park is **CHEROKEE**, where a few Cherokee managed to hang on when the tribe was "removed" along the Trail of Tears to Oklahoma in 1838 (see p.511). Now known as the "Eastern Band of the Cherokee Nation," they have a small reservation on the edge of the park, which derives its main income from tourism. As a result, Cherokee itself is a mass of fast-food restaurants, cornily named motels, moccasin retailers and tacky giftshops – and the requisite casino. It's an odd place, where the presentation of Native Americans as noble savages all but equates them with the "cuddly" bears of the park as just another novelty for tourists.

Away from the kitsch and cliché, however, the **Museum of the Cherokee Indian** at the north end of town (mid-June to Aug Mon–Sat 9am–8pm, Sun 9am–5pm; Sept to mid-June daily 9am–5pm; $4.50) has good archeological displays and sections on Cherokee arts and history – including Sequoyah's invention of a syllabary in 1821, to preserve the oral Cherokee culture in writing. Qualla Arts and Crafts, across the street, is a Cherokee-run cooperative selling traditional crafts, principally basketwork. Nearby, the **Oconaluftee Indian Village** (mid-May to late Oct daily 9am–5.30pm; $10) is a reconstruction of a mid-eighteenth-century Cherokee village. Amid the log cabins, you can see demonstrations of weaving and basketmaking, as well as crafts and skills that have long since died out, such as dugout canoe construction and blowpipe hunting. During summer months an outdoor drama *Unto these Hills*, reenacts the Cherokee plight from Hernando De Soto's arrival to the Trail of Tears (☎828/497-2111; $11–14). All three attractions can be seen by purchasing a value-ticket for $22 at any of the locations and can be spread over a series of days.

Cherokee is not much of a **place to stay**; though the motels are fine, there's not a single passable place to eat, and it's unbelievably dead between about October and March – and as a reservation town, it's also entirely dry. If you need to stay nearby, you're better driving on to Maggie Valley (see below), but if you're stuck, the **visitor center** (mid-June to Aug daily 8am–9pm; Aug–Oct daily 8am–6pm; Nov to mid-June daily 8am–5pm; ☎828/497-9195 or 1-800/438-1601), in the center of town, has lists of more than fifty motels; the central *Cherokee Plaza* (☎704/497-2301 or 1-800/535-4798; ③/④) overlooks the river. Incidentally, nearby, look out for the great sign at the *Pink Motel*, a 1950s Tinkerbell, swathed, of course, in fairytale pink.

The **Oconaluftee visitor center**, the headquarters of the North Carolina side of the park, is a short way out of Cherokee along US-441 (summer daily 8am–7pm; spring & fall daily 8am–6pm; winter daily 8am–5pm; ☎828/497-1900; free). It has good displays on Appalachian farming life, and a re-created pioneer village. Fifteen miles east, the small community of **MAGGIE VALLEY** boasts a string of motels with peaceful views over the valleys – one of the cheapest, the *Riverlet*, on US-19 (☎704/926-1900; ③), overlooks two streams and has a pool. It's all rather tranquil here, with trout farms, wooden shacks and clear, fresh air. Tourism focuses on hillbilly culture, with lots of hoedowns and the like, but if you're really desperate for kicks you could head for the nearby **Ghost Town in the Sky**, where a chairlift sweeps you up toward a hokey Wild West re-creation. During the last weekend in July, Maggie Valley hosts an **International Folk Festival**.

## Southwestern North Carolina

The area west of Asheville, and south of the national park, holds a number of dramatic **waterfalls**. **Looking Glass Falls**, about twelve miles south of the Parkway on US-276, is in a particularly beautiful section of the **Pisgah National Forest**. The falls drop 85 feet, with a great (albeit very cold) swimming hole at the bottom. **Connestee Falls**, a few miles south on US-276 toward Brevard, is a double waterfall and even higher. Unbridled optimists can pay to pan for **gemstones**, such as rubies, at outwashes of the numerous gem mines near the 250ft **Cullasaja Falls**, further west on US-64.

The far west corner of the state is famous for its superb **whitewater**, with plenty of companies offering canoeing and rafting on the **Nantahala River**. Guided raft expeditions cost around $31 for a three-hour trip; one company, Nantahala Outdoor Center (☎828/488-2175 or 1-800/232-7238), also runs a **hostel** (①). Wildwater Ltd offers a five-hour train and rafting trip along the Nantahala with the Great Smoky Mountain Railway between $55–59 depending on the type of train used (☎1-800/872-4681). Both companies offer excursions on neighboring rivers (Whitewater Ltd ☎ 1-800/451-9972).

West of the Nantahala, off US-129 almost in Tennessee, **Joyce Kilmer National Forest** is worth a final detour, as one of the last remaining stands of unlogged virgin forest in the southeastern US, with some enormous hardwood trees.

# SOUTH CAROLINA

The relatively small state of **SOUTH CAROLINA** remains, with Mississippi, one of the poorest and most rural pockets of the US, although the prime real estate along its coast has lately been developed into exclusive golf courses and tennis clubs. Politics in the first state to secede from the Union in 1860 have traditionally been conservative. Reconstruction was mired in terrible Klan violence, while c.1900 demagogues openly espoused lynching and enforced "Jim Crow" laws with frightening zeal. The state contains two of the country's most right-wing minor universities – football-fixated Clemson, and Christian Bob Jones University in Greenville, a training ground for the fundamentalist right.

South Carolina's fascinating subtropical coastline of **sea islands**, great beaches, marshes and lush palmetto groves preserves traces of a virtually independent black culture (featuring the unique patois *gullah*), from the days when slaves escaped the mainland plantations. Beyond the grand old peninsular port of **Charleston**, arguably the most elegant city in the US with its rainbow-colored old buildings and magnificent, tree-lined avenues, restored plantations stretch as far north as **Georgetown**, en route toward the poseur's paradise of **Myrtle Beach**. Inland, the rolling Piedmont and flat coastal plain hold little to see.

### Getting around South Carolina

Charleston has South Carolina's biggest **airport**, with flights to and from major towns on the East Coast. Three Amtrak routes cut through the state, stopping at Greenville and Clemson in the west, Columbia and other towns in the center and Charleston on the coast. **Buses** run along I-85 between Charlotte, North Carolina, and Atlanta, and a less regular service operates along the coast, stopping at Myrtle Beach and Charleston.

# Myrtle Beach and the north coast

Birthplace of *Wheel of Fortune* star Vanna White, **MYRTLE BEACH** is a brazen splurge of seaside fun, an unmitigated stretch of commercial development twenty miles down the coast from the North Carolina border at the center of the sixty-mile "Grand Strand." Predominantly a family resort, it's packed fit to burst during mid-term vacations with leering, jeering students in fluorescent beachwear – if you've seen the movie *Shag*, you'll know what to expect. Fans of crazy golf, water parks, factory outlet malls, funfairs and parasailing will be in heaven, and the **beach** itself isn't bad. The widest stretch is at North Myrtle Beach, a chain of small communities among which Ocean Drive is the center and Atlantic Beach is exclusively used by African-Americans.

South of Myrtle Beach lie **Murells Inlet**, a fishing port with lots of good fish restaurants, and **Pawleys Island**, a secluded resort once favored by plantation-owners and today retaining a far slower pace than its neighbors. Between the two on Hwy-17, the beautifully landscaped **Brookgreen Gardens** (summer daily 9.30am–9.30pm; rest of the year 9.30am–5pm; $8.50) hold a gathering of American figurative sculpture on the grounds of what was once a rice and indigo plantation, used as the setting for many of Julia Peterkin's novels of *gullah* life. There's also a wildlife area with alligator and deer, and an hour and a half boat tour which explores the area ($6).

### Practicalities

US or Hwy-17 (Kings Highway) is Myrtle Beach's main traffic thoroughfare, while the parallel Ocean Boulevard is lined with hotels and motels. Greyhound **buses** from Charleston and Wilmington come in at 511 7th Ave N (closed 1–3pm daily). Minimal transportation in the beach areas is provided by Coastal Rapid Public Transit buses (75¢–$2 one-way; ☎843/626-9138). Great American Trolley runs a route around the center beach area and out to the Myrtle Square Mall and Broadway at the Beach (summer 8.30am–midnight, until Oct 15 8.30am–10pm; ☎1-800/395-6629; $1.50 each way).

The main branch **visitor center** at 1200 Oak St (☎1-800/356-3016) can provide events listings and details of accommodation and there is another useful branch at 2090 Hwy 501 E in Conway. Of the countless **motels**, the *Swamp Fox*, 2311 S Ocean Blvd (☎1-800/228-9894; ①–⑥), with turquoise pools and ocean views from the more expensive tower rooms, and the similar *Sands Beach Club* further north, at 9400 Shore Drive (☎843/449-1531 or 1-800/845-2202; ④–⑦), are two solid choices. During the summer, rates increase dramatically; if traveling by yourself or with one other it may be cheaper to stay in Conway about 11 miles to the west of US-501.

With ten campgrounds and two state parks, Myrtle Beach calls itself the "Seaside Camping Capital of the World"; this might be an apt description if you have a fairly broad definition of camping. You'll find most of the commercial **campgrounds** concentrated along Kings Highway – on this road in North Myrtle Beach you'll find the *Barefoot Camping Resort,* 4825 Hwy-17 (☎1-800/272-1790). If you decide to camp make sure you check the campground's policy for returning late to avoid being locked out.

If you want burgers, standard diner meals, "surf 'n' turf" in a themed bar or any one of a zillion varieties of ethnic fast food, you'll have no problem finding places to eat. Well-prepared **seafood** can be had at the classier *Sea Captain's House* at 3002 N Ocean Blvd (☎843/448-8082), or at a number of similar establishments in Murrells Inlet; to dine on Mediterranean and look at art at the same time, stop by the *Collector's Cafe*, 7726 N Kings Hwy (☎843/449-9370).

As for **nightlife**, if you can't find anywhere to shag, Celebrity Square at Broadway at the Beach, between 21st and 29th avenues off the Hwy-17 bypass (☎843/444-3200), is a compact area of bars and clubs, while the *House of Blues*, Barefoot Landing, 4640 Hwy-17 (☎803/272-3000), attracts top national rock, reggae and roots talent. More kitsch are the glut of **country music variety shows**; the longest-running is the *Carolina Opry*, Hwy-17 N (☎803/238-8888), where powerful singers belt out corny, family-oriented rock 'n' roll, country and bluegrass with a couple of hymns for good measure. Next door at the Dolly Parton owned *Dixie Stampede*, you can see a lighthearted, surreal take on the Civil War with some impressive horsemanship all while chowing down on a huge dinner without utensils (☎1-800/433-4401; $30).

## South to Charleston: the plantations

The peaceful waterfront of **GEORGETOWN**, the first town beyond Myrtle Beach to be anything more than a beach town, makes a refreshing and quite extraordinary contrast, while the main street has a late-Fifties feel. Ask at the **visitor center**, 1001 Front St (☎1-800/777-7705), for a self-guided walking tour sheet to the fine antebellum and eighteenth-century houses in the 32-block historic district, the center. By contrast, a quick stroll down the boardwalk gives all-too-clear views of the monstrous steel works on the opposite bank. The **Rice Museum** (daily 9.30am–4.30pm; $3), in the clock tower on Front Street, tells how the cultivation of rice flourished on the coast during the slavery period. On the north side of town, turning east after the bridge, leads to the **Belle W Baruch Plantation** (June–Aug: Mon–Fri 10am–5pm, Sat 10am–2pm; tours Tues–Fri; ☎843/546-4623, reservations suggested; $10–15). Though fairly overgrown, the plantation's original "**slave street**" is still standing, complete with wooden shacks and a church. It serves as a powerful reminder of the brutal basis of antebellum southern prosperity and gentility, and an interesting look at the home of Bernard M Baruch, once called the "Park Bench Statesman," who gave economic advice to presidents Woodrow Wilson on up to JFK.

---

### KUDZU

The western Carolinas are badly afflicted by **kudzu**, a leafy climbing vine introduced from Japan in 1876 for decoration and shade. Its use was encouraged by the federal government from the 1930s to stop soil erosion. Unbelievably, it can grow as much as a foot a day in hot weather, and eventually kills trees by cutting off the sunlight. So far, it has covered about two million acres of forest. In places it's amazing, totally carpeting whole stands of trees and telegraph poles and wires. South Carolina folk poet James Dickey's poem *Kudzu* portrays it as a mysterious, evil invader from the east:

> *In Georgia, the legend says*
> *that you must close your windows*
> *at night to keep it out of the house*
> *the glass is tinged with green, even so . . .*

---

If you want to **stay** in Georgetown, the *Carolinian Clarion*, 706 Church St (☎843/546-5191; ③/④), is a good motel, with a pool. To **eat**, you don't need to stray from the motel's restaurant, *Hook, Line and Sinker*, which serves superlative crabcakes, fish stews and local Low Country Boils until 9pm daily except Sunday.

**Hopsewee Plantation**, the grand mansion home of Thomas Lynch, a signatory of the Declaration of Independence, is set in Spanish moss-draped grounds, twelve miles south of Georgetown on US-17 (March–Oct Tues–Fri 10am–4pm; house $8, grounds $2). Clouds of large and ferocious mosquitoes drift up from the adjacent river, so think twice before visiting in summer. The less manicured, and slightly less mosquito-plagued, **Hampton Plantation State Park**, further south, two miles off US-17 on Hwy-857, is probably closer to the look of a typical plantation. The grounds (Mon & Thurs–Sun 9am–6pm; free) are pretty, but the house (summer Mon & Thurs–Sun 1–4pm; rest of year Sat & Sun 1–4pm; $2) is most impressive, a huge eighteenth-century Neoclassical monolith built by Huguenots, yet while its exterior has been restored the inside is pretty bare. The plantation itself is isolated in the heart of the dense **Francis Marion National Forest**, badly damaged by Hurricane Hugo in September 1989. This heavily black area is particularly known for its sweetgrass basket-weaving, a craft that originated with the slaves in West Africa, using tight bundles of grasses to make intricate baskets and pots. In view of the enormously time-consuming work and the costs of materials, the baskets you see being made at roadside stalls here cost upward of $20.

Further south, beyond the forest a few miles north of Charleston, is the much-publicized **Boone Hall Plantation** (April to Labor Day Mon–Sat 8.30am–6.30pm, Sun 1–5pm; Labor Day to March Mon–Fri 9am–5pm, Sun 1–4pm; $12.50). A visit is a sanitized and annoying experience: the plantation may date from the late seventeenth century but the house is a twentieth-century reconstruction used for much television and movie filming. Tours are conducted by hapless young women in southern belle costumes, who rather overplay the connections with *Gone with the Wind*. The grounds are more interesting, with a long, tree-lined drive and another rare slave street, this time of small mid-eighteenth-century brick cabins that housed privileged slaves – domestic servants and skilled artisans.

# Charleston

**CHARLESTON**, one of the finest-looking cities in the US, today spreads way beyond its original confines on the tip of a peninsula at the confluence of the Ashley and Cooper rivers, roughly one hundred miles south of Myrtle Beach and north of Savannah, Georgia. It's a compelling place to visit, its historic district lined with tall, narrow hous-

**CHARLESTON**

Visitor Center
Charleston Museum
Joseph Manigault House

0          400 yds

N

Charleston Market

Waterfront Park

Heyward-Washington House

Nathaniel-Russell House

Edmonston-Alston House

Calhoun Mansion

Cooper River

*Ashley River*

*City Marina*

Colonial Lake

White Point Gardens

**ACCOMMODATION**
1 Bed no Breakfast
2 Best Western
3 Cannonboro Inn
4 Days Inn
5 Eliot House Inn
6 Maison Dupré

➤ One way street

es of peeling, multicolored stucco, adorned with wooden shutters and ironwork balconies wrought by slaves from Barbados. The Caribbean feel is augmented by palm trees, a tropical climate and easygoing atmosphere, while the town's pretty hidden gardens and leafy patios evoke New Orleans.

Founded in 1670 by a group of English aristocrats as a specifically money-making venture, Charles Towne swiftly boomed as a **port** serving the rice and cotton plantations. It became the region's dominant town, a commercial and cultural center which right from the start had a mixed population, with immigrants including French, Germans, Jews, Italians and Irish, as well as the English majority. One-third of all the nation's **slaves** came through Charleston, sold at the market on the riverfront and bringing with them their ironworking and building skills. The town had a sizeable **free black** community too, and its then unusually urban density allowed an anonymity and racial openness that, although still dominated by slavery, went a lot further than the rest of the South. Nevertheless there was still slave unrest, culminating in the abortive Veysey slave revolt of 1823, after which the city built the Citadel armory and later the military university to control future uprisings.

The **Civil War** started on Charleston's very doorstep, at Fort Sumter in the harbor. Fire swept through the city, destroying large chunks, in 1861; more damage was inflicted when it was taken by Union troops in February 1865. The decline of the plantation economy and slump in cotton prices led to an economic crash after the war, made worse by a catastrophic earthquake in 1886. As the upcountry industrialized, capital steadily deserted the city, and it only really recovered when World War II restored its importance as a port and naval base. Since then, a steady program of preservation and restoration – not helped by the devastation of Hurricane Hugo in 1989 – has made **tourism** Charleston's main focus; now *Conde Nast Traveller* regularly includes it in the world's top ten city destinations. Despite the crowds, however, it has kept its atmosphere, while maintaining all the energy and life of a real, working town. The *gullah* traditions of the sea islands are a tangible presence here, too: "basket ladies" weave their sweetgrass baskets all around the market and near the post office, and many people – black and white – possess distinctive *gullah* accents.

## Arrival, information and getting around

**Charleston International Airport** is about twelve miles north of downtown, off I-526; the airport **shuttle** (☎843/767-7111) costs $9, while a **taxi** ride with Yellow Cabs (☎843/577-6565) costs around $21. Both Amtrak – 4565 Gaynor Ave, eight miles north of downtown – and Greyhound – at 3610 Dorchester Rd, out near I-26 – are in inconvenient and potentially dangerous locations. Each is around $14 taxi ride from downtown. Local **public transportation** isn't bad, however: CARTA buses (☎843/747-0922; 75¢; day pass $2, 3-day pass $5) cover most areas, including near Amtrak (due to necessary walk down an embankment, CARTA recommends a cab at night) and in front of Greyhound, for 75¢; Downtown Area Shuttles (DASH; ☎843/724-7420) runs a variety of routes through the historic district south of Calhoun Street, which all stop at the visitor center (Mon–Fri every 15min from 8am; last bus times vary; same prices). You can rent **bikes** from The Bicycle Shoppe, 280 Meeting St (☎843/722-8168).

Charleston's huge and well-equipped **visitor center**, 375 Meeting St (summer daily 8.30am–5.30pm; rest of year daily 8.30am–5pm; ☎843/853-8000 or 1-800/868-8118), has discount coupons, leaflets and maps, and shows a film about the town ($2.50). The **post office** is at 557 E Bay St (Mon–Fri 8.30am–5.30pm, Sat 9.30am–2pm; zip code 29401).

---

### GUIDED TOURS

Charleston is ideal for **walking tours**; the visitor center has details of scores of them. Charleston Strolls (Mon–Sat 9.30am; ☎843/766-2080; $15), leave from the *Palmetto Café* at the *Charleston Place Hotel*, 130 Market St, and from *Mills House Hotel*, 115 Meeting St, thirty minutes later; the Civil War Walking Tour sets out from *Mills House Hotel* (March–Dec daily 9am; ☎843/722-7033; $15, private tours also available throughout year); Architectural Walking Tours of Charleston (Mon & Wed–Sat 10am & 2pm; ☎1-800/931-7761; $13) are specialist tours that leave from 173 Meeting St. In the fall, the Preservation Society, 147 King St (☎1-800/968-8175), organizes candlelit tours, visiting private old homes, with free champagne on Saturdays (Sept & Oct Thurs–Sat 7pm; $30).

Although much of Charleston's beauty is owed to the black slaves who built it, the town has no formal museum of black history. However, there are two good **black history tours**: Al Miller's one- or two-hour van tours leave from the visitor center, and include material on slave uprisings, the Civil War and the lives of the freed slaves (☎843/762-0051; $10/15). There are other specialized black history tours that the visitor center has details on.

**Horse and carriage** tours, among them Carolina Polo and Carriage Company (☎843/577-6767; $16), leave from the market (as a handful of other trolley tours), providing a lively, leisurely sixty-minute overview of town. *Schooner Pride* (mid-March to Oct; ☎843/559-9686; $17) offers two-hour **cruises** around the harbor in the afternoon and at sunset.

## Accommodation

Though Charleston is an expensive city, and **accommodation** options are limited if your budget's tight, it's really worth trying to stay within walking distance of downtown. As well as hotels, a lot of grand historic-district houses serve as **B&Bs**, with prices starting at around $70. Agencies include Historic Charleston B&B, 43 Legare St (☎843/722-6606). Further out, the usual **budget motels** cluster around US-17 in West Ashley and Mount Pleasant, and along I-26 in North Charleston.

**Bed No Breakfast**, 16 Halsey St (☎843/723-4450). Two-room downtown nonsmoking guesthouse. Large rooms but shared bathrooms. Coffee and tea, but, as the name says, no breakfast. ④.

**Best Western King Charles Inn**, 237 Meeting St (☎843/723-7451). Clean, cozy premises in the Historic District with pool and free various receptions. ⑤–⑦.

**Cannonboro Inn B&B**, 184 Ashley Ave (☎843/723-8572). Fine columned house, all nonsmoking, with attractive patios and gardens. Very comfortable rooms, and free bicycles. ⑤/⑥.

**Charleston Place Hotel**, 130 Market St (☎843/722-4900). Charleston's premier hotel with occasional last-minute reduced rates. ⑦–⑨.

**Days Inn Historic District**, 155 Meeting St (☎843/722-8411 or 1-800/329-7466). Standard rooms with attractive wrought-iron balconies; one of the least expensive downtown options, near the market. ⑤–⑦.

**Eliot House Inn**, 78 Queen St (☎843/723-1855 or 1-800/729-1855). Luxurious B&B in old Charleston building. Free wine and afternoon tea in a pretty courtyard, which also boasts a jacuzzi; free bicycles, good continental breakfast. ⑤–⑦.

**Holiday Inn Historic District**, 125 Calhoun St (☎877/805-7900). New downtown hotel with clean, comfortable rooms and friendly staff; rack rates are usually around $130. ⑤–⑦.

**Maison Dupre**, 317 E Bay St (☎843/723-8691). Beautiful inn in a crumbling 1804 European-style building. An idyllic garden holds fountains and a wishing well. Complimentary high teas and good continental breakfast. ⑦/⑧.

## The City

Charleston's **Historic District** is fairly self-contained, a predominantly residential area of leaning lines, weathered colors and exquisite hidden courtyards, bounded by Calhoun Street on the north and East Bay Street by the river. It's best taken in by strolling at your own pace – though that pace can get pretty slow at midday in high summer, when the heat is intense. Attractive spots to pause in the shade include the swinging benches at **Waterfront Park**, a beautifully landscaped piazza with boardwalks leading out over the river, and **White Point Gardens**, by the Battery on the tip of the peninsula, where the flower-filled lawns have good views across the water and a breeze even in summer.

Opposite the visitor center, the **Charleston Museum**, 360 Meeting St (Mon–Sat 9am–5pm, Sun 1–5pm; $7, or $18 with the Joseph Manigault House and Heyward-Washington House), is the nation's oldest, dating from 1773 (although the original building no longer stands). It's something of a ragbag of city memorabilia, with video presentations on subjects from rice growing to the Huguenots. One intriguing room holds exhibits from its early collections, where pickled snakes once shared space with Egyptian mummies and casts from the British Museum. The "head of a New Zealand chief" and "fine electrical machine," however, were destroyed in a fire of 1778.

Charleston's **market area** runs from Meeting Street to East Bay Street, centering on a long, narrow line of enclosed, low-roofed, nineteenth-century sheds, but spilling out onto the surrounding streets. Undeniably touristy, packed with hard-headed "basket ladies," this is one of the liveliest spots in town, selling junk, spices, tacky T-shirts, jewelry and rugs.

Most of the city's fine **houses** are private, and can only be admired from the outside. You're not necessarily missing all that much; the appeal of those that you can get into doesn't take long to pall. The late nineteenth-century **Calhoun Mansion**, 16 Meeting St, is among the more extreme, with its ornate plaster and woodwork, hand-painted porcelain ballroom chandeliers and other similar extravagances (Wed–Sun 10am–4pm, closed Jan; $15). The Charleston Museum's $18 combination ticket gets you into the 1803 **Joseph Manigault House**, opposite the museum, and the **Heyward-Washington House**, 87 Church St, built by a rice baron. In the heart of Catfish Row, this was the setting for Dubose Heyward's novel of black waterfront life, *Porgy*. Admission to each separately is $7 (Mon–Sat 10am–5pm, Sun 1–5pm). The stately antebellum **Edmonston-Alston House** overlooks the harbor at 21 E Battery St (Tues–Sat 10am–4.30pm, Mon & Sun 1.30–4.30pm; $7). The Neoclassical **Nathaniel-Russell House**, 51 Meeting St, is noted for its daring flying staircase, which soars unsupported for three floors; while the **Aiken-Rhett House**, 48 Elizabeth St, has its work-yard and slave quarters intact (Mon–Sat 10am–5pm, Sun 2–5pm; $7 each or $12 combination ticket). An additional source for black history is the **Avery Research Center for African-American History and Culture**, 125 Bull St (Mon–Sat noon–5pm; donation) where there is a retired nineteenth century classroom and an archive of personal papers, photographs, oral histories, and art among other items; the center has periodic films, lectures and exhibits.

## Fort Sumter

The first shots of the Civil War were fired on April 12, 1861, at **Fort Sumter**, on a small island some way out from Charleston, where the rivers meet the Atlantic. When South Carolina announced its secession, the federal government had to decide whether to reprovision its forts in the south. The commander of Fort Sumter, Major Robert Anderson, requested supplies in early 1861; when a relief expedition was sent, Confederate General Pierre Beauregard demanded the fort's surrender. In one of the ironies that so characterized the war, Beauregard, who personally coordinated the bombardment, had been the star pupil of Major Anderson's artillery classes at West Point. After a relentless barrage, the garrison gave in the next day, becoming the first prisoners of the war. The fort was retaken by Union troops on Good Friday 1865, the very day of Lincoln's assassination, and today holds a **museum** (summer daily 10am–6pm; rest of year daily 10am–5pm). Fort Sumter Tours operates **tour boats** from the City Marina, off Lockwood Boulevard and Patriot's Point in nearby Mount Pleasant, to Fort Sumter (City Marina: March–Nov daily 9.30am, noon & 2.30pm; Patriot's Point: March–Nov daily 10.45am, 1.30pm & 4pm; Dec–Feb daily 2.30pm & 4pm; ☎843/722-1691; $10.50 boat & fort).

## Eating

Though the historic district crawls with mostly undistinguished seafood places, the town's elegant ambiance lends itself very well to the classy "New" Southern **cooking** served up in a variety of innovative, upbeat restaurants. Cappuccino bars and cafes line Market and King streets.

**Bookstore Cafe**, 412 King St (☎843/720-8843). Quiet cafe near the visitor center, lined, as the name suggests, with books and newspapers. Open until 7.30pm Mon–Fri, 2pm Sat & Sun.

**Charleston Grill**, 224 King St (☎843/577-4522). Classy restaurant at the *Charleston Place* hotel with renowned chef Bob Waggoner and nightly live jazz. If you want to splurge, this is a good choice.

**Gaulart and Maliclet**, 98 Broad St (☎843/577-9797). Wonderful French bistro, seating only nine people. Fondue dinners and croissant breakfasts. Lunch only on Mon, closed Sun.

**Magnolias**, 185 E Bay St (☎843/577-7771). Splendid *nouvelle* Southern cuisine – shrimp with grits, etc – in stylish monochrome setting with a circular bar.

**Mimi's Café**, 1241 Harborview Rd, James Island (☎843/795-4090) Family-owned restaurant not associated with the popular franchise. Good value with a broad menu and hearty Sunday brunch.

**Papillon**, 32 N Market St (☎843/723-6510). Good-value pizzas and cocktail happy hour 4–7pm.

**Pinckney Cafe & Espresso**, 18 Pinckney St (☎843/577-0961). Well-prepared and inexpensive seafood, with good fresh coffee. Closed Sun and Mon.

**Poogan's Porch**, 72 Queen St (☎843/577-2337). Delicious local food in big old Charleston house; Low Country Boils, crabcakes and catfish. Very popular for Sun brunch.

**Slightly North of Broad**, 192 E Bay St (☎843/723-3424). One of the best, most fashionable restaurants in town, for truly great *nouvelle* Southern cooking – scallops with smoked sausage, Low Country sampler with Hopping John and butterbeans and the like – along with adventurous world cuisine.

## Nightlife and entertainment

Charleston has a dynamic **nightlife**, albeit one that's geared toward tourist revelers, with a wide choice of **music venues**, **clubs** and **bars**, especially around the market. Ask at the visitor center about its many festivals, or pick up the free weekly *Citypaper.* There are also lively bars out at the Isle of Palms and Sullivan's Island (see opposite). The **Spoleto Festival**, concentrating mainly on classical music, is held from late May until early June. October's **Moja Arts Festival** celebrates African/Caribbean theatre, dance and film, with all events free or low-priced.

**Blind Tiger Pub**, 38 Broad St (☎843/577-0088). Local bar away from the market area with occasional live music.

**Club Tango**, 39 John St, entrance in alley adjacent to Embassy Suites (☎843/577-2822). Hugely popular multilevel dance club, open Thurs through Sat.

**Cumberland Grill**, 26 Cumberland St (☎843/577-9469). A nice bar and sandwich shop that puts on blues, bluegrass, rock, reggae and folk.

**Henry's**, 54 N Market St (☎843/723-4363). Flash bar, with live jazz at weekends. Also serves steaks and seafood.

**Horse & Cart**, 347 King St (☎843/722-0797). Grungy bar/cafe, over 100 beers and live music (of all genres) every night.

**Music Farm**, 32 Ann St (☎843/853-FARM). Best place in Charleston to see regional and national touring bands.

**Trio Club**, 139 Calhoun St (☎843/965-5333). Another popular club, open Wed–Sat 8pm–4am with rotating live music schedule.

**Zebo**, King and Wentworth sts (☎843/577-7600). Trendy brewpub with metal and glass decor serving modern cuisine. Very popular.

## Around Charleston

The **river road**, Hwy-61, leads **west** from Charleston along the Ashley River, past a series of magnificent plantations. Many can be visited, although in best Southern tradition, house tours tend to dwell on the furniture and dining habits of the slave masters rather than any more pertinent sense of social history. **Drayton Hall**, closest to Charleston at 3380 Ashley River Rd (March–Oct daily 9.30am–4pm; Nov–Feb daily 9.30am–3pm; $8–10), is a particularly fine Georgian mansion, looking much as it did in the mid-eighteenth century with its handcarved wood and plasterwork. The nearby **Magnolia Plantation and Gardens**, ten miles from downtown Charleston, is most notable for its stunning ornamental gardens, particularly in spring when the azaleas are blooming. Tram tours cover the entire grounds (grounds daily 8am–dusk; last tickets at 5.30pm; $10; house tours daily 9.30am–4.30pm; $6; tram tours $5) but require purchase of general admission ticket. The **Audubon Swamp Garden**, a preserved swamp, complete with alligators and lush flowers has a self-guided walking tour ($5), which does not require the general admission charge. You can also rent bicycles and canoes to roam the area for $3 per three hours. Across the Ashley River, on Hwy-171, west of the Ashley River Bridge, **Charles Towne Landing** is a 663-acre state park (summer daily 9am–6pm; rest of year daily 9am–5pm; $5, tram tour $1), with a natural habitat zoo, a living history settler's village and a replica of a seventeenth-century merchant ship, as well as hiking and biking trails and bike and kayak rentals.

**East** of Charleston, **beaches** such as **Isle of Palms** and **Sullivan's Island** are heavily used by locals at weekends. The further you get from town, the more likely you are to find a stretch to yourself. The Isle of Palms **bus** (#8) from Charleston's Market Street, runs to both Isle of Palms and Sullivan's Island. If you want to stay, there are plenty of motels and eating places, and the odd decent bar, such as the *Windjammer*, 1000 Ocean Blvd, Isle of Palms (☎843/886-8596), open until 2am with live rock at weekends; *Bert's Island*, 2209 Middle St, Sullivan's Island (☎843/883-3924), is similar.

# The sea islands

South of Charleston toward Savannah, the coastline dissolves into small, marshy islands. **Edisto Island**, south of US-17 on Hwy-174, is typical: huge live oaks festooned with great drapes of Spanish moss line the roads, beside bright green marshes with rich birdlife, and great beaches on the seaward side. If you want to stay, there are no budget motels, but the **campground** at **Edisto Beach State Park** (☎843/869-2156) is near a great beach lined with palmetto trees and other semitropical plants.

**BEAUFORT** (pronounced *Byoofert*), the biggest town, has a few old houses but a slightly weird atmosphere, thanks to racial tensions and the baleful proximity of Parris Island US Marine Base, notorious for the brutality of its training regime, as mythologized in Kubrick's Vietnam film *Full Metal Jacket*. Planes roar overhead; a sign proclaims "The noise you hear is the sound of freedom." The **visitor center** at 1106 Carteret St (☎843/986-5406) has details of tours around the small historic district and discount coupons for the **motels** out on US-21. In town, the *Best Western Sea Island Inn*, 1015 Bay St (☎843/522-2090; ⑤/⑥), has nice rooms with an old-fashioned feel. The 1765 *Anchorage House*, 1103 Bay St (☎843/524-9392; closed Sun), is a romantic, candlelit **restaurant** serving reasonably priced continental and local dishes. The Greyhound **bus** station is two miles north of town on US-21.

## St Helena Island

Across the bridge to the southeast of Beaufort, **ST HELENA ISLAND** is among the least spoiled of the eastern sea islands. The **landscape** is gorgeous: amazing Spanish moss and enormous, wide views out across bright marshes, and small shrimp and oyster fishing communities. Occasionally you see what looks like a fleet of ships in the middle of a field, only to realize that in fact the boats are anchored in a small salt creek, hidden by bright green marsh reeds.

This is an area of strong **black communities**, descended from slaves, who were given parcels of land when they were freed by the Union army in February 1865 and who speak a dialect known as *gullah*, an Afro-English patois with many West African words. The **Gullah Institute** in the **Penn Center National Historic District** (☎843/838-2432), off US-21, contains the **school** started for freed slaves by Charlotte Forten, a black Massachusetts teacher, who remarked "I have never seen children so eager to learn . . . the majority learn with wonderful rapidity. Many of the grown people are desirous of learning to read. It is wonderful how a people who have been so long crushed to the earth . . . can have so great a desire for knowledge, and such a capability for attaining it." The school was an important retreat for civil rights leaders in the 1960s, used by Dr Martin Luther King Jr's SCLC and others. Set back from the road is a **museum** containing fascinating c.1900 pictures of black fishermen and farmers, plus old tools and shrimp nets, and rattlesnake skins (Tues–Fri 11am–4pm; donation). Nearby, off US-21, the ruined black **Chapel of Ease** nestles among thick Spanish moss, with seashell-adorned interior walls. Before the bridge across to Hunting Island is the *Shrimp Shack* (March–Dec Mon–Sat 11am–8.30pm), an excellent fresh **seafood** joint, where "shrimp burger" has to be seen to be believed, and should ideally be eaten at one of the trestle tables overlooking the shrimp boats bobbing in the marshy shallows.

St Helena's main **beach**, nine miles beyond the museum at **Hunting Island State Park** on the east shore (daily dawn–dusk; $2), can get crowded, but it's simply idyllic: soft white sand, wide and gently shelving, scattered with shards of pearly shells and lined with palmettos, palm trees and sea oats. The water is incredibly warm. Pelicans come in to feed, particularly in the early morning, and the shrimp fleet sails past soon after. You can **stay** near the beach in weather-beaten cabins backing onto a glassy lagoon full of jumping fat fish although you need to reserve from a year and a half to two years in advance; reserve through campground number. There's also a large **campground** (☎843/838-2011); head first to the **park office**, next to a sluggish pool complete with resident sleepy alligator (Mon–Fri 9am–5pm, Sat & Sun 11am–5pm).

# GEORGIA

Compared to the rest of **GEORGIA**, the largest of the Southern states, the bright lights of its capital **Atlanta** are a wild aberration. Apart from some beaches and towns on the highly indented coastline, this overwhelmingly rural state is composed of slow, easygoing settlements where the best, and sometimes the only, way to enjoy your time is to sip iced tea and have a chat on the porch.

Settlement in Georgia, the thirteenth British colony (named after King George II), started in 1733 at Savannah, intended as a haven of Christian principles for poor Britons, with both alcohol and slavery banned. However, under pressure from planters, **slavery** was introduced in 1752, and by the time of the **Civil War** almost half the population were black slaves. Little fighting took place on Georgian soil until Sherman's troops marched in from Tennessee, burned Atlanta to the ground and laid waste to all property on the way to the coast. The economy successfully reestablished itself after the war, however: Atlanta rose from the ashes to become the communications center of the South, and attracted substantial investment in the latter years of the nineteenth century.

Today, bustling **Atlanta** stands as the unofficial capital of the South. The city where **Dr Martin Luther King Jr** was born, preached and is buried bears little relation to *Gone with the Wind* stereotypes, and its forward-looking energy is upheld as a role model for other cities with large black populations – though it does still suffer high levels of urban poverty and violent crime.

Atlanta's main rival as a tourist destination is the **Georgia coast**, stretching south from beautiful old **Savannah** via the **sea islands** to the semitropical **Okefenokee Swamp**, inland near Florida. In the **northeast**, the **Appalachian foothills** are particularly fetching in fall, while **Athens** has a reputation for producing offbeat rock groups such as REM and the B-52's. Further **south**, the agricultural heartlands are rich in musical history, but only **Macon** and ancient **Ocmulgee** provide reasons to stop.

## Getting around Georgia
Georgia's main points of interest are easily accessible, but local transportation is poor. Amtrak **trains** from Washington DC to New Orleans and Florida call at Atlanta and Savannah respectively. **Bus** services in most areas are patchy and infrequent, though Atlanta has regular connections to the major cities, and several daily buses along the

coast call at Savannah. Atlanta has the world's largest passenger **airport**, and Savannah has a reasonable service – but airfares between the two are high.

# Atlanta

**ATLANTA** is a relatively young city: only incorporated in 1847, it was little more than a minor transportation center until the Civil War, when its accessibility made it a good site for the huge Confederacy munitions industry – and consequently a major target for the Union army. In 1864 Sherman's army **burned** the city, an act immortalized in *Gone with the Wind*. Recovery after the war took just a few years: Atlanta was the archetype of the aggressive, urban, industrial "New South," furiously championed by **"boosters"** – newspaper owners, bankers, politicians and city leaders. Industrial giants who based themselves here included **Coca-Cola**, source of a string of philanthropic gifts to the city. Heavy **black** immigration to Atlanta increased its already considerable black population and led to the establishment of a thriving community centered around **Auburn Avenue**.

Very few of Atlanta's buildings predate 1915, and nothing at all survives from before 1868. Its characters, on the other hand – politicians and newspaper people – have changed little, and the "booster" tradition has continued to the present, peaking spectacularly when Atlanta won the right to host the 1996 **Olympics**. The bid to convince the world of the city's prosperity and sophistication was led by city leaders such as ex-mayor **Andrew Young** (the first Southern black congressman since Reconstruction, who became Carter's ambassador to the UN) and flamboyant CNN magnate **Ted Turner**.

Today's Atlanta is at first glance a typical large American city. Its population has reached 3.5 million, and urban sprawl is such a problem that each citizen is obliged to travel an average of 34 miles per day by car – the highest figure in the country. Cut off from each other by roaring freeways, bright lights and an enclave mentality, its neighborhoods tend to have distinct racial identities – broadly speaking, "white flight" was to the northern suburbs, while the southern districts are predominantly black. That said, the city is undeniably progressive, with little interest in lamenting a lost Southern past. Since voting in the nation's first black mayor, Maynard Jackson, in 1974, it has remained the most conspicuously black-run city in the US, and an estimated 200,000 black families streamed in from states further north in the 1980s alone. The Olympics may not have been the triumph Atlanta so eagerly anticipated – even before the Centennial Park bombing tarnished the event itself, years of disruption and grandiose construction projects had left many Atlantans wondering whether the city had lost more than it gained – but with its ever-increasing international profile, cosmopolitan blend of cultures and hip local neighborhoods, the spirit and dynamism of modern Atlanta is a far cry indeed from its much-mythologized Deep South roots.

## Arrival, information and getting around

The colossal **Hartsfield International Airport** (☎404/530-6600), the second busiest airport in the US, is ten miles south of downtown Atlanta, just inside I-285 ("the perimeter"). Road **shuttle** services such as the Atlanta Airport Shuttle (daily every 15min 7am–11pm; ☎404/524-3400) run into the city for around $10, $17 round-trip, or a little more to get to Buckhead. The airport is also the southern terminus of the south line of the **subway**, fifteen minutes' ride from downtown ($1.50; see overleaf). If you need a **taxi** to get downtown, call Checker Cab ($18 for one passenger, $20 for two, $24 for three or more; ☎404/351-1111). The Amtrak station, at 1688 Peachtree St, is too far north of downtown to walk in: take a taxi or bus #23 to the Arts Center subway, N5 on the northern line. Greyhound **buses** arrive south of downtown at 232 Forsyth St, near the Garnett Street subway station.

Atlanta's **subway** and wide network of **buses** are run by the Metropolitan Area Rapid Transit Authority (MARTA; ☎404/848-4711), and are clean, reliable and pretty safe, operating between 5am and 1am weekdays and Saturday, and from 6am until 12.30am on Sunday. Fares are $1.50 per journey (weekly pass $11, Fri–Sun pass $7, weekend and daily pass $5).

A good way to explore the neighborhoods of Atlanta is on a ninety-minute **walking tour** with the Atlanta Preservation Center, 156 Seventh St (☎404/876-2041; $5). Destinations include the West End, Fox Theater, Sweet Auburn (with emphasis on the churches), an architectural tour of downtown and many more.

### Information

Atlanta's principal **visitor center**, in the **Peachtree Center**, 233 Peachtree St (Mon–Fri 8.30am–5.30pm; ☎404/222-6688), caters mostly to business travelers. A more useful branch for tourists, at Pryor and Atlanta streets in **Underground Atlanta** (Mon–Sat 10am–6pm, Sun noon–6pm; ☎404/222-6688), also handles bus-tour reservations and sells half-price tickets for local events. Similar offices can be found near the car rental offices in the **airport** (Mon–Fri 9am–9pm, Sat 9am–6pm, Sun 12.30–6pm; no phone); and in **Buckhead**'s Lenox Square mall (Tues–Sat 11am–5pm, Sun noon–6pm; no phone).

## Accommodation

Your best bets for somewhere to stay in **downtown** Atlanta are the chain hotels, though with so many conventions around even these aren't particularly inexpensive. **Midtown** is cheaper, and puts you nearer the nightlife, while **Buckhead** boasts some of the swankiest hotels in the country. If you're driving to Georgia, you can save a good deal of money – not just at the interstate motels around the perimeter – by picking up **discount coupons** from state welcome centers. The B&B Atlanta agency, 1608 Briarcliff Rd #5 (☎404/875-0525 or 1-800/967-3224), will reserve **B&B** rooms.

**Ansley Inn**, 253 15th St NE at Lafayette (☎404/872-9000 or 1-800/446-5416). Lovely, friendly midtown B&B, near Ansley Park, whose 33 rooms have stripped-wood floors, antique furnishings, wet bars and whirlpool tubs. ⑥.

**Atlanta Dream Hostel**, 115 Church St (☎404/370-0380). Hip private hostel near a MARTA station in the attractive Decatur district, with $15 dorm beds plus private doubles with and without baths. ①–③.

**Days Inn Downtown**, 300 Spring St NW at Baker (☎404/523-1144). Reliable chain hotel in the heart of downtown, with bar and outdoor pool. ④.

**HI-Atlanta**, 229 Ponce de Leon Ave (☎404/875-2882). Dorms ($15), with 3-day maximum stay, part of *Woodruff B&B* (see below). North Ave MARTA station. ①.

**Quality Hotel**, 89 Luckie St (☎404/524-7991). Spruced up and very central downtown hotel, with atmospheric and inexpensive diner downstairs. ④.

**Ritz-Carlton Buckhead**, 3434 Peachtree Rd NE at Phipps Drive (☎404/237-2700). Exquisite, elegant hotel, one of the finest in the Ritz-Carlton group, with Atlanta's best haute cuisine restaurant. ⑦.

**Sheraton Atlanta Hotel**, 165 Courtland St at International (☎404/659-6500). Luxury downtown hotel with wonderful indoor pool surrounded by foliage, and its own mini-shopping mall. ⑦.

**Super 8**, 111 Cone St (☎404/524-7000). Very atypical Super 8, housed in converted downtown hotel, and offering bargain rates for a great position near Peachtree Plaza, CNN and the Underground. ③.

**Travelodge Downtown**, 311 Courtland St NE (☎404/659-4545). Small, central motel, offering standard rooms on the east side of downtown. ⑤.

**Woodruff B&B**, 223 Ponce de Leon Ave (☎404/875-9449). Beautifully converted two-room former bordello; rates include full breakfast. North Ave MARTA station. ⑤.

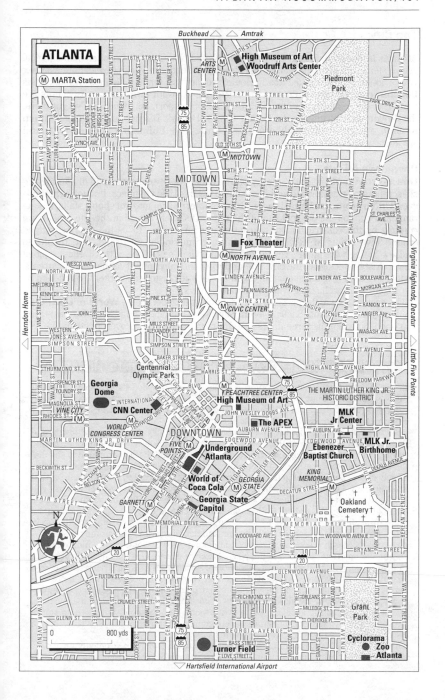

**ATLANTA**

Ⓜ **MARTA Station**

High Museum of Art
Woodruff Arts Center

Piedmont Park

MIDTOWN

Fox Theater

NORTH AVENUE

CIVIC CENTER

Centennial Olympic Park

Georgia Dome

CNN Center

WORLD CONGRESS CENTER

PEACHTREE CENTER

High Museum of Art

The APEX

DOWNTOWN

MLK Jr Center

THE MARTIN LUTHER KING JR. HISTORIC DISTRICT

FIVE POINTS

Underground Atlanta

World of Coca Cola

GEORGIA STATE

Georgia State Capitol

Ebenezer Baptist Church

MLK Jr. Birthhome

KING MEMORIAL

Oakland Cemetery †

Grant Park

0        800 yds

Turner Field

Cyclorama
Zoo
Atlanta

# The City

Atlanta's layout is confusing, following old Native American trails rather than a logical grid system, with no fewer than 32 streets called "Peachtree"; take care to note whether you're looking for Avenue, Road, Boulevard and so forth. The most important is **Peachtree Street**, which cuts a long north–south swath through the city. Sights are scattered, but relatively easy to reach on public transportation. Once you've got there, the **downtown** area, the Martin Luther King Jr Historic District ranged along **Auburn Avenue**, and the trendy neighborhoods of **Little Five Points** and **Virginia-Highland** are all easy to explore on foot.

## Downtown Atlanta

**Downtown Atlanta** is for the most part the usual big-city concentration of glimmering skyscrapers, as transformed and overhauled for the 1996 Olympics. Its highlight, however, **Underground Atlanta**, is a four-block subterranean maze of shops, stalls, restaurants and bars on the original site of the city (effectively buried in the late nineteenth century by the construction of railroad viaducts). In the 1970s the district, ranged around Five Points MARTA station, was a crime-ridden wasteland, but, thanks to Andrew Young's dream of a revitalized downtown, it's now one of the liveliest – albeit very touristy – pockets of the city. The underground labyrinth of cobbled gas-lit streets, restored to their original appearance and dotted with historical markers, is reached by steps from a piazza buzzing with street performers.

The eastern side of the piazza is dominated by the super-glossy **World of Coca-Cola** pavilion (June–Aug Mon–Sat 9am–6pm, Sun 11am–6pm; Sept–May Mon–Sat 9am–5pm, Sun noon–6pm; $6). Its three floors amount to no more than an overpriced and heavily

---

### THE BURNING OF ATLANTA AND THE MARCH TO THE SEA

In summer 1864, following the comprehensive Confederate defeats of Spotsylvania and the Wilderness in May, Union General **William Tecumseh Sherman** invaded north Georgia. Outflanking the much smaller Confederate forces, he laid siege to Atlanta; the city eventually surrendered at the start of September.

Sherman announced that the entire population of the city must leave forthwith, and that he would burn such of their property as he deemed necessary. The Confederate commander, General Hood, powerless to resist, expostulated: "Sir, permit me to say that the unprecedented measure you propose transcends, in studied and ingenious cruelty, all acts ever before brought to my attention in the dark history of war. In the name of God and humanity, I protest." Sherman responded: "In the name of common sense, I ask you not to appeal to a just God in such a sacrilegious manner . . . Talk thus to the marines, but not to me." On November 16, Sherman put a torch to the city, and set out on his notorious "**March to the Sea**." As he later exulted, "Behind us lay Atlanta, smoldering in ruins, the black smoke rising high in the air, and hanging like a pall over the ruined city."

Sherman's March is seen as an early example of total war; some accuse him of inventing the methods later followed in the Nazi *Blitzkrieg*. His explicit intention was to "make Georgia howl," via the systematic destruction of agricultural and industrial resources and terrorization of civilians. One Georgia woman recorded in her diary that "there was hardly a fence left standing all the way from Sparta to Gordon. The fields were trampled down and the road was lined with carcasses of horses, hogs and cattles that the invaders, unable either to consume or carry away with them, had wantonly shot down, to starve out the people . . . the dwellings that were standing all showed signs of pillage, and on every plantation we saw . . . charred remains."

It was the final body blow to the Southern war effort; though the Confederate armies struggled on for a few more months after Sherman took Savannah, their fate was sealed.

sanitized trawl through Coca-Cola's history, from its origins in non-air-conditioned nineteenth-century Hotlanta, with a series of dreadful videos that culminate in a "special look at those unforgettable commercials." In a surreal grand finale, space-age soda fountains jerk out a variety of sickly colas – such as raspberry Fanta, a big hit in New Guinea – for gleeful guzzling visitors.

Northwest of the Underground, the **CNN Center** – a structure that was originally an upmarket shopping mall, and still holds a few small stores – daily achieves a global penetration undreamt of by Coca-Cola's founders. The Cable News Network is just one of eleven television networks in the empire developed by Ted Turner, and sold to Time-Warner in 1995. Aptly, among the thousands of MGM classics now stamped with the Turner logo is *Gone with the Wind* – witness the plethora of Tara, Scarlett and Rhett knickknacks in the giftshop. Unlike the Coke pavilion, this is a working facility – adrenalin-fueled, forty-minute **guided tours** (daily 9am–6pm, every 15min; $7) rush past frazzled producers and toothy anchorpersons beaming across the planet, and there's no free soda at the end – but you can video yourself reading the (real) news of the day ($15 in the giftshop). If you're desperate to be on TV, time your visit to coincide with the 3.30pm filming of *Talk Back Live*, when visitors are invited to be part of the audience.

Several downtown blocks just northeast of the CNN Center were razed prior to the 1996 Olympics to make way for the open space of **Centennial Park**, intended as a focus for public festivities during the Games; forced to close almost immediately by the pipe-bombing that killed two revelers, the park has failed to find a post-Olympic identity, and rumors abound that it in turn will soon be redeveloped.

The **Atlanta Public Library**, in Margaret Mitchell Square at Carnegie Way and Forsyth Street (Mon–Thurs 9am–9pm, Fri & Sat 9am–6pm, Sun 2–6pm), has a room devoted to *Gone with the Wind* author and Atlanta-native **Margaret Mitchell**. The novel (1936) and film (1939) helped perpetuate popular images of the genteel plantation South – as well, of course, as the burning of Atlanta. Fantastically popular, the novel took just six weeks to sell enough copies to form a tower fifty times higher than the Empire State Building. The tiny downtown branch of the **Atlanta History Center** is also here, with videos on city history and information on historical tours. Midtown's **High Museum of Art** (see p.465) has a downtown outpost at 30 John Wesley Dobbs Ave at Peachtree Street, featuring smaller photography and folk art collections (Mon–Sat 10am–5pm; $5).

## Sweet Auburn

A mere half-mile east of downtown, **Auburn Avenue** provides a glimpse into Atlanta's black history. In its 1920s heyday, **"Sweet Auburn"** was a prosperous, progressive area of black-owned businesses and jazz clubs, but since the Depression it has declined, becoming yet another faceless strip of boarded-up barbers and beauty stores. Despite admirable efforts and promises of revitalization, it has yet to succeed in reincarnating itself as a living monument to black culture and heritage.

However, several blocks have been designated as the **Martin Luther King Jr National Historic Site**, in honor of Auburn's most cherished native son, the reverend who won the Nobel Peace Prize at a time when he was being actively persecuted by agents of the US government. Despite the lack of attention given to it by the city, this short stretch of road is the most visited attraction in the entire state of Georgia, and it's a moving experience to watch the crowds of schoolkids listening patiently to the guided tours and waiting in turn to take photographs. Head first for the Park Service's new purpose-built **visitor center**, 450 Auburn Ave (daily 9am–5pm), which holds a powerful exhibition entitled " Courage To Lead" that covers King's life and campaigns. Across the street at no. 449, the **Martin Luther King Jr Center for Non-violent Change** is privately run by King's family (daily 9am–5pm; free). Chiefly an educational and research facility, it also features displays of treasured artifacts such as King's Bibles and traveling case, as well as separate rooms devoted to Mahatma Gandhi and Rosa Parks. King's mortal remains were brought here from Memphis in the early 1970s, and his **memorial**, a simple slab inscribed with the words "Free at last, free at last, thank God Almighty I'm free at last," stands in the shallow, five-tiered Reflecting Pool outside, guarded by an eternal flame.

The **Ebenezer Baptist Church** next door, where King followed both his father and grandfather as pastor – and where his mother was assassinated while playing the organ in 1974 – has been converted into another museum (Mon–Sat 9am–5pm, Sun 1–5pm), while its congregation has decamped to a much larger new church over the road. Auburn remained the base for King's breathtakingly courageous campaigning during the Sixties, and his Southern Christian Leadership Conference (**SCLC**) still has its headquarters in the old Masonic building on the corner of Auburn and Hilliard.

King's **birthplace**, a block east at no. 501, is a small, neat Queen Anne-style shotgun house restored to its 1920s appearance, and now looking smarter than its neighbors. Home to Martin until he was 12, it remained in his family until 1971, since when it has been open for lively, anecdotal guided half-hour **tours** (daily 10am–5pm; free). These start from Fire Station no. 6, nearby at Auburn and Boulevard (daily 9am–5pm); you may have to be put on a waiting list, as schoolgroups often visit en masse.

Further west, at 184 Auburn, the recently reopened **Royal Peacock Club** was famed from the 1930s to the 1950s for performances by Cab Calloway, Louis Armstrong and Aretha Franklin, while the **Atlanta Life Insurance Co Building** at no. 148, from 1920 to 1980 the headquarters of the nation's largest black-owned business, now holds a small selection of African-American art in the lobby.

The privately run **African-American Panoramic Experience** (**APEX**) at 135 Auburn (Tues–Sat 10am–5pm; $3) has an eclectic collection on black history, including a reconstruction of a 1920s black-owned drugstore and an African art gallery.

## Little Five Points to Emory University

Northeast of Auburn Avenue, around Euclid and Moreland, the youthful **Little Five Points** district is the center of Atlanta's alternative community, a tangle of thrift stores, secondhand record stores, funky restaurants, body-piercing and branding parlors, bars and clubs. By way of contrast, just a few blocks north at 1 Copenhill Ave, on the hill where Sherman is said to have watched Atlanta burn, the **Carter Presidential Center** is devoted – quite literally – to the peanut farmer who rose to be Georgia state governor and the 39th president of the USA. In addition to viewing film footage and a reconstruction of his Oval Office (where he spent "tedious hours" in budget meetings, and in his final hours of office negotiated the release of the hostages in Iran), you can read the twelve-year-old Jimmy's school essay on health, in which he earnestly urges his readers to keep their teeth clean (Mon–Sat 9am–4.45pm, Sun noon–4.45pm; $5, under 17s free).

Northeast of here, beyond the yuppie **Virginia-Highland** restaurant district, the trek to **Emory University** campus is rewarded by the stylish **Michael C Carlos Museum**, 571 S Kilgo St (Mon–Sat 10am–5pm, Sun noon–5pm; $3 donation), which has a huge collection of fine art and antiquities from all continents, in an airy building designed by Michael Graves. Sub-Saharan African art is unusually well represented, including Nigerian headcrests woven with snake-like tendrils; among the extraordinary pre-Columbian collection, note the Andean *Human as a Peanut*.

## Midtown

**Midtown** stretches from Ponce de Leon Avenue, lined with funky restaurants, to 26th Street. In recent years, it has become dominated by massive skyscrapers – look out for **One Atlantic Center**, a spiky, futuristic monstrosity at 15th and Peachtree that was designed by Philip Johnson and John Burgee. The wildly flamboyant Art Deco **Fox Theater**, 660 Peachtree St at Ponce de Leon (☎404/881-2100), with its strong Moorish theme, should also not be missed. Unless you buy a ticket for one of its fairly mainstream theatrical shows, the only way to see it is on an organized tour (Mon & Thurs 10am, Sat 10am & 11.30am; $5).

A few blocks north, the huge **Woodruff Arts Center**, 1280 Peachtree St, includes the main branch of the **High Museum of Art** (Tues–Sat 10am–5pm, Sun noon–5pm; $6, free Thurs after 1pm). This stylish gallery presents excellent contemporary and non-Western exhibitions – particularly strong on African art – in a beautifully laid out, futuristic white glass-and-steel building, designed by Richard Meier. The temporary photographic shows, in particular, are usually excellent. There's a good giftshop, and a peaceful little espresso bar in the airy atrium.

## Buckhead

Even further north, the affluent white suburb of **Buckhead** is a trendy area of glitzy, youthful malls and swanky hotels. Within the space of two and a half blocks of Peachtree at Paces Ferry Road, celebrity residents such as Elton John can enjoy over a hundred top-quality restaurants. Tucked away nearby, permanent exhibits at the superb **Atlanta History Center**, 130 W Paces Ferry Rd (Mon–Sat 10am–5.30pm, Sun noon–5.30pm; $7), cover everything from Civil War black politics to women's history, while temporary installations detail city-specific events and personalities. There are also tours of two houses in the extensive grounds: the **Swan House**, a ponderous 1920s mock-classical mansion, and the **Tullie Smith Farm**, an antebellum farmhouse and garden. For a further taste of the Tara-style Old South, tour the **Governors Mansion**, 391 W Paces Ferry Rd (Tues–Thurs 10–11.30am; free).

## The West End

The **West End**, Atlanta's oldest quarter, dating from 1835, is a slightly shabby but slowly reviving district southwest of downtown. Historically a black residential area, it remains so today: a buzzy, more upbeat counterpoint to Sweet Auburn. African-American and Haitian art is displayed at the **Hammonds House**, 503 Peeples St (Tues–Fri 10am–6pm, Sat & Sun 1–5pm; $2), and you can tour the 1910 Beaux Arts **Herndon Home**, 587 University Place (Tues–Sat 10am–4pm; free), designed and lived in by Alonzo Herndon, the freed slave who became a barber, founded the Atlanta Life Insurance Company and went on to be the city's first black millionaire. Together with his wife, the director of Atlanta University's drama department, and such black luminaries as W E DuBois and Booker T Washington, he participated in setting up progressive black institutions. The mansion's grand interior, built and crafted by black artisans, contains the family's original furnishings, including some fine Venetian glass.

The fascinating **Wren's Nest**, home of *Br'er Rabbit* author Joel Chandler Harris, at 1050 R D Abernathy Blvd (Tues–Sat 10am–4pm, Sun 1–4pm; $3), shatters preconceptions about the Uncle Remus stories propagated by the racist images of Disney's *Song of the South*. Harris, a friend of Mark Twain, was a respected journalist whose column for the *Atlanta Constitution* retold the slave stories he had heard while training as a printer on a plantation newspaper; recently the dialect has been reappraised as authentically African and the stories as valuable affirmation of a black folk tradition. Regular storytelling sessions take place in the peaceful, untamed garden.

## Grant Park

Directly south of downtown, **Grant Park** is home to the **Cyclorama**, a huge circular painting (50ft by 900ft) depicting the Battle of Atlanta, executed by a group of German and Polish artists in 1885–86. Cycloramas used to travel around the country as entertainment in the days before movies; you sit inside the circle of the painting and the whole auditorium slowly rotates twice. During the second rotation, a guide provides interesting details about the painting; look out in particular for the hole in the wagon, originally used as a fire escape. In the accompanying museum, treating the war from the point of view of the average soldier, banks of distressing statistics are interspersed with photos and memorabilia (summer daily 9.20am–5.30pm; rest of year daily 9.20am–4.30pm; $5). Adjacent, **Zoo Atlanta** features such "natural habitats" as an African rainforest (daily: summer 9am–6.30pm; rest of year 9.30am–5.30pm; $10); in summer, a special "zoo shuttle" runs from Five Points MARTA station to the park.

## Eating

Atlanta has scores of good **restaurants** to suit all budgets. Most of the downtown options are quite upmarket – though with the Peachtree Center alone holding a dozen restaurants, a *Hard Rock Cafe* and a *Planet Hollywood*, and a food court, it's not hard to find something to suit any budget – while Buckhead is even glitzier. Southern **soul food** is best around Auburn Avenue, and **vegetarians** can get plenty of choice in Little Five Points and Virginia-Highland. For a good takeout lunch, try the **Dekalb Farmers' Market**, twenty minutes' drive toward Stone Mountain at 3000 E Ponce de Leon Ave, where stalls sell goat stew, tofu stir-fry and glazed duck; other goodies include fresh farm-fattened catfish and pretty blue crabs, and aromatic coffees from around the world.

**Atlanta Fish Market**, 265 Pharr Rd (☎404/262-3165). Buckhead's top seafood specialist, with ultra-fresh oysters and crabs.

**Beautiful Restaurant**, 397 Auburn Ave (☎404/233-0080). Famous down-home soul-food cafeteria – stewed chicken, corn bread, ribs and vegetable plates – near the Ebenezer Baptist Church.

**Buckhead Diner**, 3073 Piedmont Rd at E Paces Ferry (☎404/262-3336). Glitzy postmodern diner, always lively with locals enjoying *nouvelle* Southern food like crab egg-rolls, stuffed grits, veal and wild mushroom meatloaf. No reservations, so expect to wait. Around $40 for two.

**Cafe Tu Tu Tango**, 220 Pharr Rd (☎404/841-6222). Hip Buckhead cafe, where local artists make and sell their work. Serves substantial portions of eclectic, delicious snacks and tapas from around the world. Open daily from 1pm until late.

**Danté's Down the Hatch**, 86 Alabama St (☎404/577-1800). Lively, characterful, subterranean fondue restaurant in the Underground. Kitted out like an eighteenth-century sailing frigate, with wooden beams, dark nooks and crannies and a moat with live pointy-nosed crocs. Meals cost around $20, and there's nightly live jazz for an extra $5.

**Delectables**, 1 Margaret Mitchell Square (☎404/681-2909). Atlanta's public library makes an unlikely location for one of the city's best lunchtime restaurants, serving salad, soups and home-baked cakes.

**Flying Biscuit**, 1655 McLendon Ave NE (☎404/687-8888). Tiny cafe near Little Five Points, renowned for breakfasts in particular and healthy New-American food in general. Closed Mon.

**Kudzu Cafe**, 3215 Peachtree Rd (☎404/262-0661). Despite the traditional steakhouse decor, this large Buckhead restaurant serves soul food with a *nouvelle* twist. With dishes like horseradish sea bass alongside the barbecued ribs and meatloaf, it's ideal for gourmets traveling with kids.

**Mary Mac's Tearoom**, 224 Ponce de Leon Ave (☎404/876-1800). A cute, small restaurant renowned for cheap home cooking and fine soul food. Opposite the *Woodruff B&B* (see p.460). Mon–Sat 11am–9pm, Sun 11am–3pm.

**Mumbo Jumbo**, 89 Park Place (☎404/523-0330). Very chic downtown restaurant, offering an unlikely but delicious fusion of Asian and Tuscan cuisine, with an open kitchen and a bar-full of posers.

**Nava**, 3060 Peachtree Rd NW (☎404/240-1984). Spicy, modern Southwestern food plus mighty margaritas in glitzy Buckhead surroundings.

**Tamarind**, 80 14th St NW (☎404/873-4888). Stylish midtown joint with a great selection of flavorsome Thai dishes.

**Thelma's Kitchen**, 768 Marietta St NW (☎404/262-3165). Downtown soul-food institution, forced to relocate when its much-loved former home was destroyed to build Centennial Park. Everything under $8; try the fishcake and grits for breakfast. Mon–Fri 7.30am–4.30pm.

**The Varsity**, 61 North Ave NW (☎404/881-1706). Vast, packed midtown drive-in restaurant: a true Fifties throwback, complete with scuttling bellhops, where nothing costs over $5.

# Nightlife

Atlanta is a place where you can have a very good time; budget for blowing some money hopping between its bars and clubs. The **Underground Atlanta** complex comes into its own at night; otherwise the main concentrations are in the overlapping yuppie **Virginia-Highland** and punky **Little Five Points**, and the more upmarket **midtown**, the center of Atlanta's thriving **gay and lesbian** scene. **Buckhead** can be a lot of fun if you've got bags of cash. Up-to-the-minute listings for all venues can be found in the free weekly *Creative Loafing*.

**Blind Willie's**, 828 N Highland Ave NE (☎404/873-2583). The best blues venue in town, with appearances by major artists, this Virginia-Highland hangout is also a lively bar. Daily 8pm–3am.

**Eddie's Attic**, 515B N McDonough St (☎404/377-4976). Decatur bar offering nightly acoustic music, from traditional fiddlers to contemporary singer-songwriters.

**Euclid Avenue Yacht Club**, 1136 Euclid Ave (☎404/688-2582). Classic neighborhood bar in Little Five Points. Fine pork barbecue and Brunswick stew.

**Kaya Club & Bistro**, 1068 Peachtree St NW (☎404/874-4460). Midtown's hottest dance club covers the full spectrum, with Latin, reggae and "Old Skool" nights.

**Manuel's Tavern**, 602 N Highland Ave NE (☎404/525-3447). Relaxed, studenty neighborhood bar-cum-restaurant near the Carter Center. Wooden benches, ceiling fans and portraits of Jack Kennedy and Eisenhower – plus the occasional presence of Jimmy himself.

**Masquerade**, 695 North Ave (☎404/577-8026). Groovy grunge/punk hangout midtown, split into Heaven, Hell and Purgatory, with a big outdoor auditorium and regular "Foam Nights." Live bands Wed–Sun.

**Otherside**, 1924 Piedmont Rd NE (☎404/875-5238). Predominantly but not exclusively lesbian midtown joint that's a glorious melange of cozy lounges and wild dance floors, with themed nights that range from rodeo to 1970s schlock on Sun.

**The Point**, 420 Moreland Ave NE (☎404/659-4530). Hip bar and club in Little Five Points, with dismal black flyposted exterior, studenty crowd and lots of live local bands. Cover around $5. Open till 4am every night.

**Star Community Bar**, 437 Moreland Ave NE (☎404/681-9018). Enjoyable Little Five Points hangout, bursting with Elvis memorabilia, and offering food, drink and live music from country to swing, nightly except Mon.

# Stone Mountain

Just half an hour's drive east of Atlanta, **Stone Mountain State Park** (park daily 6am–midnight; attractions daily spring & summer 10am–9pm, rest of year 10am–5pm; $6 per vehicle) centers around a huge dome of granite with a five-mile circumference. You can climb it in around 45 minutes, or take a cable car, and there are various train rides and so on, but most visitors come to see the massive 90ft by 190ft relief of Confederates Jefferson Davis, Robert E Lee and Stonewall Jackson. Work on the colossal sculpture was started in 1924 by Gutzon Borglum, who went on to carve Mount Rushmore in South Dakota (see p.722), but was not completed until 1970. Concessions and giftshops down below supply endless souvenir kitsch, and the nightly lasershow in summer reaches a shuddering crescendo with Elvis' gut-wrenching rendition of *Dixie* (9.30pm; free with entrance to park).

# North from Atlanta: the mountains

Atlanta is a short drive from some spectacular **Appalachian mountain scenery**, at its best in October when the leaves turn gold and red. A drive through the mountains on the secondary roads takes you through endless hairpins and narrow passes; Hwy-348 ascends a particularly impressive pass at the White County line, crossed at the top by the **Appalachian Trail**. Of the various towns and villages, **Dahlonega** makes the best base; most of the rest – like **Helen**, 35 miles northeast, which has turned itself into a pseudo-Bavarian "theme village" – are either kitsch or downright dull. The region does, however, abound in delightful **state parks**, several of which offer both camping and hotel-style lodges.

## Dahlonega

The attractive small town of **DAHLONEGA**, in the Appalachian foothills fifty miles northeast of Atlanta on US-19, owes its origins to the first-ever **Gold Rush** in the US. Benjamin Parks discovered gold at Auraria, six miles south, in 1828; Dahlonega was established five years later, to serve as the seat of Lumpkin County. Within a further five years, enough gold had been unearthed for Dahlonega to acquire its own outpost of the US Mint, which by the time production was terminated by the Civil War had produced over $6 million of gold coin. The whole fascinating saga is recounted by videos and displays in the **Gold Museum**, housed in the handsome former courthouse on the main square (Mon–Sat 9am–5pm, Sun 10am–5pm; $3). You can also pan for gold at various small mines in the area, although you're unlikely to make your fortune. The town hosts one of Appalachia's biggest annual **bluegrass** festivals in the third week of June, and in October the **Gold Rush Days**, a real down-home hoedown, with food, crafts, clogging and music.

Dahlonega's **visitor center** is across from the courthouse (daily 9am–5.30pm; ☎706/864-3711). The *Smith House*, just down from the square at 202 S Chestatee St (☎706/867-7000 or 1-800/852-7564; ④), is a classic round-table Southern **restaurant**, serving superb all-you-can-eat meals at low prices, and also offering comfortable double **rooms**.

### Amicalola Falls State Park

Twenty miles west of Dahlonega on Hwy-52, **Amicalola Falls State Park** (daily 7am–10pm; $2 per vehicle) focuses on a dramatic multitiered waterfall that cascades down a steep wooded hillside. Having driven to the overlook at the top, continue for another half-mile to reach the park's modern **lodge** building (☎706/265-2888 or 1-800/864-7275; ④), which holds comfortable double rooms and a restaurant with panoramic views. For even more seclusion, hike for five miles toward the start of the **Appalachian Trail** from here to reach the new *Len Foote Hike Inn* (☎770/389-7275; ②), accessible only on foot, which offers basic rooms and food; you can also **camp** ($15) or stay in individual guest cabins (④) closer to the park entrance.

## Athens

The small and very likeable city of **ATHENS**, almost seventy miles northeast of Atlanta, is home to the 30,000 students of the University of Georgia, and has a liberal feel – and city government – unusual for the South. The compact downtown area north of the campus is alive with book and record stores, clubs, bars, restaurants and cafes; Broad Street in particular is lined with sidewalk tables. It may be short on formal attractions – antebellum homes, a double-barreled Civil War cannon on the grounds of city hall that never worked, and the Tree That Owns Itself – but it has achieved world fame in recent years as the home of rock groups REM and the B-52's.

Pilgrims drawn by the REM connection will want to head straight for the original home of the **Automatic for the People** slogan – *Weaver D's* soul-food cafe, well within walking distance east of downtown at 1016 E Broad St (☎706/353-7797). Unaffected by its new sideline in memorabilia, it continues to serve its delicious Southern fried chicken and vegetables on molded styrofoam plates. The group started out playing at the *40 Watt Club*, originally housed at 171 College Ave but now resurrected in its third and by far its largest premises at 285 W Washington St (☎706/549-7871), and half-owned by Barrie Buck, wife of guitarist Peter. These days the *40 Watt* doesn't put on as many local bands as its half-dozen nearby rival music clubs – such as the lively *Sugar Bowl* sports bar, 312 E Washington St (☎706/613-0021) – but it remains determinedly eclectic. Big-name bands tend to appear at the *Georgia Theatre*, 215 N Lumpkin St (☎706/353-3405), a converted movie theater that still shows films on quiet nights.

### Practicalities

Greyhound, based at 220 W Broad St, has a regular service to Atlanta, while the Athens Transit System operates buses around town (every 30min; 75¢ flat fare). The **visitor center** is in a small antebellum home a couple of blocks north of campus at 280 E Dougherty St (Mon–Sat 10am–5pm, Sun 2–5pm; ☎706/353-1820).

**Lodging** choices include the good-value, business-oriented *Courtyard by Marriott*, 166 Finley St (☎706/369-7000; ④); the *Holiday Inn Express*, 513 W Broad St (☎706/546-8122; ③); and B&B on a working horse farm at the *Hutchens-Hardeman House*, 5335 Lexington Rd (☎706/353-1855; ③). For top-quality **food**, your best bet is *Harry Bissett's New Orleans Cafe & Oyster Bar*, a simulated French Quarter restaurant at 279 E Broad St (☎706/353-7065), or the vegetarian specials at the inexpensive *Grit*, 199 Prince Ave (☎706/543-6592). The *Athens Coffee House*, 301 E Clayton St (☎706/208-9711), serves excellent coffees and desserts (though not breakfasts).

Athens' trendiest **bar** is *The Globe*, 199 N Lumpkin St (☎706/353-4721; closed Sun), where you can settle down in an old rocking chair or on a leather sofa and select from a huge array of beers.

# Central Georgia

The broad expanse of **central Georgia**, south of Atlanta, is famous more for its people than for places to see. **Otis Redding**, **James Brown**, **Little Richard** and the **Allman Brothers** were all born or grew up in the area, while peanut farmer-cum-president **Jimmy Carter** came from little Plains, roughly 120 miles due south of the capital.

Few of its small towns hold very much of interest, though vegetable fanatics may enjoy tiny **Juliette**, twenty miles north of Macon, where the *Whistle Stop Cafe* is still raking in the tourists by frying the green tomatoes celebrated in the 1991 movie *Fried Green Tomatoes* (Mon–Sat 8am–2pm, Sun noon–7pm), and **Vidalia** further east, the self-proclaimed "Sweet Onion Capital of the World." The largest communities are the dull army center of **Columbus** and the likeable town of **Macon**.

## Macon

MACON, eighty miles southeast of Atlanta on I-75, where I-16 branches off to the coast, makes an attractive stop en route to Savannah, especially when its 200,000 **cherry trees** erupt with frothy blossom (celebrated by a festival in the third week of March). As the highest navigable point on the **Ocmulgee River**, Macon was laid out in 1823 and became a major cotton port. Downtown is steadily inching towards extinction as a commercial center, particularly following the arrival of the huge **Macon Mall** near the intersection of the two freeways, but its hilly residential streets still hold more than four hundred two-story white-columned buildings. Among historic homes open to visitors, the opulent Italian Renaissance Revival **Hay House** at 934 Georgia Ave (Mon–Sat 10am–4.30pm, Sun 1–4.30pm; $6) is quite extraordinary – a vast mansion, topped by a three-storey cupola reached by a 28ft spiral staircase, where the job of restoration is endless.

Macon was home to **Little Richard, Otis Redding** (the frankly unremarkable Otis Redding Memorial Bridge is just east of downtown) and the **Allman Brothers**; Duane Allman and Berry Oakley, killed here in motorcycle smashes in 1971 and 1972 respectively, are buried in **Rose Hill Cemetery** on Riverside Drive, the inspiration for various of the band's songs. That heritage is celebrated in the exuberant **Georgia Music Hall of Fame**, next door to the visitor center at Martin Luther King Jr Boulevard and Walnut Street (Mon–Sat 9am–5pm, Sun 1–5pm; $7.50). A huge roll call of Georgian musicians are recalled by themed interactive displays that include a Gospel chapel, a rock 'n' roll soda shop and a country cafe. As well as admiring Otis Redding's trademark black sweater and the B-52's' wigs, you can watch footage of Ray Charles singing *Georgia on My Mind* to the state legislature, inspect a photo of James Brown confiding to the pope that he feels like a sex machine, and listen to seventy years' worth of jukebox recordings. On the flimsiest of pretexts, **Elvis** seems to crop up everywhere you look.

One of the best of its kind anywhere, the celebratory **Tubman African-American Museum**, 340 Walnut St (Mon–Sat 9am–5pm, Sun 2–5pm; $3), has a wonderful, eclectic collection, from African drums and textiles – which schoolchildren are encouraged to handle and play with – through intricate quilts, to angry, dazzling avant-garde work. There's a reading area, filled with black studies books, autobiographies and photograph collections, in a room quietly dominated by a heavy iron ankle brace and chain, which visitors are free to touch and lift. A few minutes north of town at 4182 Forsyth Rd, the **Museum of Arts and Sciences** (Mon–Thurs & Sat 9am–5pm, Fri 9am–9pm, Sun 1–5pm; $5, free on Mon and Fri 5–9pm) is a creative ensemble of interactive exhibits geared toward kids and an indoor "natural habitat" complete with a treehouse from which to observe the animals.

## Ocmulgee National Monument

Between 900 and 1100 AD, people of the Mississippian culture migrated from the Mississippi Valley to a spot a couple of miles east of modern downtown Macon, and leveled the site overlooking the Ocmulgee River that is now **OCMULGEE NATIONAL MONUMENT** (daily 9am–5pm; free). Their settlement of thatched huts has vanished, but two grassy mounds, each thought to have been topped by a temple, still rise prominently from the plateau. Near the informative visitor center, which holds artifacts from excavations in the area, you can enter the underground chamber of a ceremonial **earthlodge**. Modern wooden supports now hold up the roof, replacing the original timbers whose fiery destruction baked the clay floor, thereby preserving a ring of individually moulded seats, and a striking bird-shaped altar or dais.

## Practicalities

The imposing Terminal Station at the foot of Cherry Street houses Macon's **visitor center** (Mon–Sat 9am–5.30pm; ☎912/743-3401 or 1-800/768-3401); it's the base for entertaining customized two-hour **city tours** (Mon–Sat 10am & 2pm; $10).

Amtrak no longer serves Macon, but Greyhound provides good connections from 65 Spring St (where Little Richard is said to have written *Tutti Frutti* while washing dishes). Though motels surround the I-475/US-80 interchange, downtown **accommoda-**

tion is restricted to the plush B&B, *1842 Inn*, 353 College St (☎912/741-1842; ⑤), and the renovated *Crowne Plaza*, 108 First St (☎912/746-1461; ④), which also has a very fine **restaurant**. The atmospheric, wood-paneled *Len Berg's*, in Old Post Office Alley off Walnut Street (☎912/742-9255), serves down-home Southern lunches at bargain prices; the *Macon Music City Brewery and Grill*, just off I-75 at 2440 Riverside Drive, well north of downtown (☎912/741-1144), offers a menu that's several cuts above the usual brew-pub fare, as well as copious quantities of both musical memorabilia and microbrewed beers. Nearby, the outpost of *Fresh Air Barbecue* (☎912/477-7229) isn't at all bad, but for a true Southern **barbecue** experience you should drive 45 minutes' north instead to the original *Fresh Air Barbecue*, on US-23 just south of **Jackson** (☎912/775-3182): a roadside shack serving pork that's been hickory-smoked for 24 hours, along with succulent Brunswick stew and crisp coleslaw.

# Savannah

American towns don't come much nicer than **SAVANNAH**, seventeen miles up the Savannah River from the ocean, on the border with South Carolina. The appealing **Historic District**, ranged around Spanish-moss-swathed squares, formed the core of the original city, and today boasts examples of just about every architectural style of the eighteenth and nineteenth centuries, while the atmospheric cobbled waterfront on the **Savannah River**, key to the postwar economy, is edged by towering old cotton warehouses.

Savannah was founded in 1733 by James Oglethorpe as the first settlement of the new British colony of Georgia. His intention was to establish a haven for debtors, with no Catholics, lawyers or hard liquor, and above all, no slaves. However, with the arrival of North Carolinan settlers in the 1750s, plantation agriculture, based on slave labor, thrived. The town became a major export center, at the end of important railroad lines by which **cotton** was funneled from far away in the South. Sherman arrived here in December 1864 at the end of his March to the Sea; he offered the town to Abraham Lincoln as a Christmas gift, but at Lincoln's urging left it intact and set to work apportioning land to freed slaves. This was the first recognition of the need for "reconstruction," though such concrete economic provision for slaves was rarely to occur again.

The plantations floundered after the Civil War; cotton prices slumped, and Savannah went into decline. There was little industry beyond the port, and as that fell into disuse and decay so too did Savannah's graceful townhouses and tree-lined boulevards. Not until the 1960s did local citizens start to organize what has been, on the whole, the successful restoration of their town – recently, and tentatively, extended to the predominantly black **Victorian District**.

Savannah has acquired a new notoriety of late thanks to its starring role in John Berendt's best-selling *Midnight in the Garden of Good and Evil*; both book and movie detailed a delicious brew of cross-dressing, voodoo and murder. For a sense of what goes on behind closed doors in the city, it's an unbeatable read, and locals delight in making dark hints as to how much they knew, or even did, themselves. If you want to look behind the closed doors for yourself, however, few locations in "The Book" – as it's universally known – are open to the public, and none is likely to satisfy your curiosity.

## Arrival, information and getting around
Savannah's **airport**, served by several major airlines, is eight miles west of the city. A taxi downtown costs around $17. The **bus station** is on the western edge of downtown at 610 W Oglethorpe Ave, while the **train station** is about three miles southwest, at 2611 Seaboard Coastline Drive. The latter isn't served by buses; a taxi in usually costs about $7.

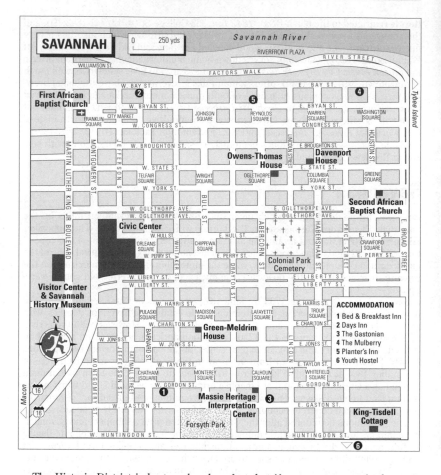

The Historic District is best explored on foot, but if you want to get further out, Chatham Area Transit (CAT; ☎912/233-5767) operates a reasonable **bus** network (75¢) and **trolleys** (50¢, $2 day pass) that run between downtown, the visitor center and the city market. Route maps are available from the **visitor center**, 301 Martin Luther King Jr Blvd (Mon–Fri 8.30am–5pm, Sat & Sun 9am–5pm; ☎912/944-0456 or 1-800/444-2427), which also has accommodation discount coupons and sells $2 DayPasses that entitle visitors to unlimited **parking** at all city meters and garages for two days. In addition, the visitor center can provide details of countless **walking tours**, and serves as the starting point for several different **trolley tours**, costing around $12 per hour. For more like $16, you can also join leisurely, breezier **horse-and-carriage tours**, most romantic by moonlight (☎912/236-6756). The best **black heritage tours** are run by the King-Tisdell Cottage (see p.474); **river cruises** start from behind City Hall, for $12.50 and up (☎912/232-6404). **Bicycles** can be rented from the Wheelman Bicycle Shop, 103 W Congress St (☎912/234-0695).

## Accommodation

By far the most appealing places to stay in Savannah are the central **B&Bs** in elegant private houses, but for those on a tight budget the usual insalubrious **hotels** congregate on and around Boundary Street near the Greyhound station, and there are chain **motels** further out on Ogeechee Road (US-17). The Last Minute Rooms service can arrange fifty percent discounts on one-night stays if you call on the day (☎912/238-1389).

The nearest **campground** is six miles southeast, at **Skidaway Island State Park** (☎912/598-2300; $17), a barrier or "sea" island, with an interesting combination of salt- and freshwater habitats.

**Bed and Breakfast Inn**, 117 W Gordon St at Chatham Square (☎912/238-0518). Great-value B&B in 1853 townhouse overlooking a shady square – reservations are essential. German-speaking owners. ⑤.

**Days Inn**, 201 W Bay St (☎912/236-4440). The most affordable hotel in the Historic District, if lacking the character of the B&Bs. ⑤.

**The Gastonian**, 220 E Gaston St (☎912/232-2869). Splendidly romantic B&B, beloved of honeymoon couples. Two-night minimum stay. ⑤.

**HI-Savannah**, 304 E Hall St (☎912/236-7744). Modernized youth hostel in a historic building, four blocks back from the river, with $15 dorms and a few basic private rooms; daytime lockout, but no curfew. Closed Jan & Feb. ①/②.

**The Mulberry**, 601 E Bay St (☎912/238-1200). Friendly Holiday Inn-owned hotel with B&B feel (free iced tea and cookies in the lounge). Rooftop jacuzzi, courtyard and luxurious riverview rooms. ⑤.

**Planters Inn**, 29 Abercorn St (☎912/232-5678 or 1-800/554-1187). Elegant, very central hotel with comfortable B&B-style rooms. ⑤.

## The Town

Savannah's **Historic District** is flanked by the river, Martin Luther King Jr Boulevard in the west, and, to the east, Broad Street, the old commercial main street, now a depressing series of boarded-up stores and offices. You can get an overview at the **Savannah History Museum**, behind the visitor center, in the restored Railroad Station at 303 Martin Luther King Jr Blvd (daily 9am–5pm; $2), where an informative jaunt through Native American culture, colonial development, the river and the Civil War is let down slightly by a slide show that is less a history lesson than a hard-sell promotion of Savannah's considerable charms.

The best way to get a feel for the place is simply to wander the "tabby" streets – made from a kind of primitive concrete mashed up with oyster shells – lined with shuttered Federal, Regency and antebellum houses adorned with intricate iron balconies, and intriguing details such as false "earthquake decorations." These sturdy iron rods embedded in the walls served no purpose, but were placed there simply to keep up with elegant South Carolina neighbor Charleston in architectural cachet. Note, too, the preponderance of light blue houses, washed in buttermilk and indigo to keep the ghosts away. The shady residential **squares**, ablaze with dogwood trees, azaleas and magnolias, offer peaceful respite from the blistering summer heat. *Forrest Gump* told his life story while seated on a bench in **Chippewa Square**; eager movie-lovers will find an imposing statue of James Oglethorpe, but no such bench.

Most visitors take in one or two of Savannah's old **mansions**, such as the classic British Regency **Owen-Thomas House**, 124 Abercorn St (tours Mon noon–5pm, Tues–Sat 10am–5pm, Sun 2–5pm; $7), or the redbrick Georgian **Davenport House**, 324 E State St (Mon–Sat 10am–4.30pm; $4). The latter, the first restoration project of the Historic Savannah Foundation, is sparsely furnished but boasts a wonderful elliptical staircase and delicate plasterwork. The **Green-Meldrim House**, on Madison Square (Tues & Thurs–Sat 10am–4pm; $4), is a splendid Gothic Revival mansion with dramatic ironwork, which General Sherman used as his headquarters. At the southern edge of the Historic District, the **Massie Heritage Interpretation Center**, 207 E Gordon St (Mon–Fri 9am–4pm; $2), is a simple, effective museum illuminating Savannah's architecture with displays on its neighborhoods and growth, and tracing influences from as far away as London and Beijing.

Though the Spanish moss of the city proper may be redolent of the Old South, Savannah's **waterfront** area, at the foot of a steep little bluff below Bay Street and reached by assorted stone staircases and atmospheric alleyways, retains the look and feel of an eighteenth-century European port. The main thoroughfare, **River Street**, is cobbled with the ballast carried by long-vanished sailing ships, while its tall brick cotton warehouses are said to be haunted by the ghosts of the slave stevedores. It's now a lively commercial district, lined with seafood restaurants and salty bars that heave with partying crowds on Saturday nights; as certain businesses target themselves ever more directly towards the "Spring Break" student crowd, however, some of its former charm is being lost. Looking out over the water from the paved **Riverfront Plaza** across the way you can appreciate just how busy the port still is.

As the one-time point of entry for many of Georgia's slaves, Savannah has a strong **black history**. The predominantly black **Victorian District**, southeast of downtown, is being slowly restored, and has a couple of good, if underfunded, museums. The nerve center of the restoration process is the **King-Tisdell Cottage**, 514 E Huntingdon St, owned by a middle-class black family c.1900 (Tues–Fri 1–4.30pm, Sat 1–4pm; $2). In addition to a fine collection of *gullah* baskets and African woodcarving, it illustrates the history of slaves and free blacks before the Civil War, and of the freed slaves after, commemorating Savannah's role as the site of Sherman's famous "**Field Order #15**," which granted each freed slave forty acres and a mule. The museum also operates excellent **black heritage tours** (leaving from the visitor center, Mon–Sat 1pm & 3pm; call a day in advance on ☎912/234-8000; $10). The two-hour tours take in the **Second African Baptist Church**, 123 Houston St, where Field Order #15 was signed; the poor black **Yamacraw** neighborhood, now sadly run-down and depressed; and the 1777 **First African Baptist Church**, the oldest black church in North America, built by slaves. This last, at 23 Montgomery St in the Historic District, can also be visited independently (daily 10am–2pm). Note the decorative carvings by the pews and diamond-shaped holes in the floor, ventilation for slaves escaping on the Underground Railroad. Back in the Victorian District, the airy **Beach Institute**, 502 E Harris St (Tues–Sat noon–5pm; $2), Georgia's first school for freed slaves, today houses an African-American art gallery with a permanent display of extraordinary woodcarvings by folk artist Ulysses Davis.

## Eating

Savannah has a large number of **restaurants**, with some great seafood places on the **riverfront**. The **City Market**, a couple of blocks south of W Factors Walk, is also a prime restaurant district, with a clutch of stylish New American places.

**Bistro Savannah**, 309 W Congress St (☎912/233-6266). Delicious Cajun and Far Eastern dishes near the City Market, with a classy menu worthy of far more expensive restaurants.

**Gallery Espresso**, 6 E Liberty St (☎912/233-5348). Dim, arty, super-hip coffee bar with exquisite cakes, crumpets, vegetarian food and soup, along with the best coffee in town (try the Iced Thai) and wine. Occasional acoustic music jams. Open until 2am Mon–Thurs, 3am Fri–Sun.

**Garibaldi's**, 315 W Congress St (☎912/232-7118). Lovely decor – cherry-red walls, pressed tin ceiling, fairy lights and gold mirrors – chatty crowd, and great Northern Italian dishes, *nouvelle cuisine* and seafood. The specialty is grilled flounder, deliciously succulent with a crispy coating. Dinner only.

**Huey's**, 115 E River St (☎912/234-7385). Riverfront restaurant, serving excellent, authentic Cajun/Creole food all day; go straight for the Oysters Rockefeller. Live music wafts in from the adjoining bar, and there's a jazz brunch at weekends.

**Mrs Wilkes' Boarding House**, 107 W Jones St (☎912/232-5997). Savannah's most famous eating place, a real Southern experience run by the redoubtable Mrs Wilkes, and serving all-you-can-eat breakfasts (8–9am; $5) and lunches (11.30am–3pm; $10) only. Everyone sits around large tables, helping themselves to delicious mounds of fried chicken, sweet potatoes, spinach, beans and spaghetti. There's no sign outside; just get there early, and join the line.

**Nita's Place**, 140 Abercorn St (☎912/238-8233). Friendly soul-food restaurant at eastern edge of downtown, open for lunch only with a fried chicken special costing $10.

**The Shrimp Factory**, 313 E River St (☎912/236-4229). Good and unusual shrimp dishes on the waterfront, with typical entrees like Shrimp Stuffed Savannah costing $20 at dinner, $15 at lunch.

**Yoshi's Downtown**, 423 W Congress St (☎912/238-5088). Very bright, spare sushi restaurant, just west of City Market; no Savannah atmosphere, but beautifully presented, affordable Japanese food. Closed Sun.

## Entertainment and nightlife

Savannah's **nightlife** is laid-back, if unusually strict about demanding ID. Everything is fairly close together, ranged between the City Market and the river. There's an annual **jazz festival** in late September. For information on this or other jazz events and venues, contact the Coastal Jazz Association at ☎912/232-2222; for **listings**, read the free *Creative Loafing* newspaper.

**Club One**, 1 Jefferson St (☎912/232-0200). Gay club, where drag acts occasionally include Lady Chablis, from "The Book."

**Crystal Beer Parlor**, 301 W Jones St (☎912/232-1153). A convivial, padded-booth bar, with moderately priced Southern food.

**Hannah's East**, *The Pirate's House*, 20 E Broad St (☎912/233-5757). Cool jazz in an informal atmosphere. Watch out for veteran piano-player Emma Kelly, who knows 6000 songs by heart. Jazz veteran Ben Tucker plays with a variety of big names after 9pm. Nightly from 6pm.

**Moon River Brewing Co**, 21 W Bay St (☎912/447-0943). Brewpub near the riverfront, with good beers and snack food.

**Savannah Blues**, 411 W Congress St (☎912/447-5044). New City Market club that features live blues nightly from 10pm.

**606 East Cafe**, 319 W Congress St (☎912/233-2887). Funky student hangout with dance floor, pool tables and drag acts, as well as inexpensive meals.

**Velvet Elvis**, 127 W Congress St (☎912/236-0665). Vintage beerhall, decorated to match the name, near City Market. Live jazz, indie, ska or R&B Wed–Sat, plus a "Steamy Seafood Patio" serving salads and shellfish.

# Out from Savannah

**Tybee Island**, eighteen miles east of the city on US-80, is served by three daily C&H buses (☎912/232-7099) from the Civic Center in Savannah. Here you'll find Savannah's best – and not too overdeveloped – **beach**, as well as a 154ft lighthouse, at 30 Meddin Drive, which dates from 1736 and houses a small museum (summer daily except Tues 10am–6pm; rest of year Mon & Wed–Fri noon–4pm, Sat & Sun 10am–4pm; $3). Abundant **accommodation** options include the *DeSoto Beach Hotel*, 212 Butler Ave (☎912/786-4542; ③). For great **Low Country food**, head for the *Chimney Creek Crab Shack*, at 404 Estill Hammock Rd (☎912/786-9857); *Spanky's Beachside* at 404 Butler Ave (☎912/786-5520) has live rock and "beach music" at weekends.

 **FORT PULASKI NATIONAL MONUMENT**, off US-80 E en route to Tybee Island, is the most interesting of several local forts (daily 8.30am–5.15pm; $2). An impressive Confederate stronghold, set on its own idyllic if rather buggy little island and ringed by a moat inhabited by the occasional alligator, it was nevertheless taken by Union troops, the first masonry fortress to be pierced by rifled cannon fire.

Ten miles south of Savannah at 7601 Skidaway Rd, **Wormsloe State Historic Site** (Tues–Sat 9am–5pm, Sun 2–5.30pm; $2) is the site of an eighteenth-century defensive plantation. The atmospheric tabby ruins of the fortified house of British settler Noble Jones are now overgrown with palms and lush forest, while the museum shows a film portraying the early settlement of Savannah, along with archeological finds and demonstrations of the skills and crafts of the first settlers.

Much of the Georgia coast is taken up by a string of **National Wildlife Refuges**, on the small marshy islands that make up the **barrier island chain**. It's well worth detouring or backtracking along the quiet side roads to cross to **Blackbeard Island**, **Wolf Island**, **Pinckney** or **Wassaw**, where tranquil swamps are filled with nesting birds and offer great fishing.

# Brunswick and the southern coast

**BRUNSWICK**, the one sizeable settlement south of Savannah, is a hop-off point for the offshore **sea islands**. It's not in itself very exciting, although the shrimp docks can be quite interesting when the catch is brought in. The wonderful *Hostel in the Forest*, reached via an inconspicuous muddy driveway on the south side of US-82, is a couple of miles west of I-95 exit 6 (☎912/264-9738; no reservations; ①); it charges $15 for dorm beds in a geodesic dome, and also boasts a couple of treehouses. In the unlikely event you'll need to stay in town, the **visitor center**, 4 Glynn Ave (daily 9am–5pm; ☎912/265-0620), has lists of budget **motels** and central **B&Bs**, such as the comfortable *Rose Manor Guest House*, 1108 Richmond St (☎912/267-6369; ④). The best **food** nearby, in an unlikely setting next to a gas station at exit 6 on I-95, not far from the hostel, is at the superlative *Georgia Pig* (☎912/264-6664), where luscious smoky barbecue comes with the local Brunswick stew, coleslaw, honey-tasting baked beans and fragrant sauce.

The **Hofwyl-Broadfield Plantation**, ten miles north of Brunswick on US-17, gives a vivid idea of life under slavery (Tues–Sat 9am–5pm, Sun 2–5.30pm; $1.50). A good exhibit covers the rice cultivation that made the planters so wealthy, and you can see the surprisingly modest plantation house where their descendants lived until the 1970s. Occasional **gospel** concerts are held here on summer Saturdays, with soul food on sale.

## The sea islands

Several of Georgia's **SEA ISLANDS**, like those of South Carolina, were divided after the Civil War between freed slaves. They remained poor, agricultural communities, however, and little now remains from those years for an outsider to see. Today they make handy alternatives to Florida as seashore breaks for tired inlanders.

### Jekyll Island

The **southern islands** are the most developed, largely due to **JEKYLL ISLAND**, originally bought in 1887 for use as an exclusive "club" by a group of millionaires, among them the Rockefellers, Pulitzers, Macys and Vanderbilts, whose opulent residences are still standing, though in a perpetual state of refurbishment. There's a small **Welcome Center** on the causeway, but the **museum orientation center** (daily 9.30am–4pm; ☎912/635-4036) gives a more useful overview of the island's history and runs guided tours of the mansions for $10; to get there, turn left after paying the toll, then head along Riverview Drive onto Stable Road. It's in the middle of the "historic district" that centers on the **Radisson**, the original club building; this is now a plush resort

(☎912/635-2600; ⑥). There are plenty more **accommodation** options strung along Beachview Drive next to the ocean: the *Ramada*, at no. 150 S (☎912/635-2111 or 1-800/835-2110; ④), has ocean views and a big Georgia-shaped pool. There's a **campground** a little further north (☎912/635-3021; $12), near the nesting sites of loggerhead turtles.

### St Simon's Island and Cumberland Island

Most of **ST SIMON'S ISLAND**, reached across a green marsh inhabited by wading birds (35¢ toll), is still an evocative landscape of marshes, palms and live oaks covered with Spanish moss. The tiny village is pleasantly quiet, little more than a handful of T-shirt shops and cafes, with a small **Museum of Coastal History** (Tues–Sat 10am–5pm, Sun 1.30–5pm; $4) concentrating on local events. You can rent **bikes** at Southeast Adventures (☎912/638-6732), which also runs bird- and dolphin-watching tours. The beach by the village is not safe for swimming due to fierce currents, but the sand is nice and firm for strolling. The best swimming is on the east side of the island, where the flat, fine sand stretches out for miles. **FORT FREDERICA NATIONAL MONUMENT**, seven miles north of the causeway (summer daily 8am–8pm; rest of year daily 8am–5pm; $4), was built in 1736 by General Oglethorpe as the largest British fort in North America; it's now an atmospheric ruin.

As well as a number of **resorts**, the nicest of which is *Sea Palms*, 5445 Frederica Rd (☎912/638-3351 or 1-800/841-6268; ⑤), with atmospheric rooms overlooking the marshes, **accommodation** options include *Saint Simon's Inn*, 609 Beachview Drive (☎912/638-1101; ③), just a block from the beach near the village. By far the best place to **eat** on the island is *Alfonza's Olde Plantation Supper Club*, 171 Harrington Lane (☎912/638-9883), where fried chicken and catfish, and a stupendous chocolate and peanut butter pie, are served deep in a Spanish-moss-shaded lane. If the mood takes them, the waiters might serenade you with gospel singing. At the **Sea Island Festival** in late August, you can hear traditional music and see folk crafts being made (☎912/638-9014).

To the south, **CUMBERLAND ISLAND** is a stunning wildlife refuge of marshes, beaches and semitropical forest roamed by wild horses, with the odd deserted planter's mansion. You can get there by ferry from the village of St Mary's, to the south near the Florida border (summer daily trips out at 9am & 11.45am, back at 10.15am, 2.45pm & 4.45pm; rest of year Thurs–Mon trips out at 9am & 11.45am, back at 10.15am & 4.45pm; 45min; $10).

## Okefenokee Swamp

The dense semitropical **OKEFENOKEE SWAMP** stretches over thirty miles down to Florida from a point roughly thirty miles southwest of Brunswick. Tucked away among its astonishing profusion of luxuriant plants and trees are something like 20,000 alligators, over thirty species of snake, as well as bears and pumas. You can only get in at the **Okefenokee Swamp Park**, a private charity-owned concession at the northeast end, on Hwy-177, off US-23/1, not served by public transportation (June–Aug daily 9am–6.30pm; Sept–May daily 9am–5.30pm; $12). The fee includes a half-hour boat trip through the swamp (slick yourself with bug repellent), a serpentarium, a good interpretive center on wildlife, an observation tower, reconstructed pioneer buildings – and a lot of placid, if cruel-grinned, alligators sunning themselves in oblivious bliss.

Unlovely **WAYCROSS**, ten miles north, holds bargain **motels** such as the *Pinecrest*, 1761 Memorial Drive (☎912/283-3580; ①). The town's **Okefenokee Heritage Center**, 1460 N Augusta Ave (Mon–Sat 9am–5pm, Sun 1–5pm; $4) has slightly erratic displays on the history of the swamp.

# KENTUCKY

Two hundred years after it was wrested from the Native Americans, **KENTUCKY** still hasn't quite made up its mind as to whether it belongs in the North or the South. Both the rival presidents in the Civil War, Abraham Lincoln and Jefferson Davis, were born here, and divisions were acute between slave-owning farmers and the merchants who depended on trade with the nearby cities of the industrial North. Officially neutral, seventy thousand Kentuckians joined the Union army and forty thousand the Confederates. After the war Kentucky sided with the South in its hostility to Reconstruction, and since then it has remained solidly Democrat.

Kentucky's rugged beauty is at its most appealing in the mountainous **east** and the small historic towns of the **Bluegrass Downs**, with visits enlivened by the varied attractions of bourbon whiskey, thoroughbred horses and bluegrass music. **Louisville**, home of the **Kentucky Derby**, is a busy manufacturing and arts center; the more reserved **Lexington**, eighty miles east, is a major horse-breeding marketplace.

### Getting around Kentucky

Kentucky's limited **public transportation** can be a real headache. There's a full Greyhound service along the interstates south of Louisville and Lexington (and both have surprisingly good city transportation), but a lot of ground is left uncovered. Amtrak doesn't operate here at all. **Cycling** is a pleasant and manageable option; if you're **driving**, be sure to keep small change for the tolls on the state highways. Lexington has its own small airport, but it's also within easy reach of the airport for Cincinnati, Ohio, which is in Covington, Kentucky (see p.270). Louisville is served by the Louisville International Airport.

# Lexington, Bluegrass and east Kentucky

The fertile **Bluegrass Downs**, just eighty miles across, form the base of America's thoroughbred racing industry, with **Lexington** quietly prospering at its heart. The name comes from the unique steel-blue sheen of the buds in the meadows, only visible in early morning during April and May. Kentucky's first white pioneers, who trekked in the 1770s through the 150 miles of wilderness now called the **Daniel Boone National Forest**, were amazed to find this "Eden" deserted while the Indians lived in much less attractive terrain. Anthropologists have now discovered that the area's twelfth-century inhabitants were plagued by fatal bone diseases, due to mineral deficiencies in the soil.

Around modern Lexington are some of the oldest towns west of the Alleghenies. However, amid the fine scenery of the **Natural Bridge** and **Cumberland Gap** districts, eastern Kentucky suffers from acute rural poverty.

## Lexington

The productivity of the bluegrass fields has kept **LEXINGTON**'s economy ticking over since 1775, though its lack of a navigable river always made its traders vulnerable to competition from Louisville. Eighty miles east of Louisville and ninety south of Cincinnati, Ohio, it still retains large numbers of fine antebellum houses. However, its current affluence dates from after World War I, when smoking caught on internationally and Lexington emerged as the world's largest burley **tobacco** market. Despite a population now exceeding 200,000, the city maintains an almost rustic atmosphere, with its most conspicuous activity the **horse** trade.

## Arrival and information

Lexington's **airport** is six miles west of town on US-60 W, near Keeneland racetrack (handy for the jets of the horse-breeders). Greyhound drops off about a mile from downtown at 477 New Circle Rd – take bus #6 to get downtown. Lex-Tran (☎606/253-4636) operates a good service to the university and suburbs, but you need a car to reach the horse-related attractions. The **visitor center** is in the Civic Center at 301 E Vine St (Mon–Fri 8.30am–5pm, Sat 10am–5pm; ☎606/233-7299 or 1-800/845-3959).

## Accommodation

Lexington has very little accommodation to offer downtown, but budget **motels** can be found around the exits from I-75. If you're stuck, the visitor center (☎606/233-7299) helps to find rooms. The best **campground** (☎606/233-4303) is at the Horse Park ($12–15 per site).

**Brand House B&B**, 461 N Limestone St (☎606/226-9464 or 1-800/366-4942). Immaculately restored antebellum house with modern amenities (including a pool table) and warm hospitality. Five blocks from the center of Lexington. ⑥.

**Homewood B&B**, 5301 Bethel Rd (☎606/255-2814). Set on a 21-acre horse farm, this is a great rural retreat. ④/⑤.

**Kimball House Motel**, 267 S Limestone St (☎606/252-9565). Much the most central option. Fifteen-room downtown boarding house/hotel with antique-furnished rooms, both single and double. ①/②.

**La Quinta**, 1919 Stanton Way, junction of I-64 & I-75, exit 115 (☎606/231-7551). Handily placed and comfortable motel rooms with free cold-buffet breakfast. ③/④.

**University of Kentucky**, 700 Woodland Ave (☎606/257-3721). A few fully equipped rooms available for short stays during the academic year, and plenty more during the summer. ①.

## Downtown Lexington

The plush hotels, glass office blocks, skywalks and shopping malls of Lexington's city center, set in a dip on the Bluegrass Downs, crowd in on fountain-filled **Triangle Park**. Despite its age, the city lacks buildings of historical interest; the early merchants threw up mostly functional structures, preferring to get on with making money. The redbrick, ivy-covered buildings of small 1780 **Transylvania University** are behind the Courthouse at N Broadway and Third Street (the name means "across the woods," an appropriate description of Kentucky at the time). At the other side of downtown, the **Art Museum** on the sprawling University of Kentucky campus displays contemporary American art and Native American artifacts (in term time Tues–Sun noon–5pm; free). The best photo opportunity comes in the form of **Thoroughbred Park**, at Main and Midland, an impressive life-size bronze sculpture of a horse race in progress.

## Lexington's horses

Along **Paris** and **Ironworks pikes**, northeast of Lexington, in an idyllic Kentuckian landscape, sleek thoroughbred horses cavort in bluegrass meadows. Some farms are still staked out by miles of immaculate white-plank fences, though most now use the cheaper but much less attractive black creosote to protect the wood. You can watch the horses' early-morning workouts at **Keeneland racetrack** to the west (April–Oct daily dawn–10am; free), and then eat a super-cheap breakfast at the adjacent *Keeneland Kitchen*. Tasteful dark-green grandstands emphasize the crisp white rails around the one-mile oval track. Until recently there was no public address system, which made for a unique atmosphere, with thousands of puzzled voices trying to work out which horse was which, breaking into cheers as they hurtled into the final furlong; even today, coverage is muted, in keeping with Keeneland tradition (racing for 3 weeks in April

Tues–Sun 7.30pm; and 3 weeks in Oct, Wed–Sun 1pm; call for reserved tickets; $2.50–25 ☎606/288-4299).

Tours of horse farms used to be very popular, but some owners have become reluctant to let the public get too close to the shy creatures. There are a handful of farms that allow visits, most are free, but you should tip the groom. One choice is **Calumet Farm** off Versailles road (☎606/231-8272; Mon–Fri at 2pm; free). **Three Chimneys** on Old Frankfort Pike is about fifteen minutes west of downtown and offers tours by appointment only (☎606/873-7053). Alternatively, try the comprehensive Blue Grass Tours (March–April 9.30am & 1.30pm; Nov–Feb by appointment only ☎606/252-5744; $20), whose three-hour itinerary includes a stop at a private farm, a drive through another, and a visit to Keeneland racetrack and other horse related areas. The **Kentucky Horse Center**, 3380 Paris Pike (Mon–Fri; tours 9am, 10.30am & 1pm; Sat 9am & 10.30am; ☎606/293-1853; $10), allows you to watch trainers at work.

The enjoyable **Kentucky Horse Park** is a little further along at 4089 Ironworks Parkway (April–Oct daily 9am–5pm; rest of year Wed–Sun 9am–5pm; $10). Its museum traces the use of horses throughout history, from Roman chariot races through cavalry regiments, commercial haulage and modern sports. The 1032-acre park also features live specimens of over thirty different breeds, a working farm, and offers guided horseback rides ($12). During May through August a special exhibit looking at the use of horses in imperial China will bump up the admission to $16. Experienced equestrians can ride unsupervised or inexperienced with a guide at Whispering Woods, in Georgetown (call for reservations ☎502/570-9663; $20 per hour).

### Eating, drinking and nightlife

Lexington's large student population means it has several lively, youth-oriented **eating places**, besides the steakhouses catering for the horse crowd and conventioneers. Fast-food cafes, open until early evening, fill the third floor of central **Festival Market**, at Main Street and Broadway; the streets around the back hold a few lively bars, which flourish despite the Baptist-inspired 1am curfew on drinking places.

**Alfalfa Restaurant**, 557 S Limestone St (☎606/253-0014). Hippyish cafe near the University of Kentucky. A wide range of international dishes, with vegetarian dishes. Lunch specials $4–9, evening meals $7–15, live music on weekends and rotating art exhibits.

**Atomic Cafe**, 265 N Limestone St (☎606/254-1969). Fun place to eat with good spicy food and potent cocktails. Live reggae Thurs–Sat.

**Cheapside Bar & Grill**, 131 Cheapside St (☎606/254-0046). Tasty food, a nice patio and good local bands make this a very popular downtown meeting spot.

**Ed and Fred's Desert Moon**, 148 Grand Blvd (☎606/231-1161). Wacky decor, good Southwestern food and pizza. If driving, though, be careful where you park, to avoid getting towed.

**Furlong's**, 735 E Main St (☎606/266-9000). Great tasting, reasonably priced Cajun cuisine.

**Kentucky Theatre**, 214 E Main St (☎606/231-6997). Evocatively restored 1920s movie palace showing offbeat and art-house films, as well as being a great venue for rock, blues and jazz concerts. Also serves alcohol and decent snacks.

**Ramsey's Diner**, 496 E High St (☎606/259-2708). Very popular and atmospheric. Tasty sandwiches, burgers and meals for $4–8. After 10.30pm cheap snacks are available from the bar, open until 1am.

## Bluegrass country

Apart from the horse farms directly to the north of Lexington, most places of interest lie to the south, like the fine old towns of **Danville** and **Harrodsburg**, and the restored **Shaker Village** at Pleasant Hill. After about forty miles, the meadows give way to the striking **Knobs** – random lumpy outcrops, shrouded in trees and wispy low-hanging clouds, that are the eroded remnants of the Pennyrile Plateau.

## The Shaker Village at Pleasant Hill

The Utopian settlement of **PLEASANT HILL**, hidden among the bluegrass hillocks near Harrodsburg, was established by **Shaker missionaries** from New England around 1805. Within twenty years, five hundred villagers were producing seeds, tools and cloth, for sale as far away as New Orleans. During the Civil War, Union and Confederate troops alike were billeted upon the pacifist Shakers. Numbers thereafter declined until the last member died in 1923, but a nonprofit organization has since 1961 returned the village to its nineteenth-century appearance.

The Shaker values of absolute celibacy, hygiene, simplicity and communal ownership have left their mark on the 27 gray and pastel-colored dwellings, which women and men entered via different doors. There are demonstrations of broom-making, weaving, quilting and other traditional crafts, and also April–October excursions on the sternwheeler *Dixie Belle* (village April–Oct daily 9.30am–5.30pm; Nov–March daily 9am–5pm; $9.50, $13.50 with *Dixie Belle*). The *Trustees Office Inn* houses a superb **restaurant** specializing in boiled ham, lemon pie and other Kentucky favorites, and also has **rooms**. Both these and the other rooms in the village should be reserved well in advance (☎606/734-5411; ④).

## Berea

Thirty miles south of Lexington, just off I-75 in the foothills where Bluegrass meets Appalachia, the unique **Berea College** gives its 1500 mainly local students free tuition in return for work in any of 120 crafts, ranging from needlework to wrought ironwork. Founded in 1855 by abolitionists as a vocational college for the young people of East Kentucky – both white and black – it was forcefully shut down four years later by mobs opposed to the board's support for John Brown's raid at Harpers Ferry (see p.399).

The college's reputation has attracted many private art and craft galleries to little **BEREA**. Free tours leave from *Boone Tavern Hotel,* a student-run hotel and restaurant at Main and Prospect streets (☎606/986-9358; ④), and explore the campus and student craft workshops.

The college runs the classy hotel, which includes the health-conscious, smoke-free **dining room** that's open to nonresidents wearing smartish clothes, and free admission to the college fitness center. If you're on a tight **budget**, the *Budget Inn,* 250 Mt Vernon Rd on US-25 (☎606/986-3771; ②/③) is a good option. You can also save a buck by eating at *Mario's Pizza,* 636 Chestnut St (☎606/986-2331).

# Daniel Boone National Forest

Almost the entire eastern length of Kentucky is taken up by the steep slopes, narrow valleys and sandstone cliffs of the unspoiled **DANIEL BOONE NATIONAL FOREST**. Few Americans can have been mythologized as much as **Daniel Boone**, said to have been one of Kentucky's earliest fur-trapping pioneers, in 1767. Perhaps the most famous legend tells of the time he was captured by Shawnee Indians and initiated as *Sheltowee,* or Big Turtle. Learning of plans to attack pioneer communities, Big Turtle escaped just in time to warn the citizens of his own settlement at **Boonesborough**, southeast of Lexington. But all did not end happily ever after. Boone failed to legalize his land claims, and lost practically all of the land in Kentucky he had claimed for himself and his sponsors. The resultant animosity forced the ageing frontiersman to press further west to Missouri in 1798, where he died in 1820 aged 86.

## Natural Bridge and around

The geological extravaganza of the **Red River Gorge**, sixty miles east of Lexington via the Mountain Parkway, is best seen by taking a thirty-mile loop drive from the **Natural**

**Bridge State Resort Park** on Hwy-77, near the village of Slade. Natural Bridge itself is a large sandstone arch surrounded by steep hollows and exposed clifflines; for the best panoramic view, continue to the solid span of **Sky Bridge**, which stretches along the top of a thin ridge. As well as hiking trails, canoeing, fishing, rock-climbing and camping, there's cottage **accommodation** in secluded *Hemlock Lodge* (☎606/663-2214; ③/④), where weekends usually fill up a year in advance.

For all its natural beauty, the **Snakey Hollow** area shows stark rural deprivation. Some tourists come here to see whether Hollywood images of backwardness, incest and violence square up in real life, but it's surely best to leave such communities undisturbed.

## Toward the southeast

In 1940, "Colonel" Harlan Sanders opened a small diner at the back of a gas station in tiny **CORBIN**, ninety miles south of Lexington on I-75. His **Kentucky Fried Chicken** empire has since spread to over sixty countries. The original 100-seat restaurant, near the junction of US-25 E and US-25 W, has been restored with 1940s decor and memorabilia (daily 9.30am–10pm; ☎606/528-2163). The bespectacled Sanders (1890–1980) was not a soldier, but a member of the Honorable Order of Kentucky Colonels.

**STEARNS**, fifty miles southwest of Corbin on Hwy-92, is a classic former mining company town, one of many such in the Appalachians, in which the company owned every building – shops, church, sheriff's office and all. As one Thirties writer put it, "with their unpaved streets and unpainted buildings (they) come into view like blighted spots on the land, with all the inconveniences and few if any of the comforts of modern towns of equal size." The **McCreary County Museum** at 1 Henderson St (Tues–Sat 9am–4pm, Sun noon–4pm; $3) takes a sanitized look at this history. The highlight for visitors is the eleven-mile trip on the **Big South Fork Scenic Railway** (April to early Nov; ☎606/376-5330 or 1-800/462-5664 for schedules; $10), which traverses deep woodlands and descends a rugged 600ft gorge to **Blue Heron**, another former mining community or to **Barthell** – where a guided tour is led through the town ($17).

On the tristate border of Kentucky, Tennessee and Virginia, the **CUMBERLAND GAP NATIONAL HISTORIC PARK** is one of the most visited parts of the area. A natural passageway used by migrating deer and bison, it served as a gateway to the west for Boone and other pioneers. **Pinnacle Overlook**, a 1000ft lookout over the three states, is near the **visitor center** (summer daily 8am–6pm; rest of year daily 9am–5pm; ☎606/248-2817) on US-25 E in **Middlesboro**.

Just outside the forest boundaries on the Virginia border, there are plenty of coalfields and lumber forests, but few people. The high death toll in underground mines and the ecological disasters of strip-mining have drawn national attention here, particularly during the violent struggles of the Thirties in places such as **Harlan County**, where striking miners were evicted from their homes and killed by armed company men.

# Louisville, central and western Kentucky

In heavily rural Kentucky, the manufacturing giant of **Louisville** stands out, with its lively cultural and racial mix. Only occasionally does it bother with the laid-back Southern image other parts of the state are so keen to promote. In the **southern** hinterland, numerous small towns retain their tree-shaded squares and nineteenth-century townhouses – and their strict Baptist beliefs – and the endless caverns of **Mammoth Cave National Park** attract spelunkers and hikers in their thousands. The west, where the Ohio River meets the Mississippi, is flat, heavily forested and generally less attractive.

# Louisville

**LOUISVILLE**, just south of Indiana across the Ohio River, is firmly embedded in the American national consciousness for its multimillion-dollar **Kentucky Derby**. Each year, the horse race attracts over 500,000 fans to this cosmopolitan and well-diversified industrial city, which still bears the traces of the early French settlers who came upriver from New Orleans. Today a third of the US's bourbon is made here.

Louisville's history revolves around a perennial rivalry with Cincinnati, a mere one hundred miles upstream. For example, despite being pro-Union during the Civil War, it promoted itself thereafter – erecting Confederate statues and so on – as the place for Southern business to invest, as opposed to Midwestern Yankee cities like Cincinnati.

As well as a lively arts scene and lots of citywide festivals, Louisville boasts an unrivaled network of public parks, many designed by Frederick Law Olmsted. One native son who took advantage of the recreation facilities was three-times world heavyweight boxing champion **Muhammad Ali**, who used to do his early-morning roadwork in the scenic environs of Chickasaw Park.

## Arrival, information and getting around

Most major US airlines fly into **Louisville International Airport** (☎502/367-4636), five miles south of downtown on I-65; take bus #2 or pay a $15 cab fare. Greyhound terminates at fairly central 720 W Muhammad Ali Blvd (☎502/585-3331). An excellent **bus** service (75¢) makes getting around easy. Some routes operate as late as 2am, and downtown **trolleys** run from 7.30am to 6pm. The useful **visitor center**, at 400 S First St (Mon–Fri 8.30am–5pm, Sat 9am–4pm, Sun 11am–4pm; ☎502/584-2121 or ☎1-800/633-3384 in-state, ☎1-800/626-5646 outside Kentucky), is the boarding point for city tours.

## Accommodation

Most of the year, Louisville's **accommodation** is plentiful and reasonably priced, though of course it's solidly booked up for the Derby Festival. You can **camp** just over the river in Indiana at the central *KOA*, 900 Marriott Drive, Clarksville, IN (☎812/282-4474).

**The Club Hotel by Doubletree**, 101 E Jefferson St (☎502/585-2200). Indoor pools. ⑤/⑥.

**The Columbine B&B**, 1707 S 3rd St (☎502/635-5000). Five rooms with private baths in this popular B&B close to the university. Great garden and gourmet breakfasts. ⑤.

**Galt House**, 140 4th St (☎502/589-5200). Huge, characterful, downtown, riverside hotel. ⑥.

**Old Louisville Inn**, 1359 S 3rd St (☎502/635-1574). Luxurious Victorian B&B with relaxed touch; whirlpool rooms available. ⑤.

**Super 8 Motel**, 927 S 2nd St (☎502/584-8888 or 1-800/800-8000). New downtown motel with a complimentary shuttle van to public transportation stations; continental breakfast and fitness room. ④.

## Central Louisville

**Downtown Louisville** rolls gently down toward Main Street, then abruptly lunges down to the river. **Riverfront Plaza**, between Fifth and Sixth streets, is a prime observation point for the natural **Falls of the Ohio**. The *Belle of Louisville*, a 1914 steam **sternwheeler**, leaves nearby for daily cruises in the summer (Tues–Sun at noon, Tues & Thurs also at 6pm; ☎502/574-2992, $10).

No matter what you think of baseball, it's hard not to be impressed by the **Louisville Slugger Museum**, at 800 W Main St (Mon–Sat 9am–5pm; $4). Frequent tours start with a short, emotive movie featuring prominent shots of Louisville Slugger bats being used to good effect, before visiting displays honoring key players, a batting cage that gives you an idea of just how rapid a 95mph fastball really is, and a working bat factory, explaining all the processes involved in the manufacturing of wooden bats. The trip ends with everyone getting a souvenir miniature bat.

The sizeable and recently overhauled **Speed Art Museum,** at 2035 S Third St on the University of Louisville campus (Tues, Wed, Fri 10.30am–4pm, Thurs 10.30am–8pm, Sat 10.30am–5pm, Sun noon–5pm; free), displays extensive collections of art and sculpture from medieval to modern times, featuring works by Picasso, Rembrandt, Rubens, Monet and Henry Moore.

## Louisville's horses: the Kentucky Derby

The **Kentucky Derby** is one of the world's premier horse races; it's also, as Hunter S Thompson put it, "decadent and depraved." Derby Day itself is the first Saturday in May, at the end of the two-week **Kentucky Derby Festival**. Since 1875, the leading lights of Southern society have gathered for an annual orgy of betting, haute cuisine and mint juleps in the plush grandstand, while tens of thousands of the beer-guzzling proletariat cram into the infield. Apart from the $36 infield tickets available on the day – offering virtually no chance of a decent view – all seats are sold out months in advance. The actual race, traditionally preceded by a mass drunken rendition of *My Old Kentucky Home*, is run over a distance of one and a quarter miles, lasts barely two minutes, and offers close to a million dollars in prize money. Only during the Superbowl do television commercials cost more. Thoroughbreds also race at **Churchill Downs**, three miles south of downtown at 700 Central Ave, in April, May, June, October and November (☎502/962-1122; $2).

The excellent hands-on **Kentucky Derby Museum** (daily 9am–5pm; $6), next to Churchill Downs at 704 Central Ave (bus #4), will appeal to horse racing enthusiasts and ignoramuses alike. Admission includes a tour of Churchill Downs, a magnificent audiovisual display captures the Derby Day atmosphere on a 360° screen.

## Eating

Louisville's **restaurants** cater for all tastes, though downtown prices are fairly high.

**Brasserie Dietrich's**, 2862 Frankfort Ave (☎502/897-6076). Atmospheric converted movie house in the Crescent Hill district, serving inventive seafood and meat dishes from a wood-burning grill. Main courses $8–22.

**Bristol Bar & Grille**, Kentucky Center for the Arts, 5 Riverfront Plaza (☎502/562-0158). Very good bistro-style salads and entrees with great desserts. A perennial Louisville favorite. Also at 1321 Bardstown Rd (☎502/456-1702) and 300 N Hurstbourne Parkway (☎502/426-0627).

**Heine Brothers Coffee**, 1295 Bardstown Rd (☎502/456-5108). Friendly espresso bar, attached to a bookstore.

**Lynn's Paradise Cafe**, 984 Barret Ave (☎502/583-EGGS). Quite simply a place that has to be visited. Friendly staff, fun decor that really has to be seen and great big portions of feelgood food and the best breakfasts in the city. In the emerging Highlands neighborhood close to downtown.

**Ramsey's Café on the World**, 1293 Bardstown Rd (☎502/451-0700) Atmospheric cafe open late with eclectic, and very tasty selections.

**Rudyard Kipling**, 422 W Oak St (☎502/636-1311). The decor has a hint of *The Jungle Book*, but the food is Mexican or French rather than Indian. Live music, usually acoustic, most nights. Closed Sun.

**Vietnam Kitchen**, 5339 S 3rd St (☎502/363-5154). A small basic joint, fifteen minutes out of downtown in the South End, but a hidden gem where the city's oriental chefs eat on their days off. Huge menu.

## Nightlife and entertainment

The **Kentucky Center for the Arts** (☎502/584-7777 or 1-800/283-7777), 5 Riverfront Plaza, between Fifth and Sixth avenues and fronted by several outlandish sculptures, is Louisville's main venue for high culture. The **Actors' Theatre of Louisville** at 316 W Main St (☎502/584-1205), meanwhile, has a national reputation for its new productions. As for **drinking** and **live music**, the two-mile strip around Bardstown Road and Baxter

Avenue (bus #17) is punctuated by fun bars and restaurants; the best **gay** clubs are on the eastern edge of downtown.

**Brewery**, 426 Baxter Ave (☎502/583-3420). Sports themed bar with live music and sand volleyball open until 4am on Thurs–Sat.

**Connections**, 130 S Floyd St (☎502/585-5742). The pick of Louisville's gay scene. At weekends this giant club, complete with terrace garden, holds over 2000.

**Molly Malone's**, 933 Baxter Ave (☎502/473-1206). Fun Irish pub and restaurant with live music on the weekends.

**Phoenix Hill Tavern**, 644 Baxter Ave (☎502/589-4957). Big bar with four different areas that gets in occasional national touring acts, Wednesday is Eighties dance night.

**Stevie Ray's**, 230 E Main St (☎502/582-9945). As the name suggests, a rocking loud blues bar.

**Twice Told Coffeehouse**, 1604 Bardstown Rd (☎502/456-0507). Cozy singer-songwriter venue that often gets noted names and surprise appearances.

# Out from Louisville

South from Louisville to Tennessee, **central Kentucky** offers great scope for a one- or two-day driving tour. There's small-town charm in **Bardstown** and Abraham Lincoln's birthplace of **Hodgenville**, while the top natural attraction is the amazing **Mammoth Cave National Park**, the largest underground cave system in the world.

Kentucky's **western** stretches don't compare with the rugged east for scenic beauty; all the significant lakes were created by damming its rivers, and much of the land is scarred by strip mines, oilfields and commercial forests. There's little of real interest here except for the **Land Between the Lakes** recreation area, squeezed between Kentucky and Barkley lakes, overlapping the Tennessee border.

## Fort Knox

Legendary **FORT KNOX** straddles 100,000 acres either side of US-31 W, thirty miles southwest of Louisville. The bomb-proof **Bullion Depository**, on Gold Vault Road, surrounded by security fences, machine-gun turrets, patrol guards and huge floodlights, stores nine million pounds of the federal gold reserve behind doors weighing twenty tons apiece. No visits are allowed at the depository; you can stop by the road for a maximum of five minutes.

## Bardstown and the bourbon distilleries

Forty miles south of Louisville on US-31 E, attractive **BARDSTOWN** is the place to get acquainted with Kentucky **bourbon whiskey**, created in earliest pioneer days, so the story goes, when Elijah Craig, a Baptist minister, added corn to the usual rye and barley. Named for Bourbon County near Lexington, Kentucky's whiskey soon gained a national reputation, thanks to crisp limestone water and the skills of small-scale distillers. Under federal law, corn must make up at least 51 percent of all solid ingredients, and the drink must mature for two years in new oak barrels with charred interiors.

Get into the spirit at Bardstown's free **Oscar Getz Museum of Whiskey History**, 114 N Fifth St (May–Sept Mon–Sat 9am–5pm, Sun 1–5pm; rest of year Mon–Sat 10am–4pm, Sun 1–4pm). Fourteen miles west at **CLERMONT**, you stop at **Jim Beam American Outpost** (Mon–Sat 9am–4.30pm, Sun 1–4pm; free), which has an informative museum, a film on the whiskey-making process, an outdoor moonshine still and barrel-making museum, and a Beam family home. **Maker's Mark Distillery**, twenty miles south of Bardstown near **Loretto**, is an out-of-the-way collection of beautifully restored black, red and gray plankhouses, in which whiskey is still made manually (Mon–Sat 10.30am–3.30pm, Sun 1.30–3.30pm; ☎502/865-2099; free). However, don't expect a sample at either distillery; like most of rural Kentucky, the area is **dry**.

## Abraham Lincoln's birthplace

On February 12, 1809, **Abraham Lincoln**, the sixteenth president of the US, was born in a one-room log cabin in the frontier wilds, son of a wandering farmer and, if some accounts are to be believed, an illiterate and illegitimate mother. The **National Historic Site** (summer daily 8am–6.45pm; rest of year daily 8am–4.45pm; free), has a symbolic cabin of his birth, three miles south of **HODGENVILLE** on US-31 E, and is enclosed in a granite and marble Memorial Building with 56 steps, one for each year of Lincoln's life. The family moved in 1811 to the **Knob Creek** area, where Lincoln's earliest memory was of slaves being forcefully driven along the road. Here you can visit another re-creation of his boyhood home (daily April–Oct varied hours; $1). Little Knob Creek, which the Lincolns left in 1816 for Indiana, doesn't overplay the presidential connection, and its down-home cafes make it a good place to stop.

## Mammoth Cave National Park

The three hundred and fifty miles of labyrinthine passages (with an average of five new miles discovered each year) and domed caverns of **MAMMOTH CAVE NATIONAL PARK** lie halfway between Louisville and Bowling Green, ten miles off I-65. Its amazing geological formations, carved by acidic water trickling through limestone, include a bewildering display of stalagmites and stalactites, a huge cascade of flowstone known as **Frozen Niagara**, and **Echo River**, 365ft below ground, populated by a unique species of colorless and sightless fish. Among traces of human occupation are Native American artifacts, a former saltpeter mine, and the remains of an experimental tuberculosis hospital, built in 1843 in the belief that the cool atmosphere of the cave would help clear patients' lungs. Access is by guided tours, available for most tastes and abilities, including the physically challenged ($7–35); tickets are available from the **visitor center** (summer daily 7.30am–7.30pm; fall daily 8am–6pm; rest of year Mon–Fri 9am–5pm, Sat & Sun 8am–5pm; ☎270/758-2328 for info and ☎1-800/967-2283 for tour reservations). Book ahead, especially in summer. Also keep in mind the temperature in the caves is a constant 54°F, so take a sweater or jacket.

The park's attractions are by no means all subterranean. The scenic **Green River** cuts through densely forested hillsides and jagged limestone cliffs; you can follow hiking trails, rent canoes, or for a more leisurely trip take the *Miss Green River II* **cruise boat** (☎270/758-2243; $5). **Camping** is free in the backcountry, however, a permit must be picked up first at the visitor center; the *Mammoth Cave Hotel* (☎270/758-2225) has cottages (③) and motel **rooms** (④).

The privately owned caves all around, many of which ruin the sights with garish light shows, and the "attractions" in nearby Cave City and Park City, are best ignored.

## Bowling Green and around

**BOWLING GREEN**'s main claim to fame is as the only place where you can buy a drink between Louisville and Nashville, just sixty miles further southwest. It's a lively enough place and offers a treat for **sports car** enthusiasts. One-hour tours of the **General Motors Corvette Assembly Plant**, on Louisville Road, off I-65, take a step-by-step look at the manufacture of one of the great symbols of the American Dream (Mon–Fri at 9am & 1pm; ☎502/745-8419; free; reservations advisable). For real Corvette junkies, there's also the **National Corvette Museum**, south of the plant at 350 Corvette Drive (April–Sept daily 8am–6pm; Oct–March daily 8am–5pm; $8).

There's another former **Shaker settlement**, with furniture displays and crafts for sale, 11 miles west of Bowling Green off US-68/80, in **SOUTH UNION** (March–Dec Mon–Sat 9am–4pm, Sun 1–4pm; $4). The 1869 *Shaker Tavern*, a **B&B** a mile or two away on Hwy-73, serves traditional Kentucky recipes such as chess pie (☎502/542-6801; ④). However, only guests and groups of six or more can eat at the tavern.

# TENNESSEE

A shallow rectangle, only one hundred miles from north to south, **TENNESSEE** stretches 450 miles from the Mississippi to the Appalachians, and divides into three distinct regions. The marshy **western** third of the state occupies a low plateau edging down toward the Mississippi. Only in the far southwest corner do the bluffs rise high enough to permit a sizeable riverside settlement – the exhilarating port of **Memphis**. Tennessee's largest city is a magnet for music fans, as the birthplace of urban blues and long-time home of **Elvis**. The fine plantation homes and tidy old towns of **middle Tennessee's** rolling farmland reflect the comfortable lifestyle of its pioneers; smack at the heart of this is **Nashville**, still **country music's** capital, despite upstart competition from Branson (see p.695) and Myrtle Beach (see p.450). The mountainous **east** shares its top attraction with North Carolina – the peaks, streams and meadows of **Great Smoky Mountains National Park.**

Tennessee's first white settlers, most of them British Protestants, appeared from across the mountains in the 1770s to settle in the hills and hollows of the Appalachians. Initially relations with the **Cherokee** were good. However, demand for land increased, and confrontations throughout the state culminated in 1838 with the forced removal of the Indians on the "Trail of Tears." One of the main congressional opponents of this process was **Davy Crockett**, familiar from legend as the heavy-drinking hunter in a coonskin cap. When **Civil War** came, the plantation owners of the west maneuvered Tennessee into the Confederacy, against the wishes of the nonslaveholding smallhold farmers in the east. The last state to secede became the primary battlefield in the west, the site of 424 battles and skirmishes.

Despite economic development to rival any in the country, soil erosion and farm mechanization led to a mass migration to the cities in the years before World War I. The fundamentalist beliefs of these transplanted hill-dwellers (whose folk and fiddle music served to spark Nashville's country scene) influenced a **prohibition** movement that kept all of Tennessee bone-dry until 1939, and still sees a majority of counties forbidding the sale of alcohol. The New Deal of the 1930s brought significant changes. In particular, the **Tennessee Valley Authority**, created in 1933, harnessed the flood-prone **Tennessee River**, providing much-needed jobs and cheap power, and ignited the transition from an agricultural to an industrial economy.

## Getting around Tennessee

For such a popular tourist destination, Tennessee has disappointing **transportation** connections. Amtrak only calls at Memphis, and while Greyhound provides a reasonable service to major towns and cities, traveling by bus through the small towns in the east is very difficult. The **airports** at Memphis and Nashville have extensive connections throughout the US, though fares between the two are high. If you cherish a fantasy of traveling by **boat** along the Mississippi, note that only luxury craft make the trip these days, at prohibitive prices (see p.491).

# Memphis

The cotton-trading capital of the Delta, **MEMPHIS**, perched above the Mississippi two hundred miles west of Nashville and three hundred south of St Louis, is one of the great destinations of the South. Visitors come from all over the world to celebrate the city that virtually invented blues, soul and rock 'n' roll as well as to chow in the unrivaled barbecue capital of the nation. A visit to Memphis, the home of the Sun and Stax record labels, with its frequent festivals and vigorous nightlife, feels like an invitation to share in a genuine and enduring local culture.

Culturally and geographically, Memphis has more in common with the deltalands of Mississippi and Arkansas than with the rest of Tennessee. Founded in 1819 and named for Egypt's ancient Nile capital, its fortunes rose and fell with **cotton**. The Confederate defeat that ended the slave trade briefly plunged it into economic chaos, and severe yellow fever epidemics didn't help, but thanks to its potential for river and rail transportation Memphis soon bounced back. The nation's second largest inland port became a major stopping-off point for **black migrants** escaping the poverty of the Delta, and many stayed, significantly shaping the city's identity.

For a couple of decades after the 1968 **assassination** of Dr Martin Luther King Jr, Memphis tottered on the brink of terminal decline, with downtown hit by a massive case of "white flight." In the past decade, however, the city has regenerated itself yet again, its new self-confidence typified by the extraordinary 321ft glossy, stainless steel **Pyramid** that now dominates the riverfront skyline. The famous **blues** corridor of **Beale Street** is booming once more, perhaps a little ersatz but always entertaining, while Elvis Presley's **Graceland** – a refreshing change from the usual "gracious southern home" – provides an intimate and exuberant glimpse of Memphis's most famous son.

## Arrival, information and getting around

**Memphis International Airport** is ten miles south of downtown – a long and complicated bus trip, but just fifteen minutes by the Yellow Cabs **limo/van** service (☎901/577-7777; $10) or **taxi** ($20–25). Greyhound **buses** stop at 203 Union Ave at Fourth Street downtown, while the Amtrak station at 545 S Main St is in a particularly seedy and unsafe area on the southern edge of downtown.

Slow and infrequent Memphis Area Transit Authority buses cover nearly all the city (☎901/274-6282); more useful is the downtown **trolley** service (☎901/274-6282) that runs along the Main Street Mall from the Pyramid to Beale Street and the Civil Rights Museum, until 6pm on Sundays and after midnight on all other days (50¢ flat fare; day pass $2).

**Carriage tours** at $30 per half-hour start from the *Peabody* and *Crowne Plaza* hotels, among others (Mon–Fri 5pm–1am, Sat & Sun 1pm–1am; ☎901/527-7542). American Dream Safari (☎901/274-1997) offers **driving tours** in a 1955 Cadillac that range from a gospel service at Al Green's church ($60 including lunch) up to week-long blues pilgrimages into the Delta. **Sternwheelers** offer ninety-minute sightseeing trips of the mighty Mississippi for $10, leaving Riverside Drive at Monroe Avenue (March–Nov daily 2.30pm; many more trips, including brunches and moonlight cruises, in season; ☎901/527-5694).

### Information

The spacious and modern **Tennessee Welcome Center** by the Pyramid, complete with 9ft bronze Elvis, facing Mud Island at river level at Riverside Drive and Adams is open 24 hours a day every day. For advance information on the city call ☎901/543-5333). The **post office** is at 555 S Third St at Calhoun (Mon–Fri 8.30am–5.30pm, Sat 10am–2pm; ☎901/521-2186; zip code 38101).

## Accommodation

Downtown Memphis has a reasonable mixture of grand hotels and inexpensive **places to stay**, though most budget motels are concentrated along Elvis Presley Boulevard to the south. The visitor center (see above) gives good advice, and is particularly helpful at busy times such as the anniversary of Elvis's death in mid-August. B&B in Memphis

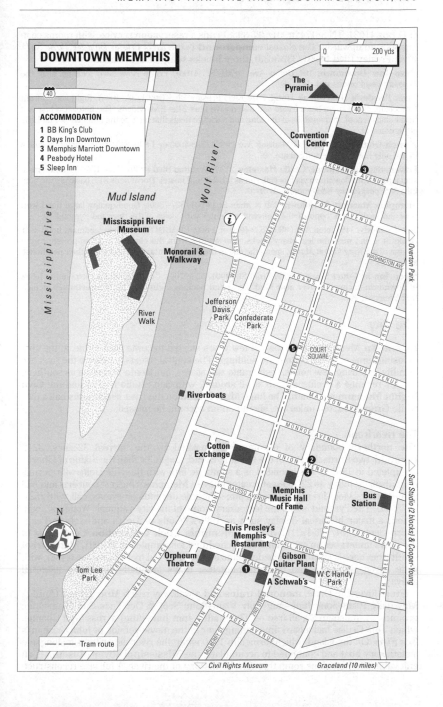

# DOWNTOWN MEMPHIS

0    200 yds

The Pyramid

Convention Center

**ACCOMMODATION**

1 BB King's Club
2 Days Inn Downtown
3 Memphis Marriott Downtown
4 Peabody Hotel
5 Sleep Inn

*Mud Island*

*Wolf River*

Mississippi River Museum

Monorail & Walkway

*Mississippi River*

River Walk

Jefferson Davis Park

Confederate Park

COURT SQUARE

Riverboats

Cotton Exchange

Memphis Music Hall of Fame

Bus Station

Elvis Presley's Memphis Restaurant

Tom Lee Park

Orpheum Theatre

Gibson Guitar Plant

W C Handy Park

A Schwab's

— · — · —  Tram route

*Overton Park*

*Sun Studio (2 blocks) & Cooper-Young*

▽ *Civil Rights Museum*      *Graceland (10 miles)* ▽

(PO Box 41621, TN 38174; ☎901/725-3958) runs a reservation service, with rooms costing $60 and upwards. The closest **campground** is the *Elvis Presley Blvd RV Park*, 3971 Elvis Presley Blvd (☎901/332-3633), three blocks south of Graceland.

**Days Inn Downtown**, 164 Union Ave (☎901/527-4100). Prime downtown location near the *Peabody*; good prices and clean. ④.

**Elvis Presley's Heartbreak Hotel**, 3677 Elvis Presley Blvd (☎901/332-1000). Right across from Graceland, every room has a fridge and microwave plus 24hr Elvis videos. The hotel also boasts a heart-shaped pool, memorabilia of the King and package deals that include the other corporate Elvis attractions. ⑤.

**French Quarter Suites**, 2144 Madison Ave (☎901/728-4000 or 1-800/843-0353). Upmarket suites in the only hotel in Overton Square. ⑥.

**Lowenstein-Long House/Castle Hostelry**, 217 N Waldran Blvd (☎901/527-7174). Victorian mansion a mile from downtown via bus #50, run as a B&B and hostel. Dorm beds $12, basic private doubles $35, plus classy B&B rooms. ①/②/④.

**Memphis Marriott Downtown**, 250 N Main St (☎901/527-7300). Good quality large hotel with pool and health club, opposite the Convention Center with views of the river and Pyramid. ⑥.

**The Peabody**, 149 Union Ave (☎901/529-4000 or 1-800/PEABODY). Opulent landmark hotel near Beale St. Don't miss the legendary ducks, who waddle from the elevator at 11am prompt to the strains of the *King Cotton March*, spend the day in the lobby fountain, and return to their penthouse at 5pm. ⑦.

**Sleep Inn at Court Square**, 40 N Front St (☎901/522-9700). Good-value new motel in the heart of downtown, facing the river near Mud Island and backing right onto Main Street; rates include free breakfast. ④.

# The City

**Downtown** Memphis has in the last few years started to come back to life, at the cost of losing some of its old cotton-era buildings. The central streets parallel to the river are steadily acquiring new hotels, restaurants and stores, but **Beale Street** on its southern fringes remains a livelier area to stroll around, with Sun Studio nearby and the **Civil Rights Museum** just south. The huge **Mud Island** on the river itself merits half a day, while **Graceland**, ten miles out, should on no account be missed.

## The riverfront

The northern boundary of downtown is marked by the surreal 32-story, 321ft **Pyramid**, two-thirds the size of the Great Pyramid, and taller than the Statue of Liberty. Completed in 1991, it was intended as a symbolic link with the Nile Delta with permanent displays; today its 22,500-seat theater puts on Memphis's biggest concerts and ball games (tours Mon–Fri noon, 1pm & 2pm; schedule depends on events, call ☎901/521-9675; $4). The Pyramid is also the temporary home of the city's annual "Wonders" exhibition, a major historical display such as 1998's "Gods of Death and Gold in Peru" (April–Sept; ☎901/576-1231), while the **Memphis Cook Convention Center** just to the south undergoes an overhaul that is scheduled for completion in 2001. **Main Street** south from here is an attractive pedestrianized mall (served by trolleys; see p.488), with wide paved sidewalks and modern fountains, that's gradually rebuilding its retail activity.

From Riverside Drive, **monorail trains** and a walkway reach **Mud Island** (April & May daily 10am–5pm; June–Aug daily 10am–8pm; Sept & Oct Tues–Sun 10am–4pm; grounds $4, museum $8, all free on Thurs after 4pm June–Aug) across Wolf Channel which Tom Cruise had a hard time getting over in the movie version of John Grisham's *The Firm*. On the island, which formed in 1910 when the river deposited silt alongside a stationary boat and continued to accumulate, the **Mississippi River Museum** is an enjoyable and ingenious romp through the history of the river. A full-size reconstruct-

## THE MISSISSIPPI RIVER

*I do not know much about gods; but I think that the river*
*Is a strong brown god – sullen, untamed and intractable.*

St Louis-born T S Eliot, *The Four Quartets*

North America's principal waterway, the **Mississippi River**, starts just ninety miles south of the Canadian border at Lake Itasca, Minnesota, and winds its way 2348 miles to the Gulf of Mexico, taking in over one hundred tributaries on the way and draining all or part of thirty-one US states and two Canadian provinces.

One of the busiest commercial rivers in the world, it's also one of the most unconventional. Only by a quirk of history does it bear the name Mississippi; if the upper Mississippi had not been discovered and charted first, geographers might well have designated the 1403-mile longer Missouri-Mississippi fork as the main stream. Instead of widening toward its mouth, like most rivers, the Mississippi grows narrower and deeper. Its **"Delta,"** over three hundred miles upstream from its mouth, is not a delta at all but an alluvial flood plain. On the other hand, its estuary deposits, which extend the land six miles out to sea every century, are comparatively paltry; Gulf currents disperse the sediment before it has time to settle.

The Mississippi is also, in the words of Mark Twain, who spent four years as a riverboat pilot, "the **crookedest** river in the world." As it weaves and curls its way extravagantly along its channel, it continually cuts through narrow necks of land to create oxbow lakes, meander scars, cutoffs and marshy backwaters. A bar could operate one day in Arkansas and then find itself in dry Tennessee the next, thanks to an overnight cutoff.

A more serious manifestation of the Mississippi's power is its propensity to **flood**. Although the river builds its own natural levees, artificial embankments have since as early as 1717 helped further to safeguard crops and homes. Since the disastrous floods of 1927, the federal government has been responsible for a wide range of flood-protection measures; virtually the entire riverfront from Cape Girardeau, Missouri, to the sea is now walled in, and it's even possible to drive along the top of the larger levees.

It's no longer feasible to sail Twain's route for yourself, though **riverboat excursions** operate in most sizeable river towns. Longer cruises, on the luxurious *Delta Queen* and *Mississippi Queen* **paddlewheelers**, are expensive; contact the Delta Queen Steamboat Company, 30 Robin Street Wharf, New Orleans, LA 70130 (☎1-800/543-1949).

ed steam packet somehow squeezes into the core of the building, a Theater of Disasters exerts a morbid fascination, and little-known characters such as keelboatman Mike Fink, who in 1830 styled himself "half-horse, half-alligator," are held up for inspection; there's also an overview of Memphis music, featuring the original sign from Stax Records and one of Elvis' Vegas-era white jumpsuits. Outside, the half-mile **River Walk** is a scale model of the river itself, complete with town grids, which ends in the "Gulf of Mexico" at a swimming pool and artificial beach. You can also visit the original **Memphis Belle**, a World War II B17 bomber, nearby.

The small, tree-shaded **Jefferson Davis** and **Confederate parks** are popular lunchtime meeting places. When the Union took Memphis during the Civil War, thousands of dismayed residents watched from these sites as seven out of eight Confederate gunboats were sunk. The imposing buildings of **Cotton Row**, halfway along Front Street, might have seen busier days, but this is still the largest spot cotton market in the country. The Cotton Exchange Building at 84 S Front St contains a small historical exhibit on the cotton trade, but visitors are not allowed into the trading area. At the south end of downtown, **Tom Lee Park**, the venue for major outdoor events such as "Memphis in May," commemorates a black boatman who rescued 32 people from a sinking boat in 1925 – despite the fact that he couldn't swim.

## Beale Street

**Beale Street** began life as one of Memphis' most exclusive enclaves; its elite residents were driven out by the yellow fever epidemics, to be replaced by a diverse mix of blacks, whites, Greeks, Jews, Chinese and Italians. But it was Beale's **black culture** that gave the street its fame. This was where black roustabouts, deckhands and travelers passing through Memphis immediately headed for; rural blacks came for the bustling Saturday market; and, in times of strict segregation, Beale acted as the center for black businesses, financiers and professionals.

As the black main street of the mid-South, Beale in its Twenties' heyday was jammed with vaudeville theaters, concert halls, bars and jook-joints (mostly white-owned). Along with the frivolity came a reputation for heavy gambling, voodoo, murder and prostitution. One appalled evangelist proclaimed that "if whiskey ran ankle deep in Memphis...you could not get drunker quicker than you can on Beale Street now."

Although Beale still drew huge crowds in the Forties, the drift to the suburbs and, ironically, the success of the **civil rights** years in opening the rest of Memphis to black businesses almost killed it off. The **bulldozers** of the late Sixties spared only the Orpheum Theatre and a few commercial buildings between Second and Fourth streets.

Beale Street has now been restored as an **Historic District**, its shops, clubs and cafes bedecked with Twenties-style facades and signs, while a Walk of Fame with brass musical notes embedded into the sidewalk honor musical greats such as BB King and Howlin' Wolf. Tourist money has led to extensive development, but with the exception of a few out-and-out souvenir shops, most of the new businesses remain in tune with the past, and for blues fans in particular its music venues showcase top regional talents. At its western end, 1997 saw the conversion of 126 Beale St – formerly home to Lansky's, tailors to the Memphis stars – into *Elvis Presley's – Memphis Restaurant* (see p.497), which now rivals *B B King's* just beyond as the street's busiest nightspot. A little further along, **A Schwab's Dry Goods Store**, at no. 163, looks much as it must have done when it opened in 1876, with an incredible array of such voodoo paraphernalia, familiar from the blues, as Mojo Hands and High John the Conqueror lucky roots in fragrant oil, as well as 99¢ neckties and Sunday School badges (closed Sun). Next door, the free **Memphis Police Museum**, open around the clock, holds an assortment of old photos, newspapers and crime-fighting accouterments – great fun at night after club-hopping.

A new arrival to the city at Beale and Third is the **Gibson Guitar Plant**, allowing visitors to watch the craftworkers construct six-string and bass guitars while upstairs is the **Rock 'n' Soul: Social Crossroads**, a permanent exhibition space curated by the Smithsonian Institution, which focuses on issues such as migration, racism, civil rights and youth culture in a musical context.

Also on Beale, the excellent **Center for Southern Folklore** (daily 10am–10pm; ☎901/525–3655; $2 donation) is a cheerful museum that tends to move every few years and celebrates the music, food, storytelling and crafts of the people of the mid-South. A small stage puts on high-quality live music most afternoons or evenings, with gospel groups and choirs on Sundays, and there's also an espresso cafe, an exhibition area, and a good giftshop that sells folk art, blues cassettes and quilts. Across the street, tree-shaded **Handy Park** – a focus for the city's many dispossessed – echoes day and night with jamming blues musicians.

A couple of blocks north of Beale Street, opposite the *Peabody Hotel* (see p.490), the **Memphis Music Hall of Fame** at 97 S Second St pays a more comprehensive homage to the musicians of Memphis (Mon–Thurs 10am–6pm, Fri & Sat 10am–9pm (summer only), Sun noon–6pm; $7.50). The jam-packed glass cabinets in this converted store are probably too dry to win new converts from casual visitors, but for aficionados the abundant photos, records, old instruments and film and TV footage, ranging from the pre-Elvis years to Sun, Stax and beyond, are sheer delight.

East along Beale at no. 352, the tiny former home of **W C Handy** (hours vary; ☎901/522–1556; $1), who was in 1910 the first man to publish blues tunes (often blues in name only; see p.522). His *Memphis Blues* – originally *Mr Crump* – was the theme song for the 1909 mayoral election of Edward H Crump, whose crooked political machine was to run the city until the early Fifties. Almost at the eastern extremity of the street, and close to Sun Studio, **the Hunt–Phelan Home**, 533 Beale (June–Aug Mon–Sat 10am–4pm, Sun noon–4pm; Sept–May Thurs–Mon 10am–4pm, Sun noon–4pm; $10), was completed in 1832 but only recently opened for public tours. It's a remarkable example of a restored antebellum home, with virtually all of the original furnishings intact and the extensive gardens restored to their original usage. Guided tours reveal some poignant Civil War stories and all in all, it lives up to the rather steep admission price.

## Sun Studio

**Sun Studio**, ten minutes' walk east of Beale at 706 Union Ave (June–Aug daily 9.30am–6.30pm, store 9am–7pm; Sept–May daily 10.30am–5.30pm, store 9am–7pm; tours $9), was where Elvis, Johnny Cash and others cut their first records (see box overleaf). Every hour, on the half-hour, twenty-minute "tours" (sic) of its single room, measuring just eighteen feet by thirty feet and focusing around Elvis' original mike stand, plus a drum kit and stand-up bass, feature tapes of legendary recording sessions. Sun Records moved out in 1959, and although the building was briefly a scuba-diving store – not surprisingly, a commercial failure – all its soundproofing remained in place when it was restored as a studio in 1987. One room of the building, which Elvis knew as *Mrs Taylor's Cafe*, still functions as an atmospheric diner, selling burgers and peanut-butter-and-banana sandwiches, and there's a well-stocked giftshop upstairs.

## The National Civil Rights Museum

The **National Civil Rights Museum**, a few blocks south of Beale Street at 450 Mulberry St (June–Aug Mon & Wed 10am–6pm, Thurs 9am–8pm, Fri & Sat 9am–6pm, Sun 1–6pm; Sept–May Mon & Wed 10am–5pm, Thurs 9am–8pm, Fri & Sat 10am–5pm, Sun 1–5pm; $6), has been built around the remains of the *Lorraine Motel*, where **Dr Martin Luther King Jr** was assassinated by James Earl Ray on April 4, 1968. In increasingly hardline speeches, Dr King had explicitly linked black poverty with military spending in Vietnam. He was killed by a single bullet the evening before he was due to lead a march in Memphis in support of a strike by black sanitation workers.

The struggle for civil rights is traced from A Philip Randolph of the Brotherhood of Sleeping Car Porters, who originally called for a march on Washington in 1941, through to the Nation of Islam and the Black Panthers. Great resources have been devoted to an impressive exposition of the movement's history, though the tone veers between the overdetailed and the banal – sitting on the front seat of a reconstructed Montgomery bus triggers a recorded message instructing you to move to the back. Tours climax with Dr King's room, preserved behind a glass screen, and the balcony where he was shot; unquestionably an emotive sight, but arguably also tasteless, if not downright exploitive. Protesters continue to charge that Memphis' role in Dr King's death should be a source of shame rather than a tourist attraction, and that his memory would have been better served if the site had been used as a facility for the poor.

## Graceland

In itself, Elvis Presley's **Graceland** was a surprisingly modest home for the world's most successful entertainer. It's certainly not the "mansion" you may have been led to expect, and while Elvis was clearly a man who indulged his tastes to the full, there's none of the pomposity that characterizes so many other showpiece Southern residences. Visits, run under the auspices of his widow Priscilla, are affectionate celebrations of the man; never exactly tongue in cheek, but not cloyingly reverential either.

Elvis was just 22 when he paid $100,000 for Graceland in 1957. It was then considered one of the most desirable properties in Memphis, though now the neighborhood is distinctly less exclusive, its main thoroughfare – **Elvis Presley Boulevard** – lined with motels, fast-food joints and surprisingly few Elvis-related souvenir shops. Tours start opposite the house in **Graceland Plaza**; excited visitors, kitted out with audio-cassette players, are ferried across the road in minibuses, which depart every few minutes and sweep through the musical gate in the "**Wall of Love**," scrawled with tens of thousands of messages from fans.

## THE SOUND OF MEMPHIS

Since the start of the twentieth century, Memphis has been a meeting place for black musicians from the Mississippi Delta and beyond. During the Twenties, its downtown pubs, clubs and street corners were alive with the sound of the blues. **Jug bands**, in which singers were given a bass accompaniment by blowing across the neck of a jug, were a specialty. Several songs by **Gus Cannon's Jug Stompers** – such as *Walk Right In* – became hits for white artists during the folk revival of the Sixties. **Bukka White, Memphis Slim** and guitarist **Memphis Minnie** appeared at nightspots like *Mitchell's Hotel* and *Pee Wee's Saloon*, all long since defunct. After World War II, young musicians and radio DJs experimented by blending the traditional blues sound with jazz, adding electrical amplification to create **rhythm 'n' blues**. Pioneers included **Bobby Bland** and **B B King**.

White promoter Sam Phillips started **Sun Records** in 1953, employing Ike Turner as a scout to comb the Beale Street clubs for new talent. Among those whom Turner helped introduce to vinyl were his own girlfriend, Annie Mae Bullock (later **Tina Turner**), **Howlin' Wolf**, and **Little Junior Parker**, whose *Mystery Train* was Sun's first great recording. Phillips' conviction that "If I could find a white man who had the Negro sound and the Negro feel, I could make a billion dollars" achieved fruition in 1954, during a coffee break, when he overheard a young white man who had hired the studio to record a disc for his mother – **Elvis Presley**. Phillips dropped his black artists right away, signing other white **rockabilly** singers like **Carl Perkins** and **Jerry Lee Lewis** to make classics such as *Blue Suede Shoes* and *Great Balls of Fire*. Elvis – who in the words of Carl Perkins had the advantage that he "didn't look like Mr Ed, like a lot of the rest of us" – was soon sold on to RCA (for just $35,000), and didn't record in Memphis again until 1969, when with songs like *Suspicious Minds* he produced the best material of his later career.

In the Sixties and early Seventies, Memphis' **Stax Records** provided a rootsy alternative to the poppier sounds of Motown. This hard-edged **southern soul** was created by a multiracial mix of musicians, **Steve Cropper's** fluid guitar complementing the blaring **Memphis Horns**. The label's first real success was *Green Onions* by studio band **Booker T and the MGs**; further hits followed from **Otis Redding** (*Try A Little Tenderness*), **Wilson Pickett** (*Midnight Hour*), **Sam and Dave** (*Soul Man*) and **Isaac Hayes** (*Shaft*). The label eventually foundered in acrimony; the last straw for many of its veteran soulmen was the signing of the British child star Lena Zavaroni for a six-figure sum.

Memphis has been renowned for its **gospel** music since the Thirties, when Rev Herbert Brewster wrote **Mahalia Jackson's** *Move On Up a Little Higher*. Following a religious revelation, the consummate soul stylist **Al Green**, who achieved chart success for **Hi Records** with *Let's Stay Together* and *Tired of Being Alone*, is now minister at the Full Gospel Tabernacle, at 787 Hale Rd in the leafy suburb of Whitehaven. Visitors are welcome at the 11am Sunday services, complete with four-piece rhythm section; continue a mile south of Graceland, then turn west (phone ahead to check he's in town; ☎901/396-9192).

---

## GRACELAND ATTRACTIONS

Graceland is ten miles from downtown Memphis, at 3734 Elvis Presley Blvd, on bus route #13 from Third and Union. The ticket office is open May & Sept daily 7.30am–6pm; June–Aug daily 7.30am–7pm; rest of year daily 8.30am–5pm. The last house tour starts at the ticket office's closing time, while the other attractions remain open for roughly two more hours. Combined ticket to all attractions (allow three hours) is $19.50; house tours only, $10 (closed Tues Nov–Feb); Automobile museum $5; airplanes $4.50; "Sincerely Elvis" $3.50; parking fee $3. Reservations are recommended, especially in August (☎901/332-3322; *www.elvis–presley.com*).

---

The audio tours, peppered with spoken memories from Priscilla and rousing choruses from the King, allow you to spend as long as you wish – and press the rewind button as many times as you like – but it's not easy to get an accurate sense of the house's size and layout, as the upstairs rooms are out of bounds to visitors. The interior is a frozen tribute to the taste of the Seventies; choice moments include the Hawaiian-themed **Jungle Room**, with its waterfall and green shag-carpeted ceiling, where he recorded *Moody Blue* and other gems from his declining years, and the navy and lemon **TV Room**, mirrored and fitted with three screens that now show 1970s talk shows. In the separate **Trophy Room**, you parade past Elvis' platinum, gold and silver records, stage costumes, outfits from many of his 31 films, and his extensive gun collection; the tour of the interior ends with the racquetball court where he played on the morning he died. Strewn with flowers and soft toys sent daily from fans, Elvis (Jan 8, 1935–Aug 16, 1977), his mother Gladys, his father Vernon and his grandmother are buried beside the swimming pool in the **Meditation Garden** outside; Elvis's body was moved here two months after his death, when the security problems inherent in keeping it in the local cemetery became obvious, though there have been recent reports that his family want to move it to a private retreat away from Graceland.

The Plaza itself, resounding with nonstop Elvis hits and lined with giftshops selling velvet Elvises and heart-shaped *Love Me Tender* "dream pillows," holds several enjoyable related attractions: don't miss the wittily edited free film *Walk A Mile In My Shoes*, the **"Sincerely Elvis"** collection of personal belongings – which features a TV punctured by a bullet fired by Elvis himself (he also shot his fridge, his stereo and even Lisa Marie's slide), as well as the King's Hai Karate and Brut aftershave – and Elvis' personal **airplanes**, including the *Lisa Marie*, customized with 24-carat gold washroom and a blue suede bathroom. End your tour with a sit-down in the **Elvis Presley Automobile Museum**, which, quite apart from a Harley Davidson golf cart and powder pink Cadillac, has a reconstructed drive-in showing motion-related clips from his movies.

### Midtown and East Memphis

The mile-long, heavily wooded expanse of **Overton Park**, three miles from downtown (#50 bus) on Poplar Avenue, holds the wide-ranging **Memphis Brooks Museum of Art** (Tues–Fri 9am–4pm, Sat 9am–5pm, Sun 11.30am–5pm; $5), and the recently modernized **Memphis Zoo and Aquarium** (March–Oct daily 9am–5pm; Nov–Feb daily 9am–4.30pm; $8). **Overton Square**, the city's top suburban entertainment, dining and shopping district, is within walking distance. Just past East Parkway, the **Memphis Pink Palace Museum and Planetarium** at 3050 Central Ave (April–Sept Mon–Wed 9am–5pm, Thurs 9am–9pm, Fri & Sat 9am–10pm, Sun noon–5pm; Oct–March Mon–Wed 9am–4pm, Thurs 9am–8pm, Fri & Sat 9am–9pm, Sun noon–5pm; $6) centers on the pink marble mansion of Clarence Saunders, who founded America's first chain of self-service **supermarkets**, Piggly-Wiggly, in 1916. Saunders went bankrupt in 1923, and never actually lived here; instead the building has acquired several new wings in the process of becoming an all-embracing museum of Memphis history, holding all kinds of stuffed animals and oddities, including an entire functioning miniature circus, an IMAX cinema and the **Sharpe Planetarium**, as well as a walk-through model of the first Piggly-Wiggly store, complete with 2¢ packets of Kellogg's Cornflakes and 8¢ cans of Campbell's Soup.

South of Overton Square, the tiny, hip **Cooper-Young** intersection is as yet little more than a handful of shops: vintage stores where the city's punks and hippies burrow through secondhand psychedelic Crimplene, and richer arty types muse over retro knickknacks. It's a lively place, quite different from downtown, where you're likely to stumble across poetry readings and yard sales, art exhibits and antique auctions. It's also home to the funky *Java Cabana*, a hugely hip coffee shop (see "Eating" below) fronted by the **Shrine of the Elvis Impersonators** (drop a quarter into the slot to see an assortment of would-be Elvises light up and revolve in a wondrous, glittery spectacle). There's a small **wedding chapel** at the back, which with its folk art and bead curtains looks more like an art student's bedroom than any place of worship. It costs $2 to have your photo taken posing in cardboard cutouts of Elvis and Priscilla, or $175 to get married. The "comments book" makes entertaining reading: in among the teenage angst, drug-fueled poetry and satirical doodles is the eternal question, "If Elvis was so great, why is he buried in the back garden like a hamster?"

# Eating

Memphians are fond of their food, proclaiming their city to be the **pork barbecue** capital of the world, with over one hundred specialist restaurants. There's also a good selection of reasonably priced soul-food cafes, and a couple of cool *nouvelle* Southern places. **Downtown** has a good choice (including some lively cafes on Beale Street); for a bit of variety, try **Overton Square** or **Cooper-Young** midtown.

**Arcade**, 540 S Main St (☎901/526–5757). Over eighty years old, this unassuming landmark (featured in Jim Jarmusch's *Mystery Train* movie) serves up no-frills Southern lunches, dinners and big breakfasts.

**Automatic Slim's Tonga Club**, 83 S 2nd St (☎901/525-7948). Trendy Southwestern restaurant/nightspot, complete with tumbleweed, opposite the *Peabody Hotel*. Excellent if pricey *nouvelle* food.

**Blues City Cafe**, 138 Beale St (☎901/526-3637). City branch of Mississippi soul-food specialist *Doe's Eat Place* (see p.522), open daily 4.30pm–4.30am. Join musicians from nearby clubs for tasty tamales, catfish and stew.

**Buntyn**, 4972 Park Ave (☎901/458-8776). Hugely atmospheric old-style diner, southeast of downtown, specializing in Southern fried chicken and an irresistible array of vegetables. Mon–Fri 11am–8pm.

**Cafe Ole**, 959 S Cooper Ave (☎901/274-1504). Very popular Mexican restaurant in Cooper-Young with good fajitas and vegetarian specialties such as spinach and mushroom quesadillas.

**Cafe Palladio**, 2169 Central Ave (☎901/276–3354). Trendy gourmet cuisine in upscale haunt that's surrounded by an expensive antiques marketplace.

**Interstate Bar-B-Que**, 2265 S 3rd St (☎901/775-2304). Legendary barbecue restaurant, south of downtown on the way to the Delta, and open daily for lunch and dinner.

**Java Cabana**, 2170 Young Ave (☎901/272-7210). *The* place in Memphis to drink coffee, in arty surroundings with a plethora of Elvis memorabilia for sale. Opens at 1pm; closed Mon.

**Little Tea Shop**, 69 Monroe Ave (☎901/525-6000). Unusual downtown soul-food cafe, serving a health-conscious version of what is traditionally a very fatty cuisine. Mon–Fri 11.15am–2.15pm; lunches cost around $5.

**Maxwell's**, 948 S Cooper St (☎901/725-1009). Stylish Cooper-Young restaurant, whose brick walls are covered with abstract art. Creative food includes Indian and Mediterranean dishes, shellfish and pasta. Main courses around $10. Dinner nightly until 2am, lunch weekdays only.

**The North End**, 346 N Main St (☎901/526-0319). Friendly bar-cum-restaurant in the emerging Pinch District opposite the Pyramid, specializing in wild-rice dishes, stir-fries and a killer hot fudge pie. Occasional live music.

**Otherlands**, 641 S Cooper Ave (☎901/278-4994). Funky midtown coffee bar with its own giftshop, colorful *naif* art works, great latte, bagels and cakes, and a laid-back crowd.

**Public Eye**, 17 S Cooper Ave, Overton Square (☎901/726-4040). Huge restaurant, popular with families, that serves superb pork ribs, all-you-can-eat deals and very cheap lunch specials.

**The Rendezvous**, General Washburn Alley, 52 S 2nd St (☎901/523-2746). Downtown Memphis' top-rated pork barbecue joint. Huge helpings and a nice atmosphere. Open Tues–Sat.

**Sleep Out Louie's**, 88 Union Ave (☎901/527–5337). Trendy oyster bar and grill that's a popular post-theater meeting point.

# Nightlife and entertainment

Though **live music** is at its best in Memphis during the city's many **festivals**, such as the month-long **Memphis in May** (which also features the Barbecue Cookout Competition) and October's **Blues Memphis Week**, the blues and soul clubs of Beale Street have plenty to offer fans all year round. The best sources of **listings** are the free weekly *Memphis Flyer*, Friday's *Memphis Commercial Appeal*, and the community **radio** station WEVL (FM 90, daily 6am–2am).

**B B King's Blues Club**, 143 Beale St (☎901/524-5464). Despite accusations from purists of having "sold out," this is justifiably Beale's most popular club. Outside there's a neon guitar; inside it's spacious and atmospheric, with barbecue ribs, catfish and beer delivered to your table, and nightly blues enjoyed by a wildly enthusiastic crowd who make good use of the dance floor. BB himself makes an appearance or two per year.

**Blues City Cafe**, 138 Beale St (☎901/526-3637). This club stays active well after the others and while the band is beating away there's a choice of well-priced ribs, catfish, tamales and gumbo to chew on.

**Elvis Presley's – Memphis**, 126 Beale St (☎1-800/238-2000). Lansky's, the tailors where Elvis bought his sharpest suits, has been transformed into a restaurant and bar with a heavily Elvis-themed menu and the financial clout to put on some of Memphis' best bands. If this new venture takes off, expect Elvis to be coming to your town shortly.

**Flying Saucer Draught Emporium**, 130 Peabody Place (☎901/523-8676). Appealingly laid-back beerhall, aimed at the grungy college crowd, just north of Beale St.

**Green's**, 2090 E Person Ave (no phone). Unpretentious, authentic neighborhood jook-joint putting on the best in Delta blues. Live music and hard dancing until 2.30am every Fri and Sat, with great house band the Fieldstones, and frequent special guests; $4 cover.

**Hernando's Hideaway**, 3210 Old Hernando Rd (☎901/398-7496). One of the region's few remaining old-style honky-tonks. A real period piece made famous by Jerry Lee Lewis's frequent visits before he became a reformed character.

**Huey's Midtown**, 1927 Madison Ave (☎901/726-4372). Popular Overton Square restaurant, famed for its great burgers, with live jazz on Sun afternoon, followed by an out-of-town blues band in the evening. There's also a downtown branch of this popular local mini-chain at 77 S 2nd St (☎901/527-2700).

**Kudzu's**, 603 Monroe Ave (☎901/525-4924). Great downtown bar with pool table and live weekend blues.

**Rum Boogie Cafe**, 182 Beale St (☎901/528-0150). Usually one of Beale's most crowded venues, with resident blues bands every night 9pm–1.30am, plus Cajun cooking and ribs; $4 cover.

**Willie Mitchell's Rhythm and Blues Club**, 326 Beale St (☎901/523-7444). One of Beale's smaller and less fancy clubs, it's owned by the daughters of legendary soul producer/songwriter Mitchell, with consistently classy blues and R&B acts. Talent search Wed nights.

## Shiloh National Military Park

Approximately 110 miles east of Memphis and twelve south of Savannah, Tennessee, via US-64 and Hwy-22, **SHILOH NATIONAL MILITARY PARK** (daily 8am–5pm; ☎901/689-5275; $2) commemorates one of the most crucial battles of the Civil War. After victories at Fort Henry and Fort Donelson, General Grant's confident Union forces were all but defeated by a surprise early-morning Confederate attack on April 6, 1862. A stubborn rump of resistance held on until around 5pm, and the Confederates elected to finish the task off the next morning rather than launching a twilight assault. However, Grant's decimated regiments were bolstered by the overnight arrival of new troops, and instead it was their dawn initiative that forced the tired and demoralized Confederates to retreat.

Shiloh was the first encounter on a scale that became common as the war continued, putting an abrupt end to the romantic innocence of many a raw volunteer soldier. Over 20,000 men in all were killed. Even the war-toughened General Sherman spoke of "piles of dead soldiers' mangled bodies . . . without heads and legs . . . the scenes on this field would have cured anyone of war."

The **visitor center** displays artifacts recovered from the battlefield and shows an informative twenty-minute film. A self-guided ten-mile driving tour takes in the **National Cemetery**, whose moss-covered walls contain thousands of unidentified graves.

# Nashville

Set amid the gentle hills and fertile farmlands of central Tennessee, **NASHVILLE** attracts six million people each year – a mixture of devoted fans and the just plain curious – to immerse themselves in **country music**. They come to enjoy themselves, and the city makes sure that they do, offering not just the relatively mainstream **Country Music Hall of Fame** and **Grand Ole Opry**, but all the wonders of "Tacksville." To make the most of this facet of Nashville, you need to abandon any idea of detachment, and get out there among the nightspots and gift emporia, joining the quest for souvenir T-shirts, Stetsons, rattlesnake belts and photos of your favorite star.

However, there is a real city beneath the rhinestone glitter. Nashville has been the leading settlement in middle Tennessee since **Fort Nashborough** was established in 1779. State capital since 1843, it is now the **financial** and **insurance** center of the mid-South, as well as a fast-growing **manufacturing** base. Giant Nissan and Saturn motor plants have been attracted to its immediate hinterland, and rapid growth since World War II has transformed a once-compact city into a sprawling conurbation stretching out in all directions along the undulating roads, here known as **pikes**.

For all its blue-collar "Nash-Vegas" image, Nashville has maintained a strong reputation for **learning** since planter times, and is home to sixteen higher education establishments, including Vanderbilt University and the renowned black colleges of Fisk University and Meharry Medical School. The city likes to see itself as the "Athens of the South" – and, endearingly, has built a replica of the Parthenon to bolster its claim. Even at night, Nashville offers more than country music, with enough going on to satisfy most tastes. It has also boosted its image by attracting an NFL team (the Tennessee Oilers) and NHL side (the Nashville Predators) here.

The other conspicuous element in Nashville's make-up is **religion**. There are over seven hundred churches, more per capita than anywhere else in the country. But what really earns it the tag of "Protestant Vatican" is the proliferation of colleges for training preachers and missionaries, church administrative offices and Bible-publishing plants.

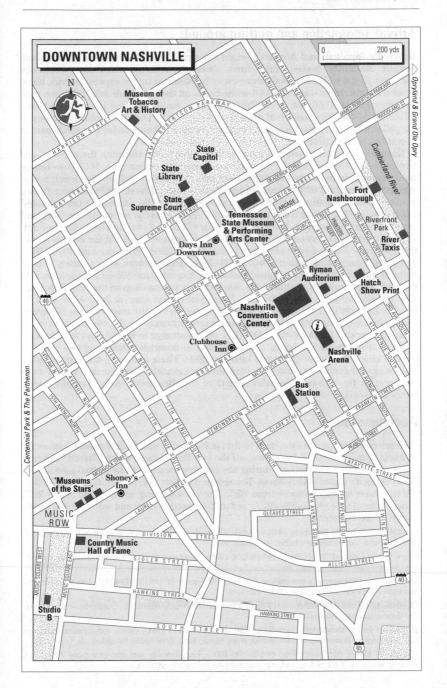

# DOWNTOWN NASHVILLE

0    200 yds

N

Opryland & Grand Ole Opry

Cumberland River

Museum of Tobacco Art & History

State Capitol

State Library

State Supreme Court

Tennessee State Museum & Performing Arts Center

Days Inn Downtown

Fort Nashborough

Riverfront Park

River Taxis

ARCADE

Ryman Auditorium

Hatch Show Print

Nashville Convention Center

Clubhouse Inn

Nashville Arena

Bus Station

Centennial Park & The Parthenon

'Museums of the Stars'

Shoney's Inn

MUSIC ROW

Country Music Hall of Fame

Studio B

HARRISON STREET

JAMES ROBERTSON PARKWAY

SHIRE N.

GAY STREET NORTH

2ND AVENUE NORTH

3RD AVENUE NORTH

WOODLAND ST.

GAY STREET

CHARLOTTE AVENUE

DEADERICK STREET

UNION STREET

CHURCH STREET

COMMERCE STREET

PRINTERS ALLEY

4TH AVENUE NORTH

5TH AVENUE NORTH

6TH AVENUE NORTH

7TH AVENUE NORTH

8TH AVENUE NORTH

9TH AVENUE NORTH

10TH AVENUE NORTH

11TH AVENUE NORTH

12TH AVENUE SOUTH

13TH AVENUE NORTH

14TH AVENUE NORTH

15TH AVENUE NORTH

BROADWAY

McGAVOCK STREET

DEMONBREUN STREET

CLARK STREET

LAUREL STREET

DIVISION STREET

SIGLER STREET

HAWKINS STREET

SOUTH STREET

GLEAVES STREET

ALLISON STREET

LAFAYETTE STREET

PEABODY STREET

FRANKLIN STREET

EWING STREET

3RD AVE. SOUTH

4TH AVENUE SOUTH

5TH AVENUE SOUTH

6TH AVENUE SOUTH

7TH AVENUE SOUTH

8TH AVENUE SOUTH

MUSIC SQUARE WEST

MUSIC SQUARE EAST

40

40

65

## Arrival, information and getting around

**Nashville International Airport** is eight miles southeast of downtown. Metropolitan Transit Authority **buses** into town (weekdays 6.45am–10.48pm; weekends 6.45am–6.05pm; ☎615/862-5950) leave every half-hour or so; the express service takes around twenty minutes and costs $4 while buses on the local route take twice the time and charge the $1.50 flat fare. The Gray Line shuttle (every 15min 6am–11pm; ☎1-800/669-9463; $9) drops off at most downtown hotels. Taxis are probably the quickest option but will set you back close to $20. Greyhound buses arrive in a seedy part of downtown at 200 Eighth Ave S; there's no Amtrak service.

Nashville is so spread out that a **car** is a very good idea. However, the one-way system can be maddening, and the roads change name without warning. MTA runs **buses** until midnight to most parts of the county, from the transit mall on Deaderick Street and Fifth Avenue ($1.50 flat fare), and **trolleys,** leaving Riverfront Park every fifteen minutes, cover the entire downtown area plus Music Row for a fare of $1 (an unlimited 1-day pass is $3; a similar 3-day pass costs $8). A nice way to get out to the Opryland area is on the Opryland US River Taxis (☎615/871-5701; $14 round-trip). Another system of trolleys runs between the theme park, the *Opryland Hotel* and the various attractions in Music Valley. Grand Ole Opry Tours (☎615/889-9490), Gray Line (☎615/883-5555) and Johnny Walker Tours (☎615/834-8585), among others, offer a variety of both cultural and specialist country music **bus tours**. Expect to pay $25 for a three-hour trip, not including admission to attractions. Alternatively you can hop on the "Big Pink Bus" with the singing guides of NashTrash Tours (Sat & Sun 11am & 2pm; other days by arrangement; ☎615/226-7300; $20) who dig up the dirt on the country stars. Nashville Black Heritage Tours offers **walking tours** concentrating on the city's considerable African-American history (☎615/890-8173; call to arrange at least 3 days in advance). The city also produces a handy CityWalk map to downtown, following two miles of painted blue lines around the major historic sights. These maps and much more information as well as discount tickets to attractions are available from the new **visitor center,** next to the massive Nashville Arena at 501 Broadway (daily daylight hours; ☎615/259-4747).

## Accommodation

Well-priced **rooms** are not too hard to find in Nashville, with budget **motels** gathering a couple of miles north of downtown, off the I-65 Trinity Lane/Brick Church Pike exit. Rates are usually higher in June during the country music Fan Fair festival (see p.504). **B&B** agencies include B&B About Tennessee, PO Box 110227, TN 37222 (☎615/331-5244), which arranges rooms from $55. There's **camping** at *Opryland KOA*, 2626 Music Valley Drive (☎615/889-0282), set in 27 attractive acres and with free live music shows in the summer.

**ClubHouse Inn**, 920 Broadway (☎615/244-0150). Realistically-priced downtown convention hotel, with pool and complimentary buffet breakfast. ⑥.

**Days Inn – Central**, 211 N 1st St (☎615/254-1551). Inexpensive hotel with good view of the city skyline and close to downtown. ③.

**Days Inn – Downtown/Convention Center**, 711 Union St (☎615/242-4311). Excellent central downtown location, and good weekend rates. ③.

**Econolodge Near Opryland**, 2460 Music Valley Drive (☎615/889-0090). Comfortable motel near the theme park and *Nashville Palace*. ④.

**Hampton Inn – Vanderbilt**, 1919 West End Ave (☎615/329-1144). Clean, comfortable lodgings, one mile west of downtown and six blocks from Music Row. Free buffet breakfast. ⑤.

**Opryland Hotel**, McGavock Pike (☎615/889-1000). Unbelievably vast and expensive 2000-room place (costing up to $2000) set out around glass-roofed courtyards. ⑦.

**Shoney's Inn – Music Row**, 1521 Demonbreun St (☎615/255-9977). Good-value rooms and free coffee close to all the record labels. ④.

## The City

**Downtown Nashville** looks much like any other regional business center, dominated by office blocks and parking lots, and dotted here and there with major new flagship structures like the gigantic **Nashville Arena** sports and entertainments complex at Fifth and Broadway and the relocated **Country Music Hall of Fame** at Fifth and Demonbreun which is due to open in mid-2001. It's perfectly possible to spend a busy day in Nashville without coming into contact with country music. A good starting point is **Riverfront Park** at First and Broadway, a thin stretch of grass and terracing dipping down to the **Cumberland River**. A replica of the wooden **Fort Nashborough** (Tues–Sun 9am–5pm; free) stands on a promontory above the river as a monument to the city's founders of 1779. A few blocks away, the worthy **Tennessee State Museum** at 505 Deaderick St (Tues–Sat 10am–5pm, Sun 1–5pm; free) is strongest on the Civil War, highlighting the hardships of the ill-clad, ill-fed soldiers, of whom 23,000 out of 77,000 died at Shiloh alone. Other displays in this huge space focus on frontier life and on black Tennesseans, looking at slavery, Reconstruction, the founding of the Ku Klux Klan and the civil rights movement.

Marking downtown's northern boundary at Sixth and Charlotte, the resplendent **Tennessee State Capitol** (Mon–Fri 9am–4pm; free), modeled on an Ionic temple, looks out across the city from its hilltop perch. Early in the twentieth century, this area was yet another "Hell's Half Acre," notorious for its drinking holes, gambling clubs, sex shows and dope dens; it's considerably tamer now, housing hotels and offices.

At the 1897 Tennessee Centennial Exposition, Nashville's "Athens of the South" exhibit featured a full-size wood-and-plaster replica of the **Parthenon**, which proved so popular with Nashville residents that the present permanent structure, in the middle of **Centennial Park** southwest of downtown at West End and 25th avenues, was built in 1931. This impressive edifice – familiar to moviegoers from the finale of Robert Altman's not-always-flattering *Nashville* – is now home to Nashville's premier **art museum** (Tues–Sat 9am–4.30pm; April–Sept also Sun 12.30–4.30pm; $2.50). The lower level contains American paintings; the upper hall is dominated by a 42ft replica of Phidias' statue of Athena.

Just across West End Avenue, weather-beaten Gothic structures sit alongside more modern utilitarian buildings on the campus of prestigious **Vanderbilt University**. This bastion of conservatism was one of the very few colleges to witness student demonstrations in *support* of US involvement in Vietnam. Nearby **Fisk University** is one of the nation's oldest black colleges, and on campus is the excellent **Van Vechten Gallery**, at Jackson Street at D B Todd Boulevard (Tues–Fri 10am–5pm, Sat & Sun 1–5pm; closed Sun in summer; donation). In addition to works by Picasso, Cézanne and Renoir, and a wide array of pieces by Georgia O'Keeffe, there are changing exhibits, many of them with an African-American theme.

Of the many buildings erected by Nashville's antebellum elite, none was more elaborate than the **Belmont Mansion**, a mile southeast of the Parthenon at 1900 Belmont Blvd (June–Aug Mon–Sat 10am–4pm, Sun 2–5pm; Sept–May Tues–Sat 10am–4pm; $5). This 36-room 1850 Italianate villa looks out across ornamented gardens that once contained a bear house and a lake stocked with alligators.

## Country music Nashville

The status of Nashville as country music's capital city dates back to the Twenties and the arrival of thousands of migrants fleeing rural poverty. The music they brought with

## THE GRAND OLD OPRY

Nashville's radio station **WSM** ("We Shield Millions," the slogan of its insurance-company sponsor) first broadcast on October 5, 1925. Two years later, at the start of his *Barn Dance* show, compere George D Hay announced "for the past hour we have been listening to music taken largely from Grand Opera, but from now on we will present *The Grand Ole Opry.*" This piece of slang became the name of America's longest-running radio show, still going out to millions every Friday and Saturday evening on WSM-AM (650m); the original "hillbilly" jam session has become country music's elite showcase.

Swiftly outgrowing the WSM studios, the show moved in 1943 to a former tabernacle – the **Ryman Auditorium**. There it acquired a make-or-break reputation; up-and-coming singers could only claim to have made it if they had gone down well at the Opry. Among thousands of hopefuls who tried to get on the show was Elvis Presley, advised by an Opry official in 1954 to stick to truck-driving. The first appearance of **Hank Williams**, in 1949, commanded an unequaled six encores. Within four years, the Opry audience was singing his evangelical *I Saw the Light* on the news of his drink- and drug-induced death.

In 1974 the show moved on again, this time to a new purpose-built 4424-seater theater in what was the **Opryland** theme park (now the **Opry Mills** mall) – one of many Opry spin-offs, including hotels, TV stations and a record label. Among more than sixty stars currently on the Opry roster are old-timers like Hank Snow and Charlie Louvin, perennial superstars like Dolly Parton, and current country chart-toppers such as Garth Brooks and Alison Krauss. However, many of the younger artists are busy touring, so most shows are dominated by stars whose best days have past.

Throughout the year, two performances on Saturday night at 6.30pm and 9.30pm and one on Friday night at 7.30pm feature up to twenty acts. During the summer there's an extra Friday-night show and matinee on Tuesday. The line-ups are usually announced on the preceding Thursday. **Tickets** are $18–20 and not too hard to get, especially if you book in advance. Contact the box office at 2808 Opryland Drive, Nashville, TN 37214 (☎615/889-3060).

them, rooted in the folk songs of Tennessee's first Irish and British settlers, soon mutated in the urban environment into something new, incorporating elements of Tin Pan Alley musicals, religious hymns and the songs of ex-slaves.

As radios and record players became widely available for the first time, the **recording industry** began to take off, and Nashville became the obvious geographical base for the musicians of the mid-South. Radio station WSM had championed the country sound since 1925, and its live weekly *Grand Ole Opry* concerts (see box above) spearheaded the city's burgeoning **live music** scene.

The first big commercial boom came in the decade of prosperity after World War II. Nashville proliferated with recording studios, publishing companies and artists' agencies. The big labels recognized that a large slice of the (white) record-buying public wanted something a bit safer than rockabilly. The easy-listening **Nashville Sound** they came up with, pioneered by Patsy Cline and Jim Reeves, perpetuated by the likes of Barbara Mandrell and Kenny Rogers and virtually preened free of twang by Shania Twain and Garth Brooks, remains the clean-cut face of country – though country music has always had its earthier side – and the concentration of stars and music-biz executives has turned Nashville into something of a downmarket Hollywood.

Though Nashville's country scene is both conspicuous and accessible, submerging yourself in it takes time and quite a lot of money; prices are set at what the industry knows enthusiastic fans will pay. In addition to the daytime attractions mentioned below, country music venues are listed in the "Nightlife" section on p.504.

**Downtown** at 116 Fifth Ave, you can do a self-guided tour of the **Ryman Auditorium** (daily 8.30am–4.30pm; $6), the former home of *The Grand Ole Opry*. With its wooden church pews and glass cases filled with flowered frocks and bootlace ties belonging to the stars, it's certainly an evocative place to visit – it also recently started presenting live performances in the evening (see p.505). Around the corner, among the Broadway honky-tonks, **Hatch Show Print** at no. 316 (Mon–Sat 10am–6pm, Sun hours vary), has been in business since 1879. It still prints and sells evocative posters from the early days of country and rock 'n' roll, using the original blocks, along with probably the best postcards in the USA. Flamboyant leather and sequined garments are sold in **Dangerous Threads**, at the foot of Second Avenue nearby at no. 105, but to see some really outlandish stage costumes, visit **Manuel's Exclusive Clothing** up toward Music Row at 1922 Broadway.

Blue route trolleys along Broadway run just over a mile southwest of downtown to the **Country Music Hall of Fame**, at 4 Music Square E (daily 9am–5pm; $10.75). This is packed with costumes, guitars and personal possessions of the stars, including Boxcar Willie's hobo hat, Gram Parsons' acoustic guitar and Elvis' gold Cadillac, whose forty coats of paint contain crushed diamonds and oriental fish scales. Film and TV clips help to clarify the arcane distinctions between bluegrass, cowboy, rockabilly, honky-tonk, Cajun and western swing. Admission also includes a **trolley tour** of Music Row that stops off for a look in at RCA's historic **Studio B**, preserved as it was when the label moved to more modern premises in 1971. The likes of Willie Nelson, Dolly Parton and Jim Reeves recorded here, as did the Monkees and the Everly Brothers, and Elvis laid down over two hundred tracks between 1957 and 1977. It's once again a working studio, so you might get to see some sessions in progress.

The surrounding area, **Music Row**, is the heart of Nashville's recording industry, with companies like Warners, Mercury and Sony operating out of plush office blocks. A minute's walk from the Hall of Fame brings you to a strip of garish souvenir shops on Demonbreun Street, and several tacky "museums." However, the Country Music Hall of Fame is due to move to a much grander downtown space at Fifth and Demonbreun in 2001, and it's very probable that these emporia of tack will follow suit.

With the exception of the **Grand Ole Opry** itself (see box, opposite), **Opryland**, the area nine miles northeast of downtown on Briley Parkway, just off the I-40 E loop isn't all that country. The old theme park has been ripped down and replaced by **Opry Mills** a giant series of malls that hold flagship stores, restaurants, cinemas and other entertainment options. Also from here are paddlesteamer trips on the beautifully restored **General Jackson Showboat** (☎615/871-6100; $33–55).

You can ride a trolley to nearby **Music Valley**, opposite the *Opryland* hotel, which boasts the popular *Nashville Palace* (see p.505), along with a museum dedicated to **Willie Nelson** plus others showcasing wax dummies and surplus cars of the stars. A factory outlet mall, various stores and theaters all compete to snatch the tourist dollar.

# Eating

Nashville has its share of awful chain restaurants, but it also offers many down-home Southern joints, as well as modern cuisine to eat up the expense accounts of music industry types who have transferred here from the West Coast. Many live music venues (see overleaf) also serve food. If you have a car, be sure to get out to *The Loveless*, quite simply one of the best **country restaurants** in the South.

**Cock o' the Walk**, 2624 Music Valley Drive (☎615/889-1930). Fantastic catfish in cheery environs. Daily until 9.30pm, until 10pm at the weekend.

**The Loveless Cafe**, Rte-5 off Hwy-100, 8 miles south of town (☎615/646-9700). Friendly motel cafe famed for its superb country food. Breakfasts are best ($8): hunks of salty ham with gravy, eggs, toast and fluffy biscuits slicked with succulent home-made jams.

**Noshville Deli**, 1918 Broadway (☎615/329-6674). Huge sandwiches and wicked shakes from 7am to midnight in this student-friendly haunt.

**Pancake Pantry**, 1796 21st Ave (☎615/383-9333). One of Nashville's most popular breakfast spots – expect to wait for a table. Close to Vanderbilt and Music Row in the likeable Hillsboro Village district. Open daily 6am–5pm.

**Prime Cut Steakhouse**, 170 2nd Ave (☎615/242-3083). Generous-sized steaks and huge portions of Texas Toast at reasonable prices in a stylish yet relaxed atmosphere.

**Sammy B's**, 26 Music Square E (☎615/256-6000). A smart-looking music industry hangout, but its great-tasting big lunch plates (around $7) are excellent value.

**Sunset Grill**, 2001a Belcourt Ave (☎615/386-3663). Stylish restaurant in Hillsboro Village, serving upmarket food such as fresh fish in smoky sauces. The terrace is great for people-watching. Around $30 per head; all food half-price after 10pm. Closed Sun.

**Wild Boar**, 2014 Broadway (☎615/329-1313). A nationally renowned French restaurant with an impressive wine list. Slightly pretentious, entree prices touching $30.

## Nightlife

Of all Nashville's country music venues, the main ones to **avoid** are the ersatz clubs along the much-hyped and tacky downtown **Printers Alley**. The **honky-tonks** on Broadway, between Second and Fourth, are more genuine and down-to-earth, though steer clear if you're on your own. Dine-and-dance places like the *Nashville Palace* offer good-quality mainstream country music (and more crowds); up-and-coming progressive country bands play smaller venues like the *Bluebird Cafe*. Every June, the **Fan Fair** is a week-long series of concerts and opportunities to meet the stars (contact 2804 Opryland Drive, Nashville, TN 37214; ☎615/889-7502). Every Thursday evening in summer, the free **Dancin' In The District** event in Riverfront Park features talent from various genres.

   For **listings** of upcoming gigs and events, check the free weekly *Nashville Scene*, Thursday's *Nashville Banner*, or Friday's and Saturday's *Tennessean*. If you're looking for music other than country, **Second Avenue** is a popular downtown hangout for both locals and tourists, offering everything from bluegrass to funk and punk, and various interesting venues can be found around Vanderbilt's campus.

   Nashville's prime venue for theater, dance and classical music is the **Tennessee Performing Arts Center** at 505 Deaderick St (☎615/741-7975). Its **symphony orchestra** also puts on weekend concerts in **Centennial Park**, at West End and 25th avenues by Vanderbilt University, between June and August.

**Bluebird Cafe**, 4104 Hillsboro Rd (☎615/383-1461). Intimate cafe, six miles west of downtown, which has become *the* place to see the latest honky-tonk and new country artists. Early evening entertainment is free, but a cover of $5–10 is charged after 9pm. Reservations recommended.

**Bourbon Street Blues & Boogie Bar**, 220 Printers Alley (☎615/242-5837). Consistently good blues in the otherwise awful downtown Printers Alley.

**Ernest Tubb's Record Store Midnight Jamboree**, Texas Troubadour Theatre, 2414 Music Valley Drive (☎615/889-2474). A live radio show, recorded every Saturday from midnight to 1am, next to the Tubb's store, in a purpose-built theater that puts out musical and other productions most evenings. Genuinely promising newcomers as well as major Opry stars. Free.

**Exit/In**, 2208 Elliston Place (☎615/321-4400). Very popular venue for beer, pizza, rock, reggae and country, with the occasional big name. Tues–Sat until 2.30am; cover $4–10 after 9pm.

### YOU'RE THE STAR

Aspirant country crooners should head for **You're the Star**, 172 Second Ave N (☎615/742-9942), where you can record your own single or video from a choice of more than 500 backing tracks. The single costs $18 to press, the video $27 (Mar–Aug Mon–Sat 10am–midnight, Sun 1–10pm; Sept–Feb Mon–Thurs 10am–6pm, Fri & Sat 10am–midnight).

**Grand Ole Opry**, 2808 Opryland Drive (☎615/889-3060). See box on p.502.

**Legends Corner**, 428 Broadway (☎615/252-4968). A new honky-tonk on the district but the decor music is old school, with live acts on stage from 11am to 2am.

**Nashville Palace**, 2400 Opryland Drive (☎615/885-1540). Opposite *Opryland Hotel*. Resident country bands, and Opry acts on summer Mon; good country food. Cover around $5.

**Pub of Love**, 124 12th Ave N (☎615/256–5683). Groovy neighborhood bar with wacky love-themed decor and live entertainemnt of an alternative bent from 10pm. Closed Sun.

**Robert's Western World**, 416 Broadway (☎615/256-7937). The best of Broadway's country music bars by far. Doubling up as a cowboy boot store, it's famous for breaking BR5-49 – similar-sounding bands play here for tips.

**Ryman Auditorium**, 116 5th Ave (☎615/254-1445). The stage that was home to The Grand Ole *Opry* between 1943 and 1974 resounds again with tributes to country singers, bluegrass reviews and other musical productions. Tickets often cost as much as $25, but it's worth it to see the "mother church of country music" in its correct context.

**Station Inn**, 402 12th Ave S (☎615/255-3307). Very popular bluegrass and acoustic venue, near Music Row. Show starts at 9pm; cover Tues–Sat, free jam sessions every Sun night.

**Tootsie's Orchid Lounge**, 422 Broadway (☎615/726-0463). Venerable downtown honky-tonk; great history but has gone downhill.

**12th and Porter**, 114 12th Ave N (☎615/254-7236). Cool restaurant/venue on the edge of downtown, noted for attracting good alternative and alternative country bands.

**Wildhorse Saloon**, 120 2nd Ave (☎615/251-1000). Popular dance hall/restaurant with big-screen transmission of TNN and Country Music Television, who film here occasionally.

# South from Nashville

As you head southeast from Nashville, large nineteenth-century plantation homes line US-31 between suburban Brentwood and the historic town of **FRANKLIN**, eighteen miles out. One of the bloodiest battles of the Civil War occurred here on November 30, 1864, when 8500 men fell in less than an hour. Despite forcing the Union troops back to Nashville, huge losses meant that the Southerners could not follow up their victory. Among several strategic buildings open for visits is **Carnton Plantation** (April–Oct Mon–Sat 9am–5pm, Sun 1–5pm; Nov–March Mon–Sat 9am–4pm, Sun 1–4pm; ☎615/794-0903; $5), about a mile southeast of the town on Hwy-431, a former Confederate hospital where bloodstains are still visible on the floor. The town's entire fifteen-block center, now full of antique and specialty shops, is listed in the National Register of Historic Places. Several country stars favor the area, among them Billy Ray Cyrus who owns a 400-acre ranch outside the town.

## Jack Daniel's at Lynchburg

The change-resistant village, **LYNCHBURG**, which seems to have a nonchanging population of 361, seventy miles southeast of Nashville, is home to **Jack Daniel's Distillery** (daily 8am–4pm; free). Founded in 1866, this is the oldest registered distillery in the country (hence the famous "No. 1" appellation). Entertaining seventy-minute tours lead you through every step of the sour-mash whiskey-making process – but you can't actually sample the stuff, as you're in a dry county, though you can buy special edition bottles of the stuff in the gift shop, every day but Sunday.

Lynchburg itself is a pretty hamlet, laid out around a neat town square with a red-brick courthouse and a number of old-fashioned stores. One enjoyable throwback is *Miss Mary Bobo's Boarding House*, which serves enormous **Southern dinners** (fried chicken, turnip greens, country ham and the like) at group tables in a lovely 1805 home (reservations essential; ☎615/759-7394).

# Eastern Tennessee

Until the creation of the Tennessee Valley Authority, the opening of Great Smoky Mountains National Park and the building of the interstate highways, life had continued in the remote hills and valleys of **eastern Tennessee** in much the same way as it had ever since the arrival of the first pioneers. Now visitors flock here for its endless expanses of natural beauty; and as a result, especially in the fall, the Smokies can get clogged with traffic. Most communities are small, and either over-touristed or just bland. The two main cities, modern **Knoxville** and picturesque **Chattanooga**, have much in common, including healthy post-World War II industrial growth, thanks to cheap TVA power.

## Knoxville

Surrounded by the backwoods wilderness of the Great Smoky, the Cumberland and the Blue Ridge Mountains, **KNOXVILLE**, the original capital of Tennessee, is a rather quiet city of 180,000. Modern skyscrapers, older brick buildings and a riverfront at the bottom of steep bluffs combine to give **downtown** an attractive edge, but specific places of interest are thin on the ground. On the northern fringe, the **Old City**, centered on Central and Jackson, is a small area of shops, galleries, restaurants and nightspots in Victorian warehouses.

On the western edge of downtown, the **World's Fair Park** is dominated by the futuristic **Sunsphere**, a huge glass ball mounted on a round concrete tower. There is an observation deck on the lower level of the sphere (Mon–Sat 9am–4.30pm; free). The **Knoxville Museum of Art**, in the park at 410 Tenth St, features a small permanent collection of paintings and a cleverly designed sculpture garden focused on a 200-year-old elm tree (Tues–Thurs & Sat 10am–5pm, Fri 10am–9pm, Sun noon–5pm; $4). Follow Cumberland Avenue up a few blocks and you come to the sprawling campus of the **University of Tennessee**. Lined with bars and diners, frequently bedecked in the orange colors of the Volunteers football team, the campus has two theaters and the **Frank H McClung Museum** at Circle Park, which features displays on the city's archeology, art and history (Mon–Fri 9am–5pm, Sat 10am–3pm, Sun 1–5pm; free).

The new **Gateway Regional Visitor Center**, 900 Volunteer Landing Lane (daily 9am–5pm; ☎1-800/727-8045; free) celebrates east Tennessee's natural resources and its technological (predominantly nuclear) achievements. It stands among the waterfalls and foliage of the revitalized Volunteer Landing, which boasts riverside restaurants and a marina complex.

### Practicalities

Greyhound **buses** stop in the Old City on North Central Street; K-Trans city buses run a free trolley to the campus. The **visitor center** is at the Sunsphere, 810 Clinch Ave (☎423/523-7263). The comfortable *Days Inn – Campus*, 1706 W Cumberland Ave (☎423/521-5000; ④), is fairly central, and there's a *Comfort Inn* further out at 5334 Central Ave (☎423/688-1010; ③), while the *Holiday Inn Select*, 525 Henley St (☎423/522-2800; ⑤) is one of the more reasonably-priced hotels near the downtown convention center. Rooms are at a premium when the Tennessee Volunteers are playing at home.

Knoxville's favorite **restaurant**, the rib specialists *Calhoun's*, overlooks the river downtown at 400 Neyland Drive (☎423/673-3355). In the Old City, the *Blue Moon*, 125 W Jackson Ave (☎423/546-0332), is a bistro-bakery with exquisite sandwiches. *Tomato Head* in the downtown Market Square Mall (☎423/637-4067) is a wildly popular place for pizza and super-stuffed sandwiches throughout the day and evening.

### DOLLYWOOD

Born in 1946, one of twelve children, **Dolly Parton** lived in several modest homes around Pigeon Forge, the most isolated of them two miles from the nearest neighbor and over four miles from the mailbox. As a child she sang every week on local radio, before leaving for Nashville on the day she finished at Sevier County High School. Her first success, duetting with Porter Wagoner, came to an acrimonious end in the early Seventies, but she scored a major country hit in 1976 with *Jolene*. She then crossed over to a poppier sound, and into Hollywood films like *9 to 5* and *The Best Little Whorehouse in Texas*. Her songs have been acclaimed for their readiness to address issues like rural poverty, and a refusal to tag along with the Nashville stereotype of subservient females.

**Dollywood**, Dolly Parton's "homespun fun" theme park, blends ersatz mountain heritage with the glamour of its celebrity shareholder. One section showcases Appalachian **crafts**, making everything from lye soap to horse-drawn carriages; a museum looks at Dolly herself in entertaining detail; and music shows are constantly on the go. The rides, however, are mostly unspectacular, and although they've moved with the times by installing the $8 million **Tennessee Tornado** roller coaster, the whole place can get insufferably twee.

Dollywood is at 700 Dollywood Lane at the north end of Pigeon Forge (April weekends 9am–6pm, May–mid-June Mon, Wed & Fri–Sun 9am–6pm; mid-June–Aug daily 9am–9pm; Sept–Nov Mon, Wed & Fri–Sun times vary; Dec daily times vary; ☎423/428-9488; $35, children (4–11) $24 Apr–Oct; Nov & Dec $25, children $12). Local **radio station** WDLY, on 105.5, is another Dolly Parton enterprise.

## Toward the Great Smoky Mountains

The usual way to approach the Smokies from the west is on the billboard-lined US-441 that sweeps past the small market center of **SEVIERVILLE**, whose well-preserved center is tucked just off the highway and evokes days gone by with its wooden-floored general stores and small cafes serving mountains of Southern food to hungry farmers. A statue of **Dolly Parton** stands on the lawn outside the courthouse. Sevierville merges almost seamlessly into the six-mile strip of motels, fast-food places, factory discount outlets, themed family attractions and souvenir shops at the dry town of **PIGEON FORGE**. This is the spot to race go-karts in places like the Rebel Yell Speedway, visit an Elvis museum and absorb regional entertainment at numerous barn-sized haunts including Elwood Smmoch's Hillbilly Hoedown. Five miles further along US-441, a heavy layer of kitsch all but submerges the genuine Germanic heritage of the more upmarket "wet" tourist town of **GATLINBURG**. The long, narrow main street is packed to the point of claustrophobia with gimmicky souvenir shops, wax museums, and stalls selling sickly sweet taffy. An alternative, if you're approaching from the east, is to drive along the pretty Foothills Parkway through woods and across misty mountains, and turn east for seven miles or so to **TOWNSEND**, a peaceful strip where the motels are laid-back and the air is clear.

### Practicalities

Gatlinburg (☎1-800/568-4748), Pigeon Forge (☎1-800/251-9100) and Sevierville (☎1-800/255-6411) all maintain toll-free **information** lines, and visitor centers on the main drag. **Accommodation** prices in the foothill towns fluctuate seasonally, from $20 up to $80 and also vary radically between weekdays and weekends.

As the furthest of the towns from the Smoky Mountains National Park, Sevierville has the best-value **motels**, and most of the major mid-price chains are represented and it also has a **youth hostel**, *HI-Great Smoky Mountain*, 3248 Manis Rd (☎423/429-8653;

$15 members, $18 nonmembers; ①). The *Calico Inn*, 757 Ranch Way (☎423/428-3833; ⑤)) is an award-winning **B&B** with great breakfasts and rural setting. The town center offers several good spots for lunch including *Virgil's*, 109 Bruce St (☎423/453-2782), a 1950s diner serving up big plates of burgers and home cooking.

**Pigeon Forge** has literally dozens of motels, such as the *Parkview*, 2806 Parkway (mid-March to Dec; ☎423/453-5051 or 1-800/239-9116; ③), and the comfortable, friendly *Shular Inn*, 2708 Parkway (☎423/453-2700 or 1-800/451-2376; ③). If you prefer neon lights to wilderness trails, you can **camp** at *Z Buda's Smokies Campground*, 705 S Parkway (April–Nov; ☎423/453-4129). A good **breakfast** place is the *Smoky Mountain Pancake House* at 4236 Parkway (☎423/453-1947).

**Gatlinburg** offers the quickest access to the park and so tends to be the most expensive place to stay, but *Bales*, 221 Bishop Lane (☎423/436-4773 or 1-800/458-8249; ③), and *Bon Air Mountain Inn*, 950 Parkway (April–Oct; ☎423/436-4857; ④), are competitively priced. There's also an unaffiliated **youth hostel**, *Wa-Floy Mountain Retreat* at 3610 E Parkway (☎423/436-7700; $11). Gatlinburg is, however, the best choice for **food**: *Linebergers,* 903 Parkway (☎423/436-9284), at traffic light #8, is strong on seafood and vegetable dishes, while *Calhoun's*, 1004 Parkway (☎423/436-4100), is a local chain renowned for decent barbecue.

In **Townsend** motels are strung along Hwy-321: try the peaceful *Highland Manor* (☎423/448-2211; ③), a friendly place with great views. Perhaps the best option in the entire area is the rustic cabins and lodges at the *Wonderland Lodge*, 3889 Wonderland Way (☎423/428-0779; ④), between Pigeon Forge and Townsend, where the idyll is maintained in the TV and telephone-free rooms. The *Hearth and Kettle*, opposite the Highland Manor motel dishes up fresh trout and crispy fried chicken in a country store atmosphere.

## Great Smoky Mountains National Park

The northern boundary of the **GREAT SMOKY MOUNTAINS NATIONAL PARK**, which stretches for seventy miles along the Tennessee–North Carolina border (see also p.447), is just two miles south of Gatlinburg on US-441. Don't expect immediate tranquility, however: the roads, particularly in the fall, can be lined almost bumper-to-bumper with cars, and if you're not staying in Gatlinburg it's best to use the well-marked bypass rather than drive through the town.

**The Smokies**, within a day's drive of the major urban centers of the East Coast and the Great Lakes – and of two-thirds of the entire US population – attract over nine million visitors per year, more than twice as many as any other national park. These heavily contorted peaks are named for the **bluish haze** that hangs over them, made up of moisture and hydrocarbons released by the lush vegetation (a mature tree emits up to 900 gallons on a summer day). Since the Sixties, however, **air pollution** has been adding sulphates to the filmy smoke, and has cut back visibility by thirty percent. More than 120 tree species and over 1400 flowering plants clothe the mountains and meadows in color from early spring to late fall. Sixteen peaks rise above 6000ft, their steep elevation accounting for dramatic changes in climate.

The most popular **times to visit** are between late March and mid-May, to see the delicate spring flowers, and during the second half of October, when the hills are shrouded in a magnificent canopy of glaring reds, subtle yellows and faded browns. During June and July, rhododendrons blaze fiercely in the sometimes stifling summer heat.

Just inside the park on US-441, the main artery running through to North Carolina, **Sugarlands Visitor Center** (summer daily 8am–7pm; fall and spring daily 8am–6pm; winter daily 8am–5pm) is a useful source of leaflets covering hiking trails, driving tours, forests and wildlife. From here a ten-mile drive rises to Newfound Gap on the state line, where a seven-mile spur road winds its way up to **Clingman's Dome**, at 6643ft the

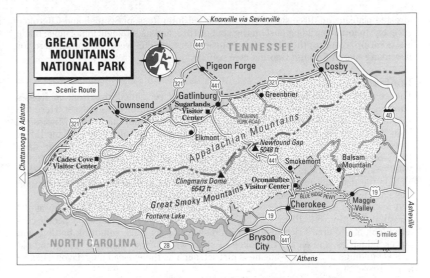

highest point in the park and in all Tennessee. A surreal concrete spiral walkway on top affords a panoramic, though hazy, view of the mountains, rather spoiled by the fact that virtually all the mature balsam firs in the area have been killed off by insect infestation.

The scenic **Little River Road** branches off back at Sugarlands toward **Cades Cove**, where another visitor center (mid-April to Oct; same hours) is situated halfway round an eleven-mile driving loop, in summer and fall always jam-packed with cars. Along the route, deserted barns, homesteads, mills and churches stand as a reminder of the farmers who carved out a living from this wilderness, before having to move out when national park status was conferred in 1934. Quieter **Hwy-321**, on the other side of Sugarlands, branches off onto a gravel road toward the beautiful Greenbrier area.

If you really want to get away from it all, escape onto the eight hundred miles of **hiking** trails. On the **Appalachian Trail**, however, you can now only camp in designated areas, caged in behind iron bars to keep out the bears.

### Practicalities

Hikers intending to stay out overnight require **backcountry permits**, available free from visitor centers (except Cades Cove). The park also has ten developed **campgrounds**, of which the three most popular – *Cades Cove, Elkmont* and *Smokemont* – are always fully booked. Reserve in advance (☎1-800/365-CAMP) if you want a space in summer or fall. For details of the North Carolina side of the park see p.447. For other enquiries contact the park headquarters (☎423/436-1230).

On Saturday, from dawn until 10am, the Cades Cove loop is reserved for **cyclists**. Bikes can be rented at the *Cades Cove Campground* (☎423/436-5615).

## Chattanooga

Few cities are so identified with a song as **CHATTANOOGA**, in the southeast corner of Tennessee. Though visitors expecting Tex Beneke and Glenn Miller's *Chattanooga Choo-Choo* may be let down to find that there is no longer even an Amtrak service, the town continues to celebrate its railroad history, and has plenty more to offer besides – not least its beautiful location on a deep bend in the **Tennessee River**, walled in by forested plateaus on three sides. This setting led John Ross, of Scottish and Cherokee ancestry, to found a trading post on the spot in 1815, and its strategic importance made it a great prize during the Civil War; victories here in 1863 were the springboard for Sherman's march through Georgia (see p.462).

## The Town

The centerpiece of Chattanooga's twenty miles of reclaimed riverfront is **Ross's Landing** (the town's original name), a park at the bottom of Broad Street. Here the splendid five-story **Tennessee Aquarium** traces the aquatic life of the Mississippi from its Tennessee tributaries to the Gulf of Mexico, and also shows giant IMAX movies (summer Mon–Thurs 10am–6pm, Fri–Sun 10am–8pm; rest of year daily 10am–6pm; $11, IMAX $7, combined ticket $15). A variety of different cruises on the *Southern Belle* **riverboat** (☎423/266-4488), from the bottom of nearby Chestnut Street, include the daunting experience of bobbing around in the bottom of a huge lock on Chickamauga Lake. Prices start from $10 for a daytime sightseeing tour.

A few blocks from the river, the **Chattanooga Regional History Museum** at 400 Chestnut St (Mon–Sat 10am–4.30pm, Sun 11am–4.30pm; $2.50) takes a people-centered look at the area's rich history, with displays on its steel, soft-drink bottling and power industries, and on the Cherokee. A short walk further along are the grand old c.1900 buildings of the lively business district, such as the eye-catching Tivoli Theatre at 709 Broad St.

The further Chattanooga sprawls back from the river, the more run-down it becomes, but it's well worth heading the two miles up to the **Choo-Choo complex**, where the 1909 Beaux Arts-style **Southern Railroad Terminal**, at 1400 Market St (☎423/266-5000), is now a *Holiday Inn* – the *Chattanooga Choo-Choo Hotel*. The impressive high-domed waiting room serves as the lobby, leading through to the former platform area, where restored carriages act as hotel suites. Giftshops and cafes share space with a steam engine similar to the original Choo-Choo (the name given by the local paper to the first passenger train to come in from Cincinnati in 1880). You're free to roam around; admission to the world's largest model railway display, on site, is $2.75. A free shuttle runs between the *Choo-Choo* and the Aquarium.

The authentic **steam trains** of the **Tennessee Valley Railroad** offer stunning six-mile rides, crossing the river, running through deep tunnels, and turning round on a giant turntable. The two main stations, restored to their 1930s look, are at 2200 N Chamberlain Ave in east Chattanooga, and 4119 Cromwell Rd (I-75 exit 4 to Hwy-153), though some weekend routes pick up at the *Choo-Choo* (summer 5 trains daily from 10.40am; for other times between May & Nov call ☎423/894-8028; $9).

## Practicalities

A taxi downtown from Chattanooga's **airport** (☎423/855-2200), three miles east, costs around $12. Greyhound connections with Nashville, Knoxville and Atlanta arrive on Broad Street downtown. The **visitor center**, adjacent to the Tennessee Aquarium (daily 8.30am–5.30pm; ☎423/756-8687 or 1-800/322-3344), provides the usual range of help, along with a useful guide for travelers with disabilities. Budget **motels** downtown, such as the *Days Inn Rivergate*, 901 Carter St (☎423/266-7331; ③), tend to be in rather dismal areas; far more atmospheric, if you can get a room on the train, is the *Choo-Choo* (☎423/266-5000 or 1-800/872-2529; ⑤), and there are countless inexpensive options along the interstates, such as the *Super 8*, off I-75 south at 1401 Mack Smith Rd (☎423/892-3888; ②). There's **camping** at *Raccoon Mountain Campground*, 319 West Hills Drive (☎423/821-9403).

The obvious place to **eat** in Chattanooga is the *Choo-Choo* complex, where the enclosed but very light *Gardens Restaurant* serves standard meals for around $10;

---

### THE CHEROKEE AND THE TRAIL OF TEARS

During the eighteenth and early nineteenth centuries, the **Cherokee** were the most powerful Indian tribe in the tristate region of Tennessee, Georgia and North Carolina. They forged close links with white pioneers, adopting white methods in schooling and agriculture, intermarrying – and owning African slaves. The only Native Americans to develop their own written language, they had a regular newspaper, *The Cherokee Phoenix*. They even supplied soldiers for Andrew Jackson's US forces against the Creek Indians and the British in 1814, hoping to buy influence with the federal government.

Thirteen years later, against a background of aggressive territorial claims by settlers, the Cherokee produced a written constitution modeled on that of the US, stating their intention to continue to be a self-governing nation. John Ross, founder of Ross's Landing, and at most one-eighth Cherokee, was elected as their first Principal Chief in 1828 in an effort to appease and negotiate with national and state governments over their lands. However, as white demand for land increased, their former ally **Jackson**, now US president, was pressurized by the Georgians into "offering" the Cherokee western lands in exchange for those east of the Mississippi. Although the tribal leadership refused, a minority faction accepted, giving the government the get-out clause they wanted. The Cherokee were ordered to leave within two years, and 14,000 of them were forcefully removed to Oklahoma in 1838 along the horrific **Trail of Tears**: 4000 died of disease and exposure on the way. In the meantime, their land was sold by lottery and Ross's Landing was renamed Chattanooga. One thousand Cherokee managed to avoid removal by escaping into the mountains, and their descendants now occupy a small reservation in North Carolina (see p.447).

The **Red Clay State Historic Park**, twenty miles east of Chattanooga off Hwy-317, recounts the old Cherokee way of life, with replica houses, tools and household implements. Its balsamic Sacred Council Spring was a meeting place for Cherokee elders.

---

the more romantic *Silver Diner* serves steaks and seafood in a railroad car permanently parked on the platform behind, and there's also an *Espresso Cafe* (all ☎423/266-5000). For inventive Southern cooking in a stylish atmosphere, try the *Southside Grill*, 1400 Cowart St (☎423/266-9211). The *Big River Grille & Brewing Works*, 222 Broad St (☎423/267-2739), is a cavernous brewpub and restaurant near the Aquarium.

## Lookout Mountain

The name Chattanooga comes from a Creek word, meaning "rock rising to a point"; six miles from downtown is the rock itself, the 2215ft **Lookout Mountain**. To reach the top, you can either drive the whole way along a complicated, poorly signed road; take a summer-only $1 shuttle from the *Choo-Choo*; or catch the world's steepest **incline railway**, which grinds its tentative way up through a narrow gash in the lush forest from 3917 St Elmo Ave near the foot of the mountain (on bus route #14), tackling nerve-racking gradients of up to 72.7 percent (summer daily 8.30am–9pm; rest of year daily 9am–6pm; 3–4 trips per hour; $8). Once there, a steep five-minute walk through **Point Park** brings you to **Point Lookout**, the northern promontory of the mountain, which commands a not-to-be-missed view of the city and the meandering Tennessee River. This is part of the **Chickamauga and Chattanooga National Military Park**, covering several sites around the city and in nearby Chickamauga, Georgia, that witnessed fierce fighting in the fall of 1863. The battle here that November, in which Confederate forces which had been besieging Chattanooga were finally forced to withdraw, was also known as the "Battle Above The Clouds"; thick mantles of fog often obscure the city below to this day. Among the many memorials in Point Park is the only statue in the country to show Union and Confederate soldiers shaking hands.

# ALABAMA

Just 250 miles from north to south, **ALABAMA** ranges from the fast-flowing rivers, waterfalls and lakes of the **Appalachian foothills** to the subtropical bayous and white beaches of the **Gulf Coast**. Most of its industry is concentrated in the **north**, around rejuvenated **Birmingham**, and **Huntsville**, first home of the nation's space program. The sun-scorched farmlands of middle Alabama envelop sober **Montgomery**, the state capital. Away from the French-influenced coastal strip around attractive **Mobile**, fundamentalist Protestant attitudes have traditionally backed a succession of right-wing demagogues, such as **George Wallace**, the four-times state governor who received ten million votes in the 1968 presidential election.

Times have moved on since the epic **civil rights** struggles in Montgomery, Birmingham and **Selma**. Monuments and civic literature celebrate the achievements of the campaigners, and even Wallace renounced his racist views, courting – and winning – black votes in his successful campaign for governor in 1982.

### Getting around Alabama

Considering its rural nature, **public transportation** is relatively good in Alabama. Daily Amtrak **trains** from New York and Atlanta to New Orleans stop at Anniston, Birmingham and Tuscaloosa, while the line from Jacksonville to New Orleans passes through Mobile; Amtrak **buses** connect Birmingham and Mobile by way of Montgomery, and Greyhound serves the major towns and cities. Mobile, Montgomery, Huntsville and Birmingham all have small airports.

# Northern Alabama

**Northern Alabama**, on the trailing edges of the Appalachians, is brightened up by the mountain lakes, rivers and canyons of the **Tennessee River Valley**. The area's first white settlers were small farmers who had little in common with the big plantation owners further south, and attempted to dissociate from the Confederacy during the Civil War. Substantial postwar mineral finds led to an industrial boom that peaked in the early Thirties.

## Huntsville

Many Southern cities aspire to blend the old with the new; few achieve it as dramatically as **HUNTSVILLE**, a hundred miles south of Nashville just inside the Alabama border. Its sleepy center still recalls the days when it was dominated by cotton merchants and railroad owners, a history absorbingly recounted in the **Huntsville Depot Museum**, 320 Church St (Mon–Sat 9am–5pm, closed Jan & Feb; $6). An excellent **trolley service** tours the town ($1 for an all-day ticket), taking in historic **Twickenham** – the community's original name in 1808, before anti-British sentiment in the run-up to the 1812 War dictated that it should be renamed for its first settler, a Virginian named John Hunt.

Time was when Huntsville was content to be the "Watercress Capital of the World"; the great leap forward came after World War II, when the army consolidated its **rocket and missile research** efforts in the city. Spearheading the project were **Dr Wernher von Braun** and 118 other German scientists, who came to Huntsville after a token period of rehabilitation. Von Braun's contribution of the V-2 ballistic missile to the Nazi war effort is ignored by the city, which prefers to laud his later space-age achievements, such as **Explorer I**, the nation's first satellite, and the mighty **Saturn V**.

The giant **US Space and Rocket Center**, five miles west of downtown on Hwy-20, off I-65 (summer daily 9am–6pm; rest of year daily 9am–5pm; $15), contains a mind-boggling array of technological exhibits, hands-on displays, and weightlessness simulators, as well as a giant IMAX cinema. Outdoors, in the surreal Rocket and Space Shuttle parks, redundant rockets protrude skywards in the blazing Alabama sunshine; the 120-yard, four-story *Saturn V* rocket is laid on its side to emphasize its immensity.

### Practicalities

Huntsville's **visitor center** is at 700 Monroe St (Mon–Sat 9am–5pm; ☎205/551-2230). Chain **motels** on the outskirts include a *Days Inn*, near the Space Center at 2201 N Memorial Parkway (☎205/536-7441; ②). Of the **restaurants**, *Ol' Heidelberg*, 6125 University Drive NW (☎205/922-0556), offers German specialties including sauerkraut and Wiener schnitzel. *Eunice's Country Kitchen*, on the western fringes of downtown at 1006 Andrew Jackson Way (☎205/534-9550; closed Tues), is an inexpensive rendezvous for home-cooked Southern breakfasts.

# Birmingham

The rapid transformation of farmland into the city of **BIRMINGHAM** began in 1870, when two railroad routes met in the Jones Valley, a hundred miles south of Huntsville. What attracted speculators was not the scenery, but what lay under it – a mixture of iron ore, limestone and coal, perfect for the manufacture of iron and steel. The expansion of heavy industry was finally brought to an abrupt halt by the Depression. Today iron and steel production account for only a few thousand jobs, but new service and medical industries have helped transform this once smog-filled metropolis into a prosperous and pleasant city.

Being known as the "Pittsburgh of the South" might seem like faint praise; however, Birmingham also earned the label of the "Johannesburg of America" for the brutality and intolerance of its police force. An intense civil rights campaign in 1963 was the turning point, setting Birmingham on the road to smoother race relations. Since 1979, under five-term black mayor Richard Arrington, the city has slowly but surely turned itself around, and the 1990s in particular saw a growing self-confidence that Birmingham is destined to be the "next Atlanta." Nonetheless, even a short stroll around downtown leaves the rather depressing impression that a lot remains to be done.

### Arrival, information and getting around

**Birmingham Airport** is just three miles from downtown, but it's not served by buses; call Yellow Cabs ($10) on ☎205/252-1131. Amtrak pulls in at 1819 Morris Ave, downtown, and the Greyhound station is at 19th Street N, between Sixth and Seventh avenues – a rough area at night. Public transportation is poor, and most of the attractions are well spread out, so you need a car to see the city properly. **Visitor centers** can be found at 2200 Ninth Ave N (Mon–Fri 8.30am–5pm; ☎205/458-8000 or 1-800/458-8085) and on the university campus at 1201 University Blvd (Mon–Sat 8.30am–5pm, Sun 1–5pm; ☎205/458-8001).

### Accommodation

Many of Birmingham's wide range of places to **stay** offer advantageous weekend rates. The nearest place to **camp** is the *Birmingham South KOA* (☎205/664-8832), eight miles south in Pelham, off I-65 S.

**Best Western Civic Center Inn**, 2230 Civic Center Blvd (☎205/328-6320). Downtown hotel opposite the Sports Hall of Fame; continental breakfast included. ④.

## CIVIL RIGHTS IN BIRMINGHAM

In the first half of 1963, civil rights leaders chose Birmingham as the target of "Project C" (for confrontation), aiming to force businesses to integrate lunch counters and employ more blacks. Despite threats from Police Chief **"Bull" Connor** that there would be "blood running down the streets of Birmingham," pickets, sit-ins and marches sparked mass arrests. Over 2000 protesters flooded the jails; one was Dr Martin Luther King Jr, who wrote his *Letter from a Birmingham Jail* after being branded as an extremist by local white clergymen. Connor's use of high-pressure hoses, cattleprods and dogs against demonstrators acted as a potent catalyst of support. Pictures of snarling German shepherds sinking their teeth into the flesh of schoolkids were transmitted throughout the world, and led to an agreement between civil rights leaders and businesses in June 1963. Success in Birmingham sparked demonstrations in 186 other cities, which culminated in the 1964 Civil Rights Act prohibiting racial segregation.

The headquarters for the campaign, the 16th Street Baptist Church, on the corner of Sixth Avenue, was the site of a sickening Klan bombing on September 15, 1963, which killed four young black girls attending a Bible class. Open daily, the church contains a small shrine dedicated to the murdered girls. Plans to erect a sculpture of them in a memorial garden have not yet been realized, though a bronze statue of Dr King stands across the road in prettily landscaped Kelly Ingram Park. Site of many huge rallies during the Sixties, the park is now home to a desultory band of – mainly African-American – dispossessed people.

Nearby, the admirable **Civil Rights Institute**, 520 16th St (Tues–Sat 10am–5pm, Sun 1–5pm; $3), is an affecting attempt to interpret the factors that led to such violence and racial hatred in the US. Exhibits re-create life in a segregated city, complete with a burned-out bus and heart-rending videos of bus boycotts and the March on Washington.

**Holiday Inn Redmont**, 2101 5th Ave N (☎205/324-2101). Modernized downtown hotel a few blocks northeast of Amtrak. ④.

**Pickwick Hotel**, 1023 S 20th St (☎205/933-9555 or 1-800/255-7304). Attractive Art Deco hotel within easy walking distance of Five Points South. ⑤.

**Radisson**, 808 S 20th St at University Blvd (☎205/933-9000). Luxury hotel in upbeat, upmarket Five Points South district. ⑤.

## The City

**Downtown Birmingham** extends north from the railroad tracks at Morris Avenue to Tenth Avenue N, bounded to east and west by 25th and 15th streets. The landscaped greenery of **20th Street**, overlooked by a collection of early skyscrapers, is not enough to save these one-hundred-plus blocks from anonymity, with shopping now firmly anchored in the malls and suburbs. If you're just passing through, you'd do better to head straight for the much livelier **Five Points South** district, a mile or so south of the tracks on 20th Street; thanks to the proximity of the university, its narrow streets and alleys are packed with bars and restaurants, and throng with revelers – mostly students – every weekend.

The concrete colossus of the Birmingham-Jefferson Civic Center, at 22nd Street and Tenth Avenue N, contains the **Alabama Sports Hall of Fame** (Mon–Sat 9am–5pm, Sun 1–5pm; $5), a tribute to sporting greats such as 1936 Olympic hero **Jesse Owens**, **Le Roy "Satchel" Paige** – the first black baseball player to appear in the World Series – and boxer **Joe Louis**. There's even a space for George Wallace, on the rather flimsy excuse that he was state amateur boxing champion. Weave your way past the monotonous white-walled legal buildings to the nearby **Museum of Art**, 2000 Eighth Ave N, which is strong on Oriental art, American landscapes and, oddly enough, Wedgwood pottery (Tues–Sat 10am–5pm, Sun noon–5pm; free).

A few blocks from the edge of downtown, at First Avenue N and 32nd Street, stand the massive sheds and tall chimney stacks of **Sloss Furnaces**, which produced pig iron to feed the city's mills and foundries from 1882 until 1971. Self-guided tours through the boilers, stoves and casting areas vividly portray the harsh working conditions endured by the ex-slaves, prisoners and unskilled immigrants. Imagining the searing heat, cramped space, the heavy loads and the putrid gaseous emissions, it's easy to appreciate why one former Sloss worker claimed "if mules had to do this work they would have banned it" (Tues–Sat 10am–4pm, Sun noon–4pm; free; guided tours Sat & Sun 1pm, 2pm & 3pm).

Atop **Red Mountain**, which rises four miles south of downtown, a 55ft iron statue of Vulcan, Roman god of the forge, is the largest cast-iron statue ever made. The chubby, rust-colored figure, perched high up on its 124ft pedestal, looks rather insignificant from ground level, but it's worth winding your way up the steep, verdant mountain road to relax in the peaceful grounds, or to ride to the top of the tower for panoramic views of the Jones Valley (daily 8am–10.30pm; $2).

## Eating and drinking

Birmingham has a couple of fantastic **barbecue** joints; for something a little more upmarket, the best bet is to ignore downtown in favor of **Five Points South**.

**Bottega**, 2240 Highland Ave S (☎205/933-2001). Elegant 1920s clothing store that now houses one of Five Points South's classiest restaurants, serving luscious, garlic-rich Mediterranean cuisine; prices are slightly lower in the adjoining *Cafe*. Closed Sun.

**Dreamland Barbecue**, 14th Ave S (☎205/933-2133). Superlative barbecue in huge, cheery restaurant. Place your order for a big plate of ribs with white sliced bread and sauce – the only dish on the menu – and watch as they barbecue in front of your eyes.

**Magic City Brewery**, 420 21st St S (☎205/328-2739). Busy brewpub, a few blocks north of Five Points South, that serves reasonable food and puts on live music at weekends.

**The Mill**, 1035 20th St S (☎205/939-3001). Bakery, brewery and general snackery, with outdoor patio, in Five Points South, that's ideal for morning coffees and inexpensive lunches.

**Ollie's Barbecue**, 515 University Blvd (☎205/324-9485). Wonderful smoky pork in a peppery sauce; unusually for this part of the country, there's beef and chicken too. Mon 10am–3pm, Tues–Sat until 8pm.

## West of Birmingham

Just west of Birmingham city limits, I-20/59 passes **BESSEMER**, a likeable small town named in 1887 after Sir Henry Bessemer, the English engineer who perfected the steel-making process. The **Hall of History Museum** here, in the 1916 Southern Railroad depot at 1905 Alabama Ave, displays Native American artifacts alongside exhibits from the industrial pioneer years (Tues–Sat 10am–4pm; free). *Bob Sykes*, 1724 Ninth Ave (☎205/426-1400), is a mouthwatering takeout **barbecue** joint in town.

**TUSCALOOSA**, home of the lively main campus of the University of Alabama, but little else of interest, lies 32 miles southwest of Bessemer. If you're hungry, combine eating with a view of the **Black Warrior River** at *Henson's Cypress Inn*, 501 Rice Mine Rd N (☎205/345-6963), which specializes in keenly priced seafood and catfish. Sixteen miles south on US-69, the **Moundville Archeological Park** preserves twenty earthen mounds, carpeted in lush grass, with the largest supporting a rebuilt Native American temple. An estimated three thousand people lived here on the banks of the Black Warrior during the twelfth century; the on-site museum (daily 9am–5pm; $4) exhibits items found in burial grounds, including jewelry, ceremonial vessels and a few skeletons.

# South central Alabama

Southern Alabama – memorably depicted in Harper Lee's child's-eye view of racial conflict, *To Kill a Mockingbird* – still consists mostly of small, sleepy, God-fearing rural communities. Only state capital **Montgomery**, with a population of just over 200,000, achieves metropolitan status. It lies in the heart of the **Black Belt**, originally named for the rich loamy soil, but these days more usually taken to refer to the region's ethnic make-up. Cotton was the major earner here until the boll weevil infestation of 1915. Now it has been supplanted (officially) by soybeans, corn and peanuts – though surveys suggest that the leading cash crop is, in fact, marijuana.

## Montgomery

**MONTGOMERY**'s Black Belt position, 90 miles south of Birmingham and 160 west of Atlanta, made it a natural political center for the plantation elite, leading to its adoption as state capital in 1846 and temporary capital of the Confederacy fifteen years later. Despite its administrative importance, Montgomery is strangely quiet, largely because many businesses have relocated to the suburbs. Most neighborhoods are either exclusively white or totally black; integration sadly does not appear to be on the social agenda in the city that saw the first successful mass civil rights activity in 1955–56.

### Arrival and information
**Dannelly Field Airport** (☎334/281-5040) is fifteen miles from downtown on US-80, but the Greyhound station is much more conveniently located at 210 S Court St.

The **visitor center** at 401 Madison Ave (Mon–Fri 8.30am–5pm, Sat 9am–4pm, Sun noon–4pm; ☎334/240-9455) is set in a grand mansion house moved here from

---

### CIVIL RIGHTS IN MONTGOMERY

During the Fifties, Montgomery's **bus system** was a miniature model of segregated society – as was the norm in the South. The regulation ordering blacks to give up seats to whites came under repeated attack from black organizations, culminating in the call by the Women's Political Council for a mass boycott after **Rosa Parks** was arrested on December 1, 1955, for refusing to give up her seat. Black workers were asked to walk to work, while black-owned taxis carried those who lived further away for the same 10¢ fare as buses. The protest attracted over ninety percent support, and the Montgomery Improvement Association (MIA), set up to coordinate activities, elected the 26-year-old **Dr Martin Luther King Jr** as its chief spokesperson. Meanwhile, the laid-off white bus drivers were employed as temporary police officials. Despite personal hardships, bombings and jailings, the boycott continued for eleven months, until in November 1956 the US Supreme Court declared segregation on public transportation to be illegal.

King remained pastor at the small brick **Dexter Avenue King Memorial Baptist Church**, surprisingly central at 454 Dexter Ave (tours Mon–Thurs 10am & 2pm, Fri 10am, Sat 10.30am & 1.30pm; donation), until his move to Atlanta in 1960. A mural along a basement wall chronicles his life, while the upstairs sanctuary, much as it was during his ministry, contains his former pulpit. One block away at the corner of Washington and Hull, in front of the Southern Poverty Law Center (which specializes in helping victims of racial attacks), the deeply moving **Civil Rights Memorial** (designed by Maya Lin) consists of a black granite table that records the names of forty martyrs murdered by white supremacists and police. Cool water pumps slowly and evenly across it, and the wall behind is engraved with the quotation used so often by Dr King, "(we will not be satisfied) until justice rolls down like waters and righteousness like a mighty stream."

Tuskegee, forty miles east. Tours start here of **Old Alabama Town**, an area of restored houses and museums immediately behind (Mon–Sat 9am–3.30pm, Sun 1–3.30pm; $6). All places of interest downtown are easily reached on foot.

## Accommodation

There are several good-value places to stay in and around downtown Montgomery: a couple of homely **B&Bs** in town and the usual **motels** alongside the highways.

**Best Western Statehouse Inn**, 924 Madison Ave (☎334/265-0741). Central if anonymous downtown hotel, with pool and restaurant. ③.

**Capitol Inn**, 205 N Goldthwaite St (☎334/265-3844). Old-fashioned motel in a somewhat bleak but central location, perched on a small hill fifteen minutes' walk from downtown. ②.

**Lattice Inn**, 1414 S Hull St (☎334/832-9931 or 1-800/525-0652). Comfortable B&B with a pool, a mile from downtown. ④.

**Red Bluff Cottage**, 551 Clay St (☎334/264-0056). Friendly B&B, with good food, near the capitol. ④.

## The City

Although 1993 saw Alabama's state flag finally replace the Confederate flag over the white-domed Greek Revival **State Capitol** at the top of Dexter Avenue, downtown Montgomery still bears reminders of its white supremacist past. A bronze star marks the spot where Jefferson Davis was sworn in as president of the Confederacy on February 18, 1861 (see p.1163). Other "attractions" in this vein include the **Alabama Department of Archives and History**, next door, notable only for the lavish use of marble in its interior (Mon–Fri 8am–5pm, Sat 9am–5pm; free), and the **First White House of the Confederacy**, 644 Washington Ave, the temporary home of Jefferson Davis, now crammed with sentimental Confederate oddments (Mon–Fri 8am–4.30pm; free).

On a different note, Montgomery was jammed with mourners in 1954 for the funeral of 29-year-old country star **Hank Williams**, who died of a heart attack on his way to a concert on New Year's Eve 1953. An Alabama native from Butler County, Williams was as famous for his drink- and drug-sustained lifestyle as he was for writing honkytonk classics like *Your Cheating Heart* and *I'm So Lonesome I Could Cry*. His hit single at the time of his death was *I'll Never Get Out of This World Alive*. The **Hank Williams Memorial**, a large white-marble headstone complete with song lyrics and an image of the singer, dominates the Oakwood Cemetery Annex, 1304 Upper Wetumpka Rd, near downtown; Hank's statue stands at Lister Hill Plaza on N Perry Street.

Reminiscent of the grounds of an English stately home, the stunningly landscaped **Blount Cultural Park** gives some credence to the city's claim to be a regional center for the arts. Situated off Woodmere Boulevard, ten miles southeast of the city, it's home to the Alabama Shakespeare Festival (Aug–Nov; ☎334/271-5353 or 1-800/841-4273), which also performs contemporary works in the sumptuous Renaissance-style Carolyn Blount Theatre. The equally slick **Montgomery Museum of Fine Arts** (Tues, Wed, Fri & Sat 10am–5pm, Thurs 10am–9pm, Sun noon–5pm; free) spans more than 200 years of American art.

## Eating and drinking

**Downtown Montgomery** is dotted with cheap cafes selling burgers or soul food; a few minutes' drive southeast, suburban **Cloverdale** offers a good selection of eating places to suit every price range. Especially in the center, things get quiet at night.

**Amy's Young House**, 231 N Hull St (☎334/262-0409). Southern cooking in an 1850 house, next to the visitor center and Old Alabama Town. Lunch only.

**Farmers' Market Cafe**, 315 N McDonough St (☎334/262-9163). Just off downtown, next to the busy marketplace; Montgomery's best spot for Southern-style breakfasts. Mon–Fri 5.30am–2pm.

**Jubilee Seafood Co**, 1057 Woodley Rd, Cloverdale (☎334/262-6224). Tiny fish restaurant serving delicious, creative food for less than $20. Closed Sun & Mon.

**Martha's Place**, 458 Sayre St (☎334/263-9135). Superb downtown Southern food, from collard greens to fried chicken. Lunch only, closed Sat.

**Vintage Year**, 405 Cloverdale Rd, Cloverdale (☎334/264-8463). One of Alabama's most highly rated restaurants, with haute cuisine for $30 plus. Dinner only, reservations necessary; closed Sun & Mon.

## Selma

The tidy market town of **SELMA**, fifty miles west of Montgomery, became in the early Sixties the focal point of a national voting rights campaign. Demonstrations, meetings and attempts to register were repeatedly met by police violence, before the murder of a black protester by a state trooper prompted the decision to organize the historic **march from Selma to Montgomery**. On "Bloody Sunday," March 7, 1965, six hundred marchers set off across the steep incline of the imposing, narrow **Edmund Pettus Bridge**. As they went over the apex of the bridge, a line of state troopers fired tear gas without warning, lashing out at the panic-stricken demonstrators with nightsticks and cattleprods. This violent confrontation, broadcast all over the world, is credited with having directly influenced the passage of the **Voting Rights Act** the following year. The full story is told in the **National Voting Rights Museum**, beside the bridge at 1012 Water Ave (Tues–Sat 1–5pm; $4). Outside the 1965 campaign headquarters at the **Brown Chapel AME Church**, 410 Martin Luther King St, a bust of Dr King forms part of a monument to the struggle that also includes explanatory plaques along the street.

Selma's history stretches back well before the Sixties; its huge arsenal and shipbuilding plant were prime targets for Union troops who looted and burned most of the buildings in March 1865. One of the few remaining plantation homes is **Sturdivant Hall**, 713 Mabry St (Tues–Sat 9am–4pm, Sun 2–4pm; $5), an attractively furnished house with an accessible cupola and lovely grounds.

Lined with independently owned stores and cafes, **Broad Street** is the town's busy main thoroughfare, running into the wide riverfront **Water Avenue**, which still feels set in the Forties with its frontier-style storefronts, seed warehouses and garages. Just a few blocks away stand the beautiful homes of the town's Historic District.

### Practicalities

Downtown Selma is very short of inexpensive places to **stay**; if the grand **St James Hotel**, close to the river at 1200 Water Ave (☎334/872-3234; ⑤), is beyond your budget, head for the *Holiday Inn*, three miles west on US-80 at 1806 W Highland Ave (☎334/872-0461; ③). The pick of the soul-food **restaurants** is the *Downtowner*, 1114 Selma Ave (☎334/875-5933), open for breakfast and lunch; *Major Grumbles*, near the *St James* at 1 Grumbles Alley (☎334/872-2006), is an upmarket riverside pub with hot sandwiches (try the almondine flounder) and a disturbing "Indian giant" skeleton draped in a Confederate flag. The **visitor center** at 2207 Broad St (Mon–Sat 8am–5pm; ☎334/875-7485), north of town at the junction with Hwy-22, has tour brochures for the Historic District and black heritage sites.

# Alabama's Gulf Coast

Alabama's narrow share of the **Gulf coastline** is blessed with an abundance of fine white-sand beaches, laundered by clear blue waters. The coast veers sharply inwards to accommodate the port city of **Mobile**, featuring hundreds of antebellum buildings in a tree-shaded center. Away from the water's edge, agriculture, dominated by pecan, peach and watermelon growing, flourishes on the gently sloping coastal plain.

# Mobile

The busy port and paper manufacturing city of **MOBILE** (pronounced *Mo-beel*) traces its origins back to a French community founded in 1702. These early white settlers brought with them **Mardi Gras**, celebrated in Mobile continuously since 1704 – several years before New Orleans. Virtually every street is transformed in early spring by the delicate colors of azaleas, camellias and dogwoods – a beautiful complement to the many early eighteenth-century Spanish and colonial-style buildings. Parallels with New Orleans are everywhere you look, from wrought-iron balconies to street names like Conti and Bienville and gumbo specials in the restaurants.

Mobile survived the torches of the Union army during the Civil War, and possesses enough antebellum buildings to designate four sizeable areas as historic districts. Even so, the city is unlikely to hold your attention for more than a day. The obvious place to start exploring is **Fort Conde** (daily 8am–5pm; free), a reconstruction of the city's 1724 French fort that was constructed to mark the Bicentennial in 1976. Dioramas in its low-ceilinged rooms cover local history, while its ramparts provide a good view of the World War II battleship **USS Alabama** permanently moored nearby (fort & ship daily 8am–sunset; $8). Fanning out north of the fort, the **Church Street Historic District** holds 59, mostly pre-Civil War, buildings, as well as two museums (both Tues–Sat 10am–5pm, Sun 1–5pm; free). The **Museum of Mobile**, 355 Government St, displays glittering Mardi Gras costumes and lavish horse-drawn carriages, while steam-powered fire engines, resplendent in original livery, shining brass bells and trumpets, are the stars of the **Phoenix Fire Museum**, 203 S Clairborne St.

Downtown Mobile's lack of action outside of Mardi Gras is made up for by an amazing display of greenery, particularly down its main thoroughfare, **Government Street**, which is shaded by a canopy of adjoining oaks, and central **Bienville Square**, a popular picnic spot with free lunchtime concerts every Wednesday during summer.

## Practicalities

Downtown Mobile is somewhat under the shadow of I-10, as it sweeps to meet I-65 a few miles west. Amtrak, 11 Government St, and Greyhound, 2545 Government St, are both central. Mobile's resourceful **visitor center**, located in Fort Conde, 150 S Royal St (daily 8am–5pm; ☎334/434-7304), can provide valuable **accommodation** discount vouchers. Downtown, the *Holiday Inn* is a very central fifteen-story round tower at 301 Government St (☎334/694-0100; ③), while the *Malaga Inn*, 359 Church St (☎334/438-4701; ④), is an 1862 twin townhouse with huge rooms, which also holds the good but expensive *Mayme's* seafood restaurant.

Unsurprisingly, Mobile abounds in **places to eat fish**: *Wintzels' Oyster House*, 605 Dauphin St (☎334/432-4605), serves good-value seafood platters and fresh oysters in a determinedly eccentric atmosphere, while the *Almost Six Cafe*, 6 N Jackson St (☎334/438-3447), has good Cajun and Creole food. At night, downtown Mobile is largely deserted with the exception of a few blocks of Dauphin Street; *G T Henry's Bar*, at no. 462 (☎334/432-0300), is a popular **pub** with a pool room, loud indie music, and a wide selection of beers, while the *Port City Brewery*, no. 225 (☎334/438-BREW), is a microbrewery that also serves food.

# Around the bay area

Twenty miles south of Mobile, off I-10, the 65 acres of landscaped color that make up **Bellingrath Gardens** – once the home of a Coca Cola magnate – include a quarter of a million azaleas (daily 8am–sunset; $8). Fifteen miles further south on Hwy-193 are the quiet beaches and undisturbed pine forest of sunny **Dauphin Island**, which has a **campground** (☎334/861-2742) on its western tip.

The Mobile Bay Ferry links Dauphin with the larger **Pleasure Island**, five miles away ($1, cars $15; ☎334/434-7345). The real gem here, and indeed on the entire Alabama Gulf Coast, lies twenty miles east, in the shape of **GULF SHORES**, a stunning **beach** where ultramarine waters sweep gently over blinding snow-white sands, just beyond the junction of Hwy-59 and Hwy-182. Although it never gets overcrowded, the beach is particularly busy on a Sunday, when young people from all over LA – as Lower Alabama is known locally – choose the resort in preference to the more expensive Florida Panhandle. A smattering of lively cafes specialize in freshly caught **shrimp**; the lurid *Pink Pony Pub* (☎334/948-6371) is the most popular place for refreshment and music.

Tourism is Gulf Shores' only trade; if you get bored with the beach and the bars, there's not a lot else to do. **Accommodation** is pricey and often booked up at summer weekends, though the *Holiday Inn on the Beach*, a mile or so west at 365 E Beach Blvd (☎334/948-6191; ③), is good value and has its own stretch of sand. Otherwise expect to pay in excess of $80 for a double, or **camp** three miles further east at the *Gulf State Park Resort* (☎334/948-7275). The Gulf Coast **CVB** (☎334/968-7511 or 1-800/745-SAND), on Hwy-59 near Gulf Shores, provides a full range of information.

# MISSISSIPPI

When cotton was king – and slavery was as yet unchallenged – **MISSISSIPPI** was the nation's fifth wealthiest state. Since the Civil War, however, it has been the poorest, its dependence on cotton now a handicap that makes it victim to the vagaries of the commodities market. Widespread poverty has long endured alongside pockets of enormous riches, and white Mississippi was notorious for violent resistance to black political participation. Not until the early Seventies did the church bombings and murders come to an end, and no one could claim that racial tension does not still exist. To some extent, the economy has regenerated since Mississippi's first Republican governor in a century, **Kirk Fordice**, decided to legalize gambling; the giant casinos may be lumbering eyesores that seem pitifully out of place on the sweeping Delta flatlands, but they're sucking considerable revenues across the state line from Memphis, Tennessee. Even today, you only have to take a detour down some rural side road to encounter pockets of truly scandalous black poverty, but with the profits from gaming being ploughed into education in Mississippi's poorest counties, the state may finally manage to shake off its appalling reputation for inequality.

While the major city is the capital, **Jackson**, historic river towns like **Vicksburg** and **Natchez** provide good reasons to stay off the interstates, and **blues** fans will need no encouragement to go exploring sleepy **Delta** settlements such as Alligator or Yazoo City.

## Getting around Mississippi

Although Greyhound serves most of Mississippi, including the Delta, only along the coastal stretch are services at all frequent. Jackson has the only **airport** of any size, while Amtrak **trains** from New Orleans head north to Memphis by way of Jackson and Greenwood; northeast to Atlanta, passing through a succession of unexciting small towns; and along the coast to Florida, stopping at Biloxi. Trips on the Mississippi itself are run on expensive luxury cruisers (see p.491).

# The Delta

*That Delta. Five thousand square miles, without any hill save the bumps of dirt the Indians made to stand on when the river over-flowed.*

William Faulkner, *Sanctuary*

"That Delta" is not in fact a delta at all; technically it's an alluvial flood plain, a couple of hundred miles short of the mouth of the Mississippi. The name stems from its resemblance to the fertile delta of the Nile (which also began at a city named **Memphis**); the extravagant meanderings of the river on its way down to **Vicksburg** deposit sufficient rich topsoil to make this one of the world's finest cotton-producing regions.

The Delta is a land of scorching sun, parched earth, flooding creeks and thickets of bone-dry evergreens, best seen at dawn or dusk, when the glassy-smooth Mississippi waters reflect the sun and the foliage along the banks. Just to contain the sheer volume of water is a never-ending battle, with giant levees struggling to protect the farmland. Though the main thoroughfare south is the legendary **Highway 61**, exploring is best done on the back roads, characterized by huge, silent empty views interrupted only by roadside shacks, tiny churches and the sound of the blues.

## Clarksdale

Unlovely **CLARKSDALE**, the first significant town south of Memphis, has an unquestionable claim to consider itself the home of the blues. Its quite phenomenal roll call of former residents – stretching from Muddy Waters, John Lee Hooker, Howlin' Wolf and Robert Johnson up to Ike Turner and Sam Cooke – is celebrated in the **Delta Blues Museum**, housed in the public library at 114 Delta Ave (Mon–Sat 9am–5pm; free). The centerpiece among the photos, instruments, personal possessions, videos and recordings is the "Muddywood" guitar, created by Z Z Top using wood from Waters' old cabin. Development has already begun for the Blues Alley Historic District, an area along the west side of the railroad tracks north of Delta Avenue, which includes a museum scheduled to move into a restored freight depot. In the meantime, blues fans can drop in at WROX radio, 127 Third St, where Early Wright has broadcast his show since 1947 (Mon–Fri 6–10pm), and the Barbershop, 317 Issaquena Ave, where recording artist Wade Walton performs for visitors when he's not cutting hair; both men are included in the museum.

### Practicalities

Clarksdale's strangest **accommodation** has to be at the *Riverside Hotel*, 615 Sunflower Ave (☎662/624-9163; ②), which until 1944 was a hospital, famous as the site of **Bessie Smith**'s death in 1937 after a car crash. Now it's an extremely basic rooming house in a run-down row – probably for blues obsessives only. If you do stay be sure to talk to "Rat" the owner and ask to see his guest book. You can find better facilities along US-61, known in town as State Street, at the *Econo Lodge* at no. 350 S (☎662/621-1110; ③) the *Hampton Inn* at no. 710 S (☎662/624-9947; ④); and the *Southern Inn* at no. 1904 N (☎662/624-6558; ①/②); a good central **restaurant** is *Abe's*, a barbecue joint at 616 S State St (☎662/624-9947).

The most famous of Clarksdale's **jook-joints**, *Smitty's Red Top Lounge*, 377 Yazoo Ave (☎662/627-4421), has live blues most weekends; on Sunday afternoon, try *Red's South End Disco*, 395–397 Sunflower Ave (☎662/627-3166).

## Delta towns

**GREENVILLE**, seventy miles south of Clarksdale, is the largest town on the Delta. Still an important riverport, it hosts the **Mississippi Delta Blues Festival** on the third Saturday of September. Tree-lined avenues lead from the characterless out-skirts into the business district, beyond which pallid warehouses stand in the shadow of a huge levee. Several of the flimsy shacks along **Nelson Street**, a run-down street in a potentially dangerous part of town, transform at night into blues joints that welcome visitors; *Perry's Flowing Fountain*, at no. 816 (☎662/335-9836), is currently the most reliable. If you wanted to **stay** the hotels near the river and the casinos would probably be the safest bet. **To eat** – arguably the best in the entire Delta for down-home cooking – is the original *Doe's*, at the safer end of Nelson at no. 502 (☎662/334-3315).

**Leland**, seven miles east of Greenville off US-82, is where Mississippi native, **Jim Henson**, created the world famous character, Kermit the Frog, naming him after his childhood playmate, Kermit Scott. The exhibit, located on the bank of Deer Creek, at the intersection of Hwy-82 and Hwy-61, is small, but well worth a stop, with displays fol-lowing Henson's life, Muppet memorabilia, and videos showing much of his work including early efforts (Mon–Sat 10am–4pm; free).

Sixteen miles farther east on US-82, **INDIANOLA** is the home of the largest catfish processing company in the world, *Delta*. **B B King**, who was born here, plays an open-

---

### THE DELTA BLUES

As recently as 1900, much of the **Mississippi Delta** remained an impenetrable wilder-ness of cypress and gum trees, roamed by panthers and bears and plagued with mos-quitoes. Bit by bit land was cleared for cotton plantations, but, though the soil was fertile, white laborers could not be enticed to work in this godforsaken backcountry. Since emancipation, the economy had come to depend on black **sharecroppers**, who would work a portion of the land on a white-owned plantation in return for a share (often piti-fully small) of the eventual crop. As a rule, this lifestyle ensured long periods of poverty and debt interspersed with occasional windfalls; but in the Delta the returns tended to be greater than elsewhere, and blacks moved here from all over Mississippi.

In 1903, W C Handy, often credited as "the Father of the Blues" but at that time the leader of a vaudeville orchestra, found himself waiting for a train in Tutwiler, fifteen miles southeast of Clarksdale. At some point in the night, a ragged black man carrying a gui-tar sat down next to him and began to play what Handy called "the weirdest music I had ever heard." Using a pocketknife pressed against the guitar strings to accentuate his mournful vocal style, the man sang that he was "Goin' where the Southern cross the Dog."

This was the **Delta blues**, characterized by the interplay between words and music, with the guitar aiming to parallel and complement the singing rather than simply provide a backing. Though a local, place-specific music – the "Southern" and the "Dog" were rail-roads that crossed a short way south at Moorhead – it did not simply appear from nowhere, but combined traditional African instrumental and vocal techniques with the "field hollers" chanted by slaves and the reels and jigs then at the basis of popular enter-tainment.

The blues started out as young people's music; the old folk liked the banjo, fife and drum, but the younger generation were crazy for the wild showmanship of men such as **Charley Patton**. Born in April 1891, Patton was the classic itinerant bluesman, moving from plantation to plantation and wife to wife, and playing Saturday-night dances with a repertoire that extended from rollicking dance pieces to documentary songs such as *High Water Everywhere*, about the bursting of the Mississippi levees in April 1927. The

air hometown show once a year under the auspices of *Club Ebony*, 404 Hannah Ave (☎662/887-9915). The *Keyhole Inn* on Church Street is an archetypal jook-joint.

**GREENWOOD**, a sleepy town of 20,000 people, forty miles east on US-82, is the country's second largest cotton exchange after Memphis. The nineteenth-century offices of downtown's Cotton Row overlook the shady Yazoo River, and graceful mansions line pretty Grand Boulevard. The **Cottonlandia Museum** (Mon–Fri 9am–5pm, Sat & Sun 2–5pm; $4), about two miles west of the town center on the US-82 W bypass, is a raggle-taggle collection of old hardware, Native American beads, stuffed birds and oddly long wooden benches polished by the tongues of mules – not one word on slavery or black history, but some intriguing artwork. Although Greenwood has recently begun to play on its Robert Johnson connection (he died here) the **Cotton Capital Blues Fest**, in the beginning of October is the city's current contribution to the Delta Blues music legacy.

Of the many **motels** along US-49 and US-82, the *Travel Inn* at no. 623 US-82 W (☎662/453-8810; ②) is basic, clean, friendly, good value with an outdoor pool. By far the best **place to eat** in Greenwood, and one of the finest in the South, is *Lusco's*, on the wrong side of the railway tracks at 722 Carrolton Ave (☎662/453-5365). Each table in this eccentric old place is hidden away in a small booth, veiled from other diners, and waiters, by chintz curtains – an arrangement dating from the days of Prohibition, when *Lusco's* was the renowned haunt of cotton barons who came here to drink moonshine. Its Italian/Cajun food is superlative, especially the pompano, lightly grilled in a garlicky lemon butter.

---

enigmatic **Robert Johnson** was rumored to have sold his soul to the Devil in return for a few brief years of writing songs such as *Love in Vain* and *Stop Breakin' Down*. His *Crossroads Blues* spoke of being stranded at night in the chilling emptiness of the Delta; themes carried to metaphysical extremes in *Hellhound on My Trail* and *Me and the Devil Blues* – "you may bury my body down by the highway side/So my old evil spirit can catch a Greyhound bus and ride."

Both Patton and Johnson died in the 1930s. However, within a few years the Delta blues had been carried north to **Chicago** by men such as **Muddy Waters** and **Howlin' Wolf**. Their electrified urban blues was the most immediate ancestor of rock 'n' roll.

In addition to towns such as Clarksdale and Helena, blues enthusiasts may want to search out the following rural sites:

**Stovall Plantation**. Stovall Road, 7 miles northwest of Clarksdale. Where tractor-driver Muddy Waters was first recorded; his cabin is still (just) standing.

**Sonny Boy Williamson's Grave**. Outside Tutwiler, 13 miles southeast of Clarksdale.

**Parchman Farm**. Junction US-49 W and Hwy-32. Mississippi State penitentiary, immortalized by former prisoner Bukka White.

**Dockery Plantation**. Hwy-8, between Cleveland and Ruleville. One of Patton's few long-term bases, also home to Howlin' Wolf and Roebuck "Pops" Staples.

**Charley Patton's Grave**. New Jerusalem Church, Holly Ridge, off US-82 6 miles west of Indianola.

**Robert Johnson's Grave**. Payne Chapel at Quito, off Hwy-7, roughly 6 miles southwest of Greenwood, where he was poisoned.

### Getting to see blues events

Managing to hear live blues music in the Delta is rarely straightforward. Half the time nobody seems to know who is playing where, let alone when, and many of the jook-joints themselves – which tend to be dark, rudimentary places, making few concessions to decor or comfort – don't have phones. Most "jookin" gets done at weekends; we've listed likely venues for each Delta town. With public transportation – even taxis – all but nonexistent, a car is essential.

# Northeastern Mississippi

Cutting its way south through Mississippi, I-55 acts as an approximate boundary between the Delta and the luscious green forests of the **northeast**. Of the area's small market towns, the most appealing are the old-style shopping center of **Columbus**, and **Holly Springs**, whose oak-lined streets hide one of the most extraordinary attractions in the state. The only other places of major interest in the region are genteel **Oxford** and tidy blue-collar **Tupelo**, birthplace of **Elvis Presley** and **John Lee Hooker**.

## Holly Springs

Centering on a neat courthouse square, **HOLLY SPRINGS** is a time-warped little town that's said to have changed hands 62 times during the Civil War; the minutiae of its otherwise uneventful history fill three splendidly eclectic floors in the local **museum** at 220 E College Ave (Mon–Fri 10am–5pm, Sat 10am–2pm; $3). Were it not for **Graceland Too**, 200 E Gholson Ave (daily noon–8pm but flexible; $5), however, Holly Springs would today be of little note. The home of Paul McLeod and his son, Elvis Aaron Presley McLeod, this shrine to the King is a quite remarkable labor of love. Walls, ceiling and stairwells are crammed with memorabilia from the kitsch to the priceless, and, just as in Graceland, the upper floor is blocked off – the stairs lined with glassy-eyed mannequins kitted out in Elvis and Priscilla outfits. The McLeods insist that this is above all an archive and research center; as well as collecting records, cuttings and books, they work around the clock to monitor and log every reference to Elvis transmitted on TV and radio. Tours last up to three hours, depending on the mood of your hosts and how busy they are compiling Elvis info; during the tour everyone has their photo taken to be entered into a record of those visited; you can also have your photo taken with both McLeods and the opportunity to buy infinitesimal snips of rug from Graceland's Jungle Room.

There's no reason to spend a night in Holly Springs, but it's well worth pausing for a **meal**. Housed in a former "blind tiger" (brothel) beside the railroad tracks east of town, *Phillips Grocery*, 541 E Van Dorn Ave (☎662/252-4671), is a ramshackle old grocery store that serves sublime fresh-ground hamburgers and Southern vegetables.

## Oxford

Twelve thousand residents and eleven thousand students enable **OXFORD**, an enclave of wealth in a predominantly poor region, to blend rural charm with a busy nightlife. Its central square is archetypal smalltown America, but the leafy streets have a vaguely European air – the town named itself after the English city as part of its campaign to persuade the **University of Mississippi**, known as Ole Miss, to locate its main campus here.

It's an undeniably pretty, appealing place today, but this leafy campus was, in September 1962, the site of the most bitter display of racial hatred ever seen in Mississippi. After eighteen months of legal and political wrangling, federal authorities ruled that **James Meredith** should be allowed to enrol as the first black student at Ole Miss. The news that Meredith had been sneaked into college by federal troops sparked a riot that left three dead and 160 injured. Despite constant threats, Meredith graduated the following year, wearing a "NEVER" badge (the segregationist slogan of Governor Ross Barnett) upside down. The university boasts a Confederate monument, but no statue, not even a plaque, mentioning Meredith. However, in recent years a group of motivated students drew attention to the fact of a missing civil rights monument, and development is currently underway of one which will include Meredith. The **Blues**

**Archive** (Mon–Fri 9am–5pm; call ☎662/232-7753 in advance) on campus holds thousands of recordings and B B King's personal memorabilia, while the **Center for the Study of Southern Culture** looks at Southern folkways (Mon–Fri 8.15am–4.45pm; free).

From Ole Miss, a ten-minute walk through lush Bailey Woods leads to secluded **Rowan Oak**, the former home of novelist **William Faulkner**, preserved as it was on the day he died in July 1962 (Tues–Sat 10am–noon & 2–4pm, Sun 2–4pm; free). The fictional Deep South town of Jefferson, where the Nobel Prize-winner set his major works, was based heavily on Oxford and its environs.

In town, a walk around the **square** brings you to Neilson's, a delightfully old-fashioned department store (the oldest in the South), little changed since 1897. You could pick up a piece of quirky Mississippi folk art at one of the offbeat giftshops, or join the students sipping lattes and reading on the balcony of the exemplary Square Books, at Van Buren and Lamar.

### Practicalities

Oxford's **visitor center** (Mon–Fri 9am–5pm; ☎662/234-4680 or 1-800/758-9177), next to Neilson's in the town square, hands out good walking tour leaflets. On weekends the tourist information center across the street opens up (Sat 10am–4pm; Sun 1–4pm). **Accommodation** options nearby include the *Downtown Inn*, 400 N Lamar (☎662/234-3031; ④), and the comfortable B&B *Oliver-Britt House*, 512 Van Buren Ave (☎662/234-8043; ③/④). The *Barksdale-Isom House*, 1003 Jefferson Ave (☎662/236-5600; ⑧) is where the University was chartered and is believed to be Faulkner's setting for *A Rose for Emily*. Nearer campus, try the *University Inn*, 2201 Jackson Ave W (☎662/234-7013; ③). Prices go up during graduation, the Faulkner Literary Festival each August, and at weekends when there are football games. You can **eat** home-cooked selections on the town square at *Ajax Diner*, 118 Courthouse Square (☎662/232-8880). Just off the town square, *Smitty's*, 208 S Lamar (☎662/234-9111), is especially famed for its country-style breakfasts; come early to people-watch and eat some of the best ham and grits anywhere.

Oxford's lively **nightlife** focuses in and around the town square with a younger crowd frequenting the eastern portion of **Harrison**. *The Gin*, in an old cotton warehouse at S 14th and Harrison (☎662/234-0024), puts on live blues and other music while nearby *Proud Larry's* on 211 S Lamar (☎662/236-0050) books popular regional acts and draws a slightly older crowd. However, there are many places to choose from, and the free *Oxford Town* paper should give a better idea of current events. Keep in mind that Sunday is a dry day.

# Tupelo

On January 8, 1935, **Elvis Presley** and his twin brother Jesse were born in **TUPELO**, an industrial town in northeastern Mississippi. Jesse died at birth, while Elvis grew up to be a truck driver. Their parents, Gladys and Vernon Presley, who lived in poor, white, East Tupelo, found it hard to make ends meet. Such was the financial strain of rearing the young Elvis that his sharecropper father was reduced to forgery in a desperate attempt to raise cash, and was jailed for three years. Their home was repossessed, and the family moved to Memphis in 1948.

Tupelo **CVB**, 399 E Main St (☎662/841-6521 or 1-800/533-0611), has details of a four-mile driving tour that takes in Elvis's first school and the shop where he bought his first guitar. The town doesn't go in for overkill, however; Main Street is a long, placid stretch of faceless buildings with not a giftshop to be seen. The actual **Elvis Presley Birthplace**, 306 Elvis Presley Drive (Mon–Sat 9am–5.30pm, Sun 1–5pm; $1), is tiny. A two-room shotgun house, built for $150 in 1934, it has been refurnished to look as it did when Elvis was born, with the judicious addition of a large can of lard in the kitchen and a love-seat swinging from the porch. The separate **museum** alongside (same hours; $4) is filled with memorabilia collected by a family friend of the Presleys, Janelle McComb, and includes her photos of, poems about, and shrines to the King, as well as selling everything from matchbooks to Elvis pendulum clocks with swinging legs (Mon–Sat 9am–5pm, Sun 1–5pm; $1). Nearby, a modern **meditation chapel** was built with donations from fans, but peculiarly the pews and altar seem to remain roped off to visitors.

Among local **motels**, there's a central *Comfort Inn*, 1190 Gloster St (☎662/842-5100; ③), and other chain accommodations close by. Main Attraction, 214 W Main St (☎662/842-9617), is a vintage clothing store with other eccentric accessories that also holds a **coffee bar**, while there's more substantial Italian and Greek **food** at *Vanelli's*, 1302 Gloster St (☎662/844-4410).

# South central Mississippi

South of the Delta, the rich woodlands and meadows of **central Mississippi** are heralded by steep loess bluffs, holding engaging historic towns such as **Vicksburg** and **Natchez**. Driving is a real pleasure, especially along the unspoiled **Natchez Trace Parkway** – devoid of trucks, buildings and neon signs – which runs through Jackson and on up to Tupelo.

## Jackson

**JACKSON**, poised two hundred miles from both Memphis and New Orleans, has been Mississippi's state capital since 1821. Only in the twentieth century, however, did it become the largest conurbation in the state, flourishing as a center for health and technological industries.

The **Old Capitol**, now the **State Historical Museum** (Mon–Fri 8am–5pm, Sat 9.30am–4.30pm, Sun 12.30–4.30pm; free), charts Mississippi's unenviable history, with excellent displays on civil rights and slavery, especially the chilling notices for slave auctions. The "new" **Mississippi State Capitol**, 400 High St (Mon–Fri 8am–5pm; free), built in 1903 as a Beaux Arts Classical showpiece, is much more ornate. In true rebel fashion, the gilt eagle on the roof looks away from Washington. A block west at 528 Bloom St, the unmissable **Smith-Robertson Museum and Cultural Center**, in Jackson's first public school for blacks (1894–1971), tells the story of black Mississippians since the French first imported slaves in 1719. Subjects covered include "folk architecture" – black homesteads built in the same period as the grand antebellum homes so beloved of the tourist boards, but left to decay unrestored – and patterns of migration after the Civil War. Photos and personal testimony show how Mississippians survived the onslaught of Jim Crow laws through their institutions of school, church and family (Mon–Fri 9am–5pm, Sat 9am–noon, Sun 2–5pm; $1).

### Practicalities
Greyhound **buses** arrive at 201 S Jefferson St, while Amtrak is at 300 W Capitol Ave. JATRAN runs a reasonable in-town bus service until 7pm (75¢ flat fare). The main **visitor center** is at 921 N President St (Mon–Fri 8.30am–5pm; ☎662/960-1891 or 1-800/354-7695).

There are central **rooms** a few blocks west of the State Capitol at the *Holiday Inn Express*, 310 Greymont Ave (☎601/948-4466; ④) or the *Hampton Inn*, 320 Greymont Ave (☎601/352-1700; ⑤). Downtown Jackson more or less closes down at 6pm, with the exception of *Hal & Mal's Restaurant & Oyster Bar*, at 200 S Commerce St (☎601/948-0888; closed Sun), which specializes in New Orleans cuisine and puts on live bands at the weekend. Out in the suburbs, *Poet's*, 1855 Lakeland Drive (☎601/982-9711; closed Sun), does great things with redfish and has live music.

# Vicksburg

The historic port of **VICKSBURG** straddles a high bluff on a bend in the Mississippi, 44 miles west of Jackson. During the Civil War, its domination of the river halted Union shipping, and led Abraham Lincoln to call Vicksburg the "key to the Confederacy." It was a crucial target for General Ulysses S Grant, who eventually landed to the south in the spring of 1863, circled inland, and attacked from the east. After a 47-day siege, the outnumbered Confederates surrendered on the Fourth of July – a holiday Vicksburg declined to celebrate for the next hundred years – and Lincoln was able to rejoice that "the Father of Waters again goes unvexed to the sea." **Vicksburg National Military Park** (summer daily 8am–7pm; rest of the year daily 8am–5pm; $4 per car), entered on US-80 (Clay St) just northeast of town, preserves the main battlefield. A sixteen-mile loop drive through the rippling green hillsides traces every contour of the Union and Confederate trenches, punctuated by statues, refurbished cannons, and over 1600 state-by-state monuments. Also at the site are the substantial remains of the iron-clad **USS Cairo**, sunk by a mine in the Yazoo River, along with artifacts found when it was salvaged a century later, and the **Vicksburg National Cemetery**, where thirteen thousand of the seventeen thousand Union graves are simply marked "Unknown."

Vicksburg today is a bare but attractive city of precipitous streets, steep terraces and wooded ravines, its Victorian riverfront as yet unaffected by the impact of at least two floating **casinos**. As well as nineteenth-century homes, it offers the fascinating **Old Court House Museum**, 1008 Cherry St (summer Mon–Sat 8.30am–5pm, Sun 1.30–5pm; rest of year Mon–Sat 8.30am–4.30pm, Sun 1.30–4.30pm; $2), focusing largely on the siege; the victorious Grant, who returned as president in 1869, addressed thousands of ex-slaves from its balcony. At 1107 Washington St, an enjoyable display of old **Coca Cola** merchandising marks the spot where the drink was first bottled (Mon–Sat 9am–5pm, Sun 1.30–4.30pm; $2.95). Three daily **hydrojet tours** explore the Mississippi and Yazoo rivers (which have changed their course since the siege), departing from the bottom of Clay Street (March to mid-Nov 10am, 2pm & 5pm; 1hr; ☎601/638-5443; $16).

## Practicalities

Vicksburg's main **visitor center** is opposite the Military Park, at Clay Street and Old Highway 27 (daily 8am–5pm, summer extended to 5.30pm; ☎601/636-9421 or 1-800/221-3536). That's also the prime area for **motels**, such as the spartan *Hillcrest*, 4503 Hwy-80 E (☎601/638-1491; ①), which has a pool, and the comfortable *Battlefield Inn*, near the park at 4137 I-20 Frontage Rd (☎601/638-5811; ③/④) which includes use of the pool, two free cocktails and a free breakfast buffet. A central **B&B**, in a historic home, is *Annabelle*, 501 Speed St (☎601/638-2000 or 1-800/791-2000; ⑤). **Camp** at the *Magnolia RV Park*, 211 Miller St (☎601/631-0388).

When it's time for **food**, tuck into superb all-you-can-eat fried chicken and other Southern delicacies from overladen Lazy Susans at lunch at *Walnut Hills*, 1214 Adams St at Clay (☎601/638-4910); *Goldie's Trail BBQ*, 4127 S Washington St near the river (☎601/636-9839), does ribs, pork, chicken and sausage. If you can resist plunking money down at the tables of the *Ameristar Casino*, 4116 Washington St (☎601/638-1000), invest it in their buffet dinner for less than $10.

# Natchez

Sixty miles south of Vicksburg, the river town of **NATCHEZ** still maintains an antebellum atmosphere, abounding in Greek Revival mansions with meticulously maintained gardens. Fourteen homes stay open all year round, including the elaborate octagonal **Longwood**, 140 Lower Woodville Rd (daily 9am–5pm; $6), with its huge dome, snow-white arches and columns, and the palatial **Stanton Hall**, 401 High St (daily 9am–5pm; $6). In March and October each year, most of the rest can be seen on the **Natchez Pilgrimage** – tours, led by women wearing massive hoopskirts, which start from 100 State St ($24 per half-day tour; ☎601/446-6631 or 1-800/647-6742). At the Presbyterian Stratton Chapel, on 405 State St, a fascinating collection of **photographs** gives an idea of life in Natchez spanning from the Civil War era to World War II (Mon–Sat 10am–5pm, Sun 1–5pm; suggested donation $3). There is also a **hot-air balloon** race in mid-October.

Down below the town proper, raucous **Natchez Under-the-Hill** was once known as the "Sodom of the Mississippi"; most of the old streets have eroded away, and the area is now choked with traffic for the 24-hour *Lady Luck* riverboat **casino**, a cacophony of slot machines and craps tables.

Ceremonial mounds, reconstructed dwellings, and a small museum can be seen at the **Grand Village**, 400 Jefferson Davis Blvd (Mon–Sat 9am–5pm, Sun 1.30–5pm; free). It commemorated the sophisticated sun-worshipping local Natchez Indians, who by the mid-sixteenth century had built a flourishing commercial empire, which they later defended in bitter running battles with the French.

### Practicalities

Natchez's **visitor center** is at 422 Main St (March–Oct daily 8.30am–6pm; rest of the year 8.30am–5pm ☎601/446-6345 or 1-800/647-6724). **Rooms** can be had at the *Days Inn*, 109 US-61 S (☎601/445-8291; ③), and *Ramada Hilltop Inn*, 130 John R Junkin Drive at the Mississippi River bridge (☎601/446-6311; ④), while the *Radisson Natchez Eola*, 110 N Pearl St (☎601/445-6000 or 1-800/888-9140; ③–⑤), is a venerable central hotel of considerable charm with occasional discounted rates during slow periods. For a quintessential Natchez experience, however, splash out on a historic **B&B**. The friendly *Highpoint*, 215 Linton Ave (☎601/442-6963 or 1-800/283-4099; ⑤), offers good-value; *Weymouth Hall*, 1 Cemetery Rd (☎601/445-2304; ⑤) has an amazing view of the river; others, such as *The Burn*, 712 N Union St (☎601/442-1344 or 1-800/654-8859; ⑥), with its beautiful pool, reach into extraordinary realms of opulence. Ratings generally will rise during the fall and spring pilgrimages and some other special events. For food, *Cock of the Walk*, on the bluff at 200 N Broadway (☎601/446-8920), serves irresistibly tasty catfish, and *Fat Mama's Tamales*, 500 S Canal St (☎601/442-4548), is a lively joint for strong drinks and fiery chili.

# Mississippi's Gulf Coast

Mississippi's hundred-mile strip of **coast** is utterly unlike the rest of the state, culturally as well as physically – a strong Mediterranean (Catholic) heritage is conspicuous amid the subtropical beauty. Some of the towns are scarred by hurricanes, but the **beaches** are often superb. Along the **Gulf Islands National Seashore**, four beautiful barrier islands boast brilliant white sand and clear blue waters, while the 26-mile artificial **Harrison County Beach** runs parallel with the busy coast road between **Biloxi**, the major resort, and laid-back **Pass Christian**, with its fine live oaks.

# Biloxi

Neon-lit **BILOXI** *(Bi-lux-ee)*, sprawling alongside a busy four-lane highway, cannot claim to be the prettiest resort in the world. But it's less expensive than Florida, it's near New Orleans, and it has sufficient diversity to satisfy local beach poseurs, senior citizens and families alike. Although Biloxi has experienced something of an economic boom since the legalization of gambling – the seafront is lined with permanently moored **casinos**, several of which have spawned large hotels on drier land nearby – it's really not a place that's likely to appeal for long to international visitors.

**Old Biloxi**, starting at the far end of Lameuse Boulevard, consists of narrow streets of stuccoed buildings, in a tree-shaded tranquility that seems miles from the hustle of US-90. Across the highway, shrimp and oyster fleets unload their catch at the **Small Crafts Harbor**. You can rent boats to visit windblown **Deer Island**, half a mile offshore, or just to go fishing (70-min shrimping tours; ☎228/385-1182; $10). A mile west, a glut of typical shops selling T-shirts, seashells, trinkets and other ephemera marks the approach to the most popular stretch of **Harrison County Beach**, in front of the *Broadwater Resort East*.

Five miles west of Main Street, the compact white raised cottage of **Beauvoir** (daily 9am–5pm; $7.50), set in beautiful wooded grounds across from the ocean, was the final home of Confederate President Jefferson Davis, who lived here until his death in 1889. Though not sponsored by the federal government, a **presidential library** has been opened in honor of Davis, and includes an interesting museum chronicling his life. The area's role as a shrine for unrepentant Confederates is typified by the grandiose title of the Civil War museum – "Experiment in Nationalism" – and a bookstore that's bursting with back issues of *Southern Partisan*, a magazine featuring such editorials as "Why the South Was Right."

## West Ship Island

Hailed by *USA Today* as one of the nation's top ten beaches, the barrier island of **West Ship** was only created in 1969, when the 200mph winds and 30ft tide of Hurricane Camille ripped Ship Island in half. It's basically a giant sandbank, dotted with inland ponds (home to a family of alligators), marshlands, sand dunes and warm tidal pools. Everywhere you come across delicate sea oats; even touching them incurs a heavy fine, as their elaborate root structure is all that holds the island together.

The small, idyllic **beach** boasts fine white sand, free showers and a reasonable cafe, though umbrella and deckchair rental is expensive. D-shaped **Fort Massachusetts** alongside was built in 1859 and captured by the Union navy early in the Civil War. Free tours give a wonderful panoramic view from its grass-topped roof.

West Ship is the only barrier island served by regular **ferry**, at **Gulfport Yacht Harbor**, at the intersection of US-90 and US-49 (summer daily 9am & noon; March to mid-May & Sept–Oct Mon–Fri 9am, Sat & Sun 9am & noon; ☎228/432-2197; $16).

## Practicalities

Biloxi's **visitor center** is at 710 Beach Blvd at Main Street (☎228/374-3105). Greyhound **buses** from New Orleans and Mobile come in at 322 Main St, very near the Amtrak station on the New Orleans–Miami line. Coast Area Transit (☎228/896-8080) runs an hourly **trolley** service, the Beachcomber line, along the coast to the unspectacular business center of Gulfport, as well as serene Pass Christian; all-day passes cost $4.

**Room** rates vary considerably according to season and ocean view, but the most convenient area to stay is near the **Loop**. Options along Beach Boulevard include the *Sun*

*Tan Motel* at no. 780 (☎228/432-8641; ④), and a good *Travelodge* at no. 2428 (☎228/385-5555; ④/⑤) You can **camp** at the *Southern Comfort Camping Resort*, 1766 Beach Blvd.

*McElroy's Harbor House*, by the harbor on Beach Boulevard (☎228/435-5001), is a cheery place for good **seafood**, and there's more excellent fish at the unglamorous *Fisherman's Wharf*, 1409 Bienville in Ocean Springs (☎228/872-6111).

# ARKANSAS

Historically, **ARKANSAS** belongs very much to the American South. It sided firmly with the Confederacy in the Civil War, and its capital, Little Rock, was in 1957 one of the most notorious flashpoints in the struggle for civil rights. Geographically, however, it marks the beginning of the Great Plains. Unlike the other Southern states, on the far side of the Mississippi River, Arkansas remained very sparsely populated until almost a century ago. Westward expansion was blocked by the existence of the Indian Territory in what's now Oklahoma, and not until the railroads opened up the forested interior during the 1880s did settlers stray in any numbers from their small riverside villages. Only once the Depression and mechanization had forced thousands of farmers to leave their fields did Arkansas begin to develop any significant industrial base. In 1992, local boy Bill Clinton's accession to the presidency jolted Arkansas into national prominence. Four towns lay claim to him: Hope, his birthplace; Hot Springs, his "home town"; Fayetteville, where he and Hillary married; and, of course, Little Rock, the state capital. Of the four, only sleepy **Little Rock** and the nearby spa resort of **Hot Springs** are worth a trip, whatever the tourist brochures may say.

Though Arkansas encompasses the **Mississippi Delta** in the east, oil-rich timber lands in the south, and the sweeping **Ouachita** (*Wash-i-taw*) **Mountains** in the west, the cragged and charismatic **Ozark Mountains** in the north are its most scenic asset, where the main attraction for tourists are the uncrowded parks and unspoiled rivers. Incidentally, "Arkansas" is a distorted version of the name of a small Indian tribe; the state legislature declared once and for all in 1881 that the correct pronunciation is *Arkansaw*.

### Getting around Arkansas

It's extremely difficult to venture beyond Little Rock and Hot Springs using public transportation. Greyhound runs intermittent services, while Amtrak cuts diagonally east–west through the state, calling at Little Rock, which also holds the only sizeable **airport**. To see the Ozarks you'll need a car.

# Eastern Arkansas

What's surprising about the eastern Arkansas deltalands is that they are far from totally flat: **Crowley's Ridge**, a narrow arc of windblown loess hills, breaks up the uniform smoothness, stretching 150 miles from southern Missouri to the atmospheric river town of **Helena**. Despite scenic rivers and sleepy bayous, the pine-clad woodlands of the Gulf Coastal Plain in southern Arkansas are of little real interest.

## Helena

The small Mississippi port of **HELENA**, roughly sixty miles south of Memphis, was once the shipping point for Arkansas's cotton crop, when Mark Twain described it as occupying "one of the prettiest situations on the river." A small historic district bordered by Holly, College and Perry streets reflects that brief period of prosperity, before the arrival of the railroad left most of the river towns obsolete; today Helena's central core is little more than the slightly run-down Cherry Street on the levee.

That said, there are three good reasons to visit Helena. Musicians among its large black population have ensured that the town is an important stop for **Delta blues** enthusiasts – no great distance from Clarksdale, Mississippi (see p.521), it hosts one of the country's leading blues festivals every October. Radio station KFFA (1360am) with living legend "Sunshine" Sonny Payne, a DJ who first began in 1941, still broadcasts the long-running *King Biscuit Time Show* (Mon–Fri 12.15–12.45pm) from the foyer of the **Delta Cultural Center**, in the old train station at 95 Missouri St, at the end of Cherry Street; visitors are welcome. Helena was for many years the home of harmonica great **Sonny Boy Williamson**, and featured in intimate detail in many of his (usually extemporized) recordings. He used to advertise Sonny Boy's Biscuit Meal on the radio show, and it continues to maintain the illusion that he is present in the studio.

The **Cultural Center** itself is excellent, covering, among other things, the first settlers of this soggy frontier, contemporary racism and, of course, the region's musical heritage (Mon–Sat 10am–5pm, Sun 1–5pm; free). You can buy – and hear – a great assortment of blues records at Bubba Sullivan's Blues Corner, nearby in the small mall at 105 Cherry St: Bubba himself is a mine of friendly information on local music gigs and events.

For some unexpected historic artifacts stop by the **Phillips County Museum** on 623 Pecan St, adjoining the library (Tues–Sat 10am–4pm; free). Here, besides paintings, period clothing, Native American arrowheads, a working model phonograph and a variety of other items are on display. You will find letters by General Lafayette, Charles Lindbergh and Robert E Lee, as well as a letter Samuel Clemens (Mark Twain) wrote when responding to a request from a library founder when asked to donate some autographed books.

### Practicalities

The best of the few places to stay, the *Edwardian Inn*, 317 Briscoe St, on the main highway into town north of the Mississippi Bridge (☎870/338-9155 or 1-800/598-4749; ④), is an opulent **B&B** with large wood-paneled rooms, slightly marred by views from the front over a chemical plant on the river. For those on a **budget** the *Lady Luck Riverbluff Hotel*, 1007 Martin Luther King St (☎870/338-6431; ①–④), has cheap rooms during the week, but you're better off opting for a **B&B** on the weekend. For **food**, *Pasquale's* (☎1-800/390-3992), opposite the Cultural Center, serves nationally marketed homemade tamales and Italian food.

# Central and west Arkansas

Quiet **Little Rock** stands right in the middle of the state, just fifty miles west of the rejuvenated spa town of **Hot Springs**, which marks the eastern gateway to the remote **Ouachita Mountains**. The rippling farmland of the **Arkansas River Valley** is sandwiched by the Ouachita crests on the south side and the craggy ridges of the Ozarks to the north. Mining and logging communities dot the east–west roads, and former frontier towns like **Fort Smith** and **Van Buren** retain their Old West flavor. Fayetteville and Hope are both in west Arkansas; there's nothing to see in either.

## Little Rock

The geographical, political and financial center of Arkansas, **LITTLE ROCK** is at the meeting point of its two major regions, the northwestern hills and the eastern Delta. The town today has a relaxed, open feel, a far cry from the dramatic events of 1957

## CONFRONTATION AT LITTLE ROCK

In 1957, Little Rock unexpectedly became the battleground in the first major conflict between state and federal government over **race relations**. At the time, the city was generally viewed as progressive by Southern standards. All parks, libraries and buses were integrated, a relatively high thirty percent of blacks were on the electoral register, and there were black police officers. However, when the Little Rock School Board announced its decision to phase in **desegregation** gradually – the Supreme Court having declared segregation of schools to be unconstitutional – James Johnson, a candidate for state governor, started a campaign opposed to interracial education. Johnson's rhetoric began to win him support, and the incumbent governor, **Orval Faubus**, who had previously shown no interest in the issue, jumped on the bandwagon himself.

The first nine black students were due to enter Central High School that September. The day before school opened, Faubus reversed his decision to let blacks enrol "in the interest of safety," only to be overruled by the federal court. He ordered state troopers to keep out the black students anyway; soldiers with bayonets forced Elizabeth Eckford, one of the nine, away from the school entrance into a seething crowd, from which she had to jump on a bus to escape. As legal battles raged during the day, at night blacks were subject to violent attacks by white gangs. Three weeks later, President Eisenhower somewhat reluctantly brought in the 101st Airborne Division, and amidst violent demonstrations the nine were at last able to enter Central High. Throughout the year, they experienced immense intimidation; when one retaliated, she was expelled. The graduation of James Green, the oldest, at the end of the year, seemed to put an end to the affair, but Faubus, up for reelection, renewed his political posturing by closing down all public schools in the city for the 1958–59 academic year – and thereby increased his majority.

The school itself is an enormous brown, crescent-shaped structure, more like a fortress, at 1500 S Park Ave, about a mile from the capitol on bus route #9. There is a visitor center across the street from Central in a historically restored former Mobil gas station that has an interesting exhibit titled, "All the World is Watching Us: Little Rock and the 1957 Crisis," (Mon–Sat 10am–4pm, Sun 1–4pm; free, call ☎501/374-1957 for special tours).

(see box, above). In the rapidly expanding **River Market District**, 400 E Markham, the **Museum of Discovery**, geared largely toward kids (Mon–Sat 10am–5pm, Sun 1–4.30pm; $5, free last Sat of each month from 10–11am), is a welcome and fun addition. This area contains the majority of Little Rock's activity, with a series of restaurants, bars and the actual farmers' market on the river. Behind the museum is **Riverfront Park**, a thin strip of greenery and fountains that runs for several blocks – here, a commemorative sign marks the "little rock" for which the city is named, which is not particularly striking.

In MacArthur Park the **Arkansas Art Center** features work by local and international artists (Mon, Thurs & Sat 10am–5pm, Fri 10am–8.30pm, Sun noon–5pm; free). Also in the park, is a newly open **Military Museum** that has exhibits from the Civil War on forward.

The white **Old State House Museum**, 300 W Markham St, surrounded by smooth lawns and shaded by evergreens, backs onto the Arkansas River (for the convenience of early politicians). Inside, displays cover all periods of Arkansas history, but the most impressive rooms are the two senate chambers, restored to their original grandeur (Mon–Sat 9am–5pm, Sun 1–5pm; free). This was where Clinton announced his bid for the presidency on October 3, 1991, and made his acceptance speech thirteen months later. There's now a special exhibit in the museum on his path to the presidency.

## Practicalities

Greyhound arrives at 118 E Washington Ave in North Little Rock. Amtrak enjoys a more central location at Markham and Victory. **Taxis** don't pick up on the street, so call Black and White (☎501/374-0333); from Greyhound to downtown costs around $7. At the **visitor center**, in the Convention Center at Markham and Main (Mon–Fri 8.30am–5pm; ☎501/376-4781 or 1-800/844-4781), you can pick up details of a self-guided walking tour of Bill Clinton's Little Rock that takes in such sights as Chelsea's high school.

Finding a **room** downtown should be no problem. The best **budget** option is just outside of downtown at the *Masters Inn*, 707 1-30 (☎1-800/633-3434; ②), while the *Quapaw Inn*, 1868 S Gaines St (☎501/376-6873; ④), is a very nice B&B. Near the River Market District is the *Doubletree*, 424 W Markham (☎501/372-4371; ④). Little Rock's finest **eating** is at the *Cafe St Moritz*, 225 E Markham St (☎501/372-0411), where the Swiss chef conjures up great continental seafood and superb desserts. *Juanita's Cantina*, 1300 S Main St (☎501/372-1228), an atmospheric and imaginative Mexican place, also hosts live bands. The *Spirit* paddlewheeler sets out on **dinner cruises** from just across the river (☎501/376-4150; $24.50).

# Hot Springs

Fifty miles southwest of Little Rock, the spa town of **HOT SPRINGS** nestles in the heavily forested Zig Zag Mountains on the eastern flank of the Ouachitas. Its thermal waters have attracted visitors since Native Americans used the area as a neutral zone to settle disputes. Early settlers fashioned a crude resort out of the wilderness, and after the railroads arrived in 1875 it became a European-style spa. During the Twenties and Thirties, the mayor reputedly ran a gambling syndicate worth $30 million per annum, and punters included Al Capone and Bugsy Malone. However, Hot Springs' popularity waned when new cures for arthritis appeared during the Fifties, and all but one of the bathhouses closed down. There was a surge of interest after Clinton's election – he lived here between 1953 and 1964 – and the **visitor center** at Central and Court provides a glossy leaflet marking his favorite haunts.

**Downtown** Hot Springs is crammed into a looping wooded valley, barely wide enough to accommodate Central Avenue. Eight magnificent buildings here, behind a lush display of magnolia trees, elms and hedgerows, make up Bathhouse Row. Between 1915 and 1962, the grandest of them all was the **Fordyce Bathhouse**, at the 300 block of Central, which reopened in 1989 as the **visitor center** for **HOT SPRINGS NATIONAL PARK** – the only national park to fall within city limits. The interior of the Fordyce is a strange mixture of the elegant and the obsolete; the heavy use of marble, mosaic-tile floors and the stained-glass ceiling of the Sun Room lend it a decadent feel (daily 9am–5pm; ☎501/624-3383; free).

It's still possible to sample the old-time luxury of Hot Springs by taking a **bath**. The only establishment on Bathhouse Row still open for business is the Buckstaff, where a thermal mineral bath costs $14 (Mon–Fri 7–11.45am & 1.30–3pm, Sat 7–11.45am; ☎501/623-2308). Full bathing facilities are also available at several hotels. To taste the water, which lacks the strong sulphuric taste often associated with thermal springs, fill up a container at the drinking fountain at Central and Reserve.

To the rear of the Fordyce, two small **springs** have been left open for viewing. The **Grand Promenade** from here is a half-mile red-and-yellow-brick walkway overlooking downtown. Trails of various lengths and severity lead up the steep slopes of **Hot Springs Mountain**. A short drive or different trails, including a testing two-and-a-half-mile hike through dense woods of oak, hickory and short-leafed pine takes you to the summit, where the observation decks of **Mountain Tower** offer superb views of the town, the Ouachitas and surrounding lakes (daily summer 9am–9pm; winter times vary; $4).

### Practicalities

Most places of interest are within walking distance of the town's central accommodation, and local **buses** provide a reasonable hourly service to most parts of the city. **Bikes** can be rented from Parkside Cycles, 719 Whittington Ave (☎501/623-6188).

Though rates rise by up to fifty percent in high season (Feb–April), luxury **accommodation** is surprisingly inexpensive. Dominating the town center, the elegant twin-towered *Arlington Resort/Sp*a at Central and Fountain is where Capone stayed when in town – and where President Clinton attended his Junior and Senior proms (☎501/623-7771; ⑨; bath and massage $42). The *Margarete Motel*, 217 Fountain St (☎501/623-1192; ②), is one of some neighboring budget motels. The nearest place to **camp** is *Gulpha Gorge Campground* (☎501/642-3383) in the national park, two miles out on Hwy-70 B, off Hwy-70 E.

Hidden among the usual family **restaurants** is the breakfast only *Pancake Shop*, 216 Central Ave (☎501/624-9465), whose stuffed pancakes make a filling start to the day. Other renowned eateries are *McClard's Bar-B-Q*, 505 Albert Pike (☎501/624-9586 or 623-9665) and *Coy's Steak and Seafood*, 300 Coy St (☎501/321-1414).

## Western Arkansas

West of Hot Springs, US-270 cuts through the **Ouachita Mountains**, unique to the continent in that they run east–west rather than north–south. On its way to Oklahoma, the road passes over uneven crests separated by wide valleys speckled with tiny communities, so isolated that, in the Thirties, hill-dwellers supposedly spoke a form of Elizabethan English. Separating the Ouachitas from the northerly Ozarks, the **Arkansas River Valley**, a natural east–west path for bison, was used for centuries by Native Americans and white hunters before steamboats arrived in the 1820s.

### Fort Smith

Now an industrial city of 70,000 people, **FORT SMITH**, on the Oklahoma border, maintains a pronounced Western feel. Until Isaac C Parker – the "Hanging Judge" – took over in 1875, this was a rowdy pioneer town uncomfortably close to Indian Territory, a sanctuary for robbers and bandits. Parker sent out 200 marshals to round up the fugitives; in 21 years he sentenced 160 to death and saw 79 go to the gallows. **Fort Smith National Historic Site** on Rogers Avenue features remains of the original fort, Parker's courtroom, the dingy basement jail and a set of gallows (daily 9am–5pm; $3). **Old Main Street** in **Van Buren**, on the opposite bank of the Arkansas River, is a stretch of over seventy restored buildings that has been used in numerous Westerns.

Fort Smith's **visitor center**, Miss Laura's, 2 North B St (Mon–Sat 9am–4pm, Sun 1–4.30pm, ☎1-800/637-1477) is oddly housed in a restored former brothel and offers $1 trolley tours of the city (Mon–Sat 9.30am–4pm; every 30min). **Lodgings** in Fort Smith include the central *Best Western*, 101 N 11th St (☎1-888/765-9467; ③). For tasty home-cooked Italian **food**, try *Taliano's*, 201 N 14th St (☎501/785-2292), where meals cost between $5 and $10.

# The Ozark Mountains

Although the highest peak fails to top 2000 feet, the **Ozark Mountains**, which extend beyond northern Arkansas into southern Missouri, are characterized by severe steep ridges and jagged spurs. Hair-raising roads weave their way over the precipitous hills, past rugged lakeshores and pristine rivers. When ambitious speculators poured into Arkansas in the 1830s, those who missed the best land etched out remote hill farms that represented no gain on what they had left behind in Kentucky or Tennessee. They remained utterly isolated until the last few decades; the Ozarks have now become the fastest-growing rural section of the US, a major tourist and retirement destination. Much-needed cash has flooded in, bringing with it the cafes and souvenir shops that have converted centers such as **Harrison** into identikit American towns.

The word *Ozark* is everywhere, used to entice tourists into music shows or gift emporia, which owe more to Nashville and Taiwan than to these mountains. With all the hype, it's getting increasingly difficult to tell the genuine article from imitations, which is a good reason for visiting the state park at **Mountain View**, a serious attempt to preserve traditional Ozark skills and music. The most visited town in the region, **Eureka Springs**, just inside the Missouri border, is a pretty mountainside Victorian spa town, though not one where you should expect to find out much about Ozark life.

## Mountain View

Roughly sixty miles due north of Little Rock, the state-run **Ozark Folk Center**, two miles north of the town of **MOUNTAIN VIEW** on Hwy-14, is a living history museum that attempts to show how life used to be in these remote hills, not reached by paved roads until the Fifties. Homestead skills are displayed in reconstructed log cabins, and folk musicians and storytellers perform throughout the park. Every weekday night in season live Ozark music concerts are held at 7.30pm (mid-April to early Nov; craft displays $7.50, concerts $7.50, combination ticket $13.25). Additionally, there are two major festivals: the **Spring Folk Festival**, around the beginning and middle of April and the **Bean Festival**, the last weekend in October; book accommodations well in advance during these times.

There are **rooms** at the *Lodge* (☎870/269-3871; ③) in the center's grounds, and the pretty *Inn at Mountain View*, 812 Washington St (☎1-800/535-1301; ④/⑤), serves a seven-course country breakfast. Good **restaurants** include the Folk Center's down-home cafe and the award winning *Tommy; Famous Pizza*, 204 Carpenter St, four blocks west of the square (☎870/269-3278). For Saturday night entertainment, even in winter, it's hard to beat the friendly jam sessions in Mountain View's town square.

The **Buffalo River** – a prime destination for whitewater canoeing – flows across the state north of Mountain View. *Buffalo Camping and Canoeing* (☎870/439-2386) provides canoes and equipment and runs a shuttle bus to the river, which is at its most spectacular around **Pruitt Landing**, thirteen miles south of unremarkable Harrison.

## Eureka Springs

Picturesque **EUREKA SPRINGS**, set on steep mountain slopes in Arkansas's northwestern corner, began life a century ago as a health center. As that role declined, its striking location turned it into a regular tourist destination, given a kitsch edge by its specializing in weddings and honeymoons. It's an enjoyable place to stroll around, filled with tasteful Victorian buildings, and you can ride on the **Eureka Springs and North Arkansas Railway** through wooded Ozark valleys. Rolling stock includes a magnificent "cabbage-head" wood-burning locomotive, and trips depart on the hour from the depot at 299 N Main St (mid-April to Oct Mon–Sat 10am–4pm; ☎501/253-9623).

Three miles east of town, an incredible religious complex includes the seven-story **Christ of the Ozarks** – a surreal statue of Jesus with a 60ft arm span – a **Bible Museum** ($2.50) and a **Sacred Arts Center** ($2.50). Elna M Smith, whose Foundation runs the whole show, was so worried that the holy sites of the Middle East would be destroyed by war that she decided to build replicas in the Ozarks, safe from Arab attacks. Minibuses whisk visitors through the **New Holy Land Tour** (Tues–Sat 9am–3.30pm; $7.50 price includes all attractions) past scaled-down versions of the Sea of Galilee, the River Jordan and Golgotha. Christ's last days on earth are reenacted with a cast of almost 200 in the **Great Passion Play** a 4100-seat amphitheater (end of April–Oct nightly except Sun and Wed 8.30pm, after Labor Day 7.30pm; ☎1-800/882-7529; $14–15).

## Practicalities
In town US-62 and Van Buren are the same road. **Accommodation** rates vary seasonally, but you can usually find inexpensive lodging just over a mile from downtown on US-62 E. More central is the *Best Western Eureka Inn* (☎501/253-9551; ③/④), at the junction of US-62 and S Main Street. The local **visitor center** is at 137 W Van Buren (daily 9am–5pm; ☎501/253-8737).

For **food**, *Sparky's Road House Cafe*, 141 E Van Buren (☎501/253-6001) is atmospheric with an inexpensive menu and good beer selection. Next door at no. 149 is the *Daily Planet Internet Cafe* (☎501/253-8984). *Pancake's Family Restaurant*, 2055 E Van Buren (☎501/253-5289) serves very well-priced, tasty food and is open late. Just off the well-worn tourist paths, *Chelsea's Corner*, 10 Mountain St, off Spring Street (☎501/253-6723), has live **music** most evenings.

# CHAPTER SEVEN

# FLORIDA

**B** rochure images of tanning flesh and Mickey Mouse give an inaccurate and incomplete picture of **FLORIDA**. Although the aptly nicknamed "sunshine state" is indeed devoted to the tourist trade, it's also among the least-understood parts of the US. Away from its overexposed resorts lie forests and rivers, deserted strands filled with wildlife, vibrant cities and primeval swamps.

In many respects Florida is still evolving. A thousand people a day move to the state, now the fourth most populous in the nation. Changing demographics are eroding the traditional Deep South conservatism: the new Floridians tend to be a younger, more energetic breed, while Spanish-speaking enclaves provide close ties to Latin America and the Caribbean – links as influential in creating wealth as the recent arrival of the movie industry in central Florida, fresh from Hollywood.

The essential stop is cosmopolitan, half-Hispanic **Miami**, from where a simple journey south brings you to the **Florida Keys**, a hundred-mile string of islands known for sports fishing, coral-reef diving, and the sultry town of **Key West**, legendary for its sunsets and anything-goes attitude. North from Miami, much of the **east coast** is disappointingly urbanized, albeit with miles of unbroken beaches flowing alongside. The residential stranglehold is lessened further north, where communities such as **Daytona Beach** have become subservient to the local sands. Farther along, historical **St Augustine** stands as the longest continuous settlement in the US.

In **central Florida** the terrain turns green, though it's no rural idyll: this is where you'll find **Walt Disney World**, where tourism is practiced on the scale of the infinite. From here it's just a skip north to the forests of the **Panhandle**, Florida's link with the Deep South, or to the towns and beaches of the west coast, which should be savored while progressing steadily south to the **Everglades**, an alligator-filled swath of sawgrass plain.

It makes little difference **when you visit**: warm sunshine and blue skies are a fact of life. Florida does, however, split into two **climatic zones**: subtropical in the south and warm temperate in the north. Orlando and points south have very mild winters (October to April), with warm temperatures and low humidity. This is the peak tourist season, when prices are at their highest. The southern summer (May to September), on the other hand, sees extremely high humidity and afternoon storms – the rewards for braving the mugginess are lower prices and fewer tourists. Winter is the off-peak period north of Orlando; while snow has been known to fall in the Panhandle, daytime temperatures are generally comfortably warm. The northern Florida summer is when

## ACCOMMODATION PRICE CODES

All accommodation prices in this book have been coded using the symbols below. Note that prices are for the least expensive double rooms in each establishment. For a full explanation see p.37 in Basics.

| | | |
|---|---|---|
| ① up to $30 | ④ $60–80 | ⑦ $130–175 |
| ② $30–45 | ⑤ $80–100 | ⑧ $175–250 |
| ③ $45–60 | ⑥ $100–130 | ⑨ $250+ |

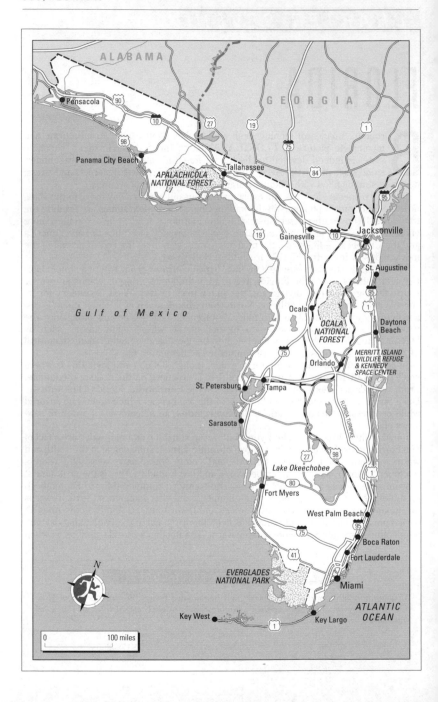

the crowds arrive, and when the days – and the nights – get hot and sticky. Aside from these differences, summer is known throughout Florida as the "**hurricane season**."

Finally, Florida is still struggling with its reputation for **crimes** against (and even murders of) tourists. While the authorities have been successful in reducing such attacks, the fact remains that planeloads of visitors who have left their cares – and sometimes their common sense – at home make an inviting target for opportunistic criminals. The odds against becoming a victim are astronomic, but it pays to be wary.

## Some history

The **first European sighting** of Florida, just six years after Christopher Columbus located the "New World," is believed to have been made by John and Sebastian Cabot in 1498, when they spotted what is now Cape Florida, on Key Biscayne in Miami. At the time, the area's 100,000 inhabitants formed several distinct **tribes**: the Timucua across northern Florida, the Calusa around the southwest and Lake Okeechobee, the Apalachee in the Panhandle and the Tequesta along the southeast coast.

In 1513, a **Spaniard**, Juan Ponce de León, sighted land during *Pascua Florida*, the Festival of the Flowers, and named what he saw *La Florida* – or "Land of Flowers." Eight years later he returned with a mandate from the Spanish king to conquer and colonize the territory, the first of several Spanish incursions prompted by rumors of gold hidden in the north of the region. When it became clear that Florida did not harbor stunning riches, interest waned; but the arrival of French Huguenots in 1562 forced the Spanish into a more determined effort at settlement. Three years later, **Pedro Menéndez de Avilés** founded St Augustine – the longest continuous site of European habitation on the continent. In 1586 St Augustine was razed by a British naval bombardment led by Francis Drake. The ensuing bloody confrontation for control of North America was eventually settled when the British captured the crucial Spanish possession of Havana, and Spain willingly parted with Florida to get it back. By this time, indigenous Floridians had been largely wiped out by disease, and Florida's Indian population was becoming composed of disparate tribes arriving from the west, collectively known as the **Seminole**, who were generally left undisturbed in the inland areas.

Following American independence, when Florida was returned to Spain, the US began to think in terms of controlling the state. In 1814 a US general, Andrew Jackson, marched south, killing hundreds of Indians and triggering the **First Seminole War** – on the pretext of subduing the Seminole but with the actual intention of taking the region. Spain formally **ceded Florida to the US** in 1819, with Jackson sworn in as Florida's first American governor and Tallahassee selected as the new administrative center. Eleven years later, the **Act of Indian Removal** decreed that all Native Americans in the eastern US should be transferred to reservations in the Midwest. Most Seminole were determined to stay and the **Second Seminole War** broke out, with the Indians steadily driven south, away from the fertile lands of central Florida and into the Everglades, where they eventually agreed to remain.

Florida **became a state** on March 3, 1845, coinciding with the prosperity brought by the railroads. As a member of the Confederacy during the **Civil War**, its primary contribution was the provision of food – a foretaste of its postwar economic role when finally readmitted to the Union. As northern speculators began to invest in Florida, the country's newspapers extolled the curative virtues of its climate. These early efforts to promote Florida as a **tourist destination** brought in the wintering rich: Henry Flagler opened luxury resorts on the northeast coast and extended his Florida East Coast Railroad south, giving birth to communities such as Palm Beach. Henry Plant connected his own railroad to Tampa, turning it into a thriving port city. Florida's climate enabled citrus fruits to be grown during the winter and sold to the cooler north, and the state became a major beef producer. After World War I, everyone in America wanted a piece of Florida, and chartered trains brought in thousands of eager buyers. But most deals were on paper only, and in 1926 the banks began to default. The **Wall Street Crash** then made paupers of the millionaires whose investments had helped shape the state.

What saved Florida was **World War II**. Thousands of troops arrived to guard the coastline, empty tourist hotels provided ready-made barracks, and – most importantly – the soldiers got a taste of Florida that would entice many of them to return. In the mid-Sixties, the state government bent over backwards to help the Disney Corporation turn a sizeable slice of central Florida into **Walt Disney World**, the biggest theme park ever known. Its enormous commercial success helped solidify Florida's place in the international tourist market: directly or indirectly, one in five of the state's twelve million inhabitants now earns a living from the tourist trade.

Behind the optimistic facade, however, lie many **problems**. There's a broadening gap between the relative liberalism of the big cities and the arch-conservatism of the Bible Belt rural area: while Miami promotes its multicultural make-up, the Ku Klux Klan holds picnics in the Panhandle. Gun laws remain notoriously lax, and the multi-million-dollar **drugs trade** shows few signs of abating – at least a quarter of the cocaine entering the US is said to arrive via Florida. **Racial issues** continue to be vexed, too, with tension on several fronts: between Anglo-Americans and nouveau riche Cubans, blacks and whites, blacks and Hispanics, police and the inner-city poor. However, increased protection of the state's **natural resources** has been a more positive feature of the last decade and impressive amounts of land are under state control – overall, wildlife is less threatened now than at any time since white settlers first arrived.

## Getting around Florida

Florida is surprisingly compact, and with a **car** you'll have few problems: crossing between the east and west coasts takes only a couple of hours, and even the longest possible trip – between the western extremity of the Panhandle and Miami – can be done in a day. **Public transportation**, on the other hand, requires adroit forward planning. Greyhound **buses** link all the major towns and cities, with both Miami and Orlando well served; but sadly, many rural areas and some of the most enjoyable sections of the coast are not covered.

Florida's **railroads** were built to service the boomtowns of the Twenties, and consequently some present-day rural nooks have rail links as good as the modern cities. Amtrak runs west from **Jacksonville** via New Orleans all the way to LA, while connections with New York remain good. However, in some areas Amtrak buses have replaced the trains; these can be very expensive, so check in advance. Passengers with cars can use the daily **Auto Train** from Lorton, Virginia (just south of Washington DC), to Sanford, north of Orlando. The southeast coast boasts an elevated **TriRail** system ferrying commuters between Miami, Fort Lauderdale, Boca Raton and Palm Beach.

Although inadvisable in the cities, **cycling** is a great way to see large parts of Florida – miles of cycle paths follow the coast, and long-distance bike trails cross the state's interior. Forget **hitching**: always dangerous (especially for women), it's illegal in Miami (where, if you did hitch, you'd be lucky to live to regret it) and on the outskirts of many other cities.

# MIAMI

Far and away the most exciting city in Florida, **MIAMI** is a stunning and often intoxicatingly beautiful place. Awash with sunlight-intensified natural colors, there are moments – when the neon-flashed South Beach skyline glows in the warm night and the palm trees sway in the breeze – when a better-looking city is hard to imagine. Even so, people, not climate or landscape, are what make Miami unique. Half of the two-million population is Hispanic, the vast majority Cubans. Spanish is the predominant language almost everywhere – in many places it's the only language you'll hear, and you'll be expected to speak at least a few words – and news from Havana, Caracas or Managua frequently gets more attention than the latest word from Washington DC.

Often tagged the most segregated city in North America, however, Miami is no melting pot. Since the black ghettos first erupted in the Sixties, violent expressions of rage – most recently among Haitians and Puerto Ricans – have made regular headlines. In 1980 it had the highest murder rate in the country, but thanks in large part to the popularity of the Eighties designer cop show Miami Vice it spent a decade or so smartening itself up considerably. South Beach in particular, the Art Deco showpiece of Miami Beach, became a regular backdrop on the fashion pages of glossy magazines.

Just a century ago Miami was a swampy outpost of mosquito-tormented settlers. The arrival of the railroad in 1896 gave the city its first fixed land-link with the rest of the continent, and literally cleared the way for the Twenties property boom. In the Fifties, Miami Beach became a celebrity-filled resort area, just as thousands of Cubans fleeing the regime of Fidel Castro began arriving in mainland Miami. The Sixties and Seventies brought decline, though with the strengthening of Latin American economic links and the upsurge in tourism, the city is now enjoying a burst of affluence.

# Arrival, information and getting around

**Miami International Airport** (☎305/876-7000) is six miles west of the city; local bus #42 goes to Miami Beach (cab fare $22–27). The 24-hour SuperShuttle minivans deliver you to any address in Miami for $8–15. From the airport, take the #7 Metrobus to downtown, taking 30 minutes or so ($1.25; every 40min Mon–Fri 5.30am–8.30pm, Sat & Sun 7am–7pm), or the 'J' Metrobus ($1.25 plus a 25¢ surcharge to South Beach; every 30min daily 5.30am–11.30pm) to Miami Beach further on. **Greyhound**'s Miami West station is a short cab ride from the airport, while the other major terminal is downtown at 700 Biscayne Blvd. The **train** station, 8303 NW 37th Ave, is seven miles northwest. To get downtown, to Coconut Grove or Coral Gables from here, take Metrobus #L to the Metrorail, eight blocks away (see below).

For free maps and leaflets, there's an information stand in **downtown Miami**, outside the Bayside Marketplace mall (daily 10am–6.30pm; ☎305/539-2980). You can also pick up information at the **Chamber of Commerce at Miami Beach**, 920 Meridian Ave (Mon–Fri 9am–6pm, Sat & Sun 10am–4pm; ☎305/672-1270), and in **South Beach** at the **Miami Design Preservation League Welcome Center**, 1001 Ocean Drive (☎305/672-2014), which has details on walking tours and events, and a great line in retro gifts.

## City transportation

**Driving** is the most practical way to get around Miami. Though the safety warnings handed to visitors as they pick up their rental cars can make unnerving reading, the much publicized tourist-targeted car-jackings of the early 1990s are now no more of an issue here than in any major city. Watch out for road signs marked with an orange sun on a blue background; they identify the most useful routes to the main attractions. Tourist police patrol in cars with the same logo.

With a lot of time and patience, it is possible to make your way around Miami on **public transportation** run by Metro-Dade Transit (☎305/638-6700 for route information). **Metrorail** trains (5.30am–midnight) run, slowly, along a single line between the northern suburbs and South Miami; useful stops are Government Center (for downtown), Coconut Grove, and Douglas Road or University (for Coral Gables). Single-journey fares are $1.25. Downtown Miami is also ringed by the **Metromover**

(6am–midnight; flat fare 25¢), a daytime monorail that doesn't cover much ground but gives a great bird's-eye view. **Metrobuses** cover the entire city, but services dwindle at night; the flat-rate single-journey fare is $1.25. **Route maps** and **timetables** for all Metro-Dade Transit services can be had at Government Center Station, and at the booth at E Flagler and E First avenues.

If you're in no great hurry, one of the most pleasant ways to get around the city is by **water taxi** (☎954/467-0008). Two routes link to provide an extensive network stretching from central Miami Beach in the north to Coconut Grove in the south. The **Shuttle Service** (daily 11am–11pm every 15–20min; $3.50 one-way, $6 round-trip, $7.50 all-day pass) runs from the Omni International Mall (north of the Venetian Causeway) to points along the Miami River. At Bayside Marketplace you can transfer to the **Beach Service** ($7 one-way, $12 round-trip, $15 all-day pass), with mooring points on the west shore of Miami Beach, Virginia Key (the Seaquarium), Key Biscayne (Crandon Park), Vizcaya and Coconut Grove.

### Taxis, cycling and tours

**Taxis** are abundant; try Central Cab (☎305/532-5555) or Metro Taxi (☎305/888-8888). Otherwise, get the free *Miami on Two Wheels* leaflet from the CVB and **rent a bike** from one of the many outlets, such as the Miami Beach Cycle Center, 601 Fifth St (☎305/531-4161). For an informed stroll, take one of **Dr Paul George's Walking Tours** (no tours June–Sept; ☎305/375-1625; $15–25), or try the various excellent **Art Deco walking tours** of South Beach (Thurs at 6pm & Sat at 10am; $10), which begin at the Miami Design Preservation League Welcome Center on Ocean Drive (see overleaf). The latter also offers a self-guided audio walking tour of the district (daily 11am–4pm; 1hr–1hr 15min; $5).

# Accommodation

**Accommodation** is not a problem in Miami except during the Boat Show (February). Otherwise, there are rooms to suit every taste and budget, with the majority of travelers opting for any one of the numerous Art Deco **South Beach** hotels. Elsewhere, **Coral Gables** is appealing but expensive; **downtown Miami** is filled with chain hotels; and the stylish high-rises of **Coconut Grove** are a jet-setter's preserve. Prices are steepest from December through April; the rest of the year you may have some luck negotiating – in any case, bargains can be found year-round in several well-run **hostels** in Miami Beach.

**Banana Bungalow**, 2360 Collins Ave, Miami Beach (☎305/538-1951 or 1-800/746-7835). Like a perpetual spring break – nightly movies in a plush video room, organized land and water tours, and the cheapest tiki bar on the strip. Choose from bunk beds or private rooms. ①/②.

**Brigham Gardens Guesthouse**, 1411 Collins Ave, South Beach (☎305/531-1331). Large rooms with either basic or fully equipped kitchens. A tropical garden patio and friendly atmosphere help make this one of the most pleasant places to stay in South Beach. ⑤/⑥.

**Clay Hotel and International Hostel**, 1438 Washington Ave, South Beach (☎305/534-2988 or 1-800/379-2529). Beautiful converted monastery serves as the city's best budget hotel and youth hostel. ①–④.

**Hotel Place St Michel**, 162 Alcazar Ave, Coral Gables (☎305/444-1666). Small, romantic hotel just off the Miracle Mile, with Laura Ashley decor and copious European antiques. Rates include continental breakfast. ④–⑥.

**Indian Creek**, 2727 Indian Creek Drive at 28th St, Miami Beach (☎305/531-2727). Fantastic restored Art Deco hotel, a 10-min walk from South Beach. Simple, stylish, comfortable rooms, a peaceful garden and pool, and fine dining in the hotel's restaurant, the *Pan Coast*. Highly recommended. ⑤.

**Leslie**, 1244 Ocean Drive, South Beach (☎305/534-2135). One of a handful of gorgeous restored South Beach hotels owned by Anglo-Jamaican entrepreneur Chris Blackwell. Great location, impeccable design and beautiful guests. ⑥–⑨.

**Marlin**, 1200 Collins Ave, South Beach (☎1-800/OUTPOST). Eleven costly but cozy suites with Caribbean-island theme, plus a rooftop sun deck. If you can't afford to stay here, at least have a drink at the futuristic bar or a jerk chicken sandwich in the haremesque *Shabeen Lounge*. ⑥–⑧.

**The Mermaid**, 909 Collins Ave, South Beach (☎305/538-5324). Tiny, sociable guesthouse with funky cabana-style rooms hidden in a lush garden. Can be noisy, but the prices and atmosphere make up for it. ④.

**Miami River Inn**, 118 SW South River Drive, downtown (☎305/325-0045). Minutes from downtown on the river, with lovely rooms in buildings dating from 1908, tropical gardens and a large pool. Don't wander round the area at night. ⑤.

**Park Central**, 640 Ocean Drive, South Beach (☎305/538-1611). Glamorous Art Deco hotel on the strip with a charismatic lobby and bar. ⑤–⑧.

**Pelican**, 826 Ocean Drive, South Beach (☎305/673-3373 or 1-800/7PELICAN). Quirkily themed rooms range from the wild "Me Tarzan, You Vain" to the bizarre dentist office "With Drill," and the most requested, "Best Whorehouse," draped in red velvet and tassels. Totally fun. ⑥/⑦.

**Shelley**, 844 Collins Ave, South Beach (☎1-800/414-0612). An original Art Deco hotel with impeccably clean rooms and just across the street from Ocean Drive and the beach. ②/③.

# The City

Many of Miami's **districts** are officially cities in their own right, and each has a background and character very much its own. Most people head straight **to Miami Beach**, specifically the **South Beach** strip, where many of the city's famed Art Deco buildings have been restored to their former stunning splendor, all pastels, neon and wavy lines. Though touted as the chic gathering place for the city's fashionable faces, it's not as exclusive as you might expect, especially on weekend afternoons when families and out-of-towners join the washboard stomachs and bulging pecs. Make time, too, for **Key Biscayne**: a smart, secluded island community with some beautiful beaches, five miles off the mainland but easily reached by a causeway.

On the mainland, **downtown** has a few good museums but little else of interest to visitors. **Little Havana**, to the west, is the best spot to head for a Cuban lunch, while immediately south the spacious boulevards of **Coral Gables** are as impressive now as they were in the 1920s, when the district set new standards in town planning. Similarly opulent **Coconut Grove**, with its trendy streetside cafes and galleries and a couple of Miami's most popular attractions, is also worth a look.

## Miami Beach

A long slender arm of land between Biscayne Bay and the Atlantic Ocean, three miles off mainland Miami, **MIAMI BEACH** was an ailing fruit farm in the 1910s when its Quaker owner, John Collins, formed an unlikely partnership with a flashy entrepreneur called Carl Fisher. With Fisher's money, Biscayne Bay was dredged. The muck raised from its murky bed provided the landfill to transform this wildly vegetated barrier island into a carefully sculpted landscape of palm trees, hotels and tennis courts.

Today Miami Beach is home to a large number of Holocaust survivors and their families. The **Holocaust Memorial** (daily 9am–9pm; free), at Dade Boulevard and Meridian Avenue opposite the visitor center, is a complex, uncompromising monument to their experience. From a distance, the impression is of a giant, defiant hand punching into the sky; as you approach, however, you make out the mass of wailing creatures scrabbling up the wrist. Following the wall of names, inscribed with a relentless list of

## THE BEACHES OF MIAMI BEACH

If you took away the Art Deco, the beautiful people and the glittering nightlife, you'd still be left with the simple truth that Miami has a fabulous **choice of beaches**, twelve miles of calm waters, clean sands, swaying palms and candy-colored lifeguard towers. The young and the beautiful soak up the rays between 5th and 21st, a convenient hop from the juice bars and cafes on Ocean Drive; **Lummus Park**, from 6th to 14th, is the heart of the South Beach scene, and there's an unofficial gay section roughly around 18th. North of 21st it's more family-oriented, with a **boardwalk** running between the shore and the hotels up to 46th. To the south, **Ocean Park** and **South Pointe** are favored by Cuban families, and are especially convivial at weekends. For **swimming**, head up to 85th, a quiet stretch that is usually patrolled by lifeguards.

Holocaust victims, brings you to the foot of the sculpture, hidden from the road, where distressing statues portray more writhing, emaciated human figures. The whole, brutal ensemble is underscored by the accompanying quote from Anne Frank: "Ideals, dreams and cherished hopes rise within us only to meet the horrible truth and be shattered."

A few blocks northeast, the prestigious **Bass Museum**, in a lovely Art Deco building at 2121 Park Ave (Tues–Sat 10am–5pm, Sun 1–5pm; $5) displays art from the fourteenth century, with a good showing of Renaissance works, Old Masters and tapestries. It also features exceptional temporary exhibitions.

### South Beach

Occupying the southernmost three miles or so of Miami Beach is gorgeous **SOUTH BEACH**, with its hundreds of dazzling pastel-colored Twenties and Thirties buildings. Concentrated between Fifth and 23rd streets, Euclid Avenue and the ocean, the area referred to as the **Deco district** actually incorporates a variety of styles: take one of the excellent walking or cycling tours from the **Miami Design Preservation League Welcome Center** (see p.541) to learn the difference between Streamline and Mediterranean, Moderne and Art Deco proper.

The most famous buildings lie along **Ocean Drive**, where a line of revamped hotels have made much of their design heritage. Swarms of photographers and film crews zoom in on what has become the hottest high-style backdrop in the world. By night, the ten blocks of Ocean Drive are the heart and soul of the biggest party in Miami, as chic terrace cafes spill across the specially widened sidewalk, sleek vintage cars prowl bumper to bumper, and Jazz Age neon illuminates the starry sky. Just a few blocks from Ocean Drive, however, the streets are much less photogenic, some still bearing the scars of the poverty-stricken Seventies; but provided you stick to the main drags and exercise the usual caution, none of South Beach is unduly dangerous. Behind Ocean Drive are **Collins Avenue**, lined with more Deco hotels and fashion chains, and **Washington Avenue**, which tends more towards funky thrift stores and cool coffee bars. At 1001 Washington, the imaginative **Wolfsonian Museum** (Tues, Wed, Fri & Sat 11am–6pm, Thurs 11am–9pm, Sun noon–5pm; $5, free Thurs 6–9pm) is one of Miami's best, a thoughtfully presented patchwork history of design and culture from the late nineteenth century up to 1945, crammed with old books, photos, paintings and posters, and all manner of domestic objects.

## Key Biscayne

A compact, immaculately manicured community, **KEY BISCAYNE**, five miles off mainland Miami, is a great place to live – if you can afford it. The moneyed of Miami fill the island's upmarket homes; Richard Nixon had a presidential winter house here. The

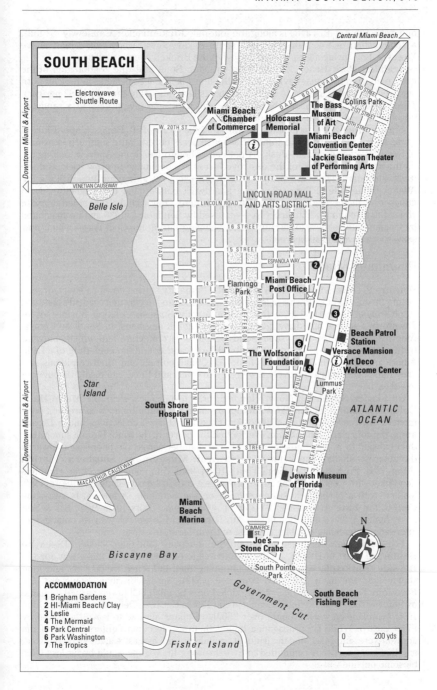

# SOUTH BEACH

- - - Electrowave
Shuttle Route

Central Miami Beach △

Downtown Miami & Airport

SUNSET DRIVE

N BAY ROAD

ALTON ROAD

N MERIDIAN AVENUE

PRAIRIE AVENUE

DADE BOULEVARD

22ND STREET

21ST STREET

Collins Park

20TH STREET

The Bass
Museum
of Art

Miami Beach
Chamber
of Commerce

W. 20TH ST

Holocaust
Memorial

ⓘ

Miami Beach
Convention Center

Jackie Gleason Theater
of Performing Arts

WASHINGTON AVE

JAMES AVE

COLLINS AVE

VENETIAN CAUSEWAY

17TH STREET

LINCOLN ROAD MALL
AND ARTS DISTRICT

Belle Isle

LINCOLN ROAD

16 STREET

PENNSYLVANIA AVE

BAY ROAD

ALTON ROAD

WEST AVENUE

15 STREET

ESPANOLA WAY

❼

❷ ❶

Miami Beach
Post Office

Flamingo
Park

14 ST.

LENOX AVENUE

MICHIGAN AVENUE

JEFFERSON AVENUE

MERIDIAN AVENUE

13 STREET

12 STREET

11 STREET

10 STREET

9 STREET

❻

The Wolfsonian
Foundation

❸

Beach Patrol
Station

Versace Mansion

ⓘ Art Deco
Welcome Center

❹

Lummus
Park

ATLANTIC
OCEAN

Star
Island

South Shore
Hospital

Ⓗ

8 STREET

7 STREET

6 STREET

WASHINGTON AVE

COLLINS AVENUE

OCEAN DRIVE

❺

5 STREET

4 STREET

3 STREET

2 STREET

MACARTHUR CAUSEWAY

ALTON ROAD

Jewish Museum
of Florida

Miami
Beach
Marina

COMMERCE
ST

Joe's
Stone Crabs

N

Biscayne Bay

South Pointe
Park

Government Cut

South Beach
Fishing Pier

0        200 yds

## ACCOMMODATION
1 Brigham Gardens
2 HI-Miami Beach/ Clay
3 Leslie
4 The Mermaid
5 Park Central
6 Park Washington
7 The Tropics

Fisher Island

only way onto Key Biscayne is along the four-mile **Rickenbacker Causeway** ($1 toll), a continuation of SW 26th Road just south of downtown, which soars high above Biscayne Bay, giving a gasp-inducing view of the Brickell Avenue skyline.

**Crandon Park Beach**, a mile along Crandon Boulevard (the continuation of the main road from the causeway), is one of the finest landscaped beaches in the city, with crystal-clear waters, barbecue grills and sports facilities (daily 8am–dusk; $2 per car). Three miles of yellow-brown beach fringe the park, and give access to a sand bar enabling knee-depth wading far from shore.

Crandon Boulevard terminates at the entrance to the **Bill Baggs Cape Florida State Recreation Area**, four hundred wooded acres covering the southern extremity of Key Biscayne (daily 8am–dusk; $4 per car). Though Hurricane Andrew took its toll on the area in 1992, most of the destroyed trees are beginning to grow back, and the trails and boardwalks have been repaired. An excellent swimming **beach** lines the Atlantic-facing side of the park, and a boardwalk cuts around the wind-bitten sand dunes towards the 1820s **Cape Florida lighthouse**. Only with the ranger-led tour can you climb through the 95ft structure – attacked by Seminole in 1836 and incapacitated by Confederate soldiers to disrupt Union shipping during the Civil War – which now serves as a navigational beacon.

## Downtown Miami

Don't try to relax in **DOWNTOWN MIAMI**: humanity storms down its short streets, easing up only to gulp down a spicy snack and a mango juice from a roadside fast-food stand. Since the early 1960s, the predominantly Spanish-speaking businesses of downtown's square mile have reaped the benefits of any boost in South or Central American economies. Only some solid US public architecture and whistle-blowing traffic cops remind you that you're still in Florida and not on the main drag of a Latin American capital. And though this fusion of Cuban culture and American ideals creates a fast pace, it has relatively few sights to offer, and those can easily be covered in a day.

On **Flagler Street**, downtown's loudest, brightest, busiest strip, the **Metro-Dade Cultural Center** is an ambitious attempt by architect Philip Johnson to create a post-modern Mediterranean-style piazza. Art shows, historical collections and a library frame the courtyard, but Johnson overlooked the power of the south Florida sun: rather than pausing to rest and gossip, most people scamper across the open space towards the nearest shade. The center's **Historical Museum of Southern Florida** (Mon–Wed, Fri & Sat 10am–5pm, Thurs 10am–9pm, Sun noon–5pm; $4, $6 combination ticket with Center for Fine Arts) provides a comprehensive peek into the region's history, with a particularly strong section on the Seminole. A few yards away, the **Center for Fine Arts** (Tues, Wed & Fri 10am–5pm, Thurs 10am–9pm, Sat & Sun noon–5pm; $5, $6 combination ticket with Historical Museum) showcases outstanding international traveling exhibits, the best of them Latin American.

The 1980s saw the destruction of the decaying buildings beside **Biscayne Boulevard** (part of Hwy-1), on the eastern edge of downtown, to make way for the **Bayside Marketplace**, a large pink shopping mall enlivened by buskers and food stands (and the main water taxi stop; see p.542). Across Biscayne Boulevard, the **Freedom Tower**, built in 1925 and modeled on a Spanish bell tower, earned its name by housing the Cuban Refugee Center in the 1960s. Between December 1965 and June 1972, ten planes a week brought over 250,000 Cubans allowed to leave the island by Fidel Castro. While US propaganda hailed them as "freedom fighters," most of the arrivals were simply seeking the fruits of capitalism, and, as Castro astutely recognized, any that were seriously committed to overthrowing his regime would be far less troublesome outside Cuba.

Fifteen minutes' walk from Flagler Street, the **Miami River** marks the southern limit of downtown. Around 1900, the millionaire oil baron Henry Flagler extended his railroad, which had opened up Florida's east coast, to reach Miami from Palm Beach. His *Royal Palm Hotel* (on the site of today's *Hotel Inter-Continental*) did much to put Miami on the map. One of the landowners was William Brickell, who ran a trading post on the south side of the river, an area now dominated by **Brickell Avenue** – *the* address in 1910s Miami. While the original grand homes have largely disappeared, money is still the avenue's most obvious asset: its half-mile parade of **bank buildings** is the largest grouping of international banks in the US. The rise of the banks was matched by new condominiums of breathtaking proportions (and expense) but little architectural merit.

## Little Havana

The impact of **Cubans** on Miami, unquestionably the largest and most visible ethnic group in the city, has been incalculable. Unlike most Hispanic immigrants to the US, who trade one form of poverty for another, Miami's first Cubans had already tasted the good life when they arrived during the late Fifties and were soon enjoying more of the same here. Some now wield considerable clout in the running of the city.

The initial home of the Miami Cubans was a few miles west of downtown in what became **LITTLE HAVANA**, whose streets, if the tourist brochures are to be believed, are filled by old men playing dominoes while puffing on fat, fragrant cigars, and exotic restaurants whose walls vibrate to the pulsating rhythms of the homeland. Naturally, the reality is quite different: Little Havana's parks, memorials, shops and food stands all reflect the Cuban experience but the streets are quieter than those of downtown Miami (except during the Little Havana Festival in early March). Make a beeline here for lunch, by all means, but don't expect a lot to do or see.

Between 12th and 13th avenues, the simple stone **Brigade 2506 Memorial** remembers those who died at the Bay of Pigs on April 17, 1961, during the abortive invasion of Cuba by US-trained Cuban exiles. Veterans of the landing, middle-aged men dressed in combat fatigues, gather here for each anniversary making all-night-long pledges of patriotism.

---

### CUBANS IN MIAMI

During the mid-Fifties, when opposition to Cuba's Batista dictatorship began to assert itself, a trickle of Cubans started arriving in a predominantly Jewish section of Miami called Riverside. The trickle became a flood when Fidel Castro took power in 1959, and the area became Little Havana, populated by the affluent Cuban middle classes who had most to lose under Communism. The second great Cuban influx into Miami, the **Mariel boatlift** bringing 125,000 islanders from the Cuban port of Mariel to Miami in May 1980, was quite different. These arrivals were poor and uneducated, and a fifth of them were fresh from Cuban jails – incarcerated for criminal rather than political crimes. Bluntly, Castro had dumped his misfits on Miami.

Many Miami Cubans still see themselves as exiles – though few would seriously think about returning, whatever regime governed Cuba. Within the complexities of **exile politics**, passions run high. In Miami, Cubans have been killed for being *suspected* of advocating dialogue with Castro, and the **Museum of Cuban Arts and Culture**, at 1300 SW 12th St (by appointment only on ☎305/858-8006), was bombed in 1989 for displaying the work of Castro-approved artists. When the Cuban-exile leadership is eventually able to return to Cuba, one might even see the feuding escalate if a post-Castro power struggle ensues.

# Coral Gables

All of Miami's constituent cities are fast to assert their individuality, but none has a greater case than **CORAL GABLES**, south of Little Havana. Twelve square miles of broad boulevards, leafy side streets and Spanish and Italian architecture form a cultured setting for a cultured community. Coral Gables' creator was a local aesthete, **George Merrick**, who raided street names from a Spanish dictionary to plan the plazas, fountains and carefully aged stucco-fronted buildings. Following the first land sale in 1921, $150 million poured in, which Merrick channeled into the biggest advertising campaign ever known. However, Coral Gables took shape just as the Florida property boom ended. Merrick was wiped out, and died as Miami's postmaster in 1942. Coral Gables never lost its good looks, though, and remains an impressive place to explore. Merrick wanted people to know they'd arrived somewhere special, and eight grand **entrances** were planned on the main approach roads (though only four were completed).

The best way into Coral Gables is along NW 22nd Street. Once across Douglas Road, this becomes the **Miracle Mile** (in fact only half a mile). Dominated by department stores, travel agents, and a staggering number of bridal shops, it gets more and more expensive and exclusive as you proceed west – note the arcades and balconies, and the spirals and peaks of the **Colonnade Building**, nos. 133–169, completed in 1926 to accommodate George Merrick's office. Further west, along Coral Way, the **Merrick House**, no. 907 (Sun & Wed 1–4pm; $2), was George's boyhood home. In 1899, when he was twelve, his family arrived here from New England to run a 160-acre farm, which was so successful that the house quickly grew from a wooden shack into an elegant dwelling of coral rock and gabled windows (thus inspiring the name of the future city).

While his property-developing contemporaries left ugly scars across the city after digging up the local limestone, Merrick had the foresight to turn his biggest quarry into a sumptuous swimming pool. The **Venetian Pool**, 2701 De Soto Blvd, opened in 1924, is today an essential stop on a steamy Miami afternoon. Its pastel stucco walls hide a fabulous spring-fed lagoon, with vine-covered loggias, fountains, waterfalls, coral caves and plenty of room to swim. The cafe isn't bad, either (hours vary; call ☎305/460-5356; $5).

Wrapping its broad wings around the southern end of De Soto Boulevard, Merrick's crowning achievement was the fabulous **Biltmore Hotel**, 1200 Anastasia Ave. With a 26-story tower visible across much of low-lying Miami, everything about the *Biltmore* was over-the-top: 25ft fresco-coated walls, vaulted ceilings, immense fireplaces, custom-loomed rugs, and a massive swimming pool hosting shows by such bathing belles and beaux as Esther Williams and Johnny Weissmuller. Today, it costs upwards of $200 a night to stay here, but a fascinating free tour leaves from the lobby every Sunday (1.30pm, 2.30pm & 3.30pm). A short way south at 130 Stanford Ave is the **University of Miami**, site of the **Lowe Art Museum** (Tues–Sat 10am–5pm, Thurs noon–7pm, Sun noon–5pm; $5), whose diverse permanent collection ranges from European Old Masters to Native American artifacts and Guatemalan textiles.

# Coconut Grove

**COCONUT GROVE** has come a long way since the 1960s, when it was peopled by down-at-heel artists and writers: these days, it is closely following in the heels of South Beach as the trendiest Miami hotspot, with a glittering cluster of art galleries, fashionable cafes and restaurants and towering bay-view apartments.

There's more to "the Grove" than people-watching, however. A century ago, a strange mix of Bahamian salvagers and New England intellectuals laid the foundations of a fiercely individual community, separated from the fledgling city of Miami by a dense wedge of tropical foliage. In 1914, farm machinery mogul James Deering blew $15 million on re-creating a sixteenth-century Italian villa within this jungle. A thousand-strong workforce completed his **Villa Vizcaya**, 3251 S Miami Ave (daily 9.30am–5pm; $10), in just two years. Deering's madly eclectic art collection, and his concept that the villa should appear to have been inhabited for four hundred years, result in a thunderous clash of Baroque, Renaissance, Rococo and Neoclassical fixtures and fittings; the fabulous landscaped **gardens**, with their fountains and sculptures, are just as excessive. Frequent **guided tours** (45min) leave from the entrance loggia and provide solid background, after which you're free to explore at leisure.

Blatant statements of wealth predominate as you approach central Coconut Grove. The marina on **Dinner Key** sports lines of million-dollar yachts, and the neighboring **Coconut Grove Exhibition Center** is usually consumed by top-of-the-range trade shows. It was at the Dinner Key Auditorium (a forerunner of the Exhibition Center) in 1969 that **Jim Morrison**, singer with the Doors, dropped his leather trousers during the band's first – and last – Florida show, bringing the band more infamy than they knew what to do with.

South along the coast, the 83-acre **Fairchild Tropical Garden**, at 10901 Old Cutler Rd (daily 9.30am–4.30pm; guided tours hourly 10am–4pm; $8), is the largest tropical botanical garden in the continental US. The entire range of tropical environments has been reproduced, and there's a good section on native south Floridian areas.

# Eating

**Cuban** food is what Miami does best, and it's not limited to the traditional haunts in **Little Havana** – the hearty, comfort food, notably rice and beans, fried plantains and shredded pork sandwiches, is found in every neighborhood. It is, however, complemented by sushi bars, American home-style diners, Haitian restaurants, Italian eateries and Indian venues, among a handful of other ethnic cuisines. **Coral Gables** stakes its claim in upmarket cafes and ethnic Italian and Greek restaurants, while **Coconut Grove** features American, Spanish, New Floridian – a mix of Caribbean spiciness and fruity Florida sauces – and even British. **Seafood** is equally abundant; succulent grouper, yellowfin tuna and wahoo, a local delicacy, are among five hundred species of fish thriving offshore. **Stone crab claws**, served from October to May, are another regional specialty. A tropical climate provides Florida with a juicy assortment of standard orange and grapefruit citrus, as well as the exotic flavors of the **lychee, mango, papaya, tamarind** and **star fruits** – many of which are used in sauces and *batidos* (light milkshakes). You'll also want to drink Cuban **coffee**: choose between *cafe cubano*, strong, sweet and frothy, drunk like a shot with a glass of water; *cafe con leche*, with steamed milk, and particularly good at breakfast with *pan cubano* (thin, buttered toast); or *cafe cortadito*, a smaller version of the *con leche*.

**Ayestaran**, 706 SW 27th Ave, Little Havana (☎305/649-4982). Sprawling Cuban restaurant, with hearty daily specials and superb *cafe con leche* that you can mix to your liking.

**Big Fish Mayaimi**, 55 SW Miami Ave, downtown (☎305/373-1770). Lively spot on the Miami River, with great fish dishes and a splendid view. Menu includes home-cooked fish sandwiches and fresh seafood chowder. Closed Sun; lunch only June–Nov.

**Big Pink**, 157 Collins Ave, South Beach (☎305/531-0888). Big portions of comfort food like mashed potatoes, ribs, macaroni and cheese, and classic "TV dinners" at 1950s prices.

**Café Tu Tu Tango**, inside CocoWalk, 3015 Grand Ave, Coconut Grove (☎305/529-2222). Quirky and entertaining spot with an artist's garret theme and quick service; good-quality and inexpensive food is served in tapas-sized portions. Try the Cajun chicken eggrolls and oriental beef skewers.

**da Leo Trattoria**, 819 Lincoln Rd, South Beach (☎305/674-0350). Friendly waitstaff, prime outdoor seating and authentic Italian fare at budget prices. Go for the beef carpaccio or veal marsala.

**Fishbone Grille**, 650 S Miami Ave, downtown (☎305/530-1915). Busy, friendly restaurant serving excellent seafood with creative starters like shrimp potato fritters and smoked fish mousse.

**Joe's Stone Crab**, 227 Biscayne St, South Beach (☎305/673-0365). Legendary restaurant, always packed for its superb stone crabs (mid-Oct to mid-May only), mustard dip, hash browns and creamed spinach. Try also the crabcakes, fresh fish and crispy fried chicken.

**Larios on the Beach**, 820 Ocean Drive, South Beach (☎305/532-9577). Better known for being owned by singer Gloria Estefan rather than for its sophisticated – and surprisingly affordable – "Nuevo Cubano" food served in a Latin nightclub atmosphere.

**News Cafe**, 800 Ocean Drive, Miami Beach (☎305/538-6397). Established, fashionable sidewalk cafe with front-row seating for the South Beach promenade. Open 24hr at weekends.

**NOA**, 801 Lincoln Rd, South Beach (☎305/925-0050). Beautiful people slurp noodle dishes served by an equally beautiful waitstaff at this Lincoln Rd newcomer; good exotic drinks, too.

**Puerto Sagua**, 700 Collins Ave, South Beach (☎305/673-1115). Cuban diner serving great, rich black bean soup and other filling meals.

**San Loco**, 235 14th St, South Beach (☎305/538-3009). Consistently rated the top spot in Miami Beach for Mexican food, their tacos are sloppy, filling and cheap.

**South Pointe Seafood House**, South Pointe Park, South Beach (☎305/673-1708). Rambling, weathered wooden restaurant with ocean views, flotsam/jetsam decor and superb reggae soundtrack. The copious Sun lunch buffet is a hit with locals, but the Caribbean entrees – paella, fresh catch, shrimp and the like – are better. They also brew their own beer.

**Tap Tap**, 819 5th St, South Beach (☎305/372-2898). Haitian food at its tastiest and most attractive in one of the best-looking restaurants in Miami Beach, hung with local art.

**Versailles**, 3555 SW 8th St, Little Havana (☎305/444-0240). A legend in Little Havana, with very little English spoken. Local families, Cuban businessmen and backpackers congregate here for the wonderfully inexpensive Cuban dishes, served by one of the friendliest waitstaffs in Miami.

**Yambo**, 1643 SW 1st St, Little Havana (☎305/642-6616). Good, inexpensive Nicaraguan food with outdoor seating and a copious buffet.

**Yuca**, 501 Lincoln Rd, South Beach (☎305/532-9822). Nuevo Cubano cooking at its best – and most expensive. Expect to pay at least $50 a head. Latin music at weekends.

# Drinking, nightlife and entertainment

Miami's nightlife is unsurpassed. **Drinking** tends to take second place to eating and partying, but a number of friendly local bars double as very good **live music** venues. **Reggae** is particularly strong; Miami has a sizeable Jamaican population, and there are regular appearances by local as well as flown-in acts. Miami's **clubs** – especially those specializing in salsa or merengue, and hosted by Spanish-speaking DJs – are among the hippest in the world, with most of the action at South Beach. Door policies are notoriously obnoxious at current in-spots; the places listed below are less about attitude and more about having a good time.

Friday's *Miami Herald* carries full weekend entertainment **listings**; the free weekly *New Times* has reliable information on cafes and clubs, while the free *TWN* (*The Weekly News*) is the key source of **gay and lesbian info**.

If you want to try out the local **sports** scene, the **Marlins** pro **baseball** team, who scored an extraordinary coup by winning the World Series in 1997 in only their fourth season, and the Dolphins, the state's only professional **football** team, play at the **Joe Robbie Stadium**, sixteen miles northwest of downtown on NW 199th St (box office Mon–Fri 10am–6pm; ☎305/620-2578).

## Bars and live music

**The Abbey Brewing Company**, 1115 16th St, South Beach (☎305/538-8110). A small yet homey spot that's South Beach's only microbrewery (try the creamy Oatmeal Stout – their best and most popular brew). Happy hour Mon–Fri 1–7pm.

**Churchill's Hideaway**, 5501 NE 2nd Ave (☎305/757-1807). A British enclave within Little Haiti with soccer and rugby matches on video and UK beers on tap.

**Clevelander**, 1020 Ocean Drive, South Beach (☎305/531-3485). Ultimate poolside sports bar, with pool tables, sports-tuned TVs and partially-clothed, well-oiled physiques attacking the brews.

**Hungry Sailor**, 3426 Main Hwy, Coconut Grove (☎305/444-9359). Unpretentious, male-dominated bar with a nautical theme and occasional live reggae.

**Lost Weekend**, 218 Espanola Way, South Beach (☎305/672-1707). Great happy hour and ladies night drink specials, with plenty of pool tables and a preppy clientele.

**Mac's Club Deuce**, 222 14th St, South Beach (☎305/673-9537). Down and dirty, no-frills bar always filled with a motley crew of local characters, cops, drag queens, models and the occasional movie star.

**Rose's**, 754 Washington Ave, South Beach (☎305/532-0228). Laid-back neighborhood bar, with great live music, DJs and pool tournaments.

**Tobacco Road**, 626 S Miami Ave, downtown (☎305/374-1198). Friendly bar – Miami's oldest – and a favorite with locals for its exceptional live blues, jazz and R&B.

**Zeke's Roadhouse**, 625 Lincoln Rd, South Beach (☎305/532-0087). Popular hangout for good, cheap beers – nightly specials start at $2.50 each.

## Clubs

**Bash**, 655 Washington Ave, South Beach (☎305/538-2274). Co-owned by Sean Penn and Mick Hucknall. Intimate bar and beckoning dance floor, though many revelers get no further than the garden. High cover on Fri & Sat.

**Club Tropigala**, *Fontainebleu Hotel*, 4441 Collins Ave, South Beach (☎305/538-2000). Superb, very popular Latin supper club featuring live acts and an orchestra. Fabulously camp decor and a friendly, varied crowd. Dress up to the nines and salsa the night away. Wed–Sun; $15.

**821**, 821 Lincoln Rd, South Beach (☎305/534-0887). Refreshingly friendly, very chatty crowd in this mostly gay club where everyone dances to anything from cabaret to Eurobeat.

**Liquid**, 1437–9 Washington Ave, South Beach (☎305/532-9154). Local club gal, Ingrid Cassares, has the hottest nightspot on the Beach. Long, long lines behind the notorious velvet rope, where Hollywood "In" stars groove next to rock stars and local clubbers. Monday is the outrageous "Fat Black Pussycat Club" night where entrance is through the side door only.

**Living Room**, 671 Washington Ave, South Beach (☎305/532-2340) A wannabe model hangout with cushy couches you have to pay money to sit in. Small dance floor packs them in when they're not posing at the boomerang-shaped bar.

**Warsaw Ballroom**, 1450 Collins Ave, South Beach (☎305/531-4555). While not exclusively gay, this is the busiest, biggest and brashest gay disco in town.

# THE FLORIDA KEYS

Fiction, films and folklore have given the **FLORIDA KEYS** – a hundred-mile chain of islands that runs to within ninety miles of Cuba – an image of glamorous intrigue they don't really deserve. Instead, this is an outdoor-lover's paradise, where fishing, snorkeling and diving dominate. Terrific untainted natural areas include the **Florida Reef**, a great band of living coral just a few miles off the coast. But for many, the various keys are only stops on the way to fascinating **Key West**. Once the richest town in the US, and the final dot of North America before a thousand miles of ocean, its lush, Caribbean-style streets hold plenty of congenial bars in which to waste away the hours, watching the famous spectacular **sunsets**.

Wherever you are on the Keys, you'll experience its distinctive **cuisine**, served for the most part in funky little shacks where the food is fresh and the atmosphere laid-back. Conch, a rich meaty mollusc, is a specialty, served in chowders and fritters. And as for the Key Lime Pie, the delicate, creamy concoction of limes and condensed milk bears little resemblance here to the lurid green imposters served in the rest of the country.

Traveling through the Keys could hardly be easier. There's just one route all the way through to Key West: the **Overseas Highway (US-1)**. The road is punctuated by **mile markers (MM)** – starting with MM127 just south of Miami and finishing with MM0 in Key West.

# Key Largo

The first and largest of the keys, **Key Largo** boasts a fine opportunity to visit the Florida Reef, at the **John Pennecamp Coral Reef State Park** at MM102.5 (daily 8am–dusk; $3.75 per car, plus 50¢ per passenger). This protected 78-square-mile section of living coral reef is rated as one of the most beautiful in the world. If you can, take the **snorkeling tour** (9am, noon & 3pm; $23.95), or the **guided scuba dive** (9.30am & 1.30pm; $37); the **glass-bottomed boat tour** (9.15am, 12.15pm & 3pm; $15) is less demanding.

Even from the glass-bottomed boat, you're virtually certain to spot lobsters, angelfish, eels and jellyfish along the reef, and shoals of silvery minnows stalked by angry-faced barracudas. The reef itself is a delicate living thing, composed of millions of minute coral polyps extracting calcium from the seawater and growing from one to sixteen feet every thousand years. Sadly, it's far easier to spot signs of death than life: white patches show where a carelessly dropped anchor, or diver's hand, has scraped away the protective mucous layer and left the coral susceptible to terminal disease.

### Key Largo and Tavernier

South of the park, the people of Rock Harbor recognized a good thing when they saw one and changed the name of their community to **KEY LARGO** after the success of the 1948 film in which Humphrey Bogart and Lauren Bacall grappled with Florida's best-known features – crime and hurricanes. Yet the movie's title was chosen for no other reason than it suggested somewhere exotic, and the film, though set here, was almost entirely shot in Hollywood. Nonetheless, Key Largo, and its neighbor **TAVERNIER**, ten miles further on, make nice enough stops on the Upper Keys, where you can almost feel urban stresses and strains slip away as the glimpses of the jewel-like turquoise sea and palms become more and more regular.

The **Florida Keys visitor center**, MM106 (daily 9am–6pm; ☎1-800/822-1088), has information on local accommodation, diving and attractions. Most **motels** offer diving packages: try *Ed & Ellen's Efficiencies*, 103365 Overseas Hwy (☎305/451-4712; ②–⑤), which has a two-night minimum; the beach cottages at the *Sea Farer*, MM97.8 (☎305/852-5349; ③–⑤); or the *Kona Kai Resort*, MM98 (☎305/852-7200; ⑤), with huge chalets and its own hotel art gallery. For fresh seafood, try *Ballyhoo's*, MM98 opposite the *Sea Farer Hotel*, Key Largo (☎305/852-0822), the *Fish House*, MM102.4 (☎305/451-4665), and the tiny *Crack'd Conch*, MM105 (☎305/451-0732).

# Islamorada

At **ISLAMORADA**, some five miles south of Tavernier on Upper Matecumbe Key, the **Theater of the Sea**, MM84.5 (daily 9.30am–6pm; $14.25; ☎305/664-2431) offers sea shows, bottomless boats, snorkel tours and swim-with-the-dolphin programs ($80; call to reserve). There's good hiking at **Long Key State Recreation Area**, MM68, a 965-acre expanse of tropical foliage and mangroves which also has one of the best beaches on the Keys (daily 8am–dusk; $3.25 per car plus 75¢ per passenger), and excellent deep-sea fishing.

Good-value **accommodation** includes the prettily landscaped *Chesapeake Bay Resort*, MM83.5 (☎305/664-4662; ⑥), with two pools, a lagoon and water sports; and the serene, oceanside *Drop Anchor* motel at MM85 (☎305/664-4863 or 1-888/664-4863; ③). For a more raucous atmosphere, try the *Holiday Isle Beach Resort*, MM84 (☎1-800/327-7070; ④–⑥), where the multilevel tiki bar provides wild nightly entertainment. As for eating, *Lazy Days*, MM79.9 (☎305/664-5256), does fabulous things with fresh fish and *Whale Harbor*, MM84 (☎305/664-4959), serves up massive nightly seafood buffets for a flat $19.95. But for a change from Keys cuisine (though they do make a delectable Key Lime Pie), try *Manny and Isa's*, MM81.6 (☎305/664-5019), a simple Cuban diner where superb Spanish food comes with copious strong, sweet sangria.

## The Middle Keys

Once over Long Key Bridge, you're into the **Middle Keys**. At the nonprofit **Dolphin Research Center**, on Grassy Key at MM59 (daily 9am–4pm; $9.50; ☎305/289-0002), you can swim with the dolphins for $90 a go (but reservations can be made only on the first day of the month, so plan ahead).

The largest of several islands, **Key Vaca** holds the nucleus of the area's major settlement, **MARATHON**. Here you'll find a couple of small beaches – rare in the Keys – and great **fishing** and **water sports**. Sombrero Beach, along Sombrero Beach Road (off the Overseas Highway near MM50), has good swimming waters and shaded picnic tables; Key Colony Beach four miles north is prettier and quieter.

An excellent introduction to the history and ecology of the Keys is presented at the **Museum of Natural History of the Florida Keys** at MM50.5 (Mon–Sat 9am–5pm, Sun noon–5pm; $7.50). Take time to follow the quarter-mile **nature trail** by the museum, as it passes through "hammock" forest, an area of dense hardwood trees characteristic of the Keys. At the end of the trail are the reconstructed remnants of a village established by settlers from the Bahamas in the nineteenth century.

Marathon has several well-equipped **resorts**, such as the lush, luxurious *Banana Bay*, MM49.5 (☎305/743-3500; ⑤–⑧), and indulgent *Cheeca Lodge*, MM82 (☎305/664-4651 or 1-800/327-2888; ⑤ñ⑧), as well as a good supply of cheaper **motels**, including the simple *Sea Cove*, MM54 (☎305/289-0800; ②–④), which has houseboat rooms. For eating, *Herbie's*, MM50.5 (☎305/743-6373), is justly busy on account of its inexpensive seafood, chowder and fritters, while the tiny, laid-back *Seven-Mile Grill*, by the bridge of the same name, serves delicious conch and creamy Key Lime Pie to a crowd of locals, seasalts and tourists (closed Wed & Thurs; ☎305/743-4481). *The Quay*, MM54 (☎305/289-1810), has good fish sandwiches for around $5 in a waterfront tiki bar behind the pricey main restaurant, and *Porky's*, MM47.5 (☎305/289-2065), offers cheap, traditional barbecue dishes and burgers, along with conch fritters and other local seafood specialties. They also have free sunset cruises whether you eat there or not.

## The Lower Keys

Starkly different to their northerly neighbors, the **Lower Keys** are quiet, heavily wooded and predominantly residential. Built on a limestone rather than a coral base, these islands have a flora and fauna all their own. It feels very quiet as you head south: everyone's gone fishing or is snoozing in a hammock.

The first place of consequence you'll hit after crossing Seven Mile Bridge is **Bahia Honda State Recreation Area** at MM37 (daily 8am–dusk; cars $5, pedestrians and cyclists $1), one of the Keys' prettiest spots. Its lagoon has a beckoning natural **beach** and pristine, two-tone ocean waters, which can be enjoyed on a leisurely kayak ride ($20 per hour). Divers should head for the **Looe Key Marine Sanctuary**, signposted from the Overseas Highway on Ramrod Key – a five-square-mile protected reef area, easily the equal of the John Pennecamp Coral Reef State Park (see p.552). The **sanc-**

**tuary office** (Mon–Fri 8am–5pm; ☎305/872-4039) can provide free maps, but to visit the reef you'll need the services of a dive shop, like the neighboring Looe Key Dive Center (☎1-800/942-5397).

In the main Lower Keys settlement, **BIG PINE KEY**, the **visitor center** is at MM31 (Mon–Fri 9am–5pm, Sat 9am–3pm; ☎305/872-2411). Of the nearby **motels**, *Looe Key Reef Resort*, MM27.5 (☎305/872-2215; ⑤), is a favorite with divers, an ideal base for visiting the marine sanctuary. There are also a couple of luxurious, secluded **B&Bs** along Long Beach Drive, off the Overseas Highway; you'll need to book ahead. Try *Deer Run*, MM32.5 (☎305/872-2015; ⑤), or *Barnacle*, MM32.5 (☎305/872-3298; ⑥). Exceptionally friendly, even for the Keys, *Mangrove Mama's*, MM20 on Sugarloaf Key (☎305/745-3030), serves stupendous local **cuisine** in a cheery shack with a tropical garden.

# Key West

Much closer to Cuba than to mainland Florida, **KEY WEST** often seems pretty tenuously bound to the rest of the US. Famed for their tolerant attitudes and laid-back lifestyles, the thirty thousand islanders seem adrift in a great expanse of sea and sky, and – despite a million tourists per year – the place resonates with an individual spirit that hits you the instant you arrive. In particular, its liberal attitudes have stimulated a large **gay** influx. Yet as wild as it may at first appear, Key West today is far from being the dropouts' mecca of a mere decade ago. Much of the sleaziness has been brushed away through a steady process of restoration, setting the course for the advent of a sizeable holiday industry. Even so, the sense of isolation from the mainland is best appreciated by adjusting to the mellow pace: amble the gorgeous, lushly vegetated streets, make meals last for hours, and pause regularly for refreshment in the numerous bars.

## Arrival, information and getting around

The **airport** (☎305/296-5439) is four miles east of town – a taxi costs $10. The **Greyhound** station is in the heart of the Old Town at 615 1/2 Duval St; confusingly, its entrance is on Simonton Street, a block east.

Both the **Welcome Center**, 3840 N Roosevelt Blvd (daily 9am–5pm; ☎305/296-4444), and the **Key West Chamber of Commerce**, Mallory Square, 402 Wall St (daily 8.30am–5pm; ☎305/294-2587), can give precise dates for Key West's annual festivals, the best being the Old Island Days (Jan–April) celebrating Key West's history; the Conch Republic Celebration in April; and the Fantasy Fest in late October, a gay-dominated version of Mardi Gras. The **Key West Business Guild**, 424 Fleming St (☎305/294-4603), is a good source of gay information.

It's best to explore the narrow streets of the mile-square Old Town – which contains virtually everything that you'll want to see – on foot. You could do it in little more than a day, though dashing about isn't the way to enjoy the place. The excellent *Sharon Wells' Walking and Biking Guide*, free in local restaurants and bars, details a number of self-guided routes through the Old Town, and lists Wells' own regular **walking tours**. **Bikes** ($10 or so per day) and **mopeds** ($15–25) can be rented from The Bike Shop, 1110 Truman Ave (Mon–Sat 9am–5.30pm, Sun 10am–5.30pm; ☎305/294-1073). For a (bright pink) **taxi**, call ☎305/296-6666.

## Accommodation

It's essential to make a **reservation** in Key West during winter; call the place directly as early as possible. In summer, competition for rooms is less fierce, and prices drop by almost fifty percent.

KEY WEST/555

**Alexander Palms Court**, 715 South St (☎305/296-6413). Gorgeous, serene small hotel with comfortable cottages ranged around a lush, fairy-lit courtyard and pool. ④–⑧.

**Angelina Guest House**, 302 Angela St (☎305/294-4480). Simple, well-priced regular rooms; spending a little more brings you kitchenettes and suites, good value for four people sharing. Rates include continental breakfast. ②–⑥.

**Bananas Foster**, 537 Caroline St (☎305/294-9061 or 1-800/653-4888). A charming, centrally located B&B with beautifully decorated rooms, delicious breakfasts, a heated spa pool and the friendliest staff in the Keys. ⑤/⑥.

**Blue Parrot Inn**, 916 Elizabeth St (☎305/296-0033). Dating from 1884, with comfortable, nicely furnished rooms, a heated pool, continental breakfast, and a "clothing optional" area. ④–⑥.

**Eden House**, 1015 Fleming St (☎305/296-6868). One of Key West's most relaxing hideaways. Peaceful rooms surround the pool and numerous giant hammocks are surrounded by lush gardens and a fish-filled pool. The cheaper rooms have shared bath; the priciest have jacuzzis. ③–⑦.

**Marrero's Guest Mansion**, 410 Fleming St (☎305/294-6977 or 1-800/459-6212). A well-known haunted guesthouse whose former owner, the late Mrs Marrero, rates guests' character by swaying the chandelier in the foyer. Outdoor hot tub and pool. ④/⑤.

**Rainbow House**, 525 United St (☎305/292-1450). Women-only accommodation with good rooms, pool, jacuzzi and continental breakfast. ④–⑦.

**Red Rooster**, 709 Truman Ave (☎305/296-6558). Friendly, comfortable, gay-oriented B&B with a good cappuccino bar and pretty garden. ④–⑦.

**Seashell Motel**, 718 South St (☎305/296-5719). If the adjoining youth hostel is full or doesn't appeal, this offers standard motel rooms at the lowest rates in the neighborhood. ①–④.

**Tropical Inn**, 812 Duval St (☎305/294-9977). Large, airy rooms in a charming restored "conch" house at the center of the action. Most of the rooms sleep three, and the more expensive ones have balconies. Ask about the neighboring cottages with hot tubs and kitchens. ③/④.

**Wicker Guesthouse**, 913 Duval St (☎305/296-4275). Very good value, simple rooms; though can be noisy at the front. Prices increase the further you get from the road. Huge garden, pool, kitchen facilities and complimentary continental breakfast. ③–⑥.

## Around the Old Town

Anyone who saw Key West two decades ago would now barely recognize the Old Town's main promenade, the mile-long swath of **Duval Street**. Teetering just on the safe side of seedy for many years, much of the street has been transformed into a tacky tourist strip of boutiques and beachwear shops. Best to foray into the side streets, where gnarled banyans, tall skinny palms, creepers and unruly exotic blooms threaten to overtake the faded wooden houses, many of them decked out in individualistic junkyard style. Make sure to get to the **Bahamian Quarter**, centering on Thomas and Petronia streets. Originally settled by Cubans and African-Bahamians, this unrestored, untouristed corner of town is an atmospheric patchwork of single-story cigar-makers' cottages, Cuban groceries and ramshackle old churches, all covered by a rich green foliage.

Numerous museums in town concern themselves with "wrecking": the salvaging of cargo from the many vessels that foundered on these treacherous shores, and the industry on which Key West's earliest good times were based. The friendly little **Wrecker's Museum**, 322 Duval St (daily 10am–4pm; $4), does a good job of illuminating the lives of the wreckers, portraying them as brave, uninsured heroes who risked all to save cargoes, ships and lives. Judging by the choice furniture that fills the house – the oldest in town – owned by Captain Watlington, the wrecker who lived here from the 1830s, they did pretty well for their pains.

Further up, at 516 Duval St, the **San Carlos Institute** (Tues–Fri 11am–5pm, Sat 11am–9pm, Sun 11am–6pm; $3) has played a leading role in Cuban exile life since it opened in 1871. Financed by a grant from the Cuban government, the present building dates from 1924 and holds a commendable account of the Cuban presence in Key West and throughout the US. Across its grounds are spread soil from Cuba's six provinces, and there is a cornerstone taken from the tomb of Cuban independence campaigner José Martí.

As you approach the southern end of Duval Street, everything, whether house, motel, gas station or restaurant, advertises itself as "the Southernmost . . ." Accurately, the **southernmost point** in Key West, and consequently in the continental US, is at the intersection of Whitehead and South streets; a daft-looking buoy marks the spot.

In the early 1800s, thousands of dollars' worth of salvage was landed at the piers, stored in the warehouses, and flogged at the auction houses on **Mallory Square**, just west of the northern end of Duval Street. By day, the square is a plain souvenir market, with overpriced ice cream, trinkets and T-shirts; at night there's an eminently missable tourist-oriented **sunset celebration**, when buskers and fire-eaters do their stuff for the crowds as the sun sets. At the adjacent **Key West Aquarium**, 1 Whitehead St (daily 10am–6pm; $8), porcupine fish and longspine squirrel fish leer out from behind glass, and small sharks are known to jump out of their open tanks during the somewhat boring **guided tours** (roughly every 2hr).

In **Mel Fisher's Treasure Exhibit**, 200 Greene St (daily 9.30am–5.30pm; $6.50), diamonds and pearls, countless vases and daggers, and an impressive emerald cross are displayed alongside the obligatory cannon, pulled up from two seventeenth-century wrecks. Fisher was running a surf shop in California before he arrived in Florida armed with ancient Spanish sea charts and, in 1985, discovered the *Nuestra Señora de Atocha* and *Santa Margarita*; both sunk during a hurricane in 1622, forty miles southeast of Key West. It's a romantic story, and a flabbergasting haul, said to be worth millions of dollars; if you're not satisfied with simply lifting a gold bar (chained to the wall, naturally), and fancy some for yourself, the giftshop sells coins and relics for $100,000 apiece.

For all the atmosphere of the streets and alleys, Key West's most popular tourist attraction is the **Hemingway House**, at 907 Whitehead St (daily 9am–5pm; $7.50). The compulsory half-hour **guided tours** deal, sadly, more in fantasy than fact: although Ernest Hemingway owned this large, vaguely Moorish house for thirty years, he lived in it for barely ten, and even the authenticity of the furnishings is disputed by his former secretary. Hemingway bought the house in 1931, when it was seriously run-down, and some of the writer's most acclaimed novels, such as *For Whom the Bell Tolls* and *To Have and Have Not*, were produced in the study (in the hayloft of a carriage house which Hemingway entered by way of a rope bridge). Divorced in 1940, Hemingway boxed up his manuscripts and moved them to a back room at the original *Sloppy Joe's* (see opposite) before heading off for a house in Cuba with his new wife, journalist Martha Gellhorn. Today some fifty cats pad contentedly around the gardens, all of them descendants of Hemingway's own; look out for those with six toes, traditionally used as ship mascots.

## Eating

In Key West, it's *de rigueur* to sample **conch fritters**; the stand at Duval and Fleming does the best in town for under two dollars. Also, don't leave without tasting **Cuban food**, as there are several excellent restaurants in town – for the best **cafe con leche** this side of Miami, try the *M&M* laundromat at Virginia and White.

**BO's Fish Wagon**, 801 Caroline St (☎305/294-9272). The over-the-counter fish'n'chips and legendary conch fritters are some of the cheapest in town.

**Blue Heaven**, 729 Thomas at Petronia, in the Bahamian Quarter (☎305/296-8666). Excellent bar and restaurant in a colorful shack where rooster chicks peck at your feet as you eat fresh fish, jerk chicken and fabulous fruit-packed breakfasts.

**Cafe des Artistes**, 1007 Simonton St (☎305/294-7100). Upscale and rather more elegant than other places, but the exquisite French-Caribbean cuisine makes it well worth a splurge. The upstairs deck is more casual, with simpler, cheaper food.

**Camille's**, 703 Duval St (☎305/296-4811). Great breakfasts and brunches; the latter might be something like shrimp cakes, blueberry pancakes or French toast with mango coconut cream sauce for $6.

**Dim-Sum**, 613 Duval St (☎305/294-6230). Serene Pan-Asian restaurant in a quiet alley off Duval, with Thai, Indonesian and Burmese specialties; reckon on spending at least $20.

**El Siboney**, 900 Catherine St (☎305/296-4184). No-frills family diner serving inexpensive traditional Cuban dishes and good daily specials. Closes 9pm.

**Half Shell Raw Bar**, Land's End Marina, at the Gulf end of Margaret St (☎305/294-7496). Dockside restaurant in an old fish market, where locals flock to eat conch fritters, smoked fish, beer-steamed shrimp and fresh catch on the breezy wooden deck.

**Island Wellness**, 530 Simonton St (☎305/296-7353). Health food store with sumptuous veggie specials including burritos and smoothies.

**Kelly's**, 303 Whitehead St (☎305/293-8484). Actress Kelly McGillis of *Top Gun* fame owns this excellent and reasonably priced restaurant featuring gourmet Floridian cuisine, an on-site microbrewery and the best Key Lime Pie in Key West – prepared with a dense crushed-Oreo base.

**Louie's Backyard**, 700 Waddell Ave (☎305/294-1061). Very popular, laid-back oceanfront restaurant, serving typical Key West cuisine. The outside deck is the place to be; Sun brunch is especially good.

**Mo's**, 1116 White St (☎305/296-8955). Locals' favorite, for inexpensive Key West food in a friendly atmosphere. Closed Sun and Mon.

**Sippin**, 424 Eaton St (☎305/293-0555). Cool cats' coffeehouse with overstuffed velvet sofas, board games, books and papers.

## Drinking and nightlife

The anything-goes nature of Key West is exemplified by the **bars** that make up the bulk of the island's nightlife. Gregarious, rough-and-ready affairs, many stay open as late as 4am and feature regular live music. The most popular places are grouped around the northern end of Duval Street, no more than a few minutes' stagger from one another. For something a little less macho, keep south of the 500 block of Duval.

**Bull & Whistle Bar**, 224 Duval St (no phone). Loud and rowdy, this bar features the best of local musicians each night. Check the list on the door to see who's playing – or just turn up to drink.

**Captain Tony's Saloon**, 428 Greene St (☎305/294-1838). Rustic fishermen's saloon. The original *Sloppy Joe's* (see below), a noted hangout of Ernest Hemingway. Live music of various kinds nightly.

**Green Parrot Bar**, 601 Whitehead St (☎305/294-6133). A Key West landmark since 1890, drawing locals to its pool tables, dartboard and pinball machine. Live music at weekends.

**Rumrunners**, 200 Duval St (☎305/294-1017). A multibar joint with reggae music until all hours. Cheap and tasty food, a big dance floor and open deck looking over Duval St.

**Sloppy Joe's**, 201 Duval St (☎305/294-5717). Despite the memorabilia and the crowds, this rowdy bar – with live music nightly – is not the one Hemingway made famous (see *Captain Tony's*, above), nor one that many locals set foot in.

# THE EAST COAST

Florida's Atlantic **east coast**, which runs for over three hundred miles from the northern fringe of Miami, is largely the sun-soaked playground of popular imagination, with palm-dotted beaches and warm ocean waves. However, the first fifty or so miles lie deep within the sway of Miami, back-to-back conurbations with little to distinguish one from the next. Despite its outdated party-town reputation, **Fort Lauderdale** these days is a sophisticated yachting center, while **Boca Raton** and **Palm Beach** to the north are even more exclusive, their Mediterranean-Revival mansions inhabited almost exclusively by multimillionaires. North of here, the coast is still substantially unspoiled, although the **Space Coast**, centering on the **Kennedy Space Center**, and **Daytona Beach**, both go all out to draw the crowds. The one genuinely characterful town in the entire stretch is **St Augustine**, still recognizable as the spot where Spanish settlers established North America's earliest foreign colony.

By car, the scenic route along the coast is **Hwy-A1A**, which sticks to the ocean side of the **intracoastal waterway**, formed when the rivers dividing the mainland from the barrier islands were joined and deepened during World War II.

# Fort Lauderdale

All it took to turn **FORT LAUDERDALE** from a mild-mannered little town that happened to adjoin seven miles of palm-shaded white sands into a byword for rumbustious beachlife was a single low-budget Hollywood film. Following the 1960 teen-exploitation movie *Where the Boys Are*, Fort Lauderdale instantly became the number-one Spring Break venue in the US, drawing hundreds of thousands of frenzied students each year. Having fueled its economic boom on underage drinking and lascivious excess, however, the city promptly turned its back on the revelers. By the end of the 1980s, it had imposed enough restrictions on boozing and wild behavior to put an end to the bacchanal, and Fort Lauderdale has now transformed itself once more, into a thriving pleasure port, catering to individual yacht-owners and major cruise liners alike, that's also one of the fastest-growing residential areas in the country.

## Arrival, information and getting around

Both Fort Lauderdale's public transit terminals are close to downtown: Greyhound **buses** pull in at 515 NE Third St, while the Amtrak and Tri-Rail **train** station is two miles west at 200 SW 21st Terrace – take bus #22 into town. The main local **visitor center** is in Port Everglades at 1850 Eller Drive (Mon–Fri 8.30am–5pm; ☎954/765-4466 or 1-800/227-8669; multilingual **entertainments/attractions hotline** on ☎954/527-5600).

**Local bus** #11 runs twice hourly along Las Olas Boulevard between downtown and the beach, and you can also call for a **water taxi** (daily 10am until late; day pass $14; ☎954/467-6677), to take you almost anywhere along Fort Lauderdale's many miles of waterfront.

## Accommodation

Although Fort Lauderdale is moving inexorably upscale, there are still plenty of **motels** near the beach where you can expect to find a reasonable room for around $50 in summer, more like $75 in winter; the tourist office's free annual *Superior Small Lodgings Guide* holds full listings.

**Floyd's Youth Hostel** (☎954/462-0631). Friendly, well-kept private hostel in central Port Everglades, which vets would-be guests on the phone before revealing its address; $16 dorms and budget private rooms. Pickup available from public transit stations during the day. ①/②.

**Ocean Hacienda Inn**, 1924 N Atlantic Blvd (☎ 1-800/562-8467). A great oceanfront hotel with a tropical garden, heated pool and surprisingly inexpensive rooms. ④/⑤.

**Pillars Waterfront**, 111 N Birch Rd (☎954/467-9639 or 1-800/800-7666). Attractive, spacious resort, facing the waterway rather than the ocean but in the heart of the beach area, with a nice pool and full breakfast included. ⑥–⑧.

**Sea View Resort**, 550 N Birch Rd at Windamar (☎954/564-3151 or 1-800/356-2326). Comfortable, well-equipped motel one block back from Fort Lauderdale Beach. ③/④.

## The Town

As far as visitors are concerned, Fort Lauderdale consists of two main areas of interest. **Downtown** focuses on a few blocks between E Broward and E Las Olas boulevards, which cross US-1 a couple of miles east of I-95. Heavily prettified with parks and promenades, it's a surprisingly pleasant place for a stroll, especially if you follow the half-mile pedestrian **Riverwalk** along the north shore of the **New River**. **Las Olas Boulevard** itself, the main shopping district, remains busy day and night, with boutiques, galleries, restaurants, bars and sidewalk cafes in abundance. It's also home to the stimulating **Museum of Art**, 1 E Las Olas Blvd (Tues–Thurs & Sat 10am–5pm, Fri 10am–8pm, Sun noon–5pm; $5), where the largely modern collection features several of the twentieth century's biggest names but also celebrates 1960s work by the CoBrA movement of artists from Copenhagen, Brussels and Amsterdam. Not far west, the simulators and interactive displays at the **Museum of Discovery and Science**, 401 SW Second St (Mon–Sat 10am–5pm, Sun noon–6pm; $6), should pacify kids pining for Disney. Blockbuster 3D IMAX theater tickets at the museum go for $9 or $12.50 with museum admission. Call 954/467-6637 for show times.

Most casual visitors, nonetheless, still come for the **beach**. Cross the arching intracoastal waterway bridge, about two miles along Las Olas Boulevard from downtown, and the mood changes appreciably. Where Las Olas ends, **beachside Fort Lauderdale** begins – T-shirt, sunscreen and beachwear stores are suddenly everywhere. Along the seafront, **Fort Lauderdale Beach Boulevard** once bore the brunt of Spring Break partying, but only a few beachfront bars suggest the carousing of the past, and the attractive new promenade draws an altogether healthier crowd of joggers, rollerbladers and cyclists.

## Eating and drinking

Beachfront Fort Lauderdale still seems to prefer boozing to **eating**; it's not hard to find a pizza or burger near the ocean, but if you want anything fancier you'll probably have to head back towards downtown, also the hub of Fort Lauderdale's nightlife.

**Casablanca Café**, intersection of Alhambra and Ocean Blvd (☎954/764-3500). An American piano bar in a Moroccan setting with a good, eclectic menu. Expect large portions.

**Mark's Las Olas**, 1032 E Las Olas Blvd (☎954/463-1000). Top-notch dinner-only downtown restaurant, serving contemporary south Floridian food – lots of sesame-crusted and pan-seared fish – at premium prices.

**Southport Raw Bar**, 1536 Cordova Rd (☎954/525-2526). Boisterous local bar, south of downtown near Port Everglades, specializing in succulent crustaceans and well-prepared fish dishes.

**Sukhothai**, at Gateway Plaza, 1930 E Sunrise Blvd (☎954/764-0148). Tasty, moderately spiced Thai dishes.

**Tom Jenkins' Bar-B-Q**, 1236 S Federal Highway (US-1) (☎954/522-5046). Outstanding barbecue and side dishes at inexpensive prices.

# Boca Raton

**BOCA RATON** (literally "the mouth of the mouse"), twenty miles north of Fort Lauderdale, is noteworthy mostly for its abundance of Mediterranean Revival architecture, a style prevalent here since the 1920s and kept alive in the **downtown** area by strict building codes. New structures must incorporate arched entranceways, fake bell towers and red-tiled roofs whenever possible, ensuring a consistent and distinctive "look." It all goes back to **Addison Mizner**, the "Aladdin of architects" (see box, p.561), who swept in to Boca Raton on the tide of the Florida property boom and bought up 1600 acres of farmland. Mizner's vision of gondola-filled canals, luxury hotels and even a great cathedral never came to fruition, but the few buildings he completed left an indelible mark. His million-dollar *Cloister Inn*, for example, grew into the present $200-a-night *Boca Raton Resort and Club*, 501 E Camino Real, a pink palace of marble columns, sculptured fountains and carefully aged wood (☎561/447-3183 or 1-800/327-0101; ⑥–⑨).

Its legendary confines at **Mizner Park**, off US-1 between Palmetto Park Road and Glades Road, and open-air plaza is adorned with palm trees and waterfalls. Amidst designer boutiques and whatnot, the **International Museum of Cartoon Art**, 201 Plaza Real (Tues–Sat 10am–6pm, Sun noon–6pm; $6), is worth a stop for its expensive collection of political cartoons and comic strip exhibits. Well worth a visit, the collection also has an interactive area geared toward kids.

A mile north of Hwy-798 (which links downtown with the beach) at 1801 N Ocean Blvd/Hwy-A1A, is **Gumbo Limbo Nature Center** (Mon–Sat 9am–4pm, Sun noon–4pm; $1 donation), a twenty-acre nature reserve inhabited by osprey, brown pelicans and sea turtles. Night turtle-watching tours are offered between May and July; book well in advance on ☎561/338-1473.

Boca Raton's most explorable **beachside** area is **Spanish River Park** (daily 8am–dusk; cars $8 Mon–Fri, $10 Sat, Sun & hols, pedestrians and cyclists free), a couple of miles north of downtown. Most of these fifty acres of vivid vegetation and highrise greenery are only penetrable on trails through shady thickets.

### Practicalities

Greyhound does not stop in Boca Raton but there is a Tri-Rail station off Yamato Road west of I-95 (☎1-800/TRI-RAIL). **The Chamber of Commerce** is at 1800 N Dixie Hwy (Mon–Thurs 8.30am–5pm, Fri 8.30am–4pm; ☎561/395-4433). The best-value **motels** near the beaches are *Shore Edge*, 425 N Ocean Blvd (☎561/395-4491; ③–⑤), and *Ocean Lodge*, 531 N Ocean Blvd (☎561/395-7772; ③–⑤).

As for **eating**, *Murphy's Ranch House*, 234 N Ocean Blvd (☎561/428-2539), in nearby Deerfield Beach, has standard American diner fare and a great view of the ocean. Boca Raton has a rather subdued **nightlife,** but local bar *Flanigan's Guppys,* 45 S Federal Hwy (☎561/395-4324), stays lively most of the week.

# Palm Beach

A small island town of palatial homes and gardens, and streets so clean you could eat your dinner off them, **PALM BEACH** has been synonymous for nearly a century with the kind of lifestyle only limitless loot can buy. The nation's nobs began wintering here in the 1890s, after Henry Flagler brought his East Coast railroad south from St Augustine and built two luxury hotels on this then-secluded, palm-filled island. Since then, tycoons, sports aces, aristocrats, rock stars and CIA directors have flocked here, eager to become part of the Palm Beach elite and enjoy its aloofness from mainland, and mainstream, life. Joe Kennedy – father of John, Robert and Edward – bought the so-called Kennedy Compound here in 1933, the focus in 1991 of much prurient interest as the scene of the events that culminated in the acquittal of his grandson William Kennedy Smith on charges of sexual battery.

Summer in Palm Beach is very quiet, and the least costly time to stay. The winter months, from November to May, see a whirl of elegant balls, fundraising dinners and charity galas, as well as the polo season – watching a chukka or two is the only time Palm Beach denizens show themselves in the less particular environs of West Palm Beach (on the mainland).

**Worth Avenue**, close to the southern tip of the island, is filled with designer stores, high-class art galleries and ultraformal restaurants, and cruised by Rolls

## ADDISON MIZNER: ARCHITECT OF PALM BEACH

A former miner and prizefighter, **Addison Mizner** was an unemployed architect when he arrived in Palm Beach in 1918. Inspired by the medieval buildings he'd seen around the Mediterranean, Mizner built the **Everglades Club**, at 356 Worth Ave – the first public building in Florida in the Mediterranean Revival style. The success of the club, and the house he subsequently built for society bigwig Eva Stotesbury, won Mizner commissions all over Palm Beach as the wintering wealthy decided to swap suites at one of Henry Flagler's hotels for a "million-dollar cottage" of their own.

Brilliant and unorthodox, Mizner's loggias and U-shaped interiors made the most of Florida's pleasant winter temperatures, while his twisting staircases to nowhere became legendary. Mizner used untrained workmen to lay crooked roof tiles, sprayed condensed milk onto walls to create an impression of centuries-old grime, and fired shotgun pellets into wood to imitate wormholes. By the mid-1920s, Mizner had created the Palm Beach Style, and he later fashioned much of Boca Raton.

Royces, Mercedes and Jaguars. Its most appealing aspect is its **architecture**: stucco walls, Romanesque facades, and passageways leading to small courtyards where miniature bridges cross nonexistent canals and spiral staircases climb to the upper levels.

Where Cocoanut Row and Whitehall Way meet, the white Doric columns fronting **Whitehall**, also known as the Flagler Museum (Tues–Sat 10am–5pm, Sun noon–5pm; $7), make it the most overtly ostentatious home on the island: a $4-million wedding present from Henry Flagler to his third wife, Mary Lily Kenan. As in many of Florida's first luxury homes, the interior design was pillaged from the great buildings of Europe: among the 55 rooms are an Italian library, a French salon, a Swiss billiard room, a hallway modeled on St Peter's, and a Louis XV ballroom. All are stuffed with ornamentation, but they lack aesthetic cohesion. Informative 45-minute **guided tours** depart continuously from the 110ft hallway and provide a background of Flaglers' fascinating rise to success and a glimpse of the Gilded Age in which he flourished.

Built in 1926 in the style of an Italianate palace, **The Breakers** hotel, on Breakers Row off the main strip, (☎1-888/273-2537; ⑧/⑨) operates as the last of Palm Beach's swanky resorts. A vision from inside and out, its decoration includes elaborate painted ceilings and huge tapestries. A guided tour is given on Wednesdays at 3pm ($10, hotel guests free; reservations ☎561/655-6611).

### Practicalities

Palm Beach's **Chamber of Commerce** is at 45 Cocoanut Row (summer Mon–Fri 10am–4.30pm, rest of year 9am–5pm; ☎561/655-3282). You'll need plenty of money to **sleep** here: prices of $200 a night are not uncommon. The elaborate, antique-furnished *Palm Beach Historic Inn*, 365 S County Rd (☎561/832-4009; ④–⑦), offers some of the best rates in town, but you'll need to book early. Otherwise come between May and December, when similarly grand options such as *The Chesterfield*, 363 Cocoanut Row (☎561/659-5800 or 1-800/243-7871; ⑤–⑧), and *The Plaza Inn,* 215 Brazilian Ave (☎561/832-8666 or 1-800/232-2632; ⑤–⑦), are at their least expensive.

As for **eating**, *TooJay's*, 313 Royal Poinciana Way (☎561/659-7232), is a bakery and deli open for breakfast onwards, with omelettes under $6, while the lunch counter at *Green's Pharmacy*, 151 N County Rd (☎561/832-0304), keeps up a steady supply of diner food. If money is no object – and you're dressed to kill – make for *Café L'Europe*, 331 S County Rd (☎561/655-4020). Spend less than $50 each in this super-elegant French restaurant and you'll still be hungry.

# The Space Coast

The so-called **Space Coast**, the base of the country's space industry, occupies a flat, marshy island bulging into the Atlantic. Many visitors are surprised to find that the land from which the Space Shuttle leaves earth is also a sizeable wildlife refuge.

## The Kennedy Space Center

Although these days NASA competes head-on with Disney for the tourist dollar, cannily seizing every opportunity to enthuse young minds with the continuing glamour of outer space, the **Kennedy Space Center** remains a working facility, where space vehicles are developed, tested, and blasted into orbit. Merritt Island has been the center of NASA's activity since 1964, when the launch pads at Cape Canaveral US Air Force base, across the water, proved too small to cope with the giant new Saturn V rockets.

Unless you have an entire day you won't be able to do everything the Space Center has to offer. Arrive early at the visitor center/museum (daily 9am–6pm or later; free), reached via Hwy-405 from Titusville or Hwy-3 off Hwy-A1A, to avoid the crowds (thinnest on weekends and during May & Sept). **Admission** to the various museums and galleries in the main complex, as well as the open-air **Rocket Garden** of spindly firework-like rockets from the 1950s, is free, as is parking. If examining their assortment of mission capsules, space suits and satellites, clambering through the mock-up Space Shuttle flight deck, and devouring a handful of Space Dots ("the ice cream of the future") doesn't sate your appetite, you can pay to see an **IMAX movie** ($7.50) or join a two-hour guided **bus tour** ($14). The bus passes the 52-story Vehicle Assembly Building and stops at the impressive **Apollo/Saturn V Center**, where multimedia displays re-create the excitement of the first moon landings and the Apollo 8 launch. For the dates and times of **launches** from the Space Center, or to arrange $10 viewing passes, call ☎407/452-2121. However, you get almost as good a view from anywhere within a forty-mile radius of the Space Center.

Near the Kennedy Space Center, at 6225 Vectorspace Blvd, Titusville, the **US Astronaut Hall of Fame** (daily 9am–5pm; $13.95) offers the full space explorer's experience, with G-force, shuttle-landing and flight simulators.

### Staying over: Cocoa Beach
The Space Center holds a number of fast-food cafes, but the closest **motels** are either back on the mainland along US-1, or, if you're looking for a bargain rates, in **COCOA BEACH**, a few miles south on a ten-mile strip of shore that's washed by some of the biggest surfing waves in Florida. Options here include a *Days Inn*, 5600 Hwy-524 (☎407/636-6500; ③), a *Motel 6*, 3701 N Atlantic Ave (☎407/783-3103; ③), and *Fawlty Towers*, 100 E Cocoa Beach Causeway (☎407/784-3870; ③).

## Merritt Island National Wildlife Refuge

NASA doesn't have Merritt Island all to itself, but shares it with the **Merritt Island National Wildlife Refuge** (daily dawn–dusk; free), reached via Hwy-402, a separate approach road from Titusville. Promoted, disconcertingly, with the slogan "Where Nature Meets Technology," this allows alligators, armadillos, racoons and bobcats – and one of Florida's greatest gatherings of birdlife – to live out their primeval existence beside some of the human world's most advanced hardware. Winter is the **best time to visit**, when the island's skies are alive with migratory birds from the frozen north, and mosquitoes are nowhere to be found. At any other period, and especially in summer, the island's Mosquito Lagoon is worthy of its name; bring repellent.

Seven miles east of Titusville on Hwy-406, the six-mile **Black Point Wildlife Drive** gives a solid introduction to the basics of the island's ecosystem; pick up the free leaflet at the entrance. Be sure to do some walking within the refuge, too. Off the wildlife drive, the five-mile **Cruickshank trail** weaves around the edge of the Indian River; or drive a few miles further east along Hwy-402 – branching from Hwy-406 just south of the wildlife drive – and tackle the half-mile **Oak Hammock trail** or the two-mile **Palm Hammock trail**, both accessible from the same parking lot.

# Daytona Beach

The consummate Florida beach town, with its T-shirt shops, amusement arcades and wall-to-wall motels, **DAYTONA BEACH** owes its existence to twenty miles of light brown sand where the only pressure is to strip off and enjoy yourself. For decades, life in this medium-paced, down-to-earth resort revolved around three major annual invasions: February's **Daytona 500**, **Bike Week** in early March, and **Spring Break**. With the latter ritual, when half a million college kids would come to indulge in underage drinking and libido liberation, now firmly discouraged (if not altogether suppressed), Daytona Beach is free to focus its attention on its true love: **motor sports** of all kinds.

Without a doubt, the best thing about Daytona Beach is the seemingly limitless **beach**: 500ft wide at low tide and fading dreamily into the heat haze. Lined with an all-but-endless procession of enormous but surprisingly low-priced **motels**, oceanfront **Atlantic Avenue** holds little to lure you away from the water. At the landward end of **Main Street Pier**, a $3 ride to the top of the candy-striped Space Needle enables you to look down on the surrounding morass of low-rent bars and tattoo parlors; you can't get to the far end of the pier, though, since Hurricane Floyd knocked out 280ft of it in September, 1999.

Pioneering auto enthusiasts such as Louis Chevrolet, Ransom Olds and Henry Ford came to Daytona's firm sands during the early 1900s to race prototype vehicles beside the ocean. The land speed record was smashed five times by millionaire British speedster Malcolm Campbell who, in 1935, roared along at 276mph. When high speeds made racing on the sands unsafe, the **Daytona International Speedway** was built, an ungainly configuration of concrete and steel three miles west of downtown along International Speedway Boulevard (bus #9AB). Opened in 1959, it has a capacity of 150,000 and hosts several major race meetings each year, starting in early February with the **Rolex 24**, a 24-hour race for GT prototype sports cars. A week or so later the qualifying races start for the biggest event of the year, the **Daytona 500** stock-car race in mid-February. Tickets sell out well in advance (from $80; ☎904/253-7223), and you should book accommodation at least six months ahead. Though they can't capture the excitement of a race, guided van **tours** (daily except race days 9.30am–4pm, every half-hour; $6) take you around the remarkable curves, whose gradients make this the fastest racetrack in the world.

Immediately outside the Speedway, **Daytona USA** (daily 9am–7pm; $12), holds one of Campbell's many *Bluebirds*, as well as interactive displays on the great races. A mile west, the **Klassix Auto Museum** at 2909 W International Speedway Blvd (daily 9am–6pm; $8.50) displays pristine examples of every Corvette design from 1953 to the present day, plus vintage motorcycles, and a 1938 Woody Wagon that boasts a top speed of 50mph.

## Practicalities

As Ridgewood Avenue, **US-1** steams through mainland Daytona Beach, passing the Greyhound station at no. 138 S. Trolleys run the length of the beach from January to September only (75¢). The **visitor center** is at 126 E Orange Ave (Mon–Fri 9am–5pm; ☎904/255-0415 or 1-800/854-1234).

Any of the following Atlantic Avenue **motels** makes a good beach base: the welcoming *Tropical Manor Motel* at 2237 S (☎904/252-4920; ②/③); *Thunderbird Beach Motel* at 500 N (☎904/253-2562 or 1-800/234-6543; ②/③); the *Best Western Mayan Inn* at 103 S (☎904/252-2378; ⑤); and *The Streamline Hotel* at 140 S Atlantic Ave (☎904/258-6937; ①).

Good places to **eat** include *Julian's*, 88 S Atlantic Ave (☎904/677-6767), a dimly lit, mock-Tahitian lounge with great food, or *Lighthouse Landing* (☎904/761-9271), beside the Ponce Inlet Lighthouse, for fresh fish. To get a sunset view, head for the west side of the island, where among several restaurants at the eastern edge of the Port Orange Bridge, *JC's Oyster Shack*, 79 Dunlawton Ave (☎904/767-1881), serves excellent, inexpensive seafood at waterfront tables. If you're looking for beachside action, the **bars** in and around the *Adams Mark Daytona Beach Resort*, 100 N Atlantic Ave, are a good bet. *The Oyster Pub*, 555 Seabreeze Blvd (☎904/255-6348), has dirt-cheap oysters and a loud jukebox.

# St Augustine

Few places in Florida are as immediately engaging as **ST AUGUSTINE**, which has the size and even some of the looks of a small Mediterranean town. The oldest permanent settlement in the US, with much from its early days still intact along its narrow streets, it also offers two alluring lengths of beach just across the bay.

Ponce de León touched ground here in 1513, but European settlement began when Pedro Menéndez de Avilés put ashore on St Augustine's Day in 1565. Sir Francis Drake's ships razed the town in 1586, the first of many battles with the British before Florida was eventually ceded to Britain in 1763. By then the town was a major social and administrative center, soon to be capital of east Florida. Subsequently, Tallahassee (see p.587) became capital of a unified Florida, and St Augustine's fortunes waned. Expansion largely bypassed the town – a fact inadvertently facilitating the **restoration program** that has turned this quiet community into a fine historical showcase.

## Arrival, information and getting around

The Greyhound station, 100 Malaga St, is a fifteen-minute walk from the center. St Augustine is best seen **on foot**, though a **sightseeing train** tours the main landmarks (daily 8.30am–5pm; $12; tickets from 170 San Marco Ave or the visitor center). There's no public transportation; if you don't have a car, you can get to the beaches, two miles away, by rented **bike** (from the youth hostel; see below) or **taxi** (Ancient City Cabs; ☎904/824-8161). The **visitor center**, 10 Castillo Drive (daily 8.30am–7.30pm; ☎904/825-1000), shows a free film on the history of the town, as well as an artsy feature-style movie (52min; $3) about the first settlers. They can also fill you in on the numerous local festivals. Harbor **cruises** ($8.50) leave five or six times a day from the City Yacht Pier, near the foot of King Street. The well-organized and informative Tour St Augustine (☎904/825-0087) leads historical **walking tours**. Colee Sightseeing & Gamsey Carriage Co. (☎904/829-2391; $15) offer horse-drawn carriage tours both day and night.

## Accommodation

Nearly thirty restored inns in the Old Town offer **bed and breakfast**, and there are cheap **motels** outside the center along San Marco Avenue. For the best prices, avoid the busy period between May and October, when rates rise by $10–20.

**Best Western**, 6 Castillo Drive (☎1-800/528-1234). Reliable chain in the Old Town, with pool and complimentary breakfast. ③–⑥.

Dallas, TX

Louisiana Cotton Field

French Quarter, New Orleans LA

Everglades National Park, FL

GREG WARD

LIFEGUARD
ON DUTY

South Beach, Miami FL

CHARLES BOWMAN

Cadillac Ranch, Amarillo TX

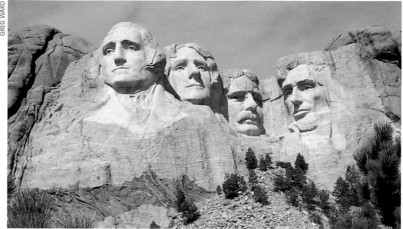

Mount Rushmore National Monument, SD

Badlands National Park, SD

EDMUND NÄGELE

Morning Glory pool, Yellowstone National Park, WY

JOHN NOBLE

JERRY DENNIS

Lone Mountain, MT

Cliff Palace, Mesa Verde National Park, CO

**Carriage Way**, 70 Cuna St (☎1-800/908-9832). One of the Old Town's best-priced B&Bs, in a pretty Victorian building. ④–⑦.

**Casa Monica Hotel**, 95 Cordova St (☎1-888/GRAND123). Elegant Spanish-style hotel, originally established in 1888 and recently reopened. ⑥–⑦.

**Coquina Gables**, 1 F St (☎904/461-8727). Beautiful and relaxing oceanfront B&B in St Augustine Beach. Pool and spa. ⑥.

**International Haus**, 32 Treasury St (☎904/808-1999). The town's only hostel accommodation, popular with travelers and very near the plaza. Dorms $15, and some private rooms. ①.

**Kenwood Inn**, 38 Marine St (☎904/824-2116). Handily positioned, sizeable Old Town inn near the waterfront. Pool and terrace, and complimentary continental breakfast. ⑤.

**Vilano Beach Motel**, 50 Vilano Rd (☎904/829-2651). Laid-back motel and a great base for enjoying the North Beach. ②–⑤.

## The Old Town

St Augustine's historic area – or **Old Town** – along St George Street and south of the central plaza holds the well-tended evidence of its Spanish period. It may be small, but there's a lot to see: an early start, around 9am, will give you a lead on the tourist crowds and should enable a good look at almost everything inside a day.

Given the fine state of the **Castillo de San Marcos** (daily 8.45am–4.45pm; $4; regular free talks on the fort and local history), on the northern edge of the Old Town beside the bay, it's difficult to credit that the fortress was started in the late 1600s. Its longevity is down to its design: a diamond-shaped rampart at each corner maximized firepower, and 14-foot-thick walls reduced vulnerability to attack. Inside, there's not a lot beyond small cases of exhibits in echoing rooms, but venturing along the 35ft ramparts gives good views across the city and the bay.

The eighteenth-century **City Gate** marks the entrance to **St George Street**, once the main thoroughfare and now a tourist-trampled pedestrianized strip. You'll find a lot of places called "The oldest . . ." in St Augustine; the **Oldest School House**, set in lush gardens at 14 George St (daily 9am–5pm; $2.50), is one of the most atmospheric, a restored wooden shack with jerky animatronic dummies portraying nineteenth-century schoolchildren. A fair-sized plot at St George and Cuna is taken up by the excellent **Spanish Quarter Living Museum** (daily 9am–6pm; $6.50). In its seven reconstructed homes and workshops, volunteers disguised as Spanish settlers go about their business at spinning wheels, anvils and foot-driven wood lathes. If you've five minutes to spare you could pop into the **Old Drugstore**, at Orange and Cordova (daily 9.30am–6pm; free), though the appeal of creepy dummies rattling their automated jaws as they tell of quack cures and herbal remedies palls quite soon. Nearby on Cordova Street, the evocative, overgrown **Tolomato cemetery** (9am–6pm) stands on the site of an eighteenth-century Christian Indian village; most graves date from the 1900s.

In the sixteenth century, the Spanish king decreed that all colonial towns had to be built around a central plaza; thus St George Street runs into **Plaza de la Constitucion**, a marketplace from 1598. On the plaza's north side, the **Basilica Cathedral of St Augustine** (guided tours Mon–Fri 9am–4.30pm, Sat & Sun 1–5pm; donation) adds a touch of grandeur, although it's largely a Sixties remake of the late eighteenth-century original. Tourist numbers lessen as you cross **south of the plaza** into a web of quiet, narrow streets, just as old as St George Street. The **Government Museum**, 48 King St (daily 9am–6pm; $3.50), gives an admirably concise and clear history of the changing demography of the colony, while nearby, opposite Flagler College, the classy **Lightner Museum** (daily 9am–5pm, last admission 4.30pm; $5) displays fine and decorative arts in the former *Alcazar Hotel*, one of the most fabulous resorts of the late nineteenth century. Rather more prosaically, the **Oldest Store Museum** at 4 Artillery Lane (Mon–Sat 9am–5pm, Sun 10am–5pm; rest of year Mon–Sat 9am–5pm, Sun

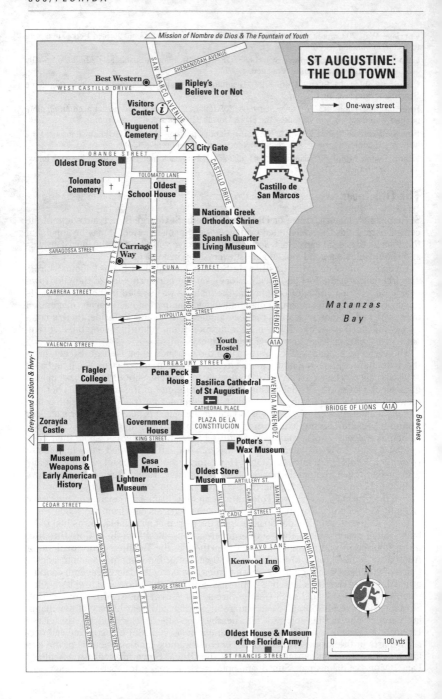

△ Mission of Nombre de Dios & The Fountain of Youth

## ST AUGUSTINE: THE OLD TOWN

→ One-way street

SHENANDOAH AVENUE

Best Western ●
■ Ripley's Believe It or Not

WEST CASTILLO DRIVE

Visitors Center ⓘ

Huguenot Cemetery †

ORANGE STREET

⊠ City Gate

Castillo de San Marcos

Oldest Drug Store ■

TOLOMATO LANE

Tolomato Cemetery †

Oldest School House ■

SAN MARCO AVENUE

CASTILLO DRIVE

■ National Greek Orthodox Shrine

■ Spanish Quarter Living Museum

SARAGOSSA STREET

Carriage Way

SPANISH STREET

CUNA STREET

CORDOVA STREET

CARRERA STREET

ST GEORGE STREET

HYPOLITA STREET

CHARLOTTE STREET

AVENIDA MENENDEZ

*Matanzas Bay*

VALENCIA STREET

Youth Hostel ●

TREASURY STREET

(A1A)

Greyhound Station & Hwy-1

Flagler College

Pena Peck House ■

Basilica Cathedral of St Augustine ✝

CATHEDRAL PLACE

Zorayda Castle

Government House ■

KING STREET

PLAZA DE LA CONSTITUCION

BRIDGE OF LIONS (A1A)

△ Beaches

■ Museum of Weapons & Early American History

Casa Monica

Lightner Museum ■

Potter's Wax Museum ●

Oldest Store Museum ■

ARTILLERY ST

CEDAR STREET

GRANADA STREET

AVILES STREET

CADIZ STREET

CHARLOTTE STREET

MARINE STREET

AVENIDA MENENDEZ

CORDOVA STREET

BRAVO LANE

Kenwood Inn ●

ST GEORGE STREET

BRIDGE STREET

ONEIDA STREET

WASHINGTON STREET

N

Oldest House & Museum of the Florida Army

0      100 yds

ST FRANCIS STREET

noon–5pm; $5) re-creates a general store of the 1880s, filled to the rafters with more than 100,000 bits and bobs from dusty top hats, bootscrapers and medicines to cigar molds and wooden washing machines.

More substantial history is unfurled a ten-minute walk away at the fascinating **Oldest House**, 14 St Francis St (daily 9am–5pm; $5), which is indeed the oldest house in town, dating from the early 1700s. Excellent guided tours take you through the different rooms, which are decorated to show how the house – and people's lives – changed as new eras unfolded.

### The beaches

Some fine **beaches** – busiest at weekends – lie just a couple of miles from the Old Town. Across the bay, **St Augustine Beach** is family terrain, with some good restaurants and a fishing pier, but the **Anastasia State Recreation Area** (daily 8am–dusk; cars $3.25, cyclists and pedestrians $1) on Anastasia Island offers a thousand protected acres of dunes, marshes and scrub, linked by nature walks. In the other direction (take May St, off San Marco Ave), the broad orange **Vilano Beach** pulls a younger crowd.

### Eating and drinking

**Eating** in the Old Town is expensive, and a number of its cafes and restaurants are closed in the evening. Many people head out to the oceanfront places for dinner, or settle instead for a long night's drinking at one of the nice old **bars**.

**A1A Ale Works**, 1 King St (☎904/829-2977) Convivial, good-looking bar/restaurant, popular with locals for its excellent, creative New World cuisine and home-brewed beers.

**Fiddler's Green**, 2750 Anahma Drive, Vilano Beach (☎904/824-8897). Big oceanfront restaurant, always full, entered by a gangplank and serving reasonably priced grilled fish, pasta and steak. Complimentary transportation to/from hotels.

**Gypsy Cab Company**, 828 Anastasia Blvd (☎904/824-8244). Reasonably priced European and New World food in a hip, urban, Art Deco setting.

**Le Pavillon**, 45 San Marco Ave (☎904/824-6202). Good Continental cuisine at fair prices and served in a semi-formal setting.

**Mill Top Tavern**, 19½ George St (☎904/829-2329). Atmospheric, historic local bar in a nineteenth-century mill; the big windows give it the feel of a treehouse, and there's deck seating. Excellent live music and raw bar make it a local favorite.

**Scarlett O'Hara's**, 70 Hypolita St (☎904/824-6535). Fun, touristy place to drink in the Old Town, with cozy rooms and a porch.

**Spanish Bakery**, 42½ St George St (no phone). Great little place where you can eat fresh Spanish soup, home-baked bread and cookies in a shady garden. Closes at 3pm.

# CENTRAL FLORIDA

Encompassing a broad and fertile expanse between the east and west coasts, most of **central Florida** was farming country when vacation-mania first struck the beachside strips. Over the last two decades, this picture of tranquility has been shattered: no section of the state has been affected more dramatically by modern tourism, and the most visited part of Florida can also be one of the ugliest. A clutter of freeway interchanges, motels and billboards arches around the small city of **Orlando**, where a tourist-dollar chase of Gold Rush magnitude was sparked off in the 1970s by **Walt Disney World**, the biggest and cleverest theme-park complex ever created. The rest of central Florida is quiet by comparison, and, north of Orlando particularly, rural towns like **Ocala** typify the state before the arrival of the highways and made-to-measure vacations.

# Orlando and the theme parks

**ORLANDO**, a quiet farming town twenty years ago, has more people passing through its environs than any other place in the state. The reason, of course, is **Walt Disney World**, which, along with **Universal Studios Escape**, **Sea World** and a host of themed attractions, pulls more than 25 million people a year to a previously featureless plot of scrubland. Few people head to Orlando proper, basing themselves in one of the countless motels along **Hwy-192**, fifteen miles south, or **International Drive**, five miles southwest, and despite enormous expansion over the last decade, the town itself remains free of the commercialism that surrounds it.

## Arrival and information

The international **airport** is nine miles south of downtown Orlando; collect brochures and discount coupons at the official **information booth** (daily 7am–11pm). Shuttle buses (24hr; best prices offered by Mears or Transtar) run to any hotel in the Orlando area for around $15, while a **taxi** to downtown, International Drive or the motels on Hwy-192 costs around $28. **Buses** and **trains** arrive downtown, at the Greyhound terminal, 555 N John Young Parkway, and the Amtrak station, 1400 Sligh Blvd.

Pick up discount coupons and promotional offers at the efficient **Visitor Information Center**, 8723 International Drive (daily 8am–7pm; ☎407/363-5872).

## Getting around: visiting the theme parks

You have to be *very* determined to get to the theme parks without a car, but it can be done. Local Lynx **buses** (☎407/841-8240) converge on the downtown Orlando terminal between Central and Pine streets; route #50 heads to Walt Disney World, but it's a somewhat patchy service and takes hours. The pricier Mears Transportation Service runs private **shuttle buses** (☎407/423-5566) between the main accommodation areas and Walt Disney World, Sea World and Universal Studios ($8–15 round-trip) – phone at least a day ahead to be picked up, or check at your hotel or hostel. **Taxis** are the best way to get around at night – try Yellow Cab Co (☎407/699-9999).

## Accommodation: outside Walt Disney World

If you're on a budget, or want to spend time visiting Universal Studios and the other parks, you'd do best to stay **outside Walt Disney World**. Once you've decided to do so, location is pretty much irrelevant – the parks and attractions are so scattered that wherever you stay you'll spend a lot of time driving back and forth between them.

Competition is fierce, and quoted **rates** can often be negotiated down; independent travelers who show up on spec during the slow winter periods may well find some bargains. The motels line **Hwy-192** between Walt Disney World and Kissimmee (10–20min drive to Walt Disney World). The chain hotels on **International Drive** (about 20min drive from Walt Disney World) are a shade more upmarket, with good restaurants and shops within walking distance. Closest to Walt Disney World are the places around **Lake Buena Vista** (5–20min drive).

**Country Hearth Inn**, 9861 International Drive (☎1-800/447-1890). Plain rooms in a kitsch building dripping with Southern Victoriana. Pool and continental breakfast. ⑤.

**HI-Orlando Resort**, 4840 W Hwy-192, Kissimmee (☎407/396-8282). Clean, friendly, efficient hostel with pool, dorms ($16) and private rooms. Lynx stops nearby and shuttles run to the parks, airport and Orlando's bus and train stations. ①/②.

**Holiday Inn Sunspree Resort Lake Buena Vista**, 13351 Hwy-535 (☎407/239-4500). Comfortable and kid-friendly, with large pool, restaurant and entertainment. ⑤.

**Howard Johnson Plaza Resort at the Universal Gateway**, 7050 Kirkman Rd (☎1-800/327-3808). A good base for exploring Universal Studios Escape. And free shuttle to other parks. ③/④.

**Sevilla Inn**, 4640 W Hwy-192, Kissimmee (☎407/396-4135). Very good-value, attractive motel with clean rooms and a nice pool. ②/③.

**Super-8**, 4840 W Hwy-192, Kissimmee (☎407/396-1144). Comfortable, clean and reliable. ②.

## Accommodation within Walt Disney World

Prices at the fabulously designed **Walt Disney World resorts** scattered around the complex (all ☎407/W-DISNEY) are much higher – sometimes over $300 per night – than you'll pay elsewhere, but the benefits (top-notch facilities; free transportation; early access to the parks; brunch with Goofy), can make it well worth the extra. Note that rates drop by $25–50 during the **"value seasons"** (roughly in January and from September to December, excluding holidays).

Though rooms may be available at short notice during the quieter times, you should book as far ahead – nine months is not unreasonable – as possible. If you do arrive on spec, the **Disney Information Center** off I-75 in Ocala (daily 9am–6pm; ☎352/854-0770) can offer discounts on rooms for that night.

A good option if you're **camping**, the *Fort Wilderness Resort and Campground* is set on a lovely 700-acre forested site near the Magic Kingdom. Here you can hook up your RV or pitch your tent for $35–54, or rent a six-berth trailer for around $204, and still enjoy the privileges of being a Disney guest.

**All-Star Resorts**. Three resorts, themed around sports, music and movies. In the Disney-MGM area, near Blizzard Beach. ④/⑤.

**Caribbean Beach Resort**. Five lodges, each with its own pool, in a lushly landscaped property. In the grounds of EPCOT. ⑥/⑦.

**Port Orleans Resort**. Gaze from your wrought-iron balcony across the mini New Orleans French Quarter re-created in this resort's courtyard, in Disney Village. ⑥/⑦.

**Wilderness Lodge**. A massive, magnificent Magic Kingdom replica of a frontier log cabin, with its own Old Faithful geyser and waterfalls. ⑦–⑨.

## Walt Disney World

As significant as air conditioning in making the state what it is today, **WALT DISNEY WORLD** turned a wedge of Florida cow fields into one of the world's most lucrative vacation venues within ten years. The immense and astutely planned empire also pushed the state's media profile through the roof: from being a down-at-heel mixture of cheap motels, retirement homes and clapped-out alligator zoos, Florida suddenly became a showcase of modern international tourism.

Walt Disney World is the pacesetter among theme parks: it goes way beyond Disney's original "theme park" – Disneyland, which opened in Los Angeles in 1955 (see p.939) – delivering escapism at its most technologically advanced and psychologically brilliant across an area twice the size of Manhattan. Its four main theme parks are quite separate entities and, ideally, you should allow a full day for each. The **Magic Kingdom** is the Disney park of popular imagination, where Mickey mingles with the crowds – very much the park for kids, though at its high-tech best capable of thrilling even the most jaded of adults. Known for its giant, golfball-like geosphere, **EPCOT Center** is

**Disney information**: ☎407/824-4321

---

## TICKETS, OPENING HOURS AND TIMING

**One-day one-park tickets** cost $44 (children aged 3–9 $35), and allow unlimited access to all shows and rides in **one park only**, for that day only. **Park-Hopper Passes** buy you entry to all four parks, in any combination, as many times as you like, over any four or five days. **Four-day passes** cost $167 ($134); **five-day passes** cost $199 ($159). A **Park-Hopper Plus Pass**, available for five ($242.76/$193.99), six ($274.57/$219.43) and seven ($306.37/$244.89) days, gives you the same options as the Park-Hopper Pass, but also features admission to the water parks, Pleasure Island or the Wide World of Sports complex, depending on the number of days on your ticket. Unused days and options never expire. If possible, buy tickets well **in advance**, over the phone or at a Disney store. If you have to buy them at the gate, arrive at least an hour before opening time. The **parking lots** cost $5 a day, but are free if you're staying at a Walt Disney World resort.

Each park is **open** daily from 9am, closing as early as 7pm and as late as midnight, depending on the time of year; pick up the current schedule when you arrive. However, all parks open earlier than the published hours, so turning up around 8am should ensure you get to see the star rides before the hordes pour in. Upon **arrival**, the best tactic is either to rush to the far end of the park and work backwards, or to head straight for the big rides, getting them out of the way before the mid-afternoon crush.

At its worst, waiting time can be well over an hour, but the excitement in the line, the atmosphere and the cleverly devised entertainment usually make the time fly by. Still, Disney recently unveiled a program called **Fastpass** to alleviate the problem of long lines, in which you place your admission ticket into a machine at the entrance of the attraction; the machine returns it with another ticket that gives you a time to return to the attraction, usually about two hours later, when you simply show up, hand your new ticket to the attendant and scoot to the front of the line.

---

Disney's celebration of science and technology; it's a sprawling area that involves a lot of walking, and can be boring for very young children. **Disney-MGM Studios** suits almost everyone: its special effects are enjoyable even if you've never seen the movies they're based on. The newest of the four, **Disney's Animal Kingdom**, brings all manner of African and Asian wildlife to the theme park setting, perhaps the lone entry that can be explored fairly quickly.

### The Magic Kingdom

The **Magic Kingdom** firmly follows the formula established by California's Disneyland, dividing into **Tomorrowland**, **Frontierland**, **Fantasyland** and **Adventureland** (roughly in declining order of merit). Some rides are identical to their Californian forebears; others are greatly improved. In Tomorrowland, old favorite **Space Mountain** offers a gut-churning roller-coaster trip around distant galaxies on a ferocious starlit switchback. More chilling is the high-tech, adrenalin-fueled **Extra TERRORestrial Alien Encounter**, where you're involved in an experiment that goes horrifically wrong. Another treat is the witty, fast-paced **Timekeeper**, where an animatronic mad professor and feisty robots take you on a dizzying trip through time, relayed convincingly on an enormous 360° cinema screen.

Rides in Frontierland are gentler, though just as much fun. On **Splash Mountain**, a lazy boat ride through Brer Rabbit land culminates in a shriek-inducing 50ft drop. People with weak hearts steer towards the less frenetic runaway train of **Big Thunder Mountain Railroad**, or, if the rides are getting too much, to the hokey **Country Bear Jamboree**, where you can hoedown with furry, dungareed grizzlies. In **Liberty Square**, between Frontierland and Fantasyland, make time for **Haunted Mansion**, a seriously spooky ghost ride with spectacular holograms.

Fantasyland, heralded by Cinderella's exceptionally pink castle, is very much old-style Disney, with a lot of stuff for kids. For adults the most striking ride is the *very* 1970s **It's a Small World**, a bizarre, almost trippy boat jaunt advocating brotherly love. Adventureland feels similarly quaint; **Pirates of the Caribbean**, a boat ride through a town invaded by debauched robotic figures, looks distinctly tame compared to the newer rides in Tomorrowland.

## EPCOT Center
Even before the new Magic Kingdom opened, Walt Disney was developing plans for **EPCOT Center**, or Experimental Prototype Community of Tomorrow, conceived in 1966 as a real community experimenting with the new ideas and materials of the technologically advancing US. The idea failed to shape up as Disney had envisioned: EPCOT didn't open its gates until 1982, when global recession and ecological concerns had put paid to utopian notions based on the infallibility of science. One drawback of this park is simply its immense size: twice as big as the Magic Kingdom and very sapping on the feet.

Inside the unmissable 180ft geosphere (unlike a semicircular geodesic *dome*, the geo*sphere* is completely round), Future World, a reminder of the park's original concept, details the history and possible advances to be made in agriculture, transportation, energy and communications. The best of the rides – all corporately sponsored, so don't expect any mention of alternative power or global warming – are the superb **Test Track**, a radical combination of simulator and switchback ride in which you test a high-speed car of the future; **Body Wars**, a fast-paced simulator voyage through the body's immune system, and the 4D cinematic thrill of **Honey, I Shrunk the Audience**. Occupying the largest area in the park is the **World Showcase**, with eleven different "countries" represented by street sets. The restaurants here are the best in Walt Disney World, and it's a great place to watch the spectacular nighttime sound and light show **Illuminations**.

## Disney-MGM Studios
When the Disney corporation began making films and TV shows for adults – most notably *Who Framed Roger Rabbit* – they also set about devising a theme park to entertain adults as much as kids. Buying the rights to the Metro-Goldwyn-Mayer (MGM)

---

### THE WORLD OF WALT DISNEY

When brilliant illustrator and animator Walt Disney devised the world's first theme park, LA's **Disneyland** (see p.939), he left himself with no control over the hotels and restaurants which quickly engulfed it, preventing growth and racking off profits Disney felt were rightly his. Determined not to let that happen again, the Disney corporation secretly bought up 27,500 acres of central Florida farmland, acquiring by the late Sixties a site a hundred times bigger than Disneyland. With the promise of a jobs bonanza for Florida, the state legislature gave the corporation the rights of any major municipality: empowering it to lay roads, enact building codes, and enforce the law with its own security force.

Walt Disney World's first park, the Magic Kingdom, which opened in 1971, was a huge success. Unveiled in 1982, the far more ambitious EPCOT Center represented the first major break from cartoon-based escapism, but its rose-tinted look at the future received a mixed response. Partly due to this, and some cockeyed management decisions, the Disney empire (Disney himself died in 1966) faced bankruptcy by the mid-1980s. Since then, the corporation has sprung back from the abyss as, with clever marketing strategies and a number of new, high-tech, young-adult-oriented rides lining up alongside the traditional favorites, it aims to increase Walt Disney World's 100,000 daily visitors and stay ahead of its rivals.

oeuvre of films and TV shows, Disney acquired a vast repertoire of instantly familiar images to mold into shows and rides. Opening in 1990, **Disney-MGM Studios** served to mute the opening of Florida's Universal Studios (see below), and at the same time found an extra use for the real film studios based here – the people you'll see laboring over storyboards aren't there for show, they really are making films.

There are more stage shows and tours than rides as such, though thrill-seekers will be more than happy with the delightfully sadistic **Twilight Zone Tower of Terror**, set in a haunted, cobweb-strewn hotel, or the new **Rock & Roller Coaster,** which, with a 2.8 second 0–60 mph launch, is Disney World's wildest ride. **Star Tours**, a flight-simulator trip piloted by *Star Wars* characters R2D2 and C-3PO, is toothless in comparison, and the **Great Movie Ride**, with actors and robotic figures re-creating scenes from classic Hollywood movies in an ersatz *Mann's Chinese Theatre*, is a tad disappointing.

Of the shows and tours, don't miss the half-hour **Backstage Studio Tour**, climaxing with the special-effects bonanza *Catastrophe Canyon*: the interest level fluctuates but you won't have had your money's worth if you miss it. The same applies to **Magic of Disney Animation**, an enlightening trip through the animation studios, and **Jim Henson's Muppet Vision 3D** show – enormous fun, with some great surprises. Capping them off is the twice-nightly **Fantasmic,** a 25-minute special effects laden show in which Mickey battles the products of his own imagination.

### Disney's Animal Kingdom

**Disney's Animal Kingdom** was opened in April 1998 as an animal-conservation theme park with Disney's patented over-the-top twist. The park is divided into five major "lands" – **Africa, Camp Minnie-Mickey, DinoLand USA, Safari Village** and **Asia** – though the true tribute here is to the versatility of concrete, which is colored, imprinted upon and formed into an endless variety of shapes to help create mock-authentic ambiances for each land.

Once within the park, visitors have four major stops. The best is **Kilimanjaro Safaris**, where "lorries" of tourists are driven past giraffes, zebras, elephants, lions, gazelle and rhinos, all passing what feels like authentic African wildlands (local oak trees have been trimmed to look like African acacias). Crossing over to "Asia," visitors can walk through dense vegetation and village ruins to see giant fruit bats, Asian birds and possibly tigers in the **Maharajah Jungle Trek.** The park's only thrill ride is in DinoLand USA: **Countdown to Extinction**, a roller-coaster-style vehicle that makes small drops and short stops in the dark as dinosaurs pop out of nowhere and roar.

The remainder of the park requires no more than casual exploration. The **Flights of Wonder** bird show exhibits parrots, hawks and other unusual birds, and classic Disney characters in appropriate attire sign autographs in **Camp Minnie-Mickey**, where you can also catch *Festival of the Lion King*, a participatory production of upbeat music with some nifty acrobatics, loosely based on its namesake film.

## Universal Studios Escape

All signs suggest that Florida will be the US moving-image capital of the next century, and the opening of **Universal Studios Escape** in 1990 has only reinforced the prediction. But it's more than just a working studio, turning out major features such as *Parenthood*, *Psycho IV* and tedious sitcoms; with the addition of the **Citywalk** and, most recently, **Islands of Adventure**, Universal has become a major player in the Orlando theme park arena. Disney still holds court, but Universal has drawn much attention and plans to expand into additional resorts in the near future. Access to all areas begins by parking in a massive parking garage (park opens daily at 9am, closing times vary; one-day pass $46.64 adults, $37.10 children aged 3–9, free for under-3s; two-day pass $84.75/$68.85; $6 parking) half a mile north of exits 29 and 30B off I-94.

## Universal Studios Florida

Like its competitor Disney-MGM, Universal is a working studio, filling more than four hundred acres with the latest in TV and movie production technology, but unlike MGM, there's more emphasis on movie-related rides than backstage shows. Currently, Universal's top rides are **Back to the Future**, a bone-shaking flight-simulator time trip from 2015 to the Ice Age (not for claustrophobes); the breathtaking **Terminator 2: 3D**, a dark, dizzying combination of high-speed live action, superb robotics and 3D morphing effects (for maximum enjoyment, aim for a seat in the middle of the auditorium, five or six rows from the front), and the flabbergasting **Twister**, where you're pitted against nature in an actual tornado. New in the summer of 2000 is **Men in Black: The Ride** that will allow you, with others, to control the fate of each ride.

Of the other rides, **Jaws**, a boat trip through shark-infested waters, plays wickedly with audience suspense; **Kongfrontation** has you scooped up and shaken by the angry six-ton brute; and **Earthquake** takes you on a subway ride through chaos, flooding and collisions. **ET** is gentler, a superb, undulating bike ride to save ET's home planet – be sure to listen when the little tyke says goodbye . . . Elsewhere, there are attempts to demystify production techniques, the most successful being **Alfred Hitchcock: The Art of Making Movies**, with surprising insights into Hitch's famed visual trickery. The two-man **Gory, Gruesome and Grotesque Horror Make-Up Show**, played for laughs, is as notable for its tour-de-force performances as for its educational content. **Woody Woodpecker's KidZone** is a good place for both adults and kids to cool off.

## Universal Studios Islands of Adventure

As the latest entry in the Orlando game of one-upmanship, **Islands of Adventure** stakes its claim as the leader in state-of-the-art, edge-of-your-seat, thrill rides. Though there are plenty of diversions for the less daring, this is what brings the crowds, and long lines are typical for many of the attractions, even if they thin out as the evening goes one.

The park is separated into five "islands" around a lagoon, each with its own theme: **Marvel Super Hero Island, Toon Lagoon, Jurassic Park, The Lost Continent** and **Seuss Landing**. Marvel Super Hero Island is home to three of the park's major rides. **The Incredible Hulk Coaster** begins with a thrust, supposedly equal to that of a US Air Force F-16 fighter jet, and continues for over two minutes of incognizant intensity. **Doctor Doom's Fearfall** provides a great panoramic view of the park before dropping 200ft, but is not worth waiting the usual half hour or so. **The Amazing Adventures of Spiderman** is arguably the best ride in the park and should not be missed, despite a not uncommon hour's wait. In a first ever combination of moving ride vehicles, filmed 3D action, and pyrotechnic special effects, you are to help Spidey get back the Statue of Liberty from a gaggle of villains. Try going during or immediately after the closing firework show, although as far as lines go, this one is the most enjoyable.

Continuing on to Toon Lagoon, **Dudley Do-Right's Ripsaw Falls** and **Popeye & Bluto's Bilge-Rat Barges** are good for getting a midday drenching. From here, Jurassic Park is a take off on the popular film and includes the visitor center used in the movie. The **Jurassic Park River Adventure** is an atmospheric trip through dino-land that ends with an 85-foot plunge – the steepest and fastest to date for a water ride. At The Lost Continent, one island over, the highlight is the intertwining set of inverted roller coasters, **Dueling Dragons**. Finally, although Seuss Landing is more directed towards kids, the playful architecture is right out of a Dr Seuss book and the firework show at the end of the night is worth sticking around for.

## Universal Studios Citywalk

Not to be outdone by Downtown Disney and Church Street Station, the **Universal Studios Citywalk** look to cash in on those lucrative evening dollars with thirty-acres

---

**THE ORLANDO FLEX TICKET**

**Universal Studios Escape, Wet 'n' Wild** and **Sea World** have teamed together to create a pass that permits access to each park over a period of seven consecutive days. The Orlando Flex-Ticket costs $169.55 ($135.63 ages 3–9), or $209.05/$167.65 including Tampa's **Busch Gardens** (see p.578), which is good for ten days.

---

of restaurants, live music, dance clubs, theaters and shops. Parrotheads not able to make it to Key West will find a safe haven at *Jimmy Buffett's Margaritaville*, while jazz lovers should take pleasure in CityJazz, a compound created in part by members of the Thelonious Monk Institute of Jazz. You can catch a flick at the **Universal Cineplex**, a twenty-screen, high-tech cineplex, or talk shop with Jeff Gordan fans at the *NASCAR Café*. Twenty-one Latin American nations offer native cuisine and music in the **Latin Quarter** or you can visit **Bob Marley – A Tribute to Freedom**, a re-creation of the Jamaican musician's home. Citywalk is free to enter but many bars and clubs will have a cover as the night progresses.

## Sea World

**Sea World**, at Sea Harbor Drive, near the intersection of I-4 and the Bee Line Expressway, the cream of Florida's sizeable crop of marine parks, should not be missed; and you should allocate a whole day to see it all (daily 9am–7pm or later; longer hours in summer; $46.64, $37.10 ages 3–9). The big event is the *Shamu Adventure* show – beginning with a pre-show film attempting to justify the twenty minutes of tricks then performed by killer whales. The **Wild Arctic** complex, complete with artificial snow and ice, shows off beluga whales, walruses and a couple of claustrophobic-looking polar bears; the experience is topped off by a thrilling simulated helicopter flight through an Arctic blizzard. The park's first thrill ride, **Journey to Atlantis**, is part fantasy, part waterslide, part roller coaster, and has a sixty-foot drop. You will get drenched – by the ride and by other tourists who pay for the privilege of spraying you. With substantially less razzmatazz, plenty of smaller tanks and displays explain more than you need to know about the undersea world. Among the highlights, the **Penguin Encounter** attempts to re-create Antarctica with scores of waddling birds scampering over an iceberg; the occupants of the **Dolphin Pool** assert their advanced intellect by flapping their fins and soaking passersby; and **Terrors of the Deep** includes a walk through a glass-sided tunnel, offering the closest eye-contact you're ever likely to have with a shark and live to tell the tale.

## Orlando's waterparks

You're spoilt for choice with superb **waterparks** in the Orlando area. Of the three Disney-owned ventures, **Blizzard Beach**, on World Drive north of the *All-Star Resorts*,

---

**DISCOVERY COVE**

**Discovery Cove** marks the second of Sea World's theme parks but is a much more exclusive venture, limiting visitors to those with reservations (and who can afford the high admission prices). This will entitle you to swim and play with dolphins, snorkel up to sharks and barracuda behind a clear partition and feed tropical birds in a resort-like setting. Call ☎1-877/4DISCOVERY for more information.

---

is the most creative, based on the fantasy that a hapless entrepreneur has opened a ski resort in Florida and the entire thing has started to melt. Star of the show is *Summit Plummet*, which shoots you down a 120ft vertical drop at more than fifty miles per hour. Gentler rides include toboggan-style slalom courses and covered raft rides. As well as the slides, **Typhoon Lagoon**, at Lake Buena Vista (one-day pass, one-park $26.95/$21.50), features geysers and a rainforest, a huge surfing pool and a shark reef, where you can snorkel among tropical fish. **River Country** is older, smaller and quieter (one-day pass $15.95/$12.50)

**Wet 'n' Wild**, 6200 International Drive (hours vary, call ☎1-800/992-9453; $28.57/$23.27, $4 parking), defends itself admirably in the face of the Disney competition, with a range of excellent slides including the challenging seven-story *Bomb Bay* and the almost vertical *Der Stuka*. Lines are shorter, too.

## Eating in the Orlando area

The only problem with **eating** in the Orlando area is wading through the choices. Downtown and its environs hold the pick of the locals' haunts; most visitors, however, head for International Drive's inexpensive all-day buffets and gourmet restaurants. Note that there's a strict embargo on taking food into any of the theme parks, where the best restaurants are to be found in **Epcot's World Showcase** – head for Japan, Morocco or Mexico.

**Lilia's Grilled Delights**, 3150 S Orange Ave (☎407/851-9087). Near downtown with good selection of inexpensive American and Polynesian fare.

**Ming Court**, 9188 International Drive (☎407/351-9988). Exceptional Chinese restaurant, serving delicious potstickers, dim sum and fragrant noodles; not as costly as you might expect.

**Numero Uno**, 2499 S Orange Ave (☎407/841-3840). Inexpensive, downtown Cuban restaurant.

**TuTu Tango**, 8625 International Drive (☎407/248-2222). Lively restaurant done out like an artist's studio, where painters and sculptors work as you eat superb pan-Asian, New World and Mediterranean food, including seared tuna sashimi or blackbean soup.

**Wild Jacks**, 7364 International Drive (☎407/352-4407). Western-style steaks, ribs and barbecue, with huge Southern helpings and Tex-Mex side dishes.

## Nightlife and entertainment

Though you'll probably be so exhausted from a long day at the parks that boozing and boogying with thousands of others will be the last thing on your mind, the Orlando area is just bursting with **themed nightspots** of every persuasion, from medieval banquets to piano bars and Country and Western clubs. It's all relentless good, clean fun, sanitized to the hilt.

From around 9pm, each Walt Disney World park holds some kind of closing-time bash, usually involving fireworks and fountains. There's also **Pleasure Island**, exit 26B off I-4 (in the Disney Village Marketplace), a remake of an abandoned island, whose pseudo-warehouses are the setting for shops, themed bars and nightclubs (daily 10am–7pm; after 7pm $19 gains access to all bars and clubs). The most enjoyable are the *Comedy Warehouse* and the *Adventurers' Club*, loosely based on a 1930s gentlemen's club. Take ID and a fat wallet.

In a similar vein, in the heart of downtown Orlando at 129 W Church St, the restored Victorian buildings of **Church Street Station** enclose a mall-like cluster of restaurants, bars, clubs and shows with a vaguely Old South theme (daily 11am–2am; after 6pm $19 gains access to all bars and clubs).

# THE WEST COAST

In three hundred miles from the state's southern tip to the border of the Panhandle, Florida's **west coast** embraces all the extremes. Buzzing, youthful towns neighbor placid fishing hamlets; mobbed holiday strips are just minutes from desolate swamplands. Surprises are plentiful, though the coast's one constant is proximity to the Gulf of Mexico – and sunset views rivaled only by those of the Florida Keys.

The largest city, **Tampa**, has more to offer than its corporate towers initially suggest – not least the exemplary nightlife scene at Cuban Ybor City and the Busch Gardens theme park. For the mass of visitors, though, the Tampa Bay area begins and ends with the **St Petersburg beaches**, whose miles of sea and sand are undiluted vacation territory. South of Tampa, a string of barrier-island beaches runs the length of the Gulf, and the mainland towns which provide access to them – such as Sarasota and Fort Myers – have enough to warrant a stop. Inland, the wilderness of the **Everglades National Park** is explorable on simple walking trails, by canoeing, or by spending the night at backcountry campgrounds with only the gators for company.

# Tampa

**TAMPA**, the business hub of the west coast, has been one of the major beneficiaries of the recent flood of money into Florida – of which it lavishes an impressive amount on a cultural diet envied by many larger rivals. A small city with an infectious, upbeat mood, it's well worth a stop: in addition to its fine **museums**, and **Busch Gardens**, one of the most popular theme parks in the state, it boasts in **Ybor City** a genuinely lively revitalized nightlife area to top the nation's best.

Tampa began as a small settlement beside a US Army base built to keep an eye on the Seminole during the 1820s. In the 1880s the railroad arrived, and the Hillsborough River on which the city stands was dredged to allow seagoing vessels to dock. Tampa became a booming port, simultaneously acquiring a major tobacco industry as thousands of Cubans moved north from Key West to the new cigar factories of neighboring Ybor City. The Depression saw off the economic surge, but the port remained one of the busiest in the country and tempered Tampa's postwar decline. While the social problems that blight any US city are evident, there seems little to stand in the way of Tampa's continued emergence as a forward-thinking and financially secure community.

## Arrival, information and getting around

The city's **airport** (☎813/870-8700) is five miles northwest of downtown: local HART bus #30 is the least costly connection (Mon–Fri every 30min 5.48am–8.18pm, weekends less frequent; $1.15; ☎813/623-5835), or use the 5am to midnight Central Florida Limo vans (☎813/396-3730; about $11 to downtown). **Taxis** (try Central Florida ☎813/253-2424) to downtown or a Busch Boulevard motel cost $13–24; to St Petersburg or the beaches, $30–46. Greyhound **buses** come in downtown at 610 Polk St; **trains** arrive at 601 N Nebraska Ave N.

The downtown **visitor center**, 111 Madison St (Mon–Sat 9am–5pm; ☎813/223-1111), and the **Ybor City Chamber of Commerce**, 1800 E Ninth Ave (Mon–Fri 9am–5pm; ☎813/248-3712) give out useful leaflets and maps.

Although both downtown Tampa and Ybor City are easily covered on foot, to travel between them without a car you'll need the HART **local buses**, ($1.15, one-day pass $2.50, five-day pass $12; ☎813/623-5835) whose route #8 passes the Florida Aquarium and Ybor City; other useful routes are #46 to Ybor City and #30 to the airport. Rush-hour commuter PSTA/HART express buses run **between Tampa and the coast** (Mon–Fri; $1.50) – #100 (PSTA ☎727/530-9911) to St Petersburg and #200 (HART) to Clearwater.

## Accommodation

Tampa is not generously supplied with low-cost **accommodation**; you'll almost certainly save money by sleeping in St Petersburg or at the beaches. There are some good deals, though, in the **motels** along Busch Boulevard, six miles north.

**Best Western All Suites – USF/Busch Gardens**, 3001 University Center Drive at 30th (☎1-800/SUNSHINE). Good value four blocks from Busch Gardens. Large suites, buffet breakfast, pool and jacuzzi. ⑤/⑥.

**Days Inn Busch Gardens/Maingate**, 2901 E Busch Blvd (☎813/933-6471). Comfortable and reliable, very good value, half a mile from Busch Gardens. ④.

**Travelodge**, 820 E Busch Blvd (☎813/933-4011). Dependable accommodation, close to Busch Gardens; with pools, jacuzzi and gym. ③–⑤.

## Downtown Tampa

Aside from riverside warehouses in various states of dilapidation around the northern end of the pedestrianized **Franklin Street** (once the district's main drag and still the best place to get your bearings), recalling the city's past is largely left to plaques detailing everything from the passage of sixteenth-century explorer Hernando de Soto to the site of Florida's first radio station. None of the contemporary buildings in downtown Tampa better reflects the city's striving for cultural articulacy than the highly regarded **Tampa Museum of Art**, on the banks of the Hillsborough River at 600 N Ashley Drive (Mon, Tues, Thurs & Sat 10am–5pm, Wed 10am–9pm, Sun 1–5pm; $5; free Wed 5–9pm & Sun). The museum specializes in classical antiquities and twentieth-century American art: selections from the permanent modern stock are cleverly blended with prime loaned specimens of recent US painting, photography and sculpture.

From **Curtis-Hixson Park** you'll see the silver minarets and cupolas on the far side of the river, sprouting from the main building of the University of Tampa – formerly the **Tampa Bay Hotel**, financed by steamship and railroad magnate Henry B Plant. To reach it, walk across the river on Kennedy Boulevard and descend the steps into Plant Park.

The structure is as bizarre a sight today as it was on its opening in 1891, when its five hundred rooms looked out on a community of just seven hundred souls. Plant had been buying up bankrupt railroads since the Civil War, steadily inching his way into Florida to meet his steamships unloading at Tampa's harbor, and was rich enough to put his fantasies of creating the world's most luxurious hotel into practice without worrying about the cost. But lack of care for the fittings (the hotel was only used during winter and left to fester during the scorching summer), and Plant's death in 1899, hastened its transformation from the last word in comfort to a pile of crumbling plaster. The city bought it in 1905 and leased it to the fledgling Tampa University 23 years later; today, in one wing, the **Henry B Plant Museum**, 401 W Kennedy Blvd (Tues–Sat 10am–4pm, Sun noon–4pm; $3 donation), holds what's left of the hotel's furnishings, which were largely the fruits of a half-million-dollar shopping trip across Europe and Asia by Plant and his wife.

The splendid **Florida Aquarium**, 701 Channelside Drive, in Tampa's dockland area (daily 9.30am–5pm; $11.95), houses lavish displays of Florida's fresh- and saltwater habitats, from springs and swamps to beaches and coral reefs. Residents include an impressive variety of fish and birds, otters, turtles and alligators.

# Ybor City

In 1886, as soon as Henry Plant's ships had ensured a regular supply of Havana tobacco into Tampa, cigar magnate Don Vincente Martinez Ybor cleared a patch of scrubland three miles northeast of present-day downtown Tampa and laid the foundations of **YBOR CITY**. Around twenty thousand migrants, mostly Cuban, settled here and created a Latin American enclave, producing the top-class, hand-rolled cigars that made Tampa the "Cigar Capital of the World." However, mass-production, the popularity of cigarettes and the Depression proved a fatal combination for skilled cigar-makers: as unemployment struck, Ybor City's tight-knit blocks of cobbled streets and redbrick buildings became surrounded by drab, low-rent neighborhoods.

Over the last few years, efforts to mold Ybor City into a tourist attraction have saved many older buildings from dereliction. Though it's best experienced at night, when the excellent restaurants and bars are heaving, you can take it in by strolling the nine blocks of Seventh and Eighth avenues east of 13th Street. The **Ybor City State Museum**, 1818 Ninth Ave (Tues–Sat 9am–5pm; $2 donation), helps you grasp the main points of Ybor City's creation and its multiethnic make-up. **Walking tours** of Ybor City (Jan–April Thurs & Sat 10.30am; May–Dec Sat 10.30am; 4$) leave from the museum. The old cigar-rolling factory is now converted into shops, restaurants and bars as **Ybor Square Mall**, between 13th and 14th streets and Eighth and Ninth avenues. Standing on the factory's steps in 1893, the Cuban poet and independence fighter José Martí called for "money, machetes and manpower" for the country's anti-Spanish struggles – expatriate cigar workers responded by contributing ten percent of their earnings.

# The Museum of Science and Industry, Busch Gardens and Adventure Island

A twenty-minute drive northeast from downtown Tampa takes you to the colossal **Museum of Science and Industry (MOSI)**, at 4801 E Fowler Ave (opening hours vary – call ☎813/987-6100; $8, $13 including IMAX), where topics such as health, the environment, and space and the stars are tackled through hands-on activities and a program of shows. Plan your day around the **Challenger Learning Center** (more Floridian space adventure where you can defy the laws of gravity), the 75mph **Gulf Coast Hurricane** and the IMAX shows.

Nearby, at Busch Boulevard and 40th Street, **Busch Gardens**, one of Florida's most popular theme parks (call for times; $46.64, $37.10 ages 3–9, parking $3; ☎813/987-5171), offers the Southeastern US's fastest, largest, most nerve-jangling roller coasters, incongruously set in an interpretation of colonial-era Africa. A sedate monorail journey allows inspection of a variety of African wildlife, but by far the most popular of the twenty-odd rides is **Gwazi**, a double wooden roller coaster that pits the two against each other in a race to finish first. Other winners include the nerve-jangling **Montu** and the enormous **Kumba**. For those weary of the G forces, the water rides **Stanley Falls** and **Congo River** are a refreshing alternative on a hot afternoon.

Opposite Busch Gardens, **Adventure Island** (call for times; $23.95, $19.95 ages 3–9; ☎813/987-5600) is a pretty good water park, with speed-slides, inner tubes and huge waves.

# Eating

There are plenty of good places to eat in Tampa, with a huge concentration of lively restaurants in **Ybor City**.

**Cafe Creole & Oyster Bar**, 1330 E 9th Ave, Ybor City (☎813/247-6283). Great Cajun dishes – try the filling seafood gumbo – in a lively, upscale atmosphere.

**Carmine's**, 1802 7th Ave, Ybor City (☎813/248-3834). Stylish Italian and Spanish restaurant with a trendy young crowd, live music at weekends, and a good nightclub upstairs.

**Cha Cha Coconuts**, 2029 E 7th Ave, Ybor City (☎813/241-2422). Caribbean/Floridian food served in a lush setting interrupted by the occasional simulated tropical storm. Live music and happy-hour drinks specials.

**Columbia**, 2117 E 7th Ave, Ybor City (☎813/248-4961). Refined Spanish and Cuban food, served on the premises since 1905, with flamenco six nights a week.

**Mise en Place**, 442 W Kennedy Blvd (☎813/254-5373). Classy New World cuisine opposite the university, with live jazz and blues.

**Ovo**, 1901 E 7th Ave, Ybor City (☎813/248-6979). Very hip, arty cafe with creative cuisine, booze and espresso.

**Shells**, 11010 N 30th St (☎813/977-8456). Convenient for the hotels near Busch Gardens, this cheap and cheerful seafood restaurant serves consistently good fresh fish to an enthusiastic crowd.

## Nightlife and entertainment

Ybor City is the only place to be at night, though new clubs open and close like wildfire. The free *Weekly Planet* has **nightlife listings**, as does the Friday edition of the *Tampa Tribune*.

**Frankie's Patio**, 1920 E 7th Ave, Ybor City (☎813/248-3337). A restaurant with a raucous rooftop bar. Live entertainment Wed–Sat.

**Irish Pub**, 1721 E 7th Ave, Ybor City (☎813/248-2099). Convivial spot for late-night drinking.

**Luna**, 1802 E 7th Ave, Ybor City (☎813/248-3460). Mixed, relaxed bar, with live music at *Zion*, downstairs.

**The Masquerade**, 1503 E 7th Ave, Ybor City (☎813/247-3319). Tampa's only purpose-built theater, hosting fringe and mainstream shows, and live music.

**Skipper's Smokehouse**, 910 Skipper Rd (☎813/971-0666). Blues and reggae rule at this family-oriented live music venue.

# St Petersburg

Declared the healthiest place in the US in 1885, **ST PETERSBURG**, twenty miles from Tampa on the eastern edge of the Pinellas peninsula, wasted no time in wooing the recuperating and the retired, at one point putting five thousand green benches on its streets to take the weight off elderly legs. By the early 1980s, few people under the age of fifty lived in the town, and no one was surprised when it became the setting for the 1985 movie *Cocoon*, in which a group of local geriatrics magically regain the vigor of their youth. Right now, St Petersburg itself seems to be emulating them. The average age of its residents has been almost halved, the revamped pier is a great place for open-air socializing, and – most remarkably of all – the town has acquired a major collection of works by Salvador Dali: reason enough to be in St Petersburg, if only as a day's break from the St Petersburg beaches, nine miles west.

The **Salvador Dali Museum**, 1000 S Third St (Mon–Wed, Fri & Sat 9.30am–5.30pm, Thurs 9.30am–8pm, Sun noon–5.30pm; $8), stores more than a thousand paintings from the collection of a Cleveland industrialist who struck up a friendship with the artist in the 1940s. **Free tours** begin whenever sufficient people gather, and trace a chronological path around the works, from early experiments with Impressionism and Cubism to the seminal Surrealist canvas *Persistence of Memory*.

Once you've done Dali, the quarter-mile-long **pier**, jutting from the end of Second Avenue N, is the town's central focus. It often hosts browsable arts and crafts exhibitions, and the inverted-pyramid-like building at its head holds five stories of restaurants, shops and fast-food counters. At the foot of the pier, the **Museum of History** (Mon–Sat 10am–5pm, Sun 1–5pm; $4) modestly recounts St Petersburg's early twentieth-century heyday as a winter resort, while nearby, the **Museum of Fine Arts**, 255 Beach Drive NE (Tues–Sat 10am–5pm, Sun 1–5pm; $6, free on Sun), holds a superlative collection ranging from pre-Columbian art through Asian and African to European Old Masters. The **Florida International Museum**, half a mile east of the pier at 100 Second St (daily during exhibition periods 9am–6pm; $14.50; reserve on ☎1-800/777-9882), occupies an entire block and, for about a year at a time, displays exhibitions from renowned museums all over the world.

## Practicalities

The Greyhound **bus** station is at 180 Ninth St N; an Amtrak bus link from Tampa pulls in someway out of town at the Pinellas mall on 7200 Hwy-19. The **Chamber of Commerce** is at 100 Second Ave N (Mon–Fri 8.30am–5pm; ☎727/821-4715). **Staying** in St Petersburg can be less costly than at the beaches. There is one **youth hostel** (members of any hostel organization pay $15): the *St Petersburg International Youth Hostel*, in the *McCarthy Hotel*, 326 First Ave N, with some private rooms (☎727/822-4141; ①/②). Of the dozens of cheap **motels** along Fourth Street (Hwy-92), good options include *The Banyan Tree* at no. 610 N (☎727/822-7072; ③) and *Kentucky* at no. 4246 (☎727/526-7373; ②). Downtown, the restored *Hotel Ponce De Leon* at 95 Central Ave (☎1-877/5-DELEON; ②/③), is good value. The *Heritage Holiday Inn* at 234 Third Ave N (☎727/822-4814; ⑤) is a stylish, comfortable, old-fashioned place; its very good **restaurant**, *Julian's* (☎727/823-6382), serves superlative New American cuisine. For great, inexpensive seafood, head for *The Shrimp Store*, 1006 Fourth St N (☎727/822-0325).

# The St Petersburg Beaches

Drab suburbs stretch west from St Petersburg, covering virtually all of the Pinellas peninsula, a bulky thumb of land poking between Tampa Bay and the Gulf of Mexico. Framing the Gulf side of the peninsula, a 25-mile chain of barrier islands forms the **St Petersburg Beaches**, one of Florida's busiest coastal strips. When the resorts of Miami Beach lost their allure during the 1970s, the St Petersburg beaches grew in popularity with domestic travelers, and more recently they've become a major destination for package-holidaying Europeans. Justifiably so; the sands are broad and beautiful, the sea is warm, and the sunsets are fabulous.

All **buses** ($1; ☎727/530-9911) to the beaches originate in St Petersburg at the **Williams Park terminal**, on First Avenue N and Third Street N; an information booth there has route details.

### The southern beaches

In twenty-odd miles of heavily touristed coast, only **PASS-A-GRILLE**, at the very southern tip of the barrier island chain, has the look and feel of a genuine community – two miles of tidy houses, cared-for lawns, small shops and a cluster of bars and restaurants. At weekends, informed locals come to enjoy one of the area's liveliest set of sands. A mile and a half north of Pass-a-Grille, the painfully luxurious **Don Cesar Hotel**, 3400 Gulf Blvd (☎727/360-1881; ⑦), is a grandiose pink castle, filling seven beachside acres. Opened in 1928, and briefly busy with the likes of Scott and Zelda Fitzgerald, its glamour was short-lived: during the Depression part of the hotel was used as a warehouse, and later as the spring training base of the New York Yankees baseball team.

Keeping to Gulf Boulevard brings you into the main section of **St Pete Beach**, a string of uninspiring hotels, motels and eating places. Further north, **Treasure Island** is even less varied tourist territory, culminating in an arching drawbridge into **Madeira Beach**, which is essentially more of the same – although, if you can't make it to Pass-a-Grille, the beach here justifies a weekend fling.

## The northern beaches
Much of the northern section of **Sand Key**, the longest barrier island in the St Petersburg chain and one of the wealthier portions of the coast, is taken up by stylish condos and time-share apartments. It ends with the pretty **Sand Key Park**, where tall palm trees frame a scintillating strip of sand. Among the nearby high-rises which somewhat mar the view is the *Sheraton Sand Key Resort*, venue of the liaison between TV evangelist Jim Bakker and church secretary Jessica Hahn in 1987, which led to the media preacher's fall from grace and, for a time, greatly boosted the hotel's custom.

Sand Key Park occupies one bank of Clearwater Pass, across which a belt of sparkling white sands characterizes the holiday town of **CLEARWATER BEACH**, whose streets still retain an endearing small-town feel. There's a well-positioned **hostel** here with a staff willing to help plan excursions around the area. *HI-Clearwater Beach,* 606 Bay Esplande (☎727/443-1211;①–③), has dorms and some private rooms. Regular buses (#80 and #60) provide links to the mainland town of Clearwater – across the two-mile causeway – where you'll find connections to St Petersburg and a Greyhound station.

## Beach practicalities
**Hotels** here tend to be filled with package tourists, and are always pricier than the **motels** that line mile after mile of Gulf Boulevard – typically $80 in the high season, anywhere between $50 and $80 in the low. Remember, too, that you'll pay $5–10 extra for a room on the beach side of Gulf Boulevard compared to an identical room on the inland side. At St Pete Beach the best bets are the luxuriously laid-back *Inn on the Beach,* 1401 Gulfway (☎727/360-8844; ③–⑥), or the secluded old *Florida Dolphin*, 6801 Sunset Way (☎727/360-7233; ③).

It's easy to find a decent place to **eat** around the beaches. *Hurricane Seafood Restaurant*, 807 Gulf Way (☎727/360-9558), has a well-priced menu of the freshest seafood; *Silas Dent's*, 5501 Gulf Blvd (☎727/360-6961), creates inspired fish dishes. In Clearwater Beach, *Frenchy's Rockaway Grill*, 7 Rockaway St (☎727/446-4844), is a fun bar and restaurant that cooks up grouper burgers and shrimp sandwiches.

# Sarasota

Rising on a gentle hillside beside the blue waters of Sarasota Bay, **SARASOTA** is one of Florida's better-off and better-looking towns, and also one of the state's leading cultural centers. It's home to numerous writers and artists, and the base of several respected performing arts companies. Despite periodic conservative flappings, the community is far less stuffy than its wealth, and the abundance of Neoclassical statues, fountains and manicured lawns decorating the town suggest. Most visitors stop by to see the **Ringling estate** on the town's northern edge – home of the art-loving millionaire from whom modern Sarasota takes its cue – and the barrier island **beaches**, a couple of miles away across the bay.

## Northern Sarasota: the Ringling Museum Complex
Don't fail to visit the house and art collections of **John Ringling**, a multimillionaire who gave Sarasota a taste for fine arts that it's never lost. One of the owners of the

fantastically successful *Ringling Brothers Circus*, which toured the US from the 1890s, Ringling acquired a fortune estimated at $200 million (see also p.334). Recognizing Sarasota's investment potential, he built the first causeway to the barrier islands and made this the winter base for his circus. His greatest gift to the town, however, was a Venetian Gothic mansion and an incredible collection of European Baroque paintings, displayed in a purpose-built museum beside the house.

The **Ringling Museum Complex**, which includes the mansion (daily 10am–5.30pm; $9, admission to the art galleries free on Sat), is at 5401 Bay Shore Rd, three miles north of downtown beside US-41. Begin your exploration by walking through the gardens to the former winter residence of John and Mable Ringling, **Ca' d'Zan** ("House of John," in Venetian dialect), a gorgeous piece of work serenely situated beside the bay and a triumph of taste and proportion. On trips to Europe to scout for new circus talent, Ringling became obsessed with Baroque art and acquired more than five hundred Old Masters: a gathering now regarded as one of the finest collections of its kind in the US. To display the paintings, a spacious **museum** was built around a mock fifteenth-century Italian palazzo. As with Ca' d'Zan, the very concept seems absurdly pretentious but, like the house, it works: the architecture matches the art with great aplomb. Five enormous paintings by Rubens, commissioned in 1625, and the painter's subsequent *Portrait of Archduke Ferdinand*, are the highlights, though there's also a wealth of talent from Europe's leading schools of the mid-sixteenth to mid-eighteenth centuries. Free guided tours depart regularly from the entrance.

### The Sarasota beaches

Increasingly the stamping ground of European package tourists spilling south from the St Petersburg beaches, the white sands of the **Sarasota beaches** are gradually losing much of their scenic appeal to towering condos. For all that, they're worth a day of anybody's time, with the two islands on which they lie, Lido Key and Siesta Key, accessible from the mainland. There is, however, no direct link between them. The third island, Longboat Key, is primarily residential.

The Ringling Causeway crosses the yacht-filled Sarasota Bay from the foot of Main Street to **Lido Key** and flows into **St Armand's Circle**, a glorified traffic circle ringed by upmarket shops and restaurants. Continuing south along Benjamin Franklin Drive you come to the island's most reachable beaches, ending after two miles at the more attractive **South Lido Park** (daily dawn–dusk; free), a belt of dazzlingly bright sand beyond a large, grassy park.

The bulbous northerly section of tadpole-shaped **Siesta Key**, reached by Siesta Drive off US-41, about five miles south of downtown Sarasota, holds the bulk of the island's residents, with streets that twist around a network of canals. To escape the crowds at **Siesta Key Beach**, beside Ocean Beach Boulevard, continue south past Crescent Beach, and follow Midnight Pass Road for six miles to **Turtle Beach**, a small body of sand that has the island's only campground.

### Practicalities

In downtown Sarasota, Greyhound **buses** stop at 575 N Washington Blvd, and the Amtrak bus from Tampa pulls up at 1995 Main St. The **local bus terminal** on Lemon Avenue, between First and Second, is where you catch the buses out to the Ringling house or the beaches. Call at the **visitor center**, 655 N Tamiami Trail (Mon–Sat 9am–5pm; ☎941/957-1877 or 1-800/522-9799), for the customary discount coupons and leaflets.

On the mainland, **motels** run the length of US-41 (N Tamiami Trail) between the Ringling estate and downtown Sarasota, typically charging $40 to $60. Prices are higher at the beaches. Try the clean, family-run *Cadillac Motel*, 4021 N Tamiami Trail

(☎941/351-4919; ②/③), or the welcoming *Surf View Resort* on Lido Key at 1121 Ben Franklin Drive (☎941/388-1818; ③), where rates include a free laundromat.

**Eating** options along Main Street include the healthful salads, sandwiches and smoothies at *Nature's Way*, no. 1572 (☎941/954-3131), and excellent pizza in uninspiring surroundings at *Patellini's*, no. 1420 (☎941/957-6433). *Cafe Kaldi*, no. 1568 (☎941/366-2326), is a hip coffeehouse with delicious pastries, Internet facilities and live music some evenings, while *Main Bar Sandwich Shop*, no. 1944 (no phone), has served great sandwiches since 1958 and *Yoder's*, 3434 Bahia Vista St (☎941/366-8817), has won awards for its old-fashioned Amish cuisine. Opposite the Ringling Museum, the friendly *Cafe of the Arts*, 5230 N Tamiani Trail (☎941/351-4304), serves good European food for lunch and dinner.

# Fort Myers

**FORT MYERS**, fifty miles south, may lack the élan of Sarasota, but it's nonetheless one of the up-and-coming communities of the southwest coast. Fortunately, most of its recent growth has occurred on the north side of the wide Caloosahatchee River, which the town straddles, allowing the traditional center, along the waterway's south shore, to remain relatively unspoiled.

Once across the river, US-41 strikes **downtown** Fort Myers, picturesquely nestled on the water's edge. Here, the **Fort Myers Historical Museum**, 2300 Peck St (Tues–Sat 9am–4pm; $4), provides thorough insights into the town's past, including the exploits of Doctor Franklin Miles, the local man who developed Alka Seltzer.

In 1885, six years after inventing the light bulb, **Thomas Edison** collapsed from exhaustion and was instructed by his doctor to find a warm working environment or face an early death. Vacationing in Florida, the 37-year-old Edison bought fourteen acres of land on the banks of the Caloosahatchee and cleared a section of it to spend his remaining winters (he lived to be 84) at what became the **Edison Winter Home**, 2350 McGregor Blvd, a mile west of downtown (Mon–Sat 9am–4pm, Sun noon–4pm; guided tours every half-hour; $10 including entrance to the Ford Winter Home, see below). The tours begin in the gardens, planted with such exotics as African Sausage trees and wild orchids. The house (which you can only glimpse through the windows), though, is an anticlimax, its plainness probably due to the fact that Edison spent most of his waking hours inside the **laboratory**, attempting to turn the latex-rich sap of *solidago Edisoni* (a strain of goldenrod weed he developed) into rubber. However, when the tour reaches the engrossing **museum** the full impact of Edison's achievements becomes apparent: a design for an improved ticker-tape machine provided him with the funds for the experiments that led to the creation of the phonograph in 1877, and financed research that resulted in the incandescent light bulb. Here, too, you'll see some of the ungainly cinema projectors derived from Edison's Kinetoscope – which brought him a million dollars a year in royalties from 1907. Next door, the uninspiring **Ford Winter Home**, bought by Henry Ford in 1915, is open for viewing (tours as for Edison Home). The banyan tree outside the ticket office is the largest tree in the state, grown by Edison from a seedling.

## The Fort Myers beaches

Still being discovered by the holidaying multitudes, the **Fort Myers beaches** on **Estero Island**, fifteen miles south of downtown, are appreciably different in character from the west coast's more commercialized beach strips, with a cheerful seaside mood. Accommodation is plentiful on and around Estero Boulevard – reached by San Carlos Boulevard, which runs the seven-mile length of the island. Most activity revolves around the short fishing pier and the **Lynne Hall Memorial Park**, at the island's north end.

Estero Island becomes increasingly residential as you press south, Estero Boulevard eventually swinging over a slender causeway onto the barely developed **San Carlos Island**. A few miles ahead, at the **Lovers Key State Recreation Area** (daily 8am–5pm; $1 walkers and bikers, $2 car, $4 car with 2–8 people), a footpath picks a trail over a couple of mangrove-fringed islands and several mullet-filled creeks to **Lovers Key**, a spectacularly secluded beach. If you don't fancy the walk, a free trolley will transport you between the park entrance and the beach.

### Practicalities

Greyhound is at 2275 Cleveland Ave; there are also Amtrak shuttles from Tampa. The **visitor center** is at Suite 100, 2180 W First St (Mon–Fri 8am–5pm; ☎941/338-3500). Distances are large, and you'll struggle without a car, though it is possible – just – to reach the beaches on local LeeTran **buses** (☎941/275-8726) whose downtown terminal is at Monroe Avenue and MLK Jr Boulevard.

**Accommodation** costs in and around Fort Myers are low between May and mid-December, when $10–20 gets lopped off the standard rates. Downtown, look along First Street – *Sea Chest*, no. 2571 (☎941/332-1545; ②/③), is among the cheapest. At the beaches, Estero Boulevard is your best bet: the *Beacon*, no. 1240 (☎941/463-5264; ②–⑤), the *Gulf*, no. 2700 (☎941/463-9247; ③–⑥), and *Laughing Gull Cottages*, no. 2890 (☎941/463-1346; three-night minimum; ③/④), sometimes offer midweek discounts. Of all the **campgrounds**, only *Red Coconut*, 3001 Estero Blvd (☎941/463-7200), is an easy walk from the beach. For downtown **food**, try the Southern home-style cooking at *Melanie's*, 2158 McGregor Blvd (☎941/334-3139). At the beaches, sample the seafood at *Top O' The Mast*, 1028 Estero Blvd (☎941/463-9424), or *The Fish Monger*, 19030 San Carlos Blvd (☎941/765-5544), and the all-you-can-eat nightly specials at *The Reef*, 2601 Estero Blvd (☎941/463-4181).

# The Everglades

Whatever scenic excitement you might anticipate from one of the country's more celebrated natural areas, there's nothing to herald your arrival in the **Everglades**, seventy miles south of Fort Myers. From the monotonous course of US-41, the most dramatic sights are small pockets of trees poking above a completely flat sawgrass plain. Yet these wide-open spaces resonate with life, forming part of an ever-changing ecosystem, evolved through a one-off combination of climate, vegetation and wildlife.

Appearing as flat as a table-top, the oolitic limestone on which the Everglades stand actually tilts very slightly towards the southwest. For thousands of years, water from summer storms and the overflow of nearby Lake Okeechobee has moved slowly through the Everglades towards the coast. The water replenishes the sawgrass, growing on a thin layer of soil formed by decaying vegetation, and gives birth to the algae at the foot of a complex food chain that sustains much larger creatures, most importantly **alligators**. After the floodwaters have reached the sea, drained through the bedrock or simply evaporated, the Everglades are barren except for the water accumulated in ponds – or "gator holes" – created when an alligator senses water and clears the soil covering it with its tail. Besides nourishing the alligator, the pond provides a home for other wildlife until the summer rains return. **Sawgrass** covers much of the Everglades, but where natural indentations in the limestone fill with soil, fertile tree islands – or "**hammocks**" – appear, just high enough to stand above the floodwaters.

Several **Native American tribes** once lived hunter-gatherer existences in the Everglades; the shell mounds they built can still be seen in sections of the park. In the nineteenth century, the Seminole, fleeing white settlers from the north, also lived peaceably in the area. By the late 1800s, a few towns had sprung up, peopled by settlers who, unlike the Indians, looked to exploit the land. As Florida's population grew, the damage caused by hunting, road building and draining for farmland gave rise to a significant **conservation** lobby. In 1947, a section of the Everglades was declared a national park, but unrestrained commercial use of nearby areas continues to upset the Everglades' natural cycle. The 1500 miles of canals built to divert the flow of water away from the Everglades and towards the state's expanding cities, the poisoning caused by agricultural chemicals from local farmlands, and the broader changes wrought by global warming could yet turn Florida's greatest natural asset into a wasteland.

# The Everglades National Park

Throughout this century the Everglades' boundaries have steadily been pushed back by urban development, and the **EVERGLADES NATIONAL PARK** bestows federal protection to only a comparatively small section around Florida's southeastern corner. It's in the park that the vital links holding the Everglades together become apparent: the all-important cycle of wet and dry seasons; the ability of alligators to discover water; the tree islands which provide sanctuaries for animals during the floods; and the forces, such as human demands for farmland and fresh water, that threaten to tear them apart.

### Everglades City and around

Purchased and named in the 1920s by an advertising executive dreaming of a subtropical metropolis, **EVERGLADES CITY**, three miles south off US-41 along Route 29, now has a population of just under five hundred. Most who visit are solely intent on diminishing the stocks of sports fish living around the mangrove islands – the aptly titled **Ten Thousand Islands** – arranged like jigsaw-puzzle pieces around the coastline.

For a closer look at the mangroves, which safeguard the Everglades from surge tides, take one of the park-sanctioned **boat trips** (April–Dec 9.30am–5pm; Jan–March irregular hours; $13–16; ☎1-800/455-7724) from the dock on Chokoloskee, a blob of land – actually a Native American shell mound – marking the end of Route 29. The dockside **Gulf Coast visitor center** (summer daily 8.30am–5pm; rest of year daily 7.30am–5pm; ☎941/695-3311) provides details on the cruises and the excellent ranger-led **canoe trips**. In Chokoloskee, you can rent an RV by the night for about $75 at Outdoor Resorts (☎941/695-2881), or in Everglades City try the clean and affordable *Everglades City Motel*, 310 Collier Ave (☎ 941/695-4224; ③).

### Shark Valley

Driven out of central Florida by white settlers, several hundred Seminole retreated to the Everglades during the nineteenth century, and their descendants – the **Miccosukee** – still live here, though the coming of US-41 brought a fundamental change in their lifestyle.

A mile east of the *Miccosukee Indian Village*, **Shark Valley** (daily 8.30am–6pm; cars $8, pedestrians and cyclists $4) epitomizes the Everglades' "River of Grass" tag. From here, dotted by hardwood hammocks, the sawgrass plain stretches as far as the eye can see. Aside from a few simple walking trails close to the **visitor center** (daily 8.30am–5.15pm; ☎305/221-8776), you can see Shark Valley only from a fourteen-mile loop road, ideally covered by renting a **bike** ($3.85 per hour, last rental at 3pm). Alternatively, a highly informative two-hour **tram tour** (winter hourly from 9am; summer at 9.30am, 11am, 1pm & 3pm; $9; reserve on ☎305/221-8455) stops frequently to view wildlife – but won't allow you to linger in any particular place, as you'll certainly want to do.

## Flamingo

The **Flamingo** section of the park – at the end of the main park road and perched on Florida's southern tip – holds virtually everything that makes the Everglades tick: spend a day or two in this southerly portion of the park and you'll quickly grasp the fundamentals of its complex ecology. From the main **park entrance** (always open; cars $10, pedestrians and cyclists $5), the road passes the main **visitor center** in the Pine Island section of the park (daily 8am–5pm; ☎305/242-7700) and continues for 38 miles to the tiny coastal settlement of **FLAMINGO**, a former fishing colony now comprising a marina, hotel and campground. A century ago, the only way to get here was by boat – it was so remote it didn't even have a name until the opening of a post office made one necessary. Then "Flamingo" was chosen, supposedly due to the abundant roseate spoonbills – pink-plumed birds which the locals failed to identify correctly as they killed them for their feathers.

Flamingo now does a brisk trade servicing the needs of sports fishing fanatics. On land, the **visitor center** (summer daily 9am–5pm, but staffed intermittently; rest of year daily 7.30am–5pm; ☎941/695-2945) and the marina of the *Flamingo Lodge*, the park's only hotel, are the activity bases. From the marina, the informative **Backcountry Cruise** ($16; reservations on ☎941/695-3101) makes a two-hour foray around the mangrove-enshrouded Whitewater Bay; the **Florida Bay Cruise** ($10; same number for reservations) is a must for bird watchers, a ninety-minute trip through the marine feeding and nursery grounds of Florida Bay.

## Park practicalities

**US-41** skirts the northern edge of the park, providing the only land access to the Everglades City and Shark Valley park entrances. To reach the Flamingo entrance, you'll need to touch the edge of Miami and head south. There's **no public transportation** along US-41, or to any of the park entrances. **Entering the park** is free at Everglades City, although you can only travel by boat or canoe; at the Shark Valley it's $8 per car and $4 for pedestrians and cyclists, at the main entrance it's $10 and $5 respectively. Tickets are valid for seven days.

The park is **open all year**, but the most favorable time to visit is **winter** (Nov–April), when the receding floodwaters cause wildlife to congregate around gator holes, ranger-led activities are frequent and the mosquitoes are bearable. In **summer** (May–Oct), afternoon storms flood the prairies, park activities are substantially reduced and the mosquitoes are a severe annoyance. Visiting between seasons is also a good bet.

There are well-equipped **campgrounds** at Flamingo and Long Pine Key ($14) and many backcountry spots on the longer walking and canoe trails (permit $10 for up to six people). Spare space at Flamingo (which fills quickly) can be checked on the board just inside the park entrance. The only **rooms** within the park are at *Flamingo Lodge* (☎941/695-3101; ④/⑤); for winter stays, make reservations months in advance. Ten miles outside the park in Florida City, *The Everglades International Hostel*, 20 SW 2nd Ave (☎1-800/372-3874), may be the best option for budget-minded travelers who want to maximize their time in the park. Dorms start at $12 and private rooms at $20.

# THE PANHANDLE

Rubbing hard against Alabama in the west and Georgia in the north, the long, narrow **Panhandle** has much more in common with the states of the Deep South than with the rest of Florida, and city sophisticates have countless jokes lampooning the folksy lifestyles of the people here. Hard to credit, then, that just a century ago, the Panhandle *was* Florida. At the western edge, **Pensacola** was a busy port when Miami was still a swamp. Fertile soils lured wealthy plantation owners south and helped establish

Tallahassee as a high-society gathering place and administrative center – a role which, as the state capital, it retains. But the decline of cotton, the chopping down of too many trees, and the coming of the East Coast railroad eventually left the Panhandle high and dry. Much of the inland region still seems neglected, and the **Apalachicola National Forest** is perhaps the best place in Florida to disappear into the wilderness. The **coastal Panhandle**, on the other hand, is enjoying better times and, despite rows of hotels, much is still untainted, with miles of blindingly white sands.

# Tallahassee and around

Briefcase-clutching bureaucrats set the mood in **TALLAHASSEE**, a provincial-feeling state capital with plentiful reminders of Florida's formative years. When the state was incorporated into the US, Tallahassee was made its administrative base – the local Native Americans, the Tamali tribe, being unceremoniously dispatched to make room for the trio of log cabins in which the first Florida government sat in 1823. However, Tallahassee's own recent fortunes have been hindered by the lightning-paced development of south Florida, and – oddly distanced from most of the people it now governs – the city remains a conservative place.

### Arrival, information and accommodation

The Greyhound **bus** terminal is at 112 S Tennessee St, within walking distance of downtown and opposite the local Taltran bus station (☎850/891-5200). You can get a **free ride** into downtown Tallahassee from the bus station on the **Old Town Trolley**, which runs to the Civic Center (near the New Capitol Building) and back (every 20min Mon–Fri 7am–6pm). Otherwise, downtown Tallahassee is best seen **on foot**. For stacks of background information, visit the **Visitor Information Center**, 106 E Jefferson St (Mon–Fri 8am–5pm, Sat 9am–1pm, closed Sun ☎1-800/628-2866). **Accommodation** in Tallahassee is only in short supply during the sixty-day sitting of the state legislature from early April, and on fall weekends during Seminoles home football games. **Hotels** and **motels** on N Monroe Street, about three miles from downtown, are far cheaper than those downtown. To get **out of the city** altogether, consider the wonderful *Wakulla Springs Lodge*, fifteen miles to the south (see overleaf).

**Governors Inn**, 209 S Adams St (☎850/681-6855). Capitol City luxury in the heart of downtown. ⑥–⑧.

**Quality Inn**, 2020 Apalachee Parkway (☎850/877-4437). Very good value, with pool, complimentary continental breakfast, free wine specials, and membership to the nearby YMCA. ④.

**Super 8**, 2702 N Monroe St (☎850/386-8818). Regular motel facilities between I-10 and downtown. ②.

### The Town

A fifty-million-dollar eyesore dominates the square mile of **downtown Tallahassee** – the vertical vents of the towering **New Capitol Building**, at Apalachee Parkway and Monroe Street (Mon–Fri 8am–5pm, Sat–Sun 9am–3pm; free). Florida's growing army of bureaucrats had previously been crammed into the 1845 **Old Capitol Building** (Mon–Fri 9am–4.30pm, Sat 10am–4.30pm, Sun noon–4.30pm; free) that stands in the shadow of its replacement. For a more rounded history – easily the fullest account of Florida's past anywhere in the state – visit the **Museum of Florida History**, 500 S Bronough St (Mon–Fri 9am–4.30pm, Sat 10am–4.30pm, Sun noon–4.30pm; free). Detailed accounts of Paleo-Indian settlements, and the significance of their burial and temple mounds – some of which have been found on the edge of Tallahassee – are valuable tools in comprehending Florida's prehistory, and the imperialist crusades of the Spanish are outlined with copious finds. There's disappointingly little on the nineteenth-century Seminole Wars – one of the bloodier skeletons in Florida's closet – but plenty on the crucial c.1900 railroads.

It's well worth making the trip out to the Florida A&M University campus west of downtown, where the **Black Archives Research Center and Museum** (Mon–Fri 9am–4pm; free) holds one of the largest and most important collections of African-American artifacts in the nation, with oral histories and music stations, as well as an awe-inspiring group of Ethiopian crosses.

## Eating

With so many politicos passing through, there's plenty of good **food** in Tallahassee; the presence of 25,000 students at its two universities keeps it affordable.

**Andrew's Adams Street Cafe/Andrew's Second Act**, 228 S Adams St (☎850/222-3444). Stylish lunch cafe, with pricier gourmet evening meals and live jazz upstairs.

**Bahn Thai**, 1319 S Monroe St (☎850/224-4765). Fresh, fragrant Thai and Chinese food and a good-value lunch buffet.

**Barnacle Bill's**, 1830 N Monroe St (☎850/385-8734). Low-cost fresh fish and seafood in a riotous atmosphere.

**The Mill**, 2329 Apalachee Parkway (☎850/656-2867). Burgers, salads, sandwiches and exquisite pizza complement *The Mill*'s home-brewed beer.

**Mom and Dad's**, 4175 Apalachee Parkway (☎850/877-4518). Delicious homemade Italian food; dinner only.

# Wakulla Springs State Park

Fifteen miles south of Tallahassee off SR-61 on SR-267, **Wakulla Springs State Park** (daily 8am–dusk; cars $3.25, pedestrians and cyclists $1.25) holds what is believed to be one of the biggest and deepest natural springs in the world, pumping up half a million gallons of crystal-clear pure water from the bowels of the earth every day – though you'd never guess it from the calm surface.

It's refreshing to **swim** in the cool pool (in a small roped-off area – this is gator territory), but to learn more about the spring, take the thirty-minute **glass-bottomed boat tour** ($4.50), and peer down to the swarms of fish hovering around the 180ft cavern through which the water comes. Forty-minute **river cruises** ($4.50) let you glimpse some of the park's inhabitants: deer, turkeys, turtles, herons, egrets and the inevitable alligators. The lovely wooden *Wakulla Springs Lodge* (☎850/224-5950; ④/⑤) is a serene 1930s **hotel**, with an excellent **restaurant** (call to reserve) serving home-baked country food, and a marble-topped soda fountain for sandwiches and coffee.

# The Apalachicola National Forest

With swamps, savannahs and springs dotted liberally about its half-million acres, the **Apalachicola National Forest** is the inland Panhandle at its natural best. Several roads enable you to drive through a good-sized chunk, with many undemanding spots for a rest and a snack, but to see deeper into the forest you'll have to make an effort: exploring at length, following one of the hiking trails, canoeing on one of the rivers, or simply spending a night under the stars at one of the basic campgrounds. Driving through the forest on Hwy-65, or around it on Hwy-319, you'll eventually pass the large and forbidding **Tate's Hell Swamp**. This is a breeding ground for the deadly water moccasin snake, and though gung-ho locals sometimes venture in hoping to catch a few to sell to the less reputable zoos, you're well advised to stay clear.

The main **entrances** to the forest are off Hwy-20 and Hwy-319; three minor roads, routes 267, 375 and 65, form cross-forest links between the two. **Accommodation** is limited to camping; apart from Silver Lake (nine miles east of Tallahassee; $4), all the campgrounds are free, with very basic facilities (no running water). For more information call the **ranger stations** at Apalachicola (☎850/643-2282) or Wakulla (☎850/926-3561).

# Panama City Beach

An orgy of motels, go-kart tracks, mini-golf courses and amusement parks, **PANAMA CITY BEACH** is entirely without pretension, capitalizing blatantly on the appeal of its 27-mile beach. The whole place is as commercial as can be, but with the shops, bars and restaurants all trying to undercut one another, there are some great bargains to be found. That said, throughout the lively summer (the so-called "100 Magic Days"), accommodation costs are high and bookings essential. In winter, prices drop and visitors are fewer; most are Canadians and – increasingly – Europeans, many of whom have no problems sunbathing and swimming in the cool temperatures.

Getting a tan, running yourself ragged at beach sports and going hammer-and-tongs at the nightlife are the main concerns in Panama City Beach. If you get restless, try go-karting, jet-skiing or parasailing; otherwise, visit one of the amusement parks (usually $18 for a go-on-everything day ticket), go on a fishing trip (from around $30 a day) or scuba-diving (several explorable shipwrecks litter the area; details from any of the numerous dive shops).

## Practicalities

Greyhound **buses** pick up and drop off near the Shell station, 17325 W Hwy-98, fifteen minutes' walk from the nearest motels. You may well, however, end up at the station in **Panama City,** eight miles east; four daily Greyhound buses (three in the morning) link the two. The **visitor center** is at 12015 Front Beach Rd (daily 8am–5pm; ☎1-800/ PCBEACH).

**Places to stay** are plentiful, but fill with amazing speed, especially at weekends. As a very general rule, **motels** at the eastern end of the beach are smarter and slightly pricier than those in the center, and those at the western end are quiet and family oriented. The *Suger Sands Motel,* 20723 Front Beach Rd (☎1-800/367-9221; ③/④), is an excellent-value oceanfront motel away from the noise. The cheapest places to **eat** are the buffet restaurants on Front Beach Road, which charge $5–12 for all you can manage. Or try one of the regular **lunch or dinner** restaurants, such as *Shuckum's Oyster Pub & Seafood Grill*, 15614 W Hwy-98 (☎850/235-3214), *Mike's Diner*, 17554 Front Beach Rd (☎850/234-1942), also open for breakfast and serving tasty Southern-style food, and *The Treasure Ship,* 3605 Thomas Drive (☎850/234-8881), a seafood restaurant that looks like a wooden sailing ship.

# Pensacola

Tucked away as it is at the western end of the Panhandle, you might be inclined to overlook **PENSACOLA**, built on the northern bank of the broad Pensacola Bay and five miles inland from the nearest beaches, particularly as its prime features are a naval aviation school and some busy dockyards. Pensacola is, however, worth a visit – its white beaches are relatively untouched, and it is a historic center: occupied by the Spanish from 1559 (only the hurricane that ended their settlement prevented it becoming the oldest city in the US), it repeatedly changed hands among the Spanish, French and British before becoming the place where Florida was officially ceded by Spain to the US in 1821.

Pensacola was already a booming port by c.1900, when the opening of the Panama Canal was expected to boost its fortunes still further. The many new buildings that appeared in the **Palafox District**, around the southerly section of Palafox Street, in the early 1900s – with their delicate ornamentation and attention to detail – reflect the optimism of the era. Between 1870 and 1930, Pensacola's professional classes took a shine to the area called **North Hill,** just across Wright Street from Palafox, commissioning elaborate homes in a plethora of fancy styles. Strewn across the fifty-block area are Neoclassical porches, Tudor Revival cottages, low-slung California bungalows, and the rounded towers of the finest Queen Anne homes. Though none is open to the public, you can see them on special tours (see below).

In earlier times, Native Americans, pioneer settlers and seafaring traders had gathered to swap, sell and barter on the waterfront of the **Seville District**, about half a mile east of Palafox Street. Those who did well took up permanent residence, and many of their homes remain in fine states of repair, forming – together with several museums – the **Historic Pensacola Village** (summer daily 10am–4pm; rest of year closed Sun; $6). One payment secures admission to all of the museums and former homes in an easily navigated four-block area. Try and time your visit to join a **tour**, which leaves from the ticket office in the Tivoli House, 205 E Zaragoza St at 11.30am and 1.30pm. Inside the US naval base on Navy Boulevard, about eight miles southwest of central Pensacola, the **Museum of Naval Aviation** exhibits US naval aircraft ranging from the first flimsy seaplane acquired in 1911 to the Phantoms and Hornets of more recent times (daily 9am–5pm; free, IMAX $5).

### Santa Rosa Island

On the other side of the bay from the city lie Pensacola's real attractions: the glistening beaches and windswept sand dunes of **Santa Rosa Island** (the barrier island that runs sixty miles from Fort Walton). **Pensacola Beach** in particular has everything you'd want from a Gulf coast beach: mile after mile of fine white sands, water sports rental outlets, a busy fishing pier and a sprinkling of motels, beachside bars and snack stands. A short way west, at the **Gulf Islands National Seashore**, on Fort Pickens Road (9am–dusk; cars $4, pedestrians and cyclists $2), vibrant white sands are walled by a nine-mile-long stretch of high, rugged dunes, and the only reminder of civilization is a foliage-encircled campground.

### Practicalities

The Greyhound station is seven miles north of the city center at 505 W Burgess Rd; bus #10 links it to Pensacola proper. Pensacola is a stop on Amtrak's *Sunset Limited* to LA; the **train station** is at 980 E Heinberg St. Local **taxi** firms include Yellow Cab (☎904/433-3333). ECAT **buses** serve the city but not the beach; the main terminal is at L Street and Fairfield (☎850/436-9383).

At the foot of the three-mile Pensacola Bay Bridge into the city (on the city side), the **visitor center**, at 1401 E Gregory St (daily 8am–5pm; ☎1-800/874-1234), has the usual worthwhile handouts. Plenty of budget chain **hotels**, all charging $30–50 per night, line N Davis and Pensacola boulevards, the main approach roads from I-10. Central options are the *Seville Inn*, 223 E Garden St (☎1-800/277-7275; ③/④), and *Days Inn*, 710 N Palafox St (☎904/438-4922; ③). At the beach try along Via De Luna Drive: the airy *Hampton Inn*, no. 2 (☎850/932-6800; ⑥), offers great value.

For **eating** in town, the always bustling *Hopkins Boarding House*, 900 N Spring St (☎850/438-3979), serves lip-smacking Deep South food family-style at big round tables; you eat your fill, then clear your plate. For beachside dining, the *Jubilee Restaurant and Entertainment Complex* (☎850/934-3108), on the boardwalk at Via De Luna Drive and Fort Pickens Road, has a selection of good places to eat, including a gourmet coffeehouse and a bar.

# CHAPTER EIGHT

# LOUISIANA

S wathed in the romance of pirates, voodoo and Mardi Gras, **LOUISIANA** is undeniably special. Its history is barely on nodding terms with the view that America was the creation of the Pilgrim Fathers; its way of life is proudly set apart. This is the land of the rural, French-speaking **Cajuns** (descended from the Acadians, eighteenth-century French-Canadian refugees), who live in the prairies and swamps in the southwest of the state, and the **Creoles** of jazzy, sassy **New Orleans**. (The term Creole covers those born in the state to French and Spanish colonists – famed in the nineteenth century for their masked balls, family feuds and duels – as well as native-born, French-speaking slaves.) Southern Louisiana's spicy home-cooked **food**, regular **festivals** and lilting French-based dialect – and above all its **music** (**jazz**, **R&B**, **Cajun** and its bluesy black counterpart, **zydeco**) – draw from all these cultures. **North Louisiana** – Protestant Bible Belt country, where old plantation homes stand decaying in vast cottonfields – feels more "Southern" than the marshy bayous, shaded by ancient cypress trees and laced with wispy trails of Spanish moss, of the Catholic south.

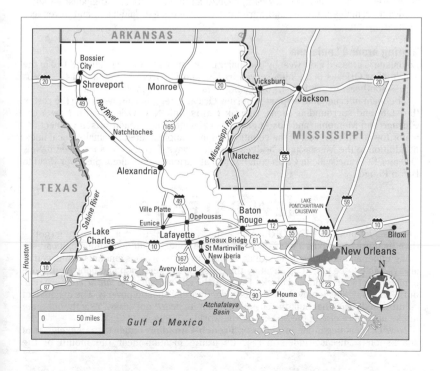

The **French** first settled Louisiana in 1682, braving swamps and plagues to harvest the abundant cypress, but the state was sparsely inhabited before its first permanent settlement, the trading post of **Natchitoches**, was established in 1714. In 1760, Louis XV secretly handed New Orleans, along with all French territory west of the Mississippi, to his **Spanish** cousin, Charles III, as a safeguard against the British. Louisiana remained Spanish until it was ceded to Napoleon in 1801, under the proviso that it should never change hands again. Just two years later, however, Napoleon, strapped for cash to fund his battles with the British in Europe, struck a bargain with president Thomas Jefferson known as the **Louisiana Purchase**. This sneaky agreement handed over to the US all French lands between Canada and Mexico, from the Mississippi to the Rockies, for a total cost of $15 million. The subsequent "Americanization" of Louisiana was one of the most momentous periods in the state's history, with the port of New Orleans, in its key position near the mouth of the **Mississippi River** growing to become one of the nation's wealthiest cities. Though the state seceded from the Union to join the Confederacy in 1861, there were important differences between Louisiana and the rest of the slave-driven South. Here, slavery was more in the West Indian mold than the Anglo-American. The **Black Code**, drawn up by the French in 1685 to govern Saint-Domingue (today's Haiti) and established in Louisiana in 1724, gave slaves rights unparalleled elsewhere, including permission to marry, meet socially and take Sundays off. The black population of New Orleans in particular was renowned as exceptionally literate and cosmopolitan.

Though Louisiana was not physically scarred by the Civil War, with few important battles fought on its soil, its economy was given a death blow. In time it recovered, benefiting from the rich agricultural land, the mighty Mississippi River and offshore oil. These days, though, the state has become dependent upon **tourism**, centred around New Orleans and Cajun country. Still, despite all its difficulties, and against all odds, Louisiana remains a unique and intriguing place – upbeat, laid-back, and never less than compelling.

### Getting around Louisiana

Louisiana is crossed east–west by two major interstates, I-20 in the north and I-10 in the south. New Orleans is the hub, served by I-55 and I-59 from Mississippi. I-49 sweeps across southeast to northwest, connecting Cajun country with the north.

The main international **airport** is in New Orleans; regional airlines serve the rest of the state and surrounding areas. Amtrak **trains** link New Orleans with New York, Chicago and Memphis, and Los Angeles via Lafayette. Greyhound **buses** connect the major towns with the rest of the country, and are supplemented by smaller local lines. In addition to the Mississippi's bridges and causeways, **ferries** cross the river at New Orleans, St Francisville in Cajun country, and at various points along the River Road to Baton Rouge.

# NEW ORLEANS

There's a lot more to **NEW ORLEANS** – the "Big Easy," the "city that care forgot" – than its tourist image as a nonstop party town. At once sordid and sublime, it careers along under an infuriating doublethink. Whilst having enormous amounts of fun, you're always liable to be pulled up short by the divisions between rich and poor (and, more explicitly, between white and black). Even so, the city's vitality and *joie de vivre* are real, buffeted but not beaten by the vagaries of commercialism and poverty. The melange of cultures and races that built the city still gives it its heart; not "easy," exactly, but quite unlike anywhere else in the States – or the world.

New Orleans began life in 1718 as a **French-Canadian** outpost, an unlikely set of shacks on a disease-ridden marsh. Its prime location near the mouth of the

**Mississippi River**, however, led to rapid development, and with the first mass importation of African **slaves**, as early as the 1720s, its unique demography began to take shape. Despite early resistance from its Francophone population, the city benefited greatly from its period as a **Spanish** colony from 1763 to 1800. By the end of the eighteenth century, the **port** was flourishing, the haunt of smugglers, gamblers, prostitutes and pirates. Newcomers included Anglo-Americans escaping the American Revolution and aristocrats fleeing revolution in France. The city also became a haven for refugees – whites and free blacks, along with their slaves – escaping the slave revolts in Saint Domingue. As in the West Indies, the Spanish, French and free people of color associated and formed alliances to create a distinctive **Creole** culture. New Orleans was thus already a many-textured city when it experienced two quick-fire changes of government, passing back into French control in 1801 and then being sold to **America** under the Louisiana Purchase two years later. Unwelcome in the French Quarter, the Americans who migrated here were forced to settle in the areas now known as the **Central Business District** (or **CBD**) and, later, in the **Garden District**. Canal Street, which divided the old Creole city from the expanding suburbs, become known as "the neutral ground" – still the name for the median strip between main roads in New Orleans.

Though much has been made of the antipathy between Creoles and Anglo-Americans, economic necessity forced them to live and work together. They fought side by side, too, in the 1815 **Battle of New Orleans**, the final battle of the War of 1812, which secured American supremacy in the States. The victorious general, **Andrew Jackson**, became a national hero – and eventually US president; his ragbag volunteer

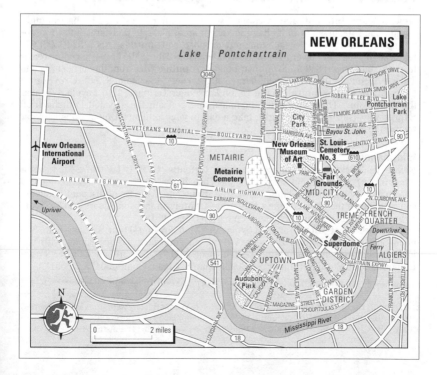

army was made up of Anglo-Americans, slaves, Creoles, free men of color and Native Americans, along with pirates supplied by the notorious **Jean Lafitte**.

New Orleans' antebellum **"Golden Age"** as a major port and finance center for the cotton-producing South was brought to an abrupt end by the Civil War. The economic blow wielded by the lengthy Union occupation – which effectively isolated the city from its markets – was compounded by the social and cultural ravages of **Reconstruction**. This was particularly disastrous for a city once famed for its large, educated, free black population. As the North industrialized and other Southern cities grew, the fortunes of New Orleans took a downturn.

**Jazz** exploded into the bars and the bordellos around 1900, and, along with the evolution of **Mardi Gras** as a tourist attraction, breathed new life into the city. And although the Depression hit here as hard as it did the rest of the nation, it also heralded the resurgence of the **French Quarter**, which had disintegrated into a slum. Even so, it was the less romantic duo of **oil** and **petrochemicals** that really saved the economy – until the slump of the 1950s pushed New Orleans well behind other US cities. The oil crash of the early 1980s gave it yet another battering, a gloomy start for a decade of high crime rates and corruption. By the end of the 1990s, however, New Orleans found itself with a strong, popular, black-dominated city government, whose highly publicized police clean-up program, in the context of a relatively stable economy based on **tourism**, lead the city into the new millennium with renewed confidence.

# Arrival, information and getting around

**New Orleans International Airport**, twelve miles northwest on I-10, has an information booth (8am–9pm) in its baggage claim area. Flat-rate **taxi** fares into town are $21 for up to two people, $8 each for three or more, and **shuttles** (☎504/522-3500) will take you to your hotel (every 10min; tickets available 24hr in the baggage claim area or from the bus driver; $10 to downtown hotels). A **public bus** from the airport goes to Tulane Avenue in the CBD (daily 6am–5.30pm; every 15–25min; $1.50). **Greyhound** buses arrive next to **Amtrak** at the Union Passenger Terminal, 1001 Loyola Ave, near the Superdome. This area, in the no-man's-land beneath the elevated Pontchartrain Expressway, is dangerous at night; take a **cab** to your lodgings. United Cabs is by far the best firm (☎504/522-9771).

## Information

Before you leave home contact the **New Orleans CVB** (☎1-800/672-6124; *www. nawlins.com*), who mail out stacks of glossy brochures. Once you've arrived, detailed information, self-guided walking tours, free **maps** and a variety of discount vouchers can be found at the **New Orleans Welcome Center**, on Jackson Square at 529 St Ann St in the French Quarter (daily 9am–5pm; ☎504/566-5031).

The official **post office** is at 701 Loyola Ave (Mon–Fri 7am–11pm, Sat 7am–8pm, Sun noon–5pm; ☎504/523-4638; zip code 70140); an equivalent service, along with fax, FedEx, photocopying and phone rental, is offered by the French Quarter Postal Emporium, 940 Royal St (Mon–Fri 9.30am–6pm, Sat 10am–3pm; ☎504/525-6551).

---

Although the heavily touristed French Quarter is comparatively safe, to wander unwittingly beyond it – even just a couple of blocks – can place your **personal safety** in jeopardy. Be careful, and at night always take a cab, however short the distance.

## CITY TOUR AND RIVER CRUISES

There is a bewildering variety of **tours** of New Orleans, from whistlestop jaunts in air-conditioned buses to preposterous moonlit ghost-hunts; stop by the Welcome Center (see opposite) to see the full range.

**Walking tours** are especially popular – notwithstanding the possibility of showers and, in summer, debilitating heat and humidity. Those led by Le Monde Creole, stopping at French Quarter sites featured in the true-life saga of a Creole family, are superb. They set off from their store at 624 Royal St (Tues–Sun 10.30am & 2.30pm; ☎504/568-1801; $16; reservations). The Bienville Foundation's French Quarter walking tours emphasize "alternative" history (schedules vary; ☎504/945-6789; $15–18), while those led by the Jean Lafitte National Park Service (☎504/589-2636) are free (French Quarter: 10.30am; Garden District: 2.30pm; reservations required). Collect a pass from the NPS office, 419 Decatur St, after 9am on the day.

If the weather's bad, you may prefer to take a **bus tour**. Gray Line (☎504/569-1401 or 1-800/535-7786) offers trips around the city (2hr; $19), to the nearby plantations (7hr 30min; $40), and the swamps (3hr 15min; $38). They also do a paddlewheeler-cruise and city-tour combination ($31). New Orleans Tours (☎504/592-0560 or 1-800/543-6332) are similar, but fractionally cheaper.

Many visitors, especially with kids in tow, take a narrated trot through the Quarter in one of the **mule-drawn carriages** that wait behind Jackson Square on Decatur. These can be fun, though you should take the "historic" running commentary with a pinch of salt. Rates range from $8 to $10 per person for 30 to 45 minutes. Another pleasant way to while away a few hours on a steamy afternoon is on a **river cruise**. The *Natchez* steamboat is by far the best. Leaving from behind Jackson Brewery, it heads downriver before turning back near the Chalmette battlefield (daily 11.30am & 2.30pm; ☎504/586-8777; $21 with lunch and live jazz). The *John James Audubon* riverboat allows you to combine a cruise with a trip to the aquarium (see p.604) or the zoo (p.605), or both. It leaves daily from the aquarium at 10am, noon, 2pm and 4pm, and from the zoo an hour later (☎504/586-8777; $10.50 one-way, $13.50 round trip)

For details on **ghost, voodoo** and **cemetery tours**, see p.601.

## City transportation

Though New Orleans' most visited neighborhoods are a dream to **walk** around, getting from one to another is not always easy on foot, and traveling anywhere outside the Quarter after dark you'd be better off calling a **cab**. The Regional Transit Authority (RTA) runs a network of **buses** (24hr information ☎504/248-3900; $1–1.25). The most useful **routes** include "Canal" (#41), which runs along Canal Street; "Magazine" (#11) from the CBD to the Garden District; and "Esplanade" (#48) from the Quarter up to City Park. You're more likely to use the handsome **St Charles streetcar** (a National Historic Monument, dating back around 100 years) that rumbles a thirteen-mile loop from Canal Street, along St Charles Avenue in the Garden District, past Audubon Park to Carrollton uptown ($1 each way; 10¢ transfers; exact fare). The cars trundle along at an average speed of 9mph; it takes about 45 minutes for a full one-way trip. Though the streetcar runs around the clock, services fall off after dark. There's a newer streetcar along the **riverfront**, where trolleys make ten stops between the Convention Center and Esplanade Avenue (Mon–Fri 6am–midnight, Sat & Sun 8am–midnight; every 15min; $1.25; exact fare). However, as it's a total trip of less than two miles, and river views are limited, there's little point using it unless you have trouble walking. VisiTour **passes**, available from major hotels, give unlimited travel on all streetcars and buses ($4 per day, $8 for three consecutive days).

# Accommodation

New Orleans has some fantastic **places to stay**, from rambling old guesthouses seeping faded grandeur to swanky tower hotels. **Room rates**, never low (you'll be pushed to find anything half decent for less than $50), increase considerably for Mardi Gras, JazzFest and the Sugar Bowl, when prices can go up by as much as 200 percent and rooms are booked months in advance. This is not a city in which you want to be stranded overnight, and though it's possible to take a chance on last-minute cancellations and deals, you should ideally make **reservations**. If you do turn up on spec, head immediately for the **Welcome Center** (see p.594), which has a room-booking service and **discount leaflets** offering savings on same-day bookings (weekdays only).

Most people choose to stay in the **French Quarter**, in the heart of things. Many accommodations here are in atmospheric **guesthouses**, most of them in old Creole townhouses. Outside the Quarter, the **Lower Garden District** offers budget options near the streetcar line, while the funky **Faubourg Marigny** specializes in bed and breakfasts and the **Garden District** proper has a couple of gorgeous old hotels. The **CBD** and **Warehouse District** are the domain of the city's upmarket chain hotels, catering mostly to conventioneers – they're much the same here as in any other American city, and contactable on the national 1-800 numbers.

## French Quarter

**Biscuit Palace**, 730 Dumaine St (☎504/525-9949). Atmospheric, friendly and spotless hotel, housed in an 1820 mansion with a flagstoned courtyard, fishpond and tropical plants. Characterful rooms, many of them suites, with balconies and antique baths. ④–⑤.

**Chateau Hotel**, 1001 Chartres St (☎504/524-9636). Simple rooms in a prime position. Some are better than others, so if you feel yours is too small or a bit dark, check to see what else is available. There's a cafe and pool, and complimentary continental breakfast. ⑤.

**A Creole House**, 1013 St Ann St (☎504/524-8076 or 1-800/535-7858). Unfussy, friendly guesthouse, bordering on shabby in places, with rooms ranging from cozy nooks with shared bath to antique-filled suites. Rates include continental breakfast and 24-hour coffee. ③–⑥.

**Dauphine Orleans**, 415 Dauphine St (☎504/586-1800 or 1-800/521-7111). Beautiful hotel, with exemplary attention to detail. Some rooms in restored brick cottages around tranquil, lush courtyards. Pretty pool, bar, library, superb complimentary breakfast and afternoon tea. ⑦.

**Olivier House**, 828 Toulouse St (☎504/525-8456). Though a bit dark, this atmospheric, rambling Creole house offers good value. The 42 rooms (all with bath) vary, but most have antique furniture, chandeliers and shuttered windows. There's a tropical courtyard, and a tiny pool, and coffee is served all day in the parlor. ④–⑨.

**Hotel Provincial**, 1024 Chartres St (☎504/581-4995 or 1-800/535-7922). Intimate, relaxed place in a quiet part of the Quarter, with antique-filled rooms opening onto peaceful, gaslit courtyards. Outdoor pool, reasonably priced restaurant, and bar on site. ⑥.

**Rue Royale Inn**, 1006 Royal St (☎504/524-3900 or 1-800/776-3901). Good-value, gay-friendly hotel. The enormous, brick-walled, high-ceilinged rooms easily sleep four, and all have bath, fridge and minibar. Rates include continental breakfast, which you can eat in the courtyard. ④.

### ACCOMMODATION PRICE CODES

All accommodation prices in this book have been coded using the symbols below. Note that prices are for the least expensive double rooms in each establishment. For a full explanation see p.37 in Basics.

| | | |
|---|---|---|
| ① up to $30 | ④ $60–80 | ⑦ $130–175 |
| ② $30–45 | ⑤ $80–100 | ⑧ $175–250 |
| ③ $45–60 | ⑥ $100–130 | ⑨ $250+ |

## Outside the French Quarter

**Columns Hotel**, 3811 St Charles Ave (☎504/899-9308). Atmospheric Garden District hotel – and great bar (see p.609) – in an 1883 mansion. Characterful rooms; some come with bath and balcony, but no TVs. Complimentary continental breakfast. Rates increase by 200 percent at Mardi Gras. ⑤–⑧.

**The Frenchmen**, 417 Frenchmen St (☎504/948-2166 or 1-800/831-1781). Gay-friendly Faubourg Marigny B&B, spread across two 1860 townhouses, overlooking a tropical patio. There's a small pool on site and a jacuzzi. ⑤–⑦.

**HI-New Orleans Marquette House**, 2253 Carondelet St (☎504/523-3014). Multi-building hostel a block from the streetcar in the Garden District. Dorm beds are $15–18, some doubles and apartments available, a few with bath. Reservations recommended; for Mardi Gras and JazzFest you'll need to pay in full in advance. No curfew. ②–④.

**La Salle Hotel**, 1113 Canal St (☎504/523-5831 or 1-800/521-9450). Reliable, popular budget option in the CBD near the Quarter. Few frills, just plain rooms – some with bath – free coffee and daily papers. The area, on the fringes of Tremé, can feel unsafe at night. ②.

**Prytania Inns**, 1415 Prytania St (☎504/566-1515 main office); also 2041 & 2127 Prytania St. German-owned houses near the streetcar in the Lower Garden District, with around one hundred varying rooms. The cheapest have shared bath; rates are often negotiable. ③/④.

**Royal Street Inn**, 1431 Royal St (☎504/948-7499 or 1-800/449-5535). Characterful Faubourg Marigny lodging above the funky *R-Bar* (see p.609), and run by the same people. The five rooms (all with bath) are decorated on themes ranging from Art Deco to bordello; the four-person suites are excellent value. Favored by a young crowd who hang out in the bar. ⑤.

**St Charles Guest House**, 1748 Prytania St (☎504/523-6556). Bohemian Lower Garden District guesthouse offering a variety of rooms, none with phone or TV. Backpackers choose the basic 6ft by 8ft cabins ($30), but for the pricier en-suite doubles you can get better value elsewhere. It's friendly enough, though, with a pool and free breakfast. They give student discounts, but ask for cash deposits with reservations. No smoking. ②–⑤.

**St Vincent's Guest House**, 1507 Magazine St (☎504/523-3411). Lower Garden District lodging, run by the same people as the *Prytania Inns*, with more than seventy simple rooms in a huge 1861 orphanage. The atmosphere is cheery, if institutional; breakfast is $10. ④.

**YMCA**, 920 St Charles Ave at Lee Circle (☎504/568-9622). Budget CBD option on the streetcar line, offering drab singles, doubles, triples and quads (with bunks) – all with TV and shared shower. There's a good veggie restaurant on site, and you can use the adjoining gym and pool. Popular during Mardi Gras, when the rooms overlooking St Charles give great parade views. No curfew. ②.

# The City

One of New Orleans' many nicknames is "the **Crescent City**," because of the way it nestles between the southern shore of Lake Pontchartrain and a dramatic horseshoe bend in the Mississippi River. This unique location makes the city's layout confusing, with streets curving to follow the river, and shooting off at odd angles to head inland. Compass points are of little use here – locals refer instead to **lakeside** (towards the lake) and **riverside** (towards the river), and, using Canal Street as the dividing line, **uptown** (or upriver) and **downtown** (downriver).

Most visitors spend most time in the surprisingly small **French Quarter** (or *Vieux Carré*), site of the original settlement. On its fringes, the funky **Faubourg Marigny** creeps northeast from Esplanade Avenue, while the Quarter's lakeside boundary, **Rampart Street**, marks the beginning of the historic, run-down African-American neighborhood of **Tremé**. On the other side of the Quarter, across **Canal Street**, the **CBD** (Central Business District), bounded by the river and I-10, spreads upriver to the Pontchartrain Expressway. Dominated by offices, hotels and banks, it also incorporates the revitalizing **Warehouse District** and, towards the lake, the gargantuan **Superdome**. A ferry ride across the river from the foot of Canal Street takes you to the suburban west bank, where old **Algiers** features the city's best Mardi Gras museum.

Back on the east bank, it's an easy journey upriver from the CBD to the rarefied **Garden District**, an area of gorgeous old mansions. (Don't confuse it with the **Lower Garden District**; creeping between the expressway and Jackson, this is quite a different creature, its run-down old houses filled with impoverished artists and musicians.) The best way to get to the Garden District is on the streetcar along swanky **St Charles Avenue**, the district's lakeside boundary; you can also approach it from **Magazine Street**, a six-mile stretch of galleries and antique stores that runs parallel to St Charles riverside. Entering the Garden District, you cross the official boundary into **uptown**, which spreads upriver to encompass **Audubon Park and Zoo**.

## The French Quarter

Heartbreakingly beautiful, depressingly tacky, the **French Quarter** is where New Orleans began in 1718. Today, battered and bohemian, decaying and vibrant, it's the spiritual core of the city, its fanciful cast-iron balconies, hidden courtyards and time-stained stucco buildings exerting a haunting fascination that has long caught the imagination of artists and writers. Official tours are useful for orientation, but it's most fun simply to wander – and you'll need a couple of days at least to do it justice, absorbing the jumble of sounds, sights and smells. Early morning, in the pearly light from the river, is a good time to explore, as sleepy locals wake themselves up with strong coffee in the neighborhood patisseries, shops crank open their shutters and all-night revelers stumble home.

The Quarter is laid out in a grid, unchanged since 1721 – bounded by the Mississippi River, Rampart Street, Canal Street and Esplanade Avenue. Its hub is Europeanate **Jackson Square**, facing the river. The **architecture** is predominantly Spanish colonial, with a strong Caribbean influence, and dates from the late eighteenth century, after most of the original buildings had been devastated by two fires in 1788 and 1794. Today the Quarter is home to offices, shops, galleries, restaurants, bars and apartments, with most of the **commercial activity** concentrated in the blocks between Decatur and Bourbon. Beyond Bourbon, up towards Rampart Street, and in the Lower Quarter, downriver from Jackson Square, things become more peaceful – quiet, predominantly residential neighborhoods that are home to many of the Quarter's **gay** community.

## Jackson Square

Ever since its earliest incarnation as the Place d'Armes, a dusty parade ground used for public meetings and executions, **Jackson Square** has been at the heart of the Quarter. Today, with its iron benches, neat lawns and blaze of flowerbeds, the square manages to stay tranquil despite the streams of photo-snapping tourists, school groups, waiters on their breaks, and the odd crashed-out casualty. Presiding over them all, an **equestrian statue** – the first in the nation, constructed by Clark Mills in 1856 – shows Andrew Jackson in uncharacteristically jaunty mode, waving his hat. It's a sculptural masterpiece, with the horse, rearing on its hind legs, perfectly balanced on the plinth. The inscription, "The Union Must and Shall be Preserved" was added by Union General "Spoons" Butler during the Civil War occupation.

St Peter, Chartres and St Ann streets are pedestrianized where they border the square. During the day, everyone passes by at some time or another, weaving their way through the tangle of artists, Lucky Dog hot dog vendors, rainbow-clad palmists, magicians, shambolic brass bands and blues musicians. A postcard-perfect backdrop for the Jackson statue, **St Louis Cathedral** is the oldest continuously active cathedral in the United States. It's the third church on this spot, built in 1794 after the first two had been destroyed by fire and hurricane. Dominated by three tall slate steeples, the facade, which marries Greek Revival symmetry with French arches, is oddly one-dimensional. Though the cathedral has always been central to the life of this very Catholic city – Andrew Jackson laid his sword on the altar in thanks for victory at the Battle of New Orleans; voodoo queen Marie Laveau (see p.600) was baptized and married here – the interior is little to shout about.

On the upriver side of the cathedral, the Hispanic **Cabildo** ($5) was built as the Casa Capitular, seat of the Spanish colonial government. Today, the building – which cuts an impressive dash with its colonnade, fan windows and wrought-iron balconies – is part of the **Louisiana State Museum** (see below). Inside, the outstanding history museum ably picks its way through the complex melange of cultures, classes and races that throng Louisiana's history, starting with the Native Americans and winding up with the demise of Reconstruction. In keeping with the city's fascination with matters morbid, there's a room devoted to disease, death and mourning, while another displays the post-Civil War cartoons put out by the Mardi Gras krewes (see p.612), revealing the racist venom with which the New Orleans elite resisted Reconstruction. Black history

## THE LOUISIANA STATE MUSEUM

The Cabildo – along with the Presbytère, 1850 House, and the Old US Mint (all p.602) – is part of the **Louisiana State Museum**. Each site is **open** Tuesday to Sunday from 9am to 5pm; buying a ticket to two or more gives a total **discount** of 20 percent.

## MACABRE NEW ORLEANS

### Voodoo

**Voodoo,** today practiced by around fifteen percent of the city's population, was brought to New Orleans by African slaves via the French colonies of the Caribbean, where tribal beliefs were mixed up with Catholicism to create a cult based on spirit-worship. French, and later, Spanish authorities tried to suppress the religion (voodoo-worshipers had played an active role in the organization of slave revolts in Haiti), but it continued to flourish among the city's black population. Under American rule, the weekly slave gatherings at **Congo Square** (in today's Louis Armstrong Park; see p.604), which included ritual ceremonies, turned into a tourist attraction for whites, fueled by sensationalized reports of hypnotized white women dancing naked.

Unlike in the West Indies, where the cult was dominated by male priests, New Orleans had many voodoo priestesses. The most famous was **Marie Laveau**, a hairdresser of African, white and Native American blood. Using shrewd marketing sense and inside knowledge of the lives of her clients, she prepared **gris-gris** – spells or potions – for wealthy Creoles and Americans, as well as Africans. Laveau died in 1881, when another Marie, believed to be her daughter, continued to practice under her name. The legend of both Maries lives on, and their **tombs** are popular tourist attractions (see opposite).

Today voodoo is big business in New Orleans, with numerous giftshops selling ersatz *gris-gris* – pouches carried for good luck, filled with amulets, charms and herbs – and exotic voodoo dolls; these can be fun, but if you're interested in the reality, you'd do better to head to the unprepossessing **Voodoo Spiritual Temple**, 828 N Rampart St (daily 10am–8pm; ☎504/522-9627), who offer tours, consultations, rituals and herbal potions; visitors are asked to make a donation.

**The Historic Voodoo Museum** (daily 10am–8pm; $6.50), 724 Dumaine St, is a ragbag collection of ceremonial objects, paintings and *gris-gris*. Its aim, to debunk the myths that surround this misunderstood religion, is undermined somewhat by the self-consciously spooky atmosphere, not to mention its resident 12ft python, crumbling rat heads and desiccated bats. The gift shop sells *gris-gris* and voodoo dolls, while the gallery features more expensive folk art.

### The Cities of the Dead

*There is no architecture in New Orleans, except in the cemeteries . . .*
Mark Twain, *Life on the Mississippi*

So much of New Orleans is at, or below, sea level that early settlers who buried their dead – and there were many of them – found that during the frequent flooding great waves of moldy coffins would float to the surface of the sodden earth. Eventually, graves began to be placed, Spanish-style, in above-ground brick and stucco vaults, surrounded by small fences. These **cemeteries** grew to resemble cities, laid out in "streets"; today, as the tombs crumble away amid the overgrown foliage, they are atmospheric places to visit. The creepiness isn't totally imaginary, either, though armed muggers, rather than ghosts, are the danger today. You should **never** venture here alone. Nearly all the city tours (see opposite) include a quick trip around one of the graveyards; some (see below) specialize in them.

**Lafayette Cemetery No. 1**, Washington Avenue and Prytania Street. Built in 1833, and filled by 1852 – the year when 2000 yellow fever victims were buried here – the Garden District cemetery is an eerie place. Many of the tombs are sinking into the ground, and some are slowly opening. It's no surprise that this decaying grandeur should capture the imagination of local author Anne Rice, who has used the place in many of her books.

**St Louis Cemetery No. 1**, 400 Basin Street between Conti and St Louis streets. The oldest City of the Dead, dating from 1789, this small graveyard is full of crooked mausolea jutting into narrow pathways. On the fringes of the Quarter, it is a regular stop on the tour bus circuit, and you will invariably come across a crowd by the tomb of "voodoo queen" **Marie Laveau**, graffitied with brick-dust crosses. They're usually being told how if you knock on the slab and mark a cross, her spirit will grant you any favor. The family who own it have asked that this bogus tradition should stop, not least because people are taking chunks of brick from other tombs to make the crosses. Voodooists – responsible for the candles, plastic flowers and rum bottles surrounding the plot – deplore the practice, too, regarding it as a desecration that chases Laveau's spirit away.

**St Louis Cemetery No. 2**, N Claiborne Avenue between Iberville and St Louis streets. One of the most desolate Cities of the Dead, hemmed in between a housing project and the interstate. Built in 1823, it's a prime example of local cemetery design, with a dead-straight center aisle lined with grandiose Greek Revival mausolea. A second Marie Laveau, thought to be *the* Marie Laveau's daughter, has a tomb here, also daubed with red-chalk crosses.

**St Louis Cemetery No. 3**, 3421 Esplanade Avenue, Mid-City. A peaceful burial ground, built in 1856 on the site of a leper colony, St Louis No.3 is mostly used by religious orders; all the priests of the diocese are buried here, and fragile angels balance on top of the tombs.

### A Haunted House

The striking French Empire **LaLaurie Home**, at 1140 Royal St on the corner with Gov Nicholls, is New Orleans' most famous **haunted house** (not open to the public). In the nineteenth century it belonged to the LaLauries, a doctor and his socialite wife Delphine, who, although seen wielding a whip as she chased a slave girl through the house to the roof, was merely fined when the child fell to her death. Whispers about the couple's cruelty were horribly verified when neighbors rushed in after a fire in 1834 – believed to have been started intentionally by the shackled cook – to find seven emaciated slaves locked in the attic. There they saw men, women and children choked by neck braces, some with broken limbs; one had a worm-filled hole gouged out of his cheek. The doctor's protestation that this torture chamber was, in fact, an "experiment," met with vitriol; the next day the pair escaped the baying mob outside their home, and fled to France. Since then, many claim to have heard ghostly moans from the building at night; some say they have seen a little girl stumble across the curved balcony beneath the roof.

### Tours

New Orleans' image as a Gothic, vampire-stalked city has really taken off in recent years, and the choice of **tours** promising **magic**, **voodoo**, **vampires** and **ghosts** has become dizzying. Among the high-camp, the overpriced and the plain silly, there are, nonetheless, a few tours worth joining: Historic New Orleans Walking Tours (☎504/947-2120) will lead you to St Louis Cemetery No. 1, Congo Square, Marie Laveau's home, and a voodoo temple; meet at *Cafe Beignet*, 334 Royal St (Mon–Sat 10am & 1pm, Sun 10am; $15; no reservations; arrive 15min before the tour is due to begin). Magic Walking Tours (☎504/588-9693) take you into the ghostly nooks and crannies of the Quarter, mixing informed historical detail with some tales quite as tall as those spun by other outfits – but without the fancy dress and to-go beers. They're run by the owner of the *Funky Butt* jazz club (see p.610), guides will happily lead you there afterwards. Meet at 8pm at *Lafitte's Blacksmith Shop* (see p.609); no reservations (2hr; $13). Finally, *Save Our Cemeteries* (☎504/525-3377; call for meeting points and to reserve) is a nonprofit restoration organization leading fascinating tours of Lafayette No. 1 (Mon, Wed & Fri 10.30am; $6 donation) and St Louis No. 1 (Sun 10am; $12 donation).

is well-represented, with as much emphasis on the free people of color as on the city's role as the major slave-trading center of the South.

On the second floor you can see the bronze **death mask of Napoleon**, along with the reconstructed **Sala Capitular**, where the Louisiana Purchase was signed in 1803, and where in 1892, the historic *Plessy vs Ferguson* case, which effectively legalized segregation throughout the South, was first argued.

Forming a matching pair with the Cabildo, the **Presbytère** ($5), on the downriver side of the cathedral, was designed in 1791 as a rectory. It was never used as such, however; and after completion in 1813 went on to serve as a courthouse. Today it's a very good decorative arts museum, full of odd treasures, including antique portraits of local dignitaries, musical instruments, maps, toys, folk art and quirky found objects.

The elegant three-story **Pontalba Buildings**, which line St Peter and St Ann streets where they border the square, were commissioned by the formidable Baroness Pontalba, who having returned from France in 1849 to find her real estate palling in comparison to the American sector across Canal Street, dreamed of replacing the shabby buildings around the Place d'Armes with elegant colonnaded structures resembling those she'd seen in Paris. Planned as both business and residential units, they are still used as such, and remain a source of pride to the city. These were not, as is commonly claimed, the first apartment buildings in the US, but they were innovative in their use of mass-produced materials and, in particular, of **cast iron** – the decorative balconies sparked off a citywide fad for lacy cast iron, which came to replace the plainer iron hand-wrought locally by African slaves. Forming another section of the state museum (see p.599), the cordoned-off rooms of the restored **1850 House** ($3), 523 St Ann St, re-create the tastes of the well-to-do Creole families who lived in these fashionable apartments. Though they draw attention to every piece of Vieux Paris china and fine crystal, the self-guided tours leave you with little sense of how the family might have lived.

## Decatur Street and Esplanade Avenue

Downriver along Decatur, the specialty shops of the restored **French Market**, said to be on the site of a Native American trading area and certainly active since the 1720s, sell overpriced tourist knickknacks; for stalls, head towards the old **Farmers' Market**, just off Decatur on N Peters Street, where fresh produce, along with foodie souvenirs are sold around the clock. Next door, the weekend **flea market** is full of bargain oddities, as are the funky thrift and **rummage stores** opposite on Decatur.

Continuing downriver, you'll come to the outer boundary of the Quarter, **Esplanade Avenue**, a broad, oak-shaded boulevard lined with crumbling nineteenth-century Creole mansions. Part of the State Museum (see p.599), the **Old US Mint**, on the 400 block near the river, houses the understated **Jazz Museum**, tracing the history of the music that New Orleans calls its own, through photographs, old letters – among them a pencil-written fan letter to pianist Amand Hug from a ten-year-old Harry Connick Jr – and advertising images. A Mardi Gras exhibit explains the complexities of carnival, with lots of splendid costumes.

Across Esplanade from the Quarter you come to hip **Faubourg Marigny**, a low-rent area of Creole cottages. Though its many excellent bars, coffee shops and restaurants are creeping further and further from the Quarter, you still need to take care when wandering beyond the blocks around Decatur and Frenchmen streets.

## Along Chartres and Royal streets

A left turn at the 600 block of Esplanade Avenue brings you to the **Old Ursuline Convent** at 1114 Chartres St (tours Tues–Fri hourly except noon 10am–3pm, Sat & Sun 11.15am, 1pm & 2pm; $5). Built in 1745, this is the only intact French colonial structure in the city, and quite possibly the oldest building in the Mississippi valley. It's one of the many structures in the Quarter that are said to be haunted, its corridors roamed by specters of the "casket girls" – white virgins shipped over in the early days of the colony, who were kept here before being sold off as wives in an attempt to stop the increasing number of couplings between French settlers and African or Native women. The **Beauregard-Keyes House**, opposite at no. 1113 (tours hourly Mon–Sat 10am–3pm; $4), owes its name to Confederate General Pierre Beauregard – who ordered the first shot of the Civil War at Fort Sumter and rented a room here during Reconstruction – and to popular novelist Frances Parkinson Keyes. She refurbished this "raised cottage" (with the basement at ground level) as her winter home in the 1940s. Her novels – including *Madame Castel's Lodger*, a romance about the house's "Beauregard period"– are on sale in the giftshop.

A block north at 1132 Royal St, the handsome **Gallier House**, dating from 1857, is a fascinating little museum (tours Mon–Sat 10am–3.30pm; $5, $8 with the Hermann-Grima House, see below). James Gallier Jr was a leading architect of the day, and the innovative features he designed for his home, such as the outdoor cistern and cooling system, indoor plumbing and above-ground storage, soon became essential for anyone wanting to live in comfort in this swampy climate.

The superb, scholarly **Historic New Orleans Collection** at 533 Royal St looks quite appropriate among the antique shops and swanky art galleries. Entry to the streetfront gallery (Tues–Sat 10am–4.45pm), which holds temporary exhibitions, is free, but to see the best of the collection you'll need to take a guided tour (10am, 11am, 2pm & 3pm; $4). These might cover the galleries upstairs, where exhibits include old maps, drawings and documents relating to the Louisiana Purchase, or the Williams House at the back. The Williamses, prominent citizens in the 1930s, filled their home with unusual, exotic objects, and the house is a must for anyone interested in design and decorative arts.

The quirky **Historical Pharmacy Museum**, in an old apothecary a block towards the river at 514 Chartres St (Tues–Sun 10am–5pm; $2), illustrates a history of medicine from the eighteenth century onwards. Hand-carved rosewood cabinets are cluttered with *gris-gris*, dusty jars of leeches for blood-letting (to remove irritability) and Creole "tonics" used to cure "all the various form of female weakness."

## Around Bourbon Street

Continuing lakeside along Conti Street, crossing Royal Street again, brings you up to **Bourbon Street**. Though you'd never guess it from the hype, there are two sides to this world-renowned drag. The touristy, booze-swilled stretch spans the seven blocks from Canal to St Ann: a frat-pack cacophony of daiquiri stalls, novelty shops, and girlie bars. This enclave is best experienced after dark, when a couple of its **bars** and **clubs** are worth a look, and the sheer mayhem takes on a life of its own. When the attraction of fighting your way through the crowds of weekending drunks starts to pall, however, it's easy to dip out again into the quieter parallel streets to regain some sort of sanity. If you manage to make it as far as St Ann, you come to a kind of crossroads, beyond where Bourbon transforms into an appealing, predominantly gay, residential area.

Half a block north of Bourbon at 820 St Louis St, the restored 1831 **Hermann-Grima House** (Mon–Sat 10am–3.30pm; $5; $8 with the Gallier House, see above) illustrates the lifestyle of middle-class Creoles in the city's golden age. Cooking demonstrations are held in the kitchen every Thursday from October to May.

## From Bourbon Street to Rampart Street

Beyond Bourbon Street, tourists are outnumbered by locals dog-walking, jogging, or chatting on stoops. Though these quiet streets are fringed by some of the Quarter's finest **vernacular architecture**, "sights" as such are few; the cheesy **Musee Conti**

---

### THE MISSISSIPPI RIVER

A resonant, romantic and extraordinary physical presence, the **Mississippi River** is New Orleans' lifeblood and its raison d'être. In the nineteenth century, as the port boomed, the city gradually cut itself off from the river altogether, hemming it in behind a string of warehouses and railroads, but as the importance of the port has diminished, a couple of downtown parks, plazas and riverside walks, accessible from the French Quarter and the CBD, have focused attention back onto the **waterfront**.

Crossing Decatur Street from Jackson Square brings you to the **Moon Walk**, a wooden promenade where buskers serenade you as you gaze across the water. Upriver from here, long thin **Woldenberg Park** is strung with benches – perfect for passing an hour or two with a picnic, watching the river traffic drift by. At the upriver edge of the park, the superb **Aquarium of the Americas**, near the Canal Street wharf (daily from 9am, closing hours vary; $11.25/children $5; IMAX $7.75/$5; aquarium and IMAX $15.50/$9; aquarium and zoo $15.50/$7.50) features a huge glass tunnel where visitors – rampaging infants, mostly – come face-to-face with rippling rays and ugly sawfish. There's also a swamp complete with white gators, along with an Amazonian rainforest, petting tank and IMAX theater.

For bird's-eye views of the dramatic bends in the river, head for the woefully drab **World Trade Center**, at the riverside edge of Canal St. There's an observation deck on the thirty-first floor (daily 9am–5pm; $2) and a kitsch revolving cocktail bar two floors above.

---

**Wax Museum** at 917 Conti St (Mon–Sat 10am–5.30pm, Sun noon–5pm; $6.50) has a variety of tableaux about the city's history, while the church of **Our Lady of Guadalupe** at 411 N Rampart St, on the corner of Conti, is notable for its statue of "Saint Expedite," mysteriously delivered here, so the legend goes, in a crate simply stamped *expedite*. **Rampart Street**, the run-down strip separating the Quarter from Tremé, is a boundary rarely crossed by tourists. Though it's home to a couple of popular clubs (*Donna's* and *Funky Butt*; see p.610, both of which are just a short walk from the heart of the Quarter), it can feel hairy at night, and only slightly less so during the day. The entrance to **Louis Armstrong Park**, a huge twinkling arch clearly visible the length of St Ann St, promises more than the desolate park itself delivers. At its upriver edge, the small paved area ringed by benches is **Congo Square**, where every Sunday African slaves would meet to trade, make music and dance.

## Outside the French Quarter

During the Civil War, the (then incomplete) grey granite **Custom House** at 423 Canal St (Mon–Fri 8am–4.30pm) was headquarters to Union General Butler, and a prison for Confederate soldiers. Inside, behind the foreboding classical exterior, there's a huge **marble hall**, illuminated by a 55ft skylight, with fourteen columns of Italian marble supporting the white and gilt ceiling.

The lakeside edge of the Central Business District or CBD, a tangle of busy gray highways, would be pretty lifeless without the colossal home of the beleagured New Orleans Saints football team, the **Superdome**. At 52 acres, with 27 stories and a diameter of 680ft, this is one of the largest buildings in the world. You can't really appreciate the sheer enormity of the place until you venture inside, either by seating yourself with 76,999 others to see a **game** (Aug–Dec $25–50), or second-best, by joining one of the superlatives- and statistics-heavy **tours** (hourly 10am–4pm; ☎504/587-3810; $6).

Spreading upriver from the World Trade Center, at the foot of Canal Street, the revitalizing **Warehouse District** is being heralded as a thriving arts community. However, though it may be a desirable place to live, the attractions are not always immediate for the visitor. Most of the sights are concentrated in the **Arts District**, the outcrop of cutting-edge galleries concentrated around Julia and Camp streets. Hub of the scene is the **Contemporary Arts Center**, 900 Camp St (Mon–Sat 10am–5pm, Sun 11am–5pm, closed July; $5), which comprises gallery and performance space, along with a cyber-cafe.

Across the road, in a gloomy Romanesque Revival hulk, built in 1891 as a place for Confederate veterans to display their mementos, the **Confederate Museum**, 929 Camp St at Lee Circle, is a relic from a bygone age (Mon–Sat 10am–4pm; $5). It can be easy to forget that freewheeling New Orleans has its roots entrenched in the Deep South, but this "Battle Abbey of the South" is no better reminder. Inside the church-like hall, glass cases are filled with flags, swords, mess-kits, uniforms and helmets. Along with affecting sepia photos, oddities include a crown of thorns hand-woven by Pope Pius IX and sent to Thomas Jefferson.

## The Garden District and Audubon Park

The **St Charles streetcar**, which runs from Canal Street to Audubon Park, offers a leisurely trip to many of New Orleans' sights. Pride of uptown New Orleans, the grand residential **Garden District** drapes itself seductively across a thirteen-block area two miles upriver from the French Quarter. It was developed as Lafayette City in the 1840s by the energetic breed of Anglo-Americans who wished to display their ever-accumulating wealth by building sumptuous mansions in huge gardens. Shaded by jungles of subtropical foliage, the glorious houses – some of them showpieces, others in ruins – evoke a nostalgic vision of the Deep South in a profusion of porches, columns and balconies. You can see the district on any number of official or self-guided tours, but the homes are only open to the public during the Spring Fiesta (see p.613).

Around 1900 saw another spate of mansion building, this time along **St Charles Avenue**. From the streetcar, look out for the **Brown House** at no. 4717, and the 1941 replica of **Tara**, the house in *Gone with the Wind*, at no. 5705. You can't miss the **Wedding Cake House** at no. 5809 – an ostentatious Colonial-Greek Revival building, frosted with a layer of balconies, cornices and columns.

Peaceful **Audubon Park** is a lovely space, shaded by Spanish moss-swathed trees, and looped by cycling and jogging paths. The admirable **Audubon Zoo**, a fifteen-minute walk or short shuttle ride from the park's St Charles entrance (daily 9.30am–5.30pm; $8.75/children $5; zoo and aquarium $15.50/$7.50) features white tigers, white alligators and Komodo dragons, along with carefully re-created habitats including a Louisiana swamp, African savannah, and "jaguar jungle."

## Algiers and Blaine Kern's Mardi Gras World

A free ferry ride from Canal Street brings you within ten minutes or so to the west bank and **Algiers**, a quiet residential neighborhood of pastel stucco Creole architecture and subtropical terraces. The main attraction is **Blaine Kern's Mardi Gras World**, 223 Newton St (daily 9.30am–4.30pm; $8.50), where year-round you can see artists preparing, constructing and painting the enormous floats used in the Mardi Gras parades. It's a surreal experience wandering these massive warehouses past piles of dusty, grimacing has-beens from parades gone by. In keeping with the carnival spirit, there is plenty of opportunity to dress up, fool about and take photos – before the tour, you're free to try on colossal Nixon and Marilyn papier maché heads, velvet cloaks and towering plumed headdresses. A complimentary minibus picks up and drops off at the ferry landing.

## Elsewhere in the city

Towards the lake, in the vast area known as **Mid-City**, New Orleans' 1500-acre **City Park** is site of the venerable **Dueling Oak**, under which Creoles and Americans met at dawn to defend their honor. The impressive collection at the nearby **New Orleans Museum of Art** (Tues–Sun 10am–5pm; $6), set among the lagoons, includes works by Degas, Picasso and Dufy, Rodin sculptures, pre-Columbian pieces, African works, Asian ceramics and paintings, and a fabulous collection of **Fabergé** jeweled eggs.

The **Chalmette battlefield** (daily 8am–5pm; free), six miles downriver from Canal Street, is where Jackson's ragbag army defeated the British at the Battle of New Orleans in 1815. There isn't much to show for it, apart from bare fields and the simple plantation home. Jean Lafitte National Historical Park rangers provide a self-guided walking tour, and give talks in the small visitor center four times daily. The plantation can be reached on the *Creole Queen* paddlewheeler or from Hwy-46.

# Eating

New Orleans is a gourmand's dream. The **food**, commonly defined as **Creole**, is a spicy, substantial – and usually very fattening – blend of French, Spanish, African and Caribbean cuisine, mixed up with a host of other influences including Native American, Italian and German. It tends to be rich, and fragrant, using heaps of herbs, peppers, garlic and onion. Some of the simpler dishes, like red beans and rice (traditional Mon lunch), reveal a strong West Indies influence, while others are more French, cooked with long-simmered sauces based on a **roux** (fat and flour heated together) and herby stocks. Many dishes are served **étouffé**, literally "smothered" in a tasty Creole sauce (a roux with tomato, onion and spices), on a bed of rice. Note that what passes for **Cajun** food in the city is often a modern hybrid, tasty but not authentic; the "blackened" dishes, for example, slathered in butter and spices, that were made famous by chef Paul Prudhomme in the 1980s.

The mainstays of most menus are **gumbo** – a thick soup of seafood, chicken and vegetables (*gumbo* comes from the Bantu for okra, a prime ingredient) – and **jambalaya**, a paella jumbled together from the same ingredients. Other specialties include **po-boys**, French-bread sandwiches crammed with oysters, shrimp or almost anything else, along with spicy sauces or gravy, and **muffulettas**, the Italian version, stuffed full of aromatic meats and cheese and dripping with olive and garlic dressing. **Seafood** is abundant and can be very cheap. Along with shrimp and soft-shell crabs, you'll get famously good **oysters**; they're in season from September to April. **Crawfish**, or mudbugs (which resemble langoustines and are best between March and October), are served in everything from omelettes to bisques, or simply boiled in a spicy stock. To eat them, tug off the overlarge head, pinch the tail and suck out the juicy, very delicious flesh.

Finally, European-influenced New Orleans has always been *the* American city for **coffee**; drunk in copious amounts, fresh, strong and aromatic, and often laced with chicory, it's been a big part of life here since long before Seattle got trendy.

## French Quarter

**Acme Oyster House**, 724 Iberville St (☎504/522-5973). Noisy, characterful neighborhood restaurant popular with tourists, cops and businesspeople alike, guzzling inexpensive po-boys, salty fresh crawfish, or plump, briny oysters. Mon–Sat 11am–10pm, Sun noon–7pm.

**Bayona**, 430 Dauphine St (☎504/525-4455). Upscale restaurant in a seventeenth-century Creole cottage with a courtyard. Chef Susan Spicer creates dazzling "New World Cuisine," giving local dishes an oriental, Southwestern or Mediterranean twist. At lunch you can get three fantastic courses for around $25. Mon–Thurs 11am–2pm & 6–10pm, Fri 11am–2pm & 6–11pm, Sat 6–11pm.

**Central Grocery**, 923 Decatur St (☎504/523-1620). Fragrant old Italian deli; the best muffulettas in town, unfeasibly overstuffed and succulent with garlic dressing. Most people take out, but there is limited counter seating. Mon–Sat 8am–5.30pm, Sun 9am–5.30pm.

**Croissant d'Or**, 617 Ursulines St (☎504/524-4663). Peaceful, absurdly cheap little local place serving the best French pastries and stuffed croissants this side of Paris, plus quiches, salads and steaming cafe au lait, in a pretty, tiled building. Daily 7am–5pm.

**Galatoire's**, 209 Bourbon St (☎504/525-2021). Splendid, top-of-the-range Creole food in landmark, mirror-lined dining room. It's best at lunchtime, on Fri or Sun especially, when long, convivial hours are spent gorging on turtle soup, oysters and filet mignon. No reservations, so expect a wait. Jacket and tie required after 5pm and all day Sun. Tues–Sun 11.30am–9pm.

**Girod's Bistro**, 500 Chartres St (☎504/522-4152). Wonderful, romantic restaurant, linked to the *Napoleon House* (see p.609) and hidden away beside its courtyard. Like the bar, the bistro is all peeling walls, candlelight and old paintings – the perfect setting to linger over robust, creative Creole food with Mediterranean and Caribbean accents. Prices are reasonable and portions are huge. Tues–Sat 6–10.30pm.

**Mr B's**, 201 Royal St (☎504/523-2078). Casually chic bistro with dark-wood booths, a relaxed, chatty buzz and excellent food. The garlic chicken is the city's finest, served with wild rice drowned in a satiny reduction. Mon–Fri 11.30am–3pm & 5.30–10pm, Sat 11.30am–3pm & 5–10pm, Sun 10.30am–3pm & 5.30–10pm.

**Peristyle**, 1041 Dumaine St (☎504/593-9535). Incongruously set on the rougher edge of the Quarter, this elegant restaurant – *very* New Orleans, all dark wood, checked tile floors and mismatched mirrors – is one of the hottest places in town to eat contemporary French–Creole–New American cuisine. Reservations are essential. Tues–Sat 6–10pm.

**Rita's**, 945 Chartres St (☎504/525-7543). Friendly, inexpensive local place for hearty soul food and Creole favorites; try a combo of jambalaya–crawfish pie–filé gumbo, and leave room for the succulent bread pudding and warm praline sauce. Daily 11am–10pm.

## Outside the Quarter

**Cafe Marigny**, 1913 Royal St (☎504/945-4472). Creative Creole cuisine with Southwestern, Mediterranean and Asian accents, served in a tranquil Faubourg Marigny corner joint. Daily specials, including inexpensive veggie options, are excellent. Mon–Thurs 11am–10pm, Fri 11am–11pm, Sat 8am–11pm, Sun 9am–8pm.

**Casamento's**, 4330 Magazine St (☎504/895-9761). Spotless, atmospheric, neighborhood oyster bar. Very cheap ice-fresh oysters and seafood; the overstuffed "loaves" are especially good. Mid-Sept to May Tues–Sun 11.30am–1.30pm & 5.30–9pm.

**Commander's Palace**, 1403 Washington Ave (☎504/899-8221). Exceptional haute Creole cuisine in a Garden District mansion. The heart-thumpingly rich food is pricey (dinner entrees $25–35), but the prix fixe ($30–35) and brunch ($25–30) menus prove good value. Jacket required for dinner and Sun lunch. Reservations essential. Mon–Fri 11.30am–1.30pm & 6–9.30pm, Sat 11.30am–12.30pm & 6–9.30pm, Sun 10.30am–1.30pm & 6–9.30pm.

**Jacques Imo's**, 8324 Oak St (☎504/861-0886). Funky restaurant with a colorful patio. The cooking, an inventive Creole–Cajun take on soul food, is astounding and good value – from the fried oysters and chicken livers to the buttery blackened redfish. It's a great place to fill up before a gig at the *Maple Leaf* a couple of doors away (see p.611), and worth a trip any time. Tues–Sat 6–10pm.

**Metro Bistro**, 200 Magazine St (☎504/529-1900). Buzzy, welcoming place for excellent French-influenced food; entrees ($9–22) include duck cassoulet, Burgundian beef stew with wild mushroom bread pudding, grilled fish on corn *choux*, and a tangy bouillabaisse. Lunch is cheaper. Daily 11am–2pm & 5–10pm.

**Mother's**, 401 Poydras St (☎504/523-9656). Though tourists go into a tizzy about *Mother's*, thrilled to be eating "N'Awlins" home cooking in a down-home ambiance, locals are drifting away as prices steadily creep up. That said, the portions are still colossal, the mood friendly and the food undeniably good. No credit cards. Daily 5am–10pm.

**Siam Cafe**, 435 Esplanade Ave (☎504/949-1750). Inexpensive Thai restaurant in the Faubourg Marigny, serving Pad Thai and zippy green and red curries in funky gamblers' den-cum-opium pit surroundings. The hot sake is a hit with the young crowd who head upstairs to the *Dragon's Den* (see p.611) after dining. Daily 6–11pm.

**Uglesich's**, 1238 Baronne St (☎504/523-8571). The "Yew-gle-sitch-es" draw on Eastern European traditions to create the best food in the city, served in a shabby Lower Garden District seafood joint.

Everything is delicious, from the oyster brie soup and crawfish *macque choux* (both $4), to the spicy "sizzling shrimp Gail" ($11). Feast on fresh oysters while you wait for a table (which can be a long time). No credit cards. No reservations. Mon–Fri 9.30am–4pm.

## Coffee bars

**Cafe du Monde**, 800 Decatur St (☎504/587-0833). Despite the hype, the crowds and the sugar-sticky table tops, this is an undeniably atmospheric place to drink steaming cafe au lait with chicory, and snack on piping hot beignets for a couple of dollars – apart from orange juice and hot chocolate, they serve little else. Daily 24hr.

**Kaldi's**, 941 Decatur St (☎504/586-8989). Spacious coffeehouse – a haven of calm opposite the French Market – serving fresh brews to a bohemian crowd. Mon–Thurs & Sun 6am–midnight, Fri & Sat 6am–2am.

**La Marquise**, 625 Chartres St (☎504/524-0420). Superb neighborhood patisserie, sister shop to the *Croissant d'Or* (see overleaf), a croissant's throw from Jackson Square. Delectable French pastries, great coffee – the cappuccinos are a work of art – and very inexpensive salads and quiches. Daily 7am–5.30pm.

**PJs**, 634 Frenchmen St; other branches all around town (☎504/949-2292). A firm favorite for its expertly made coffee, muffins, bagels and gourmet sandwiches. Mon–Fri 7am–midnight, Sat & Sun 8am–midnight.

**Rue de la Course**, 219 N Peters St; other branches all around town (☎504/523-0206). With their pressed-tin walls, cafe-au-lait decor, ceiling fans and reading lamps, the *Rue* coffee shops have an old Europe ambiance, buzzing with a mixed, local crowd. The coffee is great, and they do biscotti and bagels. Mon–Thurs & Sun 7am–11pm, Fri & Sat 7am–midnight.

# Entertainment and nightlife

New Orleans positively reels under the energy of its ever-present **live music**. From lonesome street musicians, through the shambling, joyous brass bands, to international names like Dr John and the Neville Brothers, music remains integral to the economy and the ideology of the Crescent City.

While the French Quarter has its share of atmospheric clubs and bars, there are plenty of good venues elsewhere. And visitors making a beeline for **Bourbon Street**, hoping to find it chock-a-block with cool jazz clubs, will be disappointed. That said, even this tawdriest of streets has a couple of good places to hear jazz and blues.

To decide where to go, check the **listings papers** (especially the superb music monthly *Offbeat*), collect fliers in French Quarter **record stores** such as Magic Bus, 527 Conti St, or Louisiana Music Factory, 210 Decatur St, and keep an ear tuned to the fabulous local **radio station** WWOZ (90.7 FM), which features regular gig information and ticket competitions.

Music in New Orleans often doesn't get going until late. However, many venues put on **two sets** a night, often by different performers, so with a little creative club-hopping you could easily see three outstanding gigs in one evening. Another distinctive feature of New Orleans' nightlife is that many shows can be seen – and heard – from the street. If you hear something you like, but don't want to pay the **cover charge** – low or nonexistent in bars, but as much as $20 in some clubs – it's perfectly acceptable to stand outside with a "beer to go" (see below) from another bar, moving on when the fancy takes you.

## Bars

As befits its image as a hard-drinking, hard-partying town, New Orleans has dozens of truly great **bars**. Though **24hr-drinking licences** are common, don't expect every bar to be open all night – many close whenever they empty out, which can be surprisingly early. It is also, unlike in any other American city, legal to **drink alcohol in the streets**

– for some visitors it's practically *de rigueur* – though not from a glass or bottle. Simply ask for a plastic **"to go"** cup in any bar and carry it around with you. You'll be expected to finish your drink before entering another bar, however. The **legal drinking age** in New Orleans is 21; you should carry ID, though few bartenders bother asking for it.

## French Quarter bars

**Lafitte's Blacksmith Shop**, 941 Bourbon St (☎504/523-0066). Ancient, tumbledown bar frequented by artists and writers (how they see by the candlelight remains a mystery), and a few stray tourists. A front for Lafitte's plottings, unchanged since the 1700s, with beamed ceilings and a blackened brick fireplace. In the evenings, a gloriously cheesy piano player pounds out cocktail-lounge standards.

**Molly's at the Market**, 1107 Decatur St (☎504/525-5169). Once famed for being a genuine local Irish bar, haunt of politicos and media stars, *Molly's* has been cleaned up and now pulls in a younger crowd. Still, it has its moments, and stays open during hurricane alerts, which says something.

**The Napoleon House**, 500 Chartres St (☎504/524-9752). Atmospheric bar with crumbling walls, shadowy corners and ancient oil paintings exuding a classic, relaxed New Orleans elegance. The building was the home of Mayor Girod, who schemed with Jean Lafitte to rescue Napoleon from exile.

## Bars elsewhere in the city

**Columns Hotel**, 3811 St Charles Ave (☎504/899-9308). Gorgeous hotel bar, seeping faded Southern grandeur; on warm evenings, make for the columned veranda, which overlooks the streetcar line. It's also a local favorite for occasional live modern and Latin jazz, when there's a small cover.

**R-Bar**, 1431 Royal St (☎504/948-7499). Attitude-free, bohemian Faubourg Marigny bar with funky thrift-store decor. The pool table is played by some of the coolest sharks in town, and there's a superb, eclectic jukebox. Popular with a youngish set, which includes visitors staying at the guesthouse upstairs (see p.597).

**Sazerac Bar**, *Fairmont Hotel*, 123 Baronne St (☎504/529-4733). Classy Art Deco bar in a grand old CBD hotel. Serving champagne, fine wines, cocktails and desserts, it attracts a well-dressed uptown and business traveler clientele.

**Snake and Jake's Christmas Club Lounge**, Oak St (☎504/861-2802). Dilapidated uptown bar, with perennial Yuletide decorations fading in the gloom. Nothing much happens before 2am, when it fills up with a jubilant local crowd of musicians, journalists and students.

**Top of the Mart**, World Trade Center, Canal St (☎504/522-9795). The world's largest revolving cocktail bar, on the 33rd story. Though you pay over the odds for a drink, the ambiance is appealingly kitsch, with tired red and gilt decor and bored waitresses. Each rotation takes 90min; the views are superb.

# Jazz

It is generally agreed that **jazz** was born in New Orleans, shaped in the early twentieth century by the twin talents of **Louis Armstrong** and **Joe "King" Oliver** from a diverse heritage of African and Caribbean slave music, Civil War brass bands, plantation spirituals, black church music and work songs. It suits the city well: hard to define, improvisational, and ranging from melancholic to jubilant, upmarket to downright seedy.

In 1897, in an attempt to control the prostitution that had been rampant in the city since its earliest days, a law was passed that restricted the brothels to a fixed area bounded by Iberville and Lower Basin streets. The area, which soon became known as **Storyville** after the alderman who pronounced the ordinance, filled with newly arrived ex-plantation workers, seamen and gamblers, and, from the "mood setting" tunes played in the brothels to bawdy saloon gigs, there was plenty of opportunity for musicians – in particular the solo piano players known as "professors" – to develop personal styles. Children too young to enter the bars set up makeshift "spasm bands" in the streets. Their legacy lives on in the streetwise ragamuffins on every corner, tap dancing, shoe-shining and playing trumpet.

Jazz was originally looked down upon by the white establishment as the "filthy" music of poor blacks, and, after Storyville was officially closed in 1917 – which coincided with a clampdown on live music played throughout the city – there was a mass exodus of musicians to Chicago and New York. Many more jazz artists left the city or gave up playing altogether during the Depression (King Oliver died an impoverished janitor); but in the 1950s the city fathers literally changed their tune and began to promote jazz as a tourist attraction. The double-edged nature of the music – indigenous and authentic, and at the same time a commercial construction – persists. Today it remains a living, evolving art form, and you're spoiled for choice for places to see it. The quality ranges from good to exceptional; thankfully, the best is not confined to the tourist traps.

Local, world-class, **musicians**, including the multitalented Marsalis family, trumpeters Terence Blanchard, Irvin Mayfield and Nicholas Payton, and scat singer Charmaine Neville (of the Nevilles), all perform regularly. Of the pianists, don't miss Henry Butler – whose superb, superfast modern jazz is matched by his mean R&B and blues repertoire. Two of the city's best-loved performers, trumpeters Kermit Ruffins and younger pup James Andrews, can always be counted on for a good show. Both cut their teeth in local brass bands, the ragtag groups who blast out New Orleans' homegrown party music, born from the city's long tradition of street parades. Regulars on the circuit include the ReBirth (Ruffins' old crew); the Lil Rascals, New Birth and Hot 8 brass bands, whose ear-splitting spin on traditional tunes is as big a hit in the parades as in the jazz clubs; Soul Rebel and Coolbone, who mix a cacophony of horns with hard funk, hip-hop and reggae, have a fresh "street" sound.

## Jazz Venues

**Donna's**, 800 N Rampart St (☎504/596-6914). Funky barbecue joint on the fringe of the Quarter. Hosting all the best brass bands, it feels like a locals' place – there's no stage, and you have to fight your way through the blasting horns to get to the bathroom – but it attracts a big out-of-town crowd. Cover varies; one drink minimum. Mon & Wed–Sun from 8pm.

**Funky Butt**, 714 N Rampart St (☎504/558-0872). Stylish, intimate club near *Donna's*. The eclectic decor resembles an Art Deco bordello; while the music – contemporary jazz and R&B – is exceptional. Food served. Cover varies, rising to $15, but you can drink in the bar for free.

**Palm Court Jazz Cafe**, 1204 Decatur St (☎504/525-0200). The aficionados' favorite: top-notch traditional jazz played while you dine in elegant surroundings in the French Quarter. New Orleans jazz memorabilia adds atmosphere, and they sell collectors' items and records. Reservations recommended for dinner; cover varies, but a seat at the bar costs nothing. Wed–Sun 7–11pm.

**Preservation Hall**, 726 St Peter St (☎504/522-2841). Shabby old room – with no seats, bar, air conditioning or toilets – long lauded as the best place in New Orleans to hear traditional jazz. Though the ersatz dereliction (contrary to popular belief, it's only been open since the 1960s) and over-reverent tourist crowds can be off-putting, the music, played by old pros, is superlative. Sets at 9pm and 11pm. Cover $4.

**Snug Harbor**, 929 Frenchmen St (☎504/949-0696). Friendly Faubourg Marigny jazz club in a small, vaguely nautical-looking space. Shows at 9pm and 11pm, but the restaurant (serving pasta, burgers and the like) and bar stay open late. Regulars include Astral Project, who play cool modern jazz, Charmaine Neville, and Ellis Marsalis. Cover $5–25. Daily 5pm–2am.

**Storyville District**, 125 Bourbon St (☎504/410-1000). Squeaky clean complex, with bars, dining areas and stages featuring live jazz. Geared towards tourists, it feels sanitized, with fine performers turning out background music for a low or nonexistent cover charge. Daily noon–3pm & 5.30pm–1am.

**Vaughan's**, 4229 Dauphine St, in the Bywater district (☎504/947-5562). Tiny neighborhood bar that fills on Thurs, Kermit Ruffins' night. The band is crammed up against the audience – a mixed bunch of locals, students and the players' friends and family; between sets, help yourself to free beans and rice. Take a cab. Cover $5. Daily 11am–3am.

## Other live music

There's far more to New Orleans than jazz alone. Though the **"New Orleans sound,"** an exuberant, carnival-tinged hybrid of blues, parade music and R&B, had its heyday in the early 1960s, many of its greatest stars are still going strong. Check listings papers for gigs by the Neville Brothers, the fabulous Ernie K-Doe, Eddie Bo, and "soul queen of New Orleans" Irma Thomas. Super-talented songwriter-producer Allen Toussaint, who gave many of them their big breaks, is still hard at work, too, showcasing new acts in his weekly sets at *Tipitina's French Quarter*.

In recent years, the **swing** revival has taken off in a big way in New Orleans, along with **Latin** music and **funk**. **Blues** fans should look out for guitarists Snooks Eaglin and Walter "Wolfman" Washington, the younger, Delta blues-influenced John Mooney and, for powerful gospel-blues, the formidable Marva Wright.

Though many people associate New Orleans with **Cajun** music, it's not indigenous to the city: that said, locals do love to *fais-do-do* (the Cajun two-step) and there are a couple of fantastic places to dance to **zydeco**, its bluesier black relation. The city has also taken **klezmer** to its heart, and in particular the local Klezmer Allstars, who bang out a frenzied blend of Yiddish folk, jazz and funk. Finally, for something unique, scour the listings for Mardi Gras Indians (see overleaf) such as the Wild Magnolias or Golden Eagles, whose rare gigs – you're most likely to catch them around Mardi Gras or JazzFest – are the funkiest, most extraordinary performances you're ever likely to see.

**Cafe Brasil**, 2100 Chartres St (☎504/947-9386). Minimalist, arty club at the heart of the Faubourg scene, with eclectic live music (Latin, jazz, klezmer, reggae, world), poetry readings and a small bar. The young, gorgeous crowd often spills onto Frenchmen St, mingling with the fallout from the *Dream Palace* opposite. Cover varies.

**Dragon's Den**, 435 Esplanade Ave (☎504/949-1750). Opium-den styled bar/club in the Faubourg above the *Siam Cafe* (see p.607), where bright young things loll on cushions or dance to R&B, blues, jazz and brass bands. There's a poetry slam on Thurs. Low or no cover. Daily 6pm–3am.

**Dream Palace**, 534 Frenchmen St (☎504/945-2040). Friendly, established Faubourg venue hosting reggae, Latin and world music, local funk, and brass bands. Hop between this and the *Brasil*, for a hip New Orleans night out. Cover varies. Daily 8pm–2am.

**House of Blues**, 225 Decatur St (☎504/529-2583). Sleek French Quarter venue, part of the national chain. If you can stomach its un-New Orleans attitude and high prices, it's worth checking out for big names and there's a jolly, if pricey, gospel brunch on Sun (10am & 1pm; call to reserve). Cover varies. Daily 8pm–3am.

**Lion's Den**, 2655 Gravier St, Mid-City (☎504/822-3745). Tiny club part-owned by R&B legend Irma Thomas, who performs occasionally, especially during festivals, when she may even prepare beans and rice for her devoted fans. Take a taxi. Days, hours and cover varies.

**Maple Leaf**, 8316 Oak St (☎504/866-9359). Friendly old bar with pressed-tin walls, a dance floor and a patio. A local favorite for blues, Cajun, zydeco, R&B and brass bands. There's chess and pool, too, and poetry on Sun afternoons. Cover varies. Daily 3pm–4am.

**Mid-City Lanes**, 4133 S Carrollton St, Mid-City (☎504/482-3133). Eccentric bowling alley-cum-music venue in an unprepossessing mall. Though it's especially heaving on Wed and Thurs – when the zydeco bands stir the crowd – they also book good local R&B blues and swing. Take a taxi. Cover varies. Daily noon–2am.

**Mother-in-Law Lounge**, 1500 N Claiborne Ave, in Tremé (☎504/947-1078). Difficult to categorize venue – bar/club/living room – in the home of flamboyant R&B veteran Ernie K-Doe. A great place for a drink, it's even better during one of Ernie's shows, when he invariably belts out the eponymous 1950s hit to a motley crew of die-hard fans, family and hipsters. Call to ask about music; cover around $5. Daily 6pm till late.

**The Red Room**, 2040 St Charles Ave (☎504/528-9759). Swanky, very scarlet, cocktail bar and music venue, on the fringes of the Garden District. At the forefront of the city's swing revival, it also features jazz and Latin bands, attracting a superhip uptown set. Pricey food served. Cover varies. Mon–Sat 5pm–2am.

## MARDI GRAS

New Orleans' **carnival season** – which starts on Twelfth Night and runs for the six weeks or so until Ash Wednesday – is unlike any other in the world. Though the name is used to define the entire season, **Mardi Gras** itself, French for "Fat Tuesday," is simply the culmination of a whirl of parades, parties, street revels and masked balls, all inextricably tied up with the city's labyrinthine social and political structures. Mardi Gras was introduced to New Orleans in the 1740s, when **French** colonists brought over the European custom, established since medieval times, of marking the imminence of Lent with masking and feasting. Their slaves, meanwhile, continued to celebrate **African** and **Caribbean** festival traditions, based on musical rituals and elaborate costumes, and the three eventually fused. From early days it was known for cavorting, outrageous costumes, drinking and general bacchanalia. Today, although it is the busiest tourist season – literally millions of people pack the city on Mardi Gras itself – at bottom it is ultimately an event for New Orleanians, with tourists welcomed as unofficial guests.

It was the birth of the **krewe** system – with the appearance in 1857 of a stately moonlit procession calling itself the *Krewe of Comus, Merrie Monarch of Mirth* – that really gelled Mardi Gras, bringing together the populist street festivities and the elite social functions. Initiated by a group of Anglo-Americans, the idea of secret carnival clubs was taken up enthusiastically by New Orleans aristocracy, many of them white supremacists who after the Civil War used the shroud of secrecy to mock and undermine Reconstruction. About sixty official krewes now equip colorful floats, leading huge processions on different – often mythical – themes. Each is reigned over by a King and Queen (an older, politically powerful man and a debutante), who go on to preside over the krewes' closed, masked balls. In addition to the traditional, elitist krewes there are women-only krewes; "super krewes," with members drawn from the city's new wealth (barred from making inroads into the gentlemen's club network of the old-guard krewes); gay krewes and important **black** groups. The best known is **Zulu**, established in 1909 when a black man mocked Rex, King of Carnival, by dancing behind his float with a tin can on his head; today the Zulu parade on Mardi Gras morning is one of the most popular of the season. There are also many alternative, or **unofficial krewes**, including the anarchic **Krewe du Vieux** (from Vieux Carré), whose irreverent parade and "ball" (a polite term for a wild party, open to all) is the first of the season. And then there's the parade of the **Mystic Krewe of Barkus**, made up of dogs, hundreds of whom can be seen trotting proudly through the French Quarter all spiffed up on some spurious theme.

Tourists are less likely to witness the **Mardi Gras Indians**, African-American groups who organize themselves into "tribes" and, dressed in fabulous beaded and feathered costumes, gather on Mardi Gras morning to compete in chanting and dancing. The **gay** community also plays a major part in Mardi Gras, particularly in the French Quarter, where the streets teem with strutting drag divas.

One important Mardi Gras ritual is the flinging and catching of "**throws**." Beads, beakers and doubloons (toy coins) are scattered among street revelers, who beg, plead and bargain for them. Souvenirs vary in worth: the bright, cheap strings of beads are least valuable, while the bizarrely garbed coconuts handed out by Zulu are worth their

**Tipitina's**, 501 Napoleon Ave (☎504/897-3943). Legendary uptown venue named after a Professor Longhair song. Though there's a smaller branch in the Quarter (see below), this is the original and still the best, with a consistently good funk, R&B, brass and reggae lineup, spanning the range from local favorites to national acts. The Cajun *fais-do-do* (Sun 5–9pm) is fun, too, with free red beans and rice. Cover varies. Daily 6pm–2am.

**Tipitina's French Quarter**, 233 N Peters St (☎504/566-7095). Geared towards tourists, this branch of *Tip's* lacks the atmosphere of its older sibling. It features a great lineup, though, with weekly gigs from Harry Connick Sr, Henry Butler and Kermit Ruffins, along with Allen Toussaint and Cyril Neville. Cover varies. Daily 11am–2am.

weight in gold. An offshoot of the throw tradition is the **bead-bartering** system among tourists, which in turn has given rise to the famed phenomenon of young co-eds pulling up their shirts in exchange for strings of beads and roars of boozy approval from the goggling mobs. Anyone desperate to see the show should head for Bourbon Street.

The two weeks leading up to Mardi Gras are filled with processions, parties and balls, but excitement reaches fever pitch on **Lundi Gras**, the day before Mardi Gras. Some of the city's best musicians play at **Zulu**'s free party in Woldenberg Park, which climaxes at 5pm with the arrival of the king and queen by boat. Following this, you can head to the **Plaza d'España**, where, in a formal ceremony, unchanged for over a century, the mayor hands the city to Rex, King of Carnival. The party continues with more live music and fireworks, after which people head off to watch the big **Orpheus** parade, or start a frenzied evening of clubbing. Most clubs are still hopping well into Mardi Gras morning.

The fun starts early on Mardi Gras day, with **walking clubs** striding through uptown accompanied by raucous jazz on their ritualized bar crawls. Zulu, in theory, sets off at 8.30am (but can be as much as two hours late), followed by Rex. Ironically, by the time Rex turns up, many people have had their fill of the official parades. The surreal **St Ann walking parade** gathers outside the *R-Bar* (see p.609) at around 11am, while the gay costume competition known as the **Bourbon Street awards** gets going at noon. In the afternoon, hipsters head to the Faubourg, where **Frenchmen Street** is ablaze with bizarrely costumed carousers. The fun continues throughout the Quarter and the Faubourg until **midnight**, when a siren wail heralds the arrival of a cavalcade of mounted police that sweeps through Bourbon Street and declares through megaphones that carnival is officially over.

### OTHER NEW ORLEANS FESTIVALS

**St Joseph's Day**, March 19. Italian saint's day, at the mid-point of Lent. Families build massive altars of food in their homes, inviting the public to come and admire them and to share food. The Sunday closest to St Joseph's ("Super Sunday") is the only time outside Mardi Gras that the Mardi Gras Indians (see opposite) take to the streets.

**Spring Fiesta**, March/April (week after Easter). Five-day festival when many of the loveliest homes in the French Quarter and Garden District are open to the public. It's all rather genteel, with guides rigged up in hooped skirts, a classical concert series and tours of the River Road plantations. Contact ☎504/581-1367.

**French Quarter Festival**, early April. Free three-day music festival that rivals JazzFest for the quality and variety of music on offer. Stages and food stalls, a jazz brunch in Jackson Square, tours of private patios, free evening gigs, parades and talent contests. Contact ☎504/522-5730 or *www.frenchquarterfestivals.org*

**Jazz and Heritage Festival (JazzFest)**, end of April/start of May at the Fairgrounds Race Track. Superlative, enormous festival, with stages hosting jazz, R&B, gospel, African, Caribbean, Cajun, blues, reggae, funk, Mardi Gras Indian and brass band music, with evening performances in clubs all over town. Also crafts and fantastic food stalls. Contact ☎504/522-4786 or *www.nojazzfest.com*

# CAJUN COUNTRY

**Cajun country** stretches across southern Louisiana from Houma in the east, via **Lafayette**, the hub of the region, into Texas. It's a region best enjoyed away from the larger towns, by visiting the many old-style hamlets that despite modernization can still be found cut off from civilization in soupy bayous, coastal marshes and inland swamps.

Cajuns are descended from the French colonists of Acadia, part of Nova Scotia, which was taken by the British in 1713. The Catholic **Acadians**, who had quietly fished, hunted and farmed for more than a century, refused to renounce their faith and swear allegiance to the English king, and in 1755 the British expelled them all, separating families and burning towns. About 2500 ended up in French Louisiana, where they were given land to set up small farming communities, enabling them to rebuild the culture they had left behind. Hunting, farming and trapping, they lived in relative isolation until the 1940s, when major roads were built, immigrants from other states poured in to work in the **oil** business, and **Cajun music**, popularized by local musicians such as accordionist Iry Lejeune, came to national attention. Since then, the history of the Cajuns has continued to be one of struggle. The whole region was hit hard by the oil slump; the erosion of coastal wetlands threatens the existence of towns like Houma and Morgan City; the silting up of the Atchafalaya Basin is having adverse effects on fishing and shrimping; and many coastal towns are in the firing line of the devastating hurricanes that hurtle up from the Gulf of Mexico.

However, the favorite Cajun phrase, *lache pas la patate* – "don't let go of the potato" – is an encouragement not to give up that suits this enduring culture to a tee. The popular image of the Cajuns as partying, fun-loving people is borne out at their many local dances, or *fais-do-dos*, held mostly at weekends. These singing, dancing celebrations, where everyone is welcome to trip a quick two-step, are good places to encounter this unique culture close hand, and visitors will find plenty of opportunity to join one. After Roosevelt's administration decreed that all American children should speak English in schools, French was practically wiped out in Louisiana, and the local Creole patois of the older inhabitants, with its strong African influences, was kept alive primarily by music. Since the 1980s, CODOFIL (the Council for Development of French in Louisiana), has been devoted to preserving the the the region's indigenous **language** and culture.

Although **Baton Rouge**, the capital of Louisiana, is not actually in Cajun country, heading out this way from New Orleans, via the **plantations** on the banks of the Mississippi, makes a good approach.

## Northwest from New Orleans: plantation country

The fastest roads out from New Orleans toward the west are the major I-10 and US-61; you can also drive along the **River Road**, which hugs both banks of the Mississippi all the way to Baton Rouge, seventy miles upriver. It's not a particularly eventful drive, winding through flat, fertile farmland, but a series of bridges and ferries allow you to crisscross the water, stopping off and touring several restored antebellum **plantation homes** along the way. In the nineteenth century, these spectacular homes were the focal points of the vast estates from where wealthy planters – or rather, their slaves – loaded cotton, sugar or indigo onto steamboats berthed virtually at their front doors. Today many of them offer luxurious **B&B** accommodation.

To get to the River Road from New Orleans, take I-10 west to exit 220, turn on to I-310 and follow it to **Hwy-44/48**, on the east bank. On the west bank, the River Road is **Hwy-18**. The levee runs the length of the banks, blocking the river from view, and though you'd never guess it from the tourist brochures, it's the hulking chemical plants that dominate the River Road **landscape**. There are rural stretches, where wide sugarcane fields are interrupted only by moss-covered shacks, but you'll more often find yourself driving through straggling communities of boarded-up lounges and laundromats, scarred by scrap piles and smokestacks.

From **Edgard**, 25 miles along on Hwy 18, you can cross the river to the **San Francisco House** (daily: March–Oct 10am–4.30pm; Nov–Feb 10am–4pm; $7), two miles south of **Reserve** on Hwy-44. Built in the "Steamboat Gothic" style, its rails, awnings and pillars were designed to re-create the ambiance of a Mississippi showboat, the elaborate facade is matched by a gorgeous interior – a riot of pastoral trompe l'oeils, floral motifs and Italian cherubs. A ferry at **Lutcher**, the settlement a few miles beyond San Francisco, crosses the river to Vacherie and the fascinating **Laura plantation** (daily 9.30am–5pm; $7). Rather than dwelling lovingly on priceless antiques, tours here, which draw upon a wealth of historical documents – from slave accounts and photographs to private diaries – sketch a vivid picture of day-to-day plantation life in multicultural Louisiana. Six miles upriver from Vacherie, **Oak Alley** is a Greek Revival mansion dating from 1839 – the magnificent oaks that form a canopy over the driveway are 150 years older (daily: March–Oct 9am–5.30pm; Nov–Feb 9am–5pm; $8). The **restaurant** serves Cajun lunches, and you can **stay** in pretty B&B cottages in the grounds (☎318/265-2151; ⑨).

The restored **plantation cottages** at **Tezcuco** (daily 9am–5pm; $7), about an hour's drive from New Orleans on Hwy-44, offer B&B accommodation, complete with porches, rocking chairs and, in some cases, fireplaces and libraries (☎225/562-3929; ⑦). Rates include a bottle of wine, breakfast in your room and a tour of the main house, an antebellum raised cottage built in Greek Revival style. Tezcuco is also notable for its good **African-American Museum** (Wed–Sun 1–5pm).

Eighteen miles south of Baton Rouge on the west bank, **Nottoway** is the largest surviving plantation home in the South, a huge white Italianate edifice of 64 rooms, 200 windows and 165 doors. Tours (daily 9am–5pm) cost $8, but you can get a peep at this "white castle" from the road. The house now also holds an **inn** (☎225/545-2730; ⑦) and **restaurant**.

# Baton Rouge

When French explorers first came upon the site of **BATON ROUGE** in 1699, they found poles smeared in animal blood to designate the separate hunting grounds of the Houmas and Bayougoulas Indians. The area on these shallow bluffs therefore appeared on French maps as *Baton Rouge* – "red stick." Now capital of Louisiana and the fifth biggest port in the US, Baton Rouge is an easygoing city for its size.

## Louisiana State Capitol

Surrounded by fifty acres of showpiece gardens, the magnificent Art Deco **Louisiana State Capitol** (daily 8am–4.30pm; free) serves as a monument to **Huey Long**, the "Kingfish." The larger-than-life state governor ordered its construction in 1931 and was assassinated in its corridors just four years later. First elected governor in 1928 after a vehemently anti-big-business campaign, Long swiftly concentrated power into his own hands. His massive program of public works included financing charity hospitals by levying heavy taxes on the big oil and gas corporations. Variously labeled a demagogue, communist and fascist, he set himself apart from other Southern populists of the time by refusing to exploit the race issue. Just as his appeal – with slogans like "Every Man a King" – began to reach national proportions, with a bid for the presidency in the offing, he was shot by a local doctor whose exact motives remain unknown.

Other controversial figures to have worked in the building include the segregationist country singer **Jimmie Davis**, better remembered for writing *You Are My Sunshine* and riding his horse up the steps of the capitol than for any political skills, and **David Duke**, a former Grand Wizard of the Ku Klux Klan, who was elected as a state representative in 1989 and was the unsuccessful Republican candidate for governor in 1991. Tours of this stunning building, with its huge murals and sculptures, are enlivened by Louisiana's maverick political history. Guides point out stray bullets in the marble pillars of the ground-floor corridor and a pencil embedded in the ceiling of the legislative chamber by an exploding bomb. Long decreed that nothing in Baton Rouge could be taller than the 450ft capitol, so its 27th-floor observation deck (closes 4pm) is the best vantage point to look out over miles of greenery and the sluggish Mississippi.

## The riverfront

Mark Twain referred to Baton Rouge's **Old State Capitol** (in use from 1850 to 1932) as "that monstrosity on the Mississippi." A grey crenellated structure on a lumpy mound overlooking the river, penned in by an ugly wrought-iron fence, it looks like a cross between a castle and a cathedral, without the particular merits of either. Inside, the entertaining **Center for Political and Governmental History** explores Louisiana's scandal-studded political history (Tues–Sat 10am–4pm, Sun noon–4pm; $5).

The splendid **LSU Rural Life Museum**, 4560 Essen Rd at I-10 (daily 8.30am–5pm; $5), re-creates pre-industrial Louisiana life with its carefully restored buildings – among them a plantation house, slave cottages and sugar mill – spread over 25 acres in a sultry garden setting.

One-hour harbor tours leave from the end of Florida Boulevard, passing under the **Baton Rouge Bridge**. This was perhaps the most ingenious of Huey Long's constructions; his stipulation that it should have a clearance of just 65 feet ensured that big boats

### CAJUN MUSIC

It's easy to "pass a good time" in Cajun country, especially if you're here at the weekend, when the *fais-do-dos* are traditionally held. Though things are quieter during the week, you'll still be able to enjoy authentic local music at many of the restaurants. Cajun music is a jangling, infectious melange of nasal vocals backed by jumping accordion, violin and triangle, fueled by traces of country, swing, jazz and blues. Zydeco is similar, but more blues-based, and more often played by black musicians. The patois heard in both bears only a passing resemblance to the language spoken in France. Music is never performed without space for dancing; everyone from the smallest child to most aged grandparent can join in. As well as the popular restaurants *Mulate's*, *Prejean's* and *Randol's* (reviewed on pp.619–620), venues include simple dance halls, record stores, river landings and the streets themselves. Look out for signs saying "French dance here tonight."

**Downtown Alive!**, Jefferson Ave, downtown Lafayette (☎318/291-5566). Free street concerts by rock, Cajun and zydeco artists. April–June & Sept–Nov Fri 5.30–8.30pm.

**El Sid O's Zydeco Club**, 803 Martin Luther King Drive, Lafayette (☎318/235-0647). Dances Fri & Sat, with great zydeco and blues house bands. They also serve food.

**Fred's Lounge**, 420 6th St, Mamou (☎318/468-2300). Extremely welcoming home of the locally famed live radio show (KVPI 1050 AM/92.5 FM), with music, dancing and lots of drinking. Sat only, 9am until well into the afternoon.

**Hamilton's**, 1808 Verot School Rd, beyond the airport, Lafayette (☎318/984-5583). Zydeco and reggae on Fri 9pm–2am.

**Prairie Acadian Cultural Center**, 250 W Park Ave, Eunice (☎318/457-8499). Splendid cultural center (see p.620) that hosts local musicians, storytelling and

cookery demonstrations on Sat afternoons from 3pm.

**Rendezvous des Cajuns**, Liberty Center for Performing Arts, S 2nd St and Park Ave, Eunice (☎318/457-7389). Live Cajun/zydeco radio and TV show, mostly in French, every Sat 6–8pm. Family-oriented and hugely popular. Cover $3.

**Richard's**, Hwy-190, eight miles west of Opelousas (☎318/543-6596). Popular place for zydeco bands and dancing; Fri & Sat evenings only.

**Savoy Music Center Accordion Factory**, Hwy-190, three miles west of Eunice (☎318/457-9563). Cajun record shop, with accordions made in the back room. The store is open Tues–Fri, but you should aim to be here for the joyous jam sessions on Sat 9am–noon.

**Slim's Y-Ki-Ki**, Washington Rd, Hwy-182, Opelousas (☎318/942-6242). Famed shack-style venue for zydeco music and dancing. Fri & Sat only.

could go no further north, thereby boosting the port trade of Baton Rouge several times over.

## Practicalities

Connecting **buses** from New Orleans' Amtrak station and regular Greyhound buses come in to Baton Rouge at 1253 Florida St, fifteen minutes from downtown. Local buses, run by Capital City Transportation (☎225/336-0821), are infrequent. **Information** is available at the **visitor center** in the capitol (daily 9am–4.30pm; ☎225/342-7317).

Downtown offers few decent places to **stay**; most of the chains lie along I-12 or on I-10. Large rooms at the *Best Western Chateau Louisianne Suite Hotel*, off I-10 at 710 Lobdell Ave (☎225/927-6700 or 1-800/256-6263; ④) are ranged around a pretty atrium, and there's a gym and outdoor pool on site.

Downtown, you can **lunch** with the politicos in the capitol's dining room (Mon–Fri 7am–2pm), while *Ralph and Kacoo's*, 6110 Bluebonnet Blvd (Mon–Thurs 11am–10pm,

---

### CAJUN FESTIVALS

Authentic Cajun festivals, held almost daily, it seems, to celebrate anything from frogs to new harvests, are a wonderful way to experience the food and music of the region. For some of the larger events, it's a good idea to book a room in advance; the rest of the world is catching on to the fun, and Lafayette, especially, gets crowded. The following is merely a sampler; for full details, check at any tourist office.

**Mardi Gras**, Feb/March. Second only to the New Orleans bash, this pre-Lenten party begins with street dancing on the Saturday before "Fat Tuesday." Cajun Mardi Gras differs from its city cousin; although there are private balls and parties, it is a far more pagan affair. Villages around Lafayette, like Eunice, Church Point and Mamou, are the scene of the *Courir du Mardi Gras* (see p.621).

**World Championship Crawfish Étouffé Cookoff**, last Sun in March (the Sun before if Easter falls on a Sun), Eunice. *The* place to taste the very best mudbugs, accompanied by great local music and a fierce spirit of competition among the 100 or so teams (☎318/457-2565).

**Festival International de Louisiane**, usually third week of April. Huge, six-day festival in Lafayette, with participants from all over the French-speaking world including Africa and the Caribbean. Particular emphasis on indigenous music and food (☎318/232-8086).

**Breaux Bridge Crawfish Festival**, first full weekend of May (Fri–Sun), Parc Hardy, Breaux Bridge. Crawfish-eating and peeling contests, crawfish *étouffé* cookoffs and crawfish races, along with music, crafts stalls, rides and dancing (☎318/332-6655).

**Mamou Cajun Music Festival**, Fri evening & Sat in early June. Music, dancing, competitions and crafts workshops in "Big old Mamou" (☎318/468-2258).

**Southwest Louisiana Zydeco Festival**, Sat before Labor Day at the Southern Development Farm, 457 Zydeco Rd, Hwy-167, Plaisance, near Opelousas. Top zydeco performers play "black Creole" music; with regional cuisine and African-American arts and crafts (☎318/942-2392).

**Festivals Acadiens**, third week of Sept in Lafayette. Huge three-day festival, with Cajun, zydeco and traditional French bands, along with indigenous crafts and food (☎318/232-3808).

**Prairie Cajun Folklife Festival**, in Eunice in the fall. Two days of free music, crafts, storytelling, cooking demonstrations and *Rendezvous des Cajuns* broadcasts (☎318/457-7839).

**Mamou Zydeco and Blues Festival**, first full weekend in Oct. Local music, food and dancing. Fri from 6pm, Sat from 9am (☎318/468-2370).

**Louisiana Yambilee**, last weekend in Oct. Opelousas goes all out to celebrate the sweet potato. Food stalls, sweet potato auctions, music, and Miss Yambilee and Lil' Miss Yum Yum contests (☎318/948-8848).

Fri & Sat 11am–10.30pm, Sun 11am–9pm; ☎225/766-8634), serves breaded seafood from catfish to crawfish for around $12. Further along Bluebonnet at no. 8322, *Mulate's* (Mon–Fri 11am–2pm & 5–10pm, Sat 11am–10pm, Sun 11am–9pm; ☎225/767-4794) offers fried, breaded Cajun food, plus live music and dancing nightly.

For coffee bars and funky diners, along with the bulk of the city's **nightlife**, you'll need to head for the area around the LSU campus, along College Drive and Chimes and Highland. *Bayou*, 124 W Chimes St (☎225/346-1765), is a trendy bar with pool tables and live music, as seen in the movie *sex, lies and videotape*.

# Lafayette and around

**LAFAYETTE**, 130 miles northwest of New Orleans on I-10, is geographically central in Cajun country, and is the key city for its **oil** business. Originally named Vermilionville, after the orangey bayou nearby, it was renamed in the 1880s when the railroad came to town. Today Lafayette is a quiet place, a city with a small-town feel and no real centre. It does, however, offer some lively Cajun history and good restaurants – and makes the best base for exploring the swamps, bayous and dance halls of the surrounding region.

### Arrival, information and getting around
**Greyhound** arrives in Lafayette at 315 Lee Ave and **Amtrak** a few blocks north at Jefferson and Grant. There's an **airport** south of town on the Evangeline Thruway. The **local bus** system is of little use to visitors; to get the best out of the area you'll need a **car**, as the dance halls, restaurants and hotels are spread out some distance from each other. If you need a **taxi**, try Yellow Cabs (☎318/237-9707). The Lafayette Parish **CVB** is at 1400 Evangeline Thruway at Willow (Mon–Fri 8.30am–5pm, Sat & Sun 9am–5pm; ☎318/232-3808 or 1-800/346-1958).

### Accommodation in and around Lafayette

Scores of chain **hotels** line Evangeline Thruway just south of I-10, and US-90 and Hwy-182 toward New Iberia. Alternatively, **B&Bs** are welcoming and reasonably inexpensive, but you must book ahead. You can **camp** at *KOA Lafayette*, five miles west of town, which also has a few simple cabins (☎318/235-2739; ①).

**Bayou Cabins**, 100 E Mills Ave/Hwy-94, Breaux Bridge (☎318/332-6158 or 1-800/346-1958). Three rustic nineteenth-century cabins right on Bayou Teche. Run by the owners of *Bayou Boudin and Cracklin'* (see opposite); rates include a free taster of their fantastic Cajun food and a full breakfast. ③.

**Maison des Amis**, 140 E Bridge St, Breaux Bridge (☎318/332-5273). Four B&B rooms in a Creole house on the bayou. Complimentary breakfast served at *Cafe des Amis* (see opposite). ⑤.

**Plantation Motor Inn**, 2810 NE Evangeline Thruway, Lafayette (☎318/232-7285). Motel north of town near the interstate, with plain rooms and free continental breakfast. ③.

**T'Frere's House**, 1905 Verot School Rd, 8 miles south of I-10, Lafayette (☎1-800/984-9347 or 318/984-9347). Hospitable B&B in an antique-filled, cypress-built home. Complimentary mint juleps and superb Cajun breakfast. ⑤.

### The Town

In the center of Lafayette, such as it is, stands the Romanesque **St John's Cathedral**, 914 St John St, and the old **cemetery**, where the crumbling raised graves include that of **Jean Mouton**, the town's Cajun founder. Each of the magnificent branches of the 500-year-old **St John Oak** opposite, spreading over 200ft, weighs seventy tons. Three blocks north, the small **Lafayette Museum**, at 1122 Lafayette St (Tues–Sat 9am–5pm, Sun

3–5pm; $3), was the "Sunday home" – a townhouse used after Mass, before the family returned to their plantation – of Jean's son Alexandre, Louisiana's first Democratic governor. It is filled with family memorabilia and Cajun Mardi Gras costumes.

The campus of the **University of Southwestern Louisiana**, south of the center, boasts a swamp – complete with gators, turtles, waterbirds and tattered Spanish moss – next to the Student Union. Its **art museum**, spread across two sites on Girard Park Drive, features local artists and Southern folk art (Mon–Fri 9am–4pm; $2).

The great energies Lafayette has put into tourism since the oil slump have created two excellent reconstructions of early Cajun communities. **Vermilionville**, at 1600 Surrey St across from the airport, is the easier to reach – an impressive living history exhibition set in 23 acres on the Bayou Vermilion, exploring the culture of Cajuns, Native Americans and Creoles (daily 10am–5pm; $8). Plantation slave buildings sell coffee, beignets and boudin, and stage cooking demonstrations (11.30am & 1.30pm). A large barn serves as a **theater**, with storytellers, plays and noisy *fais-do-dos* (Mon–Fri 1.30–3.30pm, Sat & Sun 2–5pm), while the **restaurant** next door serves good Cajun lunches (daily except Tues 11am–2pm). Costumed craftspeople talk to visitors about their work, and a simple chapel hosts lectures on religious traditions, from voodoo to the *traiteurs*, Cajuns who were believed to have healing powers.

Ten miles or so from the CVB, Lafayette's other folk-life museum, the smaller **Acadian Village** at 200 Greenleaf Drive (daily 10am–5pm; $5.50), depicts early nineteenth-century Cajun life along the bayous. Original structures – homes, stores and a chapel – line a sluggish bayou set in gardens and woodlands, and are filled with traditional furnishings and crafts.

## Eating in and around Lafayette

**Eating** in Cajun country is inseparable from dancing and music; evening – or afternoon, or morning – entertainment revolves around restaurants that double as impromptu dance halls. If you don't feel like two-stepping yourself, you can just watch while downing a seafood dinner.

**Cajun food** is characterized by its use of anything going (they say a Cajun cooks every part of a pig but its squeal). Basic, one-pot cooking it may be, but it's difficult to eat badly or spend over $15. At lunchtime, takeout boudin goes down a treat, as do finger-licking specialties like rich pork cracklin' washed down with frosty beer.

**Bayou Boudin and Cracklin'**, 100 Mills Ave, Hwy-94, Breaux Bridge; exit 109 from I-10 (☎318/332-6158). Nineteenth-century Cajun country cottage on Bayou Teche – the crawfish capital of the world – selling takeout po-boys, seafood boudin, hogshead cheese and crawfish balls, all prepared on the spot from traditional recipes. Tues–Sun 7am–6pm.

**Cafe des Amis**, 140 E Bridge St, Breaux Bridge (☎318/332-5273). Cozy, atmospheric country store serving tasty Cajun-Creole food. Traditional breakfasts are highly recommended. Tues & Wed 8am–3pm, Thurs & Fri 8am–10pm, Sat 7.30am–10pm, Sun 7.30am–3pm.

**Cafe Vermilionville**, 1304 W Pinhook Rd, Lafayette (☎318/237-0100). Superlative French-Cajun restaurant in an elegant 1818 building. They specialize in fresh seafood in creative sauces; try the fantastic turtle soup. Mon–Fri 11am–2pm & 5.30–10pm, Sat 5.30–10pm, Sun 11am–2pm.

**Dean-O's**, 305 Bertrand Drive, Lafayette (no phone). Unprepossessing downtown pizza joint, a local institution for its delicious pies topped with succulent shrimp and seafood. Mon–Thurs 11am–11pm, Fri & Sat 11am–1am, Sun 4–11pm.

**Mulate's**, 325 Mills Ave, Breaux Bridge (☎1-800/422-2568 or 318/332-4648). Touristy, fun Cajun restaurant. Seafood, catfish and gumbo for less than $15; the Cajun and zydeco music is thrown in for free. Dancing nightly, and daily at noon. Fifteen minutes from Lafayette on Hwy-94, a mile off I-10. Daily 11am–10pm.

**Poupart's**, 1902 W Pinhook Rd, Lafayette (☎318/232-7921). Superb French bakery serving good coffee, pastries, continental breakfasts, sandwiches and light lunches. Try the spinach-stuffed basil bread and crawfish pastries. Tues–Sat 7am–6.30pm, Sun 7am–4pm.

**Prejean's**, 3480 US-167 N, Lafayette (☎318/896-3247). Exquisite, reasonably priced, Cajun-Creole food in lively surroundings. Fish and seafood are especially good. Mon–Thurs & Sun 11am–10pm, Fri & Sat 11am–11pm; live music begins at 7pm.

**Prudhomme's Cajun Cafe**, 4676 NE Evangeline Thruway Service Rd, Carencro (☎318/896-3646). Classy place dishing up delicious shrimp *étouffé*, seafood-stuffed eggplant, sweet potato muffins and the like in a rustic 1890 home north of Lafayette on I-49, seven miles north of I-10. Mon–Sat 11am–10pm.

**Randol's**, 2320 Kaliste Saloom Rd, Lafayette (☎318/981-7080). Locally famed dance hall serving fresh steamed seafood dinners (specializing in soft-shell crabs). The nightly *fais-do-dos* are occasionally televised. Sun–Thurs 5–10pm, Fri & Sat 5–10.30pm.

# Touring Cajun country

North of Lafayette, the **Cajun Prairie** has been described by folklorist Alan Lomax as the "Cajun Cultural Heartland." A patchwork of rice and soybean fields scattered with crawfish ponds, the region has a few tiny towns where you'll be greeted with genuine warmth and interest by locals.

   **GRAND COTEAU**, off I-49 ten miles north of Lafayette, is a picture-perfect little town, with whitewashed buildings – including a dazzling white chapel – and prettily winding roads. Since 1866, when a dying woman was miraculously healed by the intercession of a saint in the **Academy of the Sacred Heart**, 1821 Academy Rd, devout Cajun Catholics have come here on pilgrimage. You can see the old classrooms of this beautifully columned school, and follow a long path through the ornate gardens, canopied by huge old oaks (Mon–Fri by appointment; ☎318/662-5275; $5).

   The 1831 **Chretien Point Plantation**, in **SUNSET**, ten miles northwest of Lafayette on Hwy-1 just off I-10, is Louisiana's oldest Greek Revival building (daily 10am–5pm; $6.50). Its main staircase was the model for Tara's in *Gone with the Wind*. Mrs Chretien, left to run the plantation after her husband's death in 1832, was very much in the Scarlett O'Hara mode. She scandalized the community by drinking, smoking, gambling and sitting with the men after dinner, and once shot an intruder, whose ghost roams the corridors. Bullet holes in the front door date from 1863, when Mrs Chretien's son showed a Masonic sign to an attacking Union general, who thereupon directed fire over the roof. The plantation has five luxurious **B&B** rooms (☎318/662-5876; ⑥).

   Predominantly French-speaking **OPELOUSAS**, twenty miles north of Lafayette on I-49, was the boyhood home of Jim Bowie, Texas Revolutionary hero and inventor of the Bowie knife. Opelousas' three other claims to fame are as the first place in the world to produce an offset newspaper (1915), as birthplace of the great zydeco musician **Clifton Chenier**, and as **yam** capital of the universe. The great little **Opelousas Museum and Interpretive Center**, 329 N Main St (Tues–Sat 9am–5pm; free), displays such relics of local history as the barber's stool on which outlaw Clyde Barrow got his last shave before being shot dead by the FBI in northern Louisiana. Stop by at the 1920s *Palace Cafe*, on the central square at 167 W Landry Ave (Mon–Sat 6am–9pm, Sun 7am–9pm; ☎318/942-2142), for shrimp, crawfish and gumbo in immaculate **diner** surroundings. There's nowhere to **stay** in town; if you're stuck, try the *Quality Inn*, five minutes or so south of town at exit 15 off I-49, which has a sauna and a pool (☎318/948-9500; ⑤).

   To learn a little about the Cajun Prairie, head for friendly **EUNICE**, about 25 miles west of Opelousas. The exemplary **Prairie Acadian Cultural Center**, 250 W Park Ave (daily 8am–5pm; free), holds far-reaching displays on local life, ranging across family, language, food and farming, with live Cajun music at weekends. If time is limited, choose this place over the **Eunice Museum**, 220 S CC Duson Drive (Tues–Sat 8am–noon & 1–5pm, Sun noon–5pm; free), an old train depot crammed with an eccentric ragbag of toys, musical instruments, farming implements and Native American artifacts. However long you're here, don't miss out on Eunice's splendid down-home **food**

## SWAMP TOURS

**Swamp tours** are available from many landings in the **Atchafalaya Basin**; you'll pass numerous signs pinned to the old cypress trees along the roadside. The basin is an eerie place: almost all its cypresses were harvested last century, and now just the twisted silhouettes of their stumps poke out of the sluggish waters. In some places cars cut right across on the enormous concrete I-10, and old houseboats lie abandoned, or get used simply for weekend retreats. The best tours take you further out, to the backwoods; wherever you go you'll see scores of fishing boats and plenty of wildlife, including sunbathing alligators. Tours are conducted by Cajuns who see the basin as more than just a tourist attraction and provide fascinating personal commentaries.

**Angelle's Atchafalaya Tours**, Whiskey River Landing, 1175 Henderson Levee Rd, Henderson (☎318/228-8567). Twenty minutes from Lafayette, along I-10 and then highways 347 and 332, this quiet landing is run by the Angelle brothers, who also own the restaurant (which hosts a great *fais do-do* Sun 4–8pm) on the bank. Daily 10am, 1pm, 3pm & (summer only) 5pm; 90min; no reservations required; $12.

**De La Houssaye's Swamp Tours**, Expeditions Atchafalaya, Lake Martin Landing, three miles south of Breaux Bridge on Hwy-31 (☎318/845-5332). Nature-watching tours leaving from Louisiana's largest rookery for wading birds. Reservations essential. Mon–Sat 10am, afternoon schedule varies; 2hr; $20.

**McGee's Swamp Tours**, McGee's Landing, 1337 Henderson Levee Rd, Henderson (☎318/228-2384). Leisurely tours run from Henderson Swamp, a top fishing spot. Daily 10am, 1pm, 3pm & (summer only) 5pm; 90min; reservations recommended; $12. No tours in Jan.

–*Johnson's Grocery,* 700 E Maple St (☎318/457-9314), serves fat, juicy boudin and spicy hogshead cheese from 6am, while *Allison's Hickory Pit*, 501 W Laurel St (Thurs–Sun; ☎318/457-9218) specializes in pork, chicken, steak and brisket smothered in a mean barbecue sauce. Although there's little else to see in Eunice, it's at the hub of the region's **music scene** (see p.616); the regular *Savoy Accordion Factory* and *Liberty Center* bashes are supplemented by the riotous annual **Courir du Mardi Gras**, when masked horsemen gallop through the countryside before parading through downtown, where the drinking and dancing continues all day. *Potier's Cajun B&B*, near the *Liberty Center* at 110 W Park Ave (☎318/457-0440; ④), is a friendly **place to stay**.

From here it's twenty miles north to **VILLE PLATTE**, and Floyd's Music Store, 434 E Main St (Mon–Fri 8.30am–5.30pm, Sun 8.30am–5pm), owned by dashing Floyd Soileau, the world's chief distributor of **South Louisiana music**, and stocking everything from zydeco reissues to contemporary swamp pop. If Mr Soileau isn't around, you could well find him listening to the rocking jukebox a couple of doors down at the *Pig Stand*, 318 E Main St (daily till late; ☎318/363-2883), where giant plates of fried chicken, smothered sausage and ribs come heaped with rice, gravy, black-eyed peas and potato salad. It's famed for its pork barbecue (served Tues, Thurs, Sat & Sun only).

## South of Lafayette

South of Lafayette the towns are less immediately welcoming than those in the Prairie, but the surroundings are undeniably atmospheric: this is **bayou country**, a marshy expanse of rivers and lakes dominated by the mighty Atchafalaya swamp, where the soupy green waters creep right up to the edges of the highway. Unsurprisingly, the economy is based on fishing and shrimping, with hunting in the forests and sugar fields, but it's also a semi-industrial landscape, with a web of oil pipelines running beneath the waterways, and refineries and corrugated-iron shacks sharing space with neat white Catholic churches.

Settled in 1765, old **ST MARTINVILLE** on the Bayou Teche, off US-90 a dozen miles south of Lafayette, was a major port of entry for exiled Acadians. The **Evangeline Oak**, on Port Street where it meets the bayou, marks where **Emmeline Labiche**, the inspiration for Longfellow's *Evangeline*, disembarked after her hard journey from Nova Scotia, only to hear that her lover, Gabriel, was engaged to another. You may find a small group of musicians or storytellers around the tree. In the nineteenth century this country town was known as "le petit Paris," filled with French Royalists fleeing the Revolution and re-creating a glittering city life of soirees and balls. It was later decimated by yellow fever, fire and hurricane, and is now a peaceful hamlet, kept going by the trickle of tourists drawn here by the Evangeline legend.

The eighteenth-century St Martin de Tours **Catholic church**, on the town square at 103 Main St, contains a gold and silver sanctuary light and intricate carved font said to have been gifts from Louis XVI and Marie Antoinette. Next door, the friendly **Petit Paris Museum** exhibits fabulous local Mardi Gras costumes (daily 9.30am–4.30pm; $2; tours of museum and church $5). Behind the church, the bronze **Evangeline Monument** was donated by the producers of the 1929 movie *The Romance of Evangeline*, and is modeled on Dolores del Rio, its star. North of town on Hwy-31, the **Longfellow-Evangeline State Commemorative Area** (daily 9am–5pm; $2 per car) on the bayou contains an 1815 **Creole Plantation House**, made with the *bousillage* mixture characteristic of early Louisianan buildings, and held together by wooden pegs. If St Martinville's sleepy charm wins you over you might want to **stay**: the *Old Castillo*, 220 Evangeline Blvd next to the Evangeline Oak (☎318/394-4010 or 1-800/621-3017; ④), is a comfortable mid-nineteenth-century B&B. The **restaurant** serves good home cooking (daily 8am–9pm).

**AVERY ISLAND**, seven miles southwest of the bayou town of **New Iberia** along a toll road, is not an island at all; it's the tip of a massive salt dome. **Tabasco sauce** is still prepared from a family recipe in the McIlhenny factory here, using the red-hot local peppers (Mon–Fri 9am–4pm, Sat 9am–noon; free). The steamy, 250-acre **Jungle Gardens** (same hours; $5.50) are full of exotic camellias, azaleas and irises, and serve as a sanctuary for blue herons, black ibises and snowy egrets.

# NORTH LOUISIANA

**North Louisiana** is at the heart of the region known as the **Ark-La-Tex**, where the cottonfields, Bible Belt mentality and soft vocal drawl of the Deep South fuse with the ranches, oil and country music of Texas and the hilly forests (resplendent in the fall) of Arkansas. Settled by the Scottish and Irish after the Louisiana Purchase, the area is strongly Baptist, with less of a penchant for fun than south Louisiana, though it does share its profusion of **festivals**.

## Natchitoches

Tiny **NATCHITOCHES** (pronounced "Nakitish"), in the sleepy cottonfields of the Cane River, is the oldest European settlement in Louisiana, having begun life as a French trading post in 1714. A Catholic oasis in a Protestant desert, it was swiftly fortified when its Spanish and Native American customers started to combine aggression with commerce.

With its lovingly restored Creole architecture, Natchitoches's exquisite **Front Street** on the river looks a lot like New Orleans' French Quarter. The lacy iron balconies, spiral staircases and cobbled courtyards are complemented by friendly, old-style stores. The 1717 **Immaculate Conception Catholic Church**, at Second and Church, has many of its original French features, including glass chandeliers and a hand-carved font. Fleur de lis on the nearby **Starwalk** commemorate celebrities with local connections, such as John Wayne, Clementine Hunter (see below), and the cast of the movie *Steel Magnolias*, which was set and filmed here in 1988. **Fort St Jean Baptiste**, at Mill and Jefferson, is a five-acre reconstruction of the town's 1716 fort, with rough wooden and adobe buildings, enclosed by a tall wooden fence (daily 9am–5pm; $2).

The quirky **Bayou Folk Museum** in novelist **Kate Chopin's** old home in **CLOUTIERVILLE** (Mon–Sat 10am–5pm, Sun 1–5pm; $5), is filled with all manner of oddities of local interest, along with exhibits relating to Chopin herself, whose nineteenth-century novel *The Awakening*, about a married woman's desire for independence, shocked the nation.

## Practicalities

Natchitoches lies seventy miles southeast of the town of Shreveport, on Hwy-6 off I-49. Greyhound comes in on the southeast side of town, on Hwy-1; the town has **no public transportation** or taxis, so to avoid being stranded, you should reserve accommodation in advance at a **B&B**, and arrange to be collected. One of the most welcoming is the Fleur de Lis, 336 Second St (☎1-800/489-6621; prepaid reservations only; ④), with its romantic veranda and huge communal breakfasts.

The **visitor center**, 781 Front St (Mon–Fri 8am–6pm, Sat 9am–5pm, Sun 10am–3pm; ☎1-800/259-1714), provides self-guided tours and can help find accommodation. The best place to **eat** is *Lasyone's Meat Pie Kitchen* (Mon–Sat 7am–7pm; ☎318/352-3353), around the corner at 622 Second St, which specializes in meat pies (spicy, flaky and lightly fried), red beans and sausage, fresh cornbread and rich cream pies.

## The Cane River plantations

The rural **Cane River roads** are dotted with ramshackle houses and small farms. As you drive past farmers sitting on porches, and women hanging out the wash, you'll come across many **plantation homes**, some overgrown and in sad disrepair, others beautifully restored.

**Melrose** (daily noon–4pm; $6), sixteen miles south of Natchitoches on Hwy-119, has a fascinating history. It was granted in 1794 to Marie Coincoin, a freed slave, by her owner, Claude Metoyer – the father of ten of her fourteen children. By the 1830s, the slave-operated plantation had grown to 12,000 acres, and Coincoin was able to buy freedom for two of her children and one of her grandchildren. Around 1900, "Miss Cammie" Henry turned the crumbling Melrose into an arts community, visited by writers such as John Steinbeck and William Faulkner. In the 1940s a black field worker, **Clementine Hunter**, started to paint vivid images of rural life, using leftover materials. She lived to be 101, and her works are on show in the 1800 **African House**, which resembles a Congo mud hut and was used as the slave jail. A short film about Melrose is shown in the **Big House** – a typical plantation home, part brick, part wood.

# Shreveport

**SHREVEPORT**, in Louisiana's northwest corner, was established in 1839, after Henry Miller Shreve had spent seven years clearing a 160-mile log jam which clogged the Red River. Built on land "given" by the Caddo Indians to Shreve's business partner Larkin Edwards (so he claimed), it was a prosperous cotton, lumber and oil port until the river rebelled, silting up so seriously that it was no longer navigable.

Despite the depression caused by the oil slump, Shreveport remains the hub of the Ark-La-Tex, flying the flags of all three states. Links with Texas are especially strong; in 1873 there was even a short-lived bid to annex Shreveport and all the land west of the Red River to the Lone Star state. Today it's a pleasant enough place to spend a night, enlivened early in October, when the eight-day **Red River Revel** puts on classical and country music, clogging and street entertainment.

**Downtown** focuses on the green riverfront, surrounded by a number of museums. The hands-on **Sci-Port Discovery Center**, 820 Clyde Fant Parkway (summer Sun 1–6pm, Mon 10am–6pm; winter Mon–Fri 10am–5pm, Sat 10am–6pm, Sun 1–6pm; $3), where you can experience a mock-tornado and try on a space suit, is fun for kids, while the **Spring Street Museum**, 525 Spring St, shows local antiques and decorative arts in the city's oldest building (Fri–Sun 1.30–4.30pm, Tues 10am–1pm; $2).

The best of the collection at the old-fashioned, doughnut-shaped **Louisiana State Museum**, 3015 Greenwood Rd (Mon–Fri 9am–4.30pm; free), are the artifacts from **Poverty Point**, in the far northeastern corner of the state. All that remains of this ancient pre-Caddoan settlement, in use from around 1700 BC and thought to be the earliest community in the Mississippi Valley, is a series of huge concentric earthern ridges. The **Stephens African-American Museum**, 2810 Lyndholm St (call ☎318/635-2147 for hours) traces three local black families through the ages, dealing with such issues as segregation, civil rights and racism.

Sixteen miles west of town, in the gardens of the **American Rose Center** (April–Oct Mon–Fri 8am–5pm, Sat & Sun 9am–dusk; $4), you can wander along serpentine paths, shaded by towering cypresses and dotted with statues and gazebos, past more than 20,000 species of fragrant rose.

## Practicalities

**Shreveport Regional Airport** is five miles southwest of town, where Greyhound arrives on Fannin Street. The city **bus** system, Sportrans, is of little use for seeing the scattered attractions, running every half-hour to Bossier and the shopping malls but to few other places. The **visitor center** at 629 Spring St (Mon–Fri 8.30am–5pm, Sat 10am–3pm; ☎318/222-9391) can provide self-guided walking tours.

Shreveport isn't blessed with good-value accommodation; the cheapest **places to stay** are near the airport on Monkhouse Drive, or on I-20 around downtown. Try the *Best Western Chateau Suite Hotel,* 201 Lake St (☎1-800/845-9334 or 318/222-7620; ⑤), with its river views, gym, spa and pool, plus free transportation to the airport and bus station; or the *Fairfield Place B&B,* 2221 Fairfield Ave (☎318/222-0048; ⑥), a luxurious Victorian inn, in an old part of town.

The city's **cuisine** pilfers elements from Southern, Tex-Mex and Louisiana cooking, resulting in delicious dishes like shrimp with guacamole and fluffy cornbread, as well as the usual gumbo and jambalaya. *Herby K's,* 1833 Pierre Ave (☎318/424-2724) serves unmissable seafood – try the shrimp buster, with special sauce, while *Karma Cup,* 2710 Centenary Blvd (☎318/221-9700), is a funky, studenty coffee bar serving cheap veggie food, muffins and the like. The **music scene** remains vibrant; bluesy, distinctly country, and quite different from the Cajun or jazz heard in south Louisiana. Standouts include *Mabel's,* 205 Texas Ave (☎318/221-7090), for jazz, by the river; *Noble Savage,* 417 Texas Ave (☎318/221-1781), for quality blues, bluegrass and R&B; and *Strand Theatre,* 619 Louisiana Ave (☎318/226-1481) which hosts blues, jazz, comedy and drama.

# CHAPTER NINE

# TEXAS

S till cherishing the memory that from 1836 to 1845 it was an independent nation in its own right, **TEXAS** stands out as distinct from the rest of the United States. While its sheer size – eight hundred miles from east to west and nearly a thousand from top to bottom – gives it a great geographical diversity, its shared history, culture and ideology bind it firmly together. Independence is key to the Texan mentality, from the overriding distrust of government – any government – to the absence of unionized labor. As the old anti-litter campaign put it, "Don't mess with Texas."

Preconceived ideas about what exactly is "Texan" are soon shattered. It's actually one of the most eclectic and cosmopolitan states in the Union and each of the major tourist destinations has its own distinct character. Hispanic **San Antonio**, for example, with its Mexican population and historic importance, has a laid-back feel absent from the big-city neurosis of **Houston** or **Dallas**, while trendy **Austin** revels in a lively music scene and intellectualism found nowhere else in the state.

Regional differences are vast. The swampy, forested **east** is more like Louisiana than the pretty **Hill Country** or the agricultural plains of the **Panhandle**, and the tropical **Gulf Coast** has little in common with the mountainous **deserts** of the west. Changes in **climate** are equally dramatic: snow is common on the Panhandle, whereas the humidity of Houston, in particular, is only made bearable by nonstop high-power air conditioning.

One thing shared by the whole of Texas is the constant boasting – everything has to be bigger and better than anywhere else. Such chauvinism is tempered both by a delight in self-parody and by the state's melting pot of cultures. The much-cited Texan **friendliness** is not imaginary; to be unwelcoming would simply be unpatriotic. Texas is, after all, named for a Native American word meaning friend, *tejas*, and a visit here, especially to the Panhandle or the Hill Country, is not for those who want to be alone.

## Some history

Early inhabitants of Texas included the Caddo in the east and nomadic Coahuiltecans further south. The **Comanche**, who arrived from the Rockies in the 1600s, soon found themselves at war when the **Spanish** ventured in, looking for gold. In the 1700s, threatened by French hopes of westward expansion from Louisiana, the Spanish began to build **missions** and forts, although these had minimal impact on the nomadic way of

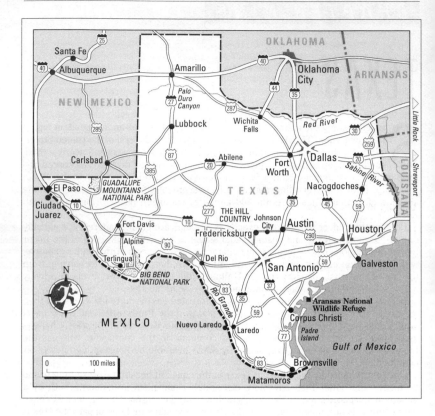

life. When Mexico won its independence from Spain in 1821, Texas was part of the deal. At first, the Mexicans were keen to open up their land, and offered generous incentives to settlers. Stephen Austin ("the father of Texas") established Anglo-American colonies in the Brazos and Colorado River valleys. However, the Mexican leader, Santa Anna, soon became alarmed by Anglo aspirations to autonomy, and his increasing restrictions led to the eight-month **Texan Revolution** of 1835–36. The romance of the Revolution draws legions of tourists to **San Antonio**, site of the legendary **Battle of the Alamo**, which, though a military disaster, presaged independence. Today's street names echo the conflict: Crockett, Travis and Bowie were all heroes at the Alamo, and Houston was the general who finally led the army to victory at San Jacinto.

The short-lived **Republic of Texas**, which included territory now in Oklahoma, New Mexico, Colorado, Kansas and Wyoming, served to define the state's identity, and in 1845 Texas joined the Union on the understanding that it could secede whenever it so wished. This is still written into its constitution, as is the proviso that it can, at any time, divide itself into five separate states. You'll see the **Lone Star** emblazoned on everything from advertising to architecture.

The influence, especially in the north and east, of settlers from the Southern states and their attendant slave-centered cotton economy resulted in Texas joining the **Confederacy**. No major Civil War battles were fought on Texan soil, however, and it remained relatively unscathed. During Reconstruction, settlers from both the North and the South began to pour in, and the phrase "Gone to Texas" was familiarly applied to anyone fleeing the law, bad debts or unhappy love affairs. This was also the period of the great cattle drives, when the longhorns roaming free in the south and west of Texas were rounded up and taken to the railroads in Kansas. The Texan – and national – fascination with the romantic myth of the **cowboy** has its roots in this era, and still prevails; today his regalia – Stetson, boots and bandana – is virtually a state costume, especially in Fort Worth and the west.

Along with ranching and agriculture, **oil** has been crucial. After the first big gusher in 1901, at Spindletop on the Gulf Coast, the focus of the Texan economy – and culture – shifted almost overnight from agriculture towards rapid industrialization. Boom towns flew up as wildcatters chased the wells, and millions of dollars were made as ranchers, who had previously thought their land only fit for cattle, sold out at vast profit. Texas today produces one-third of all the oil in the United States, and the sight of nodding pump jacks is one of the state's most potent images.

### Getting around Texas

Texan distances are best negotiated by **car**; in fact, in the larger cities like Dallas or Houston driving is all but essential. **Greyhound** routes are concentrated between the major cities of the east and the central region, though buses also serve the Gulf Coast, the Rio Grande Valley, West Texas and, to a lesser extent, the Panhandle. **Amtrak** only has one route that shuttles along the southern part of the state: the *Sunset Limited*, between Miami and LA, passes through Houston, San Antonio (in the very early hours of the morning) and El Paso three times weekly, also stopping at Alpine (for Big Bend). An Amtrak Thruway bus links Houston with Dallas, and San Antonio with Laredo. **Flying** saves time and can be very cheap; look out for price wars between airlines such as Southwest and smaller local carriers. Over thirty cities have airports.

Where Texas really falls down is on **public transportation** within the cities themselves; mass transit has proved impractical in a state where long distances – in Houston many people travel at least thirty miles to work – and low petrol prices make the love affair with the car almost inevitable. **Cycling** only really makes sense within cities like Austin and San Antonio.

# SOUTHERN TEXAS
# AND THE GULF COAST

The coastline of **south Texas**, which state residents half-jokingly refer to as the "Third Coast," curves from Port Arthur on the Louisiana border (a shipping and petrochemical town and the birthplace of Janis Joplin) on the much-touristed **Gulf Coast**, down past the urban monster of Houston, to the Rio Grande, the border with Mexico. Giant, cosmopolitan **Houston** dominates everything; its great wealth has led to a thriving arts scene, but ultimately it overpowers, rather than relates to, the rest of the region. Geographically and culturally, this area has two distinct faces. To the east are the seaside resorts of the prairie, rolling away from the hills and forests of east Texas. Much of the coast is feeling the strain of rapid property development and commercialization, but there are still unspoiled stretches along the **Padre Island National Seashore**. In the south, a Hispanic influence spreads north from the fertile Rio Grande Valley. The border towns here have little charm except as points of entry into Mexico for cheap shopping and entertainment. A hot, swampy climate is one factor uniting south Texas. Houston, especially, is unbearable in the summer, one reason for the mass exodus to the coast.

# Houston

**HOUSTON** is an ungainly beast of a city, crazed and confused by overdevelopment during the oil boom and then traumatized by the sudden slump of the early 1980s. It's a suffocating place, choking with traffic and high on humidity, yet for all this, its sheer energy, its relentless Texan pride, and above all its refusal to take itself totally seriously, give it a perverse appeal, while its well-endowed museums and rich nightlife mean there is always something to do. That Howard Hughes came from Houston makes absolute sense; eccentric, domineering and sordid, the millionaire typified all that makes the city intriguing.

There is no good reason why Houston exists at all; it was founded on a muddy mire in 1837 by two brothers from New York who hoped it would become the capital of the new Republic of Texas. For all their wild claims about its potential as a port, and its (imaginary) urban attractions, the more promising site of Austin was made capital in 1839. However, by then Houston had somehow established itself as a commercial center. Oil – discovered in 1901, and, like the city itself, unpredictable and heading for obsolescence – became the foundation, along with cotton and real estate, of vast private fortunes. Among the most famous of the philanthropists responsible for the development of downtown Houston was the cruelly named Ima Hogg. Her city improvement projects were largely cosmetic, however, and the contradictions of urban life are still writ large here, where abject poverty (not least among the blacks who migrated here from the rural South in the 1960s) coexists with ostentatious wealth.

## Arrival, information and getting around

Downtown Houston is at the intersection of I-10 (San Antonio–New Orleans) and I-45 (Dallas–Galveston), with most of what you'll want to see encircled by Loop 610, now widened on the west to include the huge Galleria mall. **George Bush Intercontinental Airport** (☎281/230-3000), 22 miles north, is the main hub for Continental Airlines, while the smaller, domestic **William P Hobby Airport** (☎713/643-3000), is seven miles southeast of downtown, just west of I-45 and a major hub for the budget Southwest Airlines. Both are served by the Airport Express **shuttle** (☎713/523-8888), which drops off at Galleria, Astrodome and downtown hotels ($18 from Intercontinental, $12 from Hobby), and Metro **buses** (Intercontinental, Mon–Fri 6–10am & 2–7pm; $1.50; Hobby, daily 5am–midnight; $1) which run downtown approximately every half-hour. **Taxis** cost $35 to $45 from Intercontinental, with the downtown fare from Hobby priced at $18 – though the fare to Galleria from here is $35. With these prices, renting a **car** makes sense for some, and all major companies are represented at the airports.

**Amtrak** arrives at 902 Washington Ave, on the western fringes of downtown. Have your camera ready for a splendid view of the skyline, though the station itself is small, isolated and barely served by taxis. Try to arrive here, or at the large and modern **Greyhound** terminal, 2121 S Main St, during daylight hours.

The main **tourist office**, a huge space with touch screen computers and other visual displays, is on the first floor of the City Hall, 901 Bagby St (Mon–Fri 8.30am–5pm Sat 9am–2pm; ☎713/227-3100 or 1-800/365-7575); there are smaller information centers at the airports.

### City transportation

There are few options for non-drivers in Houston. The Metro Buses are predominantly for commuters, **taxis** (the most reliable firm is Yellow Cabs; ☎713/236-1111) at $3 for the first mile and $1.50 for each additional mile, are expensive, and the humid climate and huge distances make walking unappealing. However, in the face of crippling traffic congestion, efforts are being made to encourage public transportation. Furious debates are raging about the possible construction of an underground rail system. Maps of the city's **bus** routes are available from the Customer Service Center, 912 Dallas Ave (Mon–Fri 10am–6pm). Local fares are $1 (with free transfers), while the downtown trolleys are free. Full information is on ☎713/635-4000.

Gray Line Tours (☎713/223-8800) and Texas Bus Lines (☎713/523-8888), which also runs scheduled services to Galveston and other regional towns, offer several **sightseeing tours** from $20.

## Accommodation

Although hostelers are reasonably well catered for, there's little call for budget **accommodation** in central Houston, where most visitors have cars; inexpensive hotels are concentrated near the Astrodome and outside the Loop, and motorists should try I-45, or the Katy or Southwest freeways.

You might also arrange **bed and breakfast** accommodation in advance; the human touch can be welcome in a city this potentially alienating and standards are high. As well as the places listed below, try the Bed & Breakfast Society of Texas (☎713/523-1114 or 1-800/553-5797).

**Angel Arbor B&B**, 848 Heights Blvd (☎713/868-4654 or 1-800/722-8788). Redbrick Georgian home just northwest of downtown which hosts "Murder Mystery Dinner Parties" and whose innkeeper writes cookbooks specializing in breakfast breads. ⑥.

**Grant Motor Inn**, 8200 S Main St (☎713/668-8000 or 1-800/255-8904). Reliable motel near the Astrodome, with a small pool but relatively large rooms. ②.

**HI-Houston International Hostel**, 5302 Crawford St (☎713/523-1009). Near Hermann Park in a pleasant neighborhood; dorm beds $14 for HI members, $17 for others. ①.

**HI-Houston (at Rice University)**, 6500 Main St (☎713/522-1096). Southwest of downtown in the Graduate House on the pleasant Rice campus. Dorm beds $14 per night. Summer only. ①.

**La Quinta**, 9911 Buffalo Speedway (☎713/668-8092). Good large rooms in close vicinity to the Astrodome. ④.

**Lancaster Hotel**, 701 Texas Ave (☎713/228-9500). Small English-flavored hotel in the Theatre District. Expensive, but weekend rates go down to around $130. ⑧.

**Lovett Inn**, 501 Lovett Blvd (☎713/522-5224 or 1-800/779-5224). Located on a leafy avenue on the edge of the Montrose district, this historic house offers first-class service and Southern hospitality. ⑤.

**Sara's Bed and Breakfast**, 941 Heights Blvd (☎713/868-1130 or 1-800/593-1130). Less than four miles northwest of downtown, near Memorial Park. A chintzy Victorian house with a fine view of downtown Houston, serving continental breakfasts on the porch. ④.

**YMCA**, 1600 Louisiana Ave (☎713/659-8501). Clean downtown rooms with shared bathrooms, a cut above the usual YMCA standards, for $18 plus a $10 key deposit. ①.

## The City

It's demoralizing and unwise to try and see too much of Houston in one go; best to concentrate on **downtown** or the **Museum District**, which can be walked around at leisure. Houston's human face is most evident in the **Montrose** area, on the way to yuppification but still home to eccentrics and bohemians.

### Downtown

Since the oil crisis in the early 1980s, the frenzy of skyscraper-building has slowed down, but Houston's skyline remains an unforgettable monument to an earlier age of certainty. Observation floors at the **Texas Commerce Tower**, 600 Travis St, and the

**Texaco Plaza** offer views of the endless plateau over which the city spreads. Just to the north, the area now covered by the reflecting pool in front of **City Hall** was granted to the city by a characterful rancher on the undertaking that no one could ever be arrested there for public intoxication, so it attracts what you might call a varied crowd.

Most people escape the Houston heat by staying underground, in the four miles of air-conditioned **tunnels** entered from the *Hyatt Regency* or the Main Street banks. However, they're a confusing and unaesthetic way to get around, despite the city's pride in their shops and restaurants. One consequence of this subterranean world is a surreal, dreamlike isolation above ground, as the plate-glass towers shimmer with reflections of the modern sculptures scattered at every turn (such as the Mirós outside the Texas Commerce Tower).

Nestling below the skyscrapers, **Sam Houston Historical Park** on Bagby Street (Mon–Sat 10am–4pm, Sun 1–5pm; $6) contains restored structures such as a church and shop, while **Market Square** features some of the original buildings at the heart of the early city, including the 1860 Creole *La Carafe*, at 813 Congress St. Once a trading post, it is now a laid-back bar complete with shadowy corners and old wooden floors.

Even if you don't make it to a performance in the **Theater District**, west of Milam Street between Preston and Rusk, visit the **Wortham Theater Center**, 500 Texas St (☎713/237-1439), which houses the city's opera and ballet. The beautifully sculpted interior, perfect acoustics and secluded private bars take the breath away, as does the knowledge that the whole set-up cost $70 million.

## The Museum District and the Rice University area

Five miles southwest of downtown, the oak-lined, student-thronged boulevards of the **Museum** and **Rice** districts are enjoyable to explore on foot, full of interesting exhibition spaces and several good bookstores.

A magnificent purpose-built gallery at 1515 Sul Ross – designed by Renzo Piano, who contributed to the Pompidou Centre in Paris – houses the private **Menil Collection** (Wed–Sun 11am–7pm; free). The superb works, gathered by oil millionaires Jean and Dominique de Menil, are displayed in spacious rooms, white-walled and naturally lit. Pieces range from paleolithic carvings dating from 15,000 BC, and a female idol from the "Mother Goddess" civilization of Catal Huyuk in Turkey, right up to modern sculptures such as John Chamberlain's *American Tableau*, made from discarded automobile parts. Artists with rooms to themselves include Max Ernst – look for the bronze *The King Playing With The Queen* – and René Magritte, while there's also a fine array of African art, including woodcarvings from Mali and ivories from Benin. One block east, the minimalist Ecumenical **Rothko Chapel**, 1409 Sul Ross (daily 10am–6pm), contains fourteen morose paintings commissioned by the Menils from Mark Rothko shortly before his death. The artist, who worked with architect Philip Johnson in designing the chapel, considered these to be his most important works, but many people today deride the building's resemblance to a nuclear bunker. The broken obelisk in the small park outside is dedicated to Dr Martin Luther King Jr. Diagonally opposite, the **Byzantine Fresco Chapel Museum**, 4011 Yupon St (Wed–Sun 11am–6pm; free) houses a pair of thirteenth-century Cypriot frescoes in a contemporary structure with a peculiarly spiritual ambiance.

At the intersection of Bissonet and Main, the **Museum of Fine Arts** (Tues, Wed, Fri & Sat 10am–5pm, Thurs 5–9pm, Sun noon–6pm; $3, free Thurs) features an eclectic collection from all eras, with Renaissance art especially well represented. Crane your neck upwards from the Matisses and Rodins in the pine-shaded **Cullen Sculpture Garden** outside to the downtown skyline. In a city with no zoning regulations, such architectural incongruity springs on you constantly.

**Hermann Park**, three miles south of downtown, is a pleasant green space with its own Japanese meditation garden. Exhibits on natural history at its excellent **Houston**

**Museum of Natural Science** (Mon–Sat 9am–6pm, Sun 11am–6pm; $4, free Thurs 9am–noon) include the recently renovated Hall of Earth Science, with its fascinating spangly array of gems and minerals. The **Cockrell Butterfly Center** (additional $3), is a giant three-story greenhouse where you can walk among lurid exotic butterflies as they flutter around an artificial waterfall, and even watch them emerge from their cocoons. There's also an IMAX theater (hourly Mon–Thurs 10am–8pm, Fri & Sat 10am–10pm, Sun noon–8pm; $6), a stunning gem collection, a good coffee shop and a sundial fountain lapping a map of the Texas coastline. The park is best avoided at night.

A short walk away, the **Contemporary Art Museum**, 5216 Montrose Blvd (Tues–Fri 10am–5pm, Sat & Sun noon–5pm; free) is worth a look if only for its huge windowless corrugated-steel wall. There is no permanent collection but the local freesheets run reviews of current exhibitions. The **Holocaust Museum Houston**, 5401 Caroline St (Mon–Fri & Sun 10am–5pm, Sat noon–5pm; free) is housed in another architecturally striking building, with a massive black funnel emerging from a triangular glass wedge. A chilling movie, *Voices*, is on permanent play and installations focus on concentration camps and those local people who survived.

### The Astrodome and the Orange Show

Around three miles further south from the Museum District, down Kirby Drive, Houston's legendary **Astrodome** was the first domed, climatized stadium in the world when it was built in 1965 and lends its name to astroturf which was first laid down here. It was home to the NFL's Oilers before they relocated to Nashville a few years ago and with the Astros playing their last baseball season here in 1999 its sparse usage is now restricted to big-wheel truck racing, trade shows and the like (daily tours 11am, 1pm & 3pm; events info on ☎713/799-9544; tours $4). A few hundred yards beyond, on the far side of the Loop, the big attraction at the **Six Flags AstroWorld** theme park is yet another mighty roller coaster, the indoor Mayan Mindbender (opening hours vary; ☎713/799-1234; $35).

Despite the dreams of its creator, the **Orange Show**, five miles east at 2401 Munger Ave, just off I-45 at the Telephone Road exit, is an altogether lower-key affair (summer Mon–Fri 9am–1pm Sat & Sun noon–5pm; rest of year closed weekends; $1). Promoted as Houston's most original piece of folk art, it's not really a show, but a suburban house transformed by the monomania of former salesman and would-be inventor Jeff McKissack into a paean to the orange. With one simple purpose – "to get more people to eat more oranges" – McKissack spent twenty years covering his home with celebratory tiles, ironmongery and slogans, with placards displayed by such oddball mannequins as the son of Santa Claus. The fabric of the place is solid ("weak construction would make the orange look weak"), but much of the mosaic work is surprisingly delicate, and it's not quite as garish as it might sound. When he finally opened it to the public in May 1979, McKissack confidently predicted that eight out of every ten Americans would visit. Depressed at the lack of crowds, the author of *How You Can Live 100 Years . . . And Still Be Spry* (in which oranges played a starring role) died in June 1980 aged 78.

### The Galleria and around

The ultramodern **Galleria** hypermall lies just west of the Loop, on Westheimer Road. Its three hundred or so smart shops, movie theaters and restaurants, plus a skating rink and a glass-floored jogging track, and ornate street lamps and signage, exemplify Houston's love of modern architecture, upmarket style and Texan tack. Across the way, a waterfall-sized fountain cascades outside the 64-story, black-glass **Transco Tower**, particularly breathtaking when lit at night.

## Montrose

Bohemian and fun **Montrose** begins at the junction of Smith and Elgin. It's all quirky sleaze, chock-full of tattoo parlors, vintage clothing stores, experimental art galleries, and junk shops selling barbed-wire cacti and other curiosities. Unfortunately, plans are afoot, spearheaded by a group of wealthy young Texans, to redevelop this as "the Old Westheimer District," complete with old-fashioned gas street lamps and similarly authentic touches. The teenagers who once cruised the streets on Saturday night have been forced elsewhere and the strip joints have closed down, but this has long been the base of a very visible **gay** community, and a high concentration of gay bars and clubs remains.

# Eating

There's plenty of variety in Houston's **food**: the large immigrant population has left its mark. Look out for Mexican, Vietnamese and even Indian restaurants, and the many good delis – such as the eight outlets of *Antone's Deli* – serving huge salads and sandwiches with an international flavor.

**Benjy's**, 2424 Dunstan Rd, off Kirby (☎713/522-7602). Modern American food with an ethnic bent and inventive desserts in a California-style environment near Rice University.

**Black Labrador**, 4100 Montrose Ave (☎713/529-1199). Open fireplaces, oak beams and superb English comfort food (bangers, shepherd's pie and the like) with great black-and-tans and imported Yorkshire bitter.

**Goode Company**, 5109 Kirby Rd (☎713/522-2530). Fabulous barbecue on the road to the Astrodome, with creative menu, outdoor seating and C&W atmosphere.

**Kim Son**, 2001 Jefferson St (☎713/222-2461). Massive Vietnamese restaurant with a long menu. Best at lunch for the good-value buffet.

**La Strada**, 322 Westheimer Rd (☎713/523-1014). Very tasty Italian dishes with an innovative and spicy Texan twist, near downtown.

**Ruggles Grill**, 903 Westheimer Rd (☎713/524-3839). One of the best places for a big night out in Montrose, with eclectic regional food at around $18 per entree. Reservations are advisable.

**Taqueria la Tapatia**, 1749 Richmond Ave (☎713/521-3144). This Mexican diner looks uninviting but its big, low-cost portions are a hit with Montrose residents.

**This Is It**, 207 W Gray St (☎713/659-1608). Heaps of soul food at budget prices in this downtown favorite.

**Treebeard's**, 315 Travis St (☎713/225-2160), and in the tunnels at 1100 Louisiana St (☎713/752-2601). Cheap and tasty Cajun food; good for a downtown lunch (stick to the veg plates rather than the stews), and also open in the evenings.

# Entertainment and nightlife

There's no shortage of things to do in Houston; just check the listings in the free *Houston Press*, or the more alternative *Public News*. **Cajun** and **zydeco** music have been significant in the city since a wave of migration from rural Louisiana in the early 1960s, and there's a strong **blues** tradition, while rootsy Texan **country** is another favorite. The Montrose area supports a very visible **gay** scene, and most of the clubs tend to be very male-dominated. **Miller Outdoor Theater** in Hermann Park, at 2020 Hermann Drive (☎713/284-8350), has free symphony concerts, ballet and opera on summer evenings, a "Juneteenth Blues" festival and a Shakespeare Festival around the end of July. Downtown's **Theatre District** holds considerable options including the nationally-renowned **Alley Theater** at 615 Texas Ave (☎713/228-8421) which offers last-minute discount seats, and the **Wortham Theater Center**, on the same street, (see p.630) is home to Houston's opera and ballet companies. **Bayou Place** at Bagby between Texas and Capitol streets, is a relatively new entertainment and restaurant complex that used to be a convention hall; one of its more interesting residents is the **Angelika Film Center** (☎713/225–5232), a multiscreen cinema complex that shows many art movies and has a good late night coffeehouse.

## Bars and clubs

**Billy Blues Bar & Grill**, 6025 Richmond Ave (☎713/266-9294). A giant sax on top of this massive club signifies that this is the joint for rocking party blues on the mile-long Richmond Strip, an "entertainment zone" made up of similarly rowdy themed bars.

**Cody's – In The Village**, 2540 University (☎713/520-5660). Above a strip mall in the Village, the top spot for jazz-blues in Houston. Their other location is *Cody's Rooftop*, 3400 Montrose Ave (☎713/522-9747).

**Continental Zydeco Ballroom**, 3101 Collingsworth St (☎713/229-8624). Possibly the best zydeco venue in the city, but not in the best of neighborhoods.

**Emo's Alternative Lounge**, 2700 Albany St (☎713/523-8503). A little hard to find on the edge of Montrose, but this slacker bar gets in the best alternative bands from the US and around the world for an unbelievable "no cover" deal. Beer prices are below average, too.

**Etta's Lounge**, 5120 Scott St (☎713/528-2611). Old blues bar-cum-diner, south of downtown – the scene of storming jam sessions.

**Fabulous Satellite Lounge**, 3616 Washington Ave (☎713/869-2665). Hosts the very best Texan roots bands and singer-songwriters.

**The Last Concert Cafe**, 1403 Nance St (☎713/226-8563). East of downtown, in an arty and isolated area. Good, cheap Tex-Mex food and live rock and roots bands in the back garden; but you can just drink all night if you prefer.

**Urban Art Bar**, 112 Milam St at Franklin (☎713/225-0500). Downtown showcase venue for breaking bands. Look for the Wednesday Buzz 107.5FM series, where admission costs just $1.07.

# Around Houston

Houston's double-edged status as having both historical importance and all the trappings of a twenty-first-century "space city" is neatly demonstrated by two possible excursions, both about twenty miles south of the city.

## San Jacinto Battleground State Historical Park

**San Jacinto Battleground**, 21 miles southeast of Houston off I-45, was the site of a fifteen-minute fight, two months after the Alamo in 1836, in which the Texans all but wiped out the superbly trained Mexican army. You see little but miles of flat land from the observation deck ($2.50) of the tallest **monument** in the world (570ft, topped by a 35ft Lone Star), but the **Museum of History** inside is more interesting, with the stirring 35-minute movie *Texas Forever!* (summer 8am–9pm, rest of year until 7pm; museum daily 9am–6pm; $3.50).

## NASA

NASA has been controlling space flight from the **Johnson Space Center**, 25 miles south of Houston off I-45 (bus #246 from downtown), since the launch of *Gemini 4* in 1965 – locals love to point out that the first word ever spoken on the moon was "Houston." As a working facility, it's not fully geared to tourists; all tours are self-guided, although you are rushed through the (tiny) Mission Control Room itself with a quick-fire lecture. Behind-the-scenes tram tours of the complex, including the Skylab training center, start with an impressive array of hands-on exhibits at the **Space Center Houston** (summer daily 9am–7pm, rest of year Mon–Fri 9am–5pm, Sat & Sun 9am–7pm; $13): you get to try on space helmets, inspect moonrocks and some remarkably cranky-looking rocket replicas, join astronauts and scientists in the cafeteria, and stock up on gimmicky space-age presents. Allow at least half a day for a visit.

# The Gulf Coast

You only have to look at the number of condo developments along the **Gulf Coast** to see that this is a major tourist destination. The climate ranges from balmy at Galveston to subtropical at the Mexican border, but everywhere it's windy: Corpus Christi rivals Chicago as the gustiest city in the States, and devastating hurricanes in the early 1900s all but ruined the traditional economy. The fierce tide, progressively gnawing away at the beaches, must place tourism itself in jeopardy; but for the moment, **Galveston** offers history, shopping and low-key relief from uptight Houston, while **Corpus Christi** to the south makes the best base for the beaches of Padre Island National Seashore. **Rockport**, a weathered resort on Hwy-35, is convenient for the **Aransas National Wildlife Refuge**, sheltering endangered whooping cranes, armadillos and alligators.

## Galveston

In 1890 **GALVESTON** – on the northern tip of Galveston Island, the southern terminus of I-45 – was a thriving port, far larger than Houston fifty miles northwest; many newly arrived European immigrants chose to stay here in the so-called "Queen of the Gulf." However, the building of Houston's Ship Canal, after the hurricanes of 1900 killed over six thousand people and washed away much of the land, left the coastal town to fade slowly away. Its recent revitalization as a historic district and beach resort has renewed spirits somewhat, but just beneath the pastel prettiness of the restored Victorian architecture and the relentless positivism of the inhabitants is a deathly stillness, as if the place is holding its breath, waiting to see if this time it can succeed without calamity or disaster.

The **Strand** downtown, once "the Wall Street of the Southwest," has been fitted with gaslights, upmarket shops, restaurants and galleries. The **Texas Seaport Museum**, in amongst a complex of shops and restaurants on Pier 21, just off Water Street (daily 10am–5pm; $5) focuses on the port's role in trade and immigration during the nineteenth century and admission also includes an opportunity to board and explore the *Elissa*, an 1877 tall ship. **Harbor tours** (Sat & Sun noon–3pm; $6) leave from the adjacent Pier 22 and offer a further 45-minute insight to the town's trading history.

Between the Strand and the beaches, old houses are everywhere, among them the ostentatious **Bishop's Palace**, 1402 Broadway (summer Mon–Sat 10am–5pm, Sun noon–5pm; rest of year daily noon–4pm; $6), with its stained glass, mosaics and marble; the antebellum **Ashton Villa**, 2328 Broadway (Mon–Sat 10am–4pm, Sun noon–4pm; $6), which shows a film about the 1900 hurricane with tours starting on the hour; the 1839 **Samuel May Williams Home**, 3601 Avenue P (Sat & Sun noon–4pm; $4.50), a New England residence moved here from Maine; and the city's oldest building, the **Michel B. Menard Home**, 1605 33rd St (Fri–Sun noon–4pm; $6), an imposing wooden structure built in 1838 which now holds a good collection of American antiques. Galveston's old Santa Fe depot, at 25th Street and the Strand, is now a **Railroad Museum** (daily 10am–4pm; $5), displaying steam trains, Pullman cars and endless train-travel-related artifacts in a skilful evocation of a lost era. Eerie white statues stand around in the waiting room; pick up a telephone and listen to their conversations.

On the west side of town, **Moody Gardens** at I-45 61st St exit (summer daily 9.30am–9pm, winter Mon–Thurs & Sun 9.30am–6pm, Fri & Sat 9.30am–9pm; $6 one attraction, $11 two, $16 three) is a floral research facility where you can happily while away a few hours. Its central focus are three giant glass pyramids; the Rainforest Pyramid houses exotic plants, birds and fish from around the world; the Discovery Pyramid is a good quality science museum that also holds a giant IMAX screen and several IMAX Ride films, and the impressive Aquarium Pyramid completed in 1999 is one of the largest such exhibits in the world. Also in the ever-developing complex are themed outdoor gardens, pleasant walking trails along the shore of scenic **Offat's Bayou**, where you can take a cruise on a paddlewheeler and Palm Beach, a popular spot for families where kids can play on a giant yellow submarine. It's worth visiting more than one attraction, especially as the box office (☎409/744-4673 or 1-800/582-4673) offers a complex variety of discounted combo tickets.

The downtown **beaches** of Seawall Boulevard are a constant reminder of Galveston's struggle simply to exist: murky, rocky and protected behind a ten-mile-long seawall from the ever-encroaching tides and the threat of further hurricanes. **Stewart Beach Park**, the most convenient curated beach for downtown, is geared towards family fun and gets very crowded; the wide **R A Apfell Park**, further east, is marginally quieter during the week, but has live music some weekends and a lively bar. Both of these beaches charge $5 per car.

## Practicalities

Greyhound takes about ninety minutes to cover the fifty miles from Houston, arriving at 4913 Broadway ($6 by taxi from the center). There is no Amtrak service. **Trolleys** (daily 6.30am–7.30pm; ☎409/763-4311; 60¢) rattle along past the historic homes and other sights between the **visitor centers** at 2016 the Strand (daily 9.30am–5pm, summer until 6pm; ☎409/765-7834) and 2106 Seawall Blvd (daily 8.30am–5pm; ☎409/763-4311 or 1-800/425-4753).

**Hotels** in Galveston are pricey in summer and at weekends, but bargains can be found at other times. The grandest place to stay on the island is the landmark *Tremont Hotel*, 2300 Ship's Mechanic Row (☎409/763-0300; ⑤–⑨) with tastefully uncluttered Victorian decor in the rooms. Rates along Seawall Boulevard can drop below $40 per night; the *Treasure Isle Inn* at no. 1002 (☎409/763-8561; ③) is one of the best value at the lower end of the spectrum, while the *Commodore on the Beach*, at no. 3618 (☎409/763-2375 or 1-800/231-9921; ④–⑤) is nicer and has a large pool; the *Hotel Galvez* at no. 2024 (☎409/765-7721; ⑤–⑦), built in 1911, is classier still. *Gaido's Seaside Inn*, at no. 3828 (☎409/762-9625 or 1-800/525-0064; ④), is another popular choice and has a good fish restaurant (see below). Within easy walking distance to the Strand, the town's **East End Historic District** holds some relaxing **B&Bs**, including the pleasant *Queen Anne B&B*, 1915 Sealy Ave (☎409/763-7088 or 1-800/472-0930; ⑥), built in 1905, and the 1887 *Garden Inn*, 1601 Ball St (☎409/770-0592; ⑤).

Other than the great seafood **restaurant** at *Gaido's* (see above), try *Yaga's Cafe*, 2314 the Strand (☎409/762-6676), which serves delicious Caribbean food in gaudy surroundings amid reggae and calypso music. For a more expensive treat, travel out to *Clary's*, 8509 Teichman Rd, off I-45 on Offat's Bayou (☎409/740-0771), and try the excellent fresh seafood. Family-run *El Napalito*, 614 42nd St (☎409/763-9815), is the pick of the town's Mexican diners, while *Phoenix*, 214 Tremont St (☎409/763-3764) is a bakery and popular breakfast spot.

**Nightlife** in Galveston basically amounts to cover bands, but there are several good noisy bars along Postoffice Street between 20th and 23rd. The *Old Quarter Acoustic Cafe*, 413 20th St (☎409/762-9199), presents hard-edged folk; the late Texan singer-songwriter Townes Van Zandt wrote *Rex's Blues* about the cafe's owner, musician Rex Bell. *Nina's Bourbon Street West*, 215 22nd St (☎409/762-8894) has live blues most nights and the *Strand Brewery & Grill*, 101 23rd St (☎409/763-4500) is a big brewpub with live music and views of the harbor.

# Corpus Christi

The unabashed and much larger resort town of **CORPUS CHRISTI** is reached along the coast on Hwy-35 from Houston or Galveston, or on I-37 from San Antonio. Originally a rambunctious trading post, it too was hit by a fierce hurricane, in 1919, but recovered, transforming itself into a center for naval air training, petroleum and shipping. Much of the population is Hispanic, and the community was devastated in March 1995, when the 23-year-old singer **Selena** was shot dead in a motel parking lot, by the former president of her fan club. Selena was on the verge of becoming the first major cross-over star of **Tejano** music, a hybrid of Mexican rhythms, German polka and reggae-influenced Colombian *cumbia*, and fifty thousand fans turned out for her funeral. The city's Bayfront Plaza Auditorium recently changed its name to the Selena Auditorium and there's been talk of a lasting monument in the shape of a Selena museum or a Tejano Hall of Fame, but so far neither have materialized.

Apart from fishing, sailing and water sports across the channel on Padre Island (see opposite), there's not a great deal to do in Corpus Christi. The impressive collection of the Philip Johnson-designed **South Texas Institute For The Arts**, 1902 N Shoreline Blvd (Tues–Sat 10am–5pm, Sun 1–5pm, Thurs until 9pm; $3), includes pieces by Monet and Picasso. Further along N Shoreline Boulevard, at no. 2710, the massive **Texas State Aquarium** (summer Mon–Sat 9am–6pm, Sun 10am–6pm; rest of year until 5pm; $9) is apparently one of the largest in the nation but feels cramped compared to the new aquarium in Galveston. Adjacent is the *USS Lexington* (summer daily 9am–6pm; rest of year until 5pm; $9) World War II aircraft carrier that's impressive to walk around although the few exhibits on board are weak. There are also plenty of interactive displays for the kids. The **Corpus Christi Museum of Science and Industry**, 1900 N Chaparral St (summer daily 9am–6pm; rest of year daily 9am–5pm; $8), specializes in hands-on natural history exhibits, including one about hurricanes, and naval aviation. Moored in the harbor a short walk from the museum, the **Columbus Fleet** (included in the museum admission) consists of life-size replicas of Christopher Columbus's *Niña, Pinta* and *Santa Maria.*

## Practicalities

Greyhound arrives at 702 N Chaparral St downtown. The **visitor center** is at 1201 N Shoreline Blvd, in the heart of all tourist activity, about a mile south of downtown (Mon–Fri 8.30am–5pm; ☎512/881-1888 or 1-800/678-6232). Daytime **buses** (☎512/289-2600; 50¢) operate downtown (except Sun) and other services include a free downtown **trolley** service and a water taxi from Peoples Street to the Texas State Aquarium ($1).

Budget **motels**, inaccessible without a car, line Leopard Street in the northwest. Along Shoreline Boulevard, the *Bayfront Inn* at no. 601 is a good deal (☎512/883-7271 or 1-800/456-2293; ③), while the *Ramada Hotel Bayfront*, 601 N Water St, offers rooms with a view of the water (☎512/882-8100; ④). Downtown Corpus's main concentration of **restaurants** is in Water Street Market at 309 N Water St, where the *Water Street Oyster Bar* (☎512/881-9448) serves fresh seafood. *Wahoos*, 415 N Water St (☎512/888-8522), serves excellent Cajun food to a background of zydeco beats. The *Lighthouse*, at 444 N Shoreline Blvd (☎512/883-3982), is pricier than downtown but serves lovely seafood in a great location on the marina.

# South towards Mexico

The disconnected islands of **Padre Island National Seashore** stretch just offshore for 110 miles south of Corpus Christi, almost down to the Mexican border. The frontier between **Brownsville** and **Matamoros** is not very interesting, however; for a brief taste of Mexico, head almost due west from Corpus one hundred miles to **Laredo**. US-83 runs along the Rio Grande between Brownsville and Laredo. Away from the coast, the fertile landscape begins to dry out and citrus groves give way to the brush and mesquite of a region of huge ranches, where Mexican *vaqueros* once held sway.

## Padre Island National Seashore and Brownsville

**Padre Island National Seashore** is not quite as unspoiled these days as its reputation might suggest, with its ranks of condos advancing steadily, but it remains a good destination for bird-watching, beachcombing and camping. Pick up details at the **park HQ**, on the main route out from Corpus Christi, at 9405 S Padre Island Drive (daily 9am–4pm; ☎512/937-2621). Infrequent buses run from Corpus Christi to the tip of Padre Island, and there is a $15 taxi shuttle service into the park. The park itself is open 24 hours, with a $10 admission charge per vehicle, good for one week, and a $5 overnight fee for its primitive campsites, or $8 for the semi-primitive *Malaquite Beach Campground*. Note that an impassable canal divides the island, meaning that the pricier and much more touristy **South Padre Island** in the south can only be accessed from the mainland.

**BROWNSVILLE**, just across from South Padre Island, is a scruffy, semitropical resort, populated by retired Texans on winter vacation, where you'll hear more Spanish spoken than English. To cross the border into **MATAMOROS**, walk across the bridge at International Boulevard (a Maxi-Taxi costs around $1). Wealthier than Brownsville, and considerably larger, the Mexican city is not terribly inspiring, but it has a good market, Mercado Juarez, on calles 9 and 10, and an untouristy main plaza at Calle 5, dominated by the cathedral. If you're intending to stay in Mexico or venture further than twenty miles or so, you must pick up a tourist card from the Mexican Consulate at Tenth Avenue and Washington Street in Brownsville.

## Laredo

The dusty, downtrodden and rather isolated smuggling center of **LAREDO**, over one hundred miles from the coast, has seen greater days even though it's the fastest-

---

### NUEVO LAREDO: MEXICAN BORDER CROSSING

It's an easy walk across the bridge from San Agustin Plaza in Laredo (see overleaf) to the typical Mexican border town of **NUEVO LAREDO**; so easy that this is the most popular crossing along the entire frontier, with most trippers coming simply for evening meals and weekend shopping. There is a lively atmosphere, with all the tourist shops and restaurants concentrated near the bridge, on "the strip," Avenida Guerrero. Most take American dollars, and bargaining is acceptable at some.

Seven blocks down Avenida Guerrero, the main plaza is the social center of town. **Hotels** include the good-value *Nuevo Romano*, at Doctor Mier 800 (☎871/12-26-94; ①) with rooms for around US$15 while the *Reforma*, on Avenida Guerrero at Calle Canales (☎871/12-26-50; ①) is cleaner and better but you'll still get change from thirty bucks. The *El Dorado Bar*, at Avenida Ocampo and Belden (☎871/12-00-15), was the first of the town's **bars** and **restaurants** to encourage tourism here, serving drinks to Texans escaping Prohibition. It's a bit tacky now; better to head for *El Rancho*, 2124 Av Guerrero (☎871/14-87-53), for *cabrito* (barbecued goat), guacamole and cold beer. For a more expensive treat, try the patio at *Victoria 3020*, 3020 Victoria St (☎871/13-30-20). As a whole, though, Nuevo Laredo lacks real charm, and can be particularly depressing after dark; have a meal but give the nightlife a miss.

As with all border crossings, expect to undergo full immigration procedures when you attempt to re-enter the United States.

growing city in the state. Santa Anna marched his troops through in 1836, and in 1840 the city was the center of Zapata's Mexican separatist protest. The capitol of Zapata's short-lived republic still stands on Zaragoza Street in the historic district, now housing the small **Republic of the Rio Grande Museum** (Tues–Sat 10am–noon, Sun 1–4pm; $1). San Agustin Plaza, the site of the original Spanish settlement, has been restored with cobbled streets and Victorian buildings, as has El Mercado, on San Agustin Avenue, the former hub of downtown activity.

Greyhound arrives at Matamoros and San Bernardo downtown. The **visitor center** is at 501 San Agustin Ave (Mon–Fri 8.30am–5.30pm; ☎956/795-2200). **Hotels** include *La Quinta*, 3610 Santa Ursula Ave (☎956/722-0511; ③), and the more central *La Posada*, 1000 Zaragoza St (☎956/722-1701 or 1-800/444-2099; ⑤), just east of the international bridge, where the dining room offers a big lunch buffet and good steaks. *Toños*, 1202 E Del Mar Blvd (☎956/717-4999) is especially popular at lunch for its Tex-Mex standards, and *Cotulla-Style Pit Bar-B-Q*, 4502 McPherson St (☎956/724-5747), specializes in a regional spicy type of barbecue as well as other Mexican dishes.

# CENTRAL TEXAS

Central Texas stretches from the prairies of the northeast through the green and fertile Hill Country into the chalky limestone landscape of the west, and includes two of Texas's most pleasant cities: San Antonio and Austin. Austin in particular, the capital city and home to the progressive University of Texas, helps to give the region an intellectual and political feel uncharacteristic of the rest of the state.

Agriculture has been the mainstay of the economy here ever since the resistant Comanche population was finally packed off to reservations in the 1840s. The slave-driven cotton plantations of the south and east have gone, but the small communities set up by Polish, Czech, Norwegian and Swedish immigrants in the **Hill Country** maintained, even until very recently, the traditions, architecture and languages of their homelands. Great cattle drives came trampling through after the Civil War and played a large part in the development of San Antonio.

## San Antonio

With neither the twenty-first-century skyline of an oil town, nor the tumbleweed-strewn landscape of the Wild West, attractive and festive **SAN ANTONIO** looks nothing like the stereotypical image of Texas – despite being pivotal in the state's history. Standing at a geographical crossroads, it encapsulates the complex social and ethnic mixes of all Texas. Although the Germans, among others, have made a strong contribution to its architecture, cuisine and music, today's San Antonio is predominantly **Hispanic**: abundant Tex-Mex restaurants, the prevalent Catholicism, a Mexican university campus and advertising billboards in Spanish all attest to a long history of "Texican" culture.

Founded in 1691 by Spanish missionaries, San Antonio became a military garrison in 1718, and was settled by the Anglos in the 1720s and 1730s under Austin's colonization program. It is most famous for the legendary **Battle of the Alamo** in 1836, when the Mexican General Santa Anna, seeking to curb the aspirations of the Anglo-Americans, wiped out a band of Texan volunteers: thus San Antonio's claim to be the "birthplace of the revolution," borne out by its role during Texas' ten subsequent years of independence. After the Civil War, it became a hard-drinking, hard-fighting "sin city," at the heart of the Texas **cattle** and **oil** empires. Drastic floods in the 1920s killed fifty people and wiped out much of the downtown area, but the sensitive WPA program which revitalized two of the city's prettiest sites, **La Villita** and the **River Walk**, laid the foundations for

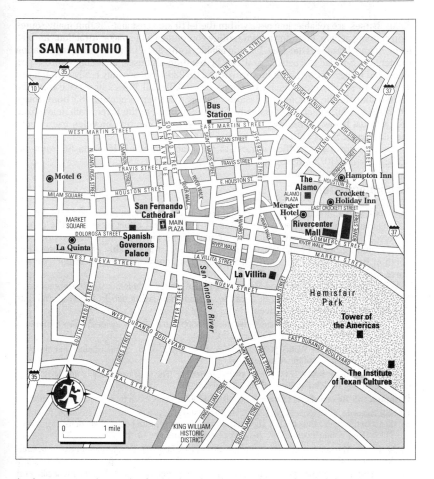

its future as a major tourist destination. San Antonio is now the ninth largest city in the US, but it retains an unhurried, organic feel, thanks to a winning combination of small town warmth, respect for diversity and a self-confidence rooted in its own history.

## Arrival, information and getting around

**San Antonio International Airport** (☎210/207-3411) is just north of the I-410 loop which encircles most of the sights. SA Trans Shuttle (☎210/281-9900) makes the twenty-minute journey downtown ($8 single, $14 round-trip; every 15min 6am–6.45pm, every 45min 6.45pm–midnight), while normal city buses run at peak times only. Taxis cost about $15 (Yellow Cabs ☎210/226-4242). Amtrak arrives centrally at 350 Hoefgen St, while Greyhound/Trailways operate from 500 N St Mary's St, supplemented by the regional Kerrville Bus Co (☎210/227-5669). Pick up information on **city transportation** from the **visitor center** at 317 Alamo Plaza directly across from the Alamo (daily 8.30am–6pm; ☎210/225-8587), or call the VIA Metropolitan Transit Service (☎210/227-

2020). **Buses** are reliable; journeys within the I-410 loop cost just 75¢, but many routes stop running at 5pm. Four downtown **trolley** routes serve the major attractions for 50¢, from Alamo Plaza. A One Day Pass available from the VIA Downtown Information Center, 112 Soledad St costs $2 and can be used on all buses, including express services, and trolleys. Gray Line's **bus tours** (☎210/226-1706) are only really of much use as a way to see the most distant missions (2hr; $20), and VIA's #40 service from the Alamo takes in the four main missions anyway. The very enjoyable $5 **boat tours** (☎210/244-5700), which do a leisurely 35-minute circuit of the River Walk, leave from the river just below the bridge on St Mary's Street. You can rent **bicycles** from Abel's Mobile Bicycle Shop, 1119 Ada St (☎210/533-9927).

The downtown **post office** is next to the Alamo at 615 E Houston St (Mon–Fri 8.30am–5pm; ☎210/227-3399; zip code 78205).

## Accommodation

The luxury of a moonlit amble along the river back to your hotel is one of the joys of visiting San Antonio, so it's worth making a determined effort to stay in the center. However, downtown is monopolized by luxury hotels, and a car is virtually a prerequisite for finding budget lodgings. There are clusters of reasonably priced **motels** just north of Brackenridge Park on Austin Highway, or, convenient for the airport, on I-35 north towards Austin.

With enough notice, Bed and Breakfast Hosts (☎210/824-8036; ③–⑥; deposit often required), can arrange rooms in a castle, a Victorian residence in the King William District, or less pricey alternatives.

**Crockett Holiday Inn**, 320 Bonham St (☎210/225-6500). Historic hotel with modern facilities, in an excellent location just opposite the Alamo. ⑦.

**Days Inn (Alamo-River Walk)**, 902 E Houston St (☎210/227-6233). Standard chain motel rooms, a few minutes' walk east of the Alamo. ⑤.

**Gatlin Guesthouse B&B**, 123 Cedar St (☎210/616-0030). The least expensive of the B&Bs in the excellent base of the King William Historic Distict. ④.

**Hampton Inn Riverwalk**, 414 Bowie St (☎210/225-8500). Good, clean rooms in central location. ⑤.

**HI-San Antonio**, 621 Pierce St (☎210/223-9426). Hostel across from Fort Sam Houston, two miles northeast of the center (bus #11). A good place to meet people, with pool and kitchens. Dorm beds are $13 ($16 for nonmembers). Call ahead to reserve in summer. ①/②.

**La Quinta – Market Square**, 900 Dolorosa St (☎210/271-0001). Decent motel next to bustling Market Square. ⑤.

**Menger Hotel**, 204 Alamo Plaza (☎210/223-4361). Texas' most famous hotel of the great cattle drives; Teddy Roosevelt recruited his "Rough Riders" here in 1898 for the Spanish-American War. The bar is inexplicably furnished to replicate the tap-room at the British House of Lords. ⑥.

**Motel 6 – Downtown**, 211 N Pecos St (☎210/225-1111). Clean but slightly worn rooms near Market Square, with a small but welcoming pool. ④.

## The Town

Since mission times, the **San Antonio River** has been the key to the city's fortunes. Destructive floods in the 1920s, and subsequent oil drilling, reduced its flow, leading to plans to pave the river over. Instead, a careful landscaping scheme, started in 1939 by the WPA, created the Paseo del Rio, or **River Walk**, now the aesthetic and commercial focus of San Antonio. Below street level, the walk is reached by steps from various spots along the main roads and crossed by humpbacked stone bridges. Cobbled paths, lined with tropical plants and shaded by pine, cypress, oak and willow, wind for two and a half miles (21 blocks) beside the jade-green water, with much of the city's eating and entertainment concentrated along the way. You can catch a river taxi at various points, but strolling is cheaper and just as much fun, watching as the river slowly changes character between the lively Rivercenter Mall and the quieter, more parklike outskirts.

While the **Alamo** (see overleaf) is the primary historical interest in the downtown area, two museums which take a pleasingly kitsch look at Americana, are also worth a visit. The surreal **Buckhorn Hall of Horns, Fins and Feathers** at the *Lone Star Brewery*, 318 E Houston St (daily 10am–5pm; ☎210/270-4000; $9.95), is a monument to Texan excess. During San Antonio's heyday as a cowtown, cowboys, trappers and traders would bring their cattle horns to the original *Buckhorn Saloon* in exchange for a drink. The entire bar has been transplanted to this downtown location that boasts an extra floor of exhibition space and as well as thousands of horns now on display, mounted as trophies, chandeliers and chairs, there are many stuffed animals including "Blondie" an unforgettable two-headed lamb. The **Cowboy Museum**, 209 Alamo Plaza (daily 10am–7pm; $3) attempts to take a look at life in the Old West but the giftshop is probably of more interest.

**La Villita** ("little town"), on the River Walk opposite Hemisfair Park, was San Antonio's original settlement, occupied in the mid- to late eighteenth century by Mexican "squatters" with no titles to the land. Only when its elevation enabled it to survive fierce floods in 1819 did this rude collection of stone and adobe buildings become suddenly respectable. It is now a National Historic District, turned over to a dubious "arts community" consisting mostly of overpriced craftshops (daily 10am–6pm). It's at its best off-season or at dusk, when the crowds dwindle and the muted colors, smells and noises are more evocative of earlier times. In contrast, the 25-block **King William Historic District** southwest, between the river and S St Mary's Street, contains the elegant late nineteenth-century homes of German merchants. A pleasant incongruity in this Mexican-feeling city, it remains a fashionable residential area and has some stylish B&Bs (see opposite).

The best of several museums in **Hemisfair Park** is the **Institute of Texan Cultures**, 801 S Bowie St (Tues–Sun 9am–5pm; $4). This maps the social histories of thirty diverse "Texan" cultures, with especially pertinent African-American and Native American sections, and an intriguing corner devoted to short-lived attempts to introduce the camel to West Texas as a beast of burden. Two of the park's other buildings house the **Mexican Cultural Institute**, filled with changing displays of historic and contemporary Mexican art (Tues–Fri 9am–5.30pm, Sat & Sun 11am–5pm; free). But for its observation deck (daily 8am–11pm; $3), the ugly 750ft **Tower of the Americas** is devoid of interest.

West of the river at 115 Main Plaza, the 1731 **San Fernando Cathedral** is the oldest cathedral in the US, though nobody really believes that the Alamo heroes are buried here, contrary to the claims of the tourist board. Mariachi Masses are held on Sunday at 9am and 12.15pm, when crowds spill outside onto the plaza. Two blocks west at 105 Plaza de Armas, the beautifully simple whitewashed **Spanish Governors Palace** (Mon–Sat 9am–5pm, Sun 10am–5pm; $1) was home to Spanish officials during the mission era. Just one story tall, it's not really what you'd call a palace, but its flagstone floors, low doorways and beamed ceilings, religious icons and ornate wooden carvings give it a wonderful atmosphere, and it provides an illuminating glimpse of the lifestyles of the civil and religious authorities in this remote outpost. Don't miss the cobbled courtyard, with its fountain, mosaic floor and lush palms.

**Market Square** (summer daily 10am–8pm; rest of year daily 10am–6pm), a couple of blocks further northwest, dates from 1840. Its outdoor restaurants and bustle are still at the heart of the city's life; fruit and vegetables are on sale early in the morning, while the shops are a compelling mix of color and kitsch. **El Mercado**, an indoor complex, is meant to resemble a traditional Mexican market, selling tourist-oriented gifts, jewelry and oddities. A few of the shops are great, even if the air conditioning and piped music undermine the authenticity of the venture.

It's also worth getting to the **McNay Art Museum**, 6000 N New Braunfels Ave at US-81 Austin Highway (Tues–Sat 10am–5pm, Sun noon–5pm; free). This exquisite Moorish-style villa, complete with tranquil garden, was built in the 1950s to house the art collection of millionaire and folk artist Marion McNay, which includes New Mexico crafts, Gothic and medieval works, as well as Post-Impressionists. Buses #11 (Nacogdoches) and #14 (Thousand Oaks) serve the museum from downtown. On the way there, bus #11 also passes the **San Antonio Museum of Art**, 200 W Jones Ave (Tues 10am–9pm, Wed–Sat 10am–5pm, Sun noon–5pm; $4, free on Tues) which occupies the old Lone Star Brewery, but it's the added Rockefeller Center For Latin American Art wing that holds most interest with a particularly fine exhibit on folk art.

## The Alamo and the other missions

**The Alamo** is the most famous – for reasons that have nothing to do with its original purpose – of a trail of Catholic missions established by the Spanish along remote stretches of the San Antonio River early in the eighteenth century. San Antonio's most distinctive landmark, it is smack in the center of downtown, but for a real sense of early Spanish influence in Texas, it's important to make an effort to get out and see the more distant, less visited missions. Each was laid out like a small fortified town, with the church as aesthetic and cultural focus. The goal was to strengthen Spanish control by "converting" the indigenous Coahuiltecan – in practice, using them as workforce and army. The missions flourished from 1745 to 1775, but couldn't survive the ravages of disease and attack from the Apache and Comanche, and fell into disuse early in the nineteenth century. To get a sense of the history of the Alamo, you could head first for the nearby **Rivercenter Mall**, where the battle is reenacted on a six-story, Texas-scale IMAX screen (call ☎210/247-4629 for showtimes; $7.50); fact and sentiment may converge during the 45-minute presentation, but it takes a callous viewer not to be affected by the rousing patriotism of the finale.

The main **visitor center** (daily 9am–5pm ☎210/932-1001) for the string of missions is next to Mission San Jose (see opposite) and contains a movie theater, small museum and giftshop.

### The Alamo

All that is left of the original fort of the **Alamo** – at the meeting of Houston, Crockett, Bonham and Alamo streets – is the **chapel**, with a large arched facade of delicately carved sandstone, and the **Long Barracks**, now a **museum** (summer Mon–Sat 9am–6.30pm, Sun 10am–6.30pm; rest of year closes at 5.30pm; free). The first of the Spanish missions, established as San Antonio de Valero in 1718, it only became known as the Pueblo del Alamo in 1801, after secularization, when it was named for the Mexican home town of a Spanish cavalry unit which used it as a base. The **Battle**, immortalized in film and song, occurred on March 6, 1836, when all of the 189 men who had held out for thirteen days against the five-thousand-strong Mexican troops were killed, a massacre dismissed by the Mexican General Santa Anna as "but a small affair." The rebels consisted of a few native – Hispanic – Texans, and a majority of volunteers (adventurers like Davy Crockett and Jim Bowie, and aspiring colonists from other states), dreaming of Texan autonomy and driven by the battle cry of "Victory or Death!"

Though a constant stream of bus tours makes visits crowded and hectic, seeing the Alamo is crucial to understanding Texan pride and stubbornness. The battle memorabilia in the **chapel** is undeniably emotive, with poignant letters sent home by soldiers preparing to die, and the **Long Barracks Museum**, hidden away southwest of the shrine's main entrance, presents two slide shows on the history of the missions and the battle. Take time also to sit in peace in the four-acre grounds, a haven from the downtown commotion just outside the walls, dotted with lush blooms, palms and cacti, and holding an irrigation ditch filled with fat fish.

### The other missions

The **Mission Trail** runs nine miles south along the river from Alamo Street, down S St Mary's Street and onto Mission Road, and can be reached by bus #40. Each of the remaining four missions has been restored to act as an **interpretive center** illustrating some aspect of mission life (daily 9am–5pm; free), while the churches themselves still serve active parishes.

**Mission Concepcion**, 807 Mission Rd, with its distinctive twin towers and cupola, was built between 1731 and 1751. Colorful scraps of original frescoes can still be seen, along with bullet holes from rougher days. Exhibits here concentrate on the religious function of the missions. The 1720 **Mission San Jose**, 6539 San Jose Drive, which interprets the mission as a social and defense center, is the most complete of all, with what is believed to be the only unrestored mission fort in the US. Other notable features include the beautiful carved-stone ornamentation, especially the ornate rose window. A Mariachi Mass is held here each Sunday at noon. Of the two smaller and more isolated missions, **Mission San Juan**, 9102 Graf Rd, has displays on the mission as economic center (as well as a unique delicate bell tower), while **Mission San Francisco de la Espada**, 10040 Espada Rd, looks back on its educational role.

## Eating

Not surprisingly, San Antonio has good **Tex-Mex** food in all price ranges. Many visitors head straight for the Mexican restaurants on the River Walk, but, charming as it is to eat alfresco beside the river, don't be seduced to such an extent that you never venture above ground. There are many good places downtown and the floor of the **Rivercenter Mall** is packed with assorted fast-food stalls.

**A H Burritos**, 516 Houston St (☎210/223-0608). Extremely inexpensive, friendly local restaurant two doors down from Woolworths in the shadow of the Alamo. Fine breakfasts of *huevos rancheros*, while for dinner, shrimp and steak are the most expensive items, at $7 a plate.

**Boudro's**, 421 E Commerce St (☎210/224-8484). One of the best places on the River Walk. Good Tex–Mex bistro food.

**Casa Rio**, 430 E Commerce St (☎210/225-6718). The oldest, most established place on the River Walk, with excellent cheap Mexican food (a huge "deluxe dinner" costs around $7).

**El Mirador**, 722 S St Mary's St (☎210/225-9444). Wonderful Mexican breakfasts and lunches for under $5, and pricier Southwestern cuisine in the evening. Specialties include *xocetl* (chicken broth) and *azteca* (spicy tomato) soups. Closed Sun and Aug.

**The Guenther House**, 205 E Guenther St (☎210/227-1061). Delicious cookies and cakes in a cool green flour mill-cum-museum in the King William District. Good breakfasts and lunches, too.

**Mi Tierra**, 218 Produce Row (☎210/225-1262). In a bustling old Market Square building, and open 24hr. Midnight snacks, or full meals. Bar until 2am.

**Paesano's**, 111 W Crockett St (☎210/227-2782). Lively Italian restaurant in the Southbank mall development. The *shrimp paesano* is delectable.

**Zuni Grill**, 511 River Walk (☎210/227-0864). Creative Southwestern food in one of the most stylish River Walk restaurants. Main courses around $14.

## Entertainment and nightlife

With its abundance of picturesque settings, San Antonio is a great city for **festivals**. The year's biggest event is May's ten-day **Fiesta San Antonio**, marking Texas' victory in the Battle of San Jacinto, with parades, cookouts and Latin music concerts filling the streets. Also in May is the **International Conjunto Festival**, at the Guadalupe Cultural Arts Center on Guadalupe Street (☎210/271-3151), west of downtown, which celebrates the German-Mexican country music of south and central Texas. During August's **Texas Folklife Festival** in Hemisfair Park, ten stages reflect the state's huge diversity of music, ranging from gospel to Lebanese. Finally, the **San Antonio Stock Show & Rodeo** in early February celebrates cowboy and King of the Hill culture with two weeks of rodeo events and country music.

Check in the free weekly *Current* for gigs, films and events. The live jazz and flamenco in the restaurants along the **River Walk** tends to be rather sanitized, while **St Mary's Street** (just beyond the bus station towards the art museum) is the main strip for college clubs and bars. The outdoor **Arneson River Theater**, opposite La Villita, where the river separates the audience from the stage, hosts Mexican folk music and dance during the summer. The outlying areas hold some great old **country dance halls**, the best of which is *Greune Hall*.

**The Blue Bonnet Palace**, 16847 I-35 N (☎210/651-6702). A bit of a trek, north of the airport, but worth it to check out urban cowboy culture at firsthand. Country bands 9pm–2am on Fri and Sat. The highlight is the live bull-riding at 10pm and 11.30pm. Cover $5–12.

**Bonham Exchange**, 411 Bonham (☎210/271-3811). Popular mixed gay club with good house and garage DJs.

**El Fandango**, 114 W Carolina St (☎210/532-0377). Hard-hitting *conjunto* sounds with occasional bursts of the poppier *tejano*.

**Floore Country Store**, 14464 Old Bandera Rd, downtown Helotes (☎210/695-8827). Old country dance hall, with outdoor dancing.

**Gruene Hall**, 1281 Gruene Rd, Gruene (☎210/606-1281). Dominating this small town (pronounced *green*), 30 miles northeast of downtown San Antonio, is the oldest remaining dance hall in Texas, with top country stars playing here at weekends.

**Jim Cullum's The Landing**, 123 Losoya St under the *Hyatt Regency* (☎210/223-7266). Traditional jazz every night in a club that's been running for over thirty years.

**Tycoon Flats**, 2926 N St Mary's St (☎210/737-1929). A variety of live music with no cover charge. Patio restaurant serves good vegetarian food for about $5. Closed Mon.

**White Rabbit**, 2410 N St Mary's St (☎210/737-2221). The main venue for touring indie bands.

# Austin

AUSTIN was only a tiny community on the verdant banks of the (Texas) Colorado River when Mirabeau B Lamar, president of the Republic, suggested in 1839 that it would make a better capital than swampy and disease-ridden Houston. Early building had to be done under armed guard, as angry Comanche watched from the surrounding hills, but despite its perilous location, the city thrived.

These days it wears its status as capital of Texas very lightly; sightseeing rates as a low priority against simply hanging out. Since the 1960s, this laid-back and progressive city has been a haven for artists, musicians and writers. Many visitors come specifically for the **music**. Local musicians are renowned for their innovative reworkings of Texas' country, folk and R&B heritage, often severing their rural roots to use Austin's enthusiastic environment as a springboard to national recognition. Janis Joplin had her start here in the early Sixties, and at the end of that decade, Austin was second only to San Francisco in its adherence to the "turn on, tune in, drop out" philosophy, with locals coining the term "headneck" to describe themselves. Musicians hungry for fame still tumble out of buses from all over Texas to seek their fortunes in the literally hundreds of live venues.

Austin is one of the few cities in the state where cycling is a viable alternative to driving. It may not have completely avoided the usual problems of urban growth – until recently it was Texas' fastest-growing city, and ugly suburbs have shot up to threaten its small-town ambiance – but it feels wonderfully safe for visitors, even women traveling alone, and the presence of the vast UT campus adds to the atmosphere, even if almost every shop and streetlamp is adorned with the unsightly brown and white colors of the college's Longhorns football team.

Within the city limits a great park system offers numerous hiking and biking trails and a wonderful spring-fed swimming pool. Looking further afield, Austin makes a fine base for exploring the green **Hill Country** that rolls away to the west.

## Arrival, information and getting around

Austin spreads about twenty miles north–south and eighteen miles east–west, severed by I-35 (between Dallas and San Antonio) to the east. The Colorado River runs south of downtown. Flights come in at the tasteful new **Austin-Bergstrom International Airport**, opened in summer. Eight miles southeast of downtown at the intersection of highways 71 and 183, it takes about twenty minutes to get downtown by **taxi** (Yellow Cabs; ☎512/462-9999; $18) or by SuperShuttle vans (☎512/258-3826; $9) while the #100 **bus** runs approximately once an hour to the campus and downtown (Mon–Fri 5am–10pm, Sat 7am–9pm, Sun 8am–9pm) for a bargain fare of 50¢.

Austin has a good **public transportation** system. The Capital METRO **bus** runs downtown, crosstown and through the campus for a flat fare of 50¢ (express services charge a dollar), with extra university shuttle routes – distinguishable by the Longhorn emblem beside the route number – during term time (Mon–Sat 6am–midnight, Sun 6am–8pm). Schedules are available from the information kiosk at Fifth Street and Congress Avenue (in front of the NCNB building; Mon–Fri 8.30am–5.30pm), or you can call the METRO information line on ☎512/474-1200. The Dillo Express, also run by METRO, is a free downtown **trolley** system, running along three routes, including one out to the UT campus, every ten to forty minutes between 6.30am and 7pm on weekdays. **Bicycles** can be rented from Bicycle Sport Shop, 1426 Toomey Rd (Mon–Fri 10am–8pm, Sat 9am–6pm, Sun 11am–5pm; ☎512/477-3472). Walking is an easy and pleasant way of getting around; organized **walking tours** leave from the south entrance of the capitol (March–Nov Sat 2pm, Sun 9am; ☎512/478-0098).

The **visitor center** is at 201 E Second St (summer Mon–Fri 8.30am–6pm, Sat & Sun 9am–6pm; rest of year closes at 5pm; ☎512/478-0098 or 1-800/926-2282), and there's a State Tourist Information Center (Tues–Fri 9am–5pm, Sat 10am–5pm; ☎512/305-8400) in the foyer of the state capitol (free), with changing exhibits of Texacana and a video presentation. The **post office** is at 300 E Ninth St (Mon–Fri 7.30am–6pm, Sat 8am–noon; ☎512/929-1252; zip code 78767).

## Accommodation

I-35 and Congress Avenue are Austin's budget **hotel** strips, but **B&Bs** are better options; there are good ones in most areas of the city.

**Austin Motel**, 1220 S Congress Ave (☎512/441-1157). Basic rooms just south of the bridge and opposite the *Continental Club*. ③.

**Carrington's Bluff**, 1900 David St (☎512/477-0711). Very good B&B, central but countrified, a block from Lamar at Martin Luther King Blvd. Shady veranda, friendly hosts and gourmet breakfast. ④.

**Driskill Hotel**, 604 E Brazos St (☎512/474-5911). Grand historic hotel in a great location. ⑥.

**HI-Austin**, 2200 S Lakeshore Blvd (☎512/444-2294). Southeast of downtown (via bus #27 to Riverside Drive) beside Town Lake. Members $14, others $17. Bike and kayak rentals available. ①.

**La Quinta Capitol**, 300 E 11th St (☎512/476-7151). Comfortable and central rooms, pool and air-port shuttle. ④.

**Woodburn House**, 4401 Ave D (☎512/458-4335). Small B&B in the leafy Hyde Park area, within walking distance of the university. Reservation and deposit required. ⑤.

# The Town

The Texas **State Capitol**, at 13th and Congress, is over 300ft high, taller than the national capitol in Washington, with a pink granite dome that dominates the downtown skyline. The chandeliers, carpets and even the door hinges of this colossal building are emblazoned with lone stars and "TEXAS" motifs, a theme continued in the new underground annex, a sleek maze of marble halls (Mon–Fri 8.30am–4.15pm, Sat & Sun 9.30am–4.15pm; public tours every 15min; free). Nearby, the antebellum **Governors Mansion**, 1010 Colorado St, contains displays on Texan history (free tours Mon–Thurs every 20min 10–11.40am). **Congress Avenue**, a stretch of 1950s shops and muted office buildings that slopes south from the capitol down to the river, is worthy of a stroll; at dusk 750,000 **bats** – the world's largest urban bat colony – emerge in a large cloud from their hangouts under the bridge. **Sixth Street**, also known as Old Pecan Street, runs west from I-35 to Congress Street, and is the focus of much of the city's nightlife, as well as featuring many renovated buildings, galleries and hip shops. The elegant Romanesque **Driskill Hotel**, on the corner with Brazos Street, has its own self-guided walking tour, with a glossy leaflet recounting the hotel's many links with government since 1886. Between Fifth and Sixth streets, just west of Lamar Boulevard, the 600-year-old **Treaty Oak** is the last of the Council Oaks where treaties were signed with Native Americans; unfortunately, someone chose to poison the tree in 1989, and only one-third of it remains.

Two interesting museums in the east of the city are the **George Washington Carver Museum** of local black history at 1165 Angelina St (Tues–Thurs 10am–6pm, Fri & Sat noon–5pm; free), which hosts free concerts on Saturdays, and the **Elizabet Ney Museum** at 304 E 44th St. This latter, a German-influenced castle-like building in a leafy, historic residential area, preserves the last studio, with marquettes and finished marbles, of Austin's most celebrated sculptor (Wed–Sat 10am–5pm, Sun noon–5pm; free).

**Zilker Park**, across the river from Amtrak and southwest of the center (bus #30 from Tenth and Congress), is one of the best of the many fine parks in the city, a perfect retreat on sweaty Austin afternoons. One of its main attractions is the spring-fed (and deliciously cold) **Barton Springs Pool**, a 1000ft turquoise rectangle shaded by pecan trees (April–Oct Mon & Thurs noon–10pm, Tues, Wed & Fri–Sun 9am–10pm; $2 Mon–Fri, $2.50 Sat & Sun). You can paddle in the pebbly creek below the pool free of charge, and you'll also find hiking and biking trails, a miniature railroad winding beside the river (daily 10am–dusk; $1.25), and, to the west, the wildlife garden of the **Austin Nature Center** (Mon–Sat 9am–5pm, Sun noon–5pm; free). South of the pool on Robert E Lee Road, the **Umlauf Sculpture Garden** (Thurs, Sat & Sun 1–4.30pm, Fri 10am–4.30pm; $2) is a tranquil, grassy enclave dotted with over one hundred works in bronze, terra cotta, wood and marble.

The **Austin Art Museum – Laguna Gloria**, 3809 W 35th St (Tues–Wed & Fri–Sat 10am–5pm, Thurs 10am–8pm, Sun noon–5pm; $1, $2 on Thurs; tours Sun 2pm), a beautiful 1916 Mediterranean villa overlooking Lake Austin in the northwest of town, was once owned by Clara Driscoll, who at 22 bought the Alamo for the Daughters of the Republic of Texas. It now features changing exhibitions of twentieth-century American art, and has a replica of the rose window at the San Jose Mission in San Antonio. Don't miss **Mayfield Park** next door, a peaceful idyll complete with water-lilies and stroppy peacocks. **Mount Bonnell**, further north on the Colorado River, gives quite spectacular views over the city and surrounding countryside.

## The University

Having its own oil well (the drilling rig Santa Rita No. 1 on San Jacinto Blvd) has made the **University of Texas** one of the world's richest universities. Its unparalleled collection of manuscripts by contemporary authors is available to scholars amid tight security in the **Harry Ransom Center**; stories abound of the sums lavished to acquire work from relative unknowns who might some day achieve fame. The Center, in the southwest corner of the campus, also houses an **art gallery** (Mon–Fri 9am–4.30pm; free), with a Gutenberg Bible as well as contemporary Latin American and American paintings. Student-guided tours of the campus and its museums leave the information center in the main building twice daily on weekdays and once on Saturday during term-time.

The stretch of **Guadalupe Street** running along campus north from Martin Luther King Boulevard to 24th Street is known as "**the Drag.**" A focus of student activity, and lined with cafes, vintage clothes shops and bookstores, it was the location for much of Richard Linklater's 1991 movie, *Slacker*.

The **LBJ Library and Museum** (daily 9am–5pm; free), on the northeast edge of campus at 2313 Red River St, traces the career of the brash and egotistical Lyndon Baines Johnson from his origins in the Hill Country to the House of Representatives, the Senate and the White House. The curious circumstances surrounding his first senatorial election in 1948 (confirmed only after some "overlooked" votes – all written in the same hand – were found three days after his opponent had been elected) go unmentioned. John Kennedy is said to have made Johnson his vice-president to avoid his establishing a rival power base; but in the aftermath of Kennedy's assassination, Johnson's administration (1963–68) was able to push through a far more radical program than Kennedy ever attempted. Johnson's nemesis, Vietnam, is presented here as an awful mess left by Kennedy for him to clear up, at the cost of great personal anguish. There's a replica of the Johnson Oval Office at the White House, as well as a wonderfully corny set of political campaign memorabilia from Roosevelt to Bush; some of the badges are for sale.

# Eating

Radical Austin has many more vegetarian and wholefood **restaurants** than is usual in Texas; even chicken-fried steak can be found prepared healthily. Add this to the fact that sitting on your own reading a book over your meal is not seen as aberrant behavior, and you have a city in which eating out can be a real pleasure. There are plenty of good budget restaurants near the university, especially along Guadalupe Street – look for the crowds. Many of the music venues also serve up decent food.

**El Sol y La Luna**, 1224 S Congress Ave (☎512/444-7700). A fun, family-run Mexican joint on the funky strip of shops and clubs just south of downtown. Great breakfasts.

**Good Eats Cafe**, 1530 Barton Springs Rd (☎512/476-8141). High-quality, reasonably priced, healthy home cooking.

**Jovita's**, 1619 S 1st St (☎512/477-7825). Reliable Tex-Mex food, with occasional sets by top local country musicians, like Don Walser, on the porch.

**Las Manitas**, 211 Congress Ave (☎512/472-9357). Authentic, great-value Mexican food and decor right downtown. Breakfast and lunch only – get there early to beat the politicians to a space.

**Magnolia Cafe**, 1920 S Congress Ave and 2304 Lake Austin Blvd (☎512/478-8645). A local favorite for breakfast. Open 24hr.

**Mezzaluna**, 310 Colorado St (☎512/472-6770). A moderate to expensive traditional Italian restaurant in the warehouse district between 6th St and the river.

**Scholz Garden**, 1607 San Jacinto Blvd (☎512/477-1958). Big portions of German sausage and Tex-Mex food at an Austin legend that also puts on good live music.

**Stubb's BBQ**, 801 Red River St (☎512/480-8341). Great Texan-style brisket, sausage and ribs, plus bands of national repute playing the indoor and outdoor stages.

**Threadgill's**, 6416 N Lamar Blvd (☎512/451-5440). An Austin institution since Kenneth Threadgill was given the first license to sell beer in the city after Prohibition. Real home cooking at bargain prices, with free seconds of vegetables like black-eyed peas and okra. Lively atmosphere, with occasional live fiddle music, folk or country-and-western bands. There's also a new downtown branch at 301 W Riverside Drive (☎512/472-9304). A must.

**West Lynn Cafe**, 1100 W Lynn (☎512/482-0950). Stylish vegetarian food from around the world and one of the city's most popular restaurants.

# Nightlife

The only problem you'll have with Austin **nightlife** is being spoiled for choice. In Sixth Street in particular, virtually every building houses a club or a bar, and many of these have become rather over-commercialized. It's much better to venture just off Sixth where you'll find some of the best clubs, or take a cab to some of the further-flung joints. Three first-rate local newspapers, the *Daily Texan*, the UT paper (Thurs), the "XL ent" supplement to the *Austin American-Statesman* (Thurs), and the *Austin Chronicle* (Fri) carry listings.

Something is always happening on campus. Big drama and dance names appear in the **Performing Arts Center**, 23rd Street and E Campus Drive (☎512/471-1444), and you can see **independent movies** at the Dobie Cinema, 2021 Guadalupe and 21st. The *Velveeta Room*, 317 E Sixth St (☎512/469-9116), showcases comedy on Wednesday and Thursday nights. The same people run *Esther's Pool*, 525 E Sixth St (☎512/320-0553; $12), home of *Esther's Follies*, Austin's hippest and funniest cabaret, which combines spoofs of local and national politicians with Texas-style singing and dancing.

## Live music

Although Austin's folk revival in the 1960s attracted enough attention to propel **Janis Joplin** on her way from Port Arthur, Texas, to stardom in California, the city first achieved prominence in its own right as the center of **"outlaw country"** music in the 1970s. **Willie Nelson** and **Waylon Jennings**, disillusioned with Nashville, spearheaded a movement which reworked sentimental country-and-western with an incisive injection of rock 'n' roll. The audiences in Austin, far removed from the hard-drinking honky-tonk crowds of West Texas, provided an environment which encouraged and rewarded risk-taking and experimentation. These days the predominant **"Austin sound"** is a melange of country, folk, blues, psychedelic and "alternative" influences, very much reliant on acoustics and guitars, though that's not to say the scene is anything but eclectic (with swing particularly popular at the moment); this, after all, is the city that spawned the Butthole Surfers.

The tradition of black Texas bluesmen such as Blind Lemon Jefferson and Blind Willie Johnson, as well as the rocking bar blues of Stevie Ray Vaughan, still lives on; *Antone's Blues Club* on Guadalupe Street is the place to hear **live blues**, while **folk** music, traditional or with a punk twist, is also thriving, with an annual **folk festival** at Rod Kennedy's *Quiet Valley Ranch* in **KERRVILLE**, a hundred miles west of Austin on I-10 (☎512/257-3600). The three-day **South by Southwest Music Conference & Festival**, held in the third week of March, features the best bands from Texas and around the world; the wristbands (about $90) that offer admission to all the shows are snapped up by locals way ahead of time, so most people now have to register as conference delegates (approximately $250 if booked in advance, if not it's a $450 walk-up; call ☎512/467-7979 for information).

**Antone's**, 213 W 5th St (☎512/474-5314). Hot, sweaty and crowded; the best blues club in the city, with big-name national and local acts nightly.

**The Back Room**, 2015 E Riverside Drive (☎512/441-4677). Texas hardcore bands in popular venue within walking distance of the youth hostel.

**Black Cat**, 309 E 6th St (no phone). Small, dark space promoting local rock and roots bands through residencies. A nicely uncommercial contrast to much of 6th St.

**The Broken Spoke**, 3201 S Lamar Blvd (☎512/442-6189). Neighborhood restaurant (good chicken-fried steak) and stomping country-music hall, with all the trappings but well away from the center. The barn-like dance floor regularly attracts the best acts on the Texas circuit. Two-stepping (line dancers are laughed out of the house) begins at 9pm.

**Cactus Cafe**, *Texas Union*, 24th and Guadalupe (☎512/471-8228). One of Austin's favorite venues. Consistently good country, rock and folk music; regular showcase for new acts.

**Club de Ville**, 900 Red River St (☎512/457-0900). Excellent cocktails and a superb patio setting in this stylish bar just a few minutes from the 6th St morass.

**Continental Club**, 1315 S Congress Ave (☎512/441-2444). The premier place to hear hard-edged country sung the Austin way. Top-notch artists.

**Electric Lounge**, 302 Bowie St (☎512/476-3873). Predominantly alternative touring bands on the edge of downtown.

**Emo's**, 603 Red River St (☎512/477-EMOS). Launchpad for Austin's best alternative bands, with a friendly, tattooed and pierced crowd. $2 cover for over-21s; minors pay $5.

**The Hole in the Wall**, 2528 Guadalupe St (☎512/472-5599). Very atmospheric, very Texan bar right next to campus, with live music ranging from reggae to jazz.

**La Zona Rosa**, 612 W 4th St (☎512/482-0662). Great venue for rootsy bands and also serves decent Southwestern food.

**Symphony Square**, Red River Rd (☎512/476-6064). Rough-hewn outdoor amphitheater, below street level on the river, hosting good jazz and classical concerts in summer.

# The Hill Country

The rolling hills, lakes and valleys of the **Hill Country**, north and west of Austin and San Antonio, were inhabited mostly by Apache and Comanche until after statehood, when German and Scandinavian settlers arrived. Many of the log-cabin farming communities they established are still here, such as **New Braunfels** (famous for its sausages and pastries) and Luckenbach. You may still hear German spoken, and the German influence is also felt in local food and music; *conjunto*, for example, is a blend of Tex-Mex and accordion music.

The whole region is a popular retreat and resort area, with some wonderful hill views and lake swimming, and a lot of good places to camp.

### The Lyndon B Johnson Historical Park

Sixty-five miles west of Austin on US-290, the **Lyndon B Johnson State and National Historical Park** preserves LBJ's birthplace (1908) and the ranch house where Lady Bird Johnson continued to live long after her husband's death in 1973 (daily 8am–5pm; 1hr 30min tours leave from the visitor center). A Living History Farmstead depicts German family life in the early 1900s.

The **visitor center** (daily 9am–5pm; ☎210/868-7128) and Johnson's boyhood home (daily 9am–5pm; free guided tours every 30min) are at sleepy **JOHNSON CITY**, fourteen miles further east; for a good lunch, stop off here at the *Hill Country Cupboard* (☎210/868-4625), at the junction of US-281 and US-290.

## Fredericksburg

**FREDERICKSBURG**, smack in the middle of the Hill Country, might at first glance look like a pastiche of a German village, overrun by Biergartens and gingerbread storefronts. In fact it's still pretty much the town founded by six hundred enterprising Germans in 1846. They managed to make – and, uniquely, keep – treaties with the local

Comanche, and their community, based on hard work and perseverance, survived through epidemics and civil war.

At the weekend, crowds of day-trippers from San Antonio and Austin visit Main Street's galleries, craftshops, antique stores and numerous fancy tearooms. Several original structures make up the **Pioneer Museum** at 309 W Main St, including a church and a store (Apr–Oct Mon & Wed–Sat 10am–5pm, Sun 1–5pm; Nov–Mar Sat 10am–5pm, Sun 1–5pm donation). The **Admiral Nimitz Museum & Historical Center**, 340 E Main St, incorporates the *Nimitz Steamboat Hotel* with its looming tower that really does look like a steamboat. What was once the last hotel on the military road to California now holds a Museum of the Pacific War (Fleet Admiral Nimitz was the grandson of the hotel's original owner, and commander of the naval forces in the Pacific in World War II), a peace garden and an historical trail that leads past aircraft, tanks and heavy artillery (daily 8am–5pm; $3). Look out also for the quirky limestone and pink-granite Bank of Fredericksburg.

### Practicalities

Like the rest of the Hill Country, Fredericksburg has no Greyhound or Amtrak service, though the occasional Kerrville Bus Company (☎1-800/231-2222) service passes through; it's reached via either US-290 from Austin or US-87 from San Antonio. The **CVB**, in the Market Square at 106 N Adams St (Mon–Fri 9am–5pm, Sat 9am–noon, Sun 1–5pm; ☎830/997-6523), has details of the budget **hotels** along E Main Street; of these, the pool-equipped *Best Western Sunday House* at no. 501 (☎830/997-4484; ⑤) is one of the more luxurious. **Bed and breakfast** is big business in historic Fredericksburg; contact B&B of Fredericksburg, 102 S Cherry St (☎830/997-4712; ②–⑥). There's **camping** in the Lady Bird Johnson Municipal Park, three miles southwest on Hwy-16 S, or in the Enchanted Rock State Natural Area.

**Restaurants** and bakeries line Main Street, many of them doing cheap lunch specials. *Dietz Bakery*, at no. 218 (☎830/997-3250), is the oldest in town, good for tasty breads and biscuits. You can eat more substantially at *Friedhelm's Bavarian Inn* at no. 905 (☎830/997-6300; closed Mon), which specializes in starchy plates of dumplings and sauerkraut.

# NORTH AND EAST TEXAS

Early immigration into **north and east Texas**, during the days of the Republic and following the devastation of the Civil War, was largely from the Southern states. In the 1930s, the northeastern oil fields near **Tyler** (a drab town only redeemed by its beautiful rose gardens) proved to be the richest ever found in the US. The whole region is now predominantly agricultural, with logging important in the densely forested east. The grand exception is, of course, the **Metroplex** – the area which includes **Dallas** and **Fort Worth**. The main tourist attractions and cultural life of the region are concentrated here; but if you enjoy exploring small-town America, and have a car, the north and east can yield more subtle pleasures. The **national forests** of Angelina, Davy Crockett, Sabine and Sam Houston in the east offer unsurpassed opportunities for outdoor living: the forest supervisor (☎713/632-4446) in Lufkin, midway between Davy Crockett and Angelina on US-59, has details of free and private **camping** facilities. Fans of the movie will want to cheout out **Paris, Texas**, northeast on US-82.

# East Texas

The tall pine forests of **east Texas** bear more relation to Louisiana than to the rest of the state; while undeniably Texan, the locals also identify themselves culturally and geographically with the adjacent corners of Arkansas and Louisiana – the **"Arklatex"** – and you'll find jambalaya and gumbo in restaurants along with standard Texan dishes.

Burial sites and reconstructed dwellings of the sophisticated **Caddo** Indians, an early southeastern mound-building culture, can be seen at the **Caddoan Mounds State Historic Site**, thirty miles west of Nacogdoches on Hwy-21. Active between the ninth and fourteenth centuries, the site includes videos on Caddoan history and a self-guided walking tour (Wed–Sun 8am–5pm; ☎409/858-3218; $3 per car, $1 for pedestrians and cyclists).

## Big Thicket National Preserve

The **Big Thicket National Preserve**, south of the Piney Woods on US-96, is a remarkable composite of natural elements from the southwestern desert, central plains and Appalachian Mountains, with swamps and bayous to boot. The area once offered ideal refuge for outlaws, runaway slaves and gamblers; now it just hides a huge variety of plant and animal life, including deer, alligators, armadillos, possums, hogs and panthers, and over three hundred species of birds. Wild flowers, orchids and towering trees share space with cacti and yucca.

Check in at the **visitor center** (daily 9am–5pm; ☎409/246-2337), south of Angelina National Forest off US-69, just south of Wildwood, before entering the site; casual rambling isn't allowed, and hiking or canoeing is best done with the Preserve guides. There is primitive **camping** in designated areas.

## Nacogdoches

**NACOGDOCHES**, north of Angelina National Forest on US-59, claims to be the oldest town in Texas. One of the state's first five Spanish **missions** was established here in 1716, to keep a watchful eye on the French in Louisiana, and a pyramidal **Caddo Indian Mound** in the 500 block of Mound Street testifies to more ancient history. The **Sterne-Hoya House**, 211 S Lanana St, the town's oldest surviving and unreconstructed home, illustrates early pioneer life (Mon–Sat 9–11.30am & 2–4.30pm; free).

*La Hacienda*, 1411 North St (☎409/564-6487), is the best place to **eat** in town, serving Mexican food in a prairie-style ranch home. If you want to **stay**, the *Little House*, 110 Sanders St (☎409/564-2735; ④), offers good **B&B** in a cottage close to downtown, while *Mound Street B&B*, 408 N Mound St (☎409/569-2211; ⑤), features big rooms in a Victorian home. The downtown **hotel**, the *Fredonia*, 200 N Fredonia St (☎409/564-1234; ④), is venerable but clean. The **Chamber of Commerce** is at 1513 North St (Mon–Fri 8am–5pm; ☎409/564-7351 or 1-888/564-7351).

# Dallas

Contrary to popular belief, there's no oil in glitzy, status-conscious **DALLAS**. Since its foundation as a prairie trading post, by Tennessee lawyer John Neely Bryan and his friend Mr Dallas in 1841, successive generations of **entrepreneurs** have amassed wealth here through trade and finance, using first cattle and later oil reserves as collateral. One early group of European settlers, the Socialist Reunion cooperative of the 1850s, had to pack up and move on due to an inability to adapt to local farming methods. The city, which has grown to become the most spread-out urban area in the world, still prides itself on their legacy of arts and high culture.

The power of **money** in Dallas was demonstrated in the late 1950s, when its financiers threw their weight behind integration. Potentially racist restaurant owners and bus drivers were pressurized not to resist the new policies, and Dallas was spared major upheavals. The city's image was, however, catastrophically tarnished by the **assassination** of President Kennedy in 1963, and it took the building of the giant DFW

International Airport in the 1960s, and the twin successes of the *Dallas* TV show and the Cowboys football team in the 1970s, to restore confidence. Then boom turned to crash once more. Unemployment and the demise of the Ewings – not to mention an appalling crime rate – all took their toll, but the indomitable entrepreneurial spirit remains and, after a slump in the late 1980s, the Cowboys are back in the big time, though their off-field antics have provided the nation's papers with some anti-Dallas copy once again.

Competitive with Houston, and smug about its cowtown neighbor Fort Worth, Dallas boasts of its "sophistication" and its "old" wealth. For all that, the stuffiness is tempered by a typically Texan delight in self-parody, and there's still fun to be had if you know where to look – especially in the alternative **Deep Ellum** district, with its superb restaurants and nightlife.

## Arrival, information and getting around

Dallas is served by two major **airports**. **Dallas/Fort Worth** (DFW; ☎972/574-4420), as big as Manhattan and the world's second busiest airport, is exactly midway between the two cities (around 17 miles from each). Telephones in the baggage claim area link up to a variety of different **shuttle buses**, such as Super Shuttle (☎817/329-2000) and Discount Shuttle (☎817/267-5150), all charging around $13; **taxis** cost around $30 (Yellow/Checker ☎214/426-6262). **Love Field** (☎214/670-6080), used mostly by Southwest Airlines, lies about nine miles northwest of Dallas, from where taxis to downtown cost around $15, shuttles charge $9, or you can take bus #539 to the DART-Rail Lovers Lane station to get into town for a total of $2. Greyhound is at 205 S Lamar St downtown, while Amtrak's 1916 Union Station is further west at 400 S Houston St. The Trinity Railway Express service goes east to Irving but will soon continue to downtown Fort Worth.

Dallas proper is circled by Inner Loop 12 (or Northwest Highway) and the Outer Loop I-635 (which becomes LBJ Freeway). A **car** makes sense in a city this size, though the main sights of downtown's Central Business District are easy to tour on foot. Get hold of the CVB's **walking** guide from the downtown **visitor center** at the "Old Red" Courthouse, 100 S Houston St in the thick of the Kennedy-related sights (Mon–Fri 8am–5pm, Sat–Sun 10am–5pm; ☎214/571-1300). The city also runs a 24-hour Events Hotline (☎214/571-1301).

DART, the Dallas Area Rapid Transit system (☎214/979-1111) operates the city's **buses** ($1 local services, $2 "express" buses and trains) and a swish new **light rail** network that links downtown and the Dallas Convention Center with the West End and various sights (fares $1 local, $2 express; all-day pass $3; three-day pass $6). Both DART buses and trains operate every day from 5.30am to 12.30am. The McKinney Trolley (☎214/855-0006) runs north from the downtown Dallas Museum of Art to the historic McKinney Avenue area (a $1.50 round-trip ticket allows one stop-off; every 30min Mon–Thurs & Sun 10am–10pm, Fri & Sat 10am–midnight). Gray Line Tours (☎214/824-2424) does all-day ($35) and half-day ($20) **city tours**, plus a $25 Saturday trip to Southfork. Finally, and on a more grisly note, the JFK Presidential Limo Tour (☎214/348-7777) will take you along the route of the infamous 1963 presidential motorcade (see box on p.655) for $25 per person.

The **post office** is at 400 N Ervay St (Mon–Fri 8am–6pm; ☎214/953-3045; zip code 75201).

## Accommodation

Room rates in downtown Dallas are firmly geared toward the business traveler, though the swanky hotels do some reasonable **weekend** deals. Chain **motels** are concentrated a long way out, on the freeways; there's a large group on LBJ Freeway near the Galleria mall, a dozen miles north, for example. **Bed and breakfast** can be arranged through B&B Texas Style (☎972/298-8586; from ③). There's **camping** in the pretty Lewisville Lake Park on the Kingfisher Trail, a mile east of I-35 in Lewisville.

**Adolphus Hotel**, 1321 Commerce St (☎214/742-8200 or 1-800/221-9083). Stunning historic hotel downtown, decorated with antiques. When built in 1912, it was said to be the most beautiful building west of Venice, Italy; today it is still by far Dallas's most glamorous place to stay. ⑧.

**Best Western Market Center**, 2023 Market Center Blvd (☎214/741-9000 or 1-800/275-7419). Two miles from downtown. Complimentary breakfast. ③.

**Dallas Grand Hotel**, 1914 Commerce St (☎214/747-7000 or 1-800/421-0011). Downtown luxury hotel. ⑤.

**La Quinta**, 10001 N Central Expressway/Hwy-75 (☎214/361-8200). Decent-priced rooms, not that far from downtown. ④.

**The Mansion on Turtle Creek**, 2821 Turtle Creek Blvd (☎214/559-2100 or 1-800/527-5432). Considered one of the finest hotels in the world, you can anticipate absolute luxury on a gorgeous landscaped hillside. ⑨.

**Ramada Plaza**, 1011 S Akard St (☎214/421-1083). Reliable rooms and a heated pool near the Convention Center. ③.

**Stoneleigh Hotel**, 2927 Maple Ave (☎214/871-7111 or 1-800/255-9299). Classy, comfortable hotel in the Turtle Creek area, three miles north of downtown. ⑥.

## The City

**Downtown Dallas** is a hymn to commerce. Many of its skyscrapers are landmarks in themselves; at night the red neon Mobil Pegasus on the 1921 Magnolia Building on Akard and Commerce appears to gallop over the city, while over two miles of green argon tubing delineate the 72-story Nations Bank. The original **Neiman Marcus** department store, set up in 1907 by sister and brother Carrie Neiman and Herbert Marcus and famed for its glamorous Christmas catalog, is still there on Main Street (Mon–Sat 10am–5.30pm). One small refuge is the quiet **Thanksgiving Square** at the intersection of Akard, Ervay, Bryan and Pacific (Mon–Fri 9am–5pm, Sat & Sun 1–5pm), with its meditation garden, descending walkways, fountains and modern spiraling chapel – though even here pealing bells boom out at regular intervals. South of the square on Ervay Street looms the precarious upside-down pyramid of **City Hall**, possibly familiar as the police station in *Robocop*.

On the north edge of downtown, the **Arts District** boasts the huge and wide-ranging **Dallas Museum of Art**, 1717 N Harwood St (Tues, Wed & Fri 11am–4pm, Thurs 11am–9pm, Sat & Sun 11am–5pm; free, around $5 for special exhibits), which has plenty of European works downstairs, including a good range of Mondrians, and an especially impressive pre-Columbian collection in the Gallery of the Americas upstairs. Two blocks east, at 2301 Flora St, the magnificent **Morton H Meyerson Symphony Center**, designed by I M Pei, is the home of the symphony orchestra. The vast geometries of glass, onyx and wood inside cost $80 million, as the tour guides won't let you forget.

Tourists flock to the restored redbrick warehouses of the **West End Historic District**, the site of the original 1841 settlement on Lamar and Munger streets, for the eighty stores and fifty restaurants here. The indoor **marketplace** has become something of an amusement arcade, with tacky giftshops, crazy golf, fast-food outlets and a ten-screen cinema.

A couple of blocks south and west of here lies **Dealey Plaza**, forever associated with the Kennedy assassination (see box on p.655). A small park beside Houston Street's triple underpass, it remains unchanged since the fateful day – in fact, since it was designed by a committee which included LBJ, in the late 1930s – and must be one of

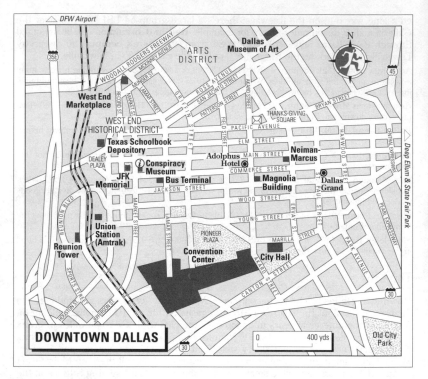

Map: **DOWNTOWN DALLAS**. Features labeled include DFW Airport, Woodall Rodgers Freeway, McKinney Avenue, ARTS DISTRICT, Dallas Museum of Art, West End Marketplace, WEST END HISTORICAL DISTRICT, Texas Schoolbook Depository, Conspiracy Museum, JFK Memorial, Bus Terminal, Union Station (Amtrak), Reunion Tower, Dealey Plaza, Adolphus Hotel, Thanks-Giving Square, Neiman-Marcus, Magnolia Building, Dallas Grand, Pioneer Plaza, Convention Center, City Hall, Old City Park, Deep Ellum & State Fair Park. Scale: 0–400 yds.

the most instantly recognizable urban streetscapes in the world. The **Texas Schoolbook Depository** itself, at 411 Elm St, is now the Dallas County Administration Building, the penultimate floor of which houses **The Sixth Floor Museum** (daily 9am–6pm; $5, or $8 with audio tour). Displays build up a suspenseful narrative, with the infamous blurred 8mm images of Kennedy crumpling into Jackie's arms left until the end, at which point there's likely to be much sobbing from moved visitors, who exorcize their grief by writing in the "memory book." The "gunman's nest" has been re-created and, whatever you feel about Oswald's guilt, it is undeniably chilling to look down at the streets below and imagine the mayhem they must have seen that day.

One block west of Dealey Plaza, in the Dallas Historical Plaza on Main and Market streets, an open cenotaph, designed by Philip Johnson and enclosing an 8ft flat granite block, stands as the **John F Kennedy Memorial**. Alongside, at 110 S Market St, the new **Conspiracy Museum** (daily 10am–6pm; $7) is a dreadful waste of money. It strives to impress with its CD-ROM technology, but in fact displays the usual amateurish hand-drawn diagrams and wild accusations, interpreting virtually every public act in America since the late 1950s as the work of the Professional War Machine. In place of hard evidence, a huge pseudo-Chinese mural features "brush-stroke interpretations" of the assassination of the Kennedys and Dr King; thus "The Three Dancing Men are the Warren Commission giving us a song and dance."

A little further south and east is the city's main business and administrative district, focused around City Hall on Marilla Street. **Pioneer Plaza**, at Young and Griffin streets, holds the world's largest bronze sculpture, a monument to the cattle drives that depicts forty longhorn steers under the guidance of three cowboys.

You can see all of these and much more from the 51st-story observation deck in the **Reunion Tower**, 300 Reunion Blvd (Mon–Thurs & Sun 10am–10pm, Fri–Sat 10am–midnight; $2), on the east side of downtown next to the Amtrak station. The *Top of the Dome Cocktail Lounge*, in the Tower, provides a good place to sip some liquor.

Further southeast, across I-30, near Harwood Street at 1717 Gano St, Dallas's first park, **Old City Park**, now serves as both recreational area and museum, charting the history of the city from 1840 to 1910 through more than thirty buildings relocated from towns in north Texas, among them farmhouses, a bank, a train station, a store, a church and a schoolhouse (daily dawn–dusk; free; tours Tues–Sat 10am–4pm, Sun 1–4pm; $6).

## Deep Ellum

Dallas's coolest district is **Deep Ellum**, five blocks east of downtown between the railroad tracks and I-30 at Elm and Main streets. Famous in the 1920s for its jazz and blues clubs (and supposedly named by Blind Lemon Jefferson, though it's more likely to stem from the Southern pronunciation of "elm"), the old warehouse district now accommodates avant-garde galleries, theaters, street-hip clothes stores and excellent restaurants and clubs. To the despair of its original inhabitants, prices are rocketing as the area drifts mainstream. However, its sense of rebellion and nonconformity makes a great antidote to the prevalent stuffiness of Dallas.

## Fair Park

Not far southeast of Deep Ellum, **Fair Park**, a gargantuan Art Deco plaza bedecked with endless Lone Stars, was built to house the Texas Centennial Exposition in 1936, and hosts the annual State Fair of Texas, the biggest event of its kind in the US. Among its plethora of fine museums are the **Dallas Museum of Natural History** (Mon–Sat 9am–5pm, Sun 11am–5.30pm; $3.50), which boasts reconstructions of a mammoth from the Trinity River and a 32ft sea snake; the hands-on **Science Place** (Mon–Thurs & Sun 9.30am–5.30pm, Fri–Sat 9.30am–10pm; $6), which sets out to teach kids and adults about physics and dinosaurs and the like, hosts lively no-expense-spared temporary exhibits, and has its own planetarium ($2) and IMAX screen ($6); and the **Dallas Aquarium** (daily 9am–4.30pm; $2).

A recent addition to Fair Park is the cross-shaped **African-American Museum** (Tues–Fri noon–5pm, Sat 10am–5pm, Sun 1–5pm; suggested donation $2). Changing

---

### THE ASSASSINATION OF PRESIDENT KENNEDY

It was 12.30pm on November 22, 1963, as John F Kennedy greeted the crowds of Dallas from his ceremonial motorcade, when the shots rang out over Dealey Plaza that killed the president and ended the "Camelot" era.

Within hours, a gunman's nest was discovered in the nearby Texas Schoolbook Depository, and one of its employees, **Lee Harvey Oswald**, was arrested. Two days later, he in turn was shot and killed in a police station by nightclub owner **Jack Ruby**, who said he wanted to spare Kennedy's wife Jackie from having to testify at Oswald's trial. The **Warren Commission**, which investigated the assassination, concluded that Oswald had acted alone, but **conspiracy** theories have flourished ever since. Most accept that Oswald (an ex-Marine who defected to Russia and returned with a Russian wife) fired the shots, but see him as the fall guy in a larger plot, variously attributed to the Mafia, anti-Castroists, Cuba, the KGB and US government agencies. Claims by witnesses to have heard shots on the famous **Grassy Knoll** on the north side of Elm Street remain unsubstantiated, but visitors can usually be found sniffing around here for clues – along with self-styled guides, ready to engage them in costly conversation. Senate inquiries were finally closed down by the Justice Department in 1988, arguing that there was no "persuasive evidence" of any plot.

exhibitions here tend to focus on African art, while the most interesting of the permanent galleries is given over to a superb collection of **folk art**, complete with detailed biographies of the artists responsible. These include Rev L T Thomas, born in 1903, who for most of his adult life has been producing minor variations of the criminals Clyde Barrow, Bonnie Parker, Pretty Boy Floyd and Frederick Thomas, all with identical hats and jackets; Charles Williams, known as Artist Chuckie, from Shreveport Louisiana, who was "discovered" in 1989 when a neighbor's house burned down and he refused to leave his mother's home until his 700 paintings were brought out; and the real stand-out, Bessie Harvey, who died aged 64 in 1994, and worked with found pieces of wood, spray-painting them and sticking on other materials to produce scenes such as the extraordinary *Jonah and the Whale* and *Two Heads Are Better Than One*.

The centerpiece of the park, however, has to be the magnificent **Hall of State Building**, an Art Deco treasure of bronze statues, blue tiles, mosaics and murals, with rooms decorated to celebrate the different regions of Texas. The park also holds the **Cotton Bowl** stadium (☎214/638-BOWL), home of the annual college football classic, while for three weeks in October Fair Park spills over with more than three million revelers enjoying the riotous **State Fair** itself.

## Southfork Ranch

The former TV home of the *Dallas* soap's wheeling-and-dealing Ewing clan, **Southfork Ranch** (daily 9am–5pm; $7) lies about 25 miles northeast of Dallas, beyond I-635 at 3770 Hogge Rd, Parker. Having lain dormant for two years from 1991, it has since been kitted out as a Western mini-theme park, with a **museum** in which you can see the gun that shot JR, and have your photo taken – wearing a cowboy hat – at JR's desk. There's also a proposed exhibit on Texas ranching, plenty of Stetson-dominated giftshops and *Miss Ellie's Deli*. The **Ranch House** itself is surprisingly small – all the show's interior scenes were shot in California, and the exterior views used a very wide-angled lens.

## Eating

Many of the less expensive – and least extravagant – of Dallas's five thousand restaurants are concentrated in **Lower Greenville Avenue**, which runs northeast of downtown parallel to I-75, and trendier **Deep Ellum**, where even the excellent New American cuisine won't break the bank.

**Aquaknox**, 3214 Knox St (☎214/219-2782). Inventive "global seafood" cuisine from Cajun to sushi. Expensive but classy.

**Blind Lemon**, 2805 Main St (☎214/939-0202). Casual Deep Ellum hangout serving a wide assortment of pizza, burgers and pasta specials, while a DJ spins Seventies funk.

**Cafe Brasil**, 2815 Elm St (☎214/747-2730). Open 24hr for great omelettes, sandwiches and enchiladas.

**Deep Ellum Cafe**, 2706 Elm St (☎214/741-9012). The first restaurant in the area and still the benchmark for the rest. Very popular, serving delicious New American food for around $10. Open until midnight on Fri and Sat.

**Dinger's Catfish Cafe**, 8989 Forest Ave (☎214/235-3251). Mesquite-grilled aquatic vertebrates with whiskers served to a hip crowd.

**Gloria's**, 600 W Davis St (☎214/948-3672). Catfish ceviche, hot banana-leaf tamales and other low-priced, top-quality El Salvadorean dishes.

**Green Room**, 2715 Elm St (☎214/748-7666). Post-modern decor, with up-to-the-minute American cuisine downstairs, and pizzas with a view across Deep Ellum to downtown from the roof.

**Mia's**, 4322 Lemmon Ave (☎214/526-1020). A family-run Mexican restaurant that's the Dallas Cowboys' favorite.

**Monica's Aca y Alla**, 2914 Main St (☎214/748-7140). Wood-grilled *nouvelle* Mexican food, with dashes of Mediterranean and Asian influences, in Deep Ellum hot spot jazzed up by its new management.

**Sonny Bryan's Smokehouse**, 2202 Inwood Rd (☎214/357-7120). The original location – it still looks like a shack – of a favorite local barbecue chain, but get there in good time as the meat can be all snapped up by early afternoon.

**Two Rows Restaurant & Brewpub**, 5500 Greenville Ave (☎214/696-2739). Better than average range of pub food in this hangout in the Old Town Shopping Mall.

## Entertainment and nightlife

The place to head for nightlife in Dallas has to be edgy, offbeat **Deep Ellum**, where among the trendy clubs the innovative **Pegasus Theater**, 3916 Main St (☎214/821-6005), puts on avant-garde and independent plays. Elsewhere nightlife is pretty formal. Mainstream attractions include the **Dallas Symphony Orchestra** at the showpiece Morton H Meyerson Symphony Center (☎214/670-3600), and the **Dallas Black Dance Theater** at 2627 Flora St (☎214/871-2376). In June and July, free **Shakespeare in the Park** performances are held in Samuell-Grand Park, east of downtown near the intersection of I-30 and Hwy-87 (☎214/954-0199).

For a real Wild West night out, head to the **Mesquite Championship Rodeo**, well out of town on I-635 at Military Parkway (April–Sept Fri & Sat 8pm; ☎972/285-8777; $12–16).

Full **listings** can be had from Thursday's *Dallas Observer*, Friday's *Dallas Morning News*, or the events information line (☎214/571-1301).

**Adair's**, 2624 Commerce St (☎214/939-9900). A country-music bar that attracts both old-timers and students with its hard-edged honky-tonk music.

**Bar of Soap**, 3615 Parry Ave (☎214/823-6617). Groovy pub-cum-laundromat on the outskirts of Deep Ellum, opposite Fair Park. Open daily noon–2am, no cover.

**Club Clearview**, 2803 Elm St (☎214/939-0077). Three-in-one Deep Ellum warehouse; a cool dance club, trippy video room with virtual reality games, ten bars, and big touring acts in *The Live Room*.

**Club DaDa**, 2720 Elm St (☎214/744-DADA). Famed Deep Ellum club where Edie Brickell and the New Bohemians began their days. Acoustic jam Sun afternoons, live bands and club nights.

**Dallas Alley**, 2019 Lamar St, West End Market Place (☎214/720-0170). One cover charge (around $8) gets you into eight very touristy clubs and five live venues.

**Muddy Waters**, 1518 Greenville Ave (☎214/823-1518). Generally acknowledged as the city's best down-home blues bar with live acts at weekends.

**Palm Beach Club**, 2807 S Crowdus St (☎214/742-4743). Reggae club in Deep Ellum, with live music every Fri and Sat, often featuring groups from Jamaica.

**Sons of Hermann Hall**, 3414 Elm St (☎214/747-4422). Delightfully old-school country venue where the Texan masters come to play as well as respectful alt/country outfits.

**Trees**, 2709 Elm St (☎214/748-5009). Deep Ellum warehouse turned auditorium, popular with up-and-coming indie bands, with pool tables upstairs.

# Fort Worth

*Yes, Dallas does have something Fort Worth doesn't have – a real city thirty miles away.*
Amon Carter, publisher, philanthropist, Fort Worthian

**FORT WORTH**, often dismissed as some kind of poor relation to Dallas, in fact has a rush and energy largely missing in its more complacent neighbor thirty miles east. Unashamed of its origins as a lawless frontier cowtown, this is one of the most "Western" cities in Texas. In the 1870s it was the last stop on the great cattle drive to Kansas, the **Chisholm Trail**; when the railroads arrived, it became a livestock market in its own right, with its own packing houses, while remaining a haven for cowboys and outlaws. The **cattle** trade is still a major industry, after aviation and defence, but the city can also pride itself on a thriving cultural life. Unlike the more anxious Dallas, Fort Worth doesn't feel the need to brag about its many excellent **museums**. For a place so wealthy (the grand **Western Hills** area claims to have proportionately more million-aires than any other US locale), it's surprisingly laid-back.

## Arrival, information and getting around

The main road between Fort Worth and Dallas, **I-30**, cuts the city north–south; Loop 820 encircles it. An Airporter express **bus** (daily 6am–11pm, every half-hour at peak times; ☎817/334-0092; $8) runs to and from DFW Airport, seventeen miles northeast (see p.652); a taxi costs around $30. Amtrak pulls in four times per week in either direction just southeast of downtown in the lovely red 1899 Santa Fe Depot, 1501 Jones St (☎817/332-2931). Greyhound operates out of the depot at 901 Commerce Street, next to the Convention Center. The city's public transportation system, **The T**, operates **free buses** downtown, running north on Throckmorton Street and south on Houston Street; fares on other T services cost 80¢ and $3 two-day Visitor passes give unlimited travel (☎817/871-6200).

There are three **visitor centers**: in the **Stockyards** at 130 E Exchange Ave (Mon–Fri 9am–6pm, Sat 9am–7pm, Sun noon–6pm; ☎817/624-4741; walking tours Mon–Sat 10am, 1pm & 3pm, Sun 1pm & 3pm; $1.50), downtown in the **CVB** at 415 Throckmorton St (Mon–Fri 8.30am–5pm; ☎817/336-8791 or 1-800/433-5747), and in the **Cultural Center Science Museum** at 3401 W Lancaster St (☎817/882-8588). The downtown Sundance Square and Stockyard areas are well patrolled and safe to walk around after dark; for a **taxi** between the two, call Yellow Cab Co ☎817/534-5555.

## Accommodation

Fort Worth is blessed with plenty of mid-priced **accommodation**, even downtown. The liveliest places to stay are around Sundance Square downtown, or in the Stockyards; more standard motel rooms can be found along I-35 both to the north and the south of the city.

**Clarion Hotel**, 600 Commerce St (☎817/332-6900 or 1-800/252-7466). Excellent location, footsteps away from Sundance Square and the bus station. ④.

**Etta's Place B&B**, 200 W 3rd St (☎817/654-0267). Ten great rooms right in the heart of the Sundance Square area, offering three-course breakfast, several patios and lounges. Named after the schoolteacher girlfriend of the Sundance Kid. ⑥.

**Miss Molly's Bed and Breakfast**, 109 W Exchange Ave (☎817/626-1522 or 1-800/996-6559). Quirkily furnished old bordello in the heart of the Stockyards, bursting with cowboy kitsch. Friendly hosts, gourmet breakfast. ⑤.

**Park Central Hotel**, 1010 Houston St (☎817/336-2011). Centrally located, convenient for downtown. ③.

**Ramada Plaza**, 1701 Commerce St (☎817/335-7000). Geared more to conference trade it's nevertheless a relatively inexpensive option on the edge of downtown. ⑤.

**Stockyards Hotel**, 109 E Exchange Ave (☎817/625-6427 or 1-800/423-8471). Historic Stockyards hotel, reputedly a favorite haunt of Bonnie and Clyde, with Western, Mountain Man, Indian and Victorian themed rooms. *Booger Red's Saloon* boasts funky saddle barstools. ⑥.

**Worthington Hotel**, 200 Main St (☎817/870-1000 or 1-800/433-5677). Large, comfortable, newly renovated hotel a short walk from Sundance Square. ⑥.

## The City

Fort Worth's main attractions fall tidily into a triangle anchored by downtown with the Cultural District and the Stockyards two miles away to the west and north respectively.

The chief focus of **downtown** Fort Worth is **Sundance Square**, a leafy, red-brick-paved fourteen-block area of shops, restaurants and bars between First and Sixth streets, ringed by glittering skyscrapers and pervaded with a genuine enthusiasm for the town's rich history. It owes its existence to vast injections of cash from the Bass family; the whole ensemble is dominated by the two gleaming glass skyscrapers of the Bass-owned **City Center Towers**, while the brand-new and extremely tasteful **Nancy Lee & Perry R Bass Performance Hall** is evidence of its continuing development. Notice the carvings of longhorn skulls everywhere, and the many trompe l'oeil murals – especially the Chisholm Trail mural on Fourth Street between Main and Houston. The **Sid Richardson Collection of Western Art**, tucked away at 309 Main St (Tues–Wed 10am–5pm, Thurs–Fri 10am–8pm, Sat 11am–8pm, Sun 1–5pm; free), has a small but excellent collection of late works by Remington, including some of his best black-and-white illustrations, and early elegiac cowboyscapes by Charles Russell. For bargain-seekers, there's a handy **outlet mall** at Throckmorton and E First with an ice rink open year round (call ☎817/878-4800 for times).

Naming the square after the Sundance Kid isn't particularly appropriate; he, and other outlaws such as Bonnie and Clyde, spent their time a few blocks south, just north of I-30 at the city's original settlement. Even into the 1950s "**Hell's Half Acre**" was renowned for bawdy lawlessness; these days it's much less exciting, although the bubbling fountains and pools of its central **Water Gardens** offer refreshing respite.

The **Cultural District**, two miles west of downtown, is an impressive area of museums and art galleries. The finest collection is at the small **Kimbell Art Museum**, 3333 Camp Bowie Blvd (Tues–Thurs 10am–8pm, Fri noon–8pm, Sat 10am–5pm, Sun noon–5pm; free, around $5 for special exhibits), a splendid vaulted, naturally lit building designed by Louis Kahn. Downstairs displays concentrate on pre-Columbian and African pieces, with some noteworthy Mayan funerary urns, while upstairs, as well as canvases by Gauguin, Cézanne, Picasso and Monet, you can admire a seventh-century Khmer figure of a Hindu deity, ancient Chinese bronzes and a fourteenth-century Japanese polychrome wood statue of En No Gyoja. The museum cafe, too, is adorned with Mayan steles and Roman-Syrian mosaics.

American art in the **Amon Carter Museum**, just up the hill at 3501 Camp Bowie Blvd (Tues–Sat 10am–5pm, Sun noon–5pm; free), includes great photographs of Western landscapes, as well as a fine assortment of Remingtons and Russells and work by Winslow Homer and Georgia O'Keeffe, while the **Modern Art Museum of Fort Worth**, 1309 Montgomery St (Tues–Fri 10am–5pm, Sat 11am–5pm, Sun noon–5pm; free), specializes in twentieth-century abstracts. South of here, the wide-ranging **Fort Worth Museum of Science and History** (Mon 9am–5pm, Tues–Thurs 9am–8pm, Fri & Sat 9am–9pm, Sun noon–8pm; free) includes a planetarium and an IMAX theater.

In the lively, interactive **Cattle Raiser's Museum**, slightly further north at 1301 W Seventh St (Mon–Fri 8.30am–4.30pm; free), the changing economic face of the cattle trade is traced from the days of the open range, via the great cattle drives, to modern ranching and latterday cowboys – with displays of spurs, assorted tangles of barbed wire and some good stuff on early women pioneers.

However, museums, no matter how good, aren't necessarily what you want from a cow-town. The ten-block **Stockyards Area**, with its wooden sidewalks and old storefronts centered on Exchange Avenue two miles north of downtown, is a glorious evocation of the days when Fort Worth's stockyards made this "the richest little city in the world." It's much more than a cynical creation for cowboy-hungry tourists and even the daily corralling of the fifteen or so Texan Longhorn cattle (with six-feet horn spans) and their driving to the Trinity River grazing spot near Northside Drive one mile toward downtown, is done in good, educational taste. The drives occur, weather permitting, between mid-March and mid-November at 11.30am from the corrals behind the Livestock Exchange Building (see overleaf) with the herd arriving back around 4pm.

Along with the restaurants and bars, the **stores** will have Western-wear obsessives in heaven. Look out for Fincher's rodeo equipment store and M L Leddy's saddle shop; and check out the Maverick Trading Post, packed with hip, bright cowgirl regalia, and with a bar serving good cold beers. They encourage you to drink first and buy later; this is not a good idea. In comparison, the shops and restaurants in the **Stockyards Station**, a brick-floored enclave in the old hog pens, are squeaky clean; one of the best is the stylish Southwestern Furniture Shop, with its own prairie dog colony. From here the magnificent *Tarantula* **steam train** puffs along a nostalgic route to Eighth Avenue downtown (departs 1.15pm, 3.30pm & 5.45pm; 30min trip; ☎817/625-RAIL; $11).

The Stockyards no longer host live **cattle auctions**; instead, images are beamed by satellite into the huge 1902 **Livestock Exchange Building** at 131 E Exchange Ave, home of the **Stockyards Collections Museum** (Mon–Sat 10am–5pm; free), packed with meaty memorabilia. The mission-style **Cowtown Coliseum** next door, used for rodeos (☎817/625-1025; good value at an average ticket price of $8) and concerts, is fronted with a bust of Bill Pickett, the black rodeo star who invented the unsavory but effective practice of "bulldogging" – stunning the bull by biting its lip. Horseback **trail rides** along the old Chisholm Trail leave from Cowtown Corrals, 500 NE 23rd St (☎817/740-0852; $22 per hour; trail camps Fri & Sat 7–11pm).

## Eating

If you love **steak**, Fort Worth is for you. Meat here is hefty, fresh and prepared with tender loving care, especially in the Stockyards area, where the many good home-cooking cafes are frequented as much by cattle ranchers as by visitors. Mex and Tex-Mex tastes are well covered though vegetarians will do less well; try the upmarket restaurants downtown. The **cafe** in the Kimbell Art Museum (see overleaf) makes for a pleasant place to snack or eat lunch.

**Angelo's Barbecue**, 2533 White Settlement Rd (☎817/332-0357). Venerable westside restaurant open for lunch and dinner and cited by locals as the best in the city.

**Cattlemen's Steak House**, 2458 N Main St (☎817/624-3945). Dim lighting and wall-sized portraits of prize steers. A Fort Worth institution thanks to its steaks and margaritas. Dinner is around $15; closed Sun lunch.

**J & J Oyster Bar**, 612 N University Drive (☎817/335-2756). If meat is murder, then try the fresh crab and oysters at this local institution near the Cultural District.

**Joe T Garcia's Mexican Dishes**, 2201 N Commerce St (☎817/626-4356). Nationally famed Mexican restaurant in the 1930s home of its owners, serving hefty set tortilla/fajita dinners ($10–15) and frosty margaritas. Outdoor seating next to the family swimming pool. There's a family-owned cafe/bakery at 2140 N Main St (☎817/626-5700), for great breakfast burritos.

**Mi Cocina**, 509 Main St (☎817/654-3600). Healthy Tex-Mex dishes in a modern, eclectically decorated joint.

**Reata**, Bank One Building, 500 Throckmorton St (☎817/336-1009). 35th-floor restaurant with views of the Fort Worth skyline and a modern Texan menu featuring good steaks and desserts.

**Star Cafe**, 111 W Exchange Ave (☎817/624-8701). Neon-lit cafe with some of the least expensive steaks – not just in the Stockyards but in the entire city. They also know how to chicken-fry steak well.

## Nightlife and entertainment

You'd be hard pushed not to find something to your taste amid Fort Worth's late-night drinking and carousing. This is a truly cosmopolitan city, where roustabouts will happily down a few beers with modern jazz fans. Bar crawling is safe and fun, and there's a great mix of live music venues (though the pick-up joints in the Stockyards are best avoided). Call ☎817/548-7337 for a telephone **listings** guide. The **Nancy Lee & Perry R Bass Performance Hall** (☎817/212-4280) is the new downtown home of the city's orchestra, opera, theater and dance companies and hosts visiting spectacles.

In addition to the regular cowboy venues below, the **Chisholm Trail Round-Up** (mid-June) and **Pioneer Days** (Labor Day weekend) are two hugely enjoyable annual Western-style celebrations in the Stockyards. *Cowtown Coliseum* holds a championship **rodeo** (Sat 8pm; $8) and special events throughout the year. There's a rodeo hotline on ☎817/336-8791.

**Billy Bob's Texas**, 2520 Rodeo Plaza (☎817/624-7117). The largest honky-tonk in the world, down in the Stockyards, with live bull-riding Fri & Sat at 9pm & 10pm, pool tables, bars, restaurants and stores, and big-name concerts. Live music nightly, and the place is open until 2am. Tours Mon–Sat 11am, 2pm & 4pm, Sun 2pm & 4pm. Cover $3–5 Mon–Thurs & Sun, $5–10 Fri & Sat.

**The Caravan of Dreams**, 312 Houston St (☎817/877-3000). One of the best spots in town, a superb downtown club in a beautiful building with a cactus garden. Attracts a friendly, stylish crowd and regular big-name acts. Cover $12–25, though access to the *Rooftop Grotto Bar* is free.

**Casa Manana Theater**, 3101 Lancaster Ave (☎817/332-6221) in the Cultural District. Live alternative comedy and plays.

**8.0**, 111 E 3rd St (☎817/336-0880). Highly popular downtown bar in Sundance Square, flamboyantly decorated inside and with sidewalk tables.

**Flying Saucer**, 201 Commerce St (☎817/877-4191). Over 200 beers, often with enticing promotional prices, in a fun Sundance Square setting.

**J&J Blues Bar**, 937 Woodward Ave (☎817/870-BEER). Westside joint with regional blues acts Wed–Sat.

**J&Js Hideaway**, 3305 W 7th St (☎817/877-3363). Good neighborhood bar in the Cultural District.

**White Elephant Saloon**, 106 E Exchange Ave (☎817/624-1887). Notoriously wild and authentic Stockyards saloon with a cowboy hat hall of fame; prop yourself up at the long wooden bar and listen to cowboy singer Don Edwards. $2 cover Fri. Open till midnight weekdays, 2am Fri & Sat.

**Wreck Room**, 3208 W 7th St (☎817/870-4900). Underground westside hangout with occasional leftfield rock bands.

# Towards the Panhandle

Routes west from central Texas lead you through the state's "backyard," where farmlands and rough-cut, juniper-covered hills give way to treeless, sandy landscapes. Of the towns, only **Abilene** and **Sweetwater**, both on I-20 towards Lubbock, are even marginally interesting enough to be possible stopovers for long-distance drivers. In theory, this is rich, oil-bearing land, but the cities have taken a battering since the slump.

## Abilene and Sweetwater

**ABILENE** has a certain curiosity value as an oppressively God-fearing Bible city with three Christian universities based here. There's not much reason to stop here, though a downtown stroll reveals a few places along **Cypress Street** worth a look. At no. 102 the **Grace Museum** (Tues–Wed & Fri–Sat 10am–5pm, Thurs 10am–8.30pm, Sun 1–5pm; $3) occupies what was once the grandest hotel in this former railroad town and is divided into three distinct sections of regional art, local history and a children's museum. The **Center For Contemporary Arts** at No. 220 (Tues–Sat 11am–5pm) holds work by local artists and is free, while the beautiful **Paramount Theatre** at no. 352 (☎915/676-9620) is open for self-guided tours of its elaborate Moorish interior on weekdays between 1pm and 5pm. Evening shows range from live theater productions to classic and art films. If you have to stay, there are plenty of interstate **motels** including the well-kept *Rodeway Inn*, 1650 I-20 E (☎915/677-2200; ②) while downtown, *BJ's*, 508 Mulberry St, offers **B&B** rooms (☎915/675-5855; ③). Cypress Street is the place to go for **food** with the *Cypress Street Station* at no. 158 (☎915/676-3463) offering a more eclectic menu than you would usually credit a restaurant in this locale for.

Dozy **SWEETWATER**, further west on I-20, began as a general store for buffalo hunters in 1877, and since 1958 has been mildly notable for its **rattlesnake round-up** on the second full weekend of March, when you can try fried snake (tough but tasty) or buy a transparent toilet seat with a rattler coiled in it. As well as the serious business of the farmers ridding their land of the diamondbacks, there are parades, cook-outs, a Miss Snake Charmer Queen contest and snake-handling demonstrations. Of the motels along Georgia Street, one of the nicest is the *Ranch House Motel and Restaurant* (☎915/236-6341; ②).

# THE PANHANDLE

The inhabitants of the **Panhandle**, the southernmost portion of the Great Plains, call it "the real Texas"; it certainly fulfils the fantasy of what Texas should look like. When Coronado's expedition passed this way in the sixteenth century, the gold-seekers drove stakes into the ground across the vast and unchanging vista, despairing of otherwise finding their way home. Hence the name *Llano Estacado*, or staked plains, which still persists today.

Once the buffalo – and the natives – had been driven away from what was seen as perilous and uninhabitable frontier country, the Panhandle began, around the 1870s, to yield great **natural resources**. Helium – especially in Amarillo – and oil, as well as **agriculture**, have brought wealth to the region, home to some of the world's largest **ranches**.

The Panhandle may hold few actual tourist attractions, but its rural charm and quirkiness is far removed from the eastern cities. **Music** has particular significance in an area famous for songwriters such as Buddy Holly, Roy Orbison, Waylon Jennings, Mac Davis, Joe Ely and Natalie Maines from the Dixie Chicks, although most musicians relocate to cosmopolitan centers like Austin. Above all, the exceptionally hospitable **people** of the Panhandle make it special, along with the starkly romantic landscape, strewn with tumbleweeds and mesquite trees.

# Lubbock

**LUBBOCK**, the largest city in the Panhandle, has long been the center of its commerce and transportation, roughly one hundred miles northwest of Abilene and the same distance south of Amarillo. At first this was cattle-grazing land, but the discovery of copious underground water made agriculture profitable.

The prosperity of the city was built on cotton; in recent years government restrictions have hit prices hard, and the days of self-sufficient farming look numbered. You may, however, still see solitary cottonfields standing defiantly on the outskirts, where farmers have refused to sell out.

With its fields, farms, lumpen bungalows and faceless block buildings, Lubbock is relentlessly ordinary-looking, its muted downtown area dotted with fading 1950s shopfronts. Which is not to say that it's dull; though Southern Baptism has left its mark and this is officially a "dry" city, Lubbock has a pervasive sense of fun that can't simply be put down to the students from Texas Tech.

### Arrival, information and getting around

Loop 289 circles Lubbock proper, with the **airport** (☎806/762-6411) a few minutes north; city buses don't come out here and taxis (☎806/765-7777) to downtown cost $10. I-127 slashes through to the west, north to Amarillo and south to Tahoka. **Buses** come

## BUDDY HOLLY

Lubbock's claim to world fame is as the birthplace of Charles Hardin Holley on September 7, 1936. Inspired by the blues and country music of his childhood – and a seminal encounter with the young Elvis Presley, gigging in Lubbock at the *Cotton Club* – **Buddy Holly** was one of rock 'n' roll's first singer-songwriters. The Holly sound, characterized by steady strumming guitar, rapid drumming and his trademark hiccoughing vocals, was made famous by hits such as *Peggy Sue, Rave On, Not Fade Away, Oh Boy!* and *That'll Be The Day*; but Buddy himself was killed at the age of 22 by the Iowa plane crash of February 2, 1959 ("the day the music died") that also claimed the Big Bopper and Ritchie Valens.

In September 1999, the city finally opened the **Buddy Holly Center** at 19th Street and Avenue G (Tues–Thurs 10am–6pm, Fri–Sat 10am–7pm), an impressive space that holds Lubbock's collection of Holly memorabilia (contracts, clothes, rare records, autographed things, and yes, those glasses) plus the Texas Music Hall Of Fame and various temporary exhibition galleries. All exhibits are free except for the Holly collection ($3).

An 8ft bronze **Buddy Holly Statue**, on Eighth Street and Avenue Q, towers over a **Walk of Fame** of plaques to local performers like Roy Orbison and Waylon Jennings (the bassist for Buddy's final concert). **Buddy's birthplace**, at 1911 Sixth St, is now a vacant lot, but more substantial sites around town include:

**J T Hutchinson Junior High School**, 3102 Canton Ave. Buddy and friend Bob Montgomery performed here in the sixth grade. Souvenirs are on sale.

**Lubbock High School**, 2004 19th St. Buddy and Bob, who graduated in 1955, won the school's "Westerners Round Up" with *Flower of My Heart*.

**Tabernacle Baptist Church**, 1911 34th St. A percentage of Buddy's royalties still go to the church that saw his baptism, wedding and funeral.

**Radio Station KRLB**, 6602 Quirt Ave. Opened in 1953, this was the first full-time country music station in the States. Buddy and Jack Neal had their own show.

**Fair Park Coliseum**, 10th St and Ave A. Where Buddy opened shows for Bill Haley and Elvis Presley. His "discovery" here in 1955 led to a contract with Decca.

**Buddy's grave**, in Lubbock cemetery at the end of 34th St. Take the right fork inside the gate, and the grave, decorated with flowers and guitar picks, is on the left.

in downtown at 1313 13th St (☎806/765-6641). The **citibus** system (☎806/762-0111) runs commuter routes within the loop, stopping at around 6pm (Mon–Sat only). The **visitor center** is at 1301 Broadway (Mon–Fri 8am–5pm; ☎806/747-5232 or 1-800/692-4035).

## Accommodation

Prices are very reasonable in this region, and rooms are plentiful, so there should be no problem finding somewhere to stay. Avenue Q has a string of good, reliable chain hotels.

**Coronado Inn**, 501 I-27 N (☎806/763-6441). Northside motel with clean rooms for thirty bucks. ①.

**Holiday Inn – Civic Center**, 801 Ave Q (☎806/763-1200). Popular downtown hotel with pool and other facilities. ④.

**La Quinta Motor Inn – Civic Center**, 601 Ave Q (☎806/763-9441). Free coffee, adjacent to a 24hr restaurant, and just across from the Buddy Holly Statue. ③.

**Lubbock Inn**, 3901 19th St (☎806/792-5181). Basic motel featuring a pool with waterfalls, and free breakfast. ③.

**Woodrow House B&B**, 2629 19th St (☎806/793-3330 or 1-800/687-5235). Eight rooms, each with a Texan theme, in a mansion-style house opposite Texas Tech. ⑤.

## The Town

Downtown Lubbock, and the university, are on the northern side of town. Few buildings of interest survive, thanks to the construction boom of the 1950s and a tornado in 1970. However, you can get a stimulating overview of local history at the university's **Ranching Heritage Center**, Fourth Street and Indiana Avenue (Mon–Sat 10am–5pm, Sun 1–5pm; free). Over thirty original ranch buildings, from simple cowboy huts to grand overseers' houses, are set in a harsh landscape spiked with cactuses and mesquite. There's an excellent museum on pioneer and cowboy history, and demonstrations on making lye soap, sourdough and quilts. The adjacent **Texas Tech Museum** (Tues–Wed & Fri–Sat 10am–5pm, Thurs 10am–8.30pm, Sun 1–5pm; free) has further Southwestern displays and a room of Buddy Holly memorabilia.

Nearby, the **Lubbock Lake Landmark State Historical Park** archeological site (Tues–Sat 9am–5pm, Sun 1–5pm; $2) has yielded an impressive array of artifacts spanning 1200 years, although to the untrained eye it resembles little more than a dry gravelly site buzzing with gigantic Texan insects. As indeed does **Prairie Dog Town**, in Mackenzie State Park, where six hundred of the cuddly little rodents (like fat barking hamsters with waggly tails) are attempting to repopulate the world and gain their revenge for the attempts of government officials and irate ranchers in the 1930s to poison them into extinction.

Three miles east of the loop on Hwy-1585, the **Llano Estacado winery** started as the hobby of two university professors. It might look incongruous, set amid scrubby pastureland and cottonfields, but its success has led Lubbock to pin great hopes on the potential of wine to revitalize and diversify its flagging economy. Visitors are given a guided tour and free tasting. Europeans, who are looked on as connoisseurs in an area where beer is the staple liquid, can expect to be questioned on their favorite vintages during the sociable and informal tasting sessions (Mon–Sat 10am–4.30pm, Sun noon–4.30pm; ☎806/745-2258).

## Eating

Lubbock has a surprising variety of **eating places**, with good barbecue and Tex-Mex and even some New American restaurants, with a particular concentration along Avenue H (Buddy Holly Avenue). However, many of even the most upmarket restaurants close before 10pm.

**Abuelo's**, 4401 82nd St (☎806/794-1762). Lubbock's best Mexican restaurant, with some great fish dishes, punch-packing margaritas, and live music on the patio in summer.

**The County Line**, half a mile west of I-27 in Escondido Canyon (☎806/763-6001). Mediterranean decor, 1940s music, and the best barbecue in Lubbock, with all-you-can-eat specials for around $15. Outside, ducks and peacocks saunter around freely.

**Hub City Brewpub**, 1807 Ave H (☎806/747-1535). Lively and youthful, with decent grill food and beers.

**LaLa's**, 1110 Broadway (☎806/765-9931). Excellent Mexican breakfasts. Mon–Sat 7am–3pm.

**Pancake House**, 510 Ave Q (☎806/765-8506). Popular downtown joint for breakfast and they also do breads to go.

**Santa Fe**, 401 Ave Q (☎806/763-6114). Bulging enchiladas, gargantuan burritos and standard Tex-Mex favorites, in a peaceful family atmosphere.

## Entertainment and nightlife

The best entertainment the Panhandle has to offer is at its **annual events**. After having been designated the "Music Crossroads of Texas" by the state legislature in 1999, the city changed the name of the annual Buddy Holly Music Festival to the catchy mouthful of the Music Crossroads of Texas Labor Day Weekend Music Festival

(MCOTLDWMF for short?) which attracts big Texan names like Joe Ely and Tanya Tucker, as well as those playing a straight homage to Mr Holly. **Rodeos** are always rip-roaring fun; Texas Tech holds one each October in Fair Park, and the **ABC Rodeo** is at Lubbock Municipal Coliseum every spring. In the same spirit, there are twirling contests, bull-riding, big-name country performers and livestock exhibits at the **Panhandle South Plains Fair** in late September and early October.

Despite its rich musical heritage there isn't a great deal of **nightlife** in Lubbock; most of the local musicians decamp to Austin. The buzz zone is the downtown Historical Depot District which spreads out for a few blocks from 19th Street and Hwy-27 and has a mix of crass chain bars, jock joints and worthy places like *Stubb's*. The oddly named *Lubbock Avalanche-Journal* carries listings.

**Cactus Theatre**, 1812 Buddy Holly Ave (☎806/747-3233). Insists on putting on a mix of variety shows as syrupy musical nostalgia shows with frequent nods to you-know-who.

**Midnight Rodeo**, 7301 University Ave at Loop 289 (☎806/745-2813). Huge C&W club: pool tables, lanky cowboys and big-haired Texan belles. Great fun. Tues–Sun until 2am.

**Stubb's BBQ**, 19th Street at I-27 (☎806/763-6001). As well as dishing out some of the best barbecue in town, *Stubb's* attracts some of the best Texan singer-songwriters around. This place has been so successful that they've opened a branch in Austin (see p.647).

# Amarillo

**AMARILLO** may seem cut off from the rest of Texas, up in the northern Panhandle, but it stands on one of the great American cross-country routes – I-40, once the legendary **Route 66** – roughly 300 miles east of Albuquerque and 250 miles west of Oklahoma City. *Amarillo* is Spanish for "yellow" – the name comes from its characteristic yellow soil. An early promoter of the city was so delighted with its potential as a site for lucrative buffalo hunting (for those who braved the Apache and Comanche threat) and as excellent ranching land that he painted all the buildings bright yellow.

Today, sitting on ninety percent of the world's helium and hosting a world-class cattle market, Amarillo is a prosperous but surprisingly uneventful city. The small "**old town**" consists of a few tree-lined streets and staid old homes; some of the less twee antique stores along **Sixth Street** (the old Route 66, known locally as "Old San Jacinto") serve equally well as museums of pioneer life. Following Sixth Street twelve miles west onto I-40 brings you to **Cadillac Ranch**. An extraordinary vision in the middle of nowhere, ten battered roadsters stand upended in the soil, their tail fins demonstrating the different Cadillac designs from 1949 to 1963. Since the cars were installed in 1974, they have been subject to countless makeovers at the hands of graffiti artists, photographers and members of the public (encouraged by owner and patron, eccentric helium millionaire Stanley Marsh III, on whose land the cars are planted); occasionally they're shiny blue or red after having been painted for a photo shoot. In 1997 the whole installation was moved two miles west to this present site as the city had begun to encroach and spoil the horizon.

Amarillo is also host to the world's stompingest, snortingest **livestock auction**, in the stockyards at S Manhattan and Third streets, on the east side of town. There are regular tours (☎806/373-7464), and the auction proper is held on Tuesday morning.

If you enjoy playing cowboys, it's fun to visit one of the many grand old Panhandle **ranches** to have diversified into tourism. Some just open for the day; others provide (usually expensive) accommodation (call Amarillo's CVB for particulars). The ranchers who entertain you are often natural showmen and women, whose welcome is utterly genuine, though they'd rather be working the animals for real than running a theme park.

## Practicalities

Amarillo has no **public transportation** to speak of, but car drivers will find it easy to navigate. Greyhound comes in downtown at 700 S Tyler St (☎806/374-5371). The **CVB** is at 1000 Polk St (Mon–Fri 8am–5pm; ☎806/374-1497 or 1-800/692-1338).

Innumerable budget **hotels** are concentrated along I-40. For a little luxury, *Ambassador Hotel*, 3100 I-40 W, is good value (☎806/358-6161; ⑤) while the *Parkview*, 1311 S Jefferson St (☎806/373-9494; ④) is a cozy and friendly **B&B**. Texana fans will love the tongue-in-cheek Western camp of the *Big Texan Steak House Motel*, 7701 I-40 E at exit 75 (☎806/372-5000 or 1-800/657-7177; ②). Its restaurant, as well as serving fried rattlesnake and buffalo chili, offers the 72oz steak challenge: if you can **eat** it all within an hour, you get it free. Other popular Amarillo restaurants include *Arnold Burgers*, 1611 S Washington St (☎806/373-1591), which serves enormous beef patties (up to 18 inches), *Cafe Americana*, 507 S Alabama Ave (☎806/373-1122), for gourmet pizza and pasta, and the self-consciously bohemian *OHMS Gallery Cafe*, 619 S Tyler St (☎806/373-3233) with an international menu.

## Canyon

The one "sight" in the former cattle town of **CANYON**, fifteen miles south of Amarillo on I-27, is a must. The **Panhandle-Plains Historical Museum** (June–Aug Mon–Sat 9am–6pm, Sun 1–6pm; rest of year Mon–Sat 9am–5pm; donation) has exhibits on restored pioneer buildings, artifacts of the Plains Indians, the history of Texas ranching, natural history displays, and a collection of Western art. Even the history of the oil and gas industry is made interesting. For **food**, head for the *Cowboy Cafe*, at 15th Street and Hwy-60 (☎806/655-9157), with giant cowboy "Tex" standing outside.

### Palo Duro State Canyon Park

**Palo Duro Canyon**, twelve miles east of Canyon and twenty miles southeast of Amarillo, is one of Texas' best-kept secrets. Plunging 1200 feet from rim to floor, it splits the plains wide open and offers breathtaking views and colors, especially at sunset and in spring, when the whole chasm is scattered with wild flowers. Pillars of sturdy sandstone loom over the flame-colored rocks, which Coronado's explorers named "Spanish Skirts" on account of their stripy flounces.

The **park** itself is located in the most scenic part of the sixty-mile canyon ($3 per person; daily 8am–10pm, visitor center closes 5pm, interpretive center June–Aug Wed–Sun 11am–7pm). You can explore the depths on **horseback** ($10 per hour; reservations ☎806/448-2231), though backpackers and hikers may want to escape the tourist busloads by following the Prairie Dog Town fork into more remote sections of the park. To **camp**, advance reservations are recommended (☎806/488-2227). The Goodnight Trading Post (daily 8am–5pm, later in summer; ☎806/488-2760), opposite the Pioneer Amphitheater at the northern end of the park, sells gasoline and snacks.

You may balk at heart-warming musical spectaculars, but the outdoor *TEXAS!* has an undeniable pull in an area not exactly throbbing with nightlife, with the dramatic prairie sky as a ceiling, a 600ft cliff as a backdrop, and genuine thunder and lightning (mid-June to late-Aug Mon–Sat 8.30pm; $8–16; pre-show chuckwagon barbecue 6pm; ☎806/655-2181).

# WEST TEXAS

**West Texas** is the stuff of Wild West fantasy: parched deserts, ghost towns, looming mesas, and above all a sense of utter isolation. Although the area south from the Panhandle down to Del Rio on the Rio Grande is, for convenience, also known as west

Texas, the fantasy really begins west of the River Pecos; you can drive for hours without a sign of life to reach **El Paso**, Texas' shabby westernmost city. Most travelers only venture into the desolation to explore **Big Bend National Park**, nearly three hundred miles southeast of El Paso in the curve of the Rio Grande.

Minimal rainfall and harsh land were not the only hindrances to settlement. The **Apache** and **Comanche**, though accustomed in the 1820s to trading with Mexican *comancheros*, were infuriated when hapless white pioneers began to trickle in during the 1830s. With their horsemanship and ability to find scarce water supplies, the Native Americans posed a real threat; upon statehood, federal money helped to set up a string of cavalry forts to protect Mexican and Anglo settlers from attack. As trading posts and cattle ranges began to spring up after the Civil War, the paramilitary **Texas Rangers** were sent out on violent vigilante missions. Eventually, as in the Panhandle, a brutal program of buffalo slaughter, supported by the US Army, starved the natives out. Not long afterwards, **oil** hit west Texas and boom towns appeared, with all the attendant lawlessness, gunslinging and brawling.

## The Davis Mountains

The temperate climate of the verdant **Davis Mountains**, south of the junction of I-10 and I-20, makes them a popular summer destination for sweltering urban Texans, while the glassy, starry nights facilitate the work of the **McDonald Observatory**, about twenty miles north of Fort Davis on Hwy-118 (tours of dome and 107-inch telescope daily 9am–5pm; $3). Nocturnal "star parties" here provide the opportunity to look at the constellations for yourself (Tues, Fri & Sun at 9pm). **Fort Davis National Historic Site** (summer daily 9am–6pm; rest of year daily 9am–5pm; $2 per person, $4 per vehicle), which starts on the northern edge of the town along Hwy-17, offers good hiking, and fishing and swimming at the foot of the canyon in Limpia Creek. Rooms at its adobe *Indian Lodge* are clean and comfortable – and often booked up, so call in advance (☎915/426-3254; ④).

**FORT DAVIS**, a one-street town with less than a thousand residents, at the junction of highways 118 and 17, is a peaceful base for exploring the state park, en route to or from Big Bend. *The Old Texas Inn*, above a wood-fronted drugstore, has clean, colorful B&B style rooms; breakfast is served in the cafe downstairs, accompanied by country tunes on the jukebox (☎915/426-3118; ③). The more expensive *Hotel Limpia*, opposite (☎915/426-3241 or 1-800/662-5517; ⑤), serves home-cooked dinners in its cozy dining room. There's pleasantly little to do in Fort Davis at night, though you can buy "membership" to the *Limpia Hotel* bar for $3. The town's **visitor center** (☎915/426-3015) offers regional information including road maps for the 75-mile scenic loop of the Davis Mountains.

# Big Bend National Park

The **Rio Grande**, flowing through 1500ft gorges, makes a ninety-degree bend south of Marathon to form the southern border of **BIG BEND NATIONAL PARK** – thanks to its isolation one of the least visited of the US national parks, and very much of a kind with the great desert parks of the Southwest.

The Apache, who forced the Chisos Indians out three hundred years ago, told that this hauntingly beautiful wilderness was used by the Great Spirit to dump all the rocks left over from the creation of the world. A breathtaking million-acre expanse of pine-forested mountains and ocotilla-dotted desert, Big Bend has been home to prospectors and smugglers, a last frontier for the true-grit pioneers at the end of the nineteenth century, who took advantage of the rich cinnabar deposits for mercury mining. Today there is camping in specific areas, and some trailer parks, but much of the park remains barely charted territory, the ruins of primitive Mexican and white settlements testament to its power to defeat earlier visitors. Wild animals have fared somewhat better: coyotes, road-runners and javelinas (an odd-looking bristly black pig with a pointy snout) all roam free. Violent contrasts in topography and temperature result in dramatic juxtapositions of desert and mountain plant and animal life. Despite the dryness, tangles of pretty wild flowers and blossoming cactuses, including peyote, erupt into color each April.

The most interesting route into Big Bend is from the west. You can't follow the river all the way from El Paso, but Hwy-170 – the **River Road**, reached on Hwy-67 south from Marfa, where James Dean made *Giant* – runs through spectacular desert scenery for around thirty miles west from Ojinaga, climbing stark buttes where you can peep down to the river below. Before reaching the park boundary just beyond Study Butte, you pass through the haunting communities of Lajitas and Terlingua (see opposite).

Once in the park, unless you're prepared to do some strenuous hiking, there are few opportunities to see the river itself; the main road is obliged to run across the desert, north of the outcrop of the Chisos Mountains. A spur road starting west of the head-quarters at **Panther Junction** leads south for six miles, up into the alpine meadows of the **Chisos Basin**, ringed by dramatic (though not amazingly high) peaks. The one gap in the rocky wall here is the **Window**, looking out over the deserts and reached by a relatively simple trail. Driving twenty miles southeast of Panther Junction brings you to the riverside **Rio Grande Village** – unless you choose to detour just before, to bathe in some rather dilapidated natural **hot springs** which feed into the river. A footbridge crosses from near the village to the Mexican hamlet of Boquillas; or you can pay $1 to be rowed across the river, then ride into Boquillas on a donkey.

At three separate stages within the park boundaries the river runs through gigantic **canyons**. The westernmost, the **Santa Elena**, is the most common **rafting trip**, being accessible from a put-in at Lajitas. Although there is virtually no whitewater, it boasts the technically challenging Rock Slide, and two ethereal Mexican side canyons that can be hiked, as well as stretches where the river swirls between awesome high rock walls, striated at an angle that makes it seem like you're plunging into an abyss. It's possible to drive within the park to the eastern end of the canyon, where the towering cliffs sud-denly come to an end and the river meanders through marshy fields; a short hike from here shows the gorge in all its splendor.

The ease of crossing the **international frontier** adds an extra frisson to the Big Bend experience, although you can get no further into Mexico than sandbanks popu-lated by browsing burros. This area is so remote that casual traffic across the river is regarded as insignificant; police checks for illegal immigrants take place roughly fifty miles north of Big Bend, on each of the main roads.

## Practicalities

The park headquarters at **Panther Junction** (daily 8am–5pm; ☎915/477-2251), where you pay the $10 per vehicle entrance fee, holds orientation exhibits and has a daytime gas station. Camping is first-come, first-served. **Rio Grande Village** has another visitor center, hot shower facilities in the grocery store, a laundry and a daytime filling station. When its 25-site $12 campground is full, there are also $7 primitive camping facilities, with pit toilets. Further free primitive **campgrounds** are scattered along the 36 marked hiking trails. These have no facilities, and you'll need a wilderness permit from Panther Junction, plus a map, compass, flashlight and first-aid kit before you can ven-ture onto the trails.

The **Chisos Basin**, which holds a visitor contact station, a store and a post office, is the site of the park's only roofed accommodation. The motel-style *Chisos Mountains Lodge* (reservations essential; ☎915/477-2291; ④) offers balcony rooms with gorgeous views; you'll often hear javelinas snuffling for food outside your door; its adequate cafe-teria restaurant closes at 7.30pm.

## Terlingua and Lajitas

Some of the long-abandoned mercury mining communities on the fringes of Big Bend are now stuttering back to life as alternative tourist centers. **TERLINGUA** in particular, a strangely appealing little ghost town scattered across the scrubby hills along Hwy-170, is populated by the adventurous types who work for the local rafting companies, along with assorted drifters lured by the solitary desert life. Near its fly-blown cemetery, against a backdrop of evocative ruins, the hugely atmospheric *Starlight Theater, Bar and Restaurant* (☎915/371-2326), with its postmodern reinterpretation of Southwestern decor, is the perfect place to enjoy a cold beer, soaking up the haunting desert view; it also serves food, and puts on evening shows in summer. A mile or so east along the highway, is the only other place to eat in the evening: *La Kiva* (☎915/371-2250), attached to the RV-oriented *Big Bend Travel Park*, is hollowed into the rock, and attracts a young crowd to its New Age bar, restaurant and evening gigs. The *Easter Egg Valley Motel* on Hwy–170 (☎915/371-2254; ③) has reasonable **rooms**.

Allow around $100 for a full day's **rafting** along Santa Elena Canyon (see opposite); further-flung canyons can cost up to $150. Far Flung Adventures, based next door to the *Starlight* in Terlingua, runs all the Big Bend routes, as well as many other Southwestern rivers, and also does memorable multiday music trips with renowned Texan musicians (☎915/371-2489 or 1-800/359-4138).

**LAJITAS**, west of Terlingua, is the main put-in for rafting trips, but has largely been taken over by the somewhat ersatz *Lajitas on the Rio Grande* resort complex, with its four separate hotels (☎915/424-3471; ⑤). However, it attempts to pull in the tourists with its distinguished mayoral figurehead – Clay Henry Jr, a beer-drinking goat in the tradition of his late father Clay Henry Sr, whose bottle-littered pen stands outside the adobe Lajitas Trading Post.

# El Paso

Back when Texas was still *Tejas*, **EL PASO**, the second oldest settlement in the United States, was the main crossing on the Rio Grande. It still plays that role today, its 600,000 residents joining with another 1.2 million across the river in **CIUDAD JUAREZ**, Mexico, to form the largest binational (and bilingual) megalopolis in North America. At first sight it's not an especially pretty place – massive railyards fill up much of downtown, the belching smelters of copper mills line the riverfront, and the northern reaches are taken up by the giant Fort Bliss military base, where two museums trace the military history of the city from adobe Spanish outpost to largest air defense center in the Western world. Its dramatic setting, however, where the Franklin Mountains meet the Chihuahua desert, gives it a certain bold, rough pioneer edge, bearing more relation to old rather than New Mexico, with little of the pastel softness of the Southwest US. Local legend has it that when Wyatt Earp arrived in sharp-shooting El Paso, he thought it too wild for him, and boarded the first train to Tombstone.

### Arrival, information and getting around

El Paso's **airport** is about twenty minutes' drive northeast of downtown; Sun Metro buses (☎915/533-3333; $1) run until 7pm each night, and it's a $12 cab fare, although most downtown hotels offer free van connections. Otherwise, shuttle services run to El Paso and Alamagordo (☎1-800/872-2702), and throughout southern New Mexico (☎1-800/288-1784). Greyhound **buses** stop at 200 W San Antonio Ave, while Amtrak **trains** pull in to the Daniel Burnham-designed Union Station at 700 San Francisco Ave, slightly to the west.

For full information on El Paso and its Mexican neighbor, contact the downtown **visitor center** (Mon–Fri 8am–5pm; ☎915/534-0653 or 1-800/351-6024), at 5 Civic Center Plaza in the Convention Center complex.

## Accommodation

Prices in El Paso tend to be reasonable and there's a good range of choices from hostels, functional old downtown hotels and swanky joints as well as the usual chain motels along the interstate.

**Camino Real Hotel**, 101 S El Paso St (☎915/534-3000). El Paso's luxury option. If you can't stay here at least visit its swanky Southwestern restaurant or the wonderfully romantic bar, topped with a colorful Tiffany dome and surrounded by rose and black marble. ⑥.

**Gardner Hotel & Hostel**, 311 E Franklin St (☎915/532-3661). Atmospheric hotel where John Dillinger bedded down in the 1920s. The hostel costs $13 for members and an extra three bucks for nonmembers. Rooms vary from singles with shared bath to clean en-suite doubles. ①/②.

**Sunset Heights B&B Inn**, 717 W Yandell Drive (☎915/544-1743). Welcoming Victorian B&B, a few minutes from downtown, that serves excellent multi-course breakfasts. ⑤.

**Travelodge City Center**, 409 E Missouri Ave (☎915/554-3333). Large, downtown motel rooms and there's a passable Mexican restaurant on the premises. ③.

## The Town

**Downtown** El Paso holds surprisingly little to see apart from a couple of worthy art and Americana museums; what character it has continues to be shaped by the **US–Mexico border**. In times past outlaws and exiles from either side of the border would take refuge across the river, and today's traffic remains considerable and not entirely uncontroversial. Manual workers come north to find undocumented jobs, and US companies secretly dump their toxic waste on the south side. The border itself, the Rio Grande, has caused its share of disagreements: the river changed course quite often in the 1800s, and it was not until the 1960s, when it was run through a concrete channel, that it was made permanent. An attractive park, the **Chamizal National Memorial** (daily 8am–5pm; free), on the east side of downtown off Paisano Drive, was built to commemmorate the settling of the border dispute and provides a pleasant place to picnic. The **Border Patrol Museum**, 4315 Transmountain Road (Mon–Fri 9am–5pm; free), is a small but engrossing museum explaining the work of the border patrollers and highlights the ingenuity of smugglers. The **Cordova Bridge** heads across the river into Mexico, where there's a larger park and a number of museums; there are no formalities, so long as you have a multiple-entry visa for the US and don't travel more than twenty or so miles south of the border. A **trolley** departs hourly across the border from the visitor center, although at $10 for a round-trip (unlimited stops, mostly at dispiriting new malls) it's no bargain.

Although El Paso is predominantly Hispanic, there is also a substantial population of **Tigua Indians**, a displaced Pueblo tribe, based in a reservation (complete with the almost statutory **casino**) on Socorro Road, southeast of downtown. The reservation's arts and crafts center is open to the public, selling pottery and textiles and hosting occasional festivals. Adjacent to the reservation, the simple **Ysleta del Sur**, the oldest mission in the United States, marks the beginning of a **mission trail** (information office ☎915/534-0677) running alongside scruffy cotton, alfalfa, chili, onion and pecan fields. Two miles east, the **Socorro mission**, moved from its original seventeenth-century site on the river, shows an unusually heavy Native American influence; the crenelation on either side of the bell tower represents a Tigua rain god. Still an active church, inside it is relatively unadorned, with hand-carved ceiling beams and lattices. Off the beaten track, six miles further along the trail, the cathedral-style **San Elizario** was the chapel for the Spanish military, with whitewashed walls, jewel-colored stained glass and a decorative tin ceiling. Splendid views of three states and two nations, especially dazzling at night, can be had from the **scenic drive** along the southern rim of the Franklin Mountains.

In **Concordia cemetery**, just northwest of the I-10 and Hwy-54 intersection, a shambling collection of crumbling stones and plain wooden crosses commemorate assorted pioneers and desperados. The grave of **John Wesley Hardin**, much romanticized gunslinger, is marked by a crooked headstone northwest of the Chinese graveyard, a section walled off since the Chinese built the railroads in the 1880s. El Paso is also the home of Tony Lama, makers of top-quality **cowboy boots**, available at substantial discounts at five outlets across town.

## Dining and Nightlife

**Dining** is understandably dominated by Mexican cuisine. **After dark**, El Paso offers an uninspiring mix of clubs and bars. The *Camino Real Hotel*'s beautiful *Dome Bar* offers a pleasant drinking atmosphere, or head across the border to **Ciudad Juarez**: the Hemingwayesque *Kentucky Club Cantina*, 629 Av Juarez, just south of the Santa Fe Street bridge, and the more touristy *Chihuahua Charlie's*, 2525 Triunfo de la Republica, near the Plaza de Toros Monumental (the main bullfight arena), are both tried and tested haunts. The latter is more comfortable for women travelers.

**Avila's Mexican Food**, 10600 Montana at Yarborough (☎915/598-3333). The Avila family have been running restaurants in El Paso for fifty years and it shows with their classic Tex-Mex dishes at this eastside location. They also have a place on the westside at 6232 N Mesa (☎915/584-3621).

**Azulejos**, *Camino Real Hotel*, 101 S El Paso St (☎915/534-3000). Without doubt the most pleasant dining space in the city though the prices of the Tex-Mex and regional fare do reflect the location.

**Cattleman's Steakhouse**, Indian Cliffs Ranch, Fabens, TX (☎915/544-3200). A regional legend about 25 miles east of El Paso, serving superb food – plus you can wander around the ranch. To get here take I-10 east to exit 49, turn right and drive a further five miles.

**H&H Coffee Shop & Car Wash**, 701 E Yandell Drive (☎915/533-1144). These adjacent businesses just off downtown work well together especially in the morning when wicked huevos rancheros are served.

**Tigua**, 9430 Socorro Rd (☎915/859-5287). Popular lunch and dinner spot on the Tigua reservation, which as well as serving Indian breads nods to both American and Mexican cultures with burgers and menudo (a chili-laden stew made from tripe and other goodies).

## Guadalupe Mountains National Park

Roughly one hundred miles east of El Paso, Hwy-62/180 climbs towards Carlsbad Caverns along the southern fringes of the **GUADALUPE MOUNTAINS**, once a stronghold of the Mescalero Apache. The national park (headquarters ☎915/828-3251) here is very much a hiking and camping destination, barely penetrated by road and without accommodation, food or even gas. It's possible to hike right to the top of Guadalupe Peak, at 8749ft the highest point in Texas, but most walkers head instead for the painlessly flat seven-mile trek through **McKittrick Canyon**, passing from bare desert into lush mountain forests beside sheer canyon walls.

# CHAPTER TEN

# THE GREAT PLAINS

T HE **GREAT PLAINS**, stretching west of the Mississippi through **OKLA-HOMA, MISSOURI, KANSAS, IOWA, NEBRASKA** and **SOUTH** and **NORTH DAKOTA**, are lumped together in the popular imagination as an unappealing expanse of unvarying flatness and conservative "Middle American" values, a huge national joke to be passed through as fast as possible. Once, however, this was the **West**, a vast empty canvas on which outlaws, fur trappers, buffalo hunters and cowboys painted their dreams. In the 1870s, the wide open range of the lone prairie, which had originally been known as the **Great American Desert** but was now promoted as a bountiful Garden of Eden, inspired such fascination that General Custer was moved to call it "the fairest and richest portion of the national domain." As well as the main routes west (the Oregon and Santa Fe trails through Missouri, Kansas and Nebraska), the plains were crisscrossed by the Pony Express, cattle trails and railroads. Today the massive Gateway Arch in **St Louis** celebrates the traders, explorers and pioneers who followed their destinies further and further west.

Early maps show the "Desert" as uninterrupted by towns or roads; even today there are fewer towns, spaced further apart, on the plains than anywhere else in the nation, and the population has steadily dropped since the 1930s. One sinister note echoes through this openness and emptiness: most of the nation's **nuclear missiles** – marked by unprepossessing concrete blocks fenced into empty fields – sit beneath a land already ravaged by greed.

The plains, today so apparently uneventful, share a troubled history. The systematic destruction by white settlers of the awesome herds of **bison** presaged the virtual eradication of the **Plains Indians**. Reservations, agencies and "assigned lands" dwindled as the natural resources of the area attracted white settlement; after 1874, when **gold** was discovered in the Black Hills, the fate of the Native Americans was practically sealed. However, thanks to warriors like **Crazy Horse** and **Sitting Bull**, the struggle for control of the plains was by no means as easy as the Hollywood Westerns imply. Today the region is ambivalent about this history: many of its museums and monuments to Native Americans seem almost like a veiled celebration of the destruction of their culture.

The plains are more comfortable playing **cowboys**, glorying in a romantic myth of the Wild West and flaunting sanitized versions of wicked old cowtowns like **Deadwood** in South Dakota, **Dodge City** (once called the "Beautiful, Bibulous Babylon of the Frontier") in Kansas, and **St Joseph**, Missouri, the birthplace of the Pony Express. **Calamity Jane, Wild Bill Hickok, Billy the Kid** and **Annie Oakley** all left their mark

## ACCOMMODATION PRICE CODES

All accommodation prices in this book have been coded using the symbols below. Note that prices are for the least expensive double rooms in each establishment. For a full explanation see p.37 in Basics.

| | | |
|---|---|---|
| ① up to $30 | ④ $60–80 | ⑦ $130–175 |
| ② $30–45 | ⑤ $80–100 | ⑧ $175–250 |
| ③ $45–60 | ⑥ $100–130 | ⑨ $250+ |

here when this was the wild frontier, and today, in the sandy scrublands of northern Nebraska and North Dakota, you can still see real cowboy and cattle country.

After Reconstruction, Southern blacks came here in search of an egalitarian future, and black colonies sprang up all around the region. The dreams soon died, though, and there are few black faces to be seen nowadays. There is, however, more evidence of nineteenth-century **Russian** and **German** settlement: many of the oldest families on the plains are descendants of European Mennonites who escaped religious persecution in the 1870s, bringing with them new farming methods that heralded the region's great agricultural prosperity. The Great Plains still provide the nation with much of its food and export two-thirds of the world's **wheat**, seas of which wave over the flat fields of Iowa, Nebraska and Kansas. The economy has also long been dependent on **oil**, especially in Oklahoma, and **gold** in the Dakotas.

Defining the geographical limits of the plains is difficult, and the term itself is almost a misnomer – there are vast flat expanses and long uninterrupted roads, but there are also canyons, forests, and splashes of unexpected color, as well as two of the nation's mightiest rivers: the **Missouri**, which weaves its course southeast from North Dakota, and the **Mississippi**, which it joins at St Louis. Since the 1950s, the siphoning of the underground Ogallala aquifer from Nebraska to Oklahoma has transformed much that was once dusty desert into verdant fields; the consequences of overuse (ensuring the depletion of the reservoir in another fifty years) remain to be seen.

The woods, caves and springs of the **Ozarks**, the lunar landscapes of South Dakota's **Badlands**, and stately **Mount Rushmore** are the region's most visited areas. Otherwise, there are few immediate attractions, and only St Louis stands out as an urban destination. Drama comes instead in the form of such unpredictable **weather** as freak blizzards, dust storms, lightning storms and the notorious "twister" tornadoes. Images of the devastating Thirties' dustbowl Depression (when topsoil was whisked as far away as Washington DC) remain as potent as the fantasy of Dorothy and Toto being swept up from Kansas by a tornado to the land of Oz, while **flooding** is a constant threat – huge swaths of Iowa and Missouri were swamped in 1993.

A **car** is practically obligatory in the plains, where distances are long, roads straight and seemingly endless, and the population sparse. The main routes (I-94, I-90, I-80, I-70, I-40) cross from east to west, making it frustratingly difficult to travel north–south. Greyhound **buses** travel the interstates, but often bypass the small towns that provide a real sense of the region. Subsidiary bus lines include Jack Rabbit in South Dakota, and the Jefferson Line, which covers Iowa, Kansas, Missouri and Oklahoma. True to their image as a crossroads rather than a destination, the plains are crossed by Amtrak **trains** almost exclusively at night, with South Dakota not covered at all. St Louis, Missouri, has the major **airport**, while Wichita, Kansas, is a regional hub.

# OKLAHOMA

Ridiculed by the rest of the nation as boring, and forever the butt of jokes at the expense of the "Okies," **OKLAHOMA** has had a traumatic and far from dull history. In the 1830s all this land, held to be useless, was set aside as **Indian Territory**; a convenient dumping ground for the so-called Five Civilized Tribes who blocked white settlement in the southern states. The Choctaw and Chickasaw of Mississippi, the Seminole of Florida, and the Creek of Alabama were each assigned a share, while the rest (though already inhabited by indigenous Indians) was given to the Cherokee from Carolina, Tennessee and Georgia, who followed in 1838 on the four-month trek notorious as "the Trail of Tears" (see p.511). Today the state has a large Native American population – *oklahoma* is the Choctaw word for "red man" – and even the smallest towns tend to have museums of Native American history.

Once white settlers realized that Indian Territory was, in fact, well worth farming, they decided to stay. The Indians were relocated once more, and in a manic free-for-all scramble in 1889, entire towns sprang up literally overnight. Those who jumped the gun and claimed land illegally were known as Sooners; hence Oklahoma's nickname, the **Sooner State**. White settlers didn't have an easy life, however, facing, after great oil prosperity in the 1920s, an era of unthinkable hardship in the 1930s. The desperate migration, when whole communities fled the dust bowl for California, has come to encapsulate the worst horrors of the Depression, most famously in John Steinbeck's novel (and John Ford's film) **The Grapes of Wrath**, but also in Dorothea Lange's haunting photos of itinerant families, hitching and camping on the road, and in the sad yet hopeful songs of Woody Guthrie. After the slump of the early Thirties, the region is now facing another crisis, and its major downtown areas are uncannily still.

Oklahoma is not the flat and unchanging expanse of popular imagination. Most of its places of interest, such as attractive **Tulsa**, lie in the hilly wooded northeast; only the sparse and treeless west is devoid of appeal, on the far side of the central "tornado alley" prairie grassland which holds the state's revitalized capital, **Oklahoma City**. The lakes and parks of the south, which bears more than a passing resemblance to neighboring Arkansas (complete with mountains, foliage and bluegrass music), have made tourism Oklahoma's second industry after oil.

### Getting around Oklahoma
**Car** travel is the only way to explore Oklahoma. Amtrak serves Oklahoma City with two trains a day from Fort Worth, Texas. Greyhound **buses** speed along I-35 and I-40, which converge on Oklahoma City, but public transportation within the towns is minimal. Tulsa and Oklahoma City have **airports**. **Route 66**, which passes through both cities on its way from Missouri to Texas, is no longer a national highway, but if you have plenty of time (and sturdy tires; much of the road is in a bad way), makes a nostalgic alternative to the interstates. A booklet is available at the Tulsa CVB detailing the small communities and ghost towns on the way.

# Eastern Oklahoma

**Eastern Oklahoma** includes the "Green Country" of the northeast, patterned with the foothills of the Ozarks, and woods, streams, lakes and rivers that make it a popular camping destination. Art Deco Tulsa is its cultural center; Tahlequah and Pawhuska are the capitals of the Cherokee and Osage nations respectively.

# Tulsa

**TULSA** is a good-looking city, thanks in part to the striking Art Deco architecture that dates from its Twenties heyday as an immensely wealthy oil town. Despite – or possibly because of – its pleasant atmosphere, two excellent museums, and thriving art scene, the city tends towards complacency. In addition, the overriding Bible Belt mentality is hard to ignore; even in the hip *Tulsa Press* a regular feature reviews local churches, whimsically entitled "Pew View."

### Arrival, information and getting around
**Tulsa International Airport** (☎918/838-5000) lies a few minutes by cab ($12) east of downtown. Hwy-169 from Kansas City skirts its eastside; I-244, which gives access from the south, is also the main route east–west across town. Greyhound comes in downtown at 317 S Detroit Ave. The **CVB**, 616 S Boston Ave (Mon–Fri 8am–5pm; ☎918/585-

1201 or 1-800/558-3311), provides a self-guided walking tour of downtown – such as it is – as well as local **bus** schedules; services operate between 5am and 8.30pm, with no Sunday service (75¢, transfers 5¢).

## Accommodation

Most of Tulsa's **budget hotels** are on the interstates and along **East Skelly Drive**, forking southwest from I-44. There's **camping** at the *KOA*, 19605 E Skelly Drive (☎918/266-4227). For details of **B&Bs**, contact Ozark Mountain Country B&B, Box 295, Branson, MO 65726 (☎417/334-4720).

**Best Western Trade Winds East**, 3337 E Skelly Drive (☎918/743-7931). Comfortable rooms. ④.

**Executive Inn**, 416 W 6th St (☎918/584-4461). Central, reasonably salubrious motel. ③.

**Lexington Hotel Suites**, 8525 E 41st St (☎918/627-0030). Luxury doubles, with breakfast. ⑤.

**YMCA**, 515 S Denver Ave (☎918/583-6201). Men-only downtown accommodation. ①.

## The City

Downtown Tulsa's most obvious landmark is the ornate Art Deco **Union Depot**, on the First Street and Boston Avenue Overpass, built in the early Thirties and now housing offices. The **320 Boston Building** on Boston Avenue, known in the Twenties as the "Oil Bank of America," is worth a look for its huge brass doors, stone archways, gargoyles and hand-painted ceilings. Further along the other side of the road, another distinctive Twenties skyscraper, the **Philtower**, 527 S Boston Ave, has a green and red tiled sloping roof and crouching gargoyles, a lobby richly decorated in brass and marble, and a small gallery of Tulsa history. **Lyon's Indian Store**, an old trading post a few blocks east at 401 E 11th St, sells authentic goods made by over thirty Oklahoma tribes, including feather headdresses, bead work, rugs and jewelry. The huge and gloriously exuberant Art Deco **Boston Avenue Methodist Church**, 1301 S Boston Ave – at 255ft in height, it's practically cathedral-sized – offers good views of the city from its fourteenth story (free tours Mon–Fri 9am–4pm, Sun at 12.15pm).

Black life in Tulsa was traditionally centered around what is now the **Greenwood Historic District**, a small section of narrow streets north of downtown. In 1921, a brutal race riot erupted outside the city courthouse after a black man was accused of assaulting a white woman in a downtown elevator. The commotion spread to Greenwood, and houses, businesses and churches were burnt to the ground. Other properties fell victim to urban renewal in the mid-1960s, but community leaders managed to save a small grouping of buildings along Greenwood Avenue and Archer Street. The **Greenwood Cultural Center**, at 322 N Greenwood Ave (Mon–Fri 9am–5pm; free), houses the **Goodwin-Chappelle Gallery**, a photographic portrait of the neighborhood's history, and the **Oklahoma Jazz Hall of Fame**, a fascinating tribute to jazz greats who were either residents of the state (Wardell Gray, Charlie Christian) or passed through on national tours (Cab Calloway, Dizzy Gillespie, Count Basie) to jam with local talent.

Outside downtown, to the south, the 75ft **Creek Council Oak**, 18th Street and Cheyenne Avenue, marks the spot where the Creek Indians ended their tortuous migration from Alabama in 1836, and founded Tulsa on the Arkansas River. The tree became a tribal meeting site, used ceremonially until 1896. The airy and stylish **Philbrook Museum of Art**, 2727 S Rockford Rd, in the house of oil man Waite Phillips in the well-heeled suburb of Mapleridge, is a Florentine-style mansion set in Gatsbyesque acres (Tues, Wed, Fri & Sat 10am–5pm, Thurs 10am–8pm, Sun 11am–5pm; tours Thurs, Sat & Sun; $4). Though displays include Native American pottery, African sculpture, Chinese jades and Renaissance paintings, the house itself is every bit as decorative as the art, with ostentatious marble floors, indoor fountains and sweeping staircases. The crumbling paths and pretty fountains of the gardens, which offer fantastic hill views, are also worth exploring.

Oral Roberts University, 7777 S Lewis Ave, is a must for kitsch obsessives. University, hospital and television station all in one, the concept was inspired by visionary Oral Roberts – who back in 1987 announced that God had decided to "call him home" unless he could raise $4.5 million before a certain deadline. Roberts retreated to a lonely vigil at the top of his **Prayer Tower**, a kind of B-movie space ship until he got his money, though his credibility was dented when the tower was struck by lightning at the moment of the deadline. You can now see a sycophantic exhibition, to the strains of a heavenly choir, on the great man's life (Mon–Sat 9am–5pm, Sun 1–5pm). There's an 80ft high pair of hands in prayer on the grass outside the **City of Faith Medical Center**, where a multimedia "journey through the Bible" (the first eight books of it) runs every twenty minutes (same hours).

The **Gilcrease Museum**, 1400 Gilcrease Museum Rd, just northwest of downtown, is set in the gently rolling **Osage Hills**, with a fine vista from the back and good view of downtown from the front. Thomas Gilcrease, of Indian heritage, grew very rich after oil was found on his land. His private collection of Western art includes Native American works, as well as excellent Remingtons, Russells and Morans (Tues, Wed, Fri & Sat 9am–5pm, Thurs 9am–8pm, Sun 1–5pm; in summer also Mon 9am–5pm; free tours daily at 2pm; $3 donation).

To experience Tulsa's cowboy history, make for the **Ted Allen Ranch**, seven miles west along 181st Street at 19600 S Memorial Drive, Bixby. This working horse ranch opens daily at 9am; activities include riding, overnight campouts, moonlit hayrides and rodeos (☎918/366-3010; prices vary). From April to September there's a music show and chuckwagon supper (steak, beans, baked potato and coffee) every Friday and Saturday at 7.30pm. The band is good, with the fastest fiddle-playing and throatiest yodeling this side of Missouri, and Ted Allen's laconic humor makes it all great fun.

## Eating

Tulsa's **restaurants** are diverse and scattered; good options can be found along E 15th Street and S Peoria Avenue in the fashionable **Brookside** district, while downtown holds several down-home diners.

**The Bistro At Brookside**, 3523 S Peoria Ave (☎918/749-7737). Inventive dishes and an extensive wine list in trendy Brookside. The Sunday brunches are well worth sampling.

**Bourbon Street Cafe**, 1542 E 15th St (☎918/583-5555). Extensive Cajun menu, featuring excellent $5 gumbos. Live jazz Thurs–Sun at 7pm.

**Camerelli's**, 1536 E 15th St (☎918/582-8900). Inexpensive but tasty Italian meats and pasta.

**Casa Bonita**, 2120 S Sheridan Rd (☎918/836-6464). Lively Mexican-themed restaurant, serving large spicy dinners in the atmosphere of your choice, from mysterious caves to rowdy Mexican villages.

**Metro Diner**, 3001 E 11th St (☎918/592-2616). Fifties-style diner east of downtown, serving good home-baked pies and chicken-fried steaks, as well as great ice cream sodas.

## Nightlife and entertainment

There is even less to do in **downtown** Tulsa after dark than during the day; 15th and Cherry streets just south, and S Peoria Avenue by the river, are much livelier. If you visit in September, try to catch the **Chilli Cookoff and Bluegrass Festival**, featuring spicy chili competitions, clogging and bluegrass gigs. Newssheets like the *Urban Tulsa Weekly*, *Tulsa World* and *Tulsa Press* (the "teepee") carry full nightlife listings.

**The Brink**, 3410 S Peoria Ave (☎918/742-4242). Hip live bands, and a youthful crowd.

**Club One**, 3200 S Riverside Drive (☎918/743-1665). R&B during the week, all-star blues jam Wed.

**Discoveryland**, 10 miles west on W 41st St (☎918/742-5255 or 1-800/338-6552). Outdoor performances of Rodgers and Hammerstein's *Oklahoma!* Mon–Sat, June–Aug; $15; pre-show barbecue 5.30pm, $8.

**Spotlight Theatre**, 1381 Riverside Drive (☎918/587-5030). This Art Deco building has been host-ing the melodrama *The Drunkard*, for the past forty years – accompanied by pretzels and sand-wiches, every Sat.

**Steamroller Blues Barbeque**, 18th and Boston (☎918/583-9520). Popular blues venue, with the best performances at weekends.

## Claremore

Thirty miles northeast of Tulsa on Route 66, **CLAREMORE**, the birthplace of **Will Rogers**, populist comedian, journalist and Twenties film star, is a shrine to a man being slowly forgotten as his films are no longer seen. His career began with a vaudeville show that included lassoing a horse and its rider, while giving a witty commentary, and he was renowned for his pithy and good-natured one-liners. Incredibly, when he died in a plane crash in 1935 there was a nationwide thirty-minute silence. One of his most famous declarations, "I never met a man I didn't like," is inscribed on his statue at the **Will Rogers Memorial**, 1720 Will Rogers Boulevard (daily 8am–5pm; free), which dis-plays his possessions, such as his "gag book," together with stills and clips from his films.

## Bartlesville

For forty miles north of Tulsa, the monotony of the plains is relieved only by clumps of spindly scrub oaks. Then comes quiet **BARTLESVILLE**, dominated by the extraordi-nary **Price Tower**, designed by Frank Lloyd Wright in 1956 – an ugly, cantilevered green oddity at Sixth and Dewey, resembling a tall tree. The **Frank Phillips Home**, 1107 SE Cherokee Ave, built in 1908 by the founder of Phillips Oil, displays oil wealth at its gaudiest, with gold faucets, mirrored ceilings and marble floors (Wed–Sat 10am–5pm, Sun 1–5pm; donation). More impressive is his **Woolaroc Ranch**, thirteen miles southwest in the Blackjack Hills, now a wildlife refuge and museum of Western art and history. Over sixty thousand artifacts are scattered through seven huge rooms. Paintings and decorative art line the walls, from Native American works to the epic Western scenes of Remington and Russell, while artifacts belonging to various tribes, pioneers and cowboys are gathered in too great an abundance to take in. Look out for the 95-million-year-old dinosaur egg, exquisite Navajo blankets, scalps taken by Native Americans, and Buffalo Bill's weathered saddle (Memorial Day to Labor Day daily 10am–5pm; rest of year Tues–Sun 10am–5pm; $5).

For **lodging**, choose between the *Travelers Motel*, 3105 SE Frank Phillips Blvd (☎918/333-1900; ③), and the more upmarket *Hotel Phillips*, 821 S Johnstone Ave (☎918/336-5600 or 1-800/331-0706; ⑤).

## Tahlequah

Forty-five minutes' drive southeast from Tulsa on Hwy-51, **TAHLEQUAH** is the capi-tal of the **Cherokee** nation, formed in 1839 when the "Trail of Tears" finally reached its end. The sophisticated Cherokee had a written constitution, published the first news-paper in Indian Territory (in both Cherokee and English) and set up the Cherokee female seminary, the first higher education school for women west of the Mississippi. The seminary stands today on the campus of **Northeastern State University** on Hwy-82, which has more Native American students than any other academic institution in the US.

Tahlequah itself is uncommercialized, and the **Cherokee Heritage Center**, three miles south off US-68 at Tsa-La-Gi, presents Native American culture with more dignity than might be expected. Historical artifacts in the museum include wooden ceremoni-al masks, and a display covers the Cherokee alphabet (May–Sept Mon–Sat

10am–4.30pm, Sun noon–4.30pm; rest of year Mon–Fri 10am–4.30pm, closed Jan & Feb; $3). A reconstructed seventeenth-century Indian village gives arts and crafts demonstrations (May–Aug Mon–Sat 10am–4.30pm, Sun noon–4.30pm; $4).

In winter, the place is pretty much dead; in summer it's not a bad idea to take a **room** in the *Tahlequah Motor Lodge*, 2501 S Muskogee Ave (☎918/456-2350; ③), or the *Lodge of the Cherokees*, south on Hwy-62 (☎918/456-0511; ③). The *Restaurant of the Cherokees* (☎918/453-9349) specializes in traditional smoked dishes.

## Muskogee

The Creek Indians, relocated to **MUSKOGEE** in the 1830s, established the town as the central meeting place of the Civilized Tribes, fifty miles southeast of Tulsa; decades later in 1905, Native American leaders gathered here to draw up a plan for their own separate state, which was never to be. The arrival of the railroad in the 1870s and the discovery of oil in 1903 both guaranteed that the town would be usurped by white settlers. The **Five Civilized Tribes Museum**, Honor Heights Drive, Agency Hill, tells the Native Americans' story through costumes, documents, photographs and jewelry, along with a reconstructed trading post and a print room (Mon–Sat 10am–5pm, Sun 1–5pm; $2).

Muskogee is an appealing place, with a dozen **motels** within a few blocks along US-69, including a *Days Inn* at 900 S 32nd St (☎918/683-3911; ③). It also makes a good base for the crystal-clear **Lake Tenkiller**, thirty miles southeast on US-64. Surrounded by woods, cliffs and quiet beaches, the lake is perfect for fishing, boating, swimming and scuba-diving, and has camping facilities, but is (unsurprisingly) very touristy; call ☎918/457-4403 for full details.

# Oklahoma City and beyond

If you're heading west, your last stop in Oklahoma is likely to be the capital, **Oklahoma City**, smack in the center of the state. Beyond here, the Great Plains stretch in all their emptiness, the endless horizons broken only by small agricultural communities. The southwest of the state is the most densely populated, as it's crossed by the two main routes to Texas – I-40 west to Amarillo, and I-44 south to Wichita Falls; to the north, in the Oklahoman Panhandle, ranches and tiny hamlets are the only signs of life.

## Oklahoma City

**OKLAHOMA CITY** was created in a matter of hours on April 22, 1889, after a single gunshot signaled the opening of the land to white settlement. What was barren prairie at dawn was by nightfall a city of ten thousand. In 1911 the capital was moved here from nearby Guthrie, and in 1928 oil was discovered. Sitting on one of the nation's largest oilfields, the city was brought up short by the slump in the Eighties, but it remains the largest stocker and feeder cattle market in the world, and is revitalizing its economy by developing tourism, aided by five years of sales tax and the revamped **National Cowboy Hall of Fame**. The capital raised by the sales tax, which was voted in by the people of Oklahoma City, is funding nine separate projects designed to help designate the city as a tourist destination.

However, the devastating **bombing** of the Alfred P Murrah Federal Building on April 19, 1995, which killed 168 people, fifteen of them infants at a day-care center, literally tore the heart out of the city, and despite the community spirit of the rescue effort it may be a long time before Oklahoma City regains its self-confidence. In June 1997, ex-military recluse Timothy McVeigh was sentenced to death for the crime; his accomplice, Terry Nichols, received life in prison. These sentences did little to relieve the city's grief. A permanent landscaped memorial has been constructed at the site of the Murrah building; while The Journal Record Building next door is to be turned into the Museum and Institute for the Prevention of Terrorism.

### Arrival, information and getting around
**Will Rogers Memorial Airport**, 7100 Terminal Drive (☎405/680-5311), lies southwest of the city, within about fifteen minutes of the hotels and motels. Airport Shuttle (☎405/681-2331) runs downtown shuttles ($10). The **CVB** is downtown at 189 W Sheridan Ave (Mon–Fri 8.30am–5pm; ☎405/297-8912 or 1-800/225-5652), not far from Greyhound at no. 427; there's also a station at the airport. Amtrak comes in twice daily from Fort Worth at historic Sante Fe Station, on Sante Fe Street. The **post office** is at 320 SW Fifth St (Mon–Fri 6am–8pm, Sat 9am–noon; zip code 73125).

The public transportation system, such as it is, is based at 20 W Reno Ave (☎405/235-7433), just north of I-40 on the east edge of downtown. **Buses** run daily except Sunday from 6am until 6pm ($1). The Oklahoma Spirit Streetcars run from the hotel strip in the Meridian and the stockyards to downtown (Mon–Sat 9am–9pm, Sun 10am–6pm; 50¢). You can rent **bikes** from Miller's Cycling and Fitness Center, 3350 W Main St (☎405/360-3838).

### Accommodation
**Rooms** are very cheap; try along the interstates, especially I-35 S, for chain motels. B&Bs are a good deal, but even the downtown luxury hotels can be affordable.

**Best Western Saddleback Inn**, 4300 SW 3rd St (☎405/947-7000). Three blocks northeast of I-40, on the west side of town. Pseudo-Indian decor, but luxurious touches like poolside service. ④.

**Howard Johnson Lodge Airport**, 400 S Meridian Ave (☎405/943-9841). Good rooms, breakfast included. ③.

**Ramada Inn Airport South**, 6800 I-35 S (☎405/631-3321). Functional accommodation directly east of the airport. ④.

**Travelers Inn**, 504 S Meridian Ave (☎405/942-8294 or 1-800/633-8300). Comfortable, inexpensive option not far south of downtown. ④.

**YMCA**, 501 Couch Drive (☎405/297-7700). Single, men-only rooms in a safe part of downtown. ①.

### The City
Urban renewal in Oklahoma City's **downtown** is based around the renovated warehouses of **Bricktown**, on Sheridan Avenue east of the Santa Fe Railroad, which is developing into a reasonable eating and nightlife center. The city's skyscrapers are low-key and old-fashioned, and there is no real sense of commercial activity; even in the middle of the day it can be depressingly quiet. **Myriad Gardens** on Sheridan Avenue, prettily landscaped with hills, gardens and waterways, gives great views across to the brick-towered downtown skyline, and on a sunny day the **Crystal Bridge** tropical botanical garden, in a glass tube in the middle of the park, abounds in garish exotic blooms (daily 9am–6pm; $4).

As well as a couple of historical museums, the **Capitol Complex**, just north of downtown, includes the unprepossessing **capitol** (free tours daily 9am–3pm), which may lack the usual dome but has a working oil well in its grounds. The **Heritage Hills** area nearby, where the cattle barons, oil millionaires and bankers used to live, is now run-down and seedy in parts, with many buildings abandoned. Of the two of its mansions open to the public, the Victorian-style **Overholser Mansion**, 405 NW 15th St (Tues–Fri 10am–4pm, Sat & Sun 2–4pm; free hourly tours), is to be preferred to the **Oklahoma Heritage Center**, 201 NW 14th St (Mon–Sat 9am–5pm, Sun 1–5pm; $3), if only because the latter holds the unrelentingly tedious "Oklahoma Hall of Fame" portrait gallery.

Two much quirkier attractions lie in the northeast of the city. **Enterprise Square USA**, on the campus of Oklahoma Christian University several miles out at 2501 E Memorial Rd, between I-35 and Eastern Avenue, is an outrageous barrage of propaganda on the glories of free enterprise – and a hallucinogenic nightmare to boot. Giant consumer products loom above your head, the George Washingtons on huge dollar bills sing the national anthem with eyes rolling and heads bobbing, and a crazed "government" computer becomes more and more manic until threatening to self-destruct (moral – don't let government interference obstruct freedom of choice). Complicated computer games gauge how successful you are in different "careers," and fragile egos should beware: it's a blow to go bankrupt setting up your gardening business when the eight-year-old on the next computer is happily balancing the economy (Wed–Sat 9am–5pm; open 2hr after last admission; $4).

The **National Cowboy Hall of Fame**, ten minutes' walk south of Enterprise Square USA at 1700 NE 63rd St, is a real treat (June–Aug daily 8.30am–6pm; Sept–May daily 9am–5pm; $6.50). Sitting atop Persimmon Hill overlooking Route 66, it combines "high art" and popular art in one loving collection. In the works of Remington and Russell – rugged landscapes, stoical cowboys with horses or in comradely groups – the link between Western art and Western movies is very clear. The paintings look like film stills, and titles such as *Waiting for Trouble* evoke the cinema's endlessly reworked myths of the West. Large exhibitions focus on contemporary Native American work, much of it colorful, bitter and subversive. John Wayne's collection is a delight for the cowboy fetishist, and the Western Performers Hall of Fame pays homage to movie cowboys and gals in hilariously reverent oil paintings and memorabilia. The poignant *End of the Trail* sculpture, 18ft high, portrays an Indian slumped exhausted – or dead – over his horse. You can also venture into Prosperity Town, a real Western town right down to hoof marks in the road, the American Rodeo Gallery, and the American Cowboy Gallery, all recent additions to the museum. In the garden, dotted with horse graves, corny epigraphs give the much-loved deceased beasts a fitting send-off to "Hoss Heaven."

Oklahoma City's **stockyards**, on Agnew Avenue and Exchange Street, are the busiest in the world, having sold over one hundred million cattle since 1910. They're well worth a visit, though vegetarians and animal-lovers should steer clear. This is the real thing, stomping, snorting and smelly, with scrawny animals shunted in and out of tiny pens for auction. The roughnecks that spend their lives here, smoking, chatting, even sleeping, take no apparent notice of the quick-fire auctioneer, but nonetheless millions of head of cattle are bought and sold each year, and it can make for addictive entertainment. Sales begin at 8am Monday to Wednesday, and fizzle out by late afternoon.

## Eating

**Beef** is, of course, good in Oklahoma City, especially around the stockyards. The warehouse restaurants of **Bricktown** are popular with the after-work and singles crowd.

**Applewoods**, 4301 SW 3rd St (☎405/947-8484). Famed in the city for its good steaks and all-you-can-eat apple fritters; they're greasy and rich, but fill you up. Closed Sat lunchtime.

**The Cattleman's Steakhouse**, 1309 S Agnew Ave (☎405/236-0416). Cattlemen from the adjacent stockyards eat in this comfortable, pub-like restaurant, which has served great steaks since 1910. (It was allegedly won in a craps game.) Lunchtime specials are a good deal.

**Sonic Drive-in**, locations everywhere, waitresses on roller skates serve up burgers and fries. Cheap and fast.

**The Spaghetti Warehouse**, 101 E Sheridan Ave (☎405/235-0402). Good-value Bricktown place (20 meals under $7), proving that there's more to Oklahoma City dining than steaks.

## Nightlife and entertainment

Oklahoma City can be pretty dodgy at night, especially in the isolated downtown – and it's a long way from the cutting edge as regards live music or dancing, although the revitalization efforts of Bricktown is hoping to fix that. For the time being, the *Black Liberated Arts Center* (☎405/424-2552) puts on a full winter season downtown at the Civic Center Music Hall on Couch Drive, otherwise you might to choose to head for the campus nightlife of **Norman**, a thirty-minute drive south, which is home to the University of Oklahoma. Wednesday's *Oklahoma Gazette*, along with lively articles, carries good listings.

**Bricktown Brewery**, 1 Oklahoma Ave (☎405/232-BREW). Large brewpub, with giant tanks of beer on show in its restaurant and live jazz most nights.

**Bricktown Jokers**, 239 E Sheridan Ave (☎405/236-5653). Live comedy performances in Bricktown; Tues–Sun 8pm, also Fri & Sat 10.30pm.

**In Cahoots**, 2301 S Meridian Ave (☎405/686-1191). Popular dance hall and saloon with nightly live music ranging from country to indie. Quite a way south of downtown.

**Oklahoma Opry**, 404 W Commerce Ave (☎405/232-8322). Authentic country shows, Sat 8pm. $6.

## Guthrie

**GUTHRIE**, thirty miles north of downtown Oklahoma City on I-35, was the capital from statehood in 1907 until 1911. Today the 1400-acre **Guthrie Historical District** forms a remarkably complete collection of restored Victorian architecture. The **State Capitol Publishing Museum**, 301 W Harrison Ave (Tues–Fri 9am–5pm, Sat 10am–4pm, Sun 1–4pm; donation), exhibits printing technology from the earliest newspaper printed in Oklahoma Territory, and the ornate Doric **Scottish Rite Masonic Temple**, 900 E Oklahoma Ave, is the largest Masonic complex in the world, featuring hundreds of bright stained-glass windows (tours Mon–Fri 10am & 2pm, Sat 10am; $5). Guthrie is also home to the **Lazy E Arena**, four miles east of downtown, a huge site which hosts world champion rodeos and roping competitions, as well as big-name concerts (☎405/282-3004).

Guthrie has two good **B&Bs** – the *Haunted Stone Lion Inn*, 1016 W Warner Ave (☎405/282-0012; ④), and *Harrison House*, 124 W Harrison Ave (☎405/282-1000 or 1-800/375-1001; ⑤), in Guthrie's first bank building. The **visitor center** is at 212 W Oklahoma Ave (☎405/282-1947 or 1-800/299-1889).

# MISSOURI

The state of **MISSOURI**, where the forest meets the prairie and the Mississippi River meets the Missouri River, has just two significant cities. Dominant **St Louis** sits midway down its eastern fringe; **Kansas City** is almost directly across on the western border. The pair are linked by I-70, but there's not much in between to warrant stopping off. In contrast, the **south** features the beautiful hillsides, streams and ragged lakes of the **Ozark Mountains**, as well as the booming country-and-western town of **Branson**, while in the **east**, small river towns such as Mark Twain's **Hannibal** and serene **Ste Genevieve** brighten the course of the Mississippi. The **northwest**, home of the Pony Express and outlaw Jesse James, still strikes up images of frontier times.

Although the first French colonists honored the claims of local Native Americans, such as the original Missouri, when the area was sold to the US in 1803 as part of the Louisiana Purchase, the Indians were driven west by a great rush of settlers. In the 1840s and 1850s immigrants from Germany and Ireland flooded into eastern Missouri. Outnumbering their pro-slavery predecessors, they swung the balance in favor of staying in the Union during the Civil War. However, Confederate guerrilla forces attracted considerable support among slave-owners in the west of the state. Meanwhile Missouri, and St Louis in particular, was establishing itself as an important gateway to the West. Today, the "**Show Me State**" (so called because of the supposed scepticism of the typical Missourian) retains a conservative air, particularly in the rural areas.

### Getting around Missouri

The central corridor between Missouri's two main cities, St Louis and Kansas City, is well served by **Greyhound**; the journey takes around six hours. Chicago and Memphis are both five hours from St Louis. Infrequent Greyhound buses run through the southeast, to Springfield and a few Ozark towns, but you'll need a car to see the mountains and the river towns in the north. St Louis (TWA's main hub) and Kansas City have major **airports**. Daily Amtrak **trains** between Chicago and LA call at St Louis, KC and assorted small towns; and two more daily Chicago trains terminate in St Louis, and one continues to Houston. Both KC and St Louis are on the daily route to New Orleans.

# Eastern Missouri

The Mississippi defines Missouri's eastern border, absorbing as major tributaries the Missouri, Ohio, Illinois and Des Moines rivers. Innumerable towns sprang up along the river, their aspirations reflected by such classical names as Alexandria, Antioch and Athens. **Hannibal**, the boyhood home of Mark Twain, is the largest in the northeast, while Gallic **Ste Genevieve** is the prettiest in the south. All have, however, decreased in size with the growing pre-eminence of **St Louis**. Away from the river, the land rises to the Ozark Plateau, whose deep green valleys are cut by swift, clear streams.

## Hannibal

**HANNIBAL** might well have been just another medium-sized river settlement, had not Samuel Langhorne Clemens, who renamed himself **Mark Twain** after the cry of pilots on the Mississippi, spent his boyhood here. Although Hannibal does have other industries, downtown is little more than a Twain theme park, with attractions such as museums, donkey rides and wax displays. Businesses include the *Clemens Hotel*, *Tom'n'Huck Motel*, *Injun Joe Campground* and even the Mark Twain Roofing Company.

Mark Twain wrote surprisingly little about his home town in his extensive non-fiction works; you could say he spoke with his feet when he left for good at seventeen to become a journeyman printer, riverboat pilot, journalist and writer. However, those of his books most specifically set in Hannibal – *The Adventures of Tom Sawyer*, and the sequel *The Adventures of Huckleberry Finn* – provide vivid accounts of growing up in the rowdy frontier riverport he renamed St Petersburg.

### The Town

Hannibal is almost disturbingly picturesque. Squeezed between two steep bluffs – Tom Sawyer's "**Cardiff Hill**" to the north and **Lover's Leap** to the south – the once-busy riverside is now largely quiet except for the occasional creaking of a crane loading grain or cement. Twain's youthful stomping ground was the short, cobbled incline of **Hill Street**, at the north end of town. Adjoining the restored **Mark Twain Boyhood Home**, a simple white-clapboard house where Twain lived between 1844 and 1853, the **Mark Twain Museum** (summer daily 8am–6pm; rest of year times vary; $6) includes such memorabilia as first editions, letters, photos, original artwork and one of his trademark white coats. Immediately opposite, there's a bookstore in the original home of Laura Hawkins (the model for Tom Sawyer's first love, Becky Thatcher), who visited Twain in Connecticut in 1908 and lived on in Hannibal until 1928. Nearby stands the law office of Twain's father, a JP who died of pneumonia while the writer was still a boy. Antique, souvenir and gift stores stretch away from here down **Main Street**, where the **New Mark Twain Museum** opened in 1995. Included in the admission price to the original museum and home, these exhibits detail the architectural and economic history of Hannibal, but more interesting are the fifteen original Norman Rockwell paintings commissioned for limited editions of Twain's most popular titles.

South of Hannibal, Hwy-79 towards St Louis offers one of the most **scenic drives** along the Mississippi, continually broken by thin, elongated, thickly wooded islands and bounded by towering limestone bluffs.

### Practicalities
Pick up full details on Hannibal from the **visitor center** at 505 N Third St (April–Oct daily 8am–6pm; Nov–March daily 8am–5pm; ☎573/221-2477). **Motel** rates vary wildly according to season. The very central *Best Western Hotel Clemens*, 401 N Third St (☎573/248-1150; ⑤), with a pool, is pretty good value, while the *Econolodge*, 612 Mark Twain Ave (☎573/221-1490; ③), on the edge of downtown, is more basic. *Lula Belle's*, 111 Bird St (☎573/221-6662 or 1-800/882-4890; ④–⑥), has B&B rooms of varying degrees of luxury, including some with river views, and serves good **food**, while the *Mark Twain Dinette & Family Restaurant*, just up from the museum at 400 N Third St (☎573/221-5300), offers Tom Sawyer burgers and Huck Finn shakes. You can **camp** at the shaded *Mark Twain Campground* (☎573/221-1656 or 1-800/527-0304; $18 for RVs, $14 for tents), a mile south of town on Hwy-79, near the **caves** made famous in *Tom Sawyer*.

# St Louis

Perched just below the confluence of the Mississippi and Missouri rivers, three hundred miles south of Chicago and north of Memphis, cosmopolitan **ST LOUIS** (pronounced, whatever any song might say, as *Lewis*) owes its vaguely European air to its history and developed cultural infrastructure. Any city capable of producing two of the twentieth century's greatest poets – T S Eliot and Chuck Berry – must have a lot going for it.

St Louis was founded in 1764 by the French fur trader **Pierre Laclede**, but the American immigration that followed its sale to the US under the Louisiana Purchase all but extinguished the refinement it had gained during French and Spanish rule. It subsequently became crucial as the major gateway for pioneers on the wagon trails westward. Transportation – first steamboats, then trains and now air haulage – has long been the basis of its considerable industrial strength. However, St Louis has not always had an easy ride. Downtown reached a nadir during the Seventies, but the years since then have seen a remarkable turnaround, with attractions on the revitalized **riverfront** including the magnificent **Gateway Arch** and the restored warehouses of **Laclede's Landing**.

Try not to leave without sampling the **suburbs**. To the west lie arty **Central West End** and studenty **University** (or "U") **City**, on either side of prodigious **Forest Park** with its museums and playing fields. The blue-collar **southside** features the markets, antique shops and jazz pubs of **Soulard** and the Italian shops and cafes of **the Hill**. Directly across the river in Illinois, **East St Louis**, once the stomping ground of jazz stars like Miles Davis and John Coltrane, has very little to offer visitors.

### Arrival, information and getting around
**Lambert-St Louis International Airport** (☎314/426-8000) is a dozen miles northwest of downtown – $25 by taxi or $3 by bus or Metro Link. Some Greyhound **buses**

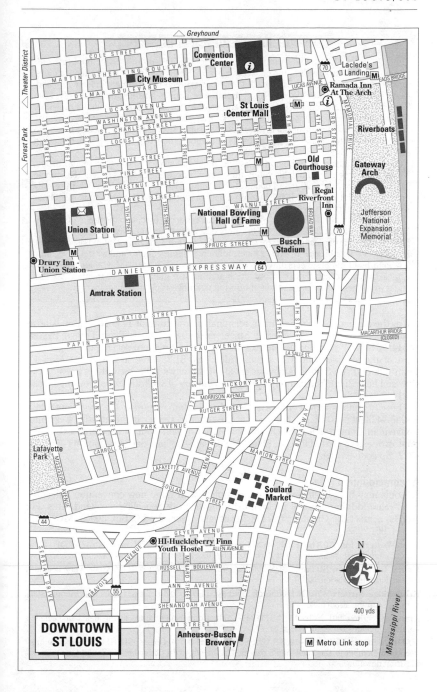

△ Greyhound

△ Theater District
△ Forest Park

COLE STREET
MARTIN LUTHER KING BOULEVARD
**City Museum**
DELMAR BOULEVARD
LUCAS AVENUE
WASHINGTON AVENUE
ST CHARLES STREET
LOCUST STREET
OLIVE STREET
PINE STREET
CHESTNUT STREET
MARKET STREET

**Convention Center** ⓘ
LUCAS AVENUE
**Ramada Inn At The Arch** ⓘ

**St Louis Center Mall**

**Old Courthouse**

Laclede's Landing Ⓜ
EADS BRIDGE

**Riverboats**

**Gateway Arch**

Jefferson National Expansion Memorial

**Union Station**
CLARK STREET
Ⓜ
**Drury Inn - Union Station**

**National Bowling Hall of Fame**
WALNUT STREET
Ⓜ
SPRUCE STREET

**Regal Riverfront Inn**
BROADWAY

**Busch Stadium**

DANIEL BOONE EXPRESSWAY 64

**Amtrak Station**

GRATIOT STREET
PAPIN STREET
CHOUTEAU AVENUE
HICKORY STREET
MORRISON AVENUE
RUTGER STREET
PARK AVENUE

MACARTHUR BRIDGE (CLOSED)

LA SALLE ST

Lafayette Park

CARROLL ST
LAFAYETTE AVENUE
SOULARD
MARION STREET

**Soulard Market**

44

**HI-Huckleberry Finn Youth Hostel**
GEYER AVENUE
ALLEN AVENUE
RUSSELL BOULEVARD
ANN AVENUE
SHENANDOAH AVENUE
LAMI STREET

SERBIAN DRIVE
GRAVOIS
55

N

**DOWNTOWN ST LOUIS**

**Anheuser-Busch Brewery**

0          400 yds

Ⓜ Metro Link stop

*Mississippi River*

---

### THE POETS OF ST LOUIS

Thomas Stearns Eliot, who as a naturalized Englishman won the 1948 Nobel Prize for Literature, was born in St Louis on September 26, 1888. His family were Unitarian aristocrats who traced their ancestry back to the earliest days of settlement in New England; his grandfather, the Rev William Eliot, founded St Louis's Washington University. Eliot lived in the city until he was seventeen, and went to school at Smith Academy on Union Avenue, a period which he later referred to as one of the happiest of his life. The "Prufrock" of his first major poem, *The Love Song of J Alfred Prufrock*, was a St Louis furniture dealer; "the yellow fog that rubs its back upon the window-panes" was the smog drifting across the Mississippi from the city's factories.

Once Eliot had moved to Boston, to attend Harvard University, and then on to Europe, he rarely returned, and he deliberately threw off his drawling St Louis accent. The house in which he was born, at 2635 Locust St, has long since been torn down, and the only memorial to him in the city is the incongruous brass star set into the sidewalk of Delmar Boulevard as part of the St Louis Walk of Fame.

Another honoree of the Walk of Fame, Chuck Berry, first saw the light of day on October 18, 1926, at 2520 Goode Ave – hence his most famous song, Johnny B Goode. Berry played his earliest gigs at the *Cosmopolitan Club* at 17th and Bond in East St Louis. Initially seen as a bizarre hybrid, a black hillbilly singing country-and-western, within a few months of his first recording for Chess Records in Chicago (Maybellene, in 1955) Chuck Berry's blend of razor-sharp lyrics and incisive guitar – not to mention his legendary business acumen – had made him the definitive rock 'n' roll songwriter.

---

call at the airport, though their main terminal is downtown at 1450 N 13th St. Amtrak stops at 550 S 16th St, at Market Street downtown. The Bi-State Transit System (☎314/231-2345) operates the Metro Link, a **light rail system** serving the airport and most of the significant tourist sights; rides cost $1.25 (free in downtown Mon–Fri 11am–1.30pm). BSTS **buses** also go to all of the city's suburbs, but services can be slow and infrequent. You can rent a **bicycle** from any of six branches of Touring Cyclist (☎314/739-4648).

The city runs **visitor centers** at 308 Washington Ave, near the riverfront (daily 9.30am–4.30pm; ☎314/241-1764), and at the America Center in the massive Cervantes Convention Center, a few blocks back (Mon–Fri 9am–5pm; ☎1-800/916-0092). The **post office** is at 1720 Market St (Mon–Fri 6.30am–2.30pm, Sat 7am–2pm; ☎1-800/275-8777; zip code 63155).

## Accommodation

St Louis may be a business center – complete with huge new convention hall – but good-value **lodging** can still be found downtown, with appealing weekend rates. For **B&Bs**, contact the Greater St Louis Reservation Service, PO Box 30069, MO 63119 (☎314/961-2252).

**Best Western Inn At The Park**, 4630 Lindell Blvd (☎314/367-7500 or 1-800/373-7501). Good motel on northeast corner of Forest Park, right by the cafes of Central West End. ⑤.

**Drury Inn – Union Station**, 201 S 20th St (☎314/231-3900 or 1-800/325-8300). Very tastefully restored accommodation. ⑥.

**Econolodge Airport**, 4575 N Lindbergh Blvd (☎314/731-3000). Clean rooms and friendly staff. Very close to the airport. ③.

**Embassy Suites**, 901 N 1st St (☎314/241-4200). Comfortable suites in the heart of Laclede's Landing. Includes buffet breakfast. ⑥.

**HI-Huckleberry Finn**, 1904–1908 S 12th St (☎314/241-0076). Dorms ($15 HI members, you must become a member to stay) and single rooms. On the edge of a dodgy area in Soulard, so take bus #73 from downtown. ①.

**Napoleon's Retreat**, 1815 Lafayette Ave (☎314/772-6979). Attractive B&B near Lafayette Square, with appealing rates. ⑤.

**Ramada Inn At The Arch**, 333 Washington Ave (☎314/621-7900). Great location at a good price. ⑤.

**Regal Riverfront Hotel**, 200 S 4th St (☎314/241-9500 or 1-800/325-7353). Ideal downtown setting; recently renovated and with all the facilities you'd expect from a hotel of its size. ⑦.

**Super Inn**, 1100 N 3rd St (☎314/421-6556). The least expensive downtown option, just a few strides from Laclede's, though it's not a pleasant walk late at night. ③.

## The riverfront

The one-and-a-half-mile cobbled granite **wharf** along the Mississippi used to lie in the shadow of a dense tangle of warehouses and factories. When river trade decreased these became an embarrassing eyesore. Though most were ripped down, some restored structures between Eads and Martin Luther King bridges now form **Laclede's Landing Historic District**, their cast-iron facades fronting antique stores, office suites, restaurants and live music venues. In late August, the district hosts the **Big Muddy Roots and Blues Festival**, featuring artists of national prominence and a great party atmosphere (information on ☎314/241-5860).

On the **waterfront** itself, where roustabouts once handled cargoes of cotton and ores, assorted permanently moored vessels hold museums, theater shows, a heliport, **casinos** and even a floating *McDonald's*. **Cruises** aboard replica paddlewheelers leave from under the Gateway Arch (April–Nov daily 10am–8pm; ☎314/621-4040 or 1-800/878-7411; $8.50).

Ten minutes' walk south, over thirty blocks of derelict buildings were torn down to clear space for the **Jefferson National Expansion Memorial**, dedicated to the US president who negotiated the Louisiana Purchase and thereby opened up the west, and to the pioneers who journeyed along the Oregon and Santa Fe trails. Its highlight, the **Gateway Arch**, designed by Eero Saarinen, was completed in 1965, a 630ft stainless steel parabola of quite majestic symmetry; in technical terms it's a weighted catenary curve, the outline formed by a heavy cable hanging freely from two points. The arch is at its most striking when its gleaming coat catches a stray reflection – perhaps a rich red sunset or a fireworks display. This unusual monument has been universally adopted as the city's emblem, used in all sorts of corporate logos and insignia.

So long as you're not claustrophobic, it's fun to take the four-minute **tram ride** up the hollow curving arch. Tiny five-seater capsules carry you to a viewing gallery, repeatedly stopping to shift position so you don't arrive at the top upside down. Unfortunately, after such an epic ride, the view is disappointing and the tiny windows are all at waist height. Lengthy queues build up during summer, but you can pick up a numbered ticket earlier in the day and come back at the allotted time (summer daily 8.30am–9.20pm; rest of year daily 9.30am–5.20pm; $6).

In a massive bunker beneath the arch, the **visitor center** (summer daily 8am–10pm; rest of year daily 9am–6pm; ☎314/982-1410; $6 one attraction, $10 two, $14 three) shows a riveting film about the construction of the monument, and another on the Lewis and Clark Expedition, which set off from St Louis in 1804 to explore the Missouri River and water communications to the Pacific Ocean. It returned two years later with details of trade routes, Native American settlements and observations on animal and plant life. The spacious **Museum of Westward Expansion** recounts the story, drawing heavily on the pair's very readable journals. The **Arch Odyssey Theater**, in the same building, beams IMAX epics onto a four-story screen.

## Central downtown

One block from the arch along St Louis's main east–west thoroughfare, Market Street, old photographs at the stately **Old Courthouse Museum** (daily 8am–4.30pm; free) record the development of the city and the settling of the West. Two restored court-rooms were the site of the trial of **Dred Scott**, a black slave who argued that having spent time with his owner in non-slave Illinois and Wisconsin, he had the right to be set free. His case was upheld in 1850, but overturned two years later. On appeal, the Supreme Court declared that Scott, born a slave in a slave state, might like any other chattel be taken anywhere his master chose to go. The decision, which meant that the US Constitution saw slaves as legitimate personal property, sent shock waves through the corridors of government and hastened the onrush of the Civil War. Scott himself, by now a nationally known figure, was voluntarily freed by his new owner, but died a year later.

The **International Bowling Hall of Fame**, at 111 Stadium Plaza (summer Mon–Sat 9am–5pm, Sun noon–5pm; rest of year daily 11am–4pm; $5, includes four free frames), is devoted to the favorite sport of such diverse figures as Martin Luther and Homer Simpson, tracing its history from ancient Egypt to the present. Bowling was not always the slick commercial sport it is today; excessive betting on games got it denounced by the Church in fifteenth-century Germany and, three centuries later, the behavior of drunken fans led to all alleys being shut down in London.

See the world's largest pair of underpants and witness the mystic power of the corndog at the whimsical **City Museum**, 701 N 15th St (Wed–Fri 9am–5pm, Sat–Sun 10am–5pm; $6). The museum is in an old parking lot and is made almost entirely of junk. The exhibits often border on the bizarre, as one floor is devoted to secret passages, which everyone can explore. On entering, you will be informed, "Have fun, and don't lose your adult." Over on Market Street at 18th Street, the focal point of the giant Romanesque **Union Station** is a 230ft clock tower. Built in 1884 and closed as a train station in 1979, it now houses a hotel and two floors of shops, cafes and bars, with an artificial lake, where you can rent boats, at the rear. The *Hyatt Hotel*'s ornate lobby, once the station's main waiting room, is well worth visiting for a coffee or just a look.

## West of downtown

The **Theater District**, three miles west of downtown, is staked out with ornate street lamps along Grand Avenue between Lindell and Delmar boulevards. Bright posters advertise the current shows at the **Fabulous Fox Theater**, 527 N Grand Ave, where you can have a look at the magnificent Siamese-Byzantine interior and massive Wurlitzer organ (tours Tues, Thurs & Sat at 10.30am; ☎314/534-1111; $5).

About a mile further west, on the edge of Forest Park, trendy shops, wine bars and c.1900 mansions line the leafy thoroughfares of the **Central West End** district. A few blocks away at 4431 Lindell Blvd, the Romanesque-Byzantine **Cathedral of St Louis**, referred to by locals as the New Cathedral, houses the world's largest collection of **mosaic art** (May–Sept daily 7am–7pm; Oct–April daily 7am–5pm; $1).

The decision to put **Forest Park** four miles directly west of downtown (served by Metrolink every ten minutes) aroused much criticism during the 1870s, opponents claiming that its inaccessibility would make it merely a pleasure ground for the local rich. It's larger than New York's Central Park, and every bit as full of attractions; in summer, the 12,000-seat amphitheater is regularly filled for the **Muny concert series** (June–Aug; ☎314/361-1900). Shuttle Bugs – bright-red buses with black spots – scurry around its roadways ($1.25).

Standing on **Art Hill** in the central western section of the park, the striking Beaux Arts **St Louis Art Museum** (Tues 1.30–8.30pm, Wed–Sun 10am–5pm; tours at 1.30pm; free), is the only surviving structure from the 1904 World's Fair. Its brief – to cover international art from prehistoric times onwards – may be ambitious, but none of the galleries can be considered as weak points or fillers. It houses one of the world's most extensive collections of **German Expressionism**, devoting an entire gallery to the powerful, spiraling and jagged images of Max Beckmann, and its **pre-Columbian art works** cover every significant style, medium and culture from Mexico to Peru.

In addition to the animals in its "cageless displays," the **St Louis Zoo** (daily 9am–5pm, in summer open until 8pm on Tues; free), set in beautiful grounds, boasts a "Living World" exhibit in which Charles Darwin has evolved into an animatronic robot giving synopses of his theories.

The main strengths of the **History Museum**, on the northern fringe of the park (Tues 9.30am–8.30pm,Wed–Sun 9.30am–5pm; free), are the thematic collections of old pictures of St Louis, documenting river life, black music in the city and Charles Lindbergh's 1927 flight in the *Spirit of St Louis* (sponsored by the city's aircraft industry) from New York to Paris. Though the main section of the **St Louis Science Center** (Mon–Wed 9am–5pm, Thurs 9am–9pm, Fri 9am–10pm, Sat 10am–10pm, Sun 10am–9pm; free) is across I-64, you can also enter it through the park; use one of the radar guns on the covered access bridge to check the speed of cars on the freeway below. General admission is free, but it costs a few dollars a time to get into the planetarium, OMNIMAX Theater and other major exhibits.

## Southside

The tens of thousands of **Germans** who came to St Louis in the mid-eighteenth century settled mostly in the **southside**, which has retained a noticeable Teutonic influence. They were skilled brewers; only one of the breweries they opened from the 1850s onwards still stands, but it does happen to be the largest in the world. The **Anheuser-Busch** plant, at Broadway and Pestalozzi (Mon–Sat 9am–4pm; free), produces a sizeable proportion of the company's 1.1 billion-plus cases of beer each year, including Budweiser and Michelob. The buildings themselves are architecturally interesting: over one hundred intricate redbrick structures. The free eighty-minute tours are mostly company PR, but they're still good fun, and you get two glasses of the company product at the end, before you're shunted into the giftshop.

A few blocks towards downtown, the colorful **Soulard Market**, at Broadway and Lafayette, is a great place to pick up picnic items and fresh fruit, especially on a Saturday. The terraced streets behind it hold the city's best **blues and jazz pubs**.

Red-, white-and-green fire hydrants let you know that you're in the nearby thirty-square-block **Hill** district, a small, neat **Italian** community. At its heart, **St Ambrose Church** displays a statue of Italian immigrants; all around, the aroma of freshly baked bread drifts out of the small specialty bakeries that share the area with one-room grocery stores and dozens of restaurants.

Further west at 4344 Shaw Blvd, the 79-acre **Missouri Botanical Garden** (summer daily 9am–8pm; rest of year daily 9am–5pm; $5) is a haven of peace and tranquility, just a few hundred yards from busy I-44. The grounds contain everything from a magnificent Japanese Garden – surrounding a small lake and adorned with stepping stones, arched bridges and wooden teahouse – through scented, rose and English woodland gardens to the Climatron, a huge greenhouse that re-creates a tropical rainforest complete with waterfalls and cliffs.

## St Charles

The beautiful little river town of **ST CHARLES**, 25 miles northwest of downtown St Louis and forever threatened by flooding – in 1993 it briefly became an island in the swirling waters – remains redolent with lazy charm, despite the advent of its first riverboat casino. Three small though distinct **historic districts** are crammed with antique shops, specialty outlets and good cafes, such as the Victorian tearoom in the *Lord Winston*, 833 S Main St (☎314/940-9550). Lewis and Clark set up strategic camp here in 1804, and are remembered in the interesting small **museum**.

St Charles's **CVB**, 230 S Main St (☎314/946-7776 or 1-800/366-2427), has details of downtown's growing range of elegant and amply porched **B&Bs**. The popular **KATY Trail**, which hugs "Big Muddy" for fifty miles along the route of an old railroad, is excellent for cycling (rent bikes from the riverfront) or even a leisurely stroll. Gambling and show boats are anchored along the riverbanks, while the *Spirit of St Louis Riverboat* operates **cruises** from 1000 Riverside Drive (☎314/946-1000).

## Eating

**Italian** food dominates St Louis cuisine, from humble salami sellers upwards. Otherwise most of the friendly Irish pubs serve beef sandwiches and stew, while University City's **Delmar Boulevard** offers African, Middle Eastern, Chinese, Indian and other ethnic places. More expensive cafes are located in Laclede's Landing, and the Central West End has acquired a scattering of upmarket espresso bars such as *Nuberry's*, 247 Euclid Ave.

**Duff's**, 392 N Euclid Ave, Central West End (☎314/361-0522). Small, relaxed and moderately priced. French-flavored international menu, homemade desserts and Sunday brunch. Outdoor seating.

**John D McGurk's Irish Pub**, 1200 Russell Blvd at 12th St, Soulard (☎314/776-8309). Fresh-baked soda bread, corned beef 'n' cabbage, Irish stew and imported Guinness. Live Irish music every night.

**O'Connell's Pub**, 4652 Shaw at Kingshighway (☎314/773-6600). The best burgers in the city, and the beef sandwiches aren't bad either. Near the Hill district.

**Red Sea**, 6511 Delmar Blvd, U City (☎314/863-0099). Cheap and cheerful Ethiopian restaurant; *berbere* sauce with everything. The decor is basic and the service slow, but the food's great.

**Rigazzi's**, 4945 Daggett Blvd, the Hill (☎314/772-4900). Popular trattoria, famous for "frozen fish bowls" of beer. Over thirty different pasta dishes, from $9, plus pizzas, veal, chicken and steak.

**Saleem's**, 6501 Delmar Blvd, U City (☎314/721-7947). "Where garlic is king" and St Louisians reckon you get the best ethnic food in the city. Lebanese and continental menu; reasonably inexpensive.

**Ted Drewe's Frozen Custard**, 6726 Chippewa Ave (☎314/481-2652) and 4224 S Grand Blvd (☎314/352-7376). A legendary slice of Americana. Try a "concrete" – an ice cream so thick it won't budge if you turn your cup upside down. March–Dec only.

## Nightlife and entertainment

Downtown St Louis's highest concentration of bars and clubs can be found in **Laclede's Landing**, with nightly jazz, blues, rock and reggae. Some of the outlying districts are well worth checking out in the evening; these include the Loop in **U City**, whose bars and cafes are not just popular with students, and the slightly more upmarket cafes and wine bars of **Central West End**. Unpretentious **Soulard** is the place to go for good jazz and blues. Every spring, the four-day **Mid-America Jazz Festival** brings the top names together for performances all over St Louis.

Don't forget also to check out the **Theater District**, centered on North Grand Boulevard in midtown, home to stage shows and the St Louis Symphony Orchestra (☎314/534-1700). Excellent listings can be found in the free weekly *Riverfront Times*.

**Blueberry Hill**, 6504 Delmar Blvd, U City (☎314/727-0880). Crammed full of memorabilia, with the downstairs dedicated to Elvis and a jukebox acclaimed by *Cashbox* as the best in the country. Live entertainment every weekend, good drinks and burgers at any time.

**Broadway Oyster Bar**, 736 S Broadway (☎314/621-8811). Cramped, crowded and dark downtown blues club, in an atmospheric old bar.

**Cicero's**, 6691 Delmar Blvd, U City (☎314/862-0009). Downstairs club putting on jazz-fusion, acoustic and "alternative" music.

**1860 Hard Shell Cafe & Bar**, 1860 S 9th St, Soulard (☎314/231-1860). One of the liveliest bars in Soulard with dancing to blues, R&B and soul bands. Also serves good Cajun and fish dishes.

**Mississippi Nights,** 914 N 1st St, Laclede's Landing (☎314/421-3853). The city's top venue for non-stadium bands.

**Pierre's,** 4th and Chestnut (☎314/342-4690). "Cigar-smoking encouraged" in this classy jazz bar in the *Adams-Mark Hotel,* downtown.

**Riddles Penultimate,** 6307 Delmar Blvd, U City (☎314/725-6985). Very lively bar in the heart of U City, with a young crowd and some sidewalk seating.

## South of St Louis

The French and German heritage of tiny **STE GENEVIEVE**, sixty miles south of St Louis, is conspicuous through its architecture, cafes and festivals, though its graceful old French homes, characterized by vertical log construction, are constantly imperiled by flooding; the damage of 1993 remains apparent. The *St Gemme Beauvais,* 78 N Main St (☎573/883-5744 or 1-800/818-5744; ⑥), is a nineteenth-century Greek Revival inn downtown, while Amish variations on catfish, chicken and seafood are on the menu in the *Anvil Saloon,* 46 S Third St (☎573/883-7323).

**CAPE GIRARDEAU,** responsible for giving Rush Limbaugh to the airwaves of the world, looks down on the Mississippi from a rocky ledge 55 miles downriver. Among its antebellum and Victorian buildings, the *Port Cape Girardeau,* 19 N Water St (☎573/334-0954), serves tasty ribs. The *Sands Motel* at 1448 N Kings Hwy (☎573/334-2828; ②), with a decent restaurant, is good value. The road continues south to Arkansas through reclaimed swamplands, rich in wheat, corn and melons, but little else.

# Kansas City

**KANSAS CITY,** 250 miles due west of St Louis, straddles the state line between Kansas and Missouri. Virtually all its main points of interest are on the Missouri side, where the fountains, boulevards, and Art Deco and Mediterranean-style buildings, and the encouraging revitalization of downtown, are unusual and welcome features in a Midwestern city. Kansas City, Kansas, on the other hand, is a dull sprawl of suburbs that doesn't have much to attract visitors.

Kansas City was a convenient staging post for 1830s wagon trains heading west. Its consequent prosperity – and rough and tumble "sin city" image – was brought to an abrupt end by the Civil War. However, its fortunes revived in the 1870s, when the railroads brought the boom in meat packing that was responsible for the development of the huge stockyards, which finally closed down in 1992.

Thanks to Mayor Pendergast, an outrageous figure with whom the city still has a love-hate relationship, its many jazz clubs continued to sell alcohol during Prohibition. As in Chicago and New Orleans, speakeasies, brothels and gambling dens went hand in hand with superlative **jazz** – and, to a lesser extent, blues – spawning the careers of Count Basie, Duke Ellington and, in the Fifties, Charlie Parker. KC's resurgent jazz scene, fine restaurants, high-spending Royals and Chiefs sports teams, and theme parks help make it a popular short-break destination for the people of the western heartland.

### Arrival, information and getting around

From the **airport** (☎816/243-5237), 25 miles northwest of downtown, a convenient forty-minute **shuttle bus** (half-hourly 6am–11.55pm; ☎816/243-5000) heads to major downtown hotels ($12) and Westport ($13). The equivalent taxi ride costs around $33 (Yellow Cab; ☎816/471-5000).

The isolated Greyhound terminal lies well out from downtown in a miserable area at 12th and Troost. Amtrak is in the newly renovated Union Station at 23rd and Main, opposite the Crown Center. The Metro Buses system (☎816/221-0660) covers downtown and routes out to Independence. In addition, except in January and February, five trolleys loop continuously between downtown, the Crown Center, Westport and the Country Club Plaza ($5 all-day pass).

The city's main **visitor center** is tucked away on the 25th floor of City Center Square at 1100 Main St (Mon–Fri 8.30am–5.30pm; ☎816/221-5242 or 1-800/767-7700); additional information offices are housed in the Country Club Plaza at 4709 W Central St (Mon–Fri 8.30am–5.30pm; ☎816/691-3800) and in the Grand Hallway of Union Station. There's also a State Welcome Center on the grounds of the Truman Sports Complex, off exit 9 on I-70 in Independence (daily 8am–5pm; ☎816/889-3330). The main **post office** is close to Amtrak at 315 W Pershing Rd (Mon–Fri 8am–6.30pm, Sat 8am–12.30pm; ☎1-800/275-8777; zip code 64108).

## Accommodation

Kansas City's budget motels lie along the interstates or out towards Independence, but reasonable central options do exist. For **B&Bs**, contact Mid-West Reservation Service, Box 636, Concordia, MO 64020 (☎816/493-7395). The most central place to **camp** is at the *Trailside Camper's Inn* (☎816/229-2267 or 1-800/748-7729) at I-70 exit 24, though there are more scenic sites thirteen miles from downtown in the 1500-acre woods of Wyandotte County Park, on N Hwy-5 at 91st Street, which also contains a 330ft lake (☎913/229-0550).

**Best Western Seville Plaza**, 4309 Main St (☎816/561-9600). Very central, close to Westport. ⑤.

**Historic Suites of America**, 612 Central St (☎816/842-6544 or 1-800/733-0612). Beautiful large rooms with fully equipped kitchens in the heart of the Garment District. Free breakfast and cocktails. ⑥/⑦.

**Holiday Inn Express Westport**, 801 Westport Rd (☎816/931-1000). Reasonable lodgings on the edge of the trendy Westport district. ⑤.

**Super 8 Independence**, 4032 S Lynn Court (☎816/833-1888). Clean budget motel, east of the city in Independence. ②.

## The City

Kansas City is doing a good job of reinvigorating its **downtown**, putting the commercial and residential needs of its citizens first. Most sights lie further south, though wandering past the restored lofts and small businesses of the **Garment District**, between Sixth and Ninth streets, makes a nice route to **City Hall**, 414 E 12th St, a fine Art Deco building with an observation deck on its thirtieth floor (Mon–Fri 8.30am–4.15pm; free). Also downtown is the redeveloped historic district known variously as **River Market** or City Market, further north in something of a no-man's-land. As well as colorful shops, cafes and a lively farmers' market at Fifth and Walnut streets, there's a good but pricey museum in the complex – "**The Treasures of the Steamboat Arabia**" – which tells the story behind the recent salvaging of a sidewheeler which sank on its way to Omaha in 1856. Perfectly preserved artifacts afford unexpected and intriguing insights into frontier life (Mon–Sat 10am–6pm, Sun noon–5pm; $7.50).

The sprawling concrete **Crown Center**, on Grand and Pershing, owned by Hallmark Cards, calls itself "a city within a city," with apartments, shops, restaurants, offices, hotels, cinemas and an ice rink. Interesting displays in its splendidly awful **Hallmark Visitors Center** (Mon–Wed & Sat 10am–6pm, Thurs–Fri 10am–9pm, Sun noon–5pm; free) trace styles of greetings cards alongside political and cultural changes, demonstrating printing processes and hand decoration, but it's a strain to keep a straight face at the sentiment that cards are "messengers of the heart" which "aid humans in their love for one another." The nearby **Union Station** is a Kansas City landmark: huge, and still riddled with the bullet holes from a Pretty Boy Floyd shoot-out.

The **18th and Vine Heritage District**, south of I-70 as it sweeps east–west, was the hub of the city's 1930s **jazz scene**. Formerly an unsafe area of empty lots and boarded-up shops, a huge revitalization project culminated in the opening of the **Negro Leagues Baseball Museum**, 1616 E 18th St (Tues–Sat 9am–6pm, Sun noon–6pm; $6), in 1997. This enthralling collection of photographs, interactive exhibits, original team uniforms and game equipment traces the turbulent history of black baseball in America, which was segregated from the white major leagues for the first half of the twentieth century. In 1920, Kansas City hosted the key meeting that founded the Negro National League – an institution that paved the way for the likes of Jackie Robinson to enter the major league. In the same complex is the **American Jazz Museum** (Tues–Thurs 9am–6pm, Fri–Sat 9am–9pm, Sun noon–6pm; $6), which tells the history of jazz through interactive exhibits; profiling some of its greatest performers, including Kansas City native, Charlie Parker, and others who cut their teeth in the smoky halls of 18th and Vine. *The Blue Room* functions as a working jazz bar, with Monday night jam sessions bringing many stars out of the woodwork.

**Westport**, an attractive district of good restaurants, cafes and trendy shops between 39th and 45th streets, was the original jumping-off point for the Santa Fe Trail. Stop off for a drink at the city's oldest building, *Kelly's Westport Inn*, 500 Westport St, a shabby but friendly redbrick bar. Five miles south of downtown, beginning at 47th and Main, the elegant **Country Club Plaza** dates from the early Twenties. Tree-shaded and upmarket (with branches of Eddie Bauer and Saks), its tiling, mosaics, fountains and orange trees evoke the streets of Spain, and a replica Sevillan tower completes the effect.

Highlights at the extensive **Nelson-Atkins Museum of Art**, a few blocks east at 4525 Oak St (Tues–Thurs 10am–4pm, Fri 10am–9pm, Sat 10am–5pm, Sun 1–5pm; $5, free on Sat), include superb Oriental exhibits, with figurines from Tang and Egyptian tombs, plus canvases by Titian, Caravaggio (*St John the Baptist*) and Monet, and twelve Henry Moore sculptures in a landscaped setting. The pretty **Toy and Miniatures Museum**, further south at 5235 Oak St (Wed–Sat 10am–4pm, Sun 1–4pm; $4), houses an offbeat collection of antique toys, games and puppets.

When the Midwestern humidity gets too much, head for the tropically themed water world **Oceans of Fun**, or the adjoining **Worlds of Fun**, with its 140-plus rides, out at exit 54 of I-435 (late May–early Sept daily, hours vary; $20.95 for Oceans, $27.95 for Worlds).

## Eating

**Barbecue**, once the unfashionable food of the poor, is big news in Kansas City – cheap, cheerful, hickory-smoked and served with tasty sauces. Restaurants in the **Crown Center** are quite good but overpriced, and many require formal dress. The **Country Club Plaza** has some great places, but again, they're expensive; relaxed Westport is a better bet.

**Arthur Bryant's**, 1727 Brooklyn Ave (☎816/231-1123). *The* place for barbecue, a mile east of downtown in a desolate area. Serving the largest portions you've ever seen of barbecue and beans; the combo plate easily feeds two hefty appetites. This is serious business – be sure not to dawdle in the queue, as novices are given short shrift.

**BroadWay Cafe**, 4106 Broadway (☎816/531-2432). Seriously trendy sidewalk cafe, offering brain-jolting espressos and light lunches in bohemian Westport.

**Hereford House**, 20th and Main sts (☎816/842-1080). KC's top steak house, in a handy downtown spot.

**Italian Gardens**, 1110 Baltimore Ave (☎816/221-9311). Seventy years serving pizzas and pastas, and still going strong.

**Jerusalem Cafe**, 431 Westport Rd (☎816/756-2770). Small Middle Eastern restaurant serving superb falafel and kebabs.

**Lucille's**, 1604 Westport Rd (☎816/561-5119). Attractive Fifties diner, open 24hr Fri & Sat. Huge portions; top-class curly fries, burgers, omelettes and malts.

**Lydia's**, 101 W 22nd St (☎816/221-3722). Popular new spot housed in an old freight house. Excellent pastas and an extensive wine selection – at an affordable price.

**Stroud's**, 1015 E 85th St (☎816/333-2132). Classic roadhouse, a long way southeast of downtown, and renowned for its fried chicken. A favorite with Rush Limbaugh among others.

### Nightlife and entertainment

Check out Kansas City's reviving **jazz** and **blues** scene, especially the authentic dives holding wonderful jam sessions into the early hours. The Friday and Sunday editions of the *Kansas City Star* carry listings, as do the freebies *Pitch Weekly* and the *New Times*. You can also call the Blues Hotline (☎913/432-KCBS) or the Jazz Hotline (☎816/753-JASS).

Downtown is otherwise pretty dead by mid-evening, and most people head to **Westport** for nightlife from country-and-western to alternative rock. In the summer, big-name bands play **free concerts** in the square at Crown Center; bring your own picnic and booze, and get there early for a good position. Showtime is 8pm Friday.

**Birdland**, 1600 E 19th St (☎816/842-8463). Seedy and authentic jazz club, in the historic 18th and Vine area.

**Blayneys**, 415 Westport Rd (☎816/561-3747). Live music in the cellar, with blues every Mon.

**Club 427**, 427 Main St (☎816/421-2582). Tremendous jazz venue in River Market, featuring local and national talent. The Friday and Saturday jam sessions are a must.

**Grand Emporium**, 3832 Main St (☎816/531-1504). R&B, blues, reggae and jazz with superb Cajun and Jamaican food. Voted the best blues club in America by the National Blues Foundation.

**Jazz Kitchen**, 1823 W 39th St (☎816/531-5556). Cajun cuisine and live jazz and blues. A classy venue, so dress well.

**Kiki's Bon Ton Maison**, 1515 Westport Rd (☎816/931-9417). Louisiana-style food, plus Cajun and zydeco music on Wed & Sat.

**Mutual Musicians Foundation**, 1823 Highland Ave (☎816/471-5212). National Historic Landmark in the 18th and Vine district. Fierce jam sessions begin 1.30am Fri & Sat, musicians competing in a frenzy for hours. It can get a bit rough, and is not recommended for women alone.

**Phoenix Piano Bar and Grill**, 302 W 8th St at Central (☎816/472-0001). Downtown jazz piano venue featuring Sat afternoon sessions.

## Independence and Liberty

Bus #24 from Kansas City goes to the small town of **INDEPENDENCE**, twenty minutes east of the city and most famous as the former home of President Harry S Truman. The **Truman Library and Museum** on US-24 and Delaware St (Mon–Wed and Sat 9am–5pm, Thurs 9am–9pm, Sun noon–5pm; $5) includes a reconstruction of his White House office, and chilling documents pertaining to the development of the atomic bomb. The Victorian Truman Home, a mile south at 219 N Delaware St, is decorated as it was when used as the summer White House (daily 8.30am–5pm, in winter closed Mon; $2).

Jesse James staged the first ever daylight bank robbery in 1866 in what's now the **Jesse James Bank Museum**, on the Old Town Square of **LIBERTY**, fifteen miles east of downtown Kansas City (Mon–Sat 9am–4pm; $3.50). Among the memorabilia and dusty relics of early banking, you can see the vault and the safe that he raided.

## St Joseph

Sixty miles north of Kansas City, **ST JOSEPH** boomed as a supply depot for the California Gold Rush, and today is still a busy manufacturing town. For a brief eighteen months, starting in 1860, it was the home of the legendary **Pony Express**, which took ten days to deliver mail all the way to Sacramento, California, by continuous horseback relay. The Pony Express was a financial disaster, driven out of business by its inability to compete with the transcontinental telegraph, but riders such as Buffalo Bill Cody remain immortal. Charlie Miller, the last of the riders, rode from New York to San Francisco in 1931, and died aged 105 in 1955. The full story is told in lively dioramas at the **Pony Express National Memorial**, 914 Penn St, attractively set in the company's original stables (June–Sept Mon–Sat 9am–6pm, Sun 1–6pm; Oct–May Mon–Sat 9am–5pm, Sun 1–5pm; $3).

It was in St Joseph, on April 3, 1882, that the notorious Jesse James was shot in the back by Robert Ford, a twenty-year-old member of his own gang who had negotiated a $20,000 reward from the governor. Countless books and films have portrayed Jesse James as a latterday Robin Hood; in fact, he spent most of the Civil War riding with a band of Confederate guerrillas. The **Jesse James Home Museum**, the one-story frame cottage where James was living incognito (naturally) while he planned his next bank job, now stands at 12th and Penn streets, having been moved closer to the main highway in the hope of attracting sightseers (June–Aug Mon–Sat 10am–5pm, Sun 1–5pm; Sept–May Mon–Sat 10am–4pm, Sun 1–4pm; $2). A ragged hole in the wall is pointed out as the spot where the bullet supposedly hit, after striking James as he was hanging a picture; you can also see where bloodstained splinters were chiseled from the floor to be sold as souvenirs. When the outlaw's property was auctioned after his death, his most valuable possession was his dog, which fetched $15. As for the assassin, Ford was himself gunned down eleven years later, and his killer in turn was also shot.

Other Jesse James museums are dotted about town, but St Joseph isn't much of a place to hang around. If you do want to leave the (tedious) drive to Kansas City or Omaha for another day, you'll find **motels** strung along I-29 as it passes east of downtown, including a *Motel 6* (☎816/232-2311; ③) and a *Days Inn* (☎816/279-1671; ②) at the intersection with Frederick Boulevard. The *Old Town Smokehouse & Pub*, 1120 Penn St (☎816/232-1899) offers huge sandwiches at appealing prices and is a must if you want **lunch** in St Joseph.

# Southwest Missouri – Ozark country

There's little to see south of Kansas City before the **Ozark Mountains**. Occupying most of southern Missouri and northern Arkansas (see p.534), the area remained frontier territory until the timber companies moved in at the end of the nineteenth century. When they moved on, the hill-dwellers were left to eke out a living from the denuded terrain. Severe droughts forced many to leave for the cities. For those who remain, fishing resorts and tourist attractions supply some work, though the region remains poor and economically backward. None of the Ozark peaks is particularly high, but the roads through switch, dip, climb and swerve to provide stunning views of steep hillsides, thick with oak, elm, hickory and redbud and quite resplendent in the fall.

**Springfield** is the region's main city, 130 miles south of Kansas City, but the gateway to the Ozarks, the country music town of **Branson**, is more popular by far.

## Branson

Nestling among beautiful Ozark lakes, the resort of **BRANSON** (year-round population 5000), forty miles south of Springfield on US-65, is, according to the AAA, the second biggest auto destination in the country after Orlando. Over five million visitors a year are attracted to what's become known as the "Ozark Disneyland" by thirty-plus music venues (almost all of a country bent), a few theme parks and lots of good ol' family fun.

"**The Strip**," until recently merely Hwy-76, abounds with theaters owned and performed in by big-name stars. The spectrum ranges from Loretta Lynn and Mel Tillis, through MOR acts like the Osmond family, Japanese fiddler Shoji Tabuchi and ancient crooner Andy Williams, to banal mountain humor joints like *Baldknobbers* and *Presleys'* (not that Presley). Lesser lights include Tony Orlando's Yellow Ribbon Theater, and Jim *Spiders and Snakes* Stafford's place. Tickets for a two-hour show are no bargain, at an average of $20, but there's no shortage of takers in summer for most, if not all, of the town's 40,000 seats – a figure said to exceed that of Nashville. Branson shows are firmly geared towards families; you won't find anything remotely progressive or avant-garde.

If you're simply intent on passing through as quickly as possible, be warned that the roads get packed, and it's not unheard of for it to take two hours to drive through Branson.

## Practicalities

Greyhound connects Branson with Springfield, Kansas City and Memphis. Call ahead, or drop in at the local **Chamber of Commerce**, at the intersection of Hwy-65 and Hwy-248 (Mon–Sat 8am–5pm, Sun 10am–4pm; ☎417/334-4136), for a copy of their show guide detailing performance schedules of all the theaters. During the main season (May–Oct), it's more or less impossible to find a **place to stay** for under $50 a night; weekend rates rise higher still. Branson Vacation Reservations (☎1-800/221-5692) will try to sell you a package deal, but can also book you into a motel, including one of five *Best Western*s (☎1-800/528-1234; ④). The Ozark Mountain Country B&B, Box 295, Branson, MO 65616 (☎1-800/695-1546) is another reliable reservation service, but if you're visiting in the main season call at least a week in advance. Most **places to eat** are of the family diner ilk, though it's worth searching out the fat-free menu at *McGuffey's on the Strip*, and the Greek cuisine at *Dimitri's*, downtown.

# KANSAS

Today's cutesy, gingham-pinafore image of **KANSAS**, associated with *Little House on the Prairie* and *The Wizard of Oz*, is a far cry indeed from the troubled history that made it known as "bleeding Kansas." It took three hundred years after Coronado came in search of gold in 1541 before pioneers established trails across the region, and Kansas's bid for statehood in 1861 is often cited as the catalyst for the Civil War. The 1854 Kansas-Nebraska Act, which gave both territories the right to self-determination over slavery, led to fierce clashes between Free Staters and pro-slavery forces. Runaway slaves from the South were given passage through the area, aided by abolitionist John Brown, and Kansas eventually joined the Union as a free state.

After the war, the mighty cattle drives from Texas made towns like Abilene, Wichita and Dodge City centers of the "**Wild West**." The debauched, male image of the West, spawning such "heroes" as Wyatt Earp and Wild Bill Hickok, is, however, challenged in Kansas, which as well as being the first state to give women the vote in municipal elections, boasts the nation's first female mayor and senator, as well as aviator Amelia Earhart and the battling Prohibitionist Carry Nation.

In 1874, Russian Mennonites brought the grain that was to transform the state into the bountiful "bread basket" that now harvests most of the nation's wheat. However, only in the west do miles of golden corn sway in Kansas's infamous gusty wind. The green and hilly northeast, patterned with woods and lakes, is home to the unattractive industrial city of Topeka, liberal college town **Lawrence**, and the dull suburbs of

Kansas City (though downtown lies across the state line in Missouri). The wild and sparse northwest is pioneer country, while the once-wicked cowtown **Dodge City** is in the southwest. **Wichita**, the state's largest city, lies in the south central area.

## Getting around Kansas

Greyhound **buses** run to all Kansas's main cities, supplemented by erratic smaller companies; services to the west and southwest are especially poor. The most frequent routes run from Kansas City to Albuquerque via Wichita (about 3 daily; 10–12hr), with one or two buses per day along I-70 to Denver. Amtrak **trains** head east–west between LA and Chicago through the center of the state, calling, usually in the middle of the night, at Lawrence, Topeka, Emporia, Newton (for Wichita, but without a connecting service), Dodge City and Garden City. Wichita has the state's biggest **airport**.

# East Kansas

Undulating **east Kansas** is laced with lakes, streams and rivers. The northeast, once crossed by the Oregon, Santa Fe and Smoky Hill trails, and now home to both Topeka and Lawrence, is more heavily visited than the southeast, where the major sight is TV's *Little House on the Prairie*, just south of Independence on SW US-75. The heritage of Kansas' four Indian tribes is still visible. Annual **powwows**, held in the major towns as well as the northwestern reservations, have become important dates in the calendar.

## Lawrence

The mellow town of **LAWRENCE** lies on the Kansas River, roughly halfway between Kansas City and Topeka, around thirty miles from either. Tree-lined streets, a welcoming historic downtown and an aura of old-hippie artsiness make it an appealing destination, with a cultural energy owed in part to the University of Kansas (home of the Jayhawk, the mythical bird which is the emblem of its sports teams), and a long liberal and intellectual history. Founded by the New England Emigrant Aid Company in 1854, and a center of Free State activities, Lawrence was the site of a violent Civil War skirmish in 1863, when Missourian Confederate guerrilla Quantrill led about 300 men on the town, killing over 150, wounding hundreds more, and setting the place alight. Rebuilding was quick, however, as evidenced by the limestone and brick buildings of today's downtown, centered on Massachusetts Street, and the State University campus, which stands on a steep, tree-covered grassy bank known as Mount Oread.

### The Town

Studded with cafes and eclectic shops, downtown Lawrence is a delight to walk around – and just as busy outside of term time, when day-trippers flock in from less congenial Kansan cities. However, most of the town's formal attractions are congregated on campus. The **University of Kansas Natural History Museum**, on Jayhawk Boulevard at 14th Street, along the crest of the hill (Mon–Fri 8am–5pm, Sat 10am–5pm, Sun noon–5pm; $2), holds a chronological panorama of North American flora and fauna, as well as Custer's beloved, enormous – and now stuffed – horse, Comanche, the centerpiece of an exhibit on the Battle of Little Bighorn. Across the road, the **Museum of Anthropology**, in Spooner Hall, presents African and Eskimo artifacts (Mon–Sat 9am–5pm, Sun 1–5pm; free). The **Spencer Museum of Art**, on Mississippi St (Tues, Wed, Fri & Sat 10am–5pm, Thurs 10am–9pm, Sun noon–5pm; free), specializes in world art, with an Oriental gallery, Old Masters and Pre-Raphaelites. Graphic art from the Sixties includes some Warhols and exceptional photographs, from Diane Arbus's disturbing portraits to Weegee's documentary exposés of New York City life. Its gift-shop does a great line in surreal and offbeat postcards.

Native American traditions are preserved and packaged for the public each year by the exhibitions of the **Lawrence Indian Arts Show**, held throughout the city from mid-September to the end of October. One venue is the Indian Nations University at 23rd and Massachusetts, where the **Hiawatha Visitor Center** and **American Indian Athletic Hall of Fame** are open year round by appointment (☎785/749-8404).

## Practicalities

Amtrak comes into Lawrence at 413 E Seventh St, and Greyhound arrives at 2447 W Sixth St. The kitsch Fifties-style Lawrence Bus Co runs local buses. The **visitor center** is north of downtown in the renovated Union Pacific Depot at N Second and Locust (Mon–Sat 8.30am–5pm, Sun 1–5pm; ☎785/865-4499 or 1-800/LAWKANS).

Adequate but dull budget **rooms** can be found near the bus station at the *Virginia Inn*, 2907 W Sixth St (☎785/843-6611; ③), while the *Super 8* at 515 McDonald Drive (☎913/842-5721; ③) is a reliable fall-back. There's a *Ramada* at 2222 W Sixth St (☎785/842-7030; ④). If you have a little extra cash, head instead to the lovely all-suite *Eldridge Hotel*, at Seventh and Massachusetts (☎785/749-5011 or 1-800/527-0909; ⑤/⑥); twice burned down by pro-slavery forces, it has been restored to an evocative faded elegance, and houses the stylish *Shalor's* restaurant (☎785/749-1005) and the atmospheric *Jayhawker* bar in the lobby. You can **camp** near downtown at *KOA*, 1473 Hwy-40 (☎785/842-3877), or three miles out along W 23rd St at Clinton Lake (☎785/843-7665).

Two healthy **places to eat** stand side by side on campus: the *Yello Sub* (☎785/841-3268) and the *Glass Onion* (☎785/841-2310), both at W Twelfth Street and Mount Oread, serve lunch in a laid-back atmosphere with sweeping views. Downtown, meat-lovers can fill up with the hickory-smoked barbecue at *Buffalo Bob's Smokehouse*, 719 Massachusetts St (☎785/841-6400), while the *Paradise Cafe*, nearby at no. 728 (☎785/842-5199), does veggie burgers, soups and salads, plus fish specials. Best of all are the nachos and gourmet pizzas at the exquisite *Teller's*, across the street in a beautifully restored bank building at no. 746 (☎785/843-4111). For a morning espresso, drop into *La Prima Tazza* at no. 638.

Lawrence's **nightlife** is dominated by students. Popular Massachusetts Street bars include the *Free State Brewing Co* at no. 636 (☎785/843-4555) and the *Jazzhaus* at no. 926 (☎785/749-3320), while the cavernous *Bottleneck*, 737 New Hampshire St (☎785/841-5483), is the place to go for live rock music. *Liberty Hall*, 642 Massachusetts St (☎785/749-1912), once a social and political center, housed Lawrence's first newspaper, until it was burned down by pro-slavery agitators in 1863. Today it puts on art-house films, plays and concerts.

# West through Kansas

Further west across Kansas, three towns re-create the state's Wild West heritage, although only in the westernmost, **Dodge City**, does the scrubby landscape conform to the cowboy-movie image. **Abilene**, if less famous than Dodge City, has as many outlaw and gunslinging stories, and **Wichita**, about 200 miles southwest of Kansas City, holds an excellent, authentic reconstruction of frontier days in its Old Cowtown museum.

## Abilene

Like all the old cattle-trail cowtowns, **ABILENE**, 115 miles west of Lawrence on I-70, claims to have been the riproaringest of the lot. By the time legendary lawman Wild Bill

Hickok became its marshal in 1871, the unruly behavior was already dying down, and little today reminds you of those raucous days. Doing its best, though, is **Old Abilene Town**, at SE Sixth and Kuney (March–Sept daily 8am–8pm; free), a replica of the town during its cattle boom, complete with stagecoach rides. Gunfights are held on Saturday and Sunday at 12.30pm, 2.15pm and 3.30pm, with cancan dancers.

These days, Abilene prefers to stress its connections with Dwight Eisenhower. The **Eisenhower Center**, 201 SE Fourth St (May–Sept daily 8am–5.45pm; Oct–April daily 9am–4.45pm), encompasses his boyhood home, with its original furnishings, the obligatory film show and many photos and papers on display in the spacious museum ($3). The former president and his wife are buried in the meditation chapel.

Abilene's **visitor center** is at 201 NW Second St (☎316/263-2231 or 1-800/569-5915). Most of the town's budget **motels** are off I-70 at Hwy-15. The very basic *Diamond*, closer to downtown at 1407 NW Third St (☎316/263-2360; ②), provides free transportation to the bus depot.

# Wichita

**WICHITA**, about 165 miles southwest of Lawrence on I-35, is the largest city in Kansas, severed by the Arkansas River, which forks just north of downtown into the Big and Little Arkansas rivers (incidentally, Kansans take umbrage if you pronounce it "Arkansaw"; pronounce it here the way it is spelled). Originally settled by the Wichita Indians, who by 1865 had been relocated to Oklahoman Indian Territory, Wichita grew up as a stop on the Chisholm Trail. Its glory days were to be short-lived, however, as farmers, angry about the damage done by stampeding cattle, erected fences which forced the drives onto different trails further west, creating new cowtowns such as Dodge City. Today three of the world's major aircraft manufacturers (Beech, Cessna and Lear) are based here, and although downtown is wilting a little, Wichita remains attractive thanks to its great museums and a rich arts scene.

## The City

**Downtown Wichita** is a rapidly emptying casualty of the exodus to the suburbs, enlivened mainly by the public art and sculpture that pops up unexpectedly all over the place, in empty lots and even in tree stumps. The exceptional **Wichita-Sedgwick County Historical Museum**, 204 S Main St (Tues–Fri 11am–4pm, Sat & Sun 1–5pm; $2), is in **Old City Hall**, a heavy stone building decorated with turrets, gargoyles and arches. The cozy interior is crammed with exhibits on everything from the Wichita Indians through decorative art to Carry Nation, whose initial zeal for singing hymns to errant drunks grew into a campaign against everything from tobacco to corsets. The stately church with vivid stained-glass windows at 601 N Water St houses the **First National Black Historical Society** of Kansas (Mon, Wed & Fri 10am–2pm, Sun 2–6pm; closed July; free), an eclectic antidote to more mainstream views of Great Plains history, with details on Buffalo Soldiers, inventors and early black Wichitans, and some African art.

Excellent museums in the **Riverside** stretch of parkland (which also holds walking and bike trails) include the **Indian Center and Museum**, 650 N Seneca Drive (Mon–Sat 10am–5pm, Sun 1–5pm; Jan–March closed Mon; $2). The 44ft *Keeper of the Plains* statue, facing east at the confluence of the Little and Big Arkansas rivers, was designed in the 1970s by a Kiowa-Comanche artist, Blackbear Bosin, and dedicated by Native Americans and city officials smoking the peace pipe. It's an eerie sight at dusk, reaching into the sky with some unknown offering. The museum itself is small, with changing exhibits of traditional and contemporary Native American art: clothing and beadwork, pottery and baskets, paintings and prints.

Western artist C M Russell is the best represented of the veritable who's who of American painters assembled at the **Wichita Art Museum**, 619 Stackman Drive

(Tues–Sat 10am–5pm, Sun noon–5pm; free); there's also a great cafe. **Old Cowtown Museum**, 1871 Sim Park Drive (March–Oct Mon–Sat 10am–5pm, Sun noon–5pm; $5), is a seventeen-acre riverside exhibit re-creating the buildings of 1870s Wichita. Looking and feeling like a movie set, the area includes – along with some docile longhorns – the city's first one-room jail, a school room, a store, a smithy, churches and stables, and old homes.

To the north of the city, the surreal geodesic **Bright Spot For Health Center**, 3100 N Hillside Ave, house the Garvey Center for the Improvement of Human Functioning, which aims, by using holistic medicine, to find a cure for cancer. It's all very worthy, but weird: road signs, for example, tell you to "de-stress to 25," and there's a 39ft food guide pyramid. Tours include a video show and individual sample "nutrient profiles" (Mon–Thurs 8am–5.30pm, Fri 9am–4pm; $4). In the southeast of the city, the products of Wichita's plane industry are on display at the **Kansas Aviation Museum**, in the old Art Deco air terminal at 3350 George Washington Blvd (Tues–Fri 9am–4pm, Sat 1–5pm; $2).

## Practicalities

Domestic **flights** arrive at the Mid-Continent Airport (☎316/946-4700), five miles southwest of downtown on Hwy-54 W (Kellogg Drive). Amtrak stops at Newton, a small Mennonite town 25 miles north, with a local bus connection to Wichita throughout the day; Greyhound comes in to 312 S Broadway Ave, two blocks east of Main Street. City transportation consists of **buses** (WMTA; ☎316/265-7221; $1 a ride), and, more appealingly, **trolleys**, which run at lunchtimes and on Saturdays for just 50¢. The resourceful **CVB** is in the heart of downtown at Douglas and Main (Mon–Fri 8am–5pm; ☎316/265-2800 or 1-800/288-9424). An additional Information Office is housed in the Wichita Boathouse at 335 W Lewis St (daily 9am–5pm; ☎316/337-9088).

Budget **lodgings** in Wichita are plentiful, especially near the airport on W Kellogg Drive – try the *Econolodge* at no. 6245 (☎316/945-5261; ③). On the opposite flank of the city is a good *Fairfield Inn* at 333 S Webb Rd (☎316/685-3777; ④). Downtown's best value is the *Guild Plaza*, 125 N Market St (☎316/265-9800; ④), with a pool and breakfast included. In the east is the *Mainstay Suites*, 9444 E 39th St (☎316/631-3773; ④), comfortable and self-contained. *USI Campgrounds*, 2920 E 33rd St (☎316/838-0435), is the closest place to **camp**.

Though filled with good **places to eat**, downtown has few options for drinking or clubbing. *Pizza Hut* started here in 1958, which explains why there are thirteen outlets, including a cafe at 7700 E Kellogg Drive (☎316/683-1311). Otherwise there's great food (try the wild mushroom strudel) at the *Old Mill Tasty Shop*, by the railroad tracks at 604 E Douglas Ave (☎316/264-6500), complete with marble soda fountain. *Willie C's Cafe and Bar*, 656 S West St (☎316/942-4077), provides a good breakfast and snack menu. *Il Primo Espresso* is a rather twee cafe redeemed by its good coffee, out to the west at Central and Woodlawn (closed Sun; ☎316/682-4884). For the best steaks in town, head out the other way to *Scotch and Sirloin*, 5325 E Kellogg Blvd (☎316/685-8701).

# Dodge City

**DODGE CITY**, 150 miles west of Wichita, is perhaps the most famous of all America's cowtowns. It has certainly been committed to celluloid more times than any other, especially in 1930s Westerns like *My Darling Clementine* and *Dodge City*. However, this wildest of Wild West cities had a heyday of only a decade, from 1875 until 1886. Established in 1872 with the Santa Fe Railroad, which transported the hides of millions of plains buffalo, by 1875 the town of traders, trappers and hunters had to find a new economic base – the buffalo had been exterminated. The era of the great cattle drives was already underway, and Dodge City became a den of iniquity where gambling, drinking and general lawlessness were the norm. Such wickedness led to gunfights galore, and the notorious Boot Hill cemetery (where the villains were buried with their boots on) was kept busy by charismatic lawmen such as Bat Masterson and Wyatt Earp.

## The Town

Dodge City today is rather more staid, with its old downtown area enveloped by a hinterland of railroad tracks and giant paint-peeling silos. Outside of the two-week Dodge City Days and Rodeo, held each July, it is content to replay its movie image in the **Boot Hill Museum**, 500 Wyatt Earp Blvd (June–Aug daily 8am–8pm; Sept–May Mon–Sat 9am–5pm, Sun 1–5pm; $7, $18 family ticket, covering admission only). The museum centers on the single-sided **Historic Front Street**, which was constructed in 1958 and has been acquiring old buildings from all over the West ever since. There's a bank and a grocer, stagecoach rides, a funeral parlor, a smithy, and even a full-sized railroad station, as well as the (alcohol-free) Long Branch Saloon, scene of a variety show with can-can dancers every night at 7.30pm ($4.75). Gunfights and showdowns break out with alarming regularity. Boot Hill cemetery itself is higher up the hill, still on museum grounds; there's just a sorry little patch of lawn on one corner of the original site, which was in any case abandoned in 1879 after just six years and thirty-four burials. The bodies were reinterred elsewhere, and the graves were never marked anyway, so the jokey wooden crosses are more than a little bogus.

Other sights in town include the **Home of Stone**, 112 E Vine St (June–Aug Mon–Sat 9am–5pm, Sun 2–4pm; free), an emotive memorial to pioneer mothers, often forgotten amid the macho Wild West myth-making. The house looks pretty much as it would have when built in 1881, with domestic memorabilia from early plainswomen. **El Capitan**, at Second Street and Wyatt Earp Boulevard, is a massive bronze longhorn, facing south towards an identical north-facing statue in Abilene, West Texas. Together they mark the beginning and the end of the cattle drives.

## Practicalities

Greyhound **buses** from Wichita arrive twice daily at 2405 W Wyatt Earp Blvd. Amtrak comes right into downtown, to the historic Santa Fe Station at Central and Front. Call the **CVB** (☎316/225-8186) for advice; they run a small information kiosk on Wyatt Earp Boulevard near the museum (daily 9am–5pm), while off-season you can drop in at their offices up the hill at Fourth and W Spruce (Mon–Fri 8.30am–5pm). There is no city transportation, but the Dodge City Trolley runs narrated town tours four times a day from a booth on the Boot Hill parking lot ($5).

Most of Dodge City's **motels** are strung out roughly a mile west of downtown along US-50, still known here as Wyatt Earp Boulevard. The *Astro* at no. 2200 (☎316/227-8146; ②) is inexpensive but a little noisy, and offers free rides to the train and bus stations; the *Dodge House* at no. 2408 (☎316/225-9900; ③), has a reliable restaurant. The newly remodeled *Econolodge* at no. 1610 has an indoor pool and sauna area (☎316/225-0231; ③). **Camping** is an option even for the carless: the lakeside *Water Sports Campground Recreation*, 500 Cherry St (☎316/225-9003), lies ten blocks south of Front Street.

As for **food**, *A Bientot*, 100 Military Ave (☎316/225-0477), occupies the center of an anonymous-looking office block; it has no views but is attractive enough inside, serving classy but inexpensive pasta dishes and fine fried chicken. *Peppercorns*, out near the motels at 1301 W Wyatt Earp Blvd (☎316/225-2335), is a conventional highway steakhouse.

# IOWA

Although at times serene, and almost always verdant, nothing about **IOWA** truly stands out: this 55,000-square-mile chunk of the Great Plains doesn't even manage to be completely flat, it just wobbles up and down a little. The state is the very essence of smalltown America, close to the geographical center of the mainland US, and coming 25th out of fifty states in size, population and level of personal income. Even the cities seem at times to be merely villages grown large.

Iowa's history, too, has been relatively uneventful. It was opened for settlement after the Black Hawk Treaty of 1832, a one-sided exercise in negotiations with the Sauk, conducted after many of them had been chased down and slaughtered in neighboring Wisconsin and Illinois. The Northern European migrants who replaced them made agricultural development their prime concern, turning Iowa into the "**Foodbasket of America**" – a role it usually achieves with scrupulous efficiency, although the severe floods of 1993 saw the entire state declared a disaster area.

Tourist attractions in Iowa are few and far between; its most visited destination is the throwback Germanic enclave of the **Amana Colonies**. However, the state does also hold a few oddball sites, such as the original locations for the movies *The Bridges of Madison County* (in south central **Winterset**, birthplace of John Wayne) and *Field of Dreams* (near Dubuque in the northeast). You can also see, but not enter, the original house that featured in Grant Wood's much-parodied *American Gothic* painting (at Eldon in the southeast, and now owned by the state).

### Getting around Iowa

Greyhound **buses** out of Chicago call at all Iowa's major towns, with at least four services per day in each direction along I-80. St Louis is also well served by six daily buses from Des Moines and Iowa City; these towns are connected less frequently with Minneapolis/St Paul. Amtrak's east–west route misses the cities, stopping instead at assorted small communities in the south, though a bus usually makes the short trip to Des Moines from Osceola. The only sizeable **airport** is in Des Moines. Somewhat surprisingly, Iowa is a good place for **cycle touring**. Each year the amazingly popular cross-state bike ride – the RAGBRAI – attracts thousands of entrants, any of whom can tell you that the plains aren't always flat (tour details ☎515/284-8000).

# Eastern Iowa

**Eastern Iowa**, in the Mississippi River hinterland, is liberally sprinkled with agribusiness towns that display the continuing influence of their central and northern European pioneers, plus **religious communities** – Amish, Mennonite and the Amana Colonies. All are easily accessible from **Iowa City**, as home to a huge university one of the state's livelier centers. Riverside towns such as northerly **Dubuque** and Burlington, near the Missouri state line, have been enlivened since 1991 by gambling, though so far low-stake poker and roulette games can only be played on board Mississippi paddlewheelers, decked out in less-than-authentic Mark Twain-era trimmings.

## Dubuque

The handsome town of **DUBUQUE**, overlooked by rocky bluffs on the Mississippi around 150 miles west of Chicago, was founded as the first white settlement in Iowa by

French-Canadian leadminers in 1788. In the nineteenth century it became a boisterous riverport and logging center. Buildings from this era still stand, but the companies that use them are now concerned with meat packing and other food industries.

A new complex of buildings at Third Street in the old Ice Harbor area, cut off from downtown by Hwy-61, includes an assortment of river-related museums (daily 10am–5.30pm; $6). Precisely which exhibits are housed in the **Mississippi River Museum**, in the **Riverboat Museum**, and in the **National Rivers Hall of Fame** (which focuses on "Pathfinders" such as Lewis and Clark, rather than the rivers themselves) seems to vary, but together they tell the story of Mississippi navigation from the days of Robert Fulton's first commercial steamboat in 1807 until the floods of 1993. The fifteen-minute introductory film **"River of Dreams"** is a good starting point for your explorations.

Once your appetite has been whetted, you can travel along the high-banked Mississippi on a *Spirit of Dubuque* **paddlewheeler** cruise (May–Sept daily; $9 for 90min; ☎319/583-8093 or 1-800/747-8093), or on board one of the more expensive gambling boats. Alternatively, what's said to be the world's shortest and steepest **cable-car** ride grinds its way in summer from Fourth Street downtown up a sheer bluff to residential Fenelon Place, for a fine view across the Mississippi to Illinois and Wisconsin (April–Nov daily 8am–10pm; 75¢). If cable cars don't appeal, then head north to the lovingly maintained, 164-acre **Eagle Point Park** (daily 7am–10pm; $1) for its sweeping vistas of the lands east of the river.

Film buffs who enjoyed 1988's baseball fantasy **Field of Dreams** can meet like-minded souls in surprising numbers at the original movie location, three miles north of Dyersville, which is 25 miles west of Dubuque on US-20. True to the movie's slogan – "if you build it they will come" – crowds still gather on the bleachers to watch phantom games at the edge of the cornfields, and buy souvenirs from two rival family concerns (April–Nov daily 9am–6pm).

### Practicalities

The **Iowa Welcome Center**, in the museum complex at Third Street and Ice Harbor (daily 9.30am–5.30pm; ☎319/566-4372 or 1-800/798-8844), is the best place to pick up information on Dubuque. Although it's in a slightly seedy part of downtown, the grand redbrick *Julien Inn*, 200 Main St (☎319/556-4200 or 1-800/798-7098; ④), is a great **place to stay** and one of the best bargains in the entire Midwest, while the *Richards House B&B*, 1492 Locust St (☎319/557-1492; ④), veers towards old-world luxury. The *Shot Tower Inn*, at the foot of the cable car at Fourth and Locust (☎319/556-1061), serves a conventional menu of pizzas and meat dishes.

## Cedar Rapids

Seventy miles southwest, **CEDAR RAPIDS**, home of Quaker Oats, is Iowa's industrial leader. In the late 1840s, a meat-packing boom lured thousands of Czechs here. The **Czech Village**, 16th Avenue SW and First Street, features the excellent Sykora's bakery, giftshops, traditional houses and a small museum of national costumes and pioneer artifacts (Tues–Sun 9.30am–4.30pm; admission varies according to exhibits; ☎319/362-8500). The very modern **Museum of Art**, 410 Third Ave SE, boasts a comprehensive collection of paintings by Grant Wood, best known for the depictions of Thirties farm-life seen in *American Gothic* (Tues, Wed, Fri & Sat 10am–4pm, Thurs 10am–7pm, Sun noon–5pm; $4).

Cedar Rapids' **CVB** is based at 119 First Ave NE, downtown (Mon–Fri 8am–5pm; ☎319/398-5009 or 1-800/523-1100). The *Best Western Cooper's Mill*, 100 F Ave NW (☎319/366-5323 or 1-800/858-5511; ④), has reasonable **rooms**.

# The Amana Colonies

The **Amana Colonies** spread from the intersection of Hwy-151 and Hwy-220, midway between Cedar Rapids and Iowa City. They were founded in 1855 by the **Community of True Inspiration**, pacifist German refugees (not linked to the Amish or Mennonites) who believed that God spoke through prophets – themselves, for example – rather than ordained ministers. Members led a simple, collective lifestyle: each family lived in its own home, but they all ate together and shared profits from the farms. During the Depression, communal ownership became increasingly difficult to maintain, and in 1932 stock was redistributed among all the adults. However, they did keep up their commitment to close family ties, a sense of community and religious principles. On Sunday mornings, you can still see women church members wearing the traditional black cap, shawl and apron, with men dressed in equally sombre attire. Church services for visitors, held in English, take place at 10am every Sunday in Middle Amana.

The Amana Colonies today, consisting of seven separate villages set in an immaculate, serene valley, feel like a cross between a ski resort with no mountains and a reservation for Midwestern pioneers. Their prosperity is very evident, though as well as tasteful clapboard houses standing on well-groomed lawns, and neat plank fences dividing rolling meadows, you'll also come across factories, pizza parlors and even a golf course. The twee streets of the largest village, **AMANA**, are lined with restaurants and craftshops, a brewery, winery and woolen mill – plus a small and somewhat self-congratulatory **Museum of History** (Mon–Sat 10am–5pm, April–Nov also Sun noon–5pm; $5 gets you into all four museums). Picturesque **HOMESTEAD** is enhanced by a walking trail around the dam on a scenic bend of the Iowa River, built centuries ago by Indians to concentrate fish into one area and thus allow them to be caught more easily.

### Practicalities

Conventional addresses are seldom used in the Amana Colonies, but points of interest are well signposted. The **visitor center**, near the junction of Hwy-151 and Hwy-220 (Mon–Sat 9am–5pm, Sun 10am–5pm; ☎319/622-7622 or 1-800/245-5465), has details of **B&Bs** such as the *Baeckerei* in the heart of Amana (☎319/622-3597; ③).

Probably the most compelling reason to visit the colonies is their undeniably excellent old-style German **food**. Apple-cheeked serving staff at the *Amana Barn Restaurant* (☎319/622-3214) in Amana village dish up huge and inexpensive portions of country ham, beef schnitzel and the like, with pickled baby vegetables; for a lighter snack, call in at *Hahn's Hearth Oven Bakery* in Middle Amana (☎319/622-3439). South Amana's *Market Place Restaurant* (☎319/622-3225) offers sausages galore. Alcohol is not proscribed.

# Iowa City

**IOWA CITY**, on I-80 55 miles west of the Mississippi, is refreshingly young at heart. The restored gold-domed **Old Capitol** is a reminder of its days as state capital, before government was transferred to the more central Des Moines. Residents were placated by getting the University of Iowa instead. The arty shops and sidewalk cafes of the compact, partly pedestrianized downtown touch the east end of campus, but its red and gray buildings, closeted by tall dark trees, remain aloof from the rest of the town.

Greyhound stops at 404 E College St, just off downtown. The **CVB** is at 408 First Ave in Coralville, a mile northeast of downtown (☎319/337-6592 or 1-800/283-6592). *Iowa House* is a comfortable central **hotel** in the Union building, beside the river on Madison Street (☎319/335-3513; ④). To the west, inexpensive **motels** in Coralville include a very clean and good-value *Super 8*, 611 First Ave (☎319/337-8388; ③). Bargain **food** is

easy to find, be it soup in a sour bread bowl at *Quinton's*, 215 E Washington St
(☎319/354-7074); the pastries and espressos served on long comfortable sofas at *Java
House*, nearby at 211 E Washington St; or the burgers at *Micky's*, 11 S Dubuque St
(☎319/338-6860), a friendly, dimly lit Irish bar.

# Central and western Iowa

Pigs outnumber people in central Iowa. The only city among the cornfields, state capital **Des Moines**, struggles to lift the monotony, and many visitors may prefer the college town of **Ames**. The humdrum west has little to offer.

## Des Moines

**DES MOINES**, near the center of Iowa amid tree-covered hills at the confluence of the
sluggish Des Moines and Racoon rivers, owes its origins to a military fort set up in
1843. It had already grown into a trading center for farmers by the time the eighteen-
year-old Frederick Hubbell arrived in 1855; within a decade he had founded the
Equitable Life and Insurance Corporation to service their need for investment capital.
Other companies soon realized the potential of agrarian business, and today the city is
the world's third largest **insurance** center, behind London and Hartford, Connecticut.
Illustrious former denizens of Des Moines include **Ronald Reagan**, who started out as
a sportscaster on Radio WHO, and **John Wayne**, born and raised in nearby Winterset.

### Arrival and information
Des Moines' Greyhound station is just northwest of downtown at 1107 Keosauqua Way.
From the very efficient transfer mall at Sixth and Walnut, MTA **buses** (☎515/283-8100)
run practically everywhere in the city. The **visitor center** occupies Suite 222, 601
Locust St (Mon–Fri 8.30am–5pm; ☎515/286-4960 or 1-800/451-2625).

### Accommodation
Downtown Des Moines caters mostly for insurance company business, but still offers
some fairly inexpensive places to stay. You can **camp** in summer at the *Iowa State
Fairgrounds Campgrounds*, E 30th Street and Grand Avenue (☎515/262-3111).

**Best Western Starlite Village**, 929 3rd St (☎515/282-5251). Reasonable downtown rooms. ⑤.

**Hotel Fort Des Moines**, 1000 Walnut Ave at 10th (☎515/243-1161 or 1-800/532-1466). Exquisite,
historical downtown gem with old-world elegance and exemplary service. The indoor swimming
pool/spa area won awards for its tasteful design. Highly recommended. ④–⑥.

**Motel 6**, 4817 Fleur Drive (☎515/287-6364). Clean rooms near the airport. ③.

**YMCA**, 101 Locust St at 1st (☎515/288-0131). Slightly faded, men-only downtown rooms for $25;
weekly rates. ①.

**YWCA**, 717 Grand Ave (☎515/244-8961). Clean, dorm-style rooms for women in a safe part of downtown; $8 per bed per night with discount for weekly stays. ①.

### The City
The steel-and-glass skyline of **downtown** Des Moines, most of which shot up during
the Eighties, is testimony to its ever-growing insurance trade. Towering above all is
the boxy, 44-story **801 Grand** building, headquarters of the Principal Financial
Company. For such a fast-track financial center, the streets are curiously empty; pedestrians instead use the **Skywalk**, a three-mile network of air-conditioned corridors linking twenty blocks of offices, banks, parking lots, restaurants, hotels and movie
theaters.

Most businesses stand on the west bank of the Des Moines River, which cuts downtown in two. In 1857, a group of speculators attempted to shift the commercial hub to the east side by bribing commissioners to site the **state capitol** at E Ninth Street and Grand Avenue. Their hopes of huge spin-offs were dashed when the nationwide financial crash later that same year saw property prices collapse. As a result, the five-domed Italian Renaissance-style mass, on the crest of a steep hill, is now detached from the heart of the city (Mon–Fri 8am–4.30pm, Sat–Sun 8am–4pm; call for tour times ☎515/281-5591; free). A short walk downhill, displays in the futuristic pink-and-brown **State of Iowa Historical Building** (Tues–Sat 9am–4.30pm, Sun noon–4.30pm; free) at E Sixth and Locust (topped by a strange neon figurine) cover Indian civilization, pioneer times and the development of Iowan farming, along with plenty of solemn portraits of former governors.

Three miles west, the impressive **Des Moines Art Center** at 4700 Grand Ave (Tues, Wed, Fri & Sat 11am–4pm, Thurs 11am–9pm, Sun noon–4pm; $4, free) is housed in a trio of buildings designed by Eliel Saarinen, I M Pei and Richard Meier. Works by Matisse, Picasso and Renoir stand alongside twentieth-century Americans such as Wood, Hopper and O'Keeffe. The most dynamic exhibits are in the mixed-media wing, and include a gigantic and disturbing Anselm Keifer canvas.

### Eating, drinking and nightlife

That Iowans eat well is reflected in the quality – and quantity – of food on offer in Des Moines' restaurants.

**Java Joe's**, 214 4th St (☎515/288-5282). Late-opening coffee bar and sandwich place attached to an artist's gallery, featuring live entertainment at weekends.

**Papa's Planet**, 208 3rd St (☎515/243-0901). Favorite weekend gathering place for young locals, with guitar bands at low cover charges and an outside street patio.

**Spaghetti Works**, 310 Court Ave (☎515/243-2195). Spacious Italian outfit with original interior decor. The all-you-can-eat pasta dishes from $4 are great value.

**Stella's Blue Sky Diner**, 400 Locust St, in Capitol Square building (☎515/246-1953). Kitsch diner decked out in lurid pinks, turquoises and yellows. Burgers and fries ($4) washed down with divine chocolate, peanut butter and banana malts. Mon–Sat 8am–6pm; a must for lunch, but be prepared for long lines.

**308 Court Ave Sports Bar**, 308 Court Ave (☎515/244-1710). Lively, reasonably priced Tex-Mex cafe.

## Around Des Moines

Thirty miles north of Des Moines, **AMES** is the home of Iowa State University. Smaller and slightly less trendy than Iowa City, it's still a lively little community (by Iowan standards at least), and has recently earned itself a place on the stadium rock roster, attracting all manner of big-name bands. The **visitor center**, 213 Duff St (☎515/232-4032 or 1-800/288-7470) can advise on upcoming concerts and area attractions. **Room** rates are reasonable out at the *Super 8*, I-35 and Hwy-30 (☎515/232-6510; ③), three miles from campus; *Godfather's Pizza*, 414 Lincoln Way (☎515/232-9000), is popular.

Ten miles west of downtown Des Moines (I-80 exit 125), the **Living History Farms** in Urbandale (May–Oct daily 9am–5pm; $8) trace the evolution of agriculture on the plains. Self-guided tours lead from the oval bark homes of an eighteenth-century Iowan settlement, through an 1850s homestead, to a look at the high-tech methods of today. If you want to continue the yokel theme, eat colossal portions of meat loaf and chops in the *Iowa Machine Shed Restaurant* (☎515/270-6818), or stay in the country-style *Comfort Suites Hotel* (☎515/276-1126; ④); both are next to the farm entrance.

## THE BRIDGES OF MADISON COUNTY

The fortunes of Winterset, the county town of Madison County, have taken an unexpected turn for the better in the years since the publication of the best-selling tearjerker **The Bridges of Madison County**. Fans attracted by 1995's movie version, which was filmed in and around Winterset and starred Clint Eastwood and Meryl Streep, will be delighted to find everything looking just as it did on screen. *National Geographic* may never have published a feature about them – fictional photographer Robert Kincaid's assignment in the book and film – but there really are six (out of an original nineteen) nineteenth-century **covered bridges** in the immediate neighborhood, of which the two that were most prominent in both book and film are most worth seeing. None charges for admission or has formal opening hours. For a full list and **driving map**, drop in at Winterset's visitor center on Courthouse Square.

**Roseman Bridge**, where Kincaid was guided by housewife Francesca Johnson, crosses the Middle River around six miles southwest of town, and can be reached via a bewildering succession of country roads (head south from Hwy-92 eight miles west of Winterset if you want to follow the undulating dirt track seen during the credits). Built on this spot in 1883, and supposedly haunted, it was restored in 1992 at a cost of over $150,000, only to be thoroughly aged again for the movie. It's far too frail to support vehicles, but you can walk out on its knotted planks, and decipher the ever-multiplying sets of carved initials on its peeling timbers.

The sturdier **Cedar Bridge**, the only one still used by traffic, was moved in 1921 from what is now Hwy-169, and today stands to one side of Hwy-G4R, a couple of miles northeast of town. The scene of Kincaid and Johnson's final tryst, it is the focus of a small county park and picnic area.

## Winterset

Until Robert Waller's *The Bridges of Madison County* changed everything, sleepy, run-down **WINTERSET**, 25 miles southwest of Des Moines, seemed a long way off the beaten track. Its one tourist attraction was the modest former home of the local pharmacist at 216 S Second St, run as a **museum** to his son, Marion Robert Morrison (daily 10am–4.30pm; $2.50). Born in 1907, he grew up to become Hollywood hardman **John Wayne**. His first lead role was in 1930 but real stardom, as the Ringo Kid in John Ford's *Stagecoach*, didn't come for another nine years. Three decades later, Wayne claimed his only Oscar as Rooster Cogburn, the drunken one-eyed marshal in *True Grit*. Among the photos, personal belongings and mementos is a glowing personal endorsement of "the Duke" from his buddy Ronald Reagan, who shared his political views, if not perhaps his acting abilities.

These days Winterset's **visitor center**, on Courthouse Square in the heart of town (Mon–Fri 9am–5pm, Sat 9am–4pm, Sun 11am–4pm; ☎515/462-1185 or 1-800/298-6119), has become accustomed to handling inquiries from all over the world about the locations for Waller's tale, including hundreds of couples wanting to marry on the bridges themselves. If you don't want to go that far, you can drive out to view the covered bridges (see box above), or at least have a meal in the old-style *Northside Cafe*, a few doors along from the visitor center, where Clint was made to feel decidedly uncomfortable in the movie. You can also visit the late 1800s homestead that was **Francesca Johnson's farm** in the movie at 3271 130th St, (May–Oct 10am–6pm or by appointment ☎515/981-5268; donation). **Accommodation** possibilities nearby include the *Village View Motel*, Hwy-92 E (☎515/462-1218 or 1-800/862-1218; ③), and *A Step Away*, 104 W Court St (☎515/462-5956; ⑤), a snug little B&B.

# NEBRASKA

*Hell, I thought I was dead too. Turns out I was just in Nebraska.*

Gene Hackman in *Unforgiven*

Though modern transcontinental travelers tend to see **NEBRASKA** in much the same light as did the early pioneers, heading west during the Gold Rush – as just another dreary expanse of prairie to get through as fast as possible – this flat and sparsely populated state in fact encompasses quite a few places of interest. However, its most appealing cities, commercial **Omaha** and the livelier state capital, **Lincoln**, are separated by a good three hundred miles of underwhelming, livestock-rearing flatlands from the western **Panhandle**, where the landscape finally erupts into giant sand hills and valleys, broken by towering rocky columns and hemmed in by sheer-faced buttes.

Western Nebraska was still embroiled in vicious and bloody battles against Native Americans long after the east had been settled; from the first serious uprising in 1854, it was 36 years before the US Army could make white control unchallengeable. Close to the South Dakota state line, **Fort Robinson**, where Crazy Horse was murdered, remains one of the West's most evocative historic sites.

Without navigable rivers, Nebraska had to rely on the **railroads** to help populate the land. During the 1870s and 1880s, rail companies, encouraged by grants that allowed them to accumulate one-sixth of the state, laid down such a comprehensive network of tracks that virtually every farmer was within a day's cattle drive of the nearest halt. Thus the buffalo-hunting country of the Sioux and Pawnee was turned into high-yield farmland, which today has few rivals in terms of **beef** production.

## Getting around Nebraska

Omaha **airport** offers the best domestic links, though planes from other cities in the region also fly to Lincoln. Several Greyhound **buses** traverse I-80 each day on the coast-to-coast marathon, stopping at all the major towns. Amtrak **trains**, traveling through the night, follow a similar route and call at Omaha, Lincoln, Hastings, Holdredge and McCook. Driving on I-80 can get tedious; if you're not in a rush, Hwy-2 is a good alternative.

# Eastern Nebraska

The silt-laden **Missouri River** separates Nebraska from Iowa and Missouri to the east. This stretch of the "Big Muddy" offers few natural ports, and **Omaha** remains the only riverfront community of any size. **Lincoln**, 58 miles southwest, is the state's capital and seat of its university.

## Omaha

Although **OMAHA**, Nebraska's largest and most easterly city, is visibly a prosperous place, with a great zoo, several museums and a lively entertainment district, the atmosphere remains sedate and predominantly suburban. As a major terminus on the first transcontinental railroad, Omaha made a logical alternative to distant Chicago as a marketplace for Wyoming and Nebraska ranchers to sell their herds of cattle. By 1900 massive stockyards had spread along the southern edge of town, and the city still handles well over one million head of livestock per year.

The broad sweeping thoroughfares of **downtown Omaha** have been all but killed off by the drift to the city's myriad malls, though you'll find good bars and cafes along the cobbled streets of the **Old Market** district, plus interesting specialist shops such as the Antiquarian Bookstore, 1215 Harney St (☎402/341-8077), packed with dusty volumes (and local bohemians). The nearby **Heartland Park of America**, at Eighth and Douglas – ideal for a picnic – holds a huge electronically controlled fountain. Behind its pink-marble Art Deco exterior, the **Joslyn Art Museum**, 2200 Dodge St (Tues–Sat 10am–4pm, Sun noon–4pm; $5, free Sat before noon), contains an interesting range of Indian art and twentieth-century American paintings.

The **Great Plains Black Museum**, in the city's predominantly black north side at 2213 Lake St (Mon–Fri 10am–2pm; $2), presents the history of African-American people on the prairies. One stimulating section focuses on blacks in the frontier army: where recently freed slaves, who could find no work in the Deep South after the Civil War, were often sent as advance parties into the most hostile and dangerous regions. It was Native American warriors who first called them "**buffalo soldiers**," because of their tightly curled hair and the color of their skin.

**Malcolm X** was born in Omaha in May 1925, though his family moved to Michigan immediately thereafter, in the face of Ku Klux Klan death threats to his father, a preacher who followed the back-to-Africa teachings of Marcus Garvey. His place of birth can be seen at 3448 Pinkney St (daily dawn–dusk; free). By way of contrast, the lavish birthplace of President **Gerald R Ford**, at 32nd and Woolworth, is also open to the public; he too moved to Michigan as an infant, after his parents separated (daily 7.30am–9pm; free).

The **Henry Doorly Zoo**, 3701 S Tenth St (daily 9.30am–5pm; $7.75), rightfully considers itself one of the best zoos in America. It started off with two buffalo borrowed from Buffalo Bill; now there's a gigantic free-flying aviary, some rare white Siberian tigers and a magnificent bear canyon, and the large Kingdoms of the Seas aquarium. Best of all is the **Lied Jungle**, an indoor rainforest housing tropical wildlife from South America, Asia and Africa: an elevated walkway, with a swaying rope bridge, leads into a world populated by pygmy hippos, gibbons, leopards, crocodiles, parrots, butterflies – and the aptly named howler monkeys.

## Practicalities

Omaha's Greyhound station is at 1601 Jackson St; Amtrak trains depart very late at night, and arrive long before the city wakes up, at 1003 S Ninth St. Both depots are well placed for downtown. Local public transportation is poor.

The **CVB**, at 6800 Mercy Rd, exit 459 from I-80 (Mon–Fri 8.30am–4.30pm; ☎402/444-4660 or 1-800/332-1819), offers discount vouchers for **motels**, which congregate around I-80 and 84th Street. There's also a **welcome center** for Nebraska as a whole, just off I-80, exit 454, across from the zoo at Tenth and Deer Park (May–Oct daily 9am–5pm; ☎402/595-3990). Rooms at the circular, almost cute, and certainly pretty unusual *Satellite Motel*, 6006 L St (☎402/733-7373; ③), come clean and at good prices. The *Riverview Garden B&B*, 9641 N 29th St (☎402/455-4623; ④) has comfortable rooms in a quiet neighborhood that overlooks the Missouri River. The well-kept *Sleep Inn*, out by the airport at 2525 Abbott Drive (☎402/342-2525 or 1-800/688-2525; ④), makes for a quiet night.

The **Old Market** district, centered on Tenth and Howard streets, has the liveliest **restaurants** and **bars**. The *Indian Oven*, 1010 Howard St (☎402/342-4856), a superb Asian restaurant, features *paneer* and vegetable dishes on its extensive menu. Both *M's Pub*, 422 S 11th St (☎402/342-2550), which serves the best bar food in town, and *The Upstream Brewing Company*, 514 S 11th St (☎402/344-0200), has excellent beers and a standard American menu, while *13th Street Coffee Co* at 519 S 13th St (☎402/345-2883) can meet your espresso requirements. Whether you fancy terrific desserts or a light meal, the *Garden Cafe*, 1212 Harney St (☎402/422-1574), won't break the bank. *Mr Toad's*, 1002 Howard St (☎402/345-4488), is a reliable **jazz venue** with good jam sessions at weekends.

# Lincoln

Were it not for Omaha, 58 miles northeast, **LINCOLN** would be in the back of beyond; the next major point of civilization to the west is Denver, Colorado, 480 miles further along I-80. As tiny Rochester, it was selected to be **state capital** in 1867 – on the condition that it change its name to Lincoln in honor of the recently assassinated president. Such was the disappointment in the territorial seat of government, Omaha, that state officials had to smuggle documents, books and office furniture out of the city in the middle of the night to avoid armed gangs.

Lincoln now serves as an oasis of culture for a large chunk of the plains. At night, when the students emerge, its compact downtown comes into its own. Of its alphabetical array of broad boulevards, O Street (the subject of Ginsberg's poem *Zero Street*) is the main drag; 13th and 14th streets are packed with bars and places to eat.

Dwarfing the rest of **downtown**, the central tower of the 1932 **Nebraska state capitol**, 1445 K St (Mon–Fri 9am–4pm, Sat 10am–4pm, Sun 1–4pm; tours every half-hour in summer; free), protrudes 400ft into the sky. Topped by a 20ft statue of a sower on a pedestal of wheat and corn, its remarkably phallic appearance – an adventurous departure from the usual architecture of state capitols – has prompted the nickname "penis of the prairies." For once there's no golden dome, and the superb iridescent murals in the foyer are a welcome alternative to old portraits, flags and emblems. From the fourteenth-floor observation deck you can survey the flatness of the surrounding farmland.

Twelve thousand years of life on the plains are covered at the **Museum of Nebraska History**, 15th and P (Mon–Fri 9am–4.30pm, Sat 9am–5pm, Sun 1.30–5pm; free), where displays focus on anthropology rather than history. The Elephant Hall, a gallery of towering mammoth, mastodon and four-tusker skeletons, is the highlight of the **U of N State Museum** at 14th and U (Mon–Sat 9.30am–4.30pm, Sun & hols 1.30–4.30pm; $2). A few blocks away, the **Sheldon Memorial Art Gallery**, Twelfth and R (Tues, Wed & Fri 10am–5pm, Thurs & Sat 10am–5pm & 7–9pm, Sun 2–9pm; free), traces the development of American art, and has a twenty-piece sculpture garden. The 76,000-seater **Memorial Stadium** (tickets ☎402/472-3111 or 1-800/8BIGRED), at the northern end of campus at the end of Vine Street, is where the brutal "Big Red" Cornhuskers invariably thrash the footballing opposition.

## Practicalities

Lincoln's Greyhound station is downtown at 940 P St, while Amtrak passes through 201 N Seventh St at crazy early-morning hours. Star-Tran (☎402/476-1234) runs good local buses (85¢). The **visitor center** is in Lincoln Station, right next to Amtrak (June–Sept Mon–Fri 9am–8pm, Sat 8am–5pm, Sun noon–5pm; rest of year Mon–Fri 9am–6pm, Sat 10am–4pm, Sun noon–5pm; ☎402/434-5348 or 1-800/423-8212). Except on football weekends, it's easy to find inexpensive **accommodation** out by the airport, off I-80 exit 399 – at the *Inn 4 Less* motel (☎402/475-4511; ②), for example. Downtown, however, has a shortage of budget rooms: the *Holiday Inn*, Ninth and O Street (☎402/475-4011 or 1-800/432-0002; ⑤), is good value; the *HI-Cornerstone* **hostel**, 640 N 16th St (☎402/476-0355; ①), in a church on the edge of campus, offers basic members-only bunks for $10.

Few of the downtown **restaurants** are desperately interesting, with grills, pizzerias and family diners predominating. *The Oven*, 201 N Eighth St (☎402/475-6118), offers Indian cuisine with a range of cheap breads and inventive specials, while the Italian menu at *Valentino's*, 232 N 13th at Q (☎402/475-1501), is not bad; both food and beer come well recommended at the *Crane River Brewpub and Cafe*, 200 N 11th at P (☎402/476-7766). *The Zoo*, 136 N 14th St (☎402/435-8754), attracts big-name jazz and blues acts who drop in en route between Chicago and Kansas City; *Duffy's Bar*, 1412 O St (☎402/474-3543), pulls in a younger crowd and some good rock bands. Across the street at 1329 O St, *O'Rourke's Lounge* (☎402/435-8052) is a lively, well-priced hangout.

The **Historic Haymarket District**, down by the Amtrak station, holds a further selection of bars and restaurants.

# Western Nebraska

After the unerringly flat journey across eastern Nebraska, the far west comes as a refreshing change. In the **Panhandle**, as it's often called, wave upon wave of rumpled sandy hills, thinly coated with prairie grass, back off towards the horizon like a sea in constant turmoil. Early pioneers wrote the area off as unproductive, and it remained barren until massive irrigation work at the start of the twentieth century enabled agricultural settlement. In the northwest the sand hills yield to classic John-Ford-style Western scenery: pancake-flat valleys, crisscrossed by dry meandering riverbeds and corralled by crusty, contorted bluffs under the constant shadow of fast-moving clouds. Emigrants on the **Oregon Trail** used the bizarre outcrops which sprout along the way as "road signs" to let them know that their trek across the plains was coming to an end.

## Along I-80

**Interstate-80** is one of the most popular coast-to-coast routes simply because it's the shortest. Scenery is not its strongest suit, and the central swath through 450 miles of Nebraskan farmland is not always a prospect drivers cherish. If time doesn't matter, then it's better to head northwest at dreary Grand Island, 93 miles west of Lincoln, onto Scenic Hwy-2 (see below) for a lonesome yet exhilarating drive through the Sandhills.

If you stick to I-80, decent pull-off points are few and far between. **KEARNEY**, a mildly interesting college town at exit 272, has a strip of inexpensive restaurants and studenty bars, but not much else. Just over halfway across the state at exit 177, **NORTH PLATTE** makes a big deal about its **Buffalo Bill Ranch Historical Park** (April–May & Sept–Oct daily 9am–5pm; June–Aug daily 10am–8pm; closed Nov–Mar; $2.50 per car), another property of the ubiquitous William "Buffalo Bill" Cody. Today the ranch is run by the state, which places more emphasis on history than tacky folklore. Cody's mansion and various barns can be examined; activities include a nightly rodeo in summer. The *Rambler Motel*, 1420 Rodeo Rd (☎308/532-9290; ③), has comfortable **rooms** and an outdoor pool, while the authentic Mexican cantina, *La Casita*, at 1911 E Fourth St (☎308/534-8077), boasts an irresistible **Elvis room**.

Thirty miles west another restaurant sets out to entertain vexed drivers, in the one-horse hamlet of **PAXTON**, off exit 145. **Ole's Big Game Lounge & Grill** (☎308/239-4500) serves tasty fried food, with over two hundred wildlife trophies from around the world mounted on walls, cabinets and shelves. Fascinating, but not a place for the animal rights activist.

**OGALLALA**, twenty miles further along, sits just nine miles south of "Big Mac" – **Lake McConaughy** reservoir, famous for fishing, water sports and the sandy beaches along its 105 miles of shoreline. From Ogallala, it's 165 miles to Cheyenne, WY, though Sidney (exit 59) takes you into the rugged Oregon Trail country (see p.712).

## Scenic Hwy-2 and Alliance

**Scenic Hwy-2** meanders and dips for over 330 miles from I-80 to South Dakota's Black Hills. It passes through the **Sandhills** – a mesmerizing landscape carpeted with short-grass prairie and softened by delicate wild flowers and shiny ponds. Apart from a few farmsteads, grain silos and tiny churches, all you're likely to see on the open road are lazing cattle, a few sluggish rivers and the occasional mile-and-a-quarter-long freight train weaving its way through the hills. It's a long, desolate yet incredibly beautiful drive through an anachronistic corner of the US, where small towns are all spick-and-span and everyone could well know each other's name; **Broken Bow**, 77 miles north of I-80, features one of the neatest town squares in the heartland.

The road dawdles for another 200 miles through scattered villages before drifting into **ALLIANCE** – a nice enough little prairie town, which pulls in over 50,000 visitors per year for its one big attraction. **Carhenge**, two miles north on Hwy-385, is a rough copy of Stonehenge, made with old cars rather than stone. Erected in a cornfield during a family reunion in 1987, this intriguing collection of Chevys, Cadillacs and Plymouths, painted a brooding battleship grey and tilted at unusual angles, has to be the best picnic site in America's heartland. To some it's an ingenious piece of Pop Art; others view it as great black humor, or an appalling eyesore; and a few fundamentalist Christians suspect it may be a Satanic shrine. Certainly, the Nebraska Department of Roads saw nothing amusing about the project. They rapidly declared it a junkyard, and ordered the City of Alliance to remove it – whereupon the city, realizing it had the only tourist attraction within a fifty-mile radius, redrew its boundaries to avoid having to enforce the order. Relentless state officials attempted to dispose of the monstrosity by ordering the construction of a slip road, parking lot and other facilities; locals rose to the challenge by forming the **Friends of Carhenge**, whose work seems to have secured the monument's future (free admission, hours vary; ☎308/762-4110).

The helpful downtown **CVB** office, 124 W Third St (☎308/762-1520) provides information and sells Carhenge souvenirs. You can get clean **rooms** at the *Days Inn*, 117 Cody Ave, just off Third St (☎308/762-8000; ③), or the *Super 8*, 1419 W Third St (☎308/762-8300; ②). *Ken & Dale's*, 123 E Third St (☎308/762-7252), serves succulent all-day breakfasts and great pecan pancakes.

## The Oregon Trail landmarks

Two of the first landmarks encountered by travelers on the Oregon Trail, which in western Nebraska paralleled the route of modern US-26, were the lumpy **Courthouse and Jail rocks**, which lie just beyond the likeable little town of **Bridgeport**, 36 miles south of Alliance. Fourteen miles west, along Hwy-92, the much-painted and photographed **Chimney Rock** rises almost 500ft above the North Platte River. Although this phallic outcrop's nineteenth-century stature may have been chipped away by erosion and lightning, it remains one of the most recognizable and memorable landmarks in the West.

The twin towns of **GERING** and **SCOTTSBLUFF**, 25 miles further west, are the commercial center for the farmlands of western Nebraska. Southwest of Gering, the rugged 800ft rampart of **Scotts Bluff National Monument** (summer daily 8am–8pm; rest of year daily 8am–5pm; $4 per car) stands like a Nebraskan Gibraltar. Known to the Sioux as *Me-a-pa-te* ("hill that's hard to get around"), it earned its anglicized name in 1828 after fur trader Hiram Scott was mysteriously found dead at its base. Treks to the top are rewarded with a magnificent view, and the entrance fee includes the absorbing **Oregon Trail Museum**, which relates the experiences of the early migrants. Just outside Gering, to the southwest, the spiky **Wildcat Hills** hold some delightful vistas and hiking terrain.

Well-kept **rooms** are available in the *Lamplighter American Inn*, 606 E 27th St, Scottsbluff (☎308/632-7108 or 1-800/341-8000; ③); the fully licensed *Woodshed*, 18 E 16th St (☎308/635-3684), is the best spot for family-style **food**. The towns' **visitor center** can be found at 1517 Broadway, Scottsbluff (☎308/632-2133).

## Fort Robinson State Park

Some eighty miles north of Scottsbluff, just west of **Crawford** village, **Fort Robinson State Park**, beside 1000ft crenelated cliffs in the inhospitable White River Valley, preserves the spot where the US Army coordinated its campaign to rid the gold-rich

---

### CRAZY HORSE

The life of Oglala Sioux leader **Crazy Horse** is shrouded in confusion, misinterpretation and controversy. So thoroughly did the most enigmatic figure in Plains Indian history avoid contact with whites outside battle that no photograph or even sketch of him exists; unlike other Indian chiefs, he refused to visit Washington DC or talk to reporters.

Crazy Horse earned his title as a youth, after he single-handedly charged rival Arapahoe and took two scalps. The finest moment in a brilliant military career came in June 1876, when he led a thousand warriors in inflicting a stinging defeat on the superior forces of General George Crook at the Battle of the Rosebud River. Only eight days later Crazy Horse headed the attack at the Battle of Little Bighorn, where Custer and his entire company were killed (see p.783).

After Little Bighorn, US Army efforts to round up the Indians redoubled. In May 1877, Crazy Horse surprised friend and foe alike by leading nine hundred of his people into Fort Robinson. They gave up their weapons and Crazy Horse, keen to stay in his native land (unlike Sitting Bull, who had retreated to Canada), demanded that the buffalo grounds along the Powder River should remain in Indian hands. Tensions at the army camp rose after a rumor went around the barracks that the Sioux chief had come to murder General Crook. Crazy Horse was arrested on September 5, 1877; during a tussle outside the fort jail, he was bayoneted three times, dying the next morning.

Quite why this undefeated warrior should have surrendered without a fight, and whether he fell victim to a deliberate assassination, remain unclear. What is certain is that his death signaled the closing chapter of the Indian Wars. The Oglala Sioux were forcibly moved to the poor hunting country of Missouri, and settlers immediately swept in their thousands into western Nebraska, South Dakota, Wyoming and Montana.

Crazy Horse, so one story goes, was buried by his family in an unmarked grave in an out-of-the-way creek called **Wounded Knee** – the very place where thirteen years later three hundred Sioux men, women and children were slaughtered in the bloody finale to over half a century of barbarism (see p.717).

---

Badlands of the native Sioux. Today, it's a cross between a dude ranch, a mini-college campus and a living history village; a cosmeticization which makes the memories of the obliteration of an entire way of native life all the more poignant.

Restored fort buildings contain period furnishings, and there are two small museums. A simple stone marks the spot where Crazy Horse was killed; the tour train (one per day; $3) acknowledges it with a mere ten-second halt. Good-value **horseback rides** pass some wondrously weird rock formations, and *Fort Robinson Lodge* (☎308/665-2660; ④) has nice **rooms** as well as bargain cottages; the *Lodge*'s restaurant serves cheap **buffalo tacos** and other beef and bison dishes.

The town of **CHADRON**, 23 miles east of Fort Robinson, is worth a visit principally for the **Museum of the Fur Trade**, three miles east on US-20 (summer daily 8am–5pm; $2.50) – a valuable historical archive illustrating the grossly unfair barter system that operated between fur traders and local Native Americans.

# SOUTH DAKOTA

The wide-open spaces of the Great Plains roll away to infinity to either side of I-90 in **SOUTH DAKOTA**. Though the land is more green and fertile east of the Missouri River, vast numbers of high-season visitors speed straight on through to the spectacular southwest, site of the **Badlands** and the adjacent **Black Hills** – two of the most dramatic, mysterious and legend-impacted tracts of land in the US. For whites, they encapsulate a wagonload of American notions about heritage and the taming of the West. To Native Americans they are ancient, spiritually resonant places.

The science-fiction severity of the Badlands resists conversion into easy tourist palatability. The bigger, more user-friendly Black Hills, home of that most patriotic of icons, **Mount Rushmore**, have been subjected to greater exploitation (dozens of physical, historical and downright commercial attractions, and the mining of gold and other metals), but encourage more active exploration (via hiking trails, mountain lakes and streams, and scenic highways).

Time and Hollywood have mythologized the larger-than-life personalities for whom the Dakota Territory served as a stomping ground: **Custer** and **Crazy Horse** battled here for supremacy over the plains, while **Wild Bill Hickok** and **Calamity Jane** were denizens of the once-notorious Gold Rush town of **Deadwood**. On a more contemporary note, Kevin Costner's award-winning 1990 **Dances with Wolves**, shot in the state, continues to boost South Dakota's tourism image, though Costner's own ambitious development plans for Black Hills mean that he himself has now fallen foul of the Sioux.

**Sioux** tribes dominated the plains from the eighteenth century, having gradually been pushed westwards from the Great Lakes by the encroaching whites. To these nomadic hunters, unlike the gun-toting Christian settlers and federal politicians, the concept of owning the earth was utterly alien. They fought hard to stay free: the Sioux are the only Indian nation to have defeated the United States in war and forced it to sign a treaty (in 1868) favorable to them. Even so, they were compelled, in the face of a gung-ho gold rush, to relinquish the sacred Black Hills, and ultimately the choice lay between death or confinement on reservations. For decades their history and culture were outlawed; until the 1940s it was illegal to teach or even speak their language, Lakota. More Sioux live on South Dakota's six reservations now than dwelled in the whole state during pioneer days, but their prospects are often grim. Nowhere is the legacy of injustice better symbolized than at **Wounded Knee**, on the Oglala Sioux **Pine Ridge Reservation** – scene of the infamous 1890 massacre by the US Army, and also of a prolonged "civil disturbance" by the radical American Indian Movement in 1973.

Native American traditions are celebrated by music, dance and socializing at **pow-wows**, held in summer on the reservations; the state tourist office can supply dates and locations. Apart from powwows, South Dakota summers are taken up with historical celebrations, volksmarches (a friendly sort of community walking exercise), ethnic festivals and rodeos. The state has 170 parks and recreation areas for hikers and campers. In winter, downhill **skiing** is limited to Terry Peak and Deer Mountain outside **Lead** in the Black Hills; cross-country and snowmobiling are more prevalent.

### Getting around South Dakota
You'll be hard put to see much of South Dakota without a car. Amtrak routes bypass the state entirely, while Greyhound and Jack Rabbit (☎1-800/678-6543) **bus** lines serve points between Rapid City and Sioux Falls, sites of the two major **airports**. Powder River buses (☎1-800/442-3682) serve Black Hills I-90 towns such as Rapid City, Spearfish and Sturgis, as well as making the two-hour trip to Cheyenne, Wyoming.

# East of the Missouri

For tourists, little in eastern or central South Dakota can be considered essential. **Sioux Falls**, the state's biggest city, is faceless but handy. As one of the country's quietest and smallest capitals, **Pierre** has its charms. **Mitchell** has a few curiosities, while **Yankton**, comfortably ensconced beside the Missouri across from Nebraska, is a gem-like historic town with the excellent Lewis and Clark Recreation Area on its doorstep. The town marks the start of an alternative cross-state route to I-90, trundling through nearby **Vermillion**, home to the exceptional Shrine to Music Museum (where the collection of musical instruments from all over the world now includes one of Bill Clinton's saxophones), plus the Rosebud and Pine Ridge reservations. About sixty miles northwest of Sioux Falls, **De Smet** is known as "Little Town on the Prairie" thanks to the autobiographical books of Laura Ingalls Wilder (though the TV location is near Independence in southeast Kansas). You can tour eighteen sites she mentions for smatterings of history, pretty scenery and homely pride. **Chamberlain**, where I-90 shoots down a steep bluff and over the Missouri River, provides the most spectacular vistas in the eastern part of the state.

## Mitchell

**MITCHELL** makes a mildly diverting stop on the seemingly endless drive along I-90. The **Corn Palace** at 604 N Main St (summer daily 8am–9pm; winter Mon–Fri 8am–5pm; free) has been pegged as "the world's largest birdfeeder;" the first Corn Palace was built in 1892 to encourage settlement and to display local agricultural products. Topped with brightly painted onion-shaped domes and minarets, this kitsch Moorish transplant to the Corn Belt is decorated annually (at a cost of about $35,000) with large murals depicting farming and other outdoor scenes. The artists' materials consist exclusively of native corn, grains and grasses of varying natural colors. Further examples of such rural folk art are found inside, along with Mitchell's **visitor center**, 601 N Main St (Mon–Fri 9am–5pm; ☎605/996-5567 or 1-800/257-CORN).

Other places where you can while away time in Mitchell include a gallery devoted to a Yanktonai Sioux painter; a surprisingly interesting museum of dolls, including a salt-carved Shirley Temple; a pioneer museum; and a prehistoric Native American village. Both the *Best Western*, 1001 S Burr St (☎605/996-5536; ④) and *Super 8* (☎605/996-9678; ③) **motels** lie just off I-90 exit 332. The railroad-themed *Depot*, 210 S Main St (☎605/996-9417), is a fun place to grab a **meal**.

## Pierre

Straggling along the east bank of the Missouri River at the center of South Dakota, **PIERRE** is the second smallest and by far the least sophisticated of all the US state capitals. With none of the plush hotels or fancy restaurants catering to power-broking politicos that you find in other capital cities, Pierre (pronounced "peer") is instead a typical South Dakota town, whose 15,000 residents do their best to ignore the fact that it's the seat of state government.

Apart from the black-domed **Capitol** itself, which sits in a pleasant park at the northeast edge of downtown and is open for tours (daily 8am–10pm; free), there's not a lot to detain you here. One exception is the worthwhile **Cultural Heritage Center** (Mon–Fri 9am–4.30pm, Sat & Sun 1–4.30pm; $3), located high on a hill, half a mile north of the capitol, and modeled on traditional Plains Indian dwellings. Repository for the usual barrage of pioneer implements and prehistoric artifacts, the museum is one of few to do more than pay lip service to the state's significant Native American cultures.

Places to eat in Pierre are limited to fast-food chains lined up along Sioux Avenue, which also holds the bulk of the town's **motels**, including the clean and comfortable *Governor's Inn*, 700 W Sioux Ave (☎605/224-4200 or 1-800/341-8000; ③). For more information, contact the **visitor center**, 108 E Missouri St (☎605/224-7361 or 1-800/962-2034).

# The Badlands

The White River **BADLANDS** could be considered a pocket-sized cousin to Arizona's Grand Canyon. Beyond the family resemblance, what's most impressive about the "Badlandscape" is not its scale, as at the Canyon, but rather its sheer strangeness. More than 35 million years ago this area of southwest South Dakota was a saltwater sea; later it became a marsh, into which sank the remains of such prehistoric mammals as sabre-toothed tigers and three-toed horses, to be covered with white volcanic ash. Drying as it evolved, the terrain became unable to support the deep-rooted shrubs or trees that might have preserved it, and over the last few million years erosion has slowly eaten away layers of sand, silt, ash, mud and gravel, to reveal rippling gradations of earth tones and pastel colors. The crumbly earth is carved into all manner of shapes: pinnacles, precipices, pyramids, knobs, cones, ridges, gorges or, if you're feeling poetic, lunar sandcastles and cathedrals. The Sioux dubbed these incredible contortions of nature *Mako Sica*, literally "land bad"; early French trappers echoed that with *Mauvaises Terres à Traverser*, or "bad lands to travel across"; they have also been aptly described as "hell with the fires out." Despite this daunting reputation, animals such as bighorn sheep, mule deer and prairie dogs are at home here, while on average a million visitors pass through each year.

The most spectacular formations can be found within the **Badlands National Park**, particularly its northern sector, while the southern stretches are encompassed by the poverty-stricken Pine Ridge Indian Reservation. Clean-cut **Wall**, just a few miles north of the park boundaries, is the most visited commercial center in the region.

## Badlands National Park

About one-tenth of the Badlands – the most amazing parts – were declared a **national park** in the Seventies (open year-round). Its two most accessible entrances are off I-90 at exits 131 (northeast entrance) and 109-110 (at the town of Wall), and connected by the forty-mile paved loop of Hwy-240, peppered with scenic overlooks. Visitors can backpack or climb just about anywhere; among the best of the marked **hiking trails** are the Door Trail, a half-hour loop that enters the eerie wasteland through a natural "doorway" in the rock pinnacles ten miles south of the northeast entrance, and the even shorter Fossil Exhibit Trail, ten miles further on, which passes a number of glass-cased fossils dug from the sandstone. The Badlands' rainbow colors are most vibrant at dawn, dusk and just after rainfall.

Adjoining the **Ben Reifel visitor center** (June–Aug daily 7am–8pm; rest of year daily 8am–5pm; ☎605/433-5361; $10 per vehicle for seven days), five miles from the northeast entrance, is the only in-park **accommodation** option. *Cedar Pass Lodge*, which has its own restaurant (mid-March to Oct; ☎605/433-5460; cabins ③, cottages ④), is operated by the Oglala Sioux, who use it as a base for assorted tours into the Pine Ridge Reservation (see opposite), and offer all-inclusive lodging-and-tour packages. Another **visitor center** – White River (June–Aug only, daily 10am–4pm) – stands on Hwy-27 in the less visited and less spectacular southern end of the park. A handful of seasonal **campgrounds** operate both in the park and in Wall. Short scenic **helicopter** rides leave from outside the northeast entrance (☎605/433-5322; from $15).

## Wall

The town of **WALL**, eight miles north of the Badlands, may look like nothing special, yet thanks to **Wall Drug**, begun modestly in 1931 as a pharmacy and veterinary supplies shop on Main Street, it's known around the world. You'll learn about Wall Drug's presence long before you reach it. Over five hundred billboards along I-90 tout its wares, including the **free iced water** that was its original sales gimmick. By the time you get to exit 110 (the one with the 85ft Wall Drug dinosaur), you'll be compelled to pull off and see what all the fuss is about.

Behind the hype lies a kitschy emporium that serves up to twenty thousand visitors per day. You can fill up on steaks or cakes in the 520-seat cafe-cum-Western art gallery, or just enjoy the wall-to-wall collection of photos, memorabilia, animal trophies and mechanical automata like the Cowboy Orchestra and the Chuckwagon Quartet. The merchandise runs the gamut from quality (an excellent Western bookstore, and a complete trail outfitters) to junk (anyone for a rattlesnake mold?). Most compelling, though, is the crackpot cornucopia atmosphere of this ultimate family store, a downmarket, down-home Disneyland wallowing in nostalgia.

There's absolutely no reason to **spend the night** in Wall, but if you're stuck try the *Best Western Plains Motel*, 712 Glenn St (☎605/279-2145; ④), or the slightly less expensive *Super 8* across the road at 711 Glenn St (☎605/279-2688 or 1-800/843-1991; ④). The *Cactus Cafe and Lounge* on Main Street (☎605/279-2561) serves reasonable food.

# Pine Ridge Indian Reservation

**Pine Ridge**, the second largest Indian reservation in the United States (after Arizona's Navajo Nation – see p.862), overlaps the southern Badlands. It is also located in the nation's poorest county. Its prefab homes and beat-up trucks blend sadly and uneasily with the surrounding dry grasslands, rocky bluffs and tree-lined creeks.

The largest town, also called **PINE RIDGE**, comprises a collection of shabby, paint-stripped structures. Just as the surrounding scrubland contrasts starkly with the former homelands of the Sioux in the lush Black Hills, these sorry communities are as far as you can get from the cozy mom-and-apple-pie atmosphere of towns like Wall. Though the emergence of the profitable *Prairie Wind* casino in Oglala has improved life here, in many ways the reservation towns are an even more bitter pill to swallow than places like the nearby site of the Wounded Knee massacre: nowhere is America's disparity of wealth and opportunity so evident as in this area, which posts the highest poverty and alcohol-related death statistics on the continent.

**Wounded Knee** is just one of several hugely significant historic sites on the reservation, marked by peeling, hand-painted tin signs as opposed to the slick decals that commemorate soldiers, bureaucrats and politicians elsewhere in the state. **Red Cloud Indian School**, a few miles west of the town of Pine Ridge on US-18, holds an Indian art show each summer featuring work by thirty different tribes. The school has a permanent display of star quilts (a Sioux tradition), paintings and a giftshop (daily 8am–5pm; free). The **Oglala Nation Fair**, on the first weekend in August, features a powwow and rodeo. For details, contact the Oglala Sioux Tribe, Box 570, Kyle, SD 57752 (☎605/455-2265). Tune in to KILI 90.1 FM, "the Voice of the Lakota Nation" for news and both traditional and contemporary music.

## Wounded Knee

No other atrocity against Native Americans remains so potent and poignant as the massacre at **WOUNDED KNEE**. On December 29, 1890, the US Army delivered a *coup de grâce* to the vestiges of Plains Indian resistance, killing several hundred unarmed Sioux men, women and children. Most were **Ghost Dancers**, followers of a messianic cult who believed that by ritualistic, trance-inducing dancing and singing they could recover their lost land, ancestors and way of life. The massacre was triggered by a misunderstanding during a tribal round-up. A deaf Indian, asked to surrender his rifle along with his peers, instead held it above his head, shouting that he'd paid a lot for it. An officer grabbed at the gun, it went off, and the troops started shooting.

A commemorative sign and a stone monument, surrounded by a chain-link fence, mark the victims' shabby collective gravesite, in a desolate spot off Hwy-27 towards the bottom of Pine Ridge Reservation. Somehow it has an intangible feeling of grief and anger, the mass murder here having left an indelible scar on all First Americans. Eighty-three years later, members of the radical American Indian Movement (AIM) grabbed headlines by occupying Wounded Knee in a dispute over the federal imposition of a tribal government; they were eventually dispersed by armed FBI agents and a paramilitary unit. More peaceably, since the mid-1980s the **Sitanka Wokiksuye** movement has organized an annual pilgrimage to the site, in which an ever-growing number of Native Americans brave the often harsh winter weather to come by horse and travois, thereby symbolically releasing the spirits of their dead ancestors and mending the sacred hoop of the Sioux nation. It's difficult to say what influence, if any, the movement has had in Washington DC, but moves are afoot to designate the gravesite a national monument.

# The Black Hills

*Our people knew there was yellow metal in little chunks up there, but they did not bother with it, because it was not good for anything.*

Black Elk, Oglala Sioux holy man

The timbered, rocky **BLACK HILLS** rise like an island from a sea of rolling hills and flat, grain-growing plains, stretching for a hundred miles between the Belle Fourche River in the north and the Cheyenne to the south, and varying in width from forty to sixty miles. For many generations of Sioux, their value was and still is immeasurable. The Hills are "the heart of everything that is," a kind of spiritual safe, a place of gods and holy mountains where warriors went to speak with Wakan Tanka (the Great Spirit) and await visions. They were dubbed *Paha Sapa*, or Black Hills, even though they are actually mountains (the highest, Harney Peak, rises 7242ft), and the blue spruce and Norway pine trees that cover them only appear to be black from a distance.

Imagining the Hills to be worthless, the United States government drew up a **treaty** in the mid-nineteenth century that gave them and most of the land west of the Missouri River to the Indians. All such treaties were destined to be broken when the discovery of gold turned the Indians' Eden into the white explorers' El Dorado, and fortune-hunters came pouring in. The story has an incomplete postscript: in 1980, the US Supreme Court ordered the federal government to pay the Sioux $105 million in **compensation** for the illegal seizure of the Hills in 1877. After heated debate among Native American representatives, this settlement was rejected and a steering committee subsequently formed to campaign for the return of the Hills themselves to the tribes. The legal battle continues, often hindered by a lack of consensus among the tribes.

The Hills these days are a major tourist destination, albeit attracting more Midwesterners, driven stir-crazy by the endless plains, than international travelers for whom forested hills may be less of a novelty. As yet, however, despite the real danger of the entire area becoming an ersatz Western theme park – as evidenced by its T-shirt stores, pseudo-historical wax museums, cowboy supper shows, and water slides – marketing and merchandising aren't so extensive as to rob the Hills of all their beauty or dignity.

The more thickly wooded north is noted more for urban activities, with the casino town of **Deadwood** its busiest spot. No place in the Hills is much more than ninety minutes from the four presidential heads carved into **Mount Rushmore**, but even more remarkable is **Crazy Horse Mountain**, the world's most ambitious work-in-progress. In the shade of these great monuments, the less spoiled southern hills are home to the

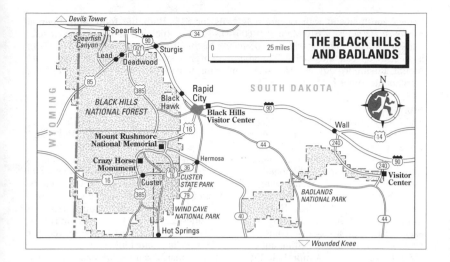

bison of **Custer State Park** and **Wind Cave National Park**, along with the town of **Hot Springs**.

Finally, a word about **gold**. Numerous outlets sell the area's distinctive grape-leaf design. The Hills variety has a frosted finish and comes in three shades – yellow, green and pink; the last two are alloys, made by mixing gold with silver and copper or zinc.

## The North Hills

The predominantly privately owned northern Black Hills are more commercialized than their southern siblings, with **Rapid City**, the hub, surrounded by more interesting smaller towns, such as **Sturgis**, **Spearfish** and **Deadwood**. The back roads, especially in the **Spearfish Canyon** area, form a network of prime driving country. The **Black Hills Information Center**, exit 61 off I-90 (June–Aug daily 8am–8pm; rest of year Mon–Fri 8am–5pm, Sat–Sun 9am–5pm; ☎605/355-3700) is just outside of Rapid City and has an abundance of information on the Black Hills, the Badlands and Native American points of interest.

### Rapid City

Though South Dakota's second largest town, **RAPID CITY**, is all but swamped with family-fun attractions, it makes a convenient base for exploring the charms of the Black Hills' lesser communities. In town, the **Journey Museum**, 222 New York St (June–Aug daily 8am–7pm, rest of year daily 10am–4pm; $5), brings together four prehistoric and historic collections to tell the complete story of the Western Great Plains. One ticket includes admission to the **Museum of Geology**, the **Archeological Research Center**, the **Sioux Indian Museum** and the **Minnilusa Pioneer Museum**.

Rapid City offers the best **lodgings** in the Black Hills, and also the cheapest, although summer rates top $50 almost everywhere. The Bavarian wood trimmings and Sioux soft furnishings of the delightful *Hotel Alex Johnson*, 523 Sixth St (☎605/342-1210 or 1-800/888-2539; ⑥), provide a great escape from dull corporate decor, while the *Stardust Motel*, 520 E North St (☎605/343-8844 or 1-800/456-0084; ③), is typical of dozens of budget **motels**. *Robert's Roost*, 627 South St (☎605/341-3434; ①) is a little-known youth hostel with comfortable beds for $15. Both the **food and beer** at *Firehouse Brewing Co*, 610 Main St (☎605/348-1915) – which has plenty of outdoor seating – are worth sampling; while *American Pie Bistro*, 710 St Joseph St (☎605/343-3773), is a classy upscale alternative. The **visitor center** is located in the Civic Center, 444 Mount Rushmore Rd N (Mon–Fri 8am–5pm; ☎605/343-1744 or 1-800/487-3223). Greyhound comes in at 333 Sixth St.

## Sturgis

The sleepy town of **STURGIS**, thirty miles north of Rapid City, comes to life in a big way during the first full week of August, when the world-famous **Sturgis Rally and Races** (PO Box 189, SD 57785; ☎605/347-6570) packs out virtually every motel and campground in the region with motorcycle enthusiasts. For the rest of the year, bikers have to make do with an abundance of **Harley souvenirs** in the downtown stores and the worthy **National Motorcycle Museum and Hall of Fame**, 1650 Lazelle St (Mon–Sat 8am–6pm, Sun 10am–6pm; $5). East of town, off Hwy-34, the volcanic outcrop which dominates **Bear Butte State Park** stands as a lonely sentinel, detached from the rest of the hills. Hundreds of Native Americans come to this site on retreat each year – to avoid disturbing anyone, check with the park's **visitor center** (☎605/347-5240) before setting out on any of its excellent short hikes.

Of the wide range of **motels** in Sturgis, the reasonably central *National 9 Junction Inn*, 1802 S Junction Ave (☎605/347-5675; ④), represents the best value. The lure of **breakfast**, burgers and overpriced souvenirs is hard to resist at the garish *Roadkill Cafe*, 1333 Main St (open only during summer ☎605/347-5675). Sturgis **visitor center** (☎605/347-2556) lies just off I-90 exit 32.

## Deadwood

One of the West's wildest Gold Rush towns, **DEADWOOD**, in a deep gulch high in the hills 42 miles northwest of Rapid City, has the rare accolade of being a National Historic Landmark in its entirety. Within a year of the discovery of **gold** here in 1876, six thousand gold-diggers had swarmed in to stake their claims; con artists, outlaws and other dubious frontier types were not far behind. Among them were James Butler, aka **Wild Bill Hickok** – sometime spy, scout, bullwhacker, stagecoach driver, sheriff and gambler, who spent only a few weeks in Deadwood prior to his murder by a young drifter named Jack McCall – and Martha "**Calamity Jane**" Canary Burke, an illiterate alcoholic whose checkered career included stints as a dishwasher, muleskinner, scout, prostitute, nurse and Wild West Show performer. She died penniless in 1903, her last wish to be buried beside Hickok high above town in **Mount Moriah Cemetery**.

**Gambling** was outlawed in Deadwood in 1889, the year South Dakota achieved statehood, but betting parlors and brothels flourished well into the twentieth century. Now the old ghosts have been revitalized, since the passing of limited-stake gambling legislation in 1989. With a residential population of only 2000, Deadwood is now booming again, but at a cost: the economy is almost totally based on gaming, and real estate prices have soared so high that there's barely a non-gambling business left on Main Street. Ill feeling is running high, focused especially on Kevin Costner's plans to construct the $140 million *Dunbar* casino and resort (named for the character he played in *Dances with Wolves*) on the edge of town.

For an overview of Deadwood past and present, start by visiting the **History and Information Center**, in the heart of town at 3 Siever St (May–Oct daily 8am–8pm; rest of year daily 9am–5pm; ☎605/578-2507). Main Street boasts two grand old **hotels**, albeit with slot machines now encroaching on their Victorian charm: the *Bullock* at no. 633 (☎605/578-1745 or 1-800/336-1876; ④–⑥), which has an elegant old-world dining room, and the *Franklin Hotel* at no. 700 (☎605/578-2241 or 1-800/688-1876; ④–⑥). The

*Penny Motel*, 818 Main St (☎605/578-1842; ①) offers brand new hostel accommodation at $12 for members and $15 for nonmembers. *Saloon #10*, 657 Main St (☎605/578-3346), has basic **food**, sawdust floors and lots of memorabilia. Above the door is the chair in which Hickok was supposedly sitting when shot dead, while holding two aces, a pair of eights and the nine of diamonds – forever after christened the Dead Man's Hand. Several casinos along Main Street aim to lure in the punters with cut-price **buffets**, but Deadwood's finest dining is at the dinner-only *Jake's*, on the top floor of Kevin Costner's *Midnight Star* casino, 677 Main St (☎605/578-1555).

## Spearfish Canyon area

Aspen, birch and white spruce spread over the towering limestone cliffs above the nineteen-mile **Spearfish Canyon National Scenic Highway**, which starts on Hwy-14A half an hour's drive west of Deadwood, and threads past sights such as Bridal Veil and Roughlock falls. The route reveals almost as many gastronomic pleasures as it does scenic ones. Twenty minutes out of Deadwood, *Latchstring Village* (☎605/584-3333) treats those who have been exploring the site of the nearby winter camp in *Dances with Wolves* with excellent trout and homemade bread. Marking the southern mouth of the canyon at Hwy-14A and Hwy-85, the *Cheyenne Crossing Country Store* (☎605/584-3510) is a must if you have a hearty appetite; popular menu items include all-day breakfasts with buffalo sausage, enormous Indian tacos and fry-bread.

Marking the canyon's north end, **SPEARFISH** itself reels in the crowds each summer for the **Black Hills Passion Play** (June–Aug Tues, Thurs & Sun 8pm; tickets $10–18; ☎605/642-2646 or 1-800/457-0160). Burgers and inventive snacks are served in the **restaurant** at *Lown House B&B* at Fifth and Jackson (☎605/642-5663; ⑤), which also has good-value **rooms** (the loft sleeps six comfortably). Other recommended accommodation options include the quiet *Best Western Downtown Spearfish*, 346 W Kansas St (☎605/642-4676 or 1-800/843-6358; ④). *Sanford's*, 545 Jackson St (☎605/642-3204), is a lively, student-oriented pub and restaurant; for a morning-after coffee, call in at *Common Grounds*, 111 E Hudson St (☎605/642-4292). The **visitor's center** is at 106 W Kansas St (☎605/642-2626 or 1-800/626-8013).

From Spearfish, the spectacular **Devils Tower** stands just an hour's drive away across the Wyoming state line (see p.768).

# The South Hills

The **southern Black Hills** encompass lower foothills and wooded pastureland; from a purely physical standpoint they are more attractive than the north, drawing visitors for their scenery and wildlife rather than kitsch or gambling. The two big mountain carvings, **Mount Rushmore** and **Crazy Horse**, mark the northern end of the region, **Custer State Park** and **Wind Cave National Park** account for much of the central zone, and the pleasant town of **Hot Springs** sits on the southern edge.

## Mount Rushmore National Memorial

America's two largest stone carvings are a mere seventeen miles apart, spitting distance when you consider the scale on which they're conceived. The better-known **Mount Rushmore National Memorial**, originally dubbed The Shrine of Democracy, is the linchpin of the Hills' tourist circuit (summer daily 8am–10pm; rest of year daily 8am–5pm; $8 to park but free parking is available away from the main entrance). It's an easy 24-mile drive southwest of Rapid City, though by far the most impressive approach is to take **Iron Mountain Road** (US-16A), from Custer State Park (see p.724), which from two miles east of the park's Game Lodge, runs for seventeen miles up and over 5500ft Iron Mountain. This engineer's nightmare is a sightseeing motorist's delight, looping over itself along three pig-tailed bridges and passing through a trio of one-lane tunnels, each of which is cleverly designed to frame the Rushmore monument for travelers heading northward.

Only New York City's Statue of Liberty rivals Mount Rushmore as a globally recognized symbol of American aspirations and ideals. In 1923, state historian Duane Robinson and the sculptor Gutzon Borglum, known for carvings such as the leaders of the Confederacy in Stone Mountain, Georgia (see p.467), talked over the possibility of turning the imposing fingers of granite known as the Needles into dramatic patriotic sculpture. They discussed depictions of such heroic figures of the West as Lewis and Clark, Buffalo Bill Cody and Jim Bridger. Borglum opted for a nearby mountain named after New York attorney Charles E Rushmore, upon which he would fashion the faces and heads of four certifiably great American presidents: **George Washington**, **Thomas Jefferson**, **Abraham Lincoln** and Borglum's buddy, **Theodore Roosevelt**.

Borglum talked, dreamed and worked big. "American art ought to be monumental, in keeping with American life," he opined. Sixty when the project began in 1927, he died fourteen years later, $200,000 in debt, just a few months prior to its final dedication. Inclement weather and uncertain funding had meant that the actual sculpting took about six and a half years, at a total cost of $989,000. Half a million tons of rock were removed to reach the softer, more malleable granite from which the heads were drilled and chiselled into recognizability. Ninety percent of the carving, however, was done with dynamite.

The Big Four gaze out impassively, cheek by jowl, arguably a greater engineering feat than an artistic one. Each head is about sixty feet from chin to crown. (The Statue of Liberty's head is only seventeen feet.) Lincoln, Borglum's favorite, has an eighteen-foot-long nose, the glint in each eleven-foot-wide eye is thirty inches, and his mole is sixteen inches in diameter. If he and his fellow presidents had been done full-figure to scale, they'd stand 465ft tall and be able to stride across the Potomac River in Washington DC without getting their knees wet.

The best time to view Rushmore is dawn or dusk, when there are fewer people and better lighting. Although there is no admission charge, by congressional decree, an $8 **parking fee** has been introduced since the construction of the hideous new multilevel parking lot and high-tech visitor center. The on-site cafe, complete with panoramic windows, as seen in Hitchcock's *North by Northwest*, serves full meals and "Presidential Breakfasts." With alternative bases such as Rapid City or Custer State Park so close to hand, there's no particular reason to stay in the nearest town, **Keystone**.

## Crazy Horse Mountain Monument

In 1939, prompted by the sight of the Rushmore monument nearing completion, Sioux leader Henry Standing Bear wrote to Korczak Ziolkowski, who had just won first prize for sculpture at the New York World's Fair, proclaiming that Indians "would like the white man to know that the red man has great heroes, too." The chief invited him to take on a similar project, and less than a decade later, with just $174 to his name, the Boston-born orphan moved permanently to the Black Hills to undertake a vastly more ambitious scheme than Rushmore – the **Crazy Horse Mountain Monument**, on US-16, six miles north of Custer (☎605/673-4681).

The subject, the revered warrior Crazy Horse on horseback (see p.713), so appealed to Ziolkowski that he set out to make his monument the biggest statue in the world, larger even than the Great Pyramid. The work he began on Thunderhead Mountain in 1948 – five Native American survivors of the battle at Little Bighorn attended the dedication ceremony – didn't stop with his death in 1982. His widow, most of their ten children, and even their children's children, continue to realize his vision. National and international interest has greatly increased as the monument finally starts to take recognizable shape; the 90ft high face was completed in time for the fiftieth anniversary celebrations in 1998, although it could well be another fifty years before the project is finished. The sheer scale of the thing is phenomenal; it's hard to believe that the main viewing terrace at the **visitor center** is a full mile from the carving itself, and that the 20ft scale model on show there is 34 times smaller than the end result, which will be 563ft high and 641ft long. An estimated four thousand people could stand atop Crazy Horse's outstretched arm, while all four Rushmore heads could fit in his head, from which will jut a 44ft stone feather. Nor do the plans stop with the carving: Ziolkowski's descendants hope to build a North American Indian museum, university and medical training center on the land stretching between the visitor center and the monument.

Ziolkowski himself raised and spent $4 million on the project. His belief in free enterprise has meant that Crazy Horse has received no federal or state funds, instead relying entirely on admissions and contributions. He twice turned down $10 million in federal funds, claiming the government had no right to be involved after all the treaties it had broken with the Sioux. The site, open dawn to dusk year-round (and illuminated for an hour each night), is free to Native Americans. Everyone else over six pays $7 each; car-loads are let in for $17. Apart from the monument, the premises contain a big barn full of Native American artifacts and crafts, a Native American Education and Cultural Center, several rooms devoted to Ziolkowski's life and work, the good *Laughing Water* cafe (May–Oct only), and an extensive giftshop. Coffee and souvenir stones are free. On the first weekend in June, the public is invited to walk to the top of the mountain and see the work close-up.

## THE BISON OF THE GREAT PLAINS

In the fifteenth century, the Great Plains were roamed by one hundred million shaggy, short-sighted **American bison** (popularly known as buffalo, a corruption of the French *boeuf*). Apart from eating their flesh, Native Americans used the fur and hide for clothing and shelter, the bones for weapons, utensils and toys, and the droppings for fuel. Eliminating the bison en masse was a mercilessly effective way to deplete the Indians as well. By 1900 there were fewer than a hundred bison left in the entire country.

**Custer State Park** was instrumental in helping to raise that meager number to today's national head count of 120,000. Its 1500 bison constitute the country's second largest publicly owned herd, beaten only by Yellowstone National Park. However, over ninety percent of bison in the US are now privately owned – the meat, higher in protein and lower in cholesterol than either chicken or tuna, is becoming something of a cross between a novelty and a delicacy item in restaurants (you can try it in burger form at the *State Game Lodge* in Custer State Park and dozens of other places around South Dakota). The *Triple U Ranch*, outside Pierre, South Dakota, boasts the largest single herd, 3500 strong, though Jane Fonda and Ted Turner own around 4000, split between their ranches in Montana and New Mexico.

The Custer State Park bison are free to roam where they please until either the last Monday of September or the first Monday in October, when the park stages its annual **round-up**. From selected viewing points, the public is welcome to witness one of the Midwest's more thrilling occasions. Modern technology has invaded cowboy territory. Helicopters, jeeps and pickup trucks, as well as riders on horseback, steer the often recalcitrant herd down a six-mile "corridor" and into a series of pens. There the calves are branded and vaccinated, and the whole herd sorted to determine which five hundred will be auctioned off on the third Saturday in November. Proceeds from the sale account for twenty percent of the park's annual revenue.

Don't let the tranquil, easygoing appearance of North America's biggest mammal lull you into a false sense of security. An average bull can stand six feet high at the hump, weigh up to a ton, outrun a horse, turn on a dime and gore a human most efficiently.

## Custer State Park

The 73,000 sublime, billboard-free acres of **Custer State Park** fill much of the southern central Black Hills, a perfect antidote to the commercial crassness elsewhere. However much of a hurry you may be in, it's worth setting aside half a day to enjoy at least one of its **scenic drives**. The **Needles Highway** (Hwy-87; open mid-April to mid-Oct), winds for fourteen miles through pine forests and past the eponymous jagged granite spires in the park's northwestern corner, between Sylvan and Legion lakes. Not far out of Sylvan Lake, as you pass close to the summit of Harney Peak, at 7242ft South Dakota's highest point, look south to spot the Needle's Eye, a slender gap in one of the pinnacles that measures three to four feet wide and fifty to sixty feet tall. The utterly different eighteen-mile **Wildlife Loop** undulates through the rolling meadows along the park's southern edge. Sunrise and sunset are prime times to spy such critters as elk, bighorn sheep, antelope, deer, burros and the most plentiful species, bison. Finally, **Iron Mountain Road** (US-16A), to the northeast, makes a dramatic route to Mount Rushmore (see p.721). This is the most likely place to bump into the park's famous "begging burros": tame and disarming four-legged panhandlers who stick their snouts through the windows of passing vehicles in search of handouts.

For a fuller appreciation of the beauty of Custer State Park, forsake your car and set off into the wilderness. Rangers at the park entrances – where you're liable for **entrance fees** of $3 per person, $8 per vehicle (the pass remains valid for a week and gets you into all other state parks) – can advise on **hiking** and **biking** trails, while concession firms offer horseback rides, boat rental and cross-country drives in open-topped jeeps. Good short hikes include the one-hour **Stockade Lake Trail** in the west, which climbs to give distant views across the lake to Harney Peak and the Needles, and the two-hour **Lovers Leap Trail**, which starts from the park's main Peter Norbeck **visitor center** (summer daily 8am–8pm; rest of year daily 9am–5pm; ☎605/255-4464) on Hwy-16A in the east.

As long as nightlife isn't high on your agenda, the park's four state-run resorts make it a splendid **place to stay** (for reservations: ☎1-800/658-3530). The finest is the *State Game Lodge* (☎605/255-4541) on Hwy-16A not far from the visitor center, which operates a motel-style lodge (⑤) and also has some lovely individual cabins (④) at the edge of the woods; the *Pheasant Dining Room* offers hearty (as opposed to heart-healthy) meaty meals. President Coolidge planned to stay for a week when he arrived here in 1927, but found it so much to his liking that he hauled his aides over from DC and ran the country from the lodge for the entire summer. You can still stay in his room. Tucked in the northwest corner on its own artificial lake, the *Sylvan Lake Resort* (☎605/574-2561; ⑤) similarly offers 31 comfy cabins, more traditional rooms in its tasteful main building, and the *Lakota Dining Room*. Custer State Park also has eight **campgrounds** (☎1-800/710-2267), costing $10–13 a night plus park entrance fees.

## Custer

In little **CUSTER**, five miles west of the park on US-16, the *Bavarian Inn* on the main highway has classic German dining and rooms (☎605/673-2802 or 1-800/657-4312; ④), while the *Custer Motel*, 109 Mount Rushmore Rd (☎605/673-2876; ③/④), is one of the cheapest in the Black Hills. Of many garish campgrounds, *Flintstones Bedrock City* (☎605/673-4664), with its own small theme park, manages to steal the show. The **visitor center** is at 615 Washington St (☎605/673-2244 or 1-800/992-9818).

## Wind Cave National Park

Beneath wide-open rangelands, **WIND CAVE NATIONAL PARK**, ten minutes north of Hot Springs, comprises over 85 miles of mapped underground passages etched out of limestone. One of the largest caves in the US, it was discovered in 1881 when a loud whistling noise on the plains led a settler to a hole in the ground – the cave's only natural opening. The wind, caused by differences between atmospheric pressures in the cave and outside, was apparently enough to blow the discoverer's hat off. Nowadays rangers lead a variety of cave **tours** ($5–20) from the **visitor center** (June–mid-Aug daily 8am–7.30pm; May & mid-Aug–Sept daily 8am–6pm; Oct–April daily 8am–4.30pm; ☎605/745-4600), pointing out delicate features such as frosting and boxwork along the way. If you come in summer, forget the standard walking tours and opt for the ones that allow you to crawl around in the smaller passages, or explore the caves by candlelight.

Even if you lack the time or inclination to delve into the Dakotas' dank bowels, simply **driving** through the park is yet another unmissable Black Hills' experience. Its classic native grass prairieland is home to deer, antelope, elk, coyote, prairie dogs and a 350-head herd of buffalo, a sizeable portion of which hangs out by the scratching posts at the junction of Hwy-385 and Hwy-87.

## Hot Springs

The Black Hills' southern anchor, **HOT SPRINGS**, differs from other regional towns in that it hasn't tarted up its downtown to look like a movie set. It doesn't need to. Several dozen utilitarian yet handsome sandstone structures dominate its center, through which flows the sprightly Fall River.

Battles over the town's thermal pools have caused as much grief as the clamor for gold. Before white settlement, the Sioux drove out the Cheyenne, and later landowners, speculators and settlers dodged and outwitted each other for ownership of the springs. The disputes ceased in 1890 when Fred Evans incorporated numerous small springs and one mammoth hot water pool into a spa center. Today, **Evans Plunge**, on the north edge of town at 1145 N River St, is a popular family-fun center, where three great slides zoom down into the 87°F waters (summer daily 6am–10pm; rest of year times vary; $8).

The unique **Mammoth Site** on Hwy-18 By-Pass is the only in situ display of mammoth fossils in the US. In 1974 building on a housing project came to an abrupt halt when a tractor driver unearthed a seven-foot tusk. Paleontologists from the University of Nebraska soon declared that the workers had discovered the 26,000-year-old grave of at least forty Columbian and Woolly mammoths. Instead of removing the bones and displaying them in some distant museum, it was decided to construct a huge hangar-like building over the site. Fascinating tours explain how these ten-ton mammoths, along with camels, bears and rodents, were trapped in a steep-sided sinkhole (a pond formed by a collapsed underground cave) and were gradually covered by sediment. Complete skeletons and tiny bones, like the delicate hyoid (a tongue bone), are easy to pick out in the excavation site, which is still being uncovered slowly by groups of summer volunteers. The museum holds interpretive displays, a fiberglass model, and an excellent book and giftshop (mid-May–Aug daily 8am–8pm; rest of year times vary; $5).

Seven miles south of Hot Springs, the huge reservoir of the **Angostura Dam State Recreation Area** ($3 per person), set against contorted sandstone bluffs, is a picture-perfect spot for boating and jet skiing. Equipment can be rented from *Breakers Beach Club*, a small hut offering beer, snacks and beach volleyball, at the north entrance.

**Information** for visitors to Hot Springs is available from the cabin at 630 N River St or from the CVB, 801 S Sixth St (May–Sept Mon–Fri 9am–7pm, Sat 9am–6pm, Sun 1–5pm; rest of year Mon–Fri 8am–5pm; ☎605/745-4140 or 1-800/325-6991). **Accommodation** rates are a bit more reasonable than in the hectic northern towns. The *Super 8 Motel*, 800 Mammoth St (☎605/745-3888 or 1-800/800-8000; ③), is unusual in having a bar and restaurant, both of which are recommended; alternatives include the old, faded, riverside *Braun Hotel*, 902 N River St (☎605/745-3187; ③–⑤), and the sumptuous *Villa Teresa B&B*, 801 Almond St (☎605/745-4633; ⑤). *Yogi's Den*, 625 N River St (☎605/745-5949), a lively lounge, fries up good burgers, while the *Elkhorn Cafe*, 310 S Chicago St (☎605/745-6556), serves sandwiches and salads on a sunny terrace.

# NORTH DAKOTA

**NORTH DAKOTA** has no nationally recognizable landmarks, nor is the state's history particularly lurid or glamorous. It seems like somebody's quiet afterthought, a place to pass through. Grain silos loom on the horizon; the haystacks resemble loaves of bread. In the summer, with the sun baking in a defiantly blue sky and the wind raking strong fingers through tall fields of golden wheat and flax, North Dakota epitomizes all things rural American. Charming, picturesque – and a bit maddening.

The influx of Europeans into the Dakota Territory, spurred by the Homestead Act of 1862, precipitated a population and agricultural boom that lasted into the twentieth century. As in South Dakota, the fertile east is more thickly settled than the west, where vast cattle and sheep ranges predominate, and it was the east that was hardest hit by the so-called **500-year flood** of 1997, when 1.7 million low-lying acres of farmland were inundated, and the entire state was declared a disaster area; visitor facilities are now even thinner on the ground than ever. From **Fargo**, the state's largest city, I-94 passes through the central capital of **Bismarck**, and on to the **Bad Lands** of the west, once cherished by President Theodore Roosevelt. Though the national park bearing his name is a key destination, Roosevelt would surely not be pleased about the continuing disfiguration of much of western North Dakota by strip mining operations.

### Getting around North Dakota

Amtrak runs one **train** per day in each direction between Fargo and Williston in the northwest, via Grand Forks. Greyhound is the major interstate **bus** operator: three buses per day make the ten-hour trip from Minneapolis/St Paul to Bismarck via Grand Forks and Fargo, before heading west along I-94 into Montana.

# East of the Missouri

Far more of North Dakota lies east of the big winding **Missouri River**, its uneven dividing line, than west. The **Red River Valley**, the state's furthest eastern strip, is home to two sizeable cities, easy-going **Grand Forks** and the less attractive **Fargo**. Pelicans, geese, swans, prairie chickens and ring-necked pheasants live off the sloughs and potholes of the rolling, glaciated prairie of south central North Dakota, while lakes and woodland dominate the north and the Canadian border. **Fort Totten Indian Reservation** at Devils Lake is midway between Grand Forks and the low-slung Turtle Mountains, which are topped by Lake Metigoshe and the **International Peace Garden** (more of a political symbol than a compelling sight).

## Grand Forks

**GRAND FORKS** sits eighty miles north of I-94, right next to Minnesota, a mere 75 miles south of the Canadian border. Even before its foundation a century ago, fur traders had used the area to rest and barter during their travels between Winnipeg and Minneapolis. It's a small, friendly, outdoorsy city, with nineteen parks and several tree-lined avenues of fine homes. The compact downtown, which lies across Kennedy Bridge from East Grand Forks, Minnesota, disappeared beneath several feet of water in April 1997, and as this book went to press it was too early to say which of its previously appealing assortment of idiosyncratic bars and cafes were going to manage to reopen.

The most interesting distractions can be found on the redbrick main campus of the **University of North Dakota**. The **North Dakota Museum of Art** (Mon–Fri 9am–5pm, Sat & Sun 1–5pm; donations) offers an eclectic assortment of contemporary art and top touring exhibits. Fascinating tours of the **Center for Aerospace Science**, one of the largest civilian pilot-training schools in the world, take in the state-of-the-art Atmospherium (by appointment at ☎701/777-2791).

### Practicalities

The **visitor center** is housed in a converted railway depot at 4251 Gateway Drive (☎701/746-0444 or 1-800/866-4566). Greyhound is at US-81 and Hwy-2; Amtrak at no. 5555. Triangle Transportation (☎701/773-2631) runs buses into Minnesota out of East Grand Forks from the Greyhound station.

Downtown's *Best Western Town House*, 710 First Ave N (☎701/746-5411; ④), is Grand Forks' most luxurious **motel**; for about $10 less you can stay in the kitsch splendor of the *Fabulous Westward Ho* on US-2 (☎701/775-5341; ④), and swim in its cowboy-boot-shaped pool, while nearby there's a *Super 8*, 1122 N 43rd St (☎701/775-8138; ③). The most serene place to **camp** is 22 miles west on US-2, in the grounds of Turtle River State Park (reservations recommended; ☎701/594-4445).

## Devils Lake

The town of **DEVILS LAKE**, ninety miles west of Grand Forks on US-2, shares its name with the state's largest natural body of water, which has four state parks and five private campgrounds along its 300 sprawling and irregular miles of shoreline. Downtown holds a smattering of nineteenth-century buildings and a few rough-and-ready bars. Most of the **places to stay**, such as the *Super 8* (☎701/662-8656; ③), are strung along US-2; more expensive resort accommodation can be found on the west side of Creel Bay, about eight miles from town, where you can also rent boats and pontoons.

**Fort Totten Indian Reservation**, fourteen miles south and site of one of the best-preserved frontier military posts (daily 7.30am–5pm; free), hosts the thrilling **Fort Totten Days Powwow and Rodeo** during the last weekend of July (daily admission $3, $5 for all three days). It's an impassioned, alcohol-free, multitribal party at which hundreds of magnificently clothed dancers of all ages compete for cash prizes.

# The West

Anyone with a hankering to play cowboy could do worse than follow in the footsteps of **Theodore Roosevelt**, who declared "I never would have been President if it had not been for my experiences in North Dakota." Roosevelt initially came to the state in search of spiritual and physical renewal after the deaths (on the same day) of his mother and first wife. He dubbed what he discovered during his few years in this "grimly picturesque" area, with its clear skies, panoramic views and weird, colorful landforms, a "perfect freedom." The national park named after him is the choicest destination in the **North Dakota Bad Lands** (distinct from South Dakota's Badlands) that dominate the state's western half.

The **Missouri River** wriggles like a giant raggedy worm out of Montana, down past the capital, **Bismarck**, and into South Dakota. En route it is transformed into Lake Sakakawea, a virtual inland sea nearly two hundred miles long that's the state's premier water playground. Scenic state **highways 1804 and 1806** follow the routes mapped out by the Lewis and Clark expedition in those respective years.

## Bismarck and Mandan

The West seems to begin as soon as you cross the Missouri River from **BISMARCK**, a capital city with a small-town feel, to Mandan. Both were founded in 1872, Bismarck as a military camp to protect railroad crews from hostile Indians and outlaws. Its original name, Edwinton, was changed by the secretary of the Northern Pacific Railroad, both in honor of German Chancellor Otto von Bismarck and in the hope of attracting Teutonic settlers. Though the scheme failed, the name stuck. The city survived an early lawless period (present-day Fourth Street was once dubbed "Murderers' Gulch") and a major fire to become first the territorial and then the state capital.

Contemporary Bismarck is pretty much contained within the oblong between I-94 in the north and Main Avenue to the south. Locals are proud of their nineteen-story limestone **Capitol**, 600 E Boulevard Ave, dating from the mid-1930s and set at the crest of a public park. The interior, a model of spatial economy and marbled Art Deco elegance, is open for free guided tours on weekdays. Across the street, the superb **North Dakota Heritage Center** (Mon–Fri 8am–5pm, Sat 9am–5pm, Sun 11am–5pm; donation) divides the state's past into six resonant sections, from the dinosaurs onwards. Look out for Sitting Bull's painted robe and the bison "smell box."

The major reason to venture into **MANDAN** is **Fort Lincoln State Park** (☎701/663-4758; $3), five miles south of downtown via Hwy-1806, where the centerpiece is the **Custer House** (May–Sept daily 9am–7pm; Oct–April daily 1–5pm; $5), an admirable reconstruction of the 1874 original designed by the brutally ambitious, indefatigable horseman himself. The guided tour supplies nuggets of quirky information about him (he loved to eat raw onions), his devoted wife Libbie (who wore wigs of his curly blond hair to fancy-dress balls), and their household prior to his death at Little Bighorn in 1876. Nearer the river, five earthlodge reconstructions stand on the site of the once-vast On-a-Slant village, occupied by the Mandan (or River Dweller) tribe from about 1610 to the late 1700s. After the Mandan abandoned On-a-Slant village, they moved upstream and settled on the site that became Fort Mandan, where in 1804 the explorers Lewis and Clark came into contact with the Shoshone woman **Sakakawea** (aka Sacajawea), who helped guide them west towards the Pacific. The site and adjacent historical museum (summer daily 9am–7pm, Sept daily 9am–5pm, Oct daily 1–5pm; Nov–Apr by appointment; free) are somewhat run-down, but be sure to make it up to the bluff above the village for fine views of the Missouri. If you don't have a car you can reach the park via **trolley** from 200 SE Third St (summer daily 1–5pm; ☎701/663-9018; $5 round-trip).

## Practicalities

Bismarck's Greyhound terminal is at 3750 E Rosser Drive; its **visitor center** is at 1600 Burnt Boat Drive (Mon–Fri 8am–5pm; ☎701/222-4308 or 1-800/767-3555). For clean, though small, downtown doubles, try the *Fleck House*, 122 E Thayer Ave (☎701/255-1450; ③). Great rooms, a pool and breakfast are on offer at *Fairfield Inn*, which has two locations, one near the airport at 135 Ivy Ave (☎701/223-9293; ④), the other near the I-94/US-83 interchange at 1120 E Century Ave (☎701/223-9077; ④). For **camping** off the beaten track, try the excellent Cross Ranch State Park (☎701/794-3731; vehicle fee $3, campsites $5–8), thirty minutes north of Bismarck on Route 112A. Overlapped by a six-thousand-acre Nature Preserve, the park features sixteen miles of trails. Alternatively you can camp in Fort Lincoln State Park (☎701/663-9571).

**Dining** and **nightlife** are plentiful in Bismarck. *Peacock Alley*, 422 E Main St (☎701/255-7917), in a downtown hotel that was once the headquarters of the progressive Non-Partisan League, serves Cajun, Italian and American cuisine, with lunch specials in the classy adjoining bar. *Fiesta Villa* (☎701/222-8075), across the street at Fourth and Main in a converted railway depot, features a patio, live music and an extensive Mexican menu. In Mandan, the *Drug Store and Soda Fountain*, 316 W Main St (☎701/663-5900), is a good place to grab a cheap lunch, espresso or ice cream.

# Theodore Roosevelt National Park

The **THEODORE ROOSEVELT NATIONAL PARK**, a huge tract of multihued rock formations, rough grassland and lazy streams, is split into north and south units approximately seventy miles apart, the area between comprising a checkerboard of federal, state and privately owned territory. Exploring the park's seventy thousand acres is like entering different rooms: from desert to woods to mountains. Both units are at their subtlest at sunrise or sundown, the best times to observe such fauna as elk, antelope, bison and several fascinating, closely knit prairie dog communities (both open daily dawn–dusk; vehicles $10, pedestrians $5).

Your first taste of the larger, more popular southern unit is likely to be at the breath-taking **Painted Canyon**, seven miles east of the town of Medora off I-94, exit 8. Here and elsewhere in the park, the land is like a sedimentary layer cake that for millions of years has been beaten by hard, infrequent rains, baked by the sun into a kaleidoscope of colors and cut through to the base by erosive streams and rivers. A mile-long nature hike begins at the end of the canyon's boardwalk.

The **southern unit**'s main **visitor center** in Medora (mid-June–Aug daily 8am–8pm; Sept–mid-June daily 8am–4.30pm; ☎701/623-4466) counts as park headquarters, and runs tours, nature walks and campfire programs in high season. Out back, the simple cabin was used by the young Roosevelt while a partner in the Maltese Cross Ranch (free guided tours daily until 4.15pm). A highlight of the scenic 36-mile loop road is the sublime view from **Wind Canyon**, ten miles out of Medora. Peaceful Valley Ranch (☎701/623-4496), six miles from Medora and a mile from the park's first-come, first-served *Cottonwood Campground* ($10), arranges **horseback tours** in summer for $12 per hour.

The northern unit, off Hwy-85 near **Watford City**, receives only a tenth as many visitors and is on the whole less spectacular, though its fifteen-mile scenic drive ends at **Oxbow Overlook**, a magnificent cul-de-sac. Its **visitor center** is open daily between May and September (9am–5.30pm; ☎701/842-2333), and at weekends and some holidays the remainder of the year.

# Medora

**MEDORA**, the southern gateway to Theodore Roosevelt National Park, languished in obscurity until the early Sixties, but has become one of North Dakota's principal attractions, an inoffensively touristy place with enough to keep you busy, and reasonably interested, for most of a day. The biggest noise in town is the **Medora Musical** (Mon–Fri 7.30pm, Sat & Sun 7pm; $15–17), a pseudo-Western, super-Americana variety show staged beneath the stars in a vast, modern amphitheater. If a man balancing on a board balanced on a bowling ball to a cover version of the *Hawaii Five-O* theme is your idea of a great time, book on ☎701/623-4444 – package tours, including accommodation, show tickets and food, offer substantial discounts.

The Medora Foundation has a monopoly on **accommodation** in Medora, operating the *Rough Riders Hotel* (☎701/623-4444; ④), which has a reliable dining room, and the *Medora* (☎701/623-4422; ④) and *Badlands* (☎701/623-4422; ③) motels, both of which have outdoor pools and are open between May and September only. The *Medora Campground* (☎701/623-4435) caters to both tents and RVs.

# CHAPTER ELEVEN

# THE ROCKIES

E xploring the Rocky Mountain states of **COLORADO, WYOMING, MONTANA** and **IDAHO** could literally take forever. Stretching over one thousand miles from the virgin forests on the Canadian border to the desert of New Mexico, America's rugged spine encompasses an astonishing array of **landscapes** – geyser basins, lava flows, arid valleys and huge sand dunes – each in its own way as dramatic as the magnificent white-topped peaks. The geological grandeur is enhanced by **wildlife** such as bison, bear, moose and elk, and the conspicuous legacy of the miners, cowboys, outlaws and Native Americans who fought over the area's rich resources during the nineteenth century.

Apart from the **Anasazi** cliff-dwellers, who lived in southern Colorado until around 1300 AD, most **Native Americans** in this region were nomadic hunters. They inhabited the western extremities of the Great Plains, the richest buffalo-grazing land in the continent. Spaniards, groping through Colorado in the sixteenth century in search of gold, were the first whites to venture into the Rockies. But only after the territory was sold to the US in 1803 as part of the **Louisiana Purchase** was it thoroughly charted, starting with the **Lewis and Clark** expedition which traversed Montana and Idaho in 1805. As a result of their reports of copious quantities of game, the fabled "**mountain-men**" had soon trapped the beavers here to the point of virtual extinction. They left as soon as the pelt boom was over, however, and permanent white settlement did not begin until gold was discovered near Denver in 1858. Within a decade, speculators were plundering every accessible gorge and creek in the four states in the search for valuable ores. The construction of transcontinental rail lines and the establishment of vast cattle ranches to feed the mining camps led to the slaughter of millions of buffalo, and conflict with the Native Americans became inevitable. The **Sioux** and **Cheyenne**, led by brilliant strategists like Sitting Bull and Crazy Horse, inflicted decisive victories over the US Army, most notably at Little Bighorn – "**Custer's Last Stand.**" However, a massive military operation cleared the region of all warring tribes by the late 1870s.

Most of those who replaced the Native Americans saw the Rockies strictly in terms of profit: they came, took what they wanted and left. Small communities in this isolated terrain remain exclusively dedicated to coal, oil or some other single commodity. All too often the uncertain tightrope walk between boom and bust is evident in their run-down facades.

Each of the four states has its own distinct character. **Colorado**, with fifty peaks over 14,000ft, is the most mountainous and populated, as well as the economic leader of the

## ACCOMMODATION PRICE CODES

All accommodation prices in this book have been coded using the symbols below. Note that prices are for the least expensive double rooms in each establishment. For a full explanation see p.37 in Basics.

| | | |
|---|---|---|
| ① up to $30 | ④ $60–80 | ⑦ $130–175 |
| ② $30–45 | ⑤ $80–100 | ⑧ $175–250 |
| ③ $45–60 | ⑥ $100–130 | ⑨ $250+ |

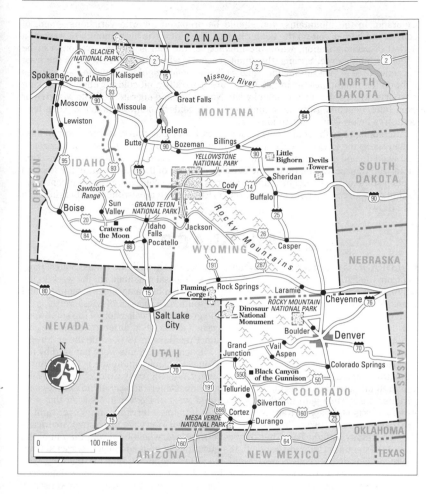

region. Friendly, sophisticated **Denver** is the only major metropolis in the Rockies. It's also the most visited, in part because it's that much more accessible, but tourist numbers remain low enough not to detract from its role as a summer paradise for cyclists and whitewater enthusiasts, and as home to the best ski resorts in the country. Less touched by the tourist circus is vast, brawny **Montana**, where the "Big Sky" looks down on a glorious verdant manuscript scribbled over with gushing streams, lakes and tiny communities.

Away from gurgling, spitting **Yellowstone**, adjacent **Grand Teton** park and the nearby **Bighorn Mountains**, vast stretches of scrubland fill **Wyoming**, the country's least populous state. Rugged, remote and desolate **Idaho** holds some of the Rocky Mountains' last unexplored wildernesses, most notably the mighty **Sawtooth** range.

You can expect **temperatures** in the high sixties all the way up to a hundred degrees Fahrenheit, between early June and early September, depending on whether you are in the high desert of Wyoming, the plains of Idaho, or the mountains of

Colorado. In the mountains, you should be prepared for wild variations – and, of course, the higher you go the colder it gets. The altitude is high enough to warrant a period of acclimatization, while the intensity of the sun at these elevations can be uncomfortably fierce. Spring (the "mud season"), when the snow melts, is the least attractive time to visit the Rockies, and while the delicate golds of quaking aspen trees light up the mountainsides in fall, things are generally a bit cold for enjoyable hiking or sports. Most **ski** runs are open by late November and operate well into March – or even June, depending on snow conditions. The coldest month is January, when temperatures below 0°F are common.

Attempting to rush around every national park and major town is a sure way to miss out on one of the Rockies' real delights – coaxing a car along the tight switchback roads that wind up and over precipitous mountain passes. At some point it's worth forsaking motorized transportation, though, to see at least some of the area by **bike**; the Rockies contain some of the most challenging and rewarding cycling terrain on the continent. And of course, you cannot count yourself a visitor to the area without embarking on a hike or two.

# COLORADO

**COLORADO** is one of the least geographically homogenous of the United States, ranging from the flat, endless plains of the east to the colossal mountains of the west. In the north, **Native Americans** hunted and trapped in lush mountain valleys in summer, and returned to the prairies for the winter; in the south, the Anasazi of Mesa Verde grew corn on their isolated mesas and shared in the great early civilization of the southwest.

Different parts of what's now Colorado accrued to the US at different times: the east and north were acquired under the **Louisiana Purchase** in 1803, while the south was won 45 years later in the war with **Mexico**. (Mexican land grants were honored by the Americans, which accounts for a still-strong Hispanic influence.) Gold-hungry Spaniards came through in the sixteenth century, and US Army Colonel Zebulon Pike ventured into the mountains in 1806, but the Native American way of life only became seriously threatened with the discovery of **gold** west of Denver in 1858. At that time Colorado was still part of Kansas Territory; it became a territory in its own right in 1861, and a state in 1876. The distractions of the Civil War gave the Native Americans the opportunity to fight back, but they were soon overwhelmed. From then until the end of the century, Colorado boomed; the quantities of gold and silver extracted from the mountains do not really compare with the riches found in California, but they were sufficient to fuel a rip-roaring frontier lifestyle. At first, too, absentee landlords attempted to exploit massive **ranches** on the plains, but their disregard for conservation ensured that the droughts and storms of 1886 and 1887 swept away the topsoil.

For the modern visitor, the obvious first port of call is **Denver**, at the eastern edge of the Rockies and basically the biggest city for six hundred miles. Outside Denver, the northern half of the state holds the most popular destinations, starting with the go-ahead college town of **Boulder** and the spectacular **Rocky Mountain National Park**. The majority of the resorts which have made Colorado the continent's foremost **skiing** destination snuggle into the mountains to the west of Denver: **Summit County** attracts the most visitors, **Vail** is considered best for terrain, and **Aspen** boasts the glitziest après-ski scene. The far west of the state stretches onto the red-rock deserts of the Colorado Plateau. **Pikes Peak** towers over the enjoyable city of **Colorado Springs**, but the rest of the state's **southeast** quarter is mostly agricultural plains. To the **southwest** untouched old mining towns like **Crested Butte** and **Durango** stand in the mountains, while **Mesa Verde National Park** preserves perhaps the most impressive of all the cliff cities left by the ancient Anasazi.

## Getting around Colorado

By far the largest **airport** in Colorado is in Denver. Shuttle buses radiate from there to all the main towns and ski resorts – as do commuter-style aircraft. Denver is also a major hub for Greyhound **buses** to all neighboring states. Amtrak **trains** run straight across the middle of Colorado, timed in both directions to pass through magnificent Glenwood Canyon in daylight hours, but little more useful in terms of getting from A to B than the hugely enjoyable Durango & Silverton Narrow Gauge Railroad (see p.75) in the southwest.

Colorado is also one of the best destinations in the world for **cyclists**, hosting numerous on- and off-road championships. The State Department of Transportation (☎719/530-0051) produces excellent **maps and guides** to cycle routes in the state.

# Denver

Its skyscrapers marking the final transition between the Great Plains and the American West, **DENVER** stands at the threshold of the **Rocky Mountains**. Despite being known as the "**Mile High City**," and serving as the obvious point of arrival for travelers heading into the mountains, it is itself uniformly flat. The majestic peaks are clearly visible, but they only begin to rise roughly fifteen miles west of downtown, and Denver has, during the last century, had plenty of room to spread out.

**Mineral wealth** has always been at the heart of the city's prosperity, with all the fluctuations of fortune that this entails. Though local resources have been progressively exhausted, Denver has managed to hang on to its role as the most important commercial and transportation nexus in the state. Its original "foundation" in 1858 was pure chance; this was the first spot where small quantities of **gold** were discovered in Colorado. There was no significant river, let alone a road, but prospectors came streaming in, regardless of prior claims to the land – least of all those of the **Arapahoe**, who had supposedly been confirmed in their ownership of the area by the Fort Laramie Treaty of 1851. Various communities had their own names for the settlement; with the judicious distribution of whiskey, one faction persuaded the rest to agree to "Denver" in 1859. The hope was to ingratiate themselves with the governor of the Kansas Territory, James Denver, but it turned out he had already resigned. The newspaperman Horace Greeley passed through in the early days, and described the place as a "log city of 150 dwellings, not three-fourths completed nor two-thirds inhabited, nor one-third fit to be."

There was actually very little gold in Denver itself; the infant town swarmed briefly with disgruntled fortune-seekers, who decamped when news came in of the massive gold strike at Central City. Denver survived, however, prospering further with the discovery of **silver** in the mountains. All sorts of shady characters made this their home; Jefferson "Soapy" Smith (see also p.1090), for example, acquired his nickname here, selling bars of soap at extortionate prices under the pretence that some contained $100 bills. When the first railroads bypassed Denver – the death knell for so many other communities – the citizens simply banded together and built their own connecting spur.

These days, Denver is a welcoming and enjoyable, though conservative city. Tourism is based on getting out into the wide open spaces rather than on sightseeing in town, but somehow its isolation, a good six hundred miles from any conurbation of even vaguely similar size, gives its two-million population a refreshing friendliness; and in a city which is used to providing its own entertainment there always seems to be something going on.

## Arrival, information and getting around

The colossal, ultra-high-tech **Denver International Airport** lies 24 miles northeast of downtown, out on the plains beyond Stapleton. Regular SkyRide **buses** can take you

### COLORADO SHUTTLES

Numerous **direct bus services** run from Denver airport to many of **Colorado's most popular resorts**, making it unnecessary to rent a car if you're based in just one place. For services to Aspen, see p.749; Boulder p.740; Colorado Springs, p.755; Estes Park (for Rocky Mountain National Park), p.743; Steamboat Springs, p.745; Summit County, p.745; Vail, p.752, and Winter Park, p.744. Note that these should be booked as far in advance as possible.

downtown ($6/$10 round-trip), and to Boulder ($8/$13 round-trip). Buses are available outside exit 506 in the East terminal, and 511 in the West Terminal. There are also a number of independent shuttle service options, which can be arranged within the terminal.

Amtrak **trains** arrive on the northwest side of downtown Denver at the beautiful old **Union Station** on Wynkoop Street, and the Greyhound **bus terminal** is every bit as close to the action at 1055 19th St.

The best place to pick up **information** about the city is the visitor information center, which can be found in the **Tabor Center**, 1668 Larimer St (Mon–Fri 8am–5pm, Sat 9am–1pm; ☎303/892-1112), though there's also an informal morning-only advice center for travelers arriving at the Greyhound terminal. The main downtown **post office** is at 951 20th St (Mon–Fri 8am–5pm; zip code 80201).

The Colorado Division of Parks and Recreation (☎303/866-3437) has information and maps for cycling in the city and the mountains, while GrayLine (☎303/289-2841) operates bus tours of Rocky Mountain National Park and the surrounding area (May 15–Oct 15).

### City transportation

Downtown Denver is fairly easily negotiated on foot, with the occasional help of the very regular **free buses** that run for a mile up and down the 16th Street pedestrian mall at its heart (daily 6am–1am). RTD **buses** (Mon–Fri 6–9am & 4–6pm, $1.25; other times, 75¢), with frequent services to Boulder, sports arenas and the airport, leave from the underground **Market Street Station** at Market and 16th. They are supplemented by a **light rail tram line** that runs five miles through downtown from I-25 and Broadway, across the 16th Street mall and up to Five Points in the northeast (same fares as buses). From June to September, you can also buy a hop-on, hop-off day pass on the **Cultural Connection Trolley** (every 30min 9.30am–10pm; $3), which links Denver's main points of interest. For information and detailed schedules of the entire RTD network, call ☎303/299-6000.

## Accommodation

Denver has a good selection of central budget **accommodation**, ranging from hostels to motels and homey B&Bs, as well as various grand historic downtown hotels. One specialist **agency** with reasonably priced properties in Denver and throughout Colorado is B&B Colorado, PO Box 6061, Boulder, CO 80306 (☎303/494-4994).

**Adam's Mark Hotel**, 1550 Court Place (☎303/893-3333). Giant, luxurious hotel with excellent facilities, adjacent to the 16th Street Mall. ⑥/⑦.

**Brown Palace Hotel**, 321 17th St (☎303/297-3111 or 1-800/321-2599). Beautifully maintained downtown landmark dating from 1892, with elegant dining rooms and public areas. Step inside and marvel at the eight-story cast-iron atrium, and relax in the comfortable red leather armchairs. ⑧/⑨.

**Capitol Hill Mansion**, 1207 Pennsylvania St (☎303/296-6666). Luxurious B&B in an old Victorian mansion. ⑤–⑦.

**Comfort Inn Downtown**, 401 17th St (☎303/296-0400). Very central comfortable chain hotel, with good continental breakfast. ⑤.

**Denver International Youth Hostel**, 630 E 16th Ave (☎303/832-9996). Dorm beds for $8.50, four blocks from the capitol, in a not entirely safe area. Office hours are 8–10am & 5–10.30pm. No curfew. ①.

**Franklin House B&B**, 1620 Franklin St (☎303/331-9106). Simple and very inexpensive rooms (one en suite) in welcoming family inn a mile east of downtown. Great value. ③/④.

**Hampton Inn DIA**, 6290 Tower Rd, next to the airport (☎303/371-0200). A comfortable place with continental breakfast and airport shuttle included. ⑤.

**HI-Denver, Melbourne Hostel**, 607 22nd St (☎303/292-6386). A run-down old hostel with no ventilation. An easy – if not all that safe – walk from the center. Dorms from $10. No curfew. ①.

**Oxford Hotel**, 1600 17th St (☎303/628-5400 or 1-800/228-5838). Very grand traditional Western hotel dating from 1891. ⑦.

**Queen Anne Inn**, 2147 Tremont Place (☎303/296-6666). Central and very hospitable nineteenth-century B&B near a peaceful park; each of the 14 rooms is tastefully decorated to an individual theme. ④–⑦.

**Standish Hotel**, 1530 California St (☎303/534-3231). Very centrally located and inexpensive. Shared or private bath. ②.

# The City

Though oil money brought a hectic spate of high-rise construction in the early 1980s, creating the "17th Street canyon," **downtown Denver** remains recognizable as the Gold Rush town of the 1860s. It's very easy to pick out the oldest sections on a map; though an endless regimental grid stretches for miles in all directions, at its heart one small area of tightly packed streets stands at a sharp angle to the rest. Much of the day-to-day activity centers on the shops and restaurants of **16th Street**, which but for its free buses is a pedestrian zone; there's also a range of galleries, brewpubs, shops and lofts in the revitalized district between 14th and 20th, Wynkoop and Larimer, known as **LoDo**, or Lower Downtown. It was in the **Larimer Square** district, around Market Street between 14th and 15th, that William Larimer built Denver's original log cabin. That burned down in a general conflagration within a few years, whereupon a city ordinance decreed that all new construction should be in brick. Restored to its late Victorian appearance, Larimer Square provides another lively focus for shops, bars and restaurants.

For a quick appreciation of Denver's geographical position, head for the **State Capitol** at Broadway and E Colfax Avenue. The thirteenth of the steps up to its entrance is exactly one mile above sea level; turn back and look west, and you get a commanding view – zealously protected by building regulations – of the Rockies swelling on the horizon. The capitol is a rather predictable copy of the one in Washington DC, but the free tours (Mon–Fri 9.30am–3.30pm) are pleasantly informal, and you can climb its dome for an even better view. The world's entire available supply of red onyx was used to make its wainscoting.

**Civic Center Park**, right in front of the capitol, contains two of Denver's finest museums. The **Denver Art Museum** at 100 W 14th Ave (Tues–Sat 10am–5pm, Sun noon–5pm; $4.50, free Sat), covered in gray-glass tiles, has paintings from around the world, but is most noteworthy for its superb examples of Native American craftwork, with marvelous pieces by the Plains and Hopi tribes. Some of the pre-Columbian art from Central America – particularly the extraordinary Olmec miniatures – is also spectacular.

The most interesting features of the **Colorado History Museum** at 1300 Broadway (Mon–Sat 10am–4.30pm, Sun noon–4.30pm; $3) are to be found in the downstairs galleries. Several dioramas, made under the auspices of the WPA in the 1930s, show

△ Coors Field

Union Station
(Amtrak)

Black American
West Museum

0      400 yds

— ○ — Light Rail Transit

Long-distance
Bus Terminal

Market Street
Station
(Local Buses)

ⓘ Visitor
Center

N

E. 20TH AVENUE

E. 19TH AVENUE

Museum of
Western Art

E. 18TH AVENUE

HG Bonfils
Theater

16TH STREET MALL

E. 17TH AVENUE

Performing
Arts Center

E. 16TH AVENUE

Colorado
Convention
Center

Civic Center
Station
(Local Buses)

COLFAX AVENUE

COLFAX AVENUE

**ACCOMMODATION**
1 Adam's Mark
2 Brown Palace
3 Comfort Inn
4 HI-Melbourne Hostel
5 Oxford
6 Standish

US Mint

Civic Center
Park

State
Capitol

E. 14TH AVENUE

**DOWNTOWN DENVER**

Denver
Art Museum

Colorado
History
Museum

E. 13TH AVENUE

historical scenes in fascinating detail, starting with the Anasazi of Mesa Verde, and following up with trappers meeting with Indians at a "fair in the wilderness" in the early 1800s, and a model of Denver in 1860. An exhaustive archive of **photographs** of the early West showcases the work of W H Jackson, who died in 1942 at the age of 99.

Free tours of the **US Mint**, a short walk northwest at 320 W Colfax Ave (Mon–Fri 8am–2.45pm; every 20min), reveal millions of fresh coins gushing from the presses in a flurry of flashing metal; avaricious fantasies are checked, though, once you notice the machine-gun turrets on the exterior, mounted in the depth of the Depression.

Many of the paintings at the small **Museum of Western Art** at 1727 Tremont Place (Tues–Sat 10am–4.30pm; $3) have more historic than artistic significance, though stimulating works by Georgia O'Keeffe hang alongside the usual pieces by Frederic Remington et al. The building itself was once Denver's leading brothel, discreetly connected by an underground passage to the grand triangular *Brown Palace Hotel* across the road.

The **Molly Brown House**, 1340 Pennsylvania Ave (June–Aug Mon–Sat 10am–3.30pm, Sun noon–3.30pm; Sept–May same schedule, closed Mon; $5) was home to the "unsinkable" Molly Brown, who is most famous for surviving the sinking of the *Titanic* (she'd already lived through a typhoon in the Pacific) and raising money for the survivors and their families. Interestingly, "Molly" is a moniker picked up after her death – she was known as Maggie during her lifetime. A poor Irish girl who went West to marry a millionaire, she ended up mixing with high society in Denver; after the *Titanic* brought her notoriety, she went on to become a suffragette and eventually ran for senator. Sadly, the house tours concentrate more on what the Browns owned and what the preservationists have managed to authenticate than on illuminating her extraordinary life.

Denver's black community is most prominent in the old **Five Points** district, northeast of downtown, created to house black railroad workers in the 1870s. The **Black American West Museum** at 3091 California St (summer Mon–Fri 10am–5pm, Sat & Sun noon–5pm; rest of year Wed–Fri 10am–2pm, Sat & Sun noon–5pm; $3) has intriguing details on black pioneers and outlaws. Perhaps the most interesting section is on cowboys, which debunks a lot of Western myths: one-third of all cowboys are thought to have been black, many of them slaves freed after the Civil War who left the South and found work as cattle hands.

Two or three miles east of downtown en route to the airport, the enormous **City Park** is home to the **Denver Museum of Natural History**, 2001 Colorado Blvd (daily 9am–5pm; museum and planetarium $6, IMAX $6, all three for $9). As with many such museums, its brief extends beyond the (very good) dinosaur exhibits and wildlife displays to include anthropological material on Native Americans, which, though fascinating, does seem rather out of place. There's also a large **zoo** nearby (daily: April–Oct 9am–6pm; rest of year 10am–5pm; $6).

Denver's **Elitch Gardens** theme park, on the western edge of downtown at 2000 Elitch Circle (summer Sun–Thurs 10am–10pm, Fri & Sat 10am–11pm; rest of year hours vary; ☎303/595-4386; $19.95 aged 6 and above), is not only unusual for being so close to the city center (accessible by a cycle path along Cherry Creek or on the Cultural Connections Trolley), but also in having a state-of-the-art **water park** attached. There are some great white-knuckle rides here, including the Mind Eraser, that catapults you at 60mph through terrifying corkscrew loops; the Tower of Doom, a freefall vertical drop of 70ft; and the Sidewinder, which spins you round an impossibly tight loop, and then, sadistically, does it again – backwards.

If you're looking for something a little quieter, the glitzy **Cherry Creek Mall**, a few miles southeast of downtown, is second only to the 16th Street mall as Denver's most popular shopping center. Opposite its main entrance is one of the best **bookstores** in the US, the Tattered Cover Bookstore at 2955 E First Ave (☎303/322-7727), which spreads over four extremely well-stocked floors. Even more tranquil is the **Denver Botanical Gardens**, 1005 York St (daily 9am–5pm; $3), where an excellent array of beautifully displayed plant life thrive, from the indigenous to the exotic.

Finally, twenty miles west of downtown, high above the Coors brewery town of Golden, **Buffalo Bill's Memorial Museum and Mountain Parks** on Lookout Mountain (May–Oct daily 9am–5pm; Nov–April Tues–Sun 9am–4pm; $3) is the final resting place of William Cody, famed frontiersman, buffalo-hunter, army scout and showman, who died in Denver in 1915 (see also p.770). Though now surrounded by huge electricity pylons, the gravesite offers great views in both directions, over the city and out to the mountains. The adjacent museum features posters, rifles, clothing, paintings and Native American artifacts.

# Eating

As well as plenty of Western-themed steak and barbecue places, Denver has a cosmopolitan selection of international restaurants. Of the several distinct restaurant districts, the **Larimer Square** area is the most easily accessible on foot and has a wide selection. Several of the city's famed **brewpubs** serve good quality meals, too.

**Brasserie Z**, 815 17th St (☎303/293-2322). Modern American cuisine in a hip atmosphere, at reasonable prices.

**Casa Bonita**, 6715 W Colfax Ave (☎303/232-5115). Absolutely wild Mexican place, seating 1200 diners, a long way out on Colfax. Gunfights, cliff divers, abandoned mines to explore . . . the only weak link is the food itself, but it's all a lot of fun (especially for kids) and far from expensive.

**Cherokee Bar & Grill**, 1201 Cherokee St (☎303/623-0346). Not far from the capitol, this local favorite dishes out great omelettes and burgers.

**The Delectable Egg**, 1625 Court Place (☎303/892-5720). Popular, friendly restaurant specializing in huge, eggy breakfasts and lunches – from Mediterranean *frittatas* to big skillet fry-ups with home fries and veggies.

**Delhi Darbar**, 1514 Blake St (☎303/595-0680). Relaxed haunt with decent Indian food and a well-priced lunch buffet.

**Kapre Lounge**, 2729 Welton St (☎303/295-9207). Exceptionally good Southern-fried chicken in old established Five Points soul-food restaurant.

**Mercury Cafe**, 2199 California St (☎303/294-9281). A lot of healthy choices, many vegetarian, but with some meat options as well. A good value.

**Rocky Mountain Diner**, 1800 Stout St (☎303/293-8383). Continental food served up in a festive Western-style atmosphere.

**St Mark's Coffeehouse**, 1416 Market St (☎303/446-2925). The small frontage of this trendy cafe hides a huge, art-filled room where regulars play chess and hang out day and night – from 7am to midnight. Excellent espresso.

**Wazee Supper Club**, 1600 15th St (☎303/623-9518). Well-established LoDo dining room, serving good cheap burgers, deli sandwiches and superb pizzas, plus a full range of beers, in an old dark-wood store. Open until 1.30am most nights.

# Nightlife and entertainment

Business is booming for **brewpubs** in downtown Denver. Following in the successful footsteps of the *Wynkoop* (see opposite), others have opened up around the 16th Street mall, and the city center is usually alive at night. For news of **musical** happenings, consult Wednesday's free *Westword*, the hip free monthly *Freestyle*, or the "Weekend" section in the *Denver Post*.

The remarkable **Red Rocks Amphitheater** (☎303/694-1234), twelve miles west of downtown Denver, has been the setting for thousands of rock and classical concerts; U2 recorded *Under a Blood Red Sky* here. This 9000-seater venue is squeezed between two 400-foot red-sandstone rocks that seem to glow in early morning and late evening. The park is open free of charge during the day.

Denver's pride and joy, the modern **Denver Performing Arts Complex** on 14th and Curtis (☎303/893-4100 or 1-800/641-1222), is home to the Denver Center Theater Company, Colorado Symphony Orchestra, Opera Colorado and the Colorado Ballet, and hosts performances nightly. Facilities in the complex include eight **theaters**, as well as the **Symphony Hall** (which is in the round, giving it superb acoustics).

**Breckenridge Brewery**, 2220 Blake St (☎303/297-3644). Atmospheric brewpub opposite Coors Field, you can watch the beers being brewed on site. Good pub grub as well.

**Brendan's**, 1624 Market St (☎303/595-0609). Good live blues in a basement club.

**Broadway Brewing Co**, 2441 Broadway at Walnut (☎303/292-2555). Excellent brewpub, a locals' favorite for interesting beer and fresh pub food.

**Cruise Room Bar**, *The Oxford Hotel*, 1600 17th St (☎303/628-5400). This place is a replica of the bar on the *Queen Mary*. Worth a stop for the atmosphere alone.

**Duffy's Shamrock**, 1635 Court Place (☎303/534-4935). Friendly local bar downtown, serving food and open till 1am daily.

**El Chapultepec**, 20th and Market sts (☎303/295-9126). Tiny, popular venue near Coors Field, with nightly live jazz and occasional big names.

**Herman's Hideaway**, 1578 S Broadway (☎303/777-5840). One of Denver's favorite rock clubs, with live music from Wed–Sat. In a homey little bar just south of I-25.

**Seven South**, 7 S Broadway (☎303/744-0513). Decent dive hosting indie rock shows.

**Wynkoop Brewing Co**, 1634 18th St (☎303/297-2700). Good home-brewed beers and bar food in the state's first brewpub, in LoDo opposite Union Station. There's an elegant pool hall upstairs, and live entertainment in the comedy lounge.

# Northern Colorado

The major attraction for visitors in the Denver area is **Rocky Mountain National Park** to the northwest. Though on the map the distances involved may not look that great, it would be a mistake to attempt to see the whole park on a day-trip from Denver. Segments of the loop drive this involves can be very slow and laborious, and in a single day it's more realistic just to dip a few miles into the park's eastern fringes.

The lively foothill town of **Boulder** can be used as a base, though the smaller mountain towns give you more time in the wilds: **Grand Lake**, near the western entrance, makes a more attractive stopover than overblown **Estes Park** on the east, while **Winter Park** is an affordable, enjoyable ski resort. Further west, midway across the state on either side of the I-70 freeway, you'll find the famous Rocky Mountain ski resorts of **Vail**, **Aspen** and the rest, and the evocative mining town of **Leadville**. Continuing towards the Utah border, the landscape rollercoasts through a patchwork of granite peaks, raging rivers and red-sandstone canyons, winding up at **Grand Junction** and the memorable scenery of **Colorado National Monument** and **Dinosaur National Monument**.

## Boulder

**BOULDER**, just 27 miles northwest of Denver on US-36, is one of the liveliest college towns in the country, filled with a young population that seems to divide its time between phenomenally healthy daytime pursuits and almost equally unhealthy nighttime activities – the town is often referred to as "7 miles surrounded by reality." It was founded in 1858 by a prospecting party who felt that the nearby Flatiron Mountains, the first swell of the Rockies, "looked right for gold"; in fact they found little, but the community grew anyway.

With an easygoing, forward-looking atmosphere and plenty of great places to eat and drink, Boulder makes an excellent place to return each night after a day in the mountains. Downtown centers on the leafy pedestrian mall of **Pearl Street**, lined with all sorts of lively cafes, galleries and stores – including several places where you can rent **mountain bikes**. The most obvious short excursion is to drive or hike up nearby **Flagstaff Mountain**, for views over town and further into the Rockies; any road west joins up with the Peak to Peak Highway, which heads through spectacular scenery to Estes Park and Rocky Mountain National Park. For rock climbing, **Eldorado Canyon State Park** (☎303/494-3943) offers many opportunities and The Boulder Mountaineer (☎303/442-8355) can answer any questions and, of course, provide gear.

The adventurous **University of Colorado** offers a mixed bag of **events**. Its mid-April Conference on World Affairs attracts an eclectic and high-powered assortment of world figures to a sort of free-for-all think tank, while it plays host each summer to the Colorado Music Festival (☎303/449-1397), in the Chautauqua Auditorium (☎303/449-2413), and the seven-week Colorado Shakespeare Festival (☎303/492-0554).

## Practicalities

Local and long-distance **buses** come into Boulder at the Transit Center, 14th and Walnut (☎303/442-1044); there are regular services from Denver and the airport (every 30min 8am–6pm, hourly 5–8am & 6–11pm; 75¢ local fare, $3 to Denver; $8 to airport; ☎303/299-6000). The Boulder Airporter also runs shuttles from Denver International Airport (hourly 8am–11pm; ☎303/444-0808; $14). Boulder's **local shuttle** bus, the HOP (every 15min Mon–Wed 7am–9pm, Thurs–Sat 7am–2.30am; 75¢), links downtown, the university and the trendy student district known as "the Hill." The hospitable **visitor center** is at 2440 Pearl St (Mon–Fri 9am–5pm; ☎303/442-2911 or 1-800/444-0447).

Even if you're not **staying** in the historic *Hotel Boulderado*, wonderfully located near Pearl Street at 2115 13th St (☎303/442-4344; ⑦), it's an atmospheric place to wander into for a drink and to listen to the free evening jazz. Nearby, in another grand old restored building, the *Pearl Street Inn*, 1820 Pearl St (☎303/444-5584 or 1-888/810-1302; ⑤), offers elegant B&B-style accommodations. The *Foot of the Mountain*, 200 Arapahoe Ave (☎303/442-5688; ④), is a friendly, log-cabin-style **motel**, nine blocks from downtown beside Boulder Creek. There's a welcoming **youth hostel** in a Victorian building at 1107 12th St, near the campus (☎303/442-0522; ②); dorm beds cost $15, and there are a few private rooms.

You won't have any problem finding **bars** and **restaurants** downtown, especially around the Pearl Street area. Two local papers, the *Boulder Planet* and the *Boulder Weekly*, are replete with dining and boozing information. *May Wah Cuisine*, 2500 Baseline Rd (☎303/499-8225), is a good-value Chinese restaurant with cheap lunch specials; *The Harvest Restaurant and Bakery*, 1738 Pearl St (☎303/449-6223) is a must for any vegetarian, or those who appreciate healthy fare, though they do serve some flesh. A good upmarket choice is the *Flagstaff House*, 1138 Flagstaff Rd (☎303/442-4640). The *Hotel Boulderado* (see above) has two popular **nighttime** haunts: the *Corner Bar,* with armchair seating, a patio and pub food, and the *Catacombs*, which features nightly live blues, jazz and acoustic music. The *West End Tavern*, 926 Pearl St (☎303/444-3535), is a great venue for live jazz and comedy, with local microbrews and spectacular **Flatiron** mountain views from the roof terrace. For getting your groove on, *Round Midnight* is your best bet. There is a packed dance floor on the weekends (1005 Pearl St, ☎303/442-2176).

## Rocky Mountain National Park

You don't have to go to **ROCKY MOUNTAIN NATIONAL PARK** to appreciate the full splendor of the Rockies; it is simply one small section of the mighty range, measuring roughly twenty-five by fifteen miles. A tenth of the size of Yellowstone, it attracts the same number of visitors – around three million per year – and with the bulk of those coming in high summer, the one main road through the mountains can get incredibly congested. However, it is undeniably beautiful, straddling the Continental Divide at elevations often well in excess of ten thousand feet. A full third of the park is above the tree line, and large areas of snow never melt; the name of the **Never Summer Mountains** speaks volumes about the long, empty expanses of arctic-style tundra. Lower down, among the rich forests, are patches of lush greenery; you never know when you may stumble upon a sheltered mountain meadow flecked with flowers. Parallels with the European Alps spring readily to mind – helped, of course, by the heavy-handed Swiss and Bavarian themes of the region's motels and restaurants.

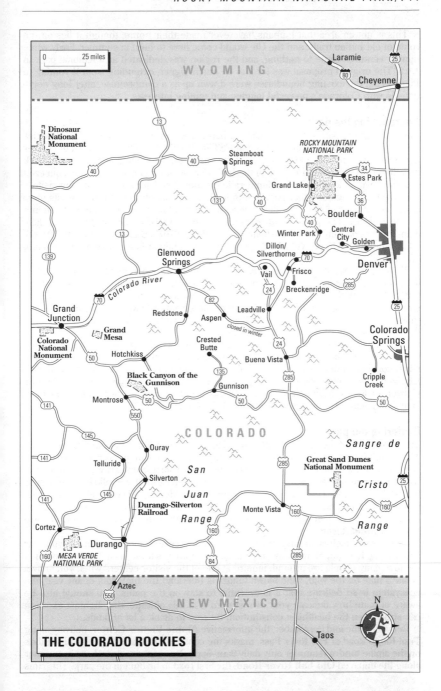

THE COLORADO ROCKIES

This is not an area that humans have ever made their home, though it lies on the route of old Indian trails, and the Ute would come here to hunt in summer. Early white mining ventures came to nothing, and the region was dedicated as a national park in 1915. The original proposal was for it to be much bigger, extending from Wyoming to Pikes Peak; the existing boundaries were drawn up as a compromise, after long negotiations with Colorado's powerful logging and mining interests.

## Approaching the park

Approaching the park from the **east**, you barely penetrate the foothills of the Rockies before you arrive at the gateway town of **ESTES PARK**, 65 miles northwest of Denver and 90 miles southwest of Cheyenne. At the end of the nineteenth century, Estes Park was the private hunting preserve of the Irish Earl of Dunraven; once he was squeezed out, the town took on the more democratic function it still serves, of providing visitors with food, lodging and other services. In itself, it's not an attractive place, but its presence does at least ensure that all the necessary evils of mass tourism are confined into one neat valley. The **park headquarters** and main **visitor center** (June–Aug daily 8am–9pm; Sept–May daily 8am–5pm; information ☎970/586-1206, weather ☎970/586-1333; admission $10 per vehicle, $5 pedestrians and bikes) is a couple of miles north, on US-36.

To reach the **western** entrance, 85 miles from Denver, turn north off I-70 onto US-40; a small detour beyond the junction takes you to the former mining community of **GEORGETOWN**, where over two hundred Victorian buildings line the immaculate streets. The **Georgetown Loop Railroad** departs from 1106 Rose St on a tortuous six-mile trip, at one point spiraling over itself (summer daily every 80min 10am–3.20pm; ☎970/569-2403 or 1-800/691-4386; $11.95).

US-40 itself negotiates **Berthoud Pass** en route to **GRAND LAKE**, a lot lower-key than Estes Park, but the same idea. This unlikely **yachting** center, high in the mountains, consists of one main boardwalk-lined street alongside the lake itself, lined with family amusements, budget lodgings and restaurants. The **Kawuneeche Visitor Center** of Rocky Mountain National Park is a mile north of town (June–Aug daily 7am–7pm; Sept–May daily 8am–5pm; ☎970/627-3471).

## Exploring the park

The showpiece of the park is **Trail Ridge Road**, between Estes Park and Grand Lake. This 45-mile stretch of US-34, said to be the highest highway in the world, affords a succession of tremendous views, and several short trails start from parking lots along the way. There are no services en route, and rangers advise that you allow three to four hours' driving time. The road is normally open from Memorial Day to mid-October. As winter progresses and the snow falls, it is blocked progressively lower down, but you can always expect to get as far as **Many Peaks Curve** from the east or the **Colorado River Trailhead** from the west.

As the road itself is so busy, the park is best appreciated by getting out of your car and **hiking**. Recommending any one trail above another is futile, as it depends so much on how many people are around; inquire at one of the visitor centers when you arrive. While a hike on the wild, wind-blown tundra is (literally) the high spot of any visit, the ecosystem is so delicate that it is essential to stay on the paths. You should also be aware of quite how delicate your own system is at this altitude: the slightest exertion can strain even the healthiest constitution. Be sure to drink a lot of fluids.

Between June and September, the informative **Alpine Visitor Center**, halfway along Trail Ridge Road at Fall River Pass, marks the center of the park; it has good exhibits on the alpine tundra (summer only daily 9am–5pm). You can also drive here in summer along the unpaved **Old Fall River Road**, the first road to be built in the park. This runs one-way only (east–west) through the bed of a valley carved by glaciers into a U-shape, so it doesn't have open mountain vistas, but it's much quieter than the Trail Ridge, and there's far more chance of spotting **wildlife**. Animals roaming the park include moose, coyote, mountain lions, beavers (often seen at work in the rivers) and a total population of perhaps thirty brown bears, which with a plentiful natural food supply tend to avoid contact with humans. The central and southern tracts of this wilderness are all but impenetrable; only a well-planned hiking expedition can get you into the remoter forests and valleys.

Just inside the park, near the Estes Park entrance, a spur road, open year-round, leads south to two small and pristine alpine lakes. On the way, the **Moraine Park Museum** (summer only daily 9am–5pm) has a well-laid out set of exhibits on the park's natural history. Beyond here, to ease the traffic in summer, a free and very regular **shuttle bus** from the Glacier Basin parking area runs the last few miles up to **Bear Lake** (every 15–30min until 5.30pm; check at the visitor centers for the day's schedule), which is the park's single most definitive viewpoint, with the mountains framed to perfection beyond the cool, still waters. **Sprague Lake**, lower down, has been landscaped to provide access for disabled visitors: a dead-level paved path encircles the shore, while the free **Handicamp** campground is exclusively for the use of wheelchair-bound travelers (contact the park HQ for details).

## Park practicalities

**Public transportation** to Estes Park from Denver International Airport is provided by Charles Tour and Travel Service (☎970/586-5151 or 1-800/950-3274; $28). To get around the park if you're not driving, you can either pick up an Estes ParkShuttle **tour** from Estes Park, which with admission (not always included in the quoted price) should cost around $60 a day or $30 a half-day, or you can do the whole thing from Denver, with Gray Line, for example (see p.734).

Five official **campgrounds**, at Moraine Park, Glacier Basin, Aspenglen, Longs Peak and Timber Creek, provide the only accommodation within the park. All fill early each day; in summer, reservations are essential. Longs Peak imposes a maximum stay of three days, the rest allow one week. They range in fees from $12–14. For **backcountry camping** you need a permit, again valid for a maximum of seven days in summer, available from the park headquarters ($15 in summer).

**Estes Park** abounds in lodges, motels and places to eat; the **Chamber of Commerce**, 500 Big Thompson Ave (☎970/586-4431 or 1-800/443-7837), has full details. Options include the *Alpine Trail Ridge Inn*, 927 Moraine Ave (☎970/586-4585 or 1-800/233-5023; ④), and the glamorous 1909 *Stanley Hotel*, in a fantastic mountainside location at 333 Wonderview Ave (☎1-800/976-1377; ⑦/⑧) – the latter is said to have been the inspiration for the big old lodge in Stephen King's *The Shining*. Dorm beds cost $9 (for members only, but you can join there), at the *HI-H-Bar-G Ranch Hostel*, five miles north of town at 3500 H-Bar-G Rd (late May–mid-Sept; ☎970/586-3688; ③). The *Colorado Mountain School* is a bargain, with dorm beds in very clean rooms for $20. There is a discount for groups of 2 or more (351 Moraine Ave; ☎970/586-5758). The relaxed *Friar's* at 157 W Elkhorn Ave (☎970/586-2806) has an extensive menu, while the buffet at the historic *Baldpate Inn*, 4900 S Colorado Ave (☎970/586-6151), is highly recommended, featuring hearty soups, fresh baked gourmet breads and cappuccino, for under $10.

**Grand Lake** has a highly recommended **youth hostel**: the gorgeous, rambling log-built *Shadowcliff*, perched high in the woods on Tunnel Road (June–Sept only; ☎970/627-9220; ①). Run by the United Methodist Church, it offers budget dorms for $10–12; clean, comfortable motel rooms with great views; big, hummingbird-visited terraces; and a serene chapel open to all. In town, note that many of the motels insist on weekly rates. One exception is the *Western Riviera Motel & Cabins*, in an attractive spot down by the lake at 419 Garfield Ave (☎970/627-3580; ④/⑤). By far the best place to eat is *EG's Garden Grill*, serving quality Mediterranean-influenced food in a cozy, colorful dining room on the boardwalk at 1000 Grand Ave (☎970/627-8404) – you can also sit in the beer garden.

# Winter Park

The former railroad center of **WINTER PARK**, 67 miles northwest of Denver, may not be Colorado's trendiest resort, but its wide, ever-expanding variety of ski and bike terrain, friendly atmosphere and good-value lodgings draw over one million visitors a year. As the only publicly owned resort in the state, it has great facilities for kids, female and disabled skiers – and the 200-acre **Discovery Park**, an excellent, economical area for beginners. Experienced skiers, in turn, relish the mogul runs on the awesome **Mary Jane Mountain**, the fluffy snows of the Parsenn Bowl, and the "backcountry" idyll of the new **Vasquez Cirque**.

In addition to skiing, you can **snowmobile** the Continental Divide on a one-hour tour with Trailblazers in Fraser (☎970/726-8452; $35), or around a 25-mile course at Mountain Madness (☎970/726-4529; $35 per hour), just north of town. **Summer** visitors can enjoy six hundred miles of **mountain bike** trails, as well as Saturday night **rodeos** ($6), chair-lift rides ($16, with room for bikes), the super-fun mile-and-a-half-long **Alpine Slide** ($6) and several contemporary music festivals.

## Practicalities

Year-round service to Winter Park is provided by Greyhound, stopping downtown outside the **visitor center** on Vasquez Road (daily 8am–5pm; ☎970/726-4118 or 1-800/903-7275), by Amtrak, five miles north in Fraser, and on Home James shuttles from Denver International Airport (☎303/726-5060 or 1-800/451-4844; $34). The **Winter Park Ski Train** does round trips from Denver every Saturday and Sunday during ski season, leaving at 7.15am and starting back at 4.15pm (☎303/296-4754; $35; 2hr; reservations required). Excellent winter **shuttle buses** mean that a car is not essential. Trail maps and general outdoor information are available at the visitor center.

Winter Park offers the best choice of **rooms** among Colorado resorts. As well as **condos** (bookable through Winter Park Central Reservations; ☎970/726-5587 or 1-800/453-2525; ④ and up), inexpensive **motels** include the downtown *Viking Lodge* (☎970/726-8885 or 1-800/421-4013; ②–④). The *YMCA Snow Mountain Ranch*, a few miles north on Hwy-40 (☎970/726-4628; ③–⑤), has good group rates, an indoor pool, library and guide-led activities. On the face of it, Winter Park's six **ski lodges**, like downtown's *Arapahoe Ski Lodge* (☎970/726-8222 or 1-800/338-2698; ④–⑦), may seem expensive, but these delightful old-style inns offer unmatched comfort, facilities and value, and are often full-board.

**Nightlife** starts at the base of the ski lifts at *The Slope* (☎970/726-5727), before progressing downtown to the likes of *Carlos and Maria's* in Cooper Creek Square, (☎970/726-9674), good for low-cost margaritas and Mexican food, and *Deno's* (☎970/726-5332) with its hundred plus beers and tasty pasta.

# Steamboat Springs

With its wide surrounding valleys, **STEAMBOAT SPRINGS**, 65 miles north of Vail, looks like no other Colorado mountain resort. Its roots are in ranching rather than mining, and its downtown area still evokes a pioneer feel – until you spot the upmarket boutiques. In this ski-mad town, rancher-types judge the quality of snowfall by the number of fence wires it covers; they're usually satisfied with a three-wire winter, which corresponds to its average snowfall of 325 inches per year.

The town's unprepossessing **ski resort** (lift tickets $46 per day), snuggled into Mount Werner five miles south of downtown, is boosted by such activities as **bobsled rides** at the small downtown, **Howelson Hill Ski Area** ($10), dogsled expeditions, hot-air ballooning and snowmobiling are all available. A favorite year-round activity is to let all the stress seep out at the secluded 105°F **Strawberry Park Hot Springs** (daily; 10am–midnight; $5–10), ten miles north of town but only accessible by 4WD in winter. If you prefer to stay in town, the **Steamboat Springs Health and Recreation Center** offers hot mineral pools, (6.30am–10pm; $5), as well as workout facilities. In the summertime, opportunities for **mountain biking**, **whitewater rafting**, and **horseback riding** abound. Outfitters throughout the town can assist you with gear and guides.

## Practicalities

Most winter visitors fly into **Yampa Valley Airport**, 22 miles out, though it's possible to drive, weather permitting, from Denver over scenic **Rabbit Ears Pass**, or take a Steamboat Express shuttle bus direct from Denver International Airport (☎970/879-3400 or 1-800/545-6050; $57).

From town, free SST **buses** (☎970/879-3717) run the five miles to the ski resort. Slopeside **lodging**, such as the comfortable *Best Western Ptarmigan Inn* (☎970/879-1730; winter ⑥, summer ④), costs more than downtown options like *Rabbit Ears Motel* (☎970/879-1150 or 1-800/828-7702; winter ⑥, summer ④/⑤), or *Nite's Rest Motel* (☎970/879-1212 or 1-800/828-1780; winter ④/⑤, summer ③). Steamboat Central Reservations (☎1-800/922-2722) can supply information on lodging and packages. You can **camp** at the *Steamboat Springs KOA Campground* (☎970/879-0273; tents $19, hookups $22–25), two miles west of downtown on US-40.

For **food**, *Cugino's*, 825 Oak St (☎970/879-5805), serves inexpensive home-style pasta and pizza; in the ski area, *La Montana* (☎970/879-5800) offers big portions of quality Southwestern and Mexican food. For a casual atmosphere and deli-bakery delights, try *Winona's* (☎970/879-2483). If you've got money to spare, try the delicious dinner at *Hazie's*, up on the mountain (open Tues–Sat for lunch and dinner during ski season, Fri and Sat nights during summer; ☎970/879-6111 ext 465), which includes a free gondola ride. Microbrews are available at the boisterous *Heavenly Daze Brew Pub* (☎970/879-8080) and *The Tugboat Grill and Pub* (☎970/879-7070), with live music and a dance floor, both located on Ski Time Square, and both of which serve good pub food.

# Summit County

The mix of purpose-built ski resorts, old mining towns, snow-covered peaks, alpine meadows and crystal lakes that make up **Summit County** lie alongside I-70, around seventy miles west of Denver. Before white settlement, the Ute hunted here every summer: the swanky Keystone Ranch Golf Club now occupies the meadow where they pitched their tepees. During the late nineteenth century the county witnessed several gold-mining booms; dilapidated **ghost towns** cling to the mountainsides, but one settlement that survived is **BRECKENRIDGE**, whose streets are lined with brightly painted Victorian houses, shops and cafes. This is the liveliest of Summit County's four towns; **FRISCO**, stretching sedately along a quiet valley, appeals to those looking for a less hectic pace. Both the other towns, **DILLON** and **SILVERTHORNE**, are dull, though the latter contains dozens of cut-price factory outlet stores. The villages at the resorts of **Keystone** and **Copper Mountain** are also unexciting.

## Arrival and information

By **car**, Summit County is about two hours from Denver. Greyhound **buses** stop in Silverthorne, at the *Alpen Hütte* ($11 one-way) and there are free buses from there to

Copper Mountain, Keystone and Breckenridge. There are also **shuttles** from **Denver International Airport**. Resort Express serves Silverthorne and Breckenridge (☎970/468-7600 or 1-800/334-7433; $40), while Supershuttle (☎1-800/258-3826) and Colorado Mountain Express (☎1-800/222-2112) run a more expensive door-to-door service to your hotel in Breckenridge. Summit Stage (☎970/453-1241) provides free **local transportation** round the county, while the Breckenridge Downtown Trolley, (☎970/453-5000) runs through town and up to the resort. The main **visitor center** (☎970/668-2051; daily 9am–5pm) stands by the lake at the end of Frisco's Main Street, and there's a small welcome center in Breckenridge at 309 N Main (☎970/453-6018).

## Accommodation

**Lodgings** in Summit County cover all price ranges, with prices doubling in winter. Frisco has the best-priced inns and **motels**, with places like the *Sky-Vue* (☎970/668-3311; ③–⑤) and *Snowshoe* (☎970/668-3444; ③–⑤) complementing the excellent *Frisco Lodge* (see below). There are a few downtown **B&Bs** in Breckenridge, where otherwise accommodation usually means a slopeside condo; The Breckenridge Resort Chamber (Mon–Fri 8am–5pm; ☎970/453-6018 or 1-800/221-1091; ☎0800/897491 in the UK) can advise on prices and package deals. Resort accommodation at both Copper Mountain (☎1-800/458-8386) and Keystone (☎1-800/222-0188; ☎0800/898727 in the UK) is first class, but so too are the prices; virtually nothing costs under $100 a night, unless you find an unusual package.

**Fireside Inn**, 114 N French St, Breckenridge (☎970/453-6456). Cozy B&B rooms, as well as a few bunk beds costing $25–30 per night in winter, $20 in summer. Winter ⑥, summer ③.

**Frisco Lodge**, 321 Main St, Frisco (☎970/668-0195). Simple, old-style accommodation in an old railroad inn. Extreme price differentials for en-suite rooms in winter. Winter ⑤, summer ③.

**HI-Alpen Hütte**, 471 Rainbow Drive, Silverthorne (☎970/468-6336). Clean bunkrooms in comfortable environs. Midnight curfew. Winter $15–25, summer $12. ①.

**Ridge Street Inn**, 212 N Ridge St, Breckenridge (☎970/453-4680). Comfortable, luxurious B&B in the heart of the historic downtown area. Winter ⑥, summer ③/④.

## Outdoor activities

Winter is still the busiest time in Summit County. **Breckenridge Ski Area**, the oldest of the four top-class resorts, spans four peaks and offers ideal terrain for all skiers – and snowboarders, with a 6-acre park with half-pipe – as does the plush **Keystone Resort**, where the biggest night-ski operation in the US permits skiing until 10pm. The smallest resort in the county, **Arapahoe Basin** (generally known as "A-Basin"), offers great above-tree line bowl skiing. All three are owned by the same company and covered by one lift ticket ($47 per day), making this one of the best-value deals in the country. The slopes at the other ski area, the ingenious **Copper Mountain** ($45 for one day), are divided into three clear sections to keep beginners, intermediates and experts out of each other's way. You can find out about conditions by calling ☎970/453-6118.

In summer, mountain-bikers and road racers alike will be happy with the opportunities for **cycling**, particularly the stretch between Frisco and Breckenridge; Racer's Edge at 114 N Main in Breckenridge (☎970/453-0995) rents out the best cycles. Each resort runs chair-lift or **gondola rides** to the top of the mountains, which, as well as stunning views, provide access to great **hiking** and cycling trails. Breckenridge also offers toboggan rides down the dry **Superslide** (summer daily 9am–5pm; $8), mini-golf ($6) and a giant maze ($4).

## Eating

With the exception of Keystone Resort, Summit County hasn't developed a reputation for fine **dining**, though there's no end of good-value places to eat, especially in Breckenridge.

**Alpenglow Stübe**, Keystone Mountain (☎970/496-4386). The best dining experience in Summit County – take the free gondola ride to the top of 11,444ft North Peak and feast on New American cuisine with a Bavarian edge in beautiful surroundings. It doesn't come cheap though.

**Blue Moose**, 540 S Main St, Breckenridge (☎970/453-4859). Inventive international menu, with lots of vegetarian dishes for well under $10.

**Bubba's Bones**, 110 S Ridge St, Breckenridge (☎970/547-9942). Authentic barbecue at reasonable prices.

**Fatty's**, 106 S Ridge St, Breckenridge (☎970/453-9802). Great pizza and pasta at good prices.

**Mi Casa**, 600 S Park Ave, Breckenridge (☎970/453-2071). The best Mexican food in the county. Fajitas are good value, as is the daily 3–6pm happy hour.

**Mountain Java**, 118 S Ridge St, Breckenridge (☎970/453-1874). Cozy, book-lined coffeehouse serving healthful lunches, low-fat muffins and gourmet breads along with steaming espresso drinks.

**Pika Bagel Bakery & Cafe**, 500 S Main St, Breckenridge (☎970/453-6246); 401 Main St, Frisco (☎970/668-0902). Friendly outlets for a fruit smoothie and a bagel sandwich.

**Rasta Pasta**, 411 S Main St, Breckenridge (☎970/453-7467). Good, cheap pasta with a Carribean twist. And of course, reggae music.

**Uptown Bistro**, 304 Main St, Frisco (☎970/668-4728). This is an elegant, upscale restaurant with seafood and Asian specialties.

## Drinking

Immediate après-ski boozing is good on the slopeside bars of all four resorts. As the night goes on, Breckenridge offers the most choice, with several late-night music venues, though Frisco too has its moments.

**Breckenridge Brewery**, 600 S Main St, Breckenridge (☎970/453-1550). Good-quality microbrews and hearty pub food.

**Gold Pan**, 103 N Main St, Breckenridge (☎970/453-5499). The only place you could get a drink in Colorado during Prohibition. Nowadays it's a lively saloon and pool hall. Daily happy hour 4–7pm, and they serve burritos, pizzas and soup.

**Matteo's**, 122 W 10th St, Silverthorne (☎970/262-6508). Super happy-hour deals and decent pizza.

**Moosejaw**, 208 Main St, Frisco (☎970/668-3931). Dark wooden bar serving great burgers until 2am.

**Shamus O'Toole's Roadhouse**, 115 S Ridge St, Breckenridge (☎970/453-2004). Dingy-looking bar attracting a motley crew of bikers, bohemians and boozers. Rowdy, fun and with a generous happy hour.

# Leadville

Standing at an elevation of over ten thousand feet, south of I-70 and eighty miles west of Denver, the wonderfully atmospheric old mining town of **LEADVILLE** is the highest incorporated city in the US, with a magnificent view across to broad-shouldered, ice-laden mounts **Elbert** and **Massive**, Colorado's two highest peaks. As you approach from the south, your first impression is of giant slag heaps and disused mining sheds, but don't let this put you off: Leadville is rich in character and romance, its old redbrick streets abounding with tales of gunfights, miners dying of exposure and graveyards being excavated to get at the seams.

In the light of this, visiting Leadville's rambling **National Mining Hall of Fame and Museum**, 120 W Ninth St (summer daily 9am–5pm; rest of year Mon–Fri 10am–2pm; $3), is a patchy experience: skip the baffling dioramas and outdated mine-shaft models in favor of the lurid globs of precious minerals and the atmospheric old photos of weather-beaten prospectors and rough-and-ready sluicers. For a more illuminating romp through the town's grim early history, head for the **Heritage Museum**, just around the corner at 102 E Ninth St (summer daily 10am–6pm; $2.50). Glass cases hold snippets on local fraternal organizations, quack doctors, music-hall stars and the like, while a host of smoky photographs portray the lawless boomtown that in two years grew from a mining camp of 200 people into Colorado's second largest city.

Of all Leadville's extraordinary tales, perhaps the most compelling is that of **Horace Tabor**, a storekeeper who supplied goods to prospectors in exchange for a share in potential profits, and hit lucky when two prospectors developed a silver mine that produced $20 million inside a year. Tabor collected a one-third share and left his wife to marry local waitress "**Baby Doe**" McCourt in the socialite wedding of 1883, attended by President Chester Arthur. By the time of his death in 1899, Tabor was financially ruined. Baby Doe took his dying injunction to "hold onto the Matchless" – his only remaining mine – literally, and she died there, emaciated and frostbitten, 36 years later. The godforsaken wooden outhouses of the **Matchless Mine** still stand, two miles out on Seventh Street, and in the crude wooden shack in which she died, guides recount the story of Baby Doe's bizarre life in full, fascinating detail (daily 9am–4.15pm; $3). Also on Seventh Street is the **Leadville, Colorado & Southern Scenic Railroad,** (depot at 326 E 7th St; ☎719/486-3936; $23), which takes passengers on a 2½-hour scenic trip to Fremont Pass.

Back in town, don't miss the **Tabor Opera House**, 308 Harrison Ave (Sun–Fri 9am–5.30pm; $4), where you're free to wander onto the stage, through the ranks of red velvet and gilt seats, and around the eerie, dusty old dressing rooms, while recorded oral histories tell tales of the grand old theater's golden days. They give no details, sadly, of the time in 1882 when Oscar Wilde, garbed in black velvet knee britches and diamonds, addressed a host of dozing miners on the "Practical Application of the Aesthetic Theory to Exterior and Interior House Decoration with Observations on Dress and Personal Ornament."

### Outdoor activities

Leadville is an ideal base for some superb **mountain** biking, hiking and skiing. Bill's Sport Shop, 225 Harrison Ave (☎719/486-0739), rents and repairs bikes, while Leadville Ski Country, 116 E Ninth St (☎719/486-3836), has the full range of ski gear and snowmobiles, and can organize local ski packages. The resort of **Ski Cooper** (☎719/486-2277), ten miles north, offers good downhill, cross-country and backcountry skiing, and lessons.

### Practicalities

Leadville's **visitor center** is at 809 Harrison Ave (summer daily 10am–5pm; ☎719/486-3900 or 1-800/939-3901). By far the best **place to stay** is the historic landmark *Delaware Hotel*, 700 Harrison Ave (☎719/486-1418 or 1-800/748-2004; ④–⑥), an atmospheric Victorian place where rates include a full breakfast; south of town on US-24 a string of cheaper motels includes the dependable *Super 8* (☎719/486-3637; ④). Leadville has a gratifying choice of places to **eat and drink**. *Cloud City Coffee House and Deli*, 711 Harrison Ave (☎719/486-1317), serves bagels, buns and espresso in a grand old hotel lobby, while further along the street at no. 612, *Columbine Cafe* (☎719/486-3599), dishes up imaginative fresh food with lots of vegetarian options, in simple diner surroundings. There's great Mexican and Southwestern food at the spartan *La Cantina*, a mile south on Hwy-24 (☎719/486-9021), which also has dancing at the weekends. Among Leadville's fine **bars**, the *Pastime Saloon*, 120 W Second St (☎719/486-9986), is a locals' favorite, with a great mountain view from its patio, and delicious wings and burgers. After his performance at the Opera House (see above) Oscar Wilde drank at the wood-paneled *Silver Dollar Saloon*, 315 Harrison Ave (☎719/486-9914); today, it's a welcoming, atmospheric place, filled with Irish memorabilia.

# Aspen

Coffee-table magazines might have you believe that a tollgate outside **ASPEN** only admits film stars and the super-rich. This elite **ski resort**, two hundred miles west of Denver via Leadville, is indeed home to the likes of Cher, Jack Nicholson and Goldie Hawn, but it can be an affordable, and very appealing place for anyone to come in summer – unless you're on an absolute shoestring budget. Visiting in winter requires more cash, though you can save money by skiing the less expensive Aspen Highlands slopes.

From inauspicious beginnings in 1879, this pristine mountain-locked town raced to become the world's top silver producer. By the time the silver market crashed fourteen years later, it had acquired tasteful residential palaces, grand hotels and an opera house. In the 1930s the population slumped below seven hundred; ironically, it was the anti-poverty WPA program that gave the struggling community the cash to build its first crude ski lift in 1936. Entrepreneurs seized the opportunity presented by the varied terrain and plentiful snow, and the first chairlift was dedicated on Aspen Mountain in 1947. Skiing has since spread to three more mountains – Aspen Highlands, Snowmass and Buttermilk Mountain, and the jet set arrived in force during the 1960s. **Development** is a burning political issue: tight architectural constraints have been put on businesses (*McDonald's* is forbidden to have a neon sign), but the last decade has seen yet more Scandinavian-style lodges, condo blocks and giant houses that remain empty for most of the year.

## Arrival and information

In winter, **Independence Pass** on Hwy-82, which provides the quickest access to Aspen, is closed, and the detour through Glenwood Springs adds an extra seventy miles to the trip from Denver. The **airport** is four miles north of town on Hwy-82, served by local buses; if you fly into **Denver**, connecting flights bought in advance only cost another $50 or so, or – again, make sure to book in advance – you can take a Supershuttle (☎1-800/258-3826) or Colorado Mountain Express (☎1-800/222-2112) shuttle bus door-to-door. Numerous airlines fly into **Eagle County Airport** near Vail, eighty minutes from Aspen by car or by Colorado Mountain Express.

Once in Aspen, there's no problem **getting around**: the Roaring Fork Transit Agency (☎970/925-8484) runs a free skiers' shuttle between the four mountains, charges nothing for journeys within the town, and also serves the airport and outlying areas. The main **Rubey Park transit center** terminal is in the center of town on Durant Avenue.

Aspen's **Chamber Resort Association** is at 425 Rio Grande Place (Mon–Fri 9am–5pm; ☎970/925-1940 or 1-800/290-1324). The free *Aspen Daily News* ("If you don't want it printed, don't let it happen") is an excellent source of local gossip, news and food and drink offers. Another helpful source of information when planning your trip is the Aspen-Snowmass **Web site**, *www.aspenonline.com*.

## Accommodation

**Aspen Central Reservations** (☎970/925-9000 or 925-4444) runs a superb service, and doesn't balk if you ask for the cheapest available room. It also arranges package deals combining accommodation with lift tickets. Rates vary considerably even in winter; the least expensive times to come are in the "**value seasons**" (last week in Nov, first two weeks of Dec and first two weeks of April). Between mid-December and January 4, you'll do well to find a double for less than $120. Money can be saved by renting a **condo**, or **camping** in summer; the ranger station, 806 W Hallam (Mon–Fri 8am–4.30pm; ☎970/925-3445), can advise on free wilderness sites and **campgrounds.** There are several campgrounds on Maroon Creek Road, south of Aspen, and some smaller options out towards Independence Pass. Call ☎877/444-6777 for reservations and information.

**Alpine Lodge**, 1240 E Hwy-82 (☎970/925-7351). Clean, friendly place a short walk out of town on Cooper Ave. En-suite or shared baths, and free continental breakfast. Winter ⑤, summer ④.

**Aspen Manor Lodge**, 411 S Monarch St (☎970/925-3001). Good clean rooms, central location, generous continental breakfast and a pool. Winter ⑦, summer ④.

**Christmas Inn B&B**, 232 W Main St (☎970/925-3822). Friendly, family-run motel, two minutes' walk from downtown. Full breakfast, free ski shuttle. Winter ⑥, summer ④.

**L'Auberge**, 435 W Main St (☎970/925-8297). Studios and cabins with kitchens and fireplaces. Winter ⑦, summer ⑤.

**Little Red Ski Haus**, 118 E Cooper Ave (☎970/925-3333). Some private rooms, plus clean dorm bunks for $40 in winter, $25 in summer. Discounts for longer stays. Winter ②–⑤, summer ①–④.

**Mountain Chalet**, 333 E Durant Ave (☎970/925-7797). Friendly, lodge-type accommodation, with large comfortable rooms, pool, jacuzzi, gym and fine buffet breakfast. Winter ⑦, summer ④.

## The town and the mountains

There's not all that much to do in Aspen, apart from sit around the leafy pedestrianized streets and watch the world go by, or browse in the chichi stores and galleries. In summer, the Aspen Historical Society Museum, 620 W Bleeker St (☎970/925-3721), offers **walking tours** of Aspen and nearby ghost towns. The **Aspen Art Museum**, at 590 N Mill St (☎970/925-8050) holds changing exhibits, lectures and special events; Aspen Center for Environmental Studies, 100 S Puppy Smith St (☎970/925-5756) is a wildlife sanctuary, which gives guided nature tours of some of the taller peaks in the Elk Mountain Range.

Three of Aspen's four mountains are run by the **Aspen Ski Co** (☎970/925-1220 or 1-800/525-6200), call ☎1/888-ASPENSNO for conditions. The mogul-packed monster of **Aspen Mountain**, looming over downtown, is for experienced skiers only; **Buttermilk** is great for beginners, with an excellent ski school that offers a three-day guaranteed "Learn to Snowboard" program; the wide-open runs of **Snowmass**, though mostly for intermediate skiers, feature some testing routes. **Aspen Highlands** has some new high-speed lifts and offers excellent extreme skiing terrain. Daily **lift tickets** for all mountains cost $39 (up to 27 years) or $59 (27 years and older). **Rental** of skis, boots and poles usually costs around $18 a day – you can also rent snowshoes in which to trek up and down the mountains. However, the town's best value has to be its fifty miles of groomed **Nordic ski trails** – one of the most extensive free cross-country trail networks in the US.

**Cycling** is the main **summer** pursuit; The Hub, 315 E Hyman Ave (☎970/925-7970), has a wide choice of bikes, while Timberline, 204 S Galena St (☎970/925-9237), is the cheapest for mountain bikes, and organizes tours. The **Roaring Fork River**, surging out of the Sawatch range, is excellent for kayaking and rafting, but sections can be dangerous and every summer sees a few fatalities. Blazing Paddles (☎970/925-5651; $50 for a half-day float trip) is not the lowest-priced company, but it does have a good safety record.

If you fancy **walking** in the mountains, a **gondola** climbs from 601 Dean St to the summit of Aspen Mountain (daily 10am–4pm; $18), where guided nature walks set off on the hour from 11am to 3pm. Occasional free lunchtime concerts and talks are held up here, and there's a good restaurant. Even more alluring is the landscape around the twin purple-gray peaks of the **Maroon Bells**, fifteen miles southwest, soaring above the dark-blue Maroon Lake. The road is closed between 8.30am and 5pm, except for overnight campers with permits, travelers with disabilities and RFTA buses, which leave daily from the Rubey Park transit center (every 30min 9am–4.30pm; $5 roundtrip, or $19 combination ticket with gondola ride). Details on hiking are available from the **ranger station** (see p.749).

## Eating and drinking

Many of Aspen's classy cafes and restaurants charge over $25 for a main course, but good budget places exist and competition is keen. New restaurants open and close with alarming regularity; the list below consists of tried and trusted favorites. Note, too, that many of Aspen's bars serve good, reasonably priced food (see below).

**Explore Booksellers and Bistro**, 221 E Main St (☎970/925-5336). Great bookstore with high-quality creative vegetarian food, good espresso and pastries, and a shady roof terrace.

**Little Annie's**, 517 E Hyman Ave (☎970/925-1098). Lively, popular and unpretentious saloon-style restaurant. Potato pancakes and hearty stews for lunch, with huge trout, chicken, beef or rib dinner platters for around $15.

**Main Street Bakery Cafe**, 201 E Main St (☎970/925-6446). Scrumptious, inventive New American cuisine, and an excellent wine list in a casual, chatty setting. Always busy in the morning for massive, fresh fruit-packed breakfasts.

**Mezzaluna,** 624 E Cooper Ave (☎970/925-5882) Mid-priced Northern Italian dishes for lunch or dinner, including wood-fired pizzas.

**Poppycocks**, 609 E Cooper Ave (☎970/925-1245). Open from 7am until 2pm, serving tasty crepes and smoothies.

**Takah Sushi**, 420 E Hyman Ave (☎970/925-8588). Phenomenally good sushi and pan-Asian cuisine, in a buzzing, cheerful atmosphere. Highly recommended yet quite expensive.

**Wienerstube**, 633 E Hyman Ave (☎970/925-3357). The best breakfast in Aspen: eggs Benedict, Austrian sausage and Viennese pastries among other things. A great value. Tues–Sun 6.30am–2.30pm.

## Entertainment and nightlife

Going out in Aspen, the capital of après-ski, is fun all year round and need not be expensive. Check the free papers for special offers. In summer, downtown hosts several top-notch festivals. The **Aspen Music Festival**, between late June and late August, features international performers (☎970/925-9042); July and early August see the **DanceAspen** festival (☎970/925-7718). Mid-January's **Winterskol** includes sporting events, parades and concerts.

**Crystal Palace Dinner Theatre**, 300 E Hyman (☎970/925-1455). Eat dinner and then watch a vaudeville-type revue. Dinner and the show cost over $50 per person.

**Double Diamond**, 450 S Galena St (☎970/920-6905). Aspen's top live music venue. Usually free before 10pm and the drink prices are reasonable.

**Flying Dog Brewpub**, 424 E Cooper (☎970/925-7464). Lively spot for microbrews and reasonably priced food; live music every Sun.

**J-Bar**, 330 E Main St in the *Jerome Hotel* (☎970/920-1000). Grand historic bar; drink and mingle with the well-heeled hotel guests.

**Red Onion**, Cooper St Mall (☎970/925-9043). Aspen's oldest bar, serving big portions of Mexican food and good burgers. A popular après-ski spot, especially for its jello shots.

**Shooters**, 220 S Galena St (☎970/925-4567). Swinging C&W bar below the *Hard Rock Cafe*.

**Woody Creek Tavern**, Upper River Rd, Woody Creek (☎970/923-4585). Seven miles north along Hwy-82, right on River Rd, and then first left. Cult bar where ranch hands and rock stars shoot pool, drink imported beers and fresh lime juice margaritas, and eat Tex-Mex. A regular haunt of gonzo journalist Hunter S Thompson.

# Vail

Compared to most other Colorado ski towns, **VAIL**, 122 miles west of Denver off I-70, is a new creation. Only a handful of farmers lived here before the resort – a collection of fake Tyrolean-style chalets and concrete-block condominiums – opened in 1952. During the Ford administration, it served as the western White House; Gerald Ford and his wife still live here, hosting annual celebrity golf and skiing competitions.

According to *SKI* magazine, Vail is the top **ski** destination in the US – but not for its aesthetic beauty. What lures the ultra-rich (more conspicuous here than in Aspen) is the exceptional quality of snow, the sheer variety of terrain, and the huge number of lifts (expensive at $48 a day, though the ticket also lets you ski Beaver Creek, ten miles west and home to America's top-rated ski school). You can also speed down a 3000ft **bobsleigh run** for $15 a time, or, in summer, go **mountain biking**: one good option is to take the gondola from Lionshead center (mid-June–Aug daily 10am–4.30pm; $12, $19 with bike) and ride down the mountain.

### Practicalities

From **Denver International Airport**, shuttles include Supershuttle (☎1-800/258-3826) or Colorado Mountain Express (☎1-800/222-2112) for door-to-door service. **Eagle County Airport**, used by American Airlines among others, lies just 35 miles from the resort. Vail spreads for eight miles along the narrow valley floor, with successive nuclei from east to west at Vail Village, Lionshead, Cascade Village and West Vail. Beaver Creek, home of the Fords, lies a further ten miles west. The entire complex is **pedestrianized**; there's no charge for the parking lots in summer, and Vail Buses run free year-round shuttles (☎970/328-8143).

For information on skiing and accommodation, contact Vail Reservations (☎1-800/427-8308; ☎0800/891772 from the UK), or call into a **visitor center** at either Vail Village (☎970/479-1394) or Lionshead (☎970/479-1385). Finding an affordable place to **stay** can be a problem. By Vail standards at least, the condos in **Avon**, just below Beaver Creek, are inexpensive. Rates in **Vail Village**, the main social center, are higher; try *Tivoli Lodge* (☎970/476-5615 or 1-800/451-4756; winter ⑦, summer ⑤), or the sumptuous *Mountain Haus* (☎970/476-2434 or 1-800/237-0922; winter ⑦, summer ⑥). The *Eagle River Inn*, 145 N Main St (☎970/827-5761 or 1-800/344-1750; winter ⑦/⑧, summer ⑤), is a B&B decked out in tasteful Santa Fe-style in the hamlet of **Minturn**, seven miles south of Vail on US-24.

**Eating out** can also prove expensive. *Jackalope* in West Vail Mall (☎970/476-4314) is a lively saloon and pool hall serving basic food, and *Vendetta's*, 291 Bridge St in Vail Village (☎970/476-5070), offers fine Italian lunch specials and pasta dinners. Both are comparatively affordable.

**Nightlife** revolves around **The Circuit** on Bridge Street, Vail Village. Most people tour between the bars and discos. The checklist of places to see and be seen includes *The Club* (live music), the *Hong Kong Cafe* (loud music), upstairs at *Vendetta's* (the ski patrol hangout) and *Nick's*, below *Russell's Restaurant*, which plays reasonable dance music.

## Glenwood Springs

Bustling, touristy **GLENWOOD SPRINGS** sits at the end of impressive Glenwood Canyon, 160 miles west of Denver and within easy striking distance of Vail and Aspen. Just north of the confluence of the Roaring Fork and Colorado rivers, the town offers endless recreational opportunities. Long used by the Ute as a place of relaxation, the **hot springs** here were the target for unscrupulous speculators who broke treaties and established resort facilities in the 1880s. The sulphurous smell that hits you on the north side of the river emanates from **Glenwood Hot Springs Pool**, 410 N River St. Billed as the "world's largest outdoor mineral hot springs pool," it sports an exhilarating hydrotube water slide and special "jacuzzi" seats (summer daily 7.30am–10pm; rest of year daily 9am–10pm; $8). Next door, you can destress in the natural subterranean steam baths of the **Yampah Spa Vapor Caves** at 709 E Sixth St (daily 9am–9pm; $8.75), with cool marble benches set deep in ancient caves.

Some of the West's most colorful characters came here in the early days, including Dr John R **"Doc" Holliday**, a dentist better known as a gambler, gunslinger and shooter in the gunfight at the OK Corral (see p.841). A chronic tuberculosis sufferer, Holliday came to the springs for a cure but died just a few months later in November 1887, at the age of 35. He is buried on a bluff overlooking the town in the picturesque Linwood Cemetery. In the paupers' section, you can find the grave of Harvey Logan, alias bank robber Kid Curry, a member of Butch Cassidy's notorious gang.

Whitewater Rafting, I-70 exit 114 (☎970/945-8477), arranges good float trips, and whitewater rides along a fairly placid twenty-mile stretch of the Colorado River. **Hiking** and **mountain biking** trails alongside streams and waterfalls crisscross the White River National Forest surrounding the town, and offer good fishing opportunities. The nearby, family-oriented Ski Sunlight complex offers some of the least expensive **skiing** in the region, accessible by shuttle from Glenwood Springs (☎970/945-7491; $1).

### Practicalities

Amtrak arrives at 413 Seventh St, at the end of a scenic route through the canyons, gorges and valleys of central Colorado. Greyhound, traveling along the less inspiring I-70, stops close to downtown. The **visitor center**, 1102 Grand Ave (24 hours; ☎970/945-6589) stocks the very useful *Glenwood Springs Official Guide*. Regular RFTA **buses** link the town with Aspen (daily 6am–10pm; 1hr; call for schedule, ☎970/925-8484; $6).

The enthusiastically run *HI-Glenwood Springs Hostel*, near downtown at 1021 Grand Ave (☎970/945-8545 or 1-800/9-HOSTEL; ①), has spacious dorms (beds $12–14), cheap private rooms, plus kitchen facilities, a giant record collection and a wealth of local knowledge. They also arrange tours and whitewater trips. They are closed from 10am–4pm. Reasonable **motels** include the *Cedar Lodge*, 2102 Grand Ave (☎970/945-6579; ③/④). The *Daily Bread Cafe and Bakery*, downtown at 729 Grand Ave (☎970/945-6253), serves delicious breakfasts, soups and salads; *Wild Rose Bakery* at 310 7th St (☎970/928-8973), is also a local favorite; and for dinner, *Rick's*, upstairs at 710 Grand Ave (☎970/945-4771), serves elegant continental food and boasts an extensive wine list. *May Palace*, at 820 Grand Ave (☎970/945-0472), serves good Chinese food while the *Glenwood Canyon Brewpu*b at the *Hotel Denver*, 402 Seventh St (☎970/945-1276), will certainly quench your thirst.

## Grand Junction

**GRAND JUNCTION**, 246 miles west of Denver on I-70, is often neglected as a destination, even though its immediate environs abound with outdoor opportunities, and within a fifty-mile stretch you can trace the transition from fertile valley to full-blown desert. Another town that sprang into life in the 1880s with the arrival of the railroads, it now makes its living primarily through the oil and gas industries. Although initial impressions are bound to be unfavorable – an unsightly sprawl of factory units and sales yards lines the I-70 Business Loop – downtown is much better, with leafy boulevards encircling a small, tree-lined, historic and retail district.

The Colorado section of Dinosaur National Monument – see p.894 – is ninety miles north of Grand Junction along Hwy-139, but the town itself holds the diverting **Dinosaur Valley Museum**, 362 Main St (summer daily 9am–5pm; rest of year Tues–Sat 10am–4.30pm; $4.50), housing realistic reconstructed reptiles along with giant bones excavated locally.

Grand Junction offers a wide range of **cycling** terrain, from canal paths to rigorous mountain trails. Bikes can be rented from the Bike Peddler, 701 First St (☎970/243-5602). There's great **hiking** beside the rippled, purple-gray **Book Cliffs**, paralleling the town on the north side, whose subtle changes of color throughout the day are a delight.

The area is also a **rock climber's** dream. Summit Canyon Mountaineering, 549 Main St (☎970/243-2847), can supply you with information and gear.

## Practicalities

Amtrak stops at Second and Pitkin. Greyhound buses serve Durango, Denver and Salt Lake City from 230 S Fifth St. The **visitor center**, 740 Horizon Drive (☎970/244-1480 or 1-800/962-2547), is very helpful. Budget **motels** on the interstate – such as the good-value *Best Western Horizon Inn*, 754 Horizon Drive (☎970/245-1410; ③), with pool, spa, and continental breakfast – offer great rates; alternatives include the downtown *HI-Grand Junction* in the historic *Hotel Melrose*, 337 Colorado Ave (☎970/242-9636 or 1-800/430-4555; ①/②), where bunks cost $12 and private rooms start at around $30. *Daniel's Motel*, at 333 North Ave, is basic but cheap, clean and convenient to downtown (☎970/243-1084; ②).

You can **eat** casually and rather inexpensively (for the area) at the *Blue Moon Bar & Grill*, 120 N Seventh St (☎970/242-5406), and at *Melissa's Table*, 319 Main St (☎970/245-8222).

## Colorado National Monument

Millions of years of wind and water erosion have gouged out the brightly colored rock spires, domes, arches, pedestals and balanced rocks of the **COLORADO NATIONAL MONUMENT**, from the edge of the cliffs just four miles west of Grand Junction. This painted desert of warm reds, stunning purples, burnt oranges and browns is also home to a high arid vegetation of piñon pine, yucca, sagebrush and Utah juniper. There's an entry fee of $4 per car, valid for seven days.

The best of many overlooks along the twisting, curving 23-mile **rim drive** (a 39-mile round trip from Grand Junction) is the **Book Cliff View**, or the **Parade of the Monoliths**, just off the rim road at the sign for Window Rock Trail. Short hikes include the one-hour **John Otto's Trail**, affording close-up views of several monoliths; longer trails get right down to the canyon floor. One of the best trails is the **Monument Canyon Trail** weaving through a series of scenic spots, while **Unaweep Canyon** is another beautiful area, with excellent **rock climbing**. You can **camp** for $7 in the park's *Saddlehorn Campground*, or pitch a tent anywhere more than a quarter of a mile off the road. Information can be found at the **visitor's center** at the north end of the park (fall–spring 9am–5pm; Memorial Day–Labor Day 8am–7pm; ☎970/858-3617).

## Grand Mesa

The **Grand Mesa**, thirty miles east of Grand Junction on Hwy-65, via I-70, is at 10,000ft the world's largest flat-topped mountain, created over a period of 600 million years by the erosion of the softer rock that surrounded a 400ft lava flow. Though its full extent can only really be grasped from thirty miles away, visitors who ascend the twisting Hwy-65 to the plateau are rewarded by a tranquil landscape, covered by pine and aspen groves with over two hundred lakes, colored by the reflections of shoreline trees. **Lands End Road**, an eleven-mile dirt track, ends at a stunning panorama: lakes, plains, sand hills and smaller mesas separate thick forest on the left from desert on the right, with the snow-crested San Juan peaks far off in the background.

Pretty campgrounds, open summer only, dot the east side near Alexander Lake (details from the ranger office at 764 Horizon Drive in Grand Junction; ☎970/242-8211), as do a motel and some basic cafes. At the bottom of the Mesa, five miles north of **Cedaredge**, the hospitable *Llama's B&B* on Hwy-65 (☎970/856-6836; ④) offers fantastic breakfasts served on a sun deck, and the chance to meet some llamas.

# Southeast Colorado

The gently undulating plains of **southeast Colorado** come as a surprise to travelers expecting the ski resorts and alpine splendor that characterize the rest of the state. Here instead are hundreds of small farming towns and endless acres of grassland, much of which looks as it did 150 years ago, when traders and early explorers crossed the region along the Santa Fe Trail, following the Arkansas River between Missouri and Mexico.

The southeast's most popular destination is the engaging small city of **Colorado Springs**, which sits at the foot of towering **Pikes Peak** and gives access to the old gold-mining country around **Cripple Creek**.

## Colorado Springs and around

Seventy miles south of Denver on I-25, **COLORADO SPRINGS** was originally developed as a vacation spot in 1871 by railroad tycoon William Jackson Palmer. He attracted so many English gentry to the town that it earned the nickname of "Little London." Despite sprawling for ten miles alongside I-25, modern Colorado Springs, a bastion of conservatism compared to liberal Denver, still retains much of Palmer's vision. Contributing factors include a high military presence, fundamentalist religious organizations, the exclusive Colorado College and a well-to-do Anglo-American community.

Motorists whisk through the incredible **Garden of the Gods**, on the west edge of town off US-24 W, without bothering to get out of their vehicles. This gnarled, twisted and warped red sandstone rockery was lifted up at the same time as the nearby mountains, but has since been eroded into finely balanced overhangs, jagged pinnacles, massive pedestals and mushroom formations. Among outstanding features are **High Point**, which has the best view, **Balanced Rock** and the **Central Garden**. The **visitor center**, at the park's eastern border (☎719/634-6666), has details on hiking and mountain biking **trails**.

At the **Pro Rodeo Hall of Fame**, 101 Pro Rodeo Drive, off I-25 exit 147 (daily 9am–5pm; $6), videos and displays explain the sport's various disciplines, other local exhibits of note include the painting and sculpture gardens of the **Colorado Springs Fine Arts Center**, 30 W Dale St (Tues–Fri 9am–5pm, Sat 10am–5pm, Sun 1–5pm; $3); the more specialized works at the **Western Museum of Mining and Industry**, east of I-25 exit 156A (Mon–Sat 9am–4pm, Sun noon–4pm; $5); and the restored courtroom at the **Colorado Springs Pioneer Museum**, 215 S Tejon St (Tues–Sat 10am–5pm, Sun 1–5pm; free).

### Practicalities

From **Denver International Airport** there are a number of inexpensive **flights**, or you can book the Colorado Springs Shuttle (☎719/578-5232; $27). Greyhound **buses** stop at 120 S Weber St downtown. Colorado Springs' **visitor center** is at 104 Cascade St (summer daily 9am–5pm; rest of year daily 10am–4pm; ☎719/635-7506 or 1-800/368-4748). The best value **accommodation** in the area is four miles west in Old Colorado City, at the neat *Amarillo Motel*, 2801 W Colorado Ave (☎719/635-8539; ②), while the lovely *Holden House B&B*, at 1102 W Pikes Peak Ave (☎719/471-3980; ⑤), is another nice option. In summer, the clean and neat *Garden of the Gods Cabins*, 3704 W Colorado Ave (☎719/475-9450; ①), has $35 cabins for two, and a $23 campground.

Appealing places to **eat** downtown include the excellent *Olive Branch*, at Boulder and Tejon (☎719/475-1199), with good vegetarian food. The *Phantom Canyon Brewing Co*, 2 E Pikes Peak Ave (☎719/635-2800), is a great place for some microbrews and authentic pub food. Out in Old Colorado City, the family-owned *Henri's Mexican*, 2427 W Colorado Ave (☎719/634-9031), pulls in the crowds for home-style food and superb margaritas. Nearby is one of the best **bars** in the city, *Meadow Muffins*, 2432 W Colorado Ave (☎719/633-0583), festooned with movie memorabilia, it serves good burgers, sandwiches and salads, hosts live music and stays open late (until 2am Fri & Sat).

## Pikes Peak

Though there are thirty taller mountains in Colorado alone, **Pikes Peak**, just west of Colorado Springs, is probably the best known – largely because the view from its summit inspired Katherine Lee Bates to write the words to *America The Beautiful*. The 14,110ft peak was first mapped by Zebulon Pike in 1806, who never climbed it himself. By the end of the century gondola trails had been built to carry rich tourists like Ms Bates to the top. In 1929 it took Bill Williams, a Texan, twenty days and 170 changes of trousers to scale the mountain, pushing a peanut with his nose.

You can reach the top by a long **hike**, or by a difficult **toll road** (summer 7am–7pm, all other times 9am–3pm; $6 per person). The thrilling **Pikes Peak Cog Railway** grinds its way up an average of 847ft per mile on its ninety-minute journey to the summit; from 11,500ft onwards it crosses a barren expanse of tundra, scarred by giant scree flows. From the bleak and windswept top, it's possible to see Denver seventy miles north, and the endless prairie to the east, while to the west mile upon mile of giant snowcapped peaks rise into the distance. The train leaves from 515 Ruxton Ave in **Manitou Springs**, six miles west of Colorado Springs (mid-May–Nov; ☎719/685-5401; $22, reservations advised).

## Cripple Creek

Fifty miles or so out from Colorado Springs, the much-chronicled gold camp of **CRIPPLE CREEK**, named for a calf that broke its leg trying to jump over a tumbling stream, nestles in a grim volcanic bowl on the west flank of Pikes Peak. In 1891, a cowhand, Bob Womack, was the first to discover gold on this poor cattle-raising land. Elated by his find, he sold his share for $500 and spent the lot on whiskey. Others were more fortunate: a total of over $500 million worth of gold was extracted. By 1900 25,000 people lived in a town boasting eight newspapers, numerous banks, splendid hotels, department stores, elegant homes and even a stock exchange. Today the main street still backs onto a forbidding rocky plateau, but since gambling was legalized in Cripple Creek in 1990 most of its Victorian buildings have been converted into casinos.

Scenic steam trains on the **Narrow Gauge Railway** (June–mid-Oct daily 10am–5pm; ☎719/689-2640; $8), trundle for four miles past abandoned mines. One mile north on Hwy-67, ex-miners take you a thousand feet underground to see gold veins in **Mollie Kathleen's Mine** (May–Oct daily 9am–5pm; $8). Built in 1896 and the only one of Cripple Creek's Gold Rush hotels still in business, the grand old *Imperial Hotel*, 123 N Third St (☎719/689-7777 or 1-800/235-2922; ④), is a unique place to **stay**. Otherwise there are anodyne casino hotels and the usual chains.

# Southwest Colorado

The high mountain passes of **southwest Colorado** are classic mining territory; dotted through the valleys you'll find all sorts of well-preserved late-Victorian frontier towns. As the pioneers moved in, first illegally and then backed by the federal government, they drove the Ute away into the poorer land of the far southwest.

From **Durango**, the main town of southwest Colorado, the dramatic **San Juan Skyway** completes a loop of over two hundred miles through the mountains, north along US-550 and then back via Hwy-145 and US-160. The stretch of road north of Durango, negotiating its way over stunning high passes, is known as the **Million Dollar Highway** for the gold-laden gravel that was used in its construction. **Crested Butte**, a gorgeous nineteenth-century mining village turned ski resort, is one of Colorado's major attractions.

## Durango

**DURANGO**, named after Durango, Mexico, and now twinned with it, too, was founded in 1880 as a rail junction for the Gold Rush community of Silverton, 45 miles further north. **Steam trains** still run the same spectacular route through the Animas Valley, and remain the foundation of Durango's tourist economy: the **Durango & Silverton Narrow Gauge Railroad** runs up to four round-trips daily between May and October, from a depot at 479 Main Ave at the south end of town (all leave in early morning; $53 round-trip; reserve tickets at least two weeks in advance; ☎970/247-2733). Shorter excursions, covering the most scenic areas of the route, run between late November and early May (daily 10am; $42).

Durango has also become one of the West's latest boomtowns, attracting a large influx of long-distance computerized teleworkers. Combine them with outdoors enthusiasts, who come to ride their mountain bikes on the grueling back roads nearby, and in the morning at least the place has a youthful, energetic buzz. In the evening, they're all a bit too wiped out to do very much.

Greyhound services between Denver and Albuquerque call in at 275 E Eighth Ave. Durango's **visitor center**, near the train station (summer Mon–Fri 8am–7pm, Sat 10am–6pm, Sun 11am–5pm; rest of year Mon–Fri 8am–6pm, Sat 8am–5pm, Sun 10am–4pm; ☎970/247-0312 or 1-800/525-8855), has full lists of **accommodation**, topped by the landmark *Strater Hotel* at 699 Main Ave (☎970/247-4431 or 1-800/247-4431 out of state; ⑥), and rounded off by the $13 dorms at the shabby *Durango Youth Hostel*, downtown at 543 E Second Ave (☎970/247-9905; ①/②). The innumerable **motels** north of town along Main Avenue double their rates in summer; try the *Siesta* at no. 3475 (☎970/247-0741; ③), or the *Vagabond Inn* at no. 2180 (☎970/259-5901; ③). The *Scrubby Oaks*, three miles east at 1901 Florida Rd (☎970/247-2176; ④), is a good-value mountain-view **B&B**. There are plenty of places to **eat** and **drink**: *Carver's Bakery & Brewpub*, 1022 Main Ave (☎970/259-2545) opens at 6.30am and keeps buzzing all day, while *Steamworks Brewing Co*, 801 E Second Ave (☎970/259-9200), also serves good food.

## Silverton

Journey's end for the narrow-gauge railroad from Durango comes at **SILVERTON**, spread across a small flat valley surrounded by high mountains. It's one of Colorado's most atmospheric mountain towns, with wide, dirt-paved streets leading off towards the hills to either side of the one main road. Silverton's zinc and copper mining days only came to an end in 1991; the population has dropped since then, but those that remain have so far resisted suggestions that its future lies in legalizing gambling to draw in the tourists. Meanwhile, the false-fronted stores along "Notorious Blair Street," paralleling the main drag, recall the days when Bat Masterson was the city marshal, and are the scene of a daily shoot-out at 5.30pm.

The majority of visitors to Silverton are day-trippers, and to spend a night here is to step back a century. Bargain **accommodation** is to be had at the *Triangle Motel*, 848 Greene St (☎970/387-5780; ③), at the south end of town, which also offers good-value two-room suites and jeep rental, though the old-style, central *Grand Imperial Hotel*, 1219 Greene St (☎970/387-5527 or 1-800/341-3340; ④), is not much more expensive.

The *French Bakery*, 1250 Greene St (☎970/387-5976), serves **food** from sandwiches through to full meals, while, *Romero's*, 1151 Greene St (☎970/387-0123), is an enjoyable Mexican cantina. The tin-walled *Silverton Hostel*, 1025 Blair St (check-in daily 8–10am & 4–10pm; ☎970/387-0015; ①), has $11 dorm beds.

## Ouray

The equally attractive mining community of **OURAY** lies 23 miles north of Silverton, on the far side of the 11,018ft **Red Mountain Pass**, where the bare rock beneath the snow really is red, thanks to mineral deposits. The Million Dollar Highway twists and turns, passing abandoned mine workings and rusting machinery in the most unlikely and inaccessible spots; back roads into the mountains offer rich pickings, for hikers or drivers with 4WD vehicles.

Ouray itself squeezes into a narrow but verdant valley, with the commercially run **Ouray Hot Springs** beside the Uncompahgre River at the north end of town. A mile or so south, a one-way loop dirt road leads to Box Cañon Falls Park (daily 8am–7pm; $2), where a straightforward 500ft trail, partly along a swaying wooden parapet, leads into the dark, narrow Box Cañon. At the far end, the falls thunder through a tiny cleft in the mountain.

The local **visitor center** is outside the hot springs (daily 8am–6pm; ☎970/325-4746 or 1-800/228-1876). At *Box Canyon Lodge*, an old-style timber **motel** at 45 Third Ave below the park (☎970/325-4981 or 1-800/327-5080; ③), you can bathe in natural hot tubs; the luxurious B&B *St Elmo Hotel*, 426 Main St (☎970/325-4951; ⑤), holds a good **restaurant**, and the *Ouray Coffee House*, next to the springs at 960 Main St (☎970/325-4001), has an appealing patio for light lunches.

## Telluride

**TELLURIDE**, 120 miles northwest of Durango on Hwy-145, is another former mining village, which in the 1880s was briefly home to the young Butch Cassidy, who robbed his first bank here in 1889. These days Telluride is better known as the home of a top-class **ski resort** that rivals Aspen as the prime winter destination for the stars. It has, however, achieved this status without losing its character – the wide main street, a National Historic District with low-slung buildings on either side, still heads directly up towards one of the most stupendous mountain views in the Rockies. Healthy young bohemians with few visible means of support but top-notch ski or snowboarding equipment seem to form the bulk of the 1200 citizens, while most of the glitzy visitors tend to hang out two miles above the town in **Mountain Village**; the two places are connected by a free year-round gondola service. In summer, the **hiking** opportunities are excellent; one three-mile round-trip walk leads from the head of the valley, where the highway ends at Pioneer Mill, up to the 365ft **Bridal Veil Falls**.

**Accommodation** is much less expensive in summer than during ski season, though prices do go up for the Bluegrass Festival in June, the Jazz Festival at the beginning of August and the Film Festival at the start of September. As well as being the town's official **information service**, Telluride Central Reservations, 666 W Colorado Ave (summer daily 9am–7pm; rest of year Mon–Fri 9am–5pm; ☎970/728-4431 or 1-800/525-3455), coordinates **lodging** and package deals, with free lift tickets for the first month of the season for guests in certain lodges. Skiing comes half-price if you stay in any of seven neighboring towns. Of specific places, the 1895 *New Sheridan Hotel*, 231 W Colorado Ave (☎970/728-4351 or 1-800/200-1891; winter ⑥, summer ③), offers some bargain rooms with shared bath, and the *Victoria Inn*, 401 W Pacific Ave (☎970/728-6601 or 1-800/611-9893; ⑤), has clean doubles.

*Eddie's*, 300 W Colorado Ave (☎970/728-5335), serves good Italian **food** and home-brewed ales; *Smugglers Brewpub and Grille*, San Juan and Pine (☎970/728-0919) is a lively evening hangout with a wide-ranging menu.

# Crested Butte

The beautiful Victorian mining village of **CRESTED BUTTE**, 150 miles northwest of Telluride and 230 miles southwest of Denver, almost died off in the late 1950s when its coal deposits became exhausted. However, the development of 11,875ft **Mount Crested Butte** into a world-class **ski resort** in the 1960s, and a **mountain-bikers'** paradise two decades later, means that today it can claim to be the best year-round resort in Colorado. The old town is resplendent with gaily painted clapboard homes and businesses, and zoning laws ensure that condos and chalets are confined to the resort area, tucked behind the foothills three miles up the road. The rapid transition from near-ghost town to sporting heaven has lured young people here from throughout the West, to produce an addictive laid-back atmosphere.

## Arrival and information
Crested Butte is not an easy place to get to, especially in winter and spring when **roads** can be cut off by snow and avalanches. Most skiers **fly** in: ten flights per day from Denver, and at least one per week from Atlanta, Dallas and Houston, touch down at **Gunnison Airport**. From here, Alpine Express (☎970/641-5074; $40 round-trip) will drive you the 28 miles to your accommodation. Once in Crested Butte there's no need for a car: **buses** ply the three-mile route between the town and resort every fifteen minutes. The **visitor center** is at Elk Avenue and Sixth (daily 9am–5pm; ☎970/349-6438 or 1-800/545-4505).

## Accommodation
The choice in Crested Butte lies between staying up at the ski area or downtown; in the end it makes little difference as you're likely to flit between the two areas every day. Crested Butte Vacations (☎970/349-2222 or 1-800/544-8448; ☎0800/894085 from the UK) can book accommodation and advise on money-saving package deals. In any case, be sure to reserve a room in advance during winter.

**Claim Jumper B&B**, 704 Whiterock Ave (☎970/349-6471). One of the most enjoyable B&Bs in Colorado. Six variously themed rooms amid a jumble of Americana. Big breakfasts; bike-friendly. ⑤.

**Crested Butte International Hostel**, 615 Teocalli Ave (☎970/349-0588). Large, friendly hostel, where dorm beds are $17 in summer, and $24 – assuming you manage to get one – in winter. ①.

**Crested Butte Lodge**, Crested Mountain Village (☎970/349-4660 or 1-800/544-8448). Built in the 1960s, this is the oldest and most characterful place to stay in the resort, with its own indoor pool and spa. Winter ⑤, summer ④.

**Forest Queen Hotel & Restaurant**, 129 Elk Ave (☎970/349-5336). Clean and basic hotel rooms. ③.

## The town and mountain
Pretty as it is, it doesn't take long to take in Crested Butte's tiny downtown during the day, leaving lots of time for exploring the mountain and environs.

In **skiing** circles, the Butte is best known for its extreme terrain, with lifts serving out-of-the-way bowls and faces that, in other resorts, would only be accessible by helicopter. While this inspires hundreds of ski rats to make Crested Butte their winter home, the combination of good runs and an easygoing attitude helps beginners get a lot better. The big deal in recent years has been the **Ski For Free** period, usually lasting a month from Opening Day in mid-November, when lift tickets (usually $49) really do cost $0.00 – no catches – and free "never-ever" lessons for absolute beginners are thrown in. Cross-country, especially telemark, skiing attracts thousands, while snow-mobiling ranks as a great way to rest your legs. For something a little different, try a **horseback ride** through the snow with Fantasy Ranch (☎970/349-5425; $85).

Summer in Crested Butte is becoming as popular as winter – during **Fat Tire Week** in early July, rooms get booked up well in advance. This is premier mountain bike country. You can spend days riding trails around the mountain, but for a special adventure hop over to Aspen on the rocky and jagged 21-mile **Pearl Pass** – 190 miles shorter than the road.

### Eating and drinking

Crested Butte lays claim to a surprising number of gourmet **restaurants**, which charge much less than their equivalents in the more glitzy resorts. Good, reasonably priced food is also easy to find; even around the ski lifts, a filling lunch can be had for $5. The early après-ski center is *Rafters*, right by the lifts. By early evening most visitors have found their way to downtown, for no-nonsense local bars such as *Kochevars* and *The Talk of the Town*.

**Bakery Cafe**, 3rd St and Elk Ave (☎970/349-7280). Best breakfast in town – oven-fresh muffins, breads and pastries, plus great selection of coffees and juices.

**Idlespur Brewpub**, 226 Elk Ave (☎970/349-5026). Definitive, cavernous Colorado microbrewery, with roaring fire in winter and inexpensive food.

**Le Bousquet**, 201 Elk Ave (☎970/349-5808). Excellent, imaginative and expensive French cuisine.

**Powerhouse**, 130 Elk Ave (☎970/349-5494). It's hard to say whether the Mexican food is better here or at nearby *Donita's Cantina*, but this restaurant's setting – a fondly restored 1880s generating station with a huge wooden bar – gives it the edge.

## Cortez

The town of **CORTEZ**, in the far southwest corner of Colorado, consists basically of one long curve of highway (US-160), roughly 25 miles up from the **Four Corners Monument** that marks the meeting place of Colorado, New Mexico, Arizona and Utah. Its primary function is as an overnight stop for visitors to Mesa Verde National Park, heading to or from the canyonlands of northern Arizona. Nothing in town commands much attention, though the giant **Sleeping Ute Mountain** to the southwest, visible from all over, makes a dramatic backdrop, looking uncannily like a warrior god asleep with his arms folded across his chest.

The **visitor center** at 928 E Main St (daily 8am–6pm; ☎970/565-4048 or 1-800/253-1616) has information on the entire state. **Motels** include the *Aneth Lodge*, 645 E Main St (☎970/565-3453 or 1-877/263-8454; ③), and *Budget Host Inn*, 2040 E Main St (☎970/565-3738; ③). *Dry Dock Restaurant*, 200 W Main St (☎970/564-9404), dishes up great seafood in its pleasant garden, while *Main Street Brewery*, 21 E Main St (☎970/564-9112), is a **brewpub** serving simple meals.

## Mesa Verde National Park

**MESA VERDE NATIONAL PARK**, the only national park in the US exclusively devoted to archeological remains, is set high in the plateaus of southwest Colorado, off US-160 halfway between Cortez and Mancos. It's an astonishing place, so far off the beaten track that its extensive **Anasazi ruins** were not fully explored until 1888.

Between the time of Christ and 1300 AD, Anasazi civilization expanded to cover much of the area known as the "**Four Corners**." Their earliest dwellings were simple pits in the ground, but before they vanished from history they had developed the architectural sophistication needed to build the extraordinary complexes of Mesa Verde.

Most of the best-preserved Anasazi relics are in modern New Mexico, Arizona and Utah; see p.813 for more background information and a list of other sites.

Mesa Verde is a densely wooded plateau, cut at its southern edge by sheer canyons that divide the land into narrow fingers. The Anasazi are thought to have been the only inhabitants the region has ever had: no one has lived here since the thirteenth century, and neither have any traces been found of a human presence before 500 AD. The people who built the first pit-houses here in the sixth century were already skilled potters leading a stable agricultural life; they owned domesticated turkeys and grew corn. After several hundred years, they moved off the mesa tops and began to construct spectacular multistory apartments and entire communities, nestling in rocky alcoves high above the canyons. Quite why they did so is not clear, though recent evidence suggests that Anasazi culture was not quite as peaceful as previously imagined; in any case the soil at Mesa Verde ultimately appears to have been depleted, and they seem to have migrated into what's now New Mexico to establish the pueblos where their descendants still live.

## Touring the park

The access road to Mesa Verde climbs south from US-160 ten miles east of Cortez. Once past the entrance station – where a fee of $10 per vehicle is payable – it twists for fifteen miles to the **Far View visitor center** (late April–late Oct daily 8am–5pm; ☎970/529-4461). Exhibits inside cover Navajo, Hopi and Pueblo crafts and jewelry.

Immediately beyond, the road divides to the two main constellations of remains: Chapin Mesa to the south, and Wetherill Mesa to the west. To tour any of the three major ruins you must buy **tickets** at the visitor center; each costs $1.75, and is valid for one specific time only. On Chapin Mesa, Cliff Palace is usually open between 9am and 5pm daily from late April until early November, and Balcony House for the same hours between late April and mid-October; at busy times, you can't tour both on the same day. On Wetherill Mesa, generally accessible between late May and early September, tours of Long House operate between 9am and 4pm daily.

Six miles towards **Chapin Mesa** from the visitor center, the **Archeological Museum** holds the park's best displays on the Anasazi, and also sells tour tickets for the remainder of the season after the visitor center closes in late fall (summer daily 8am–6.30pm; rest of year daily 8am–5pm). It's also the starting point for the short, steep hike down to **Spruce Tree House**, the only ruin that can be seen in winter – a neat little village of three-story structures, snugly molded into the recesses of a rocky alcove and fronted by open plazas.

Beyond the museum, Ruins Road (April–early Nov, daily 8am–dusk) consists of two one-way, six-mile loops. If you're pressed for time, follow the eastern one only, to reach **Cliff Palace**, the largest Anasazi cliff dwelling to survive anywhere. Tucked a hundred feet below an overhanging ledge of pale rock, its 217 rooms once housed over 200 people. Even if you don't have a tour ticket (see above), you can get a great view from the promontory where tour groups gather, below the parking lot. Entering the ruin itself, especially on a quieter day, provides a haunting evocation of a lost and little-known world, as you walk through the empty plazas, and peer down into the mysterious *kivas*. Fading murals can still be discerned inside some of the structures.

**Balcony House**, a little further on, is one of the few Mesa Verde complexes that was clearly geared towards defense; access is very difficult, and it's not visible from above. Guided tours involve scrambling up three hair-raising ladders and crawling through a narrow tunnel, teetering all the while above a steep drop into Soda Canyon. Park authorities present it as more "fun" than the other ruins, but unless you share the fearless Anasazi attitude to heights, you might prefer to give it a miss.

From the end of the tortuous twelve-mile drive onto **Wetherill Mesa** (daily late May–early Sept 8am–4.30pm; no RVs or cycles), a free miniature train loops around the tip of the mesa to reach the **Long House**. The park's second largest ruin is set in its largest cave; hour-long tours descend sixty or so steps to reach its central plaza, then scramble around its 150 rooms and 21 *kivas*.

### Park practicalities
Mesa Verde gets very crowded in high summer; the best months to visit are May, September and October. The park remains open all year, though most of the sights are inaccessible in winter, as detailed overleaf, and concessions such as gas, food and lodging only operate between late April and mid-October.

Most visitors stay in nearby towns; the only **rooms** in the park itself are at the summer-only *Far View Motor Lodge*, near the visitor center (Box 277, Mancos, CO 81328; ☎970/529-4421 or 1-800/449-2288; call ☎970/533-7731 in winter; ⑤), which has its own restaurant. **Food** is also available year-round at *Spruce Tree Terrace* near the Chapin Mesa museum. You can **camp** at the very large, never full *Morefield Campground*, four miles up from the entrance (late April–mid-Oct; ☎970/529-4421; $10), and there are also several commercial campgrounds nearby.

### Ute Mountain Tribal Park
Mesa Verde abuts against the Ute Mountain Ute reservation, to the south. Anasazi **cliff dwellings** spread over the inaccessible but utterly enthralling **Ute Mountain Tribal Park**, such as the eighty-room Lion House, and the precarious Eagle's Nest, can be seen on Ute-guided tours that start by arrangement from the tribe's visitor center-cum-museum (no fixed hours; ☎970/565-3751 ext 282 or 1-800/847-5485), housed in a former gas station at the intersection of US-160 and US-666. Full-day tours (8.30am–4.30pm) cost $30, and involve walking three miles and climbing five tall ladders; easier half-day trips, on which you see petroglyphs but no cliff dwellings are $20. Bring water and food; you're welcome to drive your own (sturdy) vehicle on the tours, but paying $5 extra entitles you to ride in the guide's jeep.

# WYOMING

Pronghorn antelope all but outnumber people in wide-open **WYOMING**, the ninth largest but least populous state in the union, with just 460,000 residents. Above all, this is classic **cowboy country** – the inspiration behind *Shane*, *The Virginian* and countless other Western novels – where the days of the open range are evoked by rodeos, country-and-western dance halls and ranchwear stores. The state emblem, seen everywhere, is a hat-waving cowboy astride a bucking bronco.

**Northern Wyoming** is the prime tourist goal, with close to three million per year heading for the simmering geothermal landscape of **Yellowstone National Park**, and the craggy mountain vistas of the adjacent, and equally outstanding, **Grand Teton National Park**. Wedged in between Yellowstone and South Dakota to the east are the helter-skelter **Bighorn Mountains**, likeable Old West towns such as **Buffalo**, and the otherworldly outcrop of **Devils Tower**.

The meager supply of buffalo in early Wyoming caused fierce intertribal wars over hunting grounds and kept the **Native American** population down to around 10,000. However, Sioux, Cheyenne and Blackfoot combined to inflict notable defeats on the US Army before it could clear the way for pioneer settlement in the 1870s. The cattle ranchers and sheep-farming homesteaders who followed engaged in violent **range wars** over grazing rights to the wiry grasslands.

Unlikely as it may seem, this rowdy, heavily male-dominated state was the first to grant women the vote in 1869 – a full half-century before the rest of the country, on the grounds that the enfranchisement of women would attract settlers and hasten statehood, which depended upon population. A year later Wyoming appointed the country's first women jurors, and the "Equality State" elected the first female US governor in 1924.

The absence of rivers to irrigate farmland has effectively put a lid on agricultural and population growth. These days, any weather-beaten, denim-clad stranger is more likely to be an oil roustabout than a genuine cowboy, fuel and mineral extraction having replaced livestock as the mainstay of the economy in the early part of the twentieth century.

### Getting around Wyoming

Amtrak **trains** cross southern Wyoming three times a week in daylight hours in each direction. Greyhound **buses** operate along I-80 through the south. The rest of the state is covered by regional bus companies; it takes considerable time and planning to get where you want to go. Jackson has the state's largest **airport**, though flights also go to Casper and Cheyenne. **Cycling** across northern Wyoming can be great fun. Check the contours for the easiest way over the Bighorn Mountains.

# South and central Wyoming

State capital **Cheyenne** is the only town of real note in the lower two-thirds of Wyoming. Set in the heart of rich prairie – a surprise after the scrubland, mountain and desert of most of the region – it has closer economic ties with Omaha or Denver than with the rest of Wyoming, a point the more northerly oil city of **Casper** stressed in its unsuccessful bids to become the seat of government. West of Cheyenne, smaller **Laramie** possesses an agreeable frontier feel, while the spectacular wilderness of the **Wind River Range**, accessible from **Pinedale** and **Lander**, accounts for most of the west central portion of the state.

## Cheyenne

The approach into **CHEYENNE**, dropping into a wide dip in the plains, leaves enduring memories for most travelers. With the snow-crested Rockies looming in the distance and short, sun-bleached grass encircling the town, the sky suddenly appears gargantuan, dwarfing the city's leafy suburbs and everything else below it.

A quick walk around reveals a diverse community, shaped by railroads, state politics, and even nuclear arms. When the Union Pacific Railroad reached this site in 1867, soldiers had to drive out the **"Hell on Wheels"** brigade of gamblers, moonshiners and hard-drinking gunmen who kept one jump ahead of the railroads, claiming land and then selling it for huge profit before moving on to the next proposed terminal. Union Pacific's sprawling yards and fine old terminus now mark the eastern edge of downtown, while to the west the city's longstanding military installation was expanded in 1957 to house the first US intercontinental ballistic missile base. Cowboy culture is big here, too, as the ranchwear stores and honky-tonks dotted around town attest. Along with the world's largest outdoor rodeo, the nine-day **Cheyenne Frontier Days** festival in late July attracts thousands of people to its concerts by top country stars, parades, chuckwagon races, air shows and free pancake breakfasts. The rest of the year, it's pretty quiet; would-be cowboys have to make do with the **Old Cheyenne Gunfight**, at 16th and Carey (summer Mon–Fri 6pm, Sat "high noon"; free), in which gunslingers act out incidents from the town's turbulent first decade.

**Sixteenth Street**, or Lincolnway, is the retail and entertainment heart of Cheyenne. Five minutes' walk north up leafy Capitol Avenue near the unspectacular State Capitol, the **Wyoming State Museum**, at no. 2320, takes a sober look at Wild West history (June–Aug Mon–Fri 8.30am–5pm, Sat 9am–4pm, Sun noon–4pm; Sept–May Mon–Fri

8.30am–5pm, Sat noon–4pm; free). The **Cheyenne Frontier Days Old West Museum**, five minutes' drive from downtown at 4501 N Carey Ave (Mon–Fri 9am–5pm, Sat & Sun 10am–5pm; $3), is more lighthearted, telling how the railroad came to town, with some great old engines and well-presented temporary exhibits. Much of the place is devoted to the Frontier Days celebrations, with photos, costumes and videos evoking the annual frenzy.

### Practicalities

Greyhound **buses** run east and west along I-80 and south to Denver, while Powder River buses (☎307/635-1327) travel through eastern Wyoming to Colorado, Montana and South Dakota. Both companies share the depot at 1209 S Greeley Hwy (US-85), along I-80 a mile south of town. The **visitor center**, 309 W Lincolnway (Memorial Day–Labor Day daily 8am–6pm; rest of year Mon–Fri 8am–5pm; ☎307/778-3133 or 1-800/426-5009; *info@cheyenne.org*), operates a two-hour **trolley tour** of Cheyenne in summer ($8 for adults, $4 for children). They also offer **ghost tours**.

Although places to **stay** are normally inexpensive, prices double during the Frontier Days festival. Budget motels line up along West Lincolnway, like the *Super 8* at no. 1900 (☎307/635-8741; ②/③), but the best value can be found downtown in the large, clean rooms of the historic *Plains Hotel*, 1600 Central Ave (☎307/638-3311; ②). The *Rainsford Inn*, 219 E 18th St (☎307/638-2337; ④/⑤), is a friendly, comfortable B&B, with superb gourmet breakfasts. **Campers** should head for *AB Camping* at 1503 W College Drive (March–Oct; ☎307/634-7035; ①).

Cheyenne has no shortage of **diners** serving cowboy-sized breakfasts, lunches and Mexican food; try *Los Amigos*, 620 Central Ave (☎307/638-8591). The *Medicine Bow Brewing Company*, 115 E 17th St (☎307/778-2739), is a big, lively **brewpub** with great food and a mixed crowd. There's comedy and live music downstairs. Between Memorial Day and Labor Day the Terry Bison Ranch, some ten miles south of town, holds a **night rodeo** on Tuesdays and Saturdays (☎307/634-4171; $6, prices vary).

## Laramie and around

**LARAMIE** lies fifty miles west of Cheyenne on I-80, or slightly further via the spectacular Happy Jack Road (Hwy-210), which slices through plains studded with bizarrely shaped boulders and outcrops. At first Laramie seems typical of rural Wyoming, but behind downtown's quaint Victorian facades lurk hard-rocking record stores, day spas, vegetarian cafes and secondhand bookstores – unusual for rodeo land, and due to the **University of Wyoming**, whose campus spreads east from the town center.

The centerpiece of the ambitious **Wyoming Territorial Park**, west of town at 975 Snowy Range Rd (mid-May–Sept daily 10am–6pm; $6.50), is the old territorial **prison**. A touch over-restored, it holds informative displays on the Old West and women in Wyoming, and huge mugshots of ex-convicts, among them Butch Cassidy, who was incarcerated here for eighteen months in 1896, for – as was the crime of most of the inmates – cattle-rustling.

The **Wyoming Children's Museum and Nature Center**, at 412 S Second St (Tues–Fri 9am–5pm, Sat 10am–4pm; 307/745-6332; $2) is a great hands-on experience for kids. The University of Wyoming visitor center, 1408 Ivinson (☎307/766-4075; Mon–Fri 8am–5pm, Sat 9am–1pm), can tell adults about several museums and sights of interest on campus, including the Anthropology Museum, the Museum of Geology, the University Art Museum and the Rocky Mountain Herbarium.

### Practicalities

Greyhound pulls in at 1358 N Second St, just north of downtown. The **visitor center** is at 800 S Third St (Mon–Fri 8am–5pm; ☎307/745-7339), supplemented during summer weekends by a small caboose on Third Street by the I-80 underpass (Sat & Sun 8am–5pm). **Room** rates are good at the downtown *Travel Inn*, 262 N Third St (☎307/745-4853; ②–④), while *Annie Moore's*, 819 University Ave (☎307/721-4177 or 1-800/552-8992; ③/④), is a very reasonably priced, comfortable B&B. *El Conquistador*, 110 Ivinson Ave (☎307/742-2377), serves authentic Mexican **food**; for a few dollars more, there's a health food and *nouvelle* menu at the buzzing *Jeffrey's Bistro*, 123 Ivinson Ave (☎307/742-7046). *Lovejoy's Bar and Grill*, at 101 Grand Ave (☎307/745-0141), has great All-American food and tasty desserts. *Coal Creek Coffee Co*, 110 Grand Ave (☎307/745-7737), serves good espresso, bagels, muffins and lunch specials, plus Internet access. The new *Sweet Melissa Vegetarian Cafe* at 213 S First St has moderately priced and quite tasty vegetarian fare. Students, yuppies and bikers pack out the frontier-style *Buckhorn Bar*, 114 Ivinson Ave (☎307/742-3554), while the friendly *Cowboy Saloon*, 108 S Second St (☎307/721-3165), is a fun place to go and hear some country music.

### The Medicine Bow Mountains
Just outside Laramie, **Hwy-130** dips into the huge wind-gouged bowl of **Big Hollow**, passes through rustic **Centennial** and starts the steep climb up the **Medicine Bow Mountains**, one of Wyoming's most picturesque drives. Overlooks at the top of the 10,847ft Snowy Range Pass (closed in winter) present picturesque alpine lakes and meadows, tight against steep mountain faces, and at lower levels there are plenty of good places to stop – pack a picnic and sit by **Marie Lake**, where the snowcapped peaks are reflected in the dark glassy waters.

Some 21 miles west of Laramie, in the shadow of the Snowy Mountain range at 2091 Hwy-130, the superb **Vee-Bar Guest Ranch** (☎307/745-7036 or 1-800/483-3227) is one of the best in the country, offering week-long summer packages for would-be cowhands of all ages ($2695 for two people). Accommodation is in luxurious log-cabins by a rushing stream, and rates include delicious all-you-can-eat meals, your own horse, a campout, mountain tours, hayrides, river tubing and fishing – or you're free simply to sit on your deck and take in the views. In winter they offer wonderful B&B (⑥).

Forty-nine miles out from Centennial, sleepy **SARATOGA** is hemmed in by the Snowy and Sierra Madre ranges. The **Hobo Hot Springs** on Walnut Ave is a free outdoor pool fed by natural 114°F springs. Easily the best place to **stay** is the antique-furnished *Wolf Hotel*, 101 E Bridge Ave (☎307/326-5525; ②/③), which has a good restaurant and bar, and you can get subs, salads and low-priced lunch specials at *Stumpy's*, 218 N First St (☎307/326-8132).

# Southwest Wyoming

The long and monotonous drive across southern Wyoming on I-80 – the route also followed by the old train track – holds little to delight the eye, though geologists and fossil enthusiasts will be in their element, and it may provide some travelers with their first introduction to the red-rock scenery of the West.

### Rawlins
There would be little reason to stop at the tiny prairie town of **RAWLINS**, a hundred miles west of Laramie, but for one extraordinary sight: the unmissable **Wyoming Frontier Prison**, at Fifth and Walnut (hourly tours 8.30am–6.30pm Memorial Day–Labor Day, by reservation only the rest of the year; ☎307/324-4422; $3.50). In service until 1981, this huge, creepy jail with dark, neglected cells, peeling walls and echoing corridors is as different from Laramie's Wyoming Territorial Park (see opposite) as it is possible to be. While the whole experience is troubling – not least due to the

fascinating life stories and anecdotes told with aplomb by the exceptional guides – the darkest moment comes as the gas chamber (in use from 1937 until 1965) is revealed. The *Sunset Motel*, 1302 W Spruce (☎307/324-3448 or 1-800/336-6752; ②/③), offers clean rooms, and there's very good authentic Mexican food at *Rose's Lariat*, 410 E Cedar St (☎307/324-5261).

Just to the west, the Continental Divide briefly splits into two in the **Great Divide Basin**. In theory, rain that falls here remains here, unable to flow towards either ocean – unfortunately virtually none does stay, and the brick-red hell of the **Red Desert** stretches implacably away to the horizon.

## Rock Springs and Green River

**ROCK SPRINGS**, the largest town in southwest Wyoming, is also unquestionably unremarkable, a down-at-heel mining community that experienced its latest short-lived boom in the 1980s. If you need to **stay**, there's the *Knotty Pine Lodge* at 1234 Ninth St (☎307/362-4515; ①/②); not far away, the *Santa Fe Trail Restaurant* at 1635 Elk St (☎307/362-5427) serves fresh Tex-Mex.

Ramshackle **GREEN RIVER** is fourteen miles west. Wedged between high buttes, and sliced through by the railroad, the interstate and the Green River itself, it's not an easy place to find your way around. *Embers*, 95 E Railroad Ave (☎307/875-9983), is the most popular **eating** spot, while the *Coachman Inn*, 470 E Flaming Gorge Way (☎307/875-3681; ②/③), is a good-value **motel**. **Campers** should note that both Green River and Rock Springs lie within easy reach of **Flaming Gorge Natural Recreation Area** (covered on p.894). Roads south from either town run through the empty hills to look down over incandescent orange rocks and a dramatic artificial lake.

## Fossil Butte National Monument

Roughly seventy miles northwest of Green River – and reached by turning north from I-80 just west of the "world's largest service station" at Little America – **Fossil Butte National Monument** preserves a fossilized cross-section of the fish population of a 50-million-year-old lake. From a distance, you can clearly see the relevant pale limestone strata on the flat-topped Butte itself, but the various trails turn out to show you less than the displays at the **visitor center** (June–Aug daily 8am–7pm; Sept–May daily 8am–4.30pm; ☎307/877-4455; free). Fossil enthusiasts will be more stimulated by the open quarry face at Dinosaur National Monument, around two hundred miles southeast (see p.894).

Twelve miles east of the monument, and isolated from the world by fifty miles of open rangeland in every direction, **KEMMERER** was the unlikely home of the first of more than 1900 J C Penney stores. It's still there on Main Street, along with assorted fossil shops.

# Casper

Dreary **CASPER**, halfway up Wyoming on I-25, may not seem an obvious place to visit, but at a good 150 miles from anywhere of similar size it makes a likely pit stop. Originally at the spot where the Oregon Trail crossed the North Platte River – you can visit a reconstruction of the 1860s **Fort Caspar** which gave it its (misspelled) name – Casper has been the center of Wyoming's oil region since 1890. Its population (and appearance) fluctuates between periods of high and low demand; right now, the economy is ticking along rather well, though with the exception of a couple of retail blocks along E Second Street downtown still hasn't shaken off the signs of harder times.

Casper's biggest bright spot is the **Nicolaysen Museum**, 400 E Collins Drive (Tues, Wed & Fri–Sun 10am–5pm, Thurs 10am–8pm; $2). Housed in a disused power station, it displays old and new art by Wyoming artists. For a portrayal of life at an Oregon Trail Outpost, visit the **Fort Caspar National Historic Place**, on the North Platte River west of downtown.

## Practicalities

Powder River **buses**, serving Cheyenne, Denver, Cody, Billings and Rapid City, pull in at 315 N Wolcott St (☎307/266-1904 or 265-2353), south of the **visitor center** at 500 N Center St (summer Mon–Fri 8am–5pm, Sat & Sun 9am—6pm; rest of year Mon–Fri 9am–5pm; ☎307/234-5311 or 1-800/852-1889; *cacc@trib.com*). Of Casper's bargain **motels**, the downtown *Showboat Motel*, 100 W F St (☎307/235-2711; ①/②), with its flashing neon lights and waterbeds, is pleasantly kitsch. *Antelope Campground* at 1101 Prairie Lane, Bar Nunn, exit 191 off I-25, offers **camping** for about $11 a tent site (☎307/577-1664), oddly, they also have a pool and hot tub to boot. The *Cheese Barrel*, 544 S Center St (☎307/235-5202), serves great breakfasts and sticky cheese bread; while *La Casacita*, at 633 W Collins Drive (☎307/234-7633), is a good bet for Mexican food.

# The Wind River range

Roads to Grand Teton and Yellowstone national parks from southern Wyoming skirt the **Wind River Mountains**, the state's longest and highest range, with some challenging backpacking terrain. No roads cross the mountains; you can either see them from the **east**, by driving through the Wind River Indian Reservation on US-26/287, or from the less accessible **west**, by taking US-191 up from I-80 at Rock Springs.

## Wind River Indian Reservation

The **Wind River Indian Reservation** occupies a large (and largely forgotten) swath of west central Wyoming, always overshadowed by the high snowcapped peaks to the west and south. It is the only Indian reservation in Wyoming, and extends roughly seventy miles from the natural spa of **Thermopolis** in the east, through arid grasslands and desiccated uranium-rich badlands, to **Dubois** in the west, with at its heart the rich fishing grounds of the cottonwood-lined Wind River itself. The reservation was created in 1863 as a permanent home for the Eastern Shoshone, but due to US government imposition, it soon came to accommodate the Northern Arapaho as well; and these days the Arapaho account for more than double the Shoshone population. Near **Fort Washakie** – named for the centenarian Chief Washakie, who held the Shoshone together throughout the period of white expansion – is the (possible) grave of **Sacagawea**, the guide of Lewis and Clark. **Powwows** – gatherings that have both spiritual and social significance to Native Americans, are held throughout the year, and are open to the public. Contact the Shoshone Tribal Cultural Center, at 15 North Fork Rd, Fort Washakie (weekdays 9am–4pm; ☎307/332-9106), for details on how to join in.

The reservation's largest town, **RIVERTON**, on US-26, 120 miles west of Casper, is still reeling from the end of the uranium boom. The friendly one-horse town of **LANDER**, southwest on US-287, makes an appealing base, with a string of cheap motels along Main Street and an excellent **B&B** at the Art Nouveau *Blue Spruce Inn*, 677 S Third St (☎307/332-8253; ④). Good places to **eat** include *The Oxbow Restaurant*, a family style place at 170 E Main (☎307/332-0233), the *Sweetwater Grille*, 148 Main St (☎307/332-7388), for upscale cuisine and microbrews, and the funky *Magpie Coffee House*, 159 N Second St (☎307/332-5565), for espresso, light breakfasts, lunches, and most useful, dessert.

In nearby **Sinks Canyon State Park**, the Popo Agie River plunges underground, only to reemerge half a mile later in a huge spring (trail information from the ranger office at 600 N US-287 in Lander).

## Dubois

The former logging town of **DUBOIS** (*"dew-boys"*), squeezed into the northern tip of the Wind River valley as the mountains begin in earnest, and an oasis among the badlands, turned to tourism after its final sawmill closed in 1987. Given a head start by being just fifty miles southeast of Grand Teton National Park (via the dramatic **Togwotee Pass**), Dubois is home to the biggest herd of bighorn sheep in the lower 48 states, and celebrates that fact with its **National Bighorn Sheep Center**, a half-mile northwest of town on US-26/287 (summer daily 9am–8pm; rest of year daily 9am–5pm, closed for part of winter; ☎307/455-3429; $2).

**Motels** such as the log-built, kitchenette-equipped *Branding Iron*, 401 W Ramshorn St (☎307/455-2893 or 1-800/341-8000; *brandingiron@wyoming.com*; ②/③)), and the historic *Twin Pines Lodge and Cabins*, 218 Ramshorn St (☎307/455-2600; *twinpines@wyoming.com*; ②/③; May–Nov), make Dubois a bargain alternative to Jackson (see p.780). Its main evening activity is watching country crooners in classic Western bars such as the *Rustic Pine*, 119 E Ramshorn St (☎307/455-2772), which also serves steaks. *The Hang-Out*, 8 Stalnaker St (☎307/455-3800), is good for sandwiches, soup and coffee.

## Pinedale

On the western side of the Wind River range, tiny well-to-do **PINEDALE** on US-191 offers unrivaled access to the mountains. Once a major logging center, it now attracts second-homeowners and backpackers. The excellent **Museum of the Mountain Man**, 700 E Hennick Rd (May–Oct daily 10am–6pm; rest of year by appointment only; ☎307/367-4102; $4), commemorates its role as a rendezvous for fur trappers in the 1830s.

A sixteen-mile road winds east from Pinedale past Fremont Lake to **Elkhart Park**, from where trails lead past beautiful **Seneca Lake** and along rugged Indian Pass to the glaciers and 13,000ft peaks; the Pinedale Ranger Station office at 210 W Pine St (Mon–Fri 8am–5pm, summer also Sat 9am–4pm; ☎307/367-4326), can give information on good hiking routes.

There are clean, basic **rooms** at the *Sun Dance Motel*, 148 E Pine St (☎307/367-4336 or 1-800/833-9178; ③/④). *The Sweet Tooth Saloon,* at 44 W Pine St, has sandwiches, outdoor seating and occasional live music. *Mc Gregor's Pub,* 21 N Franklin Ave, (☎307/367-4443) offers a good pint, a wide ranging menu and a pleasant patio.

# Northwest and north central Wyoming

Northern Wyoming has a lot more to offer than just a handy route between the Black Hills and Yellowstone. The surreal volcanic monument of **Devils Tower**, the abrupt **Bighorn Mountains** and the desertscape of the **Bighorn Basin** are the major natural attractions in a land steeped in the history of Native American wars, outlaw activity and pioneer hardships. Small towns such as unassuming **Buffalo** and the more commercialized **Cody**, developed by Buffalo Bill himself, are potential stopovers.

## Devils Tower National Monument

Though Congress designated **DEVILS TOWER**, fifty miles from South Dakota in far northeastern Wyoming, as the country's first national monument in 1906, it took Steven Spielberg's inspired use of it as the alien landing spot in *Close Encounters of the Third Kind* to make this eerie 867ft volcanic outcrop a true national icon. Plonked on top of a thickly forested hill, itself a full six hundred feet above the peaceful Belle Fourche River, it resembles a giant wizened tree stump; but, painted ever-changing hues by the sun and moon, it can be hauntingly beautiful. Sioux legend says the tower was formed after three young girls jumped onto a boulder to escape a vicious bear. They were rescued when the great god, seeing their plight, made the rock rise higher and higher; the bear's desperate efforts to climb up scored the sides of the column.

Four short trails loop the tower, beginning from the **visitor center** (mid-June–mid-Sept daily 8am–7.45pm; mid-Sept–mid-June weather dependent; ☎307/467-5283) at its base, three miles from the main gate. There will invariably be a few foolhardy souls attempting to scale the tower, despite demands from the local Native American communities to refrain from defacing their sacred place. However, if you would like to join the ranks, rockclimbing opportunities abound. For guide and route information, contact Tower Guides Climbing School (☎307/467-5659). The **entrance fee** per car is $8, and until October you can **camp** for $12 a night – arrive early or you'll end up paying more than twice that at one of the nearby commercial campgrounds.

## Buffalo

Snuggled among the southeastern foothills of the Bighorn Mountains, quiet, attractive **BUFFALO** is unaffected by the bustle of the nearby I-90/I-25 intersection. Although **Main Street**, now lined with frontier-style stores, used to be an old buffalo trail, the place was named after an early resident's home town of Buffalo, New York. The **Jim Gatchell Museum**, 100 Fort St, stacked full of Old West curiosities pertaining to soldiers, ranchers and Native Americans, is well worth a visit (June–Aug daily 8am–8pm; May, Sept & Oct Mon–Fri 8am–5pm; $2).

Pick up information from the **visitor center**, 55 N Main St (summer Mon–Fri 8am–6pm, Sat & Sun 10am–4pm; rest of year Mon–Fri 8am–5pm; ☎307/684-5544 or 1-800/227-5122; *nadgross@wyoming.com*). The **Clear Creek Trail System**, which runs through town, is a nice way to stroll through Buffalo. Decent **rooms** can be had at the cozy, log-built *Mountain View Motel*, 585 Fort St (☎307/684-2881; ②/③), and the historic *Mansion House Motel*, 313 N Main St (☎307/684-2218; ③). *The Clear Creek Cafe*, 820 N Main St (☎307/684-7755), serves exquisite seafood and meat dishes at good prices.

### Fort Phil Kearney

**Fort Phil Kearney**, the bloodiest of the western army forts, stood seventeen miles north of Buffalo, off I-90, on Hwy-193. Only operative from 1866 to 1868, it was repeatedly stormed by Sioux, Apache and Cheyenne, and destroyed by jubilant Sioux when finally abandoned in 1868. A **museum** (mid-May–Sept daily 8am–6pm; Oct–Nov & April–mid-May Wed–Sun noon–4pm; $2) tells the story of the 1866 **Fetterman Massacre**, when Captain William Fetterman (who bragged that with eighty men he could whip any Indians in battle) ignored strict orders and was lured into the path of over a thousand Sioux warriors. Fetterman and his eighty soldiers were killed, the first US Army defeat ever to leave no survivors. Monuments mark this and other battle sites.

## Through the Bighorn Mountains

Of the three scenic highways through the **Bighorn Mountains**, US-14A from **Burgess Junction**, fifty miles west of Victorian **Sheridan**, is the most spectacular. The massive and heavily wooded Bighorns soar abruptly from the plains to over 9000ft; the loftiest peaks, protruding above the timberline, seem bald beside their dark-coated neighbors. The road edges its way up **Medicine Mountain**, on whose windswept western peak the mysterious **Medicine Wheel** – the largest such monument still intact – stands protected behind a wire fence. Local Native American legends offer no clues as to the

## BUFFALO BILL

The much-mythologized exploits of **William Frederick "Buffalo Bill" Cody**, born in Iowa in 1846, began at the age of just eleven, when the murder of his father forced him to take a job as an army dispatch rider. An early escape from ambush brought Cody fame as the "Youngest Indian Slayer of the Plains"; four years later, he became the youngest rider on the legendary **Pony Express**. After a stint fighting for the Union, Cody found work – and a lifelong nickname – supplying buffalo meat to workers laying the transcontinental railroad. He killed over 4200 animals in just eighteen months, before rejoining the army in 1868 as its chief scout. In the next decade, when the Plains Indian Wars were at their peak, he earned a Congressional Medal of Honor and a remarkable record of never losing any troops in ambushes. Among battles in which he took part was the 1877 encounter with Sioux forces when he killed – and scalped – Chief Yellow Hand.

By the late 1870s, exaggerated accounts of Cody's adventures were appearing back east in the "dime novels" of Ned Buntline, and with the Indian Wars all but over he took to guiding Yankee and European gentry on buffalo hunts. He referred to the vacationers as "dudes," and called his camps "dude ranches." The theatrical productions he laid on for his rich guests developed into the world-famous **Wild West Show**. First staged in 1883, these spectacular outdoor carnivals usually consisted of a reenactment of an Indian battle such as Custer's Last Stand, featuring Sioux who had been present at Little Bighorn, trick riders, buffalo, clowns, and exhibition shooting and riding by the man himself. The show spent ten of its thirty years in Europe, and made Buffalo Bill "the most famous and recognized man in the world." Dressed in the finest silks and sporting a well-groomed goatee, Cody stayed in the grandest hotels and dined with heads of state; Queen Victoria was so enthusiastic in her admiration that rumors circulated of an affair between them.

In later life, a mellowing Cody played down his past activities, to the point of urging the government to respect all Native American treaties and put an end to the wanton slaughter of buffalo and game. Although the Wild West Show was reckoned to have brought in as much as one million dollars per year, his many investments failed badly, and, in January 1915, a penniless 69-year-old Buffalo Bill died at his sister's home in Denver. His grave can be found atop Lookout Mountain, outside Golden, Colorado (see p.737).

original purpose of these flat stones, arranged in a circular "wheel" with 28 spokes and a circumference of 245ft – the pattern suggests sun-worship or early astronomy. Even if US-14A isn't closed by snow (usually Nov–May), or if the Medicine Wheel isn't being used by local Native Americans for religious ceremonies, the precipitous dirt track (past an incongruous radar dome) along which drivers can approach to within a mile of the site, before hiking the rest of the way, may be impassable.

The route down the west side, with gradients of ten to twenty percent and three awesome runaway truck ramps, is said to have cost more to build per mile than any other road in America. Tight hairpin bends, passing almost vertical drops, keep the driver's eyes off the magnificent overlooks, but the best view comes near the bottom, when the road lets you out into the **Bighorn Basin**. At first sight, this ultra-flat, sparsely vegetated valley, walled in by mighty mountains on three sides and ragged foothills to the north, seems like a land that time forgot.

### Bighorn Canyon National Recreation Area

Before US-14A gets to Lovell, Hwy-37 turns north to the **Bighorn Canyon National Recreation Area**, an unexpected red-rock wilderness straddling the border between Wyoming and Montana. No road runs the full length of the canyon, which since being flooded by the 525ft Yellowtail Dam (only accessible from Montana) has become primarily the preserve of water-sports enthusiasts. In summer, **boat tours** leave from

**Horseshoe Bend**, where the marina (☎307/548-7230) rents out assorted equipment, and a shadeless beach of red sand offers swimming in the most bizarre of settings. The **Devil's Canyon overlook**, a few miles north, affords landlubbers a rare opportunity to gauge the hideous depth of the abyss.

A **visitor center** just east of Lovell on US-14A (daily 8.15am–5pm; ☎307/548-2251) supplies information on local activities, and has maps of the Medicine Wheel area.

# Cody

**CODY**, 79 miles east along US-14 and the North Fork of the Shoshone River from Yellowstone, was the brainchild of investors who in 1896 persuaded "Buffalo Bill" Cody to get involved in their development company, knowing his approval would attract homesteaders and visitors alike. During summer, tourism is big business, but underneath all the Buffalo Bill-linked attractions and paraphernalia, Cody manages to retain the feel of a rural Western settlement. It's certainly not a place where you would have expected avant-garde painter **Jackson Pollock** to have been born and brought up.

The wide, dusty main thoroughfare, **Sheridan Avenue**, holds an array of souvenir and ranchwear shops, and is the scene of parades and rodeos during the annual **Cody Stampede**, held on the weekend of July 4. Between June and August there's a **rodeo** every night at the open-air stadium on the road to Yellowstone, at 421 W Yellowstone Ave (8.30pm; ☎307/587-5155; $9).

## Buffalo Bill Historical Center

The nation's most comprehensive collection of Western Americana, Cody's giant **Buffalo Bill Historical Center** at 720 Sheridan Ave comprises several distinct museums (June–mid-Sept daily 7am–8pm; mid-Sept–Oct daily 8am–5pm; Nov–March to 10am–3pm closed Mondays; April daily 10am–5pm; May daily 8am–8pm; ☎307/587-4771; $10).

Artifacts from William Cody's various careers, such as guns, gifts from European heads of state, billboards, clothes and dime novels, help the **Buffalo Bill Museum** to chronicle the years of the Pony Express, Civil War, Indian Wars and Wild West shows. The lives of western Native Americans are celebrated in the **Plains Indian Museum**, which at the end of each June organizes the musical and dance performances of the **Plains Indian Powwow**. The museum's permanent historical collection is given a tragic note by the display of Ghost Dance shirts. In the late 1880s, the religious revelation of the Paiute prophet Wovoka swept the western tribes. He declared that ritual purification through song and dance would hasten the day when all whites would be buried by a heaven-sent fall of soil, and their dead warriors, along with huge herds of buffalo, would return to the Plains. The US Army condemned Ghost Dances as unacceptable shows of resistance, and mobilized troops to disrupt ceremonies.

In the beautifully laid-out **Whitney Gallery of Western Art**, the contrasting styles of Frederic Remington and Charles M Russell command most attention. The propagandist Remington dwells on conflict, depicting the Indian as a savage in the path of progress, while Russell's work shows a consistent respect for Native American life.

## Practicalities

For information and accommodation reservations, contact Cody's **visitor center** at 836 Sheridan Ave (summer Mon–Sat 8am–7pm, Sun 10am–3pm; rest of year Mon–Fri 8am–5pm; ☎307/587-2297). Cody is the site of the **Yellowstone Regional Airport**. Powder River, at 1701 Sheridan Ave (☎307/527-6316), runs one-day Yellowstone tours, and **float trips** on the Shoshone are available from, among others, Wyoming River Trips (☎307/587-6661).

Cody's showpiece Western **hotel**, the *Irma* at 1192 Sheridan Ave (☎307/587-4221 or 1-800/745-4762; ④/⑤), was named for Buffalo Bill's daughter in 1902, and retains a superb original cherrywood bar. Among good-value motels, the friendly *Skyline Motor Inn*, high above town on the main through highway at 1919 17th St (☎307/587-4201 or 1-800/843-8809; ①–④), stands out. Sheridan Avenue is very much the place for an evening's **eating** and **entertainment**. Having eaten at the always packed *Irma's*, call in for a drink at the *Proud Cut Saloon*, no. 1227. *Peter's Cafe Bakery,* at no. 1191, is the morning place for coffee or a full breakfast.

### Wapiti Valley

The drive west from Cody to Yellowstone is a superb preparation for the splendors of the park itself, skirting the artificial lake created by the Buffalo Bill Dam before running alongside the Shoshone River through the open, high **Wapiti Valley**, the heart of Wyoming's "beef country," and finally climbing through the rugged mountains to Sylvan Pass. Lodges and campgrounds appear at intervals without impinging on the magnificence of the landscape. The *Elephant Head Lodge*, along US-14/16/20 (☎307/587-3980; ④), is one such option, should you need a place to stay.

# Yellowstone National Park

Millions of visitors each year come to **YELLOWSTONE NATIONAL PARK**, America's oldest national park and the largest in the lower 48 states, to glory in its magnificent mountain scenery and abundant wildlife, and above all to witness hydrothermal phenomena on a unique scale. Measuring roughly sixty by fifty miles, and overlapping slightly from Wyoming's northwestern corner into Idaho and Montana, the park centers on a 7500ft-high plateau, the caldera of a vast volcanic eruption which occurred a mere 600,000 years ago. Into it are crammed more than half the world's **geysers**, in which the rain and snow that seep through the bedrock escape the pressure-cooker conditions under the surface in intermittent spectacular blasts, plus thousands of **fumaroles** jetting plumes of steam, **mud pots** gurgling with acid-dissolved muds and clays, and **hot springs**.

Yellowstone amounts to an extraordinary experience, combining the **colors** of the Grand Canyon of the Yellowstone, limpid Yellowstone Lake, the wild flower meadows and the rainbow-hued geyser pools; the **sounds** of subterranean rumblings, belching

## WINTER IN YELLOWSTONE

Blanketed in four feet of snow between November and April, Yellowstone takes on a whole new appearance in winter: a silent and bizarre world where waterfalls freeze in mid-plunge, geysers blast towering plumes of steam and water into the cold, crisp air, and buffalo, beards matted with ice, stand around in huddles. Only the road from Gardiner to Cooke City via Mammoth Hot Springs is kept open (the Beartooth Highway is closed), and you can only stay at the *Mammoth Hot Springs Hotel* or the *Old Faithful Snow Lodge* (accessible by snowmobile).

Winter vacationing in Yellowstone took off in a big way in the 1960s. Amfac/TW Services (☎307/344-7311) runs **snowcoach** tours of the park from West Yellowstone, Flagg Ranch at the southern entrance, Old Faithful and Mammoth Hot Springs. Alpen Guides (☎406/646-9591) runs slightly cheaper excursions out of West Yellowstone. **Snowmobile** rental, generally cheapest in West Yellowstone, costs around $115 a day. Much less expensive is **cross-country skiing**; several miles of groomed trails explore the park's west side. Call ☎307/344-7311 for full details.

mud pools, and steam hissing from the mountainsides; and the constant **smells** of drifting sulphurous fumes, with the presence of browsing bull moose, shambling bears,
heavy-bearded bison, herds of elk and ubiquitous scurrying **marmots**. It is, however,
very popular; if you let yourself get frustrated by the inevitable crowds and expense,
you'll be missing something very special. The key to appreciating the park is to take
your time, and to plan carefully; above all, try to allow for a stay of at least three days.

## Arrival and information

Two of the five main **entrances** to Yellowstone are in Wyoming, via **Cody** in the east and
**Grand Teton National Park** to the south. The others are in Montana: **West Yellowstone**
(west), **Gardiner** (north) and **Cooke City** (northeast). Most roads are open from late
May to October only (see box, opposite). **Admission** – $20 per car ($10 for pedestrians or
cyclists) – is good for seven days, and includes entry to the Grand Teton park.

The **park headquarters** are at **Mammoth Hot Springs**, near the north entrance
(June–Sept daily 8am–7pm; Oct–May daily 9am–5pm; ☎307/344-7381). Tune into 1610
AM for weather information, and consult the *Yellowstone Today* freesheet for activities
and current regulations. Other, summer-only, **visitor centers** are located approximately every twenty miles along the main **Loop Road**. Each issues backcountry hiking permits, and has an exhibit on a different aspect of the park – natural and human
history (Mammoth Hot Springs), geothermal activity (Old Faithful and Norris), the
National Park service (Norris), wilderness areas and the 1988 fires (Grant Village),
wildlife (Fishing Bridge) and bison (Canyon). Excellent National Park Service leaflets
(25¢ each), which can be found at trailheads as well as visitor centers, cover the important landmarks, marking trails and points of interest.

To get to Yellowstone by **bus**, take Karst Stage (☎406/586-8567) from Bozeman, via
West Yellowstone or Gardiner; Powder River Transportation (☎1-800/442-3682), which
runs tours and one-way trips from Cody, or Amfac/TW Services (☎307/344-7311) from
West Yellowstone, Gardiner or Billings, which also runs one-day tours inside the park
in summer. Similar services are offered by 4X4 (☎1-800/517-8243) from Gardiner,
Cooke City, West Yellowstone and Bozeman; Yellowstone Vacations (☎406/646-9564)
from West Yellowstone; Greyhound runs as far as Bozeman and West Yellowstone.

## Accommodation in the park

All accommodation within the park is run by Amfac Parks and Resorts (PO Box 165,
Yellowstone National Park, WY 82190-0165; ☎307/344-7311). **Reservations**, strongly
recommended from June through September, are essential over public holiday weekends. Prices beyond the park boundaries are a little lower, but staying inside can be
wonderfully relaxing; none of the rooms has a TV, and only a few après-hike revelers
stay up past midnight. Every location has a lodge building offering dining facilities
(closing at 9.30pm) and sometimes a laundromat, grocery store, giftshop and gas
station.

**Canyon Lodge and Cabins.** Half a mile from the Grand Canyon of the Yellowstone. Simple frame
cabins, all en-suite. ③.

**Grant Village.** Spartan en-suite rooms on the southwest shore of Yellowstone Lake; the southernmost accommodation in the park. ④.

**Lake Yellowstone Hotel and Cabins.** Grand colonial-style hotel rooms, and dark, dingy en-suite
cabins. The "Sun Room," looking over the lake, is a great place for an evening drink. ④/⑤.

**Mammoth Hot Springs Hotel & Cabins.** 1930s lodging right at the north end of the park. Very
basic cabins, without shower or toilet, en-suite cabins, and hotel rooms with or without bath.
Especially popular in winter. ①–⑧.

**Old Faithful Inn and Lodge.** The most beautiful lodge in the US and consequently very popular.
Assorted rooms in the amazing 1903 inn – said to be the world's largest log building – plus budget
and en-suite cabins. You can watch Old Faithful erupt from the terrace bar. ①–⑨.

**Old Faithful Snow Lodge and Cabins**. Cabins and rooms, most often used in winter. ③–⑤.

**Roosevelt Lodge Cabins**. The park's cheapest option, at $27 for a rustic wooden shelter with no bedding. Also Rough Rider and en-suite cabins. Cozy lounge and bar with a roaring fire. ①–④.

## Accommodation in gateway towns

In addition to **Jackson** (see p.780) and **Cody** (p.771) in Wyoming, the small towns just outside the park's western and two northern gates offer alternative and somewhat cheaper lodging, as well as more nightlife. **West Yellowstone**, the largest, at the west entrance, is disfigured by gift stores and fast-food joints, though the surrounding national forest lands are well worth exploring. **Gardiner** lies next to the northwest entrance, just five miles from Mammoth Hot Springs; prices tend to be a little higher here than elsewhere. The one-street villages of **Silver Gate** and more developed **Cooke City** are three and ten miles respectively from the northeast entrance on US-212.

**Alpine Motel**, US-212, Cooke City (☎406/838-2262). Basic but clean rooms. ②–④.

**Hoosier's Motel**, US-212, Cooke City (☎406/838-2241). Immaculate modern motel. May through October. ③/④.

**Parkview Cabins**, US-212, Silver Gate (☎406/838-2371). Cabins, with or without kitchenettes. June to early September. ②–④.

**Sleepy Hollow Lodge**, 124 Electric St, West Yellowstone (☎406/646-7707). Small yet charming log cabins with kitchenettes. ④.

**Three Bear Lodge**, 217 Yellowstone Ave, West Yellowstone (☎406/646-7353 or 1-800/646-7353). Comfortable, attractive hotel with pool and hot tub. ④.

**West Yellowstone International Hostel and Madison Hotel**, 139 Yellowstone Ave, West Yellowstone (☎406/646-7745). Clean, friendly old wooden hotel with a very odd giftshop, and $18–20 dorm beds. Rooms for slightly more. Summer only. ①/②.

**Yellowstone Village Inn**, US-89, Gardiner (☎406/848-7417). Modern motel with pool, sauna and laundromat, and spacious rooms with kitchenettes. ②–④.

## Camping

**Amfac Parks and Resorts** (☎307/344-7311) operates twelve **campgrounds** in Yellowstone, including one RV-only campground. **Fees** range from $10–15 per night for tent camping, and up to $25 for RVs. The campgrounds operate from mid-May or early June through to September, October or November.

Seven campgrounds operate on a **first-come, first-served** basis; with fewer than 2000 spaces in all, it's best to turn up very early in the morning. In the northeast of the park, Slough Creek, Tower Fall and Pebble Creek are all small, very scenic and extremely popular locations. You can also camp at Mammoth Hot Springs, Indian Creek and Norris, and at Lewis Lake in geyser country.

Sites at Madison, Canyon Village (a quarter-mile east of the village), Bridge Bay (three miles south of Lake Village), and Grant Village (near Yellowstone Lake, with the best shower and laundry facilities) can be **reserved** through Amfac (☎307/344-7311). Due to prowling bears, spaces at Fishing Bridge are restricted to hard-sided vehicles ($25; reservations essential).

To camp in the **backcountry** you need a wilderness permit, free from visitor centers or ranger stations. Camping is also possible at commercial grounds in the gateway towns, and in neighboring national forests such as Gallatin (☎307/344-7381) to the northwest and Shoshone (☎307/527-6241) to the east.

# Touring the park

All of Yellowstone's major sights are labeled and signposted within a few hundred yards of the 142-mile **Loop Road**, a figure-of-eight circuit fed by roads from the five entrances. Although the **speed limit** is a radar-enforced 45mph, the traffic makes journey times hard to predict. To get the most out of a visit, even if you're short of time, choose one or two areas to explore thoroughly.

Only in the early morning is **cycling** bearable or safe; there are no mountain bike trails. Though you can expect to **walk** considerable distances along the canyon and geyser trails, it's an idea to leave backcountry hiking for the more exciting **Grand Teton National Park**.

The following account runs clockwise around the Loop Road, from Old Faithful to the Yellowstone Lake area, both of which lie in the southern reaches of the park.

## Geyser country: from Old Faithful to Mammoth Hot Springs

For well over a century, the dependable **Old Faithful** has been the most popular geyser in the park, erupting more frequently than any of its higher or larger rivals. As a result, a half-moon of concentric benches, backed by visitor facilities including the gigantic log-built *Old Faithful Inn*, now surround it at a respectful distance on the side away from the Firehole River. On average, it "performs" for the expectant crowds every 78 minutes, with a minimum gap of half an hour and a maximum of two hours; approximate schedules are displayed in the nearby visitor center and in the lobby of the inn. The first sign of activity is a soft hissing as water splashes repeatedly over the rim. After several minutes, a column of water shoots to a height of 100 to 180ft, the geyser spurting out a total of 11,000 gallons.

---

### A BRIEF HUMAN HISTORY OF YELLOWSTONE

Although Native Americans had long hunted in what is now **Yellowstone National Park**, they were decimated by disease (and, in their absence, the wildlife was thriving) by the time the first white man arrived in 1807 – **John Colter**, a veteran of the Lewis and Clark expedition (see also p.786). His account of the exploding geysers and seething cauldrons of "Colter's Hell" was widely ridiculed. However, as ever more trappers, scouts and prospectors hit upon Yellowstone, the government eventually sent out survey teams in 1870. Just two years later, Yellowstone was set aside as the first **national park**, in part to ensure that its assets were not entirely stripped by hunters, miners and lumber companies.

At first, management of the park was beset by problems; Congress devoted enthusiasm but little funding towards its protection. Irresponsible tourists stuck soap down the geysers, ruining the intricate plumbing; bandits preyed on stagecoaches carrying rich excursionists; and the Nez Percé even killed two tourists as they raced through the park (see p.799). Congress took the park out of civilian hands in 1886, and put the army in charge. By the time they handed over to the newly created National Park Service in 1917, the ascendancy of the automobile in Yellowstone had begun.

The conflict between tourism and wilderness **preservation** has raged ever since. The elimination of predators such as mountain lions and wolves let the elk herd grow unsupportably large; the former policy of permitting bears to feed from tourist scraps resulted in maulings, a far cry from the friendly image of TV's "Jellystone" bears, Yogi and Boo Boo. Ecologists now argue that the park cannot stand alone as some pristine paradise, but must be seen as part of a much larger "Greater Yellowstone Ecosystem." In 1995, amid vociferous complaints from local ranchers fearing a subsequent loss of livestock, a pack of **wolves** was reintroduced to the park. It remains to be seen how long they can survive – one consequence of the unnaturally high elk population is the depletion of the park's smaller animals, which make up the wolves' main food source.

The **fires** that razed 36 percent of the park in 1988 also brought Yellowstone's environmental policies into focus. Despite President Reagan's dismay, park authorities insisted the burn was a natural part of the forest's ecocycle, clearing out 200-year-old trees to make way for new growth. The scarred mountainsides are now slowly but surely recovering.

Two miles of boardwalks lead from Old Faithful to dozens of other geysers in the Upper Basin. If possible, try to arrive when **Grand Geyser** is due to explode. This colossus blows its top on average just twice a day, for twelve to twenty minutes, in a series of four powerful bursts that climb to 200ft. Other highlights along the banks of the Firehole River, usually lined with browsing buffalo, include the fluorescent intensity of the **Grand Prismatic Lake** at **Midway Geyser basin**, especially breathtaking in the early evening when human figures and bison herds are silhouetted against plumes of chemical spray.

Thirty miles north of Old Faithful, in the less crowded **Norris Geyser Basin**, two separate trails explore a pallid primeval landscape of whistling vents and fumaroles. **Steamboat** is the world's tallest geyser, capable of forcing near-boiling water over 300ft into the air; full eruptions are entirely unpredictable, but it usually delivers lesser bursts of ten to forty feet a couple of times a day. The **Echinus Geyser** is the largest acid-water geyser known; every 35 to 75 minutes it spews crowd-pleasing, vinegary eruptions of forty to sixty feet. The **Emerald Spring** is a 27ft-deep pool where the vivid blue water combines with the yellow of the crater to create a stunning, jewel-like color.

At **Mammoth Hot Springs**, at the northern tip of the Loop Road, terraces of barnacle-like deposits cascade down a vapor-shrouded mountainside. Tinted a marvelous array of grays, greens, yellows, browns and oranges by algae, they are composed of travertine, a form of limestone which, having been dissolved and carried to the surface by boiling water, is deposited as tier upon tier of steaming stone.

## Tower and Roosevelt areas

The main landmark of Yellowstone's **Tower** and **Roosevelt** areas, east of Mammoth Hot Springs, is **Mount Washburn**, the park's highest peak, whose lookout tower can be reached by an enjoyable all-day hike or a grueling cycle ride. A more manageable trail leads down to the spray-drenched base of **Tower Fall**. From Tower Junction, US-212 wanders away east through the meadows of serene **Lamar Valley**, where moose and buffalo graze, towards the ice-packed peaks of the **Beartooth Mountains**.

## The Grand Canyon of the Yellowstone River

The Yellowstone River roars and tumbles for 24 miles between the sheer golden-hued cliffs of the 1540ft **Grand Canyon of the Yellowstone**, its course punctuated by two narrow but striking **waterfalls**: the 109ft **Upper Falls** and the thunderous **Lower Falls**, plummeting 308ft. Both rims of the canyon offer superb vistas, short trails and intense scenery, but the north side is the more popular, as sightseeing can be combined with a visit to the nearby stores and snack bars. To see some bears, head for the viewing area at the intersection of the Tower and Northern Rim roads at dawn or dusk.

On the south rim, **Artists' Point** looks down 700ft to the river, swirling between mineral-stained walls. Nearby, **Uncle Tom's Trail** descends steeply down into the canyon, to a gently vibrating, spray-covered platform right in the face of the Lower Falls. A few miles south, the river widens to meander over tranquil, marshy **Hayden Valley**. Buffalo, elk and deer congregate here, so it's an unsuitable place to go on foot.

## Yellowstone Lake

North America's largest alpine lake, the deep and (usually) deceptively calm **Yellowstone Lake** fills the eastern half of the Yellowstone caldera. At 7733ft above sea level it's high enough to be frozen for half the year, but in summer it's filled with tourists out on cruises (one hour; $7.30), rowboats ($5.50 per hour), motor launches ($25 per hour) and fishing expeditions ($45 per hour). Boat tours leave from the Bridge Bay Marina at **Fishing Bridge**, one of two "villages" beside the lake – the newer and much-opposed Grant Village is in the south.

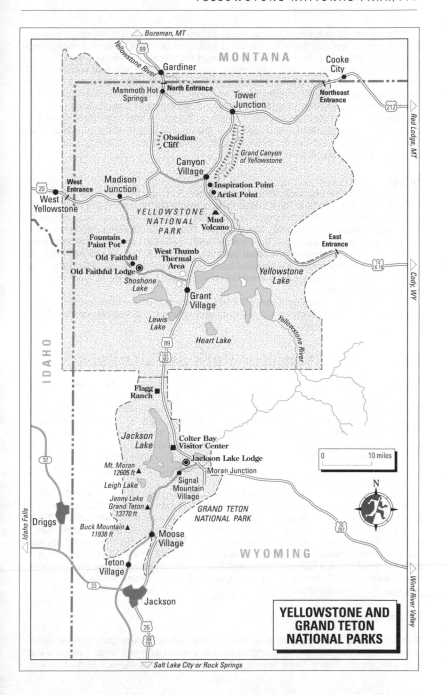

**YELLOWSTONE AND GRAND TETON NATIONAL PARKS**

At the **West Thumb Geyser** basin, north of Grant Village, hot pools empty into the tranquil waters and fizz away into nothing; early tourists took photos of themselves cooking fresh-caught fish in the boiling waters of the so-called **Fishing Cone**.

The ominous rumblings and sulphurous stench of the **Mud Volcano** area, north of the lake, make it the moodiest and ugliest of the park's thermal regions. A one-mile boardwalk winds through gurgling pools of sickly brown and yellow mud, past trees that have been steamed to death, to the bleak, barren shores of **Sour Lake**: an unnerving sight at the best of times, at dusk it makes a chemical waste dump look appealing. Joining a free ranger-led tour here gives you the chance to get off the boardwalk and into the backcountry, where the **Big Gumper**, which blew into existence in the 1970s, bubbles with big gray globs of smelly mud.

### Eating

**Snack bars** and **restaurants** inside the park aren't cheap, but are fairly reasonable and offer a varied selection. Buying food at the general stores can get pricey. The gateway towns hold few culinary delights, but do offer cheaper prices and more variety. In **West Yellowstone**, the *Running Bear Pancake House*, 538 Madison Ave (☎406/646-7703), is good for breakfast, and the *Firehole Grill*, on US-20 and Faithful Street, doles out barbecue and atmosphere in equal portions. The *Town Cafe* (☎406/848-7322) on Park Street in **Gardiner** has a huge salad bar, while the stylish *Beartooth Cafe* in **Cooke City** is probably the best place for breakfast, burgers and inexpensive dinners in any of the peripheral towns.

Within the park, the dining room at the *Old Faithful Inn* serves high-quality meals in an unforgettable rustic setting, with log walls and ceilings, and huge chandeliers lighting the elegant table settings.

# Grand Teton National Park and Jackson Hole

The classic triangular peaks of **GRAND TETON NATIONAL PARK**, which stretches for fifty miles between Yellowstone and Jackson, are every bit as dramatic as the mountains of its congested neighbor, and a visit should be more than an afterthought on the route south. Though not especially high or extensive by Rocky Mountain standards, these sheer-faced cliffs make a magnificent spectacle, rising abruptly to tower 7000ft above the valley floor. A string of gem-like lakes is set tight at the foot of the mountains; beyond them lies the broad, sagebrush-covered **Jackson Hole** (a "hole" was the pioneers' term for a flat, mountain-ringed valley), broken by the winding Snake River.

The Shoshone people knew the mountains as the *Teewinot* ("many pinnacles"), but their present name, meaning big bosom, was given by lonesome French-Canadian trappers in the 1830s. After Congress set the mountains aside as a national park in 1929, it took another 21 years of legal wrangling for Grand Teton to reach its current size – local ranchers protested that the economy of Jackson Hole would be ruined if any further land was surrendered to tourism. Meanwhile, John D Rockefeller Jr bought up a large swath of Jackson Hole and presented it to the government for free (on the condition that the Grand Teton Lodge Company, which he then owned, would be the exclusive operator of park concessions).

## Seeing the park

No road crosses the Tetons, but those that run along their eastern flank were designed with an eye to the mountains, affording stunning views at every turn. Two excellent side trips are the **Jenny Lake Scenic Loop**, leading to a face-to-face encounter with towering, partly hunchbacked **Grand Teton Mountain**, and the narrow track up **Signal Mountain**, which gives a fine view of the main Teton block and Jackson Hole.

Hiking trails, too, have been laid out so that no time is wasted in getting to the highlights. One easy and popular walk is along the sandy beaches of **Leigh Lake**, where the imposing 12,605ft **Mount Moran** bursts out dramatically from the lake shores. Also very accessible are the cascading **Hidden Falls**, reachable by a two-mile walk along the south shore of Jenny Lake; it's fun also to take the shuttle boat ($3.50 round-trip) across the lake, and walk the remaining 800 yards. For the more adventurous, the rocky nine-mile trail from Hidden Falls through U-shaped **Cascade Canyon** leads to aptly named **Lake Solitude**. Another strenuous hike, and an excellent way to reach tree line in a short distance, is the five-mile trail from **Lupine Meadows**, just south of Jenny Lake, which skirts small glacial pools like Amphitheater and Surprise lakes.

On the flat roads of the Hole, **cycling** is a joy; rent a bike down in Jackson. To admire the Tetons from **water**, take a float trip along the Snake River (see overleaf) or rent a rowing boat from Colter Bay or Signal Mountain marinas. In winter, all hiking trails are open to cross-country **skiers**, and **snowmobiles** can be rented from various outlets in Jackson. Excellent **rock climbing** opportunities exist within the park. Contact the Jenny Lake Ranger Station (☎307/739-3343 or 739-3604 for recorded information) for climbing details. **Climber's Ranch**, within the park on **Teton Park Road**, has accommodations for climbers.

## Practicalities

**Shuttle buses** to the park run from Jackson and Yellowstone. The **visitor centers** are just off the main road in **Moose** (mid-May–June daily 8am–6pm; June–Sept daily 8am–7pm; Sept–mid-May daily 8am–5pm; ☎307/739-3399) to the south, and at **Colter Bay** (May 10–May 18 & Sept daily 8am–5pm; May 18–June daily 8am–7pm; June–Aug daily 8am–8pm; ☎307/739-3594), halfway up, on the east shore of Jackson Lake. There are smaller centers at **Jenny Lake** (June–Sept daily 8am–7pm) and **Flagg Ranch** (June–Sept daily 9am–6pm). The **Indian Arts Museum** (summer daily 8am–8pm; spring & fall daily 8am–5pm; free) at Colter Bay has an extensive collection of Plains Native American craftwork.

The free *Teewinot* newspaper gives details of trails, facilities and ranger-led activities. The **entrance fee** of $20 per car ($10 for pedestrians and cyclists) also covers Yellowstone.

**Rooms**, services and activities within the park are managed by the Grand Teton Lodge Co (PO Box 240, Moran, WY 83013; ☎307/543-2811); reservations (☎307/543-3100) are essential in summer. Prices for the comfortable rooms in *Jackson Lake Lodge* (⑤–⑦) depend on whether or not you want a mountain view; *Colter Bay Village Cabins* (②, en-suite ④, four-person cabins, ⑤/⑥) are more utilitarian, and in high summer they also have $25 "tent cabins" of log and canvas – potentially pretty cold at night. On the park perimeter, there are basic cabins at *Buffalo Valley Ranch* in **MORAN** (☎307/543-2477; ③/④) or pricier motels in Jackson (see overleaf).

All of the five summer-only park **campgrounds** work on a first-come, first-served basis ($12 per site). Visitor centers or entrance stations can advise on availability, or you can call (☎307/739-3603) for recorded information. Individual campgrounds tend to fill in July and August in roughly the following order: Jenny Lake (8am; tents only), Signal Mountain (10am), Colter Bay (noon), Lizard Creek (2pm) and Gros Ventre (evening). Colter Bay is the only campground which allows RVs. For backcountry camping, you need a **permit**, available from any of the visitor centers.

The park **restaurants and snack bars**, especially at Colter Bay, are good but a little pricey. *Dornan's Original Moose Chuckwagon* (☎307/733-2415), however, just outside the southern entrance in Moose, serves all-you-can-eat pancake breakfasts and rib dinners for a song. For the ultimate in relaxation, have an early-evening **drink** in

*Jackson Lake Lodge*'s *Blue Heron Lounge*, where you can recline in comfortable chairs and watch the ever-changing blues, grays, purples and warm pinks of Mount Moran through huge picture windows.

## Jackson

The overgrown community of **JACKSON** is tucked in at the end of **Jackson Hole**, ten miles from Teton park's southern gate. Hunched around a tree-shaded square, marked by an arch of tangled elk antlers at each corner, the Old West-style boardwalks of **downtown** front designer clothes shops, craftshops and over thirty galleries. Every summer evening, except Sundays, an amateurish shoot-out is staged in the town square. In winter, time is better spent visiting the **National Elk Refuge** on the north edge of town, where you can take a horse-drawn sleigh ride among a 10,000-strong herd of elk (late Dec–late March daily 9am–5pm; sleigh rides 10am–4pm; $12 entry plus sleigh ride).

In recent years, Jackson has become the center of a **skiing** boom, with the season running from early December to early April. Summer visitors can enjoy **chairlift** rides (up 7751ft Snow King Mountain (part of the **Snow King** resort; ☎307/733-5200) from Snow King Avenue, six blocks from the town square (daily 9am–6pm; $7), coming down by hiking, cycling or the thrilling 2500ft **Alpine Slide** ($6 a go). Out at **Teton Village**, home of the **Jackson Hole** resort (☎307/733-2292), aerial **trams** swoosh their way 10,536ft to the top of Rendezvous Mountain for a spectacular panorama of the valley and mountain ranges (June–Aug daily 9am–7pm; May & Sept daily 10am–5pm; $16).

### Information, activities and transportation

Jackson's excellent **Wyoming Information Center**, 532 N Cache St (summer daily 8am–8pm; rest of year Mon–Fri 8am–5pm, Sat & Sun 10am–2pm; ☎307/733-3316; *jhchamber@sisna.com*), has detailed statewide information. Nearby, the **Bridger-Teton National Forest Headquarters**, 340 N Cache St (Mon–Fri 8am–4.30pm; ☎307/739-5500), has details of hiking and backcountry camping. START **buses** (☎307/733-4521) run to Teton Village, twelve miles northwest, while the Grand Teton Lodge Company (☎307/733-2811) operates services to the parks. For tours through the park, call Alltrans/Gray Line at Jackson Hole (☎307/733-3531).

Jackson's **airport** is actually within the national park, eight miles north; it's linked to town by the All Star Transportation van service (☎307/733-2888; $8) or $20 taxis.

Dozens of companies in Jackson offer **float trips** on the Snake River. Fort Jackson Float Trips, 315 W Broadway (☎307/733-2583), does good-value, two-hour trips including lunch, while Leisure Sports, 1075 Hwy-89 S (☎307/733-3040), offers reasonable rental rates for rafts, kayaks, tubes and bikes.

The visitor center has racks of leaflets detailing **bus tours** of Jackson and the parks: Gray Line, 330 N Glenwood St (☎307/733-4325), will pick you up at your hotel and whisk you through either Teton or Yellowstone park on a brisk one-day drive for $45. Guided **bike tours** in the area are run by Teton Mountain Bike Tours (☎307/733-0712), and cost $40 for a half-day tour including equipment.

### Accommodation

**Accommodation** in Jackson tends to come at above-average prices, though in winter motel rates are generally 25 percent lower. The closest **camping** is at the *Jackson Hole Campground* (☎307/733-2927), off West Broadway.

**Antler Inn**, 43 W Pearl St (☎307/733-2535). Very central, but reasonably quiet, with sauna and hot tub. Some rooms with log fires. ④.

**Best Western Lodge at Jackson Hole**, 80 S Scott Lane (☎307/739-9703 or 1-800/458-3866). Comfortable hotel a mile from the town center; some rooms have log fires, kitchenettes and hot tubs. Rates include an excellent, copious continental breakfast, and there's a pool and jacuzzi. Look out for the whimsical carved bears climbing all over the log-built exterior. ⑤.

**Bunkhouse in the Anvil Motel**, 215 N Cache St (☎307/733-3668). Mid-range motel that also has $22 beds in large dorm, a block and a half from the town square. No utensils in the kitchen. ①–⑤.

**Cottages at Snow King**, 470 King St (☎307/733-3480). Central motel, some rooms with kitchenettes. ③.

**Flat Creek Motel**, 1935 N Hwy-89, (☎307/733-5276 or 1-800/438-9338). Basic motel north of town, close to the Elk Refuge. ④.

**HC Richards B&B**, 160 W Deloney Ave (☎307/733-6704). Cozy bed and breakfast, within walking distance to town. ⑤.

**Hostel in Jackson Hole**, Teton Village Ski Resort (☎307/733-3415). Great location in the ski area a dozen miles northwest. Dorm beds, private rooms and nice people. ①/②.

### Eating and nightlife

The year-round tourist trade makes Jackson Wyoming's liveliest nighttime community, with an ever-changing cast of **restaurants** and **nightspots**.

**Anthony's**, 62 S Glenwood St (☎307/733-3717). Imaginative, well-priced Italian food.

**The Bunnery**, 130 N Cache St (☎307/733-5474). Great breakfasts, espressos, stuffed omelettes and sandwiches.

**Cadillac Grill**, 55 N Cache St (☎307/733-3279). Fancy Art Deco restaurant on the main square. Huge burgers, but also buffalo, wild boar, caribou, antelope and seafood entrees for $12–20. Reservations recommended.

**Harvest Natural Foods Cafe**, 130 W Broadway (☎307/733-5418). Earnest health food store with a veggie food counter: burgers, tofu, baked goods and fruit smoothies to eat in or to go.

**Mangy Moose**, Teton Village (☎307/733-4913). Antique-laden music venue, good for rock and reggae. The interesting menu is meat-heavy, with some pasta and fish.

**Million Dollar Cowboy Bar**, 25 N Cache St (☎307/733-2207). Hugely touristy Western-themed bar, with saddles for seats, a large dance floor, and big, big steaks.

**Mountain High Pizza Pie**, 120 W Broadway (☎307/733-3646). Casual, low-priced, and healthy pizza, calzones and salads.

**Off Broadway Grill**, 30 S King St (☎307/733-9777). A less pretentious setting than some of Jackson's other "grilles," with outdoor seating and creative, top-class international food (lots of Thai and Italian influences) at moderate prices.

**The Rancher**, 20 E Broadway (☎307/733-3886). Dollar drinks every Tues night at this local hangout.

**The Wort Hotel Bar**, 50 N Glenwood St (☎307/733-2190). Lively upscale bar with music nightly.

# MONTANA

**MONTANA** is Big Sky country. The nickname is no empty cliché: the entire state is blessed with a huge blue roof that both dwarfs the beautiful countryside and complements it perfectly. A magnificent northernmost cap for the US Rockies, this is a region of snowcapped summits, turbulent rivers, spectacular glacial valleys, heavily wooded forests and sparkling blue lakes, at their most dramatic in **Glacier National Park**. By contrast, the **eastern** two-thirds is high prairie: sun-parched in summer and wracked by icy blizzards each winter.

Preconceptions of a desolate land populated by cowpokes are soon shattered: each of Montana's small cities has its own proud identity. The university and sawmill community of **Missoula**, for example, possesses a high-culture feel absent from the heavily

Irish, copper-mining town and union stronghold of **Butte**, while state capital **Helena** still harks back to its prosperous gold mining years.

The fur trappers and gold miners who were the first whites to brave this inhospitable terrain soon moved on, but as white settlers invaded Native American hunting grounds, conflict was inevitable. A key plank of army strategy was to starve the Native Americans into submission: "For the sake of a lasting peace let them [professional hunters] kill, skin and sell until the buffalo are exterminated. Then your prairies can be covered by the speckled cow and the festive cowboy," declared General Philip Sheridan. By the late 1870s the buffalo were almost gone, and most of Montana had been cleared for settlement.

The speckled cow and festive cowboy were not in for an easy time. The horrendous winter of 1886 wiped out many herds, and the "sodbusters" who planted wheat in the wake of bankrupt ranchers often fared little better. Plagues of grasshoppers, droughts, falling wheat prices and erosion of the topsoil caused farms to fail everywhere in the 1920s, during which time Montana was the only state to record a population decline.

Wheat has since made a revival, and now, with lumbering and coal mining, forms the base of Montana's economy. Another significant money-earner is tourism, though apart from skiing the harsh climate restricts the season to the months between June and September.

### Getting around Montana

Considering Montana's size and sparse population, transportation connections are not bad. Greyhound and regional **bus** companies like Intermountain (north from Butte and Missoula to Glacier) and Rimrock serve towns on I-90 and I-15. Delta Air Lines and Northwest offer the most **flights** to Montana, landing in seven towns. Amtrak **trains** cross the north, stopping east and west of Glacier National Park without making it easier to see the park itself. Western Montana, in particular, is great **cycling** territory; the Adventure Cycling organization, whose national headquarters are in Missoula (see p.788), can provide special maps.

However, the best way to **get around** this huge state is by car, with practically every interstate exit in the west leading to areas of mountain solitude, interesting landmarks or small communities. Montana's "Basic Rule" used to state that, as long as you drive in a "reasonable and prudent manner," you're free to go at whatever speed you wish. However, much to the chagrin of locals, Montana now has posted speed limits, usually of 75mph.

# Eastern Montana

Before ranchers and farmers settled the flat prairie of **eastern Montana**, it was prime **buffalo** territory: one early traveler waited three nights while a massive herd crossed his path. Native Americans fought hard to hold onto their land; the crushing defeats they inflicted on the US Army include the legendary victory at **Little Bighorn**.

The eastern Montana plains are intermittently broken by mountains, of which the most impressive are the icy **Beartooth Range**, crammed between the village of Red Lodge and Yellowstone. Don't expect much from the region's towns; most are lazy farm supply centers, and down-at-heel **Billings**, Montana's largest city with a population of just over 70,000, doesn't have much more to offer.

### Little Bighorn Battlefield National Monument

In June 1876 massive US Army detachments were sent to southeastern Montana to subjugate the Sioux and Cheyenne. A key unit in the campaign was the crack **Seventh Cavalry**; at its head was the flamboyant **Lt-Colonel George Armstrong Custer**.

Few if any US soldiers have achieved the fame or opprobrium of Custer. During an erratic career, he graduated last in his class at West Point in 1861; was the US Army's youngest-ever major general; was suspended for ordering the execution of deserters from a forced march he led through Kansas primarily to see his wife; and became notorious for allowing the murder in 1868 of almost 100 Cheyenne women and children.

On June 25, 1876, Custer's was the first unit to arrive in the **Little Bighorn Valley**. Disdaining to await reinforcements, he set out to raze a tepee village along the Little Bighorn River – which turned out to be the largest-ever gathering of Plains Indians. As a party of his men pursued fleeing women and children, they were encircled by two thousand Sioux and Cheyenne warriors emerging from either side of a ravine. The soldiers dismounted to attempt to shoot their way out, but were soon overwhelmed; simultaneously, Custer's command post on a nearby hill was wiped out. Archeologists have discounted the idea of **Custer's Last Stand** as a heroic defiance in which Custer was the last cavalryman left standing; the battle lasted less than an hour, with the white soldiers being systematically and effortlessly picked off. The most decisive Native American victory in the West – led by Sitting Bull – was also their final great show of resistance. An incensed President Grant piled maximum resources into a military campaign that brought about the effective defeat of all Plains Indians by the end of the decade.

The **monument** is 56 miles southeast of Billings, with the entrance one mile east of I-90 on US-212. You can trace the course of the battle on a five-mile self-guided driving tour through the grasslands (daily: 8am–dusk; $5 per car), following the high ridge overlooking the valley, or on a narrated bus tour (spring–fall; $10) White-marble tablets mark where individual soldiers fell, and a sandstone obelisk stands above their mass grave on "Last Stand Hill" (Custer himself lies in West Point Military Academy). Dioramas in the **visitor center and museum** (mid-April–Memorial Day 8am–6pm; Memorial Day–Labor Day 8am–8pm; rest of the year 8am–4.30pm; ☎406/638-2621; $5 per vehicle) outline the battle, while the US military **cemetery** nearby holds soldiers from all America's wars (free passes available).

## Hardin

Little Bighorn is the focus of the Crow Indian Reservation. Little **HARDIN**, thirteen miles northwest, makes its living from tourists seeking authentic Native American artifacts and other Western mementos. Each year, on the weekend closest to the battle's June 25 anniversary, the **Little Bighorn Days** festival centers around reenactments of the battle at a site eight miles west of the town (*not* at the original battlefield). Other activities include Native American dancing, downtown parades, dinner dances and a rodeo.

The least expensive place to **stay** is the *Western Motel*, off Hwy-313 at 831 W Third St (☎406/665-2296; ③/④). *The Purple Cow*, Hwy-47 N (☎406/665-3601), is a cheerful family **diner** serving home-cooked feasts.

## Billings

By Montana standards, **BILLINGS** is a big city. Its dramatic setting, bounded on its north and east sides by the 400ft crumpled sandstone cliffs of the **Rimrock**, certainly makes it something more than a pockmark on the prairie. The town itself, however, consists largely of run-down housing projects and a city center whose shops have transferred out to the malls. Scarring its west side are the tracks and warehouses of the Northern Pacific Railroad, whose president, Frederick Billings, gave the city its name.

On the Rimroad, right by Logan Airport, the **Peter Yegen Jr Museum** (Mon–Fri 10.30am–5pm, Sat & Sun 2–5pm; free) is a fascinating jumble, devoted to eastern Montana pioneers. Oddities among the cabinets of weapons, fossils and domestic equipment include a stuffed two-headed calf and a display of dozens of types of barbed wire.

Billings' **bus station**, served by Greyhound along I-90 and I-15, and Powder River, heading north from Wyoming, is at 2501 First Ave N (☎406/245-5116). The *Best Western Ponderosa Inn*, next door at no. 2511 (☎406/259-5511 or 1-800/628-9081; ④), has nice **rooms**, a restaurant, pool, sauna and gym. Cheaper options line I-90, off exit 446, including a *Super 8* at 5400 Southgate Drive (☎406/248-8842; ③). Downtown, meals can be had at *Pug Mahon's*, 3011 First Ave N, an Irish pub with good food and a popular Sunday brunch. *Casey's Golden Pheasant*, 109 N Broadway (☎406/256-5200), is a jazz and blues **bar** with good Cajun food. For coffee and something sweet, try *Cafe Jones* at 2712 Second Ave (☎406/259-7676).

### Red Lodge and the Beartooth Scenic Highway

The atmospheric village of **RED LODGE**, sixty miles south of Billings at the foot of the awesome Beartooth Mountains and originally founded to dig coal for the transcontinental railroads, makes an altogether more pleasant stop. During winter, it acts as a base for skiers using the increasingly popular **Red Lodge Mountain**, six miles west on US-212 (☎406/446-2610; lodging reservation service ☎1-800/444-8977), where ski-lift passes cost $35 a day ($22 Mon & Tues from early Jan).

Red Lodge faced extinction in 1924, when its largest coal mine closed, but its future was secured by the construction of the 65-mile **Beartooth Scenic Highway** to Cooke City at the northeastern entrance to Yellowstone National Park (see p.772). Other roads in the Rockies may be higher, but none gives quite such a top-of-the-world feeling as this succession of tight switchbacks, steep grades and exciting overlooks. Even in summer the springy tundra turf of the 10,940ft **Beartooth Pass** is covered with snow that (due to algae) turns pink when crushed. All around are gem-like corries, deeply gouged granite walls, stretches of scree and huge blocks of roadside ice.

Though Red Lodge boasts plenty of reasonable **motels** grouped south of town – the *Yodeler*, 601 S Broadway (☎406/446-1435; *www.wtp.net/YODELER*; ③), is friendly, clean and central – by far the nicest place to stay is the lovely historic *Pollard Hotel*, 2 N Broadway (☎406/446-000 or 1-800/POLLARD; ⑤–⑧), with a pool, sauna, comfortable old library and superb restaurant (see below). **Camping** at the *KOA* (June–Sept; ☎406/446-2364), four miles north, costs $18. Or you can rent a cabin for $36.

Undoubtedly the best **food** in town, if not in the entire Rocky Mountain region, is served at the *Pollard*, where *Greenlee's* (☎406/446-0001) features sublime, simple, European dishes in a wonderfully serene wood-lined dining room. Also on Broadway, *Bogart's* at no. 11 S (☎406/446-1784), is popular for its Mexican and Californian cuisine. And the nearby *Mystic Mountain Pizza* is a good value. Red Lodge has a cheerful **nightlife** scene, especially in winter: the *Red Lodge Pizza Company* and *Nataly's Front Bar* at no. 115 S Broadway (☎406/446-3933) serve food and snacks all day, with beer and live music most nights at the bar. The wooden *Snag Bar*, at no. 107 S, is a friendly local haunt with a pool table (☎406/446-9923).

# Western Montana

The **western** third of Montana sees the state at its best – from Big Timber westwards, I-90 squeezes between dramatic mountain ranges, making an exhilarating approach to Yellowstone country, replete with outdoor opportunities and bustling communities. The only mining camps to grow into substantial permanent settlements were state capital **Helena** and craggy **Butte**, which made its money from copper. Between them they conjure up more of a feel for the rambunctious times, the lust for profit and the post-bust hardships of the era than all the hyped-up ghost towns in the Rockies combined.

## Bozeman

Pretty, tree-lined **BOZEMAN** lies deep in the lush Gallatin Valley, 142 miles west of Billings and a mere eighty miles north of Yellowstone. Founded by farmers in 1863, it's the only sizeable town in Montana not to owe its roots to mining, railroading or lumbering, and the absence of slag heaps, shabby warehouses or rail yards makes a refreshing change. The smart-looking storefronts along the busy Victorian Main Street just beg to be window-shopped, and you may just bump into one of the Hollywood celebrities who have set up home or business in this increasingly trendy town.

South of downtown, as **Montana State University** peters out into a beautiful wilderness in the shadow of the mountains, the huge, impressive **Museum of the Rockies** at S Seventh Avenue and Kagy Boulevard (summer daily 8am–8pm; rest of year Mon–Sat 9am–5pm, Sun 12.30–5pm; $6) holds dinosaur finds, Native American weapons and a fine selection of Western landscape paintings; there's also a **planetarium**. Though far smaller in scale, the **Pioneer Museum**, 317 W Main St (June–Sept Mon–Fri 10am–4.30pm, Sat 1–4pm; Oct–May Tues–Fri 11am–4pm, Sat 1–4pm; free) is even better, with an intriguing, well-presented selection of locally gathered historic objects, including cartoons drawn by local boy Gary Cooper in his pre-movie star days. The excellent photo selection features some great old images of early tourism at Yellowstone; many of the prints are for sale. Striking a modern note, the **American Computer Museum,** 234 E Babcock (summer daily 10am–4pm; rest of year Tues–Wed & Fri–Sat noon–4pm; $2), follows the evolution of computers, from their bulky, awkward beginnings to the modern compact incarnations of today; also on display are some well-intentioned inventions that never quite hit mainstream America.

Bozeman is well placed for those in search of **outdoor activities**. The ranger office, 3710 Fallon St (Mon–Fri 8am–5pm; ☎406/587-6920; 24hr recreation recording ☎406/587-9784), provides details of local walking trails, and Chalet Sports at 108 W Main (☎406/587-4595) rents out mountain bikes and ski equipment.

### Practicalities
Greyhound and Rimrock cruise the interstates from 625 N Seventh St (☎406/587-3110), while Amfac/TW Services runs a bus a day to Yellowstone (see p.773). **Visitor centers** are at 1001 N Seventh Ave (summer only) and **Internet** access is available at the **pubic library** at 220 E Lamme St. Central **motels** lining Seventh Avenue include the *Rainbow* at no. 510 N (☎406/587-4201; ③); the *Bozeman Inn* at no. 1235 N (☎406/587-3176 or 1-800/648-7515; ④) is more luxurious. Main Street also has a few worthy options: the rambling *Lewis and Clark*, no. 824 W (☎406/586-3341 or 1-800/332-7666; ③), though gaudy, is very good value and centrally located, with pool, sauna, gym and hot tub. The friendly *Sacajawea Backpackers Hostel*, 405 W Olive St (☎406/586-4659; ①), has bunk beds for $12 and a fully equipped kitchen.

Bozeman boasts plenty of good **places to eat**. The *Community Co-op* on Ninth and Main (☎406/587-4039) serves terrific fresh veggie food and mouth-watering desserts in its pretty roadside garden, while the *McKenzie River Pizza Co* at 232 E Main St (☎406/587-0055), pulls in a crowd with fresh and somewhat unusual toppings. The *Spanish Peaks Brewery* at 120 N 19th Ave (☎406/585-2296) offers Italian food at moderate prices alongside home-brewed beers like Black Dog Ale and Spanish Peaks Porter. For gourmet coffee or a pastry, go to *The Leaf and Bean* at 35 W Main St; other places to **drink** include *Molly Brown's* and the *Haufbrau*, both at Eighth Ave and Main St, and both good rowdy local bars. For live music, the *Zebra Lounge* on Rouse Avenue S offers an eclectic mix. The *Tributary* and *BoZone* are both good for local entertainment listings.

## Missouri Headwaters State Park

Officially, the Missouri River begins its circuitous journey to the Mississippi, and eventually the Gulf of Mexico, at the confluence of the Jefferson, Madison and Gallatin rivers. Three miles north of I-90, halfway between Bozeman and Butte, and maintained as the **Missouri Headwaters State Park** ($3 per vehicle; camping $5), these marshy grasslands beneath a shallow bluff were identified by Lewis and Clark in July 1805. Three years later, **John Colter**, a veteran of that expedition who was the first to describe Yellowstone (see box p.775), was captured here by a party of Blackfoot, who, after killing his companion, stripped him and made him run for his life. Colter killed the one pursuer who kept up with him, hid under a snag, and reached safety on the Bighorn River a week later. Fur trappers who followed in the wake of Lewis and Clark included Kit Carson; traces remain of the nineteenth-century town they created.

# Butte

Eighty miles west of Bozeman, copper-mining **BUTTE** is bunched on a steep, almost treeless hillside where massive black headframes of long-abandoned pits soar up among paint-bare homes, stark gray business premises, and a ring of surface workings and dirty-yellow slag heaps. It's an oddly compelling landscape, best appreciated at dusk, when the golden pink light casts a glow on the mine-scoured hillsides, and the old neon signs illuminate uptown's historic brick buildings.

Exploration of this friendly, atmospheric town soon reveals a community rich in ethnic and trade union culture. Among immigrants to leave their mark were the **Irish** – Butte still hosts the biggest St Patrick's Day celebrations in the Rockies, with an estimated 40,000 customers passing through the famous old *M&M Bar* every March 17 – and miners from **Cornwall**; the traditional meat-and-potato pasty is still served in most cafes.

From its early days, Butte stood out as a "Gibraltar of Unionism" in the anti-union West. Miners used their collective strength to obtain a minimum wage and an eight-hour day, and it became impossible to get work without a union card. Such confidence bred radicalism, and Butte sent the largest delegation to the founding convention of the IWW (the "Wobblies") in 1906. The eventual consolidation of mining operations under the huge Anaconda Company led to inter-union rivalries and rioting, and in 1983 the last mine closed. Today conflicts rage between the clean-up lobby (the town's largest disused mine, the Berkeley Pit, is slowly filling with heavily poisoned groundwater) and the traditionalists, keen to develop new methods to exploit the mineral-rich seams that once made Butte the "richest hill on earth." To take a look at the ecological disaster that is the 700ft by mile-long **Berkeley Pit**, head for Continental Drive. Here, a viewing platform surveys the whole horrifying mess, the most toxic stretch of water in the United States (summer daily 8am–9pm; free).

Uptown lies Butte's extensive **historic district**. On W Park Street, the excellent **World Museum of Mining** (April–mid-June & Oct Tues–Sat 10am–5pm; Memorial Day–Labor Day daily 9am–9pm; Sept daily 10am–5pm; $3) is packed with fascinating memorabilia from the boom years. Outside, beyond the scattered collection of rusting machinery – baffling to all but experts – its 37-building **Hell Roarin' Gulch** re-creates a cobbled-street mining camp, complete with saloon, bordello, church, schoolhouse and Chinese laundry. Above it all looms the blackened headframe of the Orphan Girl mineshaft.

In an old noodle parlor at 17 W Mercury St, the tiny **Mai Wah Museum** (June–Aug Tues–Sat 11am–3pm; free) focuses on the history of Butte's Chinese community with its small, intriguing collection of photos, cooking implements, kites, fireworks, menus and books. At the end of the nineteenth century the narrow strip between Galena and Mercury streets was known as China Alley, the bustling heart of a 600-strong community; by the 1940s widespread racism had reduced the number to just a few families.

At night the 90ft **Our Lady of the Rockies** statue is illuminated by floodlights. Built entirely by voluntary labor – there had just been a major lay-off at one of the mines – it was set in place on top of the Continental Divide, some 3500ft above Butte, by helicopter.

## Practicalities

Greyhound and Intermountain Transit **buses** drop off downtown at 105 Broadway. From June to September, ninety-minute **trolley tours** of town (10.30am, 1.10pm, 3.30pm & 7pm; $4) leave from the **Chamber of Commerce**, 1000 George St (May–Labor Day daily 8am–8pm; Labor Day–Oct daily 8am–5pm; Oct–May Mon–Fri 9am–5pm; ☎406/723-3177 or 1-800/735-6814). The chain **motels** line the interstate, out on the "Flat." The efficient *Best Western Butte Plaza*, 2900 Harrison Ave (☎406/494-3500 or 1-800/543-5814; ④), has good rooms, an excellent pool, steam room and gym, and generous continental breakfast; uptown, the historic *Finlen Hotel*, 100 E Broadway (☎406/723-5461; ③), has rooms in the original 1920s building and a more modern annex. The *Scott Inn*, 15 W Copper (☎406/723-7030; ④/⑤), is a charming B&B in a historic old manor.

Butte has plenty of good places to **eat and drink**, most of them uptown. The funky, friendly *Blue Venus* coffeehouse, 124 Main St, serves good espresso, light breakfasts and lunches, while *Metals Banque*, 8 W Park (☎406/723-6160), offers tasty Tex-Mex in an old bank vault complete with enormous metal safe. More upscale, though still relatively informal, the *Uptown Cafe*, 47 E Broadway (☎406/723-4735), serves fixed five-course gourmet meals, particularly strong on Mediterranean-style seafood. Savings on decor and a huge custom allow the roomy *M&M Bar*, 9 N Main St (☎406/723-7612), to serve the cheapest grease-laden breakfasts in town; it's also an atmospheric place for a beer. *The Copper King Saloon,* at 1000 S Montana St (☎406/723-9283), is a lively place to spend an evening.

# Helena and around

In 1864 a party of disheartened prospectors working over the present site of **HELENA**, more or less halfway between Yellowstone and Glacier, decided to have one final dig along a likely-looking ravine – and struck lucky on what is now **Last Chance Gulch**, the town's attractive main street. More than $20 million of gold was extracted, but Helena retained an orderly appearance, set neatly at the foot of two rounded mountains with a fine view over the golden-brown **Prickly Pear Valley**. Over fifty successful prospectors remained here as millionaires, and their palatial residences still enhance the west side of town. Hollywood star Gary Cooper was born and brought up in this quintessentially Western town; actress Myrna Loy also lived here as a child, and is commemorated by the **Myrna Loy Center for the Performing Arts** at 15 N Ewing St (☎406/443-0287).

Inside the massive Neoclassical **State Capitol**, atop a small hill surrounded by lawns at Sixth and Montana, huge murals by "cowboy artist" C M Russell depict scenes from Montana's history (daily 8am–6pm; free). You can see more of his work at the free **State Historical Museum**, 225 N Roberts St (summer Mon–Fri 8am–6pm, Sat & Sun 9am–5pm; rest of year Mon–Fri 8am–5pm, Sat 9am–5pm), as well as early photographs of pioneer life. The majestic red-tiled spires of the **Cathedral of St Helena** rise 230ft at 530 N Ewing St; elaborate Bavarian stained glass, white-marble altars and gold leaf decorate the interior. Also worth a visit is the **Holter Museum of Art**, 12 E Lawrence St (Tues–Fri 11.30am-5.30pm, Sat–Sun noon–5pm; free), which exhibits painting, sculpture, photography and ceramics. West of downtown, the **Archie Bray Foundation**, 2915 Country Club Ave (☎406/443-3502), hosts world-renowned ceramic artists who hone their craft while you watch.

## Practicalities

Between them, Intermountain and Rimrock (which links with Greyhound), offer connections throughout Montana from Helena's **bus station** at 5 W 15th St (☎406/442-5860). Between mid-May and September the Historical Society runs imitation steam train **tours** 3 times a day from the corner of Sixth Avenue and Roberts Street (☎406/442-1023 or 1-888/423-1023; $5). There's a **visitor center** at 225 Cruse Ave (Mon 9am–5pm, Tues–Fri 8am–5pm; ☎406/442-4120).

The northernmost blocks of Last Chance Gulch form a low-key pedestrianized mall, decorated with mining-themed sculptures and fountains, and enlivened by bars, sidewalk coffee shops and restaurants. The historic *Park Hotel* at no. 432 (☎406/442-0960; ③) offers simple en-suite **rooms**, but visitors looking for more comfortable lodgings should head for the *Sanders B&B*, 328 N Ewing St (☎406/442-3309; ⑤). For **breakfast** you can't do better than the scrumptious pastries, savory rolls and espresso at *Park Avenue Bakery*, 44 S Park Ave (☎406/449-8424). *Bert and Ernie's*, at 361 Last Chance Gulch (☎406/443-5680), serves classy lunches and has a popular saloon bar, while the *Windbag Saloon* at no. 19 (☎406/443-9669) is a big old barn of a place that serves a reasonable pint of Guinness, and good burgers and steaks. A little more upscale, *On Broadway*, 106 Broadway (☎406/443-1929), offers classy Italian food and wine.

## Gates of the Mountains

Sixteen miles north of Helena off I-15, you can take a two-hour **boat tour** through the **Gates of the Mountains** (daily June–Sept; ☎406/458-5241; $8.50). This dramatic stretch of the Missouri River, which enters a gorge between sheer 1200ft cliffs that rise abruptly from the northern shores of a tranquil lake, was named by Meriwether Lewis (of the Lewis and Clark expedition). This area offers excellent hiking and backpacking opportunities. The Helena National Forest Office (☎406/449-5201) can provide maps and local **camping** information.

# Missoula

Blue-collar and academic cultures converge in **MISSOULA**, framed by the Bitterroot and Sapphire mountains, to produce one of the most vibrant and friendly small towns in the country. It's a town of contrasting faces – truck sales yards and bookstores, continental cafes and gun shops – where nearly everyone seems to be connected to either the city's huge sawmills or the 10,000-student University of Montana.

The **visitor center**, across the river from the campus, at 825 E Front St (☎406/543-6623), can provide details on **trails** such as the grueling one leading from its office up **Mount Sentinel**, embellished by a huge concrete letter "M." The top gives a great view of the area, especially the rugged Hellgate River Canyon. Other worthwhile trails tra-

---

### MISSOULA AND CYCLING

Missoula has enjoyed close ties with **cycling** since 1896, when it became home to the 25th Infantry Bicycle Corps, founded to test the military potential of bikes as a means of transporting troops in mountainous regions. Its tasks included a 1900-mile ride to St Louis, where the army decided against the use of cycles and the soldiers came home by train.

Today Missoula is one of the best cities in the country for cycling, offering dozens of great road and dirt bike routes. The council even employs a bicycling coordinator (☎406/523-4626), but the best source of **information** and trail maps is Adventure Cycling (formerly Bikecentennial), 150 E Pine St (☎406/721-1776; see also p.782). The Bicycle Hangar, 1801 Brooks Ave (☎406/728-9537), rents out good-quality cycles.

verse the **Rattlesnake Wilderness**, which, despite its name, is serpent-free. The most developed of three small **ski** areas nearby is the **Snowbowl**, twelve miles northwest, which boasts a summer **chairlift** (Fri, Sat & Sun noon–5pm; ☎406/549-9777; $6, $2 for bikes). **Marshall Mountain**, 7 miles east of Missoula (☎406/258-6000), is geared toward the novice.

Tours of the Forest Service **Aerial Fire Depot and Smokejumper Center**, ten miles out of town on US-93, look at the methods used to train smokejumpers, highly skilled firefighters who parachute into forested areas to stop the spread of wildfires. A small visitor center explains their work (mid-May–mid-Sept daily 9am–5pm; ☎406/329-4934).

Missoula is home to a number of **authors**, among them Norman *A River Runs Through It* MacLean and crime writers James Lee Burke and James Crumley, and several good bookstores, including Horizon Books at 138 W Broadway.

### Practicalities
Greyhound, Rimrock and Intermountain share the **bus depot** at 1660 W Broadway (☎406/549-2339). **Motels** along East Broadway, between downtown and campus, include the *Downtown Motel* at no. 502 (☎406/549-5191; ②), the *Campus Inn* at no. 744 (☎406/549-5134 or 1-800/232-8013; ④); and, for more luxury, the spacious *Holiday Inn Express Riverside* at no. 1021 (☎406/549-7600; ④). *Goldsmith's B&B*, 809 E Front St (☎406/721-6732; ④/⑤), beside the river across from the campus, offers comfortable rooms and award-winning food. The *BirchWood Hostel*, 600 S Orange St (☎406/728-9799; ①), charges $10 a night and has lots of space for cycles; its within walking distance from downtown, however, there's a lockout from 9am–5pm.

Morning espressos and gooey pastries are the specialty at *The Break*, 432 N Higgins St (☎406/728-7300); you can pick up the best picnic lunch in town over the road at *Wordens* deli, Higgins and Spruce (☎406/549-1293). For tasty Italian food, join the inevitable line at *Zimorino's Red Pies Over Montana*, 424 N Higgins St (☎406/728-6686); try the white pizza or any of the specialty sauces. The *Mustard Seed*, 419 W Front St (☎406/728-7825), is popular for its tasty pan-Asian food, including a passable sushi – no mean feat in Montana.

### Bars and entertainment
When Milo Milodragonovitch, the heavy-drinking, coke-snorting private eye in James Crumley's *Dancing Bear*, was left battered and bleeding miles from Missoula, he was consoled by the knowledge that he would soon be back in what he considered to be "the town with the best bars in a state of great bars." It's hard to argue with either claim. Pick up a copy of the weekly *Independent* or Friday's *Missoulian* for local happenings and live music listings.

The **bar** Milodragonovitch uses as an impromptu office is based on *Charley B's*, 428 N Higgins Ave – a dark, dingy, no-frills local now known as the *Dinosaur Cafe*. The equally rough-and-ready *Top Hat*, 134 W Front St (☎406/728-9865), features live rock, blues and rockabilly bands most nights. Also worth checking out are the *Union Club*, 208 E Main St (☎406/728-7980), for C&W in an old union building, and the *Missoula Club*, hiding behind a neon "Burgers and Beer" sign at 139 W Main St (☎406/728-3740).

# The Flathead Valley

The sheer splendor of the remote 28-mile-long **Flathead Lake** provides a welcome diversion on the long route north towards Glacier National Park, reached by following US-93 north from I-90, nine miles west of Missoula, up to the Flathead Indian Reservation. Between Polson in the south and Somers in the north, US-93 follows the lake's western shore, while the smaller Hwy-36 runs up the east. Both offer superb views of the deep alpine waters; US-93's curve around Elmo in the west, where conical **Wild Horse Island** rises starkly from the crystal-blue depths, is especially memorable.

Flathead Lake is a major destination for **water-sports** enthusiasts, with the prime spot for launching fishing and pleasure boats being **Bigfork** in the northeast. If you feel more comfortable on an organized cruise, summer options include the *Far West* (☎406/857-3203) from Somers, and the *Port Polson Princess* (☎406/883-2448; $10–16) from *Best Western KwaTaqNuk Resort* at Polson.

General **information** on the Flathead Valley can be had on ☎1-800/543-3105. **POLSON** has the most extensive range of facilities. Here, the Flathead tribe owns the *Best Western KwaTaqNuk Resort*, which has a pool and its own marina with boat rentals, at 303 US-93 E (☎406/883-3636 or 1-800/882-6363; ④/⑤); the *Port Polson Inn*, also overlooking the lake from US-93 E (☎406/883-5385 or 1-800/654-0682; ③/④), is slightly less expensive. If you're passing through, it's worth pausing at *Watusi*, 318 Main St (☎406/883-6200), for its delicious, healthy lunches.

## Kalispell

Thirty miles southwest of Glacier, and fifteen miles north of Flathead Lake, largish **KALISPELL** corners a significant portion of the tourist trade en route to Glacier. There's not much to do here, but in high season it may be the closest place to the park you'll get to stay.

Stylish **accommodation** options include the venerable *Kalispell Grand Hotel*, 100 Main St (☎406/755-8100 or 1-800/858-7422; ④), and the *Creston Country Inn B&B*, 70 Creston Rd (☎406/755-7517 or 1-800/257-7517; ⑤). The clean and central *Four Seasons Motor Inn*, 350 N Main St (☎406/755-6123 or 1-800/545-6399; ③/④), is also good value. For excellent **food**, try the Chinese dishes at the *Alley Connection* in the *Kalispell Hotel*; the pizzas and sandwiches in the grand old-fashioned *Moose's Saloon*, 173 N Main St (☎406/755-2337), or *Montana Coffee Traders*, 328 W Center St (☎406/756-2326). If you're looking for a lively night out, the *Hellroaring Saloon & Eatery* on Big Mountain is the place to be – especially during ski season.

## Whitefish

The resort and lumber village of **WHITEFISH**, seventeen miles north of Kalispell, makes a more pleasant stop, though accommodation is limited. Hacked out of thick forests, it lies on the south shore of beautiful **Whitefish Lake** in the shade of the *Big Mountain Ski Resort* (☎406/862-1900). The narrow roads round the lake and foothills deserve to be **cycled**; bikes can be rented from Glacier Cyclery, 336 E 2nd St (☎406/862-6446).

Amtrak drops off downtown on Central Avenue, while Intermountain **buses** call in at Stumps Pumps gas station at 403 Second St on their way between Missoula and Glacier during summer. Of the inexpensive **motels** lining US-93, *Mountain Holiday Motel*, no. 6595 (☎406/862-2548; ③), is a decent choice a mile south of downtown; **B&Bs** in the area include the friendly little *Duck Inn*, 1305 Columbia Ave by the river (☎406/862-3825 or 1-800/344-2377; ⑤), and the rural *Crenshaw House*, three miles south of town at 5465 US-93 (☎406/862-3496 or 1-800/453-2863; ④–⑦).

For **dining**, the *Great Northern Bar and Grill*, 27 Central Ave (☎406/862-2816), is a good bar with pool tables, deli meals and live music, while *Truby's* on Central Avenue is a good place for pizza and pasta.

# Glacier National Park

Two thousand lakes and a thousand miles of rivers, threading between thick forests and glorious meadows, weave a blue-and-green carpet below the tightly packed peaks of **GLACIER NATIONAL PARK** – a haven for bighorn sheep, mountain goats, black bears and threatened grizzlies, wolves and mountain lions. Though the park still holds fifty small glaciers, its name comes from the fact that these immense valleys were carved by huge flows of ice, millennia ago. Crisp air, freezing waterfalls and year-round snow combine to give the impression of being very close to the Arctic Circle; in fact, the latitude here is lower than that of London.

## Arrival and information

There are **visitor centers** just inside the park's **western** entrance at **Apgar**, on the shores of gorgeous McDonald Lake, twenty miles east of Whitefish and just 35 miles south of the Canadian border (daily: May 9am–4.30pm; early June 8am–4.30pm; late June–Aug 31 8am–8pm; Sept–Oct 31 8am–4.30pm) and at the main **east** gate at **St Mary**, seventy miles west of **Shelby** (daily: late May–mid-June 8am–5pm; late June–July 3 8am–9pm; July 4–early Sept 7am–9pm; early Sept–Oct 17 8am–5pm). Another visitor center (daily: early June–mid-June 9am–5pm; mid-June–early Sept 9am–6pm; early Sept–Oct 17 10am–5pm) stands at the top of **Logan Pass** on the Going-to-the-Sun road – the one through-road between the two entrances, usually only passable between mid-June and mid-October. The park itself is open year-round, however, and it's well worth entering as far as Lake McDonald or St Mary's Lake even when the road is blocked and the visitor center is closed. The **entrance fee** of $10 per vehicle is good for seven days; for **park information** call ☎406/888-7800, or go to *www.nps.gov/glac/*.

Glacier combines with the adjacent, much smaller, Waterton Lakes National Park (☎403/859-2224) in Canada to form the **Waterton-Glacier International Peace Park**, though Going-to-the-Sun road does not pass that way. Both parks operate their own fees and regulations, and to get to Waterton's separate entrance, north of St Mary, you have to pass customs and pay an extra $4 a day.

The southern border of the park is skirted by the low-lying US-2, which remains open all year and constitutes an attractive alternative drive. Amtrak **trains** follow the same route, stopping at West Glacier, a short walk from the west gate, and in the south at East Glacier (thirty miles south of St Mary) and Essex Park.

Intermountain (☎406/563-5246) operates a fairly frequent summer bus service from Missoula, Kalispell, Whitefish and, to the east, Great Falls. Travelers arriving by public transportation are faced with the problem of how to see the actual park: Bright red vintage "jammer" buses (so called because of the need to jam on the brakes) run throughout the park on narrated **sightseeing tours** from the main lodges (May–Oct; ☎406/888-9817). They also offer shuttles from the Amtrak station at West Glacier to the *Village Inn* and *Lake McDonald Lodge,* hikers' shuttles from *Many Glacier Hotel* to the Siyela Bend, Logan Pass and Loop Trailheads, and a number of one-way tours and connections. Sun Tours (☎406/226-9220 or 1-800/786-9220) offers tours given by members of the Blackfeet Indian tribe, providing a historical perspective to the park's beauty.

## Accommodation within the park

**Accommodation** options within the park, along with the *Glacier Park Lodge* in East Glacier, are run by Glacier Park Inc (May–Sept: East Glacier Park, MT 59434, ☎406/226-5551; rest of year: Viad Corporate Center, Phoenix, AZ 85077; ☎602/207-6000).

Most rooms cost over $80, though you can stay more cheaply at the *Swiftcurrent Motor Inn* at Many Glacier on the upper east side (June–Sept; ④, basic cabins ②), the lakeside *Rising Sun Motor Inn* (June–Sept; ④/⑤), seven miles in from the east gate at St Mary, and the *Village Inn* (mid-May–Sept; ⑤/⑥) in Apgar, which fronts onto Lake McDonald with stunning views. Nearby, the lovely *Lake McDonald Lodge* has a few relatively affordable motel rooms (June–Sept; ⑤/⑥), but these, like the better rooms, are in the lodge itself and need to be booked well in advance. Or you could try the more upscale *Prince of Wales Hotel* in Waterton (May–Sept; ⑧/⑨) or the *Many Glacier Hotel* (June–mid-Sept; ⑥–⑧).

The park's thirteen **campgrounds** – all first-come, first-served, ranging from $10–15 – fill up by late morning during July and August; ask at any visitor center for locations and availability, or call ☎406/888-7800. For advanced reservations, call ☎1-800/365-CAMP. Most are open from late May to mid-September, though you can camp at **Apgar** through late October. For overnight backpacking, get a permit from any visitor center.

## Accommodation outside the park

Another Glacier Park Inc operation, the massive log-built *Glacier Park Lodge* (mid-May–Sept; ⑥–⑧), off US-2 at the **eastern edge** of the park, is a terrific place to stay, with simple rooms, a cozy lobby lined with enormous Douglas fir pillars, a veranda with mountain views, a swimming pool, and a very good restaurant. Though very near the lovely Two Medicine Lake area, it's a long drive from the park entrances at St Mary and Many Glacier. Two miles outside the **western entrance**, the *Vista Motel* (☎406/888-5311 or 1-800/831-7101; ③), has affordable rooms and an outdoor pool, while *West Glacier Motel* (☎406/888-5662 or 1-800/838-2363; ④) is another good choice, both inexpensive and clean. On the southern boundary at **Essex**, the *Izaak Walton Inn* (☎406/888-5700; ⑤), halfway between the east and west gates, is an atmospheric 1939 building, originally used to house railroad workers charged with keeping the lines clear in winter – to this day, Amtrak stops at the front door. There are two **hostels** in the village of **East Glacier Park**. *HI-Brownie's* at 1020 Hwy-49 (☎406/226-4426; ①), has dorms for $20 and some private doubles, while the simpler *Backpackers' Inn* (☎406/226-9392; ①), behind *Serrano's Mexican Restaurant*, offers shared dorm space for $10–12; both are near the Amtrak station. Up in **Polebridge**, the *Northfork Hostel* (☎406/888-5241) is extremely cozy, with no electricity. Beds cost $12 dollars and cabins start at $25.

Information on other **lodging in the immediate vicinity** is available from Glacier Country (☎1-800/338-5072), while popular alternative bases to the west of the park include **Whitefish** and **Kalispell** (see p.790).

## Exploring the park

Driving the fifty-mile **Going-to-the-Sun road** from west to east (which can take several hours, even when summer restrictions on vehicle size – aimed primarily at banning RVs – are in force) creates the illusion that you'll be climbing forever. After a stealthy ascent of the foothills, when the road appears to be heading straight into the huge bare mountain that fills the entire windscreen, each successive hairpin confronts you with a new colossus. At the east end of ten-mile **Lake McDonald**, the road starts to climb in earnest. Snowmelt from waterfalls gushes across the road, spilling over the sheer drops on the other side. The winding route nudges over the **Continental Divide** at **Logan Pass** (6680ft) – a bewildering area where the peaks that looked so unscaleable from the valley floor are now mere hillocks of ice. Four miles on, there's an overlook at **Jackson Glacier**, one of the few glaciers visible from the roadside. Once you get down to the east gate, continue about five miles southeast on US-89 for a stunning view of the start of the Great Plains, which stretch 1600 miles east to Chicago.

Glacier National Park is a hiker's paradise, with exceptionally beautiful views at every turn. Good short **trails** start from **Avalanche Creek** on the west flank of the Divide. The mile-long **Trail of the Cedars** loop leads through dark forest to a wall of contoured vivid red sandstone, from where a four-mile path continues gently uphill, past several waterfalls, to glacier-fed **Avalanche Lake**. The most popular trail in the park – it can be teeming at weekends and holidays – begins at Logan Pass, following a boardwalk for a mile and a half across beautiful wild flower alpine meadows framed by extraordinary craggy peaks en route to serene **Hidden Lake**.

At **Swiftcurrent Lake**, north of the east entrance and reached by the minor Many Glacier entrance, an easy two-mile loop trail runs along the lakeshore, and an exciting nine-mile trail heads to **Iceberg Lake**, so called for the blocks of ice that float on its surface even in midsummer.

From **St Mary Lake**, you can weave a mile and a half up through fir forest to the crashing, frothing **St Mary Falls** and on to the taller **Virginia Falls**; combined with an early-morning boat trip from the Rising Sun launch to the trailhead, this can be an experience verging on the sublime.

Down in the quiet southeastern end of the park, the two-mile **Aster Park** trail gives access to some of Glacier's most astounding scenery. Starting at Two Medicine Lake, framed by the ever-receding massifs, it leads through spruce forest into flower-filled meadows, passing a couple of beaver ponds before ascending steeply through the forest to a small outcrop. From here there are fantastic views of the mighty Sinopah and Rising Wolf mountains, and the calm lakes below.

**Tour boats** explore all of the large lakes, charging $8–10 for one-hour trips, including sunset cruises on Lake McDonald and St Mary Lake. You can also rent canoes, rowboats and outboards. The lakes, teeming with cutthroat trout, are excellent for **fishing**; regulations are outlined in a free pamphlet available from visitor centers.

Both Glacier Raft Co (☎406/888-5454 or 1-800/235-6781) and Wild River Adventures (☎1-800/700-7056), based outside the west gate, offer half-day (around $30) and full-day (around $70) **float trips** down the middle fork of the Flathead River, which runs along the park boundary.

### Eating and drinking
**Food** in the park, served in the various hotel dining rooms, is nothing special. The best place to head in the immediate vicinity – outside the lodges – is East Glacier Park, where *Serrano's*, 29 Dawson Ave (mid-Apri–mid-Oct; ☎406/226-9392), serves delicious Mexican food and microbrews. On the east side of Hwy-49, next to *Brownie's*, is the cozy *Whistlestop Cafe*, which has a great all-day menu and serves delicious huckleberry pie.

# IDAHO

**IDAHO**, sandwiched in between Washington, Oregon and Montana, was the last of the states to be penetrated by whites, and rivals Alaska in the sheer scale of its barely explored **wilderness** areas. Though much of its scenery amply deserves national park status, its citizens have long been suspicious of encroachment by federal government and tourism alike, and only now is its potential for adventurous travel being appreciated.

With a marked absence of urban centers (the pleasant state capital **Boise**, in the south, being the only real exception), Idaho is very much a destination for the outdoors enthusiast. Natural wonders in its five-hundred-mile stretch include **Hell's Canyon**, America's deepest river gorge, the dramatic **Sawtooth National Recreation Area** and the black, barren **Craters of the Moon**. Beyond these, **hikers** and **backpackers** have the choice of no fewer than 81 mountain ranges, interspersed with virgin forest and lava plateau, while the mighty **Snake and Salmon rivers** offer endless scope for **fishing** and **whitewater rafting**.

In 1805, **Lewis and Clark** declared central Idaho's bewildering labyrinth of razor-edge peaks and wild waterways to be the most difficult leg of their mammoth journey from St Louis to the Pacific. Only their Shoshoni guides enabled them to get through;

to this day, there is no east–west road across the heart of the state. Reports of game animals tripping over each other in their profusion attracted the usual legions of itinerant trappers, but the Gold Rush of the 1860s and white pressure for land hastened the violent end of traditional life: four hundred Shoshoni men, women and children were killed along the Bear River in 1863, the Nez Percé were driven out (see box p.799), and by the end of the 1870s the "Indian problem" had been eradicated. The name "Idaho," incidentally, was invented by a mining lobbyist, who felt it sounded Indian; it was originally proposed for what is now Colorado.

The central wilderness still divides the state into two distinct halves. The heavily forested **north**, interspersed with glacial lakes now fronted by resorts like **Sandpoint** and **Coeur d'Alene**, has always had strong trading links with Spokane in Washington; in the **south**, irrigation programs begun in the 1880s – partly instigated by Mormons – have transformed the scrubland to either side of the Snake River into the fertile fields responsible for the state's license-plate tag of "Famous Potatoes." Idaho's isolation, and small (1 million) population, have kept it largely out of the mainstream of recent US history; indeed, its remoteness has attracted assorted unwelcome guests – neo-Nazi survivalists awaiting the Second Coming and/or nuclear holocaust.

### Getting around Idaho

Bus services between north and south Idaho are nonexistent, and a car is essential for extensive travel. Two **Amtrak** routes cross the state, both ultimately linking Seattle with Chicago. Sandpoint is the only stop on the northern line, though Spokane is not far across the border. Boise and other smaller towns are served on the southerly route between Portland and Salt Lake City. Boise also has an **airport**, though Spokane and Salt Lake City can be more convenient for northern and southern Idaho respectively.

# Southern Idaho

To drivers on the interstates, **southern Idaho** appears to consist of little more than miles of vegetable fields and a few rocky or sandy desert stretches; only state capital **Boise** provides any urban interest. A trip into the interior along US-20, however, brings you to the spectacular ragged outcrops of the **Sawtooth Mountains**. During summer, the much-hyped **Sun Valley** ski resort is a good base for cyclists and canoeists, and has the best bars and restaurants in this remote zone.

## Idaho Falls

Of the two largest towns in southeast Idaho, **IDAHO FALLS** makes a better overnight stop than down-at-heel Pocatello, being approximately 100 miles from Craters of the Moon to the west and Yellowstone and Grand Teton to the northeast. The first sign you see of this likeable community, as you approach along I-15, sixty miles north of Pocatello, is its seven-tier wedding-cake Mormon temple, rising from the flat Snake River Valley. The falls for which the town was named are now entirely tamed, with a long, low concrete dam running diagonally across the river very near downtown – but they form a pleasant focus for the greenbelt of parkland that lines both banks of this agricultural town.

Much of the country en route to Yellowstone is every bit as spectacular as in the national parks, and far less crowded; the magnificent **Mesa Falls**, for example, are a worthwhile brief detour along Hwy-47, roughly forty miles short of West Yellowstone.

## Practicalities

Hotels and restaurants are congregated on the west bank of the river, near the interstate, while the old downtown area on the east side retains a fair number of shops. The visitor center at 505 Lindsay Blvd (☎208/523-1010 or 1-800/634-3246) has information on the whole area, including a large relief model of the entire valley. The bizarre towering *Holiday Inn-West Bank* at 475 River Parkway (☎208/523-8000 or 1-800/465-4329; ⑤) has some of the most expensive rooms in town. *Evergreen Gables Motel,* 3130 S Yellowstone Ave (☎208/522-5410; ②) offers inexpensive rooms, some with kitchenettes, while the larger *Days Inn Stardust* nearby at 700 Lindsay Blvd (☎208/522-2910; ③), offers cheaper accommodation and very good-value **food** at its *Snake River Smokehouse* (☎208/523-1865), where ribs are the specialty. Other good restaurant choices include the more upmarket *Jaker's Steak, Ribs & Fish House,* 851 Lindsey Blvd (☎208/524-5240). The *High Desert Rose Coffee Roasting Company and Café,* 504 Shoup Ave (☎208/528-5464), is a wonderfully quaint venue for coffee and a pastry. For a good night out you can't do better than the friendly *Lost Arts Brewery and Breadworks,* 298 D St (☎208/528-9288), which has a wide range of microbrews, great creative food and occasional live music.

## Craters of the Moon National Monument

The eerie **CRATERS OF THE MOON NATIONAL MONUMENT** is around ninety miles west of Idaho Falls, less than twenty miles beyond Arco. At first sight, these 83 square miles look like a sooty-black wasteland, but closer inspection reveals a surreal cornucopia of lava cones, tubes, buttes, craters, caves and splatter cones. Here and there, sagebrush clings to the bleak soil, and trees have been battered by the fierce winds into bonsai-like contortions. All these features were formed without the aid of a volcano as such; instead, at roughly two-thousand-year intervals over the last thirteen thousand years, successive waves of lava have oozed from gaping wounds in the earth's crust. The next wave is thought to be due any time now.

The park **visitor center** is on US-20 (summer daily 8am–6pm; rest of year daily 8am–4.30pm; ☎208/527-3257); entrance is $4 per car, and spaces at the *Lava Flow* **campground** cost $10 (May–Oct). A seven-mile loop road, open late April to mid-November, leads to assorted cones and monoliths with trails of varying difficulty – don't stray from the trails, as the rocks are razor-sharp and can reach temperatures of 200°F. In winter, the road is open for **cross-country skiing**; for a conditions report, call ☎208/527-3257. "**Caves**" formed by molten lava tubes can be explored, alone or on frequent ranger-led tours.

Halfway between the park and Idaho Falls on US-20, the unassuming redbrick Experimental Breeder Reactor No 1 (**EBR-1**) – in lay terms, the **world's first nuclear power station** – stands just south of the 890-square-mile Idaho National Engineering Laboratory. Even the first prototype nuclear submarine was built and tested here. Now decommissioned, it's a free museum.

## Sun Valley

Although these days **Sun Valley** is the common label for the entire Wood River Valley area – in the center of southern Idaho, 150 miles west of Idaho Falls and east of Boise – technically it is just the name of a **ski resort**. This was the 1930s brainchild of Union Pacific Railroad chairman Averell Harriman, who, on discovering his railroad was obliged to maintain a passenger service, decided an alpine ski center would be an ideal stimulus to tourism. His scout, Austrian ski champion Count Schaffgotsch, set out to find dry powder snow on open treeless slopes, sheltered by higher mountains and not at too strenuous an elevation. Having turned down Aspen for being too high, he decided **Dollar** and **Bald Mountains** fitted the bill, here in the relatively gentle foothills of the Sawtooths near the old sheep-ranching village of **KETCHUM**. The Sun Valley name was chosen because the snow remained even in the brightest winter sun; early brochures showed skiers stripped to the waist. The world's first chairlift was built here in 1936, and the resort was an instant success.

Sun Valley's season runs from late November through to April; as well as downhill skiing (daily lift pass $50 at Bald Mt, $24 at Dollar Mt), you can also set off cross-country. Ketchum itself is a lively little town with plenty of accommodation, and an oasis of nightlife in this otherwise thinly populated zone. Up to a point, it resembles the Colorado ski towns, though summer trade is nowhere near as busy. Among summer outdoor activities are **cycling** along thirty miles of excellent trails – including the former railroad tracks, long since paved over – and **rafting** on the rivers to the north (see opposite). The **Sports Complex** (☎208/622-2387) on Sun Valley Road, south of Dollar Road, offers a Nordic ski center, tennis, ice skating, winter sleigh rides and guided horseback rides.

**Ernest Hemingway** completed *For Whom The Bell Tolls* as a celebrity guest in the resort in 1939, and lived in Ketchum for the last two years of his life, before his suicide; his very plain grave can be found in the town cemetery.

### Practicalities

There's a free in-town shuttle service between 7.30am and midnight. Ketchum's **visitor center**, at no. 400 on the short Main Street, runs a free reservation service for **accommodation** (daily 9am–5pm; ☎208/726-3423 or 1-800/634-3347; *sunval@micron.net*). Room rates everywhere are highest in the heavy summer and winter seasons. You can save a bundle by staying in nearby Hailey, twelve miles south of Ketchum.

The luxurious 600-room *Sun Valley Lodge* resort is very expensive in season, though worth every cent in spring and fall (☎208/622-4111 or 1-800/786-8259; winter & summer ⑦/⑧, spring & fall ④); also run by the resort is the *Sun Valley Inn* (winter & summer ⑤–⑦). Cheaper options in Ketchum include the comfortable, welcoming *Lift Tower Lodge,* 703 S Main St (☎208/726-5163 or 1-800/462-8646; ③), the well-appointed *Ketchum Korral Motor Lodge* (☎208/726-3510 or 1-800/657-2657; ④/⑤), and the slightly more luxurious *Best Western Tyrolean Lodge* (☎208/726-5336 or 1-800/333-7912; ⑤). The *Dining Room* at the *Sun Valley Lodge* (☎208/622-2150) serves Idaho's best and most elegant **meals**, while *China Pepper*, in the 511 Building at Fifth and Leadville (☎208/726-0959), has superb Asian specialties, such as Thai ginger rolls. At the *Ketchum Grill*, 520 East Ave (☎208/726-4460 or 726-7434), you'll find plenty of vegetarian options for good value. The village also has a number of decent **drinking** spots. *Whiskey Jacques* at 206 N Main St (☎208/726-3200) is a good local watering hole.

## Sawtooth National Recreation Area

North of Ketchum and Sun Valley, Hwy-75 climbs through ever-larger mountains and forests – where Clint Eastwood filmed *Pale Rider* – to top out after twenty miles at **Galena Summit**, one of the most glorious panoramic viewpoints in all the Rockies. Spreading out far below, the meadows of the Sawtooth Valley stretch northwards, bearing minimal traces of the long-abandoned gold-mining settlements. The simple road meanders beside the young **Salmon River**, whose headwaters rise somewhere in the forbidding icy peaks to the south; and the serrated ridge of the **Sawtooth Mountains** forms an impenetrable barrier along the western horizon.

Backpackers are guaranteed solitude in these high fastnesses, dotted with remote lakes – pick up details of primitive **camping** sites and hiking trails at the **Sawtooth**

**National Recreation Area headquarters** (☎208/726-7672 or 1-800/260-5970), eight miles out of Ketchum.

Beside **Redfish Lake**, just east of Hwy-75, sixty miles north of Sun Valley, the attractive and deliberately low-key *Redfish Lake Lodge* offers accommodation in motel rooms and cabins (Memorial Day–early Oct; ☎208/774-3536; ③–⑤).

At tiny **STANLEY**, a few miles north, dirt roads radiate from the junction of Hwy-75 and Hwy-21, with assorted Western-style **motels** such as the historic *Sawtooth Hotel* (☎208/774-9947; ②/③) on Ace of Diamonds Avenue, which has a good **restaurant** for breakfast and lunch, and *Valley Creek Motel* (☎208/774-3606; ④/⑤). The *Rod and Gun Club Saloon*, on Ace of Diamonds Avenue, is a characterful local **bar** that also serves food. Out of season Stanley virtually closes up; in summer its main activity is organizing **rafting trips** (check in advance; weather conditions – such as heavy snowmelt – can make conditions too dangerous). Operators include The River Company (☎208/774-2244).

# Boise

Anywhere in the US, the verdant community of **BOISE** (pronounced *Boy-zee*) would come across as a bustling and likeable small city; located in arid southwestern Idaho, it's all the more appealing. The town straddles I-84, just 350 miles from Salt Lake City to the southeast and a trifling 490 miles from Seattle in the northwest.

The town grew up under the protective wing of Fort Boise, established in 1862 for the benefit of pioneers using the Oregon Trail. After adapting (or misspelling) the name originally given to the area by French trappers – *les bois*, the woods – the earliest residents boosted the town's appearance by planting hundreds more trees.

## The Town

To explore Boise's compact, friendly **downtown**, start at the central **State Capitol** at Jefferson Street and Capitol Boulevard. This squat replica of the national capitol exhibits gemstones such as the star garnet, found only in Indo-China and Idaho. **Old Boise Historic District**, nearby, is an elegant area of brick houses, shops and restaurants which has undergone major restoration. The **Idaho Basque Museum and Cultural Center** at 607 Grove St (Tues–Fri 10am–3pm, Sat 11am–2pm; free) is located in a former boarding house that was for many years home to Basque immigrants fresh from northern Spain, who came to central Idaho, with its similarly rocky terrain, to employ their shepherding skills. The museum traces the Basque cultural heritage, and hosts regular traditional dance nights.

It's impossible not to be impressed by the contrast between the urban greenery and the humpy desert hills all around. The city is rightly proud of the **Greenbelt**, almost ten miles of paths that crisscross the tranquil **Boise River** to link nine separate parks. In **Julia Davis Park**, the **Idaho Historical Museum** (Mon–Sat 9am–5pm, Sun 1–5pm; free) chronicles Native American and Basque history, as well as the experience of the Chinese miners of the 1870s and 1880s, who picked over mines long since abandoned by whites. The state legislature, controlled by unreconstructed Confederates who had fled the South after the Civil War, did nothing to stamp out racial violence, and forced the Chinese to pay $4 a month, a considerable amount at the time, just to live in the Territory.

The **Old Idaho Penitentiary** nestles beneath desert hills at 2445 Old Penitentiary Rd, off Warm Springs Avenue (summer daily 10am–6pm; rest of year daily noon–5pm; $4). This imposing sandstone-walled citadel feels like a desolate outpost, despite being just a mile from downtown. Constructed in 1870 to hold robbers, rustlers and other desperadoes, it remained open until 1974. Self-guided tours take you through the cramped solitary confinement unit, and the gallows room where the last hanging in Idaho was carried out in 1957. Restoration work has sensibly avoided trying to make this brutal prison look more palatable. A small museum displays confiscated weapons and mugshots of former inmates, including one Harry Orchard, who blew up the state governor in 1905 and served out his sentence here, dying in 1954 at the age of 88. Oddly adjacent to the penitentiary, the **Idaho Botanical Gardens** (April 15–Oct 15 Mon–Fri 10am–3pm, Sat & Sun 10am–5pm), has nine themed gardens.

### Practicalities

Greyhound **buses** stop at 1212 W Bannock St and Amtrak **trains** pull in at 1701 Eastover Terrace; both are on the edge of downtown. The **visitor center** is at 168 N Ninth St (Mon–Fri 8.30am–5pm; ☎208/344-7777 or 1-800/635-5240). Downtown's most interesting **place to stay** is the landmark *Idanha Hotel*, 928 Main St (☎208/342-3611 or 1-800/798-3611; ③), topped by a castellated mansard roof and turrets, and today owned by the Maharishi Mahesh Yogi's Heaven on Earth Inns Corp. The *Idaho Heritage Inn B&B*, 109 W Idaho St (☎208/342-8066), is a lovely place to stay in a historic building. Near the university, try the *Boisean*, 1300 S Capitol Blvd (☎208/343-3645 or 1-800/365-3645; ②/③). For a budget choice the *Seven-K Motel*, 3633 Chinden Blvd (☎208/343-7723; ②/③), isn't bad. The *Americana Kampground*, 3600 Americana Terrace (☎208/344-5733), is a little pricey at $17 but right in the heart of town, across the river from Ann Morrison Park.

You're spoilt for choice when it comes to **eating** in Boise. *Milford's Fish House* in the Eighth Street Marketplace, 405 S Eighth St (☎208/342-8382), serves good fresh fish and has a wide selection of beers, while the *Brick Oven Beanery,* on the Grove (☎208/342-3456), has a good range of down-home fare, from salads to pot pies. *Susan's*, at 219 N Tenth St (208/344-9477), is a bakery, deli and coffeehouse with Internet access. Popular among locals is *Goldy's*, 108 South Capitol (☎208/345-4100), where you can create your own breakfast combos. Of the city's many good **ethnic restaurants**, try *Aladdin*, 111 Broadway (☎208/368-0880), for Egyptian food and belly dancing on Fridays; *Bar Gernika*, 202 Capitol Blvd (☎208/344-2175), for Basque; or *Bangkok House*, 624 W Idaho St (☎208/336-0018), for Thai. Boise also has its own **microbrewery**, the happening *Table Rock* at 705 Fulton St (☎208/342-0944).

# Northern Idaho

The wilderness peaks and pinnacles of the Sawtooth, Salmon River and Clearwater mountains make traveling through the heart of Idaho impossible. There are only two routes from south to north: up the eastern fringe from Idaho Falls, or, more enjoyably, along US-95 via Hwy-55 out of Boise. At first barren and infertile, not until just before Lewiston does the scenery unfold into superb pastoral farmland. The **Nez Percé** hunted buffalo, gathered berries and fished here for hundreds of years, until gold was discovered and they were forced to beat a bloody retreat.

The heavily forested far north of the Idaho Panhandle is broken by hundreds of deep glacial lakes, the largest of which have resort towns such as **Coeur d'Alene** and **Sandpoint**. While not major destinations, they can make good one- or two-day stops.

## Hell's Canyon Region

From the busy but not over-commercialized little water-sports resort of **McCALL**, 110 miles north of Boise, Hwy-55 climbs steadily to merge with US-95 and follow the turbulent **Little Salmon River**. Just south of the hamlet of Riggins, thirty miles on, comes the only good opportunity to see **Hell's Canyon** from Idaho. With an average depth of 5500ft this is the deepest river gorge in the USA, though its low-relief formation,

## THE NEZ PERCÉ

The first whites to encounter the **Nez Percé** were the weak, hungry and disease-ridden Lewis and Clark expedition in 1805. Though the Native Americans had the explorers at their mercy, they gave them food and shelter, and cared for their animals until the party was ready to carry on westward.

Relations between the Nez Percé (so called by French-Canadian trappers because of their shell-pierced noses) and whites remained excellent for over half a century – until the discovery of gold, and white pressure for space, led the government to persuade some renegade Nez Percé to sign a treaty in 1863, taking away three-quarters of tribal land. As settlers started to move into the hunting grounds of the Wallowa Valley in the early 1870s, the majority of the Nez Percé, under the leadership of **Chief Joseph**, refused to recognize the agreement. In 1877, after much vacillation, the government decided to enact its terms and gave the tribe thirty days to leave. The Nez Percé asked for more time to round up their livestock and avoid crossing the Snake River at a dangerous time; the general in charge refused.

The ensuing tensions resulted in skirmishes that caused the deaths of a handful of settlers – the first whites ever to be attacked by Nez Percé – and a large army force began to gather to round up the Nez Percé. Chief Joseph then embarked upon the famous **Retreat of the Nez Percé**. Around 250 warriors (protecting twice as many women, children and old people) outmaneuvered army columns many times their size, launching frequent guerrilla attacks in a series of hair-breadth escapes. After four months and 1700 miles, the Nez Percé were cornered just thirty miles from the relative safety of the Canadian border. Chief Joseph then (reportedly) made his much-quoted speech of surrender:

> *Hear me my chiefs! I am tired. My heart is sick and sad. From where the sun now stands I will fight no more forever.*

The Native Americans had been told that they would be put on a reservation in Idaho; instead, they were taken to Oklahoma, where the marshy land caused a malaria epidemic. Chief Joseph died in 1904 on the Colville reservation in Washington, but decades later the Nez Percé were allowed to return to the northwest, where today some 1500 live in a reservation between Lewiston and Grangeville – a minute fraction of their original territory.

The **Nez Percé National Historic Park**, containing 24 separate sites, is spread over 12,000 square miles of north central Idaho. At the visitor center in **Spalding**, ten miles east of Lewiston (☎208/843-2261), the **Museum of Nez Percé Culture** (summer daily 8am–5.30pm; rest of year daily 8am–4.30pm; free) is good on arts and crafts but weak on history; the heavily ravined **White Bird Battlefield**, seventy miles further south on US-95, was where the Native Americans inflicted 34 deaths on the US Army at no cost to themselves, in the first major battle of the retreat. Further exhibits on Nez Percé history can be found in the Wallowa County Museum in Joseph, Oregon (see p.1073).

hemmed in by a series of gradually ascending false peaks, means that it lacks the impact of the steep-walled Grand Canyon. Nevertheless, it is impressive, with Oregon's Wallowa and Eagle Cap ranges rising behind it and the river glimmering far down below. Hwy-241 leads towards the overlooks; the final few miles of dirt road require a 4WD vehicle and permission from the Riggins forest ranger office on Hwy-95 (Mon–Fri 8am–5pm; ☎208/628-3916). The canyon is also accessible by road from Oregon (see p.1074) and by boat from Lewiston.

**RIGGINS** itself reclines in a steeply rising T-shaped canyon. This is prime **whitewater rafting** country, and outfitters, spread along a one-mile stretch of the one-street village, outnumber cafes and shops. The **Chamber of Commerce** (☎208/628-3778) has details. From Riggins, US-95 heads north along the Salmon River Valley for thirty miles to the rumpled terrain around **White Bird**, the start of Nez Percé country.

There are few compelling reasons to visit industrial **LEWISTON**, 110 miles north of Riggins (which was Territorial capital for one brief year before Boise took over). One is to drive down the old road into town from the top of Lewiston Hill, just north – what seems like an intricate network of roads crisscrossing a series of mounds is, in fact, a single tarmac ribbon, which twists and turns for several miles down the steep hillside. Another is the **Lewiston Round-up**, a massive rodeo held on the second weekend of September.

For the rest of the year, the main reason to subject yourself to the nasty smells emanating from the local paper mills is for the fantastic journey down Hell's Canyon on the Salmon River. Boats sail past abandoned mine shafts and Native American caves, with mountain goats, bobcats, snakes and birds of prey adding further interest. Of the various outfitters, Snake River Adventures, 227 Snake River Ave (☎1-800/262-8874), offers the best value: an all-day, wet-and-wild trip to Granite Creek costs around $103 including lunch. Contact the **visitor center**, 111 Main St (Mon–Fri 8am–5pm, Sat–Sun 10am–4pm; ☎208/743-3531 or 1-800/473-3543), for other options.

## Moscow

The thirty miles of US-95 between Lewiston and **MOSCOW** wind through the beautiful rolling hillsides of the fertile Palouse Valley – a patchwork of green lentils, bright yellow rape, soft white wheat and (100ft-thick) black topsoil. Roadside red barns and farmhouses complete a marvellous rural picture.

With ten thousand year-round residents and a similar number of **University of Idaho** students, Moscow is a friendly, culturally rich town that makes a good overnight stop. Bookstores, galleries, bars and sidewalk cafes line up along tree-shaded, part-pedestrianized **Main Street**, the only shopping thoroughfare. Theater, music and avant-garde cinema are on offer throughout the year, while summer sees a sprinkling of big-budget arts festivals.

The town's name might raise a few eyebrows, but it's pretty ordinary compared to the first settlers' choice of Hog Heaven. A proposal to rename it Paradise was seen as a trifle over-the-top; the present title comes from one early resident's hometown in Pennsylvania.

### Practicalities

Moscow's **visitor center** is at 411 S Main St (☎208/882-1800 or 1-800/380-1801); Northwest Trailways (a Greyhound affiliate) stops at the basic *Royal Motor Inn*, 120 W Sixth St (☎208/882-2581; ②). For a bit more comfort, try the *Mark IV Motor Inn*, 414 N Main St (☎208/882-7557 or 1-800/833-4240; ③), which has a nice pool and hot tub. The *West 4th Bar and Grill*, in the *Moscow Hotel*, 313 S Main St (☎208/882-0743), offers good **food** served in a nice atmosphere.

## Coeur d'Alene

When US Army Chief of Staff William Tecumseh Sherman set up camp in 1877 on the present site of **COEUR D'ALENE**, fifty miles north of Moscow on US-95, he found the sparkling blue lake, surrounded by wild flower borders and lush forest, so appealing that he ordered a fort to be built here. Another large structure now stands on the beautiful shoreline of long, narrow Lake Coeur d'Alene; looking not unlike an office block, the phenomenally expensive **Coeur d'Alene Resort**, which boasts the world's only floating golf green, completely dominates downtown (☎208/765-4000 or 1-800/688-5253; ⑤–⑨). Not surprisingly, it's a bitter local debating point.

**Downtown** is unremarkable, verging on tacky, with its sidewalk cafes and pricey shops. Directly east of the resort, a small public beach backs onto a balmy park area. Scenic **lake cruises** leave from the nearby City Dock (three daily in summer; $12.75; ☎208/765-4000). You can also see the lake on a twenty-minute **sea plane flight** from here, for $40 with Brooks Seaplane (☎208/664-2842).

Greyhound uses the **bus station** at 1923 N Fourth St, a mile north of downtown. There's a **visitor center** on River Bend Road, in the factory outlet complex (Mon–Sat 10am–4pm, Sun 11am–4pm; ☎208/773-4080 or 1-800/292-2553). Along Sherman Avenue, the *Flamingo Motel* at no. 718 (☎208/664-2159 or 1-800/955-2159; ④) and the *Blackwell House B&B* at no. 820 (☎208/664-0656 or 1-800/899-0656; ④–⑥) provide centrally located **rooms**. *Third Street Cantina,* at no. 201 (☎208/664-0693), serves authentic Mexican **food** in the old railway depot. *Beverly's* is an upmarket choice for seafood and meat in the *Coeur d'Alene Resort* (☎208/765-4000). *T W Fisher's* is a friendly brewpub, at 204 N Second St (☎208/664-2739).

### East from Coeur d'Alene on I-90

Fifty miles along the interstate towards Missoula, Montana (see p.788), the run-down streets, thriftshops and basic bars of **WALLACE** evoke images of its silver mining days. The 75-minute **Sierra Silver Mine Tour** leaves from 420 N Fifth St every half-hour, on a fun trolley-car trip that takes you a thousand feet underground (summer daily 9am–4pm; $7). *Sweet's Cafe and Lounge*, 310 Sixth St (☎208/556-4661), serves large **lunches** to a local crowd.

## Sandpoint

Forty-four miles north of Coeur d'Alene in the shadows of the spiky Selkirk Mountains, **SANDPOINT**, northern Idaho's most attractive resort, is at the northwestern end of Lake Pend Oreille (pronounced "Pon-duh-ray"). Smaller and less commercialized than Coeur d'Alene, Sandpoint's lazy downtown is brightened by **Cedar Street Bridge Public Market**, a covered mall of stalls, shops and cafes overlooking placid Sandy Creek. At the south end of the lake, **Farragut State Park**, 13400 Ranger Rd (☎208/ 683-2425; cars $3), a former naval training base, is a popular spot for hiking, camping and the like.

**Accommodation** possibilities include the comfortable *Lakeside Inn*, beside the lovely white sandy beach at 106 Bridge St (☎208/263-3717 or 1-800/543-8126; ④/⑤); the *K2 Inn at Sandpoint*, 501 N Fourth Ave (☎208/263-3441; ③); and the *Whitaker House B&B*, a very nice B&B on the lakefront at 410 Railroad Ave (☎208/265-7930 or 1-888/265-7930; ④). Amtrak passes through early in the morning in both directions.

# CHAPTER TWELVE

# THE SOUTHWEST

T he four sparsely populated Southwestern desert states of **NEW MEXICO, ARIZONA, UTAH** and **NEVADA** are extraordinary, unforgettable and unique. They stretch from Texas to California across an elemental landscape ranging from towering monoliths of stark red-sandstone to snowcapped mountains, on a high desert plateau that repeatedly splits open to reveal yawning canyons. The raw power of the scenery, uninterrupted from horizon to horizon, is overwhelming, and is complemented by the emphatic presence of numerous Native American cultures and the palpable legacy of America's Wild West frontier.

Among the earliest inhabitants were the **Anasazi**, the remains of whose cliff palaces and cities are scattered throughout the region. Though they abandoned these settlements around seven hundred years ago, their direct descendants, the **Pueblo** peoples of New Mexico and the **Hopi** in Arizona, still lead much the same lifestyle, in more or less the same places.

Less sedentary tribes, such as the **Navajo** and the **Apache**, began to migrate to the Southwest early in the sixteenth century. They adopted local agricultural and craft techniques and appropriated vast tracts of territory, which they in turn soon had to defend against bands of European immigrants. The first such, in 1540, was a party of **Spanish** explorers led by Coronado, who spent two years searching for mythical El Dorado-style cities of gold. Sixty years later, Hispanic colonists founded the province of **New Mexico**, an ill-defined region that covered not only all of the Southwest but much of modern California and Colorado; many of the Catholic missions they established remain intact. Not until 1848 – by which time New Mexico had spent thirty years as a neglected backwater of the newly independent nation of Mexico – was the region forcibly taken over by the **United States**. Almost immediately, large numbers of outsiders began to pass through on their way to Gold Rush California.

Thereafter, increasingly violent confrontations took place between the US government and the Native Americans. The entire **Navajo** population was rounded up and forcibly removed to the barren plains of eastern New Mexico in 1864 (though they were soon allowed to return to northeastern Arizona), and the **Apache**, under warrior chiefs Cochise and Geronimo, fought extended battles with the US cavalry. Though the nominal intention was to open up Indian lands to newly American settlers, few ever succeeded in extracting a living from this harsh terrain.

One exception were the **Mormons** (or Church of Christ of Latter Day Saints), whose flight from religious persecution brought them by the late 1840s to the alkaline basin

---

### ACCOMMODATION PRICE CODES

All accommodation prices in this book have been coded using the symbols below. Note that prices are for the least expensive double rooms in each establishment. For a full explanation see p.37 in Basics.

| | | |
|---|---|---|
| ① up to $30 | ④ $60–80 | ⑦ $130–175 |
| ② $30–45 | ⑤ $80–100 | ⑧ $175–250 |
| ③ $45–60 | ⑥ $100–130 | ⑨ $250+ |

of Utah's Great Salt Lake. Through sheer hard work, and the cooperative management of limited water resources, they established what amounted to an independent country, with outlying communities all over the Southwest. Even here they met with resistance, and until the Civil War intervened, there was a real possibility that the US might declare war on them. They still constitute seventy percent of Utah's population and maintain virtual control of the state's government.

Despite their common heritage, each of the four Southwestern states remains quite distinct. **New Mexico** bears the most obvious traces of long-term settlement, the Native American pueblos of the north coexisting alongside towns such as Santa Fe, Albuquerque and Taos, which clearly retain their Spanish colonial identity. In **Arizona**, the history of the Wild West is more conspicuous, in towns such as Tombstone, site of the legendary shoot-out at the OK Corral. Over a third of the state belongs to Native American tribes, such as the Apache, Hopi and Navajo, most of whom live in the red-rock lands of the northeast corner, on flat-topped rocky outcrops known as mesas, far out in the deserts, or amid the splendor typified by the **Canyon de Chelly** and **Monument Valley**.

The canyon country of northern Arizona – even the immense **Grand Canyon** – won't prepare you for the uninhabited but compelling landscape of **southern Utah**, where **Zion** and **Bryce Canyons** are just the best known of a string of national parks and monuments. **Moab**, poised in the east between majestic **Canyonlands** and the surreal **Arches**, has become a top destination for youthful outdoors enthusiasts. **Nevada**, on the other hand, is nothing short of desolate; gamblers are lured in the millions by the bright lights of **Las Vegas**, but away from the casinos there's little to see or do.

You can count on warm sunshine anywhere in the Southwest for nine months of the year, with incredible sunsets most evenings. Summer is the peak tourist season, for no good reason – air temperatures topping 100°F can make outdoor life unbearable, while in late summer awesome thunderstorms sweep in without warning, causing flash floods and forest fires. By October, perhaps the best time to come, the crowds are gone and in the mountains and canyons the leaves turn red and gold. Winter brings snow to higher elevations – there's excellent skiing in **northern Utah** and in the **Sangre de Cristo Mountains** of New Mexico – while spring sees wild flowers bloom in otherwise barren desert. Note that the climate varies sharply according to elevation, with mountains often 30°F cooler than the plains.

More than almost anywhere in the US, the backcountry wildernesses of the Southwest are ideal for (well-planned) **camping** and backpacking expeditions. It's vital to be prepared for the harshness of the desert, where even the most basic needs can be hard to fill: always carry water, and if you venture off the beaten track let someone know where you're going and when you'll return (see p.44 for more information).

Unless you have your own vehicle, many of the most fascinating corners of the region are utterly inaccessible. Scheduled public **transportation** runs almost exclusively between the big cities – which are not at all where you should be spending your time.

# NEW MEXICO

Settled in turn by Native Americans, Spaniards, Mexicans and Yankees, **NEW MEXICO** is among the most ethnically and culturally diverse of all the United States. Each successive group has built upon the legacy of its predecessors; their various histories and achievements are closely intertwined, and in some ways the late-coming white Americans from the north and east have had comparatively little impact. Signs of the region's rich heritage are everywhere, from ancient pictographs and cliff dwellings to the design of the state's license plates, taken from a **Zia** Indian symbol for the sun – the one near-constant fact of life in this arid land.

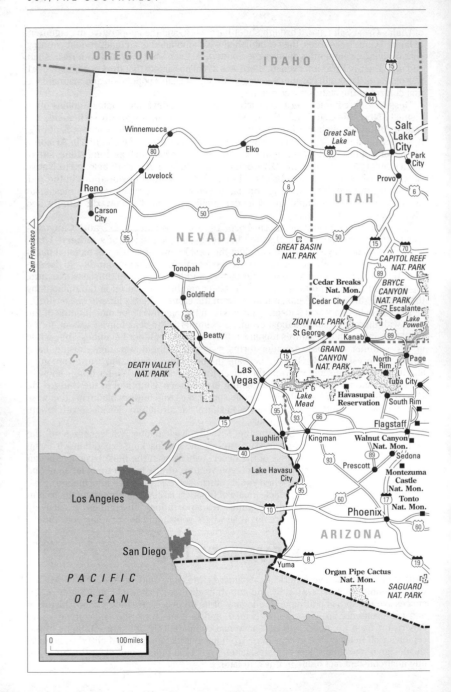

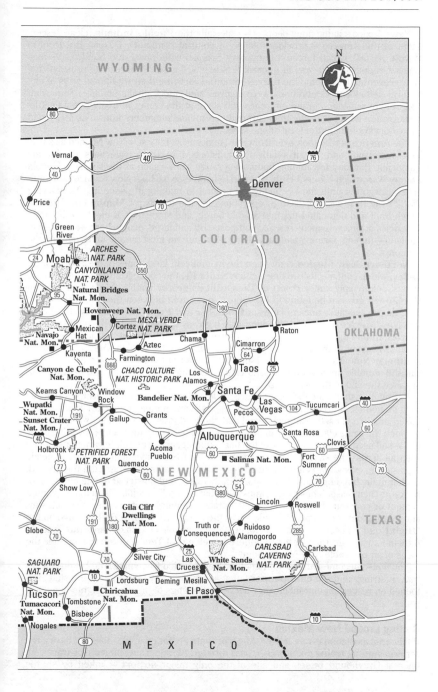

New Mexico's indigenous peoples – especially the **Pueblo Indians**, clear descendants of the **Anasazi** – provide a sense of cultural continuity. Despite the **Pueblo Revolt** of 1680, which forced a temporary Spanish withdrawal into Mexico, the missionary endeavor here was in general less brutal than elsewhere. The proselytizing padres eventually co-opted the natives without destroying their traditional ways of life, as local deities and celebrations were incorporated into Catholic practice. Somewhat bizarrely to outsiders, grand churches still stand at the center of many Pueblo settlements, often adjacent to the underground ceremonial chambers known as *kivas*, and almost always built in the local adobe style.

The Americans who took over from the Mexicans in 1848 saw New Mexico as a useless wasteland, and left it relatively undisturbed in their eagerness to develop California. But for a few mining booms and range wars – such as the so-called Lincoln County War, which brought **Billy the Kid** to fame (see p.832) – New Mexico was more or less forgotten until the US finally got around to making it a state in 1912. During World War II, it was the base of operations for the top-secret **Manhattan Project**, which built and detonated the first atomic bomb, and since then it has been home to America's premier weapons research outposts. By and large, people here work close to the land – mining, farming and ranching – with tourism increasingly underpinning the economy.

**Northern New Mexico** centers on the magnificent landscapes of the **Rio Grande Valley**, which contains its two finest cities: **Santa Fe**, the adobe-fronted capital, and the artists' colony and winter resort of **Taos**, with its nearby pueblo. More than a dozen **Pueblo** villages can be found in the mountainous area between the two, while to the west lie the evocative ancient ruins at **Bandelier** and **Puyé**. The broad swath of **central New Mexico** along I-40 – the interstate highway that succeeded the old **Route 66** – pivots around the state's biggest city, **Albuquerque**, with the extraordinary mesa-top Pueblo village of **Ácoma** ("Sky City") an hour's drive to the west. In wild and wide-open **southern New Mexico**, deep **Carlsbad Caverns** are the main attraction, while you can still stumble upon old mining and cattle-ranching towns that have somehow hung on since the end of the Wild West.

For many visitors, the defining feature of New Mexico is its **adobe architecture**, as seen on homes, churches and even shopping malls and motels. Adobe bricks are a sun-baked mixture of earth, sand, charcoal and chopped grass or straw, set with a mortar of much the same composition, and then plastered over with mud and straw. The color of the soil used dictates the color of the final building, and thus subtle variations can be seen all across the state. However, adobe is a far from convenient material: it needs replastering every few years and turns to mud when water seeps up from the ground, so that many buildings have to be sporadically raised and bolstered by the insertion of rocks at their base. These days, most of what looks like adobe is actually painted cement or concrete, but even this looks attractive enough in its own semi-kitsch way, and hunting out such superb old adobes as the remote **Santuario de Chimayó** on the "High Road" between Taos and Santa Fe, the formidable church of **San Francisco de Asis** in Ranchos de Taos, or the multitiered dwellings of **Taos Pueblo**, can provide the focus of an enjoyable New Mexico tour.

You'll also become familiar with another New Mexico trademark, the bright-red *ristras*, or strings of dried **chili peppers**, that adorn doorways throughout the state; festooned on restaurant entrances, they serve as warnings of the fiery delights that await within.

## Getting around New Mexico

Public transportation is rare in New Mexico; Santa Fe, for example, does not have a rail service. Amtrak **trains** do, however, pass through Albuquerque, pit stop for trans-continental Greyhound **buses** and site of the only major **airport** – linked by shuttle services with the rest of the state. Texas' **El Paso** (see p.669) is a more convenient transportation hub for Carlsbad. A few companies offer guided **coach tours** in the Santa Fe and Taos area, but as usual getting around is really best done by **car**.

# Northern New Mexico

New Mexico's mountainous north is the New Mexico of popular imagination, with its pastel colors, vivid desert landscape and adobe architecture. Even state capital **Santa Fe**, the one real city, is with well under 100,000 residents hardly metropolitan in scale, and the narrow streets of its small, historic center, though thronged with tourists, retain the feel of long-gone days. Ranging along the headwaters of the Rio Grande 75 miles northeast, the amiable frontier town of **Taos** – immortalized by Georgia O'Keeffe and D H Lawrence – is remarkable chiefly for the stacked dwellings of neighboring **Taos Pueblo**.

An hour's drive west from Taos or Santa Fe brings you to **Bandelier National Monument**, where ancient cliff dwellings were carved out of the same forested volcanic plateau that now holds the eerie **Los Alamos** National Weapons Lab. Alternatively, the hills to the east of the Rio Grande hold a succession of characterful Hispanic hamlets, strung along a scenic mountain highway known as the **High Road**.

## Santa Fe

Since the early 1980s, **SANTA FE** has been the chic-est destination in the US, consistently voted the country's most popular city by upmarket travelers. That appeal rests on a very solid basis: it's one of America's oldest and most beautiful cities, founded by Spanish missionaries as their northernmost colonial capital in 1609, a full ten years before the Pilgrims reached Plymouth Rock. Spread across a high plateau at the foot of the stunning Sangre de Cristo Mountains, New Mexico's capital still glories in the adobe houses and Baroque churches of its original architects, while its newer museums and galleries attract art-lovers from all over the world.

As upward of a million and a half tourists every year descend upon a town of just sixty thousand inhabitants, Santa Fe has inevitably grown somewhat overblown; long-term residents bemoan what's been lost, while first-time visitors are inclined to wonder what all the fuss is about. The depressing urban sprawl as you approach town from the interstate makes for a lousy introduction, while the rigorous insistence that every downtown building should look like a seventeenth-century Spanish colonial palace takes a bit of getting used to. This is the only city in the world where what at first glance appears to be a perfectly preserved ancient adobe turns out to be a high-rise parking lot, and it would be illegal to build a gas station that didn't resemble an Indian prayer chamber.

There's still a lot to like about Santa Fe, however. Though Santa Fe style may have become something of a cliché, that cliché is changing; the pastel-painted, wooden coyotes that were the obligatory souvenir ten years ago have for example been replaced by cast-iron sculptures of Kokopelli, the hunch-backed Anasazi flute-player. In a town where the *Yellow Pages* list over 250 art galleries, you'll get plenty of opportunities to buy one.

### Arrival, information and getting around
Despite its fame, Santa Fe is well off the beaten track. Most out-of-state visitors fly into Albuquerque, and either rent a vehicle at the airport for the hour's drive up to Santa Fe, or catch one of the half-dozen daily Gray Line shuttle vans (☎1-800/256-8991; $25). **Buses** from all over the Southwest to the Greyhound terminal at 858 St Michael's Drive, a long way from the town's central plaza, include four daily buses to and from

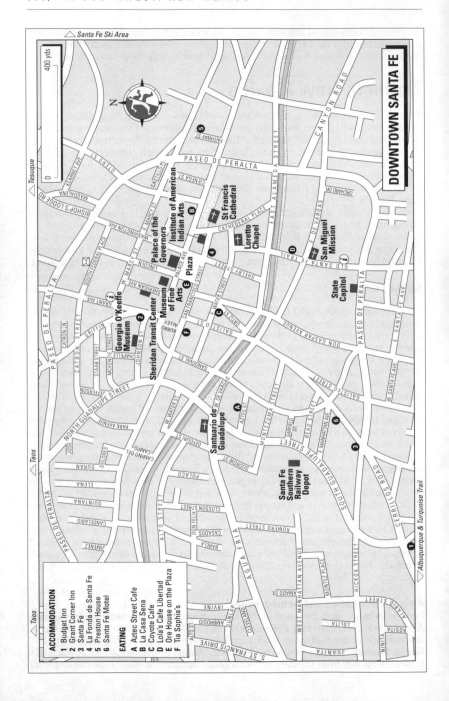

DOWNTOWN SANTA FE

△ Santa Fe Ski Area

400 yds

N

PASEO DE PERALTA

St Francis Cathedral

Institute of American Indian Arts

Loretto Chapel

San Miguel Mission

Palace of the Governors

Plaza

Museum of Fine Arts

Georgia O'Keeffe Museum

Sheridan Transit Center

State Capitol

Santuario de Guadalupe

Santa Fe Southern Railway Depot

△ Tesuque

△ Taos

△ Taos

▷ Albuquerque & Turquoise Trail

ACCOMMODATION
1 Budget Inn
2 Grant Corner Inn
3 Santa Fe
4 La Fonda de Santa Fe
5 Preston House
6 Santa Fe Motel

EATING
A Aztec Street Cafe
B La Casa Sena
C Coyote Cafe
D Lola's Cafe Libertad
E Ore House on the Plaza
F Tia Sophia's

Albuquerque (☎505/471-0008; $12). There's no direct **rail** link, but Lamy Shuttle vans (☎505/982-8829) meet Amtrak trains to Lamy, seventeen miles to the southeast.

The city **visitor center**, two blocks northwest of the plaza in the lobby of the Convention Center, 201 W Marcy St (Mon–Fri 8am–5pm; ☎505/984-6760 or 1-800/777-2489), stocks a very limited selection of brochures, but the New Mexico Department of Tourism, 491 Old Santa Fe Trail (Mon–Fri 8am–7pm; ☎505/827-4000 or 1-800/545-2040), has racks of material on the whole state.

Most of what there is to see lies within walking distance of the plaza, but it's worth knowing about the Santa Fe Trails **bus** service, based at the Sheridan Transit Center, a block northwest of the plaza on Sandoval Street (Mon–Fri 6.30am–10.30pm, Sat 8am–8pm; ☎505/438-1464; flat fare 50¢). Routes #21–23 run up Cerrillos Road, while route #10 loops between the plaza and the outlying museums, half-hourly in summer and hourly in winter. Santa Fe's only **taxi** company is Capital City Cabs (☎505/438-0000); **bikes** can be rented at Palace Bike Rentals, 409 E Palace Ave (☎505/986-0455). For a **walking tour** of town, contact Afoot in Santa Fe, based in the *Inn at Loretto*, 211 Old Santa Fe Trail (daily 9.30am & 1.30pm; ☎505/983-3701; $10).

## Accommodation

Even in winter, you won't find a **room** within walking distance of downtown for under $50, and in summer – when every bed is frequently taken – there's little under $80. The main road in from I-25, Cerrillos Road, holds most of the motels and the one hostel. If you get stuck, call Santa Fe Central Reservations (☎505/983-8200 or 1-800/776-7669) or Accommodations Hotline (daily 4–10pm; ☎505/983-6565 or 1-800/338-6877).

The most appealing **campgrounds** nearby are in the Santa Fe National Forest, starting seven miles up Hwy-475, northeast of town (summer only; ☎505/438-7840).

**Budget Inn**, 725 Cerrillos Rd at Don Diego (☎505/982-5952 or 1-800/288-7600). The most central chain motel; large, clean and a mile or so from the plaza. ⑤.

**El Rey Inn**, 1862 Cerrillos Rd at St Michael's Drive (☎505/982-1931 or 1-800/521-1349). Most characterful of the Cerrillos Rd motels, with stylish Southwestern-style rooms, nice suites and a pool. ④.

**Grant Corner Inn**, 122 Grant Ave (☎505/983-6678 or 1-800/964-9003). Incongruous downtown clapboard B&B, alongside the Georgia O'Keeffe Museum, where guests enjoy considerable luxury, and lavish breakfasts. Not all rooms are ensuite. ⑤.

**Hotel Santa Fe**, 1501 Paseo de Peralta at Cerillos Rd (☎505/982-1200 or 1-800/825-9876). Attractive, very comfortable adobe hotel (just) within walking distance of the plaza, owned and run by Picuris Pueblo Indians and featuring its own *Blue Corn Cafe*. ⑦.

**La Fonda de Santa Fe**, 100 E San Francisco St (☎505/982-5511 or 1-800/523-5002). Gorgeous old inn on the southeast corner of the plaza. Marking the end of the Santa Fe Trail, it features hand-painted murals and stained glass throughout. Each opulently furnished room is different, and there's a good restaurant, plus a lounge with live entertainment and a rooftop bar. ⑧.

**Preston House**, 106 Faithway St (☎505/982-3465). Large Queen Anne B&B inn, in a peaceful garden behind the cathedral, with a mixture of rooms (not all ensuite) and cottages. ⑤.

**Santa Fe International Hostel**, 1412 Cerrillos Rd at Alta Vista (☎505/988-1153). Old-style HI-AYH hostel, housed in ramshackle motel a couple of miles out, which can be damp and cold in winter. Dorm beds for $15, private rooms from $33 for singles to $43 for doubles. ①/②.

**Santa Fe Motel**, 510 Cerrillos Rd at N Guadalupe St (☎505/982-1039 or 1-800/745-9910). Small, quiet, pleasant adobe motel near downtown. No connection to the *Hotel Santa Fe* next door. ⑤.

**Silver Saddle**, 2810 Cerrillos Rd at Siler (☎505/471-7663). Busy, down-to-earth, but surprisingly characterful motel, well out from downtown. ④.

## Downtown Santa Fe: around the plaza

Santa Fe's old central **plaza** is still the focus of town life, especially during the annual **Indian Market** on the weekend after the third Thursday in August, when buyers and craftspeople come from all over the world, and during the Labor Day weekend for the

**Fiestas de Santa Fe**. Apart from an influx of art galleries and stylish restaurants, the web of narrow streets around the plaza has changed little through the centuries. When the Yankees took over in 1848, they neglected the adobes and chose instead to build in wood, but many of the finer adobe houses have survived, thanks in part to a 1930s preservation campaign. Since then almost every non-adobe structure within sight of the plaza has been designed or redecorated to suit the city-mandated Pueblo Revival mode, with oddly sloping, rounded, mud-colored plaster walls supporting roof beams made of thick pine logs (called *vigas*). Santa Fe today, in fact – at least at its core – looks much more like its original Spanish self than it did a hundred years ago.

The main focus of the plaza, and the principal model for Santa Fe's revived architectural unity, is the **Palace of the Governors**, which fills its entire northern side. Part of the Museum of New Mexico (see box, below), this low-slung and initially unprepossessing structure is actually the oldest public building in the US. Originally sod-roofed, it was constructed in 1610 as the headquarters of Spanish colonial administration; the name may now seem misleadingly grand, but the building was once much larger. The well-preserved interior, organized around an open-air courtyard, holds excellent displays on New Mexico's history, plus photos that show that until 1913 the palace itself looked like a typical, formal, territorial building, with a square tower at each corner. Its subsequent adobe "reconstruction" was based on pure conjecture. The arcaded adobe veranda along its front, offering protection from both sun and wind, serves as a market for local Native American crafts-sellers.

Just west of the palace, the **Museum of Fine Arts** is housed in a particularly attractive adobe, with ornamental beams and a cool central courtyard. It's also one of the few major art museums to be established by artists, as opposed to educators or collectors, and focuses on changing exhibits of contemporary painting and sculpture by mostly local artists. The showpiece **Georgia O'Keeffe Museum**, a block northwest at 217 Johnson St, owns the largest collection of O'Keeffes in the world, including many of the desert landscapes she painted near **Abiquiu**, forty miles northwest of Santa Fe, where she lived from 1946 until her death in 1986. In its permanent collection, housed in its first two galleries, some less familiar New York cityscapes make a surprising contrast among the sun-bleached skulls and iconic flowers, as sold in print galleries throughout the Southwest. However, most of the museum is given over to touring exhibitions devoted to differing aspects of O'Keeffe's work, typically on show for three to four months, so there's little guarantee as to which precise pieces may be displayed at any one time.

Across the tiny Santa Fe River to the southwest, three blocks along Guadalupe Street, you'll find a less celebrated but equally attractive little district, centered around the small **Santuario de Guadalupe** (May–Oct Mon–Sat 9am–4pm; Nov–April Mon–Fri 9am–4pm; donation). Complete with a fine Baroque reredos (altarpiece), the shrine was built at the end of the eighteenth century to mark the end of the **Camino Real** highway from Mexico City. Old warehouses and small factory premises nearby, such as the **Sanbusco Centre** on Montezuma Avenue, have been converted to house boutiques, art galleries and restaurants.

---

## THE NEW MEXICO STATE MUSEUMS

The **Museum of New Mexico** is made up of five individual museums, three – the **Palace of the Governors**, the **Museum of Fine Arts** and the **Georgia O'Keeffe Museum** – in the heart of downtown Santa Fe, the other two – the **Museum of International Folk Art** and the **Museum of Indian Arts and Culture** – close together a couple of miles away. Admission to each museum costs $5; a more economical option is a $10 ticket, valid for four days in all five museums. All are open daily except Mondays between 10am and 5pm, and also between 5pm and 8pm on Fridays, when admission is free.

Follow the river upstream, or walk two blocks east from the plaza, and you approach **St Francis Cathedral**, strangely out of place among Santa Fe's earthy adobes, looming at the top of San Francisco Street. The first church west of the Mississippi to be designated a cathedral, it was commissioned in 1869 in the formal – and, frankly, dreary – Romanesque style popular in France by **Archbishop Lamy**, the French-educated title figure in Willa Cather's novel *Death Comes for the Archbishop*. The nearby **Loretto Chapel**, a block away at the start of Old Santa Fe Trail, is known for its so-called "Miraculous Staircase," an elegant spiral built without nails or obvious means of support. During construction, the church's designer is said to have been killed by Lamy's cousin, so that for years there was no way up to the choir loft. According to legend, an unknown carpenter arrived in answer to the nuns' prayers, built the stairs and then disappeared.

Two blocks south, across the river along the Old Santa Fe Trail, is the ancient **San Miguel Mission** (Mon–Sat 10am–4pm, Sun 2.30–4.30pm). Only a few of the massive adobe internal walls survive from the original 1610 building, most of which was destroyed in the 1680 Pueblo Revolt. The chapel is the heart of the old **Barrio de Analco** workers' district, whose many two-hundred-year-old houses now form one of Santa Fe's most appealing residential neighborhoods.

Not far away to the east, gallery-lined **Canyon Road** – which stakes a claim to being the oldest street in the US, dating from Pueblo days – climbs a steady but shallow incline along the riverbed and is lined by dozens of fine adobes.

### The outlying museums

On a slightly raised plateau two miles southeast of the town center, with extensive views of the hills and mountains that almost entirely surround the city, stands Santa Fe's other concentration of museums, reachable by Santa Fe Trails bus #10. The delightful **Museum of International Folk Art**, part of the New Mexico State Museum, focuses on a huge collection of clay figurines and models from around the world, arranged in colorful dioramas that include a Pueblo Feast Day with dancing *kachinas* and camera-clicking tourists. The Hispanic Heritage Wing is an engaging reminder of just how close New Mexico's ties have always been with Mexico itself, while the museum's gift-shop sells some unusual ethnic souvenirs. The **Museum of Indian Arts and Culture**, across the parking lot, also part of the Museum of New Mexico, holds a superb array of Native American pottery, ranging from **Anasazi** and ancient **Pueblo** pieces right up to the works of twentieth-century revivalists, and covers contemporary Southwestern cultures in fascinating detail.

Fifteen miles southwest of the city, three miles from exit 276 off I-25, the **Rancho de las Golondrinas** (June–Sept Wed–Sun 10am–4pm; $4) preserves the eighteenth-century "Ranch of the Swallows." As well as the main adobe farmstead, once a fortified outpost on the Camino Real, this living-history complex includes a water mill, a Penitente chapel, and several other early Hispanic structures – and it's also a lovely spot in its own right.

### Eating

Santa Fe has been renowned as one of America's culinary hot spots since the 1980s, when a stupendous feat of marketing managed to make dishes such as banana-crusted sea bass seem quintessentially Southwestern. It now has more quality restaurants per head than any US city – which doesn't make it any easier to get a reservation at the latest hot spot in summer. Even if you don't pay the wallet-busting prices of the big-name attractions, there's some memorable dining to be had, and the sheer inventiveness of the city's menus makes up for its lack of interesting ethnic alternatives.

**Aztec Cafe**, 317 Aztec St (☎505/983-9464). Counterculture hangout off Galisteo St, offering a travelers' notice board and a nice patio, plus coffees, pastries, light meals and live music.

**Coyote Cafe**, 132 W Water St (☎505/983-1615). Celebrity chef Mark Miller's showcase restaurant, just off the plaza. The à la carte prices are ferocious, but the $40 set meal provides a good-value sampler. For a cheaper taste, try the less-expensive rooftop cafe.

**Geronimo's**, 724 Canyon Rd (☎505/982-1500). Canyon Rd's classiest option, with a streetfront patio and a cool inner courtyard, serves contemporary fusion cuisine with Mexican touches; dinner entrees are mostly $18–27.

**La Casa Sena**, 125 E Palace Ave (☎505/988-9232). Lovely courtyard restaurant, a block from the plaza; zestful Southwestern lunches, with entrees around $10, are the best deal, though the $42 set dinners are consistently good. *La Cantina*, adjoining, is a little cheaper and its staff perform Broadway showsongs as they work.

**Lola's Cafe Libertad**, 311 Old Santa Fe Trail (☎505/983-8372). Modern, attractively decorated Cuban-themed restaurant, just south of the river, offering inexpensive lunches and delicious dinners; the chocolate-flavored *mole* sauce, served on chicken or pork for $13.50, is superb. Closed Mon.

**Mu du noodles**, 1494 Cerrillos Rd (☎505/983-1411). Largely but not exclusively vegetarian place, near the hostel. Its pan-Asian menu may not always be authentic, but it's still tasty. Closed Sun.

**Ore House on the Plaza**, 50 Lincoln Ave (☎505/983-8687). "Nueva Latina" restaurant, where the menu ranges from $5 green-chili stews to elaborate $26 dinner entrees, and the on-plaza location, complete with *ristra*-garlanded balcony, is unbeatable.

**Tecolote Cafe**, 1203 Cerrillos Rd at Cordova (☎505/988-1362). Inconspicuous joint, two miles south of downtown, renowned for great breakfasts – burritos, huevos rancheros and the like. Daily except Mon 7am–2pm.

**Tia Sophia's**, 210 W San Francisco St (☎505/983-9880). Spicy, very inexpensive Mexican diner west of the plaza that's a huge hit with lunching locals. Daily except Mon 7am–2pm.

### Nightlife and entertainment

Santa Fe has the range of **nightlife** you'd expect in a small city rather than a major metropolis, though its cultural scene livens up in summer. For full listings of what's going on, check the free weekly *Reporter* or the "Pasatiempo" section of Friday's *New Mexican*. The much-anticipated Santa Fe Opera season runs through July and August in a magnificent renovated amphitheater seven miles north of town (☎505/986-5900 or 1-800/280-4654).

Some of the most atmospheric places to **drink** in town are in the old hotels – the downstairs lounge and rooftop bar of *La Fonda* on the plaza spring to mind – but otherwise conventional bars are surprisingly few and far between.

**Catamount Bar**, 125 E Water St (☎505/988-7222). Downtown bar with plenty of microbrewed beers on tap, and live rock or blues most nights.

**Cowgirl Hall of Fame**, 319 S Guadalupe St (☎505/982-2565). Very busy country-and-western-themed restaurant and bar, with regular live music.

**El Farol**, 808 Canyon Rd (☎505/983-9912). Historic bar-cum-restaurant that serves Spanish tapas to a musical accompaniment from blues to flamenco.

**Evangelo's**, 200 W San Francisco St (☎505/982-9014). The only good bare-bones bar in easy walking range of the plaza, with a pool table and a jukebox.

**The Paramount and Bar B**, 331 Sandoval St (☎505/982-8999). Cool, glamorous former restaurant that's become Santa Fe's premier venue for clubbing and alternative live music; the smaller *Bar B* programs its own specialized-appeal events.

## Bandelier National Monument

Cut into the forested mesas of the Pajarito Plateau, 35 miles northwest of Santa Fe, the cliff dwellings and Anasazi ruins of **BANDELIER NATIONAL MONUMENT** ($10 per car) are spread across fifty square miles of pine woods and deep stream-cut gorges. Named after amateur archeologist Adolph Bandelier, who publicized the place in the 1880s, they date from the very end of the Anasazi period (see opposite), around 1300 AD. Various itinerant groups of Anasazi and other tribes, seeking sanctuary from

## THE ANASAZI

Few visitors to the Southwest are prepared for the awesome scale and beauty of the desert cities and cliff palaces left by the ancient **Anasazi**, as seen all over the high plateaus of the "**Four Corners**" district, where Colorado, New Mexico, Arizona and Utah now meet.

The earliest humans reached the Southwest around 10,000 BC, but the Anasazi first appeared as the **Basket-makers**, near the San Juan River, more like two thousand years ago. Named for their woven sandals and bowls, they lived in pits in the earth, roofed with logs and mud. Over time, the Anasazi adopted an increasingly settled lifestyle, becoming expert farmers and potters. Their first freestanding houses on the plains were followed by multistoried **pueblos**, in which hundreds of families lived in complexes of contiguous "apartments." The astonishing **cliff dwellings**, perched on precarious ledges high above remote canyons, which they began to build around 1100 AD, are the first Anasazi settlements to show signs of defensive fortifications. Competition for scarce resources became even fiercer toward the end of the thirteenth century, and recent research suggests that warfare and even cannibalism played a role in their ultimate dispersal. Moving eastward, they joined forces with other displaced groups in a coming-together that eventually produced the modern **Pueblo Indians**. For that reason, the term "Ancestral Puebloan" is coming into vogue to replace "Anasazi," a Navajo word meaning "Ancient Enemies." Among the most significant **Anasazi sites** are:

**Mesa Verde**. Magnificent cliff palaces, high in the canyons of Colorado. See p.760.
**Bandelier National Monument**. Large riverside pueblos, and cave-like homes hollowed from volcanic rock. See opposite.
**Chaco Canyon**. The largest and most sophisticated freestanding pueblos, far out in the desert. See p.827.
**Wupatki**. Several small pueblo communities, built by assorted tribal groups. See p.851.
**Walnut Canyon**. Numerous canyon-wall houses above lush Walnut Creek. See p.851.
**Betatakin**. Canyon-side community set in a vast rocky alcove in the Navajo National Monument. See p.863.
**Canyon de Chelly**. Superbly dramatic cliff dwellings in glowing sandstone canyon; now owned and farmed by the Navajo. See p.865.
**Grand Gulch Primitive Area**. Barely explored ruins in the wilderness. See p.885.
**Hovenweep**. Enigmatic towers poised above a canyon. See p.886.

drought and invasion, gathered here to build a community that amalgamated their assorted cultures. At the end of the narrow switchbacking road down from Hwy-4, the **visitor center** provides an excellent overview of the site, with displays of pottery and jewelry, models of the ruins, full-scale reconstructions of pueblo interiors and fascinating photographs of local Native American life c.1900 (summer daily 8am–6pm; rest of year daily 8am–5pm; ☎505/672-3861).

Beyond the visitor center, a paved 1.5-mile trail loops through **Frijoles Canyon**. Its first stop is the remains of **Tyuonyi**, a circular, multistory village of four hundred rooms, of which only the ground floor and foundations survive. A side path leads up to dozens of **cave dwellings**, their rounded chambers scooped out of the soft volcanic rock; you can scramble up to, and even enter, some of them, to peer out across the valley. The main trail continues to the **Long House**, an 800ft series of two- and three-story houses built side by side against the canyon wall. Though most of the upper stories have collapsed, you can still see the morticed holes that held the roof beams; above these are rows of carved petroglyphs, mostly figures and abstract symbols. Half a mile beyond that, along the stream up the canyon, a reconstructed *kiva* sits in **Ceremonial Cave**, protected by a rock overhang 150ft above the canyon floor. To reach it you have to climb a succession of rickety ladders and steep stairs cut into the crumbly rock – not for the faint-hearted.

## Los Alamos

If you approach Bandelier from the east, you'll pass **Los Alamos National Laboratory**, the main US center for the research and development of **nuclear weapons** (as well as neurobiology, computer science and solar and geothermal energy). Virtually all the work at this, one of the foremost scientific research establishments in the world, is military-based, and consequently most of the complex is off limits – the small and over-simplified **Bradbury Science Museum** (Tues–Fri 9am–5pm, Sat–Mon 1–5pm; free) is the only part you can visit. What's both remarkable and unnerving about the place is that the people who work here seem oblivious to the fact that not everybody has learned to love the Bomb. The local radio station is called KBOM, and museum guides glow with excitement as they describe their weapons' devastating power. Judging by the visitors' register, a sizeable percentage of visitors come here as a sort of pilgrimage from Hiroshima and Nagasaki.

## From Santa Fe to Taos: the pueblos

The quickest route between Santa Fe and Taos follows US-84 as far as the Rio Grande, then continues northeast along the river on Hwy-68 – not that the switch from one to the other, at Española, is discernible to the naked eye. US-84 passes through the heartland of the **northern pueblos**, a cluster of tiny Tewa-speaking villages that have survived for more than five hundred years. The most interesting stops for casual visitors are **Santa Clara**, where the **Puyé Cliff Dwellings** are among the Southwest's least-known ancient ruins, and **Nambe**, near the impressive **Nambe Falls**. Other possible stops include **Pojoaque**, which operates a giftshop-cum-museum beside US-84 twelve miles out of Santa Fe, and **San Ildefonso**, five miles west, which is renowned for its pottery.

### Nambe Pueblo
The most beautifully sited of the northern pueblos is **NAMBE PUEBLO**, up the hillside five miles east of Pojoaque. Apart from a large *kiva*, not much remains in its old plaza area, but the triple-decker **Nambe Falls**, another four miles on, are well worth

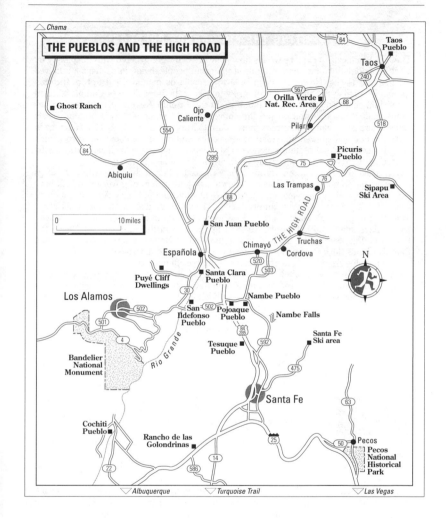

THE PUEBLOS AND THE HIGH ROAD

△ Chama

Ghost Ranch

Ojo Caliente
554

84

Abiquiu

0        10 miles

Los Alamos

Puyé Cliff
Dwellings

502
501

4

Bandelier
National
Monument

Cochiti
Pueblo

Rancho de las
Golondrinas

22        586

64        Taos
Pueblo

Taos
240

567
Orilla Verde
Nat. Rec. Area        68

Pilar        518

Picuris
Pueblo

75

Las Trampas        76        Sipapu
Ski Area

68

San Juan Pueblo

Chimayó        Truchas

Española        Cordova

520        503

Santa Clara
Pueblo        Nambe Pueblo

30

San        502        Pojoaque
Ildefonso        Pueblo        Nambe Falls
Pueblo

84
285        Santa Fe
Ski area

Tesuque
Pueblo        592

475

N

Santa Fe        63

25        50        Pecos

14        Pecos
National
Historical
Park

285

THE HIGH ROAD

Rio Grande

▽ Albuquerque        ▽ Turquoise Trail        ▽ Las Vegas

seeing (April, May & Oct daily 7am–7pm; June–Sept daily 6am–9pm; $4). There's river-side **camping** below the falls ($8).

## Santa Clara Pueblo and Puyé Cliff Dwellings

The main reason to visit **SANTA CLARA PUEBLO**, five miles north of San Ildefonso, is to see the ancestral home of its people: the dramatic **PUYÉ CLIFF DWELLINGS** in Santa Clara Canyon, an eleven-mile drive on paved roads west of the pueblo (April–Sept daily 8am–8pm; Oct–March daily 8am–4pm; $5, or $7 for a guided tour, summer Mon–Fri 9am).

Like the similar but better-known ruins at Bandelier (see p.812), the ancient community of **Puyé** was set against the south-facing cliffs at the edge of the Pajarito Plateau and was occupied between 1250 and 1550. Two tiers of "apartments" were hollowed

---

## VISITING THE RIO GRANDE PUEBLOS

The first Spaniards to explore what's now New Mexico were greeted with hospitality by a settled population of around a hundred thousand people, living in perhaps a hundred villages and towns. However, the people the Spaniards named the **Pueblo Indians** (*pueblo* is Spanish for "village") soon grew to resent the imposition of Catholicism and the virtual enslavement of Pueblo laborers. In the **Pueblo Revolt** of 1680, the various tribes banded together and ousted the entire colonial regime, killing scores of priests and soldiers and sending hundreds more south to Mexico. After the Spanish returned in 1693, the Pueblos showed little further resistance, and they have coexisted surprisingly amicably ever since, accepting aspects of Catholicism – most pueblos have a large adobe church at their core – without giving up their traditional beliefs and practices.

New Mexico is now home to around forty thousand Pueblo Indians, with each of its nineteen autonomous pueblos having its own laws and system of government. All have been modernized to some extent, and the recent explosion of Native American gaming has seen many open their own **casinos**, at sites usually located along the major highways well away from the residential areas. However, all also proudly retain the "Old Ways." Saints' days, major Catholic holidays such as Easter and the Epiphany, and even the Fourth of July, are celebrated with a combination of Native American traditions and Catholic rituals, featuring elaborately costumed dances and massive communal feasts.

Most pueblos are not the tourist attractions they're often touted to be. The best known, **Taos** and **Ácoma**, retain their ancient defensive architecture, but the rest tend to be dusty adobe hamlets scattered around a windblown plaza. Unless you arrive on a feast day, or are a knowledgeable shopper in search of Pueblo crafts (most have their own specialties), visits are liable to prove disappointing. In addition, you'll certainly be made to feel unwelcome if you fail to behave respectfully – don't go "exploring" places that are off limits to outsiders, such as shrines, *kivas* or private homes.

Fifteen of the pueblos are concentrated along the Rio Grande north of Albuquerque, with a longstanding division between the seven **southern pueblos**, south of Santa Fe, most of which speak Keresan, and the group to the north, which mostly speak Tewa (pronounced *tay-wah*) and jointly promote themselves as the **Eight Northern Indian Pueblos** (☎505/852-4265 or 1-800/793-4955). Visitors to each are required to register at a visitor center; some charge an admission fee of around $3, and all charge additional fees of up to $20 for still photography, $15–25 for video cameras and up to $100 for sketching. There's no extra charge for feast days or dances, but photography is often forbidden on special occasions.

For details of **guided tours**, contact Nambe Pueblo Tours (☎505/820-1340 or 1-800/946-2623).

---

into the upper canyon wall, while a large freestanding pueblo occupied the mesa-top just above. The trail up from the visitor center is easy at first, but eventually involves climbing at least one steep ladder, plus some deeply worn "staircases" in the rock. What seem like cozy little cave dwellings were originally interior rooms in larger complexes; each was fronted by several adobe-walled rooms, as the countless holes that once supported roof-beams now testify.

If you're reluctant to tear yourself away from this gorgeous spot, a **cafe** in the visitor center serves snacks on weekdays, and it's even possible to **camp** six miles further along Santa Clara Canyon (April–Oct; ☎505/753-7326; $8).

## The High Road

The satisfying if circuitous drive along the **"High Road"** enables you to combine a tour of the Pueblo region with the trip from Santa Fe to Taos. Leaving US-68/84 a dozen miles north of Santa Fe, near Nambe Pueblo, it leads high into the pines and aspens of the **Sangre de Cristo Mountains**, passing a number of pueblos as well as several timeless Hispanic villages. Dotted with isolated, tin-roofed shacks and barns, these hills are said to be the heartland of the secretive **Penitentes**, fanatical Catholics who in the nineteenth century were renowned, during Lent, for forming dawn processions along the ridges, flagellating themselves with yucca whips while chanting prayers.

## Chimayó

The quaint mountain village of **CHIMAYÓ**, 25 miles north of Santa Fe at the junction of Hwy-503 and Hwy-76, is the site of New Mexico's most famous Spanish colonial church, the 1816 **Santuario de Chimayó** (daily May–Sept 9am–6pm; Oct–April 9am–4pm). Known as the "Lourdes of America" for the devotion of its many pilgrims, this round-shouldered, twin-towered adobe beauty squats behind an enclosed courtyard; a small room to one side of the austere main chapel is filled with a mind-boggling array of votive offerings. A smaller and more ramshackle chapel nearby contains a diminutive statue of *Santo Niño*, the Lost Child – more of a doll, if truth be told – to whom expectant mothers bring gifts such as tiny pairs of shoes.

Two properties belonging to the Jaramillo family, resident since 1695, make Chimayó an appealing overnight destination. The *Restaurante Rancho de Chimayó*, Hwy-503 (☎505/351-4444), must be the best traditional New Mexican **restaurant** in the state, serving superb *flautas* and a mouth-watering *sopaipillas*, stuffed with meat and chilis, on a lovely sun-drenched outdoor patio. Across the road, the rambling adobe *Rancho de Chimayó* (PO Box 11, Chimayó, NM 87522; ☎505/351-2222; ④) has lovely **B&B** rooms.

## Taos

Part Spanish colonial outpost, part hangout for bohemian artists and New Age dropouts, and home to one of the oldest Native American communities in the United States, tiny **TAOS** (which rhymes with *mouse*) has become famous out of all proportion to its size. Just six thousand people live in its three component parts: **Taos** itself, around the plaza; sprawling **Ranchos de Taos**, three miles to the south; and the Native American community of **Taos Pueblo**, two miles north.

Like Santa Fe, Taos stretches languidly across a glorious high-desert plateau. The approach from the south is especially spectacular, as you cross a final bluff on Hwy-68 to be confronted by the pine-forested **Sangre de Cristo Mountains** soaring above the sun-bleached foothills. This far up, the **Rio Grande** lies deep in a craggy canyon west of town, occasionally glimpsed as a crack in the plateau.

Beyond the usual unsightly highway sprawl, Taos is a delight to visit. As well as museums, galleries and stores to match Santa Fe, it still offers an unhurried pace and charm, and the sense of a meeting place between Pueblo, Hispanic and American cultures. Its reputation as an **arts colony** began at the end of the nineteenth century, with the arrival of painter Joseph Henry Sharp. He was soon joined by two young New Yorkers, Bert Phillips and Ernest L Blumenschein; legend has it that their wagon lost a wheel outside Taos as they headed for Mexico in 1898, and they liked it so much they never got round to leaving. The three men formed the nucleus of the **Taos Society of Artists**, established in 1915. Soon afterwards, society heiress and arts patron Mabel Dodge arrived, and married an Indian from the Pueblo to become Mabel Dodge Luhan. She in turn wrote a fan letter to English novelist **D H Lawrence**, who visited three times in the early 1920s; his widow Frieda made her home in Taos after his death. New generations of artists and writers have "discovered" Taos ever since, but the most famous of all was **Georgia O'Keeffe**, who stayed for a few years at the end of the 1920s. Her renditions of the church at Ranchos de Taos in particular were a major influence on contemporary Southwestern art.

## Arrival, information and getting around

Greyhound and TNM&O **buses** from Albuquerque ($22) and Santa Fe ($17) arrive at **Taos Bus Center** (☎505/758-1144), opposite the well-equipped local **visitor center**, two miles south of the plaza at the intersection of Hwy-68 and US-64 (daily 9am–5pm; ☎505/758-3873 or 1-888/580-8267). Faust Transportation (☎505/758-3410) also connect Taos with Santa Fe ($25) and Albuquerque airport (one-way $35, round-trip $65).

**Walking** is the best way to get around the compact center, while Chile Line **buses** (☎505/751-4459) cover a twelve-mile route along the highway, and **trolley tours** visit the main attractions (Historic Taos Trolley Tours; May–Oct twice daily from visitor center and plaza; ☎505/751-0366; $25). Another option is to rent a **bike** from Cottam's, 207A Paseo del Pueblo Sur (☎505/758-2822).

## Accommodation

Taos has **accommodation** to meet all needs, at prices well below those of Santa Fe (though midwinter rates are no lower than midsummer). There are no budget options near the plaza, but a couple of local **hostels** offer bare-bones bunks. Otherwise, chain motels line Hwy-68 south of town, while three or four amusingly adobe-styled motels on Kit Carson Road just east of the plaza provide quieter alternatives. Taos Central Reservations (☎505/758-9767 or 1-800/821-2437) can reserve lodging in advance.

The best places to **camp** are the ten summer-only campgrounds in **Carson National Forest** (☎505/758-6200), reached by following Kit Carson Road east.

**Abominable Snowmansion Hostel/HI-Taos**, Taos Ski Valley Rd, Arroyo Seco (☎505/776-8298). Pleasant, friendly hostel-cum-ski lodge, at a tight curve in the road up to the ski valley, five miles north of downtown. Office hours daily 8–11am & 4–10pm; membership not required. Dorm beds $16 in summer, $22 in winter; bargain private rooms and camping space. ①–③.

**Best Western Kachina Lodge de Taos**, 413 Paseo del Pueblo Norte (☎505/758-2275 or 1-800/522-4462). Large, tasteful, family motel at the Taos Pueblo turnoff, with lots of Southwestern art, a good restaurant, live music, and nightly Pueblo dance performances in summer. There's some suggestion it may soon incorporate a casino, however; check before you book. ⑤.

**El Rincon**, 114 Kit Carson Rd (☎505/758-4874). Hispanic-flavored rooms of differing standards, in peaceful adobe B&B not far east of the plaza. ④–⑥.

**Indian Hills Inn**, 233 Paseo del Pueblo Sur (☎505/758-4293 or 1-800/444-2346). The only cheapish highway motel within walking distance of the plaza; be sure to get a room away from the street. ③.

**La Fonda de Taos**, 108 South Plaza (☎505/758-2211 or 1-800/833-2211). Throwback 1930s hotel on the plaza; neither the cheapest nor the smartest place in town, but among the most charming. The rooms lack TVs, but with their bright hand-painted furniture they're infinitely more characterful than modern motels. ④.

**Quail Ridge Inn Resort**, Ski Valley Rd (☎505/776-2211 or 1-800/624-4448). Rooms and suites in mountain-view adobe cottages 5 miles north of town, with a good on-site restaurant and pool. ④–⑨.

**Rio Grande Gorge Hostel**, Hwy-68 (☎505/758-0090). Attractive hostel-cum-B&B, perched above the Rio Grande at Pilar, 15 miles southwest of Taos. Dorm beds cost $9.50 in summer, when reservations are essential, and $11.50 in winter; private rooms are $29. ①.

**Taos Inn**, 125 Paseo del Pueblo Norte (☎505/758-2233 or 1-800/826-7466). Gorgeous – and very Southwestern – central hotel. Each of its 37 rooms plays a variation on the Pueblo theme, and both *Doc Martin's* restaurant (see p.820) and the *Adobe Bar* are packed nightly. ⑤–⑧.

## Taos plaza and the Millicent Rogers Museum

The old Spanish **plaza**, still at the heart of Taos, is now ringed by jewelry stores, art galleries and restaurants; all conform to the predominant Pueblo motif of rounded brown adobe. Specific sights are few – a small **museum** ($3) off the elderly lobby of the *La Fonda de Taos* hotel has a collection of sexy but amateurish paintings by D H Lawrence, and the tree-filled square itself is often animated by guitar-toting buskers – but the surrounding streets are perfect for an aimless stroll, and it's easy to spend half a day just mooching around. Some of the best places to eat or drink, as well as a number of top-notch art and crafts galleries, are on **Bent Street**, a block north of the plaza. Bent Street takes its name not from any irregularities, but from the first American governor of New Mexico, Charles Bent, whose house has been preserved as a **museum of frontier Taoseño life** (daily: summer 9am–5pm; winter 10am–4pm; $2).

Just east of the plaza, across the highway at the end of Taos's sole surviving stretch of wooden boardwalk, is the dusty but evocative adobe abode that was home to mountain man, mason and part-time US cavalry officer **Kit Carson** (see p.1180) for 25 years in the mid-1800s. It's now a rather flavorless **museum**, filled with saddles, rifles and Wild West paraphernalia (daily: May–Oct 8am–6pm; Nov–April 9am–5pm; $5). Two blocks south of the plaza at 222 Ledoux St, the much-restored 1790 **house** of artist and collector **Ernest L Blumenschein**, co-founder of the town's 1920s arts colony, displays paintings and furniture (daily: April–Oct 9am–5pm; Nov–March 10am–4pm; $5).

Two miles north of the Taos Pueblo turning, reached by a dirt road that angles into a tricky five-way intersection, the **Millicent Rogers Museum** (April–Oct daily 10am–5pm; Nov–March daily except Mon 10am–5pm; $6) shows off a superb collection of craft works. Objects range from **Anasazi** and **Mimbres** pottery to contemporary black-on-black ceramics from the family collection of San Ildefonso Pueblo potter **Maria Martinez**, plus **Hopi** *kachinas* (see p.868) and beautiful **Navajo** blankets. Affecting exhibits trace the development of Spanish colonial religious art in the heathen New World; the highlight is a "Death Cart," in which a skeleton holding a bow and arrow rides in a rickety wooden carriage.

## Taos Pueblo

The two multistory adobes at the flourishing community of **Taos Pueblo**, two miles north of Taos plaza and half a mile east of Hwy-68, have been continuously inhabited for perhaps eight hundred years and jointly form the most impressive Native American dwelling place still in use. The 150 full-time residents of Hlauuma, the north house, and Hlaukwima, the south house – separated by the Rio Pueblo de Taos, which flows down the hills from the sacred Blue Lake, inaccessible to outsiders – have made few concessions to the modern world, living without toilets, running water or electricity (although many others choose to live in newer homes nearby).

Each day between 9am and 6pm, whenever sufficient visitors are waiting, short **tours** of the complex provide an introduction to its traditions and culture; though you do not enter the actual adobes, several smaller buildings are open as craftshops. Car and camera fees are charged ($10, plus $10 for still photography and $20 for a video camera).

For most of the year, Pueblo life continues with scant regard for the intrusion of tourists, but feast days and dances can be spectacular. These are held regularly throughout the summer; the biggest parties are the **Corn Dances** in June and July and the **Feast of San Gerónimo** at the end of September, when hundreds and even thousands of outsiders flock to join the general revelry. The pueblo is sometimes closed during tribal events, however; telephone ☎505/758-1028 to check.

Taos Pueblo is one of the many pueblos to have rushed to build its own casino, located on the main highway (Hwy-68) several miles northwest of the pueblo itself. As one unapologetic elder remarked, "poverty was never a part of pueblo life until the Europeans came."

## Ranchos de Taos

Spreading south from the central plaza area, to either side of Hwy-68, the **Ranchos de Taos** were once the farms that fed the townspeople of Taos. Each *rancho* had its own main house, or *hacienda*; one has been restored as a **museum** of colonial life. The **Hacienda Martínez** (daily: April–Oct 9am–5pm; Nov–March 10am–4pm; $5), two miles southwest of the plaza on Ranchitos Road, was built in 1804 by Don Antonio Martínez, an early mayor of Taos. Within its thick, windowless, adobe walls – the place could be sealed like a fortress against still-prevalent Indian raids – two dozen rooms are wrapped around two separate patios, holding animal pens and a well. Trade goods of the kind Don Antonio once carried south along the Rio Grande are displayed alongside tools, looms and simple furnishings of the era.

In Ranchos' small unpaved plaza, the mission church of **San Francisco de Asis** turns its broad shoulders, or more accurately its massive adobe buttresses, to the passing traffic on Hwy-68. Built around 1776, it's one of colonial New Mexico's most splendid architectural achievements, with subtly rounded walls and corners disguising its underlying structural strength. Though the ever-changing interplay of light and shade across the church's golden exterior has fascinated painters from Georgia O'Keeffe onward, its interior is equally intriguing. Amid a clutter of devotional objects and art works, a magnificently ornate green-and-red reredos (altarpiece) frames several naive paintings. The plaza outside – remarkably peaceful considering the highway is thirty yards away – holds a handful of restaurants and giftshops.

## Taos Ski Valley

Fifteen miles north of Taos, reached via an attractive road that winds up through a narrow gap in the mountains from the village of Arroyo Seco, lie the challenging slopes of **Taos Ski Valley**. Located on the north flank of **Wheeler Peak**, the highest point in New Mexico at 13,161ft, the demanding runs are usually open to skiers between late November and early April (information ☎505/776-2291; resort reservations ☎1-800/776-1111; lift tickets $42).

## Eating, drinking and nightlife

Taos is too small to offer much **nightlife**, but it does have a fine selection of **restaurants** in all price ranges, and several coffeehouses. If your main priority is to **drink**, the *Adobe Bar* in the *Taos Inn* is the coziest spot in town, while *Eske's*, a short way south at 106 Des Georges Lane (☎505/758-1517), is a lively brewpub.

**Apple Tree Restaurant**, 123 Bent St (☎505/758-1900). Eclectic international cafe, based around a courtyard near the plaza, where the inexpensive menu ranges from Thai to Mexican.

**Bent Street Deli & Cafe**, 120 Bent St (☎505/758-5787). Airy, partly outdoor place, just north of the plaza; good-value breakfasts, sandwich lunches, and tasty dinners for under $20. Closed Sun.

**Caffe Tazza**, 122 Kit Carson Rd (☎505/758-8706). Trendy, central cafe with nice sunlit terrace, selling coffees and light veggie meals to students and assorted crazies. Next door to Taos Book Shop.

**Doc Martin's**, *Taos Inn*, 125 Paseo del Pueblo Norte (☎505/758-1977). Delicious, inventive New Mexican food in romantic adobe inn, on the main road just east of the plaza. Most dinner entrees, such as *piñon*-crusted salmon or smoked lamb sirloin, are $17–23.

**La Luna**, 223 Paseo del Pueblo Sur (☎505/751-0023). Top-quality, modern Italian-influenced cuisine a few blocks south of the plaza, past *McDonald's*. Good-value wood-fired pizzas for under $10, plus pricier specials such as wild mushroom pate or tuna steaks. Lunch Mon–Sat, dinner daily.

**Outback in Taos**, 712 Paseo del Pueblo Norte (☎505/748-3112). Hard-to-find pizzeria, a mile north of town, with a welcoming youthful ambiance and huge portions of great food – the $8 calzones are amazing.

**Stakeout Grill and Bar**, Outlaw Hill off Hwy-68 (☎505/758-2042). Well-hidden, unpretentious dinner-only restaurant in a truly stunning setting, specializing in big, good-value steaks. Only accessible by car, 4 miles south of Ranchos de Taos up a dirt track east of the highway.

# Chama

Eighty-five miles northwest of Taos on US-64 – which crosses the dramatic Rio Grande Gorge Bridge – beyond Abiquiu and the red rocks around Ghost Ranch, tiny **CHAMA** is the base for trips on the **Cumbres and Toltec Scenic Railroad** (Memorial Day–mid-Oct; ☎505/756-2151), an exhilarating high-mountain ride, following the course of the Los Piños Gorge. Daily excursions run through the High Brazos mountains on the border with Colorado; you can either take a van to Antonito, CO, and return by train (dep Chama 8am; $52), or take a round-trip for the day by train to a point halfway along (dep 10.30am; $34).

Modern timber lodges like the *Vista del Rio* (☎505/756-2138; ④) line the river south of town, while the *Gandy Dancer* is a three-bedroom B&B in a purple-clapboard mansion, near the station at 299 Maple St (☎505/756-2191 or 1-800/424-6702; ⑤).

# From Santa Fe to Albuquerque

Driving from **Santa Fe to Albuquerque**, you have three options. One route loops through the mountains to the west via **Bandelier** (see p.812) and the appealing village of Jemez Springs, while another follows the slumbering **Turquoise Trail** through the ghost towns further east. Even the most direct option, the sixty-mile sprint down **I-25**, has its moments, with views of Sandia Crest to the east and the sprawling Rio Grande to the west.

## The Turquoise Trail

The "**Turquoise Trail**," less glamorously known as Hwy-14, is a detour off I-25 that leads between the Sandia and Ortiz mountains, with one or two of the long-abandoned mining camps along the way still just about ranking as towns in their own right.

The dusty rolling hills that surround the northernmost town, **CERRILLOS**, have for centuries been known as the repository of one of the world's greatest concentrations of **turquoise**. Archeologists estimate that ninety percent of the fabled turquoise treasures seized by the Spanish when they conquered the Aztec capital of Tenochtitlan came from the mines tucked away in this unprepossessing spot. Prehistoric Indians scooped hundreds of tons of rock from the hillsides with the most basic of tools; after the **Pueblo Revolt** many shafts were buried to conceal them from the Spanish, and tales of fabulously wealthy "lost mines" still abound.

With its unpaved roads and old wooden buildings, Cerrillos made an atmospheric location for the filming of the bratpack Western *Young Guns* in 1988, though the modern gravel had to be replaced with tons of real dirt. There's still a bit of life in the old town; as recently as 1983 robbers made off with $500,000 worth of gold from the nearby Ortiz Mines. Tourists, however, have to content themselves with the **Casa Grande Trading Post, Turquoise Mining Museum and Petting Zoo**, an endearing shop-cum-museum that offers a random assortment of old bills and letters, porcupine quills, rattlesnake skins and petrified wood, plus the chance to pet a llama or pull on a string to make a plaster Indian hammer on a rock.

A dozen miles further on, the New Agey village of **MADRID** (pronounced *MAD-rid*) consists of a straggle of wooden cottages on either side of the narrow highway. Several hold genuinely interesting crafts and antiques stores; if you're close enough to home to carry furniture, there are some real bargains to be had here. Among the best stores are Primitiva, on the raised boardwalk at 500 Main St, which has two spacious floors of artifacts from around the world, and the Turquoise Trail Trading Post nearby, which concentrates more on Pueblo crafts. One attractive old mining home, *Java Junction* (☎505/438-2772; ③), houses a **coffee shop** downstairs and a **B&B** apartment upstairs, with full kitchen and bathroom facilities. Behind the lively *Mine Shaft Tavern* (☎505/473-0743), there's an accessible mine shaft.

## Coronado State Monument

If you do drive the I-25 route, be sure to stop off along the way at **Coronado State Monument**, just off the freeway on the far side of the Rio Grande, eighteen miles north of Albuquerque (daily: 8.30am–5pm; April–Oct $3, Nov–March $2). Named after the Spanish explorer who wintered here in 1540 (and who, in frustration at not finding any of the vast riches he was searching for, tortured and brutally murdered a number of local Indians), the monument consists of a large **adobe pueblo** beside the Rio Grande. You can enter its restored *kiva* to see reproductions of its multihued murals. The originals, preserved in the **visitor center**, include scenes of a rabbit hunt – the animals are still abundant in the undergrowth by the river.

The small town of **ALGODONES**, five miles north on the east bank of the river, holds one of New Mexico's most relaxing rural **B&Bs**, *Hacienda Vargas*, set in a lovely, restored adobe trading post at 1431 El Camino Real (☎505/867-9115; ④).

# Albuquerque and central New Mexico

Although to most travelers **central New Mexico** is an area to be raced through as quickly as possible, it does hold isolated pockets of interest, with the scenery, at least in the west, the main attraction. Dozens of all-American small towns hang on to the last remnants of **Route 66**, the winding old "Chicago-to-LA" transcontinental highway which has by and large been superseded by high-speed Interstate 40.

**Albuquerque** – New Mexico's largest city, with a third of the state's population – sits dead center, at the intersection of I-40 and I-25. It's also a main stop for Amtrak and Greyhound, and holds New Mexico's only major **airport**. The area **east of Albuquerque**, stretching along I-40 toward Texas, is among the most desolate parts of the Southwest, flat and dry and nearly devoid of interest. One or two towns have enough of a claim to fame to deserve a quick detour off the interstate, mostly due to **Wild West** heroes who passed through – Kit Carson and Billy the Kid, to name two. The mountainous region to the **west of Albuquerque** has more to see – above all **Ácoma Pueblo**, the mesa-top community known as "Sky City."

## East of Albuquerque: Tucumcari and Fort Sumner

The long line of truck stops, diners and motels at **TUCUMCARI**, the biggest town between Albuquerque and Amarillo, Texas (see p.665), has made it a favorite I-40 pit stop, punctuated with neon signs. During the day you can while away an hour at the mind-boggling **Tucumcari Historical Research Institute Museum**, at 416 S Adams St (Mon–Sat 9am–6pm, Sun 1–6pm; $2), which boasts one of the world's greatest collections of barbed wire. Literally hundreds of inexpensive **rooms** lie along this stretch of old Route 66; the *Rodeway Inn East*, 1023 E Tucumcari Blvd (☎505/461-0360; ②), is a cut above the many cheaper dives. The *Big Dipper*, 101 Second St at Main (☎505/461-4430), is an appealingly old-fashioned downtown diner.

**FORT SUMNER**, south of I-40 some way short of Tucumcari, means different things to different people. To the Navajo, it's where frontiersman and US Army colonel **Kit Carson** dragged them in 1864 after destroying their orchards and burning their villages in Arizona (see p.865). What little is left of the reservation is now the **Fort Sumner State Monument**, seven miles east of the modern town (daily 8.30am–5pm; $1). To Wild West fanatics, Fort Sumner is a pilgrimage spot because legendary outlaw **Billy the Kid** was gunned down here by Pat Garrett in 1881. His grave stands behind the **Old Fort Sumner Museum** (daily 9am–5pm; $3), his tombstone shielded from memento-seekers by a steel cage.

# Albuquerque

Sprawling at the heart of New Mexico, where the main east–west road and rail routes cross both the Rio Grande and the old road south to Mexico, **ALBUQUERQUE** is, with half a million people, the state's only major metropolis. Though many tourists dash straight from the airport up to Santa Fe, without a thought for Albuquerque, the "Duke City" has a good deal going for it. Like Phoenix, Arizona, it's grown a bit too fast for comfort in the last fifty years, but the original Hispanic settlement is still discernible at its core, and its diverse, cosmopolitan population gives it a rare cultural vibrancy. Even if its architecture is often uninspired, the setting is magnificent, sandwiched between the Rio Grande – lined by stately cottonwoods – and the dramatic, glowing **Sandia Mountains**. Specific highlights for visitors include the intact **Spanish plaza**, the neon-lit **Route 66** frontage of Central Avenue and the excellent **Indian Pueblo Cultural Center**, while every October Albuquerque hosts the nation's largest **hot-air balloon** rally, attracting upward of 100,000 people to its mass ascensions.

## Arrival and information

Albuquerque's **International Sunport**, New Mexico's principal airport, is four miles southeast of downtown. Mesa Airlines (☎1-800/637-2247) and Southwest (☎1-800/435-9792) run commuter flights throughout the state. All the major **car rental** chains have outlets at the airport, while a **taxi** into town with the Albuquerque Cab Co (☎505/883-4888) costs around $10, and Checker Airport Express (☎505/765-1234) runs door-to-door shuttles at similar rates. Many hotels and motels also have their own free shuttles, while half a dozen daily Gray Line vans make the 70-minute drive north to Santa Fe (☎1-800/256-8991; $25).

The modern Greyhound **bus** terminal, 300 Second St SW, is located in an otherwise deserted area, five easy minutes' walk south of downtown. It's used by long-distance east–west services, as well as four daily buses up to Santa Fe ($12) and Taos ($22), and has good-sized left-luggage lockers. Amtrak **trains** call in at a small temporary station immediately behind, at 214 First St.

Maps and free listings magazines are available from the **tourist office** downtown in the Galeria mall, 20 First Plaza at Second and Tijeras (Mon–Fri 8am–5pm; ☎505/842-9918 or 1-800/284-2282). Further information kiosks can be found in the Plaza Don Luis on Romero NW in Old Town (daily: April–Oct 9am–5pm; Nov–March 9.30am–4.30pm), and at the airport (daily 9.30am–8pm).

## Accommodation

The twenty-mile length of **Central Avenue**, the old Route 66, is lined with the flashing neon signs of dozens of $30-a-night **motels**. If you want to escape your car for a while, you'll have to pay a little extra to stay in the heart of Old Town – which holds few accommodation options – or downtown. Larger convention hotels are congregated along the interstates, and out near the airport.

**Albuquerque Hilton**, 1901 University Blvd NE (☎505/884-2500 or 1-800/274-6835). Midtown high-rise, near the intersection of I-40 and I-25. Good rooms, three restaurants – the *Casa Chaco* serves tasty Southwestern cuisine – and several busy bars. ⑥.

**Casas de Sueños**, 310 Rio Grande Blvd SW (☎505/247-4560 or 1-800/242-8987). Beautifully furnished, exotic and friendly B&B, very close to Old Town, with themed cottages and smaller rooms. One of New Mexico's most appealing places to stay. ⑤–⑨.

**Comfort Inn – Airport**, 2300 Yale Blvd SE (☎505/243-2244 or 1-800/221-2222). Good-value motel, served by free shuttles from the airport across the road, and with complimentary breakfasts. ④.

**Crossroads Motel**, 1001 Central Ave NE (☎505/255-7586). Simple, good-value budget motel, between Old Town and the university on Route 66, and complete with pool. ②.

**El Vado Motel**, 2500 Central Ave SW (☎505/243-4594). Vintage adobe Route 66 motel, within easy reach of Old Town. ②.

**La Posada de Albuquerque**, 125 2nd St NW (☎505/242-9090 or 1-800/777-5732). Historic, elegant hotel in convenient downtown location, built in Mexican style by Conrad Hilton in 1939. Plush, renovated rooms, a superb restaurant and a spacious, atmospheric bar. ⑤.

**Monterey Nonsmokers Motel**, 2402 Central Ave SW (☎505/243-3554 or 1-877/666-8379). Clean, fifteen-room motel, two blocks west of Old Town, with pool, laundry and a strict non-smoking policy. ③.

**Route 66 Hostel**, 1012 Central Ave SW (☎505/247-1813). Albuquerque's only hostel, a friendly place on the outskirts of Old Town, a mile west of downtown, offers dorm beds for $14, kitchen facilities and bargain private doubles. Office hours daily 7.30–10.30am & 4–11pm. ①.

## Old Town

Once you've cruised up and down **Central Avenue**, looking at the flashing neon and 1940s architecture of this twenty-mile stretch of Route 66 (Sun Tran buses do it all day for 75¢), most of what's interesting about Albuquerque is concentrated in **Old Town**, the recently tidied-up old Spanish heart of the city. The tree-filled **main plaza** is overlooked by the twin-towered adobe facade of **San Felipe de Neri church**, and circled by horse-drawn carriages that you can hop on for a short tour ($5). It's a very pleasant place to wander or have a meal, even if there's not a whole lot otherwise to do. One of the more bizarre of the many knickknack shops is the **Rattlesnake Museum** southeast of the plaza at 202 San Felipe St NW (daily 10am–6.30pm; $2), which has live rattlers on display. Nearby, Gus' Trading Post, at 2026 Central Ave NW, is one of the best-value shops in the Southwest for buying the perfect bolo tie or other pieces of Indian **jewelry**.

Still on Central Avenue, in the Old Town Shopping Center half a block west of the plaza, the intriguing little **Turquoise Museum** (Mon–Sat 9.30am–5.30pm; $2) may look like just another mall store, but turns out to be more of a fortified bank vault, filled with rare and beautiful turquoise nuggets. The **New Mexico Museum of Natural History**, four blocks northeast of the plaza at 1801 Mountain Rd NW (daily 9am–5pm; closed Mon in Jan & Sept; $5), has full-scale, animated models of dinosaurs, a simulated volcanic eruption and a replica of an Ice Age snow cave, as well as an engaging, touchable collection of fossils and dinosaur bones.

## The riverfront

The Rio Grande has shifted its course in the last three hundred years, so there's an unexpectedly low-key gap west of Old Town, much of it left undeveloped in deference to the unruly river. Along the wooded eastern riverbank, north of where Central Avenue crosses the river, the **Bio Park** holds two attractions that focus on the natural world. Not for the squeamish, the **Albuquerque Aquarium** (June–Aug Mon–Fri 9am–5pm, Sat & Sun 9am–6pm; Sept–May daily 9am–5pm; $6.50) offers such diverse experiences as eating in a restaurant beside a glass-walled tank filled with live sharks and walking through a tunnel surrounded on all sides by fierce-eyed moray eels. Across the way, the **Rio Grande Botanic Garden** (same hours; same ticket) consists of two large conservatories – one holding rare plants from the Sonoran and Chihuahua deserts, the other more temperate Mediterranean species – plus a series of formal walled gardens.

At the lower-key **Rio Grande Nature Center** (daily 10am–5pm; $1.50), two miles north of Old Town on Rio Grande Boulevard, informative displays describe Albuquerque's wildlife, and two short but enjoyable nature trails along the riverside feel far removed from the city.

## Indian Pueblo Cultural Center

The **Indian Pueblo Cultural Center**, at 2401 12th St NW, one block north of I-40 (daily 9am–5.30pm; ☎505/843-7270 or 1-800/766-4405; $4), is a stunning museum and crafts market owned and run as a cooperative venture by the diverse Pueblo Indians of New Mexico. Its horseshoe-shaped design deliberately echoes the architecture of the ancient Anasazi city of Pueblo Bonito, in Chaco Canyon (see p.828), and the central courtyard is the venue for free Pueblo dances, every Saturday and Sunday at 11am and 2pm.

This is New Mexico's one major museum about Native Americans to be curated by Native Americans, and the displays downstairs have a clear and distinct point of view: *Our Land, Our Culture, Our Story*, as the sign at the entrance puts it. The shared Anasazi heritage at the root of Pueblo culture is explained in detail, as is the impact of the Spanish conquistadors. Describing the **Pueblo Revolt** of 1680 as the "first civil war," it states that by allowing the defeated Spaniards to leave unharmed, the Pueblo peoples "showed them more mercy than they showed us." There's also as good an explanation as you're ever likely to get of a topic Pueblo Indians rarely discuss with outsiders: how indigenous Pueblo religion has managed to coexist with imported Catholicism. Videos illustrate modern Pueblo life, and an outstanding selection of pottery and jewelry is sold in the stores upstairs. A good-quality **cafe** serves assorted Pueblo specialties (see overleaf).

## Sandia Crest

The forested 10,500ft peaks of the **Sandia Crest** tower over Albuquerque to the east, affording particularly beautiful views from the top at and after sunset, when the city lights sparkle below. In summer it's a good 25°F cooler up here than in the valley, and in winter you can go downhill or cross-country **skiing** (lift tickets $33 per day; ☎505/242-9133). If you don't want to drive the scenic but twisting twenty-mile route from Albuquerque, take the **Sandia Peak Aerial Tram** (daily: summer 9am–10pm; rest of year shorter hours; $15), the world's longest single-span tramway at 2.7 miles; it leaves from the end of Tramway Road at the city's northeast edge.

## Eating

The chefs of Santa Fe may be trying to redefine Southwestern cuisine, but Albuquerque still knows what it likes – mountainous Mexican meals. This is the place to get to grips with what real New Mexican food is all about, with family diners all over the city competing to create the spiciest chiles rellenos, enchiladas and sopaipillas.

**Artichoke Cafe**, 424 Central Ave SE (☎505/243-0200). Simple but classy restaurant in the heart of downtown, with indoor and outdoor seating. Good, varied menu of California-influenced modern American cuisine; most entrees well under $20. Closed Sun.

**Conrad's**, *La Posada de Albuquerque*, 125 2nd St NW (☎505/242-9090). Classic Art Deco hotel diner, modernized and serving excellent Hispanic-influenced dishes, including tasty salads and tapas, plus the signature dish, a superb seafood paella, complete with lobster and saffron rice.

**Double Rainbow**, 3416 Central Ave SE (☎505/255-6633). University-district coffee bar, with a stupendous array of breads and pastries, full cooked breakfasts and a huge stock of magazines. Daily 6.30am–midnight.

**Frontier**, 2400 Central Ave SE (☎505/266-0550). Legendary 24-hour diner across from the university, where an unceasing parade of characters chows down on burgers, burritos and enchiladas.

**La Placita**, 208 San Felipe St NW (☎505/247-2204). Attractive, centuries-old adobe hacienda on the Old Town plaza, where a predominantly tourist crowd enjoy Mexican meals at surprisingly reasonable prices. Open daily 11am–9pm, with live Mexican music most evenings.

**Monte Vista Fire Station**, 3201 Central Ave NE (☎505/255-2424). Upmarket haunt, housed in a restored Art Deco Pueblo Revival fire station. Fancy grilled meats and fish at under $20 per entree, with changing specialties from around the nation.

**Pueblo Kitchen**, Indian Pueblo Cultural Center, 2401 12th St NW (☎505/843-7270). Indian fry-bread and other Pueblo specialties, plus good guacamole burgers.

**Zane Graze**, 308 San Felipe NW (☎505/243-4377). Old Town coffee bar, open for breakfast and lunch daily, with salads and desserts as well as espressos.

## Drinking and nightlife

Downtown Albuquerque has been revitalized in recent years by the emergence of a host of **bars** and **nightclubs**, many of which double as small theaters or music venues. Two free magazines, the weekly *Alibi* and the monthly *On The Scene*, can tell you all you need to know about what's coming up or going down.

**Assets Grille & Brewing Company**, 6910 Montgomery Blvd NE (☎505/889-6400). Lively micro-brewery with indoor and outdoor seating, plus Italian food – dinner nightly, lunch daily except Sun.

**Caravan East**, 7605 Central Ave NE (☎505/265-7877). Enormous honky-tonk, where tenderfeet can do the two-step with throngs of urban cowboys.

**Club 211**, 211 Gold Ave SE (☎505/766-9601). Extravagant, outrageous downtown club.

**El Rey Theater**, 620 Central Ave SW (☎505/764-2624). Live music from salsa to country and all points in between; the adjoining *Golden West Saloon* is the venue of choice for Albuquerque's metal maniacs.

**KiMo Theatre**, 423 Central Ave NW (☎505/848-1370). Gorgeous, city-owned "Pueblo Deco" the-ater, dating from the late 1920s, which puts on an eclectic program of opera, dance and theater per-formances, kids' movie shows and also regular live bands.

**The Launchpad**, 618 Central Ave SW (☎505/764-8887). Dance and live music space that showcases touring indie bands and also has a cluster of pool tables.

**University Draft House**, 318 Central Ave SW (☎505/843-7078). Hectic, no-cover downtown bar, always packed with students. Open Tues–Sat until 2am.

# West of Albuquerque: I-40 to Arizona

Driving between Albuquerque and Arizona, you could easily be so put off by the parade of billboards and hoardings offering cut-price cigarettes and Indian jewelry that you'd miss out on some of central New Mexico's most interesting places, such as **Ácoma Pueblo** and **Chaco Canyon**, which lie south and north of I-40 respectively.

## Ácoma Pueblo

The amazing **ÁCOMA PUEBLO**, south of I-40 fifty miles west of Albuquerque, encap-sulates a thousand years of Native American history. Its focus is the ancient village known as **"Sky City,"** perched atop a magnificent isolated mesa, 367ft high and 7000ft above sea level. Probably occupied by Chacoan migrants between 1100 and 1200 AD, when the great pueblos of Chaco Canyon were still in use, Ácoma has adapted to repeated waves of invaders ever since, while retaining its own strong identity. The Acomans have long been happy to take the tourist dollar – they run a large casino beside the interstate, and have hosted the Miss America Pageant – so visitors seldom feel the awkwardness possible at other pueblo communities. Nonetheless, Ácoma is the real thing, and its sense of unbroken tradition can reduce even the least culturally sen-sitive traveler to awestruck silence.

To see Sky City, you have to join one of the hour-long guided **bus tours** (April–Oct daily 8am–7pm, except July 10–13 & first or second weekend in Oct; Nov–March daily 8am–4.30pm; ☎505/470-4966 or 1-800/747-0181; $8, plus $10 for photo permit), which leave regularly from the small museum and giftshop at the base of the mesa. The main stop is at the **San Esteban del Rey** mission, a thick-walled adobe church completed in 1640. Its earthen-floored nave is capped by a roof made of pine logs, which are said to have been carried here from the top of Mount Taylor, twenty miles away, without once touching the ground. Catholicism did eventually take root among the Pueblo people, but tales of the early mission days often speak of the Spanish priests as harsh and unfeeling taskmasters, many of whom came to rather sticky ends. The sheer visual impact of the building is undeniable – due in part to its sheer incongruity – and it's striking that the Acomans obviously never felt inclined to follow its architectural example. Instead they went on constructing the multistory stone and adobe houses around which the tour then proceeds. Few of these are now lived in on any sort of permanent basis, as most Acomans prefer to reside down below, where they can get electricity and running water – and jobs. Villagers do, however, come up here during the day to sell pottery and fry-bread.

Instead of taking the bus back down, you can walk along the old path, scrambling over boulders and through narrow clefts. Away to the east, legend has it that the forbidding **Enchanted Mesa** once held its own Pueblo community; the only access to the top was via a system of ropes strung between the mesa itself and an adjoining rock pillar. When that pillar collapsed one day while the men were away from the village, the women and children were left stranded, their cries for help fading as they starved away.

## Grants

The old Route 66 town of **GRANTS**, fifteen miles west of Ácoma, holds half a dozen budget motels, including a good *Super 8*, 1604 E Santa Fe Ave (☎505/287-8811; ②), as well as *Grants Station Stockade*, a railroad-themed family restaurant at 200 W Santa Fe Ave (☎505/287-2334). The local **visitor center** doubles as the comprehensive and enjoyable **New Mexico Museum of Mining** at 100 N Iron Ave (May–Sept Mon–Sat 9am–5pm, Sun 9am–4pm; Oct–April Mon–Sat 9am–5pm; $3), offering a chance to descend into a mock-up of one of the region's many **uranium mines**.

## El Morro National Monument

Hidden away on Hwy-53 south of the Zuni Mountains, 42 miles west of Grants, **EL MORRO NATIONAL MONUMENT** feels as far off the beaten track as it's possible to be in the modern United States. Incredibly, however, this sheer sandstone cliff was a regular rest stop for international travelers before the Pilgrims landed at Plymouth Rock. It was first recorded by Spanish explorers in 1583 – *el morro* means "the headland" – and in 1605, Don Juan de Oñate, the founder of New Mexico, carved the first of many messages that earned it the American name of **Inscription Rock**.

Translations and explanations of El Morro's graffiti are displayed in the **visitor center** (daily: summer 9am–7pm; rest of year 9am–5pm; $4 per vehicle; ☎505/783-4226). You can see the real thing on a half-mile trail, which stays open until an hour before the visitor center closes.

El Morro is technically a cuesta, a long sloping mesa terminating in an abrupt bluff. The trail's first stop is the reason so many people passed this way: a cool, perennial pool of water, collected beneath a waterfall that tumbles through a cleft in the pale-pink cliffs. In such a self-evidently sacred spot, it's no surprise to see ancient **Anasazi petroglyphs** scraped into the desert varnish nearby. Not far beyond, Don Juan's chiseled signature celebrates "the discovery of the South Sea"; he was returning from an expedition that had taken him all the way to the mouth of the Colorado River. Further inscriptions follow thick and fast, some detailing the minutiae of campaigns on the Spanish frontier, others recording moments such as the Reconquest after the Pueblo Revolt.

## Chaco Canyon

For casual visitors, the long, bumpy ride to the Anasazi ruins of **CHACO CANYON**, north of I-40 between Grant and Gallup, may seem more bother than it's worth. True, the site protected as the **Chaco Culture National Historic Park** is the largest pre-Columbian city in North America; for beauty and drama, however, it can't compete with lesser settlements such as Canyon de Chelly (see p.865). The low-walled canyon is a mere scratch in the scrubby high-desert plains, and the Chaco Wash that runs through it is often completely dry.

Once you accept that you won't have amazing photos to show the folks back home, there's still plenty about Chaco to take your breath away. Over 3600 separate sites have been logged in the canyon, of which the thirteen principal ones are open to visitors. Six of these, arrayed along the canyon's north wall, are what are known as "great houses" – self-contained pueblos, three or four stories high, whose fortress-like walls concealed up to eight hundred rooms.

Both the routes to Chaco Canyon entail driving twenty miles over rough but passable dirt roads. Open all year, these should not be attempted during or within a day of a rainstorm. Whether you approach from the south – by following Hwy-57 up from **Seven Lakes**, eighteen miles northeast of **Crownpoint** – or from the north or east – by turning off Hwy-44 at **Nageezi**, 36 miles south of **Bloomfield** – you'll enter the park at its southeast corner, where the **visitor center** supplies maps and brochures, plus schedules of summer-only ranger-led tours (daily: summer 8am–6pm; rest of year 8am–5pm; ☎505/786-7014; $8 per vehicle). The basic first-come, first-served *Gallo* **campground** ($10), a short way east of the visitor center, is the only visitor facility in the park; from April to October it's usually full by 3pm.

The gates of the canyon's eight-mile one-way **loop road** are immediately north of the visitor center, and open the same hours. The major stop is at the far end, where **Pueblo Bonito** ("Beautiful town" in Spanish) can be explored on an easy half-mile trail. The largest of the great houses, Pueblo Bonito is claimed to have been the biggest single building in America until structural steel was developed in 1898. Work on this four-story D-shaped structure, which is almost perfectly aligned east–west, started in 850 AD and continued for around three hundred years. Entering the ruin via its lowest levels, the path reaches its central plaza, which held at least three **Great Kivas** – ceremonial chambers thought to have been used by entire communities rather than individual clans or families. From there, you can walk through the passageways and chambers of the pueblo proper, where the rows of neatly finished doorways, each framed by the next, are Chaco's most photographed feature.

## Gallup

Just half an hour from the Arizona border, 65 miles west of Grants, the famous **Route 66** town of **GALLUP** is a handy but uninteresting I-40 pit stop. A five-mile line of the old Route 66 frontage contains some of the least-expensive **motels** in the US, ranging from the *Ambassador*, 1601 W 66 Ave (☎505/722-3843; ①), and the *Colonial*, 1007 W Coal Ave (☎505/863-6821; ①), to the pricier national chains. Unless you're falling asleep at the wheel, the only place really worth stopping for in Gallup is the *El Rancho Hotel*, 1000 E 66 Ave (☎505/863-9311 or 1-800/543-6351; ③/④), built in 1937 by the brother of film director and producer D W Griffith as a home from home for the many Hollywood stars filming nearby. Nowadays you can ogle their photos in the spacious Spanish Revival lobby, grab a bite in the cafe or spend the night in the *Ronald Reagan Room*, the *Marx Brothers Room* or the *Mae West Room*. Some guestrooms are in the original ranchhouse, the rest in a two-story motel building alongside.

The Navajo and other local Native Americans come together in **Red Rock State Park**, four miles east, on the second weekend in August for the **Inter-Tribal Indian Ceremonial**, the largest such gathering anywhere. Four days of dances and craft shows have as their highlight a Saturday morning parade through the town.

# Southern New Mexico

Most of the travelers who come to **southern New Mexico** are here to visit **Carlsbad Caverns National Park**. Crassly commercialized it may be, but, like the Grand Canyon, it's too amazing a geological spectacle to miss. Northwest of Carlsbad, the **Sacramento** and **Jicarilla Mountains** – home to the **Mescalero Apache** reservation as well as some rough-and-ready resorts with alpine settings to match Taos – rise from the desert plains once roamed by Billy the Kid and other Wild West heroes. The desolate dunes of the **White Sands** – half national park, half missile and bombing range – spread west of the mountains with the rolling hills of the **Rio Grande Valley** beyond. The little-visited southwest corner is among the most attractive reaches of the Southwest, with dozens more ghost towns and some fine scenery, plus the undisturbed pre-Columbian remains of the **Gila Cliff Dwellings National Monument**.

## Carlsbad Caverns National Park

**CARLSBAD CAVERNS NATIONAL PARK** consists of a tract of the Guadalupe Mountains that's so riddled with underground caves and tunnels as to be virtually hollow. Tamed in classic park-service style with concrete trails and electric lighting, this subterranean wonderland is now a walk-in gallery, where tourists come in droves to marvel at its intricate limestone tracery. Though the summer crowds can get pretty intense, in a strange way that's part of the fun – coming to Carlsbad feels like a real throwback to the great 1950s boom in mass tourism. Before you decide whether to join in, however, be sure to grasp that the park is a *long* way from anywhere else – three hundred miles southeast of Albuquerque and 150 miles northeast of El Paso, Texas.

To reach the park, follow the narrow, twisting seven-mile road that leaves US-62/180 at **White's City**, twenty miles southwest of the town of **CARLSBAD**. This ends at the **visitor center** – part of a complex that includes a restaurant, a giftshop, a crèche and even a kennel – where you can pay entrance fees and pick up details of the day's schedule of tours (summer daily 8am–7pm; rest of year daily 8am–5.30pm; ☎505/785-2232).

Almost all park visitors confine their attention to the main cave, **Carlsbad Cavern** itself, and the standard park fee of $6 per person for three days covers access to this cave only; note that Golden Eagle passes (see p.41) are not accepted. Direct elevators drop to the Cavern's centerpiece, the **Big Room**, 750 vertical feet below the visitor center (summer first down 8.30am, last up 6.30pm; rest of year first down 8.30am, last up 4.55pm), but you can choose instead to walk down via the **Natural Entrance Route** (last entry summer 3.30pm; rest of year 2pm). This steep, paved footpath switchbacks into the guano-encrusted maw of the cave, taking fifteen minutes to reach the first of the formations and another fifteen to reach the Big Room. The main appeal of walking down used to be that the trail meandered through beautiful side caves such as the **King's Palace** and the **Queen's Chamber**, filled with translucent "draperies" of limestone, but these are now open to guided tours only, which start from the Big Room (daily 9am, 11am, 1pm & 3pm; $8). All visitors are obliged to ride the elevator back out.

Measuring up to 1800ft long and 250ft high, the Big Room is festooned with stalactites, stalagmites and countless unnameable shapes of swirling liquid rock. All are a uniform stone gray; the rare touches of color are provided by slight red or brown mineral-rich tinges, improved here and there with gentle pastel lighting. Most visitors take an hour or so to complete the reasonably level trail around the Room's perimeter. Whatever the weather up top – summer highs exceed 100°F – the temperature down here is always a cool 56°F, so dress warmly.

Adjoining the Big Room, the **Underground Lunchroom** is a vast formation-free side cave paved over in the 1950s to create a diner-cum-souvenir-shop that sells indigestible lunches in polystyrene containers, plus Eisenhower-era souvenirs like giant pencils and Viewmaster reels. To modern eyes, this strange installation seems absurd, but moves to close it down have been stymied by its place in popular affections.

The recesses of Carlsbad Caverns are the summer home of around a million Mexican free-tailed **bats**. Each evening, at dusk or a little later, having slept all day suspended from the ceiling of the imaginatively titled Bat Cave – to which there's no public access – they emerge in cloud-like spirals, and disperse across the desert in search of delectable insects. Park visitors watch the spectacle from the amphitheater seating that faces the cave mouth, while rangers give a free and informative "Bats aren't as bad as you think" presentation.

**Slaughter Canyon Cave**, 25 miles southwest of the visitor center, can only be explored on two-hour guided tours (usually summer daily 10am & 1pm; rest of year Sat & Sun 10am & 1pm; call for exact schedule; $15). To get there, drive five miles south of White's City on US-62/180, then eleven miles west on Hwy-418, and finally hike the steep half-mile up to the cave entrance. Slaughter Canyon Cave still appears as "New Cave" on some maps, but it's been renamed to avoid confusion since the discovery of **Lechuguilla Cave**. Revealed after cavers cleared a 30ft plug of bat dung and rubble in 1986, the astonishing Lechuguilla cave system is not only deeper than Carlsbad Cavern but, at 1600ft, has turned out to be the deepest in the US. Sixty miles of tunnels have been mapped so far, but they're so dangerous that Lechuguilla is off limits to all but the experts.

### Practicalities

No matter how you get to Carlsbad Caverns, you have to cross seemingly endless miles of the **Llano Estacado**, the deathly flat rangeland that covers southeast New Mexico and the Texas Panhandle. The route from El Paso, Texas, has the advantage of passing through **Guadalupe Mountains National Park**, a beautiful though little-visited complement to Carlsbad, which offers superb camping (see p.671).

**WHITE'S CITY** is not so much a town as a privately owned tourist complex that provides the closest **accommodation** and **camping** to the national park, including the mock-adobe *Best Western Cavern Inn* (☎505/785-2291 or 1-800/CAVERNS; ④); the *White's City RV Park* (same number), which has tent camping space; and the *Velvet Garter Restaurant* (same number). The town of **CARLSBAD** itself, 25 miles north of White's City, holds little of interest outside its many motels, such as the central *Holiday Inn*, 601 S Canal St (☎505/885-8500 or 1-800/742-9586; ⑤), and the clean, comfortable *Super 8*, 3817 National Parks Hwy (☎505/887-8888; ③). *Lucy's*, 701 S Canal St (closed Sun; ☎505/887-7714), serves good Mexican food.

## Roswell

Seventy-five miles north of Carlsbad, the small ranching town of **ROSWELL** is renowned as the spot near which an alien spaceship supposedly crash-landed on the night of July 4, 1947. The commander of the local air force base authorized a press statement announcing that they had retrieved the wreckage of a flying saucer, and despite a follow-up denial within a day – claiming that it was in fact a weather balloon – the story has kept running. In 1997, as 100,000 *X-Files* fanatics descended upon Roswell for a six-day festival to mark the "Incident's" fiftieth anniversary, the US government revealed that the errant weather balloon had crashed while monitoring the atmosphere for evidence of Soviet nuclear tests. Witnesses were also said to have confused the balloon crash with a series of parachute experiments in 1953, which involved the dropping of dummies from high-altitude planes. UFO theorists, however, remain unconvinced.

Each of the two museums in town devoted to the "Roswell Incident" has its own particular lunacies. Despite its best intentions, and the wishful thinking of the truly weird clientele who drift in from the plains, the central **International UFO Museum**, 114 N Main St (daily 10am–5pm; free), inadvertently exposes the whole tawdry business as transparent nonsense. Its showpiece is a model of the notorious "alien autopsy"; built for the movie *Roswell*, you can't help suspecting it was also featured in the grainy "documentary" autopsy footage that created a brief international sensation in 1995.

There's another chance to have your photo taken with a "little gray" at the even tackier **UFO Enigma Museum**, a long way south at 6108 S Main St (Mon–Sat 9am–5pm, Sun noon–5pm; $1). Here it's not dead on a slab, but alive and keen to make friends – unlike two of its unfortunate hand-knitted companions, which lie strewn in silver jumpsuits beside their disabled spaceship nearby.

By way of contrast, the longstanding **Roswell Museum**, 100 W 11th St (Mon–Sat 9am–5pm, Sun 1–5pm; free), boasts an excellent, multifaceted collection with nary an alien corpse to be seen. Its most sensational section celebrates pioneer rocket scientist Robert Goddard (1882–1945), while historical artifacts elsewhere range from armor and pikes brought by Spanish conquistadors to astronaut Harrison Schmitt's spacesuit. A huge gallery also displays Southwestern art by Henriette Wyeth, Peter Hurd and Georgia O'Keeffe.

Roswell's **visitor center** is at 912 N Main St (Mon–Sat 9am–5pm; ☎505/624-6860). The finest **motel** in town, the *Best Western Sally Port Inn*, 2000 N Main St (☎505/622-6430 or 1-800/600-5221; ⑤), also has a good **restaurant**; the *Super 8*, 3575 N Main St (☎505/622-8886 or 1-800/800-8000; ③), and the *Frontier Motel*, 3010 N Main St (☎505/622-1400 or 1-800/678-1401; ②), are cheaper.

## Ruidoso

The **Sacramento**, **Capitan** and **Jicarilla Mountains**, which rise at the western edge of the Llano Estacado, 85 miles northwest of Carlsbad, form a rare respite from the scrubby flatness. Spread out along winding roads that cut through dense groves of pine, fir and aspen, the main town here, **RUIDOSO**, is the fastest-growing resort in the Southwest, with dozens of motels and mountain lodges along the banks of the Ruidoso ("Noisy") River.

The **Ruidoso Downs** racetrack, just east of town, plays host to a 77-day racing season that culminates on Labor Day with the **All-American Futurity**, one of the world's richest horse races. Alongside, the **Museum of the Horse** (daily: summer 9am–5.30pm; rest of year 10am–5pm; $5) holds displays on the natural and human-related history of horses, with a selection of memorabilia from around the world such as horse-drawn Russian sleighs, English road coaches and Wild West stagecoaches.

In winter, attention turns to the 12,000ft slopes of **Ski Apache** (☎505/336-4565), a downhill ski area northwest of town where lift tickets cost around $40 per day. Though operated by the Mescalero Apache, it's not on tribal land – they bought it as a going concern.

Brochures from Ruidoso's **visitor center**, 720 Sudderth Ave (Mon–Sat 9am–5pm, Sun 1–4pm; ☎505/257-7395 or 1-800/253-2255), list dozens of **motels**, such as the inexpensive *Apache*, 344 Sudderth Ave (☎505/257-2986 or 1-800/426-0616; ②), but supply still fails to meet demand on big race days. The real local showpiece, however, is the glitzy *Inn of the Mountain Gods*, owned and run by the Mescalero Apache (PO Box 269, Mescalero, NM 88340; ☎505/257-5141 or 1-800/545-9011; ⑥), which offers ski packages, casino gambling, golf, fishing, tennis and horseback riding, plus the excellent *Dan Li Ka* **restaurant**.

## Lincoln

One of the most enduring of New Mexico's many legendary Wild West figures was a Brooklyn-born one-time bus boy named William Bonney, better known as **Billy the Kid**. Many towns lay claim to him, but he first came to fame as an eighteen-year-old in the **Lincoln County War**, which erupted in 1878 in the frontier town of **LINCOLN** – on Hwy-380 roughly halfway between Carlsbad and Albuquerque – when rival groups of ranchers and merchants fought to gain control of the town and the hundreds of square miles of grazing lands surrounding it. Since those days, no new buildings have joined the venerable false-fronted structures that line Main Street, and the entire town is now **Lincoln State Monument**. Visitors can stroll its length at any time, while admission to its various historical sites is via a joint ticket sold at each (daily 8.30am–5pm; $5; ☎505/653-4372). Displays in the modern **Lincoln County Historical Center**, at the east end of town, cover Hispanics, cowboys, "Buffalo Soldiers" – the black cavalrymen stationed at nearby Fort Stanton – and Apaches, as well as the Lincoln County War. Billy the Kid's most famous jailbreak is commemorated at the **Lincoln County Courthouse**, at the other end of the street; waiting here under sentence of death, he shot his way out and fled to Fort Sumner, where Sheriff Pat Garrett eventually caught up with him (see p.822). On the first weekend of August, the town fills up, and its streets echo with gunfire once again, during the three-day **Old Lincoln Days** festival.

Near the courthouse, the *Wortley Hotel* – once owned by Sheriff Pat Garrett – offers eight plain but appealing **hotel** rooms (PO Box 96, Lincoln, NM 88338; ☎505/653-4300; ④), and its **dining room** serves simple stews and sandwiches at lunchtime only. If you like a bit more comfort, head to the nearby *Casa de Patrón* **B&B** (PO Box 27, Lincoln, NM 88338; ☎505/653-4676 or 1-800/524-5202; ⑤/⑥).

## White Sands National Monument

Filling a broad valley west of Ruidoso and the Sacramento Mountains, the **White Sands** are 250 square miles of glistening, three-story-high dunes, not of sand but of finely ground gypsum eroded from the nearby peaks. Unfortunately, most of the desert valley is under the control of the US military, who use it as a missile range and training ground for pilots, and as a landing site for the **space shuttle**; only the southern half of the dunes is protected within **WHITE SANDS NATIONAL MONUMENT** (and even that is often closed for an hour or two at a time while missile tests are underway). The best place to start is at the **visitor center**, just off US-70, which illuminates the unique plants and animals that dwell here (daily: summer 8am–7pm; rest of year 8am–4.30pm). An eight-mile paved road ($3) stretches into the heart of the dunes, where you can scramble and slide in the sheer white landscape.

**ALAMOGORDO**, which sits at the base of the Sacramento Mountains, sixteen miles east of the Monument along US-54, holds the nearest food and lodging.

## Las Cruces and Mesilla

From White Sands, US-70 heads southwest across the Tularosa Valley to **LAS CRUCES** – "the Crosses" – a large, modern farming community on the Rio Grande at the junction of I-10 and I-25. The town takes its name from the dozens of white crosses set up in the sands to mark the graves of early travelers killed by the Apache, but any real sense of its history is pretty well buried by motels and fast-food franchises.

The little-changed Hispanic colonial village of **MESILLA**, just south of I-10 two miles west, was until the 1870s one of the Southwest's largest towns, with upward of eight thousand inhabitants. During the Civil War, it even served briefly as the Confederate capital of New Mexico and Arizona, but it went into swift decline when the railroad bypassed it in favor of Las Cruces in 1881. Mesilla's delightful Old-West **plaza** has a real frontier feel to it, even though most of the old adobes that surround it – including the former courthouse where Billy the Kid was tried and sentenced to death in 1881 – now house art galleries and souvenir shops. **Restaurants** include the steak-oriented *Double Eagle* (☎505/523-6700) and *El Patio*, a Mexican cantina (closed Sun; ☎505/524-0982), while the *Mesón de Mesilla*, 1803 Av de Mesilla (☎505/525-2380 or 1-800/732-6025; ③–⑥), a gorgeous **B&B** five minutes' walk east, has a top-class dining room.

# The southwest corner

The I-10 heads west from Las Cruces across the wide-open rangeland that fills out the southwest corner of New Mexico, also known as the "**Bootheel**" because of the way it steps down toward Mexico. It's so sparsely inhabited that there are roughly three square miles per person. Towns are few and far between: **DEMING**, sixty miles west of Las Cruces, has a few motels and cafes and is one of two places where Amtrak trains stop. Even if you're racing through on the interstate, make time for the very good **Luna Mimbres Museum** (Mon–Sat 9am–4pm, Sun 1.30–4pm; free), which relates the region's Native American and Wild West past, and has a great show of minerals and gemstones. **LORDSBURG**, too, on I-10 twenty miles before you reach Arizona, has a string of gas stations, cafes and motels but little else.

## Silver City

Rarely visited and almost entirely wilderness, the semi-arid, forested, volcanic **Mogollon** and **Mimbres Mountains** soar above the high desert plain of southwest New Mexico to over ten thousand feet. But for a number of copper mines, the area is protected within the **Gila National Forest**. The mountains are some of the most remote in the US, little altered since Apache warrior **Geronimo** was born here at the headwaters of the Gila River.

Halfway up the mountains, the biggest settlement, **SILVER CITY**, lies 45 miles north of I-10 at the junction of US-180 from Deming and Hwy-90 from Lordsburg. The Spanish came here in 1804, sold the Mimbreño Indians into slavery, and opened the **Santa Rita copper mine**, just east of town below the Kneeling Nun monolith; but the town was reestablished in 1870 as a rough-and-tumble silver camp – **Billy the Kid** spent most of his childhood here. A fine selection of ornate old buildings is scattered along elm-lined avenues and across the surrounding hills. The excellent **Silver City Museum** at 312 W Broadway (Tues–Fri 9am–4.30pm, Sat & Sun 10am–4pm; free) tells the boom-and-bust tales, and holds fine specimens of **Casas Grandes pottery**, beautiful Navajo rugs, and basketry from all the major Southwest tribes. Three blocks east, the original Main Street was washed away in a great flood and has become the cottonwood-shaded **Big Gulch Park**.

In downtown Silver City, the *Carter House*, 101 N Cooper St (☎505/388-5485; ①–④), is a HI-AYH **youth hostel** that doubles as a **B&B**, with $13 dorm beds ($16 nonmembers) and some nice little private rooms. Just outside town, however, the *Bear Mountain Guest Ranch* (☎505/538-2538 or 1-800/880-2538; ⑤) is a large 1920s ranchhouse that charges all-inclusive, full-board rates to stay in its very pleasant rooms, and offers guided bird-watching trips plus a variety of multiday cycling, mountain biking or cross-country skiing tours. Bullard Street in the heart of town holds atmospheric **saloons and cafes** like the *Silver Cafe* at 514 N Bullard (☎505/388-3480).

## Gila Cliff Dwellings National Monument

Beautiful, twisting Hwy-15 threads north from Silver City into the mountains, passing the picturesque old mining camp of Pinos Altos along its fifty-mile, two-hour climb to the **GILA CLIFF DWELLINGS NATIONAL MONUMENT**. A mile beyond the monument's **visitor center**, a further mile-long trail (daily: summer 8am–6pm; rest of year 9am–4pm; $3) sets off beside a year-round stream.

Only once you've followed the stream for half a mile do you get your first glimpse of the ancient pueblo, abandoned about seven centuries ago by the **Mogollon** peoples, who had lived here for just forty years. What look from below like three separate caves turn out, when you climb the hillside, to be a single deep, long alcove with three entrances. Each entrance was virtually sealed with stones and mortar, but behind them lay around forty interconnected rooms, sharing a communal plaza at the rear. While they may not be as architecturally impressive as those of Mesa Verde (see p.760), exploring them alone – you can wander freely through the chambers, and the chances are there will be no one else around – really allows you to imagine yourself as one of the original occupants. Keep an eye out for the pictographs that mark certain dwellings, as well as a granary that still holds a desiccated cache of tiny corn.

The monument maintains a small free **campground** beside the Gila River, equipped with running water in summer only, and there's another pretty campground at the **Gila Hot Springs Vacation Center**, eight miles south (☎505/536-9551).

# ARIZONA

The tourism industry in **ARIZONA** has, literally, one colossal advantage – the **Grand Canyon** of the Colorado River. It's the single most awe-inspiring spectacle in a land of unforgettable geology, and one of the few places in the world that you absolutely have to see at least once in your life. However, the Grand Canyon is by no means the most interesting or memorable destination in the state. Indeed, in comparison to its inhuman scale, other parts of Arizona have a more abiding emotional impact, precisely because of the sheer drama of human involvement in this forbidding but deeply resonant desert landscape.

Over a third of the state still belongs to the **Native Americans** who have lived here for centuries, and who outside the cities form the majority of the population. In the so-called **Indian Country** of northeastern Arizona, the reservation lands of the **Navajo Nation** hold the stupendous **Canyon de Chelly** and dozens of other marvellously sited **Anasazi ruins**, as well as the stark rocks of **Monument Valley**. The Navajo surround the homeland of one of the most stoutly traditional of all Native American peoples, the **Hopi**, who live in remote **mesa-top villages**. The third main tribal group are the **Apache**, in the harshly beautiful southeastern mountains – the last Native Americans to give in to the overwhelming power of the white American invaders.

Away from the reservations, **Wild West** towns like **Tombstone**, site of the famed gunfight at the OK Corral, give a clear sense of Arizona's characteristically rough-and-ready, pioneer mentality; this was the last of the lower 48 states to join the Union, in 1912. The **cities**, however, are not much fun. In **Phoenix**, the capital, well over a million souls are scattered over a 500-square-mile morass of shopping malls and tract-house suburbs; **Tucson** is a bit more civil, but still wears thin after a day or so.

Though the open spaces of southern Arizona can be harsh and violent – most of the southwestern quarter, along the parallel I-8 and I-10 highways, is used as a bombing range – the bleakness is balanced somewhat by the many nature reserves which protect its amazing flora and fauna, such as **Saguaro National Park**, just outside Tucson, with its giant cactuses, real-life roadrunners and rare Gila monsters.

## Getting around Arizona

Arizona is better served by public transportation than much of the Southwest, but it's still an effort to get around without a car. Greyhound **buses** stop at all the major cities and at most towns along the interstates, while Amtrak **trains** cross the state on two of their transcontinental routes (via Tucson in the south, or Flagstaff further north). Nava-Hopi (☎520/774-5003 or 1-800/892-8687) connect Flagstaff with the Grand Canyon, which also has a small airport; otherwise, seeing the backcountry – and especially the reservations – is all but impossible without a car. The largest airport is at Phoenix, and assorted good-value, short-hop **flights** cover the principal destinations. The only worthwhile **bus tours** visit the area around Flagstaff.

# Tucson, Phoenix and southern Arizona

Most of Arizona's compelling attractions are in its northern reaches, but the **southern** half of the state holds ninety percent of its people, all its significant cities and several important historic sites. Apart from a couple of Spanish missions, the bulk of what there is to see is frontier Americana, especially in **Tombstone**, in the southeast corner. **Phoenix**, the state capital, is huge, sprawling and dull; **Tucson** makes a better base for visiting this part of the world and for trips south of the border into Mexico.

## Tucson and around

After serving as a colonial outpost under the Spanish and Mexicans, and then as territorial capital for both the US and Confederate governments, **TUCSON** (pronounced *too-sonn*) – a mere sixty miles north of Mexico on the cross-country I-10 – has grown into a modern mini-metropolis of nearly a million people without entirely sacrificing its historic quarters. Now equal parts college town and retirement community, it's one of the more attractive big cities of the Southwest – which admittedly isn't saying much. Although it suffers from the same Sunbelt sprawl as Albuquerque and Phoenix, it does have a wanderable center, some enjoyable restaurants and a pretty good nightlife, energized by the 35,000 students at the University of Arizona. It is also redeemed by having so much superb landscape within easy reach, from the forested flanks of **Mount Lemmon** to the rolling foothills of **Saguaro National Park**.

### Arrival and information

**Tucson International Airport**, eight miles south of downtown, receives far fewer long-distance flights than Phoenix. It's connected to the city by the slow Sun Tran bus #25 (85¢), and the $12 Arizona Stagecoach shuttles (☎520/889-1000). For **taxi** service, call Allstate Cabs (☎520/798-1111). The Amtrak station, downtown at 400 E Toole Ave, is served by three **trains** weekly in each direction, with connecting buses running north to Phoenix. Greyhound **buses** also stop very centrally, at 2 S Fourth Ave.

Tucson's downtown **visitor center**, 130 S Scott Ave (Mon–Fri 8am–5pm, Sat & Sun 9am–4pm; ☎520/624-1817 or 1-800/638-8350), has free maps and information. The Southwest Parks and Monuments Association bookstore, three blocks away at 223 N Court St (☎520/792-0239), stocks Arizona's best selection of historical, hiking and wildlife guides. Tucson Tours (☎520/297-2911) offer ninety-minute city tours for $18, and an extensive program of trips further afield.

### Accommodation

Tucson offers a broader range of **accommodation** than Phoenix, with plenty of reasonably priced hotels and motels downtown, as well as some atmospheric **B&Bs** both in the historic center and out in the surrounding desert. It also has its fair share of **resorts** and **dude ranches**. Rates drop when the mercury rises, and some places are open only in the peak winter and spring seasons.

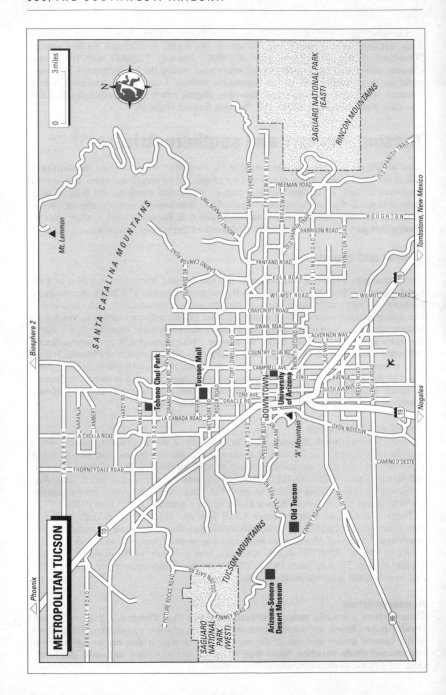

**METROPOLITAN TUCSON**

N

3 miles

0

Phoenix

Biosphere 2

Mt. Lemmon

SANTA CATALINA MOUNTAINS

SAGUARO NATIONAL PARK (EAST)

RINCON MOUNTAINS

OLD SPANISH TRAIL

Tombstone, New Mexico

FREEMAN ROAD

SPEEDWAY BLVD

BROADWAY

HOUGHTON

TANQUE VERDE BLVD

MOUNTAIN LEMMON HWY

OLD SPANISH TRAIL

HARRISON ROAD

IRVINGTON ROAD

GOLF LINKS ROAD

SABINO CANYON ROAD

PANTANO ROAD

KOLB ROAD

WILMOT ROAD

SUNRISE DR

WILMOT ROAD

CRAYCROFT ROAD

SWAN ROAD

ALVERNON WAY

SKYLINE DRIVE

COUNTRY CLUB ROAD

TWENTY-SECOND ROAD

FORT LOWELL BLVD

Tohono Chul Park

Tucson Mall

CAMPBELL AVE.

AJO WAY

ORANGE GROVE RD

RIVER ROAD

University of Arizona

FIRST AVENUE

DREXEL ROAD

HARDY RD

LA CANADA ROAD

STONE AVE

SIXTH AVENUE

VALENCIA ROAD

MAGEE RD

WETMORE RD

ROGER ROAD

ORACLE RD

DOWNTOWN

NARANJA

GRANT ROAD

LA CHOLLA ROAD

SPEEDWAY BLVD

'A' Mountain

MISSION ROAD

Nogales

LAMBERT

W. ANGLAM

THORNEYDALE ROAD

CAMINO D'OESTE

TANGERINE

TUCSON MOUNTAINS

GATES PASS RD

Old Tucson

AJO WAY

AVRA VALLEY ROAD

PICTURE ROCKS ROAD

GOLD GATE RD

KINNEY ROAD

Arizona-Sonora Desert Museum

KINNEY ROAD

SAGUARO NATIONAL PARK (WEST)

**Best Western Ghost Ranch Lodge**, 801 W Miracle Mile (☎520/791-7565 or 1-800/456-7565). Charming, old-fashioned resort, roughly ten miles north of town, with south-of-the-border stylings, a cactus-filled garden and amazingly low rates. ②.

**Clarion Santa Rita Hotel & Suites**, 88 E Broadway Blvd (☎520/622-4000 or 1-877/526-7737). Large if anonymous hotel that's an unexpected downtown bargain, and has the good Mexican *Cafe Poca Cosa* downstairs. ③.

**El Presidio Inn**, 297 N Main Ave (☎520/623-6151 or 1-800/349-6151). Three tasteful Spanish colonial suites in an historic downtown adobe B&B, with spacious wraparound veranda. ⑤.

**Flamingo Travelodge**, 1300 N Stone Ave (☎520/770-1910 or 1-800/300-3533). Attractively renovated motel, barely a mile north of downtown Tucson. Summer ②, winter ④.

**Hotel Congress**, 311 E Congress St (☎520/622-8848 or 1-800/722-8848). Central, bohemian downtown hotel, an easy walk from Amtrak, with vintage Art Deco furnishings. $15 hostel beds for HI-AYH members (no reservations) and simple private rooms for just over $30. There's a small cafe and a lively bar downstairs, and at night it's one of the hottest music venues in town. ①–③.

**Roadrunner Hostel**, 346 E 12th St (☎520/628-4709). Small and very central independent hostel in a downtown home, offering space in six-bed dorms for $13 per night or $70 per week, plus Internet access and bicycles for rent. ①.

**Tanque Verde Ranch**, 14301 E Speedway Blvd (☎520/296-6275 or 1-800/234-DUDE). Arizona's most authentic dude ranch, an irresistibly romantic 400-acre spread adjoining Saguaro National Park twenty miles east of downtown; offers luxury accommodation in individual *casitas* and a stable of over a hundred horses. Rates include all meals and a full program of rides. ⑧.

**Westward Look Resort**, 245 E Ima Rd (☎520/297-1151 or 1-800/722-2500). Plush, modern resort in attractive landscaped grounds north of the city, offering extra-large rooms and suites. ⑤–⑦.

## The Town

Tucson has two main centers: the **historic core** along the (usually bone-dry) Santa Cruz River, bisected by Congress Street, and the quarter around the **University of Arizona** campus, a mile to the east. The city was founded in the late 1700s by Catholic missionaries who came from Mexico, then a Spanish colony, to convert the Pima Indians. Nothing very substantial remains from this era, but hundreds of artifacts are now displayed inside the many historic adobe homes in and around the **El Presidio** district of cafes, art galleries and B&Bs, two blocks north of Broadway. Access to much of El Presidio is controlled by the **Tucson Museum of Art**, alongside at 140 N Main Ave (June–Aug Tues–Sat 10am–4pm, Sun noon–4pm; Sept–May Mon–Sat 10am–4pm, Sun noon–4pm; $2, free Tues). The museum itself has an excellent collection of pre-Columbian artifacts, as well as changing exhibitions of modern painting and sculpture, while the district's oldest house, **La Casa Cordova** at 175 N Meyer Ave (same hours), holds displays on the city's Mexican heritage.

Three blocks south, engulfed by the Tucson Convention Center complex, the adobe **Sosa-Carrillo-Frémont House** (Wed–Sat 10am–4pm; free) is the sole survivor of a neighborhood torn down during the 1960s. Built for merchant Leopoldo Carrillo in 1858, it was briefly rented by former explorer John C Frémont when he was Governor of Arizona in 1878. Though much restored, it offers a vivid sense of the more civilized side of frontier life, from the high-quality furniture and the saguaro-rib ceilings to the fig-tree-shaded rear courtyard gardens.

Tucson's other main area of interest, around the University of Arizona, spreads between Sixth Street and Speedway Boulevard, a mile east of downtown. Its highlight is the **Arizona State Museum** (Mon–Sat 9am–5pm, Sun 2–5pm; free), where an exceptionally comprehensive assembly of Native American artifacts from the very earliest days traces the evolution of the various Southwest tribes.

### Arizona-Sonora Desert Museum

Part zoo, part garden, the top-quality **Arizona-Sonora Desert Museum** is fourteen miles west of the university along Speedway Boulevard, in **Tucson Mountain Park** (daily: March–Sept 7.30am–6pm; Oct–Feb 8.30am–5pm; adults $8.95, ages 6–12 $1.75). Gallery displays in the museum proper explain regional geology and history, and a series of dioramas are filled with tarantulas, rattlesnakes and other creepy-crawlies. In enclosures along the looped path beyond – a hot walk in high summer – bighorn sheep, mountain lions, jaguars and other seldom-seen desert denizens prowl in credible simulations of their natural habitats, and a colony of impish prairie dogs goes about its impenetrable business. Hawks and bald eagles fly about their own large aviary, thankfully separated from a greenhouse-full of hummingbirds. The museum also serves as an animal rescue center: almost all the animals you see were injured in some way before ending up here, and would be unable to survive on their own.

## Saguaro National Park

Flanking Tucson to either side, the two sections of **SAGUARO NATIONAL PARK** offer visitors a rare and enthralling opportunity to stroll through strange desert "forests" of monumental, multi-limbed **saguaro** (pronounced *sa-wah-row*) cactuses. Each saguaro can grow up to fifty feet tall and weigh up to eight tons, but it takes around 150 years to do so. Whatever you may have seen in the movies, you can drive a long way in Arizona without seeing one; saguaro are unique to the Sonora Desert, and so the thrill when you finally encounter a thousand at once is deeply satisfying. Both segments of the park tend to be seen on short forays from the city: in summer, it's far too hot to do more than pose for photographs, dwarfed beneath some especially eccentric specimen, and there is in any case no lodging, or even permanent campground, in either segment.

The **Tucson Mountain District**, which stretches north from the Desert Museum around fifteen miles west of downtown Tucson, on the far side of the mountains, charges no admission fee. Beyond the **visitor center** (daily 8am–5pm; ☎520/733-5158), the nine-mile **Bajada Loop Drive** – not fully paved, but always passable to ordinary vehicles – loops through a wonderland of weird saguaro, offering plentiful short hiking trails and photo opportunities. Signal Hill is especially recommended, for its superb sunset views.

To reach the eastern section of the park, the **Rincon Mountain District** ($4 per vehicle), drive seventeen miles east of town, first along Broadway Boulevard and then Old Spanish Trail. Here, too, short trails such as the quarter-mile Desert Ecology Trail lead off the eight-mile **Cactus Forest Drive** (daily: April–Oct 7am–7pm; Nov–March 7am–5pm), but many visitors come specifically to hike far from the road, up into the mountains. The saguaro cactuses thin out almost as soon as you start climbing the Tanque Verde Ridge Trail, which leads in due course to a hundred-mile network of remote footpaths through thickly forested canyons.

## Eating, drinking and nightlife

Though downtown Tucson shuts down pretty early each evening – it's hard to find anywhere open after 9pm – the city has a fine selection of **restaurants**. Mexican joints and cowboy-style Wild-West steakhouses abound in the central districts, while fancier restaurants are mostly found in the exclusive St Philip's Plaza, a few miles north, as well as in the resort hotels. Most of the arty **cafes** and **nightclubs** on Congress Street downtown double as bars and restaurants, while a handful of student-oriented places can be found near the university. There are half a dozen country-and-western saloons on the outskirts of town. For a full rundown, check the listings in the free *Tucson Weekly*.

**Blue Willow**, 2616 N Campbell Ave (☎520/795-8736). Tasty, fruity breakfasts and light lunches and dinners, served on a pleasant garden patio.

**Cafe Terra Cotta**, St Philip's Plaza, 4310 N Campbell Ave (☎520/577-8100). Inventive Southwestern cuisine in a smart mall. The menu ranges from gourmet pizzas cooked in a wood-burning oven to meats grilled with chilis, all at under $20.

**Club Congress**, *Hotel Congress*, 311 E Congress St (☎520/622-8848). Hectic, trendy, late-opening bar, with live music a couple of nights each week; the *Cup Cafe*, off the hotel lobby, is a jazzy cafe, straight out of the 1930s but updated to include an espresso bar, which serves a bewilderingly broad menu from 8am until after midnight daily.

**Cottonwood Cafe**, 60 N Alvernon Way (☎520/326-6000). Top-quality Southwestern food at reasonable prices, east of downtown. If you can bear to eat a bird with eyelashes, ostrich mole *rojo* with pumpkin polenta costs $20. The same dishes are served in the adjoining *Cottonwood Club*, which features live music nightly.

**El Charro**, 311 N Court Ave (☎520/622-1922). Housed in the same El Presidio building since 1922, this claims to be the oldest Mexican restaurant in the US, and now has its own lively bar next door. The food is good, though not especially fiery; specialties include fine chimichangas.

**Gentle Ben's Brewing Co**, 865 E University Blvd (☎520/624-4177). Microbrewery serving simple food; regularly packed out with students.

**The Maverick, King of Clubs**, 4702 E 22nd St (☎520/748-0456). Old-fashioned country-music honky-tonk, well out from the center and brimming with Stetsons.

**The Rialto Theatre**, 318 E Congress St (☎520/740-0126). A 1920s vaudeville theater that's re-opened as Tucson's hottest venue for touring bands.

**Tohono Chul Tea Room**, Tohono Chul Park, 7366 N Paseo del Norte (☎520/797-1222). Attractive adobe cafe in small desert park on the northern fringes of town, operated by the *Cafe Terra Cotta* (see opposite). Open daily 8am–5pm; ideal for breakfast, a light lunch or a scones-and-jam afternoon tea.

# Biosphere 2

The giant Plexiglass bubble known as **BIOSPHERE 2** looms out of the desert thirty miles north of Tucson, in a high-security compound at mile-marker 96.5 on Hwy-77 and near the town of **Oracle**. On its completion in 1991, this vast complex was trumpeted as a major laboratory for experiments in applied environmental science. Containing five separate "biomes," or self-contained ecosystems – rainforest, marsh, savannah, desert and a 25ft-deep ocean – it was designed as a miniature working model of Biosphere 1, planet Earth itself, and stocked like a real-life Noah's Ark with almost four thousand species of plants and animals. Backed by a hundred million dollars' worth of support from Texas oil tycoon Ed Bass, this far-fetched scheme was intended as a step toward the eventual colonization of Mars.

Eight "Biospherians" were sealed into Biosphere 2 in September 1991, their "mission" being to survive in isolation for two full years. This they more or less did, although emergency oxygen twice had to be pumped in as carbon dioxide levels rose. Much of what transpired was replete with irony; hungry Biospherians soon found themselves planting bananas and papayas in what was supposed to be the inviolate wilderness of the rainforest, and destroying parts of the desert to boost oxygen, while the ocean proved impossible to keep clean. As for their fellow inhabitants, the bush babies caught the hummingbirds, and in fact the only birds to survive were unwanted sparrows that sneaked in during construction. By the time the next crew moved in, conditions at Biosphere 2 had degenerated into farce. Two of the original crew, who had been acrimoniously fired, sneaked back and broke the Biosphere's seals from the outside, thus aborting the second mission after just six months; they later sued for wrongful dismissal and won compensation. Since 1996 Biosphere 2 has operated in conjunction with Columbia University, which seems to be frantically trying to think of something to do with its vast new "campus." The line these days is that the problems are what make it interesting.

In its brief heyday, Biosphere 2 was one of Arizona's most popular tourist destinations. Now that no one is locked inside, the crowds have dwindled, but the two-and-a-half-hour guided tours are still worth taking (daily 8am–5pm; $12.95). Most of that time is spent peering into the greenhouses hoping to spot any sign of life larger than an ant, and marveling at the fact that, whatever you may have assumed, Biosphere 2 is not solar powered but depends on an external natural-gas power plant. Visitors are also allowed into the Biospherians' futuristic living quarters, tacked like a space capsule onto the back of the main block, where they appear to have suffered no privations whatsoever.

Should you arrive at the compound after 5pm, paying $5 admission entitles you to a quick look around on your own, and you can redeem your fee against purchases at its all-day *Canyon Cafe,* which serves good meals on an appealing terrace, There's also a cybercafe, and good-value **lodging** at the on-site *Inn at Biosphere 2* (☎520/825-6222; May–Sept ③, Oct–April ⑤).

## South to the border: the Mission Trail

South from Tucson, I-19 heads straight for the Mexican border, 65 miles away, passing some tangible reminders of the region's Spanish and Mexican heritage. The first of these, the **MISSION SAN XAVIER DEL BAC** – the best-preserved mission church in the United States – lies just west of the freeway, nine miles south of downtown Tucson on the fringe of the vast arid plain of San Xavier Indian Reservation. It was built for the Franciscans between 1783 and 1797, and even today its white-plastered walls and towers seem like a dazzling desert mirage; how much more dramatic they must have been two centuries ago, when to Christian missionaries and Apache warriors alike they symbolized the Spanish quest to subdue and convert the native peoples of the Southwest. No one knows the name of the architect responsible for its Spanish Baroque, even Moorish lines – it consists almost entirely of domes and arches, making only minimal use of timber – let alone the 'O'odham craftsmen who embellished its every feature. Recently restored with the help of Vatican experts previously responsible for work on the Sistine Chapel, it attracts a constant stream of tourists (daily 9am–6pm; donation). The ideal time to come is on Sunday morning, when four separate Masses draw large congregations from the reservation.

Fifty miles further south, barely twenty miles north of the border, stands the evocative ruin of another eighteenth-century mission church, preserved as **TUMACÁCORI NATIONAL HISTORICAL PARK** (daily 8am–5pm; $4), topped by a restored whitewashed dome, and home only to the birds that fly down from the Patagonia Mountains. Behind its red-tinged, weather-beaten facade, the plaster has crumbled from the interior walls to reveal bare adobe bricks. A few traces of a mural can still be discerned in the raised sanctuary, but little remains of the priests' living quarters alongside. A very good museum is housed in the small **visitor center** at the entrance, and a self-guiding tour map ($1) tells the mission story.

### Nogales, Arizona–Nogales, Mexico

Twenty miles south of Tumacácori, an hour from Tucson, sits the largest of the Arizonan–Mexican border towns, **NOGALES** – in effect two towns, one in the US and one across the border in Mexico. Known jointly as *Ambos Nogales* (both Nogales), they welcome considerable numbers of tourists, though with cheap Mexican crafts now so widely available in the US, day-trippers these days tend to be looking for cut-price medicines rather than rugs or hammocks.

There's nothing in particular to see on either side of the border, though the contrast between the sedate, ordered streets of the American town and the jumbled whitewashed houses clinging to the slopes in Mexico hits you as soon as you come in sight. Nogales, Arizona – the birthplace of iconoclastic jazz great **Charles Mingus** – is a dreary little community, while Nogales, Mexico, is basically a lively, large-scale street market.

Crossing the border is straightforward, as Mexican visas are only required by travelers heading more than 21km south of the border. US citizens should, however, ideally carry their passports or birth certificates – drivers' licenses are not always sufficient – while foreign visitors should check that their visa status entitles them to reenter the US; if you're on or eligible for the Visa Waiver Scheme (see p.10), you're fine. There's no need to change money; US dollars are freely accepted by stores and businesses in Mexico.

None of the Arizona-side **motels** stands within a mile of the border; the closest is the *Best Western Siesta Motel*, 673 N Grand Ave (☎520/287-4671; ③). Most visitors prefer to **eat** in Mexico, where abundant cafes and diners line the busy central streets. Classier dining is offered by the unusual *La Roca*, hollowed into the rocky hillside just east of the railroad, a couple of blocks from the border at c/Elias 91, where a full seafood meal costs well under $20.

## The southeast corner

Among thousands of acres of unspoiled and magnificent wilderness, southeast Arizona contains numerous well-preserved and highly atmospheric **ghost towns**. While I-10 buzzes along the New Mexico border, the more scenic US-80 makes a grand tour of the region. Even if you're racing through this barren country, set aside an hour at least for the excellent **Amerind Foundation Museum** (June–Aug Wed–Sun 10am–4pm; Sept–May daily 10am–4pm; $3), a mile from I-10 exit 318, 65 miles east of Tucson, which is one of the better anthropological museums in the US, broad in scope and focusing in turn on the diverse native cultures of the Southwest, the Pacific Northwest, and Central and South America. Nearby, the town of **BENSON** has been gearing itself up for several years for the opening of **Kartchner Caverns State Park**, a pristine labyrinth of subterranean wonders said to surpass New Mexico's Carlsbad (see p.829). The park's debut has been repeatedly postponed, but it may just happen during the lifetime of this book.

### Tombstone

Perhaps the most famous town in the Wild West, **TOMBSTONE** lies 22 miles south of I-10 on US-80, 67 miles southeast of Tucson. More than a century has passed since its mining days came to an end, but "The Town Too Tough to Die" clings to an afterlife as a tourist theme park. With its dusty streets, wooden sidewalks and swinging saloon doors, it's surprisingly unchanged. Most adults, however, have seen too many inauthentic replicas and movie re-creations for the real thing to retain much appeal, and so Tombstone is reduced to trying to divert kids with tacky dioramas and daily shoot-outs. The best time to visit is during **Helldorado Days** in late October, when the air is cooler and the sun less harsh, but the streets are full of gun-toting strangers acting out gun battles and stagecoach robberies.

Tombstone only began life as a silver-boomtown in 1877, and by the end of the 1880s it was all but deserted again. However, on the day that gave it the notoriety that's kept it alive, its population stood at more than ten thousand. It was 2pm on October 26, 1881, when **Doc Holliday**, along with **Wyatt Earp** and his brothers Virgil and Morgan (who all served as local sheriffs), confronted a band of suspected cattle rustlers, the Clantons, in the legendary **Gunfight at the OK Corral**. Within a few minutes, three of the suspects were dead. The Earps were accused of murder, but charges were eventually dropped.

Although the gunfight in fact took place on Fremont Street, the **OK Corral** itself remains the major attraction for visitors (daily 8.30am–5pm; $2.50), despite the fact that it holds little more than crude dummies that show the supposed locations of the Earps and the Clantons, in complete contradiction to contemporary reports of the fight.

A couple of blocks along Allen Street, the **Bird Cage Theater** (daily 8am–6pm; $4) was Tombstone's leading venue for entertainment of all kinds. Seven "bird cages," much like theater boxes but curtained off and said to have been used by prostitutes, hang from either side of the main hall. The theater now holds a motley collection of curiosities, including a revolting foot-long "merman" from China, while downstairs you can see the old gaming tables and bordello rooms.

Central **motels** include the *Adobe Lodge*, 505 Fremont St (☎520/457-2241 or 1-888/457-2241; ③), while the classier mountain-view *Best Western Lookout Lodge* is a mile north on US-80 W (☎520/457-2223 or 1-800/652-6772; ③). Among old-style **saloons** serving steaks and beer in as raucous an atmosphere as they can are the *Crystal Palace* at Fifth and Allen, and *Big Nose Kate's* at 417 E Allen St, where you can still join an ongoing card game.

### Bisbee

Crammed into a narrow gorge 25 miles south of Tombstone, the town of **BISBEE** is rivaled only by Jerome, near Sedona (p.852), as Arizona's most atmospheric Victorian relic. Like Jerome, its fortunes were built on a century of mining mundane, dependable copper from the surrounding mountains, rather than a few ephemeral years of gold and silver. Its solid brick buildings still stand as an enduring testament to the days when Bisbee's population of twenty thousand outstripped both Phoenix and Tucson to make it the largest city between New Orleans and San Francisco. Phelps Dodge finally closed down its Bisbee operations in 1975, having extracted more than six billion dollars' worth of metals. As the miners moved away, however, artists and retirees moved in, preserving Bisbee's original architecture while turning it into a thriving, friendly little community that caters to tourists without being overwhelmed by them.

Walking Bisbee's narrow central streets, lined with galleries and antiques stores, is a pleasure in itself, but if you'd like to know more of the background it's well worth calling in at the **Bisbee Mining and Historical Museum**, 5 Copper Queen Plaza (daily 10am–4pm; adults $3, under-18s free).

The nicest **place to stay** is the venerable *Copper Queen Hotel*, 11 Howell Ave (☎520/432-2216; ④), with a plush bar and a good **restaurant** with terrace seating.

## Southwest Arizona: Yuma

There's virtually nothing in the vast desert plain of southwest Arizona to tempt you off the twin freeways that sprint to California. The US Army stages tank battles in its Yuma Proving Grounds between I-10 and I-8, while the air force drops bombs and tests Stealth technology in the more mountainous region bordering Mexico. The largest town, **YUMA**, is little more than an oversized pit stop for freight trains and cross-country truckers. **Yuma Territorial Prison**, now a state park (daily 8am–5pm; $3) beside the Colorado River, was known a century ago as the "Hell Hole of Arizona," holding over a hundred of the Wild West's most violent criminals. Its first inmates were forced to build the adobe walls that later contained them; there's a small museum, and you can wander around the grounds and cell blocks at will.

Neon-lit budget **motels** along the main drag include the good-value *Yuma Cabana*, 2151 S Fourth Ave (☎520/783-8311 or 1-800/874-0811; ②), while the *Crossing*, 2690 S Fourth Ave (☎520/776-5551), is typical of several run-of-the-mill **diners**.

## Phoenix

The state capital and largest city in Arizona, **PHOENIX**, holds only minimal appeal for tourists. When it began life in the 1860s, it must have seemed like a good idea. The

ACCOMMODATION
1 Budget Lodge Motel
2 HI-Phoenix
3 San Carlos
4 YMCA

EATING
A Alice Cooper'stown
B Pizzeria Bianco
C Sam's Cafe

**DOWNTOWN PHOENIX**

sweltering little farming town stood in the heart of the large Salt River Valley, with a ready-made irrigation system left by ancient Indians (the name Phoenix honors the fact that the city rose from the ashes of a long-vanished **Hohokam** community). Within a century, however, Phoenix had turned into what writer Edward Abbey called "the blob that is eating Arizona," acquiring as it did so the money and political clout to defy the self-evident absurdity of building a huge city in a virtually waterless desert. Now the eighth largest city in the US, it has filled the entire valley, engulfing the neighboring towns of **Scottsdale**, **Mesa** and **Tempe** in the process, with over a million people within the city boundaries and more than two million in the metropolitan area. Arizona's financial and industrial epicenter may just be getting into its stride; boosters claim the megalopolis will one day stretch 150 miles, from Wickenburg to Tucson.

The city's phenomenal rise was originally fueled by its image as a healthy oasis, where the desert had been tamed and transformed into a suburban idyll. While retirees still flock to enclaves such as **Sun City**, however, Phoenix now has a deserved reputation as the most unpleasant city in the Southwest – Las Vegas with no casinos, or LA with no beach. Above all, it's **hot**; between June and August daytime highs average over 100°F, making it the hottest city outside the Middle East.

In winter, when temperatures rarely drop below 65°F, tourists from colder climes arrive in large numbers. They pay vast sums to warm their bones in the luxury resorts and spas, concentrated especially in Scottsdale, that are the modern equivalent of the 1930s dude ranches. Unlike golf, tennis and shopping, sightseeing rarely ranks high on the agenda – which is just as well, since there's a good deal of truth in the charge laid by Phoenix's older arch-rival, Tucson, that the city is sorely lacking in culture and history. Apart from the **Heard Museum**'s excellent Native American displays, and Frank Lloyd Wright's architecture studio at **Taliesin West**, Phoenix is short of must-see attractions. In fact, if you're on a touring vacation, you'd miss little if you bypassed it altogether; a day at one of the city's plentiful upscale malls is probably as authentic and enjoyable an experience as Phoenix has to offer.

### Arrival, information and getting around

**Sky Harbor International Airport** (☎602/273-3321), three miles east of downtown, is connected by Valley Metro **buses** (☎602/253-5000) with downtown (#13; Mon–Sat), Tempe and Mesa (Mon–Fri), but it's easier to take a door-to-door shuttle bus, at $12 for downtown destinations or around $20 for Scottsdale, with a company such as SuperShuttle (☎602/244-9000 or 1-800/BLUEVAN). Arizona Shuttle Services (☎520/795-6671 or 1-800/888-2749) run south to Tucson, while Nava-Hopi (☎520/774-5003 or 1-800/892-8687) head north to Flagstaff and the Grand Canyon.

There's no longer an Amtrak **train** service to Phoenix, but Greyhound **buses** arrive at 2115 E Buckeye Rd (☎602/389-4200 or 1-800/231-2222), close to the airport. Getting around without a car is not ideal – it can take hours to cross town – but it's not impossible. Valley Metro's commuter routes charge $1.25 per ride; pick up a schedule at the downtown terminal, at First and Washington. Tourists are more likely to use the purple DASH buses (Mon–Fri 6.30am–5.30pm; 30¢), which ply between the Arizona Center and the Capitol downtown. For a **taxi**, call Checker Cab (☎602/257-1818).

Phoenix's main **visitor center** is at Adams and Second downtown (Mon–Fri 8am–5pm; ☎602/254-6500 or 1-877/255-5749; 24hr hotline ☎602/252-5588); there's also an office at 24th Street and Camelback, at the northeast corner of the Biltmore Fashion Park (Mon–Sat 10am–9pm, Sun noon–6pm). The main **post office** is at 4949 E Van Buren St, though the branch at 522 N Central Ave is more convenient for downtown.

### Accommodation

Metropolitan Phoenix is so huge that it's worth paying a bit extra to ensure that your **accommodation** is near the places you want to visit. Oddly enough, downtown Phoenix is not one of the more expensive areas, with cheap motels lining the somewhat run-down W Van Buren Street a few blocks north of the center. The summer room rates, shown below, rise significantly in winter, when snowbirds from all over the US fill the upscale resorts of Scottsdale in particular.

**Budget Lodge Motel**, 402 W Van Buren St (☎602/254-7247). Reasonably attractive rooms at very attractive rates – not far from downtown, but you'll feel safer if you drive rather than walk. ②.

**Days Inn Resort at Fashion Square Mall**, 4710 N Scottsdale Rd, Scottsdale (☎480/947-5411 or 1-800/325-2525). Standard hotel, well priced by local standards, and handily located within walking distance of downtown Scottsdale. ④.

**HI-Phoenix**, *The Metcalf House*, 1026 N 9th St above Roosevelt (☎602/254-9803). Dorm beds at $12 for HI-AYH members, $15 others; a 15min walk north of the Arizona Center downtown. No phone reservations, but space is usually available. No curfew, cheap bike rental. ①.

**San Carlos Hotel**, 202 N Central Ave (☎602/253-4121 or 1-800/528-5446). Atmospheric, very central Twenties hotel, with tasteful good-value rooms, a nice cafe (see p.846) and a rooftop swimming pool. ④.

**Scottsdale's Fifth Avenue Inn**, 6935 5th Ave, Scottsdale (☎480/994-9461 or 1-800/528-7396, fax 947-1695). Good-value motel with pool, on the edge of Scottsdale's shopping district. ③.

**Super 8 Mesa Town Center**, 3 E Main St, Mesa (☎480/834-6060 or 1-800/800-8000). Budget motel in the heart of downtown Mesa, a couple of blocks from the Southwest Museum. ②.

**Super 8 Tempe/Scottsdale**, 1020 E Apache Blvd, Tempe (☎480/967-8891 or 1-800/800-8000). Chain motel, within half a mile of the university and 5 miles of the airport. ③.

**YMCA**, 350 N 1st Ave (☎602/253-6181). Grungy but central single rooms for men and women, with shared bathrooms. Very low weekly rates. No reservations: first-come, first-served. ①.

## Central Phoenix

**Downtown Phoenix** – defined as the few blocks east and west of Central Avenue, and north and south of Washington Street – is too hot, too run-down, and too spread out to walk around in any comfort. The latest downtown mall – the **Arizona Center**, on Van Buren Street between Third and Fifth – has finally brought some retail business back to the center, but it's still a pale imitation of the mega-malls further north.

What little remains of Phoenix's nineteenth-century architecture now constitutes **Heritage Square**, a couple of blocks southeast of the Arizona Center at 115 N Sixth St. Rather than original adobe ranchhouses, however, it preserves a quaint assortment of Victorian homes, converted into tearooms and toy museums. You can get a better impression of the early days at the new **Phoenix Museum of History**, across the street at 105 N Fifth St (Mon–Sat 10am–5pm, Sun noon–5pm; $5), which features the city's first jail – a rock with a chain attached. Twenty sun-baked blocks west, the sparkling copper dome of the disused **Arizona State Capitol** dominates the low-level sprawl. Documents in the dull, dry museum within do little to bring the state's political history to life (Mon–Fri 8am–5pm; free).

Two more significant attractions lie a mile or so north of downtown. Thanks to extensive remodeling, the **Phoenix Art Museum**, 1625 N Central Ave (Tues, Wed, Sat & Sun 10am–5pm, Thurs & Fri 10am–9pm; $6, free Thurs 5–9pm), has plenty of space to display its permanent collection, which includes paintings by Georgia O'Keeffe and Rufino Tamayo, as well as de rigueur Western art by Russell and Remington and some middleweight Old Masters, and features stimulating temporary exhibitions. Three blocks north and a block east, the **Heard Museum**, 22 E Monte Vista Rd (daily 9.30am–5pm; $7), has also been greatly enlarged, while still showcasing the lovely old buildings in which it was founded. It provides a fascinating introduction to the **Native Americans** of the Southwest, and their arts and crafts in particular. There's an especial emphasis on the Hohokam, with plenty of artifacts from the large town, now known as "La Ciudad," which occupied the site of modern Phoenix during the twelfth century. Elsewhere, the superb pottery collection ranges from stunning Mimbres bowls to modern Hopi ceramics, but the real highlight is a refrigerated room filled with *kachina* **dolls** – 400 of them donated by the late Arizona senator Barry Goldwater – arranged according to the Hopi sacred calendar.

If Phoenix gets too hot to bear, the coolest place to beat the heat is on the east side of town at the Big Surf **water park**, 1500 N McClintock Ave (May–Sept only: Mon–Sat 10am–6pm, Sun 11am–7pm; $14), where you can ride 5ft waves or careen down water-slides into a giant freshwater lagoon.

## Taliesin West and the Cosanti Foundation

Whatever its general appearance may suggest, Phoenix has managed to attract some visionary designers. Notable among them is **Frank Lloyd Wright**, who came to the city to work on the *Biltmore Hotel*, and stayed for most of the 25 years before his death in 1959. His winter studio, **Taliesin West** – located at 114th Street and Frank Lloyd Wright Boulevard, at Scottsdale's northeastern edge – is now an architecture school and a working design studio, with regular multimedia exhibits of the man's life and work (daily: June–Sept 7.30–11am; Oct–May 10am–4pm; ☎602/860-2700). It's open for up to five hour-long tours each morning ($12), followed by three 1hr 30min "Insights" on winter afternoons ($16).

Less well known, but in many ways more compelling, is the **Cosanti Foundation**, four miles west of Taliesin at 6433 Doubletree Rd (daily 9am–5pm; $1 donation). The buildings, designed by **Paolo Soleri**, an Italian-born ex-student of Wright, and constructed out of rammed earth and concrete, have a much more organic feel than Taliesin. Crafts workshops make bells and cast bronzes, and a small museum shows drawings and models of Soleri's life's work: **Arcosanti**, a space-age, environmentally sensitive project designed to be (someday) an entirely self-sufficient community of five thousand people, which emerges from the desert just an hour's drive north, a mile east of I-17 at Cordes Junction. Three-hour guided tours are given throughout the day ($5 donation; ☎520/632-7135), and an airy and spacious cafe serves healthy and tasty meals.

## Eating
Most of the **restaurants** in greater Phoenix seem to have retreated to the malls in recent years, so unless you're prepared to pay resort prices, it's hard to find a good restaurant with very much atmosphere. The mall places aren't at all bad, however, and there's plenty of variety. Apart from a block or two in central Scottsdale, no area of the metropolis is small enough to walk around while you look for a place to eat, but if you're happy to drive, neighborhood diners – especially Mexican – can still be found.

**Alice Cooper'stown**, 101 E Jackson St (☎602/253-7337). Barbecue restaurant-cum-sports bar, owned by the rock star and alongside downtown's America West Arena, where the food's better than you'd expect, and the atmosphere is fun. Lunch and dinner daily.

**Ed Debevic's Short Orders Deluxe**, 2102 E Highland Ave (☎602/956-2760). Burgers and fries, malts and cokes, served amid frenetic retro-Americana that includes a mini-jukebox on every table.

**House of Tricks**, 114 E 7th St, Tempe (☎480/968-1114). Tiny modern-American place in the university district, with lots of vegetarian options. Closed Sun.

**Monti's La Casa Vieja**, 3 W 1st St, Tempe (☎480/967-7594). Tempe's oldest adobe house, built in 1873, is now an atmospheric Western-themed diner, serving a conventional steak-and-chicken menu at extraordinarily low prices. Lunch and dinner daily, until at least 11pm.

**Pizzeria Bianco**, Heritage Square, 623 E Adams St (☎602/258-8300). Good quality pizzas in very convenient downtown location. Lunch and dinner Tues–Fri, dinner only Sat & Sun.

**Roma Coffee Co**, *San Carlos Hotel*, 202 N Central Ave (☎602/253-0410). Small downtown cafe, in an historic hotel, with some sidewalk seating.

**Roxsand**, Biltmore Fashion Park, 2594 E Camelback Rd (☎602/381-0444). Eclectic, futuristic restaurant in upmarket uptown mall. Entrees drawn from the major world cuisines – especially Asian, with plenty of spicy Thai and Chinese sauces – start at around $20.

**Roy's**, 7001 N Scottsdale Rd, Scottsdale (☎480/905-1155). Ravishing Pacific Rim restaurant in very chic dining district. Meaty entrees, mostly at $20–25, include Szechuan barbecued pork ribs or rack of lamb, while specials usually include Hawaiian fish dishes. Open daily for dinner only.

**Sam's Cafe**, Arizona Center, 455 N 3rd St (☎602/252-3545). Hectic downtown mall joint, with patio seating, that's nonetheless a great place to try out modern Southwestern cuisine at old-fashioned prices. Lunch and dinner daily.

## Nightlife, entertainment and sports
Not surprisingly, **nightlife** in Phoenix tends toward cowboy dance halls and Top 40 discos in the big hotels. For a rundown of what's on musically, pick up the free weekly *New Times* in local record- or bookstores, or check out the bars and clubs listed below. Both the Phoenix Symphony Hall, 225 E Adams St (☎602/262-7272), and the Scottsdale

Center for the Arts, 7380 E Second St (☎602/994-2787), put on **classical music, theater** and **ballet**. The **Arizona Diamondbacks** have been playing major league baseball beneath the retractable roof of the Bank One Ballpark since 1998 (☎602/514-8500), while the **Phoenix Suns** play NBA basketball at the America West Arena, 201 E Jefferson St (☎602/379-7867), and football's **Arizona Cardinals** are based at the university's Sun Devil Stadium (☎602/379-0102).

**Balboa Cafe**, 404 S Mill Ave, Tempe (☎480/966-1300). Jazz, offbeat rock and acoustic music, near the university.

**Char's Has The Blues**, 4631 N 7th Ave (☎602/230-0205). Phoenix's longest-standing, best-loved blues venue, attracting big-name touring stars.

**Coyote Springs Brewing Company**, Town & Country Shopping Center, 4883 N 20th St (☎602/468-0403). Mall microbrewery that puts on R&B several nights of the week.

**Electric Ballroom**, 1216 E Apache Blvd, Tempe (☎480/894-0707). A steady diet of rap, dance and indie rock for the college crowd.

**Mr Lucky's**, 3660 NW Grand Ave (☎602/246-0686). Massive country-music honky-tonk, featuring real-life bull-riding at weekends.

**Phoenix Live!**, Arizona Center, 455 N 3rd Ave (☎602/252-2502). Anodyne but very central alliance of three separate clubs under a single roof, with a single cover charge.

## East of Phoenix: the Superstition Mountains

Relief from the tedious Phoenix sprawl is provided by the **Superstition Mountains** that rise to the east. The main route through the angular mountains, Hwy-88 (popularly known as the **Apache Trail**), is full of cars on summer weekends; the road cuts off northeast from US-60 about ten miles east of downtown Phoenix. Despite the many dams along the Salt River, it makes for a pleasant drive, with lots of picnic spots and campgrounds. The road turns to gravel just beyond the funky hamlet of **Tortilla Flat**, before reaching the cliff dwellings of **Tonto National Monument** (daily 8am–5pm; $4 per vehicle), where the remains of a large pueblo built in the mid-fourteenth century by Salado Indians are preserved in the mouths of three distinct caves.

Hwy-88 rejoins US-60 at the nondescript mining town of **GLOBE**, on the western edge of the two-million-acre San Carlos Apache Indian Reservation, roughly sixty miles south of the awesome **Salt River Canyon**.

# Central Arizona

The interstate I-40 crosses through the center of Arizona, skirting the **Navajo Reservation** that fills the northeastern corner of the state. Though the narrow strip of land to either side can be extraordinarily beautiful, with double rainbows reaching across the desert plain and fiery dawns blazing along the horizon, it holds few specific places worth stopping for until you come to the **Flagstaff** area. Itself a pleasant town, Flagstaff makes a base for several interesting excursions – to ancient **Native American sites** and the New Age mecca of **Sedona**, but above all to the **Grand Canyon**. Beyond Flagstaff to the west, there is once again little of interest.

## East of Flagstaff

The widely touted **Meteor Crater** (daily: summer 6am–6pm, winter 8am–5pm; $8), six miles south of the interstate on a well-marked road 38 miles east of Flagstaff, might have been interesting 22,000 years ago, when a meteorite blasted a huge hole, nearly a mile across and over five hundred feet deep, into the scrubby plateau. These days, however, it's a privately run tourist operation, managed in mock-Park Service style and absurdly overpriced. Visitors cannot hike into the actual crater.

Two old Route 66 towns, **WINSLOW** and **HOLBROOK**, are kept alive by trans-continental truckers. Each town has a strip of motels – head for the *Best Western Adobe Inn* in Winslow at 1701 N Park Drive (☎520/289-4638; ③) or the concrete teepees of the *Wigwam Motel* at 811 W Hopi Drive in Holbrook (☎520/524-3048; ②) – and not much else.

## Petrified Forest National Park

At **PETRIFIED FOREST NATIONAL PARK**, which straddles I-40 a dozen miles east of Holbrook, a fossilized prehistoric forest of gigantic trees is gradually being unearthed by erosion. The original cells of the wood have been replaced by multicolored crystals of quartz. Cross-sections, cut through with diamond saws and polished, look stunning, and can be seen in the two **visitor centers**, roughly thirty miles apart at the north and south entrances. On the ground, however, the trees are not all that exciting: segmented, crumbling and very dark. Here and there rough concrete walkways have been laid over the terrain – and often over the tree trunks themselves. The **Long Logs Walk** near the southern entrance is probably the best section; but they're still just a bunch of logs lying in the sand, even if they are stone logs.

The northern section of the national park – site of the main **visitor center** and entrance station (daily 8am–5pm; ☎520/524-6228; $10 per vehicle) – is renowned for its views of the **Painted Desert**, an undulating expanse of solidified sand dunes, which at different times of day take on different colors (predominantly bluish shades of gray and reddish shades of brown). It's a godforsaken and eerie landscape, if not one that lives long in the memory.

# Flagstaff

Although some of its old streets are still redolent with Wild West charm, **FLAGSTAFF**'s real significance has always been as a center for transportation and trade. Its main thoroughfare, Santa Fe Avenue, was once **Route 66**, and before that the pioneer trail west; while for more than a century the **Santa Fe Railroad** has run right alongside.

The first white settlers arrived in 1876, lured from Boston by widely publicized accounts of mineral wealth and fertile land, but they soon moved on, disappointed, towards Prescott. However, they stayed long enough to celebrate the centenary of American independence by flying the Stars and Stripes from a towering pine tree. This flagpole became a familiar landmark on the route west, and as the community grew it inevitably became known as Flagstaff. Right from the start, it was a cosmopolitan town, with a strong black and Hispanic population working in the (originally Mormon-owned) lumber mills and in the cattle industry, and with Navajo and Hopi Indians heading in from their nearby reservations to trade. Today, Flagstaff makes an ideal base for travelers, with hotels, restaurants, bars and shops aplenty within easy strolling range of the center (and a number of food and lodging chains a couple of miles away beside the interstate). There's not all that much of interest in the town itself, but the countryside in every direction is very much worth exploring.

## Arrival and information

As the nearest town of any size to the **Grand Canyon**, seventy miles northwest, Flagstaff remains a major junction for road and rail passengers; full details of bus connections to the Canyon, which tie in with Amtrak's two daily **trains** to Flagstaff, appear on p.856. Nava-Hopi, 114 W Route 66 (☎520/774-5003 or 1-800/892-8687) also run three daily **buses** between Flagstaff and Phoenix ($22). The least-expensive **car rental**, which for a group traveling to the Grand Canyon should cost less than the bus, is Budget Rent-a-Car, 100 N Humphreys St (☎520/779-0307); Avis, Hertz and National also have outlets. Cosmic Cycles, 113 S San Francisco St (Mon–Sat 9am–6pm; ☎520/779-1092), rent out **mountain bikes** for around $20 per day, or $75 per week.

The helpful local **visitor center** adjoins the station at 101 W Santa Fe Ave (Mon–Sat 7am–6pm, Sun 7am–5pm; ☎520/774-9541 or 1-800/842-7293).

## Accommodation

Flagstaff's dozens of **motels** and **B&Bs** provide reasonable value, while **budget** travelers can choose between four hotels that offer hostel-style dorm beds as well as private rooms. Most of the chain motels are congregated well to the east, along Butler Avenue and Lucky Lane, but staying nearer downtown is much more fun.

**DuBeau International Hostel**, 19 W Phoenix Ave (☎520/773-1656, 774-6731 or 1-800/398-7112). HI-AYH hostel offering $13 dorm beds, doubles for around $27, and tent camping in the yard for $6. It also runs a $25 round-trip shuttle to the Grand Canyon (tours $38), and $20 tours down to Sedona and Montezuma Castle. ③.

**Econolodge West**, 2355 S Beulah Blvd (☎520/774-2225 or 1-800/490-6562). Relatively appealing chain motel, with good facilities, south of downtown near the interstate. ④.

**Grand Canyon International Hostel**, 19 S San Francisco St (☎520/779-9421). Independent hostel in converted motel across from Amtrak; dorm beds $12 summer, $8–10 winter, plus private rooms. Tours to the Grand Canyon ($38) and Sedona ($20), and car rental discounts. ③.

**The Inn at Four Ten**, 410 N Leroux St (☎520/774-0088 or 1-800/774-2008). Bright ranch home that's now an antique-furnished eight-room B&B. ⑥/⑦.

**Monte Vista**, 100 N San Francisco St (☎520/779-6971 or 1-800/545-3068). Flagstaff's best bargain; a very pleasant little 1920s hotel in the heart of downtown, restored to offer dorm beds ($16 summer, $10 winter) and double rooms of varying sizes, with and without attached bathrooms. Rates rise by up to $15 at weekends. ①–④.

**Motel 6**, 2440 E Lucky Lane (☎520/774-8756 or 1-800/466-8356). The cheapest of several *Motel 6s* on the outskirts of town. ②.

**Weatherford**, 23 N Leroux St (☎520/774-2731). Very central hostel, upstairs in a minimally restored railroad hotel, with $16 dorms and private doubles. ①–④.

## The Town

Flagstaff's atmospheric downtown stretches for a few redbrick blocks north of the railroad. Filled with cafes, bars, and stores selling Route 66 souvenirs and Indian crafts, it's a fun place to stroll around, even if it holds no significant tourist attractions or historic buildings. Your most lasting impression is likely to be of the magnificent San Francisco Peaks, rising smoothly from the plains on the northern horizon, and topped by a jagged ridge.

The exceptional Museum of Northern Arizona, however, three miles northwest of downtown on US-180, rivals Phoenix's Heard Museum as the best museum in the state (daily 9am–5pm; $5). Its main emphasis is on documenting Native American life, with an excellent run-through of the Anasazi past and contemporary Navajo, Havasupai and Hopi cultures, and also actively encourages the development of traditional and even new skills among Native American craftworkers. The exquisite inlaid silver jewelry now made by the Hopi, for example, is the result of a museum-backed program to find work for Hopi servicemen returning from World War II. At all times, marvellous pots, rugs and *kachina* dolls are on display – a pleasant surprise after the low standards often seen elsewhere – but the time to come is for one of the Indian Craftsmen Exhibitions each summer. The Zuni show lasts for five days around Memorial Day weekend in late May; the Hopi show is on the weekend closest to July 4; and the nine-day Navajo event is at the end of July and the start of August, with every item for sale.

### Eating and nightlife
There's enough money around in Flagstaff to support several upscale restaurants, while the area around San Francisco Street, both north and south of the tracks, must be the liveliest nightspot between Las Vegas and Santa Fe, filled with vegetarian cafes, espresso bars and pubs.

**Alpine Pizza**, 7 N Leroux St (☎520/779-4109). Raucous student hangout downtown, with decent pizzas and lots of beer.

**Beaver Street Brewery & Whistle Stop Cafe**, 11 S Beaver St (☎520/779-0079). Inventive sandwiches and salads, wood-fired pizzas, and outdoor barbecue in the beer garden in summer.

**Black Barts**, 2760 E Butler Ave (☎520/779-3142). Enjoyable Western-themed steakhouse on the east edge of town, with a delicious smell of burning wood, and waiting staff who sing and dance on stage in between serving up barbecued steaks, ribs and chickens, for $15–20.

**Cafe Espress**, 16 N San Francisco St (☎520/774-0541). Great vegetarian breakfasts, then salads, sandwiches and veggie specials for the rest of the day, plus espresso coffees.

**Charly's Pub and Grill**, *Hotel Weatherford*, 23 N Leroux St (☎520/779-1919). Cafe-restaurant that makes a classy if unlikely contrast to the hostel rooms upstairs, serving good, inexpensive meals accompanied by live music (cocktail piano at lunch, bands at night).

**Flagstaff Brewing Company**, 16 E I-40 (☎520/773-1442). Popular downtown pub, with outdoor seating, big windows, and live music Wed–Sat.

**The Museum Club**, 3404 E I-40 (☎520/526-9434). A real oddity; this log-cabin taxidermy museum somehow transmogrified into a classic Route 66 roadhouse, saloon and country music venue, that's a second home to hordes of dancing cowboys.

## Around Flagstaff

The area around Flagstaff is extraordinarily rich in natural and archeological wonders, with three national monuments – **Sunset Crater**, **Wupatki** and **Walnut Canyon** – within 25 miles. Of these, only Sunset Crater has even a campground, and none has indoor lodgings. The one alternative base to Flagstaff, Sedona (see opposite), is that bit further away and that bit more expensive, and there's no scheduled public transportation, so if you don't have your own vehicle you'll have to take a guided tour.

### Sunset Crater and Wupatki National Monuments
North of Flagstaff, the **San Francisco Volcanic Field** of around four hundred volcanoes is prominent on the western horizon from the Hopi Mesas, and its peaks are said to be the home of their powerful *kachina* spirits. At certain times of year the Hopi make pilgrimages on foot from the mesas to shrines hidden in the mountains.

Several hiking trails lead into the San Francisco Peaks, and a chairlift operates in summer (May–Oct daily 10am–4pm; $9) from the **Arizona Snowbowl** almost to the summit of Mount Agassiz (12,350ft), though you can't hike any further from there. For a brief period each winter this becomes a mildly hectic ski area.

Some of the volcanoes are still active, though the most recent eruption was that of **SUNSET CRATER** (twelve miles from Flagstaff on US-89) in around 1066 AD. Thick deposits of ash for miles around opened up previously infertile land to cultivation, accelerating if not triggering a land rush that threw different Native American cultures into contact and competition for the first time. The crater was named by John Wesley Powell for the many colors of its cone, which swells from a black base through reds and oranges to a yellow-tinged crest. It's too unstable for walkers to be allowed onto the rim, but a trail passes through lava tubes around its base. The national monument's **visitor center** is nearby (open all year, at least 8am–5pm; $3 per person), opposite the *Bonito campground* (late May to mid-Oct; ☎520/526-0866).

A dozen miles further north, the ancient ruins at **WUPATKI NATIONAL MONUMENT** appear to show different tribal groups living side by side in harmony (daily: summer 8am–6pm; rest of year 8am–5pm; same ticket as Sunset Crater). The **Sinagua** were joined here by many others, including the **Anasazi**, after the Sunset Crater explosion. When the rich new soil created by the eruption had been exhausted, around 150 years later, they all moved on once more. The specific site known as Wupatki (meaning "tall" or "big house"), standing proud on its natural foundations of red sandstone, is just the largest of innumerable sites here.

## Walnut Canyon National Monument

Between 1100 and 1250 AD, **WALNUT CANYON**, ten miles east of Flagstaff just south of I-40, was home to a thriving Sinagua community, who lived in small family groups rather than communal pueblos. Literally hundreds of their **cliff dwellings** can still be seen nestling beneath overhangs in the sides of the canyon. They simply walled off alcoves where the softer levels of the striated rock had eroded away, and then put up partitions to make separate rooms.

A large scenic window in the **visitor center** (daily: summer 8am–6pm; rest of year 9am–5pm; $3 per person) gives an excellent overall view. Beyond it, a short trail of steep steps leads across a narrow causeway to an isthmus of rock high above a gooseneck of Walnut Creek. Trees cling to the porous rock to shade the ancient dwellings, and the vegetation thickens down to a valley floor dense with black walnut and oak. Along the path, you can go inside several Sinagua homes; note the T-shaped doorways that could only be entered headfirst and the ceilings blackened by the smoke of generations of fires. There is no accommodation, and only minimal snack food, available at the canyon.

# Sedona and Red Rock Country

US-89A threads its way south from Flagstaff down the spectacular **Oak Creek Canyon** to emerge after 28 miles at **Sedona**, on the threshold of the extraordinary **Red Rock Country**. Up from the valley rise giant mesas and buttes of stark red sandstone, where Zane Grey set a number of his Wild West adventures. The boom-and-bust mining town of **Jerome** looks down from a mountainside to the south, while back beside I-17 toward Phoenix are further haunting Sinagua ruins.

## Sedona

Though local boosters make much of its setting, amid some definitive Southwestern canyon scenery, the New Age resort of **SEDONA** adds nothing to the beauty of its surroundings. Architecturally, it's a real mess, with several miles of ugly redbrick sprawl interrupted by the occasional mock-historical mall monstrosity. To the artists, healers, walking wounded and wealthy retirees who have flocked here in the last two decades, however, Sedona is "the next Santa Fe." Whether you love it or hate it will probably depend on whether you share their wide-eyed awe for angels, crystals and all matters mystical – and whether you're prepared to pay over-the-odds prices for the privilege of joining them.

Established in 1902 by one Theodore Schnebly, and named after his wife, Sedona remained for most of the twentieth century a small farming settlement, unmarked on

## VORTEX TOURS OF RED ROCK COUNTRY

As few of the side roads around Sedona are paved – in part because the town's ardent libertarians would not pay the necessary taxes – there's a booming business in **off-road tours**, run by companies such as Earth Wisdom Tours (☎520/282-4714; $40 and up), who teach their clients "the ancestral secrets of the Medicine Wheel," and the garish Pink Jeep Tours (☎520/282-5000 or 1-800/8SEDONA; $30–75). Nonetheless, a lot of the best scenery is visible from the highway, and many of the jeep roads are perfectly passable in ordinary vehicles. So long as you're happy to remain in ignorance as to which rocks are really electromagnetic tuning forks vibrating in harmony with Alpha Centauri, there's no great need to take a commercial tour. At Legends of Sedona Ranch (☎520/282-6826 or 1-800/848-7728), where "horses are free . . . but rides ain't," an hour on **horseback** costs around $40.

most maps. German surrealist painter Max Ernst moved here in the 1940s – the bizarre backdrops of his later canvases seem less surreal once you've seen where they were painted – and Hollywood movie-makers filmed in the area from the 1950s onward. However, Sedona's big break came in 1981, when Page Bryant, author and psychic, "channeled" the information that Sedona is in fact "the heart *chakra* of the planet." Since she pinpointed her first **vortex** – a point at which, it is claimed, psychic and electromagnetic energies can be channeled for personal and planetary harmony – the town has achieved its own personal growth, and blossomed as a focus for **New Age** practitioners of all kinds.

If you don't have much time to spend exploring, a cruise along US-89A enables you to see most of the sights, albeit from a distance; the best parts are south along Hwy-179 within Coconino National Forest. The closest **vortex** to town is on **Airport Mesa**; turn left up Airport Road from US-89A as you head south, about a mile past the downtown junction known as the **"Y."** The vortex is at the junction of the second and third peaks, just after the cattle grid. Further up, beyond the precariously sited airport, the **Shrine of the Red Rocks** looks out across the entire valley.

Sedona's **visitor center**, just north of the "Y," has full listings of lodgings and tour operators (Mon–Sat 8.30am–5pm, Sun 9am–3pm; ☎520/282-7722 or 1-800/288-7336). It's an expensive place to **stay**; what pass for budget **motels** include the *Sedona Motel*, close to the "Y" at 218 Hwy-179 (☎520/282-7151 or 1-800/221-2222; ④), and the renovated *Canyon Portal*, a little further north at 210 N US-89A (☎520/282-7125 or 1-800/542-8484; ③). The luxurious *Enchantment Resort*, 525 Boynton Canyon Rd (☎520/282-2900 or 1-800/826-4180; ⑧), has taken over ravishing Boynton Canyon eight miles west.

Lots of expensive Southwestern-style **restaurants** – not all of them particularly good – cater to tourists, and there's still a smattering of old-fashioned diners. *Fournos*, 3000 W Hwy-89A (reservations compulsory; ☎520/282-3331), is a lovely little Greek restaurant, open for dinner at 6pm and 8pm from Thursday to Saturday, and for brunch on Sunday at noon, while the *Sedona Coffee House & Bakery*, 293 N Hwy-89A (☎520/282-2241), is a popular breakfast hangout near the "Y," serving espresso coffees and pastries, and graduating to soup and salad later on.

### Jerome

The former mining town of **JEROME**, high above the Verde Valley on US-89A about thirty miles south of Sedona, is conspicuous from quite a distance: an enormous letter "J" is etched deep into the hillside above it, and a large chunk of that hillside is missing altogether, having been blown apart for **opencast copper mining**. This land abounds in mineral wealth – thick veins of copper are interspersed with gold and silver, and an endless supply of limestone is still extracted for cement – but serious exploitation only started in 1876. The **United Verde** mine was partly financed by New Yorker Eugene Jerome (a cousin of Winston Churchill's mother, Jennie Jerome), who insisted that the new town bear his name. Until the current tortuous road was built, the only way up to Jerome was the precipitous rail line connecting the mine with the world's largest copper smelter at Clarkdale.

From the early 1950s, when the mines closed down, until as recently as the 1970s, Jerome was a **ghost town** in which it was possible to turn up and move into an empty house. Many who did so are still here, making a living from arts and crafts, and the town itself has made a dramatic recovery. It's a bit of a tourist trap, but is nonetheless fascinating to explore. The hillside is so steep that the stone houses (it was far too expensive to haul timber up here) tend to have two stories at the front and four or five at the back. Under the repeated concussion of more than two hundred miles of tunnels being blasted into the mountainside, the whole town used to slip downhill at the rate of five inches per year, and the **Sliding Jail** on Hull Avenue came to rest 225ft from where it was built.

The old-style *Inn at Jerome*, 309 N Main St (☎520/634-5094 or 1-800/634-5094; ③), has **rooms** as well as a **bar** and operates a **cafe**, the *Jerome Grille*. The *English Kitchen* (☎520/634-2132) has been at 119 Jerome Ave since 1899. Under Chinese ownership, it was an opium den; later the Wobblies held their meetings downstairs. Now it's open for breakfast and lunch every day except Monday, and its terrace offers a commanding view of the valley. Many of the **shops** stock only souvenirs, but interesting crafts showrooms around town include the Knapp Gallery on Lower Main Street and, next door, Made in Jerome Pottery.

## Montezuma Castle National Monument

In an idyllic setting just above Beaver Creek and just east of I-17, around 25 miles from Sedona, **MONTEZUMA CASTLE NATIONAL MONUMENT** focuses on a superbly preserved Sinagua **cliff dwelling** (daily: summer 8am–7pm; rest of year 8am–5pm; $2). Filling an alcove in the hillside with a wall of pink adobe, its five stories taper up to fit the contours of the rock. Apparently, the fingerprints of the masons are still visible on the bricks, and the sycamore beams remain firmly in place, but visitors are not permitted to climb up. The ruins of an even larger dwelling "next door," which was burned out around 1400, can be examined more closely. This had 45 rooms, as well as little "cupboards" recessed into the walls.

# West of Flagstaff: I-40 to California

Everything along I-40 west of Flagstaff is dominated by the road's function as the main route between Las Vegas and the Grand Canyon. The first town you reach, **WILLIAMS**, seems to exist solely to capture the passing tourist trade, with a historic **railroad** (☎1-800/THE-TRAIN) running north to the Canyon (see overleaf for more details), though it livens up come winter, when the slopes of Mount Williams and the rest of the surrounding **Kaibab National Forest** offer good skiing, particularly for cross-country aficionados. Forty-five miles further west at the town of **SELIGMAN**, one of the longest surviving stretches of the old Route 66 heads off on a northern loop through the **Hualapai Indian Reservation** and a dozen quickly fading towns, **PEACH SPRINGS** in particular, that look like they're straight out of *The Grapes of Wrath*. This makes a great detour on what is otherwise a very dull drive; it also provides the best access to the less visited western reaches of the Grand Canyon, around **Havasu Canyon** (see p.860).

Unless you need to fill your tank, or fill up on fast food, there's little reason to stop at **KINGMAN**, the largest town in western Arizona, from where US-93 branches north to Las Vegas and I-40 continues to Los Angeles.

## Lake Havasu City

Forty miles southwest of Kingman, ten miles from the California border, a detour south brings you to one of the more bizarre sights of the American desert – the old gray stone of **London Bridge**, reaching out to an artificial island across the stagnant waters of the dammed Colorado River at **LAKE HAVASU CITY**. It has to be said that it looks a hell of a lot better here, with the Chemehuevi Mountains as a backdrop, than it ever did on the River Thames. The resort's developer, Robert P McCulloch, bought the bridge (under the impression it was Tower Bridge – or so the story goes) for 2.4 million dollars in the late 1960s, and painstakingly shipped it across the Atlantic chunk by chunk before reassembling it over a channel dug to divert water from Lake Havasu, creating an island on the other side of the bridge known as Pittsburgh Point.

**Motels** are abundant: the *Windsor Inn Motel,* 451 London Bridge Rd (☎520/855-4135; ②), has especially low rates, while the *Ramada at Lake Havasu,* 271 S Lake Havasu Ave (☎520/855-5169 or 1-800/528-5169; ③), is a little fancier. Among several good-value **restaurants** is *Shugrue's,* in the Island Fashion Mall at the end of London Bridge (☎520/453-1400), which serves fresh fish, salads and pasta.

# The Grand Canyon

Although three million people come to see the **GRAND CANYON OF THE COL-ORADO** every year, it remains beyond the grasp of the human imagination. No photograph, no set of statistics, can prepare you for such vastness. At more than one mile deep, it's an inconceivable abyss; varying between four and eighteen miles wide, it's an endless expanse of bewildering shapes and colors, glaring desert brightness and impenetrable shadow, stark promontories and soaring, never-to-be-climbed sandstone pinnacles. Somehow it's so impassive, so remote – you could never call it a disappointment, but at the same time many visitors are left feeling peculiarly flat. In a sense, none of the available activities can quite live up to that first stunning sight of the chasm. The **overlooks** along the rim all offer views that shift and change unceasingly from dawn to sunset; you can **hike** down into the depths on foot or by mule, hover above in a **helicopter** or raft through the **whitewater rapids** of the river itself; you can spend a night at **Phantom Ranch** on the canyon floor, or swim in the waterfalls of the idyllic **Havasupai Reservation**. And yet that distance always remains – the Grand Canyon stands apart.

Until the 1920s, the average **visitor** would stay for two or three weeks. These days it's more like two or three hours – of which forty minutes are spent actually looking at the canyon. The vast majority come to the **South Rim** – it's much easier to get to, there are far more facilities (mainly at **Grand Canyon Village**), and it's open all year round. There is another lodge and campground at the **North Rim**, which by virtue of its isolation can be a lot more evocative, but at one thousand feet higher it is usually closed by snow from mid-October until May. Few people visit both rims; to get from one to the other demands either a two-day hike down one side of the canyon and up the other, or a 215-mile drive by road.

Finally, there's a definite risk that on the day you come the Grand Canyon will be invisible beneath a layer of **fog**, thanks to the 250 tons of sulphurous emissions pumped out every day by the Navajo Generating Station, seventy miles upriver at Page.

**Admission** to the park, valid for seven days on either rim, is $20 per vehicle or $10 for pedestrians and cyclists.

## Getting to and around the Canyon

The vast majority of visitors make their way to the South Rim by heading north of I-17 from either **Williams** (58 miles south) or **Flagstaff** (81 miles southeast). Most of the

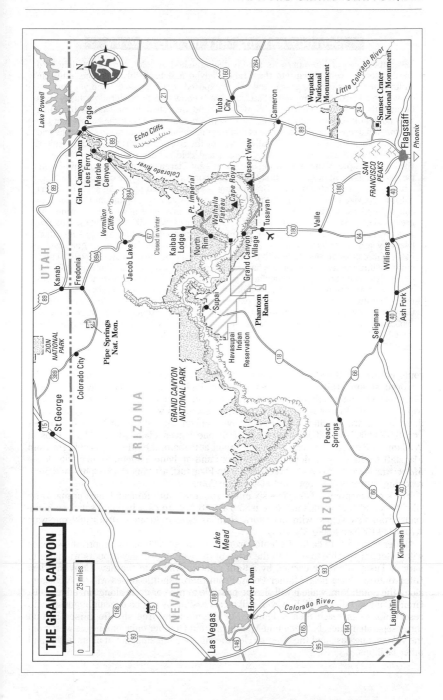

THE GRAND CANYON

0          25 miles

### GEOLOGY AND HISTORY OF THE CANYON

Layer upon layer of different rocks, readily distinguished by color, and each with its own fossil record, recede down into the Grand Canyon and back through time, until the strata at the river bed are among the oldest exposed rocks on earth. And yet how the canyon was **formed** is a mystery. Satellite photos show that the Colorado actually runs through the heart of an enormous hill (what the Indians called the *Kaibab*, the mountain with no peak); experts cannot agree on how this could happen. Studies show that the canyon still deepens, at the slow rate of 50ft per million years. Its fantastic sandstone and limestone formations were not literally carved by the river, however; they're the result of erosion by wind and extreme cycles of heat and cold. These features were named – **Brahma Temple, Vishnu Temple**, and so on – by Clarence Dutton, a student of comparative religion who wrote the first Geological Survey report on the canyon in 1881.

It may look forbidding, but the Grand Canyon is not a dead place. All sorts of desert **wildlife** survive here – sheep and rabbits, eagles and vultures, mountain lions, and, of course, spiders, scorpions and snakes. The **human** presence has never been on any great scale, but signs have been found of habitation as early as 2000 BC, and the **Anasazi** were certainly here later on. A party of **Spaniards** passed through in 1540 – less than twenty years after Cortés conquered the Aztecs – searching for cities of gold, and a Father Garcés spent some time with the Havasupai in 1776. **John Wesley Powell**'s expeditions along the fearsome and uncharted waters of the Colorado in 1869 and 1871–72 were what really brought the canyon to public attention. A few abortive attempts were made to mine different areas, but facilities for tourism were swiftly realized to be a far more lucrative investment. With the exception of the Indian reservations, the Grand Canyon is now run exclusively for the benefit of visitors; although even as recently as 1963 there were proposals to dam the Colorado and flood 150 miles of the Canyon, and the Glen Canyon dam has seriously affected the ecology downstream.

route is through thick ponderosa pine forests, so the ride up from Williams on the restored **steam trains** of the Grand Canyon Railway is not especially scenic (late March–to Oct daily, otherwise weekends only; departs Williams 9.30am; $50 round-trip; ☎520/773-1976 or 1-800/THE-TRAIN). Passengers who arrive on Flagstaff's two-daily Amtrak **trains** can reach Grand Canyon Village on connecting Nava-Hopi **buses** (☎520/774-5003 or 1-800/892-8687; $12.50); one leaves Flagstaff at 7.30am, calls at Williams at 8.20am, and arrives at the canyon at 9.45am, the other runs straight from Flagstaff to the canyon, departing at 2.30pm and arriving 4.30pm. Return trips leave *Maswik Lodge* at 10.30am – a direct service to Flagstaff, arriving at 12.30pm – and 5pm, reaching Williams at 6.15pm and Flagstaff at 7pm.

The small **airport** at Tusayan – six miles from the South Rim, and used primarily by "flight-seeing" tour companies (see p.859) – also welcomes scheduled services, especially from Las Vegas, with operators such as Scenic Airlines (from $60 one-way; ☎702/739-1900 or 1-800/634-6801).

Under plans due to be implemented from September 2000 onwards, private vehicles will no longer be able to drive to the edge of the canyon. All day-trippers will have to park at Tusayan and be carried by a light railway system to the new **Canyon View Information Plaza** near Mather Point. From there, shuttle buses will ferry visitors along the South Rim, while it will also be possible to hike or cycle along rim-edge trails. Grand Canyon Village will, however, still be accessible by car, so overnight guests with reservations can reach their lodgings. For the moment, free **shuttle buses** run on three separate routes, between mid-March and mid-October only; one heads west from the village, one east, and the other circles the village itself stopping at all its hotels and other facilities.

## Grand Canyon Village

GRAND CANYON VILLAGE is not a very stimulating place to spend any time. However, in the absence of significantly cheaper accommodation within fifty miles (for example, in **Tusayan** at the park entrance), there's little option but to stay here. The centerpiece is the magnificent **terrace** in front of *Bright Angel Lodge* (usually the liveliest spot in town) and the black-beamed 1905 *El Tovar Hotel*, which gives many visitors their only look at the canyon – though the Colorado itself is too deep in the Inner Gorge to be seen from here. Further back are more lodges and giftshops, and employee housing, while about a mile east through the woods are the informative **visitor center** (daily 8am–6pm; ☎520/638-7888), the **post office**, the **general store** and the **campground**.

## Grand Canyon accommodation

All the "lodges" in the village charge similar prices, with no budget **accommodation** alternative. To see the canyon, it makes little difference where in the village you stay. Even in the "rim-edge" places – *El Tovar Hotel* (⑥) and the *Bright Angel* (rooms ④, rimside cabins ⑤), *Thunderbird* and *Kachina* lodges (both ④) – few rooms offer much of a view, and in any case it's always dark by 8pm. Further back are *Maswik Lodge* (cabins and rooms ④), *Yavapai Lodge* near the visitor center (⑤), and *Moqui Lodge* at the park entrance (mid-Feb–Nov; ⑤).

**Camping** facilities (and a laundry) are available at the *Mather* campground and RV park ($12) near the visitor center, at least one section of which is open year-round. If you arrive on foot, you don't need a reservation; all vehicles should, however, check in well in advance (you can book through Biospherics on ☎1-800/365-2267). The summer-only *Desert View* campground, 26 miles east, is first-come, first-served, costs $10, and has no hook-ups. It's also possible to camp inside the canyon itself, if you first obtain a $20 permit from the **Backcountry Reservations Office** near *Maswik Lodge* (daily 8am–noon & 1–5pm; ☎520/638-7875); indeed, you can camp anywhere in **Kaibab National Forest** so long as you're more than 200 yards from a roadway.

If all the park accommodation is full, the nearest alternative is the underwhelming service village of **TUSAYAN**, just over a mile south of the park entrance. *Seven Mile Lodge* (☎520/638-2291; ④) offers the least expensive rooms; the new *Grand Hotel* (☎520/638-3333; ⑤) is more stylish. Much the most popular of the commercial **campgrounds** outside the park– with families, at least – is *Flintstone's Bedrock City* (mid-March to Oct; ☎520/635-2600; $12–16), 22 miles south at the junction of Hwy-64 and Hwy-180, which has its own prehistoric theme park.

## Grand Canyon eating

Thanks to the canyon's remoteness and lack of water, **food prices** tend to be well above average; if you're on a tight budget, bring your own. However, *Yavapai* and *Maswik* lodges have reasonable basic cafeterias, open until 10pm. *Bright Angel Lodge*

All in-park **accommodation reservations** – for the lodges on both the South and the North rims, as well as for Phantom Ranch and RV camping – are handled by Amfac Parks & Resorts, 14001 East Iliff, #600, Aurora, CO 80014 (same-day ☎520/638-2631; advance ☎303/297-2757; *www.amfac.com*). The best rooms are often booked as much as a year in advance, and your chances of turning up without a reservation and finding a place in summer are minimal.

has its own **restaurant**, as well as the *Arizona Steakhouse*, both also open until 10pm, and both costing $15–30. At *El Tovar*, where the dining room looks right out over the canyon, the sumptuous menu is enormously expensive. Breakfast is the most affordable meal; lunch and dinner can easily cost upwards of $40. In **Tusayan**, *We Cook Pizza & Pasta* (☎520/638-2278) is good but pricey.

## Along the South Rim

It's possible to walk along the **South Rim** for several miles in either direction from the village, the first few of them on railed and concreted pathways. The most obvious short excursions are to see the sun rise and set. At or near the village, the giant wall that reaches out in the west overshadows much of the evening view. If, however, you walk right out to **Hopi Point** at its end, looking down as you go onto the Bright Angel Trail as it winds across the Tonto Plateau, you may well see a magical **sunset**, with the Colorado – 350ft wide at this point – visible way below.

The best place within walking distance to watch the **dawn** is **Mather Point**, a mile east of the visitor center. Nearby, if you can tear your eyes away from its panoramic bay windows, the **Yavapai Observation Station** (daily 8am–6pm; free) has illuminating displays on how the canyon may have been formed.

Further dramatic views are available along the **East Rim Drive** – although, unless you take an excursion you'll need your own vehicle to see them. **Desert View**, 23 miles out from the village, is at 7500ft – the highest point on the South Rim. Visible to the east are the vast flatlands of the **Navajo Nation**; to the northeast, **Vermillion** and **Echo Cliffs**, and the gray bulk of **Navajo Mountain** ninety miles away; to the west, the gigantic peaks of **Vishnu** and **Buddha temples**. Through the plains comes the narrow gorge of the **Little Colorado**; somewhere in the depths, before it meets the Colorado itself, is the *sipapu*, the hole through which the Hopi believe that men first entered this, the Third World. The odd-looking construction on the very lip of the canyon is **Desert View Watchtower**, built by Fred Harvey in 1932 in a conglomeration of Native American styles (though a steel frame props it all up) and decorated with Hopi pictographs. It contains a **giftshop**, as does the general store a few yards away. Groups of tarantulas are often seen in the evenings at Desert View, scuttling back into the warmth of the canyon for the night.

**Tusayan Ruin**, three miles west of Desert View (and not to be confused with modern Tusayan) is a genuine Anasazi pueblo, though not comparable in scale to the relics elsewhere in this region.

## Into the Canyon

**Hiking** any of the trails that descend **into the Grand Canyon** offers something more than just another view of the same thing. Instead you pass through a sequence of utterly different landscapes, each with its own distinct climate, wildlife and topography. However, while the canyon can offer a wonderful wilderness experience, it's essential to remember that it can be a hostile and very unforgiving environment, grueling even for expert hikers.

The South Rim is 7000ft above sea level, an altitude that for most people is fatiguing in itself. Furthermore, all hikes start with a long, steep descent – which can come as a shock to the knees – and unless you camp overnight you'll have to climb all the way back up again when you're hotter and wearier.

If you're day-hiking, the golden rule is to keep track of how much time you spend hiking down, and allow twice that much to get back up again. Average summer temperatures inside the canyon exceed 100°F; to hike for eight hours in that sort of heat, you have to drink an incredible thirty pints of water. Always carry at least a quart per person, and much more if there are no water sources along your chosen trail. You must have food as well, as drinking large quantities without also eating can cause water intoxication (see p.44 of Basics).

There's only space here to detail the most popular trail, the **Bright Angel**. Many of the others, such as the **Hermit**, date from the days prior to 1928, when the obstreperous Ralph Cameron controlled access to the Bright Angel and many other rim-edge sites by means of spurious mining claims, and the Fred Harvey Company had to find other ways to get its customers down to the Colorado. These other trails tend to be overgrown now, or partially blocked by landslides; check before setting out.

### Bright Angel Trail

The **BRIGHT ANGEL TRAIL**, followed on foot or mule by thousands of visitors each year, starts from the wooden shack in the village which was once the Kolb photographic studio. The trail switchbacks for 9.6 miles down to **Phantom Ranch** beside the river, but park rangers have a simple message for all would-be hikers: don't try to hike down and back in a single day. It might not look far on the map, but it's harder than running a marathon. Instead, the longest feasible day-hike is to go as far as **Plateau Point** on the edge of the arid Tonto Plateau, an overlook above the Inner Gorge from which it is not possible to descend any further – a twelve-mile round-trip that will probably take you at least eight hours. In summer, water can be obtained along the way.

The first section of the trail was laid out by miners a century ago, along an old Havasupai route, and has two short tunnels in its first mile. After another mile, the **wildlife** starts to increase (deer, rodents and the ubiquitous ravens), and there are a few **pictographs** which have been all but obscured by graffiti.

At the lush **Indian Gardens** almost five miles down, where you'll find a ranger station and campground with water, the trails split to Plateau Point or down to the river via the **Devil's Corkscrew**. The latter route leads through sand dunes scattered with cactuses and down beside **Garden Creek** to the Colorado, which you then follow for more than a mile to get to Phantom Ranch.

### Phantom Ranch

It's a real thrill to spend a night at the very bottom of the canyon, at the 1922 **Phantom Ranch**. The **cabins** are reserved exclusively for the use of excursionists on Fred Harvey two-day mule trips ($295 per person for one night, $524 for the winter-only two-night trips). Beds in the four ten-bunk **dorms** ($22) are usually reserved way in

---

### GRAND CANYON TOURS

The Fred Harvey Company (contact the "transportation desks" in the South Rim lodges, or call ☎520/638-2401) runs at least two short daily **coach tours** along the **rim** to the west ($13.50) and east ($24.50) of the village, **sunrise** and **sunset** trips to Yavapai Point ($10), and **mule** rides to Phantom Ranch (from $295; see above). It also operates a five-hour **Smooth Water River Raft Excursion** through Marble Canyon ($80); whitewater rafting trips in the canyon proper – such as those run by Western River Expeditions (☎801/942-6669 or 1-800/453-7450) – are booked up literally years in advance, so this is probably your only chance of a trip along the river at short notice.

**Airplane tours** cost from around $65 for 30min ($45 child) up to as long as you like for as much as you've got. Operators include Air Grand Canyon (☎520/638-2686 or 1-800/AIR-GRAND) and Grand Canyon Airlines (☎520/638-2463). **Helicopter tours**, from $90 for 30min, are offered by AirStar Helicopters (☎520/638-2622) and Papillon Helicopters (☎520/638-2419), who also operate $440 day-trips to the Havasupai Reservation. Unless otherwise specified, all the companies are in **Tusayan**, at or near the airport.

advance, through Amfac (see p.857), but it's worth checking for cancellations at the Bright Angel transportation desk as soon as you reach the South Rim. Do not hike down without a reservation, and even if you do have one, reconfirm it the day before you set off. All supplies reach Phantom Ranch the same way you do (an all-day hike on foot or mule), so **meals** are expensive, a minimum of $12 for breakfast and $17 for dinner.

The **suspension bridge** here was set in place in 1928 (hanging from twin cables carried down on the shoulders of 42 Havasupai). The delta of **Bright Angel Creek**, named by Powell to contrast with the muddy **Dirty Devil** upriver in Utah, is several hundred feet wide here, and strewn with boulders. All the water used on the South Rim now comes by pipeline from the North Rim, and crosses the river on the 1960s Silver Bridge nearby.

## The Havasupai Reservation

The **HAVASUPAI RESERVATION** really is another world. A 1930s anthropologist called it "the only spot in the United States where native culture has remained in anything like its pristine condition"; things have changed a little since then, but the sheer magic of its turquoise waterfalls and canyon scenery makes this a very special place. Traditionally, the Havasupai would spend summer on the canyon floor and winter on the plateau above. However, when the reservation was created in 1882, they were only granted land at the bottom of the canyon, and not until 1975 did the concession of another 251,000 acres up above make it possible for them to resume their ancient lifestyle.

**Havasu Canyon** is a side canyon of the Grand Canyon, about 35 miles as the raven flies from Grand Canyon Village, but almost two hundred miles by road. Turn off the interstate at Seligman or Kingman, onto AZ-66, which curves north between the two, stock up with food, water and gas, and then turn on to Arrowhead Hwy-18. Plans to build a road – or even a tramway – down into Havasu Canyon have always been rejected, in part because much of the income of the five or six hundred Havasupai comes from guiding visitors on foot, mule or horseback. Instead, the road ends at **Hualapai Hilltop**, from where an eight-mile trail zigzags down a bluff and leads through the stunning waterless Hualapai Canyon to the village of **SUPAI**. Riding down costs $50 one-way, $80 round-trip, while hiking is free; all visitors, however, pay a $15 entry fee on arrival at Supai.

Beyond Supai the trail becomes more difficult, but leads to a succession of spectacular waterfalls, including **Havasu Falls**, one of the best for swimming, and **Mooney Falls**, which was named after an unfortunate prospector who dangled here for three days in the 1890s, at the end of a snagged rope, before falling to his death.

A **campground** (☎520/448-2141) stretches between Havasu and Mooney Falls, and Supai itself holds the **motel**-like *Havasupai Lodge* (☎520/448-2111; summer ⑤, winter ③), along with a **cafe**, a **general store** and the only **post office** in the US still to receive its mail by pack train. From time to time Supai is hit by freak floods, which can result in the temporary closure of the campground and hotel.

## To the North Rim

The 215-mile route by road from Grand Canyon Village to the **North Rim** follows AZ-64 along the East Rim Drive to Desert View, then passes an overlook into the gorge of the Little Colorado, before joining US-89 fifty miles later at **CAMERON**. The Cameron Trading Post has the best selection of Native American crafts in the Grand Canyon area, and remains a trading center for the **Navajo Nation** (with some of its business still conducted by barter). It also has a good-quality **motel** and **restaurant** (☎520/679-2231 or 1-800/338-7385; ⑤).

Fifteen miles north of Cameron is the junction with US-160, which heads northeast via Tuba City (where there's more accommodation; see p.864) toward Monument Valley and Colorado. Continuing north, after another 40 miles of barren wasteland, US-89 branches off to climb the mesa to the right, heading for Page and Glen Canyon Dam (see p.881).

## Lees Ferry

The direct route to the North Rim, now US-89A, crosses the Colorado at last over the single arch of **Navajo Bridge**, almost five hundred feet above the river. There are in fact two Navajo Bridges, the 1929 original, now reserved for pedestrians, having been supplanted by a wider facsimile in 1995. Until the first was built, a ferry service operated at **LEES FERRY**, six miles north. This was established in 1872, at the instigation of the Mormon Church, by John D Lee, at the only spot within hundreds of miles to offer easy access to the banks of the river on both sides. The Colorado, however, could still be a raging torrent, and the crossing was carried out in both directions by casting out and struggling across while being swept downstream, in constant danger from currents and winds. Lee himself was on the run after the **Mountain Meadows Massacre** in Utah in 1857, when a wagon train of would-be settlers was slaughtered by an armed white band clumsily disguised as Indians.

The ferry service was abandoned after a fatal accident in June 1928. Not long after, a crucial piece of equipment needed to finish the bridge on the left bank was stranded on the right bank; the only way to get it across was to take it eight hundred miles by road, via Las Vegas.

Lee's Ferry is the launching point for **whitewater rafting** trips – boats setting off from here can't leave the canyon before Diamond Creek, twelve days away by muscle power – and the end of Fred Harvey's smooth water trips from Glen Canyon Dam (see p.859). It has a few relics of Lee's days, as well as a half-sunk steamboat, hauled from San Francisco in 1911 and abandoned as a failed experiment after only five trips. There's also a **campground** (☎520/355-2334), while back on US-89A beneath the red of the **Vermillion Cliffs** you'll find a succession of **motels** – *Marble Canyon Lodge* (☎520/355-2225; ③), *Cliff Dweller's Lodge* (☎520/355-2228; ④) and the slightly lower-priced *Lees Ferry Lodge* (☎520/355-2231; ③). All have **restaurants**.

The turning south to get to the North Rim, off US-89A onto AZ-67, comes at **JACOB LAKE**, which has an *Inn* (☎520/643-7232; ④) and **campground**, but not much else. From here – along a road that's closed in winter – it's 27 miles to *Kaibab Lodge* (☎520/638-2389; ④) and another fourteen to the canyon itself.

# The North Rim

Higher, bleaker and far less accessible, the **NORTH RIM** of the Grand Canyon receives less than a tenth as many visitors as the South Rim. While that doesn't mean you'll have the place to yourself, it can still make you feel as though you're venturing into unexplored wilderness. The basic principle, however, is the same as at the South Rim, with a cluster of venerable park-service buildings where the main highway reaches the canyon, and a handful of rim-edge roads where drivers can take their pick from additional lookouts. Only one hiking trail sees much use, the **North Kaibab Trail**, which follows Bright Angel Creek down to Phantom Ranch.

Tourist facilities on the North Rim, concentrated at **Bright Angel Point**, open for the season on May 15 and close on October 15. **Accommodation** at the *Grand Canyon Lodge* (⑤) is in cabins that spread back along the ridge from the *Lodge* entrance, very few of which have canyon views. Advance reservations are essential, and are handled by the same agents as for the South Rim: Amfac Parks & Resorts, 14001 E Iliff Ave, #600,

Aurora, CO 80014 (same-day ☎520/638-2631; advance ☎303/297-2757; *www.amfac.com*). Just over a mile north is the *North Rim Campground*, where $15 spaces can be reserved – though it's not necessary for backpackers – through Biospherics (☎1-800/365-2267). The *Lodge* also holds a reasonable **restaurant**, plus a saloon and an espresso bar; ask at the information desk for details of **mule rides** (1hr $15, half-day $40, full-day canyon expeditions $95; ☎435/679-8665), and **van tours** along the rim.

The park itself remains open for day-use only after October 15, but no food, lodging or gas is available, and visitors must be prepared to leave at a moment's notice. It's shut down altogether by the first major snowfall of winter, which usually comes toward the end of October.

# Northeastern Arizona: Indian Country

The deserts of northeastern Arizona, popularly known as **INDIAN COUNTRY**, hold some of the most fascinating **pre-Columbian ruins** in North America, in the most striking settings imaginable. The cliff palaces of **Canyon de Chelly**, and **Betatakin** and **Keet Seel** in the Navajo National Monument, are among the greatest architectural achievements of the **Anasazi**, made that much more special by the fact that the lands on which they stand are still lived on and worked by their heirs, the Navajo and Hopi.

The **NAVAJO NATION**, the largest Native American reservation in the US, fills most of the region, lapping over into western New Mexico and stretching to include the majestic sandstone pillars of Monument Valley in southernmost Utah. Although the migrant Navajo have embraced the American Way – driving pickup trucks and wearing baseball caps – you get a very real sense of traveling through a foreign country here. Everyone can speak English, but Navajo, a language so complex that it was used as a secret military code during World War II, is still the lingua franca. Supermarkets mark their prices in Navajo, and the reservation follows its own rules over Daylight Savings; in frontier-style towns like Tuba City, the time on the clock can vary according to whether you're in an American or a Navajo district. Tune into the Navajo Nation **radio station**, KTNN 740AM, for a sense of the Navajo–American melange.

When white immigrants began to arrive in force during the early nineteenth century, the Navajo – who call themselves *Dineh*, "The People" – had lived in Arizona for hundreds of years; within a generation, they lost almost everything. When the Yankees took over from the Mexicans, things just got worse, hitting bottom in 1864 when Kit Carson rounded up every Navajo he could find and forced them all to move to Fort Sumner in the desolate plain of eastern New Mexico (see p.822). A few years later, the Navajo were allowed to return, the US government granting them most of the vast acreage they hold today (lawsuits arising from territorial disputes with the **Hopi**, their neighbors and predecessors, have dragged on ever since). Most of the 200,000-plus Navajo today work the land as shepherds and farmers on widely scattered smallholdings, though many craftspeople also live by selling their wares from small stands set up along highways and in tourist stops.

Visiting this region can be fascinating and rewarding, but it's important to respect the people and places you encounter. The Anasazi, the region's first occupants, have long since vanished, but many of the relics they left behind are on land that is still of spiritual significance to their modern counterparts – Native Americans come here from all over the Southwest and beyond to take pride in their heritage. Similarly, it is offensive to photograph or otherwise intrude upon people's lives without permission; one reason why the Hopi, for example, banned photography was because it was such an interfering nuisance.

On a practical note, don't expect extensive **tourist facilities**. Most towns exist solely as outposts of government bureaucracy, with little to offer visitors beyond a handful

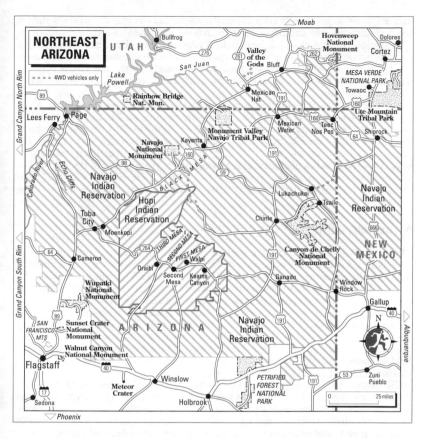

of places to eat and even fewer hotels and motels. They only come alive during the annual tribal fairs and rodeos, which are great opportunities to sample delicacies like Navajo tacos, or to buy jewelry direct from craftspeople. At other times, you may well be better off staying near I-40 to the south, in Winslow or Holbrook. For more information, call the **Navajoland Tourism Department** on ☎520/871-6436.

## Navajo National Monument

**NAVAJO NATIONAL MONUMENT**, in the northwest quarter of the reservation, protects two of Arizona's biggest and most beautifully sited cliff dwellings. From behind the good **visitor center** (summer daily 8am–6pm; rest of year daily 8am–5pm; ☎520/672-2366)) at the end of paved Hwy-564, ten miles north of US-160, a ten-minute trail crosses the plateau to a viewpoint overlooking **Betatakin**, an exceptionally well-preserved 135-room masonry structure tucked away in a large natural alcove halfway up the 700ft high, brilliant-red sandstone on the far side of a canyon. It's only possible to hike down to Betatakin – which feels as though it was abandoned seven years, not seven centuries, ago – by joining one of the unforgettable six-hour ranger-guided hikes (May–Sept; daily 9am), which leave from the visitor center. Numbers are limited, and no advance bookings are taken, so get here as early as possible on the day – or stay the previous night at the very attractive free **campground** in the forest beside the visitor center.

In summer, you can also visit the even larger Anasazi site of **Keet Seel**. However, the seventeen-mile round-trip hike from the visitor center is too grueling to attempt in a single day, so you'll have to sleep in the small **campground** near the site, having obtained a permit from the visitor center at least a day in advance. Horseback trips are also available for $55 per day.

Most people pass through this area on their way somewhere else, so there aren't many **places to stay**. TUBA CITY, west of the monument, has the large, modern *Quality Inn Tuba Trading Post* (☎520/283-4545 or 1-800/644-8383; ⑤) and $16-a-night dorm beds at the *Grey Hills High School Inn and Hostel*, which also offers budget private doubles (summer only; ☎520/283-6271; ①/②). The coal and uranium mining town of **KAYENTA**, 22 miles northeast of the monument at the junction of US-160 and US-163, holds two more expensive options: the *Best Western Wetherill Inn* (☎520/697-3231; ⑤) and the *Holiday Inn* (☎520/697-3221; ⑤), which has a distinctive and good-value **restaurant**.

## Monument Valley

The classic Wild-West landscape of stark sandstone buttes and forbidding pinnacles of rock, poking from an endless expanse of drifting red sands, has become an archetypal image. Only when you arrive at **MONUMENT VALLEY** – which straddles the Arizona–Utah state line, 24 miles north of Kayenta and 25 miles southwest of Mexican Hat – do you realize how much your perception of the West has in fact been shaped by this one spot. Such scenery does exist elsewhere, of course, but nowhere is it so perfectly concentrated and distilled. While movie-makers have flocked here since the early days of Hollywood – this was where John Ford made John Wayne a star – the sheer majesty of the place still takes your breath away. Add the fact that it remains a stronghold of **Navajo** culture, little affected by tourism, and Monument Valley can be the absolute highlight of a trip to the Southwest.

The biggest and most impressive of the monoliths are a pair called **The Mittens**, one East and one West, each of which has a distinct thumb splintering off from its central bulk. The taller of the two rises a thousand feet above the valley floor, with sand dunes lapping at its base. Over a dozen other spires are spread around nearby, along with **rock art panels** and an assortment of minor but nicely sited **Anasazi ruins**.

You can see the buttes for free, towering alongside US-163, but the four-mile detour to enter **Monument Valley Tribal Park** is rewarded with much closer views (May–Sept daily 7am–7pm; Oct–April daily 8am–5pm; $2.50). A rough, unpaved road drops from behind the visitor center to run through Monument Valley itself. The 17-mile **self-drive route** makes a bumpy but bearable ride in an ordinary vehicle, and takes something over an hour to complete (open summer daily 8am–6pm; rest of year daily 8am–4.30pm). You're allowed to stop en route to stretch your legs, but not to hike for any distance. However, the Navajo-led **jeep** or **horseback tours** into the backcountry are very much recommended; a two-hour jeep trip costs from around $20 per person from the various stalls beside the visitor center, slightly more if organized through *Goulding's Lodge* (see below). As well as stopping at such movie locations as the **Totem Pole** (atop which Clint Eastwood had some perilous moments in *The Eiger Sanction*), these pause so you can watch weavers at work in a Navajo *hogan* (traditional eight-sided dwelling).

The *Haskeneini* (☎520/871-4602) is a reasonable **restaurant** at the visitor center, not far from the very exposed *Mitten View* **campground** (first-come, first-served; summer only; $10). The only **accommodation** in the immediate vicinity is six miles west, in Utah; *Goulding's Lodge* (☎435/727-3231; ⑥), is a 1920s trading post that's now a plush resort with pricey motel rooms, a fairly good restaurant, a general store and gas station, a small movie museum and its own campground (mid-March–Oct; $14; same phone).

# Canyon de Chelly National Monument

A short distance east of **CHINLE**, sixty miles southwest of Kayenta and seventy miles north of I-40, twin sandstone walls emerge abruptly from the desert floor, climbing at a phenomenal rate to become the awesome thousand-foot cliffs of **CANYON DE CHELLY NATIONAL MONUMENT**. Between these sheer sides, the meandering course of the Chinle Wash can be discerned by its fringe of cottonwoods as it winds through grasslands and planted fields. Here and there a Navajo *hogan* stands in a grove of fruit trees, a straggle of sheep is penned in by a crude wooden fence, or ponies drink at the water's edge. And everywhere, perched above the valley on ledges in the canyon walls and dwarfed by the towering cliffs, are the long-abandoned adobe and stone dwellings of the **Anasazi**.

There are two main canyons, which branch apart a few miles upstream: **Canyon de Chelly** (pronounced *de shay*) to the south and **Canyon del Muerto** to the north. Each twists and turns in all directions, scattered with vast rock monoliths, while several smaller canyons break away. The whole labyrinth threads its way upward for thirty miles into the Chuska Mountains.

Canyon de Chelly is a magnificent place, easily on a par with the best of the Southwest's national parks. Its relative lack of fame owes much to the continuing presence of the **Navajo**, for whom the canyon retains enormous symbolic significance (although they did not themselves build its cliff dwellings). Casual visitors are restricted to peering into the canyon from above, from overlooks along the two "rim drives." There's no road in, and, apart from one short trail, you can only enter the canyons with a Navajo guide.

## Some history

The first known inhabitants of the canyon were the **Anasazi** Basketmakers, around 300 AD. During the next thousand years, before the Anasazi disappeared from history, they advanced from living in pit houses dug into the soil to building elegant cliff dwellings, and developed fine pottery and weaving (for more on the Anasazi, see p.813). For some centuries thereafter, the **Hopi** came here to farm each summer, returning for the winter to the mesas to the east, but as time went by, **Navajo** migrants from the north and west eventually displaced the Hopi altogether.

From 1583 onward, the Navajo were locked with the Spanish in a bloody cycle of armed clashes and slave raids. The US Army in turn failed in repeated attempts to dislodge the Navajo, but no treaty could restrain the rapacious hunger for land by New Mexican settlers, as well as the Ute, Paiute, Apache and Comanche. The end appeared to have come with the brutal round-up and deportation (the "**Long Walk**") of the entire Navajo people, completed by Kit Carson in 1864 when he starved the last of them down from Navajo Rock and destroyed their homes, livestock and, worst of all, their beloved peach orchards. So barbaric was the Navajo's imprisonment at Fort Sumner, however, that Congress soon allowed them to return. To this day, 25 Navajo families still farm the Canyon de Chelly in summer, the matrilineal descendants of the women between whom it was reapportioned in the 1870s.

## The view from above: the rim drives

Each of the two "rim drives" from the visitor center offers a succession of spectacular overlooks; allow two to three hours for each of the forty-mile round-trips. Thefts from cars have been a major problem, so it's wise to heed the prominent warnings.

---

**INTO THE CANYONS**

Tours of the canyon floor, organized by *Thunderbird Lodge* (see below), zigzag along the washes, which vary from two- or three-feet deep during the spring thaw to completely dry in summer. For most of the year, the bone-shaking tours are in open-top flatbed trucks, lurching over the rutted earth, and the heat can be incredible; in winter they carry on in glass-roofed army vehicles with caterpillar tracks. To reach as far as Spider Rock, you have to take the full-day tour ($55), but the half-day trip at $34 still enables you to see a wide variety of sites and terrain, including the White House Ruins.

Justin's Horse Rentals (☎520/674-5678) and Twin Trail Tours (☎520/674-8425) organize horseback trips for $8 per person per hour, plus $8 an hour for a guide.

---

The first significant stopping point along the **South Rim Drive** is **Junction Overlook**, after four miles, far above the point where the two main canyons branch their separate ways; as you scramble across the bare rocks you can see Canyon de Chelly narrowing away, with a *hogan* immediately below. Two miles further along, by which time the canyon is 550ft deep, **White House Overlook** looks down on the highly photogenic **White House Ruins**. This is the only point from which unguided hikers can descend to the canyon floor, taking perhaps 30 to 45 minutes to get down and a good hour to get back up. The beautiful if precarious trail, at times running along ledges chiseled into the slick rock, culminates with a close-up view of the ruins; the most dramatic dwellings, squeezed into a tiny alcove sixty feet up a majestic cliff, were once reached via the rooftops of now-vanished structures. Visitors are forbidden to walk for more than a hundred yards in either direction beyond the site. Back up on the South Rim Drive, twelve miles along, the view from **Sliding House Overlook** reveals more Anasazi ruins seemingly slipping down the canyon walls toward the ploughed Navajo fields below, while eight miles further on the road ends above the astonishing **Spider Rock**, where twin 800ft pinnacles of rock reach to within 200ft of the canyon rim.

The **North Rim Drive** runs twenty miles up Canyon del Muerto to **Massacre Cave**, where the Spanish expedition of 1805, led by Lieutenant Narbona, killed around one hundred Navajo women, children and old men. The "cave" is just a pitifully exposed ledge, upon which the huddled group were easily picked off by the Spanish, using ricochets off the overhang above. Visible from the nearby **Mummy Cave Overlook** is the **House Under The Rock**, with its central tower in the Mesa Verde style – the single most striking ruin in the monument. Of the two viewpoints at **Antelope House Overlook**, one is opposite Navajo Fortress, an isolated eminence atop which the Navajo were besieged for three months in 1863, while the other looks down on the ruins of Antelope House, and the **Tomb of the Weaver** across the wash, where the embalmed body of an old man was found wrapped in golden eagle feathers.

## Practicalities

For the moment, Canyon de Chelly remains remarkably unspoiled. As well as being friendly and informative guides, the Navajo are excellent stewards of the monument. However, facilities are overstretched, and it's essential to book your **accommodation** well in advance. Much the most appealing option is the *Thunderbird Lodge* (☎520/674-5841; ⑨), very near the canyon entrance, which has a good and inexpensive cafeteria and a well-stocked giftshop, and arranges the standard sightseeing tours. The adjacent (free and minimally equipped) *Cottonwood Campground* has pleasant sites among the trees. Two further motels, each with its own restaurant, stand on the road between Chinle and the canyons: the *Holiday Inn* (☎520/674-5000; ⑥) and the *Best Western Canyon de Chelly* (☎520/674-5875; ⑥). Chinle itself is a brief nondescript straggle on the highway, with service stations, *Taco Bell, Kentucky Fried Chicken,* a post office and a laundry.

The **visitor center** (May–Sept daily 8am–6pm; Oct–April daily 8am–5pm; ☎520/674-5500) on the road from Chinle has informative displays, and provides guides for unorthodox hiking or motorized expeditions. For a group, having your own personal guided tour need not be any more expensive.

# Window Rock

The seat of the Navajo Tribal Council, the reservation's governing body, is on its eastern edge, along the New Mexico border. It was based for fifty years at Fort Defiance, a US cavalry outpost, until in the 1930s **WINDOW ROCK** was established as a new capital. Named for the natural stone arch on its northern side, it's not a great place to get a grasp of Navajo culture, but it does at least have gas stations, shops and a **motel**, the showpiece *Navajo Nation Inn* at 48 W Hwy-264 (☎520/871-4108 or 1-800/662-6189; ④). The adjacent **Navajo Tribal Museum** (summer Mon–Fri 8am–5pm & Sat 10am–4pm; rest of year Mon–Fri 8am–5pm; donation) gives the background on tribal history and displays high-quality crafts.

# The Hopi Mesas

The **Hopi** people are virtually unique in the United States: they have lived continuously in the same place for over eight hundred years. Some invaders have come and gone in that time, others have stayed; but the villages on **First, Second** and **Third mesas** have endured, if not exactly undisturbed then at least unmoved.

To outsiders, it's not obvious why, with the whole Southwest to pick from, the Hopi should have chosen to live on three barren and unprepossessing fingers of rock, poking from the southern flanks of **Black Mesa** in the depths of northeast Arizona. The answer is simple. The first is that while Black Mesa has no perennial streams, its subterranean rocks are tilted at just the correct angle to deliver a tiny but dependable trickle of water, and that the "black" in its name comes from the coal that gives the Hopi limitless reserves of fuel. The second is that the Hopi used to farm and hunt across a much wider area, and have only been restricted to their mesa-top villages by the steady encroachment of their Navajo neighbors. While the Hopi are celebrated for their skill at **"dry farming,"** managing to preserve enough precious liquid to grow corn, beans and squash on hand-tilled terraces laid out beneath the villages, this precarious and difficult way of life has nonetheless been forced upon them.

By their very survival, not to mention the persistence of their ancient beliefs and ceremonies in the heart of modern Arizona, the Hopi have long been a source of fascination to outsiders. While visitors are welcome, the Hopi have no desire – or need, as the tribe has finally begun to earn considerable amounts of money from mineral leases – to turn themselves into a tourist attraction. Two motels make it possible to stay on the reservation, though, and stores and galleries provide plenty of opportunity to buy crafts such as pottery, basketwork, silver overlay jewelry and hand-carved *kachina* dolls. However, tourists who arrive in the hope of extensive sight-seeing – let alone spiritual revelations – are likely to leave disappointed, and quite possibly dismayed by what they perceive as conspicuous poverty.

## Visiting the Hopi Mesas

The essential first stop for visitors is the modern, mock-Pueblo **Hopi Cultural Center** below Second Mesa, which holds a **museum** (summer Mon–Fri 8am–5pm, Sat & Sun 9am–3pm; rest of year Mon–Fri 8am–5pm; $3), as well as a **cafeteria** and **motel**

## HOPI CEREMONIES

The Hopi feel neither the urge nor the obligation to divulge details of their religious beliefs and practices to outsiders. To that end, they have resisted attempts to make Hopi a written language, or to expose it to scrutiny by teaching it in schools. As a result, Hopi spirituality has been repeatedly misrepresented to the world, whether as barbarous devil-worship or New Age guff. There is in any case no single unified Hopi religion; ceremonials vary from clan to clan and village to village. The most basic common element is the role of the *kachinas*. These "spirit messengers," which may represent the spirits of the dead, live in the San Francisco peaks north of Flagstaff.

There are over three hundred different *kachinas*. At one time, they visited the mesas in person; now they come in the form of masked dancers. Not every village follows the same ceremonial calendar, but in general the *kachinas* arrive each year in early February for the Powamuya ceremony, or **Bean Dance**. They continue to visit throughout the growing season, before returning home after the Niman ceremony or **Home Dance** in July.

The Hopi do not worship the *kachinas*; their main significance is as examples and allegories for the children. All Hopi babies receive *tihus* – what outsiders know as *kachina* dolls, which have become very popular crafts objects – at their first Niman ceremony, and the girls receive further dolls at each Powamuya and Niman ceremony thereafter.

For much of the twentieth century, Hopi **ceremonies** were promoted as tourist attractions. Even after cameras were banned in 1916, occasions such as the **Snake Dance**, when members of the Snake clan dance with live snakes between their teeth, attracted as many as 2500 outsiders. In recent years, however, the Hopi have moved toward the exclusion of non-Native Americans. By 1989, Second Mesa had closed all its ceremonies to outsiders, and it was joined by all the First Mesa villages in 1992 after the publication of a Marvel comic that characterized the *kachinas* as violent avengers.

While spectators are now very unlikely to be allowed at any *kachina* dances, however, some **social dances**, held between August and January when the *kachinas* are away from the mesas, may still be "open." Held in the village plazas, these usually take place at the weekends, so that Hopi who live off the reservation can return. Specific timings tend not to be announced until a few days in advance; for information, ask at the Cultural Center or call ☎520/734-2441. If you do get the chance to attend, wear clothing that fully covers your body, keep your distance, and do not photograph, sketch or question either dancers or audience.

(☎520/734-2401; ④). In summer, its unexotic but adequate rooms are usually booked solid a week or more in advance.

Unless your visit coincides with a social event that's open to tourists (see box, above), the only way to see the mesa-top villages is to take a **guided tour** of the most impressive one, **WALPI** (summer Mon–Fri 9am–6pm; winter Mon–Fri 9.30am–4pm; $5). By Hopi standards, Walpi is not in fact that old; it was hastily thrown together in the immediate aftermath of the Pueblo Revolt of 1680, when the people of First Mesa decided to move to a more secure site in the face of possible Spanish or Navajo attack. The spot they chose is absolutely stunning, standing alone at the narrow southernmost tip of the mesa, and connected to the other First Mesa villages by the merest slender neck of stone, with a drop of three hundred feet to either side. It's now home to around 35 people, who do without electricity or running water.

To see Walpi, take Hwy-264 to modern **POLACCA**, at the foot of First Mesa, then drive a mile up the twisting paved road until it ends in **SICHOMOVI**. The tours assemble in Sichomovi's small community center, setting off at regular intervals for a half-hour walk to and around Walpi. Depending on the time of year, you'll either be in a group of twenty or so, or on your own, but either way there's plenty of opportunity to ask questions, and to buy pottery, *kachina* dolls, and fresh-baked *piiki*, a flatbread made with blue cornflour.

# UTAH

With the biggest, most beautiful and most pristine landscapes in North America, **UTAH** has something for everyone: from brilliantly colored canyons, across endless desert plains, to thickly wooded and snow-covered mountains. This unmatched range of terrain, almost all of which is public land, makes it *the* place to come for **outdoor pursuits** – from hiking to off-track mountain biking, whitewater rafting and skiing.

**Southern Utah** has more **national parks** than anywhere else in the US; in fact it has often been suggested that the entire area should become one vast national park. The most accessible parts – such as **Zion** and **Bryce Canyon** – are by far the most visited, but lesser-known areas like **Arches** and **Canyonlands** are every bit as dramatic. Huge tracts of this empty desert, in which beautiful pre-Columbian pictographs and Anasazi ruins lie hidden, are all but unexplored; seeing them in safety requires a good degree of advance planning and self-sufficiency.

In the **northeast** of the state, the **Uinta Mountains** remain uncrossed by road and form one of the most extensive wilderness areas in the US outside Alaska, while **Flaming Gorge** and **Dinosaur** preserve more desert splendor. Though the **northwest** is predominantly flat and dry, the granite mountains of the **Wasatch Front** tower over state capital **Salt Lake City** – a surprisingly attractive and enjoyable stopover – while Alta, Snowbird and Park City offer some of the best **skiing** in North America.

Led by Brigham Young, Utah's earliest white settlers – the **Mormons** – arrived in the Salt Lake area in 1847, and set about the massive irrigation projects that made their agrarian way of life possible. At first they provoked great suspicion and hostility back east; Congress turned down their first petition for statehood in 1850, in part because of the religious significance of the proposed name, **Deseret**, a Mormon word meaning "honeybee" (the state symbol is still a beehive, to denote industry). The Republican convention of 1856 railed against slavery and polygamy in equal measure – the potential was there for a civil war with the Mormons, had the South not intervened. Relations eased when the Mormon church realized in 1890 that it had better drop polygamy on its own terms before being forced to do so. Statehood followed in 1896, and a century on, seventy percent of Utah's two-million-strong population are Mormons. The Mormon influence is responsible for the layout of Utah's towns, where residential streets are as wide as interstates, and all are numbered block-by-block according to the same logical if ponderous system.

Despite Brigham Young's early opposition to the search for mineral wealth, Mormon businessmen became renowned as fiercely pro-mining and anti-conservation. Only since the early 1980s – once the uranium bonanza was definitely over – has tourism been appreciated as a major industry, and former mining towns such as **Moab** developed facilities for wide-eyed travelers smitten by the lure of the desert. Increased tourism has also led to a relaxation of Utah's notoriously arcane **drinking laws**; patrons of licensed restaurants can now purchase beer, wine and mixed drinks.

## Getting around Utah

It's nearly impossible to get anywhere in Utah without your own **car**. Amtrak and Greyhound serve Salt Lake City and a few provincial towns, but practically nowhere else. However, a couple of firms offer **bus tours** of the national parks, and if you're feeling adventurous, southern Utah also has an unbeatable range of mountain biking, river rafting, even hot-air ballooning opportunities: see p.883 for a list of companies.

# Southern Utah: the national parks

**Southern Utah** is a peculiar combination of the mind-boggling and the mundane. Its **scenery** is stupendous, a stunning geological freakshow where the earth is ripped bare to expose cliffs and canyons of every imaginable color, unseen rivers gouge mighty furrows into endless desert plateaus, and strange sandstone towers thrust from the sagebrush. By contrast, however, the tiny **Mormon towns** scattered across this epic landscape are almost without exception boring in the extreme, so most visitors spend as much time as possible **outdoors**.

As well as its five separate national parks, Southern Utah boasts countless lesser-known but equally dramatic wildernesses. In the southwest, **Zion National Park** centers on an awe-inspiring canyon, backed by barren highlands of white sandstone, while **Bryce Canyon** is a roaring inferno of orange pinnacles. Over to the east, **Arches** holds an eroded desertscape of graceful red-rock fins and spurs, all on a more manageable scale than the astonishing hundred-mile vistas of neighboring **Canyonlands**. Both lie within easy reach of **Moab**, a disheveled former mining town turned Utah's hippest destination. The fifth park, **Capitol Reef**, stretches through the middle of the region, pierced by slender, ravishing canyons.

The defining topographical feature of southwest Utah is the **Grand Staircase**. Named by pioneer river-runner John Wesley Powell, it consists of a series of plateaus, stacked tier upon tier, climbing from the North Rim of the Grand Canyon. The **Chocolate Cliffs**, near the border with Arizona, are followed by the dazzling **Vermillion Cliffs**, then the **White Cliffs** – a 2000ft wall of Navajo sandstone, best seen at Zion – the **Grey Cliffs**, and finally the **Pink Cliffs** of Bryce. Although it took a billion years of sedimentation for these rocks to form, the staircase itself has only been created in the last dozen million years, by the general upthrust of the **Colorado Plateau**, which stretches away to the east.

This is a tough land, and a rough one for travelers: with fewer roads than anywhere else in the US, almost nobody gets far into the deep backcountry. Even within the national parklands, overground access is more often than not limited to heavy-duty, high-clearance **four-wheel-drive vehicles, hikers** and, increasingly, to **mountain bikes**. The best way of all to experience the region is as the first explorers did: by **water**. Dozens of companies offer river-rafting trips, floating downstream and camping out under the clear night sky to experience the sights, sounds and smells of the desert.

## St George and Cedar City

Southern Utah's two biggest towns, **St George** and **Cedar City**, lie fifty miles apart on I-15 en route between Las Vegas and Salt Lake City. Both make reasonably pleasant and serviceable bases, if not ones that are likely to detain you for very long.

### St George
**ST GEORGE** was the winter home of Brigham Young and other early Mormon leaders, who basked in the comparatively mild climate of "Utah's Dixie." Set at the foot of a broad, reddish-brown sandstone cliff, it's a pretty enough town, centering around the fine 1877 **LDS Temple** at 440 South 300 East, the oldest still in use anywhere. The rest of the town holds quaint pioneer homes, including Brigham Young's much-restored **adobe house** on 200 North First West (daily 9am–dusk; free); pick up a walking tour map there or at the **visitor center**, 97 E St George Blvd (Mon–Fri 9am–5pm, Sat 9am–1pm; ☎435/628-1658).

Virtually all St George's commercial life takes place along the main drag, St George Boulevard, where **motels** include the much-patronized *Dixie Palm* at 185 E (☎435/673-

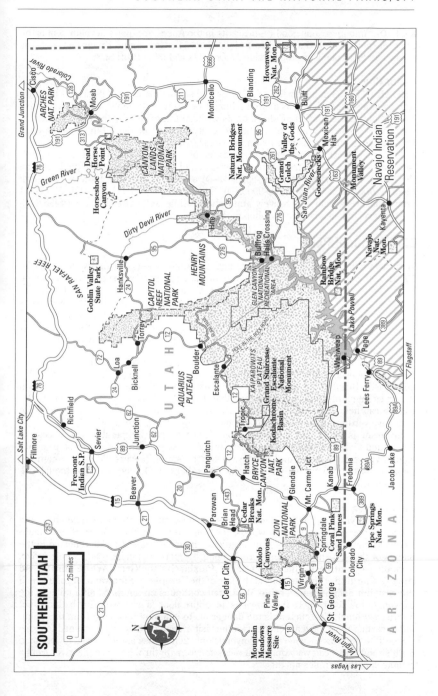

3531; ①). Among various good **restaurants** in the Ancestor Square development is the *Pizza Factory*, 1 W St George Blvd (☎435/628-1234). Greyhound **buses** between Las Vegas and Salt Lake City stop outside *McDonald's* at 1235 S Bluff St.

## Cedar City

**CEDAR CITY**, 53 miles north of St George and approximately half its size, is no more worthy of a stop. Founded as an iron mining town in the late 1850s, it's now kept alive by the Southern Utah State College on its western fringe, and by the flood of theater-goers who come to watch the enthusiastic productions of the **Utah Shakespeare Festival**, held on campus every summer (☎435/586-7878).

The large local **visitor center** stands at 581 N Main St (Mon–Fri 8am–5pm; ☎435/586-5124). **Main Street** is handy for food and lodging; motels with pools include the *El Rey Inn* at 80 S (☎435/586-6518; ③–⑥) and the smart *Best Western Town and Country Inn* at 189 N (☎435/586-9900; ④). *Godfathers Pizza* at 241 N (☎435/586-1111) offers Italian specialties in a lively atmosphere, while *Sullivan's* at 301 S (☎435/586-6761) serves up standard coffee-shop meals.

# Zion National Park

With its soaring cliffs, riverine forests and cascading waterfalls, **ZION NATIONAL PARK** is the most conventionally beautiful of Utah's parks. On first glance, it's also the least "Southwestern"; its centerpiece, **Zion Canyon**, is a lush oasis that feels far removed from the otherworldly desolation of Canyonlands or the downright weirdness of Bryce. Like California's Yosemite Canyon, it's a spectacular gorge, squeezed between mighty walls of rock and echoing to the sound of running water; also like Yosemite, it can get claustrophobic in summer, its one road clogged with traffic and its limited facilities crammed with sweltering tourists.

Too many visitors see Zion Canyon as a quick half-day detour off the interstate, as they race between Las Vegas (158 miles southwest) and Salt Lake City (320 miles northeast). Beautiful though the **Scenic Drive** through the canyon may be, Zion deserves much more of your time than that. Even the shortest hiking trail within the canyon can help you escape the crowds, while a day-hike will take you away from the deceptive verdure of the valley and up onto the high-desert tablelands beyond.

**Summer** is by far the busiest season. That's despite temperatures in excess of 100°F, and violent thunderstorms concentrated in August and a week or so to either side. If you can, come in April or May, to see the spring flowers bloom – though the mosquitoes are also at their peak – or in September and October, to enjoy the fall colors along the river.

## Zion Canyon

In **Zion Canyon**, mighty walls of Navajo sandstone rise nearly half a mile above the groves of box elders and cottonwoods that line the loping North Fork of the **Virgin River**. The awe of the early Mormon settlers who called this "Zion" is reflected in the names of the stupendous slabs of rock along the paved six-mile road, Scenic Drive, from the park entrance – the **Court of the Patriarchs**, the **Great White Throne** and **Angel's Landing**. The road ends at the foot of the **Temple of Sinawava**, beyond which the easy but delightful **Riverside Walk** trail continues on another half a mile up the canyon, to the point where the river fills the entire floor (a very welcome bathing spot in drier seasons). The current is too dangerous to continue upstream from this point, but at certain times of year (check with the visitor center), hikers determined to experience **The Narrows** – where the canyon is only 20ft across and the walls tower some 800ft straight up – can wade for eight miles *downstream* through the chilly river from a remote spot thirty miles north.

Less ambitious walkers might prefer to wander up to **Weeping Rock**, an easy half-hour round-trip from the road to a gorgeous spring-fed garden that dangles from a rocky alcove. From the same trailhead, a mile beyond *Zion Lodge*, a more strenuous and exciting route cuts through narrow **Hidden Canyon**, whose mouth turns into a waterfall after a good rain. Directly across from the lodge a short (two-mile round-trip) and fairly flat trail winds up at the **Emerald Pools**, a series of three clearwater pools, the best (and furthest) of which has a small sandy beach at the foot of a gigantic cliff; at certain times of the year a broad waterfall sprinkles down over the trail.

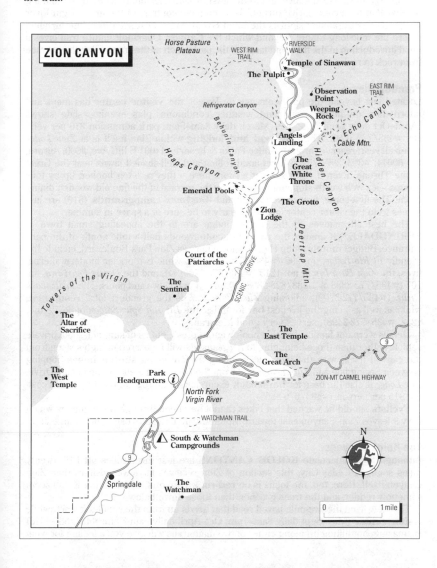

The single best half-day **hike** climbs up to **Angel's Landing**, a narrow ledge of whitish sandstone protruding some 1750ft above the canyon floor. Starting on the same route as for the Emerald Pools, the Angel's Landing trail switchbacks sharply up through the delightful coolness of **Refrigerator Canyon** before emerging on the canyon's west rim; near the end you have to cross a heart-stopping five-foot neck of rock with sheer drops to either side (there's a steel cable to grab hold of). That round-trip takes a good four hours, but backpackers can continue another twenty miles to the gorgeous Kolob Canyons district (see below).

The high dry plateau above and to the **east** of Zion Canyon, reached by continuing on Hwy-9 at the Scenic Drive turnoff, is a complete contrast to the lush Virgin River gorge. Its most dramatic sight is the blind **Great Arch**, best seen from the turnouts before the mile-long tunnel, beyond which the **Canyon Overlook** nature trail gives a good introduction to the flora and fauna of the park, such as the speedy lizards that race from rock to rock.

## Practicalities

Located just beyond the park entrance on Hwy-9, the **visitor center** has maps and information on hiking trails and weather conditions, plus evening slide shows (April–Oct daily 8am–7pm; Nov–March daily 8am–5pm; park admission $10 per vehicle; ☎435/772-3256). The only **food and lodging** within Zion itself is at *Zion Lodge* (open all year; reserve through Amfac Parks & Resorts, 14001 E Iliff Ave, #600, Aurora, CO 80014; ☎303/297-2757; ⑤), set amid rolling and well-shaded lawns near the Great White Throne. Even if you can't get a room here – they're often booked up by tour groups – it's well worth stopping for lunch on the terrace of the fine old wooden dining room. The first-come, first-served *South* and *Watchman* **campgrounds** ($10) are just across from the visitor center; get there early to be sure of a space in summer.

The best alternatives to the in-park lodge are in the appealing small town of **SPRINGDALE**, set among the riverbank cottonwoods half a mile south of the park entrance. Budget **motels** along Hwy-9, known here as Zion Park Boulevard, include the friendly *El Rio Lodge*, no. 995 (☎435/772-3205; ③), while two pricier modern alternatives, the *Zion Park Inn* at no. 1215 (☎435/772-3200; ⑥), and the *Desert Pearl Inn*, no. 707 (☎435/772-8888 or 1-888/828-0898; ④), offer good views and pools. The *Switchback Grille* (☎435/772-3700), adjoining *Zion Park Inn,* is the grandest local **restaurant**, while as well as being the liveliest **bar** for miles, the *Bit and Spur Saloon* opposite (no. 1212; ☎435/772-3498), serves very good Mexican.

Details were not finalized as this book went to press, but as of summer 2000, private vehicles other than those belonging to *Lodge* guests will be barred in high season from the canyon itself, with the only access being by foot or on **shuttle buses**, looping between Springdale and *Zion Lodge,* and from the *Lodge* to the end of the Scenic Drive. The *Lodge* is also the base for **horseback** excursions, with regular one-hour rides costing $15 per person (☎435/679-8665).

**Cyclists** should be warned that bikes cannot be ridden through the tunnel by which Hwy-9 leaves Zion Canyon east toward Mount Carmel; rangers can help arrange lifts.

## The Kolob Canyons

Although the immaculate **KOLOB CANYONS** are just three miles off I-15, twenty miles south of Cedar City, this section of Zion receives far fewer visitors than Zion Canyon itself. Here, too, the focus is on **red-rock canyons**, which in the Kolob seem somehow redder, and the trees greener, than those down below.

The view from the five-mile paved road that heads up from the small but worthwhile **visitor center** (May–Sept daily 8am–7pm; Oct–April daily 8am–6pm; ☎435/586-9548) is amazing, but hiking off along either of two main trails will give you a feeling for what makes this place so special. The first and shorter of the two starts two miles from the visitor center and follows Taylor Creek on a five-mile round-trip to **Double Arch Alcove**, a spectacular natural amphitheater roofed by twin sandstone arches; there's also a small waterfall a quarter of a mile further along. The other trail starts from the north side of the parking area at Lee Pass, four miles beyond the visitor center, and follows a well-marked route for seven miles past LaVerkin Falls to **Kolob Arch**, which at over 300ft across rivals Landscape Arch in Arches (see p.881) as the world's longest natural rock span. There are no campgrounds in the Kolob Canyons.

## Cedar Breaks National Monument

The shortest drive between Zion and Bryce, along the Virgin River and then north on US-89 across the high plain of Long Valley, is spectacular enough, but the longer route through the maple and aspen groves of the **Dixie National Forest** is even more dramatic. Halfway between Cedar City and US-89, Hwy-148 cuts sharply north through the eerie fringes of **CEDAR BREAKS NATIONAL MONUMENT** ($4 per vehicle), where the soft sandstone has crumbled away from the edge of a high wooded plateau to create a fairyland amphitheater of bizarre and brilliantly colored formations.

Cedar Breaks is in a sense just a pocket version of Bryce Canyon to the east, but that's no reason not to come. Most of the plateau is over 10,000ft high, so it's usually quite cold; in fact the roads through are often blocked by snow until June. **Point Supreme**, with a small summer-only **visitor center** (May–Sept daily 8am–6pm; ☎435/586-0787), **snack bar** and **campground** ($10), is a mile into the park from the south, and has the best view.

East of Cedar Breaks, Hwy-143 passes through pine forests and across lava flows, then drops past Panguitch Lake to reach the broad Sevier River valley at the squeaky-clean Mormon farming town of **PANGUITCH**. This holds eight gas stations (one, *Todd's Truck Stop*, is open 24hr), twenty-odd **motels**, such as the *Marianna Inn*, 699 N Main St (☎435/676-8844 or 1-800/331-7407; ②–⑤), and not much else.

## Bryce Canyon National Park

The surface of the earth can hold few weirder-looking spots than **BRYCE CANYON**. Named for Mormon settler Ebenezer Bryce, who memorably declared that it was "a helluva place to lose a cow" – it is not in fact a canyon at all. Along a twenty-mile shelf on the eastern edge of the thickly forested **Paunsaugunt Plateau**, 8000ft above sea level, successive strata of dazzlingly colored rock – yellows, reds, whites and flaming oranges – have slipped and slid and washed away to leave a menagerie of multihued and contorted **stone shapes**.

Like Cedar Breaks, the formations here have been eroded out of the muddy sandstone by a combination of icy winters (the temperature drops below freezing 200 nights out of the year) and summer rainstorms. The racks of top-heavy pinnacles known as "**hoodoos**" were formed when the harder upper layers of rock stayed firm as the lower levels were worn away beneath them. These hoodoos – **Thor's Hammer**, visible from Sunset Point, is the most alarmingly precarious – look down into technicolor ravines, all far more vivid than the Grand Canyon and much more human in scale. The whole place is at its most inspiring in winter, when the figures stand out from a blanket of snow.

The single road that runs south from Hwy-12, about twenty miles east of Panguitch, passes by the entrance station ($10 per vehicle) before arriving at the **visitor center** (April–Oct daily 8am–5pm; Nov–March daily 8am–4.30pm; ☎435/834-5322). A couple of miles south, you come to a succession of scenic overlooks, and a network of trails drops abruptly from the rim into **Bryce Amphitheater** – be prepared to walk back up the same distance that you go down. The two most popular overlooks are on either side of *Bryce Canyon Lodge* (see below): the more northerly, **Sunrise Point**, is 350yd from the parking lot and so is slightly less crowded than **Sunset Point**, where most of the bus tours stop. A good three-mile hike switchbacks steeply from Sunset Point through the cool 200ft canyons of **Wall Street**, where a pair of 800-year-old fir trees stretch to reach daylight. It then cuts across the surreal landscape into the basin known as the **Queen's Garden**, where the stout and remarkable likeness of Queen Victoria sits in majestic condescension – pointed out by a brass plaque – before climbing back up to the rim at Sunrise Point. A dozen trails crisscross the amphitheater, but it's surprisingly easy to get lost, so don't stray from the marked routes.

Sunrise and Sunset points notwithstanding, the best view at both sunset and dawn (which is the best time for taking pictures) is from **Bryce Point**, at the southern end of the amphitheater. From here, you can look down not only at the Bryce Canyon formations but also take in the grand sweep of the whole region, east to the **Henry Mountains** and north to the Escalante range. Most people only get as far as Bryce Amphitheater, but the park road climbs another twenty miles south, by way of the intensely colored **Natural Bridge**, an 85ft rock arch spanning a steep gully, en route to its dead end at **Rainbow Point**.

## Practicalities

Much the best place to **stay** in Bryce is the venerable *Bryce Canyon Lodge*, one hundred yards from the rim between Sunrise and Sunset points (April–Oct only; reserve through Amfac Parks & Resorts, 14001 E Iliff Ave, #600, Aurora, CO 80014; ☎303/297-2757; ⑤), where rustic cabins cost a few dollars more than basic doubles. It also has a **dining room**, a grocery store, a laundry and public showers. The northern approaches to the park, just off Hwy-12, are guarded (not to say disfigured) by two **motels**, both owned by the same company and open year round; the large *Best Western Ruby's Inn* (☎435/834-5341; summer ⑤, winter ③), and the cheaper, newer (and misleadingly named) *Bryce View Lodge* (☎435/834-5180; ③). *Ruby's Inn* has its own **campground** ($14) but is overall a rather dreary place to stay. There are also two first-come, first-served campgrounds within the park, which charge $10 per night; *Sunset Campground*, close to Sunset Point, and *North Campground*, near the visitor center. Backpackers can choose from dozens of sites below the rim, all south of Bryce Point; pick up the required permit at the visitor center, and take lots of water.

# Bryce Canyon to Capitol Reef: Highway 12

Turning its back on the grand amphitheater of Bryce Canyon, the tiny hamlet of **TROPIC**, which strings along Hwy-12 eight miles east of the park entrance, seems almost embarrassed about the flamboyant geological phenomena ranged along the ridge above it. The practical-minded people of this Mormon farming community (population 380) don't especially concern themselves with tourists, but they have restored Ebenezer Bryce's log cabin, which stands next to the *Pioneer Village* **motel-cum-restaurant** (☎435/679-8546; ②–④). An unmarked road heads west from the cabin two miles to the park boundary, from where it's a two-mile hike up to the main formations.

Hwy-12 then curves along the edge of the Table Cliff Plateau before dropping down into the remote canyons of the **Escalante River**, the last river system to be discovered within the continental US and site of some of the finest **backpacking** routes in the Southwest. As soon as you walk even a hundred yards off the main highway, you're in a wilderness that few travelers ever see.

**ESCALANTE**, 33 miles east of Cannonville, was just another roadside town, until it was given a new lease on life in 1996 by the surprise Presidential proclamation that created the vast new **Grand Staircase-Escalante National Monument**. The **visitor**

center at the west end of town (mid-March–Oct daily 7.30am–5.30pm; Nov–mid-March Mon–Fri 8am–4.30pm; ☎435/826-5499), is a mine of up-to-date information on all the public lands in the vicinity, and can suggest **hiking** or **mountain biking** trips into the backcountry. The most accessible local highlight is **Calf Creek**, sixteen miles east of Escalante, where a well-marked trail leads just under three miles upstream to a gorgeous shaded dell replete with a 125ft waterfall, and there's a nice undeveloped **campground** ($5). More ambitious trips start from trailheads along the dusty but usually passable **Hole-in-the-Rock Road**, which turns south from Hwy-12 five miles east of town. A trio of slender, storm-gouged **slot canyons**, including the delicate, graceful Peek-a-Boo Canyon and the downright intimidating Spooky Canyon, can be reached by a mile-long hike from the end of Dry Fork Road, 26 miles along, while from **Hurricane Wash**, 34 miles along, you can hike five miles to reach Coyote Gulch, and then a further five miles, passing sandstone bridges and arches, to the Escalante River. Under normal conditions, two-wheel-drive vehicles should go no further than **Dance Hall Rock**, 36 miles down the road, a superb natural amphitheater scuplted out of the slickrock hills. The pick of Escalante's **motels** is unquestionably the *Prospector Inn*, 380 W Main St (☎435/826-4653; ③), which adjoins the friendly, high-quality *Ponderosa Restaurant*, 400 W Main St (☎435/826-4658).

Until the mid-1980s, when it was pushed through to Capitol Reef, Hwy-12 ended at **BOULDER**, thirty miles beyond Escalante. **Anasazi State Park** (summer daily 8am–6pm; rest of year daily 9am–5pm; $2), which holds the excavated and partially reconstructed remains of a small Anasazi village, is set on a shallow knoll overlooking Boulder Creek. Beyond Boulder, Hwy-12 makes a gorgeous drive up onto the Aquarius Plateau, with marvellous vistas to the east across waves of gold- and red-sandstone outcrops; there's a lovely **campground** ($8) at Oak Creek, fifteen miles along. Due east from Boulder, all except twenty miles of the old dirt **Burr Trail** has (controversially) now been paved, providing easy access to the southern reaches of **Capitol Reef National Park** and down to **Lake Powell**.

# Capitol Reef National Park

**CAPITOL REEF** sounds more like something you'd find off the coast of Australia than in the heart of the Utah desert, but in most respects its towering ochre-, white- and red-**rock walls** and deep **river canyons** are of a piece with the rest of the region. The outstanding feature is a multilayered, 1000ft-high reef-like wall of uplifted sedimentary rock, a section of which reminded an early traveler of the grand dome of the US Capitol. Stretching for over a hundred miles north to south, but only a few miles across, the seemingly impenetrable barrier of the **Waterpocket Fold** was warped upward by the same process that lifted the Colorado Plateau, and the sharply defined sedimentary layers on display here trace over two hundred million years of geological activity. The Waterpocket Fold is sliced through in a number of places by deeply incised river canyons – some only twenty feet wide, but hundreds of feet deep – often accessible only by foot.

The one paved road through the park, Hwy-24, cuts across the northern half of the Fold, following the deep canyon of the **Fremont River**; motorists who stick to this road do not incur an entrance fee. Beneath the enormous and very prominent **Castle**, the **visitor center** (June–Sept daily 8am–7pm; Oct–May daily 8am–4.30pm; ☎435/425-3791) has explanatory exhibits and an irresistible campground ($10), set amid the orchards of the abandoned Mormon community of **FRUITA**; in season, you can pick all the fruit you can gobble down. To the west, the **Goosenecks Overlook** gazes down 500ft into the entrenched canyons cut by Sulphur Creek. Further east, beyond Fruita's former schoolhouse, are some extraordinary **Fremont petroglyphs**, figures of bighorn sheep and stylized space-people chipped into the varnished red rock a thousand years ago; a five-minute radio broadcast (AM 1540) describes their makers. Another four and a half miles along, one of Capitol Reef's best **day-hikes** heads up along the gravelly riverbed through **Grand Wash** – a beautiful (and usually quite cool) canyon where, it's said, Butch Cassidy and his gang used to hide out.

Few other paved routes run through the park, so to reach the spectacular back-country canyons you may have to put up with many miles of dusty and spine-rattling roads – renting a mountain bike is a good idea. The paved, popular **Scenic Drive** ($4 per vehicle) heads twelve miles south from the visitor center, past the top of Grand Wash to **Capitol Gorge** and back. A more adventurous sixty-mile loop trip explores **Cathedral Valley** in the north, while a 125-mile southern route starts at the foot of the volcanic **Henry Mountains**, then follows the Burr Trail through **Muley Twist Canyon**, and continues west to Boulder (see p.877).

The nearest **food and lodging** to Capitol Reef is eleven miles west, in the rapidly growing small town of **TORREY**, where options include the *Chuckwagon*, 12 W Main St (☎435/425-3335; ③–⑤), the *Wonderland Inn*, at the intersection of Hwy-12 and Hwy-24 (☎435/425-3775; ③), and the *Capitol Reef Inn*, 360 W Main St (☎435/425-3271; ③), which has a small cafe.

## Goblin Valley

Fifty fairly desolate miles east of Capitol Reef along Hwy-24, you reach the tiny cross-roads of **Hanksville**. Twenty miles north on Hwy-24, a right turn takes you onto a 32-mile dirt road to a real anthropological and artistic wonder – the rock paintings of **Horseshoe Canyon**, a remote subsection of Canyonlands National Park (see p.880).

Half a mile further north on Hwy-24, a side road to the east veers off to **GOBLIN VALLEY STATE PARK** (open 24 hr; $4), where thousands of gnome-like figures loom out of the soft Entrada sandstone. The **Carmel Canyon** trail loops for over a mile through a throng of misshapen rock pillars, many of which seem to have eyes and other human features. Stay at the well-equipped **campground** (☎1-800/322-3770; $10) if you want to see the place by moonlight, when it looks especially spooky.

## Green River

The uneventful riverside town of **GREEN RIVER**, just east of the Hwy-24 junction on I-70, is the largest community on a 200-mile stretch of interstate. One good reason to visit is the **John Wesley Powell River History Museum**, 885 E Main St (summer daily 8am–8pm; rest of year daily 8am–5pm; $2), which features the anything-but-dry personal accounts of the men who first successfully navigated the Colorado River from near its source all the way through the Grand Canyon. In summer **raft trips** from the museum – which also doubles as the local **visitor center** – float downriver to the **Crystal Geyser**, a 100ft cold-water gusher, and every Memorial Day hundreds of boats set out on weekend-long convoy trips that cruise down the Green River to its confluence with the Colorado, then head upriver to Moab.

Green River holds several bargain-priced **motels**, including the *Book Cliff Lodge*, 395 E Main St (☎435/564-3406; ④), which also has a handy **cafe**.

# Canyonlands National Park

**CANYONLANDS NATIONAL PARK**, the largest and most magnificent of Utah's national parks, is as hard to define as it is to map. Its closest equivalent, the Grand Canyon, is by comparison simply an almighty crack in an otherwise relatively flat plain; the Canyonlands area is a bewildering tangle of canyons, plateaus, fissures and faults, scattered with buttes and monoliths, pierced by arches and caverns, and penetrated only by a paltry handful of dead-end roads.

## CANYONLANDS FEES AND PERMITS

The **entry fee** for Canyonlands National Park, levied between March and October only, is $10 per vehicle, $5 for cyclists or hikers, and is valid for seven days in all sections of the park. Only limited numbers of visitors are allowed to spend a night or more in the backcountry; **backpacking permits**, covering up to seven persons in the Needles and Island In The Sky districts, or five in the Maze, cost $10, while **vehicle campsites**, issued for groups of up to three vehicles, are $25. **Reservations**, which though not compulsory are essential for the most popular areas, especially in spring and fall, must be purchased at least two weeks in advance, and picked up in person – with every member of the group present – from the appropriate park visitor center, at least one hour before it closes.

For application forms, and full details of the complex regulations, write to the National Park Service Reservations Office, 2282 S West Resource Blvd, Moab, UT 84532; call ☎435/259-4351 (Mon–Fri 8am–4pm); or contact a park visitor center.

The 527 square miles of the park are just the core of a much larger wilderness that stretches to the horizon in every direction. To nineteenth-century explorers, this was the epitome of useless desolation; only since uranium prospectors blazed crude trails across the trackless wastes in the 1950s has it become at all widely known. Even after the park was created in 1964, it took a couple of decades before tourists arrived in appreciable numbers.

Canyonlands focuses on the Y-shaped confluence of the **Green** and **Colorado Rivers**, buried deep in the desert forty miles southwest of Moab. There's only one spot from which you can see the rivers meet, however, and that's a five-mile hike from the nearest road. With no road down to the rivers, let alone across them, the park therefore splits into three major sections. The **Needles**, east of the Colorado, is a red-rock wonderland of sandstone pinnacles and hidden meadows that's a favorite with hardy hikers and 4WD enthusiasts, while the **Maze**, west of both the Colorado and the Green, is a virtually inaccessible labyrinth of tortuous, waterless canyons. In the wedge of the "Y" between the two, the high, dry mesa of the **Island In The Sky** commands astonishing views across the whole park and beyond, with several overlooks that can easily be toured by car. Getting from any one of these sections to the others involves a drive of at least a hundred miles.

Canyonlands is not a place that lends itself to a short visit. With no lodging, and little camping, inside the park, and no loop road to whisk you through it, it takes a full day to have even a cursory look at a single segment. If you're among the many visitors who find the conditions too grueling to spend much time out of your car – summer temperatures regularly exceed 100°F, and most trails have no water and little shade – then the Island In The Sky is the most immediately rewarding option. On the other hand, if you fancy a long day-hike you'd do better to set off into the Needles.

### Island In The Sky and Dead Horse Point State Park

Reached by a good road that climbs steadily up from US-191, 21 miles south of I-70, the **ISLAND IN THE SKY** district looks out over hundreds of miles of flat-topped mesas that drop in 2000ft steps to the river. Four miles along from its **visitor center** (daily 8am–5pm; ☎435/259-4712), the **Mesa Arch Trail** is the area's best short hike, looping for a mile around the mesa-top hillocks to the edge of the abyss, where long, shallow Mesa Arch frames an extraordinary view of the **La Sal Mountains**, 35 miles northeast. The definitive vantage point, however, is **Grand View Point Overlook**, another five miles on at the southern end of the road. An agoraphobic's nightmare, it commands a hundred-mile prospect of layer upon layer of naked sandstone, here stacked thousands of feet high, there fractured into bottomless canyons. The Island In The Sky's only developed **campground**, the first-come, first-served, and waterless *Willow Flat* ($5), is just back from the **Green River Overlook**, reached by forking right shortly after the Mesa Arch trailhead.

On the way in to the Island In The Sky, a turnoff long before the visitor center cuts across south to the smaller but equally breathtaking **DEAD HORSE POINT STATE PARK**, at the tip of a narrow mesa, which looks straight down 2000ft to the twisting Colorado River. Cowboys used the mesa as a natural corral, herding up wild horses then blocking them in behind a piñon pine fence that still marks its 90ft neck. One band of horses was left here too long and died – hence the name. There's a **campground** ($11) and **visitor center** (summer daily 8am–6pm; rest of year daily 8am–5pm; $5), two miles short of the point.

### The Needles and Newspaper Rock

Taking its name from the thousands of colorful sandstone pillars, knobs and hoodoos that punctuate its many lush canyons and basins, the **NEEDLES** district allows a more intimate look at the Canyonlands environment than does Island In The Sky. Here you're not always gazing thousands of feet downward or scanning the distant horizon; instead you can wander through seemingly endless acres of stone figures.

The road ends with a great collection of mushroom-shaped hoodoos at the **Big Spring Canyon Overlook**. A memorable and demanding eleven-mile round-trip hike from here remains the only way to get to the **Confluence Overlook**, 1000ft above the point where the Green River joins the muddy waters of the Colorado, to flow together, parallel but separate, toward fearsome **Cataract Canyon**. Various short walks head off the road at selected viewpoints; one of the best is **Pothole Point**, a mile before **Big Spring Canyon**. A longer day-trip, or a good overnight hike, leaves from near the *Squaw Flat* **campground** ($10 Feb–Nov, when water is available; free rest of year) to the green meadow of **Chesler Park**, cutting through the narrow cleft of the Joint Trail. Check in at the **visitor center** (daily 8am–5pm; ☎435/259-4711) near the park boundary to get up-to-date information, as well as backcountry permits if you plan to camp out. The only way to **reach the river** from within the park is by taking the hot and dry trail down through Lower Red Canyon to **Spanish Bottom**; this is the start of the Cataract Canyon rapids, so don't try to swim across.

The 35-mile drive in to the Needles from US-191 is among the prettiest in the state, winding along Indian Creek through deep red-rock canyons lined by pines and cottonwoods. **NEWSPAPER ROCK**, twelve miles in, is the best of many similarly named sites; here hundreds of tiny **petroglyphs**, many of which show deer, antelope, bear claws and helmeted human figures, have been etched in the jet-black desert varnish of a red-sandstone boulder by centuries of passing hunters and travelers. There's a lovely (free) streamside **campground** just across the road.

### The Maze and Horseshoe Canyon

Only about one in a hundred of the half-million visitors who come to Canyonlands every year makes it into the harsh backcountry of the remote **MAZE** district. Filling up the western third of the park, on the far side of the Colorado and Green Rivers, the Maze is noted for its ancient rock-art panels and for its many-fingered box canyons, accessible only by jeep or by long, dry hiking trails. If you're tempted, call into the Hans Flat **ranger station**, 46 miles east of Hwy-24.

Pretty, tree-lined **HORSESHOE CANYON**, reached halfway down a long, long dirt road that loops south from Green River itself to join Hwy-24 just south of Goblin Valley (see p.878), contains the greatest concentration of **ancient rock art** in the Southwest. Allowing at least an hour's driving from the highway both before and after, plus five hours for the six-mile round-trip hike down into the canyon itself, you'll need a full day to spare, but it's well worth the effort, both for the joy of the walk and for the sight of the **"Great Gallery"** at the far end. Hundreds of mysterious, haunting pictographs – mostly life-sized human figures, albeit weirdly elongated, or draped in robes and adorned with strange, staring eyes – were painted onto these red-sandstone walls, probably between 500 BC and 500 AD.

# Arches National Park

The writer Edward Abbey, who spent a year as a ranger at **ARCHES NATIONAL PARK** in the 1950s, wrote in *Desert Solitaire* that its arid landscape was as "naked, monolithic, austere and unadorned as the sculpture of the moon." It certainly is one of the least terrestrial places on this planet. Massive fins of red and golden sandstone stand to attention out of the bare desert plain, and over 1800 natural arches of various shapes and sizes have been cut into the rock by eons of erosive weathering. Apart from the single ribbon of black asphalt that snakes through the park, there's nothing even vaguely human about it. The narrow, hunching ridges are more like dinosaurs' backbones than solid rock, and under a full moon, at twilight, or watching the lightning strikes of a distant thunderstorm, you can't help but imagine that the landscape has a life of its own.

While you could race through in a couple of hours, to do Arches justice you should plan to spend a whole day here at the very least. A twenty-mile road cuts uphill sharply from US-191 and the park **visitor center** (mid-April–Sept daily 7.30am–6.30pm; Oct–mid-April daily 8am–4.30pm; ☎435/259-8161; $10 per vehicle), where exhibits explain the fairly simple process by which the arches are formed and point out some of the more photogenic examples. The first possible stop is the south trailhead for **Park Avenue**, an easy trail leading one mile down a scoured, rock-bottomed wash. If you stay on the road, the **La Sal Mountains Viewpoint** provides a grandstand look at the distant peaks rising over 12,000ft above the surrounding desert, as well as the huge red chunk of **Courthouse Towers** closer at hand. Beyond the Towers, the road follows the foot of the salmon-hued sandstone of the **Great Wall**.

From **Balanced Rock** – a 50ft boulder atop a slender 75ft pedestal – a turning to the right winds for two miles through the **Windows** section, where a half-mile trail loops through a dense concentration of massive arches, some over 100ft high and 150ft across. A second trail, fifty yards beyond, leads to **Double Arch**, a staunch pair of arches that together support another arch overhead.

Beyond Balanced Rock, the main road drops downhill for two miles past Panorama Point and the turnoff to **Wolfe Ranch**, where a century-old log cabin now serves as the trailhead for the three-mile round-trip to **Delicate Arch**, which as a freestanding crescent of rock, perched at the brink of a deep canyon, is by far the most impressive arch in the park. Three miles beyond the Wolfe Ranch turnoff, the deep, sharp-sided mini-canyons of the **Fiery Furnace** section form a (usually quite cool) labyrinth through which rangers lead regular hikes in spring, summer and fall ($6).

The road continues on to the **Devil's Garden** trailhead, from which an easy one-mile walk leads to a view of the astonishing 306ft span of **Landscape Arch**, now too perilously slender to approach more closely. Several other arches lie along short spur trails off the main route; seeing them all, and returning from **Double O Arch** via the longer primitive trail, requires a total hike of just over seven miles. Arches' only **campground** ($10 between mid-March and October, when water is available; $5 otherwise) is across from the trailhead; all its first-come, first-served sites tend to be occupied by early morning in season. Permits for **backcountry camping**, allowed anywhere that's a mile from the road and half a mile from any trail, are issued at the visitor center.

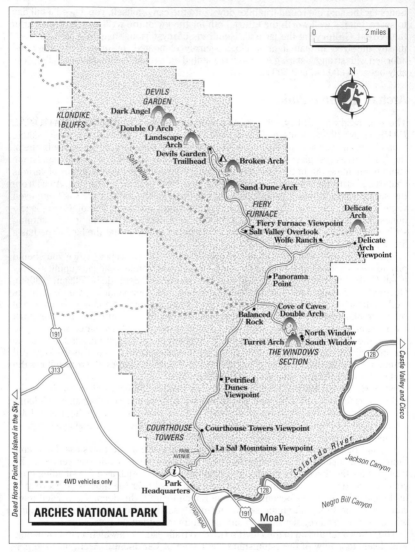

ARCHES NATIONAL PARK

## Moab

Founded in the late 1800s, **MOAB** was hardly a speck until the 1950s, when prospector Charlie Steen discovered uranium in the nearby hills. When the ensuing mining boom finally waned, the conservative hold of Moab's industrialists and landowners waned with it, and the town threw in its lot with tourism. In barely ten years, it has transformed itself into the Southwest's number-one adventure-vacation destination.

Moab still isn't a large town – the population has yet to reach ten thousand – and neither is it an attractive one. The setting is what matters. With two national parks on its doorstep, plus millions more acres of public land, Moab is an ideal base for outdoors enthusiasts. At first, it was a mecca for **mountain bikers**, lured by the legendary **Slickrock Bike Trail**. Then the **jeep** drivers began to turn up, and the **whitewater rafting** companies moved in. These days it's almost literally bursting, all year, with legions of Lycra-clad vacationers from all over the world.

## ADVENTURE TRAVEL OUTFITS IN SOUTHWEST UTAH

Moab is the main center for companies running **adventure trips** through the backcountry and along the raging waters of southwest Utah. Varying from half-day jaunts to week-long expeditions, such trips not only get you to places you'd never otherwise reach, but also provide a sense of the region's natural splendor that can't be had from a car or on foot.

### River trips
Among Moab's dozen licensed operators offering motorized one-day trips along the Colorado River for around $45 are: Western River Expeditions (☎801/942-6669 or 1-800/453-7450), Adrift Adventures (☎435/259-8594 or 1-800/874-4483) and Tag-a-Long Expeditions (☎435/259-8946 or 1-800/453-3292). The short trips start northwest of Moab, near the butte known as Fisher Towers, and arrive near town in the afternoon; many companies give passengers the chance to float quieter stretches in two-person kayaks. **Oar-powered** trips are slower but much quieter, and less expensive than motorboat trips. Longer (2- to 7-day) trips head through Cataract Canyon and other wild Canyonlands spots.

### Mountain biking
While the Moab area is ideally suited to mountain-bike touring, only experienced riders should attempt its most challenging route, the famous **Slickrock Bike Trail**. This ten-mile, half-day loop starts atop the mesa about three miles east of Moab, threading its way among the sandstone knobs with views of the La Sal Mountains and the Colorado River; wear a **helmet**, take lots of **water**, and keep an eye and an ear out for motorcyclists, who are also allowed on the trail. A more relaxing alternative is to explore the dirt roads leading through the red-rock country of Kane Creek, west of town.
  **Bike shops** offering daily rental and guided tours include Rim Tours, 1233 S Hwy-191 (☎435/259-5223 or 1-800/626-7335), Kaibab Mountain Bikes, 391 S Main St (☎435/259-7423), and Poison Spider, 497 N Main St (☎435/259-7882 or 1-800/635-1792).

### Jeep tours
Most of the thousands of miles of **jeep trails** around Moab were built years ago by miners and haven't been maintained since. The visitor center has a free map and guide to some of the more popular ones, and you can rent a 4WD jeep or pickup truck for around $100 per day from Slickrock 4x4 Rentals at 284 N Main St (☎435/259-5678). **Guided jeep tours** ($60–80 per person per day) are offered by Lin Ottinger Tours (☎435/259-7312) and Tag-a-Long Expeditions (see above).

### Scenic Flights
From a small airfield twenty miles north of Moab on US-91, Redtail Aviation (☎435/259-7421) runs **unforgettable flights** over the Canyonlands area and beyond: a perfect opportunity to appreciate the labyrinthine complexity of the Maze, to see the confluence of the two great rivers, and even to pick out inaccessible Anasazi ruins – and well worth the $75 per-person rate for a one-hour reconnaissance.

Perhaps the main reason Moab has grown so fast is that out-of-state visitors tend to find Utah's other rural communities so irredeemably boring. As soon as Moab emerged from the pack, it became a beacon in the desert, attracting tourists ecstatic to find a town that stayed up after dark. Moab amounts to little more than a few miles of motels, restaurants and bars, but that's enough to make it the only southern-Utah town where you can stay for a week and still feel that you haven't seen everything, and everyone, a dozen times. The only sight-seeing to speak of is provided by the **Moab Skyway**, an incongruous new chairlift that climbs a thousand feet above town to the northern tip of the Moab Rim, for superb views acros the Colorado to Arches and beyond (daily 9am–9pm; $7).

## Arrival and information

Moab's superb **visitor center**, in the heart of town at Center and Main (summer daily 8am–9pm; rest of year daily 8am–5pm; ☎435/259-8825 or 1-800/635-6622), carries stacks of information on Moab itself, plus brochures and maps for the nearby parks and public lands. Bighorn Express (☎801/328-9920 or 1-888/655-7433) run daily shuttle **buses** between Salt Lake City and Moab, continuing on to Blanding, while the nearest Amtrak station is at Green River.

## Accommodation

If you've already been in Utah for a while when you reach Moab, its glittering neon **motel** signs will come as a big surprise. At last count, there were 29 motels in town, but every one of the thousand-plus rooms is taken on many nights between mid-March and October – when you'd be lucky to find anything below $50 – so reservations are strongly recommended. Agencies such as Moab/Canyonlands Central Reservations (☎435/259-5125 or 1-800/748-4386) can help.

Commercial **campgrounds** nearby include the well-shaded *Slickrock Campground*, 1301 N Hwy-191 (☎435/259-7660 or 1-800/448-8873), a mile north of town; if you're happy to put up with far more primitive facilities to escape the crowds, head instead for the **Sand Flats Recreation Area**, along the top of the mesa to the east of town, near the Slickrock Bike Trail, at 1924 S Roadrunner Hill (☎435/259-6111).

**Apache Motel**, 166 S 400 East (☎435/259-5727 or 1-800/228-6882). Long-established, two-story motel – as used by John Wayne – on a backstreet east of the center. ④.

**Best Western Greenwell Motel**, 105 S Main St (☎435/259-6151 or 1-800/528-1234). Central, modern and very comfortable motel. ⑤.

**Gonzo Inn**, 100 W 200 South (☎435/259-2515 or 1-800/791-4044). Luxurious if rather self-consciously "hip" inn, complete with kitsch retro furnishings, quirky artworks, and in-house espresso bar. ⑥.

**Inca Inn Motel**, 570 N Main St (☎435/259-7261). Clean, minimally equipped but adequate budget motel. ③.

**Lazy Lizard International Hostel**, 1213 S Hwy-191 (☎435/259-6057). Amiable, very laid-back private hostel, well south of the center, with $8 beds in six-person dorms, $6 camping and private cabins for $22, plus hot tub and kitchen. No membership necessary. ①.

**Moab Valley Inn**, 711 S Main St (☎435/259-4419 or 1-800/831-6622). New, large and well-equipped motel at the south end of town, with pool, hot tub, and on-site car and 4WD rental. ⑤.

**Sleep Inn**, 1051 S Main St (☎435/259-4655 or 1-800/753-3746). Comfortable modern chain motel, whose location a mile south of downtown means it offers highly competitive rates. ④.

## Eating and drinking

Moab offers by far the greatest range of **restaurants** in southern Utah, and for once most places make the effort to cater for vegetarians. With two pubs and a winery, there's also no problem getting a **drink**, while **coffee bars** are springing up everywhere. Note that many local restaurants, tired of low-tipping foreign customers, have taken to including a fifteen percent service charge on all checks.

Downtown Los Angeles, CA

Santa Monica, CA

Transamerica Pyramid, San Francisco, CA

TONY YEATES

Monument Valley, AZ/UT

EDMUND NAGELE

Double Arch, Arches National Park, UT

Southern Oregon coast

Death Valley National Park, CA

Space Needle, Seattle WA

Waikiki Beach, HI

Snowmobiles in Alaska

**Center Cafe**, 92 E Center St (☎435/259-4295). Expensive but exquisite restaurant, offering gourmet dining with a Pacific twist. Entrees, at around $20, range from Asian barbecue salmon to rack of lamb. Open for dinner nightly, plus brunch on Sun; closed Dec–Feb.

**Mondo Cafe**, 59 S Main St (☎435/259-5911). Groovy all-day hangout next to *Eddie McStiff's* brewpub, serving espresso coffees and the odd pastry or sandwich.

**The Poplar Place**, First North and Main St (☎435/259-6018). Friendly, classy adobe bar with Anasazi-themed ironwork, serving draft beers and good pizzas. Open daily 11.30am–11pm.

**Slickrock Cafe**, 5 N Main St (☎435/259-8004). Lively central cafe, with a varied menu of $10–20 dinner entrees and burger or salad lunches. Open daily from 7am for all meals.

**Sunset Grill**, 900 N Hwy-191 (☎435/259-7146). Charlie Steen's luxury hilltop home is now a fine restaurant, with meat and seafood entrees for $13–20, great desserts and stunning views. The tortuous if short approach road from the north end of town means it's no place to drink and drive.

## Natural Bridges National Monument

One of the prettiest and least-traveled highways in southern Utah, **Hwy-95** runs for over a hundred miles southeast from Capitol Reef, through dozens of red-rock canyons and across the Dirt Devil and Colorado Rivers, before topping out on the sagebrush plains of San Juan County. It's a fine drive in itself, but it also gives access to the marvellous collection of sandstone spans at **NATURAL BRIDGES NATIONAL MONU-MENT**, forty miles west of US-191. Three canyons come together here, and at each junction the streams that carved them have also formed sandstone bridges, the largest of which, **Sipapu Bridge**, is 268ft across at its base and over 200ft high. You can see the bridge from the nine-mile paved road that loops through the monument, or walk less than a mile down into the canyon for a closer look. **Kachina Bridge**, the next along the road, is nearly as high but twice as thick, and has Anasazi pictographs at its base. The oldest, slimmest and most fragile of the bridges is **Owachomo**, a mile and a half up Armstrong Canyon or along the mesa-top road; it spans 180ft but is only nine feet thick at its thinnest point. A long and fairly strenuous eight-mile trail along the canyon bottom leads past all three bridges.

Admission to the monument is $6 per vehicle. The **visitor center** (summer daily 8am–6pm; rest of year daily 8am–4.30pm), four miles off Hwy-95, has free trail guides and a slide show explaining how the bridges are formed, as well as a brief introduction to the Anasazi sites. Camping is allowed only in the small **campground** ($6) near the visitor center, which also has the only drinkable water in the monument.

## Monticello

The small town of **MONTICELLO**, 56 miles south of Moab on US-191, sixteen miles beyond the turnoff for the Needles section of Canyonlands (see p.880), makes a much quieter alternative base. Its strip of budget **motels** includes *Canyonlands Motor Inn*, 197 N Main St (☎435/587-2266; ②), and a *Super 8*, 649 N Main St (☎435/587-2489; ④). Good, large, standard **meals** can be had at the *MD Ranch Cookhouse*, 380 S Main St (☎435/587-3299). Information on the town, and on the parks and public lands in the vicinity, can be picked up from the **visitor center** at 117 S Main St (April–Oct Mon–Fri 8am–5pm, Sat & Sun 10am–5pm; Nov–March Mon–Fri 8am–5pm; ☎435/587-3235 or 1-800/574-4386).

## Grand Gulch Primitive Area

If you share a passion for archeology with the stamina for long-distance hiking, an expedition into the **GRAND GULCH PRIMITIVE AREA**, south of Natural Bridges National Monument, can make you feel like a real-life Indiana Jones. Every twist and turn of this deep, dramatic gorge seems to be filled with relics of its thousand-year occupation by the **Anasazi**.

Grand Gulch gouges across Cedar Mesa for just over fifty miles, dropping 2700ft to meet the **San Juan River**. There's no access for vehicles; the only path in starts from **Kane Gulch Ranger Station** (March–mid-Nov; for information, call ☎435/587-1532), five miles south of the point where Hwy-261 leaves Hwy-95, two miles east of the Natural Bridges turnoff. All would-be hikers should register here, but only those planning to camp overnight are liable for the $5 fee.

The trail begins by dropping steadily down Kane Gulch to join Grand Gulch proper four miles along. **Junction Ruin** here, the largest ruin in the canyon system, makes a popular day-hike destination, though **Turkey Pen Ruin**, at 4.7 miles, and **Stimper Arch** just beyond, are also within round-trip reach. Beyond that, you can hike for up to a week, all the way to the river, though most visitors find it simpler to double back at some point en route.

## The San Juan River, Mexican Hat and Bluff

From Natural Bridges and the Grand Gulch area, Hwy-261 runs south for some 25 miles before coming to what looks like a dead end at the edge of Cedar Mesa. From here, high above the eerie sandstone towers of the **Valley of the Gods** (where much of *Thelma and Louise* was filmed), the road turns to gravel before dropping over a thousand feet in little over two twisting, hairpin-turning miles down the "**Moki Dugway.**" Six miles from the foot of the switchbacks, the barely marked Hwy-316 shoots across what seems like a flat valley floor to yet another overlook, this time high above the **SAN JUAN RIVER** at the extraordinary and aptly named **Goosenecks State Reserve** (open 24hr; free). A textbook example of what geologists call an entrenched meander, the river, a thousand feet below, snakes around in such convoluted twists and turns that it flows six miles in total for every one mile west.

Back on Hwy-261 and just south, sleepy **MEXICAN HAT**, briefly a frenzied gold-mining camp, takes its name from a riverside **sandstone hoodoo**, just north of town, that looks more than a little like a south-of-the-border sombrero. More of a cluster of buildings on the banks of the river than a town, it's good fun and makes a good base for visiting Monument Valley, twenty miles south (see p.864). The best **place to stay** is the *San Juan Inn* (☎435/683-2220; ④), right on the river, which has its own grocery store and trading post, where the amiable *Olde Bridge Bar and Grill* offers cold beers and Navajo tacos. Just up the road, *Mexican Hat Lodge* (☎435/683-2222; ④) has an atmospheric steakhouse.

The rafts you may see emerging from the water at Mexican Hat went in at **BLUFF**, twenty miles upstream. US-163, the road between, doesn't follow the river very closely but is still an enthralling drive, and when you get there the town itself has a number of **Mormon pioneer houses** along its backstreets. Places to **eat** in Bluff include the *Twin Rocks Cafe* (☎435/672-2341) and the *Cottonwood Steakhouse* (☎435/672-2282), while an excellent new motel at the south end of town, the *Desert Rose Inn*, 701 W Hwy-191 (☎435/672-2303 or 1-888/475-7673; ④), holds thirty attractively designed and well furnished rooms. *Recapture Lodge* nearby (☎435/672-2281; ③), which offers nightly slide shows and informal (and informative) guided tours of the surrounding landscape, makes a good alternative.

## Hovenweep National Monument

Hidden in the no-man's-land that straddles the Utah-Colorado border, the remote **Anasazi ruins** at **HOVENWEEP NATIONAL MONUMENT** – 25 miles east of US-191 along Hwy-262, which branches off halfway between Bluff and Blanding, and 35 miles west of Cortez, Colorado (see p.760) – offer a haunting sense of timeless isolation. Hovenweep preserves six distinct conglomerations of ruins, sprouting from the rims of shallow desert canyons and dwarfed by the distant mountains, but easy access is restricted to the **Square Tower Group**, behind the small **ranger station** (daily 8am–5pm; no phone or entrance fee). The half-mile **Tower Loop Trail**, offers good views of the largest ruins, including the grandly named **Hovenweep Castle**, constructed around 1200 AD. It may well have stood guard over a much larger pueblo complex that nestled on the sandy floor of the canyon a mere thirty feet below, clustered around a perennial spring.

The longer **Square Tower Ruins Trail** continues along the far side of the canyon, and eventually dips across it and loops back to the ranger station. Highlights along the way include a number of ruins perched on solitary boulders and pinnacles, as well as the fortress-like **Stronghold House** and the **Unit-type House**, where niches in the walls appear to line up with the angle of the sun at the summer and winter solstices.

No accommodation, gasoline or food is available at or anywhere near Hovenweep, but (funding permitting) the 31-site **campground** beside the ranger station remains open all year ($10; no reservations).

## Lake Powell and Glen Canyon Dam

The mighty rivers and canyons of southern Utah come to an abrupt and ignoble end at the Arizona border, where the **Glen Canyon Dam** stops them dead in the stagnant waters of **LAKE POWELL**. Ironically, the lake is named for John Wesley Powell, the first white man to explore the canyonlands in depth, and the first of any color to run the Colorado River through the Grand Canyon. The roaring torrents with which he battled are now lost beneath these placid blue waters, and the blocked-up Colorado, Green, Dirty Devil, San Juan and Escalante rivers are now a playground for houseboaters and waterskiers. The construction of the dam in the early 1960s outraged **environmentalists** (Edward Abbey's *Monkey Wrench Gang* made their first big splash here, sabotaging bulldozers and simulating huge cracks in the dam at the opening ceremonies) and **anthropologists** (innumerable Anasazi pictographs are submerged hundreds of feet below the surface). It has created one of the most peculiar – and utterly unnatural – landscapes imaginable, the deep and tranquil lake a surreal contrast with the surrounding dry slickrock and sandstone buttes.

Lake Powell has 1960 miles of shoreline, which is more than the entire Pacific coast of the US, and 96 water-filled side canyons. The water level fluctuates considerably, so

---

### THE RAINBOW BRIDGE NATIONAL MONUMENT

The spectacular and extremely remote **Rainbow Bridge National Monument**, the world's largest natural bridge, can be visited on **guided boat tours** from Wahweap ($83 full-day, $63 half-day), Bullfrog ($83 full-day only) and Hall's Crossing ($83 full-day only). It lies roughly fifty miles by water from either direction, including a final mile or two down the narrow, winding side channel of Forbidding Canyon. From the unappealing jetty where the boats moor, bobbing in a morass of pond scum, a ten-minute walk leads to the astonishing giant sandstone gateway, springing up nearly 300ft from just above the waterline, with Navajo Mountain visible through its magnificent smooth curve. Its upper section is composed of Navajo sandstone, while the base belongs to the harder Kayenta formation, not as easily cut by flowing water; despite the increase in tourism since the creation of the lake, it remains an inspiring sight, and a place of special importance to the Navajo. It's also possible to get here overland, on foot or horseback across (very) rough canyon country from the Navajo Reservation (call ☎602/871-6647 for the necessary permits).

for much of the time the rocks to all sides are bleached for many feet above the current waterline, with a dirty-bath tidemark sullying the golden sandstone. Most of the many summer visitors bring their own boats, or rent a vessel from one of the four marinas that fringe the lake.

If you're passing through, by far the most accessible stop is **WAHWEAP MARINA**, just off US-89 on the way between Zion and the Grand Canyon, where *Wahweap Lodge* (☎520/645-2433 or 1-800/528-6154; ⑦) has comfortable lakeside rooms and some of the best food within a day's drive. The same company arranges **houseboat rental** from Wahweap or other Lake Powell marinas; boats sleep four or more people and cost from $600 for three nights in winter, $1000 in summer. There's **camping** on the shore of the lake at each of the marinas.

The nearest **budget accommodation** is across the Arizona border in **PAGE**, home of the *Navajo Trail Motel*, 800 Bureau St (☎520/645-9508; ③), and the *HI-Lake Powell International Hostel*, 141 Eighth Ave (☎520/645-3898 or 1-800/545-5405; ①/②) – which has $15 dorm beds – plus the usual assortment of chain motels and diners.

**GLEN CANYON DAM** itself, in between Page and Wahweap, can be seen on half-hour self-guided tours that start from the **visitor center** (May–Sept daily 8am–7pm; Oct–April daily 8am–5pm; free) and climb down to the huge 1.1 million kilowatt hydro-electric turbines.

The cheapest way to get out on the waters of Lake Powell is to take the **ferry** ($9 per car) between **Halls Crossing** and **Bullfrog** marinas, two-thirds of the way up the lake; from here the Burr Trail heads west toward Capitol Reef (see p.877), while Hwy-276 runs northeast to Natural Bridges.

# Northern Utah

Compared to the scenic splendor of the southern half of the state, northern Utah holds little to interest the tourist, although Salt Lake City, the capital, is by far the state's largest and most cosmopolitan urban center. The **northeast corner** has coal mines, old railroad towns and, along the Wyoming border, the **Uinta Mountains**, uncrossed by road and showing hardly a sign of civilization. From the **northwest**, the harshly alkaline **Great Basin** plain stretches uneventfully west across Nevada to California.

## Salt Lake City

Disarmingly pleasant and easygoing, **SALT LAKE CITY** is well worth a stopover of a couple of days. It's not a particularly thrilling destination in itself, but its setting is superb, towered over by the **Wasatch Front**, which marks the dividing line between the comparatively lush eastern and the bone-dry western halves of northern Utah, and which offers great hiking or cycling in summer and fall and, in winter, some of the world's best skiing.

Salt Lake City's bid to raise its international profile by hosting the 2002 Winter Olympics has so far resulted in a major building program both in the city itself and in the surrounding ski valleys, plus an unwelcome notoriety following the taint of corruption that surrounded its selection. For the moment, however, people elsewhere in the US still tend to imagine Salt Lake City as parallel to *The Stepford Wives* in terms of spontaneous public fun, and they're not far wrong. There is a fundamental lack of things to do in the way of museums or other cultural diversions, but if you're willing to switch gears and slow down, its unhurried pace, and the positive energy and lack of pretence of its people, can make for a surprisingly enjoyable experience.

SALT LAKE CITY

N

89

500 NORTH ST.

400 NORTH STREET

400 NORTH ST.

300 NORTH ST.

200 NORTH STREET

89

NORTH TEMPLE STREET

The Tabernacle

Family History Library

Temple Square

Delta Center

100 SOUTH STREET

Salt Palace

i

Amtrak Station

500 WEST STREET

400 WEST STREET

300 WEST STREET

200 WEST STREET

CENTER STREET

N. MAIN STREET

CAPITOL ST.

400 NORTH ST.

State Capitol

CAPITOL STREET

CANYON ROAD

A STREET

FOURTH AVENUE

THIRD AVENUE

SECOND AVENUE

FIRST AVENUE

Mormon Temple

Beehive House

SOUTH TEMPLE STREET

100 SOUTH STREET

200 SOUTH STREET

300 SOUTH STREET

MAIN STREET

STATE STREET

H

400 SOUTH STREET

B

A

500 SOUTH STREET

600 SOUTH STREET

700 SOUTH STREET

89

100 EAST STREET

200 EAST STREET

300 EAST STREET

400 EAST STREET

500 EAST STREET

600 EAST STREET

WEST TEMPLE STREET

G

F E 6

5

3

C

2

4

1

0        400 yds

**EATING**
A  Bill & Nada's Cafe
B  Le Parisien
C  Market Street Grill
D  Oasis Cafe
E  Pierpoint Cafe
F  Red Rock Brewing Company
G  Rio Grande Cafe
H  Lamb's Restaurant

**ACCOMMODATION**
1  Cavanaugh's Olympus
2  Deseret Inn
3  Monaco
4  Motel 6
5  Peery
6  Shilo Inn
7  Travelodge-Temple Square

## Arrival, information and getting around

**Salt Lake City International Airport** (☎801/575-2400) is a mere four miles west of downtown. A **cab** into town costs around $12; **shuttle vans** to downtown destinations are run by Xpress Shuttles (☎801/596-1600), while Canyon Transportation (☎801/255-1841) serves the ski areas. Long-distance Greyhound-Trailways **buses**, 160 W South Temple Blvd (☎801/355-9579), and Amtrak **trains**, 320 S Rio Grande Ave, arrive downtown.

Gray Line (☎801/521-7060) offers **bus tours** ranging from city jaunts to multiday trips to the national parks. To reach the best parts of the surrounding mountains, however, you'll need a **car** – all the rental companies are represented at the airport – or a cycle and strong legs. **Bikes** can be rented from Utah Ski Rental, 134 W 100 South St (☎801/355-9088).

**Visitor centers** supplying information on the city itself can be found downtown at 90 S West Temple Blvd in the Salt Palace Convention Center (Mon–Fri 8am–5pm, Sat &

Sun 9am–5pm; ☎801/521-2822), or in Terminal 2 of the airport (daily except Sat 9am–9pm). For details on the rest of Utah, stop by the Utah Travel Council, across from the capitol at 300 N State St (Mon–Fri 8am–5pm, Sat & Sun 10am–5pm; ☎801/538-1030). The downtown **post office** is at 230 W 200 South St (Mon–Fri 8am–5.30pm, Sat 8am–1.30pm; ☎801/978-3001; zip code 84101).

## Accommodation
Salt Lake City is well equipped with **accommodation**, with downtown options that range from budget motels and B&B inns to rather more luxurious hotels, and the usual mid-range places near the airport and along the interstates.

**Brigham Street Inn**, 1135 E South Temple Blvd (☎801/364-4461 or 1-800/417-4461). Luxurious, peaceful – and inconspicuous – B&B a few blocks east of downtown toward the mountains. ⑥.

**Cavanaughs Olympus Hotel**, 161 W 600 South St (☎801/521-7373 or 1-800/325-4000). Good-value mountain-view rooms downtown, convenient for Amtrak, airport and interstates. ⑤.

**Deseret Inn**, 50 W 500 South (☎801/532-2900). This downtown motor lodge is a real throwback to a bygone era; though far from smart its rooms are clean and very inexpensive. ②.

**Holiday Inn Airport**, 1659 W North Temple Blvd (☎801/533-9000 or 1-800/HOLIDAY). Well-equipped, well-priced hotel, served by free airport shuttles and not too far from downtown. ④.

**Hotel Monaco**, 15 W 200 South (☎801/595-0000 or 1-888/294-9710). Extremely hip, very upscale downtown hotel, housed in a former bank. ⑥.

**Motel 6**, 176 W 600 South St (☎801/531-1252). Budget downtown motel, handy for Amtrak. ②.

**Peery Hotel**, 110 W 300 South St (☎801/521-4300 or 1-800/331-0073). Refurbished 1910 downtown landmark, with small but characterful rooms. ④.

**Shilo Inn**, 206 S West Temple Blvd (☎801/521-9500). Clean rooms in a downtown tower, with pool, sauna and gym. ⑤.

**Travelodge – Temple Square**, 144 W North Temple Blvd (☎801/533-8200). Most central and least expensive of three local *Travelodges*. ③.

**Ute Hostel**, 21 E Kelsey Ave (☎801/595-1645). Much the better of Salt Lake City's two hostels, this small private establishment, a few miles south of downtown, offers $15 dorm beds and a couple of private rooms, plus bike rental, a hot tub and free airport pickup. ①/②.

## Temple Square
The geographical – and spiritual – heart of Salt Lake City is **Temple Square**, the world headquarters of the **Mormon Church** (or Church of Christ of Latter Day Saints – LDS). Its focus, the monumental **Temple** itself, was completed in 1893 after forty years of intensive labor. The multispired granite edifice rises to 210ft above the city – it's not the tallest building on the mainly flat skyline but, thanks to its crisply angular silhouette, it's just about the only interesting one. Only confirmed Mormons may enter the Temple, and even they do so only for the most sacred LDS rituals – marriage, baptisms and "sealing," the joining of a family unit for eternity.

Wander through the gates of Temple Square, however, and you'll swiftly be snapped up by one of the many waiting Mormons, and shepherded to join a free 45-minute **tour** of the various sites within. As well as monuments to Mormon pioneers, you'll be ushered into the odd oblong shell of the **Mormon Tabernacle**. No images of any kind adorn its interior, which is home to the world-renowned Mormon Tabernacle Choir; a helper at the lectern laconically displays its remarkable acoustic properties by tearing up a newspaper and dropping a nail. There's free admission to the choir's 9.30am Sunday broadcast, and its rehearsals on Thursday evenings at 8pm.

The primary aim of the tours is to awaken your interest in the Mormon faith; differences from Christianity are played down in favor of a soft-focus video of Old Testament scenes. The tour ends in the northern of the Square's two **visitor centers**, where an array of touch-screen computers provide woolly answers to questions like "What is the purpose of life?" and "Who was Joseph Smith?" In the southern visitor center, a surprisingly good free movie tells the story of the arrival of Salt Lake City's first Mormon settlers.

## Downtown Salt Lake City

A block east of Temple Square along South Temple Boulevard, the **Beehive House** (Mon–Sat 9.30am–4.30pm, Sun 10am–1pm; free) is a plain white New England-style house, with wraparound verandas and green shutters. Erected in 1854 by church leader **Brigham Young**, it's now a small museum of Young's life, restored to the style of the period. Free twenty-minute tours, which you have to join to see much of the house, are given at least every half-hour.

The **Family History Library**, across West Temple Boulevard from Temple Square (Mon 7.30am–6pm, Tues–Sat 7.30am–10pm; free), is intended to enable Mormons to trace their ancestors, and then baptize them into the faith by proxy, but it's open to everyone. The world's most exhaustive genealogical library is surprisingly user-friendly, giving immediate access, through CD-ROMs and banks of computers, to birth and death records from over fifty countries, some dating back as much as five hundred years. All you need is a person's place of birth, a few approximate dates, and you're away; volunteers provide help if you need it, but leave you alone until you ask. Next door to the library, the **Museum of Church History and Art** (Mon–Fri 9am–9pm, Sat & Sun 10am–7pm; free), charts the rise of the Mormon faith in art and artifact.

The area southwest of Temple Square, now the site of the massive Salt Palace convention center and sports arena (home of the Utah Jazz basketball team), has undergone a rapid transformation. The surrounding district of brick warehouses around the Union Pacific railroad tracks is quickly filling up with designer shops and art galleries, signs that even Mormons can be yuppies.

## Capitol Hill

Quite why the Mormons chose not to put their Temple on the gentle hill that stands above today's Temple Square is anyone's guess. As a result, when Utah was granted statehood in 1896, it was free to become the site of the imposing, domed **Utah State Capitol** (summer Mon–Sat 6am–8pm; rest of year Mon–Sat 6am–6pm; free). Along with the plaques and monuments you might expect, the corridors of power are packed full of earnest and rather diverting exhibits of great Utah moments. The basement area in particular holds a fine assortment of historical whatnots, ranging from mining dioramas to the 18-cylinder, 750-horsepower *Mormon Meteor*, raced by Ab Jenkins across the Bonneville Salt Flats in the 1950s.

Now called **Capitol Hill**, the neighborhood around the capitol holds some of Salt Lake City's grandest c.1900 homes, with dozens of ornate Victorian houses lining Main Street and Quince Street to the northwest; **walking tour maps** of the district are available from the Utah Heritage Foundation, 355 Quince St. The main chamber of **Council Hall**, directly opposite the Capitol, has been restored to its period appearance, while the rest of the building houses the Utah Travel Council (see p.889).

## Eating

Though Salt Lake City has a perfectly good selection of **restaurants**, it lacks an atmospheric – let alone hip – dining district. If you like to compare menus, the only downtown area with much potential is the block or two to either side of West Temple Street, south and east of the Salt Palace.

**Bambara**, *Hotel Monaco*, 15 W 200 South (☎801/363-5454). Chic, post-Deco and pricey downtown restaurant, with a fabulous menu ranging from buffalo carpaccio or crab cakes to lamb sirloin on du Puy lentils. ⑥.

**Bill and Nada's Cafe**, 479 S 600 East (☎801/359-6984). All-American 1940s diner, open 24hr. Great for breakfast, but worth a visit anytime for its ace jukebox, the best west of Memphis – packed with Hank Williams, Patsy Cline, blues and bebop tracks.

**Lamb's Restaurant**, 169 S Main St (☎801/364-7166). Great breakfasts, best eaten at the long shiny counter, and excellent-value set meals throughout the day. Closed Sun.

**Market Street Grill**, 48 Market St (☎801/322-4668). As close as Salt Lake City comes to a New York City bar and grill. Fresh seafood, especially oysters, plus steaks in all shapes and sizes. $8 lunch specials, full dinners $15–30.

**Oasis Cafe**, 151 S 500 East (☎801/322-0404). Classy but inexpensive cafe, serving very good food (dinner entrees $12–20) with plenty of appealing vegetarian options. Live acoustic music or jazz in the evening.

**Pierpoint Cafe**, 122 W Pierpoint Ave (☎801/364-1222). Large, downtown Mexican restaurant, open for lunch Mon–Fri and dinner daily, with top-quality ceviche and gourmet dishes plus the usual standards, all competitively priced.

**Rio Grande Cafe**, 270 S Rio Grande (☎801/364-3302). Spirited and stylish Mexican cantina in the old Denver and Rio Grande railroad station, still used by Amtrak, three blocks west of downtown.

**Ruth's Diner**, 2100 Emigration Canyon Rd (☎801/582-5807). Good-value indoor and patio dining, often accompanied by live music, set in and around old railroad carriages in a narrow canyon just three miles east of town. Wide selection of fresh dishes, great salads and Utah's best breakfasts.

**Santa Fe Restaurant**, 2100 Emigration Canyon Rd (☎801/582-5888). Sophisticated upmarket sister restaurant to *Ruth's* (above). Eclectic menu of the best of Southwest cuisine; brilliantly presented grilled meats and fish, and an excellent $12 Sunday brunch.

## Drinking and nightlife

Salt Lake City doesn't roll up the sidewalks when the sun goes down. Many **drinking** venues are technically private clubs, in which a nominal membership fee entitles the cardholder and up to five guests to two weeks' use of the facilities, but there are also a handful of **brewpubs**, for which membership is not required. To find out about the broad range of **fringe** art, music and clubland happenings, pick up free papers such as *City Weekly* or the monthly *Catalyst*, or tune to radio station KRCL 91FM.

**Dead Goat Saloon**, 165 S West Temple Blvd (☎801/328-4628). Raucous, semi-subterranean saloon, with live loud music most nights.

**Squatters Pub**, 147 West Broadway (☎801/363-2739). Casual, friendly brewpub with a range of beers available until 1am every day.

**Zephyr Club**, 301 S West Temple Blvd (☎801/355-2582). Salt Lake's premier live jazz and blues venue, with semi-famous names most nights. Upmarket clientele, elegant decor, cover $5–15.

# Park City

Despite Brigham Young's strictures against prospecting for precious metals – he feared a Gentile "Gold Rush" – the first mining camp at **PARK CITY**, just thirty miles east of downtown Salt Lake City along I-80 through the mountains, was established in the late 1860s. In 1872 George Hearst laid the foundations of the Hearst media empire by paying $27,000 for a claim that became the Ontario Silver Mine, worth $50 million. These days Park City, together with adjoining Deer Valley, is Utah's largest **ski area**, with the season usually running from mid-November to mid-April. Daily lift passes are $56; equipment rental outlets include Park City Sport (☎1-800/523-3922) and Gart Brothers (☎1-800/284-4754). In addition, Park City hosts the prestigious **Sundance Film Festival**, in the second half of each January.

Park City has for many years been engulfed by an ever-growing sprawl of new condos, factory outlets and other developments, and is becoming completely unrecognizable as it prepares to host the principal skiing events for the 2002 Winter Olympics. Its restored **Main Street** now makes only token gestures towards mimicking the mountain mining community it used to be, its shops and restaurants striving instead to emulate the chic resorts of Colorado.

## Practicalities

Park City's **visitor center**, 528 Main St (May & Oct daily noon–5pm; rest of year Mon–Sat 10am–7pm, Sun noon–6pm; ☎435/658-4541 or 1-800/453-1360), doubles as an enjoyable museum of town history, and stands above the town's original jailhouse. Lewis Bros Stages (☎435/649-2256 or 1-800/826-5844) runs scheduled **shuttles** from downtown Salt Lake City ($16) and the airport ($20), and mountain **bikes** can be rented from White Pine Touring, 363 Main St (daily 10am–7pm; ☎801/649-8710).

**Accommodation** rates double in the ski season; the CVB can provide full listings of resorts and other lodgings. The *Old Miners' Lodge*, right next to the ski lift at 615 Woodside Ave (☎435/645-8068 or 1-800/648-8068; ④), is an 1893 lodge restored as a comfortable B&B; the unassuming *Chateau Apres*, 1299 Norfolk Ave (☎435/649-9372; ①–③), is a cheap, cozy alternative with some $25 dorm beds. *Morning Ray Cafe*, 268 Main St (☎435/649-5686), serves good breakfasts and has a wide-ranging lunch menu, while the dinner-only *Chimayo*, 368 Main St (☎435/649-6222), offers cutting-edge contemporary Southwestern cuisine. The *Wasatch Brew Pub*, nearby at 250 Main St (☎435/645-0900), is open until midnight daily.

# The Great Salt Lake

The **GREAT SALT LAKE**, in the barren desert west of Salt Lake City, is the last remnant of a 20,000-square-mile inland sea that once stretched into Idaho and Nevada. In the late nineteenth century, the lake's shores were lined with extravagant resorts, and steamboats and pleasure cruisers plied across its surface. After years of mysterious decline, when enough of its contents evaporated to make it the world's second-saltiest body of water – so thick with minerals as to be all but lifeless – it has since the 1980s started equally mysteriously to refill. Its level today is far higher than state planners ever bargained for, which has forced the raising of the adjacent I-80 interstate by several feet.

On the plus side, the lake's formerly abundant wildlife, and especially its migratory birds, have begun to reappear, but it's still not especially attractive to humans. **Great Salt Lake State Park**, sixteen miles west of town on I-80, is the dingiest affair imaginable (daily 8am–sunset). It marks the site of the flamboyant 1890s **Saltair** pavilion, which closed down in 1968 when the waters receded, and was promptly destroyed by fire. A smaller version reopened in 1983, just in time to be flooded out; it's now pretty decrepit and threadbare, but still gamely showing videos of the lake, while gaudy railroad cars and a lake boat outside act as giftshops.

# Into the mountains: Timpanogos Cave and the Alpine Loop

Perhaps the best way to get a feel for the bountiful wilderness that surrounds Salt Lake City is to drive the **ALPINE SCENIC LOOP BYWAY** (Hwy-92), which branches off I-15 twenty miles south of downtown to follow the American Fork River east into the **Uinta National Forest**. After ten miles, it reaches **TIMPANOGOS CAVE NATIONAL MONUMENT**, which weather permitting is normally open, for ranger-guided tours only, between mid May and October ($6; tickets sold daily 7am–4.30pm in summer, otherwise daily 8am–2.30pm; advance reservations highly recommended, call ☎801/756-1679). The hour-long underground tours start at the mouth of the caves, a moderately steep 1.5-mile hike up from the visitor center; allow three hours in total for the round-trip, plus a wait that can be as long as three hours on summer weekends. Once underground, the most spectacular of the vast array of dazzling white crystalline formations are the contorted shapes in the **Chimes Chamber** in the very heart of the mountain.

From here Hwy-92 climbs steeply up behind 11,750ft **Mount Timpanogos**, allowing access to miles of unspoiled **hiking country**. It then drops down from the ridge into

**Provo Canyon**, home of the *Sundance* ski resort and film institute, owned and run by actor Robert *Sundance Kid* Redford, who lives here as well.

The Alpine Loop ends up back on the flatlands 45 miles south of downtown Salt Lake at the tidy little town of **PROVO**, whose main feature is **Brigham Young University**, the Mormon-dominated college that has great sports teams – basketball and football especially – and such a squeaky-clean student body you'll feel like you stepped straight back into the Eisenhower years. Grab a bite to eat on campus, or in the town at *Clair's Cafe*, 154 University Ave (☎801/373-4077), which has soups, sandwiches and good burgers at fair prices. Provo also has a few inexpensive and moderately priced **motels**.

# Northeast Utah

Most of Utah's **northeastern corner** – due east of Salt Lake City, as Wyoming takes a bite out of its otherwise perfect rectangle – is taken up by the forbidding **Uinta Mountains**, very much of a piece with the rest of the Rockies. However, to the east of the mountains the terrain reverts to the classic Southwestern desert plains, with the small town of **Vernal** serving as the base for explorations of the wildernesses of **Flaming Gorge** and **Dinosaur**.

## Dinosaur National Monument

**DINOSAUR NATIONAL MONUMENT** straddles the border between Utah and Colorado in a remote area only conceivably visitable in your own vehicle. Divided into two separate sections, it was created to preserve a rock stratum in its Utah half, seven miles north of Jensen on Hwy-149, east of Vernal, which has over the years provided brontosaurus skeletons and other astonishing remains to museums around the world. Uniquely, in the **Dinosaur Quarry** building, a tilted layer of sandstone has been painstakingly exposed to display an incredible three-dimensional jigsaw of fossilized dinosaur bones, left in situ for imaginative visitors to piece together.

The other half of the monument is a 25-mile drive north of the flyblown and unattractive little town of Dinosaur, CO, the site of the main **visitor center** (summer daily 8am–7pm; winter daily 8am–4.30pm; $10 per vehicle). At the end of the road **Harpers Corner** provides a phenomenal view of the goosenecks of the Green and Yampa Rivers, approaching their confluence at imposing **Steamboat Rock**.

## Flaming Gorge

It took a major controversy in the 1950s to spare the Green and Yampa confluence from submergence by a new dam. **FLAMING GORGE**, starting around 25 miles north of Vernal, was not so lucky; the damming of the Red Canyon of the Green River in 1964 has turned it into a National Recreation Area, another "splendid recreational playground" for water-sports enthusiasts, anglers and hikers.

Ambivalence about its creation can't obscure its continuing beauty, which can be appreciated from various points on the loop drive that circles the canyon, calling at Green River, Wyoming, at its northern end (see p.766). The **Gorge** itself is an incandescent wall of red rock named by John Wesley Powell and best seen from the **Antelope Flat** marina-cum-campground on the eastern side. **Red Canyon visitor center** (summer daily 9.30am–5pm) to the west is another good stop, with a dramatic overlook and attractive nearby **campground**; the actual dam is not all that exciting.

## Vernal

Although **VERNAL**, thirty miles west of the Colorado border on US-40 as it heads to Salt Lake City, is the largest community in northeast Utah, and holds a mildly diverting dinosaur museum, for most visitors it's only significant as an overnight stop. Budget

**motels** lining Main Street include the *Sage* at no. 54 W (☎435/789-1442; ②), which has its own adjacent **restaurant**, and the *Best Western Antlers Motel* at no. 423 W (☎435/789-1202; ④).

# NEVADA

**NEVADA** is without doubt the most desolate state in the US, consisting largely of endless tracts of bleak, empty desert. Its flat sagebrush plains are cut intermittently by angular mountain ranges, and the lack of rainfall or fertile soil has ensured its maintenance as untouched wilderness. Apart from the huge acreages given over to mining and to grazing cattle and sheep, much of Nevada is under the control of the **military**, who use it to test aircraft and weapons systems, including Stealth fighters and atomic bombs. Dozens of intriguing small towns are scattered around the state, some showing signs of strong Basque influence. Many more are fairly decrepit roadside ghost towns, often little more than a gas-station-cum-general-store, flanked by a saloon and perhaps a brothel – Nevada is the only US state not to have outlawed **prostitution**, though it is illegal in Las Vegas.

Though millions of people pass through on their way to and from California, there's only one real reason why anyone ever *visits* Nevada, and that is to **gamble**: as soon as you cross the state border, you'll be attacked by a 24-hour onslaught of neon signs and gimmicky architecture, each advertising the best odds and biggest jackpots, nowhere more than in the surreal oasis of **Las Vegas**. Even the smaller and more down-to-earth settlements of **Reno** and state capital **Carson City** revolve around the casino trade. At least the casinos' energetic pursuit of passing trade keeps rooms and especially food inexpensive, so the towns make good places to break a long journey – and, with Nevada's relaxed marriage and divorce laws, make or break a relationship.

### Getting around Nevada
As there's almost nothing in Nevada outside of Las Vegas and Reno, it's hardly surprising that getting around the state's vast empty spaces is nearly impossible without a car. Las Vegas is no longer served by Amtrak, though Reno still welcomes daily trains between San Francisco and Salt Lake City; both Las Vegas and Reno have their own **airports**.

# Las Vegas

Shimmering from the desert haze of Nevada like a latter-day El Dorado, **LAS VEGAS** is the most dynamic, spectacular city on earth. At the start of the twentieth century, it didn't even exist; now it's home to over one million people, and boasts fourteen of the world's fifteen largest hotels, whose flamboyant, no-expense-spared **casinos** lure in over thirty million tourists each year. Las Vegas has been stockpiling superlatives since the 1950s, but never rests on its laurels for a moment. Long before they lose their sparkle, yesterday's showpieces are blasted into rubble, to make way for ever more extravagant replacements. A few years ago, when the fashion was for fantasy, Arthurian castles and Egyptian pyramids mushroomed along the legendary Strip; now Vegas demands nothing less than entire cities, and has already acquired pocket versions of New York, Paris, Monte Carlo and Venice.

While Las Vegas has certainly cleaned up its act since the early days of Mob domination, there's little truth in the notion that it's become a **family** destination. In fact, for kids, it's not a patch on Orlando. Several casinos have added theme parks or fun rides to fill those odd non-gambling moments, but only five percent of visitors bring children, and the crowds that cluster around the exploding volcanoes and pirate battles along the Strip remain almost exclusively adult. Neither is Vegas as consistently **cheap** as it used to be. It's still possible to find good, inexpensive rooms, and the all-you-can-eat buffets offer unbeatable value, but the casino owners have finally discovered that high-rollers happy to lose hundreds of dollars per night don't mind paying premium prices to eat at top-quality restaurants, and stay in plush hotels.

Your first hours in Las Vegas are like entering another world, where the religion is luck, the language is money, and time is measured by revolutions of a roulette wheel. Once you're acclimatized, the whole spectacle can be absolutely exhilarating – assuming you haven't pinned your hopes, and your savings, on the pursuit of a fortune. Las Vegas is an unmissable destination, but one that palls for most visitors after a couple of (hectic) days. If you've come solely to gamble, there's not much to say beyond the fact that all the casinos are free, and open 24 hours per day, with acres of floor space packed

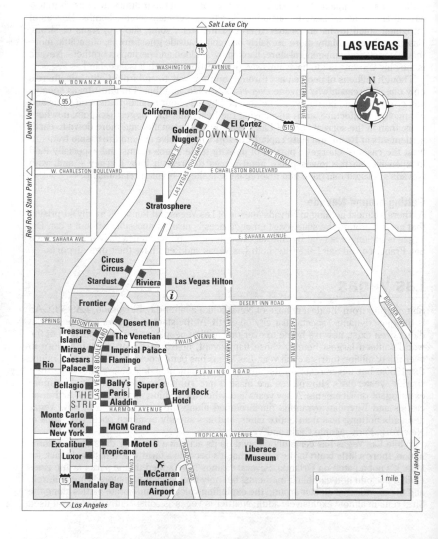

with ways to lose money: million-dollar slots, video poker, blackjack, craps, roulette wheels, and much much more.

## A history of Las Vegas

The name *Las Vegas* – Spanish for "the meadows" – was originally applied to a group of natural springs that from 1829 onwards served as a way-station for travelers on the Old Spanish Trail. In 1900, the valley had a population of just thirty people. Things changed in 1905, with the completion of the now-defunct rail link between Salt Lake City and Los Angeles.

Though Nevada was the first state to outlaw gambling, in 1909, it was made legal once more in 1931, and the workers who built the nearby **Hoover Dam** flocked to Vegas to bet away their pay-packets. Providing abundant cheap electricity and water, the dam amounted to a massive federal subsidy for the infant city. Hotel-casinos such as the daring 65-room *El Rancho* began to appear in the early 1940s, and mobster Bugsy Siegel raised $7 million to open the *Flamingo* on the Strip in December 1946.

By the 1950s, Las Vegas was booming. The military had arrived – mushroom clouds from **A-bomb tests** in the deserts were visible from the city, and visitors would drive out with picnics to get a better view – and so too had big guns like **Frank Sinatra**, who debuted at the *Desert Inn* in 1951, and **Liberace**, who received $50,000 to open the *Riviera* in 1955. As the stars gravitated towards the Vegas honeypot, nightclubs across America went out of business, and the city became the nation's undisputed live-entertainment capital.

The beginning of the end for Mob rule in Vegas came in 1966, after reclusive airline tycoon **Howard Hughes** sold TWA for $500 million and moved into the *Desert Inn*. When the owners tired of his non-gambling ways, he simply bought the hotel, and his clean-cut image encouraged other entrepreneurs to follow suit. **Elvis** arrived a little later; the young rock'n'roller had bombed at the *New Frontier* in 1956, but started a triumphant five-year stint as a karate-kicking lounge lizard at the *International* (now the *Las Vegas Hilton*) in 1969.

Endless federal swoops and stings drove the Mob out of sight by the 1980s, in time for Vegas to reinvent itself on a surge of junk-bond megadollars. The success of Steve Wynn's *Mirage* in enticing a new generation of visitors, from 1989 onwards, spawned a host of imitators. The 1990s kicked off with a spate of casino building, including *Excalibur* and the *MGM Grand*, that has barely let up since, with *Luxor* and *New York–New York* followed as the millennium approached by the opulent quartet of *Bellagio*, *Mandalay Bay*, the *Venetian* and *Paris*. Beneath the glitz, however, **gambling** remains the bedrock, and Las Vegas' pre-eminence seems little dented by the spread of casinos elsewhere in the US. City boosters point out that only fifteen percent of Americans have so far seen Vegas, and they're confidently expecting the rest to turn up any day now.

## Arrival, information and getting around

Las Vegas' busy **McCarran International Airport** is a mile east of the southern end of the Strip, and four miles from downtown (☎702/261-5743). Some hotels run free shuttle buses for guests, while Bell Trans (☎702/739-7990) run a **minibus** service to the Strip ($3.50) and downtown ($5), and a **cab** to the Strip costs from $9 for the southern end up to $15 for casinos further north.

If you plan to see more of Vegas than the Strip, a **car** is invaluable. **Public transport** does exist, however. The oak-veneered streetcars of the **Las Vegas Strip Trolley** (☎702/382-1404) ply the Strip between *Mandalay Bay* and the *Stratosphere*, for a flat fare of $1.40, while the similar **Downtown Trolley** (☎702/229-0624) loops between *Stratosphere* and downtown for 50¢. CAT buses (☎702/228-7433) serve the whole city;

## GETTING MARRIED IN LAS VEGAS

Second only to making your fortune as a reason to visit Las Vegas is the prospect of **getting married**. Over a hundred thousand weddings are performed here each year, many so informal that bride and groom just wind down the window of their car during the ceremony, and a Vegas wedding has become a byword for tongue-in-cheek chic.

You don't have to be a local resident or take a blood test to get wed in Las Vegas. Assuming you're both at least eighteen years old and carrying picture ID, and neither of you is already married, simply turn up at the Clark County Marriage License Bureau, downtown at 200 S Third St (Mon–Thurs 8am–midnight, and continuously from 8am on Fri to midnight on Sun; ☎702/455-4416), and buy a marriage license for $35 cash.

Wedding chapels claim to charge as little as $50 for their most basic ceremonies, but at that sort of rate even the minister is regarded as an "extra" costing an additional $40. Reckon on paying at least $100 for the bare minimum, which is liable to be as romantic a process as checking in at a hotel, and to take about as long. The full deluxe service ranges up to around $500.

**Candlelight Wedding Chapel**, 2855 Las Vegas Blvd S; ☎702/735-4179 or 1-800/962-1818. Busy little chapel across from Circus Circus, where you get a garter with the $169 wedding package, or two white T-shirts with the $499 option.

**Graceland Wedding Chapel**, 619 S Las Vegas Blvd; ☎702/474-6655 or 1-800/824-5732. Home of the King – an Elvis impersonator will act as best man, give the bride away or serenade you, but unfortunately he can't perform the service.

**Little Church of the West**, 4617 Las Vegas Blvd S; ☎702/739-7971 or 1-800/821-2452. Once part of the Last Frontier casino, this fifty-year-old chapel is on the National Register of Historic Places, and has moved progressively down the Strip to its current site south of Mandalay Bay. Among the more peaceful and quiet places to exchange your Vegas vows – if that's really what you want.

**Little White Chapel**, 1301 S Las Vegas Blvd; ☎702/382-5943 or 1-800/545-8111. Where Bruce Willis and Demi Moore married each other, and Michael Jordan and Joan Collins married other people. Open all day every day, with the "The One & Only 24hr Drive-Up Wedding Window," if you're in a major hurry.

#301 and #302 connect the Strip to downtown ($1.50). Greyhound's long-distance buses use a terminal at 200 S Main St downtown. Several Strip casinos are also connected by free **monorail systems**, but these don't link up with each other, and most require you to walk through the full length of the casinos in order to use them. Amtrak trains no longer serve Las Vegas, but a new high-speed service between LA and Las Vegas is rumored to be coming soon.

Any number of local freesheets and magazines provide local information. There are also **visitor centers** at 3150 Paradise Rd (Mon–Fri 8am–6pm, Sat & Sun 8am–5pm; ☎702/892-0711 or 1-800/332-5333), half a mile east of the Strip in the Convention Center, and 711 E Desert Inn Rd (Mon–Fri 8am–5pm; ☎702/735-1616). There can be no easier city in which to **change money**: the casinos gladly convert almost any currency, and their walls are festooned with every conceivable ATM machine.

## Accommodation

Although Las Vegas has well over 100,000 hotel rooms, it's best to book accommodation ahead if you're on a tight budget, or arriving on Friday or Saturday. Whatever you may have heard, Las Vegas hotels no longer offer incredibly cheap deals at the drop of a hat. It is true that serious gamblers can get their accommodation free, but to count as "serious" you'd have to commit yourself to gambling several thousand dollars, which is a strange definition of "free."

Precise **room rates** are dictated by supply and demand. Even if you stay in the same room for several consecutive days, you'll be charged a different rate for each day, depending on the day of the week, and what's going on in town. The only sure-fire way to get a cut-price room is to **visit during the week**; rates everywhere rise enormously on Friday or Saturday. On top of that, many hotels won't accept Saturday arrivals. The CVB runs a reservation service on ☎1-800/332-5333.

**Bellagio**, 3600 Las Vegas Blvd S (☎702/791-7111 or 1-888/987-6667). Extremely luxurious rooms, with plush European furnishings and marble bathrooms; amazing pool complex; and the best restaurants in town. Sun–Thurs ⑦, Fri & Sat ⑨.

**Caesars Palace**, 3570 Las Vegas Blvd S (☎702/731-7222 or 1-800/634-6661). Right in the heart of the Strip, the epitome of 1960s luxury has recently trebled in size, and offers the last word in pseudo-Roman splendor, with top-class restaurants and shops. Sun–Thurs ⑤, Fri & Sat ⑥.

**California Hotel**, 12 Ogden Ave at 1st St (☎702/385-1222 or 1-800/634-6255). Almost all the guests in this mid-range downtown casino are Hawaiian, and Hawaiian food and drink dominate the bars and restaurants. The actual rooms are plain but adequate. Sun–Thurs ③, Fri & Sat ④.

**Circus Circus**, 2880 Las Vegas Blvd S (☎702/734-0410 or 1-800/444-2472). Venerable Strip hotel popular with budget tour groups. Kids love the theme park and (almost) nonstop circus acts, adults love the low room rates. Sun–Thurs ③, Fri & Sat ④.

**El Cortez Hotel**, 600 E Fremont St (☎702/385-5200 or 1-800/634-6703). Veteran downtown casino, with adequate cut-price rooms in the main building, good-value $40 mini-suites in the new tower, and bargain-basement accommodation for $18 in *Ogden House* across the street. ①/②.

**Imperial Palace**, 3535 Las Vegas Blvd S (☎702/731-3311 or 1-800/634-6441). Behind its hideous facade, one of the Strip's best-value options. Its standard rooms are adequate if not exciting – all have balconies – while the "luv tub" suites, at $30 extra, offer huge beds, even bigger sunken baths, and mirrors everywhere you can imagine. Sun–Thurs ②, Fri & Sat ④.

**Las Vegas Backpackers Hostel**, 1322 E Fremont St (☎702/385-1150 or 1-800/550-8958). Well-kept private hostel in a grim neighborhood ten blocks east of downtown, offering dorm beds for $15 and private double rooms for $45, plus use of a good pool. ①–③.

**Las Vegas International Hostel**, 1208 Las Vegas Blvd S (☎702/385-9955). Bare-bones AAIH hostel in a small, dilapidated former motel, in an insalubrious area on the fringes of downtown. Dorm beds cost $14, rooms with shared bath under $30. Demand is heavy, especially in summer. ①.

**Luxor Las Vegas**, 3900 Las Vegas Blvd S (☎702/262-4000 or 1-800/288-1000). A night in this vast smoked-glass pyramid is one of the great Las Vegas experiences. All the 2000 enjoyably Egyptian-themed rooms in the pyramid itself face outwards, with tremendous views. Sun–Thurs ③, Fri & Sat ⑥.

**Main Street Station**, 200 N Main St at Ogden (☎702/387-1896 or 1-800/713-8933). Downtown's best-value option, two short blocks from Fremont St, with four hundred large guestrooms plus a brewpub and an assortment of good restaurants. ③.

**MGM Grand**, 3799 Las Vegas Blvd S (☎702/891-7777 or 1-800/929-1112). The world's largest hotel; waiting for any kind of service, especially check-in, can be horrendous, but you get a good standard of accommodation for the price, and it holds several of Las Vegas' finest restaurants. Sun–Thurs ④, Fri & Sat ⑤.

**New York–New York**, 3790 Las Vegas Blvd S (☎702/740-6969 or 1-800/NYFORME). Rooms at the most exuberantly enjoyable Strip casino are very nice, if a bit small, and filled with Art Deco furnishings and flourishes. Sun–Thurs ⑤, Fri & Sat ⑦.

**Paris-Las Vegas**, 3645 Las Vegas Blvd S (☎702/967-4611 or 1-888/BONJOUR). Flamboyant new casino, where the rooms and services are pitched slightly below those of Las Vegas' most upscale Vegas joints, but the location, views and general ambiance are superb. Sun–Thurs ⑤, Fri & Sat ⑦.

**The Venetian**, 3355 Las Vegas Blvd S (☎702/414-1000 or 1-888/283-6423). Even the standard rooms at this upscale Strip behemoth are split-level suites, offering antique-style canopied beds on a raised platform, plus roomy living rooms. Sun–Thurs ⑦, Fri & Sat ⑧.

# The City

Though the Las Vegas sprawl measures fifteen miles wide by fifteen miles long, most tourists stick to the six-mile stretch of Las Vegas Boulevard that includes the downtown area, slightly southeast of the intersection of I-15 and US-95, and the Strip, home to the major casinos. In between lie two somewhat seedy miles of gas stations, fast-food drive-ins and wedding chapels, while the rest of town is largely residential, and need barely concern you.

## The Strip

For its razor-edge finesse in harnessing sheer, magnificent excess to the deadly serious business of making money, there's no place like the **Las Vegas Strip**. It's hard to imagine a time when Las Vegas was an ordinary city, and Las Vegas Boulevard a dusty thoroughfare scattered with the usual edge-of-town motels. After five decades of capitalism run riot, with every new casino-hotel setting out to surpass anything its neighbors ever dreamed of, the Strip seems to be locked into a hyperactive craving for thrills and glamour, forever discarding its latest toy in its frenzy for the next jackpot.

Each casino is a self-contained fantasyland of high camp and genuine excitement. Almost against your will, huge moving walkways sweep you in from the sidewalk; once inside, it can be almost impossible to find your way out. The action keeps going day and night, and in this sealed and windowless environment you rapidly lose track of which is which. Even if you do manage to get back onto the streets during the day, the scorching heat is liable to drive you straight back in again; night is the best time to venture out, when the neon's blazing at its brightest.

As the Strip pushes deeper into the desert, the newest casinos tend to rise at its southern end, not far west of the airport. The procession kicks off with the glowing gilded tower of **Mandalay Bay**, which opened in 1999. Financed through the profits from its neighbors, *Luxor* and *Excalibur*, *Mandalay Bay* is more upmarket than either, though all it has to offer casual sightseers is the "Treasures of Mandalay Bay" museum (daily 9.30am–11pm; $7), a dull collection of old coins and banknotes. With an excellent assortment of restaurants as well as the *House of Blues* music venue, however, it's lively at night.

From the palm-fringed avenue of sphinxes guarding the entrance, to the reconstruction of Tutankhamun's tomb inside, the 36-story smoked-glass pyramid of **Luxor** next door plays endless variations upon Egyptian archeology. Three simulator rides and 3-D movies combine to reveal the *Secrets of the Luxor Pyramid*, a confusing saga of derring-do that's overpriced at $21.

*Luxor*'s architect, Veldon Simpson, had previously designed **Excalibur**, immediately north. A less-sophisticated mock-up of a medieval castle, complete with drawbridge, crenellated towers, and a basement stuffed with fairground-style sideshows for the kids, it's usually packed out with low-budget tour groups. Its brief reign as the world's largest hotel, from 1990 to 1993, ended when the five-thousand-room **MGM Grand** – another Simpson creation – opened across the street. At that time, Las Vegas was in the midst of its misguided attempt to restyle itself as a destination for kids, and the *MGM Grand* sold itself on the strength of having its own **theme park**. Not a patch on the theme parks of Orlando or LA, however, that theme park has long since been scaled down, but the *Grand* is prospering nonetheless. As well as an excellent assortment of restaurants, it has become the most prestigious big-fight venue in town. Its latest attraction, the **Lion Habitat**, is a walk-through wooded zoo near to the front entrance where real lions lounge around a ruined temple beneath a naturally-lit dome. Admission is free (daily 11am–11pm), while for $20 you can have a degrading photo taken with a cute little lion cub (daily except Tues 11am–5pm).

*Excalibur* and the *MGM Grand* are not the only giants facing off across the intersection of Las Vegas Boulevard and Tropicana Avenue, said to be the busiest traffic junction in the US. The northwest corner, diagonally opposite the veteran *Tropicana*, is occupied by the exuberantly meticulous **New York–New York**. This miniature Manhattan – created, like the original, in response to space limitations – boasts a skyline featuring twelve separate skyscrapers, and is fronted by the Statue of Liberty. Unusually, the interior is every bit as carefully realized, with a lovely rendition of Central Park at dusk. In one respect, it even surpasses New York itself; for $8 you can swoop around the whole thing at 65mph on the hair-raising *Manhattan Express* **roller coaster**.

North again, **Paris** was the 1999 handiwork of the same team of designers as *New York–New York*. With a half-size Eiffel Tower straddling the Arc de Triomphe and the Opera, it all feels a little compressed, but once again the attention to detail is a joy. Beret-wearing bread-toting bicylists whistle Gallic tunes as they scurry along its cobbled streets, dodging the stripey-shirted accordionists and smart gendarmes, and there's a fine assortment of top-notch French restaurants. Elevators soar through the roof of the casino and up to the summit of the Eiffel Tower, for stunning views of the city, at their best after dark (daily 10am–1am; $8).

The Eiffel Tower was cheekily positioned to enjoy perfect views of **Bellagio**, opposite, *Mirage* owner Steve Wynn's 1998 attempt to build the best hotel in world history. *Bellagio* is undeniably a breathtaking achievement, but Wynn set himself a pointless and self-defeating task. While casino theming has always been playful – you're not supposed to think that being in *Luxor* is like being in ancient Egypt, just that it's fun to pretend – *Bellagio* wants to be real, and somehow more authentic than its original models. The trouble is that *Bellagio* is not in Europe, it's in Las Vegas, and it's stuffed full of slot machines. Inlaid with jewel-like precision into marble counters, perhaps, but still slot machines. *Bellagio*'s proudest boasts are the **Via Bellagio**, a covered mall of impossibly glamorous designer boutiques, and its opulent **Conservatory**, where a network of flowerbeds beneath a Belle Epoque canopy of copper-framed glass, is replanted every few weeks with ornate seasonal displays. Further back, near the pool, the thirty or so pieces on display at the **Bellagio Gallery of Fine Art** (daily 8am–10pm; $12) may form a very small, "Greatest Hits"-style collection, and the admission fee is expensive, but they're uniformly excellent, ranging from a Renoir from 1874, via canvases by Picasso, Monet and Degas, to a Liechtenstein from 1995.

Across Flamingo Road from *Bellagio*, **Caesars Palace** still encapsulates Las Vegas at its best. Here the walkway delivers you past grand marble staircases that lead nowhere, and full-sized replicas of Michelangelo's *David*, into a vast labyrinth of slots and green baize, peopled by strutting half-naked Roman centurions and Cleopatra-cropped waitresses. Above the stores, restaurants and "living statues"of the extraordinary **Forum**, the blue-domed ceiling dims and glows as it endlessly cycles from dawn to dusk and back again. The Forum is also home to **Race for Atlantis**, Las Vegas' only 3-D IMAX simulator ride (Sun–Thurs 10am–11pm, Fri & Sat 10am–midnight; $9.50). What you pay is expensive for what you get – shaken to smithereens in front of a short sci-fi B-feature – but few kids leave disappointed. Caesar's itself has its own giant-screen OMNIMAX movie theater ($7), as well as the elaborate Magical Empire, a dinner-cum-magic-show for which tickets cost $75.

Nighttime crowds jostle for space on the sidewalk outside the glittering **Mirage**, beyond *Caesars*, to watch the somewhat half-hearted volcano that erupts every fifteen minutes, spewing water and fire into the lagoon below. Inside, a couple of Siegfried and Roy's white tigers lounge dopily in a glass-fronted enclosure near the main entrance. Next door, a pirate galleon and a British frigate, crewed by actors, do noisy battle outside **Treasure Island** (every ninety minutes, daily 4–11pm).

Across the Strip, the facade of another 1999 newcomer, the **Venetian**, includes loving facsimiles of six major Venice buildings. The main emphasis in the casino itself is on the lavish **Grand Canal Shoppes**, reached via a stairwell topped by vivid frescoes copied from yet more Venice originals. The ludicrous re-creation of the **Grand Canal** at the top, complete with gondolas and singing gondoliers ($10 a ride), is quintessential Las Vegas, and as such utterly irresistible – for God's sake, it's *upstairs*. Set on the second and third floors of the *Venetian*'s Library, the first US outpost of **Madame Tussaud's** renowned waxwork museum eschews boring old history in favor of styling itself as the **Celebrity Encounter** (daily 10am–10pm; $12.50, ages 4–12 $10). What that means is that visitors can pose with, touch, caress and mock effigies such as Siegfried and Roy, Liberace, Tom Jones and Frank Sinatra; the whole experience is seriously overpriced, its token animatronic showpieces not a patch on the free shows at *Caesars*.

The family-oriented **Circus Circus**, another mile north, uses live circus acts to pull in the punters – a trapeze artist here, a fire-eater there – and also has an indoor theme park, **Grand Slam Canyon** (Sun–Thurs 10am–6pm, Fri & Sat 10am–midnight), where you pay separately for each roller coaster or river-ride. If you really want to cool off, you'd do better to head on to the flumes and chutes of Vegas' one purpose-built water park, **Wet'n'Wild**, 2601 S Las Vegas Blvd (summer daily 10am–8pm; $24).

Meanwhile, the **Las Vegas Hilton**, half a mile east of *Circus Circus* at 3000 Paradise Rd, is home to the very busy **Star Trek Experience** (daily 11am–11pm; $15). In a museum-like atmosphere, glossy display panels recount a wordy Star Trek chronology that takes in World War III in 2053, and the birth of Spock in 2230, while diminutive Ferengi stroll among you. The whole thing culminates when you're sent on a mildly vomitous motion-simulator ride through deep space, to emerge in a shopping area you could have reached without paying anyway, where memorabilia prices boldly go to well over $2000 for a leather jacket.

*Circus Circus* has traditionally marked the northern limit of the Strip, though the 1996 opening of the **Stratosphere**, half a mile towards downtown, tried to change that. At 1149 feet, the *Stratosphere* is the tallest building west of the Mississippi, and the outdoor deck and indoor viewing chamber in the sphere near the summit offer amazing panoramas across the city ($5). Two utterly demented thrill rides can take you even closer to heaven; the world's highest roller coaster swirls around the outside of the sphere, while the ludicrous *Big Shot* shunts you to the very top of an additional 160-foot spire, from which you freefall back down again ($5 each).

## Downtown and the Liberace Museum

As the Strip has gone from strength to strength, **downtown** Las Vegas, the city's original core, has by comparison been neglected. Long known as "Glitter Gulch," and consisting of a few compact blocks of lower-key casinos, it has recently embarked upon a revival. Between Main Street and Las Vegas Boulevard, five entire blocks of Fremont Street, its principal thoroughfare, have been roofed with an open-air mesh to create the **Fremont Street Experience**. This "Celestial Vault" is studded with over two million coloured light bulbs, choreographed by computer in dazzling nightly displays (hourly, 8pm–midnight; free), but there's a long way to go before the district as a whole can compete with the Strip once again.

Almost all Las Vegas' handful of museums are eminently missable, with one unarguable exception: the **Liberace Museum**, two miles east of the Strip at 1775 E Tropicana Ave (Mon–Sat 10am–5pm, Sun 1–5pm; $7). Popularly remembered as a beaming buffoon who knocked out torpid toe-tappers, Liberace, who died in 1987, started out playing piano in the rough bars of Milwaukee during the 1940s. A decade later, he was being mobbed by screaming adolescents and ruthlessly hounded by the scandal-hungry press. All this is recalled by a yellowing collection of cuttings and family photos, along with electric candelabra, bejewelled quail eggs with inlaid pianos, rhinestone-covered fur coats, glittering cars and more. The music, piped into the scented toilets, may not have improved with age, but the museum is a satisfying attempt to answer the seminal question "how does a great performer top himself on stage?"

## Eating

Barely ten years ago, the **restaurant** scene in Las Vegas was governed by the notion that visitors were not prepared to pay for gourmet food, and the only quality restaurants were upscale Italian places well away from the Strip. Now, however, the situation has reversed, as the major casinos compete to attract culinary superstars from all over the country to open Vegas outlets. Many tourists now come to the city in order to eat at several of the best restaurants in the United States, without having to reserve a table months in advance or pay sky-high prices.

Nonetheless, almost every casino still features an all-you-can-eat **buffet**. The better buffets tend to be in casinos that are neither on the Strip nor downtown, and depend on locals as well as tourists. By contrast, those at the largest casinos, like *Excalibur* and the *MGM Grand*, only have to be good enough to ensure that the crowds already in the building don't leave, while also coping with a daily deluge of customers.

## Buffets

**The Buffet**, *Bellagio*, 3600 Las Vegas Blvd S (☎702/791-7111). Far and away Las Vegas' best buffet. With other buffets, you may rave about what good value they are; with this one, you'll rave about what good food it is. Breakfast is $10; lunch is $12.50, and includes sushi, sashimi and dim sum; and dinner, with choices like lobster claws, fresh oysters and venison, is $20.

**Carnival World Buffet**, *Rio*, 3700 W Flamingo Rd (☎702/252-7777). Excellent value, half a mile west of the Strip. The variety is immense, including Thai, Chinese, Mexican and Japanese stations as well as the usual pasta and barbecue, and even a fish'n'chip stand. $8 for breakfast, $10 for lunch, and $12 for dinner.

**Garden Court Buffet**, *Main Street Station*, 200 N Main St (☎702/387-1896). Downtown's best-value buffet, ranging from fried chicken and corn at "South to Southwest," to tortillas at "Ole," and pork chow mein and oyster tofu at "Pacific Rim." Breakfast is $5, lunch $7, and dinner $10.

**Le Village Buffet**, *Paris*, 3655 Las Vegas Blvd S (☎702/967-7000). Superb French-only cuisine, with great seafood, succulent roast chicken, and super-fresh vegetables. The setting is a little cramped, squeezed into a very Disneyesque French village, but the food is *magnifique*. Breakfast is $10, lunch $13, and dinner $20.

## Restaurants

**America**, *New York–New York*, 3790 Las Vegas Blvd S (☎702/740-6451). Cavernous 24-hour diner, with a vast 3-D "map" of the United States curling from the ceiling, and a staggeringly eclectic menu. At any hour of day or night, at any price there really is something for everyone, and it's all surprisingly good.

**Binion's Horseshoe Coffee Shop**, *Binion's Horseshoe*, 128 E Fremont St (☎702/382-1600). The 24-hour Las Vegas coffee shop of your dreams, in the basement of a veteran downtown casino. Between 10pm and 5am, a steak dinner costs just $3, but even at prime time, 4.45–11.45pm, a 16oz T-bone is only $6.75. Breakfast is highly recommended.

**Emeril's New Orleans Fish House**, *MGM Grand*, 3799 Las Vegas Blvd S (☎702/891-7374). An authentic slice of New Orleans in the heart of the *MGM Grand*. Cajun seafood with a modern (but never low-cal) twist is the specialty, with barbecue shrimp for $18 at lunchtime and redfish in red bean sauce for $25 at dinner.

**Il Fornaio**, *New York–New York*, 3790 Las Vegas Blvd S (☎702/740-6403). The nicest place to enjoy the atmosphere of *New York–New York*, this rural-Italian restaurant is a real joy. Grab a pizza for around $10, or linger over a full meal of soft-shell crab ($9) or carpaccio of beef ($8) to start, followed by gnocchi with smoked salmon ($14), baked seabass with cherry tomatoes ($18.50), or rotisserie chicken ($14.50).

**Margarita's Mexican Cantina**, *New Frontier*, 3120 Las Vegas Blvd S (☎702/794-8433). Appealingly old-fashioned bar-cum-restaurant, with the best-value Mexican food on the Strip.

**Mr Lucky's 24/7**, *Hard Rock Hotel*, 4455 Paradise Rd (☎702/693-5000). Stylish 24-hour coffee shop, with an open kitchen, faux-fur booths, and subdued tan-and-cream paint-job, where the food is well above average.

**Olives**, *Bellagio*, 3600 Las Vegas Blvd S (☎702/693-8181). *Bellagio*'s finest restaurant may call a $10 pizza an "individual oven-baked flatbread," and your food is more likely to be arranged vertically than horizontally, but the largely Mediterranean menu is uniformly fresh and superb. Great for lunch, at well under $20; dinner is pricier.

**Wolfgang Puck Cafe**, *MGM Grand*, 3799 Las Vegas Blvd S (☎702/895-9653). Designer-diner-cum-cafe, where they'll whisk you through your meal in the blink of an eyelid, but you won't be disappointed with the food. No reservations. Open daily for breakfast, lunch and dinner.

## Bars and clubs

Alcohol is very easy indeed to come by in Las Vegas. All the casinos have plenty of bars, but if you want a drink, there's no need to look for one; instead, a tray-toting waitress will come and find you. As for **live music**, check newspapers like *City Life* and the *Las Vegas Review Journal* to see who's appearing when you're in town, or call casinos like the *Grand* or *Caesars Palace*. In general, it'll help if your tastes are rooted in the 1960s or even earlier, but some of the newer breed of casinos are orienting themselves towards younger audiences.

**The Beach**, 365 Convention Center Drive (☎702/731-1925). 24-hour dance club, just east of the Strip, which attracts a very young crowd to the massive dance floor downstairs, and sports bar upstairs.

**Gipsy**, 4605 Paradise Rd (☎702/731-9677). High-profile gay dance club, whose success has spurred the emergence of the surrounding gay business district. There's normally some form of live entertainment, and there are beer busts most nights too. Nightly except Mon.

**House of Blues**, *Mandalay Bay*, 3950 Las Vegas Blvd S (☎702/632-7600). The Strip's premier live music venue, the voodoo-tinged, folk-art-decorated *House of Blues* has a definite but not exclusive emphasis towards blues, R&B, and black music in general. Prices range up to $65 for big-name stars.

**Triple Seven Brewpub**, *Main Street Station*, 200 N Main St (☎702/386-4442). Roomy, high-ceilinged downtown brewpub, with poor service but great beers and good food.

**VooDoo Lounge**, *Rio*, 3700 W Flamingo Rd (☎702/252-7777). Las Vegas' hottest bar, with amazing 51st-floor views and super-cool atmosphere.

## Entertainment

There was a time when Las Vegas represented the pinnacle of any showbusiness career. In the early 1960s, when Frank Sinatra's Rat Pack were shooting hit movies like *Ocean's 11* during the day then singing the night away at the *Sands*, the city could claim to be the capital of the international entertainment industry. It was even hip. Now, however, although the money is still there, the world has moved on. As the great names of the past fade from view, few of the individual performers popular with traditional Vegas visitors are considered capable of carrying an extended-run show. The tendency instead is to rely on lavish stunts and special effects. A fair number of old-style Vegas revues are still soldiering on, but there are more stimulating contemporary productions than you might imagine.

**Imagine**, *Luxor*, 3900 Las Vegas Blvd S (☎702/262-4400). A stunning array of tumblers, acrobats and contortionists, some sexy traditional showgirls and showboys, and lots of magical illusions, all accompanied by a barrage of thunderous semi-orchestral rock. Mon, Wed, Fri & Sat 7.30pm & 10pm, Sun & Tues 7.30pm. $40.

**Lance Burton**, *Monte Carlo*, 3770 Las Vegas Blvd S (☎702/730-7160). The best family show in Las Vegas, featuring master magician Lance Burton. Most of it consists of traditional but very impressive stunts with playing cards, handkerchiefs and doves, but large-scale illusions include the disappearance of an entire airplane and a narrow escape from hanging. Tues–Sat 7.30pm & 10.30pm. $35 and $40.

**Legends in Concert**, *Imperial Palace*, 3535 Las Vegas Blvd S (☎702/794-3261). Enjoyable celebrity-tribute show, with a changing roster of stars that ranges from the Righteous Brothers to Shania Twain. Daily except Sun 7.30pm & 10.30pm. $34.50, including 2 drinks, ages 12 and under $19.50.

**Mystère**, *Treasure Island*, 3300 Las Vegas Blvd S (☎702/894-7722). Fabulous Cirque du Soleil show-case, with tumblers, acrobats, trapeze artists, pole climbers, clowns and strongmen, but no animals apart from fantastic costumed apparitions. Wed–Sun 7.30pm & 10.30pm. $70, ages 12 and under $35.

**O**, *Bellagio*, 3600 Las Vegas Blvd S (☎702/693-7722). Las Vegas' most expensive show is a remark-able testament to how much is possible when the budget is barely an issue. Any part of the stage at any time may be submerged to any depth. One moment a performer can walk across a particular spot, the next someone may dive headfirst into it from the high wire. From the synchronized swimmers onwards, the Cirque du Soleil display their magnificent skills to maximum advantage. Mon, Tues & Fri–Sun 7.30pm & 10.30pm. $90 and $100.

## Lake Mead and the Hoover Dam

Almost as many people as go to Las Vegas visit **LAKE MEAD**, the vast reservoir thirty miles southeast of the city that was created by the construction of the Hoover Dam. As with the similarly incongruous Lake Powell (see p.887) it makes a bizarre spectacle, the blue waters a vivid counterpoint to the surrounding desert, but it gets excruciatingly crowded all year round.

Though the Lake Mead National Recreation Area straddles the border between Nevada and Arizona, the best views come from the Nevada side. Even if you don't need details of how to sail, scuba-dive, water-ski or fish from the marinas along the five-hundred-mile shoreline, call in at the Alan Bible visitor center (daily 8.30am–4.30pm; ☎702/293-8990), four miles northeast of Boulder City on US-93, to enjoy a sweeping prospect of the whole thing.

Eight miles on, beyond the rocky ridges of the Black Mountains, US-93 reaches the **HOOVER DAM** itself. Designed to block the Colorado River and provide low-cost electricity for the cities of the Southwest, it's among the tallest dams ever built (760ft high), and used enough concrete to build a two-lane highway from the West Coast to New York. It was completed in 1935, as the first step in the Bureau of Reclamation program that culminated with the Glen Canyon Dam (see p.887). Informative half-hour guided tours of the dam leave from the **Hoover Dam Visitor Center** on the Nevada side of the river (daily 8.30am–5.45pm; $8, plus $2 parking; ☎702/293-1824). Gray Line's five-hour **bus tours** from Las Vegas cost around $20 (☎702/384-1234).

# Crossing Nevada

The bulk of Nevada – the largest but least populated state in the Southwest – is made up of dry, flat plains sliced by knife-edge volcanic mountain ranges. Called the **Great Basin** because its rivers and streams have no outlet to the ocean, the land has a certain eerie, even hypnotic, beauty. Its attractions are hard to pinpoint, but there's an indefinable, very American sense of the endless frontier, of wide-open space.

The main route across Nevada, **I-80**, shoots from Salt Lake City to Reno, skirting dozens of bizarrely named small towns – Winnemucca, Elko, Battle Mountain – packed with casinos, bars, brothels, motels and little else. The other main route, **US-50**, has a reputation as the loneliest highway in America, with the least traffic and roadside life. Older and slower than I-80, it follows much the same route as did the riders of the Pony Express in the 1860s, though many of the towns along it have faded away, and some have been entirely abandoned. US-50 passes by Nevada's sole national park, **Great Basin National Park** in the eastern mountains, before it links up with I-80 at Reno, and then cuts off to the southwest to circuit magnificent **Lake Tahoe**, covered in the California chapter on p.1013. One last main route, **US-95**, links Reno and Las Vegas, passing near Death Valley (see p.954) as well as Nevada's most famous and most evocative ghost town, **Goldfield**.

## Great Basin National Park

Just across the border from Utah, **GREAT BASIN NATIONAL PARK** was created in 1986 by the amalgamation of the Lehman Caves National Monument with the Wheeler Peak Scenic Area. It's a distillation of the range of scenery the Nevada desert offers, from angular peaks to high mountain meadows cut by fast-flowing streams. The **Lehman Caves** are some of the most extensive and fascinating limestone caves in the country, not as big as Carlsbad Caverns (see p.829), but if anything more densely packed with intriguing formations. Daily ninety-minute tours ($4) leave every hour in summer, every two hours in winter, from the **visitor center** near the mouth of the caves (summer daily 8am–5pm; winter daily 8.30am–4.30pm), five miles west of the hamlet of **Baker**.

From the Lehman Caves, a twelve-mile road climbs the east flank of the bald and usually snowcapped **Wheeler Peak**, and trails lead past alpine lakes and through a grove of gnarled, ancient bristlecone pines to the 13,063ft summit. Few people ever come here, but in winter the mountains and meadows make for excellent off-track cross-country skiing. The nearest real town, **ELY**, an hour's drive away, has two worthwhile museums – the entertaining **Nevada Northern Railway Museum** (daily except Mon 11am–1pm; $2.50), which offers $16 rides on a restored steam train, and the **County Museum** (daily 9am–4pm; free) – as well as a dozen **motels** (try *Motel 6*, 770 Avenue O; ☎775/289-4803; ②) and a handful of **casinos** and **restaurants**.

## Elko

One of the few Nevada towns worth aiming for, if you're here at the right time of year, is **ELKO**, a straggling highway town a hundred miles from the Utah border. The self-proclaimed last real cowtown in the West is the center of one of the largest open-range cattle ranching regions in the US, and the fitting home of the annual **Cowboy Poetry Gathering**, held here every January. People get together in a sort of celebration of folk culture, telling stories around campfires, singing about the lonesome life on the range, and keeping alive the dying traditions and tales of the Wild West.

During the 72-hour party of the **National Basque Festival**, each Fourth of July weekend, hulking men throw huge logs at each other amid a whole lot of carousing and downing platefuls of Basque food. The food is available year-round in restaurants like the *Star Hotel*, two blocks south of the main drag at 246 Silver St (☎775/738-9925). Greyhound and Amtrak both stop in Elko, and there are dozens of budget motels, such as the *Holiday Motel*, 1276 Idaho St (☎775/738-7187; ②). Elko's **visitor center** is at 1601 Idaho St (Mon–Fri 9am–5pm; ☎775/738-7135 or 1-800/428-7143).

# Reno and around

If you don't make it to Las Vegas, you can get a feel for the nonstop, neon-lit gambler's lifestyle by stopping in **RENO**, on I-80, very near the California border. "The biggest little city in the world," as it likes to call itself, is a somewhat downmarket version of the glitz and glamour of Vegas, with miles of gleaming slot machines and poker tables, surrounded by tacky wedding chapels and quickie divorce courts. While the town itself may not be much to look at, its setting – at the foot of the snowcapped **Sierra Nevada**, with the Truckee River winding through the center – is superb.

There are three things to do in Reno: gamble, get married and get divorced. The **casinos** are concentrated in the downtown area, along Virginia Street either side of the railroad tracks. To get **married**, the requirements are the same as in Las Vegas (see p.898), though here you obtain your **marriage license** at the **Washoe County Court**, Virginia and Court St (daily 8am–midnight; ☎775/328-3275). Wedding chapels all around the city will help you tie the knot; across the street from the courthouse, the *Starlight Chapel* – "No Waiting, Just Drive In" – does the job for under $50, providing a pink chintz parlor full of plastic flowers and heart-shaped seats.

## Practicalities

Reno's Cannon International **airport** is a couple of miles southeast of downtown, a twenty-minute ride on local bus #24. Greyhound **buses** use the terminal at 155

Stevenson St; daily Amtrak **trains** call at 135 E Commercial Row downtown, six hours
out of San Francisco en route for Salt Lake City.

The downtown **visitor center**, in the National Bowling Stadium at 300 N Center St
(daily 8am–6pm; ☎1-800/334-2625), should be able to help you find an inexpensive
**place to stay**, though rates tend to double at weekends. All the big casinos offer
accommodation – the pick of them are the *Atlantis*, 3800 S Virginia St (☎775/825-4700;
④–⑤), *Silver Legacy*, 407 N Virginia St (☎775/329-4777 or 1-800/687-8733; ③), and
*Circus Circus*, 500 N Sierra St (☎775/329-0711 or 1-800/648-5010; ②) – while the
*Gatekeeper Inn*, 221 W Fifth St (☎775/786-3500 or 1-800/822-3504; ②), is a clean, safe
and reliable motel. Reno's best **buffet** is at the *Eldorado*, 345 N Virginia St (☎775/786-
5700 or 1-800/648-5966; ③).

# Carson City

US-395 heads south from Reno along the jagged spires of the **High Sierra**, past **Mono
Lake**, **Mount Whitney** and **Death Valley**. Just thirty miles south of Reno, **CARSON
CITY**, state capital of Nevada, is small by comparison but has a number of elegant build-
ings, some excellent historical museums and a handful of world-weary casinos.

Carson City was named after frontier explorer Kit Carson in 1858, and is still redolent with Wild West history. A good introduction is the **Nevada State Museum** at 600
N Carson St (daily 8.30am–4.30pm; $3). Housed in a sandstone structure built during
the Civil War as the Carson Mint, it covers the geology and natural history of the Great
Basin desert, from prehistoric times up through the heyday of the 1860s, when the silver mines of the nearby Comstock Lode were at their peak. Amid the many guns and
artifacts is the reconstructed **Ghost Town**, from which a tunnel allows entry down into
a full-scale model of an **underground mine**.

Greyhound **buses** between Reno and Los Angeles stop once a day in each direction,
at 111 E Telegraph Ave. Among budget **motels** are the *Westerner* at 555 N Stewart St
(☎775/883-6565; ②), behind the *Nugget* casino, and the *Hardman House Motor Inn* at
917 N Carson St (☎775/882-7744 or 1-800/626-0793; ③). The **visitor center**, on the
south side of town at 1900 S Carson St (Mon–Fri 8am–5pm, Sat & Sun 10am–3pm;
☎775/687-7410), can help with practical details and provide maps for self-guided architectural walking and driving **tours** of the town, taking in the State Capitol, the museums,
and many of the fine 1870s Victorian wooden houses and churches on the west side.

# Virginia City

Much of the wealth on which Carson City – and indeed San Francisco – was built came
from the silver mines of the **Comstock Lode**, a solid seam of pure silver discovered
underneath Mount Hamilton, fourteen miles east of Carson City off US-50, in 1859.
Raucous **VIRGINIA CITY** grew up on the steep slopes above the mines, and a young
writer named Samuel Clemens made his way here from the east with his older brother, the acting Secretary to the Governor of the Nevada Territory, to see what all the fuss
was about. His descriptions of the wild life of the mining camp, and of the desperately
hard work men put in to get at the valuable ore, were published years later under his
pseudonym, **Mark Twain**. Though Twain also spent some time in the Gold Rush towns
of California's Mother Lode, on the other side of the Sierra – which by then were all but
abandoned – his tales of Virginia City life, collected in *Roughing It*, form a hilarious eye-
witness account of the hard-drinking life of the frontier miners. There's not much to
Virginia City nowadays, since all the old storefronts have been taken over by hot-dog
vendors and tacky souvenir stands, but the surrounding landscape of arid mountains
still feels remote and undisturbed.

# CHAPTER THIRTEEN

# CALIFORNIA

P ublicized and idealized all over the world, **CALIFORNIA** really does live up
to the myth. More than just a terrestrial paradise of sun, sand, surf and sea,
it has high mountain ranges, fast-paced glitzy cities, primeval forests and hot
dry deserts. The landscape is imbued with history, ranging from rock carvings left by indigenous Native Americans to the eerie ghost towns of the Gold Rush
pioneers.

In some ways, the West Coast is the ultimate "now" society. Anywhere so vulnerable
to the constant threat of the Big One – the **earthquake** that will one day drop half the
state into the Pacific – is bound to have a sense of living for the moment. However, its
supposed superficiality is largely fictitious. Though home to such reactionary figures
as Ronald Reagan and Richard Nixon, it has also been the source of some of the country's most progressive **political movements**. The fierce protests of the Sixties may
have died down, but California remains the heart of liberal America, at the forefront in
issues such as environmental awareness, gay pride and social permissiveness.
**Economically**, too, the region is crucial, whether in the long-established film industry,
the recently ascendant music business, or even the financial markets.

California is too large to be fully explored in a single trip, but in an area so varied it's
hard to pick out specific highlights. **Los Angeles** is far and away the biggest and most
stimulating city: a maddening collection of freeways, beaches, seedy suburbs, high-
gloss neighborhoods and extreme lifestyles. From Los Angeles you can head south to
the smaller, up-and-coming city of **San Diego**, with its broad, welcoming beaches and
easy access to Mexico; or push inland to the **desert areas**, most notably **Death Valley**,
a barren and inhospitable landscape of volcanic craters and salt pans that in summer
becomes the hottest place on earth.

Most people, though, follow the shoreline north up the **central coast**: a gorgeous
run that takes in lively small towns like **Santa Barbara** and **Santa Cruz**. California's
second city, **San Francisco**, at the top end, is about as different from LA as it's possible to get: the oldest, most European-looking city in the state, set on a series of steep
hills, its wooden houses tumbling down to water on both sides. It is also well placed for
the national parks to the east, such as **Yosemite**, where waterfalls cascade into a sheer
glacial valley, and **Sequoia/Kings Canyon** with its gigantic trees, as well as the ghost
towns of the **Gold Country**. **North** of San Francisco the countryside becomes wilder,
wetter and greener, approaching Oregon through spectacular and almost deserted volcanic tablelands.

## ACCOMMODATION PRICE CODES

All accommodation prices in this book have been coded using the symbols below. Note
that prices are for the least expensive double rooms in each establishment. For a full
explanation see p.37 in Basics.

| | | |
|---|---|---|
| ① up to $30 | ④ $60–80 | ⑦ $130–175 |
| ② $30–45 | ⑤ $80–100 | ⑧ $175–250 |
| ③ $45–60 | ⑥ $100–130 | ⑨ $250+ |

The **climate** in **southern California** consists of endless days of sunshine, and warm dry nights – though LA's notorious smog is at its worst when the temperatures are highest, from July through September. All along the **coast** mornings can be hazily overcast, especially in May and June; in exposed San Francisco it can be chilly all year, and fog rolls in to ruin many a sunny day. In winter it can rain for weeks on end, causing massive mudslides that wipe out roads and hillside homes. Most hiking trails in the **mountains** are blocked between October and June by the snow that keeps California's ski slopes among the busiest in the nation.

## Some history

Around half a million people – almost half the population of what is now the US – were living in tribal villages along the West Coast when the Spaniard **Juan Cabrillo** first sighted San Diego harbor in 1542, and named **California** after an imaginary island (inhabited by Amazons) from a Spanish novel. **Sir Francis Drake** landed near Point Reyes, north of San Francisco, in 1579, where the "white bancks and cliffes" reminded him of Dover. In 1602 **Sebastián Vizcáino** bestowed most of the place-names that still survive; his exaggerated description of **Monterey** as a perfect harbor led later colonizers to make it the region's military and administrative center. The Spanish occupation began in earnest in 1769, combining military expediency with missionary zeal. Father **Junípero Serra** first established a small mission and *presidio* (fort) at San Diego, before arriving in June 1770 at Monterey. By 1804 a chain of 21 missions, each a long day's walk from the next along the dirt path of *El Camino Real* (The Royal Road), ran from San Diego to San Francisco. The labor of the Native American converts was co-opted; though not all gave up without a fight, disease ensured that they were soon wiped out.

When Mexico gained its independence in 1821, in theory it also acquired control of California. However, **Americans** were already starting to arrive, despite the immense difficulty of getting to California – three months by sea via Cape Horn, or four months overland in a covered wagon. Though the non-Native American population was a mere ten thousand in 1846, the growing belief that it was the **Manifest Destiny** of the United States to cover the continent from coast to coast soon led to the **Mexican–American War**. Virtually all the fighting took place in Texas; Monterey was captured by the US Navy without a shot being fired, and by January 1847 the Americans controlled the entire West Coast. In 1850 California became the 31st US state.

By chance, a mere nine days before the signing of the treaty that ended the war, flakes of **gold** were discovered in the Sierra Nevada. Prospectors flooded west, in the most madcap migration in history; it took just fifteen years to pick the goldfields clean. The completion of the **transcontinental railroad** in 1869, built using Chinese laborers, was a major turning point. The crossing from New York now took just five days, and a railroad rate war brought fares down to as little as $1 for a one-way ticket.

California was perceived as immune to the worst effects of the **Great Depression** of the 1930s – thanks in part to the images of prosperity promulgated by its now-established **film industry**. From the Dust Bowl Midwest, entire families of "**Okies**" packed up everything they owned and set off for the farms of the Central Valley. Heavy industry came during **World War II**, in the form of shipyards and airplane factories, and many workers and military personnel stayed on afterwards.

As home to the **Beats** in the Fifties and the **hippies** in the Sixties, and a host of radical political and ecological movements since, California was at the cutting edge of cultural change. The illusions of the Flower Power days were shattered by Charles Manson, however, and once the anti-war struggle was over, popular culture seemed to withdraw into self-satisfaction. The easy-money boom of the Eighties, however, crash-landed in a tangled mess of scandal, and for California the Nineties kicked off with a stagnant property market, rising unemployment, escalating gang violence and racial

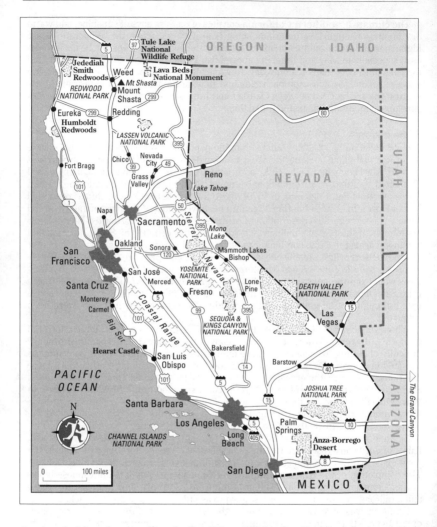

tensions in LA, and an appalling death toll from AIDS in San Francisco – compounded by earthquakes, drought and flooding. At a time when native Californians are fleeing the state in droves, some see the Golden State's golden years as past, others wait for it to reinvent itself.

## Getting around California

If you want to explore and enjoy California to the full, you'll be glad of a **car**. A city such as Los Angeles couldn't exist without the automobile, and in any case to drive down the coastal freeways invites irresistible mental images of Beach-Boys-style cruising. Car **rental** in California is some of the cheapest in the country and the savings made by easy access to campgrounds and out-of-center chain motels can easily offset the initial cost.

Frequent Amtrak **trains** connect **LA** and **San Diego**, with a stop at Fullerton for buses to Disneyland, and one daily service runs up the coast from LA, calling at **Oakland** and **Emeryville**, the nearest stations to San Francisco, and continuing via Sacramento to Seattle. Another line from Oakland runs along the Central Valley, but only connects with LA by bus. **Cross-country** routes leave LA for Florida (via Tucson, Houston and New Orleans) and for Chicago (one daily via Flagstaff, Albuquerque and Kansas City). Oakland has its own direct service to Chicago. Foreign visitors can cut fares greatly by using the **Far West Rail Pass** (see p.25). Greyhound and Green Tortoise **buses** link all the main cities.

For quick hops between the major cities – especially LA and San Francisco – you can't beat **flying**. Services are extremely frequent, and prices competitive – if your plans are flexible enough to take advantage of off-peak deals. Regular scheduled fares are high.

If you plan to do any **long-distance cycling**, traveling from north to south can make all the difference – the wind blows this way in the summer, and besides, you're on the right side of the road for the best views. Be careful if you cycle along the coast on Hwy-1: it has heavy traffic, tight curves and is prone to fog.

# SAN DIEGO

Relatively free from smog and jungle-like freeways, **SAN DIEGO**, set around a gracefully curving bay, represents the acceptable face of southern California. The second biggest city in California may be healthy, affluent and conservative, but it's also amiable, easygoing and far from smug. Though it was the site of the first mission in California, the city only really took off with the arrival of the Santa Fe Railroad in the 1880s, and in terms of trade and significance it has long played second fiddle to Los Angeles. However, during World War II the US Navy made San Diego its Pacific Command Center, and the military continues to dominate the local economy, along now with tourism.

## Arrival, information and getting around

Both **trains** and **buses** leave you in the heart of downtown San Diego: Greyhound at Broadway and First Avenue is more central than Amtrak's Santa Fe Depot. **Lindbergh Field Airport** is only two miles out, on bus #2 ($1.50).

**Getting around** without a car, by day at least, is comparatively easy. Seven companies operate an integrated **bus** system; the Transit Store, 449 Broadway (Mon–Sat 8.30am–5.30pm, Sun noon–4pm, ☎619/234-1060), has detailed timetables and sells passes such as the one-day ($5), two-day ($8) and four-day ($12) Day Tripper Transit Pass. The passes apply also to the tram-like **San Diego Trolley**, which covers the sixteen miles from the Santa Fe Depot to the Mexican border crossing at San Ysidro. It's a forty-five minute trip ($1.75; every 15min from 5am–midnight). The last trolley back leaves at 3am on Saturday night, facilitating evenings out south of the border. **Bicycle** rental shops include Rent-a-Bike, at 523 Island St (☎619/232-4700), and Hamel's Action Sport Center, 704 Ventura Place, Mission Beach (☎619/488-5050).

The **International Visitor Information Center** is downtown at 11 Horton Plaza (Mon–Sat 8.30am–5pm; ☎619/236-1212; *www.sandiego.org*). The poste restante **post office** is at 2535 Midway Drive, between downtown and Mission Beach (Mon 7am–5pm, Tues–Fri 8am–5pm, Sat 8am–4pm; ☎1-800-275-8777; zip code 92138).

# Accommodation

**Accommodation** is plentiful throughout San Diego, with budget travelers especially well catered for. The best-placed, though mall-like, **campground** is *Campland on the Bay*, 2211 Pacific Beach Drive (☎1-800/4BAY-FUN), linked to downtown by bus #30, where a basic site costs a little more than $20. For a more serene camping option, there's **San Elijo Beach State Park**, Rte-21 south of Cardiff-by-the-Sea (☎1-800/444-7275; sites from $17–23).

## Hostels

**Banana Bungalow**, 707 Reed Ave, Pacific Beach (☎619/273-3060 or 1-800/5-HOSTEL). Friendly, with slightly scruffy rooms, but the proximity to the beach – coupled with the free breakfasts, keg nights, barbecues, bonfires and other attractions – draws a party-all-night, sleep-all-day crowd. There is no better value in San Diego if you want to be right on the beach. Dorm beds for $18. Bus #34 takes you there. ①/②.

**Grand Pacific Hostel**, 726 5th Ave, downtown (☎619/232-3100 or 1-800/438-8622). Well-placed hostel on the edge of the Gaslamp District. Converted from an 1890s-era hotel, there are 6 to 8 bedrooms, with sheets and continental breakfast, for $18. Doubles for $40. Free bike use, organized tours to Tijuana, and a handy shuttle to LA. ①/②.

**HI-San Diego Downtown Hostel**, 521 Market St at 5th Ave, downtown (☎619/525-1530 or 1-800/909-4776). Handy for the Gaslamp District and Horton Plaza. $17 for HI members, $20 for others, and private doubles from $39. Free coffee and bagels. No curfew. ①/②.

**HI-San Diego (Pt Loma) Hostel**, 3790 Udall St, Ocean Beach (☎619/223-4778 or 1-800/909-4776; *www.hostelweb.com/san diego*). A couple of miles back from the beach and minus the relentless party-time atmosphere that prevails elsewhere, there is a large kitchen, patio, and common room with TV. Well-run and friendly, with $14–17 dorm beds, private rooms for three people or more, $20 each. Bus #35 from downtown. ①.

**Ocean Beach International Backpackers Hostel**, 4961 Newport Ave, Ocean Beach (☎619/223-7873 or 1-800/339-7263). Fun spot a block from the beach. Dorm beds are $14, double rooms $18 per person, with free sheets, showers and continental breakfast. Boogie board and surfboard use. ①.

## Hotels, motels and B&Bs

**Balboa Park Inn**, 3402 Park Blvd, Hillcrest (☎619/298-0823). Elegant, gay-oriented B&B, within walking distance of Balboa Park and museums. All are romantic one- and two-bedroom suites with coffee makers and mini-fridges. ⑤/⑥.

**Beach Haven Inn**, 4740 Mission Blvd, Pacific Beach (☎619/272-3812 or 1-800/831-6323). Nice rooms around a pool and spa; continental breakfast included. With air conditioning, kitchenettes, and cable TV, it's one of the best places at the beach. ⑤/⑥.

**Crystal Pier Hotel and Cottages**, 4500 Ocean Blvd, Pacific Beach (☎619/483-6983 or 1-800/748-5894). Beautiful, deluxe cottages situated on Pacific Beach pier. All units are suites with private deck, and most have kitchenettes. ⑥–⑧.

**Horton Grand**, 311 Island Ave at 3rd (☎619/544-1886 or 1-800/542-1886). Classy, modernized amalgam of two century-old hotels, with fireplaces in most rooms. ⑥/⑦.

**J Street Inn**, 222 J St, downtown (☎619/696-6922). Near the Gaslamp District, Greyhound station and waterfront, this little-known bargain has units with microwaves, refrigerator and cable TV. ④.

**Ocean Beach Motel**, 5080 Newport Ave, Ocean Beach (☎619/223-7191). Not beautiful by any means, but right across the street from the sand, with ocean-view and kitchenettes available. ③.

**Surf & Sand Motel**, 4666 Mission Blvd, Pacific Beach (☎619/483-7420). Clean, comfortable motel close to the beach; offers pool, cable TV, mini fridge or kitchenette. ⑤/⑥.

# The City

There's no pressure in San Diego to do anything other than enjoy yourself. The work-hard, play-hard ethic may be prevalent, but the accent is strongly on the second part of the equation. Indeed, the city, with its easily navigable central area, scenic bay, 42 miles of beaches and plentiful parks and museums, is hard not to like from the moment you arrive.

## Downtown San Diego and Coronado

Always vibrant and active, **downtown** San Diego is the best place to start exploring. Since the late 1970s, several blocks of Twenties architecture have been stylishly renovated, while the sleek modern bank buildings symbolize the city's growing economic significance on the Pacific Rim. Downtown is safe by day, but can be unwelcoming at night, and you should confine your after-dark visits to the restaurants and clubs of the comparatively well-lit and well-policed Gaslamp District.

The tall Moorish archways of the **Santa Fe Railroad Depot**, at the western end of **Broadway**, built in 1915, still evoke a sense of grandeur. Broadway slices through the middle of downtown, at its most hectic between Fourth and Fifth avenues. Shoppers, sailors, yuppies and street bums linger around the fountains outside **Horton Plaza** (Mon–Sat 10am–9pm, Sun 11am–7pm), San Diego's major upmarket shopping venue. Head for the open-air eating places on its top level; the food may be more expensive than in the streets, but it's fun to sit over a coffee and watch the parade go by. Take time on your way out to visit the 21ft-tall **Jessop Clock** on level one, made for the California State Fair of 1907.

South of Broadway, a few blocks and yet a world away from Horton Plaza, the sixteen-block **Gaslamp District**, heart of frontier San Diego, is now filled with smart

streets lined with classy cafes, antique stores, art galleries – and gas lamps (albeit powered by electricity). A tad artificial it may be, but its late nineteenth-century buildings are intriguing to explore. Worth a peek is the **Horton Grand**, 311 Island Ave, a reconstruction of two nineteenth-century hotels originally located a few blocks away (tours Wed 3pm; ☎619/544-1886).

West of downtown, the **Embarcadero** pathway follows the curve of the bay, and leads to the **Maritime Museum,** 1306 N Harbor Drive (daily 9am–8pm; $5), where the most interesting of three vintage sailing craft is the *Star of India*, built in 1863 and now the world's oldest still-afloat merchant ship.

Across San Diego Bay from downtown, the isthmus of **Coronado** is a well-scrubbed resort community with a major naval station occupying its western end. It's of somewhat limited interest, save for the historic **Hotel del Coronado**, around which the town grew. The massive Victorian-turreted "Del" is where Edward VIII (then Prince of Wales) first met Mrs Simpson (then a Coronado housewife) in 1920 and where *Some Like It Hot* was filmed in 1958. The simplest and most scenic way to get to Coronado is on the **San Diego Bay ferry** (☎619/234-4111; $2 each way) which leaves Broadway Pier daily on the hour between 9am and 9pm (10pm Fri & Sat). Tickets are available at **San Diego Harbor Excursion**, 1050 N Harbor Drive.

## Balboa Park and San Diego Zoo

Sumptuous **Balboa Park** contains one of the largest groups of **museums** in the US, scattered either side and to the south of El Prado, the road that bisects the park. Yet its real charm is simply itself: its trees, gardens, statues, traffic-free promenades and concentration of Spanish Colonial-style buildings. Within easy reach of downtown by **buses** #7, #16 or #25, the park is large but fairly easy to **get around on foot** – if you tire, there's a free tram. The $21 **Balboa Park Passport**, which allows admission to all twelve of the park's museums for a week, is available from the **information center** (daily 9am–4pm; ☎619/239-0512), inside the beautifully reconstructed House of Hospitality. Most of the museums are closed on Mondays; and almost all are free on varying Tuesdays.

Minor works by Rembrandt and El Greco and a stirring collection of Russian icons make the stifling formality of the **Timkin Museum of Art** (Tues–Sat 10am–4.30pm, Sun 1.30–4.30pm; closed Sept; free) worth enduring. The **San Diego Museum of Art** (Tues–Sun 10am–4.30pm; $8) has few individually striking items in its permanent collection, but it's the main venue for touring shows and offers some exquisitely crafted pieces from China and Japan. Outside, don't miss the free **Sculpture Court and Garden**, with formidable works by Henry Moore and Alexander Calder. The **Museum of Man** (daily 10am–4.30pm; $5), which straddles El Prado, veers from banal crafts demonstrations to excellent Native American displays, artifacts, folklore and physical remains.

The child-oriented science center in the **Reuben H Fleet Science Center** (Mon & Tues 9.30am–6.30pm, Wed–Sun 9.30am–9pm; science center $6 with theater or simulator $9, all three $11), close to the Park Boulevard end of El Prado, is nothing exciting, but both the Space Theater's huge, IMAX screen and virtual reality simulator take you on stomach-churning trips into outer and inner space. Across the plaza, the **Natural History Museum** (daily 9.30am–5.30pm; $6) has a great collection of fossils and pulls no punches in its coverage of threatened species. Just behind, in the **Spanish Village Art Center** (daily 11am–4pm; free), craftspeople in 37 studios and galleries practice skills such as painting, sculpture, pottery and glass-working.

The enormous **San Diego Zoo** (daily: mid-June–early Sept 7am–10pm; early Sept–mid-June 9am–dusk; last entry an hour before closing; *www.sandiegozoo.org*), immediately north of the main museums, is one of the world's best. Its wide selection of animals, many of them rare, are restrained in "psychological cages," without bars. (Don't depend on the much-hyped but usually sleeping Chinese pandas for entertainment, however). Basic **admission**, including the children's zoo, is $16; a Deluxe Tour ticket ($24) includes a bus tour and a round-trip ride on the Skyfari overhead tramway.

## Old Town San Diego and Presidio Hill
In 1769, Spanish settlers chose **Presidio Hill** as the site of the first of California's missions. They soon began to build homes at the foot of the hill, which was dominated in turn by Mexican officials and then by early arrivals from the eastern US. **Old Town San Diego**, reachable from downtown via the Trolley, is now a state historical park holding a number of original adobe dwellings, plus the inevitable souvenir shops. The stores and restaurants stay open until 10pm or later, but the **best time** to be around is during the afternoon, to enter the more interesting of the adobes on the daily **free walking tour** (2pm). Details are available from the **visitor center** at Seely Stable, off the central plaza (daily 10am–5pm; ☎619/220-5422).

The Spanish-style building now atop Presidio Hill is only a rough approximation of the original mission – moved in 1774 – but its **Serra Museum** (Fri–Sun 10am–4.30pm; $5) is an intriguing examination of Junipero Serra, the man who led the Spanish colonization of California. The **Mission San Diego de Alcalá** itself was relocated six miles north to 10818 San Diego Mission Rd (daily 9am–5pm; $3 donation), to be near a water source and fertile soils – and to be safer from attack. The present building (on bus #43 from downtown) is still a working parish church, a peaceful complex providing welcome respite from the nearby freeways. A small **museum** holds craft objects and historical articles from the mission, including the crucifix held by Junipero Serra at his death in 1834.

## Hillcrest, Ocean Beach and Point Loma
North of downtown and on the northwest edge of Balboa Park, **Hillcrest** is an increasingly lively and artsy area at the center of the city's **gay community**. Go there either for something to eat – there's a selection of interesting cafes and restaurants – or simply to stroll around the fine gathering of Victorian homes.

**Ocean Beach**, six miles northwest of downtown and reached by bus #35, rivals Pacific Beach in its surfing and partying departments, although Ocean Beach has a more down-to-earth, bohemian feel, and is replete with excellent secondhand music shops. Currently one of the most sought after addresses, the new money is barely in evidence at the main beach, or half a mile south by the pier – **Newport Street** is where most young backpackers spend their time, among rows of cheap snack bars, surf and skate shops and T-shirt stalls.

The **Cabrillo National Monument** (daily 9am–5.15pm; $5 per car) at the southern extremity of the hilly and very green peninsula of **Point Loma** stretches south from Ocean Beach. It was at its southern extremity where Cabrillo and crew became the first whites to land in California. That's as far as the historical interest goes, for they quickly reboarded their vessel and sailed away again. The startling views from this high spot, however, across San Diego Bay to the downtown skyline and right along the coast to Mexico, easily repay the journey here. From the western cliffs of the park, a platform makes it easy to view the December-to-March **whale migration**, when scores of gray whales pass by en route to their breeding grounds off Baja California, Mexico.

## Mission Bay, Mission Beach, Pacific Beach and La Jolla
North of Ocean Beach, you come to **Mission Bay** and San Diego's most popular tourist attraction. Exhibits and timetabled events at **Sea World** (mid-June–Labor Day daily 9am–dusk; rest of year 10am–dusk; $30.95, parking $5) range from "performances" by killer whales and dolphins to the eerie sight of the heads of hundreds of moray eels

protruding from the hollow rocks of the "Forbidden Reef." All manner of sharks circle menacingly in the Shark House; the Penguin Exhibit is a mock Antarctica, while the new Wild Arctic exhibit, with its polar bears and walruses, simulates the North Pole.

Anyone of a nervous disposition, or lacking a physique appropriate to bathing apparel, might find **Mission Beach**, a mile or so west – the peninsula that separates Mission Bay from the Pacific Ocean – and its seamless northern extension, **Pacific Beach** too hot to handle. On the other hand, the raver-packed sands, scantily clad torsos and surfboard-clutching hunks may be precisely what you've come to the West Coast for. Despite first impressions, the city authorities are endeavoring to limit its anarchic hedonism – more families are using the area, but little impact has been made on the beach's freewheeling character.

A much higher tone prevails in **La Jolla**, an elegant beach community just to the north. New money has made it much less stuffy than in the days when mystery writer Raymond Chandler described it as "a nice place – for old people and their parents." Stroll its immaculate, gallery-filled streets, fuel up on some California cuisine at one of the many sidewalk cafes, or visit the newly expanded La Jolla site of the **Museum of Contemporary Art**, 700 Prospect St (Tues & Thurs–Sat 10am–5pm, Wed 10am–8pm, Sun noon–5pm; $4), which has a huge – and regularly changing – stock of paintings and sculptures from 1955 onwards. On the seaward side of the museum lies the small, exquisitely tasteful **Ellen Scripps Browning Park**. Where the park meets the coast is the popular **La Jolla Cove**, with clear waters perfect for snorkeling.

## Eating

Wherever you are in San Diego, you'll have few problems finding somewhere to **eat** good food in a fun atmosphere at reasonable prices. Everything from crusty coffee shops to stylish ethnic restaurants is in copious supply, with seafood at its best around Mission Beach.

**Anthony's Star of the Sea Room**, 1360 N Harbor Drive, downtown (☎619/232-7408). Franco-California style preparations of seafood, justly famed for its freshness and variety. Terrace dining on the waterfront.

**Bella Luna**, 748 5th Ave, downtown (☎619/239-3222). This romantic, moon-adorned restaurant serves up wonderful Italian dishes to a relaxed artsy crowd.

**Berta's**, 3928 Twiggs St, Old Town (☎619/295-2343). A far cry from the area's many touristy Mexican restaurants, offering low-priced, authentic cooking from all over Latin America.

**Cafe 222**, 222 Island Ave at 2nd, downtown (☎619/236-9902). Industrially decorated cafe serving some of the city's best breakfasts and lunches at reasonable prices. Open daily from 7am–1.45pm.

**Chilango's Mexican Grill**, 142 University Ave, Hillcrest (☎619/294-8646). Gourmet Mexican food for under $8; large veggie selection, too. Tiny storefront locale is packed to the rafters in the evenings.

**Crest Cafe**, 425 Robinson Ave, Hillcrest (☎619/295-2510). Basic American food that's good and down-home, as are the prices. They also have homemade desserts.

**Croce's Restaurant & Jazz Bar**, 802 5th Ave, downtown (☎619/233-4355). Pricey but excellent range of pastas and salads; the Sunday jazz brunch is the talk of the town.

**The Field**, 544 5th Ave, downtown (☎619/232-9840). An authentic Irish restaurant and pub with a jovial atmosphere and traditional Irish dancing on Sun.

**Filippi's Pizza Grotto**, 1747 India St at Date St (☎619/232-5094). Great pizzas and a handful of pasta dishes served in a convivial small room at the back of a Little Italy grocery. A winner.

**Ichiban**, 1449 University Ave, Hillcrest (☎619/299-7203). Few better places exist in which to enjoy quality, reasonably priced Japanese cuisine.

**Kono's**, 704 Garnet Ave, Pacific Beach (☎619/483-1669). Crowded place for breakfast or lunch on the boardwalk. Inexpensive, large portions of eggs, hamburgers, sandwiches and such.

**Living Room Coffeehouse**, 1010 Prospect St, La Jolla, with three other San Diego locations (☎619/459-1187). Great sandwiches, soups, quiches and pastries in a living room-like setting.

**Mission Cafe and Coffeehouse**, 3795 Mission Blvd, Mission Beach (☎619/488-9060). Mexican-tinged breakfast and lunch type offerings, plus beer, specialty coffees, shakes and smoothies. Open late.

**Point Loma Seafoods**, 2805 Emerson St, Ocean Beach (☎619/223-1109). Fast, inexpensive counter serving San Diego's freshest fish in a basket with fries or in an oversized sandwich.

**Sammy's**, 770 4th Ave, just outside of Horton Plaza (☎619/230-8888). California cuisine in a Mediterranean-style atmosphere. Pizza, pasta, salads, seafood and chicken are the staples. Have a messy sundae for dessert.

**Taste of Thai**, 527 University Ave, Hillcrest (☎619/291-7525). Terrific Thai for reasonable prices in the center of Hillcrest; expect a wait on weekends.

## Nightlife

Though San Diego's money is lavished on **classical music, opera** and the **theatre** (most tickets and information are available at the **Times Arts Tix** booth at Horton Plaza; ☎619/497-5000), the crowds flock to beachside **discos** and boozy **music venues**. It may be narrow in scope, but at least there's plenty going on. For full listings, pick up the free *San Diego Reader* from numerous shops, bars and cafes around town.

**Barefoot Bar and Grill**, *San Diego Princess Resort*, 1404 W Vacation Rd (☎619/274-4630). Beachfront bar that attracts a lively singles scene.

**Blind Melons**, 710 Garnet Ave, Pacific Beach (☎619/483-7844). Live rock, blues and reggae bands nightly.

**Bodie's**, 528 F St, Gaslamp District (☎619/236-8988). Hosts the best local rock and blues bands, with some out-of-town guests as well.

**Cafe Sevilla**, 555 4th Ave, downtown (☎619/233-5979). Traditional Spanish cuisine upstairs, hip Latin American-flavored dance club downstairs. Brings in a trendy European crowd.

**The Casbah**, 2501 Kettner Blvd, downtown (☎619/232-4355). Varying roster of blues, funk, reggae and indie bands.

**Emerald City**, 945 Garnet Ave, Pacific Beach (☎619/483-9920). Lively disco with drink specials at weekends, and an Underworld industrial and Gothic night on Sun.

**The Flame**, 3780 Park Blvd, Hillcrest (☎619/295-4163). The city's premier lesbian club, open for dancing, pool and occasional live acts from early evening to early morning. Tues is a no-holds-barred "Boys' Night."

**Gas Haus**, 640 F St, downtown (☎619/232-5866). Alcohol-free, eclectically decorated cafe where rollerblading teenagers, students and ageing hippies coexist on deep couches, and take each other on at pool.

**Green Circle Bar**, 827 F St, Gaslamp District (☎619/232-8080) Young, European crowd. Eclectic range of acid jazz, soul and blues. Live music Wed and Thurs.

**Rich's**, 1051 University Ave, Hillcrest (☎619/295-2195). Predominantly gay club with heavy dance sessions Fri and Sat, and the more casual Hedonism night on Thursday, with house music and tribal rhythms.

**Top O' the Cove**, 1216 Prospect St, La Jolla (☎619/454-7779) Piano bar and restaurant. Old standards and show tunes from the Forties to the present.

**Winston's Beach Club**, 1921 Bacon St, Ocean Beach (☎619/222-6822). A former bowling alley, this local club has rock bands most nights, with occasional reggae and 1960s style acts as well. Close to the pier.

## Out from San Diego: the Anza-Borrego Desert

Most of eastern San Diego County, which otherwise consists largely of sleepy suburban communities, is taken up by the more than 600,000-acre **Anza-Borrego Desert**, much of it a **state park** ($5 per vehicle). Some of it can be covered by car, although four-wheel-drive vehicles are necessary for the more obscure – and most interesting – routes. The best **time to come** is winter, when daytime temperatures stay around the mid-eighties. In the fiercely hot summer, it's best left to the lizards, but when the desert **blooms**, between March and May, scarlet octillo, orange poppies, white lilies, purple verbena and other wild flowers paint a memorable, and fragrant, picture.

Historical reminders in the desert span Native American tribes, the first white trail-finders and Gold Rush times. Approaching from the west, Hwy-78 descends to Scissors Crossing, the junction with Hwy-22, which follows the line of the **Butterfield Stage Route**. This was the first regular line of communication between the East and the newly settled West, which began service in 1857. Further on, the old adobe rest stop of **Vallecito Stage Station** gives a good indication of the privations of early desert travel. To the south, around Imperial Valley in the least-visited portion of Anza-Borrego, there's a vivid and spectacular clash as gray rock rises from the edges of the red desert floor. Along Hwy-22, east of Borrego Springs, is a memorial to Peg Leg Smith, an infamous local spinner of yarns from the Gold Rush days who is celebrated by the **Peg Leg Liars Contest** on the first Saturday in April; anybody can get up before the judges and fib their hearts out.

## TIJUANA: A TASTE OF MEXICO

You could hardly find a more intriguing day-trip out from San Diego than **Tijuana**, just over the border in Mexico. It may not be the most culturally rich place in Mexico, but every year twenty million people cross here from the US. Most of them are Californians and tourists on day-long shopping expeditions, seeking somewhere cheap and colorful to spend money. And they find it: blankets, pottery, cigarettes, tequila, dentistry or car repair – everything is lower-priced in Tijuana than in the US, and all of it is hawked with enthusiasm.

Although you can't help but be made aware of the vast economic gulf separating the two countries – you're immediately confronted by shabbily dressed taco vendors and children selling woven bracelets and gum – Tijuana is, in fact, one of the wealthiest Mexican cities. Things are much safer these days than a decade or so ago, when it really was a rough border town. The main streets and shopping areas are a few blocks from the border in downtown, where the major thoroughfare is Avenida Revolución. Stroll up and down for a while to get the mood and then retire to one of the many bars and watch the throng in the company of a sizeable margarita. At night, the action mostly consists of inebriated North American youths dancing themselves silly in flashy discos and rowdy rock 'n' roll bars. **Iguanas-Ranas** (Avenida Revolución at Calle 3; ☎66/85-14-22) is a good example. For big food and revelry, check out **Tia Juana Tilly's** (Avenida Revolucion at Calle 7; ☎66/85-60-24), where you can sample traditional Mexican specialties such as roast pig, and chicken mole.

Heavy traffic, and insurance problems, make crossing into Mexico **by car** a risky business; from San Diego you can take either the Trolley (p.911) or bus #932. However, if you do decide to drive into Mexico, invest in **auto insurance,** which can be had for $5 per day in San Ysidro. Dollars are accepted as readily as pesos, so there's no need to **change money**, though prices are better if you do. **Border formalities** are minimal: you only need a Mexican Tourist Card (free from consulates in the US or at the Mexican Customs office just inside the Tijuana side of the border) if you're planning to go further than fifty-odd miles into the country. Returning to the US, however, even within a day, immigration procedures are stringent. **Hotels** are cheap, with many low-cost lodgings close to the center. At the lowest end of the price scale are *Hotel El Jaliscense,* (Calle 1 #7925; ☎66/85-34-91; ①) and *Hotel Perla de Occidente* (Mutualismo 758; ☎66/85-13-58; ①/②). Slightly more upmarket, *La Villa de Zaragoza,* Avenida Madero 1120 (☎66/85-18-32; ③) has clean rooms with air conditioning and cable TV.

The only substantial settlement in the desert is **BORREGO SPRINGS**, right in the middle, home to the state park **visitor center** (June–Sept weekends & holidays only 9am–5pm; rest of year daily 9am–5pm; ☎760/767-5311), which has details of canyon walks, some with free but waterless **campgrounds**. Camping is also available at the *Borrego Palm Canyon* campground, near the visitor center. From here, a 1.5-mile trail takes you to a mini oasis with palms and a waterfall. **Hotels** in town are fairly pricey; only the *Oasis* at 366 W Palm Drive (☎760/767-5409; ③) and *Hacienda del Sol* (☎760/767-5442; ③), on Palm Canyon Drive, are at all affordable.

# LOS ANGELES

The rambling metropolis of **LOS ANGELES** sprawls across the thousand square miles of a great desert basin, knitted together by an intricate network of high-speed freeways between the ocean and the snowcapped mountains. Its colorful melange of shopping malls, palm trees and swimming pools is at once bafflingly strange and startlingly familiar, thanks to the celluloid self-image that it has spread all over the world.

LA is a young city; in the mid-nineteenth century, it was a community of white American immigrants, poor Chinese laborers and wealthy Mexican ranchers, with a population of less than fifty thousand. Only on completion of the transcontinental railroad in the 1880s did it really begin to grow. The old ranches were subdivided, and the enduring symbol of the city became the family-sized suburban house (with swimming pool and two-car garage), set amidst the orange groves in a glorious land of sunshine. The real boom came after World War II with the mushrooming of the aeronautics industry – which, until the recent post-Cold War military cutbacks, accounted for one in four jobs.

The first-time visitor may well find Los Angeles thrilling and threatening in equal proportions; it's a place that picks you up and sweeps you along whether you want it to or not. Sure, it has its fine-art museums and so on, but what people really come here for is to experience the city that has come to epitomize the American Dream – most obviously in the fantasy worlds of **Disneyland** and **Hollywood**, but also in the half-flaunted, half-concealed opulence of **Beverly Hills** and **Malibu**.

# Arrival, information and getting around

All roads in southern California seem to lead to LA; plenty of travelers who try to avoid the city end up here anyway. Although LA is capable of bewildering people who've lived in it for years, it's really not *that* intimidating – just don't panic.

## By plane

All European and many domestic **flights** use Los Angeles International Airport – always known as **LAX** – sixteen miles southwest of downtown (☎310/646-5252). Free 24-hour **shuttle buses** (line "C") connect with the LAX Transit Center at Vicksburg Avenue and 96th Street, where you can pick up **local buses**. Minibuses such as LAX Chequer Shuttle (☎1-800/545-7745), SuperShuttle (☎310/782-6600 or 1-800/554-3146) and Coast Shuttle (☎310/417-3988) run all over town, delivering you to your door. Fares are generally around $20–25 (plus tip), with a journey time of between 30 and 45 minutes. **Taxis** from the airport are always expensive: around $25 to downtown and West LA, $30 to Hollywood and as much as $90 to Disneyland.

If you're arriving from elsewhere in the US, or from Mexico, you might just land at one of the **other airports** in the LA area – at Burbank, Long Beach, Ontario, Newport Beach or Orange County's John Wayne Airport. MTA buses (☎213/626-4455 or 1-800/COMMUTE) serve them all – phone on arrival and tell them where you are and where you're going.

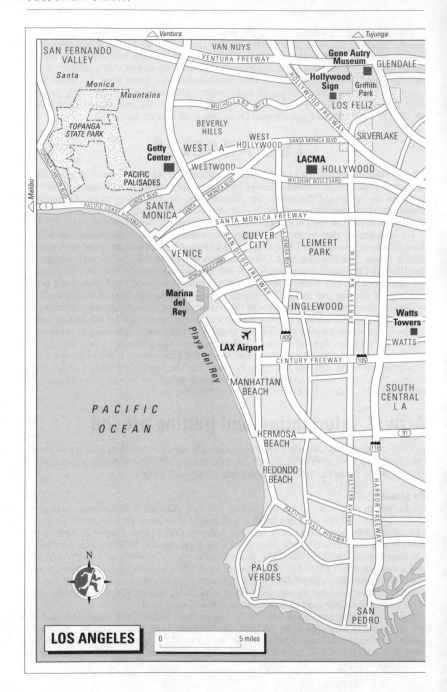

LOS ANGELES

0    5 miles

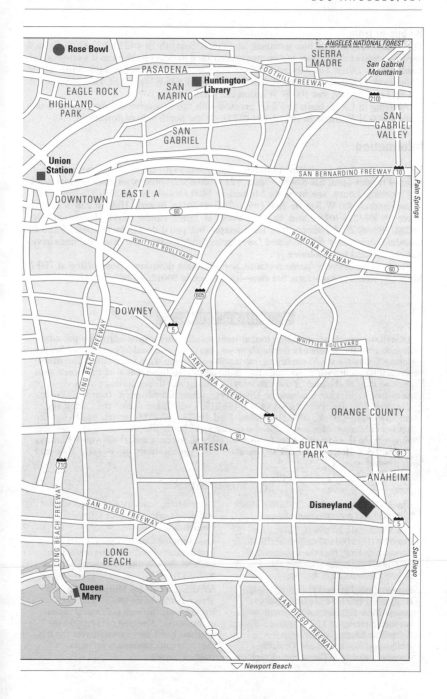

## By bus or train

The main **Greyhound** bus terminal, at 1716 E Seventh St (☎213/629-8401), is in a seedy section of downtown, but access is restricted to ticket holders so it's safe enough inside. LA's other Greyhound stations handle fewer services: 1409 Vine St, in Hollywood; 11239 Magnolia Blvd, North Hollywood; 645 E Walnut St, Pasadena; 464 W 3rd St, Long Beach; and 100 W Winston Rd, Anaheim.

Arriving in LA by **train** you'll be greeted with the expansive architecture of Union Station, 800 N Alameda St (☎213/624-0171), on the north side of downtown.

# Information

LA has a number of **visitor centers**. The downtown one is at 685 S Figueroa St (Mon–Fri 8am–5pm, Sat 8.30am–5pm; ☎213/689-8822); others, all open normal weekday working hours, are in Santa Monica at 1400 Ocean Ave (☎310/393-7593); near Disneyland at 800 W Katella Ave (☎714/999-8999); in Beverly Hills at 239 S Beverly Drive (☎301/248-1015); and in Hollywood at Janes House, 6541 Hollywood Blvd (☎323/689-8822). All supply free local **maps**, but you'd do better to spend $2.95 on Gousha Publications' fully indexed *Los Angeles CityMap*, available from machines in visitor centers and hotel lobbies.

For general delivery/poste restante, use the main downtown **post office** at 760 N Main St (Mon–Fri 8am–7pm, Sat 8am–4pm; zip code 90012; ☎1-800/275-8777).

## GUIDED TOURS

As well as downtown **walking tours**, innumerable **bus tours** introduce the city – though only the specialists below show you anything you couldn't see more cheaply yourself. Costs are $30 minimum; most will collect you from your hotel. The **mainstream** bus tours whizz you past the main sights and the **homes of the stars** (you see the gate at the end of the driveway), padding out the experience with views of palm trees and wide boulevards. Operators include **Casablanca Tours**, *Hollywood Roosevelt*, 6362 Hollywood Blvd (☎213/461-0156), which focuses on the golden age of cinema; **Tour Coach**, 6922 Hollywood Blvd (☎323/463-3333), which points out the houses of Marilyn Monroe, Barbra Streisand and Charlie Chaplin, and also runs shopping trips to the Mexican border town of Tijuana, Mexico; and **Hollywood Fantasy Tours**, 6671 Hollywood Blvd (☎323/469-8184), which shows off Beverly Hills and Hollywood only.

### SPECIALIST TOURS

**Black LA Tours** (☎213/750-9267). Black historical and entertainment tours.

**The California Native**, 6701 W 87th Place (☎310/642-1140 or 1-800/926-1140). Go sea-kayaking, tour the uninhabited islands off the coast of California. Adventure tours $175 and up.

**Grave Line Tours**, PO Box 931694, Hollywood (☎323/469-4149). Daily except Mon at 9.30am with overflow cortege running at 12.30pm and 3.30pm. A Cadillac hearse leaves from Hollywood Boulevard and Orchid Avenue, pausing at the scene of nigh-on every death, scandal, perverted sex act and drugs orgy that ever tainted Hollywood.

**Los Angeles Conservancy**, Architecture-based downtown walking tours on Sat mornings at 10am ($5; ☎213/623-CITY).

**SPARC tours: the Murals of LA**, 685 Venice Blvd, Venice (☎310/822-9560). Expert tours through the "mural capital of the world." Pointing out remarkable neighborhood landmarks all over the city, the tours put community art in its cultural context.

## MAJOR LA BUS ROUTES (MTA)

**FROM DOWNTOWN TO:**
Santa Monica #22, #434 (express).
Venice #33, #333, #436 (express).
LAX #42, #439.
Forest Lawn Cemetery, Glendale #90, #91.
Exposition Park #38, #81.
Huntington Library #79.
Burbank Studios #96.
Long Beach #60.
Disneyland #460 (express).

San Pedro #445, #446, #447 (all express), transfer to **LADOT** #142 for Catalina terminal.

**TO AND FROM DOWNTOWN:**
Along Hollywood Blvd #1.
Along Sunset Blvd #2, #3, #302.
Along Santa Monica Blvd #4, #304.
Along Melrose Ave #10, #11.
Along Wilshire Blvd #20, #21, #22, #320 (limited stops, but faster than #20).

# City transportation

The sheer scale of LA – its detractors call it "nineteen suburbs in search of a city" – means that it really *is* difficult to get around without a car. Even though the traffic is often bumper-to-bumper, the freeways are the only way to cover long distances quickly. If you're driving yourself, avoid traveling at rush hours and phone ahead for directions whenever possible. Otherwise, relax on by far the fastest alternative, **express buses**.

Some people are surprised to find sidewalks in LA, let alone pedestrians, but within districts such as downtown, Santa Monica or central Hollywood, **walking** is the best way to explore.

## Public transportation

Hampered by a series of construction scandals and budget cuts, LA's long-anticipated **Metrorail** train system is beginning to come into at least partial use. A light rail network that may one day cover the whole of Los Angeles County, it is currently made up of three lines, each distinguished by a color. Centering on the Seventh Street Metro Center Station, the **Red Line** as yet stretches only from Union Station west to Hollywood and Vine. The **Green Line** goes from Hawthorne to Norwalk along the Century Freeway. Currently the most complete route, the **Blue Line** connects downtown through Watts to the Pacific Transit Mall. Tickets cost $1.35, and trains run every five to fifteen minutes.

Car-less Angelenos are still most at ease, however, with **buses**, most of which are run by the LA County Metropolitan Transit Authority (MTA, or "Metro"), still sometimes abbreviated to its old name, the RTD. For information, phone ☎213/626-4455 or 1-800/COMMUTE (Mon–Fri 7.30am–3.30pm), or call in (Mon–Fri only) at 515 S Flower St (level C of Arco Plaza) or 6249 Hollywood Blvd (Mon–Fri 10am–6pm). Buses on the major arteries between downtown and the coast run roughly every fifteen minutes between 5am and 2am; other routes, and the **all-night services** along the major thoroughfares, are less frequent. At night, be careful not to get stranded alone downtown waiting for a connection.

The standard **single fare** is $1.35; **transfers** cost 25¢ more; **express buses**, and any others using the freeway, are $1.85 up to $3.85. A **monthly pass** costs $42, slightly more to include express buses, and a student pass is $30. Smaller **DASH** buses run five routes around downtown, and a Hollywood service weekdays and Saturdays (25¢ flat fare).

Taxis don't cruise the streets: among the more reliable companies are the Independent Cab Co (☎1-800/521-8294), LA Taxi (☎1-800/200-1085) and United Independent Taxi (☎1-800/411-0303).

## Cycling

Cycling in LA may sound perverse, but there are beach bike paths between Santa Monica and Redondo Beach, and from Long Beach to Newport Beach. Enjoyable inland routes explore Griffith Park, the mansions of Pasadena and less appealingly, along the LA River.

# Accommodation

Finding a **place to stay** in LA is easy; finding somewhere inexpensive and well located is difficult, though not impossible. Immediately beyond Customs at LAX, you'll find several interactive computer consoles with details of hotels in the LA area, including those in the vicinity of the airport that provide complimentary shuttles. You have to call the hotels for details of availability and prices; calls are dialed automatically and free of charge.

If you're not driving, choose your base carefully to avoid lengthy cross-town journeys, or divide your stay between several districts. Downtown has the best assortment of budget hotels; Hollywood is more mid-range; and West LA, Santa Monica, Venice and Malibu are predominantly mid- to upper-range. The nearest **campgrounds** to LA are along the Orange County coast.

## Hostels

**Hostels** are dotted all over the city, though some limit stays to a few nights. Colleges and fraternity houses let out space during summer; details from UCLA's Interfraternity Council (☎310/825-7878).

**Banana Bungalow**, 2775 Cahuenga Blvd W (☎323/851-1129 or 1-800/446-7835). Huge hostel in the Hollywood Hills near Hwy-101. Dorms $18–20; singles or doubles $55 and up. Free shuttle buses to Venice Beach, Magic Mountain. Every other night, you get as much beer as you can drink for $3. ①–③.

**HI-Anaheim/Fullerton**, 1700 N Harbor Blvd, Fullerton (☎323/738-3721). Spacious and comfortable, 5 miles north of Disneyland. Summer check-in 5–11pm; rest of year 4–11pm. Mornings open 7.30–10.30am. Orange County Transit Authority bus #43 stops outside. Members $11, others $13. ①.

**HI-Los Angeles/Santa Monica**, 1436 2nd St, Santa Monica (☎310/393-9913). Huge new hostel in well-restored old building, a few strides from the Santa Monica sands. $18 members, $20 others. Open 24hr. ①.

**HI-Los Angeles/South Bay**, 3601 S Gaffey St, building #613 (☎310/831-8109). In the South Bay area, overlooking the ocean. MTA bus #446 passes close by but it's a 2hr journey from downtown, or take SuperShuttle from LAX. There's a pool, and free trip to the local aquarium. Open 7am–midnight. Members $11, others $13; private rooms $27. ①.

**Hostel California**, 2221 Lincoln Blvd, Venice (☎310/305-0250). Built for the 1984 Olympics. Six-bed dorms, free shuttle bus to LAX. Big-screen TV and cable. $12 members, $14 others; $84 per week. ①.

**Huntington Beach Colonial Inn Hostel**, 421 8th St, Huntington Beach (☎714/536-3315). Four blocks from the beach; mostly double rooms. Open 8am–11pm. Key rental after 1pm $1 (plus $20 deposit). Dorms $14, private rooms $16.50 per person. ①/②.

**Jim's at the Beach**, 17 Brooks Ave, Venice (☎310/399-4018). Beachside dormitory rooms on production of a passport. $17 per night, $120 per week. ①.

**Share-Tel Apartments**, 20 Brooks Ave, Venice (☎310/392-0325). Apartments for 6 to 8 people sharing facilities and bedrooms. $15 per night including breakfast and dinner Mon–Fri. ①.

**Venice Beach Hostel**, 25 Windward Ave, Venice (☎310/399-7649). Located in historic beachside building; dorm rooms $14–17, private rooms $32–44. ①/②.

## Hotels, motels and B&Bs

There are no booking agencies, and visitor centers do not reserve accommodation, so to be sure of a **hotel** or **motel** room you should reserve direct as early as possible (and don't be afraid to haggle).

### Downtown and around

**Biltmore Hotel**, 506 S Grand Ave (☎213/624-1011 or 1-800/222-8888). Classical 1923 architecture combined with modern luxury to make your head swim. Cheaper by far at weekends. ⑧/⑨.

**City Center Motel**, 1135 W 7th St (☎213/628-7141). Small and informal, with a free continental breakfast and airport shuttle bus. ②.

**Figueroa Hotel**, 939 S Figueroa St (☎213/627-8971 or 1-800/421-9092). Well-placed mid-range hotel with pool and jacuzzi. ④/⑤.

**Hotel Inter-Continental**, 251 S Olive St (☎213/617-3300 or 1-800/327-0200). Upscale hotel atop Bunker Hill, adjacent to MOCA. Free jazz concerts Thurs evenings in summer. ⑧.

**Kawada Hotel**, 200 S Hill St at 2nd (☎213/621-4455 or 1-800/752-9232). Comfortable, clean but drab rooms in renovated hotel near Civic Center. ⑤.

**New Otani Hotel**, 120 S Los Angeles St (☎213/629-1200). Affordable luxury hotel with authentic Japanese garden. ⑥/⑦.

**Orchid Hotel**, 819 S Flower St (☎213/624-5855). Cozy place with a concierge. A simple walk to any-where in downtown. Weekly rates. ②.

**Park Plaza**, 607 S Park View St (☎213/384-5281). Sumptuous lobby (popular with filmmakers), ordinary rooms. ③.

**Westin Bonaventure**, 404 S Figueroa St (☎213/624-1000 or 1-800/228-3000). Luxury masterpiece or nightmare, depending on your point of view. Five glass towers, six-story lobby – with a lake. Suites top $2000. ⑦–⑨.

### Hollywood

**Best Western Hollywood Hills**, 6141 Franklin Ave (☎323/464-5181). Small and pleasant place with a heated pool, in the heart of Hollywood. ④.

**Chateau Marmont**, 8221 Sunset Blvd (☎323/656-1010). Former haunt of Greta Garbo et al. Largely suites. ⑦/⑧.

**Dunes Sunset Motel**, 5625 Sunset Blvd (☎323/467-5171). On the eastern side of Hollywood, also good for reaching downtown. ③.

**Holiday Inn Hollywood**, 1755 N Highland Ave (☎323/462-7181 or 1-800/462-7181). Massive, expensive, but perfectly placed. Cheaper rates if three share a room. ⑤.

**Hollywood Metropolitan Hotel**, 5825 Sunset Blvd (☎323/962-5800 or 1-800/962-5800). A recently renovated highrise with disabled access. The best at this price. ⑤.

**Hollywood Roosevelt**, 7000 Hollywood Blvd (☎323/466-7000). The first hotel built for the movie greats, lately revamped and reeking with atmosphere – though the rooms are plain. ⑥/⑦.

### West LA

**Beverly Hilton**, 9876 Wilshire Blvd (☎310/274-7777). Centrally located Beverly Hills hotel with many luxurious amenities. ⑧.

**Bevonshire Lodge Motel**, 7575 Beverly Blvd (☎323/936-6154). Well-situated motel with a pool, close to Melrose shops and Paramount Studios. ③.

**Hotel Bel Air**, 701 Stone Canyon Rd (☎310/472-1211 or 1-800/648-1097). The nicest hotel in LA bar none – and the only one in Bel Air – tucked up in a lushly overgrown canyon above Beverly Hills. Go for a beautiful brunch by the Swan pond if you can't afford the rooms, which reach a dizzying $435 a night. ⑨.

**Le Montrose**, 900 Hammond St (☎310/855-1115). West Hollywood hotel with Art Nouveau stylings, featuring rooftop tennis courts, pool and jacuzzi. Most rooms are suites. ⑧.

**Le Parc**, 733 West Knoll (☎310/855-8888 or 1-800/578-4837). Apartment hotel with studios, one-bedroom suites and rooftop pool and jacuzzi. British rock star hangout. ⑧.

**Le Reve Hotel**, 8822 Cynthia St (☎310/854-1114 or 1-800/835-7997). Gay-friendly hotel a few blocks north of Santa Monica Boulevard. Elegant suites in the style of a French provincial inn. ⑥–⑧.

## Santa Monica, Venice and Malibu

**Cadillac Hotel**, 8 Dudley Ave (☎310/399-8876). Restored 1930s Art Deco hotel and hostel right on Venice Boardwalk. Bright, airy atmosphere and friendly staff. ①–④.

**Channel Road Inn**, 219 W Channel Rd (☎310/459-1920). Fourteen-roomed romantic getaway nestled in lower Santa Monica Canyon, with ocean view, hot tub and free bike rental. ⑥–⑧.

**Loew's Santa Monica Beach Hotel**, 1700 Ocean Ave (☎310/458-6700). One of Santa Monica's newest hotels: a deluxe affair overlooking Santa Monica pier, often in demand as a film set. The best rooms top $400. ⑨.

**Malibu Riviera Motel**, 28920 Pacific Coast Hwy (☎310/457-9503). Just outside Malibu, less than a mile from the ocean. A quiet motel with a sundeck and jacuzzi. ⑤.

**Shangri-la**, 1301 Ocean Ave (☎310/394-2791). Wonderfully restored Art Deco treasure overlooking Palisades Park and the beach. ⑥.

## Near LAX

**Days Inn**, 901 W Manchester Blvd (☎310/649-0800 or 1-800/231-2508). Free parking and airport shuttle. ③–⑤.

**Howard Johnson**, 8620 Airport Blvd (☎310/645-7700). Swimming pool, whirlpool and shuttle. ③.

**Quality Inn**, 5249 W Century Blvd (☎310/645-2200 or 1-800/228-5151). Good-value motel, with ten floors of comfortable, fully equipped rooms, plus restaurant and bar. Free shuttle buses to LAX every 15min. ③.

**Travelodge LAX South**, 1804 E Sycamore Ave (☎310/615-1073). Five minutes south of LAX, ideal for South Bay. Pool, free tea, coffee and breakfast. ③.

## The South Bay and Harbor Area

**Barnabey's**, 3501 N Sepulveda Blvd, Manhattan Beach (☎310/545-8466). One of the best hotels in the area, with nice rooms, whirlpool and LAX airport transit. ⑦.

**Hotel Hermosa**, 2515 Pacific Coast Hwy (☎310/318-6000). Plush, ocean-view rooms at moderate prices. ④–⑥.

**Seahorse Inn**, 233 N Sepulveda Blvd (☎310/376-7951 or 1-800/233-8050). Clean and comfortable place a few blocks from the sands. ②.

**Vagabond Inn**, 6226 Pacific Coast Hwy, Redondo Beach (☎310/378-8555). Clean and inexpensive lodging in a beachside tourist zone. ②.

## Around Disneyland

**Anaheim Inn**, 1630 S Harbor Blvd (☎714/774-1050). One of three good-value hotels near to Disneyland, all owned by the Stovall family. The others are the *Stovall's Inn*, 1110 W Katella Ave, Anaheim (☎714/778-1880), and *Pavilions*, 1176 W Katella Ave, Anaheim (☎714/776-0140). ③–⑤.

**Desert Palm Inn and Suites**, 631 W Katella Ave, Anaheim (☎1-800/635-5423). Large, comfortable rooms feature refrigerators, microwaves, VCRs and continental breakfast. ④.

**Disneyland Hotel**, 1150 W Cerritos Ave (☎714/956-6400). The price does not include admission to the park, although the Disneyland monorail does stop right outside. Disney-themed celebrations, including fairytale weddings with Mickey and Minnie in attendance, can be arranged. ⑧.

**Holiday Inn Anaheim**, 1221 S Harbor Blvd (☎714/758–0900). Safe lodging near the Magic Kingdom. ⑤.

**Park Place Inn**, 1544 S Harbor Blvd (☎714/776-4800). Across from Disneyland. ③–⑤.

### The San Gabriel and San Fernando Valleys

**Ritz-Carlton Huntington Hotel**, 1401 S Knoll, Pasadena (☎818/568-3900). Landmark hotel, c.1900, luxuriously refurbished and discreetly tucked away in residential Pasadena. Suites start at $350. ⑧.

**Sheraton Universal**, 333 Universal Terrace, Universal City (☎818/980-1212 or 1-800/325-3535). Large and luxurious hotel with health club and outdoor pool. ⑧.

**Vagabond Inn Hotel**, 1203 E Colorado Blvd, Pasadena (☎818/449-3170). Friendly budget chain with the usual amenities. ③.

# The City

With only a finite amount of space between the desert, the mountains and the ocean, LA has long since filled in the gaps between what were once small and geographically isolated communities. As a result, it's a massive conglomeration of interconnected and not always well-defined districts, often without much in common.

If LA has a heart, however, it's **downtown**, in the center of the basin. It offers a taste of almost everything you'll find elsewhere around the city, from avant-garde art to the abject dereliction of Skid Row in the Eastside, compressed into an area of small, easily walkable blocks. The area **around downtown** contains some decaying Victorian suburbs, 1920s Art Deco buildings and the center of LA's enormous and growing Hispanic population.

A broad corridor runs 25 miles west from downtown to the coast. The first district you come to, **Hollywood**, has streets caked with movie legend – even if the genuine glamour is long gone. Adjoining **West LA** is home to the city's newest money, shown off in Beverly Hills and along the Sunset Strip. **Santa Monica and Venice** to the west are the quintessential seafront LA of palm trees, white sands and laid-back living, while the coastline itself stretches another twenty miles northwest to glorious, glamorous **Malibu**, home to the select few who've made it.

Suburban **Orange County**, to the southeast, holds little of interest apart from **Disneyland**. On the far side of the northern hills lie the **San Gabriel and San Fernando valleys**, distanced from mainstream LA life socially as well as geographically, and the butt of most Angeleno hick jokes.

## Downtown LA

**Downtown LA** embraces LA's every social, economic and ethnic division. It's not the highrise megalopolis you might expect; relatively few towering office blocks punctuate its low and level skyline. During the postwar boom, as businesses spread out across the basin, it seemed to be heading for dilapidation and decay, but the corporate revitalization of the Eighties has given it a new life, at least economically.

The whole area can easily be seen in a day on foot, aided by the odd 25¢ ride on a DASH **bus** (☎213/808-2273). LA's original settlement on the **Northside** is the obvious first stop, before crossing into the brasher and more modern **Westside**, and continuing through the chaos along **Broadway**.

### The Northside: Olvera Street

To see downtown LA, begin at the beginning. **El Pueblo de Los Angeles**, off Alameda Street and south of **Chinatown**, was the site of the initial late eighteenth-century

△ *Gateway Intermodal Transit Center*

SUNSET BOULEVARD

**Union Station**

**El Pueblo de Los Angeles**

HOLLYWOOD FREEWAY

SANTA ANA FREEWAY

LA River

**Ahmanson Theatre**

TEMPLE STREET

**Mark Taper Forum**

**LA Children's Museum**

**Dorothy Chandler Pavilion**

**City Hall**

**New Otani Hotel**

**The Geffen Contemporary**

**LA Times**

2ND STREET

**Japanese Village Plaza**

LITTLE TOKYO

❺

**MOCA**

BROADWAY

SPRING STREET

3RD STREET

**Wells Fargo Museum**

OLIVE STREET

❹

**Bradbury Building**

4TH STREET

**SKID ROW**

**Grand Central Market**

5TH STREET

CENTRAL AVENUE

❶ PERSHING SQUARE

6TH STREET

WILSHIRE BOULEVARD

ⓘ

Red Line Metrorail

**Los Angeles Theater**

SAN PEDRO STREET

❷

7TH STREET

GARMENT DISTRICT

**Flower Markets**

❼ ❻

8TH STREET

BROADWAY

❸

HARBOUR FREEWAY

FIGUEROA STREET

Blue Line Metrorail

9TH STREET

OLYMPIC BOULEVARD

HOPE STREET

GRAND AVENUE

**ACCOMMODATION**
1 Biltmore
2 City Center Motel
3 Figueroa
4 Inter-Continental
5 Kawada
6 Orchid
7 Westin Bonaventure

● Metro Stations
--- Dash Mini-Bus Routes

0          500 yds

**LA Convention Center**

12TH STREET

PICO BOULEVARD

SAN PEDRO STREET

VENICE

**DOWNTOWN LOS ANGELES**

Mexican settlement of Los Angeles, and a few evocative early buildings remain in situ. The **plaza church**, the city's oldest, has served as a sanctuary for Central American refugees. **Olvera Street**, which runs north from the plaza, contrived in part as a pseudo-Mexican village market, is saved only by its cheery grouping of food and craft stalls and by the historic **Avila Adobe** (daily Mon–Sat 10am–5pm; free), the city's oldest building.

The magnificent mission-style **Union Station** nearby is chiefly used as a Metrorail and Amtrak terminal. Across the Santa Ana Freeway at the **Civic Center**, plodding office buildings surround the lifeless plaza of the Music Center, home to LA's high-art investments. The one exception is the Art Deco **City Hall**; the city's tallest structure as late as 1960, it has a 360° view from its 28th-story observation deck (Mon–Fri 10am–4pm). On the south side of the plaza, free tours of the **Los Angeles Times** building (Mon–Fri 11.15am; ☎213/237-5757) show how the West Coast's biggest newspaper is put together.

## The Westside: Bunker Hill

Until a century ago the area south of the Civic Center, **Bunker Hill**, was LA's most elegant neighborhood, its elaborate Victorian mansions and houses connected by funicular railroad to the growing business district down below. Now it's been subsumed into the amorphous **Financial District**, sprouting colossal new fifty-story towers. The largest and most ambitious of these, the billion-dollar **California Plaza** on Grand Avenue, is based around the playfully colorful **Museum of Contemporary Art** (or **MOCA**), designed by showman architect Arata Isozaki as a "small village in the valley of the skyscrapers" (Tues, Wed & Fri–Sun 11am–5pm, Thurs 11am–8pm; $6, free Thurs 5–8pm). MOCA opened at the end of 1986, funded by a one-percent tax on all new downtown construction. In addition to work by Franz Kline, Mark Rothko, Robert Rauschenberg and Claes Oldenburg, and the impressive multimedia memorials of Antoni Tapiès, it houses a compelling collection of paintings and sculpture by the rising stars you're likely to come across in trendy city galleries. A ticket also entitles you to same-day entry into **The Geffen Contemporary**, 152 N Central Ave, adjacent to Little Tokyo, 55,000 square feet of a former police garage initially used to display MOCA overspill, now a more raw-edged exhibition space , designed by LA's own Frank Gehry. Across from the Geffen, the Japanese Village Plaza is a pleasantly appealing collection of historic sites, restaurants and galleries.

If MOCA's highbrow tone gets too demanding, there's relief in the shallow but amusing **Wells Fargo Museum** (Mon–Fri 9am–5pm; free) at the base of the shiny red towers of the Wells Fargo Center, which tells the story of the bank of Gold Rush California. A block away rise the unmistakeable shining glass tubes of the **Westin Bonaventure Hotel**. Its lobby doubles as a shopping mall and office complex – a disorienting Escher-style labyrinth of spiraling ramps and balconies that can only be negotiated with frequent recourse to the color-coded map.

## Broadway

Though it's hard to picture now, **Broadway** was once LA's most fashionable shopping and entertainment district. Today it's largely taken over by the cash-rich hustle and bustle of Hispanic clothing and jewelry stores, all to a soundtrack of blaring salsa music. Its most vivid taste is to be had amid the pickled pigs' trotters and sheep's brains inside the **Grand Central Market**, on Broadway between Third and Fourth streets. Right alongside, the whimsical terra-cotta facade of the 1918 **Million Dollar Theater**, seen like its neighboring Bradbury Building in the film *Blade Runner*, mixes buffalo heads with bald eagles. The moviehouse has since become a church, though the **Los Angeles Theater** at 615 S Broadway is still in use, albeit for special events, and is even more extravagant, built in ninety days for the world premiere of Charlie Chaplin's *City Lights* in 1931.

# Around downtown

The LA sprawl begins as soon as you leave downtown, whose diverse environs tend to be forgotten quarters, scythed by freeways and with large distances separating their few points of interest. They are too widely separated for it to make sense to try to see them consecutively; each is ten to thirty minutes by car or bus from the next.

## MacArthur Park and around

Reachable on the new Red Line subway, the dilapidated patches of green and large lake of **MacArthur Park** are the nearest open spaces to the sidewalks of downtown. Half a mile west, the seminal **Bullocks Wilshire** department store is the most perfectly realized example of late 1920s Art Deco in LA and has recently been reincarnated as the law library of adjacent **Southwestern University**.

Inside the **Ambassador Hotel**, 3400 Wilshire Blvd, the *Cocoanut Grove* club flourished from the Twenties to the Forties, and the large ballroom (now closed) featured in the first two versions of *A Star is Born*. The kitchen, however, was the scene of the hotel's most notorious event. **Bobby Kennedy** was fatally shot here on June 5, 1968, the day of his greatest political triumph – his victory in the California Democratic Primary. Converted into a filmmaking location, nowadays the *Ambassador* is also closed to public view.

The so-called "Miracle Mile" (see p.933) continues west from the *Ambassador*. South of Wilshire, along Olympic Boulevard between Vermont and Western, **Koreatown** is five times larger – and far more genuine and lively – than the more tourist-oriented Chinatown and Little Tokyo combined, and is home to the largest concentration of Korean people outside Korea.

## Exposition Park

Across Exposition Boulevard from the USC campus, south of downtown, is the sizeable **Exposition Park**, one of the most appreciated parks in LA. It retains a real sense of community, bolstered by its function as favorite lunchtime picnic place. The **California Science Center** here, off Figueroa Street (daily 10am–5pm; free), contains enjoyable working models and thousands of gadgets – recently improved thanks to a multimillion-dollar renovation, though the museum remains as familiar as other science-and-industry museums around the US. Just outside, an IMAX Theater attracts youthful patrons of nature documentaries; while nearby, the **Aerospace Hall** recalls LA's once-dominant industry, though the building is more notable for its architect, Frank Gehry. Exhibitions on the history, art and culture of America's black communities are at the **California African-American Museum** (daily except Mon 10am–5pm; free).

The **Natural History Museum of Los Angeles County** (Mon–Fri 9.30am–5pm, Sat & Sun 10am–5pm; $8) is the nicest building in the park, with its echoey domes and travertine columns. Its tremendous stock of dinosaur skeletons includes the skull of a Tyrannosaurus Rex, and a Diatryma – a huge flightless bird. Other displays include Mayan pyramid murals and the complete contents of a Mexican tomb (albeit a reconstruction).

## South Central LA

**South Central LA** hardly ranks on the tourist circuit, but it's a large and integral part of the city, whatever wealthy white LA might prefer to think. The population has tradi-

---

### THE GANGS OF LOS ANGELES

South Central LA is the heartland of LA's infamous **gangs**, said to number over one hundred thousand members. The gangs have existed for forty years, but only in the last fifteen, with the massive influx of drug money, has violence escalated and automatic weaponry (not least Uzi machine guns) become commonplace. Most fatalities (there are about 350 a year) are a direct result of drug-trade rivalry, though there are also occasional "drive-by shootings," in which pedestrians are sprayed with bullets from a passing car and the victims are often bystanders. Recent clampdowns have made little real headway in tackling the problem.

Although the black Crips and Bloods gangs were once LA's most prominent, that title is increasingly being assumed by Hispanic groups like the huge and ever-growing 18th Street Gang – visible like other gangs with widespread graffiti, illegible to most outsiders, denoting certain gangs by letters and symbols. Fortunately there's even less chance of witnessing inter-gang warfare. As for personal danger, passing through South Central LA by car is safe during the day, but definitely not a good idea after dark.

tionally been mostly black, but is increasingly Hispanic and Asian, joined here and there by bottom-of-the-heap, working-class whites. It doesn't look so terribly run-down at first sight, mostly made up of detached bungalows enjoying their own patch of palm-shaded lawn, but just about all its people get an abysmal deal in schooling and work, and have little chance of climbing the social ladder and escaping. If you pass through, what's most striking is the sheer monotony: every block for twenty-odd miles looks much like the last, enlivened periodically by fast-food outlets, noxious liquor stores and abandoned factory sites, with burned-out, vacant lots still undeveloped almost a decade after the 1992 **riots**.

The district of **Watts**, on the southernmost fringe of downtown, achieved notoriety as the scene of the six-day **Watts Riot** of August 1965, which left 36 dead and innumerable buildings in charred ruins, and of the 1975 gun battle which put an end to the Symbionese Liberation Army (SLA), kidnappers of publishing heiress Patti Hearst. It's also the site of the Gaudiesque **Watts Towers**, striking pieces of folk art which stand alongside railroad tracks at 1765 E 107th St. The towers are usually open on Saturdays, but the schedule can be erratic; call the adjacent Watts Tower Arts Center, 1727 E 107th St (☎213/847-4646), for more details. Recently celebrated as the home of the tennis phenoms, the Williams sisters, **Compton** is renowned worldwide as the home of many of LA's **rappers** – NWA made their reputation with *Straight Outta Compton*. However, outsiders should not attempt to sniff out the local music scene.

The **Dunbar Hotel** at 4225 S Central Ave marks the first US hotel built specifically for blacks and patronized by almost every prominent African-American during the Thirties, Forties and Fifties. Unfortunately, you can only see the hotel's restored lobby and facade, as the structure is now used for elderly housing; for information call the Dunbar Economic Development Corporation at ☎213/234-7882.

# Hollywood

If a single place-name encapsulates the LA dream of glamour, money and overnight success, it's **Hollywood**. Millions of tourists arrive on pilgrimages; millions more flock here in pursuit of riches and glory. Hollywood is a weird combination of insatiable optimism and total despair. It really does blur the edges of fact and fiction, simply because so much seems possible – and yet so little, for most people, actually is. Those who do strike it rich here get out as soon as they can, just as they always have; the big film companies, too, long ago relocated well away, leaving Hollywood in isolation, with prostitution, drug dealing and seedy bookstores as the reality behind the fantasy.

## Central Hollywood

The myths, magic, fable and fantasy splattered throughout the few short blocks of **Central Hollywood** would put a medieval fairytale to shame. A rich sense of nostalgia pervades the area, giving it an appeal no measure of tourists or souvenir postcard stands can diminish. Although you're much more likely to find a porno theater than spot a real star, the decline which blighted Hollywood from the early 1960s is fast receding, with all manner of new investment and redevelopment projects, which may have at least a chance of success. Nevertheless the place still gets hairy after dark, with adolescents cruising Hollywood Boulevard in customized cars and occasional petty criminals on the prowl for the odd pocketbook.

The natural place to begin exploring Hollywood Boulevard is the junction of **Hollywood and Vine** – the classic location for budding stars to be mythically "spotted" by big-shot directors and whisked off to fame and fortune. At 6608 Hollywood Blvd, the purple and pink **Frederick's of Hollywood** has been (under-) clothing Hollywood's sex goddesses since 1947, as well as mortal bodies all over the world via mail order. Inside, the **lingerie museum** (daily 10am–6pm, Fri open until 9.45pm; free) displays

---

### A BRIEF HISTORY OF HOLLYWOOD

Hollywood started life as a temperance colony in 1887, intended to provide a sober, God-fearing alternative to raunchy downtown LA, eight miles away by rough country road. The film industry was drawn here from the East Coast by the guaranteed sunshine, low taxes, cheap labor and diverse assortment of natural locations, and as a way of dodging restrictive patent laws. Although nearby Silverlake was the first – temporary – location for the movie business, the first permanent studio opened in Hollywood in 1911, and within three years the place was packed with filmmakers – such as Cecil B DeMille, who shared his barn-converted office space with a horse.

The ramshackle industry expanded fast, and eager new arrivals soon swamped the original inhabitants, outraging them with their hedonistic lifestyles. Once movie-making had proved itself to be a financially secure business – with the success of D W Griffith's *The Birth of a Nation* in 1915 – film production became highly specialized. Small companies either went bust or were incorporated into big studios. Hollywood's enduring success is in making slick, pleasurable movies that sell – from the hard-bitten film noir of the 1940s to the new creativity of filmmakers such as Francis Ford Coppola and Quentin Tarantino. Ultimately, though, it's been big names, big bucks and conservatism that have kept Hollywood alive, and with a careful eye trained on the box office, the modern American film industry rarely even thinks about taking artistic risks – even though financial ones are constant and often foolhardy.

---

some of the company's best corsets, bras and panties, donated by happy big-name wearers ranging from Lana Turner to Cher.

A little further on, the **Egyptian Theater** at no. 6708 was financed by impresario Sid Grauman, in a modest attempt to re-create the Temple of Thebes. The very first Hollywood premiere (*Robin Hood*) took place here in 1922. Now owned by the city, Grauman's Thebes has recently been reborn as home to American Cinematheque, a film preservation and exhibition group that presents film festivals and hourly showings of a touristy documentary extolling the fact and fantasy behind Hollywood. No Hollywood visitor will want to miss the mundane yet magical foot and hand prints in the concrete concourse of the 1927 Mann's **Chinese Theatre** at 6925 Hollywood Blvd. Actress Norma Talmadge (supposedly by accident) trod in wet cement while visiting the construction site, and the practice has continued ever since, starting with Mary Pickford and Douglas Fairbanks Sr, at the opening of *King of Kings*, and recently involving stars such as Al Pacino. Through the halcyon decades, this was the spot for movie first-nights. As for the building, it's an odd Western version of a classical Chinese temple, replete with dodgy Chinese motifs and upturned dragon tail flanks.

The **Roosevelt Hotel** opposite was movieland's first luxury hotel, its *Cinegrill* restaurant hosting the likes of W C Fields and F Scott Fitzgerald, not to mention hangers-on like Ronald Reagan and the alleged ghost of 1950s-era actor Montgomery Clift. In 1929 the first Oscars were presented here, beginning the long tradition of Hollywood rewarding itself in the absence of honors from elsewhere.

Despite the beliefs of some of their loopiest fans, even the biggest Hollywood stars have been mortal; the many LA cemeteries that hold their tombs get at least as many visitors as the city's museums. In the southeast corner of the **Hollywood Memorial Cemetery**, near Santa Monica Boulevard and Gower Street, a mausoleum contains the resting place of **Rudolph Valentino**, the celebrated screen lover who died aged just 31 in 1926. To this day on each anniversary of his passing (August 23), at least one "Lady in Black" – as his posthumous devotees are known – will likely be found mourning. The achingly ostentatious memorial to **Douglas Fairbanks Sr**, who with his wife Mary Pickford did much to introduce social snobbery among movie-making people, is just outside. Also on view are the graves of Hollywood's more recently deceased inhabitants: an increasingly large population of Russian and Armenian immigrants.

## Griffith Park

The gentle greenery and rugged mountain slopes that make up vast **Griffith Park** northeast of Hollywood (daily 5am–10.30pm, mountain roads close at dusk; free) are a welcome escape from the mind-numbing hubbub of the city. The landmark **Observatory** (Tues–Fri 2–10pm, Sat & Sun 12.30–10pm; free) here has been seen in innumerable Hollywood films, most famously *Rebel Without a Cause*, and the surrounding acres add up to the largest municipal park in the country, one of the few places where LA's multitude of racial and social groups at least go through the motions of mixing together. Above the landscaped flat sections, the hillsides are rough and wild, marked only by foot and bridle paths, leading into desolate but appealingly unspoiled terrain that gives great views over the LA basin and out to the ocean, provided the city smog isn't too thick. One way to explore is on a **rented bike** from Woody's Bicycle World, 3157 Los Feliz Blvd (☎213/661-6665), a short distance away. Definitely worth a look is the **Gene Autry Museum of Western Heritage**, 4700 Western Heritage Way, devoted to true Wild West history and its Hollywood interpretation (Tues–Sun 10am–5pm; $7.50). The park is safe enough by day, but its reputation for after-dark violence is well founded.

## The Hollywood Hills

The views from the **Hollywood Hills** take in a bizarre assortment of opulent properties. Around these canyons and slopes, which run from Hollywood itself into Benedict Canyon above Beverly Hills, mansions are so commonplace that only the half-dozen fully blown castles (at least, Hollywood-style castles) really stand out. On Mulholland Drive are Rudolph Valentino's extravagant **Falcon Lair** (1436 Bella Drive) and Errol Flynn's **Mulholland House** (7740 Mulholland Drive). Guided tours (see box p.922) can point out which is which, but for the most part you can't get close to the most elaborate dwellings anyway, and none is open to the public.

From more or less anywhere in Hollywood, you can see the **Hollywood Sign**, erected as a property advertisement in 1923 (when it spelt "Hollywoodland"; the "land" was removed in 1949). The sign is also famous as a suicide spot, though few have followed the 1932 example of would-be movie star Peg Entwhistle. Hers was no mean feat, the sign being as hard to reach then as it is now: from the end of Beachwood Drive (a route that affords a fine view of the sign) she picked a path slowly upwards through the thick bush, to leap to her death from the 50ft "H." For the first time in its sixty-five-year existence, the sign is being insured against earthquake damage. Infra-red cameras and radar-activated zoom lenses have been installed to catch graffiti writers. Innocent tourists who can't resist a close look are also liable for the $103 fine.

# West LA

LA's so-called "Westside" begins immediately beyond Hollywood in **West LA**, bordered by the foothills of the Santa Monica Mountains to the north and the Santa Monica Freeway to the south. West LA is at the sharp end of all that's new and happening in the city, though tucked away behind the showcase streets, the usual long residential blocks are only marginally less drab than is normal in LA.

## The LA County Museum of Art

The **Miracle Mile** which stretches between La Brea and Fairfax avenues along Wilshire Boulevard was the premier property development of the 1930s. Many of the businesses have moved out, but recent development has created a "Museum Mile" in their place. Though the enormous **LA County Museum of Art** or **LACMA** (Mon–Tues 10am–5pm, Thurs noon–8pm, Fri noon–9pm, Sat & Sun 11am–8pm; $6, free second Wed in the month) is one of the least impressive of its buildings, some of the collections here are among the best in the world. Despite the loss of Armand Hammer's stock of paintings to his own museum in Westwood (see opposite), it justifies a lengthy visit. The **Fearing Collection** of funereal masks and sculpted guardian figures from pre-Columbian Mexico is highly impressive, but where the museum really excels is in its specializations, notably the **German Expressionist** prints and drawings and the scrolls and ceramics in the **Pavilion for Japanese Art**. An astonishing assortment of bones has been recovered from the adjacent **La Brea Tar Pits**. For thousands of years animals who tried to drink from the deceptive layer of water that covers this pool of smelly and still-seeping tar have found themselves stuck fast; it is now surrounded by life-size models of such victims as mastodons and sabre-toothed tigers. If you're interested, the site's **George C Page Museum** (Tues–Sat 10am–5pm; $6) will tell you all you want to know.

The baby of media mogul Robert Petersen, the **Petersen Automotive Museum**, 6060 Wilshire Blvd, pays sumptuous if superficial homage to the automobile (Tues–Thurs, Sat & Sun 10am–6pm, Fri 10am–9pm, also open Mon during holidays; $7). It fails to explain the reasons behind the collapse of LA's early public transportation system and the city's subsequent obsession with what Tom Wolfe called the "Tangerine-flake Kandy-Kolored Streamline Baby," but it has enough mint-condition classic models to make the car-crazy delirious with joy.

## West Hollywood

Between Fairfax Avenue and Beverly Hills, **West Hollywood** was for many years notorious for after-hours vice clubs and general debauchery. Since its 1984 incorporation as a city, however, it's become much more upmarket, home to Los Angeles' prominent – and affluent – gay community. **Melrose Avenue**, LA's trendiest shopping street, runs parallel to the main drag, **Santa Monica Boulevard**, looking at times like something out of a low-budget 1950s sci-fi feature. Neon and Art Deco abound among a fluorescent rash of designer and secondhand boutiques, exotic antique shops, and avant-garde galleries.

Above West Hollywood, on either side of La Cienega Boulevard, is the two-mile-odd conglomeration of restaurants, plush hotels and nightclubs on Sunset Boulevard known as the **Sunset Strip**, which remains one of LA's best areas for nightlife. These establishments first appeared in the early Twenties, along what was then a dusty dirt road linking the Hollywood movie studios with the West LA "homes of the stars." With the rise of TV the Strip declined, only reviving in the Sixties when a scene developed around the landmark *Whisky-a-Go-Go* club, which featured seminal psychedelic rock bands such as The Doors, Love and Buffalo Springfield.

Greta Garbo was only one of many stars to appreciate the quirky Norman castle that is the **Chateau Marmont Hotel**, towering over the east end of the Sunset Strip at no. 8221. Howard Hughes used to rent the entire penthouse so he could keep an eye on the bathing beauties around the pool below, and comedian John Belushi died of a heroin overdose here, in the hotel bungalow he used as his LA home.

## Beverly Hills

Though **Beverly Hills** must be one of the world's wealthiest residential areas, the money is discreet rather than vulgar, revealed more by the immaculate shops (like the high-fashion showcase of **Rodeo Drive**) and squeaky-clean streets than ostentatious displays, although the mock-European shopping alley **Rodeo Two** is the height of pretension. However, the city has been trying harder in recent years to be more visitor-friendly. The **Museum of Television and Radio** (Wed–Sun noon–5pm; $6), is a welcome addition, chronicling fifty years of the boob tube, while the **Beverly Hills Trolley** (daily during summer, otherwise Sat; $5) offers tourists a forty-minute glimpse of the city's highlights, departing hourly from the corner of Dayton Way and Rodeo Drive.

Palatial estates lie hidden behind landscaped security gates in the verdant canyons and foothills above Sunset Boulevard. **Benedict Canyon Drive** climbs past a good number, beginning with the site of the most famous: the lavish **PickFair** mansion at 1143 Summit Drive, built for Mary Pickford and Douglas Fairbanks in 1919 and unceremoniously demolished by Pia Zadora in the 1980s. Further up, Harold Lloyd's **Green Acres** (1740 Green Acres Drive), with its secret passageways and large private screening room, survives intact, although the grounds, which contained a waterfall and a nine-hole golf course, have been broken up into smaller lots.

Just outside Beverly Hills, in LA's Jewish heartland, the $50 million **Simon Wiesenthal Center, Beit HaShoa Museum of Tolerance**, at 9786 W Pico Blvd, is an extraordinary interactive resource centre aimed at exposing the lies of revisionist historians (April–Oct Mon–Thurs 10am–4pm, Fri 10am–3pm, Sun 10.30am–5pm; Nov–March closes 1pm on Fri; $8). The most technologically advanced institution of its kind, it uses videotaped interviews to provide LA's frankest examination of the 1992 riots, and leads the visitor through reenactments outlining the rise of Nazism to a harrowing conclusion in a replica gas chamber.

## Westwood Village

Just west of Beverly Hills, on the north side of Wilshire Boulevard, **Westwood Village** is one of LA's more user-friendly neighborhoods, a grouping of low-slung redbrick buildings that went up in the late 1920s around the central Broxton Avenue, along with the nearby campus of the University of California at Los Angeles (UCLA). It's an area that's easily explored on foot, and one very much shaped by the proximity of the university campus, which is really the lifeblood of the area. Once LA's prime movie-going district, Westwood Village has lost its cinematic eminence due to a 1980s gang scare and a real lack of parking, but remains the most densely packed movie-theater district in the country, and its 1931 "Village" cinema is still often used for premieres or special "sneak" previews to gauge audience reactions.

South of the Village, Wilshire Boulevard exploded in the 1970s with oil-rich highrise developments; now modest detached houses sit next to twenty-story condominium towers in which penthouse apartments with private heliports sell for upwards of $12 million. Inside one such tower, on the corner with Westwood Boulevard, is the **Armand Hammer Museum of Art and Culture Center** (Tues, Wed, Fri & Sat 11am–7pm, Thurs 11am–9pm, Sun 11am–5pm; $4.50, free Thurs 6–9pm), amassed over seven decades by the flamboyant late boss of Occidental Petroleum. Its Rembrandts and Rubens are less than stunning, but Van Gogh's intense and radiant *Hospital at Saint Rémy* is a real jewel.

Outside the museum, behind the tiny Avco cinema, Hammer's marble tomb in **Westwood Memorial Park** stands near the lipstick-covered plaque that marks the resting place of **Marilyn Monroe**.

## The Getty Center

Opened at the end of 1997, the new **Getty Center** near the Sepulveda Pass north of Wilshire Boulevard (Tues–Wed 11am–7pm, Thurs–Fri 11am–9pm, Sat–Sun 10am–6pm; free) towers over the surrounding area. Designed by Richard Meier at a cost of $1 billion, the museum is LA's most recent, and most obvious, attempt to make a mark on the international art scene. Drivers must reserve parking space in advance and pay a $5 parking fee; otherwise, take MTA bus #561, which stops on Sepulveda Boulevard.

Two years after the original Malibu museum opened in 1974 (see p.937), oil magnate John Paul Getty died, leaving it $1.3 billion. Obliged to spend a set percentage of its now $3 billion endowment every year, it can outbid anyone to get what it wants. Hence the inflation in international art prices – and allegations of shady behavior among the museum's suppliers.

The quality of the **exhibits** is extraordinary, including a feast of ornate French furniture and decorative arts from the reign of Louis XIV, with clocks, chandeliers, tapestries and gilt-edged commodes, which fills several overwhelmingly opulent rooms. Although Getty himself was much less interested in painting, a large collection has been amassed since his death, featuring all the major names from the thirteenth century to the present, including Vincent Van Gogh's *Irises* and several Rembrandt portraits. Photography is represented by the works of Man Ray, Moholy-Nagy and others.

# Santa Monica, Venice and Malibu

Set along an unbroken twenty-mile strand of clean, white-sand beaches, the small, self-contained communities that line the **Santa Monica Bay** feature some of the best Los Angeles has to offer, with none of the smog or searing heat that can make the rest of the metropolis unbearable. The entire area is well served by public transportation, near (but not too near) the airport, and a wide selection of accommodation makes it a good base for seeing the rest of LA.

## Venice
**Venice** was laid out in the marshlands of Ballona Creek in 1905 by developer Abbot Kinney as a romantic twenty-mile network of canals, lined by sham palazzos and waterfront homes. The original plan to create a West Coast art-and-culture zone failed, followed by a more successful turn as an amusement park; however the coming of the automobile finished it off altogether. Many of the canals were filled in, and the area fell into disrepair, being taken over by oil wells. Orson Welles' film *Touch of Evil* starred the then-derelict Venice as a seedy Mexican border town. Kinney was, however, ahead of his time. A fair bit of the original plan survives, and the pseudo-European atmosphere has made Venice one of the coast's trendiest spots. Chic cafes and restaurants abound near the beach, and a strong alternative arts scene centers on the Beyond Baroque Literary Arts Center in the old City Hall at 681 Venice Blvd.

The town's main artery, **Windward Avenue**, runs from the beach into what was the Grand Circle of the canal system. Its original Romanesque **arcade**, around the intersection with Pacific Avenue, is alive with health-food shops, secondhand record stores and roller-skate rental stands, although less and less of the arcade remains with each passing year. Nearby, having just undergone several years' worth of renovation, the few remaining **canals** display their original quaint bridges and pedestrian-friendly footpaths. A single street from outside the canals, **Dell Avenue**, enters the area from its intersection at Washington Boulevard.

Southerly **Venice Beach** itself is the reason most people come here. Nowhere else does LA parade itself quite so openly as along the wide pathway of **Venice Boardwalk**, ever packed with jugglers, fire-eaters, roller-skating guitar players or just people-watchers. South of Windward is **Muscle Beach**, a legendary outdoor weightlifting centre where serious-looking hunks of muscle pump serious iron, and high-flying gymnasts swing on the adjacent rings and bars. Spend ten minutes watching and you'll find Narcissus is alive and well, and working on his biceps. Outlets along Washington Street near the pier – such as Spokes'n'Stuff (☎310/395-4748) – rent out **bikes**.

**At night** Venice Beach is taken over by street gangs and drug dealers. Walking on the beach after dark is illegal, and you should be very cautious in the vicinity.

## Santa Monica

Immediately north of Venice, **Santa Monica** is the oldest and biggest of LA's resort areas, perched on palm-tree-shaded bluffs above the blue Pacific. Once a wild beach-front playground, it's now a self-consciously healthy and liberal community, with a large expatriate British contingent of writers and rock stars, ranging from Rod Stewart to John Lydon.

The Santa Monica beachfront grew into a giant funfair city when it was linked to downtown LA by the suburban streetcar system. It was the location for many of the underworld stories of Raymond Chandler, most memorably as "Bay City" in *Farewell My Lovely*, but today Chandler wouldn't recognize the place. The gambling ships and bathing clubs have gone, and Santa Monica is now well known for its effective rent control policy and its stringent planning and development regulations. For these perceived infractions, local right-wingers refer sneeringly to the city as the "People's Republic."

Santa Monica reaches nearly three miles inland, but most things of interest are within a few blocks of the beach. The **visitor center** (daily 10am–5pm; ☎310/393-7593), in a kiosk just south of Santa Monica Boulevard, along Ocean Boulevard in Palisades Park (the cypress tree-lined strip along the top of the bluffs), makes a good first stop. Two blocks east of Ocean Boulevard, the **Santa Monica Promenade**, a pedestrianized stretch popular with buskers and itinerant evangelists, is the closest LA comes to having an urban energy, though it has been losing some of its steam lately with the arrival of colorless chain stores, which are crowding out the quirky boutiques and oddball shops. On weekend nights this three-block strip hosts a pleasant *passeggiata* bringing together Angelenos of all ages and accents, and it's by far the best place to come for alfresco dining, beer-drinking or simply people-watching.

The real focal point of Santa Monica life is down below, on the **beach** and around the once-decaying and recently refurbished **Santa Monica pier**, which boasts a giant helter-skelter and a well-restored 1922 wooden **carousel** – featured, along with Paul Newman, in the 1973 movie *The Sting*. The grand beach houses just to the north of the pier were known as Hollywood's "Gold Coast"; the largest, now the **Sand and Sea** beach club, was built as the servants' quarters of a massive 120-room house, now demolished, that belonged to William Randolph Hearst. In the adjacent villa of MGM boss Louis B Mayer, the Kennedy brothers were later rumored to have had liaisons with Marilyn Monroe.

Five miles along the curving **Pacific Coast Highway (PCH)** from Santa Monica, a huge mock French chateau inadvertently marks the easily missed entrance to the **Getty Villa**, once the site of the Getty museum, at 17985 PCH. A fake Roman villa poised high above the ocean, the complex is currently closed until 2001, when it will re-emerge as a showcase for Getty antiquities.

## Malibu

**Malibu**, at the top of the bay twenty miles north of Santa Monica, is a whole other world, its beach-colony houses owned by those famous enough to need privacy and rich enough to afford it. It's not all that impressive on arrival, however, with ramshackle surf shops, fast-food stands and real-estate agents scattered along PCH around the graceful **Malibu Pier**. **Surfrider Beach** here was the surfing capital of the world in the Fifties and early Sixties, as seen in the *Beach Blanket Bingo* movies of Annette Funicello and Frankie Avalon (the surf is at its best in late summer). Just beyond is Malibu Lagoon State Park, a nature reserve and bird refuge, and nearby is the Adamson House, a stunning Spanish Colonial home with opulent decor and colorful tilework.

Most Malibu residences are tucked away in an insular community in the narrow canyons on the fringes of town. There's very little to see; if you must, you can enter on foot or cycle a mile or so along PCH, on the other side of the hill. You'd do better, though, to visit **Malibu Colony Plaza**, near the gated entrance to the colony – good both for star-spotting and stocking up on food and drink before a day on the sands.

Much of **Malibu Creek State Park**, at the crest of Malibu Canyon Road, well to the north along Mulholland Drive, used to belong to 20th Century Fox, who filmed many Tarzan pictures here, as well as the TV show *M.A.S.H.* The 4000-acre park includes a large lake, some waterfalls and nearly fifteen miles of hiking trails.

Five miles along the coast from Malibu Pier, **Zuma Beach** is the largest and most crowded of the Los Angeles County beaches. Adjacent **Point Dume State Beach**, below the bluffs, is a lot more relaxed, and the rocks at its southern tip, **Pirate's Cove**, are a good place to look out for seals and migrating gray whales in winter.

# The South Bay

South of Venice, Marina del Rey and the declining resort town of Playa del Rey, the coast is dominated by the runways of LAX and the oil refineries of El Segundo. Beyond here begins the eight-mile coastal strip of the quieter, more suburban and less pretentious South Bay beach towns: **Manhattan Beach**, **Hermosa Beach** and **Redondo Beach**. Each has a beckoning strip of white sand, and Manhattan and Hermosa especially are well equipped for surfing and beach sports. They're also well connected by regular buses to downtown LA. To the south are **Long Beach** and **Catalina Island**.

## Long Beach

Thanks to a billion-dollar clean-up, downtown **Long Beach** is not the seedy stamping ground of off-duty sailors that it was twenty years ago. **Pine Avenue** is an enjoyable stretch of restored architecture and bargain antique stores, but the only reason you're likely to consider crossing to the far side of LA's massive harbor is to see the **Queen Mary** (daily 10am–6pm; $12). The Cunard flagship from the 1930s until the 1960s, the *Queen Mary* is now a luxury hotel, and guided tours present a sentimentalized version of its days of elegance and refinement. The huge geodesic dome nearby housed Howard Hughes's *Spruce Goose* airplane until it was sold in 1992, but this tourist loss has been more than remedied by the recent opening of the **Aquarium of the Pacific** (daily 10am–6pm; $14), along Shoreline Drive, a terrific exploration of aquatic flora and fauna in three distinct geographic and climatic zones from around the world.

## Santa Catalina Island

The enticing island of **Santa Catalina**, twenty miles offshore, has been in private ownership since 1811, when the Gabrileño Indians were forced to resettle on the mainland. It remains a wilderness, devoted to the conservation of unique species such as the **Catalina shrew** (so rare that it's only been sighted twice), and tourism has been held largely at bay. Hotels are unobtrusive among the whimsical architecture, and cars are largely forbidden; the two thousand islanders walk, ride bikes or drive electric mokes. Return **ferry** trips to Catalina run several times daily from San Pedro and Long Beach ($25–35; operators are Catalina Cruises, ☎1-800/464-4228, and Catalina Express, ☎562/519-1212 or 1-800/995-4386). From Newport Beach, the Catalina Passenger Service (☎714/673-5245) runs a $30 daily round-trip.

The island's one town, **AVALON**, can be fully explored on foot in an hour. Begin at the sumptuous Art Deco **Avalon Casino**, built in the 1920s by William Wrigley Jr (of the Chicago chewing-gum dynasty), which runs regular movie showings and irregular silent film displays. The collections at the adjoining **museum** (daily 10.30am–4pm; $1.50) include Native American artifacts from Catalina's past. On the slopes above, the **Zane Grey Pueblo Hotel** (☎310/510-0966; ④–⑥) is the former home of the Western author, who visited Catalina to film *The Vanishing American* and liked the place so much he never left. The hotel's seventeen rooms are each themed around a Zane Grey story, and there's a pool in the shape of an arrowhead.

The **Chamber of Commerce** (☎310/510-1520) has more detailed information on visiting Catalina; mokes and bikes can be rented from the stand on Bay Shore Drive.

Hotel **accommodation** in Avalon is much in demand, and pricey – upwards of $85: the least expensive is usually the *Atwater* (☎1-800/446-0271 or 626-1496; ③/④). The only budget options are three seaside and one mountainside **campgrounds**; call ☎310/510-0303 for details.

# Anaheim: Disneyland and around

In the early 1950s, Walt Disney conceived a theme park where his already hugely popular cartoon characters – Mickey Mouse, Donald Duck and the rest – could come to life, to enchant children and make their Uncle Walt even richer. **ANAHEIM** was chosen as the location for **Disneyland** on the basis that these acres of orange groves, thirty miles southeast of downtown, would become LA's next focus of population growth – which indeed they did. The whole area is now overrun with hotels and restaurants (when Disney opened his next theme park, in Florida – see p.569 – he made sure he owned all of them too, thus retaining total corporate control), and the boom doesn't look like slowing, although the surrounding area has generally become seedier and more prone to crime. If you're not coming to visit Disneyland, or the creakier rides at nearby Knott's Berry Farm (8039 Beach Blvd; $35), you may as well give the place a miss: it hasn't an ounce of interest in itself.

### Disneyland

To make the most of **Disneyland** – the ultimate escapist fantasy and the blueprint for imitations worldwide – throw yourself right into it. Don't think twice about anything and go on every ride you can. The high admission price ($38) includes them all, although during peak periods each one can entail hours of waiting on line. Remember, too, that the emphasis is on family fun; the authorities take a dim view of anything remotely antisocial and eject those they consider guilty.

Over four hundred "Imagineers" worked to create the *Indiana Jones Adventure*, Disneyland's biggest opening in years. Two hours of waiting are built into the ride, with an interactive archeological dig and 1930s-style newsreel show leading up to the main feature – a giddy journey along 2500ft of skull-encrusted corridors in which you face fireballs, falling rubble, venomous snakes and, inevitably, a rolling boulder finale. Disney claims that, thanks to computer engineering, no two *Indiana Jones* rides are ever alike. Judge for yourself.

Among the best of the older **rides** are two in **Adventureland**: the *Pirates of the Caribbean*, a boat trip through underground caverns, singing along with drunken pirates; and the *Haunted Mansion*, a riotous "doom buggy" tour in the company of the house spooks. While **Fantasyland** consists mainly of low-tech fairy-tale rides that won't scare the kiddies, **Tomorrowland** is Disney's vision of the future, where the *Space Mountain* roller coaster zips through the pitch-blackness of outer space, and the *Star Tours* ride simulates a journey into the world of George Lucas. This section of the park has been updated in the last few years with space probes and "rocket rods," which underscores once again how Cold War-era this area still remains in its outlook.

As for **accommodation**, try to visit Disneyland just for the day and spend the night somewhere else. Most of the hotels and motels nearby cost well in excess of $70 per night (see p.926). You're not permitted to bring your own **food** to the park; you can only consume the fast food sold on the premises.

Disneyland is at 1313 Harbor Blvd, Anaheim, 45 minutes by **car** from downtown using the Santa Ana Freeway. In summer, the park is open daily between 8am and 1am;

otherwise opening hours are weekdays 10am to 6pm, Saturday 9am to midnight, and Sunday 9am to 10pm. Arrive early; traffic and ride queues quickly become nightmarish, especially in the summer. For further **information**, including public transportation details, call ☎714/781-4565.

### Yorba Linda: the Richard Nixon Library and Birthplace

Mickey Mouse may be its most famous resident, but conservative Orange County's favorite son is former president **Richard Milhous Nixon**, born in 1913 in what's now the freeway-caged **Yorba Linda**, about eight miles northeast of Disneyland at 18001 Yorba Linda Blvd (Mon–Sat 10am–5pm, Sun 11am–5pm; $5.95). His birthplace – and final resting place; he's buried in the grounds – is a shrine to a man who forged a career from lies and secrecy, and finally resigned from the world's most powerful job in total disgrace. In the shadow of a 12ft high, 600lb chunk of the Berlin Wall, oversized gifts from world leaders, amusing campaign memorabilia, and a laugh-a-line collection of obsequious letters written by and to Nixon form the core of the exhibition, but the man's distinctive persona is best enjoyed in the constantly running archive radio and TV recordings.

Nixon's face leers down in Big Brother fashion from almost every wall, but only inside the **Presidential Auditorium** do you get the chance to ask him a question, although the choice is limited to a small pre-programed selection. Nixon's gaunt features fill the overlarge screen and provide the stock replies – as endearingly and believably as ever.

## The San Gabriel and San Fernando valleys

The northern limit of LA is defined by two long, wide valleys lying over the hills from the central basin, starting close to one another a few miles north of downtown and spanning outwards in opposite directions – east to the deserts around Palm Springs, west to Ventura on the central coast. You wouldn't miss an awful lot by not visiting the valleys at all, but they do give a picture of life in LA's suburbs.

### The San Gabriel Valley

Spreading east from Pasadena, ten miles north of Los Angeles, the **San Gabriel Valley** was settled by farmers and cattle ranchers on the lands of the eighteenth-century Mission San Gabriel. **PASADENA** itself is as much the home of the *grandes dames* of LA society as it is to the "little old lady from Pasadena" of the Jan and Dean song. A luxury resort in the 1880s, it then became a residential area and underwent a major renovation in the 1980s, with modern shopping centres slipping in behind Edward Hopperish 1920s facades, and the blocks around the "Old Town" of Colorado Boulevard now fashionable with early-evening diners and kids cruising in heavily chromed lowrider cars. Maps and booklets are available at the **Convention and Visitors Bureau**, 171 S Los Robles Ave (Mon–Fri 8am–5pm, Sat 10am–4pm; ☎626/795-9311).

The **Norton Simon Museum** at 411 W Colorado Blvd (Thurs–Sun noon–6pm; $4) is not one of LA's better-known museums, but its collection – ranging from paintings by Rembrandt and Frans Hals to Monet's *Mouth of the Seine at Honfleur* and Picasso's extraordinary *Woman with Book* – is consistently excellent. Your ticket stub entitles you to a pre-selected print from the superb museum **bookshop**. The nearby **Gamble House** (Thurs–Sun noon–3pm; $5) allows an hour-long tour through one of the country's best examples of Craftsman architecture, a rugged building style popular around 1900.

South of Pasadena, in the dull, upper-crust little suburb of **San Marino**, the **Huntington Museum and Library**, off Huntington Drive at 1151 Oxford Rd (Tues–Fri noon–4.30pm, Sat–Sun 10.30am–4.30pm; suggested donation $8.50), contains numerous manuscripts and rare books, such as a Gutenberg Bible and the **Ellesmere Chaucer**, an illuminated manuscript of *The Canterbury Tales* from around 1410. Paintings include Gainsborough's *Blue Boy* and Reynolds' *Mrs Siddons as the Tragic Muse*, and the whole ensemble is set off by acres of beautiful themed **gardens**.

## The San Fernando Valley

The San Fernando Valley, spreading west, is *the* valley to most Angelenos: a sprawl of tract homes, mini-malls, fast-food drive-ins and auto parts stores. It has more of a middle-American feel than anywhere else in LA, inhabited – at least, in the popular LA imagination – by macho men and bimboesque "Valley Girls," speaking their own dialect, "Valley Talk." In the gateway town of **GLENDALE**, eight miles north of downtown, **Forest Lawn Cemetery** at 1712 S Glendale Ave (daily 9am–5pm; free) was immortalized with biting satire by Evelyn Waugh in *The Loved One*. Those buried here include Errol Flynn, Walt Disney (contrary to urban legend, not frozen), Clara Bow, Nat King Cole, Chico Marx, Clark Gable, and Jean Harlow, in a marble-lined room paid for by her fiancé William Powell. If seeing the gravesites of the famous isn't enough for you, check out the **replicas** of the highlights of art history, all rendered with maximum vulgarity.

### Burbank and the studios

The name of Hollywood may be synonymous with the movies, but the studios themselves, if they were there at all, moved out of Tinseltown long ago; the nitty-gritty business of actually making films goes on over the hills in otherwise boring **Burbank**.

Studios offering tours include **NBC**, at 3000 W Alameda St (Mon–Fri 9am–3pm; ☎818/840-3537; $7), and the technically oriented **Warner Bros Studios** (Mon–Fri 9am–4pm; ☎818/954-1744; $30). The largest of the old backlots belongs to **Universal Studios**, whose four-hour tours (summer daily 8am–10pm; rest of year daily 9am–7pm; ☎818/508-9600; $38) are more like a trip around an amusement park, with high-tech rides and "evening spectaculars" often based on current movies. The shows are without exception cheesy, but for fans of fireworks or high kitsch, they're an absolute must.

# Eating

LA **eating** covers every extreme: whatever you want to eat and however much you want to spend, you're spoiled for choice. Try to take at least a few meals in the more exotic restaurants, if only to watch the city's many self-appointed food snobs going through their paces. If you simply want to fill up quickly and inexpensively, the options are almost endless, and include free food available for the price of a drink at numerous happy hours. Catering appears to be the movie stars' sideline of choice these days, and LA is littered with **celebrity-owned** outfits – like Steven Spielberg's submarine-shaped sandwich store *Dive!* and *Planet Hollywood* (where displays include Forrest Gump's box of chocolates) in Beverly Hills – but the food is usually unremarkable, as many visitors are quickly discovering.

### Downtown

**Bella Cucina**, 949 S Figueroa St (☎213/623-0014). Fabulous pizzas and homemade pastas, with the accent on Northern and rural Italian cuisine.

**Buffet Palace**, 3014 Olympic Blvd (☎213/480-8949). Korean restaurant, strong on spicy barbecued beef.

**Clifton's Cafeteria**, 648 S Broadway (☎213/627-1673). A cafeteria complete with redwood trees and a waterfall; the food is inexpensive, and good too.

**El Cholo**, 1121 S Western Ave (☎323/734-2773). One of LA's first big Mexican restaurants and still one of the best, despite the drunken frat-rats from USC.

**Ocean Seafood**, 750 N Hill (☎213/687-3088). Cavernous and often crowded restaurant serving low-priced, excellent food.

**The Original Pantry**, 877 S Figueroa St (☎213/972-9279). Mayor Riordan owns this diner serving huge pork chops and classic American breakfasts 24 hours a day.

**Pacific Dining Car**, 1310 W 6th St (☎213/483-6000). Starched linen and expensive steaks in a former railroad carriage styled after the hushed tones of an English supper club. Good-value breakfasts.

**Philippe's Original**, 1001 N Alameda St (☎213/628-3781). Since 1908, the home of delicious French "dipped" sandwiches; invented right here as well.

## Hollywood

**Casita de Campo**, 1920 Hyperion Ave (☎323/662-4255). Great Mexican food, comfortable atmosphere in the heart of the Silverlake district.

**French Quarter**, 7985 Santa Monica Blvd (☎323/654-0898). Inside the French Market Place, a gay-run, New Orleans-themed restaurant that's at least as much fun as Disneyland.

**Gloria's Cafe**, 3603 W Sunset Blvd (☎323/664-5732). Popular, gay-friendly local hangout that's great for dinner, especially Cajun food.

**Hampton's**, 1342 N Highland Ave (☎323/469-1090). Over fifty styles of gourmet hamburger.

**Mexico City**, 2121 Hillhurst Ave (☎323/661-7227). Spinach enchiladas and other Californian versions of Mexican standards. Red booths, a great view of the street from the wall-length window and a young crowd. You're allowed to smoke in the adjoining bar, a rarity in LA.

**Musso and Frank Grill**, 6667 Hollywood Blvd (☎323/467-7788). Since it opened in 1919, all the Hollywood bigwigs have frequented this landmark restaurant and bar – but at $15 for bacon and eggs, you pay for the atmosphere.

**Shibucho**, 3114 Beverly Blvd (☎323/387-8498). Excellent sushi bar in the heart of Little Tokyo; go with someone who knows what to order, as no one seems to speak English.

**Tommy's**, 2575 Beverly Blvd (☎310/389-9060). Often called LA's best burgers: loaded with thick beef, toppings and most importantly, grease.

**Yukon Mining Co**, 7328 Santa Monica Blvd (☎323/851-8833). Excellent coffee shop catering to the local gay community and the neighboring senior citizens' home. Open 24hr.

## West LA

**Apple Pan**, 10801 W Pico Blvd (☎310/475-3585). Grab a spot at the counter and enjoy great pies and the best hamburgers in the world.

**Campanile**, 624 S La Brea Ave (☎323/938-1447). Upmarket Italian restaurant with indoor fountain and pleasing pastries from La Brea Bakery next door.

**Canter's Deli**, 419 N Fairfax Ave (☎323/651-2030). Infamous older waitresses in pink uniforms and running shoes serve kosher soup and sandwiches in a kitsch, white-vinyl setting.

**Casa Carnitas**, 4067 Beverly Blvd (☎323/667-9953). Tasty Mexican food from the Yucatan Peninsula: the dishes are unmistakeably inspired by Cuban and Caribbean cooking; lots of seafood, too.

**Chung King**, 11538 W Pico Blvd (☎310/477-4917). The best neighborhood Chinese restaurant in LA, serving spicy Szechuan food: don't miss out on the *bum-bum* chicken.

**Citrus**, 6703 Melrose Ave (☎323/857-0034). Trendy, upmarket restaurant, serving good California cuisine in an outdoor setting indoors. Reservations are essential; lunch for two will be at least $60.

**El Coyote**, 7312 Beverly Blvd (☎323/939-2255). Satisfying portions of genuine Mexican home-cooking in a gloomy setting. Watch soccer and down the legendary cheap margaritas in the bar.

**Georgia**, 7250 Melrose Ave (☎323/933-8420). Down-home Southern cooking, about $25 for a main course. Part-owned by Denzel Washington. Be prepared to tip like you've never tipped before.

**The Gumbo Pot**, 6333 W 3rd St in the Farmers' Market (☎323/933-0358). Delicious and dirt-cheap Cajun cooking; try the *gumbo yaya* of chicken, shrimp and sausage, and the fruit-and-potato salad.

**Mishima**, 8474 W 3rd St (☎323/782-0181). Some of LA's best miso soup and *udon* noodles, at afford-able prices.

**Shamshiry**, 1916 Westwood Blvd (☎310/474-1410). The best of the Iranian restaurants that have been established in Hollywood since the fall of the Shah, offering kebabs, pilafs and exotic sauces.

**Swingers**, 8018 Beverly Blvd (☎323/653-5858). Basic and cheap American food served in a strangely trendy motel environment.

**Tommy Tang's**, 7313 Melrose Ave (☎323/937-5733). Excellent Thai food in very popular, medium-sized restaurant. Incongruous biweekly drag nights.

## Santa Monica, Venice and Malibu

**Cafe 50s**, 838 Lincoln Blvd, Venice (☎310/399-1955). No doubts about this place: Ritchie Valens on the jukebox and burgers on the tables.

**Cafe Montana**, 1534 Montana Ave, Santa Monica (☎310/829-3990). Good breakfasts and excellent salads and grilled fish in this art gallery-cum-cafe on the new upmarket strip.

**Chaya Venice**, 110 Navy St (☎310/396-1179). Coolly elegant culinary crossroads serving Japanese and Mediterranean foods to a smart clientele. Try the huge California roll platter between two.

**Chinois on Main**, 2709 Main St, Santa Monica (☎310/392-9025). LA's most popular restaurant, run by the city's best-known chef, Wolfgang Puck, and serving Chinese-style dishes like fresh fish in garlic and ginger. Very expensive, with lunches from $25.

**Inn of the Seventh Ray**, 128 Old Topanga Canyon Rd, just off Topanga Canyon (☎310/455-1311). The ultimate New Age restaurant, serving vegetarian and wholefood dishes in a relatively secluded environment. Excellent desserts, too.

**Lighthouse Buffet**, 201 Arizona Ave, Santa Monica (☎310/451-2076). All-you-can-eat sushi is a long-accepted concept in LA; indulge to your heart's content for under $10 at lunchtime or $20 in the evening.

**Norm's**, 1601 Lincoln Blvd, Santa Monica (☎310/450-0074). The prototypical LA diner, with 1950s architecture and $4 breakfasts.

**Versailles**, 1000 N Sepulveda Blvd, Manhattan Beach (☎310/558-3168). Packed and noisy Cuban restaurant with a sibling on La Cienega. Fried bananas, steaks and "Moors and Christians" (black beans and rice) for about $10.

## Disneyland and around

**Angelo's**, 511 S State College Blvd, Anaheim (☎714/533-1401). Straight out of *Happy Days*, drive-in complete with roller-skating car-hops and good burgers. Open until 1am at weekends.

**Belisle's**, 12001 Harbor Blvd, Garden Grove (☎714/750-6560). Open late for filling sandwiches, and sweet and meat pies.

**Knott's Chicken Dinner Restaurant**, 8039 Beach Blvd, located just outside Knott's Berry Farm (☎714/220-5080). Famous for delicious fried chicken long before Disneyland was around – serving cheap and tasty chicken dishes for over 65 years.

## The San Gabriel and San Fernando valleys

**Dr Hogly-Wogly's Tyler Texas Bar-B-Q**, 8136 Sepulveda Blvd, Van Nuys (☎626/782-2480). Queue up for the chicken, sausages, ribs and beans, some of the best in LA.

**Genmai Sushi**, 4454 Van Nuys Blvd, Van Nuys (☎626/986-7060). Japanese-style vegetarian restau-rant with brown rice, sushi and seasonal macrobiotic dishes.

**Merida**, 20 E Colorado Blvd, Pasadena (☎626/792-7371). Unusual Mexican restaurant, featur-ing dishes from the Yucatan Peninsula; try the spicy pork wrapped up and steamed in banana leaves.

**Sea Star**, 2000 W Main St, Alhambra (☎626/282-8833). Dim sum at its best: pork, *baos*, potstickers and dumplings, and delicious sweets.

**Wolfe Burger**, 46 N Lake St, Pasadena (☎626/792-7292). A great place for chili, tamales and burg-ers, with huevos rancheros served for breakfast.

# Nightlife and entertainment

Exploring the jungle of LA's **nightlife** can be great fun. Everyone you meet claims to be either a rock star or in the movies; half of them aren't lying. Even the quietest venue offers a chance to eavesdrop on a bit of vapid *Less Than Zero* dialogue; the most raucous ones will take your breath away. In all the pubs, clubs and discos, you'll need to be 21 and will almost certainly be asked for ID.

The best sources of **listings** are *LA Weekly* and the "Calendar" section in the *LA Times* at the weekend.

## Bars, pubs and coffeehouses

LA's **bars and pubs** are rarely the scruffy boozing places found elsewhere in the US, due at least in part to the generally high degree of health consciousness – not to mention the very early (daybreak) starting time of the movie business working day. **Coffeehouses** are a newer phenomenon, but are now established all over the city as popular meeting places.

**Al's Bar**, 305 S Hewitt St, downtown (☎213/625-9703). Post-apocalyptic place in a gritty part of town, with cheap beer and smoke-filled rooms. Best appreciated when there's a good live line-up. Don't go if you can't deal with paying someone to make sure your car isn't stolen.

**Barney's Beanery**, 8447 Santa Monica Blvd, West Hollywood (☎213/654-2287). Well-worn poolhall bar, stocking over 200 beers. It also serves food, often of marginal quality.

**Boardners**, 1652 N Cherokee Ave, Hollywood (☎323/462-9621). A likeably unkempt neighborhood bar – a rarity in the heart of Hollywood.

**Cat'n'Fiddle**, 6530 Sunset Blvd, Hollywood (☎323/468-3800). Boisterous British expat pub with good beers and live music.

**Dragonfly**, 6510 Santa Monica Blvd, Hollywood (☎323/466-6111). Disco and house music, with the odd bit of rock at this established hipster hangout.

**The Dresden Room**, 1760 N Vermont Ave, Hollywood (☎323/665-4294). Wed night is open-mike, otherwise the resident husband-and-wife lounge act takes requests from the crowd of old-timers and hipsters.

**King's Road Espresso House**, 8361 Beverly Blvd, Hollywood (☎323/655-9044). Sidewalk cafe popular day and night with West Hollywood's *nuovo* beatnik crowd.

**Lava Lounge**, 1533 N La Brea, Hollywood (☎323/876-6612). Cheesy, retro decor, glowing cocktails and plenty of rock and surf music.

**The Novel Cafe**, 212 Pier Ave, Santa Monica (☎310/396-8566). Considering the name and the trendy environs, this is a remarkably unpretentious cafe, with good coffees, teas and pastries.

**The Powerhouse**, 1714 N Highland Ave, Hollywood (☎213/463-9438). Enjoyable heavy-rockers' watering hole just off Hollywood Blvd; few people get here much before midnight.

**The Red Setter Irish Pub**, 2615 Wilshire Blvd, Santa Monica (☎310/449-1811). Formerly *McGinty's*, this pub features plenty of darts and beer.

**Tiki-Ti**, 4427 W Sunset Blvd, Hollywood (☎323/669-9381). Tiny grass-skirted cocktail bar straight out of *Hawaii Five-0*. The Filipino owners mix deadly concoctions at about $5 a hit.

## Clubs and discos

LA's **clubs** are among the wildest in the country, ranging from absurdly faddish hangouts to industrial noise cellars. The trendier side of the club scene is, as always, hard to pin down; check the *LA Weekly* before setting out.

**Florentine Gardens**, 5951 Hollywood Blvd, Hollywood (☎323/464-0706). A fun, unpretentious dance club catering to the under-21 set.

**Mayan**, 1038 S Hill St, downtown (☎213/746-4287). Latin, fusion and salsa. Get past the doorman and you're in with LA's coolest, eager to shake a leg in gorgeous and historic surrounds. Open Fri and Sat; $12. Dress to impress.

## LESBIAN AND GAY LA

Although proportionately not as big as that of San Francisco, the **gay scene** in LA is far from invisible, and gay people are prominent right across the city. West Hollywood has a gay-led council and has become synonymous with the (affluent white) gay lifestyle, not just in LA but all over California. The other overtly gay community is Silverlake, most evidently along Hyperion Boulevard. We've listed gay accommodation, restaurants, bars and clubs in the relevant listings sections.

The city's best known gay and lesbian **bookshop** is A Different Light, 8853 Santa Monica Blvd (☎310/854-6601). Magazines with good **listings** sections include *Compass*, *Dispatch*, *Edge* and *Lesbian News*. The *Gay Community Yellow Pages* (☎323/469-4454) is a comprehensive annual directory ($5) of gay businesses, publications, services and gathering places; it also publishes a gay restaurant guide. **The Gay and Lesbian Community Services Center**, 1625 N Schrader Blvd (☎323/993-7400), is the community's prime resource for counseling, health testing and information.

**Union**, 8210 Sunset Blvd, West Hollywood (☎323/654-1001). Relaxed supper club with funk, soul and R&B groove room. Frequented by the young actor crowd on Tues nights.

**The Viper Room**, 8852 Sunset Blvd, West Hollywood (☎310/358-1881). Stellar live acts and a famous owner. Best known as the spot where River Phoenix met his end. Cover varies.

### Gay and lesbian bars and clubs

**Arena**, 6655 Santa Monica Blvd, Hollywood (☎323/462-0714). Many clubs under one huge roof, large dance floors throbbing to funk, Latin and hi-NRG grooves. Also called *Circus*, it's mostly men at the Pink Feather on Tues; gay men and women on Fri. Cover $8–12.

**Detour**, 1087 Manzanita, Silverlake (☎323/664-1189). A friendly and quite inexpensive denim and leather bar.

**Jewel's Catch One**, 4067 W Pico Blvd, Mid-Wilshire (☎323/734-8849). Sweaty dance barn, packed with gay men on Wed, women on Thurs.

**The Palms**, 8572 Santa Monica Blvd, Hollywood (☎310/652-6188). Mostly house and dance nights at West Hollywood's longest-established lesbian bar.

**Rage**, 8911 Santa Monica Blvd, West Hollywood (☎310/652-7055). Very flash gay men's club playing the latest hi-NRG hits. Drinks are inexpensive, the cover varies. Great Forties tea dance on Sun (no cover).

**Rudolpho's**, 2500 Riverside Drive, Silverlake (☎323/662-4021). Every second Sat of the month the "dress up, drag down" dance club, Drag Strip 66, has a different theme. Dressed $10, out of drag $20.

**7969**, 7969 Santa Monica Blvd, Hollywood (☎323/654-0280). West Hollywood's longest running gay and lesbian disco with drag shows, New Wave, techno and disco and more. Cover $6–10.

### Live music

LA has a near-overwhelming choice if you're looking for **live music**. Ever since the nihilistic punk bands – Circle Jerks, X, Black Flag – drew the city away from its cocaine-sozzled laid-back West Coast image in the late Seventies and early Eighties, LA's **rock music** scene has been excellent. **Country music** is also fairly prevalent, at least away from trendy Hollywood, and the valleys are hotbeds of country-folk and newly resurgent swing. **Jazz**, too, is played in a few genuinely authentic downbeat dives, though more commonly found being used to improve the atmosphere of a restaurant. **Reggae**, though popular with many, is much less common. **Salsa** is pervasive among LA's Hispanic population, and is found mostly in the bars of East LA; it's worth saying that (aside from the places we've listed) these are very male-oriented, and female visitors may well feel out of place.

**Anti-club**, 4658 Melrose Ave, Mid-Wilshire (☎323/661-3913). Located in one of the truly abysmal corners of the city sprawl, this is the other end of the world from upmarket Melrose, with inexpensive beer and an adventurous booking policy.

**The Baked Potato**, 3787 Cahuenga Blvd, North Hollywood (☎818/980-1615). A small but near-legendary contemporary jazz spot, where many reputations have been forged; $8, or $5 Thurs.

**Bar Deluxe**, 1710 N Las Palmas, Mid-Wilshire (☎323/469-1991). Bare-bones crimson-lit atmosphere, and a suspended 125-gallon aquarium. Sake and beer served to the beat of live rockabilly.

**B B King's Blues Club**, 1000 Universal Center Drive, Universal City (☎818/6-BBKING). Once past the garish exterior of Universal's CityWalk, it's all catfish, deep-fried pickle and Southern hospitality. *Lucille's* features acoustic blues at the weekend. Full bar, no age limit, low cover.

**The Conga Room**, 5364 Wilshire Blvd (☎323/938-1696). A high-profile celebrity investment results in a surprisingly appealing feast of Cuban food and Latin music. Cover varies.

**The Derby**, 4500 Los Feliz Blvd, Los Feliz (☎323/663-8979). Not the original hat-shaped bar on Wilshire, but a throwback to its 1940s heyday. Retro jazz, rockabilly and bebop, with dance lessons to get you up to speed. Drinks are club-pricey, but the circular bar, domed wooden ceiling and swing are hard to resist. Open nightly, music starts at 9pm; $5, free Tues.

**Doug Weston's Troubadour**, 9081 Santa Monica Blvd, West Hollywood (☎310/276-6168). Less heavy metal than of old, but still the club for the heaviest riffs and shaggiest manes. $6–15.

**The Foothill Club**, 1922 Cherry Ave, Signal Hill (☎562/984-8349). A glorious country dance hall from the days when hillbilly was cool. Punk, surf and roots-rock Thurs to Sat. Cover varies.

**Golden Sails Hotel**, 6285 E Pacific Coast Hwy, Long Beach (☎562/596-1631). Has some of the best reggae bands from LA and beyond on Fri and Sat. $8.

**House of Blues**, 8430 Sunset Blvd, West Hollywood (☎323/848-5100). Incongruous mock sugar shack, with excellent but pricey live music nightly. Good local-name hip-hop, R&B and blues. Very popular with tourists.

**Kingston 12**, 814 Broadway, Santa Monica (☎310/451-4423). Nightly reggae; nice and small. $10–15.

**Largo**, 432 N Fairfax Ave, Mid-Wilshire (☎323/852-1073). Intimate cabaret venue with some of LA's more interesting bands. 18 and over. Cover varies.

**Luminarias**, 3500 Ramona Blvd, Monterey Park, East LA (☎323/268-4177). A hilltop restaurant where the live salsa is reckoned to be as good as the Mexican food. Fri and Sat; $5.

**McCabe's**, 3103 W Pico Blvd, Santa Monica (☎310/828-4497). The back room of LA's premier acoustic guitar shop; long the scene of excellent and unusual folk and country shows. $10–20.

**Opium Den**, 1605 1/2 N Ivar Ave, Hollywood (☎323/466-7800). A strip club turned nightclub with an array of upcoming rock and punk acts taking turn on the overly small stage.

**The Palomino**, 6907 Lankershim Blvd, North Hollywood (☎818/764-4010). Firmly established as the best place to catch visiting C&W singers, also good for R&B and the odd goth gig. $10. Thurs is talent night.

**The Roxy**, 9009 Sunset Blvd, West Hollywood (☎310/276-2222). The showcase of the rock industry's new signings, intimate and with a great sound system. Cover varies.

**Whisky-a-Go-Go**, 8901 Sunset Blvd, West Hollywood (☎310/535-0579). Recently done up after many years as LA's most famous rock 'n' roll club, nowadays mainly hard rock. $10–20.

## Classical music, opera and dance

Considering its size and stature in the other arts, LA has very few outlets for **classical music**. The **Los Angeles Philharmonic** (☎213/850-2000), the city's only major name, performs regularly during the year, and the **Los Angeles Chamber Orchestra** (☎213/622-7001) appears at assorted venues. San Francisco has more of an opera scene (see p.999), although LA's **Music Center Opera** (☎213/972-7211) stages productions between September and June, as does Orange County's **Opera Pacific** (☎949/474-4488, based in distant Irvine), which performs both grand opera and operettas. Prices range from $10 to $120.

The last twenty years or so have seen an increase in **dance** activity in LA, with major ballet companies like the **Joffrey Ballet** (☎213/563-3739) relocating on the West Coast

## A CALENDAR OF LA'S FESTIVALS

**January**

**1** Tournament of Roses in Pasadena. A parade of floral floats and marching bands along Colorado Boulevard.

**February**

**First full moon after 21st** Chinese New Year. Three days of dragon-float street parades, based in Chinatown.

**March**

**17** St Patrick's Day. Related events all over the city, with some bars serving green beer.

**End** The Academy Awards are presented at the Shrine Auditorium or Dorothy Chandler Pavilion; legendary citywide parties ensue.

**April**

**Early** The Blessing of the Animals. A long-established Mexican-originated cere- mony thanking animals for their services to humans. Pets are blessed in Olvera Street, followed by a parade.

**May**

**5** Cinco de Mayo. Day-long commemora- tion of the Mexican victory at the battle of Puebla. With several blocks closed to downtown traffic, the celebration features a spirited parade in Olvera Street and cel- ebrations with Mexican food, drink and music in most LA parks.

**June**

**Late** Gay Pride. Parade on Santa Monica Boulevard in West Hollywood. Carnival atmosphere and an all-male drag football cheer team. Other events in various parts of the city.

**July**

**Independence Day (4th)** *The Queen Mary* in Long Beach hosts a particularly

large fireworks display, as well as colorful entertainment.

**August**

**First two weeks** Culmination of the South Bay's International Surf Festival, where globally famed surfers compete amid crowds of tourists and beach volley- ball players.

**September**

**4** LA's birthday. A civic ceremony and assorted street entertainment around El Pueblo de Los Angeles to mark the founding of the original pueblo in 1781.

**Last two weeks** LA County Fair in dis- tant Pomona, in the San Gabriel Valley. The country's biggest; livestock shows, eating contests and fairground rides.

**October**

**Second weekend** LA Street Scene. Free rock music, fringe theater and comedy on the streets of downtown. Usually running at the same time is the West Hollywood Street Festival, a display of handmade arts and crafts and a general slap on the back for LA's newest constituent city, founded in 1984.

**Middle** Watts Jazz Festival. Two days of free music with the Watts Towers as a backdrop.

**November**

**End** Hollywood Christmas Parade. The first and best of the many Yuletide events, with a cavalcade of mind-boggling floats.

**December**

**13th** Christmas Boat Parade. A flotilla of yachts and powerboats gets decorated in bright holiday lights and cruises around Marina del Rey.

after making their name in New York, accompanied by the growth of a number of small modern ensembles and regular visits by international companies.

**The Dorothy Chandler Pavilion**, in the Music Center, 135 N Grand Ave, downtown (☎323/972-7211 or 972-7460). Home to the LA Philharmonic from Oct until May. Also used by the Joffrey Ballet, the Music Center Opera and other top names.

**The Hollywood Bowl**, 2301 N Highland Ave, Hollywood (☎323/850-2000). The LA Philharmonic gives open-air concerts Tues–Sat evenings from July to Sept.

**Japan America Theatre**, 244 S San Pedro St, downtown (☎323/680-3700). Dance and performance works drawn from Japan and the Far East.

**John Anson Ford Theater**, 2850 Cahuenga Blvd (☎323/461-3673). As well as the summer "Dance Kaleidoscope," this open-air venue also has one-off productions by local groups.

**Orange County Performing Arts Center**, 600 Town Center Drive, Costa Mesa (☎714/556-ARTS). Home of the Pacific Symphony Orchestra.

**The Pacific Amphitheater**, 100 Fair Drive, Costa Mesa (☎310/740-2000). A big open-air venue, Orange County's answer to the Hollywood Bowl.

**Royce Hall**, on the UCLA campus (☎310/825-9261 or 825-2101). Classical concerts throughout the college year, often involving big names.

**The Shrine Auditorium**, 665 W Jefferson Blvd (☎213/749-5123), box office at 655 S Hill St (☎213/749-5123). A distinctive building that hosts regular performances by choral gospel groups and alternate Academy Awards ceremonies.

**UCLA Center for the Performing Arts** (☎310/825-4401). Coordinates a wide range of touring companies, and also runs the experimentally inclined "Art of Dance" series between Sept and May.

## Comedy clubs
Although the **comedy** scene in LA is pretty much what you'd get elsewhere in the US, it's a good place to catch live performances by established television names like Jay Leno and Drew Carey.

**Comedy & Magic Club**, 1018 Hermosa Ave, Hermosa Beach (☎310/372-1193). Strange couplings of naff magic acts and good-quality comedians.

**The Comedy Store**, 8433 W Sunset Blvd (☎323/656-6225). Popular comedy showcase spread over three rooms; you can usually turn up on spec at weekends. Always a good line-up, too.

**Groundlings Theater**, 7307 Melrose Ave (☎323/934-9700). Only the gifted survive at this pioneering improvisation venue.

**The Ice House**, 24 N Mentor Ave, Pasadena (☎626/577-1895). The comedy mainstay of the valley, very established and fairly safe.

**The Improvisation**, 8162 Melrose Ave (☎323/651-2583). Prime destination for out-of-town comedy-lovers – so book ahead.

**LA Connection**, 13442 Ventura Blvd, Sherman Oaks (☎818/784-1868). An improvisation showcase for highly rated obnoxiousness specialists. Seldom less than memorable.

## Theater
We've listed a few selections from LA's very active (and very changeable) **theater** scene; Theatrix (☎323/466-1767) handles reservations and provides details on what's playing at several of the smaller venues. The *LA Weekly* and the *LA Times* "Calendar" section both have full listings and reviews.

**Coronet Theater**, 368 N La Cienega Blvd (☎310/657-7377). Home of the LA Public Theater; productions include the odd famous name. Also home to the Youth Academy of Dramatic Arts.

**Geffen Playhouse**, 10886 Le Conte Ave, Westwood (☎310/208-5454). Small theater across from UCLA with frequent one-person shows.

**Mark Taper Forum**, 135 N Grand Ave, downtown (☎323/972-0700). Theater in the three-quarter round, frequently putting on innovative new plays.

**Powerhouse Theater**, 3116 2nd St, Santa Monica (☎310/396-3680). Experimental shows.

**Shubert Theater**, 2020 Avenue of the Stars, Century City (☎1-800/447-7400). The only good thing about Century City is that you can come here to ogle the razzmatazz musicals.

## Film
Many major feature films are released in LA months (or years) before they play anywhere else in the world. Short seasons of **foreign-language films** are often screened

at the eight Laemmle Theaters. If you're after a golden-years-of-film **atmosphere**, head for one of the historic downtown movie palaces along Broadway, where the delirious furnishings may hold your attention longer than the all-action triple bills. Otherwise, catch **new releases** in one of the many mall-based multiplexes, like the Beverly Center Cineplex (☎310/652-7760), the AMC Century 14 (☎310/553-8900), or the eighteen-screen Universal City complex (☎818/508-0588).

**Bing Theater**, at the LA County Art Museum, 5905 Wilshire Blvd (☎323/857-6010). Afternoon screenings of many neglected Hollywood classics. Matinees cost just $2, evening shows $7.

**Chinese Theatre**, 6925 Hollywood Blvd (☎323/464-8186). Landmark Art Deco cinema. Giant screen and six-track stereo sound make this absolutely the best place to see a big-budget flick, egged on, on opening weekends, by a cheering and whistling crowd.

**Egyptian Theater**, 6712 Hollywood Blvd (☎323/466-FILM). Newly reopened showcase for classic and foreign films, in the middle of Old Hollywood.

**El Capitan Theater**, Hollywood Blvd at Highland Ave (☎323/467-7674). Another legendary Hollywood venue, restored to full glory and recently renovated for a second time.

**New Beverly Cinema**, 7165 Beverly Blvd (☎323/938-4038). Imaginative cult double bills.

**Nuart Theater**, 11272 Santa Monica Blvd (☎310/478-6379). Rare classics, foreign films and documentaries. Be prepared for a lengthy line outside.

**Silent Movie**, 611 N Fairfax Ave (☎323/655-2520). As its name suggests, silent Chaplin, Laurel and Hardy, Ramon Navarro thrillers and so on. Every show accompanied by an organist.

# Shopping

You can buy virtually anything, anywhere, anytime in LA. The big **department stores** or the thoroughly exclusive **Rodeo Drive** (see p.934) will have it if the ubiquitous run-of-the-mill retailers don't, and if all else fails try LA's massive **malls**, which often resemble self-contained city suburbs as much as shopping precincts. The newish **CityWalk** mall at Universal Studios distills a dozen LA neighborhoods into cutout facades fronting all the national chain stores, complete with a sandy beach – safe shopping for the 1990s. At the central seven-acre **Beverly Center**, bordered by Beverly and La Cienega boulevards, San Vicente Boulevard and Third Street, you'll find designer stores, fourteen cinemas and ample opportunities for star-spotting. West Hollywood, and Melrose Avenue in particular, hold many of the city's trendier boutiques, but if you're after a first edition of Shirley MacLaine's autobiography, old movies stills or a *Buffalo Springfield* album in mint condition, try one of the places listed overleaf.

## Books

**Acres of Books**, 240 Long Beach Blvd, Long Beach (☎562/437-6980). LA's largest, and most disorganized, secondhand collection – well worth a trip down the Blue Line.

**Bodhi Tree**, 8585 Melrose Ave (☎310/659-1733). New and used New Age, occult and Philip K Dick books, in a garden setting along an exclusive section of Melrose.

**Either/Or**, 950 Aviation Blvd, Hermosa Beach (☎310/374-2060). Known for its fiction and New Age sections. Open until 11pm nightly.

**Hennessey and Ingalls**, 1254 3rd St Promenade, Santa Monica (☎310/458-9074). An impressive range of hard-to-find art and architecture books, plus rare posters and catalogs.

**Koma Books**, 1764 N Vermont Ave (☎323/665-0956). Mayhem, true crime, fanzines and neuropolitics; everything the others are too shocked to sell. A small shop with a large mail-order clientele, favored by tabloid TV researchers. Now publishing its own authors.

**Larry Edmunds Book Shop**, 6644 Hollywood Blvd (☎323/463-3273). Stacks of books on every aspect of film and theater, plus movie stills and posters.

**Midnight Special**, 1318 3rd St Promenade, Santa Monica (☎310/393-2923). Excellent for politics and social sciences; open late.

**Norton Simon Museum Bookstore**, 411 W Colorado Blvd, Pasadena (☎626/449-6840). Very inexpensive prices for art books, given the spendy LA market. Good selection, too.

**Sisterhood Bookstore**, 1351 Westwood Blvd (☎310/477-7300). Westside landmark. Music, cards, jewelry and of course books, pertaining to the national and international women's movement.

## Records

**Aron's Records**, 1150 N Highland Ave (☎323/469-4700). The best place in LA for secondhand discs – huge stock, all styles, all prices.

**Moby Disc**, 28 E Colorado Blvd, Pasadena (☎818/449-9975). Secondhand and deletions.

**Music and Memories**, 5057 Lankershim, North Hollywood (☎818/761-9827). 300 Sinatra LPs and 30,000 records that sound like he should be on them.

**Poo-Bah Records**, 1101 E Walnut Ave, Pasadena (☎626/449-3359). American and imported New Wave.

**Rhino Records**, 1720 Westwood Blvd (☎310/474-8685). The biggest selection of international independent releases.

**Vinyl Fetish**, 7305 Melrose Ave (☎323/935-1300). Besides the punk and post-punk merchandise, a good place to discover what's new on the LA music scene and purchase a cheesy Gen-X T-shirt or two.

# THE DESERTS

The **deserts** of Southern California occupy a quarter of the state. Untouched but for the three million acres used for military bases, this hot and often inhospitable wilderness exerts a powerful fascination. There are two distinct regions: the **Colorado** or **Low Desert** in the south, which is the most easily reached from LA, containing the opulent artificial oasis of **Palm Springs** and the primeval expanse of **Joshua Tree**; and the **Mojave** or **High Desert**, dominated by **Death Valley** and stretching along Hwy-395 up the sparsely populated **Owens Valley**.

It is impossible to do any justice to this area without your own wheels. Palm Springs can be reached on public transportation, but only the periphery of Joshua Tree is accessible and it's a long hot walk to anywhere very interesting. You can get as far as Barstow on Greyhound and Amtrak, but no transportation traverses Death Valley, leaving only the Owens Valley with its daily Greyhound service between LA and Reno.

# The Low Desert

Most visitors to the Low Desert have no intention of getting away from it all. They head straight for where it's at – the irrefutable capital of the desert, **Palm Springs**. In these few square miles, overrun with the famous and the star-struck, the average age and average temperature are said to be about the same – a steady 88. Still, it's got a gorgeous setting and you'll find it hard to avoid: it's the first stopping point east from LA on I-10, at the centre of the **Coachella Valley**, part of the most intensively productive agricultural area in the world, growing dates, oranges, lemons and grapefruits in vast quantities.

The sublime landscape of **Joshua Tree National Park**, well worth a weekend spent taking in the sunsets and the howl of coyotes at twilight, lies one hour's drive east of Palm Springs, three and a half from LA.

## Palm Springs

Sitting in lush farming land, replete with manicured golf courses, condominiums and millionaires, **PALM SPRINGS** does not conform to any typical image of the desert. The massive bulk of Mount San Jacinto looms over its low-slung buildings, casting an instantaneous and welcome shadow over the town in the late afternoon. Ever since Hollywood stars first came here in the 1930s, the clean dry air and sunshine, just 120 miles east of LA, have made Palm Springs irresistible. For years, high-school kids arrived in their thousands for the drunken revelry of Spring Break, until civic zeal ran them out of town, while others come specifically to sober up: the **Betty Ford Center** in nearby Rancho Mirage draws a star-studded patient list to its booze- and drug-free environment, attempting to undo a lifetime's behavioral disorders in a $11,000 28-day stay. The town is also regarded as the country's largest **gay** resort.

Palm Springs wasn't always like this. Once it was the domain of the **Cahuillan Indians**; they were allocated this land in the 1890s, but exact zoning wasn't settled until the 1940s, by which time the development of hotels and leisure complexes was well under way. Under an odd checkerboard system, every other square mile of Palm Springs forms part of the **Agua Caliente Indian Reservation**, and high rents have made this the second richest tribe in America, worth more than $2 billion, wealth that's been increasing with the new Casino Morongo, right in the heart of town.

### Arrival, information and getting around

Arriving by **car**, you drive into town on N Palm Canyon Drive, passing the **visitor center** at no. 2781 (daily 9am–5pm; ☎(1-800/34-SPRINGS). Greyhound **buses** (nine daily from LA) come in at 311 N Indian Canyon Drive. **Trains** from LA (three per week) stop just south of I-10 at N Indian Avenue, about ten minutes from downtown. Sun Buses (4am–10pm; ☎760/343-3451), circulate all the local resort towns.

Companies such as Palm Springs Celebrity Tours, 4751 E Palm Canyon Drive (☎760/770-2700), offer **celebrity tours** from $12. You could do it yourself, with a map of the stars' homes from the visitor center – but you'd miss out on the sharp anecdotal commentary.

### Accommodation

Luxury **hotels** outnumber the affordable variety in Palm Springs, but prices drop by as much as seventy percent as temperatures rise in summer. The north end of town, along Hwy-111, holds many of the lower-priced places, virtually all of which have pools. The prices below are **summer rates**.

**Bee Charmer Inn**, 1600 E Palm Canyon Drive (☎760/778-5883). Lesbian motel a mile or so south of downtown, offering continental breakfast, pool, and mini-fridges and microwaves in the room. ④–⑤.

**Casa Cody**, 175 S Cahuilla Rd (☎760/320-9346 or 1-800/231-2639). Attractive, well-located Southwestern-style B&B in a shady garden. ③–⑥.

**Desert Lodge**, 1177 S Palm Canyon Drive (☎760/325-1356 or 1-800/385-6343). Spacious motel-style place with free continental breakfast and in-room movies. Closed July and Aug. ③/④.

**Hampton Inn**, 2000 N Palm Canyon Drive (☎760/320-0555). Has a beautiful outdoor pool, a must-have in the desert, plus free continental breakfast and comfortable rooms. ③/④.

**Ingleside Inn**, 200 W Ramon Rd (☎760/325-0046 or 1-800/772-6655). Expensive downtown option, but one with real class – as evidenced by a guest list including Dalí, Garbo and Brando. Many rooms have antiques, fireplaces, whirlpool tubs and patios. A Palm Springs historic building. ⑤–⑨.

**Mira Loma**, 1420 N Indian Canyon Drive (☎760/320-1178). Small, welcoming place with well-appointed rooms around a central pool. In 1949 Marilyn Monroe stayed in Room Three. ②.

**Vagabond Inn**, 1699 S Palm Canyon Drive (☎760/325-7211). Clean, small rooms in a centrally located, comfortable motel. Coffee in the room, refrigerators available. ②.

## Downtown Palm Springs

**Downtown Palm Springs** stretches for half a mile along **Palm Canyon Drive**, a wide, bright and modern strip of boutiques that's engulfed the town's original Spanish village-style structures. Shops run the gamut from Saks Fifth Avenue to tacky T-shirt emporia and bookstores devoted exclusively to Hollywood stars.

The luxuriously housed **Desert Museum**, 101 Museum Drive (Tues–Sat 10am–5pm, Sun noon–5pm; end of July through the end of September, Fri–Sun only, 10am–5pm; $7.50), is strong on Native American and Southwestern art, though its only permanent display is the late actor William Holden's collection of Asian and African works. Some interesting natural science exhibits focus on the animal and plant life of the desert, demonstrating that it's not all sandstorms and rattlesnakes. There is a modern art gallery and some lovely sculpture courts on the museum grounds and the museum hosts performances in the 450-seat Annenberg Theater. The major cultural center in the desert is the McCallum Theater, at 73-000 Fred Waring Drive, Palm Desert, presenting films, live music, opera, ballet and plays (☎760/340-2787). There's an anarchic piece of landscape gardening at **Moorten's Botanical Gardens**, 1701 S Palm Canyon Drive (Mon–Sat 9am–4.30pm, Sun 10am–4pm; $2), a bizarre cornucopia of every desert plant and cactus, in settings designed to simulate their natural environments.

## Around Palm Springs

Most visitors to Palm Springs never leave the poolside, but desert enthusiasts still visit to **hike** and **ride** in the **Indian Canyons** (fall & winter daily 8am–5pm; spring & summer daily 8am–6pm; $5), three miles southeast of downtown along S Palm Canyon Drive. Centuries ago, ancestors of the Cahuilla developed extensive communities here, growing melons, squash, beans and corn. The canyons are about fifteen miles long, and can be toured by car, although it's worth walking at least a few miles; the easiest trails lead past the waterfalls, rocky gorges and palm trees of **Palm Canyon** and **Andreas Canyon**. Some areas are set aside for the specific lunacy of **trailblazing** in jeeps and four-wheel-drives; rent a vehicle from Off-Road Rentals, four miles north of town at 59-755 Hwy-111 (around $30 per hour; Sept–June only; ☎760/325-0376), or take a guided jeep adventure around the Santa Rosa Mountains with Desert Adventures, 67-555 E Palm Canyon Drive, Cathedral City (☎760/324-JEEP; around $70 for 2hr).

If the desert heat becomes too much to bear, large cable cars grind and sway over eight thousand feet up the **Palm Springs Aerial Tramway**, Tramway Road, just off

Hwy-111 north of Palm Springs (Mon–Fri 10am–8pm, Sat–Sun 8am–8pm; ☎760/325-1391; $18), passing through five climatic zones on the way to the top of Mount San Jacinto, where there's a **bar** and **restaurant** at the Mountain Station.

## Eating and Drinking
The stifling desert heat suppresses even the healthiest of appetites; most people go all day on nothing, to find themselves suddenly ravenous at dusk. Although most of the more famous **restaurants** in Palm Springs are ultra-expensive, more reasonable options can be found with a little effort; alternatively, head to gay-oriented **Cathedral City** ("Cat City"), five miles east along Hwy-111.

**El Gallito Cafe**, 68820 Grove St, Cathedral City (☎760/328-7794). Busy Mexican cantina that has the best food for miles and often a wait to match – get there around 6pm to avoid the crowds. Closed in Aug.

**Le Vallauris**, 385 W Tahquitz Way, next to Desert Museum (☎760/325-5059 – reservations only). Excellent Californian/French/Italian food, though the price is around $80 per head. You're likely to run into one or two once-renowned stars.

**Mykonos**, 139 E Andreas Rd (☎619/322-0223). A family-run Greek joint downtown offering large portions of simple, excellent food.

**Shame on the Moon**, 69-950 Frank Sinatra Drive, Rancho Mirage (☎760/324-5515). Pasta, seafoods and meats, on a mid-priced menu in a contemporary setting. Excellent service.

**Thai Smile**, 651 N Palm Canyon Drive (☎760/320-5503). Uninspiring decor but great, authentic Thai food at very reasonable prices. Open daily.

# Joshua Tree National Park

In a unique transitional area, where the lower Colorado Desert meets the high Mojave northeast of Palm Springs, **JOSHUA TREE NATIONAL PARK** protects 986 square miles of grotesquely gnarled and ragged trees. The trees can reach up to forty feet in height, but they have to contend with extreme aridity and rocky soil, and the strain of their struggle to survive is evident. All around lie great heaps of boulders, pushed up by the Pinto Mountain fault, their edges rounded and smoothed by flash floods and winds.

This unearthly landscape is ethereal at sunrise or sunset, when the desert floor is bathed in red light; at noon it can be a threatening furnace. The name "Joshua Tree" was given by Mormons in the 1850s, who saw the craggy branches of the trees as the arms of Joshua leading them to the promised land. Nowadays, Joshua Tree is appreciated by campers, daytrippers and rockclimbers for its unspoiled beauty, gold mine ruins, ancient petroglyphs and incredible rock formations.

Be selective in your explorations. As with any desert area, the heat can be punishing and, for a good part of the year, an ambitious schedule is impossible. Brief yourself at the visitor centers, and never venture anywhere without a map. On unmarked roads restricted to four-wheel-drive vehicles, don't think about taking a normal car – you'll soon grind to a halt, and it could be quite a few panic-stricken hours before anybody finds you. When hiking, **stick to the trails**. Joshua Tree is full of abandoned gold mines: watch for loose gravel around openings, stay away from the edges, never trust the safety of ladders or timber, and bear in mind that the rangers rarely check mines for casualties. Even on the simpler trails, allow around an hour per mile.

One of the easiest hiking routes leads one and a half miles from Canyon Road, six miles from the visitor center at Twentynine Palms, to **Fortynine Palms Oasis** (2–3hr). To the west of the oasis, quartz boulders tower around the *Indian Cove* campground; a trail from the eastern branch of the campground road heads to **Rattlesnake Canyon**, where, after rainfall, the streams and waterfalls break an otherwise eerie silence among the monoliths.

Moving south into the main body of the park, follow the trails through **Hidden Valley** (1hr), where cattle rustlers used to hide out; and to the rain-fed **Barker Dam** to the east (1hr): Joshua Tree's crucial water supply, built by cattlemen c.1900. One negotiable trail climbs past abandoned mining sites, where some buildings and equipment are still intact, to **Lost Horse Mine** (3hr), 450ft up – which once produced an average of $20,000 worth of gold a week.

A brilliant desert panorama of badlands and mountains is to be had from the 5185ft **Key's View** nearby, from where Geology Tour Road leads down to the east through the best of Joshua Tree's **rock formations**.

### Practicalities

Hwy-62 from Palm Springs leads to the West Entrance, near the town of Joshua Tree, and the North Entrance, close to the **Oasis Visitor Center**, 74485 National Park Drive (daily 8am–5pm, ☎760/367-5500) at Twentynine Palms. There's another entrance and visitor center at **COTTONWOOD**, seven miles north of I-10 (daily 8am–4pm).

The park has nine established **campgrounds**, all in the northwest except for one at Cottonwood. Only two have water – *Black Rock Canyon* ($10) and *Cottonwood* ($8) – and except for *Indian Cove* ($10) all the others are free. You can reserve sites at *Black Rock* and *Indian Cove* by calling Destinet (☎1-800/365-2267); the rest are operated on a first-come, first-served basis. Come prepared – gathering firewood is not allowed, and you should stock up on water. There are good **motels** – and decent restaurants – in **TWENTYNINE PALMS**, just two minutes' drive from the park: the best is the historic *Twentynine Palms Inn*, 73950 Inn Ave (☎760/367-3505; ④–⑤). You can grab a snack at *The Finicky Coyote*, 73511 Twentynine Palms Hwy (760/367-2429). Morongo Basin Transit Authority **buses** (☎760/367-7433 or 1-800/794-6282) run from Palm Springs to Twentynine Palms, but not into the park.

# The High Desert

The stretches of the **Mojave Desert** that most people tend to see from the road conform to the stereotype of the earth's arid regions – barren, lifeless and desolate. Consequently, visitors tend to zip through, not inspired to explore further. However, because much of this area is High Desert – that is, it lies at an elevation of at least 2,000ft – it also offers some of the most dramatic scenery in the southern part of the state, rolling with lush grasses, startling volcanic formations, large stands of Joshua trees, and even, in some spots, piñon pines.

### Barstow

**BARSTOW**, the one stopoff along the dusty, endless I-15 – served by both Greyhound and Amtrak – is a lackluster small town. During the hottest season it seems perpetually empty; everyone hides in their air-conditioned homes. The one main road, formerly Route 66, is lined with **motels** – such as the *Budget 8 Motel*, 1271 E Main St (☎760/256-2204; ③) – and **restaurants**, like *Carlos and Toto's*, at 901 W Main St (☎760/256-7513). At the junction of Barstow Road and I-15, the **Barstow Chamber of Commerce** at 409 E Fredricks (daily 9am–5pm; ☎760/256-8617) has a good selection of maps, lodging and restaurant guides. You can **camp** ($18) in shaded canyons at the contrived **Calico Ghost Town** (daily 8am–dusk; $6), ten miles north along I-15.

## Death Valley National Park

**DEATH VALLEY** is utterly inhuman: the hottest place on earth and almost entirely devoid of shade, much less water – carry plenty for both car and body. Its sculpted rock layers form deeply shadowed, eroded crevices at the foot of sharply silhouetted hills, their exotic mineral content turning million-year-old mudflats into rainbows of sunlit phosphorescence. It was named by a party of white settlers who stumbled through in 1849, looking for a short cut to the Gold Rush towns; they survived despite running out of food and water.

Throughout the summer, the air temperature in Death Valley averages 112°F, and the ground can reach near boiling point. Better to come during the spring, when the wild flowers are in bloom, or from October to May, when it's generally mild and dry.

The central north–south valley for which the park is named contains its two main outposts: **Stovepipe Wells** and **Furnace Creek**, where the **visitor center** (daily 8am–6pm; ☎760/786-2331; *www.nps.gov/deva*) is located. A $10 entrance fee (valid for seven days) is payable at the **park entrance ranger stations**, close to the park boundaries, which provide free maps and information on tours and activities.

Many of the most unusual sights are located south of Furnace Creek. A good first stop, seven miles along Hwy-178/Badwater Road, is the **Artist's Palette**, an eroded hillside covered in an intensely colored mosaic of reds, golds, blacks and greens. Ten miles further south, **Badwater** is an unpalatable but non-poisonous 30ft wide pool of water, loaded with chloride and sulphates, that's the only home of the soft-bodied Death Valley snail. A four-mile hike across the hot valley floor drops a further two feet down to the **lowest point in the western hemisphere**, 282ft below sea level.

**Zabriskie Point**, overlooking Badwater and the Artist's Palette off Hwy-190, four miles south of Furnace Creek, was the inspiration for Antonioni's eponymous 1960s film. The view is best during the early morning, when the pink-and-gold Panamint Mountains across the valley are highlighted by the rising sun.

Near Stovepipe Wells, some thirty miles northwest of Furnace Creek, spread fifteen rippled and contoured square miles of ever-changing **sand dunes**. A ten-mile dirt road west of the campground leads to sheer black-walled **Marble Canyon**, scratched with mysterious ancient petroglyphs.

Hordes of overheated tourists wait patiently to wander through the surreal luxury of **Scotty's Castle**, forty miles north of Stovepipe Wells. It was built in the 1920s as the desert retreat of Chicago insurance broker Albert Johnson, but named after "Death Valley" Scotty, who managed the construction and claimed the house was his own, financed by a hidden gold mine. **Tours** (daily on the hour 9am–5pm; $8) take in the ornate wooden ceilings, indoor waterfalls and a remote-controlled player piano. The house remains as it was when Johnson died in 1948. Scotty himself lived here until 1954, and is buried just behind the house.

Eight miles west gapes the half-mile-wide **Ubehebe Crater**, the rust-tinged result of a massive volcanic explosion; half a mile south sits its thousand-year-old younger brother, **Little Hebe**. Beyond the craters the road continues south for another twenty dusty miles to **Racetrack Valley**, a two-and-a-half-mile mudflat across which giant boulders seem slowly to be racing, leaving faint trails in their wake.

## Practicalities

Death Valley is a long way from anywhere and has no scheduled public transportation. If you plan to **stay**, you must reserve ahead. Amfac (☎1-800/236-79167 or 760/786-2345; *www.furnacecreekresort.com*) operates two overpriced hotels on natural oases at Furnace Creek – the plush *Furnace Creek Inn* (⑦), and the very ordinary *Furnace Creek Ranch* (⑤), about half a mile north, which has two **restaurants** and a nice bar. Far more reasonable is *Stovepipe Wells Motel* (☎760/786-2387, fax 786-2389; ③) on Hwy-190 about thirty miles northwest of Furnace Creek. **Camping** in one of the many National Park Service campgrounds costs $6–16 depending on facilities and location, or is free if you don't mind being up in the Panamint Range, far from the valley's sights: the only campground to take reservations is *Furnace Creek* (☎1-800/365-2267).

# The High Sierra and the Owens Valley

The towering **eastern** peaks of the **High Sierra** drop abruptly to the empty landscape of the **Owens Valley**, sixty miles west of Death Valley. Almost the entire range is wilderness: well-maintained roads lead to trailheads at over ten thousand feet, providing access to the stark terrain of spires, glaciers and clear mountain lakes. US-395 is the lifeline of the area, traveled daily by Greyhound and with plenty of budget motels. There are always shuttle services available to the trailheads.

## Mount Whitney and Lone Pine

Rising out of the northern Mojave Desert, the Sierra Nevada Mountains announce themselves with a bang two hundred miles north of Los Angeles at 14,494ft **Mount Whitney**, the highest point in the lower 48 states. A silver-gray ridge of pinnacles forms a nearly sheer wall of granite, dominating the small roadside town of **LONE PINE** eleven thousand feet below. **Motels** here include the *Dow Villa Motel/Historic Dow Hotel* at 310 S Main St (☎1-800/824-9317 or 760/876-5521; ②), where John Wayne always stayed when filming in the area, and the *Best Western Frontier Motel*, 1008 S Main St (☎760/876-5571 or 1-800/528-1234; ③). You can **camp** at *Tuttle Creek* campground (free; no water) on Horseshoe Meadow Road some four miles west of town beyond the Alabama Hills (see below). The *Pizza Factory*, 301 S Main St (☎760/876-4707), and the diner-style *Mt Whitney Restaurant*, 227 S Main St (☎760/876-5751), are decent places to **eat**. The **Eastern Sierra Interagency Visitor Center**, a mile south of town on US-395 at the junction of Hwy-136 (daily: June–Aug 8am–6.50pm; Sept–May 8am–5.50pm; ☎760/876-6222), is a great source of information about the Owens Valley.

Many early Westerns, and the epic *Gunga Din*, were filmed in the **Alabama Hills** to the west, a rugged expanse of bizarrely eroded sedimentary rock. Some of the oddest formations are linked by the **Picture Rocks Circle**, a paved road that loops around from Whitney Portal Road, passing rocks shaped like bullfrogs, walruses and baboons.

Two thousand eager souls make the strenuous 22-mile round-trip **hike** (12–16hr; 6500ft ascent) to the summit of Mount Whitney each summer. Permits are needed and should be reserved well in advance from Inyo National Forest Wilderness Reservation Service (PO Box 430, Big Pine, CA 93513; ☎760/938-1136 or 1-888/374-3773; *www.sierrawilderness.com*). No-shows are occasionally available on weekdays; line up at the Mount Whitney Ranger Station, 1452 S Main St in Lone Pine before 7am the morning before you want to start hiking. One-day ascents start at dawn from the **campground** (mid-May–mid-Oct; ☎1-800/280-2267; $12) at the end of twisting Whitney Portal Road, reachable via trailhead shuttle (☎760/876-5518). The trail cuts up to boulder-strewn Trail Crest Pass, the southern end of the 220-mile John Muir Trail to Yosemite, then climbs along the top of vertical cliffs. At the rounded summit, a stone cabin serves as an emergency shelter – though not one you'd choose to be in during a lightning storm.

## Big Pine and the White Mountains

Nearly fifty miles north, hikes lead from the end of Glacier Lodge Road, ten miles west of nondescript **BIG PINE**, up to the **Palisades Glacier**, the southernmost glacier in the northern hemisphere. Along the opposite wall of the five-mile-wide Owens Valley, the ancient, bald and dry **White Mountains** are home to the gnarled **bristlecone pines**, the oldest living things on earth. Occupying a narrow band at around ten thousand feet, and often covered in snow until mid-June, some of these gnarled trees have been alive for over four thousand years. Battered and beaten by the harsh environment into contorted but beautiful shapes, even when dead they hang on without decaying for upwards of another thousand years, slowly being eroded by wind-driven ice and sand.

**Schulman Grove** ($2) was named after dendrochronologist Dr Edmund Schulman, who revealed the extreme longevity of the trees in the mid-1950s. It is the most accessible collection, 24 twisting but paved miles from Big Pine off Hwy-168, and centers on the newly enlarged **visitor center** (late May–Aug daily 10am–5pm or later; Sept & Oct Sat & Sun 10am–5pm; ☎760/873-2503). Two trails radiate from here: the mile-long **Discovery Trail**, which passes some photogenic examples; and a longer loop which passes but intentionally fails to identify the oldest tree, the 4700-year-old Methuselah. **Patriarch Grove**, twelve miles further, along a dusty dirt road that gives spectacular views of the Sierra Nevada and the Great Basin ranges, contains the largest and comparably ancient bristlecone.

In the White Mountains there's the free, waterless *Grandview* **campground**, or you can retreat to the **motels** along US-395 in Big Pine – the *Big Pine Motel*, 370 S Main St (☎760/938-2282; ②), and the *Starlight Motel*, 511 S Main St (☎760/938-2011; ②).

# Bishop

**BISHOP**, to a Californian, means outdoor pursuits. The largest town (population 3500) in the Owens Valley, it's an excellent base for cross-country skiing, fly-fishing and especially rock-climbing. Furthermore, it's easy to get to with Reno–LA Greyhound buses (one a day in either direction) stopping at 201 S Warren St. **Motels**, such as the *El Rancho*, 274 W Lagoon St (☎760/872-9251; ②), the *Thunderbird*, 190 W Pine St (☎760/873-4215; ②), and bargain restaurants can be found within a block of US-395. The **visitor center** at 690 N Main St (Mon–Fri 9am–5pm, Sat & Sun 10am–4pm; ☎760/873-8405) can provide details of the many **adventure travel specialists** based in town. For **hiking** and **camping** information, the White Mountain Ranger Station, 798 N Main St (July & Aug daily 8am–5pm; rest of year Mon–Fri 8am–4.30pm; ☎760/873-2500), will be more use.

# Mammoth Lakes

Forty miles north along US-395 from Bishop then five miles west on Hwy-203, the resort town of **MAMMOTH LAKES** offers the state's premier ski slopes outside the Lake Tahoe basin, and in summer hosts on- and off-road bike races. The setting is stunning, but the town is pricey and prone to testosterone overload. To ski **Mammoth Mountain** (*www.mammoth-mtn.com*), which looms up behind the resort, pick up **lift tickets** ($49 per day) from the Main Lodge on Minaret Road, where you can also rent **equipment** ($20 for basic skis, boots and poles), and book **lessons** ($32 per half-day). In summer, fifty miles of snow-free slopes transform themselves into the 3500-acre **Mammoth Mountain Bike Park** ($20 a day for trail access, $25 for trails and cable car, $35 a day for bike rental; two-hour all-in midweek taster $30).

One appealing summer-only destination is the **DEVIL'S POSTPILE NATIONAL MONUMENT**, seven miles southwest of the bike park, reached by shuttle bus ($9). A collection of slender, blue-gray basaltic columns, some scaling sixty feet, the Postpile was formed as lava from a volcanic eruption cooled and fractured into multisided forms. From here, a two-mile hike along the San Joaquin River leads to **Rainbow Falls** which refract the midday sun perfectly.

### Practicalities

The daily Greyhound stops in the *McDonald's* parking lot on Hwy-203. During the ski season, get around on the four-line Mammoth Shuttle (☎760/934-3030). For information, go to the combined US Forest Service and Mammoth Lakes **visitor center** (daily 9am–5pm; ☎1-888/466-2666 or 760/924-5500) on the main highway half a mile east of the town center.

Mammoth's plentiful **accommodation**, which includes two hostels, are costliest in winter. *Mammoth Mountain Inn* on Mammoth Mountain (☎760/934-2581 or 1-800/228-4947; ⑥), is a touch sterile but it's at the heart of all the ski and bike action, while the *White Stag Inn*, at Main and Minaret (☎1-800/376-4134 or 760/934-7507; ④), is reasonably priced and central. *Davison St Guesthouse*, 19 Davison St (☎760/544-9093, fax 544-9107; ①), offers mountain views from its four-bed rooms and dorms. There are **camp-grounds** ($12) close to Devil's Postpile National Monument, and free waterless sites in the Inyo National Forest off US-395 around eleven miles north.

**Restaurants** tend to be expensive but casual: *Giovanni's*, in the Minaret Village Mall (☎760/934-7563), is popular for pasta and pizza, with great lunchtime deals; *Good Life Cafe*, at the Mammoth Mall (☎760/934-1734), serves burgers, egg dishes and vegetarian staples at modest prices on the sunny deck; and *The Lakefront Restaurant*, at Tamarack Lodge (☎760/934-3534), offers superb lake views and good food – for a price. *Whiskey Creek*, at Main and Minaret (☎760/934-2555), is a lively **bar** and restaurant, with its own good microbrews.

## Mono Lake, Lee Vining and Bodie Ghost Town

The blue expanse of **Mono Lake** sits in the midst of a volcanic desert tableland at the north end of the valley. It looks like a science-fiction landscape, with two large islands, one light colored, the other black, surrounded by salty, alkaline water. Strange sand-castle-like formations of **tufa** (calcium deposited from springs) have been exposed over the fifty years since the City of Los Angeles extended an aqueduct into the Mono Basin through an eleven-mile tunnel, dropping the **water level** by over forty feet and creating the biggest environmental controversy in California. Mono Lake is the primary nesting ground for the state's **California gull** population – twenty percent of the world total – and a prime stopover point for thousands of migratory geese, ducks and swans. As the water levels dropped, the islands in the middle of the lake, where the seagulls lay their eggs, became peninsulas, and the colonies fell prey to coyotes and other mainland predators. The landlocked water became increasingly alkaline, threatening the unique ecosystem. Though the California Supreme Court ruled in 1983 that Mono Lake must be saved, it wasn't until 1991 that emergency action was taken.

For more details about Mono Lake and the fight for its survival, stop by the **Mono Lake Committee Information Center** (daily 9am–5pm, often until 9pm in July & Aug; ☎760/647-6595; *www.leevining.com*), in the small town of **LEE VINING** on US-395, or a mile north at the excellent **Mono Basin Scenic Area Visitor Center** (May–Sept daily 9am–5.30pm; Oct–April Thurs–Mon 9am–4.45pm; ☎760/647-3044). Greyhound buses from the south stop here daily at 2.30am, while the bus from Reno in the north comes in at the more reasonable 11am. **Motels** along US-395 include *El Mono Motel* (☎760/647-6310; ③) and *Murphey's* (☎760/647-6316 or 1-800/334-6316; ④). *Nicely's Restaurant* (☎760/647-6477) is a Fifties vinyl palace that opens at 6am; the more upscale *Mono Inn Restaurant*, five miles north along US-395 (☎760/647-6581), is owned by Ansel Adams' granddaughter.

Northeast of Lee Vining, in a remote, high desert valley, stands a well-preserved and evocative relic of the gold-mining 1870s. The **Bodie State Park** (open all year but often inaccessible by car in winter; $2 per person; ☎760/647-6445) is perhaps the best **ghost town** in the US, with many of its structures still intact but not gussied up for tourists. With thirty saloons and dance halls and a population of ten thousand, it was once the raunchiest and most lawless mining camp in the west; over 150 wooden buildings survive in a state of arrested decay around the intact town center, littered with old bottles, bits of machinery and old stagecoaches. The ruins of the mines themselves, in the hills east of town, are off limits to visitors except on the frequent tours.

# THE CENTRAL COAST

After the hustle of LA and San Francisco, the four hundred miles of coastline in between – the **central coast** – can seem like the land that time forgot. Sparsely populated outside the few medium-sized cities, and lined by clean sandy beaches, it is at its most dramatic along **Big Sur**, one of the most savagely beautiful stretches of coastline in the world, where the brooding Santa Lucia Mountains rise steeply out of the thundering Pacific surf. The two largest towns are poles apart: **Santa Barbara** in the south is a wealthy resort, **Santa Cruz** in the north is a coastal town redolent of the Sixties. In between, languorous **San Luis Obispo** makes a good base for visiting **Hearst Castle**, the hilltop palace of publishing magnate William Randolph "Citizen Kane" Hearst.

Almost all of the towns grew up around Spanish **missions**, each a long day's walk from the next, and once-upon-a-time enclosed within thick walls to prevent Native American attack. **Monterey**, a hundred miles south of San Francisco, was California's capital under Spain and Mexico, and still has attractive early nineteenth-century architecture.

Amtrak's *Coast Starlight* **train** runs along the coast up to San Luis Obispo before cutting inland north to San Francisco; Greyhound **buses** stop at most of the towns, especially along the main highway, US-101.

## Santa Barbara

The six-lane coastal freeway that races past oil wells and offshore drilling platforms slows to a leisurely pace a hundred miles north of Los Angeles at **SANTA BARBARA**. This conservative town – home to Ronald Reagan – is beautifully sited, on gently sloping hills above the Pacific. The insistent red-tiled roofs and white stucco walls of its low-rise buildings form a backdrop to some fine Spanish Revival architecture, while the golden beaches are wide and clean, lined by palm trees along a curving bay. Although a large portion of downtown has been replaced by a vast upscale, shopping mall, Santa Barbara has managed to retain its quaintly upscale yet relaxed character.

The mission-era feel of Santa Barbara is no accident. Following a devastating earthquake in 1925, the entire town was rebuilt in the image of an apocryphal Spanish Colonial past, with numerous arcades linking shops, cafes and restaurants. **State Street**, the main drag, is home to a friendly assortment of diners, bookshops, coffee bars and nightclubs. The few remaining genuine mission structures are preserved as the **Presidio de Santa Barbara** (daily 10.30am–4.30pm; donation). At its center, the 200-year-old barracks, **El Cuartel**, stand two blocks off State Street on Perdido Street; the second oldest building in California, it now houses historical exhibits and a scale model of the small Spanish colony. The more recent past is recounted in the nearby **Santa Barbara Historical Museum** at 136 E de la Guerra St (Tues–Sat 10am–5pm, Sun noon–5pm; donation).

State Street leads half a mile down from the town center to wooden **Stearns Wharf**. Built in 1872, it was nearly destroyed in November 1998, when a third of the pier was engulfed in flames; restoration efforts are still progressing. In the meantime, you can still walk along the remaining pier to explore its seafood restaurants and ice-cream stands, while magnificent **beaches** stretch in either direction.

In the hills above the town is the beautiful **Mission Santa Barbara** (daily 9am–5pm; $3), the so-called "Queen of the Missions," with its colorful twin-towered facade. A small **museum** displays historical artifacts from the mission archives. Other mission stops in the area are Santa Inés just outside the kitsch Danish town of **Solvang** heading north on US-101 and *La Purísima*, the most completely restructured of all the California missions, about twenty miles northwest of Solvang on Hwy-1.

## Practicalities

Greyhound **buses** from LA and San Francisco stop every two hours downtown at 34 W Carrillo St; **trains** call at the old Southern Pacific station at 209 State St, a block west of US-101. The **visitor center** is at 1 Garden St (Mon–Sat 9am–5pm, Sun 10am–5pm; ☎805/965-3021). Hot Spots, is a 24-hour hotel reservation center and espresso bar at 36 State St (☎805/564-1637 or 1-800/793-7666). You can walk to most places, although a frequent, quarter-a-ride **shuttle bus** loops around Santa Barbara during the day, with the Santa Barbara Metropolitan Transit District (☎805/683-3702) covering the outlying areas into the evening.

Dorm **beds** at the relaxed *Banana Bungalow Hostel*, 210 E Ortega St (☎805/963-0154 or 1-800/3HOSTEL; ①), are both cheap and comfortable. Otherwise, rooms are generally expensive and hard to find; low-priced options include the characterful old mission-style *Hotel State Street*, 121 State St (☎805/966-6586; ②), near the beach. For something more upscale, two casually luxurious options are *The Cheshire Cat* B&B, 36 W Valerio St (☎805/569-1610; ⑥), and *The Harbor View Inn*, 28 W Cabrillo Blvd (☎805/963-0780 or 1-800/755-0222; ⑦). The nearest useful **camping** spot is ten miles south of Santa Barbara at Carpinteria State Beach (☎805/684-2811 or 1-800/444-7275; $17).

Among fine Santa Barbara **restaurants** are *El Paseo*, 10 El Paseo (☎805/962-6050), an upscale Mexican restaurant with a festive fountain courtyard; *Pascucci*, 729 State St (☎805/963-8123), serving tremendous portions of innovative Italian cuisine at reasonable prices; the *Natural Cafe*, 508 State St (☎805/962-9494), offering scrumptious veggie meals and a prime spot for people watching; *Chad's*, 625 Chapala St (☎805/568-1876), with modern American cuisine in the intimate atmosphere of an historic Victorian home; and *Mousse Odile*, 18 E Cota St (☎805/962-5393), the locals' latest favorite for French cuisine with a California flair.

**Cafes**, **bars** and **clubs** line State Street; *Coffee Bean & Tea Leaf* at 811-A (☎805/966-2442) is a great place to watch the partygoers parade back and forth on the strip. If you'd rather actually enter a club, *Zelo*, at no. 630 (☎805/966-5792), is a popular restaurant and club hosting alternative DJs, while *Fathom*, at no. 423, bills itself as a gay disco, making it all the more popular with trendy college students of all persuasions.

# San Luis Obispo

**SAN LUIS OBISPO**, 160 miles north of Santa Barbara and halfway between LA and San Francisco, is a few miles inland, but makes the best base for exploring the surrounding coastal regions. Still primarily an agricultural market center, it holds more nineteenth-century architecture than any other Californian city, plenty of good restaurants, a couple of pubs, and – outside summer holiday weekends – lots of accommodation.

The compact core of San Luis is eminently walkable, centered around the late eighteenth-century **Mission San Luis Obispo de Tolosa** (daily: late May–early Sept 7am–5pm; early Sept–late May 7am–4pm; donation), a dark and unremarkable church that was the prototype for the now ubiquitous red-tiled roof, developed to replace the original, flammable thatch in response to Native American arson attacks.

Between the mission and the visitor center, **Mission Plaza**'s terraces step down along San Luis creek, along which footpaths meander, crisscrossed by bridges every hundred feet and overlooked by shops and outdoor restaurants on the south bank.

**Higuera Street**, a block south of Mission Plaza, is the main drag, and springs to life on Thursday afternoons for the **Farmers' Market**, when the street is closed to cars and filled with vegetable stalls, mobile barbecues and street-corner musicians.

## Practicalities

Greyhound is at 150 South St, while Amtrak trains stop at the end of Santa Rosa Street, half a mile south of the business district. The **chamber of commerce** is at 1039 Chorro St (☎805/781-2777). Monterey Street was the site of the world's first (long gone) **motel** – the *Motel Inn*. Rates in its modern counterparts are generally low: *The Economy Motel* at 652 Morro St (☎805/543-7024; ②) is a particularly good value. A landmark in itself, the *Madonna Inn*, 100 Madonna Way (☎805/543-3000 or 1-800/543-9666; ⑥), was featured in the cult classic *Aria*, but the "theme" rooms in this shocking kitsch monstrosity are a big disappointment after touring the pink, chalet-style lobby, especially at such inflated prices. With that much to spend, you're better off taking a short drive south to stay in a room with a view: *The Best Western Shorecliff Lodge*, 2555 Price St, Pismo Beach (☎805/773-4671; ⑥) has a dramatically situated swimming pool and a cliff-hugging gazebo over the Pacific.

Higuera Street is the place to **eat**, especially during the farmers' market on Thursday. For other eating options try *Buona Tavola*, 1037 Monterey St (☎805/545-8000), for a great selection of Northern Italian bistro-style food and wine; *Taj Palace*, 795 Foothill Blvd (☎805/543-0722) is the city's Indian choice; and the *SLO Brewing Company*, 1119 Garden St (☎805/543-1943), is the first brewery/restaurant in the city since prohibition. For something more seafood-oriented, head to Pismo Beach for the clam chowder at *Splash Cafe*, Pomeroy Avenue (☎805/773-4653).

# Hearst Castle

Forty-five miles northwest of San Luis Obispo, the hilltop **Hearst Castle** is one of the most extravagant houses in the world. The home where publisher **William Randolph Hearst** held court over such guests as Winston Churchill, Charlie Chaplin, George Bernard Shaw and Charles Lindbergh now brings in over a million visitors a year. Its interior combines walls, floors and ceilings torn from European churches and castles with Gothic fireplaces and Moorish tiles, while nearly every

---

### W.R.HEARST – CITIZEN KANE

Often portrayed as a power-mad monster – most memorably by Orson Welles in his thinly veiled *Citizen Kane* – **William Randolph Hearst** seems in retrospect more like a very rich, overindulged little boy. Born in 1863 as the only son of a multimillionaire mining engineer, he learned his trade in New York working for Joseph Pulitzer, the inventor of "Yellow Journalism." When he published his own *Morning Journal*, Hearst took Pulitzer's advice to heart, fanning the flames of American imperialism to ignite the Spanish-American War of 1898. As he told his correspondents in Cuba: "You provide the pictures, and I'll provide the war." Hearst eventually controlled an empire that during the 1930s sold twenty-five percent of the nation's newspapers – and sixty percent in California.

Despite his war-mongering and nationalism, Hearst was middle-of-the-road politically, a lifelong Democrat who served two terms in the House of Representatives but failed to be elected as Mayor of New York, let alone President. Besides his many newspapers, Hearst owned eleven radio stations and two movie studios, which he used to make his mistress, Marion Davies, a star. The Depression forced him to sell off most of his holdings, but he continued to exert power and influence until his death in 1951, aged 88.

room bursts with Greek vases and medieval tapestries. Ironically, the same financial power and public infamy which allowed Hearst to hoard these artifacts to himself have made them viewable to more people than had they remained in the lands in which they were created.

Work on Hearst's 250,000-acre ranch began in 1919, managed by architect Julia Morgan, who designed each room and building in the spirit of the works destined to be housed inside. The castle was never truly completed: rooms were torn out as soon as they were finished in order to accommodate yet more acquired treasure. The main facade, a twin-towered copy of a Mudejar cathedral, stands at the top of steps which curve up from a swimming pool (the most photographed in the world) filled with spring water and lined by a Greek colonnade.

Four different two-hour guided **tours** (summer daily 8am–4pm; rest of year daily 8am–3pm; ☎1-800/444-4445; $14) leave from the visitor center just off Hwy-1. A tour is essential, as are reservations. The most dramatic time to visit is first thing in the morning when the coastal fog hides the castle from the world below. Another magic event at the castle is the evening tour series in spring and fall, when docents in period dress take visitors through the castle, speaking of Hearst in the present tense.

## The Big Sur coast

Starting just north of Hearst Castle, the ninety wild and undeveloped miles of rocky cliffs of the **Big Sur coast** form a sublime landscape at the edge of a continent, where redwood groves line river canyons and the Santa Lucia Mountains rise straight out of the blue-green Pacific. Only the occasional outpost interrupts the tortuous, exhilarating route of **Hwy-1**, carved out of bedrock cliffs 500ft above the ocean, and **public transportation** is limited to the MST bus which runs south from Monterey to Nepenthe twice daily during the summer. Hardly anyone braves the turbulent winters, when violent storms can sweep sections of the highway into the sea. Summer weekends see the roads and campgrounds packed to overflowing, but a mile or two's walk still gets you away from it all.

The southern coastline of Big Sur is relatively gentle, with sandy beaches hiding below crumbling yellow-ochre cliffs. **ESALEN** is named after the Native Americans who once enjoyed its natural **hot spring**, on a clifftop high above the raging Pacific surf. Since the 1960s, when people came to Big Sur to smoke pot and get back to nature, Esalen has been at the forefront of the "New Age" movement, and the spring is now owned and operated by the Esalen Institute which offers workshops on "potentialities and values of human existence" (by reservation only; ☎831/667-3005).

Three miles north on Hwy-1, **Julia Pfeiffer Burns State Park** (daily dawn–dusk; $6 parking), has some of the best day-hikes in the Big Sur area, including a ten-minute walk along the cliffs to see McWay Falls crashing down onto the beach. Seven miles further on, the lovely old *Deetjen's Big Sur Inn* (☎831/667-2377; ⑤/⑥) has rooms handcrafted from thick redwood planks, and excellent food. The privately operated *Ventana Campground* (☎831/667-2331 or 624-4812) offers full facilities and campsites for $25 a night.

Further north, at **NEPENTHE**, the rooftop *Nepenthe* restaurant offers pricey steaks and seafood, and the same impressive views as from the more affordable *Cafe Kevah*, serving breakfast and lunch on a terrace below. Just across the highway, at the **Henry Miller Library**, works by the author, who lived in the area on and off until the 1960s, are displayed and sold. Two miles north along Hwy-1, the unmarked Sycamore Canyon Road leads a mile west to Big Sur's best beach, **Pfeiffer Beach**; the white sand here is dominated by a hump of rock whose color varies from brown to red to orange in the changing light.

### Big Sur river valley

Immediately north of the Pfeiffer Beach turnoff, and 65 miles north of Hearst Castle, Hwy-1 drops into the valley of the Big Sur River, where the majority of the accommodation and restaurants are dotted sporadically along six miles of the highway. First stop should be at the US Forest Service **ranger station** (daily 8am–6pm; ☎831/667-2315), which handles the camping permits that are required for the Ventana Wilderness in the mountains above.

In sheltered **Pfeiffer Big Sur State Park**, deep, clear swimming holes form in the steepwalled river gorge during late spring and summer, and a hiking trail leads half a mile up a canyon shaded by redwoods to the sixty-foot **Pfeiffer Falls**. The **campgrounds** here charge $17 and are often full on summer weekends; book through the California State Parks' Reservation Service (☎1-800/444-7275).

The cluster of shops, lodgings and restaurants known as **The Village**, sited just north of Pfeiffer Big Sur State Park, is the most feasible base for seeing Big Sur. **Accommodation** fills up in summer, but if you can afford it, it's worth spending a night in one of the rustic riverside rooms at the *Big Sur River Inn Resort* (☎831/667-2700 or 1-800/548-3610; ④–⑦), which has a very good **restaurant**. There are also good-sized cabins in the *Big Sur Lodge* (☎831/667-3100 or 1-800/424-4787; ④). Alternatively try the cabins at *Big Sur Campgrounds and Cabins*, a mile north of Pfeiffer Big Sur (☎831/667-2322; ②).

# The Monterey Peninsula

The rocky headlands of the **Monterey Peninsula**, where gnarled cypress trees amplify the collision between the cliffs and the thundering sea, mark the northern edge of the Big Sur coast, a hundred miles south of San Francisco. The lively harbor town of **Monterey** was the capital of California under the Spanish and Mexicans, and retains many old adobe houses and places of genuine historic appeal alongside some overstated tourist traps. **Carmel**, on the other hand, three miles to the south, is a self-consciously quaint village of million-dollar holiday homes.

### Arrival, information and getting around

If you're coming from the south, Greyhound **buses** will drop you at the Exxon station on the Monterey waterfront, while Amtrak requires you to change in the sprawling agricultural town of **Salinas** inland, and take a further 55-minute trip on the hourly local bus #21 into Monterey. **Getting around** the peninsula itself is surprisingly easy, on Monterey-Salinas Transit (MST) buses (☎831/899-2555). The most useful routes are #4 and #5 (Monterey–Carmel), #21 (Monterey–Salinas), and #1 (Monterey–Pacific Grove); there's also a free shuttle bus from downtown to the Aquarium on Cannery Row. Bus #22 runs along the Big Sur coast to Nepenthe twice a day, in summer only.

Another option is to **rent a bike**: good-quality mountain bikes are offered by Adventures by the Sea, 201 Alvarado Mall (☎831/372-1807) and outside the Maritime Museum, or Bay Bikes, 640 Wave St on Cannery Row (☎831/659-5824).

The Monterey **Visitors Center** is at Camino El Estero at Franklin St on Lake El Estero (summer Mon–Sat 9am–6pm, Sun 9am–5pm; winter Mon–Sat 9am–5pm, Sun 10am–4pm; ☎831/649-1770). Both it and the less busy Chamber of Commerce **tourist office** at 380 Alvarado St (Mon–Fri 8.30am–5pm) can help with accommodation. In Carmel, the Monterey County **Visitors Center**, 137 Crossroads Blvd (Mon–Fri 10am–6pm, Sat 10am–6pm, Sun 11.30am–5.30pm; ☎831/626-1424), has information on the entire peninsula and will help with hotel reservations.

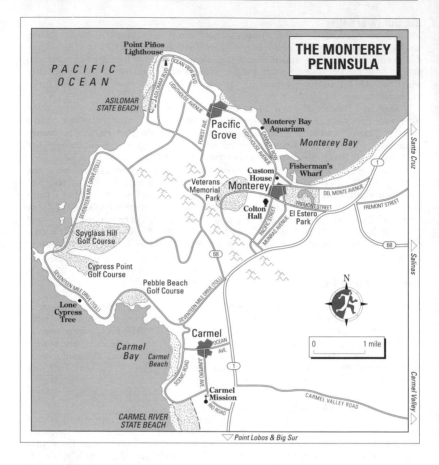

## Accommodation

**Hotel** and **B&B** rates average $120 a night, but cheaper **motels** gather along Fremont Street and Munras Avenue, two miles north of the center. The nearest **camping** is in Veteran's Memorial Park, site of Steinbeck's fictional *Tortilla Flat*, in the hills above town.

**Bide-a-Wee Motel**, 221 Asilomar Ave, Pacific Grove (☎831/372-2330). Excellent value, no-frills rooms, a few with kitchenettes. A 2min walk to the ocean. ③.

**Carmel Resort Inn**, Carpenter and 2nd Ave, Carmel (☎831/624-3113 or 1-800/454-3700). One of the least expensive properties in town; cottage rooms with fireplaces. ⑤.

**Del Monte Beach**, 1110 Del Monte Ave, Monterey (☎831/649-4410). A bargain B&B close to the center of Monterey. All the usual trappings for half the normal cost. ③.

**El Dorado Inn**, 900 Munras Ave (☎1-800/722-1836). Cheap, basic accommodation at budget rates. ③.

**Green Gables Inn**, 104 5th St, Pacific Grove (☎831/375-2095 or 1-800/722-1774). Plush doubles in one of the prettiest homes in town, on the waterfront just a few blocks from the Aquarium. ⑥.

**Mariposa Inn**, 1386 Munras Ave (☎831/649-1414 or 1-800/283-5663). The best deal in town. Cozy rooms with fireplaces and full amenities at reasonable rates. ③/④.

**Pacific Grove Motel,** Lighthouse Ave at Grove Acre (☎831/372-3218 or 1-800/858-8997). Basic, small motel in marvelous setting, 100 yards from the sea. ③.

## Monterey

Though named by Vizcaino in 1602, **MONTEREY** was not colonized until 1770, as the military, administrative and commercial center of a territory that extended east to the Rockies and north to Canada (with a nonnative population of less than seven thousand). With the conjunction of the US takeover and the Gold Rush, Monterey suddenly became a backwater, hardly affected by the waves of immigration that followed.

Impressive vernacular colonial **buildings** now stand unassumingly in the compact town center, within a few blocks of the tourist-thronged waterfront. A loosely organized **Path of History** connects the 37 sites of the **Monterey State Historic Park.** Most can't be entered unless you're part of a ninety-minute guided historic **walking tour** (daily every hour from 10am–3pm; $5), leaving from the Maritime Museum, near the waterfront at the foot of Alvarado Street.

The best place to get a feel for life in old Monterey is the **Larkin House,** on Jefferson Street a block south of Alvarado (entered only as part of a tour), home of the first and only American Consul to California. The New England-born Thomas Larkin, who was influential in persuading the Californians to turn towards the US and away from the erratic government of Mexico, is credited with developing the now-common Monterey style of architecture, combining local adobe walls and the balconies of a Southern plantation home with a puritan Yankee's taste in ornament. The house, the first two-story adobe in California, is filled with millions of dollars' worth of antiques, and the gorgeous surrounding gardens are open all day.

The **Stevenson House,** a short way east at 530 Houston St (entry as for Larkin House, above), is filled with memorabilia of Robert Louis Stevenson, who passed through in 1879 and foresaw that Monterey's Mexican-influenced lifestyle was no match for the "Yankee craft" of the "millionaire vulgarians of the Big Bonanza." At the foot of the otherwise tacky **Fisherman's Wharf,** the **Pacific House** (daily 10am–5pm; free) has been a courthouse, a rooming house and a dance hall in the years since its construction in 1847, and is now the best of the local **museums,** with displays on Monterey history and a pretty fair collection of Native American artifacts. While in the area, wander by the balconied **Customs House** (daily 10am–5pm; free), the oldest governmental building on the West Coast, with portions built by Spain in 1814, Mexico in 1827, and the US in 1846.

A **bike path** runs the two miles to Pacific Grove, along **Cannery Row** – named after John Steinbeck's portrait of the rough-and-ready workers of its fish canneries. During World War II some 200,000 tons of sardines were caught and canned each year, but the stocks were exhausted by 1945. The abandoned canneries reopened in the 1970s as malls and restaurants, which now teem with tourists.

The engaging **Monterey Bay Aquarium,** a mile west of town at the end of Cannery Row (daily 10am–6pm; ☎831/648-4888 or 1-800/756-3737; $15.95), is one of the largest, most stunning displays of underwater life in the world. Book tickets well in advance and allow a day for your visit. Museum highlights include a 335,000 gallon Kelp Forest tank, a touch pool where you can pet bat rays, a pool of sea otters, and a stunning jellyfish exhibit which uses the latest lighting technology to bring out the creatures' myriad colors.

## Pacific Grove

**PACIFIC GROVE** – or "Butterfly Town USA," as it likes to call itself – began as a campground and Methodist retreat in 1875, and still holds ornate wooden **cottages** from those days. **Ocean View Boulevard** circles the coast around the town, passing the headland of **Lovers Point** – originally called Lovers of Jesus Point – where preachers used to hold sunrise services. Surrounded in early summer by the colorful red-and-purple cloaks of blooming ice plant, it's one of the peninsula's best **beaches**. Every year, from November through early March, hundreds of thousands of golden Monarch **butterflies** come to Pacific Grove to escape the winter chill, forming orange and black blankets on the **Butterfly Trees**, on Ridge Road, inland along Lighthouse Avenue towards the 150-year-old **Point Piños** lighthouse (Thurs–Sun 1–4pm; free), the oldest continuously operating lighthouse on the California coast.

## Carmel

Set on gently rising headlands above a sculpted rocky shore, **CARMEL**'s biggest crime is its unmitigated cuteness. Were it not for ridiculously inflated prices, the neat rows of quaint shops and miniature homes, which run along either side of Ocean Avenue towards the largely untouched coastline, might seem almost charming. **Carmel Beach** is a tranquil cove of blue water bordered by soft white sand and cypress-covered cliffs; the tides are deceptively strong and dangerous, so be careful if you chance a swim.

**Point Lobos State Reserve** (daily: summer 9am–7pm; winter 9am–5pm; $7 per vehicle), two miles south of Carmel on Hwy-1, has plenty of natural justifications to support its title of "the greatest meeting of land and water in the world." There are over 250 bird and animal species along the hiking trails in the area, and the sea here is one of the richest underwater habitats in California. Gray whales are often seen offshore, migrating south in January and returning with young calves in April and early May. Because the point juts so far out into the ocean, chances are good of seeing them from as little as a hundred yards away.

## Eating

There are many excellent places to **eat** all over the peninsula. If you're on a tight budget, the best cheap eats are on the north side of Monterey, along Fremont Street and just south of Cannery Row on and around Lighthouse Avenue.

**Bookworks**, 667 Lighthouse Ave, Monterey (☎831/372-2242). Cafe frequented by locals, serving light lunch fare at reasonable prices.

**Fishwife Restaurant**, 1996 Sunset Drive at Asilomar, Pacific Grove (☎831/375-7107). Longstanding local favorite, serving great food at reasonable prices – about $10 a plate – in cozy surroundings.

**Old Monterey Cafe**, 489 Alvarado St, Monterey (☎831/646-1021). More-than-you-can-eat breakfasts, plus tasty sandwiches. Closed Mon.

**Paolina's**, San Carlos between Ocean & 7th, Carmel (☎831/624-5599). Fresh homemade pastas in a casual courtyard setting.

**Papa Chano's Taqueria**, 462 Alvarado St, Monterey (☎831/646-9587). Delicious and cheap Mexican food, featuring burritos.

**Pasta Mia Trattoria**, 481 Lighthouse Ave, Pacific Grove (☎831/375-7709). Tasty homemade pastas, grilled seafood and veal in a rustic, homey setting.

**Pepper's Mexicali Cafe**, 170 Forest Ave, Pacific Grove (☎831/373-6892). Gourmet Mexican seafood Californified into healthy, high-style and reasonably priced dishes.

**Sardine Factory**, 701 Wave St, Monterey (☎831/373-3775). California seafood cuisine served in French château splendor – costs less then you might expect too.

**Schooners**, in the *Monterey Plaza Hotel*, 400 Cannery Row, Monterey (☎831/372-2628). Colorful California bistro in an historic hotel with views over the bay.

## Drinking and nightlife

Monterey has always been better known as a sleepy, romantic getaway than as a hub of hip nightlife, but the **Monterey Jazz Festival** in mid-September (☎1-800/307-3378) is the oldest continuous jazz festival in the world and draws crowds from afar.

**Franco's Norma Jean Club**, 10639 Merritt St, Castroville (☎831/633-2090). Heading towards Santa Cruz, this disco serves up Latin, house and techno to local trendsters.

**Lighthouse Bar & Grill**, 281 Lighthouse Ave (☎831/373-4488). Friendly gay pub where the locals hang.

**The Mucky Duck**, 479 Alvarado St (☎831/655-3031). Sip a 20oz Guinness around the fire, at the bar, or at a table on the patio out back. Occasional live folk, Celtic and rock music; DJ on back patio.

**Planet Gemini**, 625 Cannery Row (☎831/373-1449). Mixed music and comedy venue usually with a $6–8 cover. Closed Mon.

# Santa Cruz

After the overcharged tourism of Monterey, the unassuming (if somewhat seedy) community of **SANTA CRUZ**, 75 miles south of San Francisco, comes as a surprise. Although in many ways the quintessential Californian coastal town, spread at the foot of thickly wooded mountains beside a clean sandy beach, it has grown considerably in the last few years, having recovered from the destruction wrought by the 1989 earthquake. In the Sixties, the Merry Pranksters turned the local youth on to LSD long before it defined a generation, and the area is still among the most politically and socially progressive in California. It's also surprisingly untouristy. No hotels spoil the miles of coastline; most of the land is agricultural; and roadside stands are more likely to sell apples or sprouts than postcards and souvenirs.

The **Santa Cruz Boardwalk**, one of the last surviving beachfront amusement parks on the West Coast, is the main focus for visitors (May–Sept daily 11am–10pm; rest of year hours vary; $1.50–3 per ride, unlimited rides $19.95). Although it can get packed on weekends with teenagers on the prowl, most of the time it's a friendly funfair, where barefoot hippies mix with mushroom farmers. The star attraction is the 75-year-old **Giant Dipper**, a wild and rickety wooden roller coaster that has been ridden by more than 45 million people.

The **beach** next to the boardwalk is good but can get rowdy (and dirty). For more peace and quiet, follow the coast out of town to one of the smaller beaches such as Capitola or New Brighton. From **West Cliff Drive**, you'll see some of the biggest waves in California, not least at **Steamer Lane**, beyond the Municipal Pier. Cowell's Beach, just north of the Municipal Pier, is the best place to give surfing a try; Club Ed (☎831/459-9283) in the parking lot, will rent boards and assist with lessons. The ghosts of surfers past are animated at the **Surfing Museum** (daily except Tues noon–4pm; donation) in the old lighthouse on the point, where surfboards range from early 12ft redwood planks to modern high-tech multifinned cutters. A clifftop cycle path runs two miles to **Natural Bridges State Park** (daily 8am–dusk; $6 per car), where waves have cut holes through the coastal cliffs, forming delicate stone arches (though three of its four eponymous bridges have now collapsed).

Twenty-five miles up the coast from Santa Cruz, the beginning of the San Francisco Peninsula is marked by **Pigeon Point Lighthouse** (☎650/879-0633; ①/②), where you can spend the night in the old lighthouse keeper's quarters and soak your bones in a hot tub, cantilevered out over the rocks. Dorm beds cost from $12 and there are also private doubles. Pigeon Point took its name from the clipper ship *Carrier Pigeon*, which broke up on the rocks off the point, one of many shipwrecks that led to the construction of the lighthouse in the late nineteenth century.

Just before Pigeon Point, at the foot of beautiful **Big Basin Redwoods State Park** giant blubbery elephant seals congregate every December and January to mate in the **Ano Nuevo State Reserve**. Even without the spectacle of the seals, the surrounding coastal area has beautiful **hiking**; when the fog rolls in (as it often does), head for the redwood tree-shaded trails of Big Basin.

## Practicalities

Greyhound **buses** from San Francisco, Oakland and San Jose stop five times a day at 425 Front St, in the center of town. Santa Cruz has an excellent **public transportation** system on which the basic fare is $1 and an all-day pass $3. Bicycle Rental Center, 131 Center St (☎831/426-8687), rents **bikes** from $20 a day. The **Santa Cruz Visitors Council** is at 701 Front St (Mon–Sat 9am–5pm, Sun 10am–4pm; ☎831/425-1234 or 1-800/833-3494).

Off season, Santa Cruz has plenty of inexpensive places to **stay**, though rates can be much higher on weekends. Cheapest of the lot, with beds from $12, is the well-sited *HI-Santa Cruz* **hostel**, 321 Main St (☎831/423-8304; ①). *Capri Motel*, 337 Riverside Ave (☎831/426-4611; ②), is the cheapest motel near the boardwalk; the 1887 *Cliff Crest B&B Inn*, 407 Cliff St (☎831/427-2609; ⑤), at the top of Beach Hill, is more luxurious. The best **campground** is at *New Brighton State Beach* (☎831/464-6330 or 1-800/444-7275), three miles south on the edge of the beachfront village of Capitola. The *Miramar Fish Grotto*, 45 Municipal Wharf (☎831/423-4441), is one of several good seafront **restaurants**; *Gabriella Cafe*, 910 Cedar St (☎831/457-1677), has elegant Californian cuisine; *Zachary's* at 819 (☎831/427-0646) and *Zoccoli's* (☎831/423-1711) are just two of the many casual cafes along the main drag of Pacific Avenue, the best spot in town for watching locals parade past.

Santa Cruz has the central coast's rowdiest **nightlife**, ranging from coffeehouses to bars and nightclubs where the music varies from surf-thrash to reggae to the rowdy rock of local resident Neil Young and sometimes all on the same dance floor. *The Catalyst*, 1011 (☎831/423-1336), and *Palookaville*, 1133 Pacific Ave(☎831/454-0600), are the best bets for catching big-name touring artists and up-and-coming locals (consult the free *Good Times* magazine for what's on), while the friendly and intimate *Kuumbwa Jazz Center*, 320 Cedar St (☎831/427-2227), showcases modern jazz. *Blue Lagoon*, 923 Pacific Ave (☎831/423-7117), and *Club Dakota*, Pacific Avenue near Lincoln (☎831/454-9030), are each two popular gay and lesbian hangouts.

# THE CENTRAL VALLEY

The vast **interior** of California is split down the middle by the Sierra Nevada Mountains. The wide **Central Valley** (aka the San Joaquin Valley) in the west was made super-fertile by irrigation projects during the 1940s, and is now almost totally agricultural. Even if the nightlife begins and ends with the local ice-cream parlor, after the big cities of the coast it can all be quite refreshing. However, the real reason to come here is to reach the **national parks** of **Sequoia** and **Kings Canyon** – whose huge trees form the centerpiece of a rich natural landscape – and **Yosemite**, where towering walls of silvery granite are invigorated by waterfalls. No roads penetrate the hundred miles of wilderness to the east, but the entire region is crisscrossed by hiking trails leading up into the pristine alpine backcountry of the **High Sierra**. Seen from the east side, their Spanish name, *Sierra Nevada* ("snowcapped sawblade"), perfectly describes the sharply serrated ridges that stand high above the semi-desert of the Owens Valley (see p.956).

The arrow-straight I-5 barrels straight up from LA to San Francisco. Four daily **trains** and frequent Greyhound **buses** run through the valley, calling at the towns along Hwy-99, in particular Fresno and Merced, which both have bus connections to Yosemite but otherwise don't merit a look-in.

## Bakersfield

The first town you come to across the rocky peaks north of Los Angeles, looming unappealingly out of a forest of oil derricks, is the flat and featureless **BAKERSFIELD**. This is the unlikely home of one of the liveliest **country music** scenes in the nation, stemming from the arrival during the Depression of Midwestern farmers, with their hillbilly instruments and campfire songs. In the mid-Sixties, the gutsy honky-tonk style of Bakersfield artists such as Merle Haggard and Buck Owens challenged the slick commercial output of Nashville, but hopes of luring the major country music record labels to "Nashville West" foundered with the emergence of rivals like Austin, Texas.

Nevertheless, the numerous honky-tonks of Bakersfield are still jumping every Friday and Saturday night. There's seldom a cover charge, and live sets usually entail one band playing for four or five hours from around 8pm, with a fifteen-minute break every hour. Stetson hats and flouncy shirts are the sartorial order of the day, and audiences span generations. Most **venues** are hotel lounges or restaurant backrooms; don't miss the country bar *Trouts*, 805 N Chester Ave (☎661/399-6700). Closer to town, you might also try the *Buck Owens Crystal Palace*, 2800 Buck Owens Boulevard (☎661/328-7560), where the $6 cover includes a museum of Buck Owens memorabilia, or the clubbier *Rockin' Rodeo*, 3745 Rosedale Hwy (☎805/323-6617), with a New Country or rock DJ every night.

### Practicalities

You have to come to Bakersfield from LA by Amtrak Thruway bus to catch the train through the valley to San Francisco and northern California. Several Greyhound routes require changes here too, calling at 1820 18th St. The handiest **visitor center** is at 1725 Eye St (Mon 9am–5pm Tues–Fri 8am–5pm; ☎661/327-4421). Bargain **overnight stays** include the *EZ-8*, 2604 Pierce Rd (☎661/322-1901 or 1-800/326-6835; $35), and the adjacent *La Quinta*, 3232 Riverside Drive (☎1-800/531-5900 or 661/325-7400; $65); both pool-equipped and a short stagger from Buck Owens Crystal Palace. For **eating**, *Zingo's* at 2625 Pierce Rd (☎661/324-3640) is a 24-hour truckstop where frilly-aproned waitresses deliver plates of diner staples; *24th Street Cafe*, 1415 24th St, does top-rate breakfasts; *Joseph's*, hidden back off the road at 3013 F St (☎661/322-7710), serves huge calzone and other Italian dishes; and the *Noriega Hotel*, 525 Sumner St (☎661/322-8419), offers excellent all-you-can-eat Basque meals at long communal tables.

# Sequoia and Kings Canyon

The southernmost of the Sierra Nevada national parks, preserving ancient forests of giant sequoia trees, are Sequoia and Kings Canyon. As you might expect, **Sequoia National Park** contains the thickest concentration – and the biggest specimens – of sequoias to be found anywhere, tending (literally) to overshadow its assortment of meadows, peaks, canyons and caves. **Kings Canyon National Park** has few big trees but compensates with a gaping canyon gored out of the rock by the Kings River as it cascades down from the High Sierra. The few established sights of both parks are near the main roads, leaving the vast majority of the landscape untrammeled and unspoiled, but well within reach for willing hikers.

### Arrival and information

No **public transportation** of any kind serves the parks, but by **car** things are simple: the closest large town is **Visalia**, just under fifty miles distant on Hwy-198, or a slightly longer, but faster, drive uses Hwy-180 from Fresno. Collected at the park's entrance stations, there is a **fee** of $10 per car, or $5 per person for those on foot or bike, you'll be given a detailed map of the paired parks, a copy of *Sequoia Bark*, detailing accommodation, **guided hikes** and other activities, and free rein in the parks for a week. The two parks are separate but jointly run; for activities, **road** and **park information** call ☎559/565-3341 or look at *www.nps.gov/seki*.

## Sequoia National Park

While trees are seldom scarce in **SEQUOIA NATIONAL PARK** – where the giant sequoias can't grow there are thick swaths of pine and fir – the scenery varies. Paths lead through forests and meadows; longer treks rise above the tree line to the barren peaks of the High Sierra. Soon after entering the park from the south, Hwy-198 becomes the **Generals' Highway** and climbs swiftly into the dense woods of the aptly labeled **Giant Forest**, from where you can explore along Crescent Meadow Road, which spurs east here. A short distance along, you pass the **Auto Log**, a fallen sequoia chiseled flat for motorists to drive onto. Just beyond, a loop road leads to the granite monolith of **Moro Rock** (a three-mile marked trail leads from Giant Forest), which streaks wildly upward from the green hillside. Views from its remarkably level top can stretch 150 miles. A hewn staircase makes it easy to climb the rock in fifteen minutes, although the altitude can be a strain.

Continuing east along Crescent Meadow Road, you pass under the **Tunnel Log**, which fell across the road in 1937 and had a vehicle-sized hole cut through it. At the end of the route, **Crescent Meadow** is, like other grassy fields in the area, more accurately a marsh, too wet for the sequoias that form an impressive boundary around. A perimeter trail leads to **Tharp's Log**, a cabin hollowed out of a fallen sequoia by Hale Tharp who, while searching for a summer grazing ground for his sheep, was led here by Native Americans in 1856. He was not only the first white man to see the giant sequoias but the first to live in one. Just north of Giant Forest, back on the Generals' Highway, is the biggest sequoia of them all, the 3000-year-old, 275ft **General Sherman Tree**. While it's certainly a thrill to see what is held to be the largest living thing on the planet, its extraordinary dimensions are hard to grasp alongside the almost equally monstrous sequoias around.

Whatever your plans, you should stop at **Lodgepole Village**, three miles north of the Sherman Tree, for the geological displays and film shows at the **visitor center** (mid-May–Aug daily 8am–6pm; rest of year daily 8am–5pm). You can explore the glacial canyon on the **Tokopah Valley Trail** (2hr), which leads to the base of Tokopah Falls, beneath the 1600ft **Watchtower** cliff. The top of the Watchtower is accessible by the fatiguing but straightforward seven-mile **Lakes Trail**.

## Kings Canyon National Park

**Kings Canyon National Park** is wilder and less visited than Sequoia, with a maze-like collection of canyons and a sprinkling of isolated lakes – the perfect environment for careful self-guided exploration. To reach the main canyon proper, you have to pass through the hamlet of **Grant Grove**, where there's a useful **visitor center** (daily: mid-May–Aug 8am–6pm; rest of year 8am–5pm) and the 2.5-mile **Big Stump Trail** shows off the remains of the logging which took place in the 1880s. Several massive trees from these parts were sliced up and sent to the Atlantic seaboard to convince cynical easterners that such enormous trees really existed. A mile west of Grant Grove, a large stand of sequoias contains the **General Grant** and **Robert E Lee** trees, which rival the General Sherman further south.

**Kings Canyon Highway** (Hwy-180; May–Oct only) descends from Grant Grove into the steep-sided Kings Canyon, cut by the furious gushings of various forks of the Kings River. Whether or not this is the deepest canyon in the US, as some would have it, its wall sections of granite and gleaming blue marble and the yellow pockmarks of yucca plants are magnificent. It's extremely perilous to wade into the river: people have been swept away even when paddling close to the bank in a seemingly placid section.

Once into the national park proper, the canyon sheds its V-shape and gains a floor. **Cedar Grove Village** here is named for its proliferation of incense-cedars. There's a

**ranger station** across the river (June–Aug daily 9am–5pm; May, Sept & Oct hours reduced). Apart from the scenery, you should look out for the **flowers** – leopard lilies, shooting stars, violets, lupins and others – and **birdlife**. The longer hikes beside the creeks, many seven or eight miles long, are fairly strenuous. An easy alternative is to wander around the green **Zumwalt Meadow**, four miles from Cedar Grove Village and a short walk from the road, beneath the forbidding gray walls of Grand Sentinel and North Dome.

Just a mile further on, Kings Canyon Road comes to an end at **Copper Creek**. Thirty years ago it was decided that vehicles should not be allowed to penetrate further. Instead the multitude of canyons and peaks which constitute the Kings River Sierra are networked by **hiking paths**, almost all best enjoyed armed with a tent, provisions and a wilderness permit from the trailhead ranger station.

## Accommodation and eating in the parks

The least expensive **rooms** are in the motels near the park entrances: *Sierra Inn Motel* (☎559/338-2144, fax 338-0789; ④) fourteen miles west of the Big Stump entrance on Hwy-180 and, near the southern entrance on Hwy-198, *Gateway Lodge* (☎559/561-4133, fax 561-3656; ④). Inside the parks, all facilities are managed by Kings Canyon Park Services (KCPS; ☎559/335-5500; ⑤/⑥) who operate in Kings Canyon; and Delaware North Parks Services (DPNS; ☎1-888/252-5757 or 559/565-3301; ⑥/⑦) who cover Sequoia, with cabins and hotel units at Wuksachi, Stony Creek, Grant Grove and Cedar Grove. Space is at a premium during the high season (May–mid-Oct), but you can usually pick up cancellations on the day. Summer prices range from $45 for basic cabins without bath to $155 for stylish modern hotel rooms. In winter the cheaper cabins are too cold; and only those at Grant Grove drop their prices below $40.

Recorded **camping** information for both parks is on ☎559/565-3341. Campgrounds are dotted all over both parks, charging an average of $14 a pitch, though there are a couple of free, waterless sites in the national forest between the two. In **Sequoia**, the busiest is *Lodgepole*, which you can book up to eight weeks in advance through the National Park Reservation System (☎1-800/365-2267; *www.reservations.nps.gov*). In **Kings Canyon**, the bulk of the sites are around Grant Grove, with another at Cedar Grove – again, all cost around $14. For **backcountry** camping, get a free permit from a visitor center or ranger station. And remember this is **bear country**: in established campgrounds use the bearproof food boxes, in the backcountry rent bear canisters from the stores in Cedar Grove, Grant Grove and Lodgepole.

There are pricey **food** markets and cafeterias in the various villages, and a couple of restaurants, notably bargain buffets at the *Montecito-Sequoia Lodge* in the national forest between the two parks. Three Rivers, on the southern approach to Sequoia, has the best range of places to eat nearby.

## The Sierra National Forest

The entire gaping tract of land between Kings Canyon and Yosemite is taken up by the less-visited **Sierra National Forest**. If you want to hike and camp in complete solitude, this is the place to do it. But don't try lone exploration without thorough planning – public transportation is nonexistent, and roads and trails are often closed due to bad weather. The best-placed source of information is the **Pineridge Ranger Station** (daily 8am–4.30pm; ☎559/855-5360), located along Hwy-168 at Prather, five miles west of the forest entrance.

Of the forest's two main regions, the **Pineridge** district, forty miles east from Fresno using Hwy-168, is the best to explore. The popular **Shaver Lake** and **Huntington**

**Lake**, rich in campgrounds (reserve in summer on ☎1-800/280-2267), soon give way to the isolated alpine landscapes beyond the 9200ft Kaiser Pass. The sheer challenge posed by the rugged, unspoiled terrain of the adjoining **John Muir Wilderness** can make the national parks look like holiday camps. You can bathe outdoors at the nearby **Mono Hot Springs**, although the *Mono Hot Springs Resort* here (mid-May–mid-Oct; ☎559/325-1710; ②/③) has indoor mineral baths along with its self-catering cabins. The road narrows and twists on to **Edison Lake** and the *Vermillion Valley Resort* (☎559/855-6558; ②/③), from where you can catch a small ferry across the lake to the trailheads. **Ranger stations** (daily 8am–4.30pm) at Huntington Lake on Hwy-168, and another twenty miles east at Shaver Lake issue free backcountry permits and have camping and wilderness information.

# Yosemite National Park

More gushing adjectives have been thrown at **YOSEMITE NATIONAL PARK** (*www.nps.gov/yose*) than at any other part of California. However excessive the hyperbole may seem, the instant you turn the corner that reveals **Yosemite Valley**, you realize it's actually an understatement – this is one of the world's most dramatic geological spectacles. Just seven miles long and at most one mile across, it is walled by near-vertical mile-high cliffs, streaked by tumbling waterfalls and topped by domes and pinnacles that form a jagged silhouette against the sky. At ground level, grassy meadows are framed by oak, cedar and fir trees; deer, coyotes and even black bears are not uncommon. Tourists are even commoner, but the park is big enough to absorb the crowds: you can visit at any time of year, even in winter when the waterfalls turn to ice and the trails are blocked by snow, and out of summer the valley itself is rarely overcrowded.

Yosemite Valley was made by glaciers gouging through the canyon of the Merced River: the ice scraped away the softer granite but only scarred the harder sections, which became the present cliffs. The lake which formed when the glaciers melted eventually silted up to create the present valley floor. Native Americans lived here in comparative peace until the mid-nineteenth century, when the threatening approach of Gold Rush settlers led them to launch raiding parties. In 1851 Major James Savage's Mariposa Battalion trailed the Native Americans into the foothills and beyond, becoming the first whites to set foot in Yosemite Valley, and the native community soon moved out to make way for farmers, foresters and tourists. In 1864 Yosemite became the country's first state park.

**John Muir**, a Scottish immigrant who traveled the entire area on foot, spearheaded the conservation movement that led to the founding of the Sierra Club, with the express aim of preserving Yosemite. In 1913, the construction of a dam in the Hetch Hetchy Valley just north, to provide water for San Francisco, was a setback; but the publicity actually aided the formation of the present National Park Service in 1916, which promised – and has since provided – greater protection.

## Getting there

**Getting to Yosemite** by car is straightforward, though the only road in from the east, Hwy-120 from Lee Vining, is closed from late October to late June. **Gas** is pricey in the park and unavailable in Yosemite Valley. **Public transportation** runs from two points in the Central Valley, both easily accessible by train. VIA Yosemite Connection (☎1-888/727-5287) has a once-daily service (April–Sept; $25 one-way, $48 for a one-day round-trip) from Fresno, and runs three or four times a day (year-round; $20 one-way and $38 round-trip) from **Merced**. Fares are inclusive of **park entry**, which otherwise costs $20 per vehicle, $10 per cyclist or hiker, and is valid for seven days. If you need somewhere to stay overnight before heading to Yosemite, the cheapest options are the

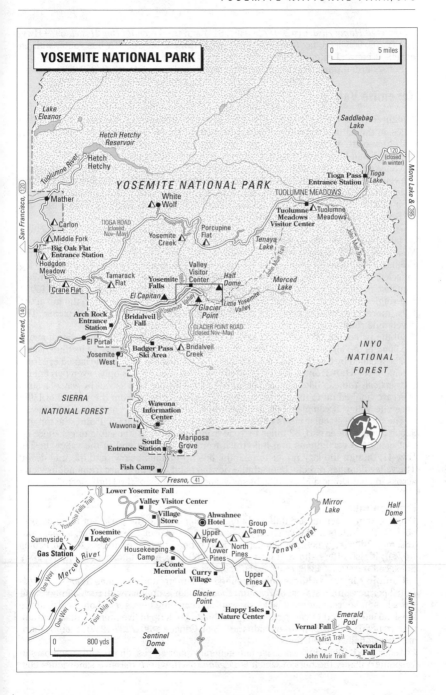

*HI–Merced Home Hostel* (☎209/725-0407; $14) and the *Yosemite Bug Hostel*, 6979 Hwy-140 (☎209/966-6666, fax 966-6667; $15), at **Midpines**, on the VIA bus route, with an excellent bar and cafe.

For recorded **park**, **road** and **weather information** phone ☎209/372-0200.

# Yosemite Valley

The three roads from the Central Valley end up in the center of the park's 1200 square miles, in the natural splendor of **Yosemite Valley**. This is the busiest part of Yosemite, with **Yosemite Village** holding the main shops and the useful **visitor center** (daily: mid-June–mid-Sept 8am–7pm; mid-Sept–mid-June 8.30am–5pm; ☎209/372-0265).

There's little in the village of any great interest; the reason to come here is to explore the valley itself. One of the most popular short walks is to the sensual **Bridalveil Falls**, a slender ribbon at the valley's western end. The falls, like all those in the valley, are at their most dramatic during the meltwater period of April and May; by August they can be reduced to a trickle or disappear altogether.

While you'll never be alone on the valley floor, most of the crowds can be left behind by taking any path that contains a slope. Perhaps the best of these leads to the **Upper Yosemite Falls** along a steep switchback path from behind the *Sunnyside* campground, near *Yosemite Lodge*. This almost continuous ascent is very sapping on the leg muscles, but you get fine views over the valley on the way up, and after about two miles, a chance to appreciate the power (and volume) of the water as it crashes almost 1500ft in a single cascade. A mile and a half further on the same trail, you reach the top of the falls, more spectacular views and riverside spots for a much deserved picnic. The seven-mile round-trip walk will take around five or six hours.

Of the two major cliffs visible from the valley, **El Capitan**, rising some 3500ft above the floor, is the biggest piece of exposed granite in the world. A sense of its dimensions can be gleaned by the fact that rock-climbers fast become invisible to the naked eye from ground level. **Half Dome**, the sheerest cliff in North America, is only seven percent off the vertical. You can hike up past Vernal Falls, making the final ascent by way of a steel staircase hooked on to its curving back (May–mid-Oct only) from the far end of Little Yosemite Valley; if you plan a one-day assault, you'll need to start at the crack of dawn.

The most spectacular views of Yosemite Valley are from **Glacier Point**, the top of a 3200ft almost-sheer cliff, 32 miles by road from the valley. It's possible to get there on foot using the vertiginous four-mile track from the western end of the valley, beside Hwy-41, though the lazy prefer to take the bus up (details below) and the trail down. The valley floor lies directly beneath the viewing point, and there are tremendous views across to Half Dome and the distant snowcapped summits of the High Sierra.

## Practicalities

Prices within Yosemite are uniformly higher than outside the park, but not unaffordable. Of the **hotels** in the valley, try *Yosemite Lodge* (⑤) or *Curry Village*, a mile from Yosemite Village, which has similarly priced rooms, plus fixed tents (②) and cabins (④/⑤); it also offers showers for nonguests ($2). For hotel information and reservations, call ☎209/252-4848; *www.yosemitepark.com*.

**Camping in the valley** is only permitted in campgrounds, such as *Sunnyside Walk-In* ($3 per person), just west of *Yosemite Lodge*, which is popular with rock-climbers and has a bohemian reputation; it lacks showers and can only be reserved on the day at the kiosk on site. For other campgrounds, you should book up to five months ahead in summer (☎1-800/436-7275; from outside the US or Canada ☎301/722-1257), though there are occasionally cancellations.

As for **food**, there are expensive and generally poor stores, diners and snack bars in Yosemite Village, the best of which is *Degnan's Deli*, where massive sandwiches cost around $5. The *Mountain Room Broiler* at *Yosemite Lodge* is good but fairly pricey, while the baronial *Ahwahnee Dining Room* (☎209/372-1489) has the best (and most expensive) food in Yosemite: jacket and tie preferred. *Curry Village* has a great deck where you can order pizza, and margarita pitchers.

Once in Yosemite Valley, **getting around** is easy. Frequent, free **shuttle buses** loop around the valley in summer (daily 7.30am–10pm), calling at all points of interest. **Cars** spoil everybody's fun; if you drive in for the day, park at the *Curry Village* lodge. A number of **bicycle paths** cross the valley floor but **bike rental** is limited to outlets at *Yosemite Lodge* and *Curry Village* ($20 a day). There are also **guided tours** (☎209/372-1240), **hikes** and **horseback trips**.

## Outside the valley

The **Mariposa Grove**, three miles east of Hwy-41 on a small road that cuts off just past the park's southern entrance, is the biggest and best of Yosemite's groves of **giant sequoia** trees. To get to the towering growths, walk the 2.5-mile loop trail from the parking lot at the end of the road, which is also served by a free tram from the entrance. The most renowned of the grouping, well marked along the route, is the **Grizzly Giant**, thought to be 2700 years old.

On the eastern edge of the park, the **Tuolumne Meadows** have an atmosphere quite different from the valley; here, at 8500 feet, you almost seem to be level with the tops of the surrounding snow-covered mountains. The air always has a fresh, crisp bite, and early summer reveals a plethora of colorful wild flowers. It's a better starting point than the valley for backcountry hiking into the High Sierra, where seven hundred-odd miles of trails, both long and short, crisscross their way along the Sierra Nevada ridges. To use any of the primitive **backcountry campgrounds**, you must get a free **wilderness permit**, available by post from the Wilderness Office, Box 577, Yosemite National Park, CA 95389, or no more than 24 hours in advance from the nearest visitor center. In summer canvas **tent cabins** are available in Tuolumne only for around $35.

# SAN FRANCISCO

SAN FRANCISCO proper occupies just 48 hilly square miles at the tip of a slender peninsula, almost perfectly centered along the California coast. Arguably the most beautiful, certainly the most liberal city in the US, it remains true to itself: a funky, individualistic, surprisingly small city whose people pride themselves on being the cultured counterparts to their cousins in LA – the last bastion of civilization on the lunatic fringe of America. It's a compact and approachable place, where downtown streets rise on impossible gradients to reveal stunning views of the city, the bay and beyond, and blanket fogs roll in unexpectedly to envelop the city in mist. This is not the California of monotonous blue skies and slothful warmth – the temperatures rarely exceed the seventies, and even during summer can drop much lower.

The original inhabitants of this area, the **Ohlone Indians**, were all but wiped out within a few years of the establishment in 1776 of the **Mission Dolores**, the sixth in the chain of Spanish Catholic missions that ran the length of California. Two years after the Americans replaced the Mexicans in 1846, the discovery of gold in the Sierra foothills precipitated the rip-roaring **Gold Rush**. Within a year fifty thousand pioneers had traveled west, and east from China, turning San Francisco from a muddy village and wasteland of sand dunes into a thriving supply center and transit town. By the time the **transcontinental railroad** was completed in 1869, San Francisco was a lawless, rowdy boomtown of bordellos and drinking dens, something the monied elite – who hit it big on the much more dependable silver Comstock Load – worked hard to mend, constructing wide boulevards, parks, a cable car system and elaborate Victorian redwood mansions.

In the midst of the city's golden age, however, a massive **earthquake**, followed by three days of fire, wiped out most of the town in 1906. Rebuilding began immediately, resulting in a city more magnificent than before, in the decades that followed, writers like Dashiell Hammett and Jack London lived and worked here. Many of the city's landmarks, including Coit Tower and both the Golden Gate and Bay bridges, were built in the 1920s and 1930s. By World War II San Francisco had been eclipsed by Los Angeles as the main West Coast city, but it achieved a new cultural eminence with the emergence of the Beats in the Fifties and the hippies in the Sixties, when the fusion of music, protest, rebellion and, of course, drugs that characterized 1967's "Summer of Love" took over the Haight-Ashbury district.

In a conservative America, San Francisco's reputation as a liberal oasis continues to grow, attracting waves of resettlers from all over the US. It is estimated that over half the city's population originates from somewhere else. It is a city in a constant state of evolution, fast gentrifying itself into one of the most high-end towns on earth – thanks, in part, to the disposable incomes pumped into its coffers from its sizeable singles and gay contingent. Gay capital of the world, San Francisco is also at the heart of the Information Revolution, and the resultant wealth has made housing prices skyrocket – often at the expense of the city's middle and lower classes. Despite this stratification, and a growing homeless population, your impression of the city likely won't be altered – it remains one of the most proudly distinct places to be found anywhere.

## Arrival and information

All international and most domestic flights arrive at **San Francisco International Airport** (SFO), inconveniently located about fifteen miles south of the city. San Mateo County Transit (SamTrans) **buses** leave every half-hour from the upper level of the airport; the #KX express ($3) takes around 25 minutes to reach the Transbay Terminal downtown, while the slower #292 ($1.10) stops everywhere and takes nearly an hour. On the #KX, you're allowed only one carry-on bag; on the #292, you can bring as much as you want provided you can carry it onto the bus yourself. The SFO Airporter bus ($10) picks up outside each baggage claim area every fifteen minutes and travels to Union Square and the Financial District. The blue **Supershuttle**, **American Airporter Shuttle** and the **Yellow Airport Shuttle** minibuses depart every five minutes from the upper level of the circular road and take passengers to any city-center destination for around $12 a head. Be ruthless – competition for these and the several other companies running shuttle service is fierce and queues nonexistent. **Taxis** from the airport cost $25–30 (plus tip) for any downtown location, more for East Bay and Marin County – definitely worth it if there is more than one of you. If you're planning to drive, the usual **car rental** agencies operate free shuttle buses to their depots, leaving every 15 minutes from the upper level, but you have to load and unload your bags yourself. The car rental depot is located north of SFO and is too far to walk to. A shuttle train, now under construction, will alleviate this inconvenient system.

Several domestic airlines (America West and Southwest are two) and United fly into **Oakland International Airport** (OAK; see p.1002 for details), across the bay. This is actually closer to downtown San Francisco than SFO, and is efficiently connected with the city by the $2 AirBART shuttle bus, which drops you at the Coliseum BART station. Get on BART and San Francisco's downtown stops are fifteen minutes away ($2.75).

### By bus and train
All San Francisco's **Greyhound** services use the **Transbay Terminal** at 425 Mission St, south of Market Street, near the Embarcadero BART station. **Green Tortoise** buses

stop behind the Transbay Terminal on First and Natoma. **Amtrak** trains stop across the bay in **Richmond** (with easy BART transfers) and continue to **Oakland**, from where free shuttle buses run across the Bay Bridge to the Transbay Terminal, or you can take BART. Though technically closer to San Francisco, don't get off at the stop before Oakland, **Emeryville**, as consistent public transportation to the city doesn't exist.

## Information

The **San Francisco Visitor Information Center**, on the lower level of Hallidie Plaza at the end of the cable car line on Market Street (Mon–Sat 9am–5pm, Sun 9am–3pm; ☎415/391-2000), has free maps of the city and the Bay Area, and can help with lodging and travel plans. Its free *San Francisco Book* and *Lodging Guide* provide detailed, if somewhat selective, information about accommodation, entertainment, exhibitions and stores.

San Francisco's two main **post offices**, with telephone and general delivery facilities, are at Sutter Street Station, 150 Sutter St (Mon–Fri 8.30am–5pm), and Rincon Finance Station, 180 Steuart St (Mon–Fri 7am–6pm, Sat 9am–2pm).

## City transportation

San Francisco is a rare American city where you don't need a car to see everything. In fact, given the chronic shortage of parking downtown, horrible traffic and zealous

---

### SAN FRANCISCO PUBLIC TRANSPORT

**USEFUL BUS ROUTES**

**#5** From the Transbay Terminal, west alongside Haight-Ashbury and Golden Gate Park to the ocean.

**#7** From the Ferry Terminal (Market St) to the end of Haight St and to Golden Gate Park.

**#15** From Third St (SoMa) to Pier 39, Fisherman's Wharf, via the Financial District and North Beach.

**#20 (Golden Gate Transit)** From Civic Center to the Golden Gate Bridge ($1.75).

**#22** From the Marina up Pacific Heights and north on Fillmore.

**#28** and **#29** From the Marina through the Presidio, north through Golden Gate Park, the Richmond and the Sunset.

**#30** From the CalTrain depot on Third Street, north to Ghiradelli Square, via Chinatown and North Beach, and out to Chestnut Street in the Marina district.

**#38** From Geary St via Civic Center, west to the ocean along Geary Blvd through Japantown and the Richmond, ending at Cliff House.

**MUNI TRAIN LINES**

**Muni F-MARKET LINE** Restored vintage trolleys from other cities run downtown from the Transbay Terminal up Market Street and into the heart of Castro.

**Muni J-CHURCH LINE** From downtown to Mission and the edge of the Castro.

**Muni K-INGLESIDE LINE** From downtown through the Castro to Balboa Park.

**Muni L-TARAVAL LINE** From downtown west through the Sunset to the zoo and Ocean Beach.

**Muni M-OCEAN VIEW** From downtown west by the Stonestown Galleria shopping center and San Francisco State University.

**Muni N-JUDAH LINE** From downtown west through the Inner Sunset and to Ocean Beach, via the outer Haight.

From the Muni N-Judah line or buses #5 and #38, you can connect to **bus #44** which goes by the **De Young Museum, Asian Art Museum, Japanese Tea Garden, California Academy of Sciences** and **Steinhart Aquarium** in Golden Gate Park. A Muni transfer will get you **discounts** at these places.

meter maids who love to give expensive parking tickets, going carless makes sense. The public transportation system, **MUNI**, though much maligned by locals for its unpredictable schedule, covers every neighborhood inexpensively via its system of cable cars, buses and trolleys. Bikes are a good option, as marked bike routes – with lanes – direct riders to all major points of interest. Walking the compact metropolis is the best bet, with each turn revealing surprises. Often these are in the form of stunning homes and bustling marketplaces, but on killer hills, some angled at 30 degrees and all punishment on the legs. Wear comfortable shoes.

## Muni
The city's public transportation is run by the **San Francisco Municipal Railway**, or Muni (☎415/673-6864). A comprehensive network of **buses, trolleybuses** and **cable cars** run up and over the city's hills, while the underground **trains** become **streetcars** when they emerge from the downtown metro system to split off and serve the suburbs. On buses and trains the flat **fare** (correct change only) is $1; with each ticket you buy, ask for a **free transfer** – good for another two rides on a train or bus, and a fifty-percent reduction on cable cars if used within ninety minutes. Local groceries have begun to vend **single-ride tokens** ($.80), which save money and take care of the annoyance of not having correct change. Cable cars cost $2 one-way (no transfers).

If you're staying a few days, the Muni **Passport** is available in one-day, three-day, and seven-day denominations ($6, $10, $15) and is valid for unlimited travel on the Muni system and BART stations (see below) within the city limits. A **Fast Pass** costs $35 for a full calendar month. Muni trains run **throughout the night** on a limited service, except those on the M-Ocean View line, which stop around 1am. **Buses** run all night, but services are greatly reduced after midnight. For **more information**, pick up the handy Muni map from the Visitor Information Center or bookstores.

**Bikes** are allowed on MUNI buses equipped with bicycle racks (on the front of the bus) and on Bay Area Rapid Transit, **BART**, except during peak commute hours.

## Other transportation services
Various other public transportation networks serve San Francisco and the Bay Area. Along Market Street downtown, Muni shares the station concourses with BART, which runs to the East Bay – including downtown Oakland and Berkeley – and outer suburbs. The **CalTrain** commuter railway (depot at Fourth and Townsend, South of Market) links San Francisco along the peninsula south to San Jose. **Golden Gate Ferry** boats (☎415/923-2000) leave from the Ferry Building at the Embarcadero, crossing the bay past Alcatraz to Sausalito and Larkspur in Marin County. **Blue & Gold Fleet** (☎415/773-1188) sail to Sausalito and Tiburon from Pier 41 at Fisherman's Wharf. The **Alameda–Oakland ferry** (☎510/522-3300) sails between Oakland's Jack London Square, the Ferry Building and Fisherman's Wharf ($4.50 one-way) and, in summer, to Angel Island (daily May–Oct; $13 round-trip).

**Taxis** ply the streets, and you can flag one down (especially downtown), but finding one can be a pain. Phoning around, try Veterans (☎415/552-1300) or Yellow Cab (☎415/626-2345). Fares (within the city) are roughly $1.70 to start the meter, $1.80 for the first mile and $1.50 per mile thereafter.

If you fancy **cycling**, Park Cyclery, 1749 Waller St (☎415/751-7368) in the Haight, near Golden Gate Park, rents mountain bikes for $5 per hour, $25 per day. Downtown, for Golden Gate Bridge rides, try American Bicycle Rental, 2715 Hyde St, near Fisherman's Wharf (☎415/931-0234), and Blazing Saddles, 1095 Columbus in North Beach (☎415/202-8888); both rent bikes for $5 per hour, $25 per day.

## Organized tours

One way to orient yourself is an **organized tour**. Gray Line Tours (☎415/558-9400), for example, take you around the city in three-and-a-half fairly tedious hours for around $28 a head. Considerably more exciting are the 75-minute **bay cruises** operated by the Blue & Gold Fleet (☎415/705-5555; $16) from pier 39 and pier 41 – though be warned that everything may be shrouded in fog. Excruciatingly expensive **aerial tours** of the city and Bay Area in light aircraft are available from several operators, such as Bay Aero Tours (☎510/632-6763), which offers spectacular flights over the Bay Area for $55 per passenger – the third passenger goes free.

The best of the **walking tours** include City Guides, sponsored by the San Francisco Public Library and free (☎415/557-4266); Cruisin' the Castro (☎415/550-8110; $35), an absorbing and witty tour of the gay community; Beatnik Walking Tour (☎415/522-9621; $10), hosted by an Englishman beginning at the *Vesuvio Cafe*; and All About Chinatown (☎415/982-8839; $25), an insider's cultural perspective on this lively quarter (optional dim sum lunch, $10 extra). There are also special mural tours of the Mission, taking in the district's distinctive street art (see p.989 for details).

# Accommodation

Annual visitors far outnumber San Francisco's 750,000 people, and the city isn't short on lodging. Some thirty thousand beds are available in the city, at prices ranging from $15 for dormitory-style accommodation to a whopping $575 for a suite at the *Ritz*. The **hotels and motels** have a good reputation for comfort and cleanliness. Hotels in the developing South of Market area and the very seedy Tenderloin start at around $30 per night or $120 a week, without a private bath or even a toilet. In the groomed areas around Union Square and Nob Hill it's hard to find a place for under $125 a night.

For **B&Bs**, the city's fastest-growing source of accommodation, consult the list below, or contact a specialist agency such as Bed and Breakfast California (12711 McCartysville, Saratoga, CA 95070; ☎408/867-9662 or 1-800/872-4500; *www.bbintl.com*) or Bed and Breakfast San Francisco (PO Box 420009, San Francisco, CA 94142; ☎415/931-3083). British visitors can reserve rooms through **Colby International** (☎0151/220 5848.)

San Francisco Reservations (22 Second St, Fourth Floor, San Francisco, CA 94105; ☎1-800/677-1500 or 415/227-1500; *www.hotelres.com*) will find you a room from around $80 a double. If all else fails and you've got a car, **motels** are legion along the highways and bigger roads throughout the Bay Area, at a standard rate of $35–45 a night. In all cases, bear in mind that all quoted room rates are subject to a **fourteen percent room tax**.

**Camping** isn't an option in San Francisco itself, though throwing down a bag in Golden Gate Park or the Presidio may seem tempting. Camping is illegal within the city, and can be dangerous, as well.

## Hostels and YMCAs

**Green Tortoise Hostel**, 494 Broadway (☎415/834-1000). Funky North Beach hostel amongst strip clubs. Dorm beds $16–19 per night, double rooms $42–48; both options include complimentary breakfast, use of sauna and Internet access. They also run a daily bus to Seattle, departing at 8pm (24hrs; $59). ③/②.

**HI-San Francisco Downtown**, 312 Mason St (☎415/788-5604). Large, newish downtown hostel with dorm beds from $14–16 and twins $28–32. Members only; day membership costs $3. The cleanest and most central of the bunch. ③.

**Interclub/Globe Hostel**, 10 Hallam Place (☎415/431-0540). Lively South of Market hostel with young clientele and no curfew. $15 per person; doubles $36. ①/②.

**Pacific Tradewinds Guesthouse**, 680 Sacramento St (☎415/433-7970). Great location in Chinatown, no curfew, laundry and a host of other services. $14–16 per person. ①.

**San Francisco International Guest House**, 2976 23rd St (☎415/641-1411). Popular with European travelers, this Mission District Victorian house has dorms and a few private rooms. $15 per person daily, 5-day minimum stay; $13 a day if you stay a month. Two kitchens; no curfew, and no reservations accepted. ①.

**San Francisco International Youth Hostel**, Building 240, Fort Mason (☎415/771-7277). On the waterfront between the Golden Gate Bridge and Fisherman's Wharf. One of the most comfortable and convenient hostels around. Open 24hr, 150 beds, free parking. From $16 per person, $32 for a twin. Includes breakfast, and because it is on federal land, no membership fee. ①.

**YMCA Central Branch**, 220 Golden Gate Ave (☎415/885-0460). Good central single and double rooms, two blocks from Civic Center. Rates include breakfast and use of gym, pool and sauna. $30 single, $40 double. ①/②.

## Hotels, motels and B&Bs

**Abigail**, 246 McAllister St (☎415/861-1560). Comfortable, stylish and affordable, this Civic Center hotel caters to travelers performing at the nearby arts centers. ⑤.

**Andora Inn**, 2438 Mission at 20th (☎415/282-0337 or 1-800/967-9219). Fully restored 12-room Victorian manor located in the heart of the Mission with an awesome staff. Shared ④/⑤, deluxe room and suites for $119 to $169. ④.

**Archbishop's Mansion**, 1000 Fulton St (☎415/563-7872). Grandly camp Alamo Square mansion that was once a school for wayward Catholic boys and is now a really interesting, gay-friendly B&B. Attentive personalized service, a variety of "theme" rooms, the ballroom chandelier from *Gone With the Wind*, and everything from fitness training to image consulting. ⑥/⑦.

**Beresford Arms**, 701 Post St (☎415/673-2600). Luxury B&B in the heart of town. ⑤/⑥.

**Clarion-Bedford**, 761 Post St (☎415/673-6040). Charming old-world mid-sized hotel offering tremendous value in the traditionally pricey Theater District. ⑥/⑦.

**Del Sol**, 3100 Webster St (☎415/921-5520). Bright, sunny refurbished 50s motor lodge in the heart of the Marina, near Union and Fillmore St shopping. A delight to the eye. ⑥–⑧.

**Fairmont**, 950 Mason St (☎415/772-5000). Most famous of the top-notch hotels, an over-ornate palace with four restaurants and lounges, and fantastic views from the rooms. Site of US TV series *Hotel*. Don't miss the terrace garden, overlooking Powell and the splendor of the Tonga Room, in the basement. ⑧/⑨.

**Grant Plaza**, 465 Grant Ave (☎415/434-3883). Clean, comfortable Chinatown hotel. One of the best values in San Francisco. ③.

**Harbor Court**, 165 Steuart St (☎415/882-1300). Smart hotel in the Embarcadero district. On the waterfront; bay-view rooms get a panorama. ⑦/⑧.

**Huntington**, 1075 California St (☎415/474-5400). Understated and quietly elegant compared to its Nob Hill counterparts, this is *the* hotel for the wealthy who don't need to flash it about. ⑧/⑨.

**Inn at the Opera**, 333 Fulton St (☎415/863-8400). Very fancy, small hotel with a classical music theme. Across the street from the Opera House. ⑥.

**Jackson Court**, 2198 Jackson St (☎415/929-7670). Lovely converted Pacific Heights mansion. ⑥–⑨.

**La Quinta Inn**, 20 Airport Blvd (☎650/583-2223). Overnight laundry service and a pool make this a comfortable stopover near the airport. Free shuttle service to the airport. ④.

**Mansions**, 2220 Sacramento St (☎415/929-9444). Luxurious Victorian mansion, perched high up in the fancy reaches of Pacific Heights. ⑥–⑨.

**Monaco**, 501 Geary St (☎415/292-0100). Best of the new wave of San Francisco hotels offering great style and decor. Unfortunately, prices have risen in recent years. ⑦/⑧.

**Nob Hill,** 835 Hyde St (☎415/885-2987 or 877/NOBHILL). Inexpensive accommodation in the lower Nob Hill area. Small, clean and comfortable rooms with shared bath; private bath available. ⑥–⑨. $89 a night for six days or more.

**Pension San Francisco,** 1668 Market St (☎415/864-1271). A good, clean and basic base near the Civic Center, walkably close to SoMa and the Castro. ③–⑥.

**The Phoenix,** 601 Eddy St (☎415/776-1380). Converted Fifties-style motel in a slightly dodgy neighborhood on the edge of the Tenderloin, but the hip music-biz crowd who lounge around the pool drinking cocktails don't seem to mind. Next to the hip *Backflip* (see p.996). ⑤–⑦.

**The Red Victorian Bed, Breakfast and Art,** 1665 Haight St (☎415/864-1978). Bang in the middle of Haight-Ashbury, a lively New Agey B&B, which also calls itself the *Peace Center*, with a hippie art gallery. A real Sixties relic. ⑤–⑦.

**Renoir,** 45 McAllister between 7th and Market sts (☎415/626-5200). Good location just opposite the Civic Center. Glitzy lobby and large, comfy rooms. ⑤–⑦.

**Ritz-Carlton,** 600 Stockton St (☎415/296-7465). Incredible Beaux Arts structure – immaculate, expensive and yet somehow soulless. ⑨.

**San Remo,** 2237 Mason St (☎415/776-8688 or 1-800/352-7366). Pleasant, old-fashioned rooms (shared bath) in nice North Beach Victorian house. Friendly staff, good bar and restaurant. ④.

**Sir Francis Drake,** 450 Powell St (☎415/392-7755 or 1-800/227-5480). Don't be put off by the Beefeaters outside, this is a colonial California hotel whose greatest attraction is the 21st-floor *Harry Denton's Starlight Room,* offering jazz, smart drinks and great views to a good-time crowd. ⑦–⑨.

**Stanyan Park,** 750 Stanyan St (☎415/751-1000). Gorgeous small Victorian hotel in a great setting across from Golden Gate Park, with friendly staff and free continental breakfast. ⑥/⑦.

**Triton,** 342 Grant Ave (☎415/394-0500 or 1-888/364-2622). Very stylish, very comfortable and very central hotel, across from the Chinatown Gateway, two blocks from Union Square. ⑧/⑨.

**Washington Square Inn,** 1660 Stockton St (☎415/981-4220). Cozy B&B right on North Beach's lovely main square. Nonsmokers only. ⑥–⑧.

**Westin St Francis,** 335 Powell St (☎415/397-7000 or 1-800/WESTIN1). This completely renovated landmark hotel has a sumptuous lobby, five restaurants, two bars and a disco on the 32nd floor, but disappointingly plain rooms. ⑦–⑨.

**York,** 940 Sutter St (☎415/885-6800 or 1-800/808-9675). Quiet, older hotel on the western edge of downtown; location for the dramatic stairway scenes in *Vertigo.* ⑦–⑨.

## Women's and gay men's accommodation

**Andora Inn** 2434 Mission St at 21st (☎415/282-0337). Lovingly restored Victorian manor in the lively Mission district. Free continental breakfast, and wine and cheese in the evenings. ④.

**Archbishop's Mansion,** 1000 Fulton St (☎415/563-7872). See listing opposite.

**Hayes Valley,** 417 Gough St (☎415/431-9131). Bit of a flop-house, but popular with a rowdy crowd. ④/⑤.

**Inn on Castro,** 321 Castro St (☎415/861-0321). Luxury B&B; well worth the price for the large rooms and good breakfasts. Smack in the middle of the Castro. ⑤–⑦.

**Mary Elizabeth Inn,** 1040 Bush St (☎415/673-6768). Run by the United Methodist Church; a safe but unexciting place for women. Weekly rates available, breakfast and dinner included. ③.

**Queen Anne,** 1590 Sutter St (☎415/441-2828). Very much a gay hotel with overdone decor and complimentary afternoon tea and sherry. ⑥/⑦.

**24 Henry,** 24 Henry St (☎415/864-5686). Quiet, intimate guesthouse near the heart of the Castro. ④ with shared bath, ⑤ with private bath.

**24 Henry Village Guesthouse,** 4080 18th St (☎415/864-0994). Branch of the above. Right in the heart of the Castro. ⑥.

**The Willows,** 710 14th St (☎415/431-4770). Affordable, well furnished and near the Castro. ⑥/⑦.

**Women's Hotel,** 642 Jones St (☎415/775-1711). Comfortable, secure, women-only building, unfortunately situated in the shabby Tenderloin district. Weekly rates only: singles $185 per week, doubles $235. ①/②.

# The City

San Francisco is a city of hills and distinct neighborhoods. As a general rule, geographical elevation means wealth – the higher up you are, the less fog you endure, resulting in better views. Commercial square-footage is surprisingly small and mostly confined to the downtown area, and the rest of the city is made up of primarily resi-

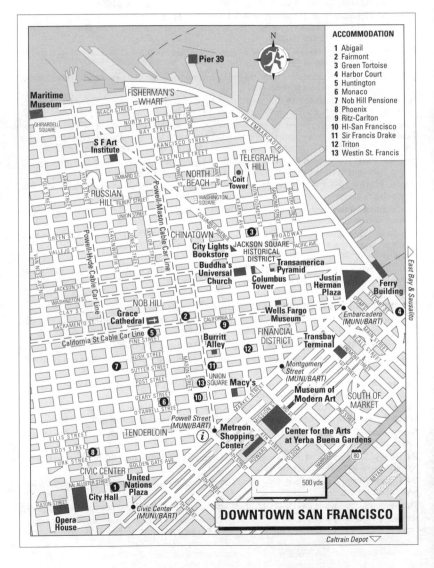

**ACCOMMODATION**

1 Abigail
2 Fairmont
3 Green Tortoise
4 Harbor Court
5 Huntington
6 Monaco
7 Nob Hill Pensione
8 Phoenix
9 Ritz-Carlton
10 HI-San Francisco
11 Sir Francis Drake
12 Triton
13 Westin St. Francis

**DOWNTOWN SAN FRANCISCO**

dential neighborhoods with street-level shopping districts, easily explored on foot. Armed with a good map and strong legs, you could plough through much of the city in a day, but the best way to get to know San Francisco is to dawdle.

## Union Square

The city's heart can be found around **Union Square**, located north of Market Street and bordered by Powell and Stockton streets. Cable cars clank past bustling shoppers and theater-goers who gravitate to the district's many upscale hotels, department stores and boutiques. The statue in the center commemorates Admiral Dewey's success in the Spanish–American War, though the square takes its name from its role as gathering place for stumping speechmakers during the US Civil War. (The woman who posed for the monument became a local celebrity, marrying into the wealthy Spreckels family.) The square witnessed the attempted assassination of President Gerald Ford outside the **St Francis Hotel** in 1975, and was also the location of Francis Ford Coppola's film *The Conversation*, where Gene Hackman spied on strolling lovers. Many of **Dashiell Hammett's** detective stories, such as *The Maltese Falcon*, are set partly in the *St Francis*, in which he worked as a Pinkerton detective during the Twenties. Hammett fans should check out *John's Grill*, 63 Ellis St, for Sam Spade's favorite eating spot, and **Burritt Alley**, two blocks north of the square on Bush Street, near Stockton Street. Here's where Spade's partner, Miles Archer, met his end, shot by Brigid O'Shaughnessy. A plaque marks the spot.

On Geary Street, on the south side of the square, the **Theater District** is a pint-sized Broadway of restaurants, tourist hotels and serious and "adult" theaters. On the eastern side of the square, **Maiden Lane** is a chic urban walkway that before the 1906 earthquake and fire was one of the city's roughest areas, where homicides averaged around ten a month. Nowadays, aside from some prohibitively expensive boutiques, its main feature is San Francisco's only **Frank Lloyd Wright** building (now occupied by the Xanadu ethnic art gallery), an intriguing circular space which was a try-out for the Guggenheim in New York.

---

### THE CABLE CARS

It was the invention of the **cable car** that made high-society life on San Francisco's hills possible and practical. Since 1873, these little trolleys have been an integral part of life in the city, thanks to Scots-born Andrew Hallidie's concern for horses. Having watched a team struggle and fall, breaking their legs on a steep San Franciscan street, Hallidie designed a pulley system around the thick wire rope his father had patented in England. A transportation revolution followed. At their peak, just before the 1906 earthquake, over six hundred cable cars traveled 110 miles of track throughout the city; over the years, usage dwindled and, in 1964, nostalgic citizens voted to preserve the last seventeen miles (now just 10) as a moving historic landmark.

Today there are three lines. Two of them, the Powell & Mason and the Powell & Hyde lines run from Hallidie Plaza off Union Square at Powell and Market streets to Fisherman's Wharf. The Powell & Hyde is the steepest, reaching a hair-raising 21-degree grade between Lombard and Chestnut streets. The oldest route, the California line, climbs Nob Hill along California Street from the Embarcadero, rattling past the fanciest hotels in the city. The cars fasten onto a moving two-inch cable, which runs beneath the streets, gripping on the ascent then releasing at the top and gliding down the other side. You can see the huge motors that power these cables in the **Cable Car Museum and Powerhouse**, at 1201 Mason at Washington Street (daily 10am–5pm; free).

## The Financial District

North of the city's main artery, Market Street, the glass-and-steel skyscrapers of the **Financial District** have sprung up in the last twenty years to form its only real high-rise area. Sharp-suited workers clog the streets and coffee kiosks during business hours, but after 6pm, the area pretty much shuts down. Stop at the corner of Kearny and Market streets to admire the just-refurbished **Lotta's Fountain**, San Francisco's most treasured artifact. It was around here that people gathered to here news following the 1906 earthquake and fire, and also where famed soprano Luisa Tetrazinni gave a free concert on Christmas Eve, 1910.

Once cut off from the rest of San Francisco by the double-decker Embarcadero Freeway – damaged in the 1989 earthquake and finally torn down in 1991 – the **Ferry Building**, at the foot of Market Street, was modeled on the cathedral tower in Seville, Spain. Before the bridges were built in the 1930s it was the arrival point for fifty thousand cross-bay commuters daily. A few ferries still dock here (see p.978), but the characterless office units inside do little to suggest its former importance. The area in front of the Ferry Building is the site of the much-loved **Ferry Plaza Farmers' Market** (Sat 8.30am–2pm), a great place to buy or merely gawk at the colorful local produce.

Since the freeway was pulled down, the area around it, known as **The Embarcadero**, has experienced a dramatic renaissance – from an area of charmless office blocks into a swanky waterfront district with the city's most fashionable restaurants and hotels springing up beside palm trees and views of the bay.

From the vast and unimaginative **Embarcadero Center** shopping mall and the fountains of **Justin Herman Plaza** at the foot of Market it's a few blocks down to **Montgomery Street**, where the grand pillared entrances and banking halls of the post-1906 earthquake buildings era jostle for attention with a mixed bag of modern towers. For a hands-on grasp of modern finance, the **World of Economics Gallery** in the **Federal Reserve Bank**, 101 Market St (Mon–Fri 9am–6pm), is unbeatable: computer games allow you to engineer your own inflationary disasters, while exhibits detail recent scandals and triumphs. The **Wells Fargo History Museum**, 420 Montgomery St (Mon–Fri 9am–5pm; free), traces the far-from-slick origins of San Francisco's big money, right from the days of the Gold Rush, with mining equipment, gold nuggets, photographs, and a genuine retired stagecoach. Tucked discreetly in a nondescript building at 121 Steuart St is the little-known **Jewish Museum San Francisco** (Mon–Wed & Sun noon–5pm, Thurs noon–8pm; $5, free first Mon of month), which far from being the somber trudge through history its name suggests, has an impressive collection of contemporary work by Jewish artists.

## Jackson Square and the Barbary Coast

A century or so ago, the eastern flank of the Financial District formed part of the **Barbary Coast**, an area of land that grew due to the hundreds of ships that lay abandoned by sailors heading for the Gold Rush. Enterprising San Franciscans used the dry ships as hotels, bars and stores. This then-rough-and-tumble waterfront district gave The City an unsavory reputation as **Baghdad by the Bay**, packed as it was with saloons and brothels where hapless young males were given Mickey Finns and shanghaied into involuntary servitude on merchant ships. William Randolph Hearst's *Examiner* lobbied frantically to shut down the quarter, resulting in a 1917 California law prohibiting prostitution. Remains of the cradle of San Francisco can be seen in the **Jackson Square Historic District**, not an actual square but an area bordered by Washington, Columbus, Sansome and Pacific streets.

The landmark **Transamerica Pyramid**, at the foot of diagonal Columbus Avenue and Washington serves as a useful dividing point between the various downtown areas.

The 48-story structure, capped by a colossal 212ft hollow spire, arose amid a city-planning furor that earned it the name of "Pereira's Prick," after its LA-based architect William Pereira. Since then its been indisputably the signature of San Francisco's skyline, in these days of plump speculative buildings, a rare example of architecture that sacrifices the pragmatic for the symbolic. From a real-estate perspective, the building is a nightmare – as the structure tapers upward, the floors that fetch the highest rents diminish in area – the pyramid would be far more valuable upside down. Rudyard Kipling, Robert Louis Stevenson, Mark Twain and William Randolph Hearst all rented office space in the Montgomery Block that originally stood on this site, and regularly hung around the notorious *Bank Exchange* bar within. Legend also has it that Sun Yat Sen – whose statue is in Chinatown, three blocks away – wrote the Chinese constitution and orchestrated the successful overthrow of the Manchu Dynasty from his second-floor office here. Next door is a pleasant **redwood tree park** with fountains perfect for an outdoor lunch. Across the street from the park, **Hotaling Place**'s winding brickwork and antique lamps recall the past, and some original redbrick buildings can be seen, now serving as office space for upscale design firms. Heading west on Jackson or Pacific Streets from the area leads you back to Columbus and the green-copper siding of the **Columbus Tower**, 906 Kearney, the de facto beginning of North Beach. Director and San Francisco native Francis Ford Coppola owns the building, and his *Neibaum-Coppola Cafe* on the ground floor serves sandwiches, pasta and his wine from the nearby vineyards.

## Chinatown

Its 24 square blocks smack in the middle of San Francisco make up the second-largest Chinese community outside Asia. Almost entirely autonomous, with its own schools, banks and newspapers, it has its roots in the migration of Chinese laborers to the city after the completion of the transcontinental railroad, and the arrival of Chinese sailors keen to benefit from the Gold Rush. The city didn't extend much of a welcome: they were met by a tide of vicious racial attacks and the 1882 Chinese Exclusion Act. Nowadays they have been joined by Vietnamese, Koreans, Thais and Laotians: by day the area seethes with activity, by night it's a blaze of neon. Overcrowding is compounded by a brisk tourist trade – sadly, however, Chinatown boasts some of the tackiest stores and facades in the city, making it more similar to shopping in a bad part of Hong Kong than in Beijing. Indeed, Chinese tourists are often disappointed in the neighborhood's disorder, and the new, some say true, Chinese neighborhood is in the Richmond district along Clement Street.

Gold ornamented portals and brightly painted balconies sit above the souvenir shops and restaurants of narrow **Grant Avenue**, pass under the entrance arch at Bush Street to be met by an assault of plastic Buddhas, cloisonné "health balls," noisemakers and chirping mechanical crickets in every doorway. **Old St Mary's Church**, on Grant and California, was one of the few San Francisco buildings to survive the 1906 fire, and they have a good photo display of the damage to the city in the entranceway of the beautiful church.

Parallel to Grant Avenue, **Stockton Street** is crammed with exotic fish and produce markets, bakeries and herbalists. Inside the **Ellison Herb Shop** at no. 805 Stockton St, Chinatown's best-stocked herbal pharmacy, you'll find clerks filling orders the ancient Chinese way – with hand-held scales and abacuses – from drug cases filled with dried bark, roots, sharks' fins, cicadas, ginseng and other staples. Here, between Grant and Stockton, jumbled alleys hold the most worthwhile stops in the area. The best of these is Waverly Place, a two-block corridor of brightly painted balconies that was lined with brothels before the 1906 catastrophe and now home to three opulent but skillfully hidden **temples** (nos. 109, 125 and 146), their interiors a riot of black, gold and vermillion, still in use and open to visitors. North of Waverly Place, between Jackson and Washington streets, Ross Alley features the **Golden Gate Fortune Cookie Company**, no. 56, specializing in X-rated fortunes, and, next door, a barber who will cut your hair to resemble that of any Hollywood star's.

Some of the hundred-plus **restaurants** (see p.993 for recommendations) are historical landmarks in themselves. *Sam Woh*, at 813 Washington St, is a cheap and churlish exhaunt of the Beats where Gary Snyder taught Jack Kerouac to eat with chopsticks and had them both thrown out with his loud and passionate interpretation of Zen poetry.

## North Beach

Resting in the hollow between Russian and Telegraph hills, and split by Columbus Avenue, **North Beach** likes to think of itself as the happening district of San Francisco. It has been a focal point for anyone vaguely alternative ever since the **City Lights Bookstore** opened in 1953. The first paperback bookstore in the US stands amid the flashing neon and sleazy clubs of Columbus Avenue at Broadway, open until midnight seven days a week, and is still owned by poet and novelist Lawrence Ferlinghetti. The **Beat Generation** made this the literary capital of America, achieving overnight notoriety when charges of obscenity were leveled at Allen Ginsberg's poem *Howl* in 1957, which he first performed over in Cow Hollow at 3119 Fillmore St. It was the hedonistic antics of the Beats, as much as their literary merits, that struck a chord, and North Beach came to symbolize a wild and subversive lifestyle. The roadtrips and riotous partying, the drug-taking and embrace of Eastern religions were emulated nationwide; tourists poured into North Beach for "Beatnik Tours."

Next to the bookstore, **Vesuvio's**, an old North Beach bar where the likes of Dylan Thomas and Kerouac would get loaded, remains a haven for the lesser-knowns to pontificate on the state of the arts. At the crossroads of **Columbus and Broadway**, poetry meets porn in a raucous assembly of strip joints, coffeehouses and drag queens. Most famous, the *Condor Club* was where Carol Doda's revealing of her silicone-implanted

---

### ALCATRAZ

Before the rocky islet of **Alcatraz** became America's most dreaded **high-security prison**, in 1934, it had been home to little more than the odd pelican (*alcatraz* in Spanish). Surrounded by the freezing, impassable water of San Francisco Bay, it made an ideal place to hold the nation's most wanted criminals – men such as Al Capone and Machine Gun Kelly. The conditions were inhumane: inmates were kept in solitary confinement, in cells no larger than nine by five feet, most without light. They were not allowed to eat together, read newspapers, play cards or even talk; relatives could visit for only two hours each month. Escape really was impossible. Nine men managed to get off the rock, but there is no evidence that any of them made it to the mainland.

Due to its massive running costs, the jail finally closed in 1963. The island remained abandoned until 1969, when a group of Native Americans staged an occupation as part of a peaceful attempt to claim the island for their people, citing treaties which designated all federal land not in use as automatically reverting to their ownership. Using all the bureaucratic trickery it could muster, the government finally ousted them in 1971, claiming the operative lighthouse qualified it as active.

At least 750,000 tourists each year take the excellent hour-long, self-guided audio **tours** of the abandoned prison, which include some sharp anecdotal commentary and even the chance to spend a minute (it feels like forever) locked in a darkened cell.

**Boats** to Alcatraz leave from pier 41 (frequent departures from 9.30am, last boat back at 4.30pm; $11 including audio tour, $7.75 without). Advance reservations strongly recommended, especially in peak tourist season (allow two weeks; ☎415/705-5555).

breasts started the topless waitress phenomenon. Now reincarnated as the (fully-clothed) *Condor Sports Bar*, the landmark site still preserves her nipples, once immortalized in neon above the door, in its museum, along with photos and clippings from the *Condor Club's* heyday.

As you continue north on Columbus Avenue, you enter the heart of the old **Italian neighborhood**, an enclave of narrow streets and leafy enclosures. Explorations lead to small landmarks like the **Cafe Trieste**, where the jukebox blasts out opera classics to a heavy-duty art crowd, toying with cappuccinos and browsing slim volumes of poetry. From Columbus' **Washington Square**, head up the very steep steps on Filbert Street to reach Telegraph Hill and the **Coit Tower**, featuring grand views of the city and beyond.

To the west of Columbus, **Russian Hill** was named for Russian sailors who died here in the early 1800s. In the summer, there's always a long line of cars waiting to drive down the tight curves of **Lombard Street**. Surrounded by palatial dwellings and herbaceous borders, Lombard is an especially thrilling drive at night, when the tourists leave and the city lights twinkle below. Even if you're without a car, the journey up here is worth it for a visit to the **San Francisco Art Institute**, 800 Chestnut St (Tues–Sat 10am–5pm; free), the oldest art school in the west, where the **Diego Rivera Gallery** has an outstanding mural created by the painter in 1931. Walking south from the institute for four blocks on Jones Street, you'll find **Macondray Lane**, a pedestrian-only "street" thought to be one of the inspirations for Armistad Maupin's *Tales of the City* (see p.1179).

## Fisherman's Wharf

San Francisco rarely tries to pass off pure, unabashed commercialism as a worthy tourist attraction, but with **Fisherman's Wharf**, and the nearby waterfront district, it makes an exception.

An inventive use of statistics allows the area to proclaim itself the most-visited tourist attraction in the entire country; in fact, this crowded and hideous ensemble of waterfront kitsch and fast-food stands makes a sad and rather misleading introduction to the city. It may be hard to believe, but this was once a genuine fishing port; the few fishing vessels that can still afford the exorbitant mooring charges are usually finished by early morning and get out before the tourists arrive. The shops and bars here are among the most overpriced in the city, and crowd-weary families do little to add to the ambiance.

If you wish to get out on the water, 75-minute **bay cruises** depart several times a day from piers 39 and 41 (see p.979). Better instead to head to the museums of **Fort Mason** and on to the expanse of green parkland along the **Marina district**, affording excellent views of the Golden Gate Bridge.

## Nob Hill

*From Nob Hill, looking down upon the business wards of the city, we can decry a building with a little belfry, and that is the stock exchange, the heart of San Francisco; a great pump we might call it, continually pumping up the savings of the lower quarter to the pockets of the millionaires on the hill.*

Robert Louis Stevenson

If the Financial District is representative of new money in the city, the posh hotels and Masonic institutions of **Nob Hill** exemplify San Francisco's old wealth; it is, as Joan Didion wrote, "the symbolic nexus of all old California money and power." Once you've made the stiff climb up (or taken the California cable car), there are very few real sights as such, but nosing around is pleasant enough, taking in the aura of luxury and enjoying the views over the city and beyond.

The area became known as Nob Hill after the robber-baron industrialists who came to live here while running the Central Pacific Railroad. **Grace Cathedral** here is one of the biggest hunks of sham-Gothic architecture in the US. Construction began soon after the 1906 earthquake, but most of it was built, of faintly disguised reinforced concrete, in the early Sixties. The entrance is adorned with faithful replicas of the fifteenth-century Ghiberti doors of the Florence Baptistry. A block east, be sure to go inside the **Fairmont Hotel**, 950 Mason St, to get a sense of the opulence that once ruled the hill. Take its elevators up for a great view of the city. Across from the *Fairmont*, the brownstone of the **Pacific Union Club** was the only original Nob Hill structure left standing after the 1906 fire.

## The Tenderloin, Civic Center and South of Market

While parts of San Francisco can almost seem to be an urban utopia, the adjoining districts of **the Tenderloin** and **Civic Center** reveal harsher realities and are a gritty reminder that not everybody has it so easy. However, **South of Market** (aka SoMa) has, like the Embarcadero, taken a previously unimaginable upswing. A new entertainment complex surrounding Yerba Buena Gardens – anchored by the high and low culture appeals of the San Francisco Museum of Modern Art and Sony's Metreon mall – has transformed it from a bleak post-industrial wasteland into a thriving extension of the crowded downtown area.

The majestic federal and municipal buildings of **Civic Center**, squashed between the Tenderloin and SoMa, can't help but look strangely out of sync, both with their immediate neighbors and with San Francisco as a whole. Their grand Beaux Arts style is at odds with the quirky wooden architecture of the rest of the city. At night, when the ritzy **War Memorial Opera House**, 301 Van Ness Ave, and the aquarium-like **Louise M Davies Symphony Hall**, Grove Street at Van Ness Avenue, swarm with well-heeled patrons of the ballet, opera and symphony, it all looks distinctly more impressive than by day.

It was at the huge, green-domed **City Hall**, on the northern edge of the dismal **United Nations Plaza**, that Mayor George Moscone and gay supervisor Harvey Milk were assassinated in 1978 (see p.990). The recently restored gold plate dome is an impressive relic of Gold Rush-era largess.

Formerly one of San Francisco's least desirable neighborhoods, **SoMa**, the district South of Market, has been enjoying a renaissance since the 1980s. It's reminiscent in a way of New York's SoHo several years ago: many of its abandoned warehouses have been converted into studio spaces and art galleries, and the neighborhood is now home to artists, musicians, hep-cat entertainers and trendy restaurants. This may well be short-lived, however: SoMa is a prime piece of central real estate, and it's only a matter of time before the bulldozers move in and the artists are squeezed out. Indeed, the new home of the **SF Museum of Modern Art**, 151 Third St (Mon, Tues & Fri–Sun 11am–6pm, Thurs 11am–9pm; $8, free first Tues of month), opened here in January 1995. Major works include paintings by Jackson Pollock, Frida Kahlo and Diego Rivera. The temporary exhibitions are the museum's strongest suit; with newly acquired financial muscle it can snap up the better touring works. However, the allegation that the building, designed by Swiss architect Mario Botta, is far more beautiful than anything inside, is pretty hard to dispute – flooded with natural light from a soaring, truncated, cylindrical skylight, it's a sight to behold.

Opposite the museum is the other totem of civic pride, the **Center for the Arts at Yerba Buena Gardens** (daily except Mon 11am–6pm; $5, free first Thurs of month 6–8pm), bounded by Third and Fourth streets, Mission and Folsom. A spectacular $44 million project featuring a theater and three galleries, the center's best feature is its parklike setting – five and half acres of lovely gardens with a 50ft Sierra granite waterfall memorial to Martin Luther King Jr. Dominating the Gardens' south side is the **Sony Metreon**, a combination movie theater and multimedia entertainment mall.

A brand new addition to the city's waterfront is **Pac Bell Park**, down Third Street at King, home to the **San Francisco Giants**. The faux-old brick building offers views of the bay beyond the outfield fences to distract you during particularly dull ballgames.

Above all, SoMa is the nucleus of **clubland**, where the city's wildlife is at its best. Folsom Street was until recently a major gay strip, the center for much lewder goings-on than the Castro; in recent years the mix has become pretty diverse, though never tame.

## The Mission

Vibrant, hip and ethnically mixed, **the Mission** is easily San Francisco's funkiest neighborhood. A mile or so south of downtown, it is also the warmest, eluding the summer fogs. As the traditional first stop for immigrants, the Mission serves as a microcosm of the city's history and, for the time being, ensures that the neighborhood never transcends the "transitional" stage it has been in for years.

The area takes its name from the old **Mission Dolores**, at 16th and Dolores (daily 9am–4.30pm; $2), the oldest building to survive the 1906 earthquake and fire. Founded in 1776, it was the sixth in a series of missions built along the Pacific coast as Spain staked its claim to California; the graves of the Native Americans it tried to "civilize" can be seen in the cemetery next door, along with those of white pioneers. Go early in the morning to avoid the tour buses.

The heart of the Mission lies east of Mission Street between 16th and 24th streets. Here you'll absorb the district's original Latin flavor, with Nicaraguan, Salvadoran, Costa Rican and Mexican stores and restaurants, along with markets selling tropical fruits and *panaderias* baking traditional pastries.

In the last few years, however, the "in" crowd has descended on a strip of Valencia south of 16th, site of a new crop of hip bars, cafes and restaurants. The profusion of independent bookstores and thrift stores around here makes for heavenly browsing and the vicinity of 22nd Street has become a new gourmet-dining ghetto. At the **Levi Strauss & Co** factory at 250 Valencia St (free tours on Wed 10am & 1pm; reserve on ☎415/565-9159), you can see how the world's most famous jeans are made.

What really sets the Mission apart from other neighborhoods, though, are its **murals** – there are over two hundred in all. A brilliant tribute to local hero **Carlos Santana** adorns three buildings where 22nd Street meets South Van Ness, while every possible surface on **Balmy Alley**, between Folsom and Harrison off 24th Street, has been covered with murals depicting the political agonies of Central America. The mural organization Precita Eyes hosts weekend **mural tours** by foot, bike or bus (☎415/285-2287; $4 to $30).

## The Castro

Progressive and celebratory, but also increasingly comfortable and wealthy, **the Castro** is the city's gay capital, providing a barometer for the state of the grown-up and sobered gay scene. Some people insist that this is still the wildest place in town, others reckon it's a shadow of its former self; all agree that things are not the same as ten or even five years ago, when a walk down the Castro would have had you gaping at the revelry. Most of the same bars and hangouts still stand, but these days they're host to an altogether different and more conservative breed. Cute shops and restaurants lend a young professional feel to the place. A visit to the district is a must if you're to get any idea of just what San Francisco is all about, though in terms of visible street life, the few blocks around Castro and Market streets contain about all there is to see.

### GAY AND LESBIAN SAN FRANCISCO

San Francisco is still the undoubted **gay capital of the world**, but the gay scene hasn't had much to celebrate in the last few years and there's been a definite move from the outrageous to the mainstream. The increasing number of gay activists in public office have become more conservative in approach, if not in policy. However, gay parties, parades and street fairs still swing better than most. If you're here in June, you'll coincide with the Gay and Lesbian Film Festival, Gay Pride Week and the Gay Freedom Day Parade. Come October, the street fairs are in full swing and Halloween, for years the zenith of the Castro's social calendar, traditionally sees the beautiful of body and ballgown out in force – although in the last couple of years city officials have tried to move it to Civic Center, where there's better crowd control and safety.

Although the 1980s saw the flowering of a **lesbian** culture to rival the male 1970s upsurge, the bars for women have all but closed down (the exception being the Mission's *Lexington Club*, see p.997) and the nightlife revolves around a handful of women's club nights. Lesbian culture is more in evidence in the bookstores.

*The Sentinel*, *Oblivion*, *The Bay Area Reporter* and *Gay Times* are all free **publications** listing events, services, clubs and bars, found in Castro bars and cafes. *On Our Backs* and *Bad Attitude* are of particular use to lesbians. Gay men could not do better than purchase a copy of *Betty and Pansy's Severe Queer Review* ($11), available in gay bookstores – as is *The Lavender Pages*, a free telephone-cum-resource book. The AIDS Hotline (☎415/863-2437) and the Lavender Line, a lesbian and gay switchboard (☎510/841-6224), provide counseling and advice. You'll find gay **accommodation** and **bars** listed on pp.981 and 997 respectively.

**Harvey Milk Plaza**, by the Castro Muni station, is dedicated to the assassinated gay supervisor (or councilor), who owned a camera store in the Castro. The man who shot Milk and Mayor George Moscone, Dan White, was a disgruntled ex-supervisor who resigned in protest at their liberal policies. At the trial, his plea of temporary insanity caused by harmful additives in his fast food – the "Twinkie defense" – won him a sentence of five years' imprisonment for manslaughter. The gay community reacted angrily; the riots that followed were among the most violent San Francisco has ever witnessed, with protesters marching into City Hall, burning police cars as they went.

Before heading down Castro Street into the heart of the neighborhood, take a short walk to the visitor center of the **Names Project** at 2363A Market St (daily 10am–7pm; ☎415/863-1966) which sponsored the creation of "**The Quilt**" – a gargantuan blanket in which each panel measures six feet by three feet (the size of a grave site) and bears the name of a person lost to AIDS. Made by lovers, friends and families, the panels are stitched together and regularly tour the country and the world; it has been spread on the Mall in Washington DC several times to dramatize the epidemic. Inside the workshop, you can see thousands of panels stored on shelves, and a few are hung up for display. Those interested in making their own panel can do so at the Quilting Bee held every Wednesday evening from 7pm to 10pm.

The junction of **Castro and 18th Street**, known as the "gayest four corners of the earth," marks the Castro's center, cluttered with bookstores, clothing stores, cafes and bars. The side streets offer a slightly more exclusive fare of exotic delicatessens, fine wines and fancy florists, and enticingly leafy residential territory.

## Haight-Ashbury

The fame of **Haight-Ashbury**, two miles west of downtown San Francisco, far outstrips its size. No more than eight blocks in length, centered around the junction of Haight and Ashbury streets, "The Haight" was a run-down Victorian neighborhood until it transmogrified into the epitome of cool during the 1960s. Since then the area has become gentrified, but it retains a collection of radical bookstores, laid-back cafes, record stores and secondhand clothing emporia, not to mention a collection of characters still flying the counterculture's rather worn flag.

All there is to do in the Haight today is to stroll around what is one of the best areas in town to **shop**. It shouldn't take more than a couple of hours to update your record collection, dress yourself up and blow money on books and beer. The eastern end of Haight Street, around the crossing with Fillmore Street, is the funkiest corner of the district. Known as the **Lower Haight**, and for decades a primarily black neighborhood, it was reborn a few years ago – thanks to low rents – as a stomping ground for young hipsters. Though its trend appeal has since been surpassed by the Mission, it remains home to a small glut of DJ shops and a boisterous Brit-heavy population of club kids.

## Golden Gate Park

In a city with an abundance of green space, **Golden Gate Park** stands out as not just the largest, but also the most beautiful, and safest, of its parks. Spreading three miles or so west from the Haight as far as the Pacific, it was constructed on what was then an area of wild sand dunes, buffeted by the spray from the ocean. Despite the throngs of joggers, polo players, roller-skaters, cyclists and strollers, it never seems to get over-crowded and you can always find a spot to be alone.

Of the park's several museums, the **M H de Young Museum** (Wed–Sun 9.30am–5pm; $7, $2 discount with Muni transfer; free first Wed of month) has a large and diverse range of painting and sculpture, while the soon-to-move **Asian Art Museum** (same times; ticket included with de Young fee) is exhaustingly thorough. The **California Academy of Sciences** (summer daily 9am–6pm; rest of year daily 10am–5pm; $8.50, $1 discount with Muni transfer, free first Wed of month) opposite is a good place to amuse restless children, with its 30ft dinosaur skeleton, life-size replicas of elephant seals and other California wildlife, and live colony of twenty black-footed penguins. Over 14,500 specimens of aquatic life can be viewed in its **Steinhart Aquarium** (daily 10am–5pm; entry included with above admission); the best are the alligators and other reptiles lurking in a simulated swamp. Slightly to the west is the **Japanese Tea Garden** (daily 9am–5.30pm; $2.50), dominated by a massive bronze

---

### THE HIPPIES

During the heady days of the massive "be-in" in Golden Gate Park in 1966 and the so-called "Summer of Love" the following year, no fewer than 75,000 pilgrims turned the busy little intersection of Haight-Ashbury into the mecca of alternative culture.

Where Beat philosophy had emphasized self-indulgence, the **hippies**, on the face of it at least, stressed such concepts as "universal truth" and "cosmic awareness." Characters like Ken Kesey and his Merry Pranksters set a precedent of wild living and challenging authority. The use of drugs was seen as an integral – and positive – part of the movement. **LSD**, especially, which was not then illegal, was claimed as an avant-garde art form, pumped out in private laboratories and distributed by Timothy Leary and his supporters with a prescription – "Turn on, tune in, drop out" – that galvanized a generation into inactivity. Life in the Haight took on a theatrical quality: Pop Art found mass appeal, light shows became legion and dress flamboyant. The psychedelic music scene, spearheaded by the Grateful Dead, Jefferson Airplane and Janis Joplin, became a genuine force nationwide, and it wasn't long before kids from all over America started turning up in Haight-Ashbury for the free food, free drugs and free love. Money became a dirty word, the hip became "heads," and the rest of the world were "straights."

Buddha. Bridges, footpaths, pools filled with carp, bonsai and cherry trees lend a peaceful feel. Busloads of tourists pour in; by far the best idea is to get here early for a breakfast of tea and fortune cookies in the tea house ($2.50 anytime).

## The Golden Gate Bridge and Beyond

The orange towers of the **Golden Gate Bridge**, perhaps the best-loved symbol of San Francisco, are visible from almost every high point in the city. The bridge, which spans 4200ft, had taken only 52 months to design and build when it was opened in 1937. Some quarter of a million people turned up for a sunrise party to celebrate its fiftieth anniversary in 1987; the winds were strong and the bridge buckled, but fortunately did not break. **Driving** across is a real thrill, racing under the towers, while the half-hour **walk** across allows you to take in its enormous size and absorb the views. It's also a favorite with the suicidal – in a typical year dozens jump to their deaths. Those jumping are said to hit the water at a speedy 80mph – few have survived the leap.

The **Fort Point National Historic Site** beneath the bridge gives a good sense of the place as the westernmost outpost of the nation. This brick fortress, built in the 1850s, has a dramatic site, the surf pounding away beneath the great span of the bridge high above – a view made famous by Kim Novak's suicide attempt in Alfred Hitchcock's *Vertigo*. A small **museum** (Wed–Sun 9am–4pm; free) inside the fort displays some rusty old cannons and artillery.

San Francisco's best waters are to be found at the **beaches** at the tip of the peninsula, but beach culture doesn't exist here the way it does in southern California. Dangerous riptides and excruciatingly cold water make it impossible to swim with any confidence, and nude sunbathing is about as adventurous as things get.

Inland, **Lincoln Park**, at 34th Avenue and Clement Street, primarily an unusually dramatic golf course, offers striking views of the Marin headlands and is home to the remote, white-pillared **California Palace of the Legion of Honor** (daily except Mon 9.30am–5pm; $7, $2 off with Muni transfer, surcharge for special exhibitions). Reopened in late 1995 after extensive renovation, the museum is arguably San Francisco's best and most staggeringly majestic building. Its isolated, windswept location, high on a bluff overlooking the ocean, is unsurpassably romantic, and deters the hordes that swarm the MoMA and the museums in the park. The emphasis is on fine art, with the **Renaissance** represented by the works of Titian and El Greco, hung in spacious, high-ceilinged, well-lit marble halls. Some great canvases by Rembrandt and Hals, as well as Rubens' magnificent *Tribute Money*, are highlights of the seventeenth-century **Dutch** and **Flemish** collection. The **Impressionist** and **Post-Impressionist** galleries contain works by Courbet, Manet, Monet, Renoir, Degas and Cézanne. Several galleries are devoted to **Rodin** sculptures – bronze, porcelain and stone pieces including *The Athlete*, *Fugit Amor* and a small cast of *The Kiss*.

# Eating

With well-over three thousand restaurants crammed onto the small peninsula, and scores of bars and cafes open all day, **eating** in San Francisco is never difficult. Eating is *the* culture in this town, with excellent food often at modest prices. Be warned, though – San Francisco closes early, and you'll be struggling to get served much after 10pm. **Mexican** food is big in the Mission, **Italian** places abound in North Beach, and, of course, Chinatown naturally has plenty of **Chinese**, while **Japan Center** – the heart of Japantown, located at Post between Geary, Laguna and Fillmore, a mile west of Union Square – boasts a few fine Japanese places. In health-conscious San Francisco you'll find **vegetarian** entrees on every menu and quite a few entirely vegetarian restau-

## LATE-NIGHT EATING

For that midnight snack or 3am binge, check out the following **24-hour** dependables.

**Allstar Pastry & Donuts**, 2095 Chestnut St at Steiner, Marina (☎415/441-9270).

**Bagdad Cafe**, 2295 Market St at 16th, Castro (☎415/621-4434).

**Denny's**, 1700 Post St at Webster, Japantown (☎415/563-1400) and 495 Beach St at Jones, Fisherman's Warf (☎415/776-3700)

**International House of Pancakes**, 2299 Lombard St at Pierce, Marina (☎415/921-4004).

**Lori's Diner**, 336 Mason St at Geary and O'Farrell, Downtown (☎415/392-8646).

**Orphan Andy's**, 3991 17th St at Market and Castro, Castro (☎415/864-9795).

**Pine Crest**, 401 Geary St at Mason, Downtown (☎415/885-6407).

**Sparky's**, 242 Church St, Castro (☎415/621-6001).

rants. With the vineyards of Napa and Sonoma Valley on the city's doorstep, quality **wines** have a high profile in most San Francisco restaurants. State law prohibits **smoking** in all restaurants, cafes and bars, as evidenced by crowds of people puffing illicitly on the pavements.

### Downtown

**Boulevard**, 1 Mission St (☎415/543-6084). Outstanding French/California cuisine in this chic brasserie catering to a smart crowd. Prices keep it a special occasion for most. Reservations strongly recommended.

**Cafe Claude**, 7 Claude Lane, Union Square (☎415/392-3505). More than any of the other imitations in town, the great old furnishings of this one make it *feel* like Paris. A young, loose crowd listens to jazz with their $20 dinners.

**Farallon**, 450 Post St, Union Square (☎415/956-6969). Brand-new and sumptuously styled as an undersea grotto, serving highly creative seafood dishes in small portions. Definitely worth a splurge if you're into elegant dining experiences.

**House of Nanking**, 919 Kearny St (☎415/421-1429). One of the city's most popular Chinese restaurants, despite the lack of decor and elbow room. You wait ages for a table, but the inexpensive food doesn't disappoint.

**Plouf**, 40 Belden Place, off Bush between Kearny and Montgomery (☎415/986-6491). Convivial South-of-France seafood bistro, with sidewalk seating in good weather. The garlicky mussels – the house specialty – are the best in the city.

**Tadich Grill**, 240 California St (☎415/391-2373). The oldest restaurant in California, and a wood-paneled San Francisco institution. Grilled fresh seafood and excellent desserts.

### The Marina, Embarcadero, Fisherman's Wharf, North Beach and Chinatown

**Cafe Marimba**, 2317 Chestnut St (☎415/776-1506). Not a bad choice if you're down in the Marina district, *Marimba* tries to replicate authentic Mexican regional cuisine, achieving excellent salsas and moles. Packed with young professionals.

**Capp's Corner**, 1600 Powell St (☎415/989-2589). Funky, family-style Italian restaurant in North Beach, with a fashionable clientele lining up for the big portions.

**Cypress Club**, 500 Jackson St (☎415/296-8555). Jackson Square hot spot. Delicately presented, inventive Californian cuisine served up in one of SF's most stylish dining rooms – a cross between a *Ritz-Carlton* and a Bedouin tent. Pricey.

**Empress of China**, 838 Grant Ave (☎415/434-1345). The poshest Chinese place in town. An incredible selection of dishes and amazing views over North Beach. $13–18 for a main course.

**Fior d'Italia**, 601 Union St (☎415/986-1886). This is where to go when you're tired of trendy Italian cooking with attitude and just want the real thing. Good old-timer scene at the bar.

**Gaylord**, Ghirardelli Square, 900 North Point, Fisherman's Wharf (☎415/771-8822). The best of San Francisco's very few Indian restaurants. Expect to pay around $15 for a main course.

**Greens**, Building A, Fort Mason Center, Fort Mason (☎415/771-6222). The city's only Zen Buddhist restaurant, with delicious macrobiotic and vegetarian food, plus a gorgeous view of the bay. Book ahead; $38 for a five-course dinner.

**Little Joe's**, 523 Broadway (☎415/433-4343). Always a line for tables, but worth it for the low-cost, enormous portions of well-cooked food in this North Beach institution.

**Mayes Oyster House** 1233 Polk St (☎415/474-7674). One of the oldest restaurants in town still serves classic seafood dishes such as Oysters Rockefeller, along with hearty Italian dishes.

**Rose Pistola**, 532 Columbus (☎415/399-0499). A staple of North Beach's "Cal-Ital" dining scene, headed by one of the city's hottest chefs. Menu selections include a range of eclectic tapas and thin-crust pizzas that won't break the bank.

**Sam Woh**, 813 Washington St (☎415/982-0596). The space is unpleasantly cramped, the food is mediocre and the service downright unpleasant. So why bother? It's open late and back in the Fifties this was the spot Jack, Allen and the rest of the Beats used to come when they were too wired to go to bed.

**Washington Square Bar & Grill**, 1707 Powell St (☎415/982-8123). Stylish grill – *the* place to see San Francisco media power-lunching with a few cocktails. Food cooked to rich and heavy perfection; $30 a head.

**Yank Sing**, 427 Battery St (☎415/781-1111). A cavernous spot that regularly tops locals' list for the best dim sum in the city. Despite being routinely packed during lunch hours, the waitstaff can almost always find a spot for you in the seemingly endless warren of dining rooms. You might need their help to get out, as well.

**Yuet Lee**, 1300 Stockton St (☎415/982-6020). Cheap and cheerful Chinese restaurant with a good seafood menu and enthusiastic diners. Surprisingly good food served as late as 3am.

**Zinzino**, 2355 Chestnut St (☎415/346-6623). Lively Marina bistro done out like a Roman piazza, combining tasty Italian cuisine – try the wild mushroom lasagne – with San Francisco pizzazz.

## Civic Center, Tenderloin, SoMa and the Mission

**Asia SF**, 201 9th St (☎415/255-2742). More of an "experience" than a restaurant, this only-in-San Francisco spot features an all-drag queen staff who put on a nightly revue. Though it can't compete with the show, the food's not half bad, either.

**Cafe Delle Stelle**, 395 Hayes St (☎415/252-1110). Serving strong renditions of the hearty cooking of northern Italy, with an emphasis on rich flavors and roasted meats.

**Flying Saucer**, 1000 Guerrero St (☎415/641-9995). This quirky bistro attracts fans from far and wide with inventive, exquisitely presented continental cuisine.

**Hamburger Mary's**, 1582 Folsom St (☎415/626-1985). Rowdy restaurant, where punky waiting staff serve up burgers, sandwiches and several vegetarian options for less than $8.

**La Rondalla**, 901 Valencia St (☎415/647-7474). Lively, late-night Mission Mexican festooned in Christmas lights. Killer margaritas and good live mariachi music. Open till 3am.

**La Taqueria**, 2889 Mission St (☎415/285-7117). The best place in town for a taco. Slightly pricier than average, it still consistently packs in a crowd by simply focusing on the basics and getting them right every time.

**Manora's Thai Cuisine**, 1600 Folsom St (☎415/861-6224). Massively popular: you may have to wait, but it's worth it for light, spicy and fragrant Thai dishes at around $7 each.

**Millennium**, 246 McAllister St (☎415/487-9800). You'd swear it couldn't be done, but this restaurant has managed to make delicious meals for vegans. Stylish decor too.

**Pancho Villa**, 3071 16th St (☎415/864-8840). Though locals tend to scoff at the largely out-of-neighborhood clientele, the Mexican food here is consistently fresh and flavorful.

**Shalimar**, 532 Jones St (☎415/982-0333). A happy find in the downtrodden Tenderloin, this divey spot serves delicious, cheap Indian food, all of it made to order before your eyes, so you know it's fresh.

**Slanted Door**, 584 Valencia St (☎415/864-8032). One of the trendiest restaurants in town, serving upscale Vietnamese to customers thankful for having successfully made reservations.

**Suppenküche**, 601 Hayes St (☎415/252-9289). Satisfying and delicious German cooking near Civic Center in a loud, lively bar/restaurant decked out like a traditional Bavarian pub. Don't miss the potato pancakes appetizer – it's enough alone for a light supper.

**Truly Mediterranean**, 3109 16th St (☎415/252-7482). Fast-threatening to overtake the beloved burrito as the locals' favorite portable dinner item, this hole-in-the-wall's version of the falafel comes wrapped in thin, crispy bread.

**Tu Lan**, 8 6th St (☎415/626-0927). If you can brave the seedy Tenderloin neighborhood, you can stuff your face with fresh Vietnamese food for $4. Open daytime only.

**Vicolo**, 20 Ivy St, off Franklin (☎415/863-2382). Superlative pizza in a crowded, cafe-like place in Hayes Valley, near Civic Center.

**Zuni Cafe**, 1658 Market St (☎415/552-2522). Chic place to be and be seen, with California cuisine portions as minimal as the decor for around $30 with wine. The staff can be a bit snooty.

## The Castro, Haight-Ashbury and Japantown

**Axum Cafe**, 698 Haight St (☎415/252-7912). Neighborhood coffee shop where you can chow down on well-made Ethiopian specialties in a relaxed, homey atmosphere.

**Cha Cha Cha**, 1805 Haight St (☎415/386-5758). Bright, colorful, noisy Cuban restaurant that serves up delicious dishes and great cocktails at reasonable prices.

**Chow**, 215 Church St (☎415/552-2469). New eatery serving wonderful, lovingly made, eclectic Italian dishes on the cheap – a real find. Entrees $8 and under.

**Kabuto Sushi**, 5116 Geary Blvd (☎415/752-5652). Japantown favorite whose eccentric owner prepares sushi at manic speed. Perfect for sitting at the bar and picking.

**Spaghetti Western**, 576 Haight St (☎415/864-8461). Best breakfasts in town and a lively Lower Haight crowd to look at while you chow down.

**Thep Phanom**, 400 Waller St (☎415/431-2526). Delicate decor and beautifully prepared Thai dishes in the Lower Haight. Only $7 for a main course, but expect to wait for a table.

**Yoshida-Ya**, 2909 Webster St (☎415/346-3431). Genuine sushi bar; kick off your shoes and eat at low tables on futon floors. Expect to pay around $25 a head, with a few drinks.

## The Sunset and Richmond

**Beach Chalet**, 1000 Great Hwy (☎415/386-8439). A combination brewpub and restaurant located in a pretty WPA-era building along the windy stretches of Ocean Beach.

**Coriya Hot Pot**, 852 Clement St (☎415/387-7888). Also in Richmond, this popular Chinese restaurant lets you load up all you can eat and cook it yourself at the table. Go early to avoid disappointment.

**Ebisu**, 1283 9th Ave (☎415/566-1770). Generally considered the best sushi in town. They don't take reservations and standing out in the evening breeze can get more than chilly, but the freshness of the fish should more than compensate.

# Nightlife and entertainment

Compared to many US cities, where you need money and attitude in equal measure, San Francisco's **nightlife** scene demands little of either. It is not unusual for restaurants to provide live music and you can often eat and be entertained for no extra cost. This is no 24-hour city, and the approach to socializing is often surprisingly low-key, with little of the pandering to fads and fashions that goes on in New York or LA. For $30 you can get a decent night out, including cover charge and a few drinks. Always have your ID with you, otherwise you cannot get past the bouncers at all clubs and music venues. Though smoking is technically illegal in all bars and clubs, the law is routinely flouted by locals willing to risk a ticket.

The Sunday *Chronicle*'s "Pink Pages" supplement, along with the free weekly *Bay Guardian* or the *San Francisco Weekly*, are the best sources of **listings**. BASS (☎510/893-2277) is the major **ticket** agency.

## Bars

Since its lawless, boomtown days, San Francisco has been a **drinking** town. Even as the rest of California cleans up its act, San Franciscans continue to indulge; the city's bars vary from seedy late-night dives to rooftop piano lounges touting glittering views.

**Backflip**, *Phoenix Hotel*, 601 Eddy St, Tenderloin (☎415/771-3547). Fantastically retro bar adjacent to the hotel's pool patio. Black-vinyl-clad waitstaff, entirely blue decor and a menagerie of bizarre and lively patrons. To write home about.

**Brainwash**, 1122 Folsom St, SoMa (☎415/861-FOOD). Great idea – cafe/bar and laundromat where you can have breakfast and beer while you do your washing. Popular with the young and novelty-conscious.

**Gordon Biersch Brewery**, 2 Harrison St, Embarcadero (☎415/243-8246). Bayfront microbrewery in a converted coffee warehouse. Great selection of beers pulls in a downtown twentysomething crowd.

**Harry Denton's Starlight Room**, top floor, *Sir Francis Drake Hotel*, 450 Powell St, downtown (☎415/395-8595). Join the dressed up, grown up, moneyed crowd and drink martinis to live-jazz accompaniment.

**Occidental Grill,** 453 Pine St, downtown (☎415/834-0484). This Barbary Coast-style den is supposedly the birthplace of the martini, though that's open to more than some debate. However, they certainly do make a mean one.

**Red Room**, 827 Sutter St, Tenderloin (☎415/346-7666). Like the name implies, everything – including the walls, the furniture, the glasses and many of the drinks – is red in this popular faux-dive.

**The Tonga Room**, basement of the *Fairmont*, 950 Mason St, Nob Hill (☎415/772-5278). A must for fans of the ludicrous or just the very drunk. It's decked out like a Polynesian village, complete with a pond and simulated rainstorms, and a grass-skirted band plays terrible jazz and pop covers from a raft in the middle of the water. Cover $3, outrageously priced cocktails, but worth every cent.

**Tosca Cafe**, 242 Columbus St, North Beach (☎415/391-1244). A beautiful old bar with tiled floors, bow-tied bartenders and opera as the soundtrack. Come early as the bass from the *Palladium* nightclub upstairs can be bothersome.

**The Up & Down Club**, 1151 Folsom St, SoMa (☎415/626-2388). This small, popular split-level club-cum-bar has earned a solid reputation for first-rate drinks and live music.

**Vesuvio's**, 255 Columbus St, North Beach (☎415/362-3370). Legendary Beat haunt in the Fifties, next to City Lights Bookstore. Still draws an arty, friendly crowd who prop up the bar into the small hours.

## WOMEN'S SAN FRANCISCO

The flip side of San Francisco's gay revolution has in some women's circles led to a separatist culture, and women's resources and services are sometimes lumped together under the lesbian category. While this may be no bad thing, it can be hard to tell which organizations exist irrespective of sexuality. Don't let this stop you checking out anything that sounds interesting; nobody is going to refuse you entry or help if you're not a lesbian.

### CONTACTS AND RESOURCES

**Osento Bathhouse**, 955 Valencia St (☎415/282-6333). More than a bathhouse, this is the heart of San Francisco's women's community. Girls of all shapes, sizes, colours and persuasions.

**Rape Crisis Line** (☎415/647-7273 or 647-RAPE). 24-hour switchboard.

**Women's Building**, 3543 18th St (☎415/431-1180). Central stop in the Mission for women's art and political events. A very good place to get information – the women who staff the building are happy to deal with the most obscure of inquiries.

**Women's Needs Center**, 2166 Hayes St (☎415/487-5607). Low-cost health care and referral service.

**Zeitgeist**, 199 Valencia, the Mission (☎415/255-7505). A biker bar largely populated with nonmotorized bicycle messengers. A large patio makes it a haven for smokers.

## Gay and lesbian bars

San Francisco's **gay and lesbian bars** are many and varied, ranging from cozy cocktail lounges to no-holds-barred leather-and-chain hangouts. The scene may no longer be quite as wild as its reputation would have you believe, but at its best it can still be hard to beat.

**Cafe Flore**, 2298 Market St (☎415/621-8579). Very much the "in" spot before dark. Attractive cafe with leafy outdoor area and no shortage of people sizing each other up.

**The Castro Station**, 456 Castro St (☎415/626-7220). Noisy disco bar that packs 'em in even in the middle of the day. Very much the die-hard 1970s scene, with a fair number still in leather gear.

**Coco Club**, 139 8th St (☎415/626-2337). A low-key lesbian dive, with art on the walls and a convivial crowd. Dancing on weekends and occasional performances.

**Esta Noche**, 3079 16th St (☎415/861-5757). Gay discomania Latin-style. Young men and their admirers dance to a hi-NRG disco beat.

**Harvey's**, 500 Castro St (☎415/431-HARV). The Castro's newest gay bar, a convivial place drawing a friendly, community-oriented mixed gay and lesbian crowd. Serves food, too.

**Hole in the Wall**, 289 8th St (☎415/431-HOWL). A biker and rock club that deliberately recalls the days when gay bars hid in dark alleys. Generally all in good fun (and quite popular), but occasionally a little rough.

**Lexington Club**, 3464 19th St at Lexington (☎415/863-2052). The first neighborhood bar for women in a long time, packed with lesbians of all stripes and their male friends. Good jukebox.

**Midnight Sun**, 4067 18th St (☎415/861-4186). Young, white boys dressed to the nines and cruising like maniacs in this noisy Castro video bar.

**The Mint**, 1942 Market St (☎415/626-4726). The best karaoke bar in the city, packed with a boisterous, thirtysomething crowd of songsters.

**Rawhide**, 280 7th St (☎415/621-1197). If men in chaps are your scene, look no further than this dimly lit SoMa bar/dance club that plays country-and-western and bluegrass favorites. A legendary SF venue.

**SF Eagle**, 389 12th St (☎415/626-0880). Legendary SoMa biker bar. Not for wimps.

**The Stud**, 399 9th St (☎415/252-STUD). An oldie but a goodie. A favorite gay dancing spot with lesbian nights on certain days. Energetic, uninhibited dancing and good times.

## Live music: rock, jazz and folk

San Francisco's **music scene** reflects the character of the city: laid-back, eclectic and not a little nostalgic. The options for catching live music are wide and the scene is definitely on the up and up, with the city regularly spawning good young bands. Check the *San Francisco Bay Guardian* and *SF Weekly* free weeklies, and the *San Francisco Chronicle*, for listings.

**Bahia Cabana**, 1600 Market St (☎415/861-4202). Expensive, yuppie hangout and supper club with good Brazilian and samba bands. Cover $6–10.

**Bimbo's 365 Club**, 1025 Columbus Ave (☎415/474-0365). Classy lounge with tableside drink service (2 minimum) and a varied high quality menu of music styles from jazz to ska.

**Biscuits & Blues**, 401 Mason St (☎415/292-BLUE). Lively blues supper club with inexpensive Southern cuisine and hot blues acts nightly. Reservations recommended for dinner shows.

**Blue Lamp**, 561 Geary St (☎415/885-1464). Quintessential dive close to downtown that features good acoustic acts (blues & jazz).

**The Boom Boom Room**, 1601 Fillmore St (☎415/673-8000). Owned by blues legend John Lee Hooker, this small, intimate bar delivers straight-ahead jazz or classic blues acts nightly; no cover Sun & Tues, otherwise $3 cover weekdays and $7 weekends.

**Bottom of the Hill**, 1233 17th St (☎415/621-4455). Potrero Hill hangout for rock & country music, live seven nights a week, drawing a late-twenty- to thirtysomething crowd. There's an outdoor all-you-can-eat barbecue on the patio Sun. Cover for shows $4–7.

**Bruno's**, 2389 Mission St (☎415/550-7455). Swank new jazz bar/restaurant pulling the kind of attractive young things who are titillated to be in the Mission's seedy section. Cover about $5.

**Cafe du Nord**, 2170 Market St (☎415/979-6545). This popular bar is quite the place to experience live swing, jazz, Latin and blues over good food, or just have a beer and shoot some pool.

**Club 181**, 181 Eddy St (☎415/673-8181). Dreadful location in the vortex of the Tenderloin, but one of San Francisco's coolest nightspots. Acid-jazz, funk, house and soul and a good-time crowd. Highly recommended, but take a cab.

**Elbo Room**, 647 Valencia St (☎415/552-7788). The birthplace of acid jazz, a smoothed out instrumental sound that provides upbeat background music for an intense pick-up scene.

**Great American Music Hall**, 859 O'Farrell St (☎415/885-0750). Historic former bordello and saloon that has been converted into a popular venue for rock, blues, and world music acts.

**Lou's Pier 47**, 300 Jefferson St (☎415/771-0377). An old favorite, and about the only decent place on the Wharf. Lou's blues pulls a good crowd most nights.

**Mick's Lounge**, 2513 Van Ness Ave (☎415/928-0404). Local bands ranging from rock and funk to Seventies retro and alternative. Cover $4–8.

**Paradise Lounge**, 308 11th St (☎415/861-6906). Good SoMa venue to see up-and-coming rock bands (usually three per night), or take a break for a game of pool upstairs.

**The Saloon**, 1232 Grant St (☎415/989-7666). North Beach's best spot for R&B. Always packed, it creaks nightly as blues bands and crowds of enthusiastic dancers do their thing.

## Clubbing

While **clubbing** in San Francisco may not have the feverish following of other cities, the clubs that exist are encouragingly inexpensive, and you can leave your attitude at home. A recent spate of police raids has put something of a damper on the scene and forced several popular spaces to shut down. But with a population as young and hip as this city's, odds are it will be impossible to keep a good party down for long. The greatest concentration of clubs is in **SoMa** and, recently, the **Mission**. You must bring your ID to get in to all clubs; most require you to be at least 21 except for a few 18-and-over clubs. Expect to pay a cover charge ranging anywhere from $3 to $7 and up to $15 for the huge dance caverns like *Ten15*.

**Club Townsend**, 177 Townsend St (☎415/974-6020). Site of long-running gay and lesbian dance parties (Club Q for women, Club Universe and Pleasuredome for men) on Fri, Sat and Sun respectively. Call their information line for the latest events.

**DNA Lounge**, 375 11th St (☎415/626-1409). The music changes nightly, but the young hipsters are the same. Large dance floor downstairs, comfy sofas in the mezzanine.

**DV8**, 540 Howard St (☎415/777-1419). Huge, ornate and fashionable, about the only club in town worth dressing up for. High-energy funk and house music. Open Wed–Sat.

**El Rio**, 3158 Mission St (☎415/282-3325). Mixed crowds gather for changing nightly entertainment and some great giveaways, like oysters on the half-shell on a Friday. The popular live salsa on summer Sun afternoons draws a predominantly female crowd.

**EndUp**, Harrison and 6th St (☎415/357-0827). Long after other places close, this is where everyone ends up. Certain nights attract gay or lesbian crowds like Girl Spot (Sat) and Fag (Fri). Good for the hardcore party animal – especially the all-day, all-night Sunday T-dance beginning at 5am.

**Justice League**, 628 Divisadero St (☎415/289-2038). Hosting top-notch hip-hop and salsa acts, in addition to regular stints by adventurous DJs.

**Nickie's**, 460 Haight St (☎415/621-6508). This place rocks every night. Whether it's Grateful Dead night, African, Latin or Seventies funk, *Nickie's* is for the very lively.

**Sol y Luna**, 475 Sacramento St (☎415/296-8191). Latin supper club featuring live flamenco dinner shows on Wed, Fri and Sat, plus nightly DJ dancing on the smallish floor (and patio in good weather) to salsa, tango and flamenco-rumba. The crowd of young professionals is well-dressed and usually looking to score.

**Sound Factory**, 525 Harrison St (☎415/979-8686). Huge multilevel 18 and over place with three rooms for simultaneous house, hip-hop and Latin dance parties.

**Ten15**, 1015 Folsom (☎415/431-0700). Another huge club for serious sweating: 6 rooms with different music in each, especially deep jungle house, and cool laser light shows. You may have to wait in a long line Thurs–Sat.

**330 Ritch**, 330 Ritch St (☎415/541-9574). Low-ceilinged and crowded with slender SoMa types. Serves food until 10pm, then DJs spin funk, soul, disco and British pop music on different nights. Live jazz on Sat and a live swing band and free swing lessons on Wed.

## Classical music, opera and dance

Though the San Francisco arts scene has a reputation for provincialism, this is the only city on the West Coast to boast its own professional **symphony, ballet** and **opera** companies. These companies rely entirely on private contributions for their survival and low-priced tickets are rare, if not nonexistent. Look out in summer for the **free concerts in Stern Grove** (at 19th Ave and Sloat Blvd), where the symphony, opera and ballet give open-air performances for ten successive Sundays (starting in June). Last-minute standing room tickets provide a cheaper option for those on a budget.

The **San Francisco Opera Association** (ticket and schedule information ☎415/864-3330) has been performing in the opulent **War Memorial Opera House**, 301 Van Ness Ave at Grove, since the building opened in 1932, pulling in big names like Placido Domingo and Kiri Te Kanawa on a regular basis. Its main season runs from the end of September for thirteen weeks, and its opening night is one of the principal social events on the West Coast. Also housed here is the **San Francisco Ballet** (tickets ☎415/865-2000; information ☎415/861-5600), whose regular season starts in February, while performances of *The Nutcracker* occur during the Christmas season.

The **Louise M Davies Symphony Hall**, 201 Van Ness Ave (☎415/431-5400), is the permanent home of the San Francisco Symphony, hosting a year-round season of classical music and sometimes performances by other, often offbeat musical and touring groups.

## Theater

The majority of the **theaters** in downtown's Theater District are not especially innovative, but tickets are reasonably inexpensive – up to $20 a seat – and there's usually good availability. The TIX Bay Area ticket booth in Union Square (Tues–Thurs 11am–6pm, Fri–Sat 11am–7pm; ☎415/433-7827) regularly has day-of-performance tickets for half price and full-price advance sales.

**American Conservatory Theater**, Geary Theater, 415 Geary St (☎415/749-2228). The Tony award-winning ACT puts on eight major plays each season in the city's best serious theater venue.

**Beach Blanket Babylon**, Club Fugazi, 678 Green St (☎415/421-4222). Legendary musical spoof in tribute to San Francisco recently celebrated its quarter century. Highly recommended, but remember to book in advance.

**Exit Theatre**, 156 Eddy St (☎415/673-3847). Avant-garde and experimental, the Exit is the place to go when you've wearied of the Broadway retreads.

**Golden Gate Theater**, 1 Taylor St (☎415/551-2000). San Francisco's most elegant theater, with marble flooring, Rococo ceilings and gilt trimmings. A pity the program doesn't live up to the surroundings – generally a mainstream diet of touring musicals.

**Lorraine Hansberry Theater**, 620 Sutter St (☎415/474-8800). The mainstay of African-American theater in San Francisco. Traditional theater as well as contemporary political pieces and jazz/blues musical revues.

**The Magic Theater**, Fort Mason Center, Building D (☎415/441-8822). Specializes in contemporary American playwrights and emerging new talent: Sam Shepard premieres his work here.

**Theatre Rhinoceros**, 2926 16th St (☎415/861-5079). San Francisco's leading gay theater group. Lighter, humorous productions, as well as those that confront gay issues.

**Theatre on the Square**, 450 Post St (☎415/433-9500). Converted Gothic theater with drama, musicals, comedy and mainstream theater pieces. San Francisco's main fringe venue.

## Comedy Clubs

**Cobb's Comedy Club**, *The Cannery*, 2801 Leavenworth St (☎415/928-4320). Pricey and usually full of tourists, but the standard of the acts is fairly consistent. Worth a look if everything else is booked up.

**Josie's Cabaret and Juice Joint**, 3583 16th St (☎415/861-7933). Good all-rounder offering a mixed menu of gay cabaret and comedy during the week, and live music and dancing weekends. The bill changes weekly.

**Punchline Comedy Club**, 444 Battery St (☎415/397-7573). Frontrunner of the city's "polished" cabaret venues. Intimate, smoky feel; ideal for downing expensive cocktails and laughing your head off. The bigger names in the world of stand-up perform here, and it's always packed.

# Shopping

While boasting the large-scale facilities and international names you'd expect in a major city, San Francisco's shopping scene is low-key and unpretentious. This means prices are slightly lower, and shopping here is a pleasant, relatively stress-free activity.

If you want to run the gauntlet of designer labels, or just watch the style brigade consume, **Union Square** is the place to be. The heart of the city's shopping territory, it has a good selection of big-name and chic stores – Neiman Marcus, whose prices have earned it the nickname "Needless Markup," Nordstrom, Saks Fifth Avenue, Gump's and a completely redesigned Macy's – worth a few hours if you're into serious dollar-dropping.

SoMa is home to the new Sony Metreon mall at Fourth Street and Mission, a form of "shopper-tainment" with its technolog-driven stores and state-of-the-art movieplex.

## Books

**The Booksmith**, 1644 Haight St (☎415/863-8688). Good general Haight-Ashbury bookstore with an excellent stock of countercultural titles.

**Borders Books and Music**, 400 Post St (☎415/399-1633). Massive, emporium-style bookstore stocking over 160,000 book titles as well as a music department with over 60,000 choices. It's a day's work getting through this lot, but there's a cafe within the store to refresh yourself.

**Bound Together Anarchist Collective Bookstore**, 1369 Haight St (☎415/431-8355). Haight-Ashbury store specializing in radical and progressive publications.

**City Lights Bookstore**, 261 Columbus Ave (☎415/362-8193). America's first paperback bookstore, and still San Francisco's best. The range of titles includes house publications.

**A Different Light**, 489 Castro St (☎415/431-0891). Well-stocked and diverse gay bookstore.

**Good Vibrations**, 1210 Valencia St (☎415/974-8980). A comfortable, decidedly unsleazy place to buy sex books and erotica, specializing in women's sexuality. Also sells a bewildering array of sex toys, condoms and the like.

**Green Apple Books & Music**, 506 Clement (☎415/387-2272). In the heart of the Richmond district, this relaxed and welcoming store features new and used books (rare-out-of print volumes as well as standards) plus a well-priced selection of CDs and vinyl recordings.

**Modern Times**, 968 Valencia St (☎415/282-9246). Alternative community bookstore in the Mission. Good selection of Latin American literature, women's issues and hard-to-find contemporary cultural studies.

**Rand McNally**, 595 Market St at 2nd (☎415/777-3131). Travel guides, maps and paraphernalia for the person on the move.

**Tillman Place Bookstore**, 8 Tillman Place, off Grant Ave, near Union Square (☎415/392-4668). Downtown's premier general bookstore, with a beautifully elegant feel.

## SPORTS IN SAN FRANCISCO

San Francisco's dedication to its **professional sports** teams can verge on the obsessive. Tickets for the big events can sell out, but it's usually possible to show up on the day, and it needn't cost all that much: an outfield seat to watch baseball from the "bleachers" goes for around $7, with seats closer-in topping the scale at around $15. The Oakland team runs a promotion called "Buck Days" when select seats and all hot dogs are $1 on Wednesdays. However, the year 2000 opening of the new Pac Bell Ballpark downtown's China Basin mean **tickets** for San Francisco Giants games will be hard to come by for awhile. Advance tickets for all Bay Area sports events are available through the BASS charge-by-phone ticket service (☎510/762-BASS), or through the teams' headquarters.

**Baseball**: The **Oakland A's** play at the usually sunny Oakland Coliseum (☎510/638-0500), which has a BART stop in front. The **San Francisco Giants** play at the beautiful new Pac Bell Park, where homeruns will splash into the bay (☎1-800/5-GIANTS).

**Football**: The **San Francisco 49ers**, many-time Super Bowl champions, also play at 3Com Park, where you may have to pay as much as $100 (☎415/468-2249), and the **Oakland Raiders**, blue-collar heroes, bash heads at the Oakland Coliseum (☎510/864-5000).

**Basketball**: The annually awful **Golden State Warriors** play at newly renovated Oakland Arena (☎510/986-2200).

**Ice hockey**: The **San Jose Sharks** (☎408/287-4275), one of the NHL's newer teams, play at their own arena in San Jose.

**Soccer**: The **San Francisco Seals** play at Kezar Stadium in the Haight. The **San Jose Clash** (☎408/260-6300), a new-comer to Bay Area professional sports, draw large crowds at San Jose State's Spartan Stadium.

**Stanford Stadium**, scene of six matches in soccer's **1994 World Cup**, is on the campus of Stanford University, 27 miles south of San Francisco and not far north of San Jose.

## Music

**Aquarius Records**, 3961 24th St (☎415/647-2272). Small neighborhood store with friendly, knowledgeable staff and a good range of indie rock, jazz and things experimental and obscure.

**CD & Record Rack**, 3897 18th St (☎415/552-4990). Castro emporium with a brilliant selection of dance music including a few 1970s 12-inch singles.

**Jack's Record Cellar**, 254 Scott St (☎415/431-3047). The city's best source for American roots music – R&B, jazz, country and rock 'n' roll.

**Mission Music Musica Latina/American Music Store**, 2653 Mission St (☎415/664-5554). Mission store selling music from all over the continent, but especially South America.

**Reckless Records**, 1401 Haight St at Masonic (☎415/431-3434). Specializes in independent music, buys and sells new and used stuff.

**Rooky Ricardo's**, 448 Haight St (☎415/864-7526). Secondhand store specializing in soul, funk and jazz from the Fifties to the Seventies. Vinyl only.

**Streetlight Records**, 3979 24th St (☎415/282-3550). A great selection of used records, tapes and CDs. The perfect opportunity to beef up your collection on the cheap.

**Virgin Megastore**, 2 Stockton at Market (☎415/397-4525). As the name implies, it is a big shop. Three floors of books, videos and music.

# The Bay Area

Of the six million people who make their home in the vicinity of San Francisco, only a lucky one in eight lives in the city itself. Everyone else is spread around the **Bay Area**, a hodgepodge of either very rich or very poor towns located down the peninsula or across one of the two impressive bridges that span the chilly waters of the exquisite natural harbor. In the **East Bay** are industrial Oakland and intellectual Berkeley. To the south lies the gloating new wealth of the **Peninsula**, known as "Silicon Valley" because of its multi-billion-dollar computer industry. Across the Golden Gate Bridge to the north is the woody, leafy landscape and rugged coastline of **Marin County**, America's richest suburb.

# The East Bay

The largest and most-traveled bridge in the US, the **Bay Bridge** heads east from San Francisco, part graceful suspension bridge and part heavy-duty steel truss. Now recovered from its partial collapse during the 1989 earthquake, the Bay Bridge works a lot harder for a lot less respect than the more famous (and better-loved) Golden Gate: a hundred million vehicles cross it each year. The heart of the East Bay is **Oakland**, a blue-collar city that was badly scarred by the firestorm of October 1991. Just north is the image-conscious, progressive university town of **Berkeley**; the two communities all but merge into one city, with the hills above them topped by a twenty-mile string of forested **regional parks**.

## Arrival, information and getting around

Flights direct to the East Bay touch down at **Oakland Airport**, just outside town. The AirBART Shuttle van (every 15min; $2) runs to the Coliseum BART station, and there are also door-to-door shuttle buses such as Bayporter ($15; ☎415/467-1800). The **Greyhound** station is in a dodgy part of northern Oakland on San Pablo Avenue at 21st Street. **Amtrak** terminates at Second Street near Jack London Square in West Oakland, but a better option is to get off at Richmond and change onto the ultramodern **BART** trains. Three of these underground lines link San Francisco with the East Bay (Mon–Sat 6am–midnight, Sun 9am–midnight; fares $1.10–4.45), heading their separate ways from downtown Oakland. The revamped AC Transit (☎510/839-2882) buses cover the entire East Bay area, with a more limited service running to Oakland and Berkeley from the Transbay Terminal in San Francisco.

There are **visitor centers** at 550 Tenth St near the 12th Street BART station in downtown Oakland (Mon–Fri 8.30am–5pm; ☎510/839-9000), and in Berkeley at 2015 Center St (Mon–Fri 9am–5pm; ☎510/549-7040).

## East Bay accommodation

The East Bay's **motels** and **hotels**, at between $60 and $90 a night, are barely better value for money than their San Francisco equivalents. However, they give visitors the chance to stay just outside of the city's hubbub whilst affording easy access to it.

**Bancroft Hotel**, 2680 Bancroft Way, Berkeley (☎1-800/549-1002 or 510/549-1000). Small hotel – just 22 rooms – with good location and service. Breakfast included. ⑤–⑦.

**Berkeley YMCA**, 2001 Allston Way at Milvia St, a block from Berkeley BART (☎510/848-6800). Berkeley's best bargain accommodation; rates include use of gym and pool. ②.

**The Claremont Resort & Spa**, 41 Tunnel Rd (☎1-800/551-7266 or 510/843-3000) The lap of luxury among Berkeley hotels in a 1915 building. $235–395 for double rooms; spa session begin at $95/hour for facials or massages. ⑨.

**Dean's Bed and Breakfast**, 480 Pedestrian Way, Rockridge (☎510/652-5024). A hidden gem with swimming pool and Japanese garden. $85 with breakfast, $80 without. ④/⑤.

**Durant**, 2600 Durant Ave, Berkeley (☎1-800/238-7268 or 510/845-8981). Fairly plain but well worn and comfortable, and very handy for the UC Berkeley campus. ⑥.

**Jack London Inn**, 444 Embarcadero W (☎510/444-2032). Kitschy motorlodge located next to Jack London Square. ⑤/⑥.

**Shattuck**, 2086 Allston Way, Berkeley (☎510/845-7300). Comfortable, central rooms in a well-restored older hotel. ⑥.

**Waterfront Plaza Hotel**, 10 Washington St, Oakland (☎510/836-3800 or 1-800/729-3638). Plush, modern hotel moored on the best stretch of the Oakland waterfront. ⑥–⑨.

## Oakland

OAKLAND, the workhorse of the Bay Area, is one of the largest ports on the West Coast. It has also been the breeding ground of revolutionary **political movements**. In the Sixties, the city's fifty percent black population found a voice through the militant Black Panthers, and in the Seventies the Symbionese Liberation Army, kidnappers of heiress Patty Hearst, obtained a ransom of free food for the city's poor. It's not all hard graft, though: the climate is often sunny and mild when San Francisco is cold and dreary, and there's great hiking in the redwood- and eucalyptus-covered hills above the city.

Despite this, there's not all that much to see within the city, the major concession to the tourist trade being the waterfront Jack London Square, an aseptic collection of national chains that have nothing to do with the writer. At the far eastern end of the promenade however, you will find **Heinhold's First and Last Chance Saloon**, a slanting tiny bar built in 1883 from the hull of a whaling ship. Jack London really did drink here, and the collection of yellowed portraits of him on the wall are the only genuine thing about the writer you'll find on the square. A half-mile north up Broadway from the waterfront, Oakland's restored downtown is anchored by chain stores and the gargantuan open-air **City Center** complex of offices and fast food. Beside it, at Broadway and 14th Street, the massive green-space of **Frank Ogawa Plaza** offers a good place for people-watching. A bit west on Tenth and Oak streets, the **Oakland Museum of California** (Wed–Sat 10am–5pm, Sun noon–5pm) has a good exhibit of California history, including the Beat Generation.

**Gertrude Stein**, who was born in Oakland at around the same time as the macho and adventurous London, is barely commemorated – perhaps because she wrote "what was the use of me having come from Oakland, it was not natural for me to have come from there yes write about it if I like or anything if I like but not there, *there is no there there*" – a quote which has haunted Oakland ever since. Nonetheless, the majority of Oakland residents are proud of their city, and would argue that there is indeed a *there* there, notably in the small and trendy communities of **Rockridge** and **Piedmont Avenue**, and the lively **Grand Avenue** neighborhood.

**Joaquin Miller Park**, the most easily accessible of Oakland's hilltop parks, stands above East Oakland. It was once home to the "Poet of the Sierras," Joaquin Miller, who made his name playing the eccentric frontier American in the salons of 1870s London. His poems weren't exactly acclaimed (his greatest poetic achievement was rhyming "teeth" with "Goethe"), but his prose account of the time he spent with the Modoc Indians near Mount Shasta (see p.1022) remains invaluable. His house, a small white cabin called **The Abbey**, still survives, as do the thousands of trees he planted.

## Berkeley

BERKELEY (pronounced as for Busby, though named after the English philosopher-theologian George Berkeley) is dominated by the **University of California**, one of America's most famous – and infamous – universities. Its grand buildings and thirty thousand students give off an energy that spills south down raucous **Telegraph Avenue**, where ageing hippies peddle rainbow bracelets in front of vegetarian restaurants, music stores and pizza joints. The very name of Berkeley conjures up images of dissent. **Sproul Plaza**, in front of the school's entranceway, Sather Gate, is where the Free Speech Movement began, and, too, argue some historians, the experience known as the Sixties. Among the sites of the almost-daily pitched battles of the Sixties and early Seventies, part of the broad campus revolt against the Vietnam War, was the now-seedy **People's Park**. Things have calmed down considerably, and now the campus prides itself on its high academic rankings and Nobel-laureate-laden faculty. In recent years, the biggest cause celebre on campus was the plight of Naked Man, an undergraduate who refused to wear clothing while attending class, and the attempted shutting down of local radio station KPFA. Today's students yell profanities and shout down Bible-thumpers on Sproul Plaza, unaware of the irony of it all; feel free to stroll around the campus's tree-shaded pathways and contemplate the dissent of years long gone.

Telegraph Avenue holds most of the student hangouts, and several excellent bookstores. Older students congregate in **Northside**, popping down from their woodsy hillside homes to partake of goodies from "Gourmet Ghetto" – the restaurants, delis and bakeries on Shattuck Avenue. North of here, on the hills, **Tilden Regional Park** has good trails and a fine rose garden. Along the bay itself, at the **Berkeley Marina**, you can rent windsurfing boards and sailboats, or just watch the sun set behind the Golden Gate.

## Eating

As befits the birthplace of California cuisine, the East Bay offers a choice of good **restaurants**. Berkeley is both an upmarket diner's paradise and a student town where you can eat cheaply and well, especially on and around Telegraph Avenue.

**Cafe Intermezzo**, 2442 Telegraph Ave near Haste, Berkeley (☎510/849-4592). Huge sandwiches on homemade bread, even bigger salads, and great coffee.

**Cafe Rouge**, 1782 4th St, Berkeley (☎510/525-1440). Southern French and Northern Italian food specializing in delicately prepared organic meats. They have their own butcher shop. Dinner entrees are about $16; lunch is cheaper.

**Cha-Am**, 1543 Shattuck Ave, North Berkeley (☎510/848-9664). Climb the stairs up to this unlikely, always crowded small restaurant for deliciously spicy Thai food at bargain prices.

**Cheeseboard Pizza**, 1512 Shattuck Ave, North Berkeley (☎510/549-3055). Incredibly good designer pizza at incredibly low prices: $1.75 a slice.

**Chez Panisse**, 1517 Shattuck Ave, North Berkeley (☎510/548-5525). The first and still the best of the modern Californian cuisineries – although at $45, $55 and $65 a head prix fixe (plus wine) on Mon, Tues–Thurs and Fri respectively, you may prefer to try the comparatively inexpensive *Cafe* upstairs, especially if you don't have the obligatory three-months-in-advance reservation.

**Genova**, 5095 Telegraph Ave, Oakland (☎510/652-7401). Friendly deli serves up some of the best sandwiches in the world. 7am–7pm daily.

**Homemade Cafe**, 2454 Sacramento St, Berkeley (☎510/845-1940). Non-traditional Californian-style Mexican and Jewish food served for breakfast and lunch – at shared tables when it's crowded.

**Juan's Place**, 941 Carlton St, West Berkeley (☎510/845-6904). The original Berkeley Mexican restaurant, with great food (tons of it) and an interesting mix of people.

**La Mediterranee**, 2936 College Ave, Berkeley (☎510/540-7773). Great Middle Eastern food in a relaxed atmosphere.

**La Note**, 2377 Shattuck Ave, Berkeley (☎510/843-1535). The appropriately sunny cuisine of Provence isn't the only flavor you'll find in this petite dining room: students and teachers from the jazz school next door routinely stop in for casual jam sessions.

**Tropix**, 3814 Piedmont Ave, Oakland (☎510/653-2444). Large portions of fruity Caribbean delicacies at reasonable prices, with authentic jerk sauce and thirst-quenching mango juice.

## Cafes and bars

The many bohemian **cafes** of Berkeley are full from dawn to near midnight with earnest characters wearing their intellects on their sleeves; if you're not after a caffeine fix, you can generally get a glass of beer or wine. For serious drinking you're better off in one of the many **bars**, particularly in rough-hewn Oakland. Grittier versions of what you'd find in San Francisco, they're mostly blue-collar, convivial, and almost always less expensive.

**Bison Brewing Company**, 2598 Telegraph Ave, Berkeley (☎510/841-7734). Eat and drink at great prices on the terrace, where some of the best Bay Area beers are brewed. Noisy bands on weekends.

**Cafe Mediterraneum**, 2475 Telegraph Ave, Berkeley (☎549-1128). Berkeley's oldest cafe, straight out of the Beat generation archives: beards and berets optional, books de rigueur.

**Heinhold's First and Last Chance Saloon**, Jack London Square, Oakland (☎510/839-6761). Authentic waterfront bar that's hardly changed since around 1900, when Jack London himself drank here. They've never even bothered to fix the slanted floor that was caused by the 1906 earthquake.

**Jupiter**, 2181 Shattuck Ave, Berkeley (☎510/843-8277). Many, many beers to select from at this local favorite. Live jazz on weekends and an outdoor beer garden.

**Mama Bear's**, 6536 Telegraph Ave, North Oakland (☎510/428-9684). Women's bookstore, doubling as a cafe and meeting place. Open daily 10.30am–7pm, later for regular author readings.

**Pyramid Brewery**, 901 Gilman St, Berkeley (☎510/528-9880). Great microbrewed beers in a popular pub.

**Starry Plough**, 3101 Shattuck Ave, Berkeley (☎510/841-2082). Convivial Irish bar where you can argue the latest cease-fire over darts. Bargain-price live rock and country many evenings.

**The White Horse**, 6551 Telegraph Ave at 66th St, North Oakland (☎510/652-3820). Oakland's oldest gay bar – a smallish, friendly place, with mixed dancing for men and women nightly.

## Live music and entertainment
**Nightlife** is where the East Bay really comes into its own. **Discos** are virtually nonexistent; however, dance music – this is, after all, the home of Hammer, En Vogue and Digital Underground – is thriving, and **live music venues** range from smoky jazz cafes to sweaty R&B dives.

Berkeley's **Pacific Film Archives** at 2621 Durant Ave (☎510/642-1412), perhaps the best **cinema** in California, puts on contemporary international films, plus old favorites. The free *East Bay Express* has the most comprehensive **what's** on listings.

**Ashkenaz**, 1317 San Pablo Ave, Berkeley (☎510/525-5054). World music and dance cafe. Acts from modern Afrobeat to the best of the Balkans. Kids and under-21s welcome. Cover $5–8.

**Eli's Mile High Club**, 3629 Martin Luther King Jr Way, North Oakland (☎510/655-6661). One of the best Bay Area blues clubs. Cover $5–8.

**Freight and Salvage**, 1111 Addison St, West Berkeley (☎510/548-1761). Singer-songwriters in a coffeehouse setting. Cover $6–12.

**Gilman Street Project**, 924 Gilman St, West Berkeley (☎510/525-9926). On the outer edge of the hardcore punk, indie, and experimental scene. No booze, all ages, cover $3–6.

**Kimball's East**, 5800 Shellmound, off Powell St, Emeryville (☎510/658-2555). The prime jazz and blues venue in the entire Bay Area, with big-name players in an intimate setting. Cover $12–20.

**Yoshi's Restaurant and Nitespot**, 510 Embarcadero W, Oakland in Jack London Square. The centerpiece of Oakland's newly revived Jack London Square, this combination jazz club and sushi bar routinely attracts the biggest names in jazz. Cover $15–25.

# The Peninsula

The city of San Francisco sits at the tip of a five-mile-wide neck of land commonly referred to as the **Peninsula**. Home of old money and new technology, the peninsula stretches for fifty miles of relentless suburbia south from San Francisco along the bay, winding up in the futuristic roadside landscape of the so-called "Silicon Valley" near **San Jose**.

There was a time when the region was largely agricultural, but the continuing computer boom – spurred by Stanford University in **Palo Alto** – has replaced the orange groves and fig trees of yesteryear with office complexes and parking lots. Surprisingly, however, most of the land along the **coast** – separated from the bayfront sprawl by a ridge of redwood-covered peaks – remains rural and undeveloped; it also contains some of the best **beaches** in the Bay Area, well worth a day-trip from San Francisco.

## Palo Alto

In recent years, **Palo Alto**, home of high-brow **Stanford University**, has become somewhat a social center for Silicon Valley's nouveaux riches, as evidenced by the trendy cafes and chic new restaurants that have popped up along its main drag, **University Avenue**. The town doesn't offer a lot in terms of sights other than Spanish colonial homes, but it's a great place for a lazy stroll and a gourmet meal. Wash down a California-style Greek dish from *Evvia*, 420 Emerson St (☎650/326-0983), or a heaping plate of Cajun-influenced food from *Nola*, 535 Ramona St (☎650/328-3726), with a microbrewed beer from the *Gordon Biersch Brewery*, 640 Emerson St (☎650/323-7723), or a latte from *Caffe Verona*, 236 Hamilton Ave (☎650/326-9942). The old-style malt and burger joint, *The Peninsula Creamery*, Hamilton and Emerson streets, is a favorite with Apple cofounder Steve Jobs. *MacArthur Park*, 27 University Ave (☎650/321-9990), is a great barbecue restaurant with more than two hundred wines on offer. Surprisingly affordable **rooms** are available at the *Cardinal Hotel*, 235 Hamilton Ave (☎650/323-5101; ④–⑦).

## San Jose

Burt Bacharach could easily find **SAN JOSE** today simply by heading south from San Francisco and following the heat and smog. The fastest-growing city in California, is not strong on identity – though in area and population it's close to twice the size of San Francisco. Sitting at the southern end of the peninsula, San Jose has in the past 25 years emerged as the civic heart of Silicon Valley, surrounded by miles of faceless high-tech industrial parks where the next generations of computers are designed and crafted. Ironically, it's also acknowledged as the first city in California, though the only sign of this is the eighteenth-century **Mission Santa Clara de Asis**, on the pleasant campus of the Jesuit-run University of Santa Clara.

Its most famous landmark is the **Winchester Mystery House**, 525 S Winchester Blvd, just off I-280 near Hwy-17 (daily 9.30am–4.30pm; $12.95). Sarah Winchester, heiress to the Winchester rifle fortune, was convinced upon her husband's death that he had been taken by the spirits of men killed with Winchester rifles, and believed that unless a room was built for each of the spirits and the sound of hammers never ceased, the same fate would befall her. Work on the mansion went on 24 hours a day for the next thirty years – stairs lead nowhere, windows open on to solid brick. The **Rosicrucian Museum**, 1342 Naglee Ave (daily 9am–5pm; $6), houses a brilliant collection of Assyrian and Babylonian artifacts, while the revamped **Tech Museum of Innovation** (Tues–Sat 10am–5pm, Sun noon–5pm; $8), downtown at 202 Market St contains hands-on displays of high-tech engineering.

San Jose's **visitor center** is at 333 W San Carlos St (Mon–Fri 8am–5.30pm, Sat & Sun 11am–5pm; ☎408/295-9600 or 1-800/SAN-JOSE) and also has a branch in the convention center across the street. Downtown **accommodation** is grossly overpriced, serving as it does high-tech executives and conventioneers. Options include the *Valley Inn*, 2155 The Alameda (☎408/241-8500; ⑤), and the slightly more expensive *Best Western San Jose Convention Inn*, 455 S Second St (☎408/298-3500; ④–⑥). The *Executive Inn*, 3930 Monterey Rd (☎408/281-8700; ⑤), offers basic rooms fifteen minutes outside downtown. Good old-fashioned American **food** is dished up at *Original Joe's*, 301 S First St (☎408/292-7030). Grab a stool at the counter or settle into one of the comfy booths and enjoy a burger or a plate of pasta at this San Jose institution, where $10 goes a long way. For fresh coffee and pastries, head to *Cafe Matisse*, 371 S First St (☎408/298-7788), in the heart of the popular "SOFA" district.

## The coast

The **coastline** of the peninsula south from San Francisco is a world away from the valley of the inland: mostly undeveloped, with a few small towns, and countless beaches that run 75 miles south to the mellow cities of Santa Cruz and **Capitola**. Past Daly City just south of San Francisco, Hwy-1 hugs the precipitous cliffs of Devil's Slide to the clothing-optional sands of **Gray Whale Cove State Beach** (daily dawn–dusk; $5 to park). Despite the name, it's not an especially great place to look for migrating gray whales, but there is a stairway from the bus stop down to a fine strand of sand. Two miles south, the red-roofed buildings of the 1875 **Montara Lighthouse**, set among the windswept Monterey pine trees at the top of a steep cliff, have been converted into a **youth hostel** (☎650/728-7177; ①). Just south of the hostel, on California Street, the **Fitzgerald Marine Reserve** (☎650/728-3584; free) has three miles of diverse oceanic habitat, peaceful trails, and, at low tide, the best tidal pools. Continuing a few miles south on Hwy-1, the hamlet of **El Grenada** has good roadside lunch stops like the *Highway One Diner*, and its beaches are always clogged with surfers and crowds of spectators watching them. There's a long breakwater here you can walk out on. The next town, sleepy **Half Moon Bay**, allows camping on some of its beaches ($16). Gas up here; fuel stations are rare for the next fifty miles to Santa Cruz.

# Marin County

Across the Golden Gate from San Francisco, **Marin County** is an unabashed introduction to Californian self-indulgence: a pleasure zone of conspicuous luxury and abundant natural beauty, with sunshine, sandy beaches, high mountains and thick redwood forests. Often ranked as the wealthiest county in the US, Marin has attracted a sizeable population of wealthy young professionals to its swanky waterside towns, though in the past the region served as logging headquarters.

The modern **ferries** that travel across the bay from San Francisco can make a great start to a day out. Boats to the chic bayside settlement of **Sausalito** leave from the Embarcadero (Golden Gate Transit; 5.30am–8.30pm, half-hourly during rush hour, less often during the rest of the day, and every two hours on weekends; ☎415/923-2000; $4.25 each way) or Pier 41 at Fisherman's Wharf (Blue & Gold Fleet Ferries; 5 daily; ☎415/773-1188; $11 round-trip). **Biking** over here makes for a beautiful ride over the Golden Gate Bridge and allows you to explore the headlands freely. Bikes are allowed on the ferry back to San Francisco.

### Across the Golden Gate: the Marin Headlands

The largely undeveloped **Marin Headlands**, across the Golden Gate from San Francisco, afford some of the most impressive views of the bridge and the city behind. The coastline is much more rugged than it is on the San Francisco side, and it makes a great place for an isolated clifftop scramble, in among the concrete remains of old forts and gun emplacements. Heading west on Bunker Hill Road takes you up to the brink of the headlands before snaking down to Fort Barry, and wide, sandy **Rodeo Beach**, from which numerous hiking trails branch out. Check in at the Marin Headlands Information Center (daily 9.30am–4.30pm; ☎415/331-1540) alongside Rodeo Lagoon for free maps. The largest of the fort's old buildings has been converted into the spacious but homey *HI-Marin Headlands* **hostel** (☎415/331-2777; ①), an excellent base for more extended explorations of the inland ridges and valleys.

### Sausalito

Pretty, smug little **SAUSALITO**, along the bay below US-101, was once a gritty community of fishermen and sea traders, full of bars and bordellos. Now exclusive restaurants and pricey boutiques line its picturesque waterfront promenade, and expensive, quirky houses climb the overgrown cliffs above Bridgeway Avenue, the main road and bus route through town. Ferries from San Francisco arrive next to the Sausalito Yacht Club in the town center. If you have **sailing** experience, split the $130 daily rental fee of a four- to six-person sailboat at Cass's Marine, 1702 Bridgeway (☎415/332-6789).

Aside from walking, shopping and sucking in the sea air, Sausalito has a one-of-a-kind exhibit in the **Bay Model Visitor Center**, 2100 Bridgeway (Tues–Sat 9am–4pm; donation), where elevated walkways in a huge building lead you around a scale model of the entire bay, surrounding deltas and its aquatic inhabitants.

*Casa Madrona* at 801 Bridgeway Ave (☎415/332-0502; ⑦), a deluxe **hotel** hideaway in the hills above the bay, also houses *Mikayla*, a delectable seafood **restaurant**. Less expensive food can be found near the waterfront; *Gatsby's*, 39 Caledonia St (☎415/332-4500), at the north end of town, is a reasonably priced pizza parlor, while *Caledonia Kitchen*, 400 Caledonia St (☎415/331-0220), serves a tasty variety of salads, sandwiches and fresh pastries. The *no name bar*, 757 Bridgeway Ave (☎415/332-1392), is a smoky ex-haunt of the Beats hosting frequent live jazz.

## Mount Tamalpais and Muir Woods

**Mount Tamalpais** dominates the skyline of the Marin peninsula, hulking over the cool canyons of the rest of the county in a crisp yet voluptuous silhouette, and dividing the county into two distinct parts: the wild western slopes above the Pacific coast and the increasingly suburban communities along the calmer bay frontage. The Panoramic Highway branches off from Hwy-1 along the crest above Mill Valley, taking ten miles to reach the center of **Mount Tamalpais State Park**, which has some thirty miles of hiking trails and many campgrounds. While most of the redwood trees that once covered its slopes have long since been chopped down to build San Francisco's Victorian houses, one towering grove remains, protected as the **Muir Woods National Monument** (daily 8am–sunset; $2). It's a tranquil and majestic spot, with sunlight filtering three hundred feet down from the treetops to the laurel and fern-covered canyon below. Being so close to San Francisco, Muir Woods is a popular target, and the paved trails nearest the car park are often packed with coach-tour hordes; more secluded hiking paths include the Matt Davis Trail, leading south to Stinson Beach and north to Mount Tamalpais.

## Mill Valley

From the east peak of Mount Tamalpais, a quick two-mile downhill hike follows the Temelpa Trail through velvety shrubs of chaparral to the town of **MILL VALLEY**, the oldest and most enticing of the inland towns of Marin County. This was originally a logging center, from where the destruction of the surrounding redwoods was organized, but for many years the town has made a healthy living out of tourism and October's annual Mill Valley Film Festival, which draws area stars and up-and-coming directors alike.

The restored town centers today around the redwood-shaded square of the *Depot Bookstore and Cafe* (Mon–Sat 7am–10pm, Sun 8am–10pm; ☎415/383-2665), a popular bookstore, cafe and meeting place at 87 Throckmorton Ave; there's a small **visitor center** next door (Mon, Tues, Thurs & Fri 11am–4pm; ☎415/388-9700). Far and away the best place to **stay**, if you can afford it, is the *Mill Valley Inn*, 165 Throckmorton Ave (☎415/389-6608 or 1-800/595-2100; ⑦–⑨), a gorgeous European-style inn with elegant rooms and two private cottages. They've just opened a branch along the waterfront: sumptuous *Acqua Hotel,* 555 Redwood Hwy (☎415/380-0400; ⑦) on Richardson Bay. *Piazza D'Angelo*, at 22 Miller Ave (☎415/388-2000), has very good pizzas and pastas.

*Sunnyside Cafe*, 31 Sunnyside Ave (☎415/388-5260), claims "the customers are rarely right" but serves large, affordable breakfasts and lunches nonetheless. *Sweetwater*, at 153 Throckmorton Ave (☎415/388-2820), is a comfortable saloon which doubles as Marin's prime **live music** venue, with gigs ranging from jazz and blues all-stars to Jefferson Airplane survivors.

## Point Reyes National Seashore

The westernmost tip of Marin County comes at the end of the **Point Reyes National Seashore**, a near-island of wilderness bordered on three sides by over fifty miles of isolated coastline – pine forests and sunny meadows hemmed in by rocky cliffs and sandy, windswept beaches. This wing-shaped landmass is a rogue piece of the earth's crust that has been drifting steadily northwards along the San Andreas Fault, having started out some six million years ago as a suburb of Los Angeles. When the great earthquake of 1906 shattered San Francisco, the land here, at the epicenter, shifted over sixteen feet in an instant, though damage was confined to a few skewed cattle fences.

The **visitor center** (Mon–Fri 9am–5pm, Sat, Sun & hols 8am–5pm; ☎415/663-1092), two miles southwest of Point Reyes Station, has engaging displays on local geology and natural history, plus details of hiking trails. Just to the north, Limantour Road heads six miles west to the *HI-Point Reyes* **hostel** (closed 9.30am–4.30pm; ☎415/663-8811; ①) in an old ranch house. Nearby **Limantour Beach** is good for swimming.

Eight miles west of the hamlet of Inverness, a small road leads down to **Drake's Beach**, the presumed landing spot of Sir Francis Drake in 1579. Appropriately, the coastline resembles the southern coast of England – cold, wet and windy, with chalk-white cliffs rising above the wide sandy beach. The road continues southwest another four miles to the very tip of Point Reyes. A precarious-looking **lighthouse** (Thurs–Sun 10am–5pm) stands firm against the crashing surf, and the bluffs are excellent for watching sea lions and, from mid-March to April and late December to early February, migrating gray whales.

# THE GOLD COUNTRY

About 150 years before international techies invaded California in search of Silicon gold, rough and ready **49ers** came to the **Gold Country** of the Sierra Nevada, 150 miles east of San Francisco, to look for the real thing. The area ranges from the foothills near Yosemite to the deep gorge of the Yuba River two hundred miles north, with **Sacramento** as its largest city. Many of the mining camps that sprung up around the Gold Country vanished as quickly as they appeared, but about half still survive. Some are bustling resorts, standing on the banks of whitewater rivers in the midst of thick pine forests; others are just eerie ghost towns, all but abandoned on the grassy rolling hills. Most of the mountainous forests along the Sierra crest are preserved as near pristine wilderness, with excellent hiking, camping and backpacking. There's great skiing in winter, around the mountainous rim of **Lake Tahoe** on the border between California and Nevada, aglow under the bright lights of the nightclubs and casinos that line its southeastern shore.

## Sacramento

California's state capital, **SACRAMENTO**, in the flatlands of the Central Valley, was founded in 1839 by the Swiss John Sutter. He worked hard for ten years to build a busy trading center and cattle ranch, only to be thwarted by the discovery of gold at a nearby sawmill in 1848. His workers quit their jobs to go prospecting, and thousands more flocked to the goldfields of the Central Mother Lode, without any respect for Sutter's claims to the land. Sacramento became the main supply point for the miners, and remained important as the western headquarters of the transcontinental railroad. Flashy office towers and hotel complexes have now sprung from its rather suburban streetscape, enlivening the flat grid of leafy, tree-lined blocks, and going some way towards resurrecting the rowdy, free-for-all spirit of the city's Gold Rush past.

Sacramento is not especially prominent on most travelers' itineraries. There's not a great deal to see, though the wharves, warehouses, saloons and stores of the historic core along the **riverfront** have been restored and converted into the touristy shops and restaurants of **Old Sacramento**. On the northern edge of the old town, the **California State Railroad Museum** (daily 10am–5pm; $6) brings together a range of lavishly restored 1860s locomotives, with "cow-catcher" front grilles and bulbous smokestacks. The old passenger station and freight depot, a block south, now serve as the summer depot for a refurbished **steam train** (summer weekends 10am–5pm; $6), which makes a seven-mile, 45-minute round-trip along the river.

Further east, and isolated from downtown, the dome of the **state capitol** stands proudly in a spacious green park two blocks south of K Street Mall. Recently restored to its original elegance, and still the seat of state government, the luxurious building brims over with finely crafted details. Although you're free to walk around, you'll see a lot more if you take one of the free hourly **tours** (daily 9am–5pm).

**Sutter's Fort State Historic Park** (daily 10am–5pm; $3–6), on the east side of town at 27th and L streets, is a re-creation of Sacramento's original settlement. An adobe house displays relics from the Gold Rush, and on summer weekends volunteers dress up and act out scenes from the 1850s.

### Practicalities

Most tourists arrive in Sacramento by car, taking a logical break from driving on Rte-80. **Trains** come in at Fifth and I streets, near Old Sacramento, while an almost continuous stream of Greyhound **buses** arrives at Seventh and L streets. The **airport** is twelve miles northwest: Super Shuttle Sacramento vans (☎1-800/BLUE-VAN; $12) take you directly to your downtown destination.

Sacramento's most accessible **visitor information center** is at 1101 Second St (daily 10am–5pm; ☎916/442-7644). Besides the central *Sacramento Hostel*, 900 H St (☎916/443-1691; ①), there are plenty of **places to stay** within walking distance of the city center – the best value is the *Econolodge*, 711 16th St (☎916/443-6631 or 1-800/553-2666; ②), while *Abigail's*, 2120 G St (☎916/441-5007 or 1-800/858-1568; ⑥), and *Hartley House Inn*, 700 22nd St (☎916/447-7829 or 1-800/831-5806; ⑥), both offer nineteenth-century elegance in the heart of Sacramento's liveliest local neighborhood. *Paesano's*, at 1806 Capitol Ave (☎916/447-8646), is a delicious and popular pizza **restaurant**; *Virga's*, at 1501 14th St near O (☎916/442-8516) offers scrumptious Italian fare and was selected best restaurant in local polls; *Centro Cocina Mexicana*, 454 28th St near J Street (☎916/442-2552), offers innovative Californian-Mexican fusion cuisine. Local indie bands play at the down-to-earth *Cafe Paris*, 2326 K St (☎916/442-2001).

# The Mines

In the romantically rugged landscape of the **Gold Country**, overshadowed by the 10,000ft granite peaks of the Sierra Nevada, fast-flowing rivers cascade through steeply walled canyons. During the fall, the flaming reds and golds of poplars and sugar maples on the slopes stand out against an evergreen background of pine and fir. The camps of the **southern mines** of the Gold Country were the liveliest and most uproarious of all the Gold Rush settlements, and inspired most of the popular images of the era: Wild West towns full of gambling halls, saloons and gunfights in the streets. Freebooting prospectors in these "placer" mines sometimes panned for nuggets of gold in the streams and rivers; further **north**, the diggings were far richer and more successful, but the gold was (and is) buried deep underground, and had to be pounded out of hardrock ore.

## Sonora, Columbia, Jamestown and Mariposa

The center of the southern mining district is **SONORA**, set on steep ravines roughly a hundred miles east of San Francisco. This friendly and animated logging town boasts numerous Victorian houses and false-fronted buildings on its main **Washington Street**. The Tuolumne County Visitors Bureau, 542 West Stockton Rd off Hwy-49 (☎209/533-4420 or 1-800/446-1333), is the best source of **information**.

Sonora's onetime arch-rival, **COLUMBIA**, three miles north on Parrots Ferry Road, is now a ghost town (and a state historic park), with a carefully restored Main Street that gives an excellent – if slightly contrived – idea of what Gold Rush life might have been like. In 1854 it was California's second largest city, and it missed becoming the state capital by two votes – just as well, since by 1870 the gold had run out and the town was abandoned.

The **Railtown 1897 State Park**, four blocks east of Main Street in **JAMESTOWN**, holds an impressive collection of old steam trains including the one used in *High Noon* (daily 9.30am–4.30pm). Further south, after a breathtaking drive over the Don Pedro Lake and Merced River, is **MARIPOSA**, gateway to Yosemite and one of the last gold rush towns on Hwy-49. Its **California State Mining & Mineral Museum** (Wed–Sun 10am–4pm; summer Wed–Mon 10am–6pm, $3.50), just south of the historic downtown, has a working 1860s stamp mill model and hundreds of mineral samples.

### Practicalities

In downtown Columbia, the best **place to stay** is right on the historic Main Street in the balconied *City Hotel* (☎209/532-1479 or 1-800/532-1479; ⑤); in Sonora the *Ryan House* is a comfortable B&B at 153 S Shepherd St (☎209/533-3445 or 1-800/831-4897; ⑤); motels on Hwy-49 between Sonora and Jamestown include the good-value *Miner's Motel* (☎209/532-7850 or 1-800/451-4176; ③). Jamestown's Main Street is lined by old Gold Rush hotels such as the *Jamestown Railroad Hotel* (☎209/984-3332 or 1-800/252-8299; ④). Sonora has a wide variety of **places to eat** along Washington Street: locals love *Alfredo's* for Mexican food at no. 123; for Italian, *Carmela's* at no. 301 is the old standby.

## Grass Valley, Nevada City and Downieville

The compact communities of **GRASS VALLEY** and **NEVADA CITY**, four miles apart in the Sierra Nevada Mountains, were the most prosperous and substantial of the gold-mining towns. Since the 1960s, artists and craftspeople have settled in the elaborate Victorian homes of the surrounding hills and gorges. In Grass Valley, the **North Star Mining Museum** (May–Oct daily 10am–5pm; donation) at the south end of Mill Street is housed in what used to be the power station for the North Star Mine. Its giant water-driven **Pelton wheel**, fitted with a hundred or so iron buckets, once powered the drills and hoists of the mine. Dioramas show the day-to-day working life of the miners, three-quarters of whom had emigrated here from the depressed tin mines of Cornwall (bringing the Cornish pasty with them).

The last mine in California to shut down was its richest, the **Empire Mine**, now preserved as a state park in the pine forests a mile southeast of Grass Valley (daily 10am–5pm; summer 9am–6pm; $3). It closed in 1956, after more than six million ounces of gold had been recovered, when the cost of getting the gold out of the ground exceeded $35 an ounce, the government-controlled price at the time. Machinery sold off when the mine closed has been replaced from other disused workings and now augments the excellent and very informative **museum** at the entrance.

The Grass Valley **visitor center** at 248 Mill St (☎530/273-4667 or 1-800/655-4667) is in a house replicating that of Lola Montez, an Irish entertainer and former mistress of Ludwig of Bavaria, who retired here after touring America with her provocative "Spider Dance" and kept a grizzly bear in her front yard.

Towns don't get much quainter than **Nevada City**. Amid all the shops and restaurants in the city center, the newly restored **Old Firehouse** at 214 Main St, a lacy, balconied and bell-towered piece of gingerbread, houses a small **museum** of local social history (May–Oct daily 11am–4pm; Nov–April Thurs–Sun 11am–4pm; donation).

Several daily Amtrak Thruway **buses** from Sacramento and Auburn stop on Sacramento Street in Nevada City and on West Main Street in Grass Valley. The Gold Country Stage connects the two towns every half-hour (Mon–Fri 8am–5pm, Sat 9.15am–5.30pm; ☎530/477-0103; $1, $2 for a day-pass).

North on Hwy-49, an hour's drive from Nevada City, you'll head into the most rugged and beautiful part of the Gold Country, where waterfalls tumble over black rocks bordered by pines and maples. **DOWNIEVILLE** is in the midst of such an idyllic setting. As the only mining camp to have ever hanged a woman, the town has, oddly enough, restored a gallows to commemorate that grisly passage of its history.

## Accommodation

Accommodation in the revamped old Gold Rush **hotels** doesn't come cheap, but if you can afford to splash out on a B&B, Nevada City has some excellent options.

**Airway Motel**, 575 E Broad St, Nevada City (☎530/265-2233). Quiet, 1940s motel with swimming pool, a 10min walk from the center of town. No credit cards. ②.

**Downey House**, 517 W Broad St, Nevada City (☎530/265-2815 or 1-800/258-2815). Pretty 1870s Victorian home at the top of Broad St, looking out over the town and surrounding forest. ④.

**Holbrooke Hotel**, 212 W Main St, Grass Valley (☎530/273-1353 or 1-800/933-7077). Historic hotel, once visited by Mark Twain, and right in the center of town. ④.

**Holiday Lodge**, 1221 E Main St, Grass Valley (☎530/273-4406). Comfortable, basic accommodation with perks such as a swimming pool, free breakfast and free local calls. ②.

**Swan-Levine House**, 328 S Church St, Grass Valley (☎530/272-1873). Attractively decorated, sunny rooms in an old Victorian hospital. ④.

## Eating and drinking

Both Grass Valley and Nevada City have good places to eat, as well as many bars and saloons, where you'll often be treated to free live music.

**Broad Street Books**, 426 Broad St, Nevada City (☎530/265-4204). Pastries, light fare, and espresso with wonderful tree-shaded outdoor seating.

**Cafe Mekka**, 237 Commercial St, Nevada City (☎530/478-1517). Relaxed, fabulously decorated coffee shop.

**Main Street Cafe**, 213 W Main St, Grass Valley (☎530/477-6000). Casual but refined and slightly expensive restaurant. An eclectic menu, from pastas to Cajun specialties. Recommended for grilled meats and fresh fish.

**Marshall's Pasties**, 203A Mill St, Grass Valley (☎530/272-2844). Vast array of fresh takeout pasties.

# Lake Tahoe

One of the highest, largest, deepest, cleanest and coldest lakes in the world, **Lake Tahoe** is perched high above the Gold Country in an alpine bowl of forested granite peaks. Longer than the English Channel is wide, and more than a thousand feet deep, it's so cold that perfectly preserved cowboys who drowned over a century ago have been recovered from its depths. The lake lures weekenders from the Bay Area and beyond with sunny beaches in the summer, snow-covered slopes in the winter and bustling casinos year round.

### Arrival, information and getting around

Daily Greyhound buses from San Francisco and Sacramento stop at *Harrah's* casino in **Stateline**, Nevada. From there, local STAGE **buses** serve the communities of Tahoe City and South Lake Tahoe. Amtrak Thruway buses arrive several times daily from Sacramento, heading for Carson City. You can rent **bicycles** from the Mountain Sports Center (☎530/542-6584) in South Lake Tahoe and from Olympic Bike Shop (☎530/581-2500) in Tahoe City. There are **visitors centers** around the lake, in California at 13066 US-50 (☎530/541-5255), and at 245 North Lake Blvd in Tahoe City (☎530/581-6900 or 583-3494); in Nevada at 969 Tahoe Blvd in Incline Village (☎775/832-1606 or 831-4440) and at 195 Hwy-50 (☎775/588-4591).

### Accommodation

There are dozens of bargain **motels** along the Southshore, though weekday rates from $40 can easily double at weekends and in summer. In Tahoe City, there are fewer budget choices, but as prices skyrocket around the lake, you'll rarely find a great deal in any direction. The South Lake Tahoe Visitors Authority (☎1-800/288-2463) runs a free **room reservation service**, which can also help you with Northshore and Reno reservations.

**Doug's Mellow Mountain Retreat**, 3787 Forest Ave, South Lake Tahoe (☎530/544-8065). A relaxed, if cramped, hostel where beds are $15 a night. ①.

**Red Carpet Inn**, 4100 Lake Tahoe Blvd (Hwy-50), South Lake Tahoe (☎530/544-2261 or 1-800/336-5553). Basic, but has a pool and is right on the Nevada border. ③.

**River Ranch**, Hwy-89 and Alpine Meadows Rd, Tahoe City (☎530/583-4264 or 1-800/535-9900). Historic lodge on the Truckee River with one of the lake's best restaurants. ⑥.

**Sierrawood Guest House**, 12 miles from Southshore, Tahoe Paradise (☎530/577-6073 or 1-800/700-3802). This is just a few minutes drive from the casinos' glitter. Jacuzzi, exercise room, fireplace and free snowmobiling on premises. ⑥.

**Tahoe City Inn**, 790 North Lake Blvd, Tahoe City (☎530/581-3333 or 1-800/800-8246). This place can cost as little as $60 midweek. ③.

**Tamarack Lodge**, 2311 North Lake Blvd, Tahoe City (☎530/583-3350 or 1-888/824-6323). The best deal anywhere on the lake. Comfortable and clean. ③.

### South Lake Tahoe and around

In **South Lake Tahoe**, the lakeside's largest community, ranks of restaurants, modest motels, and pine-bound cottages stand cheek by jowl with the high-rise gambling dens of Stateline, just across the border in Nevada. If you happen to lose your money at the tables and slot machines, you can always explore the beautiful hiking trails, parks and beaches that populate the surrounding area.

Not far away, the prettiest part of the lake is along the southwest shore, at **Emerald Bay State Park**, ten miles from South Lake Tahoe, which has a number of good shoreline **campgrounds**. A mile from the parking lot, **Vikingsholm** is an unlikely reproduction Viking castle (summer daily 10am–4pm, hourly tours; $2). In **D L Bliss State Park**, two miles north, the huge **Ehrman Mansion** (daily 11am–4pm; free) is decorated in Thirties-era furnishings; the extensive lakefront grounds were seen in *The Godfather II*.

The rest of the 75-mile **drive** is lovely enough, though certainly not the "most beautiful drive in America" as one locally produced brochure touts; a better way to see it is to take a **paddlewheel boat cruise** on either the *Tahoe Queen* from South Lake Tahoe (three departures daily, call for times; ☎1-800/238-2463; $18–45;) or the *MS Dixie II*, from Zephyr Cove (three departures daily, call for times; ☎775/588-3508; $17–42), reached on a free shuttle from South Lake Tahoe.

## Tahoe City

**Tahoe City**, the hub on the lake's northwestern shore, does not escape the tourists, but nevertheless manages to retain a more relaxed small-town attitude. Hwy-89 meets Hwy-28 at Lake Tahoe's only outlet, the **Truckee River**. The **Gatekeeper's Museum** (daily 11am–5pm; $2), at the mouth of the river, is a well-presented hodgepodge of artifacts from the nineteenth century, and has a good collection of native basketware. **Rafting** down the Truckee is a common activity in summer.

## LAKE TAHOE SKIING

Lake Tahoe has some of the best **downhill skiing** in North America, with some of its larger resorts rivaling their Rocky Mountain counterparts. Although skiing is certainly not cheap – the largest ski areas charge $50 for the privilege of using their mountain for a single day – many resorts offer decent-valued rental/lift ticket/lesson packages or multiday discounts. **Snowboarding** has, of course, caught on in a big way, and the same resorts that once scoffed at the sport have now installed massive snow parks with radical half-pipes and jumps. **Cross country skiing** is also popular. Most resorts **rent** skis for about $25 and snowboards for $35.

### DOWNHILL SKIING

**Squaw Valley USA**, Squaw Valley Rd, halfway between Truckee and Tahoe City (☎530/583-6985 or 1-800/766-9321). Thirty lifts service over 4000 acres of unbeatable terrain at the site of the 1960 Winter Olympics. Nonskiers can take the cable lift ($14) and use the ice-skating/swimming pool complex for the day. Lift tickets are $49.

**Heavenly**, reachable by shuttle from Southshore, two miles from the casinos, (☎775/586-7000 or 1-800/243-2836). Prime location and sheer scale (82 runs and 27 lifts) makes this one of the lake's most frequented resorts. Nonskiers can take the aerial tram for the view ($12.50). Lift tickets are $54.

**Homewood**, 6 miles north of Tahoe City on Hwy-89 (☎530/525-2992 or 1-800/824-6348). Smaller and more relaxed than its massive resorty neighbors, Homewood boasts some surprisingly good skiing

with unbeatable views of the lake and reasonable prices. Lift tickets go for $36.

**Kirkwood Ski Resort**, 35 miles south of South Lake Tahoe on Hwy-88 (☎209/258-6000). A bit out of the way if you're in Tahoe but worth the trip as a destination in itself for numerous recreational possibilities including excellent hiking and biking trails. Lift tickets are $45.

### CROSS-COUNTRY SKIING

**Royal Gorge**, in Soda Springs, 10 miles west of Truckee (☎530/426-3871 or 1-800/500-3871). The largest and best of Tahoe's cross-country resorts has 204 miles of groomed trails. $19.50 trail fee, $16.50 rental fee, and $18 for lessons.

**Spooner Lake**, in Nevada at the intersection of Hwy-50 and Hwy-28 (☎775/749-5349). The closest cross-country resort to South Lake Tahoe has lake views and 63 miles of groomed trails. Trail fees are $15, rentals are $15, and lessons are $34.

A couple of miles south along Hwy-89, 500 yards past the Kaspian picnic grounds, **hike** ten minutes up the unmarked trail to the top of **Eagle Rock** for amazing panoramic views of the royal-blue lake. Several miles further along the highway is popular **Chamber's Beach**.

**Squaw Valley**, the site of the 1960 Winter Olympics, is situated five miles west of Tahoe City off of Hwy-89, although the original facilities (except the flame and the Olympic rings) are now swamped by the rampant development which has made this California's largest ski resort (see box opposite).

### Eating and drinking

Fast food and casino all-you-can-eat buffets are standard in Southshore. Tahoe City has a better range of moderately priced restaurants as well as a couple of good bars, all within a few minutes of each other.

**Lakehouse Pizza**, 120 Grove St, Tahoe City (☎530/583-2222). Tahoe's best place for pizza is also a popular spot for cocktails on the lake at sundown.

**Pierce Street Annex**, in the back of the Lighthouse Center, Tahoe City (☎530/583-5800). The place for drinking and dancing on the Northshore.

**Red Hut Waffle Shop**, 2723 Lake Tahoe Blvd, South Lake Tahoe (☎530/541-9024). Ever-popular coffee shop, justifiably crowded early winter mornings with carbo-loading skiers.

**River Ranch**, Hwy-89 and Alpine Meadows Rd, Tahoe City (☎530/583-4264 or 1-800/535-9900). Historic lodge on the Truckee River with excellent New American cuisine served in a relaxed comforting atmosphere.

**Rosie's Cafe**, 571 North Lake Blvd, Tahoe City (☎530/583-8504). Cozy restaurant with a vaulted ceiling and fireplace serving delicious grilled meats, fresh sandwiches and filling breakfasts.

**Sprouts**, 3123 US-50 near Alameda Ave, South Lake Tahoe (☎530/541-6969). Almost, but not completely, vegetarian, with good organic sandwiches, burritos and smoothies.

**Sunnyside**, 1850 West Lake Blvd, Tahoe City (☎530/583-7200). One of the most popular places to have cocktails at sunset on the deck overlooking the lake.

**Tahoe Restaurant & Bäckerei**, Hwy-89, 1/2 mile south of Hwy-28, Tahoe City (☎530/583-1377). Family style bakery and restaurant that's popular with locals.

**Taj Mahal**, 3838 Lake Tahoe Blvd, South Lake Tahoe (☎530/541-6495). Basic Indian fare with a daily 11-course lunch buffet.

**Tep's Villa Roma**, 3450 Hwy-50, South Lake Tahoe (☎530/541-8227). Longstanding Southshore institution serves large portions of hearty Italian food.

### Donner Lake

Twenty-five miles north of Lake Tahoe, **Donner Lake**, surrounded by alpine cliffs of silver-gray granite, was the site of a gruesome tragedy in 1846, when the **Donner Party**, heading for the Gold Rush, found their route blocked by early snowfall. They stopped and built crude shelters, hoping that the snow would melt; it didn't. Fifteen of their number braved the mountains in search of help from Sutter's Fort in Sacramento; only two men and five women made it, surviving by eating the bodies of the men who died. A rescue party set off immediately, only to find more of the same: thirty or so half-crazed survivors, living off the meat of their fellow travelers. The horrific tale is recounted in the small **Emigrant Trail Museum** (daily 10am–4pm; $2), just off Donner Pass Road.

# NORTHERN CALIFORNIA

The massive and eerily silent volcanic lands of **northern California** have more in common with Oregon and Washington than with the rest of the state. Its small settlements live by logging, fishing and farming, though locals have been joined in recent years by New Agers, ex-hippies, and an ever-growing contingent of tourists. Once you're past the atypically lush valleys of the **Wine Country**, the **coast** stretches for four hundred miles of rugged bluffs and forests. Aside from the beautiful deserted beaches that stripe the coast, trees are the big attraction, thousands of years old and hundreds of feet high, dominating a landscape swathed in swirling mists. The **Redwood National Park** teems with campers and hikers in summer, but out of season it can be idyllic. The remote wildernesses of the **interior** can be enchanting, especially around the **Shasta Cascade** and **Lassen Volcanic National Park**.

**Public transportation** is, not surprisingly, scarce, though Greyhound buses run from San Francisco and Sacramento up and down I-5 and US-101.

# The Wine Country

The warm and sunny hills of **Napa** and **Sonoma valleys**, an hour north of San Francisco, are by reputation if not statistically at the center of the American wine industry; their 29,000 grape-acres turn out vintages to satisfy a snobbery every bit as rampant as in Europe. In summer, cars jam Hwy-29 through its heart, as visitors embark on a day's free drinking, thinly disguised as an avid interest in wine.

## The Napa Valley

A thirty-mile strip of gently landscaped hillsides, the **Napa Valley** looks more like southern France than a near-neighbor of the Pacific Ocean. The one anomaly is the town of **Napa** itself, a sprawling, ungainly city of 60,000 best avoided in favor of the wineries and small towns north on Hwy-29. Nine miles north, first up is **YOUNTVILLE**, named in honor of the valley's pioneer, George C Yount. Today the town is anchored by **Vintage 1870**, 6525 Washington St (daily 10.30am–5.30pm), a shopping and wine complex in a converted winery that rents bikes, helmets and a map of wine country for $20/day.

Of the large wineries at the valley's southern end, **Robert Mondavi**, at 7801 St Helena Hwy in Oakville (daily 10am–4.30pm; free), offers the most informative and least sales-driven tours and tastings.

A little further up the valley in the pretty village of **ST HELENA**, **Beringer Vineyards,** at 2000 Main St (daily 9.30am–5pm; free) is modeled on a German Gothic mansion and has graced the cover of many a wine magazine. Spacious lawns and a grand tasting room, heavy on the dark wood, make for quite a regal experience.

Homely **CALISTOGA**, at the very tip of the valley, is well known for its mud baths, whirlpools and mineral water, though its wineries are just as appealing. South of town, **Clos Pegase**, 1060 Dunaweal Lane (daily 10.30am–5pm; ☎707/942-4981), is a flamboyant, high-profile winery that emphasizes the link between fine wine and fine art, with an excellent sculpture garden around buildings designed by postmodern architect Michael Graves. Tastings are $2.50, and there are tours at 11am and 2pm. The **Chateau Montelena**, 1429 Tubbs Lane, just north of town, is one of the valley's oldest and smallest wineries, with an impressive medieval facade. A mile further up the road, the **Old Faithful Geyser** (daily 9am–6pm; $6) spurts boiling water sixty feet into the air at forty-minute intervals. The water source was discovered while drilling for oil here in the 1920s, when search equipment struck a force estimated to be up to a thousand pounds per square foot.

### Practicalities
From San Francisco there are daily Gray Line **bus tours** (☎415/558-9400) to the Wine Country; otherwise take the Blue & Gold Fleet tour which leaves daily from Fisherman's Wharf and includes a ferry trip across the bay past Alcatraz as well as a

bus trip through Napa and Sonoma valleys with stops at three wineries (☎415/705-8500; $52). Napa itself doesn't offer much for budget lodging; you're better off in Sonoma, where at least the cost of a room is offset by a pleasant surrounding.

In **St Helena**, *Hotel St Helena*, 1309 Main St (☎707/963-4388; ⑥–⑨) provides cozy rooms right in the center of town. Also a working vineyard set on 26 acres of grapes, *Sunny Acres Bed & Breakfast*, 397 Main St (☎707/963-2826; ⑦), continually books its three sumptuous rooms. St Helena's restaurants range from the California fusion cooking of *Pinot Blanc*, 614 Main St (☎707/963-6191), to the 400-plus list of wines at the gigantic *Wine Spectator Greystone Restaurant*, 2555 Main St (☎707/967-1010).

In **Calistoga**, *Dr Wilkinson's Hot Springs*, 1507 Lincoln Ave (☎707/942-4102; ⑤), is a legendary health spa and hotel; less expensive lodgings (and spa facilities) lining the main drag, Lincoln Avenue, include the quiet, modern *Comfort Inn* at no. 1865 (☎707/942-9400; ⑤ weekdays, ⑥ weekends). Downtown's most enticing hotel can be found at 1457 Lincoln in the historic *Mount View Hotel and Spa* (☎707/942-6877; ⑦ double, ⑨ cottage with patio and jacuzzi). Creative cuisine featuring unheard-of combinations such as chile rellenos with walnut pomegranate sauce make dining at the *Wappo Bar Bistro*, 1226 Washington St (☎707/942-4712), a delicious adventure. The *Calistoga Inn*, 1250 Lincoln Ave (☎707/942-4101), serves great seafood appetizers, including spicy Cajun prawns and crispy crabcakes, plus a wide range of wines, microbrewed beers and excellent desserts. *Brannan's Grill,* 1374 Lincoln Ave (☎707/942-2233) serves fresh oysters, salmon and pecan-stuffed quail in an airy wood-interior bistro.

## The Sonoma Valley

On looks alone, the crescent-shaped **Sonoma Valley** beats Napa hands down. This altogether more rustic valley curves between oak-covered mountain ranges from the Spanish colonial town of **SONOMA** to Glen Ellen, a few miles north along Hwy-12. It's far smaller than Napa, and many of its wineries are informal, family-run businesses, where a charge for tasting is still frowned upon and visitors are few.

The restored **Mission San Francisco Solano de Sonoma** (daily 10am–5pm; $3), just east of the spacious plaza in Sonoma, was the last and northernmost of the California missions, and the only one established in northern California by the nervous Mexican rulers, who were fearful of expansionist Russian fur traders. The plaza was also the sight of the Bear Flag Revolt, the 1846 action that propelled California into independence from Mexico, and then statehood. Sonoma's wineries are concentrated a mile east, within walking distance, and include the grand old **Buena Vista Winery**, 18000 Old Winery Rd (free tasting daily 10.30am–4.30pm; historical tours daily 2pm), which has champagne cellars, tunnels of oak caskets and a high-ceilinged tasting room. A 10-minute drive further north, in charming Glen Ellen, takes you to the **Benziger Family Winery**, 1883 London Ranch Rd (free tasting daily 10am–5pm). A do-it-yourself tour explains how wine grapes are cultivated and flavored, and four times daily a free tractor ride tour takes you around the vineyard along the side of Mount Sonoma. A half-mile up London Ranch Road begins **Jack London State Park** (daily 9.30am–6pm; $6 per car), which holds the author's final resting place along with a decent museum that houses a collection of souvenirs he picked up while traveling the globe.

### Practicalities
On weekdays, Sonoma County Transit (☎707/576-7433) **buses** link the town to Napa, and to Santa Rosa in the north. **Accommodation** is pricey, though the *Sonoma Hotel*, 110 W Spain St (☎707/996-2996; ⑦), has antique-crammed doubles and a good bar, and

the *Swiss Hotel*, 18 W Spain St (☎707/938-3298; ⑤) is both historical and whimsical. Good shopping and cafes abound on the square; *La Casa*, 121 E Spain St (☎707/996-3406), is a friendly, festive and inexpensive Mexican **restaurant** across from the mission, while next door, at 400 First St E, *Lo Spuntino* vends Italian ingredients perfect for putting together a picnic basket.

# The northern coast

The fog-bound towns and windswept, craggy beaches of the **northern coast** couldn't be farther removed from Southern California's sandy, sunny strip of ocean. Stretching north of San Francisco to the Oregon border, the area is better suited for hiking and camping than sunbathing, with a climate of cool temperatures year-round and a huge network of national, state and regional parks preserving magnificent **redwood** trees. Throw on your hiking boots and get out onto the trails that sweep past lolling seals, migrating whales, and some of the oldest, tallest trees on Earth.

### The Sonoma coast and Russian River

Despite the weekend influx from San Francisco, the villages of the **Sonoma coast** and **Russian River Valley** seem all but asleep for most of the year. Tucked along the slow, snaking Hwy-1, towns include **BODEGA BAY**, where Hitchcock filmed *The Birds*. From here, a great thirteen-mile hike leads along the rugged cliffs to busy **Goat Rock Beach**, where the Russian River joins the ocean. A prime seal and whale-watching spot, the beach is less than a mile from equally pleasing **JENNER**, which is a good place for clam chowder and ocean-staring.

About ten miles inland on Hwy-116, towards the warm and pastoral Russian River Valley, **GUERNEVILLE** is a well-established gay resort. It offers plenty of **places to stay** – though many are expensive. *The Willows*, 15905 River Rd (☎707/869-2824; ④–⑤), provides luxurious rooms alongside the river, while the **campground** at *Johnson's Resort* on First Street has cabins, as well as a lively nightlife (☎707/869-2022; ①). The *Russian River Resort ("Triple R")*, 16390 Fourth St (☎707/869-0691), and *River Business Inc*, 16225 Main St (☎707/869-3400), are both popular places to eat and drink. The **Armstrong Redwoods State Reserve** ($6 per car, pedestrians free), two miles north, contains 750 very dense acres of enormous redwoods, interspersed by trails – horseback riding is particularly recommended. Guided expeditions run by the Armstrong Woods Pack Station (☎707/887-2939) vary in length from half a day ($40) to three-day pack trips ($450).

**MONTE RIO**, three miles back down the river towards the coast, is a lovely old resort town, at the entrance to the 2500-acre **Bohemian Grove**, where the richest and most powerful men in the country traditionally gather in privacy each July for a week of (supposedly male-only) high jinks.

### The Mendocino coast

The coast of **Mendocino County**, 150 miles north of San Francisco, is a dramatic extension of the Sonoma coastline – the headlands a bit sharper, the surf a bit rougher, but otherwise more of the same. **MENDOCINO** itself looks like a transplanted New England fishing village: weathered and charming, with plenty of art galleries and boutiques. Just south of town, hiking and cycling trails weave through the unusual **Van Damme State Park**, on Hwy-1 (☎707/937-5804; $6), where the ancient trees of the **Pygmy Forest** are stunted to waist height because of poor drainage and soil chemicals. Two-hour sea cave tours through the park are available through Lost Coast Kayaking (three times daily; ☎707/937-2434; $45).

The *Sea Gull Inn*, 44960 Albion St (☎1-888/937-5204 or 707/937-5204; ③–⑥), is the best of the affordable accommodations in the center of town, though the antique-filled rooms at *The Mendocino Hotel*, 45080 Main St (☎1-800/548-0513 or 707/937-0511; ④–⑧), are more luxurious. The town's oldest **bar** is *Dick's Place* on Main Street, the closest thing you'll find to a local hangout. Of Mendocino's **restaurants**, the best and most famous is *Cafe Beaujolais*, 961 Ukiah St (☎707/937-5614), which specializes in organic California cuisine. *955 Ukiah Street* (☎707/937-1955) serves some of the best food in town, entrees are considered a steal for $15–20 a plate (Wed–Sun from 6pm). For slightly cheaper fare, try the *Mendocino Cafe*, 10485 Lansing St (☎707/937-0836), serving an eclectic mix of salads, pastas, and sandwiches daily until 9pm. *Tote Féte Bakery*, behind the deli of the same name at 10450 Lansing St (☎707/937-3383; daily until 7pm), produces delicious breads, pastries and muffins, which you can eat outside on the tree-shaded deck.

## The Humboldt coast

Humboldt is by far the most beautiful of the coastal counties: almost entirely forestland, overwhelmingly peaceful in places, in others plain eerie. The impassable cliffs of **Kings Range** prevent even the sinuous Hwy-1 from reaching the "Lost Coast" of its southern reaches. To get there you have to travel US-101 through the deepest redwood territory as far as **GARBERVILLE**, a one-street town with a few good bars, at the center of the "Emerald Triangle" that produces the majority of California's largest cash crop, marijuana. Every August, the town hosts the enormous **Reggae on the River** festival (information on ☎707/923-3368).

Redwood country begins in earnest a few miles north, at the **Humboldt Redwoods State Park**. The serpentine **Avenue of the Giants** weaves for 33 miles through trees that block all but a few strands of sunlight, but you can exit at numerous points to get back on US-101. This is the habitat of *sequoia sempervirens*, the coastal redwood, with ancestors dating back to the dinosaurs. Some are over 350ft tall. Three campgrounds fill up quickly in summertime ($16; reserve through Parknet at ☎1-800/444-7275 or call ☎707/946-2409 for information).

Tiny **SAMOA**, a few minutes by car over the bay from **EUREKA**, holds the last remaining cookhouse in the west. Lumbermen came to the *Samoa Cookhouse* (☎707/442-1659) to eat gargantuan meals after a day of felling redwoods; the oilskin tablecloths and burly workers have gone, but the lumber-camp style remains, with long tables and colossal portions of red meat.

**ARCATA**, twelve miles north of Eureka, a small college town with an earthy, mellow pace, has a grassy central plaza surrounded by good restaurants, and some excellent white-sand, windswept beaches to the north. Three blocks from the Greyhound station on Tenth Street, the *Arcata Youth Hostel*, 1390 I St (late-June–late Aug; ☎707/822-9995; ①), has $15 dorm beds; not far away is the *Fairwinds Motel*, 1674 G St (☎707/822-4824; ②). The working *Humboldt Brewery*, 856 Tenth St, has its own bar and low-priced restaurant.

## Redwood National Park

Thirty miles north of Arcata, the small town of **ORICK** marks the southern limit, and busiest section, of the **Redwood National Park. Tall Trees Grove** here is home to one of the world's tallest trees – a mighty 367-footer. Many visitors hike to it on the 8.5-mile trail from the **information center** (daily 9am–6pm; ☎707/488-3461), from which you can obtain the needed free permit to drive and camp the back roads leading to the tree.

Of the three state parks within the Redwood National Park area, **Prairie Creek** is the most varied and popular, and while bear and elk roam in plain sight, you can also be taken around here by the rangers for a **tour** of the wild and damp profusion. Highlights include the meadows of **Elk Prairie** in front of the **ranger station** (summer daily 8am–6pm; rest

---

### BIGFOOT COUNTRY

**Willow Creek**, forty miles east of Arcata, is the self-proclaimed gateway to "**Bigfoot Country**." Reports of giant 350- to 800-pound humanoids wandering the forests of northwestern California have circulated since the late nineteenth century, fueled by long-established Indian legends, but weren't taken seriously until 1958, when a road maintenance crew found giant footprints. Thanks to their photos, the Bigfoot story went worldwide. Since then, there have been over forty separate sightings of Bigfoot prints. At the crossroads in Willow Creek is a huge wooden replica of the man-ape, with slanted forehead, flared nostrils and short ears, an identikit of the creature who in recent years has added kidnapping to his list of alleged activities. A small **visitor center** here has details of Bigfoot's escapades, as well as information on the adjacent **Hoopa Valley Indian Reservation**, which has often been the site of violent confrontation between Native Americans and whites over fishing territory.

---

of year daily 8am–5pm; ☎707/488-2171), where herds of Roosevelt Elk, massive beasts weighing up to four hundred pounds, wander freely, protected from poachers.

Spectacular coastal views can be had from trails in the **Klamath** area, especially the **Klamath Overlook**, on Requa Road about three-quarters of a mile down to the sea. You can drive through, jump over, or lumber under all the sculpted **Trees of Mystery** (daily 8am–6pm; $6.50), except the impressive **Cathedral Tree**, where nine trees have grown from one root structure to form a spooky circle. The *HI-Redwood National Park* **hostel** (☎707/482-8265; ①) on US-101 has dorm beds from $12–14.

The park headquarters are in **CRESCENT CITY** at 1111 Second St (daily 8am–5pm ☎707/464-6101), but you can pick up information all over the park. There are **campgrounds** everywhere; three that have showers and water are *Prairie Creek* on US-101; *Mill Creek*, eight miles south of Crescent City; and *Jedediah Smith*, five miles north of Crescent City on the Smith River. If you must come in summer, make reservations through PARKNET; ☎1-800/444-7275; and if things get really desperate, head up US-101 and look for **motels** around Crescent City.

# The northern interior

The remote **northern interior** of California, cut off from the coast by the **Shasta Cascade** range and dominated by forests, lakes and mountains, is largely uninhabited too, and infrequently visited. I-5 leads through the heart of this near wilderness, forging straight through the unspectacular farmland of **Sacramento Valley** to **Redding** – the region's only buses follow this route. Redding isn't much of a place in itself, but it's a good base for the **Whiskeytown-Shasta-Trinity area** and the more demanding **Lassen National Volcanic Park**. Mountaineers and the spiritually-minded flock to **Mount Shasta**, which is close enough to the volcanic **Lava Beds** at the very northeastern tip of the state for them to be a long but feasible day's car trip.

## Chico

Charming little **CHICO**, about midway between Sacramento and Redding, some twenty miles east of I-5, is a good stop-off if you don't want to attempt to cover the whole valley from top to bottom in one day, or if you're here to visit Lassen Volcanic National Park (see opposite) and need somewhere to stay. Home to **Chico State University**, the laid-back town is loved by mountain bikers for its many trails. Cheap rooms downtown exist at *Days Inn*, 740 Broadway (☎530/343-3286; ②), and there are several good restaurants, notably *La Hacienda Inn*, 2635 Esplanade (☎530/893-8270), a Mexican spot famed for its special pink sauce, known as "Heroin Sauce" for its addictive sweet flavor.

## Redding and Shasta

A sprawling expanse of chain stores with a shopping mall in its heart and a poured-concrete convention center at its gate, **REDDING** sticks out as an anomaly amidst the natural splendor that makes up the northern interior. The region's largest city, with 70,000 people, it's acted as a northern nexus since the late-nineteenth century, when the Central Pacific railroad came through. Today it remains a crossroads, bulging with cookie-cutter motels and diners. Along Market Street (Hwy-273) and Pine Street, four blocks from the Greyhound station: *Budget Lodge*, 1055 Market St (☎530/243-4231; ②), is a typical cheap option; the *Redding Lodge*, 1135 Market St (☎530/243-5141; ③), is slightly more luxurious.

**SHASTA**, four miles west of Redding and not to be confused with Mount Shasta, is more appealing, though barely. These half-ruined brick buildings were once a booming gold-mining town, literally at the end of the road from San Francisco and on the very edge of the wilderness. The **courthouse** has been turned into a museum (Wed–Sun 10am–5pm; $2) full of mining paraphernalia; the gallows and prison cells are a grim reminder of the once daily executions.

Precipitous Hwy-299 climbs from Shasta into the **Whiskeytown-Shasta-Trinity National Recreation Area**, where the artificial beaches, forests and camping facilities at three lakes – Clair Eagle, Whiskeytown and Shasta – meet the needs of waterskiers, sailors and wilderness hikers. Sadly, during summer it's completely congested, as windsurfers, motorboats, jet skis and recreational vehicles block the narrow routes which serve the lakes. An extensive system of tunnels, dams and aqueducts directs the plentiful waters of the Sacramento River in to California's central valley to irrigate cash crops. The lakes are pretty enough, but residents complain they're not a patch on the wild waters that used to flow from the mountains before the Central Valley Project came along in the 1960s.

## Lassen National Volcanic Park

About fifty miles over gently-sloping plains east from Red Bluff on Hwy-36, or forty miles east from Redding on Hwy-44, the 106,000 acres that make up the pine forests, crystal-green lakes and boiling thermal pools of the **LASSEN VOLCANIC NATIONAL PARK** are one of the most unearthly parts of northern California's forbidding climate, which brings up to fifty feet of snowfall each year, keeps the area pretty much uninhabited outside the brief summer season. **Mount Lassen** itself last erupted in 1915, when the peak blew an enormous mushroom cloud some seven miles skyward, tearing the summit into chunks that landed as far away as Reno; scientists predict that it is the likeliest of all the West Coast volcanoes to blow again.

The thirty-mile tour of the park along Hwy-89 from **Manzanita Lake** in the north should take no more than a few hours. The Mount Lassen explosion denuded the devastated area, ripping out every tree and patch of grass. Slowly the earth is recovering a green blanket, but the most vivid impression is one of complete destruction. Marking the halfway point, **Summit Lake** is a busy camping area set around a beautiful icy lake, close to which are the park's most manageable hiking trails. From a parking area to the south (8000ft up), the steep, five-mile ascent to Lassen Peak begins. Experienced hikers can do it in four hours, but wilderness seekers will have a better time pushing east to the steep trails of the **Juniper Lake** area.

Continuing south along Hwy-89, Lassen's indisputable show-stealers are **Bumpass Hell** and **Emerald Lake**, the former (named after a man who lost a leg trying to cross it) a steaming valley of active pools and vents which bubble away at a low rumble all around. The trails are sturdy and easy to manage, but you should never venture off them. The crusts over the thermal features are often brittle, and breaking through could plunge you into very hot water. Before leaving the park at **Mineral**, make an effort to stop at **Sulphur Works**, an acrid cauldron of steam vents. A magnificent but grueling trail leads for a mile around the site to the avalanche-prone summit at **Diamond Peak**, with great views over the entire park and forestland beyond.

The Park Service has its **headquarters** in Mineral (daily 8am–4.30pm; PO Box 100, Mineral, CA 96063; ☎530/595-4444), where you can get free maps and information (there's a box outside when it's closed, and they'll leave your backcountry permits here if you arrive late), including the *Lassen Park Guide*. The main **visitor center** (summer daily 9am–5pm; ☎530/595-4444 ext 5180) is at Manzanita Lake, just inside the northern entrance.

## Mount Shasta City and Mount Shasta

Roughly sixty miles north of Redding, a scenic road branches off I-5 to the tiny town that describes itself as "the best kept secret in California": **MOUNT SHASTA CITY**, hard under the enormous bulk of the 14,162ft **Mount Shasta**. Still considered active despite not having erupted for two hundred years, this lone peak dominates the landscape for a hundred miles around, and its "energies" attract New Agers by the score. If you want to climb to the summit (10hr; crampons and ice axe needed most of the year), or simply to explore the flanks of the mountain along the many trails, you must obtain a free permit from the **ranger district office**, 204 W Alma St (summer daily 8am–4.30pm; rest of year Mon–Fri 8am–4.30pm; ☎530/926-4511), or you can self-issue one at the main trailheads.

Greyhound buses on the Redding–Oregon run stop on N Mt Shasta Blvd, a couple of blocks from the **Chamber of Commerce**, 300 Pine St (Mon–Sat 9am–5pm, Sun 10am–4pm; ☎530/926-4865 or 1-800/926-4865). There's budget **accommodation** at the excellent *Alpenrose Cottage Hostel*, 204 E Hinkley St (☎530/926-6724; ①), and the *Best Western Tree House Motor Inn*, 111 Morgan Way (☎1-800/545-7164 or 530/926-3101, ④–⑥). Nicer still, the *McCloud Hotel*, 408 Main St, McCloud (☎1-800/964-2823 or 530/964-2822), has rooms with jacuzzis (⑦) and without (⑤). *Lake Siskiyou Campground* (☎530/926-2618) is four miles west of town.

Some of the town's best food can be found at *Willy's Bavarian Kitchen*, 107 Chestnut St (☎530/926-3636), which serves sausage, sauerkraut and, surprisingly, a wide range of vegetarian dishes, fruit smoothies and good beer on its terrace. For Italian and cocktails, head for *Mike and Tony's*, 501 S Mount Shasta Blvd (☎530/926-4792). Breakfast, or bagels anytime, can be found at the New Agey *Bagel Cafe and Natural Bakery*, 105 E Alma St (☎530/926-1414).

## Lava Beds National Monument

**Lava Beds National Monument**, in the far northeastern corner of the state, is the most remote and forgotten of California's parks, and also one of its most interesting. The history of these volcanic caves and huge black lava flows is as violent as the natural forces that created them. Before the Gold Rush the area was home to the **Modoc** Indians, but repeated and bloody confrontations with miners led the government to order them into a reservation shared with another, traditionally enemy, tribe. After only a few months the Modocs drifted back to the isolation of the lava beds, and in 1872 the army was sent in. Fifty-two Modoc warriors, under the leadership of "Captain Jack," held back an army twenty times the size of theirs for five months from a natural fortress of passageways now known as **Captain Jack's Stronghold**, at the park's northern tip. You can retrace the conflict and the US press' pressure on the Army to abandon its cause, through well-detailed self-guided trails in the park as well as an exhibit at the **visitor center** (summer daily 8am–6pm; rest of year daily 8am–5pm; ☎530/667-2282).

The bulk of the lava tube caves are close to the visitor center from where you can opt for the free ranger-led tours (daily 9am & 2pm) or, with some nerve and a good light source (free to borrow from the visitor center), explore the caves alone. You can camp near the visitor center, but there are no shops nearby so bring everything you need with you. Nearby is the **Modoc Ranger Station** (Mon–Fri 8am–4.30pm; ☎530/667-2248) with general information on the Modoc National Forest. North and west of Lava Beds, the **Klamath Basin National Wildlife Refuge** hosts millions of birds migrating along the Pacific Flyway. The **visitor center** (Mon–Fri 8am–4.30pm, Sat & Sun 10am–4pm; ☎530/667-2231), off Hill Road near the northwest entrance for Lava Beds, issues permits for the bird-watching and hunting blinds ($5): call ahead to be sure of getting one. Surprisingly, the best way of spotting the wildlife is by driving along designated routes ($3); getting out of the car and walking scares the birds off.

# CHAPTER FOURTEEN

# THE PACIFIC NORTHWEST

The two northern Pacific states of **WASHINGTON** and **OREGON** are similar in both topography and climate. Significantly cooler than California to the south – and hence spared most of the damaging effects of overtourism – both are split in half by the great north–south spine of the Cascade Mountains, with their western sides more appealing by far.

Throughout these hilly **western** regions, the ocean rains, if not quite as unceasing as local folklore might suggest, have created a verdant landscape, thick with woodlands that on the **Olympic Peninsula** become mini-rainforests. This fertile land is where the population is most heavily concentrated, although the principal cities are not along the exposed coast itself, which remains – in Oregon at least – remarkably pristine, scattered with remote beaches. Both **Seattle** and **Portland** lie roughly fifty miles from the open Pacific along the I-5 highway, which runs from Canada to California. Seattle, the commercial and cultural capital of the Northwest, is nonetheless a major port, perched on the edge of the beautiful, island-strewn **Puget Sound**, with a busy network of local and long-distance ferries among the container traffic. Portland lies adjacent to the rich farmlands of the Willamette Valley, long the historic heartland of Oregon.

Across the Cascades, the **east** is far drier and less hospitable, sometimes verging on desert. Of the towns, only **Spokane** is of any appreciable size, though the booming resort town of **Bend**, within easy distance of both mountains and desert, is a far more appealing target, and a useful base for sampling the wide-skied, empty landscapes of the east, at their most beautiful along the **Columbia River Gorge**. Of outstanding interest also is the scarred territory between Seattle and Portland around **Mount St Helens**, which erupted to devastating effect in 1980.

## Some history

The first inhabitants of the Pacific Northwest are believed to have reached the continent across a land bridge over what is now the Bering Strait between Siberia and Alaska. Archeological evidence of Plains tribes dates back thousands of years and artifacts recently unearthed from the perfectly preserved five-hundred-year-old settlement

---

### ACCOMMODATION PRICE CODES

All accommodation prices in this book have been coded using the symbols below. Note that prices are for the least expensive double rooms in each establishment. For a full explanation see p.37 in Basics.

| | | |
|---|---|---|
| ① up to $30 | ④ $60–80 | ⑦ $130–175 |
| ② $30–45 | ⑤ $80–100 | ⑧ $175–250 |
| ③ $45–60 | ⑥ $100–130 | ⑨ $250+ |

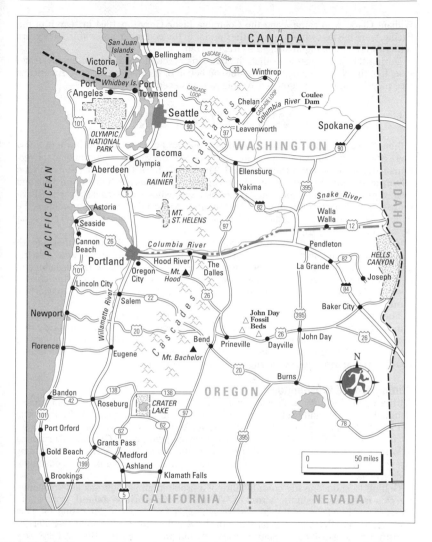

at **Makah Bay** provide a great opportunity to appreciate how this local population once lived.

Not until early in the nineteenth century was there a significant white presence in the region, and even that was very much confined to trading and exploration along the coast rather than permanent settlement. Russian trappers began to make their way down from the north, Canadians from the northeast, while European sea captains such as Cook and Vancouver came in search of the **Northwest Passage**, an ice-free route between the Atlantic and the Pacific. A brief period of hectic competition, in which entrepreneurs of many nationalities vied for fur-trading profits, only came to an end when the whole coast was all but "trapped out." Explorers Meriwether Lewis and

William Clark, who came along the Columbia River Gorge in 1804 in search of the Pacific, were the first whites to cross the interior of the continent, and within forty years settlers were streaming in along the Oregon Trail.

During the forty years after that, the railroads reached Portland and Seattle, Chief Joseph of the Nez Percé made his last bid on behalf of the displaced Native Americans (see p.799), and both Oregon and Washington achieved statehood.

# WASHINGTON

Although **Seattle** is one of America's most likeable and vibrant cities, well **worth a few days** of anybody's time, perhaps its greatest asset for the tourist is proximity to the glorious rural scenery of the **Puget Sound**. The islands here are stepping stones to the **Olympic Peninsula** to the west, whose rugged mountains are home to rare elk and lush vegetation that merges into rainforest, and whose wilderness beaches have remained unchanged for centuries. The **Olympic National Park**, which occupies the bulk of the peninsula, is dazzling, and a hike along one of its clearly laid-out trails can be a highlight of any trip.

The problem here is the **weather**: as the clouds sweep in off the Pacific, they deposit bucketloads of rain on the western part of the state, and only in the summer are the odds on for warm weather and blue skies. Further south, the **lower coast** is flatter and more accessible but not as appealing, splodged with industrial towns and glum holiday resorts. It's much better to spend time inland, amidst the wasted volcanic scenery of **Mount St Helens**.

The sprawling prairie-plateau that makes up most of **eastern Washington** is a real grind to drive across and frankly there's little to enthrall, though if a cross-country trek takes you through **Spokane**, the **Grand Coulee Dam** is worth a detour; otherwise you're only likely to come out here if you're traveling the Cascade loop, a spectacular 400-mile round-trip through the rugged **Cascade Mountains**.

## Getting around Washington

All the main cities of the Pacific Northwest are served by both **trains** and **buses**. Roughly four trains and twelve buses per day make the four-hour journey from **Seattle** to **Portland** along the route of the I-5 interstate. Amtrak and Greyhound run east from Seattle across the Cascades to **Spokane** and beyond, with other Greyhounds running to Wenatchee (for Chelan), Ellensburg, Yakima and Walla Walla. Areas not covered by Greyhound are usually accessible on local buses, though this can be time-consuming and inconvenient.

Getting to and along the coast is more of a problem and requires a little planning. **Ferries** from Seattle shuttle across to Winslow, on **Bainbridge Island**, from where Kitsap Transit services link with Jefferson Transit for access to Port Angeles, Port Townsend and Olympic National Park. In the Seattle and Puget Sound area, ferries (mostly run by Washington State Ferries; Washington: ☎206/464-6400 or 1-888/808-7977; British Columbia: ☎250/381-1551; *www.wsdot.wa.gov/ferries*) are a reliable and enjoyable method of getting to such places as Whidbey Island and the San Juan Islands. There are also long-distance services, to Canada from Seattle, Anacortes and Port Angeles, and to Alaska from Bellingham; see p.1036.

# Seattle

Curved around the shore of Elliott Bay, with Lake Washington behind and the snowy peak of Mount Rainier hovering faintly in the distance, **SEATTLE** has a magnificent setting. The insistently modern skyline of glass skyscrapers gleams across the bay, an emblem of three decades of vigorous urban renewal.

Seattle's beginnings were inauspiciously muddy. Flooded out of its first location on the flat little peninsula of Alki Point, the town shifted in the 1850s to what's now Pioneer Square, renaming itself after the Native American Chief Sealth (aka Seattle). This was soggy ground, and the small logging community built its houses on stilts. As the surrounding forest was gradually felled and the wood shipped out, Seattle grew slowly until the Klondike Gold Rush of 1897 put it firmly on the national map. World War I boosted shipbuilding, and the city was soon a large industrial center. Trade unions, based around the shipworkers, grew strong, and the Industrial Workers of the World, or "Wobblies," coordinated the US's first general strike here on February 6, 1919.

Since the beginning of the twentieth century, the **Boeing** airline corporation has been crucial to the city's well-being, booming during World War II and employing one in five of Seattle's workforce by the 1960s. The prosperity that Boeing and more recent success stories such as computer software giant **Microsoft** and Internet shopping site **Amazon.com** have brought the city is obvious, reflected in a restored old center, a nationally acclaimed arts scene with vibrant movie and music industries, and a flood of coffeehouses and excellent seafood restaurants. No longer overshadowed by the two big Californian conurbations, Seattle now regularly tops magazine surveys of desirable places to live, attracting migrants across the social and economic spectrum.

Despite the dizzying expansion, the city's more established neighborhoods remain distinctive and Seattle has a pleasantly down-to-earth ambiance, although its new-found affluence jars uncomfortably with a visible street community of teenage runaways and homeless people.

## Arrival, information and getting around

Flights land at Seattle/Tacoma's **Sea-Tac Airport** (☎206/431-4444), out on Hwy-99 (the Pacific Highway) fourteen miles south of downtown. Outside, the Gray Line Airport Express bus (☎206/626-6088; $7.50 one-way, $13 round trip) leaves every twenty minutes for the 25-minute journey to various hotels downtown. ShuttleExpress (☎206/622-1424 or 1-800/487-RIDE) offers a door-to-door service for $16–30). The Metro express city bus #194 ($1.10, during peak hours $1.60) takes thirty minutes to reach downtown's Transit Tunnel. A **taxi** to downtown will cost around $25.

The Amtrak station at Third and Jackson, just south of downtown, and the Greyhound bus terminal at Eighth and Stewart, to the east, are both an easy bus ride from downtown. Green Tortoise drops off and picks up at Ninth and Stewart. A couple of blocks towards downtown from Greyhound is the **visitor center**, on the Galleria level inside the Washington State Convention Center at Seventh and Pike (Mon–Fri 8.30am–5pm, Sat–Sun 10am–4pm; ☎206/461-5840). The main **post office** is at Union Street and Third Avenue downtown (Mon–Fri 8am–5.30pm; ☎1-800/275-8777; zip code 98101).

### City transportation

It's best to **get around** either on foot or on the free downtown buses. Cross out of the free zone, and you pay as you get off; come back in and you pay as you enter. Single fares vary between $1 and $1.75, and tickets are valid for an hour. **Day-passes** ($1.70; bought from the driver) are available on weekends and holidays: ticket books (for 10 and 20 rides) can be purchased from the **Metro Customer Assistance Offices** at the Metro Transit Tunnel, Westlake Mall, Fifth Avenue and Vine Street, or in the Exchange Building, Second and Marion in downtown Seattle (Mon–Fri 9am–5.30pm; call 24-Hour Rider Information ☎206/553-3000, or Bus-Time ☎206/287-8463 for automated schedule), and can be used on the overhead monorail (otherwise $1) between downtown and the Seattle Center, and on the waterfront streetcar (85¢ off-peak, $1.10 peak).

Washington State **ferries** run to Bainbridge Island and Bremerton; tickets from Pier 52, Colman Dock (☎206/464-6400). Gray Line (☎206/626-5208) organizes guided half-day **bus tours** ($26), and is among several operators of **boat tours**, of which the best is the Argosy's Locks Cruise tour from Pier 57 (3hrs; ☎206/623-4252; $28).

## Accommodation

While there's no shortage of hotel space in Seattle, it can be difficult to find the middle ground between smart, expense-account-type places and seedy dives. The best choices are downtown and the city's hostels are of good value. Three specialist **B&B agencies** are A Pacific Reservation Service (☎206/784-0539 or 1-800/684-2932; *www.seattlebedandbreakfast.com*), Washington Bed and Breakfast Guild (2442 NW Market St, #355, Seattle, WA 98107; ☎1-800/647-2918), and Travelers' Reservation Service (PO Box 492, Mercer Island, WA 98040; ☎206/232-2345); all have places throughout the state.

**Ace**, 2423 1st Ave (☎206/448-4721). Elegant and practical lodgings in chic Belltown that feature sleek, loft-like rooms with hardwood floors. ③.

**Alexis**, 1007 1st Ave (☎206/624-4844 or 1-800/426-7033). A posh nineteenth-century hotel situated between Pike Market and Pioneer Square. Aveda spa, fitness center and cigar bar. ⑧.

**American Backpackers Hostel**, 126 Broadway Ave E (☎206/720-2965). Near the busiest corner in Capitol Hill. Four-bed dorms and a few private rooms. No curfew, free breakfast, downtown pickup, club passes, and parking (during off-season). ①/②.

**Claremont**, 2000 4th Ave (☎206/448-8600 or 1-800/448-8601). An intimate, European-style hotel in downtown Seattle. Complimentary continental breakfast. ⑤.

**Green Tortoise**, 1525 2nd Ave, between Pike and Pine (☎206/340-1222 or 1-888/424-6783). Old-style hotel digs now functioning as a hostel with some private rooms. Free breakfast, Internet access, and pickups at Amtrak, Greyhound or ferries. ①/②.

**HI-Seattle**, 84 Union St, behind Pike Place Market (☎206/622-5443 or 1-888/662-5443). Modern and well-equipped hostel that is popular with families. Open 24hr. Reservations are strongly advised in summer. ①.

**Hotel Seattle**, 315 Seneca St (☎206/623-5110). A good deal for those looking for a central location and modern, but not antiseptic, ambiance in the upper-middle price range. ⑤.

**Kings Inn**, 2106 5th Ave (☎206/441-8833 or 1-800/546-4760). Clean and basic downtown motor lodge with some large suites. ④.

**Monaco**, 1101 4th Ave (☎206/621-1770 or 1-800/945-2240). A luxurious "boutique" hotel in the old Pacific Northwest Bell switching office. Pet goldfish included. ⑧.

**Pioneer Square Hotel**, 77 Yesler Way (☎206/340-1234). A restored nineteenth-century hotel in Pioneer Square. Inexpensive accommodation with a good level of comfort. ⑤.

**Sorrento**, 900 Madison St (☎206/622-4400 or 1-800/426-1265). Seattle's oldest hotel is a small luxury accommodation on the east side of I-5 from downtown. The regal exterior surrounds a circular courtyard with palm trees. ⑧.

**University Inn**, 4140 Roosevelt Way NE, University District (☎206/632-5055 or 1-800/733-3855). Average modern hotel just off University Way. Some rooms have kitchens; there's also a pool and whirlpool spa. ⑥.

**Vincent's Backpackers Guest House**, 527 Madison Ave E (☎206/323-7849). Comfortable house on a quiet tree-lined street in Capitol Hill has 38 beds, most in six-bunk dorm rooms ($12), as well as a few doubles for $45. Bathroom with shower in all rooms, abundant kitchen facilities and a backyard with picnic tables. Free pickup from Greyhound and Amtrak, ferry terminals and anywhere downtown if you call in advance. ①/②.

**YWCA**, 1118 5th Ave (☎206/461-4888). Large, clean women-only singles and doubles. ②.

## The City

Downtown Seattle's main attractions are the busy stalls and cafes of **Pike Place Market** and the restored nineteenth-century **Pioneer Square**, lined with restaurants

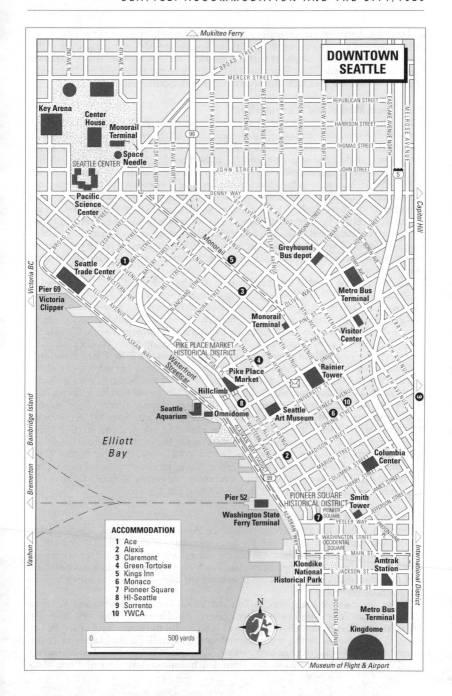

and taverns. A stroll along the **waterfront** lets you enjoy fabulous views of Elliott Bay. At the **Seattle Center** in the north, the **Space Needle** presides over a collection of theaters and museums. A couple of outlying districts are often livelier than downtown: **Capitol Hill**'s cafes and bars form the heart of the city's gay scene, and the **University District** is a student area with inexpensive cafes and uptempo nightlife.

### Pike Place Market and the waterfront

**Pike Place Market** is the oldest continuous working public market in the US. Farmers first brought their produce to the market in 1907, lowering food prices by selling straight from the barrow. The market prospered during the Depression, but by the 1960s it was shabby and neglected, and the authorities decided to flatten the area altogether. Following vigorous protests, Seattlites voted overwhelmingly to preserve this as the affordable domain of the elderly and poor. The restoration has been highly successful: the whole place, stretched over several city blocks, bustles with energy, and a real attempt has been made to keep it true to its roots, even if upscale restaurants are inevitably creeping in. Street entertainers play to busy crowds, the aroma of coffee drifts from the cafes, and stalls are piled high with lobsters, crabs, salmon, vegetables, fruit and flowers. Further into the long market building, handmade jewelry, woodcarvings and silk-screen prints are on sale, while small shops close by stock a massive range of ethnic foods.

Also nearby, the **Seattle Art Museum** at 100 University and First (Tues, Wed & Fri–Sun 10am–5pm, Thurs 10am–9pm; $7 ticket includes entry to the Seattle Asian Arts Museum on Capitol Hill; free first Thurs of month) occupies a new Robert Venturi-designed building, a lavish setting for contemporary art, international touring exhibitions and eclectic collections of African, Pacific and Native American work. Outside the main entrance is the 48ft "Hammering Man," a motion sculpture by Jonathan Borofsky.

Stairs in the market lead down to the steep staircase of the **Pike Place Hillclimb**, and to the waterfront below. No longer deep enough for oceangoing ships, much of this has become cluttered with tourist shops while the port's real business goes on to the north and south. Almost opposite the Hillclimb, **Pier 59**, an old wooden jetty that once served the tall ships, now houses the underwater viewing dome of the **Seattle Aquarium** (summer daily 10am–7pm; rest of year daily 10am–5pm; $8). A combined ticket also admits you to the 3-D **Omnidome** next door (daily shows starting 10am; $6.95; combined ticket $13), where 70mm films on the huge screen include the award-winning *Eruption of Mount St Helens*. On Pier 54 to the south, the most famous of the waterfront's fish-and-chip stands, *Ivar's Acres of Clams*, has its own special stop ("Clam Central Station") on the restored vintage **waterfront streetcar**. **Colman Dock** at Pier 52 is the terminal for Washington State Ferries (see p.1028).

### Pioneer Square and around

A few blocks inland from the ferry terminal, the **Pioneer Square** area, Seattle's oldest district, also had a close brush with the demolition balls of the 1960s. The restoration work is a little glossier here, with bookshops and galleries adding a veneer of sophistication to the old red-brick, wrought iron and shady trees. Things get a bit more raucous at night, when rock music booms out from assorted taverns and panhandlers become more persistent.

By far the most amusing way to find out about the city's seamy past is on an **Underground Tour** from *Doc Maynard's* tavern, 610 First Ave (☎206/682-4646; $8). After a disastrous fire in 1889, this area was rebuilt with the street level raised by one story, so what used to be the ground-level floors of its brick buildings are now underground, linked by subterranean passageways. A couple of blocks from *Doc Maynard's*, at 117 S Main St, the free **Klondike Gold Rush National Historical Park** (daily

9am–5pm) is not a park at all, but a small museum. It celebrates the days when, thanks to a formidable campaign to promote Seattle as the gateway to Alaskan gold, prospectors streamed in, and traders (and con artists) made their fortunes. The dog population fared less well as many a hapless mutt was harnessed to a sledge so that gold-seekers could practise "mushing" up and down Seattle's streets before facing Alaskan snow (see Jack London's novel *The Call of the Wild*).

The large cobblestoned square of **Occidental Park**, between Main and Washington streets at Occidental, holds four totem poles carved with mythical creatures from Northwest Native American legends.

## The Museum of Flight

The best and biggest of Seattle's museums, the **Museum of Flight**, a twenty-minute bus ride (#174) south of downtown at 9404 E Marginal Way (daily 10am–5pm, until 9pm on Thurs; $8), is partly housed in the magnificently restored 1909 "Red Barn" that was the original Boeing manufacturing plant. Displays lead from the dreams of the ancients, via the Wright brothers, to the growth of Boeing itself, culminating in the Great Gallery, hung with twenty full-sized aircraft and a replica of John Glenn's 1962 Mercury space capsule.

## Belltown

The resurgently chic **Belltown** area (also referred to as the Denny Regrade), has left its grunge legacy behind and is now choked with bohemian cafes, vintage clothing stores, used record shops and alternative galleries. Belltown casually blends the swank and avant-garde, beginning just to the north of Pike Street Market and extending one mile in the same direction towards the Seattle Center, with the heart of Belltown the five-block area of Second Avenue between Stewart and Battery. Many of the customers (and even proprietors) in this area affect a slacker pose that belies the hard work they've put into reviving the neighborhood. Godfathers of the neighborhood, **Sub Pop Records**, famous for promotion of the grunge scene with early releases by Nirvana, Mudhoney and Soundgarden, began its operations on the edge of Belltown, where it still occupies several floors of the Terminal Sales Building. Near its offices, the company has opened a tiny retail store, the ironically named **Sub Pop Mega Mart** at 1928 Second Ave, which mostly sells Sub Pop records and memorabilia.

## The Seattle Center

The **Seattle Center** dates from the 1962 World's Fair, whose theme was "Century 21" (hence the spindly, 600ft flying-saucer-tipped Space Needle tower, now the symbol of Seattle). Since then the 74-acre site has become a sort of culture park staging major sporting events, concerts, performing arts and annual festivals. The Pacific Northwest Ballet, Opera House, the Pacific Science Center, Children's Museum, various theaters, and a small amusement park are here. The Center is best reached by the **monorail**, which runs from the third floor of Westlake Center at Fifth and Pine downtown ($2.50 round-trip) and drops you close to the **Space Needle**, which now feels oddly dated, but still exudes a fair amount of glamour, especially at night, when it's lit up. The panoramic view from the observation deck, where there's a bar, is unmatched (summer daily 8am–midnight; $9).

Southwest of the needle, the **Pacific Science Center** (mid-June–Labor Day daily 10am–6pm; rest of year Mon–Fri 10am–5pm, Sat–Sun 10am–6pm; $7.50) is easily recognizable by its white arches. The hands-on adventure park is full of innovative exhibits for children on science-based topics, sometimes linked to cultural issues. The center also has a planetarium and IMAX theater. A nine-day **CityPass** ticket booklet for $26.50 saves you 50 percent on admission to six famous Seattle attractions – Woodand Park

Zoo, Space Needle, Pacific Science Center, Seattle Aquarium, Seattle Art Museum and Museum of Flight. Passes are sold at each attraction.

Between the Space Needle and the Pacific Science Center, the Frank Gehry-designed **Experience Music Project** (*www.experience.org*), demands a turn of the head for its undulating, colorful frame. Beset by problems that have delayed the opening, like a falling out between the museum and the Jimi Hendrix estate – initially the museum was to be a celebration of the Seattle native – the project is now slated to debut in mid-2000, focusing more generally on American popular music.

## Capitol Hill

A fifteen-minute bus ride to the top of a steep hill east of downtown takes you to **Capitol Hill**, the city's alternative center since young gays, hippies and assorted radicals moved in during the 1960s and 1970s; today, it exemplifies the city's diverse lifestyles. The shops and cafes around **Broadway** are a great place to watch the constant stream of tattooed, pierced and multicolored-haired youth (Kurt Cobain used to slink around Broadway), not to mention drink a good latte or two. The **Pike/Pine Corridor**, which extends from Twelfth to about Ninth Avenue, is filled with all-night coffeehouses, live music venues and some of Seattle's most happening nightspots.

The northern end of the district is quietly wealthy. Mansions built on Gold Rush fortunes sit sedately around **Volunteer Park**, where the **Conservatory's** hothouses contain flowers, shrubs and orchids from jungle, desert and rainforest (daily 10am–4pm, in summer till 7pm; free). The **Seattle Asian Art Museum**, 1400 E Prospect St (Tues, Wed & Fri–Sun 10am–5pm, Thurs 10am–9pm; $3 ticket includes entry to Seattle Art Museum downtown; free first Thurs of month), housed in a tasteful Art Deco building, boasts a 7000-piece collection of ceramics, jade and snuff bottles from Japan, China, Korea and Southeast Asia. Be sure to visit the Kado Tea Garden in the basement. Ten blocks east, **Washington Park** stretches to the north, encompassing the **Arboretum**, a lush showcase for indigenous Puget Sound vegetation. At the south end of the park, the immaculately landscaped **Japanese Gardens** flash banks of pink flowers beside neat little pools with exotically colored carp (March–Nov daily, opens 10am, closing times vary; $2.50).

## The University District

Across Union Bay from the park, the **University (or "U") District**, a busy hotchpotch of coffeehouses, cinemas, clothes, book and record stores caters to the University of Washington's 35,000 students. The area centers on University Way, known as "the Ave," and is lined with inexpensive ethnic restaurants and the cavernous University Bookstore. Although the sidewalks are always bustling, the area lacks the late-opening clubs and music venues of nearby Capitol Hill.

On campus, the **Henry Art Gallery**, at 15th Avenue and NE 41st Street, (Tues & Fri–Sun 11am–5pm, Wed–Thurs 11am–8pm; $5, free Thurs 5–8pm), houses American and European paintings and photography from the last two centuries, as well as contemporary exhibitions. **The Burke Museum**, at 17th Avenue and NE 45th Street (daily 10am–5pm, Thurs 10am–8pm; $5.50), presents exhibits on the natural and cultural history of the Pacific Rim, and has plenty of Northwest Native American art.

## Ballard and the Ship Canal

The "U" District and Seattle's other northern neighborhoods are sliced off from the rest of town by water; the **Lake Washington Ship Canal** connects Lake Union with the sea to the west and Lake Washington to the east. The procession of boats passing through the locks near the mouth of the canal is a captivating scene (bus #17 from downtown). Migrating salmon bypass the locks via a **fish ladder**, laid out with viewing windows. In season (late summer for salmon, fall and early winter for trout) the water is full of enormous leaping fish.

Behind the locks is Salmon Bay, with **Fisherman's Terminal** on its south side, crowded with Seattle's fishing fleet and stalls selling freshly caught fish. On the northern side of Salmon Bay, the blue-collar neighborhood of **BALLARD** (reached by several buses from downtown) is undergoing gentrification and the historic Old Town, on Ballard Avenue, is now home to galleries, bars and restaurants. Originally settled by Scandinavian fishermen in the late nineteenth century, their cultural impact remains intact and is celebrated at the **Nordic Heritage Museum**, 3014 NW 67th St (Tues–Sat 10am–4pm, Sun noon–4pm; $5).

## Fremont

**Fremont** is a consciously hip, mostly white middle-class area, with more than a touch of bohemia in its used bookshops and artsy cafes. The hub is the stretch of Fremont Avenue N that runs, beginning at the Fremont Bridge, from N 34th to N 37th streets, where the **Fremont Sunday Market** (Apr–Nov 10am–5pm) fills up a parking lot with produce stalls and a flea market. In the summer the lot doubles as Seattle's most unusual movie venue when **Fremont Outdoor Cinema** projects classics against the building wall on Saturdays at dusk, with live music and entertainment before all shows. A big attraction in Fremont's industrial section is the *Trolleyman Pub* at **The Redhook Brewery**, 3400 Phinney Ave N, where you can order a pint of your favorite Redhook beer or taste three to four samples to find your match (Mon–Thurs 2pm & 5pm, Fri 2pm, 5pm & 6pm, weekends 1–5pm hourly; free).

# Eating

You won't have to spend a fortune in Seattle's elegant French restaurants to eat well: among the numerous coffee shops of Capitol Hill, the ethnic restaurants of the University district, and above all Pike Place Market, there are some excellent pickings. **Seafood** is the specialty, ranging from salmon and crab to fish and chips or clam chowder. Most social interaction in the city seems to be fueled with copious quantities of **coffee**, and we list some of the best places to get the buzz below; although some of these establishments serve desserts and snacks, they're essentially somewhere to hang out (an alternative to the tavern) rather than a place to go for a proper meal.

## Restaurants and cafes

**Blowfish**, 722 Pine St in the *Paramount Hotel* (☎206/467-7777). Good pan-Asian restaurant with an accent on tapas-style dishes, such as the grilled chicken *yakisoba*, marinated in a spicy Korean red bean paste.

**Cafe Septieme**, 214 Broadway E (☎206/860-8858). A trendy, bustling European-style bistro. Sophisticated and imaginative homemade food, at moderate prices. Great desserts.

**Cascadia**, 2328 1st Ave (☎206/448-2242). An upscale restaurant serving sophisticated dishes featuring fresh regional ingredients. Decor includes a wall of water sculpture.

**Crocodile Cafe**, 2200 2nd Ave (☎206/448-2114). Best known as Belltown's prime nightlife haunt for alternative music, it is also a diner by day serving the biggest breakfasts in town for about $6.

**Dahlia Lounge**, 1904 4th Ave (☎206/682-4142). Beautifully presented regional seafood dishes, and the prices to match – dinner will cost around $50 per person.

**The 5 Spot**, 1502 Queen Anne Ave N (☎206/285-SPOT). This Southern-style diner is a favorite breakfast spot. Specialties include a platter of corn-vegetable patties, the Truck Stop Pork Chop sandwich and the Coca-Cola cake.

**Gravity Bar**, 415 Broadway E (☎206/325-7186). Described as a "fern bar on smart drugs," this industrial chic spot is the last word in postmodern vegetarian cuisine.

**LushLife**, 2331 2nd Ave (☎206/441-9842). Italian cuisine is the main feature in this sexy, dimly lit Belltown eatery. Moderate to expensive.

**McCormick's Fish House and Bar**, 722 4th Ave (☎206/682-3900). Seattle's classic fish house boasts a 43-item menu printed daily. Lively bar and oyster bar with stunning views.

**Noodle Ranch**, 2228 2nd Ave (☎206/728-0463). Good pan-Asian cuisine in the $10 range lures in the hungry and the budgeted.

**The Pink Door**, 1919 Post Alley (☎206/443-3241). Tucked away in Pike Place Market (no sign, just a pink door), this contemporary and moderately priced eatery serves traditional Italian dishes while also mixing a mean martini.

**Wild Ginger**, 1400 Western Ave (☎206/623-4450). An extremely popular, well-designed, upscale restaurant with an extensive menu of fiery dishes from Southeast Asia, India and China.

## Coffeehouses

The Seattle coffee craze goes beyond the desire for a caffeine hit: the city's myriad **coffeehouses** host much of its social scene, with places to suit all tastes, and are inexpensive places in which to while away the time.

The two big players are *Starbucks*, which started here in the early 1970s and has now spread as far as Europe, and the equally established *SBC* (short for both *Seattle's Best Coffee* and *Stuart Bros*). The original locations are in Pike Place Market. A few smaller roasting firms, such as *Torrefazione Italia*, at 320 Occidental Ave S (☎206/624-5847) and 622 Olive Way (☎206/624-1429), have their fans. If you haven't time to sit down, one of Seattle's 200-plus espresso carts is sure to be close at hand.

**Bauhaus Books & Coffee**, 301 E Pine St (☎206/625-1600). A Capitol Hill hangout for the dressed-in-black crowd with large tables, an artsy used-book section and good coffee.

**Espresso Vivace Roasteria**, 901 East Denny Way (☎206/860-5869). A giant espresso bar and roasterie packs in the Capitol Hill locals, plus the skilled baristas design "rosettas" or unique patterns out of textured milk in your *caffè latte*.

**Last Exit on Brooklyn**, 5211 University Way SE (☎206/526-9155). Longtime hangout in the U District where the hippie/slacker crowd philosophizes in sparse decor. Opens late.

**Macrina Bakery and Cafe**, 2408 1st Ave (☎206/448-4032). Much-loved stylish cafe with excellent baked goods, impressive homemade breads, salads, ciabatta sandwiches and small pizzas, in comfortable Belltown. Weekend brunch.

**Online Coffee Company**, 1720 E Olive Way (☎206/328-3731). Check your email or surf the Web here on Capitol Hill – large black monitors and stylish wooden desks set the tone for serious surfing. First 30 minutes free with a coffee purchase.

**Still Life in Fremont Coffeehouse**, 709 N 35th (☎206/547-9850). As expected in Seattle the coffee is excellent; plus *Still Life* serves up great baked goods, hearty fritatta breakfasts, and lunch specials like corn tortilla pies.

# Entertainment and nightlife

Seattle's **nightlife** doesn't quite live up to the expectations aroused by the city's musical notoriety, but it's convivial enough and there's usually something happening most nights of the week. It's not bad for a **beer** or two, either – like other West Coast cities, Seattle boasts an excellent selection of microbrewed beers. *Redhook Brewery,* 3400 Phinney Ave N in Fremont, *The Pike Pub & Brewery,* 1415 First Ave, and *Pyramid Brewery & Ale House,* 1201 First Ave S, all make unique hand-crafted brews, and the Irish pubs, *Kells* and *Tir na nog,* serve great pints of Guinness plus the usual selection of European ales. **Taverns** in Washington sell beer and wine but not spirits, while **bars** sell everything but must be attached to a restaurant. The tavern scene is at its most accessible (and touristy) in **Pioneer Square** downtown, where lively establishments like *Doc Maynard's, Old Timer's Cafe* and the *Central Saloon* host jazz, reggae and blues bands. Look out for "joint cover nights" ($8 weekends/$5 weeknights), when you can get into about ten different live music venues. Although Seattle's grunge heyday is long gone, there's still a buzz about the place and a thriving and original **music** scene. The better-known bands play at the atmospheric old **Moore Theater** downtown or the **Seattle Center Arena**.

For what's on **listings**, *Seattle Weekly*, free from boxes on the streets and many cafes and stores, is good for reviews and theater, cinema and arts listings, as is the Friday edition of the *Seattle Post Intelligencer*. Free papers *The Stranger* and *The Rocket* provide excellent coverage of the regional music scene.

## Drinking and clubs

**Alibi Room**, 81 Pike St (☎206/623-3180). Swank martini bar popular with Seattle's film community, tucked in a dramatic alley behind the Pike Street Market. Excellent food, DJs and library of film scripts.

**Baltic Room**, 1207 E Pine St (☎206/625-4444). Stylish Capitol Hill jazz salon selling beer, wine and cigars.

**The Capitol Club**, 414 E Pine St(☎206/325-2149). An intimate casbah-style lounge popular with a youthful, well-heeled Capitol Hill crowd. Excellent Morrocan-flavored food.

**ChaCha Lounge**, 504 E Pine St (☎206/329-1101). Dark, smoky, alternative place with good cheap drinks.

**Comet Tavern**, 922 E Pike St (☎206/323-9853). The oldest bar on Capitol Hill, and a grunge institution, is not surprisingly a smoky dive and a bit of a rocker's hangout with pool tables.

**Linda's Tavern**, 707 E Pike St (☎206/325-1220). Immensely popular with musicians mainly for its jukebox stocked with classics and current indie rock acts.

## Music venues

**Central Saloon**, 207 1st Ave S, Pioneer Square (☎206/622-0209). Claiming to be the oldest tavern in the city, the *Central* was an important breaking ground for Nirvana et al, though nowadays the emphasis is more on R&B.

**Crocodile Cafe**, 2200 2nd Ave (☎206/441-5611). A hip alternative club in Belltown promoting everything from rock to avant-garde jazz and spoken word.

**Dimitriou's Jazz Alley**, 2033 6th Ave (☎206/441-9729). Best jazz joint in town, showcasing international jazz acts, as well as up-and-coming brilliants.

**Doc Maynard's Public House**, 610 1st Ave (☎206/682-4649). Fun, restored 1890s saloon featuring live reggae, classic and alternative rock music.

**Fenix/Fenix Underground**, 2nd Ave (☎206/467-1111). Hip by Pioneer standards, a nightclub that often books high-profile regional and national bands.

**OK Hotel Cafe**, 212 Alaskan Way S (☎206/621-7903). Once the mosher's favorite, this lively venue near Pioneer Square, mixes grunge with avant-garde and poetry. Good for local bands and new jazz. Also worth a note, this is where Nirvana first performed *Smells Like Teen Spirit* in April 1991.

**Old Timer's Tavern**, 620 1st Ave S (☎206/623-9800). Narrow and crowded tavern with nightly blues and jazz acts.

**Tractor Tavern**, 5213 Ballard Ave NW (☎206/789-3599). A popular live music venue in Ballard with great character.

## Dance, classical music, opera, theater and film

The **Seattle Center** is the base for most of the city's cultural institutions: the **Pacific Northwest Ballet** (☎206/292-ARTS) and the **Seattle Opera** (☎206/389-7676 or 1-800/426-1619) take turns performing in the Opera House. Tickets tend to sell out in advance, but there are sometimes half-price tickets on the day of performance, for students and seniors. The **Seattle Symphony Orchestra** has a new stylish home in the Benaroya Concert Hall (☎206/215-4747).

Seattle has more equity **theaters** and more theater performances than any city except New York. The longest-established small company is the **Seattle Repertory**

Company (☎206/443-2220) at the Seattle Center which mixes revivals of classics with contemporary work. Next door, the **Intiman Theater Company** (☎404/815-1888 or 206/269-1900), performs classics and premieres of innovative new works. **A Contemporary Theater (ACT)**, (☎206/292-7676) is more mainstream; while **On the Boards** presents contemporary dance, music, theater and multimedia performance at Queen Anne Hall (☎206/217-9888).

**Bumbershoot**, the Seattle Arts Festival, hosts more than 2000 artists from around the world at 25 stages, exhibit halls and performance venues on Labor Day weekend. ($32 four-day pass; *www.bumbershoot.org*). In May, the **Seattle International Film Festival** centers on independent venues such as the Art Deco Egyptian, in an old Masonic temple at 801 E Pine St (☎206/323-4978), and the Harvard Exit on 807 E Roy near Broadway on Capitol Hill (☎206/323-8986). **Seafair**, held from late July to early August, is Seattle's answer to Mardi Gras, complete with pirates, parades and the gay-inspired "Unofficial Seafair Tacky Tourist Queen City Cruise" through the Ship Canal.

## Out from Seattle: Bainbridge and Vashon islands

For a brief escape from Seattle, **Bainbridge Island**, a serene half-hour ferry ride across Elliott Bay, is well worth the trip. Washington State Ferries leave from Pier 52 ($3.70 round-trip for foot passengers, $8.25 round-trip per car; hourly – avoid rush hours) for the 35-minute journey, docking in the town of **BAINBRIDGE ISLAND** (formerly Winslow), which is so small that once you've admired the harbor and had lunch you'll probably be ready to head back. This green and rural island, occupying less than fifty square miles, is mostly private land; if you want to pitch a tent, there's **camping** at the far end in Fay Bainbridge State Park. Otherwise, accommodation is limited to **B&Bs**, details of which can be obtained from the **visitor center** at 590 Winslow Way E (☎206/842-3700). The *Streamliner Diner*, 397 Winslow Way (☎206/842-8595), with its huge breakfasts and sandwiches, is the best place to **eat** in the daytime.

Nine Washington State Ferries from Seattle's Pier 50, West Seattle and Tacoma also make the short trip to the pleasant, cyclable **Vashon Island** every day (car and driver $8.25 round-trip; passengers $3.70 round-trip). A few beaches are dotted around the coastline of this twelve-mile-long island where the main community of **VASHON** is little more than a hamlet.

The *HI-Vashon Island AYH Ranch Hostel* at 12119 SW Cove Rd (☎206/463-2592; ①), six miles from the Seattle–Vashon ferry dock at the north end of the island, is a lyrical location surrounded by a forest with log cabins, covered wagons, or teepees as accom-

---

### ONWARDS TO CANADA AND ALASKA

**Victoria** on Vancouver Island in Canada is just two-to-three hours by the high-speed passenger-only *Victoria Clipper* from Seattle's Pier 69 (summer 4 daily, winter 1 daily; ☎206/448-5000; $54–66 one-way, $89–109 round-trip; *www.victoriaclipper.com*.) The same company operates a luxury **car ferry service**, *Princess Marguerite III*, from Pier 48 with a daily crossing (4hr 30min) each way. One-way fares are $54 for a car and driver and $29 per passenger. Other services to Vancouver Island from Washington State run out of Anacortes (see p.1039), Port Angeles (see p.1043) and Bellingham (see p.1041). Kenmore Air schedules five flights daily from downtown Seattle on Lake Union to Victoria (☎1-800/543-9595; $85 one-way $145 round-trip), as well as flights to the San Juan Islands.

The much more expensive **Alaska Marine Highway** (☎360/676-0212 recorded schedule information, ☎360/676-8445 administrative office) is a three-day ferry ride that winds between islands and a fjord-lined coast from **Bellingham**, ninety miles north of Seattle, to Skagway, Alaska.

modation. Phone ahead to make a reservation and arrange a free pickup at the jetty. There are also a number of reasonably priced **B&Bs**, among them *Artist's Studio Loft,* 16592 91st Ave SW (☎206/463-2583; ④), and the *Swallow's Nest Guest Cottages,* 6030 SW 248th St (☎206/463-2646; ④).

Good **places to eat** are *Emily's Cafe,* 17530 Vashon Hwy SW (☎206/463-9404), an espresso bar and bakery with good vegetarian meals, or *Rock Island Pub & Pizza,* 17322 Vashon Hwy SW which has gourmet pizzas and microbrews.

# The Puget Sound

The broad and deep **Puget Sound** hooks far into Washington, a clutter of tiny islands and ragged peninsulas teeming with yachts, oceangoing ships, fishing trawlers and even nuclear submarines. At first, the dense forest deterred homesteaders, but soon small logging communities sprang up, and the Sound became a vital waterway. As more and more settlers arrived, the demand for land grew, and in the 1850s treaties confining Native Americans to reservations were put before tribal leaders. Some signed, including Chief Seattle of the Suquamish, but others refused and accusations of forgery flew. A legacy of injustice was created, with which modern courts still struggle.

The southern end of the Sound is increasingly urban. There's little to attract visitors to industrial **Tacoma** or even the small state capital of **Olympia**, but all around are mountains, forests and lakes. Popular weekend escapes include the rural parts of **Whidbey Island**, and the beautiful **San Juan Islands** further north.

## Tacoma

Its hard to avoid passing through **TACOMA** on the main Seattle–Portland route, and passing through may be all you wish to do, though the city has worked hard to overcome its bad reputation as a polluted industrial town with a strong military presence. In recent years, the downtown historical district has received funding from the state, and the two-block-long **Antique Row** on Ninth Avenue and Broadway features some great Victorian buildings worth perusing if you have the time.

Among the smattering of new galleries and theaters in the city center is the **Tacoma Art Museum**, 1123 Pacific Ave (Tues, Wed, Fri & Sat 10am–5pm, Thurs 10am–7pm, Sun noon–5pm; $4, free third Thurs of month), which hosts decent touring exhibitions but has a pedestrian permanent collection. Another attraction of sorts is the copper-domed **Union Station**, built in 1911, which has been impressively restored and worthy of a quick look around. Next door at 1911 Pacific Ave, the huge new **State History Museum** (summer Mon–Wed & Fri–Sat 10am–6pm, Thurs 10am–8pm, Sun 11am–6pm; rest of year Tues–Wed & Fri–Sat 10am–5pm, Thurs 10am–8pm, Sun 11am–5pm; $7), has fine exhibits on frontier towns, railroads, logging, Native American and twentieth-century history.

**Hotels** tend to be either too smart or too grim, but are usually significantly less expensive than their counterparts in Seattle. The downtown *Tacoma Sheraton,* 1320 Broadway (☎253/572-3200 or 1-800/325-3535; ⑦), has the best rooms in town. The usual **motel** chains line the freeways, or you can **camp** in the **Dash Point State Park**, 5700 SW Dash Point Rd, Federal Way, five miles northeast of Tacoma, which has wide beaches and some hiking trails. For **B&Bs**, contact the Greater Tacoma Bed & Breakfast Reservation Service (☎253/759-4088 or 1-800/406-4088) or the Bed & Breakfast Association of Tacoma and Mt Rainier (☎253/593-6093 or 1-888/593-6098). The *Ram Restaurant and Big Horn Brewery,* 3001 Ruston Way (☎253/756-7886), has better than average pub **food**. *Antique Sandwich Shop,* 5102 N Pearl St (☎253/752-4069), near the large Point Defiance Park, is an authentic luncheonette filled with locals;

*Grounds for Coffee,* 764 Broadway (☎253/627-7742), is a funky downtown espresso bar with good sandwiches and live jazz or blues every Friday and Saturday night.

## Olympia and around

Just a muddy little logging community when picked as Washington's territorial capital in 1853, **OLYMPIA** has never really become the metropolis its founders had hoped. Its downtown area is small, with a few blocks of stores and restaurants presided over by the chateau-like **Old Capitol** at Seventh Avenue between Washington and Franklin. Nevertheless, it's quite a busy little place, with state employees knocking around during the day and students from the Evergreen State College, a popular liberal arts school, pepping up the nightlife. There's a well-established **Farmers' Market** downtown at 401 N Capitol Way (April–Dec weekends, and occasional weekdays), north of which is a boardwalk with several decent places to **eat**.

The state offices are arranged around neat lawns on the **Capitol Campus**, just south of downtown. It's worth taking a tour of the imposing Romanesque **Legislative Building** (daily 8am–4.30pm; free) completed in 1927, if only to wonder at the sheer energy of the pioneers who set out to construct a close replica of the Capitol Building in Washington DC in what was then a backwoods on the far side of the continent. Eight blocks south, the small **State Capitol Museum**, 211 W 21st Ave (Tues–Fri 10am–4pm, Sat & Sun noon–4pm; admission by donation), juxtaposes a restored dining room with displays of Native American basketwork and local natural history.

A short drive south of Olympia, tiny **TUMWATER** was Washington's first pioneer community, settled in 1845 by a group that included Bing Crosby's grandparents. Its name comes from the tumbling water of the Deschutes River, which now goes into the making of Olympia beer at the **Olympia Brewing Company**, by the Tumwater turning (exit 103) off I-5. The brewery overlooks **Tumwater Falls**, now enclosed in a park but once a rich salmon-fishing site for the Nisqually tribe.

### Practicalities

The Greyhound station is at 107 Seventh Ave at Capitol Way about five blocks north of the Capitol Campus; the Amtrak station is about eight miles southeast and not on the bus route. Intercity Transit (IT) (☎360/786-1881) runs **local buses**, providing a free service between downtown and the Capitol Campus.

Olympia's **visitor center** (Mon–Fri 8am–5pm; ☎360/586-3460) is on the Capitol Campus near the Legislative Building. In-town **accommodation** is geared towards business visitors; the *Golden Gavel Motor Hotel*, 909 Capitol Way S (☎360/352-8533; ③), usually has the best deals, while the *Harbinger Inn*, 1136 E Bay Drive (☎360/754-0389; ④), is a pleasant nineteenth-century **B&B** a mile from downtown. For real budget rooms you'll have to go further out to Tumwater's *Motel 6*, 400 W Lee St (☎360/754-7320; ②), or the *Holly Motel*, 2816 Martin Way (☎360/943-3000; ②), east of town at exit 109 off I-5. There's **camping** at forested **Millersylvania State Park**, 12245 Tilley Rd, south of Olympia, two miles east of I-5 (exit 99).

Of places to **eat**, the *Urban Onion,* 116 Legion Way (☎306/943-9242), has delicious burgers for the vegetarian and carnivore alike, while a few blocks away, *The Spar* at 114 Fourth Ave (☎360/357-6444), is a diner which has catered to Olympia's working class since 1935.

## Whidbey Island

With sheer cliffs and craggy outcrops, rocky beaches and prairie countryside, **Whidbey Island** is a favorite retreat for Puget Sound's city-dwellers. In its north is a large naval base, but in the southern and central parts, narrow country roads wind through farmland and small villages.

Although it's possible to reach the island by road – Hwy-20 off I-5 drops into the north end of Whidbey, some 85 miles north of Seattle – the **ferry** is often a better option. The quickest route from Seattle is to head thirty miles north to Mukilteo and catch the ferry to Whidbey's southern tip (every half-hour; $4.50 one-way for driver and vehicle, $2.50 per person round-trip). From Port Townsend on the Olympic Peninsula (see p.1042) an hourly ferry goes to **Keystone**, in the middle of the island just south of the town of Coupeville (one-way $1.85 per person, $6.50 with a car). Whidbey's own (erratic) **bus** system, Island Transit (☎360/321-6688), runs the length of the island for free.

The Mukilteo ferry lands at the small town of Clinton, but **LANGLEY**, further around the east coast, makes a better first stop, with its main street of old-West wooden storefronts set on a bluff overlooking the water. The **visitor center** is at 208 Anthes St (Mon–Fri 9am–5pm; ☎360/221-6765). If you're here in the evening, the *Dog House Tavern* at First and Anthes streets (☎360/221-9996) is a convivial gathering place and **restaurant**.

The middle part of the island is a National Historic Reserve called **Ebey's Landing**, where charming **COUPEVILLE**, with its nineteenth-century sea captains' houses, is of most appeal – and certainly preferable to **OAK HARBOR**, Whidbey's largest town and the site of most of its motels. To the north, at **Deception Pass State Park**, a steel bridge arches gracefully over the narrow gorge between Whidbey and Fidalgo Island, connecting point for the San Juans beyond.

On the edge of Coupeville, you'll find the budget *Tyee Motel*, 405 S Main St, by Hwy-20 (☎360/678-6616; ②). The *Captain Whidbey Inn*, 2072 W Captain Whidbey Inn Rd, two miles west of Coupeville on Penn Cove (☎360/678-4097; ⑥), is a lovely **hotel** serving superb food, though the *Anchorage Inn*, 807 N Main St (☎360/678-5581; ④), is more central. The local **Chamber of Commerce**, at 302 N Main St (☎360/678-5434), has lists of **B&B**, or visit the Whidbey Island Bed & Breakfast Association Web site at *www.whidbeyisland.com/bandb*. As well, you can **camp** in any of Whidbey's four state parks.

# The San Juan Islands

North and west of Whidbey Island, midway between Seattle and Vancouver, the beautiful **San Juan Islands** scatter across the northern reaches of the Puget Sound, and entirely upstage the rest of the inlet. Every summer brings more visitors than the islands can really accommodate, especially on the largest, San Juan and Orcas. You'll need to book somewhere to stay in advance, though even in July and August peaceful corners can easily be found.

## Getting there

Washington State Ferries runs a dozen boats per day, more in summer, to the islands from the harbor a few miles west of **ANACORTES** – a gritty port and fishing town at the end of Hwy-20, about 75 miles north of Seattle. The ferry only stops at four of the 172 islands (Lopez, Shaw, Orcas and San Juan), but the slow cruise through the archipelago is a delight. Motorists should get to the port early (there's often an hour's wait or more to get vehicles onto a summer crossing); pedestrians and cyclists have less of a hassle. Summer fares – $22.25 for a car and driver, $5.30 for foot passengers on a round-trip to San Juan – are collected only on the westbound journey and there is no charge for foot passengers on inter-island trips; the driver fare drops by about fifteen percent in winter. One ferry a day (two in summer) goes on to Sidney in British Columbia. A **passenger-only** service to Orcas and San Juan islands runs from Bellingham (see opposite) during the summer months. Kenmore Air (☎206/486-1257 or 1-800/543-9595) runs scheduled **seaplane flights** from Seattle to five harbors in the San Juans for $85 (one-way) and $125–165 (round-trip). Harbor Airlines (☎253/851-2381 or 1-800/359-3220) offer flights from Sea-Tac Airport to Friday Harbor Municipal Airport, and West Isle Air (☎360/293-4691 or 1-800/874-4434) flies between Anacortes or Bellingham and San Juan and Lopez islands.

If you want to catch an early ferry (the first one leaves before 6am) from Anacortes, you may as well stay the night. The *Islands Motel*, 3401 Commercial Ave (☎360/293-4644; ④), is one of several roadside **motels**, while the grand old *Majestic*, 419 Commercial Ave (☎360/293-3355 or 1-800/950-3323; ⑤), has the best restaurant (and bar) in Anacortes. Gas on the islands is considerably more expensive than on the mainland.

## San Juan Island

**San Juan**, the ferry's last stop before Canada, is the only island where the ferry drops you in what can be called a town. Though small, **FRIDAY HARBOR** is the only incorporated town in the archipelago and the best place to sort out the necessary transportation. SJ Island Shuttle circles between twelve communities and points of interest on the island, and a daily hop-on, hop-off pass costs a reasonable $10. *The Inn* at Friday Harbor, 680 Spring St (☎360/378-3031 or 1-800/752-5752), rents out **cars** and runs tours, while **bikes** can be had from Island Bicycles at 380 Argyle St (☎360/378-4941), and **mopeds** from Susie's Mopeds at First and A streets (☎360/378-5244 or 1-800/532-0087). Maps, essential on such twisting and badly marked roads, are available at the unattended **tourist information booth** on A Street, just across from where the cars line up for the ferry. Further information can be had at the main office of the San Juan Island Historical Park at First and Spring streets (summer daily 8am–5pm; rest of year daily 8am–4pm; ☎360/378-2240).

Friday Harbor's cafes, shops and waterfront make for pleasant wandering. There's a small **Whale Museum** on First Street, but to see the real thing, head past the coves and bays on the island's west side to **Limekiln Point State Park**. Orca ("killer") whales come here in summer to feed on migrating salmon, and there's usually at least one sighting a day. San Juan Tours (☎360/378-3499) is one of several companies offering three-hour **whale-watching cruises** for $39.

**Camping** is an obvious way to stay on San Juan Island; there's a very pleasant cyclists-only campground, the *Pedal Inn* at 1300 False Bay Drive (☎360/378-3049), and *Lakedale Campground* (☎1-800/717-CAMP) is six miles from the ferry on Roche Harbor Road, accessible by bus. In Friday Harbor, *Friday's*, 35 First St (☎360/378-5848 or 1-800/352-2632; ⑤), is a cozy central inn, or you can stay in one of two rooms on the *Jacquelyn*, a disused sailing boat on Slip K-13 in the port (☎360/378-5661; ⑤). *Blair House* at 345 Blair Ave (☎360/378-5907 or 1-800/899-3030; ④) is a few blocks from the ferry and comfortably isolated from the street by surrounding trees. The Bed & Breakfast Association of San Juan Island (PO Box 3016, Friday Harbor, WA 98250; ☎360/378-3030) can hook you up with a room, though most places start at around $100 in high season. It's essential to **book ahead** in summer for rooms in Friday Harbor, especially during the biggest part of the year, **San Juan Island Jazz Festival** (☎360/378-5509), the last weekend in July.

Of Friday Harbor's plentiful places to **eat**, *Duck Soup Inn,* 3090 Roche Harbor Rd (☎360/378-4878), is an expensive award-winning restaurant with excellent seafood and wine; the *Electric Company*, 175 First St (☎360/378-4118), has good pastas and live music on the weekends; the *Hungry Clam*, 130 First St (☎360/378-FISH), serves excellent fish 'n' chips and burgers; and the *San Juan Donut Shop*, 225 Spring St (☎360/378-2271), offers hefty breakfasts from 5am.

## Orcas Island

Horseshoe-shaped **Orcas Island** is quieter than San Juan, its several holiday resorts tucked away in distant coves. Tiny **ORCAS** itself, where the ferry lands, holds little beyond the grand Victorian *Orcas Hotel* (☎360/376-4300; ⑤). You can rent **bicycles** and **mopeds** (around $25 and $45 per day respectively) around the ferry dock area.

Most visitors head ten miles north through the farmlands to the main town, **EAST-SOUND**, where the **visitor information kiosk** on North Beach Road, just past Eastsound Square, can provide maps. Places to **eat** include the diner *Doty's A-1 Cafe & Bakery* (☎360/376-2593), a block inland from the waterfront, and the more eclectic and upscale restaurant at the venerable *Outlook Inn* (☎360/376-2200; ⑤), west of the center. Two miles west, at the end of West Beach Road, the *Beach Haven Resort* (☎360/376-2280; ④) is a great place to **stay**, its 50-year-old beachfront log cabins lined up along a densely wooded, sunset-facing cove; in summer they are only available by the week.

The island's real highlight is **Moran State Park**, where over thirty miles of hiking trails wind through dense forest and open fields to freshwater lakes, and to the summit of 2409ft **Mount Constitution**, where there are great views to be had from an observation tower. The park's four **campgrounds** fill up early in summer; reserve at Reservations Northwest ☎360/376-2326.

The lovely *Doe Bay Village Resort & Retreat,* Star Rte-86, eighteen miles east of Eastsound on Horseshoe Hwy (☎360/376-2291; campsites and dorms ①, yurts ②, and cabins ③), is tucked into a secluded bay and offers primitive to modern accommodation. *Cafe Doe Bay* specializes in excellent vegetarian dishes, seafood and a good selection of beer on tap. Nearby, in tiny **Olga**, *Cafe Olga* (☎360/376-5098) serves great pies, but is often swamped by parties visiting the art gallery to which it belongs.

## Lopez Island

Much more tranquil than the two larger atolls is modest **Lopez Island**, whose rolling hills also make it the most enjoyable place to cycle. The delightful *Islander Lopez* resort hotel (☎360/468-2233 or 1-800/736-3434; ⑤) sits on the edge of Lopez Village, about four miles from the ferry dock, and not far from the excellent *Bay Cafe Restaurant* (☎360/468-3700). The ultilitarian *Lopez Lodge* (☎360/468-2233 or 1-800/736-3434; ④) offers good value accommodation.

# Bellingham

**BELLINGHAM** – a happy blend of industry, Victorian architecture and college-town liveliness – lines up for over ten miles along a broad curve of Bellingham Bay, around 85 miles north of Seattle and just eighteen miles south of the Canadian border. Its place on the tourist map is largely due to the presence of the southern terminal of the **Alaska Marine Highway** (see box, p.1036). The ferries sail from the gleaming Cruise Terminal on the edge of the **Fairhaven** district, three miles south of downtown – take I-5 exit 250, which with its hip bookstores, cafes and clothing stores, is easily Bellingham's most appealing area. In contrast, **downtown** (I-5 exit 253) is fairly mundane, but likeable enough and has a few good restaurants.

Bellingham's chief attraction, however, is its convenience as a touring base for the surrounding countryside. Parks, set among the bluffs and forests surrounding the city, are laid out with hiking trails, and beyond them to the east are the foothills of **Mount Baker**, 56 scenic miles along Hwy-542. Lummi tribal mythology has this as a sort of Ararat, surviving the Great Flood to provide sanctuary for a Native American Noah in his giant canoe, but it's better known today for its skiing, with a seven-month season from early November until late May, and the best early snow in the Northwest (ski information on ☎360/734-6771).

## Practicalities

Greyhound **buses** and Amtrak **trains** pull in at the **Bellingham Cruise Terminal** in Fairhaven. San Juan Island Shuttle Express (☎360/671-1137) runs a passenger-only service to Orcas and San Juan Island in summer, and Victoria-San Juan Cruises (☎360/738-8099 or 1-800/443-4552) operates a similar summer service to San Juan Island and Victoria in British Columbia. Local **buses** (☎360/676-RIDE) ply 22 routes for a maximum fare of 35¢. The **visitor center** is at 904 Potter St, off I-5 exit 253 (☎360/671-3990 or 1-800/487-2032).

The best **rooms** in Bellingham are at the *North Garden Inn*, 1014 N Garden St (☎360/671-7828 or 1-800/922-6414; ④), a beautiful B&B next to downtown and just off I-5, with first-class breakfasts and a great view of the bay. Also off I-5 (exit 253) is the reliable *Best Western Lakeway Inn*, 714 Lakeway Drive (☎360/671-1011; ④). There's also the *HI-Bellingham Hostel* in Fairhaven, 107 Chuckanut Drive (☎360/671-1750; ①). The best place to **camp** is **Larrabee State Park**, seven miles south of Bellingham on Hwy-11, but there are numerous campgrounds along the highway to Mount Baker.

Downtown has several decent places to **eat** and **drink**, including *Il Fiasco Cucina Italiana,* 1309 Commercial St (☎360/676-9136), a gourmet Italian affair with terrific seafood. **Fairhaven** is the best bet for whiling away a few hours: *Tony's*, at 1101 Harris Ave (☎360/733-6319), is a hip coffee shop, sometimes hosting live music, while inside Village Books at 1208 Eleventh St is the *Colophon Cafe* (☎360/647-0092), which is open in the evening until 9 or 10pm and serves good meals and great desserts.

# The Olympic Peninsula

The broad mass of the **Olympic Peninsula** projects across the Puget Sound, sheltering Seattle from the open sea. Small towns are sprinkled sparingly along US-101, which loops the peninsula's coast, but at the core the Olympic Mountains thrust upwards, shredding rain clouds as they drift in from the Pacific and drenching the surrounding area. In the western river valleys, the dense vegetation thickens into rainforest, and the forests and unspoiled Pacific beaches provide cover for a huge variety of wildlife and seabirds.

Much of the peninsula is protected land, and large areas of national forest surround **Olympic National Park**. Outside of those areas, much of the landscape has been devastated by clear cuts. The timber trade brought settlers here in the first place, almost every town has a sawmill, and logging still provides many local jobs, but the industry is in crisis and ecologists favor tourism as the lesser environmental evil.

## Port Townsend

With its brightly painted Victorian mansions, convivial cafes and vigorous cultural scene, **PORT TOWNSEND** has always had aspirations beyond its small-time logging roots. Gothic mansions sprang up above the flourishing port in the 1890s, when confident predictions of a railroad terminus lured in the rich. Unfortunately for the investors, the trains never arrived, and the town was left with a glut of stylish residences and a very small business district.

Port Townsend's physical split – half on a bluff, half at sea level – reflects nineteenth-century social divisions, when wealthy merchants built their houses uptown, well above the noise and brawl of the port. The downtown area is at the base of the hill, its shops and pleasant cafes centering on **Water Street** – lined with proud 1890s brick and stonework. In recent times the old mansions have been restored, and the town has mellowed into an artsy community with hippie undertones and a fair amount of charm.

During the annual **music festivals** at **FORT WORDEN**, two miles north of town – principally Jazz Port Townsend, towards the end of July, and American Fiddle Tunes in early July – you should book accommodation well ahead.

## Practicalities

Pick up a map and information in Port Townsend at the helpful **visitor center**, 2437 E Sims Way (☎360/385-2722 or 1-888/365-6978), just west of the town center on Hwy-20. There's a good choice of **places to stay** in town, but prices are fairly high – with the exception of the *HI-Olympic Hostel*, 272 Battery Way (☎360/385-0555 or 1-800/909-4776 ①), in Fort Worden State Park – and vacancies rare in the height of summer. The town's specialty is its **B&Bs**, the best of which occupy grand Victorian mansions uptown, such as the *James House*, 1238 Washington St (☎360/385-1238 or 1-800/385-1238; ④–⑦), the exceptional 40-room mansion, *Manresa Castle*, 7th and Sheridan (☎360/385-5750 or 1-800/732-1281; ④–⑥); or the delightful *Quimper Inn*, 1306 Franklin St (☎360/385-1060 or 1-800/557-1060; ④–⑦). There are also a couple of nineteenth-century downtown **hotels** – try the recently renovated *Palace Hotel*, 1004 Water St (☎360/385-0773 or 1-800/962-0741; ③–⑧) – and several handy **motels**, including *The Tides Inn,* 1807 Water St (☎360/385-0595 or 1-800/822-8696; ④–⑥), a modern motel on the waterfront.

Port Townsend is the peninsula's best place to **eat and drink** and there is no shortage of excellent restaurants. The *Salal Cafe*, 634 Water St (☎360/385-6532), is a local favorite with excellent omelettes and lunches at a modest price, while the best baked goods are at *Bread & Roses Bakery,* 230 Quincy St (☎360/385-1044), serving great sandwiches on seven different kinds of breads. More upmarket alternatives include *The Fountain Cafe*, 920 Washington St (☎360/385-1364), with innovative regional cuisine, and the *Silverwater Cafe*, 237 Taylor St (☎360/385-6448), which consistently wins awards for its fresh seafood. In the nearby beach community of **Port Hadlock**, the nostalgic *Ajax Cafe*, on Lower Haddock Road (☎360/385-3450), serves up inventive Northwest cuisine specializing in seafood dishes, amid eclectic decor and occasional live music.

# Port Angeles

Originally named "Puerto de Nuestra Señora de los Angeles" by the Spanish in 1791 (the post office later insisted one Los Angeles was enough), **PORT ANGELES** is the peninsula's main town and the most popular point of entry into the Olympic National Park. Though its setting is lovely, this deepwater port is very much a working town, the main strip of motels and restaurants making few concessions to quaintness. Timber is Port Angeles' real business, and the harbor is streaked with industrial chimneys backdropped by mountains, while out in the bay cormorants fly over the fishing boats.

Though it's preferable to stay inside the park, Port Angeles is a cheaper option, and has a number of inexpensive chain **motels** strung along its two parallel one-way main drags, First Street and Front Street, try *Aggie's Inn*, 602 E Front St (☎360/457-0471; ③), *All View Motel,* 214 E Lauridsen Blvd (☎360/457-7779; ②) and the *Traveler's Motel,* 1133 E First St (☎360/452-2303; ②). For more upscale accommodation, try the smart *DoubleTree Hotel*, by the waterfront at 221 N Lincoln St (☎360/452-9215 or 1-800/222-8733; ④–⑥). *Domaine Madeleine,* 146 Wildflower Lane (☎360/457-4174; ⑥), is a B&B with a lovely five-acre garden. To get to any of the excellent **campgrounds** in Olympic National Park, you need your own vehicle. Try *Heart o' the Hill,* six miles south of Port Angeles, along Hurricane Ridge Road, or further west, *Elwah* and *Altaire* campgrounds are equally good with access to the numerous hiking trails in Olympic National Park.

For **breakfast or lunch**, head for the tiny *First Street Haven*, 107 E First St and Laurel (☎360/457-0352); for **dinner**, the upscale *Bella Italia*, 117-B E First St (☎360/457-5442), has seafood and authentic Italian cuisine.

Port Angeles has the peninsula's best **transportation connections**. Olympic Bus Lines (☎360/452-3858) offers daily trips to Seattle and Sea-Tac Airport, while Clallam Transit buses (☎360/452-4511 or 1-800/858-3747) go west from Port Angeles around the peninsula to Lake Crescent, Neah Bay and Forks and east to Sequim, connecting with Jefferson Transit (☎360/385-4777) buses to Port Townsend. Black Ball Transport (☎360/457-4491 or 250/386-2207) runs **ferries** to Victoria in Canada (except in Feb) for a bargain $6.75 walk-on one-way fare, $28.50 for a car) and Victoria Express (☎360/452-8088 or 1-800/633-1589) operates a faster passenger-only service for $25 from late May to mid-October, $20 rest of the year. The **visitor center**, at 121 E Railroad St, beside the ferry terminal (summer daily 7am–10pm; rest of year Mon–Fri 10am–4pm; ☎360/452-2363), stocks information on the entire peninsula and can put you in touch with local river-rafting and sea-kayaking firms.

## Neah Bay, the Makah Indian Reservation and Cape Flattery

Although US-101 takes a turn inland from Port Angeles to skirt the Olympic National Park (see below), Hwy-112 clambers along the coast for seventy miles to **NEAH BAY**, the tiny, tattered fishing village that is home to the **Makah Nation**, a seagoing Native American people almost wiped out by a smallpox epidemic in 1850. "Makah," a name given to the tribe by their neighbors, means "generous with food."

In 1970, tidal erosion near Cape Alava uncovered an ancient Makah settlement that had been buried, Pompeii-like, by a mudslide some 500 years ago. The first witnesses encountered bizarre scenes of instantaneous ageing – green alder leaves, lying where they had fallen centuries ago, shriveled as soon as they were exposed. The Ozette Dig, one of the most significant archeological finds in North America, uncovered thousands of artifacts: harpoons, intricately carved seal clubs, watertight boxes made without the use of metal, bowls, toys – all belonging to a period before trade with Europeans. The site itself was reburied in 1981, but the finds are displayed at Neah Bay's **Makah Museum** (summer daily 10am–5pm; rest of year Wed–Sun 10am–5pm; $4), a superbly curated center which includes marine dioramas, dugout cedar canoes and a life-size replica of a fifteenth-century Makah longhouse.

At the northern corner of the Makah Reservation is **Cape Flattery**, a remote headland accessible on an unpaved road from Neah Bay. From the road, a half-mile hike through the rainforest leads to the cape which once "flattered" Captain Cook with the hope of finding a harbor. It is the continental US's northwesternmost point. Below the cape, the waves have worn caves into the sheer rock of the cliff face, while opposite, on Tatoosh Island, coastguards run a remote lighthouse.

With only the drab **motels** of Neah Bay as competition. *Van Riper's Resort,* on the corner of Front and Rice streets (☎360/963-2334; ③), seventeen miles back east in **SEKIU**, a popular sports fishing town, can just about claim the best accommodation in the vicinity. A better selection can be found further south near Forks, or in Port Angeles. Clallam Transit buses (see above) connect Makah and Port Angeles.

## Olympic National Park

The stunning **OLYMPIC NATIONAL PARK** – covering much of the peninsula's mountainous interior and a detached 57-mile strip of the Pacific coast – was created in 1938 by Franklin D Roosevelt partly to ensure the survival of the rare Roosevelt elk; it now has the largest remaining herd in the US. Over 200 miles of wild rivers exist in the park, while the valleys of the Quinault, Queets and Hoh rivers contain sizeable chunks of temperate **rainforest** .

The main **visitor center**, just outside Port Angeles, 600 East Park Ave at the top of Race Street en route to Hurricane Ridge (summer daily 8.30am–6pm; rest of year daily 9am–4pm; ☎360/452-0330), has useful maps and trail leaflets; there are smaller centers at **Hurricane Ridge, Hoh Rainforest, Kalaloch** and **Quinault Lake**. The weather can be dodgy, so carry rainwear; there's a fair amount of snow even as late as June.

No roads cross the park, but many run into it, so you'll probably end up making several forays into different sections around the peninsula's western rim.

## Hurricane Ridge and Lake Crescent

The main visitor center marks the start of a sheer road that climbs eighteen miles to **Hurricane Ridge**, where the jagged peaks and sparkling glaciers of the Olympic Mountains are spread majestically before you. A new **day lodge** on the ridge (May–Oct) has tourist facilities and information. Where the road ends, the hiking trails begin. Hurricane Hill Trail (1.5 miles), a moderate hike, climbs through wild-flower meadows to the peak where, on a clear day, Cape Flattery, the Straits of Juan de Fuca, Vancouver Island and the Cascade Mountains are all in view. In winter, Clallam Transit **buses** (☎360/452-4511) climb up to the ridge for excellent cross-country skiing.

Ten miles west of Port Angeles, the glacially carved **Lake Crescent** is popular for fishing and has some good shoreline trails. *Lake Crescent Lodge* (May–Oct; ☎360/928-3211; ⑥) is superbly located amongst dense forest on the lake's south shore. The lodge is perhaps the best place to stay on the peninsula, though the *Sol Duc Hot Springs Resort* (early-April–late Sept; ☎360/327-3583; ⑨), set deep in the park twelve miles off US-101, is a close rival. The resort, built in 1912, has an excellent restaurant and the **Sol Duc Hot Springs**, mineral-rich waters which bubble out of the ground to be channeled into three pools. Guests have free use of the pools, visitors pay $6.75.

## Forks

Beyond the Sol Duc turning, US-101 cuts across the Olympic National Forest on its way to the dreary logging town of **FORKS**, nestled between the Olympic Mountains and coastal sections of the park. This commercial hub is famous for its temperate rainforests draped with moss, and world-class river fishing. There's reasonably priced **accommodation** here at the *Miller Tree Inn*, 654 E Division St (☎360/374-6806; ③), a relaxed country homestead on three acres, and at the large, functional *Olympic Suites*, 800 Olympic Drive (☎360/374-5400 or 1-800/262-3433; ③), on the north side of town. The town's **visitor center** is at 1411 S Forks Ave (☎360/374-2531 or 1-800/44-FORKS).

## The Hoh Rainforest

The most popular of the park's rainforest areas, the **Hoh Rainforest** is situated nineteen miles along Upper Hoh River Road, which branches off from US-101 twelve miles south of Forks. There are two short **trails** to explore the rainforest: the Hall of Mosses Trail, and the slightly longer Spruce Trail, following along the glacier-fed Hoh River. More energetic hikers can undertake the 36-mile Hoh River Trail up to the base of 8000ft Mount Olympus. Climbing the ice-covered peak is a major undertaking; if you just want to camp along the route, check in with the rangers and get a free backcountry permit. Cougars and other beasts are still very much present in the park and in winter Roosevelt elk from higher elevations gather here. Nineteen miles inland is the Hoh Rainforest Visitor Center (daily: summer 9am–6.30pm; winter 9am–4pm; ☎360/374-6925).

## South to Kalaloch: the peninsula's ocean beaches

Beyond the Hoh turning, US-101 dips down to the Pacific coast where the wild and lonely **beaches** still look exactly as they did before the pioneers got here: black rocks point up out of a gray sea, populated mostly by seabirds. With their strong currents, floating tree trunks and dramatic tides, these beaches are not suitable for swimming, but the hiking between them can be magnificent, and a series of short and enjoyable trails threads down to and along the seashore – Ruby Beach, named for the garnet-colored sand, is one of the most scenic. Near the end of the park's coastal strip, **KALALOCH** has a couple of campgrounds and the impressive *Kalaloch Lodge* (☎360/962-2271; ③–⑥), which has a good restaurant and large ocean-view rooms. The ranger station here has lots of information and suggestions for hiking trips.

## Queets River Rainforest

South of Kalaloch, US-101 turns inland to circumvent the Quinault Indian Reservation before reaching the 25-mile dirt road that branches northeast to the **Queets River Rainforest**, the least visited of the three main rainforest areas. The luxuriant flora and fauna along the well-marked trail at the end of the turning includes the **world's tallest Douglas fir tree** – 220ft tall and 45ft in circumference.

## Lake Quinault and the Quinault Rainforest

The most accessible, and beautiful, of all the rainforests is the **Quinault Rainforest**, around the shores of glacier-carved Lake Quinault just off US-101. The lake itself was already a popular resort area when Teddy Roosevelt visited in the 1900s and decided to proclaim it part of an expanded Olympic National Park. Thick and impressive groves fan off from the road explored by a series of hiking trails: one of the best is the half-mile Maple Glade Trail on the north shore, leading through some textbook rainforest vegetation. Longer and more difficult trails take hikers up the forested river valley and into the Olympic Mountains.

Of the three **hotels** at Lake Quinault, the pick of the bunch is the charming *Quinault Lodge* (☎360/288-2900 or 1-800/562-6672; ⑤), a National Historic Landmark built in 1926 on the shores of Lake Quinault. There are also several lakeside **campgrounds**. The **ranger station** is footsteps from the lodge.

# South to Aberdeen

Heading south on US-101 from Lake Quinault, leaving the national park behind, it's little more than forty hilly miles through privately-owned timber land, thinned by logging and punctuated by bald patches of "clear-cutting," to industrial **ABERDEEN**. Once a major seaport, Aberdeen has seen better days and you'll not want to linger except perhaps to note that this was the hometown of Nirvana. Immediately following Kurt Cobain's suicide there was talk of erecting a statue of him in the waterfront park, but the idea was rejected as tasteless.

At Aberdeen there's a choice of routes: US-12/Hwy-8 lead east towards Olympia (see p.1038), whilst Hwy-101 pushes on south over the hills and then threads along the shore of muddy Willapa Bay on its way to the mouth of the wide Columbia River, the boundary with Oregon, and the bridge over to Astoria (see p.1065).

# The Cascade Mountains

The serene beauty of the snowcapped and pine-covered **Cascade Mountains** conceals awesome volcanic power – as demonstrated by the 1980 explosion of **Mount St Helens**. But away from the gray scar left by the blast, the Cascades offer mile upon mile of forested wilderness, stretching from Canada down to Oregon, traversed by a skein of beautiful trails – which, for all but a few summer months, you'll need snowshoes to follow. Deservedly the most popular access point is **Mount Rainier**, set in its own national park some ninety miles southeast of Seattle. Further north, the **North Cascades National Park** demands more time; Hwy-20, the high mountain road that crosses the Cascades, is by far the most spectacular route to eastern Washington.

## The North Cascades and the Cascade Loop

When Hwy-20 opened up the rugged **North Cascades** to an admiring public in 1972, the towns of the eastern foothills got together and came up with the **Cascade Loop**, a 400-mile round-trip that channeled tourist traffic their way, along highways 20, 153, 97 and 2. The complete trip is only feasible during the summer, since at other times snow closes the mountain passes. The towns themselves – with the possible exception of Chelan – are best taken simply as bases between trips into the gorgeous scenery, despite some rather frantic efforts to attract visitors: the economy is none too healthy in these parts, and the tourist dollar has become crucial.

Hwy-20 begins its long journey inland at **Anacortes**, from where it crosses the coastal flatlands – passing the **North Cascades National Park Headquarters** (Mon–Fri 8am–4.30pm; ☎360/856-5700) in Sedro Woolley – before threading through high mountain passes to tiny **WINTHROP**, an old mining town dressed up in Wild West regalia (befitting its status as the original setting for Owen Wister's *The Virginian*). The Western theme has proved popular with passing motorists, and it's certainly worth stopping at the *Winthrop Brewing Co* (☎509/996-3183) to sample the excellent, unpasteurized *Outlaw Pale Ale*. There are some good places to **stay** and **eat** in, and around, Winthrop. The cozy and inexpensive *Duck Brand Hotel & Cantina* (☎1-800/996-2192 or 509/996-2192; ③), and the comfortable *Hotel Rio Vista*, 285 Riverside Ave (☎509/996-3535 or 1-800/398-0911; ④), are both pleasant lodges. Check also with the **Chamber of Commerce** on the main drag (☎509/996-2125) for a list of lodgings. The nearby **visitor center** (☎509/996-4000) has information and backcountry permits.

The trim resort of **CHELAN**, some sixty miles south of Winthrop, nestles at the foot of Lake Chelan, a spectacular lake set in a glacially-carved trough deep in the mountains. Of several lakeside **lodgings**, *Campbell's Resort*, 104 W Woodin Ave (☎509/682-2561 or 1-800/553-8225; ④–⑧), is the pick, though cheaper accommodation is available at the *Apple Inn Motel*, 1002 E Woodin Ave (☎509/682-4044; ②). Spots to **eat and drink** include *Local Myth Pizza*, 514 E Woodin Ave (☎509/682-2914), and *Deepwater Brewing & Public House*, 225 Highway-20 (☎509/682-2720). The **ranger station** is at 428 W Woodin Ave (☎509/682-2576).

The Lake Chelan Boat Company (☎509/682-2224 info, ☎509/682-4584 reservations) runs a ferry and high-speed catamaran service to the head of Lake Chelan with scheduled stops at Field's Point, Lucerne and Stehekin. All boats leave Chelan's Boat Dock, located one mile south of downtown on Hwy-97A, and from Field's Point Landing, 30 minutes from Chelan on South Lakeshore Drive (Hwy-971). *Lady of the Lake II* ferry takes four hours to cruise the 55 miles of the nation's deepest gorge, leaving daily in summer at 8.30am and returning early evening ($22 round-trip); there's also the *Lady Express* ($41 round-trip) which reaches Lake Chelan's mountainous western tip in half the time. It's a delightful cruise with a 90-minute layover at **STEHEKIN** (population 70), an isolated village otherwise accessible only by air-taxi ($80 each way from Chelan; ☎509/682-5555). At Stehekin there are **campsites** and trailheads leading to superb hiking and backpacking in the North Cascades. Bikes and canoes are available from the *North Cascades Stehekin Lodge* (reserve well ahead; ☎509/682-4494 or 682-4584; ⑤). If you're hungry, *Stehekin Pastry Company* (☎509/682-7747) makes excellent cinnamon buns, fresh breads and berry pies. For camping and hiking **information** (and, for some of the trails, a wilderness permit), visit the ranger stations in Stehekin or Chelan.

A few miles south of Chelan, the Cascade Loop turns west along US-2 at the apple-growing center of **Wenatchee**, heading for pocket-sized **LEAVENWORTH**, a Bavarian theme town where even Safeway and *McDonald's* are decked out in high gables and fancy woodwork. It only takes about an hour to explore the town, but there are plenty of outdoor activities to be had in the spectacular mountain setting. The **ranger station**, just off US-2 at 600 Sherbourne St (daily 7.45am–4.30pm; ☎509/782-1413), provides trail guides and hiking information, whilst **bikes**, **canoes** and **kayaks** can be rented from several outlets. The town's **visitor center**, 894 Hwy-2 (☎509/548-5807), has listings of local accommodation. Downtown options include the emphatically alpine *Edel Haus Inn*, 320 Ninth St (☎509/548-4412 or 1-800/487-3335; ④) and the comparable *Enzian Motor Inn*, 590 Hwy-2 (☎509/548-5269 or 1-800/223-8511; ④). The *Innsbrucker Inn*, 703 Hwy-2 (☎509/548-5401; ③), has literary theme rooms, and the *All Seasons Cafe* (☎509/548-5460), down the street, serves up a good lunch inspired by various authors.

West of Leavenworth, US-2 crosses the mountains over Stevens Pass, but the principal east–west highway, I-90, lies further to the south, connecting Seattle with the fertile Yakima Valley. Near I-90, is the 268-foot **Snoqualmie Falls** and the impressive *Salish Lodge*, 6501 Railroad Ave SE (☎425/888-2556 or 1-800/826-6124; ⑧), where much of David Lynch's *Twin Peaks* was filmed.

## Mount Rainier National Park

Set in its own national park, glacier-clad **MOUNT RAINIER** is the highest (14,410 feet) and most accessible peak in the Cascades. Recurrent jokes characterize its name as a description of its weather: often very wet, with heavy snowfalls during the long winter season. Not until midsummer does the snowpack melt enough to unblock roads and reveal a web of hiking trails. Then, the deer, mountain goats and marmots reappear, the alpine meadows are ablaze in dazzling wild flowers, and Mt Rainier makes for some perfect – and not always tough – hiking.

**Admission** to the park is $10 per vehicle, $5 per person. It's possible to **stay** in the park at one of two national park lodges: *National Park Inn* (☎360/569-2275 or 569-2411; ④), nestled in a forest at Longmire, is a small, rustic lodge open year-round; and further up the mountain, *Paradise Inn* (mid-May–early Oct; ☎360/569-2275 or 569-2413; ④), is a massive 1917 wooden lodge. Make reservations well in advance. *Cougar Rock* and *Ohanapecosh* **campgrounds** are available by reservation only from July to Labor Day (☎1-800/365-CAMP; ①), while *White River, Sunshine Point* and *Ipsut Creek* campgrounds are first-come, first-served. For overnight backpacking, pick up a wilderness permit, free from Longmire, White River or Paradise ranger stations (☎360/569-2211).

There are four entrances to the park – **Nisqually Entrance** in the southwest corner, **Stephen's Canyon Entrance** in the southeast, **White River Entrance** in the northeast, and **Carbon River Entrance** in the northwest corner. Only the **Nisqually Entrance** is open year-round (for cross-country skiing; the others open in about May). During the summer, it's possible to drive the 240 miles of roads that almost circumnavigate Mount Rainier National Park to the various entrances. The **Nisqually Entrance** is the only part serviced by public transportation – either on a day-trip with Gray Line from Seattle (May–Oct; ☎1-800/426-7532 or 206/626-5208), or from Sea-Tac Airport to Paradise with Rainier Shuttle (☎360/569-2331) or Rainier Overland (☎360/569-2604) from mid-May to Oct. There is no public transportation within the park.

If you only have a day to explore Mount Rainier National Park, consider traversing the south and east sides of the park from Nisqually Entrance to **Paradise**, with a side trip to **Sunrise**. The stunning 80-mile drive winds through river valleys and lowland forests with glaciated peaks and magnificent vistas. There are numerous trails radiating from Paradise. The 5-mile Skyline Trail to Glacier Overlook is the perfect spot to ponder the awesome ice-fall on Nisqually Glacier.

There are over 300 miles of **trails** in Mount Rainier National Park, ranging from short interpretive walks to the 93-mile Wonderland Trail that circumnavigates Mount Rainier. The Pacific Crest Trail cuts through the eastern edge of the park. For map and trail conditions, visit the Hiker Information Centers at Longmire, Paradise or White River. Climbing Mount Rainier is hazardous and should only be undertaken by experienced climbers with the necessary equipment, and who are physically fit. The long-established guide service, Rainier Mountaineering Inc, in Paradise (☎360/569-2227 or 253/627-6242 in winter), offers climbing courses and guided climbs – one day's practice, then the two-day climb – and rents equipment for around $300.

## Mount St Helens

The Klickitat Indians who called **Mount St Helens** *Tahonelatclah* ("Fire Mountain") knew what they were talking about. A perfect snowcapped peak, long popular with scout camps and climbing expeditions, Mount St Helens erupted on May 18, 1980, leaving a charred area of almost total destruction. The force of the eruption flattened the forests for miles around; heavy clouds of ash choked an even larger area; and a massive lateral blast threw an avalanche of debris down the Toutle River Valley. Slowly but surely, the forests are starting to grow again, and the ash is being reinhabited, but the scarred landscape bears witness to the awesome force of the eruption. In the meantime, Mount St Helens has become a major attraction.

Located in a remote pocket of Gifford Pinchot National Forest, there are three entry routes into the region. Most visitors arrive along Hwy-504, off I-5 roughly halfway between Olympia and Portland. The road snakes through dark green forests, until bald, spiky trees signal a sudden change: thousands of gray tree-skeletons lie in combed-looking rows, knocked flat in different directions as the blast waves bounced off the hillsides.

---

### THE ERUPTION OF MOUNT ST HELENS

From its first rumblings in March 1980, **Mount St Helens** became a big tourist attraction. Residents and loggers working the forests were evacuated and roads were closed, but by April the entrances to the restricted zone around the steaming peak were jammed with reporters and sightseers. But the mountain didn't seem to be doing much, and impatient residents demanded to be allowed back to their homes. Even the official line became blurred when Harry Truman, a local pensioner who refused to move out, became a national celebrity and was, incredibly, congratulated on his "common sense" by Washington's governor.

A convoy of homeowners was waiting at the barriers, about to go and collect their possessions, when the explosion finally came on May 18 – not upwards but sideways, ripping a great chunk out of the mountainside. An avalanche of debris slid into Spirit Lake, raising it by two hundred feet and turning it into a steaming cauldron of mud. Heavy clouds of ash suffocated loggers on a nearby slope, and drifted east where several inches of ash settled between Yakima and Spokane.

Fifty-seven people died on the mountain: a few were there officially, but most, like Harry Truman, had ignored the warnings. The wildlife population was harder hit: about a million and a half animals – deer, elk, mountain goats, cougar and bears – were killed, and thousands of fish were boiled alive in sediment-filled rivers. There were dire economic effects, too, as falling ash devastated the land, and millions of feet of timber were lost.

At the end is **Johnson Ridge Observatory** (May–Sept daily 10am–6pm; ☎360/274-2140) with breathtaking views of the still-steaming lava dome and crater, plus state-of-the-art interpretive displays, an exciting film of the eruption of Mount St Helens and powerful testimonials by blast survivors. The main disadvantage with the Hwy-504 approach to Mount St Helens is its popularity – you can expect long tailbacks on any sunny summer's day.

An alternative is to take Hwy-503 from Portland (or I-5) to **COUGAR**, on the mountain's southern periphery, from where challenging, summer-only forest roads, USFS-90, 25 and 99, wriggle along its flanks to **Windy Ridge** viewpoint on the northeast side of the mountain. Windy Ridge can also be accessed from the north from **RANDLE**, along USFS-25 and 99, which provides access to Spirit Lake and passes through desolate lava flows with numerous viewpoints en route. There are fewer cars on this side, consequently Windy Ridge is a more natural environment to view the destruction.

Mount St Helens National Monument charges an $8 admission fee which allows visitors access to all the sites, good for one week. En route to **Windy Ridge** from Hwy-503, is the **Mount St Helens Volcanic Monument Headquarters** (☎360/247-5473) in Amboy, which has information and issues backcountry permits. Just off the I-5 near Castle Rock is the **Mount St Helens Visitor Center** (daily 9am–5pm; ☎360/274-2103) which has interpretive exhibits. The **Coldwater Ridge Visitor Center** (April 26–Sept 26 10am–6pm; Sept 27–April 25 9am–5pm; ☎360/274-2131), focuses on the ways plants and animals have recolonized in the blast zones. There are also areas in the Monument where you can **hike** and **camp**. Contact Monument Headquarters (☎360/247-3900; *www.fs.fed.us/gpnf*) or visitor centers for information.

# Eastern Washington

Big, dry and hot, **eastern Washington** has more in common with neighboring Idaho than with the green, western side of the state. Faded olive-colored sagebrush covers miles of land, and huge reddish rocks loom over the prairies – the powerful landscape of a thousand Westerns. Further south, the lower Yakima Valley is a vast agricultural belt with miles of orchards and farms that flank the Yakima River. With over 300 sunny days a year, this region is the largest producer of apples in the world, and in the last 20 years, has become one of the Northwest's major wine areas. The area towns are agricultural and commercial centers, and only **Spokane** has any degree of cultural life. Nevertheless, some are excellent bases for winery tours or outdoor activities such as rafting, fishing, hiking, paragliding and skiing.

## Ellensburg

If you're traveling by Greyhound east beyond the mountains along I-90, your first major stop will be **ELLENSBURG**, a dusty little town with fetching nineteenth-century architecture in the redbrick core. The home of the state police training academy, Ellensburg is dependent on the students from the Central Washington University for any vitality. The town comes into its own on Labor Day weekend, when the **Ellensburg Rodeo** fills the streets with Stetsoned cowhands who rope steers, ride bulls and sit on bucking broncos, accompanied by much pageantry. For tickets, call the Rodeo Ticket Office (☎509/962-7831 or 1-800/637-2444).

Greyhound stops at Okanogan and Eighth Avenue. The **visitor center**, a short walk away at 436 N Sprague St (Mon–Fri 9am–5pm; ☎509/925-3137), can provide a downtown map and advice on accommodation; a budget option is *Harold Motel*, 601 N Water St (☎509/925-4141; ②). The art-deco *Valley Cafe*, 103 W Third Ave (☎509/925-3050), is the nicest place in town to eat.

## Yakima and Toppenish

YAKIMA, to the south, the sprawling urban hub for the surrounding agricultural area, is not about to win any beauty contests: the railroad yard, busy with freight trains, is pretty much its aesthetic high point. Though its attractions are few, it is an excellent base to visit a few tasting rooms of the award-wining wineries scattered through the Yakima Valley to the east. The part of downtown that hasn't been absorbed into the downtown-cum-mall development is enlivened by the brightly painted railroad cars, **Track 29** at Yakima Avenue and N First Street, which house a small collection of shops and food stalls. Opposite, **Yesterday's Village and Antique Mall** is a nostalgic antiques-and-crafts mall in what was once the old Fruit Exchange. The **Yakima Farmer's Market** on Sundays (10am–2pm), in front of the Capitol Theater, sells an awesome variety of fresh local produce.

Wine tour maps, lodgings and local information can be had from the **visitor center**, 10 N Eighth St at E Yakima Avenue (Mon–Fri 8am–5pm, Sat hours vary; ☎509/575-1300 or 1-800/221-0751). Greyhound stops nearby at 602 E Yakima Ave. Motels and diner-style **restaurants** abound along N First Street. Located in the old train depot is America's first brewpub, *Grant's Brewery Pub*, 32 N Front St (☎509/575-2922), which serves quality hand-crafted ales and tasty pub-type food. *Deli de Pasta*, 7 N Front St (☎509/453-0571), is a small Italian bistro with a gourmet edge. *Santiago's*, 111 E Yakima Ave (☎509/453-1644) is a favorite Mexican restaurant, but for the real thing, super cheap, check out *Salsita Antojitos Mexicanos,* 902 S Fair Ave #A (☎509/425-9515). There's **camping** across the Yakima River on Hwy-24 at **Sportsman State Park** (☎509/575-2774 or 1-800/562-0990).

Twenty miles south of Yakima, **TOPPENISH**, the primary town on the Yakima Indian Reservation, has a Wild West feel that is heightened by buildings displaying historical Western murals. The **visitor center**, 11 S Toppenish Ave (☎509/865-3262), supplies brochures on the murals and has a list of local **accommodation**. The modern and comfortable *Toppenish Inn Motel*, 515 S Elm St (☎509/865-7444 or 1-800/222-3161; ②–⑤), is the best choice. There are a few good Mexican restaurants; the authentic *Esther's El Paso Cafe,* 5 W First Ave (☎509/865-2066), is popular with locals. In nearby Sunnyside, *Snipes Mountain Brewery & Restaurant,* 905 Yakima Valley Hwy (☎509/837-BREW), serves great regional food, select ales and local valley wines.

## Walla Walla: the Whitman Mission

WALLA WALLA, about 120 miles east of Yakima along I-82 and US-12, is an uneventful college and agricultural town, known best for its sweet onions, eaten raw like apples. There's little to see now, but this was the place where the missionary **Dr Marcus Whitman** arrived from the East Coast in 1836. He was unsuccessful in his bid to convert the local Cayuse into crop-growing Christian citizens, and soon turned his attention to white settlers. In 1843, Whitman helped guide the first wagon-train across the Oregon Trail: his mission became a refuge for sick and orphaned travelers. The Cayuse eyed the ever-increasing emigrants warily, and when measles spread among the tribe, suspicions grew that they were being poisoned, particularly as Dr Whitman could help (some) whites but few of the Indians – who had no natural immunity to the disease. Half the tribe died. Whitman must have been aware of the tribal tradition that medicine men were liable for the deaths of their patients, but continued to take on even hopeless cases. In November 1847, a band of Cayuse murdered Whitman, his wife and eleven others. Fifty more, mostly children, were taken captive, and although they were later released, angry settlers raised volunteer bands against the Cayuse. When the story hit the newspapers back east, it generated such a tide of fear about Native American uprisings that the government finally declared the Oregon land (then including Washington) a US territory, which meant the army could be sent in to protect the settlers – with drastic implications for the Native Americans.

The site where the **Whitman Mission** was burned down (daily 8am–4.30pm; ☎509/522-6360; $2), in a lovely little dell seven miles west of town off US-12, is bare but effective. Simple marks on the ground illustrate its layout, and a visitor center shows a film on Whitman's life and exhibits the weapon thought to have polished him off.

Greyhound stops at 315 N Second St, a couple of blocks from the **visitor center** at Sumach and Colville (Mon–Fri 9am–5pm; ☎509/525-0850 or 1-800/743-9562). The *Whitman Motor Inn*, 107 N Second Ave (☎509/525-2200; ③), has an excellent restaurant, while the *Tapadera Budget Inn*, 211 N Second Ave (☎509/529-2580 or 1-800/722-8277; ②), offers lower rates. The *Green Gables Inn*, 922 Bonsella St (☎509/525-5501; ⑤), is a comfortable **B&B** in an old mansion, with private baths in all rooms, on the east side of town. There are a few decent eateries: *Merchants Ltd French Bakery,* 21 E Main St (☎509/525-0900) is a good spot for espresso and pastries.

# Spokane

The wide open spaces and plain little towns of eastern Washington don't really prepare you for **SPOKANE**. Just a few miles from the Idaho border, it's the region's only real city, and its scattering of grandiose late nineteenth-century buildings – built on the spoils of the Coeur d'Alene silver mines, just across the state divide – sport some unexpectedly elegant touches. But its heyday came and went, and shades of the down-at-heel freight town it became haunt the modern city. It's not a place to linger long, but its pleasant parks and unusual architecture can easily fill a day or so.

In summer, the town's focal point is the hundred-acre **Riverfront Park**. Sprawling over two islands in the middle of the Spokane River, the park was originally planned by Frederick Olmsted of Central Park fame, though it was not laid out as specified until just before Spokane hosted the 1974 EXPO. Bisecting the park, the river tumbles down a series of rocky shelves known as **Spokane Falls**, once a fishing site for the Spokanee peoples and later the home of the first pioneers. Attractions include an ice-skating rink which shares space with the IMAX theater, the charming hand-carved Looff Carousel, and the **Gondola Skyride** cable cars (summer Sun–Thurs 11am–8pm, Fri & Sat 11am–10pm; $3) which run above the falls from the west end of the park.

Most of the relics of Spokane's early grandeur can be found several blocks southwest on W Riverside Avenue, where Neoclassical facades cluster around Jefferson Street. Renowned architect Kirtland K Cutter designed many nineteenth-century Spokane buildings including the **Davenport Hotel**, the **Clark Mansion**, and the Tudor Revival-style **Campbell House**, which is part of the **Cheney Cowles Museum** at 2316 W First Ave, a regional history museum holding an impressive collection of artifacts.

### Practicalities
Greyhound, Northwestern Trailways (☎509/838-5262) and local **bus** lines share the Spokane Intermodal Transportation Center alongside the Amtrak station at 221 W First Ave and Bernard Street. The **visitor center** is at 201 W Main St (Mon–Fri 8.30am–5pm; ☎509/747-3230 or 1-800/248-3230). Central, moderately-priced **accommodation** options include the basic *Suntree Inn*, S 211 Division St (☎509/838-6630; ②), the *Shilo Inn* at 923 E Third Ave (☎509/535-9000 or 1-800/222-2244; ④), and the *West Coast Ridpath Hotel*, W 515 Sprague Ave (☎509/838-2711 or 1-800/426-0670; ⑤), a big 350-room hotel with good views over the city. There's also a string of standard motels along I-90. There's **camping** in Riverside State Park (☎509/456-3964), six miles northwest off Hwy-291.

Downtown, there's great Greek **food** at *Niko's*, 725 W Riverside Ave (☎509/624-7444), and innovative vegetarian cuisine at *Mizuna Restaurant & Wine Bar*, 214 N Howard St (☎509/747-2004).

## The Grand Coulee Dam and around

The huge **Grand Coulee Dam** – the largest concrete structure in the world – is around eighty miles west of Spokane. When work began in 1933, it was as much a political icon as an engineering feat. Probably the most ambitious scheme of the New Deal, this symbol of hope provided jobs for hundreds of workers from all over the country, notably the dust-bowl regions further east. Folk singer **Woody Guthrie**, who worked on the Bonneville Dam lower down the river, was commissioned to write some twenty songs about the Columbia project. These were originally played at local rallies, held to raise investment money and combat propaganda from the private power companies that wanted to keep power production in their own hands. Glowing with optimism, the songs underline the promise the dam held for impoverished working people.

Grand Coulee Dam is now the world's biggest producer of hydroelectricity, and has certainly controlled flooding lower down the Columbia. But the power-guzzling demands of industry switched attention and resources from irrigation, and Guthrie's vision of "green pastures of plenty from dry desert ground" has been much slower to get under way – even now, only half the area originally planned has been irrigated.

The whole story is detailed in the **visitor center** (☎509/633-9265), on Hwy-155 on the west side of the dam, which also runs tours of the dam and its generating plants (summer daily 9am–9pm; rest of year daily 9am–5pm). The **dam** itself is initially something of an anticlimax; it just doesn't look that big, a trick of the huge-scale scenery that surrounds it. At night it's lit up by a laser show that takes place at 8.30 or 9.30pm, depending on the time of year.

The neighboring towns of **Coulee Dam**, **Grand Coulee** and **Electric City** have a few **motels** and fairly dire **restaurants**. More appealingly, over thirty **campgrounds** are scattered around the long, spindly reservoir of Lake Roosevelt, which becomes more woody and secluded as you get further north.

# OREGON

For nineteenth-century pioneers, driving in covered wagons over the mountains and deserts of the Oregon Trail, the **Willamette Valley** was the promised land. Rich and fertile, it became the home of Oregon's first settlements and towns, and the valley is still the heart of the state's social, political and cultural existence, its citizens proud of their traditions and keen to keep the worst excesses of West Coast development at bay. **Portland**, the biggest city, has a cozy European feel; **Salem**, the state capital, maintains the air of a small town; and **Eugene**, at the foot of the valley, with its hippies, jogging trails and modern downtown, is a likeable college community.

Just east of Portland, waterfalls cascade down mossy cliffs along the **Columbia River Gorge**, south of which the twisting path of an old pioneer road leads through more beautiful scenery around **Mount Hood**. Central Oregon, and the hip sport town, **Bend**, is located on a high chaparral desert with sage and juniper trees, with close access to the southern Cascades, numerous lakes and rivers dropping into impressive canyons. Further south, around **Grant's Pass** the major rivers drain to the Pacific carving steep gorges making for some excellent white-water rafting. Several highways link the Willamette Valley to the rugged coast, whose most northerly town, **Astoria**, enjoys a magnificent setting and is strewn with imposing Victorian homes. South along the coast, wide expanses of sand are broken by jagged black monoliths; white lighthouses look out from stark headlands; and rough cliffs conceal small, sheltered coves. With its sand dunes, dense forests, and sheer variety, the coast is every bit as appealing as its Californian counterpart, albeit not as warm. Along the coast are a couple of working ports and several small resorts, busy in summer, half-deserted and lashed by waves and wind out of season.

**Eastern Oregon** is more remote and was only settled on any scale once the prime land in the west had already been taken, and the process involved not only ferocious "Indian campaigns" but also the bitterly violent "range wars" between sheep-farmers and terrorist "sheep-shooters" (associations of cattle ranchers). Sheep and cows now graze in peace, and some small towns still celebrate their cowboy roots with annual rodeos.

### Getting around Oregon

**Portland** is well connected by **train** and **bus** along the line of I-5 to **Seattle** in the north and California to the south. Bus routes radiate from Portland out to Spokane in Washington, across **southern** and **central Oregon** and to the coast. There's also a twice-daily service from Portland to San Francisco along US-101, and another following the line of I-84 east from Portland as far as Pendleton, and then south towards Boise in Idaho. Trains running between Seattle and California stop at Portland, Salem, Eugene, and a few other Oregon towns.

**Local bus** companies serve communities north of Lincoln City in sporadic fashion, but the coast is also excellent for **cycling**, if a bit windy. If you want to get any distance off the beaten track – and certainly if you plan to **hike** – having your own vehicle can make all the difference. **Hitching**, inadvisable anywhere in the US, is illegal in Oregon.

# Portland

Amiable **PORTLAND** is a pleasant surprise. It's not the most obvious tourist destination – there are no major sights – but its bookstores, galleries, parks and restaurants should keep most people going for a few days. In addition the city is an excellent base for touring the surrounding coast and mountains.

The city was named after Portland, Maine, following a coin toss between its two East Coast founders in 1845. Its location on a deep part of the Willamette River, just 78 miles from the Pacific and surrounded by fertile valleys, made it a perfect trading port, and it grew fast, gentrifying quickly and replacing its clapboard houses with ornate Florentine facades and Gothic towers and gables. Nevertheless, throughout the nineteenth century it remained a raunchy, bawdy place, notorious for gambling, prostitution and opium dens.

However, when the new ports of Puget Sound – principally Seattle – gained ascendancy, Portland declined, leaving behind huge swaths of derelict riverside warehouses and rail yards. City planners in the 1970s faced a downtown in tatters, its historic buildings decayed or sacrificed to parking lots and expressways. Portland scrupulously salvaged what was left of its past, replacing concrete with red brick, while risking the odd splash of postmodernist architectural color and introducing folksy statues and murals. There's been much assiduous gap-filling since, and today downtown Portland is a place of attractive squares, meeting places and fountains.

### Arrival, information and getting around

**Portland International Airport (PDX)** is a thirty-minute drive from downtown, by either the RAZ express bus (every 30min 6am–midnight; $7), which drops off at major hotels, or the cheaper local Tri-Met bus #12 (2–5 hourly, 6am–11.30pm;

$1.35), which runs to the transit mall at Fifth Avenue and Stark. A **cab** from the airport into town costs around $25. Greyhound at 550 NW Sixth Ave at Glisan and Amtrak close by at 800 NW Sixth Ave, are conveniently situated within easy walking distance of the center; if you arrive at night take a cab – this part of town is not safe after dark. Pacific Trails (☎503/292-4437) runs buses from Portland to the Oregon Coast.

Though you can see much of the compact city center on **foot**, Portland has an excellent public transportation network. Portland's **light rail transit system,** Metropolitan Area Express (MAX), shunts tourists around downtown and the old town, and carries commuters over the river to the suburbs, also tunneling under Washington Park (and the zoo) en route to Hillsboro. The Tri-Met **bus system** is based at the downtown **transit malls** along Fifth Avenue (southbound) and Sixth Avenue (northbound). Each bus shelter is labeled with a symbol – brown beaver, blue snowflake and so on – which serves as a code for a block of bus routes in a particular area of the city. The **Tri-Met Info Bureau** on Pioneer Courthouse Square (Mon–Fri 8am–5pm; ☎503/238-7433; for disabled customers ☎503/238-4952) offers free transit maps and route-planning advice, and sells all-zone day tickets ($3.60) and books of ten tickets ($9.50). Buses and MAX trains are **free** in the downtown zone – "Fareless Square" – edged by the Willamette to the north and east, and I-405 to the south and west. Outside here, fares are between $1.05 and $1.35 – pay the bus driver exact change; **transfers** for onward travel within the same zone (there are three fare zones altogether) are free.

During the daytime, vintage **trolley cars** use the more central MAX lines. Portland's **taxis** don't stop in the street; you'll have to either get one at a hotel or call (Broadway Cabs ☎503/227-1234; Portland Taxi Co ☎503/256-5400).

The **visitor center,** by the river in the World Trade Center, 26 SW Salmon St at Front (May–Aug Mon–Fri 9am–5pm, Sat 10am–4pm, Sun 10am–2pm; Sept–April Mon–Fri 9am–5pm, Sat 10am–4pm; ☎503/275-9750 or 1-800/962-3700), has plenty of maps and information on both the city and the state. Portland's main **post office** is at 715 NW Hoyt St (☎503/294-2124 zip code 97205).

## Accommodation

Dozens of **motels** line the interstates and Sandy Boulevard northeast of the city center, but – for a few dollars more – you're far better staying downtown, where you'll find **hostels**, **B&Bs**, and a good range of **hotels**, the pick of which occupy grand and elegantly restored old buildings. Portland also has more than its share of downtown flophouses, but these are best avoided.

**Benson**, 309 SW Broadway (☎503/228-2000 or 1-800/426-0670). Classy hotel with a superb walnut-paneled lobby dating from 1912. Extremely comfortable bedrooms with modern furnishings. All facilities. ⑦.

**Days Inn City Center**, 1414 SW 6th Ave (☎503/221-1611 or 1-800/899-0248). Great location and smart, well-tended motel-style rooms. Excellent value for downtown. ⑤.

**General Hooker's House B&B**, 125 SW Hooker St (☎503/222-4435 or 1-800/745-4135). Four guestrooms in an attractive Victorian home, a 20-min walk from downtown. The host is a fourth generation Portlander who really knows her city. ④.

**Heathman Hotel**, 1001 SW Broadway at Salmon (☎503/241-4100 or 1-800/551-0011). Portland's top hotel, the *Heathman* occupies a finely restored old building, with an elegant, teak-paneled interior and much marble and brass. Splendid rooms, excellent restaurant. ⑦.

**Heron Haus**, 2545 NW Westover Rd (☎503/274-1846). Enough cannot be said about this romantic, stylish 1904 Tudor B&B. The large suites, each with fireplace and cozy sitting areas, sweeping breakfast room and airy-sunroom all add to the grand experience of staying here. Excellent continental breakfast is served by the charming owner and host. ⑦.

**HI-Portland**, 3031 SE Hawthorne Blvd (☎503/236-3380). Hostel facilities in a cheery Victorian house, well located in the heart of "alternative" Hawthorne District. Occasional live performances. ①.

**HI-NW Portland International Hostel**, 1818 NW Glisan (☎503/241-2783). A new hostel located in a nineteenth-century home in upscale Nob Hill district. Espresso bar. ①.

**McMenamins Edgefield**, 2126 SW Halsey Rd (☎503/669-8610 or 1-800/669-8610). Fifteen minutes east of the airport, *Edgefield* is a unique resort brewpub that features a Georgian Manor, B&B, restaurants, authentic bars, brewery, winery and tasting room, distillery, movie theater, gardens, and an 18-hole British golf course. ③–⑤.

**McMenamins Kennedy School**, 5736 NE 33rd St (☎503/249-3983 or 1-888/249-3983). Thirty-five B&B rooms, each in a refurbished schoolroom with chalkboards and cloakrooms, plus modern conveniences. Excellent breakfast, bars, movie theater and pool. ⑤.

**Vintage Plaza**, 422 SW Broadway (☎1-800/243-0555). An intimate boutique hotel with oversized rooms – and a calm, relaxed atmosphere throughout. Wine is offered in the afternoons in the lobby. ⑤–⑥.

## The City

The Willamette River divides Portland in half: the downtown area, where you'll probably spend most time, is on the west bank and forms the bulk of the city's southwest quadrant; the east is mostly residential. When the sun shines, **Pioneer Courthouse Square** is downtown Portland's focal point, its amenable curving steps filled with music and people. Within easy walking distance are the city's leading department stores, theaters and museums – a harmonious melange of old and new, where fading plasterwork and terracotta reliefs face concrete and glass, punctuated by small grassy parks.

Broadway epitomizes Portland's mix of early grandeur and new wealth, with prestigious hotels sharing space with great white movie palaces, such as the grand *Portland* restored as part of the impressive **Portland Center for the Performing Arts**. One block west, is the long, low facade of **Portland Art Museum** (Tues–Sun 10am–5pm; $7.50), which hosts international touring exhibitions, plus a wide-ranging collection of Northwest Native American masks, squat Mexican statues, ancient Chinese figures – and one of Monet's *Water Lilies*. Next door, the old **Masonic Hall** now serves as an annex to the museum, its spacious interior used for exhibitions of contemporary, mostly local art. Beside an old, ivy-covered church, the **Oregon History Center**, 1200 SW Park (Tues–Sat 10am–5pm, Sun noon–5pm; $6) is primarily a research facility, but has some imaginative exhibits exploring different facets of the state's history. **Nike Town**, 930 SW Sixth Ave, is the flagship store of this sportswear giant whose corporate headquarters are just southeast of Portland in Beaverton.

A five-minute walk away, at the junction of Madison and Fifth, is Portland's one sight of renown – Michael Graves' **Portland Building**, a monumental concrete, tile and glass edifice, adorned with rosettes and pink and blue tiling, that looks like a gift-wrapped box. America's first postmodern building, its reworking of classical and other motifs outraged conservatives and delighted the avant-garde. Portland relished the controversy, going so far as to hoist a 36ft-high kneeling copper figure of *Portlandia* above the main entrance.

A few blocks further east, the riverfront has been rescued from over a century of burial beneath wharves, warehouses and, more recently, an express highway, and is now lined by the two-mile-long **Tom McCall Waterfront Park**, on Willamette River. Just behind the park at First and Salmon, the modern, gray and glassy **World Trade Center** looms over the gushing fountains of the Salmon Street Springs. A couple of blocks over, the small **Yamhill Historic District** is lined with 1890s buildings. **Yamhill**

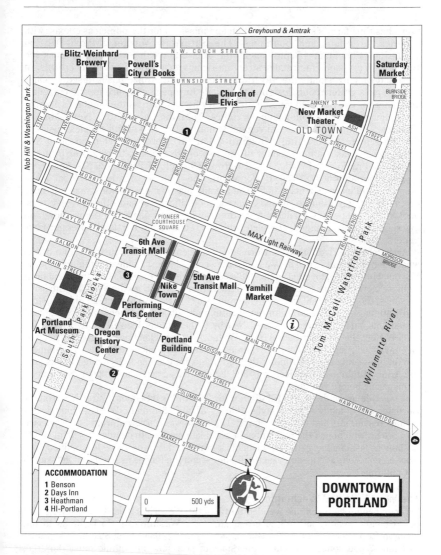

△ *Greyhound & Amtrak*

Blitz-Weinhard Brewery

Powell's City of Books

N.W. COUCH STREET

BURNSIDE STREET

Saturday Market

BURNSIDE BRIDGE

Church of Elvis

OAK STREET

New Market Theater

ANKENY ST

OLD TOWN

STARK STREET

PINE STREET

ASH STREET

❶

WASHINGTON ST

13TH AVENUE

12TH AVENUE

11TH AVENUE

9TH AVENUE

PARK AVENUE

BROADWAY

6TH AVENUE

5TH AVENUE

4TH AVENUE

3RD AVENUE

2ND AVENUE

1ST AVENUE

FRONT AVENUE

ALDER STREET

MORRISON STREET

YAMHILL STREET

PIONEER COURTHOUSE SQUARE

MAX Light Railway

Tom McCall Waterfront Park

MORRISON BRIDGE

TAYLOR STREET

SALMON STREET

6th Ave Transit Mall

MAIN STREET

❸

Nike Town

5th Ave Transit Mall

Yamhill Market

South Park Blocks

Performing Arts Center

Portland Art Museum

Oregon History Center

Portland Building

MADISON STREET

MAIN STREET

ⓘ

Willamette River

❷

JEFFERSON STREET

COLUMBIA STREET

CLAY STREET

HAWTHORNE BRIDGE

MARKET STREET

❹

**ACCOMMODATION**
1 Benson
2 Days Inn
3 Heathman
4 HI-Portland

0        500 yds

N

**DOWNTOWN PORTLAND**

Nob Hill & Washington Park △

---

**Marketplace** (actually built in 1982) has a couple of produce stalls and cafes, though most of its interior has been turned into a gym.

## Old Town, Chinatown, Pearl District and Nob Hill

**Old Town**, north along the river between the Morrison and Burnside bridges, is where Portland was originally founded in 1843. The area tended to flood, however, and when the railroad came in 1883 the town center soon shifted away; its big, ornate buildings became warehouses and it plummeted down the social scale. Old

Town has thus far resisted gentrification and missions for the homeless coexist with galleries, brewpubs and boutiques. The **Saturday Market** (March–Dec Sat 10am–5pm, Sun 11am–4.30pm) packs the area around the west end of Burnside Bridge with arts and crafts stalls, street musicians, spicy foods and lively crowds. At First and Ankeny, stands the **Skidmore Fountain**, a bronze basin raised by cary-atids above a granite pool, designed to provide European elegance for the citizens – and water for hard-worked nineteenth-century horses. Across the fountain's angular plaza, an ornamental colonnade stretches from the side of the **New Market Theater**, a restored theater-cum-vegetable market that is now full of cafes. Inside is the **American Advertising Museum** (Mon–Fri appt only; Sat noon–5pm; $3), which gives a fascinating account of the rise of advertising, from poster prints to tapes of old radio and TV ads. The **24-Hour Church of Elvis**, 720 SW Ankeny St ("most hours"; ☎503/226-3671; donation), the chaotic creation of local artist Stephanie G Pierce, is a maze of Styrofoam and plastic monstrosities, many dedicat-ed to Mr Presley. Church of Elvis marriage certificates – and other Presley para-phernalia – are usually available from the coin-operated display in the window, and marriages can be arranged, complete with a serenade from Portland's premier Elvis impersonator.

Away from the river, up West Burnside, the oriental gate at Fourth Avenue marks what's left of **Chinatown**. This was once the second largest Chinese community in the US, but white unemployment in the 1880s led, as elsewhere, to racist attacks, and most Chinese workers were forced to leave. The further west you go the shabbier Burnside becomes, though it's well worth pushing on into chic **Pearl District**, an old industrial and warehouse section now converted to upscale loft development, galleries, stylish restaurants, and designer boutiques. Nearby is the famous **Powell's City of Books**, 1005 W Burnside St (daily 9am–11pm). With over one million books, Powell's occupies an entire block, as well as separate theme annexes, and issues free maps so customers can find their way around. Among the highlights are used and discounted books, and the **Anne Hughes Coffee Room** (☎503/228-4651), a great place to pour over a book or magazine before you buy.

A bus ride away, the **Nob Hill** district (or "North West Section") stretches from W Burnside Street along a dozen stylish blocks of NW 23rd and NW 21st, choked with serious restaurants and designer shops. The name was borrowed from San Francisco by a grocer who hoped the residential heart of late nineteenth-century Portland would become as fashionable as the Nob Hill back home. It did, almost, the few multicolored wooden mansions add a San Franciscan tinge – and the food is as good as it gets north of California.

### The West Hills and Washington Park

Directly behind Nob Hill, the wooded bluffs of the West Hills hold the elegant houses of Portland's wealthy as well as green and leafy **Washington Park**, home to the **Oregon Zoo** (Apr 1–Sept 30, 9am–6pm; Oct 1–Mar 31, 9am–4pm; $5.50). In summer, Rhythm & Zoo concerts feature superstars of jazz, folk and ethnic music for free; 7–9pm. Close by, the **World Forestry Center** (daily 9am–5pm; $3.50) uses interactive exhibits to explain forest management.

### East of the river

While the west side of the Willamette River provided a deep port, the east side was too shallow for shipping and the area remained undeveloped for the first fifty years of Portland's life. The Morrison Bridge crept across at the end of the nineteenth cen-tury, since then most of Portland's population has lived here, in various neighborhoods that are almost entirely residential. The **Hawthorne District**, however, is Portland's most alternative and diverse neighborhood. Hawthorne Boulevard, between 30th and 45th, is choked with bookstores, hip cafes, divey bars and cheap ethnic restaurants. Belmont and Clinton avenues are also trendy pockets. The lavish **Oregon Museum of Science and Industry** (summer daily 9.30am–7pm; rest of year Tues–Sun 9.30am–5.30pm; $6.50), at 1945 SE Water and Clay, is the thing to see. Hundreds of interactive exhibits and space artifacts are gathered here, such as the excellent Flight Simulator. There's also an OMNIMAX theater, the **Murdock Planetarium** and a submarine docked in the Willamette; these incur additional charges.

## Eating

If the Southwest can claim its own cuisine, then so too can the Northwest. Like in Seattle, Pacific Northwest cuisine – a mix of international cooking styles and fresh regional produce – is served at Portland's most fashionable restaurants. Portland is bursting with excellent dining options for all palates and pocketbooks. Downtown, Pearl Town and Nob Hill have unlimited swank cocktail bars, sedate bistros, brewpubs and Pacific-fusion and vegan-friendly restaurants, while Hawthorne Boulevard has the best inexpensive grub, and ethnic restaurants. Stylish cafes know no boundaries. At the *Metro on Broadway*, 911 SW Broadway, a dozen low-priced outlets offer food from around the world under one roof. Downtown also has an abundance of **mobile kitchens**, that crank out authentic Mexican food, Italian paninis, vegetarian Indian cuisine, Philly cheesesteak sandwiches, gourmet pizzas and bentos – which often make a better lunch than you'll find for the same money in restaurants.

**Acropolis**, 8325 SE McLoughlin Blvd (☎503/231-9611), is carnivore headquarters. Meaty burgers that start at a whopping full pound and swell bigger than your head. Open till 2am daily.

**Bombay Cricket Club**, 1925 Hawthorne Blvd (☎503/231-0740). Not just another excellent Indian restaurant, there's a Muslim-inspired Middle Eastern element to the usual fare. Cricket matches on video, too.

**Dot's Cafe**, 2521 SE Clinton Ave (☎503/235-0203). An inexpensive late-night spot decked out in primo garage-sale decor, with a diner menu that includes the classic bacon cheeseburger, Vegan Vavoom, burritos and the best grilled-cheese sandwich in Portland.

**Fernando's Hideaway**, 824 SW 1st Ave (☎503/248-4709). Popular Spanish restaurant and cavernous Madrid-style tapas bar. Latin dance classes and a good singles scene.

**Jake's Famous Crawfish**, 401 SW 12th Ave (☎503/226-1419). Portland's landmark restaurant has remained a classic for 106 years. An ever-changing menu with a staggering choice of fresh fish, including Columbia River Sturgeon, Depot Bay Dungeness Crab, or spicy Crawfish cakes with rémoulade.

**McCormick and Schmick's**, 235 SW 1st Ave at Oak (☎503/224-7522). Excellent fish restaurant, with ultrafresh nightly specials, and a lively oyster bar with a happening single's scene. Entrees around $15.

**Montage**, 301 SE Morrison (☎503/243-1324). A very popular Creole bistro, open late, with moderately-priced dishes and long communal tables.

**Oba**, 555 NW 12th (☎503/228-6161). Flashy, *nuevo latino* eatery in the Pearl District that fuses flavors from all over Latin America to create food you won't find anywhere else in Portland.

**Toney Bento**, 1423 SE 37th Ave (☎503/234-4441). A lively Hawthorne spot with giant bowls of tasty and inexpensive noodle concoctions, and sushi – plus an endless variety of chili, Thai peanut, ginger and wasabi condiments.

**Wildwood**, 1221 NW 21st Ave (☎503/248-9663). Upscale Nob Hill restaurant in a warm bright interior, friendly staff, and imaginative food will delight the most jaded Northwest palate. Fresh local ingredients rule.

# Drinking and nightlife

Portland's smart cocktail lounges and divey bars easily rival those in hip Seattle. The city is a beer-drinker's heaven, with over thirty local **microbreweries**. *BridgePort Ale House*, 3632 SE Hawthorne Blvd (☎503/233-6540), *BridgePort Brewing Co*, 1313 NW Marshall St (☎503/241-3621), and *Blitz-Weinhard Brewery*, 1133 W Burnside (☎541/222-4351) are worth checking out. *McMenaman's* "concept" brewpubs sell their own locally-brewed ales in unique settings. The book-browsing, **coffee**-swilling scene looms large. The ubiquitous *Starbuck's* is everywhere, as is the locally-owned *Coffee People*. For **music**, the place to head is downtown, on- and off-Broadway.

The comprehensive *Willamette Week*, available free on any street corner, carries up-to-the-minute **listings** of what's on and where, as does the Friday edition of *The Oregonian*, the leading local newspaper. *Just Out* is the gay/lesbian publication.

## Bars, brewpubs and coffeehouses

**Bar of the Gods**, 4801 SE Hawthorne (☎503/232-2037). A very cool dive populated by Hawthorne youth. Malted beverages and extensive wines. Free pool.

**Biddy McGraw's**, 3518 SE Hawthorne (☎503/233-1178). Revered by locals, Portland's most authentic Irish pub is a time-warp to Dublin. Celtic music and perfect pints of Guinness.

**Cafe Lena**, 2239 SE Hawthorne Blvd (☎503/238-7087). Food fit for a revolution and an authentic crowd; open-mike poetry and acoustic guitar. Late-night weekend menu served until 1am.

**Cobalt Lounge**, 32 NW 3rd (☎503/225-1003). A fun, retro-style club in Old Town with stiff drinks and a party crowd. Breakfast served from 4pm to 2am daily.

**Coffee People**, 506 SW 6th at Washington (☎503/226-3074). Splendid range of coffees – arguably the best in town. Also at 737 Salmon at Park and 817 NW 23rd Ave.

**Ember's**, 11 NW Broadway (☎503/222-3082). A gay bar with drag shows on the runway in the front bar and high-energy dancing in the club. Cool fish-tank bar top.

**Huber's**, 411 SW 3rd Ave (☎503/228-5686). Portland's oldest bar is an elegant room with arched stained-glass skylight, mahogany paneling and terrazzo floor. Famous for roast turkey and flaming Spanish coffees.

**Lucky Lab Brewpub**, 915 SE Hawthorne Blvd (☎503/236-3555). An unpretentious brewpub in a huge warehouse with an outdoor patio. Fresh ales, great sandwiches, BBQ specials, and a peanut curry bento to die for.

**Ohm**, 31 NW 1st Ave (☎503/223-9919). A high-energy dance club with a state-of-the-art sound system. DJs and bands. Artful decor, great lighting.

**Ringler's Annex**, 1223 SW Stark St (☎503/525-0520). Great people-watching in the cavernous basement of the ornate wedge-shaped 1917 Flatiron Building.

**Shanghai Tunnel**, 211 SW Ankeny (☎503/220-4001). A subterranean bar popular with hipsters. Asian-style soul food.

**Space Room**, 4800 SE Hawthorne (☎503/235-8303). The Jetson-era decor, black lights and big booths draw in a devoted local crowd.

**The Tao of Tea**, 3430 SE Belmont St (☎503/736-0119). More than 120 different kids of teas are served in an exquisite room with Zen-like decor. Elegant meals of vegan and Indian food.

**Tiger Bar**, 317 NW Broadway (☎503/222-7297). An uber-hip, swank lounge with a tiger-striped bar and long banquettes. Dark, sultry and smoke-friendly. Late-night food.

## Music venues

**Brasserie Montmarte**, 626 SW Park St (☎503/224-5552). A Portland institution, this upscale joint is famous for its late-night jazz and table-crayon drawing competitions. Good French cuisine.

**Crystal Ballroom**, 1332 W Burnside St (☎503/225-0047). An elegant nineteenth-century dance hall with a "floating" floor and on-site brewery. Bands range from hippie to hip-hop, local to national, and feature the best of Portland's indie rock.

**East Avenue Tavern**, 727 E Burnside St (☎503/236-6900). Nightly Irish, folk or bluegrass music half a mile east of the river.

**Jazz de Opus**, 33 NW 2nd Ave (☎503/222-6077). Cozy, low-key atmosphere with excellent live jazz and grilled food. No cover most nights.

**Mt Tabor Pub & Cinema**, 4811 SE Hawthorne Blvd (☎503/238-1646). Live bands, jam sessions, movies, pool and pizza.

**Parchman Farm**, 1204 SE Clay St (☎503/235-7831). Intimate club; good pizza, great jazz, no cover.

**Satyricon**, 125 NW 6th Ave (☎503/243-2380). Diverse acts with an emphasis on punk rock. Good bar food.

### Classical music, theater and cinema

Portland's arts scene revolves around the **Portland Center for the Performing Arts**, 1111 SW Broadway, a dynamic complex comprised of three main buildings – The **Civic Auditorium**, at SW 3rd between Market and Clay; the **Arlene Schnitzer Concert Hall**, at SW Broadway and Main; and the New Theater Building, containing the **Dolores Winningstad Theater** and **Newmark Theater**, at SW Broadway and Main. The Arlene Schnitzer Concert Hall is a sumptuously restored 1928 vaudeville and movie house that presents big musical extravaganzas, opera and one-off theater productions. These venues host performances by the **Oregon Symphony Orchestra**, **Portland Opera**, **Oregon Ballet Theater**, **Portland Center Stage** and **Tygres Theater**, to name a few. For tickets to PCPA events, call ☎503/224-4000; Events hotline ☎503/248-4335.

The Portland State University hosts the **Portland International Performance Festival** in mid-July. **Free concerts** are held on Pioneer Courthouse Square, the Tom McCall Waterfront Park, and at the zoo during the summer.

# Around Portland: the Columbia River Gorge and Mount Hood

The **Columbia River Gorge**, to the east of Portland, was scoured deep and narrow by huge glaciers during the Ice Age. Now it's covered with green fir and maple trees, which turn fabulous shades of gold and red in the fall, and narrow white waterfalls tumble down its sides.

The most dramatic part of the gorge, between Troutdale and the town of Hood River, lies in the shadow of snow-tipped Mount Hood. The ideal way to explore it is by driving along the **Historic Columbia River Highway** (accessed at exits 22 or 35 off I-84), which boasts several excellent vantage points, the best at Crown Point Vista House and the Portland Women's Forum Overlook. The most spectacular of the waterfalls en route is **Multnomah Falls**, whose waters plunge over 530ft down a rock face before collecting in a pool and dropping a further seventy feet. But be warned: this is the state's most popular attraction and the crowds can get too much.

Early British explorers such as Cook and Vancouver either missed or under-estimated the importance of the Columbia River. It was left to the American trader Robert Gray to cross the sand bar at its mouth in 1792 and sail into Oregon's interior. More interested in buying furs than making maps, he didn't follow the river very far, and its first non-native explorers came down the Columbia the other way – a tired Lewis and Clark, on the last stage of their 1804 trek. Forty years later, the Gorge became the final leg of the Oregon Trail, negotiated by pioneer families on precarious rafts.

**Mount Hood**, a dormant volcano rising some eleven thousand feet, is the tallest of the Oregon Cascades. The **Mount Hood Loop** takes in both mount and gorge, but you should not attempt to drive it in a day; one of the joys of the area is to explore it by foot along some of the trails. The highest point on the loop, **Barlow Pass**, is named after Samuel Barlow, a wagon-train leader who blazed the first trail around the mountain.

Much of the Barlow Road is still followed by Hwy-35/US-26, including the steep ridges where wagons frequently skidded out of control and plummeted downhill. You can still see deep gashes on some of the trees where ropes were fastened to check the wagons' descent.

Near the intersection of Hwy-35 and US-26, a turning up the mountain leads to the solid stone *Timberline Lodge* (☎503/272-3311 or 1-800/547-1406; ④), a New Deal structure which is now a year-round ski resort, and the setting for Stanley Kubrick's *The Shining*. Two other downhill ski areas – Mount Hood Meadows and Mount Hood SkiBowl – offer nighttime **skiing** during the regular November to April season. There are also many miles of cross-country skiing trails throughout the **Mount Hood National Forest**.

### Hood River

Although nothing much to look at, the town of **HOOD RIVER** is a busy center for windsurfing and mountain biking, with outfitters' shops lining the streets. It's a good base for exploring the gorge; one of the most exquisite **places to stay** in the entire region is the *Columbia Gorge Hotel* (☎541/386-5566 or 1-800/345-1921; ⑧), whose gorgeous rooms and garden overlook the gorge just off I-84 at the extreme west end of town. More central, and less expensive, options include the *Hood River Hotel*, 102 Oak Ave (☎541/386-1900 or 1-800/386-1859; ⑤), built in 1913 and featuring a good Italian restaurant, and the basic but clean *Love's Riverview Lodge*, 1505 Oak St (☎541/386-8719 or 1-800/789-9568; ④). The *Hood River Brewing Co*, 506 Columbia St (☎541/386-2247), is a popular spot in the evening and there are several inexpensive places to **eat**. The town's **visitor center** is down by the river at the east end of town in the Port Marina Park (☎541/326-2000 or 1-800/366-3530).

# South through the Willamette Valley

South of Portland, I-5 threads towards the Californian border along a series of inland valleys, bypassing historic **Oregon City**, the first state capital, at the end of the Oregon Trail. Today, the split-level town consists of a short modern main street, connected by steps, steep streets and a cliff-face elevator to an uptown area of old wooden houses set on a bluff.

The Willamette Valley has perhaps the world's most diverse agriculture. Hwy-99 W, the scenic route through wine country, takes you across more than two dozen acclaimed **wineries,** most of which pour superb Pinot noirs, Chardonnays and Rieslings. Pick up a wine country driving tour map from any local visitor center. The Willamette Valley also has some of the best examples of **covered bridges**. There are thirty-four in the area; many span creeks near Scio, Albany and Cottage Grove.

## Salem

The build-up of motels and fast-food chains that ushers you into **SALEM** is deceptive, as this is in fact a small and rather staid little town, content to dutifully point visitors around its quota of attractions, but not expecting them to linger. Its showpiece is the tall, white Vermont-marble **Capitol Building** whose cupola is surmounted by a large gold-leaf pioneer, axe in hand, eyes towards the West. At the entrance, there's a marble carving of explorers Lewis and Clark processing regally towards (presumably) the Willamette Valley. There are regular **tours** round the building – the information desk inside the rotunda has the times. Next to the capitol, tree-lined **Willamette University** is the oldest university in the West. Elsewhere, the historic **Mission Mill Village** is a collection of pioneer buildings off 12th Street.

Greyhound is convenient at 450 Church St NE and Amtrak at 13th and Oak. The **visitor center**, at 1313 Mill St SE (☎503/581-4325 or 1-800/874-7012), is part of the Mission Mill Village. There are plenty of budget **motels**, among them the central *Grand Motel*, 1555 State St (☎503/581-2466; ②), and *City Center Motel*, 510 Liberty St SE (☎503/364-0121 or 1-800/289-0121; ②). *The Marquee House*, 333 Wyatt Court NE (☎503/391-0837 or 1-800/949-0837; ④), is a good-value **B&B** close to downtown. If you're **camping**, head for the waterfalls and lush forests of **Silver Falls State Park** (☎503/873-8681), 26 miles east of Salem via highways 22 and 214.

The area around the university is not the busy **food** scene you might expect, and you're better off downtown, where the *Dairy Lunch Cafe*, 347 Court St at Liberty (☎503/363-6433), is a classic 1960s diner with food that's both good and inexpensive. *Jonathan's Oyster Bar and Long Bar*, 120 Liberty St (☎503/362-7219), an affordable downtown classic for 20 years, serves fresh seafood, Cajun and Southwestern cuisine. The hip *Coffee House Cafe*, 135 Liberty St (☎503/371-6768), has organic coffee, natural foods and live music.

# Eugene

Oregon's second largest city, **EUGENE** dominates the lower end of the Willamette Valley – a lively social mix of students, professionals, hippies and blue collars. Truly a fun town, this is where Ken Kesey and some of the Merry Pranksters came to live in the woods after tiring of the California scene; it's where the famous Nike running shoe was first tried and tested by University of Oregon athletes; and it's where much of *Animal House* was filmed.

Though short on sights, Eugene is an energetic cultural center, to which the **University of Oregon** campus in the city's southeast corner lends a youthful feel. The University's **Museum of Art** (Wed–Sun noon–5pm; $3), has a strong Asian collection and regional contemporary art. The **Hult Center for Performing Arts** at Sixth Avenue and Willamette Street (concert line ☎541/682-5746; for tickets ☎541/687-5000) is the home to several local arts organizations including the Eugene Opera, Eugene Symphony, Eugene Ballet Company, Oregon Bach Festival and Willamette Repertory Theater.

The city has two big markets: the weekly **Saturday Market** around Eighth and Oak (from 10am–5pm, between April and Christmas) is something of a carnival, thanks to the live music and street performers, and an institution – it's been going for nearly thirty years. Tie-dye and wholefoods set the tone, but rastas, skateboarders, punks and students join in, too. **Fifth Street Market** is more upscale, essentially a boutique mall, that sells arts, crafts and clothes.

Eugene is a center of sporting activity. Trails and paths abound for runners and cyclists, both in the city center and along leafy river banks; bikes can be rented from Pedal Power, 535 High St (☎541/687-1775).

## Practicalities

The Greyhound terminal is at 987 Pearl and Tenth, Amtrak pulls in at Fourth and Willamette. Green Tortoise passes through Eugene twice-weekly on its trip up the coast. There's a **visitor center** downtown at 115 W Eighth Ave (Mon–Fri 8.30am–5pm; ☎541/484-5307 or 1-800/547-5445). The best **rooms** in town are at the resort-style *Valley River Inn*, 1000 Valley River Way (☎541/687-0123 or 1-800/543-8266; ⑦), set by the Willamette River about a mile from downtown, while *Campbell House*, 252 Pearl St (☎541/343-1119 or 1-800/264-2519; ⑤), offers great hospitality in an elegant eighteen-room restored 1892 Victorian home. *Franklin Inn*, 1857 Franklin Blvd (☎541/342-4804; ③), has reasonably priced rooms near the university, and *Downtown Motel*, 361 W Seventh Ave (☎541/345-8739 or 1-800/648-4366; ②), offers attractive and centrally located rooms. *Eugene International Hostel,* 2352 Willamette St (☎541/349-0589; ①), is clean, safe and comfortable.

With over fifteen thousand students to feed, Eugene has plenty of places to **eat**. *Cafe Zenon,* 8998 Pearl St (☎503/343-3005), is the best restaurant around, with an eclectic menu filled with various international dishes; *Chanterelle,* 207 E Fifth Ave (☎541/484-4065), is an intimate French bistro; *Morning Glory Bakery & Cafe,* 450 Willamette (☎541/687-0709) serves hearty vegan-style breakfast dishes all day. *Full City Coffee Roaster's,* 842 Pearl St (☎541/344-0475), has the best java in town.

The live **music** scene is big in Eugene. *Jo Federigo's Restaurant and Jazz Club,* 259 E Fifth Ave, has nightly jazz and serves Italian and Northwest cuisine in a great late-night atmosphere. *Sam Bond's Garage,* 407 Blair Blvd (☎541/431-6603), hosts live music and specializes in exotic pizzas by the slice, and hard-to-find microbrews.

The **Oregon Country Fair** (☎541/343-4298) is a big hippie-flavored festival of music, arts, food and dancing, held in **VENETA**, ten miles west on US-126, during the second weekend in July. Traffic then is heavy, and even if you have a car it's easier to travel there by bus – Eugene's LTD system operates special services.

## South to California

South of Eugene along I-5, not too far from the California border, the unenticing town of **GRANTS PASS** lies on the Rogue River, which tumbles vigorously from the Cascades. It earns its living mainly from taking visitors **whitewater rafting**. Half a day will cost around $45, a full day $60 – the **visitor center**, just off I-5 at 1501 NE Sixth St (☎1-800/547-5927 or 541/476-7717), can provide brochures from more than two dozen licensed (and so safer) river guides. Beyond Grants Pass, I-5 dips southeast through **Ashland** on an inland route to California, whilst US-199 heads southwest to the California (and Oregon) coast, passing near the **Oregon Caves**.

### Oregon Caves National Monument

Some thirty miles southwest of Grants Pass along US-199, at the hamlet of **CAVE JUNCTION**, Hwy-46 veers east twenty miles to the **OREGON CAVES NATIONAL MONUMENT**. Tucked in a wooded canyon at the end of a narrow, twisting road, it's actually one enormous cave, with smaller passages leading off. The dripping marble walls are covered with elaborate stalactites, stalagmites and flowstone. Organized (and very cold) tours of the caves run year-round (75min; ☎541/592-3400 for schedule; $6).

Close to the cave entrance, surrounded by forest, is the first-class *Oregon Caves Lodge,* 2000 Caves Hwy (mid-March–Sept; ☎541/592-3400; reservations advised; ④), an elegant 1930s structure with baronial public rooms. Alternatively, there are more modest lodgings back in Cave Junction – try the *Holiday Motel* (☎541/592-3003; ③), on US-199 – and several **campgrounds** dotted along Hwy-46 (☎541/592-3400 for reservations).

### Ashland and the Shakespeare Festival

Throughout Oregon, small **ASHLAND**, forty miles southeast of Grants Pass, is identified with William Shakespeare – a real anomaly among the timber and dairy-farming towns. Since 1945, the **Oregon Shakespeare Festival** has been held here between February and October, packing audiences into the half-timbered **Elizabethan Theatre** in Lithia Park. It may all be a bit contrived, but Ashland is no more tacky than Shakespeare's real birthplace, and in some ways has the distinct edge. Its setting, between the Cascade and the Siskiyou mountains, is magnificent; there's good skiing in the winter and river rafting in summer; there's some excellent contemporary fringe theater – not to mention pleasant cafes, galleries and a young, friendly atmosphere when the nearby college is in session.

The **Angus Bowmer Theatre**, adjacent to the Elizabeth Theatre in Lithia Park, stages both Shakespearean and more contemporary works, while the smaller **Black Swan**, off Pioneer Street, has an exclusively modern repertoire. The three theaters share the same box office (☎541/482-4331) and tickets average around $25, sometimes half-price on the day; standing room at the Elizabethan Theatre costs $10. For a further helping of contemporary drama, try the **Actors' Theater**, three miles north in the tiny town of **TALENT**, at Main and Talent (☎541/535-5250), or the **Oregon Cabaret Theater**, in a renovated pink church at First and Hargadine (☎541/488-2902).

The **visitor center** is at 110 E Main St (Mon–Fri 9am–5pm; ☎541/482-3486) and there's a seasonal information kiosk – with longer hours – on the plaza at the entrance to Lithia Park; Greyhound **buses** drop passengers on the edge of town near the I-5 freeway exit. Ashland has over sixty **B&Bs** (④–⑥), most of which are in charming Victorian homes. Ashland B&B Network (☎1-800/944-0329; *www.abbnet.com*) or Southern Oregon Reservation Center (☎541/488-1011 or 1-800/547-8052), can hook you up with a room and theater tickets. One of the most central, is the plush *Winchester Country Inn*, 35 S Second St (☎541/488-1113 or 1-800/972-4991; ⑥), which serves excellent breakfasts. *The Ashland Hostel,* 150 N Main St (☎541/482-9217; ①), is a friendly, clean and well-located hostel. Failing that, there are several **motels** out along Siskiyou Boulevard – try the no-frills *Palm Motel*, at no. 1065 (☎541/482-2636; ②).

Good places to **eat and drink** range from the popular *Ashland Bakery Cafe*, 38 E Main St (☎541/482-2117), to more upscale haunts like *The Firefly*, 15 N First St (☎541/488-3212), and *Primavera,* 241 Hargadine (☎503/488-1994), both of which have innovative fusion menus and stylish decor. The *Standing Stone Brewing Co,* 101 Oak St (☎541/482-2448), has excellent hand-crafted ales, above-average pub food and nightly live music.

# The Oregon Coast

Although the **Oregon coast** is as beautiful as any stretch of America's Pacific seaboard, the Californian sun draws off the tan-seeking masses (summer temperatures here stay in the sixties and seventies), leaving Oregonians to hike and clam-dig along their own four hundred miles, most of it public land. State park after state park lines the shore, with campgrounds scattered thickly; while extensive and often isolated beaches offer a multitude of free activities, from beachcombing to shell-fishing and whale-watching. This isn't to say that Oregon has escaped commercialism: small fishing towns, hard-hit by decline, are jumping onto the tourism bandwagon as fast as they can, and it's a lucky traveler who finds a budget room without booking ahead in July and August.

About a dozen of the state parks along the Oregon coast offer novel accommodation in the form of **yurts** – domed circular tents with wooden floors, electricity and lockable doors. Yurts come equipped with bunk beds and a futon couch, and cost $25 per night for five people; in nine coastal state parks, details from the **State Park Campsite Information Line** (☎1-800/452-5687).

The coast is perfect for **cycling** (pick up the *Coast Bike Route Map* from any major visitor center). US-101 follows the coastline to the California border, and you can escape onto the many smaller "scenic loop" roads.

## Astoria

Set near the mouth of the Columbia River, **ASTORIA** was founded as a private commercial venture by the millionaire John Jacob Astor in 1811. The idea was to gather furs here from all over the Northwest and then export them to Asia, where demand verged on the feverish. In the event, "Fort Astoria" survived for just a painful year and a half, beset by natural disasters and internal feuding, before it was sold to the British: Washington Irving made the best of the saga in his novel *Astoria*. A small replica of the old fort stands at 15th and Exchange, but nowadays Astoria is really a working port, with enough history and ornate Victorian architecture to attract a few visitors, but little of the hype of communities to the south.

Arriving from Portland, the main road into Astoria, **Marine Drive**, runs parallel with the waterfront – crammed with saloons and brothels in the nineteenth century, many equipped with built-in trap doors for "shanghaiing" drunken customers, who might wake up halfway across the Pacific. The situation got so out of hand at one point that workers at quayside canneries carried guns to get themselves safely through the night shift. Things are much tamer now, but exhibits from Astoria's seafaring past are on display at the **Columbia River Maritime Museum**, 1792 Marine Drive (daily 9.30am–5pm; $5).

From Marine Drive, numbered streets climb towards the fancy Victorian mansions of the uptown area. Beyond, on top of Coxcomb Hill, is the **Astoria Column**, coated with a mural depicting the town's early history, and offering superb views. The concrete replica of a Native American burial canoe near the base of the column is a memorial to Chief Comcomly of the Chinook. He was on amiable terms with the first settlers, one of whom married his daughter, until he caught his son-in-law hoeing potatoes (women's work in the chief's opinion). Comcomly's son, on the other hand, is said to have proposed to **Jane Barnes**, a barmaid from Portsmouth who arrived on an English ship in 1814 to become, Astorians claim, the first white woman in the Northwest. Jane turned him down, which wrought havoc with local race relations, but for many years local taverns still nominated honorary barmaids to take part in Jane Barnes Day.

A few miles southwest of town is **Fort Clatsop** (daily: summer 8am–6pm; rest of year 8am–5pm; $2 in summer, otherwise free), a reconstruction of the stockade-cum-winter quarters Lewis and Clark built here in 1808. The visitor center has an outstanding display on the explorers' expedition and is set deep in the forest by the ocean. Further west, also off US-101, **Fort Stevens State Park**, with its trails, camping and miles of beaches, occupies the tapering peninsula that nudges into the mouth of the Columbia. Fortifications were first put up at Fort Stevens to guard against Confederate raiders during the Civil War, though **Battery Russell**, the most significant military relic, was part of its World War II defenses. The fort was shelled one night by a passing Japanese submarine, which makes it, incredibly, the only military installation on the mainland US to have been fired on by a foreign power since 1812.

## Practicalities

Pierce Pacific Stages (☎503/338-6757) operates a once-daily bus service from Portland to Astoria (and subsequently Seaside and Cannon Beach). The **visitor center**, at 111 W Marine Drive (summer daily 8am–6pm; winter Mon–Fri 9am–5pm, Sat & Sun 1–5pm; ☎503/325-6311), is near the base of the US-101 bridge over the Columbia. You can **camp** at Fort Stevens State Park (see above), or stay in one of the mundane **motels** along Marine Drive, but the town's most distinctive offerings are its **B&Bs**, the pick of which occupy splendidly refurbished Victorian mansions. *Franklin St Station*, 1140 Franklin St (☎503/325-4314 or 1-800/448-1098; ④), has seven guestrooms and balconies overlooking the town. *Rosebriar Hotel,* 636 14th St (☎503/325-7427 or 1-800/487-0224; ③), is a renovated 1902 convent with excellent views of the Columbia River.

Downtown has its share of good places to **eat**. *Columbian Cafe*, 1114 Marine Drive (☎503/325-2233), offers gourmet seafood and vegetarian meals, plus a good-value daily special. *Shark Rock Cafe*, 1092 Marine Drive (☎503/325-7720), packs in a loyal crowd with its imaginative menu; while the *Home Spirit Baking Company*, 1585 Exchange (☎503/325-6846), serves hearthstone-baked sourdough and homemade ice cream in a lovely Victorian home.

# Seaside

Seventeen miles down the coast from Astoria, **SEASIDE** is an endearingly tacky family resort, with a long sandy beach paralleled by a concrete walkway known as **The Prom**. It was here that every member of the Lewis and Clark expedition had to take a tedious turn boiling down seawater to make salt – vital to preserve meat for the return journey. The reconstructed **salt works** – a few boulders and pans – are located near the south end of the Prom and there's a commemorative statue of Lewis and Clark halfway along The Prom at the Turnaround traffic circle.

The most expensive **places to stay** are those along The Prom, such as the *Shilo Inn Oceanfront*, 30 N Prom (☎503/738-9571 or 1-800/222-2244; ⑤). Further from the ocean, the *Riverside Inn*, 430 S Holladay Drive (☎503/738-8254 or 1-800/826-6151; ③), officially a B&B, is a good cut above the average motel; the *Mariner Motel*, 429 S Holladay Drive (☎503/738-3690; ②), next door, is less expensive. There's also the *HI-Seaside Hostel*, 930 N Holladay Drive (☎503/738-7911; ①), just four blocks from the ocean. Places to **shop** and **eat** are concentrated along Broadway, which meets The Prom at the Turnaround. Seaside is on the once-daily Pierce Pacific Stages (☎503/338-6757) bus route south from Astoria. The **visitor center** is at 7 N Roosevelt Ave (☎503/738-6391 or 1-800/444-6740).

# Cannon Beach

Nine miles south from Seaside, the more upmarket and pleasant **CANNON BEACH** is at its liveliest during the great annual **Sandcastle Competition**, a one-day event held late May or early June: what Cannes is to film, Cannon Beach is to sandcastle-building, and past themes have included dinosaurs, sphinxes, even the Crucifixion. At heart, though, Cannon Beach remains a sedate and prosperous resort, with a long, wide, sandy beach where the 240ft **Haystack Rock**, a black monolith crowned with nesting seagulls, is accessible at low tide. It's crowded in season; to escape the crush, head four miles north to **Ecola State Park**, where dense conifer forests decorate the basaltic cliffs of Tillamook Head, or south to **Oswald West State Park** where there is a beautiful beach, rocky headland and coastal rainforest. *Oswald West* (☎1-800/551-6949), a tent-only campground popular with surfers, has wheelbarrows to transport your gear to the site.

**Accommodation** is tight, especially at competition time. *Cannon Beach Hotel,* 1116 S Hemlock St (☎503/436-1392; ⑤), is a petite, European-style hotel, while the much-in-demand *Waves Motel* is right on the seafront at 188 W Second St (☎503/436-2205 or 1-800/822-2468; ⑤). For **food**, *Midtown Cafe,* 1235 S Hemlock St (☎503/436-1016) has the best breakfast in town. Down the road *Heather's Cafe,* 271 N Hemlock (☎503/436-9353), does perhaps the best grilled-cheese sandwich on the Oregon coast.

# Lincoln City

There's no avoiding **LINCOLN CITY** if you're driving; probably the ugliest town on the Oregon coast, it sprawls along the highway for seven congested, motel-lined miles. In the unlikely event you decide to stay, there's plenty of cheap **accommodation** to choose from – the **visitor center**, on US-101 (☎541/994-8378 or 1-800/452-2151), has the full list. For somewhere to **eat**, the *Bay House*, 5911 SW US-101 (☎541/996-3222), does fine seafood in a Northwestern style and great desserts.

# Newport

Thirty miles south of Lincoln City, **NEWPORT** is one of several Oregonian fishing towns laboring to turn itself into a resort – more successfully than most, integrating pieces of the past with the more recent development. The place also has an artsy undertone, manifest in a pair of **arts centers** – one performing, the other visual – on long, uncrowded **Nye Beach**. A more traditional attraction is the large and impressive **Oregon Coast Aquarium**, across the river at 2820 SE Ferry Slip Rd (summer daily 9am–6pm; rest of year daily 10am–5pm; $8.50), home to sea otters and seals, the tufted puffin, and all sorts of aquatic species.

The Greyhound station is just off the main drag (US-101) on SW Bayley Street, and the **Chamber of Commerce** is at 555 SW Coast Hwy (☎541/265-8801 or 1-800/262-7844). The best place to **stay** is the *Sylvia Beach Hotel*, perched on a cliff overlooking Nye Beach at 267 NW Cliff St (☎541/265-5428; ①–⑥). An attractive Edwardian building, the hotel is named after the owner of the Shakespeare & Co bookstore in Paris of the Twenties and Thirties, and each of the twenty rooms bears the name of a famous writer; it also has dorm beds and a good restaurant. Less distinctive lodgings include the *Penny Saver Motel*, 710 N Coast Hwy (☎541/265-6631; ③), and the *Puerto Nuevo Inn*, 544 SW US-101 (☎541/265-5767 or 1-800/999-3068; ④). There's a cluster of first-rate **cafes** and **restaurants** in Historic Bayfront along Bay Boulevard, among them the *Whale's Tale* (☎541/265-8660), with a varied menu and occasional live music, and *Mo's Original* (☎541/265-2979) and *Mo's Annex* (☎541/265-7512), two popular seafood restaurants.

## Bandon

Further along, at the mouth of the Coquille River, 20 miles south of industrial Coos Bay, easygoing, likeable **BANDON** (or Bandon-by-the-Sea, as it's known in the brochures) combines old town restoration with a strong New Age presence, making it something of an arts and crafts center. It was originally a Native American settlement, which was swamped by the onset of the Gold Rush. The twentieth century began rather ominously, when townsfolk dynamited Tupper Rock, a sacred tribal site, to build the sea wall, and the town was cursed to burn down three times: it's happened twice so far, in 1914 and 1936, and the superstitious are still waiting.

Bandon's main attraction today is its rugged beach, strewn with unusual rock formations and particularly magnificent in stormy weather, when giant tree stumps are tossed up out of the ocean like matchsticks. In calmer conditions, clammers head off to the mudflats of the river, crabbers gather at the town dock, and the whole scene makes for a delightful stroll.

The **visitor center** is centrally located at 300 SE Second St (☎541/347-9616). There's oceanfront **accommodation** just south of town at the outstanding *Sunset Motel*, 1755 Beach Loop Drive (☎541/347-2453 or 1-800/842-2407; ③–⑦), which comprises motel rooms, condo units and, best of all, seafront cabins – it's well worth paying the extra. In town, the place to stay is the *Sea Star Guest House*, 375 Second St (☎541/347-9632; ③), part of which is given over to the *HI-Sea Star Hostel* (①), which incorporates a friendly cafe. Two blocks away, there's great **seafood** at *Andrea's Old Town Cafe* on Baltimore Street (☎541/347-3022).You can **camp** just north of town at **Bullards Beach State Park** (☎541/347-2209), where the Coquille River Lighthouse stands guard over miles of windswept wilderness.

## South to California

Towns are fewer and farther between as you travel south along US-101, with the coastline at its prettiest beyond **PORT ORFORD** where forested mountains sweep smoothly down to the sea. These mountains mark the western limit of the **Siskiyou**

National Forest, a vast slab of remote wilderness best explored by boat along the turbulent Rogue River from workaday **GOLD BEACH**. The town's **visitor center**, on the main road at 1225 S Ellensburg (☎541/247-7526 or 1-800/525-2334), has details of rafting and powerboat excursions plus prices for the town's various motels and hotels.

# Central and eastern Oregon

Once you cross the Cascades, Oregon, like Washington, grows warmer, drier and wilder; green valleys give way to the high desert with scrubby sageland, juniper trees, bare hills and stark rock formations broken up by the occasional tract of pine forest. The landscape is volcanic and often alien, with cracked lava flows, abrupt cone-like hills, and high craters such as beautiful **Crater Lake** in the south. The east, though seldom visited, can be surprisingly beautiful, the **John Day Fossil Beds** along US-26, and the remote, snowcapped **Wallowa Mountains** overlooking the deep slash of **Hell's Canyon** are both overwhelmingly dramatic landscapes, not to be dismissed.

## Bend and around

**BEND** is easily the most useful base for visiting central Oregon, giving access both to Cascade grandeur and the eerie landscape of Oregon's Lava Lands. Crammed with stylish restaurants, microbreweries and outdoor gear shops, its roots are still firmly set in outdoor pursuits. Greyhound buses from Portland and Eugene arrive a mile or so east of town at Hwy-20. **The Chamber of Commerce** is on Hwy-97, just north of the center (☎541/382-3221 or 1-800/905-2363). **The Central Oregon Welcome Center**, 63085 N US-97 (☎541/389-8799 or 1-800/800-8334) has brochures and accommodation listings.

Budget **motels** – often full – are strung out along the unenticingly modern Third Street (US-97), including the straightforward *Dunes Motel* at no. 1515 NE (☎541/382-6811; ③). However, the compact town center, with its old villas dotting the banks of the Deschutes River, is a much more attractive destination, home to several smart **B&Bs**: try the *Lara House*, 640 NW Congress St (☎541/388-4064; ④), or the slightly pricier *Sather House*, 7 NW Tumalo Ave (☎541/388-1065 or 1-888/388-1065; ④). The *Bend Cascade Hostel*, 19 SW Century Drive (☎541/389-3813; ①), is only a short walk from the free ski shuttle to Mount Bachelor (see below). You can camp in **Tumalo State Park** (☎541/382-3586), a wooded dell by the Deschutes River five miles northwest along US-20.

Bend has some great restaurants and **microbreweries**. *Pine Tavern,* 967 NW Brooks St (☎541/382-5581), *Deschutes Brewery and Public House*, 1044 NE Bond St (☎541/382-9242), and *Bend Brewing,* 1019 NW Brooks St (☎541/383-1599), all serve a wide range of microbrewed ales and stouts and innovative cuisine. *West Side Cafe & Bakery*, 1005 NW Galveston (☎541/382-3426), boasts the best breakfast in town and *Cup of Magic*, 1304 NW Galveston (☎541/330-5539), has great coffee and baked goods.

### Mount Bachelor and the Cascades Lake Highway

The largest ski resort in the Northwest is at **Mount Bachelor** (☎541/382-2442 or 1-800/829-2442), 22 miles southwest of Bend, its Olympic-standard facilities open from mid-November to as late as July, snowfall permitting. Mount Bachelor is also the first stop on the **Cascade Lakes Highway**, known as "Century Drive" – a hundred-mile mountain loop road which gives access to trailheads into the **Three Sisters** or, further south, the **Diamond Peak** wilderness areas, and a sprinkling of campgrounds. Get details from **Deschutes National Forest Ranger Station** at Deschutes, 1645 E Hwy-20 (☎541/388-2715), or Bend, 1230 NE 3rd St (☎541/388-5664).

## The Lava Lands

The so-called **Lava Lands** cover a huge area of central Oregon, though the greatest concentration of sizeable lava formations – neat conical buttes, caves and the frozen forms of trees – is in the Bend area. They date back seven thousand years to the eruptions of Mounts Newberry and Mazama, which dumped enormous quantities of ash and pumice across the region. The **Lava Lands visitor center** (summer daily 9.30am–5pm; ☎541/593-2421; $5) is an excellent source of maps and information on hiking trails; it's eleven miles south of Bend on US-97, near the spectacular dark cinder cone of **Lava Butte**.

A mile south, off US-97, the **Lava River Cave** (summer daily 9am–5pm; $2, plus $1 for a lamp), is a subterranean passage into the volcanic underworld. Most of the lava that created the cave eventually cooled and hardened around the still-molten center of the flow. When this drained away, it left an empty lava tube, over a mile long, discovered only when part of the roof fell in. There are all kinds of formations along the chilly cave, but even if you have a lantern it's hard to see much beyond the next few steps.

## Crater Lake National Park

The Northwest's best-looking volcanic crater, now protected as Oregon's only national park, is just over a hundred miles south of Bend. The shell of Mount Mazama holds the blue, deep and resoundingly beautiful **CRATER LAKE**, formed after an explosion 42 times greater than the Mount St Helens blast (see box, p.1049); the two islands you see in it are the tips of two mini-volcanoes which began to grow again within the hollowed mountaintop. In its snow-covered isolation, the lake, which plunges to a depth of nearly two thousand feet, is awe-inspiring; in summer too it's spectacular, when wild flowers bloom along the severe and desolate rim.

You need a car to get there, though only the southern roads (the US-62 from Medford off of I-5 or Klamath Falls off US-97) are kept open year-round. The northern access road (off Hwy-138) is closed from mid-October to June, as is the spectacular, 33-mile "Rim Drive" around the crater's edge. Regular **boats** cruise the lake (late June–mid-Sept daily 10am–4pm; $12), reached via the sheer, mile-long **Cleetwood Cove trail**, which provides the only access to the lakeshore. The trail is on the north shore, but visitor facilities are clustered on the south at tiny **RIM VILLAGE**, where the summer-only **visitor center** is a few steps from *Crater Lake Lodge* (mid-May–mid-Oct; ☎541/830-8700; ⑥), a grand old lodge that's recently been refurbished at massive expense; ask for a room overlooking the lake – the lodge perches on the rim of the caldera. *Mazama Village* (early June–mid-Oct; ☎541/830-8700; ①–④) is a combined **campground** and **motel** in a quiet wooded setting about seven miles south of the rim. There are also several wilderness campsites. The **park headquarters** are at the Steel Information Center (☎541/594-2211), an all-year facility a couple of miles south of the rim on the main access road.

## Klamath Falls

Just sixty miles to the southeast of Crater Lake, the industrial town of **KLAMATH FALLS** makes an easy day-trip – a useful option if the weather deteriorates in the mountains. It's not particularly pretty, but it does boast the **Flavell Museum**, 125 W Main St (Mon–Sat 9.30am–5.30pm; $4), housing an extraordinary collection of Native American artifacts, and a large collection of Western (frontier) paintings.

Klamath Falls sits in the middle of **Klamath Basin**, whose low-lying lakes and marshes once formed a vast wetland stretching far beyond the Californian border. Much of the basin has been drained for cattle pasture, but six areas are now protected as **national wildlife refuges**, with the resident bird population increased to upwards of a million during spring and fall migrations. The town's **visitor center** at 1451 Main

St in the Klamath County Museum (daily 9am–5pm; ☎541/884-0666), issues detailed maps of the basin and its bird sanctuaries.

## East on US-26: the John Day Fossil Beds

Hwy-140 continues on from Klamath Falls into southeast Oregon, but it's a numbingly boring journey. If instead you follow US-97, then Hwy-126/26 from Bend, you'll emerge from a brief green passage through the **Ochoco National Forest** into a bare, sun-scorched landscape of ochre and beige. Many features of the area are named after **John Day**, an employee of fur trapper John Jacob Astor (see p.1065) who was left behind on the journey out west when he became too exhausted to continue. Remarkably, he recovered just enough to stagger to the Columbia River, where he was promptly robbed of everything he had. His luck finally changed when, lost and naked, he stumbled into a group of trappers who carried him on to Astoria. Of special importance are the **John Day Fossil Beds**, which hold some of the most revealing fossil formations in the US. These were preserved in a layer of volcanic ash as the Cascades sputtered into being, just after the extinction of the dinosaurs.

There are three separate fossil-bed sites, the most westerly of which is the **Painted Hills** unit, six miles off US-26 down a paved side road. Striped in shades of rust and brown, the hills look like sandcastle mounds, the smooth surface quilted with rivulets worn by draining water. Back on US-26, it's a further thirty miles east to the **Sheep Rock** unit, just north of the junction with Hwy-19. Here, the main **visitor center** (Mon–Fri 8am–4.30pm; ☎541/987-2333) is housed in an old cattle rancher's homestead and exhibits a modest selection of recovered fossils. A mile or so further to the north lies the **Blue Basin**, a natural amphitheater where a mile-long trail leads past Perspex-covered fossil exhibits, including a tortoise that hurtled to its death millions of years ago, and a sabre-toothed cat.

### John Day town

The peaceful little village of **DAYVILLE**, nestling in the valley just six miles east of the Sheep Rock unit on US-26, is the best spot to break your journey – though by default rather than merit: the handful of settlements between here and Baker City (see below), some 120 miles to the east, are far from enticing, and Dayville itself has only one place to stay, the *Fish House Inn B&B* (☎541/987-2124; ②).

The largest town along this portion of the US-26 is charmless **JOHN DAY**, whose only noteworthy sight is the fascinating **Kam Wah Chung & Co Museum** (May–Oct Mon–Thurs 9am–noon & 1–5pm, Sat & Sun 1–5pm; $2), once the home-cum-opium den and general store of a famed Chinese herbalist whose mistrust of his white neighbors induced him to heavily reinforce his doors and windows.

### Baker City

In the forested foothills east of John Day, US-26 turns southeast for the long run down to Idaho. Much more enjoyable is the far shorter drive on Hwy-7 through the southern reaches of the **Wallowa-Whitman National Forest** to the more substantial redbrick community of **BAKER CITY**, which flourished during the Gold Rush and now ticks over as the commercial center for the surrounding cattle lands. The **National Historic Oregon Trail Interpretive Center** (May–Sept daily 9am–6pm; Oct–April daily 9am–4pm; ☎541/523-1843; free) at **Flagstaff Hill**, five well-signposted miles east of town, was built to commemorate the 150th anniversary of the trail in 1993. As well as first-rate audiovisual displays, the complex has over four miles of original trails featuring some well-preserved wagon ruts and other points of interest. Back in town, the **Oregon Trail Regional Museum**, at Grove and Campbell (May–Oct daily 10am–4pm;

$1.50), has some artifacts from pioneer days, including good Native American pieces, but is more notable for its massive collection of rocks and semiprecious stones glowing under an ultraviolet light.

Baker's Main Street possesses a string of handsome early twentieth-century buildings, but the bulk of the available **accommodation** is on the peripheries of town in routine motels dotted along Tenth or Campbell: the *Quality Inn*, 810 Campbell St (☎541/523-2242 or 1-800/228-5151; ③), and the *Eldorado Inn*, 695 Campbell St (☎541/523-6494 or 1-800/537-5756; ③), are typical. The vast Wallowa-Whitman National Forest, which stretches both to the east and west of Baker City, is sprinkled with **campgrounds**; details from the **visitor center**, 490 Campbell St, beside I-84's exit 304 (☎541/523-3356 or 1-800/523-1235). **Restaurants** along Main Street include the cheap *Front Street Cafe* at no. 1840 (☎541/523-0223) and the popular, but predictable, *Brass Parrot* at no. 2190 (☎541/523-4266). Greyhound, 515 Campbell St, and Amtrak, 2803 Broadway, both run to Portland.

## North on I-84: La Grande and Pendleton

The **Grande Ronde Valley**, north of Baker City on I-84 through cattle-grazing rangeland, is large, round, flat and rimmed by mountains. Now mostly drained to become farmland, this was once a marsh, fatally boggy to pioneer wagons, forcing the Oregon Trail to keep to the higher but tougher ground around the hills as it headed northwest towards the Blue Mountains.

### THE OREGON TRAIL

Between the 1840s and 1870s, upwards of a quarter of a million Americans journeyed by wagon train from the Midwest to Oregon in search of a new start. Ever since Lewis and Clark completed their successful reconnaisance of the Oregon Country (as the coastal region between Russian Alaska and Spanish California was then known) in 1806, both politicians and prospective settlers were keen to see their country expand from coast to coast.

The first migrants – or **movers** – were also inspired by the missionaries who went to Christianize the "Indians" in the 1830s, and sent back glowing reports of the region's fine climate, fertile soil, dense forests, fish-rich rivers and absence of malaria.

With the promise of generous land grants on offer, in spring 1843 over one thousand would-be migrants gathered at Independence and Westport on the banks of the Missouri, to prepare for the **"Great Migration."** The pioneers were a remarkably homogenous bunch, nearly all experienced farmers, traveling with their families in ox-pulled wagons with flimsy canvas roofs.

Traversing almost two thousand miles of modern Missouri, Nebraska, Wyoming and Idaho, the movers cajoled their wagons across rivers, over mountain passes and through virgin forests, pausing at the occasional army frontier fort or missionary station to recuperate, and bartering supplies with Native Americans in return for rafts and local knowledge. After three months on the trail, they arrived at what is now the town of The Dalles. From here they had a difficult choice to make before they reached the lush Willamette Valley: either build rafts and risk the swirling currents of the Columbia River or take the hazardous Barlow Trail around Mount Hood, notorious for its swiftly changing weather.

Over the next thirty years further waves of settlers swelled the population of the Willamette Valley by some fifty thousand, with others moving into Washington and California. The migration spawned a minor industry of specialist supply companies and wagon builders, and the traffic on the trail was such that the route was miles wide in parts. Inevitably, there are precious few surviving signs of the passing of the migrants, but they are commemorated by a handful of museums, the best of which is outside Baker City, where you can still see the deep ruts made by their wagon wheels.

The hub of the valley is **LA GRANDE**, a simple lumber-and-railroad town linked with Portland by Greyhound and Amtrak. The **Chamber of Commerce**, 1912 Fourth St (☎541/963-8588 or 1-800/848-9969), has maps and information. Inexpensive **motels** include the *Greenwell Motel*, 305 Adams Ave (☎541/963-4134 or 1-800/772-0991; ②), and the *Royal Motor Inn*, 1510 Adams Ave (☎541/963-4154 or 1-800/990-7575; ②). **Restaurants** also line up on Adams Avenue; *Mamacita's*, off Adams Avenue at 110 Depot St (☎541/963-6223), is best for Mexican food.

### Pendleton

From La Grande, I-84 follows the route of the Oregon Trail northwest to **PENDLE-TON**. Stetsons and pick-up trucks proliferate in this quintessential Western town, befitting its status as home of the immensely popular annual four-day **Pendleton Round-Up** in mid-September, which combines traditional rodeo with extravagant pageantry; tickets can be had from the Round-Up Association, PO Box 609, Pendleton, OR 97801 (☎541/276-2553 or 1-800/45-RODEO; $8–15 per rodeo session). The **Round-Up Hall of Fame**, on Court Avenue at the rodeo grounds (summer Mon–Fri 1–4pm; free), is stuffed with associated memorabilia.

The hugely enjoyable **Pendleton Underground**, 37 SW Emigrant at First Street (Mon–Sat 9am–5pm; $10), is a tour of the town's extensive network of subterranean passageways, used during Prohibition as saloons, card rooms and brothels, and as a refuge for the area's much-abused Chinese population.

Pendleton's **Chamber of Commerce** is at 501 S Main St (Mon–Fri 9am–5pm; ☎541/276-7411 or 1-800/547-8911), a short walk from the Greyhound station. Accommodation options include the no-frills *Long Horn Motel*, 411 SW Dorion Ave (☎541/276-7531; ②), and the similarly plain *Chaparral Motel*, 620 SW Tutuilla St (☎541/276-8654; ②). Book early at Round-Up time.

## Joseph and the Wallowa Mountains

The **Wallowa Mountains**, reached by leaving I-84 at La Grande and heading east on Hwy-82, make up one of eastern Oregon's loveliest and least-discovered areas. Set at the northern tip of glacially carved Wallowa Lake, the mountains rearing behind, the tiny town of **JOSEPH** is a perfect spot to spend the night. **Motels** such as the *Indian Lodge Motel*, 201 S Main St (☎541/432-2651; ③), are inexpensive, but for just a little more money the friendly *Chandlers' Bed, Bread and Trail Inn*, 700 S Main St (☎541/432-9765; ④), offers a big morning feed. Also on the main street are lots of antique and craft stores and the small **Wallowa County Museum** (officially daily in summer 10am–5pm; but in practice less often; donation), where the story of the Nez Percé (see p.799) is detailed alongside an attic-like collection of pioneer bits and pieces.

A mile or so south of Joseph, mountain-rimmed **Wallowa Lake** is supposedly inhabited by a Native American version of the Loch Ness monster. At its far end, the state park has **camping**, and the **Mount Howard cable car** whisks visitors to the top of the mountain, where short trails lead to magnificent overlooks (June–Aug daily 10am–4pm; weekends only in May & Sept; $12). Much of the mountain scenery behind Joseph belongs to the **Eagle Cap Wilderness**, whose lakes, streams and peaks are accessible only along trails (no roads). Backcountry hiking and camping here really is remote – contact the **Wallowa-Whitman National Forest Office** by Hwy-82 in Enterprise (☎541/426-5546) for details of the Eagle Cap and Hell's Canyon (see below).

## Hell's Canyon

East of Joseph, along the Idaho border, the Snake River has gouged the deepest canyon on the continent, a thousand feet deeper than the Grand Canyon, with the Seven Devils mountains rising behind and the river glimmering in its depths. **Hell's Canyon** is what's known as a low-relief canyon, edged by a series of gradually ascending false peaks – so it doesn't have the overwhelming impact of the steep-walled Grand Canyon. This used to be a winter retreat for the Nez Percé: stone tools and rock carvings have been found at several old village sites.

The canyon and its immediate environs are now preserved as the **Hell's Canyon National Recreation Area**: deer, otters, mink, black bears, mountain lions and elk live here, along with rattlesnakes and black widow spiders. Mechanical vehicles are banned above water-level in much of the canyon (boats along the Snake are allowed), so you can only explore on foot or horseback. The forest roads that skirt the recreation area tend to be rough and slippery, and many are closed by snow for much of the year: if you intend to use them, check with the **rangers** in Enterprise (☎541/426-5546) or Baker City (☎541/523-6391) before you set out; bear in mind also that high-summer temperatures in the canyon regularly reach 100°F.

Of the two ways to approach the canyon from Oregon, the first and more difficult begins in Joseph. From here, Little Sheep Creek Highway leads to **IMNAHA** where a narrow and extremely precipitous, graveled Forest Service road leads to the ultimate view from **Hat Point**, the site of a campground and lookout tower. Beyond Hat Point, the road fades into a trail that leads down to the bottom of the canyon, but to undertake this trek you must be very fit and properly equipped. The second (and much easier) approach is at the south end of the canyon, along Hwy-86 east from Baker City. On the way, tiny tin-roofed **HALFWAY** makes a good stop-off, with rooms at *Halfway Motel*, 170 S Main St (☎541/742-5722; ②), and the rural *Clear Creek Farm B&B* (☎541/742-2238; call for directions from the town; ③).

Pressing on from Halfway, Hwy-86 winds towards the canyon, meeting the Snake River at Oxbow Dam, where a rough Forest Service road leads on to Hell's Canyon Dam, the launching-point for jet boat and raft trips through the canyon. Hell's Canyon Adventures Inc (☎541/785-3352 or 1-800/422-3568; reservations required) and other companies run sightseeing **tours** in summer, costing from $30 per person for a two-hour trip. Skimming over whitewater rapids, the boats take you between the deceptively low, bare hills, to an old pioneer homestead. They also operate a "drop-off" service, taking you to hiking trails along the canyon and picking you up either the same day or later in the week (fee from $25 per person).

# CHAPTER FIFTEEN

# ALASKA

N o other region in North America possesses the mythical aura of **ALASKA**; even the name – a derivation of *Alayeska*, an Athabascan word meaning "great land of the west" – fires the imagination. Few who see this land of gargantuan ice fields, sweeping tundra, glacially excavated valleys, lush rainforests, deep fjords and occasionally smoking volcanoes leave unimpressed. **Wildlife** may be under threat elsewhere, but here it is abundant, with grizzly bears standing twelve feet tall, moose stopping traffic in downtown Anchorage, wolves prowling through national parks, bald eagles circling over the forests and fifty-pound-plus salmon leaping upstream.

The sheer size of Alaska is hard to comprehend: America's **northernmost, westernmost** and, because the Aleutian Islands stretch across the 180th meridian, its **easternmost** state would, if superimposed onto the "Lower 48" (the rest of the continental United States) stretch from the Atlantic to the Pacific. This vast expanse covers more than double the area of Texas, and its coastline is longer than the rest of the US combined. All but three of the nation's twenty highest peaks are found within its boundaries and one glacier alone is twice the size of Wales.

A mere 600,000 people live in this huge state – over forty percent of them in **Anchorage** – of whom only one-fifth were born here. As a rule of thumb, the more winters you have endured, the more Alaskan you are, and recent arrivals are known by the mildly abusive nickname of *cheechako*. Often referred to as the **"Last Frontier,"** Alaska in many ways mirrors the American West of the nineteenth century: an endless, undeveloped space in which to stake one's claim and set up a life without interference. Or at least that's how Alaskans would like it to be. Throughout this century tens of thousands have been lured by the promise of wealth, first by gold and then by fishing, logging and, most recently, oil. However, Alaska's 86,000 **Native peoples**, who don't have the option of returning to the Lower 48 if things don't work out, have been greatly marginalized, though Native corporations set up as a result of pre-pipeline land deals have increasing economic clout.

Traveling around Alaska still demands a spirit of adventure. To make the most of the state you need to have an enthusiasm for striking out on your own, and to be prepared to rough it. If you plan to camp, you'll need the best possible gear. Binoculars are an absolute must, as, rather more mundanely, is bug spray; the **mosquito** is referred to as the "Alaska state bird" and only a repellent with 100 percent DEET keeps it away. On top of that, of course, there's the **climate**, though Alaska is far from

## ACCOMMODATION PRICE CODES

All accommodation prices in this book have been coded using the symbols below. Note that prices are for the least expensive double rooms in each establishment. For a full explanation see p.37 in Basics.

| | | |
|---|---|---|
| ① up to $30 | ④ $60–80 | ⑦ $130–175 |
| ② $30–45 | ⑤ $80–100 | ⑧ $175–250 |
| ③ $45–60 | ⑥ $100–130 | ⑨ $250+ |

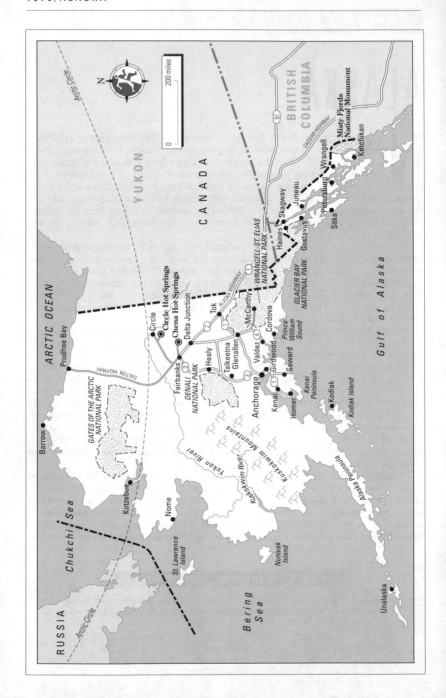

the popular misconception of being one big icebox. While winter temperatures of -40°F in Fairbanks are commonplace and northern towns like Barrow see no sunlight for nearly three months each year, its most touristed areas, the southeast and the Kenai Peninsula, enjoy a maritime climate (45–65°F in summer) similar to that of the rest of the Pacific Northwest, meaning much more rain (in some towns 180-plus inches per year) than snow. Remarkably, the summer temperature in the Interior often reaches 80°F.

Experiencing Alaska on a low budget is possible, but requires a lot of planning. The peak period of June to August sees crazy room prices; May and particularly September, when tariffs are relaxed and the weather only slightly chillier, are just as good times to go, and in April or October you'll have the place to yourself, albeit with a smaller range of places to stay and eat. Except for around forty summertime **hostels**, mostly in the major towns or popular regions, there's little budget accommodation; ground **transportation**, despite the long distances, is less expensive, with backpacker shuttles ferrying budget travelers between major centers; but **eating** and **drinking** are at least twenty percent more expensive than in the Lower 48, and perhaps fifty percent in more remote regions. **Winter**, when hotels drop their prices by as much as half, is becoming an increasingly popular time to visit, particularly for the dazzling **aurora borealis**.

## Some history

Alaska has been inhabited for longer than anywhere else in the Americas; it was here, across the broad plains of the "land bridge" that is now submerged below the Bering Sea, that humans first reached the "New World," most likely around 14,000 years ago. These first settlers can be classified into four groups, which lived within well-defined regions until whites arrived. The **Aleut**, in the inhospitable Aleutian Islands, built underground homes and hunted sea mammals such as walrus for food and clothing, while the nomadic **Athabascan** herded caribou in the Interior. The warrior **Tlingit** lived in the warmer coastal regions of the southeast, where food was plentiful, in contrast to the **Eskimos** (or, more correctly, Yup'ik and Inupiak), who inhabited the northwestern coast, living off fish and larger marine life.The famed **igloo** ice houses were almost unknown in Alaska, and where they existed were used only as temporary lodging during hunts. Descendants of all these groups remain in Alaska today; a few live in much the same way as their ancestors, though most have been integrated into the modern American way through conquest, rape, marriage and religion.

In 1741, Danish explorer, **Vitus Bering**, working for the Tsar of Russia, sailed into Prince William Sound and became the first Caucasian to set foot on Alaskan soil. He died before he could return to Russia, but his crew reported huge numbers of fur seals and **sea otters** – whose pelts were ideal for making hats – in Alaska's coastal waters. Russians, and later Britons and Spaniards, joined in the ensuing slaughter, both of the otters and the Aleut, who were enslaved and forced to hunt on behalf of the fur traders. By 1799 the Russians had established their Alaskan capital at present-day Sitka, pushed down the coast as far as northern California and, in the process, decimated the sea otter colonies.

During the 1860s, when Russia experienced a recession, it proposed the sale of its lands to America. On October 18, 1867, Secretary of State William Seward purchased Alaska for $7,200,000 – less than 2¢ per acre. Although the unpopular deal was referred to as "**Seward's Folly**" or "Seward's Icebox," Alaska soon turned out to be a literal **gold mine**. Gold was discovered in 1880 at Juneau, eighteen years later near Nome on the Bering Strait, and subsequently outside Fairbanks in 1902. With logging companies and commercial fishing operations also descending upon Alaska, the government began to take a more active interest in its affairs. In 1912 the Territory of Alaska was set up, and in 1959 it became the 49th state.

In 1942, after the Japanese bombed Dutch Harbor and occupied two of the Aleutian Islands, the huge **US military** build-up that was to last all through the Cold War began with the construction of the Alaska Highway to link the state with the rest of America. Alaska's next boom followed the discovery of oil at Prudhoe Bay on the Arctic Ocean, and fortune-seekers headed to Alaska in the mid-1970s to construct and work on the **trans-Alaska pipeline**, which runs to Valdez on Prince William Sound. Today, despite price fluctuations, Alaska still derives about eighty percent of its wealth from oil and gas; indeed, each resident receives an annual dividend check of $1000 or so. But the state is still in economic transition and continues to be prone to extreme boom-and-bust cycles. The once lucrative fishing and lumber industries are fast giving way to tourism as the state's second most important source of income, and the ethical question of how best to use Alaskan lands in the future has led to bitter controversy.

Alaska is so thinly populated that the single telephone area code ☎907 is used throughout the state, and must precede the number when dialing outside the immediate local area.

# Getting to Alaska

Alaska is a long way from the rest of the United States, and whichever way you get there is going to be **expensive**. Once you accept that, however, there is no question as to which is the most **enjoyable** method – the memorable sea trip on the Alaska Marine Highway.

### By air
Anchorage is no longer the major air crossroads it once was, but it's still easy to **fly** to Alaska. It is, however, very expensive. Most but not all flights from the Lower 48 are routed through Seattle. The most frequent service from the West Coast is operated by Alaska Airlines/ERA Aviation (☎1-800/426-0333; *www.alaskaair.com*), whose money-saving package enables you to fly to towns like Juneau, Sitka, Cordova and Fairbanks at little extra cost. Round-trip fares from Seattle are around $500, but occasional deals turn up for as little as $199. Better still, foreigners traveling from outside North America can make use of Alaska Airlines' pre-purchased "Best of the West" airpass (see p.1080) and fly LA–Anchorage for $149 each way.

### By sea – the Alaska Marine Highway
The ferries of the state-run **Alaska Marine Highway** cover many areas unreachable by car, currently operating in two separate regions with an occasional "inter-tie" trip linking them. The most popular route, in the **southeast**, runs for more than a thousand miles from Bellingham, Washington, just north of Seattle, through a wonderland of pristine waters, towering glaciers and untouched forests to Skagway, at the northern end of **the Inside Passage**. Stops on the principal route are Ketchikan, Wrangell, Petersburg, Juneau and Skagway, though many other communities, including Sitka, are served by smaller ferries in the fleet. The whole trip takes three days and costs $246 for walk-on passengers, $581 for a small car, $208 for a motorbike and $40 for "other means of transportation" which covers bicycles and canoes. It is possible to sleep – and even to pitch a tent – on the "solarium," a covered, heated upper deck, while a two-berth cabin costs from $227. The **southwest** ferry system, which charges slightly higher fares, connects the Kenai Peninsula and Prince William Sound to the Aleutians. The new Kennicott ferry now links the two systems by running between Juneau and Seward once a month in summer.

While the ferry is a bargain for foot passengers prepared to rough it, an extended voyage with vehicle and an overnight cabin becomes very expensive. If you're driving up from the Lower 48, consider boarding a ferry at Prince Rupert in British Columbia, a day's drive north of Seattle. This saves the cost of an extra two days at sea from Bellingham without missing out on any of the natural spectacle.

For **information** on either route, contact the Alaska Marine Highway System, PO Box 25535, Juneau, AK 99802-5535 (☎907/465-3941; or call the countrywide central reservations line: ☎1-800/642-0066). Book ahead in summer; standby space is available, but such passengers risk being off-loaded at each port of call.

### By road

For many people, the drive up to Alaska through Canada is one of the major highlights of a visit to the state. Originally built by the military in just eight months, the **Alaska Highway**, which can be accessed from Washington, Idaho and Montana, used to consist of 1520 fearsome miles of dirt, gravel, steep descents and thick mud. These days all but a small section of the route is paved, with sufficient service stations, campgrounds and hotels along the way, but it remains as beautiful as ever, and still demands a spirit of adventure from drivers who attempt it.

The unwieldy *Milepost* (Vernon Publications; $24) provides comprehensive mile-by-mile information on the Alaska Highway and all roads within Alaska, but almost exclusively plugs its advertisers – unless you're traveling the Alaska Highway, it's a rather bulky luxury.

No direct **buses** run to Alaska, though for around $380 in total you can hop on a Greyhound in Seattle, and, after a few transfers, reach Whitehorse in the Yukon, from where local companies such as Alaskon Express continue to Haines or Skagway in the southeast, or on the longer haul to Fairbanks and Anchorage. Green Tortoise (see p.26) runs a month-long trip ($1500 plus $250 for food) each July from San Francisco traveling up the Inside Passage and around the Alaskan roads before flying back.

## Getting around Alaska

Getting around Alaska on the cheap can be tough; **public transportation** is limited, and many areas are only accessible by boat or plane, which is quick and convenient but invariably pricey. **Hitching** is hard work, simply due to the lack of traffic, but, with enough time, it can be done, and is more acceptable, and safer, here than elsewhere.

**Anchorage** is very much the hub of Alaska; **buses** run from the city to Haines and Skagway via Whitehorse, Yukon (see above), and also to Denali, Fairbanks, Valdez and the Kenai Peninsula (Seward Bus Line; ☎907/224-3608; and Kachemak Bay Transport ☎1-877/235-9101). The "big city" is also the base for tour operators such as Gray Line of Alaska (☎1-800/544-2206).

---

**THE ALASKA PASS**

If you are planning to keep up a frenetic pace you may make savings by buying an **Alaska Pass** (*www.alaskapass.com*), which allows unlimited surface transport on participating ferries, trains and buses throughout Alaska and Yukon Territory. There are two types of Alaska Pass: one is valid for a number of **consecutive days of travel** (8 days for $499, 15 days for $699, 22 days for $799 and 30 days for $949); the **Alaska Pass Flexible** covers a number of travel days over a longer period (12 days in a 21-day period for $729 or 21 days in a 45-day period for $999). Contact PO Box 351, Vashon, WA 98070-1351 (☎206/463-6550 or 1-800/248-7598; UK ☎0800/898285).

The **Alaska Railroad**, constructed between 1915 and 1923 to transport supplies to the mines in the Interior, runs nearly five hundred miles north from Seward on the Kenai Peninsula through Anchorage to Fairbanks. Another service from Anchorage to Whittier connects with ferries to Valdez.

Visitors intending to **drive** around Alaska should bring an **emergency kit**, particularly essential in winter, as traffic can be sparse even on major routes. Conditions on the roads can change rapidly – for information, call ☎907/243-7675. Avalanches are a serious threat, as are collisions with wild animals, especially moose. Drivers unused to gravel roads should keep to speeds below 50mph, as sliding out on bends or hard braking often mean losing control.

Travel by **plane** is not always more expensive than other methods, especially if you can map out your itinerary in advance with the state's largest operator, Alaska Airlines (☎1-800/426-0333), which flies to most major communities and uses subcontractors such as ERA Aviation (☎907/683-2574) to get to bush towns in the Interior, or LAB (☎907/789-9160 or 1-800/426-0543) to communities in the southeast. If you are traveling from outside North America, consider pre-purchasing an Alaska Airlines "Best of the West" **airpass** which allows you to reserve up to ten one-way flights either within Alaska ($99 each leg), or from outside the state (essentially Seattle or LA to Anchorage; $149), or any combination of these.

For short-haul flights, **chartering a plane** might sound extravagant but can actually be an inexpensive alternative for groups of four or more, and in remote parts may be the only option. Many travelers get nervous after hearing stories about **bush planes**, which serve remote communities. Sure they can be scary at times: Alaskan conditions are demanding and accidents do happen, but remember that the pilot wants to crash just as much as you do. A trip on a light aircraft can be the crowning glory of an Alaskan vacation.

Now that there's a link between Bellingham all the way to Seward (see p.1078) the **Alaska Marine Highway** is an even more practical and enjoyable way of exploring the towns lining the Gulf of Alaska; as it's bound to become popular with local drivers looking to avoid the four-day drive to the lower states, book ahead to be sure of a place.

# Southeast Alaska

**Southeast Alaska** – also known as the panhandle – may lack the vast openness of the Interior, but the fjords, mountains, glaciers and thick conifer forests lining the **Inside Passage** are awesome in their own right. All of its communities have their economic base in lumber, fishing and tourism and are set amid magnificent scenery. The state's southernmost town, **Ketchikan**, rich in native heritage, makes a pretty introduction, tiny **Wrangell** emits a pioneer air, while **Petersburg** and **Sitka** retain the respective influence of Norway and Russia. Further north are swanky **Juneau**, the capital; **Haines**, with its mix of old-timers and arty newcomers; and **Skagway**, at the northern end of the Inside Passage and thoroughly redolent of the old gold-mining days.

Although this six-hundred-mile panhandle, looking out towards over a thousand rugged islands, can take months to explore, it holds surprisingly few "sights." With the exception of the **Mendenhall Glacier**, many of the most beautiful spots are expensive jaunts – none more so than **Glacier Bay National Park**.

The region's first settlers, the **Tlingit** (*Hlin-git*),were joined somewhat violently by Russian expansionists at the end of the eighteenth century. A steady stream of free-lance profiteers, keen on tapping the region's gold, fur, fish and lumber, soon followed, and today its small communities resound with tales of endurance, folly and cruelty.

By far the best way to travel is on **Marine Highway ferries**, though at some stage make sure you take a **floatplane** ride. No roads connect the major towns except

Haines and Skagway, which are linked to the US highway system after long drives through British Columbia. For a true outdoor adventure, you can rent a **cabin** in the huge Tongass National Forest – which encompasses most of southeast Alaska – for $25 per night; details from the visitor centre in Juneau (see p.1084) or Ketchikan (see below).

# Ketchikan and around

**KETCHIKAN**, the sole community on Revillagigedo Island, five hundred miles north of Seattle, likes to be known as Alaska's "first city." As the first port of call for many cruise ships, its historic downtown, wedged between the waters of the Tongass Narrows and forested Deer Mountain, becomes saturated in summer with elderly tourists. But beyond the souvenir shopping it can be a delight, built into steep hills and partly propped on wooden pilings, with boardwalks and wooden staircases common thoroughfares, and totem poles dotted throughout.

White settlers reached Ketchikan in the early 1880s. By 1886 the first of dozens of canneries had opened in what was soon to be the "salmon capital of the world." Tall forests of cedar, hemlock and spruce, which had provided timber for Tlingit homes and totems, also fed the town's sawmills. The timber and fishing industries have declined, and with the closure of the antiquated pulp mill in 1997 the town's economy is in a state of flux.

The state's fourth largest city is a strong contender for the nation's wettest; annual precipitation averages 165 inches. The tourist board shrugs it off as "liquid sunshine" and, indeed, Ketchikan's perennial drizzle and sporadic showers won't spoil your visit.

## Arrival and information

Alaska Marine Highway **ferries** (☎907/465-3941 or 1-800/642-0066) dock two miles north of downtown on Tongass Highway; city **buses** stop here every 40 minutes until 9.30pm. On the other side of the Narrows is the **airport**, served by Alaska Airlines, linked to town by half-hourly ferries ($2.50). The renovated **visitor center** stands downtown at 131 Front St (Mon–Fri 8am–5pm or when a cruise ship's in; ☎907/225-6166 or 1-800/770-3300; *www.visit-ketchikan.com*). Close by, on Main Street, is the **Southeast Alaska Visitor Center** (summer daily 8am–5pm; rest of year Tues–Sat only; ☎907/225-3101; *www.fs.fed.us/r10/ketchikan;* $4 in summer, otherwise free), one of the town's "must-sees," a striking cedar-framed building housing an absorbing display of the region's natural habitats, native culture and natural resources.

**Bikes** can be rented from The Pedalers at 330 Spruce Mill Way (☎907/225-0440), on the dock behind the information center. Scores of companies run **sightseeing excursions**, among them Alaska Sourdough Tours (☎907/225-4081) which takes you around town and to the two major totem pole sites at Saxman and Totem Bight. Island Wings (☎907/225-2444 or 1-888/854-2444), Promech Air (☎907/225-4845) and Taquan Air (☎907/225-8800 or 1-800/770-8800) offer **floatplane** trips from just $60, while Southeast Sea Kayaks (☎907/225-1258 or 1-800/287-1607) or Southeast Exposure, 507 Stedman St (☎907/225-8829), will take you **sea kayaking** along the fjords; a six-hour trip costs around $80 with day rental for experienced paddlers from $40.

### Accommodation

**Hotels** in Ketchikan vary widely; Ketchikan Reservation Service (☎907/247-5337 or 1-800/247-5337) can arrange accommodation as well as car rentals and tours. The closest **campgrounds** to town are in the attractive Ward Lake Recreation Area, five miles northwest of the ferry terminal.

**HI-Ketchikan**, in the United Methodist Church, 400 Main St (☎907/225-3319). Very basic youth hostel with beds for $8, June–Aug only. ①.

**Innside Passage B&B**, above the main road just north of town (☎907/247-3700). Rooms and apartments close to the ferries, with good views across the Narrows. ④–⑥.

**The New York Hotel**, 207 Stedman St (☎907/225-0246). Nicely restored eight-room hotel with a good cafe overlooking the small-boat harbor. ⑤.

**Shoreline B&B**, 5237 Shoreline Drive (☎907/225-5233). Large home two miles north of town, looking right over the Narrows. ④.

## The Town

The bulk of Ketchikan's historic buildings lie on **Creek Street**, a rickety-looking boardwalk along Ketchikan Creek. This was a red-light district until 1954; now all the former houses of ill-repute are given over to giftshops and arty cafes. Dolly's House, 24 Creek St, once the home and workplace of Dolly Arthur, the town's most famous madam, is now a small museum stuffed with saucy memorabilia (hours vary; $3).

While most of the totem poles you see around town are replicas, the **Totem Heritage Center**, 601 Deermount St (Mon–Sat 8am–5pm, Sun 9am–4pm; $2, free Sun noon–4pm and winter), exhibits a few genuine nineteenth-century examples, recovered from abandoned Native villages. Fourteen of the best replica totem poles and a rebuilt tribal house stand in **Totem Bight State Park**, breathtakingly set on a forested strip of coast overlooking the Narrows, ten miles north of town on the Tongass Highway. The Tlingit-run **Saxman Totem Park**, three miles south of town, displays the world's largest standing collection of poles and an authentic tribal house. Admission, including a chance to see sculptors at work, is free, but full **guided tours** will help to decipher the images (daily 8.30am–5pm; $15–35). On the way back from Totem Bight, take some time out to do the easy but enjoyable boardwalk trail up to **Perseverance Lake**, starting at Ward Cove, four miles north of town.

A Marine Highway ferry (almost daily during summer) connects Ketchikan with Prince of Wales Island, less than fifty miles west, where 650 miles of dirt road make for superb explorations by 4WD or mountain bike. There's nowhere to stay in **Hollis**, the ferry terminal, some forty miles east of the main town of **CRAIG**; if you don't have transportation, ask about the current status of the shuttle van service before setting off.

## Misty Fjords National Monument

Twenty-two miles east of Ketchikan on the mainland, the awe-inspiring **MISTY FJORDS NATIONAL MONUMENT** consists of 2.3 million acres of deep fjords flanked by sheer 3000ft glacially scoured walls topped by dense rainforest. As befits its name, the monument is at its most atmospheric when swathed in low-lying mists. No roads lead here, but the kayak and floatplane operators listed overleaf all do. Fly-in/cruise-out tours are run by Alaska Cruises (☎907/225-6044 or 1-800/225-1905; $185). Fourteen rustic cabins are rented out by the Forest Service (☎907/225-3101; ①).

## Eating and drinking

Inexpensive **food** in Ketchikan tends to be rather good, a rare combination in Alaska. The place is also renowned for its hard **drinking**. Steer clear of the *First City Tavern*, a favorite with commercial fishers and cannery workers eager to forget the sight and smell of raw fish.

**Annabelle's Keg & Chowder House**, 326 Front St (☎907/225-6009). Classy but relaxed atmosphere. Good espresso, sourdough pancakes and seafood.

**Cape Fox**, Westmark Lodge, 800 Venetia Way (☎907/225-8001). Accessed via a fixed tram above Creek Street, this is the town's latest upmarket eating venue.

**Chico's**, 435 Dock St (☎907/225-2833). Great Mexican food and pizza, dinners starting at $9.

**Diaz Chinese Restaurant**, 335 Stedman St (☎907/225-2257). Good-value, tasty Filipino dishes.

**5 Star Cafe**, 5 Creek St (☎907/247-7827). Popular with an arty crowd who come to sip great coffee and munch on the tasty health-oriented fare.

**Potlatch Bar**, 126 Thomas St (☎907/225-4855). Lively, no-frills pub by the small-boat harbor.

**Steamers**, 76 Front St (☎907/225-1600). Locally popular restaurant opposite the cruise-ship dock with great views and seafood to match – not to mention a well-stocked bar with a plethora of beers on tap.

## Wrangell and Petersburg

**WRANGELL**, the second stop on the Marine Highway system and, with a population of just 2600, altogether quieter than Ketchikan, has a distinctly old-fashioned feel. Right in the busy harbor, accessible by a short boardwalk, **Chief Shakes Island** holds an excellent collection of totem poles and a replica tribal house filled with Tlingit blankets. The ancient rock carvings at **Petroglyph Beach**, a mile north of town on Evergreen Road, which date back as far as 7500 years, are only obscured during high tide.

**Ferries** dock right in town and usually stop over long enough to allow explorations of Chief Shakes Island. The **airport**, with daily connections to other Southeastern towns, is a mile and a half north of town. The nearest **campground** is at **City Park**, two miles south on Zimovia Highway. Of **motels**, the comfortable *Thunderbird* at 223 Front St (☎907/874-3322; ④) is the least expensive option. The First Presbyterian Church at 220 Church St sometimes runs a summer-only **hostel** in town (☎907/874-3534; ①). You'll find the **visitor center** (Mon–Fri 10am–4pm; ☎907/874-3901) inside the *Sitkine Inn* on Front Street; if it's closed pick up a free *Wrangell Guide* from the ferry terminal or the museum.

One of the highlights of an Inland Passage ferry ride is sitting up front watching the boat negotiate the 46 tight turns of the 22-mile-long **Wrangell Narrows**. At times it feels like you can reach out and touch the steep-walled shore, and the whole deal is even more spectacular at night when the channel is floodlit. Cruise ships can't squeeze through the Narrows, thus saving the pretty fishing town of **PETERSBURG**, at the north end, invariably referred to as "Alaska's Little Norway," their hit-and-run attentions. The best times to come are during the summer halibut season, when the largest fleet in the nation takes to the sea, and the annual **Little Norway Festival** (held the weekend nearest Norwegian Independence Day, May 17). In the absence of budget **accommodation** scooped up by summertime cannery workers, choices include the 33-room *Scandia House*, 110 N Nordic Drive (☎907/772-4281 or 1-800/722-5006; ④), and *Nordic House B&B*, 806 S Nordic Drive (☎907/772-3620; *www.nordichouse.net*; ⑤). For **food**, the excellent *Pellerito's Pizza*, opposite the ferry terminal (☎907/772-3662), and the health-food-oriented *Helse Cafe*, Sing Lee Alley, downtown (☎907/772-3444), are recommended. The **visitor center** is at First and Fram (Mon–Fri 8am–5pm, Sat 9am–5pm, Sun noon–4pm; ☎907/772-4636).

## Juneau

The sophisticated and vibrant city of **JUNEAU** is unlike any other state capital in the nation. Accessible only by sea or air, it is exceptionally picturesque, hard against the **Gastineau Channel**, with steep, narrow roads clawing up into the rainforested hills behind. Gold features heavily in its history. In 1880, two prospectors – one of them Joe Juneau – made **Alaska's first gold strike** in the rainforest along the banks of the Gastineau Channel. Named Gold Creek, the camp grew rapidly. Until the last mine was shut down in 1944, this was the world's largest producer of low-grade ore – all the flat land in Juneau, stretching from downtown to the airport, is landfill from mine tailings.

## Arrival, information and getting around

The **Marine Highway ferry terminal** (☎907/465-3940) is fourteen miles northwest of downtown at Auke Bay. Because the daily ferries often arrive at unearthly hours, getting into town can be a problem. In summer a Mendenhall Glacier Transport **shuttle bus** (☎907/789-5460) leaves the terminal about fifteen minutes after the ferry arrives, dropping off at the airport and downtown (both $5). At other times you'll have to take a **taxi** ($25) or walk a mile and a half right along the road and catch the Capital Transit (☎907/789-6901; fixed fare $1.50) bus #3 or #4 at Mendenhall Loop Road. It's part of the town **bus service** which runs daily (limited on Sun) every hour from 7am until 11.30pm. The ferry dock is not to be confused with the **cruise-ship terminal**, right downtown. Alaska Airlines land daily at Juneau's **airport**, nine miles out towards the ferry terminal; express buses (Mon–Fri 8am–11pm hourly; $1.50) take you downtown; at other times catch buses from the nearby Nugget Mall (details and schedules at the Juneau Visitors Information desk on the ground floor). From here, a taxi downtown costs around $20.

The **Davis Log Cabin**, 134 Third St, carries information about Juneau and the surrounding area (June–Sept Mon–Fri 8.30am–5pm, Sat & Sun 9am–5pm; Oct–May Mon–Fri 9am–5pm; ☎907/586-2201 or 1-888/581-2201), and when a cruise ship's in there are **information booths** at Marine Park on the waterfront, and by the cruise-ship dock. The **visitor center** at 101 Egan Drive (summer daily 8am–5pm; rest of year closed Sat & Sun; ☎907/586-8751) has exhibits and videos on the region's ecology and is the place to book forest cabins.

Popular hikes from **Juneau** include the undemanding Perseverance Trail and, over the bridge on Douglas Island, the Treadwell Mine Historic Trail. Mountain Gears, 126 Front St (☎907/586-4327), rents out **mountain bikes** and offers customized area tours. Alaska Discovery (☎907/780-6226 or 1-800/586-1911) or Auk Ta Shaa (☎907/586-8687 or 1-800/820-2628) organizes **sea-kayaking trips** amid wondrous scenery from around $100 per day.

## Accommodation

There are plenty of **motels** near downtown, though it's worth trying one of Juneau's many good **B&Bs**; the B&B Association of Alaska (☎907/789-8822) or Juneau B&B (☎907/586-2959) reserves rooms for $50 and up. The remodeled *Mendenhall Lake Campground*, accessible by buses #3 or #4 and a short hike, is spectacularly situated near the glacier, but gets cold even in summer.

**Alaskan Hotel and Bar**, 167 S Franklin St (☎907/586-1000 or 1-800/327-9374). Pleasant old hotel with a salacious past in the heart of downtown, with a fine bar and a sauna. Twelve doubles with shared or private bath. ④.

**Cashen Quarters B&B**, 315 Gold St (☎907/586-9863 or 1-888/543-5701). Five rooms with continental breakfasts. Located close to downtown. ④.

**Driftwood Lodge Motel**, 435 Willoughby Ave (☎907/586-2280 or 1-800/544-2239). One block from the waterfront, with large rooms including kitchenettes. Courtesy bus to airport and ferry. ④.

**HI-Juneau**, 614 Harris St (☎907/586-9559). Clean and comfortable hostel, in an old home near downtown, with dorm beds for $7. Daytime lock-out and 11pm curfew. ①.

**Pearson's Pond Luxury B&B**, 4541 Sawa Circle (☎907/789-3772 or 1-888/658-6328). Three comfortable rooms in a spacious modern house a mile from Mendenhall Glacier, with CD and VCR, personal gyms, modem plugs, computer, kitchenettes with self-serve breakfasts, hot tubs, boating, bikes, tour bookings and visiting yoga instructors. ⑨.

## Downtown Juneau

From the kiosk in Marine Park, it takes an hour and a half to follow the self-guided Juneau **walking tour**. Many original buildings stand in the **South Franklin Street Historic District** – Juneau managed to avoid the fires that destroyed many other gold towns in Alaska. The onion-domed **St Nicholas Russian Orthodox Church**, on Fifth and Gold, contains icons and religious treasures, while the excellent **Alaska State Museum**, 395 Whittier St, covers native culture, the Russian heritage and the first gold strikes. Its pride and joy is the logbook in which Bering reported his first sighting of Alaska (summer Mon–Fri 9am–6pm, Sat & Sun 10am–6pm; rest of year Tues–Sun 10am–4pm; $4). The smaller **City Museum** at 155 S Seward St displays relics from the mining era (summer Mon–Fri 9am–5pm, Sat & Sun 10am–5pm; rest of year Fri & Sat noon–4pm; $2).

## Tracy Arm Fjord and Mendenhall Glacier Area

One of the best day-trips out of Juneau is up the narrow, twisting **Tracy Arm Fjord**, with waterfall-fringed cliffs and common sightings of whales and seals. Day-long **cruises** with Auk Nu Tours' stable twin-hulls (☎907/586-8687 or 1-800/820-2628) or Adventure Bound Alaska (☎907/463-2905 or 1-800/228-3875) go from $110.

There are certainly bigger and more spectacular glaciers in Alaska, but the twelve-mile-long, one-and-a-half-mile-wide **Mendenhall Glacier**, thirteen miles from downtown, is easily the most accessible. Should your knowledge of cirques and striations be a little rusty, the **visitor center** (on a point this receding glacier occupied as recently as 1940) has all you need to know (summer daily 9am–5pm; rest of year Sat & Sun only; ☎907/789-0097). Hiking trails include the West Glacier Trail, on which, with extreme caution and without official approval, you can explore the ice caves.

Capital Transit buses leave for Mendenhall hourly from downtown; get off at Glacier Spur Road for the visitor center, or Montana Creek Road for the West Glacier trail. Alaska Travel Adventures runs three-hour **float trips** on the Mendenhall River (☎907/789-0052 or 1-800/791-2673; $90); Coastal Helicopters (☎907/789-5600; $140) offers one-hour trips with 25 minutes on the glacier itself.

## Eating and drinking

Downtown's excellent places to **eat and drink** fill up very quickly when cruise ships are in town.

**Alaskan Hotel and Bar**, 167 S Franklin St (☎907/586-1000). Great old bar, with occasional live music.

**Armadillo Tex-Mex Cafe**, 431 S Franklin St (☎907/586-1880). Huge plates of nachos start at $6, or try the Enchiladas Azteca, served with beans, rice and guacamole for $12.

**Channel Bowl Cafe**, 608 W Willoughby Ave (☎907/586-6139). Unpretentious breakfast spot attached to a bowling alley just off downtown.

**Chan's Thai Kitchen**, 11806 Glacier Hwy (☎907/789-9777). Up in Auke Bay but well worth the trek and possible wait (no reservations). Open Tues–Sat for lunch and dinner.

**Fiddlehead Restaurant and Bakery**, 429 W Willoughby Ave (☎907/586-1042). Known throughout the state for wholesome food. Most main dishes are under $10. One of Juneau's best places to eat with fine dining upstairs.

**Heritage Coffee and Cafe**, 625 W 7th St (☎907/586-1087). Great coffee and huge sandwiches are a promise at this cozy local hangout.

**Red Dog Saloon**, S Franklin St (☎907/463-3777). Touristy bar opposite the cruise-ship terminal, with a carefully fabricated olde-worlde ambiance. At night there's a much younger crowd and live music.

# Glacier Bay National Park

When Captain George Vancouver sailed through Icy Strait in 1794, **GLACIER BAY** was no more than a dent in the ice-packed coastline. Since then the Grand Pacific Glacier has receded 65 miles, to reveal a tranquil "land that time forgot" of deep fjords lined by rock walls and fed by fifteen other receding tidewater glaciers. The flora of the bay ranges from mature spruce forests to delicate plant life, while brown and black bear, moose, mountain goats, sea otters, humpback whales, porpoise, seals and a colorful array of birds have made the area their home. Most, if not all, of them can be seen on a **day-cruise** through Glacier Bay (the only way to access the area). The most spectacular moment comes when the boat, having negotiated its way through three miles of icebergs, comes face to face with the massive wall of the Grand Pacific Glacier.

Auk Nu Tours operates a daily **ferry** from Juneau to Gustavus (2hr 15min; ☎907/586-8687 or 1-800/586-2628; $45 one-way, bikes $10, kayaks $40), the nearest town to the otherwise inaccessible park. In summer, LAB (☎907/766-2222 or 1-800/426-0543) makes three daily **flights** from Juneau to Gustavus **airport** for around $140 round-trip, and once daily (a little more expensively) from Skagway and Haines. In summer larger Alaska Airlines planes also touch down once a day, flying between Juneau and Anchorage. You can charter a plane from LAB or Air Excursions (☎907/697-2375 or 1-800/354-2479) from around $209 each way for up to four people. **Buses** from the airport to the **park headquarters** in Bartlett Cove cost $10; otherwise it's a ten-mile walk, while the **cruise** itself – the principal way of experiencing the park's wonders short of paddling – costs $158.

**Accommodation** within the park ranges from a pleasant **campground** to $28 dorm beds and tasteful rooms at the *Glacier Bay Lodge* (☎1-800/451-5952; ①–④). The concession company, Glacier Bay Tours (☎1-800/451-5952), handles bookings for park accommodation and cruises and also offers a bewildering number of packages. If you want a roof over your head, the best bet lies in **GUSTAVUS**, a hamlet occupying a sand spit that tapers its way into Icy Strait, where *A Puffin's B&B Lodge* (☎907/697-2260 or 1-800/478-2258; ⑨) consists of half a dozen modern cabins in a forest clearing.

# Sitka

Perched on the seaward edge of the Inside Passage, **SITKA** ranks as one of Alaska's prettiest and most historic towns. The Fuji-like **Mount Edgecumbe** volcano rises menacingly across Sitka Sound from the spot where Russian colonists established a fort in 1799. Three years later Tlingit warriors massacred the imperialist troops and their Aleut slaves, but were themselves cannoned into submission in 1804. Under Russian occupation the town was rebuilt and christened **Novaya Archangelsk** (New Archangel), the capital of Russian America – a role it retained beyond the 1867 transfer of ownership to the US, until federal powers passed control to Juneau in 1906. Sitka today earns its keep from logging, fishing and tourism; it's all too keen to flog tacky "Russiocana" – you'll find more nesting dolls here than the rest of the US put together – but the town also has a wealth of great outdoor opportunities and commands a fine reputation for its festivals, especially the chamber-oriented **Summer Music Festival** each June. Working-class culture is celebrated in the same month with the **All-Alaska Logging Championships**.

## Arrival, information and getting around

Marine Highway **ferries** pass through five times per week, dropping anchor seven miles northwest of town on Halibut Point Road (☎907/747-3300). Sitka Tours **shuttles** (☎907/747-8443) will take you downtown for $3; it also does short tours of town ($10). Alaska Airlines runs a daily service on the Seattle–Juneau–Anchorage route from the airport on Japonski Island, just under two miles from downtown, across the suspension bridge. Again, Sitka Tours meets all flights (same prices) for the run downtown, which can be a pleasant half-hour walk. The **CVB** office is in the Centennial Building, 330 Harbor Drive (Mon–Fri 8am–5pm; ☎907/747-5940; *www.sitka.org*).

## Accommodation

Sitka has a good range of **accommodation**, with a fine hotel, two dorm-style lodgings and several B&Bs. If you're looking for something a bit different, *Middle Island Kayak Cabin* (☎907/747-5169; ⑦), on a quiet cove five miles from Sitka, sleeps six. The rustic *Starrigavan* **campground** (☎907/747-4216; $8) is a mile north of the ferry.

**HI-Sitka**, 303 Kimshan St (☎907/747-8661). Spartan hostel in a Methodist church, a mile from downtown. June–Aug only; $9 for members, $12 for nonmembers. ①.

**Karra's B&B**, 230 Kogwanton St (☎907/747-3978). Stunning view of the sea, great breakfasts. ④.

**My View B&B**, 201 Cascade Creek Rd (☎907/747-8966). Huge house with five rooms and full breakfasts. ⑤.

**Sitka Hotel**, 118 Lincoln St (☎907/747-3288). Renovated historic town-center hotel offering good-value rooms with and without bathrooms and a touch of old-fashioned class. ⑤.

**Westmark Shee Atika**, 330 Seward St (☎907/747-6241 or 1-800/544-0970). Top-quality hotel tastefully decked out with Native paintings and trimmings. ⑥.

## The Town

Getting a grasp of Sitka's Russian past doesn't take much time. The best place to start is from the vantage point of **Castle Hill**, a rocky knob where Alaska was officially transferred to the US on October 18, 1867; a plaque marks the spot. A two-minute stroll to the heart of downtown leads to **St Michael's Cathedral** on Lincoln Street. A fine piece of rural Russian church architecture, completed in 1848 and rebuilt after a disastrous fire in 1966, it displays priceless original icons (Mon–Sat 7.30am–5.30pm, and when cruise ships are in town, otherwise 1.30–5.30pm; $2 donation). Free tours take in the restored chapel, schoolroom and living quarters of the large mustard-colored **Russian Bishop's House**, by the harbor – a log structure that is the oldest standing building in Alaska (summer daily 9am–1pm & 2–5pm; rest of year by appointment; ☎907/747-6281; free).

Four blocks further along at 104 College Drive, the **Sheldon Jackson Museum** (summer daily 9am–5pm; rest of year Tues–Sat 10am–4pm; $3) houses the most extensive accumulation of Native artifacts in the state. All of the tools, utensils and craft objects from Aleut, Athabascan, Tlingit and especially Inuit peoples were collected by the Rev Dr Sheldon Jackson on his wide-ranging travels throughout Alaska as a missionary and the territory's first General Agent of Education.

At the end of Lincoln Street, in a verdant copse between ocean and creek, **Sitka National Historic Park** embraces both the town's Tlingit heritage and its days of Russian rule. When Tsarist troops attacked a Tlingit fort on this site in 1804, the natives withstood bombardment for six days, but after running out of gunpowder, decided to abandon the fort silently at night. The next day Russians stormed the stockades only to find them empty except for a few dead children, whom they alleged were murdered to accomplish the retreat in complete silence. Nothing remains of the fort but a grassy clearing, but the evocative air is enhanced by several vividly painted **totem poles** alongside the footpaths. A **visitor center** features good interpretive displays on what is commonly called the "Battle of Sitka," as well as hosting Native craft workshops (summer daily 8am–5pm; rest of year Mon–Fri 8am–5pm; free). On the way back consider a visit to the **Alaskan Raptor Rehabilitation Center** on Sawmill Creek Road (summer daily 8am–5pm; tours $10). Here, eagles and other wounded birds of prey are cared for and released back into the wilds or sent south for breeding.

Sitka's **trail system** ranges from shoreside strolls to harder climbs up Gavan Hill and steep Mount Verstovia. Three of the nineteen Forest Service cabins (office, 201 Katlian St; ☎907/747-4220; ①) in the area are reachable by trail, but are twenty to forty miles from town, making it easier to pedal there; **mountain bike** rental costs $30 per day from Yellow Jersey Cycles, 805 Halibut Point Rd (☎907/747-6317). If you fancy some marine recreation, Baidarka Boats, 201 Lincoln St (☎907/747-8996), rents **kayaks** from $35 per day and also organizes tours in the Sound.

## Eating
Sitka's **restaurants** aren't exactly going to set gourmet tongues wagging, though there are several unusual places to dine out. For evening drinks, join the crowds in the *Westmark Shee Atika's* bar, or the down-to-earth *Pioneer Bar* on colorful Katlian Street.

**Back Door Cafe**, behind Old Harbor Books, 201 Lincoln St (☎907/747-8856). Great coffee, plus tasty sandwiches, pastries and light lunches. Daytime only.

**Bayview Restaurant**, upstairs at 407 Lincoln St (☎907/747-5440). Burgers, Russian specialties, chowders and white salmon dishes. Reasonably priced. Open 6.30am–8pm in summer.

**Marina**, 205 Harbor Drive (☎907/747-8840). Good pizzas and Mexican food. Open until 11pm.

**Nugget Restaurant**, Sitka Airport Terminal (☎907/966-2480). Not the first place you'd look for good food but the *Nugget* is well worth a visit – especially for its famous fruit pies.

# Haines

Although it lacks the fascinating history of other southeastern communities, **HAINES**, at the northern end of the Lynn Canal fjord on a peninsula between the Chilkat and the Chilkoot inlets, is a real "Alaskan experience." When the weather is clear, it is nothing short of spectacular, with snow-covered **Mount Ripinsky** rising up behind, the **Chilkoot and Chilkat mountains** hemming it in on either side, and glaciers spilling out into the deep fjord. The community itself is an interesting mix of unreconstructed rednecks along with urban escapees from the Lower 48.

The Tlingit fished and traded here for years before 1881, when the first missionaries arrived and renamed the settlement for a prominent Presbyterian, Mrs F Haines. Today Haines survives on fishing and tourism, and though cruise ships tend to press on to Skagway, it remains a popular spot, which in mid-August hosts the cookouts, crafts and log-rolling of the **Southeast Alaska Fair**. The fairgrounds also hold **Dalton City**, a small pioneer theme park notable only in that its buildings came from the movie sets of Jack London's *White Fang*, which was filmed in the Haines area in 1989.

### Arrival, information and getting around
Haines' **Marine Highway** terminal (☎907/766-2113) is five miles west of town, with a near daily service to and from Juneau and Skagway. Local **taxis** meet all ferry arrivals; downtown costs $6. Alaskon Express **buses** (☎1-800/544-2206) leave Haines three times a week in the summer for the 150-mile trip to Haines Junction in Canada, Anchorage and Fairbanks. Two private ferry operators, Haines Water Taxi (☎1-888/766-3395) and Chilkat Cruises (☎1-888/766-2103), undertake the one-hour run up the fjord to Skagway (359 miles by road) for around $32 round-trip.

The **visitor center**, at Second and Willard (summer daily 8am–8pm; rest of year Mon–Fri 8am–5pm; ☎907/766-2234 or 1-800/458-3579; *www.haines.alaska.us*), has all kinds of maps and information.

### Accommodation
As well as the usual mid-range **accommodation**, Haines has nearly a dozen **campgrounds**, such as the spotless *Haines Hitchup Park*, half a mile west on Main Street, and *Portage Cove*, on a great beach less than a mile from Fort Seward on S Front Street (no vehicles).

**Bear Creek Camp and Hostel**, 2 miles south on Small Tract Rd (☎907/766-2259). Dorm beds ($14) and four-person cabins ($38); $2 pickup from ferry. ①/ ②.

**Chilkat Eagle B&B**, Fort Seward (☎907/766-2763, fax 766-3677; *eaglebb@kcd.com*). Central B&B in old Fort Seward building offering separate kitchen, TV lounge and full breakfasts. ④.

**Hotel Haslingland**, Fort Seward (☎907/766-2000; ☎1-800/478-6363 in US; ☎1-800/478-2525 in Canada & AK). Choice of grand old hotel or B&B in the center of the old barracks. ③–⑥.

**Mountain View Motel**, Mud Bay Rd, Fort Seward (☎907/766-2900 or 1-800/478-2902). Nine comfortable rooms, some with kitchenettes. ④.

## The Town

Apart from a few art galleries and craftshops, concentrated around the visitor center, downtown Haines holds little interest. Instead, an exciting agenda of outdoor pursuits makes it a must on an Inside Passage itinerary. Two great, wild **state parks** – Chilkoot Lake and Chilkat – are a mere half-hour cycle ride to the north and south of town respectively. Chilkat in particular has some good trails and vistas, while well-tramped treks lead from town to the summits of Mount Riley and the much more difficult Mount Ripinsky. Haines is also a popular starting point for **rafting trips**: Chilkat Guides on Beach Road (☎907/766-2491, *raftalaska.com*), is one of many operators to offer four-hour **float trips** ($80) down the Chilkat River, ideal for viewing eagles and other wildlife.

Each fall, the world's largest gathering of **bald eagles** flocks to the banks of the Chilkat River to feed on an unusually late chum salmon run (delayed by an alluvial fan that keeps the river from freezing). By November over three thousand of these once endangered rare birds – as many as two dozen to a tree – are gathered along a five-mile sand bar at the **Chilkat Bald Eagle Preserve**, nine miles north of town on the Haines Highway. If you're here at the wrong time of year, you can see plenty of stuffed baldies at **American Bald Eagle Foundation** on Second and Haines Hwy (summer daily 9am–5pm; $2).

Half a mile west of downtown, **Fort William H Seward** was established in Haines in 1903 in response to the general lawlessness of the Gold Rush era, and territorial disputes with Canada. In summertime it buzzes with a small fairground and a reconstructed Totem Village, as well as replicas of a Tlingit tribal house and a trapper's cabin. This is also your chance to see the Chilkat Dancers perform in traditional costumes at the **Chilkat Center for the Arts**, in Fort Seward's recreational center (☎907/766-2160; $10).

### Eating and drinking

Haines's most exciting **bars** and **restaurants** can be found in the Fort Seward area. In the evening visitors converge on the friendly bar at the *Hotel Haslingland* while some locals stick to the more raucous joints downtown.

**Bamboo Room**, 2nd Ave near Main St (☎907/766-2800). Seafood, steaks and burgers in what is also a favorite late-night drinking hole for locals.

**Chilkat Restaurant and Bakery**, 5th Ave and Main St (☎907/766-2120). Reasonably priced, freshly made breads, breakfasts and lunches.

**Dejon Delights**, Portage St, Fort Seward (☎907/766-2505). Take the best smoked or pickled salmon in the state and fresh bread for the price of burger and fries.

**Fort Chilkoot Potlatch**, Parade Grounds, Fort Seward (☎907/766-2003). All-you-can-eat salmon bake on summer evenings.

## Skagway

**SKAGWAY**, the northernmost stop on the Marine Highway, sprang up overnight in 1897, as a trading post serving **Klondike Gold Rush** pioneers about to set off on the five-hundred-mile ordeal. It was also the last stop before the harrowing White Pass Trail, known as the "Dead Horse Trail," on which over three thousand horses perished during the winter of 1897–98 from severe weather, rugged ground and exhaustion. Having grown from one cabin to a town of twenty thousand in three months, Skagway, rife with disease and desperado violence, was reported to be "hell on earth." It boasted over seventy bars and hundreds of prostitutes, and was controlled by organized criminals, including the notorious **Jefferson "Soapy" Smith**, renowned for cheating hapless prospectors out of their gold (see also p.733). One of his scams was to operate a bogus telegraph office through which he concocted false messages from loved ones in the Lower 48 urgently demanding money, which Soapy, of course, took responsibility for sending. He finally met a nasty end in 1898 after a shoot-out with Frank Reid, head of a vigilante group.

By 1899, the Gold Rush was over, but the completion in 1900 of the White Pass and Yukon Railway from Skagway to Whitehorse, the Yukon capital, ensured Skagway's survival. The 816 residents have gone to great lengths to maintain the original appearance of their town, much of which lies in the **Klondike Gold Rush National Historic Park**, and in summer as many as five ships a day call in to appreciate the effort. However, from mid-September to early May the town ticks over much more sedately.

### Arrival, information and getting around

**Marine Highway ferries** (☎907/983-2229) arrive daily a short walk from the main thoroughfare, Broadway Street. Two to five trains a day run from the **train station**, a block off Broadway Street on Second Avenue, the White Pass Summit and Fraser, British Columbia, where you can connect with buses to Whitehorse, Yukon. Alaska Direct **buses** (☎1-800/780-6652) also run daily in summer to Whitehorse ($35), from where trips run to Anchorage ($145) and Fairbanks ($120) three times a week; Alaskon Express offers a similar service from the *Westmark Inn* on Third Avenue (☎907/983-2241). The daily Marine Highway ferry is the cheapest way to get here from Haines, though two independent operators (see p.1088) come here too.

Skagway is very compact, and most of the sights can easily be seen on foot. The Klondike Gold Rush National Park **visitor center**, on the corner of Second Avenue and Broadway Street, holds talks, leads walking tours, and has historical displays and an impressive movie about the Gold Rush, as well as maps and information on the Chilkoot Trail (June–Aug daily 8am–7pm; May & Sept daily 8am–6pm; ☎907/983-2921). **Skagway's** visitor center is on Broadway between Second and Third avenues in the Arctic Brotherhood Hall building (summer daily 8am–5pm; ☎907/983-2854 or 1-888/762-1898).

### Accommodation

In such a touristy little town, prices run a little higher, with places booked up in advance. There's a pleasantly secluded **campground** ($7) at 14th and Broadway.

**Gold Rush Lodge**, 6th Ave and Alaska St (☎907/983-2831). Twelve rooms located five minutes from the town center, with free pickups and continental breakfast. ④.

**Golden North Hotel**, Broadway St at 3rd Ave (☎907/983-2294). Alaska's oldest and Skagway's most famous hotel. All rooms feature Gold Rush antiques and large cast-iron bathtubs. ③–⑤.

**Skagway Home Hostel**, 3rd Ave and Main St (☎907/983-2131). Traditionally run hostel in a century-old building shared with its owners and open all year. Luggage storage facility for overnight hikes. $15 per night. ①.

**Skagway Inn B&B**, 7th Ave and Broadway (☎907/983-2289). Lovely ambiance and fresh-baked breakfasts in one of Alaska's very best small inns, with very reasonable rates. ④.

**Wind Valley Lodge**, 22nd Ave and State St (☎907/983-2236). Clean, modern alternative if the *Golden North Hotel* or *Skagway Inn* are full. ④.

### The Town

The eye-catching facade of the **Arctic Brotherhood Hall**, on Broadway Street between Second and Third, built in 1899 by gold miners who paid their dues in nuggets, is decorated with over twenty thousand pieces of driftwood and houses the Skagway Visitor Center. Three blocks away, at the corner of Sixth and Broadway, the *Days of 98 Show* is an entertaining historical musical about Soapy Smith ($12).

About one and a half miles north of town, the **Gold Rush Cemetery** is the final resting place of many of the stampeders. Among them are Soapy Smith and Frank Reid, who according to his gravestone "gave his life for the honor of Skagway"; a local prostitute, on the other hand, is remembered for "giving her honor for the life of Skagway."

If you've had enough of Soapy and his cronies, you may feel like **hiking**; one of the best short trails leads from the cemetery to the 300ft high Reid Falls. The useful *Skagway Trail Map*, available from the visitor center, details other walks in the area, including those in the Dewey Lakes system, which pass pretty subalpine lakes and tumbling waterfalls, and the more difficult scramble uphill to Denver Glacier. Sockeye Cycles, next to the visitor center (☎907/983-2851), rents out well-maintained **mountain bikes**, and the neighboring Mountain Shop (☎907/983-2544) rents and sells backpacking supplies.

The lazy – and very popular – way to take in the scenery is on **the White Pass and Yukon Railway** (mid-May–late Sept; up to seven departures daily; ☎907/983-2217 or 1-800/343-7373), which follows the gushing Skagway River upstream past waterfalls and ice-packed gorges and over a 1000ft high wooden trestle bridge, stopping at the Canadian border ($78 round-trip) before occasionally continuing on to Lake Bennett, British Columbia ($128). It's not inexpensive, but there's no shortage of takers; get there early and grab a seat on the left-hand side going up. The company also offers a through bus service to Whitehorse after a train ride to Fraser, British Columbia ($65 one way).

### The Chilkoot Trail

Alaska's most famous and popular trail, the 33-mile **Chilkoot Trail**, is one huge "wilderness museum." Following in the exact footsteps of the original Klondike prospectors, it is strewn with haunting reminders of the past, including old mining dredges and Gold Rush ghost towns. Starting in **DYEA**, nine miles from Skagway, and ending in **BENNETT** in Canada, the trail climbs through rainforest to tundra with fast-flowing streams and waterfalls in evidence for much of the way.

The three- to five-day hike can be strenuous, especially the final ascent up from Sheep Camp (1000ft) to Chilkoot Pass (3550ft). You must be self-sufficient for food, fuel and shelter, and be prepared for foul weather. Campgrounds line the trail, as well as emergency shelters with stoves and firewood. There are also ranger stations at Dyea, Sheep Camp and Lindeman City. Dyea is accessible by road, and the White Pass and Yukon Railway runs a service for hikers returning to Skagway for $65.

Numbers on the trail are limited, so before setting off, you must make a reservation at the **NPS visitor center** in Skagway (☎1-800/661-0486), where rangers make sure you watch an instructional video and provide information on weather conditions and current bus and train schedules for the trip back to Skagway. While here you must also pay out a rather extravagant Can$35 for a Canadian permit (there is a bank in town). Be warned that mountain-top Mounties issue citations for transgressors.

## Eating and drinking

Most of Skagway's **bars** and **restaurants** lie in the touristy part of Broadway Street. The best snacks, in the form of smoked salmon, are on offer at *Dejon Delights*, next to the popcorn wagon on Broadway.

**Corner Cafe**, 4th and State sts (☎907/983-2155). New alternative to the established *Sweet Tooth*.

**Dee's Restaurant**, 2nd Ave, off Broadway (☎907/983-2200). Salmon and halibut bakes, burgers and decent salads, with indoor and outdoor seating.

**Northern Lights**, Broadway, between 4th and 5th aves (☎907/983-2225). Good Italian food, with pizza from $12 and pasta from $8, in a pleasant setting.

**Red Onion Saloon**, 2nd Ave and Broadway (☎907/983-2222). The best bar in town. Live music, excellent pizza, and Alaskan Amber on tap.

**Sweet Tooth Cafe**, 3rd Ave and Broadway (☎907/983-2405). Skagway's top traditional American-style cafe, serving breakfast, burgers and ice cream.

# Anchorage

Wedged between the two arms of Cook Inlet and the imposing Chugach Mountains to the east, **ANCHORAGE** is home to over forty percent of Alaska's population, and serves as the transportation center for the whole state. This sprawling conurbation on the edge of one of the world's great wildernesses often gets a bad press from those who live elsewhere in Alaska – derided as being "just half an hour from Alaska" – but it has its attractions, and with its beautiful setting can make a pleasant one- or two-day stopover.

By the time Captain James Cook came up what is now Cook Inlet in 1778, in search of a Northwest Passage to the Atlantic, Russian fur trappers had already started to settle the area, trading copper and iron for fish and furs with the Indians. Though Cook was sure that the inlet was not the Passage, he sent boats out in a southeasterly direction to investigate. When they were forced to turn back by the severe tides, Cook named this gloriously scenic stretch **Turnagain Arm**.

Anchorage itself began life in 1915 as a tent city for construction workers on the Alaska Railroad. During the 1930s, hopefuls fleeing the Depression came pouring in from the Lower 48, and World War II – and the construction of the Alaska Highway – further boosted the city's size and importance. The opening of the airport established Anchorage – equidistant between New York and Tokyo – as the "Crossroads of the World," and statehood in 1959 brought in yet more optimistic adventurers.

## Arrival, information and getting around

Anchorage International Airport lies seven miles southwest of town, served, in the early morning and late afternoon, by the People Mover urban transit service (see below). Alternatively, the Borealis shuttle service (☎907/276-3600 or 1-888/436-3600) costs $8 to downtown and a taxi costs around $15. The **train station** is on the north edge of downtown at 411 W First Ave (☎907/265-2494 or 1-800/544-0552).

Most of the major sights downtown are easily reached on foot. People Mover **buses** cover the city and the surrounding area – known together as the "Anchorage bowl" – daily between 6am and 10pm, for a $1 flat fare ($2.50 day-pass from the Transit Center, downtown at 6th Ave and G St), though they're a rare sight on Sundays. A free downtown shuttle service runs up and down Fifth and Sixth avenues as far as Cordova Street.

### Information

The main information office downtown is the diminutive **Log Cabin Visitor Center**, at Fourth and F (daily: May & Sept 8am–6pm, June–Aug 7.30am–7pm, Oct–April 9am–4pm; ☎907/274-3531; *www.anchorage.net*), which has an annex full of brochures and details of an easy self-guided downtown walking tour.

Diagonally across the street from the Log Cabin, the **Alaska Public Lands Information Center** (June–Aug daily 9am–5.30pm; rest of year Mon–Fri 10am–

5.30pm; ☎907/271-2737; *www.nps.gov/aplic/center*) has an excellent natural history display plus maps and more brochures. It can help plan trips into the Interior, and make reservations both for accommodation and the shuttle bus to Denali National Park – important in summer.

## Accommodation

Inexpensive **accommodation** in Anchorage can be hard to find, especially in summer, and many places are reserved months in advance. Downtown, the hotels are nearly all prohibitively expensive from June to September, though at other times they reduce their prices by as much as half. The most convenient **campgrounds** are *Lion's Campground* (☎907/333-9711) in Russian Jack Springs Park, half a mile south from Glenn Highway on Boniface Highway and, a little further out at *Centennial Park* (☎907/333-9711), five miles north on Glenn Highway. Free **B&B** reservation services include Alaska Private Lodgings (☎907/258-1717), AAA B&B (☎907/344-4676) and Alaska Sourdough B&B Association (☎907/563-6244).

**Alaskan Samovar Inn**, 720 Gambell St (☎907/277-1511 or 1-800/478-1511, fax 272-5192). No-nonsense motel with jacuzzis in most rooms and free airport pickups. ⑤.

**Copper Whale Inn**, 440 L St (☎907/258-7999, fax 258-6213; *cwhalein@alaska.net*). Welcoming cross between a B&B and a small hotel with a knowledgeable owner, central location and great view at breakfast. ⑥.

**Earth B&B**, 1001 W 12th Ave (☎907/279-9907, fax 279-9862; *earthtrs@alaska.net*). A B&B unlike any other, enthusiastically and liberally run by multilingual Dutch émigré, Margriet, who makes the place a home from home for Denali-bound climbers during the season and a broad cross-section of folk for the rest of the year. Bus #6, #36 or #60 from downtown. ⑤.

**HI-Anchorage**, 700 H St (☎907/276-3635, fax 276-7772; *hipat@servcom.com*). Cozy and central hostel, opposite the Transit Center, but persists with afternoon lockout, chores and midnight curfew. Dorm beds are $16 for members, $19 for nonmembers. Reserve well ahead in summer. ①.

**Inlet Inn**, 539 H St (☎907/277-5541, fax 277-3108). The cheapest rooms downtown, though the decor leaves a bit to be desired. ④.

**International Backpackers Inn**, 3601 Peterkin Ave (☎907/274-3870). Five suburban homes operated as a hostel three miles east of downtown (bus #45), with beds $12–15 and good weekly rates; $10 camping. No lockout but a daily chore. ①.

**Qupqugiac Inn**, 640 W 36th Ave at Arctic Blvd, midtown (☎907/562-5681; *qupq@alaska.net*). Somewhere between a hostel and a hotel with clean double rooms and a communal area with self-catering facilities. Rates include a bagel-and-latte breakfast in the cafe downstairs. Bus #9 from downtown passes within a block, along Arctic Blvd. ②/③.

**Spenard Hostel**, 2845 W 42nd Place (☎907/248-5036, fax 248-5063; *hostel@alaskalife.net*). Set in a residential suburb with nearby mall just a mile and a half from the airport (bus #6): $13 winter; $16 summer. ①.

**12th and L**, 1134 L St (☎907/276-1225, fax 276-1224; *arcticimages@customcpu.com*). Central and tastefully furnished B&B with a self-serve continental breakfast, liberal daytime use of kitchen, and half-price bikes from Downtown Bicycle Rental. Bus #6, #36 or #60 from downtown. ⑥.

## The City

Travelers eager to rush off into the "real" Alaska tend to overlook cosmopolitan Anchorage – a blend of old and new, urban blight and rural parks – as a destination. There is, however, plenty to see in town, and it's worth spending some time here experiencing big-city Alaska, as uncompromisingly "real" as the rest of the state. The city is laid out on a grid; numbered avenues run east–west, lettered streets north–south.

If you only see two things in Anchorage, visit the Alaska Native Heritage Center (see below) and the **Anchorage Museum of History and Art**, 121 W Seventh Ave (mid-

May–mid-Sept daily 9am–6pm, mid-Sept–mid-May Tues–Sat 10am–6pm, Sun 1–5pm; $5), an excellent overview of the state and its history told through intricate dioramas, alongside beautiful examples of carved ivory and basketware. The gallery is noted for works by Alaska's best known painter, Sydney Laurence, particularly his monumental oil painting of Mount McKinley.

The **Imaginarium**, 737 W Fifth Ave (June–early Sept daily 10am–6pm; early Sept– May Mon–Sat 10am–6pm, Sun noon–5pm; $5), is exciting, with hands-on displays telling you all about glaciers, the Northern Lights, polar bears and the private life of the dopey-looking moose. At the **Alaska Experience Center**, Sixth Avenue and G Street (summer daily 9am–9pm; $10), forty minutes of Alaska's best scenery, shot from choppers, is beamed onto a 180° wraparound screen and can be enough to make you nauseous. The Center's **Earthquake Theater** is showing its age, however, with an unremarkable film on the 1964 disaster and a feeble simulation of a 4.6 tremor.

Despite some of the most garish T-shirt designs on the planet, Anchorage is home to some very good **shopping**. The not-for-profit giftshop in the **Alaska Native Medical Center**, on Tudor Avenue and Bergall Street (Mon–Fri 10am–2pm), has a fine selection of authentic Native crafts for sale, including jackets and moccasins. For a non-garish shirt, head for the giftshop in the **4th Avenue Theatre**, 630 W Fourth Ave.

Originally a firebreak for the town site, downtown's **Delaney Park**, running parallel to Ninth Avenue from A to L streets, has also served as an airstrip and golf course. Today it's a popular spot to play baseball, tennis, soccer and basketball, or simply hang out. West of the city, the almost eerie tranquility of Earthquake Park, at the end of Northern Lights Boulevard, offers restorative views of the mountains, and an interpretive display provides an inkling of the havoc wrought by the earthquake of Good Friday 1964, which devastated much of downtown, and at 9.2 on the Richter scale remains North America's strongest ever **earthquake**.

Six miles to the east on the outskirts of town lies the **Alaska Native Heritage Center**, Muldoon Road exit from the Glenn Hwy (May–Sept daily 9am–9pm; $20). It is expensive, new and still finding its feet, but provides an excellent introduction to the state's five main ethnic groups. Each is represented by a typical house where Native guides interpret their culture. Throughout the day, cultural groups perform in the main auditorium where there is also an instructive introductory film. The Fourth Avenue Trolley runs here hourly from downtown for an additional $2.

Just fifteen minutes' drive east from Anchorage, the mountains and lakes of the 495,000-acre **Chugach State Park** make for great moose-spotting territory. Challenging trails traversing the park include an often treacherous scramble to the summit of the 4500ft Flattop Mountain, a spectacular vantage point from which to view the city and Cook Inlet.

# Eating

Nowhere in Alaska will you find a more diverse range of places to eat – restaurants, cafes, bars and brewpubs – than those dotted around Anchorage. That's not to say you'd make a special journey for its culinary wonders, but only the pickiest eaters would find the city wanting, and after a few weeks in the interior it can seem like heaven. Downtown has a good selection of reputable places, though many of the spots popular with locals are scattered far and wide. For groceries, make for Carr's supermarket at the junction of Northern Light Boulevard and Minnesota Drive (bus #3, #4 or #36) which has a good deli section.

**Corsair**, 944 W 5th St (☎907/278-4502). Not much of a view inside the basement, but the best French continental food in town.

**The Federal Building Cafeteria**, 222 W 7th at C St (☎907/277-6736). Breakfast and lunch cafeteria that's about the best budget value downtown, certainly a cut above the fast-food joints and more filling. Steaming clam chowder for $3 and entrees start at around $5.

**Glacier Brewhouse**, 737 W 5th St (☎907/274-2739). Hugely popular restaurant, bar and microbrewery, lacking a bit in ambiance, but serving wonderful food and drink. At least half a dozen toothsome house-brewed beers to accompany alder-wood baked gourmet pizza ($10), spit grilled three-peppercorn prime rib ($20), or steamed Alaskan King crabs ($30).

**Humpy's**, 610 W 6th Ave (☎907/276-2337). Though it functions primarily as a bar (see below), *Humpy's* also produces some of the best value meals in town: the likes of charbroiled salmon, burgers, soups and salads. Cajun halibut focaccia with a small caesar salad will only set you back $10 or so.

**L'Aroma at New Sagaya's City Market**, 900 W 13th Ave at I St (☎907/274-6173). Trendy and spendy grocery store, deli and cafe with a great selection from organic veges and great cheeses to pizza, wraps, Thai dishes and good coffee. The nearest groceries to downtown.

**Moose's Tooth**, 3300 Old Seward Hwy at 33rd Ave (☎907/258-2537). A perennial favorite, always alive with diners tucking into some of the town's best gourmet pizza.

**Snow City Cafe**, 1034 W 4th Ave (☎907/272-6338). Foremost among the city establishments that successfully manage to combine several roles drawing in the coffee set, lunching office workers and pre-theater diners. All-day breakfast – French toast for $5, granola for $3 – are supplemented by Thai halibut, rosemary chicken, cedar plank salmon or vegetarian meatloaf. Live music on Fri night.

**Surf City: an Internet Cafe**, 415 L St (☎907/279-7877). Primarily an Internet cafe but also a good place to hang out on the couches or on the sunny veranda, and play chess and backgammon over a coffee and muffin.

**Thai Cuisine Too**, 328 G St (☎907/277-8424). Central Thai restaurant that's a little light on Siamese ambiance but good value. Dishes are tasty and handily graded for spiciness. The $9 lunches including rice, house soup and salad are a bargain.

## Entertainment and nightlife

Good **bars** abound in downtown Anchorage, and the atmosphere varies as much as the clientele. Late at night, the main drag of **Fourth Avenue** can seem like a surreal slalom course as you swerve to avoid the terminally drunk. The other sleazy area – **Spenard**, on Spenard Road between Northern Lights Boulevard and International Airport Road – can be fun as long as you're careful. Women travelers may not find the "bohemian" side of macho Anchorage quite as endearing as many locals seem to think it is, with some innocent-looking bars turning out to be strip joints.

Not much can lure Alaskans indoors during the summer, so there are few summer performances, but for the rest of the year the **Center for Performing Arts** (☎907/263-2787) has a huge variety of shows, plays, opera and concerts.

**Bernie's Bungalow**, 626 D St at 7th Ave (☎907/276-8808). A very un-Alaskan hangout featuring the "lounge-a-licious" Martini and a cocktail bar fashioned from an old wooden house. Latin and jazz grooves the smartly dressed set. Stylish seating is in short supply so come early.

**Chilkoot Charlie's**, 2435 Spenard Rd (☎907/272-1010). Sawdust-strewn barn that packs them in nightly for pricey drinks, pool, foosball, two floors of DJ-led dance and live music from 9.30pm.

**Darwin's Theory**, 426 G St at 4th Ave (☎907/277-5322). Straightforward local bar for moderately priced boozing and neighborly encounters with colorful local characters.

**Humpy's Great Alaskan Alehouse**, 610 W 6th Ave at F St (☎907/276-2337; see "Eating" above). Popular watering hole with a strong college bar feel and lots of local microbrews plus English and Belgian bottled beers, and over thirty top-shelf single malts. Live music nightly, often acoustic or Irish.

**Mr Whitekey's Fly By Night Club**, 3300 Spenard Rd at 32nd Ave (☎907/279-7726). Zany cabaret and live music venue which, throughout summer, hosts *The Whale Fat Follies* (June–mid-Sept Tues–Sat 8pm; $12–18; 16 and over only), a satirical and occasionally bawdy slant on Alaska.

## South of Anchorage

All that stands on the original site of **GIRDWOOD**, 37 miles south of Anchorage and destroyed by the 1964 earthquake, is an ordinary strip mall. The village now lies two miles inland in the shade of the **Alyeska Ski Resort**, Alaska's largest winter sports complex and the lowest-elevation ski resort in the world – Mount Alyeska's 3939ft summit rises from just 270 feet above sea level. Until 1993 Alyeska resembled one of the small municipal resorts in the Rockies, but a huge investment from its Japanese owners has since given it many new downhill runs, a first-class hotel and an extensive night-skiing operation. In summer, this is prime mountain biking terrain, and Alyeska's cable car or "tram" ($16) provides access to a stunning view of Turnagain Arm and a high-altitude eatery. For full details on the skiing opportunities here, get a copy of *Skiing in Alaska* (Epicenter Press; $12.95).

The *Alyeska Prince Hotel* (☎907/754-1111 or 1-800/880-3880; winter ⑥, summer ⑦) is a grand ski lodge and one of Alaska's finest hotels with half a dozen good restaurants and service to match. At the other end of the price range, but equally good value, is the *Alyeska Home Hostel* (☎907/783-2099; ①), with $10 loft beds; to get there, turn right on Timberline and right again on Alpina. For **B&B** reservations (the woods all around are crammed with inviting timber homes) call Girdwood's B&B Network (☎907/222-4858). There's inexpensive **food** at *Chair Five* in Girdwood (☎907/783-2500; daily 11am–2am) or the unmissable *Double Musky Inn* on Crow Creek Road (☎907/783-2822); budget on $25 a head and a meal to remember. *Max's Bar* next door to the *Musky* is lively in the evenings.

Eleven miles south of Girdwood, a five-mile road leads to **Portage Glacier**, an unbearably popular day-tour from Anchorage. Frustratingly, you can't see the glacier from the parking lot; instead you must pay Gray Line $25 for a cruise around the lake's corner to the glacier's snout. Take some solace inside the fascinating **visitor center** (mid-May–mid-Sept daily 9am–6pm, mid-Sept–mid-May Sat & Sun 10am–4pm; ☎907/783-2326) while you're waiting, with its mock-up walk-through ice cave and observation decks. Two USFS **campgrounds** ($10) can be found a mile or two back down the road.

# Kenai Peninsula

Beyond Portage, the Seward Highway skirts the south shore of Turnagain Arm and enters the **Kenai Peninsula**, "Anchorage's playground." At over nine thousand square miles, the peninsula is larger than many states in the Lower 48, and offers an endless diversity of activities and scenery. Most of the major communities are accessible by public transportation, including **Homer**, at the end of the highway. Cruises leave this artsy little town for glorious **Kachemak Bay State Park**, while on the more mountainous east coast, **Seward** is the base for boat trips along the shores of the inspirational **Kenai Fjords National Park**.

Throughout the peninsula, trails branch off all along the highway to provide excellent hiking in the Kenai Mountains; the 38-mile Resurrection Trail (allow 4 days; USFS cabins available) begins at the wonderful gold-mining village of **Hope**, and comes out on the Sterling Highway near the rafting hub of **Cooper's Landing**.

Most Alaskans who come to the Kenai Peninsula do so to **fish**. Cast aside preconceptions of this as a tranquil activity – "combat fishing," when thousands of anglers stand elbow to elbow along the Kenai, Russian and Kasilof rivers, is intense stuff, and it takes strength and know-how to pull in a thirty-pound king salmon. **Campgrounds** along the rivers fill up fast, but in July and August hungry bears join in the fun and games, so most people opt to stay elsewhere.

# Seward

SEWARD, 127 miles south of Anchorage, sprang to life in 1903 after engineers declared this ice-free port the ideal starting point for railroad tracks to the Interior. Since then it has been a key freight terminal, but tourism – particularly cruises into Kenai Fjords National Park – is now its most conspicuous business.

Seward fronts onto a classic view of the Gulf of Alaska, and is ringed by glaciers and mountains. In 1909 two "sourdough pioneers" (old-time Alaskan frontiersmen who subsisted on bread made from sour dough) bet each other to run up and down the 3022-foot **Mount Marathon**; this masochistic dare has developed into an annual Fourth of July race (current record 43 minutes 23 seconds). Most athletes accomplish the descent in ten minutes by launching themselves down the sleep slope on their bottoms. A more moderately paced four-hour **hiking trail** leads to the top for a glorious view down the bay.

Seward's main activities are enjoying the scenery and visiting the wonders at the **SeaLife Center** at the bottom of Fourth Avenue (May–mid-Sept daily 9am–9.30pm; rest of year Wed–Sun 10am–5pm; $12.50), a successful marriage of marine research and visitor education – partly funded by the Exxon Valdez oil spill settlement. The center offers the chance to watch ongoing cold water research in action and marvel at the underwater antics of stellar sea lions, harbor seals and adorable puffins.

## Kenai Fjords National Park

Beginning just south of Seward, **KENAI FJORDS NATIONAL PARK** is a magnificent 580,000-acre region of peaks, glaciers and craggy coastline. Its towering mountains are mantled by the prodigious three-hundred-square-mile Harding Icefield, feeding the three dozen retreating glaciers which have exposed the dramatic fjords after which the park is named.

Eight of these tidewater glaciers "calve" icebergs into the sea with thunderous booms (though not always with the drama that brochures and videos might suggest), and the fjords also hold a wealth of **marine wildlife** – sea otters, porpoises, seals, stellar sea lions, plus orca, gray, humpback and minke whales – as well as the seabird rookeries on the cliffs of the Chiswell Islands. The best of the **cruises** from Seward is conducted aboard the large boats of Kenai Fjords Tours (☎1-800/468-8068; $54–139); pay out for the longer day-tours which go right up to the calving tidewater glaciers.

Back on land, **Exit Glacier**, down a road which starts at Mile 3.7 Seward Hwy, is the section of the park you can see without spending lots of money or walking for days. From the ranger station at the end of the track, a short stroll leads to the still-active glacier, though signs warn you back from the ice wall and its inviting blue clefts. If you have five hours to spare, walk up the steep three-mile trail to the edge of the Harding Icefield. The effort is rewarded with an adjective-defying vantage point out over isolated mountain peaks – **nunataks** – interrupting the almost completely flat virgin-white surface of the ice field.

The park's **visitor center**, 1212 Fourth Ave in Seward's small-boat harbor (summer Mon–Fri 8am–6pm, Sat 9am–5pm, Sun 9am–4pm; rest of year Mon–Fri 8am–5pm; ☎907/224-8051), provides maps, film shows and details on regional hikes.

## Practicalities

In summer, **Alaska Railroad** trains from Anchorage arrive and depart daily (☎1-800/544-0552; $86 round-trip) at the depot next to the tour boats. **Marine Highway ferries** between Valdez and Kodiak dock nearby (☎907/224-5485). Seward Bus Line (☎907/224-3608) charges $30 for a one-way ride from Anchorage.

Seward's two hubs of activity, the small-boat harbor and downtown, are joined by the mile-long Fourth Avenue; if you don't feel like walking, hop on the local trolley (daily 10am–7pm every 30min; $1.50, day-pass $3).

The main **visitor center** is at Mile 2 Seward Hwy (mid-May–mid-Sept Mon–Fri 8am–6pm, Sat 9am–5pm, Sun 9am–4pm; mid-Sept–mid-May Mon–Fri 8am–5pm; ☎907/224-8051, *www.seward.net/chamber*). The US Forest Service (USFS) office, 334 Fourth at Jefferson (Mon–Fri 8am–5pm; ☎907/224-3374) has details on trails, campgrounds and bookable cabins in the Chugach National Forest.

A couple of old downtown **hotels** that are good value spots are the clean *New Seward Hotel*, 217 Fifth Ave (☎907/224-8001; ⑤), and the historic *Van Gilder Hotel*, 308 Adams St (☎907/224-3079; ⑥). Out on Exit Glacier Road, the thoroughly relaxing *Le Barn Appetite B&B* (☎907/224-8706; ④) has rooms in a big rustic barn, and a superb cafe serving fresh crepes, quiches and deli sandwiches. The lovely log *Alaska's Treehouse B&B*, off Timber Street at Mile 7 Seward Hwy (☎907/224-3867; ④), offers a hot tub and sauna and great breakfasts. Downtown **hostel** accommodation is provided by *Moby Dick Hostel*, 432 Third Ave (☎907/224-7072; ①–③), handily sited on the trolley route with bunks ($16.50), limited kitchen facilities, and private rooms (some with kitchenettes). There's also *Kate's Roadhouse*, Mile 5.5 Seward Hwy (☎907/224-5888; ①) and *Snow River Hostel*, way out at Mile 16 Seward Hwy (☎907/276-3635; ①), with $13 dorm beds.

**Eating** in Seward is fairly reasonably priced: for a coffee or light meal make for *Resurrect Art*, 320 Third Ave, a coffeehouse and gallery in a former church. More substantial eating is best done at the seafood oriented *Harbor Dinner Club* on Fifth Avenue (☎907/224-3012), or the upscale *Ray's Waterfront Bar and Grill*, by the harbor (summer only; ☎907/224-3012), which has nice views and big steak and seafood dinners for around $20.

# Homer

At the end of the Sterling Highway, **HOMER**, 226 miles from Anchorage, is the Kenai Peninsula's southernmost town that's accessible by road. It commands a truly magnificent setting, spread beneath gently sloping verdant bluffs with a five-mile finger of land – **The Spit** – slinking out into the dark waters of Kachemak Bay, into which flow crystal-blue glaciers, framed by dense black forest. It's so appealing that you can forgive the tourist board for billing it the "Shangri-la of Alaska," while its activities and lively nightlife make this a place to scrap your itinerary and linger a few days.

Russians, drawn by the abundance of coal, were the first whites to reach the area, and by the mid-1800s several American companies had followed suit. In 1896, **Homer Pennock**, a gold-seeker from Michigan, set up the community that still bears his name. Every summer in recent years, young people from the Lower 48 have arrived here in droves to work on the halibut boats or in the cannery, though this tradition may disappear with the recent decline in the quantity and price of salmon in Alaska.

Homer's other main industry, **tourism**, is under no such threat. Due to its dramatic surroundings and "mild" winters (temperatures average 25°F), visitors flock and Anchorites are relocating to this pretty fishing village. The resident population, younger and more mixed than elsewhere in the state, supports a thriving arts community.

## Arrival, information and getting around

The **Alaska Marine Highway** office (Mon–Fri 8.30am–4pm or when the boat's in; ☎907/235-8449) stands at the end of the Spit; **ferries** usually go to Seldovia, Kodiak and Seward once a week, and to the Aleutian Islands once a month during the summer.

Kachemak Bay Transit (☎1-877/235-9101) runs a daily service between Anchorage and Homer (via Seward) for $45 each way. ERA and Southcentral Air fly in from Anchorage for around $90 one-way.

Most hotels, restaurants and shops are in town, while almost all of the fishing charter and tour operators can be found along the twee boardwalks of the Spit. In summer Day Breeze shuttles between the two locations ($2) or you can rent mountain bikes from Homer Saw & Cycle, 1532 Ocean Drive (☎907/235-8406; $25 per day). The main visitor center is at 135 Sterling Hwy (late May–early Sept Mon–Fri 9am–8pm, Sat & Sun 10am–6pm; ☎907/235-7740; *www.homeralaska.org*). KBBI (890 AM; ☎907/235-7721) broadcasts a "Ride Line," useful for offering or requesting lifts back up north.

## Accommodation

Homer's good-value **hotels** and **B&Bs** can be fully booked in midsummer; the visitor center can help. There's **camping** in town, across the bay, or in an exposed and noisy location on the Spit.

**Driftwood Inn**, 135 W Bunnel Ave (☎907/235-8019 or 1-800/478-8019). Near downtown on the edge of the bay, the inn hosts barbecue and shellfish cookouts, plus a good bar opposite. ④–⑥.

**Heritage Hotel**, 147 E Pioneer Ave (☎907/235-7787 or 1-800/380-7787). Fifty-year-old log-built hotel downtown; rooms without baths in the original wing, or within the extension. ⑤.

**Ocean Shores Motel**, 451 Sterling Hwy (☎907/235-7775 or 1-800/770-7775). Just off the highway coming into town with spacious new kitchenettes offering views right into the bay and older rooms at good rates. ⑥/⑦.

**Seaside Farms Hostel**, Mile 5 East End Rd (☎907/235-7850). Great place to meet backpackers. Clean dorms $15, tent sites $10, with discount for long stays. You can also work off part of the cost by doing a stint on the farm. Plenty of lifts to town. ①.

**Sun Spin**, 358 Lee Drive (☎907/235-6677 or 1-800/391-6677). Quiet and central guesthouse with a couple of bunkrooms ($28 per person including breakfast) and private rooms, some with sauna. ④/⑤.

## The Town

The downtown **Pratt Museum**, 3779 Bartlett St (daily 10am–6pm; $5), features high-quality works by local craftspeople, as well as Inuit and other Native artifacts, aquariums and historic Homer oddities. Many of Homer's most popular activities, however, revolve around the Spit. To Alaskan anglers, Homer is "**Halibut Central**": a full day's excursion with any of the charter companies costs from $130. If you don't mind joining the crowds, it's cheaper and simpler to visit the **Fishing Hole**, a tiny bight on the Spit, which is stocked with salmon and offers good fishing from mid-May to mid-September.

**Skyline Drive**, which runs along the top of a bluff above the town, offers glorious views of glaciers spilling into Kachemak Bay; the twenty-odd miles of the dead-end **East End Road** provide similarly good views.

## Kachemak Bay State Park

The prime tourist attraction in the Homer area is exploring the 250,000 acres of forested mountains, glaciers, pristine fjords and inlets that comprise **Kachemak Bay State Park**, directly across the bay from Homer. Bird species here include puffin, auklets, kittiwakes and storm petrels, and marine creatures such as seals, sea otters and whales are also plentiful. Rainbow Tours on Cannery Row (☎907/235-7272) operates two-hour sightseeing cruises to **Gull Island** – a 15,000-strong rookery. However, a longer stay reaps rewards. The area's best trails, most of them manageable in a day, originate from the gorgeous hamlet of **Halibut Cove**. The most-traveled route, up to **Grewingk Glacier**, is an easy three-and-a-half-mile trek above the spruce and cottonwood forest to the foot of the glacier, from where you get splendid views of the bay.

The *Danny J* **ferry** (☎907/235-7847) makes two daily trips to Halibut Cove, on the south shore of the bay, via Gull Island rookery, for around $40 round-trip, while Central Charters (☎907/235-7847 or 1-800/478-7847) runs several excursions. Pick up maps and information from the **Alaska National Marine Wildlife Refuge**, 202 Pioneer Ave in Homer (☎907/235-6546).

## Eating and drinking

Downtown Homer offers some of the best **meal** deals for budget travelers in Alaska: all-you-can-eat specials are the order of the day. For **nightlife**, head for the colorful bars, or to the relaxed **Pier One Theater** (May–Sept; ☎907/235-7333), next to the fishing hole on the Spit.

**Cafe Cups**, 162 Pioneer Ave (☎907/235-8330). Relaxing yet vibrant cafe serving some of the best coffee and great sandwiches.

**Duncan House Diner**, 125 E Pioneer Ave (☎907/235-5344). Traditional, down-home diner open daily for breakfast, lunch and dinner.

**Fresh Sourdough Express Bakery and Cafe**, 1316 Ocean Drive (☎907/235-7571). Mouthwatering breads and pastries, plus all-you-can-eat breakfast for $10.

**The Homestead**, Mile 8.2, East Rd (☎907/235-8723). Open for dinner nightly for crab-and-shrimp cakes ($13) followed by Mediterranean pasta ($20), half a pound of King crab ($23) or sautéed scallops ($21).

**Lands End Resort**, at the end of the Spit (☎907/235-0400 or 1-800/478-0400). Plush and pricey restaurant offering an absolutely wonderful view of the bay. Breakfast is a must.

**Pioneer Building Pizzeria**, 265 E Pioneer Ave (☎907/235-3663). Drab family pizza restaurant mainly of interest for the $5 pizza-and-soda lunchtime specials and the $8 all-you-can-eat buffet (Mon–Sat evenings only).

**Smoky Bay Co-op Natural Food Store**, Pioneer Ave and Bartlett St (☎907/235-7242). Wholefood shop and cafe with great lunches from $7.

**Young's**, 565 E Pioneer Ave (☎907/235-4002). One of the best and least expensive all-you-can-eat Chinese (with a Japanese twist) buffets that you're likely to find anywhere.

# Kodiak Island

Known as the "Emerald Isle" for its thick spruce forests in the north and an interior carpeted by wild grasses studded with marshes, lumpy knolls and reeded lakes, **KODIAK ISLAND** offers some of Alaska's most uncommon and pleasing landscapes. The dominant landmass in a small Gulf of Alaska archipelago some hundred miles southwest of the Kenai Peninsula, this is the second largest island in the US (after Hawaii's Big Island). Despite its size, no point lies more than fifteen miles from the ocean.

The island is renowned as the home of the **Kodiak bear**, a subspecies of the brown/grizzly, which weighs up to 1500 pounds. Streams chock-full of spawning salmon allow these monsters to thrive in the **Kodiak National Wildlife Refuge**, covering the southwestern two-thirds of the island. Roughly ten bears inhabit each square mile around Red and Fraser lakes, and bear-watching trips are big business. In addition to *Ursus*, the Emerald Isle provides a favorable habitat for **bald eagles**, and as many as two million seabirds nest along the fjords, bights and bays. Accommodation in the nine **wilderness cabins** ($25 a night) dotted throughout the island is drawn by lottery each year; details from Kodiak NWR, 1390 Buskin River Rd, Kodiak, AK 99615 (April–Sept Mon–Fri 8am–4.30pm, Sat noon–4.30pm; ☎907/487-2600).

The **Japanese Current** supports a mild maritime climate along with plenty of rain and fog, creating poor flying conditions and the distinct possibility that your stay could be extended by a day or two. If you want to avoid peak-season prices, May and June are notoriously wet but September weather is usually fairly reliable.

# Kodiak

All but two thousand of the island's 15,000 inhabitants live in and around its only major town, the likeable and busy fishing port of **KODIAK** on the northeastern tip. Before Russian explorers established a community here in 1792, Aleut and Alutiiq had fished the area for millennia. After Alaska was transferred to the US, Kodiak survived as a center for trappers, whale-hunters and salmon-fishers, and in 1939 was just another sleepy Alaskan village when a massive war base was established here and the population rocketed to around 50,000. However, most of Kodiak's wealth comes from fishing the rich waters of the Gulf, and the town maintains a fleet of over 2700 fishing vessels. Tourism definitely plays second fiddle; few cruise ships stop, but this bustling little town has a splendid range of activities, good B&Bs and a lively nightlife.

### Arrival, information and getting around

Marine Highway **ferries** on the Seward–Homer route dock once weekly at Center Avenue and Marine Way downtown (☎907/486-3800), taking ten hours from Homer. Alaska Airlines (☎1-800/252-7522) and ERA Aviation (☎907/683-2574) jointly dispatch eight one-hour flights a day from Anchorage at around $290 round-trip. The local bus runs five miles into town roughly every ninety minutes (not Sun) for $2.

Except for Port Lions, which is served by ferry, the most practical way to explore the island is to **fly**; Uyak Air's Kodiak trips (☎907/486-3407 or 1-800/303-3407), which guarantee close-up views of bears or your money back, have never had to refund the $400-plus fee.

The helpful **visitor center** is by the ferry dock at 100 Marine Way (June–Aug daily 8am–5pm and longer if there is a late ferry arrival; Sept–May Mon–Fri 8am–5pm; ☎907/486-4782, fax 486-6545; *kicvb@ptialaska.net*; *www.kodiak.org*) and there is the **Kodiak National Wildlife Refuge Visitor Center**, close to the airport, four miles south of town (April–Sept Mon–Fri 8am–4.30pm, Sat noon–4.30pm; ☎907/487-2600), which stocks a wealth of information on bears and the backcountry.

### Accommodation

Most **lodging** in Kodiak is expensive, but the hotels and B&Bs are generally very good. The best place to **camp** is in **Fort Abercrombie State Park** (see overleaf), for $10.

**Buskin River Inn**, 1395 Airport Way (☎907/487-2700 or 1-800/544-2202, fax 487-4447; *brikiua@ptialaska.net*). Good independent hotel next to the airport, five miles outside of town. Excellent dining, a good bar and sightseeing packages. ⑥.

**Harborview**, 312 W Rezanof Drive (☎907/486-2464 or 1-888/283-2464, fax 486-3486; *kodiakfk@ptialaska.net*). Downtown B&B with good home-cooked breakfast, cable TV, and one large room ($110) with wonderful harbor views. ⑤.

**Kalsin Bay Inn**, Mile 29, Chiniak Hwy (☎907/486-2659). Small rustic hotel, with a bar, restaurant and good-value rooms, thirty miles south of Kodiak. Reservations advisable. ④.

**Shelikof Lodge**, 211 Thorsheim Ave (☎907/486-4141, fax 486-4116; *shelikoflodge@usa.net*). The best of the budget downtown motels with basic but clean rooms. ④.

**Wintel's B&B**, 1723 Mission Rd (☎907/486-6935, fax 486-6935; *awintels@ptialaska.net*; *www.wintels.com*). Kodiak's premier B&B. Big yet cozy home overlooking the channel, a twenty-minute walk from downtown. ⑤.

### The Town and around

**Downtown Kodiak** is usually lively, with plenty of comings and goings in the small-boat harbor and adjacent bars and cafes on Marine Way. The small **Baranov Museum** (June–Aug Mon–Fri 10am–4pm, Sat & Sun noon–4pm; Sept–Jan, March–May Mon–Wed & Fri 10am–4pm, Sat noon–3pm; $2), in an old Russian house opposite the dock, holds Aleut, Russian and American pioneer artifacts, including an impressive collection of whale bones. Nearby, the small but beautifully formed **Alutiiq Museum**, 218 Mission Rd (June–Aug Mon–Sat 10am–6pm, Sun 11am–4pm; Sept–May Tues–Sat 10am–4pm; $2) showcases the life and culture of the island's native people.

Etched out of lush rainforest, less than four miles north, **Fort Abercrombie State Historical Park** is a great place to do some seabird- and **whale-watching**, camp or take a shoreline hike: a meadow at the north end provides a dazzling blaze of color in summer. Other moderately easy **hiking trails** originating near town go to the top of Pillar Mountain and Termination Point. However, most trails are unmaintained and can be confusing; get precise details from the visitor center or the rangers at Fort Abercrombie. The undulating and unpaved **Chiniak Highway** runs for 48 miles to Cape Greville and the *Road's End Cafe*, sweeping through tightly bunched spruce and passing many abandoned World War II defenses plus prime vistas of Chiniak Bay.

### Eating and drinking

Food in Kodiak is generally good, and not overpriced. Junk-food connoisseurs should be aware that the town's *McDonald's* serves a unique delicacy: **Salmon McNuggets**.

**Beryl's Sweet Shop**, 202 Center St (☎907/486-3323). Although its known for its great shakes and ice cream, it also serves good stews, sandwiches and snacks.

**Buskin River Inn Restaurant**, 1395 Airport Way (☎907/487-2700). Where the locals go for top-class seafood and steak. Inventive dishes (average $15), big desserts and a long wine list.

**El Chicano**, 103 Center Ave (☎907/486-6116). Good value and only marginally Americanized Mexican restaurant serving basic fare at reasonable prices (huevos rancheros for around $9).

**Harborside Coffee & Goods**, 216 Shelikof St (☎907/486-5862). Best spot for coffees, pastries and shakes.

**Henry's Great Alaskan Restaurant**, 512 Marine Way (☎907/486-3313). Downtown entertainment hub, open from 11am until the fun runs out.

# Prince William Sound

**Prince William Sound**, a largely unspoiled wilderness of steep fjords and mountains, glaciers and rainforest, rests calmly at the head of the Gulf of Alaska. Sheltered by the Chugach Mountains in the north and east, and the Kenai Peninsula in the west, and with its sparkling blue waters full of whales, porpoise, sea otters and seals, the Sound has a relatively low-key tourist industry. The only significant settlements, spectacular **Valdez**, at the end of the trans-Alaska oil pipeline, and to a lesser extent **Cordova**, a fishing community only accessible by sea or air, are the respective bases from which to see the **Columbia** and **Childs glaciers**. Just behind the Chugach peaks lies the vast and untrammeled world of **Wrangell-St Elias National Park**. Let others throng to Kenai, Denali and the Inside Passage: for unparalleled scenic grandeur and the true solitude of the wilderness, this park is the place to come.

The region's first settlers, the Chugach Eskimos, were edged out by the more aggressive Tlingit, who in turn were displaced first by Russian trappers in search of sea otter pelts, and then by American gold prospectors and fishers. The whole glorious show was very nearly spoiled forever on Good Friday 1989, when the **Exxon Valdez** spilt its cargo of 11 million gallons of crude oil. Although the long-term effects have yet to be fully determined, the spill fortunately affected just a fifth of the Sound and today no surface pollution is visible, safety precautions against a similar event (small spillages still occur regularly) are conspicuously second to none.

# Valdez

**VALDEZ**, 304 road miles from Anchorage and the northernmost ice-free port in the western hemisphere, lies at the head of a fjord that reaches inland twelve miles from Prince William Sound. Known as "Little Switzerland" due to its stunning backdrop of steep mountains, glaciers and waterfalls, and a record annual snowfall of over forty feet, Valdez (pronounced *Valdeez*) offers great hiking, rafting, sea kayaking, wildlife-viewing and, of course, fishing.

The 1890s **Gold Rush** transformed Valdez from a remote whaling station into a flourishing settlement, when thousands of prospectors arrived to head up the Valdez Trail to the mines in the Yukon and Alaskan Interior. They arrived in 1898 to find that no trail existed and that the roughly mapped-out "all-American route" crossed the deadly Valdez and Klutina glaciers. Only an estimated three hundred of the 3500 miners who set out made it to the goldfield – those that did not perish from frostbite and starvation gave up. The gold boom passed as miners found alternative routes, and Valdez came to depend on fish canneries, logging and occasional military use for its economic survival. Nature conspired to finish it off on Good Friday 1964: the epicenter of North America's largest **earthquake** (see p.1094) was just 45 miles away. Shockwaves turned the ground to quivering jelly, snapping roads, toppling buildings, and killing 33 residents. A 30ft wave set off by submarine landslides completed the devastation. However, the citizens of Valdez refused to be intimidated, and moved around sixty buildings to the more stable present site four miles away.

The town's fortunes rose again during the 1970s, when oil was found beneath Prudhoe Bay, and Valdez became the southern terminus of the 800-mile **trans-Alaska pipeline**, which carries up to two million barrels of oil per day. Although winds and tides ensured that no oil from the *Exxon Valdez* made it into the port of Valdez, the spill ironically triggered an economic boom for the city as it was the most accessible site from which to direct the massive **cleanup**. The operation, which lasted into 1991, cost Exxon and the government over one hundred billion dollars. Eleven thousand workers in over one thousand boats and three hundred planes scoured the beaches.

## Arrival and information

One of the most exciting things about Valdez is getting here; both car and ferry rides are unforgettable. The turnoff at Glenallen takes you onto the scenic **Richardson Highway** and the remaining 115 miles hold epic scenery: restful alpine meadows, angry-looking waterfalls, mountain glaciers and the icy summit of **Thompson Pass**. After another twenty miles you pass through the waterfall-fringed **Keystone Canyon** and finally you've reached Valdez and can give your camera a rest.

Alaskon Express, based at the *Westmark Hotel*, 100 Fidalgo Drive (☎907/835-4391), plies the ten-hour route to Anchorage daily in high season for $68. Many visitors arrive on the **Alaska Marine Highway** from either Whittier or Seward at the city dock at the end of Hazelet Avenue (☎907/835-4436). If the weather is clear, the ride offers superb views of the Columbia Glacier. ERA/Alaska Airlines flies two to four times daily to Anchorage (one-way $85) from the **airport** five miles north; **taxis** (☎907/835-2500; $5) run downtown, or you could visit the Alaskan Cultural Center (see overleaf) and use their shuttle to get into town.

The **visitor center** (late May–early Sept daily 8am–8pm; ☎907/835-4636 or 1-800/770-5954, fax 835-4845; *valdez@alaska.net*; *www.alaska.net/~valdezak*) is at 200 Fairbanks St.

## Accommodation

Valdez has very little inexpensive **accommodation**, and what there is gets snapped up pretty quickly, though a free phone (summer only) outside the visitor center connects with some of the fifty-plus **B&Bs**. If you want to **camp**, the *Valdez Glacier Campground*, ($10) seven miles from town past the airport, is somewhat impractical for those without transportation, while the small *Bear Paw* campground (☎907/835-2530; ①), close to the ferry terminal, gets booked up very quickly.

**Casa de La Bellezza B&B**, 333 Oumalik St (☎907/835-4489). Comfortable, oak-floored home with a grand mountain view from the rear deck. Alasko-Italian breakfast and evening snacks. ⑤.

**Downtown B&B**, 113 Galena Drive (☎907/835-2791 or 1-800/478-2791). Don't be fooled by the name – it's more like a small motel – but it enjoys a good location, near the waterfront. ④.

**Keystone Hotel**, 144 Egan Drive (☎907/835-3851 or 1-888/835-0665; *keyston@alaska.net*). Recently renovated hotel with industrial looking steel-clad exterior, but well appointed, comfortable rooms with private bathrooms and a complimentary continental breakfast. ⑥.

**L&L's B&B**, 533 W Hanagita St (☎907/835-4447; *mrlou@alaska.net*). Huge, barn-like home in the posh part of town. Five rooms with shared bathroom. Close to Mineral Creek hikes. ④.

**Valdez Hostel**, 139 Altina St (☎907/835-2155; *vhostel@pobox.alaska.net*). The only hostel in town. A little cramped but there's only three bunks to a room and excellent cooking facilities. Some bedding available for rent but it's best to bring your own. ①.

## The Town

The town's major events are covered in just the right amount of detail in the small but surprisingly absorbing **Valdez Museum**, 217 Egan Drive (summer daily 8am–6pm; $3). They include the Gold Rush, glaciation, the 1964 earthquake, plenty on the oil pipeline which supports the town's economy and a new and long-overdue display on the *Exxon* oil spill. The **Alaskan Cultural Center** (June–Aug daily 9am–6pm; May & Sept Mon–Sat 9am–6pm; $5), out at the airport but with a shuttle bus from town (☎907/834-1690), is concerned with artifacts, notably an astounding collection of carved ivory and an assortment of dead beasts including a couple of moose hides with Alaskan scenes burnt into them by an early pioneer.

A nose around the $1.4 billion Alyeska pipeline terminal, on the other side of the fjord, is recommended. Hot, crude oil arrives at the terminal after a week-long journey from Prudhoe Bay, its passage smoothed to a friction- and turbulence-free surge by an ingenious additive. Along the way it's boosted by eight jet-engine-powered pumping stations which keep it moving at around 7mph. The thick sludge is then stored in eighteen huge tanks before being pumped into the seventy tankers which visit Valdez each month. Tours of the facility are run by Valdez Tours (☎907/835-2686) for $15.

If you fancy something more active, **mountain bikes** can be rented at Beaver Sports, 316 Galena St (☎907/835-4727), and Keystone Raft and Kayak Adventures, at Mile 17 on the Richardson Highway (☎907/835-2606 or 1-800/328-8460; $50) can take you **rafting** along the Lowe River as it surges through Keystone Canyon. Out in the Sound, Anadyr Adventures (☎907/835-2814) offers **sea kayaking** among the ice floes and whales from around $90.

## The Columbia Glacier

Nearly four miles wide at its face and towering three hundred feet above the sea, **Columbia Glacier** is particularly spectacular when huge blocks of ice crash into the water. Unfortunately it is receding by half a mile a year and the fjord is now so choked with ice that you can't get close to the face. You can see it at long range from the Alaska Marine Highway **ferries** running between Valdez and Whittier, but for a closer look at this calving giant contact experienced operators like Stan Stephens (☎907/835-4731 or 1-800/992-1297), who pick their way through a floating icefield and point out such sights as Bligh Reef, where the *Exxon Valdez* ran aground. Choose between an eight-hour cruise, which includes a salmon bake, for $109, and a six-hour cruise at $69.

## Eating

Don't schedule a gourmet night out while in Valdez. Considering its size and wealth, the town's **dining** options are disappointing.

**Alaska Halibut House**, 208 Meals Ave (☎907/835-2788). Fast food, but for the most part fresh (fried) local seafood: catch of the day and fries from $7. Treat yourself to a halibut basket.

**Mike's Pizza Palace**, 210 N Harbor Drive (☎907/835-2365). Despite the name, this is the best place in town for steak and seafood – try the Goldrush Seafood Platter. Great view of the harbor from the bar.

**Oscar's**, 143 N Harbor Drive (☎907/835-4700). Next to *Mike's*, this hangout is a combination of diner, fast-food-joint, coffee shop and ice-cream parlor. Summer only.

**The Pipeline Club**, at the *Pipeline Inn*, 136 Egan Drive (☎907/835-4332). Reasonable steak and seafood dinners in a dark bar reminiscent of Alaska in the 1970s.

# Cordova

Far quieter than Valdez, and only accessible by sea or air, **CORDOVA** is an unpretentious fishing community set in forests and mountains on the southeastern edge of the Sound. In 1906, the Irish engineer **Michael J Heney** (who made a name for himself by building the White Pass and Yukon Railway over "impassable" terrain out of Skagway) chose Cordova as the port from which to ship the copper mined in Kennicott, a hundred miles northeast. The government labeled it a foolhardy idea (his proposed Copper River and Northwestern Railroad – the CR&NW– was ridiculed as "Can't Run & Never Will") and commissioned a syndicate headed by Guggenheim to lay tracks over an easier but longer route to Katalla, near Valdez. Heney, who had rejected Katalla as being prone to winter storms, and gambled on trying to cut a path between two active glaciers, was vindicated when a huge gale wrecked the Katalla pier. His crew won the race, but only after completing the elaborate **"Million Dollar Bridge"** across the glacier-walled Copper River in 1911.

Ironically after such effort, the mines became exhausted just 27 years later. Cordova shifted its dependency to fishing, but this was also dealt a potentially fatal blow in 1989 with the grounding of the *Exxon Valdez*. For the next two seasons, the community reeled from the effects of the **oil spill**. Fortunately, it now seems that most of the salmon and halibut have survived, though fishers still bear a grudge against the oil companies – just read their bumper stickers.

Today the "Million Dollar Bridge," heavily battered by the 1964 earthquake, cuts a lonely figure at the end of the Copper River Highway, a gravel road that traverses the wondrous **Copper River Delta**, a major homing ground for America's migratory birds. Right next to the bridge is the incredibly active **Childs Glacier**. The delta and glacier rank as two of Alaska's very best sights – few tourists get to see them, but if current plans to overhaul the bridge and build a road over the old railroad tracks to Chitina are realized, you can be guaranteed that this desolate area will be mobbed out.

There are few sights in Cordova; the **small-boat harbor** is the core of the town's activity, particularly when the fleet is in, from May until September. The **Cordova Historical Museum** on First and Adams (late May–early Sept Mon–Sat 10am–6pm, Sun 2–4pm; rest of year Tues–Fri 1–5pm, Sat 2–4pm; $1 donation) has quirky exhibits on local history, including the evolution of the little **ice worm** that lives in the glaciers, and the funky annual festival that celebrates its existence.

## Practicalities

There is no road access to Cordova; **flights** land at the airport twelve miles down the Copper River Highway. Alaska Airlines has daily flights from Anchorage, for around $90 or $120 APEX round-trip. A **bus** from the airport costs $9. Most people get to

Cordova on the Alaska Marine Highway's *Tustumena* or *Bartlett* **ferries**, which visit Cordova thrice weekly. The ferry dock lies a mile north of downtown (☎907/424-7333). The tiny **Chamber of Commerce** office is on First Street (summer only Mon–Fri 10am–5.30am; ☎907/424-7260).

Most of Cordova's **hotels** get fully booked in summer, but **B&Bs** are a good option – try the *Northern Nights Inn*, 501 Third Ave (☎907/424-5356; ③), or the *Cordova Rose Lodge*, 1315 Whitshed Rd, a mile east of downtown (☎907/424-7673; ③), built into a permanently dry-docked barge filled with nautical artifacts. There are USFS forest **cabins** (☎907/424-7661; $25 per night) throughout the Copper River Delta. The nearest **campground** is the scruffy *Odiak Camper Park* on Whitshed Road, half a mile south of town. To **eat**, check out the popular *Killer Whale Cafe* on First Street above the *Orca Bookshop* (☎907/424-7733), or the superb seafood at the pricier *Reluctant Fisherman Inn*, 407 Railroad Ave (☎907/424-3272 or 1-800/267-3682; $85–125). Wash it all down afterwards, at the *Alaskan Hotel*'s **bar**.

## Copper River Delta

A superb 48-mile drive along the mostly unpaved Copper River Highway leads through the incredible wetlands of the **Copper River Delta**, a fascinating tapestry of marshes, sluggish streams, glacial sloughs and shallow ponds, all backed by the heavy-shouldered Chugach Mountains. This is also one of the continent's best sites for bird-watching. Common mammals include moose, beaver and mountain goat, while bears can often be seen feasting upon berries or fishing out salmon in summer. In all, it's a wonderful – and tranquil – site for fishing, bird-watching or **hiking** along many of the excellent trails, such as the difficult trek up to Crater Lake.

A visit to Cordova simply has to incorporate a trip along the entire length of the Copper River Highway to **Childs Glacier**. By far the best way to experience it is in your own vehicle rented (for around $75 a day, unlimited mileage) from either the *Reluctant Fisherman Inn* (☎907/424-3272) in town or Cordova Car Rental (☎907/424-5982) at the airport. Alternatively, Copper River/Northwest Tours (☎907/424-5356) runs a six-hour tour to the bridge for $45 including lunch.

# Wrangell-St Elias National Park

As Denali becomes more crowded, people are increasingly making the trip to more out-of-the-way **WRANGELL-ST ELIAS NATIONAL PARK**, in the extreme southeast corner of the Interior. Just over the (inaccessible) peaks from Valdez and Cordova, the park is where four of the continent's great mountain ranges – the Wrangell, St Elias, Chugach and Alaska – cramp up against each other. Most of the eastern border is shared with the adjoining Kluane National Park in Canada. Even the usually reserved National Park Service literature breaks ranks by saying, "Incredible. You have to see Wrangell-St Elias . . . to believe it – and even then you won't be so sure."

Everything in Wrangell-St Elias is writ large: peak after peak (including nine of the sixteen highest in the US), glacier after enormous glacier, canyon after dizzying canyon – all laced together by braided rivers, massive moraines and idyllic lakes, with the volcanic monster of Mount Wrangell still steaming on in the background. Vegetation struggles to take hold in much of the park, though does enough to support mountain goats, Dall sheep, bears and moose throughout its environs, while the silty lowlands are traversed by sizeable herds of caribou.

Wrangell-St Elias, created in 1980, is very much in a stage of development, with a lot of the land still privately owned although projects are underway to improve the track to

McCarthy and facilities at Kennicott. The first whites in the area came in search of gold but instead hit upon one of the continent's richest copper deposits. The mines closed in 1938, after 27 frantic years of production, and today **Kennicott**, with over thirty creaking, disused buildings, looks like a ghost town, save for the *Kennicott Glacier Lodge* which accounts for most of the population. The railroad once ran all the way from here to Cordova, via Chitina, and sections of it make a great bike ride, though collapsed bridges prevent a full traverse.

**McCarthy**, the main social hub and base for outfitters, lies at the end of the entrance road. Its main feature is the old *McCarthy Lodge* with rooms, and a lively bar (see below for details). Wrangell-St Elias is a trailless park, so in theory you can head off near enough anywhere, but St Elias Alpine Guides (☎907/277-6867) offers a number of hikes, ice climbing, mountain bike rides, raft trips and even glacier skiing.

## Practicalities

Getting here is half the fun. From Glenallen, travel 32 miles along the Edgerton Highway to Chitina, from where a car-wide defile frames the spectacle ahead: the start of the rough, 58-mile dirt road to McCarthy. Running along an old railway line (rail spikes can still cause punctures), hemmed in by trees which obscure the fantastic scenery, allow at least three hours and patience with other road users. The rickety, 90-year-old rail bridge 400ft above the Kuskulana River at Mile 17 is a highlight not for the faint of heart – the guard rails are only a recent addition.

The road ends at the Kennicott River, which you cross via a footbridge. From here it's a half-mile walk to the hamlet of McCarthy, from where a shuttle bus runs along the rough five-mile dirt road to Kennicott.

Hitching along the McCarthy road can be a hit-or-miss affair; if you haven't got a vehicle you can take a McCarthy Kennicott Shuttle (mid-May–mid-Sept Mon–Sat; ☎907/822-5292 or 1-800/478-5292) from Glenallen ($105 round-trip) on the main Anchorage–Valdez bus route, or from Chitina ($70). Alternatively, you can enjoy a great **flight** into McCarthy from Glenallen or Chitina with Wrangell Mountain Air (☎1-800/478-1160; $130 round-trip).

Due to their remoteness, McCarthy and Kennicott are not cheap places to **stay**, though more affordable in the shoulder season. The budget options are all along the final quarter-mile of road and include **camping**, either at the free campground (no water) a mile before the road end, or on the gravel parking lot at the road end ($10). In the same area is *Kennicott River Lodge and Hostel* (☎907/554-4441; *krlah@polarnet.com*; ①), a newish house with large common area and sauna surrounded by four-bunk cabins and a sleeping loft. Showers cost $5; bring a sleeping bag and food to prepare. The best bet actually in McCarthy is the very pleasant *Ma Johnson Hotel/McCarthy Lodge* (☎907/554-4402; ⑥), which evokes the atmosphere of its 1916 construction date. In Kennicott there's the upscale *Kennicott Glacier Lodge* (☎907/554-4477, fax 248-7975; ⑥), and *Historic Kennicott B&B*, 14 Silk Stocking Row (☎907/554-4469; *kennicottbb@aol.com*; ⑤) in a former mill managers' cottage.

The park's **visitor center** is at the Copper Center turnoff at Mile 111 on the Richardson Hwy (late May–early Sept daily 8am–6pm; early Sept–late May Mon–Fri 8am–5pm; ☎907/822-7261, fax 822-7216) with another summer-only facility at Chitina.

Another, less well-known track, the **Nabesna Road**, cuts 45 miles into the northern fringe of the park from the village of **Slana** on the Tok cutoff between Glennallen and Tok. A summer-only ranger station operates at Slana (mid-May–mid-Sept daily 8am–7pm; ☎ & fax 907/822-5558) and you'll find a few cabins and campgrounds nearby, but nothing except a lodge with fuel at Mile 28 all the way to **Nabesna**, a moribund mining community.

# INTERIOR ALASKA

Falling roughly within a triangle outlined by the Glenn, Parks and Alaska highways, **Interior Alaska** cannot fail to live up to expectations of the Great Land. For the most part it's a rolling plateau in between the Alaska and Brooks ranges, crisscrossed by river valleys, punctuated by glaciers and with views of imposing peaks, including ever present Mount McKinley, the nation's highest. Even in high summer, when RVs clog the Parks Highway, people are still hugely outnumbered by game: moose, Dall sheep, grizzly bears and herds of caribou sweep over seemingly endless swathes of taiga (birch woodland) and tundra.

Tourists speeding north from Anchorage to Denali tend to overlook the magnificent glacially contorted **Mat-Su Valley**, thirty-odd miles north. Stop by antiquated **Palmer**, heart of the state's most concentrated agricultural region, then follow the scenic summer-only Fishhook–Willow Road which runs high over 3886ft **Hatcher Pass** through the Talkeetna Mountains, twisting and weaving for 32 unpaved miles across the ranges, past old mines and memorable vistas, to join the Parks Highway for the run north to Denali.

The jewel of the Interior is **Denali National Park**, some one hundred miles south of **Fairbanks**, a jumping-off point for the roadless and virtually uninhabited **Alaskan Bush**. Weather can vary enormously from day to day, with even greater seasonal variations: in winter temperatures can drop to -50°F for days at a time, while summer days reach a sweltering 90°F. However, the major problem during the warmer months is huge mosquitoes – with attitude. Don't leave without insect repellent.

## Talkeetna

At Mile 98.7 on the Parks Highway comes the fourteen-mile turnoff to tiny **TALKEETNA**, the center for climbers attempting Mount McKinley, and an idyllic example of a pleasant Bush community. Its log cabins and smalltown-Alaska feel, combined with an international flavor as mountaineers from all over the world gather to prepare for their assaults on McKinley, make it an unusual if not downright essential stop. The view of "the Mountain" from the overlook as you descend into town cannot fail to impress, especially when you realize that McKinley is still sixty miles away. Rumor has it that this eclectic hamlet was the model for Cicely in *Northern Exposure*, but to its credit Talkeetna doesn't use this as tour-bus bait.

The major summer celebration – the **Moose Dropping Festival** – falls on the second weekend of July; little brown balls can be purchased (with a sanitary coat of varnish) for use as earrings, necklaces and so on, throughout the town. In addition to these highly desirable lumps of Alaskana, the festival features dancing, drinking and a moose-dropping throwing competition and some more drinking.

**Trains** en route between Anchorage and Denali stop half a mile south of the center of Talkeetna once a day. Hitching the fourteen miles to and from the Parks Highway rarely poses any problems, but Talkeetna Shuttle Services (☎1-888/288-6008 or 907/733-1725) run daily from Anchorage for $40. Information is widely available from the gas station, various giftshops, the laid-back Museum of Northern Adventure (daily summer 11am–7pm; $2.50) or, more conventionally, the **Talkeetna Ranger Station**, on B Street (late April–early Sept daily 8am–6pm; early Sept–late April Mon–Fri 8am–5pm; ☎907/733-2231, fax 733-1465).

For a town of just three hundred ("and one grouch," the sign proclaims) Talkeetna teems with good **accommodation**, the cheapest being the central *Talkeetna Hostel* on I St (☎907/733-4678, fax 733-4679; *www.akhostel.com*; bunks ①, rooms ②). Dating back to 1917, the central *Talkeetna Roadhouse* (☎907/733-1351, fax 733-1353; *rdhouse@ alaska.net*; ④), bolsters its old-style atmosphere with some great home cooking and rooms with shared bathrooms. Rooms at the *Swiss Alaskan Inn* (☎907/733-2424; ⑤) near the air strip, include authentic jacuzzis, and *Belle's Cabin* on Main Street (☎907/733-2414; ⑤) serve Denali-sized breakfasts. **Campers** can stay at the *Talkeetna River Park* ($8), at the western end of main street, but most tenters stroll a hundred yards further west from the latter and (unofficially) pitch on the river flats.

Good places to **eat** include the *McKinley Deli* at Main and C streets (☎907/733-1234) which serves pizza, and the *Latitude 62* motel (☎907/733-2262; ④), for steak and seafood dinners. And make sure you have a **drink** in the wonderfully ancient *Fairview Inn* on Main Street (☎907/733-2423; ③).

## Denali National Park

The six-million-acre wildlife reserve of **DENALI NATIONAL PARK**, beginning 237 miles north of Anchorage, is named after the Athabascan word for its most famous denizen, **Mount McKinley**. However, the mountain is far from being the park's only attraction. In fact it's frequently surrounded by a thick blanket of cloud, and only around one-quarter of visitors actually get to see the snow-covered massif. Don't let this put you off, as a ride through Denali on a shuttle bus guarantees a chance to glimpse a vast world of tundra and taiga, glaciers and U-shaped valleys, still lakes and other huge mountains in the Alaska range. Best of all is the park's prolific wildlife population – most visitors return with tales of sighting grizzlies, caribou, moose and Dall sheep.

Visiting Alaska without trying to see Denali is unthinkable for most travelers, and therein lies the park's problem. In the height of summer, the visitor center and the service hotels out on the Parks Highway are a stream of campervans, tour buses and the like. Things pick up in the park itself, and backcountry hiking, undertaken by only a tiny fraction of visitors, remains a wonderfully solitary experience.

---

### MOUNT McKINLEY/DENALI – THE GREAT ONE

Long before whites reached Alaska, Athabascan natives referred to **Mount McKinley** as **Denali**, "the Great One." Although an early adventurer renamed the mountain after the governor of Ohio who later became the 25th US president, Alaskans have never really taken to the name, and still refer to both the mountain and the park by their original title. Whatever you choose to call it, North America's tallest mountain rises from 2000ft lowlands to a height of 20,320ft, and on a clear day its white glow, in sharp contrast to the warm colors all around, makes for a transcendent experience.

The ice-covered giant dominates life in the village of **Talkeetna**, 153 road miles south of the park entrance, during the climbing season of mid-April to mid-July. Only 45 percent of the one thousand mountaineers who annually tackle McKinley, "the coldest mountain in the world" – and the highest from base to peak (Everest et al start off from a high plateau) – succeed in the ascent, thanks largely to extreme weather conditions. Swirling ice storms can trap climbers for days, and almost every season sees at least one fatality.

Several companies based in Talkeetna will whisk you on a 120-mile, ninety-minute "Circle McKinley" flight over moose-grazing lowlands, past ugly moraines, alongside dazzlingly blue glaciers and (weather permitting) the peak, from $140. Less ambitious flights, still closely approaching the mountain go from $95. K2 Aviation (☎907/733-2291 or 1-800/764-2291, fax 733-1221; *flyk2@alaska.net*; *www.alaska.net/~flyk2*), the choice of most climbing expeditions, offers the widest range of options, including a glacier landing at base camp in planes fitted with skis.

## Getting to the park

Driving to the Denali Park entrance (Mile 237.3 Parks Hwy) takes about five hours from Anchorage, three from Fairbanks. **Hitching** along the Parks Highway is quite easy, especially during the summer when there are more than twenty hours of daylight. Alternatively, the convenient and comfortable trains of the **Alaska Railroad** leave Anchorage daily in summer at 8.15am; the trip to the station at Denali, one and a half miles inside the park entrance, takes almost eight hours and costs $102 one-way ($84 in shoulder season). The 8.15am departure from Fairbanks is $54 one-way ($44 in shoulder season) and pulls in at noon. The luxurious way to arrive is in one of the (expensive) glass-domed railroad cars operated from Anchorage by Princess Tours (☎1-800/835-8907) and Gray Line (☎1-800/544-2206).

Several Anchorage-based companies such as Alaska Backpacker Shuttle (☎1-800/266-8625; $40) run shuttles to Denali; Parks Highway Express (☎1-888/600-6001) charges $35 for the park and runs on to Fairbanks ($49).

## Accommodation

With the exception of several exclusive lodges deep in the heart of the park, there are no hotels in Denali, and most unimaginative souls head for the busy summer-only gaggle of hotels and cabins a mile or so north of the park entrance. You can do better than this: ten miles further up the road, the little coal-mining town of **HEALY** boasts three motels which stay open all year and the compact, spotless and very popular *Denali Hostel*, Mile 1.3 Otto Lake Rd (☎907/683-1295, fax 683-2106; ①) which has a complimentary shuttle run to the park twice a day. There is also a number of good **B&Bs** – such as the comfortable *Alaskan Chateau*, Sulphide Road (☎907/683-1377, fax 683-1380; *chepoda@mtaonline.net*; ⑤), and the multilevel geodesic *Dome Home B&B*, E Healy Spur Road, just off Mile 248.8 Parks Hwy (☎907/683-1239, fax 683-2322; *denalidome@alaskaone.com*; ⑤).

**Camping** is the best way to experience Denali up close, with most of the park's eight campgrounds open from mid-May to mid-September. The best sites are at **Wonder Lake**, with a stunning view of McKinley; failing that, **Igloo Creek** is good for spotting Dall sheep, while **Riley Creek** near the entrance is open all year. All sites cost $12, and all (except the $6 *Morino* walk-in, where you can self-register) are bookable at the main visitor center or on ☎1-800/622-7275. If you don't do this you may have to wait for up to three days to get a spot.

The best alternative is *Denali Grizzly Bear Cabins & Campground*, Mile 231.1, seven miles south of Denali (☎907/683-1337, fax 683-2697; ①–④), set in the trees close to the Nenana River with simple but attractive cabins all around. A number of private campgrounds line the Parks Highway north and south of the entrance; most are gravel lots geared towards RVs and wholly unappealing for tenting. If pushed try *Denali Rainbow Village RV Park*, Mile 238.6 (☎907/683-3362, fax 683-7275; ①), a mile north of the entrance.

## Sightseeing, hiking and other activities

Bar a few tour companies and those with special permits, the only vehicles allowed on Denali's narrow, unpaved 97-mile road are green **shuttle buses**, a policy that ensures that the native flora and fauna remain, for the most part, undisturbed. Buses costs $21 to the Eielson Visitor Center and $27 to Wonder Lake; reserve on ☎907/622-7275 or 1-800/622-7275) plus the $5 park entrance fee which is good for a week, but, and it's a big but, you may have to wait up to three days to get on one. Tickets are available up to two days in advance from the **Visitors Access Center (VAC)**, just inside the park entrance (late April–late Sept daily 7am–8pm; closed in winter; ☎907/683-1266, or ☎452-PARK for recorded information). The VAC also stocks a wide range of literature, and each visitor receives a copy of the *Denali Alpenglow* paper; ranger-led activities include short hikes and the popular, and free, dogsled demonstration held daily at 10am, 2pm and 4pm.

Shuttle buses run to either the **Eielson Visitor Center** at Mile 66, where rangers lead one-hour tundra tours each day at 1.30pm, or to the aptly named **Wonder Lake** at Mile 84; round-trips take about eight and ten hours respectively. You can, of course, jump off the bus at any point along the route for a hike and return to the road and flag down the next bus to the VAC if it has room. Though the shuttle bus drivers do not give guided tours, with up to forty pairs of watchful eyes on board, you're almost guaranteed to see the big mammals; a recent park questionnaire revealed that 95 percent of visitors saw **bear, caribou** and **Dall sheep**, 82 percent moose, and over one-fifth **wolves**. Other regularly sighted creatures include porcupine, snowshoe hare and red foxes, while over 160 bird species populate the park.

**Backcountry hiking** represents the best way to appreciate Denali's scenery and its inhabitants. Don't expect it to be easy though, there are no formal trails and, what with thick spongy tundra and frequent river crossings, even hardy hikers find themselves limited to five miles a day. The park is divided into 43 units and only a designated number of hikers is allowed into each section at a time. Free permits are available, one day in advance, from the VAC's **Backcountry Desk** (daily 7am–8pm), though high demand means you should be prepared to hike in the less popular areas. The backcountry desk will also issue you with bear-resistant food containers: the idea is to disassociate human smells and food, thus sparing bears from becoming dependent on hikers, and hikers from becoming food for bears. It's also compulsory to view the five backcountry simulator programs in the VAC before you set out across fast-flowing rivers and within sniffing distance of the grizzlies. Special camper buses – reserved for those with campground or backcountry permits – head into the park; riders are free to get off in their assigned section and start hiking. It's not a bad idea to reconnoitre the park on a full-day bus trip in order to choose where you might like to hike on subsequent days. If there's room, buses also carry bikes; cyclists can be dropped off wherever they like, but are obliged to keep to the road.

An alternative to going it alone is to join a **narrated tour** (☎1-800/276-7234) along the park road: either the three-hour Natural History Tour for $35; or the full-day Wildlife Tour ($61) which penetrates as far as Mile 53 stopping frequently to observe wildlife.

Just outside the park entrance, several **rafting** companies offer two-hour trips down the Nenana River: all offer a gentle "scenic float," and an eleven-mile "Canyon Run" through Class III and IV rapids – they cost around $45 individually and $60–65 for a joint run. Denali Outdoor Center (☎907/683-1925 or 1-888/303-1925; *docadventure@ hotmail.com*) charge a couple of dollars more than some of the others but offer a quality experience and the luxury of dry-suits. For close-up views of Mount McKinley, hourlong **flight-seeing tours** cost about $170 with companies such as Peré Air (☎907/683-6033); though flights from Talkeetna are better value.

In **winter**, Denali is transformed into a ghostly, snow-covered world. Motorized vehicles are banned and transportation, even for park personnel, is by snowshoe, skis or dogsled as temperatures dive and northern lights glitter over the snows.

# Fairbanks

**FAIRBANKS**, 358 miles north of Anchorage, is at the end of the Alaska Highway route from Canada and definitely at the end of the road for most tourists. Its central location makes it the focal point for the tiny villages scattered around the surrounding wilderness, and a staging post for North Slope villages such as **Barrow** and the oil community of **Prudhoe Bay**. These northern areas are all accessible by air, but only the latter can be reached by the region's only road, the **Dalton Highway**, also known as the Haul Road in honor of its stop-for-nothing trucks.

The town was founded accidentally when, in 1901, a steamship carrying E T Barnette, a merchant with all his wares on board, ran aground in the shallows of the Chena River. Unable to transport the supplies he was carrying, Barnette set up shop in the wilderness and catered to the few trappers and prospectors trying their luck in the area. The following year, with the beginnings of the **Gold Rush**, a tent city sprang up on the site, and Barnette made a mint.

In 1908, at the height of the gold stampede, Fairbanks had a population of 18,500. Due to the difficulty in retrieving gold from the frozen bedrock, most independent miners gave up, and by 1920 the population had dwindled to only 1100. The community sputtered along until World War II, when several huge **military bases** were built to thwart possible Japanese attacks. Many bases remained after the war (and still do today), and the town received another major boost in the mid-1970s when it became the transportation center for the **trans-Alaska oil pipeline** project: construction and other oil-related activities brought a rush of workers seeking wages of up to $1500 per week and the population reached an all-time high. The city's economy dropped dramatically with the oil crash, and unemployment hit twenty percent before government spending put the city back on track.

Fairbanks may be flat and somewhat bland, but it's bang in the middle of Alaska and makes a good base for exploring a hinterland of gold mines, hot springs and bush communities, and is surrounded by rolling hills beyond which roll the Alaska and Brooks ranges. Tourism is becoming an increasingly important earner. The spectacular **aurora borealis** is a major winter attraction, as is the **Ice Festival** in mid-March, when the North American Open Sled Dog Championships take place on the frozen downtown streets. The festival is perhaps most famous for its ice-sculpting competition; the extraordinary design and detail that go into these large works makes it well worth braving the breath-freezing temperatures.

Summer visitors should try to catch the three-day **World Eskimo-Indian Olympics** in mid-July. Competitors from around the state compete in the standard dance, art and sports competitions, as well as some unusual ones like ear-pulling, knuckle hop, high kick and the blanket toss, where age and wisdom often defeat youth and strength.

Fairbanks suffers remarkable extremes of climate. Temperatures can drop to -70°F, yet rise to over 90°F in summer. Because the city sits just 188 miles south of the Arctic Circle, where the sun neither sets during the summer solstice nor rises during the winter solstice, Fairbanks also has very long days. The shortest day of the year has fewer than three hours of sunlight, the longest has over 21. Both can be disconcerting, and residents suffer from a high rate of depression. In summer, midnight baseball games under natural light are great fun, but stumbling out of a bar at 2am into bright sunshine can be really perturbing.

## Arrival, information and getting around

Alaska Airlines, Delta and United all offer daily services from Anchorage to **Fairbanks International Airport** which lies four miles southwest of downtown; the MACS **bus** Yellow Line (not Sun; $1.50) runs downtown but the long wait between services means you'll probably want to grab a **taxi** (around $12), or the GO Shuttle (☎907/474-3847) which charges $7 per person to your accommodation. The airport also acts as a gateway for flights into the bush; Frontier Flying Service (☎907/474-0011) operates a reliable service, weather permitting.

By road, Fairbanks is 653 miles from Haines via the Alaska Highway, and 348 miles north of Anchorage along the scenic Parks Highway. **Alaska Railroad trains**, stopping downtown at 280 N Cushman Rd, offer a more relaxing way of enjoying the landscape between Anchorage and Fairbanks, for $154 one-way in peak season, $120 in shoulder season (daily in summer; once or twice weekly in winter). Several very competitive minibus companies run here from Anchorage (around $65 one-way), all stopping at Denali: try Parks Highway Express (☎1-888/600-6001), Alaska Backpacker Shuttle (☎1-800/344-8775) and Fireweed Express (☎907/458-8267). Alaskon Express (☎1-800/544-2206) makes the trip four times a week from Haines ($180) and Skagway ($205) via Whitehorse, Canada. The two-day bus trip stops overnight at Beaver Creek in the Yukon, where you make your own sleeping arrangements (motel rooms $43 per person and up; camping $20).

Sprawling Fairbanks belies its meager population of 45,000; having a vehicle is a good idea. Five **bus lines**, run by MACS (☎907/459-1011), provide a reasonable service, but routes and schedules change frequently; call for information or collect a schedule from the visitor center (see below) or the Transit Center at N Cushman Street and 5th Avenue (Mon–Fri 6.30am–8pm, Sat 10am–6pm). GO Shuttle Service (☎907/474-3847 or 1-800/478-3847) offers transport to sights within the city for $5, and outside for $15 – considerably cheaper than going by taxi. Several other companies can whisk you off into the bush and Alaska's far west. The Northern Alaska Tour Company (☎907/474-8600) is the specialist for the Arctic Circle and Prudhoe Bay, while Gray Line operates tours to Denali, Barrow and the Yukon. Unashamedly touristy but great fun and very popular is a four-hour **cruise** down the Chena River on the *Riverboat Discovery* (☎907/479-6673; $40), which includes a visit to a mock Native village.

Numbered avenues in Fairbanks run parallel to the Chena River, getting higher as you head south. The **visitor center**, 550 First Ave (mid-May–early Sept daily 8am–8pm; early Sept–mid-May Mon–Fri 8am–5pm; ☎907/456-5774 or 1-800/327-5774), stores a vast amount of information on lodging and activities. For information on the area's parks, including Denali, the useful **Alaska Public Land Information Center** (APLIC) is at 250 N Cushman St (June–early Sept daily 9am–6pm; early Sept–May Tues–Sat 10am–6pm; ☎907/456-0527).

## Accommodation

The motels and hotels in downtown Fairbanks tend to be either quite pricey or pretty dodgy. **B&B**s are plentiful, with rooms from $65; the visitor center offers free phone calls and all the brochures. Thankfully there are plenty of hostels, all close to a good bus route. For campers, the best choice is the tranquil *Tanana Valley Campground*, 1800 College Rd at Aurora Drive (mid-May–mid-Sept; ☎907/456-7956; $6) on the MACS bus Red line (hourly or better) and with free bikes for guests' use.

**Ah, Rose Marie**, 302 Cowles St at 3rd Ave (☎907/456-2040, fax 456-6193). Justly popular B&B that's a little cramped but imaginatively decorated and well-run by the charming host, John. Some rooms have private facilities and a hearty breakfast is served on the glassed-in veranda. Some single rooms for ③, shared facilities ④, private ⑤.

**Alaska Heritage Inn B&B and Hostel**, 1018 22nd Ave (☎907/451-6587, fax 456-6511). Inexpensive B&B rooms ($54) with continental or Alaskan breakfast, dorm beds from $16, and camping for $10. ①–③.

**A B&B Inn on Minnie Street**, 345 Minnie St (☎907/456-1802 or 1-888/456-1849, fax 451-1751; *minniebb@mosquitonet.com*). Top-line B&B with every luxury taken to the nth degree. Some rooms share a bathroom, but you always get bathrobes which you can wear down to the communally served full breakfast. Shared bath ⑤, private bath ⑥.

**Billie's Backpackers**, 2895 Mack Rd (☎ & fax 907/479-2034). Welcoming though somewhat cramped hostel, in a nice area and handily placed on the bus route between downtown and the university. Bikes available at $25 a day. Bunks and camping available. ①.

**Fairbanks Hotel**, 517 3rd Ave (☎907/456-6411, fax 456-1792; *fbxhotl@alaska.net*). Good-value downtown hotel done in ersatz Miami Beach Deco style, featuring small but cheerily decorated rooms each with cable TV and a washstand, and some with private bath. Shared bath ④, private bath ⑤.

**Golden North Motel**, 4888 Old Airport Way (☎1-800/447-1910, fax 907/479-5766). Spotlessly-clean motel with neat rooms (some with separate bedroom) which come with cable TV and a complimentary continental breakfast. Located out towards the airport, they do courtesy train station and airport pickups, but it is inconvenient without your own wheels. ⑤.

**Grandma Shirley's**, 510 Dunbar St (☎907/451-9816). Clean and tidy hostel run by Grandma Shirley who makes up the beds on arrival (linen provided), and generally runs a tight ship. Guests get the use of the family kitchen, bikes are available and they'll store bags if you are away hiking. The MACS bus Purple line passes within a block. Dorms ①.

**Midge's Birch Lane B&B**, 4335 Birch Lane (☎907/388-8084 or 1-800/479-4895; *midge@alaska.net*). Relaxed, welcoming, spacious house in the quiet University district. Rooms with and without private bathrooms. ④.

**A Taste of Alaska Lodge**, Eberhardt Rd, Mile 5.3 Chena Hot Springs Rd (☎907/488-7855). Somewhere in between a B&B and a small country lodge. Sumptuous decor and a good view of McKinley. ⑥.

## The Town

**Downtown Fairbanks** shouldn't take up much of your time. Besides the **visitor centers**, the only real stop of interest is the small **Fairbanks Community Museum**, 450 Cushman St at 5th Avenue (June–early Sept Mon–Sat 10am–5pm; $1 donation requested), containing locally-donated trapping, mining and dogsled racing equipment along with a mock-up of a trapper's cabin, assorted prospecting implements and a handmade Athapascan birch sled lined up next to its modern racing equivalent. Nearby, **Yukon Quest**, 558 2nd Ave at Cushman acts as the public face of the Yukon Quest dogsled race – a grueling thousand-mile marathon between Fairbanks and Whitehorse, Yukon – and sells related books, videos and T-shirts. A similarly wintry theme is pursued at the **Ice Museum**, 500 2nd Ave at Lacey Street (June–mid-Sept daily 10am–6pm; $6), a year-round chance to get a flavor of the annual Ice Sculpting competition by means of a slide show and walk in refrigerators housing some small ice carvings.

A couple of miles west on Airport Way, the forty-acre **Alaskaland** complex on the banks of the Chena River celebrates Alaskan history in a very touristy, but not unpleasant way; admission is free, though different attractions charge small fees. Two reasonable **museums** cover the early pioneering days, and the **Crooked Creek and Whiskey Island Railroad** encircles the entire park. A carousel, playgrounds and crazy golf course account for the rest of the space. Numerous free shuttle buses head out from the major hotels in town, and there is sometimes a bus from the visitor center.

The **University of Alaska-Fairbanks (UAF) Museum** (May & Sept daily 9am–5pm; June–Aug daily 9am–7pm; Oct–April Mon–Fri 9am–5pm, Sat & Sun noon–5pm; $5), occupying a corner of the attractive campus on the northeastern edge of town, houses some of the best examples of Native artifacts and pioneer relics, as well as natural and human history displays, in Alaska.

## Eating

You should be able to find pretty much any food you want in Fairbanks, not least inexpensive Thai cuisine at restaurants and the *Bahn Thai* takeaway wagon on 2nd Avenue. Broadly, the cheaper places congregate around the western end of College Road towards the university, and the pricier places are further out, with the gaps being plugged by mid-range places and all the franchise joints you could ask for – especially along Airport Way. For groceries try the 24-hour Carr's supermarket downtown at 526 Gafney Rd.

**Gambardella's Pasta Bella**, 706 2nd Ave, downtown (☎907/456-3417). Fairbanks' best Italian and not wildly expensive, with a pleasant outdoor area for those endless summer evenings.

**Gulliver's Books Cafe**, 3525 College Rd (☎907/474-9574). Pleasant spot above a bookstore, serving chicken tarragon wraps for under $5, pesto turkey melts, bagels, biscotti and coffee all at reasonable prices, and free Internet access to boot.

**Pump House**, Mile 1.3 Chena Pump Rd (☎907/479-8452). A local favorite in a historic pumphouse stuffed with gold mining paraphernalia and set by the Chena River with a deck to watch river life go by. Great for steak, seafood and burgers, and also pulls in a substantial drinking crowd.

**Souvlaki**, 310 1st Ave, downtown (☎907/452-5393). Bargain Greek and American dishes served in spartan surroundings. Stuffed vine leaves are only 50¢ each, Greek salad and *spanakopita* are both under $4 and crab quiche and souvlaki barely break $6. Closed Sun.

**Thai House**, 526 5th Ave, downtown (☎907/452-6123). A small but ever-popular restaurant serving the usual range of Thai dishes, but all done to perfection and at very modest prices around the $9 mark. The green and red curries with zucchini, peas and peppers are especially good. Closed Sun.

**Two Rivers Lodge**, Mile 16 Chena Hot Springs Rd (☎907/488-6815). A fair way out of town, but it's a pleasant drive and you'll be well rewarded with a huge menu stretching to spicy Louisiana alligator tail ($11) followed by Mediterranean linguini and shrimp ($17).

**Whole Earth Grocery and Deli**, 1157 Deborah St near University Ave and College Rd (☎907/479-2052). Healthy and creative takeout and eat-in meals, juices, smoothies, coffee and fresh baked goods near the university, everything meat-free and most organic.

## Nightlife

Fairbanks has its decent **nightspots**, though none lies in hard-drinking downtown. You'll find the nine-screen **Goldstream Cinema** (☎907/456-5113) on the south side of Airport Way.

**Blue Loon**, Mile 353.5 Parks Hwy (☎907/457-5666). Late-closing hot spot five miles west of Fairbanks that's always good for a convivial drink, hosts local and touring bands (sometimes a DJ) several nights a week, and screens cult and art-house movies. At weekends a bus runs here from outside *The Marlin*. Closed Mon.

**Howling Dog Saloon**, junction of Elliot and Steese hwys, Fox (☎907/457-8780). An inconvenient eleven miles north of town, but perhaps the best bar in the entire North Country – unassuming, unpretentious and fun. Live rock and R&B bands and the ideal place to play volleyball under the midnight sun.

**Into the Woods**, 3569 College Rd (☎907/479-7701). A combined bookshop and relaxed coffeehouse fashioned from an original pioneer cabin that hosts regular acoustic events such as bluegrass performances, Celtic jams and poetry evenings.

**The Marlin**, 3412 College Rd (☎907/479-4646). Poky wood-paneled cellar bar that defines the cutting edge of Fairbanks' music scene with live bands – blues, jazz and rock – playing most evenings from around 9pm and only a small cover charge, if any.

# Around Fairbanks: two hot springs

**Chena Hot Springs**, the most accessible and developed resort, stands in a clearing, sixty miles east of Fairbanks in the Chena River State Recreation Area – a wonderfully bucolic swath of **muskeg** (grassy swampland) and forest traversed by good hiking trails and teeming with moose. Rooms at the fully equipped resort are pricey but worth it (☎907/452-7867 or 1-800/478-4681, fax 356-3122; ④–⑥), and camping costs $16. Walking in the area is especially enjoyable after a soak in the steaming natural spring waters; if you're not staying at the resort, it costs $8 per day to use the indoor pool and hot tubs. The resort also rents out canoes and mountain bikes, as well as offering rafting float trips.

The traditional favorite for folks from Fairbanks has been the more rustic **Circle Hot Springs**, 130 miles northeast of the city along scenic Steese Highway. It's a long drive but you pass through some pristine scenery, alongside the Chatanika River and over the 3624ft Eagle Summit. To get to the resort, take a right at the mining village of **Central** and carry on for eight miles. Accommodation ranges from $20 dorm beds right up to deluxe rooms (☎907/520-5113; ①–④).

Don't confuse the resort with the town of **CIRCLE** – a 34-mile drive over very rough roads from Central on the banks of the broad Yukon River. The name was given by prospectors, who in 1893 thought they were establishing a community on the Arctic Circle; it's actually fifty miles south. Today Circle is a classic end-of-the-road community numbering seventy souls, from where you can join Yukon River Tours (☎ & fax 907/773-8439) who run **boat charters** (half-day $250, full day $500) for up to five people either upstream into the Yukon-Charley National Preserve, or downstream through the **Yukon Flats National Wildlife Refuge** to Fort Yukon on the **Arctic Circle**.

## The Dalton Highway

Built in the 1970s to service the **trans-Alaska pipeline**, the gravel-surfaced **Dalton Highway**, or Haul Road, runs from Fairbanks five hundred miles to the oil facility of Prudhoe Bay on Alaska's north coast, some three hundred miles beyond the Arctic Circle. It is a long, bumpy and demanding drive, so be prepared with spare tires, gas, provisions and, ideally, a sturdy 4WD: regular rentals aren't permitted up here. Just beyond the Fairbanks city limits you start to get glimpses of the pipeline snaking up hills and in and out of the ground. At 188 miles north of Fairbanks is **The Sign**, with an observation platform and picnic area, which alerts you to the fact that you've just crossed the **Arctic Circle**.

Most people are happy to return south at this point, but the highway plugs on through increasingly barren territory, finally dispensing with trees as you climb through the still largely unmapped and unexplored **Brooks Range**, a nine-thousand-foot chain mostly held within the **Gates of the Arctic National Park**. From the crest at Atigun Pass you descend through two hundred miles of grand glaciated valleys and blasted arctic plains to the end of the road at dead-boring **Deadhorse**. You can't stroll by the ocean or camp here so your choices are confined to staying in one of the $110 per night hotels and taking a tour of the adjacent – and otherwise off-limits – **Prudhoe Bay** oil facility. The basic $20 affair takes you to a jetty on the shores of the Arctic

### THE NORTHERN LIGHTS

The **aurora borealis**, or "Northern Lights," an ethereal display of light in the uppermost atmosphere, give their brightest and most colorful displays in the sky above Fairbanks. For up to one hundred winter nights, the sky appears to shimmer with dancing curtains of color, ranging from luminescent monotones – most commonly green or dark red – to fantastic veils that run the full spectrum. The display becomes more animated as it proceeds, twisting and turning in patterns called "rayed bands," and as a finale a corona sometimes appears in which rays seem to flare in all directions from a central point.

Named after the Roman goddess of dawn, the aurora was long thought to be produced by sunlight reflected from polar snow and ice, or refracted light produced in the manner of a rainbow. It now seems they are caused by an interaction between the earth's magnetic field and the **solar wind**, an invisible stream of charged electrons and protons continually blown out into space by the innate violence of the sun. The earth deflects the solar wind like a rock in a stream, the magnetic field channeling the charged particles down towards the earth's magnetic poles. Here the protons and electrons release some of their energy as visible light – much like a neon sign. Auroras become more distinctive and are spread over a larger area two days after intense solar activity, the time it takes the "solar wind" to arrive.

The Northern Lights, at their most dazzling from December to March, when nights are longest and the sky darkest, can usually be seen even as far south as Juneau. First sightings are eagerly reported on the front page of the *Alaska Daily News* around mid-October.

Ocean, while the $50 deluxe version additionally tours the exterior of the assorted pumphouses and workers accommodation blocks.

Even driving the relatively short stretch to the Arctic Circle poses its problems with trucks and the rough road. Nevertheless, going to the Arctic Circle commands an irresistible pull, no matter how pointless it is. By far the best way to do it is with the **Northern Alaska Tour Company** (☎907/474 8600), who'll drive you up in a minibus, supply commentary and video films (but no lunch), and fly you back down to Fairbanks for around $160 (you can save money by taking the minibus back, but it makes for a long day). The company also runs a three-day tour to Prudhoe Bay for around $590 as well as other flying tours to the west.

# CHAPTER SIXTEEN

# HAWAII

The islands of **HAWAII**, with their **volcanoes**, palm-fringed **beaches**, verdant **valleys**, glorious **rainbows** and awesome **cliffs**, hold some of the most spectacularly beautiful scenery on earth. However, despite their isolation, two thousand miles out in the Pacific, they belong very definitely to the United States. If you expect your South Seas idyll to be completely unspoiled, forget it; the fantasy of a dream holiday in Paradise remains firmly rooted in the creature comforts of home. With six million tourists per year, including honeymooners from all over the world, frequent fliers cashing in their mileage, and more than a million Japanese, the islands can seem like a gigantic theme park. Resort development may have slowed in the last few years, but you can't help but be aware of how much of what was unique has gone.

**Honolulu,** by far the largest city of the fiftieth state, and with its resort annex of **Waikiki** also the main tourist center, is on **Oahu**. The biggest island, **Hawaii** itself, is known as the **Big Island** in a vain attempt to avoid confusion. **Maui** and **Kauai** also attract mass tourism, while smaller **Molokai** remains far quieter. All the islands share a similar topography and **climate**. Ocean winds from the northeast shed their rain on the **windward** coast, keeping it wet and green; the southwest, **leeward** (or "Kona") coasts can be almost barren, and so make ideal locations for big resorts. Rainfall is heaviest from December to March, but temperatures remain consistent throughout the year at between 70°F and 85°F. Christmas and midsummer are far more expensive times to visit than the "off-seasons" of September to December and April to May, with

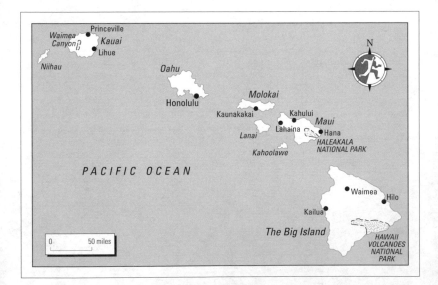

top-range hotels charging as much as fifty percent extra. A visit to Hawaii doesn't have to cost a fortune, however; there are plenty of **budget** facilities if you know where to look. The one major expense you really can't avoid, except possibly on Oahu, is car rental – rates are very reasonable, but gas is pricey.

## Some history

Each of the Hawaiian islands was forced up like a vast mass of candle drippings by submarine volcanic action, all fueled by the same "hot spot" below the sea bed, which has remained stationary as the Pacific plate drifted above. The oldest islands are now mere atolls way off to the northwest; the process is continuing at Kilauea on the Big Island, with lava exploding into the sea to add new land day by day. Until two thousand years ago, these unknown specks in the ocean were populated only by the mutated descendants of what few organisms had been carried here by wind or wave. The first known human inhabitants were the **Polynesians**, who arrived in two separate migrations: one from the Marquesas in the eighth century, and another from Tahiti four or five hundred years later.

Incredibly, no Western ship chanced upon Hawaii until **Captain Cook** arrived at Kauai in January 1778. He was amazed to find a civilization sharing a culture – and language – with the peoples of the South Pacific. The Hawaiians, too, were amazed, having long since lost contact with the outside world. Cook himself was killed in Hawaii in 1779 (see p.1138), but he had started an irreversible process of change. The first Polynesians had brought the plants and animals necessary to create a self-sufficient way of life. Westerners took things further, and in reshaping the islands to suit their economic and agricultural needs decimated most of the indigenous flora and fauna – as well as the Hawaiians themselves. Cook's men estimated that there were a million islanders; the population today is roughly the same, but a mere eight thousand **pure-blood Hawaiians** are left.

As well as bringing venereal and other diseases, Cook's voyage opened the fur trade between the Pacific Northwest and China. Passing ships regularly traded arms to the Hawaiians, and within a few years, chief **Kamehameha** of the Big Island became the first king to unite all the islands. The sudden advent of capitalism was devastating. When the fur traders realized that Hawaiian **sandalwood** fetched enormous prices in China, the mass of the population abandoned taro-farming and fishing. The great forests were almost entirely denuded by the end of the 1820s, at which point a replacement industry appeared – **whaling** (see p.1143).

With the dislocation of traditional ways, Hawaiian **religion** fell apart. After the death of Kamehameha in May 1819, the female regent Kaahumanu set out to break the **kapu** (*tabu*) system that held society together. Her public defiance of the injunctions forbidding women to eat alongside men, or to eat bananas or pork, threw the islands into moral anarchy – just as the first Puritan **missionaries** arrived from New England in 1820, determined to turn Hawaii into the Promised Land. Their wholehearted capitalism and harsh strictures on the easygoing Hawaiian lifestyle might have been calculated to compound the chaos. White advisers and ministers soon dominated the government, and the missionaries amassed vast acreages, with the result that their children became Hawaii's wealthiest and most powerful class.

While the Civil War severely disrupted whaling, it triggered a Hawaiian **sugar** boom, to replace Southern sugar in the markets of the north. From then on, the machinations of the sugar industry to get favorable prices on the mainland moved Hawaii inexorably towards **annexation** by the US. In 1887 an all-white group of "concerned businessmen" forced King David Kalakaua to surrender power to an assembly elected by property owners (of any nationality) rather than citizens. When, after his death, his sister Liliuokalani announced her desire to proclaim a new constitution, the businessmen called in the US warship *Boston* and declared a provisional government. US President

Cleveland (a Democrat) responded that "Hawaii was taken possession of by the United States forces without the consent or wish of the government of the islands . . . (It) was wholly without justification . . . not merely a wrong but a disgrace." With phenomenal cheek, the provisional government rejected his demand for the restoration of the monarchy by saying the US should not "interfere in the internal affairs of their sovereign nation." It found defenders in the Republican US Congress, and declared itself a republic on July 4, 1894.

On August 12, 1898, Hawaii was formally **annexed** as a territory of the United States. At this point there was no question of Hawaii becoming a state; the whites were outnumbered ten to one, and had no desire to afford the natives the protection of US labor laws, let alone to give them the vote. Furthermore, as the proportion of Hawaiians of Japanese descent (*nisei*) increased, Congress feared the prospect of a state whose people might consider their primary allegiance to be to Japan.

Consequently, Hawaii was for the first half of the twentieth century the virtual fiefdom of the **Big Five**, conglomerations started by the missionary families and rooted in their massive landholdings (still-familiar names include Castle & Cooke – now Dole – and Alexander & Baldwin). By controlling agriculture, they also dominated transportation, banks, utilities, insurance – and government. The inevitable integration of Hawaii into the American mainstream was hastened by its crucial role in the war against Japan – with the clear support of the *nisei* – and the expansion of tourism thereafter. The islands finally became the fiftieth of the United States in 1959, after a plebiscite showed a seventeen-to-one majority in favor. The only group to oppose statehood were the few remaining native Hawaiians.

Support has been growing over the last couple of decades for the concept of **Hawaiian sovereignty**, on the basis that those of Hawaiian descent should gain at least the rights already held by Native American nations on the mainland. In 1993, the US Congress and President Clinton issued a formal apology to native Hawaiians "on the occasion of the 100th anniversary of the illegal overthrow of the Kingdom of Hawaii"; debate rages as to what form restitution might take, with some campaigners arguing for a complete restoration of **independence**.

## Modern Hawaii

Roughly sixty percent of the million-plus modern Hawaiians were born here. Around one-third are Caucasian (many of them US military personnel), one-third Japanese and one-sixth Filipino, with 200,000 claiming at least some Hawaiian ancestry. The traditional reliance on agriculture seems to be in terminal decline, with sugar and pineapple plantations – unable to compete with Third World wages – closing one after the other, and only coffee production, thanks to the gourmet status of the Kona name, on the increase. The need to import virtually all the basics of life has resulted in an extraordinarily high **cost of living** (the Paradise Tax, as it's called). In particular, the cost of housing is so high that many islanders find themselves either obliged to work at two jobs, or simply to sleep on the beaches.

---

### ACCOMMODATION PRICE CODES

All accommodation prices in this book have been coded using the symbols below. Note that prices are for the least expensive double rooms in each establishment. For a full explanation see p.37 in Basics.

| | | |
|---|---|---|
| ① up to $30 | ④ $60–80 | ⑦ $130–175 |
| ② $30–45 | ⑤ $80–100 | ⑧ $175–250 |
| ③ $45–60 | ⑥ $100–130 | ⑨ $250+ |

Visitors in search of the **ancient Hawaii** will find that few vestiges remain. What is presented as "historic" usually postdates the missionary impact. The "old towns" are pure nineteenth-century Americana, with false-front stores and raised wooden board-walks. The ruins of temples (*heiaus*) to the old gods still stand in some places – notably on the Big Island – and committed campaigners work to revive traditional philosophies, but the closest Hawaii comes to a state religion now appears to be Elvis-worship. The two biggest **festivals** are the Big Island's week-long **Merrie Monarch Festival**, honoring King David Kalakaua (mid-April), and the statewide **King Kamehameha** events (around June 11). Authentic **hula** dancing is a powerful art form, but you're far more likely to encounter it bastardized in some kind of "Polynesian spectacular" – perhaps a **luau** or "traditional feast." Primarily tourist money-spinners, *luaus* provide an opportunity to sample Hawaiian **foods** such as *kalua* pig, baked underground, and local fish such as *ono, ahi, mahi mahi* and *lomi-lomi* (raw salmon). *Poi* – a paste made from mashed taro root – remains a staple of the diet, much as it was when one of Captain Cook's men described it as "a disagreeable mess."

The Hawaiian **language** endures in place names and music. At first glance it looks unpronounceable – especially as it is written using a mere twelve letters (the five vowels, plus *h, k, l, m, n, p* and *w*). Usually, each letter is enunciated individually – glottal stops indicate a pause for breath. Long words often break down into repeated sounds, such as "*meha-meha*" in "Kamehameha." Hawaii itself is more correctly written (and pronounced) *Hawai'i*, but for visual clarity we've omitted the glottal stops in this book.

## Getting to and around Hawaii

Honolulu, just under six hours by plane from the US West Coast, is one of the world's busiest centers for air traffic; return fares from **LA**, **San Francisco** and **Seattle** start at around $300. There are also direct flights from the mainland to Maui and the Big Island. Many flights to the US from **Australia** – such as those on Continental – include free stopovers in Hawaii. **European** travelers should buy all-inclusive tickets from Europe.

The principal **inter-island carriers** are Hawaiian Airlines (Oahu ☎808/838-1555; US ☎1-800/367-5320) and Aloha Air (Oahu ☎808/484-1111; US ☎1-800/367-5250), together with its subsidiary Island Air (Oahu ☎808/484-2222; US ☎1-800/323-3345). They connect all the major islands several times per day, with standard one-way fares of around $80; special discount offers, on the first or last flights of each day, or for booklets of perhaps a dozen tickets, are constantly advertised.

All the airports have car rental outlets; with the exception of Oahu, **bus** services on the islands barely exist. No **ferry** services connect the major islands.

# OAHU

Three-quarters of Hawaii's population live on **OAHU**, which has monopolized the islands' trade and tourism since the first European sailors realized that **Honolulu** offered the safest in-shore anchorage in thousands of miles of ocean. Over eighty percent of visitors to Hawaii still arrive in **Honolulu** – albeit by air now, rather than by sea – and most remain for their entire vacation. Oahu effectively confines tourists to the tower-block enclave of **Waikiki**, just east of downtown Honolulu; there are few rooms anywhere else. In much the same way, the **military** are closeted away in relatively inconspicuous camps. On any one day, the numbers of military personnel and tourists on Oahu are roughly the same.

Overcrowding and rampant development mean Oahu can't be recommended over the **Neighbor Islands** (as the other Hawaiian islands are known), but it can still give

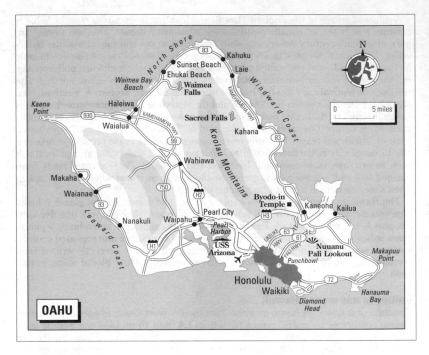

a real flavor of Hawaii. There are some excellent **beaches**, with those on the north shore a haven for **surfers** and campers, and the **cliffs** of the windward side are awesome.

# Honolulu

Until the Europeans came, **HONOLULU** was insignificant; soon so many foreign ships were frequenting its waters that it had become King Kamemeha's capital, and it remains the economic center of the island. The city covers a long (if narrow) strip of southern Oahu, but **downtown** is a manageable size, and a lot quieter than its glamorous image might suggest. The tourist hotels, and most of Honolulu's hustle, are concentrated among the skyscrapers of very distinct **WAIKIKI**, a couple of miles east.

The setting is beautiful, right on the Pacific and backed by dramatic cliffs (*pali*) and the extinct volcanoes of **Punchbowl** (a military cemetery) and **Diamond Head**; but then beauty is not so rare a commodity on Hawaii, and you can see this sort of scenery in plenty of other places without a city slapped down in the middle of it. What attracts most visitors to stay in Honolulu, and especially Waikiki, is the sheer **hedonism** of shopping, eating and generally hanging out in the sun. Hawaii's broad ethnic mix, and Honolulu's status as a major world crossroads, make it a cosmopolitan place where something is always happening (and everything is for sale). It's also the center of an exemplary **public transportation** system, facilitating exploration of the whole island.

# Arrival, information and getting around

The runways of Honolulu's **International Airport**, just west of downtown, extend out to sea on a coral reef. **Car rental** outlets abound, but a car is not especially desirable in Honolulu, what with city traffic and hefty parking fees in Waikiki. The ABC **shuttle service** (☎808/988-9293; one-way $7, round-trip $12) is typical of the many minivan services that run on request to any Waikiki hotel. Regular buses **#19** and **#20** connect Waikiki with the airport, but don't allow large bags, cases or backpacks (there are left-luggage lockers at the airport). A **taxi** will cost around $20. The nine-mile – not at all scenic – drive to Waikiki takes anything from 25 to 75 minutes.

## Information

The **Hawaii Visitors Bureau** runs an information office on the fourth floor of the Royal Hawaiian Shopping Center in Waikiki, at Kalakaua Avenue and Lewers Street (Mon–Fri 8am–5pm; ☎808/923-1811), but you're unlikely to need it: racks of free listings magazines and leaflets are everywhere you turn, and all the hotels have information desks. Kiosks around Kalakaua Avenue offer greatly discounted rates for the various "**activities**" on offer – island tours, helicopter rides, dinner cruises, surfing lessons and so on.

The only **post office** that takes general delivery (poste restante) mail is at the airport (3600 Aolele St, Honolulu, HI 96820), but there is a post office in Waikiki at 330 Saratoga Rd.

## Getting around

A network of over sixty **bus** routes, collectively named TheBus, covers the whole of Oahu. All journeys, however long, cost $1, with free transfers onto any connecting route if you ask as you board (enquiries ☎808/848-5555). The most popular routes with Waikiki-based tourists are **#2** to downtown, **#8** to Ala Moana Shopping Center, **#20** to Pearl Harbor, **#22** to Hanauma Bay, and the bargain "**Circle Island**" buses (**#52** clockwise and **#55** counterclockwise), which take four hours to loop around the central valley and the east coast, passing the legendary North Shore surf spots, still for just $1.

In Waikiki, Aloha Funway (☎808/942-9696) offers **bicycle rental** at seven locations, charging $20 for 24 hours. Among companies running **city and island bus tours** for around $55 for a full day, as well as off-island packages, are Polynesian Adventure Tours (☎808/833-3000) and Roberts (☎808/539-9400). Honolulu TimeWalks (☎808/943-0371) runs a changing program of themed **walking tours** of the city.

# Accommodation

All the accommodation listed below is in or near **Waikiki**; very little is available in central Honolulu. Waikiki accommodation covers a wide range, and the highest rates will bring absolute luxury, but it's possible to pay much less. It's also such a tiny place that there's little point paying the $50-plus premium on top of usual rates that it takes to get an ocean view.

**Aloha Punawai**, 305 Saratoga Rd (☎808/923-5211). Miniature hotel, opposite the post office, offering kitchenette apartments and studios with and without air-conditioning. ③.

**Hale Pua Nui**, 228 Beachwalk (☎808/923-9693). Small, clean hotel that's among central Waikiki's best deals. Simple studio apartments with two twin beds, kitchenettes and free local calls. Reserve well ahead. ③.

**HI-Waikiki**, 2417 Prince Edward St (☎808/926-8313). Official but informal youth hostel in the heart of Waikiki, a couple of minutes from the beach. Open to HI-AYH members only, charging $16 for a dorm bed. Reserve in advance, especially for the four private double rooms. ①/②.

**Hotel Honolulu**, 376 Kaiolu St (☎808/926-2766 or 1-800/426-2766). Hawaii's only hotel specifically catering for gays and lesbians, with stylish studios and one-bedroom suites. ⑤.

**InterClub Waikiki Hostel and Hotel**, 2413 Kuhio Ave (☎808/924-2636). Incongruous light-blue motel-style place tucked in a block from the ocean, offering $15 dorm beds, plus $45 private en-suite rooms. ①/③.

**Island Hostel**, Hawaiian Colony Building, 1946 Ala Moana Blvd (☎808/924-8748). Unofficial, ramshackle but good-value hostel in western Waikiki. No curfew, dorm beds $15, plus doubles with kitchenette and TV. ①/③.

**New Otani Kaimana Beach Hotel**, 2863 Kalakaua Ave (☎808/923-1555 or 1-800/356-8264). Intimate beachfront hotel half a mile east of central Waikiki. ⑤.

**Outrigger**, numerous locations around Waikiki, mostly skyscrapers (reservations ☎1-800/688-7444). Choices include the *Maile Sky Court*, 2058 Kuhio Ave (④), or the slightly more luxurious *Waikiki Surf*, 2200 Kuhio Ave (⑤); most of the others will have rooms for around $75. On request, a free Dollar rental car is provided for every day of your stay. ④–⑨.

**Polynesian Hostel Beach Club**, 2584 Lemon Rd (☎808/922-1340). Clean private hostel, a block from the sea. Some rooms have en-suite bathrooms; some hold four $16 bunk beds, some serve as good-value private doubles. Free snorkels and boogie board, and meals are served in the communal area some nights. ①–②.

**The Royal Hawaiian**, 2490 Kalakaua Ave (☎808/922-7311 or 1-800/782-9488). 1920s "Pink Palace," commanding the beach, which is one of Waikiki's best-loved landmarks. The original building looks out across terrace gardens to the sea, but is now flanked by a less atmospheric tower block, which holds the most expensive suites. ⑧.

# The City

**Downtown Honolulu** is surprisingly small, set back a little from the sea and centering around a spacious plaza on King Street which includes **Iolani Palace** and the **state capitol**. The palace was built for King David Kalakaua in 1882, but, apart from its *koa*-hardwood floors, contains little that is distinctively Hawaiian (Tues–Sat 9am–2.15pm; $10). Across the road is a colorful statue of Kamehameha I.

To reach the nearby ocean, pedestrians have to negotiate fearsome traffic. Although the sea may be turquoise, the shorefront is concrete, not beach, and you can't wander along it for any distance. The **Aloha Tower** on Pier 9 used to be the city's tallest building; the area around its base has just been converted into an expensive shopping and dining mall, fronting onto the city docks. The view from the top of the tower is little short of ugly, but is good for orientation (Sun–Thurs 9am–9pm, Fri & Sat 9am–10pm; free). The **Hawaii Maritime Center** (daily 8.30am–5pm; $8), just east of Aloha Tower, documents Hawaii's seafaring past in superb detail, from ancient migrations through to white contact, nineteenth-century trade and twentieth-century cruises. A stunning film from 1922 (with Clara Bow in a bit part) shows the true-life drama of whaling, and there's a wall of gigantic historic surfboards. In the adjacent dock are the fully rigged four-master *Falls of Clyde* and the replica Polynesian canoe *Hokulea*, whose voyages to Tahiti and New Zealand over the last two decades have inspired a huge revival of interest in traditional methods of navigation.

Though few tourists seem to know about it, Honolulu residents take great pride in the stunning fine art on display at the **Academy of Arts**, half a mile east of the capitol at 900 S Beretania St (Tues–Sat 10am–4.30pm, Sun 1–5pm; $5). Highlights of the superb collection of paintings include Van Gogh's *Wheat Field*, Gauguin's *Two Nudes on a Tahitian Beach* and one of Monet's *Water Lilies*. The Academy also holds some fascinating depictions of Hawaii by visiting artists, including a pencil sketch of Waikiki drawn in 1838, and vivid, stylized studies of Maui's Iao Valley and Hana coast by Georgia O'Keeffe, plus magnificent ancient **Chinese** ceramics and bronzes.

## Chinatown

TheBus #2 from Waikiki drops you at Hotel and Bishop, outside the gleaming high-tech Executive Center in downtown Honolulu. Just five minutes' walk away down Hotel Street, the fading green-clapboard storefronts of **Chinatown** seem like another world. Traditionally the city's red-light district, the narrow streets leading down to the Nuuanu Stream are still characterized by pool halls, massage parlors and heavy-duty bars.

It's well worth strolling around, delving into inconspicuous alleyways to explore the area's history. Some of the old walled courtyards are now converted into open modern malls, but the businesses remain much the same as ever, and you can still find herbalists weighing out dried leaves in front of vast arrays of bottles and wooden cabinets. Pig snouts and salmon heads are among the Oriental food specialties at **Oahu Market**, on N King and Kekaulike.

## Bishop Museum

The anthropological collection at the **Bishop Museum**, back from the ocean at 1525 Bernice St (daily 9am–5pm; $15), demonstrates the reality of Polynesian culture, as opposed to the fakery of Waikiki. Three floors of one of Hawaii's oldest houses display magnificent feather cloaks and Japanese samurai armor, and a full-size sperm whale hangs in the central well. There are also excellent special exhibitions for kids, and a planetarium. TheBus #2 from Waikiki stops two blocks away on Kapalama Street.

## Punchbowl

High above Honolulu, lush lawns growing in the caldera of an extinct volcano are the emotive setting for the **National Memorial Cemetery of the Pacific** (daily: March–Sept 8am–6.30pm; Oct–Feb 8am–5.30pm), in which are buried the dead of all US Pacific wars, including Vietnam. The Hawaiian shuttle astronaut Ellison Onizuka is also here. This spot is said to have held an ancient sacrificial temple, and is on TheBus route #15 from town.

## Waikiki

Built on a reclaimed swamp, **Waikiki** is very nearly an island, all but separated from Honolulu between the sea and the Ala Wai canal (which provides the drainage to make its incredible highrise profusion possible). Once home to King Kamehameha I, the site may be venerable, but these days its *raison d'être* is rampant commercialism. You could, just about, survive here with very little money, buying snacks from the omnipresent ABC convenience stores, but there would be no point – there's nothing to see, and the only thing to do apart from surf and sunbathe is to stroll along the seafront **Kalakaua Avenue** and shop.

The most striking thing about the parallel **Waikiki Beach** is how narrow it is, a thin but somehow attractive strip of shipped-in sand. Compared to other Hawaiian beaches, it's overcrowded and small, but then it serves a different function; no one is trying to "get away from it all," they're there to be seen.

Two possible diversions on the eastern fringes of Waikiki are **Honolulu Zoo** (daily 9am–5.30pm; $6), where you can walk through a mock African savannah set against the magnificent backdrop of Diamond Head, and the more expensive oceanfront **Waikiki Aquarium** (daily 8.30am–5pm; $6), which as well as holding sharks and monkfish seals has a tank devoted to the many-hued reef fish of Hanauma Bay (see overleaf).

## Diamond Head

Waikiki's most famous landmark is the pinnacle of **Diamond Head**, just to the east. Named for the erroneous belief of a party of English sailors that they'd found diamonds

**WAIKIKI**

*Ala Wai Canal*

ALA WAI BOULEVARD

KUHIO AVENUE

KALAKAUA AVENUE

KALIA ROAD

KAPIOLANI BOULEVARD

ALA MOANA BOULEVARD

KAPAHULU AVENUE

◁ *Downtown Honolulu*

Fort DeRussy
Military Camp

International
Market
Place

Royal Hawaiian
Shopping Center

*Waikiki Beach*

*Gray's Beach*

*Kuhio Beach*

*Kapiolani Beach*

Honolulu
Zoo

Waikiki
Aquarium

PACIFIC OCEAN

| ACCOMMODATION | RESTAURANTS |
|---|---|
| 1 Aloha Punawai | A Arancino |
| 2 Hale Pua Nui | B Internet Cafe |
| 3 Honolulu | C Oceanarium |
| 4 InterClub Waikiki | D Perry's Smorgy (two locations) |
| 5 Island Hostel | E Caffe Pronto |
| 6 Outrigger Maile Sky Court | F Texas Rock 'n' Roll Bar |
| 7 Outrigger Waikiki Surf | |
| 8 Polynesian Hostel Beach Club | |
| 9 Royal Hawaiian | |
| 10 HI - Waikiki | |

0          300 yds

on its slopes, it's another extinct volcano. The lawns of the crater interior are oddly bland, almost suburban in fact, but a straightforward hiking trail leads up a mile or so to the summit, and a panorama of the whole coast, passing through a network of tunnels built by the military during World War II. TheBus #22 and #58 stop on the road nearby.

## Hanauma Bay

A few miles further on, the magnificent crescent-shaped **Hanauma Bay**, formed when the wall of a crater collapsed to let in the sea, is renowned as Oahu's best place to **snorkel**. It makes a nice excursion, and the sea is full of brightly colored fish; but overuse has killed off most of the coral near the shore, and the feeding of fish with food sold at the bay has led to a decline in the range of species. Tour parties were banned in 1991, and attempts are now made to educate visitors about the fragile ecology of the shallow bay; the daily fee of $3 for non-Hawaiian visitors helps to keep the numbers down as well. Patches of living coral, and bigger fish, can be seen if you swim out to the deeper waters beyond the inner reef, but the currents can be strong, and you invite coral cuts that can take weeks to heal. Snorkeling equipment can be rented for $6 (bring a deposit in the form of your passport, credit card or a large amount of cash). The beach is closed on Wednesday mornings. TheBus #22 ("The Beach Bus") runs by the bay from Waikiki every forty minutes.

## Pearl Harbor

Almost the whole of **Pearl Harbor**, the principal base for the US Pacific fleet (just over one hour from Waikiki, beyond the airport, on TheBus #20), is off limits to visitors. However, the surprise Japanese attack of December 7, 1941, which an official US enquiry called "the greatest military and naval disaster in our nation's history," is commemorated by a simple white memorial set above the wreck of the battleship **USS Arizona**, still discernible in the clear blue waters. More than 1100 of its crew – who had earned the right to sleep in late that Sunday morning by coming second in a military band competition – are entombed there.

Free tours to the ship operate between 8am and 3pm each day, but it can be two or three hours after you pick up your numbered ticket at the **Pearl Harbor visitor center** (daily 7.30am–5pm) before you are called to board the ferry across the bay. Many of the 1.5 million annual visitors are Japanese; a surprisingly even-handed twenty-minute film pays tribute to "one of the most brilliantly planned and executed attacks in naval history," and books and charts are on sale telling the Japanese side of the story. The *USS Arizona* memorial was partly financed by Elvis Presley's 1961 Honolulu concert, his first show after leaving the army.

The huge **USS Missouri**, which survived the attack and was used four years later for the ceremony in Tokyo Harbor that ended World War II, is now moored alongside the *Arizona*. It can be visited in conjunction with the veteran submarine *USS Bowfin*; guided tours include the actual surrender site as well as sweeping views of the harbor from the *Missouri*'s bridge (daily 9am–5pm; $10).

## Eating

Honolulu and Waikiki offer so many **food** possibilities that recommendations are inevitably highly personal. For fine dining, all the larger Waikiki hotels have good restaurants, and **Restaurant Row** near the harbor in Honolulu is a good bet. There are excellent **fast-food malls** in the **Ala Moana Center**, and the much cheaper and more exotic **Maunakea Marketplace** on Maunakea Street in Chinatown, while Waikiki's Kuhio Avenue is lined with snack outlets and fast-food franchises.

**Arancino**, 255 Beach Walk, Waikiki (☎808/923-5557). Good Italian trattoria in the heart of Waikiki, with plenty of pasta, pizza and seafood specialties.

**Caffe Pronto**, 131 Kaiulani Ave, Waikiki (☎808/923-0111) and 1778 Ala Moana Blvd (☎808/949-0844). Bright, cheerful takeout with a small seating area, best for its fine early-morning coffees. Daily 6.30am–11pm.

**Canellia Buffet**, 930 McCully St (☎808/951-0511). Korean buffet restaurant a mile north of Waikiki, where you select slices of marinated beef, chicken or pork and grill it yourself at the gas-fired burners set into each table. Open daily for lunch ($13) and dinner ($18).

**Indigo**, 1120 Nu'uanu Ave (☎808/521-2900). Top-quality restaurant in Honolulu's Chinatown, specializing in a delicious *nouvelle* Chinese–Californian melange, and featuring inventive dim sum.

**Internet C@fe**, 559 Kapahulu Ave, Waikiki (☎808/735-JAVA). 24-hour coffee shop that serves great cinnamon buns and offers Internet access and even "psychic nights."

**Maxime**, 1134 Maunakea St (☎808/545-4188). Bright, clean, pastel-pink Chinatown restaurant serving very inexpensive Vietnamese food, especially *pho* (noodle soups).

**Oceanarium**, *Pacific Beach Hotel*, 2490 Kalakaua Ave, Waikiki (☎808/922-1233). Simply furnished restaurant with a big gimmick: you gorge yourself beneath the goggling eyes of 400 live fish, plus the occasional scuba diver. Open for all meals, with noodles, burgers and sandwiches, and full surf 'n' turf dinners.

**A Pacific Cafe – Oahu**, Ward Center, 1200 Ala Moana Blvd (☎808/593-0035). Magnificent Pacific Rim dining in a very stylish setting, not far from Ala Moana mall; the sampler menu costs around $35.

**Perry's Smorgy**, 2380 Kuhio Ave, Waikiki (☎808/926-0184). All-you-can-eat buffets, indoors and alfresco (with hordes of scavenging birds). Bargain prices – $5 breakfast (7–11am), $6 lunch (11.30am–2.30pm), $9 dinner (5–9pm) – but the food is bland in the extreme. A second location is at the *Outrigger Coral Seas*, 250 Lewers St.

**Sam Choy's Breakfast, Lunch & Crab**, 580 N Nimitz Hwy (☎808/545-7979). Copious quantities of modern Hawaiian cuisine, plus a microbrewery, a mile or two west of downtown Honolulu.

**Texas Rock 'n' Roll Sushi Bar**, *Hyatt Regency Hotel*, 2424 Kalakaua Ave, Waikiki (☎808/923-7655). High concept, postmodern restaurant-bar, with a bizarre menu that combines traditional sushi at reasonable prices with duck, barbecued beef and chicken – there's even BLT sushi rolls.

# Entertainment and nightlife

Most of Honolulu's **nightlife** is concentrated in Waikiki, where fun-seeking tourists set the tone. On the whole, the available entertainment is on the bland side. Hawaii tends to be off the circuit for touring musicians, so if you enjoy live music you'll probably have to settle for little-known local performers (rising stars of contemporary Hawaiian music tend to prefer to keep their credibility by not playing in Waikiki too often). Look out also for special events at downtown's beautifully restored Hawaii Theater, 1130 Bethel St (☎808/528-0506). As for **bars**, Chinatown has the most raucous in town, but they're way too hair-raising for most tastes.

## SEA AND SURF SAFETY

**Drownings** in Hawaii are all too common. In many places the waves come sweeping in from two thousand miles of open ocean, onto beaches magnificent to look at but unprotected by any reef. Not all beaches have lifeguards and warning flags; unattended beaches are not necessarily safe. Look for other bathers, but whatever your experience elsewhere, don't assume you'll be able to cope with the same conditions as the local kids. Don't rush into the water, watch the sea carefully before going in, and never take your eyes off it thereafter. Fierce **rogue waves** can appear from the blue to drag waders – or even those walking along the shore – far out to sea in seconds, and powerful **undertows** may not be detectable until too late. If you do get swept out, wait until the big waves die down, even if it takes hours. Never attempt to swim where waves are breaking right on the reef.

Sea creatures to avoid include *wana* – black spiky **sea urchins** – Portuguese men-of-war **jellyfish**, and **coral** in general, which can give painful infected cuts. **Shark attacks** are much rarer than popular imagination suggests; those which do occur are usually due to "misunderstandings," such as spear-fishers inadvertently keeping sharks from their catch, or surfers idling on their boards looking a bit too much like turtles from below.

If you're keen to get a **tan**, take exposure to the harsh tropical **sun** in moderation; a mere twenty minutes is the safe recommendation for the first day. Even on overcast days human skin still absorbs most of the harmful UV rays.

### Ocean Fun

The nation that invented **surfing** – long before the whites came – remains its greatest arena. The sport was popularized early in the twentieth century by Olympic swimmer Duke Kahanamoku, using a 20ft board; these days most are around six foot. Smaller **boogie boards**, which you don't stand on, make an exhilarating initiation. **Windsurfing**, too, is rapidly growing, using the same favorite beaches, usually on the north shore of each island. **Snorkeling** and **diving** are top-quality, although Hawaii's **coral** has fewer brilliant hues than in warmer equatorial waters – and in places it's just plain dead. Two-day diving courses cost around $300. **Snuba**, basically snorkeling with a longer tube, is less demanding. For the sedentary, **submarines** are in action on Oahu and Hawaii.

**Anna Banannas**, 2440 S Beretania St (☎808/946-5190). Reasonable bar, with live R&B and reggae most nights. $4 cover.

**Duke's Canoe Club**, *Outrigger Waikiki on the Beach*, 2335 Kalakaua Ave (☎808/922-2268). Smooth Hawaiian sounds wash over this oceanfront Waikiki cocktail bar nightly from 6pm and 10pm to midnight – including big-name "Concerts on the Beach" Fri–Sun 4–6pm – with no cover charge.

**Hula's Bar and Lei Stand**, Kalakaua Ave and Kapahulu (☎808/923-0669). Waikiki's most popular gay venue, offering videos and dance music inside and outdoors. Open daily 10am–2am.

**La Mariana Sailing Club**, 50 Sand Island Access Rd (☎808/848-2800). Waterfront restaurant with a wonderful 1950s feel, hidden away amid Honolulu's docks, and featuring live Hawaiian music at weekends.

**Moose McGillycuddy's**, 1035 University Ave (☎808/944-5525). Trendy students flock to this no-cover Honolulu rock 'n' roll venue on weekends, but there's something on most nights. The Waikiki branch, at 310 Lewers St, features mainstream sounds, with a $3 cover charge on weekends.

**Wave Waikiki**, 1877 Kalakua Ave (☎808/941-0424). Loud heavy rock, live and on record, 9pm–4am.

# Windward Oahu

Much the most spectacular moment of a tour of Oahu comes as you cross the Koolau Mountains on the **Pali Highway** (Hwy-61) to see the sheer green cliffs of the windward side of the island, swirling with mists. The highest spot, just four miles out of Honolulu heading northeast, is the **Nuuanu Pali Lookout**. King Kamehameha finalized his conquest of Oahu here in 1795, forcing hundreds of enemy warriors over the edge of the cliffs; Mark Twain saw the battlefield seventy years later, littered with skulls.

The wide highway is barely adequate for its role as a major commuter thoroughfare connecting Honolulu with **Kailua** and **Kaneohe**, and a new tunnel is being dug which will inevitably bring further "development" to the windward side. Apart from the Japanese Buddhist **Byodo-In Temple**, in a spectacular setting hard against the mountains off Hwy-83 (daily 8.30am–4.30pm; $2), there's little worth seeing. The best way to get a close-up view of the inaccessible inland cliffs is on the attractive hiking trails in **Kahana Valley State Park** (no opening hours or fee), a dozen miles short of the island's northernmost tip.

Oahu's leading paying attraction, with one million annual visitors, is the **Polynesian Cultural Center**, slightly further north at Laie (Mon–Sat 12.30–9pm; $27). This haphazard mixture of real and bogus Polynesia – in which the history is firmly on the bogus side – is owned by the Mormons, and staffed by students from Brigham Young University right behind it. The imposing white **Mormon Temple** nearby was the first to be built outside the continental United States. TheBus #52 takes roughly two hours to get this far.

# North Shore Oahu

The **surfing beaches** of northern Oahu are famous the world over, but they're barely equipped for tourists. **Waimea**, **Sunset** and **Ekuhai** beach parks (the latter is home of the Banzai Pipeline, the most famous surfing spot in the world) are all laid-back roadside stretches of sand, where you can usually find a quiet spot to yourself. Sunset is best for savoring the atmosphere, though surfers can be an exclusive bunch. The tame summer waves may make you wonder what all the fuss is about; if you see them at full tilt in the winter, you'll have no doubts.

**HALEIWA** is the main surfers' hangout, combining alternative shops and cafes with upfront tourist traps. Most of the **food** around is vegetarian; at the back of the Celestial Natural Foods store, 66-443 Kamehameha Hwy, the *Paradise Found Cafe* (☎808/637-

4640) serves breakfast and lunch for about $6 a time, while the friendly *Coffee Gallery*, in the North Shore Marketplace across the street (☎808/637-5571), has occasional live music to go with its espressos and sandwiches.

For **accommodation**, you have to head five miles northeast to reach the *Backpacker's Vacation Inn*, at 59-788 Kamehameha Hwy by Waimea Bay (☎808/638-7838; ①–④), which has dorm beds for $17 a night, as well as some great-value ocean-view private rooms and studios. Nearby, **Waimea Falls Park** is a commercial exploitation of what is nonetheless a beautiful valley, replete with waterfalls and river (daily 10am–5.30pm; $20 per person).

# Leeward Oahu

The leeward (Waianae) coast of Oahu, customarily dismissed as "arid," is only so by Hawaiian standards. It certainly has its share of fine beaches, the best being **Makaha** beach park (served by TheBus #51). However, the traditionally minded inhabitants of towns such as **NANAKULI** don't welcome the encroachment of hotels and golf courses, and visitors tend to be treated with a degree of suspicion. In the southwest corner of the island, two unlikely neighbors stand side by side next to their own neat beaches; the relentlessly tacky *Paradise Cove luau* site (see p.1121), and Oahu's most luxurious resort, the *Ihilani Resort and Spa* (☎808/679-0079 or 1-800/626-4446; ⑨).

The further north you go, the stronger the military presence becomes, with soldiers in camouflage blending into the green valleys. It's possible to hike from both the Leeward and North shores to bleak, windswept **Kaena Point**, at the northwestern corner – where the waves in winter are said to be the highest in the world – but the road is barred to vehicles.

# THE BIG ISLAND

The **Big Island** of **HAWAII** is well named – it could accommodate all the other islands with room to spare. With a population of only 130,000, half what it was in Captain Cook's day, and a comparatively low level of tourism, there's far more space than on Oahu or Maui. The development that will surely come may put an end to that, but for the moment there are sleepy old towns all over the island, unchanged for a century. The few resorts are in the least beautiful areas, built on the barren lava flows of the **Kona** coast to catch maximum sunshine.

What's more, the Big Island is still growing. The southern shore is inching ever further out to sea, thanks to the **Kilauea** volcano, still destroying roads and even towns and spewing out pristine beaches of jet-black sand. **Hawaii Volcanoes National Park**, which includes **Mauna Loa** as well as Kilauea (though not **Mauna Kea**, higher than either at 13,796ft), is absolutely compelling; you can explore steaming craters and cinder cones, venture into the rainforest, and at times approach within feet of the eruption itself. The summits of Mauna Loa and Mauna Kea have the clearest air on earth – and astronomical observatories to take advantage of it – but down below, when the tradewinds drop, the island is prone to a choking sulphurous haze known as "**vog.**"

As befits the birthplace and base of **King Kamehameha**, more of the ancient Hawaii survives on the Big Island than anywhere else. **Puuhonua O Honaunau** National Historical Park preserves a temple complex which served as a "place of refuge" for *kapu*-breakers and defeated warriors, just a few miles from the site of Captain Cook's death, and there are further temples north along the Kohala coast. **Waipio Valley**, where Kamehameha spent his youth, remains as lush and green as

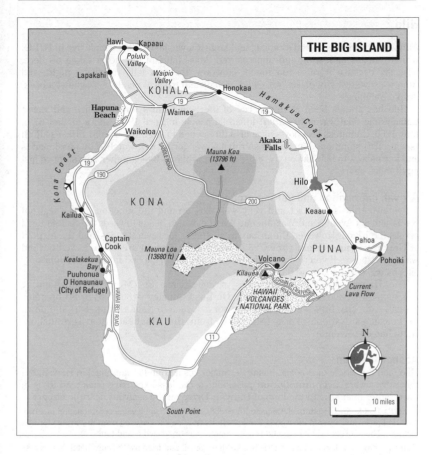

ever, all the more magical for the knowledge that six further impenetrable valleys lie beyond it.

Flights to the Big Island arrive at **Hilo** on the rainy east coast, or the much less genuine but inoffensive resort of **Kailua** (often referred to as Kona) on the west. If you don't rent a **car**, you may not get to the interesting sites; one bus daily links Hilo and Kailua, and organized bus tours go to specific attractions, but public transportation is all but nonexistent.

# Windward Hawaii

Almost all the rain that falls on the slopes of Mauna Kea flows down to the sea on the eastern side of the Big Island. Numerous streams and waterfalls nourish dense jungle-like vegetation; the main road north along the coast from Hilo is alive with colorful orchids, and most of the state's commercial tropical gardens are in this area. Hilo is the only sizeable base for travelers, though several places have small hotels.

# Hilo

Although it's the Big Island's capital, and largest town, just 45,000 people live in **HILO**, which remains endearing and unpressured. Mass tourism has never taken off here, basically because it rains too much. However, the rain falls mostly at night, and America's wettest city blazes with wild orchids and tropical plants, set against a backdrop of rainbows.

Hilo has always been at the mercy of the twin natural forces of fire and water. Cataclysmic tidal waves (*tsunami*) killed 96 people in April 1946, and a further 61 in May 1960. Countless lava flows have also threatened to engulf it; in 1881 Princess Ruth (see p.1136) summoned up all her spiritual power (or *mana*), watched by missionaries and journalists, to halt one on the edge of town, while in 1984 another flow stopped just eight miles short.

## Arrival, information and getting around

Downtown Hilo is compact and very walkable, around the junction of the seafront Kamehameha Avenue and Waianuenue Avenue, which heads towards the Saddle Road across the island. However, the urban area extends for several miles, and the **airport** at **General Lyman Field** (☎808/935-4782), on the eastern outskirts, is well beyond walking distance. If you're not renting a car at the airport, a taxi into town is your only alternative, costing around $5.

The **Hawaii Visitors Bureau** is at 250 Keawe St (Mon–Fri 8am–noon & 1–4.30pm; ☎808/961-5797). Hilo's Hele On Bus Company (☎808/961-8744) operates a small-scale **city bus** service, plus one service each to Kailua (Mon–Sat) and down to Volcanoes National Park (Mon–Fri) from the Mooheau Bus Terminal on Kamehameha Avenue.

## Accommodation

Hilo, and the whole east coast, has fewer major resort hotels than usual in Hawaii, but there are several **accommodation** possibilities; the less expensive ones tend to be in town rather than around the loop of **Banyan Drive** on the seafront near the airport.

**Arnott's Lodge and Hostel**, 98 Apapane Rd (☎808/969-7097). Laid-back accommodation in a two-story lodge, tucked away in the woods 2 miles southeast of downtown. Call from the airport for free pickup. 12-bed dorms ($17 a bed) and private rooms, plus organized island tours. ①/②.

**Dolphin Bay Hotel**, 333 Iliahi St (☎808/935-1466). Small and friendly 18-room hotel, just across the river from downtown. One- and two-bedroom suites with kitchens. ③.

**Uncle Billy's Hilo Bay Hotel**, 87 Banyan Drive (☎808/961-5818 or 1-800/367-5102). Family-run hotel, the oldest on Banyan Drive, with pleasantly relentless Polynesian decor and budget restaurant. ④.

**Wild Ginger Inn**, 100 Puueo St (☎808/935-5556 or 1-800/882-1887). Near the *Dolphin Bay* in a quiet residential area, this is one of the Big Island's best bargains – a quiet, renovated inn in tropical gardens just across the Wailuku River from downtown. ②.

## Downtown Hilo

There is a simple and tragic reason why **downtown Hilo** looks so appealingly low-key, with its modest streets and wooden stores: all the buildings which stood on the seaward side of Kamehameha Avenue were destroyed by the two *tsunami*. After 1960, no attempt was made to rebuild the "little Tokyo" that had housed Hilo's predominantly Japanese population, and the seafront is now occupied by a succession of pleasant gardens. Besides plenty of conventional shopping, Hilo has a seafront **market** on Wednesday and Saturday mornings. If you want to **swim**, follow Kamehameha Avenue for four miles beyond Banyan Drive to tiny **Richardson's Beach**.

The focus of the two-part **Lyman Museum** at 276 Haili St (Mon–Sat 9am–4.30pm; $4.50) is the original 1830s **Mission House**, furnished in dark *koa* wood, which belonged to Calvinist missionaries David and Sarah Lyman. Their congregation numbered merely twenty until the charismatic Titus Coan arrived in 1835 and, aided by a fortuitous tidal wave in 1837, started a Revival – complete with speaking in tongues – which baptized thousands of ordinary Hawaiians but antagonized his superiors. The museum next door starts with a fascinating set of ancient weapons and then documents Hawaii's various ethnic groups, including the Portuguese shipped in 1878 from the overpopulated but similarly volcanic Azores, who brought the *braginha* which became the ukelele, and the first Japanese arriving from Hiroshima, Hilo's sister city.

A couple of miles up Waianuenue Avenue, at **Rainbow Falls**, just to the right of the road, a spectacular wide waterfall plummets 100ft across the mouth of a huge cavern. Continue another two miles to reach the bubbling natural jacuzzis of the **Boiling Pots**.

The **Hilo Tropical Gardens** at 1477 Kalanianaole Ave (daily 8.30am–5pm; $3) are the best of the commercial gardens. To admire extraordinary plants in a less formal setting, take a self-guided tour through the rainforest of the **Hawaii Tropical Botanical Gardens** (daily 8.30am–5.30pm; $15), which sweep down to the sea at Onomea Bay, seven miles north of town on the lovely **Peepeekeo Scenic Drive**.

### Eating and nightlife

Most of Hilo's (eminently missable) **nightlife** is in the Banyan Drive hotels, though there are a few shows at downtown's restored Palace Theater. As well as its **restaurants**, early risers will enjoy the daily 7am **Suisan Fish Auction**, at Banyan and Lihiwai, where you can buy from the night's catch of marlin and other big fish.

**Bears Coffee**, 110 Keawe St (☎808/935-0708). Hilo's coolest breakfast hangout, one block back from the ocean in the heart of downtown.

**Cafe Pesto**, 130 Kamehameha Ave (☎808/969-6640). Large, Pacific-influenced Italian restaurant, facing the ocean from downtown Hilo. Tasty calzones and pizzas.

**Pescatore**, 235 Keawe St (☎808/969-9090). Formal Italian dining opposite the visitor center, with lunch specials and wonderful fish stews for dinner.

**Reubens**, 336 Kamehameha Ave (☎808/961-2552). Inexpensive but tasty Mexican food, with dinner entrees costing under $10.

# North from Hilo

The **Belt Road** (Hwy-19) follows the **Hamakua coast** north of Hilo, clinging to the hillsides and crossing ravines on slender bridges. At first the fields are crammed into narrow rain-carved "gulches"; further north the land spreads out. For a glimpse into the interior, head into the mountains after fifteen miles to the 450ft **Akaka Falls**. A short loop trail through the forest, festooned with wild orchids, offers views of Akaka and other jungle-like tropical waterfalls.

### Waipio Valley

Hwy-240, which turns north off the Belt Road at **HONOKAA**, comes to an abrupt end after nine miles at the edge of **Waipio Valley**. As the southernmost of six successive sheer-walled valleys, this is the only one accessible by land – and it's as close as Hawaii comes to the classic South Seas image of an isolated and self-sufficient valley, dense with fruit trees and laced by footpaths leading down to the sea. Just off the gray-sand beach of his boyhood home, Kamehameha the Great fought Kahekili of Oahu in 1791's inconclusive but bloody "Battle of the Red-Mouthed Gun," in which for the first time Hawaiian fleets were equipped with cannons, operated by foreign gunners. Spectacular waterfalls cascade down the valley's flanks, but recurrent tidal waves have ensured that only a few taro farmers now live here.

It's perfectly possible to walk down the steep, mile-long track into Waipio, but most visitors take tours, either in the four-wheel-drive vehicles of the Waipio Valley Shuttle (Mon–Sat 9am–4pm; ☎808/775-7121; $35), at the Waipio Valley Art Works in Kukuihaele, a mile from the end of the road, in horse-drawn wagons (☎808/775-9518; $40), or on horseback (☎808/775-0419; $40). It's permissible to **camp** discreetly on the beach, for which you need a permit from the Bishop Estate (☎808/776-1104), or to stay in the spartan $15 rooms at *Tom Araki's Hotel* (☎808/775-0368; ①), which is so remote it doesn't have electricity. Rough-and-tumble Honokaa itself has dorm beds and private rooms at the *Hotel Honokaa Club* on Mamane Street (☎808/775-0678; ①–③), and the *Waipio Wayside B&B* (☎808/775-0275; ④).

# North Kohala

On the green slopes of **Kohala Mountain**, at the northern tip of the Big Island, old-style plantation towns such as **HAWI** survive virtually unchanged – run-down in an appealing sort of way, the all-purpose general stores' still floored with creaking planks. Call in at the spacious *Bamboo Restaurant and Bar* (☎808/889-5555), converted from a former hotel, to enjoy one of the friendliest and most Hawaiian restaurants in the state.

In **KAPAAU**, the birthplace of Kamehameha (who was brought up in Waipio Valley, hidden from his enemies) is marked by his statue. Identical to that in Honolulu, this is in fact the original, lost at sea near the Falklands, and then miraculously recovered after the insurance money had paid for a new one. *Jen's Kohala Cafe* opposite (☎808/889-0099) does basic snacks, with vegetarian options.

**Polulu Valley** at the road's end is the last of the chain of inaccessible valleys, and for the moment is every bit as pristine as Waipio. The fear of *tsunami*, which led the Hawaiians to abandon these once densely populated valleys, is probably their best defense against the rapacity of the developers.

# Waimea and the interior

The **interior** of the Big Island comes as a surprise: pastoral meadows roll over gentle hills where once stood forests of sandalwood. This is cattle-ranching country, most of it – ten percent of the island – owned by the United States' largest private ranch, the **Parker Ranch**.

**WAIMEA** (also known as **Kamuela**) is not the company town it once was – the Parker Ranch now employs just one hundred of its eight thousand inhabitants – but more of a sophisticated country-town resort, which retains traces of its cowboy past. Though you can no longer tour the ranch itself, there's an interesting **visitor center** (Mon–Sat 9am–4pm; $5) in town; the nearby **Kamuela Museum** is enjoyably eclectic and eccentric (daily 8am–5pm; $5).

## Waimea practicalities

**B&B** is booming in Waimea; in fact there's little else. Barbara Campbell runs her own very appealing *Waimea Gardens Cottage* (☎808/885-4550 or 1-800/262-9912; ⑥), and also coordinates Hawaii's Best B&Bs (PO Box 563, Kamuela, HI 96743), a selection of properties on all the islands costing from $70 to $100 per night. The main alternative is the refurbished *Kamuela Inn* (☎808/885-4243; ③), which is part inn, part luxury hotel. *Merriman's* in Opelo Plaza (☎808/885-6822) wins awards for its innovative **cuisine**, but if paying $20 for an entree puts you off, cross the street and walk a few yards to the

*Waimea Coffee Co* in Parker Square (☎808/885-4472), which offers good coffees and vegetarian specials.

## The Saddle Road

The fifty-mile **Saddle Road** cuts across the Big Island from Hilo to Kona, between Mauna Kea and Mauna Loa. Even locals consider it dangerous, especially at night, as there are no facilities, and it's a winding, foggy drive. If you do choose to chance it (in the daytime), you get some great views of the volcanoes – and a good deal of mist even then. Strictly speaking, you're forbidden to drive it in a rental car.

# The Kona coast

Hawaii's leeward **Kona coast** divides into two distinct areas. To the north of its only sizeable community, **Kailua**, a long bleak slope of barren lava trails down to the sea from the third of the Big Island's volcanoes, Hualalai. Thanks to the relentless sun on its magnificent beaches, luxury hotels dot the shoreline, incongruous green patches in the wasteland. To the south, the hillsides are more fertile, and although the condos are spreading, you can still get a real feel of the old Hawaii, in the land where Captain Cook met his end.

## North Kona and the resorts

The best of the spectacular sandy beaches along the Kona coast – safe for summer swimming, though with tempestuous winter surf – lie to the north of Kailua. **Hapuna Beach**, almost forty miles up the coast, is deservedly the most famous; it's still possible to rent $20 cabins here (☎808/974-6200), but since the opening of the giant *Hapuna Prince Beach Hotel* (☎808/880-1111 or 1-800/882-6060; ⑨) in 1994 it has lost some of its charm. For real idyllic seclusion, head instead for **Kona Coast State Park** (daily except Wed 9am–8pm; free), reached via a bumpy dirt road just a couple of miles north of Keahole Airport.

Several extraordinary **resort hotels** lie in the district of South Kohala, thirty miles north of Kailua. Three separate enclaves – Waikoloa, Mauna Kea and Mauna Lani – have been landscaped out of this inhospitable lava desert, each one a self-contained oasis holding two or three hotels, a beach or two, and nothing else. Although **Waikoloa** is the least exclusive of the three, it's home to the ludicrously ostentatious, mile-long *Hilton Waikoloa* (☎808/886-1234; ⑨), said to consume seven percent of all the island's energy. Guests travel to and from their rooms by electric boats or monorail. The adjoining *Royal Waikoloan* (☎808/886-6789; ⑥) is half the price, and has two good restaurants, as well as its own field of petroglyphs.

## Kailua (Kona)

Although the Big Island's main resort is officially called **KAILUA**, and its postal address is "Kailua-Kona," you're likely to hear it referred to as **Kona** as often as not. It's reasonably attractive, and has played its part in Hawaiian history, but its summer-holiday seafront of fast-food restaurants and souvenir shops could be anywhere; and the wind-borne "vog" means that the atmosphere can be as bad as in Los Angeles or London.

### Arrival and information

Open-plan **Keahole Airport**, on a field of black lava nine miles north of Kailua, has the usual car rental places; otherwise the Speedi Shuttle (☎808/329-5433) into town costs around $16 per person. Once in Kailua, a regular **shuttle bus** runs the six-mile length of Alii Drive every ninety minutes (8.30am–9.30pm; $2). One daily bus follows Hwy-11 around the north of the island to Hilo, leaving Kailua just before 6am and returning in the evening.

The **Hawaiian Visitors Bureau** is in Kona Plaza on Alii Drive (Mon–Fri 8am–noon & 1–4.30pm; ☎808/329-7787), as is the well-stocked Middle Earth bookstore. **Bicycles** can be rented from Hawaiian Pedals in the Kona Inn Shopping Village (☎808/329-2294).

## Accommodation

Alii Drive is lined for about five miles south from Kailua with hotels and condos, but none offers much by way of budget accommodation. The listings below therefore include a couple of places a bit further along the coast.

**King Kamehameha's Kona Beach Hotel**, 75-5660 Palani Rd (☎808/329-2911 or 1-800/367-6060). Long-established landmark hotel at the northern end of oceanfront Kailua, centered around a picturesque little beach and the Ahuena Heiau (see below). ⑤.

**Kona Seaside Hotel**, 75-5646 Palani Rd (☎808/329-2455 or 1-800/560-5558). Six floors of reasonable air-conditioned rooms, with and without kitchens, plus discounted car rental. ④.

**Kona Tiki Hotel**, 75-5968 Alii Drive (☎808/329-1425). Bargain little three-story motel, on the ocean a mile south of central Kailua. No phones or TVs. ③.

**Patey's Place**, 75-195 Ala Ona Ona (☎808/326-7018, or on Big Island ☎1-800/972-7408). Chaotic, ramshackle budget hostel, up from the town center, and dominated by backpackers and surf freaks. $18 beds in 4-person dorms, plus some private rooms with shared bath. ①/②.

**Uncle Billy's Kona Bay Hotel**, 75-5739 Alii Drive (☎808/329-6488 or 1-800/367-5102). Friendly central hotel, run by the same family as *The Hilo Bay* in Hilo. Simple but comfortable rooms arranged around a small pool and the *Banana Bay* buffet restaurant. ④.

## The Town

**Hulihee Palace** (daily 9am–4pm; $4) stands square-on to the ocean in the middle of Kailua. Built as the governor's residence in 1838, it's not all that imposing from the outside. Within, it's notable for massive *koa*-wood furnishings, made to fit the considerable girth of the various members of the Hawaiian royal family who later lived here, such as the redoubtable 400-pound Princess Ruth. The 1836 **Mokuaikaua Church** opposite was the first in Hawaii, and acts in part as a museum of the early days of Hawaiian Christianity, setting out to debunk the popular notion of the missionaries as having been primarily concerned with feathering their own nests. A peculiar "sausage-tree" from Mozambique stands in the grounds. Nearby, *King Kamehameha's Kona Beach Hotel* (listed above) dominates the northern end of the bay. King Kamehameha's funeral rites were performed in the **Ahuena Heiau** which juts into the sea in front of its beach.

Some of the world's best fishing, snorkeling or scuba spots are approached by sea from Kailua. Expensive two-hour tours on Atlantis Submarines (☎808/329-6626; $85, under-12s half-price) descend one hundred feet to a coral reef, accompanied by the *Star Wars* theme, to see a frenzy of feeding fish and the occasional lurking shark. The catamaran *Fair Wind* (☎808/322-2788; $75) goes to Kealakekua Bay, for snorkeling and a bit of scuba. If you fancy chartering a boat to fish for the big ones, contact the Charter Locker (☎808/329-5603); rates start at $75 for a half-day.

## Eating and drinking

Competition ensures that the bars and restaurants of central Kailua – especially those along the seafront – are well priced, though the relentless vacation atmosphere means the place can seem a bit unreal.

**Cassandra's Greek Taverna**, Kona Plaza, 75-5719 Alii Drive (☎808/334-1066). Delicious and inexpensive Greek food, from light salads to substantial moussakas.

**Huggo's**, on the beach at 76-6828 Kuhakai St (☎808/329-1493). Lunch and dinner only on a large ocean-view terrace; burgers, salads and sandwiches, plus live evening entertainment.

**Island Lava Java Bakery & Bistro**, Alii Sunset Plaza, 75-5799 Alii Drive (☎808/327-2161). Seafront cafe/bakery just south of central Kailua, with delicious Kona coffee, fresh-baked bread, and live acoustic music in the evening.

**Ocean View Inn**, 75-5683 Alii Drive (☎808/329-9998). Very inexpensive Hawaiian and Asian diner overlooking the sea; traditional fish dishes. Closed Mon.

**Oodles of Noodles**, Crossroads Shopping Center, 75-1027 Henry St (☎808/329-2222). Pan-Asian noodle joint a mile up from the ocean near the highway; great dinners from around $15.

**Su's Thai Kitchen**, 74-5588A Pawai Place (☎808/326-7808). Kailua's best Thai restaurant; hard to find, but also hard to beat, tucked away behind the North Kona mall. Red- or green-curry specials for around $6, Pad Thai noodles for under $10.

## Kealakekua Bay

**Kealakekua Bay**, a dozen miles south of Kailua, was where Captain Cook was killed on his second voyage to Hawaii (see box overleaf). One of ancient Hawaii's major population centers, it's now barely inhabited, and the white **obelisk** on the death site – legally a small piece of England – is all but inaccessible. You can only get to within a mile of it by car, to the beach at **Napoopoo** across the bay, though you'll glimpse it from the road on the way down. The bay itself is the best place on the Big Island for **snorkeling**, even if there are sharks further out. It's also possible to hike down to the monument, but it's a grueling four-hour round-trip, for which you need to carry all your water and supplies. The trail starts just before the town of **CAPTAIN COOK**, which is also home to the bargain *Manago Hotel* (☎808/323-2642; ①/②), which offers comfortable ocean-view rooms amid flowering Japanese gardens.

South Kona is the prime source of **Kona coffee**, which sells here for around $20 a pound (including shipping). You can tour the restored **Old Hawaiian Coffee Plantation**, reached via a one-track rutted road four hundred yards from Marker 105 outside Captain Cook, and buy the produce of its five thousand coffee trees and macadamia nut trees.

## Puuhonua O Honaunau – "The City of Refuge"

**Puuhonua O Honaunau National Historical Park** (daily 7.30am–5.30pm; $4), four miles on from Kealakekua, is the single most evocative historical site in all the Hawaiian islands, jutting into the Pacific on a small peninsula of jagged black lava. The grounds include a palace, with fishpond and private canoe landing, and three *heiaus*, guarded by large carved effigies of gods – reproductions, but still eerie in their original setting. An ancient "**place of refuge**" lies firmly protected behind the mortarless masonry of the sixteenth-century **Great Wall**. Those who broke ancient Hawaii's intricate system of *kapu* (*tabu*) – perhaps by treading on the shadow of a chief, or fishing in the wrong season – could expect summary execution unless they fled to the sanctuary of such a place as this. As chiefs lived on the surrounding land, transgressors had to swim through the shark-infested seas. If successful, they might be absolved and released overnight. In times of war, noncombatants came here to sit out the conflict.

# Hawaii Volcanoes National Park

The Big Island's southernmost volcanoes, **Mauna Loa** and **Kilauea**, jointly constitute **HAWAII VOLCANOES NATIONAL PARK**, thirty miles from Hilo and eighty from Kailua. It's possibly the most dramatic of all the US national parks; as well as two active

## THE DEATH OF CAPTAIN COOK

When **Captain James Cook** sailed into Kealakekua Bay on January 17, 1779, he was on his second visit to Hawaii, making his way home after a year spent searching for the Northwest Passage. As he anchored the *Resolution* in this sheltered harbor, a vast crowd of Hawaiians had gathered to greet him – eyewitnesses claim that as many as ten thousand were out on the water. For three weeks, he was fed and feted by chief Kalaniopuu and his priests, attending temple ceremonies and wrestling matches, observing the life of the island, and replenishing his supplies.

The departure of the *Resolution*, amid declarations of friendship, might have been the end of things, had it not been forced to return just a week later, following a storm that left the ship in tatters. This time the islanders were not so hospitable, far from keen to part with further scarce resources. On February 14, Cook led a landing party of nine men in a bid to kidnap Kalaniopuu and effect the return of a stolen small boat. In an undignified scuffle, surrounded by thousands of hostile warriors including the future Kamehameha the Great, he was stabbed, and died at the water's edge, unable as a non-swimmer to reach safety. His body was treated as appropriate for a dead chief: the skull and leg bones were kept, and the rest cremated.

The legend soon grew that the Hawaiians had taken Cook to be the great god **Lono**; but Hawaiian commentators now argue that such tales say more about European attitudes to Cook than about Polynesian perceptions. To the European mentality of the time, it was self-evident that a noble figure of the Enlightenment such as Captain Cook must appear god-like to superstitious "natives." The fact that Cook was called Lono, the name of a historic chief as well as a god, could not be an allusion or metaphor, but only a literal declaration of his godhood. That Hawaiians prostrated themselves on the ground in front of Cook could only mean that they were worshipping him as a god – even though commoners were obliged to do so before any of their chiefs. It was in England, not Hawaii, that popular images appeared showing his ascent to heaven, borne by angels.

The major anomaly in the Cook-as-Lono legend is quite why the Hawaiians would have killed this "god." Some proponents say it was a ritual sacrifice, even though it happened in battle, while others argue that the man who struck the final blow had only just arrived from upcountry, and "didn't know." The usual explanation, that it was simply an accident, serves both to perpetuate the idea of Hawaiians as "innocent" savages, and to absolve Cook himself of any responsibility for his fate. What seems more likely is that his actions in peremptorily dismantling a temple at Napoopoo for use as firewood antagonized the priests, and when he infuriated the chiefs as well by seizing Kalaniopuu, deference finally gave way to defiance.

Voyages such as Cook's were intended to bring civilization and order to blighted heathen lands. The record of British violence – from the shooting of a Hawaiian at the very moment of first contact, on Kauai in 1778, to the brutal massacre that followed Cook's death, in which the village at Napoopoo was set ablaze, old and young alike were bayoneted, and severed Hawaiian heads were impaled on poles – was all but deleted from official accounts.

volcanoes, of which at least one is likely to be erupting, it includes desert, arctic tundra, and the Wao Kele O Puna rainforest (where a much-opposed project is attempting to tap geothermal energy).

Evidence is everywhere of the awesome power of the volcanoes to create and destroy; no map can keep up with the latest whims of the lava flow. Whole towns have been engulfed, and what were once prized beachfront properties lie buried hundreds of yards back from the sea. No one knows quite where they are – there's nowhere for surveyors to get their bearings. There are no towns left on the southern coast. The Hawaiians abandoned their villages 150 years ago, after a succession of terrible tidal waves; now the Americans too have been driven out.

## Kilauea Caldera

The park headquarters is on the rim of **Kilauea Caldera**, where the **visitor center** (daily 7.45am–5pm; ☎808/967-7311; $10 per vehicle), and the fascinating **Jaggar Museum** of geology (daily 8.30am–5pm; free), on the eleven-mile **Crater Rim Drive**, offer basic orientation.

Kilauea is said to be the home of the volcano goddess **Pele**, who has followed the "hot spot" from island to island. In 1824 Queen Kapiolani, a recent convert to Christianity, defied her by descending into the crater, reading aloud from her Bible, eating the *tabu* red ohelo berries, and throwing stones into the pit. When Mark Twain came here, he saw a dazzling lake of liquid fire; since a huge explosion in 1924 it's been shallower and quieter, a black dusty expanse dotted with hissing steam vents. Enthusiastic hikers should set time aside to follow the long trails that explore the caldera floor, now (mostly) solid. Both the **Halemaumau Trail**, a seven-mile round trip, and the **Kilauea Iki Trail**, a total of five miles, involve picking your way from cairn to cairn across an eerie landscape of cracked and jagged lava.

Among shorter routes, the mile-long **Devastation Trail** is a boardwalk laid across the scene of a 1959 eruption; scientists are monitoring how long vegetation takes to re-establish itself. Most of what you see is new growth – fresh lava is full of nutrients, and rainwater and seeds soon collect in the recesses – but a few older trees survived partial submersion in ash by growing "aerial roots" some way up their trunks. Around the cinder cone of **Puu Puai** the land is utterly barren, scattered with bleached dead branches.

A short drive from *Volcano House* (see overleaf), and across the road from the crater, is a rainforest. A ten-minute walk takes you through **Thurston Lava Tube**, created when the surface of a lava stream, exposed to the air, hardened. Just below, the now-protected lava was able to keep flowing 28 miles to the sea with only a slight loss of temperature. It's now a damp empty tunnel, an illuminated segment of which is open. Gigantic ferns grow over the top, and a few roots have worked their way through cracks in the rock to dangle from the ceiling. Outside, the native red-billed *iiwi* bird can always be heard, if not seen.

Stretching away southwest of Kilauea, the **Kau Desert** receives plenty of rainfall – but it's a naturally sulphurous acid rain, composed of volcanic fumes carried by the tradewinds, and far too noxious to support life.

## Chain of Craters Road

**Chain of Craters Road** winds down to the sea from Crater Rim Drive, sweeping around a succession of cones and vents where an occasional dead, white tree trunk or flowering shrub pokes up. Fresh sheets of lava constantly ooze down the slopes to cover the road. When a new road is built on top of the flow, more lava covers it. Along the coast, the scale of the damage since 1983 has been too great to repair – over seven miles have been lost – so now the road is a dead end, and getting shorter year by year. One by one the landmarks along its seafront stretch – such as **Wahaula Heiau**, a temple where human sacrifice may have been introduced to Hawaii – have been destroyed, and before long it may not follow the shoreline at all.

Check current conditions at the visitor center when you arrive, and make sure you have enough gas. The end of the road is a fifty-mile round-trip from the park entrance, and there are no facilities of any kind along the way. For several years, depending on where current activity is concentrated, it has been possible at times to walk across the congealed lava blocking Chain of Craters Road to see molten rock gush from the earth – sometimes directly into the sea. A **Volcano Update** information line (☎808/985-6000) has the latest details; for information on ranger-led tours, call the visitor center.

## Practicalities

The national park operates two free **campgrounds** on a first-come, first-served basis, while the famous *Volcano House*, on the very edge of the crater within the park (PO Box 53; ☎808/967-7321; ⑤), has spectacular views, and good food in the evening, although the prices for its simple motel-style rooms are a little over the odds. Otherwise, the small and inconspicuous town of **VOLCANO**, just before the park entrance on the Hilo side, provides the best places to **stay** in the vicinity, with B&Bs such as *Hale Ohia* (PO Box 758; ☎808/967-7986; ⑤). *Kilauea Lodge*, on the leafy main street (☎808/967-7366; ⑤), is a comfortable inn with a good **restaurant**, and there's also good food at *Surt's* nearby (☎808/985-6711).

## Pahoa and the southeast

The southeastern corner of the Big Island is off the usual tourist trail. **PAHOA** in particular has gone its own sweet way, its distinctive blend of lawless cowboy town and hippie hangout probably due to its alleged role as the island's main marijuana-growing area. Businesses along the rudimentary boardwalks include a handful of New Age bookstores and cafes. Among the best **restaurants** are *Sawasdee* (☎808/965-8186), serving plenty of Thai vegetarian dishes, and the Italian *Godmother* (☎808/965-5055). The central *Village Inn* is a small and friendly **B&B** (PO Box 1987; ☎808/965-6444; ②).

# MAUI

The island of **MAUI**, the second largest in the Hawaiian chain, is Oahu's fastest-growing rival, attracting roughly a third of all visitors to the state. Some would say that things have gone too far. What were remote, unspoiled beaches twenty years ago, around **Kaanapali** and **Kihei** for example, have been swamped by ugly, sprawling

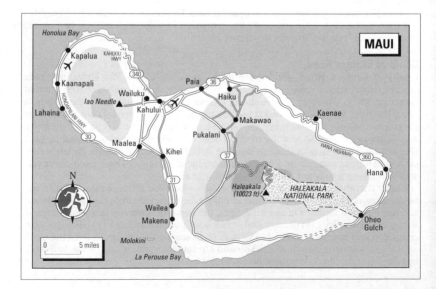

resorts, and **Lahaina**, once "whaling capital of the world," is now just another tourist trap. Traffic clogs the roads, and most towns consist of little more than a succession of malls.

On the other hand, the crowds come to Maui for the good reason that it's still beautiful. This is probably the best equipped of all the islands for **activity** holidays – whale-watching, windsurfing, diving, sailing, snorkeling and cycling. Temperatures along the coast can be searing, especially at Lahaina, but it's always possible to escape to somewhere cooler. **Upcountry Maui**, on the slopes of the mighty **Haleakala** volcano, is a delight, well away from the bustle; **Makawao** and **Paia** here make good alternative hangouts, although they're short on accommodation. The tortuous road out west to **Hana** does not quite merit its legendary status, but with its waterfalls and ravines it outclasses anything on Oahu.

# Kahului and Wailuku

Half of Maui's 91,000 inhabitants – the workers who keep this fantasy island going – live in the twin towns of **KAHULUI** and **WAILUKU**, to the north of the "neck" connecting its two mountainous sections. The land here can be so flat you fear the waves will wash right over it. Kahului is the main commercial center; Wailuku, if not aesthetically pleasing, is unusual for Maui in feeling like a genuine community, and with its budget hotels and restaurants – and the stunning **Iao Needle** nearby – it makes a good central base.

### Arrival and information
Virtually all visitors to Maui arrive at **Kahului Airport**, which is well placed for all the major destinations and has an information booth. Maui Airporter Shuttle **buses** (☎808/877-7308) connect the airport regularly with Lahaina and Kaanapali, for $13 per person, while TransHawaiian (☎808/877-0380) provide similar services to the rest of the island.

The offices of the **Maui Visitors Bureau** are hard to find, at 1727 Wili Pa Loop in Wailuku (Mon–Fri 8am–4.30pm; ☎808/244-3530); it's easier simply to pick up information in major hotels.

### Accommodation
As most of the Maui resorts are long oceanfront strips of expensive hotels, where you have to drive just to get to a shop or restaurant, there's a lot to be said for a simple room in Wailuku.

**Banana Bungalow**, 310 N Market St, Wailuku (☎808/244-5090 or 1-800/746-7871). Extremely convivial budget hotel with Maui's least expensive accommodation. $16 for a dorm bed; also some bare, basic doubles. Informal meals, organized trips, cut-price car rental. ①/②.

**Maui Seaside Hotel**, 100 W Kaahumanu Ave at the harbor (☎808/877-3311 or 1-800/560-5552). Good-value rooms in a far from attractive setting, plus discounted car rental. ④.

**Northshore Inn**, 2080 Vineyard St, Wailuku (☎808/242-8999). $15 dorms, plus some private rooms. Much the same communal feel as *Banana Bungalow*. ①/②.

### Exploring Kahului and Wailuku
There's no sightseeing to speak of in either Kahului or Wailuku, though you may well become familiar with both while shopping for food and other necessities, better value here than elsewhere on the island. **Market Street** in Wailuku contains several interesting curio and souvenir shops, and commands a view across to Haleakala.

Wailuku's Main Street heads straight into the **West Maui Mountains**, stopping three miles in at **Iao Needle**, a stunning 1200ft pinnacle of green-clad lava. It stands, head usually in the clouds, at the intersection of two lush valleys; you can't climb the needle itself, but hiking trails lead off in all directions, and as very few visitors follow them for any distance you can soon be alone in the wilderness. King Kamehameha won control of Maui here in 1790, in a battle determined by a cannonade directed by two captured European gunners. On the road up, a natural rock formation has become known for fairly – but not very – obvious reasons as the **John F Kennedy Profile**.

### Eating

Kahului has recently acquired a number of classy **restaurants**, while Wailuku has a handful of good-value alternatives, though nothing that could be considered fine dining.

**Maui Coffee Roasters**, 444 Hana Hwy, Kahului (☎808/877-2877). Good breakfasts, lunch specials and espresso coffees.

**Saeng's**, 2119 Vineyard St (☎808/244-1567). Pleasant, plant-filled restaurant, serving top-quality Thai food at bargain prices.

**Sam Choy's**, Kaahumanu Mall, Kahului (☎808/893-0366). Trendy mall restaurant serving giant portions of contemporary Hawaiian favorites, with dinner entrees at $20–25.

# West Maui

Despite the guaranteed sunshine that draws the vacationers, you can feel somewhat cut off if you choose to stay on Maui's **west coast**, while the prices are higher, and the long drive around is worsened by heavy traffic. The expensive air-conditioned hotels and shopping centers are concentrated in the two main resorts, **Lahaina** and **Kaanapali** (an Amfac development), although development has sensibly been restricted to the *makai* (oceanward) side of the Honoapiilani Highway, leaving the inland hills and valleys largely untouched except by drifting rainbows.

## Lahaina

The square at the heart of modern **LAHAINA** is all but filled by a magnificent **banyan tree**, its aerial roots pushing down into the earth to become sturdy additional trunks. Just in front, in the small harbor, the replica square-rigged *Carthaginian* houses a not wildly interesting **maritime museum** (daily 10am–5pm; $4). The **Pioneer Inn** nearby is Lahaina's main social center, great for a convivial, if not quiet, beer.

Otherwise, a walk up Front Street and back down Wainee Street covers most of what Lahaina has to offer. It does hold some appealing nineteenth-century buildings, but the concentration of tourist shops and fast-food places is phenomenal. The view out to sea, towards the island of **Lanai**, is a welcome respite. If you have the time, consider taking a ferry over there for the day; there's little to see, but the main beach, at Hulopoe Bay, is a delight. Expedition provide five sailings daily, from the seafront at Lahaina (☎808/661-3756; $50 round-trip).

### Accommodation

If you have the money to spend on resort-style **accommodation**, Lahaina and the coast to the north have some good options, but there's very little available for under $90 per night.

**Aloha Lani Inn**, 13 Kauaula Rd (☎808/661-8040). Simple but comfortable B&B near the beach. ④.

**Maui Islander**, 660 Wainee St (☎808/667-9766 or 1-800/367-5226). Very central, low-key, mid-range accommodation. ④.

**Pioneer Inn**, 658 Wharf St (☎808/661-3636 or 1-800/457-5457). Characterful and very lively old hotel, right in the thick of things. ⑤.

### WHALE-HUNTING AND WHALE-WATCHING

The first **whaling ships** arrived in Hawaii in 1820, the same year as the missionaries – and had an equally dramatic impact. With the ports of Japan closed to outsiders, Hawaii swiftly became the center of the industry. Any Pacific port of call must have seemed a godsend to the whalers, who were away from New England for three years at a time, and paid so badly that most were either fugitives from justice or just plain mad (see p.198). Hawaii was such a paradise that up to fifty percent of each crew would desert, to be replaced by native Hawaiians, born seafarers eager to see the world. Soon King Kamehameha IV had established his own whaling fleet, and the economy adapted to meet the sailors' needs. Cattle-raising began on the Big Island, and vegetables were grown on Maui.

Until the 1840s, Honolulu, which permitted drinking, was the whalemen's favorite port. Then potatoes and prostitution lured them to **Lahaina** as well, which by 1857 stretched for several miles. The sea was calm enough for ships to dock along the open road, and a grassy marketplace stood beside a central canal. Both Lahaina and Honolulu became notorious for such diseases as syphilis, influenza, measles, typhoid and smallpox.

At the peak of the trade, almost six hundred whaling vessels docked in Honolulu in a single year. Decline came with the Civil War – when many ships were bought up in order to be sunk as a blockade of Confederate ports – and an 1871 disaster, when 31 vessels lingered in the Arctic too long, became frozen in, and had to be abandoned.

#### Whale-watching

Ironically, the waters just off western Maui now rate among the world's best areas for whale-watching and research. Between January and March each year, and for up to a month either side of that, **humpback whales** use the ocean channels here as both sanctuary and playground. They did not do so in the nineteenth century, although they would have been safe enough, as humpbacks were not then hunted. When caught with the old technology, they sank uselessly to the bottom of the sea.

The whales are often clearly visible from the shore, but specific whale-watching trips can take you much nearer (with money-back guarantees if you don't see one). Operators include the nonprofit Pacific Whale Foundation (☎808/879-8811; $31).

## Food and nightlife

Lahaina's harborside malls contain a tremendous selection of restaurants, national and local chain outlets (including a *Hard Rock Cafe* and a *Planet Hollywood*) and takeaways, not all of them good by any means, but covering a wider spectrum than the hotels.

**Cheese Burger in Paradise**, 811 Front St (☎808/661-4855). Busy, crowded seafront restaurant, perched on stilts above the water. Very much what the name suggests, though as well as meaty $7–8 cheeseburgers they have fish sandwiches and spinach nutburgers at similar prices.

**David Paul's Lahaina Grill**, *Lahaina Inn*, 127 Lahainaluna Rd (☎808/667-5117). Upmarket dinner-only restaurant with Maui's finest Pacific Rim cooking; it's slightly cramped and unatmospheric, but the food is great.

**Pacific 'O**, 505 Front St (☎808/667-4341). Pacific Rim cuisine served in an attractive oceanfront mall setting; try the amazing $28 Shrimp Nui.

**Sunrise Cafe**, 693A Front St at Market (☎808/661-8558). Small, laid-back and very central cafe, with outdoor seating beside its own tiny patch of beach. Espressos, smoothies, salads, sandwiches and daily specials, with prices starting at well under $5.

## Kaanapali

**KAANAPALI**, just a few miles north of Lahaina but reliably cooler, was never a town; fields of sugar cane here were replaced in the 1960s by high-rise hotels and condos,

---

### MAUI ACTIVITIES

Promotional handouts, and free newspapers such as *Maui Beach Press*, will familiarize you with a wide range of possible tours and activities. Agencies throughout the island, especially along Front Street in Lahaina, offer deals well below advertised rates.

**Molokini**
Maui's best-known **snorkeling** and **diving** spot is the tiny crescent of **Molokini**, all that's left poking above the sea of a once-great volcano. There's no beach, or landfall of any kind, but you do see a lot of fish, including deep-water species. Countless cruises leave early each morning (to avoid the worst of the heat) from Maalea Harbor. Vessels range from the forty-passenger sailing ship *Silent Lady* (☎808/875-1112; $67) up to the 150-seater *Prince Kuhio* (☎808/242-8777; $76).

**Downhill Cycle Rides**
One of Maui's more unusual opportunities is to be taken by van to the top of **Haleakala**, watch the sun rise, and then ride a bicycle 39 miles down to Paia by the sea – without pedaling once. Even Dan Quayle managed it, accompanied by six Uzi-toting Secret Service men on mountain bikes. Serious cyclists may find the slow pace of the trip frustrating; complete novices or the unfit shouldn't try; the in-betweens will think it's great. Companies running trips for around $80 (including pickups) include Haleakala Bike Co (☎808/572-2200 or 1-800/922-2453).

---

each no doubt comfortable enough but soulless en masse. Besides several perfect family **beaches** – swimming and snorkeling are best at **Black Rock**, in front of the *Sheraton* – the main attraction is the two-part **whaling museum** in the Whalers Village mall (daily 9.30am–10pm; free). Grisly but fascinating exhibits include a cast-iron "try pot," used for reducing whale blubber at sea; such pots gave rise to the stereotyped but not entirely fictitious image of cannibals cooking missionaries in big black cauldrons.

A free shuttle bus connects Kaanapali with Lahaina, and a trolley operates within the resort. The warnings of the car rental companies concerning the **Kahekili Highway**, which on the map looks like a good route to continue around northwest Maui and back to Wailuku, should be taken seriously: it's an exceptionally dangerous drive. Two of Maui's most famous **surfing** spots, at Mokuleia Bay and Honolua Bay, are a few miles along, however, before the road gets too hair-raising.

# Kihei and Wailea

Maui's other main resort area is south of Kahului, across the isthmus. The long strip of hotels, malls and condos begins at **KIHEI**, with the road heavily built up on both sides, but thins out beyond the manicured lawns of **WAILEA**, near some superb beaches. **Paluea Beach** is ideal for families, while **Little Beach**, reached by a trail from cactus-lined **Makena (or Big) Beach**, is famous for (illegal) nudism. A very rough one-lane track, with minimal visibility, peters out altogether just before **La Perouse Bay**. Once a significant population center, the beach here is good for snorkeling, and **dolphins** regularly come to play with swimmers, though you're forbidden to encourage them.

Few of the **accommodation** options are geared towards budget travelers; *Hale Kai O Kihei*, 1310 Uluniu Rd (☎808/879-2757 or 1-800/457-7014; ③) is good value, while *Maui Vista*, 2191 S Kihei Rd (☎808/879-7966 or 1-800/535-0085; ⑥), is a bit more luxurious. For **food**, the *Pacific Cafe Maui*, 1279 S Kihei Rd (☎808/879-0069), offers some great Pacific Rim concoctions, while *Kihei Caffe*, 1945 S Kihei Rd (☎808/878-2230), has smoothies and inexpensive snacks.

# Upcountry Maui

Hawaii is not always a land tarnished by civilization. **Central Maui**, in the nineteenth century "a dreary expanse of sand and shifting sandhills, with a dismal growth . . . of thornless thistles," is now a pastoral idyll, thanks to an ingenious system of irrigation channels.

The highway to the top of **Haleakala** rises higher, at a faster rate, than any road on earth, starting in the rich meadows where Jimi Hendrix's *Rainbow Bridge* concert was filmed. Beyond the exclusive homes and white-clapboard churches, it climbs past purple-blossoming jacaranda, firs and eucalyptus to reach open ranching land, and then ascends in huge curves to the volcanic desert and the crater itself.

## Haleakala

Though **HALEAKALA** – "the House of the Sun" – is the world's largest dormant volcano, you may not appreciate its full ten thousand feet until you're at the top. Shield volcanoes are not as dramatic as the classic cones, as lava oozes from fissures along broad flanks to create a long, low profile, and the summit is often obscured by cloud. That it hasn't erupted for two hundred years doesn't necessarily mean it won't ever again – in 1979, for example, Haleakala was thought more likely to explode than Mount St Helens (see p.1049).

The higher reaches of the mountain are a **national park**, which never closes (admission $10). Manhattan would fit comfortably into the awe-inspiring **crater**, almost eight miles across, which was for the ancient Hawaiians a site of deep spiritual power. The most popular time to come is for the **sunrise**; the **visitor center** at the top operates from just before dawn until 3pm (weather ☎808/572-7749, information ☎808/572-9306). Hiking trails of varying difficulty cross the crater floor, where **camping** is permitted in three remote cabins, awarded by lottery two months in advance, that require a hike of four to ten miles and a $40 fee per night. In addition, fifteen to twenty-five free tent sites outside the crater are available every day (first-come, first-served).

On the way up or down, stop to eat and admire the view at the *Kula Lodge*, 3200ft up (☎808/878-1535; ⑥), which serves all meals and also offers some pricey cabin accommodation.

## Makawao and Paia

Coming down from Haleakala, Hwy-365 leads north to two laid-back little country towns, populated mainly by old Californian hippies: **MAKAWAO**, five miles up from the ocean, and **PAIA**, Maui's first plantation town, near the surfing beach of **Hookipa**. Neither has much accommodation, though advertisements at Paia's wholefood store Mana Foods, 49 Baldwin Ave (☎808/579-8078), offer rooms from around $25 per night. In the center of Makawao, the friendly Italian restaurant *Casanova's,* 1188 Makawao Ave (☎808/572-0220), puts on live music at night, courtesy of the local community of rock exiles. Fresh fish is the specialty in Paia, at *Paia Fishmarket*, 101 Hana Hwy (☎808/579-8030), and the more expensive but greatly recommended *Mama's Fish House*, 799 Poho Place (☎808/579-8488), set next to the sea a mile along the Hana Highway. Vegetarians will be glad of the *Vegan*, at 115 Baldwin Ave, Paia (closed Mon; ☎808/579-9144).

# The road to Hana

The rains which fall on Haleakala cascade down Maui's long windward flank, covering it in thick, jungle-like vegetation. Convicts in the 1920s hacked out a road along the coast that has become a major tourist attraction in its own right, twisting tortuously in and out of gorges, past innumerable waterfalls, and over more than fifty tiny one-lane bridges. All year round, and especially in June, the route is ablaze with color, from orchids up to rainbow eucalyptus and African tulip trees with their orange blossom.

The usual day's excursion is roughly fifty miles (three hours) each way from Paia, to **Oheo Gulch** just past Hana. Don't attempt it if it's raining; in good weather, this road of hairpin turns, while not too difficult, is not recommended for the potentially carsick. Drivers can miss much of the scenery, and may prefer to take an **organized tour** (around $70 for a full day) with No Ka Oi Scenic Tours (☎808/871-9008) or Alii Coach Service (☎808/875-7178).

## Keanae

Halfway along the Hana Highway, a side road down to the peninsula of **KEANAE** brings you to a small Hawaiian village with taro fields and a fine old church. Banana trees and birds of paradise abound, and the ocean surf crashes onto sharp headlands of prickly black *aa* lava. *YMCA Camp Keanae*, on the highway just before the turning, is a **youth hostel** (once a prison) with dorm beds at $10 per night, for a maximum of three days. Book ahead via Maui YMCA (250 Kanaloa Ave, Kahului, HI 96732; ☎808/242-9007).

## Hana

The former sugar town of **HANA** itself might seem a disappointment at the end of the road; really it's a pleasant enough little community that isn't especially interested in attracting tourists. Hasegawa's General Store is a friendly place to pick up supplies, and a delightful **red-sand beach** can be reached by a precarious trail from the end of Uakea Road. Rooms at the deluxe *Hotel Hana-Maui* (☎808/248-8211 or 1-800/3215-4262; ⑨) *start* at around $400; *Joe's Place* on Uakea Road is a rudimentary but affordable alternative (☎808/248-7033; ②).

## Beyond Hana

A mile or two past Hana, a dirt track leads to the banyan-shaded oceanside cemetery of **Palapala Hoomau** church, where **Charles Lindbergh** was buried in 1974. The first man to fly across the Atlantic (in 1927), who retired to Maui for privacy, was a notorious Nazi sympathizer who once told the *Reader's Digest* that aviation is "one of those priceless possessions which permit the White Race to live at all in a sea of Yellow, Black, and Brown."

The gorgeous scenery of **Oheo Gulch** – part of Haleakala National Park, although admission is free – is ten miles out of Hana. Waterfalls tumble down the hillside to oceanfront meadows. If you hike up, you soon escape the crowds and reach cool rock pools which are ideal for swimming; most visitors stroll down to an attractive spot the tour operators persist in calling the **Seven Sacred Pools** – a groundless label which in its time has been attached to other features along the way, and is discouraged by Hawaiians.

If you're averse to going back the same way you came, in normal conditions (but *not* rain) it is possible with four-wheel-drive to follow the road right around southern Maui, although it has several rocky and unpaved stretches which invalidate rental-car insurance. At first the countryside is lovely, dotted with exclusive homes whose owners would prefer this not to become a standard tourist loop. Beyond a small black-sand beach, the 1859 church at **Huailoha**, and the Last Chance Store at **Kaupo**, the road climbs thirty miles up bleak lava fields and rounds the corner to give spectacular views out to the island of **Kahoolawe** (a naval bombing range until 1990, which has now been returned for restoration to the Hawaiians). You're now back in upcountry Maui, and soon come to the **Tedeschi Winery** (daily 9am–5pm; free), Hawaii's only vineyard.

# MOLOKAI

Halfway between Oahu and Maui, little **MOLOKAI** is the least visited of the major Hawaiian islands. It doesn't have a single traffic light or elevator; a brief visit is a chance to feel how Hawaii must have been fifty years ago. The capital, **Kaunakakai**, is one dusty street of wooden false-front stores, the scenery of **Kalaupapa Peninsula** and **Halawa Valley** is unspoiled, and gigantic **Papahoku Beach** is usually deserted. The downside is that agriculture is on the decline, and Molokai has the highest unemployment in the United States; some islanders have to commute to factory jobs in Maui.

## Eastern Molokai

**Halawa Valley** is perhaps the finest of all Hawaii's "lost valleys," an absolute gem and a laborious hour's drive east of Kaunakakai. The first view from the **overlook** is staggeringly beautiful, with Moaula Falls high in the distance half-hidden by clouds and the rich-green valley with its black-sand beach below. You can continue down to the **beach**, where the shore is taken up with lush meadows filled with bright wild flowers.

The highest **sea cliffs** in the world, at four thousand feet, are further around the northern coast. The best way to see them is by air – scheduled flights south from Molokai pass over them, as do helicopter trips.

## Kalaupapa peninsula

King Kamehameha IV set aside the flat peninsula of **Kalaupapa** in northern Molokai, created by a lava flow at the base of a colossal cliff, as a **leper colony**. Sufferers from all the islands were banished here to live out their days, separated forever from their homes and families, and without help until 1873, when a Belgian priest, **Father Damien**, began to improve their living conditions. Robert Louis Stevenson sprang to his defence when his reputation was maligned; he eventually succumbed to the disease himself and is now a likely candidate for sainthood. In the 1940s, when new drugs made leprosy no longer contagious, the need for isolation ended, but many patients remain. The peninsula can only be seen on guided tours (Damien Tours; ☎808/567-6171; $30), and you have to make your own way down, either on foot, by air (Molokai Air Shuttle; ☎808/567-6847; $52 round-trip), or by mule (Molokai Mule Ride; ☎808/567-6088; $120 including ground tour).

## Western Molokai

The few hotels at the west end of Molokai are a surreal testament to the wonders a bit of water can work in a volcanic wasteland. They may lack character, but **Papahoku Beach**, on the other hand, is phenomenal. Stretching for miles of empty white sand and magnificent pounding surf, it's so massive that unscrupulous developers were able to cart much of it off to Waikiki before anyone realized.

**Mauna Loa**, on the road down, used to be a Dole pineapple town, and in antiquity was the birthplace of *hula*, but it's now the domain of the **Molokai Ranch** (☎808/552-2741 or 1-800/254-8871), which operates phenomenally expensive camping trips into rarely seen parts of the island, charging a minimum $185 per person per night to sleep in its semi-permanent "tentalows."

## Practicalities

Molokai's **airport** is in the center of the island, with Dollar and Budget rental cars and taxis but no public transportation. **Rooms in Kaunakakai** can be had at the *Pau Hana Inn* (☎808/553-5347 or 1-800/423-MOLO; ③), with its spreading banyan tree and low-slung buildings, or for a little more at the pseudo-Polynesian but comfortable *Hotel*

*Molokai* (same phone; ③). **B&Bs** in superb settings along the road to Halawa, **east** of Kaunakakai, include the *Kamalo Plantation* after ten and a half miles (☎808/558-8236; ③), and the *Honomuni House* after eighteen miles (☎808/558-8383; ④). In the **west**, there's the large oceanfront *Kaluakoi Hotel* (☎808/552-2555; ⑤), and the appealing *Ke Nani Kai* (☎808/552-2761; ⑤) condo development.

Kaunakakai offers reasonable **food** at the *Pau Hana Inn*, and wholefood snacks and smoothies at *Outpost Natural Foods* (☎808/553-3377), behind the Chevron garage. The only restaurant at the west end is in the *Kaluakoi Resort*.

# KAUAI

Although no point on the tiny island of **KAUAI** is as much as a dozen miles from the sea, the variety of its landscapes is quite incredible. This is the oldest of the major islands, and erosion has had that many more million years to sculpt it into fantastic shapes. The mist-shrouded extinct volcano **Mount Waialeale** at its heart is the world's wettest spot, draining into a high landlocked swamp, full of unique plants and animals. Nearby is the chasm of **Waimea Canyon**, while the north shore holds the vertiginous green cliffs of the awe-inspiring **Na Pali** coast, familiar to millions from films such as *Jurassic Park* and *South Pacific* but the sole preserve of adventurous **hikers**. Kauai is a place to be active, on sea and land; and if you only go on one **helicopter** flight in your life, this is where to do it, despite recent restrictions on how low they can fly.

On September 11, 1992, **Hurricane Iniki** slammed into Kauai; along with 300,000 tons of debris, it created a unique opportunity for the island and its tourism industry to rebuild from the ground up. That process is now all but completed; visitor facilities may

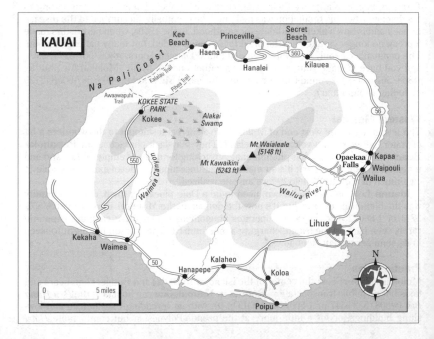

not be quite on the same scale as the other major islands, but in many ways Kauai is once again the most idyllic vacation destination of all the Hawaiian islands.

# Lihue

Flights to Kauai arrive at the capital, **LIHUE**, which stands slightly inland of lovely little Nawiliwili Harbor. It's roughly at the midpoint of the round-island highway (prevented from completing a loop by the Na Pali cliffs), but as a base it's pretty undistinguished. The population is just five thousand, and downtown consists of a few tired plantation-town streets, well back from the sea and surrounded by anonymous malls.

The small **Kauai Museum** at 4428 Rice St (Mon–Fri 9am–4pm, Sat 10am–4pm; $5) traces the island's history from the mythical *menehune* through Captain Cook's 1778 landfall and on to its sugar-growing heyday. Kauai was the one island not conquered by Kamehameha the Great; he spent six years amassing a fleet which never sailed, and settled in the end for accepting economic tribute.

### Practicalities

Lihue's **airport** is only two miles from downtown ($8 by **taxi**; Wailua or Kapaa cost more like $20). Along with the usual **car** rental outlets, it also has **helicopters** – Safari Helicopter Tours (☎808/246-0136) is typical in offering basic tours from $109. Shopping around in the malls, and checking freesheets like *Kauai Beach Press*, you'll find discounts. The **Hawaii Visitors Bureau** is in town at 3016 Umi St (Mon–Fri 8am–4pm; ☎808/245-3971).

Since Iniki, Lihue's range of budget **rooms** is not what it was, and there's no real point staying here rather than along the coast. However, the *Garden Island Inn*, near the harbor at 3445 Wilcox Rd (☎808/245-7227 or 1-800/648-0154; ④), is a lovely refurbished three-story motel, dripping with purple bougainvillea. For a quick meal in the heart of town, call in at *Hamura Saimin*, 2956 Kress St (☎808/245-3271), a family-run communal Japanese food counter, open very late and specializing in bowls of *saimin* (noodles) for $3.50. The *Hanamaulu Restaurant and Tea House* (☎808/245-2511), a mile or two east, is a delightful old place, complete with fishponds, that serves both Chinese and Japanese food.

# East Kauai

Most Kauaians live between Lihue and the overlapping communities of **WAILUA**, **WAIPOULI** and **KAPAA**, whose malls, condos and hotels blend into each other a few miles north of the capital. All the way along there's an exposed thin strip of beach; only Wailua is especially aesthetic, and you have to go further north for snorkeling.

The most popular tourist attraction here is the excursion from Wailua up the Wailua River, the only navigable river in all Hawaii, to **Fern Grotto**. This large, damp and dull cave – immortalized by Elvis Presley in *Blue Hawaii* – is only accessible on $15 tours in large, open-topped barges, run by Smith's (☎808/821-6892) and Waialeale Boat Tours (☎808/822-4908). Following Hwy-580 brings you to the spectacular **Opaekaa Falls**.

### Accommodation

Most east-coast **hotels** are in the luxury bracket, but there are many possibilities on a more manageable scale.

**Aston Kauai Beachboy Hotel**, Coconut Plantation, Kapaa (☎808/922-7866 or 1-800/847-7417). High lava-rock walls make this property look a little forbidding, but lawns lead down from the comfortable rooms to an open beach. ⑥.

**Kauai International Hostel**, 4532 Lehua St, Kapaa (☎808/823-6142). Kauai's only hostel, across from Kapaa Beach and open to everyone except Hawaiian residents, with a maximum one-week stay. $16 dorm beds and a few private rooms. ①/②.

**Lae nani**, 410 Papaloa Rd, Wailua (☎808/822-4938 or 1-800/367-7052). Irresistible complex of oceanfront apartments and condos, with lovely swimming alongside. ⑤.

**Royal Drive Cottages**, 147 Royal Drive, Kapaa (☎808/822-2321). Very friendly, very secluded B&B, just beyond Opaekaa Falls. ⑤.

## Eating

**Kapaa** is the only one of the towns with anything like a center; you can windowshop for **restaurants** along its street of wooden stores, fronted by a beach park.

**Korean Bar-B-Q Restaurant**, 4-3561 Kuhio Hwy, Wailua (☎808/823-6744). Unassuming barbecue diner serving excellent grilled meats and chickens; the best bet for a bargain meal, with large combos for under $7. Closed Tues.

**Mema**, 4-361 Kuhio Hwy, Wailua (☎808/823-0899). Large, attractive Thai/Chinese restaurant; great curries with fresh spices for around $10.

**A Pacific Cafe**, 4-831 Kuhio Hwy, Kapaa (☎808/822-0013). Very popular for its exotic and utterly wonderful (if expensive) Pacific cuisine. Dinner only.

# North Kauai

That part of northern Kauai which is unique and unspoiled seems to be diminishing all the time. The astonishing valleys of the **Na Pali coast** itself must surely remain inviolate – though accessible enough by canoe to sustain large Hawaiian populations, their awesome walls shield them from any attempt to build roads in. But the bulldozers are inching ever closer. Only temporarily did Iniki manage to slow the growth of the resort of **Princeville**, which began life as a sugar plantation in 1860.

Long, golden **Secret Beach**, hidden away from the road up from Kapaa, is among Kauai's best-looking beaches, though swimming is usually unsafe. It's an unofficial center for campers and nudists, though landowners are cracking down on long-term stays. Driving up Hwy-56 from the south, pass **Kilauea** and then turn right at Kalihiwai. Take the second right, which is a dirt track leading to a parking area, and the beach is a ten-minute walk down through the woods. At the far end there's a waterfall of beautiful fresh mountain water, and there are often spinner dolphins just offshore, especially around the picturesque 1913 Kilauea **lighthouse**. The cliffs above are a bird sanctuary.

## Hanalei

For the moment, major development stops beyond Princeville, mainly because the road then crosses seven successive one-lane bridges. The first is over the Hanalei River, where the valley stretching away inland is a National Wildlife Refuge. Here endangered Hawaiian ducks, coots and stilts are protected by the preservation of their major habitats – natural wetlands and taro ponds. As a result, this is a rare chance to see a Hawaiian landscape relatively unchanged since ancient times.

The small town of **HANALEI**, set around a magnificent bay, has some low-key apartments for rent, but otherwise little formal accommodation. Of local **restaurants**, the *Tahiti Nui* (☎808/826-6277) is particularly nice, with authentic Tahitian decor, rattan screens and old prints. In the **Hanalei Center** mall, the busy *Hanalei Gourmet* (☎808/826-2524) is the ideal stop for breakfast or a sandwich lunch, and also has live music every night.

Gorgeous **Lumahai Beach**, at the western edge of Hanalei Bay, has starred in countless movies, such as *South Pacific*, but is too treacherous for swimming. All the roadside beaches from here on, however, are good for snorkeling. Just two miles from the start of the Na Pali coast, the *Hanalei Colony Resort* (☎808/826-6235 or 1-800/628-3004; ⑥) is Kauai's most dramatic waterfront property, within a few feet of the pounding surf; its units all have two bedrooms. The road finally comes to an end at **Kee Beach**, perhaps the loveliest spot of all.

## The Na Pali coast

The lush valleys of the **Na Pali coast**, separated by knife-edge ridges of rock often thousands of feet high but just a few feet thick, make Kauai one of the world's great hiking destinations. Although many of the best views (other than from a helicopter) are from the trails in Kokee State Park (see overleaf) or boat trips out at sea, the **Kalalau Trail** along the shore is unforgettable. The full eleven miles to Kalalau Valley is arduous and gets progressively more dangerous; in places you have to scramble along a precipitous (and shadeless) wall of crumbly red rock.

However, the first two miles of the trail, to **Hanakapiai Beach**, are probably the most beautiful. They're steep but straightforward, passing through patches of dense vegetation where you clamber over the gnarled root systems of the baffling *hala* (or pandanus) tree. Creepers and vines hang down, and it's all exposed to the sun. From the beach, a further hour's arduous hike (off the main trail) leads inland to the natural amphitheater of the towering **Hanakapiai Falls**. It takes at least four and a half hours to get to the falls and back from the trailhead at Kee Beach, opposite the ten-mile marker at the end of the road. Hikers and campers doing anything more than a day-hike must obtain (free) permits from the State Parks Office (3060 Eiwa St, Lihue zip code 96766; Mon–Fri 8am–4.15pm; ☎808/274-3444). Accidents and drownings are not uncommon, and the staff need a record of who may be missing.

Until recently, **boat excursions** along the Na Pali coast were a major attraction for visitors to Hanalei. Fears that such trips were causing irreparable environmental damage have resulted in their suspension, however.

# South Kauai

POIPU, Kauai's principal beach resort, was hard hit by Iniki, but is now finally back to normal, offering great surfing and snorkeling. Its finest **hotel** is the sumptuous *Hyatt Regency*, 1571 Poipu Rd (☎808/742-1234 or 1-800/233-1234; ⑨), while Poipu Vacation Rentals (☎808/742-7220 or 1-800/325-5701; ⑤–⑨) quotes much lower prices for condos in the area than you'll be offered by individual properties. The best restaurants are in the Poipu Shopping Village mall. *Roy's Poipu Bar & Grill* (☎808/742-5000) is a very fashionable, dinner-only place specializing in what celebrity chef Roy Yamaguchi calls "Euro-Asian" cuisine, while *La Griglia* (☎808/742-2147) serves Italian snacks, pizzas and coffees in the open air.

# West Kauai

Two of the major scenic attractions in all Hawaii, the gorge of **Waimea Canyon** and **Kokee State Park**, with its views of the Na Pali cliffs to one side and the sodden Alakai Swamp to the other, can only be reached from the **west coast** of Kauai. The coast itself, however, is nondescript. WAIMEA, the largest town, is just one short street at the foot of the poorly marked road up to the canyon. The statue of **Captain Cook**, which commemorates his "discovery" of Hawaii here on January 20, 1778, is an exact replica of one in Cook's home town of Whitby, England. *Waimea Plantation Cottages* (☎808/338-1625; ⑥)

are exactly what they sound like: self-contained cottages for rent, set in an attractive
coconut grove and with an excellent restaurant in the main plantation house.

# Waimea Canyon and Kokee State Park

It's not unreasonable to call **Waimea Canyon** the "Grand Canyon of the Pacific." At
three thousand feet, it may not be quite as deep, but the colors – all shades of green
against the bare red earth – are absolutely breathtaking. The road from Waimea climbs
beside the widening gorge, until after eight miles the mile-wide canyon can be seen in
all its splendor. Each of the roadside lookouts is worth stopping for. Erosion by torrential rains created this landscape, but the process began when a massive geological fault
almost split Kauai in two.

Explore Kokee Park as early in the day as possible; by late morning the valleys may
be filled with mist and cloud. Trails head off to both sides of the highway. Although the
ranger station at **KOKEE**, the park headquarters, is often unstaffed, you can pick up
detailed information from the small but informative **Kokee Museum** nearby (daily
10am–4pm; $1 donation), where displays center on the indigenous wildlife. Kauai is the
only island where mongooses have not killed off most native **birds**, and at this height
mosquitoes are no threat either, so some of the world's rarest species (such as the *o'o
a'a*) survive here and nowhere else.

*Kokee Lodge Housekeeping Cabins*, next to the park headquarters, are rented by the
day (PO Box 819, Waimea, Kauai, HI 96796; ☎808/335-6061; ②), and there's free **camping**, with permits from the parks office in Lihue (see overleaf). *Kokee Lodge* has lunch
specials for around $7.

## Awaawapuhi Trail

The **Awaawapuhi Trail** drops steeply from the road beyond Kokee, passing through
three miles of dense forest before emerging abruptly to provide a staggering view of a
valley open only to the ocean, tucked between the Na Pali cliffs. The sheer razorback
ridges are almost vertical, though somehow covered with clinging vegetation.

## Kalalau Lookout and Pihea Trail

A few miles further up, **Kalalau Lookout** stands over the valley where the Kalalau
Trail ends (see overleaf) – though to attempt a descent would be certain suicide. The
**Pihea Trail** follows the course of a lunatic attempt to extend the road beyond its current end. At times it narrows to a few feet, with precipitous drops to either side, and visibility can drop to nothing as the clouds siphon across the ridges. Inland lies the **Alakai
Swamp**, where the heaviest rainfall on earth collects in the volcanic rock; standing
here above, you can listen to the shrills and whistles and buzzes of a jungle without
mammals or snakes, and watch the darting flashes of color. Since Iniki, the trail
through the swamp has had a boardwalk laid for almost its entire six-mile length,
though in places the planks just rest on cloying black swamp mud. Giant ferns dangle
above the trail, and orchids gleam from the undergrowth, while the trees – especially
in June – erupt into brilliant flowering displays. If you make it all the way to the end,
you're rewarded with a stupendous panorama of Hanalei Bay.

PART THREE

THE

# CONTEXTS

# A BRIEF HISTORY OF NORTH AMERICA

There's no room in these few pages to do more than briefly survey the peopling and political development of the disparate regions that now form the USA, and to show that there's much more to the history of America than the history of the United States alone. Many of the events and issues discussed below are covered in more detail in the relevant chapters, while the books listed on p.20 are invaluable resources for serious students.

## FIRST PEOPLES

The true pioneers of America, the first settlers to enter the pristine continent, are thought to have been nomadic **mammoth-hunters** from Siberia. Around 14,000 years ago, they gradually worked their way into Alaska, along the "**land-bridge**" that then followed the line of what is now the Bering Strait. The entire region was treeless tundra, no more appealing than it is today, but it supported sufficient quantities of large mammals to make hunting worthwhile. It's quite possible that only a small band of perhaps fifty individuals completed the journey; that could have been enough to spread and populate the entire continent. Their descendants advanced so quickly through the new territory that they had reached the southernmost

tip of South America within a couple of thousand years. That may well be because everywhere they went, they swiftly drove the indigenous fauna – not just the mammoths, but also such defenceless creatures as giant ground sloths – to extinction, and they were forever obliged to press onwards in search of new sources of food. Behind them, several thousand years later, came at least two further groups, the Athapascans who harried the descendants of their predecessors all the way into the Great Plains, and the ancestors of the modern Inuit, who found their own niche in the frozen Arctic north.

Distinct groups settled in specific areas, and adapted to the challenges of their local environment. The first definite signs of a human presence in the territory of the modern United States, dating back 12,000 years, have been uncovered at Meadowcroft in southwest Pennsylvania. Five hundred years later, a homogenous culture can be identified by their characteristic arrowheads (named **Clovis** points, after Clovis, New Mexico) as inhabiting much of the Southwest. Subsequent subgroups ranged from the Algonquin farmers of what's now New England to peoples such as the Chumash and Macah, who lived by catching fish, otters and even whales along the coasts of the Pacific Northwest.

Nowhere did a civilization emerge that could rival the wealth and sophistication of the great cities of ancient Mexico, such as Teotihuacan or Tenochtitlan. However, the influence of these far-off cultures does seem to have filtered north; the cultivation of crops such as beans, squash and maize made the development of large communities possible, and northern religious cults, including human sacrifice, are thought to owe much to Central American beliefs. The so-called **Moundbuilders** of the **Ohio** and **Mississippi** valleys developed sites such as the Great Serpent Mound in modern Ohio and Poverty Point in Louisiana. The most prominent of these early societies, now known as the **Hopewell** culture, flourished between around 1 and 400 AD. Later on, **Cahokia** just outside modern St Louis became the largest pre-Columbian city in North America, centered on a huge mound topped by some form of temple, and reaching its peak between 1050 and 1250 AD.

In the deserts of the **Southwest**, the Hohokam settlement of Snaketown, near modern-day Phoenix in Arizona and complete with Central American-style ball courts, set about grappling with the same problems of water management that plague the region today. Nearby, the **Anasazi** "Basketmakers" developed the art of pottery around 200 AD, and began to gather into the walled villages later known as pueblos, possibly for protection against the threat of Athapascan invaders who were arriving from the north, such as the Apache. Anasazi "cities," such as Pueblo Bonito in New Mexico's Chaco Canyon – a center for the turquoise trade with the mighty Aztec – and the "Cliff Palace" at Mesa Verde in Colorado, are the most impressive monuments to survive from ancient America. Although the Anasazi are no longer identifiable as a group after the twelfth century – they probably dispersed after a devastating drought – many of the settlements created by their immediate descendants have remained in use ever since. Through centuries of migration, war and changes of government, the desert farmers of the **Hopi Mesas** in Arizona (see p.867), and the pueblos of **Taos** and **Acoma** in New Mexico, have never been dispossessed of their homes.

While estimates of the total indigenous population before the arrival of the Europeans vary widely, the figure of twelve million is generally thought to be reasonable.

## EUROPEAN CONTACTS

The greatest seafarers of early medieval Europe, the **Vikings**, are known to have established a colony in Greenland around 982 AD. Under the energetic leadership of Erik the Red, this became a base for voyages of exploration and even colonization along the mysterious coastline that lay to the west. Traces of permanent Viking occupation have been uncovered at L'Anse aux Meadows in Newfoundland, though the exact location of their southernmost outpost, **Vinland**, will probably never be known. It seems likely, however, that they ventured as far as Maine, and that while the Algonquin may have been inquisitive enough to trade, they forcibly prevented permanent settlement.

The Vikings remained a presence in Greenland until about 1500 AD, by which time it appears that European **fishermen**, such as the British and the Spanish Basques, were already familiar with the cod-rich seas off Newfoundland. The world first took notice of such vague reports when organized voyages dispatched in search of China began to return with news of a new continent. **Christopher Columbus** reached San Salvador in the Bahamas on October 12, 1492, and a mere four years later the English navigator John Cabot officially "discovered" Newfoundland. Soon British fishermen in particular were beginning to set up makeshift encampments in what became known as **New England**, to spend the winter curing their catch.

Over the next few years various expeditions mapped the eastern seaboard. In 1524, for example, the Italian **Giovanni Verrazano** sailed past Maine, which he characterized as the "Land of Bad People" thanks to the inhospitable and contemptuous behavior of its natives, and reached the mouth of what was to become the Hudson River. The great hope at first was of finding a passage between the "islands" that might lead to China. To the French **Jacques Cartier**, the St Lawrence Seaway seemed a real possibility, and successive expeditions explored and even unsuccessfully attempted to settle the northern areas of the Great Lakes region from the 1530s onwards. Intrepid trappers and traders began to venture ever further west.

To the south, the Spaniards had started to nose their way up from the Caribbean in 1513, when **Ponce de Leon**'s expedition in search of the Fountain of Youth landed at what is now Palm Beach, and named the region of **Florida**. Spanish attentions for the next few years were devoted to the lucrative conquest of Mexico, but in 1528 they returned under Narvaez, whose voyage ended in shipwreck somewhere in the Gulf. One of his junior officers, **Cabeza de Vaca**, managed to survive, and together with three shipmates spent the next six years on an extraordinary odyssey across Texas into the Southwest. Sometimes held as slaves, sometimes revered as seers, they finally managed to get back to Mexico in 1534, bringing tales of golden cities deep in the desert, known as the **Seven Cities of Cibola**.

One of Cabeza de Vaca's companions was a black African slave called **Estevanico the Moor**, a giant of a man who had amazed the native peoples they encountered. Rather than return to a life of slavery, he volunteered to map the route for a new expedition; racing alone into the interior, with two colossal greyhounds at his side, he was killed in Zuni Pueblo in 1539. The following year, **Francisco de Coronado**'s full party managed to prove to everyone's intense dissatisfaction that the Seven Cities of Cibola did not exist, encountering the Hopi and other pueblo peoples along the way before being brought up short by the Grand Canyon. Hernan Corteés, the conqueror of the Aztec, had meanwhile traced the outline of the peninsula of Baja California, and in 1542 Juan Cabrillo sailed right up the coast of California, failing to spot San Francisco Bay in the usual mists.

It was the Spanish who established the **first permanent settlement** in the present United States, when they founded **St Augustine** on the coast of Florida in 1565 – not that it seemed all that permanent when it was burned to the ground by Sir Francis Drake in 1586. In 1598 the Spanish also succeeded in subjugating the pueblo peoples, and founded the colony of **New Mexico** along the Rio Grande. This was more of a missionary than a military enterprise, and its survival was always rendered precarious by its separation by vast tracts of empty desert from the rest of Mexico. Nonetheless, the construction of a new capital, **Santa Fe**, began in 1609 (see p.807).

## THE GROWTH OF THE COLONIES

The great rivalry between the English and the Spanish in the late sixteenth century extended right around the world. Freebooting English adventurers-cum-pirates contested Spanish hegemony along both coasts of North America. Sir Francis Drake staked a claim to California in 1579, five years before **Sir Walter Raleigh** claimed **Virginia** in the east, in the name of his Virgin Queen, Elizabeth. The party of colonists he sent out in 1585 established the short-lived settlement of **Roanoke**; they were still there three years later, when they were reinforced, but the only trace of them left in 1590 was a single mysterious word carved on a tree – "Croatoan."

The Native Americans encountered by the earliest settlers were seldom hostile at the outset. To some extent the European newcomers were obliged to make friends with the locals; most had crossed the Atlantic to find religious freedom or to make their fortunes, and lacked the experience or even the inclination to make a success of the mundane business of subsis-

tence farming. Virginia's first enduring colony, **Jamestown**, was founded by Captain John Smith on May 24, 1607. He bemoaned "though there be Fish in the Sea, and Foules in the ayre, and Beasts in the woods, their bounds are so large, they are so wilde, and we so weake and ignorant, we cannot much trouble them"; six out of every seven colonists died within a year of their arrival in the New World.

Gradually, however, the settlers learned the techniques necessary to cultivate the strange crops that grew in this unfamiliar terrain. As far as the English government was concerned, the colonies were strictly commercial ventures, intended to produce crops that could not be grown at home. There was no conception that the colonists might have goals of their own. After early failures with sugar and rice, Virginia finally found its feet with its first **tobacco** harvest in 1615 (the man responsible, John Rolfe, is now better known as the husband of Pocahontas). A successful tobacco plantation requires two things in abundance: land, which intensified the pressure to dispossess the Indians, and labor. No self-respecting Englishman came to America to work for others; when the first **slave** ship called in at Jamestown in 1619, the captain found an eager market for his cargo of twenty African slaves. By that time there were already a million slaves in South America.

The 102 **Puritans** known to history as the **"Pilgrim Fathers"** were deposited on Cape Cod by the *Mayflower* in late 1620, and soon moved on to set up their own colony at Plymouth (see p.188). Fifty of them died during that winter, and the whole party might well have perished but for the fortuitous emergence from the woods of the extraordinary **Squanto**. This Native American had twice been kidnapped and taken to Europe and succeeded in making his way home; during his wanderings he had spent four years working as a merchant in the City of London, and had also lived in Spain. Having recently come home to find his entire tribe exterminated by smallpox, he decided to throw in his lot with the English. With his guidance, they finally managed to reap their first harvest, celebrated with the mighty feast of **Thanksgiving** that is still commemorated today.

Of greater significance to the history of New England was the founding in 1630 of a new colony, further up the coast at Naumkeag (which became Salem), by the Massachusetts Bay Company. Its governor, **John Winthrop**, soon moved to establish a new capital on the Shawmut peninsula – the city of **Boston**, complete with its own university of Harvard. His vision of a Utopian "City on a Hill" did not extend to sharing Paradise with the Indians; he argued that they had not "subdued" the land, and it was therefore a "vacuum" for the Puritans to use as they saw fit. While their faith helped individual colonists to endure the early hardships, the colony as a whole failed to maintain a strong religious identity (the Salem witchtrials of 1692 did much to discredit the idea that the New World had any moral superiority to the Old), and breakaway groups soon left to create the rival settlements of Providence and Connecticut.

Between 1620 and 1642, a total of sixty thousand migrants left England for America – which amounted to 1.5 percent of the population. Those who came in pursuit of economic opportunities tended to join the longer-established colonies, where they served to dilute the religious zeal of the Puritans. Groups hoping to find spiritual freedom were more inclined to start afresh; thus **Maryland** was created as a haven for Catholics in 1632, and fifty years later **Pennsylvania** was founded by the Quakers.

The English were not alone, however. After Sir Henry Hudson rediscovered Manhattan in 1609, it was "bought" by the **Dutch** in 1624 – though the Indians who took their money were passing nomads with no claim to it either. The Dutch colony of New Amsterdam, founded in 1625, lasted less than forty years before it was captured by the English and renamed **New York**; by that time, there was a strong Dutch presence on the lower reaches of the Hudson River.

From their foothold in the Great Lakes region, meanwhile, the **French** sent the explorers Joliet and Marquette to map the course of the Mississippi in 1673. They turned back once they had established that the river did indeed flow into the Gulf of Mexico, but their trip cleared the way for the foundation of the huge and ill-defined colony of **Louisiana** in 1699. The city of **New Orleans**, at the mouth of the Mississippi, was created in 1718.

While the Spanish remained firmly ensconced in Florida, things were not going so smoothly in the Southwest. In the bloody **Pueblo Revolt** of 1680, the pueblo peoples briefly managed to drive the Spanish out of New Mexico altogether; they returned in force a dozen years later. Thereafter, a curious synthesis of traditional and Hispanic religion and culture began to evolve, and, but for hostile raids from the north, the Spanish presence was not seriously challenged.

With the arrival of the foreigners, things were also changing in the unknown hinterland. The frontier in the east was pushing steadily forward, as colonists seized Indian land, with or without the excuse of an "uprising" or "rebellion" to provoke them into bloodshed. The major killer of the indigenous peoples, however, was **smallpox**, which worked its way deep into the interior of the continent long before the Europeans did so in person. (Scientists speculate that the Native Americans may have had no equivalent "new" diseases to inflict on the newcomers because of the long period their ancestors had spent crossing the Arctic in subzero temperatures.) As populations were decimated, great migrations took place. In addition, around this time the **horse** arrived on the Great Plains. The original inhabitants of the region were sedentary farmers, who also hunted buffalo by driving them over rocky bluffs. The bow and arrow was discovered around the fifth century, but the acquisition of horses (probably captured from the Spanish, and known at first as "mystery dogs") made possible the emergence of an entirely new, nomadic lifestyle. Groups such as the Cheyenne and the Apache swept their rivals aside to dominate vast territories, and eagerly seized the potential offered by firearms when they followed in due course. This created a very dynamic, but fundamentally unstable culture, as they became dependent on trade with Europeans for the necessities of life.

## THE AMERICAN REVOLUTION

The American colonies prospered during the **eighteenth century**, with the cities of Boston, New York and **Philadelphia** in particular becoming home to a wealthy, highly educated and highly articulate middle class. A sense of frustration began to mount at the inequities of the colonies' relationship with Britain. While they were allowed to trade among themselves, the Americans could otherwise only sell their produce to the British, and all transatlantic commerce had to be undertaken in British ships.

Although full-scale independence was not an explicit goal until late in the century, the main factor in making it possible was the economic impact of the pan-European conflict known as the **Seven Years War**. Officially, the war in Europe lasted from 1756 to 1763, but fighting among the English, French and Spanish in North America broke out a little earlier. Having started in 1755 by expelling the French settlers en masse from Acadia in Nova Scotia (triggering their epic migration to Louisiana, where as the **Cajuns** they remain to this day), the British went on to conquer all of Canada. In forcing the **surrender of Québec** in 1759, General Wolfe brought the war to a close; the French ceded Louisiana to the Spanish rather than let it fall to the British, while Florida passed into British control for a year before reverting to the Spanish. All the European monarchs were left hamstrung by debts, and it was becoming apparent to the British that colonialism in America was not such a profitable business as it was in those parts of the world where the native populations could be coerced into working for their overseas masters.

There was one further major player on the scene – the **Iroquois Confederacy**. Iroquois culture, characterized by military expansionism and even human sacrifice, can first be identified in the Great Lakes area from around 1000 AD onwards. Forever in competition with the Algonquin and the Huron, the southern Iroquois had by the eighteenth century resolved themselves into a League of Five Nations – the Seneca, Cayuga, Onondaga, Oneida and Mohawk, all in what's now upstate New York. Wooed by both French and British, the Iroquois for most of the century charted an independent course between the two. During negotiations with the colonists in 1744, an Onondaga chief, unimpressed by the squabbling representatives of Pennsylvania, Virginia and Maryland, had recommended "by your observing the same methods our wise forefathers have taken, you will acquire fresh strength and power." Benjamin Franklin, who was present, wrote in 1751 that "It would be a very strange thing if . . . ignorant savages should be capable of forming a scheme for such a union . . . that has subsisted ages and appears indissoluble; and yet that a like union should be impracticable for ten or a dozen English colonies."

Shortly after the Seven Years War, an unsuccessful insurrection by the Ottawa tribe in 1763, led by their chief **Pontiac**, encouraged the cash-strapped British to feel that, while America needed its own standing army, it was not unreasonable to expect the colonists to pay for it.

Events began to move very fast. In 1765, the British introduced the **Stamp Act**, which required duty on all legal transactions and printed matter in the colonies to be paid to the British Crown. Firm in the belief that there should be "no taxation without representation," delegates from nine of the colonies met in the Stamp Act Congress in October 1765 – the first time the colonies had assembled as a recognized entity. By that time, however, the British prime minister responsible for the Act had already been dismissed by King George III. Only briefly, in Georgia, were the offending stamps ever distributed, and the Act was repealed in 1766.

However, in 1767, Chancellor Townshend made political capital at home by proclaiming "I dare tax America" as he introduced a program of legislation that included the broadly similar Revenue Act. That led the merchants of Massachusetts, inspired by **Samuel Adams**, to vote to boycott English goods; they were subsequently joined by all the other colonies except New Hampshire. Townshend's Acts were repealed in turn by a new prime minister, Lord North, on March 5, 1770. By chance, on that same day a stone-throwing mob surrounded the Customs House in Boston; shots from the guards killed five people, including Crispus Attucks, in what became known as the **Boston Massacre**. Even so, most of the colonies resumed trading with Britain, and the crisis was postponed for a few more years.

In May 1773, Lord North's **Tea Act** relieved the debt-ridden East India Company of all need to pay duties on exports to America, while still requiring the Americans to pay duty on tea. Massachusetts called for the colonies to unite in action, and its citizens took the lead on December 16 in the **Boston Tea Party**, when three tea ships were boarded and 342 chests thrown into the sea. As John Adams put it, "to let it be landed would be giving up the principle of taxation by Parliamentary authority."

The infuriated British Parliament thereupon began to pass a program of legislation collectively known as both the "Coercive" and the "Intolerable" Acts, which included closing the port of Boston and disbanding the government of Massachusetts. Thomas Jefferson retaliated that the acts amounted to "a deliberate and systematical plan of reducing us to slavery." To discuss a response, the first **Continental Congress** was held in Philadelphia on May 5, 1774, and attended by representatives of all the colonies except Georgia.

War finally broke out on April 18, 1775, when General Gage, the newly imposed governor of Massachusetts, dispatched four hundred British soldiers to destroy the military store at **Concord**, in order to prevent weapons falling into rebel hands. Silversmith **Paul Revere** was dispatched by the citizens of Boston on his legendary ride to warn the rebels, and the British were confronted en route at Lexington by 77 American "Minutemen," who fired the "shot heard round the world."

Congress set about forming an army at Boston, and decided for the sake of unity to appoint a Southern commander, **George Washington**. One by one, as the war raged, the colonies set up their own governments and declared themselves to be states, and the politicians set about defining the society they wished to create. The writings of pamphleteer Thomas Paine – especially *Common Sense* – were, together with the *Confederacy of the Iroquois*, a great influence on the **Declaration of Independence**. Drafted by Thomas Jefferson, this was accepted in Philadelphia on July 4, 1776. The anti-slavery clauses originally included by Jefferson – himself a slave-owner – were omitted to spare the feelings of the Southern states, though the section that denounced the King's dealings with "merciless Indian Savages" was left in.

At first, the Revolutionary War went well for the British. General Howe crossed the Atlantic with around twenty thousand men, took New York and New Jersey, and ensconced himself in Philadelphia for the winter of 1777–78. Washington's army was encamped not far away at Valley Forge, freezing cold and all but starving to death. However, General Burgoyne's expedition, which set out from Canada to march on New England, was so harried by rebel guerrillas that he found himself obliged to surrender at Saratoga in October 1777. As the logistical difficulty of maintaining the British war effort

became ever more apparent, other European powers took delight in coming to the aid of the Americans. Benjamin Franklin led a wildly successful delegation to France to request support, and soon the nascent American fleet was being assisted in its bid to cut British naval communications by both the French and the Spanish. The end came when Cornwallis, who had replaced Howe, was instructed to dig in at Yorktown and wait for the Royal Navy to come to his aid, only for the French to seal off Chesapeake Bay and prevent reinforcement. Cornwallis surrendered to Washington on October 17, 1781, just fifteen miles from the site of the first English settlement at Jamestown.

The ensuing **Treaty of Paris** granted the Americans their independence on generous terms – the British completely abandoned their Native American allies, including the Iroquois, to the vengeance of the victors – and Washington entered New York as the British left in November 1783. The Spanish were confirmed in their possession of Florida.

The victorious US Congress met for the first time in 1789, and the tradition of awarding political power to the nation's most successful generals was instigated by the election of George Washington as the first president. He was further honored when his name was given to the new capital city of **Washington DC**, deliberately sited between the north and south.

## THE NINETEENTH CENTURY

In its first century, the territories and population of the new **United States of America** expanded at a phenomenal rate. The white population of North America in 1800 stood at around five million, and there were another one million African slaves (of whom thirty thousand were in the north). Of that total, 86 percent lived within fifty miles of the Atlantic, but no US city could rival Mexico City in having 100,000 inhabitants. (Both New York and Philadelphia reached that figure within twenty years, however, and New York had passed a million fifty years later.)

It had suited the British to discourage settlers from venturing west of the Appalachians, as beyond the mountains they would be far beyond the reach of British power and become inclined to carry on independent existences. For George Washington, however, any agreement to follow such a policy had been a "temporary expedient to quieten the minds of the Indians."

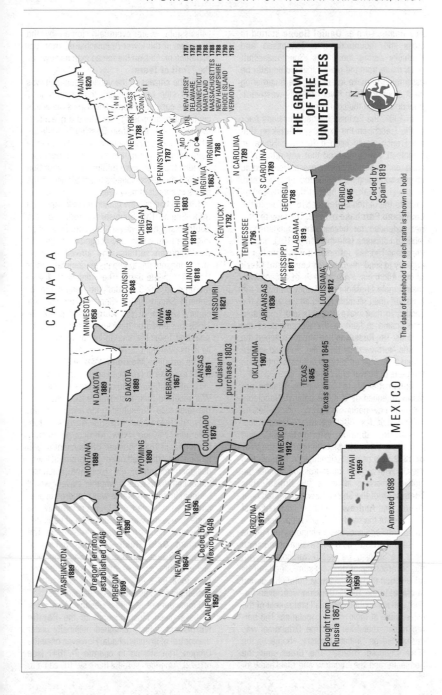

THE GROWTH OF THE UNITED STATES

N

NEW JERSEY 1787
DELAWARE 1787
CONNECTICUT 1788
MARYLAND 1788
MASSACHUSETTES 1788
RHODE ISLAND 1790
VERMONT 1791

MAINE 1820

VT N H

NEW YORK 1788

MASS

CONN

R I

N J

PENNSYLVANIA 1787

MD

DEL

D C

W. VIRGINIA 1863

VIRGINIA 1788

OHIO 1803

KENTUCKY 1792

N CAROLINA 1789

S CAROLINA 1789

GEORGIA 1788

FLORIDA 1845

Ceded by Spain 1819

CANADA

MICHIGAN 1837

INDIANA 1816

ILLINOIS 1818

TENNESSEE 1796

ALABAMA 1819

MISSISSIPPI 1817

WISCONSIN 1848

MINNESOTA 1858

IOWA 1846

MISSOURI 1821

ARKANSAS 1836

LOUISIANA 1812

N DAKOTA 1889

S DAKOTA 1889

NEBRASKA 1867

KANSAS 1861

OKLAHOMA 1907

Louisiana purchase 1803

TEXAS 1845

Texas annexed 1845

MONTANA 1889

WYOMING 1890

COLORADO 1876

NEW MEXICO 1912

MEXICO

The date of statehood for each state is shown in bold

WASHINGTON 1889

OREGON 1859

Oregon Territory established 1846

IDAHO 1890

UTAH 1896

NEVADA 1864

CALIFORNIA 1850

ARIZONA 1912

Ceded by Mexico 1848

HAWAII 1959

Annexed 1898

Bought from Russia 1867

ALASKA 1959

Adventurers such as **Daniel Boone** started to cross the mountains into Tennessee and Kentucky during the 1770s. Soon makeshift rafts, made from the planks that would later be assembled to make log cabins, were careering west along the Ohio River (the only westward-flowing river on the continent).

In 1801, the Spanish handed Louisiana back to the French, on the express undertaking that the French would keep it for ever. However, Napoleon swiftly realized that any attempt to hang on to his American possessions would involve spreading his armies too thinly. Instead, he chose to make the best of things by selling them to the United States for $15 million, in the **Louisiana Purchase** of 1803. The new territories extended far beyond the boundaries of modern Louisiana (see map on p.1161), and for President Thomas Jefferson it was a matter of urgency to send the explorers **Lewis and Clark** to map them out. With the help of Sacagawea, their female Shoshoni guide, they followed the Missouri and Columbia rivers all the way to the Pacific; in their wake, trappers and "mountain men" came to hunt in the wilderness of the Rockies. The **Russians** had already reached the Pacific Northwest by this time, and had established a network of fortified outposts to trade in the pelts of beaver and otter.

British attempts to blockade the Atlantic, primarily intended as a move against Napoleon, gave the new nation its first chance to flex its military muscles. Although British raiders succeeded in capturing Washington DC, and burned the White House to the ground, the **War of 1812** was of most significance in providing the US with a cover for aggression against the Native American allies of the British. Thus **Tecumseh** of the Shawnee was defeated near Detroit, and **Andrew Jackson** moved against the Creek of the southern Mississippi. Jackson's campaign against the Seminole in Florida enabled the US to gain possession of the state from the Spanish; he was rewarded first with the governorship of the new state, and later by his election to the presidency. During his period in office, in the 1830s, Jackson went even further, and set about clearing all states east of the Mississippi of their native population. The barren region that later became Oklahoma was designated as "Indian Territory," home to the "Five Civilized Tribes." The Creek and the Seminole, and the Choctaw and Chickasaw of

Mississippi, were eventually joined by the Cherokee of the lower Appalachians, after four appalling months on the forced march known as the "**Trail of Tears**."

For the citizens of the young republic, it was a small step from realizing that their country might be capable of spreading across the whole continent to supposing that it had a quasi-religious duty – a "**Manifest Destiny**" – to do so. At its simplest, that doctrine amounted to little more than a belief that might must be right, but the idea that they were fulfilling the will of God inspired countless pioneers to set off across the plains in search of new lives.

Mexico had by now gained its independence from Spain. The Spanish territories of the Southwest had never attracted enough migrants to turn into fully-fledged colonies, and the American settlers who arrived in ever-increasing numbers began to dominate their Hispanic counterparts. The Anglos of **Texas** rebelled in 1833, under the leadership of General Sam Houston. Shortly after the legendary setback at the **Alamo** (see p.642), in 1836, they defeated the Mexican army of Santa Ana, and Texas became an independent republic in its own right.

The ensuing **Mexican War** was a barefaced exercise in American aggression, in which most of the future leading figures of the Civil War received their first experience fighting on the same side. It resulted in the acquisition not only of Texas, but also of Arizona, Utah, Colorado, Nevada, New Mexico and finally California, in 1848. A token US payment of $15 million to the Mexican government was designed to match the Louisiana Purchase. Initial controversy as to whether slavery would be legal in the new states was rendered academic when it turned out that, on virtually the same day as the war ended, gold had been discovered in the Sierra Nevada of California. The resultant **Gold Rush** was the making of California's first significant city, San Francisco, and brought a massive influx of free white settlers to a land that was in any case utterly unsuitable for a plantation-based economy.

Proponents of Manifest Destiny seem never to have given much thought to the **Pacific Northwest**, which remained nominally under the control of British Canada. However, once the Oregon Trail started to operate in 1841 (see p.1072), American settlers there swiftly came to outnumber the British. In 1846, a surprisingly amicable treaty fixed the border as running along the 49th parallel, just as it already did across eastern Canada, with the single exception of allowing the British to keep all of Vancouver Island.

## THE CIVIL WAR

From the moment of its inception, the unity of the United States had been based on shaky foundations. Great care had gone into devising a **Constitution** that balanced the need for a strong federal government with the aspirations for autonomy of its component states. That was achieved by giving Congress two separate chambers – the **House of Representatives**, in which the number of representatives from each state depended upon its population, and the **Senate**, in which each state, regardless of size, had two members. Thus, although in theory the Constitution remained silent on the issue of **slavery**, it allayed the fears of the less populated Southern states (where, of course, the slaves themselves did not have the vote) that the voters of the North might destroy their economy by forcing them to abandon their "peculiar institution." However, it gradually became apparent that the system only worked so long as there were roughly equal numbers of "Free" and slave-owning states. At first it seemed possible that the balance could be maintained – in 1820, under the Missouri Compromise, Missouri was admitted to the Union as a slave-owning state simultaneously with Maine as a free one.

Abolitionist sentiment in the North was not all that great before the middle of the nineteenth century. At best, after the importation of slaves from Africa ended in 1808, Northerners probably hoped rather vaguely that slavery was an anachronism which might simply wither away. In fact, however, the profitability of the Southern plantations was dramatically boosted by the development of the cotton gin, and the increased demand for manufactured cotton goods triggered by the **Industrial Revolution**. What really changed the situation was the rapid growth of the nation as a whole, making it ever more difficult to maintain a political balance between North and South.

There was a clear difference between tacitly acknowledging the existence of slavery in the Southern states as a matter for those states to decide, and being obliged to let it spread into

one out of every two new states that joined the Union. In 1854, the **Kansas-Nebraska Act** brought matters to a head, sparking off guerrilla raids and mini-wars between rival settlers by allowing both prospective states self-determination on the issue. That same year, the **Republican Party** was founded, on the platform of resisting the further expansion of slavery. Escaped former slaves such as Frederick Douglass were by now inspiring Northern audiences to moral outrage, and Harriet Beecher Stowe's *Uncle Tom's Cabin* achieved an unprecedented readership.

In October 1859, **John Brown** – a white-bearded, wild-eyed veteran of some of Kansas's bloodiest infighting – led a dramatic raid on the US Armory at Harpers Ferry, West Virginia, intending to secure arms for a slave insurrection (see p.399). Swiftly captured by forces under the command of Robert E Lee, he was hanged within a few weeks, proclaiming that "I am now quite certain that the crimes of this guilty land will never be purged away but with blood."

The Republican candidate for the presidency in 1860 was the little-known **Abraham Lincoln** from Kentucky; he won no Southern states, but with the Democrats split into Northern and Southern factions he was elected with 39 percent of the popular vote. Within weeks, on December 20, South Carolina became the first state to secede from the Union; the **Confederacy** was declared on February 4, 1861, when it was joined by Mississippi, Florida, Alabama, Georgia, Louisiana and Texas. Its first (and only) president was Jefferson Davis, also from Kentucky; at their inauguration, his new vice-president remarked that their government was "the first in the history of the world based upon the great physical and moral truth that the negro is not equal to the white man." Lincoln was inaugurated in turn in March 1861, proclaiming that "I have no purpose, directly or indirectly, to interfere with the institution of slavery in the States where it exists. I believe I have no lawful right to do so, and I have no inclination to do so." He was completely inflexible, however, on one paramount issue: the survival of the Union.

The **Civil War** began just a few weeks later. The first shots were fired on April 12, when a much-postponed federal attempt to resupply Fort Sumter, in the harbor at Charleston, South Carolina, was greeted by a Confederate bombardment that forced its surrender. Lincoln's immediate call to raise an army against the South was greeted by the further secession of Virginia, Arkansas, Tennessee and North Carolina. Within a year, both armies had amassed 600,000 men; Robert E Lee had been offered command of both and opted for the Confederacy, while George McLellan became the first leader of the Union forces.

Although the rival capitals of Washington DC and Richmond, Virginia, were a mere one hundred miles apart, over the next four years operations of war reached almost everywhere south of Washington and east of the Mississippi. As in any civil war, the motivations of the individual soldiers were manifold, with loyalty to one's family or home, the desire for adventure or the lust for blood as likely to determine their involvement as the overt principles.

Tracing the ebb and flow of the military campaigns – from the Confederate victories of the early years, via Grant's successful siege of Vicksburg in 1863 and Sherman's devastating March to the Sea in 1864, to Lee's eventual surrender at Appomattox in April 1865 – it's easy to lose sight of the fact that it was not so much generalship as sheer economic power that won the war for the Union. It was the North that could maintain full trading with the rest of the world while diverting spare resources to the production of munitions, and could go on doing so despite matching Southern losses man for man. Conversely, defeat for the South spelt destruction for its economy; two-thirds of its wealth was lost, its share of national assets collapsed from thirty percent in 1860 to twelve percent in 1870, and one in four Southern white males of military age had been killed. Moreover, when Lincoln's wartime proclamation emancipating the slaves achieved full legal force under the Thirteenth Amendment in 1865, the plantation system was rendered inoperable.

Lincoln himself was assassinated within a few days of the end of the war, a mark of the deep bitterness that would almost certainly have rendered successful **Reconstruction** impossible even if he had lived. There was a brief period, after black men were granted the vote in 1870, when the Southern states elected black political representatives, but without a sustained effort to enable former slaves to acquire land, social relations in the South swiftly deteriorated. Thanks to white suprema-

cist organizations such as the Ku Klux Klan, nominally clandestine but brazenly public, Southern blacks were soon effectively disenfranchised once more. Anyone working to transform the South came under attack either as a carpetbagger (a Northern opportunist who headed South for personal profit) or a treacherous scalawag (a Southern collaborator).

The aftermath of the Civil War can almost be said to have lasted for a hundred years. While the South condemned itself to a wasted century as a backwater, the rest of the re-United States embarked on a period of expansionism and prosperity.

## THE INDIAN WARS

With the completion of the transcontinental railroad in 1867, Manifest Destiny became an unarguable reality. Among the first to head west were the troops of the federal army, with Union and Confederate veterans alike marching under the same flag to do battle with the remaining Native Americans. Treaty after treaty was signed, only to be broken as it became expedient to do so (usually upon the discovery of gold or precious metals). When the whites overreached themselves, or when driven to desperation, the Indians were capable of fighting back. The defeat of **General George Custer** at Little Bighorn in 1876, by **Sitting Bull** and his Sioux and Cheyenne warriors (see p.782), provoked the full wrath of the government. Within a few years, leaders such as **Crazy Horse** of the Oglala Sioux and **Geronimo** of the Apache had been forced to surrender, and their people were confined to reservations. One final act of resistance came in the form of the visionary, messianic cult of the **Ghost Dance**, whose practitioners hoped that by correct ritual observance they could win back their lost way of life, in a land miraculously free of white intruders. Such aspirations were regarded as hostile, and military harassment of the movement culminated in the massacre at **Wounded Knee** in South Dakota in 1890.

A major tactic in the campaign against the Plains Indians was to starve them into submission, by eliminating the vast herds of bison that were their primary source of food. As General Philip Sheridan put it, "For the sake of a lasting peace . . . kill, skin and sell until the buffalo are exterminated. Then your prairies can be covered by the speckled cow and the festive cowboy."

More significant than the activities of the much-mythologized cowboys, however, was the back-breaking toil of the miners up in the mountains, and the homesteading families out on the plains.

## INDUSTRY AND IMMIGRATION

The late nineteenth century was an era of massive **immigration** to North America from the rest of the world, with influxes from Europe to the East Coast paralleled by those from Asia to the West. As in colonial times, national groups tended to form enclaves in specific areas – examples range from the Scandinavian farmers of Minnesota and the northern Plains, to the Basque shepherds of Idaho, and the Cornish miners of Colorado. In the Southwest, where individual hard work counted for less than shared communal effort, the **Mormons** of Utah had fled persecution further east to become the first white settlers to manage to eke a living from the unforgiving desert.

The fastest growth of all was in the nation's greatest **cities**, especially New York, Chicago and Boston. Their industrial and commercial strength enabled them to attract and absorb migrants not only from throughout Europe but also from the old South – particularly in the shape of the ex-slaves, who could now at least vote with their feet.

Now that it stretched "from sea to shining sea," the territorial boundaries of the US had reached almost their current form. In 1867, however, Secretary of State William Seward agreed to buy **Alaska** from the crisis-torn Russian government for $7.2 million. The purchase was at first derided as "Seward's Folly," but it was not long before the familiar Midas touch of the Americans was revealed by the discovery of gold there as well. Finally, the Kingdom of **Hawaii**, far out in the Pacific, was annexed in 1898 following the 1894 "Revolution," led by white American business-men, which even then-President Cleveland condemned as "wholly without justification . . . not merely wrong but a disgrace."

The various US presidents of the day, from the victorious General Grant (a man palpably out of his depth) onwards, now seem anonymous figures compared to the industrialists and financiers who manipulated the national economy. These "**robber barons**" included such men as John D Rockefeller, who controlled

seventy percent of the world's oil almost before anyone else had realized it was worth controlling; Andrew Carnegie, who made his fortune introducing the Bessemer process of steel manufacture; and J P Morgan, who went for the most basic commodity of all – money. Their success was predicated on the willingness of the government to cooperate in resisting the development of a strong labor movement. A succession of widely publicized strikes – such as those on the railroads in 1877, in the mines of Tennessee in 1891, and in the steel mills of Pittsburgh in 1892 – were forcibly crushed.

The nineteenth century had also seen the development of a distinctive American voice in **literature**, which rendered increasingly superfluous the efforts of passing English visitors – such as Charles Dickens, and the Trollopes, mother and son – to "explain" the United States. From the 1830s onwards, a wide range of writers set out to find new ways to describe their new world, with results as varied as the introspective essays of Henry Thoreau, the morbid visions of Edgar Allan Poe, the all-embracing novels of Herman Melville, and the irrepressible poetry of Walt Whitman, whose endlessly revised *Leaves of Grass* was an exultant hymn to the young republic. Virtually every leading participant in the Civil War wrote at least one highly readable volume of memoirs, while public figures as disparate as Buffalo Bill Cody and the showman P T Barnum also produced lively autobiographies. The boundless national self-confidence found its greatest expression in the vigorous vernacular style of **Mark Twain**, whose depictions of frontier life, whether in the journalistic *Roughing It* and *Life on the Mississippi*, or fictionalized in novels like *Huckleberry Finn*, gave the rest of the world perhaps its most abiding impression of the American character.

At the end of the century, despite an erratic boom-and-bust cycle that hit its lowest point in 1893, the United States had advanced to the point that it knew, even if the rest of the world wasn't yet altogether sure, that it was the strongest, wealthiest country on earth. As the empires of Europe embarked upon their long, slow disintegration, it was even toying with **colonialist ventures** of its own. For a brief period it seemed as if the Philippines might pass into permanent US control, while the escapades of Teddy Roosevelt's Rough Riders in

Cuba presaged a century of ongoing US involvement in Latin America.

## THE TWENTIETH CENTURY

It may not have been apparent to everyone at the time, but the first few years of the twentieth century witnessed the emergence of many of the features that came to characterize modern America. In 1903 alone, Wilbur and Orville Wright achieved the first successful powered **flight**, and Henry Ford established his Ford Motor Company. Ford's enthusiastic adoption of the latest techniques of mass production – the assembly line – gave Detroit a head start in the new **automobile** industry, which swiftly became the most important business in America. Both **jazz** and **blues** music came to the attention of a national audience for the first time during that same period, while Hollywood acquired its first **movie** studio in 1911, and its first major hit in 1915 with D W Griffith's unabashed glorification of the Ku Klux Klan in *Birth Of A Nation*.

This was also a time of growing **radicalism**. Both the NAACP (National Association for the Advancement of Colored People) and the socialist International Workers of the World ("the Wobblies") were founded in the early 1900s, while the campaign for women's suffrage also came to the forefront. Writers such as Upton Sinclair, whose *The Jungle* exposed conditions in Chicago's stockyards, and Jack London proselytized to the masses; contemporary improvements in the educational system mean this may well have been the most literate period in US history.

President Wilson managed to keep the US out of the **Great War** for several years but, when it came, American intervention was decisive. With the Russian Revolution illustrating the dangers of anarchy, the US also took charge of supervising the peace. However, although Wilson presided over the postwar negotiations that resulted in the Treaty of Versailles in 1919, isolationist sentiment at home kept the US out of his pet scheme to preserve future world peace, the League of Nations.

Back home, the Eighteenth Amendment to the Constitution, in 1920, forbade the sale and distribution of alcohol, while the Nineteenth finally gave all American women the vote. Quite how **Prohibition** ever became the law of the land is something of a mystery; certainly, in the buzzing metropolises of the Roaring Twenties, it enjoyed little conspicuous support. There was no noticeable elevation in the moral tone of the country, while Chicago in particular became renowned for the street wars between bootlegging gangsters such as Al Capone and his rivals.

### THE DEPRESSION AND THE NEW DEAL

By the middle of the 1920s, the US was enough of an industrial powerhouse to be responsible for more than half the world's output of manufactured goods. From leading the way into a new era of prosperity, however, it suddenly found itself dragging the rest of the world down into economic collapse. It's hard to say exactly what triggered the **Great Depression**; the consequences were out of all proportion to any one specific cause. Possible factors include American overinvestment in the floundering economy of postwar Europe, combined with high tariffs on imports that effectively precluded European recovery, as well as a quasi-superstitious faith in the stock market that had seen interest rates rise to a minimum of twelve percent in 1928. That faith was shattered by the **Wall Street Crash** of October 1929. On "Black Tuesday" alone, enough stocks were sold to produce a total loss of ten thousand million dollars – more than twice the total amount of money in circulation in the US. Within the next three years, industrial production was cut by half, the national income dropped by 38 percent, and, above all, unemployment rose from 1.5 million to 13 million.

National self-confidence, however shaky its foundations, has always played a crucial role in US history, and President Hoover was not the man to restore it. Matters only began to improve in 1932, when the patrician figure of **Franklin Delano Roosevelt** accepted the Democratic nomination for president with the words "I pledge myself to a new deal for America," and went on to win a landslide victory. At the time of his inauguration, early in 1933, the banking system had all but closed down; it took Roosevelt the now-proverbial "Hundred Days" of vigorous legislation to turn around the mood of the country.

Taking advantage of the new medium of radio, he used his "Fireside Chats" to cajole America out of crisis; among his earliest observations was that it was a good time for a beer, and that therefore the experiment of Prohibition was over. The **New Deal** took many forms and worked through many newly created agencies, but was marked throughout by a massive growth in the power of the federal government, which only now seems to be under threat. Among its accomplishments were the National Recovery Administration, which created two million jobs; the Social Security Act, of which Roosevelt declared "no damn politician can ever scrap my social security program"; the Public Works Administration, which built dams and highways the length and breadth of the country; the Tennessee Valley Authority, which by generating electricity under public ownership for the common good was probably the closest the US has ever come to institutionalized socialism; and measures to legitimize the role of the unions and revitalize the "Dust-bowl" farmers out on the plains.

Roosevelt originally saw himself as a populist who could draw support from every sector of society. By 1936, however, business leaders were making it clear that as far as they were concerned he had done more than enough already to kick-start the economy. From then on, as he secured an unprecedented four consecutive terms as president, he was firmly cast in the role of the champion of the little man.

After the work-creation programs of the New Deal had put America back on its feet, the deadly pressure to achieve victory in **World War II** spurred industrial production and know-how to new heights. Once again the US stayed out of the war at first, until it was finally forced in by the high-stakes gamble of the Japanese, who launched a pre-emptive strike on Hawaii's Pearl Harbor in December 1941. In the Pacific and in Europe alike, American manpower and economic muscle eventually carried all before it. Roosevelt died early in 1945, after laying the foundations for the postwar carve-up with Stalin and Churchill at Yalta, and thus was spared having to make his successor Harry Truman's fateful decision to use the newly developed atomic bomb on Hiroshima and Nagasaki.

## THE COMING OF THE COLD WAR

With the war won, the United Nations was created amid much hopeful rhetoric, and the Marshall Plan was set up to speed the recovery of Europe, a goal in which it was far more suc-

cessful than its predecessors 25 years earlier. However, as Winston Churchill announced in Missouri in 1946, an "Iron Curtain" had descended upon Europe, and Joseph Stalin was transformed from ally to enemy almost overnight.

The ensuing **Cold War** lasted for over four decades, at times fought in ferocious combat in scattered corners of the globe, and during the intervals absorbing colossal resources in the stockpiling of ever more destructive arsenals. Some of its ugliest moments came in its earliest years; Truman was still in office in 1950 when war broke out in **Korea**. A dispute over the arbitrary division of the Korean peninsula into two separate nations, North and South, soon turned into a stand-off between the US and China (with Russia, in theory at any rate, lurking in the shadows). Two years of bloody stalemate ended with things pretty much as they were before it all happened, except that Truman had by now been replaced by the genial **General Eisenhower**, the latest war hero to turn president.

The Eisenhower years have become a byword for bland complacency. Once Senator **Joseph McCarthy**, the "witch-hunting" anti-Communist scourge of the State Department and Hollywood, had finally discredited himself by attacking the army as well, the country is generally regarded as having lapsed into a sort of wilful suburban stupor. Great social changes were starting to take shape, however. World War II had introduced vast numbers of women and members of ethnic minorities to the potential rewards of factory work, and it had shown many Americans the lifestyle that was attainable in other parts of their own country. With the development at last of a national highway system, and a huge increase in automobile ownership, people felt able to pursue their version of the American Dream wherever they chose, and this led to another **mass migration** of blacks from the rural South to the cities of the North. The cities of **California** entered a period of exponential growth, with the aeronautical industries of Los Angeles in particular attracting thousands of prospective workers.

It was also during the 1950s that **television** reached every home in the nation. Together with the LP record, it created an entertainment industry that might at first have seemed designed to promote mass conformity but swiftly showed itself capable of addressing the needs of individual groups of consumers that had previously been barely identified. **Youth culture** burst into public prominence from 1954 onwards, with Elvis Presley's recording of *That's Alright Mama* appearing within a few months of Marlon Brando's moody starring role in *On the Waterfront* and James Dean's in *Rebel Without a Cause*.

## THE CIVIL RIGHTS YEARS

**Racial segregation** of public facilities, which had remained the norm in the South ever since Reconstruction, was in 1954 finally declared illegal by the Supreme Court ruling on *Brown vs Topeka Board of Education*. Just as a century before, however, the Southern states saw the issue more in terms of states' rights than of human rights, and attempting to implement the law, or even to challenge the failure to implement it, required supreme individual courage. The action of Rosa Parks in refusing to give up her seat to a white man on a bus in Montgomery, Alabama, in December 1955 triggered a successful mass boycott (see p.516), and pushed the 27-year-old **Rev Dr Martin Luther King Jr** straight to the forefront of the civil rights campaign. Further confrontation took place at the Central High School in Little Rock, Arkansas, in 1957 (see p.532), when the reluctant Eisenhower found himself forced to call in federal troops to counter the state's unwillingness to integrate its education system.

The election of **John F Kennedy** to the presidency in 1960, by the narrowest of margins, marked a sea-change in American politics, even if in retrospect his policies do not seem exactly radical. At 43 the youngest ever president, and the first Catholic, he was prepared literally to reach for the moon, urging the US to victory in the Space Race in which it had thus far lagged humiliatingly behind the Soviet Union. Kennedy had won in part thanks to his spurious allegations concerning the "missile gap," and after years of peace under Eisenhower the Cold War soon began to hot up again. Fortunately, the US military spotted Soviet missile bases in Communist Cuba in 1962 before the missiles themselves had been installed, and Kennedy insisted that they were withdrawn. Kennedy had had rather less success the previous year, however, in launching the abortive **Bay of Pigs** invasion of Cuba, and he also managed to embroil America in the ongoing war in Vietnam, by sending "advisers" to Saigon.

Although another factor in Kennedy's election success had been a much-publicized telephone call to the wife of Dr King, during one of King's many sojourns in Southern jails, as president he was rarely keen to identify himself with the civil rights movement. The campaign nonetheless made headway, given extra momentum by the impact on global television news programs of such horrific images as Birmingham police chief "Bull" Connor turning water cannon and dogs on peaceful demonstrators in 1963. Its defining moment came with Dr King's eloquent "I Have a Dream" speech during the "March on Washington for Jobs and Freedom" later that summer. For his unwavering espousal of Gandhian principles of non-violence, King was awarded the Nobel Peace Prize the next year. Nonetheless, part of the reason that middle America came to accept that the time had come to address racial inequalities was the threat it perceived in the rhetoric of **Malcolm X**, who argued that black people had the right to defend themselves against aggression.

After Kennedy's assassination in November 1963 (see p.655), his successor **Lyndon Johnson** ("LBJ," in conscious homage to Roosevelt's "FDR") was responsible for pushing through a program of legislation that enacted most of the primary demands of civil rights campaigners. Violent white resistance in the South continued, however, and only the long, painstaking and dangerous work of registering Southern black voters en masse eventually forced Southern politicians to mend their ways.

Johnson won a landslide victory over Republican Barry Goldwater in the elections of 1964, but whether his dream of being the architect of a "Great Society" could ever have come to fruition is impossible to know. Instead he was soon brought low by the war in **Vietnam**, where American involvement had escalated beyond all reason or apparent control. Broad-based popular opposition to the conflict grew in proportion to the death toll of American soldiers, and the threat of the draft gave a new focus to the mood of youthful rebellion. San Francisco in particular responded to psychedelic prophet Timothy Leary's call to "turn on, tune in, drop out"; 1967's Summer of Love saw the lone beatniks of the Fifties transmogrify into an entire generation of hippies.

From the earliest days of the civil rights struggle, Dr King had argued that social justice could only be achieved through economic equality. That message was given a new urgency by riots in the ghettos of Los Angeles in 1965 and Detroit in 1967, and the emergence of the Black Panthers, an armed defence force in the tradition of the now-dead Malcolm X. King also began to denounce the Vietnam War, while, after refusing the draft with the words "No Vietcong ever called me nigger," Muhammad Ali was stripped of his title as world heavyweight boxing champion.

In 1968, the US reached the brink of collapse. Not long after his plummeting popularity led LBJ to announce that he would not run again for the presidency, Dr King, in Memphis to support a garbage workers' strike, was gunned down in his motel. Shortly after that, JFK's brother and former Attorney General Robert, who had managed to redefine himself as spokesman for the nation's dispossessed, was shot on the night that he emerged as Democratic front-runner. It didn't take a conspiracy theorist to believe that the spate of deaths reflected a malaise in the soul of America.

## *RICHARD NIXON TO JIMMY CARTER*

Somehow – perhaps because the brutally suppressed riots at the Chicago Democratic convention raised the specter of anarchy – the misery of 1968 resulted in the election of the Republican **Richard Nixon** as president. Eisenhower's vice-president while still in his thirties, Nixon had famously told the press after his failure to become governor of California in 1962 that "you won't have Richard Nixon to kick around any more." Now he was back, and it soon became apparent that he had scores to settle with his countless perceived enemies, above all in the media. Nixon's impeccable conservative credentials enabled him to bring the US to a rapport with China, but the war in Vietnam dragged on, to claim a total of 57,000 American lives. Attempts to win it included the secret and illegal bombing of Cambodia, which raised opposition at home to a new peak, but ultimately it was simpler to abandon the original goals in the name of "peace with honor." The end came either in 1972 – when Henry Kissinger and Le Duc Tho were awarded the Nobel Peace Prize for negotiating a treaty, and Tho at least had the grace to decline – or in 1975, when the Americans finally withdrew from Saigon.

During Nixon's first term, many of the disparate individuals politicized by the events and undercurrents of the 1960s coalesced into activist groupings. Native Americans occupied the island of Alcatraz in San Francisco, in the genesis of the American Indian Movement; gay men in New York's *Stonewall* bar fought back after one police raid too many; feminists united to campaign for abortion rights and an Equal Rights Amendment; and even the prisoners in America's jails attempted to organize themselves, resulting in such bloody debacles as the 31 prisoners killed when the military stormed Attica prison in September 1971. Nixon directed various federal agencies to monitor the new radicalism, but his real bugbear were the anti-war protesters. Increasingly ludicrous covert operations against real and potential opponents culminated in the botched attempt to burgle Democratic National Headquarters in Washington DC's **Watergate** complex in 1972. It took two years of investigation and exposure before Nixon was demonstrated to have conspired to thwart the processes of justice. He resigned in 1974, one jump ahead of impeachment by the Senate, to be succeeded by vice-president Gerald Ford.

With the Republicans briefly discredited, former Georgia governor Jimmy Carter was elected to the presidency as a clean-handed outsider in the nation's bicentennial year of 1976. His victory showed how far the US had come in a decade, let alone two centuries; a crucial element of the support for this new-style Southern Democrat was the recently enfranchised black population of the South. Carter's enthusiastic attempts to put his Baptist principles into practice on such issues as global human rights soon came to be perceived as naive, if not un-American. Misfortune followed misfortune. Not only was he attacked by a giant rabbit while rowing on a lake in Georgia, but he had to break the unpleasant news to the nation that it was facing an energy crisis, following the formation of the OPEC cartel of Middle East oil producers. Worse still, the Shah of Iran, a close American ally, was overthrown, and the staff of the US embassy in Teheran were taken hostage by Islamic revolutionaries. Carter's failed attempts to get the hostages released was seized upon by the Republicans as a sign of his weakness as a leader and all but destroyed his hopes of winning reelection in 1980. In fact, the tenacious refusal of the Iranians to release the hostages while Carter was still President, holding them until the very day that he left office and was replaced by the former "B" movie star Ronald Reagan, led to accusations that the Republicans had struck a secret deal with the hostage-takers. Whatever the truth, the facts are that Carter's Presidency ended with the taint of the hostage crisis still present and Reagan's term started free of that burden and in an aura of celebration at their final return home.

## THE REAGAN–BUSH YEARS

Ronald Reagan was a new kind of president. Unlike the obsessive workaholic Carter, he made a virtue of his hands-off approach to the job, joking for example that "they say hard work never killed anybody, but I figured why take the risk?" This laissez-faire attitude extended to his domestic economic policies, under which the rich were left to get as rich as they could manage, and his successors were left to cope with the explosion in the national debt that followed deregulation of the financial markets and the collapse of the Savings and Loans system. Somehow, the common perception that Reagan was unaware of what went on around him meant that his personal popularity remained undented through a succession of scandals, and reelection in 1984. He did have his pet projects, however, such as the enormously expensive attempt to seal off American skies with the Strategic Defense Initiative ("Star Wars"), and a personal vendetta against Colonel Gaddafi of Libya. Persistent maneuverings to destabilize the left-wing Sandinista government in Nicaragua culminated in the labyrinthine "Iran-Contra" affair, under which the profits from illegal arms sales to Iran were equally illegally siphoned into buying arms for the Contra rebels in Nicaragua (unbeknownst to Congress or the public). Like other conservatives before him, Reagan was adept at the posturing of Cold War superpower politics, and was allowed greater leeway by his electorate than a Democrat might have been in arms-control negotiations with Mikhail Gorbachev, the new leader of what he called the "Evil Empire."

In 1988, Reagan was replaced in office by his vice-president **George Bush**. It had briefly seemed that Jesse Jackson, at the head of his multiracial "Rainbow Coalition," might become the first black presidential candidate of a major

party, but after an early strong showing in the Democratic primaries, he lost the nomination to a more traditional – and, it was thought, more "electable" – Democrat, Massachusetts governor Michael Dukakis. During the ensuing race, Bush succeeded in labeling Dukakis a "card-carrying liberal," and voters responded to Bush's pledge to "read my lips – no new taxes," a vow that would help undo him a few years later.

Bush's one term in office was marked by the increasing influence of the US in foreign affairs, largely made possible by the sudden end of the Cold War, brought on by the collapse of the communist governments in Eastern Europe. He watched as the Berlin Wall came down in 1989, and the Soviet Union crumbled away to give what the US was happy to see as final victory in the Cold War. He was also president when Operation Desert Storm required 100 hours and virtually no American lives to drive the Iraqis out of Kuwait in February 1991. Bush's unprecedented level of popularity at the moment of triumph in Kuwait convinced many that he was certain of a second term in office – but his success was short-lived. During the 1992 election campaign it became clear that Americans were more concerned with domestic affairs than with what was happening overseas, and Bush seemed woefully out of touch with the common man when he was confused by the technology of the cash register at a supermarket during a campaign appearance. Twelve years of Republican government came to an end with the election of the Arkansas governor **Bill Clinton** in 1992.

## CLINTON AND THE END OF THE CENTURY

Bill Clinton's first term as president was characterized by his failure to deliver on specific campaign promises – most obviously, his pledge to reform the nation's health-care system. His resultant unpopularity helped the Republican opposition to win sweeping victories in the 1994 congressional elections and made it nearly impossible for him to pass any of his favored legislation. The remaining years of his first term were characterized by repeated and protracted struggles with the Republican-dominated Congress, just the sort of "gridlock" that both parties had pledged to avoid. Through a better grasp of the popular mood, Clinton managed to assign most of the blame for the resultant nonfunctioning of the government to the Republicans and was eventually elected to a second term with surprising ease.

But the "Comeback Kid" was to find holding on to his office somewhat more challenging than that reelection. Persistent allegations of adulterous liaisons finally came to a head in early 1998 with the revelation that Clinton had carried on an affair with a young White House intern named Monica Lewinsky. To make matters worse, he engaged in a series of dubious actions and misleading statements that Republicans, behind appointed Special Prosecutor Kenneth Starr, interpreted as a far-reaching cover-up of the scandal. Starr's exhaustive investigation led to the technical **impeachment** of the President, on grounds of perjury and abuse of power. Despite being convicted by the lower house of Congress, Clinton was eventually saved by a close vote in the upper house of the Senate – largely because the American people were tired of the scandal, and did not feel Clinton's indiscretions were serious enough to merit removal. In fact, it was the Republicans that suffered losses in the 1998 congressional elections, while the President's popularity remained surprisingly high.

## THE NEW MILLENNIUM

Clinton talked often during his tenure about "building a bridge to the new millennium," political speak for not much of anything, really. His legacy more rests in turning over the reins of power to his vice-president, **Al Gore**, though Gore's election in 2000 is certainly no foregone conclusion. In any case, Clinton did oversee a booming economy in the Nineties, one that showed exceptional strength in the technology industry. A landmark antitrust case against computer giant **Microsoft**, won by the US government in 1999, has shaken up that field a bit, and there are always the worried prognosticators, waiting for the inevitable recession, but America shows no signs of giving up its self-proclaimed "leader of the free world" position as the next millennium begins.

# BOOKS

It would be futile to attempt to provide a comprehensive overview of American literature in the limited space available. The following bibliography is, therefore, a personal selection of those books which proved most useful or enjoyable during the preparation of this guide.

## HISTORY AND SOCIETY

**James Baldwin**, *No Name on the Street*, *The Fire Next Time*, *Evidence Of Things Not Seen*, and many others. The most brilliant prose stylist of twentieth-century America. Stunningly incisive accounts of the black experience in the cities of the USA, although Baldwin was such a powerful polemicist that he was occasionally swept away by his own rhetoric.

**John Berendt**, *Midnight in the Garden of Good and Evil*. Voodoo, transvestism and murder; best-selling true-life tales of life and death in contemporary Savannah – see p.471.

**Center of the American West**, *Atlas of the New West*. Admirable, well-illustrated volume, full of quirky facts, figures and personal essays to reveal the true colors of one of the most mythologized, rapidly changing regions in the nation.

**Hugh Brogan**, *Penguin History of the USA*. Good, up-to-date and very complete history of the United States.

**Dee Brown**, *Bury My Heart at Wounded Knee*. A quarter of a century on from its first publication, this remains the best narrative of the impact of white settlement and expansion on Native Americans across the continent.

**Bill Bryson**, *Made in America*. A compulsively readable history of the American language, packed with bizarre snippets, which does much to illuminate the history of the nation.

**Peter Carroll and David Noble**, *The Free and the Unfree: a New History of the USA*. A good interpretive history of American political development, focusing on the wide gap between those who hold power and those who are disadvantaged on grounds of race, sex or class.

**Alston Chase**, *Playing God in Yellowstone*. Taking Yellowstone as his example, the iconoclastic Chase explores the truth behind the National Park Service's rhetoric.

**Jill Ker Conway (ed)**, *Written by Herself*. Splendid anthology of women's autobiographies from the mid-1800s to the present, including sections on African-Americans, scientists, artists and pioneers.

**Mike Davis**, *City of Quartz*. City politics, neighborhood gangs, unions, film noir and religion are drawn together in this award-winning, leftist, hyperbolic history of Los Angeles.

**Joan Didion**, *The White Album*, *Slouching Toward Bethlehem*, *Miami* and others. Essays on the American way of life, drawing heavily on the late Sixties. A respected social commentator, Didion spoils the act at times by dropping too many names.

**Frederick Douglass et al**, *The Classic Slave Narratives*. Compilation of ex-slaves' autobiographies, ranging from Olaudah Equíano's kidnapping in Africa and global wanderings to Frederick Douglass' eloquent denunciation of slavery. Includes Harriet Jacobs' story of her escape from Edenton, North Carolina – see p.432.

**Brian Fagan**, *Ancient North America*. Archeological history of America's native peoples, from the first hunters to cross the Bering Strait up to European contact.

**Frances Fitzgerald**, *Cities on a Hill*. Intelligent, sympathetic exploration of four of the odder corners of American culture, including San Francisco's gay Castro district and the Rajneeshi community in eastern Oregon.

**Shelby Foote**, *The Civil War: a Narrative*. Epic, three-volume account containing anything you could possibly want to know about the War Between the States.

**U S Grant**, *Personal Memoirs*. Encouraged by Mark Twain, the Union general and subsequent president wrote his autobiography just before his death, in a (successful) bid to recoup his horrendous debts. At first the book feels oddly downbeat, but the man's down-to-earth modesty grows on you.

**James R Grossman**, *Land of Hope*. Scholarly yet moving account of the exodus of Southern blacks to Northern cities, specifically Chicago, during the early twentieth century. Though it focuses on the broader social and economic issues, it also manages to bring to life the individual stories involved.

**Tony Horwitz** *Confederates in the Attic: Dispatches from the Unfinished Civil War*. Strange meld of past and present, as journalist Horwitz explores the places in the South where die-hards keep the Civil War very much alive.

**Frederick Hoxie (ed)**, *Indians in American History*. Eye-opening collection of essays focusing on the role of Native Americans in US history, presenting them as active and aware (if hopelessly outgunned) players rather than passive victims. Filled with illustrations and extensive quotes from journals and contemporary accounts of Native Americans from across the US.

**J B Jackson**, *American Space*. Engagingly written work which traces the transition of America from a rural to an urban and industrialized nation in the crucial decade immediately after the Civil War.

**William Loren Katz**, *The Black West*. Fascinating, scholarly and long-overdue exploration of the African-American experience of the opening of the West.

**Roger G Kennedy**, *Rediscovering America*. Collected essays by one of America's most readable historians, appointed by Clinton to run the National Park Service. Kennedy looks behind the gloss of conventional tellings to reveal something of the real story of how America came to be.

**Meriwether Lewis and William Clark**, *The Original Journals of the Lewis and Clark Expedition, 1804–1806*. Eight volumes of meticulous jottings by the Northwest's first inland explorers, scrupulously following President Jefferson's orders to record every detail of flora, fauna and native inhabitant.

**Clyde A Milner II, Carol A O'Connor and Martha A Sandweiss**, *The Oxford History of the American West*. Fascinating collection of essays on Western history, covering topics ranging from myths and movies to art and religion.

**James M McPherson**, *Battle Cry of Freedom*. Extremely readable history of the Civil War, which integrates and explains the complex social, economic, political and military factors into one concise volume. Highly recommended.

**James Mooney**, *The Ghost Dance Religion and The Sioux Outbreak of 1890*. An extraordinary Bureau of Ethnology report, first published in 1890 but still available in paperback. Mooney persuaded his Washington superiors to allow him to roam the West in search of first-hand evidence, and even interviewed Wovoka, the Ghost Dance prophet, in person.

**Stephen Plog**, *Ancient Peoples of the Southwest*. Much the best single-volume history of the pre-Hispanic Southwest, packed with diagrams and color photographs.

**Marc Reisner**, *Cadillac Desert*. Compendious but compulsive account of the environmental and political impact on the West of this century's mania for dam-building and large-scale irrigation projects.

**Hunter S Thompson**, *The Great Shark Hunt* and *Songs of the Doomed*. Accessible and varied collections of the maverick Dr Gonzo's journalistic rantings on contemporary American life and politics. Spiced up by tales of his own anarchic love of good times, guns and gambling.

**Sun Tracks & University of Arizona Press**, *Between Sacred Mountains*. Superb overview of Navajo history, culture and politics, written by Navajo teachers and parents as a sourcebook for Navajo students.

**Stephen Trimble**, *The People*. Excellent introduction to all the Native American groups of the Southwest, bringing the history up to date with contemporary interviews.

**Mark Twain**, *Roughing It, Life on the Mississippi*, and many others. Mark Twain was by far the funniest and most vivid chronicler of nineteenth-century America. *Roughing It*, which covers his early wanderings across the continent, all the way to Hawaii, is absolutely compelling.

**John Unruh**, *The Plains Across*. A history of the wagon trains, drawing heavily on pioneer journals.

**Mariann Voller**, *Ghosts in Mississippi*. This horrific account of the 1963 murder of civil rights leader Medgar Evers, and quite why it took thirty years to convict his self-proclaimed assassin, provides fascinating insights into how the Deep South has and has not changed.

**Geoffrey C Ward, with Ric and Ken Burns**, *The Civil War*. Marvelous illustrated history of the Civil War, designed to accompany the TV series and using hundreds of the same photographs.

**Richard White**, *It's Your Misfortune and None of My Own*. Dense, authoritative and all-embracing history of the American West, that debunks the notion of the rugged pioneer by stressing the role of the federal government.

**Juan Williams**, *Eyes on the Prize*. Informative and detailed accompaniment to the excellent TV series, covering the Civil Rights years from the early 1950s up to 1966, with lots of rare and some very familiar photos.

**Edmund Wilson**, *Patriotic Gore*. Fascinating eight-hundred-page survey of the literature of the American Civil War, which in its own right serves as an immensely readable narrative of the conflict.

## BIOGRAPHY AND ORAL HISTORY

**Maya Angelou**, *I Know Why the Caged Bird Sings*. First volume of an autobiographical sequence which provides an ultimately uplifting account of how a black girl transcended her traumatic childhood in 1930s Arkansas.

**William F Cody**, *The Life of Hon William F Cody, Known As Buffalo Bill*. Larger than life autobiography of one of the great characters of the Wild West. Particularly treasurable for the moment when he refers to himself more formally as "Bison William."

**Henry Hampton and Steve Fayer**, *Voices of Freedom*. Hugely impressive oral history of the Civil Rights movement, heavily drawn from the TV series.

**Joyce Johnson**, *Minor Characters*. Johnson, Jack Kerouac's girlfriend and "muse," tells her own story and those of the other women in the 1950s East Village scene, revealing the stiflingly reactionary male elitism of the Beats.

**Florence King**, *Confessions of a Failed Southern Lady*. Hilarious autobiography of a girl who grows up with her faded Southern belle grandmother, and foul-talking, heavy-smoking mother, only to effect the greatest rebellion of all by falling in love with a woman.

**Malcolm X, with Alex Haley**, *The Autobiography of Malcolm X*. Searingly honest and moving account of a progress from street hoodlum to political leadership. Written on the hoof over a period of years, it traces the development of Malcolm X's thought before, during and after his split from the Nation of Islam. The conclusion, when he talks about his impending assassination, is painful in the extreme.

**Muhammad Ali**, *The Greatest*. Powerful and entertaining autobiography of the Louisville boy who grew up to become world heavyweight boxing champion. The most memorable parts deal with his fight against the Vietnam draft and the subsequent stripping away of his world championship status.

**Tony Parker**, *A Place Called Bird*. Fascinating oral history based on interviews with the inhabitants of a tiny town in the very center of Kansas, the heartland of the Midwest.

**Ishbel Ross**, *Rebel Rose*. Evocative rebel-yelling biography of Rose Greenhow, glamorous Washington socialite and remarkably brave Confederate spy. Works equally well as an exciting tale of political espionage and an impeccably detailed historical document.

**Quinta Scott and Susan Croce Kelly**, *Route 66*. Moving oral histories and monochrome photographs trace the life span of the now abandoned 2000-mile highway immortalized in film, novels and song.

**Annick Smith**, *Homestead*. Beautifully written episodes of a Montana life. A host of characters, personal and cultural insights, all offset by Smith's tangible passion for that huge, awesome landscape.

**Ralph Steadman**, *Scar Strangled Banner*. Warped, cynical and crazy underview of America, full of sketches and hacked-about photos, from sometime Hunter S Thompson collaborator and illustrator.

**Joanna L Stratton**, *Pioneer Women*. Original memoirs of women – mothers, teachers, homesteaders and circuit riders – who ventured across the Plains from 1854 to 1890. Lively, superbly detailed accounts, with chapters on journeys, homebuilding, daily domestic life, the church, the cowtown, temperance and suffrage.

**Studs Terkel**, *American Dreams Lost and Found*. Interviews with ordinary American citizens. As illuminating a guide to US life as you could hope for.

**Frank Waters**, *Book of the Hopi*. Extraordinary insight into the traditions and beliefs of the Hopi, prepared through years of interviews and approved by tribal elders.

## ENTERTAINMENT AND CULTURE

**Kenneth Anger**, *Hollywood Babylon*. A vicious yet high-spirited romp through Tinseltown's greatest scandals, amply illustrated with gory and repulsive photographs, and always inclined to bend the facts for the sake of a good story. A shoddily researched second volume covers more recent times.

**Charlotte Greig**, *Will You Still Love Me Tomorrow?* Enthusiastic feminist appraisal of (predominantly American) girl groups from the 1950s (the Chantels and the Crystals) through to 1980s rap stars like Salt'n'Pepa. Lots of photos and personal recollections make it a great read.

**Peter Guralnick**, *Lost Highways*, *Feel Like Going Home* and *Sweet Soul Music*. Thoroughly researched personal histories of black popular music, packed with obsessive detail on all the great names. His more recent Elvis biographies, *Last Train to Memphis* and *Careless Love*, trace the rise and fall of the iconic star in a non-sensational but nonetheless gripping documentary manner, while also performing the rare trick of evaluating him seriously as a musician.

**Gerri Hershey**, *Nowhere To Run: the History of Soul Music*. Definitive rundown on the evolution of soul music from the gospel heyday of the 1940s through the Memphis, Motown and Philly scenes to the sounds of the early 1980s. Strong on social commentary and political background and studded with anecdotes and interviews.

**Greil Marcus**, *Dead Elvis*. Vastly entertaining overview of the many Elvis myths, if a little hastily put together from previously published articles. Marcus' *Mystery Train* is an intelligent and absorbing overview of American popular music, from Robert Johnson to Elvis Presley and Randy Newman.

**Dave Marsh**, *Louie, Louie*. This unusual biography of a song traces the way *Louie, Louie* transcends American society, and goes into hilarious detail about kazoo parades, various radio station bans and the campaign to make it the state song of Washington.

**Robert Palmer**, *Deep Blues*. Readable history of the development and personalities of the Delta Blues.

**Randall Reise**, *Nashville Babylon*. Thrashes the squeaky-clean image of the country music scene. Cocaine, whiskey, infidelity, murder, rape and other skeletons are dug up from the closets of some unlikely characters.

**Henry Rollins**, *Get in the Van*. Illustrated diary of a trek round the US and Europe with punk band Black Flag during the early 1980s. Rollins lives up to his malcontent reputation by criticizing almost everywhere he visits; Madison, Wisconsin, being about the only place he seems to like.

**David E Stanley**, *The Elvis Encyclopedia*. It might lack the authoritative analysis of Peter Guralnick's book (see above), but this well-illustrated tome, by Presley's stepbrother, is the most enjoyable of the many coffee-table trivia books on the subject. Interesting oddments include "Elvis's Iron Constitution."

**John Williams**, *Into The Badlands*. Williams' interviews with a batch of America's very best crime writers build a picture of the underbelly of US society from the Montana mountainsides of James Crumley to the mean streets of Elmore Leonard's Detroit. He lapses into sexism, however, when dealing with Chicago's Sara Paretsky, who "is learning as she goes along."

## TRAVEL WRITING

**Edward Abbey**, *The Journey Home*. Hilarious accounts of whitewater rafting and desert hiking trips alternate with essays, by the man who inspired the radical environmentalist movement Earth First! All of Abbey's many books, especially *Desert Solitaire*, a journal of time spent as a ranger in Arches National Park, make great traveling companions.

**James Agee and Walker Evans**, *Let Us Now Praise Famous Men*. A deeply personal but also richly evocative journal of travels through the rural lands of the Depression-era Deep South, complemented by Evans' powerful photographs.

**Stephen Brook**, *New York Days, New York Nights*. An Englishman's drily witty impressions of the Big Apple, with chapters on every aspect of the place from flotation chambers to Jewish restaurants. Brook's *Honky Tonk Gelato* treats Texas in a similar, if sometimes patronizing, vein.

**Bill Bryson**, *The Lost Continent*. Using his boyhood home of Des Moines in Iowa as a benchmark, the author travels the length and breadth of America to find the perfect small town. Hilarious, if occasionally a bit smug. His latest, *A Walk in the Woods*, applies his trademark irony to the Appalachian Trail from Georgia to Maine, but suffers from too much nature and too few quirky characters.

**J Hector St-John de Crèvecoeur**, *Letters from an American Farmer and Sketches of Eighteenth-Century America*. First published in 1782, a remarkable account of the complexities of Revolutionary America.

**Robert Frank**, *The Americans*. The Swiss photographer's brilliantly evocative portrait of mid-century American life from coast to coast, with striking images contextualised by an introductory essay from Jack Kerouac.

**Ian Frazier**, *Great Plains*. An immaculately researched and well-written travelogue containing a wealth of information on the people of the American prairielands from Native Americans to the soldiers who staff the region's many nuclear installations.

**Jack Kerouac**, *On the Road*. Definitive account of transcontinental Beatnik wanderings, which now reads as a curiously dated period piece. Not as incoherent as you might expect.

**Irma Kurtz**, *The Great American Bus Ride*. Account of Kurtz's journey crisscrossing the country on Greyhound. At times frustratingly insubstantial, it does give a pertinent, relevant account of the strange limboland of bus stations and the etiquette, camaraderie and unwritten rules of bus travel.

**James A MacMahon (ed)**, *Audubon Society Nature Guides*. Attractively produced, fully illustrated and easy-to-use guides to the flora and fauna of seven different US regional ecosystems, covering the entire country from coast to coast and from grasslands to glaciers.

**Virginia and Lee McAlester**, *A Field Guide to American Houses*. Well-illustrated and engagingly readable guide to America's rich variety of domestic architecture, from pre-colonial to postmodern.

**Melanie McGrath**, *Motel Nirvana*. Entertaining account of a British traveler's experiences in the Southwest, with some enjoyable swipes at various New-Age nonsense.

**John McPhee**, *Encounters with the Arch Druid*. In three interlinked narratives, environmental activist and Friends of the Earth founder David Brower confronts developers, miners and dam builders, while trying to protect three different American wilderness areas – the Atlantic shoreline, the Grand Canyon and the Cascades of the Pacific Northwest.

**William Least Heat Moon**, *Blue Highways*. Account of a mammoth loop tour of the US by back roads, in which the author interviews ordinary people in ordinary places. A good overview of rural America, with lots of interesting details on Native Americans. His next book, *Prairyerth*, opted for the microcosmic approach, taking six hundred loving pages over the story of Chase County, Kansas.

**Jonathan Raban**, *Old Glory*. A somewhat pompous though always interesting account of Raban's journey on a small craft down the Mississippi River from the headwaters in Minnesota to the bayous of Louisiana.

**Bernard A Weisberger (ed)**, *The WPA Guide to America*. Prepared during the New Deal as part of a make-work program for writers, these guides paint a fairly comprehensive portrait of 1930s and earlier America. Also available are state-by-state guides, most of them out of print but easily found in US libraries and secondhand bookshops.

**Edmund White**, *States of Desire: Travels in Gay America*. A revealing account of life in gay communities across the country, focusing heavily on San Francisco and New York.

## FICTION

### GENERAL AMERICANA

**Raymond Carver**, *Will You Please Be Quiet Please?* Stories of the American working class, written in a distinctive sparse, almost deadpan style that perhaps owes something to Hemingway and certainly influenced untold numbers of contemporary American writers. The stories served as the basis for Robert Altman's film *Short Cuts*.

**Don DeLillo**, *White Noise* and *Underworld*. The former is his best, a funny and penetrating pop culture exploration, while the latter is one of those typically flawed attempts to pack the twentieth-century American experience into a great big novel. Worthwhile, though.

**John Dos Passos**, *USA*. Hugely ambitious novel (originally a trilogy) which grapples with the US in the early decades of the twentieth century from every possible angle. Gripping human stories with a strong political and historical perspective.

**Dennis Johnson**, *Jesus' Son*. Junkies and thieves and all the usual trappings of a Beat-era collection of stories, but from 1990s urban America.

**Herman Melville**, *Moby Dick*. Compendious and compelling account of nineteenth-century whaling, packed with details on American life from New England to the Pacific.

**E Annie Proulx**, *Accordion Crimes*. Proulx's latest book comes as close to being the fabled "Great American Novel" as anyone could reasonably ask, tracing a fascinating history of immigrants in all parts of North America through the fortunes of a battered old Sicilian accordion.

### NEW YORK CITY

**Paul Auster**, *New York Trilogy*. Three Borgesian investigations into the mystery and madness of contemporary New York. Using the conventions of the detective novel, Auster unfolds a disturbed and disturbing picture of the city.

**Truman Capote**, *Breakfast at Tiffany's* and *In Cold Blood*. The first story is about a fictional social climber in New York called Holly Go-Lightly; the second concerns the true life stories of two serial killers in the heartland. The subject matter of these two stories could hardly be much different, but the degree of insight provided into two uniquely American stories is equally high in both accounts.

**Chester Himes**, *Cotton Comes to Harlem*, *Blind Man with a Pistol*, and many others. Action-packed and uproariously violent novels set in New York's Harlem, starring the much-feared detectives Coffin Ed Johnson and Grave Digger Jones.

**Grace Paley**, *Collected Stories*. Shrewd love–hate stories written over a lifetime by the daughter of Russian-Jewish immigrants, who published dead-on accounts of New York life in three installments: her first book of stories came out in the 1950s, her second in the early 1970s and her third in the late 1980s.

**J D Salinger**, *The Catcher in the Rye*. Classic novel of adolescence, tracing Holden Caulfield's sardonic journey through the streets of New York.

### NEW ENGLAND

**George V Higgins**, *Penance for Jerry Kennedy*. Crime thriller written almost entirely in the dialogue of Boston lowlifes and crooked lawmen.

**John Irving**, *The Cider House Rules*. One of Irving's more successful sprawling novels, weaving themes of love, suffering, and the many facets of the abortion debate against a shifting Maine backdrop.

**H P Lovecraft**, *The Best of HP Lovecraft: Bloodcurdling Tales of Horror and the Macabre*. Creepy New England stories from the author Stephen King called "the twentieth century's greatest practitioner of the classic horror tale."

### FLORIDA, THE SOUTH

**William Faulkner**, *The Reivers*. The last and most humorous work of this celebrated Southern author. *The Sound and the Fury*, a fascinating study of prejudice, set like most of his books in the fictional Yoknatapawpha County in Mississippi, is a much more difficult read.

**Carl Hiaasen**, *Double Whammy*, and many others. Hiaasen is the funniest crime writer on the scene – and a razor-sharp chronicler of Florida's weirder, wilder side. This one sees rednecks/bass fishermen and religious sects caught up in a fast-moving and hilarious plot.

**Zora Neale Hurston**, *Spunk*. Short stories celebrating black culture and experience from around the country, by a writer from Florida who became one of the bright stars of the Harlem cultural renaissance in the 1920s.

**Harper Lee**, *To Kill a Mockingbird*. Classic tale of racial conflict and society's view of an outsider, Boo Radley, as seen through the eyes of children.

**Cormac McCarthy**, *Suttree*. McCarthy is better known for his "modern Western" works like *Blood Meridian* and *All the Pretty Horses*, but this beautifully written tale, of a Knoxville, Tennessee scion opting for a hard-scrabble life among a band of vagrants on the Tennessee River, is his best.

**Carson McCullers**, *The Heart is a Lonely Hunter*. McCullers is unrivaled in her sensitive treatment of misfits, in this case the attitude of a small Southern community to a deaf mute.

**Margaret Mitchell**, *Gone With the Wind*. Worth a read even if you know the lines of Scarlett and Rhett off by heart.

**Toni Morrison**, *Beloved*. Exquisitely written ghost story by the Nobel Prize-winning novelist, which traces the painful lives of a group of freed slaves after Reconstruction, and the obsession a mother develops after murdering her baby daughter to spare her a life of slavery.

**Flannery O'Connor**, *A Good Man is Hard to Find*. Short stories, featuring strong, obsessive characters, that explore religious tensions and racial conflicts in the Deep South.

**Alice Walker**, *In Love and Trouble*. Moving and powerful stories of black women in the South, from the author of the much-acclaimed *The Color Purple*.

**Eudora Welty**, *The Ponder Heart*. Quirky, humorous evocation of life in a backwater Mississippi town. Her most critically acclaimed work, *The Optimist's Daughter*, explores the tensions between a judge's daughter and her stepmother.

**Bailey White**, *Mama Makes Up Her Mind* and *Sleeping at the Starlight Motel*. Witty, touching tales of Georgian life. The eponymous, eccentric mother is the delightful central character of the former, while the fond portrayal of White's small home-town in the second is spot-on.

## LOUISIANA

**James Lee Burke**, *Black Cherry Blues*. Cajun cop Dave Robicheaux sets out to expose alliances between government and organized crime in the beautiful environs of Louisiana and Montana. A detective book that has it all.

**George Washington Cable**, *The Grandissimes*. Romantic saga of Creole family feuds, written c.1900 but set during the Louisiana Purchase. Superb evocation of steamy Louisiana elite, the Creole lifestyle and the resistance of New Orleans to its Americanization. Apparently shocking at the time for its sympathetic portrayal of blacks.

**Kate Chopin**, *The Awakening*. Subversive story of a bourgeois married woman whose fight for independence ends in tragedy. Swampy c.1900 Louisiana is portrayed as both a sensual hotbed for her sexual awakening and as her eventual nemesis.

**John Kennedy Toole**, *A Confederacy of Dunces*. Anarchic black tragicomedy in which the pompous and repulsive anti-hero Ignatius J Reilly wreaks havoc through an insalubrious and surreal New Orleans.

## THE GREAT LAKES, THE GREAT PLAINS

**Willa Cather**, *My Antonia*. Stunning book set in Nebraska that provides a great sense of pioneer hardships on the Plains.

**Louise Erdrich**, *The Beet Queen*. Offbeat tale of passion and obsession amongst poor white North Dakota folk – particularly women – set against the backdrop of an economy and culture changing with the introduction of sugar beet as a crop in the 1940s. Erdrich's other novels play through the tensions between tradition and "progress" in Native American communities.

**Garrison Keillor**, *Lake Wobegon Days*. Wry, witty tales about a mythical Minnesota small town. Pokes fun at the rural Midwest with an affectionate finger.

**Elmore Leonard**, *Freaky Deaky*. One of the funniest of Leonard's many tough, brutal thrillers. Set in Detroit, it follows two former Sixties radicals who turn to crime.

**Mari Sandoz**, *Old Jules*. Written in 1935, this fictionalized biography gives a wonderful insight into the life of the author's pioneer Swiss father on the Nebraskan plains. Sandoz's other major work, *Crazy Horse*, contains great historical overviews but is spoiled somewhat by her insistence on narrating it through Sioux eyes.

**Richard Wright**, *Native Son*. The harrowing story of Bigger Thomas, a black chauffeur who accidentally kills his employer's daughter. The story develops his relationship with his lawyer, the closest he has ever come to being on an equal footing with a white.

## THE ROCKIES, THE SOUTHWEST

**James Crumley**, *The Wrong Case*. The lack of an intricate plot is more than compensated for by accounts of Montana scenery and the hapless detective Milo Milodragonovic, a man with a drink problem and a knack for doing things the hard way. An enjoyable, easy read.

**A B Guthrie Jr**, *Big Sky*. When first published in the Thirties it shattered the credibility of the mythical West peddled by Hollywood. Realistic historical fiction at its very best, following desperate mountain man and fugitive Boone Caudill, whose idyllic life in Montana was ended by the arrival of white settlers.

**Tony Hillerman**, *The Dark Wind*, and many others. The adventures of Jim Chee of the Navajo Tribal Police on the reservations of northern Arizona, forever dabbling in dark and mysterious forces churned up from the Anasazi past.

**Norman MacLean**, *A River Runs Through It*. Unputdownable – the best ever novel about fly-fishing, set in beautiful Montana lake country.

## CALIFORNIA

**Raymond Chandler**, *The Big Sleep* and *Farewell My Lovely*. The original incarnations of archetypal tough guy and iconic private eye Philip Marlowe are far more complex and beautifully written than the caricature movies made out of them with Humphrey Bogart would lead you to expect. This is pulp fiction at its finest – written by an American raised in London.

**Armistead Maupin**, *Tales of the City*. Long-running saga comprising sympathetic and entertaining human tales of life in San Francisco, that also work surprisingly well as suspenseful stand-alone novels. The fact that many of its key characters are gay meant that over the years the series became a chronicle of the impact of AIDS on the city. Maupin's *Maybe the Moon* is the equally humanist, poignant true-life story of his friend, the short person who played ET in the movie but was never allowed to reveal her true identity.

**Thomas Pynchon**, *The Crying of Lot 49*. Shorter, funnier and more accessible than *Gravity's Rainbow*, this novel of techno-freaks and pot-heads in Sixties California reveals, among other things, the sexy side of stamp collecting.

**Douglas Ruskoff**, *The Ecstasy Club*. Dark, chemical comedy about a group of young San Franciscans who set up a rave club which gradually turns into a big, long and bad trip.

**John Steinbeck**, *The Grapes of Wrath*. The classic account of a migrant family forsaking the Midwest for the Promised Land. Steinbeck's lighthearted but crisply observed novella *Cannery Row* captures daily life on the prewar Monterey waterfront, and the epic *East of Eden* updates and resets the Bible in the Salinas Valley and details three generations of familial feuding.

**Nathanael West**, *The Day of the Locust*. West wrote dark novels wholly vested in the American experience; this one, set in LA, is an apocalyptic story of fringe characters at the edge of the film industry.

## PACIFIC NORTHWEST

**David Guterson**, *Snow Falling on Cedars*. Gripping, atmospheric, mystery novel, evocatively capturing interracial tensions in the postwar Pacific Northwest.

**Tobias Wolff**, *This Boy's Life*. A memoir that reads more like a novel, this mournful book – leavened by self-deprecating humor – recounts his tough upbringing in a small Washington State town.

## ALASKA

**Tom Bodett**, *The End of the Road*. First novel by broadcaster from Homer, Alaska, who shot to fame as the voice on *Motel 6* radio commercials. Funny, witty and certainly better than his often shallow collections of essays (viz. *As Far As You Can Go Without a Passport*), but for the best value invest in some of his taped books.

**Jack London**, *The Call of the Wild and Other Stories*. London's classic tale, of a family pet discovering the ways of the wilderness while forced to pull sleds across Alaska's Gold Rush trails, is still essential reading before a trip to the far north.

# *BIOGRAPHIES*

The following are some of the many personalities from American history whose names recur throughout this book. You can find detailed page references for all of them in the main index, which begins on p.1186.

**Susan B Anthony** (1820–1906). Pioneer suffragette and president of the US suffragist society from 1892 to 1900, Anthony began her campaigning career in the temperance movement. She was also a committed abolitionist, published the New York liberal paper *The Revolution* (1868–70), and advocated equal pay for women, as well as donning bloomers to protest against the constrictive nature of women's clothing.

**Louis Armstrong** (1900–1971). New Orleans-based jazz trumpeter, known as Satchmo (from "satchel mouth"). Credited with devising the scat style of improvisational singing, and for his individualistic style, which foregrounded the solo performance above that of the band. Well known for his humor and affability, Armstrong also appeared in a number of Hollywood films.

**Benedict Arnold** (1741–1801). Revolutionary commander who shifted his allegiance to the British in 1779, but soon lost popularity with loyalists for leaving his British contact, Major John Andre, to be captured and hanged as a spy.

**Chuck Berry** (born 1926). Rock 'n' roll pioneer born in (*Johnny B*) Goode Street, St Louis. Consummate lyricist, red-hot guitarist and sharp businessman.

**Billy the Kid** (1859–1881). The subject of innumerable Wild West legends, former busboy William Bonney made his name in the Lincoln County Wars in New Mexico. His brief and bloody career ended at the hands of Pat Garrett.

**Daniel Boone** (1735–1820). Legendary hunter, trapper and explorer. One of the first whites to cross the Appalachians and stake out Kentucky for settlement.

**John Brown** (1800–1859). Fervent white abolitionist who, as part of a grand plan to set up a free state for escaped slaves, seized the US Armory at Harpers Ferry. After a short battle, Brown was captured, tried and hanged for treason.

**Calamity Jane** (1852–1903). Bawdy frontierswoman, cook, dancer, prostitute and camp follower, who in 1876 took up as bullwhacker for the Gold Rush camps in South Dakota. "Calam" traveled with Wild West shows but was fired for boozing and brawling.

**Al Capone** (1899–1947). Bootlegger and gangster who controlled the Chicago underworld during the 1920s, and later died in Florida of syphilis.

**Andrew Carnegie** (1835–1919). Scots-born industrialist and philanthropist, responsible for major innovations in the steel industry. By the close of the nineteenth century, when US steel production outdid that in Britain, most of it came from Carnegie's "vertically integrated" company – which owned the coalfields and the ships and railroads for transport of the supplies to the mills.

**Kit Carson** (1809–1868). Carson, who moved to Taos in 1826 and became a guide on the Santa Fe Trail and "mountain man," was later instrumental in rounding up the Navajo from Canyon de Chelly.

**William "Buffalo Bill" Cody** (1846–1917). Pony Express rider and Indian scout immortalized by the dime novels of Ned Buntline. His Wild West show toured all over the world.

**Francisco Vázquez de Coronado** (1510–1554). Spanish explorer who traveled through the Southwest as far as Kansas in search of cities of gold. When he eventually threw in the towel in 1542 and returned to Mexico, he faced a series of indictments for his lack of success.

**Crazy Horse** Ta-Sunko-Witko (1842?–1877). Oglala Sioux leader, and one of the most able and determined Native American warriors.

Prominent in the Fetterman Massacre, Battle of the Rosebud and Custer's Last Stand. Murdered at Fort Robinson, Nebraska.

**Davy Crockett** (1786–1836). Frontiersman, Indian fighter and Tennessee politician, who perished at the Alamo with all the other American volunteers. Popularly represented as a backwoods boy in a raccoon hat, with no education but the gift of the gab, Crockett was, in fact, less unconventional than his legend suggests.

**George Armstrong Custer** (1839–1876). Legendary US Cavalry general whose first big mistake – leading over two hundred troops into an ambush at Little Bighorn – was his last.

**John Dillinger** (1902–1934). Bank robber whose criminal activities earned him the title of Public Enemy Number One. After being set up by the legendary "Lady in Red," Dillinger was killed by FBI agents outside a Chicago movie theater.

**Walt Disney** (1901–1966). Inventor of Mickey Mouse, Donald Duck and Disneyland, Disney was also Hollywood's Last Tycoon, singlehandedly controlling a vast media and entertainment empire.

**Frederick Douglass** (1817?–1895). Escaped slave who rose to prominence as a writer and orator in the abolitionist movement.

**W E B DuBois** (1868–1963). Black intellectual and civil rights activist best known for his debates with Booker T Washington (see p.1185) in the early part of the twentieth century, and his role in forming the National Association for the Advancement of Colored People. A longtime campaigner for the independence of African colonies, he joined the Communist Party in 1961 and emigrated to Ghana, where he renounced his US citizenship.

**Bob Dylan** (born 1941). North-country Minnesota boy who redefined himself first as Woody Guthrie-style folkie and later as enigmatic rock star. The endearing elliptical games of his youth have long since grown wearisome in a man in his fifties, but he can still write songs to equal his best.

**Amelia Earhart** (1897–1937). Pioneer aviatrix, the first woman to fly solo across the Atlantic (in 1932), and the first person ever to fly the perilous route from Hawaii to California (1935). Both she and her navigator vanished without trace on an attempted round-the-world flight, and were last contacted just near the international date line.

**Thomas Edison** (1847–1931). Mercurial inventor and entrepreneur who developed the light bulb, motion pictures and phonograph records. He also founded General Electric, still one of the largest US corporations.

**Thomas Stearns Eliot** (1888–1965). Born beside the Mississippi in St Louis, Eliot reversed the usual American pattern and moved east, first to Harvard and then England, where he was awarded the Nobel Prize for Literature for a body of poetry including *The Waste Land* and *The Four Quartets*.

**Henry Ford** (1863–1947). Michigan farmer's son and industrial genius who pioneered assembly-line production in his car factories. A vehement right-winger, particularly on trade union and racial issues.

**Benjamin Franklin** (1706–1790). Printer, inventor, diplomat and politician, responsible amongst other things for publishing *Poor Richard's Almanac* (a litany of mottoes advocating prudence and honesty), setting up America's first public library, the invention of bifocal glasses and early experiments with electricity. Franklin also helped draft the Declaration of Independence, and went to France to seek aid for the revolutionary cause.

**Geronimo** (1829–1909). Brilliant Chiricahua Apache leader who battled the US Army in Arizona and New Mexico throughout the 1880s. Despite US promises, after surrendering he and his people were deported to Florida.

**Ulysses Simpson Grant** (1822–1885). At the start of the 1860s, the 38-year-old Ulysses Grant was finding it difficult to hold down a part-time job in his brother's saddle shop; within ten years he had led the Union armies to victory in the Civil War and become president of the US.

**William Randolph Hearst** (1863–1951). Publishing magnate and role model for *Citizen Kane*, whose inflammatory "yellow journalism" kindled public support for the Spanish–American War.

**Billie Holiday** (1915–1959). Definitive song stylist – not quite blues, not quite jazz – who made her greatest recordings with Lester Young and Duke Ellington.

**Buddy Holly** (1936–1959). Bespectacled kid from Lubbock, Texas, who died at 22 but was the first and the greatest of rock's singer-songwriters.

**Henry Hudson** (1565–1611). English explorer whose expedition for the Dutch East India Company to find a route from Europe to Asia through the Arctic led to the discovery of the Hudson River in 1609 – which he mistakenly believed would lead to the Pacific – and formed the basis for Dutch colonization in the New World.

**Howard Hughes** (1905–1976). Business magnate and Hollywood film producer (*Hell's Angels*, 1930; *Scarface*, 1932), who became increasingly eccentric after an aircraft crash in 1946. Twenty years later, he sold his majority holding in TWA for $500,000,000 and lived from then on in complete seclusion in sealed-off hotel suites.

**Andrew Jackson** (1767–1845). Military general who was a major light in the Revolutionary War. His defeat of the British in New Orleans in 1815 led to huge popular support, and he was elected seventh US president (Democrat) in 1829. The first president from west of the Appalachians, Jackson had much grass-roots support in Tennessee, and his election is seen as the first truly democratic choice in the nation's history.

**Rev Jesse Jackson** (born 1941). Black religious and political leader whose Rainbow Coalition seemed briefly during the late 1980s to represent the most viable progressive alternative to the centrist Democratic Party.

**Thomas Jefferson** (1743–1838). Author of the Declaration of Independence, third US president, and slave-owner, Jefferson was a strong advocate of freedom of the press and of religion, as well as being an accomplished architect.

**Lyndon Baines Johnson** (1908–1973). Brash Texan Democrat sworn in as president two hours after John Kennedy's assassination in 1963. Johnson pushed through liberal civil rights and social welfare bills, but his failure to deal with the increasingly horrific mess of Vietnam left him obliged not to seek reelection in 1968.

**Robert Johnson** (1911?–1938). Seminal Delta bluesman, whose songs were imbued with such a brooding aura that he was rumored to have sold his soul to the Devil. The clearest, earliest forerunner of rock 'n' roll.

**Kamehameha the Great** (1760?–1819). The first man to unite the Hawaiian islands – by terror, force of personality and shrewd exploitation of European expertise.

**Helen Keller** (1880–1968). Despite being struck blind and deaf by scarlet fever as an infant, Keller's writings and activism made her an inspirational early leader in the movement for equal rights for disabled people.

**John Fitzgerald Kennedy** (1917–1963). When elected in 1960, Kennedy was the youngest ever, and the first Catholic, president. His liberal domestic policies (known as "new frontier" programs) and success in securing the nuclear test ban treaty with the USSR and Britain won him huge popularity, as did his superficially glamorous life with wife Jackie. His assassination in Dallas, on November 22, 1963, might be said to mark the beginning of a long period of disillusionment and hopelessness in the American psyche.

**Dr Martin Luther King Jr** (1929–1968). Baptist minister who was the main black spokesperson during the Civil Rights years, and was awarded the Nobel Peace Prize after his "I have a dream" speech. Remembered by a public holiday in most states, and a street name in most major cities.

**General Marie Joseph Paul Yves Roch Gilbert du Motier Lafayette** (1757–1834). French aristocrat, known as "the hero of two worlds" for supporting the Americans in the Revolutionary War, who went on to fight with the revolutionary bourgeoisie in France. A great friend of George Washington, Lafayette advocated religious tolerance and the abolition of slavery.

**Robert Edward Lee** (1807–1870). Confederate Civil War general, considered one of the outstanding military strategists of all time. Enjoyed early success by whipping the vastly superior Union forces under the incompetent McClellan, but crashed to defeat at Gettysburg.

**Meriwether Lewis** (1774–1809) and **William Clark** (1770–1838). Jointly famed as leaders of the first exploratory expedition west from the Mississippi to the Pacific in 1804–1805. Lewis's journals and Clark's drawings are invaluable documents of the pre-conquest western US.

**Rush Limbaugh** (born 1951). Ultraconservative loudmouth turned political powerbroker, with daily talk-radio and TV shows.

**Abraham Lincoln** (1809–1865). To northerners at least, the most revered of all US presidents. The son of a Kentucky backwoodsman, he taught himself law and later entered Illinois politics, beating better-known opponents for the 1860 Republican presidential nomination. He led the Union through the Civil War, but was shot five days after the Confederate surrender.

**Charles Lindbergh** (1902–1974). In 1927, Lindbergh became the first person to complete a solo flight across the Atlantic, in the *Spirit of St Louis*, named for his home town. Ticker-tape parades feted him across the continent, and the "Lindy Hop" was named for him. The kidnapping and murder of his infant son was one of the most notorious crimes of the 1930s, but his pronounced Nazi sympathies lost him public support.

**Huey Long** (1893–1935). Flamboyant, populist governor of Louisiana known as the "Kingfish." His radical social welfare policies and tax reforms boosted the morale of poor rural whites during the Depression, and as senator, in the last three years of his life, he claimed his "Share the Wealth" program would make "every man a king." However, his corrupt and intimidating style of government made him plenty of enemies, and he was eventually assassinated in still-mysterious circumstances in Baton Rouge.

**Joe Louis** (1914–1981). Black Detroit heavyweight boxer who took the world championship from Mussolini-sidekick Primo Carnera in 1937 and retained it for twelve years.

**Malcolm X** (1925–1965). Not so successful burglar who came into contact in prison with the teachings of Elijah Muhammad's Nation of Islam, rose to become its leading minister and spokesperson, and then broke with the organization after a trip to Mecca and tour of Africa. Malcolm occasionally worked with Dr Martin Luther King Jr during his Civil Rights campaigns, and for many people his militant approach remains more persuasive than Dr King's.

**Joseph McCarthy** (1909–1957). Republican Senator for Wisconsin, notorious for his hysterical and unproven charges of Communist subversion in high government circles. President Truman called him a "pathological character assassin" and his career was ended when the Senate censured him for unconstitutional behavior.

**J Pierpoint Morgan** (1837–1913). The quintessential New York financier, Morgan achieved sufficient wealth to buy out Andrew Carnegie and served as a broker between world governments.

**Muhammad Ali** (born 1941). Heavyweight boxer who upon winning the world title from Sonny Liston in 1964 announced that he was a member of the Nation of Islam. Within three years his anti-war stance – "no Vietcong ever called me nigger" – had cast him into the wilderness, but eventually America took him to its bosom once more.

**Carry Nation** (1846–1911). Temperance activist and suffragette whose tendency to take an axe to saloons after storming in, singing hymns and bellowing biblical insults, won her no popularity with the official temperance movement (although she made lots of money on lecture tours). Frequently imprisoned, she paid her fines from souvenir axe sales.

**Richard Nixon** (1913–1995). From his earliest days as Eisenhower's vice-president – a position obtained with the help of his maudlin "Checkers" speech, about his little puppy dog – Nixon was the man American liberals most loved to hate. That he emerged from the turmoil of 1968 as America's president made a mockery of the idea that the 1960s would turn out to be a progressive decade. The seemingly relentless progress of his rehabilitation following the disgrace of Watergate has much to do with an enduring and perverse media fondness for him.

**Annie Oakley** (1860–1926). Performer with Buffalo Bill's Wild West show. Nicknamed "Little Miss Sure Shot," she once shot the cigar from the mouth of Kaiser Wilhelm.

**Georgia O'Keeffe** (1887–1986). Prolific painter whose stark, brightly colored abstractions of flowers and the Southwest desert won her acclaim as one of the greatest modern US artists.

**Dolly Parton** (born 1946). Country singer, movie star, perennial talk-show guest and part-owner of a theme park.

**William Penn** (1644–1718). British Quaker, often imprisoned in England for his beliefs. He gradually softened towards other doctrines, and campaigned strongly against any form of persecution, eventually establishing the colony of Pennsylvania as a refuge for religious minorities.

**Pocahontas** (1597?–1617). Daughter of a Native American Chief, Pocahontas was instrumental in the successful establishment of the English colony at Jamestown, Virginia. After sparing the life of the captive Captain John Smith, in 1614 Pocahontas married colonist John Rolfe, who brought her (and tobacco) to England, where she died.

**John Wesley Powell** (1834–1902). After losing an arm in the Civil War, Powell headed west to lead the first group of white men through the rivers and canyons of the Colorado Plateau.

**Elvis Presley** (1935–1977). Poor white boy from Tupelo, Mississippi, who moved to Memphis and became the first and the greatest white rock 'n' roll star. Whether you blame Colonel Tom Parker or Elvis himself, within a couple of years he was throwing away his magnificent voice on empty show-tunes, and embarking on the long road to Hamburger Heaven.

**Paul Revere** (1735–1818). Silversmith and unofficial political leader of the mechanic class in Boston in the period leading up to the Revolutionary War. As principal rider for Boston's Committee of Safety, in April 1775 he made the famed horseback journey from Boston to Concord to warn the rebels that the British were coming; thus started the War of Independence.

**John D Rockefeller** (1839–1937). Petroleum magnate whose Standard Oil company dominated the US and international markets from the 1880s to 1911, when the government dissolved his monopoly. Also a great philanthropist, in his later years he gave away his money – over half a billion dollars.

**Franklin Delano Roosevelt** (1882–1945). Four-term Democratic president, crippled by polio in 1920, who steered the country through the Depression with the closest the US has ever come to having socialist policies: his "New Deal" provided work for the unemployed and enforced collective bargaining with unions. His wartime leadership was often criticized, especially, with hindsight, his appeasement of Stalin.

**Theodore (Teddy) Roosevelt** (1858–1919). Explorer, writer, soldier and Republican president from 1901 to 1909. His "square deal" policies, which included "trust busting" and government arbitration in wage disputes, were seen to serve the public interest over Big Business, and he won the Nobel Peace Prize in 1906 for mediating an end to the Russo-Japanese War. In 1912 he founded the Progressive Party and ran (unsuccessfully) for president as an independent, advocating a strong social service state.

**Sacagawea** (1788?–1812). A legendary figure in American history, Sacagawea was a young Shoshone woman who accompanied the Lewis and Clark expedition across the continent in 1805. Only seventeen years old, and carrying her newborn baby boy, "Pomp," she and her French fur-trapper husband Charbonneau were indispensable members of the "Corps of Discovery," and their presence helped convince the natives of the explorers' peaceful intentions.

**Dred Scott** (1795?–1858). Black slave who made constitutional history as the plaintiff in a widely publicized but unsuccessful test case, in which he sought his freedom on the grounds that his master had taken him to live in a free state. The ruling effectively allowed slavery in US territories and was a leading factor in the build-up to the Civil War.

**William Tecumseh Sherman** (1820–1891). The Union general who burned Atlanta and boasted about it in his memoirs, and invented the blitzkrieg by laying waste to Georgia. The bane of his later life was to be greeted at all official functions with *Marching through Georgia*, a song he detested. His son, a Jesuit priest, had to be forcibly disuaded from attempting his own march thirty years later.

**Frank Sinatra** (1915–1998). Italian boy from Hoboken, New Jersey, who made his name thrilling bobby-soxers with New York's Tommy Dorsey Band in the early 1940s and went on to become the most beloved voice of the century. One of the few singers to turn into a decent movie actor.

**Sitting Bull** Tatanka Iyotake (1834–1890). Chief of the Dakota Sioux and leader of the Native American forces at the Battle of Little Bighorn. Pursued by the army, he escaped to Canada but surrendered in 1881. He was killed by police in the attempt to suppress the 1890 Ghost Dance movement.

**Bruce Springsteen** (born 1949). New Jersey singer-songwriter known as "the Boss." His energetic and poignant articulations of white, male, working-class America are often dismissed as machismo; President Reagan missed the point completely in the 1980s and announced his approval of Springsteen's *Born in the USA*, mistaking its ironic blue-collar disillusionment for reactionary blue-eyed patriotism.

**Harriet Beecher Stowe** (1811–1896). Though she had little firsthand experience of the South, Stowe's *Uncle Tom's Cabin* aroused the world in fierce opposition to slavery. Abraham Lincoln greeted her with the words "so this is the little lady that made this big war."

**Peter (Petrus) Stuyvesant** (1592–1672). Early governor of all Dutch colonies in North America, known as "Peg-leg Pete" for his wooden leg. He arrived in New Amsterdam (now New York) in 1647, doubling the colony's size and population, but was so unpopular, ignoring all appeals for self-government, that in 1664 he was forced to surrender the colony to the British. His farm, the Bowerie, gave the district in New York City its name.

**Harriet Tubman** (1820–1913). Escaped from slavery in Maryland in 1849 to become the leading abolitionist voice in the pre-Civil War years. Led hundreds of slaves to freedom on the Underground Railroad and served as a nurse and spy for Union forces during the war.

**Nat Turner** (1800–1831). Black preacher who led five Virginia slaves on a murderous rampage, killing over fifty whites, mostly with knives and axes, in a single day. In reaction, whites murdered hundreds of blacks and enacted an even more repressive regime.

**Mark Twain** (1835–1910). The great humorist and novelist, whose works provide the most vivid imaginable account of pioneer days across the continent, was also a powerful polemicist for liberal causes, and pioneered white-suit chic long before Tom Wolfe. He pursued his desire to typeset his own books, and break free from the evil machinations of self-important publishers, almost to the point of bankruptcy.

**George Wallace** (born 1919). Segregationist three-times Alabama governor; received 13 percent of the popular vote in the 1968 presidential election and looked set to increase his tally in the 1972 race before he was shot and paralyzed. Towards the end of his political career he eschewed his previous racist policies and was reelected governor in 1982.

**Booker Taliaferro Washington** (1856–1915). Controversial self-taught black educationalist who founded Tuskegee University. His 1901 book *Up From Slavery* proposed that blacks should abandon campaigns for voting rights and instead gain skills to work for economic gains.

**John Wayne** (1907–1979). Alias "the Duke": movie macho man, legendary boozer, Reagan role model and right-wing crank.

**Walt Whitman** (1819–1892). Writer and poet whose *Leaves of Grass*, first published in 1848, is among the most original and passionate works of American literature.

**Hank Williams** (1923–1953). Country music legend whose compositions (*I Saw the Light*, *Jambalaya*, etc) are still Nashville standards. A drink- and drug-sodden lifestyle accounted for his premature death.

**Frank Lloyd Wright** (1867–1959). Prolific architect who came to prominence around 1900 with a series of prototypical suburban houses and went on to design such landmarks as New York's Guggenheim Museum.

**Wilbur** (1867–1912) and **Orville** (1871–1948) **Wright**. Bicycle shop proprietors from Dayton, Ohio, who went on to greater things at Kitty Hawk, North Carolina, when they made the world's first powered flight on December 17, 1903 – it lasted twelve seconds.

**Brigham Young** (1801–1877). The son of near-illiterate Vermont farmers, Young led the Mormons to Utah following the assassination of Joseph Smith in 1844. More of a pragmatist than a theologian, he confronted the full force of the US to establish a permanent home for his people.

# INDEX

Glen, NH 225
Glen Arbor, MI 287
Glen Canyon Dam, UT 887
Glendale, CA 941
Glenwood Springs, CO 752
Globe, AZ 847
Gloucester, MA 186
Goblin Valley State Park, UT 878
Gold Beach, OR 1069
Golden Access Passport 32
Golden Age Passport 33
Golden Eagle Pass 41
Golden Gate Bridge, The, CA 992
**Goosenecks State Park**, UT 886
Gordy, Berry Jr 278
**Graceland**, TN 494
Grafton, VT 227
**Grand Canyon, The**, AZ 854
Grand Coteau, LA 620
Grand Coulee Dam, WA 1053
Grand Forks, ND 726
Grand Gulch, UT 885
Grand Haven, MI 286
Grand Junction, CO 753
Grand Lake, CO 742
Grand Marais, MI 291
Grand Marais, MN 345
Grand Mesa, CO 754
Grand Ole Opry, The 502
Grand Portage, MN 346
Grand Staircase, The, UT 870
**Grand Staircase-Escalante National Monument**, UT 875
**Grand Teton National Park**, WY 778
Grandfather Mountain, NC 446
Grant, Ulysses S 325, 498, 527, 1164, 1172, 1181
Grants, NM 827
Grants Pass, OR 1064
*Grapes of Wrath, The* 675
Grass Valley, CA 1011
Great Basin National Park, NV 905
**GREAT LAKES, THE** 253–349
Great Neck, NY 115
**GREAT PLAINS, THE** 672–729
Great Salt Lake, UT 893
**Great Smoky Mountains National Park** 447, 508

Green, Rev Al 494
Green Bay, WI 329
Green Mountains, The, VT 228
Green River, UT 878
Green River, WY 766
Green Tortoise 26
Greenport, NY 116
Greenville, ME 251
Greenville, MS 522
Greenwood, MS 523
**Greyhound** 26
Groton, CT 212
Guadalupe Mountains National Park, TX 671
Guerneville, CA 1018
Gulf Islands National Seashore, FL 590
Gulf Shores, AL 520
Gunflint Trail, MN 346
Gustavus, AK 1086
Guthrie, OK 682
Guthrie, Woody 1053

# H

Hackman, Gene 708
Haines, AK 1088
Halawa Valley, HI 1147
Haleakala National Park, HI 1145
Haleiwa, HI 1129
Halfway, OR 1074
Hamlin Beach State Park, NY 130
Hammett, Dashiell 983
Hammocks Beach State Park, NC 437
Hampton Beach, NH 217
Hana, HI 1146
Hanakapiai Beach, HI 1151
Hanakapiai Falls, HI 1151
Hanalei, HI 1150
Hanauma Bay, HI 126
Hancock Shaker Village, MA 201
Hannibal, MO 683
Hanover, NH 226
Harbor Springs, MI 289
Hardin, MT 783
Hardin, John Wesley 671
Harlan County, KY 482
Harmony, MN 348
Harpers Ferry, WV 398

Harris, Joel Chandler 465
Harrisburg, PA 148
Harrison, AR 535
Harrodsburg, KY 480
Hartford, CT 213
Harvard University, MA 182
Havasupai Reservation, AZ 860
**HAWAII** 1118–1152
**Hawaii Volcanoes National Park**, HI 1137
Hawi, HI 1134
Hawthorne, Nathaniel 188
Hayward, WI 331
Health 14
Healy, AK 1110
Hearst, William Randolph 960–961, 1181
Hearst Castle, CA 960
Helen, GA 467
Helena, AR 530
Helena, MT 787
Hell's Canyon, ID 798
Hell's Canyon, OR 1073
Hemingway, Ernest 556, 796
Henry, Patrick 382
Henson, Jim 522
Hershey, PA 149
Hibbing, MN 346
Hickok, Wild Bill 672, 699, 720
High Sierra, The, CA 956
Highway 61, MN 345
**Hiking** 44
Hillsboro, WV 402
Hilo, HI 1132
Hinton, WV 403
Historic Triangle, VA 383
History 1155
Hitchhiking 30
Hodgenville, KY 486
Hoh Rainforest, WA 1045
Holbrook, AZ 848
Holiday, Billie 1181
Holidays 53
Holland, MI 286
Holliday, Doc 753, 841
Holly, Buddy 662, 663, 1182
Holly Springs, MS 524
**Hollywood**, CA 931
Homer, AK 1098
Homestead, IA 704
Honokaa, HI 1133
**Honolulu**, HI 1122
Hood River, OR 1062

| ROUGH GUIDE FAVORITES Scenic Drives | |
| --- | --- |
| Blue Ridge Parkway, VA | →p.397 |
| Going-to-the-Sun Road, MT | →p.792 |
| Hatcher Pass, AK | →p.1108 |
| Moki Dugway, UT | →p.886 |
| Pictured Rocks National Lakeshore, MI | →p.1291 |
| Red Mountain Pass, CO | →p.758 |
| River Road, TX | →p.668 |
| The Road to Hana, HI | →p.1145 |
| The Sandhills, NE | →p.711 |
| Sawtooth National Recreation Area, ID | →p.796 |
| St Charles Streetcar, LA | →p.595 |
| Wapiti Valley, WY | →p.722 |

INDEX/1201

Washington, George 350,
357, 360, 364, 367, 377,
387, 396, 399, 400, 415,
1160
Washington Island, WI 330
WASHINGTON STATE 1026-
1053
Waterbury, VT 231
Waters, Muddy 521
Watford City, ND 729
Waycross, GA 477
Wayne, John 705, 707, 1185
Weather 55
Weirs Beach, NH 221
Wenatchee, WA 1048
West Point Military Academy,
NY 118
West Quoddy Head, ME 248
West Ship Island, MS 529
WEST VIRGINIA 398–404
West Yellowstone, MT 774,
778
Weston, VT 228
Whales 189, 198, 1143
Whidbey Island, WA 1038
Whiskey 48, 485, 505
Whiskeytown-Shasta-Trinity
National Recreation Area,
CA 1021
White Mountains, CA 956
White Mountains, NH 222
White Pass and Yukon Railway,
AK 1091
White River Junction, VT 230
White Sands National
Monument, NM 832
White Sulphur Springs, WV
403

White's City, NM 802
Whitefish, MT 790
Whitman, Dr Marcus 1051
Whitman, Walt 140, 1165,
1185
Whitney, Eli 214
Wichita, KS 699
Wildlife 45
Willamette Valley, OR 1062
Williams, AZ 853
Williams, Hank Sr 502, 517,
1185
Williamsburg, VA 384
Williamson, Sonny Boy 531
Williamstown, MA 200
Wilmington, DE 421
Wilmington, NC 438
Wind Cave National Park, SD
724
Wind River Indian Reservation,
WY 767
Window Rock, AZ 867
Windsor, Ontario 282
Wine 48
Winkle, Rip van 117
Winona, MN 348
Winslow, AZ 848
Winston–Salem, NC 442
Winter Park, CO 744
Winterset, IA 707
Winthrop, WA 1047
Wiscasset, ME 241
WISCONSIN 325–335
Wisconsin Dells, WI 332
Wizard of Oz, The 696
Wobblies, The (International
Workers Of The World) 786,
1027

Wolf, Howlin' 494, 521
Wolfe's Neck Woods State
Park, ME 240
Wolfeboro, NH 220
Women Travelers 35
Women, National Hall of Fame,
NY 126
Wonder, Stevie 278
Woods Hole, MA 191
Woodstock, NY 119
Woodstock, VT 229
Woolwich, ME 241
Worcester, MA 199
Working in the US 12
Wormsloe State Historic Site,
GA 476
Wounded Knee, SD 717
Wrangell, AK 1083
Wrangell-St Elias National
Park, AK 1106
Wright, Frank Lloyd 300,
304, 313, 324, 334, 678, 845,
1185
Wright, Wilbur and Orville 363,
434, 1185
Wrightsville Beach, NC 438
Wupatki National Monument,
AZ 851
WYOMING 762–781

X
X, Malcolm see Malcolm X

Y
Yakima, WA 1051
Yale University, CT 214
Yankton, SD 714
Ybor City, FL 578
Yellowstone National Park,
WY 772–778
YMCAs 39
Yorba Linda, CA 940
York, ME 236
York, PA 149
Yorktown, VA 387
Yosemite National Park, CA
972
Yosemite Village, CA 974
Young, Andrew 459
Young, Brigham 870, 1185
Young, Neil 968
Yountville, CA 1016

| ROUGH GUIDE FAVORITES Movie Locations | |
|---|---|
| Alice's Restaurant | →p.201 |
| The Birds | →p.1018 |
| Bridges of Madison County | →p.707 |
| Close Encounters of the Third Kind | →p.768 |
| The Eiger Sanction | →p.864 |
| Field of Dreams | →p.703 |
| Giant | →p.668 |
| Mystic Pizza | →p.211 |
| Rocky | →p.141 |
| The Shining | →p.1062 |
| Thelma and Louise | →p.886 |
| Witness | →p.145 |

# ROUGH GUIDES: Travel

# the perfect getaway vehicle

## low-price holiday car rental.

rent a car from holiday autos and you'll give yourself real freedom to explore your holiday destination. with great-value, fully-inclusive rates in over 4,000 locations worldwide, wherever you're escaping to, we're there to make sure you get excellent prices and superb service.

what's more, you can book now with complete confidence. our £5 undercut* ensures that you are guaranteed the best value for money in holiday destinations right around the globe.

drive away with a great deal, call holiday autos now on **0990 300 400** and quote ref RG.

# holiday autos
miles ahead

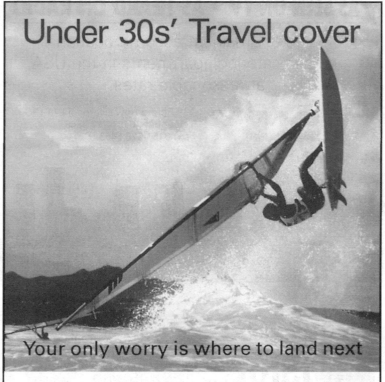 

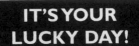

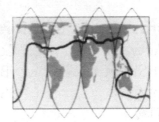